Encyclopedia of

HISTORIANS

AND

HISTORICAL WRITING

Volume 2

Encyclopedia of

HISTORIANS

AND

HISTORICAL WRITING

Volume 2
M–Z

Editor

KELLY BOYD

FITZROY DEARBORN PUBLISHERS
LONDON CHICAGO

British Library Cataloguing in Publication Data
Encyclopedia of historians and historical writing
   1. Historians – Encyclopedias
   I. Boyd, Kelly
   907.2′02

ISBN 1–884964–33–8

Library of Congress Cataloging in Publication Data is available.

First published in the USA and UK 1999

Typeset by The Florence Group, Stoodleigh, Devon
Printed by Vail-Ballou Press, Binghamton, New York

Cover design by Philip Lewis

CONTENTS

ALPHABETICAL
LIST OF ENTRIES

THEMATIC LIST

Entries by Category

REGIONS AND PERIODS

Africa
Ancient World
Asia
    1) China
    2) India
    3) Japan and Korea
    4) Middle East
    5) Southeast Asia and Australasia
Byzantium
Europe
    1) Medieval
    2) Early Modern and Modern
    3) Britain
    4) Eastern and Central
    5) France
    6) Germany
    7) Ireland
    8) Italy
    9) Low Countries
    10) Russia and Central Asia
    11) Scandinavia
    12) Spain and Portugal
North and South America
    1) Canada
    2) Latin America
    3) United States

TOPICS

Art History
Cultural History
Demographic History
Diplomatic History
Economic History
Intellectual History
Jewish History
Legal History
Military History
Periods, Themes, Branches of History
Political History
Religion
Science, Medicine, Technology, and Ecology
Social History
Theories and Theorists
Women's and Gender History

REGIONS AND PERIODS

Africa

Afigbo, A.E.
Africa entries
African Diaspora
Ajayi, Jacob F. Ade
Ayandele, Emmanuel Ayankami
Bernal, Martin
Boahen, A. Adu
Coquery-Vidrovitch, Catherine
Davidson, Basil
Diop, Cheikh Anta

Egypt: since the 7th Century CE
Feierman, Steven
Gallagher, John
Gsell, Stéphane
Hargreaves, John D.
Iliffe, John
Julien, Charles-André
Laroui, Abdallah
Lovejoy, Paul E.
Marks, Shula

Mazrui, Ali A.
Ogot, Bethwell A.
Oliver, Roland
Ranger, Terence O.
Rodney, Walter
South Africa
Thompson, Leonard
Vansina, Jan

Ancient World

Ammianus Marcellinus
Bauer, Walter
Beloch, Karl Julius
Bernal, Martin
Breasted, James Henry
Brown, Peter
Caesar, Julius
Cassiodorus
Cassius Dio
Daube, David
Diodorus Siculus
Dionysius of Halicarnassus
Droysen, J.G.
Egypt: Ancient
Eusebius of Caesarea

Finley, M.I.
Fustel de Coulanges, Numa
Gibbon, Edward
Greece: Ancient
Herodotus
Jones, A.H.M.
Josephus
Livy
Meyer, Eduard
Momigliano, Arnaldo
Mommsen, Theodor
Near East: Ancient
Niebuhr, B.G.
Plutarch
Polybius

Roman Empire
Rostovtzeff, M.I.
Sallust
Sanctis, Gaetano de
Scriptores Historiae Augustae
Suetonius
Syme, Ronald
Tacitus
Thucydides
Velleius Paterculus
Vernant, Jean-Pierre
Watson, Alan
Wilamowitz-Möllendorff, Ulrich von
Xenophon

Asia : 1) China

Ban Gu
Chen Yinke
China entries
China: Historical Writing entries
Eberhard, Wolfram
Fairbank, John K.
Gu Jiegang

Kong-zi
Liang Qichao
Liu Zhiji
Ma Huan
Maspero, Henri
Mongol Empire
Naitō Torajirō

Needham, Joseph
Pelliot, Paul
Sima Guang
Sima Qian
Spence, Jonathan D.
Wang Fuzhi
Zhang Xuecheng

Asia: 2) India

Bīrūnī, Abū Rayhān al-
Chaudhuri, K.N.
Dutt, R.C.

Eaton, Richard Maxwell
Gopal, Sarvepalli
Guha, Ranajit

India: since 1750
Kosambi, D.D.
Thapar, Romila

Asia: 3) Japan and Korea

Arai Hakuseki
Boxer, C.R.
Gunki monogatari
Hayashi School
Japan

Japanese Chronicles
Kitabatake Chikafusa
Korea
Maruyama Masao
Mito School

Niida Noboru
Otsuka Hisao
Shigeno Yasutsugu
Shiratori Kurakichi

Asia: 4) Middle East

Bartol'd, Vasilii Vladimirovich
Browne, Edward G.
Byzantium
Cahen, Claude
Eberhard, Wolfram
Hodgson, Marshall G.S.
Hourani, Albert
Ibn al-Athīr, 'Izz al-Dīn
Ibn Khaldūn

Inalcık, Halil
Iran:: since 1500
Issawi, Charles P.
Kasravi, Ahmad
Kedourie, Elie
Köprülü, M.F.
Lewis, Bernard
Massignon, Louis
Middle East: Medieval

Naima, Mustafa
Near East: Ancient
Ottoman Empire
Rashīd al-Dīn, Fazlallah
Rodinson, Maxime
Said, Edward
Watt, W. Montgomery
Zaydān, Jurjī

Asia: 5) Southeast Asia and Australasia

Ali Haji, Raja
Anderson, Benedict
Australia
Babad
Beaglehole, John C.
Bean, C.E.W.
Blainey, Geoffrey
Bugis and Makasar Chronicles
Clark, Manning

Dening, Greg
Furnivall, J.S.
Grimshaw, Patricia
Ileto, Reynaldo Clemeña
Indian Ocean Region
Lake, Marilyn
Le Quy Don
Malay Annals
New Zealand

Pacific/Oceanic History
Ranggawarsita, Raden Ngabei
Raniri, Nur ud-Din ar-
Scott, James C.
Southeast Asia
Vietnam
Vietnamese Chronicles
Wood, G.A.
Yamin, Muhammad

Byzantium

Brown, Peter
Bury, J.B.
Byzantium
Cameron, Averil

Kazhdan, A.P.
Komnene, Anna
Obolensky, Dimitri
Ostrogorsky, George

Procopius
Psellos, Michael
Runciman, Steven
Vasiliev, A.A.

Europe: 1) Medieval

Anglo-Saxon Chronicle
Annales regni Francorum
Barraclough, Geoffrey
Bede
Bloch, Marc
Bolland, Jean
Burns, Robert Ignatius
Byzantium
Cam, Helen
Camden, William
Castro, Américo
Cheney, C.R.
Crusades
Delisle, Léopold
Duby, Georges
Einhard
Froissart, Jean
Ganshof, F.L.
Giesebrecht, Wilhelm von
Gilson, Etienne
Gregory of Tours
Guichard, Pierre
Gurevich, Aron

Haller, Johannes
Haskins, Charles Homer
Hilton, Rodney
Holy Roman Empire
Hughes, Kathleen
Huizinga, Johan
Janssen, Johannes
Kantorowicz, Ernst H.
Knowles, David
Krusch, Bruno
Lea, Henry Charles
Lévi-Provençal, Evariste
Levison, Wilhelm
Leyser, Karl
Lopez, Roberto S.
Mabillon, Jean
Maitland, F.W.
Medieval Chronicles
Medieval Historical Writing
Muratori, L.A.
Orderic Vitalis
Otto of Freising
Paris, Matthew

Pirenne, Henri
Postan, M.M.
Power, Eileen
Roger of Wendover
Rörig, Fritz
Salvemini, Gaetano
Savigny, Friedrich Karl von
Saxo Grammaticus
Schramm, Percy Ernst
Snorri Sturluson
Southern, R.W.
Switzerland
Thietmar
Thorne, Samuel E.
Ullmann, Walter
Vernadsky, George
Villani, Giovanni
Waitz, Georg
White, Lynn, Jr.
Widukind of Corvey
William of Malmesbury
William of Tyre

Europe: 2) Early Modern and Modern

Blum, Jerome
Boxer, C.R.
Braudel, Fernand
Brenner, Robert
Broué, Pierre
Burckhardt, Jacob
Burke, Peter
Carr, E.H.
Chartier, Roger
Cipolla, Carlo M.
Darnton, Robert
Davies, Norman
Davies, R.W.
Davis, Natalie Zemon
Delbrück, Hans
Delumeau, Jean
Deutscher, Isaac
de Vries, Jan
Dickens, A.G.
Elliott, J.H.
Enlightenment Historical Writing
Europe: Modern

European Expansion
Froude, J.A.
Fruin, Robert
Gallagher, John
Gay, Peter
Geyl, Pieter
Gilbert, Felix
Ginzburg, Carlo
Giovio, Paolo
Greece: Modern
Guicciardini, Francesco
Hobsbawm, E.J.
Howard, Michael
Hufton, Olwen H.
Hunt, Lynn
Joll, James
Kelly-Gadol, Joan
Kennedy, Paul M.
Kristeller, Paul Oskar
Machiavelli, Niccolò
McNeill, William H.
Mahan, Alfred Thayer

Marrus, Michael R.
Mattingly, Garrett
Mayer, Arno J.
Mosse, George L.
Motley, John Lothrop
Parker, Geoffrey
Raynal, Guillaume-Thomas
Renaissance Historical Writing
Robinson, James Harvey
Rostow, W.W.
Schama, Simon
Schorske, Carl E.
Scott, Joan Wallach
Scribner, R.W.
Switzerland
Thorne, Samuel E.
Ullman, Berthold L.
Venturi, Franco
Vergil, Polydore
Wallerstein, Immanuel
Wedgwood, C.V.
Yates, Frances A.

Europe: 3) Britain

Acton, Lord
Anderson, Perry
Anglo-Saxon Chronicle
Bede
Briggs, Asa
Britain entries
British Empire
Buckle, Henry Thomas
Butterfield, Herbert
Cam, Helen
Camden, William
Carlyle, Thomas
Carr, E.H.
Chadwick, Owen
Cheney, C.R.
Clapham, J.H.
Clark, Alice
Cole, G.D.H.
Davidoff, Leonore
Dickens, A.G.
Dyos, H.J.
Elton, G.R.
Engels, Friedrich
Foxe, John
Froude, J.A.
Gallagher, John
Gardiner, Samuel Rawson
Habakkuk, H.J.

Halévy, Elie
Hammond, J.L. and Barbara
Hexter, J.H.
Hill, Christopher
Hilton, Rodney
Hobsbawm, E.J.
Holdsworth, W.S.
Holinshed, Raphael
Howard, Michael
Hughes, Kathleen
Hume, David
Jones, Gareth Stedman
Knowles, David
Landes, David
Macaulay, Thomas Babington
Maitland, F.W.
Milsom, S.F.C.
Namier, Lewis
Paris, Matthew
Pinchbeck, Ivy
Plucknett, T.F.T.
Plumb, J.H.
Pocock, J.G.A.
Radzinowicz, Leon
Roger of Wendover
Rostow, W.W.
Rowbotham, Sheila
Russell, Conrad

Samuel, Raphael
Scotland
Seeley, J.R.
Selden, John
Skinner, Quentin
Southern, R.W.
Stenton, F.M.
Stone, Lawrence
Stubbs, William
Tawney, R.H.
Taylor, A.J.P.
Thirsk, Joan
Thomas, Keith
Thompson, E.P.
Thompson, F.M.L.
Thorne, Samuel E.
Trevelyan, G.M.
Trevor-Roper, Hugh
Vergil, Polydore
Walkowitz, Judith R.
Webb, Beatrice and Sidney
Wedgwood, C.V.
William of Malmesbury
Williams, Raymond
Wilson, Charles H.
Wrigley, E.A.

Europe: 4) Eastern and Central

Austro-Hungarian Empire
The Balkans
Barkan, Ömer Lütfi
Blum, Jerome
Brunner, Otto
Central Europe
Davies, Norman
East Central Europe
Fügedi, Erik

Halecki, Oskar
Jelavich, Barbara and Charles
Kołakowski, Leszek
Kula, Witold
Lelewel, Joachim
Macartney, C.A.
Marczali, Henrik
Palacký, František
Pekař, Josef

Poland entries
Polanyi, Karl
Rothschild, Joseph
Seton-Watson, Hugh
Seton-Watson, R.W.
Srbik, Heinrich von
Stavrianos, Leften Stavros
Sugar, Peter F.
Szekfű, Gyula

Europe: 5) France

Annales regni Francorum
Ariès, Philippe
Bloch, Marc
Bodin, Jean
Chartier, Roger
Cobb, Richard
Cobban, Alfred
Corbin, Alain
Darnton, Robert
Davis, Natalie Zemon
Delisle, Léopold
Delumeau, Jean
Duby, Georges
Einhard
Febvre, Lucien
Foucault, Michel
France entries

Froissart, Jean
Furet, Francois
Fustel de Coulanges, Numa
Gilson, Etienne
Godechot, Jacques Léon
Gregory of Tours
Guizot, François
Henry, Louis
Hufton, Olwen H.
Hunt, Lynn
Labrousse, Ernest
Lavisse, Ernest
Lefebvre, Georges
Le Roy Ladurie, Emmanuel
Marrus, Michael R.
Mathiez, Albert
Michelet, Jules

Mousnier, Roland
Ozouf, Mona
Renouvin, Pierre
Rudé, George
Scott, Joan Wallach
Seignobos, Charles
Simiand, François
Soboul, Albert
Thierry, Augustin
Tilly, Charles
Tilly, Louise A.
Tocqueville, Alexis de
Voltaire
Vovelle, Michel
Weber, Eugen
Zeldin, Theodore

Europe: 6) Germany

Barraclough, Geoffrey
Bock, Gisela
Bracher, Karl Dietrich
Broszat, Martin
Conze, Werner
Delbrück, Hans
Dopsch, Alfons
Droysen , J.G.
Engels, Friedrich
Ennen, Edith
Fischer, Fritz
Gall, Lothar
Gatterer, Johann Christoph
Germany entries
Giesebrecht, Wilhelm von
Haller, Johannes
Hartung, Fritz
Hausen, Karin
Hillgruber, Andreas

Hintze, Otto
Janssen, Johannes
Joll, James
Kehr, Eckart
Kocka, Jürgen
Koonz, Claudia
Koselleck, Reinhart
Krusch, Bruno
Kuczynski, Jürgen
Lamprecht, Karl
Levison, Wilhelm
Lüdtke, Alf
Mason, Tim
Meinecke, Friedrich
Miller, Susanne
Mommsen, Hans
Mommsen, Wolfgang J.
Mosse, George L.
Niethammer, Lutz

Otto of Freising
Ranke, Leopold von
Ritter, Gerhard A.
Rörig, Fritz
Rosenberg, Arthur
Rosenberg, Hans
Schieder, Theodor
Schnabel, Franz
Schramm, Percy Ernst
Scribner, R.W.
Sudhoff, Karl
Sybel, Heinrich von
Thietmar
Treitschke, Heinrich von
Vagts, Alfred
Waitz, Georg
Weber, Hermann
Wehler, Hans-Ulrich
Widukind of Corvey

Europe: 7) Ireland

Froude, J.A.
Green, Alice Stopford

Ireland
Lecky, W.E.H.

Lyons, F.S.L.
Moody, T.W.

Europe: 8) Italy

Baron, Hans
Cantimori, Delio
Chabod, Federico
Cipolla, Carlo M.
Croce, Benedetto
De Felice, Renzo
De Sanctis, Francesco
Garin, Eugenio
Giannone, Pietro
Gilbert, Felix
Ginzburg, Carlo

Giovio, Paolo
Gramsci, Antonio
Guicciardini, Francesco
Italy entries
Kelly-Gadol, Joan
Machiavelli, Niccolò
Mack Smith, Denis
Manzoni, Alessandro
Martines, Lauro
Momigliano, Arnaldo
Pieri, Piero

Pieroni Bortolotti, Franca
Portelli, Alessandro
Procacci, Giuliano
Renaissance Historical Writing
Romeo, Rosario
Salvemini, Gaetano
Sarpi, Paolo
Spriano, Paolo
Ullman, Berthold L.
Villani, Giovanni
Villari, Pasquale

Europe: 9) Low Countries

de Vries, Jan
Fruin, Robert
Geyl, Pieter

Low Countries
Motley, John Lothrop
Parker, Geoffrey

Pirenne, Henri
Schama, Simon

Europe: 10) Russia and Central Asia

Bartol'd, Vasilii Vladimirovich
Blum, Jerome
Carr, E.H.
Central Asia
Davies, R.W.
Deutscher, Isaac
Karamzin, N.M.

Kliuchevskii, V.O.
Lewin, Moshe
Medvedev, Roy
Miliukov, Pavel
Pipes, Richard
Platonov, S.F.
Poliakov, Léon

Raeff, Marc
Russia entries
Solov'ev, Sergei
Vasiliev, A.A.
Vernadsky, George
Vinogradoff, Paul
Zaionchkovskii, P.A.

Europe: 11) Scandinavia

Gurevich, Aron
Heckscher, Eli F.

Saxo Grammaticus
Snorri Sturluson

Sweden

Europe: 12) Spain and Portugal

Boxer, C.R.
Braudel, Fernand
Burns, Robert Ignatius
Carr, Raymond
Domínguez Ortiz, Antonio

Elliott, J.H.
Guichard, Pierre
Lea, Henry Charles
Lévi-Provençal, Evariste
Maravall, José Antonio

Menéndez Pidal, Ramón
Parker, Geoffrey
Sánchez-Albornoz, Claudio
Spain entries
Thomas, Hugh

North and South America: 1) Canada

Canada
Creighton, Donald Grant
Eccles, W.J.
Frégault, Guy

Groulx, Lionel
Innis, Harold A.
Lower, A.R.M.
Morton, W.L.

Ormsby, Margaret A.
Ouellet, Fernand
Séguin, Maurice
Trigger, Bruce G.

North and South America: 2) Latin America

Argentina
Basadre, Jorge
Bolton, Herbert E.
Borah, Woodrow
Boxer, C.R.
Brazil
Castro, Américo
Central America
Chevalier, François
Cosío Villegas, Daniel
Cuba
Díaz del Castillo, Bernal
Freyre, Gilberto
Garcilaso de la Vega
Germani, Gino

Gibson, Charles
Góngora, Mario
González Casanova, Pablo
Halperín-Donghi, Tulio
Hanke, Lewis
Holanda, S.B. de
Las Casas, Bartolomé de
Latin America entries
Lavrin, Asunción
León-Portilla, Miguel
Levene, Ricardo
Mexico
Mitre, Bartolomé
Moreno Fraginals, Manuel
O'Gorman, Edmundo

Ortiz, Fernando
Pérez, Louis A., Jr.
Prado Júnior, Caio
Prebisch, Raúl
Prescott, William H.
Raynal, Guillaume-Thomas
Rock, David
Rodrigues, José Honório
Romero, José Luis
Scobie, James R.
Stein, Stanley J.
Tannenbaum, Frank
Varnhagen, Francisco Adolfo de
Williams, Eric

North and South America: 3) United States

Adams, Henry
African American History
African Diaspora
Ambrose, Stephen E.
Andrews, Charles McLean
Axtell, James
Bailyn, Bernard
Bancroft, George
Beard, Charles A. and Mary Ritter Beard
Becker, Carl L.
Boorstin, Daniel J.
Chandler, Alfred D., Jr.
Commager, Henry Steele
Commons, John R.
Cott, Nancy F.
Crosby, Alfred W., Jr.
Curti, Merle
Curtin, Philip D.
Davis, David Brion
Debo, Angie
Degler, Carl N.
Du Bois, W.E.B.
Dunning, William A.
Elkins, Stanley
Fogel, Robert William
Foner, Eric
Foner, Philip S.
Franklin, John Hope
Genovese, Eugene D.
Goldman, Eric
Gordon, Linda
Greene, Jack P.

Gutman, Herbert G.
Handlin, Oscar
Hartz, Louis
Hine, Darlene Clark
Hofstadter, Richard
Horwitz, Morton J.
Hughes, Thomas P.
Jensen, Merrill
Jordan, Winthrop D.
Kerber, Linda K.
Kessler-Harris, Alice
Kolko, Gabriel
LaFeber, Walter
Lasch, Christopher
Lerner, Gerda
Leuchtenburg, William
Levine, Lawrence W.
Lewis, David Levering
Link, Arthur S.
Litwack, Leon F.
Mahan, Alfred Thayer
Malin, James C.
Meier, August
Merchant, Carolyn
Miller, Perry
Montgomery, David
Morgan, Edmund S.
Morison, Samuel Eliot
Mumford, Louis
Nash, Gary B.
Nevins, Allan
Osgood, Herbert Levi

Owsley, Frank Lawrence
Painter, Nell Irvin
Parkman, Francis
Parrington, Vernon Louis
Pessen, Edward
Phillips, Ulrich Bonnell
Potter, David M.
Prucha, Francis Paul
Quinn, David B.
Schlesinger, Arthur M., Jr.
Scott, Anne Firor
Semple, Ellen Churchill
Smith, Henry Nash
Smith, Merritt Roe
Smith-Rosenberg, Carroll
Spruill, Julia Cherry
Stampp, Kenneth M.
Takaki, Ron
Tocqueville, Alexis de
Turner, Frederic Jackson
Ulrich, Laurel Thatcher
United States entries
United States: Historical Writing, 20th Century
Wiebe, Robert H.
Williams, William Appleman
Wood, Gordon S.
Woodson, Carter G.
Woodward, C. Vann
Worster, Donald
Zinn, Howard

TOPICS

Art History

Art History
Burckhardt, Jacob
Gombrich, E.H.

Huizinga, Johan
Panofsky, Erwin
Pevsner, Nikolaus

Schama, Simon
Winckelmann, J.J.

Cultural History

Anthropology, Historical
Art History
The Body
Bourdieu, Pierre
Braudel, Fernand
Burckhardt, Jacob
Burke, Peter
Chartier, Roger
Chevalier, François
China: Modern
Consumerism and Consumption
Corbin, Alain
Cultural History
Darnton, Robert
Davis, David Brion

Davis, Natalie Zemon
Europe: Modern
Freyre, Gilberto
Garin, Eugenio
Gay, Peter
Ginzburg, Carlo
Hanke, Lewis
Herder, J.G.
Huizinga, Johan
Hunt, Lynn
Intellectual History
Köprülü, M.F.
Lamprecht, Karl
Mentalities, History of
Miliukov, Pavel

Mosse, George L.
Mumford, Lewis
Ozouf, Mona
Ranger, Terence O.
Schorske, Carl E.
Soboul, Albert
Theatre
Thomas, Keith
Thompson, E.P.
Vico, Giambattista
Vovelle, Michel
Williams, Raymond
Zeldin, Theodore

Demographic History

Annales School
Cambridge Group
Cipolla, Carlo M.

Demography
de Vries, Jan
Henry, Louis

Migration
Wrigley, E.A.

Diplomatic History

Ambrose, Stephen E.
Annales regni francorum
Butterfield, Herbert
Carr, E.H.
Chabod, Federico
Diplomatic History
Droysen, J.G.
Elliott, J.H.
Europe: Modern

Fischer, Fritz
Gilbert, Felix
Intelligence and Espionage
Jelavich, Barbara and Charles
Kedourie, Elie
Kennedy, Paul M.
Kolko, Gabriel
LaFeber, Walter
Mattingly, Garrett

Mayer, Arno J.
Motley, John Lothrop
Ranke, Leopold von
Renouvin, Pierre
Rodrigues, José Honório
Taylor, A.J.P.
Vagts, Alfred
Williams, William Appleman

Economic History

Beard, Charles A. and Mary Ritter Beard
Business History
Cardoso, Fernando Henrique
Cipolla, Carlo M.
Cole, G.D.H.
Economic History

Hammond, J.L. and Barbara
Hill, Christopher
Hilton, Rodney
Hobsbawm, E.J.
Industrial Revolution
Otsuka Hisao

Polanyi, Karl
Postan, M.M.
Power, Eileen
Tawney, R.H.
Thompson, E.P.
Vinogradoff, Paul

Intellectual History

Berlin, Isaiah
Dilthey, Wilhelm
Foucault, Michel
Intellectual History

Lovejoy, Arthur O.
Meinecke, Friedrich
Pocock, J.G.A.
Skinner, Quentin

Weber, Max
White, Hayden V.

Jewish History

Baron, Salo Wittmayer
Braham, Randolph L.
Dubnov, Simon
Goitein, S.D.

Graetz, Heinrich
Hilberg, Raul
Holocaust
Jewish History

Josephus
Katz, Jacob
Marrus, Michael R.

Legal History

Bodin, Jean
Daube, David
Góngora, Mario
Hargreaves, John D.
Holdsworth, W.S.
Horwitz, Morton J.

Legal History
Maitland, F.W.
Milsom, S.F.C.
Plucknett, T.F.T.
Radzinowicz, Leon
Savigny, Friedrich Karl von

Simpson, A.W.B.
Sinclair, Keith
Vinogradoff, Paul
Watson, Alan

Military History

Delbrück, Hans
Howard, Michael
Keegan, John
Kennedy, Paul M.
Mahan, Alfred Thayer

Mattingly, Garrett
Military History
Napoleonic Wars
Naval History
Pieri, Piero

Schramm, Percy Ernst
Thorne, Samuel E.
Vagts, Alfred

Periods, Themes, Branches of History

African American History
African Diaspora
Agrarian History
America: Pre-Columbian
Archaeology
Art History
Astrology
The Body
Business History
Childhood
Comparative History
Computers and Computing, History of
Computing and History
Consumerism and Consumption
Counter-Reformation
Crime and Deviance
Crusades
Cultural History
Demography
Design History
Diplomatic History
Documentary Film
Dress
Eastern Orthodoxy
Ecclesiastical History
Ecology
Economic History
Environmental History
Ethnicity
Ethnohistory
European Expansion
The Family
Feminism

Feudalism
Film
Frontiers
Gender
Historical Geography
Historical Maps and Atlases
Historiology
History Workshop
Holocaust
Homosexuality
Imperialism
Indian Ocean Region
Indigenous Peoples
Industrial Revolution
Intellectual History
Intelligence and Espionage
Islamic Nations and Cultures
Labor History
Legal History
Leisure
Literature and History
Local History
Maritime History
Marriage
Marxist Interpretation of History
Masculinity
Media
Medicine, History of
Memory
Mentalities, History of
Metahistory
Migration
Military History

Musicology
Napoleonic Wars
Nationalism
Native American History
Natural Sciences, Historical
Naval History
Oral History
Orientalism
Orthodoxy, Eastern
Pacific/Oceanic History
Philosophy of History
Political and Constitutional History
Popular History
Prehistory
Prosopography
Protestantism
Quantitative Method
The Reformation
Religion
Religions, Comparative History of
Rhetoric and History
Science, History of
Sexuality
Slavery entries
Social History
Sociology and History
Sport, History of
The State
Theatre
Urban History
World History
World War I
World War II

Political History

Althusser, Louis
Beard, Charles A. and Mary Ritter Beard
Elton, G.R.
Foner, Eric
Furet, François
Genovese, Eugene D.
Guizot, François
Jones, Gareth Stedman
Hartz, Louis

Hofstadter, Richard
Legal History
Leuchtenburg, William
Macaulay, Thomas Babington
Maitland, F.W.
Namier, Lewis
Pocock, J.G.A.
Political and Constitutional History
Russell, Conrad

Schama, Simon
Schlesinger, Arthur M., Jr.
Seeley, J.R.
Skinner, Quentin
The State
Stubbs, William
Trevelyan, G.M.

Religion

Bauer, Walter
Bolland, Jean
Brown, Peter
Bultmann, Rudolf
Catholicism/Catholic Church
Chadwick, Owen
Cheney, C.R.
Christianity
Counter-Reformation

Delumeau, Jean
Dickens, A.G.
Eastern Orthodoxy
Foxe, John
Janssen, Johannes
Lea, Henry Charles
Mansi, Giovanni Domenico
Pagels, Elaine
Protestantism

Ranke, Leopold von
The Reformation
Religion
Religions, Comparative
Sarpi, Paolo
Troeltsch, Ernst
Ullmann, Walter
Wellhausen, Julius

Science, Medicine, Technology, and Ecology

Crosby, Alfred W., Jr.
Dilthey, Wilhelm
Duhem, Pierre
Fleck, Ludwig
Garin, Eugenio
Heilbron, J.L.
Hughes, Thomas P.
Kuhn, Thomas S.
Mach, Ernst
Malin, James C.

Medicine, History of
Merchant, Carolyn
Merton, Robert K.
Mumford, Lewis
Needham, Joseph
Rosenberg, Charles E.
Sarton, George
Sauer, Carl O.
Science, History of
Semple, Ellen Churchill

Sigerist, Henry E.
Smith, Merritt Roe
Sudhoff, Karl
Technology
Temkin, Owsei
Trigger, Bruce G.
Vico, Giambattista
Whewell, William
White, Lynn, Jr.
Worster, Donald

Social History

Althusser, Louis
Annales School
Bloch, Marc
Braudel, Fernand
Cobb, Richard
Cole, G.D.H.
Conze, Werner
Corbin, Alain
Gutman, Herbert G.
Hammond, J.L. and Barbara
Hill, Christopher
Hilton, Rodney
History Workshop

Hobsbawm, E.J.
Hunt, Lynn
Lamprecht, Karl
Lefebvre, Georges
Marx, Karl
Marxist Interpretation of History
Mathiez, Albert
Montgomery, David
Pinchbeck, Ivy
Plumb, J.H.
Power, Eileen
Scott, Joan Wallach
Seignobos, Charles

Simiand, François
Soboul, Albert
Social History
Tawney, R.H.
Thomas, Keith
Thompson, E.P.
Thompson, F.M.L.
Tilly, Charles
Trevelyan, G.M.
Webb, Beatrice and Sidney
Weber, Max

Theories and Theorists

Althusser, Louis
Anderson, Benedict
Anderson, Perry
Annales School
Anthropology, Historical
Ariès, Philippe
Barraclough, Geoffrey
Begriffsgeschichte
Berlin, Isaiah
Bernal, Martin
Bloch, Marc
Bodin, Jean
Bourdieu, Pierre
Braudel, Fernand
Buckle, Henry Thomas
Burckhardt, Jacob
Butterfield, Herbert
Cambridge Group
Cardoso, Fernando Henrique
Carlyle, Thomas
Carr, E.H.
Cassirer, Ernst
Chandler, Alfred D., Jr.
Chartier, Roger
Cipolla, Carlo M.
Collingwood, R.G.

Comte, Auguste
Croce, Benedetto
Dening, Greg
Dilthey, Wilhelm
Engels, Friedrich
Erikson, Erik H.
Foucault, Michel
Freud, Sigmund
Gatterer, Johann Christoph
Gay, Peter
Geertz, Clifford
Gramsci, Antonio
Habermas, Jürgen
Hegel, G.W.F.
Henry, Louis
Herder, J.G
History from Below
James, C.L.R.
Kiernan, V.G.
Kong-zi
Lovejoy, Arthur O.
McLuhan, Marshall
Marx, Karl
Montesquieu
Moore, Barrington, Jr.
Nietzsche, Friedrich

Popper, Karl
Postcolonialism
Postmodernism
Ranke, Leopold von
Rhetoric and History
Said, Edward W.
Schlözer, August Ludwig von
Schorske, Carl E.
Scott, James C.
Simiand, François
Spengler, Oswald
Subaltern Studies
Tilly, Charles
Todorov, Tsvetan
Toynbee, Arnold J.
Turner, Victor
Universal History
Villari, Pasquale
Voltaire
Vovelle, Michel
Weber, Max
Whig Interpretation of History
White, Hayden V.
Williams, Raymond

Women's and Gender History

Bock, Gisela
Clark, Alice
Cott, Nancy F.
Davidoff, Leonore
Davis, Natalie Zemon
Gordon, Linda
Grimshaw, Patricia
Hausen, Karin
Hine, Darlene Clark
Hufton, Olwen H.

Kelly-Gadol, Joan
Kerber, Linda K.
Kessler-Harris, Alice
Koonz, Claudia
Lake, Marilyn
Lavrin, Asunción
Lerner, Gerda
Painter, Nell Irvin
Pieroni Bortolotti, Franca
Pinchbeck, Ivy

Rowbotham, Sheila
Scott, Anne Firor
Scott, Joan Wallach
Smith-Rosenberg, Carroll
Spruill, Julia Cherry
Tilly, Louise A.
Ulrich, Laurel Thatcher
Walkowitz, Judith R.
Women's History entries

CHRONOLOGICAL LIST
OF HISTORIANS

551–479 BCE	Kong-zi [Confucius]	1276–1348	Giovanni Villani
c.484–after 424 BCE	Herodotus	1293–1354	Kitabatake Chikafusa
c.460/455–c.399 BCE	Thucydides	1332–1406	Ibn Khaldūn
c.428–c.354 BCE	Xenophon	c.1337–after 1404	Jean Froissart
c.200–c.118 BCE	Polybius	fl.1413–33	Ma Huan
c.145–c.87 BCE	Sima Qian	1469–1527	Niccolò Machiavelli
c.104–c.20 BCE	Diodorus Siculus	1470(?)–1555(?)	Polydore Vergil
100–44 BCE	Julius Caesar	1474–1566	Bartolomé de Las Casas
86–35 BCE	Sallust	1483–1540	Francesco Guicciardini
c.60–after 7 BCE	Dionysius of Halicarnassus	c.1486–1552	Paolo Giovio
59 BCE–c.17 CE	Livy	c.1492–1584	Bernal Díaz del Castillo
c.20/19 BCE–after 30 CE	Velleius Paterculus	1516–1587	John Foxe
c.32–92 CE	Ban Gu	1529/30–1596	Jean Bodin
37/8–c.94 CE	Josephus	1539–1616	Garcilaso de la Vega
before 50–after 120 CE	Plutarch	1551–1623	William Camden
c.56–after 118 CE	Tacitus	1552–1623	Paolo Sarpi
c.70–c.140 CE	Suetonius	fl.1560–80	Raphael Holinshed
c.150–235 CE	Cassius Dio	1584–1654	John Selden
c.265–339 CE	Eusebius of Caesarea	1596–1665	Jean Bolland
c.330–c.395 CE	Ammianus Marcellinus	1619–1692	Wang Fuzhi
c.487–c.585	Cassiodorus	1632–1707	Jean Mabillon
c.500–after 542	Procopius	1655–1716	Mustafa Naima
538/9–594/5	Gregory of Tours	1657–1725	Arai Hakuseki
661–721	Liu Zhiji	d. 1658	Nur ud-Din ar-Raniri
c.672/3–735	Bede	1668–1744	Giambattista Vico
c.770–840	Einhard	1672–1750	L.A. Muratori
c.925–after 973	Widukind of Corvey	1676–1748	Pietro Giannone
973–c.1050	Abū Rayhān al-Bīrūnī	1689–1755	Montesquieu
975–1018	Thietmar, bishop of Merseburg	1692–1769	Giovanni Domenico Mansi
1018–after 1081	Michael Psellos	1694–1778	Voltaire
1019–1086	Sima Guang	1711–1776	David Hume
1075–1142/3	Orderic Vitalis	1713–1796	Guillaume-Thomas Raynal
1083–c.1153/4	Anna Komnene	1717–1768	J.J. Winckelmann
c.1090–c.1143	William of Malmesbury	c.1726–c.1784	Le Quy Don
c.1114–1158	Otto of Freising	1729–1799	Johann Christoph Gatterer
c.1130–1186	William of Tyre	1735–1809	August Ludwig von Schlözer
1160–1233	'Izz al-Dīn Ibn al-Athīr	1737–1794	Edward Gibbon
1178/9–1241	Snorri Sturluson	1738–1801	Zhang Xuecheng
fl.1185–1208	Saxo Grammaticus	1744–1803	J.G. Herder
c.1200–c.1259	Matthew Paris	1766–1826	N.M. Karamzin
d. 1236	Roger of Wendover	1770–1831	G.W.F. Hegel
1247–1318	Fazlallah Rashīd al-Dīn	1776–1831	B.G. Niebuhr

1874–1945	Ernst Cassirer	1892–1982	E.H. Carr
1874–1934	Alice Clark	1892–1968	Erwin Panofsky
1874–1959	Georges Lefebvre	1892–1986	Alfred Vagts
1874–1932	Albert Mathiez	1893–1980	Gu Jiegang
1875–1950	Carter G. Woodson	1893–1979	James C. Malin
1876–1958	Mary Ritter Beard	1893–1974	Piero Pieri
1876–1947	Wilhelm Levison	1893–1974	Pierre Renouvin
1876–1962	G.M. Trevelyan	1893–1984	Claudio Sánchez-Albornoz
1877–1960	Walter Bauer	1893–1969	Frank Tannenbaum
1877–1934	Ulrich Bonnell Phillips	1894–1952	Harold A. Innis
1878–1956	Lucien Febvre	1894–1956	Evariste Lévi-Provençal
1878–1960	J.S. Furnivall	1894–1970	Percy Ernst Schramm
1878–1967	Lionel Groulx	1895–1989	Salo Wittmayer Baron
1878–1945	Paul Pelliot	1895–1980	F.L. Ganshof
1878–1951	Heinrich von Srbik	1895–1963	Ernst H. Kantorowicz
1879–1968	C.E.W. Bean	1895–1988	Ernest Labrousse
1879–1952	Eli F. Heckscher	1895–1978	C.A. Macartney
1879–1951	R.W. Seton-Watson	1895–1990	Lewis Mumford
1880–1971	Lawrence Henry Gipson	1896–1961	Ludwig Fleck
1880–1936	Oswald Spengler	1896–1974	David Knowles
1880–1967	F.M. Stenton	1897–1996	Merle Curti
1880–1962	R.H. Tawney	1897–1965	T.F.T. Plucknett
1881–1969	Fernando Ortiz	1898–1982	Otto Brunner
1882–1952	Fritz Rörig	1898–1976	Daniel Cosío Villegas
1882–1965	Berthold L. Ullman	1898–1982	Ivy Pinchbeck
1883–1967	Fritz Hartung	1899–1981	M.M. Postan
1883–1945	Henri Maspero	1899–1986	Julia Cherry Spruill
1883–1962	Louis Massignon	1899–1981	Frances A. Yates
1883–1955	Gyula Szekfű	1900–1988	Hans Baron
1884–1976	Rudolf Bultmann	1900–1979	Herbert Butterfield
1884–1978	Etienne Gilson	1900–1987	Gilberto Freyre
1884–1956	George Sarton	1900–1980	S.D. Goitein
1885–1968	Helen Cam	1900–1962	Garrett Mattingly
1885–1972	Américo Castro	1900–1995	Joseph Needham
1885–1959	Ricardo Levene	1901–1971	John C. Beaglehole
1886–1944	Marc Bloch	1901–1960	Federico Chabod
1886–1964	Karl Polanyi	1901–1968	Alfred Cobban
1887–1966	Pieter Geyl	1901–1989	C.L.R. James
1887–1976	Samuel Eliot Morison	1901–1986	Raúl Prebisch
1887–1966	Franz Schnabel	1902–1985	Fernand Braudel
1887–1973	George Vernadsky	1902–1998	Henry Steele Commager
1888–1960	Lewis Namier	1902–1979	Donald Grant Creighton
1888–1967	Gerhard A. Ritter	1902–1994	Erik H. Erikson
1889–1959	G.D.H. Cole	1902–1982	S.B. de Holanda
1889–1943	R.G. Collingwood	1902–1933	Eckart Kehr
1889–1988	A.R.M. Lower	1902–1976	George Ostrogorsky
1889–1940	Eileen Power	1902–1983	Nikolaus Pevsner
1889–1943	Arthur Rosenberg	1902–1994	Karl Popper
1889–1975	Carl O. Sauer	1902–	Owsei Temkin
1889–1975	Arnold J. Toynbee	1903–1980	Jorge Basadre
1890–1988	Angie Debo	1903–	Steven Runciman
1890–1946	Ahmad Kasravi	1903–1989	Ronald Syme
1890–1966	M.F. Köprülü	1903–1962	Muhammad Yamin
1890–1971	Allan Nevins	1904–	C.R. Boxer
1890–1956	Frank Lawrence Owsley	1904–1966	Delio Cantimori
1890–1969	Chen Yinke	1904–1970	A.H.M. Jones
1891–1937	Antonio Gramsci	1904–	Jacob Katz
1891–1973	Oskar Halecki	1904–1997	Jürgen Kuczynski
1891–1989	Charles-André Julien	1904–1966	Niida Noboru
1891–1957	Henry E. Sigerist	1904–1988	Hans Rosenberg

1904–1983	P.A. Zaionchkovskii	1912–	R.W. Southern
1905(?)–1979	Ömer Lütfi Barkan	1912–	Kenneth M. Stampp
1905–1991	Felix Gilbert	1913–1993	Jerome Blum
1905–1993	Lewis Hanke	1913–	V.G. Kiernan
1905–1980	Merrill Jensen	1913–	Barrington Moore, Jr.
1905–	Paul Oskar Kristeller	1913–1987	José Honório Rodrigues
1905–1963	Perry Miller	1913–	Leften Stavros Stavrianos
1906–1987	C.R. Cheney	1914–1984	Philippe Ariès
1906–1995	Edmundo O'Gorman	1914–	Daniel J. Boorstin
1906–	Leon Radzinowicz	1914–	François Chevalier
1906–1986	Henry Nash Smith	1914–	Basil Davidson
1906–1990	A.J.P. Taylor	1914–1996	Maruyama Masao
1907–1967	Isaac Deutscher	1914–1982	Albert Soboul
1907–	Edith Ennen	1914–	Hugh Trevor-Roper
1907–1991	John K. Fairbank	1914–	Franco Venturi
1907–1989	Jacques Léon Godechot	1914–	Jean-Pierre Vernant
1907–1966	D.D. Kosambi	1914–1991	Charles H. Wilson
1907–1984	T.W. Moody	1915–1991	Manning Clark
1907–1993	Roland Mousnier	1915–	John Hope Franklin
1907–1996	Otsuka Hisao	1915–1989	Eric Goldman
1907–1990	Caio Prado Júnior	1915–1985	Mario Góngora
1907–	Samuel E. Thorne	1915–	H.J. Habakkuk
1907–1987	Lynn White, Jr.	1915–	Oscar Handlin
1908–1984	Geoffrey Barraclough	1915–1993	Albert Hourani
1908–	Fritz Fischer	1915–	Susanne Miller
1908–1987	Arnaldo Momigliano	1915–	Maxime Rodinson
1908–1980	W.L. Morton	1915–	Carl E. Schorske
1908–1984	Theodor Schieder	1916–	Owen Chadwick
1908–	C. Vann Woodward	1916–1993	Erik Fügedi
1909–1997	Isaiah Berlin	1916–	Rodney Hilton
1909–1991	Claude Cahen	1916–1970	Richard Hofstadter
1909–	David Daube	1916–	Halil Inalcık
1909–	Antonio Domínguez Ortiz	1916–	Charles P. Issawi
1909–1989	Wolfram Eberhard	1916–1988	Witold Kula
1909–	Eugenio Garin	1916–	Bernard Lewis
1909–	E.H. Gombrich	1916–	Edmund S. Morgan
1909–1996	Margaret A. Ormsby	1916–	W.W. Rostow
1909–	David B. Quinn	1916–1984	Hugh Seton-Watson
1909–1977	José Luis Romero	1916–	Leonard Thompson
1909–	W. Montgomery Watt	1917–1996	Richard Cobb
1910–1986	Werner Conze	1917–	W.J. Eccles
1910–	A.G. Dickens	1917–	E.J. Hobsbawm
1910–1994	Philip S. Foner	1917–	William H. McNeill
1910–1996	J.H. Hexter	1917–	Arthur M. Schlesinger, Jr.
1910–1986	Robert S. Lopez	1918–1990	Louis Althusser
1910–	Robert K. Merton	1918–	Alfred D. Chandler, Jr.
1910–1997	Léon Poliakov	1918–1977	Guy Frégault
1910–1971	David M. Potter	1918–1994	James Joll
1910–1993	George Rudé	1918–	George L. Mosse
1910–1983	Walter Ullmann	1918–	Dimitri Obolensky
1910–1997	C.V. Wedgwood	1918–1984	Maurice Séguin
1911–1979	Gino Germani	1919–	Raymond Carr
1911–1991	Louis Henry	1919–1996	Georges Duby
1911–1980	Marshall McLuhan	1919–1980	John Gallagher
1911–1986	José Antonio Maravall	1919–1986	Louis Hartz
1911–	J.H. Plumb	1919–	Lawrence Stone
1911–1981	Eric Williams	1919–	Peter F. Sugar
1912–	Woodrow Borah	1920–1985	Charles Gibson
1912–1986	M.I. Finley	1920–	Gerda Lerner
1912–	Christopher Hill	1920–1992	Karl Leyser

1920–	Arthur S. Link	1926–1989	Martin Broszat
1920–	Denis Mack Smith	1926–	Robert William Fogel
1920–	Manuel Moreno Fraginals	1926–1984	Michel Foucault
1920–1992	Edward Pessen	1926–	Clifford Geertz
1920–	Stanley J. Stein	1926–	Tulio Halperín-Donghi
1920–1983	Victor Turner	1926–	Raul Hilberg
1921–	Asa Briggs	1926–1977	Kathleen Hughes
1921–	Robert Ignatius Burns	1926–1992	Elie Kedourie
1921–	Carl N. Degler	1926–	Miguel León-Portilla
1921–1978	H.J. Dyos	1926–	Arno J. Mayer
1921–1994	G.R. Elton	1926–	Fernand Ouellet
1921–	Moshe Lewin	1926–	Giuliano Procacci
1921–	Francis Paul Prucha	1927–	David Brion Davis
1921–	Anne Firor Scott	1927–1997	François Furet
1921–1990	William Appleman Williams	1927–	Leszek Kołakowski
1921–1988	Raymond Williams	1927–	Lauro Martines
1922–	Bernard Bailyn	1927–	David Montgomery
1922–	Karl Dietrich Bracher	1928–	Natalie Zemon Davis
1922–	Randolph L. Braham	1928–1985	Herbert G. Gutman
1922–	Carlo M. Cipolla	1928–1982	Joan Kelly-Gadol
1922–	Philip D. Curtin	1928–	Hermann Weber
1922–	Pablo González Casanova	1928–	Hayden V. White
1922–	Ranajit Guha	1929–	Jacob F. Ade Ajayi
1922–1968	Marshall G.S. Hodgson	1929–1996	Renzo De Felice
1922–	Michael Howard	1929–	Jürgen Habermas
1922–	Charles Jelavich	1929–	Emmanuel Le Roy Ladurie
1922–1997	A.P. Kazhdan	1929–	Leon F. Litwack
1922–1996	Thomas S. Kuhn	1929–	Bethwell A. Ogot
1922–	William E. Leuchtenburg	1929–	Terence O. Ranger
1922–1993	Keith Sinclair	1929–1981	James R. Scobie
1922–	Joan Thirsk	1929–	Charles Tilly
1922–	Howard Zinn	1929–	Jan Vansina
1923–	Jean Delumeau	1930–	Geoffrey Blainey
1923–1985	Cheikh Anta Diop	1930–	Pierre Bourdieu
1923–	Peter Gay	1930–	J.H. Elliott
1923–	Sarvepalli Gopal	1930–	Eugene D. Genovese
1923–	Thomas P. Hughes	1930–	Hans Mommsen
1923–1995	Barbara Jelavich	1930–	Wolfgang J. Mommsen
1923	Reinhart Koselleck	1930–	Louise A. Tilly
1923–1983	F.S.L. Lyons	1930–	Immanuel Wallerstein
1923–	August Meier	1930–	Robert H. Wiebe
1923–	S.F.C. Milsom	c.1930s	Asunción Lavrin
1923–	Roland Oliver	c.1930s	Mona Ozouf
1923–	Richard Pipes	1931–	Fernando Henrique Cardoso
1923–	Marc Raeff	1931–	Alfred W. Crosby, Jr.
1924–	Aron Gurevich	1931–	Greg Dening
1924–	John D. Hargreaves	1931–	Jack P. Greene
1924–	David S. Landes	1931–	Winthrop D. Jordan
1924–	J.G.A. Pocock	1931–	Joseph Rothschild
1924–1987	Rosario Romeo	1931–	A.W.B. Simpson
1924–1993	E.P. Thompson	1931–	Romila Thapar
1925–	R.W. Davies	1931–	Hugh Thomas
1925–	Stanley Elkins	1931–	Hans-Ulrich Wehler
1925–1989	Andreas Hillgruber	1931–	E.A. Wrigley
1925–	Roy Medvedev	1932–	A. Adu Boahen
1925–1985	Franca Pieroni Bortolotti	1932–	Leonore Davidoff
1925–1988	Paolo Spriano	1932–	Gabriel Kolko
1925–	F.M.L. Thompson	1932–1994	Christopher Lasch
1925–	Eugen Weber	1933–	Walter LaFeber
1926–	Pierre Broué	1933–	Abdallah Laroui

1933–	Lawrence W. Levine	1939–	Lutz Niethammer
1933–	Ali A. Mazrui	1939–	Ronald Takaki
1933–	Gary B. Nash	1939–	Tsvetan Todorov
1933–	Keith Thomas	1940–	Averil Cameron
1933–	Michel Vovelle	1940–	Richard Maxwell Eaton
1933–	Alan Watson	1940–	Steven Feierman
1933–	Gordon S. Wood	1940–	Linda Gordon
1933–	Theodore Zeldin	1940–	Linda K. Kerber
1934–	K.N. Chaudhuri	1940–1990	Tim Mason
1934–	J.L. Heilbron	1940–	Quentin Skinner
1934–	John Keegan	1940–	Merritt Roe Smith
1934–1996	Raphael Samuel	c.1940s	Claudia Koonz
1935–	Peter Brown	1941–	James Axtell
1935–	Catherine Coquery-Vidrovitch	1941–	Alice Kessler-Harris
1935–	Edward W. Said	1941–	Jürgen Kocka
1936–	Stephen E. Ambrose	1941–	Michael R. Marrus
1936–	Benedict Anderson	1941–	Joan Wallach Scott
1936–	Emmanuel Ayankami Ayandele	1941–1998	R.W. Scribner
1936–	Alain Corbin	1941–	Donald Worster
1936–	Lothar Gall	1942–	Gisela Bock
1936–	David Levering Lewis	1942–	Gareth Stedman Jones
1936–	Shula Marks	1942–	Nell Irvin Painter
1936–	Carolyn Merchant	1942–	Alessandro Portelli
1936–	Charles E. Rosenberg	1942–1980	Walter Rodney
1936–	James C. Scott	1943–	Robert Brenner
1936–	Carroll Smith-Rosenberg	1943–	Jan de Vries
1936–	Jonathan D. Spence	1943–	Eric Foner
1937–	A.E. Afigbo	1943–	Paul E. Lovejoy
1937–	Martin Bernal	1943–	Alf Lüdtke
1937–	Peter Burke	1943–	Elaine Pagels
1937–	Conrad Russell	1943–	Geoffrey Parker
1937–	Bruce G. Trigger	1943–	Louis A. Pérez, Jr.
1938–	Perry Anderson	1943–	Sheila Rowbotham
1938–	Patricia Grimshaw	1945–	Roger Chartier
1938–	Karin Hausen	1945–	Nancy F. Cott
1938–	Morton J. Horwitz	1945–	Lynn Hunt
1938–	Olwen H. Hufton	1945–	Paul M. Kennedy
1938–	Laurel Thatcher Ulrich	1945–	David Rock
1939–	Robert Darnton	1945–	Simon Schama
1939–	Norman Davies	1945–	Judith R. Walkowitz
1939–	Carlo Ginzburg	1946–	Reynaldo Clemeña Ileto
1939–	Pierre Guichard	1947–	Darlene Clark Hine
1939–	John Iliffe	1949–	Marilyn Lake

M

Ma Huan *fl.* 1413–33

Chinese traveler, interpreter, and journalist

The diarist Ma Huan is remembered chiefly for his participation in one of the greatest but least heralded achievements of the Ming dynasty (1368–1644) – the launching of an unprecedentedly ambitious series of maritime expeditions between the years 1405 and 1433. The leader of these expeditions was the grand eunuch-admiral Zheng He. Ma Huan became attached to the voyages by imperial decree because of his reputed knowledge of Arabic and Persian languages. He accompanied Zheng He's fleet on three of its seven expeditions across the "Western Ocean" – the fourth, in 1413–15; the sixth, in 1421–22; and the seventh, in 1431–33.

The most impressive fact about the Ming naval expeditions was their astonishing scale. Zheng He's flotillas, each of which had more than 25,000 men, comprised the largest peaceful expeditions ever launched by the Chinese traditional empire. Over the course of the seven voyages, the immense Chinese ships (the largest of which perhaps approached 300 feet in length) landed at all the major territories of the Indian Ocean and even called at the Arabian ports of Hormuz and Jidda as well as at several ports along the northeastern coast of Africa, as far south as modern-day Kenya's Malindi.

Immediately upon his return from his first expedition in 1415, Ma Huan arranged the notes of his observations in the form of the book *Yingyai shenglan* (*Ying-yai sheng-lan: The Overall Survey of the Ocean's Shores*, 1433, 1970), to which he added much more material from his two subsequent expeditions. Ma Huan was probably at least 25 years old when he received his first assignment in 1413. Thus, when his book was finally published in 1451, Ma Huan, if still alive, was possibly 80 years old.

Ma Huan's is neither the only account of Zheng He's expeditions nor even the first. Earlier reports were assembled by his contemporaries Gong Zhen and Fei Xin, both of whom accompanied Ma Huan on the seventh and last expedition. But Ma Huan's account is by far the lengthiest – being twice as long as Fei Xin's – and the most thorough. It provides information drawn from visits to 21 "countries" under nearly as many separate headings. While his work, like those of his fellow authors, contains many mistakes and distortions, Ma Huan's observations are, by and large, offered in relative fairness and with the least degree of prejudice. We are also indebted to Ma Huan for furnishing us with logistical details of the expeditions that are to be found nowhere else. From his account alone, for instance, we learn that squadrons were specifically detached from main fleet of each expedition and dispatched on subsidiary voyages to prescribed sites.

Through its descriptions of foreign lands like Java, Malacca, the Nicobar, Maldive, and Laccadive islands, Sri Lanka, and the port of Mogadishu in Somalia, Ma Huan's *Overall Survey* not only affords us information about places and peoples never before visited or commented on by the Chinese but also not yet encountered by European travelers. However, the single most important explanation that is absent from Ma Huan's account (as well as those of all others) is why the expeditions were undertaken in the first place. Religion was clearly a personal impetus for both Zheng He and Ma Huan. As devout Muslims, both men naturally desired to make the meritorious pilgrimage to Mecca, though it is questionable whether either ever succeeded. One of the main responsibilities of the fleets – which were after all led by "treasure ships" – was to secure exotic objects, animals, spices, and other curiosities for the personal amusement of the Chinese throne. But it would hardly seem necessary to send missions of such grand size to accomplish this particular task. In short, the most plausible motivation for the expeditions seems to have been quasi-diplomatic and closely linked to Chinese notions of a hierarchical world order. The mobilization of such huge spectacles of seapower, sent to what were then so many unknown corners of the world, clearly enhanced the prestige of the Ming emperors Yongle (1403–24) and Xuande (1426–35) who were responsible for them. Yongle – who authorized the first six missions – was especially expansionist-minded and though the missions were expressly non-belligerent, one aim of such enormous displays of Chinese seapower was no doubt to awe the foreign monarchs visited, commit them to the reciprocal exchange of tribute gifts, and extract from them either real or nominal acknowledgments of the suzerainty of the Chinese emperor.

Despite its flaws, the value of Ma Huan's *Overall Survey* remains incontestable. Its misinformation and occasional flights into fantasy notwithstanding, Ma Huan's Chinese record supplies much reliable, firsthand data on customs and conditions prevailing among the peoples of southern Asia, the Arabian peninsula, and the eastern coastline of Africa some eighty years before the Portuguese observations attributed to Vasco da Gama. The great pity is perhaps that the early investigation of these unknown regions by Chinese explorers did not continue beyond a single generation. The remarkable Ming voyages were terminated because of their expense, their non-productivity, and the

743

consuming desire of the dominating literati class to undermine any achievements that glorified their perennial eunuch enemies. Thereafter, China's dynastic rulers never again launched ships for the purpose of promoting cultural exploration or interchange.

DON J. WYATT

Biography

Attached to Zheng He's imperial voyages, 1413–15; 1421–22; and 1431–33.

Principal Writings

Yingyai shenglan, written 1415–33, published 1451; in English as *Ying-yai sheng-lan: The Overall Survey of the Ocean's Shores, 1433*, 1970

Further Reading

Anderson, Mary M., *Hidden Power: The Palace Eunuchs of Imperial China*, Buffalo, NY: Prometheus, 1990

Levathes, Louise, *When China Ruled the Seas: The Treasure Fleet of the Dragon Throne, 1405-1433*, New York: Simon and Schuster, 1994

Mirsky, Jeannette, ed., *The Great Chinese Travelers*, New York: Pantheon, 1964; London: Allen and Unwin, 1965

Swanson, Bruce, *Eighth Voyage of the Dragon: A History of China's Quest for Seapower*, Annapolis, MD: Naval Institute Press, 1982

Wolf, Ken, *Personalities and Problems: Interpretive Essays in World Civilizations*, vol. 1, New York: McGraw-Hill, 1994

Mabillon, Jean 1632–1707

French document collector and critic

Soon after his ordination to the priesthood in the Benedictine order, Jean Mabillon was assigned to the order's house at Saint-Germain-des-Prés which boasted one of the best libraries in Europe, a circle of scholars which included Luc d'Achéry, Charles Du Fresne Du Cange, Thierry Ruinart, and others, as well as weekly gatherings of scholars and connoisseurs the likes of Bossuet and Colbert. Within three years he had completed the project of editing the complete works of Bernard of Clairvaux, an edition he would revise in 1690 and 1701 and which remained the standard until the middle of the 20th century. He also began assisting d'Achéry in a collection of the lives of saints of the Benedictine order for which he wrote brilliant prefaces and critical essays and which was published in nine volumes from 1668 to 1701. Forced to defend the excellent critical apparatus of the early volumes against attacks from within his order, Mabillon wrote a spirited defense of his historical methods and prevailed on his order to vindicate him. This exercise served him in good stead when the Bollandist Daniel Papebroch claimed that the Benedictine charters of St. Denis were not authentic. In response, Mabillon published in 1681 his *De re diplomatica* (The Science of Diplomatic), which, in elaborating and justifying a sounder set of methodological principles than Papebroch's for determining the date and authenticity of medieval manuscripts and charters, virtually created the discipline of diplomatics and the scientific study of Latin paleography. The book was a text for two centuries

and some of its principles remain key to the study of medieval paleography to this day. Marc Bloch called the year 1681 "a truly great one in the history of the human mind, for the criticism of documents of archives was definitely established." Mabillon contended that documents must be carefully scrutinized not merely for specific verbal formulae, as Papebroch was wont to do, but for general style, provenance, external and internal clues to age, orthography, etc. He presented a taxonomy of charters, discussions, and examples of different scripts, materials, formulae, seals, and an entire volume of chronologically arranged documents as exemplars. Papebroch conceded the superiority of Mabillon's scholarship.

This modest man was dogged by controversies that had the fortunate effect of eliciting from him distinguished contributions to the development of rigorous and sophisticated historical methods. When the Trappist reformer Armand de Rancé asserted that study played no essential part in monastic spirituality, Mabillon replied with his 1691 *Traité des études monastiques* (Treatise on Monastic Studies) that not only justified study as a mode of worship but prescribed a curriculum that included study of the documentary and traditional sources of theology as well as sacred and secular history. In another instance, controversy over a spurious relic led to his writing a 1698 dissertation on the cult of unknown saints, which explored the problems of authentication of the lives of saints and their relics.

These and other of Mabillon's considerable researches, such as his pioneer works in liturgical history, *De liturgia gallica* (On the Gallican Liturgy, 1685) and *Musaeum Italicum* (The Italian Library, 1687–89), and his *Annales ordinis sancti Benedicti* (Annals of the Benedictine Order), which he began publishing in 1703, were immeasurably improved by the three great journeys he undertook in search of manuscript resources: to Burgundy in 1682; Germany, Austria, and Switzerland in 1683; and to Italy in 1685–86. On the last of these, financed by the royal purse, he spent 6096 francs purchasing 2192 manuscripts and books to send back to France. Lesser bibliographical journeys took him at various times to Flanders, Alsace and Lorraine, Tours and Angers, and Champagne and Normandy. As a result, he achieved a breadth and depth of historical knowledge rare in his own, or indeed any, age.

Oblivious to his physical surroundings except when discomfort hindered his work, indifferent to the monuments of pagan antiquity, Mabillon was unexcelled in his knowledge of the 7th through 12th centuries, though uninformed about earlier and later ages. His contributions to textual criticism were crucial to the development of historical method.

JOSEPH M. MCCARTHY

See also Catholicism; France: to 1000; France: 1000–1450; Historiology; Knowles

Biography

Born Saint-Pierremont, 23 November 1632. Studied at Reims; master of arts, 1652. Entered the Order of Saint Benedict, 1654; ordained a priest, 1660. Assisted in editing the works of Bernard of Clairvaux and in collecting documents relative to saints of his order, organizing the search of manuscript depositories in western Europe. Admitted to the Royal Academy of Inscriptions, 1701. Died Saint-Germain-des-Prés, 27 December 1707.

Principal Writings

With Jean Luc d'Achéry, *Sancti Bernardi opera omnia* (Complete Works of St. Bernard), 1667; revised 1690, 1701

With Thierry Ruinart, *Acta sanctorum ordinis sancti Benedicti* (Acts of the Benedictine Saints), 9 vols., 1668–1701

Vetera analecta (Collections of Ancient Writings), 4 vols., 1675–78

De re diplomatica (The Science of Diplomatic), 1681

De liturgia gallica (On the Gallican Liturgy), 3 vols., 1685

Itinerarium Burgundicum, Itinerarium Germanicum (The Burgundian Journey, The German Journey), 1685

Musaeum Italicum (The Italian Library), 2 vols., 1687–89

Traité des études monastiques (Treatise on Monastic Studies), 1691

Eusebii Romani ad Theophilum Gallum Epistola de Cultu Sanctorum Ignotorum (The Letter of Eusebius the Roman to Theophilus the Gaul Concerning the Unknown Saints), 1698

With R. Massuet and Edmond Martène, *Annales ordinis sancti Benedicti* (Annals of the Benedictine Order), 6 vols., 1703–39

Ouvrages posthumes de D. Jean Mabillon et D. Thierry Ruinart (Posthumous Works of Mabillon and Ruinart), 3 vols., 1724

Further Reading

Aris, Rutherford, "Jean Mabillon (1632–1707)," in Helen Damico and Joseph B. Zavedil, eds., *Medieval Scholarship: Biographical Studies in the Formation of a Discipline*, New York: Garland, 1995

Barrett-Kriegel, Blandine, *Jean Mabillon*, Paris: Presses Universitaires de France, 1988

Bauckner, A., *Mabillons Reise durch Bayern im Jahre 1683* (Mabillon's Journey Through Bavaria in 1683), Munich: Wild, 1910

Baumer, Suitbert, *Johannes Mabillon: ein Lebens- und Literaturbild aus dem XVII. und XVIII. Jahrhundert* (Jean Mabillon: A Biographical and Literary Portrait from the 17th and 18th Centuries), Augsburg: Seitz, 1892

Bergkamp, Joseph U., *Dom Jean Mabillon and the Benedictine Historical School of Saint-Maur*, Washington, DC: Catholic University of America Press, 1928

Besse, Jean Martial Léon, *Les Etudes ecclésiastiques d'après la méthode de Mabillon* (Ecclesiastical Studies According to Mabillon's Method), Paris: Bloud et Barral, 1900

Broglie, Emmanuel de, *Mabillon et la société de l'abbaye de Saint-Germain-des-Prés à la fin du dix-septième siècle 1664–1707* (Mabillon and the Community of the Abbey of Saint-Germain-des-Prés at the End of the 17th Century, 1664–1707), 2 vols., Paris: Plon, 1888

Denis, Paul, *Trois dissertations de Dom Mabillon* (Three Essays on Mabillon), Vienne: Aubin, 1909

Denis, Paul, *Dom Mabillon et sa méthode historique* (Dom Mabillon and His Historical Method), Paris: Jouve, 1910

Deries, Léon, *Un moine et un savant: Dom Jean Mabillon, religieux bénédictin de la Congrégation de Saint-Maur (1632–1707)* (A Monk and a Scholar: Dom Jean Mabillon, Monk of the Congregation of Saint-Maur), Vienne: Abbaye Saint-Martin, 1932

Didiot, Henri, *La Querelle de Mabillon et de l'Abbé de Rancé* (The Dispute of Mabillon and the Abbé de Rancé), Amiens: Rousseau-Leroy, 1892

Heer, Gall, *Johannes Mabillon und die schweizer Benediktiner* (Jean Mabillon and the Swiss Benedictines), St. Gallen: Leobuchhandlung, 1938

Jadart, Henri, *Dom Jean Mabillon (1632–1707): étude suivie des documents inédits sur sa vie, ses oeuvres, sa mémoire* (Dom Jean Mabillon: A Study of His Life, His Works, and His Memory, Based on Some Unpublished Documents), Reims: Deligne et Renart, 1879

Knowles, David, "Jean Mabillon," in his *The Historian and Character*, Cambridge: Cambridge University Press, 1963

Knowles, David, "The Maurists," in his *Great Historical Enterprises*, London and New York: Nelson, 1963

Leclercq, Henri, "Mabillon," in *Dictionnaire d'archéologie chrétienne et de liturgie*, Paris: Letouzey, 1907–53

Leclercq, Henri, *Mabillon*, 2 vols., Paris: Letouzey et Ané, 1954–57

Mélanges et documents publiés à l'occasion du deuxième centenaire de la mort de Mabillon (Miscellanies and Documents Published on the Second Centenary of Mabillon's Death), Paris: Veuve Poussielique, 1908

Rosenmund, Richard, *Die Fortschritte der Diplomatik seit Mabillon* (The Development of Diplomatics since Mabillon), Munich: Oldenbourg, 1897

Ruinart, Thierry, *Abrégé de la vie de dom Jean Mabillon, prêtre et religieux bénédictin de la congrégation de Saint-Maur* (Summary of the Life of Jean Mabillon, Priest and Benedictine Monk of the Congregation of Saint-Maur), Paris: Muguet et Robustel, 1709

Valery, M., *Correspondance inédite de Mabillon et Montfaucon avec l'Italie* (Unpublished Correspondence of Mabillon and Montfaucon with Italy), 3 vols., Paris: Labitte, 1846–47

Macartney, C.A. 1895–1978

British historian of Eastern Europe

For most of the 20th century C.A. Macartney was the principal western historian of the Danube region at a time when the region was being racked with change. His interests ranged from the early medieval period to the Habsburg empire, and culminated in his engagement with the reshaping of Central and Eastern Europe in the post-Habsburg period. Macartney's interest sprang from his experiences during World War I, when he volunteered for service in the army and rejected a fellowship at Trinity College, Cambridge, from which he had recently received his degree. After the war his credentials resulted in his posting to Vienna as vice-consul, then to the League of Nations in Geneva. He began to write on the region before returning to academic life in 1936 as a research fellow at Oxford University. His expertise was also used by the Foreign Office during World War II.

Macartney's first book, *The Social Revolution in Austria* (1926), dealt with conditions in postwar Austria, and drew upon his considerable knowledge of the country. His next work, *The Magyars in the Ninth Century* (1930), focused its attention on the problem of the Magyars' migration in this crucial period of their history, using as its basis an analysis of Greek and Arabic sources in order to understand the peculiarities of the future Hungarian oligarchic political system, a theme that his *Hungary* (1934), continued to pursue. *Hungary and Her Successors* (1937) was a comprehensive analysis of the nationalities question in the region, and was a work in which Macartney supported the claims of the losers of the post-1918 settlements. He regarded the Treaty of Trianon, which had handed over nearly one third of Hungary's population to the successor states, as unfair, and advocated border revisions to redress the balance. His hungarophile attitude did not, however, cause him to lose sight of the wider problems of contemporary European security, a subject discussed in *Problems of the Danube Basin* (1942).

Macartney's 2-volume *October Fifteenth* (1961, 1st edition as *A History of Hungary, 1929–1945*) dealt with German-Hungarian relations in the 15 years leading to the thwarted attempt by the regent to end the alliance with Hitler. It contained illuminating portraits of the principal personalities and is regarded as the principal western language history of Hungarian politics in the 1930s. Macartney's *magnum opus* is perhaps also his best known work. *The Habsburg Empire, 1790–1918* (1968) is a comprehensive narrative account of the political and social history of the empire, although it has been criticized for focusing its attention upon the German and Hungarian elements that made up the population, at the expense of the Slavs. Despite this mild criticism, it is a huge achievement, and stands as a fitting monument to its author.

MICHAEL ALMOND-WELTON

See also Central Europe; Germany: 1450–1800; Seton-Watson, R.

Biography

Carlile Aylmer Macartney. Born in Kent, 24 January 1895. Educated at Winchester College; Trinity College, Cambridge. Served in the British Army, 1914–18. Acting British vice-consul, Vienna, 1921–25; staff member, *Encyclopaedia Britannica*, 1926–28; Intelligence Department, League of Nations Union, 1928–36; and Research Department, Foreign Office, 1939–46. Research fellow, All Souls College, Oxford, 1936–65; taught at Edinburgh University, 1951–57. Married Nedella Mamarchev. Died 18 June 1978.

Principal Writings

The Social Revolution in Austria, 1926
The Magyars in the Ninth Century, 1930
Refugees: The Work of the League, 1931
World Labour Problems, 5 vols., 1932–36
Hungary, 1934
National States and National Minorities, 1934
With Maurice Fanshawe, *What the League Has Done, 1920–1932*, 1936
Hungary and Her Successors: The Treaty of Trianon and Its Consequences, 1919–1937, 1937
Studies on the Earliest Hungarian Historical Sources, 3 vols., 1938–51
Problems of the Danube Basin, 1942
The Medieval Hungarian Historians: A Critical and Analytical Guide, 1953
A History of Hungary, 1929–1945, 2 vols., 1956–57; 2nd edition as *October Fifteenth: A History of Modern Hungary, 1929–1945*, 2 vols., 1961
Hungary: A Short History, 1962
Independent Eastern Europe: A History, 1962
The Habsburg Empire, 1790–1918, 1968; revised abridgement as *The House of Austria: The Later Phase, 1790–1918*, 1978
Maria Theresa and the House of Austria, 1969
Editor, *The Habsburg and Hohenzollern Dynasties in the Seventeenth and Eighteenth Centuries*, 1970

Macaulay, Thomas Babington 1800–1859

British historian

Thomas Babington Macaulay was born in 1800, the eldest child of Zachary Macaulay (1768–1838), of Scots Presbyterian descent, a leader of the Evangelical Clapham Sect and anti-slavery campaigner. An infant prodigy who wrote an epitome of a universal history, Macaulay went up to Trinity College, Cambridge in 1818, where he was converted from his family Toryism to Whiggery. His honors included a college prize essay on the hero of his later *History of England*, William III.

Macaulay was elected a fellow of Trinity in 1824, and became a barrister in 1826. His first great literary triumph was an article in 1825 on Milton in the Whig *Edinburgh Review*, in which he had already perfected his incomparable prose style, with its "Ciceronian antithesis and Augustan balance," stirring rhythms, surface glitter, and dogmatic tone. He attacked the Tories Robert Southey and John Wilson Croker in the *Edinburgh*, and as MP for Calne, made his famous speech in 1831 in defence of the First Reform Bill. In 1832 he was returned for Leeds, but then became a member of the Supreme Council of India from 1834, where he recommended an educational system based on English rather than Oriental studies, and drafted an Indian criminal code.

In 1839, Macaulay was elected MP for Edinburgh and became secretary at war in the Whig administration. In 1842 came the triumphant publication of his *Lays of Ancient Rome* and in 1843 the first official edition of his collected *Essays*. Like his battle poems "Ivry" and "The Battle of Naseby," the *Lays* drew on his immense classical erudition and his Italian journey of 1838–39 for their re-creation of Roman republican balladry, in vigorous, technically faultless verse. The essays, ostensibly book reviews, transcend the works that occasioned them: those on English themes are a major contribution to the study of 17th- and 18th-century history and literature, partly making up for the closure of the later *History of England* in 1702. They tend to a one-sided view of the English past: Protestants, Puritans, and Whigs were right, while Catholics, Cavaliers, Tories, and High Churchmen were wrong. Yet Macaulay had a tenderness for a good man on the wrong side. His romantic vision of social history was inspired by the High Tory Sir Walter Scott; his love of historic grandeur appears in the depiction of the Catholic church in his review of Ranke's *History of the Popes*, where his belief in progress disappears in the image of a future New Zealand Maori standing on a broken arch of London Bridge to sketch the ruins of St. Paul's.

Macaulay was defeated at the hustings in Edinburgh in 1847, and though Edinburgh returned him unopposed in 1852, his gradual withdrawal from politics enabled him to concentrate on his *The History of England from the Accession of James II*, which he conceived in 1838 as lying between the Whig achievements of the Glorious Revolution of 1688 and the Reform Bill of 1832. The first two volumes were published to great critical and popular acclaim in 1849. The first chapter of volume 1 surveys English history to 1660, the second deals with the reign of Charles II, and the third paints a famous social portrait of England in 1685. The narrative then slows to a snail's pace, and only reaches William III's death in 1702. Macaulay used the work of other Whig scholars: the forty volumes of papers transcribed from continental archives for Sir James Mackintosh and the French ambassador Barillon's despatches copied for Charles James Fox and loaned to him by his friend Lord Holland. Yet Macaulay's Whiggery was that of the militant middle, between radical and Tory, as the Church of England stood between Rome and Dissent, as the Marquess of Halifax "trimmed" between Whigs and Tories, and as William was (in the words of Macaulay's Trinity prize essay) "a sovereign, yet the champion of liberty; a revolutionary leader, yet the supporter of social order." The third and fourth volumes of the *History* appeared in 1855, the fifth posthumously in 1861, edited by Macaulay's sister Hannah, Lady Trevelyan.

Macaulay combined a robust Georgian rationalism with a Romantic imagination. His Whiggery was magnified by his biographer George Otto Trevelyan, who mangled his letters for literary convenience, but supplied a brilliant and indispensable picture of the man. His defect was stridency: he was too sure of everything. Charles Williams said that "His only real instrument was the trumpet; his only good colour was purple." Carlyle thought his style like living under Niagara; Lytton Strachey mocked its metallic exactness and its fatal efficiency as "one of the most remarkable products of the Industrial Revolution." G.P. Gooch called Macaulay "the greatest of party writers, not the greatest of historians." Like a caricaturist, he heightened the villainy of his villains, James II and John Churchill, and the heroism of his heroes like William III. His optimistic Victorian vision is no more, suggesting that his *History* has dated as badly as the Victorian prejudices that informed it. Herbert Butterfield's polemic against Whig historiography is a warning against such prejudices, and the attempts by Marxists and the school of Sir Lewis Namier to expel idealism from history are fatal to Macaulay's heroic conception of a humanity moved by principle as well as interest. On points such as his assault on the Quaker William Penn, he was wrong and impervious to criticism.

Yet he was too interested in the complexity of personality and in the cunning twists in his story to be a consistent partisan. His pioneering ventures into social history, as in his use of broadsides and street balladry, have borne an enormous fruit in our own time, while his universal humanity usually raises his writing above Whig confessionalism. In its literary brilliance, its panoramic sweep, its mastery of sources from state papers to penny pamphlets hitherto assumed to be beneath the dignity of Clio, it remains compulsively readable, and sets standards of clarity, accessibility, and narrative skill at which modern scholars can only wonder.

SHERIDAN GILLEY

See also Britain: 1066–1485; Europe: Modern; Gardiner; Literature; Niebuhr; Political; Popular; Trevelyan; Whig

Biography
Born Rothley Temple, Leicestershire, 25 October 1800. Educated privately; at Trinity College, Cambridge, BA 1822, MA 1825; fellow, 1824–31. Called to the Bar, 1826. Member of Parliament, 1830–34, 1839–47, 1852–56. Legal adviser to the Supreme Council of the East India Company, Calcutta, 1834–38. Created Baron Macaulay of Rothley, 1857. Died Kensington, 28 December 1859.

Principal Writings
Critical and Historical Essays Contributed to the Edinburgh Review, 1843
The History of England from the Accession of James II, 5 vols., 1849–61

Further Reading
Burrow, John Wyon, *A Liberal Descent: Victorian Historians and the English Past*, Cambridge and New York: Cambridge University Press, 1981
Clive, John, and Thomas Pinney, eds., *Thomas Babington Macaulay: Selected Writings*, Chicago and London: University of Chicago Press, 1972
Clive, John, *Macaulay: The Shaping of the Historian*, New York: Knopf, and London: Secker and Warburg, 1973
Edwards, Owen Dudley, *Macaulay*, London: Weidenfeld and Nicolson, and New York: St. Martin's Press, 1988
Firth, C.H., *A Commentary on Macaulay's History of England*, London: Macmillan, 1938
Gay, Peter, *Style in History*, New York: Basic Books, 1974; London: Cape, 1975
Gilley, Sheridan, "Macaulay as Historian," *The Australian Journal of Politics and History* 29 (1983), 328–43
Hamburger, Joseph, *Macaulay and the Whig Tradition*, Chicago: University of Chicago Press, 1976
Knowles, David, *Lord Macaulay, 1800–1859: A Lecture*, Cambridge: Cambridge University Press, 1960
Millgate, Jane, *Macaulay*, London and Boston: Routledge, 1973
Pinney, Thomas, ed., *The Letters of Thomas Babington Macaulay*, 6 vols., Cambridge: Cambridge University Press, 1974–81
Stunt, Timothy C.F., "Thomas Babington Macaulay and Frederick the Great," *Historical Journal* 23 (1980), 939–47
Trevelyan, George Otto, *The Life and Letters of Lord Macaulay*, 2 vols., New York: Harper, 1875; London: Longmans, 1876

Mach, Ernst 1838–1916
Austrian physicist

Ernst Mach, for whom Mach-bands and the measure of supersonic speed are named, was a noted physicist and philosopher. He also was interested in the history of physics. Mach was a positivist who restricted true science to the search for general laws through empirical experiments, and a phenomenalist, for whom observation only reflected the sensory experiences of scientists instead of absolute reality. As a result Mach believed scientists should simply describe and relate these experiences, and not speculate, pitting him against the dominance in physics of Newtonian mechanics and atomic theory, which were both based on theoretical deduction.

Mach studied the history of physics to understand how people acquired scientific concepts, and to convince others that the prominence of Newtonian physics was the result of contingency. He also took his role as teacher of physics uncommonly seriously, and worried that the prevailing method of introducing physics through logical abstractions repelled college students. He showed them how past scientists had grappled with a problem, in order to sustain their interest and spur their understanding, until they were ready to tackle abstractions. Most of his works were primarily intended for students. They were widely read at German-speaking universities from the 1880s to World War I, and also by the general public.

In his first major work, *Die Geschichte und die Wurzel des Satzes der Erhaltung der Arbeit* (1872; *History and Root of the Principle of the Conservation of Energy*, 1911), Mach disputed the contention of Hermann von Helmholtz and Rudolf Clausius that Rudolf Mayer's 1842 statement of the first thermodynamic law showed the deductive prowess of Newtonian physics, arguing that its general principle had been known since early times. The structure of his other works was similar: to show that a given principle, presented as new pinnacle of truth, had been known in some form much earlier, and that other theories about it had been made into paradigms through misreadings and chance, and later rejected not so much out of superior insight as from the same random factors that had elevated it. In *Die Mechanik in ihrer Entwickelung: historisch-kritisch dargestellt* (1883; *The Science of Mechanics*, 1911), Mach suggested that a close reading of Newton showed that he had believed in absolute reality much less than his followers claimed. As Mario Bunge and John Blackmore have noted, Mach had misread Newton. He also argued against the reification of mechanics and atomic theory in other fields of physics in *Die Principien der Wärmelehre* (1896; *Principles of the Theory of Heat*, 1986), *Die Prinzipien der physikalischen Optik* (finished in 1913, published in 1921; *Principles of Physical Optics*, 1926), and *Kultur und Mechanik* (Culture and Mechanics, 1915). More explicitly philosophical were *Beiträge zur Analyse der Empfindungen* (1886; *Contributions to the Analysis of the Sensations*, 1887), and *Erkenntnis und Irrtum* (1905; *Knowledge and Error*, 1976), which showed parallels to Buddhist thinking.

Though his works were styled "historical-critical," and despite his reputation as historian of science, Mach was not a historian. He always clearly stated that he wrote about contemporary physics. In *Theory of Heat* he stressed: "Although a great many sources have been used, one should not expect in this work the results of archival research. The focus is much more on the coherence and growth of thought than on interesting curiosities." Uninspired by the particulars of history of science or individual scientists, he did no work in archives, contributed little new material, and raised no debates among historians. He simply cited from scientific writings to narrate the transmission of ideas.

Yet Mach wrote at a time when historical influences on scientific knowledge were neglected by scientists, and he wrote well. As the physicist Selig Brodetsky declared in 1926, he had made reading the rise and fall of ideas "as fascinating as a romance." Albert Einstein stressed in 1916 how much his textbooks "had great influence on our generation of natural scientists." They fostered interest in physics among generations of students, and inspired physicists such as the French Pierre Duhem and the Japanese Ayao Kuwaki; both of whom became noted historians of science.

Mach applied his contemplative and undogmatic philosophy of science to life in general. He was an atheist, who denied the objective existence of human ego or immortal soul. His works, translated into English, Russian, and other languages, made him by 1900 a thinker of world reknown. His popularity waned after World War I, partly because his central assumption, that sensations were absolute, was found to be incorrect. His legacy was indirect, through his influence on thinkers as diverse as Sigmund Freud, William James, Sinhalese Buddhists, Bolshevik leaders such as Alexander Bogdanov, and Ludwig Wittgenstein.

Mach's writings helped speed the demise of Newtonian mechanics as the paradigm in physics, but his opposition to atomic theory delayed its acceptance in Central Europe. The acceptance of the theory served to undercut his influence as philosopher of science. But he raised awareness about the transiency of scientific knowledge, and popularized interest in the history of science at a time when little attention was paid to it. Though Mach was not a great academic historian, he was a great teacher of history. And in the past two decades the rise of postmodern distrust in the triumphalism of the materialist conception of Western science has revived interest, especially in Central Europe, in the gentle approach to knowledge of this Sudeten German scientist.

THOMAS REIMER

See also Duhem; Heilbron

Biography
Born Chirlitz-Turas, near Brno, Moravia (now in Czech Republic), 18 February 1838. Educated at home to age 14, attended high school briefly, then studied at University of Vienna, PhD in physics, 1860. Taught mechanics and physics, Vienna, 1860–64; professor of mathematics, University of Graz, 1864–67; professor of experimental physics, Charles University, Prague, 1867–95; professor of inductive philosophy, University of Vienna, from 1895: suffered a stroke, 1897, and retired 1901. Entered Austrian Parliament, 1901. Married Ludovica [Luise] Marussig, 1867 (4 sons, 1 daughter). Died Vaterstetten, near Haar, Germany, 19 February 1916.

Principal Writings
Die Geschichte und die Wurzel des Satzes der Erhaltung der Arbeit, 1872; in English as *History and Root of the Principle of the Conservation of Energy*, 1911
Die Mechanik in ihrer Entwickelung: historisch-kritisch dargestellt, 1883; in English as *The Science of Mechanics: A Critical and Historical Account of Its Development*, 1911
Beiträge zur Analyse der Empfindungen, 1886; in English as *Contributions to the Analysis of the Sensations*, 1887
Die Principien der Wärmelehre, 1896; in English as *Principles of the Theory of Heat: Historically and Critically Elucidated*, 1986
Erkenntnis und Irrtum: Skizzen zur Psychologie der Forschung, 1905; in English as *Knowledge and Error: Sketches on the Psychology of Enquiry*, 1976
Kultur und Mechanik (Culture and Mechanics), 1915
Die Prinzipien der physikalischen Optik: historisch und erkenntnispsychologisch entwickelt, 1921; in English as *The Principles of Physical Optics: An Historical and Philosophical Treatment*, 1926

Further Reading
Blackmore, John T., *Ernst Mach: His Work, Life, and Influence*, Berkeley: University of California Press, 1972
Blackmore, John T., ed., *Ernst Mach – A Deeper Look: Documents and Perspectives*, Dordrecht and Boston: Kluwer, 1992
Bunge, Mario, "Mach's Critique of Newtonian Mechanics," *American Journal of Physics* 34 (1966), 585–96
Cohen, Robert S., and Raymond Seeger, eds., *Ernst Mach: Physicist and Philosopher*, Dordrecht: Reidel, 1970
Gamptier, P., "Mach and Freud: A Comparision" *Zeitgeschichte* 17 (1990), 291–330
Haller, Rudolf, and Friedrich Stadler, eds., *Ernst Mach: Werk und Wirkung*, Vienna: Holder Pichler Tempsky, 1988
Hiebert, Erwin N., "Ernst Mach," *Dictionary of Scientific Biography*, New York: Scribner, 1970–80, vol. 8, 595–607
Hiebert, Erwin N., "The Influence of Mach's Thought on Science," *Philosophia Naturalis* 21 (1984), 598–615
Hoffmann, Dieter, and Hubert Laitko, eds., *Ernst Mach: Studien und Dokumente zu Leben und Werk*, Berlin: Deutscher Verlag der Wissenschaften, 1991
Mayerhoefer, Josef, "Ernst Mach as a Professor of the History of Science," *Proceedings of the 10th International Congress of the History of Sciences*, vol. 2, 337–339
Thiele, Joachim, *Wissenschaftliche Kommunikation: Die Korrespondenz Ernst Machs* (Scientific Communication: The Correspondence of Ernst Mach), Kastellaun: Henn, 1978

Thornton, Russell, "'Imagine Yourself Set Down . . .': Mach, Frazer, Conrad, Malinowski and the Role of Imagination in Ethnology," *Anthropology Today* 1 (October 1985), 7–14

Zahar, Elie, "Mach, Einstein, and the Rise of Modern Science," *British Journal for the Philosophy of Science* 28 (1977), 195–213

Machiavelli, Niccolò 1469–1527

Florentine humanist historian

By the end of August 1520 Niccolò Machiavelli had finished his brief biography of Castruccio Castracani, written over a few weeks in free moments on an embassy to Lucca. Reminiscent of Plutarch, it consciously echoed Diodorus Siculus and Diogenes Laertius. Machiavelli essentially rewrote in classical guise one main source, *Castruccio Castracani vita* by the Luccese jurist Niccolò Tegrimi (first printed in 1496), and culled information from Villani's *Chronicle*, incorporating sentiments borrowed from Livy and from the *Cyropaedia* (*On the Education of Cyrus*) of Xenophon in Jacopo Poggio's Latin translation. The theme selected was innocuous in terms of both the Medici and Florence, and Machiavelli's purpose in composing the work had been to furnish testimony of his potential as a historian; sending it to friends of influence in Florence he declared it to be "a model for history." Two months later he achieved his objective in becoming official historiographer of Florence. He took his consequent *Istorie fiorentine* (*The History of Florence*), which ended with the death of Lorenzo de' Medici in 1492, to Pope Clement VII (Giulio de' Medici) in Rome, presenting it probably early in June 1525. Yet 40 years ago Ferdinand Schevill in his *Six Historians*, one of whom was Machiavelli, paradoxically opened the relevant chapter with "Machiavelli was not a historian," explaining that "what he offers as history is largely free invention, lacking a solid indispensable substructure of tested events." It is a mistake to judge Machiavelli's history against a present-day definition; rather, Schevill should have considered his work in the context of what was deemed history in the Italian Renaissance. To his contemporaries Machiavelli was a historian.

Moreover, there is a caveat in making an assessment of Machiavelli's writings. Within a few years of his death there had come into being the pejorative adjective "machiavellian," meaning expediency before Christian morality, duplicity rather than keeping faith, principles associated with his *Il principe* (*The Prince*), his best-known work, infamous since its printing in 1532. It had been written in two bursts between 1513 and 1516, the year Machiavelli presented it to Lorenzo de' Medici. From the early 1530s Machiavelli's name was generally held in abhorrence in his native city of Florence, particularly because of the writings of Giovanni Battista Busini, who believed *The Prince* to be the inspiration for Alessandro de' Medici's tyranny as duke of Florence. For 500 years polemic regarding Machiavelli's writings has been to the fore, and his writings themselves seldom been examined as an entity or in context. Schevill's comments are symptomatic of that polemical tradition.

Recognized today as Machiavelli's most profound historical study is his *Discorsi sopra la prima Deca di Tito Livio* (1512–18; *The Discourses on Livy*). The thrust of the argument is that Rome was greatest when a republic with a citizen army, and hence republican government was to be preferred. This appeared in sharp contrast to the supposed teaching of *The Prince*, which overlapped work on *The Discourses*. From what follows it will be suggested that there was no such contradiction. Fifteenth-century Italian humanists looked to the classical world for models, and acknowledged the preeminence of Livy and Sallust as historians. These historians were seen as detached from the events described, as excelling in eloquence, in clarity, and in style; Caesar, though held in esteem, was flawed as a historian since he was personally involved in the circumstances narrated. From the age of 17, if not earlier, Machiavelli had available a printed text of Livy, and when in 1503 he wrote his report "On the Method of Dealing with the Rebels of the Val di Chiana," he quoted from Livy a passage *in extenso*. The initial version of his *Discourses* can be dated to between 1512 and 1518, when it was essentially a commentary on all Livy's known *Decades*, and not just on the first as the published title of 1531 implies. There was emphasis on what may be termed Machiavelli's laws of social science, a feature he was elaborating when he died; the published text represents an unfinished work. It reveals, in conformity with his other mature writing, that rather than accepting the traditional classical and humanistic cyclic view of history, Machiavelli had come to adopt an evolutionary one: primitive society, which comprised tribes each under a leader or king, evolved to the zenith of civilization as exemplified in the Italian city-state. In terms of government the process of development was from princely rule to republican. Once this final stage was reached any attempt to revert to the earlier mode of rule brought the society's disintegration in its wake. Drawing on Livy and his knowledge of Florentine history, Machiavelli believed he could identify the factors that produced the evolutionary process, what stimulated it and what could retard it. The root cause of incessant strife on the Italian peninsula Machiavelli believed to be factional rivalry. In the shorter term this helped to perpetuate princely rule, as a prince promoted faction so as to remain in power – in other words "divide and rule"; but in the longer term the consequence was civil war and the creation of republican rule. All in all *The Discourses* was an embryonic Arnold J. Toynbee's *A Study of History*.

Humanists in Machiavelli's day divided histories into two categories, which they considered had existed in antiquity. First there was the raw material that gave details of historical events, such as annals or chronicles; second, there was true history like that of Livy and Sallust, which through interpretation furnished a guide for living. In the period now called the "Middle Ages," the former had proliferated and tended to be ignored by humanists concerned with true history. The humanists, in taking Livy and Sallust as models for their own historical writings, thought that they had returned to a true history. Machiavelli's *The Prince* was intended as a guide to teach a prince how to retard the process of a state's inevitable evolution to a republic. This could be done only if the prince ruled as a "civil" prince in the best interest of most of his subjects; a tyrant would accelerate the evolution. This was entirely the opposite of what Busini and his followers read into the work. Viewed in this light there was no conflict between *The Prince* and the conclusions advanced in *The Discourses*.

CECIL H. CLOUGH

See also Baron, H.; Burke; Chabod; De Sanctis; Ecclesiastical; Gilbert; Italy: Renaissance; Pieri; Pocock; Renaissance Historical Writing; Skinner; Villari

Biography
Born Florence, 3 May 1469. Began learning Latin aged 7 and arithmetic aged 11; aged 12 was preparing Latin compositions with the Florentine teacher Paolo da Ronciglione; this and his subsequent training was to prepare him for the profession of Florentine notary, like his father; he never learned Greek. In 1498 designated second chancellor of the Florentine Republic established in 1494: secretary and envoy to states of the Italian peninsula and beyond; following the return of the Medici to power in Florence in September 1512 was dismissed from his post early in November, confined to the Florentine state, and excluded from the Palazzo della Signoria in Florence; in February 1513, accused (almost certainly unjustly) of involvement in an anti-Medicean plot, he was imprisoned and tortured; in March after a heavy fine he was released, thereafter devoting himself to writing; by 1520 he had sufficiently ingratiated himself with the Medici to become historiographer of Florence; subsequently he undertook for the Medici various administrative tasks including a mission to Carpi and the supervision of a survey of Florence's fortifications. Married Marietta Corsini, 1501 (5 children). Died Florence, 21 June 1527.

Principal Writings
Discorsi sopra la prima Deca di Tito Livio, 1512–18; printed 1531; in English as *The Discourses on Livy*, 1636
Il principe, written 1513–16, printed 1532; in English as *The Prince*, 1640
Dell'arte della guerra, 1519, printed 1521; in English as *The Art of War*, 1560
Istorie fiorentine, 1520–25, printed 1532; as *Florentine History*, 1595, and *The History of Florence*, 1675
Machiavelli and His Friends: Their Personal Correspondence, edited by James B. Atkinson and David Sices, 1996

Further Reading
Anselmi, Gian Mario, *Ricerche sul Machiavelli storico* (Studies on Machiavelli the Historian), Pisa: Pacini, 1979
Clough, Cecil H., *Machiavelli Researches*, Naples: Università degli studi, Istituto universitario orientale, 1967
Clough, Cecil H., "Niccolò Machiavelli's Political Assumptions and Objectives," *Bulletin of the John Rylands Library* 53 (1970), 30–74
Clough, Cecil H., "Father Walker's Presentation and Translation of Machiavelli's *Discourses* in Perspective," in Niccolò Machiavelli, *The Discourses*, 2 vols., London: Routledge, 1975
Cochrane, Eric, *Historians and Historiography in the Italian Renaissance*, Chicago: University of Chicago Press, 1981
Fryde, Edmund B., *Humanism and Renaissance Historiography*, London: Hambledon Press, 1983
Gilbert, Allan H., "Machiavelli on Firepower," *Italica* 23 (1946), 275–85
Gilbert, Felix, "Machiavelli: The Renaissance Art of War," in Edward M. Earle, ed., *Makers of Modern Strategy: Military Thought from Machiavelli to Hitler*, Princeton: Princeton University Press, 1941
Gilbert, Felix, *Machiavelli and Guicciardini: Politics and History in Sixteenth-Century Florence*, Princeton: Princeton University Press, 1965
Marietti, Marina, "Machiavel historiographe des Médicis" (Machiavelli, Historian to the Medici), in André Rochon, ed., *Les Ecrivains et le pouvoir en Italie à l'époque de la Renaissance*, Paris: Université de la Sorbonne Nouvelle, 1974
Reynolds, Beatrice, "Shifting Currents in Historical Criticism," in Paul Oskar Kristeller and Philip P. Weiner, eds., *Renaissance Essays*, New York: Harper, 1968
Whitfield, John H., "Machiavelli and Castruccio," in his *Discourses on Machiavelli*, Cambridge, MA: Heffer, 1969
Wilcox, Donald J., *The Development of Florentine Humanist Historiography in the Fifteenth Century*, Cambridge, MA: Harvard University Press, 1969

Mack Smith, Denis 1920–
British historian of modern Italy

Denis Mack Smith's formidable reputation among modern Italian historians was established with the publication of his first book, *Cavour and Garibaldi, 1860* in 1954. As a number of reviewers remarked at the time, the history of Italy's Risorgimento was never to be the same again. In *Cavour and Garibaldi*, Mack Smith used a combination of official documents and private papers in a meticulous reconstruction of the political events surrounding Italian unification in 1860. The book is designed, in Mack Smith's words, "as a study in revolutionary politics during a civil war." His choice of words is not accidental. Hitherto, Italian unification had been seen as a complex jigsaw where every piece fitted together. On the basis of the evidence used in *Cavour and Garibaldi*, Mack Smith demonstrates that the unification of Italy was in fact the accidental outcome of bitter conflict. In other ways too, he alters the established orthodoxy of many generations. Cavour – once the supreme example of a hard-headed, practical politician – emerges from Mack Smith's study as wily, impulsive, and often unrealistic in his aims. Garibaldi – the epitome of a romantic, impractical hero – comes out as a leader of good sense with limited ambitions. "With brilliant, though well-founded, perversity," A.J.P. Taylor remarked, "Mr. Mack Smith turns things upside down."

English historians had been taught by Trevelyan to admire the achievements of Italian liberalism and to enthuse about the exploits of its heroes. In *Cavour and Garibaldi*, Mack Smith was writing for this readership. However, as he admitted in a new preface written for the second edition, the book's "biggest impact was in Italy." Before *Cavour and Garibaldi* was published in Italy, Mack Smith had published a study of the Sicilian peasantry which emphasized the role of the peasantry in the 1860 revolution and detailed their final betrayal at the hands of the revolutionaries. Apparently unwittingly, Mack Smith had stepped into a major historical (and political) controversy raging in Italy. His critical approach to Cavour and to the conflicts of 1860 was welcomed by a new generation of left-wing historians in Italy. Mack Smith's work appeared to endorse a view of the Risorgimento as a "failed revolution." This same approach earned Mack Smith the lasting enmity of some prominent liberal historians, notably Rosario Romeo.

In many respects, both the arguments and the public reception of *Cavour and Garibaldi* set the tone for Mack Smith's whole career. The controversy caused in Italy by his first book became nothing less than a furore with *Italy: A Modern History* (1959), and this continued with *Mussolini's Roman Empire* (1976), *Mussolini* (1981), and *Italy and Its Monarchy* (1989).

It is not difficult to see why Mack Smith's approach so often offends. Like his heroes, Garibaldi and Mazzini, Mack Smith has steadfastly refused to conform to current orthodoxies or to accept established narratives. In *Victor Emanuel, Cavour and the Risorgimento* (1971) and again in *Italy and Its Monarchy*, Mack Smith quotes the Italian prime minister, Giovanni Giolitti, that "beautiful historical legends" should not be "discredited by historical criticism." From *Cavour and Garibaldi* to his recent book *Mazzini* (1994), Mack Smith has set out to undermine this view of history and to prove the value of a critical approach based on documentary research. "There is no necessary reason" he writes in *Victor Emanuel, Cavour and the Risorgimento*, "why truth should be beautiful or simple."

At its best, as in *Cavour and Garibaldi*, Mack Smith's critical approach produces brilliant and thought-provoking history. His books can also be a delight to read. As Davis and Ginsborg have written, Mack Smith has the rare talent "of writing original, serious, and scrupulously researched history which none the less remains accessible and attractive to the non-specialist." If the truth in Mack Smith's work is seldom beautiful or simple, the same cannot be said for the quality of his prose.

At times, however, Mack Smith's insistence on unravelling the nationalist myths of Italian historiography has tended to overwhelm his scholarship. His critical approach can become merely a patronizing one. In *Italy: A Modern History*, Mack Smith's analysis is heavily weighted towards proving the link between the Risorgimento and fascism; this focus obscures a much more complex reality. Similarly, his *A History of Sicily* (1968) concentrates overwhelmingly on what Raymond Grew calls Sicily's "frustrated modernization" and its uninterrupted decline. His judgments of Italian political leaders in *Cavour* (1985) and *Italy and Its Monarchy* are, even to the hardened cynic, unduly harsh. Thus, his criticisms of Italian national myths become on occasion inseparable from criticisms of Italians themselves.

Mack Smith belongs to the generation of postwar Cambridge historians, based largely at Peterhouse, who were taught to respect the primacy of documentary evidence. The influence of a Whig concept of history is also apparent in Mack Smith's attempts to explain what went "wrong" with the Risorgimento and to discover the roots of Italy's (or Sicily's) economic "backwardness." This kind of history is currently very unfashionable. Neither of Mack Smith's recent biographies, of Cavour and Mazzini respectively, nor his study of the Italian monarchy, have been particularly well received. Yet, there is in the best of Mack Smith's writing a passionate edge and an acute sense of the convolutions of history which take it beyond its immediate subject matter. Like his predecessor Trevelyan, Mack Smith conveys in his writing the excitement of Italian history. It is this, at least in part, that continues to inspire successive generations of historians to study modern Italy. And it is in this, as well as in his personal commitment to historical research and unfailing courtesy to the views of other historians, that Mack Smith's importance as a historian should be judged.

LUCY RIALL

See also Italy: since the Renaissance

Biography

Born 3 March 1920. Educated at St. Paul's Cathedral Choir School; Haileybury College; Peterhouse, Cambridge, MA. Assistant master, Clifton College, 1941–42. Posted to cabinet offices, 1942–46. Fellow of Peterhouse, Cambridge, 1947–62, tutor, 1948–58; university lecturer, Cambridge, 1952–62; fellow, All Souls College, Oxford, 1962–87 (emeritus). Married Catharine Stevenson, 1963 (2 daughters).

Principal Writings

"Cavour's Attitude to Garibaldi's Expedition to Sicily," *Cambridge Historical Journal* 9 (1949), 359–70
"The Peasants' Revolt in Sicily, 1860," *Studi in onore di Gino Luzzato*, 1950; reprinted in *Victor Emanuel, Cavour and the Risorgimento*, 1971
Cavour and Garibaldi, 1860: A Study in Political Conflict, 1954
Garibaldi, 1957
Italy: A Modern History, 1959; revised 1969
"The Latifundia in Modern Sicilian History," *Proceedings of the British Academy* 51 (1965), 85–124
A History of Sicily, vols. 2–3, 1968
The Making of Italy, 1796–1870, 1968
Victor Emanuel, Cavour and the Risorgimento, 1971
"Benedetto Croce: History and Politics," *Journal of Contemporary History* 8 (1973), 41–61
Mussolini's Roman Empire, 1976
Storia di cento anni di vita italiana visti attraverso il "Corriere della Sera" (One Hundred Years of Life seen by the *Corriere della Sera*), 1978
Mussolini, 1981
Cavour, 1985
Italy and Its Monarchy, 1989
Mazzini, 1994
Modern Italy: A Political History, 1997

Further Reading

Bosworth, Richard J.B., "Denis Mack Smith and the Third Italy," *International History Review* 12 (1990), 782–92
Davis, John A., and Paul Ginsborg, eds., *Society and Politics in the Age of the Risorgimento: Essays in Honour of Denis Mack Smith*, Cambridge: Cambridge University Press, 1991
Graw, Raymond, "A History of Sicily" *American Historical Review* 75 (1970), 536–38 [review]
Taylor, A.J.P., "Cavour and Garibaldi," in his *From Napoleon to the Second International: Essays on Nineteenth-Century Europe*, edited by Chris Wrigley, London: Hamish Hamilton, 1993; New York: Allen Lane, 1994

McLuhan, Marshall 1911–1980

Canadian communications theorist

Almost two decades after his death, the work of Marshall McLuhan is currently enjoying a resurgence. This Canadian academic achieved instant international recognition as the media sage of the "swinging" sixties. The coiner of the concept of "the global village," McLuhan was regarded as a communications guru and his name became irrevocably linked with such catch phrases as "the medium is the message." His work has acquired new relevance in our own electronic age, where so many of his predictions concerning the development and power of mass communications appear to have come true.

He is best known as an analyst of the role of media in modern society, and those casually aware of McLuhan's work may wonder if he warrants a place in a collection devoted to the study of historians. However, a reading of any of his major works will clearly establish that McLuhan's studies of the role of communications in contemporary society developed from a profound historical sensibility, and one that was also distinctively Canadian.

Starting from the perspective of literary analysis, McLuhan's early writings followed the predictable path of a literary critic attempting to understand and interpret the cultural climate of past and present societies. *The Mechanical Bride* (1951) may be seen as McLuhan's first systematic attempt to interpret what Dennis Duffy has called "the dissociated world produced by the disjunction between intellect and emotion," and although it seems to progress naturally from his earlier studies, this work may be seen also as the first step in the evolution of McLuhan's technique of media analysis which would emerge, fully developed, during the 1960s with *Explorations in Communication* (1960), *The Gutenberg Galaxy* (1962), and *Understanding Media* (1964).

It is not coincidental that McLuhan's *Mechanical Bride* appeared one year after *Empire and Communications* (1950) and during the same year as *The Bias of Communication* (1951), two late works by the Canadian historian, Harold Adams Innis (1894–1952). Innis' early writings had explored the significance of the fur and cod trades to Canada's development and had documented the history of the Canadian Pacific Railway. From the descriptive, narrative history of the role of economic staples in Canada's development, the later Innis moved to the consideration of systems of communication as equally significant forces in the history of the development of western civilization. He became convinced that analysis of communications media provided the most valuable insight into understanding societies of the past and also those of the present. It was this interpretive key that McLuhan was to develop as an essential part of his own efforts to probe the mysteries of cultural meaning.

In two brief essays, McLuhan clearly delineated the links that are implicit throughout his major writings. In a 1953 article entitled "The Later Innis" and, a decade later, in the introduction to a new edition of Innis' *The Bias of Communication*, McLuhan identified the shaping of his own approach to history. "Flattered by the attention that Innis had directed to some work of mine," he observed in the introduction, "I turned for the first time to his work." Generous in his praise of what he found, McLuhan declared that "I am pleased to think of my own book *The Gutenberg Galaxy* as a footnote to the observations of Innis on the subject of the psychic and social consequences, first of writing and then of printing."

There were many elements in the work of Innis that resonated for the younger scholar: both were attempting to achieve what Bertrand Russell had called "a change in our imaginative picture of the world." Believing an insight to be "the sudden awareness of a complex process of interaction," McLuhan had no higher praise than to view Innis as "above all a recognizer of patterns" using history "as a scientific laboratory, as a set of controlled conditions within which to study the life and nature of forms," with "the bias of culture and communication as an instrument of research." Even Innis' writing style was to find echoes in McLuhan's work; in his later books, McLuhan observed in 1953, Innis abandoned "the linear development of paragraph perspectives," in favor of "the rapid montage of single shots." This was a technique that McLuhan himself was increasingly to favor.

As it was for the later Innis, McLuhan's notion of historical periodization, even his concept of history itself, was defined by shifts – he called them "explosions" – in communications media. The phonetic alphabet gave rise to the concept of Euclidian space, the Roman empire sprung from the ability to employ the alphabet on light papyrus, rather than heavy clay or stone, and Gutenberg's introduction of moveable type to the West in the 15th century heated up the medium of writing "to repeatable print intensity" which, in turn, "led to nationalism and the religious wars of the 16th century." This aspect of his work has been criticized as technological determinism and, because of its inevitable simplifications and "mosaic" approach, even dismissed by one critic, Sidney Finkelstein, as a "bizarre substitution of fiction for history."

It may be said that McLuhan's writing combined the historical analysis of Innis with the investigative techniques of the literary critics I.A. Richards and William Empson, for McLuhan noted that the importance of language as the greatest medium of communication and the most significant barometer of change had eluded Innis. In answer to those who caviled at inaccuracies in his periodizations, McLuhan claimed that he was constructing "probes," mechanisms for investigating ambiguity. He infuriated his critics by insisting that he had no "point of view"; he became himself, as he had described Innis, "a roving mental eye, an intellectual radar screen on the alert for objective clues to the inner spirit or core of our time" ("The Later Innis"). Always impish and irreverent, he resisted categorization. A reincarnated McLuhan, upon finding himself canonized as the patron saint of the new information age, would certainly question his old answers or, more probably, would immediately begin the search for new questions.

KATHLEEN E. GARAY

See also Media

Biography
Herbert Marshall McLuhan. Born Edmonton, Alberta, 21 July 1911. Studied at University of Manitoba, BA 1932, MA 1934; Trinity Hall, Cambridge, BA 1936, MA 1939, PhD 1942. Taught at University of Wisconsin, 1936–37; St. Louis University, 1937–44; Assumption College, Windsor, Ontario, 1944–46; and St. Michael's College, University of Toronto, 1946–80; director, Centre for Culture and Technology, 1963–80. Married Corinne Keller Lewis, 1939 (2 sons, 4 daughters). Died Toronto, 31 December 1980.

Principal Writings
The Mechanical Bride: Folklore of Industrial Man, 1951
"The Later Innis," *Queen's Quarterly* (Autumn 1953), 365–94
Editor with Edmund Carpenter, *Explorations in Communication: An Anthology*, 1960
The Gutenberg Galaxy: The Making of Typographic Man, 1962
Introduction, in *The Bias of Communication* by Harold A. Innis, 1964
Understanding Media: The Extensions of Man, 1964
Essential McLuhan, edited by Eric McLuhan and Frank Zingrone, 1995

Further Reading
Curtis, James M., "McLuhan: The Aesthete as Historian," *Journal of Communication* 31 (1981), 144–52
Duffy, Dennis, *Marshall McLuhan*, Toronto: McClelland and Stewart, 1969

Finkelstein, Sidney, *Sense and Nonsense of McLuhan*, New York: International, 1968

Gordon, W. Terrence, *Marshall McLuhan: Escape into Understanding*, New York: Basic Books, 1997

Gordon, W. Terrence, *Marshall McLuhan for Beginners*, New York: Writers and Readers, 1997

Stamps, Judith, *Unthinking Modernity*, Montreal: McGill-Queens University Press, 1994

McNeill, William H. 1917–

US (Canadian-born) world historian

William H. McNeill's greatest contribution to the historical field has been his promotion of world history. Influenced by Arnold Toynbee's *A Study of History* (1934) and Oswald Spengler's *The Decline of the West* (1918) in their sweeping ecumenical views of history, but not subscribing to their notions of internal cycles of civilization, McNeill presented the development of civilizations as a series of interactions. As McNeill wrote in *Mythistory and Other Essays* (1986), he proposed to turn Spengler and Toynbee on their heads, for both of them had asserted that separate civilizations borrowed nothing of importance from one another. This proposal led to his classic *The Rise of the West* (1963), where he affirmed the idea of a progressive, secular history of the human community, as opposed to the cyclical and religious views put forward by Spengler and Toynbee respectively, and where he suggested that the current Western predominance in the world is the result of the process of entire world history. McNeill's concentration on encounters as the driving force of civilizations and ultimately history, has led him to concentrate on frontier areas, particularly in the Eurasian realm. In *The Rise of the West*, he identified the center of highest skill in a given age, and the cultural flow outwards from it, correspondingly demonstrating the importance of communications and transportation on historical development. In McNeill's words, "the history of civilization is a history of the expansion of particularly attractive cultural and social patterns through the conversion of barbarians to modes of life they found superior to their own." An underlying Darwinianism pervaded his analyses.

With *The Rise of the West* as a foundation, McNeill in his later works explored individual topics and their associated international phenomena, constituting, in his own words, extended footnotes to *The Rise of the West*. His interest in broad trends in historical development was clear in *The Pursuit of Power* (1982) where he examined the influence of warfare as a catalyst for industrial development. With *Plagues and Peoples* (1976), McNeill introduced an ecological dimension to world history, in which he brought out the interrelation of separate disease pools, population die-offs, and socioeconomic relationships. In *Plagues and Peoples*, for example, McNeill pointed to the direct relationship between the rise of various religions and population die-offs.

McNeill's research was influenced by both anthropological method, emphasizing the role of diffusion – the adoption from other societies of technologies, skills, customs, and social arrangements perceived as useful or empowering – and by Marc Bloch and the Annales school with its emphasis on long-term trends.

McNeill's passion for world history came from a conviction that the enormous problems the world confronted could be lessened with the promotion of a global consciousness. This promotion, he felt, should be the moral duty of the historical profession, which had, in any case, been seeking purpose since the demise of Whig history after World War I. McNeill felt that historians necessarily wrote of the past in a way that provided an intellectual basis for the present. By writing a broad, meaningful interpretation of the past, historians would contribute to the view of the unity of humanity and give history-writing a clear *raison d'être*.

Because McNeill points to the importance of the unconscious processes that cross both political and temporal boundaries, he has not been without his detractors. Arguments against McNeill's conception of history point to his generalizations as unscientific, and far removed from the historicist roots of modern historiography. His seeming contempt for the close scrutiny of documents and detailed studies comes under criticism in this regard. McNeill would counter that all historians select their facts differently, and therefore all history is generalization. His emphasis on underlying trends has also been criticized as downplaying the role of the individual in history. Lastly, McNeill's views have been criticized for their apparent ethnocentrism, as his approach seems to suggest that Western society is the cumulative product of history.

GARY S. BRUCE

See also Curtin; Environmental; European Expansion; Migration; Military; World

Biography

William Hardy McNeill. Born Vancouver, Canada, 31 October 1917. Received BA, University of Chicago, 1938, MA 1939; PhD, Cornell University, 1947. Taught at University of Chicago, 1947–87 (emeritus). Took US citizenship. Married Elizabeth Darbishire, 1946 (2 sons, 2 daughters).

Principal Writings

The Greek Dilemma: War and Aftermath, 1947

America, Britain, and Russia: Their Co-operation and Conflict, 1941–1946, 1953

Past and Future, 1954

Greece: American Aid in Action, 1947–1956, 1957

The Rise of the West: A History of the Human Community, 1963

Europe's Steppe Frontier, 1500–1800, 1964

A World History, 1967

Editor/compiler with others, *Readings in World History*, 10 vols., 1968–73

The Shape of European History, 1974

Venice: The Hinge of Europe, 1081–1797, 1974

Plagues and Peoples, 1976

Editor with Ruth S. Adams, *Human Migration: Patterns and Policies*, 1978

The Metamorphosis of Greece since World War II, 1978

The Pursuit of Power: Technology, Armed Force, and Society since AD 1000, 1982

The Great Frontier: Freedom and Hierarchy in Modern Times, 1983

Mythistory and Other Essays, 1986

Polyethnicity and National Unity in World History, 1986

Arnold J. Toynbee: A Life, 1989

Population and Politics since 1750, 1990

"The Rise of the West after Twenty-Five Years," *Journal of World History* 1 (1990), 1–22

Hutchins' University: A Memoir of the University of Chicago,
   1929–1950, 1991
Keeping Together in Time: Dance and Drill in Human History,
   1995

Further Reading

Adelson, Roger, "Interview with William McNeill," *Historian* 53
   (1990), 1–16
Costello, Paul, "William McNeill's Ecological Mythistory: Toward
   an Ambiguous Future," *Historical Reflections* 18 (1992), 99–119
McDougall, Walter, "Mais ce n'est pas l'histoire! Some Thoughts on
   Toynbee, McNeill, and the Rest of Us," *Journal of Modern
   History* 58 (1986), 19–42
Roland, Alex, "Technology and War: The Historiographical
   Revolution of the 1980s," *Technology and Culture* 34 (1993),
   117–34
"William H. McNeill: Bibliography," *Journal of Modern History* 58
   (1986), 3–18

Mahan, Alfred Thayer 1840–1914

US naval historian

Alfred Thayer Mahan's reputation as the most famous naval historian of the late 19th and early 20th centuries rests on two major works: *The Influence of Sea Power upon History, 1660–1783* (1890) and *The Influence of Sea Power upon the French Revolution and Empire, 1793–1812* (1892). All told, Mahan wrote 20 books and 137 articles.

The major thrust of Mahan's works was that naval superiority and shipping are instrumental in determining the power and wealth of nations. This idea, however, did not originate with him; naval strategists such as Rear Admiral John Rodgers and Robert Schufeldt had already propagated these ideas long before Mahan. Mahan's great contribution was his ability to analyze systematically naval history and to define clearly what he saw as its lessons. As he himself put it in *The Influence of Sea Power upon History*, his object was to estimate "the effect of sea power upon the course of history and the prosperity of nations."

Mahan emerged from the relative obscurity of a naval career to become one of the best known historians of his era. After first attending Columbia College in New York City, he enrolled at the US Naval Academy in Annapolis, Maryland, against the advice of his father, Dennis Hart Mahan, a professor of civil and military engineering at the US Military Academy in West Point, New York. Despite his father's reservations, the younger Mahan excelled at Annapolis and graduated second in his class in 1859.

Following his graduation from Annapolis, Mahan rose through the naval ranks, eventually becoming Lieutenant Commander. His naval service in the US Civil War was unexceptional. However, due to his high rank, the 26-year-old Mahan decided, despite reservations, to remain in the navy where he served in navy shipyards, on the Naval Academy staff, and on cruises to the Asiatic Station and to the west coast of South America. It was while commanding the steam sloop *USS Wachusett* off the coast of Peru that Mahan received an invitation from his old friend Commodore Stephen B. Luce to join the faculty of the newly founded Naval War College.

Mahan's only major qualification for this position was his short book, *The Gulf and Inland Waters* (1883), a Civil War naval history, which he had recently completed. Mahan accepted Luce's offer, and, after some delay, reported to Newport, Rhode Island, for duty in the summer of 1886. When he arrived at the Naval War College, Mahan, now a newly promoted Captain, found to his dismay that Luce had been ordered back to sea. It therefore fell to Mahan to lecture on strategy and naval history and to assume the presidency of the Naval War College. This was the turning point in his career.

Mahan served two terms as president of the Naval War College (1886–89 and 1892–93) and during his first term, he organized his lectures into book form which resulted in the publication of *The Influence of Sea Power upon History, 1660–1783*. In 1893, Mahan was ordered to take command of the *USS Chicago* and, on his arrival in the English port of Southampton in late July of that year, was hailed as a hero by the British for his praise of British sea power and the British navy.

Mahan's work was controversial in its day. His critics claimed that he was reactionary and impractical while his supporters touted the virtues of his theory that control of the seas was the key to empire. At the beginning, Mahan himself claimed to be an anti-imperialist, but he argued for the construction of an Isthmian canal in Panama and for use of the Hawaiian Islands as a refueling station for US ships. Later historians have found great fault with Mahan's analysis of sea power, a term that Mahan invented, mostly on the basis of oversimplification by omission. These critics claimed that Mahan's theories do not account for the rise of such nonmaritime empires as Austria-Hungary, Germany, Russia and Turkey. Mahan has also been criticized for failing to emphasize the interrelationship between naval and land operations, especially amphibious warfare. Particularly glaring was Mahan's omission of the years 1784–93 in his histories.

Despite their flaws, the profound impact of Mahan's writings on the study of naval history has been compared by the historian Louis M. Hacker to the effect of Darwin's *The Origin of Species* on 19th-century scientific study. In Mahan's own day, the London *Times* compared his work to the revolution "effected by Copernicus in the domain of astronomy."

GREGORY WEEKS

See also Military; Naval

Biography

Born West Point, New York, 27 September 1840, to a military family. Graduated US Naval Academy, 1859; served as naval officer, 1859–86; naval instructor and president, Naval War College, 1889–96. Retired from navy to write and to serve as governmental naval adviser. Married Ellen Lyle Evans, 1872 (2 daughters, 1 son). Died Washington, DC, 1 December 1914.

Principal Writings

The Gulf and Inland Waters, 1883
The Influence of Sea Power upon History, 1660–1783, 1890
Admiral Farragut, 1892
*The Influence of Sea Power upon the French Revolution and
   Empire, 1793–1812,* 2 vols., 1892
The Interest of America in Sea Power, Present and Future, 1897
*The Life of Nelson: The Enlightenment of the Sea Power of Great
   Britain,* 2 vols., 1897

Lessons of the War with Spain, and Other Articles, 1899

The Problem of Asia and Its Effects upon International Policies, 1900

The Story of War in South Africa, 1899–1900, 1900

Retrospect and Prospect: Studies in International Relations, Naval and Political, 1902

Sea Power in Its Relations to the War of 1812, 2 vols., 1905

From Sail to Steam: Recollections of Naval Life, 1907

Naval Administration and Warfare, 1908

The Harvest Within: Thoughts and Life of a Christian, 1909

Naval Strategy: Compared and Contrasted with the Principles and Practice of Military Operations on Land, 1911

Armaments and Arbitration; or, The Place of Force in the International Relations of States, 1912

The Major Operations of the Navies in the War of American Independence, 1913

Further Reading

Pratt, Julius, "Alfred Thayer Mahan," in William T. Hutchinson, ed., *The Marcus W. Jernegan Essays in American Historiography*, Chicago: University of Chicago Press, 1937

Puleston, William D., *Mahan: The Life and Work of Captain Alfred Thayer Mahan, USN*, New Haven: Yale University Press, and London: Cape, 1939

Seager, Robert II, and Doris D. Maguire, eds., *Letters and Papers of Alfred Thayer Mahan*, 3 vols., Annapolis, MD: Naval Institute Press, 1975

Seager, Robert II, *Alfred Thayer Mahan: The Man and His Letters*, Annapolis, MD: Naval Institute Press, 1977

Taylor, Charles Carlisle, *The Life of Alfred Thayer Mahan, Naval Philosopher*, New York: Doran, and London: Murray, 1920

Maitland, F.W. 1850–1906

British medievalist

F.W. Maitland was one of the generation of late 19th-century historians following William Stubbs, whose work dominated English medieval history and focused it on constitutional issues for much of the 20th century. Eight years as a practicing lawyer gave him a different perspective and methodology from his contemporaries. He set the standard for professional historical scholarship through his careful study of legal records and shrewd identification of major themes. Maitland worked mainly on the 12th and 13th centuries: his view of the age of Henry II as that of the development of the Common Law, and the 13th century as the age of its codification, has been challenged in detail, but not in outline.

At Cambridge Henry Sidgwick, a student of John Stuart Mill, was an influential teacher. Maitland shared their liberal intellectual outlook and support for women's education. Like many educated people of his generation, his Protestant upbringing gave way to agnostic anticlericalism. He was a friend of Leslie Stephen, editor of the *Dictionary of National Biography* and father of Virginia Woolf. Maitland's wife Florence was a relative of Stephen and sister of H.A.L. Fisher the historian. Marital happiness sustained him through the chronic ill-health of his adult life. In 1885 he became reader in English law at Cambridge through Sidgwick's patronage, and in 1888 professor.

The wealth of documents in the Public Record Office was as yet little explored, and Maitland shared the general enthusiasm for its systematic ordering and publication. Unlike Stubbs whom he greatly admired, or his contemporaries, he did not construct a grand narrative of the past: instead he traced the development of governmental institutions through close analysis of legal terminology. In *The History of English Law* (1895), published with Frederick Pollock, who wrote only one chapter on Anglo-Saxon law, Maitland refused to go beyond the reign of Edward I, because subsequent records had been insufficiently digested. However, his belief that the Angevin laws of the 12th and 13th centuries had a simplicity distorted by later medieval developments reflected the contemporary romantic notion that the high Middle Ages was followed by inevitable decline. *The History of English Law* represents his most lasting achievement, particularly his clear explanation of the complexity of land law and of the writ, the legal form that governed the availability of remedies for wrongs at Common Law. Maitland provided the groundwork on which others built, notably S.F.C. Milsom, also lawyer turned historian, and H.G. Richardson and G.O. Sayles in their history of Parliament.

His lawyer's tendency to argue his case from a narrow base of evidence led to flaws in other works. In *Domesday Book and Beyond* (1897) Maitland followed Round's theory that it was a geld, or tax book, a theory subsequently overturned by V.H. Galbraith, who saw it as a more wide-ranging enquiry. Maitland's methodological innovation, however, was to use the Domesday Book to shed light on the "beyond," or on the pre-conquest period. In *Township and Borough* (1898), another pioneering work, he underestimated the role of trade in the development of pre-conquest towns, focusing instead on the "garrison theory," and in *Roman Canon Law in the Church of England* (1898) his anticlericalism led him to overemphasize conflict between church and crown.

Maitland was fascinated by the shadowy figure of Henry de Bracton, a judge on King's Bench and supposed author of a 13th-century legal treatise. He associated other documents with this text, including *Bracton's Note Book* which he published in 1897. The evidence was later reworked by Samuel Thorne, who found that the case-materials contained in it were collected not by one man but over a number of generations. In his last years Maitland was preoccupied by the yearbooks recording legal precedents from the reign of Edward I. He overestimated their significance but his work identified them as student compilations made from notes taken in court. He edited three volumes of this material from Edward II's reign.

Maitland's most widely-read book, *The Constitutional History of England* (1908), was published posthumously from lecture notes and reprinted many times. His influence resulted from the clarity and breadth of his scholarship. His comparative knowledge of French and German law was considerable and he translated Otto Gierke's *Political Theories of the Middle Age* (1900). His only research student was the distinguished scholar Mary Bateson, whose early death three weeks before his own deeply affected him. Despite ill-health, in 22 years of academic activity he published many works. He was a founder of the Selden Society, dedicated to the publication of legal records, and his valuable introductions to these volumes, as well as his main writings, have been of lasting significance.

VIRGINIA R. BAINBRIDGE

See also Agrarian; Britain: 1066–1485; Cam; Legal; Milsom; State

Biography

Frederic William Maitland. Born London, 28 May 1850. Educated at Eton College; Trinity College, Cambridge, BA 1873, MA 1876. Barrister, Lincoln's Inn, 1876–84; reader in English law, Cambridge University, 1885–88, professor, 1888–1906. Married Florence Henrietta Fisher, 1886 (2 daughters). Died Las Palmas, Canary Islands, 19 December 1906.

Principal Writings

With Frederick Pollock, *The History of English Law before the Time of Edward I*, 2 vols., 1895; revised 1898

Editor, *Bracton's Note Book: A Collection of Cases Decided in the King's Courts during the Reign of Henry the Third*, 3 vols., 1897

Domesday Book and Beyond: Three Essays in the Early History of England, 1897

Roman Canon Law in the Church of England: Six Essays, 1898

Township and Borough, 1898

Translator, *Political Theories of the Middle Age*, by Otto Gierke, 1900

The Constitutional History of England, edited by H.A.L. Fisher, 1908

The Collected Papers of Frederic William Maitland, edited by H.A.L. Fisher, 3 vols., 1911

Further Reading

Bell, Henry Esmond, *Maitland: A Critical Examination and Assessment*, London: A. & C. Black, and Cambridge, MA: Harvard University Press, 1965

Cameron, James Reese, *Frederic William Maitland and the History of English Law*, Norman: University of Oklahoma Press, 1961

Elton, G.R., *F.W. Maitland*, London: Weidenfeld and Nicolson, and New Haven: Yale University Press, 1985

Fifoot, Cecil Herbert Stuart, and P.N.R. Zutshi, eds., *The Letters of Frederic William Maitland*, 2 vols., London: Selden Society, 1965–95

Fifoot, Cecil Herbert Stuart, *Frederic William Maitland: A Life*, Cambridge, MA: Harvard University Press, 1971

Hudson, John, ed., *The History of English Law: Centenary Essays on "Pollock and Maitland,"* Oxford and New York: Oxford University Press, 1996

Milsom, S.F.C., *F.W. Maitland*, Oxford: Oxford University Press, 1982

Malay Annals (Sejarah Melayu)

The *Malay Annals*, known in the Malay world as the *Sejarah Melayu* or the *Sululatus Salatin*, was called "the most famous, distinctive and best of all Malay literary works" by Sir Richard Winstedt, one of the most prominent scholars to study this work in detail during the last hundred years. Though Winstedt's assessment of the value of the work represents the personal view of a Western scholar, its popularity and widespread distribution in various forms throughout the Malay world indicates that Malays have held it in similar esteem since its original composition.

There is some debate regarding both the identity of the original author of the *Malay Annals*, as well as its date of composition. Western philologists have used critical techniques in attempting to identify the oldest form of the text and to develop a theory for the stages in compilation of the *Malay Annals* as it currently exists. In this endeavor, the almost thirty extant manuscripts have been consulted, as have the various printed editions which have appeared since the first version was published by Abdullah Munshi around 1931. Nevertheless, there is still no critical edition of the text.

The core of the *Malay Annals* purports to record the history of the Malay Sultanate of Malacca from the time of its establishment in the late 14th century to its fall to the Portuguese in 1511. Later versions also include historical accounts relating to other Malay kingdoms, including Johor and Siak, which postdated that of Malacca. As such, the *Malay Annals* represents a composite work in terms of both authorship and contents. Indeed, Roolvink has argued that the work was originally conceived as a list of the kings of Malacca. With the subsequent insertion of narrative sections, the *Malay Annals* developed into both a short and long version, and these came to form the basis of the various manuscript and printed editions in current circulation.

The value of the work as a historical document has been debated at some length by both Western and Asian scholars. Western scholarship has tended to regard it as an idealized account of events in the medieval Malay world, rather than as a product of critical historiography as it is understood in the West. Detailed studies, such as that by Walls, have argued that the *Malay Annals* represented more a didactic tool for imparting behavioral principles (the need for rulers to be just and subjects to be loyal) rather than serving primarily to record objectively a series of historical events. Walls shows that the authors used the work to demonstrate the lesson that disaster (such as the fall of Malacca to the Portuguese) results directly from ignoring the balance between reciprocal loyalty (of subjects) and justice (of rulers). The validity of these principles is established by reference to Islamic scripture; thus, Malay history, tradition, and Islam are seen as completely complementary in this framework. In this context the work's approach to history would be seen to be interpretive; the authors of the *Malay Annals* fine-tuned historical records in order to serve moral, ethical, and religious purposes.

The Asian view of the work as a record of historical events tends towards diversity. Certain scholars such as Umar Junus argue that the *Malay Annals* presents a more reliable historical account than many of its literary contemporaries, such as the various *hikayat*, while still stopping short of claiming that its primary function is to record and present historical events. In contrast, school history curricula in Malaysia have at times accepted the work uncritically as a factual account of events as they occurred in Malacca during the 14th century. Attention has been refocused on the work in recent years in Asia, and new editions have been produced by Asian scholars (A.S. Ahmad 1979) to supersede the earlier Western studies by Shellabear (1898) and Winstedt (1938) and to re-establish Southeast Asia as the center of expertise on this important work. Thus the work is increasingly coming to assume a role in Malay identity formation and nation building.

Nevertheless, regardless of whether events are related in the work with absolute accuracy, there is little doubt that the *Malay Annals* provides a valuable window onto life in the Malay Kingdoms of Malacca and Johor during the 15th century and subsequently. Malacca is depicted as a multicultural, thriving trading entrepôt, with contacts with China, India, and other regions in Southeast Asia. Islamic scholars are shown to visit from other parts of the Muslim world, and Sufi beliefs and practices appear to have been firmly established in the community depicted in the work. The work also demonstrates that Malay literary classics broadly contemporaneous with the *Malay Annals* were popular in Malacca, including Muslim works imported from other regions, such as the *Story of Muhammad Hanafiyyah* and the *Bustanus Salatin* (Garden of Kings). The work is also important in contributing to our understanding about the spread of Islam to Southeast Asia. It suggests that Islam was already established in the region prior to the conversion of Malacca's rulers. Moreover, the *Malay Annals* provides an insight into popular belief about the impetus for conversion, in portraying Malacca's rulers choosing to convert in response to the appearance of the prophet Muhammad in dreams. Thus, the *Malay Annals* serves as an important testament to community life in the medieval Malay world, although its reliability as a record of specific historical events and personalities is open to question.

PETER G. RIDDELL

See also Yamin

Further Reading

Ahmad, A.S., *Sulalatus Salatin (Sejarah Melayu)*, Kuala Lumpur: Dewan Bahasa dan Pustaka, 1979

Blagden, C.O., "An Unpublished Variant of the Malay Annals," *Journal of the Malayan Branch of the Royal Asiatic Society* 3 (1925), 10–52

Brown, C.C., "Sejarah Melayu or Malay Annals: A Translation of Raffles MS 18," *Journal of the Malayan Branch of the Royal Asiatic Society* 25 (1952)

The Certificate History of Malaya, 1400–1965, Kuala Lumpur: Preston, 1971

Gibson-Hill, C.A., "The Malay Annals: The history brought from Goa," *Journal of the Malayan Branch of the Royal Asiatic Society*, 29 (1956), 185–88

Hooykaas, Christiaan, *Perintis Sastera* (Guide to Literature), Jakarta: Wolters, 1953

Iskandar, Teuku, "Three Malay Historical Writings in the First Half of the 17th Century," *Journal of the Malay Branch of the Royal Asiatic Society* 40 (1967), 38–53

Josselin de Jong, P.E. de, "The Character of the Malay Annals," in John Bastin, and Roelof Roolvink, eds., *Malayan and Indonesian Studies*, Oxford: Clarendon Press, 1964

Junus, Umar, *Sejarah Melayu: Menemukan Diri Kembali* (The Malay Annals: Rediscovering Itself), Kuala Lumpur: Fajar Bakti, 1984

Kamaruzzaman Shariff, "Sejarah Melayu as a Historical Source," *Journal of the Historical Society* 2 (1963–64), 41–50

Linehan, W., "Notes on the Text of the Malay Annals," *Journal of the Malayan Branch of the Royal Asiatic Society* 20 (1947), 107–16

Roolvink, Roelof, "The Variant Versions of the Malay Annals," *Bijdragen tot de Taal-, Land- en Volkenkunde* 123 (1967), 301–24

Shellabear, William Girdlestone, ed., *Sejarah Melayu, or the Malay Annals*, Singapore: American Mission Press, 1898

Situmorang, T.D., and A. Teeuw, *Sejarah Melayu menurut terbitan Abdullah (ibn Abdulkadir Munsji)* (The Malay Annals According to the Edition of Abdullah ibn Abdulkadir Munsji), Jakarta and Amsterdam: Djambatan, 1952

Sweeney, P.L. Amin, "The Connection between the Hikayat Raja Pasai and the Sejarah Melayu," *Journal of the Malayan Branch of the Royal Asiatic Society* 40 (1967), 94–105

Walls, Charles Bartlett, *Legacy of the Fathers: Testamentary Admonitions and the Thematic Structure of the Sejarah Melayu*, Ann Arbor, MI: Xerox University Microfilms, 1974

Winstedt, Richard O., "The *Malay Annals* or *Sejarah Melayu*: The Earliest Recension from MS No. 18 of the Raffles Collection, in the Library of the Royal Asiatic Society, London," *Journal of the Malayan Branch of the Royal Asiatic Society* 16 (1938)

Winstedt, Richard O., *A History of Classical Malay Literature*, Kuala Lumpur: Oxford University Press, 1969

Malin, James C. 1893–1979

US environmental historian

University of Kansas historian James C. Malin was one of the most prolific historians of his generation, publishing more than 15 books and 80 journal articles. Writing from the 1920s through the 1970s, he was a pioneer in the methodology and theory of local history, environmental history, demographic studies, and interdisciplinary research. Malin applied knowledge of plant and animal ecology, climatology, geology, geography, soil science, and anthropology to his historical studies thirty years before the modern subfield of environmental history caught up. He focused his research and writing exclusively on the Great Plains, and stands with Frederick Jackson Turner and Walter Prescott Webb as the third member of a triumvirate whose explanations have shaped our understanding of grassland history.

Malin was at his best analyzing human adaptation to the prairie. In *Winter Wheat in the Golden Belt of Kansas* (1944), he presented the themes that underlay most of his work. Malin described an evolution of agricultural land use in the decades after initial settlement of the Great Plains. Farmers first attempted to replicate the crops and land management of the forested eastern US from which they had come. Because of much lower rainfall in Kansas, crops like corn failed repeatedly. Farmers experimented with various alternatives, eventually selecting soft spring wheat, and then hard winter wheat. As time went by they gave up their illusions of recreating eastern farms and adapted their planting to a new geographical setting.

In spite of this emphasis on adjustment to environment, Malin was vehement in his dislike of determinism. He criticized Walter Prescott Webb's monumental *The Great Plains* (1931) as too rigid in attributing all human adjustments to climate. Malin, asserting the theory of possibilism, argued that while geography might limit human choices, it did not determine unique historical outcomes. People always have latitude for choice, he felt, and within any given environment may take many different paths. This "open space" approach meant that adaptation was indeterminate and never-ending. Human cultures do not simply adjust until they reach some ultimate and final life-way, but go on forever changing along with their world.

During the 1940s Malin wrote his most important books. They describe folk innovation as an attempt to adjust to low rainfall grassland environments in a context of open-ended possibilities. *Essays on Historiography* (1946), *The Grassland of North America* (1947), and *Grassland Historical Studies* (1950) form a trilogy which remain essential reading for grassland historians.

The methods Malin employed to tease out the history of common farmers were truly original. He relied primarily on small local newspapers from the 19th century, manuscript census schedules of population and agriculture, and minutes of agricultural societies. He discovered that farmers discussed crop varieties, pest problems, farm machinery, and many other land management concerns in the pages of their village newspapers and at regular agricultural society meetings. Malin employed historical demographic techniques to link individual families in the population census to their farm records in the agricultural census, then traced those families – at five- or ten-year intervals – through consecutive censuses. In this way he recreated a web of individuals one township at a time, and was able to outline agricultural change, demographic turnover, and community evolution. He relied on these demographic studies to launch an attack on Frederick Jackson Turner's frontier thesis, demonstrating that immigration to new frontiers did not follow the progression Turner had predicted.

In many ways Malin was ahead of his time. His interest in the lives of obscure farm families predated the 1960s historical reorientation toward a "new social history." His use of scientific literature to connect past generations to the physical world around them anticipated precisely, in both method and theory, environmental history written since the late 1970s. Yet today Malin is little known to students of the American past.

His obscurity stems from several quirks of character. Malin was a biting critic of many accepted historical doctrines. He openly indicted ideas and scholars he disagreed with. Beyond that, he was unwilling to work with publishers. Early in his career Malin decided that editors should not tell him how to write his books, and proceeded to publish the remainder of his work privately. These books tended to be too long, and their typescript text has an unfinished feel. What is more, Malin's corpus was not as widely distributed as it might have been by a regular press. Finally, Malin was a political maverick. At the height of his career he was at odds with Franklin Roosevelt's New Deal, and openly attacked its policies in his writing. He especially disliked the brain trust's application of what he considered fallacious history. According to Malin, New Dealers used inaccurate Turnerian "closed space" ideas to defend a replacement of farming on the Dust Bowl-ridden plains with "better adapted" ranching. Malin's crotchety personality, the disadvantage of self-publication, and the taint of political bias all have conspired to obscure what are in fact solid historical contributions.

Still, James Malin is not forgotten. Historians of agriculture have recalled his influence from time to time, most recently in *History and Ecology: Studies of the Grassland* (1984), an anthology of Malin's most important articles edited by Robert P. Swierenga. Environmental historians also pay Malin his due. Richard White followed the Kansan's methodological lead in his acclaimed *Land Use, Environment, and Social Change: The Shaping of Island County, Washington* (1980). No one has so far superseded Malin's analysis of America's vast grassland interior.

GEOFF CUNFER

See also Environmental

Biography

James Claude Malin. Born Edgley, North Dakota, 8 February 1893. Received BA, Baker University, 1914; MA, University of Kansas, 1916, PhD 1921. Taught at University of Kansas, 1921–63. Died Lawrence, Kansas, 26 June 1979.

Principal Writings

An Interpretation of Recent American History, 1926
The United States after the World War, 1930
John Brown and the Legend of Fifty-six, 1942
Winter Wheat in the Golden Belt of Kansas: A Study in Adaption to Subhumid Geographical Environment, 1944
Essays on Historiography, 1946
The Grassland of North America: Prolegomena to Its History, 1947
Grassland Historical Studies: Natural Resources Utilization in a Background of Science and Technology, 1950
The Nebraska Question, 1852–1854, 1953
On the Nature of History: Essays about History and Dissidence, 1954
The Contriving Brain and the Skillful Hand in the United States: Something about History and the Philosophy of History, 1955
Confounded Rot about Napoleon: Reflections upon Science and Technology, Nationalism, World Depression of the Eighteen-Nineties and Afterwards, 1961
A Concern about Humanity: Notes on Reform, 1872–1912 at the National and Kansas Levels of Thought, 1964
Ironquill: Paint Creek Essays, 1972
Doctors, Devils, and the Women: Fort Scott, Kansas, 1870–1890, 1975
H.H. Sargent and Eugene F. Ware on Napoleon, 1980
Power and Change in Society, 1981
History and Ecology: Studies of the Grassland, edited and introduced by Robert P. Swierenga, 1984

Further Reading

Bell, Robert Galen, "James C. Malin and the Grasslands of North America," *Agricultural History* 46 (1972), 414–42
Johannsen, Robert W. "James C. Malin: An Appreciation," *Kansas Historical Quarterly* 38 (1972), 457–66
LeDuc, Thomas H, "An Ecological Interpretation of Grasslands History: The Work of James C. Malin as Historian and as Critic of Historians," *Nebraska History* 31 (1950), 226–33
White, Richard, *Land Use, Environment, and Social Change: The Shaping of Island County, Washington*, Seattle: University of Washington Press, 1980
Williams, Burton J., ed., *Essays in American History in Honor of James C. Malin*, Lawrence, KS: Coronado Press, 1973

Mansi, Giovanni Domenico 1692–1769
Italian theologian and editor

Early in Giovanni Domenico Mansi's career, he ran afoul of ecclesiastical censors when his first book, *Tractatus de casibus et excommunicationibus episcopis reservatis* (Treatise on Cases and Excommunications Reserved to Bishops, 1724) drew charges of a lack of rigor. Chastened, he turned from writing to translating and editing, producing a Latin translation of Calmet's *Dictionnaire de la Bible* (1725–38), a new edition of Caesar Baronius's *Annales ecclesiastici* and the companion *Continuatio annalium* by Odoricus Raynald (38 vols., 1738–59), and an edition of Noël Alexandre's *Historia ecclesiastica* (9 vols., 1749). In 1758 he incurred the wrath of pope Clement VIII by participating in a project to annotate Diderot's *Encyclopédie* so as to render it harmless to faith and morals. Pressed by the pope to concentrate on safer projects, he pointed to his *Sanctorum conciliorum et decretorum collectio nova* (The New Collection of the Holy Councils and Decretals, 1748–52) updating and extending collections of materials on the Ecumenical Councils. From that time to his death Mansi concentrated on conciliar documents, the work for which he is remembered.

Mansi was an indefatigable collector, journeying throughout Italy and maintaining correspondence with agents in Vienna, Rome, and Milan to seek materials. Yet he was also occupied throughout his life with pastoral duties, including archiepiscopal responsibilities after 1765. When he turned to his *chef d'oeuvre*, the *Sacrorum conciliorum nova et amplissima collectio* (The New and Most Complete Collection of the Sacred Councils), his scholarly shortcomings became glaringly evident. By reproducing editions of earlier compilers without providing tables or indices, he produced an unwieldy mass of documents to which he added errors rather than correcting the flaws in earlier editions. Delighted to be able to unite so many documents in a single compilation, he overlooked the need for critical editing, avoided revising or correcting, had little appreciation of the significance of variant readings, and provided a system of noting them that was more confusing than enlightening. In some places, he seems to have missed the point of commentaries by previous redactors and occasionally omitted documents, seemingly due to carelessness rather than to any sinister purpose. In using David Wilkins' *Concilia Magnae Brittaniae et Hiberniae*, for example, he omitted copying the sentence in which Wilkins gave the date of a council held at London in 1268 with the papal legate Ottoboni presiding. Wilkins included Ottoboni's constitutions in some manuscripts but not in the edition of his work published by Coleti. Mansi included extracts of the constitutions from Wilkins' manuscripts in his first collection, but in his second collection reproduced the Coleti version omitting the constitutions. When reporting the 1271 Council of Reading, Mansi included mention of a meeting held by the bishops of the Canterbury province to contest the claims of the metropolitan chapter regarding procedures to be followed when the see was vacant. Unlike Wilkins, however, Mansi did not describe the agreement reached between the bishops and the chapter in 1278 settling the question. In using Edmond Martène's *Veterum scriptorum amplissima collectio*, Mansi failed to include more than half the documents of the Council of Pisa given in volume 7. From Martène's *Thesaurus novus anecdotorum* Mansi reproduced some synodal statutes while excluding others just as interesting and significant, with no mention of how or why he was making his choices (or, indeed, that he was making them at all). Even when transcribing a document as well-known as *The Rule of St. Benedict*, Mansi lapsed repeatedly. For all of this, his collection rendered conciliar documents more accessible than earlier collections because of its scope and completeness and it is significant that modern scholars preferred to carry on his work rather than revise it from the outset.

JOSEPH M. MCCARTHY

See also Catholicism; Muratori

Biography

Born Lucca, 16 February 1692. Entered the Marian Fathers, 1708; professed, 1710. Taught moral theology in Naples before founding an academy for church history and liturgy in Lucca. Considered by Clement XIII for elevation to the cardinalate in 1758. Created archbishop of Lucca in 1765. Died Lucca, 27 September 1769.

Principal Writings

Tractatus de casibus et excommunicationibus episcopis reservatis (Treatise on Cases and Excommunications Reserved to Bishops), 1724
Sanctorum conciliorum et decretorum collectio nova (The New Collection of the Holy Councils and Decretals), 6 vols., 1748–52
Sacrorum conciliorum nova et amplissima collectio (The New and Most Complete Collection of the Sacred Councils), 31 vols., 1759–98 [reprinted and continued by L. Petit and J.B. Martin, 53 vols., Paris: 1901–27]
Carmen elegiacum de vita sua, edited by Aldo Marsili, 1984

Further Reading

Leclercq, Henri, "Jean-Dominique Mansi," *Dictionnaire d'archéologie chrétienne et de liturgie*, Paris: Letouzey, 1907–53
Quentin, Henri, *Jean-Dominique Mansi et les grandes collections conciliaires* (Mansi and the Great Concilian Collections), Paris: Leroux, 1900

Manzoni, Alessandro 1785–1873

Italian poet and novelist

One of the most renowned Italian authors of the 19th century and an impassioned patriot for a unified Italy, Alessandro Manzoni is most famous for his historical novel *I promessi sposi* (1827; *The Betrothed*, 1844), which had immense appeal to the nationalist sentiments of the Risorgimento and is considered a masterpiece of world literature. His use of history to construct works of fiction went beyond the adaptation of myths or legends to suit a particular theme. Instead he sought to use "real" history as derived from documentary sources to create dramatic works that placed individual characters in a concrete historical setting furnished with an unprecedented accuracy of detail and brought fiction to a higher level of historical consciousness.

Manzoni was born into an intellectual and politically-minded Milanese family of the lesser nobility. Educated in a series of religious boarding schools in the Lombardy region, he returned to Milan in 1801 to gravitate around republican intellectual circles and befriend the likes of the poet Vincenzo Monti and the revolutionary historian Vincenzo Cuoco. This early period was to produce in Manzoni the strong humanitarian ideals and historical sensitivity that would characterize his future literary achievements. From 1805 to 1810 he lived in Paris where he met *Idéologues* philosophers and engaged in philosophical and political debate. Some time during this period he was converted to the Roman Catholicism he had denied and criticized strongly in his youth. His conversion and subsequent Christian fervor led him to admire the idealism of Romantic writers as an antidote to what he saw as the barren rationalism and empty skepticism of Enlightenment thought.

Like many Romantics of his time, Manzoni greatly admired the works of Shakespeare and Walter Scott for their use of historical themes to create great dramas, and he drew on the German Romantic theorist August Schlegel for ideas of organic form. He was also influenced by the new French historiography represented by such figures as Guizot and Augustin Thierry who proclaimed their discipline a "science" and focused on the history of the lower classes, and on art and customs, rather than that of kings and battles. Such influences were to produce in Manzoni a preoccupation with finding universal and "poetical" truths in the particularism provided by historical study.

Manzoni wrote his greatest works precisely in the early years of the Risorgimento when Italians were searching for a national identity to which history and historical subjects could contribute. The historical tragedy *Il conte di Carmagnola* (The Count of Carmagnola, 1820), which recounted the story of the life of a 15th-century soldier of fortune unjustly executed for treason, illustrated a general theme that reflected Manzoni's observation of Italy's national political scene – innocence crushed by the sheer weight of political power. The tragic play *Adelchi* (1822), clearly influenced by the works of Shakespeare, was likewise fused with nationalist sentiments as it focused on themes of the Italian race conquered and oppressed by more powerful neighboring forces. (It might be noted that Manzoni refused all official honors offered to him until the Austrians no longer dominated the peninsula in 1860).

To this first "Romantic" period of his writing, which extended from around 1810 to the commencement of the linguistic revisions of *The Betrothed* in 1827, belongs his *Discorso sopra alcuni punti della storia longobardica* (A Discourse on Some Points of Lombard History, 1822), Manzoni's first and perhaps best contribution to Italian historiography, which served as a historical supplement to *Adelchi*. Here Manzoni identified the outstanding historians of the Middle Ages and ranked the meticulously factual Ludovico Muratori alongside the more philosophically speculative Giambattista Vico, encouraging the union of the two different styles. In the *Lettre à M. Chauvet* (1820; published in Paris, 1823), an essay on the use of history in literary works written in response to a Paris review of *Il conte di Carmagnola*, Manzoni equated the "historical" with the "Romantic," using the terms interchangeably, and he observed that historiography was about to become a science, destined to affect the literary arts profoundly. He defined history as documented facts interpreted and shaped by more universal principles of human thought, proposing that the historian and poet share a single methodology of organizing facts around (Kantian) categories already formed in the human mind, such as cause and effect, space and time.

His later writing moved away from literary creativity and further toward theoretical issues of literature and art, including more profound attempts to identify historical truth. This is exemplified in the *Storia della colonna infame* (1840–42; *The Column of Infamy*, 1845) which consisted of a digression that begins from within the story of *The Betrothed*, but moves further away from the fictionalism of the novel and is more a judicial-style narrative inquiry, informed by well-documented research and conducted by a dramatized narrator with a strong ideological bent. His later long essay, *Del romanzo storico* (1845; *On the Historical Novel*, 1984), represented Manzoni's more mature thought on the subject, deeply probing the relationship of history to literature and ruminating on the popularity of the historical novel during his lifetime in a discourse infused with classic Aristotelian understandings of history and poetry in the pursuit of truth. The more profound appreciation of the divergence between the requirements of literary form and those of historical accuracy expounded in *On the Historical Novel* somewhat contradicts many of the optimistic statements of the possibilities of "historical poetry" found in the earlier *Lettre à M. Chauvet*, concluding here that, "A great poet and a great historian may be found in the same man without creating confusion, but not in the same work."

Manzoni often used the device of authorial commentary within the text in challenging the reader to verify the truthfulness of his account of events or historical personages. Examples of this can be found in the first chapter of *The Betrothed* when Manzoni describes the dress of the Lombard Bravi, a certain type of bandit that flourished in the 16th and 17th centuries in northern Italy, and then continues to give two and a half pages of quotations from historical documents to justify his description to the reader. The same technique is applied in his account of the plague. In *Il conte di Carmagnola*, Manzoni supplied a special explanatory preface containing historical information not included in the drama. Such techniques stemmed from Manzoni's desire to communicate with complete honesty and truthfulness to his audience and served to elevate the latter from the role of passive spectator to companion of the author, forced to consider and judge the events as the author himself has witnessed them from documentary sources.

Manzoni's romanticism and religiosity led him not to an overwhelming providentialism, but instead to a more anthropological gaze on the general principles governing human conduct which were to be understood without needing insights into divine Providence. He accepted Vico's position that history, although consisting primarily as an idea in the mind of God which is realized in the course of time, was also committed to the psychology of human choice for its full realization. When it came to understanding historical development, Manzoni's theological fatalism was too tempered by his belief in individual human responsibility for it to intrude.

Manzoni's later years were devoted more to linguistics and the problem of standardizing the Italian language, for which he was made president of an official commission by the Italian government in 1868, culminating in such works as *Dell'unità della lingua e dei mezzi di diffonderla* (On the Unity of the Language and the Means to Diffuse It, 1868), *Lettera intorno al vocabulario* (On Vocabulary, 1868), and a series of similar essays intended to be synthesized into a larger work, "Della Italiana" (On the Italian Language). Manzoni's fame is owed more to his fiction than his historiographical speculations. However the sense of historical inquiry evident in his literary creations and theoretical treatises not only signified new attitudes on behalf of the author to the past and the representation of it, but also reflected his audience's growing preoccupation with understanding historical development.

NICHOLAS EVERETT

Biography

Alessandro Francesco Tommaso Antonio Manzoni. Born Milan, 7 March 1785; from a family of lesser nobility and conservative politics; his parents separated in 1792. Educated in religious boarding schools at Merate, Lugano, Magenta, and Milan. Returned to Milan in 1801 and began friendship with Vincenzo Monti before living in Paris, 1805–10; converted to Catholicism; returned to Milan, 1810. Made Senator, 1860. President of commission for a unified Italian language, 1868. Granted honorary Roman citizenship, 1872. Married 1) Henriette Blondel, 1808 (died 1833; 8 children survived infancy); 2) Teresa Borri, 1837. Died Milan, 22 May 1873.

Principal Writings

Il conte di Carmagnola (The Count of Carmagnola), 1820
Lettre à M. Chauvet (Letter to M. Chauvet), written 1820; published 1823
Adelchi, 1822
Discorso sopra alcuni punti della storia longobardica in Italia (A Discourse on Some Points of Lombard History in Italy), 1822
I promessi sposi, 1827; in English as *The Betrothed*, 1844
Storia della colonna infame, 1840–42; in English as *The Column of Infamy*, 1845
Del romanzo storico e, in genere, de' componimenti misti di storia e d'invenzione 1845; in English as *On the Historical Novel*, 1984
L'opera di Alessandro Manzoni, edited by Alberto Chiari, 2nd edition revised, Turin: Eri, 1967

Further Reading

Barricelli, Jean Pierre, *Alessandro Manzoni*, Boston: Twayne, 1976
Battaglia, Salvatore, *Il realismo dei "Promessi sposi"* (Realism in *The Betrothed*), Naples: Liguori, 1963
Bermann, Sandra, Introduction, to Alessandro Manzoni, *On the Historical Novel*, Lincoln: University of Nebraska Press, 1984
Cavallini, Giorgio, *Lettura dell' "Adelchi" e altre note manzoniane* (A Reading of *Adelchi* and Other Notes on Manzoni), Rome: Bulzoni, 1984
Ceroni, Vittorio, *The Italian Thinker of the Nineteenth Century: Alessandro Manzoni (1785–1873)*, New York: La Lucerna, 1945
Chandler, S. Bernard, *Alessandro Manzoni: The Story of a Spiritual Quest*, Edinburgh: Edinburgh University Press, 1974
Colombo, Umberto, *Alessandro Manzoni*, Rome: Paoline, 1985
Colquhoun, Archibald, *Manzoni and His Times*, London: Dent, 1954
De Lollis, Cesare, *Alessandro Manzoni e gli storici liberali francesi della Restaurazione* (A. Manzoni and the French Liberal Historians of the Restoration), Bari: Laterza, 1926; reprinted Rome: Istituto storico italiano per l'eta moderna e contemporanea, 1987
Gabbuti, Elena, *Il Manzoni e gli Ideologi francesi* (Manzoni and the French Idéologues), Florence: Sansoni, 1936
Gentile, Francesa, ed., *Manzoni, il suo e il nostro tempo* (Manzoni, His Time and Labors), Milan: Electa, 1985
Getto, Giovanni, *Manzoni europeo* (Manzoni the European), Milan: Mursia, 1971
Ginzburg, Natalia, *La famiglia Manzoni*, Turin: Einaudi, 1983; in English as *The Manzoni Family*, New York: Seaver, and Manchester: Carcanet, 1987
Lukács, Georg, *A Történelmi regény*, Budapest: Magveto Kiado, 1947; in English as *The Historical Novel*, London: Merlin Press, 1962; Boston: Beacon Press, 1962
Matteo, Sante, and Larry H. Peer, eds., *The Reasonable Romantic: Essays on Alessandro Manzoni*, New York: Lang, 1986
Ulivi, Ferruccio, *Manzoni*, Milan: Rusconi, 1985

Maravall, José Antonio 1911–1986

Spanish intellectual historian

The immensely prolific José Antonio Maravall was the leading Spanish historian of ideas of his generation and a major figure in the intellectual life of Spain during the half-century that encompassed the Civil War, the Franco regime, and the transition to democracy following the dictator's death in 1975. Although three of his nearly thirty books as well as numerous occasional pieces dealt with more recent historiography and literature, the bulk of Maravall's work focused on Spanish thought and culture in the 15th through 18th centuries. His

central concern, as perhaps befits a scholar trained in law and the social sciences rather than in history, was to trace the origins of modernity in the intellectual, ideological, literary, and scientific writings of the Renaissance and Golden Age. While this quest for the emergence of the modern state and the modern mind sometimes lent a teleological cast to Maravall's enterprise, his works were based on an incomparable breadth of reading in the literary production of early modern Spain. Political and legal treatises, polemics and pamphlets, institutional regulations, devotional and theological works, histories and genealogies, plays, poems, *autos*, and novels, of good, bad, or indifferent quality – these were the voluminous and varied sources of Maravall's histories, and few historians of any nationality could match his facility in drawing together disparate contemporary writings to illustrate a larger vision of the mentality of an age.

All subsequent students of early modern Spain are in Maravall's debt for his manifold contributions to the field. Whether it is a question of understanding the guiding ideas of Habsburg statecraft, of tracing the vicissitudes of the idea of progress in a society that treasured custom and continuity, or of linking picaresque literature to a specific social context, Maravall's books abound with shrewd delineations and analyses of problems lying at the confluence of social, cultural, political, and intellectual history. Perhaps more significant in the long run, however, are the attitudes and approaches that he bequeathed to scholars in his own country and beyond.

First, and against powerful scholarly and ideological opposition, Maravall asserted throughout his long career that Spain could be understood only in the context of Europe. In this, he followed the Europeanizing intellectual lead of José Ortega y Gasset, the pre-eminent figure of Spanish letters in his youth and early maturity, and briefly his own teacher in 1933–34. In his approach to history, though, Maravall rejected Ortega's judgment – most forcibly expressed in *España invertebrada* (1921) – that through the centuries Spain had been crippled by congenital historical defects. Rather than viewing Spain as a deficient and peripheral European nation, Maravall made a powerful case for his country's role in the forefront of Western development, and particularly in the elaboration of the modern state. His related insistence that the study of the Spanish past should no longer be obscured by quasi-historical notions of a unique destiny, or of an immutable national character, or of a centuries-long cultural dysfunction stemming from self-defeating intolerance, brought Maravall into conflict – amicable but nonetheless sharply expressed – with two more intellectual giants of the preceding generation, Claudio Sánchez-Albornoz and, especially, Américo Castro. In a barbed rebuke to scholars who prided themselves on their opposition to rightist obscurantism, Maravall spoke (to M.C. Iglesias in 1983) of the phenomenon of "américo-castrismo," whose academic devotees "have displayed a tendency to gaze at their navels and to believe that everything in Spain is utterly distinct. One could even say that the lamentable slogan 'Spain is different,' that the Ministry of Tourism came up with in the Francoist era, really contains a philosophy that is that of américo-castrismo."

Second, Maravall championed and pursued in his own major works an approach that he came to call "historia de las mentalidades" – quite distinct, in its overwhelming concentration on literate elites, from the social history of *mentalités* – which produced striking insights into early modern culture. This method entailed extracting not just individual ideas but more general preconceptions from the array of contemporary texts that were Maravall's primary sources, to the end of determining how, in a given context, mental processes shaped behavior and material reality. His most ambitious work in this vein was *La cultura del barroco* (1975; *Culture of the Baroque*, 1986). Here he attempted a general interpretation of the Spanish and European culture of the 17th century, conceived as a multi-faceted unity, a "historical structure" in the book's subtitle. By this term, Maravall meant "the image – or mental construction – which shows us a linked array of incidents endowed with an internal articulation, a framework that systematizes and captures the meaning of the complex network of relationships between such incidents." For Maravall, the historical structure of the Baroque was a near-seamless web of control exerted by the supreme absolutist state acting in concert with church and aristocracy to shape mental and cultural resistance to the turmoil threatened by economic depression and sharpening social conflict. Like any grand interpretation, Maravall's Baroque has come in for criticism, primarily that he overstated elite cohesion and the possibility of dictating culture from above. Despite its flaws, however, the book has been widely influential, not least as a catalyst of the recent restoration of the concept of the Baroque to the vocabulary of historians after its long exile among literary critics and art historians.

Finally, by his example of intellectual distinction and probity in an academic environment depleted by the loss of talent to post-Civil War exile and tarnished by the political promotion of sycophants and mediocrities, Maravall helped to sustain serious intellectual life in Spain during the long decades of the Franco era. During his extended sojourns as a visiting professor in France and the United States, Maravall broadened his own horizons while nurturing institutional connections and personal contacts that proved useful to younger Spanish scholars. His legacy extends beyond his impressive body of published scholarship; as John Elliott observed in 1987, Maravall "did much to liberalize intellectual life during the later years of the Franco regime and to prepare a new generation for the restoration of democracy."

JAMES M. BOYDEN

Biography

José Antonio Maravall Casenoves. Born Játiva near Valencia, 1911. Taught at University of Madrid, 1932–36, 1944–49, 1955–81 (emeritus); director, Colegio de España, University of Paris, 1949–54. Married María Teresa Herrero (1 daughter, 3 sons). Died Madrid, 19 December 1986.

Principal Writings

Teoría del estado en España en el siglo XVII (The Theory of the State in 17th-Century Spain), 1944
El concepto de España en la Edad Media (The Idea of Spain in the Middle Ages), 1954; 3rd edition 1981
Teoría del saber histórico (A Theory of Historical Knowledge), 1958
Carlos V y el pensamiento político del Renacimiento (Charles V and the Political Thought of the Renaissance), 1960
Velázquez y el espíritu de la modernidad (Velázquez and the Spirit of Modernity), 1960
Las Comunidades de Castilla: una primera revolución moderna (The Comuneros of Castile and the First Modern Revolution), 1963

Antiguos y modernos: la idea de progreso en el desarrollo inicial de una sociedad (Ancients and Moderns: The Idea of Progress in the Development of a Society), 1966
Estudios de historia del pensamiento español (Studies in the History of Spanish Thought), 3 vols., 1967–84
Estado moderno y mentalidad social (siglos XV a XVII) (The Modern State and Social Mentality from the 15th through the 17th Centuries), 2 vols., 1972
La oposición política bajo los Austrias (The Political Opposition under the Spanish Habsburgs), 1972
La cultura del barroco: análisis de una estructura histórica, 1975; in English as *Culture of the Baroque: Analysis of a Historical Structure*, 1986
Utopía y contrautopía en el Quijote, 1976; in English as *Utopia and counterutopia in the "Quixote,"* 1991
La literatura picaresca desde la historia social (siglos XVI y XVII) (The Picaresque Literature of the 16th and 17th Centuries from the Perspective of Social History), 1986

Further Reading

Elliott, J.H., "Concerto Barocco," *New York Review of Books* 34/6 (9 April 1987), 26–29
Iglesias, María del Carmen, "Conversación con José Antonio Maravall" (Conversation with José Antonio Maravall), *Cuadernos hispanoamericanos* 400 (October 1983), 53–74
Iglesias, María del Carmen, "Noticia biográfica" (Biographical Notice) and "Bibliografía" (Bibliography), in María del Carmen Iglesias, Carlos Moya, and Luis Rodríguez Zúñiga, eds., *Homenaje a José Antonio Maravall*, 3 vols., Madrid: Centro de Investigaciones Sociológicas, 1985, vol. 1, 17–41
Maravall, José Antonio, "Cómo he visto y sigo viendo nuestros *Cuadernos*" (How I Have Seen and Continue Seeing Our *Cuadernos hispanicos*), *Cuadernos hispanoamericanos* 400 (1983), 47–52

Marczali, Henrik 1856–1940
Hungarian historian

A student and great admirer of Leopold von Ranke, and a disciple of Macaulay, Henrik Marczali was the first outstanding Hungarian historian with the ability, the broad knowledge, and the professionalism to write useful general accounts of both European and Magyar history. He was a specialist in early medieval history, particularly the rule of the Arpád dynasty from the 10th to the 13th centuries. He has been most acclaimed, however, as an expert on 18th-century Hungary. In 1910 the English version of his book on the age of Joseph II was hailed in Britain as "the highest achievement of Magyar scholarship."

In addition, he wrote extensively on European history from the Reformation to the 19th century. In a unique work of Hungarian historiography, *A Legújabb Kor Története* (History of Our Times, 1898), he ventured a synthesis of contemporary international and Hungarian history in the period from 1820 to 1880. Although the elaborate and more original Hungarian chapters are not woven seamlessly into the main narrative, Marczali was able to give a coherent liberal view of both Magyar and World history.

He began his academic career as a scholar of geography. In the early 1870s Budapest offered no specialist university training for historians, and it was as a result of his studies in German, French, and English universities that Marczali changed his discipline. He was especially fortunate to receive instruction from the leading experts on the critical analysis of primary sources, just at the time when the first archives were opened in Budapest and the papers of the state administration were made available to researchers. The humble son of a village rabbi, Marczali had one-to-one tutorials from the German "historian-king" Ranke. The young scholar's academic mentors encouraged his zealous pursuit of archival work and his keen interest in primary sources, which included both medieval manuscripts and modern papers. Although some Marxist critics labeled Marczali as "positivist," recent works explain his obsession with original material in terms of his professionalism.

His first scholarly achievement was an essay on the *Gesta Hungarorum*, a crucial but disputed source on the early history of the Magyars. With the comparison of various chronicles he proved that the author, known in Hungarian historiography by the Latin name Anonymus, was the notary of King Béla IV (1235–70). The essay was written during Marczali's studies in Berlin and it was first published in Germany as a fine example of the comparative method in the historical analysis of medieval sources. It was characteristic of Marczali that in parallel to his studies of the Middle Ages he began to work on modern history and researched Prussian-Hungarian relations in 1789–90 in German archives. From the very beginning of his career, he evenly divided his attention between medieval and modern topics.

Marczali's reputation in Hungary was established by his 3-volume *Magyarország története II. József korában* (History of Hungary during the Reign of Joseph II, 1885–88), the fruit of ten years of archival research. In the introduction, the young author claimed to have consulted about 70,000 files from a collection that was only one of his major sources. For all that, the originality of his work lay as much in interpretation as in its vast documentation. He argued that the 18th century was a crucial period in which Hungary was able to gather strength and make economic progress. He later developed this theme in his biography of Maria Theresa, portraying the reign of the empress as an era of peace and calm. In *Az 1790–1791 országgyűlés története* (History of the Diet of 1790–1791, 1907), he praised the quiet and little acknowledged work of two generations living before the national reawakening. At the same time Marczali was the first historian to propose that economically Hungary was no more than a colony of Austria. As a supporter of the *Ausgleich*, he tried to strike a balance between pro-Austrian and Magyar nationalist views. He sided neither with the Protestant nor with the Catholic schools of traditional Hungarian historiography. Consequently, he was described by English liberals such as G.P. Gooch as the first Magyar scholar who "broke the shackles of narrow patriotism."

Marczali's career reached its peak towards the end of the 19th century. He wrote three of the ten volumes of *A magyar nemzet története* (History of the Hungarian Nation), the most monumental project in Magyar historiography to date, to coincide with the millennial celebrations of the foundation of the Hungarian kingdom. He then wrote half of a 12-volume illustrated world history single-handedly. In addition he became a professor and held the first and most popular history seminar at the university in Budapest. Yet, in the early years of the 20th century his popularity gradually waned.

After World War I Marczali came to be marginalized both politically and professionally, ultimately losing his university post and pension. In the early 1920s he even came into conflict with some of his former students. He criticized them for founding a Magyar school of the history of ideas. Notwithstanding this academic debate, on his death Marczali's scholarly credentials and accomplishments were reassessed and celebrated by a prominent historian of ideas, the most famous of his ex-students, Gyula Szekfű.

GÁBOR BÁTONYI

Biography

Born Marcali, 1856. Studied at University of Budapest, then studied in Vienna, Paris, and Berlin. Professor, University of Budapest, from 1895. Dismissed because of political views, 1918. Died Budapest, 1940.

Principal Writings

Magyarország története II. József korában (History of Hungary during the Reign of Joseph II), 3 vols, 1885–88; abridged in English as *Hungary in the Eighteenth Century*, 1910
Mária Terézia, 1717–1780, 1891
A magyar nemzet története (History of the Hungarian Nation), 1895–98 [3 vols. of 10]
A Legújabb Kor Története (History of Our Times), 1898
Az 1790–1791 országgyűlés története (History of the Diet of 1790–1791), 2 vols., 1907
Hungary in the Eighteenth Century, 1910

Further Reading

Gunst, Péter, Introduction to Marczali's *Világtörténelem / Magyar történelem* (World History / Hungarian History), Budapest: Gondolat, 1982
Gunst, Péter, *A magyar történetírás története* (The History of Hungarian Historiography), Debrecen: Csokonai Kiadó, 1995
Lederer, Emma, "Marczali Henrik helye a magyar polgári történettudományban" (Henrik Marczali's Place in the Hungarian Bourgeois Historiography), *Századok*, 3–4 (1962)

Maritime History

"The sea isolates and connects at the same time," declared Michel Mollat du Jourdin in *L'Europe et la mer* (1993; *Europe and the Sea*, 1993), an observation true of maritime history itself. The field's origins, especially in Britain and North America, lay in the belief that naval and non-naval maritime activities should be separate. The British journal *Mariner's Mirror*, for example, was founded in 1911 to promote support for a strong Royal Navy. The *Mirror* now carries articles on all aspects of maritime enterprise, but earlier non-naval specialists felt marginalized; this led to the establishment of a "maritime history" dedicated to the economic and social features of humanity's interaction with the sea. A comparison between Oppenheim's *Maritime History of Devon* (1922) and Duffy et al.'s *New Maritime History of Devon* (1992) tells the story. Oppenheim's work focused entirely on the naval establishments of the south Devon coast, whereas the authors of the *New Maritime History* described activities from smuggling and privateering to marine science and labor relations throughout the region.

In Britain and the United States before the 1960s, professional maritime historians studying non-naval subjects tended to identify with economic or transport history, while seafaring reminiscences and narratives enjoyed great popular interest. Here were two problems: the identification of "maritime history" as a distinct field, and the defence of its academic credibility. During the rise of business history in the 1950s, some economic historians began focusing on the study of shipping companies; in Britain, Hyde's *Blue Funnel* (1957) founded a "Liverpool school" of maritime business history. An emphasis on corporate organization and tactics still characterizes Japanese maritime history, as in Tsunehiko Yui and Keiichiro Nakagawa's *Business History of Shipping* (1985).

Other economic historians, notably Davis in *The Rise of the English Shipping Industry* (1962), noted the absence of detailed primary research and quantitative analysis in the business studies approach, and called for a study of maritime labor as well as corporate strategy. In North America too, economic historians lamented the lack of original research on the American and Canadian merchant marine. Change began in the 1960s and 1970s under Ernest Dodge's 18-year editorship of *The American Neptune*, a journal that began to reflect Dodge's belief, quoted in Runyan's "*The American Neptune*" (1991), that "maritime history bridges the spaces between academia, sport, and industry."

European maritime history avoided many of these methodological and identity problems, mainly because naval history did not predominate at the expense of other specialties. In the Netherlands, an officially sponsored "Committee for Sea History" was inaugurated in 1933, at a time when most governments in the English-speaking world funded only naval history. Paris hosted the first International Maritime History Symposium in 1956, and French maritime historian Michel Mollat du Jourdin was president of the International Commission for Maritime History for 25 years.

The establishment in 1986 of the International Maritime Economic History Association helped emphasize the field's growing stature, and prompted the launch of an *International Journal of Maritime History* in 1989. Its articles reflected the international, interdisciplinary approach of historians such as Rediker, whose *Between the Devil and the Deep Blue Sea* (1987) did much to bring neglected aspects of social and labor studies to the fore while sparking a lively debate about Marxist methodology. Other historians have questioned gendered assumptions about maritime enterprise, and balanced a swashbuckling popular literature with the quantitative analysis of whaling, tramp shipping, and privateering.

The most notable recent development has been the study of ever-larger maritime environments. In the comparative study of port towns, or in regional history, political and economic issues are fleshed out by studies of marine science, family life, and historical geography. Quantitative analysis is combined with the written and oral records in collaborative works such as Fischer and Minchinton's *People of the Northern Seas* (1992), a comparison of maritime social histories from the north Pacific to the Baltic, or in team-produced studies of southwest England and Atlantic Canada.

Not all maritime regions have prompted such interest, or been so suitable for unified study. Australian historians, preoccupied by the frontier thesis, have only recently begun to explore the history of Australia as an island. Only after Blainey's *The Tyranny of Distance* in 1966 did debate begin about the effect of ocean transport on the development of Australia's economy. Australian historians have also worked with South Asian colleagues on Indian Ocean history, but unlike the Mediterranean or Atlantic, this ocean is bounded by countries with radically different maritime histories. Here Broeze's *Brides of the Sea* (1989) suggested the comparative study of port cities, rather than a unified economic or social analysis.

This raises one of the most pressing questions facing maritime historians today: is there a distinctiveness about seafarers and their communities that can be identified and analyzed? Like all other historical fields, maritime history has been influenced by cultural studies, and Scandinavian historians have led the way in blending anthropological and historical techniques to uncover a "maritime culture," as in Weibust's *Deep Sea Sailors* (1969). Meanwhile, the relatively new field of marine archaeology is adding material evidence of shipbuilding techniques and shipboard life to the interdisciplinary brew. The sea connects more than it isolates; Philip D. Curtin, in his introduction to Knight and Liss' *Atlantic Port Cities* (1991), invoked a "web of solidarity" that defines and links the identity of maritime communities. At a time when global perspectives, international collaboration, and interdisciplinary flexibility are often sought but seldom found, maritime history is seizing the opportunities of a subject that recognizes few boundaries.

JANE SAMSON

See also European Expansion; Indian Ocean; Mahan; Naval; Southeast Asia

Further Reading
Bach, John, *Maritime History of Australia*, Melbourne: Nelson, 1976
Bass, George F., ed., *Ships and Shipwrecks of the Americas: A History Based on Underwater Archaeology*, London and New York: Thames and Hudson, 1988
Blainey, Geoffrey, *The Tyranny of Distance: How Distance Shaped Australia's History*, Melbourne: Sun, 1966, London: Macmillan, and New York: St. Martin's Press, 1968; revised 1982
Broeze, Frank, ed., *Brides of the Sea: Port Cities of Asia from the 16th–20th Centuries*, Kensington: New South Wales University Press, and Honolulu: University of Hawaii Press, 1989
Broeze, Frank, ed., *Maritime History at the Crossroads*, St. John's, Newfoundland: International Maritime Economic History Association, 1995
Davies, Peter N., and Sheila Marriner, "Recent Publications and Developments in the Study of Maritime Economic History," *Journal of Transport History* 9:1 (1988), 93–108
Davis, R., *The Rise of the English Shipping Industry in the Seventeenth and Eighteenth Centuries*, London: Macmillan, and New York: St. Martin's Press, 1962
Duffy, Michael, Stephen Fisher, Basil Greenhill, David J. Starkey, and Joyce Youings, eds., *The New Maritime History of Devon*, 2 vols., London: Conway, 1992
Fischer, Lewis R., and Helge W. Nordvik, eds., *Shipping and Trade, 1750–1950: Essays in International Maritime and Economic History*, Pontefract: Lofthouse, 1990
Fischer, Lewis R., and Walter Minchinton, *People of the Northern Seas*, St. John's, Newfoundland: International Maritime Economic History Association, 1992
Fisher, Stephen, ed., *Man and the Maritime Environment*, Exeter: Exeter University Press, 1994
Hasslof, Olof, Henning Henningsen, and Arne Emil Christensen, eds., *Ships and Shipyards, Sailors and Fishermen: Introduction to Maritime Ethnology*, Copenhagen: Scandinavian Maritime History Working Group, 1972

Hattendorf, John B., *Ubi Sumus? The State of Naval and Maritime History*, Newport, RI: Naval War College Press, 1994

Henderson, Graeme, *Maritime Archaeology in Australia*, Nedlands: University of Western Australia Press, 1986

Hyde, Francis, *Blue Funnel: A History of Alfred Holt and Company of Liverpool, 1865–1914*, Liverpool: Liverpool University Press, 1957

Knight, Franklin W., and Peggy K. Liss, eds., *Atlantic Port Cities: Economy, Culture, and Society in the Atlantic World*, Knoxville: University of Tennessee Press, 1991

Mollat, Michel, *L'Europe et la mer*, Paris: Seuil, 1993; in English as *Europe and the Sea*, Oxford and Cambridge, MA: Blackwell, 1993

Nadel-Klein, Jane, and Dona Lee Davis, *To Work and to Weep: Women in Fishing Economies*, St. John's, Newfoundland: Institute of Social and Economic Research, 1988

Oppenheim, Michael M., *The Maritime History of Devon*, written 1922; first published, Exeter: Exeter University Press, 1968

Rediker, Marcus, *Between the Devil and the Deep Blue Sea: Merchant Seamen, Pirates, and the Anglo-American Maritime World, 1700–1750*, Cambridge: Cambridge University Press, 1987

Runyan, Timothy J., "*The American Neptune*: A Half Century of Maritime History," *American Neptune* 51 (1991), 45–48

Starkey, David J., *British Privateering Enterprise in the Eighteenth Century*, Exeter: Exeter University Press, 1990

Tsunehiko Yui and Keiichiro Nakagawa, eds., *Business History of Shipping: Strategy and Structure*, Tokyo: University of Tokyo Press, 1985

Weibust, Knut, *Deep Sea Sailors: A Study in Maritime Ethnology*, Stockholm: Nordiska Museet, 1969

Williams, David M., "The Progress of Maritime History, 1953–93," *Journal of Transport History* 14 (1993), 126–41

Marks, Shula 1936–
South African social historian

Shula Marks' reputation as a leading Marxist or "revisionist" South African historian was in large part shaped by living abroad in Britain, rather than in the somewhat parochial isolation of her homeland. Her background in Natal influenced a lifelong passion for Zulu history, and surely influenced the topic of her University of London dissertation, published as *Reluctant Rebellion* (1970). Superficially a traditional political history, this now classic study of the Bambatha Revolt, South Africa's last "premodern" black rebellion, showed early signs of identifying with broader new scholarly trends, such as the emerging "resistance and collaboration" school pioneered by Terence Ranger and John Iliffe in studies on Zimbabwe and Tanzania. Here too was a motif that recurred in Marks' later work: a preoccupation with greys, rather than simple blacks and whites, with ambiguity and the need to probe into the multiple meanings behind evidence. Already, she clearly strove to get beyond the emotionally engaged, but often superficial discussions that she perceived in too much liberal writing on South Africa, to what she thought was a more detached, balanced, and deeper understanding of the dynamics of racism.

In the same year she discussed this last concern in a critical review of the second volume of the *Oxford History of South Africa*, which stressed interaction between racial and ethnic groups, and marked the apogee of the liberal Africanists, led by Leonard Thompson. Marks was soon the leading figure in a British-based group of mainly expatriate scholars which, in opposition to the Africanists, stressed the significance of class more than race.

In a long career at the School of Oriental and African Studies and at the Institute for Commonwealth Studies at the University of London, latterly as director of the Institute, Marks was as important for her supervision of numerous path-breaking doctoral dissertations and her pioneering seminars, which produced a flood of much-cited papers, as for her own work. Among her students were Phil Bonner, William Beinart, Tim Keegan, Peter Delius, and Baruch Hirson. The work developed under her sponsorship and that of her longtime Oxford associate and fellow expatriate Stanley Trapido, dramatically reshaped South African historiography, exploring topics ranging from precolonial political economy to the role of capital in the development of apartheid. Her heavy teaching and administrative responsibilities limited time for on-site research in South Africa, restricting her own writing primarily to a remarkably steady flow of articles and chapters in anthologies and, at longer intervals, some notable books.

The collections she co-edited are perhaps her best-known publications, providing the readiest access to the work of the emerging revisionist school, which often appeared only as unpublished papers. For instance, seminal articles rejecting the frontier as the crucible of apartheid, suggesting ecological factors in the rise of the Zulu empire, and analyzing the hypocrisies of 19th-century British liberalism, appeared in the now standard collection, *Economy and Society in Pre-Industrial South Africa* (1980). This volume was co-edited with Anthony Atmore, with whom Marks had written her probably most influential piece, a 1974 article reassessing the "imperial factor" in 19th-century South Africa, and suggesting that much of what passed for philanthropism was a thin disguise for expanding British economic domination at the expense of the Afrikaners, who were rescued from black African wrath when they served British interests and swept aside when they did not.

Although such themes had been developed long before by relatively obscure radicals such as Hosea Jaffe and Dora Taylor, Marks' position in a world-class graduate center, attracting many disaffected young South Africans, brought such ideas before a far broader audience. The prestigious Oxford-based *Journal of Southern African Studies*, of which she was a founder, provided a further avenue for disseminating the revisionists' work.

If sometimes seen as the leading Marxist historian of South Africa, Marks never succumbed to economistic structuralism, despite a tendency to give overall primacy to class. Yet her differences from structuralists such as Martin Legassick and Daniel O'Meara were never made explicit. They were all committed to overturning the liberal paradigm, but Marks was always far closer to the transparent, fundamentally traditional, social-historical empiricism of E.P. Thompson and Eric Hobsbawm than to the arcane theoretical complexities of an Althusser or Poulantzas.

Nor did Marks focus on class to the exclusion of race. As early as 1971 she had co-edited the *Journal of African History*, which put blacks at the center of African historiography. Many of her students worked on Africanist themes that might have attracted Thompsonian liberals. Only the manner of treatment differed, locating African struggle in the context of resistance to proletarianization and subjection to large-scale capitalist interests.

Equally rooted in the liberal tradition was her interest in individuals as expressive of larger themes, dating back to a 1963 article on 19th-century pro-Zulu activist Harriette Colenso. This commitment to biography as a legitimate "radical" vehicle, but with a revisionist twist stressing the intersection of race, class, and gender, led to two books. *The Ambiguities of Dependence in South Africa* (1986) was a parallel treatment of three Zulu political figures in modern Natal province, while *Not Either an Experimental Doll* (1987), marking a return to the neglected area of South African women's history, was an inventive narrative woven around edited correspondence between three women. Most recently, Marks' interest in women, as well as health issues, led to *Divided Sisterhood* (1994), a history of South African nursing.

Marks has remained at the forefront of South African scholarship in other ways, for instance co-editing with Trapido a landmark 1987 anthology on constructing ethnic identity, a theme which, with the end of both Soviet communism and apartheid, increasingly overshadows the old focus on class. But, despite current uncertainty about the future direction of "leftist" research, the revisionists' work has unquestionably changed the whole direction of South African historiography, and contributed to an explosion in scholarly work on South Africa. Marks' key role in establishing this school and disseminating its findings will likely be her most important contribution to historical studies.

Patrick J. Furlong

See also Labor; South Africa

Biography

Shula Eta Winokur Marks. Born Cape Town, South Africa, 14 October 1936. Received BA, University of Cape Town, 1959; PhD, University of London, 1967. Taught at School of Oriental and African Studies and Institute of Commonwealth Studies, from 1963: professor of commonwealth history, 1983–93, professor of southern African history, from 1993; director, Institute of Commonwealth Studies, 1985–93. Married Isaac M. Marks, 1957 (1 son, 1 daughter: historian Lara Marks).

Principal Works

Reluctant Rebellion: The 1906–08 Disturbances in Natal, 1970
With Anthony Atmore, "The Imperial Factor in South Africa: Towards a Reassessment," *Journal of Imperial and Commonwealth History* 3 (1974), 105–39
Editor with Anthony Atmore, *Economy and Society in Pre-Industrial South Africa*, 1980
Editor with Richard Rathbone, *Industrialisation and Social Change in South Africa: African Class Formation, Culture, and Consciousness, 1870–1930*, 1982
Edited with Peter Richardson, *International Labour Migration: Historical Perspectives*, 1984
The Ambiguities of Dependence in South Africa: Class, Nationalism, and the State in Twentieth-Century Natal, 1986
Editor, *Not Either an Experimental Doll: The Separate Worlds of Three South African Women*, 1987
Editor with Stanley Trapido, *The Politics of Race, Class, and Nationalism in Twentieth-Century South Africa*, 1987
Editor with Hugh Macmillan, *Africa and Empire: W.M. Macmillan, Historian and Social Critic*, 1989
Editor with Dagmar Engels, *Contesting Colonial Hegemony: State and Society in Africa and India*, 1994

Divided Sisterhood: Race, Class, and Gender in the South African Nursing Profession, 1994

Further Reading

Bozzoli, Belinda, and Peter Delius, "Radical History and South African Society," *Radical History Review* 46 (1990), 13–45
Foner, Eric, "'We Must Forget the Past': History in the New South Africa," *South African Historical Journal* 32 (May 1995), 163–76
Murray, Martin J., "The Triumph of Marxist Approaches in South African Social and Labour History," *Journal of Asian and African Studies* 23 (1988), 79–101
Posel, Deborah, "Rethinking the 'Race-Class Debate' in South African Historiography," *Social Dynamics* 9/1 (1983), 50–66
Saunders, Christopher, *The Making of the South African Past: Major Historians on Race and Class*, Cape Town: David Philip, and Totowa, NJ: Barnes and Noble, 1988
Wright, Harrison M., *The Burden of the Present: Liberal-Radical Controversy over South African History*, Cape Town: David Philip, and London: Rex Collings, 1977

Marriage

Marriage has always been a part of historical inquiry, if only as part of the investigation of elite dynastic problems. However, in the last few decades, interest has expanded to an examination not only of the rest of society but also the reasons for marriage, the rituals involved, the expectations of the participants, and the means of resolving problems within it. In order to understand the history of marriage, it is necessary to comprehend that it is heavily embedded in legal systems and in the customs of people. For this reason studies have focused not only on what is seen as the ideal union but on the way that ideal has been tested. Although marriage since ancient times has been studied in great detail, the greatest attention has been on northwest Europe and the societies it spawned.

Marriage in pre-Reformation Europe was based upon two principles. The parties had to consent freely to the union, and the union, once formed, could not be legally dissolved. This emphasis on individual choice led C.S. Lewis to argue in *The Allegory of Love* (1936) that a fundamental change in the way men and women felt toward each other took place in the 12th century. Lewis claimed that the characteristics of courtly love – the exaltation of the loved one, the subservient position of the lover, the lover's duty to serve his lady – were the constituent elements of a "real change in human sentiment" Lewis' seductive prose and the superficially convincing nature of his argument made his book one of the most influential works on the topic of love and Western society. The book heralded the beginnings of the modern preoccupation with romance in marriage and contrasted this with a previous European tradition in which "marriage was the drab background against which this new love stood out."

Although Lewis' work was influential among literary scholars, it was not until almost thirty years later that the study of marriage began in earnest among historians. Two strands of inquiry have been dominant. One strand has concentrated on the demographic consequences of the marriage regime found in Western Europe, the other has focused on the development and application of a specifically European ideology of marriage. For the demographic study of marriage in Europe, John Hajnal's identification of a specific European marriage pattern was crucial. He argued that marriage in the European past had two main characteristics: people married relatively late and a large proportion of the population never married at all. Hajnal's study coincided with the formation of the Cambridge Group for the History of Population and Social Structure, and among the important works on the early history of European marriage to emerge from this group was Richard Smith's article "Hypothèses sur la nuptialité en Angleterre aux XIIIe–XIVe siècles" (Hypotheses on Nuptiality in England in the 13th and 14th Centuries, 1983) which argued that the European marriage pattern was discernible much earlier than argued by Hajnal. Smith also argued that the European marriage pattern was mainly found in northern Europe and that the Mediterranean countries were characterized by a relatively early age at marriage and a high age differential between spouses. In this insight Smith was supported in particular by the results of studies by David Herlihy and Christine Klapisch-Zuber Other scholars, such as Goldberg and Outhwaite, have argued for the existence of a European "marriage market" that was subject to the same fluctuations as the rest of the economy.

The other line of inquiry into marriage in the European past has dealt with the role of ecclesiastical and legal institutions in the development of a European ideology of marriage. Although small in volume, the contribution of Michael M. Sheehan has been crucial to the development of the field. Among his essays, "The Formation and Stability of Marriage in Fourteenth-Century England" (1971) is a classic study of how a canon law court dealt with marriage, as are the three papers "Marriage and Family in English Conciliar and Synodal Legislation" (1974), "Marriage Theory and Practice in the Conciliar Legislation and Diocesan Statutes of Medieval England" (1978) and "Choice of Marriage Partner in the Middle Ages" (1978) in which he outlined the way in which the medieval church came to insist on the individual's free choice of marriage partner. The research of James Brundage and Charles Donahue, Jr. has added to Sheehan's insights, but his work has not yet been superseded. A survey of surviving marriage litigation in England was performed by Richard Helmholz, who concluded that the medieval church courts provided a speedy remedy for those who felt they had a genuine complaint against an alleged spouse and Helmholz have agreed that by the 14th century the laity understood at least the basic principles of the canon law of marriage.

The medieval church's insistence on individual choice meant that a new social reality emerged. The implications of this change were discussed in Georges Duby's *Le Chevalier, la femme et le prêtre* (1981; *The Knight, the Lady, and the Priest*, 1983) and his *Medieval Marriage* (1978), and in Jack Goody's *The Development of the Family and Marriage in Europe* (1983). Duby revealed a struggle between two models of marriage, the lay and the ecclesiastical, which took place in the 12th century. The lay model emphasized the continuation of the blood line and concerned itself with the preservation of the male seed and the estate of the family. The ecclesiastical model denied the possibility of divorce and stressed the partners' mutual obligation to fidelity. The ecclesiastical model also aimed to limit sexual activity to within marriage.

Seeking to assess the social and political consequences of these changes in the church's rules of incest, the Cambridge anthropologist Jack Goody argued that the church enforced its rules of exogamy to facilitate the transfer of land to the church by making it increasingly difficult for laymen to marry a member of their kin and by introducing a general ban on adoption. Thus the church wished to prevent a concentration of land among a few powerful families. Goody did not concern himself with the psychological needs and the emotions that bound a couple to each other, but it is implicit in his argument that he believed that family solidarity would tend to limit the choice of partner to the family within the forbidden degrees and thus also to limit the free choice of marriage partner. Goody's book has sparked vigorous debate. The theory has been criticized for being over-elaborate and based on an analysis of Western Christianity at a time when both Jewish and other Christian churches introduced similar rules of exogamy, and upon a misunderstanding of the rules of the canon law on adoption

Scholars of the early modern period have largely ignored the questions about the interaction between religious ideology and the practice of marriage. Instead, they have returned to the question of how love influenced marital choices. On this score, Lawrence Stone's *The Family, Sex and Marriage in England, 1500–1800* (1977) is outstanding. Stone argued that the kind of change in emotional involvement in marriage that Lewis saw in the high Middle Ages actually took place about 400 years later. His thesis has not gone unchallenged, especially by the demographer Peter Laslett in several articles in the *Times Literary Supplement*. John Gillis' *For Better, For Worse* (1985) extended the examination to all classes, and turned a keen eye on the actual rituals involved in courtship. Tracing marriages from 1660 to the present, he chronicled the increasing influence that individuals had on their marriage choices. He also demonstrated that the "white wedding" so popular today is of relatively recent invention.

Ironically, the study of marriage has increased at a time when the institution of marriage is allegedly breaking down. More attention is being paid to the dissolution of marriage. Lawrence Stone's *Road to Divorce* (1990) illuminated the changes in Britain since the 16th century, while Nelson Manfred Blake's *The Road to Reno* (1962) and Glenda Riley's *Divorce: An American Tradition* (1991) did the same for the US. The stresses on families forbidden to form long-term ties were a central theme in Herbert Gutman's *The Black Family in Slavery and Freedom* (1976). Non-European marriage has also been studied recently in Barbara MacGowan Cooper's *Marriage in Maradi* (1997) and Richard Boyer's *Lives of the Bigamists* (1995).

FREDERIK J.G. PEDERSEN

See also Cambridge Group; Demography; Duby; Gutman; Stone

Further Reading

Adair, Richard, *Courtship, Illegitimacy, and Marriage in Early Modern England*, Manchester: Manchester University Press, and New York: St. Martin's Press, 1996

Blake, Nelson Manfred, *The Road to Reno: A History of Divorce in the United States*, New York: Macmillan, 1962

Boyer, Richard E., *Lives of the Bigamists: Marriage, Family, and Community in Colonial Mexico*, Albuquerque: University of New Mexico Press, 1995

Brundage, James A., *Law, Sex, and Christian Society in Medieval Europe*, Chicago: University of Chicago Press, 1987

Brundage, James A., *Medieval Canon Law*, London and New York: Longman, 1995

Cooper, Barbara MacGowan, *Marriage in Maradi: Gender and Culture in a Hausa Society in Niger, 1900–1989*, Oxford: Currey, 1997

Dixon, Chris, *Perfecting the Family: Antislavery Marriages in Nineteenth-Century America*, Amherst: University of Massachusetts Press, 1997

Donahue, Charles, Jr., "The Policy of Alexander the Third's Consent Theory of Marriage," in Stephan Kuttner, ed., *Proceedings of the Fourth International Conference of Medieval Canon Law*, Vatican City: Bibliotheca Apostolica Vaticana, 1976

Donahue, Charles, Jr., "The Canon Law on the Formation of Marriage and Social Practice in the Later Middle Ages," *Journal of Family History* 8 (1983), 144–58

Duby, Georges, *Medieval Marriage: Two Models from Twelfth-Century France*, Baltimore: Johns Hopkins University Press, 1978

Duby, Georges, *Le Chevalier, la femme et le prêtre: le mariage dans la France féodale*, Paris: Hachette, 1981; in English as *The Knight, the Lady, and the Priest: The Making of Modern Marriage in Medieval France*, New York: Pantheon, 1983, London: Allen Lane, 1984

Frost, Ginger Suzanne, *Promises Broken: Courtship, Class, and Gender in Victorian England*, Charlottesville: University Press of Virginia, 1995

Gillis, John R., *For Better, For Worse: British Marriages, 1600 to the Present*, Oxford and New York: Oxford University Press, 1985

Goldberg, P.J.P., *Women, Work, and Life Cycle in a Medieval Economy: Women in York and Yorkshire c.1300–1520*, Oxford and New York: Oxford University Press, 1992

Goody, Jack, *The Development of the Family and Marriage in Europe*, Cambridge and New York: Cambridge University Press, 1983

Grubbs, Judith Evans, *Law and Family in Late Antiquity: The Emperor Constantine's Marriage Legislation*, Oxford and New York: Oxford University Press, 1995

Gutman, Herbert G., *The Black Family in Slavery and Freedom, 1750–1925*, New York: Pantheon, and Oxford: Blackwell, 1976

Hajnal, John, "European Marriage Patterns in Perspective," in D.V. Glass and D.E.C. Eversley, eds., *Population in History: Essays in Historical Demography*, London: Arnold, and Chicago: Aldine, 1965

Helmholz, R.H., *Marriage Litigation in Medieval England*, Cambridge and New York: Cambridge University Press, 1974 [Cambridge Studies in English Legal History, vol. 11]

Herlihy, David, and Christiane Klapisch-Zuber, *Les Toscans et leurs familles: une étude du catasto florentin de 1427*, New Haven: Yale University Press, 1987; in English as *Tuscans and Their Families: A Study of the Florentine Catasto of 1427*, New Haven and London: Yale University Press, 1985

Lewis, C.S., *The Allegory of Love: A Study in Medieval Tradition*, Oxford and New York: Oxford University Press, 1936

Molho, Anthony, *Marriage Alliance in Late Medieval Florence*, Cambridge, MA: Harvard University Press, 1994

Outhwaite, R.B. *Clandestine Marriage in England, 1500–1850*, London: Hambledon Press, 1995

Pedersen, Frederik, "Did the Medieval Laity Know the Canon Law Rules on Marriage: Some Evidence from Fourteenth-Century York Cause Papers," *Medieval Studies* (1994), 111–52

Poos, L.R., Michael Mitterauer, Richard P. Saller, Michael M. Sheehan, and Lloyd Bonfield, "Legal Systems and Family Systems: Jack Goody Revisited," *Continuity and Change* 6 (1991), 285–374

Riley, Glenda, *Divorce: An American Tradition*, Oxford and New York: Oxford University Press, 1991

Riley, Glenda, *Building and Breaking Families in the American West*, Albuquerque: University of New Mexico Press, 1996

Sheehan, Michael M., "The Formation and Stability of Marriage in Fourteenth-Century England: Evidence of an Ely Register," *Medieval Studies* 33 (1971), 228–63

Sheehan, Michael M., "Marriage and Family in English Conciliar and Synodal Legislation," in J. Reginald O'Donnell, ed., *Essays in Honour of Anton Charles Pegis*, Toronto: Pontifical Institute of Medieval Studies, 1974

Sheehan, Michael M., "Choice of Marriage Partner in the Middle Ages: Development and Mode of Application of a Theory of Marriage," *Studies in Medieval and Renaissance History*, new series 1 (1978), 1–34

Sheehan, Michael M., "Marriage Theory and Practice in the Conciliar Legislation and Diocesan Statutes of Medieval England," *Medieval Studies* 40 (1978), 408–60

Sheehan, Michael M., "Theory and Practice: Marriage of the Unfree and the Poor in Medieval Society," *Medieval Studies* 50 (1988), 457–87

Sheehan, Michael M., and Jacqueline Murray, eds., *Domestic Society in Medieval Europe: A Select Bibliography*, Toronto: Pontifical Institute of Medieval Studies, 1990

Sheehan, Michael M., *Marriage, Family, and Law in Medieval Europe: Collected Studies*, edited by James K. Farge, Toronto and Buffalo: University of Toronto Press, 1996

Smith, Richard M., "Hypothèses sur la nuptialité en Angleterre aux XIIIe–XIVe siècles" (Hypotheses on Nuptiality in England in the 13th and 14th Centuries), *Annales: ESC* 38 (1983), 107–36

Stone, Lawrence, *The Family, Sex and Marriage in England, 1500–1800*, London: Weidenfeld and Nicolson, and New York: Harper, 1977

Stone, Lawrence, *Road to Divorce: England, 1530–1987*, Oxford and New York: Oxford University Press, 1990

Wagner, William G., *Marriage, Property, and Law in Late Imperial Russia*, Oxford and New York: Oxford University Press, 1994

Marrus, Michael R. 1941–

Canadian historian of modern Europe

During his academic career, Michael R. Marrus has contributed greatly to French and Jewish social history. His first contribution was in 1980, when, greatly influenced by Hannah Arendt, he delved into the problems of modern anti-Semitism in relation to the implications of Jewish assimilation. Unlike Arendt, however, Marrus focused solely on France during the end of the 19th century. Specifically, he probed the incident involving Captain Alfred Dreyfus, the highest ranking Jewish officer in the French army, who was falsely accused of treason and sentenced to Devil's Island for life imprisonment. As a result, Marrus' first book established him as the world authority on the Dreyfus Affair and a specialist on French anti-Semitism.

After his early work on Dreyfus, Marrus expanded his research on French Jews when Robert O. Paxton, an American scholar of Vichy France, invited him to be co-author of *Vichy France and the Jews* (1981). Paxton asked Marrus to contribute to the book because the material was too depressing for him to write about it single-handedly. Using their meticulous research, Marrus and Paxton confirmed the responsibility of the government of Vichy France in the destruction of French Jews. The authors argued that governmental policies towards Jews in Vichy France were actually harsher than in other European countries. In fact, Marrus and Paxton emphasized that Vichy France initiated autonomous acts that were at times more brutal than those of German forces in occupied France. Additionally, the authors weakened the stance of "apologists" for Vichy France by demonstrating that Pétain and Laval, the two bureaucratic leaders of the regime, along with many

French anti-Semites actually facilitated the process by which French Jews were killed. For their book Marrus and Paxton received the National Jewish Book award in 1982 in the category of Holocaust Studies.

In 1987, Marrus completed the first comprehensive historiography of the vast literature on the Holocaust. In *The Holocaust in History,* he attempted to bring the subject of the Holocaust into the "modern historical experience." He wanted the history of the Holocaust to be seen as more than just a part of the history of the Jewish people. While presenting historical disputes on specific issues, Marrus offered historical, sociological, and political analyses in his historiography. He often synthesized historians' opposing views, and presented his own conclusions. The book was well received by historians, although Marrus received some criticism for not presenting American policy regarding the Holocaust.

Marrus is responsible for expanding historical knowledge of anti-Semitism, Vichy France, and the Holocaust in general. There is no doubt that he will be remembered for his extraordinary scholarly work in *Vichy France and the Jews* and the debates generated by his claims about bureaucracy and the nonchalant attitudes of the French towards the Jews.

LAURIE ROBYN BLUMBERG

See also France: since the Revolution; Holocaust

Biography
Michael Robert Marrus. Born Toronto, 3 February 1941. Received BA, University of Toronto, 1963; MA, University of California, Berkeley, 1964, PhD 1968. Taught at University of Toronto (rising to professor), from 1968. Married Randi Greenstein, 1971 (2 sons, 1 daughter).

Principal Writings
The Politics of Assimilation: The French Jewish Community at the Time of the Dreyfus Affair, 1980
With Robert O. Paxton, *Vichy France and the Jews,* 1981
The Unwanted: European Refugees in the 20th Century, 1985
The Holocaust in History, 1987
Editor, *The Nazi Holocaust: Historical Articles on the Destruction of European Jews,* 9 vols., 1989
Samuel Bronfman: The Life and Times of Seagram's Mr. Sam, 1991
"Reflections on the Historiography of the Holocaust," *Journal of Modern History* 66 (1994), 92–116

Martines, Lauro 1927–
US historian of the Italian Renaissance

Lauro Martines is one of the leaders of the new school of Anglo-American scholars who from the late 1950s combined major archival research with social history to reshape fundamentally our vision of the Italian Renaissance. Essentially, they reformulated the Burckhardtian paradigm that focused on high culture in terms of a more nuanced and inclusive social and political history. Martines was perhaps more interested in literature, art, and interdisciplinary methodology than many of his peers, and his work added a significant cultural dimension to theirs. Especially important was his fascination with the interplay between power and imagination in the Renaissance – the way social and political forces were intimately intertwined with culture.

His first book brilliantly showed his range and the impact of these interests. *The Social World of the Florentine Humanists* (1963) was at one level a massive archival research endeavor that reconstructed the social profiles of the main figures associated with humanism in Florence between 1390 and 1460. But it was much more than a collective biography, for Martines demonstrated that Florentine humanists, rather than being the wandering scholars seeking patronage imagined by tradition, were overwhelmingly important men from major families, and in the process mapped out a sophisticated vision of the social divisions of Renaissance Florence. Without falling into social reductionism, he illuminated a more complex cultural world where power and imagination reinforced and fed off each other in ways that helped send a generation back to the archives to re-examine the social world and writings of humanists and intellectuals.

Martines' second book, *Lawyers and Statecraft in Renaissance Florence* (1968), moved his fascination with the relationship between social class, ideas, and power to the heart of official power in the Renaissance – urban government. At a time when archival studies of the political workings of Florence were revitalizing the understanding of the Renaissance city and scholars were evermore concerned with discovering how governments actually worked, Martines saw that lawyers and notaries were the crucial players in virtually everything from the everyday operation of government to the justification of that operation and government itself. Based again on magisterial archival research, but moving further to examine the massive contemporary literature on the craft of lawyers and notaries, he developed a rich study of the way those two groups underlay the workings of government – a study that still informs much of the ground-breaking work on Renaissance government.

At much the same time that *Lawyers and Statecraft* was published, Martines gathered together at UCLA a group of some of the most important leaders of the new archival history, including Gene Brucker, David Herlihy, John Hale, and J.K. Hyde to consider the largely unstudied issue of violence and civil disorder in the Renaissance. *Violence and Civil Disorder in Italian Cities, 1250–1500* (1972), the volume that came out of that conference, was again path-breaking: it played an important role in problematizing the relationships between rulers and ruled, power and ideology, and opened up new areas of research. In those same years, and again with an eye to expanding the range of historical inquiry, Martines began working on women's history and what would become the history of gender. With his wife, the noted novelist Julia O'Faolain, he published *Not in God's Image: Women in History from the Greeks to the Victorians* (1973), a book that studied the history of women in the West with suggestive texts and keen critical insight.

The work that in many ways summed up his earlier studies and integrated them with his broader understanding of the cultural world of the Renaissance was *Power and Imagination: City-States in Renaissance Italy* (1979). Designed to be read by an educated public, this extended essay reconceptualized the Renaissance as a social, cultural, and political phenomenon with tremendous power and imagination itself. In many ways it is the summation of the insights and innovations of that generation of archival scholars of which Martines was a leader. But unlike many summations, *Power and Imagination* did not merely look back; in fact, it could be read as a research agenda for the future – each chapter ripe with suggestions for research, especially on the relationship between government and structures of power and ideas and realms of imagination. In many ways almost twenty years after its publication it remains the most powerful reformulation of the paradigm of the Italian Renaissance.

After *Power and Imagination*, Martines returned to an early interest of his and one that had always been an important, if largely unremarked, component of his work, his interest in poetry. Renaissance poetry for him was never just an elegant play of words, allusions, and metaphors – although his fine sense of style as a writer reflects his appreciation of these elements – but more importantly poetry was another realm where the social and the cultural intertwined. Revealing once again his innovative flair and his interdisciplinary range, he published *Society and History in English Renaissance Verse* (1985), a work that took him far afield from his formally recognized expertise in the Italian Renaissance and serves as a model for the critical use of poetry for understanding the social and visa versa. With *An Italian Renaissance Sextet: Six Tales in Historical Context* (1994), he returned to his interest in the reading of literature during the Italian Renaissance, using six Italian *novelle* of the 15th century as a base for a close historical analysis of social and cultural life. Fascinating reading, these studies are yet another model for historians interested in reintegrating literature into the discipline in more subtle and methodologically sophisticated ways. Martines, now officially retired and living in London, continues to teach occasionally in Paris, Britain, and the US, and to lecture widely, and is working on a long-term project on the relationship between poetry, power, and society in the Italian Renaissance.

GUIDO RUGGIERO

See also Italy: Renaissance

Biography
Born Chicago, 22 November 1927. Received BA, Drake University, 1950; PhD, Harvard University, 1960. Taught at Reed College, 1958–62; and University of California, Los Angeles, from 1966 (emeritus). Married Julia O'Faolain, novelist, 1957 (1 son).

Principal Writings
The Social World of the Florentine Humanists, 1390–1460, 1963
Lawyers and Statecraft in Renaissance Florence, 1968
Editor, *Violence and Civil Disorder in Italian Cities, 1250–1500*, 1972
Editor, with Julia O'Faolain, *Not in God's Image: Women in History from the Greeks to the Victorians*, 1973
Power and Imagination: City-States in Renaissance Italy, 1979
Society and History in English Renaissance Verse, 1985
An Italian Renaissance Sextet: Six Tales in Historical Context, 1994

Maruyama Masao 1914–1996
Japanese intellectual historian

A leading scholar of Japanese political thought, Maruyama played a key role in setting the agenda for intellectual historians of early modern and modern Japan in the postwar decades. From his father Maruyama Kanji, a liberal political journalist, he inherited a skepticism about any "grand theory." Under the influence of Nanbara Shigeru (1889–1974), his adviser at Tokyo Imperial University and a neo-Kantian, however, he encountered German idealism and was attracted enormously by Hegel's works. He also had a baptism in Marxism, which was an influential current in Japan in the late 1920s. Maruyama's early intellectual life thus became the object of a tug of war between the two contradictory attitudes of positivism and idealism. He eventually realized, as he stated in his introduction to the English version of *Gendai seiji no shisō to kōdō* (1956–57; *Thought and Behavior in Modern Japanese Politics*, 1969), that "in the field of social and political studies the thinkers who take a middling position between German 'historicism' and English 'empiricism,' men like Max Weber, Hermann Heller, and Karl Mannheim, are the ones whom I always found most sympathetic and stimulating."

Maruyama's monumental work, *Nihon seiji shisōshi kenkyū* (1952; *Studies in the Intellectual History of Tokugawa Japan*, 1974), included three articles published in the early 1940s. Through documenting the development of modernity in Tokugawa (17th to mid-19th centuries) ideas, he intended to combat from an academic standpoint the wartime ideological currents, including ultranationalism and totalitarianism. By linking the internal logical and the external sociological perspectives on the major Tokugawa intellectual currents, he was successful in explaining how the division of the twin concepts of "norm" and "nature" in orthodox Neo-Confucianism had prepared the ground for the mode of thought of the scholars of National Learning, and how the transition from the idea of a natural to that of an artificial social order had emerged as an "unintended consequence." Thus he made a decisive departure from traditional and current research methods. Maruyama also devoted much time to the study of Fukuzawa Yukichi (1835–1901), Meiji Japan's foremost thinker and an advocate of westernization, in an attempt to reject the Japanese "national polity" theory.

After the war, Maruyama continued his criticism of the Japanese emperor system and wartime fascism, trying to shed light on the pathological aspects of Japanese society. He described in many of his articles the underlying value-system of the Japanese, especially that of the ruling elites, and its effect on political leaders and their discussion. In examining contemporary politics, he attempted to show how ideological tensions had been aggravated by the refusal of both sides to recognize the political features common to all societies which, in a given situation and irrespective of ideology, made certain patterns of behavior inevitable. Meanwhile, Maruyama further studied Japanese intellectual history from antiquity, in an effort to clarify its frame and characteristics.

DE-MIN TAO

Biography
Born Osaka, 22 March 1914. Attended school in Tokyo; studied political science at Tokyo Imperial University, BA 1936. Taught (rising to professor), Tokyo Imperial University (renamed Tokyo University in 1945), 1936–71. Enlisted toward the end of World War II and stationed at Hiroshima. Married (2 sons). Died 15 August 1996.

Principal Writings

Nihon seiji shisōshi kenkyū (A Study of the History of Japanese Political Thought), 1952; in English as *Studies in the Intellectual History of Tokugawa Japan*, 1974

Gendai seiji no shisō to kōdō, 2 vols., 1956–57; expanded in English as *Thought and Behavior in Modern Japanese Politics*, 1969

Nihon no shisō (The Japanese Thought), 1961

Maruyama Masao shū (Complete Works of Maruyama Masao), 16 vols., 1995–96

Further Reading

Imai Hisaichiro and Kawaguchi Shigeo, *Zohoban Maruyama Masao chosaku nōto* (A Chronology of Maruyama Masao's Works, expanded edition), Tokyo: Gendai no riron sha, 1987

Koschmann, J. Victor, "Maruyama Masao and the Incomplete Project of Modernity," in Masao Miyoshi and H.D. Harootunian, eds., *Postmodernism and Japan*, Durham, NC: Duke University Press, 1989

Sasakura Hideo, *Maruyama Masao ron nōto* (Essays on Maruyama Masao), Tokyo: Misuzu shobo, 1988

Marx, Karl 1818–1883

German political theorist and historian

Friedrich Engels was the first to credit Karl Marx as originator of a new theory of history. This theory, which was developed in concert with Engels, usually goes by the name of the "materialist conception of history" or "historical materialism." Put simply, Marx held that history could be best understood through examination of the material conditions of a society rather than studying only the prevailing ideas or ideologies. Among the most important factors for Marx were: 1) the economic level of development in any given society; 2) changes in the mode of production and exchange; 3) the various class divisions within society; and 4) the extent and nature of the class struggle.

Marx's theory of history denies the primacy of ideas in history. This is not to say he considered ideas as being without force in history. Rather, material conditions are always more significant than abstract philosophical thoughts. Moreover, all historical research has to be based on a solid factual basis instead of theoretical conjecture. This may well seem commonplace among late 20th-century historians but was iconoclastic in the context of a discipline which, at the time of Marx's contribution, was often little more than a subfield of philosophy.

Although Marx is popularly viewed as a proponent of deterministic economic elements, central concerns in Marx's theory of history includes the cardinal importance of human activity in the development of history, and the idea that labor is crucial to the transformation of social relations in history. That is, he presents "real human activity" as the driving force of history, while stressing that how people work helps mold any given society. Marx also emphasized the relation of humans with nature, in which he held that humans are dependent on nature while nature is independent of humanity. The importance of these aspects of his historical worldview is not widely discussed because of his greater emphasis on the centrality of the class struggle within human society.

Marx, along with Engels, appears to have first begun to articulate this historical approach in the 1845 "Die deutsche Ideologie" (*The German Ideology*, 1964). Instead of resting on a set of philosophical assumptions, Marx sought to ground his theory in empirical observations and data. He argued that history could best be understood by the realization that the economic structure of society was the ultimate – but not the only – basis of human history. From this arises everything else: law, religion, politics, culture, and "definite forms of social consciousness." As the productive forces expand or change so too does history become transformed. Moreover, as outlined in his *Der achtzehnte Brumaire des Louis-Bonaparte* (1869; *The Eighteenth Brumaire of Louis Bonaparte*, 1898) Marx contended that class position would normally tend to determine worldview. This being the case, as the economy changes and class structure is altered, consciousness will inevitably change as well. As expressed in a famous passage in his preface to *Zur Kritik der politischen Ökonomie* (1859; *A Contribution to the Critique of Political Economy*, 1904), Marx argued that it is not the consciousness of men which determines their being but "their social being that determines their consciousness."

From such an approach, it would be easy to conclude that the "materialist conception of history" holds to a rigid and fatalistic interpretation of human affairs. In the Soviet Union – and among its more uncritical supporters – this fatalistic interpretation was promoted and history reduced to a series of discernible and infallible "laws." This view – many would say distortion – of Marx's theory of history left little room for human activity or initiative. Although widely accepted – particularly during the Cold War period – this approach contradicts some of Marx's most loudly proclaimed doctrines.

Witness Marx in *Die heilige Familie* (1845; *The Holy Family*, 1956) where he declared that "History does *nothing* . . . it is *man*, real living man, that does all . . . history is *nothing but* the activity of man pursuing his own aims." Later, in an 1871 letter, Marx noted that history would be easy to make if there were infallibly favorable conditions and if there were no "accidents." He even concluded that if there were no accidents history would "be of a very mystical nature."

Instead of mysticism, Marx promoted a dialectical view of world history, rejecting both the unscientific idealism of "great man" theories and the mechanical materialism that would leave humanity out of history. For him, humanity is both object and subject of history. Both molded by historical developments and the molders of those very same developments, humans make their own history but not in conditions of their own choosing.

Marx's method of historical investigation has had a deep influence on countless historians throughout the late 19th and 20th centuries. Some have been primarily political activists in the socialist movement such as, for example, Karl Kautsky. Kautsky, considered the leading theoretician of the Second International, wrote a number of historical studies including *Die Vorläufer des neueren Sozialismus* (1895; *Communism in Central Europe at the Time of the Reformation*, 1897) and *Thomas More und seine Utopie* (1890; *Thomas More and His Utopia*, 1927). While others may have held equally strong left-wing views, their work lies chiefly within the field of history.

Notable among those are the British Marxist historians including Christopher Hill, George Rudé, Rodney Hilton, Eric

Hobsbawm, and E.P. Thompson, whose work has had a profound impact on western – and particularly English-speaking – historians. These historians broke the conventional habits of historiography, injecting materialist analysis, class analysis, and the idea of human agency into their works. For example in his *The Crowd in the French Revolution* (1959), Rudé re-examined the long accepted idea of the irrational "mob" running wild in the streets of Paris. Using a wealth of primary evidence, Rudé built a convincing case that the "crowd" was far more rational than historical tradition would admit. Within Western Europe, the Marxist approach to history – while never truly what one could term mainstream – has reached a level of acceptance that means even Marx's critics have to take his arguments seriously.

Nor was Marx's influence absent even in the politically inhospitable climate of the United States. It was Marx's writings which swayed Philip S. Foner to write a new American labor history that put conflict – rather than accommodation – at the heart of labor's story. Herbert Apetheker broke new ground in revealing the deep history of slave resistance and struggle because of his Marxist training, while later, Eugene Genovese would utilize Marxist tools to reinterpret the history of American slavery.

WILLIAM A. PELZ

See also Engels; Foner, P.; Genovese; Hilton; Hobsbawm; Rudé; Thompson, E.

Biography

Karl Heinrich Marx. Born Trier, 5 May 1818, son of a lawyer. Studied in Bonn and Berlin, 1835–41; PhD, University of Jena, 1841. Editor, *Rheinische Zeitung für Politik, Handel und Gewerbe*, 1842–43; lived in Paris (where he became lifelong friends with Friedrich Engels), 1843–44, and Brussels, 1845–47; chief editor, *Neue Rheinische Zeitung*, Cologne, 1848–49; expelled from Germany and lived in London from 1849. Married Jenny von Westphalen, 1843 (3 daughters, 1 son). Died London, 14 March 1883.

Principal Writings

With Friedrich Engels, "Die deutsche Ideologie," written 1845–46; published in *Historisch-kritische Gesamtausgabe: Werke, Schriften, Briefe*, vol. 5, edited by David Rjazanov and V.V. Adoratskij, 1932; in English as *The German Ideology*, 1964

With Friedrich Engels, *Die heilige Familie, oder Kritik der kritischen Kritik*, 1845; in English as *The Holy Family; or, Critique of Critical Critique*, 1956

Zur Kritik der politischen Ökonomie, 1859; in English as *A Contribution to the Critique of Political Economy*, 1904

Das Kapital, 3 vols., 1867–94; in English as *Capital*, 3 vols., 1887–1909

Der achtzehnte Brumaire des Louis-Bonaparte, 1869; in English as *The Eighteenth Brumaire of Louis Bonaparte*, 1898

With Friedrich Engels, *Collected Works*, 1975–

Further Reading

Aguirre Rojas, Carlos Antonio, "Between Marx and Braudel: Making History, Knowing History," *Review* (Fernand Braudel Center) 15 (1992), 175–219

Fischer, Ernst, *Was Marx wirklich sagte*, Vienna: Molden, 1968; in English as *Marx in His Own Words*, London: Allen Lane, 1970; revised as *How to Read Karl Marx*, New York: Monthly Review Press, 1996

Kaye, Harvey J., *The British Marxist Historians: An Introductory Analysis*, Cambridge: Polity Press, 1984; New York: St. Martin's Press, 1995

Mahon, Joseph, "Marx as a Social Historian," *History of European Ideas* 12 (1990), 749–66

Murray, Patrick, "Karl Marx as a Historical Materialist Historian of Political Economy," *History of Political Thought* 20 (1988), 90–105

Vadász, Sándor, "Marx mint történetíro" (Marx as a Writer on History), *Századok* (Hungary) 117 (1983), 1225–45

Marxist Interpretation of History

For Marx, the role of material production was an essential fact of human history. Human beings always require food and shelter in order to exist. The ways in which these means of subsistence are produced by individuals and groups working together – "the social production of their existence" – involves some division of labor and hence some kind of social hierarchy. Since production – work – is so central a part of daily life, social relations have a material element. This had been elaborated in the first part of "Die deutsche Ideologie" (*The German Ideology*, 1964), drafted by Marx and Engels between November 1845 and the autumn of 1846.

In his 1859 preface to *Zur Kritik der politischen Ökonomie* (*A Contribution to the Critique of Political Economy*, 1904) Marx presented a widely-quoted summary of the working principles of what subsequently became known as the materialist interpretation of history, or historical materialism:

> In the social production of their existence, men inevitably enter into definite relations, which are independent of their will, namely relations of production appropriate to a given stage in the development of their material forces of production. The totality of these relations of production constitutes the economic structure of society, the real foundation, on which arises a legal and political superstructure and to which correspond definite forms of social consciousness. The mode of production of material life conditions the general process of social, political, and intellectual life. It is not the consciousness of men that determines their existence, but their social existence that determines their consciousness. At a certain stage of development, the material productive forces of society come into conflict with the existing relations of production, or – this merely expresses the same thing in legal terms – with the property relations within the framework of which they have operated hitherto. From forms of development of the productive forces these relations turn into their fetters. Then begins an era of social revolution. With the change of the economic foundations the entire immense superstructure is more or less rapidly transformed.

Following from this, these social relations of production and their connected hierarchies change as the material forms of production change. The evolving relations between forms of material production, the division of labor and social structure – together constituting "the mode of production" – thus provide a way of periodizing history. In the 1859 preface Marx further emphasized the determining role of the *forces* of production. Productive forces can be defined as elements of the process of production: technology, raw materials, sources of energy, scientific knowledge, the skills of the workforce, etc. The combination of these elements in the specific process of production, the technical organization of production, is itself connected to the wider social relations of production, defined as the relations of property which hold between the producers and the owners of the means of production. Here, and elsewhere, Marx suggested that the forces of production have their own power and dynamic.

Periods of development and gradual change are punctuated by periods of crisis, revolution, and rapid transformation. These occur when relations of production become incompatible with changing forces of production. They become "fetters" and are broken open, to be replaced by new relations of production which encourage a further period of development. Hence the rise and fall of successive forms of society – slave societies, feudalism, and, ultimately, capitalism. This pattern of historical change from the ancient world to industrial capitalism had been sketched out in the first part of *Manifesto der kommunistischen Partei* (1848; *The Communist Manifesto*, 1888).

If the social relations of production are underpinned by a dynamic economic structure, they themselves in turn underpin a further set of institutional relations – "a legal and political superstructure." This is the space within which specific forms of consciousness move. Just as the social relations of production change in response to the pressures of the productive forces, so in turn the legal and political superstructure and forms of consciousness have to adapt and change. Moments of crisis, when forces and relations of production are in conflict, will generate conflict within the legal and political superstructure and within consciousness.

This passage from the 1859 preface is the most succinct statement of the guiding principles of Marx's approach to history. Here in condensed form he summarized, developed, and clarified some of the central arguments of his earlier writings. He provided a schema for analyzing long-term historical change based on the dynamic axis of forces and relations of production. And he supplied a model – economic foundation / legal and political superstructure – of the totality of interconnections within a specific historical moment. But this is where the problems begin. What is the theoretical status of these propositions? "A few indications concerning the course of my own politico-economic studies" was how Marx introduced the 1859 preface, and he went on to describe this passage (and it is no more than a single paragraph in a brief preface) as "a guiding thread for my studies" and a "sketch." Marx's rare summaries of his theory of history, part 1 of *The German Ideology*, the introduction to *Grundrisse der Kritik der politischen Ökonomie* (1939–41; *Grundrisse: Foundations of the Critique of Political Economy*, 1973) as well as the 1859 preface to *A Critique of Political Economy*, have been deservedly influential. But they should not be taken as his final (much less his only) word. As Etienne Balibar observed in *Lire le Capital* (1967; *Reading Capital*, 1970): "These are very general, prospective or summary texts; texts in which the sharpness of the distinctions and the peremptoriness of the claims are only equalled by the brevity of the justifications, the elliptical nature of the definitions." Such

texts need to be read critically and in relation to other texts by Marx – and in particular, the substantial amount of his writing that engaged in empirical analysis. If the 1859 preface was a "sketch" it was also, he observed, "the result of conscientious investigation lasting many years."

In more than 300 articles for the New York *Daily Tribune*, more than 100 for *Neue Rheinische Zeitung* and around 175 for *Die Presse*, all written between 1852 and 1862, Marx gave some proof of his "conscientious investigation," often on historical materials. In 1858 Marx was planning a historical work on the development of different modes of production. The so-called *Grundrisse*, seven notebooks from 1857–58, contained in notebook 4 a lengthy section on precapitalist modes of production, presumably a preliminary draft of this work. The *Grundrisse* was first published in full in English only in 1973, but this historical section was published separately as *Pre-Capitalist Economic Formations* in 1964. In his lengthy introduction, Eric Hobsbawm noted the importance of this material. It marked a considerable refinement in periodizing historical development and in specifying historical forms of the division of labor.

The first volume of *Das Kapital* (1867–94; *Capital*, 1887–1909) was the summa of Marx's effort to produce an effective critique of political economy. As such, it is not in any very obvious sense a work of history but, again, it is grounded in immense empirical research and there is much historical material in its pages. For instance, chapter 10, "The Working Day," provided a detailed historical account of the contest between employers and workers over the length of the working day. Chapters 14 and 15 offered a detailed account of the transition from manufacture to modern industrial production. Chapters 26–33 used the historical case of England to focus on "primitive accumulation."

Problems may arise from focusing narrowly on the 1859 preface without examining these more empirically-focused writings. First, on the issue of periodization, Marx's linear model of economic and social change through a sequence of stages apparently leaves little scope for historical specificity or contingency. In the preface to the first edition of volume 1 of *Capital*, complacent German readers were warned that "the natural laws of capitalist production" worked themselves out "with iron necessity": "The country that is more developed industrially only shows, to the less developed, the image of its own future." In chapter 26 the expropriation of the English peasantry and creation of a landless rural labor force is represented as a process inevitably repeated in all the countries of Western Europe. But here Marx qualified his argument: "The history of this expropriation assume[d] different aspects in different countries, and [ran] through its various phases in different orders of succession, and at different historical epochs." Now the English case was, he said, exceptional, though it was also "the classic form" of the process. It is difficult here to understand precisely what "classic form" means. Was the English case unique or exemplary? How significant were the differences in historical sequence from country to country? Are we looking at a single underlying process that simply takes different national forms? Are we looking at one history or several histories? Confusion seems unavoidable for even the attentive reader and, in an unsent letter of November 1877, Marx reprimanded one of them for extrapolating his account to Russia: "He insists on transforming my historical sketch of the genesis of capitalism in Western Europe into an historico-philosophic theory of the general path of development prescribed by fate to all nations, whatever the historical circumstances in which they find themselves." The account in *Capital* had become merely a "historical sketch," and "iron necessity," "natural" or inevitable laws of development, and all the rest are downplayed. "Historical circumstances" now played a crucial determining role. Marx concluded this long and important letter with a discussion of the dispossession of the free peasants of ancient Rome, which gave rise not to capitalism but to slavery: "Thus events strikingly analogous but taking place in different historical surroundings led to totally different results. By studying each of these forms of evolution separately and then comparing them one can easily find the clue to this phenomenon, but one will never arrive there by using as one's master key a general historico-philosophical theory, the supreme virtue of which consists in being supra-historical." This is just one of a number of instances in which the austere logic of the 1859 preface is severely qualified when Marx changed focus, engaged with problems of historical specificity, and examined particular processes of change.

Another set of problems stems from ahistorical applications of the so-called "base/superstructure model." It was never, of course, merely "the economic" as such that was determining for Marx. It was always a historically-specific matrix of forms of productive activity and social relations that was decisive. This is indicated in an important passage in volume 3 of *Capital* (chapter 47):

> It is in each case the direct relationship of the owners of the conditions of production to the immediate producers . . . in which we find the innermost secret, the hidden basis of the entire social edifice, and hence also the political form of the relationship of sovereignty and dependence, in short, the specific form of the state in each case. This does not prevent the same economic basis – the same in its major conditions – from displaying endless variations and gradations in its appearance, as the result of innumerable empirical circumstances, natural conditions, racial relations, historical influences acting from outside, etc., and these can only be understood by analyzing these empirically given conditions.

Thus Marx insisted that material production must be understood in its specific historical form and not applied as a general category. We are a long way here from any kind of mechanical base/superstructure model.

In a note in the first volume of *Capital* Marx responded to one criticism of the 1859 preface – that the overwhelming centrality of the economic in social life may be applicable to the 19th century but not to the ancient world or the Middle Ages. First he reaffirmed that material production of food, shelter, clothing, and so on was a precondition of human existence in all periods of history: "the Middle Ages could not live on Catholicism, nor the ancient world on politics." But he went on to distinguish between the determining role of the economic and the dominant role of religion or politics: "it is the mode in which they gained a livelihood that explains why here politics, and there Catholicism, played the chief part." In *Capital*, and elsewhere, Marx acknowledged that in precapitalist modes of

production forms of extra-economic coercion were crucial elements of the social relations of production. In other words, political structures were constitutive of the economic sphere. Marx also qualified the synchronic model of social totality, recognizing that there were historical lags and patterns of uneven development (see, for instance, the discussion of Greek art in the introduction to *Grundrisse*).

Many other issues are raised by juxtaposing summary texts, such as the 1859 preface, with others of Marx's writings. "The history of all hitherto existing societies is the history of class struggles," *The Communist Manifesto* declared in its opening sentence. But the 1859 preface did not mention class struggles, or even class. Whether or not this silence was a way of evading the Prussian censor, it leaves unexplored some central questions. If the forces/relations of production matrix is the dynamic core of historical change, what is the role of class struggle? What is the relative force of conscious social agency and economic structures? And following on from this, there are a whole cluster of questions about the definition of social class, the causal connections between class location, class consciousness, and political action.

Two brilliant pieces of historical analysis of a specific historical moment, *Die Klassenkämpfe in Frankreich 1848 bis 1850* (written 1850, first published 1895; *The Class Struggles in France, 1848–1850*, 1924) and *Der achtzehnte Brumaire des Louis-Bonaparte* (written 1852, first published 1869; *The Eighteenth Brumaire of Louis Bonaparte*, 1898), exemplified the ways in which Marx grappled with some of these problems. The former was, Engels later said, "Marx's first attempt to explain a section of contemporary history by means of his materialist conception." In handling the complexities of a precise sequence of events in France in the 1830s and 1840s, both studies abandoned big generalizations and simple models. Especially in *The Eighteenth Brumaire*, Marx developed a very careful and empirically-controlled periodization of recent French political history. He accepted that capital and labor did not appear on the political stage "in person." Contending political groupings "represented" wider social forces in different ways – and these forces were not limited to capitalists and workers. Constitutions, political alliances, electoral procedures, traditions, and ideologies – the whole terrain of political life – had their own material effects and were never merely the shadowy reflection of some prior economic reality. And again, the power of history is addressed in the opening pages of *The Eighteenth Brumaire*: "The tradition of the dead generations weighs like a nightmare on the minds of the living."

The model of base and superstructure is, then, no more than a useful and flexible device for thinking about the relative pressure of different elements within a social totality at a particular moment. Here, as in the case of the forces and relations of the production axis, Marx is making analytical distinctions that are provisional and exploratory. They are signposts, not empirical descriptions. As *The German Ideology* had emphasized: "Empirical observation must in each separate instance bring out empirically, and without any mystification and speculation, the connection of the social and political structure with production."

Interrupted by political activity, especially his involvement in the International Working Men's Association (the so-called First International), and plagued by poor health, by the time of his death in 1883 Marx had not provided an extended theoretical account of historical materialism. The published oeuvre of Karl Marx today consists of letters, working drafts, notebooks, and manuscripts never finalized for publication, as well as newspaper articles, political speeches, and documents, local polemics, and a few major studies, notably the first volume of *Capital*, which he did see through the press himself. His partnership with Engels, who not only cooperated in the writing of several texts but was responsible for editing and rewriting several of Marx's works after the latter's death – outstandingly, volumes 2 and 3 of *Capital* – adds further complications. It is hardly surprising that this collection of writings bearing the name "Karl Marx" is fragmentary and discrepant.

This issue, however, involves more than Marx's peculiar publication history. The major themes of this body of work – the determining pressures exerted by the forces of production in long-term historical change, the pivotal role of class struggle in history, the profound connections between forms of economic production and political structures, and so on – were developed by Marx in summaries and extended analyses which were often inconsistent, or at least pointed in different directions. The forms in which "the legal and political superstructure" were "conditioned" by, or "represented," socioeconomic processes were formulated and reformulated in several ways. The central concept of social class received various definitions and, crucially, in chapter 52 of volume 3 of *Capital*, was abandoned to silence. At the very core of Marx's work there were unresolved tensions: between, for instance, a stress on social agency, whereby men (and women) make their own history through conscious collective activity, and a countervailing stress on overpowering structural constraints; or between the creation of coherent and overarching conceptual models and empirical analysis of specific histories. Marx said of Adam Smith's inconsistencies in his theory of value, that they were "natural in a writer who is the founder of political economy and is necessarily feeling his way, experimenting, and struggling with a chaos of ideas." So too in the case of Marx the price of his conceptual innovation was a body of work riddled by uncertainties and provisionalities. It was precisely his dogged refusal to systematize prematurely or to foreclose on inconsistencies that was to make his influence so productive.

As socialist parties responsive to Marx's ideas began to be established in Europe in the 1880s, it fell to Engels to systematize and clarify "historical materialism." This was in a context in which key texts were unavailable. *Economic and Philosophic Manuscripts of 1844* (1959), *The German Ideology*, and *Grundrisse* were unpublished and forgotten. Many of Marx's important newspaper articles were undiscovered, and even major works were untranslated into English or French, much less other languages. It is clear from his correspondence in these years that Engels was anxious to avoid over-simplification, and impatient with those who adopted a mechanical economic reductionism. As he quipped to one of his correspondents in 1890: "the materialist conception of history ... has a lot of friends nowadays to whom it serves as an excuse for *not* studying history." And yet Engels' own widely circulated writings – *Anti-Dühring* (1878) and *Ludwig Feuerbach und der Ausgang der klassischen deutschen Philosophie* (1888; *Ludwig Feuerbach and the Outcome of Classical German Philosophy*, 1934) – did in crucial respects encourage the idea that historical materialism

was a coherent and finished theoretical system that could be applied to empirical reality.

In the hands of a new generation, especially in Germany, dazzled by the high status of the natural sciences and persuaded of the deep affinity of Darwin and Marx – again encouraged by Engels (and sometimes Marx) – historical materialism was represented as a positivist method based on the model of the natural sciences and imbued with the idiom of Darwin. Karl Kautsky and Georgii Plekhanov were the most authoritative of the second generation of interpreters of Marxism and received the imprimatur of Engels. Kautsky's *Die materialistische Geschichtsauffassung* (1927; *The Materialist Conception of History*, 1988) and Plekhanov's *K voprosu o razvitii monisticheskogo vzgliada na istoriiu* (1919; *In Defence of Materialism*, 1947) were vigorous assertions of the scientific credentials and the materialism of the Marxist approach to history. Both followed closely the text of the 1859 preface to elaborate a universal history grounded in the development of the forces of production, now narrowly understood in terms of technological relations to the material environment. History appeared as a more or less inexorable and cumulative process of technical mastery over nature. Despite the violent political differences of Kautsky and Plekhanov, the dominant version of the Marxist-Leninist interpretation of history in the Soviet Union remained committed to the same kind of productive forces determinism – see Bukharin's *Teoriia istoricheskogo materializma* (1923; *Historical Materialism*, 1925) or Stalin's admittedly succinct "Dialectical and Historical Materialism" (1938).

This is not to say that this second generation did not make a valuable contribution to the development of Marxist historical writing. In the years before 1914 there was a proliferation of historical work throughout Europe, generally outside the academy, influenced to varying degrees by a "Marxist" approach. Kautsky himself wrote historical studies of the origins of Christianity and of Thomas More. Eduard Bernstein, literary executor of Engels and the major political voice of revisionist Marxism in the pre-1914 SPD, did pioneering research on the English revolution of the 1640s and 1650s, rescuing the Levellers from obscurity in his *Cromwell and Communism*. At the same time, for this politically-engaged generation of Marxists, historical materialism was not merely a philosophy of history or a way of writing about the past. It was a source of knowledge capable of informing current political practice and directed towards the present and the future. Works such as Kautsky's *Die Agrarfrage* (1898; *The Agrarian Question*, 1988) or Lenin's *Razvitie kapitalizma v Rossii* (1899; *The Development of Capitalism in Russia*, 1960) – concerned with the transformative impact of capital on precapitalist forms of agriculture – Hilferding's *Das Finanzkapital* (1923; *Finance Capital*, 1981) or Bukharin's *Mitovoe khoziaistvo i imperializm*, 1923; *Imperialism and World Economy*, 1929) – focused on the replacement of laissez-faire capitalism by a new forms of state capital – were not historical studies in any narrow sense. They were analyses of contemporary issues with immediate political purpose. But they necessarily involved historical periodization and appropriated key concepts from Marx precisely in order to analyze change over time. There is a narrow dividing line between utilizing a historical perspective to inform political practice and exploiting it to justify a political policy. In the Soviet Union, especially from the later 1920s, the Marxist interpretation of history, in its most narrow determinist form, became part of state doctrine. It reached its nadir in the Boshevik Central Committee's 1938 *History of the Communist Party of the Soviet Union: Short Course*, written under Stalin's supervision, with its blatant distortions of history to justify the Soviet regime.

From the 1920s in Western Europe quite different variants of Marxism emerged, breaking decisively from the productive forces/technological determinism of the Second International and Soviet Marxism-Leninism. The Italian Communist leader Antonio Gramsci saw the Bolshevik revolution as a revolution *against* Marx's *Capital*, or at least against the sometimes rigid historical schemas derived from it by Kautsky, Plekhanov, and others. But he was similarly critical of a Bolshevik such as Bukharin for reducing the Marxist approach, in his *Historical Materialism*, "to a mechanical formula which gives the impression of holding the whole of history in the palm of its hand." Gramsci insisted on the value of the idealist prehistory of Marxism with its emphasis on consciousness, culture, and human agency, as against what he termed "the positivist and naturalist incrustations" that "contaminated" some of Marx's later writings. A prisoner of Mussolini from 1926, Gramsci, in difficult conditions, patiently outlined an innovative programme for historical research. The insights and new concepts sketched out in the *Prison Notebooks* were not, however, to reach a wider readership until the 1950s.

A complementary project to reassert the antipositivist strand within historical materialism, subsequently called "Western Marxism," emerged in the 1920s. The seminal text was *Geschichte und Klassenbewusstsein* (1923; *History and Class Consciousness*, 1971), a collection of essays by Georg Lukács which elaborated some startling and brilliant new perspectives on Marx. In particular, it retrieved the importance of Marx's brief discussion of commodity fetishism in volume 1 of *Capital* and connected it to the notion of reification, derived from Max Weber. But, despite its title, the book had little to say about most of the major themes of historical materialism or about specific economic and social histories. Condemned by the Comintern and subsequently renounced by Lukács himself, *History and Class Consciousness* was a founding text for Walter Benjamin, Herbert Marcuse, Theodor Adorno, Max Horkheimer, and others who constituted "the Frankfurt school" in the early 1930s. Its Hegelian affinities reinforced by the discovery in 1932 of Marx's *Economic and Philosophic Manuscripts of 1844*, "Western Marxism" tended to replace concrete historical research with philosophical reflection and cultural critique. Nevertheless, between the 1930s and the 1960s the Frankfurt school and a parallel generation of French leftists, notably Lucien Goldmann, Maurice Merleau-Ponty and, especially, Jean-Paul Sartre – in critical dialogue with Freud, Weber, and phenomenology – made valuable contributions to Marxist approaches to the historical analysis of culture and of politics.

Elsewhere between the 1930s and 1950s, despite a degree of political and intellectual isolation, and despite the limitations of the Soviet paradigm of historical materialism, various kinds of creative historical work influenced by Marx did proceed within the orbit of European communist parties. Some of this writing laid the groundwork for the massive explosion of Marxist historiography in the 1960s and 1970s. Maurice Dobb's *Studies in the Development of Capitalism* (1946) was an extremely influential historical study by a British Communist party (and Cambridge University) economist which broke new ground in using Marx's categories to examine the historical transition from feudalism to capitalism. It triggered an international debate in the pages of the American journal *Science and Society*, subsequently collected together in *The Transition from Feudalism to Capitalism: A Symposium* edited by Rodney Hilton in 1954. Subsequent work by Hilton, Witold Kula, Immanuel Wallerstein, Perry Anderson, Robert Brenner, Guy Bois, and others has made this one of the most productive and international areas of Marxist historical work in the postwar period. Here there were significant convergences with the theoretical work of Louis Althusser, especially *Lire le Capital* (1965; *Reading "Capital"*, 1970), which was focusing attention on relevant concepts in Marx dealing with the transition between modes of production. Hindess and Hirst's *Pre-Capitalist Modes of Production* (1975) was an important, if much disputed, Althusserian intervention in this historiography.

Labor history and the history of working-class political organizations was another important field of Marxist historical work developing from the interwar years. In France, inevitably, this was centered around the Revolution, the understanding of which was dominated for several generations by a Marxist framework associated with the writing of Albert Mathiez, Georges Lefebvre, and Albert Soboul. In Britain strong traditions of labor history and radical cultural criticism, developed further in the interwar years by communists such as A.L. Morton, Dona Torr, Edgell Rickword, and Jack Lindsay, laid the groundwork for a group of historians who were to have a massive international influence from the 1960s. Christopher Hill, E.P. Thompson, and Eric Hobsbawm in particular – but also George Rudé, Victor Kiernan, and John Saville – contributed to the emergence of a new social history of the working class and, increasingly, of other subaltern social groups. In fact, by the 1970s a more or less Marxian agenda was shaping historical work in many different fields and periods in Western Europe and the United States. At the same time the writings of Marx and some of the key figures of Western Marxism were being translated, debated, and appropriated for the first time. There were probably more exegeses and more theoretical debates around the Marxist interpretation of history between 1970 and 1985 than at any time in the previous century.

Especially in these years, in field after field of historical research, questions and perspectives derived from Marx have set agendas, provoked debates, and reshaped important historical territories. The renaissance of Marxism is now over. New radical theories associated with French poststructuralism and feminism are now setting the pace across the human sciences, sometimes in open critical dialogue with the Marxist tradition, sometimes in profoundly uncritical hostility (in both directions). The revolutions of 1989 and the collapse of Soviet communism have challenged not only the Marxist world but its intellectual edifice. For better or worse, the Marxist interpretation of history remains a problematic and highly politicized issue.

JOHN SEED

See also Anderson, P.; Althusser; Brenner; Furet; Gramsci; Hilton; Hill; Hobsbawm; Kula; Labor; Subaltern; Thompson, E.; Wallerstein

Further Reading

Althusser, Louis, Etienne Balibar *et al.*, *Lire le Capital*, Paris: Maspero, 1965; abridged edition (by Althusser and Balibar only) in English as *Reading "Capital"*, London: Verso, 1970, New York: Pantheon, 1971

Anderson, Perry, *Considerations on Western Marxism*, London: NLB, 1976

Baron, Samuel H., *Plekhanov: The Father of Russian Marxism*, London: Routledge, and Stanford, CA: Stanford University Press, 1963

Bernstein, Eduard, *Sozialismus und Demokratie in der grossen englischen Revolution*, 2nd ed., Stuttgart: Dietz, 1908; in English as *Cromwell and Communism*, London: Allen and Unwin, 1930; New York: A.M. Kelley, 1963

Bolshevik Central Committee, *History of the Communist Party of the Soviet Union: Short Course*, Moscow: Foreign Language House, 1938; New York: International Publishers, 1939; London: Cobbett, 1943

Brenner, Robert, "The Origins of Capitalist Development: A Critique of Neo-Smithian Marxism," *New Left Review* 104 (July–August 1977), 25–92

Brewer, Anthony, *A Guide to Marx's "Capital,"* Cambridge and New York: Cambridge University Press, 1984

Bukharin, Nikolai, *Mirovoe khoziaistvo i imperializm*, Petrograd: Priboi, 1923; in English as *Imperialism and World Economy*, New York: International Publishers, 1929, London: Merlin Press, 1972

Bukharin, Nikolai, *Teoriia istoricheskogo materializma: populiarnyi uchebnik marksistskii sotsiologii*, Moscow, 1923; in English as *Historical Materialism: A System of Sociology*, New York: International Publishers, 1925, London: Allen and Unwin, 1926; reprinted Ann Arbor: University of Michigan Press, 1969

Cohen, Gerald Allan, *Karl Marx's Theory of History: A Defence*, Oxford: Oxford University Press, and Princeton: Princeton University Press, 1978

Cottrell, Allin, *Social Classes in Marxist Theory*, London and Boston: Routledge, 1984

de Ste. Croix, G.E.M., *The Class Struggle in the Ancient Greek World: From the Archaic Age to the Arab Conquests*, London: Duckworth, and Ithaca, NY: Cornell University Press, 1981

Dobb, Maurice, *Studies in the Development of Capitalism*, London: Routledge, 1946; New York: International Publishers, 1947

Elster, Jon, *Making Sense of Marx*, Cambridge and New York: Cambridge University Press, 1985

Engels, Friedrich, *Herrn Eugen Dührings Umwälzung der Wissenschaft [Anti-Dühring]*, Leipzig: Genossenschafts-Buchdruckerei, 1878; in English as *Herr Eugen Dühring's Revolution in Science [Anti-Dühring]*, New York: International Publishers, 1894, London: Lawrence and Wishart, 1931

Engels, Friedrich, *Der Ursprung der Familie, des Privateigenthums und des Staats*, Hottingen-Zurich: Schweizerische Volksbuchhandlung, 1884; in English as *The Origin of the Family, Private Property, and the State*, Moscow: Foreign Languages Publishing House, 1891, Chicago: Kerr, 1902, London: Lawrence and Wishart, 1940

Engels, Friedrich, *Ludwig Feuerbach und der Ausgang der klassischen deutschen Philosophie*, Stuttgart: Dietz, 1888; in English as *Ludwig Feuerbach and the Outcome of Classical German Philosophy*, London: Lawrence, and New York: International Publishers, 1934

Forgacs, David, ed., *A Gramsci Reader: Selected Writings, 1916–1935*, London: Lawrence and Wishart, 1988

Furet, François, *Marx et la Révolution française*, Paris: Flammarion, 1986; in English as *Marx and the French Revolution*, Chicago: University of Chicago Press, 1988

Godelier, M,. "Infrastructures, Society and History," *New Left Review* 112 (1978), 84–96

Gramsci, Antonio, *Quaderni del carcere*, 6 vols., written 1926–37, published Turin: Einaudi, 1948–51, critical edition, 4 vols., 1975; in English as *Selections from the Prison Notebooks,* London: Lawrence and Wishart, 1971, New York: International Publishers, 1972

Hilferding, Rudolf, *Das Finanzkapital: eine Studie über die jüngste Entwicklung des Kapitalismus*, Vienna: Wiener Volksbuchhandlung, 1923; in English as *Finance Capital: A Study of the Latest Phase of Capitalist Development*, London and Boston: Routledge, 1981

Hilton, Rodney, ed., *The Transition from Feudalism to Capitalism: A Symposium*, New York: Science and Society, and London: Fore, 1954; revised London: New Left Books, and Atlantic Highlands, NJ: Humanities Press, 1976

Hindess, Barry, and Paul Q. Hirst, *Pre-Capitalist Modes of Production*, London: Routledge, 1975

Holton, R.J., "Marxist Theories of Social Change and the Transition from Feudalism to Capitalism," *Theory and Society* 10 (1981), 805–32

Jones, Gareth Stedman, "Engels and the Genesis of Marxism," *New Left Review* 106 (1977), 79–104

Kautsky, Karl, *Thomas More und seine Utopie*, Stuttgart: Dietz, 1890; in English as *Thomas More and His Utopia*, New York: International Publishers, and London, A. & C. Black, 1927; reprinted 1979

Kautsky, Karl, *Die Agrarfrage: eine Übersicht über die Tendenzen der modernen Landwirtschaft und die Agrarpolitik der Sozialdemokratie*, Stuttgart: Dietz, 1898; in English as *The Agrarian Question*, London: Zwan, 1988

Kautsky, Karl, *Die materialistische Geschichtsauffassung*, 2 vols., Berlin: Dietz, 1927; in English as *The Materialist Conception of History*, New Haven: Yale University Press, 1988

Labriola, Antonio, *Essays on the Materialistic Conception of History*, Chicago: Kerr, 1904 [Italian original]; reprinted 1966

Lenin, V.I., *Razvitie kapitalizma v Rossii: protsess obrazovaniia vnutrennego rynka dlia krupnoi promyshlennosti*, St. Petersburg, 1899; in English as *The Development of Capitalism in Russia*, vol. 3, Moscow: Progress, and London: Lawrence and Wishart, 1960

Lukács, Georg, *Geschichte und Klassenbewusstsein: Studien über marxistische Dialektik*, Berlin: Malik, 1923; in English as *History and Class Consciousness: Studies in Marxist Dialectics*, London: Merlin, and Cambridge, MA: MIT Press, 1971

Marx, Karl, and Friedrich Engels, "Die deutsche Ideologie," written 1845–46; published in *Historisch-kritische Gesamtausgabe: Werke, Schriften, Briefe*, vol. 5, edited by David Rjazanov and V.V. Adoratskij, Frankfurt: Marx-Engels-Archiv, 1932; in English as *The German Ideology*, Moscow: Progress, 1964, London: Lawrence and Wishart, 1970, and in Marx and Engels, *Collected Works*, New York: International Publishers, 1975–, vol. 5: 19–539

Marx, Karl, and Friedrich Engels, *Manifesto der kommunistischen Partei*, London: Burghard, 1848, Chicago: Hofmann, 1871; in English as *Manifesto of the Communist Party*, London: Reeves, 1888, Chicago: Kerr, 1902; generally known as *The Communist Manifesto*

Marx, Karl, *Zur Kritik der politischen Ökonomie*, Berlin: Duncker, 1859; in English as *A Contribution to the Critique of Political Economy*, New York: International Publishers, and London: Kegan Paul Trench Trübner, 1904

Marx, Karl, *Das Kapital*, 3 vols., Hamburg : Meissner, 1867–94; in English as *Capital*, 3 vols., vol. 1: London: Sonnenschein Lowrey, 1887, New York: Appleton, 1889; vols. 2 and 3: Chicago: Kerr, 1907–09; vols. 1–3: London: Penguin, 1976–81

Marx, Karl, *Der achtzehnte Brumaire des Louis-Bonaparte*, Hamburg: Meissner, 1869; in English as *The Eighteenth Brumaire of Louis Bonaparte*, New York: International Publishers, 1898, London: Allen and Unwin, 1924

Marx, Karl, *Die Klassenkämpfe in Frankreich, 1848 bis 1850*, Berlin: Glocke, 1895; in English as *The Class Struggles in France, 1848–1850*, New York: New York Labor News, 1924, London: Lawrence, 1934

Marx, Karl, *Grundrisse der Kritik der politischen Ökonomie*, 2 vols., Moscow: Verlag für fremdsprachige Literatur, 1939–41; section in English as *Pre-Capitalist Economic Formations*, edited by Eric J. Hobsbawm, London: Lawrence and Wishart, 1964, New York: International Publishers, 1965; full translation as

Grundrisse: Foundations of the Critique of Political Economy, New York: Random House, and London: Penguin, 1973

Marx, Karl, and Friedrich Engels, *Karl Marx and Friedrich Engels on Britain*, Moscow: Foreign Publishing House, 1953

Marx, Karl, *Economic and Philosophic Manuscripts of 1844*, Moscow: Foreign Languages Publishing House, 1959; New York: International Publishers, 1964

Marx, Karl, *Political Writings*, edited by David Fernbach, 3 vols., London: Allen Lane, 1973; New York: Random House, 1974

Marx, Karl, and Friedrich Engels, *Collected Works*, London: Lawrence and Wishart, and New York: International Publishers, 1975–

Oakley, Allen, *The Making of Marx's Critical Theory: A Bibliographical Analysis*, London and Boston: Routledge, 1983

Plekhanov, Georgii Valentinovich, *K voprosu o razvitii monisticheskogo vzgliada na istoriiu*, Moscow, 1919; in English as *In Defence of Materialism: The Development of the Monist View of History*, London: Lawrence and Wishart, 1947

Rigby, Stephen Henry, *Marxism and History: A Critical Introduction*, Manchester: Manchester University Press, and New York: St. Martin's Press, 1987

Sartre, Jean-Paul, *Critique de la raison dialectique*, 2 vols., Paris: Gallimard, 1960–85; in English as *Critique of Dialectical Reason*, 2 vols., London and New York: Verso, revised edition, 1976–90

Sartre, Jean-Paul, *Search for a Method*, New York: Knopf, 1963 [French original]

Shaw, W.H., *Marx's Theory of History*, London: Hutchinson, 1978

Stalin, Joseph, "Dialectical and Historical Materialism" (1938) in *The Essential Stalin: Major Theoretical Writings, 1905–52*, edited by Howard Bruce Franklin, Garden City, NY: Anchor, 1972; London: Croom Helm, 1973

Masculinity

Since the mid-1970s, both social theorists and historians have come to see the importance of the analysis of men's gendered behavior. The impact of second-wave feminist theory was profound during the emergence of men's studies as a discrete area within the broader study of gender during the 1970s. Perhaps the most important American work to incorporate masculinity into the study of history during the 1970s was Joe Dubbert's *A Man's Place* (1979), which analyzed the US frontier of the 19th century. His case studies of exemplary male heroes of the mythologized West scrutinized the role of both 19th-century racial theories and popular culture in the creation of models of male behavior.

By 1980 masculinity had become identified as a culturally and historically constructed phenomenon. Moreover, the acquisition of the traits of conventional masculinity was no longer seen as easy, let alone automatic. While sex-role theory was not eliminated, a more complicated theory was evolving that emphasized lived experience and men's agency. Typical of this new approach was D.H. Bell's *Being a Man* (1982) which used oral history to uncover some of the complexities of growing up male. During the early 1980s changes in feminist theory also began to have an impact on the study of masculinity, particularly in relation to historical studies. Sylvia Strauss' book *Traitors to the Masculine Cause* (1982), for example, examined men's role in first-wave feminist campaigns for female suffrage in the US and Britain. Strauss studied both individual men, such as John Stuart Mill, and pro-suffrage men's organizations such as the Men's League for Women's Suffrage. Importantly, this study demonstrated that men did not always act as a gender, but as individuals responding to historical events.

Strauss' work was one of several historical studies that focused on the 19th and early 20th centuries in Britain and the United States. These studies have presented that period as being central to the construction of modern dominant masculinity. Mangan and Walvin's edited collection, *Manliness and Morality* (1987), for example, is typical of this approach. The various contributors placed the Victorian/Edwardian concept of manliness at the center of the creation, transmission, and social reproduction of dominant masculinity. This volume is important for the historical study of masculinity because it emphasized the sociopolitical and ideological context within which dominant masculinity arose. For example, many of the contributors, especially Mangan and Rotundo, were careful to highlight the significance of social class in relation to the creation of gender norms in the 19th century. The interpenetration of masculinity and femininity was also emphasized in this book, although in an uneven fashion. That is, while some of the essays highlighted the role of enhanced femininity on the development and changes in masculinity, others ignored it. Allen Warren's chapter on Baden-Powell and the connections between scouting, imperialism, and "manliness," for example, left women out of its analysis.

By contrast, Arthur Brittan's *Masculinity and Power* (1989) portrayed the 1890s as a period of crisis in masculinity precisely because of men's decidedly mixed reaction to first-wave feminism and changing definitions of femininity. The author was particularly careful to distinguish between masculinity, a changeable set of characteristics, and "masculinism," an ideology that justified male domination. Importantly, both "masculine" character traits and masculinist ideology were presented as historical constructs.

Carnes and Griffin's *Meanings for Manhood* (1990) is another collection of essays focusing on masculinity in the Victorian era. The editors emphasized the need for a gendered history of men's lives and foregrounded their debt to both feminism and women's history. The editors stressed that one of the lessons gained from women's history was the need for some single-sex analyses. Their collection therefore included studies of the law as a masculine profession, and an examination of 19th-century printing apprenticeships as case-studies of masculinized workplaces.

Other contributions to this collection offer a more interactive gendered approach, for example, Margaret Marsh's study of suburban men and changing definitions of masculinity and domesticity in the late Victorian and Edwardian periods. In such a highly theorized area as gender and men's studies, this collection is notable for its commitment to historical tasks and skills. The editors maintained, for example, that, "Theory may enrich research, and political values and personal interests give it passion . . ., but in the end we depend on what the historical record may yield."

A similar concern with empirically-based analysis was emphasized in Michael Roper and John Tosh's collection, *Manful Assertions* (1991). Although the various contributors provided interesting accounts of various aspects of masculinity ranging from a gendered re-reading of Thomas Carlyle through to the role of boys' story papers in the interwar period, its strongest contribution is in the introductory chapter. In this essay, the editors outlined the development of the field of men's studies especially as it relates to history. Undermining essentialist concepts, Roper and Tosh stated that their object "is to demonstrate that masculinity has a history, that it is subject to change and varied in its forms."

Mary Ryan's *Cradle of the Middle Class* (1981) remains one of the few studies of a sociohistorical character that has focused on a particular place and time and thoroughly integrated the analysis of gender in an interactive manner. That is, her study focused on the interaction and dynamics present in changing definitions and expressions of both masculinity and femininity.

Of all the historical works to have emerged from the various calls from theorists for concrete histories, perhaps the most ambitious to date has been Jock Phillips' 1987 study of masculinity in post-settlement New Zealand, *A Man's Country? The Image of the Pakeha Male: A History* (1987). Though the title suggests an analysis centered on "images," the subject matter is, in fact, much more broadly based. Phillips studied the pioneer experience in fact and in subsequent legend; he also decoded New Zealand's obsession with rugby, placing the question of masculinity at the center of its deconstruction. Phillips charted the role of war in the creation and transmission of dominant masculinity. His analysis emphasized the role of men in the family and in postwar reconstruction and suburbia. The book's resonances for the historical analysis of analogous white settler colonies/countries such as Australia, South Africa, and Canada are obvious, but to date histories on this scale from those countries have yet to emerge.

Masculinity continues to be a somewhat marginalized field within historical study. Generally, these works are catalogued in the psychology section of libraries, which is fair enough in a work such as Klaus Theweleit's path-breaking *Männerphantasien* (1977–78; *Male Fantasies*, 1987–88), which explored the fiction popular with the men who came to make up the shock troops of Nazi Germany. More recently, works such as Mrinalini Sinha's *Colonial Masculinity* (1995) and Gail Bederman's *Manliness and Civilization* (1995) have sought to uncover the links between cultural constructions of masculinity and the suppression of subaltern cultures. These complex works suggest new ways for the field to develop.

ROSS LAURIE

See also Davidoff; Gender; Hausen; Koonz; Lake; Military; Scott, Joan; Smith-Rosenberg; Women's History: Africa

Further Reading

Almeida, Miguel Vale de, *The Hegemonic Male: Masculinity in a Portuguese Town*, Providence, RI: Berghahn, 1996

Bederman, Gail, *Manliness and Civilization: A Cultural History of Gender and Race in the United States*, Chicago: University of Chicago Press, 1995

Bell, Donald H., *Being a Man: The Paradox of Masculinity*, Lexington, MA: Lewis, 1982

Black, Daniel P., *Dismantling Black Manhood: An Historical and Literary Analysis of the Legacy of Slavery*, New York: Garland, 1997

Bourke, Joanna, *Dismembering the Male: Men's Bodies, Britain, and the Great War*, Chicago: University of Chicago Press, 1996

Brittan, Arthur, *Masculinity and Power*, Oxford and New York: Blackwell, 1989

Budd, Michael Anton, *The Sculpture Machine: Physical Culture and Body Politics in the Age of Empire*, New York: New York University Press, and Basingstoke: Macmillan, 1997

Carnes, Mark C., and Clyde Griffin, *Meanings for Manhood: Constructions of Masculinity in Victorian America*, Chicago: University of Chicago Press, 1990

Chapman, Rowena, and Jonathan Rutherford, eds., *Male Order: Unwrapping Masculinity*, London: Lawrence and Wishart, 1988

Cohen, Michele, *Fashioning Masculinity: National Identity and Language in the Eighteenth Century*, London and New York: Routledge, 1996

Connell, Robert W., *Masculinities*, St. Leonard's, New South Wales: Allen and Unwin, and Berkeley: University of California Press, 1995

Dawson, Graham, *Soldier Heroes: British Adventure, Empire, and the Imaginings of Masculinities*, London and New York: Routledge, 1994

Dixon, Robert, *Writing the Colonial Adventure: Race, Gender, and Nation in Anglo-Australian Popular Fiction, 1875–1914*, Cambridge and New York: Cambridge University Press, 1995

Dubbert, Joe, *A Man's Place: Masculinity in Transition*, Englewood Cliffs, NJ: Prentice Hall, 1979

Ehrenreich, Barbara, *The Hearts of Men: American Dreams and the Flight from Commitment*, New York: Doubleday, 1983

Hearn, Jeff, and David H.J. Morgan, *Men, Masculinities and Social Theory*, London and Boston: Unwin Hyman, 1990

Hoch, Paul, *White Hero, Black Beast: Racism, Sexism and the Mask of Masculinity*, London: Pluto, 1979

Kimmel, Michael, ed., *Changing Men: New Directions in Research on Men and Masculinity*, Newbury Park, CA: Sage, 1987

Kimmel, Michael, *Manhood in America: A Cultural History*, New York: Free Press, 1996

Lees, Clare A., Thelma Fenster and Jo Ann McNamara, eds., *Medieval Masculinities: Regarding Men in the Middle Ages*, Minneapolis: University of Minnesota Press, 1994

McLaren, Angus, *The Trials of Masculinity: Policing Sexual Boundaries, 1870-1930*, Chicago: University of Chicago Press, 1997

Mangan, J.A., and James Walvin, eds., *Manliness and Morality: Middle-Class Masculinity in Britain and America, 1800–1940*, Manchester: Manchester University Press, and New York: St. Martin's Press, 1987

Marsh, Margaret S., *Suburban Lives*, New Brunswick, NJ: Rutgers University Press, 1990

Mosse, George L., *The Image of Man: The Creation of Modern Masculinity*, New York: Oxford University Press, 1996

Nye, Robert A., *Masculinity and Male Codes of Honor in Modern France*, New York: Oxford University Press, 1993

Phillips, Jock, *A Man's Country? The Image of the Pakeha Male: A History*, Auckland: Penguin, 1987; revised 1996

Roper, Michael, and John Tosh, eds., *Manful Assertions: Masculinities in Britain since 1800*, London and New York: Routledge, 1991

Rotundo, E. Anthony, *American Manhood: Transformation in Masculinity from the Revolution to the Modern Era*, New York: Basic Books, 1993

Ryan, Mary P., *Cradle of the Middle Class: The Family in Oneida County, New York, 1790–1865*, Cambridge and New York: Cambridge University Press, 1981

Seidler, Victor J., *Unreasonable Man: Masculinity and Social Theory*, London and New York: Routledge, 1994

Sinha, Mrinalini, *Colonial Masculinity: The "Manly Englishman" and the "Effeminate Bengali" in the Late Nineteenth Century*, Manchester: Manchester University Press, and New York: St. Martin's Press, 1995

Strauss, Sylvia, *Traitors to the Masculine Cause: The Men's Campaign for Women's Rights*, Westport, CT: Greenwood Press, 1982

Theweleit, Klaus, *Männerphantasien*, 2 vols., Frankfurt: Peter Stern, 1977–78; in English as *Male Fantasies*, 2 vols., Cambridge: Polity Press, and Minneapolis: University of Minnesota Press, 1987–88

Tolson, Andrew, *The Limits of Masculinity*, London: Tavistock, 1977; New York: Harper, 1979

Waters, Karen Volland, *The Perfect Gentleman: Masculine Control in Victorian Men's Fiction, 1870–1901*, New York: Lang, 1997

Mason, Tim 1940–1990
British historian of Germany

Tim Mason was Britain's most significant historian of the Third Reich. The originality of his work sparked important debates and he intervened with skill in others. A Marxist historian, he was concerned with developing an approach to history that was undogmatic, analytical, humanistic. He participated in the History Workshop at Ruskin College, Oxford, and was a founding editor of *History Workshop Journal* – projects aimed at developing the approaches of socialist and feminist historians. He was a key advocate of history from below.

Mason's work can be understood as the intersection of two historiographical trends. First, he followed the generation of the Marxist historians that emerged in the 1950s and 1960s. Mason became a historian at a time when many western Marxist historians exorcised the determinism of earlier Marxist, in particular Stalinist, versions of history. Second, Mason's work coincides with a rejuvenation of interest, an intensification of debate, and a series of revised assumptions about the Third Reich in particular and fascism in general.

Mason was not responsible for this rejuvenation of interest but he did significantly contribute to it. *Social Policy in the Third Reich* (1977, translated 1993) was the centerpiece of Mason's work. In this meticulously detailed and thoughtful study he focused on the relationship between the working class and the Nazi state. Far from being a description of the activities of proscribed underground organizations, as much of the East German scholarship had been, Mason widened the perspective to the working class as a whole and in particular to how it was viewed from above by the regime itself. Hitler and other leading Nazis, Mason argued, had been profoundly shaken by the November Revolution of 1918 when the deprivations and suffering of war led to a popular revolt of soldiers, sailors, and workers that put a stop to the faltering military campaign and the Kaiserreich itself. This scenario haunted an insecure Nazi leadership that countenanced war but feared a repetition of 1918. As a result, the regime was willing to make considerable concessions to the working class in terms of social policy, was reluctant to demand material sacrifices during war, and was slow to implement the policy of a total war economy.

Also, Mason uncovered a pattern of workers' opposition that was molded to conditions of full employment and repression. Workers moved from one employer to another in search of the highest wages. Moreover, Mason argued this necessarily individualized response was profoundly influenced by a sense of distinct class interests and therefore should be considered as a form of opposition to the regime. Here he undermined the notion that the Nazis "conquered the soul of the German workers" and indeed his work encouraged further investigation of the German working class. The work of Kershaw and Peukert, for example, importantly complemented Mason's deepening historical understanding of a working class which the regime was able to contain, but never fully convince.

Consequently, according to Mason, in conditions of rapid rearmament, precarious economic recovery, and nationalist posturing by the regime, this opposition brought about a domestic crisis for the regime which forced Hitler into a "flight forwards," into hurried external expansion, and ultimately, into an early war. The regime was driven, therefore, not by the interests of "the most reactionary, most chauvinist, and most imperialist elements of finance capital" of Dimitrov's official Comintern formulation, but by an autonomous Nazi leadership that was able to act outside, and to some extent against, the interests of the ruling class. This is what Mason famously called the "primacy of domestic politics." It is this element of his case that has attracted the greatest controversy and made the least headway among historians. He was criticized by East German historians for his abandonment of Marxism, and by western academics for underplaying the fundamental reasons for launching war, that is, the relative national scale of rearmament, and Hitler's intentions. Mason's phrase has unfortunately been set up as an academic straw man. Perhaps the most telling criticism is that the concept too neatly divided politics and economics in a situation where the state took on an increasing role within the territorially expanded German economy, thus blurring that very division.

Mason contributed widely to other questions concerning the Third Reich. In his many articles he dealt with the role of women within the Third Reich, and the weaknesses of the intentionalist case, and he defended using fascism as a generic analytical device.

Mason's work is an impressive attempt to use history to make sense of the barbarity of the Third Reich and to salvage the German working class from the crimes of their tormentors. His aim was to forego moralistic simplifications but he was simultaneously committed to rejecting any notion that the Third Reich should be treated dispassionately or "normally." His approach is perhaps best summed up by his own words in response to the public argument between West German historians that erupted in 1986: "If historians do have a public responsibility, if hating is part of their method and warning part of their task, it is necessary that they should hate precisely."

MATT PERRY

See also Germany: 1800–1945; History Workshop

Biography

Timothy Wright Mason. Born Birkenhead, 2 March 1940, of schoolteacher parents. Studied at Oxford University; then held a research fellowship, St. Antony's College, Oxford, PhD 1971. Fellow and tutor, St. Peter's College, Oxford, 1971–85. Settled in Rome, 1984. Married 1) Ursula Vogel, 1970 (marriage dissolved); 2) Simonetta Piccone, 1987. Died Rome, 5 March 1990.

Principal Writings

"Some Origins of the Second World War," *Past and Present* 29 (1964), 67–87

"Labour in the Third Reich," *Past and Present* 33 (1966), 112–41

"Nineteenth Century Cromwell," *Past and Present* 40 (1968), 187–91

"Primacy of Politics: Politics and Economics in Nationalist Socialist Germany," in Stuart J. Woolf, ed., *The Nature of Fascism*, 1968

Arbeiterklasse und Volksgemeinschaft: Dokumente und Materialien zur deutschen Arbeiterpolitik, 1936–1939 (The Working Class and the National Community: Documents and Material on German Worker Politics), 1975

"Women in Germany, 1925–40: Family, Welfare and Work," parts 1–2, *History Workshop Journal* 1 (1976), 74–113; and 2 (1976), 5–32

"National Socialism and the German Working Class, 1925–May 1933," *New German Critique* 11 (1977), 49–93

Sozialpolitik im Dritten Reich: Arbeiterklasse und Volksgemeinschaft, 1977; in English as *Social Policy in the Third Reich: The Working Class and the National Community*, edited by Jane Caplan, 1993

"Worker's Opposition in Nazi Germany," *History Workshop Journal* 11 (1981), 120–37

"Injustice and Resistance: Barrington Moore and the Reaction of the German Workers to Nazism," in R.J. Bullen, Hartmut Pogge von Strandmann, and A.B. Polonsky, eds., *Ideas into Politics: Aspects of European History 1880–1950*, 1984

"Massenwiderstand ohne Organisation: Streiks im faschistischen Italien und NS-Deutschland" (Mass Resistance Without Organization: Strikes in Fascist Italy and Nazi Germany), *Gewerkschaftliche Monatshefte* 32 (1984), 197–212

"Arbeiter ohne Gewerkschaften: Massenwiderstand im NS-Deutschland und im faschistischen Italien" (Workers without Trade Unions: Mass Opposition in Nazi Germany and Fascist Italy), *Journal für Geschichte* (1985), 28–35

"History Workshop," *Passato e Presente* 8 (1985), 175–86

"Il nazismo come professione" (Nazism as a Profession), *Rinascita* 18 (18 May 1985), 18–19

"The Great Economic History Show," *History Workshop Journal* 21 (1986), 129–54

"Italy and Modernisation," *History Workshop Journal* 25 (1988), 127–47

"Gli scioperi di Torino del Marzo '43," (The Turin Strikes of March 1943) in Francesca Ferratini Tosi, Gaetano Grasso, and Massimo Legnani, eds., *L'Italia nella seconda guerra mondiale e nella resistenza* (Italy and Its Resistance Movement During World War II), 1988

"Debate: Germany, 'Domestic Crisis and War in 1939': Comment 2," *Past and Present* 122 (1989), 205–21

"Whatever Happened to 'Fascism'?" *Radical History Review* 49 (1991), 89–98; reprinted in Thomas Childers and Jane Caplan, eds., *Reevaluating the Third Reich*, 1993

"The Domestic Dynamics of Nazi Conquests: A Response to Critics," in Thomas Childers and Jane Caplan, eds., *Reevaluating the Third Reich*, 1993

Nazism, Fascism and the Working Class: Essays by Tim Mason, edited by Jane Caplan, 1995

Further Reading

Caplan, Jane, ed., "Introduction," *Nazism, Fascism and the Working Class: Essays by Tim Mason,* Cambridge and New York: Cambridge University Press, 1995

DiCori, Paola, Raphael Samuel, and Nicola Gallerano, "Tim Mason: l'uomo, lo studioso" (Tim Mason: The Man, the Scholar), *Movimento Operaio e Socialista* 13 (1990), 267–86

Kershaw, Ian, *The Nazi Dictatorship: Problems and Perspectives of Interpretation*, London: Arnold, 1985; 3rd edition 1993

Peukert, Detlev, *Volksgenossen und Gemeinschaftsfremde: Anpassung, Ausmerze und Aufbegehren unter dem Nationalsozialismus*, Cologne: Bund Verlag, 1982; in English as *Inside Nazi Germany: Conformity, Opposition, and Racism in Everyday Life*, New Haven: Yale University Press, and London: Batsford, 1987

Samuel, Raphael *et al.*, "Tim Mason: A Memorial," *History Workshop Journal* 30 (1990), 129–88 [includes bibliography]

Maspero, Henri 1883–1945

French historian of China

Henri Maspero was the foremost Western historian of China in the early 20th century. Working before the current infrastructure of research aids and typeset modern editions had come into being, he produced not only pioneering research, but also a synthesis of existing scholarship on early China which is still worth reading today. His posthumously published writings on the history of Chinese religion introduced to scholars Eastern and Western a mass of information concerning a tradition – Taoism – that had hitherto been almost totally ignored.

Maspero was the son of an Egyptologist, and his first published work was on Egypt. By 1907, however, he had acquired a sinological training from Edouard Chavannes (1865–1918), the first man to introduce the teaching of history into Western study of China, though then the study of Asia was far less specialized than at present, and throughout his life Maspero made contributions not simply to historical research but also to the study of the Chinese language, and to the study of Indochina. But despite showing a certain flair as an ethnographer, his chief interests (even his linguistic interests) were historical. He soon showed this while working in Hanoi, with a series of articles on the sources for the early history of Vietnam and on the history of Chinese Buddhism. After his return to France, he set to work on producing the first general history of China based on modern critical scholarship in a Western language, and by 1927 had completed *La Chine Antique* (China in Antiquity, 1978). Though this predated the flowering of critical history in China itself in the 1930s, and the more recent rise of archaeology as a source of information on early China, it still remains a masterly survey, combining a wide reading of early Chinese sources with a careful use of modern ethnographic insights derived from study of the minority groups of Indochina, which, as Marcel Granet noted, showed features reminiscent of the civilization of early China.

As Maspero's reading advanced following the publication of *La Chine Antique* to cover the early imperial period of Chinese history, he encountered a type of source material never used before: the scriptures of the Taoist religion. The Taoist canon, a repository of well over a thousand texts, was before its printing by photolithographic reproduction in 1927 an exceptionally rare work, and even the very incomplete copy which already had been brought to Paris and used by Chavannes was almost the only substantial portion of the work existing outside East Asia. Gradually Maspero began to sort through this new treasure trove of information, and to work out which materials dated back to the formative phase of the religion in the 4th and 5th centuries CE. Other aspects of history still continued to occupy him, including the preparation for publication of an archive of early administrative documents retrieved from the sands of Central Asia by the British explorer Sir Aurel Stein (1862–1943). As a result of these diverse projects and of the onset of war, no further monograph by Maspero saw print during his lifetime, though the volume of Stein documents was ready for publication in 1936, save for the necessary funding from the India Office and the British Museum; in fact it appeared only in 1953.

By that time three volumes of posthumous works gathering together a number of unpublished writings and reprints on Chinese religion, on Taoism, and on early history had already been complied and published by Paul Demiéville in 1950. Further pieces followed for up to ten years after his death, and even thereafter anthologies or reprints of his writings have been produced in France, and latterly in English and other translations. Maspero's research had been translated into other languages ever since his early work on Chinese Buddhism had been rendered into Japanese before World War I, but from 1966 onwards, when his second posthumous collection on Taoism was translated into Japanese, entire volumes started to be published in foreign languages.

In part this continued interest in Maspero's work testifies to the energies on his behalf of his executor Demiéville, like him a historian of religion (Buddhism) with a strong interest in language, but the number of younger scholars who gathered to celebrate the centenary of his birth in 1983 covered a wide spread of expertise from France and beyond, ample testimony to an influence undiminished by his tragic premature death. Together with Chavannnes, Pelliot, Demiéville, and others of like stature, Maspero helped to achieve such a dominance for French-language studies of Chinese civilization that up to World War II students at Harvard were obliged to learn French before starting their Chinese studies. In retrospect the scope of his achievements looks even more amazing when set against the rudimentary state of the field at the start of his career.

T.H. BARRETT

See also China

Biography

Born Paris, 15 December 1883, son of the Egyptologist Gaston Maspero (1846–1916). Educated in sinology at the Collège de France, to 1907. Apart from brief periods of leave and war service as an interpreter, attached to the Ecole Française d'Extrême-Orient, Hanoi, doing full-time research in Indochina or China itself, 1908–20; chair in sinology at the Collège de France, 1921–45. Arrested and deported because of his son's resistance work; died Buchenwald, 17 March 1945.

Principal Writings

La Chine Antique, 1927; in English as *China in Antiquity*, 1978
Mélanges posthumes sur les religions et l'histoire de la Chine (Posthumous Writings on the Religions and History of China), 3 vols., 1950
Les Documents chinois de la troisième expédition de Sir Aurel Stein en Asie Centrale (Chinese Documents on Sir Aurel Stein's Third Expedition to Central Asia), 1953
Le Taoïsme et les religions chinoises, 1971; in English as *Taoism and Chinese Religion*, 1981

Further Reading

Kierman, Frank A., Jr., Introduction, to Maspero, *China in Antiquity*, Amherst: University of Massachusetts Press, 1978 [includes bibliography]
Kierman, Frank A., Jr., Introduction to Maspero, *Taoism and Chinese Religion*, Amherst: University of Massachusetts Press, 1981

Massignon, Louis 1883–1962

French Islamic historian

One of the last of the major European Orientalists in the line of the Hungarian Ignace Goldziher and the Dutch C. Snouck Hurgronje, Louis Massignon established with his pioneering research into the language, history, and literature of Islamic mysticism the scientific basis for Islamic study. His *Essai* (1922) on the origins of the technical language of Muslim mysticism and, especially, his *magnum opus*, the 2-volume study of a 10th-century mystic and martyr, *La Passion d'al-Hallaj* (1914–21; *The Passion of al-Hallaj*, 1982), earned him election in 1924 to the Royal Asiatic Society of London and the Academy of Sciences of the USSR, and led to his appointment in 1926 to the chair in sociology and sociography of Islam at the Collège de France, a position he held until his retirement in 1954.

Massignon's magisterial study of Hallaj in its enlarged posthumous edition of 1975 from Gallimard, and in its English edition of 1982 in the Bollingen series of Princeton University Press, was a work of four volumes and nearly 2000 pages. In his preface designed for the new edition Massignon set forth his methodology and working hypotheses for situating Hallaj's life historically and establishing his place in Islamic intellectual history and mystical tradition: a painstaking authentication of the texts, a complete annotated translation, and the minute examination of "testimonial chains" showing direct traces of Hallaj's influence upon others' literature and art. Essential for Massignon, however, from his earliest exposure to Hallaj in 1907, was "an intellectual affinity by friendship of the spirit, entirely disinterested and supraracial." Given that "there remained the preparation of a body of explicative annotation for the entire work, which was indispensable for rendering it intelligible to the non-Muslim reader."

The three substantive volumes, concentrating respectively on the "Life," "Survival," and "Teaching" of Hallaj, were completed by a fourth, "Bibliography and Index," the most exhaustive compendium of primary and secondary sources found in any work of Islamic studies, including particularly Arabic, Iranian, and Turkish authors along with European authors. Its index of sects, schools, and technical terms has been an essential resource ever since its shorter 1922 edition for anyone doing advanced research in early and medieval Islam.

Volume 1 is a truly awesome historical reconstruction of Islamic civilization as it was in the century of Hallaj's life, imprisonment, politically motivated trial, and execution for "heresy," roughly the mid-9th to mid-10th century CE. Based on primary sources drawn from all spheres of economic and social life, religious and political institutions, the volume offers dramatic evidence of Massignon's linguistic range and erudition. Volume 2 focuses on the evolution of Hallaj's influence on other mystical thinkers and establishes, as Massignon argues, his central place within the Muslim mystical tradition down to the present day. This reveals Massignon the classical Orientalist, verifying the chains of authority from generation to generation and collecting thereby a wealth of living anecdotal history not found in the works of generalists. Finally, volume 3 concentrates on the history of Muslim philosophical and theological thought and Hallaj's contribution to it. Here Massignon, a leading Catholic thinker, shows his remarkable ability to translate himself into an Islamic intellectual framework and to argue persuasively for the authenticity of Qur'anic inspiration. In volume 3, especially, Hallaj's own extant works of poetry and prose are translated with exceptional skill, penetration, and lyric power by Massignon. It is clear to the specialists in Islamic studies that no one among Western experts before or since brought to his subject such a combination of mastery of languages, control of texts, singular and comparative perspective, interpretive subtlety, and literary gifts. This work is, as Julian Baldick wrote in his *Times Literary Supplement* review of the English edition, "a very great book by France's most famous Islamic specialist of our century."

Both in his Paris professorship and in his long standing association with the New Egyptian University of Cairo as professor in Arabic of Muslim philosophical doctrines and language, Massignon influenced several generations of European and Muslim students who have had distinguished academic careers. Included among those who have pursued and extended various aspects and methods of Massignon's research have been the French Iranianist Henry Corbin, himself later of the Collège de France, in his insightful studies of Avicenna and Ibn 'Arabi; Ibrahim Madkour of the New Cairo University in his major contributions to the study of Muslim theology; George Makdisi, the noted Arabist historian of the University of Pennsylvania, in his 2-volume study of the 11th-century traditionalist Ibn 'Aqil; Annemarie Schimmel, professor of Indo-Islamic cultures at Harvard and Bonn, whose studies of Rumi, Ghalib, and others in the long tradition of Islamic mysticism follow both the rigorous textual precision and the spiritual devotion to Islam of Massignon. Among Americans influenced directly by Massignon were James Kritzeck and Marshall Hodgson, whose 2-volume *Venture of Islam* many consider the most ambitious undertaking by an American in the field of Islamics. Under the influence of the noted Persian philosopher and historian of science Seyyed Hossein Nasr, himself directly linked to Massignon through Corbin, a host of young British and American scholars of Sufism has emerged in recent times with indebtedness to the linguistic range and textual fidelity established by the Orientalists of Europe particularly through Massignon. In terms of serious re-examination of Massignon's studies of Qur'anic and mystical language and of Hallaj himself and his works, Volume 4 includes an "Ultima Hallagiana" section of works through 1979; but special attention should be paid to the exegetical work of Paul Nwyia of the University of Paris and to the careful editing and study of Hallaj's poetry by Kamil M. al-Shaibi of the University of Baghdad.

Massignon spent the last years of his life, following his retirement from teaching, in the service of Muslim-Christian dialogue and writing numerous papers in pursuit of peace between Western and Islamic countries. He continued to guide students informally in areas of Islamic and comparative Semitic studies, Arabic and Persian textual exegesis, and comparative histories of religion. But most of his energy was devoted to the completion of his work on Hallaj and to his activism against the war in Algeria, which ended just prior to his death in 1962. His legacy both as a scholar and as an ecumenical thinker was recognized in 1983 on the occasion of the centenary of his birth when he was honored by UNESCO as one of Europe's seminal intellectuals of the 20th century.

HERBERT W. MASON

See also Near East

Biography

Born Nogent-sur-Marne, 1883. Educated at Lycée Louis-le-Grand, Paris; traveled to Algeria while working on his diploma, which he received in 1905. Joined Institut Française d'Archéologie Orientale, Cairo, 1906; remained in Middle East studying and teaching at the newly founded University of Cairo, 1912–13. During World War I, served in the Middle East, eventually as high commissioner in Palestine and Syria. Returned to Paris and taught at Collège de France, from 1919: chair in sociology and sociography of Islam, 1926–54. Died Paris, 1962.

Principal Writings

Mission en Mésopotamie (1907–1908) (Mission to Mesopotamia), 2 vols., 1910–12
La Passion d'al-Hosayn-ibn-Mansour al-Hallaj, martyr mystique de l'Islam, exécuté à Baghdad le 26 mars, 922, 4 vols., 1914–21, abridged, 1922, enlarged 1975; in English as *The Passion of al-Hallaj*, 4 vols., 1982, abridged, 1994
Essai sur l'origines du lexique technique de la mystique musulmane, 1922; in English as *Essay on the Origins of the Technical Language of Muslim Mysticism*, 1997
La Mubâhala de Médine et l'Hyperdulie de Fatima, 1955
Opéra Minora, 3 vols., 1963, and *Parole donnée*, 1987; selections in English as *Testimonies and Reflections: Selected Essays of Louis Massignon*, 1989

Further Reading

Basetti-Sani, Giulio, *Louis Massignon: orientaliste cristiano*, Milan: Vita e Pensiero, 1971; in English as *Louis Massignon, Christian Ecumenist: Prophet of Inter-Religious Reconciliation*, Chicago: Franciscan Herald, 1974
Destremau, Christian, and Jean Moncelon, *Louis Massignon*, Paris: Plon, 1994 [includes bibliography]
Gude, Mary Louise, *Louis Massignon: The Crucible of Compassion*, Notre Dame, IN: University of Notre Dame Press, 1996
Hourani, Albert, "T.E. Lawrence and Louis Massignon," in his *Islam in European Thought*, Cambridge and New York: Cambridge University Press, 1991
Mason, Herbert, *Memoir of a Friend: Louis Massignon*, Notre Dame, IN: University of Notre Dame Press, 1988
Monteil, Vincent, *Le Linceul de feu: Louis Massignon, 1883–1962* (The Shroud of Fire: Louis Massignon), Paris: Vegapress, 1987
Moubarac, Youakim, *L'Oeuvre de Louis Massignon: Bibliographie Complétée et refondue (1906–1962)* (The Works of Louis Massignon: Revised and Completed Bibliography), Beirut: Edition du Cénacle Libanasis, 1972–73
Rocalve, Pierre, *Louis Massignon et l'Islam* (Louis Massignon and Islam), Damascus: Institut Français du Damas, 1993
Waardenburg, J., "Massignon: Notes for Further Research," *Muslim World* 56 (1966)

Mathiez, Albert 1874–1932
French religious historian

Albert Mathiez is probably best remembered as the expert on religious questions during the French Revolution. His doctoral thesis on Theophilanthropy (1904) and his book published in 1911 – *Rome et le clergé français sous la Constituante* (Rome and the French Clergy under the Constituent Assembly) – placed him clearly at the heart of the development of revolutionary studies set up by F.-A. Aulard. His conclusions outlined the hesitations of the Catholic clergy faced with the Civil Constitution in 1790. He showed that 18th-century philosophers and Constituent members alike had no inkling of the emergence of a secular state; at the same time he insisted that financial issues tended to dominate the religious debate. In that respect, Mathiez illustrates the preoccupations of the generation who had fought for the creation of a secular parliamentary democracy in the 1880s.

Mathiez's early contributions to revolutionary studies followed Aulard's political republican stance, concerned with creating a republican tradition for the Third Republic. This included the emergence of history as an academic discipline, breaking away from literary studies, and attempting to acquire a new methodology based on textual analysis of sources, but concerned with political developments from above. Indeed, Mathiez devoted an entire volume of his *La Révolution française* (1922–27; *The French Revolution*, 1929) to events between 10 August 1792 and 3 June 1793, highlighting the importance of the struggle between Girondins and Montagnards in their attempts to control power. Yet Mathiez is more than a simple political historian. He stands as the first revisionist of the republican orthodoxy elaborated by Aulard. For Aulard, Danton had provided a symbol of republican and lay patriotism, untouched by accusations of betrayal and conveniently detached from the episode of the September massacres in 1792. In contrast, Robespierre was viewed in a variety of ways; sometimes clerical because of his involvement in the Cult of Supreme Being, sometimes dictatorial because of the Terror, sometimes egalitarian because of his support for the Constitution of 1793, the Maximum and the Ventose decrees. Though Mathiez remained concerned with leaders and continued to perceive history as written from above, he nevertheless brought a new dimension to the debate. He questioned the relative significance of the events of 1789 and 1793. He asked what was the nature of the Republic in 1793–94 and at the end of the 19th century. Mathiez's answer is a clear cut rehabilitation of Robespierre, hence an acknowledgement that the Revolution is One. In the tradition of Guizot and other 19th-century writers, he accepted the Terror as part and parcel of revolutionary history, while Aulard had played down revolutionary violence to create a moderate republican consensus. In fact, Mathiez amplified the dictatorial tendencies of the Revolution in his writings, which he saw as reflecting Sans Culotte pressure on the government and which he identified as going back to 1789.

It can be argued that Mathiez's stance on Robespierre reflects Jean Jaurès' influence. In his introduction to Jaurès' *Histoire socialiste de la Révolution française* (Socialist History of the French Revolution, 8 vols., 1922–27), the socialist leader attempted to conciliate socialism to a republican tradition that would include "democracy and social dimensions" (Jaurès). Thus Robespierre is revealed as the precursor of socialism in a republican context, while Danton is denounced as a traitor to the Republic, who attempted to delay the war effort, hesitated in relation to the king's trial, and indulged in dishonest dealings in association with Lameth and Fabre d'Eglantine. Mathiez devoted a lot of energy to this particular polemic, which led to a lasting legacy for future revolutionary studies. He created the Société des Etudes Robespierristes (Society of Robespierrist Studies) and the *Annales Historiques de la Révolution française* (AHRF). Both still exist today and are responsible for many of historical publications on the Revolution.

However, this change of emphasis, from Danton to Robespierre, did not bring a new kind of historical writing. Mathiez also assessed the importance of economic and social issues. This was partly as a result of Jaurès' influence. It was also because of the experiences of World War I! In *La Vie chère et le mouvement social* (The High Cost of Living and the Social Movement, 1927) Mathiez showed how economic problems influenced Parisian and provincial politics in relation to the establishment of the revolutionary government, and their relation to the decisions taken by the Committee of Public Safety. However, he ignored the peasants and retained more interest in government reactions to economic problems than in the predicaments of the people when faced with them.

Mathiez's contribution to French historiography is vast and reflects the activities of a remarkable scholar whose archival finds were numerous and used with great imagination. His writings on religious issues remain a point of reference, though he did not persevere with a sociological analysis of the revolutionary cults which he had hinted at in his *Origines des cultes révolutionnaires* (Origins of the Revolutionary Cults, 1904). He was thus reflecting his fear that the use of sociological methods could lead to generalizations achieved at the expense of patient and methodical research. This can also be seen in his role in developing history as an academic discipline rooted in archival research. A tireless researcher, Mathiez left Aulard behind and charted the way for future economic and social historians.

MARTINE BONDOIS MORRIS

See also France: French Revolution; Furet; Godechot; Hufton; Marxist Interpretation; Soboul; Social

Biography

Albert Xavier Emile Mathiez. Born La Bruyère, Haute Saone, 10 January 1874, to a peasant family. Educated at Lure, Vesoul, and Lycée Lakanal, Sceaux, near Paris; entered the Ecole Normale Supérieure, 1894, agrégation 1897. Taught away from Paris for a while, before receiving his doctorate in 1904, then occupied various posts at universities in Caen, Nancy, Lille, Besançon, and Dijon before moving to the Sorbonne, 1926–32. From 1924, editor of the journal *Annales Révolutionnaires* which was renamed *Annales Historiques de la Révolution française*. Died Paris, February 1932.

Principal Writings

Les Origines des cultes révolutionnaires (1789–1792) (Origins of the Revolutionary Cults), 1904; reprinted 1977

La Théophilanthropie et le culte décadaire, 1796–1801: essai sur l'histoire religieuse de la révolution (Theophilanthropy and Revolutionary Cults), 1904; reprinted 1975

Le Club des Cordeliers pendant la crise de Varennes et la massacre du Champ de Mars (The Cordeliers Club), 1910

Rome et le clergé français sous la Constituante: la constitution civile du clergé, l'affaire d'Avignon (Rome and the French Clergy under the Constituent Assembly), 1911

La Révolution et les étrangers: cosmopolitisme et défense nationale (The Revolution and Foreigners), 1918

Danton et la paix (Danton and Peace), 1919

L'Affaire de la Compagnie des Indes (The Affair of the Company of the Indies), 1921

Robespierre terroriste (Robespierre as Terrorist), 1921
La Chute de la royauté (The Fall of the Monarchy), 1922
La Révolution française, 3 vols, 1922–27; in English as *The French Revolution*, 1929
Autour de Robespierre, 1925; in English as *The Fall of Robespierre, and Other Essays*, 1927
Autour de Danton (On Danton), 1926
La Vie chère et le mouvement social sous la Terreur (The High Cost of Living and the Social Movement during the Terror), 1927
La Réaction thermidorienne, 1929; in English as *After Robespierre: The Thermidorian Reaction*, 1931

Further Reading

Caillet-Bois, Ricardo Rodolfo, *Bibliografia de Albert Mathiez*, Buenos Aires: Buenos Aires University Press, 1932
Lefebvre, Georges, *Etudes sur la Révolution française* (Studies on the French Revolution), Paris: Presses Universitaires de France, 1954

Mattingly, Garrett 1900–1962

US historian of early modern Europe

Garrett Mattingly, an American historian of early modern Europe, was one of the rare modern scholars who have enjoyed both professional esteem and popular acclaim. He was the author of three classic books, each of which grew out of his abiding interest in the diplomatic relations between England and Spain. The master of a lean and elegant prose style, he had an unerring eye for illuminating detail, a powerful grasp of character, and a gift for lucid generalization. His command of the archival sources in his field was unrivaled, but he tended to minimize the scholarly apparatus of his books. Each of them was aimed at the widest possible audience, and each offered an exemplary combination of engaging narrative and incisive analysis.

One of Mattingly's mentors was the Harvard historian Roger Merriman, who introduced him to the field of early modern Spanish history; another was Bernard De Voto, who nourished his interest in literature and problems of narration. De Voto was an extraordinary figure, something like a combination of H.L. Mencken and Francis Parkman: a curmudgeonly man of letters and a romantic historian of America's westward expansion. De Voto's *The Year of Decision: 1846* (1943) offered an example of how to keep multiple story lines advancing simultaneously through the course of a single eventful year. It was a technique that De Voto learned from his experience as a novelist, and one that Mattingly would employ brilliantly in *The Armada* (1959). As a popular historian, De Voto rejected the conventions of monographic history in favor of a narrative of epic sweep studded with dramatic vignettes. Wallace Stegner, De Voto's biographer, called this strategy "history by synecdoche, the illumination of whole areas and periods through concentration upon one brief time, one single sequence, a few representative characters." Mattingly too learned how to make the rush of events comprehensible through an almost novelistic presentation of the predicaments of individual characters.

Mattingly's first book, *Catherine of Aragon* (1941), already combined the craft of the historian with the gifts of the novelist. The book restored to Henry VIII's first queen both agency and dignity, and showed how the personal, political, and ideological conflicts of the period were fought out in the language of conscience. It was, he wrote in his foreword, "the story of a life which shaped history by not moving with its flow." Throughout his career, Mattingly was attracted to persons of stubborn integrity torn by divided loyalties and caught in situations of crisis. In describing with meticulous care the accumulation of circumstances and grievances that led to the royal divorce, Mattingly not only shed new light on the origins of the English Reformation, he also produced one of the great modern biographies.

Mattingly's *Armada* (1959), is a work of wider scope than *Catherine of Aragon*, though it used the same strategy of evoking character and conflict through an accumulation of incidents: some dramatic, like the unforgettable account of the execution of Mary Stuart with which the book opens; others rescued from obscurity, like Drake's little-noticed but crucial destruction of the Armada's supply of barrel staves. The originality of the book lay not only in the use of previously overlooked archival sources (principally Italian), but in the European framework of the analysis and the rapid shifts of scene and perspective. Equally impressive is the unobtrusive mastery of technical details relating to ship construction, gunnery, and naval tactics. In the final reckoning Mattingly's 1588 (unlike De Voto's 1846) appears not so much as a "decisive" year, but rather as the first episode in a long war of attrition. Mattingly's broadly European perspective enabled him to puncture a number of myths about the defeat of the Armada, to offer a realistic analysis as well as a complex and stirring narrative. Some of his conclusions have been revised by recent scholarship, but the book retains its extraordinary stature and appeal.

The Armada was Mattingly's most popular book, but *Renaissance Diplomacy* (1955) was his masterpiece. The book began as an analysis of the institution of the resident ambassador, but it blossomed into a full-scale history of European diplomatic practices and of Renaissance statecraft. Here again Mattingly shuttled back and forth from the revelatory incident to the panoramic view, always setting intellectual developments and institutional innovations against a complex and shifting background of social and political change. "There are half a dozen chapters," J.H. Hexter wrote in one of the best appreciations of Mattingly's work, "that for sheer brilliance, for depth of insight, for concise easy statement of complex and fundamental truths about the age they deal with, have few peers in historical literature."

Toward the end of his career Mattingly produced a series of remarkable essays: two provocative contributions to Machiavelli studies, a portrait of Prince Henry the Navigator, a survey of Renaissance attitudes towards the state, and a brilliant 30-page distillation of his work on the Armada. But the three great books, with their wonderful combination of scrupulous scholarship and narrative flair, are his lasting legacy. They meet the sternest test of the classic histories: one can return to them again and again for both pleasure and instruction.

BRUCE THOMPSON

Biography

Born Washington, DC, 6 May 1900. Moved with his family to Kalamazoo, Michigan, where he attended high school before serving in the US Army, 1918–19. Trained by Charles Homer Haskins, Charles Howard McIlwain, and Roger B. Merriman at Harvard

University, BA 1923, MA 1926, PhD 1935. Taught at Northwestern University, 1926–28; and Long Island University, 1928–42, before serving in the US Navy, 1942–46; taught at Cooper Union, 1946–48; and Columbia University, 1948–62. Married Gertrude McCollum, 1928. Died 18 December 1962.

Principal Writings

"An Early Nonaggression Pact," *Journal of Modern History* 10 (1938), 1–30

"The Reputation of Doctor De Puebla," *English Historical Review* 60 (1940), 27–46

Catherine of Aragon, 1941

Renaissance Diplomacy, 1955

"Machiavelli's Prince: Political Science or Political Satire?," *American Scholar* 27 (1958), 482–91

The Armada, 1959; in UK as *The Defeat of the Spanish Armada*, 1959

"Changing Attitudes towards the State during the Renaissance," in William H. Werkmeister, ed., *Facets of the Renaissance*, 1959

"Navigator to the Modern Age," *Horizon* 3 (November 1960), 72–83

"Some Revisions of the Political History of the Renaissance," in Tinsley Helton, ed., *The Renaissance: A Reconsideration of the Theories and Interpretations of the Age*, 1961

The "Invincible" Armada and Elizabethan England, 1963

"Machiavelli," in J.H. Plumb, ed., *The Penguin Book of the Renaissance*, 1964

Further Reading

Carter, Charles Howard, ed., *From the Renaissance to the Counter-Reformation; Essays in Honor of Garrett Mattingly*, New York: Random House, 1965

Gilbert, Felix, "Sixteenth-Century Unlimited," *New York Herald Tribune* (13 April 1965)

Stegner, Wallace, *The Uneasy Chair: A Biography of Bernard DeVoto*, New York: Doubleday, 1974

Mayer, Arno J. 1926–

US (Luxembourg-born) historian of modern Europe

Arno J. Mayer's work has focused on the way in which the legacy of *ancien régime* Europe shaped the first half of the 20th century. His theoretical starting point is radical, describing himself at times as either left dissident or Marxist to indicate his non-doctrinaire flexibility and eclecticism. Thus, he freely and significantly borrowed from Joseph Schumpeter in his analyses of *fin-de-siècle* and interwar Europe. His concern was to demonstrate that the convulsions of this period emerged from the contradiction between the dynamism of industrialization on the one hand and the stagnation of the governing classes and their methods of rule on the other. His two major works dealt with how this relationship was reflected in, first, the peace settlement of 1919 and, second, the period 1914–45, or as Mayer calls it: the Thirty Years Crisis.

In *Politics and Diplomacy of Peacemaking* (1967), Mayer contrasted new and old diplomacy. New diplomacy, represented by the Bolshevik's Peace Decree and Woodrow Wilson's Fourteen Points (which were a hurried response to the Bolsheviks), was concerned with rational, open, and peaceful international relations. For old diplomacy, represented by the secret treaties and the Alliance system, war was a justifiable goal of imperialism and dynastic rivalry. This cleavage is explained by the aristocratic retention of state power in Europe and its absence or failure in Russia and the United States. Mayer characterized Wilsonian diplomacy as a counterrevolutionary but "new" alternative to Lenin's. Hence, Versailles, for Mayer, was a fudged settlement with an "old" diplomatic core, a "new" Wilsonian gloss, and counterrevolutionary intent.

Mayer followed a similar line of reasoning in *The Persistence of the Old Regime* (1981). He constructed a hypothesis that World War I and II and interwar instability were linked by "an umbilical chord." This era, the Thirty Years Crisis, was the progeny of the continued political domination of the old ruling classes in spite of industrialization and the rise of the bourgeoisie. Indeed, World War I demonstrated "The forces of the old order were sufficiently willful and powerful to resist and slow down the course of history, if necessary by recourse to violence." The aristocracy was able to survive economically as a class through ownership of the still predominant agricultural sectors of most European economies. It was treated with deference and imitated by a politically subordinate, immature, and fragmented bourgeoisie. Within this interpretive framework, the governing elites, faced with the challenge of the modern world, took to increasingly reactionary ideas (Social Darwinism and Nietzsche), and political formations (dictatorship and fascism). The contradictions that characterized the Thirty Years Crisis were resolved only by the convulsions of World War II. "It would take two world wars and the Holocaust . . . finally to dislodge the feudal and aristocratic presumption from Europe's civil and political societies." Mayer developed this theme in his study of the Holocaust – *Why Did the Heavens Not Darken?* (1988).

Mayer is not alone in this interpretation of the role of the aristocracy in the 20th century. In different guises it is common to Perry Anderson, Ralph Dahrendorf, and Barrington Moore. Their position was criticized most trenchantly by E.P. Thompson in reply to Anderson, and by Geoff Eley and David Blackbourn on the German case. According to this critique, the modernization theory underplays the extent to which members of the aristocracy adapted themselves to capitalist development and capitalist interests. Second, it has been argued that to divide the propertied classes of *fin-de-siècle* Europe into aristocrat and capitalist misleadingly obscures the degree of interpenetration of large landlords, state officials, and leading industrialists. Third, it overplays the role played by the nobility in the reaction of the early 20th century while exonerating industrial capitalism without which World War I and fascism could not have been possible, at the very least in a narrow technological sense. By exclusively focusing on class formation and action *from above*, the defining character of 20th-century reaction as being in response to working class challenge *from below* is not fully explored.

Modernization theory, such as that of Mayer, did gain considerable influence, particularly in the interpretation of fascism. However, by the mid-1980s and 1990s such broad interpretations had lost favor to more focused, less overarching explanations of the first half of the 20th century. Despite this, Mayer's work is generally received as an important and provocative contribution to our understanding of the 20th century.

MATT PERRY

See also Europe: Modern

Biography

Arno Joseph Mayer. Born Luxembourg, 19 June 1926. Received BBA, City College of New York, 1949; MA, Yale University, 1950, PhD, 1954. Taught at Wesleyan University, 1952–53; Brandeis University, 1954–58; Harvard University, 1958–61; and Princeton University, from 1961. Married (2 children).

Principal Writings

Political Origins of the New Diplomacy, 1917–1918, 1959

"Post-War Nationalisms, 1918–19," *Past and Present* 34 (1966), 114–26

Politics and Diplomacy of Peacemaking: Containment and Counter-Revolution at Versailles, 1918–19, 1967

Dynamics of Counter-Revolution in Europe, 1870–1956: An Analytical Framework, 1971

"Lower Middle Class as Historical Problem," *Journal of Modern History* 47 (1975), 409–36

"Internal Crisis and War since 1870," in Charles L. Bertrand, ed., *Revolutionary Situations in Europe, 1917–22*, 1977

The Persistence of the Old Regime: Europe to the Great War, 1981

Why Did the Heavens Not Darken? The "Final Solution" in History, 1988

"Memory and History: On the Poverty of Forgetting and Remembering about the Judeocide," *Radical History Review* 56 (1993), 5–20

Further Reading

Blackbourn, David and Geoff Eley, *Mythen deutscher Geschichtsschreibung: die gescheiterte bürgerliche Revolution von 1848*, Frankfurt: Ullstein, 1980; revised in English as *The Peculiarities of German History: Bourgeois Society and Politics in Nineteenth-Century German History*, Oxford: Oxford University Press, 1984

Fry, Michael G., and Arthur M. Gilbert, "A Historian and Linkage Politics: Arno J. Mayer," *International Studies Quarterly* 26 (1982), 425–44

Lundgreen-Nielsen, Kay, "The Mayer Thesis Reconsidered: The Poles and the Paris Peace Conference, 1919," *International History Review* 7 (1985), 68–102

Righart, Hans, "'Jumbo-History': perceptie, anachronisme en 'hindsight' bij Arno J. Mayer en Barrington Moore" (Jumbo History: Reception, Anachronism, and Hindsight in the work of Arno J. Mayer and Barrington Moore), *Theoretische Geschiedenis* 17 (1990), 285–95

Thompson, E.P., *The Poverty of Theory and Other Essays*, London: Merlin Press, and New York: Monthly Review Press, 1978

Mazrui, Ali A. 1933–

Kenyan historian

Ali Mazrui was born in Mombasa, Kenya, and spent a good deal of his youth attempting to integrate his Swahili cultural heritage with the newly imposed Western culture. Mazrui and his family tried to preserve as much as they could of their culture, but also took advantage of European culture when possible, especially in secular education. Mazrui did not treat education lightly, as it had important connections to culture and identity. In *Political Values and the Educated Class in Africa* (1978), Mazrui stated that all educated Africans are cultural captives. Their differences only lie in the degree to which they are captives. This is how Mazrui saw lived experience fitting into the culture and ideology of the lived Africa.

Mazrui and his peers grew up during the era of nationalist agitations. Although he was not a fervently active member of nationalist movements, the independence era did affect his thinking. He has often been criticized for overemphasizing how his life has influenced his writing. Yet, much of his writing involves the negotiation of cultures, and it seems only appropriate to describe one's life experiences in such an investigation. In addition, being forthright about one's possible biases should not be the occasion for criticism.

Following his postgraduate education in the US and Britain, Mazrui returned to Africa as a lecturer at Makerere University in Kampala, Uganda. There, he became a supporter of academic freedom and was even publicly denounced by president Obote for his support of a jailed editor, Rajat Neogy. Mazrui was in trouble with the government for some time, but he managed to weather the storm of indignation.

Mazrui has been an instrumental figure in defining what it means to be an African. Much like Kwame Nkrumah of Ghana, he has battled to define the idea of Africanness in the broadest sense possible. That is, he defined an African as anyone who supports Africa and its people. This is the classic Pan-Africanist definition of an African that incorporates Africans and people in diaspora, which he elaborated in *Towards a Pax Africana* (1967). Because Mazrui defined an African in this way, he encouraged the study of the African diaspora and its cultures in African universities. In his mind, not only was it important for Africans currently living on the continent to uncover their own past, it was also important for these same Africans to understand everyone who identified themselves as Africans. Consistent with his Pan-African thinking, Mazrui was also a supporter of the East African federation.

Among Mazrui's most enduring legacies, and one to which he has devoted much energy, has been his discussion of the warrior tradition in African politics. While his argument has been much questioned, it remains an important part of African historiography. Mazrui's belief was that the cultural legacy and imperialism of Europe could be broken if a political system based on indigenous ideas of the warrior could be implemented. An elaboration of this idea may be found in several works, beginning with *On Heroes and Uhuru-Worship* (1967). Mazrui was among the pioneers in investigating African politics and African indigenous political systems as they related to the modern world. He envisioned an Africa where respectable and responsible leaders would lead Africans; they would integrate the idea of ancestor or grandfather with that of parent or father-figure. This new brand of African leader would then be able to lead Africans in the contemporary world through an integration of past/indigenous ideals and contemporary interpretations of what a leader should be.

Another area in which Mazrui has published widely concerns Africa and its place in the world. Many of these works look at the negotiation of cultures and identities. Mazrui has helped make the world realize that Africa has to contend with numerous heritages, which have only begun to be negotiated. But, until Africa begins to address questions of identity, it will always remain weak in global diplomatic terms. There are points of contact between assumptions about African diplomatic behavior and traditional norms of Western international conduct. They need to be found and negotiated in order for Africa to assert its proper place in the world.

TOYIN FALOLA and JOEL E. TISHKEN

See also Afigbo; Africa: West

Biography

Ali Al'Amin Mazrui. Born Mombasa, 24 February 1933. Worked in
various jobs and traveled in Africa, 1948–55. Studied at
Huddersfield College of Technology, England 1955–57; University of
Manchester, BA 1960; Columbia University, MA 1961; Oxford
University, PhD 1966. Taught at Makerere University, Kampala,
Uganda, 1963–73; research professor, University of Jos, Nigeria,
1981–87; professor of political science and of Afroamerican and
African studies, University of Michigan, 1974–91; professor-at-large,
Cornell University, 1986–92; Albert Schweitzer professor in the
humanities, State University of New York, Binghamton, from 1989.
Divorced (5 children).

Principal Writings

On Heroes and Uhuru-Worship: Essays on Independent Africa,
  1967
Towards a Pax Africana: A Study of Ideology and Ambition, 1967
Editor with Robert I. Rotberg, *Protest and Power in Black Africa*,
  1970
The Trial of Christopher Okigbo, 1971
*The Political Sociology of the English Language: An African
  Perspective*, 1975
*Soldiers and Kinsmen in Uganda: The Making of a Military
  Ethnocracy*, 1975
Political Values and the Educated Class in Africa, 1978
Editor with T.K. Levine, *The Warrior Tradition in Modern Africa*,
  1978
*Nationalism and New States in Africa from about 1935 to the
  Present*, 1984
The Africans: A Triple Heritage, 1986
Cultural Forces in World Politics, 1990
Africa since 1935, 1993 [UNESCO General History of Africa, vol. 8]

Further Reading

Mazrui, Ali A., "The Making of an African Political Scientist,"
  International Social Science Journal 25 (1973), 101–16
Nyang, Sulayman S., *Ali A. Mazrui: The Man and His Works*,
  Lawrenceville, VA: Brunswick, 1981

Media

The subject of the media occupies a central place in contemporary societies, and media historiography has grown rapidly
in the last several decades, cross-fertilized by social theories,
communication research, and cultural studies. It has covered
such diverse subjects as the uses of photography, propaganda,
censorship, the role of the media in cultural integration, the
mass media as social systems, and the effects of advertising.

The origins of communication research in Europe can be
traced to the late 19th century with literary, legal, and historical
inquiries about the press that were influenced by theories of mass
society. In the age of the mass press and the metropolis, Auguste
Comte's conception of the collective organism, Ferdinand
Tönnies' contrast of *Gemeinschaft* and *Gesellschaft* (community
and society), Werner Sombart's polemic about advertising and
publicity, and Gabriel Tarde's analysis of public opinion were all
part of an ongoing philosophical speculation about the effects
of modern, urban society said to be marked by the erosion of
traditional bonds. Max Weber, in his remarks to the first meeting
of German sociologists in 1910, pointed to the press as a main
area for a systematic study that would involve empirical research

of contents and quantification of data and would provide an
overall assessment of the role of the press in the "making of
modern man."

After World War I, propaganda analysis emerged as a new
activity. Walter Lippmann in *The Phantom Public* (1925)
argued that the public's action might be in response to "pseudo-
environments" communicated through the media. This coincided with a shift from a philosophical approach toward
behavioral science and empirical analysis. Methods of institutional analysis and audience research popular in the 1920s and
1930s were replaced by quantification in the 1940s. After World
War II the Chicago school led by Robert Park focused on the
sociological study of media organizations and the nature of
news. Functionalism based on the tendency of society toward
stability and equilibrium was also influential. Researchers
rescrutinized the role of the state in order to define the government as a regulatory or facilitating agency.

At the same time, early historical studies of the media emphasized a linear development of technologies and the internal
dynamic of institutions shaped by heroic journalists and editors.
This "Whiggish" view has since been criticized for naively defining the media as objective and progressive, for emphasizing
success stories and for neglecting the social and cultural contexts of the press in the past. Critics have also argued that the
tight association of the media and commercial interests meant
that such research was often aimed at promoting particular
branches of the media.

A significant contribution came from the Frankfurt school
and its associates. While arguing that postwar mass culture
was dominated by the culture industry, Theodor Adorno advocated empirical and dialectical methodologies for the study of
social phenomena. Jürgen Habermas likewise emphasized
critical and historical methods. In the seminal *Strukturwandel
der Öffentlichkeit* (1962; *The Structural Transformation of the
Public Sphere*, 1989) he argued that in the course of the 18th
century French political discourse emerged separate from the
state and civil society, and that the realm of private life –
including literary salons and coffee houses – provided a new
public sphere. According to him, after a momentous expansion during the French Revolution, the public sphere has since
lost its independence as part of the media's loss of immediate
relationship to the state and civil society. Although historians
have since modified such theses, the concept of the public
sphere remains influential.

In the 1950s and the 1960s the Canadian critic Marshall
McLuhan provided a radical critique of the media. He argued
that the media contain inherent biases that powerfully manipulate the public through physiological and psychological
impact. While such a holistic critique appeared to be a contemporary phenomenon, the thesis of manipulation has been
continually tested in studies of reception. Scholars have
contrasted the diversity of the 19th-century media with the
dominance of media corporations in the 20th century.

The construction of identities and the role of ideology have
also been important themes. Benedict Anderson in *Imagined
Communities* (1983) emphasized the profound impact of the
press in the formation of national and cultural identities in
the modern world. Scholars of China point to the role of the
media in the remarkable integration of the country in the 20th
century, an integration built upon achievements of the late

imperial period. The homogeneous, high-context cultural identities of Japan have been reflected in very subtle advertisements. Studies of the radio have revealed that radio programs sought to reinforce gender and national identities. The study of minority presses, the relationship of religion and the media, and the historical analysis of radio programs have contributed to understanding the formation of cultural identities.

In the last three decades the study of advertising has come into its own, stimulated by broad theoretical works such as Raymond Williams' *Problems in Materialism and Culture* (1980) or Daniel Boorstin's *The Image* (1962) which took the domination of the visual as a crucial aspect of modern life. Analyses of the visual content of advertising such as Judith Williamson's *Decoding Advertisements* (1978) and Stuart Ewen's *All Consuming Images* (1988) underlined the importance of "image management." The cultural history of advertising revives the original contexts and perceptions of advertising. Jackson Lears in *Fables of Abundance* (1994) pointed out that William James at the turn of the century saw advertising not as advocating hedonism and materialism but as a part of the routinization of modern life that was transforming American society through economic rationalization. Other important themes in the study of the media include theories of "hypermedia" – nonlinear media – first advanced in the 1960s and associated with the electronic revolution, economic logic, and utopian aspirations.

H. Hazel Hahn

See also Anderson, B.; Boorstin; Briggs; Film; Habermas; McLuhan; Williams, R.

Further Reading

Anderson, Benedict, *Imagined Communities: Reflections on the Origin and Spread of Nationalism*, London and New York: Verso, 1983; revised 1991

Baughman, James L., *The Republic of Mass Culture: Journalism, Filmmaking, and Broadcasting in America since 1941*, Baltimore: Johns Hopkins University Press, 1992

Bellanger, Claude, *et al.*, eds., *Histoire générale de la presse française* (General History of the French Press), 5 vols., Paris: Presses Universitaires de France, 1969–76

Boorstin, Daniel J., *The Image; or, What Happened to the American Dream*, New York: Atheneum, and London: Weidenfeld and Nicolson, 1962

Censer, Jack R., *The French Press in the Age of Enlightenment*, London and New York: Routledge, 1994

Cole, Robert, *Propaganda in Twentieth Century War and Politics: An Annotated Bibliography*, Lanham, MD: Scarecrow Press, 1996

Crowley, David, and Paul Heyer, *Communication in History: Technology, Culture, Society*, New York and London: Longman, 1991

DeFleur, Melvin Lawrence, *Theories of Mass Communication*, New York: McKay, 1966; London: Longman, 1977

Eisenstein, Elizabeth L., *The Printing Press as an Agent of Change: Communications and Cultural Transformations in Early-Modern Europe*, 2 vols., Cambridge and New York: Cambridge University Press, 1980

Ewen, Stuart, *All Consuming Images: The Politics of Style in Contemporary Culture*, New York: Basic Books, 1988

Habermas, Jürgen, *Strukturwandel der Öffentlichkeit: Untersuchungen zu einer Kategorie der bürgerlichen Gesellschaft*, Neuwied: Luchterhand, 1962; in English as *The Structural Transformation of the Public Sphere: An Inquiry into a Category of Bourgeois Society*, Cambridge, MA: MIT Press, and London: Polity Press, 1989

Hardt, Hanno, *Social Theories of the Press: Early German and American Perspectives*, Beverly Hills, CA: Sage, 1979

Hesse, Carla, and Randolph Starn, eds., "The Future Library," *Representations* 42 (1993) [special issue]

Horkheimer, Max, and Theodor W. Adorno, *Dialektik der Aufklärung*, Amsterdam: Querido, 1947 [revised edition of *Philosophische Fragmente*; 1944]; in English as *Dialectic of Enlightenment*, New York: Seabury Press, 1972, London: Allen Lane, 1973

Høyer, Svennik, Epp Lauk, and Peeter Vihalemm, eds., *Towards a Civic Society: The Baltic Media's Long Road to Freedom: Perspectives on History, Ethnicity and Journalism*, Tartu: Nota Baltica, 1993

Ivy, Marilyn, *Discourses of the Vanishing: Modernity, Phantasm, Japan*, Chicago: University of Chicago Press, 1995

Johnson, David G., Andrew J. Nathan, and Evelyn S. Rawski, eds., *Popular Culture in Late Imperial China*, Berkeley: University of California Press, 1985

Kittler, Friedrich A., *Aufschreibesysteme, 1800/1900*, Munich: Fink, 1985; in English as *Discourse Networks, 1800/1900*, Stanford, CA: Stanford University Press, 1985

Lacey, Kate, *Feminine Frequencies: Gender, German Radio, and the Public Sphere, 1923–1945*, Ann Arbor: University of Michigan Press, 1996

Landow, George, *Hypertext: The Convergence of Contemporary Critical Theory and Technology*, Baltimore: Johns Hopkins University Press, 1992; revised 1997

Lears, T.J. Jackson, *Fables of Abundance: A Cultural History of Advertising in America*, New York: Basic Books, 1994

Leiss, William, Stephen Kline, and Sut Jhally, eds., *Social Communication in Advertising: Persons, Products and Images of Well-Being*, London and New York: Methuen, 1986; revised 1990

Lent, John A., *Third World Mass Media and Their Search for Modernity: The Case of the Commonwealth Caribbean*, Lewisburg, PA: Bucknell University Press, 1977

Lippmann, Walter, *The Phantom Public*, New York: Harcourt Brace, 1925

McCauley, Elizabeth Anne, *Industrial Madness: Commercial Photography in Paris, 1848–1871*, New Haven and London: Yale University Press, 1994

McLuhan, Marshall, *Understanding Media: The Extensions of Man*, New York: McGraw Hill, and London: Routledge, 1964

Marchand, Roland, *Advertising the American Dream: Making Way for Modernity, 1920–1940*, Berkeley: University of California Press, 1985

Nunberg, Geoffrey, ed., *The Future of the Book*, Berkeley: University of California Press, 1996

Pharr, Susan J., and Ellis S. Krauss, eds., *Media and Politics in Japan*, Honolulu: University of Hawaii Press, 1996

Poster, Mark, *The Second Media Age*, Cambridge: Polity Press, and Cambridge, MA: Blackwell, 1995

Roeder, George H., Jr., *The Censored War: American Visual Experience during World War Two*, New Haven and London: Yale University Press, 1993

Schiller, Herbert I., *Culture, Inc.: The Corporate Takeover of Public Expression*, Oxford and New York: Oxford University Press, 1989

Shaw, Tony, *Eden, Suez and the Mass Media: Propaganda and Persuasion during the Suez Crisis*, London: Tauris, 1996

Solomon, William S., and Robert W. McChesney, eds., *Ruthless Criticism: New Perspectives in US Communication History*, Minneapolis: University of Minnesota Press, 1993

Tunstall, Jeremy, *The Media in Britain*, London: Constable, and New York: Columbia University Press, 1983

Warner, Michael, *The Letters of the Republic: Publication and the Public Sphere in Eighteenth-Century America*, Cambridge, MA: Harvard University Press, 1990

Wicke, Jennifer, *Advertising Fictions: Literature, Advertisement, and Social Reading*, New York: Columbia University Press, 1988

Williams, Raymond, *Problems in Materialism and Culture: Selected Essays*, London: Verso, 1980; New York: Schocken, 1981

Williamson, Judith, *Decoding Advertisements: Ideology and Meaning in Advertising*, London: Boyars, 1978

Medicine, History of

The history of medicine or medico-history began as illustrative historical accounts intended to inform the practice of contemporary physicians. This work usually exhibited a straightforward, positivist point of view with little context or interpretation, and was essentially focused on great healers and their methods. This remained true until well into the 20th century, when the nature and scope of medical education became more structured through scientific advances. As a result, fewer and fewer physicians have had either the general educational background or, perhaps more crucially, the leisure to produce significant works on the history of medicine. As medical practice relied more on laboratory findings, lessons for the present became more difficult to discern in examples from the past.

Since the Enlightenment, there has been a direct shift from these doxographical studies, to an emphasis on the history of specific diseases, on the effect of the environment on health, on different branches of medicine such as epidemiology or psychiatry, on biological factors in history, on nutrition, on public health, and perhaps most importantly and most radically, on the patient. All this reflects the increasing influence of social history in the 20th century, and also the spread of interdisciplinarity among historians of medicine who routinely use the methodology and ideas of anthropology, linguistics, and demography among other disciplines, to explore the history of medicine. Also influential has been the expansion of empirical sources interrogated about the history of medicine. From the study of ancient medical texts, modern historians have moved on to the inclusion of clinical notes, legal records, topographical maps, and a variety of other sources.

This change did not come quickly. The European schools of the history of medicine, especially the Germans, were influenced by Kurt Sprengel's *Versuch einer pragmatischen Geschichte der Arzneykunde* (Essay on a Pragmatic History of Medicine, 1803). Sprengel related medicine to its surrounding culture, thereby revealing it as a branch of intellectual history. Karl Sudhoff controlled the history of medicine in Germany at the beginning of the 20th century through his periodical *Sudhoffs Archiv* or *Zeitschrift für Geschichte der Medizin*. His pupils were physician-historians with sufficient knowledge in the humanities to sow the seeds of what would become the social history of medicine later in the 20th century. Henry Sigerist, Sudhoff's successor at the University of Leipzig's Institute for the History of Medicine (and later briefly director of the Johns Hopkins University Institute for the History of Medicine), made the first clear call for historians of medicine to see their subject as social history. Despite Sigerist's sojourn at Johns Hopkins, medical historians in the United States were slow to adopt interdisciplinary methods. While research in continental Europe and in Britain was incorporating the insights of demographers, anthropologists, sociologists, and economists, the history of medicine remained the province of physicians in the United States until the 1970s.

Twentieth-century historians Henry Sigerist, Richard Shryock, George Rosen – who used the term *iatrocentric* to describe previous history of medicine – and Erwin Ackerknecht all envisioned a history of medicine going beyond the chronologies, hagiographic biographies, and bio-bibliographies that had dominated the history of medicine since Le Clerc's *Histoire de la médecine* (1696; *The History of Physick*, 1699). Le Clerc had infused the history of medicine with Renaissance humanist ideals. Unlike the history of science – where Kuhn's *The Structure of Scientific Revolutions* (1962) was a landmark work – there has been no one work that was the turning point for the path of the historiography of the history of medicine.

However, Michel Foucault's *Folie et déraison* (1961; *Madness and Civilization*, 1965) and *Naissance de la clinique* (1963; *The Birth of the Clinic*, 1973) called attention to the language surrounding medical events. Foucault exerted tremendous influence on the developing group of historians of medicine who were in reality historians of health care and all of its practitioners.

Since the 1950s the history of medicine has enriched itself by its seemingly endless efforts to become multidisciplinary. The sudden influx of researchers not trained in applied medicine sparked criticism that the new scholars left medicine and doctors out of the history of medicine. This has led to a further tension between the medically trained historians who, for example, have sought to explain how the treatment of a certain disease has evolved over time, and researchers whose training rejects a narrowly scientific reading of the evidence. This has been most noticeable in the response to François Delaporte's claim that disease has no meaning apart from that assigned by society. This poststructuralist reading of the history of medicine has puzzled researchers more wedded to the empirical tradition, who would argue that diseases and medical problems are not shaped by discourse, but by their biological and physiological imperatives. Other difficulties have emerged from the difficulty of incorporating many excellent studies of isolated phenomena in small populations into a larger vision of the changing priorities of healthcare around the world and since the time of Hippocrates.

Scholars have called for these diverse studies to be gathered together and synthesized. To date, no one scholar has attempted a single-volume history of medicine reflecting the issues raised by the social historian, but two works published in 1993 attempted to begin the task, if not always with the conciseness needed to explicate the topic. The *Companion Encyclopedia of the History of Medicine*, edited by W.F. Bynum and Roy Porter, brought together essays on both the traditional history of medicine and topics suggested by the social history of medicine. *The Cambridge World History of Human Disease*, edited by Kenneth Kiple and the product of the Cambridge History and Geography of Human Disease Project, endeavored to bridge the chasm that opened between the medically trained and the historically trained historians of medicine in the last fifty years. Their bibliographies offer the researcher items from a full spectrum of approaches: literary, medical, social history, anthropology, geography, and area studies. A truly interdisciplinary list of contributors points to the future of medical history and biomedical history.

NANCY PIPPEN ECKERMAN

See also Crosby; Foucault; Kuhn; Rosenberg, C.; Science; Sigerist; Sudhoff; Temkin

Further Reading

Ackerknecht, Erwin H., *A Short History of Medicine*, New York: Ronald Press, 1955; revised Baltimore: Johns Hopkins University Press, 1982

Boyden, Stephen, *Western Civilization in Biological Perspective: Patterns in Biohistory*, Oxford and New York: Oxford University Press, 1987

Brieger, Gert H., "History of Medicine," in Paul T. Durbin, general editor, *A Guide to the Culture of Science, Technology, and Medicine*, New York: Free Press, 1980

Brumberg, Joan Jacobs, *Fasting Girls: The Emergence of Anorexia Nervosa as a Modern Disease*, Cambridge, MA: Harvard University Press, 1988

Bynum, William F., "Health, Disease and Medical Care," in G.S. Rousseau and Roy Porter, eds., *The Ferment of Knowledge: Studies in the Historiography of Eighteenth-Century Science*, Cambridge: Cambridge University Press, 1980

Bynum, William F., and Roy Porter, eds., *Companion Encyclopedia of the History of Medicine*, 2 vols., London and New York: Routledge, 1993

Carmichael, Ann G., *Plague and the Poor in Renaissance Florence*, Cambridge and New York: Cambridge University Press, 1986

Clarke, Edwin, ed., *Modern Methods in the History of Medicine*, London: Athlone Press, 1971

Crosby, Alfred W., Jr., *The Columbian Exchange: Biological and Cultural Consequences of 1492*, Westport, CT: Greenwood Press, 1972

Delaporte, François, *Disease and Civilization: The Cholera in Paris, 1832*, Cambridge, MA: MIT Press, 1982

Dwyer, Ellen, *Homes for the Mad: Life Inside Two Nineteenth-Century Asylums*, New Brunswick, NJ: Rutgers University Press, 1987

Evans, Richard J., *Death in Hamburg Society and Politics in the Cholera Years 1830-1910*, Oxford and New York: Oxford University Press, 1987

Foucault, Michel, *Folie et déraison*, Paris: Plon, 1961, abridged as *Histoire de la folie*, Paris: UGE, 1961; in English as *Madness and Civilization: A History of Insanity in the Age of Reason*, New York: Pantheon, 1965, London: Tavistock, 1967

Foucault, Michel, *Naissance de la clinique: une archéologie du regard médical*, Paris: Presses Universitaires de France, 1963; in English as *The Birth of the Clinic: An Archaeology of Medical Perception*, New York: Pantheon, and London: Tavistock, 1973

Kiple, Kenneth F., ed., *The Cambridge World History of Human Disease*, Cambridge: Cambridge University Press, 1993

Kleinman, Arthur, *Patients and Healers in the Context of Culture: An Exploration of the Borderland Between Anthropology, Medicine, and Psychiatry*, Berkeley: University of California Press, 1982

Kuhn, Thomas S., *The Structure of Scientific Revolutions*, Chicago: University of Chicago Press, 1962; revised 1970

Leavitt, Judith Walzer, *The Healthiest City: Milwaukee and the Politics of Health Reform*, Princeton: Princeton University Press, 1982

Le Clerc, Daniel, *Histoire de la médecine*, Geneva: Chouët et Ritter, 1696; in English as *The History of Physick; or, An Account of the Rise and Progress of the Art, and the Several Discoveries therein from Age to Age: with Remarks on the Lives of the Most Eminent Physicians*, London: Brown Roper Leigh and Midwinter, 1699

Loudon, Irvine, *Medical Care and the General Practitioner, 1750-1850*, Oxford and New York: Oxford University Press, 1986

MacDonald, Michael, *Mystical Bedlam: Madness, Anxiety and Healing in Seventeenth-Century England*, Cambridge and New York: Cambridge University Press, 1984

McKeown, Thomas, *The Role of Medicine: Dream, Mirage or Nemesis?*, London: Nuffield Provincial Hospital Trust, 1976; Princeton: Princeton University Press, 1979

Pernick, Martin S., *A Calculus of Suffering: Pain, Professionalism and Anesthesia in Nineteenth-Century America*, New York: Columbia University Press, 1985

Porter, Roy, "The Patient's View: Doing Medical History from Below," *Theory and Society* 14 (1985), 175-98

Porter, Roy, and Andrew Wear, *Problems and Methods in the History of Medicine*, London: Croom Helm, 1987

Reverby, Susan B., *Ordered to Care: The Dilemma of American Nursing, 1850-1945*, Cambridge: Cambridge University Press, 1987

Riley, James, *Sickness, Recovery, and Death: A History and Forecast of Ill Health*, Iowa City: University of Iowa Press, 1989

Risse, Guenter B., *Hospital Life In Enlightenment Scotland: Care and Teaching at the Royal Infirmary of Edinburgh*: Cambridge: Cambridge University Press, 1986

Rosenberg, Charles E., *The Cholera Years: The United States in 1832, 1849, and 1866*, Chicago: University of Chicago Press, 1962; revised 1987

Rosenberg, Charles E., *The Care of Strangers: The Rise of America's Hospital System*, New York: Basic Books, 1987

Shryock, Richard H., *The Development of Modern Medicine: An Interpretation of the Social and Scientific Factors Involved*, Philadelphia: University of Pennsylvania Press, and London: Oxford University Press, 1936

Shryock, Richard H., *Medicine in America: Historical Essays*, Baltimore: Johns Hopkins Press, 1966

Sigerist, Henry, *A History of Medicine*, 8 vols., New York: Oxford University Press, 1951-61

Sigerist, Henry, *Landmarks in the History of Hygiene*, London and New York: Oxford University Press, 1956

Siraisi, Nancy, *Medieval and Early Renaissance Medicine: An Introduction to Knowledge and Practice*, Chicago: University of Chicago Press, 1990

Slack, Paul, *The Impact of Plague in Tudor and Stuart England*, London and Boston: Routledge, 1985

Sprengel, Kurt Polycarp Joachim, *Versuch einer pragmatischen Geschichte der Arzneykunde* (Essay on a Pragmatic History of Medicine), 6 vols. in 8, 3rd edition, Halle: Gebauer, 1821-28 [1st edition 1803]

Temkin, Owsei, *The Falling Sickness: A History of Epilepsy from the Greeks to the Beginnings of Modern Neurology*, Baltimore: Johns Hopkins Press, 1945; revised 1971

Temkin, Owsei, *The Double Face of Janus, and Other Essays in the History of Medicine*, Baltimore: Johns Hopkins University Press, 1976

Ulrich, Laurel Thatcher, *A Midwife's Tale: The Life of Martha Ballard, Based on Her Diary, 1785-1812*, New York: Knopf, 1990

Medieval Chronicles

Although scholars are agreed that chronicles, annals, and histories rank among the richest sources for medieval history, more than a century and a half of study and discussion has failed to produce a consensus as to the basis for differentiating these from one another. Prior to the 14th century, writers tended to use the term almost interchangeably. Modern historians have tended to see chronicles as more general in scope, with annals primarily treating local events in a series of chronological notations. World chronicles certainly fit the usage. They may be traced to Eusebius of Caesarea's Chronicle (written in Greek, *c.*303 CE, Latin version by Jerome, *c.*380) and generally follow the Eusebian approach, focusing on the history of salvation since the Creation (often calling attention to this theme in a preface) and arranged in books and chapters. The earliest chroniclers simply rewrote Eusebius or Eusebius-Jerome and added material to bring the account to the chronicler's own time. These chronicles were in turn rewritten in later ones. Nonetheless, a great many chronicles are limited in scope to a single region, locality, or institution. In one famous instance, the monk Orderic Vitalis set out to write a chronicle of his monastery, expanded it to include the history of the Normans, then to the history of western Christianity. Annals began only in the 7th or 8th centuries as annotations in Paschal tables that established the annual dates for the celebration of Easter. In the sometimes large blank space between years, Anglo-Saxon monks began noting the significant events of the year. Missionaries introduced the practice on the Continent, where it became the dominant mode of contemporary history. The form became so successful during the Carolingian Renaissance that from the 10th century some Latin chronicles began to adopt a chronological/annalistic arrangement and the two genres converged. To further complicate the situation, *gesta*, genealogies, and hagiography may embrace background or records that are more properly annals or chronicles, and many writings referred to as histories would better be termed chronicles or annals.

Both chronicles and annals are rich mines of specific information on medieval life. Since they embrace treatments of regions, cities and towns, rulers, popes, bishops, abbots and abbesses, monastic orders and individual institutions, they contain a variety of valuable details and insights about popular culture, rituals, procedures, mentalities, and the like. Of course, any portion of a chronicle that treats of times more than two generations removed from its writing is not to be trusted in matters of fact or detail, however interesting it may be by virtue of its theme, mode of expression, or affiliation. The clergy were most often the authors of these works, which therefore reflect the ecclesiastical point of view and defend church interests. Though the authors were literate, they were not often very perceptive or critical in their approach to reality and sometimes seemed to regard their task as unredeemed drudgery, a mental state in which neither linguistic nor conceptual rigor flourished. Moreover, annals, *gesta*, and genealogies are to be systematically interrogated rather than taken at face value because they are often concerned only with celebrating the virtues and achievements of a person, trumpeting the greatness of an institution, or establishing a claim to title or property and not to what later times would consider even minimal objectivity.

JOSEPH M. McCARTHY

See also Medieval Historical Writing

Further Reading

Archambault, Paul, *Seven French Chroniclers: Witnesses to History*, Syracuse: Syracuse University Press, 1974
Balzani, Ugo, *Le cronache italiane nel medio evo* (Italian Chronicles of the Middle Ages), Milan: Hoepli, 1884; reprinted Hildesheim: Olms, 1973
Bauer, Adolf, *Ursprung und Fortwirken der christlichen Weltchronik* (Origin and Continuity of the Christian World Chronicle), Graz: Leuscher & Lubensky, 1910
Bodmer, Jean Pierre, *Chroniken und Chronisten im Spätmittelalter* (Chronicles and Chroniclers in the Late Middle Ages), Bern: Francke, 1976
Boulay, F.R.H. du, "The German Town Chronicles," in R.H.C. Davis and J.M. Wallace-Hadrill, eds., *The Writing of History in the Middle Ages: Essays Presented to Richard William Southern*, Oxford and New York: Oxford University Press, 1981, 445–69
Brincken, Anna-Dorothee von den, *Studien zur lateinischen Weltchronistik bis in das Zeitalter Ottos von Freising* (Studies on the Latin World Chronicle from the Era of Otto von Freising), Düsseldorf: Triltsch, 1957
Centro italiano di studi sull'alto Medioevo, *La storiografia altomedievale*, 2 vols., Spoleto: Presso la Sede del Centro, 1970
Genicot, Léopold, *Les Généalogies* (Genealogies), Turnhout: Brepols, 1975
Goetz, H.W., "Zum Geschichtsbewusstsein in der alemannisch-schweizerischen Klosterchronistik des hohen Mittelalters, 11.–13. Jahrhundert" (On Historical Consciousness in the German-Swiss High Medieval Chronicles of Monasteries), *Deutsches Archiv* 44 (1988), 455–88
Gransden, Antonia, "The Chronicles of Medieval England and Scotland," *Journal of Medieval History* 16 (1990), 129–50; 17 (1991), 217–43
Green, Louis, *Chronicle into History: An Essay on the Interpretation of History in Florentine Fourteenth-Century Chronicles*, Cambridge: Cambridge University Press, 1972
Grundmann, Herbert, *Geschichtsschreibung im Mittelalter: Gattungen, Epochen, Eigenart* (History Writing in the Middle Ages: Types, Eras, Individuality), Göttingen: Vandenhoeck & Ruprecht, 1965
Guenée, Bernard, "Histoires, annales, chroniques: essai sur les genres historiques au Moyen Age" (Histories, Annals, Chronicles: Essay on the Historical Genres of the Middle Ages), *Annales: ESC* 28 (1973), 997–1016
Guenée, Bernard, "Documents insérés et documents abrégés dans la Chronique du religieux de Saint-Denis (Documents Inserted and Abridged in the Chronique . . .)," *Bibliothèque de l'Ecole des Chartes* 152 (1994), 373–428
Hay, Denys, *Annalists and Historians: Western Historiography from the Eighth to the Eighteenth Centuries*, London: Methuen, and New York: Harper, 1977
Hoffmann, Hartmut, *Untersuchungen zur karolingischen Annalistik* (Research on the Writing of Carolingian Annals), Bonn: Röhrscheid, 1958
Huyghebaert, Nicolas N., *Les Documents nécrologiques* (Necrologies), Turnhout: Brepols, 1972
Jones, Charles W., *Saints' Lives and Chronicles in Early England*, Ithaca, NY: Cornell University Press, 1947
Krüger, Karl Heinrich, *Die Universalchroniken* (Universal Chronicles), Turnhout: Brepols, 1976
Landsberg, Fritz, *Das Bild der alten Geschichte in mittelalterlichen Weltchroniken* (The Portrayal of Ancient History in Medieval World Chronicles), Berlin: Streisand, 1934
Levison, Wilhelm, and Heinz Löwe, eds., *Deutschlands Geschichtsquellen im Mittelalter: Vorzeit und Karolinger* (Germany's Historical Sources of the Middle Ages: Antiquity and the Carolingians), Weimar, 1952–73 [revision of Wilhelm Wattenbach's edition]
McCormick, Michael, *Les Annales du haut Moyen Age* (Annals of the High Middle Ages), Turnhout: Brepols, 1975
McGuire, Martin R.P., "Annals and Chronicles," *New Catholic Encyclopedia*, vol.1, New York: McGraw Hill, 1967, 551–56
Patze, Hans, "Klostergründung und Klosterchronik" (The Founding and Chronicling of Monasteries), *Blätter für deutsche Landesgeschichte* 113 (1977), 89–121
Patze, Hans, ed., *Geschichtsschreibung und Geschichtsbewusstsein im späten Mittelalter* (History Writing and Historical Consciousness in the Late Middle Ages), Sigmaringen: Thorbecke, 1987

Peixoto da Fonseca, Fernando Venancio, "Les Chroniques portugaises de *Portugalie Monumenta Historica*" (The Portuguese Chronicles in PMH), *Revue des Langues Romanes* 77 (1967), 55–84

Poole, Reginald Lane, *Chronicles and Annals: A Brief Outline of Their Origin and Growth*, Oxford: Oxford University Press, 1926

Randa, Alexander von, ed., *Mensch und Weltgeschichte: Zur Geschichte der Universalgeschichtsschreibung* (Man and World History: On the History of Universal History Writing), Munich: Pustet, 1969

Schmale, Franz-Joseph, ed., *Frutolfs und Ekkhards Chroniken und die anonyme Kaiserchronik* (Frutolf's and Ekkehard's Chronicle and the Anonymous Kaiserchronik), Darmstadt: Wissenschaftliche Buchgesellschaft, 1972

Schmidt, H.J., *Die deutschen Stadtchroniken als Spiegel des bürgerlichen Selbstverständnisses im Spätmittelalter* (German City Chronicles as a Mirror of Bourgeois Self Images in the Late Middle Ages), Göttingen: Vandenhoeck & Ruprecht, 1958

Schneider, J., "Grundlagen und Grundformen der Geschichtsschreibung im lateinischen Mittelalter" (Fundamentals and Primary Forms of History Writing in the Latin Middle Ages), *Wissenschaftliche Zeitschrift der Universität Rostock* 18 (1969), 483–92

Schnith Karl *et al.*, "Chronik" (Chronicles), in *Lexikon des Mittelalters*, 2, 954–1028

Schulz, Marie, *Die Lehre von der historischen Methode bei den Geschichtsschreibern des Mittelalters, 6.–13. Jahrhundert* (The Teaching of Historical Method by the Historians of the Middle Ages), Berlin: Rothschild, 1909

Sot, Michel, *Gesta episcoporum, gesta abbatum* (Episcopal and Abbatial Gesta), Turnhout: Brepols, 1981

Spörl, Johannes, *Grundformen hochmittelalterlicher Geschichtsanschauung: Studien zum Weltbild der Geschichtsschreiber des 12. Jahrhunderts* (Primary Forms of the High Medieval View of History: Studies on the View of Life of the Historians of the Twelfth Century), 2nd edition, Darmstadt: Wissenschaftliche Buchgesellschaft, 1968

Taylor, John, *The Use of Medieval Chronicles*, London: Historical Association, 1965

Tout, Thomas Frederick, "The Study of Medieval Chronicles," *Bulletin of the John Rylands Library* 6 (1921–22), 414–38

Van Houts, Elisabeth M.C., *Local and Regional Chronicles*, Turnhout: Brepols, 1995

Wattenbach, Wilhelm, and Robert Holtzmann, eds., *Deutschlands Geschichtsquellen im Mittelalter: die Zeit der Sachsen und Salier* (Germany's Historical Sources of the Middle Ages: The Era of the Saxons and Salians), new edition, 3 vols., Darmstadt: Wissenschaftliche Buchgesellschaft, 1967–71

Medieval Historical Writing

Historical writing, like other literature in the Middle Ages, was almost entirely the work of clerics, and was imbued with religious thought and biblical imagery. At the same time it was conducted in the setting of a strong oral culture. Books of all kinds might be used for private study, but they were commonly meant to be read aloud, to audiences with a prodigious memory and appetite for detail, and with a strong preference for verse and rhythmic patterns of prose. The oral and written cultures first met in the monastic refectory and the royal court, and fused there. The universities subsequently both refined and broadened literary skills, but folk history and myth – such traditions as the Merovingian kings' descent from a seagod, or the foundation of Albion, prehistoric Britain, by Brutus of Troy – became and long remained components of the written history of every country.

Historical writing of all kinds flourished in classical antiquity, but the Middle Ages had in effect to recreate it. Medieval historians did so mainly through the medium of annals, a simple year-by-year record of events for which the church provided the expertise and the setting. As the date of Easter is determined each year by the incidence of the first full moon after the vernal equinox, and the other moveable feasts such as Whitsun accord with Easter, every church needed tables from which those dates could be calculated or read, and also an annual calendar to record saints' days and the obituaries of benefactors. Such documents naturally attracted and accumulated notes of other events, especially the lives and deeds and deaths of the sovereigns, lords, and ladies who were the clergy's patrons.

Down to the 11th century texts of that kind were mainly to be found in monastic houses, which commanded much of the wealth and almost all the intellectual power of the western church. In the absence of any systematic archival sources, such works as the annals of the abbey of Fulda, or the annals of St. Bertin from St. Omer, published in the *Monumenta Germaniae Historica*, provide essential guides to western and central European history for several centuries. The annals known as the *Anglo-Saxon Chronicle*, compiled in the interests of the West Saxon monarchy under the stress of the Scandinavian invasions, were one of the longest-lived of such enterprises, which all served political as well as pietistic purposes. The *Grandes Chroniques de France* compiled at St-Denis provide an encomium of the later Capetian kings.

The examples of history and biography available from the classical world were taken as literary rather than methodological models. Biography was largely subsumed in lives of saints and martyrs, such as St. Martin of Tours and St. Edmund of East Anglia, and narrative history almost disappeared. One notable early exception was Bede's account of the conversion of the English, *Historia ecclesiastica gentis Anglorum* (Ecclesiastical History of the English People), completed in 731, pious in its purpose, but lucidly written and critically directed, with a careful attention to sources. The survival of almost 800 manuscript copies shows how widely and long it was admired and studied, but it had few effective imitators. On the other hand, hagiography in its turn bred political biography, as in the life of Louis VI (1081–1137) of France by Abbot Suger of St-Denis, or the life of St. Louis, Louis IX (1215–70) by Jean de Joinville.

The most distinctive kind of historical writing in the Middle Ages was the chronicle, which developed from annalistic notes into a general narrative. The transition was not sudden, and was a product of many forces. From c.1000 a remarkable growth in population, sustained by a corresponding surge of economic activity, worked great changes in the social and intellectual life of western Europe. One consequence was that the secular clergy, those who worked among the laity, came to provide expert services for kings and princes who found their authority enhanced by the written word. Although most chronicles were written in the monasteries, from the 12th century onward the growth of secular government produced clerks who subsequently drew on their experiences to write accounts of their own times. Ralph Diceto and Roger Howden were two such ministers of Henry II of England (reigned 1154–89), who wrote what were in effect historical memoirs.

There were two manifestations of the chronicle that were highly characteristic of the time. The first was the universal history, and the second its local continuations. The universal history took various forms, but it commonly began with the creation of the world and its cosmography, a framework into which what would now be called geography and science was introduced, and went on to demonstrate the working of God's purpose toward mankind down to some particular place and time. It drew freely upon the Bible, and went on through the history of Rome to the Christianization of the west, and to the emergence of the papacy and the German empire. The most popular work of that kind in the later Middle Ages was the world chronicle of Martin von Troppau, also known as Martinus Polonus, a Dominican who died at Bologna in 1278. His chronicle circulated in several vernacular translations as well as its original Latin. The continuations were added to suit local purposes wherever copies of the chronicle came to rest. England produced its own master narrative in the *Polychronicon* of Ralf Higden of Chester (d. 1364), which then formed the basis of most English chronicles until the end of the Middle Ages. The universal chronicle had a wide appeal, but it was principally sustained by the schools of divinity in the universities, which used it for exegetic studies.

The Italians first coined the expression Middle Ages (*medio aevo*) to describe the period of uncritical belief from which they perceived themselves emerging in the late 12th century. For the most part they wrote history in the intense context of life in the city state, when Florence and Venice were worlds of their own, though the chronicle of the Franciscan friar known as Salimbene (1221–90) is a valuable source for French and German history. Their critical acumen was exercised first upon the writings of classical antiquity which they greatly admired, but spread to theological studies and on to secular history. The Middle Ages came to an end when those habits of thought spread into northern Europe in the movement called the Renaissance, and the past was seen in a new perspective.

GEOFFREY H. MARTIN

See also Anglo-Saxon Chronicle; Bede; Britain: 1066–1485; France: 1000–1450; Germany: to 1450; Knowles; Medieval Chronicles; Spain: to 1450

Further Reading

Chaytor, Henry John, *From Script to Print: An Introduction to Medieval Literature*, Cambridge: Cambridge University Press, 1945; reprinted 1974

Galbraith, Vivian Hunter, *Historical Research in Medieval England*, London: Athlone Press, 1951

Gransden, Antonia, *Historical Writing in England*, 2 vols., London: Routledge, and Ithaca, NY: Cornell University Press, 1974–82

Hay, Denys, *Annalists and Historians: Western Historiography from the Eighth to the Eighteenth Centuries*, London: Methuen, and New York: Harper, 1977

Knowles, David, *Great Historical Enterprises* [and] *Problems in Monastic History*, London and New York: Nelson, 1963

Poole, Reginald Lane, *Chronicles and Annals: A Brief Outline of Their Origin and Growth*, Oxford: Oxford University Press, 1926

Taylor, John, *English Historical Literature in the Fourteenth Century*, Oxford and New York: Oxford University Press, 1987

Medvedev, Roy 1925–

Russian historian

The nonconformist historian, prolific writer, and leading Soviet dissident, Roy Medvedev stands apart from many of his contemporaries in that he remained loyal to the paradigm of socialism in his criticism of Stalinist rule. Despite police harassment, Medvedev remained a citizen of the former Soviet Union, who, in his allegiance to the socialist idea, has refused to live in exile.

His most acclaimed work, *K sudu istorii* (1971; *Let History Judge*, 1971), chronicles Stalin's origins, his gradual emergence from Lenin's shadow, his rise to absolute power, and then the growth of Stalinism and of the personality cult. This was the main work of his life and took years of research and revision. The crux of this text rests on Medvedev's commitment to exposing the political realities of a ruling strata whose survival was rooted in the mass deception of its society. His analysis of Stalin was, therefore, central, as it was through this ruler that total control was implemented. His 1989 revision stresses the continued need to challenge persistent myths about Stalin, that often continue to portray him "as a 'wise statesman,' a 'prudent manager,' an 'experienced politician,' and an 'outstanding military leader'."

Many Western commentators and soviet émigrés perceive Medvedev's account of Stalinism to be somewhat misguided in his emphasis on Stalin, the leader, as opposed to the political system that created him. Medvedev's notion that Stalinism was Marxism gone wrong and his commitment to Lenin and Leninist ideals pervades much of his work. Yet, Medvedev has written extensively on major areas of the corrupt Soviet system which locates fault not just in Stalin and his entourage but the sociopolitical and economic conditions that underpinned him, as in *All Stalin's Men* (1983) and *Kniga o sotsialisticheskoi demokratii* (1972; *On Socialist Democracy*, 1975).

Medvedev's dual stance of maintaining a pro-Soviet line while fearlessly exposing and criticizing the previously taboo areas of crime, corruption, and injustice that were common practice under Stalin, has attracted mixed reactions. Medvedev's ability to provide in-depth, and often extensive "inside" information on Stalin, without access to archives, and also – unlike his brother Zhores, who was unjustly placed in a psychiatric hospital – to escape severe persecution, has often led to the accusation that he was in some way collaborating with the KGB. It is important to stress that, even when derived from suspect sources, like the recollections of old Bolsheviks, Medvedev's use of the material, once obtained, clearly illustrated his intentions as a dissident to expose aspects of Soviet society that were purposefully hidden from the majority in the interests of the party.

Another major feature of his work was his advocacy of gradual democratic socialist reform from above. The idea that true democratic reform could emerge only from a renovated Communist party was a fundamental denial of the traditional Marxist idea that change could come only from the mass mobilization of the proletariat. Furthermore, contrary to Western Marxist perspectives, Medvedev believed that, although the Stalin and post-Stalin periods were fundamental in the formation of a central bureaucracy, the Soviet state machine did not constitute a ruling class. Instead he saw bureaucracy as balancing on a fragile political equilibrium in which bureaucrats had no access to the ownership of the means of production or possession of lands that could be bequeathed to their children.

This argument is indicative of his stance as an alternative Soviet dissident. That neither socialism nor capitalism had been achieved in the Soviet Union was a controversial line of argument. What is explicit in his work is the idea that it was the malpractice of the party elite, and in particular Stalin, that had led to the erosion of the socialist idea. The recognition of this was seen to be vital if socialism was to remain viable. As Medvedev writes in his preface to the 1989 edition of *Let History Judge*, in order for socialism as "a scientific social doctrine" to survive it was necessary to "explain the socio-historical, economic, and political processes that under specific circumstances led to the degeneration of the socialist state and to tyranny by specific individuals in socialist countries." This independent and powerful indictment of a debased socialism has had a penetrating effect on historical debates resulting in both widespread criticism and worldwide praise.

The role of Medvedev, as a key Soviet historian, has been further enhanced by his keeping alight the ideas and lives of other heroic dissidents who otherwise would have remained effectively invisible in official Soviet history. For example, in "Bukharin's Last Years," published in *New Left Review* in 1978, Medvedev perceptively unfolded the elusive character of one of the greatest dissidents of the Communist party, who, for Medvedev, represents a dignified and loyal opposition from within.

Medvedev often saw himself as breaking out of his academic mold in his quest to reveal and influence his political surroundings. In his 1989 preface to *Let History Judge* he wrote, "It long ago became my primary aim and the driving motive of my life and work to orient myself in the contradictory reality around me and to find a way of changing it for the better, including changes in the prevailing ideological conceptions."

In his quest to defend socialism Medvedev had only one solution, "to speak the truth". Whether this is possible is debatable, but Medvedev did to a large extent give fresh insight into the essence of Soviet society in his exposure of "that serious and prolonged disease . . . which has been given the name Stalinism."

KATHERINE PINNOCK

See also Russia: Modern

Biography
Roy Alexandrovich Medvedev. Born Tbilisi, 14 November 1925. Educated at Leningrad State University; Academy of Pedagogical Sciences of the USSR; received PhD. Worked in a factory, 1943–46; taught history at the Ural Secondary School, 1951–53; director of a secondary school in the Leningrad region, 1954–56; deputy to editor-in-chief, Textbook Publishing House, Moscow, 1957–59; department head, Research Institute of Vocational Education, USSR Academy of Pedagogical Science, 1960–70, and senior scientist, 1970–71; freelance writer from 1972. Until 1969, was a member of the Communist party; reactivated his party membership, 1981–91, and served in various political posts; co-chairman, Socialist Party of Labor, from 1991. Married Galina A. Gaidina, 1956 (1 son).

Principal Writings
K sudu istorii: genezis i posledstviia stalinizma, 1971; in English as *Let History Judge: The Origins and Consequences of Stalinism*, 1971, revised 1989

With Zhores Medvedev, *Kto sumasshedshii?*, 1971; in English as *A Question of Madness*, 1971
Kniga o sotsialisticheskoi demokratii, 1972; in English as *On Socialist Democracy*, 1975
N.S. Khrushchev: gody u vlasti, 1975; in English as *Khrushchev: The Years in Power*, 1976
Intervista sul dissenso in URSS, edited by Piero Ostellino, 1977; in English as *On Soviet Dissent*, 1980
Editor, *The Samizdat Register*, 2 vols., 1977–81
The October Revolution, 1979
On Stalin and Stalinism, 1979
Nikolai Bukharin: The Last Years, 1980
Leninism and Western Socialism, 1981
An End to Silence: Uncensored Opinion in the Soviet Union from Roy Medvedev's Underground Magazine Political Diary, edited by Stephen F. Cohen, 1982
Khrushchev, 1982
All Stalin's Men, 1983
China and the Superpowers, 1986

Further Reading
"Détente and Socialist Democracy: A Discussion with Roy Medvedev: Essays," *European Socialist Thought* 6, Nottingham: Foundation for Spokesman, 1975
Medvedev's Notion of Stalinism, Belfast: British and Irish Communist Organization, 1980
Pons, Silvio, "Roy Medvedev: Storico dello stalinism" (Roy Medvedev: Historian of Stalin), *Passato e Presente* 3 (1983), 115–34

Meier, August 1923–
US historian

A leading authority on 20th- and late 19th-century African American history, August Meier began his professional life as a historian in the 1940s, at Tougaloo, a small black college in Mississippi. At this time most black educational institutions in the United States lacked the intellectual prestige of their white counterparts, and few other white historians took much active interest in African American society as a serious area of research.

Meier's unusual choice of career path owed much to his early family life and upbringing. The son of a German father and East European Jewish mother, he was initially drawn to the study of race by the rise of Nazism and anti-Semitism in Germany during the 1930s. This concern was reinforced by the political radicalism of his parents who at this time were, as Meier himself described it in *A White Scholar and the Black Community, 1945–1965* (1992), "left wing New Dealers."

Meier is a lifelong liberal himself, and his many academic writings have been inspired not just by scholarly curiosity but a personal commitment to bring about a greater understanding of, and improvement in, the pattern of race relations in the United States. A grassroots civil rights activist as well as a historian, Meier participated in many of the protests of the civil rights movement during the 1950s and 1960s. He enjoyed personal contact with many African American spokesmen of the time, including Stokely Carmichael, Bayard Rustin, and Malcolm X, which provided him with invaluable insights for his academic research.

In collaboration with the historian Elliott Rudwick, Meier published *CORE: A Study in the Civil Rights Movement* (1973), which has become a standard authority on the origins, character, and development of the Congress of Racial Equality, one of the most prominent civil rights organizations of the 1960s. His scholarly partnership with Rudwick has played an important part in Meier's career. Since the 1970s they have jointly written or edited several important studies on African American history.

Among Meier's earlier, but most influential, writings on the civil rights movement was a 1965 article for *New Politics*, "On the Role of Martin Luther King." Examining criticisms made by radical activists, that King was too accommodationist to white society, Meier advanced the view that this "moderation" was actually a key asset. It enabled King to occupy the "vital center" of the civil rights movement, uniting both militant and conservative civil rights organizations behind his leadership. The last three years of King's life, 1965–68, when many historians believe King went through a process of radicalization, subsequently created the need for a reassessment of Meier's analysis. Despite this, his seminal study is still a key starting point for any understanding of the life and career of King.

Although himself a liberal integrationist, Meier has won respect for his knowledge and understanding of black nationalist groups in the United States, such as the Black Muslims or Nation of Islam. In this context during 1962, at Morgan State College, Maryland, he once famously participated in public debate, with the then Black Muslim leader Malcolm X, on the merits of integrationism versus separatism.

Meier is well regarded for his work on early 20th-century black civil rights leadership, and his first book, *Negro Thought in America, 1880–1915* (1963), remains a major work on this subject. Particularly important have been Meier's writings on the accommodationist African American leader Booker T. Washington, who dominated black American life between 1895 and 1915. Meier's insights into Washington's motives and strategies provided key foundations for later revisionist historians such as Louis Harlan.

Since the mid-1960s the emergence of Black Power, and other developments in race relations, resulted in a general sense of disillusionment in the United States with the liberal values associated with Meier. Paradoxically, the substantial awakening of interest in African American history that also occurred in these years has led to a much greater and widespread recognition of the work of Meier the historian. He is now justly recognized as one of the foremost thinkers and researchers in his field of study.

KEVERN J. VERNEY

See also African American; Franklin; Hine

Biography
Born New York City, 20 April 1923. Received BA, Oberlin College, 1945; MA, Columbia University, 1948, PhD 1957. Taught at Tougaloo College, 1945–49; Fisk University 1953–56; Morgan State College, 1957–64; Roosevelt University, 1964–67; and Kent State University, 1967–93 (emeritus).

Principal Writings
Negro Thought in America, 1880–1915: Racial Ideologies in the Age of Booker T. Washington, 1963
"On the Role of Martin Luther King," *New Politics* 4 (Winter 1965), 1–8

With Elliott M. Rudwick, *From Plantation to Ghetto: An Interpretive History of American Negroes*, 1966; 3rd edition 1976
With Elliott M. Rudwick, *The Making of Black America: Essays in Negro Life and History*, 1969
With Elliott M. Rudwick, *CORE: A Study in the Civil Rights Movement, 1942–1968*, 1973
With Elliott M. Rudwick, *Along the Color Line: Explorations in the Black Experience*, 1976
Black Detroit and the Rise of the UAW, 1979
With Elliott M. Rudwick, *Black History and the Historical Profession, 1915–1980*, 1986
A White Scholar and the Black Community, 1945–1965: Essays and Reflections, 1992

Meinecke, Friedrich 1862–1954
German historian

Friedrich Meinecke was one of the most influential German historians in the first third of the 20th century. He was editor of the prestigious *Historische Zeitschrift* from 1896 to 1935 and chaired the Historische Reichskommission in the Weimar republic. In his historiographical work he broke new ground with contributions to the intellectual history of the 18th and 19th centuries. Meinecke was also an influential analyst of contemporary history and contributed to the political and intellectual reorientation after the cataclysms of two world wars.

Meinecke had already published widely when, in 1908, his *Weltbürgertum und Nationalstaat* (*Cosmopolitanism and the National State*, 1970) had an immediate impact on German historiography. The synthesis of political and intellectual history that Meinecke achieved in depicting the intricate relation between nation and state in 19th-century Germany had, as Ludwig Dehio later remembered, the effect of a spring rain on the younger generation of historians. The theme of the book is Germany's development from a *Kulturnation* (cultural nation) to a *Staatsnation* (nation-state) as reflected in the publications of authors and politicians from Humboldt to Ranke and Bismarck. A subsequent large part of the book deals with the relation between the Prussian nation-state and the German nation-state.

In his *Die Idee der Staatsräson* (1924; *Machiavellism*, 1957), Meinecke focused on the relation between power and morality, between *kratos* and *ethos*. He highlighted the development of the idea of the reason of state (*raison d'état*), from Machiavelli and the age of emerging absolutism, to the era of mature absolutism, culminating with Frederick the Great and his attempt to bridge the gap between the philosopher and the king. A final chapter is devoted to the idea of the state in 19th-century Germany (Hegel, Fichte, Ranke, and Treitschke). Much more pessimistic in outlook than in his previous book, Meinecke underlined the dualism of the law of states on the one side and the natural law on the other side, the perennial struggle between both realms and the reason of state as the bridge between power impulses and moral responsibilities. The reason of state thus is not politics solely based on power, but the attempt to bring together *kratos* and *ethos* for the best of the state.

In 1936, when the balance of *kratos* and *ethos* was already upset in Germany, Meinecke published *Die Entstehung des Historismus* (*Historism*, 1972), where he interpreted the origins of historism as a concept opposed to the universalism of the Enlightenment. Meinecke argued that historism is deeply rooted in European intellectual history and can be found in the writings of English and French writers. The cultural concept of historism in Germany is represented by Lessing, Winckelmann, Möser, Herder, and Goethe. With Goethe, historism reached its fullest cultural potential and subsequently became a political concept, serving as a justification for the German *Sonderweg* in the 19th century.

Immediately after World War II Meinecke wrote a short book entitled *Die deutsche Katastrophe* (1946; *The German Catastrophe*, 1950) in which he interpreted Hitler in the context of German history. Hitler, according to Meinecke, had no organic ties to German history and German history did not inevitably result in the National Socialist catastrophe. Meinecke pointed to the mass Machiavellism as a European phenomenon since the French Revolution and to coincidences that facilitated the rise of Hitler. His liberal-conservative interpretation of the German catastrophe concluded with a call to go back to the roots of German cultural identity to build a better future.

Meinecke always had political influence, whether in supporting the Weimar republic or in attempting to contribute to the intellectual reorientation after World War II. In 1948 he became one of the founders of the Free University of Berlin; the university's Department of History was named after him in 1951. Meinecke did not found a school of historiography, but his emphasis on the history of ideas and how they shaped politics influenced generations of scholars in Europe and America. With the advent of the social sciences within historical research and its emphasis on the meticulous analysis of facts, rather than on intuitive understanding or on colorful and atmospheric portrayals, Meinecke's influence considerably abated. It remains to be seen if his deep insights into history will be rediscovered by the post-modern approaches to history.

MATTHIAS ZIMMER

See also Begriffsgeschichte; Fischer; Gatterer; Germany: 1800–1945; Gilbert; Intellectual; Kehr; Rosenberg, H.; Schnabel; Srbik

Biography

Born Salzwedel, Prussia, 30 October 1862. Studied at universities of Bonn and Berlin, 1882–86. Archivist, German State Archives, Berlin, 1887–1901; professor, University of Berlin, 1896–1901; University of Strasbourg, 1901–06; University of Freiburg, 1906–14; and University of Berlin, 1914–32. Editor, *Historische Zeitschrift*, 1896–1935. Chairman, Historische Reichskommission, 1928–35. Rector, Free University of Berlin, 1948. Died Berlin, 6 February 1954.

Principal Writings

Das Leben des Generalfeldmarschalls Hermann von Boyen (The Life of Fieldmarshal General Hermann von Boyen), 2 vols., 1896–99
Das Zeitalter der deutschen Erhebung, 1795–1815, 1906; in English as *The Age of German Liberation, 1795–1815*, 1977
Weltbürgertum und Nationalstaat: Studien zur Genesis des deutschen Nationalstaates, 1908; in English as *Cosmopolitanism and the National State*, 1970
Radowitz und die deutsche Revolution (Radowitz and the German Revolution), 1913
Die Idee der Staatsräson in der neueren Geschichte, 1924; in English as *Machiavellism: The Doctrine of Raison d'Etat and Its Place in Modern History*, 1957

Geschichte des deutsch-englischen Bündnisproblems, 1890–1901 (History of the Anglo-German Alliance Problem, 1890–1901), 1927
Staat und Persönlichkeit (State and Personality), 1933
Die Entstehung des Historismus, 2 vols., 1936; in English as *Historism: The Rise of a New Historical Outlook*, 1972
Die deutsche Katastrophe: Betrachtungen und Erinnerungen, 1946; in English as *The German Catastrophe: Reflections and Recollections*, 1950
1848: Eine Säkularbetrachtung, 1948; in English as "The Year 1848 in German History: Reflections on a Centenary," in Herman Ausubul, ed., *Making of Modern Europe: Waterloo to the Atomic Age*, 1951
Werke (Major Works), 9 vols, 1957–79

Further Reading

Erbe, Michael, ed., *Friedrich Meinecke heute: Bericht über ein Gedenk-Colloquium zu seinem 25, Todestag am 5. und 6. April 1979* (Friedrich Meinecke Today), Berlin: Colloquium Verlag, 1981
Hofer, Walther, *Geschichtsschreibung und Weltanschauung: Betrachtungen zum Werk Friedrich Meineckes* (Historical Thought and Ideology: Observations on the Work of Friedrich Meinecke), Munich: Oldenbourg, 1950
Iggers, Georg G., *The German Conception of History: The National Tradition of Historical Thought from Herder to the Present*, Middletown, CT: Wesleyan University Press, 1968; revised 1983
Meineke, Stefan, *Friedrich Meinecke: Persönlichkeit und politisches Denken bis zum Ende des ersten Weltkrieges* (Friedrich Meinecke: Personality and Political Thinking to the End of World War I), Berlin: de Gruyter, 1995
Pois, Robert A., *Friedrich Meinecke and German Politics in the Twentieth Century*, Berkeley: University of California Press, 1972
Schulin, Ernst, "Friedrich Meinecke," in Hans-Ulrich Wehler, ed., *Deutsche Historiker*, vol. 1, Göttingen: Vandenhoeck & Ruprecht, 1971
Sterling, Richard W., *Ethics in a World of Power: The Political Ideas of Friedrich Meinecke*, Princeton: Princeton University Press, 1958

Memory

The French sociologist Maurice Halbwachs (1877–1945) was the first scholar to discuss systematically the relation between history and "memory," and his studies on the subject, *Les Cadres sociaux de la mémoire* (The Social Frameworks of Memory, 1925), *La Topographie légendaire des évangiles en Terre Sainte* (The Legendary Topography of the Gospels in the Holy Land, 1941), and *La Mémoire collective* (1950; *The Collective Memory*, 1980), remain classics in the field. But "memory" began to emerge as an issue of serious and widespread concern in history and related areas only in the 1980s. There are a number of reasons for increased interest in the subject: a growing fascination with the *experience* of history, supplementing more traditional concerns with sociopolitical events and structures; a growing willingness to link historical writing explicitly (rather than only covertly) to the identities of particular groups; and a growing sense that the modern social and cultural order has a tendency, which needs to be actively resisted, to obliterate consciousness of the past from people's minds.

The scare quotes around memory are needed because the term, as currently employed in historical and metahistorical writing, refers to a number of different phenomena. "Memory" as understood by historians has little relation to psychological or neurobiological conceptions. It does, however, have an important relation to psychoanalysis. Sigmund Freud discovered in his therapeutic practice that memories become, under certain conditions, pathogenic, and he aimed to get his patients through and beyond memory, or at any rate beyond its bad consequences. His was a common 19th- and early 20th-century view, found, as Ian Hacking noted, in such therapists as Pierre Janet and H.H. Goddard; it was also articulated by Friedrich Nietzsche in "Vom Nutzen und Nachtheil der Historie für das Leben" (1874; "On the Use and Disadvantage of History", 1909) and other works. Such writers held that memory is something to be overcome, by hypnosis, analysis, courage in facing the future, or other means. Currently, however, many therapists and others influenced by psychoanalysis take a different view: while acknowledging that memories may be traumatic, they also see memory as a marker of the lived experience through which the self's identity has come into being, and hence as possessing an authenticity and value of its own, however distressing its contents.

In one of its meanings, closely akin to psychoanalytic conceptions, "memory" denotes the recovery and conversion into narrative of the experience of historical agents and sufferers. Beginning in the late 1970s, memory in what we might call its "experiential" sense became an issue in Holocaust studies, when scholars and others started to come to grips with the fact that the generation of Holocaust survivors would soon die out. Saul Friedlander is one among many historians for whom Holocaust memory, and its integration into historical research and writing, have been important concerns. Also worth noting is the videotaping of the recollections of Holocaust survivors, undertaken at the Fortunoff Video Archive for Holocaust Testimonies (established 1982) at Yale University, as well as elsewhere. Such taping goes far beyond what is needed for historical documentation alone; it thus illustrates the positive valuation that "memory" has acquired in contemporary culture. The concern with memory in its experiential sense also enters into many other domains and genres of history, including "history from below" and *Alltagsgeschichte* or "history of everyday life."

Second, "memory" has come to denote knowledge or tradition. In the 1980s scholars could still think about knowledge or tradition without any important evocation of memory, as illustrated by E.D. Hirsch, Jr.'s widely noted *Cultural Literacy: What Every American Needs to Know* (1987), but by the early 1990s the notion of "cultural" or "public" memory began to acquire some currency as a stand-in for cultural knowledge. "Memory" is widely assumed to connote something living and authentic; hence, "cultural memory" seems to manifest a wish for an authentic, as distinguished from a dead or oppressive, tradition or knowledge. In historical and metahistorical writing, memory in this second, cognitive sense is often said to be "collective." Sometimes "collective memory" refers to the memories that a group of people, such as Holocaust survivors, have of the historical experience that they underwent, in which case the first, experiential sense of historical memory is in play. But the term is also used to refer to the memories that people have of participating in such tradition-manifesting rituals as the Seder, Christmas, or Bastille Day. Memory of participation in cultural practices that *refer* to an alleged historical past is not the same as memory that is *of* that historical past, although in contemporary culture there is a tendency to blur the two.

Collective memory of participation in rituals easily tips over into a third sense, in which "memory" denotes commemoration. What distinguishes many memorials and museums constructed or redesigned in the 1970s and later is the concern they manifest with giving visitors an experience putatively similar to the experience of people in the past. On the basis of such simulated experience, some sites attempt to offer a commemoration of the past rivaling the directness and vividness that is often attributed to the memory of the past: the United States Holocaust Memorial Museum in Washington, DC, which opened in 1993, and Steven Spielberg's film *Schindler's List* are good examples of memorials of this type.

Memory in its various senses has an important role to play in history. For clarity, it is important to distinguish among the different senses. It is also important to be aware of memory's limitations. Near the beginning of Western historiography, Thucydides reacted against Herodotus, whom he saw as excessively reliant on oral tradition. Instead, he resolved to write his history of the Peloponnesian War on the basis of eyewitness accounts – that is, on the basis of the recounted memories of historical participants. The memories were also, in part, Thucydides' own, since he was himself a participant in the war. Our modern view of memory is more chastened. Memory has a close relation to various subjectivities, including those of historical participants, of the historian, and of the audience addressed by the historian. Recognizing the uncritical character of subjectivity, R.G. Collingwood insisted, in *The Idea of History* (1946), that memory be confirmed by material traces. Collingwood's rule remains a good one, since in its absence history risks being displaced by unchecked desire.

ALLAN MEGILL

See also Collingwood; Freud; Holocaust; Nietzsche; Oral

Further Reading

Anderson, Benedict, *Imagined Communities: Reflections on the Origin and Spread of Nationalism*, London and New York: Verso, 1983; revised 1991

Carruthers, Mary J., *The Book of Memory: A Study of Memory in Medieval Culture*, Cambridge and New York: Cambridge University Press, 1990

Collingwood, R.G., *The Idea of History*, edited by T.M. Knox, Oxford: Oxford University Press, 1946, New York: Oxford University Press, 1956; revised edition, with *Lectures 1926–1928*, edited by Jan van der Dussen, Oxford: Clarendon Press, 1993, New York: Oxford University Press, 1994

Farmer, Sarah, *Oradour: arrêt sur mémoire* (Oradour: Focus on Memory), Paris: Calmann-Lévy, 1994

Freud, Sigmund, *The Standard Edition of the Complete Psychological Works*, 24 vols., London: Hogarth Press, and New York: Macmillan, 1953–74

Freud, Sigmund, "On the Psychical Mechanism of Hysterical Phenomena: A Lecture" (1893), in Freud, *Early Psycho-Analytic Publications, 1893–1899* [*The Standard Edition*, vol. 3]

Freud, Sigmund, "Project for a Scientific Psychology" (1895), in Freud, *Pre-Psycho-Analytic Publications and Unpublished Drafts* [*The Standard Edition*, vol. 1]

Freud, Sigmund, "Screen Memories," (1899), in Freud, *Early Psycho-Analytic Publications, 1893–1899* [*The Standard Edition*, vol. 3]

Freud, Sigmund, "Remembering, Repeating and Working-Through (Further Recommendations on the Technique of Psycho-Analysis II)" (1914), in Freud, *The Case of Schreber: Papers on Techniques and Other Works* [*The Standard Edition*, vol. 12]

Freud, Sigmund, "A Note upon the 'Mystic Writing Pad'" (1925), in Freud, *The Ego, The Id and Other Works* [*The Standard Edition*, vol. 19]

Friedlander, Saul, *Quand vient le souvenir*, Paris: Seuil, 1978; in English as *When Memory Comes*, New York: Farrar Straus, 1979

Friedlander, Saul, *Memory, History, and the Extermination of the Jews of Europe*, Bloomington: Indiana University Press, 1993

Funkenstein, Amos, "Collective Memory and Historical Consciousness," *History and Memory: Studies in Representation of the Past* 1 (1989), 5–27

Hacking, Ian, *Rewriting the Soul: Multiple Personality and the Sciences of Memory*, Princeton: Princeton University Press, 1995

Halbwachs, Maurice, *Les Cadres sociaux de la mémoire* (The Social Frameworks of Memory), Paris: Alcan, 1925; abridged in English in his *On Collective Memory*, edited by Lewis A. Coser, Chicago: University of Chicago Press, 1992

Halbwachs, Maurice, *La Topographie légendaire des évangiles en Terre Sainte: étude de mémoire collective* (The Legendary Topography of the Gospels in the Holy Land: A Study in Collective Memory), Paris: Aubier, 1941; reprinted 1971

Halbwachs, Maurice, *La Mémoire collective*, Paris: Presses Universitaires de France, 1950, reprinted 1968; in English as *The Collective Memory*, with an introduction by Mary Douglas, New York: Harper, 1980

Hirsch, E.D., Jr., *Cultural Literacy: What Every American Needs to Know*, Boston: Houghton Mifflin, 1987

History and Memory: Studies in Representation of the Past, Bloomington: Indiana University Press, 1989–

Hutton, Patrick H., *History as an Art of Memory*, Burlington: University of Vermont Press, 1993

Huyssen, Andreas, *Twilight Memories: Marking Time in a Culture of Amnesia*, New York: Routledge, 1995

Kammen, Michael G., *Mystic Chords of Memory: The Transformation of Tradition in American Culture*, New York: Knopf, 1991

Langer, Lawrence L., *Holocaust Testimonies: The Ruins of Memory*, New Haven: Yale University Press, 1991

Le Goff, Jacques, *Storia e memoria*, Turin: Einaudi, 1986; in English as *History and Memory*, New York: Columbia University Press, 1992

Lipsitz, George, *Time Passages: Collective Memory and American Popular Culture*, Minneapolis: University of Minnesota Press, 1990

Middleton, David, and Derek Edwards, eds., *Collective Remembering*, London: Sage, 1990

Nietzsche, Friedrich, "Vom Nutzen und Nachtheil der Historie für das Leben," in *Unzeitgemässe Betrachtungen*, vol. 2, Leipzig: Fritzsch, 1874; in English as "On the Use and Disadvantage of History," in *Complete Works*, edited by Oscar Levy, vol. 5, New York: Macmillan, and Edinburgh: Foulis, 1909, and as "On the Uses and Disadvantage of History for Life," in *Untimely Meditations*, edited by R.J. Hollindale, Cambridge: Cambridge University Press, 1983

Nora, Pierre, ed., *Les Lieux de mémoire*, 3 vols., Paris: Gallimard, 1984–92; abridged in English as *Realms of Memory: Rethinking the French Past*, 2 vols., New York: Columbia University Press, 1996–97

Samuel, Raphael, *Theatres of Memory*, London and New York: Verso, 1994

Santner, Eric L., *Stranded Objects: Mourning, Memory, and Film in Postwar Germany*, Ithaca, NY: Cornell University Press, 1990

Schacter, Daniel L., *Searching for Memory: The Brain, the Mind, and the Past*, New York: Basic Books, 1996

Vansina, Jan, *Oral Tradition as History*, Madison: University of Wisconsin Press, and London: Currey, 1985

Yerushalmi, Yosef Hayim, *Zakhor: Jewish History and Jewish Memory*, Seattle: University of Washington Press, 1982

Young, James, *The Texture of Memory: Holocaust Memorials and Meaning*, New Haven: Yale University Press, 1993

Zerubavel, Yael, *Recovered Roots: Collective Memory and the Making of the Israeli National Tradition*, Chicago: University of Chicago Press, 1995

Menéndez Pidal, Ramón 1869–1968
Spanish medievalist and literary historian

Ramón Menéndez Pidal studied with Marcelino Menéndez y Pelayo at the University of Madrid. When the latter became director of the National Library in 1899 his chair was abolished and Menéndez Pidal won the successor position in comparative philology. In 1910 Menéndez Pidal became director of the newly-founded Center for Historical Studies, devoted mainly to the historical development of Spanish language and literature. There he trained an extraordinary group of scholars and the Center became a haven for European Hispanists. Américo Castro, as professor of the history of the Spanish language, was a key figure at the Center, as was the institutional historian Claudio Sánchez-Albornoz, founder and editor of the *Anuario de Historia del Derecho Español*.

In *Orígenes del español* (Origins of Spanish, 1926), Menéndez Pidal laid out the cultural and ethnic history of Castile and León through the 11th century, made a case for the strong influence of Mozarabic culture brought there by Christians fleeing al-Andalus (Islamic Spain), and also theorized on the emergence of Romance dialects out of vulgar Latin. Here he applied the neo-Lamarckian evolutionism of August Schleicher by asserting that the Castilian language stabilized early by defeating competing dialectal norms. Menéndez Pidal's notion of the *convivencia* (coexistence) of norms struggling with each other was to become, in Castro's work, a general model of sociocultural interaction.

Menéndez Pidal's controversial method of reconstructing medieval epic poetry from chronicles nevertheless placed him admirably for the writing of chronicle-based history. *La España del Cid* (1929; *The Cid and His Spain*, 1934) was his primary contribution to medieval historiography. Here, he attacked Dutch Arabist Reinhart Dozy's portrayal of the Cid as a kind of noble brigand and made him into the paladin of Castilian and Leonese imperialism, the very spirit of the struggle against the Muslims, and a model of feudal virtue. In spite of the nationalistic overlay, the book was a model piece of research, emerging from the considerable documentary evidence amassed in the Center. It laid the groundwork for further discussions of political and social interaction among the Taifa states of Islamic and the Christian kingdoms of the 11th century.

Menéndez Pidal spent most of the period of the Spanish Civil War (1936–39) in New York (as visiting professor at Columbia University) and in Paris, returning to Spain soon after the defeat of the Republic. The nationalist political ideology of Francoism was based on regionalist – particular Castilian – medievalism in which certain of Menéndez Pidal's ideas played major roles. Not only did heroes of important epics and chronicles, such as Fernán González and the Cid, assume gigantic proportions in the new nationalism, so also did the "Reconquest," viewed as

Castile's "manifest destiny." Patriotism based on anything else was false. The Goths had made no cowardly retreat, and the basic rationale for Reconquest was religious. Although Menéndez Pidal rejected the notion of implacable and permanent hostility between Christians and Muslims, he did so on the false premise that the latter were "racially" Spaniards. On the other hand, he not only vouched for Christianity's superiority, but promoted the legitimacy of Castile's title to "a Leonese notion of Empire." Near the end of *The Cid and His Spain*, he asserted the existence of a popular nationalism in medieval Castile, led by classless elites. His historically-based political views appeared between 1944 and 1950 in a series of articles in the *Revista de Estudios Políticos*, the ideological voice of the Franco regime, where his accounts of the originality of Castile's vision and the reality of Castilian hegemony among the other Spanish kingdoms were quickly raised to the level of nationalist dogma. Menéndez Pidal's leadership in Castilian medievalism was at the center of ideas expressed in the official 1944 celebration of the "Millennium of Castile."

Nevertheless when, in 1947, Menéndez Pidal revived the notion of "two Spains" to explain modern Spanish politics in terms of a struggle between progressive and conservative fractions of a disunified bourgeoisie, Francoist intellectuals regarded his position as nearly treasonable.

Menéndez Pidal finished his active life as a scholar in the 1960s with his participation in two significant scholarly debates. The first involved the polemic between Américo Castro and Claudio Sánchez-Albornoz on the origins of Spanish culture and nationality, which Castro attributed to the centuries-long contact among Christians, Muslims, and Jews. Here Menéndez Pidal came down squarely on the traditionalist side which held that Spanish culture was inherent in the land and its population and that therefore "Al-Andalus . . . had Hispanified its Islam; the scant Asiatic and African racial elements had been almost completely absorbed within the indigenous elements, so that the great majority of Spanish Muslims were simply Ibero-Romans or Goths reshaped by Islamic culture, and who could easily enough come to an agreement with their brothers to the north." This radical denial of the authenticity of Al-Andalus as a normative Arabic Islamic country placed him on the side of Sánchez-Albornoz and severely strained his relationship with his former student Castro. In the second polemic he opposed Sánchez-Albornoz's notion of the complete depopulation of the Duero valley in the early Middle Ages which rested in part on a literal reading of portions of the Chronicle of Alfonso III alleging that Alfonso I had removed all the Christians to the north. Menéndez Pidal argued (correctly) that *poblar, populare* did not mean "to populate" but rather to reduce a disorganized zone to administration (a usage found elsewhere in medieval Europe) and that, in any case, place-name evidence suggested continuity in settlement. His participation in these controversies revealed his continuing engagement with critical historiographical debates whose concerns persist to this day.

THOMAS F. GLICK

See also Castro; Spain: to 1450

Biography

Born La Coruna, 13 March 1869. Professor of Romance philology, University of Madrid, 1899–1939; founder, Madrid Center for Historical Studies, 1907. Founder/editor, *Revista de filología española*, 1914. Died Madrid, 14 November 1968.

Principal Writings

Editor, *Primera Crónica General: estoria de España que mondó componer Alfonso el Sabio y se continuaba bajo sancho 4 en 1289* (First General Chronicle), 1906

Orígenes del español estado linguistico de la Peninsula iberica hasta el siglo XI (Origins of Spanish), 1926

La España del Cid, 2 vols., 1929; in English as *The Cid and His Spain*, 1934

Historia de España, 1947; partially translated as *The Spaniards in Their History*, 1950

"Repoblación y tradición de la cuenca del Duero," in *Enciclopedia lingüística hispánica*, vol. 1, 1960

Further Reading

Brown, Catherine, "The Relics of Menéndez Pidal: Mourning and Melancholia in Hispanomedieval Studies," *La Corónica* 24 (1995), 15–41

Lacarra, María Eugenia, "La utilización del Cid de Menéndez Pidal en la ideología militar franquista" (The Use of Menéndez Pidal's *The Cid* in pro-Franco Military Ideology), *Ideologies and Literature* 3/12 (March–May 1980), 95–127

Pérez Villanueva, Joaquín, *Ramón Menéndez Pidal: su vida y su tiempo* (Ramón Menéndez Pidal: His Life and Times), Madrid: Espasa Calpe, 1991

Portoles, José, *Medio siglo de filología española (1896–1952): positivismo e idealismo* (Half a Century of Spanish Philology: Positivism and Idealism), Madrid: Cátedra, 1986

Mentalities, History of

The history of mentalities is an approach to cultural history that focuses on the attitudes of ordinary people toward their everyday lives. Popularized during the 1960s and 1970s, it is identified especially with French historical scholarship, although it eventually influenced historians everywhere, notably in Britain (Peter Burke, Keith Thomas), the United States (Natalie Zemon Davis, Robert Darnton, Lawrence Stone), Germany (Ulrich Raulff), and Italy (Carlo Ginzburg).

The history of mentalities might be characterized as a reinvention of the history of ideas in a more democratic guise. Historians of ideas had been largely interested in the outlook and influence of the most illustrious philosophers and writers, especially as they engaged in intellectual innovation. Historians of mentalities, by contrast, have been more concerned with customs and tacit understandings as they are woven into the fabric of popular traditions. Mentalities presented a repertoire of fascinating topics little studied before: attitudes toward children and family life; growing up, growing old, and dying; eccentric, deviant, criminal, and nonconformist behavior; manners and social mores; religious piety and devotional practices. In addressing such topics, its historians redirected attention from the high discourse of intellectuals to the popular idiom of ordinary people. The historians of ideas had been interested in the way ideas circulate among elites before being more widely disseminated in popular culture. The historians of mentalities studied the environments in which people form their attitudes, and observed how tenacious can be the modes of resistance to intellectual change – the inertial power of habits of mind, conventions of speech, and visceral convictions that inhere in the common sense of tradition. Accordingly, historians of mentalities sought to locate and describe the deep structures of culture – the mental imagery, collective memories, and linguistic forms that frame the dimensions of our mental universe. Concomitantly, their work charted the possibilities of a non-psychoanalytic approach to historical psychology. They studied the interplay of thought and emotion, habit and innovation, poetical and refined speech, orality and literacy in ways that revealed historically significant changes in the organization of the human psyche, even in relatively recent times.

The rise of mentalities as a historiographical interest has important sources in the French Annales school of historical writing, and for some scholars represents a stage in its evolution. As early as the 1920s, Lucien Febvre and Marc Bloch wrote pioneering studies on the collective psychology of people living in traditional European society. Febvre proposed an agenda for a new field of historical inquiry that would inventory the "mental equipment" and identify reconfigurations in the emotional life of human societies across the ages. But their appeal elicited few followers until the 1960s. One connection between the work of these Annales pioneers and the renascent interest in mentalities among a younger generation of historians was a study by one of Febvre's students, Robert Mandrou. Working with a manuscript left by Febvre at his death in 1956, Mandrou wrote *Introduction à la France moderne* (1961; *Introduction to Modern France*, 1975), a history of French culture in the 16th and 17th centuries that underscored the importance of environmental, social and cultural constraints on intellectual innovation. It provided an important model for investigations in this field.

But the question remains, why did mentalities arouse such widespread historical interest in the 1960s whereas it had elicited so little before? Some scholars point to the relationship between mentalities and the evolution of more sophisticated research techniques, particularly those that employ quantitative analysis. They argue that such historical research had by the 1960s arrived at a stage of development in which quantitative methods could at last be applied to cultural data. But the best known and most popular studies were appreciated not only for their data-gathering, but also for the interesting long-range trends in the evolution of popular attitudes that they identified. Others evoked poignant issues about popular culture through micro-histories of particular events – Natalie Davis's *The Return of Martin Guerre* (1983), which explored the hallmarks of personal identity, for example, or Carlo Ginzburg's *Il formaggio e i vermi* (1976; *The Cheese and the Worms*, 1980), which considered the relationship between literacy and the formulation of religious concepts. Certainly, mentalities was attuned to the keen interest in historical psychology during the 1960s, and in many ways it dealt more successfully with issues of collective psychology than did its psychoanalytic alternative, psychohistory, based on the model of Erik Erikson's *Young Man Luther* (1958).

One might also argue that mentalities reflected the changing culture of the postwar era. In many ways, this new cultural history represented the historians' response to issues raised by

the coming of the welfare state in Western civilization, for which problems of the quality of life were as important as those of its material condition. In the affluent society of the late 20th century, the politics of ideology was giving way to a politics of culture. The interest in mentalities reflected that reorientation, and permitted a "postmodern" cultural critique of the "modern" era of history that was being left behind.

Particularly important in this respect is the work of Philippe Ariès, one of the most original and widely read historians in this field during the 1960s. In his *L'Enfant et la vie familiale sous l'Ancien Régime* (1960; *Centuries of Childhood*, 1962), he addressed the topic of family history with an interpretation about the way long-term changes in attitudes toward childhood reveal the historical emergence of a developmental conception of the human life cycle. Ariès had important ties to the royalist Action Française and to right-wing educational movements under Vichy. In juxtaposing everyday life in traditional society to that in the modern world, he offered a subtle critique of the shortcomings of modern mass culture, with its stress upon material affluence, conformity, and consumerism. Ariès sought to expose the present disillusionment with this cultural ideal, particularly among the young, and the ways in which the mores of the old regime were germane as a reference point in the search for postmodern alternatives. Emmanuel Le Roy Ladurie, the author of *Montaillou* (1975; translated 1978), a portrait of everyday life in a medieval village and the most popular study in this genre, found his way to mentalities as a saving shore from his youthful flirtation with the Communist party.

Mentalities effected a rendezvous for such historians, many of whom were disillusioned with the timeworn ideologies of the modern age. In its way, this historiographical movement evinced the historians' effort to put the modern age in a postmodern historical perspective. From this vantage point, the seemingly diverse topical interests of the historians of mentalities converged toward a common preoccupation with traditional ways of life that were disappearing in modern culture. In their histories of everyday life in the modern world, they explored the moving boundary between rising expectations about cultural change in the public sphere and the profound resistance of traditional attitudes in the private one. They traced the dynamics of the historical relationship between the two, thereby shedding light on some of the most poignant issues of modern culture: the trend from extended toward nuclear families (Ariès), the appropriation of an aristocratic code of manners by the bourgeoisie (Norbert Elias), the retreat of sociability into the realm of privacy (Christopher Lasch), the institutionalization of nonconformists in asylums and prisons (Michel Foucault), the psychological and cultural nurturing of personality attending the rise of literacy (Robert Darnton), and the evolution of rituals of commemoration (Maurice Agulhon, Michel Vovelle).

Such studies thereby highlighted dilemmas of the postmodern age: the crisis of the family, the disappearance of rituals to ease the process of dying, the beguiling demands of public authority for social and psychological conformity, the decline of civility, anxieties over the fate of literary culture in the face of the new technologies of electronic communication, and the waning of civic responsibility in a culture of narcissism. The interpretations offered tended to subvert nearly all of the assumptions of an earlier generation of political historians about the course of modern civilization toward some higher destiny.

While the history of mentalities inspired intense interest, it enjoyed an ephemeral reign as the principal forum for cutting edge historical research. As a movement, its unity was in the issues it addressed rather than in the methods or the models of its practitioners. The term itself began to be abandoned by the 1980s in favor of that of the "new cultural history" (Roger Chartier) or the "history of private life" (Georges Duby). Indeed, the 5-volume anthology, *Histoire de la vie privée* (1985–87; *A History of Private Life*, 1987–91), edited by Ariès and Duby, attempted a synthesis of work in the field and in its way represented the denouement of this approach to historical scholarship. By then, the interest of historians looking for new terrain was turning from mentalities to memory, signifying the historiographical need to understand the unraveling of the conceptual web of modern history that mentalities had helped to untie (Pierre Nora).

Mentalities, therefore, is an approach to historical scholarship that can be nested in the historiography of the late 20th century. It contributed to the larger movement among historians away from the old narrative political history while introducing new conceptions of the structural foundations of culture. It provided an historical perspective that proved more effective than "psychohistory" in interpreting collective psychology. It also signifies the degree to which culture has displaced economics in the historians' search for meaning in the late 20th century.

PATRICK H. HUTTON

See also Annales School; Ariès; Bloch; Burke; Chartier; Darnton; Davis, N.; Duby; Erikson; Febvre; Foucault; Ginzburg; Lasch; Le Goff; Le Roy Ladurie; Stone; Thomas, K.; Vovelle

Further Reading

Agulhon, Maurice, *Marianne au combat: l'imagerie et la symbolique républicaines de 1789 à 1880*, Paris: Flammarion, 1979; in English as *Marianne into Battle: Republican Imagery and Symbolism in France, 1789–1880*, Cambridge and New York: Cambridge University Press, 1981

Ariès, Philippe, *L'Enfant et la vie familiale sous l'Ancien Régime*, Paris: Plon, 1960; in English as *Centuries of Childhood*, New York: Knopf, and London: Cape, 1962

Ariès, Philippe, "L'Histoire des mentalités" (The History of Mentalities), in Jacques Le Goff, ed., *La Nouvelle Histoire*, Paris: Pretz, 1978

Ariès, Philippe, and Georges Duby, eds., *Histoire de la vie privée*, 5 vols., Paris: Seuil, 1985–87; in English as *A History of Private Life*, 5 vols., Cambridge, MA: Harvard University Press, 1987–91

Burguière, André, "The Fate of the History of *Mentalités* in the *Annales*," *Comparative Studies in Society and History* 24 (1982), 424–37

Burke, Peter, *Popular Culture in Early Modern Europe*, London: Temple Smith, and New York: New York University Press, 1978

Burke, Peter, "Strengths and Weaknesses of the History of Mentalities," *History of European Ideas* 7 (1986), 439–51

Burke, Peter, *The French Historical Revolution: The Annales School, 1929–89*, Cambridge: Polity Press, and Stanford, CA: Stanford University Press, 1990

Chartier, Roger, "Intellectual History or Sociocultural History? The French Trajectories," in Dominick LaCapra and Steven L. Kaplan, eds., *Modern European Intellectual History: Reappraisals and New Perspectives*, Ithaca, NY: Cornell University Press, 1982

Chartier, Roger, *Cultural History: Between Practices and Representations*, Ithaca, NY: Cornell University Press, and Cambridge: Polity Press, 1988

Darnton, Robert, *The Great Cat Massacre and Other Episodes in French Cultural History*, New York: Basic Books, and London: Allen Lane, 1984

Darnton, Robert, *The Kiss of Lamourette: Reflections in Cultural History*, New York: Norton, and London: Faber, 1990

Davis, Natalie Zemon, *The Return of Martin Guerre*, Cambridge, MA: Harvard University Press, 1983

Dosse, François, *L'Histoire en miettes: des "Annales" à la "nouvelle histoire,"* Paris: La Découverte, 1987; in English as *New History in France: The Triumph of the Annales*, Urbana: University of Illinois Press, 1994

Duby, Georges, "L'Histoire des mentalités" (The History of Mentalities), in Charles Samaran, ed., *Histoire et ses méthodes*, Paris: Gallimard, 1981

Elias, Norbert, *Über den Prozess der Zivilisation: Soziogenetische und Psychogenetische Untersuchungen*, 2 vols., Basel: Falken, 1939; in English as *The Civilizing Process*, 2 vols., New York: Urizen (vol. 1) and Pantheon (vol. 2), and Oxford: Blackwell, 1978–82

Erikson, Erik H., *Young Man Luther: A Study in Psychoanalysis and History*, New York: Norton, 1958; London: Faber, 1959

Febvre, Lucien, *Le Problème de l'incroyance au XVIe siècle: la religion de Rabelais*, Paris: Michel, 1942; in English as *The Problem of Unbelief in the Sixteenth Century: The Religion of Rabelais*, Cambridge, MA: Harvard University Press, 1982

Febvre, Lucien, *A New Kind of History: From the Writings of Febvre*, edited by Peter Burke, London: Routledge, and New York: Harper, 1973

Foucault, Michel, *Folie et déraison*, Paris: Plon, 1961, abridged as *Histoire de la folie*, Paris: UGE, 1961; in English as *Madness and Civilization: A History of Insanity in the Age of Reason*, New York: Pantheon, 1965, London: Tavistock, 1967

Ginzburg, Carlo, *Il formaggio e i vermi: il cosmo di un mugnaio del '500*, Turin: Einaudi, 1976; in English as *The Cheese and the Worms: The Cosmos of a Sixteenth-Century Miller*, Baltimore: Johns Hopkins University Press, and London: Routledge, 1980

Hunt, Lynn, ed., *The New Cultural History*, Berkeley: University of California Press, 1989

Hutton, Patrick H., "The History of Mentalities: The New Map of Cultural History," *History and Theory* 20 (1981), 237–59

Hutton, Patrick H., "The Psychohistory of Erik Erikson from the Perspective of Collective Mentalities," *Psychohistory Review* 12 (1983), 18–25

Lasch, Christopher, *Haven in a Heartless World: The Family Besieged*, New York: Basic Books, 1977; London: Norton, 1995

Le Goff, Jacques, "Les Mentalités: une histoire ambigüe" (Mentalities: An Ambiguous History), in Jacques Le Goff and Pierre Nora, ed., *Faire de l'histoire*, Paris: Gallimard, 1974

Le Goff, Jacques, *La Naissance du purgatoire*, Paris: Gallimard, 1981; in English as *The Birth of Purgatory*, Chicago: University of Chicago Press, and London: Scolar Press, 1984

Le Roy Ladurie, Emmanuel, *Montaillou: village occitan de 1294 à 1324*, Paris: Gallimard, 1975; in English as *Montaillou: The Promised Land of Error*, New York: Braziller, 1978, and as *Montaillou: Cathars and Catholics in a French Village, 1294–1324*, London: Scolar Press, 1978

Mandrou, Robert, *Introduction à la France moderne, 1500–1640: essai de psychologie historique*, Paris: Michel, 1961; in English as *Introduction to Modern France, 1500–1640: An Essay in Historical Psychology*, London: Arnold, 1975, New York: Holmes and Meier, 1976

Mandrou, Robert, "L'Histoire des mentalités" (The History of Mentalities), *Encyclopaedia universalis* 8 (1968 edition), 436–38

Nora, Pierre, ed., *Les Lieux de mémoire*, 3 vols., Paris: Gallimard, 1984–92; abridged in English as *Realms of Memory: Rethinking the French Past*, 2 vols., New York: Columbia University Press, 1996–97

Raulff, Ulrich, ed., *Mentalitäten-Geschichte: zur historischen Rekonstruktion geistiger Prozesse* (Mentalities-History: Toward an Historical Reconstruction of Intellectual Processes), Berlin: Klaus Wagenbach, 1987

Stone, Lawrence, *The Family, Sex and Marriage in England, 1500–1800*, London: Weidenfeld and Nicolson, and New York: Harper, 1977

Stone, Lawrence, "The Revival of Narrative: Reflections on a New Old History," *Past and Present* 85 (1979), 3–24

Thomas, Keith, *Religion and the Decline of Magic: Studies in Popular Beliefs in Sixteenth- and Seventeenth-Century England*, London: Weidenfeld and Nicolson, and New York: Scribner, 1971

Vovelle, Michel, *La Mentalité révolutionnaire: société et mentalités sous la Révolution française* (The Revolutionary Mentality: Society and Mentalities during the French Revolution), Paris: Messidor, 1985

Merchant, Carolyn 1936–

US environmental historian

A scholar of wide-ranging interests whose work explores the intersection of science, feminism, and ecology, Carolyn Merchant helped to establish the field of environmental history in the 1980s, and she remains one of its leading practitioners. Best known for her first, highly influential book, *The Death of Nature* (1980), Merchant has also published an environmental history of New England, a study of contemporary responses to the ecological crisis, and a collection of essays on feminism and the environment. She has also edited two anthologies: a collection of documents and essays on environmental history, and a theoretical exploration of the concept of ecology.

Strongly influenced by both Thomas Kuhn's theory of scientific revolution and Karl Marx's theory of social revolution, Merchant advocates a structural theory of ecological revolution, which she details most fully in her second book, *Ecological Revolutions* (1989). Ecological revolutions, she argues, initiate from two sets of tensions – tensions between production and local ecological conditions, and tensions between production and reproduction – both of which bring about transformations in consciousness. The major theoretical contribution of this framework is the emphasis it places on gender in the sphere of reproduction. Merchant identifies four manifestations of reproduction in environmental history: two biological (reproduction of population and reproduction of daily life) and two social (reproduction of social norms and reproduction of legal-political structures). Each of these forms of reproduction exists in dynamic relationship with local ecological conditions, and each relationship is also mediated by a particular mode of production (subsistence production or market-oriented production). A simultaneous examination of these relationships (between production, reproduction, and ecology) can reveal how changing forms of patriarchy affect human interactions with nature in different cultures.

Although Merchant published her first explanation of this theory in 1987, its outlines were already visible in *The Death of Nature*, in which she offered a detailed analysis of the shift from an organic to a mechanistic worldview during the 16th and 17th centuries. Central to this shift, according to Merchant, was the association of female images with natural systems, an association that not only facilitated the scientific revolution but also encouraged the exploitation of nature and the subjugation of women. One of the strengths of Merchant's analysis is her desire to avoid a deterministic explanation of this transformation; although *The Death of Nature* is primarily an intellectual history, Merchant attempts to link this shift in ideology to a parallel set of social, scientific, and ecological changes. In particular, she examines the scientific revolution in terms of the emergence of the capitalist system, claiming in a key chapter that 1) this new economic and scientific order valorized the concepts of "passivity" and "control," and that 2) "the controls of the experimental method and technological advance" sanctioned a transformation in women's roles from active participants in economic life to passive dependants in production and reproduction.

Merchant's theory of ecological revolutions received its most rigorous application in her second book, *Ecological Revolutions*, in which she shifted focus from intellectual to social history and from Europe to the United States, offering a detailed study of environmental changes in New England from the arrival of Europeans to the mid-19th century. The "ecological revolutions" of her title – the colonial ecological revolution of the 17th century, and the capitalist ecological revolution of the late 18th and early 19th centuries – each resulted in new constructions of nature, both materially and ideologically. Although *Ecological Revolutions* covers some of the same ground as William Cronon's *Changes in the Land* (1983), Merchant moves beyond Cronon's more descriptive account in her analysis of how changes in human and nonhuman populations altered and were altered by changes in food intake, land use, and other economic and social factors, as well as by the same change in worldview she describes in *The Death of Nature*.

Critics have faulted Merchant for not fully elaborating the connections that lie at the heart of her arguments in both *The Death of Nature* and *Ecological Revolutions*: connections between the domination of the earth by humans and the domination of women by men, and connections between human representations of nature and human behavior toward nature. Some have also questioned her interpretation of evidence, particularly regarding Sir Francis Bacon, whose inquisition of witches and interrogation of nature, Merchant says, share a common metaphorical foundation. While each of these criticisms may have merit, they do not fundamentally alter what may be the most significant contribution of both books: Merchant's reconstruction of neglected traditions of resistance to environmentally destructive ideologies, a subject she explores further in *Radical Ecology* (1992).

A taxonomy of responses to the contemporary environmental crisis, *Radical Ecology* lacks the comprehensive analysis characteristic of Merchant's previous books. Nevertheless, *Radical Ecology* is a valuable survey text, especially notable for its evenhanded approach to a complex series of issues, its excellent classification of the varieties of ecofeminism, and its sustained discussion of the environmental concerns of developing nations. If Merchant fails to distinguish fully between the categories of "problems," "thought," and "movements" into which she places such diverse topics as deep ecology, environmental ethics, spiritual ecology, green politics, and social ecology, it may be due in part to the inherent disorderliness of ecological ideas, an issue she examines in greater detail in *The Death of Nature*.

Merchant's most recent book, *Earthcare* (1996), collects her major statements on the theory, history, and practice of feminism and the environment, including two important articles on the contributions of women reformers to the progressive conservation and modern environmental movements. Although almost all of its chapters have been previously published, *Earthcare* is a useful introduction to Merchant's varied interests, a clear illustration of the continuities of her thought, and a visible testament to her influence in defining the scope of the emerging discipline of environmental history.

DANIEL J. PHILIPPON

See also Ecology; Environmental; Native American

Biography

Born Rochester, New York, 12 July 1936. Studied chemistry at Vassar College, BA 1958; graduate study in physics, University of Pennsylvania, 1958–59; MA in history of science, University of Wisconsin, Madison, 1962, PhD 1967. Taught history of science, University of San Francisco, 1969–78; professor of environmental history, philosophy, and ethics, University of California, Berkeley, from 1979.

Principal Writings

The Death of Nature: Women, Ecology, and the Scientific Revolution, 1980
Ecological Revolutions: Nature, Gender, and Science in New England, 1989
Radical Ecology: The Search for a Livable World, 1992
Editor, *Major Problems in American Environmental History: Documents and Essays*, 1993
Editor, *Ecology: Key Concepts in Critical Theory*, 1994
Earthcare: Women and the Environment, 1996

Further Reading

Gross, Paul R. and Norman Levitt, *Higher Superstition: The Academic Left and Its Quarrels with Science*, Baltimore: Johns Hopkins University Press, 1994
Soble, Alan, "In Defense of Bacon," *Philosophy of the Social Sciences* 25 (1995), 192–215

Merton, Robert K. 1910–

US sociologist and historian of science

Robert K. Merton was attracted to Harvard as a student by Pitrim Sorokin, a sociologist with a civilizational perspective, and became interested in the history of science through his participation in a famous seminar given on the subject by L.J. Henderson and George Sarton. The latter guided him through his dissertation and published it in his journal *Osiris* in 1938 as *Science, Technology, and Society in Seventeenth-Century England*. The work became a landmark in the relatively new academic field of the history of science and also launched Merton on his career as a sociologist of science.

Merton builds his argument on two separate spheres of interaction between science and society. The first describes a chain of economic events and stimuli: population growth creates demand for more consumer products which, because of the promise of immediate economic rewards, causes a favorable climate for technological innovation which, in turn, stimulates the practice of science by enhancing its prestige. The second sphere is that of values, in particular the relationship between science and religion. In this view, the practice of science was further stimulated by the Puritan work ethic which placed a positive value on the exploitation of the natural world, its active observation, and pursuit of knowledge through experimentation. The structural flow-chart describes the economic stimulus to science perfectly well without any allusion to the Puritan value system, and, while there may be a presumption of interaction between values and structural trends, the correlation is difficult to prove. Indeed Merton would at best establish a functional relationship between social structure and utilitarian values, without stating any causal relationship, and there is no support in his analysis for the "strong program" in the sociology of knowledge, which assumes a causal relationship between socioeconomic infrastructure and science, as an ideological system.

Merton's study was, of course, inspired by Max Weber's *The Protestant Ethic and the Spirit of Capitalism* (1904, translated 1930). Weber himself discussed the relationship between ascetic Protestant values and empiricism and recognized that physics was the science most favored by Puritans. From Weber, too, Merton appropriated the notion of unanticipated consequences: science, just like capital accumulation, was an unanticipated consequence of the Protestant ethic, inasmuch as, although there was a higher incidence of Puritans in the Royal Society than in the general population, the latter was notable for a strong current of anti-intellectualism.

The connection between science and ascetic Protestantism is based, in Merton's argument, on the presumed effect that the Puritan exaltation of reason had on the creation of a positive climate for science, a belief in progress that fostered the cultivation of utilitarian science, and statements by Robert Boyle and few other prominent actors to the effect that there was a religious commandment to study God's handiwork as revealed in the "book of nature."

Merton's study caused a sensation because it had been widely presumed that science and religion were antithetical worldviews and there was no case for any functional relationship between them. Although Merton had avoided asserting a causal relation between Puritan values and the cognitive structure of science, much of the ensuing debate assumed that he had. Therefore, a great part of the scholarly polemic that the Merton thesis ignited was fought on the narrow ground of the role of scientific values or practice within the context of the sociology, theology, or ideology of Puritanism. Even so, the vast literature that the thesis spawned had the positive result of forcing intellectual and political historians to consider the role of science and scientists in 17th-century England, while in the history of science itself Merton became the central referent for those who, in the 1960s and 1970s, worked to expand the horizons of the social study of science.

Merton's second historical classic is the raucous, free-form *On the Shoulders of Giants* (1965) in which he traces the aphorism ascribed to Sir Isaac Newton – "If I have seen further it is by standing of ye shoulders of Giants" – backwards (to the medieval cleric, Bernard of Chartres), forwards, and laterally to discover the changing contexts and uses of the aphorism, an illustration of the contingency of ideas. The aphorism's history served to illustrate a number of themes that Merton developed in sociological articles. One is the perceived relationship between ancient and modern thought: are ancients always giants, moderns the dwarves who stand on their shoulders? The matter becomes significant in establishing the originality of ideas. Similar social environments, Merton argues, produce independent scientific inventions, discoveries, or observations, which inevitably generate priority disputes. Such disputes are about prestige, not about material reward. Newton used the aphorism in the context of a priority dispute with Robert Hooke over the law of universal attraction. Thus the aphorism and concepts related to it constitute a convenient metaphorical language with which to situate one's own ideas with respect to those of others, past and present.

In many other articles and books, Merton analyzes the social patterning of science, frequently in historical context or using historical examples. In addition to multiple discoveries and priority disputes, he has written on the related issues of how scientific reputations are made and how power is allocated within scientific communities. His definition of science as "organized skepticism" encapsulates his ability to conjoin the social with the cognitive facets of systems of knowledge.

THOMAS F. GLICK

See also Hofstadter; Sarton; Science

Biography
Robert King Merton. Born Philadelphia, 4 July 1910. Educated at Temple University, BA 1931; Harvard University, MA 1932, PhD 1936. Taught sociology, Harvard University, 1936–39; taught at Tulane University, 1939–41, Columbia University (rising to professor), 1941–79 (emeritus). Associate director, Bureau of Applied Social Research, 1942–71. Married 1) Suzanne Carhart, 1934 (separated 1968, died 1992; 1 son, 1 daughter); 2) Harriet Zuckerman, 1993.

Principal Writings
Science, Technology, and Society in Seventeenth-Century England, 1938, reprinted 1970 [originally published in Osiris, 4, pt.2 (1938), 360–632]
On the Shoulders of Giants: A Shandean Postscript, 1965, post-Italianate edition, 1993

Further Reading
Clark, Jon, Celia Modgil, and Sohan Modgil, eds., Robert K. Merton: Consensus and Controversy, London and New York: Falmer Press, 1990
Cohen, I. Bernard, ed., Puritanism and the Rise of Modern Science: The Merton Thesis, New Brunswick, NJ: Rutgers University Press, 1990
Coser, Lewis A., The Idea of Social Structure: Papers in Honor of Robert K. Merton, New York: Harcourt Brace, 1975
Merton, Robert K., A Life of Learning, New York: American Council of Learned Societies, 1994

Metahistory

The label Metahistory was coined by R.G. Collingwood to refer to what philosophers of history such as Karl Popper then called the "material philosophy of history" or "historicism," and what might today be termed metanarratives or upper case History; that is, those overarching, totalizing theories of, say, Hegel or Marx or Spengler. Such theories suggested that it was possible to find immanent in the past a true or real direction, plan, or pattern, whose discovery allowed various legitimations of the then present or, in other cases, predictions as to the future. In this usage the term carried with it pejorative overtones: "proper," professional historians were concerned with studying the past on its own terms and for its own sake. This ruled metanarratives as illegitimate "impositions," which could only ever be ideological projections of the historians' own position. Such proper historians have rarely gone on to see that the study of the past on its own terms and for its own sake (own-sakism) is also ideological: to imagine that the past has any terms "of its own" is as much an imposition as any other. However, given the lack of reflexivity of "proper" historians, and given their powerful role in our social formation, the terms metahistory and metanarrative still retain their pejorative, ideological taint.

There is, however, a different and extremely constructive use of the term metahistory in a non-pejorative way, as popularized above all by the American historian Hayden White. In his book Metahistory (1973) White argued that in attempting to make sense of a past that has actually neither rhyme nor reason in it, all historians' narrative orderings – in both the (allegedly) ideological upper case and the (ostensible) proper lower case – have to organize and structure historical constructions in identical ways. Irrespective of the substantive historical content, the form of making sense of it is the same. All historians, in order to put the past into something it itself never was – a history – have to use a combination of one of four modes of argument (formism, organicism, mechanism, and contextualism); one of four modes of emplotment (romance, comedy, tragedy, and satire); one of four ideological modes (anarchism, radicalism, liberalism, and conservatism); and, because all historians have to use figurative language for their narratives, one of the four organizing rhetorical tropes (metaphor, metonymy, synecdoche, and irony), such tropes being basic – even foundational – for historical creations. In that sense, White saw all histories as linguistic, tropical constructions, such linguistic products being anterior to and thus constitutive of "reality" and the "reality of things past," so that the allegedly independent referent of both upper and lower case histories (the past) is collapsed into the metahistorical mode of representation. In this way White's notion of metahistory ("every history presupposes a metahistory in the way that every physics presupposes a metaphysics") connects up to contemporary ideas constitutive of poststructuralism and postmodernism, and it is probably in this sense – as a linguistic, a priori structuring of the historian's field as opposed to a synonym for metanarrative – that metahistory occupies a place in current theorizing vis-à-vis the nature of history.

KEITH JENKINS

See also Historiology; Literature; Philosophy of History; Rhetoric; White, H.

Further Reading

Ankersmit, F.R., *Narrative Logic: A Semantic Analysis of the Historian's Language*, The Hague: Nijhoff, 1983

Ankersmit, F.R., *History and Tropology: The Rise and Fall of Metaphor*, Berkeley: University of California Press, 1994

Appleby, Joyce, Lynn Hunt, and Margaret Jacob, *Telling the Truth about History*, New York: Norton, 1994

Attridge, Derek, Geoff Bennington, and Robert Young, eds., *Post-Structuralism and the Question of History*, Cambridge and New York: Cambridge University Press, 1987

Bann, Stephen, *The Inventions of History*, Manchester: Manchester University Press, 1990

Bennett, Tony, *Outside Literature*, London and New York: Routledge, 1991

Bertens, Hans, *The Idea of the Postmodern: A History*, London and New York: Routledge, 1995

Bolla, Peter de, "Disfiguring History," *Diacritics* 16 (1986), 49–58

Callinicos, Alex, *Theories and Narratives: Reflections on the Philosophy of History*, Durham, NC: Duke University Press, and Oxford: Polity Press, 1995

Canary, Robert H., and Henry Kozicki, eds., *The Writing of History: Literary Form and Historical Understanding*, Madison: Wisconsin University Press, 1978

Collingwood, R.G., *The Idea of History*, edited by T.M. Knox, Oxford: Oxford University Press, 1946, New York: Oxford University Press, 1956; revised edition, with *Lectures 1926–1928*, edited by Jan van der Dussen, Oxford: Clarendon Press, 1993, New York: Oxford University Press, 1994

Jenkins, Keith, On *"What Is History?" From Carr and Elton to Rorty and White*, London and New York: Routledge, 1995

Kansteiner, Wulf, "Hayden White's Critique of the Writing of History," *History and Theory* 32 (1993), 273–95

Kellner, Hans, *Language and Historical Representation: Getting the Story Crooked*, Madison: University of Wisconsin Press, 1989

"Metahistory: Six Critiques," *History and Theory* 19 (1980), Beiheft

Popper, Karl, *The Poverty of Historicism*, London: Routledge, and Boston: Beacon Press, 1957

Veeser, H. Aram, ed., *The New Historicism*, London and New York: Routledge, 1989

White, Hayden V., *Metahistory: The Historical Imagination in Nineteenth-Century Europe*, Baltimore: Johns Hopkins University Press, 1973

Mexico

The history of Mexico has attracted a great number of Latin Americanists. A quick glance at leading scholarly journals tells us that Mexico was and remains a privileged area of study. For many reasons Mexican historiography is one of the most sophisticated and developed in the field of Latin American history. In the colonial era, it was Spain's most important colony because of its mines of silver and its large indigenous population. Mexico's long border with the United States ensured not only constant political interference, but scholarly attention from US academics. Its agrarian revolution in 1910 also commanded the attention of scholars.

An important trend in the historiography of colonial Mexico has been the blurring of disciplinary boundaries. History and anthropology are virtually indistinguishable. This has entailed a growth of microhistories that have used both archival research and oral interviews. Increasingly historians are writing regional histories. For the 16th century, the debate continues to revolve around the conquest of Mexico. The central question

that recurs is: how did a small number of European soldiers achieve mastery over a large indigenous population? The simple assertion that the Europeans conquered Mexico because of their technological superiority no longer satisfies the scholarly community. In the search to find new answers, historians have adopted other tactics. Tzvetan Todorov's *La Conquête de l'Amérique* (1982; *The Conquest of America*, 1984) inspired a new debate by suggesting that Europeans possessed a superior system of communication that allowed them to be flexible and innovative during the conquest of Mexico, while the highly ritualized and collectively based systems of communication of the Aztecs impeded their defenses. New approaches that began to appear in the late 1960s sought to rescue the indigenous people's perspectives on the arrival of the Spaniards. Miguel León-Portilla's *Visión de los vencidos* (1959; *The Broken Spears*, 1962) exemplified this approach with his careful presentation of indigenous perspectives. Debates have also revolved around land patterns and the birth of the hacienda. As Eric Van Young pointed out in a seminal article, "Mexican Rural Historiography since Chevalier" (1983), the debate between François Chevalier who characterized the Mexican hacienda as feudal versus Charles Gibson who suggested it was commercial, endures to this day albeit in a different form.

The historiography on the era previous to Díaz's regime, 1876–1910, is relatively little studied. Some historians see the roots of Mexican independence from Spain in the Bourbon reforms while others have emphasized the external nature of the independence with the demise of Spanish royalty in Spain. The failure of Father Hidalgo's agrarian rebellion of 1810 has led historians to debate whether this movement was a precursor to independence or just an agrarian rebellion. The conservative nature of Mexican independence, including its domination by elites, has led historians such as Jan Bazant to argue that the grievances of peasant communities were shelved, only to erupt one hundred years later. Charles Hale provided an interesting analysis to Mexico's loss of territory during the 19th century.

Since the Revolution of 1910 broke out during Porfirio Díaz's government, his era has enjoyed considerable attention. State formation and economic processes are themes that occupy the center stage of the analysis of Díaz's era. Coatsworth's *Growth Against Development* (1981) and Vanderwood's *Disorder and Progress* (1981) are examples of such approaches. The heart of the debate centers on whether the state under Díaz was modern or feudal. This question, of course, is closely linked to whether the origins of the modern Mexican state lie in Díaz's regime or in the Mexican Revolution. Those who stress continuities clash with those who emphasize change. The nature of the economic development is also a much debated topic. Should the origins of the dependent nature of the economy of Mexico be located in the Díaz era or after the Revolution? The author most helpful for understanding Mexico's intellectual history is D.A. Brading. His work has centered on the creole elites and their elaboration of Mexican nationalism.

The Mexican Revolution of 1910–20 is the central focus for numerous narratives and numerous debates. As Charles Hale pointed out in a historiographical essay, Frank Tannenbaum was the historian who introduced the Mexican Revolution to the US scholarly public. His monographs *The Mexican Agrarian Revolution* (1929), *Peace by Revolution* (1933), and *Mexico*

(1950) are today considered the starting point for scholarly research about Mexico. Hale noted that Tannenbaum characterized the Mexican Revolution as a spontaneous community-based peasant movement that arose against the "feudal haciendas." This narrative of the insurrection and victory of peasant communities underwent revision, but the notion of popular participation during the Revolution endures.

The state that emerged from the Revolution also had an important effect on the historiography of Mexico. The revolutionary state provided the funds and moral support to historians with the object of elaborating a collective memory. The large body of work produced by Mexican historians distinguishes it from other Latin American countries. Institutional frameworks such as INAH (Instituto Nacional de Antropologia y de Historia) were set up to provide the opportunities for Mexicans to write their own history. Daniel Cosío Villegas and his colleagues assembled volumes of bibliography designed to help scholars to do further research. The Revolution also shaped the questions that historians brought to the history of Mexico regardless of the era they were studying. Whether studying peasant communities in the 19th century or in the colonial era, the historian is unavoidably affected by the Revolution of 1910.

A more recent turning point in the historiography occurred in 1968 when the Mexican official revolutionary party severely repressed student protests in Mexico City. The government of the Revolution was clearly not always on the side of the masses. No longer could scholarly studies aim only at explaining why and how the Revolution happened, but they had to ask whether a revolution had ever happened. Following the lead of Mexican historians, US historians began to do regional studies in an effort to understand the authoritarian character that the revolutionary party assumed in the late 1960s. The outcome of these numerous regional monographs was that "the Revolution" was very different in the various regions. Mark Wasserman with his focus on Chihuahua and Gilbert Joseph's monograph on the Yucatan, *Revolution from Without* (1982), are examples of this new trend toward regionalism. Alan Knight's *The Mexican Revolution* (1986) argued that it was a revolution because of the spontaneous uprising of peasant communities, but that ironically its outcome was to accelerate Mexico's process of modernization, with detrimental consequences for peasant communities. Historians such as John Tutino undertook to analyze the Mexican Revolution from a *longue durée* perspective. Tutino's *From Insurrection to Revolution in Mexico* (1986) argued that the origins of the Revolution lay in a long process of change in land tenure patterns which had begun in the 18th century. Florencia Mallon's comparative approach in *Peasant and Nation* (1995) provided the insight that Mexico's distinct historical development had incorporated peasants more successfully than had other countries in Latin America.

While economic histories such as Haber's *Industry and Underdevelopment* (1989), continue to play a role in the discussion about Mexican history, some historians have turned to what has become known as the "New Cultural History." This attempts to address the subaltern's perspective and to explore issues of gender and ethnicity. In the words of a "postrevisionist" historian/anthropologist, Ana Maria Alonso – referring to Joseph and Nugent's collection, *Everyday Forms of State Formation* (1994) – "In contrast to revisionists, post revisionists make popular social memory and discourses of resistance

central to their analyses while eschewing the romanticism of the populists." The focus of this history is indeed on the discourse and on the negotiation of power between subaltern groups and elites. Some historians have criticized this approach for its prose style that they maintain obfuscates rather than clarifies the narrative. Other scholars have claimed that the "New Cultural History" fails to provide sufficient economic and social background for the analysis of discourse. However, it is certain that this new approach has brought to life topics and aspects of Mexican history that were previously overlooked.

BRETT TROYAN

See also America: Pre-Columbian; Borah; Chevalier; Cosío Villegas; Crime; Díaz; European Expansion; Gibson; González Casanova; Latin America: Colonial; Latin America: National; Lavrin; Léon-Portilla; O'Gorham; Prescott; Spain: Imperial; Tannenbaum; Thomas, H.; Women's History: Latin America

Further Reading

Alonso, Ana Maria, *Thread of Blood: Colonialism, Revolution, and Gender on Mexico's Northern Frontier*, Tucson: University of Arizona Press, 1995

Bartra, Roger, *La Jaula de la melancolía: identidad y metamorfosis del mexicano*, Mexico: Grijalbo, 1987; in English as *The Cage of Melancholy: Identity and Metamorphosis in the Mexican Character*, New Brunswick, NJ: Rutgers University Press, 1992

Bazant, Jan, "From Independence to the Liberal Republic, 1821–1867," in Leslie Bethell, ed., *Mexico since Independence*, Cambridge and New York: Cambridge University Press, 1991

Becker, Marjorie, "Black and White and Color: Cardenismo and the Search for a Campesino Ideology," *Comparative Studies in Society and History* 29 (1987), 453–65

Brading, David A., *The First America: The Spanish Monarchy, Creole Patriots, and the Liberal State, 1492–1867*, Cambridge and New York: Cambridge University Press, 1991

Chevalier, François, *La Formation des grands domaines au Mexique: terre et société aux XVIe–XVIIe siècles*, Paris: Institut d'Ethnologie, 1952; in English as *Land and Society in Colonial Mexico: The Great Hacienda*, Berkeley: University of California Press, 1963

Coatsworth, John H., "Obstacles to Economic Growth in Nineteenth Century Mexico," *American Historical Review* 83 (1978) 80–91

Coatsworth, John H., *Growth Against Development: The Economic Impact of Railroads in Porfirian Mexico*, DeKalb: Northern Illinois University Press, 1981

Collier, George Allen, and Elizabeth Lowery Quaratiello, *Basta! Land and the Zapatista Rebellion in Chiapas*, Oakland, CA: Food First, 1994

Conrad, Geoffrey W., and Arthur A. Demarest, *Religion and Empire: The Dynamics of Atzec and Inca Expansionism*, Cambridge and New York: Cambridge University Press, 1990

Díaz del Castillo, Bernal, *Historia verdadera de la conquista de la Nueva España*, written 1568, published c.1575; in English as *The Discovery and Conquest of Mexico, 1517–1521*, New York: Harper, and London: Routledge, 1928, and as *The Conquest of New Spain*, London: Penguin, 1963

Graham, Richard, ed., *The Idea of Race in Latin America, 1870–1940*, Austin: University of Texas Press, 1990

Haber, Stephen H., *Industry and Underdevelopment: The Industrialization of Mexico, 1890–1940*, Stanford, CA: Stanford University Press, 1989

Hale, Charles, *Mexican Liberalism in the Age of Mora, 1821–1853*, New Haven: Yale University Press, 1968

Hale, Charles, *The Transformation of Liberalism in Late Nineteenth Century Mexico*, Princeton: Princeton University Press, 1989

Hamilton, Nora, *The Limits of State Autonomy: Post-Revolutionary Mexico*, Princeton: Princeton University Press, 1982

Joseph, Gilbert M., "Mexico's 'Popular Revolution': Mobilization and Myth in Yucatan, 1910–1940," *Latin American Perspectives* 6 (Summer 1979), 46–65

Joseph, Gilbert M., *Revolution from Without: Yucatan, Mexico, and the United States, 1880–1924*, Cambridge and New York: Cambridge University Press, 1982

Joseph, Gilbert M., and Daniel Nugent, eds., *Everyday Forms of State Formation: Revolution and Negotiation of Rule in Modern Mexico*, Durham, NC: Duke University Press, 1994

Katz, Friedrich, *The Secret War in Mexico: Europe, the United States and the Mexican Revolution*, Chicago: University of Chicago Press, 1981

Knight, Alan, "The Mexican Revolution: Bourgeois?, Nationalist?, or Just a 'Great Rebellion'?" *Bulletin of Latin American Research* 4 (Spring 1985), 1–37

Knight, Alan, *The Mexican Revolution*, 2 vols., Cambridge and New York: Cambridge University Press, 1986

León-Portilla, Miguel, ed., *Visión de los vencidos: relaciones indígenas de la conquista*, México City: UNAM, 1959; in English as *The Broken Spears: The Aztec Account of the Conquest of Mexico*, Boston: Beacon Press, 1962

Mallon, Florencia E., *Peasant and Nation: The Making of Postcolonial Mexico and Peru*, Berkeley: University of California Press, 1995

Seed, Patricia, *To Love, Honor, and Obey in Colonial Mexico: Conflicts over Marriage Choice, 1574–1821*, Stanford, CA: Stanford University Press, 1988

Tannenbaum, Frank, *The Mexican Agrarian Revolution*, New York: Macmillan, 1929

Tannenbaum, Frank, *Peace by Revolution: An Interpretation of Mexico*, New York: Columbia University Press, 1933

Tannenbaum, Frank, *Mexico: The Struggle for Peace and Bread*, New York: Knopf, 1950

Todorov, Tsvetan, *La Conquête de l'Amérique: la question de l'autre*, Paris: Seuil, 1982; in English as *The Conquest of America: The Question of the Other*, New York: Harper, 1984

Tutino, John, *From Insurrection to Revolution in Mexico: Social Bases of Agrarian Violence, 1750–1940*, Princeton: Princeton University Press, 1986

Vanderwood, Paul J., *Disorder and Progress: Bandits, Police, and Mexican Development*, Lincoln: University of Nebraska Press, 1981; revised and enlarged, Wilmington, DL: SR Books, 1992

Van Young, Eric, "Mexican Rural History since Chevalier: The Historiography of the Colonial Hacienda," *Latin American Research Review* 18 (1983), 5–62

Wasserman, Mark, *Persistent Oligarchs: Elites and Politics in Chihuahua, Mexico, 1910–40*, Durham, NC: Duke University Press, 1993

Werner, Michael S., *Encyclopedia of Mexico: History, Society, and Culture*, 2 vols., Chicago and London: Fitzroy Dearborn, 1997

Meyer, Eduard 1855–1930

German historian of the ancient world

Remarkably proficient both in Greek and Latin as a child, Eduard Meyer decided to study ancient history as a means to writing "universal history." To that end, he began the study of Hebrew and Arabic even before leaving Hamburg for his university studies in Bonn and Leipzig. At Leipzig he intently studied the ancient Near East, as well as classical Greece and Rome, and conceived of antiquity as a unity throughout his career. Meyer's scholarship, however, was as diverse as it was wide-ranging: he published more than 500 works, some of them works of synthesis, but many of them monographs on disparate topics. Self-conscious about methodology, as many historians of the time were, Meyer also wrote on the philosophy of history, notably in his *Zur Theorie und Methodik der Geschichte* (On the Theory and Method of History, 1902).

This diversity of publication was a result of deliberation as well as immense native energy. "History," Meyer wrote, "is not an exact science. Its task is the discovery and narration of those prior things that formerly were part of the real world. For that reason . . . it can never escape the infinite variety of the individual which is enclosed in everything real, in everything that we call fact." Meyer accordingly paid particular attention to establishing exact chronologies in areas of ancient history. He also followed carefully the increasing flood of new publications, with the lamentable exceptions of recent works in modern economic theory and the rich archaeological research of the early 20th century. As a result, he was continually involved in extensive revision. For example, his magisterial *Geschichte des Alterthums* (History of Antiquity), published in five volumes between 1884 and 1902, had to be researched anew and wholly rewritten for the second edition. Meyer deeply believed that individual data were important not by themselves but as particles of a "universal history."

This pursuit of universalism showed in the variety of his major books. Aside from his synthetic *Geschichte des Alterthums*, his *Geschichte des alten Ägyptens* (History of the Ancient Egyptians, 1887) was the first comprehensive work on ancient Egypt. Meyer also wrote major synoptic histories on the Sumerians in his *Sumerier und Semiten in Babylonien* (Sumerians and Semites in Babylon, 1906) and the Hittites with his *Reich und Kultur der Chetiter* (Empire and Culture of the Hittites, 1914). Both works were based far more on written sources than new archaeological evidence. In his celebrated 1896 work *Die Entstehung des Judenthums* (The Origin of Judaism) he accepted Wellhausen's claim that the legal, pentateuchal texts came after the lively biblical narratives associated with Samuel. He sharply rejected, however, Wellhausen's use of the documents in the "Book of Ezra" and of the name list in "Nehemiah" because Wellhausen's interpretation made the origination of Judaism too rapid and too late. Meyer was both respectful and convincing in his treatment of Jewish prophecy, but in his later 3-volume work on Christianity – *Ursprung und Anfänge des Christenthums* (Origin and Beginnings of Christianity, 1921–23) – he regrettably continued the Christian stereotype of rabbinical Judaism as rigid and outdated.

Meyer turned to Greek history in his "Alexander der Grosse und die absolute Monarchie" (Alexander the Great and Absolute Monarchy, 1910), in which he differed significantly with J.G. Droysen's classic account. Meyer also applied himself to Roman history in *Kaiser Augustus* (Caesar Augustus, 1903) and *Caesars Monarchie und das Principat des Pompeius* (Caesar's Monarchy and Pompey's Principate, 1918). These works, especially the last which was written at the end of World War I, were deeply tinged by a defensive monarchism that Meyer imported from the politics of his own age. In his study of the *princeps* Augustus, for example, Meyer challenged Mommsen's favorable treatment of Caesar and praised his successor for bringing to Rome the stability of managed constitutional life. The parallels between antiquity and his own age were all the clearer to him for his influential belief, articulated in his work on

Alexander the Great, that the ancient world was like the modern in important ways. Meyer's polemical edge in the service of conservative German nationalism became more pronounced, indeed vociferous in his old age. Thus, he was openly expansionist and xenophobic in his World War I essays gathered in his *Weltgeschichte und Weltkrieg* (World History and World War, 1916). After the war he made a point of tearing up the honorary degrees received from Chicago, Harvard, and Oxford and called publicly for the exclusion of foreign students from German universities. By then, of course, Meyer was on the verge of retirement, so this late stridency remained outside his major works.

ROBERT FAIRBAIRN SOUTHARD

See also Plutarch; Roman; Rostovtzeff; Wilamovitz-Möllendorff

Biography

Born Hamburg, 25 January 1855, son of a teacher. Educated at Gymnasium Johanneum; University of Bonn, 1872; University of Leipzig, 1875. Professor of ancient history, University of Leipzig, 1884–85; University of Breslau, 1885–89; University of Halle, 1889–1902; and University of Berlin, 1902–23. Married Rosine Freymond, 1884 (3 sons, 4 daughters). Died Berlin, 31 August 1930.

Principal Writings

Geschichte des Alterthums (History of Antiquity), 5 vols., 1884–1902 [and subsequent revisions]

Geschichte des alten Ägyptens (History of the Ancient Egyptians), 1887

Die Entstehung des Judenthums: eine historische Untersuchung (The Origin of Judaism), 1896

Zur Theorie und Methodik der Geschichte (On the Theory and Method of History), 1902

Kaiser Augustus (Caesar Augustus), 1903

Sumerier und Semiten in Babylonien (Sumerians and Semites in Babylon), 1906

"Alexander der Grosse und die absolute Monarchie" (Alexander the Great and Absolute Monarchy), in his *Kleine Schriften*, 1910

Reich und Kultur der Chetiter (Empire and Culture of the Hittites), 1914

Weltgeschichte und Weltkrieg (World History and World War), 1916

Caesars Monarchie und das Principat des Pompeius: innere Geschichte Roms von 66 bis 44 v. Chr. (Caesar's Monarchy and Pompey's Principate: The Core of Roman History from 66 to 44 BCE), 1918

Ursprung und Anfänge des Christenthums (Origin and Beginnings of Christianity), 3 vols., 1921–23

Further Reading

Christ, Karl, "Eduard Meyer," in his *Von Gibbon zu Rostovtzeff: Leben und Werk führender Althistoriker der Neuzeit* (From Gibbon to Rostovtzeff: The Life and Work of the Leading Ancient Historians of Modern Times), Darmstadt: Wissenschaftliche Buchgesellschaft, 1972

Marohl, Heinrich, *Eduard Meyer: Bibliographie*, Stuttgart: Cotta, 1941 [also includes Meyer's autobiography]

Michelet, Jules 1798–1874
French historian

"Others have taught us as much of how mankind acted," John Stuart Mill declared in an 1844 article on Jules Michelet, "but no one makes us so well comprehend how they felt." Born to working-class parents in Paris in 1798, Michelet rose to become one of his country's greatest historians. Some have gone so far to call him *the* historian of France. Never before and rarely since has a historian possessed such passion for his subjects – especially in the case of his nationalist fervor for *le peuple*, the French people – and expressed it in such empathic, emotive, and dramatic writing.

An early influence on Michelet's ideas about history was the 18th-century Italian thinker Giambattista Vico, whose writings Michelet discovered around 1824, and whose *New Science* he translated in a much-admired edition in 1827. Explaining Vico's impact, Eugen Weber summarized in a 1991 essay: "Vico turns history from would-be science into art ... Vico's 'new science' pays little heed to dates and heroes, much attention to popular psychology and what we now describe as *mentalités*: that spirit of time and place of which significant anecdotes, customs, laws, and legends are more expressive, hence significant, than political events." In this respect, it seems reasonable to think of Michelet as Vico's heir, and the 20th-century *Annaliste* Lucien Febvre and his disciples as Michelet's.

Michelet was a prolific and wide-ranging writer who produced textbooks, popular tracts about women and religion, and nature studies as well as sophisticated historical works. His two most important efforts are the 17-volume *Histoire de France* (1833–67; *History of France*, 1844–46) – which took him 34 years to complete – and the *Histoire de la Révolution française* (1847–53; *History of the French Revolution*, 1848–). Scholars generally look more favorably on the first six volumes of the *Histoire de France* than on their successors: there was an eleven-year time gap between the publication of the sixth and seventh volumes. The early series dealt with French history through the end of the Middle Ages and celebrated France's gradual progress toward political, social, and psychological unity. Within this unified nation, however, Michelet valued the rich diversity of its people. The second volume contained a remarkable and oft-cited "Tableau de France" in which Michelet highlighted the psychological particularities of the country's various geographic regions.

The Revolution study, which was published in seven volumes between 1847 and 1853, was, in the words of Ceri Crossley, "intended to revive the memory of the Revolution in the hearts of a divided people and spur them to reconciliation and to action." Again Michelet produced a dramatic societal story, a far cry from traditional political accounts. "The people" were the heroes of Michelet's Revolution, and this distinguished his work from the many other Revolution studies of his time.

In his professorial life Michelet earned a reputation as an enormously popular lecturer. His career received a considerable boost when he was appointed to teach history and philosophy at the Ecole Normale in 1827. He later substituted at the Sorbonne for another eminent historian, François Guizot – at Guizot's request – when Guizot became occupied with government service. In 1838 Michelet obtained his coveted post at the Collège de France. During the 1840s, his job was endangered by the political controversies in which he, along with his colleagues Edgar Quinet and Adam Mickiewicz, was embroiled. At first the conflict focused on a Catholic campaign against university teaching; the professors reacted, in lectures and in print, to what they saw as a threat to their academic freedom. Later, however, Michelet was viewed as simply too inflammatory and influential, and when, in 1852, he refused to swear allegiance to the Second Empire ruler Louis Napoleon, he was stripped of his position.

At that time Michelet lost another part of his professional identity: his responsibilities in archival administration. Early in the July Monarchy, Michelet had been appointed to direct the historical section of the National Archives. He served in this position for nearly 22 years. His own research benefited from his access to rich stores of source material, and he assisted others among his contemporaries as well. Michelet's *Histoire de la Révolution française*, in particular, is distinctive for its incorporation of many archival materials that were lost to history when they burned during the 1871 Commune.

Still, it is for his passionate nationalism and the emotion with which he infused his work that Michelet is most remembered. Perhaps it is Michelet himself who best captured the essence of his unique historical contributions. Among his contemporaries and mentors, Michelet said, Augustin Thierry wrote history as narrative, Guizot as analysis. His own efforts, Michelet declared, produced a resurrection of the past, a revival of silenced actors and episodes in the vast canvas of humanity.

ERIKA DREIFUS

See also Europe: Modern; Italy: Renaissance; Nationalism; Reformation; Thierry; Tocqueville; Vico

Biography

Born Paris, 21 August 1798, son of a printer. Attended Collège Charlemagne, then university where he graduated with highest honors, 1821. Taught history, Collège Rollin, 1821–26; lecturer in ancient history, Ecole Normale, 1827–38; assistant to François Guizot, at the Sorbonne, 1834–35, professor of history and morals, Collège de France, 1838–51; head, history section, National Archives, 1830–52; lost his posts under the Second Empire. Married 1) Pauline Rousseau, 1824 (died 1839; 1 son, 1 daughter); 2) Athénaïs Mialaret, 1849. Died Hyères, 9 February 1874.

Principal Writings

Histoire de France, 17 vols., 1833–67; abridged in English as *History of France*, 2 vols., 1844–46
Histoire de la Révolution française, 7 vols., 1847–53; abridged in English as *History of the French Revolution*, 1848–; new translation, 1967

Further Reading

Barnes, Harry Elmer, *A History of Historical Writing*, Norman: University of Oklahoma Press, 1937
Barthes, Roland, *Michelet par lui-même*, Paris: Seuil, 1954; in English as *Michelet*, New York: Hill and Wang, and Oxford: Blackwell, 1987
Calo, Jeanne, *La Création de la femme chez Michelet* (The Creation of Women in Michelet's Works), Paris: Nizet, 1975
Crossley, Ceri, *French Historians and Romanticism: Thierry, Guizot, the Saint-Simonians, Quinet, Michelet*, London and New York: Routledge, 1993
Gooch, G.P, *History and Historians in the Nineteenth Century*, London and New York: Longman, 1913; revised 1952
Haac, Oscar A., *Jules Michelet*, Boston: Twayne, 1982
Kippur, Steven A., *Jules Michelet: A Study of Mind and Sensibility*, Albany: State University of New York Press, 1981
Mill, John Stuart, *Collected Works*, vol. 20: *Essays on French History and Historians*, edited by John M. Robson, Toronto: University of Toronto Press, and London: Routledge, 1985
Mitzman, Arthur, *Michelet, Historian: Rebirth and Romanticism in Nineteenth-Century France*, New Haven: Yale University Press, 1990
Monod, Gabriel, *La Vie et la pensée de Jules Michelet* (The Life and Thoughts of Jules Michelet), 2 vols., Paris: Champion, 1923
Rudler, Gustave, *Michelet, historien de Jeanne d'Arc* (Michelet, Historian of Joan of Arc), 2 vols., Paris: Presses Universitaires de France, 1925–26
Thompson, James Westfall, *A History of Historical Writing*, vol. 2, *The Eighteenth and Nineteenth Centuries*, New York: Macmillan, 1942
Viallaneix, Paul, *La "Voie Royale": essai sur l'idée de peuple dans l'oeuvre de Michelet* (The "Royal Way": Essay on the Notion of the People in Michelet's Works), Paris: Delagrave, 1959
Weber, Eugen, "Great Man at Work: Michelet Reconsidered," *American Scholar* 60 (1991), 53–72

Middle East: Medieval

From the historical point of view, the medieval Middle East is the area conquered by the Arabs in the 7th and 8th centuries, and incorporated into their empire under the Umayyads of Damascus, 661–750, and the 'Abbasids of Baghdad, 750–945. Its political history is that of the formation and breakup of this empire into a shifting pattern of localized states subject to fresh waves of invasion and conquest. Its economic history, on the other hand, is that of the constitution of a commercial empire based on the long-distance trade that followed the original routes of the Arab conquest and the tribute that flowed back to Damascus. Its social history is that of the creation of an overwhelmingly Muslim population in town and countryside, corresponding to a cultural history of the rise of Islam as a religion, a way of life, and a civilization.

As a source, the 14th-century historian Ibn Khaldun is both primary and secondary. Few modern books, however, treat the subject by itself and as a whole. Gustave von Grunebaum's *Classical Islam* (1970) and J.J. Saunders' *A History of Medieval Islam* (1965) go up to 1258; Hugh Kennedy's *The Prophet and the Age of the Caliphates* (1986) is good on the period to 1050; P.M. Holt's *The Age of the Crusades* (1986) is short but to the point. *The Cambridge History of Islam* (edited by Holt *et al.*, 1970) and Ira Lapidus' *A History of Islamic Societies* (1988) examined the overall history of Islam, while Gerhard Endress' *An Introduction to Islam* (1988) was just that. Stephen Humphreys' *Islamic History* (1988) was technical and selective, but good. Marshall Hodgson's *The Venture of Islam* (1974) was the most satisfying. Philip Hitti on the Arabs is informative, but, like Bernard Lewis, concentrated on the period to 1050; Albert Hourani is good but general. On the Iranian world, the *Cambridge History of Iran* (1968–91) is excellent but dense. For Anatolia, see Claude Cahen's *Pre-Ottoman Turkey* (1968), Georges Ostrogorsky's *History of the Byzantine State* (1940, translated 1956), Colin Imber's *The Ottoman Empire* (1990), and Halil Inalcık's *The Ottoman Empire* (1973); for the Maghrib, see Jamil Abun-Nasr's *A History of the Maghrib in the Islamic Period* (1971), Michael Brett and Elizabeth Fentress' *The Berbers* (1996), and Charles-André Julien's *Histoire de l'Afrique du Nord* (1931; *History of North Africa*, 1970). Neither W. Montgomery Watt's *A History of Islamic Spain* (1965) nor Anwar Chejne's *Muslim Spain* (1974) is satisfactory, while Evariste Lévi-Provençal's *Histoire de l'Espagne musulmane* (A History of Muslim Spain, 1945) is incomplete. C.E. Bosworth's *The New Islamic Dynasties* (1996) is an indispensable guide to the various dynasties and their histories.

Controversy initially centered around the origin and development of Islam, with Western scholars torn between acceptance of the historical veracity of the Muslim tradition, and skepticism in accordance with the principles of biblical criticism. The first tendency is notably represented by Watt's *Muhammad* (1961) and most recently by Kennedy's *The Prophet and the Age of the Caliphates* (1986). But from Ignaz Goldziher onwards, through Robert Brunschvig and Joseph Schacht, to John Wansbrough, and Michael Cook and Patricia Crone, the view has been taken that the evidence of the sources is evidence only of the beliefs of the 9th and 10th centuries, to be used with the greatest care for the events they purport to relate: the approach, for example, of G.R. Hawting's *The First Dynasty of Islam* (1986). The argument is not simply about the detail of the first two centuries of Islam, but whether the religion and its civilization should be seen, not as a process of exponential growth out of the revelation to Muhammad, but as a reformulation of previous elements in the civilization of the Near and Middle East under the rubric of the Prophet and the Book.

Whatever the process, it was evidently linked to the growth of the Muslim population from a minority into the great majority of the population of the Arab empire. For this, the evidence is inadequate, but Richard Bulliet has proposed an S-curve of conversion passing the halfway mark in the 9th century, and suggested that the resultant creation of large and vigorous Muslim communities in the provinces of the Arab empire in place of a thin layer of conquerors was responsible for the final disintegration of the Arab empire in 945. This view is echoed by Kennedy, who proceeded to describe a "Muslim commonwealth" of states in the 10th and 11th centuries, a time commonly regarded as the golden age of medieval Islamic literature, philosophy, and science: compare *The Genius of Arab Civilization* (1975) edited by John R. Hayes, S.H. Nasr's *Islamic Science* (1976), and *The Cambridge History of Arabic Literature* (1990). *Islam dans sa première grandeur* (1971; *The Golden Age of Islam*, 1975) is Maurice Lombard's description of the society and economy of this civilization, which he sees as an urban network spread over the vast distances of Marshall Hodgson's "Arid Zone" of mountain and desert from North Africa to Central Asia. That network, in his and K.N. Chaudhuri's formulation, became the center of the intercontinental economy of Africa and Asia in the Middle Ages.

Problems arose from the 11th century onwards, when the Middle East was invaded from Central Asia by the Seljuk Turks followed by the Mongols, and attacked in Spain, Sicily, and the Levant by Christian Europeans. The longstanding view represented by H.A.R. Gibb was that this amounted to a comprehensive disaster, in which government fell into the hands of barbarian warriors, towns decayed, religion became either sterile or superstitious, science dried up, and the political, economic, and cultural initiative passed to the growing civilization of western Europe. S.D.F. Goitein and Eliyahu Ashtor endeavored to prove the case economically, while J.J. Saunders pointed to the Mongols, and M.W. Dols to the Black Death. As an explanation of the weakness of the region in the face of European pressure in the 19th century, this view has been overtaken by the work of André Raymond and his pupils on the growth of towns and trade in the Ottoman empire. Meanwhile Hodgson had pointed on the one hand to the essential fragility of the prosperity of the "golden age," but on the other to the enormous expansion of Islam in the second half of the Middle Ages, out of the lands of the old Arab empire into Africa and Asia, well described by Ross Dunn in his account of Ibn Battuta. If the problem will not go away, it may well be relegated to the background by the spate of research into the late medieval period made possible by the increasing quantity of surviving material from Egypt and Syria in particular. Humphreys' *Islamic History: A Framework for Inquiry* not only provides a wide review of the literature and the problems with which it wrestles, but does indeed map out the trends of current scholarship.

MICHAEL BRETT

See also Goitein; Inalcık; Islamic; Julien; Lévi-Provençal; Lewis, B.; Ostrogorsky; Ottoman; Watt

Further Reading

Abun-Nasr, Jamil M., *A History of the Maghrib in the Islamic Period*, Cambridge and New York: Cambridge University Press, 1971

Ashtor, Eliyahu, *A Social and Economic History of the Near East in the Middle Ages*, Berkeley: University of California Press, and London: Collins, 1976

Bosworth, Clifford Edmund, *The New Islamic Dynasties: A Chronological and Genealogical Manual*, Edinburgh: Edinburgh University Press, and New York: Columbia University Press, 1996

Brett, Michael, and Elizabeth Fentress, *The Berbers*, Oxford and Cambridge, MA: Blackwell, 1996

Brunschvig, Robert, "Ibn Abdal'hakam et la conquête de l'Afrique du Nord par les Arabes" (Ibn Abdal'hakam and the Conquest of North Africa by the Arabs), in his *Etudes sur l'Islam classique et l'Afrique du Nord*, London: Variorum, 1986

Bulliet, Richard W., *Conversion to Islam in the Medieval Period: An Essay in Quantitative History*, Cambridge, MA: Harvard University Press, 1979

Cahen, Claude, *Pre-Ottoman Turkey: A General Survey of the Material and Spiritual Culture and History, c.1071–1330*, London: Sidgwick and Jackson, and New York: Taplinger, 1968

The Cambridge History of Arabic Literature, vol. 1: *'Abbasid Belles-Lettres*, edited by Julia Ashtiany, and vol. 2: *Religion, Learning and Science in the 'Abbasid Period*, edited by M.J.L. Young, John Derek Latham, and Robert Bertram Serjeant, both vols. Cambridge and New York: Cambridge University Press, 1990

The Cambridge History of Iran, 7 vols., Cambridge: Cambridge University Press, 1968–91

Chaudhuri, K.N., *Trade and Civilisation in the Indian Ocean: An Economic History from the Rise of Islam to 1750*, Cambridge and New York: Cambridge University Press, 1985

Chejne, Anwar G., *Muslim Spain: Its History and Culture*, Minneapolis: University of Minnesota Press, 1974

Cook, Michael, and Patricia Crone, *Hagarism: The Making of the Islamic World*, Cambridge and New York: Cambridge University Press, 1977

Crone, Patricia, and Martin Hinds, *God's Caliph: Religious Authority in the First Centuries of Islam*, Cambridge and New York: Cambridge University Press, 1986

Dols, Michael W., *The Black Death in the Middle East*, Princeton: Princeton University Press, 1971

Dunn, Ross E., *The Adventures of Ibn Battuta: A Muslim Traveler of the 14th Century*, Berkeley: University of California Press, 1980; London: Croom Helm, 1986

Endress, Gerhard, *Einführung in die islamische Geschichte*, 2 vols., Munich: Beck, 1982; in English as *An Introduction to Islam*, Edinburgh: Edinburgh University Press, and New York: Columbia University Press, 1988

Gibb, H.A.R., "An Interpretation of Islamic History," in his *Studies on the Civilization of Islam*, London: Routledge, and Boston: Beacon Press, 1962

Goitein, S.D., *Studies in Islamic History and Institutions*, Leiden: Brill, 1966

Goitein, S.D., *A Mediterranean Society: The Jewish Communities of the Arab World as Portrayed in the Documents of the Cairo Geniza*, 6 vols., Berkeley: University of California Press, 1967–93

Goldziher, Ignaz, *Muhammedanische Studien*, 2 vols., Halle: Niemeyer, 1888–90; in English as *Muslim Studies*, 2 vols., London: Allen and Unwin, 1961–71, Chicago: Aldine, 1967

Grunebaum, Gustave E. von, *Der Islam*, Ullstein: Propyläen, 1963; in English as *Classical Islam: A History, 600–1258*, London: Allen and Unwin, and Chicago: Aldine, 1970

Hawting, Gerald R., *The First Dynasty of Islam: The Umayyad Caliphate AD 661–750*, London: Croom Helm, 1986

Hayes, John R., ed., *The Genius of Arab Civilization: Source of Renaissance*, New York: New York University Press, 1975, Oxford: Phaidon, 1976; 3rd edition, 1992

Hitti, Philip Khuri, *History of the Arabs*, London and New York: Macmillan, 1937

Hodgson, Marshall G.S., *The Venture of Islam: Conscience and History in a World Civilization*, 3 vols., Chicago: University of Chicago Press, 1974

Holt, Peter Malcolm, Ann K.S. Lambton, and Bernard Lewis, eds., *The Cambridge History of Islam*, 2 vols., Cambridge: Cambridge University Press, 1970; revised in 4 vols., 1978

Holt, Peter Malcolm, *The Age of the Crusades: The Near East from the Eleventh Century to 1517*, London and New York: Longman, 1986

Hourani, Albert, *A History of the Arab Peoples*, Cambridge, MA: Harvard University Press, and London: Faber, 1991

Humphreys, R. Stephen, *Islamic History: A Framework for Inquiry*, Minneapolis: Bibliotheca Islamica, 1988; revised Princeton: Princeton University Press, and London: Tauris, 1991

Ibn Khaldūn, *Muqaddima*, written 1375–78; in English as *The Muqaddimah: An Introduction to History*, 2nd edition, Princeton: Princeton University Press, 1967, London: Routledge/Secker and Warburg, 1978

Imber, Colin, *The Ottoman Empire, 1300–1481*, Istanbul: Isis Press, 1990

Inalcık, Halil, *The Ottoman Empire: The Classical Age, 1300–1600*, London: Weidenfeld and Nicolson, and New York: Praeger, 1973

Julien, Charles-André, *Histoire de l'Afrique du Nord: Tunisie, Algérie, Maroc*, Paris: Payot, 1931; in English as *History of North Africa: From the Arab Conquest to 1830*, London: Routledge and Kegan Paul, and New York: Praeger, 1970

Kennedy, Hugh N., *The Prophet and the Age of the Caliphates: The Islamic Near East from the Sixth to the Eleventh Century*, London and New York: Longman, 1986

Lapidus, Ira Marvin, *A History of Islamic Societies*, Cambridge and New York: Cambridge University Press, 1988

Lévi-Provençal, Evariste, *Histoire de l'Espagne musulmane*, vol. 1: *De la conquête à la chute du Califat de Cordoue (710–1031 J.C.)* (A History of Muslim Spain: From the Conquest to the Fall of the Caliphate of Cordoba), Cairo: Institut Français d'Archéologie, 1945; Paris: Maisonneuve, 1950

Lewis, Bernard, *The Arabs in History*, London and New York: Hutchinson, 1950; 6th edition 1993

Lombard, Maurice, *Islam dans sa première grandeur, VIIIe–XIe siècle*, Paris: Flammarion, 1971; in English as *The Golden Age of Islam*, Amsterdam and Oxford: North Holland, and New York: American Elsevier, 1975

Nasr, Seyyed Hossein, *Islamic Science: An Illustrated Study*, London: World of Islam Festival Publishing, 1976

Ostrogorsky, George, *Geschichte des byzantinischen Staates*, Munich: Beck, 1940; in English as *History of the Byzantine State*, Oxford: Blackwell, 1956, New Brunswick, NJ: Rutgers University Press, 1957; revised 1968

Raymond, André, *Grandes villes arabes à l'époque ottomane* (Great Arab Cities in the Ottoman Period), Paris: Sindbad, 1985

Saunders, J.J., *A History of Medieval Islam*, London: Routledge, and New York: Barnes and Noble, 1965

Schacht, Joseph, *The Origins of Muhammadan Jurisprudence*, Oxford: Oxford University Press, 1950; revised 1967

Wansbrough, John, *Quranic Studies: Sources and Methods of Scriptural Interpretation*, Oxford: Oxford University Press, 1977

Wansbrough, John, *The Sectarian Milieu: Content and Composition of Islamic Salvation History*, Oxford and New York: Oxford University Press, 1978

Watt, W. Montgomery, *Muhammad at Mecca*, Oxford: Clarendon Press, 1953

Watt, W. Montgomery, *Muhammad at Medina*, Oxford: Clarendon Press, 1956

Watt, W. Montgomery, *Muhammad: Prophet and Statesman*, London and New York: Oxford University Press, 1961

Watt, W. Montgomery, *A History of Islamic Spain*, Edinburgh: Edinburgh University Press, and Chicago: Aldine, 1965

Migration

At its most ambitious the historical treatment of human migration encompasses movement across the globe since prehistoric times. Archaeologists and anthropologists have established patterns of expansion and retreat over several millennia as the oceans were crossed and the continents populated. Often – as McNeill and Adams showed – migration is associated with demographic and technological changes, with war, and with the elimination of income differentials between regions, countries, and continents. Migration takes many forms: long and short distance; peaceful and disruptive; temporary, seasonal, and permanent; free and coerced; individual, family, and communal. The mechanisms and motivations of migration have required historians to draw on the work of economists, demographers, geographers, and sociologists. Migration has been one of the vital dimensions of modernization, both cause and consequence, and is central to any study of historical change.

Most historical attention has been devoted to European migration from early modern times. From Europe emerged the dynamism for the so-called great "re-shuffling" of humanity by means of international migration from the time of Columbus onwards. This eventually shifted the balance of the world's populations, starting slowly in the 17th century and eventually accelerating to a torrent by the mid-19th century. The chronology, scale, composition, and facilities of the movements are only now being established. The relationship between these mainly European outreaches and internal mobilities has been a contentious question in recent historiography. The old notion that preindustrial societies were immobile has been greatly undermined by evidence of much short-distance, annual, circular migration, often related to hiring practices. But the radius was usually less than 30 miles in a lifetime. Longer-distance migration (to large cities especially) usually involved professional or subsistence needs. These movements probably lengthened and intensified during industrialization when increased labor flexibility became an urgent requirement of the new economy. Precensus sources include legal and apprenticeship records and even the data of convict transportees. The systematic statistical study of British migration began with Ravenstein in the 1880s, was taken up by Arthur Redford in the 1920s, and elaborated by economic and social historians such as John Saville, Michael Anderson, and W.A. Armstrong. Work in Europe has been well surveyed by Leslie Page Moch.

The British Isles figured prominently in the early phases of European emigration and immigration. Bernard Bailyn's synthesis, *Voyagers to the West* (1986), portrayed the Atlantic outreach as an extrapolation of internal systems; in other work – for example, Cinel on Italy – external migration was interpreted as a substitute for older traditions of internal mobility within Europe. Seminal work by Frank Thistlethwaite hypothesized great internal structural forces generating the European outflows of the 19th century. In reaction against the earlier dominance of saga-like American accounts of the Atlantic migration – notably Oscar Handlin's *The Uprooted* (1951) – Thistlethwaite argued persuasively for more sophisticated analyses of conditions in the European homelands to be integrated into a fully sequential account of the entire transatlantic migration. Hence the best modern work has concentrated with almost microscopic precision on local context, sometime using individual level data. By contrast, Brinley Thomas employed statistical data to measure emigrations within a reciprocating relationship between the two sides of the Atlantic economy in the second half of the 19th century.

As Dudley Baines emphasized, there is no agreed account of emigration and there are several historiographical traditions that tend not to connect. The aggregative statistical approach has been dominated by economic historians and has sought correlation of long series of data on movements of labor, with changes on income, prices, fertility, and investment. Williamson tested hypotheses about the role of migration in the convergence of trends in the international economy in the past 150 years, as part of incipient globalization. Mobility involved vast numbers of people, generates much statistical data of highly variable reliability, and lends itself naturally to quantitative methods. Another approach, associated especially with Charlotte Erickson, establishes the collective identity of migrants from individual-level data to draw deductions concerning the selectivity of emigration. Baines used cohort-depletion methods employing census data. Another school, best exemplified by Erickson, Fitzpatrick, and Miller, has used emigrant letters to explore mentalities and family strategies, achieving almost ethnographic levels of insight. The comparative richness of some European documentation, especially that of the Dutch and Scandinavia, has produced some of the most precise and distinctive of modern studies of international migration.

European emigration of the 19th century has dominated, but research in other areas has shifted the historiographical perspective significantly. Eltis, extending the work of Curtin, has shown that slavery out of Africa was the greatest migration system until the 1830s. Indentured migration from Europe before 1815 and then out of Asia, were also dominant flows,

while convict transportation provided ancillary contributions. Just as important were the mainly uncharted movements within Asia. The study of 20th-century migration contends with radical changes in the political context, the re-direction of migration flows, new means of mobility, a great increase in numbers of refugees, and the evolution of global labor markets.

Within the historiography of migration great strides have been made in the study of the economic impact of emigration on donor and receiving countries, especially in the Irish case. Emigration is portrayed as a conveyor of culture and capitalism, disease and technology, as an adjunct of imperialism, and as a means of global income equalization. Its influence on questions of national identity (see, for example, Nugent) and the relative success of migrants in terms of assimilation and social mobility (see Bodner and Thernstrom) have been central concerns, together with the study of reverse migration and the role of emigrant remittances for the maintenance of family welfare in the countries of origin. Historians continue to examine fundamental propositions about emigration as a "safety valve" for political and economic problems, and the impact of colonial settlement on indigenous patterns of mobility. Historians of migration mentality inevitably encounter some of the most vital issues of modern times. These entail, for instance, the record of circumstances that have governed the freedom of movement across frontiers, the treatment and status of aliens, and, ultimately, the global distribution of humanity.

ERIC RICHARDS

See also Bailyn; Curtin; Demography

Further Reading

Anderson, Michael, *Family Structure in Nineteenth-Century Lancashire*, Cambridge: Cambridge University Press, 1971

Armstrong, Alan, *Stability and Change in an English County Town: A Social Study of York, 1801–51*, Cambridge: Cambridge University Press, 1974

Bailyn, Bernard, *Voyagers to the West: A Passage in the Peopling of America on the Eve of the Revolution*, New York: Knopf, 1986; London: Tauris, 1987

Baines, Dudley E., *Migration in a Mature Economy: Emigration and Internal Migration in England and Wales, 1861–1900*, New York and Cambridge: Cambridge University Press, 1986

Bodnar, John, *The Transplanted: A History of Immigrants in Urban America*, Bloomington: Indiana University Press, 1985

Brettell, Caroline B., *Men Who Migrate, Women Who Wait: Population and History in a Portuguese Parish*, Princeton: Princeton University Press, 1986

Cinel, Dino, *From Italy to San Francisco: The Immigrant Experience*, Stanford, CA: Stanford University Press, 1982

Clark, Peter, and David Souden, eds., *Migration and Society in Early Modern England*, London: Hutchinson, 1988

Curtin, Philip D., *The Atlantic Slave Trade: A Census*, Madison, University of Wisconsin Press, 1969

Eltis, D., "Free and Coerced trans-Atlantic Migration: Some Comparisons," *American Historical Review* 88 (1983), 251–80

Erickson, Charlotte, ed., *Invisible Immigrants: The Adaptation of English and Scottish Immigrants in Nineteenth-Century America*, London: London School of Economics/Weidenfeld and Nicolson, and Coral Gables: University of Miami Press, 1972

Erickson, Charlotte, *Leaving England: Essays on British Emigration in the Nineteenth Century*, Ithaca, NY: Cornell University Press, 1994

Ferenczi, Imre, and Walter Willcox, eds., *International Migrations*, 2 vols., New York: National Bureau of Economic Research, 1929–31

Fitzpatrick, David, ed., *Oceans of Consolation: Personal Accounts of Irish Immigration to Australia*, Ithaca, NY: Cornell University Press, 1994

Gjerde, Jon, *From Peasants to Farmers: The Migration from Balestrand, Norway, to the Upper Middle West*, Cambridge and New York: Cambridge University Press, 1985

Gould, J.D., "European Inter-Continental Emigration, 1815–1914: Patterns and Causes," *Journal of European Economic History* 8 (1979), 593–679

Gould, J.D., "European Inter-Continental Emigration, 1815–1914: The Road Home: Return Migration from the USA," *Journal of European Economic History* 9 (1980), 41–112

Gould, J.D., "European Inter-Continental Emigration: The Role of 'Diffusion' and 'Feedback'," *Journal of European Economic History* 9 (1980), 267–315

Handlin, Oscar, *The Uprooted: The Epic Story of the Great Migrations That Made the American People*, Boston: Little Brown, 1951, revised 1973; as *The Uprooted: From the Old World to the New* London: Watts, 1953

Hansen, Marcus Lee, *The Atlantic Migration, 1607–1860: A History of the Continuing Settlement of the United States*, Cambridge, MA: Harvard University Press, 1940

Hatton, Timothy, and Jeffrey G. Williamson, eds., *Migration and the International Labor Market, 1850–1939*, London and New York: Routledge, 1994

Hoerder, Dirk, ed., *Labor Migration in the Atlantic Economies: The European and North American Working Classes during the Period of Industrialization*, Westport, CT: Greenwood Press, 1985

McNeill, William H., and Ruth Adams, eds., *Human Migration: Patterns and Policies*, Bloomington: Indiana University Press, 1978

Miller, Kerby A., *Emigrants and Exiles: Ireland and the Exodus to North America*, Oxford and New York: Oxford University Press, 1985

Moch, Leslie Page, *Moving Europeans: Migration in Western Europe since 1650*, Bloomington: Indiana University Press, 1992

Mokyr, Joel, *Why Ireland Starved: A Quantitative and Analytical History of the Irish Economy, 1800–1850*, London: Allen and Unwin, 1983

Nugent, Walter, *Crossings: The Great Transatlantic Migrations*, Bloomington: Indiana University Press, 1992

Ravenstein, E.G., "The Laws of Migration," *Journal of the Royal Statistical Society*, 48 (1885), 167–227

Redford, Arthur, *Labour Migration in England, 1800–1850*, Manchester: Manchester University Press, 1926

Thernstrom, Stephan, *Poverty and Progress: Social Mobility in a Nineteenth Century City*, Cambridge, MA: Harvard University Press, 1964

Thistlethwaite, Frank, "Migration from Europe Overseas in the Nineteenth and Twentieth Centuries" and "Postscript," in Rudolph J. Vecoli and Suzanne M. Sinke, eds., *A Century of European Migrations, 1830–1930*, Urbana: University of Illinois Press, 1991

Thomas, Brinley, *Migration and Economic Growth: A Study of Great Britain and the Atlantic Economy*, Cambridge: Cambridge University Press, 1954

Military History

The history of warfare can lay claim to great antiquity, for its earliest practitioners (Thucydides, Herodotus, Xenophon, and Vegetius) were among the first historians. Yet, despite its impressive pedigree, military history has only been grudgingly and belatedly accepted as a legitimate topic for historical research by professional historians. Prior to 1945, self-styled military historians were generally employed outside universities, either as journalists or as lecturers attached to the staff colleges and training academies of the world's navies and armies. Military history, when it was addressed by professional historians, was at best a footnote to the bigger political developments historians were attempting to portray. Military historians as a whole would not be welcomed into universities until after World War II and, even then, they have frequently complained of their marginalization within the profession. Instead, military history's greatest triumphs have been secured outside academe, where popular military history continues to outsell most other historical fields. With a few notable exceptions (here one can point to writings by John Keegan, John Terraine, and Bruce Catton), such popular treatments are rarely satisfactory from a scholarly point of view. They are generally antiquarian and descriptive in nature, militaristic in tone, and with a propensity to go hardware-happy.

The integrity of military history has also been compromised by its often didactic purpose. Much of the military history that has been written was driven by the need to identify axioms to guide future commanders rather than to understand the roles played by warfare and its associated institutions within the broader processes of history. And while historians often admire the research that underpins the many official histories produced in the aftermath of the two world wars, nagging questions remain as to whether these really are scholarly productions, given that not only were they funded by the belligerent powers, but they were frequently produced by retired or seconded officers. Consequently, the scholarly integrity of military history has been compromised by its unfortunate association with either the "drum and trumpet" histories written for military enthusiasts, or the instructional works prepared by military professionals for the education of their colleagues. Since the 1970s, however, military history has begun to win over some of the skeptics by proving that it no longer necessarily treats armies and navies in isolation, but situates them within the wider society.

The scholarly tradition of writing military history, as distinguished from popular works or the simple chronicling of campaigns, can be safely traced back to the late 18th and early 19th centuries. The combined impact of the Enlightenment and the Napoleonic Wars prompted a number of intellectuals to seek out explanations for the cause of war, and whether there were any underlying laws or principles that could be said to govern its conduct. The Enlightenment's emphasis on reason had two tremendous effects insofar as military history was understood. First, it was increasingly argued that war was not necessarily a permanent condition of humankind. As Michael Howard has convincingly argued in *What Is History Today?* (1988), to talk of military history before the Enlightenment is anachronistic since societies prior to the 18th century did not distinguish as we do now between war and peace. The Enlightenment's faith in reason, which led many to believe that war could at least be controlled if not rendered extinct, encouraged a number of intellectuals to try to establish systematically the causes of war. Not surprisingly they turned to history. A second offshoot of the Enlightenment was a common belief that the conduct of war, like other human activities, could be reduced to a set of principles. Military intellectuals such as the Swiss writer A.H. Jomini then turned to history in their search for these elusive rules of war. This didactic tradition would live on in the writings of the 19th-century American naval historian (and one-time president of the American Historical Association) Alfred Thayer Mahan, who produced several works that elegantly though misleadingly reduced Britain's rise to naval domination to a few rules governing naval policy. Memories of World War I, and the desire to ensure that future wars would not get bogged down into battles of attrition, lay behind the didactic works of B.H. Liddell Hart and J.F.C. Fuller. Yet despite the polemical quality of their writings, their descriptions and analysis of western warfare over the centuries still offered many insights.

Not all of military history was swept up in the positivist search for the rules and truths of warfare. An alternative strategy was established by the writings of Carl von Clausewitz, particularly *On War* (1832). Unlike Jomini and his heirs, Clausewitz situated war within a much broader context, one that conceded the importance of intangibles such as morale in accounting for success or defeat. Furthermore, Clausewitz did not try and isolate military actions and decision-making from their political and economic surroundings. Clausewitz has been credited with laying the foundations for a much broader definition of military history, one that has been labelled "war and society" or sometimes the "new military history." Clausewitz's insistence that military forces cannot be understood in isolation from their historical circumstances was expanded on at the beginning of the 20th century in the works of Hans Delbrück. Delbrück sought to professionalize military history by subjecting it to the same rigors as other fields of history. He hoped that his 4-volume study of the history of war would convince skeptics that the "Recognition of the reciprocal effects of tactics, strategy, political institutions, and politics throws light on the interconnections in universal history, and has illuminated much that until now lay in darkness or was misunderstood. This work was not written for the sake of the art of war, but for the sake of world history" (quoted by Peter Paret, 1971).

Delbrück's plea that armed conflict, its origins, conduct, and consequences be treated as an integral part of human history struck a responsive chord with many historians in the aftermath of World War II. As the historical profession expanded in numbers and opened up new areas of specialization, the study of warfare found new niches. In Britain, the development of the war studies program at King's College under Michael Howard provided a powerful impetus to scholars working on a number of topics relating to warfare and society in 19th- and 20th-century Europe. Coinciding with this flurry of activity on warfare in modern European history came Michael Roberts' seminal study of technology and the military revolution in early modern Europe. Roberts' interest was not simply limited to detailing the impact of infantry firepower; he also began to flesh out its political and economic consequences. Permanent armies of disciplined soldiers recruited for long periods necessitated the modern absolutist state as the manpower and material demands of such forces lay beyond the financial and organizational capacity of its predecessors. Roberts' demonstration of the tremendous impact that military developments had upon various sectors of early modern society has inspired other historians to refine and extend his arguments – most notably Geoffrey Parker, who has applied

the idea of a military revolution in an effort to account for the success of European expansion between 1500 and 1800.

Another variant on the military revolution thesis was developed by the American historian William H. McNeill who, though not a self-styled military historian, examined the interconnections between armed forces, society, and technology in an effort to chart out the fluctuations in the global distribution of power over the last millennium.

Military history also gained credibility in the United States with scholars such as John Shy, Peter Paret, and Edward Coffman. A striking characteristic of much American scholarship is the degree to which it has been willing to employ the insights, models, and modes of analysis developed in other branches of the social sciences. "War and society" means something quite different in the US, and scholarly journals such as *Armed Forces and Society* deliberately cut across disciplinary boundaries with issues containing articles by historians, political scientists, psychologists, anthropologists, and sociologists. In such a situation, it is not surprising to see that military historians in the US are as likely to be intellectually indebted to sociologists such as Charles Tilly and Morris Janowitz or political scientists such as Samuel Huntington as they are to Liddell Hart or Delbrück.

The post-World War II era also saw military history making considerable gains in France and Germany. André Corvisier and Philippe Contamine in France have between them produced several important works (some of which have been translated) which explore the relationship between armies and society from the Middle Ages to the modern era. In Germany, the writing of an official history of World War II has been entrusted to a team of professional historians (Militärgeschichtliche Forschungsamt). Working at arm's length from the state and the armed forces, these scholars have been able to write much more objectively and dispassionately about Germany's experiences during World War II than was the case with many other official histories.

The scope of military history during this period not only broadened to incorporate political and economic perspectives, but also deepened as it began to explore the social and cultural parameters of armies and societies. John Keegan's *The Face of Battle* (1976) was without a doubt a major breakthrough; Keegan reconstructed the experience of battle from the perspective of those on the firing line, which counterbalanced the numerous battle studies written from the commander's vantage point. Paul Fussell's *The Great War and Modern Memory* (1975) was another milestone. Fussell used literature to probe the responses of European society (principally Britain) to the traumas of World War I. While Fussell's conclusions are the subject of considerable debate, he has nevertheless prompted others to begin tracking the many pathways through which war and the military have come to be embedded in popular culture.

The recent revival of interest in the history of the state and of the processes and ideologies of state formation by such scholars as Charles Tilly and John Brewer has suggested yet more opportunities for military history to move beyond the battlefield. As their work and that of others has made clear, the will to monopolize the means of coercion lurked at the heart of most modern states, and consequently armies and navies were often in a position to exploit such agendas to serve their own interests. However, the resources to sustain such grabs for power were not always in place. Paul Kennedy's massive work on the rise and fall of empires provides clear evidence of the dangers caused when military and political ambitions outpace the state's capacity to support them materially.

Despite the very impressive gains made by military historians in further developing traditional areas of enquiry, such as the origins and conduct of wars as well as the opening up of new lines of enquiry, sizeable gaps remain. Military historians, like historians in general, have tended to clump around certain topics. The two world wars, the American Civil War and the Napoleonic Wars have all been minutely explored. With respect to themes, there has been considerable interest in the evolution of strategic thought, in the impact of technological development on warfare, and on the relationship between military force and diplomacy (at least for the West in the modern era). There has also been considerable work on the impact of intelligence on the planning and conduct of military operations, spurred on by newly declassified documents. The social history of armies and navies and the societies with which they were in contact has been slower to develop, though there are promising signs that this is changing.

There remain several areas of military history that either languish or have yet to take off. Perhaps the best example of the former is the current state of naval history. Earlier in this century, naval historians such as Mahan, Julian Corbett, and Herbert Richmond were powerful figures within the historical establishment, but naval history has since sailed into the doldrums. Why this is the case is not completely clear, though the level of technical competency needed to understand naval operations may help explain it. It also may be that as air forces have overtaken navies as the prime instrument through which states project their power beyond their boundaries, there is consequently no longer the same apparent need or interest in naval history.

For fields that have been slow to develop, we need look no further than the military history of the non-European world. There are numerous popular accounts of colonial wars, but these are with few exceptions potboilers that too often reproduce European prejudices and inaccuracies. Even those works which seek to account for military developments in Africa, Asia, and the Americas in a more sophisticated manner, for example comparing military technologies and organizations, often rely implicitly upon an idea of European exceptionalism (such as the paradigm of the military revolution). In other words, non-European armies, like non-European societies, are defined in terms of their differences from their European counterparts. Fortunately, more nuanced interpretations of warfare and society outside Europe are being written. James Belich wrote an important study of the New Zealand Wars which has shattered many existing stereotypes and assumptions, and David Ralston has looked closely at how European military institutions and practices were assimilated by countries outside Europe and what the consequences were to them.

Notwithstanding these lacunae, it is quite clear that as military history gains credibility within the historical profession, its scope will broaden, and there will be increasing opportunities for the exchange of ideas and perspectives between various fields of history. Novel approaches to the rise of the state, on how masculinity was constructed through the centuries, and on the impact and application of new technologies are just some examples of the possibilities gained through dialogue between military historians and their colleagues in other fields.

DOUGLAS PEERS

See also Delbrück; Herodotus; Howard; Keegan; Kennedy; McNeill; Mahan; Napoleonic Wars; Naval; Parker; Thucydides; Tilly, C.; World War I; World War II; Xenophon

Further Reading

Belich, James, *The New Zealand Wars and the Victorian Interpretation of Racial Conflict*, Auckland: University of Auckland Press, 1986

Bond, Brian, *Liddell Hart: A Study of His Military Thought*, London: Cassell, and New Brunswick, NJ: Rutgers University Press, 1977

Bucholz, Arden, *Hans Delbrück and the German Military Establishment: War Images in Conflict*, Iowa City: University of Iowa Press, 1985

Clausewitz, Carl von, *Vom Kriege*, 3 vols., Berlin: Dümmler, 1832–34; in English as *On War*, London: Trübner, 1873; edited by Michael Howard and Peter Paret, Princeton: Princeton University Press, 1976

Contamine, Philippe, *Le Guerre au Moyen Age*, Paris: Presses Universitaires de France, 1980; in English as *War in the Middle Ages*, Oxford and New York: Blackwell, 1984

Corvisier, André, *Armées et sociétés en Europe de 1914 à 1789*, Paris: Presses Universitaires de France, 1976; in English as *Armies and Societies in Europe, 1494–1789*, Bloomington: Indiana University Press, 1979

Delbrück, Hans, *Geschichte der Kriegskunst im Rahmen der politischen Geschichte*, 4 vols., Berlin: Stilke, 1900–20, reprinted Berlin: de Gruyter, 1962–66; in English as *History of the Art of War within the Framework of Political History*, 4 vols., Westport, CT: Greenwood Press, 1975–85

Fuller, J.F.C., *The Decisive Battles of the Western World and Their Influence on History*, 3 vols., London: Eyre and Spottiswoode, 1954–56

Fussell, Paul, *The Great War and Modern Memory*, Oxford and New York: Oxford University Press, 1975

Howard, Michael, *War in European History*, Oxford and New York: Oxford University Press, 1976

Howard, Michael, *The Causes of War, and Other Essays*, Cambridge, MA: Harvard University Press, and London: Temple Smith, 1983; revised 1984

Howard, Michael, Brian Bond, J.C.A. Stagg, David Chandler, Geoffrey Best, John Terraine, "What Is Military History?" in Juliet Gardiner, ed., *What Is History Today?*, London: Macmillan, and Atlantic Highlands, NJ: Humanities Press, 1988

Keegan, John, *The Face of Battle*, London: Cape, and New York: Viking, 1976

Kennedy, Paul M., *The Rise and Fall of the Great Powers: Economic Change and Military Conflict from 1500 to 2000*, New York: Random House, 1987; London: Unwin Hyman, 1988

Liddell Hart, B.H., *The Real War, 1914–1918*, London: Faber, and Boston: Little Brown, 1930

McNeill, William H., *The Pursuit of Power: Technology, Armed Force, and Society since AD 1000*, Chicago: University of Chicago Press, 1982; Oxford: Blackwell, 1983

Mahan, Alfred Thayer, *The Influence of Sea Power upon History, 1660–1783*, Boston: Little Brown, and London: Sampson Low, 1890

Paret, Peter, "The History of War," *Daedalus* 100 (1971), 376–96

Paret, Peter, *Clausewitz and the State*, Oxford and New York: Oxford University Press, 1976

Paret, Peter, ed., *Makers of Modern Strategy from Machiavelli to the Nuclear Age*, Princeton: Princeton University Press, 1986

Parker, Geoffrey, *The Military Revolution: Military Innovation and the Rise of the West, 1500–1800*, Cambridge and New York: Cambridge University Press, 1988

Ralston, David, *Importing the European Army: The Introduction of European Military Techniques and Institutions into the Extra-European World, 1600–1914*, Chicago: University of Chicago Press, 1990

Roberts, Michael, *The Military Revolution, 1560–1660*, Belfast: Queen's University, 1956; reprinted in his *Essays in Swedish History*, London: Weidenfeld and Nicolson, and Minneapolis: University of Minnesota Press, 1967

Shy, John, *A People Numerous and Armed: Reflections on the Military Struggle for American Independence*, New York: Oxford University Press, 1976; revised 1990

Strachan, Hew, *European Armies and the Conduct of War*, London: Allen and Unwin, 1983

Miliukov, Pavel 1859–1943

Russian economic historian

Pavel Miliukov's scholarly prowess was noted and encouraged at the Historical-Philological Faculty of Moscow University, where he studied with Pavel Vinogradov and Vasilii Kliuchevskii. Upon graduation, he remained at Moscow University as a *Privatdocent* in the Department of Russian History, teaching and simultaneously researching and writing his doctoral dissertation, an analysis of Russian economic history during the reign of Peter I. Defended and published in 1892, *Gosudarstvennoe khoziaistvo Rossii v pervoi chetverti XVIII stoletiia i reforma Petra Velikogo* (Russia's State Economy in the First Quarter of the 18th Century and the Reforms of Peter the Great) argued that Russia's Europeanization was not a product of borrowing from or imitation of the West, but rather a result of the country's internal evolution – developments that were fundamentally similar to those in Western Europe, but retarded by specific conditions of the Russian environment. Thus contradicting to a significant degree Kliuchevskii's views, Miliukov's findings caused a certain coolness in his relationship with his mentor. In this study, Miliukov was also very critical of the financial policies of Peter the Great and concluded that "Russia had been raised to the rank of a European power at the cost of the country's ruin."

Although overloaded with statistics, as well as somewhat cumbersome and convoluted explication, Miliukov's treatise is a major contribution to historiography; it opened the field of economic history to academic scrutiny in Russia. His study also remains important for the scholarly debate concerning Russia's modernization, despite the fact that later in his life Miliukov largely modified his interpretation in favor of Peter the Great.

Dismissed from his post at Moscow University for his protest against suspension of a number of politically active students in 1895 and forbidden employment in any educational institution in the Russian empire due to his "harmful influence" on the youth, Miliukov remained active as an original scholar. During a two-year exile in Riazan' he began a series of publications entitled *Ocherki po istorii russkoi kul'tury* (1896–1903; *Outlines of Russian Culture*, 1942). These essays originally appeared in the journal *Mir Bozhii* (*God's World*) and eventually comprised three full-length volumes, published in several editions in Russia and abroad.

The *Outlines of Russian Culture* series is generally considered to be Miliukov's main scholarly achievement. It is the most lucid and popular of his works, intended as much for a broad circle of educated readers as for specialists. Indeed, to a large extent the *Outlines* were a result of Miliukov's effort to contribute to public education by popularizing his area of expertise.

The study presupposed a comprehensive approach, since, according to Miliukov, cultural history "encompasses all aspects of internal history: economic, social, political, intellectual, moral, religious and esthetic." The first volume represents Miliukov's continued attempt to work on general problems of Russian economic history, while avoiding the deterministic and materialistic approach of the Marxists. Indeed, at least in the Russian setting, it was the state, and not the economic base, that, in Miliukov's view, exerted the primary influence on the country's social organization. Analyzing what may be called "spiritual culture" in the second volume, Miliukov focused his attention on the Orthodox church and the Russian school. He considered these two factors instrumental in determining the development of spiritual differences between the people and the intelligentsia. Addressing the disparity between the way Russian educated society dissociated itself from its past, and the way in which a similar process had occurred in Western Europe, the historian attributed it to the "dissimilarity in the cultural role of religious beliefs." Finally, Miliukov, who considered Russia to be part of Europe yet stressed the importance of its unique national features, devoted the third part of his *Outlines* to the question of nationalism. In his opinion, the Russian national consciousness gradually evolved into a social phenomenon, presupposing greater public attention to domestic policies, as well as broader and more active participation in current affairs.

In 1903 Miliukov was invited to give lectures on Russian history at the University of Chicago, and this academic experience earned him a distinguished reputation in the United States. In the following year he went to Boston, where, under the auspices of the Lowell Institute, he delivered another lecture series under the general title "The Russian Crisis," later published as *Russia and Its Crisis* (1905).

In the period following the outbreak of the 1905 Revolution, Miliukov devoted his primary efforts to politics, serving as the leader of the Constitutional Democratic party, as a prominent Duma deputy, and eventually as a minister in the provisional government. After the Bolshevik takeover in 1917, Miliukov left Russia never to return. Although he was still active in politics, his primary occupation in exile was that of a historian who sought to integrate personal experiences during and after the crisis of 1917 and its scholarly interpretation.

ANNA GEIFMAN

See also Russia: Medieval; Russia: Early Modern; Russia: Modern

Biography

Pavel Nikolaevich Miliukov. Born Moscow, 28 January 1859, son of an architect. Educated at University of Moscow, BA 1886, PhD 1892. A student activist, he was arrested and imprisoned, 1881; on release studied art in Italy for a year. Taught at the University of Moscow, but was removed from post and exiled internally briefly before choosing to take a post first at the University of Sofia, Bulgaria, then in Turkey; rearrested in Moscow, 1901; from this time he worked for reform as a founder of the Constitutional Democratic party and member of the Duma; served as foreign minister in the provisional government, 1917, but resigned protesting extremist domination; settled in Paris, 1917, where he edited an émigré newspaper. Married twice (3 daughters from first marriage). Died Aix-les-Bains, France, 31 March 1943.

Principal Writings

Gosudarstvennoe khoziaistvo Rossii v pervoi chetverti XVIII stoletiia i reforma Petra Velikogo (Russia's State Economy in the First Quarter of the 18th Century and the Reforms of Peter the Great), 1890–92

Ocherki po istorii russkoi kul'tury, 3 vols., 1896–1903, revised 1930–64; in English as *Outlines of Russian Culture*, 3 vols., 1942, abridged as *The Origins of Ideology*, 1974, and *Ideologies in Conflict*, 1975

Glavnye techeniia russkoi istoricheskoi mysli (The Main Trends in Russian Historical Thought), 1897

Iz istorii russkoi intelligentsii; sbornik statei i etiudov (From the History of the Russian Intelligentsia: A Collection of Articles and Studies), 1903

Russia and Its Crisis, 1905

Constitutional Government for Russia, 1907

Balkanskii krizis i politika A. P. Izvol'skogo (The Balkan Crisis and the Politics of A.P. Iavol'skii), 1910

Russian Realities and Problems, 1917

Bolshevism, An International Danger: Its Doctrine and Its Practice Through War and Revolution, 1920

Istoriia vtoroi russkoi revoliutsii, 1921–24; in English as *The Russian Revolution*, 3 vols., 1978–87

Russia Today and Tomorrow, 1922

Zhivoi Pushkin, 1837–1937: istoriko-biograficheskii ocherk (Living Pushkin, 1837–1937: A Historical-Biographical Sketch), 1937

Vospominaniia, 2 vols., 1955; in English as *Political Memoirs, 1905–1917*, 1967

Further Reading

Riha, Thomas, *A Russian European: Paul Miliukov in Russian Politics*, Notre Dame, IN: University of Notre Dame Press, 1969

Stockdale, Melissa Kirschke, *Pavel Miliukov and the Quest for a Liberal Russia, 1880–1918*, Ithaca, NY: Cornell University Press, 1996

Miller, Perry 1905–1963

US intellectual historian

Perry Miller declared in *Errand into the Wilderness* (1956) "that the mind of man is the basic factor in human history." He traced this history in philosophy, literature, theology, painting, science, law, rhetoric, and many other channels. Having missed World War I, the young scholar sought adventure in the merchant marine, traveled to Tampico, Mexico (the opening scene in *Treasure of the Sierra Madre*), the Mediterranean, and the African coast at Matadi on the Congo River. There he received an "epiphany . . . for expounding my America to the twentieth century."

As originally conceived, Miller planned a "massive narrative of the movement of European culture into the vacant wilderness of America." Early volumes on Puritanism triumphantly provided a beginning. His studies on Transcendentalism mapped out another field but remained incomplete at his death. And another work on Darwininism and modernism left behind many suggestions awaiting completion by others.

Kenneth Murdock, Samuel Eliot Morison, and Perry Miller have sometimes been linked as the three M's in the recovery of 17th-century New England Puritans from their debunkers. Murdock tackled the literature, Morison the history, and Miller combined the two. Miller, however, departed significantly from the ancestor worship of his two Harvard colleagues. They admired the Puritans as white Anglo-Saxon Protestants; Miller as an atheist admired them for their determination and integrity.

The theologian Reinhold Niebuhr recognized that Miller, an unbelieving believer, could find in Jonathan Edwards, the 18th-century brimstone preacher, "a superior guide to the labyrinths of the human heart." Miller's study of Jonathan Edwards (1949) was his most heartfelt work. If Miller's understanding of Edwards was imperfect, his understanding of himself was not. Edwards had, he wrote, "early conceived his resolution to present ideas naked."

In 1941, Miller began teaching a course at Harvard on Romanticism in American literature. He started by quoting a letter from A.O. Lovejoy (whom Miller called "one of the great philosophic minds of the century"). Lovejoy, the analyst of "romanticisms," warned that the student must define which ideas Americans chose from the continent and how Americans used and transformed them. Miller began by presenting Kant's analysis of the sublime. He applied that to descriptions of American landscapes, Niagara Falls, Kentucky caves, senatorial oratory, and even the apocalypse of the Civil War.

Miller generally abjured psychological interpretations in history, but he provided pioneering studies in his analysis of Henry David Thoreau, where he first identified homoerotic themes in *Consciousness in Concord* (1958). Miller's last lecture at Harvard (7 December 1963) analyzed the place of Whitman's homosexuality in his becoming the poet and celebrator of America. In *Margaret Fuller* (1963) Miller hinted at lesbian themes in Fuller's work and entertained her own estimate that she possessed the greatest mind among the Transcendentalists.

Miller demanded close readings of the writings of those he studied. For him, the text came first. His gathering of writings *The Puritans* (with Thomas H. Johnson, 1938) remains comprehensive. *The Transcendentalists* (1950) identified authors and writers virtually unknown even to specialists. *American Thought* (1954) indicated the direction his research might have gone had he lived longer.

While Miller figures as a giant among historians, he occupies an equally eminent position among literary critics. He edited works of Washington Irving (1961), Henry David Thoreau (1958, 1960), and Charles Dickens (1962), as well as *Major Writers of America* (1962). He taught in the English department at Harvard where his student Alan Heimert continued his work after Miller's death. Sacvan Bercovitch, also teaching in the Harvard English department, considers Miller to be America's greatest intellectual historian.

Miller's political position resembled that of nonseparating Puritanism: he wanted to purify Anglicanism without abandoning it. Likewise he enthusiastically supported war efforts and served as an officer in the OSS during World War II, yet joined with Archibald MacLeish against the excesses of Macarthyism and 1950s conformity. He was a keen admirer of John F. Kennedy, who had been a student in his course at Harvard and who had quoted John Winthrop's famous "city on the hill" in his farewell to Massachusetts in 1960. Miller died of a heart attack only two weeks after Kennedy's assassination.

Miller influenced a multitude of students and fellow scholars. Donald Fleming carried on work in intellectual history at Harvard. The late Nathan Huggins applied Miller's principles to the Harlem Renaissance. Bernard Bailyn reconceptualized the American Revolution by actually reading the pamphlets of the time. Ann Douglas applied the same techniques to New York City during the 1920s.

Some might cringe at Miller's easy use of words like "essence" or "essential." There is now less talk of the "vacant wilderness of America." Seventeenth-century Puritans certainly knew that their wilderness was no blank slate as they battled the indigenous inhabitants. Nevertheless, one cannot read the American Puritans or the Transcendentalists without Miller. His close textual analysis has stood the test of time and his reputation has been strengthened not weakened by his failure to finish a master narrative.

CHARLES SHIVELY

See also Curti; Gilbert

Biography

Perry Gilbert Eddy Miller. Born Chicago, 25 February 1905, son of a doctor. Attended Tilton School and Austin High School, Chicago; and University of Chicago, 1922. Traveled to Colorado before moving to Greenwich Village, New York, where he wrote for pulp magazines and occasionally acted in plays, before becoming a sailor, and eventually working for an oil company in the Belgian Congo, 1923–26. Re-entered University of Chicago, BA 1928, PhD 1931; at Harvard University, 1930–31, studying with Kenneth Murdock and Samuel Eliot Morison. Taught American literature (rising to professor), Harvard University, 1931–63. Served in the US Army, 1942–45, working in the Office of Strategic Services (OSS). Married Elizabeth Williams, 1930. Died Cambridge, Massachussetts, 9 December 1963.

Principal Writings

Orthodoxy in Massachusetts, 1630–1650: A Genetic Study, 1933
Editor with Thomas H. Johnson, *The Puritans*, 1938
The New England Mind, 2 vols., 1939–53
Jonathan Edwards, 1949
Editor, *The Transcendentalists: An Anthology*, 1950
Roger Williams: His Contribution to the American Tradition, 1953
Editor, *American Thought: Civil War to World War I*, 1954
Errand into the Wilderness, 1956
Editor, *Consciousness in Concord: The Text of Thoreau's Hitherto "Lost Journal" (1840–1841) Together with Notes and a Commentary*, 1958
Editor, *Margaret Fuller, American Romantic: A Selection of Her Writings and Correspondence*, 1963
The Life of Mind in America: From the Revolution to the Civil War, 1965
The Responsibility of Mind in a Civilization of Machines: Essays, edited by John Crowell and Stanford J. Searl, Jr., 1979

Further Reading

Bercovitch, Sacvan, "Investigations of an Americanist," *Journal of American History* 78 (1991), 972–87
Douglas, Ann, "The Mind of Perry Miller," *New Republic*, 186 (3 February 1982), 26–30
Middlekauff, Robert, "Perry Miller," in Marcus Cunliffe and Robin Winks, eds., *Pastmasters: Some Essays on American Historians*, New York: Harper, 1969

Schlesinger, Stephen, ed., "Perry Miller and the American Mind: A Memorial Issue," *Harvard Review* 2 (1964)
Skotheim, Robert Allen, *American Intellectual Histories and Historians*, Princeton: Princeton University Press, 1966, 453–64

Miller, Susanne 1915–
German (Bulgarian-born) historian

Susanne Miller is a leading scholar of the German Social Democratic Party (SPD), whose works have emphasized the ethical foundations of social democratic theory and practice. Miller wrote major investigations of the SPD during and immediately after World War I, when the party found itself profoundly challenged by the immense difficulties of governing a defeated and traumatized nation.

Miller became a historian later in life, having had her education interrupted by fascism and war in the 1930s and 1940s. Born Susanne Strasser in Bulgaria in 1915 into a wealthy family of the Austrian Jewish upper bourgeoisie (her father was a banker whose business interests were in Vienna and Sofia), she grew up in a post-1918 Vienna that was materially impoverished but retained much of its prewar artistic and intellectual brilliance. Young Susanne, alert to the world around her, soon became aware of her own privileged status and the poverty and insecurity of the working classes. At the same time, living in a "Red Vienna" controlled by a militant Social Democratic party, she came to realize that social injustices could indeed be rectified if individuals and groups were committed to bring about change for the better.

As a student at the University of Vienna in the early 1930s, Miller was confronted by the brutal ugliness of fascism. Nazi students supported by much of the faculty dominated this venerable institution, attacking Jewish, socialist, and liberal students at will. Fascinated by history, she was at the same time acutely aware of contemporary events in Central Europe, and by her late teens was moving in militantly antifascist circles. One of her Bulgarian teachers, the philosopher Zeko Torbov, introduced her to the writings of the German socialist Leonard Nelson. Nelson's vision of socialism was ethically based, essentially Kantian, and strongly elitist in its political conception. For the rest of her life, Miller's socialist ideal would be based on ethics rather than economics, on freedom instead of compulsion.

The year 1933 saw the collapse of democracy in Germany and the rapid erosion of parliamentary rule in Austria. For a young woman of the Jewish bourgeoisie, the future was a bleak one, and the vicious spirit that dominated the University of Vienna only deepened her despair about her own and her generation's prospects for the future. In February 1934, she witnessed the Austro-Fascist regime's bloody suppression of social democracy, becoming personally involved in relief efforts for impoverished Viennese working-class families. After spending the summer of 1934 in London as an au pair studying English, she severed her ties to Vienna and began to live mostly in England. Poor but free, Miller moved in émigré circles linked to an elitist organization inspired by Leonard Nelson's ideals, the International Socialist League of Struggle (ISK).

Miller earned her living for the next decade by working in a vegetarian restaurant located between Leicester Square and

Piccadilly Circus. In her free time, she gave talks about the menace of fascism to women's groups linked to the Labour party. Frustrated in her plans for higher education, she read voraciously and closely followed the rapidly deteriorating political landscape.

During World War II Miller entered into a pro forma marriage with Labour Party activist Horace Miller. The acquisition of a British passport would prove essential later on, when she carried out her plans to return to the continent after the defeat of Nazi Germany. During this period, she was deeply involved in the affairs of London's German-speaking émigré circles, with the small but enthusiastic ISK organization remaining at the center of her political and personal life.

In 1944 Miller became the personal secretary as well as companion of Willi Eichler. Berlin-born Eichler served as Leonard Nelson's private secretary during the last years of his life, and succeeded him as the undisputed leader of the hierarchically organized ISK. Although pitifully tiny in numbers (perhaps two dozen active members) in London, the ISK made up in militancy and confidence what it lacked in numerical weight. Brilliant and indefatigable, Eichler advocated an idealistic vision of socialism that went far beyond the drab Marxism of the communists and the faded bureaucratic notions of the social democratic leadership. Miller's developing concept of socialism – idealistic and universal in scope – was enhanced during these years of professional collaboration and personal ties to the charismatic Eichler.

The defeat of Nazi Germany in the spring of 1945 released Miller's pent-up hopes of returning to the continent to help in the creation of a free and democratic society built on the ruins of fascism. Before her return, she supported Eichler in his tireless efforts to bring about the unification of the often bitterly hostile factions among Britain's German social democratic emigrant community. This major task achieved, they moved to occupied Germany in 1946, where they married. Settling in the devastated city of Cologne, he became chief editor of the *Rheinische Zeitung*, while she plunged enthusiastically into SPD organizational work among women.

Undiscouraged by the moral as well as physical destruction of Germany, Miller worked tirelessly to spread socialist ideals among the population of Cologne. Popular among her fellow-SPD members, she was elected, first to the Cologne district council and then to the middle Rhenish district of the party. By 1952 her talents brought her to the attention of the national SPD leadership, who selected her to work in the national executive committee in Bonn. Here she participated in the internal debates that led in 1959 to the adoption of the landmark Bad Godesberg declaration, which finally severed the last ties of the SPD to Marxist ideology, including the idea of class struggle and dictatorship of the proletariat. Serving as secretary of the program commission that drafted the declaration, Miller played a significant role in the extended and sometimes acrimonious internal debates that resulted in a new party firmly based on ideals of ethically grounded democratic socialism.

Decades of political turmoil and personal insecurity behind her, in 1959 Miller activated her long-delayed plans for an academic career, enrolling in the University of Bonn. By 1963 she had earned a doctorate in history under the direction of Karl Dietrich Bracher. Miller's dissertation was published in 1964 as *Das Problem der Freiheit im Sozialismus* (The Problem

of Freedom in Socialism), a broadly conceived study of the "problem of freedom" in the first four decades of the social democratic movement in Germany. Superbly researched and clearly written, it illuminated the essential dilemmas faced by a mass movement in an imperial Germany that remained stubbornly antidemocratic in spirit. Her thesis, that German social democracy had since 1848 carried the double burden of fighting not only for the economic and social advancement of the proletariat but also for the achievement of bourgeois liberty and republican virtue in a profoundly authoritarian society, would be a major theme in all of Miller's subsequent research.

Miller's next three books were all editions of documents. Appearing in 1966 was her edition of the World War I diary of SPD Reichstag deputy Eduard David, which was hailed as a significant contribution to historical understanding of the motives for social democratic support of the war, David revealing in his diary his belief that the German proletariat's support of the imperial regime in the conflict would not only result in accelerated democratization but a final integration of long-alienated workers into the national political culture.

After preparing an edition of Willi Eichler's speeches which appeared in 1967, Miller and her colleagues Erich Matthias and Heinrich Potthoff published in 1969 a massive 2-volume edition of documents from the crucial period of November 1918 through February 1919 when the post-Hohenzollern German state struggled to achieve democracy and come to terms with the reality of military defeat. Published under the auspices of the Commission for the History of Parliamentarianism and Political Parties, the volumes were hailed by reviewers as a major feat of scholarship, making possible for the first time objective assessments by other historians of the activities of the revolutionary Council of People's Representatives during a crucial period of modern German history.

In 1974 Miller published another major work, her study of the SPD during World War I. Once again reviewers noted the excellence of her research, which utilized not only printed and archival sources but oral testimony as well. Socialist historian Carl Landauer, writing in the *American Historical Review*, praised the book as "a great contribution to the history of socialism." Four years later, in 1978, Miller published another massive volume, this time investigating the "burden of power" shouldered by the SPD from October 1918 through June 1920, when the party bore the immense responsibility of governing a defeated and demoralized German Reich. Based on research in 15 archives scattered over six countries, Miller's work was again highly praised. Werner Angress noted in the *American Historical Review* that not only was her research "exemplary," but her assessment of the first German experiment in socialism had been able to strike an admirable balance between narrative and interpretation, noting both SPD achievements and shortcomings.

In her major books Miller exhibited the confidence of a historian who could make controversial judgments when she felt they were appropriate. Her studies of the post-1918 SPD are strongly critical of a political party increasingly out of touch with the masses, who during this crucial period yearned for both a thoroughgoing socialization of the economy and a fundamental democratization of the bureaucracy and military. Social democratic failure to achieve these goals allowed the mental and institutional structures of reactionary Germany to remain largely intact and in time made it possible for them to gather strength and eventually to attack and destroy the Weimar republic. The gradualism of the SPD was more a reflection of the ideological exhaustion of its leaders than a reflection of a clear strategy on their part.

Miller's strong personal commitment to the ideals of democratic socialism, which can be traced back to her earliest political involvement in Vienna, underlies her basic interpretations of modern German history. Her telling criticisms of the social democratic leadership during the period 1914–20 when they reluctantly assumed the "burden of power" in the German Reich emphasized the passivity of the party leadership in pursuing power or pressing for internal reforms, their lack of a strong policy concept, and their growing isolation from the workers who formed the great majority of their party.

Believing that history must be made accessible to a mass audience, Miller wrote books, pamphlets, and articles that contributed to popular awareness of the legacy of democratic socialism, and also helped to strengthen humane, democratic ideals in Germany. Convinced that "objective history" does not exist, Miller studied and wrote history in order to assist the working class and the democratic party that best represented its interests to learn from the mistakes of the past. She regarded her work as part of the democratic reconstruction of post-1945 Germany that of necessity had to study the causes for the failure of democracy in the Weimar republic. Avoiding the turgidity characteristic of much of German scholarly prose, Miller's books are characterized by a clear prose style, a reflection of her belief that history must be comprehensible to the average educated citizen of a democracy who can only engage in effective political discourse when properly armed with the facts of history. A powerful inspiration for Miller's style and approach to historical writing was the socialist historian Gustav Mayer.

In collaboration with Heinrich Potthoff, she published in 1981 a compact history of the German social democratic movement. In this primer aimed at non-specialists, Potthoff covered the years 1848 through 1945, while Miller's contribution was a concise survey of the successes and failures of the SPD in the Federal Republic of Germany from the end of the Third Reich in 1945 to the unification of Germany in 1990. The socialist values she discussed in this book were grounded not in Marxist notions of revolutionary inevitability but instead were an expression of the unrelenting struggle for personal and political freedom waged not only by workers but progressive-minded Germans of all classes.

Because of the dramatic and sudden nature of European political changes of the 1980s, which culminated in German unification in October 1990, Miller has been kept busy adding new materials to the SPD history primer. The book, which surprised its authors by becoming a bestseller, went through a number of editions, including a well-received English-language edition in 1986. The 7th edition (1991) chronicled the dramatic events of 1989–90 which led to the demise of the totalitarian state socialism practiced in the German Democratic Republic and validated Miller's strongly held belief that to be viable, socialism had to be inseparably linked to democracy.

Although she officially retired in 1978, Miller remained active into the 1990s, serving on various panels (including serving from 1982 through 1989 as chair of the SPD Executive Committee's Historical Commission), continuing to publish for a broad audience, and occasionally participating as a citizen in mass rallies for democracy and against the dangers of ethnic intolerance and neo-Nazism. In a 1985 speech on the occasion of Miller's 70th birthday, Willy Brandt noted that what had always inspired her work was the will to assist in the creation of a better society in which working people would be able to live "good, meaningful and fulfilled lives."

JOHN HAAG

Biography

Susanne Strasser Miller. Born Sofia, Bulgaria, 14 May 1915, daughter of a wealthy Austrian Jewish banker. Grew up in Vienna and Sofia; studied briefly, University of Vienna, 1932; lived mostly in England, 1934–46; returned to Germany, 1946. Involved in German Social Democratic party politics from 1946. Received PhD, University of Bonn, 1963. Member, Commission for the History of Parliamentarianism and Political Parties, 1963–78; retired. Married 1) Horace Miller; 2) Willi Eichler, 1946.

Principal Writings

Das Problem der Freiheit im Sozialismus: Freiheit, Staat und Revolution in der Programmatik der Sozialdemokratie von Lassalle bis zum Revisionismusstreit (The Problem of Freedom in Socialism: Freedom, State and Revolution in the Social Democratic Party Program from Lassalle to the Debates over Revisionism), 1964

Editor with Erich Matthias, *Das Kriegstagebuch des Reichstagsabgeordneten Eduard David 1914 bis 1918* (The War Diary of Reichstag Deputy Eduard David 1914 to 1918), 1966

Editor with Gerhard Weiser, *Willi Eichler, Weltanschauung und Politik: Reden und Aufsätze* (World View and Politics: Addresses and Essays by Willi Eichler), 1967

Editor with Gerhard A. Ritter, *Die deutsche Revolution, 1918–1919: Dokumente* (The German Revolution, 1918–1919: Documents), 1968; revised 1975

Editor with Erich Matthias and Heinrich Potthoff, *Die Regierung der Volksbeauftragten 1918/19* (The Government of the People's Representatives 1918/19), 2 vols., 1969

Burgfrieden und Klassenkampf: Die deutsche Sozialdemokratie im Ersten Weltkrieg (Internal Truce and Class Struggle: The German Social Democratic Movement in World War I), 1974

Die Bürde der Macht: Die deutsche Sozialdemokratie, 1918–1920 (The Burden of Power: German Social Democracy, 1918–1920), 1978

With Heinrich Potthoff, *Kleine Geschichte der SPD: Darstellung und Dokumentation, 1848-1980*, 1981, revised 1991; in English as *A History of German Social Democracy from 1848 to the Present*, 1986

Sozialistischer Widerstand im Exil: Prag, Paris, London (Socialist Resistance in Exile: Prague, Paris, London), 1984

The Germans and Their History: Landmarks of Ideological Change: Two Essays, 1989

"England: An Eyewitness Report," in Sibylle Quack, ed., *Between Sorrow and Strength: Women Refugees of the Nazi Period*, 1995

Susanne Miller: Sozialdemokratie als Lebenssinn: Aufsätze zur Geschichte der SPD. Zum 80. Geburtstag herausgegeben von Bernd Faulenbach (Susanne Miller: Social Democracy as Life's Meaning: Essays on the History of the SPD, Presented on her 80th Birthday by Bernd Faulenbach), 1995

Further Reading

Rosch-Sondermann, Hermann, and Rüdiger Zimmermann, eds., *Susanne Miller: Personalbibliographie zum 75. Geburtstag überreicht von der Bibliothek der Sozialen Demokratie/Bibliothek* der *Friedrich-Ebert-Stiftung* (Susanne Miller: Bibliography of Works Presented on the Occasion of her 75th Birthday by the Library of Social Democracy and the Library of the Friedrich Ebert Foundation), Bonn: Forschungsinstitut/Friedrich Ebert Stiftung, 1990

Milsom, S.F.C. 1923–
British legal historian

S.F.C. Milsom, perhaps more than any other living English legal historian of the 20th century, has secured a formidable reputation as the leading authority on the medieval history of the English common law. He is widely regarded as the intellectual successor to Maitland and Plucknett (his distinguished predecessor in the chair of legal history in the University of London). In a now famous metaphor, Milsom characterized his craft as being "not unlike that children's game in which you draw lines between numbered dots, and suddenly from the jumble a picture emerges: but our dots are not numbered."

During his period as literary director of the Selden Society (1965–81), Milsom commissioned many annual volumes and initiated the Society's Supplementary series. He also made a most notable contribution to the publishing program in 1963 when he edited a collection of precedents of oral pleadings in various common-law actions from the time of Edward I for the Society (*Novae Narrationes*), an enterprise that required considerable work translating the Anglo-Norman texts. In his introduction to these texts, a taste of things to come, Milsom provided a consideration of the place of the texts and an extended commentary on the forms of action represented by the pleadings.

Milsom's scholarly reputation, however, derives largely – but by no means exclusively – from his two principal works of scholarship, *Historical Foundations of the Common Law* (1969) and *The Legal Framework of English Feudalism* (1976), the latter being the published text of his Maitland lectures at Cambridge in 1972. But not to be forgotten is Milsom's magisterial introduction to the reissue of the second edition of Pollock and Maitland's *History of English Law* (1968). In his "essay in heresy, pious heresy, intended to suggest the kind of doubt which it seems possible to have about Maitland's picture," Milsom articulated modifications to the picture of medieval English legal history as presented by Pollock and Maitland, most especially that concerning the development of land law between the accession of Henry II and the reign of Edward I. His main thesis was that Maitland had underestimated the role of the local courts, at the expense of exaggerating the role played by the curia regis, most especially in his analysis of property. For Milsom, the real property actions formed a part of the feudal landscape whereas Maitland overemphasized the proprietary characteristics of these actions, "working as it were backwards from Bracton." Milsom returned to his challenge of the Maitland view in his important scholarly monograph on feudalism. While prepared to acknowledge that feudalism had indeed begun to decline during the reign of Henry II, Milsom declined the Maitland view that Henry II had consciously attempted to defeudalize the law: "Great things happened; but the only intention behind writ of right, mort d'ancestor, and novel disseisin was to make the seignorial [feudal] structure work according to its own assumptions." This revised view of the course of English feudalism has not been seriously challenged.

A reviewer of the first edition of Milsom's *Historical Foundations* predicted that it would "come to be placed beside Holdsworth and Plucknett as one of the great post-Maitland contributions to the study of the history of the common law." Milsom did not here set out to cover the whole field of the common law; indeed this would not have been compatible with his aim, which was "to give a single picture of the development of the common law." The two substantively influential sections of the book concern "property in land" and "obligations" and it is these, perhaps more so than the other parts, that have challenged certain widely-held orthodoxies, a theme suggested in the introductory essay to Pollock and Maitland the previous year and to which Milsom was to return again in his Maitland lectures. Although intended "to draw the main outlines of the subject," the book's sophisticated and epigrammatic style, a hallmark of all Milsom's work, demands a considerable familiarity with the subject matter before it can be tackled with profit. For this, one can fortunately turn to Milsom's equally well-known pupil, John H. Baker.

Milsom's distinctive contribution to English legal historical scholarship is not restricted to his books. His illuminating and scholarly articles on such diverse topics as "trespass," "sale of goods in the 15th-century," "reason in the development of the common law," "law and fact in legal development," and "the nature of Blackstone's achievement," appeared in the leading English law journal, the *Law Quarterly Review* and elsewhere. Several of these were gathered together and published separately in one volume as *Studies in the History of the Common Law* (1985).

STEPHEN D. GIRVIN

See also Legal

Biography

Stroud Francis Charles Milsom. Born 2 May 1923. Educated at Charterhouse School; Trinity College, Cambridge, MA 1948. Called to the Bar, Lincoln's Inn, 1947. Commonwealth Fund fellow, University of Pennsylvania, 1947–48; fellow/lecturer, Trinity College, Cambridge, 1948–55; tutor/fellow/dean, New College, Oxford, 1956–64; professor of legal history, University of London, 1964–76, and Cambridge University, 1976–90; fellow, St. John's College, Cambridge, from 1976. Queen's Counsel, 1985. Married Irène Szreszewski, 1955.

Principal Writings

Editor, *Novae Narrationes*, 1963
Theodore Frank Thomas Plucknett, 1897–1965, 1965
Editor, *The History of English Law*, by Frederick Pollock and F.W. Maitland, 1968
Historical Foundations of the Common Law, 1969, 2nd edition 1981
The Legal Framework of English Feudalism, 1976
F.W. Maitland, 1982
Studies in the History of the Common Law, 1985
Editor with J.H. Baker, *Sources of English Legal History: Private Law to 1750*, 1986

Further Reading

Baker, J.H., and D.E.C. Yale, *A Centenary Guide to the Publications of the Selden Society*, London: Selden Society, 1987

Hudson, John, "Milsom's Legal Structure: Interpreting Twelfth-Century Law," *Tijdschrift voor Rechtsgeschiedenis* 59 (1991), 47–66

Palmer, Robert C., "The Feudal Framework of English Law," *Michigan Law Review* 79 (1981), 1130–64

Palmer, Robert C., "The Origins of Property in England," *Law and History Review* 3 (1985), 1–50

Mito School

The Mito school (*Mitogaku*) was a Japanese school of historical, moral, and political thought sponsored by the *daimyō* (barons) of the Mito domain (present-day Ibaraki Prefecture in central Honshu) during the Tokugawa period (1603–1868). These *daimyō* belonged to a branch of the ruling Tokugawa family of shoguns and therefore promoted scholarship which, like that of the rival Hayashi school, was designed to legitimize the existing political order. However, the Mito scholars were more inclined to produce historical writing in which individuals were strictly judged according to neo-Confucian moral standards.

The school was founded in 1657 by the second *daimyō* of the Mito domain, Tokugawa Mitsukuni (1628–1700), who invited Japanese and Chinese scholars to his mansion in Edo (modern Tokyo) to compile a comprehensive history of Japan from the earliest times. By Mitsukuni's death more than 130 scholars had participated in the effort, which absorbed about one-third of the domain's annual budget.

Mitsukuni was the third son of the first Mito *daimyō*, who passed over both him and the first son (Mitsukuni's full biological brother) in favor of a son by a different mother when determining the succession. With the death of this half-brother, however, Mitsukuni was made heir. Guilt-stricken by his selection (over his elder brother who should have been chosen under Confucian rules of precedence), Mitsukuni began to study the Chinese historical texts that specified appropriate moral behavior. This was the inception of the *Dai Nihon shi* (History of Great Japan) project; it eventually consisted of 397 volumes, and was completed only in 1906. Rooted in Mitsukuni's own soul-searching, this and other projects of the Mito school were intended to awaken in the national military government a commitment to self-rectification.

Among the noted scholars involved in the first stage of compilation (to 1720) were the Chinese exile Shu Shunsui (1600–82), a scholar of the Zhu Xi [Chu Hsi] school; Asaka Tanpaku (1656–1737); Kuriyama Senpo (1671–1706); Miyake Kanran (1674–1718); and Mitsukuni's heir Tokugawa Tsunaeda (1656–1718). These scholars followed the format of official Chinese histories, including in the *Dai Nihon shi* annals, biographies, treatises and charts, and combining neo-Confucian ethical and historiographical principles with native Shinto influences.

The divine origins of the imperial institution are assumed in this work, and the imperial regalia are invested with mystical significance. Nevertheless, the emperors are depicted as having "lost the Mandate of Heaven" from the 14th century. The Tokugawa leaders, descended from a branch of the imperial line, had, like the Ashikaga and Minamoto shoguns before them, inherited this mandate.

The treatises (*ronsan*) explicitly indicated the historian's judgment about a particular event. These judgments were conspicuously absent from the Hayashi school project, *Honcho tsugan*; they provided a distinctive moralistic tone to the first version of the *Dai Nihon shi*, covering the period to the early 15th century, presented to the shogunate in 1720. Most of the treatises were written by Asaka; on his death the historical work fell into abeyance until it was resumed under the leadership of Tachihara Suiken (1744–1823) in 1786. Thereafter the school was torn by factional quarrels, in which Fujita Yūkoku (1774–1826), his son Fujita Tōko (1806–55), and the *daimyō* Tokugawa Harutoshi and Nariaki played important roles.

During this "later period" of the Mito school, its scholars shifted their attention from moral commentary on the past to examination of laws and institutions. Asaka's *ronsan* were deleted from the *Dai Nihon shi* text at the request of Fujita Yūkoku, on the grounds that Mitsukuni had never authorized them. During a period of extraordinary internal stresses, and military pressure from Western countries, Mito school scholars came to emphasize the need for major political change to protect the national polity (*kokutai*), and to re-articulate a vision of Japan as the "country of the gods" (*shinkoku*). Thus what had originated as a school for historical inquiry became transformed into a hotbed of antiforeign activism, particularly following the signing of the unequal treaties with Western powers in the 1850s.

GARY P. LEUPP

See also Arai; Japan

Further Reading

Blacker, Carmen, "Japanese Historical Writing in the Tokugawa Period," in William G. Beasley and Edwin G. Pulleyblank, eds., *Historians of China and Japan*, London: Oxford University Press, 1961

Koschmann, J. Victor, *The Mito Ideology: Discourse, Reform, and Insurrection in Late Tokugawa Japan, 1790–1864*, Berkeley: University of California Press, 1987

Nakai, Kate Wildman, "Tokugawa Confucian Historiography: The Hayashi, the Early Mito School, and Arai Hakuseki," in Peter Nosco, ed., *Confucianism and Tokugawa Culture*, Princeton: Princeton University Press, 1984

Webb, Herschel, "What Is the *Dai Nihon Shi*?" *Journal of Asian Studies* 19 (1960), 135–49

Mitre, Bartolomé 1821–1906

Argentine historian

Like most Latin American historians of the 19th century Bartolomé Mitre participated in a variety of other careers and, in fact, his political and military activity overshadowed his historiographic work for a time. He also worked as a journalist while in exile in Chile and after he returned to his home in Argentina he was elected president. As an officer he was naturally interested in military leaders and his first work in 1859 was a 2-volume biography of General Manuel Belgrano, an outstanding leader in the Argentine independence struggle. The laudatory nature of the biography led Mitre into two historiographic polemics not only revolving around his treatment of Belgrano but also on how history should be written. The Argentine scholar Dalmacio Velez Sarsfield took exception to Mitre's argument that Belgrano virtually had to drag the people to the battlefield to get them to support independence. Velez charged that this view was based on only one letter Belgrano wrote to a friend during the struggle and that it was not supported by other evidence. Velez and others charged that the people of Argentina were committed to independence and leaders like Belgrano were of secondary importance to the acquisition of freedom. This charge led Mitre to insist that his critics were moved more by emotion than by careful scholarship. He maintained that biography and history had to be based on documents that were compared and tested and winnowed until the final truth was found. He reiterated that he had used primary documents and tested them against other evidence such as oral tradition, whereas Velez relied upon patriotic myths and stories passed on from the independence age that went untested. But when Velez continued his charges in subsequent articles Mitre broadened the debate. He claimed that Velez had now introduced the concept that the mass of the Argentine population had won the independence struggle alone without the guidance of a group of educated, economically elite leaders. Mitre argued that, historically, in any significant military encounter it required both the leaders and the fighting men to achieve victory. Therefore, he could not understand Velez's attempt to belittle the efforts of Belgrano and other officers. Velez countered that Mitre simply gave too much credit to Belgrano and too little to the fighting men who confronted the Spanish on the battlefield.

Despite their differences on historiographic method, both Mitre and Velez had opened a discussion that influenced later historians in Argentina by emphasizing careful examination of primary materials. Beyond that, Velez ultimately conceded that Mitre's book on Belgrano was the best account of that period of Argentine history despite his slighting the Argentine people who fought in and supported the war. For his part Mitre insisted to the conclusion of the polemic that he had used primary sources and that he never encountered any other documentation that contradicted his position on Belgrano or on Argentine society. Both men expressed the hope that their differences would aid the development of Argentine historiography.

In a later polemic in 1881 and 1882 Mitre clashed with Vicente Fidel López while both were in exile in Chile. This discussion was more impassioned and the participants were more willing to use harsh language to attack each other. Once again the crux of the argument was Mitre's biography of Belgrano. Mitre reverted to his insistence that history had to be written from a careful screening of primary documentation. This time he was more critical of his opponent whom he characterized as using too few tested documents and relying instead on ideas and concepts that López already held when he initiated his histories. This historiographical technique Mitre came to call philosophical history. In the heat of this discussion Mitre also criticized a number of other Argentine historians for the same methodology. López argued that this public criticism of him and his countrymen was unforgivable. If he wished to criticize another's work Mitre should have done it personally and certainly not in a foreign journal or with a foreign publisher, in this case Chilean. Nationalism was a powerful force to which

Mitre also subscribed, but true history was, for him, more important. López argued that Mitre's history was too detailed and too bound to the documents. López's view was that such history was uninteresting and that the reader could glean much more about his country's history if the work were readable and exciting. Style, therefore, was an important ingredient which Mitre relegated to a level below painstaking research in documents. Mitre insisted that Lopez wrote his histories from the works of others, with only a modicum of primary research. His chief concern was that Argentine historiography was not yet ready for that type history when so much basic research was still required – he did not object to writing philosophical history so long as it was based on fact. His complaint was with those histories that were based on too little primary research at a time when there was still so much yet to learn of a basic nature.

After some 800 pages written by each man, Argentine historiography was the primary beneficiary. From this clash of ideas Argentines could clearly evaluate two different types of historical method, archival research and synthesis on the one hand and analysis of secondary sources on the other. This was one of Mitre's great contributions to Argentine historiography. His adversaries too must be praised for their contribution, but the historiographic polemics centered around Mitre's book on the role of General Belgrano in the Argentine independence wars.

JACK RAY THOMAS

See also Argentina; Latin America: National; Levene; Scobie

Biography

Born Buenos Aires, 1821. Graduated from a military academy, Montevideo, 1839. Involved in independence movements in Uruguay, Bolivia, Peru, and Chile. Director, Bolivian Military Academy, 1849; journalist in Chile; fought in Uruguayan battle of Caseros, 1852; governor, Buenos Aires Province, 1860; opposition to Urquiza resolved with Mitre's battlefield victory, Pavón, 1861; president, unified Argentine Republic, 1862–68; unsuccessful rebellion after election defeat led to capture and imprisonment, but later pardoned, 1874. Founder, *La Nación* newspaper, 1870. Died Buenos Aires, 1906.

Principal Writings

Historia de Belgrano y de la independencia argentina (History of Belgrano and of Argentine Independence), 1859
Historia de San Martín y de la emancipación sudamericana, 3 vols., 1887–90, abridged in English as *The Emancipation of South America*, 1893
Archivo del general Mitre (Archive of General Mitre), 28 vols., 1911–14
Obras completas (Complete Works), 18 vols., 1938–72

Further Reading

Acuña, Ángel, *Mitre historiador* (Mitre Historian), 2 vols., Buenos Aires: Coni, 1936
Barager, Joseph R., "The Historiography of the Rio de la Plata Area since 1830," *Hispanic American Historical Review* 39 (1959), 587–642
Burns, E. Bradford, "Bartolomé Mitre: The Historian as Novelist, The Novel as History," *Inter-American Review of Bibliography* 32 (1982), 155–67
Caillet-Bois, Ricardo Rodolfo, *El americanismo de Mitre y la crítica histórica*, Buenos Aires, 1971

Carbia, Rómulo D., *Historia crítica de la historiografía argentina desde sus orígenes en el siglo XVI* (Critical History of Argentine Historiography from its Origins in the 16th century), Buenos Aires: Lopez, 1939

Jeffrey, William, *Mitre and Argentina*, New York: Library Publishers, 1952

Levene, Ricardo, *Las ideas históricas de Mitre* (The Historical Ideas of Mitre), Buenos Aires: Coni, 1940

Levene, Ricardo, *Los estudios históricos de la juventud de Mitre* (Historical Studies of the Young Mitre), Buenos Aires: Emece, 1946

Pla, Alberto J., *Ideología y método en la historiografía argentina* (Ideology and Method in Argentine Historiography), Buenos Aires: Nueva Vision, 1972

Robinson, John L., *Bartolomé Mitre, Historian of the Americas*, Washington, DC: University Press of America, 1982

Momigliano, Arnaldo 1908–1987

Italian ancient historian

Every historian has a favorite vehicle, and for Arnaldo Momigliano it was the lecture or essay, a piece of brief compass in which he could raise very general questions. This was clear even in his first book, a study of the emperor Claudius that was really a series of essays. Published in Italian in 1932, it already revealed many of the characteristics of Momigliano as a mature scholar: a taste for pithy aphorisms, an extraordinary control of modern scholarship, an interest in Judaism, and a quality of being responsive to his surroundings; it may not be accidental that a book published after a decade of fascist power culminated in a discussion of Claudius' policy of centralization. But as time passed, particularly after Momigliano's migration to England in 1939, it became apparent that his interests were far broader than those of a conventional ancient historian. While he would always remain at home in the world of classical studies, being a contributor to both the first and second editions of the Cambridge Ancient History, it eventually became clear that his interests were far broader than those of conventional historians of the ancient world.

One result of his coming to live in England was the developing of contacts with the Warburg Institute in Bloomsbury, which had been founded for the study of cultural and intellectual history in 1921. These bore fruit in 1963 with the publication of a series of lectures he had arranged, *The Conflict Between Paganism and Christianity in the Fourth Century*. Momigliano contributed an introduction to the volume in which he reopened the old question of the connection between the rise of Christianity and the decline of the Roman empire. He argued that as the church developed into a powerful structure it undermined the empire. The case he developed showed lightness of touch and an ability to offer novel hypotheses based on mastery of a huge body of scholarship. These qualities were also displayed in a classic paper "The Fault of the Greeks," in which he suggested that the Greeks were less interested in other peoples than were the Jews and Romans with whom they shared the Hellenistic world, and that this had massive consequences for the way the West has looked at other cultures.

A man of breadth of vision, Momigliano had a genuine passion for the life of the mind. He was fascinated by the western historiographical tradition, and moved with assurance among the works of historians from Herodotus to those of his contemporaries writing in half a dozen languages. It was a degree of knowledge that lent itself to displays of erudition and to a love of detail which led one distinguished Roman historian to refer to him as a pedant. While some of his published work had a slender footnote apparatus, there is no mistaking the learning behind it, while the piling up of references in his more heavily documented work can certainly alarm beginners. But it can also open new horizons. His uncanny ability to use the particular and the general to illuminate each other was seen to great advantage in a lecture read before the British Academy in 1955, a monumental paper on the 6th-century author Cassiodorus which summed up centuries of scholarship. Beginning with an unforgettable throwaway sentence ("When I want to understand Italian history I catch a train and go to Ravenna"), Momigliano went on to offer a novel hypothesis on the relationship between Cassiodorus and Jordanes which continues to provoke discussion.

In one of his most influential essays, an analysis of Edward Gibbon, Momigliano remarked that the work of this scholar combined two different traditions which had developed by his time, the learning of the antiquarian *érudits* and the broad interests of philosophical historians. It was a comment that could have been applied to himself with equal force. The mixture of an exhilarating depth of scholarship with the most provocative broad ideas will continue to challenge and inspire.

JOHN MOORHEAD

See also Poliakov; Roman

Biography

Arnaldo Dante Momigliano. Born Caraglio (Cuneo), Italy, 5 September 1908, to Jewish intellectual family. Studied with Gaetano De Sanctis, University of Turin, received degree 1929. Taught at University of Rome, 1932–36; professor of Roman history, University of Turin, 1936–38: dismissed under Mussolini's race laws. Moved to England and lived in Oxford, 1939–47; taught at University of Bristol, 1947–51; professor of ancient history, University College, London, 1951–75. Married Gemma Segre, 1932 (1 daughter). Died London, 1 September 1987.

Principal Writings

Prime linee di storia della tradizione Maccabaica (Outlines of the History of the Maccabaean Tradition), 1930, reprinted 1968

L'opera dell'imperatore Claudio, 1932; in English as *Claudius the Emperor and His Achievement*, 1934

Filippo il Macedone, saggio sulla storia greca del 4 secolo AC (Philip of Macedon: Essay on Greek History in the 4th Century BC), 1934, reprinted 1987

Contributo alla storia degli studi classici, 9 vols. to date, 1955–; selected essays in English as *Essays in Ancient and Modern Historiography*, 1977

Editor, *The Conflict Between Paganism and Christianity in the Fourth Century*, 1963

Studies in Historiography, 1966

The Development of Greek Biography, 1971; expanded 1993

Alien Wisdom: The Limits of Hellenization, 1975

The Classical Foundations of Modern Historiography, 1990

Further Reading

Bowersock, Glen Warren, and Tim J. Cornell, eds., *A.D. Momigliano: Studies on Modern Scholarship*, Berkeley: University of California Press, 1994

Brown, Peter, "Arnaldo Dante Momigliano," *Proceedings of the British Academy*, 74 (1988), 405–42

Crawford, Michael H., and C.R. Ligota, eds., *Ancient History and the Antiquarian: Essays in Memory of Arnaldo Momigliano*, London: Warburg Institute, 1995

Dionisotti, Carlo, *Ridordo di Arnaldo Momigliano* (Recollections of Arnaldo Momigliano), Bologna: Mulino, 1989

Rivista Storica Italiana 100 (1988) [special issue]

Steinberg, Michael P., ed., *The Presence of the Historian: Essays in Memory of Arnaldo Momigliano*, Middletown, CT: Wesleyan University Press, 1991

Mommsen, Hans 1930–

German historian

Hans Mommsen is one of the leading German historians of the 20th century. Mommsen, who has held a chair for modern history at the Ruhr-Universität Bochum since its foundation, has made his scholarly contribution in 20th-century German history. Based on his rigorous analysis of this era, Mommsen has also become one of the leading political figures of the German republic.

In much of his early work Mommsen addressed the history of the working class, both as an interest group itself, and also as a group of actors on the larger political stage. *Arbeiterbewegung und nationale Frage* (The Labor Movement and the National Question), a collection of Mommsen's essays published in 1979, represents the culmination of his research in this area. Mommsen's growing interest in the fate of the working class and its political and union representation during the National Socialist period led him to become an expert on the Third Reich.

During the 1960s, Mommsen worked with Martin Broszat of the Institute of Contemporary History, Germany's foremost research institution for the history of National Socialism. Broszat and Mommsen were among the first to reveal the contradictions between the historical evidence on the one hand and on the other the totalitarian model of National Socialist rule and its intentionalist approach to the Holocaust. Mommsen himself developed the concept of the "weak dictator" to show the limited role that Hitler – as a single individual – played in the catastrophe of the Third Reich. Mommsen showed how broad-ranged complicity and even apathy among various social groups contributed to the development of National Socialist rule. Mommsen's first significant work in this regard was *Beamtentum im Dritten Reich* (The Institution of the Civil Service in the Third Reich, 1966).

Mommsen's insistence on clear historical proof as the basis of any discussion about the Third Reich has done much to limit contemporary ideological abuse of the Third Reich. For example, Mommsen was the first historian to defend Fritz Tobias' work on the Reichstag fire of 1933. In "Der Reichstagsbrand und seine politischen Folgen" (The Reichstag Fire and Its Political Consequences, 1964), Mommsen argued convincingly against both right- and left-wing conspiracy theories. While Tobias proved the historical case that a lone arsonist set the fire, it was Mommsen who addressed the contemporary political implications of Tobias' findings by showing the political capital at stake in dismantling the myths that had arisen around the fire.

Mommsen has also published extensively on the social composition of the German resistance to Hitler. In this area, too, he has contributed to a much more differentiated understanding of the role both of former labor leaders and of different circles within the conservative resistance.

Mommsen has preferred publishing essays rather than larger works. On the occasion of his 60th birthday, many of his most important essays were collected in *Der Nationalsozialismus und die deutsche Gesellschaft* (1991), some of which have been translated in *From Weimar to Auschwitz* (1991). In his history of the Weimar republic, *Die verspielte Freiheit* (1989; *The Rise and Fall of Weimar Democracy*, 1996), Mommsen argues that the conflict between conservatives and socialists caused the republic's collapse, for which he ultimately blames the conservatives.

Unlike most Anglo-American historians, German historians play a significant role in public discourse and Mommsen is no exception. Through his essays, which are frequently published in popular journals and newspapers, he has contributed much to maintaining a vibrant dialogue about the lessons on democracy to be learned from the first fifty years of the 20th century. Mommsen displays a healthy if un-German distrust for the personified state. In the *Historikerstreit*, the debate about historicizing the Holocaust and the National Socialist regime, Mommsen deftly undermined arguments from both extremes. Rejecting the efforts of conservative politicians and historians to "close the books" on the period, in *Auf der Suche nach historischer Normalität* (In Search of Historical Normalcy, 1987), Mommsen argued that only a continuing dialogue with the past could provide the basis for a healthy, ever-evolving national identity. The goal should not be the creation of a "usable," consensus-driven German past. For Mommsen, a vigilant citizenry is the only sure defense of democracy. Thus, any tendency toward complacency or toward government's detachment from the people suffers harsh criticism at the hands of this combative political thinker. In a recent *Festschrift* for Mommsen, published on the occasion of his 65th birthday, *Von der Aufgabe der Freiheit: politische Antwortung und bürgerliche Gesellschaft im 19. und 20. Jahrhundert* (The Task of Freedom: Political Responsibility and Civil Society in the 19th and 20th Centuries), leading German historians and public figures paid tribute to Mommsen as an important if uncomfortable practitioner of his craft and a model of the historian as citizen.

MARTIN R. MENKE

See also Broszat; Germany: 1800–1945

Biography

Born Marburg, 5 November 1930, son of historian Wilhelm Mommsen and twin brother of historian Wolfgang J. Mommsen. Studied history, German language, and philosophy at universities of Marburg, Tübingen, and Heidelberg; PhD, University of Tübingen, 1959. Taught at Tübingen, 1960–61, Heidelberg, 1963–68, and Bochum, from 1968. Married Margaretha Reindl, 1966.

Principal Writings

Die Sozialdemokratie und die Nationalitätenfrage im habsburgischen Vielvölkerstaat (Social Democracy and the Nationalities Question in the Multi-Ethnic Hapsburg Empire), 1963

"Der Reichstagsbrand und seine politischen Folgen" (The Reichstag Fire and Its Political Consequences), *Vierteljahreshefte für Zeitgeschichte* 12 (1964), 351–413

Beamtentum im Dritten Reich: Mit ausgewählten Quellen zur nationalsozialistischen Beamtenpolitik (The Institution of the Civil Service in the Third Reich: With Selected Sources on National Socialist Civil Service Policy), 1966

Editor with Dietmar Petzina and Bernd Weisbrod, *Industrielles System und politische Entwicklung in der Weimarer Republik* (Industrialism and Political Development of the Weimar Republic), 1974

Editor, *Sozialdemokratie zwischen Klassenbewegung und Volkspartei* (Social Democracy Between Class Movement and Populist Party), 1974

Editor, *Arbeiterbewegung und industrieller Wandel: Studien zu gewerkschaftlichen Organisationsproblemen im Reich und an der Ruhr* (Labor Movement and Industrial Change: Problems in Union Organizing in the Reich and in the Ruhr), 1978

Klassenkampf oder Mitbestimmung: zum Problem der Kontrolle wirtschaftlicher Macht in der Weimarer Republik (Class Struggle or Co-Determination: Issues in Controlling Economic Influence the Weimar Republic), 1978

Arbeiterbewegung und nationale Frage: Ausgewählte Aufsätze (The Labor Movement and the National Question: Selected Essays), 1979

Editor with Ulrich Borsdorf, *Glück Auf, Kameraden! Die Bergarbeiter und ihre Organisationen in Deutschland* (Good Luck, Comrades! Miners and Their Organizations in Germany), 1979

Editor with Winfried Schulze, *Vom Elend der Handarbeit: Probleme historischer Unterschichtenforschung* (Concerning the Misery of Piece-Work: Problems in Conducting Historical Research about the Underclass), 1981

Editor with Isabella Acker and Walter Hummelberger, *Politik und Gesellschaft im alten und neuen Österreich: Festschrift für Rudolf Neck zum 60. Geburtstag* (Politics and Society in the Old and the New Austria: *Festschrift* for Rudolf Neck on the Occasion of his 60th Birthday), 2 vols., 1981

Auf der Suche nach historischer Normalität: Beiträge zum Geschichtsbildstreit in der Bundesrepublik (In Search of Historical Normalcy), 1987

Editor with Susanne Willems, *Herrschaftsalltag im Dritten Reich: Studien und Texte* (Everyday Rule in the Third Reich: Studies and Texts), 1988

Die verspielte Freiheit: der Weg der Republik von Weimar in den Untergang, 1918 bis 1933, 1989; in English as *The Rise and Fall of Weimar Democracy,* 1996

Der Nationalsozialismus und die deutsche Gesellschaft, 1991; abridged in English as *From Weimar to Auschwitz: Essays in German History,* 1991

Editor with Wolfgang Benz and Hans Buchheim, *Der Nationalsozialismus: Studien zur Ideologie und Herrschaft* (Studies in National Socialist Ideology and Rule), 1993

Editor with Jiří Kořalka, *Ungleiche Nachbarn: demokratische und nationale Emanzipation bei Deutschen, Tschechen und Slowaken (1815–1914)* (Unequal Neighbors: Democratic and National Emancipation of Germans, Czechs, and Slovaks, 1815–1914), 1993

"Adolf Hitler und der 9. November 1923" (Adolf Hitler and the 9th of November 1923), in Johannes Willms, ed., *Der 9. November: Fünf Essays zur deutschen Geschichte,* 1994

Widerstand und politische Kultur in Deutschland und Österreich (Resistance and Political Culture in Germany and Austria), 1994

Further Reading

"Einleitung" (Introduction), in Lutz Niethammer and Bernd Weisbrod, eds., *Der Nationalsozialismus und die deutsche Gesellschaft: Ausgewählte Aufsätze* (National Socialism and German Society: Selected Essays), Reinbek: Rowohlt, 1991

Jansen, Christian, Lutz Niethammer, and Bernd Weisbrod, eds., *Von der Aufgabe der Freiheit: politische Antwortung und bürgerliche Gesellschaft im 19. und 20. Jahrhundert: Festschrift für Hans Mommsen zum 5. November 1995* (The Task of Freedom: Political Responsibility and Civil Society in the 19th and 20th Centuries), Berlin: Akademie, 1995

Niethammer, Lutz, and Bernd Weisbrod, eds., *Der Nationalsozialismus und die deutsche Gesellschaft: Ausgewählte Aufsätze* (National Socialism and German Society: Selected Essays), Reinbek: Rowohlt, 1991

Mommsen, Theodor 1817–1903
German historian of the ancient world

Theodor Mommsen was an extraordinarily productive and wide-ranging scholar. The Protestant pastor's son from southern Schleswig loyally trained as a jurist at the nearby University of Kiel, and his dissertation in Roman law and history attracted favorable attention at once. But he worked harder in his philology courses with Otto Jahn and – with Jahn and his own brother Tycho – published some passable lyric poetry. He was especially gifted as a writer of prose: his scholarly bibliography lists 1500 items and, in 1902, his *Römische Geschichte* (1854–56; *The History of Rome,* 1864–75), though long in print, won the Nobel prize for literature. Mommsen had, really, two academic careers. First, he was a professor of Roman law at Leipzig and – after his dismissal on political grounds after 1848 – at Zürich and Breslau. Then, because of his distinguished work with Roman inscriptions, he was appointed professor of Roman history at the University of Berlin.

A numismatist of distinction, Mommsen was also a talented administrator: he knew how to initiate and manage large-scale, long-term academic projects, specifically in the collection and study of ancient inscriptions, the location and study of Roman coin hordes in Germany, and the study of the Roman *limes* – the wall and forts at the northern limit of Roman territory in Germany. Mommsen himself labelled such projects "large-scale scholarship" (*Grosswissenschaft*). He was also an active political liberal in 1848 and later in the Chamber of Deputies in Prussia. Prusso-German liberals tended to moderation, and although Mommsen applauded Bismarck's application of force to German unification, he more often criticized than condoned Bismarck's policies. Thus, Mommsen helped found the left-liberal Progressive party (*Fortschrittspartei*) and energetically defended Jews against his famed colleague Heinrich von Treitschke. He conducted the defense in print, and resigned his secretaryship in the Prussian Academy of Sciences when Treitschke's membership at last became inevitable.

The renewal of Mommsen's reputation in post-1945 Germany resulted in large part from his modeling of a decent, liberal political career. Mommsen was decent beyond any doubt, but his political attitude was not very different from his colleagues'. He merely swam on the left side of the main stream, and by his own declaration was no philo-Semite. Jews as fellow citizens deserved defense from abuse, and Mommsen paid them the odd compliment of claiming that in 19th-century Germany they could again do what they had done for Julius Caesar, namely act as the "ferment of decomposition" by subverting old loyalties and undercutting particularism. In private correspondence he admitted what was implicit in his public utterances: ultimately Jews would have to cease to be Jews in order to become Germans. This was a logical conclusion from his basic political premise. Modern men – he did not think of women as full citizens – were properly members of self-governing, free, yet powerful nation-states. Their citizenries therefore required a high degree of national homogeneity.

He wrote history, in good part, to train such a citizenry; and the history that won him a popular reputation (and his Nobel prize) was his *The History of Rome*. This work, which is now a classic and was an almost immediate success, is a product of an age when synthetic histories graced the homes of educated middle-class families who sometimes read them. Mommsen had these readers in mind when, in the political reaction after 1848 he published volumes 1, 2, and 3 in, respectively, 1854, 1855, and 1856. (He never completed his projected volume 4 on the age from Augustus to Diocletian, though – curiously – in 1885 he published a masterful volume 5 on the Roman provinces.) When he conceived and wrote the first three volumes, Mommsen was still a law professor in his early thirties.

He was also a recently disappointed political advocate. Like other disappointed liberal nationalists in those years, he saw the need to ready Germany for its historical future by writing for its vicarious political instruction a narrative history that was intellectually rigorous yet readable and accessible to the lay public. Droysen and Sybel in particular charted this path. Mommsen's mastery of prose style and knowledge of Latin sources let him perform this task with distinction, even though he did not much consult the work of other recent scholars. *The History of Rome* is a work of limpid, graceful prose, marked by meticulous and persuasive personality sketches of major actors in an account of political and cultural history. The hostile sketches of Cicero as an empty, ineffectual phrase-maker and of Caesar as idealistic opportunist are genial whether right or not. That is why they remain the most read pages that Mommsen wrote.

He intended these sketches as political education not in some crude allegory whereby Cicero simply stood for 1848 liberal chatterboxes and Caesar for Bismarck. Mommsen did not write crudely and, in any case, his opinion of Bismarck was not very flattering, just as his sense of self-reproach as an 1848 liberal was not very intense. He wanted to educate by making Germans understand how politics worked. That meant knowing why a Caesar won. Moreover, the Roman principate, as Mommsen saw, was not a "dyarchy" of *princeps* and Senate but the rule of the *princeps* at most helped by the Senate. Caesar was justified as the creator of the coming thing. Mommsen did not believe in fighting historical success. Despite this strongly political bent, he did not wish partisanship to overcome scholarship. It was Mommsen who made current the demand for "presuppositionless scholarship" (*vorrausset-zungslose Wissenschaft*) while defending a colleague against dismissal on religious grounds.

Mommsen's reputation with his colleagues rested less on *The History of Rome* than on his more specialized, more monographic works – in addition, of course, to the large-scale, ongoing projects that he launched, joined in, and superintended. These included a series of published collections of Roman inscriptions. The earliest of these, the 1852 *Inscriptiones regni Neapolitani Latinae* was instrumental in establishing firmly his academic reputation. There are, in addition, the many essays and articles gathered in the topically organized eight volumes of the *Gesammelte Schriften* published between 1905 and 1913. His most important purely scholarly work was his *Römisches Staatsrecht* (Roman Constitutional Law). He published this huge, technical work section by section and volume by volume between 1871 and 1888 and then issued it in a revised, complete edition in 1893. The work is clearly written, comprehensive, and systematic. As such, it displays Mommsen's celebrated though occasionally criticized power to abstract. Roman law, after all, was made piece by piece, and the Roman codifications came late and after the fact. Mommsen, however, was able to find and express an inner coherence in Roman law that let him infer a Roman constitution from its bits and pieces. The result, arguably, is an inferred clarity and consistency greater than what original Roman institutions actually possessed.

ROBERT FAIRBAIRN SOUTHARD

See also Beloch; Delbrück; Germany: to 1450; Meyer; Niebuhr; Pekař; Religion; Roman; Syme; Wilamovitz-Möllendorff

Biography
Christian Matthias Theodor Mommsen. Born Garding, Schleswig-Holstein, 30 November 1817, son of a Protestant minister. Studied at the Gymnasium Christianeum Altona; University of Kiel, 1838–44. Traveled in Italy, 1844–47. Professor of law, University of Leipzig, 1848–51; University of Zurich, 1852–54; and University of Breslau, 1854–58; professor of Roman history, University of Berlin, 1858–1903. Appointed editor-in-chief, *Corpus Inscriptionum Latinarum*, 1858. Member, Prussian Chamber of Deputies. Awarded Nobel prize for literature, 1902. Married Marie Reimer, 1854 (16 children). Died Charlottenburg, near Berlin, 1 November 1903.

Principal Writings
Editor, *Inscriptiones regni Neapolitani Latinae*, 1852
Römische Geschichte, 3 vols., 1854–56, in English as *The History of Rome*, 4 vols., 1864–75; vol. 5 as *Die Provinzen von Caesar bis Diocletian*, 1885, in English as *The Provinces of the Roman Empire from Caesar to Diocletian*, 1886
Römisches Staatsrecht (Roman Constitutional Law), 3 vols., 1871–88; revised 1893
Römisches Strafrecht (Roman Penal Law), 1899
Gesammelte Schriften (Complete Writings), 8 vols., 1905–13

Further Reading
Christ, Karl, "Theodor Mommsen," in his *Von Gibbon zu Rostovtzeff: Leben und Werk führender Althistoriker der Neuzeit* (From Gibbon to Rostovtzeff: Lives and Work of the Leading Ancient Historians of Modern Times), Darmstadt: Wissenschaftliche Buchgesellschaft, 1972
Heuss, Alfred, *Theodor Mommsen und das 19. Jahrhundert* (Theodor Mommsen and the 19th Century), Kiel: Hirt, 1956
Wickert, Lothar, *Theodor Mommsen: Eine Biographie* (Theodor Mommsen: A Biography), 4 vols., Frankfurt: Klostermann, 1959–80
Wucher, Albert, *Theodor Mommsen: Geschichtsschreibung und Politik* (Thedor Mommsen: Historian and Politics), Göttingen: Musterschmidt, 1956

Mommsen, Wolfgang J. 1930–

German historian

Throughout his long and distinguished academic career Wolfgang J. Mommsen produced an extensive body of work that defies any evident categorization. As a historian, he transcended traditional barriers between social, economic, political, and intellectual history; between continental and British history; between 19th- and 20th-century history; even between history and political philosophy. The result of this constant diffusion of interest and experimentation with new areas of research has been work of both remarkable breadth and fascinating depth, characterized by methodological clarity and interpretive originality.

Mommsen's contribution to the study of 19th- and 20th-century history is attested by the diversity of his themes. His writings have covered such areas as modern German history, imperialism, Max Weber, trade unionism, social protest, and appeasement. In spite of his initial emphasis on German history, he also developed an interest in comparative analysis, either by collating the British and the German models of socioeconomic development or by assessing the impact of key issues (e.g., social protest, appeasement) throughout Europe. His contribution to the analysis of social institutions has been significant, not simply from a historical point of view but also because of his interest in examining them in the present context and in weighing their future prospects.

Mommsen's main area of research has been Bismarckian and Wilhelminian Germany. Among his many writings on this period, the recently published collection *Der autoritäre Nationalstaat* (1990; *Imperial Germany, 1867–1918*, 1995) epitomized the key points in Mommsen's analysis of imperial Germany. He emphasized the tension between persisting authoritarian structures of the German state and the introduction of parliamentary politics, highlighting the failure of constitutional arrangements to regulate political change. He also underlined the inherent social and economic contradictions of the new state, its inability to respond constructively to the new challenges of mass politics and modernization. Mommsen attached particular importance to the period between 1909 and 1914 as the culmination of all the unresolved tensions of unified Germany. He focused his attention on the domestic factors that brought the German state to crisis shortly before the outbreak of World War I. Contrary to the traditional concept of the primacy of foreign affairs, Mommsen argued that the crisis of imperial Germany was mainly a domestic issue. Undoubtedly, lack of program and direction in the Wilhelminian foreign policy aggravated the situation. It was, however, the complete detachment of government from parliament, the ensuing loss of political legitimacy, and the failure of German imperialism to foster economic development or to appease the nationalists that created the domestic deadlock and established war as a solution to crisis.

In order to complement his social and political analysis of German history until 1914, Mommsen also turned to intellectual history and political philosophy. His editorial work on *Intellektuelle im Deutschen Kaiserreich* (Intellectuals in the German *Kaiserreich*, 1993) highlighted the emergence of a new generation of intellectuals in 19th-century Germany who questioned traditional concepts of German culture and put forward a more pluralistic model for a German mass society. He also produced a poignant analysis of Max Weber's thought in *Max Weber und die deutsche Politik, 1890–1920* (1959; *Max Weber and German Politics, 1890–1920*, 1984). Mommsen's interest in Weber has not been mainly philosophical. As a historian, he has incorporated Weber's ideas into the political context of imperial Germany, assessing their inherent contradictions but uncovering their consistent radical-liberal reasoning as a powerful antidote to the official ideology and politics of the Wilhelminian establishment.

Mommsen's interest in modern German history, however, is not confined to the pre-1918 period. He argued that the revolution of 1918 in Germany failed to transform the authoritarian structures of the state. In spite of the introduction of the republic, the position of traditional elite groups was not seriously challenged. He also co-edited *The Fascist Challenge and the Policy of Appeasement* (1983), which analyzed Nazi foreign policy in the context of European appeasement. The volume highlighted the willingness of all European powers to "tame" the emerging fascist challenge by granting concessions, in the hope that they would eventually avoid another military conflict. It also located the fundamental flaws in the political and military doctrines of appeasement, arguing instead that the belated adoption of appeasement policies coincided with an unprecedented increase in Germany's military power. In this sense, it was ill-timed, insufficient for the Nazi leadership, and dangerously deceptive for the rest of Europe.

The comparative dimension in Mommsen's work is manifested in his research on the development of social institutions in Britain and Germany. In *The Emergence of the Welfare State in Britain and Germany, 1850–1950* (1981) he examined how the two countries influenced each other in the construction of welfare state during the 19th and 20th centuries. On a general level, he believed that the comparison between the British and the German models of socioeconomic development was an extremely constructive exercise in comparative history. He also never hesitated to use his historical analysis of welfare state in order to put forward radical ideas about introducing a model of solidarity in the international system, whereby welfare policies would guarantee aid from rich to developing countries.

Mommsen's overall work reflects three major shifts in postwar German historiography. First, as the primacy-of-domestic-policy thesis gained ground, Mommsen placed particular emphasis on the domestic factors that influenced policymaking under the Bismarckian, the Wilhelminian, and the Third Reich. Second, by using his experience from the study of imperial Germany to shed light on the problems of interwar Germany, he underlined continuities in German history and contributed to the historicization of the Third Reich. Finally, although Mommsen located certain peculiarities in the German state and society, he treated German history not in isolation from, but in firm connection with historical developments in the rest of Europe.

ARISTOTLE A. KALLIS

See also Labor

Biography

Wolfgang Justin Mommsen. Born Marburg, 5 November 1930, son of historian Wilhelm Mommsen and twin brother of historian Hans

Mommsen. Attended University of Marburg, 1951–53; PhD, University of Cologne, 1958; post-doctoral study, University of Leeds, 1959. Taught at University of Cologne, 1959–67; and University of Düsseldorf, from 1968; director, German Historical Institute, London, 1978–85. Married Sabine von Schalburg, 1965 (3 daughters, 1 son).

Principal Writings

Max Weber und die deutsche Politik, 1890–1920, 1959, revised 1974; in English as *Max Weber and German Politics, 1890–1920*, 1984

"The Debate on German War Aims," *Journal of Contemporary History* 1 (1966), 47–74

"Die latente Krise des Deutschen Reiches, 1909–1914" (The Latent Crisis of the German Reich, 1904–1914), in *Handbuch der deutschen Geschichte*, vol. 4: *Deutsche Geschichte der neuesten Zeit von Bismarcks Entlassung bis zur Gegenwart*, part 1: *Von 1890 bis 1933*, 1973

The Age of Bureaucracy: Perspectives on the Political Sociology of Max Weber, 1974

Imperialismustheorien, 1977; in English as *Theories of Imperialism*, 1980

Der europäische Imperialismus: Aufsätze und Abhandlungen, 1979

Editor with Wolfgang Mock, *The Emergence of the Welfare State in Britain and Germany, 1850–1950*, 1981

Editor with Gerhard Hirschfeld, *Sozialprotest, Gewalt, Terror: Gewaltanwendung durch politische und gesellschaftliche Randgruppen im 19. und 20. Jahrhundert*, 1982; in English as *Social Protest, Violence, and Terror in Nineteenth- and Twentieth-Century Europe*, 1982

Editor with Lothar Kettenacker, *The Fascist Challenge and the Policy of Appeasement*, 1983

Editor with Hans-Gerhard Husung, *The Development of Trade Unionism in Great Britain and Germany, 1880–1914*, 1985

Editor with Jürgen Osterhammel, *Imperialism and After: Continuities and Discontinuities*, 1986

Editor with Stig Förster and Ronald E. Robinson, *Bismarck, Europe, and Africa: The Berlin Africa Conference, 1884–1885, and the Onset of Partition*, 1988

The Political and Social Theory of Max Weber: Collected Essays, 1989

Der autoritäre Nationalstaat: Verfassung, Gesellschaft und Kultur des deutschen Kaiserreiches, Frankfurt: Fischer, 1990; in English as *Imperial Germany, 1867–1918: Politics, Culture, and Society in an Authoritarian State*, London and New York: Arnold, 1995

Editor with Gangolf Hubinger, *Intellektuelle im Deutschen Kaiserreich* (Intellectuals in the German *Kaiserreich*), 1993

Mongol Empire

The history of the Mongol empire dates back to 1206 when Temüjin was proclaimed Genghis Khan or Great Khan of all the Mongols, establishing a united Mongol feudal state. The first major studies of the history of the empire were not undertaken until the 19th century. Since then practically all historians have focused mainly on reproducing a narrative of Mongolian history based on various contemporary chronicles, such as *Niguca Tobchiyan* and *Yüan ch'ao pi shih* (The Secret History of the Mongols, 1982). There have been several controversial areas that have attracted the attention of scholars and given rise to discussion. The first revolved around the social and political organization of the nomadic peoples of the Mongol plain. Soviet and Mongolian historians in *Istoriia*

Mongolskoi Narodnoi Respubliki (History of the Mongolian People's Republic, 1954) emphasized that the unification of different Mongolian tribes was the final stage in the formation of a feudal state on the territory of present-day Mongolia. Boris Vladimirtsov in *Obschestvennyi stroi mongolov* (The Social System of the Mongols, 1934) and Ralph Fox in *Genghis Khan* (1936) pointed out that Mongolian feudal lords (*noyod*), who opted to keep their private herds separately and to lead a nomadic life based around a clan (*ayil*), required a centralized and powerful state to provide for their security and well-being, as well as to give them means to keep their vassals, and to strengthen their power over the common nomad (*arat*). Moreover, all these historians stressed the important role of the *nökör* – "free companions" who abandoned their own clan to obligate themselves to each other – whose activities also stimulated the formation of the empire. What is more, Genghis Khan's charismatic personality and his success as a military leader helped to recruit new followers. In *Turkestan v epokhu mongol'skogo nashestviia* (1898–1900; vol. 2 as *Turkestan Down to the Mongol Invasion*, 1928) Vasilii Bartol'd postulated that the rise of Genghis Khan could be explained by the policy of "divide and rule." This had long been the practice of the Chinese towards their nomadic tribesmen neighbors, and their initial response to the success of Temüjin was seen in this context. They believed the warring among the Mongols would waste energy better turned against China itself.

A second problem centered on the figure of Genghis Khan himself. Historians have recognized Genghis Khan's decisive role in Mongolia's history as the founder of a unique nomadic empire, but assessing the long-term results of his vision of a Mongol empire has been harder. His administrative and military reforms could have promoted the prosperity of Mongolia, but instead he chose to continue with a state based around constant warfare. Vladimirtsov, the contributors to the *Istoriia Mongolskoi Narodnoi Respubliki*, and the Mongolian historian Chuluung Dalai in his *Mongolia v XIII–XIV vekah* (Mongolia in the 13th–14th Centuries, 1983) all maintained that the Mongols' campaigns were pernicious not only for the conquered nations but for the conquerors as well, since the population of Mongolia considerably decreased as a result of permanent warfare which also dissipated plundered wealth.

Genghis Khan and his successors are notorious for their military campaigns against other nations. The reason for these campaigns, as Soviet historians have put it, was the limited economic basis of cattle-breeding. The pastoral economy of the Mongols could not satisfy the growing needs of the *noyod*, and conquests were necessary to smooth over inner contradictions in Mongol society. Moreover, Fox argued that Genghis Khan had no opportunity to conduct profitable trade with his neighbors because all were in decay. Less economic approaches have included that of the English historian Henry Howorth who, in his *History of the Mongols from the 9th to the 19th Century* (1876) painted Genghis Khan as the scourge of God. Howorth was merely repeating a traditional idea expressed in various Armenian annals such as *Istoriia mongolov inoka Magakii, XIII veka* (History of the Mongols by the 13th-Century Monk, Magakia, 1871). In *The Mongols and Russia* (1953) George Vernadsky also spoke about the divine mission of Genghis Khan, whom Vernadsky saw as imbued with an imperial idea and the wish to unite all nomads of the steppes.

This is similar to the position of Nikolai Veselovskii in *Lektsii po istorii mongolov* (Lectures on History of the Mongols, 1909). He considered Genghis Khan to be the only person capable of awakening the Mongols and harnessing their belligerent spirit in order to push them towards conquering new lands. Bartol'd concluded that Genghis Khan cared little about the well-being of the Mongols, but rather was preoccupied with increasing his own wealth and the living standards of his relatives and close friends.

A third problem dealt with approaches to the rapid decline of the empire after Genghis Khan's death. Vladimirtsov pointed out that the new state system was not strong enough to withstand challenges. Genghis Khan had seized power and then legitimized it at the *kuriltai* (tribal council). This led to conflict among his descendants and undermined the strength of the subsequent rulers. By the 1360s such provinces as the Golden Horde and the Mongol state in Iran and the Transcaucasian region had severed their ties to the central power and begun to pursue their own policies. Vladimirtsov and Fox attributed the disintegration of the empire to a lack of clan unity and the increasing influence of the non-Mongol peoples. According to Veselovskii, after Genghis Khan's grandson Kublai Khan conquered China in 1271, the Chinese simply assimilated the Mongols and made them submit to the huge Chinese bureaucratic machine. Chinese historians, such as Yui Bayan in his 1955 biography of Genghis Khan, have denied that the period of 1271–1368 was a period of Mongolian dominance; instead they have deemed it to be a footnote to Chinese history. In this connection Chuluung Dalai has emphasized the progressive role of Kublai's brother Arigböge, and of his cousin Kaidu, who each fought against him in order to keep the political center of the empire in Mongolia, fearing its relegation to the periphery. According to both Veselovskii and to Bira in *Mongolskaia istoriografiia* (Mongolian Historiography, 1978), the Yüan dynasty collapsed under the religious influence of the Buddhists whose intrigues and conspiracies weakened Mongol authority. The Mongols were also strained by the need to maintain a large army to suppress the uprisings of the peoples they had conquered. As the empire was based on a military force, their economy was quickly exhausted by military expenditures, and there was no common economic basis that could integrate the peoples of this multinational state. In 1368 the Yüan dynasty was overthrown, putting an end to the Mongol empire while the core of it – Mongolia – lapsed into tribal disunity and feudal wars.

DMITRI POLIKANOV

See also Bartol'd; China: Late Imperial; China: Historical Writing, Late Imperial; Ibn Khaldūn; Korea; Middle East; Paris; Pelliot; Rashīd; Russia: Medieval; Russia: Early Modern; Vernadsky

Further Reading

Akademiia Nauk SSSR, *Istoriia Mongolskoi Narodnoi Respubliki* (History of the Mongolian People's Republic) Moscow: Nauka, 1954; Cambridge, MA: Harvard University Press for the East Asian Research Center, 1976

Bartol'd, Vasilii, *Turkestan v epokhu mongol'skogo nashestviia*, 2 vols., St. Petersburg: Akademiia Nauk, 1898–1900; vol. 2 in English revised as *Turkestan Down to the Mongol Invasion*, London: Luzac, 1928; revised with additional chapter, London: Luzac, 1968, Philadelphia: Porcupine, 1977

Bira, Sh., *Mongolskaia istoriografiia (XIII–XVII veka)* (Mongolian Historiography, 13th–17th centuries), Moscow: Nauka, 1978

Brent, Peter L., *The Mongol Empire: Genghis Khan, His Triumph and Legacy*, London: Weidenfeld and Nicolson, 1976

Dalai, Chuluung, *Mongolia v XIII–XIV vekah* (Mongolia in the 13th–14th Centuries), Moscow: Nauka, 1983

Dalai, Chuluung, "Chingishan i velikoe mongolskoie gosudarstvo" (Genghis Khan and the Great Mongol State), *Problemy Dal'nego Vostoka* 6 (1992)

Fox, Ralph, *Genghis Khan*, London: Lane, 1936

Grousset, René, *L'Empire des steppes: Attila, Genghis-Khan, Tamerlan*, Paris: Payot, 1939; in English as *The Empire of the Steppes: A History of Central Asia*, New Brunswick, NJ: Rutgers University Press, 1970

Grousset, René, *Le Conquérant du monde: la vie du Gengis-khan*, Paris: Michel, 1944; in English as *Conqueror of the World*, New York: Orion, 1966, London: Oliver and Boyd, 1967

Gumilev, Lev Nikolaevich, "Ludi i priroda velikoi stepi" (People and Nature of the Great Steppe), *Voprosy istorii* 11 (1987)

Howorth, Henry Hoyle, *History of the Mongols from the 9th to the 19th Century*, London: Longman, 1876

Istoriia mongolov ot drevneishikh vremen do Tamerlana (History of the Mongols from Ancient Times to Tamerlane), St. Petersburg, 1834

Istoriia mongolov inoka Magakii, XIII veka (History of the Mongols by the 13th-Century Monk, Magakia), St. Petersburg, 1871

Kapitsa, Mikhail Stepanovich, "Esche raz o roli Chingishana v istorii" (Once Again about the Role of Genghis Khan in History), *Voprosy istorii* 7 (1988)

Lister, Richard Percival, *Genghis Khan*, New York: Stein and Day, 1969; published in the UK as *The Secret History of Ghengis Khan*, London: Davies, 1969

Mailla, Joseph-Anne-Marie de Moyriac de, *Histoire générale de la Chine ou annales de cet Empire* (General history of China; or, The annals of This Empire), vols. 9–11 of 13, Paris: Clousier, 1777–85

Martin, Henry Desmond, *The Rise of Chingis Khan and His Conquest of North China*, Baltimore: Johns Hopkins Press, 1950

Ohsson, Constantin d', *Histoire des Mongols depuis Tchinguiz-khan jusqu'à Timour Bey ou Tamerlan* (History of the Mongols from Genghis Khan up to Timur-bei or Tamerlane), 4 vols., The Hague: Van Cleef, 1834–35

Pelliot, Paul, and Louis Hambis, trans., *Histoire des campagnes de Gengis-khan* (History of the Genghis Khan's campaigns), Leiden: Brill, 1951

Phillips, E.D., *The Mongols*, New York: Praeger, and London: Thames and Hudson, 1969

Prawdin, Michael, *The Mongol Empire: Its Rise and Legacy*, London: Allen and Unwin, and New York: Macmillan, 1940

Rachewiltz, Igor de, *Papal Envoys to the Great Khans*, Stanford, CA: Stanford University Press, and London: Faber, 1971

Saunders, J.J., *The History of the Mongol Conquest*, London: Routledge, 1971

Smirnov, K., *Armiia mongolov v XIII veke. Po zapiskam sovremennika-evropeitsa* (The Mongol Army in the 13th Century as Described by a European Contemporary), St. Petersburg, 1903

Vernadsky, George, *The Mongols and Russia*, New Haven: Yale University Press, 1953

Vladimirtsov, Boris, *Chingis-khan*, St. Petersburg: Grzhebin, 1922; in English as *The Life of Chingis-Khan*, London: Routledge, and Boston: Houghton Mifflin, 1930

Vladimirtsov, Boris, *Obschestvennyi stroi mongolov: Mongol'skii kochevoi feodalizm* (The Social System of the Mongols: Mongolian Nomadic Feudalism), Leningrad, 1934; in French as *Le Régime social des Mongols: le féodalisme nomade*, Paris: Musée Guimet, 1948

Yüan ch'ao pi shih; in English as *The Secret History of the Mongols*, edited and translated by Francis Woodman Cleaves, Cambridge, MA: Harvard University Press, vol. 1, 1982

Montesquieu 1689–1755

French philosopher

Montesquieu was one of the first, if not the very first, of the 18th-century philosophical historians. Although his most famous work, *De l'Esprit des lois* (1748; *The Spirit of the Laws*, 1748) influenced the development of political and sociological thought, especially among English writers, Montesquieu began his attempt to explain the causes of social change with the publication of the *Considérations sur les causes de la grandeur des romains et de leur décadence* (1734; *The Greatness of the Romans and Their Decline*, 1965). That historical study was philosophical because it sought to explain history by connecting historical events to changes in social and legal structures. The lives of heroes and the exposition of divine purposes were abandoned in favor of the pursuit of secular causes of historical events. This new method of history, therefore, was philosophical in the sense that it was critical and in the sense that it was empirical, or scientific. In writing the history of Rome's decline, Montesquieu hoped to discover the laws of history. Law, to Montesquieu, was "that which arranges things." So the laws of history, in contemporary historiographical terms, would be discovered by investigating the relations between state and society.

Montesquieu's history of Rome is the least known of his works today, yet it was in the *Considérations* that he developed the method that would influence Hume, Gibbon, Raynal, and others. Roman history was known to his readers, it offered the opportunity to investigate both a republic and an empire, and its historical record was relatively complete, so it was a logical subject for the new kind of history. After considering Rome's transformation from a republic into an empire, Montesquieu developed a general theory of causation:

> It is not fortune that rules the world. On this point, consult the Romans who enjoyed a series of consecutive successes when their government followed one policy, and an unbroken set of reverses when it adopted another. There are general causes, whether moral or physical, which act upon every monarchy, which advance, maintain, or ruin it. All accidents are subject to these causes. If the chance loss of a battle, that is, a particular cause, ruins a state, there is a general cause that created the situation whereby this state could perish by the loss of a single battle.

Thus, for Montesquieu, historical knowledge did not depend on understanding the role of political or military heroes or even political or military events, but on understanding the significance of social, economic, and institutional changes.

The importance of Montesquieu's new philosophical, or scientific, method was recognized in Diderot's *Encyclopédie*, where the article "Observation" compared Montesquieu's empirical method to that of natural philosophy. Montesquieu's history of Rome was offered as the example of the superiority of the method of observation, "the primary foundation of all the sciences . . . the principal means of extending the circumference of scientific knowledge." Montesquieu had done more than accumulate and record the facts. He had revealed the relations between the facts and shown how they were connected. By doing

so, the encyclopedist declared, his history of Rome had made a significant contribution to the new "human sciences."

HUGH L. GUILDERSON

See also Gatterer; Historical Geography; Niebuhr; Raynal

Biography

Charles-Louis de Secondat, Baron de la Brède et de Montesquieu. Born La Brède, Bordeaux, 18 January 1689, to an aristocratic family; inherited La Brède after his mother's death in 1695. Educated at Collège de Juilly, near Paris, to 1705; then in the faculty of law, University of Bordeaux. Called to the Bar, 1708; practiced in Paris, 1708–13; had a judicial career as councillor, Bordeaux parlement, 1714–16, president, 1716–26, before retiring to travel to Germany, Austria, Italy, Switzerland, Holland, and England, 1728–31. Wrote on a variety of philosophical, legal, and historical topics from 1721. Married Jeanne de Lartigue, 1715 (2 daughters, 1 son). Died Paris, 10 February 1755.

Principal Writings

Lettres persanes, 1721; in English as *The Persian Letters*, 1961
Considérations sur les causes de la grandeur des romains et de leur décadence 1734; in English as *The Greatness of the Romans and Their Decline*, 1965
De l'Esprit des lois, 1748; in English as *The Spirit of the Laws*, 1748

Further Reading

Althusser, Louis, *Montesquieu: la politique et l'histoire*, Paris: Presses Universitaires de France, 1959; in English as *Politics and History: Montesquieu, Rousseau, Hegel, and Marx*, London: NLB, 1972
Aron, Raymond, *Les Etapes de la pensée sociologique*, enlarged edition, Paris: Gallimard, 1967; in English as *Main Currents in Sociological Thought*, vol. 1, New York: Basic Books, 1965
Barckhausen, Henri-Auguste, *Montesquieu: ses idées et ses oeuvres*, Paris: Hachette, 1907
Hampson, Norman, "Montesquieu," in his *Will and Circumstance: Montesquieu, Rousseau, and the French Revolution*, Norman: University of Oklahoma Press, and London: Duckworth, 1983
Hulliung, Mark, *Montesquieu and the Old Regime*, Berkeley: University of California Press, 1976
Keohane, Nannerl O., *Philosophy and the State in France: The Renaissance to the Enlightenment*, Princeton: Princeton University Press, 1980
Neumann, Franz, "Introduction," to Montesquieu, *The Spirit of the Laws*, New York: Hafner, 1949
Richter, Melvin, ed., *The Political Theory of Montesquieu*, Cambridge and New York: Cambridge University Press, 1977
Shackleton, Robert, *Montesquieu: A Critical Biography*, Oxford: Oxford University Press, 1961
Shklar, Judith, *Montesquieu*, Oxford and New York: Oxford University Press, 1987
Starobinski, Jean, *Montesquieu*, Paris: Seuil, 1953

Montgomery, David 1927–

US labor historian

Regarded as the pre-eminent historian of the United States workplace, David Montgomery is perhaps more rightly associated with the depth of his knowledge of class formation in America and his grasp of international issues and historiographies. Few historians of the United States working class have ranged as broadly over the course of the 19th and 20th centuries; fewer still can punctuate their writings with references to studies in Italian and French, alluding to transatlantic migrations, European social democratic traditions, and the militant stands of Canadian miners. Montgomery continually reaches for understanding of the "big picture" and, if his books and essays occasionally fall short of sustaining an assertive thesis, they nevertheless always illuminate obscured histories of central importance in the making of working-class America.

Schooled in the Communist party, the machinist's trade, and labor unions, as well as in traditional academic training, Montgomery brings deep commitments and vital sensitivities to his studies of workers. Montgomery is attracted to the mechanisms by which workers exert limited control over their lives, which are often governed by imperatives not of their making; he is necessarily concerned with the economics of production, the politics of opposition, and the culture of class institutions, from neighborhoods and families to taverns and leisure activities.

Intrigued by the post-Civil War clash of Radical Republicans, struggling to resolve the question of race in American political economy, and labor reformers, who demanded that "class" inequality be addressed as well, Montgomery's early research produced a stunningly original account of the years immediately preceding the depression of the 1870s. Breathtaking in its interpretive boldness, Montgomery's *Beyond Equality* (1967) lured students into the world of working-class institutions ideas and industrial struggles via a contentious thesis that Radical Republicanism foundered on the shoals of class conflict.

Before turning to the history of the workplace in the later 19th and 20th centuries, Montgomery produced much-read articles on workers and the preindustrial city, and on artisans and nativism. Appearing at just the moment that many "new left" graduate students began research projects that would later flourish as the "new labor history," these studies, as well as Montgomery's Radical America pamphlet, *What's Happening to the American Worker* (1969), established his reputation in the overlapping circles of activist and academic labor history. A late 1960s stint working alongside E.P. Thompson at the University of Warwick consolidated this prestige, and many graduate students were drawn to Montgomery's imaginatively constructed working-class history seminars at the University of Pittsburgh.

It was in this period that Montgomery began the studies of shopfloor practices that consolidated forms of workers' control at the very peak of American capitalism and managerial innovation (Taylorism and other rigorous efforts to curb the craftsman). These essays eventually appeared in *Workers' Control in America* (1979). Montgomery wove together accounts of 19th-century union work rules, immigrant workers, managerial reform, machinists and the Socialist party, and the World War I battle over whose standards – workers' or employers' – would prevail in industry. He closed the collection with a synthetic *tour de force,* a suggestive account of the state and the workplace that drew on his own researches as well as firsthand experiences with movements that attempted to transcend the coercions and concessions of Washington's ongoing "New Deal Formula." Criticized for his romanticization of craft sectionalism and his inattention to the powerful fragmenting forces of race and gender, Montgomery continued to research and think

through the nature of workplace/state relations and class struggle. His 1987 book *The Fall of the House of Labor* presented a brilliant reconstruction of the layering of working-class America, the first three chapters outlining the experiences of skilled workers, common laborers, and semi-skilled operatives in ways that incorporated race and gender into an appreciation of the pervasive class struggle endemic to the late 19th century. The latter half of the book traced the theme of working-class political and industrial opposition through to the mid-1920s, offering readers a cascade of insights and imaginative interpretations scaffolded on wide reading and empirically researched case studies.

Many critics thought the book less than they had been waiting for, but in looking for the focused thesis, convincingly packaged, they were perhaps expecting what Montgomery rarely produced. His strength as a historian seldom manifested itself in the routine narrative and narrowly-construed academic project. Rather, Montgomery's range across boundaries – both geographic and analytic – and his refusal to be cornered into a particularity meant that he wrote with the intention of graphic generalization, the suggestive parts of the whole often, in the end, outweighing in significance the concluding arguments.

Montgomery's latest book, *Citizen Worker* (1993), returns to themes he first addressed in his studies of Radical Republicanism in the 1960s. Perplexed by the ease with which market "freedoms" and the supposed "values" and citizenship practices of "representative" democracy were ideologically conflated in the 1990s, Montgomery looked to the experience of workers in the 19th-century United States with the economic and political realities of bourgeois order. He found a paradox. Popular democracy expanded in the formal sense, but grew at the same time as the substantive restrictions of exploitative "free" market relations circumscribed its material meanings, narrowing the role of "government." Studies of master-servant doctrine and the bondage of African American workers, the policing of the dangerous classes, and labor's relation to the established political party system provide the substance of his commentary.

To appreciate Montgomery is to appreciate the complexity and combativeness of American workers. His texts are never far from the workplace, where so much of class antagonism is born, but they are not removed from other spaces where identities and understandings are also forged. No historian of United States workers can capture the lived experience of labor as Montgomery has for the last thirty years. Watching him perform in a public lecture has always been observing a theatrical act of reconstruction: the text unfolds as Montgomery revels in the culture of the Chicago anarcho-communist milieu, parading across the stage in ribald ribbing of the 19th-century bourgeoisie, or bends over the arduous tasks of rough canal navvies or sweat-drenched puddlers. Whatever his subject, his concern is work and the politics of change. Quoting Samuel Gompers at the end of *Citizen Worker,* Montgomery summarizes his own perspective: "There never yet existed coincident with each other autocracy in the shop and democracy in political life."

BRYAN D. PALMER

See also Commons; Labor; Social; United States: Historical Writing, 20th Century

Biography

Born Bryn Mawr, Pennsylvania, 1 December 1927. Received BA, Swarthmore College, 1950; MA, University of Minnesota, 1960, PhD 1962. Taught at Hamline University, 1962–63; University of Pittsburgh, 1963–77; University of Warwick, 1967–69; State University of New York, Buffalo, 1977–78; and Yale University from 1979. Married (2 children).

Principal Writings

Beyond Equality: Labor and the Radical Republicans, 1862–1872, 1967

Labor History, 1968

What's Happening to the American Worker, 1969

Workers' Control in America: Studies in the History of Work, Technology, and Labor Struggles, 1979

The Fall of the House of Labor: The Workplace, the State, and American Labor Activism, 1865–1925, 1987

Citizen Worker: The Experience of Workers in the United States with Democracy and the Free Market During the Nineteenth Century, 1993

Further Reading

Abelove, Henry *et al.*, eds., *Visions of History*, by MARHO: The Radical Historians Organisation, Manchester: Manchester University Press, and New York: Pantheon, 1983

Brody, David, "The Old Labor History and the New: In Search of an American Working Class," *Labor History* 20 (1979), 111–26

Kealey, Gregory S., "Gutman and Montgomery: Politics and Direction of Labor and Working-Class History in the United States," *International Labor and Working-Class History* 37 (1990), 58–68

Monds, Jean, "Workers' Control and the Historians: A New Economism," *New Left Review*, 97 (May 1976), 81–100

Montgomery, David, "Thinking about American Workers in the 1920s," with responses by Susan Porter Benson and Charles S. Maier, *International Labor and Working Class History*, 32 (1987), 4–38

"A Symposium on *The Fall of the House of Labor*," *Labor History* 30 (1989), 93–137

Wiener, Jonathan M., "Radical Historians and the Crisis in American History," in his *Professors: Politics, and Pop*, London and New York: Verso, 1991

Moody, T.W. 1907–1984

Irish historian

T.W. Moody was a leading historian of Ireland, and was perhaps the leading promoter of modern Irish historical practice. In his many roles as mentor, historian, editor, and public cultural figure Moody had an impact on the practice of Irish history that is without equal. In the process Moody's legacy has become the source of some controversy within Ireland, as his emphasis on demythologizing Ireland's past through detailed research in primary sources, and his disinterest in theoretical problems, played a major role in the development of a selfconsciously "revisionist" history of Ireland.

Perhaps because of Moody's lack of interest in theory it is not easy to characterize his research interests and publications. Author of three major books, *The Londonderry Plantation, 1609–41* (1939); *Queen's Belfast, 1845–1949* (1959); and *Davitt and Irish Revolution, 1846–82* (1981), as well as co-author/editor of the most widely read Irish history text, *The*

Course of Irish History (1967), Moody's writings all bear the hallmark of extensive research into primary documents and a rich awareness of the historiography of his various subjects. Despite the step forward his *Londonderry Plantation* came to represent in Irish social history, it is not Moody's research that reveals the important place he came to have in the practice of Irish history. Moody's significance is due more to his promotion of his profession and his general cultural and pedagogical influence over large numbers of graduate students than it is to his particular skill as a historian.

Along with his former student Robert Dudley Edwards, Moody played the decisive role in the founding of two historical societies, one in Belfast in 1936 and another in Dublin in 1937, with the expressed goal of creating a more formal academic tone in the practice of Irish history. This was followed by the establishment of the first Irish historical journal, *Irish Historical Studies*, in 1938 with Moody and Edwards as co-editors. The editors hoped to emulate the standards of journals such as the *English Historical Review* or the *Historische Zeitschrift* to encourage archival research into unused sources at the same time that they acknowledged that the project intended to increase knowledge of Ireland's past among teachers and the public. Critical to this effort was confronting historical "myth" and fostering the "revision" of that history. Moody and Edwards admitted that what they had in mind was an agenda akin to that of the London-based Historical Association, founded on the notion of "fact"-driven history, dedicated to increasing accurate public understanding of the past.

This project moved beyond the usual work of academic historians. With time Moody came to take a pivotal role on a number of governmental and quasi-governmental bodies focused on disseminating Irish history through radio and television broadcasts both in Northern Ireland and in the Republic. Out of a series of 21 television lectures came *The Course of Irish History*, co-authored/edited with F.X. Martin, which has remained in print in revised editions ever since.

In academic history Moody's accomplishments with *Irish Historical Studies* were paralleled in his role in the 1940s in developing monograph series publishing dissertations in Irish history, first with the publishers Faber and Faber and then with Routledge and Kegan Paul. He followed this with his grandly envisioned *A New History of Ireland*. In his 1967 presidential address to the Irish Historical Society, Moody announced a monumental multivolume and multi-author project to create a standard history of Ireland conceived along the lines of the Cambridge histories. This project was slow to develop and resulted in only one published volume and the completion of another at the time of Moody's death in 1984. Nonetheless, the project continues to publish additional volumes in the series.

Moody's writing was varied, detailed, archivally driven, and bears the marks of a considerable stylist. But his agenda was much more theoretically determined than he was aware of or willing to admit. The focus on myth and demythologizing, and the assumption of a more "objectively based" history, particularly in the Irish context, has led to criticism that Moody and his students were and are revisionists determined to deny the nationalist vision of the Irish past – a debate with profound implications for present-day Irish politics and culture. While this criticism of many of those who followed his lead has merit, Moody's own work was notable for its tolerance and openmindedness. His work on the Irish landowning classes anticipated much of the literature that followed him in its insistence on a broader, and less hostile, approach to the oft-maligned landowners. However, his work on the radical land agitator Michael Davitt is open to criticism as too accepting of Davitt within a legal and constitutional tradition in 19th-century politics – it is clearly the work of an admirer who wished Davitt to be seen as an exemplar.

Moody's accomplishment has been a profound one. In many respects he made the practice of Irish history what it is today and because of it deserves praise and criticism. Without *Irish Historical Studies* it is difficult to see how Irish history would have moved past a 19th-century nationalist agenda, but with it, the criticism that Irish history is now mainly revisionist and positivist, often imitative of British historical models, and with little awareness of the theoretical problems inherent in a practice of "scientific" history, seems hard to refute. Nevertheless, as a part of a tradition in European historiography, and more specifically as a part of the British tradition of historiography, Moody's career and influence in Irish history are almost without equal.

SEÁN FARRELL MORAN

See also Ireland; Lyons

Biography

Theodore William Moody. Born Belfast, 26 November 1907, son of an engineer. Educated at Royal Academical Institution, Belfast; BA, Queen's University, Belfast, 1930; PhD, Institute of Historical Research, 1934. Taught at Queen's University, Belfast, 1932–39; fellow/professor, Trinity College, Dublin, 1939–77 (emeritus). Married Margaret C.P. Robertson, 1935 (1 son, 4 daughters). Died 11 February 1984.

Principal Writings

The Londonderry Plantation, 1609–41: The City of London and the Plantation in Ulster, 1939
Thomas Davis, 1814–45, 1945
Editor with J.C. Beckett, *Ulster since 1800: A Political and Economic Survey*, 1954
"Twenty Years After," *Irish Historical Studies* 11 (1958–59), 1–4
With J.C. Beckett, *Queen's Belfast, 1845–1949: The History of a University*, 2 vols., 1959
Editor with Francis X. Martin, *The Course of Irish History*, 1967
"Thirty Years' Work in Irish History (I)" *Irish Historical Studies* 15/60 (September 1967), 359–90
"A New History of Ireland," *Irish Historical Studies* 16 (1969), 241–57
Editor, *Irish Historiography 1936–1970*, 1971
The Ulster Question, 1603–1973, 1974
Editor with others, *A New History of Ireland*, 1976–
"Irish History and Irish Mythology," *Hermathena* 124 (1978), 7–24
Editor, *Nationality and the Pursuit of National Independence*, 1978
Davitt and Irish Revolution, 1846–82, 1981
Editor with Richard Hawkins and Margaret Moody, *Florence Arnold Foster's Irish Diary*, 1988

Further Reading

Brady, Ciaran, "'Constructive and Instrumental': The Dilemma of Ireland's First 'New Historians,'" in Ciaran Brady, ed., *Interpreting Irish History: The Debate on Historical Revisionism*, Dublin: Irish Academic Press, 1994

Lyons, F.S.L., and R.A.J. Hawkins, eds., *Ireland under the Union: Varieties of Tension: Essays in Honour of T.W. Moody*, Oxford and New York: Oxford University Press, 1980
Mulvey, Helen F., "Theodore William Moody (1907–1984): An Appreciation," *Irish Historical Studies* 24 (1984–85), 121–30

Moore, Barrington, Jr. 1913–

US sociologist and political theorist

Barrington Moore, Jr. is the author of seminal books on an astonishing variety of topics, from specific studies of Soviet politics and society to a wide-ranging investigation of the origins of conceptions of privacy in antiquity. All of his work, as James J. Sheehan has observed, combines the conservative's sense of the harsh limits of the human condition with the radical's anger at the persistence of injustice. But one book stands out as his masterpiece: *Social Origins of Dictatorship and Democracy* (1966) is among the most influential and widely cited works of the 1960s. Moore is a sociologist and political theorist with intellectual debts to both Marx and Weber, and he is skilled in the art of using historical studies for comparative purposes. His great book combined a global thesis about the social origins of political regimes with extensive case studies of specific patterns of development in England, France, the United States, China, Japan, and India.

Moore argued that in order to understand why certain social and political alignments have proven more favorable to democratic outcomes than others, it is essential to investigate agrarian social relations, and particularly the fates of landlords and peasants during the process of modernization. If a powerful class of privileged nobles presides over the transition to commercial agriculture, they are likely at some stage to form antidemocratic coalitions with large industrialists: the result may be some form of fascist dictatorship (Japan, Germany). If oppressed peasants persist in large numbers, and the landlord class succeeds in inhibiting the development of a bourgeoisie, the eventual result may be a peasant revolution that issues in a communist dictatorship (China, Russia). Only if the combination of labor-repressive landlords and non-commercial peasants is dissolved in the course of historical development is a democratic outcome likely. But such a consummation is rarely achieved, according to Moore, without some episode of violence (the French Revolution, the American Civil War) or some measure of coercion (the English enclosure movement). And where no dissolution of the backward agricultural sector occurs, the result is stagnation (India).

This bold argument elicited cloudbursts of criticism – from specialists who questioned Moore's grasp of the literatures of their particular fields, from conservatives who objected to his neo-Marxian emphasis on conflicts and coalitions between social classes, and from liberals who objected to his suggestion that social revolution has been a prerequisite for democracy. Ten years after *Social Origins* appeared, Jonathan Wiener published a brilliant survey of several dozen substantial critiques. And thirty years after its initial publication, the book is widely recognized as a classic contribution to modern historical sociology, a provocative stimulus to further comparative analysis by admirers and critics alike.

In subsequent books Moore continued to pose large questions and to examine the causes, costs, and limits of revolutionary action. In *Reflections on the Causes of Human Misery, and upon Certain Proposals to Eliminate Them* (1972), a small book with a grand 18th-century title, he examined the structural bases of predatory politics in the contemporary world. In *Injustice* (1978), he turned to the case of German workers in the 19th and 20th centuries, looking for the factors that determined either revolutionary action or political passivity at critical points in modern German history. Here the emphasis was on working-class consciousness and agency, and Moore's conclusions about the efforts of German workers at once to preserve and to renegotiate the terms of the social contract ran very close (though in a more pessimistic key) to E.P. Thompson's conclusions about the making of the English working class.

Like Thompson, Moore tended increasingly in his later work to draw on the insights of anthropology. But whereas Thompson (the romantic) used anthropological concepts to illuminate specific aspects of a particular culture, Moore (the rationalist) was in search of certain universal features of the human condition: conceptions of injustice, of reciprocity, of privacy, that transcend the limits of any one culture. Hence his use of the comparative method and his willingness to pursue data and to draw conclusions from very diverse types of societies. The result has been an extraordinary body of work, which continues to stimulate bold approaches to comparative historical studies.

BRUCE THOMPSON

See also Mayer; Sociology; Tilly, C.; World

Biography

Born Washington, DC, 12 May 1913, son of a forestry engineer. Received BA, Williams College, 1936; PhD, Yale University, 1941. Research analyst, US Justice Department, 1941–43; and Office of Strategic Services, 1943–45. Taught at University of Chicago, 1945–48; professor, Harvard University, from 1948. Married Elizabeth Carol, 1944.

Principal Writings

Soviet Politics – The Dilemma of Power: The Role of Ideas in Social Change, 1950
Terror and Progress USSR: Some Sources of Change and Stability in the Soviet Dictatorship, 1954
Political Power and Social Theory, 1958
Social Origins of Dictatorship and Democracy: Lord and Peasant in the Making of the Modern World, 1966
Reflections on the Causes of Human Misery and upon Certain Proposals to Eliminate Them, 1972
Injustice: The Social Bases of Obedience and Revolt, 1978
Privacy: Studies in Social and Cultural History, 1984
Moral Aspects of Economic Growth, and Other Essays, 1998

Further Reading

Sheehan, James J., "Barrington Moore on Obedience and Revolt," *Theory and Society* 9 (1980), 723–34
Smith, Dennis, *Barrington Moore: Violence, Morality and Political Change*, London: Macmillan, 1983; as *Barrington Moore, Jr: A Critical Appraisal*, Armonk, NY: Sharpe, 1983
Stone, Lawrence, "Revolution and Reaction," in his *The Past and the Present Revisited*, London: Routledge, 1987
Wiener, Jonathan M., "Review of Reviews: *Social Origins of Dictatorship and Democracy*," *History and Theory* 15 (1976), 146–75

Zelnik, Reginald, "Passivity and Protest in Germany and Russia: Barrington Moore's Conception of Working-Class Responses to Injustice," *Journal of Social History* 15 (1982), 485–512

Moreno Fraginals, Manuel 1920–
Cuban historian of Latin America

Few historians of Latin America have had the enormous influence of Manuel Moreno Fraginals, born in Cuba in 1920 and still active in research, teaching, and writing in 1998. His has been an unusual and extraordinary career. After a degree in law at the University of Havana, Moreno studied history with the eminent Silvio Zavala and Rafael Altamira at the Colegio de México in the mid-1940s. In Mexico he began a steady stream of publications that explored several aspects of Mexican and Cuban history and society, notably *¿Nación o plantación?* (Nation or Plantation?, 1948), *Augustín de Iturbide: Caudillo* (Augustín de Iturbide: Caudillo, 1950), and *Misiones cubanas en los archivos europeos* (Cuban Missions to European Archives, 1951). With a boundless intellectual curiosity, tireless energy, and focused attention, Moreno began a lifelong professional interest in Cuban society in all its varied dimensions, but especially the impact of the slave labor-based plantation society that developed in the later 18th and 19th centuries.

Exiled by the dictator Fulgencio Batista in the early 1950s, Moreno spent several years in Venezuela, where he engaged in a variety of lucrative businesses. He would bring to his later histories, when he returned to that vocation after 1959, valuable insights from the world of commerce, especially the way in which businessmen deal with investments and production. His scholarly production has been prodigious. Moreno has also contributed more than a hundred scholarly articles to journals published in dozens of countries in dozens of languages.

Moreno's major contribution to the historiography, however, derives from his various studies of Cuban slave society, none more insightful than *El ingenio* (1964; *The Sugarmill*, 1976). Much more than a narrow study of sugar and slavery, it is a complex and magisterial analysis that seamlessly combines economics, politics, anthropology, labor management principles, social mores, and general culture into a multifaceted study illustrative of the overall changing mentality of Cuban society throughout the 19th century. *The Sugarmill* elevated studies of American slave societies to a higher plane by demonstrating their inherent dynamism and flexibility. After its publication, studies that saw a simple, polarized world of mutually antagonistic masters and slaves no longer proved acceptable. Moreno's works gave greater agency to slaves in the day-to-day operation of Cuban plantations and argued that slave owners were not inhumane simpletons. That observation has contributed much to the understanding of the operation of slave plantations in the 19th century. His other main thesis, that slavery and technological innovation were incompatible, has not withstood the test of further research as well. Nevertheless, *The Sugarmill* was sufficiently path-breaking to gain for its author in 1982 the prestigious Clarence Haring award of the American Historical

Association for the best publication from Latin America in the previous ten years.

FRANKLIN W. KNIGHT

See also Cuba

Biography

Born Cuba, 1920. Received law degree, University of Havana, 1944; then studied with Silvio Zavala and Rafael Altamira at the Colegio de México, MA 1947. Exiled from Cuba, and worked in Venezuela before taking up research/writing career from 1959. Distinguished visiting professor, Florida International University, 1997–98.

Principal Writings

¿Nación o plantación? (Nation or Plantation?), 1948

Augustín de Iturbide: Caudillo (Augustin de Iturbide: Caudillo), 1950

Misiones cubanas en los archivos europeos (Cuban Missions to European Archives), 1951

José Antonio Saco: estudio y bibliografía (José Antonio Saco: Studies and Bibliography), 1960

El ingenio: el complejo económico social cubano del azúcar, 1760–1860, 1964, revised in 3 vols., 1978; vol. 1 in English as The Sugarmill: The Socioeconomic Complex of Sugar in Cuba, 1760–1860, 1976

Editor, Africa en America Latina, 1977; in English as Africa in Latin America: Essays on History, Culture, and Socialization, 1984

Editor with Stanley L. Engerman and Frank Moya Pons, Between Slavery and Free Labor: The Spanish-Speaking Caribbean in the Nineteenth Century, 1985

La historia como armas y otros estudios sobre esclavos, ingenios y plantaciones, 1983

Cuba a través de su moneda, 1985

Guerra, migración y muerte: el ejército español como vía migratoria, 1993

Cuba/España España/Cuba: Historia común (Cuba/Spain, Spain/Cuba: A Common History), 1995

Further Reading

Ribeiro Júnior, José, "Entrevista/Interview: Manuel Moreno Fraginals," Historia [Brazil] 11 (1992), 51–56

Morgan, Edmund S. 1916–

US historian of early America

Edmund S. Morgan's career as a historian of early America has spanned more than half a century. From assessing Puritan beliefs and behavior in 17th-century New England to understanding the rise of slavery in the South to pinpointing the ideological forces undergirding the American Revolution, Morgan has investigated a variety of topics covering more than two centuries of early American history. In the process, he has resisted being categorized into a historiographical slot. This, however, has not dissuaded certain members of the academy from trying. While some have argued that Morgan is a "Niebuhrian," others have labeled him as a "left-liberal" housed under a consensus roof. Rising out of his exhaustive quest to study the primary source material, Morgan's prose does demonstrate one indisputable pattern: an empathy for

people and a fascination with their ideas. Assisting him with his intellectual forays into the past was his wife and sometimes co-author, Helen M. Morgan.

Trained under Perry Miller at Harvard University, Morgan completed his doctoral degree in 1942. Morgan's dissertation, a study of the Puritan New England family, called attention to the paucity of scholarship on what went on inside the household. Remedying this omission, Morgan's work considered covenant theology's effects on such matters as child rearing, affective emotions, marriage, and household management. His dissertation published as The Puritan Family (1944) and numerous articles and books published afterwards revealed his continued interest in New England Puritanism. Subsequent studies published by Morgan urged his readers to consider the political activism of a Roger Williams or an Anne Hutchinson, not to mention the brooding poetry of a Michael Wigglesworth or the intellectual vision of an Ezra Stiles.

Morgan's early scholarship revealed his unwillingness to join with Progressive historians such as Vernon Parrington who had cast Puritans in an unsavory light. Rather, Morgan's work humanized the intense intellectual and emotional energy that went into what he referred to as the "Puritan Dilemma," namely the struggle of the godly to wrestle with inner- and other-worldly demands. Countless students have pondered this conflict as they traced the life of the Bay Colony's first governor, John Winthrop, in Morgan's elegantly written volume The Puritan Dilemma (1958). Five years later, Morgan completed perhaps his most substantial work, Visible Saints (1963). Dedicated to Perry Miller, it was an important reinterpretation of a Puritan ideal: the church of the Elect. Disputing the contention that the criterion for church membership was fixed prior to their departure from English ports of call, Morgan argued that a short time after their arrival New Englanders had altered membership to a gathered church composed exclusively of tested Saints.

Intrigued by what people were doing outside the confines of New England, Morgan's efforts to reconstruct life in Virginia produced what was arguably his most controversial book: American Slavery, American Freedom (1975). In his analysis of how African slavery replaced indentured servitude as the dominant form of labor in the Chesapeake, Morgan argued that the rise of slavery and the concomitant espousal of liberty and equality by Virginia planters was the "central paradox of American history." As the imperial crisis deepened in the 1760s and 1770s, Morgan's research revealed Virginians to be remarkably comfortable in their ability to express republican ideas arising out of the freedom they enjoyed and the enslavement they imposed on their workers.

Morgan's interest in the rhetoric of revolutionaries began long before American Slavery, American Freedom appeared in print. Investigating the deepening chasm between the American colonies and Britain prompted Morgan and his wife to write The Stamp Act Crisis (1953). Through a series of biographical sketches, the Morgans put human faces on a political crisis. Three years later, Morgan completed a narrative survey of the Revolutionary period in The Birth of the Republic, 1763–1789 (1956). Because he discounted the notion that class conflict held as much significance as republican ideals in the march toward revolution, some of Morgan's readers placed him in a "Neo-Whig" school of post-World War II historians. Nonplussed by this attempt to label him, in *The American Revolution* (1958), Morgan decided to categorize others, offering his candid assessment of the work of past historians and the various schools of interpretation. He then challenged his peers to delve deeper into the Revolutionary generation for new clues and insights.

Morgan's clarion call fell on a ready audience of scholars, including himself. In a prize-winning essay published in 1967 entitled "The Puritan Ethic and the American Revolution," Morgan discussed the linkages between the revolutionaries and their Puritan forebears. As America's bicentennial approached, a plethora of studies on the American Revolution and republican ideology appeared. Morgan contributed to this scholarship, publishing a collection of essays entitled *The Challenge of the American Revolution* (1976). Another book published that year, *The Meaning of Independence*, was a chance for Morgan to illuminate the beliefs of the first three presidents of the United States: George Washington, John Adams, and Thomas Jefferson.

Although Morgan retired from his post as Sterling professor at Yale University in 1986, his affection for Clio still continues. A coterie of former graduate students, many of whom are distinguished professors in their own right, produced *Saints and Revolutionaries* (1983) in his honor. In 1988, Morgan published a provocative study entitled *Inventing the People*. Morgan's study charted the ideological shift from the divine right of kings embraced by the early Stuarts to the triumph of the sovereignty of the people by the time of the American Revolution. After investigating these two extremes, a questioning Morgan claimed that divine right kingship and popular sovereignty were both a "necessary fiction" created by political elites. With some calling him "Whiggish" and others calling him "impish," Morgan's latest work has once again caused historians to mine the primary sources to see if he is right.

ELIZABETH T. VAN BEEK

See also Gipson; Slavery: Modern

Biography

Edmund Sears Morgan. Born Minneapolis, 17 January 1916, son of a lawyer. Received BA, Harvard University, 1937, PhD 1942; studied at the London School of Economics, 1937–38. During World War II worked as machinist, Massachusetts Institute of Technology radiation laboratory. Taught at University of Chicago, 1945–46; Brown University, 1946–55; and Yale University, 1955–86 (emeritus). Married Helen Theresa Mayer, 1939 (2 daughters).

Principal Writings

The Puritan Family: Essays on Religion and Domestic Relations in Seventeenth-Century New England, 1944; revised and enlarged 1966
The Stamp Act Crisis: Prologue to Revolution, 1953; revised with Helen M. Morgan, 1963
The Birth of the Republic, 1763–1789, 1956; 3rd edition 1992
The American Revolution: A Review of Changing Interpretations, 1958
The Puritan Dilemma: The Story of John Winthrop, 1958
Visible Saints: The History of a Puritan Idea, 1963
Roger Williams: The Church and the State, 1967
"The Puritan Ethic and the American Revolution," *William and Mary Quarterly* 24 (1967), 3–43
American Slavery, American Freedom: The Ordeal of Colonial Virginia, 1975

The Challenge of the American Revolution, 1976
The Meaning of Independence: John Adams, George Washington, and Thomas Jefferson, 1976
The Genius of George Washington, 1980
Inventing the People: The Rise of Popular Sovereignty in England and America, 1988

Further Reading

Courtwright, David T., "Fifty Years of American History: An Interview with Edmund S. Morgan," *William and Mary Quarterly* 44 (1987), 336–69
Hall, David D., John M. Murrin, and Thad W. Tate, eds., *Saints and Revolutionaries: Essays in Early American History*, New York: Norton, 1983
Liddle, William D., "Edmund S. Morgan," in Clyde N. Wilson, ed., *Twentieth-Century American Historians*, Detroit: Gale 1983 [*Dictionary of Literary Biography*, vol. 17]

Morison, Samuel Eliot 1887–1976
US historian

Disavowing any allegiance to particular philosophies of history, unaffiliated with specific schools of historical thought, and having trained few graduate students in any definite historical methodology, Samuel Eliot Morison is nonetheless considered by many the "dean of twentieth-century American historians." His renown derived from the longevity and the prolific quality of his career as well as from his ability to reconcile the scholarly objectives of his profession with the popular demands of lay audiences. Primarily a historian of the sea and of intellectual history, Morison gained notoriety by restoring the reputations of fallen historical figures such as John Paul Jones, William Bradford, and Matthew C. Perry, heroes who had been "taken from the people" in Morison's estimation by irreverent professional historians of the early 20th century. Some viewed the resurrections of these "dead, white males" as undesirable – reversions back to the patriarchal traditions of 19th-century "romantic" historians such as Parkman, Prescott, and Motley – while others considered them as necessary correctives to the iconoclastic revisionism of 20th-century historians. Morison cared little for such methodological debates, however: he simply wished to attract readers of all types to his balanced and highly readable books, which he inevitably did.

Morison's intellect was shaped by the "great triumvirate" of American historians at Harvard University at the beginning of the 20th-century – Edward Chaining, Frederick Jackson Turner, and Albert Bushnell Hart – who instilled in him a love for social history, regionalism, and cultural history. This wide-ranging training enabled Morison to pursue an awesome array of scholarly interests, including in the first twenty years of his career major works on such diverse topics as 17th-century Puritanism, the tercentenary history of Harvard, the maritime history of Massachusetts, and a biography of Christopher Columbus. In this last work, *Admiral of the Ocean Sea* (1942), Morison reversed the prevailing negative portrait of Columbus in the works of Henry Vignaud and others by employing a historical technique patterned after the participatory models of Thucydides and Parkman. Resailing Columbus' sea voyages, Morison attempted to answer certain perplexing questions about the discoverer by identifying self-consciously with him. This empathetic approach to historical inquiry was praised by some as "controlled imagination" and criticized by others as "reckless subjectivity," but most readers agreed that Morison's dramatic narrative style made the biography worthy of its Pulitzer prize.

The most extensive use of this participatory technique came in the field of military history, where Morison's struggles against debunkers had crucial implications for foreign policy. Historian Charles Beard had argued in *The Devil Theory of War* (1936) that reluctant Americans had been drawn into World War I by disreputable leaders motivated purely by selfish political and economic concerns. When Beard advanced a similar argument in the early 1940s with regard to Franklin D. Roosevelt's decision to enter World War II, Morison labeled him a "dialectical materialist," a bitter, contemptuous historian who was capable of seeing the world only in conspiratorial terms. In an inflammatory article facetiously titled "History Through a Beard" (1948), Morison argued that his nemesis was practicing history with the "economic autarchy" of a Hitler by "endeavoring to inculcate in the rising generation the same self-pity about being tricked into war that bedeviled the generation of the 1920s and 30s." Determined to uncover the true story of the coming of the war and to chronicle its activities from a firsthand perspective, Morison secured a commission from Roosevelt to serve as the "official" historian of naval operations during the war. He gained berths on patrol boats, destroyers, and heavy cruisers; participated in planning sessions for invasions; witnessed sea battles; narrowly escaped death at the hands of a Japanese kamikaze pilot; and conducted post-operational interviews with commanders in the Pacific theater. The result of his labors and those of his hardworking assistants was a 15-volume study which took him nearly two decades to complete.

The History of United States Naval Operations in World War II (1947–62) not only argued against the economic determinism of debunkers such as Beard, whom Morison derided as "armchair historians" who had never "seen" war, the series also challenged many of the standard interpretations of military history. Refusing to adopt the congratulatory tone of traditional government-sponsored military histories, Morison pointed to deficiencies in US naval operations where evident. He also rejected the conventional notion advanced by 19th-century historians such as Jacob Burckhardt that only absolutist regimes made effective fighting nations, arguing instead that "the history of modern warfare proves that they cannot win over representative governments in the long run." And Morison was one of the first military historians of note to popularize (without glamorizing) the story of naval operations in war, sailing a path between the excesses of Winston Churchill's "Hornblower" treatment and the obsessive detail of Admiral Richard Bates' Naval War College history of battle strategies.

The capstone of Morison's scholarly career, a 1-volume survey of United States history entitled *The Oxford History of the American People* (1965), was a highly subjective assessment of his nation's past. As with nearly all of Morison's works, it challenged the "bland concoction of orthodoxies known as 'standard history,'" not by providing any thematic unity or alternative hypothesis to the prevailing interpretations of the American past, but by injecting Morison's "distinctive personality" into a compelling and highly readable narrative grounded in sound scholarship and decades of personal participation in American life. Although historians such as Daniel Boorstin accused Morison of avoiding explanatory theories by plunging "without direction into the dark and muddied well of personal feelings, hobbies and prejudices," Morison preferred to think of the volume as the crowning moment in a long career devoted to making the past accessible and enjoyable to a people jaded by the "dull pedantry" of traditional scholarship.

GREGORY M. PFITZER

See also Commager; Latin America: Colonial; Miller, P.; Parkman; Popular; United States: Historical Writing, 20th Century

Biography

Born Boston, 9 July 1887. Attended Noble's School, Boston; St. Paul's School, Concord, New Hampshire; BA, Harvard University, 1908, MA 1909, PhD 1912; also studied at the Sorbonne, Ecole des Science Politiques, Paris, and University of Grenoble. Taught briefly at Radcliffe College and the University of California; joined Harvard faculty, 1915. Served in the US army during World War I; delegate to the Paris Peace Conference. Harmsworth professor of American History, Oxford University, 1922–25; professor, Harvard University, 1925–55. Historian of naval operations during World War II, and served in many theaters of operation. Married 1) Elizabeth Shaw Green, a painter, 1910 (died 1945; 3 daughters, 1 son); 2) Priscilla Barton, 1949 (died 1974). Died Boston, 15 May 1976.

Principal Writings

The Maritime History of Massachusetts, 1783–1860, 1921
Oxford History of the United States, 2 vols., 1927
Builders of the Bay Colony, 1930
The Growth of the American Republic, with Henry Steele Commager, 1930; 5th edition 1962
The Puritan Pronaos: Studies in the Intellectual Life of New England in the Seventeenth Century, 1935; as *The Intellectual Life of Colonial New England,* 1960
Admiral of the Ocean Sea: A Life of Christopher Columbus, 2 vols., 1942; as *Christopher Columbus: Admiral of the Ocean Sea,* 1942
The History of United States Naval Operations in World War II, 15 vols., 1947–62; condensed as *The Two-Ocean War: A Short History of the United States Navy in the Second World War,* 1963
John Paul Jones: A Sailor's Biography, 1959
One Boy's Boston, 1962
The Oxford History of the American People, 1965
The European Discovery of America, 2 vols., 1971–74

Further Reading

Cunliffe, Marcus, and Robin Winks, eds., *Pastmasters: Some Essays on American Historians,* New York: Harper, 1969
Loewenberg, Bert J., *American History in American Thought: Christopher Columbus to Henry Adams,* New York: Simon and Schuster, 1972
Pfitzer, Gregory M., *Samuel Eliot Morison's Historical World: In Quest of a New Parkman,* Boston: Northeastern University Press, 1991
Skotheim, Robert Allen, *American Intellectual Histories and Historians,* Princeton: Princeton University Press, 1966
Taylor, P.A.M., "Samuel Eliot Morison: Historian," *Journal of American Studies* 11 (1977), 13–26

Morton, W.L. 1908–1980

Canadian historian

W.L. Morton was a dominant figure in the writing of Canadian history, working at a time when three men – Morton, A.R.M. Lower and Donald Creighton – cast a large shadow over the historical profession in the country. Morton brought a conservative, western perspective to Canadian history, his work best summarized by Carl Berger's description as a "delicate balance of region and nation." A westerner by birth and conviction, Morton nonetheless took an active role in the sweeping debates about the origins and meaning of Canada.

Morton's first major contribution to Canadian historical scholarship came through the publication of *The Progressive Party in Canada* (1950). This work, part of a series of studies on the emergence of the Social Credit phenomenon in western Canada, was a detailed and insightful investigation of the roots of western alienation and protest. It offered an important counterbalance to the prevailing tendency to interpret western political uprisings in personal and radical terms, and instead provided a perceptive analysis of the broad-based support for non-mainstream parties in the region and of the many regional contradictions that prevented the Progressive movement from becoming a lasting national force. Perhaps his most notable work, and the one that established him as the leading historian of the west, was the monumental *Manitoba: A History* (1957). Morton's *Manitoba* revealed both the passion of a regional advocate and the insight of the scholar. Arguably, it was also his best written work, evoking time and place in a way that remains unique in the writing of Canadian history.

Regional concerns played a major role in Morton's work throughout his career. His introduction to Alexander Begg's *Red River Journal* (1956) is one of the best pieces of writing on the western fur trade. His work, particularly in his books on Manitoba, and, more generally, in his seminal article, "The 'North' in Canadian Historiography," revealed his conviction that the environment played a major role in shaping of Canadian history and regional societies. Throughout this writing, and perhaps in reaction to the continued assertiveness of western Canadian politicians, Morton sought to explicate the important connections between regional distinctiveness and the essence of being Canadian. While he found much that was unique in being western Canadian, he consistently argued that too much could be made of the differences and that the west was an inherently Canadian place.

This conviction that Canada could not be understood without reference to its regions and the regions had to be explained in a national context, pushed Morton to tackle broader, national topics. He became the executive editor of the Canadian Centenary series, a consciously nation-building act of scholarship, designed to explore Canada's historical roots, and contributed a key volume on the years surrounding Confederation in 1867. Morton continued his search for the broader "relevance" of Canadian history and believed that he found it in the country's curious combination of commitment to the British crown, its northern location, its legacy of dependence, and its emerging international role. In a survey text, *The Kingdom of Canada* (1963), Morton shaped these ideas into a detailed narrative. A more accessible publication, *The Canadian Identity* (1961), provided a powerful statement of Morton's conservative, environmentalist, and emphatically nationalistic view of Canada. While his approach fell from favor in the more historiographically divisive era of the 1960s and 1970s, Morton remained convinced that the special character of Canada could be best explained through broad patterns and national-level analysis.

Toward the end of his career, Morton turned his attentions to the link between the fur trade and the development of Canada. He was, at the time of his death, working on a biography of Donald A. Smith, fur trader and railway developer, and one of the key figures in the integration of the prairie west into Confederation. Perhaps his greatest intellectual legacies were his constant effort to bring the west to the attention of the nation's historians, no easy feat in the 1950s and 1960s, and his search for broad patterns in the study of Canada's past. A passionate nationalist, disturbed by the disintegrative impulses that rocked the country in the 1960s and 1970s, Morton believed that historians had a major public role to play in contemporary political debates. He played a significant intellectual role as a counterbalance to the liberal ideas that dominated Canada after the 1960s. Canadian historians shifted their attentions to what J.M.S. Careless described as the nation's "limited identities," the bonds of region, race, class, and gender that played such an influential role in shaping the country's past; Morton's emphasis on national themes and processes seemed out of step with historiographical realities, but he persisted in his belief that region and nation were not inherently in conflict.

Morton's scholarship both reflected and influenced the changing nature of Canadian scholarship. He is remembered best for his regional histories, which set high standards for their depth of research, quality of writing, and sensitivity of analysis. Much of this work, on the Métis, Manitoba, the fur trade, and western protest, remains of considerable significance. His national-level analyses have not held the attention of the country's historians in the same manner, for the metahistorical analysis that Morton offered does not find much favor in these more context-driven and theoretical times. Morton's most enduring legacy, however, may yet prove to be his struggle to explain the uniqueness of Canada as a political and social experiment. His belief in the importance of Canada being a northern nation, his conviction that the struggle between region and nation need not wreck the national fabric, and his belief in the continuing importance of Canada's British connections as a counterbalance to American influences speak to issues of continuing importance in Canada.

KEN COATES

See also Canada; Ormsby

Biography

William Lewis Morton. Born Gladstone, Manitoba, 13 December 1908, son of a farmer. Received BA, University of Manitoba, 1935; Rhodes scholar, Oxford University, BA 1934, MA 1937. Served in the Canadian Army Reserve, 1940–45. Taught at St. John's College, Winnipeg, 1935–38; United College, Winnipeg, 1938–39; University of Manitoba, 1939–40 and 1942–67; Brandon College, 1940–42; and Trent University, Peterborough, 1966–69. Married Margaret Orde, 1936 (2 sons, 1 daughter). Died Medicine Hat, Alberta, 1980.

Principal Writings

The Progressive Party in Canada, 1950

Editor, *Red River Journal*, by Alexander Begg, 1956

Manitoba: A History, 1957; revised 1967

The Canadian Identity, 1961; revised 1972

With Martha Arnett MacLeod, *Cuthbert Grant of Grantown: Warden of the Plains of Red River*, 1963

The Kingdom of Canada, 1963

The Critical Years: The Union of British North America, 1857–1873, 1964

Contexts of Canada's Past: Selected Essays of W.L. Morton, edited by A.B. McKillop, 1980 [includes "The 'North' in Canadian Historiography"]

Further Reading

Berger, Carl, ed., *The West and the Nation: Essays in Honour of W.L. Morton*, Toronto: McClelland and Stewart, 1976

Mosse, George L. 1918–

US (German-born) intellectual/cultural historian

As a teacher and scholar, George Mosse has posed challenging questions about what it means to be an intellectual engaged in the world. The central problem Mosse has examined throughout his career is: how do intellectuals relate their ideas to reality or to alternative views of that reality? In other words, how do intellectuals adjust their ideas and beliefs to everyday life? In order to answer these questions, Mosse has chosen to focus on intellectuals and the movements with which they were often connected at their most intemperate. He does this in order to compel individuals to confront the implications of ideas and movements, for Mosse feels that it is the historian's task to force people to face reality. For Mosse, the role of the historian is one of political engagement; he or she must delineate the connections (and disconnections) between myth and reality.

Mosse's priorities as a scholar may well stem from his youth as an assimilated German Jew. His family owned the Mosse publishing house in Berlin (publishers of the *Berliner Tageblatt*), and they were forced into exile with Hitler's ascension to power. While not allowing his status as an erstwhile refugee to generate self-pity, Mosse's experience of the National Socialist regime and his Jewishness seem to explain his focus as a scholar.

In his work Mosse eschewed a more traditional approach to intellectual history, preferring to concentrate on intellectual history as a cultural phenomenon. His approach demanded that he not confine himself to the giants of intellectual history, but to focus also on the works of secondary thinkers, popular writers, polemicists, and pamphleteers. In this way Mosse hoped to see how ideas make their way through popular thought and, more specifically, how ideas devolved from elite culture to National Socialism.

Mosse's career has had two parts, the later study of modern nationalism, National Socialism, and the position of Jews in modern society and an earlier engagement with the early modern period. It should be said that although he has studied two very different eras, Mosse's theoretical focus has remained much the same. He has always been interested in the way symbols mediate between intellectual elites and the masses and how this applied to the functioning of everyday life. One of his first major works, *The Holy Pretence* (1957), was an examination of how Puritans, while sincere in their beliefs, made compromises with everyday life.

In switching his focus to modern Europe, Mosse attempted to determine the place of political symbols in mass politics, including how they are appropriated on a popular level. He saw this process as a secularization of religious impulses, with political leaders (as opposed to clerics) using symbols to draw people into political movements (as opposed to religious organizations). In one of his most important works, *The Nationalization of the Masses* (1975), Mosse showed how symbols impose form and, as such, disguise reality, within a more general study of how nationalism and politics in Germany became mass politics and the role of mass political rituals in this process. He cited many examples of how people in power manipulated symbols for their own ends. Mosse revealed this process as one of "mystification," arguing that it is the historian's job to disconnect symbols from reality in a process of demystification. Mosse qualified his view of mystification somewhat when he stated in *Nazism* (1978) that leaders of fascist and National Socialist movements did not merely manipulate their followers but captured in rhetoric what their followers already felt. Mosse also pointed out how, while leaders shaped symbols and language to their own agenda, they were also constrained by the same symbols and language. In other words, they were compelled to become their own ideologies.

In *The Nationalization of the Masses*, Mosse concluded that one cannot understand history as a reasonable progression, fitting easily into rational structures. Movements such as National Socialism and fascism were, for Mosse, more attitudes than rational political systems, focusing on feelings rather than on ideas. Despite this, Mosse has not been dismissive of these movements or their adherents as he saw that perceptions of reality, no matter how skewed, were as concrete for those who held them as reality itself.

In *Nazism* Mosse expressed the idea that people, for the most part, have false rather than true consciousness. He recognized this falseness as arising from a faulty match between interests and perceptions. To get at this, he examined how interests are expressed within the interplay of symbols, myths, and ideas. An example of this is anti-Semitism, which Mosse in several of his books has seen less as an actual fear or hatred of Jews *per se* than as an abstraction of middle-class angst over economic and social insecurity. This theme was also taken up in *The Nationalization of the Masses*, wherein Mosse pointed out how seemingly irrational beliefs have been used to rationalize mundane problems.

Another major theme of Mosse's work has been the brutalization of politics. Mosse understood the National Socialist corruption of traditions and values as part of this brutalization, but he also realized that the process predated the Nazis. As he stated in *Nazism*, "It's part of a growing brutalization – a part of the idea of a total war which you already have in World War I: The enemy must be killed and to kill the enemy is a good act."

In *Fallen Soldiers* (1990), Mosse examined how the dual themes of brutalization and manipulation of symbols interact to produce the "Myth of the War Experience." By this, Mosse referred to a system of beliefs prevalent after World War I in which death in war, through apotheosis of the war dead, redeemed the nation as a whole in a way similar to Christian beliefs in Christ's crucifixion and resurrection. As such, death in war was seen as transcendent. Mosse argued that the peoples of Europe required such a myth to deal with the impact of the mass carnage of World War I. However, a political movement like National Socialism used the myth for its own ends as a glorification of war and the German nation, as defined by Nazi racial doctrine.

Some cultural historians have criticized Mosse for implying that myth is a manifestation of false consciousness, arguing that there is no such thing as a true, unmediated consciousness. Also, Mosse has tended to focus most acutely on those ideas and movements that played out into the National Socialist period. As such, some of Mosse's critics have claimed to detect a sense of teleologism in his work. Mosse has addressed this criticism in *Confronting the Nation* (1993), a study of how nations manifest themselves and how Jews have reacted to this. In this work, he emphasized that nationalism was, at its inception, the intellectual property of the Western liberal tradition and that nationalism only gradually became co-opted by irrational and extremist thinkers and politicians. In the book's introduction, Mosse calls for us all to remember this fact and for Western liberalism to reclaim nationalism in the name of liberal humanist principles.

JAMES E. FRANKLIN

See also Masculinity; Nietzsche; World War I

Biography

George Lachmann Mosse. Born Berlin, 20 September 1918, to a publishing family. Emigrated to the US, 1930s. Received BS, Haverford College, 1941; PhD, Harvard University, 1946. Taught at University of Michigan, 1944; University of Iowa, 1944–55; and University of Wisconsin, Madison, from 1955 (emeritus).

Principal Writings

The Struggle for Sovereignty in England, From the Reign of Queen Elizabeth to the Petition of Right, 1950

The Holy Pretence: A Study in Christianity and Reason of State from William Perkins to John Winthrop, 1957

The Culture of Western Europe: The Nineteenth and Twentieth Centuries, an Introduction, 1961

The Crisis of German Ideology: Intellectual Origins of the Third Reich, 1964

Editor, *Nazi Culture: Intellectual, Cultural, and Social Life in the Third Reich*, 1966

Editor with Walter Laqueur, *1914: The Coming of the First World War*, 1966

Editor with Walter Laqueur, *Literature and Politics in the Twentieth Century*, 1967

German and Jews: The Right, the Left, and the Search for a "Third Force" in Pre-Nazi Germany, 1970

Editor with Walter Laqueur, *Historians in Politics*, 1974

Editor with Bela Vago, *Jews and Non-Jews in Eastern Europe, 1918–1945*, 1974

The Nationalization of the Masses: Political Symbolism and Mass Movements in Germany from the Napoleonic Wars Through the Third Reich, 1975

With Michael A. Ledeen, *Nazism: A Historical and Comparative Analysis of National Socialism*, 1978 [interview]

Toward the Final Solution: A History of European Racism, 1978

Editor, *International Fascism: New Thoughts and New Approaches*, 1979

Masses and Man: Nationalist and Fascist Perceptions of Reality, 1980

German Jews beyond Judaism, 1985

Nationalism and Sexuality: Middle-Class Morality and Sexual Norms in Modern Europe, 1985

Fallen Soldiers: Reshaping the Memory of the World Wars, 1990

Confronting the Nation: Jewish and Western Nationalism, 1993

The Image of Man: The Creation of Modern Masculinity, 1996

Further Reading

Aschheim, Steven E., "Between Rationality and Irrationalism: George L. Mosse, the Holocaust, and European Cultural History," *Simon Wiesenthal Center Annual* 5 (1988), 187–202

Drescher, Seymour, David Warren Sabean, and Allan Sharlin, eds., *Political Symbolism in Modern Europe: Essays in Honor of George L. Mosse*, New Brunswick, NJ: Transaction, 1982

Motley, John Lothrop 1814–1877

US historian of early modern Europe

One of the leading American historians of Europe during the 19th century, John Lothrop Motley's dramatic narrative, his love of liberty, and his emphasis on heroic characters make his work a classic example of American Romanticism. His *The Rise of the Dutch Republic* (3 vols., 1856) met with popular acclaim, but was flawed by its Protestant bias and inadequate research. Later works reflected a more sophisticated methodology, but were less successful with the reading public.

Motley entered Harvard at the age of 13, and, drawn to the German Romantic writers, published a translation of Goethe while still a student. After graduating, he traveled to Germany, obtaining a doctorate from Göttingen. There he began a life-long friendship with Otto von Bismarck, who became the model for a character in one of Motley's two novels, *Morton of Morton's Hope* (1839). After serving in the US legation to the court of St. Petersburg and a term in the Massachusetts legislature, Motley began work on a history of the Dutch revolt against Spain in the 16th century, a topic to which he was drawn by his interest in the writings of the German Romantics, notably Goethe and Schiller.

Motley's account of the revolt, *The Rise of the Dutch Republic*, was constructed as if it, too, were a novel, one which centered on the epic clash between two giants: the noble William the Silent and the nefarious Philip II of Spain. His comic passages and powerful characterization produce an absorbing work, but critics have found fault with his bias against Catholicism and his projection of 19th-century republican sentiments onto 16th-century burghers. Motley had to underwrite the publication of *The Rise of the Dutch Republic* himself, but it became an immediate bestseller and critical success, winning praise from Washington Irving and François Guizot, among others. It remained in print for more than a century.

The Dutch translation of *The Rise of the Dutch Republic* won generous praise from Dutch historians, notably Bakhuizen van den Brink, Groen van Prinsterer, and Robert Fruin, despite the fact that their analyses and use of sources were far more sophisticated than Motley's. Indeed, Dutch historiography at this time was nearly as advanced as that of German historians. Fruin did mix criticism with his praise, noting that Motley's description of the siege of Leiden contained a number of inaccuracies.

Motley's next project was the *History of the United Netherlands* (4 vols., 1860–67), which carries his account of the revolt up to the 1609 truce between the Dutch and the Spanish. Possibly influenced by the professionalism of Dutch historians, Motley based this work on research in French, Spanish, Dutch, and British archives. No longer celebrating the triumph of liberty, he now aimed to place the revolt in its wider European context, demonstrating its effects on British and on French history. Recasting himself as a diplomatic historian made his position as an outsider an advantage, but his scholarly approach was less popular than his earlier style, and sales of *History of the United Netherlands* never matched *The Rise of the Dutch Republic*.

Motley's diplomatic career took precedence over his scholarly one for some time after the publication of *History of the United Netherlands*. He was appointed minister to the Habsburg court in Vienna, and later minister to London, but was caught in a power struggle between Hamilton Fish, the secretary of state, and Charles Sumner, the chairman of the Senate Foreign Relations Committee, and this led to his dismissal. He spent the remainder of his life in England, where he wrote *The Life and Death of John of Barneveld, Advocate of Holland* (2 vols., 1874). This was his most scholarly work, written after Motley had reviewed stacks of documents in Oldenbarneveldt's nearly illegible handwriting, most of them neglected by historians to that point. He championed Oldenbarneveldt in this account, casting Maurice of Nassau in an unfavorable light. That made him the object of harsh criticism from a former friend, Groen van Prinsterer, defender of the royal House of Orange-Nassau.

Motley died in 1877, still intending to write a history of the Thirty Years' War. His pioneering use of a variety of national archives had played a key role in winning respect for the work of American historians abroad, and his lively style attracted several generations of Americans to an interest in European history.

MARYBETH CARLSON

See also Fruin

Biography

Born Dorchester, Massachusetts, 15 April 1814, to a well-off merchant family. Received BA, Harvard University, 1831; then postgraduate study at Göttingen and Berlin. Unsuccessful as a novelist, he served as a diplomat and turned to writing history. Married Mary Benjamin, 1837 (3 daughters, 1 son). Died Kingston Russell, near Dorchester, England, 29 May 1877.

Principal Writings

The Rise of the Dutch Republic, 3 vols., 1856
History of the United Netherlands, 4 vols., 1860–67
The Life and Death of John of Barneveld, Advocate of Holland, 2 vols., 1874
The Writings of John Lothrop Motley, 17 vols., 1973

Further Reading

Blok, Petrus Johannes, "John Lothrop Motley as Historian (1814–1877)," in his *Lectures on Holland for American Students*, Leiden: Sijthoff, 1924

Fruin, Robert, "Motley's Geschiedenis der Vereenigde Nederlanden" (Motley's History of the United Netherlands) in his *Verspreide geschriften*, 11 vols., The Hague: Nijhoff, 1900–05, vol. 3, 118–224.
Geyl, Pieter, "Motley's Rise of the Dutch Republic," in his *Encounters in History*, Cleveland: Meridian, 1961; London: Collins, 1963
Gooch, G.P., *History and Historians in the Nineteenth Century*, London and New York: Longman, 1913; revised 1952
Guberman, Joseph, *The Life of John Lothrop Motley*, The Hague: Nijhoff, 1973
Holmes, Oliver Wendell, *John Lothrop Motley: A Memoir*, London: Trübner, 1878; Boston: Houghton Osgood, 1879
Levin, David, *History as Romantic Art: Bancroft, Prescott, Motley, and Parkman*, Stanford, CA: Stanford University Press, 1959

Mousnier, Roland 1907–1993
French political/institutional historian

Roland Mousnier was a distinguished historian of the highest rank who is best known for his institutional histories of early modern French government and society. Mousnier holds an interesting place in the hierarchy of French historians because he eschewed the Annales school of social history at the height of its 20th-century popularity and pursued a more traditional, often highly narrative, approach to historical analysis. He also vehemently rejected Marxist reductionism and any notion that class was a useful method of analysis for early modern society. Mousnier was thus something of an outsider among his scholarly peers. While it was fashionable to study peasants, he concentrated on nobles. While it was common to search for conflict between those who controlled the means of production and exploited workers, Mousnier focused on tensions he perceived between elites in French society: the traditional nobility of the sword and the administrative nobility of the robe. Because of these differences Mousnier stimulated many historical debates during his long career and was well known to British and American audiences through the translation of many of his works into English.

Mousnier published his doctoral thesis in 1945, *La Vénalité des offices sous Henri IV et Louis XIII* (The Venality of Offices under Henry IV and Louis XIII), and first introduced his interpretation of early modern social stratification as a "society of orders." According to Mousnier early modern Europeans most valued status, honor, and social esteem so that their "society of orders," was divided vertically by ranks as opposed to horizontally by classes. Mousnier incorporated this theme with single-minded certainty into most of his publications. It was fully elaborated in his 2-volume work, *Les Institutions de la France sous la monarchie absolue, 1598–1789* (1974–80; *The Institutions of France under the Absolute Monarchy*, 1979–84).

In the 1950s and 1960s Mousnier launched a critical attack on Boris Porchnev, a Soviet Marxist historian who used class as an explanation for 17th-century French popular revolts. Mousnier denounced the idea of class warfare in preindustrial society and even argued in *Les Hiérarchies sociales de 1450 à nos jours* (1969; *Social Hierarchies, 1450 to the Present*, 1973) that societies based on orders were historically more common and numerous than societies based on class or caste. In volume 2 of *The Institutions of France*, however, Mousnier modified his thesis somewhat to emphasize transition and change. He concluded that in the 18th century France evolved from a society of orders to a society of classes as attitudes changed and the country moved closer to a market-based economy.

Although not part of the Annales school, Mousnier was very interested in social history and traveled to the United States to study anthropology and sociology. He even turned away briefly from his study of the nobility and published a work on the peasantry in 1968, *Fureurs paysannes* (*Peasant Uprisings in Seventeenth-Century France, Russia, and China*, 1970). His work in the 1960s and 1970s grew more multidisciplinary and comparative, but the results were not entirely satisfactory. In *Social Hierarchies*, for example, Mousnier used Bernard Barber's functional theory of social stratification to examine various societies across time in (among others) France, Russian, China, Tibet, and Nazi Germany. Mousnier did all this in under 200 pages so that most of his discussion was far too generalized. Theodore Rabb and Charles Tilly both criticized him for oversimplifying the societies he examined and the social theory he used. Mousnier was an outspoken right-wing conservative and a devout Roman Catholic, and many thought he wrote *Social Hierarchies* to warn the world against communism and/ or "technocratic orders."

One of Mousnier's most successful books examined the assassination of France's popular king, Henry IV. The work, *L'Assassinat d'Henri IV* (1964; *The Assassination of Henry IV*, 1973) delineated two themes. First it considered the society that produced the assassin, François Ravaillac, and the forces that drove him to murder his king. Mousnier uncovered societal angst surrounding Henry IV's kingship by showing that many of his subjects disapproved of his actions and policies. Mousnier concluded that there were many "potential Ravaillacs" in French society ready to do away with the king. The author's second theme hypothesized that the impact of Henry's assassination strengthened the "triumph of absolutism in France." Mousnier produced this work long before revisionists began to attack the very idea of "absolutism" and rendered his discussion outdated. The book remains highly useful, however, for Mousnier's insight into the tensions that divided early modern French society.

Perhaps Mousnier's most lasting contribution to early modern French scholarship concerns his recognition of the importance patronage and clientage played in the early modern world. His "society of orders" included an understanding of the complicated ties that bound social superiors and inferiors in reciprocal relationships. Mousnier termed these linkages *maître-fidèle* relations and explained they involved ties of total devotion between kings and subjects, and between gentlemen and their patrons. Mousnier contended that fidelity was the definitive characteristic of patronage ties. Although his definition of fidelity was later criticized as too narrow by American scholars such as Sharon Kettering and Robert Harding, his exploration of patronage fostered numerous studies of the issue by French, British, and American scholars, most notably by Yves Durand, Arlette Jouanna, and Jean-Marie Constant.

In developing a model of 17th-century French society, Mousnier's "society of orders" often overlooked merchants, artisans, peasants, and women. He never incorporated economic differences as elements of classification in his social model, and he too readily accepted the words of legal jurists as perfect indicators of how French society functioned. Whether historians agree with his "society of orders" or not, however, they are still indebted to Mousnier for his investigations of institutions and the social relationships they encompassed. Peter Burke commented in 1992 that Mousnier's arguments are dated, but they provoked useful inquiry and forced a generation of post-World War II scholars to re-think assumptions about old regime society.

ANNETTE FINLEY-CROSWHITE

See also France: 1450–1789

Biography

Roland Emile Mousnier. Born Paris, 7 September 1907. Attended lycée in Paris and studied at the Ecole Pratique des Hautes Etudes, PhD 1931. Taught at Lycée Corneille, Rouen, 1932–37; Lycée Janson-de-Sailly, Paris, 1937–40; and Lycée Louis-le-Grand, Paris, 1940–47. Joined the French Resistance during World War II. Professor, Faculty of Letters and the Institute of Political Studies, Strasbourg, 1947–55, and Faculty of Letters, Sorbonne, 1955–77. Founded Centre de Recherches sur l'Histoire de la Civilisation de l'Europe moderne, 1958, and Institut de Recherches sur les Civilisations de l'Occident moderne, 1970; president, Comité français des Sciences historiques, 1971–75. Married Jeanne Lecacheur, 1934. Died 9 February 1993.

Principal Writings

La Vénalité des offices sous Henri IV et Louis XIII (The Venality of Offices under Henry IV and Louis XIII), 1945; revised 1971

Les Réglements du Conseil du Roi sous Louis XIII (The Statutes of the Kings Council under Louis XIII), 1949

Les XVIe et XVIIe siècles: la grande mutation intellectuelle de l'humanité: l'avènement de la science moderne et l'expansion de l'Europe (The 16th and 17th Centuries: The Great Intellectual Awakening of Humanity: The Beginning of Modern Science and the Expansion of Europe), 1953

L'Assassinat d'Henri IV, 1964; revised in English as *The Assassination of Henry IV: The Tyrannicide Problem and the Consolidation of the French Absolute Monarchy in the Early Seventeenth Century*, 1973

Lettres et mémoires adressées au chancelier Séguier (1633–1649) (Letters and Memoires addressed to Chancelier Séguier), 2 vols., 1964

Fureurs paysannes: les paysans dans les révoltes du XVIIe siècle (France, Russie, Chine), 1968; in English as *Peasant Uprisings in Seventeenth-Century France, Russia, and China*, 1970

Les Hiérarchies sociales de 1450 à nos jours, 1969; in English as *Social Hierarchies, 1450 to the Present*, 1973

"French Institutions and Society, 1610–1661," in J.P. Cooper, ed., *The New Cambridge Modern History*, vol. 4: *The Decline of Spain and the Thirty Years War*, 1970

La Plume, la faucille et le marteau: institutions et société en France du Moyen Age à la Révolution (The Pen, the Sickle, and the Hammer: Institutions and Society in France from the Middle Ages to the Revolution), 1970

Les Institutions de la France sous la monarchie absolue, 1598–1789, 2 vols., 1974–80; in English as *The Institutions of France under the Absolute Monarchy, 1598–1789*, 2 vols., 1979–84

Paris capitale au temps de Richelieu et de Mazarin (Paris as Capital in the Era of Richelieu and Mazarin), 1978

"Les Fidélités et les clientèles en France aux XVIe, XVIIe et XVIIIe siècles" (Patron-Client Relations in France in the 16th, 17th, and 18th Centuries), *Histoire sociale/Social History* 15 (1982), 35–46

L'Homme rouge, ou la vie du cardinal de Richelieu, 1582–1642 (The Man in the Red Robe; or, The Life of Cardinal Richelieu), 1992

Further Reading

Durand, Yves, ed., *Hommage à Roland Mousnier: clientèles et fidélités en Europe à l'époque moderne* (Hommage to Roland Mousnier: Patron-client relations in Europe to the Modern Era), Paris: Presses Universitaires de France, 1981

Hayden, J. Michael, "Models, Mousnier and *Qualité*: The Social Structure of Early Modern France," *French History* 10 (1996), 375–398

Mumford, Lewis 1895–1990

US architectural and cultural historian

Lewis Mumford belonged to a rare and declining species in 20th-century America: the public intellectual. Living into his tenth decade, Mumford published thirty books and thousands of articles. Although he never earned a college degree or held a long-term academic post, he extended and deepened public awareness about the importance of architecture, cities, and technology to culture, thought, and everyday life.

In 1916 at the age of 21, Mumford dropped out of college. He aimed instead to make New York his university. "My present interest in life," the young Mumford wrote, "is the exploration and documentation of cities." And while his interests influenced the formation of two scholarly disciplines – American Studies and the history of technology – his most significant contributions came as a writer about cities and architecture. Through his "Sky Line" column in the *New Yorker*, which he wrote from 1931 to 1963, and *The Culture of Cities* (1938), his most important book, he helped define the debates over urban development and city planning.

More than just a history of urban places, *The Culture of Cities* contains plans for future cities, attacks the megalopolis, and calls for regional planning. In fact, Mumford first entered public prominence when, in 1923, he joined with a group of architects, planners, and environmentalists to form the Regional Planning Association of America (RPAA). The group planned to advocate the building of several garden cities, an idea borrowed from British planners. Mumford, his biographer notes, acted as the RPAA's spokesperson and theoretician.

While the RPAA captured limited attention during the New Deal years of the 1930s, their ideas never won widespread appeal. Mumford's regionalism did not reflect nostalgia for smalltown life. Rather, Mumford, a resident of New York City for his first forty years and of a small upstate New York town for the remainder of his life, thought planning could disperse and thus preserve the benefits of urban life. He contended that a "polynucleated" city was superior to a "mononucleated" city. He wanted cities to remain manageable in size and scope.

Throughout much of his life, Mumford appeared out of step with American society. One notable instance was his powerful denunciation of American neutrality as Europe drifted toward war in the late 1930s. His stance, articulated in *Men Must Act* (1939) and *Faith for Living* (1940), ruptured several friendships with other intellectuals.

Mumford's thoughts about technology matched his views on planning. During the 1930s, the decade in which Mumford had his greatest influence, he published *Technics and Civilization* (1934), a path-breaking study of the history and culture of technology. In the book he argued that mega-machines of the day represented a dangerous abandonment of limitations in modern society. Mumford, who distrusted specialization, searched and pleaded for holistic solutions to renew and balance American culture.

His vision darkened in the postwar years, when he spent a good deal of his time assailing the development of American society. He continued to write and publish books about cities, architecture, culture, and technology, in particular his multi-volume "Renewal of Life" series (1934–51), *The City in History* (1961), and the 2-volume *The Myth of the Machine* (1967–70). Mumford, the citizen, helped defeat the New York City planners who wanted to build an expressway that would have decimated a vibrant city neighborhood. His concerns were global as well. He worked in the movement against nuclear proliferation and he protested the war in Vietnam.

A great irony in Mumford's life was that admirers honored him with awards in his later years even as they (and mainstream American culture) ignored or forgot his ideas. America's messy urban sprawl and its fascination with and dependence on technology and machines have obliterated Mumford's social vision.

CHRISTOPHER MACGREGOR SCRIBNER

See also Hughes, T.; Sauer; Technology; Urban; United States: Historical Writing, 20th Century

Biography

Born Flushing, New York, 19 October 1895, illegitimate son of a New York lawyer. Studied at City College of New York; New School for Social Research; Columbia University. Served as radio operator, US Navy, 1918. Associate editor, *Fortnightly Dial*, 1919; acting editor, *Sociological Review*, London, 1920; co-editor, *American Caravan*, 1927–36; independent author. Married Sophia Wittenberg, 1921 (1 son, 1 daughter). Died Amenia, New York, 26 January 1990.

Principal Writings

The Brown Decades: A Study of the Arts in America, 1865–1895, 1931

Technics and Civilization, 1934

The Culture of Cities, 1938

Men Must Act, 1939

Faith for Living, 1940

Art and Technics, 1952

The City in History: Its Origins, Its Transformations, and Its Prospects, 1961

The Myth of the Machine, 2 vols., 1967–70

Further Reading

Carrithers, Gale, Jr., *Mumford, Tate, and Eiseley: Watchers in the Night*, Baton Rouge: Louisiana State University Press, 1991

Fried, Lewis, *Makers of the City*, Amherst: University of Massachusetts Press, 1990

Goist, Park Dixon, *From Main Street to State Street: Town, City, and Community in America*, Port Washington, NY: Kennikat Press, 1979

Hughes, Thomas P., and Agatha C. Hughes, eds., *Lewis Mumford: Public Intellectual*, New York: Oxford University Press, 1990

Krueckeberg, Donald A., ed., *The American Planner*, New York: Methuen, 1983

Miller, Donald L., *Lewis Mumford: A Life*, New York: Weidenfeld and Nicolson, 1989

Novak, Frank G., *The Autobiographical Writings of Lewis Mumford: A Study in Literary Audacity*, Honolulu: University of Hawaii Press, 1988

Muratori, L.A. 1672–1750

Italian medievalist

Every present-day student researcher into medieval Italian history rapidly becomes acquainted with the name of Muratori, probably first by encountering the 25 volumes of *Rerum Italicarum Scriptores* (Writers or Historians of Italian Affairs, 1723–51). This immense compilation, the fruits not only of Muratori's own labors but of his collaboration and correspondence with a network of scholars in Italy and beyond (more than 6000 of his letters survive), made available works, both Latin and Italian, which in many instances had lain for centuries unpublished or even if published, in the obscurity of long-forgotten editions. The day is still far distant when the original *Scriptores* will be superseded either by the new edition, initiated in 1900 under the editorship of Giosuè Carducci, or by piecemeal re-editions elsewhere. The new *Scriptores* (commonly referred to together with the old under Muratori's name) has combined the re-editing of many of the texts he published with editions of others unknown to or untouched by him, but the works for which we still have recourse to the original are numerous and considerable. Eric Cochrane professed himself content if his *Historians and Historiography in the Italian Renaissance* (1981) should be used as "a guide to Muratori."

Muratori of course had his progenitors both as "Italian" historian and more generally as a pioneer of the study and publication of sources. His Italian medieval agenda was in large part set by the *De Regno Italiae* of Carlo Sigonio (1523–84), of whom he wrote an appreciative biographical sketch. Sigonio helped to focus Muratori's attention not only on the period of the "kingdom of Italy" (as distinct from the empire of Rome) but on the sources for its study. Around the time of Muratori's birth both the compilation and the criticism of the sources for ecclesiastical history were becoming established scholarly activities on a large scale; it is sufficient to mention the Bollandists and the Maurists. Of significance for Muratori were Cardinal Baronius (1538–1607), whose *Annales Ecclesiastici* was updated by a series of continuators including Muratori's younger contemporary Mansi, and the Cistercian Ferdinando Ughelli (1596–1670), whose *Italia Sacra*, a compendium of historical information arranged by province and diocese, appeared originally between 1644 and 1662 and was revised by Nicolò Coleti (1723–33).

Muratori's *Scriptores* are an almost everyday resource for the medieval Italian researcher; the 6-volume *Antiquitates Italicae Medii Aevi* (Ancient Italy in the Middle Ages, 1738–42) occupies a particular place in the regard of modern scholars as a pioneering work that breaches the limits of narrative history to take notice of other documentary sources and of such physical mementoes of the past as coins, seals, and medals. The work consists of 75 "dissertations" on topics which range from the ranks of society and the structure of government to coinage, heresy, poetry, hospitals, and parishes; each topic is illustrated by extensive quotation of sources and by engravings where appropriate. Less used today, perhaps, are the twelve volumes of *Annali d'Italia* (Annals of Italy, 1744–49), in which Muratori endeavored to extrapolate a chronological survey of Italian history from the sources.

The coverage attempted in the *Annali* continued down to 1749; by contrast, both the *Scriptores* and the *Antiquitates* are monuments to a still-familiar concept of the "Middle Ages" which Muratori helped to establish, to the point that he enforced a cut-off date of 1500 on the chronicles he published in the former. Even if the date seems, and is, arbitrary, it is understandable that an Italian should feel that the history of his country had reached an epoch at the end of the 15th century, with the imposition on the peninsula of a framework of "foreign" rule within which native powers, including the papacy, were to function down to Muratori's own time and for the foreseeable future. By extension, the history of the centuries before 1500, which had witnessed the formation of a distinctive Italian civilization in the aftermath of the fall of Rome, had an identity that deserved study and commemoration in greatly changed times.

This assertion, which still needed making in face of the long dominance of historical interests by Greece and Rome, also had a clear political resonance, insofar as it implied an ongoing historical identity for "Italy." In that sense, Muratori was compiling materials for the use of the Risorgimento as well as for the more disinterested purposes of modern scholarship. Felix Gilbert saw him as among the foremost of those intellectuals who between the 16th and 18th centuries upheld the sense of an Italian identity. This did not, however, necessarily or obviously imply opposition to the existing system of Italian states. As librarian of the dukes of Este at Modena, one of the oldest of Italy's native ruling dynasties, who had found their niche within the Habsburg system, Muratori too enjoyed the favor and protection of the imperial house on those occasions when he threatened to fall foul of Rome as his works enjoyed considerable fame and influence in Austrian Enlightenment circles. Rather, it was in the nature of his scholarly enterprise that he drew to the attention of contemporary Italians, and their rulers, the historical record of their past, of both the intimate and complex interrelationships of the states in which their predecessors had lived and their jealous pursuit of independence. Several possible blueprints for Italy's future, as the next century would show, could be derived from the contemplation of its history.

Towards the end of his life Muratori rendered the *Antiquitates* into a 3-volume Italian edition, implying a bid for an educated readership which lay beyond the confines of the narrow scholarly community. He was an advocate of the vernacular reading of the scriptures to the people, and even published a translation of the Catholic Mass to aid understanding. To be aware of his activity as a moderate Catholic reformer, who became embroiled in controversies over the reality of witchcraft and the abolition of excessive saints' days, is to supply a context in which his historical scholarship takes on a fuller meaning.

DIANA WEBB

See also Historiology; Italy: since the Renaissance; Manzoni

Biography

Ludovico Antonio Muratori. Born Vignola in Modena, 21 October 1672, to a poor family. Educated by the Jesuits, then at the state school of Modena; took minor orders and received degree in canon and civil law, 1688. Ordained priest, 1695; nominated curator, Ambrosian Library, Milan, 1695; chief archivist, court of Modena, 1700–50. Died Modena, 23 January 1750.

Principal Writings

Primi disegni della Repubblica letteraria d'Italia (First Designs for a
  Literary Republic of Italy), 1703
Riflessioni sopra il buon gusto nelle scienze e nella arti (Reflections
  on Good Taste in the Sciences and the Arts), 1708
Rerum italicarum scriptores (Writers or Historians of Italian
  Affairs), 25 vols., 1723–51
Antiquitates Italicae Medii Aevi (Ancient Italy in the Middle Ages),
  6 vols., 1738–42
Annali d'Italia (Annals of Italy), 1744–49

Further Reading

Bertelli, Sergio, *Erudizione e storia in L.A. Muratori* (Erudition and
  History in L.A. Muratori), Naples: Nella sede dell'Istituto, 1960
Carpanetto, Dino, and Giuseppe Recuperati, *Italy in the Age of
  Reason, 1685–1789*, London and New York: Longman, 1987
Chadwick, Owen, *The Popes and European Revolution*, Oxford and
  New York: Clarendon Press, 1981
Cochrane, Eric, *Historians and Historiography in the Italian
  Renaissance*, Chicago: University of Chicago Press, 1981
Dupront, Alphonse, *L.A. Muratori et la société européenne des pré-
  lumières: essai d'inventaire et de typologie d'après l'Epistolario*
  (L.A. Muratori and European Society before the Enlightenment),
  Florence: Olschki, 1976
Gilbert, Felix, "The Historian as Guardian of National
  Consciousness: Italy between Guicciardini and Muratori," in his
  History: Choice and Commitment, Cambridge, MA: Harvard
  University Press, 1977
Rosa, Mario, *Riformatori e ribelli nel '700 religoso italiano*
  (Reformers and Rebels in 18th-Century Italian Religious History),
  Bari: Dedalo, 1969
Venturi, Franco, *Italy and the Enlightenment: Studies in a
  Cosmopolitan Century*, New York: New York University Press,
  and London: Longman, 1972
Woolf, Stuart, *A History of Italy, 1700–1860: The Social
  Constraints of Political Change*, London and New York:
  Methuen, 1970

Musicology

Musicology is the scholarly study of music. In its modern guise,
it began in the 19th century, prior to which there was little
interest in the historical study of music, since the music
performed was largely that of the present (although past ideas
and certain theoretical concepts from the past were often part
of current thought about music). The first music to remain in
the repertory a generation beyond its composition was that of
Ludwig van Beethoven; since the middle of the 19th century,
performers have continually reached further back in time to
revive older musical works, developing in the process a canon
of "masterpieces." That this phenomenon should have begun
in the 19th century is not surprising, for it was part of the
historicizing tendency prevalent in that century; it also reflected
the growing interest in the notion of genius. Hence, until
recently, much of the focus of musicological work has been on
archival research, textual criticism, problems concerning
performance, the broad delineation of style based on the canon,
and biographical studies.

The attempts to systematize the discipline were by Germans,
notably by Guido Adler. These early musicologists used the term
Musikwissenschaft to encompass all thinking about music.
Adler proposed two divisions to be made within the discipline:
the "historical" and the "systematic" (the second encompassing acoustics, psychology, aesthetics, theory, pedagogy, and the
study of non-western musics). In the later 20th century, especially in North America, musicologists have been most concerned with Adler's first category, and also to some extent with
aesthetics, while music theorists have dealt with theoretical matters, and ethnomusicologists have studied non-western musics.

Throughout the history of the discipline, archival research
and the editing of musical texts and musico-theoretical documents have been the occupation of many prominent scholars
and have resulted in critical editions of certain repertories (14th-
century polyphony, for example), of the works of certain composers (the Bach-Gesellschaft's edition of the works of J.S. Bach
beginning in 1851 being the earliest example), of works deemed
of national importance (the German and Austrian *Denkmäler*
series), and of facsimile editions (the Solesmes monks' *Paléographie musicale*, 1899–, which reproduces the earliest notated
music in the West). Many medieval and Renaissance theoretical writings have been edited and published, especially in the
series *Corpus scriptorum de musica* (1950–); these works are
now appearing in a computer data base called *Thesaurus
musicarum latinarum*.

As far as performance practice is concerned, fewer problems
surround music that has never left the current repertory (such
as much 19th-century music) than music more removed from
the present. In some cases, it is extremely difficult to recover
lost performance traditions. Landmarks in the study of historical performance include work on the performance of baroque
music. For medieval and Renaissance music, a great deal of
effort was at first expended on deciphering archaic notation
systems, but also on questions of text underlay, tuning, and
more recently, the range and quality of singers' voices.

Broad-based discussions of musical style, which move
chronologically, have also been the purview of musicologists,
for example Jan LaRue's *Guidelines for Style Analysis* (1970).
Periods in music history (which correspond roughly to those
of art history) have been delineated on the basis of major stylistic shifts, and so there have also been important works
devoted to the music of each period, for example the series
published by Norton, which includes books on Medieval,
Renaissance, Baroque, Classical, Romantic and 20th-century
music, each by a specialist in the music of that period. There
are a vast number of studies of the music and biography of
individual composers: Alexander Thayer's *Life of Beethoven*
(1866–79) is an early example on which many subsequent
studies have been based.

There continue to be valuable studies such as these made
in the field of musicology, but since the 1960s several musicologists have called into question the aims and methods of
musicological enquiry, and there was a decisive shift in the
discipline with the publication of Joseph Kerman's *Contemplating Music* (1985). Kerman called for musicologists to move
away from "positivistic" studies towards "criticism"; not only
did the majority of musicological studies up until this time
concentrate on the "objective" search for historical truth, but
there was also a long tradition of regarding musical works as
transcending the people, places, and times from which they
came. Debates concerning music's autonomy were prevalent in
the mid-19th century (see, for example, the writings of the
music critic Eduard Hanslick), and this idea has been carried

into the 20th century, albeit tacitly. A new generation of musicologists responded to Kerman with works in which the production of social meaning through music became the focus, drawing for models (belatedly, compared to other disciplines) on poststructuralist cultural criticism. Addressing social and political meaning – indeed meaning of any kind – in music is particularly difficult, since music is not a language in the ordinary sense, but "new musicology," as it is being called, holds that particular sound structures (melodic, rhythmic, harmonic, timbral, etc.) are, indeed, socially determined. Watershed studies in this new direction have come from Susan McClary, whose work has focused on music, gender, and sexuality (for example, she has studied the opera *Carmen* to reveal how the characters' masculine and feminine qualities are depicted in the music) and Lawrence Kramer, who has drawn on, among other writings, Foucault's theory of cultural archaeology to determine how music of certain historical moments reflects other cultural concerns of the time and place. Collaborative volumes of essays have also appeared, for example Solie's *Musicology and Difference* (1993) and Brett, Wood and Thomas' *Queering the Pitch* (1994), the former concerned with gender studies, the latter exploring homosexual composers and issues in music. Works such as these have gone far to recover composers who have been marginalized. In Bergeron's *Disciplining Music* (1992), the issue of the musical canon is addressed: musicologists have traditionally been exclusively concerned with western "classical" music, and even this tradition has been stratified into acceptable and less-acceptable composers and works to study; but recently musics that have hitherto been neglected have begun to receive critical attention, including popular music (sociologists have long studied it, but without much discussion of the music itself). Richard Middleton's theoretical work, *Studying Popular Music* (1990) has been very important in this respect. Jazz has, for the past twenty years, enjoyed comparatively wide acceptance as an area for serious enquiry and many fine musicological works have been produced, notably Gunther Schuller's *The Swing Era* (1989). Traditional musicology has concentrated on the notated score, but now performance (both live and recorded) is receiving attention, not only with respect to the sound made, but with the relationship of musical production to the body (see, for example, Carolyn Abbate's *Unsung Voices*, 1991).

SUSAN FAST

Further Reading

Abbate, Carolyn, *Unsung Voices: Opera and Musical Narrative in the 19th Century*, Princeton: Princeton University Press, 1991

Adler, Guido, "Umfang, Methode und Ziel der Musikwissenschaft" (Scope, Methods, and Aim of Musicology), *Vierteljahresschrift für Musikwissenschaft* 1 (1885), 5–20

Adler, Guido, and E. Schenk, eds., *Denkmäler der Tonkunst in Österreich* (Monuments of Austrian Music), Vienna, 1894

Allen, Warren Dwight, *Philosophies of Music History*, New York: American Book Company, 1939

Apel, Willi, *The Notation of Polyphonic Music, 900–1600*, Cambridge, MA: Medieval Academy of America, 1953

Bach, Johann Sebastian, *Werke*, ed. Bach-Gessellschaft, Leipzig, 1851–99

Bergeron, Katherine, ed., *Disciplining Music: Musicology and Its Canons*, Chicago: Chicago University Press, 1992

Brett, Philip, Elizabeth Wood, and Gary C. Thomas, eds., *Queering the Pitch: The New Gay and Lesbian Musicology*, New York and London: Routledge, 1994

Dolmetsch, Arnold, *The Interpretation of the Music of the Seventeenth and Eighteenth Centuries Revealed By Contemporary Evidence*, London: Novello, 1915; revised 1946

Gochring, Edmund J., issue ed., "Approaches to the Discipline," *Current Musicology* 53 (1993) [special issue]

Hanslick, Eduard, *Vom musikalisch-schönen: ein Beitrag zur Revision der Aesthetik der Tonkunst*, 2 vols., Leipzig: Weigel, 1858; in English as *The Beautiful in Music: A Contribution to the Revisal of Musical Aesthetics*, London: Novello, 1891

Haydon, Glen, *Introduction to Musicology: A Survey of the Fields, Systematic and Historical, of Musical Knowledge and Research*, Chapel Hill: University of North Carolina Press, 1941

Kerman, Joseph, *Contemplating Music: Challenges to Musicology*, Cambridge, MA: Harvard University Press, 1985

Knighton, Tess, and David Fallows, eds., *Companion to Medieval and Renaissance Music*, London: Dent, and New York: Schirmer, 1992

Kramer, Lawrence, *Music as Cultural Practice, 1800–1900*, Berkeley: University of California Press, 1990

Kramer, Lawrence, *Classical Music and Postmodern Knowledge*, Berkeley: University of California Press, 1995

LaRue, Jan, *Guidelines for Style Analysis*, New York: Norton, 1970

McClary, Susan, *Feminine Endings: Music, Gender, and Sexuality*, Minneapolis: University of Minnesota Press, 1991

Mathiesen, Thomas, project director, *Thesaurus musicarum latinarum*, Bloomington, IN: The Thesaurus, 1991–

Middleton, Richard, *Studying Popular Music*, Milton Keynes: Open University Press, 1990

Mocquereau, André, and Joseph Gojard, eds., *Paléographie musicale: les principaux manuscrits de chant grégorien, ambrosien, mozarabe, galbéan*, 2 vols., Solesmes: St. Pierre, 1899–

Reaney, Gilbert, ed., *Corpus scriptorum de musica*, Rome: American Institute of Musicology, 1950

Recent Researches in Music of the Middle Ages, Renaissance . . ., Madison, WI: AR Editions, 1964

Riemann, Hugo, *Grundriss der Musikwissenschaft* (History of Music Theory), Leipzig: Quelle & Meyer, 1908

Schrade, Leo, ed., *Polyphonic Music of the Fourteenth Century*, 24 vols., Monaco: Editions de l'Oiseau-Lyre, 1956–91

Schuller, Gunther, *The Swing Era: The Development of Jazz, 1930–1945*, New York: Oxford University Press, 1989

Solie, Ruth A., ed., *Musicology and Difference: Gender and Sexuality in Music Scholarship*, Berkeley: University of California Press, 1993

Spiess, Lincoln, *Historical Musicology: A Reference Manual for Research in Music*, Brooklyn: Institute of Medieval Music, 1963

Thayer, Alexander, *Ludwig van Beethovens Leben*, edited by H. Dieters, 3 vols., Berlin, 1866–79; in English as *The Life of Ludwig van Beethoven*, 3 vols., New York: Beethoven Association, 1921

Waite, William, *The Rhythm of Twelfth Century Polyphony*, New Haven: Yale University Press, 1954

N

Naima, Mustafa 1655–1716

Ottoman political historian

Naima was the most well known and popular historian of the late 17th and early 18th centuries of the Ottoman empire. He was born in Aleppo, Syria and arrived in Istanbul sometime after 1683 where he became a halberdier (*teberdar*) and rose quickly to become secretary of the council (*divan*) of Kalaylıkoz Ahmed Pasha who subsequently was appointed Grand Admiral (*kapu-dan-ı derya*) of the empire. Naima then embarked on the career path of a bureaucrat (*kalem*) as a member of the imperial secretarial service (*hacegan*) affiliated with the treasury-chancellery which at this time was developing into an embryonic foreign ministry.

Naima's service brought him to the attention of Hüseyin Köprülü, scion of the famous Köprülü family, who became grand vizier from 1697 to 1702. Hüseyin Köprülü appointed Naima official historian (*vak'anüvis*) in 1700. Up to the time of Naima's appointment, the term *vak'anüvis* had generally meant recorder-of-events, but due to Naima's interpretation of his job, the *vak'anüvis* began to be recognized as someone who interpreted events and did not just record them. Naima's contribution to his craft is that his work fundamentally changed the Ottoman perception of the historian. His work contributed to the recognition by imperial officials of the need to develop an accurate historiography in order better to administer the empire and to enhance its legitimacy.

Naima served as imperial historian for only two years, but this period was crucial to the subsequent evolution of the empire. It was just prior to the revolution of 1703 in which Sultan Mustafa II (1695–1703) was deposed and Ahmed III (1703–30) became Sultan. Ahmed III inaugurated a period of Ottoman history known as the Tulip Period (*Lâle Devrî*) in which the empire sought political, intellectual, and cultural rapprochement with Europe. Naima's career as historian coincided with these crucial years of imperial history.

Naima seems to have stopped writing around 1704. He held a series of important imperial posts until his death in 1716 at the age of 62. In addition to his history, some scholars attribute the section on the deposition of Şeyhülislam Feyzullah in the history of Raşid, his successor as official historian, to Naima. Naima apparently made notes on the period 1660 to 1698/99 that he intended to include in his history, but they were not included in Ibrahim Müteferrika's 1733 printed version of his work.

Naima's fame rests on his multivolume work dealing with the period from October 1591 to April 1660, a span of 71 years and 7 months in the Muslim lunar calendar. Entitled *Ravzat el-hüseyin fi hulâsât ahbâr el-hâfikayn* (The Garden of al-Hüseyin, Being the Choicest of News of the East and West), and sometimes known as *Tarih-i vaka'i* (History of Events) it came gradually to be called simply *Naima's History*. Hüseyin in the original title referred to Hüseyin Köprülü, Naima's patron and grand vizier. Münir Aktepe argues on the basis of three additional manuscripts (out of a total of 40) of Naima's work that he found in Istanbul libraries that Naima's history commenced 18 years earlier than the 1591 date suggested by Lewis V. Thomas in *A Study of Naima* (1972). Naima's history covers the reigns of eight Sultans: from Murad III (1574–95) to Mehmed IV (1648–87).

Naima's history is in the tradition of Islamic scholarship and heavily dependent on the work of his predecessors. In many instances Naima copied verbatim and at some length from scholars such as Kâtip Çelebi (*Fezleke/Treatises*) and Şarih al-Manarzade whose work was subsequently lost. He also relied on Hüseyin Maanoğlu, the son of the famous Druze Amir Fakr ad-Din who attained political autonomy from the Sublime Porte in the middle of the 17th century, for his knowledge of events in the Arab provinces. Naima also plagiarized and quoted extensively from the works of his predecessors: Ibrahim Peçevi, Vechihî, Kara Çelebîzade Tevki'i Abdî, and Abdülaziz Efendi among others.

Like many of the learned men of his time Naima was a disciple of the famous North African scholar Ibn Khaldūn, and followed his five theories regarding the characteristics of the rise and fall of empires: 1) the heroic age of the establishment and expansion (*nümüv*); 2) the consolidation of the state and its slave-servant hierarchy; 3) the heyday of the state characterized by stability; 4) the period of stagnation (*vüküf*) and; 5) disintegration (*inhitat*). In his history, Naima stated that he thought the Ottoman empire was in the fourth stage of the cycle.

In the introduction to his work, Naima stated his nine principles for writing good history: 1) tell the truth and substantiate it; 2) disregard the false tales of the common folk; 3) be as objective (*dehrin*) as possible; 4) let the reader draw the moral for himself; 5) use plain language and do not sacrifice clarity for literary affection; 6) use appropriate embellishment such as verses from Arabic and Persian to increase appeal; 7) discuss astrology, but only when the historian can prove that astrological causes created certain consequences; 8) recognize that people who do not know history are reckless; 9) strive to write history in order to comprehend the work of preceding historians.

Naima followed his own advice well. Given the traditions of the time in which he wrote, he was more objective not only than many of his predecessors, but than many of his successors. A telling comment on his methodology, however, is that he did not see the contradiction between his objective criteria and his belief in the efficacy of the explicative power of astrology to provide an explanation for historical developments. Naima did adhere to his admonition to write more plainly and clearly, and this is the greatest contribution of his work. He wrote in a much more simple style than the customarily bombastic Arabic and Persian writing of his time. His engaging style was the reason that his history was one of four historical works to be printed by Ibrahim Müteferrika which contributed to his continuing appeal.

Salim Efendi, one of Naima's contemporaries, characterized him as "a witty scoundrel of a devil-may-care nature and a poet of broad talent. But he was skillful in his own branch of knowledge and an able writer of prose and verse. In the field of Ottoman history, he is perfect and detailed." Naima's appeal bridged the centuries. In her *Memoirs* (1926), Halide Edip, the foremost woman of letters of modern Turkey, whose life spanned both the 19th and 20th centuries as well as the Arabic and Latin scripts used for writing Turkish, noted the appeal of Naima to her generation: he was a "wonderful Turkish chronicler who reaches to levels of Shakespearian psychological penetration in his simple yet vivid descriptions" and provides "a wonderful vision of individual souls, large crowds, and revolutions in life and actions."

ROBERT OLSON

See also Ibn Khaldūn; Ottoman; Rashīd

Biography

Mustafa Naima (Na'īma). Born in 1655; raised in Aleppo, Syria in an established military family. Went to Istanbul some time after 1683 where he became in succession a halberdier, a secretary to the Istanbul council (*divan*) and a member of the elite *hacegan* (scribal service); official court historian, 1700–02; held a series of important imperial posts, 1702–16. Died c.1 September 1716, in Patras, Greece; survived by one son, Ramiz, who was a member of the *ulama* (clergy).

Principal Writings

Ravzat el-hüseyin fi hulâsât ahbâr el-hâfikayn (The Garden of al-Hüseyin, Being the Choicest of News of the East and West); also known as *Tarikh-i vaka'i*, and *Tarih-i Naima*, 2 vols., 1733; in English as *Annals of the Turkish Empire from 1591–1659 of the Christian Era*, 1832; and as *Naima's History*
Resail-i siyasiya (Political Treatises), manuscript in Süleymaniye Library Esad Efendi collection, Istanbul

Further Reading

Abou-el-Haj, Rifa'at Ali, *The 1703 Rebellion and the Structure of Ottoman Politics*, Leiden: Nederlands Historisch-Archeologisch Instituut te Istanbul, 1984
Aktepe, Münir, "Naîmâ Tarihi'nin Yazma Nüshaları Hakkında" (Concerning the Manuscripts of Naima's History), *Tarih Dergisi* 1 (1949), 35–52

Babinger, Franz, *Die Geschichtsschreiber der Osmanen und Ihre Werke* (Ottoman Historians and Their Works), Leipzig: Harrassowitz, 1927, 245–49
Cânib, Ali, ed., *Nâimâ Tarihi* (The History of Naima), Istanbul: Devlet matbaasi, 1927
Çelebi, Âsaf Hâlet, *Naîmâ: hayatı, san'atı, eserleri* (Naima: His Life, Artistry and Works), Istanbul: Varlık Yayı nevi, 1953
Çelebi, Kâtip, *Fezleke* (Summation), 2 vols., Istanbul: Ceride-i Havadis Matbaasi, c.1870
Edip, Halide, *Memoirs*, New York: Century, and London: Murray, 1926
Encyclopaedia of Islam, Leiden: Brill, 1913–36, vol. 7, 917–18
Hammer-Purgstall, Joseph von, *Geschichte des Osmanischen Reiches* (History of the Ottoman Empire), 10 vols., Budapest: Hartleben, 1827–1935
Islam Ansiklopedisi (version of *Encyclopaedia of Islam* in Turkish), Istanbul, 1941–, vol. 9, 44–49
Peçevî, Ibrahim, *Peçevî tarihi* (Peçevî's History), edited by Murat Uroz, 2 vols., Istanbul: Nesrivat Youdu, 1968–69
Raşid, Mehmed, *Tarih-i Rashid* (Rashid's History), 2nd ed., 6 vols., Istanbul: Matbaa-yi Amire, 1865
Refik, Ahmet, *Alimler ve sanatkârlar* (Scholars and Artists), Istanbul: Kitaphane-yi Hilmi, 1924
Salim, Mehmed Emin, *Tezkire-i Salim* (Memories of Salim), Istanbul: Matbaasi, 1896–97
Süreyyâ, Mehmed, *Secill-i Osmânî* (Ottoman Register), 4 vols., Istanbul: Matbaa-yi Âmire, 1890–93
Tahır, Bursalı Mehmed, *Osmanlı müellifleri* (Ottoman Authors), 3 vols., Istanbul: Matbaa Âmire, 1915–19
Tayyarzade, Ahmed Atâ, *Tarih-i Âta* (History of Âta), 5 vols., Istanbul: Yahya Efendi Matbaasi, 1844–46
Thomas, Lewis Victor, *A Study of Naima*, edited by Norman Izkowitz, New York: New York University Press, 1972

Naitō Torajirō 1866–1934
Japanese historian of China

Naitō Torajirō, formally known as Naitō Konan, was the foremost interpreter of Chinese history in Japan during an era when his country moved steadily towards a deeper imperialist involvement in Chinese affairs. The tragic consequences of this brought, after 1945, a fierce criticism of his views from a younger generation of scholars keen to exorcise the past, but some of his ideas concerning the periodization of Chinese history have outlasted those of his critics, and gained a yet wider influence as Western scholars, almost entirely absent from his field of study during his lifetime, have come to examine the problems that he first described.

Naitō came from a samurai background in which the study of Chinese literature formed a major part of the curriculum. Though he also studied English a little, it was his prose style in Japanese that marked him out as destined for a life of influence from very early in his career. His scholarship ranged widely, in the manner of his generation, yet despite early years employed as a journalist rather than as an academic, his achievements, particularly as a teacher at Kyoto University, were often substantial. Though he asked his son to translate for him a classic study on early China by Henri Maspero, he soon told him to stop, because he himself knew much more than Maspero – despite the fact that much of his published research focused on the Qing period (1644–1911). One of his main achievements as a teacher was to put the study of the documents of this period, which drew to a close during his own lifetime, on a firm foundation.

Naitō's most lasting influence, however, especially beyond the confines of Japanese China studies, has been due to his periodization of Chinese history into the equivalents of ancient, medieval, and modern. This scheme is already apparent in his *Shinaron* (On China) of 1914, which set the medieval/modern divide at *c*.800–1000 CE, the "Tang-Song transition," in contemporary parlance. It was more novel than one might imagine: before his time the notion of a "Golden Age" in Chinese antiquity followed by long decline had been widespread in East Asia, and had been taken up with a vengeance by Westerners, who saw their own arrival in China as the stimulus that would arouse that country from complete torpor.

Naitō's tripartite division is open to the objection that it fostered similar self-regarding sentiments in Japan, in that the "modern" era was held to have run its course, so that China now required renewal with outside help. But Naitō was never a simple apologist for Japanese expansion; he could not, for instance, countenance Japanese military aggression in China, since the military could not understand his own view of the importance of Japanese cultural leadership. From the start he saw republicanism as inevitable in China, and his emphasis on the importance of local society in China picked up anti-autocratic arguments already apparent in 17th-century Chinese writings. But equally he could not abide the rise of a new, Western-educated Chinese leadership who knew less of their own history than he did. Like many pundits on foreign affairs, his chief fault was an unwillingness to accept that the country on which he had staked his career could develop in ways other than those he himself thought ideal.

The great merit of his periodization, by contrast, was its recognition of a pattern of development in the Chinese past which others had been unwilling to see. In fact, though he may have derived some hints from Japanese discussions of the term "medieval" in relation to their own history, his scheme reflects a longstanding awareness on the part of traditional Chinese historians that the period from early in the Common Era to the 11th century had been marked by cultural influences, such as the importation of Buddhism, that gave way to a re-evaluation of the purely Chinese culture of antiquity. It is perhaps significant that Naitō, a Buddhist, started his journalistic career writing for a Buddhist periodical, but his delineation of the medieval period actually concentrates on its distinctive sociopolitical history in a way that has far fewer precedents than the characterization of the time span in religious terms.

Since 1945 Naitō's most famous idea has been subjected to various modifications: a "recent modern" period was soon tacked onto the end, to meet the charge that Naitō's scheme implied recent stagnation, while most current writing in the West would see the period 800–1000 as but a phase in longer-term or successive changes, rather than a brief but completely exceptional episode. Even so, the "Tang-Song transition" remains a notion which it is difficult to do without, and it now seems that whatever his demerits, the credit due to Naitō for raising a generation of scholars who took change in Chinese history seriously will never be taken from him.

T.H. BARRETT

See also Maspero

Biography

Born Kemanai, Akita prefecture, 18 July 1866. Educated in Osarizawa, and at Akita Normal School, 1883–85. Elementary school principal, Tsuzureko, Akita, 1885–87; journalist specializing in Chinese issues, in Tokyo, and later Osaka (also visiting Taiwan and China), 1887–1907; first professor of East Asian history, Kyoto University, 1907–27. Died Mikanohara, Kyoto prefecture, 26 June 1934.

Principal Writings

Shina shigakushi (History of Chinese Historical Writing), 1949
Naitō Konan zenshū, 14 vols., 1969–76. This collection of Naitō's writings includes all his best-known publications; *Shinaron* (On China, 1914), which first made known his thoughts on periodization is in vol. 5. For a listing of articles not included in this collection, see pp.335–44 of Fogel, *Politics and Sinology*, below.

Further Reading

Fogel, Joshua A., *Politics and Sinology: The Case of Naitō Konan, 1866–1934*, Cambridge, MA: Harvard University Press, 1984
Miyakawa Hisayuki, "An Outline of the Naitō Hypothesis and Its Effects on Japanese Studies of China," *Journal of Asian Studies* 14 (1955), 533–52
Okamoto, Shumpei, "Japanese Response to Chinese Nationalism: Naitō (Ko'nan) Torajirō's Image of China in the 1920s," in F. Gilbert Chan and Thomas H. Etzold, eds., *China in the 1920s: Nationalism and Revolution*, New York: New Viewpoints, 1976
Tam, Yue-him, "An Intellectual's Response to Western Intrusion: Naitō Konan's View of Republican China," in Akira Iriye, ed., *The Chinese and the Japanese: Essays in Political and Cultural Interactions*, Princeton: Princeton University Press, 1980

Namier, Lewis 1888–1960

British (Polish-born) historian

Lewis Namier, born Ludwik Niemirowski to Polish parents, was educated at Balliol College, Oxford. As a youth he was influenced by attending lectures by Vilfredo Pareto at Lausanne. He was employed in the political intelligence department of the British Foreign Office before serving as political secretary of the Jewish Agency for Palestine in 1929–31. In 1931 he was elected to the chair of history at Manchester University, which he occupied until 1953.

Namier not only changed his name and embraced Anglicanism, but became firmly part of the British Establishment, including among his achievements membership in the Athenaeum and a knighthood in 1952, although he was a lifelong Zionist. His fame as a historian is founded on two books, *The Structure of Politics at the Accession of George III* (1929) and *England in the Age of the American Revolution* (1930), and on his editorship of the History of Parliament series.

Namier's research often used prosopography or collective biography, a technique that worked extremely well for studying elites and small groups. From common education, membership in the same clubs and lodges, and other similarities it is possible to discern a "group mind." As a research technique, prosopography as he employed it frequently revealed that local interests, not broad national issues, determined political behavior. For his pains Namier was accused of taking ideas out of history and claiming that principles did not count in politics, but in actual fact he was much less a cynic than he was a zealous collector of facts and believer in meticulous research rather than jumping to generalizations. He did not trust grand narrative and opposed what he regarded as mythmaking, which he felt could be curbed by the study of such neglected materials as wills and tax records. He was not a "number cruncher" or mindless advocate of quantification, although there is some substance to the charge that he did not "believe in belief."

Namier's name is often invoked when the old question of whether history can be a science is discussed. While he took advantage of the growth of reference sources and boom in the publication of records which would have made an earlier generation of historians envious, he would have been aghast at any assertion that prosopography would work in every circumstance. When a group such as members of the House of Commons was readily identifiable and ample biographical material was available, a prosopographical approach was eminently useful and remains so. His work on Parliament in the 18th century and Europe in the 19th century has already become somewhat outdated, so it is as the modern father of prosopography that Namier perhaps has earned his permanent place in historical discussions.

PAUL JOHN RICH

See also Britain: 1485–1750; Britain: since 1750; Butterfield; Central Europe; Hargreaves; Macaulay; Political; Prosopography; Rosenberg, H.; Rudé; Seton-Watson, R.; Taylor

Biography
Lewis Bernstein Namier. Born Ludwik Niemirowski in Wola Okrejska, Poland, June 1888, to a secular Jewish family. Educated privately, then briefly at the universities of Lvov and Lausanne, and the London School of Economics; studied at Balliol College, Oxford, BA 1911. Came to Britain, 1906; naturalized 1913. Served as private, 20th Royal Fusiliers, 1914–15; in Department of Propaganda, 1915–17, Department of Information, 1917–18, and Political Intelligence department, Foreign Office, 1918–20. Taught modern history, Balliol College, 1920–21; in business, 1921–23; engaged in historical research, 1923–29; political secretary, Jewish Agency for Palestine, 1929–31; professor of modern history, Manchester University, 1931–53; editorial board member, History of Parliament series. Married 1) Clara Sophie Poniatowski Edeleff, 1917 (died 1945); 2) Julia Kazarin de Beausobre, 1947. Knighted 1952. Died 19 August 1960.

Principal Writings
The Structure of Politics at the Accession of George III, 1929
England in the Age of the American Revolution, 1930
In the Margin of History, 1939
Conflicts: Studies in Contemporary History, 1942
1848: The Revolution of the Intellectuals, 1944
Facing East, 1947
Europe in Decay: A Study in Disintegration, 1936–1940, 1950
Avenues of History, 1952
Basic Factors in Nineteenth-Century European History, 1953
Vanished Supremacies, 1958 [collected essays]
Crossroads of Power, 1962 [collected essays]

Further Reading
Colley, Linda, *Lewis Namier*, New York: St. Martin's Press, and London: Weidenfeld and Nicolson, 1989

Namier, Julia, *Lewis Namier: A Biography*, London and New York: Oxford University Press, 1971
Pares, Richard, and A.J.P. Taylor, eds., *Essays Presented to Sir Lewis Namier*, London: Macmillan, and New York: St. Martin's Press, 1956

Napoleonic Wars (1800–1815)

Few events, or series of events, have generated quite as much writing as the Napoleonic Wars. The number of countries involved, the chronological scope, and the far-reaching effects of the wars have spurred the production of a truly daunting number of works.

Works on the wars were published while the conflicts still raged. Much of this early writing took the form of journalistic reportage (what might now be termed journalistic or contemporary history). A good example of such writing is Robert Ker Porter's *Letters from Portugal and Spain*, published in 1809. Many such works suffered from the shortcomings of most journalistic writing, that is a lack of in-depth background and often premature analyses.

After the end of the Napoleonic Wars in 1815, interest in works on the period continued, though many of these works were limited in scope, in part due to the sheer vastness of the subject. Some of the most valuable and interesting works of the early 19th century are the memoirs of erstwhile combatants. Some of the better-known memoirs were written by high-ranking commanders. Many of these were French marshals and generals, who sought to establish their places within the Napoleonic legend. One of the best memoirs written by a high-ranking officer is *Opérations du 3e Corps, 1806–1807* (Operations of the Third Corps, 1806–1807) by Marshal Davout (1896), a painstaking account of the battle of Auerstädt and the operations of Davout's army corps, emphasizing Davout's important role in the defeat of the Prussians. Other commanders (on all sides) wrote memoirs that are often amusing for the lengths to which the writers go in order to demonstrate their indispensability to the course of history. Some of these are examples of pure self-aggrandizement, such as Marshal Macdonald's literary reshaping of his poor generalship and an attempt to convince the restored Bourbons of his repentance for one-time loyalty to Napoleon in *Souvenirs* (Memoirs, 1892).

Numerous memoirs were also written by relatively minor figures and sought to give an accurate accounting of battles, military life, and the feeling of participating in great events. Many memoirs were written to promote agendas or particular views of the meaning of the Napoleonic era for subsequent generations. For example, many German accounts emphasized the nationalist notion of a popular German war against the French invader. One of the best analyses of these writings is Hans Kohn's *Prelude to Nation-States* (1967), in which the author examined the polemic prevalent amongst early nationalists in Germany and France. This trend was also evident in the attempts at hagiography involving Napoleon. A major source in this is Napoleon's memoirs, as dictated to his servant in exile Las Cases. Napoleon portrayed himself as a child of the French Revolution who tried to preserve its ideals, while introducing them to a benighted Europe like a modern Prometheus. A very good modern commentary on the legends surrounding Napoleon's memory is H.A.L. Fisher's *Bonapartism* (1980), which sought to separate myth from the reality of Napoleon's remarkable life.

There were few works that attempted to encompass the full course and scope of the subject; however, some of those that did make the attempt are among the classic studies of Napoleonic warfare. The 19-volume study by Mathieu Dumas, *Précis des événements militaires, ou essais historiques sur les campagnes de 1799 à 1814* (Summary of Military Events, or Historical Essays on the Campaigns of 1799 to 1814, 1816–26), demonstrated the difficulty of handling such a vast topic as the Napoleonic Wars; despite the amount of textual space, Dumas was able to cover only up to the year 1807 with any kind of comprehensiveness. Other writers of the early 19th century, such as Antoine Henri Jomini in *Vie politique et militaire de Napoléon* (The Political and Military Life of Napoleon 1827), limited the scope of their work to examining individual commanders or the operations of single armies.

Much of the writing of the early 19th century was intended for a military audience, slanted to the instruction of military officers. These tended to take the form of campaign histories and military analyses. One of the most cited writers in either genre is Carl von Clausewitz, whose body of work was compiled into *Hinterlassene Werke des Generals Carl von Clausewitz über Krieg und Kriegführung* (Posthumous Works of General Carl von Clausewitz on War and Warfare, 1832–1937). In looking back on the military events of his epoch, Clausewitz posited war as an instrument of state policy. He also argued that armies, in their forms, organizations, and operations, were dependent on their particular contexts, reflecting the political cultures and societies that engendered them. Clausewitz saw the nation-states of post-French Revolutionary Europe as producing the modern nation-in-arms, making possible for the first time mass armies backed by the full resources of their nations. He posited the difference between what he called "real war" and "true war," the former being primitive, heroic warfare; the latter was, for Clausewitz, the state of modern warfare. In "true war," the enemy's will to resist was eliminated through the battlefield annihilation of its forces; thus Clausewitz's emphasis was on battle, the decisive clash of large, well-organized armies. Clausewitz's writings were to have a deep effect on military history in general, and the history of the Napoleonic Wars in particular, well beyond the 19th century.

Following Clausewitz, most historians of the Napoleonic Wars have concentrated on major battles and great commanders in a way that demonstrates the influence of the Prussian theorist. One may see evidence of this influence in a number of campaign and battle histories, as well as in general works on military theory. Surprisingly, perhaps, Clausewitz's work did not receive a positive reception immediately in his native Prussia. Many members of official ruling circles were wary of the populist implications of mass armies discussed by Clausewitz, preferring to rely on military professionals to preserve the position of the monarchy. However, as the 19th century wore on, political elites were tempted to co-opt nationalist sentiment for their own ends. For these leaders, Clausewitz's ideas on mass armies and the army as a school of the nation became more attractive. In *Geschichte der Kriegskunst im Rahmen der politischen Geschichte* (1900–20; *History of the Art of War within the Framework of Political History*, 1975–85), Hans Delbrück cast the history of the evolution of warfare in Clausewitzean terms. Like Clausewitz, Delbrück saw armies and the conduct of war as tied to political organization, with the modern Western mode of war as the apogee of armed conflict.

In the latter half of the 19th century and into the early 20th century, many European military establishments utilized Clausewitzean or similar ideas to justify their positions *vis-à-vis* state and society. Much of the Napoleonic military history of this period was written, in part, to justify this relation, and much of it written by military officers or published by military presses. One of these works was Alembert-Goget and Colin's *La Campagne de 1805 en Allemagne* (The Campaign of 1805 in Germany, 1902–08), published by the historical section of the French high command. Besides producing a detailed account of the campaign that included the French victories over the Austrians at Ulm and Austerlitz, the authors sought to enhance the image of the French army, which had suffered defeat during the Franco-Prussian War at the hands of Austria's closest ally, Germany.

Other militaries sought to use the history of the Napoleonic Wars in a similar manner. Several campaign histories were published in the Habsburg monarchy under the auspices of the army, which was trying to recover a glorious image damaged by defeats in the middle of the 19th century. Two good examples of such work are *Krieg, 1809* (War, 1809, 1907–10) and *Befreiungskrieg, 1813 und 1814* (Austria in the Wars of Liberation, 1913), both of which were written under the rubric of the Austro-Hungarian Kriegsarchiv (war archive). Like most of the official histories, those works are valuable sources of material on the Austrian military establishment. However, beyond that they are fairly unreliable due to their ignoring of unsuccessful operations and the problems present within the Austrian military establishment. The Austrian army was seen, with some justification, as the main support of the monarchy and the unity of the empire, so it was unlikely for an official history to pursue a critique of the army.

Some writing on the Napoleonic Wars was meant not for military aggrandizement, but for the promotion of an ideology. This was especially true in the Soviet Union, where, in *Diplomatiia i voiny tsarkoi Rossii v. XIX stoletii* (Diplomacy and the Wars of Tsarist Russia in the 19th Century, 1923), Mikhail Pokrovskii wrote that the wars were merely a means by which France attempted to defend and extend its economic system. Napoleon's invasion of Russia was explained, not as a national struggle, but as the conflict between two classes from differing countries. However, this approach was officially attacked during the late 1930s because of Soviet uneasiness over the aggressive foreign policies of Nazi Germany. During World War II, the idea of a national resistance against Napoleon was revived in order to exhort the Soviet populace to resist the Germans.

In the 20th century, the study of the Napoleonic Wars has become more objective, while the emphasis still remains on battles, commanders, and military establishments. David Chandler wrote a very good book along these lines entitled *The Campaigns of Napoleon* (1966), which managed in one volume to give an informative account of Napoleon's conduct of warfare, along with an analysis of military strategy and the armies of the period. Gunther Rothenberg has written a general examination of the armies of the period entitled *The Art of Warfare in the Age of Napoleon* (1977). In this work, Rothenberg detailed the organization of the various major armies, as well as their strategy and tactics. A more recent book by Owen Connelly, *Blundering to Glory* (1987), offered a less than flattering portrait of Napoleon, in which the emperor is seen as talented at rescuing himself from his own mistakes but not at enacting any sort of carefully planned action.

Connelly's book, while proposing an alternative to the dominant view of Napoleon as great captain, also demonstrated the continued reliance of Napoleonic military history on traditional subjects. Very little has been written on the so-called minor theaters of Napoleonic warfare such as Sweden, Illyria, or the Low Countries. Some innovation in the study of the Napoleonic Wars is to be found in the section on Waterloo in John Keegan's *The Face of Battle* (1976). While Keegan did relate a general account of the course of the battle, he does so as a framework for his main project, which was to attempt to discover the experience and feeling of the battle on the part of its lower-ranking participants.

Keegan's work suggests the possibilities of combining military history with some of the newer approaches of social and cultural history. An early attempt in this regard was Jean Morvan's *Le Soldat impérial* (The Imperial Soldier, 1904), a study of the Grande Armée's rank and file, rather than its commanders. Other areas of research are suggested by Stuart Woolf's *Napoleon's Integration of Europe* (1991), in which Woolf examines the process by which France attempted to integrate its satellites and the relations between subalterns and metropolitan France. While Woolf focuses on civilian, as well as military service, his approach is applicable to the study of the military culture of the satellites in the Napoleonic orbit.

JAMES E. FRANKLIN

See also Delbrück; Keegan; Military

Further Reading

Alembert-Goget, Paul Claude, and Jean L.A. Colin, *La Campagne de 1805 en Allemagne* (The Campaign of 1805 in Germany), 4 vols., Paris: Chapelot, 1902–08

Barnett, Correlli, *Bonaparte*, London: Allen and Unwin, and New York, Hill and Wang, 1978

Brett-James, Antony, *Life in Wellington's Army*, London: Allen and Unwin, 1972

Bryant, Arthur, *Years of Victory, 1802–1812*, London: Collins, 1944; New York: Harper, 1945

Chandler, David G., *The Campaigns of Napoleon*, New York: Macmillan, and London: Weidenfeld and Nicolson, 1966

Clausewitz, Carl von, *Hinterlassene Werke des Generals Carl von Clausewitz über Krieg und Kriegführung* (Posthumous Works of General Carl von Clausewitz on War and Warfare), 10 vols., Berlin: Dümmler, 1832–1937

Clausewitz, Carl von, *Vom Kriege*, 3 vols., Berlin: Dümmler, 1832–34; in English as *On War*, London: Trübner, 1873; edited by Michael Howard and Peter Paret, Princeton: Princeton University Press, 1976

Connelly, Owen, *Blundering to Glory: Napoleon's Military Campaigns*, Wilmington, DE: Scholarly Resources, 1987

Davout, Louis Nicolas, duc d'Auerstadt et prince d'Eckmuhl, *Opérations du 3e Corps, 1806–1807* (Operations of the 3rd Corps, 1806–1807), Paris: Levy, 1896

Delbrück, Hans, *Geschichte der Kriegskunst im Rahmen der politischen Geschichte*, 4 vols., Berlin: Stilke, 1900–20, reprinted Berlin: de Gruyter, 1962–66; in English as *History of the Art of War within the Framework of Political History*, 4 vols., Westport, CT: Greenwood Press, 1975–85

Dumas, Mathieu, *Précis des événements militaires, ou essais historiques sur les campagnes de 1799 à 1814* (Summary of Military Events, or Historical Essays on the Campaigns of 1799 to 1814), 19 vols., Paris: Treuttel et Würtz, 1816–26

Ellis, Geoffrey, *The Napoleonic Empire*, London: Macmillan, and Atlantic Highlands, NJ: Humanities Press, 1991

Elting, John R., *Swords around a Throne: Napoleon's Grande Armée*, New York: Free Press, 1988

Fisher, H.A.L., *Bonapartism*, Oxford: Clarendon Press, 1908

Horward, Donald D., ed., *Napoleonic Military History: A Bibliography*, New York: Garland, and London: Greenhill, 1986

Jomini, Antoine Henri, *Vie politique et militaire de Napoléon* (The Political and Military Life of Napoleon), 4 vols., Paris: Anselin, 1827

Keegan, John, *The Face of Battle*, London: Cape, and New York: Viking, 1976

Kohn, Hans, *Prelude to Nation-States: The French and German Experience, 1789–1815*, Princeton, NJ: Van Nostrand, 1967

Kriegsarchiv, *Krieg, 1809* (War, 1809), 4 vols., Vienna: Seidel, 1907–10

Kriegsarchiv, *Befreiungskrieg, 1813 und 1814* (Austria in the Wars of Liberation), 5 vols., Vienna: Seidel, 1913

Macdonald, Jacques Etienne Joseph Alexandre, duc de Tarante, *Souvenirs du maréchal Macdonald, duc de Tarente* (Memoirs), Paris: Plon, 1892

Morvan, Jean, *Le Soldat impérial (1800–1814)* (The Imperial Soldier), 2 vols., Paris: Plon, 1904

Palmer, Alan W., *Napoleon in Russia: The 1812 Campaign*, New York: Simon and Schuster, and London: Deutsch, 1967

Pokrovskii, Mikhail N., *Diplomatiia i voiny tsarskoi Rossii v XIX stoletii* (Diplomacy and the Wars of 19th-Century Tsarist Russia), Moscow: Krasnaia nov', 1923

Porter, Robert Ker, *Letters from Portugal and Spain*, London: Longman, 1809

Rothenberg, Gunther, *The Art of Warfare in the Age of Napoleon*, London: Batsford, 1977; Bloomington: Indiana University Press, 1978

Rothenberg, Gunther, *Napoleon's Great Adversaries: Archduke Charles and the Austrian Army, 1792–1814*, London: Batsford, and Bloomington: Indiana University Press, 1982

Weller, Jac, *Wellington in the Peninsula, 1808–1814*, London: Vane, 1962

Woolf, Stuart, *Napoleon's Integration of Europe*, London and New York: Routledge, 1991

Nash, Gary B. 1933–

US historian

Gary B. Nash is one of the foremost exponents of that "rediscovery of complexity in American history" which, according to Richard Hofstadter, characterized the discipline from the 1970s on. In a period that emphasized the historical role of the dispossessed and of groups previously overlooked, including women, African Americans, nonwhite ethnic groups, and labor, and which focused on social history, Nash produced major pioneering works examining urban and African-American history, whose breadth of vision and sophistication are entitled to stand beside any products of previous eras of US historiography. As such, he is a leading proponent of what became known as the "new social history."

Nash chose to concentrate his scholarly endeavors on pre-Civil War United States history. His first major work, *The Urban Crucible* (1979), was a reinterpretation of the part the city played in early American political change and ideology. In particular, it drew attention to the role of urban class formation and class conflict in bringing on the American Revolution. Nash looked at "[t]he narrowing of opportunities and the rise of poverty" in three colonial American cities, New York, Boston, and Philadelphia, and suggested that such deprivation was a major causative factor in the American Revolution. He also traced the concurrent development of a sense of class consciousness during this period, which he suggested could not be ignored. He did not suggest that ideology was simply "a reflection of economic interests," nor that there was a "unified laboring class," but he did focus on previously ignored groups, particularly slaves and poor laborers, and argued that the role of women also required further investigation. This work won wide acclaim, and is justly regarded as a key work on the history of the revolutionary period. In his book of collected essays, *Race, Class, and Politics* (1986), Nash carried these themes further. These essays were painstaking, immensely well-researched pieces of scholarship, whose existence proved that a preoccupation with social history and the study of non-elites could be combined with the highest academic standards.

His next monograph, *Forging Freedom* (1988), concentrated on a particular community in one major city, Philadelphia. Again, it focused on the dispossessed and ignored. It also traced the growing transformation of white Philadelphians' sentiments toward free blacks, from racial harmony in the early 1790s to antagonism and outright hostility in the early 1830s. Initially Philadelphia had one of the largest free black communities, which served as a model of what such groups might accomplish, but by 1820 race relations had deteriorated to the point where blacks would face discrimination and racial injustice for more than a century to come. Sympathetic Philadelphian whites proved unable to assist the black community, which nonetheless remained vital, united, and vibrant in its opposition to slavery and discrimination.

Nash also edited a textbook and several collections of readings, designed for undergraduate audiences. Again, such works highlighted the role of groups previously ignored or dismissed by historians. His influential co-authored textbook, *The American People* (1986), stressed class conflict and the political, social, and economic achievements and role of industrial workers, trade unionists, blacks, and women, while tending to minimize and discount the centrality of middle-class reformers and such liberal presidents as Theodore Roosevelt, Woodrow Wilson, and Franklin D. Roosevelt. *The Great Fear* (1970), co-authored with Richard Weiss, was an early effort not only to deal with race, but also to make whites aware of and to implicate white society in prevailing American racism. *The Private Side of American History* (1975) attempted to "provide a fresh perspective from which to view such vital but often neglected aspects of American history as work; family life, childbirth, child rearing, and sex; education and entertainment; religion; health, disease, and death; and conflicts created by encounters between diverse population groups – Native Americans and colonists, blacks and whites, and immigrants and established residents." This description neatly encapsulates the preoccupations of the new social history, of which Nash is such a distinguished and well-qualified

avatar. Yet it does not fully describe his own work, which often transcends its subgenre to cross the boundaries between social, urban, ethnic, and political history. In this respect, Nash's *oeuvre* perhaps represents the future direction which the best of United States history will take.

PRISCILLA M. ROBERTS

See also Native American; United States: American Revolution

Biography

Born Philadelphia, 27 July 1933. Received BA, Princeton University, 1955, PhD 1964. Taught at University of California, Los Angeles, from 1964. Married 1955 (4 children).

Principal Writings

Quakers and Politics: Pennsylvania, 1681–1726, 1968
Class and Society in Early America, 1970
With Richard Weiss, *The Great Fear: Race in the Mind of America*, 1970; 3rd edition 1991
Red, White, and Black: The Peoples of Early America, 1974; 3rd edition 1991
The Private Side of American History: Readings in Everyday Life, 1975
The Urban Crucible: Social Change, Political Consciousness, and the Origins of the American Revolution, 1979; abridged as *The Urban Crucible: The Northern Seaports and the Origins of the American Revolution*, 1986
Editor with others, *The American People: Creating a Nation and a Society*, 2 vols., 1986
Race, Class, and Politics: Essays on Colonial and Revolutionary Society, 1986
Forging Freedom: The Formation of Philadelphia's Black Community, 1720–1840, 1988
Race and Revolution, 1990

Further Reading

American Historical Review 94 (June 1989), 581–698
Hamerow, Theodore S., *Reflections on History and Historians*, Madison: University of Wisconsin Press, 1987
Kraus, Michael, and Davis D. Joyce, *The Writing of American History*, revised edition, Norman: University of Oklahoma Press, 1985
Novick, Peter, *That Noble Dream: The "Objectivity Question" and the American Historical Profession*, Cambridge and New York: Cambridge University Press, 1988
Stearns, Peter N., "Toward a Wider Vision: New Trends in Social History," in Michael G. Kammen, ed., *The Past Before Us: Contemporary Historical Writing in the United States*, Ithaca, NY: Cornell University Press, 1980
Thelen, David P., Jonathan Wiener, John D'Emilio, Herbert Aptheker, Gerda Lerner, Christopher Lasch, John Higham, Carl Degler, and David Levering Lewis, "A Round Table: What Has Changed and Not Changed in American Historical Practice?" *Journal of American History* 76 (1989), 393–478
Veysey, Laurence R., "The 'New' Social History in the Context of American Historical Writing," *Reviews in American History* 7 (March 1979), 1–12

Nationalism

Nationalism as a discourse is inextricably linked with the history, and evolution of, the idea of the nation. Nations, nationalists argue, constitute the optimum form of social organization, and possess specific, distinctive characteristics which can be utilized to include or exclude, and to provide defining roles for the individuals and groups that comprise the nation. The nation is envisaged (sometimes alongside religious belief) as the highest and most important object of allegiance.

Although nationalism as a concept for serious historical inquiry emerged in the interwar period, the concept began to receive serious scholarly attention in the 1960s, when historians joined scholars from other disciplines in order to study the subject. The time scale given for the emergence of a specifically national consciousness varies between historians and according to country. For example, while Liah Greenfeld pointed to 16th-century England, Linda Colley has located the formation of British nationalism in the 18th century. For most historians of the subject, nationalism, and national feeling, first emerged during the time of the French Revolution. According to this interpretation, nationalism emerged as a liberal doctrine of popular sovereignty and freedom from external influence. This phase of nationalism was evident in Western Europe during periods of aspiration to nationhood, or the internal unification of existing nations. Peter Sugar, for example, has seen nationalism as a revolutionary force aiming to transfer sovereignty from rulers to the people, and was ideologically informed by the work of Jean-Jacques Rousseau and later theorists such as Giuseppe Mazzini. In contrast, the concept of uniqueness was an early and integral component of nationalism in Central and Eastern Europe. Johann Herder cited language as a factor of national uniqueness. Language is communal, and reflects thought. Languages are different, therefore communities are different. For Johann Gottlieb Fichte, language mirrored the national soul (*Volksgeist*) and, for its protection, needed periodic cleansing of alien elements. This line of reasoning could be used to justify the exclusion of perceived alien inhabitants of the nation.

Historians have distinguished between different types of nationalism, which emerged as a result of local needs and conditions. Hans Kohn differentiated between Western and Eastern nationalism, and Isaiah Berlin discriminated between cultural and political nationalism. Western European (political, or "subjective") nationalism, was seen as the rational organization of the state and the advancing of citizenship rights, emphasizing individual freedom within the framework of the nation, and tending to be urban and middle-class. Eastern European (cultural, or "objective") nationalism, which emerged without an urban middle class, was characterized by a mystical bond between the land and people, and was a reaction to western ideas of modernization. It was believed that "the people" were infused with a creative force, of which nations were the expression. For cultural nationalists, race, language, and an apparent shared community of descent are important ideological factors. An influential three-phase model for national consciousness was offered by Miroslav Hroch. The first stage was based upon a cultural renaissance, usually manifesting itself as a search for folklore and customs. The second stage witnessed the emergence of activists calling for the establishment of a nation. Stage three saw mass support for the national idea, which was often evident during periods of rapid modernization.

Historians of nationalism have sought to define the meaning of the concept, and have questioned the legitimacy of the central tenets of nationalist ideology. Nationalism has therefore been variously analyzed as an ideological vehicle for the mobilization of popular support for bourgeois goals; as a tool to be used to enrol the masses into politics; as a secular form of religion, in which individuals achieve freedom and fulfillment through the cultivation of their unique national identity; and, conversely, as a by-product of the urge, during certain periods of a nation's history, for cultural homogeneity. Eric Hobsbawm, however, in *Nations and Nationalism since 1780* (1990) posited the thesis that, as national languages emerged only from the confusion of local dialects as a result of mass literacy and education, nations and national feeling were largely invented, or imposed from above. This imposition has been legitimated by the use of invented histories, traditions, and symbols, such as national anthems and national flags. This approach has also been used by Benedict Anderson and Ernest Gellner, studying the functions of nationalist discourse within rapidly modernizing societies.

Writers of national histories were invariably nationalists, informed by the pervading cultural ethos of the time, which drew heavily upon nationalist discourse. See, for example, George Bancroft's *History of the United States from the Discovery of the American Continent* (1834–74); František Palacký's *Geschichte von Böhmen* (History of Bohemia, 1836–67); Jules Michelet's *Histoire de France* (1833–67; History of France, 1844–46); Heinrich von Treitschke's *Deutsche Geschichte im neunzehnten Jahrhundert* (1879–94; History of Germany in the Nineteenth Century* (1879–94); and William Stubbs' *Constitutional History of England* (1874–78). Early national historians essentialized supposed national characteristics, and sought to trace these national markers into the distant past, thereby placing the nation in a long-term historical framework, and legitimizing the idea of the nation. This reciprocity between nationalism and the writing of national history informed the culture of the time, and resulted in constructions of the nation and national identity which many modern historians now question. Early nationalists emphasized national characteristics in order to call for the forging of nations (for example, in the case of Italy and Germany), to glorify and to eulogize the nation, or to redefine or reassert national character. The glorification of the historical "achievements" of some nations was even echoed by Marx and Engels, who argued that the Slavonic peoples of Eastern Europe were *geschichtslos* (without history) and that their languages and cultures would die out with the march of progress.

The later 19th century saw biological ethnicity emerge as a central factor of belonging to, or exclusion from, the nation. This was due to Darwinian evolutionary ideas, and their application to human society by thinkers such as Comte de Gobineau, Vacher de Lapouge, and Houston Stewart Chamberlain. The uniqueness of "races" was stressed, as well as their phenotypical classification into a hierarchy of worth and ability. Again this classification tended to favor "historic" nations such as the English, Germans, and French, and created a vast category of subaltern peoples from the Irish through to the Turks and the Bantu. Later, fascist ideology demanded the submerging of the individual in the totality of the nation (*Volksgemeinschaft*), with national goals defined by a dictator, and popular support roused for the pursuit of those goals. Nazism added to this ideology many of the ideas to be found in the cultural nationalism model, with its emphasis on racial exclusivity and superiority, and the perceived biological basis of national characteristics. Michael Burleigh has argued that an entire discipline – *Ostforschung* (study of Eastern Europe) – emerged during the Third Reich, which attempted to reinterpret the historical role of the Germans in Eastern Europe as one of natural dominance over "inferior, historyless" peoples. Eric Hobsbawm has challenged the notion of specific national characteristics and the replacement of group allegiance for national allegiance; he has also questioned ethnicity as a founding factor of nationhood, and has cited migration and the existence of multi-ethnic regions in his defence.

Just as Western nationalism has affected the construction of histories, so in turn the emergence of an intelligentsia claiming in some way to represent African, Asian, and South American indigenous populations has led to the creation of new histories. In some of these histories the construction of the subject is mimetic. The work of Basil Davidson on Africa is largely a hermeneutic inversion of Western nationalist historiography. Some scholars have made methodological innovations. Gayatri Chakavorty Spivak has questioned the ability of the scholar to represent the "subaltern" historical subject and Edward Said has argued that the concept of the "Orient" and the whole discipline of "Oriental Studies" was constructed by Western scholars (particularly the British, French, and Germans) during the era of the growth of their own national consciousness.

Much of the recent research by historians of nationalism has also focussed upon the interrelationship between gender and nationalism. Anthias and Yuval-Davis have highlighted the role assigned to women as producers in the nation-state. They have asserted that women are assigned the role as the nation's biological reproducers, and, in their role as mothers, of perpetuating the culture of the nation/ethnic group through the socialization of future generations during children's formative years. Feminine symbolism has also been addressed, for example, the image of "vulnerable" womanhood needing male protection during periods of war. Nationalist discourse is seen to have encouraged the division of male and female into separate spheres – the private and the public – with the effect that the "natural" female role has been perceived as passive domestic provider, while the male performed the duties of the active citizen in service of the nation.

Nationalism as a subject for research appears to exert an enduring interest, with the revival of nationalism, and the creation of new nation-states, especially in Eastern Europe and the former Soviet Union. The debate concerning the creation of a United Europe will also serve to question current theories of nationalism, and the applicability, indeed relevance, of the role of nationalism to such a supra-state. The role of rival forms of allegiance (gender, sexuality, race, class), and their reciprocal relationship with nationalism also continues to be a lively source of debate.

CATHERINE CARMICHAEL
and MICHAEL ALMOND-WELTON

See also Anderson, B.; Balkans; Bancroft; Berlin; Davidson; East Central Europe; Hobsbawm; Michelet; Palacký; Said; Stubbs; Sugar; Treitschke

Further Reading

Anderson, Benedict, *Imagined Communities: Reflections on the Origin and Spread of Nationalism*, London and New York: Verso, 1983; revised 1991

Anthias, Floya and Nira Yuval-Davis, *Woman, Nation, State*, Basingstoke: Macmillan, and New York: St. Martin's Press, 1989

Bancroft, George, *History of the United States from the Discovery of the American Continent*, Boston: Little Brown, 10 vols., 1834–74

Berlin, Isaiah, *Vico and Herder: Two Studies in the History of Ideas*, London: Hogarth Press, and New York: Viking, 1976

Breuilly, John, *Nationalism and the State*, Manchester: Manchester University Press, and New York: St. Martin's Press, 1982

Burleigh, Michael, *Germany Turns Eastwards: A Study of Ostforschung in the Third Reich*, Cambridge and New York: Cambridge University Press, 1988

Chamberlain, Houston Stewart, *Die Grundlagen des neunzehnten Jahrhunderts*, Munich: Bruckmann, 1899; in English as *Foundations of the Nineteenth Century*, 2 vols., London: Lane, 1910

Colley, Linda, *Britons: Forging the Nation, 1707–1832*, New Haven and London: Yale University Press, 1992

Curthoys, Ann, Carroll Smith-Rosenberg, Mary Poovey, Catherine Hall, Samita Sen, Beth Baron, Joanna de Groot, and Eleni Varikes, "Gender Nationalisms and National Identities," *Gender and History* 5 (1993), 159–83 [special issue]

Darwin, Charles, *On the Origin of Species by Means of Natural Selection; or, The Preservation of Favoured Races in the Struggle for Life*, London: Murray, 1859, New York: Appleton, 1860; 6 revisions, 1860–76

Darwin, Charles, *The Descent of Man, and Selection in Relation to Sex*, 2 vols., London: Murray, and New York: Appleton, 1871

Davidson, Basil, *The Story of Africa*, London: Mitchell Beazley, 1984

Fichte, Johann Gottlieb, *Reden an die deutsche Nation*, Berlin: In der Realschulbuchhandlung, 1808; in English as *Addresses to the German Nation*, Chicago: Open Court, 1922

Gellner, Ernest, *Nations and Nationalism*, Oxford: Blackwell, and Ithaca, NY: Cornell University Press, 1983

Gobineau, Comte de, *Essai sur l'inégalité des races humaines*, 4 vols., Paris: Firmin Didot, 1853–55; in English as *The Inequality of Human Races*, New York: Putnam, and London: Heinemann, 1915

Greenfeld, Liah, *Nationalism: Five Roads to Modernity*, Cambridge, MA: Harvard University Press, 1992

Hayes, Carlton J.H., *Essays on Nationalism*, New York: Macmillan, 1926

Hayes, Carlton J.H., *The Historical Evolution of Modern Nationalism*, New York: Macmillan, 1931

Herder, J.G., *Ideen zur Philosophie der Geschichte der Menschheit*, 4 vols., 1785–91; in English as *Outlines of a Philosophy of the History of Man*, London: Hansard, 1800; abridged as *Reflections on the Philosophy of the History of Mankind*, Chicago: University of Chicago Press, 1968

Hobsbawm, Eric J., *Nations and Nationalism since 1780: Programme, Myth, Reality*, Cambridge and New York: Cambridge University Press, 1990

Hroch, Miroslav, *Social Preconditions of the National Revival in Europe: A Comparative Analysis of the Social Composition of Patriotic Groups among the Smaller European Nations*, Cambridge and New York: Cambridge University Press, 1985

Hutchinson, John, *The Dynamics of Cultural Nationalism: The Gaelic Revival and the Question of the Irish Nation State*, London and Boston: Allen and Unwin, 1987

Hutchinson, John, and Anthony D. Smith, eds., *Nationalism*, Oxford and New York: Oxford University Press, 1994

Kedourie, Elie, *Nationalism*, London: Hutchinson, and New York: Praeger, 1960; revised 1993

Kemiläinen, Aira, *Nationalism: Problems Concerning the Word, the Concept and Classification*, Jyvaskyla, Finland: Jyväskylvfän Kasvatusapillinen Korkeakoulu, 1964

Kohn, Hans, *The Idea of Nationalism*, New York: Macmillan, 1944

Michelet, Jules, *Histoire de France*, 17 vols., Paris: Hachette, 1833–67; abridged in English as *History of France*, 2 vols., London: Chapman and Hall, 1844–46; New York: Appleton, 1845–47

Minogue, Kenneth R., *Nationalism*, New York: Basic Books, and London: Batsford, 1967

Nairn, Tom, *The Break-up of Britain: Crisis and Neo-Nationalism*, London: NLB, 1977; revised 1981

Palacký, František, *Geschichte von Böhmen* (History of Bohemia), 5 vols., Prague: Kronberger & Weber, 1836–67

Rosdolsky, Roman, *Zur Nationalen Frage: Friedrich Engels und das Problem der "Geschichtslosen" Völker*, Berlin: Olle & Wolter, 1979; in English as *Engels and the "Nonhistoric" Peoples: The National Question in the Revolution of 1848*, Glasgow: Critique, 1986

Said, Edward W., *Orientalism*, New York: Pantheon, and London: Routledge, 1978

Spivak, Gayatri, *In Other Worlds: Essays in Cultural Politics*, London and New York: Methuen, 1987

Stubbs, William, *The Constitutional History of England in Its Origin and Development*, 3 vols., Oxford: Oxford University Press, 1874–78

Sugar, Peter F., and Ivo J. Lederer, eds., *Nationalism in Eastern Europe*, Seattle: University of Washington Press, 1969

Treitschke, Heinrich von, *Deutsche Geschichte im neunzehnten Jahrhundert*, 5 vols., Leipzig: Hirzel, 1879–94; in English as *History of Germany in the Nineteenth Century*, 7 vols., London: Jarrold, and New York: McBride, 1915–19

Vacher de Lapouge, Georges, *Race et milieu social: essais d'anthroposociologie* (Race and Social Milieu: Essays on Anthropological Sociology), Paris: Rivière, 1909

Native American History

The late 1960s and early 1970s can be seen as a watershed within Native American history. A shift significant in scope, methodology, and perspective accompanied an upsurge in publication and scholarship. Prior to this, native peoples had a limited and circumscribed role within histories of the United States, whose direction and leadership were firmly European. In 1893 when Frederick Jackson Turner delivered his famous lecture, "The Significance of the Frontier in American History," he positioned the frontier and the Indian firmly within the nation's past. The Indian's characterization as a "vanishing" and/or a "noble savage" solidified within contemporary discourse and within United States history. Subsequent early 20th-century historical studies that focused on Native Americans, dismissed as "myth" a rich native oral tradition, and based research upon European sources laden with mediations of translation, male bias, and cultural incomprehension. The University of Oklahoma Press did, however, pioneer Native American history publication, beginning a Civilization of the American Indian series in 1932 which included Grant Foreman's series of texts on Indian removal. Like Angie Debo's work in the 1940s, Foreman's texts remain valuable standard tribal-history subject studies concerned with native experience. Yet it was the fascination of frontier conflict which retained most popularity with the reading public up until the middle decades of the 20th century in texts by scholars such as George T. Hunt and Howard Peckham. Nevertheless, as late as the mid-20th century Native Americans remained essentially marginalized figures within the broad range of interpretations of American history.

These developments within the field up until the watershed years have been divided by Frederick Hoxie into three neat categories: "the history of Indian policy, the history of frontier conflict (including white settlement and warfare), and tribal histories whose narratives usually ended around 1900" with historians dominating the first two categories and anthropologists the last. Anthropology had of course provided a bedrock for scholarship on Native Americans, its most significant early publication being Lewis Henry Morgan's 1851 *The League of the Iroquois*. A useful overview of the discipline and its theoretical development has been provided by Marvin Harris. Even after the reorientation in Indian scholarship stemming from the 1960s, scholarship on Indian policy did not disappear: its foremost practitioner remains Francis Paul Prucha. But after the early 1970s, debate moved beyond consideration of the construction or merits of specific policy and increasingly focused instead on how such policy was administered and experienced by native peoples. Scholars, benefiting from institutional developments such as the foundation of the D'Arcy McNickle Centre in 1972, began to move beyond the insidious stereotype of the "vanishing American." They began to frame research around questions of cultural survival and persistence, and new recognition of the actuality of cultural continuity and creative adaptation to another culture came to the fore. As the "conflict" and "consensus" paradigm which had been applied to American history lost intellectual currency, the Indian voice became more significant in the construction of the American past. Instead of casting American Indians as either the nation's chief victims or as marginal "exotics," historians began to address the complexities of Indian-white relations across time.

While Dee Brown created a popular but one-sided version of white-Indian relations for the Vietnam and Civil Rights generation, texts such as Angie Debo's *A History of the Indians of the United States* (1970) and Wilcomb E. Washburn's *The Indian in America* (1975) aimed toward more or less comprehensive overviews. The most broad-ranging body of studies were published by the Smithsonian from 1978 as the multivolume *Handbook of North American Indians* (general editor William C. Sturtevant) which gave an encyclopedic summary of knowledge of the prehistory, history, and cultures of the aboriginal peoples of North America.

After 1970, pre-Columbian history assumed a new significance within US history and US history textbooks, and pre-Columbian culture gained a global context. The essay collection edited by Alvin M. Josephy, Jr., *America in 1492* (1992) engaged in the contested area of pre-Columbian population estimate, an issue developed by Russell Thornton in *American Indian Holocaust and Survival* (1987).

Since the 1970s, "discovery" as the founding myth of the United States has remained a fascination for scholars, together with the implications and complexities of early contact. Recent approaches have tended to present fluid, reciprocal, mutual encounters whose nature remains dependent on the distribution of power within and between each group. Since 1991, there has been a welcome deluge of "Columbian Encounter" scholarship, parts of which are of particular value to students of indigenous America. The compilation *New World Encounters* (1993) edited by Stephen Greenblatt is one particularly useful New Historicist group of studies that gives discourse a determining role in the process of colonialism. A refreshing recent archaeological approach to contact and post-contact trade relations can be found in the twelve essays in *Ethnohistory and Archaeology* (1993), edited by J. Daniel Rogers and Samuel M. Wilson. Spanish conquest of the Indies has received much varied and diverse attention ranging from the quirky and romantic *The Conquest of Paradise* (1990) by Kirkpatrick Sale to the careful arguments housed within the anthology of Western understandings of the Island Caribs by Peter Hulme and Neil L. Whitehead. Conquest of the South and Southeast is discussed within the essay collection, *The Forgotten Centuries* (1994) edited by Charles Hudson and Carmen Chaves Tesser.

The biological impact of "discovery" has been traced by Alfred W. Crosby, Jr., in *The Columbian Exchange* (1972). Crosby's work can be juxtaposed to that of William Cronon and of Carolyn Merchant. Such work has problematized any idealized picture of an Indian Eden prior to contact, especially the idea of virgin land, and shown clear connections between environmental degradation and native conquest. The associated myth of a disease-free pre-contact America received similar treatment in *Disease and Demography in the Americas* (1992), edited by John W. Verano and Douglas H. Ubelaker. Male and female cross-cultural mediators post-contact were the focus of the collection *Between Indian and White Worlds* (1994), edited by Margaret Szasz. Indian academic voices which consider the role and significance of Columbus and "discovery" included *Confronting Columbus* (1992), edited by John Yewell, Chris Dodge, and Jan DeSirey and *The Unheard Voices* (1994), edited by Carole M. Gentry and Donald A. Grinde, Jr.

New approaches have developed the history of contact during the 17th and 18th centuries, for which limited records exist. "Ethnohistory," pioneered during the late 1950s and 1960s by anthropologists such as Anthony F.C. Wallace, attempted to present an Indian-oriented perspective within a marriage of disciplinary categories and concepts. An excellent introduction to the approach is James Axtell's *The European and the Indian* (1981). Historians such as Neal Salisbury, Gary B. Nash, and Richard White have brought a new understanding of the specificity of cultural perspective and of the extent of native peoples' adaptation to European influence. The Iroquois nation's significance within colonial politics has become another focus for scholars such as Daniel K. Richter, Francis Jennings, Barbara Graymont, and contributors to the compilation edited by Oren Lyons and John Mohawk. Dean Snow's comprehensive history, *The Iroquois* (1994) provided special, field-based insight to this group of peoples from 900 CE to the present. Debate continues over the nature of Indian cultural change which accompanied the fur trade. Key players in this debate include George R. Hammell and Christopher L. Miller, Calvin Martin, Arthur J. Ray, and contributions to the critique of Martin's text edited by Shepard Krech.

The perception of Indians held by Jefferson and his contemporaries has been studied by Bernard W. Sheehan who has related conceptions of native peoples in the late 18th and early 19th centuries to policy shifts designed to amalgamate and "civilize" them. Aspects of Jeffersonian thinking carried forward into the Jacksonian era where two recent texts stand out. The first is Satz's *American Indian Policy in the Jacksonian Era* (1975) and the second Rogin's *Fathers and Children* (1975).

Twentieth-century Indian studies remains a developing field. The late Hazel W. Hertzberg provided an excellent foundation stone for further study with her 1971 *The Search for an American Indian Identity*. Hertzberg characterized the Native American church as an example of modern religious "pan-Indianism." As a combination of Indian and non-Indian traditions, it has received further discussion within Omer C. Stewart's *Peyote Religion* (1987) and David F. Aberle's *The Peyote Religion among the Navaho* (1966). A useful overview of specific Native American 20th-century figures can be found in *American Indian Intellectuals* (1978), edited by Margot Liberty, while Indian leadership across both the 19th and 20th centuries receives consideration within *Indian Lives* (1985) edited by L.G. Moses and Raymond Wilson.

Scholars have found little positive to write about Indian education until the growth of Indian-oriented education in the 1970s. This aspect of Indian affairs remains a developing avenue of research, although there are useful broad-based texts by Margaret Szasz and by Estelle Fuchs and Robert J. Havinghurst. Authors such as Lomawaima and Mihesuah have also investigated how public and boarding school student experience affected Indian tribal and pan-tribal identity. To date, the 20th-century urban Indian experience has not received broad-ranging or comprehensive attention, although groundwork has been laid by Bernstein, Fixico, Sorkin, and Hauptman.

A further developing area of research, most of which is found within essays and journal articles, is that of the histories of Native American women. In 1984 Gretchen Bataille and Kathleen Sands provided an overview of biographical studies of 20th-century Native American women and more recently Nancy Shoemaker has edited a much-needed essay collection. The Indian "princess" Pocahontas alias "Matoaka," daughter of the Indian leader Powhatan, is a dominant symbol of 17th-century contact, and remains a focus of study surrounding native women. This can be related to the fact that she is probably the ultimate native subaltern, given that she left no verifiable words of her own. Recently, Robert S. Tilton has charted the powerful contrasting representations of her made possible by her silence; Karen Ordahl Kupperman provided an earlier study.

Indian art is inseparable from other aspects of native culture. From George Catlin's best-selling 1841 work to Lawrence Abbott's 17 interviews with practicing Native American artists, texts on this topic have yielded insight into issues of "authenticity" and native interaction with the non-Indian world. Correspondingly, Indian literatures have much to teach students of both the Indian past and Indian future. The work of critics such as Arnold Krupat have brought a new complexity to understanding the nature of the US literary canon and have developed understandings of the significance of the recent success of Indian writers. An excellent access to the motivation and agendas of Indian writers has been provided by Laura Coltelli in her 1990 interview compilation.

One of the most recent and interesting developments within Native American Studies is the increasing research on mestizo culture, that is, the product of racial intermixture of all kinds. Jacqueline Peterson and Jennifer S.H. Brown have edited a useful introduction to the developing research on the Métis, and Maria Root has edited a more general text, *Racially Mixed People in America* (1992). Gary B. Nash is concerned to see that the "hidden history" of a Mestizo America gains its proper historical significance, while studies of Afro-Indian intercultural relations, by Jack D. Forbes and Theda Perdue, have caused a series of older assumptions to be questioned.

Indian historical writing has been forced to address issues that overlap with subaltern and postcolonial studies. Issues of power, agency, "Indian voice," and audience for Indian scholarship await productive resolution. Although excellent work such as Robert Berkhofer's *The White Man's Indian* (1978) has demonstrated the invented nature of so much of Indian representation, native scholars and commentators remain critical of the fact that much scholarship is discrete from central concerns of Native American Indian experience. It is to be hoped that the growing body of Native American authorship will further the rich possibilities of peaceful coexistence and communication which the current erosion of orthodoxy within United States history seems to promise.

JOY PORTER

See also Axtell; Crosby; Debo; Ethnohistory; Frontier; Nash; Prucha; Turner

Further Reading

Abbott, Lawrence, ed., *I Stand in the Center of the Good: Interviews with Contemporary Native American Artists*, Lincoln: University of Nebraska Press, 1994

Aberle, David F., *The Peyote Religion among the Navaho*, Chicago: Aldine, 1966

Axtell, James, *The European and the Indian: Essays in the Ethnohistory of Colonial North America*, New York: Oxford University Press, 1981

Axtell, James, *Beyond 1492: Encounters in Colonial North America*, New York: Oxford University Press, 1992

Bataille, Gretchen M., and Kathleen Mullen Sands, *American Indian Women: Telling Their Lives*, Lincoln: University of Nebraska Press, 1984

Berkhofer, Robert, Jr., *The White Man's Indian: Images of the American Indian from Columbus to the Present*, New York: Knopf, 1978

Bernstein, Alison R., *American Indians and World War II: Toward a New Era in Indian Affairs*, Norman: University of Oklahoma Press, 1991

Brown, Dee, *Bury My Heart at Wounded Knee: An Indian History of the American West*, New York: Holt Rinehart, and London: Barrie and Jenkins, 1971

Catlin, George, *Letters and Notes on the Manners, Customs and Conditions of North American Indians*, 2 vols., New York: Wiley and Putnam, and London: Catlin, 1841; reprinted Minneapolis: Ross and Haines, 1965

Coltelli, Laura, *Winged Words: American Indian Writers Speak*, Lincoln: University of Nebraska Press, 1990

Cronon, William, *Changes in the Land: Indians, Colonists, and the Ecology of New England*, New York: Hill and Wang, 1983

Crosby, Alfred W., Jr., *The Columbian Exchange: Biological and Cultural Consequences of 1492*, Westport, CT: Greenwood Press, 1972

Crosby, Alfred W., Jr., *Germs, Seeds, and Animals: Studies in Ecological History*, Armonk, NY: Sharpe, 1994

Debo, Angie, *And Still the Waters Run: The Betrayal of the Five Civilized Tribes*, Princeton: Princeton University Press, 1940; reprinted 1984

Debo, Angie, *The Road to Disappearance*, Norman: University of Oklahoma Press, 1941; reprinted 1979

Debo, Angie, *A History of the Indians of the United States*, Norman: University of Oklahoma Press, 1970; reprinted 1989

Fixico, Donald Lee, *Termination and Relocation: Federal Indian Policy, 1945–1960*, Albuquerque: University of New Mexico Press, 1986

Forbes, Jack D., *Black Africans and Native Americans: Color, Race and Caste in the Evolution of Red-Black Peoples*, Oxford and New York: Blackwell, 1988; revised as *Africans and Native Americans: The Language of Race and the Evolution of Red-Black Peoples*, Urbana: University of Illinois Press, 1993

Foreman, Grant, *Indian Removal: The Emigration of the Five Civilized Tribes of Indians*, Norman: University of Oklahoma Press, 1932; reprinted 1976

Foreman, Grant, *The Five Civilized Tribes*, Norman: University of Oklahoma Press, 1934; reprinted 1972

Fuchs, Estelle, and Robert J. Havinghurst, *To Live on This Earth: American Indian Education*, Garden City, NY: Doubleday, 1972

Gentry, Carole M., and Donald A. Grinde, Jr., eds., *The Unheard Voices: American Indian Responses to the Columbian Quincentenary, 1492–1992*, Los Angeles: American Indian Studies Center, University of California, 1994

Graymont, Barbara, *The Iroquois in the American Revolution*, Syracuse, NY: Syracuse University Press, 1972

Greenblatt, Stephen, ed., *New World Encounters*, Berkeley: University of California Press, 1993

Harris, Marvin, *The Rise of Anthropological Theory*, New York: Crowell, 1968

Hauptman, Laurence M., *The Iroquois and the New Deal*, Syracuse, NY: Syracuse University Press, 1981

Hauptman, Laurence M., *The Iroquois Struggle for Survival: World War II to Red Power*, Syracuse, NY: Syracuse University Press, 1986

Hertzberg, Hazel W., *The Search for an American Indian Identity: Modern Pan-Indian Movements*, Syracuse, NY: Syracuse University Press, 1971

Hoxie, Frederick E., *A Final Promise: The Campaign to Assimilate the Indians, 1880–1920*, Lincoln: University of Nebraska Press, 1984; Cambridge: Cambridge University Press, 1989

Hoxie, Frederick E., "The View from Eagle Butte: National Archives Field Branches and the Writing of American Indian History," *Journal of American History* 76 (1989), 172–80

Hudson, Charles, and Carmen Chaves Tesser, eds., *The Forgotten Centuries: Indians and Europeans in the American South, 1521–1704*, Athens: University of Georgia Press, 1994

Hulme, Peter, and Neil L. Whitehead, *Wild Majesty: Encounters with Caribs from Columbus to the Present Day*, Oxford and New York: Oxford University Press, 1992

Hunt, George T., *The Wars of the Iroquois: A Study in Intertribal Relations*, Madison: University of Wisconsin Press, 1940; reprinted 1994

Jennings, Francis, *The Invasion of America: Indians, Colonialism, and the Cant of Conquest*, Chapel Hill: University of North Carolina Press, 1975

Josephy, Alvin M., Jr., *America in 1492: The World of the Indian Peoples before the Arrival of Columbus*, New York: Knopf, 1992

Krech, Shepard III, ed., *Indians, Animals, and the Fur Trade: A Critique of Keepers of the Game*, Athens: University of Georgia Press, 1981

Krupat, Arnold, *The Voice in the Margin: Native American Literature and the Canon*, Berkeley: University of California Press, 1989

Kupperman, Karen O., *Settling with the Indians: The Meeting of English and Indian Cultures in America, 1580–1640*, Totowa, NJ: Rowman and Littlefield, 1980

Liberty, Margot, ed., *American Indian Intellectuals*, St. Paul, MN: West, 1978

Lomawaima, K. Tsianina, *They Called It Prairie Light: The Story of Chilocco Indian School*, Lincoln: University of Nebraska Press, 1994

Lyons, Oren, and John Mohawk, *Exiled in the Land of the Free: Democracy, Indian Nations, and the US Constitution*, Sante Fe: Clear Light, 1992

Martin, Calvin, *Keepers of the Game: Indian-Animal Relationships and the Fur Trade*, Berkeley: University of California Press, 1978

Merchant, Carolyn, *Ecological Revolutions: Nature, Gender, and Science in New England*, Chapel Hill: University of North Carolina Press, 1989

Mihesuah, Devon A., *Cultivating the Rosebuds: The Education of Women at the Cherokee Female Seminary, 1851–1909*, Urbana: University of Illinois Press, 1993

Miller, Christopher L., and George R. Hammell, "A New Perspective on Indian-White Contact: Cultural Symbols and Colonial Trade," *Journal of American History* 73 (1986), 311–28

Morgan, Lewis Henry, *The League of the Ho-dé-no-sau-nee or Iroquois*, Rochester, NY: Sage and Brother, 1851; reprinted as *League of the Iroquois*, New York: Corinth, 1962

Moses, Lester George, and Raymond Wilson, eds., *Indian Lives: Essays on Nineteenth and Twentieth Century Native American Leaders*, Albuquerque: University of New Mexico Press, 1985

Nash, Gary B., *Red, White, and Black: The Peoples of Early America*, Englewood Cliffs, NJ: Prentice Hall, 1974; 3rd edition, 1991

Nash, Gary B., "The Hidden History of Mestizo America," *Journal of American History* 82 (1995), 941–64

Peckham, Howard, *Pontiac and the Indian Uprising*, Princeton: Princeton University Press, 1947; reprinted 1994

Perdue, Theda, *Slavery and the Evolution of Cherokee Society, 1540–1866*, Knoxville: University of Tennessee Press, 1979

Peterson, Jacqueline, and Jennifer S.H. Brown, eds., *The New Peoples: Being and Becoming Métis in North America*, Lincoln: University of Nebraska Press, 1985

Prucha, Francis Paul, ed., *Documents of United States Indian Policy*, Lincoln: University of Nebraska Press, 1975

Prucha, Francis Paul, *The Great Father: The United States Government and the American Indians*, 2 vols., Lincoln: University of Nebraska Press, 1984; abridged 1986

Prucha, Francis Paul, *American Indian Treaties: The History of a Political Anomaly*, Berkeley: University of California Press, 1994

Ray, Arthur J., *Indians in the Fur Trade: Their Role as Trappers, Hunters, and Middlemen in the Lands Southwest of Hudson Bay, 1660–1870*, Toronto: University of Toronto Press, 1974

Richter, Daniel K., *The Ordeal of the Longhouse: The Peoples of the Iroquois League in the Era of European Colonization*, Chapel Hill: University of North Carolina Press, 1992

Rogers, J. Daniel, and Samuel M. Wilson, eds., *Ethnohistory and Archaeology: Approaches to Postcontact Change in the Americas*, New York: Plenum Press, 1993

Rogin, Michael Paul, *Fathers and Children: Andrew Jackson and the Subjugation of the American Indian*, New York: Knopf, 1975

Root, Maria P.P., ed., *Racially Mixed People in America*, Newbury Park, CA: Sage, 1992

Sale, Kirkpatrick, *The Conquest of Paradise: Christopher Columbus and the Columbian Legacy*, New York: Knopf, 1990

Salisbury, Neal, *Manitou and Providence: Indians, Europeans, and the Making of New England, 1500–1643*, New York: Oxford University Press, 1982

Satz, Ronald N., *American Indian Policy in the Jacksonian Era*, Lincoln: University of Nebraska Press, 1975

Sheehan, Bernard W., *Seeds of Extinction: Jeffersonian Philanthropy and the American Indian*, Chapel Hill: University of North Carolina Press, 1973

Shoemaker, Nancy, ed., *Negotiators of Change: Historical Perspectives on Native American Women*, London and New York: Routledge, 1995

Snow, Dean R., *The Iroquois*, Oxford and Cambridge, MA: Blackwell, 1994

Sorkin, Alan L., *The Urban American Indian*, Lexington, MA: Lexington, 1978

Stewart, Omer C., *Peyote Religion: A History*, Norman: University of Oklahoma Press, 1987

Sturtevant, William C., general editor, *Handbook of North American Indians*, Washington, DC: Smithsonian Institution Press, 1978–

Szasz, Margaret, *Education and the American Indian: The Road to Self-Determination, 1928–1973*, Albuquerque: University of New Mexico Press, 1974

Szasz, Margaret, *Between Indian and White Worlds: The Cultural Broker*, Norman: University of Oklahoma Press, 1994

Thornton, Russell, *American Indian Holocaust and Survival: A Population History since 1492*, Norman: University of Oklahoma Press, 1987

Tilton, Robert S., *Pocahontas: The Evolution of an American Narrative*, Cambridge and New York: Cambridge University Press, 1994

Turner, Frederick Jackson, *The Significance of the Frontier in American History*, Madison: State Historical Society of Wisconsin, 1894 [as lecture 1893]

Verano, John W., and Douglas H. Ubelaker, eds., *Disease and Demography in the Americas*, Washington, DC: Smithsonian Institution Press, 1992

Wallace, Anthony F.C., *The Death and Rebirth of the Seneca*, New York: Knopf, 1970

Washburn, Wilcomb E., ed., *The American Indian and the United States: A Documentary History*, 4 vols., New York: Random House, 1973

Washburn, Wilcomb E., *The Indian in America*, New York: Harper, 1975

White, Richard, *The Roots of Dependency: Subsistence, Environment, and Social Change among the Choctaws, Pawnees, and Navajos*, Lincoln: University of Nebraska Press, 1983

White, Richard, *The Middle Ground: Indians, Empires, and Republics in the Great Lakes Region, 1650–1815*, Cambridge and New York: Cambridge University Press, 1991

Yewell, John, Chris Dodge, and Jan DeSirey, eds., *Confronting Columbus: An Anthology*, Jefferson, NC: McFarland, 1992

Natural Sciences, Historical

The history of historical natural sciences (i.e., geology, paleontology, mineralogy, botany, and zoology, as well as other fields formerly emcompassed by natural history) has a pattern of development very similar to that of the history of sciences in general. The first historical accounts were written by 19th-century scientists involved in the very constitution of these disciplines, mainly as part of a strategy of social and academic legitimization. An excellent example would be the introductory chapters of Charles Lyell's *Principles of Geology* (1830–33), in which he gives his version of the birth of geology as a modern science and establishes the "heroes" and the "villains," obviously placing himself among the former. This kind of exposition was responsible for the transmission of a "received view," that is still very common in textbooks and secondary papers on the history of science.

In the 1930s the first works focusing especially on the history of historical natural sciences appeared; these indubitably echoed the new level of institutionalization being experienced at that time by the history of sciences in general, due to the efforts of scholars such as George Sarton and Paul Tannery. At the institutional level there was the creation in 1936 of the international Society for the Bibliography of Natural History (from 1983 Society for the History of Natural History). This society embraces all aspects of the history and bibliography of the set of disciplines within the biological and earth sciences and publishes a regular and comprehensive journal.

On the thematic level, a good example of a text specific to the area is Adams' *The Birth and Development of the Geological Sciences* (1938). Its evident "internalistic" approach emphasizes tracing ideas and concepts supposed to be non- or pre-scientific back to their roots, as well as identifying the precursors or far-sighted individuals considered to have had insights beyond their time. This kind of work usually combined certain elements of erudite scholarship made necessary by consultation of some of the original sources (classical, medieval, or early modern works), and a philosophical framework – even if this is better used to judge than to elucidate "the strange explanations which were put forward by ancient writers." Such an intellectual history of scientific rationality has flourished up until today, as can be seen in Ellenberger's or Gohau's histories of geology.

On the other hand, the "externalistic" approach – the other side of the theoretical debate that arose in the 1930s – resulted in another trend of historiographical production which has also extended up to present. Using historical materialism more or less explicitly, these works were produced mainly by Eastern European historians of science, although some Chinese have also worked along this line. Emphasis was placed on a description and analysis of the material conditions of a given time and society, stressing its economy and needs, and then establishing links with scientific achievements and ideas. Fine representative papers, to quote a few, are those by Tikhomirov and Guntau. Part of the writings along this line were also contained in introductory chapters with a nationalistic view in scientific textbooks, whose main purpose is to carve a niche for outstanding countrymen in the general standard history of the sciences.

It is important to mention that not all of the historiography produced up to the beginning of the 1970s followed these general trends. Books by Hooykaas, Davies, and Rudwick, are probably better fitted within the framework of a social history of historical natural sciences. Hoykaas was especially skilled in his connection of philosophy, science, religion, and literature. Rudwick, on the other hand, pioneered the use of iconographical sources in the history of sciences.

From the 1970s onwards, the development of the social studies of science opened a rich arena for work in this field, allowing for the flourishing of a diversified historiography, which has increased since the 1979 publication of Barnes and Shapin's *Natural Order*. Demystifying and reconceiving naturalism and natural sciences has led the studies to focus on the relationships between these disciplines and imperialism, on the contradictory processes involved in the "mundialization" of sciences, on the construction of our image of nature (and the very shaping of our knowledge about it), and on minor actors such as insect collectors, women scientists, mineral dealers, or amateur botanists. Former "peripheral" themes or countries (in Latin America or Africa) have come to receive more attention over the years, too. Hence, it seems that a broader and more accurate picture of the history of historical natural sciences is emerging.

SILVIA FIGUEIRÔA

See also Archaeology; Sarton; Science

Further Reading

Adams, Frank D., *The Birth and Development of the Geological Sciences*, New York: Dover, 1938

Albritton, Claude C., Jr., *The Abyss of Time: Changing Conceptions of the Earth's Antiquity after the Sixteenth Century*, San Francisco: Freeman Cooper, 1980

Barnes, Barry, and Steven Shapin, eds., *Natural Order: Historical Studies of Scientific Culture*, London: Sage, 1979

Davies, Gordon L., *The Earth in Decay: A History of British Geomorphology, 1578–1878*, New York: American Elsevier, and London: Macdonald, 1969

Ellenberger, François, *Histoire de la géologie* (The History of Geology), 2 vols., Paris: Lavoisier, 1988–94

Geikie, Archibald, *The Founders of Geology*, New York and London: Macmillan, 1905

Gohau, Gabriel, *Histoire de la géologie*, Paris: La Découverte, 1987; in English as *A History of Geology*, New Brunswick, NJ: Rutgers University Press, 1990

Gould, Stephen J., *Time's Arrow, Time's Cycle: Myth and Metaphor in the Discovery of Geological Time*, Cambridge, MA: Harvard University Press, 1987

Guntau, Martin, *Die Genesis der Geologie als Wissenschaft* (The Genesis of Geology as a Science), Berlin: Akademie, 1984

Hooykaas, Reijer, *Natural Law and Divine Miracle: A Historical-Critical Study of the Principle of Uniformity in Geology, Biology, and Theology*, Leiden: Brill, 1963

Kumar, Deepak, *Science and Empire: Essays in Indian Context, 1700–1947*, Delhi: Anamika, 1990

Lyell, Charles, *Principles of Geology*, 3 vols., London: Murray, 1830–33

MacKenzie, John M., ed., *Imperialism and the Natural World*, Manchester: Manchester University Press, 1990

Porter, Roy, *The Making of Geology: Earth Science in Britain, 1660–1815*, Cambridge and New York: Cambridge University Press, 1977

Rossi, Paolo, *I segni del tempo: storia della Terra e storia delle nazioni da Hooke a Vico* (Signs of Time: History of the Earth and History of Nations from Hooke to Vico), Milan: Feltrinelli, 1979

Rudwick, Martin J.S., *The Meaning of Fossils: Episodes in the History of Palaeontology*. New York: American Elsevier, and London: Macdonald, 1972

Rudwick, Martin J.S., *The Great Devonian Controversy: The Shaping of Scientific Knowledge among Gentlemanly Specialists*, Chicago: University Chicago Press, 1985

Rudwick, Martin J.S., *Scenes from Deep Time: Early Pictorial Representations of the Prehistoric World*, Chicago: University Chicago Press, 1992

Secord, Anne, "Science in the Pub: Artisan Botanists in Early Nineteenth-Century Lancashire," *History of Science* 32 (1994), 269–315

Secord, James, *Controversy in Victorian Geology: The Cambrian-Silurian Dispute*, Princeton: Princeton University Press, 1986

Sheets-Pyenson, Susan, *Cathedrals of Science: The Development of Colonial Natural History Museums during the Late 19th Century*, Montreal: McGill–Queen's University Press, 1989

Tikhomirov, Vladimir V., "An Attempt to Analyse the Development of Geology as a Science," *International Geological Review* 13 (1971)

Torre, Alejandro R.D., Tomás Mallo, and Daniel P. Fernández, eds., *De la ciencia ilustrada a la ciencia romántica* (From Enlightened Science to Romantic Science), Madrid: Doce Calles, 1995

Torrens, Hugh S., "Women in Geology 2: Etheldred Benett," *Open Earth* 21 (1985), 12–13

Torrens, Hugh S., and Michael A. Taylor, "Saleswoman to a New Science: Mary Anning and the Fossil Fish *Squaloraja* from the Lias of Lyme Regis," *Bulletin, Dorset Natural Historical and Archaeological Society* 105 (1989), 135–48

Naval History

The study of naval history involves the use of modern historical methods to examine the naval dimension of the past in breadth, depth, and context. Practitioners require specific skills in addition to those commonly required of historians, including knowledge of maritime technology, tactics, and strategy. The significance of naval history lies in the extent to which it can contribute to the development of mainstream history. For many years the study of navies, and other aspects of the history of war, has been ignored or denigrated, to the detriment of historical understanding. There remains a critical dichotomy at the heart of naval history, which reflects its origins. It has always been subject to the divergent demands of academic communities attempting to raise the standard of scholarship, and armed services seeking a relevant educational tool. In consequence it has received only fitful support from either community. It is indicative of the present-mindedness of naval history that there is no sustained historiography, and little interest in the objects and methods of the pioneers.

The professional study of naval history was developed by Professor Sir John Knox Laughton (1830–1915), a Cambridge mathematics graduate and naval instructor. Laughton argued that an accurate understanding of the past was the basis for the development of contemporary naval doctrine. His self-devised "scientific" approach to the sources paralleled the Rankean methodology promoted by his friend and colleague Samuel Rawson Gardiner. Appointed professor of modern history at King's College, London in 1885, Laughton brought naval history into the academic mainstream, contributing to the *English Historical Review* and *The Cambridge Modern History*. He enlisted the academic community to interpret the past for the Royal Navy, founding the Navy Records Society in 1893 to print archival material that would illuminate contemporary strategic debates. He stressed the importance of the context within which naval activity took place, and founded the study of imperial history at King's College. Laughton's aims and methods dominated the naval history in Britain and America. His most prominent followers were Captain Alfred Thayer Mahan USN (1840–1914) and Sir Julian Corbett (1854–1922). Mahan used history to support theories on the role of naval power in world history, and the primacy of sea-control strategies, in order to raise support for battlefleet seapower to his countrymen. Although he served as president of the American Historical Association, Mahan was more propagandist than scholar, subordinating the evidence to the message. His work was premature and unreliable. By contrast Corbett developed Laughton's approach, providing a succession of wide-ranging studies for the contemporary Royal Navy. However, Laughton had no successor in a British university. The Royal Navy, which had gained much from the professional study of history before 1914, founded a chair at the Naval College in 1919, but appointed a lightweight professor, revealing a careless approach. Without an academic base, and deprived of Laughton's intellectual drive, the subject slipped into a narrowly focused backwater, occasionally illuminated by the work of an isolated individual.

A similar pattern was repeated around the world. In the United States early interest, prompted by Mahan, soon withered. By the 1930s the subject had disappeared from university teaching, although a few seminal theses were written at this time, notably those of Robert Albion, Theodore Ropp, Arthur Marder, and James Baxter, all based on European archives. A strong naval institutional base preserved the subject, but the academic history of war has been marginalized, and with it the scholars who work in the field. There are more naval historians teaching in American universities than anywhere else, but there is no recognized school, no core debate, and little optimism. In France the study of war was a prominent target of the Annales school, and, lacking an institutional base, journals, and a coherent school, naval history remains marginal. Building on the educational traditions of the mid-19th century, high quality work was produced as part of naval education, and in staff histories, notably Edouard Desbrière's work on Napoleon's plans to invade Britain. But the French Navy lost interest in the 1950s and the subject withered. Modern work, attempting to link into the core discipline, has concentrated on ports and logistics. The most prominent individual scholar, Jean Boudriot, has devoted a lifetime to the study of the wooden warship. French naval archives remain popular, but published French-language material is poorly integrated into the field. The brief naval history of Germany, 1848–1945, has encouraged a more focused approach, concentrating on key debates, notably on the purpose of the Tirpitz program, discussed by Jonathan Steinberg and Volker Berghahn, among others, the degree of continuity between the Imperial and Nazi navies, and the impact of politics. Linked to a strong British field, these works offer the closest approximation in naval history to a major debate. It is significant that the history of the German navy is closely integrated into a dynamic historical mainstream. However, naval history in Germany is taught only in naval academies.

John Hattendorf's *Ubi Sumus?* (1994) provides an overview of the current state of the art. It is necessarily defensive. Across the world naval history is struggling for recognition in universities, and for survival in naval education. It is still trying to walk the fine line between the divergent demands that faced John Laughton in the 1870s; his methodology remains the benchmark for naval history, combining broadly based historical scholarship with the publication of primary source material, to expand the educational potential of the subject.

Naval history has rarely been able to afford the luxury of an internal debate. In order to be noticed naval historians have to work in the mainstream. Recently Jan Glete's outstanding *Navies and Nations* (1993) addressed the role of navies in the formation of modern nation-state. The early naval historians had little overlap as to subject. Their debates were methodological, reflecting the problem of combining scholarship and relevance. This was resolved by the universal acceptance of Laughton's "scientific" approach over Mahan's subordination of evidence to message. Perhaps more than any other branch of history the work of naval historians has reflected present concerns. Where Laughton sought to build naval doctrine, and Corbett a national strategy, the post-1918 work of Robert Albion reflected American antitrust legislation, and that of Arthur Marder the "merchants of death" campaign against the private manufacture and sale of arms. The disastrous losses inflicted on British and allied merchant shipping by U-boats in the two world wars prompted a wide ranging debate on the reasons why the Royal Navy was so ill-prepared. Until recently this produced more repetition and polemic than wisdom, because the prospect of a third such struggle seemed all too immediate. The rise of the Soviet navy prompted a rash of interest, addressing the basic question of whether Russia was, or had ever been, a naval power, a question addressed in John Daly's recent study. Most of the material was too present-minded to survive the collapse of the Soviet Union, but it has contributed to the wider debate about naval power as a historical phenomenon. The "natural" sea-powers are usually given as Athens, Carthage, Venice, and Britain, although Japan and the United States, which are essentially continental military powers, have been included. These are contrasted with Sparta, Rome, the Ottoman empire, Spain, France, Russia, and Germany. In addition the naval history of smaller states has been considered, necessarily in a context far removed from that normally applied to the Royal Navy; Lawrence Sondhaus' two volumes on the Habsburg Navy contributed a notable example. By contrast Iain Hamilton's *The Anglo-French Naval Rivalry, 1840–1870* (1993) provided a model comparative analysis of two services dominated by their perceptions of each other and engaged in a series of arms races and crises. Paul Halpern's work on the Mediterranean spread the research base wider still.

Naval history can be broken down by period and by subject. It is now possible to examine the historiography, and see signs of development, but the coverage is inconsistent. The development of warships, both as technical history and operational analysis, has a strong following, Jon Sumida's *In Defence of Naval Supremacy* (1989) being a highlight because it expanded the boundaries of the subject. Sumida examined critical aspects of the pre-1914 Royal Navy, calling into question the validity of Arthur Marder's *From the Dreadnought to Scapa Flow* (1961–70). Nicholas Rodger's *The Wooden World* (1986) examined the old image of life afloat in the sailing navy, revealing how the mid-18th-century Royal Navy functioned. This important book revised popular images dating back to the campaign against corporal punishment in the first half of the 19th century. Paul Kennedy's seminal *The Rise and Fall of British Naval Mastery* (1976) – an ambitious single-volume survey integrating naval, economic, and international history to revise the image created by Mahan – played a large part in reviving the academic study of naval history in Britain.

Significantly the strongest institutional supporter of naval history in the past thirty years has been the interdisciplinary Department of War Studies at King's College, London. From 1970 Bryan Ranft, professor of history at the Royal Naval College, Greenwich, returned the subject to the academic mainstream. It is now approximately where John Laughton left it in 1915, and will make little more progress without a permanent academic base. Until the subject can offer career opportunities and promotion it will remain marginal. Few historians study navies, fewer still teach naval history, and hardly any are specialist naval history teachers. Without the support of non-academic scholars the subject would long ago have died out. Naval history should make better use of the talents of those outside the academic mainstream; the subject is innately popular, and need not apologize for that, if best practice is employed. Critically naval history must reintegrate itself into the academic mainstream, to further the development of scholarship, without losing the support of navies. This *caveat* is critical, for navies still provide the greatest number of teaching posts. The key question for the subject is how to define naval historical expertise. Is it to be found in the most encyclopedic conception of the naval past, or in the detailed understanding of a specific period, in breadth, depth, and context? The latter offers the best hope for reintegration in a monograph-led profession, notably by encouraging those with period-specific expertise to examine naval issues, as seen in Bernard Capp's important study of the Cromwellian navy; but in doing so it risks losing sight of naval continuities and long-term comparisons.

ANDREW LAMBERT

See also Mahan; Maritime

Further Reading

Albion, Robert Greenhalgh, *Forests and Sea Power: The Timber Problem of the Royal Navy 1652–1862*, Cambridge, MA: Harvard University Press, 1926

Baugh, Daniel A., *British Naval Administration in the Age of Walpole*, Princeton: Princeton University Press, 1965

Baxter, James Phinney, *The Introduction of the Ironclad Warship*, Cambridge, MA: Harvard University Press, 1933

Berghahn, Volker, *Der Tirpitz Plan: Genesis und Verfall einer innenpolitischen Krisenstrategie unter Wilhelm II* (The Tirpitz Plan), Dusseldorf: Droste, 1971

Boudriot, Jean, *Le Vaisseau de 74 canons*, 4 vols., Paris: Boudriot, 1976–78; in English as *The Seventy-four Gun Ship: A Practical Treatise on the Art of Naval Architecture*, 1986–88

Capp, Bernard, *Cromwell's Navy: The Fleet and the English Revolution, 1648–1660*, New York and Oxford: Oxford University Press, 1989

Corbett, Julian S., *England in the Seven Years' War: A Study in Combined Strategy*, London: Longman, 1907

Corbett, Julian S., *Some Principles of Maritime Strategy*, London: Longman, 1911; reprinted London: Conway, 1972

Daly, John Charles Kennedy, *Russian Sea Power and "The Eastern Question," 1827–41*, Annapolis: Naval Institute Press, and London: Macmillan, 1991

Desbrière, Edouard, *1793–1805: projets et tentatives de débarquement dans les îles britanniques* (1793–1805: Plans to Invade the British Isles), 5 vols., Paris: Chapelot, 1901–02

Ehrman, John, *The Navy in the War of William III, 1689–1697: Its State and Direction*, Cambridge: Cambridge University Press, 1953

Friedmann, Norman, *British Carrier Aviation: The Evolution of the Ships and Their Aircraft*, London: Conway, 1988

Glete, Jan, *Navies and Nations: Warships, Navies, and State Building in Europe and America, 1500–1860*, 2 vols., Stockholm: Almqvist & Wiksell, 1993

Graham, Gerald Sandford, *The Politics of Naval Supremacy: Studies in British Maritime Ascendancy*, Cambridge: Cambridge University Press, 1965

Grove, Eric J., *Vanguard to Trident: British Naval Policy since World War II*, London: Bodley Head, 1987

Halpern, Paul G., *The Naval War in the Mediterranean, 1914–1918*, Annapolis: Naval Institute Press, and London: Allen and Unwin, 1987

Halpern, Paul G., *A Naval History of World War I*, Annapolis: Naval Institute Press, and London: University of London Press, 1994

Hamilton, C. Iain, *The Anglo-French Naval Rivalry, 1840–1870*, Oxford: Clarendon Press, and New York: Oxford University Press, 1993

Hattendorf, John B., *Ubi Sumus? The State of Naval and Maritime History*, Newport, RI: Naval War College Press, 1994

Hattendorf, John B., *Doing Naval History: Essays Towards Improvement*, Newport RI: Naval War College Press, 1995

Hunt, Barry Dennis, *Sailor-Scholar: Admiral Sir Herbert Richmond, 1871–1946*, Waterloo, Ontario: Wilfrid Laurier University Press, 1982

Kennedy, Paul M., *The Rise and Fall of British Naval Mastery*, London: Allen Lane, 1976

Lambert, Andrew, *The Crimean War: British Grand Strategy, 1853–1856*, Manchester: Manchester University Press, 1990

Laughton, John Knox, "The Scientific Study of Naval History," *Journal of the Royal United Services Institute* 18 (1874), 508–26

Laughton, John Knox, *Studies in Naval History: Biographies*, London: Longman, 1887

Lavery, Brian, *The Ship of the Line*, 2 vols., London: Conway, 1983–84

Mackay, Ruddock F., *Fisher of Kilverstone*, Oxford: Clarendon Press, 1973

Mahan, Alfred Thayer, *The Influence of Sea Power upon History, 1660–1783*, Boston: Little Brown, and London: Sampson Low, 1890

Marder, Arthur Jacob, *The Anatomy of British Sea Power: A History of British Naval Policy in the pre-Dreadnought Era, 1880–1905*, New York: Knopf, 1940

Marder, Arthur Jacob, *From the Dreadnought to Scapa Flow*, 5 vols., Oxford: Oxford University Press, 1961–70

Meyer, Jean, and Martine Acerra, *Marines et révolution*, Rennes: Ouest-France, 1988

Milner, Marc, *North Atlantic Run: The Royal Canadian Navy and the Battle for the Convoys*, Toronto: University of Toronto Press, 1985

Navy Records Society, London, 1894–, 150+ volumes published

Nicolas, Nicholas Harris, *A History of the Royal Navy from the Earliest Time to the Wars of the French Revolution*, 2 vols., London, 1847

Ranft, Brian M., ed., *Technical Change and British Naval Policy, 1860–1939*, London: Hodder and Stoughton, 1977

Rodger, N.A.M., *The Wooden World: An Anatomy of the Georgian Navy*, London: Collins, 1986

Ropp, Theodore, *The Development of a Modern Navy: French Naval Policy, 1871–1904*, Annapolis: Naval Institute Press, 1987

Schurman, Donald M., *The Education of a Navy: The Development of British Naval Strategic Thought, 1867–1914*, London, Cassell, 1965

Schurman, Donald M., *Julian S. Corbett, 1854–1922: Historian of British Maritime Policy from Drake to Jellicoe*, London: Royal Historical Society, 1981

Seager, Robert II, *Alfred Thayer Mahan: The Man and His Letters*, Annapolis, MD: Naval Institute Press, 1977

Sondhaus, Lawrence, *The Habsburg Empire and the Sea: Austrian Naval Policy, 1797–866*, West Lafayette, IN: Purdue University Press, 1989

Sondhaus, Lawrence, *The Naval Policy of Austria-Hungary, 1867–1918: Navalism, Industrial Development and the Politics of Dualism*, West Lafayette, IN: Purdue University Press, 1994

Steinberg, Jonathan, *Yesterday's Deterrent: Tirpitz and the Birth of the German Battlefleet*, London: Macdonald, 1965

Sumida, Jon Tetsuro, *In Defence of Naval Supremacy: Finance, Technology and British Naval Policy, 1889–1914*, London, Allen and Unwin, and Boston: Unwin Hyman, 1989

Tunstall, W.C. Brian, *The Realities of Naval History*, London: Allen and Unwin, 1936

Zimmerman, David, *The Great Naval Battle of Ottawa*, Toronto: University of Toronto Press, 1989

Near East: Ancient

The ancient Near East, that region that lies between the Mediterranean Sea and the Iranian plateau and includes Palestine and Mesopotamia, the fertile valleys of the Tigris and the Euphrates rivers, and Egypt, has inspired historians since Herodotus. The inquiry by historians into the past of the region has been a grand enterprise, but one the results of which must be judged critically as subjective and provisional at best.

The western historian's passion for Greco-Roman grandeur has remained virtually intact through the modern inquiries based on linguistic expertise and on more scientific methods of research, but the ancient Near East and its legacy of secrets have remained elusive, haunting, and mysterious. However, much that is known and understood about the region and its peoples today is indebted to western support for archaeological excavations, restoration of monuments, and the collection and deciphering of artifacts and recorded texts.

The best summaries of current knowledge range from James Breasted's classic and still valuable *A History of Egypt from the Earliest Times to the Persian Conquest* (1905) to Thomas Levy's *The Archaeology of Society in the Holy Land* (1995). Other helpful works include John A. Wilson's *The Burden of Egypt* (1951); S.N. Kramer's *The Sumerians* (1963); Georges Roux's *Ancient Iraq* (1964); W.W. Hallo and W.K. Simpson's *The Ancient Near East: A History* (1971); David Oates and Joan Oates' *The Rise of Civilization* (1976); Bruce Trigger's *Ancient Egypt* (1983); Gösta Ahlström's *The History of Ancient Palestine from the Paleolithic Period to Alexander's Conquest* (1993); and the latest edition of H.G. May's *Oxford Bible Atlas* (1984). These are among the most comprehensive and readable "histories" of the region available in English, although all remain subject to revision due to the continuing flow of discoveries. Also of value to students are "time line" graphs, among the most useful of which is Ian Shaw's *Time Line of the Ancient World: 3000 BC–AD 500* (1994).

It must be emphasized that today historians of these and other such soundly researched overviews are dependent on geographers and meteorologists, archaeologists and sociologists, paleographers and philologists, paleontologists and mineralogists, to say nothing of mythologists, comparative religionists, and theologians, and they draw conclusions for consumption by the general reader only very cautiously. Many have discovered that the overriding theme and principal characteristic of the historical source material of the ancient Near East (and even the medieval and modern Middle East) is a passion for continuity, not critical interpretation.

For example, in Mesopotamia, from Babylonian to Sassanian-Persian times, the preponderance of historical writing consists of lists of kings, annals of their reigns, and the names of the gods they served, preserved in temple and other monumental inscriptions and in constructed archives for administrative documents and records. Most notable is the Sumerian king list, compiled from various sources by Thorkild Jacobsen; it is a source that has yielded important information on a Sumerian heroic age and of an uninterrupted monarchy and a governing system of elders centered in Uruk that lasted from the mid-3rd millennium to the 18th century BCE. The discovery in Nineveh of the library of Ashurbanipal (668–627 BCE) yielded 20,000 clay tablets, including an Akkadian recension of earlier Babylonian and Hittite versions of the much older Sumerian pictographic record of heroic stories associated in myth with king Gilgamesh of Uruk, whom scholars now believe existed.

Two invaluable collections available in English bring the general reader in close touch with primary textual sources and, as much as is possible, with the thinking and beliefs of ancient

Near East peoples. The first is J.B. Pritchard's *Ancient Near Eastern Texts* (1950), which includes translations of the Epic of Gilgamesh, the Code of Hammurabi, and important texts from Akkad, Egypt, and Palestine, with marginal concordances of sacred Egyptian and biblical sources. The second is the richly interpretive yet soundly informed *Before Philosophy* (1946), edited by Henri Frankfort, which includes Jacobsen's brilliant essay on Mesopotamia, with its depiction of Gilgamesh's time.

Prior to our more scientific age and as recently as the late 19th century, information about the ancient Near East came to us through "genial amateurs," to use George Roux's phrase; prior, that is, to the discovery in 1946 by C.W.F. Libby of the University of Chicago of the radiocarbon method of dating ancient and prehistoric artifacts. Among those scholars of Mesopotamia noted by Roux were the explorer and philologist Sir Henry C. Rawlinson and the Italian-born French consul of Mosul, Paul E. Botta, who in 1843 led the first serious archaeological team to excavate Assyrian sites in Iraq, most notably at Nineveh and Nimrud. This paved the way for the discovery in 1845 of the Akkadian Semitic version of the Gilgamesh epic by two scholars from the British Museum, A.H. Layard and George Smith, and the Turkish archaeologist Hormuzd Rassam.

Between 1835 and 1847 the deciphering of the Assyro-Babylonian language (Akkadian) was assured by Edward Hincks of Ireland, Jules Oppert of France, and Rawlinson, who contributed to the 5-volume collection *The Cuneiform Inscriptions of Western Asia* (1861–1909). By 1900 the other Mesopotamian language, Sumerian, was at least provisionally understood, and the process of collecting the multitude of texts for museums and university libraries in Europe, America, and Turkey was underway. More careful scientific methods of excavation and research by the later German archaeologists Robert Koldewey and Walter Andrae at particular sites, such as Babylon and Assur respectively, were followed by other Europeans, such as Sir Leonard Woolley at Ur, A. Parrot at Mari, and British and American teams at Kish and other sites in the 20th century. Armed with modern technology, the heirs of these scholars and explorers have attempted to penetrate back into the 4th and 5th millennia BCE and into the Stone Age of ancient Iraq.

In the study of Egypt certain western names stand out, especially in terms of the unraveling of hieroglyphics and the establishment of the science of Egyptology. Most prominent is J.F. Champollion, who in 1821 deciphered the 604 ideogram signs, phonogram consonants, and determinative symbols of the Rosetta Stone, which was unearthed by Napoleon's troops near the Egyptian city of Rosetta in 1799 and is now in the British Museum. Gaston Maspero, founder of the French school of Oriental Archaeology at Cairo, excavated at Luxor and Karnak. His work, *Histoire ancienne des peuples de l'orient* (1874–1908; *The Dawn of Civilization*, 1894; *The Struggle of the Nations*, 1896; and *The Passing of the Empires*, 1900), remains a classic in the field. Breasted carried out research in both Egypt and Mesopotamia; his translations of historical records and his books, including *History of Egypt* and *The Dawn of Conscience* (1933), are essential reading.

Egyptian funerary literature – including the famous Book of the Dead, with its recorded charms, spells, formulas for use in the afterlife, prophecies, wisdom verse, hymns, and songs –

was set down in inscriptions first, and later on papyrus scrolls placed in tombs with the mummies. The earliest collection dates from the 18th dynasty (1580–1350 BCE). John A. Wilson's admirable translations are available in Pritchard's *Ancient Near Eastern Texts*.

Many western readers are familiar with the biblical literature associated with the history of the Israelites. Abraham, it is generally believed, came with his family from Ur in Sumer to Hebron in Canaan around 1850 BCE, and Joseph's migration to Egypt occurred during the Hyksos period (1700–1580). The encounters between the Israelites from Egypt and the Canaanites of Lebanon and Syria (Phoenicians to later Greek and Roman historians) occurred around 1290 as a result of the Exodus led by Moses. The conquest of Canaan, undertaken by Joshua, took approximately a hundred years by successive chiefs (or Judges) of the twelve tribes; finally David (c.1010–955) united the kingdom under a single authority on behalf of the progeny of Abraham. The capital city was Jerusalem and remained so until Solomon's death in 935, when the kingdom was divided into two parts: Israel in the north, Judah in the south. Jerusalem continued as the capital of Judah. Phoenicia, with its port cities of Sidon and Tyre, was the first to fall to the Israelites, although eventually it rose to eminence as a trading and maritime power throughout the eastern Mediterranean, particularly with the founding of Carthage in 814. The historic importance of Phoenicia derives from its invention of the alphabet. Later adopted and modified by the Greeks and the Aramaeans of central Syria, it supplanted all previous writing systems developed in the Near East. The region of the divided kingdom of the Jews was conquered first by the Assyrians (neo-Babylonians c.580), which marked both the cultural apogee of Babylon, with its famous hanging gardens under Nebuchanezzar, and the captivity of the Jews, 586–538. The Assyrians were followed by the Achaemenid Persians (539–331), the Greeks and Romans, and in 640 CE the Muslims.

Greater attention focused on the region of Palestine in 1947 and 1948, with the discovery in the Qumran caves of the Dead Sea Scrolls, dating from c.140 BCE, and with the founding of the state of Israel. Millar Burrows' *The Dead Sea Scrolls* (1955) remains a readable and balanced historical account and assessment of the discovery of the scrolls and of their importance to Jewish and Christian religious understanding. Numerous books have appeared on the subject, and controversies from various quarters surround the discovery, claim to ownership, and interpretation of the scrolls. One of the best non-textual sources for the sites of ancient Palestine, as for Egypt and Mesopotamia, is the series of educational films produced by the National Geographic Society for dissemination in schools and colleges. Gösta Ahlström and Thomas Levy have provided two fine general studies of the archaeology and history of ancient Palestine.

In summary, a few points need reiteration. Although the ancient Near East is distant in time, that distance has been greatly shortened in the last two centuries through the efforts of both amateur explorers and scientists. Long-buried monuments and texts have been uncovered, deciphered, and critically assessed. The modern historian has found guidance both from the learning and observations of the Greek writer Herodotus and from the carbon-14 dating of the American scholar Libby. The content and inspirational origin of the familiar old texts considered sacred and authoritative have been subjected to comparison with the content and non-monotheistic perspective of still older texts, such as the secular Mesopotamian Epic of Gilgamesh (with its detailed account of a Great Flood), the 2nd-millennium Code of Hammurabi, and the Egyptian Book of the Dead, each a testimony of distinct and parallel development throughout the ancient Near East. The Epic of Gilgamesh gives a sophisticated picture of the human concerns, particularly of what Jacobsen called "the revolt against death," that drove the Babylonian people of the 2nd millennium to affirm a world-view whose central idea was human justice rather than the whims of gods. Further, although rich in its mythopoetic consciousness, it also depicted the ancient Near East as a place of continuing dialectic between unsettled nomadic steppe and desert peoples and the builders of the great cities who guarded the sacred and encouraged civilization. The distinguished Muslim social historian and philosopher Ibn Khaldūn (1332–1406) demonstrated that this dialectic continued through pre-Islamic Arabian times and on through Islamic history.

The contemporary traveler both to the older surviving cities and to the more rural regions of the Middle East discovers a continuity difficult to comprehend from the perspective of modern western consciousness. The ancient Near East continues to hold secrets of experience and wisdom mirroring the desires and needs of many beyond its boundaries of place and time, and the spirit of inquiry and passion to understand still invite the historian to journey there, and to return to communicate to others what remains to be learned.

HERBERT W. MASON

See also Breasted; Egypt: Ancient; Massignon; Trigger

Further Reading

Ahlström, Gösta W., *The History of Ancient Palestine from the Paleolithic Period to Alexander's Conquest*, Minneapolis: Fortress Press, and Sheffield: JSOT Press, 1993

Breasted, James Henry, *A History of Egypt from the Earliest Times to the Persian Conquest*, New York: Scribner, 1905, revised 1909; London: Murray, 1938

Breasted, James Henry, *The Dawn of Conscience*, New York: Scribner, 1933

Burrows, Millar, *The Dead Sea Scrolls*, New York: Viking, 1955; London: Secker and Warburg, 1956

Frankfort, Henri, general editor, *Before Philosophy: The Intellectual Adventure of Ancient Man: An Essay on Speculative Thought in the Ancient Near East*, Baltimore: Penguin, 1946; Harmondsworth: Penguin, 1949

Hallo, William W., and William Kelly Simpson, *The Ancient Near East: A History*, New York: Harcourt Brace, 1971

Jacobsen, Thorkild, *Sumerian King List*, Chicago: University of Chicago Press, 1939

Kramer, Samuel Noah, *The Sumerians: Their History, Culture, and Character*, Chicago: University of Chicago Press, 1963

Levy, Thomas E., ed., *The Archaeology of Society in the Holy Land*, New York: Facts on File, and Leicester: Leicester University Press, 1995

Maspero, Gaston, *Histoire ancienne des peuples de l'orient*, Paris: Hachette, 1874–1908; in English as *The Dawn of Civilization: Egypt and Chaldaea*, London: SPCK, and New York: Appleton, 1894; *The Struggle of the Nations: Egypt, Syria and Assyria*, 1896; and *The Passing of the Empires: 850 BC to 330 BC*, 1900

May, Herbert G., ed., *Oxford Bible Atlas*, 3rd edition, Oxford and New York: Oxford University Press, 1984

Oates, David, and Joan Oates, *The Rise of Civilization*, Oxford: Elsevier Phaidon, 1976

Pritchard, James Bennett, ed., *Ancient Near Eastern Texts Relating to the Old Testament*, 2 vols., Princeton: Princeton University Press, 1950; 3rd edition 1969

Rawlinson, Henry C., Edwin Norris, George Smith, and T.G. Pinches, *The Cuneiform Inscriptions of Western Asia*, 5 vols., London: British Museum, 1861–1909

Roux, Georges, *Ancient Iraq*, London: Allen and Unwin, 1964, Cleveland: World, 1965; revised 1980

Shaw, Ian, *Time Line of the Ancient World: 3000 BC–AD 500*, London: British Museum Press, 1994

Trigger, Bruce G. *et al.*, *Ancient Egypt: A Social History*, Cambridge and New York: Cambridge University Press, 1983

Wilson, John A., *The Burden of Egypt: An Interpretation of Ancient Egyptian Culture*, Chicago: University of Chicago Press, 1951; reprinted as *The Culture of Ancient Egypt*, 1956

Needham, Joseph 1900–1995
British historian of Chinese science

Ever since the late Enlightenment and into the 20th century, Western science and technology have reinforced the Western conviction of cultural superiority. Joseph Needham's clearest mission was to attack Western complacency by showing just how many crucial scientific advances had in fact been imported from China. Famously, he cited Francis Bacon to the effect that the history of the Western world had been changed irrevocably by the three inventions of printing, gunpowder, and the magnetic compass, and went on to show how all three of these had been discovered in China significantly in advance of the European scientific revolution. Needham portrayed science as the source and inspiration for a new, ecumenical world community. He is best known for his massive *Science and Civilization in China* (1954–94); its seven large, multi-part volumes covering science, technology, and medicine throughout Chinese history. This history provided examples of Chinese science in extraordinary detail. The amassing of scientific achievement in China to the point where it was superior to Europe throughout the Middle Ages and until at least the 16th century prompted the so-called "Needham question": why did the scientific revolution take place in Europe and not in China? Needham's answer (in grossly oversimplified terms) was that only capitalism could have bred modern science. Needham's impact has been considerable. In China he has been widely seen as a champion of Chinese culture by the standards of modernity; in the West, Needham has contributed to a reconceptualization of non-European cultures as capable of science and rationality. His work has been eagerly adapted and emulated in decolonized countries such as India.

Needham started his career as a biochemist/embryologist at Cambridge University and it was not until after World War II that he began to publish on China. He was a successful scientist, having been elected fellow of the Royal Society by the time he shifted to the history of Chinese science. Throughout his life, he argued that science provided the means for the improvement of human life. A devout Anglican, he associated the Regnum Dei with the society that science could and would create.

In the 1920s and 1930s, Needham published on the philosophy of biology and also looked at the history of science and religion. He developed a florid style in keeping with his High Church leanings. When writing an embryology textbook, he dealt first with the history of that subject, producing his first properly historical monograph, *History of Embryology*. It was a straightforward history of ideas showing the progress of scientific thought.

During the late 1920s and 1930s, Needham became a socialist in the Wellsian mould, and associated with other socialist scientists, such as Desmond Bernal, J.B.S. Haldane, Hyman Levy, Lancelot Hogben, Julian Huxley, and J.G. Crowther. The socialism of the time fitted well both with Needham's conception of the Regnum Dei and with the supposedly superior role given to science in the Soviet Union. Needham joined a chorus arguing that science had been supported by capitalistic structures as long as it was small scale, but was now frustrated in its chiliastic role, and only socialist structures could provide the necessary degree of organized rationality for the prosperity of humanity.

When a high-powered Soviet delegation lectured on history of science from a Marxist perspective in London in 1931, many socialist scientists took note. Selfconsciously externalist history of science in Britain dates from this encounter. Needham also began to embed his history of ideas within the society in which they were put forward. But he remained wedded to the conception of good science as independent of culture. He employed this conception in indignant rebuttals of Nazi scientists who made distinctions between German and degenerate Jewish science.

In 1937, three Chinese students came to Cambridge, including Lu Gwei-Djen, who was to become Needham's main collaborator in his *magnum opus* and also his second wife. They surprised him with reports of science-like activity in the Chinese past and he began to study Chinese. China was not only a country with a highly literate classical culture comparable to that of ancient Greece, it could also provide material for the argument for universal science. In addition China already attracted the sympathy of Western socialists, faced as it was with Japanese imperialism.

Needham spent 1942–46 in the Kuomintang-held parts of the Chinese hinterland as head of the Sino-British Science Cooperation Office which aimed to help Chinese science in its anti-Japanese war effort. In this period he collected many of the materials for *Science and Civilization in China*. After 1946, Needham began work on the history of Chinese science, while remaining active in both local and international politics. He was famously instrumental in putting the S (for science) in UNESCO. This UN body initiated work on a multivolume history of humanity. In the committee work the Annales historian, Lucien Febvre, convinced the committee and Needham of the need to feature not only the accomplishments of all cultures, but also the exchanges and transmissions between them.

Most historiographical features of the *Science and Civilization in China* can be located in Needham's experience from the late 1920s to the late 1940s: universalism and cooperation in science, interest in China, concern with the transmission of science, and an interest in the inhibiting factors in historical development. Universalism was common in science apologetics, as was the contention that scientific government would eliminate social strife, specifically class struggle; interest in China was common in socialism, the transmission mechanism in science was an explicit part of the UNESCO project, and the

inhibitor was a concept to be found both in biological sciences and in the "frustration of science" apparent to the self-styled advocates of a greater role for science in society.

Needham's historiography now seems dated, and few Western historians accept the validity of the Needham question. But the monumentality of his resurrection of a non-Western scientific heritage, along with his commitment to a non-Eurocentric and anti-racist history of science, remain extraordinary.

ARNE HESSENBRUCH

See also Science

Biography
Noel Joseph Terence Montgomery Needham. Born near London, 9 December 1900, son of a doctor. Educated at Oundle School; studied medicine and science, Gonville and Caius College, Cambridge. Fellow, Gonville and Caius College, from 1924; demonstrator, then reader in biochemistry, Cambridge University, 1928–66; director, Needham Research Institute, Cambridge University, 1976–90. Married 1) Dorothy Mary Moyle, biochemist, 1924 (died 1987); 2) Lu Gwei-Djen, 1989 (died 1991). Died Cambridge, 24 March 1995.

Principal Writings
History of Embryology, 1934; revised 1959
Science and Civilisation in China, 6 vols., 1954–94
The Development of Iron and Steel Technology in China, 1958
With others, *Heavenly Clockwork: The Great Astronomical Clocks of Medieval China*, 2nd edition, 1986

Further Reading
Goldsmith, Maurice, *Joseph Needham: 20th-Century Renaissance Man*, Paris: UNESCO Publishing, 1995
Nakayama, Shigeru, and Nathan Sivin, eds., *Chinese Science: Explorations of an Ancient Tradition*, Cambridge, MA: MIT Press, 1973
Teich, Mikuláš, and Robert Young, eds., *Changing Perspectives in the History of Science: Essays in Honour of Joseph Needham*, London: Heinemann, and Boston: Reidel, 1973

Nevins, Allan 1890–1971
US historian

Allan Nevins was one of the best-known, most prolific, and versatile 20th-century historians of the United States. His prodigious output included more than 50 books, at least another 75 edited volumes, and around a thousand articles, essays, and reviews. Nevins' workaholic habits, his industry, energy, and determination to spend every possible minute on research and writing were legendary among his peers. C. Vann Woodward described him as "a one-man history-book industry, a phenomenon of American productivity without parallel in the field."

A farmer's son, Nevins was born in Camp Point, Illinois, and quickly acquired a lifelong habit of omnivorous reading. He took his bachelor's and master's degrees in English literature at the University of Illinois, publishing the thesis he produced for the latter degree, but he never obtained a doctoral degree. For fifteen years, until he reached his late thirties, he was employed as a journalist, producing editorials and literary articles for the liberal periodicals the *Nation* and the New York *Evening Post*. While thus employed, he produced several books, among them histories of the *Evening Post* (1922) and *The American States during and after the Revolution, 1775–1789* (1924). Nevins' historical studies and his close connections with New York literary and intellectual figures helped to win him academic recognition. In 1927 he joined Cornell University's history department. A year later he moved to Columbia University, where he remained until 1958, when he reached the mandatory retirement age of 68.

Nevins' journalistic experience helped to account for both his productivity and his insistence that history should be appealing to the public. He was firmly committed to the belief that history should be accessible and entertaining to the general reader; not only should it be based upon exhaustive research and embody high standards of detailed accuracy, it should also be well written and entertaining. His historical models were the great 19th-century narrative historians, such as Thomas Carlyle, Thomas Babington Macaulay, and Francis Parkman. His own works, predominantly in biography and narrative history, exemplified these demanding standards, and some were immensely popular, gaining several prizes. Nevins' memories of interviewing subjects for newspaper articles, obtaining otherwise unrecorded information, also played a role in his establishment, in 1948, of the Columbia Oral History Program, an enterprise that was the first such in the United States, and which has since spawned many imitators. Nevins' belief that academic historians were inaccessible and unsympathetic to the man in the street also led him to establish the journal *American Heritage*, designed to interest the general reader rather than the specialist historian.

Nevins' work also embodied mid-20th-century liberal American values. He was a strong supporter of the New Deal, of civil rights, and of American intervention in World War II. In the late 1940s he spent three summers as chief public affairs officer at the United States Embassy in London. These values came through particularly strongly in *Ordeal of the Union* (1947–71), his 8-volume history of the American Civil War, in which he condemned slavery, ascribing the responsibility for the war to its existence, and argued that war was on occasion justified. Nevins' passionate belief that history was not simply for specialists was rooted in his sense that the study of the past was essential to the understanding of the present.

Nevins' work, particularly *The Emergence of Modern America, 1865–1878* (1927) and his biographies of inventors and businessmen, helped to bring about a reassessment of 19th-century American industrialization and its architects. Nevins argued that economic development in the United States caused relatively little human suffering, while raising the general standard of living and making the United States a great industrial power capable of defeating Germany in both world wars. The great capitalists of that period should, he argued, be viewed, not as "robber barons," but as men whose economic self-interest had played an essentially positive role in American history, and who had done nothing criminal by the standards of their time.

Nevins' *magnum opus* was *Ordeal of the Union*, his narrative history of the Civil War, completed only after his death.

This work emphasized political, social, administrative, cultural, and economic, rather than purely military history. The later volumes stressed the manner in which the changes resulting from the Civil War laid the foundations of future industrial development. He also published several political biographies, including studies of John C. Frémont, Hamilton Fish, Grover Cleveland, and the diplomat Henry White. All were fairly balanced works, although Nevins was sometimes criticized for aligning himself too closely with the status quo and with his subjects. Overall, it can justly be said that Nevins lived up to the criteria he set himself, and was a worthy successor to those 19th-century narrative historians whom he tried to emulate.

PRISCILLA M. ROBERTS

See also Commager; United States: 19th Century; United States: Historical Writing, 20th Century

Biography

Born Camp Point, Illinois, 20 May 1890. Received BA in English, University of Illinois, 1912, MA 1913. Traveled to Europe after graduation. Editorial writer, New York *Evening Post*, 1913–23, and *Nation*, 1913–18; literary editor, New York *Sun*, 1924–25; staff member, New York *World*, 1925–27, 1928–31. Taught at Cornell University, 1927–28; and Columbia University, 1928–58. Married Mary Fleming Richardson, 1916 (2 daughters). Died Menlo Park, California, 5 March 1971.

Principal Writings

The Evening Post: A Century of Journalism, 1922
The American States during and after the Revolution, 1775–1789, 1924
The Emergence of Modern America, 1865–1878, 1927
Grover Cleveland: A Study in Courage, 1932
Abram S. Hewitt: With Some Account of Peter Cooper, 1935
Hamilton Fish: The Inner History of the Grant Administration, 1936
John D. Rockefeller: The Heroic Age of American Enterprise, 2 vols., 1940
America: The Story of a Free People, with Henry Steele Commager, 1942
The Ordeal of the Union, 8 vols., 1947–71; includes *The War for the Union*, 4 vols., 1959–71
The Emergence of Lincoln, 1950
With Jeanette Mirsky, *The World of Eli Whitney*, 1952
Study in Power: John D. Rockefeller, Industrialist and Philanthropist, 2 vols., 1953
Ford, 3 vols., 1954–63
Allan Nevins on History, edited by Ray Allen Billington, 1975

Further Reading

Billington, Ray Allen, "Allan Nevins, Historian: A Personal Introduction," in Ray Allen Billington, ed., *Allan Nevins on History*, New York: Scribner, 1975
Kraus, Michael, and Davis D. Joyce, *The Writing of American History*, revised edition, Norman: University of Oklahoma Press, 1985
Lowery, Charles D., "Nevins, Joseph Allan," in *Dictionary of American Biography: Supplement Nine, 1971–1975*, New York: Scribner, 1994
McMurry, Richard M., "Allan Nevins," in Clyde N. Wilson, ed., *Twentieth-Century American Historians*, Detroit: Gale, 1983 [*Dictionary of Literary Biography*, vol. 17]
Sheehan, Donald, and Harold C. Syrett, eds., *Essays in American Historiography: Papers Presented in Honor of Allan Nevins*, New York: Columbia University Press, 1960

Terry, Robert J., "The Social and Intellectual Ideas of Allan Nevins," MA thesis, Cleveland: Western Reserve University, 1958

Wish, Harvey, *The American Historian: A Social-Intellectual History of the Writing of the American Past*, New York: Oxford University Press, 1960

New Zealand

The first significant history of New Zealand, Arthur S. Thomson's *The Story of New Zealand: Past and Present, Savage and Civilized* (1859), emphasized, like most other 19th-century chronicles, the successful nature of British colonization. In *The Long White Cloud: Ao Tea Roa* (1898), the former Liberal cabinet minister William Pember Reeves provided a narrative of exploration and settlement that culminated in the progressive Liberal legislation of the 1890s. Reeves' interpretations of political history influenced many later historians, and his colorful and compact account remained the standard history for some sixty years. Pakeha (that is, settlers of European ancestry) amateur ethnologists, most notably S. Percy Smith in *Hawaiki* (1898), created a history for New Zealand before the European intrusion by textualizing and chronologizing traditions of the indigenous Maori people.

In the first third of the 20th century, journalists such as Lindsay Buick and James Cowan compiled popular accounts of episodes connected with the establishment of British sovereignty; Cowan, who was bilingual, was unusual in drawing upon oral testimonies from both Maori and Pakeha, particularly in his government-commissioned *The New Zealand Wars* (1922–23). The centennial of British colonization in 1940 provided the occasion for a great deal of historical writing and research, much of it celebrating Pakeha achievements; the government-sponsored centennial surveys prepared through the Historical Branch of the Department of Internal Affairs included some distinguished short historical works, among them J. C. Beaglehole's *The Discovery of New Zealand* (1939). Two versions of a history of social services by W.B. Sutch commissioned for the same series were rejected, the second apparently at the instigation of the prime minister, but both manuscripts were subsequently published by private firms: *Poverty and Progress in New Zealand* (1941) and *The Quest for Security in New Zealand* (1942) provided a left-wing account of New Zealand's history that received a further lease of life in the 1960s when the books were reissued in amplified editions.

The involvement of the state in the production of historical works continued in the postwar period, particularly through the War History Branch which was responsible for the publication of more than forty campaign, unit, and service histories commemorating New Zealand activities in World War II. There was also an increasing number of histories, of varying size and sophistication, published to mark provincial, regional, and local anniversaries of Pakeha settlement; one of the most notable and scholarly was Philip Ross May's *The West Coast Gold Rushes* (1962). Public interest in New Zealand history was further stimulated by the activities of the Historic Places Trust, established in 1954.

Until the 1950s, most of the research into aspects of New Zealand history carried out by the few academic historians in the small university colleges was pursued within an imperial framework. In the 1950s and 1960s, however, as the universities expanded, there was a growing emphasis on teaching and researching New Zealand history for its own sake, and the publication of Keith Sinclair's *A History of New Zealand* (1959) and W.H. Oliver's *The Story of New Zealand* (1960) provided an important impetus in this process. As well as a large increase in the number of students carrying out research for MA theses (both Sinclair and Oliver had drawn on the unpublished labors of earlier MA students for their histories), a significant number of students from around 1970 onwards undertook doctoral research in New Zealand topics. The scope and strengths of all this essentially empirical endeavor were reflected in the multi-authored *The Oxford History of New Zealand* (1981), edited by W.H. Oliver with B.R. Williams.

Partly reflecting developments in historical scholarship elsewhere and partly in response to political changes within New Zealand itself, New Zealand historians during the 1970s and 1980s added enquiry into social, cultural, and intellectual aspects of the past to their more traditional concerns with political and economic affairs. As a result, issues of gender, class, and the nature of the colonial encounter have become much more prominent. Raewyn Dalziel's 1977 article "The Colonial Helpmeet" was especially important in stirring debate about the social roles of women; and two volumes of essays edited by Barbara Brookes, Charlotte Macdonald, and Margaret Tennant indicate the dimensions of this research. Erik Olssen has been the leading analyst of class; his *Building the New World* (1995) describes in rich detail social and political transformations in a Dunedin working-class suburb. In contrast, Miles Fairburn's *The Ideal Society and Its Enemies* (1989) argues that "the typical colonist was a socially independent individual," while Rollo Arnold, in *New Zealand's Burning* (1994), depicts a "yeoman world" built upon family and community life.

Perceptions of the colonial encounter were significantly changed by James Belich's *The New Zealand Wars and the Victorian Interpretation of Racial Conflict* (1986) and Claudia Orange's *The Treaty of Waitangi* (1987). The establishment of the Waitangi Tribunal in 1975, and the extension of its jurisdiction back to 1840 a decade later, have resulted in hundreds of Maori claims for loss of land and other possessions and a greatly increased demand for historical researchers, Maori and Pakeha. The Tribunal's published reports are revealing a "hitherto largely submerged Maori history." Judith Binney's *Redemption Songs* (1995) is an excellent recent illustration of the extent to which Pakeha historians now draw upon Maori traditions and perspectives as well as documentary materials. In *Making Peoples* (1996) James Belich attempts a major reinterpretation of New Zealand history, emphasizing bicultural perspectives. A second volume will carry the story through the 20th century.

The editors of *The Dictionary of New Zealand Biography* (1990–), a government project designed as a sesquicentennial commemoration, mirrored contemporary concerns about the inclusiveness of the historical record by setting targets for representation of women and Maori, while Maori subjects also appear in a companion series in the Maori language, *Ngā Tāngata Taumata Rau* (1990–). Many of the contributors to the *Dictionary* have been amateur historians whose expertise was developed through compiling local and family histories;

academics and amateurs have also shared the growing enthu-siasm for the preservation and use of oral testimony. At the same time the chief historian, Jock Phillips, has reinvigorated the Historical Branch and increased opportunities for profes-sional historians through launching a major program of public history.

PETER GIBBONS

See also Beaglehole; British Empire; Grimshaw; Masculinity; Military; Pacific; Popular; Sinclair; Women's History: Australia and New Zealand

Further Reading

Arnold, Rollo, *New Zealand's Burning: The Settlers' World in the mid-1880s*, Wellington: Victoria University Press, 1994

Beaglehole, John C., *The Discovery of New Zealand*, Wellington: Department of Internal Affairs, 1939

Belich, James, *The New Zealand Wars and the Victorian Interpretation of Racial Conflict*, Auckland: Auckland University Press, 1986

Belich, James, *Making Peoples: A History of the New Zealanders from Polynesian Settlement to the End of the Nineteenth Century*, Auckland: Allen Lane, and Honolulu: University of Hawaii Press, 1996

Binney, Judith, *Redemption Songs: A Life of Te Kooti Arikirangi Te Turuki*, Auckland: Auckland University Press, 1995; Honolulu: University of Hawaii Press, 1997

Brookes, Barbara, Charlotte Macdonald, and Margaret Tennant, eds., *Women in History: Essays on European Women in New Zealand*, Wellington: Port Nicholson Press, 1986

Brookes, Barbara, Charlotte Macdonald, and Margaret Tennant, eds., *Women in History 2*, Wellington: Bridget Williams Books, 1992

Cowan, James, *The New Zealand Wars: A History of the Maori Campaigns and the Pioneering Period*, 2 vols., Wellington: Government Printer, 1922–23

Dalziel, Raewyn, "The Colonial Helpmeet: Women's Role and the Vote in Nineteenth-Century New Zealand," *New Zealand Journal of History* 11 (1977), pp. 112–23

The Dictionary of New Zealand Biography, 3 vols to date, Wellington and Auckland: Allen and Unwin/Auckland University Press – Department of Internal Affairs, 1990–96

Fairburn, Miles, *The Ideal Society and Its Enemies: The Foundations of Modern New Zealand Society, 1850–1900*, Auckland: Auckland University Press, 1989

Kawharu, Ian Hugh, ed., *Waitangi: Maori and Pakeha Perspectives of the Treaty of Waitangi*, Auckland: Oxford University Press, 1989

May, Philip Ross, *The West Coast Gold Rushes*, Christchurch: Pegasus, 1962

Ngā Tāngata Taumata Rau, 3 vols. to date, various publishers, 1990–96

Oliver, W.H., *The Story of New Zealand*, London: Faber, 1960

Oliver, W.H., with Bridget R. Williams, eds., *The Oxford History of New Zealand*, Wellington: Oxford University Press, and Oxford: Clarendon Press, 1981; 2nd edition, Geoffrey W. Rice, ed., Auckland: Oxford University Press, 1992

Olssen, Erik, "Where To from Here: Reflections on the Twentieth-Century Historiography of Nineteenth-Century New Zealand," *New Zealand Journal of History* 26 (1992), 54–77

Olssen, Erik, *Building the New World: Work, Politics and Society in Caversham, 1880s–1920s*, Auckland: Auckland University Press, 1995

Orange, Claudia, *The Treaty of Waitangi*, Wellington: Allen and Unwin, 1987

Phillips, Jock, "Of Verandahs and Fish and Chips and Footie on Saturday Afternoon," *New Zealand Journal of History* 24 (1990), 118–34

Pickens, Keith, "The Writing of New Zealand History: A Kuhnian Perspective," *Historical Studies: Australia and New Zealand* 17 (1977), 384–98

Reeves, William Pember, *The Long White Cloud: Ao Tea Roa*, London: Horace Marshall, 1898

Rice, Geoffrey, ed., *The Oxford History of New Zealand*, Oxford and New York: Oxford University Press, 1992

Sinclair, Keith, *A History of New Zealand*, Harmondsworth: Penguin, 1959; 4th edition 1991

Sinclair, Keith, "New Zealand," in Robin Winks, ed., *The Historiography of the British Empire-Commonwealth: Trends, Interpretations, Resources*, Durham, NC: Duke University Press, 1966

Smith, S. Percy, *Hawaiki: The Whence of the Maori*, Christchurch: Whitcombe and Tombs, 1898; revised 1904, 1910, 1921

Sutch, William Ball, *Poverty and Progress in New Zealand*, Wellington: Modern Books, 1941; revised 1969

Sutch, William Ball, *The Quest for Security in New Zealand*, Harmondsworth: Penguin, 1942; revised 1966

Thomson, Arthur S., *The Story of New Zealand: Past and Present, Savage and Civilized*, 2 vols., London: Murray, 1859; reprinted 1970

Ward, Alan, "History and Historians before the Waitangi Tribunal," *New Zealand Journal of History* 24 (1990), 150–67

Niebuhr, B.G. 1776–1831
German (Danish-born) historian

Overshadowed by Theodor Mommsen, the other great 19th-century historian of Rome, Barthold Georg Niebuhr – states-man, diplomat, financier, and official historian at the Prussian court – was largely forgotten after the later 19th century. However, he was one of the founders of German historicism, of attempts to make historical thinking follow the laws of natural science, and of modern source criticism. This may even be why Niebuhr was displaced, as he himself helped to achieve a radical critique of sources and of earlier historical writing. He was once characterized by Wilhelm von Humboldt as a scholar among statesmen and a statesman among scholars.

Niebuhr's fame has been restored over the last two decades, and rests on his studies of Roman history. He was active in organizing academic enterprises such as a publication of all Greek inscriptions (*Corpus Inscriptionum Graecarum*), his initiative for the *Corpus Scriptorum Historiae Byzantinae*, and his foundation of the philological journal *Rheinisches Museum* (1827). His university lectures in Bonn, which also covered the history of Greece and the Orient, demonstrated the univer-sality of his knowledge. He believed that all other histories led up to Roman history, and this underpinned his universal concept of history. In this respect Burckhardt and Ranke agreed with Niebuhr. In contrast to Bossuet's theological under-standing of history, Niebuhr tried to find a "philological" method that would allow him to interpret ancient history as a discipline of classical philology. He caused a sensation with his "theory of songs": he was convinced that a large part of Roman history could best be understood through the inter-pretation of Roman songs, which he saw as an essential element in a plebeian tradition distinct from the official annals of the patricians.

August Wilhelm von Schlegel and Mommsen, both among his fiercest critics, firmly rejected Niebuhr's theory. After his death it became obvious that Niebuhr's methods were too personal to have produced a school. Schlegel found his style too complicated. Contemporaries criticized the mixture of personal reflection, historical and literary analogies, and highly detailed descriptions. In this context Macaulay said that Niebuhr did not distinguish clearly enough between historical truth and what could be called a hypothesis. Generally, however, the Roman history was praised more in England than anywhere else outside Germany. Mommsen's masterly history of Rome, which should be seen in the context of Niebuhr's historical writing, emphasized the nobility's achievements and interpreted Roman history as the archetype of national unity.

Coming from a northern German rural background Niebuhr early on showed interest in the agrarian conditions of his country and in questions of land ownership. The ideas of the French Revolution, especially of Gracchus Babeuf concerning the equal distribution of land and harvests, made a considerable impact on Niebuhr at the time of the Danish and later Prussian liberation of the peasants. As the meaning of Roman agricultural structures and their laws played an important role in the discussion of the legitimacy of contemporary agricultural claims, Niebuhr soon became interested in the history of the early Roman republic, particularly in the struggle between the patricians and the plebeians. He identified completely with the latter. This does not mean that he was a revolutionary: on the contrary, it meant first that Niebuhr had high regard for the balance that had been achieved between the two Roman classes, and second that his preference was for a constitutional monarchy based on the social and constitutional harmony of the estates. Between 1803 and 1806 he wrote his *Zur Geschichte der Römischen Staatsländereien* (On the History of the Roman Landed Estates), a preparation for his famous history of Rome.

In his *Römische Geschichte* (1811–32; *History of Rome*, 1828–42), without doubt Niebuhr's greatest historical work, he stressed the relevance of the Roman tribunes whom he saw as the representatives of the people. Thus it was the institution of the tribunes that supported the interests of the estates. In these books he studied the Roman state and its culture. They were published after Niebuhr had lectured on Roman history at the newly founded University of Berlin. His lectures, and later his books, were so successful and popular that Savigny claimed that Niebuhr was opening a new era for Roman history, and Goethe proclaimed that all history should be written in the same manner. Here Niebuhr projected his contemporary political ideal of a harmony between the estates into the Roman past. This led to a highly idealized picture of Roman history and the Roman constitution. According to Niebuhr, this constitution was based on liberty, morality, and honesty, and its strength lay in its gradual development and continuity. He claimed that Rome was an example of political perfection and of the combination of power with mind.

In order to prevent revolutionaries from using those ideas for their own political ends, Niebuhr had to demonstrate, drawing closely on the sources, that Roman agricultural laws had hitherto been wrongly reconstructed and that Livy and Cicero, and even Montesquieu, had misinterpreted them. No one before Niebuhr had looked at the coherence of the Roman state with its successive institutional, political, and legal changes. His investigation of the Roman republic was the equivalent of Grote's study of Athenian democracy. The early history of a nation, Niebuhr argued, was a history of institutions not events, and of classes not individuals. Niebuhr compared Roman history with the development of English history, which he saw from a somewhat Whiggish standpoint as a process of steady constitutional perfection from 1688. His detestation of revolution led him to admire a Burkian reformist political system.

Friedrich Engels was one of the first to see that Niebuhr's history, because it emphasized the plebeian aspects, could have social implications, but it was certainly far from propagating a revolution. Niebuhr discussed the agricultural and social constitution of the Roman republic, and he called for a liberal constitution for his own times, although he was aware of the contradictions between the ideal and reality. Niebuhr contributed to the development of German classical studies in the early 19th century by bringing together the collection of classical texts with the interpretation and the description of their historical settings. Further, Niebuhr first formulated the connections between the historian's personal experiences in his time and his understanding of the past; consequently he considered it essential for historians to have practical experience of politics and administration.

BENEDIKT STUCHTEY

See also Byzantium; Sanctis; Whewell

Biography

Barthold Georg Niebuhr. Born Copenhagen, 27 August 1776, son of an engineer/explorer. Studied at Kiel University, 1794–96. Private secretary to Danish minister of finance, 1796–98. Completed education, University of Edinburgh, 1798–99. Joined Danish civil service, 1800; director, National Bank, 1804; moved to Prussia, 1806; served as privy state councillor and head of banks and state debt section, resigned 1810; appointed state historian, 1810; taught at University of Berlin, 1810, and later at University of Bonn; Prussian ambassador to the Vatican, 1816–23; taught at University of Bonn, 1823–31. Member, Prussian State Council, 1823. Married Amélie Behrens, 1800. Died Bonn, 2 January 1831.

Principal Writings

Zur Geschichte der Römischen Staatsländereien (On the History of the Roman Landed Estates), written 1803–06

Römische Geschichte, 3 vols., 1811–32; in English as *History of Rome*, 1828–42

Kleine historische und philologische Schriften (Small Historical and Philological Writings), 2 vols., 1828–43

Nachgelassene Schriften nichtphilologischen Inhalts (Posthumous Non-Philological Writings), edited by Marcus Niebuhr, 1842

Geschichte des Zeitalters der Revolution (History of the Age of Revolutions), edited by Marcus Niebuhr, 2 vols., 1845

Vorträge über römische Geschichte (Lectures on Roman History), edited by Meyer Isler, 3 vols., 1846–48

Vorträge über alte Geschichte, an der Universität zu Bonn gehalten (Lectures on Ancient History Held at the University of Bonn), edited by Marcus Niebuhr, 3 vols., 1847–51

Vorträge über alte Länder- und Völkerkunde (Lectures on Ancient Geography and Ethnology), edited by Meyer Isler, 1851

Vorträge über römische Alterthümer (Lectures on Roman Antiquities), edited by Meyer Isler, 1858

Further Reading

Bridenthal, Renate, "Was there a Roman Homer? Niebuhr's Thesis and Its Critics," *History and Theory* 11 (1972), 193–213

Christ, Karl, *Von Gibbon zu Rostovtzeff: Leben und Werk führender Althistoriker der Neuzeit* (From Gibbon to Rostovtzeff: The Life and Work of the Leading Ancient Historians of Modern Times), Darmstadt: Wissenschaftliche Buchgesellschaft, 1972

Christ, Karl, "Barthold Georg Niebuhr," in Hans-Ulrich Wehler, ed., *Deutsche Historiker*, vol. 6, Göttingen: Vandenhoeck & Ruprecht, 1980

Hanns Reill, Peter, "Barthold Georg Niebuhr and the Enlightenment Tradition," *German Studies Review* 3 (1980), 9–26

Heuss, Alfred, *Barthold Georg Niebuhrs wissenschaftliche Anfänge: Untersuchungen und Mitteilungen über die Kopenhagener Manuscripte und zur europäischen Tradition der lex agraria (loi agraire)*, Göttingen: Vandenhoeck & Ruprecht, 1981

Rytkönen, Seppo, *Barthold Georg Niebuhr als Politiker und Historiker* (Barthold Georg Niebuhr as Politician and Historian), Helsinki: Suomalainen Tiedeakatemia, 1968

Straub, Johannes, "Barthold Georg Niebuhr 1776–1831," in *Bonner Gelehrte: Beiträge zur Geschichte der Wissenschaften in Bonn* (Scholars from Bonn: Contributions to the History of the Arts and Sciences in Bonn), Bonn: Röhrscheid, 1968

Walther, Gerrit, *Niebuhrs Forschung* (Niebuhr's Research), Stuttgart: Steiner, 1993

Wirth, Gerhard, ed., *Barthold Georg Niebuhr, Historiker und Staatsmann: Vorträge bei dem anlässlich seines 150. Todestages in Bonn veranstalteten Kolloquiums 10.–12. November 1981* (Niebuhr, Historian and Statesman: Lectuers Given at the Colloquium Held in Bonn on the 150th Anniversary of His Death), Bonn: Röhrscheid, 1984

Witte, Barthold C., *Der preussische Tacitus: Aufstieg, Ruhm und Ende des Historikers Barthold Georg Niebuhr, 1776–1831* (The Prussian Tacitus: The Rise, Glory, and Fall of the Historian Barthold Georg Niebuhr), Düsseldorf: Droste, 1979

Niethammer, Lutz 1939–

German oral historian

Lutz Niethammer, a German philologist, is best known for his work in German oral history and he has spent the greater part of his career conducting research into the lives of average people from the 1930s to the present. Recently Niethammer published several important studies on the social history of East Germany, the impact of the postwar occupation, and East Germany's role within the general context of German history. His ground-breaking studies have forced historians to rethink earlier interpretations of social conditions and living standards under Hitler and have shed immense light on postwar German history.

Niethammer's earlier works dealt with the Allied occupation of Germany. In 1982 he published *Die Mitläuferfabrik* (The Fellow-Traveler Factory), an expanded version of his doctoral dissertation. Herein Niethammer examined the relationship between the American forces of occupation and the Germans who were forced to endure it. The Germans, in time, developed a form of passive resistance to American occupation and denazification methods. The work is noteworthy for its even-handed treatment of both American and German reactions to the war and the occupation.

With the publication in 1983 of the first volume of *Lebensgeschichte und Sozialkultur im Ruhrgebiet 1930 bis 1960* (Life Histories and Social Culture in the Ruhr Region, 1930–1960), Niethammer established himself in the field of oral history. The volume includes eight essays which examined

the living conditions and experiences of average Germans in the Ruhr area between 1930 and 1960. Niethammer interviewed approximately 200 people between the ages of 55 and 80 from 1980 to 1982. His research led him to the conclusion that average Germans accepted Nazi rule rather compliantly, largely motivated by the desire for stability and security.

Niethammer's historiographical study, *Posthistoire: ist die Geschichte zu Ende?* (1989; *Posthistoire: Has History Come to an End?*, 1992) is one of his few works available in English. In this short, analytical study, Niethammer examined the notion of the collapse of historicism in the face of mass-produced culture and society. This theme is traced from its adoption by western intellectuals in the 19th century through its absorption, in the modern era, into mainstream culture. Niethammer criticized the whole method of historical treatment as being derived from an elitist conception that portrays history as a simple process of fulfillment.

Recently Niethammer produced a study on East Germany, *Die volkseigene Erfahrung* (National Experience, 1991). Niethammer explored the social norms and culture which existed within East Germany during the Cold War, basing his study on a vast array of interviews conducted in 1987, with additions being added after German unification in 1989. The study attempts to place East Germany within the overall framework of German history and come to terms with how East Germans dealt with the collapse of the Third Reich and the occupation that followed.

STEPHEN K. CHENAULT

Biography
Born Stuttgart, 26 December 1939. Studied history, theology, and social sciences at the universities of Heidelberg, Bonn, Cologne, and Munich, receiving his PhD from Heidelberg, 1971. Fellow, St Antony's College, Oxford University, 1972–73; taught at University of Essen, 1973–82; Fernuniversity, Hagen, 1982–93; professor, University of Jena, from 1993. Married Regina Schulte, 1990 (2 daughters).

Principal Writings
Entnazifizierung in Bayern: Säuberung und Rehabilitierung unter amerikanischer Besatzung (Denazification in Bavaria under the American Occupation Forces), 1972; doctoral thesis reprinted as *Die Mitläuferfabrik: die Entnazifizierung am Beispiel Bayerns* (The Fellow-Traveler Factory: Denazification in the Case of Bavaria), 1982

Zwischen Befreiung und Besatzung: Analysen des US-Geheimdienstes über Positionen und Strukturen deutscher Politik 1945 (Between Freedom and Occupation: An Analysis of US Intelligence Positions and Structures within German Politics), 1976

Editor with Werner Trapp, *Lebenserfahrung und kollektives Gedächtnis: die Praxis der "Oral History"* (Life Experience and Collective Memory: The Practice of Oral History), 1980

Lebensgeschichte und Sozialkultur im Ruhrgebiet 1930 bis 1960 (Life Histories and Social Culture in the Ruhr Region, 1930–1960), 3 vols., 1983–86

Editor with Othmar Nikola Haberl, *Der Marshall-Plan und die europäische Linke* (The Marshall Plan and the European Link), 1986

Die volkseigene Erfahrung: eine Archäologie des Lebens in der Industrieprovinz der DDR: 30 biografische Eröffnungen (National Experience: Archeology of Life in the Industrial Province of the German Democratic Republic), 1991

Posthistoire: ist die Geschichte zu Ende?, 1989; in English as
   Posthistoire: Has History Come to an End?, 1992
Editor, *Der "gesäuberte" Antifaschismus: die SED und die roten
   Kapos von Buchenwald: Dokumente* ("Cleansed" Antifascism:
   The SED [Socialist Unity Party of Germany] and the Red NCOs
   of Buchenwald: Documents), 1994

Nietzsche, Friedrich 1844–1900

German historical philosopher

Friedrich Nietzsche's innovative blend of philology and philosophy with cultural history drove modern European society and its leading thinkers into a crisis of modernity. Exemplified through his work "Vom Nutzen und Nachtheil der Historie" (1874; "On the Use and Disadvantage of History," 1909) Nietzsche rejected the scientism typifying Rankean and Hegelian forms of historical analyses. Nietzsche contended that scientism (or historicist positivism) had overpowered the creative, spontaneous forces of history within us. Building on Arthur Schopenhauer's denunciation of history as a science, Nietzsche demanded of historians a greater sense of moral responsibility and intellectual cultivation.

Nietzsche belonged to a new generation of 19th-century German thinkers who changed the character of historical and philosophical inquiry. Rejecting Leopold von Ranke's dispassionate view of historical analysis, Nietzsche joined with his contemporary Jakob Burckhardt in emphasizing deeply imbedded cultural and social values inhibiting the individual's creative impulses. Historians tend toward two interpretations of Nietzsche. For one group, Nietzsche remains a challenge and inspiration; Hajo Holborn, Gordon Craig, and Karl Dietrich Bracher interpreted Nietzsche as the cultural critic attempting to steer European society *away* from its self-destruction in the modern age. For another group, Nietzsche symbolizes Europe's self-destructive cultural and political evolution in the 20th century. For example, George L. Mosse interpreted Nietzsche as a warning of the residual barbarism and anti-intellectualism within the western soul.

Steven E. Aschheim's *The Nietzsche Legacy in Germany, 1890–1990* (1992) traced the early appeal of Nietzsche's critiques of liberalism and contemporary society on Austrian intellectual circles of the 1870s, particularly on Gustav Mahler and Viktor Adler. A decade later, Nietzsche's echo expanded into Europe's radical fringes. Within *Ecce Homo* (1887), Nietzsche commented on his peculiar popularity among "Socialists, Nihilists, Anti-Semites, Christian-Orthodox, [and] Wagnerians." Nietzsche rose in national prominence in the 1890s only after the publication of *Also Sprach Zarathustra* (1883–85; *Thus Spake Zarathustra*, 1896). He became an integral component of mainstream intellectual discourse by the turn of the century, the year of his death. In his eulogy, the historian Kurt Breysig equated Nietzsche's reputation with that of Jesus Christ and the Buddha. In George L. Mosse's *The Crisis of German Ideology* (1964), Nietzschean hero-worship combined with a romanticized German Volkisch movement early in the 20th century. Hans Günther's *Ritter, Tod, und Teufel* (Knights, Death, and Devils, 1920) and Walther Darré's *Das Bauerntum als Lebensquelle der nordische Rasse* (The

Farming Community as the Life-Source of the Northern Race, 1929) exemplified the dangerous intellectual currents which freely merged with the doctrines of National Socialism.

Nietzsche's cultural pessimism found expression in a variety of intellectual circles in Weimar Germany. As depicted in Peter Gay's *Weimar Culture* (1968), Aby Warburg's *Kulturhistorische Bibliotek Warburg* in Hamburg attracted historians, philosophers, and philologists anxious to apply the ideas of Burckhardt and Nietzsche in more creative historical analyses. Sponsored by the Warburg Institute, Ernst Cassirer, Paul Lehmann, Erwin Panofsky, and Eduard Norden contributed important works breaking with German historical tradition by blending a socio-philosophical approach into the more traditional emphasis on political history. As tuberculosis in Thomas Mann's *Der Zauberberg* (1924; *Magic Mountain*, 1927) symbolized society in decay, Weimar historians applied Nietzschean ideas to larger studies of history. Oswald Spengler's popular *Der Untergang des Abendlandes* (1918–22; *The Decline of the West*, 1926–28) used Nietzschean notions of social decay, militarism, and changing social values in order to understand the decline of western civilization. While cultural critics such as Berlin's Kurt Tucholsky used Nietzsche to attack German militarism, Arthur de Gobineau and Houston Stuart Chamberlain's racist histories drew heavily from Nietzsche's condemnation of Christianity and his posthumously published notes in *Der Wille zur Macht* (1901; *Will to Power*, 1909–10). Coupled with Nietzschean impulses in Alfred Rosenberg's *Mythus des 20. Jahrhunderts* (1925; *Myth of the Twentieth Century*, 1982) and Martin Heidegger's *Sein und Zeit* (1927; *Being and Time*, 1962), Hitlerism's intellectual foundation was complete. George L. Mosse's *Germans and Jews* (1970), however, observed that European fascists, such as the Italian poet Gabriel D'Annunzio, drew strength from Nietzsche's ecstatic pagan primitivism driving the emergence of the *new man*, one worthy of worship – the *Übermensch* or Overman.

Nietzsche's writings were highly instrumental in motivating the growth of Zionism. Aschheim's *The Nietzsche Legacy* and Nahum Glatzer's *Franz Rosenzweig* (1953) explored the origins of classical Zionism in Rosenzweig's adoption of Nietzsche's radical individualism to breathe a new vitality into Jewish life, evident in Rosenzweig's work *Der Stern der Erlösung* (1921; *The Star of Redemption*, 1971). Paralleling his thoughts on Hasidism, Martin Buber focused Nietzschean individualism onto Zionist/Jewish national aspirations. Finally, Micha Josef Berdichevsky moved Zionist/Jewish historiography out of its religious and apolitical tendencies toward a reinvigorated self-confidence in Jewish cultural and political emancipation.

For historians seeking the motivating forces within the personalities of historical figures, Nietzsche's *Zarathustra* gave a certain impetus to psychoanalysis and psychohistory. Sigmund Freud and Carl Jung found an inspiration in Nietzsche's desire to release unconscious passionate desires and escape the limitations imposed upon the individual by society. Erik H. Erikson's *Young Man Luther* (1958) blended Freud and Nietzsche into an analysis of Luther, while Robert G.L. Waite's *The Psychopathic God: Adolf Hitler* (1977) applied this form of historical analysis to uncover the pathological drives behind Hitler's rise to power.

Directed toward contemporary western civilization, Francis Fukuyama's *The End of History and the Last Man* (1992)

reflected the continued influence of Nietzsche's *Thus Spake Zarathustra*. While praising the spread of liberal democracy, Fukuyama lamented contemporary liberal society's devaluation of egoistic individualism. Fukuyama endows Nietzsche with a prophetic capacity, as Nietzsche had interpreted liberal democracy as the victory of moral passivity and relativism over the struggle for recognition and self-respect. In parallel with Nietzsche, Fukuyama sees history, or the consciousness of historical evolution, as a constant inspiration to push on to new horizons. Beyond the realm of historical inquiry, Geoff Waite's *Nietzsche's Corps/e* (1996) stands as a powerful reminder of Nietzsche's impact on philosophical and literary circles from deconstructionism to postmodernism and in artistic circles from aestheticism to surrealism. For better or worse, Nietzsche has become an integral component of modern intellectual discourse.

DAVID A. MEIER

See also Burckhardt; Cultural; Foucault; Historiology; Joll; Mayer; Memory; Spengler; Weber, M.; White, H.; Wilamovitz-Möllendorff

Biography
Friedrich Wilhelm Nietzsche. Born Röcken, Prussia, 15 October 1844, son of a Lutheran minister who died when Nietzsche was five. Educated by tutors then attended local school, transferring to Schulpforta, 1858; studied philology with Ritsch, University of Bonn, 1864–65; studied at University of Leipzig, 1865–67, PhD 1869. Compulsory military service, 1867–68. Taught Greek, University of Basel, 1869–79; retired on medical pension. After a series of physical and mental breakdowns, died Weimar, 25 August 1900.

Principal Writings
"Vom Nutzen und Nachtheil der Historie für das Leben," in *Unzeitgemässe Betrachtungen*, vol. 2, 1874, definitive edition in *Werke: Kritische Gesamtausgabe*, edited by Giorgio Colli and Mazzino Montinary, 1967; in English as "On the Use and Disadvantage of History," in *Complete Works*, edited by Oscar Levy, vol. 5, 1909, and as "On the Uses and Disadvantage of History for Life," in *Untimely Meditations*, edited by R.J. Hollindale, 1983

Also Sprach Zarathustra, 4 vols., 1883–85; in English as *Thus Spake Zarathustra*, 1896

Ecco Homo, written 1887; published in German, 1908; published in English, 1911

Der Wille zur Macht, 1901; in English as *The Will to Power*, 2 vols., 1909–10

Further Reading
Aschheim, Steven E., *The Nietzsche Legacy in Germany, 1890–1990*, Berkeley: University of California Press, 1992

Heller, Erich, *The Importance of Nietzsche: Ten Essays*, Chicago: University of Chicago Press, 1988

Megill, Allan, *Prophets of Extremity: Nietzsche, Heidegger, Foucault, Derrida*, Berkeley: University of California Press, 1985

Mosse, George L., *The Crisis of German Ideology: Intellectual Origins of the Third Reich*, New York: Grosset and Dunlap, 1964; London: Weidenfeld and Nicolson, 1966

Pasley, Malcolm, ed., *Nietzsche: Imagery and Thought: A Collection of Essays*, Berkeley: University of California Press, and London: Methuen, 1978

Solomon, Robert C., ed., *Nietzsche: A Collection of Critical Essays*, Notre Dame, IN: University of Notre Dame Press, 1980

Niida Noboru 1904–1966
Japanese historian of Chinese legal history

The pioneer and founder of modern studies of Chinese legal history in Japan, Niida produced numerous valuable works. He was nicknamed Mencius by his high school classmates due to his excellent understanding of Chinese classics. He studied Chinese philology and institutional history during his university years under the supervision of Nakada Kaoru (1877–1967), the founder of modern studies of Japanese legal and institutional history, which prepared solid foundations for his future research.

At age of thirty, Niida established himself as a leading scholar in the field by publishing *Tōrei shūi* (Reconstruction of the T'ang Administrative Statutes, 1933), an epoch-making work of over a thousand pages based on extensive reading and careful textual study, for which he received a prize from the Imperial Academy of Japan the following year. Three years later, Niida received a doctorate from Tokyo Imperial University for *Tō-Sō hōritsu bunsho no kenkyū* (A Study of Legal Documents of the T'ang and the Sung, 1937), in which he made detailed analyses of medieval Chinese written contracts on sales, rents, employment, inheritance, and adoption. *Chūgoku mibunhōshi* (A History of Chinese Statutes on Status, 1942), however, which looked systematically into the Chinese legal history on the clan, the family, the relative, and the slave, can be considered as his representative work because of its significance in understanding traditional Chinese social organization as a whole.

During World War II, Niida was associated with a large-scale survey of customary law in North Chinese village society, the results of which were published later in six volumes under his editorship. He also conducted – with the help of a young Japanese scholar and interpreter – investigations into the industrial and commercial guilds in the Peking area, which opened up a new field of interest. The early postwar period saw a series of fundamental changes in China, especially due to land reform and the establishment of the new marriage laws. Niida was sympathetic to the Chinese revolution and deeply involved in the revival of Marxist interpretation of Chinese history. *Chūgoku no shakai to girudo* (Chinese Society and the Guild, 1951) and *Chūgoku no nōson kazoku* (China's Rural Families, 1954), the two studies based on his wartime survey and investigation, showed this transformation in his scholarship. The best expression of his general view of Chinese history can be found in a book published around the same time, *Chūgoku hōseishi* (A History of the Chinese Law, 1952).

In the late 1950s Niida returned to the subject on which much of his prewar work had been concentrated – the interpretation of the institutional manuscripts discovered at Tunhuang and of the documents discovered at Turfan. Following Nakada's example he brought together his life's research in the 4-volume set, *Chūgoku hōseishi kenkyū* (Studies in Chinese Legal History, 1959–64).

DE-MIN TAO

Biography
Niida Noboru. Born 1 January 1904. Attended school in Tokyo; studied law at Tokyo Imperial University, BA 1928, doctorate 1937.

Researcher, Tokyo Institute of the Academy of Oriental Culture, 1929–39; professor, later director of the Institute of Oriental Culture at Tokyo University, 1942–64. Died 22 June 1966.

Principal Writings

Tōrei shūi (Reconstruction of the T'ang Administrative Statutes), 1933

Tō-Sō hōritsu bunsho no kenkyū (A Study of Legal Documents of the T'ang and the Sung), 1937

Chūgoku mibunhōshi (A History of Chinese Statutes on Status), 1942

Chūgoku no shakai to girudo (Chinese Society and the Guild), 1951

Chūgoku hōseishi (A History of the Chinese Law), 1952

Chūgoku no nōson kazoku (China's Rural Families), 1954

Chūgoku hōseishi kenkyū (Studies in Chinese Legal History), 4 vols., 1959–64

Chūgoku no dentō to kakumei: Niida Noboru shu, 1974 [includes bibliography]

Further Reading

Ikeda On, "Niida Noboru," in Egami Namio, ed., *Tōyōgaku no keifu* (A Genealogy of the Oriental Studies in Japan), vol. 2, Tokyo: Taishūkan shoten, 1994

Oyama Masaaki, "Niida Noboru," in Nagahora Kieji and Kano Masanao, eds., *Nihon no rekishika* (The Historians of Japan), Tokyo: Nihon hyōronsha, 1976

O

Obolensky, Dimitri 1918–

Russian historian of Byzantium

Dimitri Obolensky has specialized in Byzantine cultural and religious history. His work on religion made him a recognized expert on all aspects of Orthodox church history, although his major contributions to the field have concerned Orthodoxy's impact in the Byzantine empire's provinces. For example, he increased our understanding of the significance of Cyril and Methodius' missionary activities among the West Slav Moravians and the Bulgars, as well as the influence those actions had much later on the Russians. His most important study on the history of the Byzantine Orthodox church is his 1948 monograph *The Bogomils: A Study in Balkan Neo-Manichaeism*, which has become the standard work on this heresy. Besides eliminating misconceptions concerning the Bogomils, Obolensky's research differentiated them from neo-Manichaen sects, and treated them as a distinct phenomenon in the Balkans between the 10th and the 14th centuries.

The other major contribution Obolensky has made to Byzantine studies is his somewhat controversial theory of the Byzantine commonwealth. He developed this thesis in several publications collected in *The Byzantine Inheritance of Eastern Europe* (1982) and *Byzantium and the Slavs* (1971). The monograph *The Byzantine Commonwealth* (1971) contains the fullest presentation of his thesis. In these books Obolensky argued that common cultural traditions derived from the richness of Byzantine civilization developed among the people who invaded the Byzantine empire between the 6th and the 8th centuries. Such a view clashes with the nationalism that has dominated the work of most East European historians since the latter part of the 19th century. It also underscored the fact that 20th-century Byzantine historiography, which has involved many disciplines, has largely remained international in approach. Obolensky's thesis concentrated on the Serbs, Croats, and Bulgarians who settled in the Balkans. At the extremes of Byzantine influence he included the Moravians and non-Slavic Magyars in the west, and the Russians and Khazars in the east. For some reason, Obolensky omitted Italy, Sicily, the Caucasus, and the Arab lands, all of which experienced Byzantine culture to some degree.

In the *Byzantine Commonwealth* Obolensky defined their commonalty as a "supranational community of Christian states of which Constantinople was the center and Eastern Europe the peripheral domain." At first the invaders sought to plunder the empire, but soon turned from attacking it to emulating its culture, primarily due to the work of Orthodox missionaries such as Cyril and Methodius. The resulting single cultural community held together by the common bonds of geographical contiguity, political exchange, cultural values, artistic styles, and, above all, Orthodox Christianity, laid the foundation of Eastern Europe by molding undisciplined tribes into nations. The commonwealth's zenith came in the 11th century, although it lasted from the mid-9th century until Constantinople fell to the Ottomans in 1453. Even after that date its influence persisted in Eastern Europe until the 18th century, although Obolensky refuted the Russian contention that they were the successors (the Third Rome) to the Roman and Byzantine empires. A remnant of the commonwealth survives today in the practices of the Orthodox church.

Byzantium's most significant gift to these peoples was writing and literature, the very basis of civilization. However, the Bulgars, Serbs, and Russians never copied the Byzantine educational system, and consequently monks and clerics, rather than laymen, monopolized learning and literature. Byzantine officials and clerics also taught the princes of these tribes how to govern, and transmitted Byzantine political institutions to them without erasing their individuality. Perhaps Byzantium's greatest source of influence on the Balkan Slavs was its legal system, although the Russians completely avoided it.

Russian historians praised Obolensky's conclusion that the links between the Russians and Byzantium were cultural not political, unlike those that bound the Bulgars and – to a lesser extent – the Serbs to the Byzantine empire. Although united by a common religion, Orthodoxy, the Kievan Rus borrowed much more from Byzantine models than did the Muscovites, due mainly to Kiev's closer proximity to Constantinople; this accounts for many of the differences between the Kievan Rus and Muscovite Russians. In the final analysis, Obolensky's importance rests on his conclusion that the Byzantine empire integrated most East Europeans into western civilization through the powerful influence of its religion and culture.

ROBERT F. FORREST

See also Byzantium; Russia: Early Modern

Biography

Born Petrograd, 1 April 1918. Educated at Lycée Pasteur, Paris; Trinity College, Cambridge, BA 1940, PhD 1943. Fellow, Trinity College, Cambridge, 1942–48: lecturer, 1945–46; fellow, Christ Church, Oxford, 1950–85: reader in Russian and Balkan medieval history, Oxford University, 1949–61, professor, 1961–85 (emeritus). Married Elisabeth Lopoukhin, 1947 (marriage dissolved 1989).

Principal Writings

The Bogomils: A Study in Balkan Neo-Manichaeism, 1948
"Byzantium, Kiev and Moscow: A Study in Ecclesiastical Relations," *Dumbarton Oaks Papers* 11 (1957), 23–78
"The Heritage of Cyril and Methodius in Russia," *Dumbarton Oaks Papers* 19 (1965), 45–65
With David Knowles, *The Middle Ages*, 1968 [*The Christian Centuries*, vol. 2]
The Byzantine Commonwealth: Eastern Europe, 500–1453, 1971
Byzantium and the Slavs: Collected Studies, 1971
Editor with Robert Auty, *An Introduction to Russian History*, 1976
The Byzantine Inheritance of Eastern Europe, 1982
Six Byzantine Portraits, 1988

O'Gorman, Edmundo 1906–1995

Mexican historian

Although he is a lawyer by profession, Edmundo O'Gorman's pastime as a young man was literature. In 1932 he published a short story "El caballo blanco" (White Horse) and a few poems. However, literature was not to become his calling, although his elegant prose as a historian was to reflect his fondness for writing.

O'Gorman was an assiduous reader of the Spanish philosopher and essayist José Ortega y Gasset. Under his influence and that of another Spanish philosopher, José Gaos, a refugee from Spain after 1938, O'Gorman was set on the road to the history of ideas. In order to be able to devote all his time to his intellectual pursuits, O'Gorman gave up his career as a lawyer. During the following years, he wrote, co-directed Mexico's national archives, and studied for his master's and doctoral degrees, which he received in 1946 and 1951 respectively.

In 1951 O'Gorman published *La idea del descubrimiento de América* (The Idea of America's Discovery). This work marked the beginning of O'Gorman's long career analyzing and arguing about this topic. O'Gorman contended that Columbus did not discover America because, seeking east Asia, he did not realize what he had really found. Americo Vespucci came closer to this realization, and so did those who named the New World after him.

O'Gorman was a powerful polemicist. Throughout his lifetime he engaged in scholarly polemics with fellow historians such as Silvio Zavala, Lewis Hanke, Marcel Bataillon, Octavio Paz, Jacques Lafaye, and Miguel León-Portilla, to name just a few. In the early 1950s, he sustained a dialogue with the French historian Bataillon on the idea of the discovery of America. The scholarly exchange was published under the title *Dos concepciones de la tarea histórica con motivo de la idea del descubrimiento de América* (Two Conceptions of the Historical Task of Defining the Idea of America's Discovery, 1955). Bataillon disagreed with O'Gorman's interpretation of the idea of discovery because his reading of the sources was different from that of O'Gorman. Bataillon's exposition of his differences with O'Gorman comprised the first part of the book. In the second part O'Gorman replied to Bataillon defending his

idea of the discovery of America. The book concluded with exchanges of letters between Bataillon and O'Gorman from June to September 1954.

In *La invención de América* (1958; *The Invention of America*, 1961), O'Gorman reiterated his thesis and took one step further in developing his theory that America could not have been discovered because it had no existence as America in the minds of men in 1492 and subsequently. The concept of America dawned slowly and did not fully exist until well into the 16th century. In this work O'Gorman also reviewed the voyages of Columbus and Vespucci and the changing geographical concepts of the two navigators. O'Gorman's thesis was that America's historical meaning derived from Western consciousness, that the West provided Americans with points of reference to think of themselves historically. He argued that the idea of discovery was meaningless because only that which fully existed could be discovered. In the 1961 English edition of the book he added a chapter in which he distinguished two traditions in Mexico's history: the Anglo-Saxon, derived from the Reformation, and the Hispanic, stemming from the Counter-Reformation, two traditions that stood in dire opposition to each other in one historical subject.

O'Gorman's study of Mexico's history led him to reflect on the theory of history, on the relationship between the historical subject and object, and the problem of truth in history. In these reflections, he adopted a historicist, relativist, and idealist standpoint. In addition to the theoretical reflection, he inquired into what elements constituted Mexican historical awareness. In several works he examined in great depth the racial and religious underpinnings of the cult of the Mexican Virgin of Guadalupe.

As the preparations for the celebration of the 500th anniversary of Mexico's discovery by Europeans were underway, O'Gorman became involved in a sharp public debate with Miguel León-Portilla who had proposed the substitution of the notion of discovery for that of an encounter of the Old and the New worlds. O'Gorman objected to this vision of the conquest. He argued that the idea of an encounter did not correspond to the historical truth and was too superficial. When in 1492 the Europeans came into contact with the moral and physical environment of the New World, there was a profound transformation of both. The result was an "ontological assimilation of American to European reality." O'Gorman maintained that the world is one and could not be divided into separate entities. Because his disagreements with León-Portilla did not lead to a change in the concept of the celebration, in 1987 O'Gorman resigned from the Mexican Academy of History. The debate has not been resolved.

DANIELA SPENSER

See also Latin America: Colonial; León-Portilla

Biography

Born Coyoacán Federal District, Mexico, 1906, son of an English mining engineer and painter. Educated at Colegio Franco Inglés, 1922; received law degree, Escuela Libre de Derecho, 1928; MA in philosophy, National Autonomous University, 1948, PhD in history, 1951. Practiced law, 1928–38; taught (rising to professor), National Autonomous University, 1940–78. Worked at National Archives, 1938–52. Married Ida Rodríguez. Died 1995.

Principal Writings

La idea del descubrimiento de América: historia de esa interpretación y crítica de sus fundamentos (The Idea of America's Discovery: History of Its Interpretation and the Criticism of its Foundations), 1951

With Marcel Bataillon, *Dos concepciones de la tarea histórica con motivo de la idea del descubrimiento de América* (Two Conceptions of the Historical Task of Defining the Idea of America's Discovery), 1955

La invención de América: el universalismo de la cultura de Occidente, 1958; in English as *The Invention of America: An Inquiry into the Historical Nature of the New World and the Meaning of Its History,* 1961

Meditaciones sobre el criollismo (Meditations on Creolism), 1970

México, el trauma de su historia (Mexico: The Trauma of Its History), 1977

Destierro de sombras: luz en el origen de la imagen y culto de Nuestra Señora de Guadalupe de Tepeyac (Shadows in Exile: Light in the Image and Cult of Our Lady of Guadalupe Tepeyac), 1986

Further Reading

Florescano, Enrique, and Ricardo Pérez Montfort, eds., *Historiadores de México en el siglo XX* (Mexican Historians of the 20th Century), Mexico City: FCE & CONACULTA, 1995

La obra de Edmundo O'Gorman (The Works of Edmundo O'Gorman), Mexico City: UNAM, 1968 [includes bibliography]

Ortega y Medina, Juan, ed., *Conciencia y autenticidad históricas: escritos en homenaje a Edmundo O'Gorman* (Historical Consciousness and Authenticity: Writings Dedicated to Edmundo O'Gorman), Mexico City: UNAM, 1968 [includes bibliography]

Ogot, Bethwell A. 1929–

Kenyan historian of Africa

Bethwell Ogot has been a tireless supporter of African history. He has supervised more than 60 MA and Ph.D theses written at universities in Kenya, Tanzania, Ghana, Nigeria, Botswana, and Sweden. Perhaps most noteworthy among his numerous achievements has been his work with the International Scientific Committee for the Preparation of the UNESCO History of Africa (1971–to date), as president of the Committee from 1978 to 1984, and as editor of the fifth volume, *Africa from the Sixteenth to the Eighteenth Century* (1992). His promotion of cultural awareness does not stop at the boundaries of Africa: Ogot has also served as the UNESCO consultant on culture from 1980 to 1984 and as a member of the International Commission for the Preparation of a History of the Scientific and Cultural Development of Mankind since 1980.

Ogot has earned the reputation of being a staunch defender and promoter of oral traditions as historical sources. While others before him, such as Jan Vansina and Basil Davidson, employed oral traditions, no one had used oral traditions as their primary form of evidence for a professional degree. His dissertation on the precolonial history of the Luo was eventually published as *A History of the Southern Luo* (1967) and remains a seminal example of oral historiography. Ogot has persisted in his belief that African history should be based primarily on African historical sources, not on colonial sources. Doing so, he claims, purges African history of most of its racist connotations, such as those developed during the colonial era.

He has stuck to a liberal mode of interpretation throughout his career, striving to raise awareness of Africa's place in world history, without becoming caught up in ideological rhetoric.

Kenya has been the main focus of Ogot's scholarship. He was the founder and chairman of the Historical Association of Kenya from 1966, served as editor of the association's proceedings, *Hadith,* and published widely on Kenyan history. In fact, so strong is the link between Ogot and Kenya's history that, with few exceptions, every scholar writing on Kenya in the past two decades is either a former student of his or a foreign student who has had the advantage of his supervision.

Two subfields of African history especially benefited from Ogot's work. The first, military history, was a timely subject of study given its prevalent role in postcolonial politics. Ogot stated in the introduction of *War and Society in Africa* (1972), that in order to understand the role of the military in contemporary Africa, scholars must study the role of the military in precolonial and colonial Africa. Much of the current role of the military in Africa has connections to much older traditions concerning African views of the military and of violence. To attribute the current role of the military solely to the events of the postcolonial situation is to lack a clear understanding of African history and culture.

The second subfield cultivated by Ogot was ecological history. Much of the foundation for study of the African environment was laid in the introduction of *Hadith 7: Ecology and History in East Africa.* Here Ogot stated that ecological history is the story of man's efforts to adapt himself to his environment and his environment to himself. But human culture and society are not determined by environment. The physical environment is passive, human activity is not. Humans have spatial alternatives, and human societies could have evolved in a number of ways. What we must understand is why they evolved in the way they did. Another key issue in studying the environment is understanding environmental change over time: the Sahara being an excellent example for study. Finally, Ogot encouraged ecological historians to borrow from other disciplines, especially geography, in developing a methodology for studying the environment.

TOYIN FALOLA and JOEL E. TISHKEN

See also Africa: Eastern; Oliver

Biography

Bethwell Allan Ogot. Born 3 August 1929. Educated at Makerere University College, Kampala, Uganda, 1950–52, diploma in education, 1952; St. Andrew's College, Canada, 1955–59; University of London, 1960–61. Taught mathematics, Alliance High School, Kikuyu, 1953–55; lecturer in history, Makarere University College, 1959–64; secretary-general, East African Institute of Social and Cultural Affairs, 1963–68; taught (rising to professor), University of Nairobi, 1964–66; director, Institute of African Studies, 1965–75. Editor, *East African Journal,* 1964–74, and *Trans Africa Journal of History,* from 1970. Married Grace Emily Akinyi, 1959 (3 sons, 1 daughter).

Principal Writings

"Oral Traditions and History," in Merrick Posnansky, ed., *Prelude to the African Past,* 1966

A History of the Southern Luo, 1967

Editor with J.A. Kieran, *Zamani: A Survey of East African History,* 1968

"Historians and East Africa." in John Donnelly Fage, ed., *Africa and Its Past*, 1969
Editor, *Politics and Nationalism in Colonial Kenya*, 1972
Editor, *War and Society in Africa*, 1972
Editor, *Kenya before 1900*, 1976
Editor, *Ecology and History in East Africa*, 1979
Historical Dictionary of Kenya, 1981
"History, Ideology and Contemporary Kenya," *Kenya Historical Review* 7 (1982)
Editor, *Kenya in the Nineteenth Century*, 1985
Editor, *Africa from the Sixteenth to the Eighteenth Century*, 1992 [UNESCO General History of Africa, vol. 5]
Editor with W.R. Ochieng, *Decolonization and Independence in Kenya, 1940–93*, 1995
The Making of Kenya: A Hundred Years of Kenya's History, 1895–1995, 1995

Further Reading

Ochieng, W.R., ed., *A Modern History of Kenya, 1895–1980: Essays in Honour of B.A. Ogot*, Nairobi: Evans, 1989

Oliver, Roland 1923–

British historian of Africa

Between 1948 and his retirement in 1986, Roland Oliver progressed from the first lectureship in African history at the University of London's School of Oriental and African Studies to its first professorship. As co-founder of the *Journal of African History*, and subsequently of the *Cambridge History of Africa*, he not only provided historians of Africa with the first forum for their subject, but also with its fullest complete account. As a teacher, he was in effect the founder of that subject as it is taught today, drawing together the European-centered histories of the colonial period, the findings of social anthropologists and linguists, the evidence of archaeologists, and the regional studies of his early contemporaries in Britain, France, and North America together with those of the first generation of African historians into a comprehensive discipline for the continent as a whole.

His own published work began with studies of the colonial period: *The Missionary Factor in East Africa* (1952) and *Sir Harry Johnston and the Scramble for Africa* (1957), but in the first volume of the Oxford *History of East Africa* (1963) – co-edited with Gervase Mathew – he dealt with the precolonial period which he had come to see as the key to the entire project. In *The Dawn of African History* (1961), and still more in *A Short History of Africa* (1962) – written in collaboration with John Fage – he showed the way to write the history of the whole of Africa from the beginning, from an African-centered point of view.

It was unfortunate that the fourth chapter ("The Sudanic Civilisation") of this brilliant little book, in which he attempted to show the spread of divine kingship across the continent from a base in ancient Egypt, should have exposed him to criticism as an exponent of the infamous "Hamitic hypothesis" of the civilization of black Africans by whites. What it did reveal was his inevitable dependence, in his quest for the early history of Africa, upon the works of scholars who for the most part were not historians, in this case ethnologists. In a heroic struggle to convert their findings into history, he found himself repeatedly overtaken by fresh evidence and fresh conclusions, notably in the case of the spread of the Bantu languages as described by Guthrie. In the same way, the rapid but patchy growth of African archaeology, which provided him with the bulk of his material, allowed him only provisional conclusions. In collaboration with the archaeologist Brian Fagan, he nevertheless published *Africa in the Iron Age, c.500 BC to AD 1400* (1975), followed by *The African Middle Ages, 1400–1800*, with Anthony Atmore (1981), together with articles and chapters in the *Journal of African History* and the *Cambridge History*. What really mattered was the vision which governed the effort, and which ensured that history remained in control of the whole range of African studies in its quest for comprehensiveness.

Five years after Oliver's retirement, however, *The African Experience* (1991) appeared, the product of his reflections on the state of African history today. Its approach was thematic, bringing out the common factors in the history of the continent since the emergence of humanity, as seen by an author who could indeed place them in the context of the whole. It is ironic, therefore, that he should once again be involved in controversy, this time over his view of the colonial period. In *Africa since 1800* (1967), also written in collaboration with Anthony Atmore, he had argued that African nationalism did not spring from African resistance to colonial conquest, but from its acceptance as an avenue to real advancement. In his 1985 *Times Literary Supplement* review of volume 7 of the UNESCO *General History of Africa*, he sharply criticized the contributors, and in particular the editor, Adu Boahen, for their denunciation of the colonial period as one of exploitation and impoverishment. In Bethwell Ogot's review of *The African Experience* Oliver was in turn criticized for a benign view of the colonial conquest and subsequent colonial rule, as well as for his refusal to confront the causes of contemporary crisis in the continent. It would be a pity if a lifetime's successful struggle for the African past were to be clouded by the unfashionableness of his opinions on the merits of that short period which the preface to *A Short History* declared was no longer the be-all and end-all of history on the continent.

MICHAEL BRETT

See also Africa: Eastern

Biography

Roland Anthony Oliver. Born Srinigar, Kashmir, 30 March 1923. Attended Stowe School; King's College, Cambridge MA and PhD. Attached to Foreign Office, 1942–45. Junior research fellow, King's College, Cambridge, 1946–48; taught (rising to professor), School of Oriental and African Studies, University of London, 1948–86 (emeritus). Married 1) Caroline Florence Linehan, 1947 (died 1983; 1 daughter); 2) Suzanne Doyle, 1990.

Principal Writings

The Missionary Factor in East Africa, 1952
Sir Harry Johnston and the Scramble for Africa, 1957
The Dawn of African History, 1961
With J.D. Fage, *A Short History of Africa*, 1962; 6th edition, 1986
Editor with others, *History of East Africa*, 3 vols., 1963–76
With Anthony Atmore, *Africa since 1800*, 1967
With Brian Fagan, *Africa in the Iron Age, c.500 BC to AD 1400*, 1975

General editor with J.D. Fage, *The Cambridge History of Africa*, 8
vols., 1975–86
With Anthony Atmore, *The African Middle Ages, 1400–1800*, 1981
General editor with Michael Crowder, *The Cambridge Encyclopedia
of Africa*, 1981
The African Experience, 1991

Further Reading

M.C. (Michael Crowder), "Roland Oliver," *Journal of African
History*, special issue in honour of Roland Oliver, 29 (1988), 1–4
Ogot, Bethwell A., "Review of R.A. Oliver, *The African
Experience*," *Journal of African History* 33 (1992), 477–82

Oral History

Perhaps because the practice had its origins outside of or on
the fringes of professional "respectability" in terms of sources,
methods, and practitioners, oral history seems to defy precise
definition. When oral historians, or those who use the term
"oral history" in their writings, describe what it is they do,
they mix genres with abandon. Sometimes what is being
described is oral tradition; at others life history, life review, or
life course. For some oral historians the practice is the collection of interviews for archival purposes, to provide a record
for the future. For others it is the conduct of interviews for
particular publications or public history projects, and for still
others it is a pathway to "community empowerment." In addition the term "oral historian" is applied with great looseness.
Some argue that the oral historian is the person who conducts
the interview, others that the oral historian is the person being
interviewed – the narrator who tells the history. Neither is
there any agreement on what to call people being interviewed:
they can be interviewees, narrators, subjects, respondents. In
recent years oral history has become a noun, the thing itself
is the thing being collected, rather than the activity of interviewing for historical purposes. Indeed there is even debate
over whether oral historians simply collect oral histories, or
create them.

Such imprecision is at once liberating and confusing: liberating in the sense that traditional disciplinary and sub-disciplinary
boundaries are of little meaning and are crossed with impunity;
confusing in the sense that it is almost impossible from the name
itself to understand the practice. Work in oral history, as
described by practitioners, published in a variety of forms, or
presented at various meetings of oral historians, varies from
detailed empirical case studies, to methodological analyses, to
folkloric or linguistic studies, and from the presentation of
collected testimony to the analysis of conversation. Because the
phenomena itself is so universal – people talking to other people
about what happened in the past, and what meaning that past
has – Latin American testimonials, Scandinavian life histories,
small group conversations, consciousness-raising groups, one on
one interviews, survey interviews, Holocaust memories, and
African oral traditions are all fair game for the oral historian.

If form is irrelevant, the subject of analyses is enormously
wide. Originating in many areas as a way to fill in the gaps
in the written record, either as archival practice or because
that written record simply ignored so much of the daily life
of so many people, oral history has outgrown its roots in the
search for data and has become an activity seeking to understand all forms of subjectivity: memory, ideology, myth,
discourse systems, speech acts, silences, perceptions, and consciousness in all its multiple meanings. The search is not only
to document the past but to reveal how the past lives on in
daily life; what people do with what has been given to them
as a historical heritage.

Despite the confusion over terms and the scale of the task
they have set for themselves, oral historians seem to go about
their work untroubled by this imprecision. Aside from a few
attempts within the American oral history movement to come
to some consensus on goals and guidelines, and a few articles
seeking to define the relationship between oral history and the
life history method, or oral history and oral traditions, most
oral historians have not found it necessary to be overly
concerned with careful distinctions. Reflecting the status of oral
history, bridging the gap between the academic discipline of
history and the work of local or community historians,
archivists, public historians, or simply collectors with no well
defined position in the traditional academic hierarchy, it has
not been possible or, in many cases, necessary to devote the
kind of effort needed to construct boundaries.

Yet, a community of oral historians has evolved, both on a
number of national levels and internationally. Formal oral history societies and associations have existed since the 1960s in
most of the English-speaking world, and new national organizations have been founded in Argentina, Brazil, Mexico, Russia,
and other countries. There are also informal oral history sections within formal organizations such as the History Workshop
in South Africa and ASEAN (Association of South East Asian
Nations) archivists. On the international level there have now
been nine official and several interim international conferences
that have brought together oral historians from many different
national and scholarly traditions. In their membership and programs these organizations reflect the openness of the field itself.
At the most recent international conference held in Sweden an
international association was formed and officers elected, with
board members from six continents. The association plans a
series of publications and will hold its next meeting – the first
outside of Europe or the United States – in Rio de Janeiro. The
combination of national, regional, and international organizations is the most significant structuring of the oral history movement, and by its very nature will probably impose some more
or less consistent definition of the practice.

The oral history movement has, over the past twenty years,
produced its own rich and varied bibliography. The basic text
and primer in the field is Paul Thompson's *The Voice of the Past*
(1978). Reflecting the origins of the British oral history movement in the "new" social history, *The Voice of the Past* is deeply
informed by both the empiricist and positivist bent of that historiography, and its commitment to uncover the history of those
who have heretofore been ignored by professional historians. It
is an invaluable starting point for anyone interested in oral
history. A more structuralist presentation of the theoretical and
methodological problems of oral history is Ronald Grele's
Envelopes of Sound (1991). Far and away the most insightful
and complex work to date in oral history is *The Death of Luigi
Trastulli, and Other Stories* (1991) by Alessandro Portelli.
Combining Italian traditions of historiography harkening back
to Croce, Gramsci, and Carlo Ginzburg, and more recent work

on narrativity, *Trastulli* is a series of reflections on issues raised by Portelli's fieldwork experiences interviewing Italian workers and members of various Appalachian communities in the United States. Cross-cultural and cross-disciplinary it reveals the potential of the practice of oral history to open up and redefine the nature of the historical process itself. *A Shared Authority* (1990) by Michael Frisch moves from issues of the creation of oral documents to questions of use in a variety of public venues. *Women's Words*, edited by Sherna Gluck and Daphne Patai (1991), contains a number of essays attempting to apply feminist theory to oral history.

There are also several publications of essays on oral history in different nations, such as *Oral History*, edited by David K. Dunaway and Willa K. Baum (1984, revised 1996) on oral history in the United States, and *(Re)introduzindo história oral no Brasil* by José Carlos Sebe Bom Meihy (1996) on the Brazilian movement. Articles on oral history and news of events, conferences, and bibliographies are most easily found in the various journals published by national organizations such as the Oral History Association of Australia's *Journal*, the *Oral History Review* of the [United States] Oral History Association, and especially, *Oral History*, the journal of the British Oral History Society. A special edition of *Bios: Zeitschrift für Biographie Forschung und Oral History* (1990) contained a series of essays on the state of the field in the Americas, China, Eastern Europe, and Western Europe.

The exciting possibilities of merging careful empirical studies with newer questions of subjectivity raised by the use of oral histories can be found in such works as *Fascism in Popular Memory* (1984, translated 1987) by Luisa Passerini; *Dark Sweat, White Gold* by Devra Weber (1994); *Trade Unionists Against Terror* by Deborah Levenson-Estrada (1994); and *Righteous Lives* (1993) by Kim Lacy Rogers.

Interesting works attempting to apply philosophical hermeneutics to oral history can be found in *Elite Oral History Discourse* (1989) by Eva McMahan, and in some of the essays in *Interactive Oral History Interviewing* (1994), edited by McMahan and Rogers.

A steady stream of first-rate article literature can be found in the past issues of the *International Journal of Oral History* (1980–89), which first attempted to create an international forum for oral history, and in the three volumes published to date as the International Yearbook of Oral History: *Memory and Total Totalitarianism*, edited by Luisa Passerini (1992); *Between Generations*, edited by Daniel Bertaux and Paul Thompson (1993); and *Migration and Identity* edited by Rina Benmayor and Andor Skotnes (1994). The Yearbook is no longer published but a successor series is planned. "Subjectivity and Multiculturalism in Oral History," an issue of the *International Journal of Oral History* (1990), edited by Ronald Grele, contains a number of essays from a broad range of perspectives from various parts of the world.

The most important Spanish-language journal is *Historia y Fuente Oral*, whose director, Mercedes Vilanova, is the first president of the International Oral History Association. Founded in 1989 the journal offers a mix of original and translated essays. Other publications have been issued in Portuguese by the Brazilian Oral History Association.

Lastly, the brilliant *Theatres of Memory* (1994) by Raphael Samuel showed the wide influence of oral history in opening new questions about the traditional practice of history. In all of these works one can see the continuity of thinking about oral history despite the broad range of interests among oral historians.

The major creative tension in the field of oral history is that between the concern to develop a scholarship equal in richness to the documents, and the concern with community history. That tension can be seen in the project listings of the Singapore national archives, in the debates within the South African History Workshop movement, in the early issues of the *History Workshop Journal* in Britain, in the programs of the American Oral History Association, in the work done at Fernuniversität (Open University) in Germany, and in debates in Mexico and Brazil. The practice of oral history, by its very nature, raises questions about where history is practiced, who practices it, and to what end since it is a form of historical work not limited to traditional sites. Oral history also raises questions about the personal relations between the historian and the object of investigation. There is no question that the oral historian, here considered as the interviewer, is intimately involved in the creation of the document he or she then goes on to interpret (no matter what the setting for the interpretation). There is also no question that both the person being interviewed and the interviewer bring to the interview a complex and textured sense of history. In both community history and more traditional publications this is the crux of the issue of presentation. The interaction between interviewer and interviewee as each struggles to understand the other is what raises the theoretical questions at the heart of oral history, and it is this interaction that gives the promise of a new history from the bottom up – not just the creation of documents of the heretofore ignored populations but the ways in which those in the community become their own historians and present their history. Both on a theoretical level and as a form of practice, oral history brings into question the assumptions of professionalism among historians. This is, at once, the great promise and the great divide.

While future trends are difficult to predict, two trajectories seem clear. More and more oral historians, in particular in Europe and the United States, are experimenting with new technologies to organize, present, and make interviews and finding aids available to wider audience. There are also attempts to use the Internet to enlarge the practice of oral history. Though still experimental, the intersections of oral history and the virtual text are clear.

Also more and more work is being done in radio programming and video interviewing. Examples of video interviews from Europe, the United States, Brazil, Asia, and Africa have been presented at a variety of conferences, as has radio use of oral history. Radio programming has long been a tradition in places such as Canada and the United Kingdom and has now spread widely. In the United States the work of Charles Hardy III and Pamela Hensen has been of particular note.

Oral History has been a particularly creative practice over the past twenty years, and the growth of interest and activity shows no sign of diminishing. As more historians from the academy and among the citizenry turn to oral history as part of their historical practice, and as new fora are founded for the practice, one can expect new ways of thinking about what is being done to emerge.

RONALD J. GRELE

Further Reading

Benmayor, Rina, and Andor Skotnes, eds., *Migration and Identity*, Oxford and New York: Oxford University Press, 1994

Bertaux, Daniel, and Paul Thompson, eds., *Between Generations: Family Models, Myths, and Memories*, Oxford and New York: Oxford University Press, 1993

Bios: Zeitschrift für Biographie Forschung und Oral History, Leverkusen: Leske & Budrich, 1988–

Dunaway, David K., and Willa K. Baum, eds., *Oral History: An Interdisciplinary Anthology*, Nashville: American Association for State and Local History, 1984; revised 1996

Frisch, Michael H., *A Shared Authority: Essays on the Craft and Meaning of Oral and Public History*, Albany: State University of New York Press, 1990

Gluck, Sherna Berger, and Daphne Patai, eds., *Women's Words: The Feminist Practice of Oral History*, London and New York: Routledge, 1991

Grele, Ronald J., ed., "Subjectivity and Multiculturalism in Oral History," *International Journal of Oral History*, 1990 [special issue]

Grele, Ronald J., *Envelopes of Sound: The Art of Oral History*, New York: Praeger, 1991

Historia y Fuente Oral, Barcelona: University of Barcelona, 1989–

International Journal of Oral History, Westport, CT: Meckler, 1980–89

Levenson-Estrada, Deborah, *Trade Unionists Against Terror: Guatemala City, 1954–1985*, Chapel Hill: University of North Carolina Press, 1994

McMahan, Eva, *Elite Oral History Discourse: A Study of Cooperation and Coherence*, Tuscaloosa: University of Alabama Press, 1989

McMahan, Eva, and Kim Lacy Rogers, eds., *Interactive Oral History Interviewing*, Hillsdale, NJ: Erlbaum, 1994

Meihy, José Carlos Sebe Bom, *(Re)introduzindo história oral no Brasil*, São Paulo: USP, 1996

Oral History, British Oral History Society, Colchester: University of Essex Press, 1972–

Oral History Association of Australia *Journal*, Neutral Bay, NSW: Association, 1978–

Oral History Review, Fullerton, CA: Oral History Association, 1973–

Passerini, Luisa, *Torino operaia e fascismo: una storia orale*, Rome: Laterza, 1984; in English as *Fascism in Popular Memory: The Cultural Experience of the Turin Working Class*, Cambridge and New York: Cambridge University Press, 1987

Passerini, Luisa, ed., *Memory and Total Totalitarianism*, Oxford: Oxford University Press, 1992

Portelli, Alessandro, *The Death of Luigi Trastulli, and Other Stories: Form and Meaning in Oral History*, Albany: State University of New York Press, 1991

Rogers, Kim Lacy, *Righteous Lives: Narratives of the New Orleans Civil Rights Movement*, New York: New York University Press, 1993

Samuel, Raphael, *Theatres of Memory*, London and New York: Verso, 1994

Thompson, Paul, *The Voice of the Past: Oral History*, Oxford and New York: Oxford University Press, 1978

Vansina, Jan, *Oral Tradition as History*, Madison: University of Wisconsin Press, and London: Currey, 1985

Weber, Devra, *Dark Sweat, White Gold: California Farm Workers, Cotton, and the New Deal*, Berkeley: University of California Press, 1994

Orderic [Ordericus] Vitalis 1075–1142/3
Anglo-Norman monastic historian

Orderic Vitalis, best known for his *Historia ecclesiastica* (*Ecclesiastical History*), is one of our most valuable literary sources for the Anglo-Norman period. In addition, we can learn much about 12th-century monastic historiography from his work. Writing at the direction of successive abbots between about 1114 and 1141, he produced 13 books of lively narrative, incorporating eyewitness accounts of current events and invented speeches to illustrate character and purpose, his intent to edify and entertain apparent on every page.

His *Ecclesiastical History* began as a history of his monastery of Saint-Evroult, but during the approximately ten years taken to write the first book, it expanded to become a discussion of "the chances and changes of English and Normans alike." Despite the avowedly ecclesiastical focus, Orderic wrote of and in feudal Europe, with much of his narrative dealing with the period prior to the Gregorian reform. Since the temporal world and the church were deeply intertwined at all levels of society, Orderic discussed the politics and culture of the world in which he lived. Starting from the birth of Christ, he covered topics ranging from the foundation and growth of Saint-Evroult, with its various possessions, to the political history of the Anglo-Norman kings up to 1141. Along the way, he wrote on subjects such as the history of the Giroie, Grandmesnil, and Bellême families and their feudal relationships, the development of the new monastic orders, fashions at court, the crusades, miracle stories and wonderful events such as fires and thunderstorms. Many vivid portraits of individuals from all social ranks enliven his narrative.

Orderic, clearly a committed historian, based his history on extensive research, using more than 100 literary sources, monastic documents, and eyewitness accounts, taking notes and making extracts from borrowed books, for a time with the help of assistants. He took advantage of occasional travel to interview possible informants and to investigate other libraries. There are, nevertheless, some factual errors in his work. Conservative in his outlook as 12th-century monks frequently were, he had a firmly theocratic worldview (see Ray, 1974) and a belief in the rightness of the feudal order of his day, which colored his writing. Aside from this bias, he has been accused of deliberately creating villains, usually members of the Bellême family, to allow other men, often anointed kings, to stand as heroes. Thompson (1994) has suggested that the accuracy of the *Ecclesiastical History* and Orderic's judgments be reassessed with this stricture in mind.

Orderic had a vision of his role as a historian. Recounting the actions of famous men made their examples available to be followed, while lists of monastic donors and their gifts would remind monks of their own good fortune and of the recipients of their prayers. The present could be better understood with a knowledge of the past, the future faced similarly equipped, and all stories of human activity showed the working out of God's will on this earth. His vision of universal history appears to be derived from that of Bede. If miracles and examples of holiness had not been so rare in Orderic's lifetime, he would have preferred to concentrate on such edifying stories. "But we must write truthfully of the world as it is," and so he recounted the good with the bad, the heroic with the cowardly, the political with the spiritual. He strove to back up his stories with reliable evidence and to arrive at the truth as he saw it. To the modern historian, the *Ecclesiastical History* is infinitely rich in detail but infuriating: Orderic included few dates, pursued only an approximately chronological narrative, and seized many opportunities to digress, often at considerable length.

Despite Orderic's hopes of an audience wider than the members of his own monastery, extending to readers and listeners of the Norman world and even further afield, the *Ecclesiastical History* was little known in the Middle Ages. Chibnall ascribed this neglect to its individuality and personal nature, and also to the sheer size of the work. Ironically more medieval copies survive of his earlier, and much less important, interpolations in William of Jumièges' *Gesta Normannorum Ducum* than of the *Ecclesiastical History*. However, it was widely circulated from the 16th century, published by Duchesne a century later, and has been a basis for modern Anglo-Norman political, social, and cultural history. Marjorie Chibnall's English translation has increased the work's accessibility, as is demonstrated by increasingly frequent references to it. Thus, Orderic is now recognized, along with William of Malmesbury, as one of the foremost Anglo-Norman historians.

KATHLEEN TROUP

See also Delisle; Medieval Chronicles; Thietmar

Biography
Born Atcham, near Shrewsbury, England, 16 February 1075, son of a Norman priest who had taken an English wife. Sent to become a monk at St. Evroult in Normandy in 1085; ordained priest, 1107. Occasionally traveled, but remained at St. Evroult to his death, 13 July 1142/3.

Principal Writings
Historia ecclesiastica, 13 vols., written 1114–41; in English as *The Ecclesiastical History of Orderic Vitalis*, edited by Marjorie Chibnall, 6 vols., 1969–80

Further Reading
Chibnall, Marjorie, "Orderic Vitalis and Robert of Torigni," in *Millénaire monastique du Mont Saint-Michel*, Paris: Lethielleux, 1966

Chibnall, Marjorie, "General Introduction," in Marjorie Chibnall, ed., *The Ecclesiastical History of Orderic Vitalis*, 6 vols., Oxford: Oxford University Press, 1969–80

Chibnall, Marjorie, "Feudal Society in Orderic Vitalis," in R. Allen Brown, ed., *Proceedings of the Battle Abbey Conference on Anglo-Norman Studies 1, 1978*, Ipswich, Suffolk: Boydell, and Totowa, NJ: Rowman and Littlefield, 1979

Chibnall, Marjorie, *The World of Orderic Vitalis*, Oxford and New York: Oxford University Press, 1984

Chibnall, Marjorie, "Anglo-French Relations in the Work of Orderic Vitalis," in J.S. Hamilton and Patricia J. Bradley, eds., *Documenting the Past: Essays in Medieval History Presented to George Peddy Cuttino*, Woodbridge, Suffolk: Boydell, 1989

Chibnall, Marjorie, "Orderic Vitalis on Castles," in Christopher Harper-Bill, Christopher J. Holdsworth, and Janet L. Nelson, eds., *Studies in Medieval History Presented to R. Allen Brown*, Woodbridge, Suffolk: Boydell, 1989

Chibnall, Marjorie, "Women in Orderic Vitalis," *Haskins Society Journal* 2 (1990), 105–21

Delisle, Léopold, *Notice sur Ordéric Vital* (Notice on Orderic Vitalis), 1855

Gransden, Antonia, *Historical Writing in England*, vol. 1: *c.550 to c.1307*, London: Routledge, and Ithaca, NY: Cornell University Press, 1974

Holdsworth, Christopher, "Orderic, Traditional Monk and the New Monasticism," in Diana Greenway, Christopher Holdsworth, and Jane Sayers, eds., *Tradition and Change: Essays in Honour of Marjorie Chibnall Presented by Her Friends on the Occasion of Her Seventieth Birthday*, Cambridge and New York: Cambridge University Press, 1985

Petry, Ray C., "Three Medieval Chroniclers: Monastic Historiography and Biblical Eschatology in Hugh of St. Victor, Otto of Freising, and Ordericus Vitalis," *Church History* 34 (1965), 282–93

Ray, Roger D., "Orderic Vitalis and His Readers," *Studia monastica* 14 (1972), 17–33

Ray, Roger D., "Orderic Vitalis on Henry I: Theocratic Ideology and Didactic Narrative," in George H. Shriver, ed., *Contemporary Reflections on the Medieval Christian Tradition: Essays in Honor of Ray C. Petry*, Durham, NC: Duke University Press, 1974

Smalley, Beryl, *Historians in the Middle Ages*, London: Thames and Hudson, and New York: Scribner, 1974

Thompson, Kathleen, "Orderic Vitalis and Robert of Bellême," *Journal of Medieval History* 20 (1994), 133–41

Wolter, Hans, *Ordericus Vitalis: ein Beitrag zur kluniazensischen Geschichtsschreibung* (Orderic Vitalis: An Article on Cluniac Historical Writing), Wiesbaden: Steiner, 1955

Orientalism

Orientalism has only recently become a contentious term: since the late 18th century it has been shorthand for the various scholars and disciplines engaged in the study of the peoples and cultures of Asia. Scholars such as William Jones, Max Müller, and the savants who accompanied Napoleon to Egypt laid the foundations for the systematic inquiry into the literature, religions, cultures, and philosophies of Asia by emphasizing the mastery of local languages and the close scrutiny of indigenous and often sacred texts. They were spurred on by the Enlightenment's fascination with the wider world, and in some cases were individually driven by a sympathetic reading of Asian culture. Their methods and perspectives would eventually influence many disciplines, including history, literature, anthropology, and sociology, and would also culminate in the founding of specialist institutes of Oriental study in London, Oxford, Cambridge, Leiden, Paris, Brussels, Heidelberg, and in many universities in the United States. Even with such growth and diversification, Orientalism remained anchored in philology and hermeneutics.

However, since the publication of Edward Said's *Orientalism* (1978), the motives and consequences of Oriental scholarship have become hotly contested. Said insisted that scholars, including historians, re-examine not only what they knew about the "Orient," and how they knew it, but why they knew it. He coupled together the anti-imperialism of Frantz Fanon, as well as Fanon's insights into the psychological trauma unleashed by colonial rule, with Michel Foucault's emphasis on discourse as the means through which knowledge is transformed into power. Said exposed Orientalism's complicity in Western domination by uncovering the processes and motives that underpinned European efforts to produce authoritative knowledge of the East. He demonstrated that it was not simply a case of bias and stereotypes in need of correction. Instead, the very act of representation was called into question, particularly as it was accompanied by Europe's growing political, economic, and cultural domination over Asia, Africa, and the Middle East. Knowledge of the Orient became power over the Orient, for Orientalist discourses shaped not only our impressions of nonwestern peoples, but also helped to forge the tools through which they were subjugated. Novels, travelogues, and historical works about the lands of the "other," and later censuses, district reports, and other forms of textual information were as important, if not more so, than the Gatling gun or the steamship in accounting for European domination. This command over information was to persist after the formal ending of empires, ensuring the conditions necessary for what has been termed neocolonialism.

The production of this authoritative discourse rested upon the application of European models, terminology, and theories. This allowed the distinction between the European self and the conquered other to be rigidly demarcated through binary oppositions: masculine vs. feminine, progress vs. stagnation, adulthood vs. childhood, reason vs. superstition, and so on. Such oppositions bolstered colonial hierarchies and rationalized colonial rule. Said's powerful denunciation of the will to power implicit in Orientalism has inspired others to conduct detailed inquiries into other manifestations of Western knowledge about lands beyond Europe. Other scholars have begun to explore in more detail the manner in which Orientalism helped shape European culture, showing the extent to which many domestic ideologies and values were influenced by Orientalist knowledge. Said returned to this debate with *Culture and Imperialism* (1993), a work that ranges widely through Western literature, historical writings, and even music in such a way as to extend his earlier insights to the world beyond the Middle East. His conclusions in this work are breathtaking – imperialism is everywhere, it can be found in nearly every conceivable nook and cranny of Western culture over the past two centuries.

Said's work has without doubt forced Western scholarship in general to reflect on its intellectual heritage, and prompted many scholars to re-examine the assumptions which had hitherto guided their work. However, postorientalism, a term which refers to work which takes Said's critique as its point of departure, has not met with universal approval. Interest seems to vary somewhat by discipline, by region of study, and even by country. Literature and cultural studies have proven to be the most receptive to postorientalism, not surprisingly given postorientalism's emphasis on the production of texts and discourses, and its affinities with other forms of critical theory, including poststructuralism and the new historicism. Scholars such as Homi Bhabha, Sara Suleri, Mary Louise Pratt, and Gayatri Spivak have opened up new perspectives on the manifestations and consequences of Orientalism. It can also be argued that enthusiasm seems stronger in the United States than in Britain. This can best be accounted for by the kinship that connects postorientalism with other manifestations of American intellectual radicalism, particularly feminist studies, Afro-American studies and multiculturalism. All these movements question our faith in objectivity and expose the linkages between elite domination and Western intellectual traditions.

The responses by historians to the postoriental manifesto have generally been more muted, though there are important exceptions at both ends of the spectrum. While many now concede that imperialism was undeniably bolstered by Oriental scholarship, postorientalism's potential to deny the validity of any representation, on the grounds that representations are invariably the product of unequal power relationships, threatens to subvert the foundations of many disciplines, including

history. If we accept that Orientalism is thoroughly implicated in the rise and consolidation of Western imperialism, then we must also consider whether there can be any form of knowledge about another society that does not depend on domination.

Opposition to postorientalism also stems from the empirical tradition within Western historiography. Empirical approaches sit uneasily with the demands of theory. Scholars such as John M. MacKenzie, David Kopf, and Bernard Lewis insist that postorientalist scholarship is far too selective in its choice of examples, and that in order to make the evidence fit the theory, the wider context is often overly simplified. Critics have also pointed to what they see as an overly rigid distinction between colonizer and colonized in this production of knowledge. They note for example that the production of this Orientalist discourse was frequently dependent on local intermediaries and translators who were in a position to propound their own interpretations. Other historians, such as Rosalind O'Hanlon and David Washbrook, who emphasize materialist explanations of history, have also been reluctant to subscribe to postorientalism, arguing that its emphasis on representation as the foundation of power neglects material reality.

Objections have also been made to the conclusion that the self/other dichotomy could only be worked out within an extra-European empire. Internal colonization, the conquest and subordination of Britain's Celtic fringes, was instrumental in defining what it meant to be British. And as Linda Colley has recently argued in *Britons* (1992), the "other" that was so crucial to forging the British character in the 18th and early 19th centuries tended to be European and Catholic, and not Indian and Hindu, or Arab and Muslim. There is also the awkward task of accounting for the great depths of Oriental scholarship undertaken in countries which had no obvious interest in building up an Asian empire. German Orientalism is perhaps the best example here.

These criticisms notwithstanding, one can question MacKenzie's claim that neither *Orientalism* nor *Culture and Imperialism* have had the impact on historians that might have been otherwise assumed. A special issue of *Annales* in 1980 attests to the interest of French historians in this topic, not surprisingly given that *Orientalism* dwelled at length on French Orientalists. South Asian historiography has been especially influenced by such scholars as Ronald Inden, Gauri Viswanathan, Sara Suleri, Javed Majeed, and Gyan Prakash, as well as those associated with the most recent volumes of *Subaltern Studies*, who have illuminated how the British came to know India and the manner in which such representations contributed to the rise of the Raj. Postorientalism has also had an impact on the study of African, Chinese, Japanese, Southeast Asian, and Latin American scholarship. Writings by V.Y. Mudimbe, and the essays edited by Gyan Prakash in *After Colonialism* (1995) indicate the potential for much further work in this direction.

Few would deny the importance of the controversies triggered by Said's *Orientalism*. While not all historians are willing to subscribe completely to its agenda, the debates it has unleashed and its insistence that scholars reflect upon what we know of the world and how we have come to know it, have forced many to reconceptualize their historical scholarship.

DOUGLAS PEERS

See also Anderson, B.; Indigenous; Lewis, B.; Postcolonialism; Rodinson; Said; Southeast Asia; Women's History: Asia; Xenophon

Further Reading

Ahmad, Aijaz, *In Theory: Classes, Nations, Literatures*, London and New York: Verso, 1992

Barkan, Elazar, "Post-anti-colonial Histories: Representing the Other in Imperial Britain," *Journal of British Studies* 33 (1994), 180–203

Bhabha, Homi K., ed., *Nation and Narration*, London and New York: Routledge, 1990

Breckenridge, Carol A., and Peter van der Veer, eds., *Orientalism and the Postcolonial Predicament: Perspectives on South Asia*, Philadelphia: University of Pennsylvania Press, 1993

Inden, Ronald, *Imagining India*, Oxford and Cambridge, MA: Blackwell, 1990

Kopf, David, "Hermeneutics versus History," *Journal of Asian Studies* 39 (1980), 495–506

Lewis, Bernard, *Islam and the West*, Oxford and New York: Oxford University Press, 1994

Lewis, Reina, *Gendering Orientalism: Race, Femininity, and Representation*, London and New York: Routledge, 1996

MacKenzie, John M., "Edward Said and the Historians," *Nineteenth-Century Contexts* 18 (1994), 9–25

MacKenzie, John M., *Orientalism: History, Theory and the Arts*, Manchester: Manchester University Press, 1995

Majeed, Javed, *Ungoverned Imaginings: James Mill's The History of British India and Orientalism*, Oxford and New York: Oxford University Press, 1992

Melman, Billie, *Women's Orients: English Women in the Middle East, 1718–1918: Sexuality, Religion and Work*, London: Macmillan, 1990; Ann Arbor: University of Michigan Press, 1992

Mudimbe, V.Y., *The Idea of Africa*, Bloomington: Indiana University Press, and London: Currey, 1994

O'Hanlon, Rosalind, and David Washbrook, "After Orientalism: Culture, Criticism, and Politics in the Third World," *Comparative Studies in Society and History* 34 (1992), 141–67

Prakash, Gyan, ed., *After Colonialism: Imperial Histories and Post-colonial Displacements*, Princeton: Princeton University Press, 1995

Pratt, Mary Louise, *Imperial Eyes: Travel Writing and Transculturation*, London and New York: Routledge, 1992

Said, Edward W., *Orientalism*, New York: Pantheon, and London: Routledge, 1978

Said, Edward W., *Culture and Imperialism*, New York: Knopf, and London: Chatto and Windus, 1993

Schwab, Raymond, *La Renaissance orientale*, Paris: Payot, 1950; in English as *The Oriental Renaissance: Europe's Rediscovery of India and the East, 1680–1880*, New York: Columbia University Press, 1984

Spivak, Gayatri, *In Other Worlds: Essays in Cultural Politics*, London and New York: Metheun, 1987

Sprinker, Michael, ed., *Edward Said: A Critical Reader*, Oxford and Cambridge, MA: Blackwell, 1992

Suleri, Sara, *The Rhetoric of English India*, Chicago: University of Chicago Press, 1992

Viswanathan, Gauri, *Masks of Conquest: Literary Study and British Rule in India*, New York: Columbia University Press, 1989

Young, Robert, *White Mythologies: Writing History and the West*, London and New York: Routledge, 1990

Ormsby, Margaret A. 1909–1996
Canadian historian

The best known historian of British Columbia, Margaret Ormsby was a native of Canada's westernmost province. She was among the first generation to graduate from the University of British Columbia and returned to teach at her alma mater after completing a PhD at Bryn Mawr College in Pennsylvania. Ormsby became the first woman to head a history department at a Canadian university when she stepped into the position at University of British Columbia. As a teacher and publishing historian for over half a century, Ormsby helped establish British Columbia history as a viable field of academic historical study.

Ormsby's most important work was *British Columbia: A History* (1958), published as part of the celebrations marking the establishment of British Columbia as a colony one hundred years earlier. The first provincial history written since World War I, *British Columbia* stood as the standard in the field for decades – in many aspects, it still has not been surpassed. The text gave structure to the province's past through a series of oppositions that animated the narrative: the ongoing pull between maritime and continental forces; the opposition between a "closed," hierarchical model of society represented by the Hudson's Bay Company and colonial officials, and the "open," egalitarian vision of English and Canadian settlers; and regional tensions, between Vancouver Island and mainland, metropolitan Vancouver and the hinterland interior. Throughout, Ormsby drew upon her own experiences growing up in British Columbia's interior to craft a distinct vision of the province's past and identity: the sharp juxtaposition of civilization (community, intellectual life, etc.) and natural wilderness distinguished British Columbia, and it was in the hinterland that this juxtaposition was clearest. Indeed, Ormsby tackled an abiding issue in North American historiography, namely the perennial tension between a new environment, and the cultural baggage of people only recently claiming that environment as their own. While acutely aware of the power of British Columbia's forbidding topography and geographic isolation, Ormsby did not adopt Frederick Jackson Turner's frontier thesis; like other Canadian historians, she tended to see people rather than environment as determinative in the end.

In *British Columbia* and in her other work, Ormsby contributed to an emerging tradition of provincial historiography while introducing new themes that would be picked up later. As with other British Columbia historians, there was an underlying materialism to Ormsby's work, both in its concern for economic growth through the exploitation of British Columbia's rich natural resources, and through the impact of the province's topography and isolating geography. Meanwhile, influenced by American Progressive historians and their definitions of "interests" and "class," Ormsby placed faction and conflict at the heart of provincial history. Finally, Ormsby pointed the way to the study of aspects of British Columbia's social history; but while she wrote of the province's "social life," mentioned the perspective and place of women within that, and departed from previous historians in welcoming cultural and racial pluralism, Ormsby did not anticipate the "bottom up" social history that emerged in the 1960s.

Ormsby's writing was marked by its elegance and accessibility, which helps explain the popularity of *British Columbia* among both general and academic readers. Praising the example of Donald Creighton, Ormsby stressed the importance of narrative and of the individual in history. She was particularly interested in bringing out the uniqueness and diversity of characters in history, and her work made use of political leaders as representative figures. As such, it was consistent with the general move to political biography in post-World War II Canadian historiography, but Ormsby rejected the latter's centrist, "national" focus. Along with W.L. Morton (*Manitoba: a History*, 1957), Ormsby directed historians' eyes toward the more "limited identities" of Canada's regions.

CHAD REIMER

See also Canada

Biography

Margaret Anchoretta Ormsby. Born Quesnel, British Columbia, 7 June 1909. Received BA, University of British Columbia, 1929, MA 1931; PhD, Bryn Mawr College, 1937. Taught at Sarah Dix Hamlin School, San Francisco, 1937–40; McMaster University, 1940–43; University of British Columbia (rising to professor), 1943–74 (emeritus). Died Coldstream, British Columbia, 2 November 1996

Principal Writings

"The History of Agriculture in British Columbia," *Scientific Agriculture* 20 (1939), 61–72
"Prime Minister Mackenzie, the Liberal Party and the Bargain with British Columbia," *Canadian Historical Review* 26 (1945), 148–73
British Columbia: A History, 1958
"Humanized History," *Canadian Literature* 3 (Summer 1961), 53–56
"T. Dufferin Pattulo and the Little New Deal," *Canadian Historical Review* 43 (1962), 277–97
"A Horizontal View: Presidential Address," Canadian Historical Association, *Historical Papers* (1966), 1–13
Editor, *A Pioneer Gentlewoman in British Columbia: The Recollections of Susan Allison*, 1976

Further Reading

Norris, John, "Margaret Ormsby," *BC Studies* 32 (Winter 1976–77), 11–27
Woodward, Frances, "Margaret Anchoretta Ormsby: Publications," *BC Studies* 32 (Winter 1976–77), 163–66

Ortiz, Fernando 1881–1969

Cuban historian, sociologist, anthropologist, and linguist

The founder of Afro-Cuban studies, Fernando Ortiz began his professional life as a law student at the University of Havana and in Barcelona, Spain before serving a short term as consular official in Italy in the early 1900s. His early contact with Europeans and European thought had a profound influence on the future direction of Ortiz's work; he studied sociology and penal science under Manuel Sales y Ferré who convinced him that crime was a socially-produced phenomenon, and also met the Italian social theorists Cesare Lombroso and Enrico Fermi. Using the scientific methodology and objective observation techniques he had absorbed while in Europe, Ortiz returned to Cuba to publish his first major book, *Los negros brujos* (The Black Warlocks, 1906), a study of primitive psychology and its effects on criminal behavior, in which the early stages of Ortiz's unique investigative style were already discernible. In *Los negros brujos* Ortiz adopted the form of a scientific study, complete with charts, tables, and figures, to investigate a social and cultural phenomenon; in fact, his work was highly narrative and interpretive, utilizing a broad array of sources from popular culture, mythology, and historical chronicles, as well as empirical data. He was able to situate Afro-Cuban culture in its original context, and therefore introduce a new perspective to the discussion of its current condition. Ortiz developed this theme throughout the rest of his long, varied, and remarkably productive career.

From the earliest days, Ortiz was concerned with the elaboration of a Cuban national identity which incorporated all its diverse elements, but particularly the Hispanic and the African, into a unique society. His collection of constructively critical essays entitled *Entre Cubanos: psicología tropical* (Among Cubans: Tropical Psychology, 1913) revealed Ortiz's fundamental positivism, and suggested improvements in government and social administration that would help Cuba attain its full potential. The author even joined the Liberal party and entered government as a reform candidate. By 1919 Ortiz was frustrated with the corruption and official lethargy, and as a response he published *La crisis política cubana* (The Cuban Political Crisis) in which he criticized Cubans' apathetic ill-preparedness for participatory democracy, the creoles' general pessimism and malaise, and foreign domination of his country's economy. He founded the Junta for Civic Renovation in the 1920s and urged immediate reforms, including industrial protectionism, reciprocity in trade agreements, expanded health services, prison reform, an end to graft and corruption, a reorganized judiciary, and a reduction of US influence in Cuban society and its economy. He was exiled by the Machado government in 1931 and spent two years in the United States studying, researching, and publishing articles on Cuba.

In his most famous and influential work, *Contrapunteo cubano del tabaco y el azúcar* (1940; *Cuban Counterpoint: Tobacco and Sugar*, 1947), Ortiz used an allegorical contrast between tobacco and sugar production to discuss the types of societies produced by each, and to reveal how these two distinct types of agricultural culture affected the development of Cuban national identity. Ortiz argued that "Tobacco and sugar are opposed to each other in the economic as in the social field" with "highly antithetical characteristics and effects." Where the sugar industry was seasonal, mechanized, capital-intensive, and required little human creativity, tobacco production was almost an artistic enterprise, requiring individual talent and assessment, skill, and nurture. Ortiz discussed the types of labor systems adopted by each, investment and capital strategies, immigration and family structures produced, and the literary or cultural mythology spawned. Not surprisingly, Ortiz condemned the harshness of the foreign-owned sugar mills, something that endeared him to Marxists and the future revolutionary regime, while celebrating tobacco and cigar-smoking as "the most typical and autochthonous custom left to us."

Cuban Counterpoint had broader significance than its socio-economic analysis of Cuban society; it also introduced Ortiz's concept of "transculturation" into general usage to replace previously used terms such as cultural exchange, acculturation, diffusion, and migration of cultures, all of which were ethnocentric and implied that others had to adapt themselves to the dominant Western European culture. The anthropologist Bronisław Malinowski, in his introduction to the English edition, enthusiastically adopted Ortiz's idea of transculturation as "a source of pleasure and profit to me." In *Cuban Counterpoint*, Ortiz discussed the transculturation of Cuban society, noting that the "result of every union of cultures is similar to that of the reproductive process between individuals: the offspring always contains something of both parents but is always different from each of them." His all-encompassing narrative touched on all aspects of Cuban folk society: religion, ethics, morality, sexual behavior, artistic endeavors, language, the economy, and collective psychology. He made an eloquent plea for the recognition and preservation of a unique Cuban national identity in the face of encroaching foreign domination which, Ortiz pointed out, has been a facet of Cuban political existence since the arrival of Columbus.

Ortiz's discussion of transculturation and the incomplete migration of cultures to Cuba found great acceptance among Malinowski's followers, the school of social science known as functionalism. He continued his investigations into the religion, language, and psychology of Afro-Cubans and brought that previously ignored element of Cuban society into the realm of legitimate subjects for study. He also founded several important journals and cultural associations to promote his investigations, most notably *Ultra* (1936–47), *Estudios afro-cubanos* (Afro-Cuban Studies, 1937–40, 1945–46), *Revista Bimestre Cubana* (1910–60), the Hispano-Cuban Cultural Institute (1926), the Afro-Cuban Studies Society (1936), and the International Afro-American Studies Institute (1934). Always politically active, Ortiz directed the Cuban Alliance for a Free World Against Fascism, and wrote *El engaño de las razas* (The Hoax of Races, 1945) to counteract Aryan claims to racial superiority. In this forcefully argued book he maintained that races did not exist, that one could distinguish nations, cultures, and classes, but there was no commonly accepted division of people into races.

Fernando Ortiz was a dominant intellectual figure in 20th-century Cuban life. He singlehandedly raised Afro-Cuban culture to a national prominence and placed a new emphasis on scientific and rigorous investigation into social phenomenon. His argument that Cuban identity had been conditioned by the transculturation of various people, by slavery, abolition and racism, and foreign economic imperialism were embraced by reformists and revolutionaries alike and had a resonance beyond the shores of his island. Ortiz emphasized the interrelationship between culture and politics and believed that salvation would come only with a knowledge and acceptance of Cuban national identity.

KAREN RACINE

See also Cuba; Latin America: National

Biography

Fernando Ortiz Fernández. Born Havana, 16 July 1881. Attended University of Havana; then studied in Barcelona, Madrid, and Italy. Originally member of diplomatic corps, before joining University of Havana law faculty. Married Esther Cabrera (1 daughter). Died Havana, 10 April 1969.

Principal Writings

Hampa afro-cubana: los negros brujos (apuntes para un estudio de etnología criminal) (Afro-Cuban Criminality), 1906

Los negros brujos (The Black Warlocks), 1906
Entre Cubanos: psicología tropical (Among Cubans: Tropical Psychology), 1913
La crisis política cubana: sus causas y sus remedios (The Cuban Political Crisis), 1919
Contrapunteo cubano del tabaco y el azúcar, 1940; in English as *Cuban Counterpoint: Tobacco and Sugar*, 1947
El engaño de las razas (The Hoax of Races), 1945
La africanía de la música folklórica de Cuba (The Africanness of the Folkloric Music of Cuba), 1950

Further Reading

Argüelles Espinosa, Luís, "Correspondencia mexicana de Fernando Ortiz" (The Mexican Correspondence of Fernando Ortiz), *Revista de la Biblioteca Nacional "José Martí"* 25/3 (1983), 97–109

Argüelles Espinosa, Luís, "Significación política de Fernando Ortiz" (The Political Significance of Fernando Ortiz), *Universidad de La Habana* 221 (1983), 40–50

Barnett, Curtis Lincoln, "Fernando Ortiz and the Literary Process," unpublished PhD dissertation, Columbia University, 1986

Castells, Ricardo, "Ficción y nacionalismo en el *Contrapunteo cubano* de Fernando Ortiz" (Fiction and Nationalism in *Cuban Counterpoint* by Fernando Ortiz), *Journal of Interdisciplinary Literary Studies* 4 (1992), 55–70

Catzaras, Marina, "Negrismo y transculturación en Cuba: El pensamiento de Ortiz y las obras tempranas de Carpentier y Guillén" (Negrism and Transculturation in Cuba: The Thought of Ortiz and the Early Works of Carpentier and Guillén), unpublished PhD dissertation, University of Pittsburgh, 1990

Coronil, Fernando, "Challenging Colonial Histories: *Cuban Counterpoint*, Ortiz's Counterfetishism," in Steven Bell, ed., *Critical Theory, Cultural Politics, and Latin American Narrative*, Notre Dame, IN: University of Notre Dame Press, 1993, 61–80

Gárciga, Orestes, "El archivo de Fernando Ortiz: acerca de su estructuración metodológica y fin práctico" (The Archive of Fernando Ortiz: On its Methodological Structure and Practical End), *Santiago* 58 (1985), 63–83

Ibarro, Jorge, "La herencia científica de Fernando Ortiz" (The Scientific Heritage of Fernando Ortiz), *Revista Iberoamericana* 56 (1991), 122–53, 1339–51

Lamore, Jean, "La obra antiracista de Fernando Ortiz: el caso de la revista Ultra" (The Antiracist Work of Fernando Ortiz: The Case of the Review Ultra), *Santiago* 58 (1985), 45–62

Le Riverend, Julio, "Ortiz y sus contrapunteos" (Ortiz and his Counterpoints), *Islas* 70 (1981), 7–35

Moore, Robin, "Representation of Afro-Cuban Expressive Culture in the Writing of Fernando Ortiz," *Latin American Music Review* 15 (1994), 32–54

Muller, Edward J., "Los negros brujos: A Re-examination of the Text" (The Black Warlocks), *Cuban Studies* 17 (1987), 111–29

Nodal, Roberto, "The Black Man in Cuban Society: From Colonial Times to the Revolution," *Journal of Black Studies* 16 (1986), 251–67

Serrano, Carlos, "Fernando Ortiz y Miguel de Unamuno: un episodio de regeneracionismo tránslatlantico" (Fernando Ortiz and Miguel de Unamuno: an Episode in Transatlantic Regeneration), *Revista de la Biblioteca Nacional "José Martí"* 29 (1987), 7–22

Suret-Canale, Jean, "En el homenaje a Fernando Ortiz: observaciones críticas en torno de los conceptos de la cultura africana" (In Homage to Fernando Ortiz: Critical Observations Around the Concepts of African Culture), *Revista de la Biblioteca Nacional "José Martí"* 1-2 (1982), 97–104

Toro González, Carlos del, "Fernando Ortiz y el encuentro de dos culturas" (Fernando Ortiz and the Encounter of Two Cultures), *Revista de la Biblioteca Nacional "José Martí,"* 1992

Osgood, Herbert Levi 1855–1918

US historian of colonial America

Described by admirers as a historian's historian, Herbert Levi Osgood saw himself as a scientific scholar who pioneered the study of the political and institutional history of the American colonies within the framework of the British empire during their first 150 years, a period he considered as significant in the country's development as the momentous decades of the later 18th century. Educated at Amherst, Yale, Berlin, and Columbia, he came under the influence of Germanic and German-educated scholars who had learnt from philologists how to authenticate and evaluate documentary sources. Based on extensive research in British archives and state and local depositories in the United States, and assisted by graduate students at Columbia University who perpetuated his influence long after his death, Osgood's multivolume histories of the American colonies in the 17th and 18th centuries were the first to place their development in an imperial context. However, unlike other imperial historians, his vantage point was colonial not metropolitan. As a professional historian, employed at one of America's leading universities, Osgood's career differed significantly from that of the generation which preceded his, dependent on the lecture circuit, and exemplified by John Fiske.

Presaged by a series of articles which appeared in the *Political Science Quarterly* and the *American Historical Review* in the late 1890s, two volumes of the first of Osgood's key works, *The American Colonies in the Seventeenth Century*, were published in 1904; the third volume appearing in 1907. At his death in 1918 he had virtually completed his 4-volume study *The American Colonies in the Eighteenth Century*. Only the chapter on slavery was missing but, doubtful of the popular appeal of a work allegedly devoid of human interest and heroic deeds, his publishers did not go ahead with it until 1924.

The principal theme of Osgood's first two volumes was the transition of the colonies from largely private hands, and corporate or proprietary government, to royal government. In taking this approach he eschewed the geographical division of the colonies adopted by some writers to focus on the degree of autonomy, relative or absolute, that the early settlers enjoyed. More importantly, in volume 3 he examined the centralizing and autocratic tendencies of the later Stuarts as they sought to transform the nature of colonial government through policies that were "in violent opposition to colonial and English traditions." When James II fell from power, former colonial boundaries and institutions were restored. Even so, the trend towards uniformity was irreversible.

Osgood regarded the period from 1690 to 1763, during which the colonies gradually coalesced into one system under the control of the British government, itself part of a much larger system, as "the unknown period" of American history. No one, he claimed, had previously studied the internal development of each of the continental colonies, their relationship with one another, and the institutions and processes by which they were joined to the government of Britain. In structuring the *American Colonies in the Eighteenth Century* Osgood gave priority to the succession of colonial wars with the French from which the British emerged triumphant. Through an analysis of the relationship between colonial assemblies, "the embodiment

of colonial self government," and royal appointees, Osgood examined royal government to reveal the encroachment of the former on the putative powers of the latter and the steady erosion of royal authority. This history became more American than British with each decade. Despite a substratum of British law, Americans had in fact created a distinct type of society and government.

Osgood brought a new sophistication to the study of colonial relations posing the question from an institutional perspective, of how the Atlantic was bridged. He was the first American historian to recognize the complexity of imperial structures, the experimental character of the empire, and the contradictions between theory and practice that gave rise, on both sides of the Atlantic, to inconsistencies and misunderstandings. Yet despite the focus of his work, it was American factors rather than imperial influences that in his view shaped the development of the colonies. Osgood's work still has value for professional historians interested in the nature of the colonies' place in the early British empire, and their internal political development. Not all would subscribe to his view that colonial society and politics grew increasingly distinctive during the colonial period, or his implicit denial of human agency, while his concept of national stock and assumption of Indian savagery would find little echo among today's historians. In other respects, especially with regard to the central role of colonial assemblies in Virginia, New York, and South Carolina, and of the importance of demographic factors and non-British migration which he raised but did not pursue, Osgood anticipated the direction of much recent work.

GWENDA MORGAN

See also United States: Colonial

Biography

Born Canton, Maine, 9 April 1855. Educated at Wilton Academy, Andover, Maine; BA, Amherst College, 1877, MA 1880; postgraduate study, Yale University, 1881; University of Berlin, 1882–83; PhD, Columbia University, 1889. Taught (rising to professor) at Columbia University, 1891–1918. Married Caroline Augusta Symonds, 1885 (2 sons, 1 daughter). Died 11 September 1918.

Principal Writings

"The Corporation: A Form of Colonial Government," *Political Science Quarterly* 11 (1896), 259–77, 502–33, 694–715
"The Proprietor Provinces as a Form of Colonial Government," *American Historical Review* 2 (1897), 644–64; 3 (1898), 31–55, 244–65
"The American Revolution," *Political Science Quarterly* 13 (1898), 41–59
The American Colonies in the Seventeenth Century, 3 vols., 1904–07
The American Colonies in the Eighteenth Century, 4 vols., 1924–25

Further Reading

Fox, Dixon Ryan, *Herbert Levi Osgood: An American Scholar*, New York: Columbia University Press, 1924
Kraus, Michael, and Davis D. Joyce, *The Writing of American History*, revised edition, Norman: University of Oklahoma Press, 1985
Wish, Harvey, *The American Historian: A Social-Intellectual History of the Writing of the American Past*, New York: Oxford University Press, 1960

Ostrogorsky, George 1902–1976

Russian historian of Byzantium

Russian-born George Ostrogorsky played a major role in overcoming the negative stigma that had attached to Byzantine studies prior to the 1920s. He received his elementary and secondary education in Russia before obtaining his university degrees at Heidelberg where the great German medievalist, Percy Schramm, encouraged him to pursue a career in Byzantine studies. After a brief stay in Paris, where he worked with all the important French Byzantine specialists, including the most outstanding, George Diehl, Ostrogorsky received a doctorate from the University of Heidelberg in 1925. In 1927 his dissertation, *Die ländliche Steunergemeinde des Byzantinisches Reiches im X. Jahrhundert* (The Rural Tax Community of the Byzantine Empire in the Tenth Century), became the first of his more than 180 publications. His painstaking analysis of primary sources, both narrative and archival, which he employed to research his dissertation served him well throughout his career. One of his great strengths was the ability to deduce general aspects of Byzantine civilization from evidence relating to very specific cases. The conclusions he reached on the 7th century, and on what he called Byzantine feudalism, remain at the center of historical debate on Byzantine institutions.

In addition to such important technical articles as his early investigation of Theophanes' chronology, Ostrogorsky focused his research on three main fields. The first, inaugurated by his dissertation, concerned economic, social, and institutional history, with special emphasis on the Byzantine peasantry. The second encompassed Byzantine theology and imperial ideology, while the third embraced Byzantine-Slavic relations, especially in the Balkans.

The first topic included Ostrogorsky's most significant work for specialists. It derived from his thesis that the Byzantine empire had a dependent peasantry comparable to, yet different from, that found in western Europe. After establishing in his dissertation that peasant communes had existed in the Byzantine empire before the Slavs entered it at the end of the 6th century, he studied the difficulties peasants faced during the turbulent times of the 7th to the 10th centuries, and introduced new information concerning the effect of conflicts between the Byzantine imperial court and the bureaucracy on peasants living in the empire. The culmination of this line of research, and Ostrogorsky's most important contribution to Byzantine history, was his analysis of the *pronoia*, a type of military landholding that resembled the medieval western European fief. In two books, *Pronija* (Pronoia, 1951) and *Pour l'histoire de la féodalité byzantine* (On the History of Byzantine Feudalism, 1954), based on the Acts of Mount Athos and the inventories of peasants, he concluded that between the 10th and 12th centuries holders of *pronoia* had interposed themselves between the state and its peasant militia. Although his thesis has undergone extensive revision, partly by Ostrogorsky himself, no one has offered a better alternative.

Ostrogorsky's work on institutional history concentrated on the *themes*, which were Byzantine provincial administrative units through which the emperor's officials recruited troops, collected taxes, and enforced imperial laws. Based on his analysis of the sources, Ostrogorsky determined that the *themes* had existed earlier than historians had believed, probably as early as the reign of the emperor Heraclius (610–41). Not content with establishing the origins of the *themes*, he also traced their evolution through the 9th century. As regards religious and imperial intellectual history, he wrote on iconoclasm and the imperial coronation ceremony, although his major contribution to this field was his analysis of the medieval conception of the hierarchy of states. His work on Byzantine-Slavic relations devoted attention to Byzantium's impact on Kievan Russia, but mostly concentrated on the links between Byzantium and the Serbs. A study of the Chronicle of the Serbian Princes in Constantine Porphyrogennetos, an article on the struggle against the Byzantine empire of Stephen Dušan and the Serbian nobility, and on the principality of Serres after Dušan's death, constitute his main contributions to this field.

Ostrogorsky's most influential work was his *Geschichte des byzantinischen Staates* (1940; *History of the Byzantine State*, 1956). It was reprinted in two German editions (1952 and 1963), two English ones (1956 and 1969), and was translated into some ten other languages. The book remains the best general survey of Byzantine political institutions in print, although it is now outdated in places. While it includes little on Byzantine society, and nothing on art, literature, religion, science, or philosophy, Ostrogorsky does provide some detail on economics.

In addition to his publications, Ostrogorsky's importance stems from his role as an educator. He taught at Belgrade for forty years, founded the Institute of Byzantine Studies of the Serbian Academy in 1948, and served as its director until his death. He also edited the Institute's journal until 1975 and supervised its monograph series. Because of his efforts, the Institute became one of the world's leading centers of Byzantine studies, and provided Yugoslav historians with contacts in the world community of scholars.

ROBERT F. FORREST

See also Byzantium; Middle East; Vasiliev

Biography

Georgii Aleksandrovich Ostrogorskii. Born St. Petersburg, 6 January [19 January] 1902. After early education in St. Petersburg, left with family during Russian Revolution. Studied philosophy, sociology, and economics, University of Heidelberg, 1921–24, PhD 1925; studied Byzantine history and art with Charles Diehl and Gabriel Millet, Paris, 1924–25. Taught at University of Wrocław [Breslau], 1928–33; professor of Byzantine history, University of Belgrade, 1933–76. Founder/director, Institute of Byzantine Studies, Serbian Academy of Sciences and Arts, 1948. Married. Died Belgrade, 24 October 1976.

Principal Writings

Die ländliche Steunergemeinde des Byzantinisches Reiches im X. Jahrhundert (The Rural Tax Community of the Byzantine Empire in the Tenth Century), 1927

Geschichte des byzantinischen Staates, 1940; in English as *History of the Byzantine State*, 1956, revised 1968

Pronija (Pronoia), 1951

Pour l'histoire de la féodalité byzantine (On the History of Byzantine Feudalism), 1954

"The Byzantine Emperor and Hierarchical World Order," *Slavonic and East European Review* 35 (1956), 1–14

Quelques problèmes d'histoire de la paysannerie byzantine, 1956

Editor, *Zur byzantinischen Geschichte: Ausgewählte kleine Schriften* (On Byzantine History: Selected Essays), 1973

Further Reading

Ferluga, J., "Georg Ostrogorsky (1902–1976)," *Jahrbuch für Geschichte Osteuropas*, new series 25 (1977), 632–36

Ševčenko, Ihor, *Byzantium and the Slavs in Letters and Culture*, Cambridge, MA: Harvard Ukrainian Research Institute, 1991

Otsuka Hisao 1907–1996

Japanese economic historian

A leading economic historian, Otsuka Hisao is also a prominent non-church Christian who was considerably influenced by the Bible class led by Uchimura Kanzō (1861–1930) and Yanaihara Tadao (1893–1961) in the early Showa period. Supported partly by his religious belief, Otsuka was tireless and fearless in dealing with important and serious social issues from his academic standpoint. He thought that the study of modern Western economic history was indispensable because it could provide an excellent contrast to contemporary Japanese economic society, which was a complex amalgamation of very advanced capitalism and a very old social system. He believed that it was possible to synthesize through proper translation and connection the concepts of Marxist economics and Max Weber's sociology in order to form an effective analytical methodology.

Otsuka's first book *Kabushiki-gaisha hassei shiron* (On the History of the Development of the Joint Stock Company, 1938), made a clear distinction between preindustrial capital and industrial capital. It was a case study of early English and Dutch joint stock companies and their transition from private companies to public ones with shareholders. Implicit in this study was his criticism of prewar Japanese financial combines. Meanwhile, he helped to translate Weber's "Die protestantische Ethik und der Geist des Kapitalismus" (1904–05, revised 1920; *The Protestant Ethic and the Spirit of Capitalism*, 1930), in order to search for the subjective force and ethos of modern European capitalism.

The immediate postwar period saw a series of reforms in Japan including land reform and the dissolution of the financial combines, for which Otsuka had hoped. In order to construct a new Japan, he began to advocate modernization and democracy and published several influential books on this subject, including *Kindaika no ningenteki kiso* (The Human Foundations of Modernization, 1948) and *Shūkyo kaikaku to kindai shakai* (The Religious Reformation and Modern Society, 1948). While continuing his writings and publications on Western economic history, Otsuka began to refine his theoretical framework and research methods. *Kyōdōtai no kiso riron* (Basic Theories on the Community, 1955) and *Shakai kagaku no hōhō* (Methodology of the Social Science, 1966) displayed his insights on universal law in the development of human societies and on scientific methods of analyzing social and economic phenomena. Otsuka was also concerned about underdeveloped countries, and edited *Kōshin shihonshugi no tenkai katei* (The Developing Process of Backward Capitalism, 1973) in order to help establish a scientific understanding of the

economic reality in those countries and to suggest proper ways to change it. In the late 1970s he further turned to the question of anomie in contemporary society caused by modern bureaucratic rationalization, and tried to construct his own typology of human beings.

DE-MIN TAO

Biography

Born 3 May 1907. Attended school in Kyoto; studied economics at Tokyo Imperial University, BA 1930, doctorate in economics 1949. Taught at Tokyo Imperial University, 1930–33; Hosei University, 1934–38; Tokyo University, 1947–68; professor, International Christian University, 1968–78. Died 9 July 1996.

Principal Writings

Kabushiki-gaisha hassei shiron (On the History of the Development of the Joint Stock Company), 1938
Kindai Oshū keizaishi josetsu (An Introduction to Modern European Economic History), 1944
Kindaika no ningenteki kiso (The Human Foundations of Modernization), 1948
Shūkyo kaikaku to kindai shakai (The Religious Reformation and Modern Society), 1948
Kyōdōtai no kiso riron (Basic Theories on the Community), 1955
Shakai kagaku no hōhō (Methodology of the Social Science), 1966
Otsuka Hisao chosakushū (Complete Works of Otsuka Hisao), 1969–76
Editor, *Kōshin shihonshugi no tenkai katei* (The Developing Process of Backward Capitalism), 1973
The Spirit of Capitalism: The Max Weber Thesis in an Economic Historical Perspective, 1982

Further Reading

Iinuma Jiro, "Otsuka Hisao to sono jidai" (Otsuka Hisao and His Time), in *Shisō no kagaku* (The Science of Thought), 36, 1974

Ota Hidemichi, "Otsuka Hisao," in Nagantora Keiji and Kano Masanao, eds., *Nihon no rekishika* (The Historians of Japan), Tokyo: Nihon hyōronsha, 1976

Ueno Masaharu, *Otsuka Hisao chosaku nōto* (A Chronology of Otsuka Hisao's Works), Tokyo: Tosho shibunsha, 1965

Otto of Freising c.1114–1158

German chronicler

Otto wrote two major histories, one partly for the instruction and the other partly at the urging of his powerful and celebrated nephew, emperor Frederick I Barbarossa. Otto brought to both works a mind trained both by study in Paris, the intellectual center of 12th-century northern Europe, and by first-hand experience in lay and ecclesiastical governance. He had been abbot of a major Cistercian monastery in Burgundy, been elected bishop of Freising in Bavaria, and had accompanied emperor Conrad III on the unsuccessful Second Crusade before beginning his chronicles. The first history, the *Chronicon*, is customarily entitled *De duabus civitatibus* (c.1146; *The Two Cities*, 1928). The portion that Otto wrote chronicled world history to 1146 – the year before the Second Crusade – in eight books. About ten years later, Otto wrote the first half of the *Gesta Friderici imperatoris* (1157; *The Deeds of Frederick Barbarossa*, 1953); Rahewin continued and completed it after

Otto's death in 1158. In consequence of their sharply varying implications for Frederick Barbarossa's rulership and for understanding the meaning of history, these texts – and, in particular, their relationship to each other – have attracted the attention of those interested in the philosophy and theology of history.

The Two Cities, as its title suggests, was inspired by St. Augustine's *The City of God* and, less visibly, Orosius' *Seven Books against the Pagans* and Boethius' *On the Consolation of Philosophy*. Otto's book, therefore, is a *Heilsgeschichte* – a chronicle of world history in terms of its presumed congruence with divine

providence – of the respective careers of Augustine's heavenly city and earthly city. In treating these careers, however, Otto blurred the fine distinctions that Augustine made between them. His purposes, after all, were not Augustine's. In the interest of the young emperor's education, Otto had three didactic aims. First, he wanted Frederick to see the long-term origins of current affairs. Second, he sought to increase Frederick's sophistication by engrossing him in past politics. Third, and theologically most interesting, Otto tried to show that the world's, or the worldly city's, time had nearly expired. In keeping with the Four Monarchies Theory, the Assyrian, Persian, and Greek monarchies had passed while the current age was still in the final, Roman monarchy. Now, however, rulership had moved to the west where, of course, the sun set. This was a symbol for what many events portended, the imminent end of time. Otto foreshadowed the tenor of the work in the beginning of his Prologue: "In pondering long and often in my heart upon the changes and vicissitudes of temporal affairs and their varied and irregular issues, even as I hold that a wise man ought by no means to cleave to the things of time, so I find that it is by the faculty of reason alone that one must escape and find release from them."

The Two Cities, therefore, can variously seem either a pessimistic or an optimistic history. It seems pessimistic because it portrays secular history as merely a sequence of vanities now drawing to a close. Conversely, it appears optimistic because it portended the final reckoning with the evil world and, with it, the long-awaited triumph of the heavenly city. This ambivalence is characteristic of Augustinian historians, but it seems very remarkable in view of Otto's subsequent *The Deeds of Frederick Barbarossa* which celebrated the emperor's brilliance and success in a world that showed no sign of ending. Thus, Otto's works flatly contradicted each other with respect to the meaning of history. Commentators have suggested three possible solutions to this problem. First, Otto may have himself been confused by seemingly final portents followed by promising signs. Second, he may have believed both that the world was soon to end and that the worldly rule of his nephew was a short-lived, prosperous hiatus in a headlong rush to destruction. Third, he may just have changed his mind over ten years. Each hypothesis has something to recommend it and something to undercut it.

Each interpretation implies an intimate relationship in Otto's mind between long-term and contemporary history. Otto's continual musings in the histories and his surviving correspondence with emperor Frederick rather intensify than remove the difficulty of interpretation. Otto, however, is important not solely as a specimen of Augustinian historiography. His careful narrations are indispensable as documents in medieval imperial history, and

for that reason were edited and published in 1868 by Julius Ficker in volume 20 of the *Monumenta Germaniae Historica*. His stylistic clarity, and keen interest in classical antiquity, are also strong evidence for a renaissance in the 12th century.

ROBERT FAIRBAIRN SOUTHARD

Biography
Born c.1114, descended from the Holy Roman emperor Henry IV and half-brother of the Hohenstaufen king Conrad III. Studied in Paris and entered Cistercian order, 1133. Abbot of Morimund monastery, 1137; later bishop of Freising. Fought Guelphs with Conrad III; went on Second Crusade, 1147; celebrated mass in Jerusalem, 1148; adviser to Frederick I, 1152–58. Died Morimund, 22 September 1158.

Principal Writings
Chronicon or *De duabus civitatibus*, c.1143–46; in English as *The Two Cities: A Chronicle of Universal History to the Year 1146 AD*, 1928

With Rahewin, *Gesta Friderici I imperatoris*, 1157–58; in English as *The Deeds of Frederick Barbarossa*, 1953

Further Reading
Faussner, Hans Constanin, *Die Königsurkundenfälschungen Ottos von Freising: aus rechtshistorischer Sicht* (Otto of Freising's Falsifications of Royal Documents in Legal Perspective), Sigmaringen: Törbecke, 1993

Funkenstein, Amos, *Heilsplan und natürliche Entwicklung: Formen der Gegenwartsbestimmung im Geschichtsdenken des hohen Mittelalters* (Divine Plan and Natural Development: Forms of Certifying the Present in the High Middle Ages), Munich: Nymphenburger Verlanshandlung, 1965

Lammers, Walther, *Weltgeschichte und Zeitgeschichte bei Otto von Freising* (World History and Contemporary History in Otto of Freising), Wiesbaden: Steiner, 1977

Schürmann, Brigitte, *Die Rezeption der Werke Ottos von Freising im 15. und frühen 16. Jahrhundert* (The Receiption of the Works of Otto of Freising in the 15th and 16th Centuries), Stuttgart: Steiner, 1986

Ottoman Empire

A good portion of the historiography of the last quarter of the 20th century has been devoted to the problems and questions of the origins of the Ottoman empire, explanations of its expansion, its supposed zenith in the 16th century epitomized by the reign of Süleyman the Magnificent (Kanunî Süleyman), the commencement and periodization of its supposed decline, and its incorporation into the world capitalist economy before becoming a victim of European colonization.

After decades of relative consensus, the study of the origins of the empire was rejuvenated by Rudi Lindner who argued in *Nomads and Ottomans in Medieval Anatolia* (1983) that tribes did play an important role in the success of the Ottoman emirate (princedom) as opposed to the dozen or so other emirates that existed in 13th-century northwestern Asia Minor. But Lindner's definition of a tribe is that of an inclusive non-tribal organization which incorporated many non-Turks and non-Muslims. This view is contrary to that of Fuad Köprülü in *Les Origines de l'Empire Ottoman* (1935; *The Origins of* the Ottoman Empire, 1992) who stressed the tribal and ethnic Turkish origin of the empire, and of Paul Wittek, who assigned the dominant role to ghazis or warriors fighting for the causes of Islam. Lindner's work also took issue with Halil Inalcık who, while discounting Köprülü's emphasis on ethnicity, did accept Wittek's argument that the gazi element was significant. Inalcık's contribution regarding the origins of the empire is his stress on the role of demographic changes in the 13th-century eastern Mediterranean. In Between Two Worlds: The Construction of the Ottoman State (1995), Cemal Kafadar synthesized the works on the origins of the empire over the past half century and concluded that the debate over the normative "Muslimness" of the ghazis obscured the historical realities of the distinctive heterogeneity of the culture and ethos of the march environment in which the empire developed.

The historiography of the expansion of the Ottomans into the Balkans was also rejuvenated in the 1990s as a result of war in the former Yugoslavia. The starting point of all works dealing with the expansion of the Ottomans into the Balkans is Ömer Lûtfi Barkan's series of essays on deportations as a method of settlement and colonization in the Ottoman empire (1946–54) which documented the demographic changes accompanying the Turkification and Islamization of the Balkans. Two books written in the 1970s, Peter F. Sugar's Southeastern Europe under Ottoman Rule, 1354–1804 (1977) and Charles Jelavich and Barbara Jelavich's, The Establishment of the Balkan Nation States, 1804–1920 (1977), incorporated research done by Ottoman scholars of the Balkans, and are immeasurably better than prior works written primarily by Christian, anti-Ottoman scholars, many of whom originated from countries of southeastern Europe. Bistra Cvetkova and Nikolai Todorov each demonstrated the vitality of the cities and the non-Muslim contributions to the development of urban life in the Ottoman Balkans. Both demonstrated the great contributions that Marxist historians have made to the historiography of the Balkans under Ottoman rule.

But many Marxist paradigms collapsed along with the collapse of the Soviet Union and its satellite states. This is especially true regarding the controversies over the extent of and reasons for the Islamization of the Balkans. Three essay collections edited by Mark Pinson and by Daniel Panzac argued persuasively for the deep and profound influence of Islamic practices and forms on urban life in the Balkans. H.T. Norris' Islam in the Balkans (1993) took the revisionist trend a step further in demonstrating convincingly that Muslim culture among both the Slavs and the Turks was much fuller and richer than hitherto acknowledged in Western and Christiancentric Western historiography. A Bosnian Muslim scholar, Adem Handzíç, affirmed Norris' conclusions. Machiel Kiel demonstrated the innovative and original, but eclectic and diverse input, including Christian, of the constructs and structure of Islamic architecture in the Balkans.

Three major syntheses of the Ottoman political economy, with emphases on the Balkans, appeared in the 1980s and 1990s. John Lampe and Marvin Jackson's Balkan Economic History, 1550–1950 (1982) stressed the interconnections between the peoples of the Habsburg and Ottoman empires, but they utilized almost no Ottoman sources. This lacuna was corrected by the appearance of Bruce McGowan's Economic Life in Ottoman Europe (1981) which utilized Ottoman sources to

establish the crucial role of the growth of private commercial farming (çiftliks) which contributed to increased trade between the two empires. This increased privatization also contributed to the rise of nationalism. McGowan brought his research up to date in his contribution to Inalcık's An Economic and Social History of the Ottoman Empire, 1300–1914 (1994).

One of the quests of Ottoman historians from the 1970s through the 1990s was the attempt to find common historical dimensions with the history of early modern Europe. These efforts were intended to break from the dominant view that the Ottoman polity was an entity sui generis, especially regarding the Ottoman land control practices as exemplified by the timar system, as being quite different from European feudalism. This view was held by Ömer Lûtfi Barkan and Halil Inalcık who squashed the thesis of Sencer Divitçioğlu that the Asiatic Mode of Production had any relevance in explaining the economic and class system of the empire. Barkan and Inalcık's influence was successful in limiting the impact of Marxist and Marxian paradigms as instruments for analyzing the political economy of the empire, which discouraged young scholars from further comparisons of the Ottoman political economy with that of European societies. In New Approaches to State and Peasant in Ottoman History (1992) Halil Berktay went so far as to accuse Barkan of "document fetishism" and "state fetishism." Such characterizations imply that Barkan had no adequate explicative base for his work and that he was supportive of the authoritarian state.

The monolithism of the "difference" construct between the Ottoman empire and Europe was contested steadily and brilliantly in a remarkable series of books and articles in the 1980s and 1990s by Suraiya Faroqhi, who effectively demolished it. She demonstrated the many common dimensions of Ottoman and European socio-economic structures, while acknowledging that both experienced profound internal differences. Faroqhi argues that to discuss common dimensions the historian must not compare the 16th- and 17th-century Ottoman empire with the northern European countries, but rather with Spain, the Italian principalities, and the German states which, like the Ottomans, experienced declining populations, economic involution, and political dislocation.

Palmira Brummett argued in Ottoman Seapower and Levantine Diplomacy in the Age of Discovery (1994) that the Ottoman empire was a major player in the 16th-century world economy and that it was the challenge of the Ottomans as the "other" that compelled the Europeans to obstruct it as a competitor and to eliminate it as a challenger for world hegemony. In The Forgotten Frontier: A History of the 16th-Century Ibero-African Frontier (1978) Andrew Hess agreed with Faroqhi and Brummett on the existence of shared economic conjunctures between Europe and the Ottomans, but he insisted that their cultural, social, and technological history was "quite separate" and not comparable either in the 16th century or subsequently. But Faroqhi and her disciples, who stressed the porosity of boundaries and rejected essentialization of contract, dominated the historiography of the 1980s and 1990s.

Faroqhi and those she influenced also questioned the supposed "decline" paradigm that dominated Ottoman studies up to the 1970s. Cornell H. Fleischer attempted to elucidate the problem of decline – whether it was the socioeconomic reality or bureaucratic imaginings of lost power – through an in-depth study of a 16th-century high Ottoman official and intellectual. Fleischer concluded from his study that Mustafa Ali's work reflected real decline. Mustafa Ali's work is representative of an entire genre of literature known as *nasihatname* (advice) which has been used to support the decline paradigm by various Ottoman historians such as Bernard Lewis, I. Metin Kunt, and Madeline C. Zilfi. In *Formation of the Modern State: The Ottoman Empire, Sixteenth to Eighteenth Centuries* (1991), Rifa'at Abou-el-Haj argued vociferously against the utilization of the *nasihatname* literature to elucidate the true state of affairs, especially with regard to the political economy. He concluded that most of the *nasihatname* literature was self-serving and was a result of its authors' inability to understand the changes taking place. The empire was not declining, it was changing as more grandees (*ayan*s, *eşref,* and pashas), both from the center and periphery clamored to be part of the action. Abou-el-Haj suggested that class and not nation-state models should be the vehicle to explain Ottoman history. Nation-state models stress that it was inevitable that the empire become more Western and evolve into a secular state. Based on a class model, Abou-el-Haj suggested that it is possible that a non-secular, Islamic state could have emerged in Turkey and in the Arab portions of the empire. Abou-el-Haj's objections that the Tanzimat period (1839–76) cannot be studied as an evolving western state was brilliantly vindicated by Butrus Abu-Manneh in "The Islamic Roots of the Gülhane Rescript" (1994), in which he argued that the rescript was declared not solely because of European pressure or a desire to institute a government based on the French Rights of Man as emphasized by Roderic H. Davison in *Reform in the Ottoman Empire, 1856–1876* (1963). The rescript was issued rather as an attempt to reinvigorate the orthodox Sunni ideals as expressed through the Muslim brotherhood of the Naqsbandi-Mujaddi. Abu-Manneh's study profoundly revised the current history of the Tanzimat period and will influence all subsequent research on this period.

Criticism and advocacy of the "decline" paradigm continued to focus research in the 1990s. Karen Barkey's *Bandits and Bureaucrats* (1994) portrayed the capabilities of the state in the 17th century to co-opt and to absorb the rebellious peasants, bandits, and the disgruntled high office holders in ways reminiscent of the British elite's success in warding off the charges of "old Corruption" in the first half of the 18th century. The traditional view as posited in 1914 by Ahmet Refik – one that prevailed up to the 1990s – was that imperial women contributed to the decline of the empire; this was demolished by Leslie P. Peirce in *The Imperial Harem* (1993) which showed convincingly that imperial women made an essential contribution to strengthening the Sultanate from the late 16th through the 17th centuries. The Queen Mother became in effect the "glue which held the dynasty together." The power of the dynasty and the contribution of imperial women were strengthened further by the utilization of architecture and ceremony to symbolize in form and manner the absolute sovereignty of the dynasty, as Gülrü Necipoğlu's *Architecture, Ceremonial, and Power* (1991) vividly depicts.

Another way in which the Ottoman elite maintained power up through the mid-19th century was through the "privatization" of land and other state resources: a practice that spread rapidly throughout the 18th century. Ariel Salzmann posited that privatization and the long-term institutional decentralization of a previously highly centralized state was a strategy for the socio-organizational evolution of the empire that allowed the elite to maintain legitimacy. Rifa'at Abou-el-Haj in *The 1703 Rebellion and the Structure of Ottoman Politics* (1984) suggested that it was the relative weakness of the dynasty after its wars with the Habsburgs (1683–99) that allowed Ottoman elites (viziers and pashas) to play decisive roles in the coalitions that ruled the empire in the late 17th and 18th centuries. In addition to the debilitating effects of European wars, Robert W. Olson in *The Siege of Mosul and Ottoman-Persian Relations, 1718–1743* (1975) was the first to argue that the Ottoman wars (1727–47) with the Safavid empire also played a major role in the necessity of the dynasty to renegotiate relations with the cultural and political elite. Such realignments of power led to the revolution that deposed Ahmet III (1703–30): brought to power by one coalition, he was deposed by another. These shifting currents of power finally resulted in a "peace policy" originating at the end of the wars with the Safavids, but reaching its peak after the Russo-Ottoman war of 1768–74. The results of the weakening of the empire, its pursuit of a peace policy and the development of a "Foreign Office" to carry out this policy is the subject of Virginia H. Aksan's *An Ottoman Statesman in War and Peace* (1995). Aksan's work suggested that is was only during the last quarter of the 18th century that the Ottoman elite resolved to pursue policies to stem their increasing weakness.

But the internal renegotiation of political and economic power was not sufficient to stave off the economic and trade onslaught of the Europeans in the 19th century, as Roger Owen in *The Middle East in the World Economy, 1800–1914* (1981) emphasized. He suggested that the dramatic impact on the redistribution of economic power was a result of the incorporation of the Middle East into the European-dominated capitalist world economy of the 19th century. While there was growth in some parts of the empire, it was due, argued Owen, to European demands. The colonial presence shifted economic power to the coast where non-Muslim minorities were able to take greater advantage of their European connections. This development also increased the differences and hostilities between the Muslims and non-Muslims, contributing subsequently to the development of nationalism. Donald Quataert acknowledged Owen's thesis of pervasive European dominance, but argued that small-scale manufacturing and technology transfer did take place. But Quataert failed to establish that such developments provided any means for an Ottoman economic take-off. Şevket Pamuk agreed with Owen that the Ottoman empire was dependent on the European capitalist core, but using per capita indices of foreign trade and foreign investment, he concluded that the degree of integration of the empire into the world economy was still below that of medium-sized countries of the Third World. This Pamuk attributed to the strength of the central bureaucracy *vis-à-vis* both the European powers and the internal interest groups such as merchants and landlords. Taking up where Owen, Quataert, and Pamuk left off, Reşat Kasaba acknowledged that the Ottoman empire was peripheralized in the world economy of the 19th century, but made the case that the non-Muslims were mainly intermediaries, brokers, and beneficiaries, and not, as is generally assumed, compradors: they opposed the hegemonic power of the capitalist world economy, but, for their own benefit and not for that of the state, and pre-empted the last possible opportunity for Ottoman capitalist development. The centralization of the Muslim-led bureaucracy in opposition to the non-Muslim policies also, argued Kasaba, impeded the growth of a civil society and democratized developments epitomized by the reign of Abdülhamid II (1876–1909).

In a brilliant study, Şükrü Hanioğlu showed just how unsuccessful the Tanzimat and Abdülhamid's reforms were. He demonstrated convincingly that materialism-positivism, combined with Turkish nationalism as the ideology created by the Young Turks during the last decade of the 19th century, was implemented during the Young Turk period (1908–18) in power, and persisted in influencing the ideology of the Turkish republic through most of the 20th century. Hanioğlu emphasized, contrary to previous histories, that the Young Turks were not "liberals" or "constitutionalists"; they were anti-parliament and never envisioned the participation of the masses in policy-making or administration. Prior to the appearance of Hanioğlu's book, Erik J. Zürcher's *The Unionist Factor* (1984) had already argued for the continuity between the policies of the Committee of Union and Progress (CUP) and republican politics. A view thought heretical as late as the 1970s, it is now part of mainstream historiography. Zürcher is also the author of *Turkey: A Modern History* (1993) in which he integrated his ideas within the *longue durée* context of Ottoman and Turkish history. Another good essay emphasizing the impact of empire on republic is Feroz Ahmad's *The Making of Modern Turkey* (1993) which focused on the attempts of both the Young Turks and the republicans to create a Turkish bourgeoisie class to facilitate modernization policies. Both Zürcher's and Ahmad's work demonstrate conclusively the strong ideological, economic, and political cultural continuity between the late Ottoman empire, the Young Turks, and the republic of Turkey.

ROBERT OLSON

See also Balkans; Barkan; Browne; Byzantium; Cahen; Crusades; Eastern Orthodoxy; Egypt: since the 7th Century; Germany: to 1450; Greece: Modern; Hourani; Inalcık; Issawi; Jelavich; Jewish; Kedourie; Köprülü; Lewis, B.; Middle East; Naima; Ranke; Runciman; Spain: Imperial; Sugar; Zāydan

Further Reading

Abou-el-Haj, Rifa'at Ali, *The 1703 Rebellion and the Structure of Ottoman Politics*, Leiden: Nederlands Historisch-Archeologisch Instituut te Istanbul, 1984

Abou-el-Haj, Rifa't Ali, *Formation of the Modern State: The Ottoman Empire, Sixteenth to Eighteenth Centuries*, Albany: State University of New York Press, 1991

Abu-Manneh, Butrus, "The Islamic Roots of the Gülhane Rescript," *Die Welt des Islams* 34 (1994), 173–203

Ahmad, Feroz, *The Making of Modern Turkey*, London and New York: Routledge, 1993

Aksan, Virginia H., *An Ottoman Statesman in War and Peace: Ahmed Resmi Efendi, 1700–1783*, Leiden: Brill, 1995

Barkan, Ömer Lûtfi, "Osmanlı imparatorluğunda bir iskân ve kolonizasyon metodu olarak sürgünler" (Deportations as a Method of Settlement and Colonization in the Ottoman Empire), *Iktisat Facültesi Mecmuası* 11 (1946–50), 524–69; 13 (1951–52), 58–79; 15 (1953–54), 209–329

Barkan, Ömer Lûtfi, *Toplu eserler* (Collected Works), Istanbul: Gözlem, 1980

Barkey, Karen, *Bandits and Bureaucrats: The Ottoman Route to State Centralization*, Ithaca, NY: Cornell University Press, 1994

Berktay, Halil, and Suraiya Faroqhi, eds., *New Approaches to State and Peasant in Ottoman History*, London: Cass, 1992

Braude, Benjamin, and Bernard Lewis, eds., *Christians and Jews in the Ottoman Empire: The Functioning of a Plural Society*, New York: Holmes, 1982

Brummett, Palmira, *Ottoman Seapower and Levantine Diplomacy in the Age of Discovery*, Albany: State University of New York Press, 1994

Cvetkova [Tsvetkova], Bistra, *Vie économique des villes et ports balkaniques aux XVe et XVIe siècles* (The Economic Life of Balkan Cities and Ports in the 15th and 16th Centuries), Paris: Geuthner, 1971

Dadian, Vahakn, "The Armenian Genocide in Official Turkish Records," *Journal of Political and Military Sociology* 22 (1994), 1–201

Davison, Roderic H., *Reform in the Ottoman Empire, 1856–1876*, Princeton: Princeton University Press, 1963

Divitçioğlu, Sencer, *Asya üretim tarzı ve Osmanlı toplumu* (Ottoman Society and the Asiatic Mode of Production), Istanbul: Istanbul History Faculty, 1967

Faroqhi, Suraiya, *Towns and Townsmen of Ottoman Anatolia: Trade, Crafts, and Food Production in an Urban Setting, 1520–1650*, Cambridge and New York: Cambridge University Press, 1984

Faroqhi, Suraiya, *Men of Modest Substance: House Owners and House Property in Seventeenth-Century Ankara and Kayseri*, Cambridge: Cambridge University Press, 1987

Faroqhi, Suraiya, *Pilgrims and Sultans: The Hajj under the Ottomans, 1517–1683*, London: Tauris, and New York: St. Martin's Press, 1994

Fleischer, Cornell, *Bureaucrat and Intellectual in the Ottoman Empire: The Historian Mustafa Âli, 1541–1600*, Princeton: Princeton University Press, 1986

Gibb, H.A.R., and Harold Bowen, eds., *Islamic Society and the West: A Study of the Impact of Western Civilization on Moslem Culture in the Near East*, 2 vols., London: Oxford University Press, 1950–57

Goffman, Daniel, *Izmir and the Levantine World, 1550–1650*, Seattle: University of Washington Press, 1990

Goodwin, Jason, *Lords of the Horizons: A History of the Ottoman Empire*, London: Chatto and Windus, 1998

Handzić, Adem, *Studije o Bosni: historijski prilozi iz Osmansko-Turskog peroda* (Studies on Bosnia: Historical Contributions of the Ottoman-Turkish Period), Istanbul: Research Center for Islamic History, Art, and Culture, 1994

Hanioğlu, Şükrü M., *The Young Turks in Opposition*, Princeton: Princeton University Press, 1995

Hasluck, Frederick W., *Christianity and Islam under the Sultans*, 2 vols., Oxford: Clarendon Press, 1929

Hess, Andrew, *The Forgotten Frontier: A History of the 16th-Century Ibero-African Frontier*, Chicago: University of Chicago Press, 1978

Imber, Colin, *The Ottoman Empire, 1300–1481*, Istanbul: Isis Press, 1990

Inalcık, Halil, *The Ottoman Empire: The Classical Age, 1300–1600*, London: Weidenfeld and Nicolson, and New York: Praeger, 1973

Inalcık, Halil, with Donald Quataert, *An Economic and Social History of the Ottoman Empire, 1300–1914*, Cambridge and New York: Cambridge University Press, 1994

Islamoğlu-Inan, Huri, ed., *The Ottoman Empire and the World Economy*, Cambridge and New York: Cambridge University Press, 1987

Issawi, Charles, ed., *The Economic History of Turkey, 1800–1914*, Chicago: University of Chicago Press, 1980

Jelavich, Charles, and Barbara Jelavich, *The Establishment of the Balkan Nation States, 1804–1920*, Seattle: University of Washington Press, 1977

Kafadar, Cemal, *Between Two Worlds: The Construction of the Ottoman State*, Berkeley: University of California Press, 1995

Kasaba, Reşat, *The Ottoman Empire and the World Economy: The Nineteenth Century*, Albany: State University of New York Press, 1988

Kiel, Machiel, *Studies on the Ottoman Architecture of the Balkans*, Aldershot: Variorum, and Brookfield, VT: Gower, 1990

Köprülü, M.F., *Les Origines de l'Empire Ottoman*, Paris: Boccard, 1935; in English as *The Origins of the Ottoman Empire*, Albany: State University of New York Press, 1992

Kunt, I. Metin, *The Sultan's Servants: The Transformation of Ottoman Provincial Government, 1550–1650*, New York: Columbia University Press, 1983

Lampe, John R., and Marvin R. Jackson, *Balkan Economic History, 1550–1950: From Imperial Borderlands to Developing Nations*, Bloomington: Indiana University Press, 1982

Lewis, Bernard, *The Emergence of Modern Turkey*, London and New York: Oxford University Press, 1961; revised edition 1968

Lindner, Rudi P., *Nomads and Ottomans in Medieval Anatolia*, Bloomington: Indiana University Press, 1983

McGowan, Bruce, *Economic Life in Ottoman Europe: Taxation, Trade, and the Struggle for Land, 1600–1800*, Cambridge and New York: Cambridge University Press, 1981

Marcus, Abraham, *The Middle East on the Eve of Modernity: Aleppo in the Eighteenth Century*, New York: Columbia University Press, 1989

Masters, Bruce, *The Origins of Western Economic Dominance in the Middle East: Mercantilism and the Islamic Economy in Aleppo, 1600–1750*, New York: New York University Press, 1988

Mutafchieva, Vera P., *Agravnite otnosheniia v Osmanskatu imperiia prez XV–XVI v.*, Sofia: Bilgradska, 1962; in English as *Agrarian Relations in the Ottoman Empire in the 15th and 16th Centuries*, New York: Columbia University Press, 1988

Necipoğlu, Gülrü, *Architecture, Ceremonial, and Power: The Topkapı Palace in the Fifteenth and Sixteenth Centuries*, Cambridge, MA: MIT Press, 1991

Norris, H.T., *Islam in the Balkans: Religion and Society Between Europe and the Arab World*, London: Hurst, and Columbia: University of South Carolina Press, 1993

Olson, Robert W., *The Siege of Mosul and Ottoman-Persian Relations, 1718–1743: A Study of Rebellion in the Capital and War in the Provinces of the Ottoman Empire*, Bloomington: Indiana University Press, 1975

Ortaylı, Ilber, *Imparatorluğun en uzun yüzyıl* (The Empire's Longest Century), Istanbul: Hil, 1983

Owen, Roger, *The Middle East in the World Economy, 1800–1914*, London and New York: Methuen, 1981

Pamuk, Şevket, *Oslmanlı ekonomisi ve dunya kapitalizmi (1820–1913)*, Ankara: Yurt yayınevi, 1984; in English as *The Ottoman-Empire and European Capitalism, 1820–1913: Trade, Investment, and Production*, Cambridge and New York: Cambridge University Press, 1987

Panzac, Daniel, *La Peste dans l'Empire Ottoman* (The Plague in the Ottoman Empire), Leuven: Peeters, 1985

Panzac, Daniel, ed., *Les Villes dans l'Empire Ottoman: activités et sociétés* (Cities in the Ottoman Empire: Social and Cultural Structures), 2 vols., Paris: Editions du Centre National de la Recherche Scientifique, 1991–94

Panzac, Daniel, ed., *Les Balkans à l'époque ottomane* (The Balkans during the Ottoman Period), La Calade, France: Edisud, 1993

Peirce, Leslie P., *The Imperial Harem: Women and Sovereignty in the Ottoman Empire*, New York: Oxford University Press, 1993

Pinson, Mark, ed., *The Muslims of Bosnia-Herzegovina: Their Historic Development from the Middle Ages to the Dissolution of Yugoslavia*, Cambridge: Cambridge University Press, 1994

Quataert, Donald, *Manufacturing and Technology Transfer in the Ottoman Empire, 1800–1914*, Istanbul: Isis, 1992

Refik [Altınay], Ahmed, *Kadınlar Sultanatı* (The Sultanate of Women), 4 vols., Istanbul: Hilmi, 1914–23

Salzmann, Ariel, "An Ancien Régime Revisited: Privatization and Political Economy in the Eighteenth Century Ottoman Empire," *Politics and Society* 21 (1993), 393–423

Sugar, Peter F., *Southeastern Europe under Ottoman Rule, 1354–1804*, Seattle: University of Washington Press, 1977

Thobie, Jacques, *Intérêts et impérialisme français dans l'Empire Ottoman, 1895–1914* (French Interests and Imperialism in the Ottoman Empire, 1895–1914), Paris: Sorbonne, 1987

Todorov, Nikolai, *The Balkan City, 1400–1900*, Seattle: University of Washington Press, 1983 [Russian original]

Toprak, Zafer, *Türkiye'de "Milli Iktisat," 1908–1918* (The "National Economy" in Turkey), Ankara: Yurt, 1982

Wittek, Paul, *The Rise of the Ottoman Empire*, London: Royal Asiatic Society, 1938

Zilfi, Madeline C., *The Politics of Piety: The Ottoman Ulema in the Post-Classical Age, 1600–1800*, Minneapolis: Bibliotheca Islamica, 1988

Zürcher, Erik J., *The Unionist Factor: The Role of the Committee of Union and Progress in the Turkish Nationalist Movement*, Leiden: Brill, 1984

Zürcher, Erik J., *Turkey: A Modern History*, London and New York: Tauris, 1993

Ouellet, Fernand 1926–

French Canadian historian

In the aftermath of World War II, Fernand Ouellet was one of a number of historians at the Université Laval in Quebec City who developed a new way of looking at the French Canadian past. Along with Marcel Trudel and Jean Hamelin, Ouellet largely focused upon the factors that had been responsible for the economic inferiority of French-speakers since the conquest of Quebec by the English in the late 18th century. Previous historians, most of whom had been priests with little professional training, had largely concentrated upon such cultural issues as the survival of the French language and the well-being of the Catholic church. However, in the aftermath of World War II, as French-speakers' standard of living improved quite markedly, there was a growing interest in material advancement, and historians such as Ouellet reflected this new orientation by turning to economic issues.

In making this shift, Ouellet and his Laval colleagues developed a point of view that differed from that of their contemporaries at the other Canadian French-language university, the Université de Montréal. While all of the postwar historians were united by the fact that they were laymen who had received appropriate professional training, they were divided when it came to attributing responsibility for the long-standing economic weakness of French-speakers. While the+ Montreal historians such as Guy Frégault focused on the devastating impact of the conquest, the Laval historians emphasized the internal weaknesses of French Canadian society that had inhibited economic success.

Ouellet, for his part, contributed to the Laval interpretation by looking at various aspects of the social and economic behavior of French-speakers in the late 18th and early 19th centuries. Over the course of the 1950s, 1960s, and 1970s he wrote numerous articles and two highly influential books that showed how the arrival of British rule had provided an expanded market for the goods produced by French-speaking farmers, who made up the bulk of the population. By and large, Ouellet found that French-speakers had failed to respond to the available opportunities, thus leading him to the conclusion that they had been the agents of their own misery. He made this point most emphatically in his most important work, *Histoire économique et sociale du Québec* (1966; *Economic and Social History of Quebec, 1760–1851*, 1980), in which he blamed French Canadian farmers for lavish spending instead of wise investment, and the French Canadian bourgeoisie for maintaining social structures that impeded economic advancement instead of supporting projects that might have created wealth. Along the way Ouellet was particularly critical of French Canadians' Catholic heritage which he viewed as an impediment to their economic success.

While many of Ouellet's claims regarding the outdated *mentalité* of French-speakers were little more than assertions based upon relatively little evidence, there were other aspects of his work that were both innovative and based upon painstaking research. Ouellet first received the taste for historical research from an early encounter with the French historian Ernest Labrousse, and many of Ouellet's works were marked by Labrousse's concern for the use of serial data to understand economic change. Moreover, Ouellet made frequent use of the terms "structure" and "conjoncture," popularized by Labrousse, to distinguish the relatively permanent features of a given socioeconomic situation from ones of a shorter duration. In more concrete terms, Ouellet used serial data to indicate that the major watershed in Quebec history came not with the conquest, as most previous historians had argued, but rather with a variety of economic changes in the early 19th century. From Ouellet's perspective, the great disaster for French Canadians came with their failure to take advantage of these structural changes, which might have offered them the means for economic gain. In this regard, he was particularly critical of the leaders of French Canadian society who took part in armed uprisings in 1837–38 instead of tending to the real economic problems at hand.

Ouellet was in good company in the immediate postwar era in pointing to the self-inflicted problems faced by French Canadians. A number of Laval professors in other disciplines were arguing along much the same lines, as was Pierre Elliott Trudeau, a future prime minister of Canada, who wrote extensively about French Canadian society in the 1950s and 1960s. Over the past thirty years, however, Ouellet has not been particularly kindly treated by French-speaking historians who have not appreciated the suggestion that French Canadians had been the agents of their own difficulties. Ouellet's self-critical approach has been particularly resented since the 1970s as the economic and political power of French Canadians has been on the rise. In this context, recent French Canadian historians, instead of dwelling on economic problems, have stressed the deep roots of French Canadian modernity, a position that Ouellet has bitterly attacked in a number of historiographical essays. In one such essay, he insisted that Quebec history offers much "more support for the thesis of backwardness than for that of modernization" (*Economy, Class and Nation in Quebec*, 1991). Ouellet's isolation from most French Canadian historians stands in stark contrast with his kind treatment at the hands of English-Canadian colleagues, who have had little reason to be troubled by Ouellet's negative view of his own society.

RONALD RUDIN

See also Canada

Biography

Born Lac-Bouchette, Quebec, 6 November 1926. Received BA Université Laval, 1948, L ès L 1950, D ès L, 1965. Assistant archivist, Quebec province, 1956–61; taught at Laval University, 1961–65; Carleton University, 1965–75, University of Ottawa, 1975–85, and York University, Downsview, Ontario, from 1986 (professor of history). Married Thérèse Roy, 1956.

Principal Writings

Histoire économique et sociale du Québec, 1760–1850, 1966; in English as *Economic and Social History of Quebec, 1760–1850*, 1980

Eléments d'histoire sociale du Bas-Canada (Elements of Social History in Lower Canada), 1972

Le Bas-Canada, 1791–1840: changements structuraux et crise, 1976; in English as *Lower Canada, 1791–1840: Social Change and Nationalism*, 1980

L'Etude des religions dans les écoles: l'expérience américaine, anglaise et canadienne (The Study of Religion in Schools: The American, English and Canadian Experiences), 1985

The Socialization of Quebec Historiography since 1960, 1988

Economy, Class and Nation in Quebec: Interpretive Essays, 1991

Further Reading

Behiels, Michael, *Prelude to Quebec's Quiet Revolution: Liberalism versus Neo-Nationalism, 1945–1960*, Kingston, Ontario: McGill-Queen's University Press, 1985

Berger, Carl, *The Writing of Canadian History*, 2nd edition, Toronto: University of Toronto Press, 1986

Cook, Ramsay, *Canada, Quebec and the Uses of Nationalism*, Toronto: McClelland and Stewart, 1986

Dubuc, Alfred, "The Influence of the Annales School in Quebec," *Review* 1 (1978), 123–46

Fournier, Marcel, *L'Entrée dans la modernité* (Entering Modernity), Montreal: Editions St-Martin, 1986

Gagnon, Serge, *Le Québec et ses historiens*, Quebec: Presses de l'Université Laval, 1978; in English as *Quebec and Its Historians, 1840–1920*, Montreal: Harvest House, 1982, and *Quebec and Its Historians: The Twentieth Century*, Harvest House, 1985

Lamarre, Jean, *Le Devenir de la nation québécoise selon Maurice Séguin, Guy Frégault et Michel Brunet, 1944–1969* (The Future of the Quebec Nation According to Maurice Séguin, Guy Frégault, and Michel Brunet, 1944–1969), Sillery, Quebec: Septentrion, 1993

LeGoff, T.J.A., "The Agricultural Crisis in Lower Canada, 1802–12: A Review of a Controversy," *Canadian Historical Review* 55 (1974), 1–31

Rudin, Ronald, "Revisionism and the Search for a Normal Society: A Critique of Recent Quebec Historical Writing," *Canadian Historical Review* 73 (1992), 30–61

Trudel, Marcel, *Mémoires d'un autre siècle* (Memoirs of Another Century), Montreal: Boréal, 1987

Owsley, Frank Lawrence 1890–1956
US historian

Frank Owsley, born in Alabama to an old plantation family, spent his career in the American South and devoted it to developing a revisionist interpretation of the history of the South and the Civil War, an enterprise intended to rehabilitate the South's past, rescue its history from quasi-colonial status, instill a sense of Southern identity, and regain the respect of Americans from other sections for his native region. From 1920 to 1948 Owsley taught at Vanderbilt University, where he built up a graduate program in history, with a strong concentration upon the history of the South. In 1949 he took an endowed chair at the University of Alabama at Tuscaloosa, and as he had done at Vanderbilt he again helped to found a new graduate program in history and directed many theses on southern history. In 1940 Owsley, undoubtedly the leading southern historian of his generation, served as president of the Southern History Association; he was also offered many prestigious visiting appointments at leading institutions in the United States and abroad. His influence continued long after his death; his numerous students themselves constituted almost a school of southern historians, and many of them achieved prominent positions in the profession, particularly in southern institutions.

Owsley's first book, *State Rights in the Confederacy* (1925), suggested that the South lost the Civil War not so much through the North's military superiority but because the governors of southern states were unwilling to cooperate fully with Jefferson Davis' Confederate government in the common cause. His second work, *King Cotton Diplomacy* (1931), was a study of the attitude of Britain and France toward the Confederacy. It argued that, although the British government hoped for a southern victory, which would have permanently weakened a divided United States, at no time were its officials prepared to risk northern disfavor by siding openly with the South, an outlook that was understood by northern leaders but not by their southern counterparts.

By 1930 Owsley was associated with a group of southerners known as the Nashville Agrarians, many of them members of Vanderbilt's English department, who engaged in a strongly partisan defense of their region and its interests. In several collections of essays, notably *I'll Take My Stand* (1930), and *Who Owns America?* (1936), they argued that agrarian and southern interests were ignored by a centralized government dominated by urban, business, and trade union interests. Owsley, who himself owned a farm for many years, reiterated these themes in many political essays, which also extolled the agrarian lifestyle as a democratic, Jeffersonian, and fundamentally virtuous enterprise, one that instilled in men respect both toward each other and for the limits of nature.

These political interests almost certainly helped to impel Owsley to devote his mature academic career to the study of the rural middle class of the antebellum South, which resulted in his most influential work, *Plain Folk of the Old South* (1949). It suggested that the South's middle-class yeomanry, the majority of whites in that section, enjoyed a relationship of mutual respect with the gentry and planters of the region and a common commitment to the South's existing socioeconomic system which united all of them. Increasingly vitriolic abolitionist attacks on slavery by northerners during the 1850s threatened the South's identity and domestic independence, to the point that such "plain folk" felt that, in defending their section, they were defending the same liberties that the thirteen colonies had defended in 1776: a viewpoint with which Owsley clearly sympathized. Owsley's own work was supplemented by monographs on the yeomen freeholders of individual states undertaken by his students, and although critics have queried his interpretation of the politics of the period and the attitudes of the "plain folk," his finding that most whites in the South belonged to this class has not been challenged – a tribute to the meticulous research underpinning it.

Although much of Owsley's work clearly had an underlying social and political objective, and he wrote extensively on current politics, he based his scholarly works on diligent and thorough research in primary sources. His career was notable not merely for his productivity but also for his role in restoring the serious study of the South's past to the agenda of the American historical profession.

PRISCILLA M. ROBERTS

Biography

Born Montgomery County, Alabama, 1890. Attended Fifth District Agricultural School, Wetumpka, Alabama; received BA, Alabama Polytechnic Institute (later Auburn University), 1911, MA 1912; PhD, University of Chicago, 1924. Taught at Fifth District Agricultural School, 1912–14; Alabama Polytechnic Institute, 1914–15; Birmingham Southern University, 1919–20; Vanderbilt University, 1920–48; University of Alabama, 1949–56. Served in World War I. Married Harriet Fason Chappell, 1920 (1 son, 1 daughter). Died Winchester, England, 21 October 1956.

Principal Writings

State Rights in the Confederacy, 1925
Contributor, *I'll Take My Stand: The South and the Agrarian Tradition*, 1930
King Cotton Diplomacy: Foreign Relations of the Confederate States of America, 1931
Contributor, *Who Owns America? A New Declaration of Independence*, edited by Herbert Agar and Allen Tate, 1936
Plain Folk of the Old South, 1949
The South: Old and New Frontiers: Selected Essays of Frank Lawrence Owsley, edited by Harriet Chappell Owsley, 1969

Further Reading

Binkley, William C., "Frank Lawrence Owsley, 1890–1956: A Memorial Foreword," in Owsley's *King Cotton Diplomacy*, Chicago: University of Chicago Press, 1959.
Bradford, M.E., "What We Can Know for Certain: Frank Owsley and the Recovery of Southern History," *Sewanee Review* 78 (1970), 664–69
Bradford, M.E., "Frank L. Owsley," in Clyde N. Wilson, ed., *Twentieth-Century American Historians*, Detroit: Gale, 1983 [*Dictionary of Literary Biography*, vol. 17]
Cresap, Bernarr, "Frank L. Owsley and King Cotton Diplomacy," *Alabama Review* 26 (1973), 235–51
Hyde, Samuel C., Jr., ed., *Plain Folk of the South Revisited*, Baton Rouge: Louisiana State University Press, 1997
Lytle, Andrew, "Foreword," in Harriet Chappell Owsley, ed., *The South: Old and New Frontiers: Selected Essays of Frank Lawrence Owsley*, Athens: University of Georgia Press, 1969
O'Brien, Michael, *The Idea of the American South, 1920–1941*, Baltimore: Johns Hopkins University Press, 1979
Owsley, Frank L., Jr., "Frank Lawrence Owsley," in John R. Wunder, ed., *Historians of the American Frontier: A Bio-Bibliographical Sourcebook*, New York: Greenwood Press, 1988
Owsley, Harriet Chappell, *Frank Lawrence Owsley: Historian of the Old South: A Memoir*, Nashville: Vanderbilt University Press, 1990
Shapiro, Edward, "Frank L. Owsley and the Defense of the Southern Identity," *Tennessee Historical Quarterly* 36 (1977), 75–94

Ozouf, Mona

French social historian

French historian Mona Ozouf began *L'Ecole de la France* (The School of France, 1984) by reminiscing about her childhood experiences as the daughter of a village schoolteacher in Brittany. She recalled the secret joys of being the teacher's child, sitting at her father's desk after school hours and dipping his pen into the mysterious red ink. We sense that out of these stolen hours in the classroom, Ozouf developed her love of learning and of scholarship. Ozouf also described how her childhood was divided between three worlds: the schoolhouse, where her anticlerical and left-wing father spoke only French; her home, where her parents insisted the family speak Breton and filled their shelves with books celebrating regional identity; and the church, where her grandmother led her for Thursday catechism and Sunday mass. She depicted a childhood of "multiple codes" and eccentricity, which led her to dream of harmonious unity. "With pieces from these three worlds . . . how could one hope to make a single fabric? How to build unity out of so much diversity?" These were the questions, Ozouf noted, that bound together the essays in *L'Ecole de la France*, but they are also the questions that underlie all of Mona Ozouf's scholarship.

With her first book, *L'Ecole, l'Eglise et la République, 1871–1914* (The School, the Church, and the Republic, 1963), Ozouf began a career-long exploration into the meaning and role of secular education in the Third Republic, an intellectual interest that she shares with her husband, historian Jacques Ozouf, author of the 1973 collective autobiography, *Nous les maîtres d'école* (We, the Schoolmasters). In numerous books and essays, together and separately, the Ozoufs have surveyed the social, cultural, and political role that teachers have played in French national life. In *La Classe ininterrompue* (The Uninterrupted Class, 1979), Mona Ozouf used memoirs from four generations of schoolteachers from a single family to illustrate the social history of teaching from the French Revolution to World War I. Similarly, the Ozoufs' most recent collaborative project, *La République des instituteurs* (The Republic of Schoolteachers, 1992), provided an in-depth look at the experiences, values, and beliefs of French schoolteachers of the early 20th century, based on some 4000 questionnaires that Jacques Ozouf collected from former teachers in the 1960s. Finally, in essays on education in *L'Ecole de la France* and elsewhere, Ozouf scrutinized the ideological values that animated the first generations of Third Republic schoolteachers: fervent patriotism and a certain idea of France that was deeply rooted in the revolutionary principles of liberty, equality, and fraternity. These principles, and the Revolution of 1789 that put them on the political map, have been, in fact, the second subject at the center of Ozouf's scholarship.

Ozouf is best known as a scholar of the French Revolution. Along with François Furet, she helped to define a new revisionist interpretation of the revolutionary period. Reacting against Marxist historiography that focused on economic and social change, Ozouf and other revisionists have sought to privilege questions of culture and politics in their analysis. This reorientation is clear in Ozouf's seminal book, *La Fête révolutionnaire, 1789–1799* (1976; *Festivals and the French Revolution*, 1988). In this book, Ozouf analyzed the flurry of festivals that marked the revolutionary period, from the most organized and staged Parisian affairs – such as the Festival of the Supreme Being – to the most raucous provincial celebrations, where spontaneity and violence often lurked just below the surface. Ozouf focused on the common threads that tied all festivals together, showing that revolutionaries of widely varying political beliefs all tried to stage festivals in open fields unscarred by symbols of the monarchy or the church. They all paid close attention to the timing of festivals, making them a regular and customary part of seasonal rhythms. Similarly, they all saw festivals as an opportunity to teach French people about patriotism and republican loyalty. Ozouf's careful analysis of symbols, images, and other cultural representations in revolutionary festivals has had a profound influence on the historiography of the Revolution and on the field of cultural history more broadly.

Ozouf followed her study of festivals with a number of other books and essays on the politics and culture of the Revolution, many of them collaborative projects with François Furet. Among these works, the *Dictionnaire critique de la Révolution française* (1988; *A Critical Dictionary of the French Revolution*, 1989) has evoked much interest and acclaim, though some historians have been disappointed by the degree to which the book ignored older social and economic historiography. The volume offered critical essays on the events, actors, institutions, ideas, and interpretations of the revolutionary period, and with 21 entries to her credit, Ozouf's intellectual influence is felt throughout the book. Other essays on politics, culture, and social expression in the French Revolution were presented in the collection *L'Homme régénéré* (Regenerated Man, 1989).

More recently, Ozouf turned her attention to the history of women in *Les Mots des femmes* (Women's Words, 1995). Focusing on intellectual portraits of ten prominent women in French history – including Madame de Staël, George Sand, and Simone de Beauvoir – Ozouf explored the anxieties and passions of French women for 200 years. In a controversial concluding essay, Ozouf advanced an explanation for why French feminism has historically been less confrontational than its Anglo-Saxon counterpart.

Whether she has focused on educators, revolutionaries, or women, the question, "How to build unity out of so much diversity?" continues to haunt Ozouf's historiography. Her intellectual quest, which originated as a personal self-exploration of sorts, has ultimately embraced the very essence of French culture and political life.

MONA L. SIEGEL

See also Social; Theatre

Biography

Director of research, Centre Nationale de la Recherche Scientifique, Paris. Married historian Jacques Ozouf.

Principal Writings

L'Ecole, l'Eglise et la République, 1871–1914 (The School, the Church and the Republic), 1963

La Fête révolutionnaire, 1789–1799, 1976; in English as *Festivals and the French Revolution*, 1988

La Classe ininterrompue: cahiers de la famille Sandre, enseignants, 1780–1960 (The Uninterrupted Class: Notes on the Sandre Family, Teachers, 1780–1960), 1979

L'Ecole de la France: essais sur la Révolution, l'utopie, et l'enseignement (The School of France: Essays on the Revolution, Utopia and Teaching), 1984

With Jacques Ozouf, "Le Tour de la France par deux enfants (The Tour of France by Two Children)," in Pierre Nora, ed., *Les Lieux de mémoire*, 1984, 1:291–321

Editor with François Furet, *Dictionnaire critique de la Révolution française*, 1988; in English as *A Critical Dictionary of the French Revolution*, 1989

L'Homme régénéré: essais sur la Révolution française (Regenerated Man: Essays on the French Revolution), 1989

Editor with François Furet, *Terminer la Révolution: Mounier et Barnave dans la Révolution française* (Ending the Revolution: Mounier and Barnave in the French Revolution), 1990

Editor with François Furet, *La Gironde et les Girondins* (The Gironde and the Girondins), 1991

Editor with François Furet, *The French Revolution and the Creation of Modern Political Culture*, vol. 3: *The Transformation of Political Culture, 1789–1848*, 1991

With Jacques Ozouf, *La République des instituteurs* (The Republic of Schoolteachers), 1992

Editor with François Furet, *Le Siècle de l'avènement républicain* (The Century of Republican Accession), 1993

Les Mots des femmes: essai sur la singularité française (Women's Words: An Essay on French Singularity), 1995

P

Pacific/Oceanic History

Pacific history covers the Pacific islands, sometimes including precolonial New Zealand, but excluding Australia. As with so many other "area studies" programs during the 1960s, Pacific specialists wished to break with Eurocentric political and imperial history in favor of a regional view and islanders' own perspectives. To that end J.W. Davidson founded the Research School of Pacific Studies at Canberra, Australia, in 1954 and the *Journal of Pacific History* in 1966. His team of historians and anthropologists pioneered interdisciplinary methods to uncover Pacific islanders' own accounts of their history. Elsewhere in the south Pacific, the founding of new universities in Papua New Guinea and Fiji in 1966 encouraged the growth of island-oriented research. Through the 1970s, fieldwork in the islands was the basis for publications that emphasized Pacific islanders' energetic and creative response to the problems posed by European explorers, missionaries, and traders. The later colonial period, shunned because of its association with British imperial history, remained largely unexamined: culture contact dominated the agenda. One of the most innovative members of the Davidson school, Greg Dening, described the beach as a zone of interaction where islanders and Europeans negotiated the complexities of culture contact in *Islands and Beaches* (1980).

The first general history of the islands appeared in Howe's *Where the Waves Fall* (1984), reflecting the desire for a broader, comparative approach to Pacific history. The anthropological approach of Davidson and his colleagues was often narrow, focusing on the history of a single island or region; Howe has remarked in Lal's *Pacific Islands History* (1992) that "we were learning more and more about less and less." Other general histories followed Howe's, and the increasing involvement of American historians prompted a movement outward from familiar areas such as Fiji and French Polynesia to the neglected north and central Pacific. Douglas Oliver's *The Pacific Islands* (1951) urged attention to American involvement in the Pacific in the wake of World War II; Americans are so prominent in the field today that the anthropologists Sahlins and Obeyesekere dominate the current debate about Captain Cook's explorations and death in Hawaii.

German and French activities in the Pacific began receiving greater attention in the 1980s, and the field began to re-engage issues of imperialism. Australian rule in Papua and New Guinea has been a particularly fruitful subject, as have studies of colonial resistance in various island groups. Interest in the decolonization process, and the continuing involvement of former colonial or mandate powers in bodies such as the South Pacific Commission, is growing as well.

The 1980s also saw the emergence of wide-ranging, comparative studies such as Moore, Leckie, and Munro's *Labour in the South Pacific* (1990) or Jolly and Macintyre's *Family and Gender in the Pacific* (1989). These studies joined international debates about labor migration and gender relations, unlike earlier work which had often treated islanders in isolation. Corris' *Passage, Port and Plantation* (1973) focused on the labor trade, or "blackbirding" in islanders of the late 19th century; more recent studies include the migration of various groups such as indentured Indian laborers in Fiji. Likewise, Jolly and others relate the Pacific experience to widespread changes in family and gender relations under European influence. Missionary records, once used almost exclusively to explore early contact issues, are now mined for information about the attempted acculturation of islanders and their appropriation and adaptation of European cultural forms.

The 1987 Fijian coups provided a pointed reminder that the study of race relations could not be confined to interaction between Europeans and islanders, and debate about romanticism and isolationism in island-oriented Pacific history grew. Kelly's *A Politics of Virtue* (1991) lamented the neglect of subaltern studies, especially with regard to Fiji Indians, and called for a greater awareness of recent developments in South Asian and British imperial historiography. Studies of postcolonial island governments began grappling with the issue of lingering European influence, and the "invention of tradition": the means by which colonial rule had reshaped many aspects of island culture. A greater interest in contemporary history has prompted the launch of new journals, notably *The Contemporary Pacific* and *Pacific Affairs*. Howe, Kiste, and Lal were invited to compile *Tides of History: The Pacific Islands in the Twentieth Century* (1994) with an eye to international issues such as nationalism and regionalism.

Meanwhile, postmodernism and deconstruction theory have invited a return to the European records, and a re-examination of the way Europeans imagined and interpreted the Pacific. Thomas' *Colonialism's Culture* (1994) adds a Pacific perspective to the burgeoning literatures on European discourses about Africa or South Asia. New theories have also questioned traditional assumptions in the field of anthropology, inviting less side-taking – European v. island viewpoints – and more multivocal interpretations of culture contact such as Neumann's *Not the Way It Really Was* (1992).

JANE SAMSON

See also Anthropology; Beaglehole; Dening; Indian Ocean; Southeast Asia

Further Reading

Aldrich, Robert, *The French Presence in the South Pacific, 1842–1940*, Basingstoke: Macmillan, and Honolulu: University of Hawaii Press, 1990

Boyd, Mary, *New Zealand and Decolonisation in the South Pacific*, Wellington: New Zealand Institute of International Affairs, 1987

Corris, Peter, *Passage, Port and Plantation: A History of Solomon Islands Labour Migration, 1870–1914*, Melbourne: Melbourne University Press, 1973

Davidson, J.W., "Problems of Pacific History," *Journal of Pacific History* 1 (1966), 5–21

Daws, Gavan, *A Dream of Islands: Voyages of Self-Discovery in the South Seas*, New York: Norton, 1980

Dening, Greg, *Islands and Beaches: Discourse on a Silent Land, Marquesas 1774–1880*, Carlton: Melbourne University Press, and Honolulu: University of Hawaii Press, 1980

Downs, Ian, *The Australian Trusteeship: Papua New Guinea, 1945–75*, Canberra: Australian Government Publication Service, 1980

Fitzpatrick, Peter, *Law and State in Papua New Guinea, 1945–75*, London and New York: Academic Press, 1980

Gunson, Niel, *Messengers of Grace: Evangelical Missionaries in the South Seas, 1797–1860*, Melbourne and New York: Oxford University Press, 1978

Hempenstall, Peter J., and Noel Rutherford, eds., *Protest and Dissent in the South Pacific*, Suva, Fiji: Institute of Pacific Studies of the University of the South Pacific, 1984

Howe, K.R., *Where the Waves Fall: A New South Sea Island History from First Settlement to Colonial Rule*, Sydney and London: Allen and Unwin, and Honolulu: University of Hawaii Press, 1984

Howe, K.R., Robert C. Kiste, and Brij V. Lal, eds., *Tides of History: The Pacific Islands in the Twentieth Century*, Honolulu: University of Hawaii Press, 1994

Jolly, Margaret, and Margaret Macintyre, eds., *Family and Gender in the Pacific: Domestic Contradictions and the Colonial Impact*, Cambridge and New York: Cambridge University Press, 1989

Kelly, John D., *A Politics of Virtue: Hinduism, Sexuality, and Countercolonial Discourse in Fiji*, Chicago: University of Chicago Press, 1991

Lal, Brij V., ed., *Pacific Islands History: Journeys and Transformations*, Canberra: Journal of Pacific History, 1992

Macdonald, Barrie, *Cinderellas of the Empire: Towards a History of Kiribati and Tuvalu*, Canberra: Australian National University Press, 1982

Maude, H.E.O., *Of Islands and Men: Studies in Pacific History*, Melbourne and New York: Oxford University Press, 1968

Moore, Clive, Jacqueline Leckie, and Doug Munro, eds., *Labour in the South Pacific*, Townsville: James Cook University of Northern Queensland, 1990

Moses, John A., and Paul M. Kennedy, eds., *Germany in the Pacific and Far East, 1870–1914*, St. Lucia: University of Queensland Press, 1977

Neumann, Klaus, *Not the Way It Really Was: Constructing the Tolai Past*, Honolulu: University of Hawaii Press, 1992

Newbury, Colin Walter, *Tahiti Nui: Change and Survival in French Polynesia, 1767–1945*, Honolulu: University of Hawaii Press, 1980

Obeyesekere, Gananath, *The Apotheosis of Captain Cook: European Mythmaking in the Pacific*, Princeton: Princeton University Press–Honolulu: Bishop Museum Press, 1992

Oliver, Douglas, *The Pacific Islands*, Honolulu: University of Hawaii Press, 1951; revised 1989

Peattie, Mark R., *Nan'yo: The Rise and Fall of the Japanese in Micronesia, 1885–1945*, Honolulu: University of Hawaii Press, 1988

Sahlins, Marshall, *How "Natives" Think: About Captain Cook, for Example*, Chicago: University of Chicago Press, 1995

Scarr, Deryck, *Fragments of Empire: A History of the Western Pacific High Commission, 1877–1914*, Canberra: Australian National University Press, 1967

Smith, Bernard, *European Vision and the South Pacific 1768–1850*, Oxford: Clarendon Press, 1960

Spate, O.K.H., *The Pacific since Magellan*, 3 vols., London: Croom Helm, 1979–88

Thomas, Nicholas, *Colonialism's Culture: Anthropology, Travel and Government*, Cambridge: Polity Press, and Princeton: Princeton University Press, 1994

Pagels, Elaine 1943–

US historian of religion

Elaine Pagels is a professor of religion who studies early Christian texts. Her writings have informed scholarly debate while at the same time being accessible, indeed popular, with an audience of non-specialists. In spite of her interest in topics that seem at first obscure (Gnosticism or Pelagianism), her approach is not that of an antiquarian. Pagels places the texts under consideration in their cultural contexts, and this historical approach allows her to ask unusual questions of texts familiar to scholars. Her fresh vision draws very old texts into contemporary debates where they shed light on modern problems.

In the 1970s, Pagels worked on editing technical editions of the Coptic Gnostic Gospels, and published two scholarly monographs on these texts: *The Johannine Gospel in Gnostic Exegesis* (1973) and *The Gnostic Paul* (1975).

The work that first brought Pagels broad-based acclaim was *The Gnostic Gospels* (1979). In this work she recreates the diversity of the early centuries of Christianity by an exploration of some of the central themes in the Gnostic texts discovered at Nag Hammadi. By looking at the contrast between the Gnostic and the orthodox positions on such things as bodily resurrection, gender, and martyrdom, the author illuminates not only the orthodox and heretical positions, but also the political and cultural implications of both.

In *Adam, Eve, and the Serpent* (1988), Pagels looks closely at interpretations and implications of the biblical story of the Fall. Pagels argues that Christians saw in the Genesis account an affirmation of the intrinsic value of every person and of human moral freedom. Thus, many used this text as a justification for a revolutionary rejection of traditional pagan social values. The book concludes with an analysis of Augustine's views on the subject, and his repudiation of the freedom that some Christians had read into the verses. Pagels emphasizes the questions of free will that were implicit in Augustine's thought but were seldom analyzed in the context of his views on sexuality. Consistent with her pattern of making the seemingly obscure immediately relevant, Pagels includes a sympathetic analysis of Pelagius, Augustine's opponent and perhaps the last Christian advocate for human free will.

In *The Origin of Satan* (1995), Pagels explores the roots of western culture's tendency to demonize opponents, and she finds them in the Judeo-Christian texts that have been so influential to subsequent western thought. Pagels brings a number of fresh insights to the often-studied questions of evil and the devil. Not only does she show that Judeo-Christian texts expressed the idea of an evil entity to embody opposition to God, but that in its origins this evil was perceived not primarily outside the Jewish and Christian communities, but within them. In looking for the enemy, Pagels discovers that it is an "intimate enemy" within each religious group that people most readily demonize. The early Jewish communities were plagued with division over issues of assimilation to Gentile culture or maintaining religious separation from it, and they attributed the power of Satan to their adversaries. The writers of the Gospels saw Satan less in the pagan world than in those Jews who did not accept their Messiah, and who sometimes persecuted their supporters. Early Christians saw Satan in the diverse opinions that threatened to split their communities. Pagels shows that we are harshest on those who are closest to us, and in that harshness we see not differences of opinion, but the devil.

Some historians have disagreed with the conclusions that Pagels draws from her fresh readings of these texts, and some dispute the value of the questions she asks. However, there can be no doubt that her works have advanced the study of religion and have brought to the fore texts and ideas frequently forgotten. The impact of Pagels' work was recognized as early as 1981, when she was awarded a MacArthur fellowship, and her subsequent work has not disappointed.

JOYCE E. SALISBURY

Biography

Born Palo Alto, California, 13 February 1943. Educated at Stanford University, BA 1964, MA 1965; Harvard University, PhD 1970. From 1970, taught at Barnard College (rising to professor), then Princeton University. Married Heinz Pagels, physicist, 1969 (died 1988; 1 daughter, 2 sons, 1 died 1986).

Principal Writings

The Johannine Gospel in Gnostic Exegesis, 1973
The Gnostic Paul: Gnostic Exegesis of the Pauline Letters, 1975
The Gnostic Gospels, 1979
Adam, Eve, and the Serpent, 1988
The Origin of Satan, 1995

Painter, Nell Irvin 1942–

US historian

Nell Irvin Painter is one of the foremost American historians of the African American experience. Her work is part of the scholarship on African American history and culture that has flourished since the 1960s, a historiographical tradition that ranks as a major collective achievement of an entire generation of historians and critics. In *Exodusters* (1976), Painter chronicled the travails of thousands of black southerners who voted with their feet against the white supremacist governments that returned to power across the South little more than a decade after Appomattox. In her edition of *The Narrative of Hosea Hudson* (1979), she recovered the story of one black man's struggle against the oppressions of the 20th-century South. Her scholarly revisionist biography, *Sojourner Truth* (1996), has attracted widespread attention.

Painter says that she has never felt entirely comfortable as a historian. She did not want to have anything to do with US history when she was a student at Berkeley in the early 1960s: "I thought it was a pack of lies," said Painter, who was interested in segregation and racial oppression, but found nothing in US history on those topics. However, by the early 1970s historical scholarship had changed enough to accommodate her version of US history.

In her book, Painter agrees that many of the stories about Sojourner Truth are false, but that is what she finds interesting. Her focus is on how – and why – Truth and others remade Truth's image: "I'm as much interested in the symbol of Sojourner Truth as in her life," she says, "It tells you a lot about the way race functions in our society." For that, she has had to go beyond the written sources. One approach that she used was to draw on psychology. For example, in discussing psychological theories about the impact of abuse on children, Painter interpreted the phrasing and structure of Truth's *Narrative* to argue that she was probably sexually abused. And, to flesh out Truth's interior life, Painter also looked at the *cartes-de-visite* that became popular in the United States in the 1860s – small black-and-white photographs bought and sold like popular stories.

Painter believes that although black women scholars have written critically of the work of other black men and women, for the most part they have embraced rather then censured their biological and intellectual foremothers. As a result of having flourished during the late 20th century, black women's studies is likely to find more grounds for hope. Linda Kerber noted that "For the last 20 to 30 years, a whole generation of historians has been at pains to stress the strengths and agency of black people, to see the strategies that they forged to survive the brutality of slavery. Then here comes Nell saying, that's good, but let's not gloss over the damage."

As disparate as her works seem, for Painter they possess a common thread. "I think the thing I've always tried to do is deal with people as individuals, not as integers of race," she says. "Race does matter, but it's not all there is. I look carefully at other factors, including gender and class, but especially psychology and family dynamics, for motivations." This approach, increasingly informed by feminist theory and criticism, has distinguished her from many of her colleagues. For Painter, focusing on Truth's image has spurred an interest in cultural representation. She is now at work on how Americans produced concepts of beauty in the late 19th and early 20th centuries.

LAUREN COODLEY

See also United States: 19th Century; United States: 20th Century

Biography

Born Houston, 2 August 1942, daughter of a chemist and a personnel officer. Received BA, University of California, Berkeley, 1964; MA, University of California, Los Angeles, 1967; PhD, Harvard University, 1974. Taught at University of Pennsylvania, 1974–80; professor, University of North Carolina, Chapel Hill, 1980–88; Hunter College, City University of New York, 1985–91; and Princeton University, from 1991.

Principal Writings

Exodusters: Black Migration to Kansas after Reconstruction, 1976
Editor, *The Narrative of Hosea Hudson: His Life as a Negro Communist in the South*, 1979

Standing at Armageddon: The United States, 1877–1919, 1987
"Soul Murder and Slavery: Toward a Fully-Loaded Cost
  Accounting," in Linda Kerber, Alice Kessler-Harris, and Kathryn
  Kish Sklar, eds., *US History as Women's History: New Feminist
  Essays*, Chapel Hill: University of North Carolina Press, 1995
Sojourner Truth: A Life, a Symbol, 1996

Palacký, František 1798–1876
Czech historian

František Palacký was an extremely influential Czech nationalist and historian. In the opinion of the distinguished Habsburg historian Robert Kann, Palacký was the finest historian in the entire Austrian empire during the 19th century. Josef Dobrovsky (1753–1829), a Czech devotee of the Enlightenment, introduced Czech intellectuals to high standards of textual criticism, which greatly influenced the self-trained Palacký. Consequently much of his work consists of critical editions of historical texts and documents. Early in his career he edited the *Stari letopisové cesti od r. 1527* (Old Bohemian Chronicles, 1829) and the *Würdigung der alten böhmischen Geschichtsschreiber* (Assessment of the Old Bohemian Chroniclers, 1830), and he concluded that without exception these primary sources for Czech history were badly flawed. Between 1840 and 1872, he also prepared a new 6-volume edition of Czech documents on the Hussite period and the Reformation entitled *Archiv cesky* (The Bohemian Archiv). In 1848 he produced *Popis královstvi českého* (Description of the Bohemian Kingdom), an important work on medieval Bohemian genealogy and topography. Finally, between 1857 and 1873, he contributed material on the Hussite period from foreign archives for publication in several large collections of documents.

Rather than the Enlightenment's rationalism, Palacký's view of history owed more to the romanticism that he absorbed from his early 19th-century intellectual milieu. Many romantic historians focused on the ancient and medieval periods in which they used the increasingly popular concept of nationalism to explore the origins of nations. Palacký's deep attachment was to Bohemia, where the Czechs, a branch of the West Slavs, resided, and writing a history of Bohemia became his main goal in life. He completed it only to 1526, which was the year when the Habsburg dynasty obtained Bohemia as a hereditary possession. As the best history of the Czechs written to that date, it had a powerful influence on the Czech national revival movement that ended successfully with the creation of Czechoslovakia in 1919. The work consists of five volumes published in German and Czech editions between 1836 and 1876. The first volume appeared in German as the *Geschichte von Böhmen* (History of Bohemia), but for political reasons in 1848 he switched to the Czech language and subtly changed the title to *Dějiny národu českého v Čechách a v Morave* (History of the Czech Nation in Bohemia and Moravia). The theme of Palacký's monumental history of Bohemia is the usurpation of the peaceful and democratic Czechs' homeland by an aggressive German ruling elite encouraged by the Roman Catholic hierarchy. German intervention in Bohemia also introduced social and legal inequality into a Czech society where equality had flourished due to the Slavs' democratic nature. Curiously, his romantic determination to polarize his topic between the good Czechs and the evil Germans and Roman Catholic church led him to accept two manuscripts discovered in 1817 and 1818 that Dobrovsky had exposed as forgeries. Furthermore, the romantic thesis of the peace-loving democratic Slavs, accepted by many romantic Slavic nationalists, has subsequently been exposed as a myth. Habsburg critics of Palacký's interpretation of Bohemian history also devised a counterargument that Germans had colonized Bohemia before the Slavs arrived, which ignited a polemic between adherents of this theory and Czech defenders of Palacký's version that endured until the Habsburg empire disintegrated during World War I. On a more positive note, his view that the Hussite Revolution was the most important event in European history, while exaggerated, did correct the overemphasis on Luther as the principal cause of the Reformation.

Palacký the nationalist politician contributed much less to the formation of Czech national consciousness than did Palacký the historian. His most important political argument, announced as early as 1848, was that the Habsburg empire was necessary, but needed to transform itself into a multinational federation of peoples equal before the law in order for it to survive. He summarized this theory, which made him the spokesman of all the Habsburg's non-German and non-Magyar peoples, in an often quoted statement that "Truly if the Austrian empire had not already existed for a long time, the interests of Europe and the interests of humanity would demand its speedy creation." Not only could such a state enhance the lives of its citizens, but it would also provide the West with a bulwark against Russian expansionism. After the creation in 1867 of the Dual Monarchy of Austria-Hungary, Palacký gave up all hope of ever realizing his dream of a federated Habsburg empire. His intellectual and moral legacy continued to influence the Czechs until the 1930s, while his historical writings remain important for the study of medieval Bohemia.

ROBERT F. FORREST

See also Europe: Modern; Nationalism; Pekař

Biography
Born Hodslavice, Northern Moravia, 14 June 1798, to a Bohemian Protestant family. Educated in Latin and German, Pressburg evangelical lyceum. Tutor in Vienna, 1818–23; moved to Prague, 1823; appointed editor of the Czech museum journal, *Casopis Ceského Muzea*, 1827, and historiographer of the Bohemian kingdom, 1831; archivist of the Sternberg family; leader of the Czech national movement, from 1840; member, Austrian parliament upper house, 1861. Married daughter of a Prague lawyer and landowner. Died Prague, 26 May 1876.

Principal Writings
Editor, *Stari letopisové cesti od r. 1527* (Old Bohemian Chronicles), 1829
Editor, *Würdigung der alten böhmischen Geschichtsschreiber* (Assessment of the Old Bohemian Chroniclers), 1830
Geschichte von Böhmen (History of Bohemia), 5 vols., 1836–67
Editor, *Archiv cesky* (The Bohemian Archiv), 6 vols., 1840–72
Dějiny národu českého v Čechách a v Morave (History of the Czech Nation in Bohemia and Moravia), 8 vols., 1848–76

Popis královstvi českého (Description of the Bohemian Kingdom), 1848

Further Reading

Hlaváček, Ivan, and Vladimír Kaiser, eds., "Bibliografie tisteného literarniho dila Frantiska Palackého po r.1876" (A Bibliography of František Palacký's Published Literary Works up to 1876), *Acta Universitatis Carolinae Philosophica et Historia 5* (1982), 119–50

Kann, Robert A., *The Multinational Empire: Nationalism and National Reform in the Habsburg Monarchy, 1848–1918*, 2 vols., New York: Columbia University Press, 1950

Kann, Robert A., *A History of the Habsburg Empire, 1526–1918*, Berkeley: University of California Press, 1974

Zacek, J.F., *Palacký: The Historian as Scholar and Nationalist*, The Hague: Mouton, 1970

Panofsky, Erwin 1892–1968

US (German-born) art historian

Born in Germany, Erwin Panofsky was already a well-respected scholar when he first came to the United States in 1931. Through his appointments at New York University and the Institute for Advanced Study in Princeton, and his many public lectures, he became a leader in the development of art historical thought in his adopted homeland as well; he is, in fact, widely acknowledged as the most influential art historian of the 20th century.

Panofsky's major contribution is his direct linkage of art history with cultural history. His philosophy served as a bridge between many disciplines, influencing not only art history but many other fields as well. Even in his work as a specialist on Renaissance art, Panofsky revealed this broader philosophy. When considering the art of Albrecht Dürer, for instance (the topic of his doctoral dissertation and a later monograph), he discussed contemporaneous aspects of philosophy, literature, and mathematics not only as influences on Dürer's art, but as parallel entities that reflected the same culture. This philosophical approach to art led to his development of a methodological approach which he called "iconology," for which he is best known. He employed it in articles such as "Hercules am Scheidewege" (Hercules at the Crossroads, 1930) and "Jan van Eyck's Arnolfini Portrait" (1934); his masterly explanation of the theory appeared in the introduction of his *Studies in Iconology* (1939).

In iconology one can encounter a work of art (or any visual phenomenon) on three levels, all of which focus on subject matter. The first and most basic is that of Natural Subject Matter. This is the level of pre-iconographical description and entails the recognition of formal aspects (line, color, shape, etc.) as configurations that represent a specific object (i.e., human being, plant, house, etc.) or a specific event (i.e., man raising his hat in the street), concepts that are common to virtually all human beings.

The level of Secondary or Conventional Subject Matter involves identification of an object or event in light of concepts common only to a specific culture, i.e., that a male figure with a knife represents St. Bartholomew, that a group of figures seated around a dinner table in a certain arrangement represents the Last Supper, that a man raising his hat represents a greeting. It is this level that is normally associated with the term *iconography*, the study of subject matter (as opposed to the study of form).

The third level deals with Intrinsic Meaning or Content; this is the realm of *iconology*, a term that Panofsky described as "iconography turned interpretive." This third level, then, was significantly different than the other two: it involved synthesis rather than analysis. By using an iconological approach (which depends on accurate analysis on the first two levels) the art historian seeks to view the work of art as a part of a larger picture. Leonardo's *Last Supper* is understood as a document of Leonardo's personality, of a specific religious attitude, or of the civilization of the High Renaissance in Italy; the greeting presented by a man raising his hat is understood not only as a greeting but as part of his personality, which includes his nationality, his social and educational background, his philosophy. Panofsky acknowledged that all of these aspects of character cannot be discerned through a single painting or one man's action, but he argued that a man's personality would be reflected in his every single action, and that a piece of art would, in the same way, incorporate the personality of its maker and the historical/cultural situation that informed that artist. Each piece of art, therefore, can be treated as a product of that historical/cultural situation. Considered along with a large number of other objects and events similarly symptomatic of the same culture, a comprehensive view of the culture begins to appear.

In developing this approach, Panofsky clearly acknowledged his borrowings from Ernst Cassirer's philosophy of symbols. He also built on ideas developed by Alois Reigl and Heinrich Wölfflin, pioneers in art historical theory. He followed the latter two in trying to seek out a recognizable system that addresses the relationship between art and history, and he adopted their establishment of alternating polar extremes to and from which art continually moves. Panofsky, however, was more concerned with the process by which art moved between those poles within a specific timeframe, and how an art historian bridges the gap between the work of art and the culture that produced it. His iconological method is an attempt to systematize that process.

In that iconology is, by definition, tied to culture, it is not as abstract an art historical construct as the models of Reigl and Wölfflin's are. It is more subjective in nature, but it can still be applied to different contexts and periods throughout history, and, to that extent, has an abstract/objective aspect to it. Moreover, although Panofsky's system deals directly with subject matter whereas Reigl and Wölfflin deal directly with form, iconology does not exclude formalist issues; rather, it deals with them in the same way that it deals with issues of philosophy or literature – as symbols of a culture that, taken together, give meaning to the visual arts.

In *Studies in Iconology* Panofsky noted that many of the symbolic aspects of art are unconscious on the part of the artist, while in his *Early Netherlandish Painting* (1953) he demonstrated that symbolic meaning was sometimes very consciously included as well. This conflict was not resolved in his work and gave rise to criticism; however, it shows that Panofsky was considering the role of the psychology of the artist. It was an issue ignored by his predecessors, but one that became central to many of those who followed him. In moving away from a strictly formalist approach, Panofsky lent credence to art historical approaches – such as the psychological approach (see Gombrich) – that seek to explain or illuminate a work of art through outside sources and materials (as opposed to sources/materials found within a work of art itself); and, in fact, a multitude of such approaches flourished in the second half of the 20th century. His lasting legacy, however, may be his gift for combining approaches that look both inside and outside of the sphere created by an individual work of art. Indeed, Panofsky's art historical philosophy pulled together many seemingly disparate elements and united them to present a more complete picture of both art and culture.

JULIET GRAVER ISTRABADI

See also Art; Burke; Gombrich; Schramm

Biography

Born Hannover, Germany, 30 March 1892, to a wealthy family. Attended Joachimsthalsches Gymnasium, Berlin; University of Munich; University of Berlin; PhD, University of Freiburg (Baden), 1914. Lecturer, University of Hamburg, 1921, full professor, 1926–33 when dismissed by Nazis; emigrated to US, 1934 (naturalized later). Visiting professor, New York University, 1931–34 and Princeton University, 1934–35; professor, Institute for Advanced Study, Princeton, 1935–62; Samuel F.B. Morse professor, New York University, 1962–68. Married 1) Dora Mosse, 1916 (died 1965; 2 sons); 2) Gerda Sörgel, art historian, 1965. Died Princeton, 14 March 1968.

Principal Writings

"Idee": Ein Beitrag zur Begriffsgeschichte der älteren Kunsttheorie, 1924; in English as Idea: A Conception in Art History, 1968
Hercules am Scheidewege und andere antike Bildstoffe in der neueren Kunst (Hercules at the Crossroads of Life and Other Ancient Themes in Contemporary Art), 1930
Studies in Iconology: Humanistic Themes in the Art of the Renaissance, 1939
Albrecht Dürer, 1943; as The Life and Work of Albrecht Dürer, 1955
Editor, Abbot Suger on the Abbey Church of St-Denis and Its Art Treasures, 1946
Early Netherlandish Painting: Its Origins and Character, 2 vols., 1953
Meaning in the Visual Arts: Papers in and on Art History, 1955
With Dora Panofsky, Pandora's Box: The Changing Aspects of a Mythical Symbol, 1956
Renaissance and Renascences in Western Art, 1960
Three Essays on Style, edited by Irving Lavin, 1995

Further Reading

Holly, Michael Ann, *Panofsky and the Foundations of Art History*, Ithaca, NY: Cornell University Press, 1984
Oberer, Hariolf, and Egon Verheyer, eds., *Erwin Panofsky: Aufsätze zu Grundfragen der Kunstwissenschaft* (Erwin Panofsky: Essays on the Fundamental Questions of Art Theory), Berlin: Hessling, 1974 [includes bibliography]

Paris, Matthew c.1200–c.1259
English historical writer

Matthew Paris is one of the most famous and controversial of English medieval historians. A monk at the Benedictine abbey of St. Albans, Hertfordshire, he began his independent writing career between 1235 and 1240 when he took over the role of abbey chronicler following the death of Roger of Wendover. From then until his death in 1259 his output was prolific, comprising three major histories and numerous shorter historical works such as a history of his own abbey, in addition to a variety of illustrated saints' lives written for noble laypersons. He has been admired for his outspoken criticism of authority, his powers of observation and description, and his enthusiasm in collecting information from every available source. However, perhaps his greatest value to modern historians lies in the vast number of contemporary documents he included in his work and in the insight he gives to his own fears, opinions, and prejudices.

His greatest historical work was the *Chronica majora* (Greater Chronicle) which began with the Creation and came down to his own day. From 1250 Matthew was recording events almost as they happened, writing more as a commentator on current events than as a historian. He gave a lively and generally well-informed account of the uneasy relations between Henry III and his magnates, which were to culminate after Matthew's death in the revolt of Simon de Montfort. For the period c.1228–59 the chronicle is also an important source for the history of the European territories in Palestine and Syria, and for the wars between the emperor Frederick II and the papacy in Europe. Matthew also described the Mongols and their invasions of the Middle East and Eastern Europe. Certain themes run through this vast and rambling collection: Matthew's opposition to any form of authority, especially the king and pope; and his dislike of taxation, foreigners, and innovative religious orders such as the military orders and the friars.

To make his vast history more accessible, Matthew produced selective summaries known as the *Flores historiarum* (Flowers of History), the *Historia anglorum* (History of the English) and then the *Abbreviatio*, a summary of the *Historia*. It was not his great chronicle but its summary in the *Flores* that won Matthew most fame in his own century. Copies circulated to many other monasteries, where they were added to as the years passed. For this reason, the identity of the author, "Matthew," became obscured, and not until the work of V.H. Galbraith in *Roger of Wendover and Matthew Paris* (1944) was Matthew Paris shown conclusively to have been the first author.

Matthew's bitter criticism of the papacy of his own day was an important factor in the survival of his reputation after the dissolution of the monasteries. In the wake of the break with Rome, his work received praise from John Bale in *Scriptorum illustrium majoris Britanniae* (Illustrious Writers of Great Britain, 1557) for its description and condemnation of the "avarice, frauds, lies … and worst deeds of certain Roman pontiffs." For the same reason, archbishop Matthew Parker relied heavily upon Matthew's account of the years 1206–59 in his *De antiquitate Britanniae ecclesiae* (The Antiquity of the Church in Britain, 1605). Parker published Matthew's works; his edition was reprinted by William Wats in 1640.

By the 19th century improving standards of critical scholarship found this edition inadequate, and Matthew's historical works were re-edited. Matthew's 19th-century editors admired his patriotism and saw in his fearless outspokenness against incompetent authority the foreshadowing of the constitutional, democratic citizen concerned for the well-being of his nation. Matthew was clearly a mouthpiece of general informed opinion: "The 13th-century editor of the Times," as Augustus Jessopp called him (*Studies by a Recluse*, 1893). It was known that he made errors, but he wrote in good faith.

Historians' increasing use of documentary and other forms of historical evidence to supplement Latin chronicles has made possible a reassessment of Matthew's picture of 13th-century Europe and the Middle East. In *Matthew Paris* (1958), Richard Vaughan showed that Matthew was far from being a truth-seeking, critical historian. He added to his material, he invented material, he reported rumor as truth, and his account was heavily distorted by his own well-entrenched prejudices. His patriotism was simply a hatred of foreigners. His hostility to the king was not "constitutional" but based on his innate dislike of authority. Although he claimed to represent general opinion, in fact he spoke only for himself. From being "editor of the Times," such modern reassessments have reduced Matthew to the level of a gutter-press gossip columnist.

Yet today historians remain divided over Matthew. The debate continues as to how far his personal piety affected his work, and how far he spoke for the "man in the street." In any case his work is still of immense value, even if it is regarded more as a window into the mind of one well-informed 13th-century man than as a critical analysis of events. In recent years he has received increasing acclaim as an artist, and his saints' lives and shorter histories are being re-evaluated as valuable historical records in their own right; again, not as a factual record but as a guide to the values and attitudes of Matthew and the audience for which he wrote. A new edition of his works is currently in progress, with a modern translation into English.

HELEN J. NICHOLSON

See also Britain: 1066–1485; Roger; William of Tyre

Biography

Born *c.*1200. Entered St. Albans Benedictine abbey as monk, 1217; visited Westminster Abbey, 1247; sent by pope Innocent III to St. Benet Holm abbey, Nidarholm, Norway, 1248. Died St. Albans, Hertfordshire, *c.*1259.

Principal Writings

Chronica majora (Greater Chronicle; revision and continuation of Roger of Wendover's *Flores historiarum*), written from *c.*1235; edited by Henry R. Luard, 7 vols., 1872–84, reprinted 1964; partially translated as *Matthew Paris's English History, from the Year 1235 to 1273*, 3 vols., 1852–54, reprinted 1968

Historia anglorum (History of the English), edited by F.H. Madden, 3 vols., 1866–69

Further Reading

Bulst-Thiele, Mary Luise, "Zur Geschichte der Ritterorden und des Königreichs Jerusalem im 13. Jahrhundert bis zur Schlacht bei La Forbie am 17. Oktober 1244" (On the History of the Order of the Knights and Kingdom of Jerusalem in the 13th Century, until the Battle of La Forbie, 17 October 1244), *Deutsches Archiv für Erforschung des Mittelalters* 22 (1966), 197–226

Galbraith, Vivian Hunter, *Roger of Wendover and Matthew Paris*, Glasgow: Jackson, 1944

Gransden, Antonia, *Historical Writing in England*, vol. 1: *c.550 to c.1307*, London: Routledge, and Ithaca, NY: Cornell University Press, 1974

Hahn, C., "Proper behaviour for Knights and Kings: The Hagiography of Matthew Paris, Monk of St. Albans," *Haskins Society Journal* 2 (1990), 237–46

Holt, J.C., "The St. Albans Chroniclers and Magna Carta," *Transactions of the Royal Historical Society* 5th series, 14 (1964), 67–88

Keynes, Simon, "A Lost Cartulary of St. Alban's Abbey," *Anglo-Saxon England* 22 (1993), 253–79

Legge, Mary Dominica, *Anglo-Norman in the Cloisters: The Influence of the Orders upon Anglo-Norman Literature*, Edinburgh: Edinburgh University Press, 1950; St. Clair Shores, MI: Scholarly Press, 1971

Lewis, Suzanne, *The Art of Matthew Paris in the Chronica Majora*, London: Scolar Press, and Berkeley: University of California Press, 1987

McCulloch, Frances, "Saints Alban and Amphibalus in the work of Matthew Paris," *Speculum* 56 (1981), 761–85

Menache, Sophie, "Rewriting the History of the Templars According to Matthew Paris," in Michael Goodich, Sophie Menache, and S. Schein, eds., *Cultural Convergences in the Crusader Period: Essays Presented to Aryeh Grabois*, New York: Lang, 1995

Nicholson, Helen J., "Steamy Syrian Scandals: Matthew Paris on the Templars and Hospitallers," *Medieval History* 2 (1992), 68–85

Saunders, J.J., "Matthew Paris and the Mongols," in T.A. Sandquist and Michael R. Powicke, eds., *Essays in Medieval History Presented to Bertie Wilkinson*, Toronto: University of Toronto Press, 1969

Thomson, W.R., "The Image of the Mendicants in the Chronicles of Matthew Paris," *Archivum Franciscanum Historicum* 70 (1977), 3–34

Vaughan, Richard, *Matthew Paris*, Cambridge: Cambridge University Press, 1958

Vaughan, Richard, *The Chronicles of Matthew Paris: Monastic Life in the Thirteenth Century*, London: Sutton, and New York: St. Martin's Press, 1984

Parker, Geoffrey 1943–
British historian of early modern Europe

Although Geoffrey Parker holds the Robert A. Lovett chair of military and naval history at Yale University, the breadth of his scholarship suggests that his title is not restrictive. Parker's work addresses Europe's transition from the chaotic early modern period to the establishment of European hegemony (1500–1800). Few historians have been able to come to grips with the dynamics of early modern Europe and identify patterns of change as effectively and eloquently as Parker. He is both a skilled researcher and a great thinker, a rare combination that explains his success as a historian. Whether it is his famous critique of Michael Roberts' theory of the military revolution or his insight into the trials and tribulations of the Habsburg empire, Parker's scholarship is provocative, comprehensive, and reflective.

Parker began his intellectual journey at Cambridge University under the direction of John Elliott. His dissertation was the basis of his first book, *The Army of Flanders and the Spanish Road, 1567–1659* (1972). Here the historian demonstrated a remarkable mastery of the Spanish archives and provided answers to the question of how the Spanish army managed to wage a lengthy war in the Netherlands given the enormous logistical problems that faced early modern armies. Michael Roberts was an external examiner of Parker's dissertation, in which Parker first challenged Roberts' theory of the military revolution. The military revolution centers on the idea that tactical changes between 1560 and 1660 necessitated an increase in the size of armies. Larger armies meant more ambitious strategies and ambitious strategies required state centralization to finance military expansion. Roberts regarded the military revolution as the impetus for Europe's transformation into competitive nation-states. Parker, while not discounting the military revolution, cited such events as the Battle of Nordlingen (1634) in which a conservative Spanish army routed a supposedly tactically innovative Swedish army and proved that Roberts' theory was not flawless. Parker also noted that military expansion stretched early modern governments to the breaking point, because they were ill-equipped to support large armies. Roberts urged Parker to develop his critique further, marking the beginning of Parker's enduring interest in the military revolution.

The setting of the military revolution, the pervasive conflict between Spain and the Netherlands that eventually spilled over into the Thirty Years' War, continued to occupy Parker's attention during the 1970s and 1980s. Parker's 1978 biography of Philip II remains the definitive work because of its reliance on personal letters and diaries that give insight into the personality of one of early modern Europe's most important figures. With the assistance of nine other historians, Parker published the extensive volume *The Thirty Years' War* (1984). Within this work above all others one discerns Parker's depth as a scholar. Parker unraveled the complex political maneuvering before, during, and after the war, dividing the war into phases and providing a sense of historical order to one of history's most confusing periods. The most compelling chapter is the final one which dealt with the conduct and legacy of the war. Parker described the fate of the soldier, the peasant, and the systematic destruction of the Germanies – topics inadequately covered by most Thirty Years' War scholarship.

The military revolution has been the focal point of Parker's delineation of early modern European history, and in 1988 he revised not only Roberts' interpretation, but expanded upon his own by postulating that the military revolution fueled European imperialism. *The Military Revolution* (1988) outlined a "gunpowder revolution," proposing the notion that technological change was responsible for instigating state centralization. For Parker, innovations in fortress construction and artillery increased the significance of siege warfare and required larger armies. Parker's insistence on placing technology at the forefront of the military revolution provoked extensive debate among military historians, historians of technology, and other early modern Europeanists. Parker extended the military revolution from land armies to naval warfare. Technological innovation in ship construction and artillery meant that the impasse on land forced states to seek a decision at sea. The naval dimension of Parker's military revolution is fully examined in *The Spanish Armada* (1988). After analyzing the military revolution in Europe, Parker suggested that Europe achieved global hegemony by unleashing the fruits of its military revolution on the rest of the world.

Parker once worked with Fernand Braudel, the distinguished historian from the Annales school, with hopes of writing a quantitative "total history" of the Habsburg empire. Parker quickly realized the limitations of Annales methods, however,

when they are applied to early modern Europe. The sources are simply too few and problematic, but Parker comes close to writing "total history" by treating each subject comprehensively. Historians have criticized the "technological determinism" central to Parker's interpretation of the military revolution, and like most historians writing about war, he devotes insufficient attention to women. Nevertheless, Parker poses compelling questions and develops innovative theories which he supports with exhaustive research and an impressive writing style. He is currently (1998) completing a book on the grand strategy of Philip II, continuing a career already filled with definitive works on numerous aspects of early modern Europe.

BRIAN CRIM

See also Crime; European Expansion; Germany: 1450–1800; Military

Biography

Noel Geoffrey Parker. Born 25 December 1943. Attended Nottingham High School; received BA, Cambridge University, 1965, MA, PhD 1968. Fellow, Christ's College, Cambridge, 1968–72; taught at Cambridge University, 1972–78; and University of St. Andrews, 1982–86; professor, University of Illinois, Urbana, 1986–93 and Yale University from 1993. Married 1) Angela Maureen Chapman (1 son, 1 daughter); 2) Jane Helen Ohlmeyer (1 son).

Principal Works

The Army of Flanders and the Spanish Road, 1567–1659: The Logistics of the Spanish Victory and Defeat in the Low Countries' Wars, 1972

The Dutch Revolt, 1977

Philip II, 1978; 3rd edition 1995

Europe in Crisis, 1598–1648, 1979

Spain and the Netherlands, 1559–1659: Ten Studies, 1979

Editor with V.A.C. Gatrell and Bruce Lenman, *Crime and the Law: The Social History of Crime in Western Europe since 1500*, 1980

Editor, *The Thirty Years' War*, 1984; revised 1997

The Military Revolution: Military Innovation and the Rise of the West, 1500–1800, 1988

With Colin Martin, *The Spanish Armada*, 1988

Editor, *The Cambridge Illustrated History of Warfare: The Triumph of the West*, 1995

Editor with Richard L. Kagan, *Spain, Europe, and the Atlantic World: Essays in Honour of John. H. Elliott*, 1995

Editor with Robert Cowley, *The Reader's Companion to Military History*, Boston: Houghton Mifflin, 1996

Parkman, Francis 1823–1893
US historian of the frontier

One of America's greatest narrative historians, Francis Parkman overcame poor health and failing vision to build a brilliant career over a half century as an independent historian of the British and French contest for control of the North American frontier.

In 1846 Parkman spent six months on the Great Plains researching his classic *The Oregon Trail* (1849), first published in 1847 as a magazine series. Travelling on the frontier with his cousin Quincy Adams Shaw and a French Canadian guide, Parkman lived with hunters, trappers, voyageurs, soldiers, and a Sioux tribe, using this experience to inform his later work, most clearly in *The Conspiracy of Pontiac and the Indian War after the Conquest of Canada* (1851).

Parkman's *magnum opus* was *France and England in North America* (1865–92), seven separate studies of French and British exploration, empire and conflict in North America, which concluded with an epic account of the French and Indian War (1754–63). Parkman was the first American to combine the new methods of German scholarship with the narrative art of romantic writing, winning a place as the foremost North American historian of his era.

Despite recognition by Herman Melville, Henry Adams, Henry James, Theodore Roosevelt, William Dean Howells, and Frederick Jackson Turner, in the 20th century Parkman was often overlooked, or consigned to literary and historiographical surveys. This may be due to his image as a conservative "dilettante" and Beacon Hill aristocrat, and to his fluid narrative method, as well as his penchant for martial subjects, heroic noblemen, and epic sagas, and a pronounced rationalist bias.

However, by the 1950s, sympathetic studies by scholars such as Samuel Eliot Morison, Howard Doughty, David Levin, William R. Taylor, and Mason Wade had redressed this neglect. Far from limiting or prejudicing his work, Parkman's privileged origins invigorated his scholarship. Spurning a gentleman's career, as a boy Parkman hunted and fished in pockets of forest near Boston, and later explored northern New England, developing his woodcraft and a taste for personal experience in the wilderness. While he was still an undergraduate, his love of the frontier and passion for history converged on a lifelong theme – the history of French and British explorers in North America. Like those other genteel Bostonians, William H. Prescott and John Lothrop Motley, Parkman found in history a manly profession, active life, patriotic impulses, and recognition as an author. Parkman's example would influence other Harvard College aristocrats who studied the frontier, Owen Wister and Theodore Roosevelt.

After his Oregon Trail expedition, Parkman's health and eyesight failed, but private resources permitted him to continue his work and to travel in North America and Europe, employing researchers in libraries and archives. Extensive and critical reliance on documentation was a hallmark of his work, together with broad research, deep understanding of human nature, an interest in the new science of ethnology, and a lucid literary style, all of which made Parkman America's foremost historian in the 19th century.

Parkman's productivity was remarkable. When Paris archives became available, due in part to a $10,000 appropriation Parkman obtained from Congress, he published a revision of *Discovery of the Great West* (1869) entitled *La Salle and the Discovery of the Great West* (1879). Before his books were published in new editions, Parkman often revised and rewrote, seeking always the highest standards of accuracy and literary skill.

During his lifetime, Parkman was hailed as the American Herodotus or another Thucydides, extravagant praise perhaps, but an indication of his high standing in the emerging discipline. At a time when history was still a literary endeavor, Parkman was a scientific scholar collecting manuscript materials and visiting historic locations. He made repeated research trips to Canada from 1843 to 1886, as he wrote, to "imbue himself with the life and spirit of the time." He relied less on books than on personal experience identifying him with his subjects.

His journals were published in 1947, and his letters in 1960. Parkman's work remains a valid, vivid and authentic contribution, and his position as a founding father of American history is secure.

PETER C. HOLLORAN

See also Eccles; Morison; Schama; Trigger

Biography

Born Boston, 16 September 1823, to a wealthy family. Educated at Harvard College, BA 1844, and Harvard Law School, LLB 1846. Traveled from St. Louis along the Oregon Trail, 1846. Professor of horticulture, Harvard University, 1871; president of the Massachusetts Horticultural Society; a founder of the Archaeological Institute of America, 1879. Married Catherine Scollay Bigelow, 1850 (2 daughters, 1 son). Died Boston, 8 November 1893.

Principal Writings

The California and Oregon Trail, 1849; revised as *The Oregon Trail*, 1872
The Conspiracy of Pontiac and the Indian War after the Conquest of Canada, 1851; published in Britain as *History of the Conspiracy of Pontiac, and the War of the North American Tribes against the English Colonies after the Conquest of Canada*, 1851
France and England in North America, 9 vols., 1865–92
The Journals of Francis Parkman, edited by Mason Wade, 1947
The Letters of Francis Parkman, edited by Wilbur R. Jacobs, 1960

Further Reading

Doughty, Howard M., *Francis Parkman*, New York: Macmillan, 1962; reprinted Cambridge, MA: Harvard University Press, 1983
Farnham, Charles Haight, *A Life of Francis Parkman*, Boston: Little Brown, 1900
Gale, Robert L., *Francis Parkman*, New York: Twayne, 1973
Jacobs, Wilbur R., *Francis Parkman, Historian as Hero: The Formative Years*, Austin: University of Texas Press, 1991
Levin, David, *History as Romantic Art: Bancroft, Prescott, Motley, and Parkman*, Stanford, CA: Stanford University Press, 1959
Morison, Samuel Eliot, ed., *The Parkman Reader*, Boston: Little Brown, 1955
Pease, Otis A., *Parkman's History: The Historian as Literary Artist*, New Haven: Yale University Press, 1953
Schama, Simon, *Dead Certainties: Unwarranted Speculations*, New York: Knopf, and London: Granta, 1991
Schramm, Wilbur J., ed., *Francis Parkman: Representative Selections*, New York: American Book Company, 1938
Wade, Mason, *Francis Parkman, Heroic Historian*, New York: Viking, 1942

Parrington, Vernon Louis 1871–1929

US intellectual historian

Vernon Louis Parrington is remembered for one book, the three volumes – the last uncompleted at his death – of *Main Currents in American Thought* (1927–30). An important work in the already well-established tradition of Progressive history of the United States, whose most notable exponents included Frederick Jackson Turner, Charles A. Beard, Carl Becker, and James Harvey Robinson, Parrington's *magnum opus* also gave new credibility to the then poorly regarded field of American literature. As the first attempt at any comprehensive interpretive synthesis of the subject, it broke new ground, and even in the 1950s a survey of one hundred historians still cited Parrington's study as the single work of American history they "most preferred."

Parrington spent his career in relative obscurity, teaching literature at, successively, the College of Emporia, Kansas, the University of Oklahoma, and the University of Washington in Seattle, where he spent most of his career. Unhappy during his undergraduate years at Harvard, he gravitated toward midwestern dissent and radicalism, and in 1897, led a delegation to a Kansas Populist convention. Something of a romantic, throughout his life Parrington remained an admirer of the social thought of John Ruskin and William Morris, particularly drawn by both the latter's cult of craftsmanship and his criticism of the materialism of big business. In the early 20th century he was much influenced by the radical scholarship of the Progressive period, particularly that of his Washington colleague, the political scientist James Allen Smith, who like Beard considered the American Constitution a "reactionary" document designed to maintain the status quo and subvert majority rule.

Although Parrington began work on *Main Currents* in 1913, he could not find a publisher until 1927, when the appearance of the first two volumes created an immediate sensation. In a fine and polished style that greatly enhanced the book's appeal, Parrington analyzed American literary and political writing from the perspective of the intellectual, social, and economic ideas which it represented, largely ignoring any artistic content. He portrayed the entire history of the United States as a battle between the values of Jeffersonian democratic idealism and Hamiltonian conservatism, making it clear that he strongly favored the Jeffersonian tradition and its exponents. Following the approach taken in Beard's historical writings, Parrington depicted political ideas, especially those he found unsympathetic, as the product of the environment in which their proponents lived rather than of any universal principle. Of purely literary work, representing no strong political viewpoint, such as the writings of Edgar Allan Poe and Henry James, Parrington clearly disapproved. Parrington's work was characterized by numerous striking individual studies of particular writers and political figures, which added to his survey's popularity. Immediately hailed as a masterpiece, during the 1930s, when the Depression discredited big business and capitalism, Parrington's work became the standard account of its subject. In later years, however, his treatment of numerous aspects of United States history, in particular his interpretation of Puritan figures and the colonial period, would be subjected to heavy criticism as being inaccurate and distorted to fit into his overriding thesis that the entire history of the United States was the story of the contest between democratic and conservative values. Today, Parrington is little read and regarded largely as a historical curiosity. Even so, *Main Currents* was one of the first and most ambitious attempts to provide an interdisciplinary perspective melding together history, literature, economics, politics, and geography, and as such may be regarded as one of the founding texts of American studies.

PRISCILLA M. ROBERTS

See also Curti; Hofstadter; LaFeber; Morgan; United States: 19th Century; United States: Historical Writing, 20th Century

Biography

Born Aurora, Illinois, 3 August 1871, son of a judge. Studied at College of Emporia, Kansas; Harvard University, BA 1893. Taught English and French at College of Emporia, 1893–97; English and modern languages (rising to professor), University of Oklahoma, 1897–1908; and English at University of Washington, 1908–29. Married Julia Rochester Williams, 1901 (2 sons, 1 daughter). Died Winchcomb, Gloucester, England, 16 June 1929.

Principal Writings

Main Currents in American Thought: An Interpretation of American Literature from the Beginnings to 1920, 3 vols., 1927–30

Further Reading

Colwell, James L., "The Populist Image of Vernon Louis Parrington," *Mississippi Valley Historical Review* 49 (1962), 52–66

Ekirch, Arthur A., Jr., "Parrington and the Decline of American Liberalism," *American Quarterly* 4 (1951), 295–308

Gabriel, Ralph H., "Vernon Louis Parrington," in Marcus Cunliffe and Robin Winks, eds., *Pastmasters: Some Essays on American Historians*, New York: Harper, 1969

Harrison, Joseph B., *Vernon Louis Parrington: American Scholar*, Seattle: University of Washington Book Store, 1929

Hofstadter, Richard, *The Progressive Historians: Turner, Beard, Parrington*, New York: Knopf, 1968; London: Cape, 1969

O'Brien, Michael, "Vernon L. Parrington," in Clyde N. Wilson, ed., *Twentieth-Century American Historians*, Detroit: Gale, 1983 [*Dictionary of Literary Biography*, vol. 17]

Peterson, Merrill D., "Parrington and American Liberalism," *Virginia Quarterly Review* 30 (1954), 35–49

Skotheim, Robert Allen, and Kermit Vanderbilt, "Vernon Louis Parrington: The Mind and Art of a Historian of Ideas," *Pacific Northwest Quarterly* 53 (1962), 100–13

Utter, William T., "Vernon Louis Parrington," in William T. Hutchinson, ed., *The Marcus W. Jernegan Essays in American Historiography*, Chicago: University of Chicago Press, 1937

Pekař, Josef 1870–1937

Czech historian

Josef Pekař was perhaps the most influential Czech historian after František Palacký, and was the leading member of the Goll school in Czech historiography that set out to revise Palacký's romantic nationalistic historiography through rigorous criticism of historical sources. Trained by Jaroslav Goll in Prague and abroad in historical seminars in Erlangen and Berlin, Pekař went beyond historical positivism to achieve mastery in combining political and economic themes through the medium of his cultivated prose. He soon became involved in major academic controversies dominating Czech intellectual life, especially with T.G. Masaryk, the future founder of the Czechoslovak Republic. Pekař's tastes were distinctly conservative, molded by agrarian Catholicism; he detested growing proletarianization and feared revolutionary socialism.

Pekař's baptism of fire was in connection with his critical analysis of the so-called Manuscript Forgeries "discovered" in 1817 and 1818. Even the great Palacký did not dare to touch upon their dubious authenticity. The next two generations, however, including Goll, Masaryk, and the young Pekař, willing to risk becoming outcasts in the polarized Czech society, did dare. Pekař's next significant public controversy was his rebuttal of the renowned German historian Theodor Mommsen for the latter's vilification of the Czechs as "apostles of barbarism" (*Neue Freie Presse*, 31 October 1897). Mommsen, "without knowing our history," Pekař complained, had decided to throw in his name behind the Bohemian Germans in their fight for the maintenance of language privileges. In *Nejstarší kronika česká* (The Oldest Czech Chronicle, 1903), and in *Die Wenzels- und Ludmila-Legenden und die Echtheit Christians* (The Wenceslas and Ludmila Legends and their Authenticity as Christians, 1906), Pekař challenged many established views on the earliest Czech legends and chronicles. In 1909 his finest book, *Kniha o Kosti* (The Book of Kost) came out. Here Pekař captured the complex relationship between man and land in his native region of north-western Bohemia during and after the Thirty Years' War. Pekař's continuous immersion in social and agrarian history resulted in the publication of *České katastry, 1654–1789* (Bohemian Land Registers, 1913), in which he proved that the Czech lands had carried the major burden of taxation for the Habsburg monarchy during the Turkish Wars.

In 1912 Pekař published the article "Masarykova česká filosofie" (Masaryk's Czech Philosophy), considered his finest polemic, convincingly destroying as teleological mystification of the Czech past the views of his professorial colleague, T.G. Masaryk, on the pseudohistorical connection between Hussitism and the Czech Reformation. During World War I, Pekař, always a staunch defender of the historical Czech Constitution (Böhmisches Staatsrecht), hoped that loyalty to the Habsburg dynasty would be rewarded by an increase in Czech autonomy against the forces of Pan-Germanism. He could never conceive the emergence of a sovereign and independent Czech State with Slovakia. Thus, the three most prominent Czech historians, Pekař himself, his teacher Jaroslav Goll, and fellow-historian Josef Šusta, refused to sign the 1917 Declaration of Czech Writers demanding self-determination. However, when the creation of the Czechoslovak Republic became irreversible, Pekař performed a mental somersault and in his December 1918 address greeted the independent Czechoslovak state "with the most jubilant cry," explicitly saying that the new state was the fruit of the systematic work of Czech historians over generations – and not the product of Masaryk's recent foreign action.

Pekař's political conservatism became more pronounced, and he criticized the new land reform in Czechoslovakia, which divided large aristocratic estates for the benefit of smallholders. In press articles he blamed the Bolsheviks and Jews alike for the collapse of the old order. He was opposed to the one-sided cult of Hussitism, which now received official support from the government. His favorite era was the Baroque, stigmatized by the Catholic Counter-Reformation in the language of Czech patriots as the "Epoch of Darkness," but seen by Pekař as the birthplace of modern Czech nation. Hence Pekař's last major work, on the Hussite period, *Žižka a jeho doba* (Žižka and His Era, 1927–33), and numerous smaller monographs dealt with the

significance of the Battle of the White Mountain and the cult of Bohemian saints such as St. Wenceslas and St. John of Nepomuk. The polemics with Jan Slavík and other historians over Žižka and Hussitism overlapped with the renewed debate on "the meaning of Czech history" and its periodization. In a lecture in 1928 Pekař reminded his audience that he, alone among the Goll school of empirical historians, had actually written a book with a philosophy of Czech history. He meant his textbook for Czechoslovak high schools, originally published under the *ancien régime* in 1914 as *Dějiny naší říše* (History of Our Empire, 1914) – in which he emphasized the decisive influence of Europe via Germany as the central factor in Czech history – just as Western Europe had been decisively influenced by the Orient and antiquity during earlier centuries. In 1935, on President Masaryk's 85th birthday, Pekař appeared for the last time as the grand interpreter of Czech destiny, graciously forgiving Masaryk his past methodical mistakes. Though considered by many as the only plausible rival of Masaryk, Pekař never showed ambition to become the presidential candidate of the Catholic right during the 1935 campaign.

In his endeavor to improve Czech-German relations, Pekař underrated the brutal nature of Hitler's dictatorship. He thus fell an easy prey to unscrupulous manipulators such as Josef Pfitzner, a history professor from the German University of Prague and a Sudeten German activist. Pekař did not live to witness the tragic year of 1938, but during the German occupation his name was misused by Nazi propaganda to foster collaboration with the Reich and to outweigh the legacy of Palacký and Masaryk. After the war communist propagandists condemned Pekař as the leading ideologue of counterrevolution. Since the "Prague Spring" of 1968, however, Pekař's work has enjoyed a remarkable recovery among the Czech public, partly because of the official anathema that lasted until the end of 1989, but mostly because of the extraordinary range and quality of his historical analysis, combined with a rare gift for a balanced synthesis, both of which make his work unusually fresh and insightful in the present crisis of statehood and national identity in Eastern Europe.

MILAN HAUNER

Biography

Born 12 April 1870. Educated at Czech University, Prague; postgraduate study, University of Erlangen and University of Berlin; Habilitation, 1895. Taught at Czech University, Prague, 1897–1937: professor of Austrian history, 1905–18, then professor of Czech history, 1918–37. Elected rector of Charles University, Prague, 1931. Editor, *Český časopis historický* (Czech Historical Journal), 1897–1937. Died 23 January 1937.

Principal Writings

Dějiny Valdštejnského spiknutí 1630–1634 (History of the Wallenstein Conspiracy), 1895; second edition 1934; in German as *Wallenstein: Tragödie einer Verschwörung*, 1936

Nejstarší kronika česká (The Oldest Czech Chronicle), 1903

Die Wenzels- und Ludmila-Legenden und die Echtheit Christians (The Wenceslas and Ludmila Legends and Their Authenticity as Christians), 1906

Kniha o Kosti (The Book of Kost), 2 vols., 1909–11

"Masarykova česká filosofie" (Masaryk's Czech Philosophy), *Český časopis historický* (Czech Historical Journal) 18 (1912); special issue Prague 1927

České katastry, 1654–1789 (Bohemian Land Registers), 1913
Dějiny naší říše (History of Our Empire), 1914
Bílá Hora (The White Mountain), 1921
Dějiny československé (Czechoslovak History), 1921; in German as *Tschechoslowakische Geschichte*, 1988
Tři kapitoly z boje o svatého Jana Nepomuckého (Three Chapters from the Struggle of St. John of Nepomuk), 1921
Žižka a jeho doba (Žiška and His Era), 4 vols., 1927–33
Svatý Václav (St. Wenceslas), 1929, 1932
O smyslu českých dějin (On the Meaning of Czech History), 1977

Further Reading

Hanzal, Josef, ed., *Josef Pekař: na cestě k samostatnosti* (Josef Pekař: On the Road to Independence), Prague: Mlada Fronta, 1993

Hauner, Milan, "The Meaning of Czech History: Masaryk versus Pekař," in Harry Hanak, ed., *T.G. Masaryk: Statesman and Cultural Force*, 3 vols., London: Macmillan, 1987; New York: St. Martin's Press, 1989–90

Hauner, Milan, "Josef Pekař: Interpreter of Czech History," *Czechoslovak and Central European Journal* 10 (1991), 13–35

Kanturková, Eva, ed., *Pekařovské studie* (Essays on Pekař), 2 vols., Prague: Academia, 1995

Klik, Josef, ed., *Listy úcty a přátelství* (Letters of Reverence and Friendship), Prague, 1941

Kučera, Martin, *Pekař proti Masarykovi* (Pekař contra Masaryk), Prague: Masaryka, 1995

Kutnar, František, ed., *Josef Pekař: Postavy a problémy českých dějin* (Personalities and Problems of Czech History), Prague: Vyšehrad, 1970

Kutnar, František, *Přehledné dějiny českého a slovenského písemnictví* (Historical Survey of Czech and Slovak Historiography), vol.2, Prague: SPN, 1978

Masaryk, Tomáš, *The Meaning of Czech History*, edited by René Wellek, Chapel Hill: University of North Carolina Press, 1974

Pachta, Jan, *J. Pekař: ideolog kontrarevoluce* (J. Pekař: The Ideologue of Counterrevolution), Prague, 1948

Pachta, Jan, *Pekař a pekařovština v českém dějepisectvi* (Pekar and His Pseudo-Science in Czech Historiography), Brno: Rovnost, 1950

Plaschka, Richard G., *Von Palacký bis Pekař: Geschichtswissenschaft und Nationalbewusstsein bei den Tschechen* (From Palacký to Pekař: Czech Historiography and National Consciousness), Wiener Archiv für Geschichte des Slawentums und Osteuropas, vol.1, Graz: Böhlaus, 1955

Slavík, Jan, *Pekař contra Masaryk* (Pekar Against Masaryk), Prague: Ein, 1929

Pelliot, Paul 1878–1945

French historian of China

Paul Pelliot's career and his scholarly activities fall more or less neatly into two parts. Born in Paris in 1878, he graduated in Sanskrit and Chinese at the Sorbonne, where he studied under Sylvain Lévi, the leading French sinologist of the period, before joining the Mission archéologique d'Indochine in Hanoi in 1899. This institution was in the process of changing its title to the Ecole française d'Extrême Orient and expanding the geographical range of its activities accordingly. It needed to enhance the size and increase the range of its library, and Pelliot made annual journeys into China from 1900 to 1902 to acquire books for it. He also started publishing the substantial body of articles on a wide range of Chinese and Southeast Asian topics that would mark the whole of his scholarly career.

Among the earliest of these was his 1903 study of the Cambodian kingdom of Fu-nan.

Pelliot's proven skills as book collector and experience of travel in China made him, despite his relative youth, the obvious leader for a three-man mission, sent in 1906 under the aegis of the Academie Française to try to obtain books and manuscripts in China, and in particular in Chinese Turkestan, following the recent great success of the British expedition led by Aurel Stein. Pelliot's extraordinary linguistic gifts – he had a capacious memory and would become fluent in 13 languages – gave him considerable diplomatic advantages, and at Tunhuang enabled him to select the printed books and manuscripts, which were in Tibetan, Uighur, Tokharian, Sogdian, and Sanskrit, as well as Chinese, with particular skill, despite the secretive and pressured nature of the conditions under which he had to work. On his return to Paris in 1909 he brought with him more than 30,000 books and between 4000 and 5000 manuscripts. Subsequent personal attacks on his integrity and on the account that he gave of his activities were dispelled, not least by Stein's endorsement and the account that he gave of the difficulties he too had faced when working at Tun-huang. Pelliot in turn inspected Stein's more substantial – if less discriminatingly selected – haul of manuscripts in London, with a view to cataloguing them. This, like many of his other projects, was to prove abortive.

The second phase of Pelliot's career began in 1911 with his appointment, in recognition of his achievements in China, to a specially created chair in the Collège de France. Here, apart from a brief period of diplomatic service during World War I, he would remain teaching up to his death. Additional honors that he received included election to the Academie des Inscriptions et Belles Lettres in 1921 and to the presidency of the Société Asiatique in 1936. He was long recognized as France's foremost sinologist and East Asian specialist, and taught most of the leading scholars in these fields of the next generation. His own work was particularly concerned with the western border provinces and with the neighbors of China rather than with the heartlands of the empire. As a scholar Pelliot was particularly noted for his insistence upon the inclusion of full and detailed source references in his work, something that had previously not been taken so seriously. While he continued to publish numerous articles on a wide range of historical, literary, and linguistic topics, notably in the *Journal Asiatique*, the *Bulletin de l'Ecole française d'Extrême Orient*, and *T'oung-pao* (of which he became joint editor in 1920 and sole editor in 1925), he completed very few larger-scale projects. While eight volumes of catalogues of the materials that he brought back from his 1906–09 mission to China were published between 1914 and 1918, he himself failed to produce any substantial text to accompany the four books of photographs of the expedition that appeared as *Les Grottes de Touenhouang* (The Grottoes of Dunhuang, 1920–24). Likewise, although he agreed in 1926 to produce a revised and expanded edition of the book on the early history of printing in China by the American sinologist Thomas Francis Carter, this was eventually reprinted with only a short introduction by Pelliot. He had, however, devoted a course at the Collège de France to the subject and begun work on a book of his own. This, like the materials for ten other books, was found unfinished at his death. It has been suggested that the requirement for professors at the Collège de France to produce an entirely new course of lectures each year explains the large number of such books that he was writing and his failure to publish them. To this should be added the very wide range of the subjects that he was working on, apparently simultaneously. These included editions of the Mongol *Secret History* of c.1240, of a 14th-century Arab-Mongol dictionary, and of a Cambodian descriptive text. The first of these was to be accompanied by a translation, and he was also working on a French version of the first part of the history of the Mongols of Rashid al-Din. There were also monographs in preparation on the Kalmuks, on T'ang dynasty sources relating to the history of Tibet, on the history of the Golden Horde, and on the famous Nestorian inscription at Si-ngan-fu. In his own lifetime Pelliot had produced a well-regarded historical survey, *Haute Asie* (Inner Asia, 1931), but much of his major scholarly work would be published only posthumously. This began almost immediately after his death, under the auspices of the Academie des Inscriptions. Not all of the manuscripts were far enough advanced for publication and the process faltered after the fourth volume of his posthumous works appeared in 1953. One or two more, notably the *Notes critiques d'histoire kalmouke* (Critical Notes on Kalmuk History, 1960) and the *Recherches sur les Chrétiens d'Asie Centrale et d'Extrême-Orient* (Researches on the Christians of Central Asia and the Far East, 1973) followed later.

ROGER COLLINS

See also Maspero; Mongol

Biography

Born Paris, 28 May 1878. Studied Sanskrit and Chinese at the Sorbonne. Member, Mission archéologique d'Indochine (later the Ecole française d'Extrême Orient), Hanoi, 1899–1909; traveled extensively in China buying books and manuscripts, 1900–09; chair in Chinese history, Collège de France, 1911–45. Served in World War I in military and as a diplomat. Died Paris, 26 October 1945.

Principal Writings

Les Grottes de Touen-houang (The Grottoes of Dunhuang), 6 vols., 1920–24
Haute Asie (Inner Asia), 1931
Editor and translator, *Histoire secrète des Mongols* (Secret History of the Mongols), 1949
Translator with Louis Hambis, *Histoire des campagnes de Genghis Khan*, vol. 1, 1951
Editor and translator, *Mémoires sur les coutumes du Cambodge*, by Chou Ta-kuan, revised edition, 1951; abridged in English as *Notes on the Customs of Cambodia*, 1967
Notes on Marco Polo, 3 vols., 1959–73
Notes critiques d'histoire kalmouke (Critical Notes on Kalmuk History), 1960
Histoire ancienne du Tibet, 1961
Recherches sur les Chrétiens d'Asie Centrale et d'Extrême-Orient (Researches on the Christians of Central Asia and the Far East), 1973

Further Reading

Hopkirk, Peter, *Foreign Devils on the Silk Road: The Search for Lost Cities and Treasures of Chinese Central Asia*, London: Murray, 1980

Pérez, Louis A., Jr. 1943–

US historian of Latin America

Louis A. Pérez, Jr. is the leading contemporary historian of Cuba writing in the English language. Since the 1976 publication of his first major work, *Army Politics in Cuba, 1898–1958*, Pérez has continued to produce solid scholarly works dealing with Cuban politics and society since 1875. In this regard, he has successfully led the movement, particularly in the United States, of reviving an interest in Cuban historical issues outside the 1959 Castro Revolution.

Pérez has incorporated into his writings various groups who have traditionally been minimized in the histories of Latin America, especially blacks and women. In addition, his writings tend to share a common theme: Cuban history has been a history of revolution, and that revolutionary impulse has been shaped and determined by the actions of others – notably Spain and the United States. While this statement surely seems to fit most of the islands of the Caribbean, what Pérez and the "revisionist" Cuban historians have argued is that the actions by the United States stifled a modern nationalist revolution in Cuba toward the end of the 19th century.

Pérez's works have complemented, and eclipsed, Hugh Thomas' monumental *Cuba: The Pursuit of Freedom* (1971), which set the standard for authoritative English-language histories of the Caribbean island and its people. Historiographically, Pérez has provided the English-speaking world with both monographs and bibliographic collections, thus enriching the field of Cuban history. Pérez's works on Cuba have focused primarily on the late colonial to pre-1959 Revolution period of Cuban history, an area that is generally neglected by international historians. Cuban historians, especially since the Revolution, have tended to write overtly nationalist and Marxist interpretations of Cuban history after independence, while North American scholars have tended to focus on either social or diplomatic history. In this regard, Pérez has produced materials in both social and diplomatic history, having published works on banditry, education, Cuban exiles at the beginning of the century, and Protestant missionaries on the island. In general, Pérez's works are objective in that they provide a balanced analysis and interpretation of the facts. His works are well researched, utilizing archival materials both inside and outside of Cuba.

H. MICHEAL TARVER

See also Cuba; Latin American: National

Biography

Born New York City, 5 June 1943. Received BA, Pace University, 1965; MA, University of Arizona, 1966; PhD, University of New Mexico, 1970. Taught (rising to professor), University of South Florida; and University of North Carolina. Married 1965 (2 children).

Principal Writings

Army Politics in Cuba, 1898–1958, 1976
Intervention, Revolution, and Politics in Cuba, 1913–1921, 1978
Cuba Between Empires, 1878–1902, 1983
Cuba under the Platt Amendment, 1902–1934, 1986

Cuba: Between Reform and Revolution, 1988
Lords of the Mountain: Social Banditry and Peasant Protest in Cuba, 1878–1918, 1989
Cuba and the United States: Ties of Singular Intimacy, 1990
A Guide to Cuban Collections in the United States, 1991
Essays on Cuban History: Historiography and Research, 1995

Pessen, Edward 1920–1992
US social historian

Edward Pessen belonged to a generation of historians who redefined American social history, challenging accepted verities concerning the United States and relying heavily upon the use of quantitative data. A native of New York City, where except for a two-year period at Fisk University during the 1950s and occasional years abroad later, he spent his entire life, he was educated at Columbia University in the late 1940s and early 1950s. Pessen was much influenced by and a product of the "Columbia group" of anticommunist New York liberal intellectuals centering around Lionel Trilling, Daniel Bell, Richard Hofstadter, and the journals *Partisan Review* and *Commentary*. In many ways he represented the group's left-wing, critical aspects rather than its endorsement, however qualified, of the status quo, an outlook which meant that he bridged the often yawning chasm between the New York intellectuals on the one hand and the New Left and proponents of the "new" social history on the other. Unlike many of the latter, however, he not only demanded meticulous accuracy of himself, but also followed his mentors in laying great stress upon style and literacy. In his *Who's Who in America* entry, Pessen wrote: "I have made trans-Atlantic calls to check the accuracy of a footnote. As author, I love writing sentences that communicate my thoughts clearly and interestingly. Since good writing, like good pitching, requires a change of pace, I try to vary the rhythm, mood, and length of my sentences. As an iconoclastic historian, I feel a special obligation to say what I have to say lucidly and attractively in order to gain a sympathetic hearing for what I have been told are my provocative ideas."

Because of heavy teaching commitments, Pessen began to publish extensively relatively late in his career, when he reached his late forties. Initially, he concentrated upon the Jacksonian period, publishing articles and a well-received book, *Most Uncommon Jacksonians* (1967), on radical labor leaders of the time, whom he characterized as "atypical men whose denunciations of society testified . . . more to their radical state of mind than to the actual state of things in America." Several edited collections of readings and essays and the synthesis *Jacksonian America* (1969), a volume described by a reviewer as "an updated codification of the Columbia School," were marked by their readiness to regard politics as an expression of the broader society, rather than the reverse. Pessen suggested that Jacksonian America was relatively inegalitarian and exhibited pronounced differences in income, themes that he explored further in *Riches, Class and Power before the Civil War* (1973). In this book Pessen employed a wealth of statistical analysis to challenge the hallowed Tocquevillian assumptions that the United States was characterized by high social mobility and relatively limited income differentials.

Pessen then proceeded to turn a skeptical floodlight upon another hallowed American belief, the idea that presidents generally enjoyed fairly humble origins and that a disadvantaged background was a positive asset in attaining the presidency. *The Log Cabin Myth* (1984) scrutinized the antecedents of all occupants of that office from George Washington to Ronald Reagan, discovering that, although aspirants to the presidency often claimed modest origins, in reality most came from relatively well-to-do and many from wealthy families.

In his later years Pessen wrote many short pieces on sports, particularly baseball, an abiding passion, but his somewhat selfconsciously iconoclastic outlook remained. His final work, *Losing Our Souls* (1993), published posthumously, was highly critical of American tactics in the Cold War, condemning what he saw as inflated US rhetoric, exaggerations of the Soviet threat, the undermining of democratic freedoms at home and abroad, the growth of an expensive and economically unsound military-industrial complex, and thousands of unnecessary deaths in Third World countries. He argued that, although Soviet behavior was often "deplorable" and unpleasant, this had not constituted a threat to United States security sufficient to justify the military buildup and excessively antagonistic attitudes that his country displayed during the Cold War. By the end of his life Pessen, though trained in the Columbia school, had essentially accepted the New Left outlook. Challenging US triumphalism at the ending of the Cold War, he remained a dissenter to the last.

PRISCILLA M. ROBERTS

See also Prucha; United States: 19th Century

Biography
Born New York City, 31 December 1920. Worked as a welder before serving in the US Army infantry, 1944–45. Received BA, Columbia University, 1947, MA 1948, PhD 1954. Taught at City College of New York, 1948–54; Fisk University, 1954–56; Staten Island Community College, 1956–70; and Baruch College and City University Graduate Center, 1970–92. Married Adele Barlin, 1940 (3 daughters, 2 sons). Died Miami, 22 December 1992.

Principal Writings
Most Uncommon Jacksonians: The Radical Leaders of the Early Labor Movement, 1967
Jacksonian America: Society, Personality, and Politics, 1969; revised 1978
Riches, Class, and Power before the Civil War, 1973
Editor, *Three Centuries of Social Mobility in America*, 1974
The Log Cabin Myth: The Social Backgrounds of the Presidents, 1984
Losing Our Souls: The American Experience in the Cold War, 1993

Further Reading
Hamerow, Theodore S., *Reflections on History and Historians*, Madison: University of Wisconsin Press, 1987
Jacoby, Russell, *The Last Intellectuals*, New York: Basic Books, 1987
Jumonville, Neil, *Critical Crossings: The New York Intellectuals in Postwar America*, Berkeley: University of California Press, 1991
Kraus, Michael, and Davis D. Joyce, *The Writing of American History*, revised edition, Norman: University of Oklahoma Press, 1985
Novick, Peter, *That Noble Dream: The "Objectivity Question" and the American Historical Profession*, Cambridge and New York: Cambridge University Press, 1988

Thelen, David P., Jonathan M. Wiener, John D'Emilio, Herbert
Aptheker, Gerda Lerner, Christopher Lasch, John Higham, Carl
N. Degler, and David Levering Lewis, "A Round Table: What
Has Changed and Not Changed in American Historical Practice?"
Journal of American History 76 (1989), 393–478
Veysey, Laurence R., "The 'New' Social History in the Context of
American Historical Writing," *Reviews in American History* 7
(March 1979), 1–12

Pevsner, Nikolaus 1902–1983
British (German-born) architectural historian

Nikolaus Pevsner was one of the century's most well-known
historians of art and architecture. One of the first to turn a
critical eye on contemporary creations, he was particularly
influential in helping a modern audience comprehend the
historical background of his subject. Educated in Leipzig,
Pevsner settled in England in 1935. He was the editor of the
Pelican History of Art series from its inception in 1953, and
of the 46 volumes of *The Buildings of England*, of which he
wrote 38. His *Pioneers of the Modern Movement from William
Morris to Walter Gropius* (1936) constructed a lineage of the
Modern movement that was rooted in the English Arts and
Crafts movement, included Art Nouveau and architects such
as Frank Lloyd Wright, Tony Garnier, Adolf Loos, and Peter
Behrens, and culminated in the Bauhaus. He viewed modernism
as the style that expressed the essence of the 20th century
and considered the triumph of rationalism, functionalism, and
streamlined design as inevitable. His emphasis on the social
role of design also led him to *An Enquiry into Industrial Art
in England* (1937), an empirical study partly based on interviews. In the 1950s Pevsner toned down his rigorous advoca-
tion of modernism and announced that the "style of the straight
line and the annihilated ornament is not the whole modern
style of design." Indeed, in *The Englishness of English Art*
(1955) he declared picturesque informality as the essence of
British culture. *Architectural Review*, of which Pevsner, along
with J.M. Richards, was the most active editor, also supported
such "new humanism."

Pevsner popularized art history. *An Outline of European
Architecture* (1942) was aimed at a broad public as was the monumental *The Buildings of England* (1951–74), which covered all
the English counties. This was based on the German Dehio guide
and was of methodical thoroughness based on countless histories,
local guides, and Pevsner's firsthand visual survey.

Architectural history provided a foundation of fact and
theory for the English conservation movement that swelled in
the 1960s, and Pevsner supported the cause by becoming the
chairman of the Victorian Society in 1963. The sudden surge
of interest in Victorian architecture, however, took him somewhat aback as did the popularity of Neo Art Nouveau. Pesvner
criticized the return of historicism – the interest in imitating
past styles – which he considered outmoded. However, he also
recognized his neglect of certain Art Nouveau architects by
featuring Antoni Gaudí and Antonio Sant'Elia in the new
edition of *Pioneers of the Modern Movement*.

With the publication of David Watkin's *Morality and
Architecture* (1977) a bitter controversy erupted. Watkin
argued that the ideological base of *Pioneers* was the Hegelian

Geistesgeschichte, an interpretation of history as the unfolding
of the will of the spirit. Such historicism considered artistic
expression as one manifestation of the "spirit of the age," or
Zeitgeist. Watkin's critique coincided with the development of
postmodernism. Some criticized the destructive effect of
modernism on many cities and towns. Others noticed how
Pevsner's political stance caused him to ignore important
aspects of architectural history, such as the role of patronage
and the relationship between interior decoration and architecture. Almost everyone agrees however on the immense contribution of Pevsner not only in making Britain a center of art
history, but also in greatly popularizing the field.

H. HAZEL HAHN

See also Design

Biography

Nikolaus Bernhard Leon Pevsner. Born Leipzig, Germany,
30 January 1902, son of a fur trader. Educated at St. Thomas's
School, Leipzig; attended universities of Leipzig, Munich, Berlin, and
Frankfurt; received PhD in history of art and architecture, University
of Frankfurt, 1924. Assistant keeper, Dresden Gallery, 1924–28;
lecturer in history of art and architecture, Göttingen, 1929–33; left
Germany, 1933; settled in England (naturalized 1946); taught
history of art, Birkbeck College, London, 1942–69; Slade professor
of fine art, Cambridge University, 1949–55; fellow, St. John's
College, Cambridge, 1950–55; Slade professor of fine art, Oxford
University, 1968–69. Married Karola Kurlbaum, 1923 (died 1963;
2 sons, 1 daughter). Knighted 1969. Died London, 18 August 1983.

Principal Writings

Barockmalerei in den romanischen Ländern (Baroque Art in the
    Latin Countries), 1928
*Pioneers of the Modern Movement from William Morris to Walter
    Gropius*, 1936; reprinted as *Pioneers of Modern Design from
    William Morris to Walter Gropius*, 1949
An Enquiry into Industrial Art in England, 1937
Academies of Art, Past and Present, 1940
An Outline of European Architecture, 1942; 7th edition, 1968
High Victorian Design: A Study of the Exhibits of 1851, 1951
General Editor, *The Buildings of England*, 46 vols., 1951–74
General Editor, *The Pelican History of Art*, 1953–
The Englishness of English Art, 1955
With Jean Cassou and Emile Langui, *The Sources of Modern Art*,
    1962
With John Fleming and Hugh Honour, *The Penguin Dictionary of
    Architecture*, 1966
The Sources of Modern Architecture and Design, 1968
The History of Building Types, 1976

Further Reading

Banham, Reyner, *Theory and Design in the First Machine Age*,
    London: Architectural Press, and New York: Praeger, 1960
Harbison, Robert, "With Pevsner in England," *Architectural Review*
    176 (1984), 1052
Irace, Fulvio, ed., *Nikolaus Pevsner: la trama della storia* (Nikolaus
    Pevsner: The Thread of a Story), Milan: Guerinie, 1992
Madge, Pauline, "An Enquiry into Pevsner's Enquiry," *Journal of
    Design History* 1/2 (1988), 113–26
Muthesius, Stefan, "Nikolaus Pevsner," in Heinrich Dilly, ed.,
    Altmeister moderner Kunstgeschichte, Berlin: Reimer, 1990
Porphyrios, Demetri, ed., *On the Methodology of Architectural
    History*, London: Architectural Design Profile, and New York: St.
    Martin's Press, 1981

Phillips, Ulrich Bonnell 1877–1934

US historian of the American South

Over the first half of the 20th century Ulrich Bonnell Phillips reigned as the premier historian of the antebellum American South and black slavery. Influenced by his family's Georgia plantation background, and his graduate training under Frederick Jackson Turner and William A. Dunning, Phillips wrote about his native region with affection, and interpreted slavery as a paternalistic, though economically flawed, institution.

Phillips' *Georgia and State Rights* (1902) analyzed his state's antebellum political system by mapping changing political allegiances over time. This study won the American Historical Association's Justin Winsor prize. Over the next seven years Phillips dug deeply into the South's primary sources – plantation and census records, diaries, newspapers, and government documents. He utilized these rich sources effectively, publishing the path-breaking *A History of Transportation in the Eastern Cotton Belt to 1860* (1908) and 15 articles in the leading historical and economic journals of his day. Phillips' pioneer scholarship dealt with previously unexplored economic themes – capitalization of the region's railroads, plantation operations, the unprofitability of black slave labor, and slavery's long-term ill effects on the South's economy. In these years Phillips also labored in the cause of Progressivism, publishing widely in popular magazines and newspapers in favor of southern agricultural reform.

Always enamored of primary sources, in *Plantation and Frontier* (1909) Phillips amassed a vast documentary collection of excerpts gleaned from planters' diaries, travelers' journals, and merchants' account books. He also edited *The Correspondence of Robert Toombs, Alexander H. Stephens, and Howell Cobb* (1911) and published his only biography, *The Life of Robert Toombs* (1913). During his career Phillips contributed many important articles on comparative systems of slavery, slave economics, and slave crime. His most significant and controversial essay, "The Central Theme of Southern History," appeared in 1928. According to Phillips, one theme – the desire to keep their region "a white man's country" – solidified white southerners throughout their history. Despite his many writings, Phillips' reputation rests on his two best-known works, *American Negro Slavery* (1918) and *Life and Labor in the Old South* (1929).

American Negro Slavery was the first systematic analysis of slavery in the entire South. It surpassed in focus and content previous books on North American slavery, and has influenced virtually all subsequent books on the subject. His chapters on West African culture, the slave trade, Caribbean slavery, and slavery in the North actually added little to previous scholarship, but Phillips' use of the comparative method to examine slavery in the West Indies offered a fresh perspective to American historians. Phillips also made penetrating observations regarding the mechanics of plantation agriculture, the South's plain folk, and overseers. He focused predominantly, however, on the masters and their slaves.

He identified a sense of fellowship between the two, a relation characterized by "propriety, proportion and cooperation." Through years of living together, Phillips maintained, blacks and whites developed a rapport not between equals, but between dependent unequals. Under slavery the two racial groups became interdependent – the blacks "always with the social mind and conscience of the whites, as the whites in turn were within the minds and conscience of the blacks." Though masters controlled the privileges that the slaves enjoyed, Phillips considered blacks "by no means devoid of influence." Phillips thus interpreted slavery as a labor system "shaped by mutual requirements, concessions and understandings, producing reciprocal codes of conventional morality" and responsibility.

Life and Labor in the Old South added little that was new to his interpretation of slavery. Again he described slavery as an economic cancer but a vital mode of racial control. These themes can be traced back to his earliest writings. In this book Phillips modified neither his view that blacks were inherently inferior nor his belief that they retained few of their African cultural traits after enslavement. "The bulk of the black personnel," Phillips explained, "was notoriously primitive, uncouth, improvident and inconstant, merely because they were Negroes of the time." Less detailed and presented in a more attractive literary style than *American Negro Slavery*, Phillips's *Life and Labor in the Old South* was a general synthesis rather than a monograph. He devoted considerable space to the different groups that lived in the South, including "Redskins and Latins," "The Plain People," and "The Gentry."

In his last years, he began what he often called his "big job" – a 3-volume history of the South. The first volume, *Life and Labor in the Old South*, was so well received by reviewers that it was awarded a large cash prize from the publishers Little Brown. The volume's success also earned Phillips the year-long Albert Kahn traveling fellowship: in 1929–30 he used it to observe blacks and other laborers in tropical climates worldwide.

Phillips never lived to complete his trilogy on the South and his research on the region's political history went unpublished. Scholars remember him for his original use of plantation and other manuscript sources, for his interpretation of slavery as a benign yet unprofitable institution, and for his condescending and patronizing descriptions of blacks as childlike inferiors.

JOHN DAVID SMITH

See also African American; Fogel; Genovese; Slavery: Modern; Stampp; United States: 19th Century

Biography

Born La Grange, Georgia, 1877. Received BA, University of Georgia, 1897, MA 1899; PhD, Columbia University, 1902. Taught at University of Wisconsin, 1902–08; Tulane University, 1908–11; University of Michigan, 1911–29; and Yale University, 1929–34. Married Lucie Mayo-Smith, 1911 (2 sons and 1 daughter survived childhood). Died New Haven, Connecticut, 21 January 1934.

Principal Writings

Georgia and State Rights: A Study of the Political History of Georgia from the Revolution to the Civil War, with Particular Regard to Federal Relations, 1902

A History of Transportation in the Eastern Cotton Belt to 1860, 1908

Plantation and Frontier, 2 vols., 1909

Editor, *The Correspondence of Robert Toombs, Alexander H. Stephens, and Howell Cobb*, 1911

The Life of Robert Toombs, 1913

American Negro Slavery: A Survey of the Supply, Employment, and Control of Negro Labor as Determined by the Plantation Regime, 1918

"The Central Theme of Southern History," *American Historical Review* 24 (1928), 30–43

Life and Labor in the Old South, 1929

The Course of the South to Secession, edited by E. Merton Coulter, 1939

The Slave Economy of the Old South: Selected Essays in Economic and Social History, edited by Eugene D. Genovese, 1968 [includes bibliography]

Further Reading

Dillon, Merton, *Ulrich Bonnell Phillips: Historian of the Old South*, Baton Rouge: Louisiana State University Press, 1985

Gray, Wood, "Ulrich Bonnell Phillips," in William T. Hutchinson, ed., *The Marcus W. Jernegan Essays in American Historiography*, Chicago: University of Chicago Press, 1937

Landon, Fred, and Everett E. Edwards, "A Bibliography of the Writings of Professor Ulrich Bonnell Phillips," *Agricultural History* 8 (1934), 196–218

Roper, John Herbert, *U.B. Phillips: A Southern Mind*, Macon, GA: Mercer University Press, 1984

Smith, John David, *An Old Creed for the New South: Proslavery Ideology and Historiography, 1865–1918*, Westport, CT: Greenwood Press, 1985

Smith, John David, "The Historian as Archival Advocate: Ulrich Bonnell Phillips and the Records of Georgia and the South," *American Archivist* 52 (1989), 320–31

Smith, John David, and John C. Inscoe, eds., *Ulrich Bonnell Phillips: A Southern Historian and His Critics*, Westport, CT: Greenwood Press, 1990

Smith, John David, "Ulrich Bonnell Phillips' *Plantation and Frontier*: The Historian as Documentary Editor," *Georgia Historical Quarterly* 77 (1993), 123–43

Smith, John David, "U.B. Phillips's World Tour and the Study of Comparative Plantation Societies," *Yale University Library Gazette* 68 (1994), 157–68

Philosophy of History

The word "history" has two meanings – what historians write or speak, and what historians write or speak about (in German the meanings are marked, although imperfectly, by two separate words, *Historie* and *Geschichte*). Correspondingly, the term "philosophy of history" means an attempt to give a general, theoretical account either of history itself (*Geschichte*) or of historical thinking and writing (*Historie*). The first project is sometimes referred to as synthetic or speculative philosophy of history and the second as analytic or critical philosophy of history. Because *Geschichte* becomes known to us only by the intellectual processes that generate *Historie*, the distinction between the two projects is not as sharp as it seems initially. But it nonetheless remains an essential starting point for thinking about "philosophy of history," because historically two different projects have gone under that name, and because the question of the relation between the two is itself a theoretical issue of some significance. The present article surveys the project of offering a theory of history itself. Philosophy of history understood as an attempt to address historical thinking and writing is surveyed separately in the article Historiology.

The term "philosophy of history" was invented by Voltaire, who in 1765 published *La Philosophie de l'histoire* (*The Philosophy of History*, 1766). Although Voltaire invented the term he did not invent the thing, for he had no conception of history as a coherent, rational process: instead, he saw it as largely a story of human crimes and follies. A precondition for philosophy of history is the view that history is a rational process and not just a collection of contingencies, for only then can one describe and explain history in the universal theoretical terms of philosophy. Additionally, there needed to be some distance from the view that history is ordained by God, for such a view favored not a philosophy of history but a theologically grounded narrative.

Philosophy of history as understood here is associated above all with 19th-century European thought, although there are earlier foreshadowings of it, as in the *La scienza nuova* (1730; *The New Science*, 1948) of the Neapolitan philosopher Giambattista Vico. Shaken by the upheavals of the French Revolution and of the Napoleonic period, 19th-century intellectuals were deeply interested in history, and especially in historical change. Their interest need not have led to philosophy of history, for the two fields of inquiry had traditionally been distant from each other. Aristotle himself had held that philosophy deals with universals, whereas history deals only with particulars. In the 19th century, however, the distance was lessened by the widespread conviction that history is indeed a rational process.

Nineteenth-century philosophy of history usually involved the belief that progressive tendencies are embedded in history – a view that we can call "embedded progress." As Maurice Mandelbaum pointed out, belief in an inherently progressive tendency in history had precursors in 18th-century thought. First, the belief was rooted in a late 18th-century organicism that viewed the world on the model of a living being, developing over time. When combined with another late 18th- and early 19th-century view, namely, that the world is a unified whole, the notion that history has a single overall tendency was an obvious conclusion. An influential figure along this line was the philosopher and critic Johann Gottfried von Herder. Already in his *Auch eine Philosophie der Geschichte zur Bildung der Menschheit* (1774; *Yet Another Philosophy of History for the Education of Humanity*, 1968), responding to Voltaire, Herder treated individual ages and nations as organic unities whose diversity is to be respected; later, in his *Ideen zur Philosophie der Geschichte der Menschheit* (1785–91; *Reflections on the Philosophy of the History of Mankind*, 1968), he portrayed human history as advancing by a kind of natural evolution, in which different nations pass through different processes of development while nonetheless contributing to the realization of a common humanity. G.W.F. Hegel, most famously in his *Vorlesungen über die Philosophie der Geschichte* (1837; *Lectures on the Philosophy of World History*, 1975), articulated a view of history akin in its holism to the organicist view, with the state passing through stages in which, successively, one man is free, some are free, and finally all are free.

Belief in embedded progress was also rooted in mainstream Enlightenment social theory. Eighteenth-century Enlightenment thinkers had, at best, a tenuous belief in progress, Voltaire being a typical case. Even the marquis de Condorcet (1743–94), in his classic *Esquisse d'un tableau historique des progrès de l'esprit humain* (1795; *Sketch for a Historical Picture of the Progress of the Human Mind*, 1955), did not argue that anything embedded in history guarantees progress. But early in the 19th century the idea of progress came to be linked to the idea of social science. Some Enlightenment social theorists believed that one ought to be able to discover social laws analogous to the laws of nature. A number of influential post-Enlightenment thinkers, beginning with the comte de Saint-Simon (1760–1825), looked for laws of social development, not just for laws of social order. The result was a notion of embedded progress. One important proponent of the idea was Auguste Comte, the founder of the positivist school, in his *Cours de philosophie positive* (1830–42; *The Positive Philosophy*, 1853); another was Herbert Spencer, the British positivist. Especially after the publication of Charles Darwin's *Origin of Species* (1859), which was widely (and wrongly) read as articulating a notion of biological progress, the idea that history has an inherently progressive character was widespread, even pervasive.

The French *La Grande Encyclopédie* (1894) defined "philosophy of history" as "the search for . . . general causes . . . applied to the development of human societies"; it rightly concluded that philosophy of history "still hardly exists as a science." So conceived, philosophy of history was and remained an abject failure. Historians (most notably Leopold von Ranke and Jacob Burckhardt) were deeply hostile to it. Historians rightly saw that a completed philosophy of history would be antithetical to professional historiography, for if one knows the general causes of history one would have little need for the kind of detailed research into particular facts that historians do. In its aims, philosophy of history is closer to social science than to history, but in the 20th century, professionalized social science gave up the attempt to explain society and history generally, and focused instead on specific problems and "middle-range" theories. As for professional philosophers, some addressed issues of historical understanding and explanation, which are matters having to do with *Historie*, but few attended to history itself (*Geschichte*) and one of the most original philosophical minds of the century, Martin Heidegger (1889–1976), went beyond both to a concern with "historicity" (*Geschichtlichkeit*).

To be sure, some 20th-century thinkers – among them, Pitirim Sorokin, Oswald Spengler, and Arnold Toynbee – kept up the quest for general causes, but by the 1990s their efforts had been passé for decades. The most resilient of the 19th-century philosophies of history, the historical materialism of Karl Marx and Friedrich Engels, continued to be seriously defended as late as the 1980s, but communism's collapse and much skeptical and corrosive thinking on the part of intellectuals meant that by the mid-1990s its prestige as a general view of history was very low.

Yet philosophy of history still persists as a ghostly presence behind other projects. As Hayden White showed in *Metahistory* (1973), works of history presuppose philosophies of history, even though historians characteristically refuse to articulate them. Similarly, the philosopher Haskell Fain (1970) pointed out that analytic philosophy of history (concerned with historical thinking and writing – with *Historie*) poses questions of meaning and interpretation that only speculative philosophy of history (concerned with the historical process itself – with

Geschichte) can answer. Finally, even the project of reflecting on the failure of the search for the "general causes" of history comes close to articulating a philosophy of history in its own right.

ALLAN MEGILL

See also Comte; Engels; Hegel; Herder; Historiology; Marx; Spengler; Toynbee; Universal; Vico; Voltaire; White, H.

Further Reading

Barnard, Frederick M., ed., *J.G. Herder on Society and Political Culture*, Cambridge: Cambridge University Press, 1969

Barnard, Frederick M., "Natural Growth and Purposive Development: Vico and Herder," *History and Theory* 18 (1979), 16–36

Comte, Auguste, *Cours de philosophie positive*, 6 vols., Paris: Bachelier, 1830–42; in English as *The Positive Philosophy of Auguste Comte*, London: Chapman, 1853

Condorcet, Marie Jean Antoine Nicolas de Caritat, marquis de, *Esquisse d'un tableau historique des progrès de l'esprit humain*, Paris: Agasse, 1795; in English as *Sketch for a Historical Picture of the Progress of the Human Mind*, New York: Noonday, and London: Weidenfeld and Nicolson, 1955

Fain, Haskell, *Between Philosophy and History: The Resurrection of Speculative Philosophy of History within the Analytic Tradition*, Princeton: Princeton University Press, 1970

Hegel, G.W.F., *Vorlesungen über die Philosophie der Geschichte*, Berlin: Humblot, 1837; in English as *Lectures on the Philosophy of World History: Introduction: Reason in History*, Cambridge and New York: Cambridge University Press, 1975

Herder, J.G., *Ideen zur Philosophie der Geschichte der Menschheit*, 4 vols., 1785–91; in English as *Outlines of a Philosophy of the History of Man*, London: Hansard, 1800; abridged as *Reflections on the Philosophy of the History of Mankind*, Chicago: University of Chicago Press, 1968

Mandelbaum, Maurice, *History, Man, and Reason: A Study in Nineteenth-Century Thought*, Baltimore: Johns Hopkins University Press, 1971

Marx, Karl, and Friedrich Engels, "Die deutsche Ideologie," written 1845–46; published in *Historisch-kritische Gesamtausgabe: Werke, Schriften, Briefe*, vol. 5, edited by David Rjazanov and V.V. Adoratskij, Frankfurt: Marx-Engels-Archiv, 1932; in English as *The German Ideology*, Moscow: Progress, 1964, London: Lawrence and Wishart, 1970, and in Marx and Engels, *Collected Works*, New York: International Publishers, 1975–, vol. 5: 19–539

Meyerhoff, Hans, ed., *The Philosophy of History in Our Time: An Anthology*, Garden City, NY: Doubleday, 1959

Mortet, Ch. and V., "Histoire," *La Grande Encyclopédie* (Paris, 1886–), vol. 20 (1894): 121–50

Vico, Giambattista, *La scienza nuova*, 1725, revised 1730; in English as *The New Science*, Ithaca, NY: Cornell University Press, 1948

Voltaire, *La Philosophie de l'histoire*, 1765; in English as *The Philosophy of History*, London: Allcock, 1766; reprinted 1965

Walsh, W.H., *An Introduction to Philosophy of History*, London: Hutchinson, 1951; revised 1967

White, Hayden V., *Metahistory: The Historical Imagination in Nineteenth-Century Europe*, Baltimore: Johns Hopkins University Press, 1973

Pieri, Piero 1893–1974

Italian military historian

Piero Pieri came to the fore as a military historian after the publication in 1934 of his volume on the reasons for the defeat of the Italian states in the wars that commenced in 1494; a second much amplified version appeared in 1952. Initially his publications were determined by the exigencies of an academic career with but a slight emphasis on war; his breadth of vision tempered his eventual concentration on military matters. A disciple of Gaetano Salvemini, Pieri was to collaborate in editing his master's writings on the Risorgimento. His first publication in 1922 had been on the restoration of the grand-duke of Tuscany in 1814 and its aftermath, which was followed in 1927 by a study of the Arte della Seta of Florence. The former was instrumental in his appointment, originally as professor of 19th-century history, at the University of Naples. There his archival researches produced significant monographs on the defeat of the Neapolitan fleet on 8 January 1799, on the vicissitudes of the government of the kingdom of Naples from July 1799 to March 1808, on the inception of British control of Malta, 1798–1803, on the part played by secret societies in the disturbances of 1820 and 1830, and on the Piedmontese army's campaign of 1849. His history of Messina as a commune (1939) was the outcome of his chair in that city's university.

From 1939, when he moved to the University of Turin, Pieri claimed to be a military historian, focusing on the Renaissance, the 19th century and World War I. However, his *Guerra e politica negli scrittori italiani* (Italian Writers' Views on War and Politics, 1955) spanned the five centuries from Machiavelli to Marselli. He had edited the former's *Arte della guerra* (Art of War) in 1938, and also the correspondence relating to the 1706 Italian campaign of Prince Eugène of Savoy (1936). Pietro Badoglio's rise to general in World War I was the theme of Pieri's last major work in 1974. Previously in 1947 he had published a study on World War I, examining problems inherent in writing its military history, while his *Storia militare del Risorgimento* (A Military History of the Risorgimento, 1962) remains essential reading in its field. His 1938 reconstruction of the Battle of Garigliano of 1503 is a model of its kind, and his excellent *Intorno alla politica estera di Venezia al principio del Cinquecento* (A Study of Venetian Foreign Policy in the Early 16th Century, 1934) serves as testimony that diplomacy can be judged as integral to war studies.

It is Pieri's work on the military crisis of the Italian Renaissance that is most stimulating, original, and influential, although untypically somewhat inadequately documented. Pieri, like several predecessors, sought to explain why, despite the exceptional economic and artistic flowering of the Italian states in the 15th century, these rapidly passed through conquest to foreign domination – itself the prelude to the peninsula's rapid decline. Charles VIII's invasion in 1494 was punctuated by a series of Italian military reverses, usually viewed as the consequence of Italian military inferiority. Pieri deemed that war should not be studied in isolation, or merely in terms of military campaigns. For him war had political ends and was conducted by a state as a last resort, economic and diplomatic endeavors having failed. Accordingly for Pieri war was to be related to the civilization of the states involved, notably their economic, political, and social developments. In practice a historian could but make a selective analysis, which was what Pieri attempted in 1934. There his conclusion was that the Italian crisis occurred essentially because in 1494 and thereafter the Italian powers lacked the political will to survive. Pieri sought to demonstrate this by revealing the political ineptitude of the Italian states, first in the face of a united French nation under a king and, subsequently, when opposed by Ferdinand, king of Aragon, and then by Charles V. His examination of several significant battles showed, he believed, that what determined victory was not Italian military incompetence or cowardice. This view was in conflict with that of Machiavelli who indicated that mercenaries doomed the Italian states to foreign domination. Pieri neglected the fact that Italian commanders fought by "Italian" rules of war, based on Christian morality and supposedly justified by classical models, whereas for the Ultramontanes war was to be won by any means, including surprise attack, giving no quarter (even to the wounded), terrorism, and violence against civilians. It is evident, also, that Pieri underestimated the technological advantages of the French in 1494, in particular the superiority of their mobile cannons.

CECIL H. CLOUGH

Biography

Born Sondrio, 20 August 1893. Studied with Gaetano Salvemini, Scuola Normale Superiore di Pisa, 1912–15. Commissioned in the Alpini, wounded, and twice decorated for valor during World War I. Taught at University of Naples, 1922–35; University of Messina 1936–39; and University of Turin, 1939–74. Arrested by Salò regime, 1945. Married Maria Isotta Bortolotti, 1942. Died Turin, 1974.

Principal Writings

La restaurazione in Toscana (1814–1821) (The Restoration of the Grand Duchy of Tuscany, 1814–1821), 1922
Intorno alla storia dell' arte della seta in Firenze (Aspects of the History of the Silk Guild of Florence), 1927
Le società segrete ed i moti degli anni 1820–21 e 1830–31 (Secret Societies and the Riots of 1820–21 and 1830–31), 1931
La crisi militare italiana nel rinascimento nelle sue relazioni con la crisi politica ed economica (The Italian Military Crisis in Relation to Those Political and Economic Crises in the Renaissance), 1934; revised as *Il rinasciemento e la crisi militare italiana* (The Renaissance and the Italian Military Crises), 1952
Intorno alla politica estera di Venezia al principio del Cinquecento (A Study of Venetian Foreign Policy in the Early 16th Century), 1934
L'Italia nella prima guerra mondiale (1915–1918) (Italy in World War I), 1947
Guerra e politica negli scrittori italiani (Italian Writers' Views on War and Politics), 1955
Editor with Carlo Pischedda, *Scritti sul Risorgimento* (Writings on the Risorgimento), by Gaetano Salvemini, 1962
Storia militare del Risorgimento: guerre e insurrezioni (A Military History of the Risorgimento: The Wars and Insurrections), 1962
With Giorgio Rochat, *Pietro Badoglio*, 1974

Further Reading

Clough, Cecil H., "The Romagna Campaign of 1494," in David Abulafia, ed., *The French Descent into Renaissance Italy, 1494–95: Antecedents and Effects*, Aldershot: Variorum, 1995

Pieroni Bortolotti, Franca 1925–1985
Italian historian of the women's political movement

With her pioneer work *Alle origini del movimento femminile in Italia, 1848–1892* (The Origins of the Women's Movement in Italy, 1963), Franca Pieroni Bortolotti initiated studies on Italian feminism, rediscovering events and personalities that had been ignored both as political subjects and as objects of historical inquiry, despite the numerical strength and widespread diffusion of the suffragist and feminist associations that sprang up in late 19th- and early 20th-century Italy. Many things account for this: the crisis into which feminist organizations had fallen from World War I onward contributed to the process, as later did the fascist regime which dissolved the suffragist organizations or attempted to *fascistizzare* (fascistize) those few that survived. However, the main factor contributing to the oblivion into which the women's movement was consigned was the view, expressed both by Right and Left, that it was politically and socially irrelevant.

In her research Pieroni Bortolotti revealed that, to the contrary, the women's movement was central to any critical reappraisal of the political and social processes that during the Risorgimento and the early years of this century had led to the formation of what has been called the "imperfect democracy" of the contemporary Italian political system. In so doing, she brought a radical innovation to Italian historiography: in seeing events, personalities, and political movements in terms of the place occupied therein by women or hypotheses posited about the role of women in society, Pieroni Bortolotti not only contributed to a deepening of knowledge but brought about a qualitative change in the overall picture of concepts and events. This in turn encouraged a rethinking of analyses, hierarchies of problems, evaluations, and even information pure and simple, regarding the processes through which the identity of post-unitary Italy came to be defined – bringing to light a web of connections and ruptures that had hitherto gone unnoticed by even the most alert historiography. The value of her work, however, went beyond the domain of historical research, extending to the present-day political debate, since it provided the contemporary women's movement and feminist historiography with roots and, thus, historical legitimacy.

The approach adopted by Pieroni Bortolotti, who as a very young woman had participated in the Resistance and was an active member of the Communist party, derived from Togliatti's definition, dating from 1944, of the relationship between women's emancipation and the development of democracy. In addition to this, Pieroni Bortolotti inquired into the profound nature of the process through which, after the "second Risorgimento" – the Resistance – as after the first, Italian women had found themselves pushed to the margins of political life. Her interest in 19th-century democracy also found support in the post-World War II historiographical climate, with its revival of interest in the Risorgimento on the part of many scholars, based on Gramsci's analysis of the formation of the Italian national state. Pieroni Bortolotti's approach followed the teachings of Carlo Morandi, Gaetano Salvemini, and Delio Cantimori. The influence of these masters had found fertile terrain in their pupil, already oriented in two directions that she considered interdependent – the development of an authentic democracy, namely socialism, and the development of a new relationship between the sexes – which were in her view the twin hallmarks of the "profound meaning of anti-Fascism."

Despite its foundational value, *Alle origine del movimento femminile* went almost unnoticed at the time of its publication. Italian culture and society in the 1960s projected a future of progress in which it was claimed that women too would come into their own. They were reluctant to pay too much attention to the limitations and contradictions in the development of what was, after all, a fragile politico-economic system. Pieroni Bortolotti's work was rediscovered more than a decade later, following the appearance of the second of her books devoted to the history of feminism, *Socialismo e questione femminile in Italia* (Socialism and the Woman Question in Italy, 1974) and after the publication of *La liberazione della donna* (The Liberation of Women, 1975), her selection from the writings of the most important exponent of 19th-century feminism, Anna Maria Mozzoni. Those works appeared at the height of the new feminist wave, and thus intersected several questions that Italian women were asking themselves about their history. However, Pieroni Bortolotti's relationship with new feminism was no easy one. To her, the initiator of an important line of research, "the history of women" as a field of inquiry seemed "a nonsense," because "one cannot have a history of one undifferentiated half of the earth's population." It was in these terms that she polemicized against a social history of women severed from the history of society, ideas, economics, and so forth. Once again, this position went against the stream of the growing, Anglophone-inspired, appreciation accorded to the historiography of women, and contributed to the further isolation of Pieroni Bortolotti, viewed by Italian feminists as an academic diehard. The academic establishment, for its part, paid scant attention to her studies, considering women irrelevant as a subject of historical inquiry, so that her career was studded with rejections, despite her many years of teaching at the University of Siena.

In actual fact, her position regarding the history of women was not very distant from what Joan Kelly Gadol or Natalie Zemon Davis were writing at the time about the history of women as a history of sexual roles and of the relationship between the sexes. What Pieroni Bortolotti was proposing was, in fact, a history of women as not only a topic of study, but a perspective from which – starting from the historical experience of women and their condition – she surveyed the entire social, political, and cultural process.

Following her studies of pacifist communist figures and of aspects of the history of the international workers' movement, she developed in the early 1980s a new rapport with the younger generation of feminists. It was to her reading of Sheila Rowbotham's early essays that Pieroni Bortolotti attributed her renewed interest in the comparative investigation of pacifist feminism and workers' internationalism – a theme to which she dedicated her last book, *La donna, la pace, l'Europa* (Women, Peace, Europe), published a week after her death in 1985.

Recognition, albeit tardy, came to Bartolotti, both from academe and from feminist historians, with the relatively widespread diffusion of her writings, now used as university set texts, and with the development of research in sectors of inquiry to which she had pointed the way in her works.

ANNARITA BUTTAFUOCO

Biography

Born Florence, 1925. Received PhD, University of Florence, 1950. Professor of history, University of Siena. Died Florence, 1985.

Principal Writings

Alle origini del movimento femminile in Italia, 1848–1892 (The Origins of the Women's Movement in Italy, 1848–1892), 1963

Francesco Misiano: vita di un internazionalista (Francesco Misiano: Life of an Internationalist), 1972

Socialismo e questione femminile in Italia, 1892–1922 (Socialism and the Woman Question in Italy, 1892–1922), 1974

Editor, *La liberazione della donna* (The Liberation of Women) by Anna Maria Mozzoni, 1975

With Nicola Badaloni, *Movimento operaio e lotta politica a Livorno* (Working-Class Movement and Political Struggle in Livorno), 1977

Le donne della Resistenza antifascista e la questione femminile in Emilia Romagna, 1943–1945 (Women in the Antifascist Resistance and the Woman Question in the Emilia Romagna, 1943–1945), 1978

Femminismo e partiti politici in Italia, 1919–1926 (Feminism and Party Politics in Italy, 1919–1926), 1978

La donna, la pace, l'Europa (Women, Peace, Europe), 1985

Sul movimento politico delle donne: scritti inediti (On the Women's Political Movement: Unpublished Essays), edited by Annarita Buttafuoco, 1987

Pinchbeck, Ivy 1898–1982
British economic historian of women

First published in 1930, and reprinted in 1969, Pinchbeck's pioneering study, *Women Workers and the Industrial Revolution, 1750–1850*, focused on the changes wrought by the Industrial Revolution on the working lives of British women. This study represented the first serious exploration of the work undertaken by women during a period that witnessed rapid agricultural and manufacturing innovation. The importance of this work to the study of British women working within the wage economy cannot be overstated, and as such provided a solid foundation for subsequent scholarship in this challenging and contentious area. Pinchbeck's 2-volume *Children in English Society* (1969–73), co-authored with Margaret Hewitt, detailed the conditions of primarily poor and orphaned children from the 16th to 20th centuries and offered a context for understanding the evolution of legislative and voluntary responses throughout the period.

Pinchbeck was a student of Lilian Knowles (author of *The Industrial and Commercial Revolutions in Great Britain during the Nineteenth Century*, 1921) and Eileen Power, and a younger contemporary of Alice Clark at the London School of Economics, and her work was at the forefront of the emerging academic discipline of economic history. In *Women Workers*, Pinchbeck arrived at the conclusion that women, overall, gained more than they lost from the Industrial Revolution. By contrasting the unsanitary, dangerous, and harsh working conditions of the pre-industrial domestic economy with the factory system and the subsequent protective legislation it engendered, Pinchbeck saw progress in the material condition of women's work. This conclusion was supported by her belief that married women's labor within the home came to be regarded as a sufficient contribution to the family economy, and recognized through the payment of a "family wage" to the male breadwinner. For single women, employment outside the home supplied economic and social independence, and contributed toward the push for greater educational access and female suffrage. Pinchbeck, therefore, falls squarely on the "optimistic" side in the debate over the impact of the Industrial Revolution. She effectively established the intricate relationship between women's domestic labor and the waged economy. Her analysis of household budgets presented as evidence demonstrated not only the monetary value of women's contribution to the household economy, but also the growing reliance on wages over household production.

Pinchbeck produced an impressive amount of information concerning the nature of women's work culled from manuscript sources, copious government reports, and contemporary literature, supplemented by a wide range of secondary readings. However, the dearth of statistical information available for the late 18th and early 19th century resulted in an inability to establish a reliable quantitative database for the study of the impact of the Industrial Revolution upon women workers. Instead, there was a reliance on contemporary literature, such as the 18th-century writings of Daniel Defoe and Arthur Young, whose rambles about the countryside documented how a woman's waged and domestic economies were integrally linked. These accounts were set against the 19th-century testimonies garnered through numerous government-sponsored commissions investigating the status of working women and children, the Poor Laws, and social conditions. In addition, periodical publications and newspapers dating from the mid-18th century furnished contemporary accounts of women's work throughout the period.

Subsequent scholars who have turned their attention to the study of working women have utilized Pinchbeck's impressive collection of facts while not necessarily agreeing with her conclusions. In "Women and the British Economy since 1700," published in *History* in 1974, Eric Richards credited Pinchbeck as the "best source" for her account of the harsh physical conditions of women's work in the pre-industrial period. However, Richards argued that employment opportunities for women contracted during the Victorian period and continued to do so well into the first half of the 20th century. More recently, Deborah Valenze in *The First Industrial Woman* (1995) has contributed to the debate by analyzing the gendered ideology surrounding women's productivity and the rhetoric employed by contemporary commentators to illustrate the process by which women's work, and working women, came to be devalued throughout this period, thereby challenging Pinchbeck's optimistic conclusion.

The impact of the Industrial Revolution on women has come to the fore of academic scholarship only within the last 25 years. Informed by strands in women's and social history, historians have turned their attention to the exploration of the nature of women's work and its changes over time. Pinchbeck was the first to supply a systematic exploration of the economic lives of women during a crucial period in British history. Her work reflects the movement toward the historical contextualization of the socio-economic condition of British women underway in the 1920s and 1930s. By exploring the evidence provided by government commissions such as those investigating the Poor Laws and factory abuses, Pinchbeck was able to paint a compelling picture of female employment in the fields, farms, and workshops of Great Britain.

MARGARET SHKIMBA

See also Childhood; Clark; Social

Biography

Born 9 April 1898. Studied at University College, Nottingham, BA 1920; London School of Economics, MA 1927, PhD 1930. Taught history, Queen Mary's High School, Walsall, 1921–25; lecturer, Workers' Educational Association, London branch, 1929–30; taught (rising to reader) in Department of Sociology, Social Studies and Economics, Bedford College, University of London, 1929–61. Died 10 May 1982.

Principal Writings

Women Workers and the Industrial Revolution, 1750–1850, 1930
With Margaret Hewitt, *Children in English Society*, 2 vols., 1969–73

Pipes, Richard 1923–

US (Polish-born) historian of the Soviet Union

The two major historiographical questions regarding the Russian Revolution – the legitimacy of the Revolution itself and whether or not there was continuity between Lenin and Stalin – have divided Sovietologists along partisan lines. According to Russian historian Stephen F. Cohen in *Rethinking the Soviet Experience: Politics and History since 1917* (1985), "the less empathy a [Western] historian has felt for the Revolution and original Bolshevism, the less he or she has seen meaningful distinctions between Bolshevism and Stalinism." In the 1940s Western historians adopted a totalitarian model that viewed the Revolution as a Bolshevik coup that destroyed the growing constitutional democratic movement and created an "evil empire." According to that Cold War model, Lenin's dictatorship led directly to Stalin's excesses. Both were totalitarian in nature and the logical result of communism's dark beginnings. During the 1960s a modernization model became popular among Western historians. Russia was not an evil empire, for the Revolution was popularly based and the Bolsheviks unorganized and democratic in nature. Totalitarianism was a temporary measure implemented in order to industrialize and to educate the masses. Russia would someday become "democratic," revisionists claimed, if the Cold War would only end and allow the Soviet Union to develop peacefully.

Despite changing trends in the historiography of the Revolution, historian Richard Pipes has consistently promoted a modified totalitarian model of Russian history which has received increasing attention in the light of the recent collapse of the Soviet Union. Born in Poland in 1923, Pipes became a US citizen in 1943. Among his many activities Pipes has served on the executive committee of the Committee on Present Danger (1977–92) and was president Reagan's director of East European and Soviet Affairs for the National Security Council (1981–82). Pipes also holds membership on the Council on Foreign Relations (a semiofficial advisory and negotiating committee closely related to the State Department) and was a leading opponent of detente – a policy Pipes claims was "inspired by intellectual indolence. [and] based on ignorance of one's antagonist and therefore inherently inept."

Pipes is a hard-line cold warrior who agreed that the Reagan administration's view of the Soviet Union as "a totalitarian state driven by a militant ideology and hence intrinsically expansionist" was the correct one and that the president's determined confrontation of the Soviet Union was responsible for ending the Cold War. Pipes has been called a warmonger by many; his earliest works demonstrated his conservatism and passionate anticommunism during an era of historical revisionism.

Pipes' version of totalitarianism, or "patrimonialism" as he calls it, differs from that of other orthodox historians. According to Pipes, Russian history has been a more-or-less continuous process, and the seeds of Stalin were sown much farther back than the October Revolution. Pipes claims that historians must go all the way back to Muscovy to understand Soviet politics. Because of its geography and climate, Russia was backward and developed as a patrimonial (traditional domination) state devoid of Western feudalism. The Revolution occurred, according to Pipes, when Russia left its traditional practices in society, culture, and economics, in order to westernize and compete with Europe, yet retained patrimonial politics. In the beginning the intelligentsia hoped for a democratic constitution, but were forced to resort to revolution when they could not rally the peasants to their banner. In response to this "unfortunate" radicalism, the autocracy created a police state and the stage was set for a coup.

Other conservative historians argue that the Revolution was preventable because Stolypin's reforms promised a better and more judicial Russia. Historian Peter Kenez claims, however, that Pipes took a Dostoevskian point of view and saw little value in Stolypin's reforms, for "it is wrong to rebel whoever the regime and however little hope there is for improvement. Presumably all that a human being can do under the circumstances is to cultivate his own soul."

Pipes loathes the fanaticism of the intelligentsia and blames them for the Revolution and for not planning a viable government to replace autocracy. He gives little credit to the workers and the soldiers in the movement and ignores completely the concept of a larger social revolution accompanying the political coup. To Pipes socialism meant "all power to the intellectuals" and little if any to the people.

Pipes blames Bolshevism on the Enlightenment idea that "man is merely a material compound, devoid of either soul or innate ideas, and as such a passive product of an infinitely malleable social environment." If so, then the American experiment must be examined, for it too tried to rationalize politics and cultures. Pipes implied that all revolution is bad when he claimed that "the tragic and sordid history of the Russian Revolution . . . teaches that political authority must never be employed for ideological ends. It is best to let people be."

LORI LYN BOGLE

See also Russia: Modern; Russia: Russian Revolution

Biography

Richard Edgar Pipes. Born Cieszyn, Poland, 11 July 1923. Emigrated to the US, 1940; naturalized 1943. Studied Muskingum College, Ohio; received BA, Cornell University, 1945; MA, Harvard University, 1947, PhD 1950. Taught (rising to professor), Harvard University, from 1950 (emeritus). Member, National Security Council, 1981–82. Married Irene Eugenia Roth, 1946 (2 sons).

Principal Writings

The Formation of the Soviet Union: Communism and Nationalism,
1917–1923, 1954; revised 1964
The Russian Intelligentsia, 1961
Social Democracy and the St. Petersburg Labor Movement,
1885–97, 1963
Struve, 2 vols., 1970–80
Russia under the Old Regime, 1974
US–Soviet Relations in the Era of Detente, 1981
Survival Is Not Enough: Soviet Realities and America's Future, 1984
The Russian Revolution, 1990; concise version, 1995
Russia under the Bolshevik Regime, 1993

Further Reading

Kenez, Peter, "The Prosecution of Soviet History: A Critique of
    Richard Pipes' *The Russian Revolution,*" *Russian Review* 50
    (1991), 345–351
Malia, Martin Edward, "The Hunt for the True October,"
    Commentary 92 (1991), 21–28
Somin, Ilya, "Riddles, Mysteries, and Enigmas: Unanswered
    Questions of Communism's Collapse," *Policy Review* 70 (1994),
    84–88
Stent, Angela E., review of *US Soviet Relations in the Era of
    Detente, Russian Review* 41 (1982), 91–92
Szeftel, Marc, "Two Negative Appraisals of Russian Pre-
    Revolutionary Development," *Canadian-American Slavic Studies,*
    1980, 74–87

Pirenne, Henri 1862–1935

Belgian medievalist

Henri Pirenne's reputation as one of the most significant
western European historians of his time is based on the breadth
of his thinking about historical problems and on his two
greatest achievement: the "Pirenne thesis" on the importance
of international trade in the formation of medieval Europe;
and his *Histoire de Belgique* (The History of Belgium,
1899–1932) in seven volumes.

Pirenne, a French-speaking Belgian, was for most of his
career professor of medieval history at the University of Ghent.
In the 1880s he studied in Germany at Leipzig and Berlin and
had close links throughout his career with the University of
Paris. He maintained a vast correspondence with scholars from
many countries and served as president of various international
scholarly committees. Both his work and his network of
contacts made him one of the most influential historians of his
generation.

In the 1890s Pirenne was appointed by the ambitious
monarch Leopold II to write a history of the recently formed
Belgian state, created after the 1830 revolution. Pirenne forged
a national historical identity from the histories of the fragmented territories that make up this border region between
French and Germanic language groups. Frequently a war zone,
these lands were always under the overlordship of foreign powers, lastly the Dutch. Into this story, Pirenne incorporated the
history of the county of Flanders. Its cities were the greatest
centers of trade and manufacturing in medieval northern
Europe, dominated by powerful guilds. Flanders' wealth
financed the glittering court of Burgundy and many cultural
achievements of what has been termed the northern renaissance.

Pirenne's work is an example of the appropriation of the histories of past cultures to serve subsequent nationalistic ends.

Nationalism was to cause problems for Europe's historians,
among whom there was a widespread exchange of ideas before
World War I. Pirenne published in German and enjoyed friendships with many German colleagues, notably Karl Lamprecht.
However, after his experiences in the war, he became hostile
to Germany. He despised the uncritical support for the
emperor's war policies among German intellectuals. One of
Pirenne's sons died on active service in 1914 and he himself
was interned for refusing to work in the German-controlled
University of Ghent when the city was under occupation.
Pirenne's writings during internment considered broader
themes in history as a way of transcending national limitations. From 1921 to his death in 1935 he guided the young
historians Lucien Febvre and Marc Bloch in the foundation of
the celebrated journal *Annales d'histoire économique et sociale.*
Unfortunately, continuing suspicion of the German academy
made this a predominantly French publication. The *Viertel-
jahrschrift für Sozial und Wirtschaftsgeschichte,* with which
Pirenne had been associated before the war, resumed publication of German research on these themes.

In the 1920s and 1930s Pirenne published his mature works,
which incorporated the ideas that made up the "Pirenne thesis." He sought to explain the shift of the center of European
economic and cultural life from the Mediterranean basin to the
plains of northern Europe, a shift that marked the transition
from antiquity to the Middle Ages. *Medieval Cities* (1925)
explored the idea that the growth of towns in early medieval
Europe was stimulated by long-distance trade. Pirenne put forward the related hypothesis that Roman civilization in the former western empire did not collapse in the 5th century with the
Germanic invasions, as Edward Gibbon had proposed: instead
it continued to be significant until the Arabs under the influence of Islam came to dominate the Mediterranean in the 8th
and 9th centuries, thus isolating northwest Europe. *Mahomet
et Charlemagne* (1937; *Mohammed and Charlemagne,* 1939),
published posthumously after extensive editing, developed this
idea most fully.

The "Pirenne thesis" has long been debated, but not discredited. Challenges have come from economic historians, notably
experts on the circulation of coinage. However Pirenne's ideas
injected new life into early medieval studies, stimulating extensive research that is a tribute to the scope of his historical
vision. He was one of the greatest urban and economic historians of the 20th century, and he inspired historians such as
those of the Annales school with a broader view of history.

VIRGINIA R. BAINBRIDGE

See also Bloch; Cipolla; Duby; Ennen; France: to 1000; Ganshof;
Geyl; Lopez; Power; Rörig; Urban

Biography

Jean Henri Otto Lucien Marie Pirenne. Born Verviers, Belgium,
23 December 1862, son of an industrialist. Studied with Godefroid
Kurth (Gottfried Kurth) at University of Liège, PhD 1883; with
Gustav Schmoller in Leipzig and Berlin, 1883–84; and with Arthur
Giry, Ecole des Chartes and Ecole Pratique des Hautes Etudes, Paris,
1884–85. Professor, University of Ghent, 1885–1935. Elected to
Royal Commission of History, Royal Academy of Belgium, 1891:

secretary, 1907–35. Interned by the Germans, 1916–18. Married Jenny-Laure Vanderhaegen, 1887 (4 sons). Died Uccle, near Brussels, 24 October 1935.

Principal Writings

Histoire de Belgique (History of Belgium), 7 vols., 1899–1932
Les Anciennes démocraties des Pays-Bas, 1910; in English as *Belgian Democracy: Its Early History*, 1915, and *Early Democracies in the Low Countries*, 1963
Medieval Cities: Their Origins and the Revival of Trade, 1925; French version as *Les Villes du Moyen-Age: essai d'histoire économique et sociale*, 1927
Histoire de l'Europe des invasions au XIVe siècle, 1936; in English as *A History of Europe from the Invasions to the XVI Century*, 1939
Mahomet et Charlemagne, 1937; in English as *Mohammed and Charlemagne*, 1939

Further Reading

Havighurst, Alfred F., ed., *The Pirenne Thesis: Analysis, Criticism and Revision*, Boston: Heath, 1958; revised 1969
Lopez, Robert S., "Mohammed and Charlemagne: A Revision," *Speculum* 18 (1943), 14–38
Lyon, Bryce, *Henri Pirenne: A Biographical and Intellectual Study*, Ghent: Story-Scientia, 1974
Lyon, Bryce, and Mary Lyon, *The Birth of Annales History: The Letters of Lucien Febvre and Marc Bloch to Henri Pirenne 1921–1935*, Brussels: Academie Royale de Belgique, 1991

Platonov, S.F. 1860–1933
Russian social historian

S.F. Platonov was one of the most prominent representatives of the St. Petersburg historical school at the end of 19th and the beginning of the 20th century; his field of study was mainly 16th- and 17th-century Russian history. This era, generally known as the "Time of Troubles," was remarkable for its social upheaval and political collapses, changes of ruling dynasty, usurpers to the throne, and a foreign invasion. Platonov's first extended piece of work, which also served as his master's thesis, was a critical historigraphical survey of this period. *Drevne-russkie skazaniia i povesti o smutnom vremeni* (Ancient Russian Legends and Tales about the Time of Troubles, 1888) surveyed the major historical documents available. In addition to his analysis of the documents, Platonov examined them to determine their authenticity. Scholars still use the biographical studies he made of the documents' authors.

Platonov's second monograph *Ocherki po istorii smuty v moskovskom gosudarstve XVI–XVII vekov* (Essays on the Time of Troubles, 1899) won him his doctorate and presented his basic interpretation of the significance of the period. Platonov's analysis was similar to that of V.O. Kliuchevskii and other liberal historians. Abandoning older literary traditions, he dedicated himself to archival research, and concluded that Russian history needed to be grounded in a precise historical analysis of its political, social, and economic realities. He was also motivated by a desire to see the Russian state modernized, but within a context of gradualist reform and the retention of the monarchy.

Next Platonov turned to the social and political conflicts of different classes under the 16th- and 17th-century Muscovite

state. The origins of Russia's failure to develop a modern state were rooted, in Platonov's mind, in the tyranny of Ivan the Terrible and the regime of political terror established by him. The *oprichnina* itself was the tsar's domain; he both expelled the hereditary aristocracy from it, and used the land to reward newly-elevated noblemen who were giving him military support. The word *oprichnina* (administrative elite, and the territory assigned to this elite) came to stand for the tyranny associated with it. Platonov argued that the *oprichnina* was instituted as a response to the political tensions between the hereditary *boyar* (nobleman) aristocracy and tsarist autocracy. The necessity for the constant expansion of the army resulted in a major redistribution of land among new soldiers, causing tension in society. Furthermore, it reinforced the growing discontent of the peasants, who recognized themselves as pawns. In their eyes, peasant labor was the source of the nation's prosperity, which was under threat due to the civil war which the *oprichnina* precipitated.

Platonov viewed the Time of Troubles as a period when all the contradictions that lay deeply hidden in Russian society erupted, causing an upheaval at every level of society. In his analysis, the only things that prevented the collapse of the nation were the authority of the church and the firm action taken by the conservative section of society, both within the traditional nobility, but also the growing urban merchant class. Dedicated to the idea of a strong central state, they organized a people's army which placed a new dynasty on the throne. Platonov's interpretation, which essentially saw the Time of Troubles as an aberration, was deemed conservative and anti-materialist under the Soviet state.

From his professorship at the University of St. Petersburg, Platonov published several basic textbooks which helped to focus thinking about Russian history. His *Lektsii po russkoi istorii* (1899; *History of Russia*, 1925) and *Uchebnik russkoi istorii dlia srednei shkoly* (Textbook on Russian History for Secondary Schools, 1900) are the most distinguished of these. After the October Revolution Platonov initially concentrated on administrative work at the various Soviet scientific and archival institutes and universities with which he was associated, and formalized his historical theories in a series of books on Boris Godunov, Ivan the Terrible, and Peter the Great. However, in 1929 he was accused of anti-Soviet activities, and eventually transported to Samara where he died in 1933.

DMITRY A. GOUTNOV

See also Russia: Medieval; Russia: Early Modern

Biography

Sergei Fedorovich Platonov. Born Chernigov, 16 June 1860. Received secondary education, St. Petersburg, 1870–79; studied with K.N. Bestuzhev-Riumin, V.G. Vasilevskii, and A.D. Gradovskii, Department of History and Philology, University of St. Petersburg. Taught history at a St. Petersburg secondary school, 1882–89; University of St. Petersburg, 1888–1917 (dean of history and philology, 1900–05); director, Women's Teacher Training College, 1905–16. After the October Revolution, appointed director, Archaeological Institute, 1918–23; chairman, Archaeographical Commission at the Academy of Sciences of USSR, 1918–29; director, Petrograd Central Record Office, 1918–23; director, Pushkin House; director, Library of the Academy of Sciences, 1925. Accused without evidence of anti-Soviet activities, 1929; held until

1931 when transported to Samara where he died, 10 January 1933. Posthumously pardoned by USSR Supreme Court, 20 July 1967.

Principal Writings

Drevnerusskie skazaniia i povesti o smutnom vremeni XVII veka (Ancient Russian Legends and Tales about the Time of Troubles), 1888

Lektsii po russkoi istorii, 3 vols. in 1, 1899; in English as *History of Russia*, 1925

Ocherki po istorii smuty v moskovskom gosudarstve XVI–XVII vekov (Essays on the Time of Troubles and the Muscovite State in the 16th and 17th Centuries), 1899

Uchebnik russkoi istorii dlia srednei shkoly: kurs sistematicheskii (Textbook on Russian History for Secondary Schools), 1900

Stat'i po russkoi istorii (1883–1902) (Articles on Russian History), 1903; revised and expanded 1912

Boris Godunov, 1921; in English as *Boris Godunov, Tsar of Russia*, 1973

Ivan Groznyi, 1923; in English as *Ivan the Terrible*, 1974

Smutnoe vremia, 1923; in English as *The Time of Troubles: A Historical Study of the Internal Crises and Social Struggle in Sixteenth- and Seventeenth-Century Muscovy*, 1970

Moskva i zapad, 1926; in English as *Moscow and the West*, 1972

Petr Velikii: lichnost' i deiatelnost' (Peter the Great), 1926

"Avtobiografiia akademika Platonova, napisannaia dlia Ogon'ka (An Autobiography of the Academic Platonov Written for Ogonek Magazine)," *Ogonek* 35 (1927), 10–27

Further Reading

Brachev, V.S., "'Delo akademika S.F. Platonova" (The Case of Academician S.F. Platonov), *Voprosy Istorii* 5 (1989), 117–29

Ivanov, Ia.A., "O formirovanii vzgliadov S.F. Platonova" (On the Formation of the Ideas of S.F. Platonov), *Vestnik LGU* 20 (1983), 92–94

Kolobkov, V.I., ed., *Arkhiv akademika Platonova v Otdele Rukopisei Rossiiskoi Natsional'noi Biblioteki, Katalog* (Catalog of Platonov's Archive), St. Petersburg: Izd-vo Rossiiskoi natsional'noi biblioteki, 1994

Sbornik statei po russkoi istorii, posviashchennykh S.F.Platonovu (Articles on Russian History devoted to S.F. Platonov), Petrograd: Ogni, 1922; reprinted Würzburg: Jal, 1978

Sergeiu Fedorovichu Platonovu, ucheniki, druz'ia i pochitateli, sbornik statei (To S.F. Platonov from Students and Admirers), St. Petersburg, 1911; reprinted Düsseldorf: Brucken, 1970

Plucknett, T.F.T. 1897–1965

British legal historian

One of the major legal historians of the first half of the 20th century, T.F.T. Plucknett was a precocious scholar. Known early in his student days as a constitutional historian, he was a fellow of Emmanuel College, Cambridge, where he wrote a thesis on statutes in the early 14th century for his LLB in 1920, which was soon published (1922). His law degree took him to Harvard University, where he worked with Roscoe Pound, becoming a historian of private law and writing his most lasting work, *A Concise History of the Common Law* (1929). The reputation of this book brought his appointment to the first chair of legal history in England at the London School of Economics in 1931.

Professionally, Plucknett was the literary director of the Selden Society (1937–63), elected fellow of the British Academy in 1946, president of the Royal Historical Society (1948–52)

and of the Society of Public Teachers of Law (1953–54), and received several honorary doctorates. He was elusive both professionally and personally. A formal, solitary man, he had only a few close friends, who were all historians. He was also aloof as a teacher, with a few dedicated students who appreciated his detailed, analytical approach to the sources as the grist of the historian's mill.

Plucknett was not a prolific writer. Most of his books were published lectures: his Ford lectures at Oxford became *Legislation of Edward I* (1949), his Creighton lecture *The Medieval Bailiff* (1954), his Maitland lecture *Early English Legal Literature* (1958), and his Wiles lectures *Edward I and the Criminal Law* (1960). Other works were introductory texts for law students, such as the *Readings on the History and System of the Common Law* (1927) and *The English Trial and Comparative Law* (1952). The core of his academic career was at the Selden Society, which he almost single-handedly kept alive in the 1940s and 1950s when there was little demand for legal history. His dedication to the field led him to complete volumes that others had started and left unfinished, to add notes and explanations to other editions, and in general to maintain a flow of commissioned works by encouraging his editors.

As a scholar of legal history, Plucknett was not perhaps of the first tier himself. Lacking extensive legal and historical training, and eschewing assistance from others, he became (as was his idol F.W. Maitland) primarily his own critic. His most famous work, *A Concise History*, underwent five editions by 1956. Written as 745 pages of one-page subject-item descriptions, it was more a dictionary than a history. On the other hand, his more obscure introduction to Thomas Pitt Taswell-Langmead's *English Constitutional History from the Teutonic Conquest to the Present Day* had ten editions by 1946. Plucknett's goal was to make legal history relate to real problems of real people, but his writings did not always succeed in this regard. He came closest in his studies of the reigns of Edward I (1272–1307) and Edward II (1307–27).

Plucknett prided himself in the belief that the legal history of the past should be taught and written as the study of law in the present: as "a school of living law." In his work on the early literature of the law, he makes the medieval law school come alive with teachers putting questions and students answering them, dissecting the didactic legal literature of the era. In his work on the early statutes, he wrote persuasively that Edward I should be remembered not for his wars, battles, and politics, but as a man who had a vocation as a legislator, one who saw "the law as a mass of technicalities which might be ingeniously combined to secure his ends." The highly technical research to which Plucknett committed himself, trying to piece together the early history of lawyers and legislators, remains valuable. His early history of parliamentary legislation, in particular, is still part of the foundation for the study of the origins and early history of statute law.

LOUIS A. KNAFLA

See also Holdsworth; Milsom

Biography

Theodore Frank Thomas Plucknett. Born Bristol, 2 January 1897. Educated at Alderman Newton's School, Leicester; Bacup and Tawtenstall School, New Church, Lancashire (University of London external degree in history, 1915); University College, London, MA 1918; research fellow, Emmanuel College, Cambridge, LLB 1920; Choate fellow, Harvard Law School, 1921–22. Taught at Radcliffe College, 1923–24; and Harvard Law School, 1923–31; professor of legal history, London School of Economics, University of London, 1931–63: dean, faculty of law, 1954–58. Married Marie Guibert, 1923 (1 son). Died Wimbledon, 14 February 1965.

Principal Writings

Statutes and Their Interpretation in the First Half of the Fourteenth Century, 1922
Editor with Roscoe Pound, *Readings on the History and System of the Common Law*, 3rd edition, 1927
A Concise History of the Common Law, 1929; 5th edition, 1956
Editor, *English Constitutional History from the Teutonic Conquest to the Present Time*, by Thomas Pitt Taswell-Langmead, 10th edition, 1946
Legislation of Edward I, 1949
With Charles John Hamson, *The English Trial and Comparative Law: Five Broadcast Talks*, 1952
The Medieval Bailiff, 1954
Early English Legal Literature, 1958
Edward I and the Criminal Law, 1960
Studies in English Legal History, 1983

Further Reading

Milsom, S.F.C., *Theodore Frank Thomas Plucknett, 1897–1965*, Oxford: Oxford University Press, 1965

Plumb, J.H. 1911–
British political historian

One of the more influential British historians of the 1950s, 1960s and 1970s, J.H. Plumb was a major figure in the Cambridge History Faculty who influenced the work of a large number of younger protégés and sought to break free from the conventional mold of 18th century British political history.

From an affluent background in Leicester, Plumb was educated at the University College there and then at Christ's College, Cambridge. Beginning research on the social structure of the House of Commons in the reign of William III, Plumb worked in British Intelligence during World War II, before returning to Cambridge where he was appointed to a university post and to a college fellowship at Christ's. Thereafter, he rose through the Cambridge system becoming eventually a professor and master of Christ's College. By 1950 he had decided to work on the transition of English political life from the violence and civil strife of the 17th century to the more settled world of the 18th, a period bridged by the life of Sir Robert Walpole, and to focus on the question of the rise of political stability and oligarchy. In 1949 Plumb decided to work on a life of Walpole and also on the growth of stability.

The Walpole biography brought Plumb fame but was never finished, and remains curiously emblematic of Plumb's entire career. The two volumes that appeared were popular works and attracted much attention, but their long-term impact has been minimal. Plumb's other biographical work, his treatment of William Pitt the Elder, 1st Earl of Chatham, displayed a similar acuteness in the distinction of character but was a shorter and lesser work.

Plumb's study of the rise of political stability, originally the Ford lectures at Oxford, was important in its discussion of political structures and shifts, a world away from the minutiae of political maneuvers, but he underrated Jacobitism and the post-1715 Tory party, and his decision to concentrate on England rather than the British Isles provided a misleading perspective, not least because developments in Ireland and Scotland were crucial to the situation in England.

After the lectures were published in 1967, Plumb did not make any more important contributions to scholarship on the period. His published lecture on the commercialization of leisure in 18th-century England was interesting, but he failed to follow it up. Instead, as with his work on Walpole, there was a curiously unfinished feel to his career. He was an active lecturer in America, a frequent reviewer, and general editor of a number of important series, but his own work diminished. In contrast, for example, with John Ehrman who in retirement wrote the third of his major 3-volume biography of Pitt the Younger, or Plumb's Cambridge rival, Sir Geoffrey Elton, who continued publishing books in his retirement, Plumb made little impact after retirement. As with Elton, Plumb's influence rested in large part on the fact that he was powerful in Cambridge at a time when the profession was expanding, and he was therefore in a position to help the careers of protégés. Many leading scholars of the period were trained or influenced by him, including John Brewer, David Cannadine, and Linda Colley. Plumb, however, would not have wished to be seen as Walpole was by his critics – as a master of patronage – but rather would have preferred his own portrayal of Walpole, one that is in fact more accurate, as a statesman who had ideas as well as interests, and supported policies as well as patronage.

JEREMY BLACK

See also Britain: 1485–1750; Consumerism; Jordan; Schama; Social; Trevelyan

Biography

John Harold Plumb. Born 20 August 1911. Attended Alderman Newton's School, Leicester; studied at University College, Leicester, receiving external BA degree from London University, 1933; research student, Cambridge University, 1934–36, PhD 1936. War service in British Intelligence, 1940–45. Taught at Cambridge University (rising to professor), 1939–82. Fellow, later master, Christ's College, Cambridge, 1946–82. Knighted 1982.

Principal Writings

England in the Eighteenth Century, 1950
G.M. Trevelyan, 1951
Chatham, 1953
The First Four Georges, 1956
Sir Robert Walpole, 2 vols., 1956–60
Men and Places, 1963, in US as *Men and Centuries*, 1963
The Growth of Political Stability in England, 1675–1725, 1967; in US as *The Origins of Political Stability: England, 1675–1725*, 1967
The Death of the Past, 1969
In the Light of History, 1972
The Commercialisation of Leisure in Eighteenth-Century England, 1973
Royal Heritage: The Story of Britain's Royal Builders and Collectors, 1977; in US as *Royal Heritage: The Treasures of the British Crown*, 1977
Georgian Delights, 1980

Royal Heritage: The Reign of Elizabeth II, 1981
With Neil McKendrick and John Brewer, *The Birth of a Consumer Society: The Commercialization of Eighteenth-Century England*, 1982
The American Experience, 1988
The Collected Essays of J.H. Plumb, 2 vols., 1988
The Making of an Historian, 1989

Further Reading

Kammen, Michael G., "On Predicting the Past: Potter and Plumb," *Journal of Interdisciplinary History* (1974), 109–18
McKendrick, Neil, ed., *Historical Perspectives: Studies in English Thought and Society in Honour of J.H. Plumb*, London: Europa, 1974
Roberts, Clayton, "The Growth of Political Stability Reconsidered," *Albion* 25 (1993), 237–77

Plutarch before 50–after 120 CE

Greek essayist and historian

Plutarch, son of Aristobulus of Chaeronea, was a prolific essayist and biographer whose influence on the literature of western Europe has been enormous. The "Lamprias catalogue," supposedly compiled by a son of Plutarch, but probably dating to late antiquity, lists 227 titles, some spurious. He studied philosophy in Athens where he must have attended lectures by the famous sophists of the time though he mentions only one, the Egyptian Platonist, Ammonius, and in his youth he traveled widely, visiting Alexandria and journeying to Rome at least twice. But he spent most of his life quietly at Chaeronea where he resided and kept a private school, and at Delphi where he held a priesthood, and where he probably died. Plutarch had a wide circle of friends, including both Greek notables and Roman imperial administrators, and he himself acquired Roman citizenship, which brought him influential friends, equestrian rank, and eventually the *ornamenta consularia* and the post of imperial procurator in Achaea. Proud though he was of the Greek past, he accepted Greece's subject status in the Roman empire and was happy to collaborate with Greece's conquerors. His corpus of more than seventy miscellaneous essays is usually called the *Moralia*, a title used in the medieval period for a group of essays dealing with practical ethics. Their subjects range from the education of children and the intelligence of animals to a collection of Spartan apophthegms, advice on marriage, and an essay on the myth of the Egyptian gods Isis and Osiris, which was a major source for our knowledge of Egyptian religion until Egyptian hieroglyphs were deciphered. A small group deal with philosophy: Plutarch was a Platonist and averse to Stoicism. His interest in Delphi is reflected in three treatises, *The Decline of Oracles*, *The Delphic "E,"* and *The Pythia's Prophecies*, and one essay, *On the Malignity of Herodotus*, is important evidence for Herodotus' reputation for mendacity which he acquired in the ancient world.

Plutarch himself considered his major work the *Parallel Lives*, which was dedicated to Quintus Sosius Senecio, twice consul in the reign of the emperor Trajan. This work paired biographies of great public figures, one Greek, the other Roman, and all but four of the extant pairs concluded with a formal comparison. Plutarch was the heir of the Greek biographical tradition that went back to the 4th century BCE and was a product of both rhetoric and philosophy. Great men were treated as paradigms and held up for praise or criticism. Plutarch added to the tradition the notion of pairing a Greek with a Roman counterpart: Theseus with Romulus, both founding heroes, Nicias with Crassus, both generals whose careers ended in disaster, Lycurgus with Numa, both lawgivers, and so on. The *Lives* are based on wide and not uncritical reading, but historical exactitude was not Plutarch's major goal; rather, he was selective and used personal details only as indicators of character. The same technique colored Plutarch's *Lives of the Caesars*, a series stretching from the emperor Augustus to Vitellius, of which only the *Galba* and *Otho* have survived.

Plutarch's popularity continued in late antiquity and the Byzantine world, and in the 15th century, the *Lives* rapidly found readers in western Europe. Jacques Amyot (1513–93) produced a French translation of both the *Lives* and the *Moralia*, which in turn were translated into English, the *Lives* by Thomas North and the *Moralia* by Philemon Holland. Plutarch in North's translation was one of Shakespeare's sources of inspiration: *Julius Caesar*, *Coriolanus*, *Antony and Cleopatra*, and *Timon of Athens* all come from the *Lives*. In France, Michel de Montaigne (1533–92) drew on Plutarch's *Moralia* as a model for his essays and quoted him 398 times. But it was in the 18th-century Enlightenment that the idealized portraits drawn in the *Lives* had their greatest influence. Jean-Jacques Rousseau (1712–78) knew Amyot's translation by heart by the age of eight; he identified with Plutarch's heroes and particularly admired Plutarch's description of the early Roman republic and the virtues and laws of Sparta. Plutarch's essay *On Superstition* was quoted by Pierre Bayle and through him passed into the mainstream of Enlightenment thought, and with the French Revolution, the creative influence of Plutarch as a political philosopher reached its height. Before Charlotte Corday's assassination of Marat, she spent the day reading Plutarch.

In the 19th century, historians put Plutarch's research methods under scrutiny and found them wanting. Plutarch quoted no fewer than 150 historians, including 40 who wrote in Latin, but the suspicion developed, particularly among German historians, that he got most of his information at second hand: Eduard Meyer even took the extreme view that he did not use Herodotus, Thucydides, and Xenophon directly. This hypothesis has now been overturned by A.W. Gomme. But the doubts were founded on valid grounds: how could Plutarch find all the works he quoted in a small place like Chaeronea? The answer seems to be that he quoted a great deal from memory, or from notes from books he had previously read. He has little claim to originality, though he drew his portraits skillfully, and his value to the historian depends partly on the amount of other source material available. Thus his life of Alexander the Great is carefully studied; his *Julius Caesar* is not. But he continues to attract a great deal of attention in modern classical scholarship.

J.A.S. EVANS

See also Christianity; Egypt: Ancient; Herodotus; Kasravi; Religion; Roman

Biography

Born Chaeronea, Boeotia, near Thebes, before 50 CE. Traveled extensively in Egypt and Italy, but remained mainly in Chaeronea, where he taught. Served as priest at Delphi for 30 years and helped to revive the shrine there. Married Timoxena (at least 4 sons, 1 daughter). Died after 120.

Principal Writings

Plutarch's Lives (Loeb edition), translated by Bernadotte Perrin, 11 vols., 1914–26

Moralia (Loeb edition), translated by F.G. Babbitt *et al.*, 15 vols., 1927–69

Further Reading

Aalders, Gerhard Jean Daniël, *Plutarch's Political Thought*, Amsterdam and New York: North-Holland, 1982

Barrow, Reginald Haynes, *Plutarch and His Times*, London: Chatto and Windus, and Bloomington: Indiana University Press, 1967

Gomme, Arnold Wycombe, *A Historical Commentary on Thucydides 1*, Oxford: Clarendon Press, 1945

Jones, Christopher Prestige, *Plutarch and Rome*, Oxford: Clarendon Press, 1971

Russell, Donald Andrew, *Plutarch*, London: Duckworth, 1972; New York: Scribner, 1973

Scardigli, Barbara, ed., *Essays on Plutarch's Lives*, Oxford and New York: Oxford University Press, 1995

Stadter, Philip A., ed., *Plutarch and the Historical Tradition*, London and New York: Routledge, 1992

Pocock, J.G.A. 1924–

British historian

As a proponent of studying the ideas of the past in the context of their own period, J.G.A. Pocock has been one of the primary figures involved in a bringing a clear historical examination to the intellectual tradition of civic humanism. Through demonstrating the changes and alterations that must be taken into account when following the development of such a tradition, he has enabled researchers to extend the precepts of this approach to their own field of study, and has facilitated the advancement of historical research into the formation of concepts of political theory during the political and intellectual ferment of 17th-century Britain.

Pocock taught in universities in Britain and New Zealand prior to moving to the United States in 1966, where he eventually obtained a post at Johns Hopkins University. Along the way he undertook a comparative study of the political structures in these nations which would no doubt have its own effect upon his understanding of political change. But long before he arrived in America, he had already published, in 1957, what may be one of his greatest works, *The Ancient Constitution*, a study of the notion of an ancient, unwritten English constitution dating back to the pre-migration tribes of Germany. In *The Ancient Constitution*, Pocock used what has come to be his trademark, a clear-visioned insight into what this notion meant for those who expressed it – in this case the parliamentary politicians of early 17th-century Britain – rather than an attempt to define the mythical constitution in modern terms or through a modern filter. This study opened new areas for research and examination, and forced a re-examination of

the basis for some of the ideological proposals submitted during that period.

Throughout his career Pocock pursued this theme, isolating the basic ideas and proposals from the ideological embellishments added by later political theorists, and by isolating the germ of the idea to illustrate how it was transmitted and transformed. In his varied studies and examinations of James Harrington (a 17th-century British political theorist) and those who later adopted Harrington's political theories, the so-called Neo-Harringtons, Pocock demonstrated how the latter's opinions should be distinguished from the former's, how what they believed Harrington stated was not always what he actually wrote or intended to imply. In pointing out this distinction, Pocock illustrated the division that must exist between one time and another, and joined with other historians in arguing against applying contemporary beliefs, opinions, or standards to the events, thoughts, or actions of the past. After all, as Pocock ably demonstrated in his study of Machiavellian political theory, what Machiavelli proposed had little in common with what later political writers would have thought of as purely Machiavellian.

Pocock is a notable historian of political theory, but in some ways he has been something much more important: an exemplar of clear-headed research, who has shown all who read his writing how to apply some of the tenets of historical research. While his work in the history of British political theory has been very important for that field and should not be overlooked, it is essential to remember that this was only one of the factors that have added to the lustre of his reputation as a necessary figure in the development of historical writing; Pocock has been an important and persuasive instrument in illustrating how failure to recognize our own prejudices can warp our view of the past; by so doing he helped to establish a template by which other historical developments may be observed and better understood.

His body of work will ensure that his legacy in this area is not forgotten, but it is an area of historical thought that must be constantly reinforced and re-emphasized. One hopes that Pocock's research and writing will continue to demonstrate this fact, not only within his own discipline, but to all others who essay to study the past.

DANIEL M. GERMAN

See also Baron, H.; Intellectual; Italy: Renaissance; Political; Quinn; United States: American Revolution

Biography

John Greville Agard Pocock. Born London, 7 March 1924. Received BA, Canterbury University, New Zealand, 1945, MA 1946; PhD, Cambridge University, 1952. Taught at Canterbury University, 1946–48; and University of Otago, 1953–55; research fellow, Cambridge University, 1956–58; rose to professor of political science, Canterbury University, 1959–65; professor of history and political science, Washington University, 1966–74; professor of history, Johns Hopkins University, 1974–94 (emeritus). Married Felicity Willis-Fleming, 1958 (2 sons).

Principal Writings

The Ancient Constitution and the Feudal Law: A Study of English Historical Thought in the Seventeenth Century, 1957; revised 1987

*Politics, Language, and Time: Essays on Political Thought and
   History,* 1971
*The Machiavellian Moment: Florentine Political Thought and the
   Atlantic Republican Tradition,* 1975
*Virtue, Commerce, and History: Essays on Political Thought and
   History, Chiefly in the Eighteenth Century,* 1985

Further Reading

Geerken, John H., "Pocock and Machiavelli: Structuralist
   Explanation in History," *Journal of the History of Philosophy* 17
   (1979), 309–18
Goodale, J.R., "J.G.A. Pocock's Neo-Harringtons: A
   Reconsideration," *History of Political Thought* 1 (1980), 237–59
Janssen, Peter L., "Political Thought as a Traditionary Action: The
   Critical Response to Skinner and Pocock," *History and Theory*
   24 (1985), 115–46
Landau, Norma, "Eighteenth Century England: Tales Historians
   Tell," *Eighteenth-Century Studies* 22 (1988–1989), 208–18
Lockyer, Andrew, "Pocock's Harrington," *Political Studies* 28
   (1980), 458–64

Poland: to the 18th Century

The academic discipline of medieval and early modern history
in Poland dates back to about the mid-19th century. Ever since
its beginnings, the historiography has been affected by three
features of the contemporary general political and intellectual
scene: the absence of an independent Polish state, especially
during the Partition period (1791–1918) and World War II and
its aftermath (1939–89); the generational disruptions of both
world wars, especially the Second; and religious and ethnic
diversity that had characterized the Polish territories until
1945, and situated Poland as a frontier region within Europe.
These three features have shaped the basic questions posed by
Polish historians, affected the quality and survival of the available archival evidence and institutions of higher learning, and
made periodic recovery of knowledge, sources, and syntheses
the central project of several generations of historians over the
past century. Polish medieval and early modern historiography
has specialized in three broad directions: 1) source criticism
and editions (and other auxiliary disciplines of history);
2) focus on statecraft, and the relationship of the medieval and
early modern "state" to social groups and the economy, as the
central conceptual issue; and 3) several other areas of inquiry
that had originally been related to that relationship but have
emerged as interesting and important on their own terms.

The 19th century was the heroic age of the source edition
and criticism in the territories of partitioned Poland. The source
editions that originated between the middle of the century and
1914, and continued thereafter, fall into three categories: 1) a
comprehensive edition of diplomatic evidence from each of the
major regions of historical Poland (Great Poland, Little Poland,
Masovia, Cuiavia, Silesia, and parts of Pomerania); 2) an
authoritatively edited miscellany of narrative sources, modeled
directly or indirectly on the Monumenta Germaniae Historica;
3) an authoritatively edited miscellany of legal sources; and
4) occasional publications of various kinds of sources,
including facsimiles. The first years of the 20th century and
the interwar period were a time of preparation for a new generation of source editions of the entire corpus of sources edited

between the 1850s and 1914. The planned initial step was
several volumes of extensive registers of the entire diplomatic
evidence with the apparatus and critique lacking in the older
editions, pending a full set of re-editions; of which only the
first, concerning 12th-century sources, appeared before 1939
(Kozłowska-Budkowa, 1938). Despite the destruction of much
of the actual documentation during World War II, these plans
were implemented briskly after 1945. As a result, source criticism is a distinctive feature of postwar Polish scholarship, with
its main venue the *Studia Źródłoznawcze* (Studies in Source
Criticism, 1957–), a journal of interdisciplinary history as well
as source studies. Although the comprehensive register of the
interwar period (Kozłowska-Budkowa, 1938) has been discontinued, two guides to published and manuscript sources have
appeared (Płaza, 1974, 1980), as well as a series of studies
and a textbook in diplomatics and codicology (Maleczyński,
1971; Maleczyński, Bielińska, and Gąsiorowski, 1971), and in
the remaining auxiliary disciplines (Szymański, 1972, 1993).

The interest of the pioneering generation of Polish historians in the pathology and demise of Polish statecraft affected
several specific areas of inquiry. The first was a search for a
theory of origins of the Polish state and society that might
explain the fate of both. In the 19th century, such "theories"
were usually anchored in contemporary ethnography and
comparative social evolution. One early theory attributed
the origins of kinship and social stratification in Poland to the
conquest of the Slavic population by Scandinavians in the 9th
and 10th centuries; another explained the origins of kinship,
lordship, property, and other elements of the social order in
terms of the Slavic extended family, and viewed "kinship" relations as a vague counterpart to Western "feudalism." Although
the "Norman" (or "conquest") and "kinship" theories have
been either rejected or revised beyond recognition, both served
to focus attention on what was viewed as the base of the royal
(or seigneurial) power, namely the village, peasantry, and the
rural estate.

The pioneer of this new social and economic history, and its
relationship to ducal (or royal) power, was Stanisław Smolka
followed by Franciszek Bujak. The interwar period witnessed
the first, brief but very fruitful, burst of reconstructions of the
history of the rural economy and society to be conceptually and
methodologically removed from issues of statecraft. In addition
to continued output by Bujak, the contributions to the social
and economic history of medieval and early modern Poland
(and, since the 15th century, Poland-Lithuania) consisted of the
early 'works by Roman Grodecki, Kazimierz Tymieniecki,
Henryk Łowmiański; and above all in the mature works of Jan
Rutkowski, which included several detailed studies on the structure of the medieval and early modern Polish agrarian estate –
and directly contributed to Witold Kula's theory of "feudal
system" later. Rutkowski was also a founding editor of the
Roczniki Historii Społecznej i Gospodarczej (Annals of Social
and Economic History), a journal founded in Warsaw in close
association with, and nearly at the same time as, the *Annales
d'Histoire Sociale et Economique* in Paris.

During the postwar period, these contributions were complicated by ideological factors. In its focus on the peasantry and
other laboring groups, its basic paradigm of the medieval and
early modern "state" (and lordship) as essentially exploitative,
and its close contact with the first Annales generation, the

interwar Polish school of social and economic history had been situated within one of the mainstreams of the European left, with close affinities to Marxist analysis though of course free of claims to "scientific" accuracy or dogma that characterized orthodox (especially Leninist) Marxism. Like their Russian predecessors, authors of the left-leaning generation that matured in the 1930s found it extremely difficult to continue to publish without espousing the conceptual tools of Marxism-Leninism that became mandatory in the later 1950s. The result was a silencing of the output of this group in particular – and of the innovative brand of social and economic history it had pioneered – until the later 1950s; qualified, however, by a number of important developments.

The first was continued activity in research and teaching of a handful of senior- or intermediate-level scholars who continued to train skilled medievalists and early modernists, edited the primary sources whose re-edition had long been planned, and channelled their areas of specialization in new directions that were favored by the new regime with a relatively light requirement of the otherwise obligatory ideological straitjacket imposed after 1950. The published results were scarce and uneven between 1953 and 1957, but thereafter reflected several interesting – and, again politically less encumbered – directions of specialization. Thus, the first postwar work by Henryk Łowmiański (1953) is an early example of a careful study of the "economic base" and – above all – demography of the Piast kingdom and principalities between the 10th and 13th centuries. In 1956 Jerzy Kłoczowski revived the heretofore barred subject of church history with a superb study of the Dominicans of the Polish province in Silesia in the 13th and 14th centuries; Tadeusz Ładogórski provided a major contribution to the demographic history of 14th-century Poland with a very careful and innovative methodology; Karol Maleczyński embarked on a series of articles on source analysis, criticism, and editions; while Tadeusz Manteuffel and Aleksander Gieysztor each launched publications on a wide range of subjects concerning medieval and early modern Poland in a comparative context, as well as other regions and issues of medieval Europe.

In contrast to what happened in most other communist countries, this generation preserved the interwar tradition of moderately left-wing, pioneering social and economic history from oblivion; and enabled its development in directions that, while compatible with Marxist analysis, retained their intellectual excitement and freedom from dogma. Against enormous odds, these scholars created a dynamic intellectual environment for other colleagues interested in all aspects of early Piast history, notably including Gerard Labuda, Witold Hensel, Wacław Korta, Karol Buczek, and their own students, and ultimately trained the first generation of students to reach scholarly maturity in the 1970s and 1980s. This unexpectedly continuous lineage of scholarship, and the high standards of historical craft and intellectual rigor it reproduced, ushered in a remarkable effervescence of Polish medieval and early modern historiography when the research students produced a corpus of work, and re-established very strong patterns of international contacts, especially – once again – with the editors and contributors to the *Annales*.

The historiographic output produced in Poland since the 1960s, especially during the 1970s and 1980s, spanned a wide range of specializations that, as earlier, tied in with the interests of Polish historiography since its 19th-century beginnings, above all the relationship of economy, society, and royal (or ducal) power. This subject has provided occasion for the most significant single dispute among Polish medievalists since the war, between Karol Buczek, active between the late 1950s and his death in 1983, and a younger scholar Karol Modzelewski, who produced most of his output between 1964 and 1987. Although the core of the controversy concerned the rather abstruse issue of whether the rulers of the Piast kingdom between the 10th and the 12th centuries maintained themselves from a network of "castellanies" (Modzelewski) or of "estates" (Buczek), their polemics raised fundamental issues about the structure of Polish society and economy, the nature of royal and seigneurial power within both, and the place of Polish society, economy, and lordship in a broader European context between the 10th and 13th centuries.

Social and economic history, broadly conceived, has remained the core specialization of Polish medievalists and early modernists. A very large number of scholars – perhaps best typified by Benedykt Zientara, active between the 1970s and his death in 1983 – have produced a series of works contributing to social, political, cultural, and economic history, as well as the history of ethnic relations – especially the historiographically thorny issues of Slavs and Germans, and Slavs and Jews – during the period of transition from what Modzelewski considered the exceptionally strong first Polish state of the 10th century, to the Piast duchies of the later 12th, 13th, and early 14th centuries. Unlike Modzelewski, Zientara and others avoid historical explanation in terms of any particular, supposedly unusual model or paradigm, and instead portray the Polish duchies as part of a broader European story of settlement and economic expansion, proliferation of types of peasants and of lordship, and integration of peripheral regions into a common framework of cultural, economic, and demographic contact and exchange.

The Polish noble estate has continued to attract attention. Building on Jan Rutkowski's work of the interwar period, Witold Kula has constructed an economic model of the noble agrarian estate in medieval and early modern Poland, Marian Małowist has contrasted Poland and Western Europe in the early modern period in terms of the economic and social significance of the noble estate – with special focus on the issue of "second serfdom," while Andrzej Wyrobisz has examined the noble estate as a unit of entrepreneurship and specialized production. Kula and Małowist have been important sources for Immanuel Wallerstein's world-system model, and for his debate with Robert Brenner; and a useful sample of the school of agrarian, social, and economic history that traces its descent to Rutkowski was subsequently published in English (Mączak, Samsonowicz, and Burke, 1985).

Urban history is especially informed by archaeology and the study of material culture. In 1926 Karol Maleczyński, and in 1964 Karol Buczek each reconsidered early towns in terms of urbanizing processes, above all the emergence and function of marketplaces, and by the 1970s systematic archaeological excavations enabled Polish historians such as Leciejewicz to reconstruct a general history of the Polish urban space, its functions and settlement patterns, and social stratification – the "sociotopography" of Polish towns throughout the medieval and early modern periods – and to integrate these findings with changes in the legal status of towns expressed in charters of franchise, usually modelled on German law. Recent syntheses of this subject include a general survey by Bogucka and Samsonowicz of Polish urban history between its 10th-century origins and the Partitions; a collection of essays by Wyrobisz and others concerning urban conceptions of space and time; several histories of specific towns, most recently of Kraków by Wyrozumski; and several works in the western languages on Kraków, and on Polish urban historiography by Ludwig, Knoll, and Carter.

Interdisciplinary study of material culture and its historical and social significance has been facilitated by a specialized journal, *Kwartalnik Historii Kultury Materialnej* (Quarterly of the History of Material Culture), which after 1954 rapidly evolved toward a broad focus ranging from the technical through social, economic, political, and cultural analysis (of which urban "sociotopography" is an example). The interest in archaeology and material culture is especially well reflected by numismatics, which has emerged as perhaps the most important, and internationally the most visible, of the specialized (or auxiliary) disciplines of medieval and early modern Polish historiography. Here the focal forum has also been a specialized journal, *Wiadomości Numizmatyczne* (Numismatic News), another technical and interdisciplinary publication, and the work of two scholars, Stanisław Suchodolski and Ryszard Kiersnowski.

Despite Adamus' blistering critique of the old "kinship theory," historians have remained interested in the history of family groups – especially the "knightly" and noble family – as an important, though not vaguely unique or essential, source of social cohesion. Family history has proceeded in two directions: prosopographic reconstruction over long periods; and intensive study of particular types of familial groups, above all the conjugal and the stem family. Polish prosopography was pioneered between the late 19th century and the interwar period by Władysław Semkowicz, in monographs on the genealogical origins of the Polish nobility, and has been continued above all by Janusz Bieniak and Marek Cetwiński. Interest in smaller familial groups largely concerns their proprietary functions; Juliusz Bardach and others have sought to reconstruct the breadth of familial groups that possessed rights of ownership, including issues of "divided" and "undivided" estates, incidence and significance of "individual" versus "undivided" landholding, and familial practices of alienation. Maria Koczerska has applied life-cycle analysis to marriage, (Koczerska, 1975), which has been the main context for the study of women's history in medieval and early modern Poland (Lesiński, 1956), although more recently Andrzej Karpiński has situated women's history in the very different context of urban social and economic history (Karpiński, 1990). Gender history has been virtually unexplored.

Legal and ecclesiastical history were pioneered during the 19th century and the interwar period, but have remained rather distinct fields, until relatively recently uninformed by the interdisciplinary approaches that have long distinguished political, social, and economic history. With a few exceptions, emphasis in Polish legal history has been formalist and norm-centered, largely divorced from social history and practice. There have been a very large number of works (for example by Julius

Bardach) on the substance and procedure of Polish "private" law, as well as analysis of the written evidence of Polish law, and several historical legal textbooks. This careful work has made possible the ultimate integration of legal history into a broader social and interdisciplinary inquiry by the current generation, especially by Hanna Zaremska.

Although medievalists and early modernists from all universities inevitably touch on all aspects of religious history, the center of inquiry into ecclesiastical history – and its gradual integration into social, economic, and political history – has since 1945 been the Catholic University of Lublin, under continuous leadership of Jerzy Kłoczowski. Since his early work on Polish Dominicans, Kłoczowski has been at the forefront of the study of religion – in the total sense of beliefs, practices, and institutions, and as an aspect of social, economic, and cultural history. In addition to continued focus on the mendicants (and older orders), he is general editor of the major 3-volume history of the Polish church, author of two major syntheses integrating the Polish duchies with other areas of "Latin" Europe in terms of education, cultural change, and religious institutions and practices, general editor of a forthcoming atlas of religious history in East Central Europe, and colleague and teacher of a large number of specialists in several areas of ecclesiastical history informed by anthropology, historical geography, and other interdisciplinary perspectives.

The intersection of material culture, social and religious history, and source analysis, has since the 1970s led to a specialization in the history of mentalities, that – as in other European historiographies – transcends the historical fields to which it is related. This field reflects close postwar bilateral contacts between Polish medievalists and the Annales school, involving Jacques Le Goff, Aron Gurevich, Bronisław Geremek, Aleksander Gieysztor, Jerzy Kłoczowski, and, more recently, Henryk Samsonowicz, Jacek Banaszkiewicz, Stanisław Bylina, Hanna Zaremska, Roman Michałowski, and a large number of other scholars. Their interests include: 1) basic ontological categories, such as conceptions of time and space, the group and the self, the sacred and the profane; 2) the psychological dimensions of social divisions, including social marginality and deviance; 3) social specificity of religious, cultural, and economic experience; 4) sacral dimensions of royal power; and 5) constructions of the past and collective identities – which, though expressed in Polish as a history of "national consciousness," are quite similar to those studies of collective memory that have now emerged as an exciting subject in English-language scholarship.

PIOTR GÓRECKI

See also Davies, N.; East Central Europe; Gurevich; Kula

Further Reading

Abramsky, Chimen, Maciej Jachimczyk, and Antony Polonsky, eds., *The Jews in Poland*, Oxford and New York: Blackwell, 1986

Adamus, Jan, *Polska teoria rodowa* (Polish Kinship Theory), Łódź: Ossolińskich, 1958

Aubin, Hermann, "Medieval Agrarian Society in Its Prime: The Lands East of the Elbe and German Colonisation Eastwards," in M.M. Postan and H.J. Habakkuk, eds., *The Cambridge Economic History of Europe*, 2nd edition, vol.1, Cambridge: Cambridge University Press, 1966

Banaszkiewicz, Jacek, *Kronika Dzierzwy: XIV-wieczne kompendium historii ojczystej* (Dzierzwa's Chronicle: A 14th-Century Compendium of Native History), Wrocław: Ossolińskich, 1979

Banaszkiewicz, Jacek, *Podanie o Piaście i Popielu: studium porównawcze nad wczesnośredniowiecznymi tradycjami dynastycznymi* (The Tale of Piast and Popiel: A Comparative Study of Early Medieval Dynastic Traditions), Warsaw: Państwowe Wydawnictwo Naukowe, 1986

Bardach, Juliusz, *Historia państwa i prawa Polski* (History of the State and Law in Poland), vol.1, Warsaw: Państwowe Wydawnictwo Naukowe, 1964

Bardach, Juliusz, Bogusław Leśnodorski, and Michał Pietrzak, *Historia państwa i prawa polskiego* (History of the Polish State and Law), Warsaw: Państwowe Wydawnictwo Naukowe, 1976

Bardach, Juliusz, "L'Indivision familiale dans les pays du Centre-Est européen" (The Familial Undivided Estate in the Countries of East-Central Europe), in Georges Duby and Jacques Le Goff, eds., *Famille et parenté dans l'Occident médiéval* (Family and Kinship in the Medieval West), Rome: Ecole française de Rome, 1977

Bieniak, Janusz, "Clans de chevalerie en Pologne du XIIIe au XVe siècle" (Knightly Clans in Poland, from the 13th to the 15th Centuries), in Georges Duby and Jacques Le Goff, eds., *Famille et parenté dans l'Occident médiéval* (Family and Kinship in the Medieval West), Rome: Ecole française de Rome, 1977

Bieniak, Janusz, "Knight Clans in Medieval Poland," in Antoni Gąsiorowski, ed., *The Polish Nobility in the Middle Ages*, Wrocław: Ossolińskich, 1984

Bogucka, Maria, and Henryk Samsonowicz, *Dzieje miast i mieszczaństwa w Polsce przedrozbiorowej* (History of the Towns and the Bourgeoisie in Pre-Partition Poland), Wrocław: Ossolińskich, 1986

Buczek, Karol, *Targi i miasta na prawie polskim (Okres wczesnośredniowieczny)* (Markets and Towns Established According to Polish Law [The Early Medieval Period]), Wrocław: Ossolińskich, 1964

Buczek, Karol, "Gospodarcze funkcje organizacji grodowej w Polsce wczesnofeudalnej (wiek X–XIII)" (The Economic Functions of the Castle Organization in Early Feudal Poland between the 10th and 13th Centuries), *Kwartalnik Historyczny* 86 (1979), 364–84

Bujak, Franciszek, *Wybór pism* (Selected Writings), Warsaw: Państwowe Wydawnictwo Naukowe, 1976

Burke, Peter, Antoni Mączak, and Henryk Samsonowicz, eds., *East-Central Europe in Transition: From the Fourteenth to the Seventeenth Century*, Cambridge and New York: Cambridge University Press, 1985

Bylina, Stanisław, *Człowiek i zaświaty* (Man and the Supernatural), Warsaw: Upowszechnianie Nauki-Oswiata, 1992

Carter, F.W., *Trade and Urban Development in Poland: An Economic Geography of Cracow, from Its Origins to 1795*, Cambridge and New York: Cambridge University Press, 1994

Cetwiński, Marek, *Rycerstwo śląskie do końca XIII wieku: Pochodzenie, gospodarka, polityka* (Silesian Knighthood Through the End of the 13th Century: Origins, Economy, Politics), Wrocław: Ossolińskich, 1980

Cetwiński, Marek, *Rycerstwo śląskie do końca XIII wieku: qiogramy i rodowody* (Silesian Knighthood Through the End of the 13th Century: Biograms and Genealogies), Wrocław: Ossolińskich, 1982

Christiansen, Eric, *The Northern Crusades: The Baltic and Catholic Frontier, 1100–1525*, Minneapolis: University of Minnesota Press, and London: Macmillan, 1980

Davies, Norman, *God's Playground: A History of Poland*, 2 vols., Oxford: Oxford University Press, and New York: Columbia University Press, 1982

Duby, Georges, and Jacques Le Goff, eds., *Famille et parenté dans l'Occident médiéval* (Family and Kinship in the Medieval West), Rome: Ecole française de Rome, 1977

Fryde, M.M., "The Population of Medieval Poland," in Josiah Cox Russell, ed., *Late Ancient and Medieval Population*, Philadelphia: American Philosophical Society, 1958

Gąsiorowski, Antoni, "Rex ambulans," *Quaestiones Medii Aevi* 1 (1977), 139–62

Gąsiorowski, Antoni, ed., *The Polish Nobility in the Middle Ages*, Wrocław: Ossolińskich, 1984

Geremek, Bronisław, *Les Marginaux Parisiens aux XIVe et XVe siècles* (Parisians on the Margins in the 14th and 15th Centuries), Paris: Flammarion, 1976

Geremek, Bronisław, ed., *Kultura elitarna a kultura masowa w Polsce późnego średniowiecza* (Elite Culture and Mass Culture in Medieval Poland), Wrocław: Ossolińskich, 1978

Geremek, Bronisław, *Litość i szubienica: dzieje nędzy i miłosierdzia*, Warsaw: Czytelnik, 1989; in English as *Poverty: A History*, Oxford and Cambridge, MA: Blackwell, 1994

Gieysztor, Aleksander, "Les Origines de la ville slave" (The Origins of the Slavic Town), *Settimane di studio del Centro Italiano di Studi sull'Alto Medoevo* 6 (1959), 279–315

Gieysztor, Aleksander, "En Pologne médiévale: problèmes du régime politique et de l'organisation administrative du Xe au XIIIe siècles" (Medieval Poland: Problems of Political and Administrative Organization from the 10th to 13th Centuries), *Annali della Fondazione Italiana per la storia amministrativa* 1 (1964), 135–56

Gieysztor, Aleksander, "Le Lignage et la famille nobiliaire en Pologne au XIe, XIIe et XIIIe siècles" (The Noble Lineage and Family in Poland in the 11th, 12th and 13th Centuries), in Georges Duby and Jacques Le Goff, eds., *Famille et parenté dans l'Occident médiéval* (Family and Kinship in the Medieval West), Rome: Ecole française de Rome, 1977

Gieysztor, Aleksander, ed., *History of Poland*, Warsaw: Państwowe Wydawnictwo Naukowe, 1979

Gieysztorowa, Irena, "Research into the Demographic History of Poland: A Provisional Summing-up," *Acta Poloniae Historica* 18 (1968), 5–17

Górecki, Piotr, *Economy, Society, and Lordship in Medieval Poland, 1100–1250*, New York: Holmes and Meier, 1992

Górecki, Piotr, *Parishes, Tithes, and Society in Earlier Medieval Poland, c.1100–1250*, Philadelphia: American Philosophical Society, 1993

Górski, Karol, *L'Ordine Teutonico alle origini dello stato prussiano* (The Teutonic Order until the Origins of the Prussian State), Turin: Einaudi, 1971

Grodecki, Roman, "Książęca włość trzebnicka na tle organizacji majątków książęch w Polsce w XII w." (The Ducal Estate at Trzebnica in the Context of Ducal Estates in Poland in the 12th Century), *Kwartalnik Historyczny* 26 (1912), 433–75 and 27 (1913), 1–66

Grodecki, Roman, *Polska Piastowska* (Piast Poland), Warsaw: Państwowe Wydawnictwo Naukowe, 1969

Grüger, Heinrich, *Heinrichau: Geschichte eines schlesischen Zisterzienserklosters, 1227–1977* (Henryków: A History of a Silesian Cistercian Monastery, 1227–1977), Cologne and Vienna: Böhlau, 1978

Heck, Roman, ed., *Dawna świadomość historyczna w Polsce, Czechach i Słowacji* (Former Historical Consciousness in Poland, Bohemia, and Slovakia), Wrocław: Ossolińskich, 1978

Heck, Roman, "The Main Lines of Development of Silesian Medieval Historiography," *Quaestiones Medii Aevi* 2 (1981), 63–87

Hensel, Witold, *U źródeł Polski średniowiecznej* (At the Roots of Medieval Poland), Wrocław: Ossolińskich, 1974

Hoffmann, Richard C., *Land, Liberties, and Lordship in a Late Medieval Countryside: Agrarian Structures and Change in the Duchy of Wrocław*, Philadelphia: University of Pennsylvania Press, 1989

Karpiński, Andrzej, "Przekupki, kramarki, straganiarki: zakres feminizacji drobnego handlu w miastach polskich w drugiej połowie XVI i w XVII wieku" (Huckstresses, Sellers, Street-Vendors: The Scale of Feminization of Petty Trade in Polish Towns in the Second Half of the 16th and the 17th Century), *Kwartalnik Historii Kultury Materialnej* 38 (1990), 81–91, English summary

Kiersnowski, Ryszard, *Pieniądz kruszcowy w Polsce wczesnośredniowiecznej* (The Coin in Early Medieval Poland), Warsaw: Państwowe Wydawnictwo Naukowe, 1960

Kiersnowski, Ryszard, *Wstęp do numizmatyki polskiej wieków średnich* (Introduction to Polish Numismatics of the Middle Ages), Warsaw: Państwowe Wydawnictwo Naukowe, 1964

Kiersnowski, Ryszard, *Moneta w kulturze wieków średnich* (Coin in Medieval Culture), Warsaw: Państwowe Wydawnictwo Naukowe, 1988

Kłoczowski, Jerzy, *Dominikanie polscy na Śląsku w XIII-XIV wieku* (Polish Dominicans in Silesia in the 13th and 14th Centuries), Lublin: Towarzystwo Naukowe Katolickiego Uniwersytetu Lubelskiego, 1956

Kłoczowski, Jerzy, ed., *Kościół w Polsce* (The Church in Poland), 3 vols., Kraków: Znak, 1966

Kłoczowski, Jerzy, "Les Cisterciens en Pologne, du XIIe au XIIIe siècle" (The Cistercians in Poland from the 12th to the 13th Centuries), *Cîteaux* 28 (1977), 111–34

Kłoczowski, Jerzy, "Le Développement de la civilisation en Europe Centrale et Orientale au XIVe et XVe siècles" (The Development of Civilization in Central and Eastern Europe in the 14th and 15th Centuries), *Quaestiones Medii Aevi* 1 (1977), 111–38

Kłoczowski, Jerzy, ed., *The Christian Community of Medieval Poland*, Wrocław: Ossolińskich, 1981

Kłoczowski, Jerzy, *Europa słowiańska w XIV-XV wieku* (Slavic Europe in the 14th- 15th Centuries), Warsaw: Państwowy Instytut Wydawniczy, 1984

Kłoczowski, Jerzy, *Dzieje chrześcijaństwa polskiego* (History of Polish Christianity), vol. 1, Paris: Editions du Dialogue, 1987

Kłoczowski, Jerzy, ed., *Uniwersalizm i swoistość kultury polskiej* (Universality and Distinctiveness of the Polish Culture), 2 vols., Lublin: Wydawnictwo Katolickiego Uniwersytetu Lubelskiego, 1989

Kłoczowski, Jerzy, *La Pologne dans l'Église médiévale* (Poland in the Medieval Church), Aldershot: Variorum, 1993

Knoll, Paul, *The Rise of the Polish Monarchy: Piast Poland in East Central Europe, 1320–1380*, Chicago: University of Chicago Press, 1972

Knoll, Paul, "The Urban Development of Medieval Poland, with Particular Reference to Kraków," in Bariša Krekić, ed., *Urban Society of Eastern Europe in Premodern Times*, Berkeley: University of California Press, 1987

Koczerska, Maria, *Rodzina szlachecka w Polsce późnego średniowiecza* (The Noble Family in Poland in the Later Middle Ages), Warsaw: Państwowe Wydawnictwo Naukowe, 1975

Korta, Wacław, *Rozwj wielkiej wlasnosci feudalnej na Slasku do polowy XIII wieku* (The Development of the Great Feudal Properties in Silesia through the mid-13th Century), Wrocław, 1964

Kossmann, Oskar, *Polen im Mittelalter* (Poland in the Middle Ages), 2 vols., Marburg: Herder Institute, 1971–85

Kozłowska-Budkowa, Zofia, *Repertorium polskich dokumentw doby piastowskiej*, vol. 1: *Do konca wieku XII* (Inventory of Polish Documents of the Piast Period, vol. 1: Through the End of the 12th Century), Kraków, 1938

Kula, Witold, *Teoria ekonomiczna ustroju feudalnego*, Warsaw: Książka i Wiedza, 1962, revised 1983; in English as *An Economic Theory of the Feudal System: Towards a Model of the Polish Economy, 1500–1800*, London: NLB, 1976

Kula, Witold, *Miary i ludzie*, Warsaw: Państwowe Wydawnictwo Naukowe, 1970; in English as *Measures and Men*, Princeton: Princeton University Press, 1986

Kürbis, Brygida, *Dziejopisarstwo wielkopolskie XIII i XIV wieku* (Great Polish Historical Writing of the 13th and 14th Centuries), Warsaw: Państwowe Wydawnictwo Naukowe, 1959

Kutrzeba, Stanisław, *Historja źródeł dawnego prawa polskiego* (History of the Sources of Old Polish law), 2 vols., Lwów and Kraków: Ossolińskich, 1925–26

Labuda, Gerard, "Miasta na prawie polskim" (Towns Established According to Polish Law), in Aleksander Gieysztor, ed., *Studia historica: w 35-lecie pracy naukowej Henryka Łowmiańskiego*,

Warsaw: Państwowe Wydawnictwo Naukowe, 1958

Ładogórski, Tadeusz, *Studia nad zaludnieniem Polski XIV wieku* (Studies in the Population of Poland on the 14th Century), Wrocław: Ossolińskich, 1958

Leciejewicz, Lech, "Early-medieval Sociotopographical Transformations in West Slavonic Urban Settlements in the Light of Archaeology," *Acta Poloniae Historica* 34 (1976), 29–56

Lekai, Louis J., "Germans and the Medieval Cistercian Abbeys in Poland," *Cîteaux* 28 (1977), 121–32

Lesiński, Bogdan, *Stanowisko kobiety w Polskim prawie ziemskim do połowy XV wieku* (The Position of the Woman in Polish Common Law until the mid-15th Century), Wrocław: Ossolińskich, 1956

Łowmiański, Henryk, *Podstawy gospodarcze formowiania się państw słowiańskich* (The Economic Base for the Formation of Slavic States), Warsaw: Państwowe Wydawnictwo Naukowe, 1953

Łowmiański, Henryk, *Początki Polski* (The Origins of Poland), 6 vols., Warsaw: Państwowe Wydawnictwo Naukowe, 1963–73

Łowmiański, Henryk, ed., *Polska w okresie rozdrobnienia feudalnego* (Poland during the Period of Feudal Fragmentation), Wrocław: Ossolińskich, 1973

Łowmiański, Henryk, *Studia nad dziejami Wielkiego Księstwa Litewskiego* (Studies in the History of the Grand Duchy of Lithuania), Poznań: Wydawnictwo Uniwersytetu im. Adama Mickiewicza, 1983

Ludwig, Michael, *Tendenzen und Erträge der modernen polnischen Spätmittelalterforschung unter besonderer Berücksichtigung der Stadtgeschichte* (Tendencies and Results of the Modern Polish Late Medieval Scholarship, with Particular Consideration of Urban History), Berlin: Duncker & Humblot, 1983

Ludwig, Michael, *Besteuerung und Verpfändung königlicher Städte im spätmittelalterlichen Polen* (Taxation and Pawning of Royal Towns in Late Medieval Poland), Berlin: Duncker & Humblot, 1984

Maleczyński, Karol, *Najstarsze targi w Polsce i stosunek ich do miast przed kolonizacją na prawie niemieckim* (The Oldest Marketplaces in Poland and Their Relationship to Towns before Colonization According to German Law), Lwów: Nakładem Towarzystwa Naukowego, 1926

Maleczyński, Karol, Maria Bielińska, and Antoni Gąsiorowski, *Dyplomatyka wieków średnich* (Diplomatics of the Middle Ages), Warsaw: Państwowe Wydawnictwo Naukowe, 1971

Maleczyński, Karol, *Studia nad dokumentem polskim* (Studies on the Polish Document), Wrocław: Ossolińskich, 1971

Małowist, Marian, *Croissance et régression en Europe, XIVe–XVIIe siècles* (Growth and Regression in Europe, the 14th-17th Centuries), Paris: Colin, 1972

Manteuffel, Tadeusz, "Polska w okresie prawa książęcego, 963–1194," in his *Historyk wobec historii: rozprawy nieznane, pisma drobne, wspomnienia*, Warsaw: Państwowe Wydawnictwo Naukowe, 1976; in English as *The Formation of the Polish State: The Period of Ducal Rule, 963–1194*, Detroit: Wayne State University Press, 1982

Matuszewski, Józef, *Najstarsze polskie zdanie prozaiczne i jego tło historyczne* (The Oldest Polish Sentence in Prose and Its Historical Background), Wrocław: Ossolińskich, 1981

Matuszewski, Jacek, *Vicinia id est . . .: Poszukiwanie alternatywnej koncepcji staropolskiego opola* (Vicinia id est . . .: A Search for a New Conception of the Old Polish "Neighborhood"), Łódź: Wydawnictwo Uniwerystetu Łódzkiego, 1991

Michałowski, Roman, *Princeps fundator: Studiurn z dziejów kultury politycznej w Polsce X-XIII wieku* (*Princeps fundator*: A Study in the History of Political Culture in Poland from the 10th to the 13th Century), Warsaw: Arx Regia, 1993

Modzelewski, Karol, "La Division autarchique du travail à l'échelle d'un état: l'organisation 'ministérielle' en Pologne médiévale" (The Autarchic Division of Labor in the Hierarchy of a State: The "Ministerial" Organization in Medieval Poland), *Annales: ESC* 19 (1964), 1125–38

Modzelewski, Karol, *Organizacja gospodarcza państwa piastowskiego, X–XIII wiek* (The Economic Organization of the Piast State, 10th-13th Centuries), Wrocław: Ossolińskich, 1975

Modzelewski, Karol, "The System of the *Ius Ducale* and the Idea of Feudalism," *Quaestiones Medii Aevi* 1 (1977), 71–99

Modzelewski, Karol, "L'organizzazione dello stato polacco nei secoli X–XIII: la società e le strutture del potere" (The Organization of the Polish State in the 10th–13th Centuries: Society and the Structure of Power), *Settimane di studio del Centro Italiano di Studi sull'Alto Medioevo* 30 (1983), 557–99

Modzelewski, Karol, *Chłopi w monarchii wczesnopiastowskiej* (Peasants in the Early Piast Monarchy), Wrocław: Ossolińskich, 1987

Mularczyk, Jerzy, *Władza książęca na Śląsku w XIII wieku* (Ducal Power in Silesia in the 13th Century), Wrocław: Wydawnictwo Uniwersytetu Wrocławskiego, 1984

Myśliwski, Grzegorz, "Powstanie i rozwój granicy liniowej na Mazowszu (XII-poł. XVI w.)" (The Origins and Development of the Linear Boundary in Masovia Between the 12th and mid-16th Centuries), *Kwartalnik Historyczny* 101 (1994), 3–24

Płaza, Stanisław, *Źródła drukowane do dziejów wsi w dawnej Polsce: studium bibliograficzno-źródłoznawcze* (Printed Sources for the History of the Village in Old Poland: A Bibliographic and Source Study), Warsaw and Kraków: Nakładem Uniwersytetu Jagiellońskiego, 1974

Płaza, Stanisław, *Warsztat naukowy historyka wsi Polski feudalnej* (The Research Workshop of the Rural Historian of Feudal Poland), Warsaw: Państwowe Wydawnictwo Naukowe, 1980

Polonsky, Antony, Jakub Basista, and Andrzej Link-Lenczowski, *The Jews in Old Poland, 1000–1795*, New York: Tauris, and Oxford: Institute for Polish-Jewish Studies, 1993

Postan, M.M., and H.J. Habakkuk, eds., *The Cambridge Economic History of Europe*, 2nd edition, vol. 1., Cambridge and New York: Cambridge University Press, 1966

Rabęcka, Irena, "The Early Medieval Tavern in Poland," *Ergon* 3 (1962), 372–75

Roman, Stanisław, *Geneza statutów Kazimierza Wielkiego: studium źródłoznawcze* (Genesis of the Statutes of Casimir the Great: A Source-Critical Study), Kraków: Nakładem Uniwersytetu Jagiellońskiego, 1961

Rutkowski, Jan, "Medieval Agrarian Society in Its Prime: Poland, Lithuania, and Hungary," in M.M. Postan and H.J. Habakkuk, eds., *The Cambridge Economic History of Europe*, 2nd edition, vol. 1., Cambridge: Cambridge University Press, 1966

Rutkowski, Jan, *Wokół teorii ustroju feudalnego: Prace historyczne* (Toward a Theory of the Feudal System: Historical Essays), edited by Jerzy Topolski, Warsaw: Państwowy Instytut Wydawniczy, 1982

Sedlar, Jean W., *East Central Europe in the Middle Ages, 1000–1500*, Seattle: University of Washington Press, 1994

Semkowicz, Władysław, "Ród Pałuków" (The Pałuka Clan), *Rozprawy Akademii Umiejętności: Wydział Historyczno-Filozoficzny* 2nd series, 24 (1907), 151–268

Semkowicz, Władysław, *Ród Awdańców w wiekach średnich* (The Awdaniec Clan in the Middle Ages), Poznań, 1920

Smolka, Stanisław, *Mieszko Stary i jego wiek* (Mieszko the Old and His Age), Warsaw: Nakł Gebethnera i Wolffa, 1881; reprinted Warsaw: Państwowe Wydawnictwo Naukowe, 1959

Spufford, Peter, *Money and Its Use in Medieval Europe*, Cambridge and New York: Cambridge University Press, 1988

Suchodolski, Stanisław, "*Renovatio monetae* in Poland in the Twelfth Century," *Wiadomości Numizmatyczne* 10 (1961), 57–75

Szymański, Józef, *Nauki pomocnicze historii* (Auxiliary Sciences of History), Warsaw: Państwowe Wydawnictwo Naukowe, 1983

Szymański, Józef, *Herbarz średniowiecznego rycerstwa polskiego* (Crests of the Medieval Polish Knighthood), Warsaw: Państwowe Wydawnictwo Naukowe, 1993

Topolski, Jerzy, *Zarys dziejów Polski*, Warsaw: Interpress, 1982; in English as *An Outline History of Poland*, 1986

Topolski, Jerzy, *The Manorial Economy in Early-Modern East-Central Europe*, Aldershot: Variorum, 1994

Tymieniecki, Kazimierz, *Historia chłopów polskich* (History of Polish Peasants), vol. 1, Warsaw: Państwowe Wydawnictwo Naukowe, 1965

Urban, William, *The Prussian Crusade*, Lanham, MD: University of America, 1980

Vetulani, Adam, "The Jews in Medieval Poland," *Jewish Journal of Sociology* 4 (1962), 374–94

Vetulani, Adam, "Über den Ursprung des Polenspiegels aus der Mitte des XIII. Jahrhunderts" (On the Origins of the Polish Mirror at the mid-13th Century), *Studia Gratiana* 9 (1966), 171–88

Vetulani, Adam, *Z badań nad kulturą prawniczą w Polsce piastowskiej* (Studies on the Legal Culture in Piast Poland), Wrocław: Ossolińskich, 1976

Wasilewski, Tadeusz, "Poland's Administrative Structure in Early Piast Times," *Acta Poloniae Historica* 44 (1981), 5–31

Wyrobisz, Andrzej, and Michal Tymowski with Wojciecha Falkowskiego, *Czas, przestrzeń, praca w dawnych miastach: studia ofiarowane Henrykowi Samsonowiczowi w sześDdziesiątą rocznicę urodzin* (Time, Space, and Labor in Former Towns: Studies Offered to Henryk Samsonowicz on His 60th Birthday), Warsaw: Państwowe Wydawnictwo Naukowe, 1991

Wyrozumski, Jerzy, *Kazimierz Wielki* (Casimir the Great), Wrocław: Ossolińskich, 1982

Wyrozumski, Jerzy, *Dzieje Krakowa: Kraków do schyłku wieków średnich* (A History of Kraków: Kraków until the End of the Middle Ages), Kraków: Wydawnictwo Literackie, 1992

Zaremska, Hanna, *Niegodne rzemiosło: kat w społeczeństwie Polski, XIV–XVI w.*, (An Unworthy Craft: The Executioner in Polish Society from the 14th to the 16th Century), Warsaw: Państwowe Wydawnictwo Naukowe, 1986

Zaremska, Hanna, *Banici w średniowiecznej Europie* (Outlaws in Medieval Europe), Warsaw: SEMPER, 1993

Zientara, Benedykt, *Henryk Brodaty i jego czasy* (Henry the Bearded and His Times), Wrocław: Państwowy Instytut Wydawniczy, 1975

Zientara, Benedykt, "Socio-economic and Spatial Transformations of Polish Towns during the Period of Location," *Acta Poloniae Historica* 34 (1976), 57–84

Zientara, Benedykt, "Über ius Theutonicum in Schlesien" (On the *ius Theutonicum* in Silesia), *Acta Poloniae Historica* 42 (1980), 231–46

Poland: since the 18th Century

In the late 18th and early 19th centuries, at a time when the historical sciences were in their infancy, the Polish state ceased to exist. The partitions of Poland had a profound impact on the development of Polish historiography, and the study of history took on new meaning for society at large. After 1795, when the nation existed only "in spirit," historical writing in Poland had an effect on the nation's social and political consciousness that was exceeded in few other nations. The central question of how the Polish-Lithuanian Commonwealth, which had once thoroughly dominated Eastern Europe, fell into ruin was played out against a historiographic backdrop that emphasized the rise, development, and fall of nations. Many Polish thinkers sought to reconcile their country's past with prevailing historical theories and to provide hope that the nation might regain its independence.

Both the Enlightenment and Romanticism had a vital impact on Polish historiography. The short-lived Polish Enlightenment of the late 18th century that succeeded, however briefly, in restructuring the Polish state, also brought forth the first critical analyses of Poland's past. Nevertheless, Romanticism had the most profound effect on the writing of Polish history. Poland's 19th century was marked by two major revolts against Russian rule (1830–31 and 1863) and by the development of a messianic nationalism. Led by Romantic writers such Adam Mickiewicz, this nationalism, in its most extreme form, portrayed Poland as "the Christ among nations," suffering for the sins of the world. Following the failure of the 1863 uprising, however, Romanticism was eclipsed by a strong Positivist movement.

The true father of modern Polish history was Joachim Lelewel (1796–1861) who reperiodized the Polish past. Instead of an emphasis on the reigns of kings as put forward by earlier chroniclers, Lelewel divided Polish history into four parts: 1) a pre-Christian period in which Slavic tribes lived in a kind of democratic state of grace; 2) a medieval period characterized by the corruption of the church and magnate rule; 3) a golden period of noble democracy; and 4) a corruption of these democratic ideals fostered by the country's rulers which ultimately led to Poland's demise. Lelewel rehabilitated Poland's republican past, portraying it as a wellspring of future strength for the nation. His view of the past had obvious similarities to the views of Russia's Slavophiles.

From this intellectual milieu developed two basic schools of Polish historical thought: the Kraków school and the Warsaw school. Both were affected by positivism and by German historiography, but adopted different views of Poland's past.

The Kraków school, which arose in the relatively free Austrian partition of Poland, put forward an important critique of Lelewel's history. Michał Bobrzyński's *Dzieje Polski w Zarysie* (Outline of Polish History), published in 1880, saw Poland's decline as a consequence of the failure to develop a centralized monarchy. The nobles' republic had not provided a basis for lasting freedoms, and the partitions were largely the result of Poland's inherent weakness, not the machinations of outsiders. This "pessimistic" view of the Polish past, in which Poland's development was seen in contrast to that of the rest of Europe, set off fierce debates among literate Poles of all classes.

The Warsaw school, led by Szymon Askenazy (1866–1935) and others, questioned the uniqueness of Poland's experience. In contrast to the Kraków historians, the Warsaw school tried to see Poland in its European context and put forward the view that Poland was neither the "Christ" nor the "Devil" of Europe. This school also argued that it was unrealistic to place all the blame for Poland's fall on the Poles themselves.

The re-emergence of an independent Polish state in 1918 brought major changes to the historiographic landscape. No longer could historians simply debate the reasons for Poland's collapse at the end of the 18th century without reference to its rebirth at the beginning of the 20th century. Historians emphasized the continuity of Polish traditions and the underlying strength of the nation. This view was also reflected in works by non-Polish writers such William J. Rose and Robert Machray.

At the same time, independence provoked a debate over the nature of the new Poland that reflected deeply divergent views of the past. On one hand there were those who wished for a smaller, more ethnically homogeneous state that would supposedly harken back to the Piast kingdoms of the early Middle Ages. Proponents of this vision tended to see in that ancient state a golden age; they also tended to be more anti-German and politically more conservative. On the other hand, many Poles wished for a return to the old multi-ethnic Commonwealth. Proponents of this vision looked to the Polish-Lithuanian Commonwealth for inspiration, and tended to be politically more liberal and more anti-Bolshevik – that is, anti-Russian. The former view was more closely aligned with the Kraków school, while the latter more closely reflected the Warsaw school. In the end, the interwar Polish state fulfilled neither of these visions.

The 1920s and 1930s saw a flowering and maturing of the Polish historical sciences. Higher education was freed from the repressive policies of the partitioning powers and scholarship was placed on a more rational basis, while there was an increase and improvement in basic education and literacy. There were important, but as yet imperfectly studied, influences from the French Annales school on Polish history writing. New students emerged in the fields of political and military history (Oskar Halecki, Marian Kukiel, Władysław Konopczynski, to name a few), economics (such as Franciszek Bujak), culture (Stefan Czarnowski), law (Stanisław Kutrzeba), and religion and culture (Stanisław Kot). Many of these scholars, combined with contributors from the West, wrote chapters for Reddaway *et al.*'s *The Cambridge History of Poland* (which did not appear in complete form until after World War II), the first attempt at a comprehensive compendium of writings on Polish history in English.

The German and Soviet occupations of Poland during and after World War II had a devastating impact on Polish academe, as many scholars were executed or forced into exile. Communist rule proved equally deleterious for historiography, as doctrinaire Marxism was strongly enforced through the early years of the Polish People's Republic. New works of merit emerged from Poland in the 1970s and 1980s, although topics such as Polish-Soviet relations were strictly circumscribed. Following the collapse of communism and the installation of a democratic government, the historical sciences were freed from ideological constraints. Reflecting the importance history had played in refuting the falsehoods of totalitarianism and in keeping alive the "national spirit," historians played key leadership roles in some of Poland's post-1989 governments.

Outside of Poland, Western and Polish émigré historians produced a steady stream of noteworthy works in the postwar period. These include important syntheses in English by Oskar Halecki, Norman Davies, and, most recently, Piotr Wandycz.

For the early modern period, important scholarship has appeared from Maria Bogucka on towns, and cultural history; from Janusz Tazbir on religion; Jerzy Topolski on economics; and Andrzej Wyczanski on politics, to mention just a few of the notable names. Jerzy Lukowski has argued that the Polish Enlightenment restored the foundation for a vibrant national culture, while Bartłomiej Szyndler has produced new works on Tadeusz Kościuszko and his 1794 uprising. For the partition era, Piotr Wandycz's *Lands of Partitioned Poland* (1975) stands out as a superior work. Andrzej Walicki's political-intellectual histories have also proven noteworthy.

Works on the 20th century include Antony Polonsky's *Politics in Independent Poland* (1972), and Jan Karski's *The*

Great Powers and Poland (1985), as well as a number of biographies of Józef Pilsudski. Military and political affairs have been well represented for the interwar Polish state, which continues to be the subject of a debate reminiscent of the debate over the Polish-Lithuanian Commonwealth. Works on Poland's ethnic minorities are not as numerous, although there is new interest in Poland's Jewish legacy. Earlier work on Polish Jewry include Aleksander Hertz's classic *Żydzi w kulturze polskiej* (1961; *The Jews in Polish Culture*, 1988). A tremendous volume of literature has been produced on Poland in World War II, ranging from military histories of Polish forces in exile, and works on the Warsaw Uprising and the underground movement, to studies of Polish society under German rule and Polish responses to the German extermination of the Jews.

During the Cold War, a wide range of works appeared in the West on communist Poland, some quite good but many rather superficial. The post-1989 period has seen attempts to fill in the "blank spots" of Polish history including the previously taboo subjects of Polish-Soviet relations, anti-regime demonstrations and actions, and the deportation of Rusyn communities during Poland's undeclared civil war in 1946–56. Since the 1970s there has also been important work on Polish immigrant communities around the world, led by the Institute for the Study of Poles Abroad in Kraków and the Polish American Historical Association in the US. Among the notable works on this topic are English-language syntheses by Andrzej Brożek (1985), John Bukowczyk (1988), and James S. Pula (1995). Also important in this area have been the works of Ewa Morawska (1985) and Adam Walaszek (1988).

Polish history has always been influenced by, and been a part of the mainstream of European historiography. The period 1939–89 proved something of an exception to that, albeit an artificially created one. Recent trends seem to indicate that Polish history writing is rejoining that mainstream, which, as Piotr Wandycz has pointed out, it never really left.

JOHN RADZILOWSKI

See also Conze; Davies, N.; East Central Europe; Halecki; Holocaust; Nationalism

Further Reading

Barnett, Clifford R., *Poland: Its People, Its Society, Its Culture*, New York: Grove Press, 1958

Beauvois, Daniel, *Le Noble, le serf et le revizor: la noblesse polonaise entre le tsarisme et les masses ukrainiennes, 1831–1863*, Paris: Edition des Archives Contemporaines, 1985; in English as *The Noble, the Serf, and the Revizor: The Polish Nobility Between Tsarist Imperialism and the Ukrainian Masses (1831–1863)*, New York: Harwood, 1991

Blobaum, Robert, *Rewolucja: Russian Poland, 1904–1907*, Ithaca, NY: Cornell University Press, 1995

Bobrzyński, Michał, *Dzieje Polski w Zarysie* (Outline of Polish History), 1880

Bogucka, Maria, *Dzieje Kultury Polskiej do 1918 roku* (History of Polish Culture to 1918), Wroclaw: Ossoliskich, 1987

Bogucka, Maria, "Gesture, Ritual, and Social Order in Sixteenth- to Eighteenth-Century Poland," in Jan Bremmer and Herman Roodenburg, eds., *A Cultural History of Gesture from Antiquity to the Present Day.* Cambridge: Polity Press, 1991; Ithaca, NY: Cornell University Press, 1992

Braun, Jerzy, ed., *Poland in Christian Civilization*, London: Veritas, 1985

Brock, Peter, *Polish Revolutionary Populism: A Study in Agrarian Socialist Thought from the 1830s to the 1850s*, Toronto: University of Toronto Press, 1977

Bromke, Adam, *The Meaning and Uses of Polish History*, Boulder, CO: East European Monographs, 1987

Brożek, Andrzej, *Polonia amerykańska, 1854–1939*, Warsaw: Interpress, 1977; in English as *Polish Americans, 1854–1939*, Warsaw: Interpress, 1985

Buell, Raymond Leslie, *Poland: Key to Europe*, New York: Knopf, 1939

Bukowczyk, John J., *And My Children Did Not Know Me: A History of the Polish-Americans*, Bloomington: Indiana University Press, 1987

Burke, Peter, Antoni Mączak, and Henryk Samsonowicz, eds., *East-Central Europe in Transition: From the Fourteenth to the Seventeenth Century*, Cambridge and New York: Cambridge University Press, 1985

Ciechanowski, Jan M., *Powstanie Warszawskie: Zarys podłoża politycznego i dyplomatycznego*, London: Odnova, 1971; in English as *The Warsaw Rising of 1944*, Cambridge and New York: Cambridge University Press, 1974

Czarnowski, Stefan, *Kultura* (Culture), Warsaw: Ksixaz, 1946

Davies, Norman, *White Eagle, Red Star: The Polish–Soviet War, 1919–20*, London: Macdonald, and New York: St. Martin's Press, 1972

Davies, Norman, *God's Playground: A History of Poland*, 2 vols., Oxford: Oxford University Press, 1981; New York: Columbia University Press, 1982

Davies, Norman, *Heart of Europe: A Short History of Poland*, Oxford and New York: Oxford University Press, 1984

Davies, Norman, "Sobieski's Legacy: Polish History 1683–1983," London: Orbis, 1985

Engel, David, *Facing a Holocaust: The Polish Government in Exile and the Jews, 1943–1945*, Chapel Hill: University of North Carolina Press, 1993

Fedorowicz, J.K., ed., *A Republic of Nobles: Studies in Polish History to 1864*, Cambridge and New York: Cambridge University Press, 1982

Gierowski, Józef Andrzej, *W Cieniu Ligi Północnej* (In the Shadow of the Northern League), Wrocław: Ossolińskich, 1971

Gross, Jan Tomasz, *Polish Society under German Occupation: The Generalgouvernement, 1939–1944*, Princeton: Princeton University Press, 1979

Gross, Jan Tomasz, *Revolution from Abroad: The Soviet Conquest of Poland's Western Ukraine and Western Belorussia*, Princeton: Princeton University Press, 1988

Gutman, Israel *et al.*, eds., *The Jews of Poland Between the Two World Wars*, Hanover, NH: University Presses of New England, 1989

Hagen, William W., *Germans, Poles, and Jews: The Nationality Conflict in the Prussian East, 1772–1914*, Chicago: University of Chicago Press, 1980

Halecki, Oskar, *La Pologne de 963 à 1914: essai de synthèse historique*, Paris: Alcan, 1933; in English as *A History of Poland: An Essay in Historical Synthesis*, New York: Roy, and London: Dent, 1942, 9th edition, New York: McKay, 1976, London: Routledge, 1978

Hertz, Aleksander, *Żydzi w kulturze polskiej*, Paris: Instytut Literacki, 1961; in English as *The Jews in Polish Culture*, Evanston, IL: Northwestern University Press, 1988

Kapiszewski, Andrzej, *Hugh Gibson and a Controversy over Polish-Jewish Relations after World War I: A Documentary History*, Kraków: Jagiellonian University, 1991

Karski, Jan, *The Great Powers and Poland, 1919–1945: From Versailles to Yalta*, Lanham, MD: University Press of America, 1985

Kieniewicz, Stefan, *The Emancipation of the Polish Peasantry*, Chicago: University of Chicago Press, 1969

Kieniewicz, Stefan, *Historia Polski, 1795–1864*, Warsaw: Państwowe Zakłady Wydawn, 1956; in English as *History of Poland*, Warsaw: PWN, 1979

Klimaszewski, Bolesław, ed., *Outline History of Polish Culture*, Warsaw: Interpress, 1984

Konopczybnski, Władysław, *A Brief Outline of Polish History*, Geneva: Atar, 1919

Korbonski, Stefan, *Wimieniu Rzeczypospolitej*, Paris: Instytut Literacki, 1954; in English as *Fighting Warsaw: The Story of the Polish Underground State, 1939–1945*, New York: Macmillan, and London: Allen and Unwin, 1956

Korbonski, Stefan, *Miedzy młotem a kowedłem*, London: Gryf, 1969; in English as *Between the Hammer and the Anvil*, New York: Hippocrene, 1981

Korbonski, Stefan, *Polskie państwo podziemne: przewodnik po Podziemiu z lat, 1939–1945*, Paris: Instytut Literacki, 1975; in English as *The Polish Underground State, 1939–1945: A Guide to the Underground*, Boulder, CO: East European Monographs, 1978

Kuchowicz, Zbigniew, *Obyczaje i postacie Polski szlacheckiej XVI–XVIII wieku* (The Customs and Character of the Polish Szlachta in the 16th through 18th Centuries), Warsaw: Wydawnictwo Polonia, 1993

Kukiel, Marian, *Czartoryski and European Unity, 1770–1861*, Princeton: Princeton University Press, 1955

Lelewel, Joachim, *Polska, dzieje i rzeczy jej* (Poland, Her History and Everything about Her), 13 vols., Pozna: Zupanskiego, 1853–64

Leslie, R.F., *Polish Politics and the Revolution of November 1830*, London: Athlone Press, 1956

Leslie, R.F., *Reform and Insurrection in Russian Poland, 1856–1865*, London: Athlone Press, 1963

Levine, Hillel, *The Economic Origins of Anti-Semitism: Poland and Its Jews in the Early Modern Period*, New Haven: Yale University Press, 1991

Lewis, Richard D., "Revolution in the Countryside: Russian Poland, 1905–1906," *The Carl Beck Papers in Russian and East European Studies*, no. 506, University of Pittsburgh, 1986

Łojek, Jerzy, *Geneza i Obalenie Konstytucji 3 Maja: Polityka Zagraniczna Rzeczypospolitej, 1787–1792* (The Origins and Overthrow of the Constitution of the 3rd of May: The Political Limits of the Polish Republic, 1787–1792), Lublin: Wydawnictwo Lubelskie, 1986

Lukas, Richard C., *Forgotten Holocaust: The Poles under German Occupation, 1939–1944*, Lexington: University Press of Kentucky, 1986

Lukas, Richard C., ed., *Out of the Inferno: Poles Remember the Holocaust*, Lexington: University Press of Kentucky, 1989

Lukas, Richard C., *Did the Children Cry? Hitler's War Against Jewish and Polish Children, 1939–1945*, New York: Hippocrene, 1994

Lukowski, Jerzy, *Liberty's Folly: The Polish-Lithuanian Commonwealth in the Eighteenth Century, 1697–1795*, London and New York: Routledge, 1991

Machray, Robert, *Poland, 1914–1931*, New York: Dutton, 1932

Morawska, Ewa, *For Bread with Butter: The Life Worlds of East Central Europeans in Johnstown, Pennsylvania, 1890–1940*, Cambridge and New York: Cambridge University Press, 1985

Okęcki, Stanisław, Witold Biegański, and Mieczysław Juchniewicz, ed., *Polacy w ruchu oporu narodów Europy, 1939–1945*, Warsaw: PWN, 1977; in English as *Polish Resistance Movement in Poland and Abroad, 1939–1945*, Warsaw: PWN, 1987

Olszer, Krystyna M., ed., *For Your Freedom and Ours: The Polish Progressive Spirit from the Fourteenth Century to the Present*, revised edition, New York: Ungar, 1981

Opalski, Magdalena, and Israel Bartal, *Poles and Jews: A Failed Brotherhood*, Hanover, NH: University Presses of New England, 1992

Polonsky, Antony, *Politics in Independent Poland, 1921–1939*, Oxford: Oxford University Press, 1972

Polonsky, Antony, ed., *"My Brother's Keeper?" Recent Polish Debates on the Holocaust*, London and New York: Routledge, 1990

Pula, James S., and Mieczysław B. Biskupski, eds., *Polish Democratic Thought from the Renaissance to the Great Emigration: Essays and Documents*, Boulder, CO: East European Monographs, 1990

Pula, James S., *The Polish Americans: An Ethnic Community*, New York: Twayne, and London: Prentice Hall, 1995

Reddaway, William, J.H. Penson, Oskar Halecki, and Roman Dybaski, eds., *The Cambridge History of Poland*, 2 vols., Cambridge: Cambridge University Press, 1950–51

Roos, Hans, *Geschichte der polnischen Nation, 1916–1960: von der Staatsgründung im Ersten Weltkrieg bis zur Gegenwart*, Stuttgart: Kohlhammer, 1961; in English as *A History of Modern Poland: From the Foundation of the State in the First World War to the Present Day*, London: Eyre and Spottiswoode, and New York: Knopf, 1966

Rose, William J., *The Rise of Polish Democracy*, London: Bell, 1944

Rutkowski, Jan, *Histoire économique de la Pologne avant les partages* (An Economic History of Poland before Its Division), Paris: Champion, 1927

Shelton, Anita Krystyna, *The Democratic Idea in Polish History and Historiography: Franciszek Bujak (1875–1953)*, Boulder, CO: East European Monographs, 1989

Skurnowicz, Joan S., "Joachim Lelewel and the Partitions of Poland: A Two Hundred Year Perspective," *Polish Review* 40 (1995), 433–42

Suchodolski, Bogdan, *A History of Polish Culture*, Warsaw: Interpress, 1986

Sukiennicki, Wiktor, *East Central Europe during World War I: From Foreign Domination to National Independence*, 2 vols., Boulder, CO: East European Monographs, 1984

Swiecicka, Maria A.J., ed. and trans., *The Memoirs of Jan Chryzostom z Gosławic Pasek*, New York: Kosciuszko Foundation, 1987

Szyndler, Bartłomiej, *Powstanie Kościuszkowskie, 1794* (Kościuszko's Uprising, 1794), Warsaw: Ancher, 1994

Tazbir, Janusz, *Państwo bez stosów: szkice z dziejów tolerancji w Polsce XVI i XVII w.* Warsaw: Państwowy Instytut Wydawniczy, 1967; in English as *A State Without Stakes: Polish Religious Toleration in the Sixteenth and Seventeenth Centuries*, New York: Kosciusko Foundation, 1973

Topolski, Jerzy, *Zaryś dziejow Polski*, Warsaw: Interpress, 1982; in English as *An Outline History of Poland*, 1986

Wagner, Wenceslas J., ed., *Polish Law Throughout the Ages: 1,000 Years of Legal Thought in Poland*, Stanford, CA: Hoover Institution Press, 1970

Walaszek, Adam, *Polscy Robotnicy, Praca, i Związki Zawodowe w Stanach Zjednoczonych Ameryki, 1880–1922* (Polish Workers, Labor, and Trade Unions in the US, 1880–1922), Wroclaw: Ossolisich, 1988

Walicki, Andrzej, *Philosophy and Romantic Nationalism: The Case of Poland*, Oxford and New York: Oxford University Press, 1982

Walicki, Andrzej, "National Messianism and the Historical Controversies in the Polish Thought of 1831–1848," in Roland Sussex and J.C. Eade, eds., *Culture and Nationalism in Nineteenth-Century Eastern Europe*, Columbus, OH: Slavica, 1983

Wandycz, Piotr S., *Lands of Partitioned Poland, 1795–1918*, Seattle: University of Washington Press, 1975

Wandycz, Piotr S., "Historiography of the Countries of Eastern Europe: Poland," *American Historical Review* 97 (1992), 1011–25

Wandycz, Piotr S., *The Price of Freedom: A History of East Central Europe from the Middle Ages to the Present*, London and New York: Routledge, 1992

Wynot, Edward D., *Polish Politics in Transition: The Camp of National Unity and the Struggle for Power, 1935–1939*, Athens: University of Georgia Press, 1974

Wyrozumski, Jerzy, Józef Andrzej Gierowski, and Józef Buszko, *Historia Polski* (History of Poland), Warsaw: PWN, 1978

Zaloga, Steven, and Victor Madej, *The Polish Campaign of 1939*, New York: Hippocrene, 1985

Zawadzki, W. H., *A Man of Honour: Adam Czartoryski as a Statesman of Russia and Poland, 1795–1831*, Oxford and New York: Oxford University Press, 1993

Zawodny, Janusz Kazimierz, *Nothing but Honor: The Story of the Warsaw Uprising, 1944*, Stanford, CA: Hoover Institution Press, and London: Macmillan, 1978

Zebrowski, Rafal, and Zofia Borzyminska, *Po-Lin: Kultura Żydów Polskich w XX wieku* (Po-Lin: Polish-Jewish Culture in the 20th Century), Warsaw: Amarant, 1993

Polanyi, Karl 1886–1964

Hungarian political economist and economic historian

Karl Polanyi's writings have one central preoccupation: to demonstrate the destructive social and cultural implications of the emergence of a modern "disembedded" market economy and the associated triumph of free market ideology. He saw the Industrial Revolution (the great transformation) as setting in motion the operation of an autonomous free market system and the need for society to regain control of economic forces to avoid the political extremes (of both communism and fascism) that could result from a market society out of control. He was influenced by the interwar period's interest in the sociology of knowledge and by the contemporaneous debate on planning and freedom. The breakdown of international trading and financial mechanisms in the interwar period was the background to Polanyi's search for a degree of state intervention that was compatible with basic human freedoms. He attempted to distinguish between the economic realm, which required planning and control, and the cultural and social spheres, where freedom was important.

In search of a holistic understanding of economic life both in the present and in the past, Polanyi's historical work was concerned with the material existence of earlier – including ancient and primitive – civilizations, and with the transformation of the West in the 18th and 19th centuries. His method was cross-temporal and cross-cultural. Influenced by social anthropology, German historicism, Aristotelian ideas, and Marxism, and by the work of Hegel, Maine, Tönnies, Durkheim, Weber, and Malinowski, Polanyi explored the logic of material life and culture in contexts far removed from Western capitalist societies of the 20th century. In so doing he highlights those features of economic life that are temporally and culturally specific to modern industrial and market economies. His purpose was to provide an understanding of the place of the economy in society that avoided the ethnocentric "economistic fallacy" of perceiving all economies, past and present, as crude variants or precursors of the advanced market form. Polanyi challenged the assumption that calculative gain-oriented economic behavior was prevalent and intrinsic to all human societies, and showed that the pursuit of gain through exchange is an institutionally-enforced pattern of behavior.

The key to his analysis is the distinction between formal and substantive economics. Formal economics denoted the interplay of free market forces in advanced capitalism, driven by calculative economizing behavior and understood within a paradigm emphasizing scarcity, rationality, and choice. Substantive economics was the rest of human behavior, which involved and influenced the material world but which was largely excluded from the "economic sphere," as conventionally understood, even though it was fundamental to the livelihood of man. Substantive economics included relationships and institutions based upon kinship, religion, family, and community, which organized economic production and distribution in non-market ways, particularly through *reciprocity*, *redistribution*, and *householding*, which were governed by notions of provisioning and sufficiency rather than scarcity. Polanyi showed that trade and money had very different functions in non-market and in market contexts. The value of his insights for the study of economic and social history lies in the emphasis he placed upon the need to understand the functioning of past economies on their own terms and as systems of both market and non-market transactional modes embedded in and inseparable from specific cultural and institutional environments. Polanyi rejected the deductive and psychological approach that saw man as a creature of limitless wants, preferring an empirical and cultural approach that did not start with an unchanging and intrinsic view of human nature. His ideas in relation to modern economic life have, however, been criticized for neglecting the extent and the degree of non-market behavior and the cultural and institutional embeddedness of advanced western economies themselves.

Polanyi's work has had a marked though diffuse and frequently uncited influence upon approaches to economic history, particularly those that stress the very different nature of markets, money, and trade in early societies from today, the fragility of market society, and the cultural catastrophe of the Industrial Revolution. Fernand Braudel, Moses Finley, Paul Veyne, Eric Hobsbawm, and Immanuel Wallerstein are among those who cite his influence, but many others appear to have absorbed his ideas or to have misinterpreted them and treated them with condescension. Economic and historical sociology and cultural geography have also been affected by Polanyi: the notion of the economy as an instituted or embedded process has been particularly influential, as has his insistence that calculative behavior is not spontaneous but instituted through acculturation and state policy. The main impact of Polanyi's work has been upon economic anthropology, especially in the United States, where the development of a substantivist school formed an important break with economic determinism.

PAT HUDSON

See also Economic; Rostovtzeff

Biography

Born Vienna, 25 October 1886; grew up in Budapest. Studied at Budapest Gymnasium; University of Budapest; University of Kolosvar, Romania, received law degree 1909. Called to the Bar, 1912. Served in the Hungarian Army during World War I. Staff member, *Der österreichische Volkswirt*, Vienna, 1924–33; moved to England to escape rise of fascism, and taught for the Workers' Educational Association, Oxford, 1937–40; moved to US, 1940; taught at Bennington College, 1940–43; and Columbia University, 1947–60. Married Ilona Duczynska, 1923 (1 daughter). Died Pickering, Ontario, 23 April 1964.

Principal Writings

The Great Transformation: The Political and Economic Origins of Our Time, 1944; in UK as *Origins of Our Time: The Great Transformation*, 1945

"On Belief in Economic Determinism," *Sociological Review* 39 (1947), 95–102

"Marketless Trading in Hammurabi's Time"; "Aristotle Discovers the Economy"; and "The Economy as Instituted Process," in Karl Polanyi, Conrad M. Arensberg, and Harry W. Pearson, eds., *Trade and Market in the Early Empires: Economies in History and Theory*, 1957

"Ports of Trade in Early Societies," *Journal of Economic History* 23 (1963), 30–45

"Sortings and 'Ounce Trade' in the West African Slave Trade," *Journal of African History* 5 (1964), 381–94

Dahomey and the Slave Trade: An Analysis of an Archaic Economy, 1966

Primitive, Archaic, and Modern Economies: Essays of Karl Polanyi, edited by George Dalton, 1968

The Livelihood of Man, edited by Harry W. Pearson, 1977

Further Reading

Block, F., and M. Sommers, "Beyond the Economistic Fallacy: The Holistic Social Science of Karl Polanyi" in Theda Skocpol, ed., *Vision and Method in Historical Sociology*, Cambridge and New York: Cambridge University Press, 1994

Dalton, George, "Primitive, Archaic, and Modern Economies: Karl Polanyi's Contribution to Economic Anthropology and Comparative Economy," in June Helm, ed., *Essays in Economic Anthropology, Dedicated to the Memory of Karl Polanyi*, Seattle: American Ethnological Society, 1965

Humphreys, S.C., "History, Economics and Anthropology: The Work of Karl Polanyi," *History and Theory* 8 (1969), 165–212

Mendell, Marguerite, and Daniel Salée, eds., *The Legacy of Karl Polanyi: Market, State and Society at the End of the Twentieth Century*, Basingstoke: Macmillan, and New York: St. Martin's Press, 1991

Polanyi-Levitt, Kari, ed., *The Life and Works of Karl Polanyi*, New York: Black Rose, 1990

Stanfield, J. Ron, *The Economic Thought of Karl Polanyi*, Basingstoke: Macmillan, 1986

Poliakov, Léon 1910–1997

Russian-French historian of anti-Semitism

Léon Poliakov was a pioneering postwar historian of European Jewry. Poliakov's interest in the history of anti-Semitism came at a time when the field of Jewish history had little place in academic history, and he had little training as a historian. While Poliakov was raised in a secular Jewish family, his interest in tracing the roots of anti-Semitism stemmed from his involvement in the founding in 1944 of the Centre de Documentation Juive Contemporaine (CDJC, organized by Isaac Schneersohn). It gained impetus during Poliakov's later preparation of testimony at Nuremberg on the basis of Gestapo archives left in Paris. Poliakov had trained in law in Paris after emigrating with his family from Russia; his work was informed by Enlightenment values, but was driven by a strong moral commitment to understanding, documenting, and tracing European anti-Semitism through its intensification in the early 20th century. His work as a journalist for an anti-Nazi newspaper through 1939 was a political education. In the course of preparing and presenting evidence for the Nuremberg trials, he gained a clearer sense of the nature, immensity, and atrocity of the "final solution," and found the moral commitment that informed his work.

His work spanned large periods attempting a "total history" of attitudes toward European Jewry, but it remained outside purely religious systems. "The history of antisemitism," he was to repeat, "is not only Jewish history." While his works ranged widely chronologically, seeking to demystify the intertwining of race, country, and nation that underlay the failure of Jewish assimilation in Europe, they returned to the perpetuation of the image of Jew as "other" to understand the resurgence of anti-Semitism in the Holocaust. Poliakov returned to the Holocaust as a touchstone through his life, grasping the extermination of Jews as a human drama in terms of the new tenor of anti-Semitism, which in the 20th century led to Nazi genocide. The ties between anti-Semitism and modernization are an implicit riddle in Poliakov's many works. At a time when the Enlightenment could no longer be understood as a basis for Jewish assimilation, Enlightenment principles provided a position from which to confront the position of Jews in postwar Europe.

The question of how man can turn against man, rather than the social marginalization of Jews, animated Poliakov's groundbreaking multivolume *Histoire de l'antisémitisme* (1955–77; *The History of Anti-Semitism* 1965–85). Expressing Poliakov's commitment to the moral, ethical, and historical importance of a secular history, these volumes traced the marginalization of Jews in European society up to the 20th century. He saw the project as recuperating the memory of an insidious strand that itself lacked any comprehensive account. Indeed, his work was colored by a strong sense of human drama and belief in the benefit of tracing the myths, charges, and persecutions that Jews faced as they remained on the margins of European society. Poliakov's contact with Fernand Braudel and other members of the *Annales* school encouraged him to cross traditional divisions in academic works, often traversing boundaries to synthesize social, economic, and intellectual history in order to provide a more satisfying record of his subject. Frequently, it pushed him into new camps, and new ranges of documentation, as in his exploration of the archives of Rome's Jewish ghetto.

The *History* was planned at an important time in postwar France, where his work at the CDJC sought to repair divisions between French and Jews. Indeed, his work's broad scope fulfilled a need to trace a strand of history that extended from the Dreyfus affair to Vichy France. After his contemporary Jules Isaac had pointed to the responsibility of Christianity for European anti-Semitism, Poliakov provided a social and psychological narrative of the long-standing secular roots of these attitudes. In questioning the place of religion in his narrative, Poliakov's interpretation contrasted with the recent work of Fadiey Lovsky, which argued that anti-Semitism was a manifestation of moments of crisis in Christianity and other religions, and the resurgence at those moments of hostility toward a religion that refused to worship or tolerate other gods. If Isaac and Lovsky emphasized the presence of religion at the basis of anti-Semitic accusations, Poliakov directed attention to the mythic qualities of anti-Semitic discourse. Rather than seeing the blood-definition of Jews as animating modern anti-Semitism, he argued that it was woven to fit the myths of its makers.

The *History* traced a documentary record of anti-Semitism from the time of Christ, but it resisted easy generalization or simple historical conclusions. Poliakov wrote a "detailed history of hostility to the Jews" not from a position of moral judgment, but as a basis for understanding how the "anti-Semitic problem that is intrinsic to our entire Western civilization" was not "an aberrant phenomenon" but "came to lie at the center of the 1939–45 catastrophe." In 1951, he prefaced a small history of the policies of the Nazi state toward the Jews and the decision to proceed with their extermination as offering the opportunity that "with this record in hand, the reader may . . . judge for himself and draw his own conclusions" about the war crimes. Such hopes for objectivity and the search for the objective reader are reflected in his repeated urging that the problem of anti-Semitism, while directed in his account toward the Jews, needed to be studied from the point of view and in the interest of all mankind. The animus for the destruction of Jews was a "beast" that inhabited Germany, that must be historicized in order to be understood. Whereas many earlier studies of attitudes toward the Jews were written in terms of their exclusion from nations, Poliakov focused in later work on the construction of social and cultural myths about the Jews in order to historicize anti-Semitism's animus, and the basis for the exclusion of the Jew from the social body.

His work was not only engaged in a broader desire to understand European anti-Semitism after the war. In part, Poliakov saw the value of his research as revealing the biases that motivated anti-Semitic accusations. In doing so, it recovered the humanity of its victims, but also the biases that underlay the relations of Jews and Christian society in Europe from the classical to early modern periods. Classical historians such as Arnaldo Momigliano or S.D. Goitein had pointed to the coexistence of religions in the late classical period, while Poliakov's work focused on their points of tension and interruption. The groundwork he laid provided an empirical and theoretical basis for much work on the history of Jews in the Middle Ages and modern period, from Shlomo Simonsohn on the relation of Jews to the Apostolic See, to Gavin Langmuir's work on the persecution of Jews in the Middle Ages, from relations of anti-Semitism to fears of heresy, to a range of more specialized studies of the Inquisition. In trying to trace a broad narrative of anti-Semitism's specific manifestations, his surveys and specific studies emphasized the relevance of examining it through its particular manifestations. Through Vatican briefs on the status of Jewish bankers, he analyzed the image of the Jew and lives of Jews at the intersection of social and economic history and of theology. By joining the Christian image of the Jews and attitudes toward the Jew as a legal actor, he approached the notion of a "total history" of the place of Jews on the margins of society in earlier cultures.

While commitment to documenting and describing the development of anti-Semitism characterized most of his work, Poliakov grew dissatisfied toward the end of his life with a rational frame of interpretation of anti-Semitism, and his work gained a broader philosophical nature. He began to work on the possibilities of a history of anti-Semitism within a history of persecution, taking bearings from psychology and anthropology to understand the irrational origins of social demonization. He transformed his studies of anti-Semitism into a history of persecution, and the irrational basis of the thought of the persecutor and anti-Semitic belief, influenced by Leszek Kołakowski's notion of "cultural regression" as a tool to understand the psychology of the persecutor and character of persecution. His 2-volume study, *La Causalité diabolique* (Diabolical Causality, 1980–85), examined the irrational basis of charges

directed toward Jews. Poliakov's emphasis on the irrational character of social demonization in history reframed the relation of modernity to anti-Semitism's resurgence in Russia during the revolution, tracing it through projections since the 13th century of conspiracies and social dangers onto Jews. The book's range suggested a retreat from combating anti-Semitism with rational arguments or objective research, and an expansion of the analytic interrogation of sources. Poliakov had indeed always applied new analytic models as his work required and his interests changed; in focusing on the irrational, he abandoned the hope for a purely logical explanation or account of anti-Semitic beliefs. Drawing heavily on earlier and other printed work, Poliakov responded to this through a new historiography of the irrational processes of thought and the accusations that undergirded social marginalization.

In spite of the range of his research and his changing methodological approach, Poliakov saw his work both as a documentation of persecution and a clarification of historical memory. His influence on the history both of Judaism and of persecution was considerable in France and the United States, and the decades over which he published marked a period of renewed interest in and expansion of engagement with Jewish history in the academy and among professional historians. Poliakov was an important point of reference among French intellectuals, and was himself involved with a range of scholars of political thought and historical theorists such as Raymond Aron and François Furet. His moral importance to postwar French historiography was illustrated by the open response he wrote in 1979 to the revisionist Robert Faurisson, co-signed by Pierre Vidal-Naquet and other historians, affirming the historical undeniability of the Nazi death camps.

DANIEL BROWNSTEIN

See also Hilberg; Holocaust

Biography
Born St. Petersburg, Russia, 25 November 1910 to a secular Jewish family. Left Russia with his family, 1917; settled in Paris, 1920. Studied at Goetheschule, Berlin, 1921–24, Lycée Janson-de-Sailly, Paris, and in the law faculty, University of Paris; awarded doctorate in history, 1965. After university, wrote for family-owned newspaper, the anti-Nazi *Pariser Tageblatt*, to 1939 when it folded. Served in French Army: captured and escaped imprisonment; served in the Resistance from 1941: member, Association de Israélites pratiquants resistance unit; founding member, 1944, and director of research, Centre de Documentation Juive Contemporaine; from Nazi archives in Paris assembled documents for use at Nuremberg trials. Research fellow, Centre Nationale du Recherche Scientifique; director of studies and teacher, Ecole des Hautes Etudes, University of Paris, 1954–79. Married 1) Nathalie Poliakov [no relation] (marriage dissolved 1937); 2) 1941 (3 children); 3) Germaine Rousso, 1952 (1 son). Died Paris, 6 December 1997.

Principal Writings
La Condition des Juifs en France sous l'occupation italienne, 1946; in English as *Jews under the Italian Occupation*, 1955
L'Etoile jaune (The Yellow Star), 1949
Bréviaire de la haine: le IIIe Reich et les Juifs, 1951; in English as *Harvest of Hate: The Nazi Program for the Destruction of the Jews of Europe*, 1954
Histoire de l'antisémitisme, 4 vols., 1955–77; in English as *The History of Anti-Semitism*, 4 vols., 1965–85

Les Banquiers Juifs et le Saint-Siège du XII au XVII siècles, 1965;
   in English as *Jewish Bankers and the Holy See from the
   Thirteenth to the Seventeenth Century*, 1977
*Le Mythe aryen: essai sur les sources du racisme et des
   nationalismes*, 1971, expanded and revised 1987; in English as
   *The Aryan Myth: Essay on the Sources of Racism and
   Nationalisms*, 1974
Le Causalité diabolique (Diabolical Causality), 2 vols., 1980–85
L'Auberge des musiciens: mémoires (The Musicians' Inn: Memoirs),
   1981
With Jean-Pierre Cabestan, *Les totalitarismes du XXe siècle*
   (Totalitarianisms of the 20th Century), 1987
Editor, *Histoire de l'antisémitisme, 1945–1993* (History of Anti-
   Semitism), 1994

Political and Constitutional History

Political history may be understood as the history of public
life and institutions as well as the study of the operation of
power at all levels of society. It is particularly concerned with
the way in which society acquires structure. Political history
therefore includes within it administrative history and has links
to diplomatic, legal, and military history, as well as to the
study of political thought. Its influence is such that many of
the forms of periodization that historians employ are derived
from it. Slightly unfashionable in the immediate post-1945
period, the subject has come to enjoy a renaissance.

The Victorian historian John Seeley wrote: "History is past
politics and politics is present history." Given that most history
until recently was political history, it is not altogether surprising
that political historians have been extremely reticent about
discussing the specifics of their methodology or craft. Political
history has often been solidly empirical, lending itself to a
narrative form. It therefore privileges events and individuals
rather than deeper social processes. It frequently tends to be
the kind of history that is written first, partly because it benefits from the abundance of sources. Social history usually
requires a certain amount of distance from the period under
review so that historical patterns can be discerned. The first
wave of political history includes memoirs by participants and
journalists' accounts of recent events. The release of all public
records (the British Public Record Office operates a 30-year
rule, for example) allows for more considered historical interpretations with a fuller range of source material. From the time
of Ranke onwards, political history has been characterized by
the meticulous scrutiny of public and private archives.

Perhaps the dominant form of political history has been
constitutional history. This was to some extent coterminous
with the rise of the nation-state. Historians allocated themselves the task of explaining how nations came about and the
distinctiveness of their political order. For example, the great
historians of Victorian Britain (Macaulay, Stubbs, Maitland)
documented the emergence of its constitution. While his
famous third chapter has some claims to launching social
history, Macaulay saw his task as explaining Britain's tolerant
and liberal regime in terms of the emergence of the modern
constitution (following the Glorious Revolution of 1688), part
of what came to be known as the "Whig interpretation of
history." His great nephew, George Macaulay Trevelyan,
retained in his writings on the later Stuarts the classic Whig

stories of the struggle for religious freedom and progress.
As David Cannadine observed in his study of Trevelyan, this
kind of history was intended to promote the values of good
citizenship.

In the United States, the Constitution of 1787 received similarly adulatory treatment. It was not until Charles Beard's *An
Economic Interpretation of the Constitution* (1913) that a more
skeptical interpretation set in. Beard held that the founding
fathers of the American Constitution were not patriots so much
as self-serving plutocrats. Historians inspired by Progressivism,
such as Beard, tended to interpret politics in terms of social conflict. After the end of the Progressive era in the United States,
the most influential book in the Progressive tradition was
Arthur M. Schlesinger, Jr.'s *The Age of Jackson* (1945), which
viewed Jacksonian Democracy as an example of lower-class
mobilization against the business community. In the 1950s,
there was a shift away from examining conflict in American
political history and back toward focusing on consensus, evident in Richard Hofstadter's *The American Political Tradition*
(1948) and *The Age of Reform* (1955), and Louis Hartz's *The
Liberal Tradition in America* (1955), all works concerned with
the contribution of ideology to politics.

The importance of constitutional history partly explains why
political history has always been seen as a valuable training for
future politicians and other public officials. Many historians
have had political careers themselves. Macaulay was a Whig MP
in the British House of Commons and an advocate of parliamentary reform during the debates over the passing of the 1832
Reform Act. Schlesinger was close to the Kennedy administration, while the best examples of politicians who took the role of
historian seriously are François Guizot, Winston Churchill, and
Theodore Roosevelt. Political history has given historians a
public role in interpreting the developments of their times.

One of the most influential of 20th-century political historians was Lewis Namier, who rejected the notion that ideas
played a part in 18th-century British politics and instead
devoted *The Structure of Politics at the Accession of George
III* (1929) to a dissection of the interplay between interest
groups in Hanoverian politics. Namier abandoned the Whig
theory of history; his version of 18th-century politics had little
time for ideology or the idea of politicians as bearers of
progress. Instead, politicians were portrayed as essentially
careerists. Namier had a deep impact on the history of high
politics, particularly in Britain where he is associated with the
structural analysis of politics and the collective biography
(prosopography) of political elites. His influence can be
detected in the work of British historians of later periods such
as Norman Gash and John Vincent. Namier also initiated the
History of Parliament project which is assembling biographical data on every member of the British House of Commons.
Paradoxically, Namier's methodology, investigating the background of MPs, amounts to an elaborate form of social history.

A popular form of political history has been the biography
(including the official biography where a historian is granted
privileged access to a subject's papers). Most great figures of
state receive biographical treatment, of which good examples
would be John Morley's Gladstone, Robert Blake's Disraeli,
Ben Pimlott's Harold Wilson and Schlesinger's Robert Kennedy.

Politics has provided historians with an easy form of
chronology, with dates derived from the tenure of power by

heads of state. In 1948, Thomas C. Cochran complained about the American version of this, the presidential synthesis, which neatly divided history into four-year sections. Instead, he called for a political history that would be wider in orientation, deriving its methodology from the social sciences. This coincided with the rise of the systematic study of voter behavior, particularly at Columbia University in New York.

The discipline nurtured political science, which was originally taught as part of history. In the 1950s, the relationship between political scientists and historians was extremely close, particularly at Columbia University and at Nuffield College, Oxford, where David Butler pioneered the study of elections (psephology). Many political scientists (such as Robert McKenzie and V.O. Key) made what were in effect distinguished contributions to political history. Lee Benson's *The Concept of Jacksonian Democracy* (1961) epitomized a new political history that derived from the methodology of political science, characterized by quantification and the study of electoral behavior as well as the inclusion of cultural factors such as religion.

The shift toward quantification was particularly evident among historians such as William O. Aydelotte, who examined patterns in the Victorian House of Commons. In Britain and America, this school of electoral sociology viewed popular politics as the product of deeper social trends that found their expression in political parties. H.J. Hanham's *Elections and Party Management* (1959) described the construction of the political machine in Britain following the introduction of mass democracy in the 1870s and 1880s. Peter Clarke's *Lancashire and the New Liberalism* (1971) examined the consequences for the Edwardian Liberal party of the rise of class voting. The role of sociology was evident in much of this work. For example, John Vincent's *Pollbooks* (1967) drew on Ralf Dahrendorf's *Soziale Klassen und Klassenkonflikt in der industriellen Gesellschaft* (1957; *Class and Class Conflict in Industrial Society*, 1959). In the United States, Richard Hofstadter's work was distinguished by its borrowing from the social sciences, particularly the idea of status anxiety, in order to understand the mentality of reform movements. Thus it is quite erroneous to suggest that political history has lacked ideas.

However, in the 1960s, political history fell out of favor as social history increasingly gained its ascendancy. The Annales school had been notoriously dismissive of the narratives of events associated with political history. The disenchantment of the 1960s New Left with the political system generated the idea that politicians did not make much difference to everyday life and were therefore unimportant. The field was considered antiquated, narrow, elitist, and dry as dust. It was criticized for its top-down focus and concern with a small circle of policymakers which denied the subaltern classes any kind of agency. For Marxists, politics was merely an example of society's superstructure. Political history appeared to lack any reference to profound historical forces. The field did have its defenders, the most prominent of whom, G.R. Elton, considered it the only kind of history worth writing: "historians who can muster no interest for the active political lives of past societies have no sense of history at all." Another British exponent was Maurice Cowling, whose work on high politics emphasized its autonomy and militantly rejected the kind of determinist approaches common in social history. Moreover, political history continued to be heavily taught in schools.

Sellar and Yeatman's wonderful parody of school history, *1066 and All That* (1930), and its many imitators are largely concerned with the kind of stories told to illustrate political history.

More recently the subject has begun to acquire a new respectability. It has focused increasingly on the psychology of elites and considered the role of politics in society. Alongside this there have been debates over the revival of the narrative art that was so integral to political history, signalled by the success of Simon Schama's chronicle of the French Revolution, *Citizens* (1989). François Furet's *Penser la Révolution française* (1978; *Interpreting the French Revolution*, 1981) suggested that the Revolution could not be understood outside of its purely political meaning. Profound economic causes for events were rejected by historians in favor of explanations that stressed political factors, an example of which would be the revisionist arguments about the English revolution initiated by Conrad Russell in the 1970s. The concern with problems of state formation and the growth of the public sphere rendered politics problematic and therefore important. William Leuchtenburg argued that, in the 20th century, few people have been isolated from the state, making political history a pertinent subject. Following the 1960s' insight that "the personal is political," everything became political. Ideas began to matter once more, reflecting the influence of the new intellectual history associated with J.G.A. Pocock and Quentin Skinner.

Eric Foner's masterly study of the ideology of the American Republican party in the 1850s, *Free Soil, Free Labor, Free Men* (1970) represented a new sense that ideology had to be taken seriously. Historians of the right and the left attacked social history for ignoring politics. Curiously, their arguments could be very similar. Tony Judt, Geoff Eley and Keith Nield, and Eugene Genovese and Elizabeth Fox-Genovese (on the left) and Gertrude Himmelfarb (on the right) all noted that its bias against political history rendered social history incapable of dealing fully with important questions of power. Himmelfarb echoed G.R. Elton's defence of political history by calling for the "restoration of reason to history," that is: "the reason embodied in the polity, in the constitutions and laws that permit men to order their affairs in a rational manner – or, on occasion, in an irrational manner, which other men perceive as such and rationally, often heroically struggle against." For Himmelfarb, politics for ordinary people is "what elevated them above the ordinary," something that social historians chose to ignore. Perhaps the finest criticism of the restrictiveness of social history in ignoring politics was produced on the left by Gareth Stedman Jones in his article "Rethinking Chartism." This argued that the Chartist movement in early Victorian Britain could not be understood simply with reference to social and economic forces. Instead, a close reading of its political ideology suggested that it was rooted not in a new class consciousness but in a traditional radical critique of "Old Corruption." This meant that its diagnosis of the state was inadequate at a time when the state was becoming more liberal, explaining Chartism's ultimate failure. Jones therefore restored the political dimension to Chartism.

Politics required attention because of the way in which it made sense of the social structure. Historical actors, it was understood after Furet, became political in a framework derived from politics. The revisionist literature on the French

Revolution downgraded economic and social causes in favor of examining the way in which politics provided a language and ideology that permitted the Revolution to take place. Following the work of the philosopher Louis Althusser, it became common for historians to talk about the "relative autonomy of the political," focusing on the essential strangeness of the political process and the way in which it transformed social phenomena. It is now understood that the political context is indispensable for both social and economic history (see Adrian Wilson, ed., *Rethinking Social History*, 1993). At the same time, political scientists have increasingly turned to history in the construction of their arguments about state formation, evident in Theda Skocpol's *States and Social Revolutions* (1979) and in Richard Bensel's *Yankee Leviathan* (1990). Politics is no longer seen as merely the expression of broader social trends. Revisionists such as those in Jon Lawrence and Miles Taylor's collection, *Party, State, and Society* (1997), have focused on the way in which politicians create rather than reflect their own constituency. The contingencies associated with the political process have been restored as an important factor. Political history has therefore re-emerged as an important discipline with an armory of ideas that can explain change.

ROHAN McWILLIAM

See also Althusser; Beard; Elton; Foner, E.; Furet; Genovese; Guizot; Hartz; Hofstadter; Jones, G.; Leuchtenburg; Macaulay; Maitland; Pocock; Schama; Schlesinger; Seeley; Skinner; State; Stubbs; Trevelyan

Further Reading

Aydelotte, William O., "Voting Patterns in the British House of Commons in the 1840s," *Comparative Studies in Society and History* 5 (1963), 134–63

Beard, Charles, *An Economic Interpretation of the Constitution of the United States*, New York: Macmillan, 1913

Bensel, Richard, *Yankee Leviathan: The Origins of Central State Authority in America, 1859–1877*, Cambridge: Cambridge University Press, 1990

Benson, Lee, *The Concept of Jacksonian Democracy: New York as a Test Case*, Princeton: Princeton University Press, 1961

Blake, Robert, *Disraeli*, London: Eyre and Spottiswoode, 1966; New York: St. Martin's Press, 1967

Bogue, Allan G., "The New Political History in the 1970s," in Michael G. Kammen, ed., *The Past Before Us: Contemporary Historical Writing in the United States*, Ithaca, NY: Cornell University Press, 1980

Cannadine, David, *G.M Trevelyan: A Life in History*, London: HarperCollins, 1992; New York: Norton, 1993

Clarke, Peter F., *Lancashire and the New Liberalism*, Cambridge: Cambridge University Press, 1971

Cochran, Thomas C., "The 'Presidential Synthesis' in American History," *American Historical Review* 53 (1948), 748–59

Cowling, Maurice, *1867: Disraeli, Gladstone and Revolution: The Passing of the Second Reform Bill*, Cambridge: Cambridge University Press, 1967

Dahrendorf, Ralf, *Soziale Klassen und Klassenkonflikt in der industriellen Gesellschaft*, Stuttgart: Enke, 1957; in English as *Class and Class Conflict in Industrial Society*, London: Routledge, and Stanford, CA: Stanford University Press, 1959

Eley, Geoff, and Keith Nield, "Why Does Social History Ignore Politics?," *Social History* 5 (1980), 249–71

Elton, G.R., *Political History: Principles and Practice*, London: Allen Lane, and New York: Basic Books, 1970

Foner, Eric, *Free Soil, Free Labor, Free Men: The Ideology of the Republican Party before the Civil War*, Oxford and New York: Oxford University Press, 1970

Fox-Genovese, Elizabeth, and Eugene D. Genovese, "The Political Crisis of Social History: A Marxian Perspective," *Journal of Social History* 10 (1976), 205–20

Furet, François, *Penser la Révolution française*, Paris: Gallimard, 1978, revised 1983; in English as *Interpreting the French Revolution*, Cambridge and New York: Cambridge University Press, 1981

Gash, Norman, *Politics in the Age of Peel: A Study in the Technique of Parliamentary Representation, 1830–1850*, London and New York: Longman, 1953

Hanham, H.J., *Elections and Party Management: Politics in the Time of Disraeli and Gladstone*, London: Longman, 1959; Hamden, CT: Archon, 1978

Hartz, Louis, *The Liberal Tradition in America: An Interpretation of American Political Thought since the Revolution*, New York: Harcourt Brace, 1955

Hays, Samuel P., "Politics and Social History: Towards a New Synthesis," in James B. Gardner and George Rollie Adams, eds., *Ordinary People and Everyday Life: Perspectives on the New Social History*, Nashville: American Association for State and Local History, 1983

Himmelfarb, Gertrude, "History with the Politics Left Out" in her *The New History and the Old*, Cambridge, MA: Harvard University Press, 1987

Hofstadter, Richard, *The American Political Tradition and the Men Who Made It*, New York: Knopf, 1948; London: Cape, 1962

Hofstadter, Richard, *The Age of Reform: From Bryan to FDR*, New York: Knopf, 1955; London: Cape, 1962

Jones, Gareth Stedman, "Rethinking Chartism" in his *Languages of Class: Studies in English Working-Class History, 1832–1982*, Cambridge and New York: Cambridge University Press, 1983, 90–178

Judt, Tony, "A Clown in Regal Purple: Social History and the Historians," *History Workshop Journal* 7 (1979), 66–94

Katznelson, Ira, "The State to the Rescue? Political Science and History Reconnect," *Social Research* 59 (1992), 719–37

Key, Valdimer Orlando, Jr., *Southern Politics in State and Nation*, New York: Knopf, 1949

Lawrence, Jon, and Miles Taylor, eds., *Party, State, and Society: Electoral Behavior in Britain since 1820*, Aldershot: Scolar Press, and Brookfield, VT: Ashgate, 1997

Leuchtenburg, William, "The Pertinence of Political History: Reflections on the Significance of the State in America," *Journal of American History* 73 (1986), 585–600

Macaulay, Thomas Babington, *The History of England from the Accession of James II*, London: Longman, 5 vols., 1849–61

McKenzie, Robert, *British Political Parties: The Distribution of Power within the Conservative and Labour Parties*, London: Heinemann, 1955

McWilliam, Rohan, *Popular Politics in Nineteenth-Century England*, London and New York: Routledge, 1998

Morley, John, *The Life of William Ewart Gladstone*, London and New York: Macmillan, 1903

Namier, Lewis, *The Structure of Politics at the Accession of George III*, London: Macmillan, 1929; New York: St. Martin's Press, 1957

Namier, Lewis, and John Brooke, *The House of Commons, 1754–1790*, 3 vols., London: HMSO, 1964

Pimlott, Ben, *Harold Wilson*, London: HarperCollins, 1992

Pocock, J.G.A., *The Ancient Constitution and the Feudal Law: A Study of English Historical Thought in the Seventeenth Century*, Cambridge: Cambridge University Press, 1957; revised 1987

Pocock, J.G.A., "Political History in the 1980s," in Theodore K. Rabb and Robert I. Rotberg, eds., *The New History: The 1980s and Beyond*, Princeton: Princeton University Press, 1982

Russell, Conrad, *Parliaments and English Politics, 1621–1629*, Oxford and New York: Oxford University Press, 1979

Schama, Simon, *Citizens: A Chronicle of the French Revolution*, New York: Knopf, and London: Viking, 1989

Schlesinger, Arthur M., Jr., *The Age of Jackson*, Boston: Little Brown, 1945; London: Eyre and Spottiswoode, 1946

Schlesinger, Arthur M., Jr., *Robert Kennedy and His Times*, Boston: Houghton Mifflin, and London: Deutsch, 1978

Sellar, Walter Carruthers, and Robert Julian Yeatman, *1066 and All That: A Memorable History of England*, London: Methuen, 1930; New York: Dutton, 1931

Skinner, Quentin, *The Foundations of Modern Political Thought*, 2 vols., Cambridge and New York: Cambridge University Press, 1978

Skocpol, Theda, *States and Social Revolutions: A Comparative Analysis of France, Russia and China*, Cambridge and New York: Cambridge University Press, 1979

Trevelyan, G.M., *England under Queen Anne*, 3 vols., London and New York: Longman, 1930–34

Vandermeer, Philip R., "The New Political History: Progress and Prospects," in Georg G. Iggers and Harold T. Parker, eds., *International Handbook of Historical Studies*, London: Methuen, and Westport, CT: Greenwood Press, 1979

Vincent, J.R., *Pollbooks: How the Victorians Voted*, Cambridge: Cambridge University Press, 1967

Wilson, Adrian, ed., *Rethinking Social History: English Society 1570–1920 and Its Interpretation*, Manchester: Manchester University Press, 1993

Polybius *c.*200–*c.*118 BCE

Greek historian of Rome

Born in Megalopolis in Arcadia, Polybius was the son of a prominent leader of the Achaean league and so lived the privileged life of a young Greek aristocrat. He received an education as well as military training and by 181–82 he was considered a strong candidate for domestic and international leadership. That Greece was, in his day, dominated by the emerging power of Rome became evident in a purge of the Greek leadership after the weak Achaean support of the Romans against Macedonia in 168. In this upheaval the skills, nobility, and military office of Polybius worked against him, causing the Romans to be suspicious. He was taken, among a thousand Achaean noblemen, to Rome for safekeeping and examination. These factors would all serve to mould his historiography.

Of his literary accomplishments only the *Histories* survives. This work of 40 books (of which only five books and some fragments are known) was designed to be a "universal" history, covering the entire "inhabited world." In this account Polybius was critical of previous historians whom he found too emotional, sensational, or rhetorical. Rather, his history was to be "pragmatic," focusing mainly on political and military material. Polybius sought to provide statesmen, military leaders, and his general readers the moral training and lessons of history. According to his account, the historian should be one who has a passion for truth, should gather firsthand knowledge of political life as well as of the countries being described and, finally, the historian should seek eyewitness accounts of the events in question. Above all, Polybius asserted that the historian should explain the causes of events, particularly in the rise and fall of nations.

Polybius stated that his work was meant to relate "by what means and under what system of government the Romans succeeded in less than 53 years in bringing under their rule almost the whole inhabited world." This promise is particularly fulfilled in book 6 of the *Histories* wherein he described the mixed constitution of kingship, aristocracy, and democracy that informed the Roman rise to power. This he compared to the flawed constitutions of other states such as Athens, Thebes, Crete, Sparta, and Carthage; all but one being Greek. Polybius saw further evidence of Rome's success in the merits and piety of its people as compared to the decadence and, therefore, failure of the Greeks. On occasion he was quite petty in his description of other Greeks who were hostile to the Achaeans.

This causal approach to history has often been viewed by modern historians as rather enlightened. However, in the historiography of Polybius there was also a further agenda designed to impart more than political lessons. Though his philosophical skills were questionable, in the undercurrent of his *Histories* was his description of the various reactions by historical figures to the shifting of fortune. His expression of *Tyche* (fortune), was, at times, orderly and providential. On other occasions it served as an expression of simple chance, while elsewhere it was completely rejected. Such ambiguity was common in the Hellenistic literary expressions of the day, but for Polybius this ambiguity played a more significant role. His "universal" *Histories* was also designed as an account of fortune's "greatest achievement," that is, its ability to unite the whole world under Roman hegemony. Therefore, the ambiguity of fortune in Polybius reflected a general Greek anxiety regarding the new Roman world order.

In the historiography of Polybius the manifestations of fortune must be regarded as primary causations. In addition, his comparison of various governments with Rome's mixed constitution also included an alternate, cyclical view of history wherein kingship, tyranny, aristocracy, oligarchy, democracy, mob-rule, monarchy, and, again, kingship succeeded one another. These elements, and his boast of writing a universal history, all strongly suggest that Polybius was providing a work that had a greater message, a universal model, beyond the simple study of material causation. His *Histories*, describing the rise of Rome, was not a wholehearted acceptance of Roman hegemony, but a subtly reactionary account that affirmed the nonmaterial causation that might possibly provide a future demise of Rome in the movement of history.

While in Rome, Polybius was employed as a tutor to the young aristocrat Scipio Aemelianus who, with Polybius and others, constituted a "circle" of Roman intellectuals. This relationship with Scipio later provided Polybius with opportunities to travel and aided him in the writing of his *Histories*. It probably also brought him into contact with the Stoic philosopher Panaetios who wrote about duty and the movement of providential forces. Polybius wrote his *Histories* partly as an expression of Roman political ideology but also as an expression of Greek hopes. That he wrote in *koine* (common) Greek suggests that his work was accessible to Greek readers as well as Roman aristocrats who could appreciate this less elegant style. On at least one occasion, Polybius found himself acting as mediator between the Romans and his fellow Achaeans. Therefore, his work, aimed at both groups, was at once a subtle affirmation of both Roman triumphalism and Greek angst.

KENNETH R. CALVERT

See also Diodorus; Dionysius; Greece: Ancient; Guicciardini; Roman

Biography
Born Megalopolis in Arcadia, southern Greece, *c*.200 BCE; son of a nobleman, Lycortas. Received education and military training. Appointed Hipparch (military commander) of the Achaean League, 169; one of the thousand prominent Achaeans deported to Rome: held there, 168–150; accompanied Scipio Aemilianus in the siege of Carthage, 147–146; on voyages in the Atlantic, 146. Died *c*.118

Principal Writings
The Histories (Loeb edition), translated by W.R. Paton, 6 vols., 1922–27

Further Reading
Dörrie, Heinrich, "Polybius über Pietas, Religio und Fides" (Polybius on Piety, Religion and Belief), in *Mélanges de philosophie, de littérature et d'histoire ancienne offerts à Pierre Boyancé*, Rome: Ecole Française de Rome, 1974
Fowler, William Warde, "Polybius' Conception of Tyche," *Classical Review* 17 (1903), 445–49
Pédech, Paul, *La Méthode historique de Polybe* (The Historical Method of Polybius), Paris: Belles Lettres, 1964
Walbank, Frank W., *A Historical Commentary on Polybius*, 3 vols., Oxford: Oxford University Press, 1957–79
Walbank, Frank W., *Polybius*, Berkeley: University of California Press, 1972

Popper, Karl 1902–1994
British (Austrian-born) philosopher and historical theorist

As one of the most important philosophers of the 20th century, Karl Popper's name is recognized worldwide. He is, however, less well known in his role as a historical theorist.

Popper's notoriety in the field of history is based almost entirely upon his book *The Poverty of Historicism* (1957), the central thesis of which arose out of his disagreement with a 1944 seminar lecture given by F.A. von Hayek at the London School of Economics. In this lecture, Hayek had argued that laws of historical development exist which the great powers used to legitimize their claims to power. Popper disagreed with the theory that history is governed by laws similar to those in the physical sciences and resisted Hayek's deterministic approach. This became important for him not only in developing his conception of natural philosophy but also in shaping his views on individual psychology.

As Popper began to write down the reasons for his disagreement with Hayek, he ended up with two different manuscripts: *The Poverty of Historicism* and *The Open Society and Its Enemies*. *The Poverty of Historicism* appeared in three parts in the periodical *Economica* in 1944 and then in book form in 1957. In this work, Popper's most important contribution was his recognition of the inability of historians to explain events by means of logic. In Popper's eyes, Hayek's steadfast, but untenable, assertion that there were logical historical laws that could be used to explain historical events, needed to be corrected, and he took it upon himself to set the record straight. Popper advocated an interdisciplinary approach to offer a broader perspective. His unusual understanding of history based on philosophy enabled him to show that historians who claimed to identify historical laws were misleading the public and themselves. For Popper, the beauty of history lay in man's inability to explain all of its facets. His recognition of the flaws of historical research has become an integral part of modern historiography and through his arguments, historians have been forced to be more honest with themselves and their readers.

In his second book, *The Open Society and Its Enemies* (1945), Popper argued, on the basis of Plato, Marx, and Hegel, his idea of an "open society" in the spirit of the Enlightenment which is directed against every form of totalitarianism. This second book established Popper's reputation as a social philosopher and, as a result, he was invited to teach at the London School of Economics and Political Science in 1945, where he remained until his retirement.

Popper's social philosophy was greatly influenced by the rise of totalitarianism in Europe. The hunger and suffering experienced by large portions of the Vienna population following World War I interested him in socialism. However, he quickly realized that there was a huge gap between the promises of the socialists and communists to better the lot of the downtrodden, and their actions. Popper himself experienced the divergence between doctrine and practice when he decided to become a manual laborer in order to resolve his intellectual dilemma. After a short time, Popper realized that he was not up to the physical demands of this type of work, and he enrolled full time at the University of Vienna as an education major with certification in math and physics, completing his degree in 1924.

During this time, Popper had contact with Heinrich Gomperz, a well known student of Greek philosophy, and Karl Bühler, a developmental and Gestalt psychologist. It was under Bühler's direction that Popper completed his dissertation *Zur Methodenfrage der Denkpsychologie* (On the Methods Question in the Psychology of Thought, 1928).

In 1930, Popper first met Herbert Feigl, a member of the Wiener Kreis (Vienna Circle), who convinced him to write down his ideas about scientific theory. The result was Popper's manuscript "Die beiden Grundprobleme der Erkenntnistheorie" (The Two Basic Problems of Epistemology) which long remained unpublished because of its complexity and length. After several friends had read the manuscript, Popper decided to shorten it. This version was published in 1934 as *Logik der Forschung* (*The Logic of Scientific Discovery*, 1959). In *The Logic of Scientific Discovery*, Popper outlined his theory of falsification in the philosophy of science. Here, Popper contended that scientific theories are never more than provisionally adopted and remain acceptable only as long as scientists devise new experiments to test (falsify) them. *The Logic of Scientific Discovery* took an emphatic counterposition to the philosophy of logical empiricism, thus assuring it major influence in philosophical circles. The success of *The Logic of Scientific Discovery* brought Popper invitations to visit London and Brussels in 1935 and 1936. This led to his professorship at the University of Christchurch in New Zealand in 1937, one year before Hitler seized power in Austria.

Although *The Poverty of Historicism* was important for Popper's development as a philosopher, the arguments expressed in *The Logic of Scientific Discovery* remained the basis of his philosophy. In 1961 Popper, in conjunction with

Theodor Adorno, made a speech "On the Logic of the Social Sciences." This began a controversy that appeared in book form under the title *Der Positivismusstreit in der deutschen Soziologie* (The Positivism Debate in German Sociology, 1969), This debate occupied the German academic community for many years afterwards.

In a number of treatises, Popper developed his philosophical positions still further. These were collected as *Conjectures and Refutations* (1963). A further collection of essays, *Objective Knowledge* (1972), directed itself against subjectivism in episte- mology which resulted in a "Theory of the Objective Spirit." On the subject of the "body-soul problem," Popper developed ideas about the interaction between consciousness and processes in the human neural system in conjunction with the neuropsychologist John C. Eccles which led to the publication of *The Self and Its Brain* (1977).

As can be seen from these works, Popper steered away from historical arguments in later years and spent his time investi- gating scientific and psychological questions. Despite this shift, his *Poverty of Historicism* still holds an important place as a work of historical theory.

GREGORY WEEKS

See also Gombrich; Metahistory

Biography

Karl Raimund Popper. Born Vienna, 28 July 1902. Received PhD, University of Vienna 1928. Emigrated to New Zealand, 1937. Senior lecturer in philosophy, Canterbury University College, Christchurch, 1937–45; reader in logic and scientific method, London School of Economics, 1945–49, professor, 1949–69. Married Josefine Anna Henninger, 1930 (died 1985). Knighted 1965. Died Croydon, London, 17 September 1994.

Principal Writings

Zur Methodenfrage der Denkpsychologie (On the Methods Question in the Psychology of Thought), 1928
Logik der Forschung, 1934; in English as *The Logic of Scientific Discovery*, 1959; revised 1980
The Open Society and Its Enemies, 2 vols., 1945; revised 1950
The Poverty of Historicism, 1957
Conjectures and Refutations: The Growth of Scientific Knowledge, 1963
Der Positivismusstreit in der deutschen Soziologie (The Positivism Debate in German Sociology), 1969
Objective Knowledge: An Evolutionary Approach, 1972
Philosophy and Physics: Essays in Defence of the Objectivity of Physical Science, 1974
The Philosophy of Karl Popper, edited by Paul Arthur Schilpp, 2 vols., 1974; portion reprinted as *The Unended Quest: An Intellectual Autobiography*, 1976
With John C. Eccles, *The Self and Its Brain*, 1977
Die beiden Grundprobleme der Erkenntnistheorie (The Two Basic Problems of Epistemology), 1979 [written 1930–33]
Postscript to The Logic of Scientific Discovery, edited by W.W. Bartley, 3 vols., 1982–83

Further Reading

Alt, Jürgen August, *Karl R. Popper*, Frankfurt and New York: Campus, 1992
Döring, Eberhard, *Karl R. Popper: Einführung in Leben und Werk* (Karl R. Popper: Introduction to his Life and Work), Hamburg: Hoffmann & Campe, 1987

Fahny-Eid, Nadia, "Histoire, objectivité et scientificité: jalons pour une reprise du débat épistémologique" (History, Objectivity, and Being Scientific: Foundations for a Resumption of the Epistemological Debate), *Social History* [Canada] 24 (1991), 9–34
Levinson, Paul, *In Pursuit of Truth: Essays on the Philosophy of Karl Popper on the Occasion of His 80th Birthday*, Brighton: Harvester Press , and Atlantic Highlands, NJ: Humanities Press, 1982
Salamun, Kurt, ed., *Schriftenreihe zur Philosophie Karl R. Poppers und des kritischen Rationalismus* (Publication Series about Karl R. Popper's Philosophy and Critical Rationalism), 7 vols., Amsterdam: Rodopi, 1991–
Schäfer, Lothar, *Karl R. Popper*, Munich: Beck, 1992
Skagestad, Peter, *Making Sense of History: The Philosophies of Popper and Collingwood*, Oslo: Universitetsforlatget, 1975
Triki, Fathi, "Popper et la philosophie de l'histoire" (Popper and the Philosophy of History), *Cahiers de Tunisie* 28 (1980), 221–35
Wilkins, Burleigh Taylor, *Has History any Meaning? A Critique of Popper's Philosophy of History*, Ithaca, NY: Cornell University Press, 1978

Popular History

Popular history undoubtedly exists, but since there are so many varieties of it, it is difficult to define. Its existence points out, moreover, the fact that the opposite must also exist – not, one hopes, "unpopular" history, but the kind of history that is written for a specialist rather than a wide audience, the kind of writing often called "academic" history.

From the earliest times until close to the end of the 19th century – from Herodotus through Gibbon to Macaulay and Carlyle – the distinction between popular and academic histo- rian did not exist: all historians were popular, in the sense that they all wrote for a general literate public rather than for other historians. Gibbon, Macaulay, and Carlyle wrote in an era when the audience for serious writing in the English-speaking world was numbered only in the tens of thousands, yet their books sold well, were widely discussed, and had considerable influence on public thinking. Their audience was the privileged classes, the beneficiaries of a classical education, who recog- nized the Latin tags that every reader was expected to under- stand. They wrote from particular perspectives, of course: Gibbon's *Decline and Fall of the Roman Empire* (1776–88) was written under the influence of the Enlightenment and was markedly anticlerical; Gibbon's famous judgment was that the fall was "the triumph of barbarism and Christianity." Carlyle and Macaulay also had their axes to grind.

Popular history is mostly a creation of the late 19th and 20th centuries, tied to the professionalization of historical writing that began when history became a subject taught in universities. When possession of a doctorate supplanted book sales as the goal of some historians, the craft was split into two factions: one that wished to please the public, and one that wished to please peer review boards and promotion committees. Only a very few managed to please both.

Perhaps the most common variety of popular history is that which deliberately sets out to reach as wide an audience as possible, and to illustrate a historical period or episode through good narrative writing and compelling characterization. The writer usually seeks to accomplish this goal by concentrating on the anecdotal and colorful aspects of the topic. "Bringing the past to life" and "telling a good story" are emphasized, and there is usually a total absence of analysis. The result can often be almost indistinguishable from historical fiction. One of the most famous practitioners of this latter craft was James A. Michener, whose many works, notably *Hawaii* (1959), *Chesapeake* (1978), and *Alaska* (1988), sold millions of copies, and gave a sense of the history of the regions about which he wrote to readers unlikely to read academic history.

In the hands of a writer such as Michener, who put much effort into getting his facts right and had the skill to write compelling prose, popular history is at once engaging and convincing. When practiced by one who is less talented or less concerned about authenticity, popular history can descend to the level of purple prose and fabricated conversations. At the worst it becomes the sort of romantic fiction, sometimes called a "bodice ripper," in which history is merely a stage setting for softcore pornography. At best it becomes the kind of fiction that gives a real sense of place and time, as well as telling a gripping tale; the Horatio Hornblower series of C.S. Forester is a fine example. At a more "literary" level still it is exemplified by the works of the poet and novelist Robert Graves, notably *I, Claudius* (1934), and of Gore Vidal, author of *Burr* (1973) and *Julian* (1964). Both writers give a sense of time and place that most academics cannot match, and have a strong effect on shaping the general understanding of the past.

Another kind of popular history might be termed "panoramic." Here the writer attempts to paint on a very wide canvas, often with the goal of explaining all of history to a popular audience. Sometimes this is attempted in a single volume, as for example by H.W. Van Loon in *The Story of Mankind* (1921), and by H.G. Wells in *The Outline of History* (1920). At other times the history of humanity requires many volumes, most spectacularly in the work of Will and Ariel Durant, whose *The Story of Civilization*, begun in 1935, ran eventually to eleven volumes written over many decades, of which only the first, *Our Oriental Heritage*, dealt with anything beyond western Europe.

The Durants' work was like the famous "five-foot shelf" of great books; it was meant to serve as a work of self-education, to be read by ordinary people who wanted to know the roots of their civilization. As such, it was often bought in sets, and individual volumes were sold throughout the years by the Book of the Month Club in the United States to people interested in self-improvement. It is difficult to believe that many read all or even very much of it.

Such was not the case with Winston Churchill, whose 4-volume *A History of the English-Speaking Peoples* (1956–58) profited by the fame and prose style of its author, which reminded readers of his sonorous and orotund speaking style. To read the work, with its appeal to the unity of the old British empire and America, was to hear his wartime speeches once more; it spoke to its time, and was popular history at its best.

A category that probably has more titles in print than all the others combined is local history. These histories are narratives of events or biographies of people who were important to their region or locality: pioneers, ranchers, doctors, miners, schoolteachers, "colorful characters," and others. Sometimes they are histories of small towns or municipalities, and include a brief sketch of every citizen, past and present; sometimes they are histories of mines, railroads, hospitals, or schools.

They are often compiled by amateur historians with a strong dedication to the personalities and artifacts of the past.

Popular history at the end of the 20th century is alive and flourishing, both outside the universities and to some extent within them. Lamentably, however, the gulf between popular and academic history seems to be widening with each decade. In the past fifty years the number of historians working in universities has increased tremendously, and so has their output, most of which does not fall into the popular category. In many countries, subsidized university presses produce hundreds of works of history every year, flooding the libraries (whose budgets shrink as the flood increases). Freed from the imperatives of the marketplace, academic historical writing is now often produced with less attention to the audience than to professional or methodological and doctrinal considerations.

Because book sales are of secondary importance, historians can concentrate on conceptual frameworks, some old (Marxist), some newer (feminist, postmodernist), on new historical methods (quantitative history, prosopography), and on carefully nuanced historical debates. In contrast, the works of popular historians must stand on their own in this regard. With the expansion of numbers in the historical profession, buttressed by new or expanded universities, the development of new subdisciplines, some with their own special language, and the proliferation of university presses, there was sufficient interest inside the academy to make it possible to spend one's career writing only for other historians. The result has been the division of popular and academic scholarship into two distinctive, only occasionally overlapping streams of historical writing.

Only a few university-based intellectuals, such Henry Reynolds of Australia, author of *The Other Side of the Frontier: Aboriginal Resistance to the European Invasion of Australia* (1981) and Keith Sinclair of New Zealand, author of *A Destiny Apart: New Zealand's Search for National Identity* (1986), have made a conscious effort to write history for a general audience. (Here the colon, the invariable mark of an academic title, is a warning signal of a book with academic roots.) In the previous generation, the American Samuel Eliot Morison was a fine scholar, giving due care to detail and evidence, who could at the same time interest a wide public audience by his brilliant evocation of time and place, and his lucid prose style. His many works, the last of which was his 2-volume *The European Discovery of America* (1971–74), are good as popular and academic history.

Works of historians such as these draw on years of scholarship. They pay careful attention to the rules of historical evidence, thus ensuring that their books will withstand historical assessment, while at the same time their spirited prose and powerful sense of nationalism, historical grievance, or whatever their focus may be attract popular interest. Some of these writers have deliberately set out to bridge the gap between popular and academic history, demonstrating that solid works of historical scholarship can, if well written, argumentative, and focused, serve both Clio and the bookseller. In effect, they maintain the tradition of Gibbon and the rest as both figures of literary renown and important historical analysts.

Academic historians sometimes disparage popular historians, even the good ones, such as Barbara Tuchman, whose books *The Guns of August* (1962), *A Distant Mirror: The Calamitous Fourteenth Century* (1978), and *The March of Folly: From Troy* to *Vietnam* (1984) are, despite the suspicious colons in the titles, excellent popular histories, have sold widely, and have been well-reviewed in the press. By the methodological and theoretical standards employed by many in university history departments, however, the emphasis by Tuchman and writers like her on individuals in history (the much-disparaged "great man" approach) and on the forces of contingency seem like quaint affectations of an earlier age. The very fact of their popularity has been sufficient to earn the enmity of some academics, and because they usually have a wide focus, they invariably contain specific errors that are gleefully seized upon by those whose expertise is much deeper, though much more narrow.

In fairness to the critics of popular history, some of its writers are more interested in popularity than in history, and sometimes substitute illustrations for text, anecdote for evidence, generalization for interpretation, and secondary research for archival study. The result is well-exemplified in a long-standing dispute around Peter C. Newman, a Canadian journalist and historian, whose history of the Hudson's Bay Company infuriated the historical profession, and set off a shouting match in which the scholars were accused of nit-picking and envy, and Newman derided for distorting and sensationalizing the past.

Happily such quarrels are the exception. The list of thoughtful and careful writers who flourish outside the universities is a long and distinguished one. In the United States Shelby Foote's books on the Civil War are authoritative as well as popular, and Daniel Boorstin's 3- volume work *The Americans* (1958–73) is an excellent attempt to explain the republic to its citizens. In an earlier generation, the journalist Frederick L. Allen's history of the 1920s, *The Big Change*, published just after the decade ended, is so perceptive and engaging that it is still required reading in undergraduate university classes, surely one of the toughest audiences for popular history. William Manchester's biography of General MacArthur, *American Caesar* (1978), illustrates the strength and worth of the popular history genre, though his excessively detailed *Death of a President* (1967) illustrates some of its weaknesses.

In Britain the list of excellent popular historians is even longer, for that country, for whatever reason – a greater sense of its own past, higher standards in its education system – has produced many excellent writers of popular history. Lytton Strachey was perhaps more polemicist than historian, but his *Eminent Victorians* (1918) was both widely read and influenced perceptions of the Victorian age. The 20th century has produced so many good British popular historians that it would be impossible to name even a fraction of them. A good representative is Antonia Fraser, whose specialty is biography; she has tackled such disparate subjects as Boadicea, Charles II, Mary Queen of Scots, and the wives of Henry VIII, as well as writing books on the Gunpowder Plot and the role of women in the 17th century, all with style, grace, and accuracy.

Fraser's career is an example of the fact that popular historians have in the past generation or two largely taken over the field of biography, a field that many academics have abandoned, partly because the "great man/woman" approach to history is no longer academically fashionable, and partly because biography does not fit well into new trends in academic thinking. Much popular history has always centered on the lives of kings and queens, politicians, soldiers, and captains of industry, for there is fascination with the lives of those in high places, even if, like Edward VIII, they were weak or unattractive as people. Both Frances Donaldson and Philip Ziegler, among others, wrote sensitive biographies of this unlucky monarch, proof of the continuing appeal of the genre.

One of the best examples of a popular historian is perhaps the Australian Robert Hughes. As well as many works of journalism and criticism, he has written an important study of the origins of Australia. *The Fatal Shore* (1987) is a compelling work, serious, thorough, and highly interpretive. It is based on a careful reading of both primary and secondary materials, and yet is so well written that it has become a bestseller in several countries.

With the advent of television and motion pictures, the popularization of history has spread further afield. Though it is difficult to think of a historical movie that does not invite criticism, some television has combined new technology with decent scholarship. In Britain, Peter Watkins' treatment of the 17th-century battle of Culloden won professional as well as popular acclaim. In the United States, Ken Burns has produced excellent documentary series on the Civil War, the American West, and the history of baseball for the public television network. The highly popular television serialization of Graves' *I, Claudius* undoubtedly was the definitive word on Rome for thousands of viewers.

At present, popular history and academic historical writing seem destined to continue to move in different directions. The fascination on the part of many academic historians with new theories, and the difficult jargon associated with postmodernism and deconstruction, have strengthened a new public perception of academic history as aloof, confusing, and irrelevant. It has also created tensions in the historical profession between the practitioners of the new art and those who consider it gibberish. Television has created a proliferation of competing versions of the past. In the United States, the History Channel mingles fairly serious historical documentaries with dubious motion pictures and endless rubbish about the "mysteries" of the past: were the pyramids built by gods from outer space? where is the lost continent of Atlantis? what is the magical power of the Bermuda Triangle? and so on. The danger is that Gresham's law will prevail, and that bad history will drive out good.

But the very popularity of popular history is a hopeful sign, for it would not be good for the discipline to have it confined to university campuses. From the earliest days of human literacy, people have been intensely interested in historical writing. Historical works, whether judged good or bad by the professionals, have always appeared on bestseller lists, and have been fodder for Hollywood. Popular historians know that there is a good market for their work, and if the academic historians have retreated to the university presses and the academic journals, it is their loss and the profession's.

KEN COATES and WILLIAM MORRISON

See also Boorstin; Carlyle; Gibbon; Herodotus; Macaulay; Morison; Sinclair; Stone; Universal

Further Reading

Allen, Frederick Lewis, *The Big Change: America Transforms Itself, 1900–1950*, New York: Harper, and London: Hamish Hamilton, 1952

Boorstin, Daniel J., *The Americans*, 3 vols., New York: Random House, 1958–73; London: Cardinal, 1988

Carlyle, Thomas, *A Carlyle Reader: Selections from the Writings of Thomas Carlyle*, edited by G.B. Tennyson, New York: Modern Library, 1969; Cambridge: Cambridge University Press, 1984

Churchill, Winston, *A History of the English-Speaking Peoples*, 4 vols., London: Cassell, and New York: Dodd Mead, 1956–58

Donaldson, Frances, *Edward VIII*, London: Weidenfeld and Nicolson, and Philadelphia: Lippincott, 1974

Durant, Will, and Ariel Durant, *The Story of Civilization*, 11 vols., New York: Simon and Schuster, 1935–75; abridged edition, London: Benn, 1947

Foote, Shelby, *The Civil War*, 3 vols., New York: Random House, 1958–74; London: Bodley Head, 1991

Forester, Cecil Scott, *The Happy Return*, London: Joseph, 1937; as *Beat to Quarters*, Boston: Little Brown, 1937 [and 10 further Horatio Hornblower novels, 1938–67]

Fraser, Antonia, *Mary Queen of Scots*, London: Weidenfeld and Nicolson, and New York: Delacorte Press, 1969

Fraser, Antonia, *King Charles II*, London: Weidenfeld and Nicolson, 1979; as *Royal Charles: Charles II and the Restoration*, New York: Random House, 1979

Fraser, Antonia, *The Weaker Vessel: Woman's Lot in Seventeenth Century England*, London: Weidenfeld and Nicolson, and New York: Knopf, 1984

Fraser, Antonia, *Boadicea's Chariot: The Warrior Queens*, London: Weidenfeld and Nicolson, 1988; as *The Warrior Queens*, New York: Knopf, 1989

Fraser, Antonia, *The Six Wives of Henry VIII*, London: Weidenfeld and Nicolson, and New York: Knopf, 1992

Fraser, Antonia, *The Gunpowder Plot: Terror and Faith in 1605*, London: Weidenfeld and Nicolson, 1996

Frisch, Michael H., *A Shared Authority: Essays on the Craft and Meaning of Oral and Public History*, Albany: State University of New York Press, 1990

Füredi, Frank, *Mythical Past, Elusive Future: History and Society in an Anxious Age*, London: Pluto Press, 1992

Gibbon, Edward, *The History of the Decline and Fall of the Roman Empire*, 6 vols., London: Strahan and Cadell, 1776–88

Graves, Robert, *I, Claudius*, London: Barker, and New York: Smith and Haas, 1934

Hughes, Robert, *The Fatal Shore: A History of the Transportation of Convicts to Australia, 1787–1868*, New York: Knopf, and London: Collins, 1987

Leffler, Phyllis K., *Public and Academic History: A Philosophy and Paradigm*, Malabar, FL: Krieger, 1990

Macaulay, Thomas Babington, *The History of England from the Accession of James II*, 5 vols., London: Longman, 1849–61

Manchester, William, *The Death of a President*, New York: Harper, and London: Joseph, 1967

Manchester, William, *American Caesar: Douglas MacArthur, 1880–1964*, Boston: Little Brown, 1978; London: Hutchinson, 1979

Michener, James A., *Hawaii*, New York: Random House, 1959; London: Secker and Warburg, 1960

Michener, James A., *Chesapeake*, New York: Random House, and London: Secker and Warburg, 1978

Michener, James A., *Alaska*, New York: Random House, and London: Secker and Warburg, 1988

Morison, Samuel Eliot, *The European Discovery of America*, 2 vols., Oxford and New York: Oxford University Press, 1971–74

Newman, Peter C., *Company of Adventurers*, 3 vols., New York and London: Viking, 1985–91

Reynolds, Henry, *The Other Side of the Frontier: Aboriginal Resistance to the European Invasion of Australia*, Ringwood and Harmondsworth: Penguin, 1981

Sinclair, Keith, *A Destiny Apart: New Zealand's Search for National Identity*, Wellington and London: Allen and Unwin, 1986

Stone, Lawrence, *The Past and the Present Revisited*, London: Routledge, 1987

Strachey, Lytton, *Eminent Victorians: Cardinal Manning, Florence Nightingale, Dr. Arnold, General Gordon*, London: Chatto and Windus, and New York: Putnam, 1918

Tuchman, Barbara, *The Guns of August*, New York: Macmillan, 1962; as *August 1914*, London: Constable, 1962

Tuchman, Barbara, *A Distant Mirror: The Calamitous Fourteenth Century*, New York: Knopf, and London: Macmillan, 1978

Tuchman, Barbara, *The March of Folly: From Troy to Vietnam*, New York: Knopf, and London: Michael Joseph, 1984

Van Loon, Hendrik Willem, *The Story of Mankind*, New York: Boni and Liveright, 1921; London: Harrap, 1922

Vidal, Gore, *Julian*, Boston: Little Brown, and London: Heinemann, 1964

Vidal, Gore, *Burr*, New York: Random House, 1973; London: Heinemann, 1974

Wells, Herbert George, *The Outline of History*, 2 vols., London: Newnes, and New York: Macmillan, 1920 [and later revisions]

Ziegler, Philip, *King Edward VIII: The Official Biography*, London: Collins, 1990; New York: Knopf, 1991

Portelli, Alessandro 1942–

Italian oral historian

Although Alessandro Portelli is not a historian by training, Italian historiography owes him a great deal because of his original and innovative research, especially in the field of oral history where his contribution has been outstanding.

In the early 1960s, while studying for a law degree, then a degree in foreign languages at the University of Rome, Portelli began a productive collaboration with Gianni Bosio and the Istituto Ernesto de Martino in Milan. Each was concerned with gathering and publishing songs of the class struggle from the preceding two centuries. Portelli joined in the enterprise and began publishing on the subject in the journal *I giorni cantati*, which he also edited from 1972 to 1995. This drew him deeper into questions about popular memory, which he began to exploit in his formal writings.

Portelli's most important contribution to historical research, and a landmark in Italian oral historiography, is without doubt *Biografia di una città* (Biography of a City, 1985), which emerged in a period when oral history was achieving acceptance as an academic discipline. Portelli's work injected new life into oral history, breaking the very close tie of historiographical representation with pure orality. The wide time-span covered by the research, starting from the memory of the post-Napoleonic commotions in the then sleepy provincial papal town of Terni, is a clear example of his new approach. *Biografia di una città* was also a demonstration of Portelli's ability to exploit disparate sources such as archival material, printed material (especially newspaper reports), daily discourse, oral tradition, and mass culture, and to interweave them with direct testimonies. He reconstructed in this way 150 years of history, from the Risorgimento to the transformation of a small country town into a major heavy industrial center, and finally the collapse of an industrial economy.

His exploitation of oral sources masterfully linked people's memories with formal historical writing, validating the importance of memory, language, and imagination. Portelli extracted the recollections of a wide spectrum of people born between 1886 and 1966, from peasants to politicians, from industrial workers to priests, and demonstrated that collective memory was well equipped not only to survive, but also to function effectively in an environment where the balance of power leaned toward official memory. Singularly relevant in this respect was his analysis of the so-called "creative errors" by which people manipulated their memory and reconstructed their judgment about individual or collective events by using fantasy as an interpretive tool.

Portelli also argued that oral history was no less reliable than other forms of memoir, and that the way in which people reconstructed events in their mind could allow historians to appreciate better the way people interpreted the past. Portelli set out his arguments in "Sulla specificità della storia orale" (1979; "The Peculiarities of Oral History," 1981), and used his own work on Terni to illustrate his point. He had found that interviewees had often misremembered the year of the killing of Luigi Trastulli, a local political activist, as they had shaped the narrative of postwar events. Rather than seeing this as negating their testimony, Portelli suggested that it could help clarify our understanding of how they interpreted the events of the period.

Portelli's contribution is also relevant in other areas of research, and his specialist attention to language has favored avenues of research that might have been left unexplored by more conventional historians. His innovative use of language is a case in point, as he ventured that the relationship between interviewees and dialect was one of consciousness and self-denigration. The dialects of Terni – in fact all dialects of Umbria and the Marches regions – are generally considered in Italy unattractive and inferior to others regarded as more noble and beautiful. The people of Terni feared sounding uncultured when speaking; that attitude exemplified Terni's liminal status between town and countryside, dialect and national language, working class and middle class, oral tradition and schooling, and the invasion of the mass media.

That image of transition is perhaps one of the most interesting contributions of Portelli's multifaceted work, linking linguistic uncertainty to the tension that is primarily one of social status.

GENNARO CAROTENUTO

See also Oral

Biography

Born Rome, 4 July 1942. Educated at Liceo Classico, Terni; received law degree, University of Rome, 1966, foreign languages degree 1973. Taught at University of Siena at Arezzo, 1975–81; professor of Anglo-American literature, University of Rome from 1981. Married Mariella Eboli, economist (2 sons).

Principal Writings

"Sulla specificità della storia orale," *Primo Maggio* 13 (1979), 54–60; in English as "The Peculiarities of Oral History," *History Workshop Journal* 12 (1981), 96–107; reprinted in his *The Death of Luigi Trastulli*, 1991

With others, *Racconto: tra oralità e scrittura* (Tales: Oral and Written), 1983

Biografia di una città: storia e racconto: Terni 1830–1985 (Biography of a City: Stories and Tales, Terni, 1830–1985), 1985

The Death of Luigi Trastulli, and Other Stories: Form and Meaning in Oral History, 1991

The Battle of Valle Giulia: Oral History and the Art of Dialogue, 1997

Postan, M.M. 1899–1981

British (Russian-born) medievalist

Michael Postan was one of the leading figures in the emerging field of medieval economic history during the interwar period. The 19th-century application of scientific principles to historical data continued with the application of economic theory. Economics was then perceived to be the most scientific of the social sciences.

Postan's exact date of birth and details of his early life in Russia before his arrival in Britain were for long unclear, as the stories he told varied. He enrolled as a mature student at the London School of Economics, then a vibrant intellectual center, from which professors R.H. Tawney and Eileen Power were challenging the dominant emphasis on political and constitutional history, through the use of new theoretical approaches and documentary sources.

Postan's abilities as a scholar were noticed by Eileen Power. He became her research assistant and subsequently her husband. She fostered his career, helping him to obtain a lectureship at the London School of Economics and later declining an invitation to apply for the chair of economic history at Cambridge to ensure his success. They were both powerful personalities and formed a close intellectual partnership. Power's strength lay in her ability to construct a conceptual framework for her subject. Inspired by Henri Pirenne and Marc Bloch, she set out to develop a broad social and economic history of Europe. Her abilities were complemented by Postan's knowledge of European social theory, especially the Russian and German literature, and his stronger emphasis on detail. After Power's early death, aged 51, Postan continued many of the projects she had initiated. These included editing the *Economic History Review* and *The Cambridge Economic History of Europe*, of which their edited volume *Studies in English Trade* (1933) was a forerunner.

Postan's initial interests were in medieval capital formation, as his early essays, collected in *Medieval Trade and Finance* (1973), illustrate. Later he turned his attention to manorial records and made important contributions to our understanding of agrarian economy and demographic change. Today his thesis that the population was already in decline before the Black Death of 1347–49 is widely accepted. However, his emphasis on the Malthusian theory of population crisis, an aspect of his economic determinism – the view that society was at the mercy of abstract economic forces – was criticized by Marxist historians such as Kosminsky and Hilton. They believed that collective struggle against feudal lords was significant in improving the lives of the majority of the peasantry in the course of the Middle Ages.

Postan insisted on tackling the intellectual problems that arose as he was applying economic theory to historical data. He found these equally challenging whether he was thinking about the Middle Ages or his own times, as in *An Economic History of Western Europe, 1945–1964* (1967). He wrote no major work on medieval economic history because of this attention to detail. *The Medieval Economy and Society* (1972) is only a brief overview of his researches at the end of a long life of study. Postan's contemporaries were disappointed that his publications were not more extensive, considering his early promise. Nevertheless, his contribution to history was the application of economic theory to the Middle Ages, a large number of articles, mainly on English agrarian history, and his editorship of *The Cambridge Economic History of Europe* and the *Economic History Review*.

VIRGINIA R. BAINBRIDGE

See also Britain: 1066–1485; Economic; Habakkuk; Hilton; Power

Biography

Michael Moïssey Postan. Born Tighina, Bessarabia, Russia, 24 September 1899. Came to England, 1920; naturalized 1926. Received BA, London School of Economics, 1924. Taught at University College, London, 1927–31; London School of Economics, 1931–35; and Cambridge University (rising to professor), 1935–65 (emeritus): fellow, Peterhouse, Cambridge, 1935–65. Head of Russian section, Ministry of Economic Warfare, 1939–42; official historian of munitions, Offices of War Cabinet, 1942. Knighted 1980. Married 1) Eileen Power, historian, 1937 (died 1940); 2) Lady Cynthia Rosalie Keppel, 1944 (2 sons). Died Cambridge, 12 December 1981.

Principal Writings

Editor with Eileen Power, *Studies in English Trade in the Fifteenth Century*, 1933
General editor with H.J. Habakkuk, *The Cambridge Economic History of Europe*, 2nd edition, 1966–89
An Economic History of Western Europe, 1945–1964, 1967
The Medieval Economy and Society: An Economic History of Britain in the Middle Ages, 1972; in US with subtitle *An Economic History of Britain, 1100–1500*, 1972
Essays on Medieval Agriculture and General Problems of the Medieval Economy, 1973
Medieval Trade and Finance, 1973
Editor, *Medieval Women* by Eileen Power, 1975

Further Reading

Berg, Maxine, *A Woman in History: Eileen Power, 1889–1940*, Cambridge: Cambridge University Press, 1996

Postcolonialism

Postcolonialism is an elusive and contested term that refers to the multifaceted project of examining the complex and unequal relationships between the imperial European powers and their generally, though not exclusively, non-European subjects before and after formal political independence. A particular focus has been on the use of literature and language as means of political control. Postcolonial theorists have argued that imperialist texts – novels, travelers' accounts, histories – contain seemingly immutable and unquestioned assumptions regarding race, gender, ethnicity, religion, nation, and nationalism that serve to marginalize and objectify subject peoples.

Postcolonialists argue that the colonizers, by naming, defining, categorizing, mapping, and dividing peoples, places, languages, and cultures, created new social forms that furthered their own imperial interests. Postcolonial writers are now challenging these names, definitions, and categories, in new and highly creative literatures. Salman Rushdie's novels *Midnight's Children* (1981) and *The Moor's Last Sigh* (1995) exemplify this approach.

Edward Said's *Orientalism* (1978) has been pivotal in demonstrating the extent to which European representations of "the Orient" have been distorted by unequal power relations. Postcolonialist historians have expanded on Said's project of undermining the binarism of self/other, us/them, advanced/aboriginal, male/female, rational/irrational, modern/traditional, developed/underdeveloped, center/margin, core/periphery, by emphasizing instead the intricacy and complexity of the relations between the colonizer and the colonized. Instead of such binarism, postcolonial theorists have posited a hybridity in which individuals in colonial and neocolonial societies, or individuals from the colonies living in the West, participate in complex, fluid, and unequal combinations of indigenous and imperial cultures. This hybridity can lead to the creation of new concepts and literatures that are themselves sites of resistance.

Postcolonial theorists argue that imperial powers have attempted to impose their languages and cultures through education and other means of cultural diffusion because of their unquestioned assumption of cultural superiority and of the universality of human concerns. In resisting universalistic assumptions, postcolonial theorists celebrate diversity, pluralism, and cultural syncretism.

Postcolonial historians focus on reconceptualizing history as a process in which successive generations have written their lived experiences, rather than as a chronological, purposeful narrative that progresses from primitive to advanced stages. Postcolonial historians construct their own histories by challenging notions of cultural purity that have served to remove the indigenous subject, the "other," from history. The postcolonial historian has taken an active role in challenging unequal power relations through this process of interrogating and rewriting the historical narratives canonized by the imperial powers and taught in Western-style schools. The new histories subvert unequal colonial relationships by rewriting notions of time and place and by writing in the marginalized who are both the products and the creators of the new hybrid cultures.

NANCY GALLAGHER

See also Anderson, B.; Orientalism; Said

Further Reading

Anderson, Benedict, *Imagined Communities: Reflections on the Origin and Spread of Nationalism*, London and New York: Verso, 1983; revised 1991
Ashcroft, Bill, Gareth Griffiths, and Helen Tiffin, eds., *The Empire Writes Back: Theory and Practice in Postcolonial Literatures*, London and New York: Routledge, 1989
Ashcroft, Bill, Gareth Griffiths, and Helen Tiffin, eds., *The Postcolonial Studies Reader*, London and New York: Routledge, 1995
Babha, Homi, ed., *Nation and Narration*, New York and London: Routledge, 1990
Boehmer, Elleke, *Colonial and Postcolonial Literature: Migrant Metaphors*, New York and Oxford: Oxford University Press, 1995
Lewis, Reina, *Gendering Orientalism: Race, Femininity, and Representation*, London and New York: Routledge, 1996

McClintock, Ann, "The Angel of Progress: Pitfalls of the Term
'Post-colonialism,'" in Patrick Williams and Laura Chrisman,
eds., *Colonial Discourse and Post-colonial Theory: A Reader*,
New York: Harvester Wheatsheaf, 1993

Mitchell, Timothy, *Colonising Egypt*, Cambridge and New York:
Cambridge University Press, 1988

Mohanty, Chandra Talpade, Ann Russo, and Lourdes Torres, eds.,
Third World Women and the Politics of Feminism, Bloomington:
Indiana University Press, 1991

Mudimbe, V.Y., *The Idea of Africa*, Bloomington: Indiana University
Press, and London: Currey, 1994

Rushdie, Salman, *Midnight's Children*, London: Cape, and New
York: Knopf, 1981

Rushdie, Salman, *The Moor's Last Sigh*, London: Cape, and New
York, Pantheon, 1995

Said, Edward W., *Orientalism*, New York: Pantheon, and London:
Routledge, 1978

Said, Edward W., "Representing the Colonized: Anthropology's
Interlocutors," *Critical Inquiry* 15 (1989), 205–25

Said, Edward W., *Culture and Imperialism*, New York: Knopf, and
London: Chatto and Windus, 1993

Turner, Bryan S., *Orientalism, Postmodernism, and Globalism*,
London and New York: Routledge, 1994

Williams, Patrick, and Laura Chrisman, eds., *Colonial Discourse
and Post-colonial Theory: A Reader*, New York: Harvester
Wheatsheaf, 1993

Young, Robert, *White Mythologies: Writing History and the West*,
London and New York: Routledge, 1990

Postmodernism

It is usual in the literature to distinguish between postmodernity (as referring to our current socioeconomic-political condition) and postmodernism (as referring to ways of making sense of various "expressive" intellectual changes *vis à vis* postmodernity at the level of theory), a distinction captured by J.F. Lyotard (*The Postmodern Condition*, 1979, translated 1984): "our working hypothesis is that the status of knowledge is altered as societies enter what is known as the post-industrial age and cultures enter what is known as the postmodern age." It is also useful – if not so usual – to distinguish between deconstructionism (a method of reading associated most closely with Jacques Derrida and Paul de Man), which exposes the limits and inconsistencies of texts, not least by demonstrating how the attempt to make them internally coherent by bracketing out inconvenient elements is impossible, so that by making them visible the text is rendered problematic, indeterminate and thus ultimately undecidable at the level of its meaning; and poststructuralism (the arguments associated with Roland Barthes, Michel Foucault, Jacques Lacan, and others) that language is anterior to the world it carves up and shapes so that "reality" is never known "in and for itself," but is a linguistic affect of the language system inhabited by the speaker. This is not to deny the actuality of the world (or of worlds past) but is simply to say that it is human discourse that appropriates it and gives it all the meanings it can be said to have.

Postmodernism, as a more general cultural condition, uses the insights of deconstructionism and poststructuralism to argue that there is no necessary or entailed correspondence between world and word, that the world is to be read on its surfaces for its created significances as a text with no meanings outside of such texts; that we know not the world as such but only our narratives of it; that ultimately we cannot reach the truth of the world unless that truth is restricted to acceptance of the internal coherences within and between various language games, the way the world has always already been put under a description, and so on.

In addition to this, postmodernism has (in the hands of, say, Lyotard, Richard Rorty, Jean Baudrillard, and others) placed these arguments in a larger context. Thus it has attacked any idea that we can find in, say, history, any overarching metanarrative that would guarantee immanent meanings (ideas of progress, etc.), Lyotard defining postmodernism as "incredulity towards metanarratives"; that we have to understand that there are not, and nor have there ever been, any real foundations of the kind alleged to underpin the "experiment of modernity" (i.e., foundations from which could be extrapolated, in positivistic manner, various laws, predictions and so on). Postmodernism also asks that we recognize that we live, and have always lived, amidst social formations that have no legitimating ontological, epistemological, methodological, or ethical grounds for our beliefs or actions beyond the status of an ultimately self-referencing, rhetorical conversation. As far as history is concerned, such thinking undercuts any idea of our finding a meaning in the past, present, or future of the sort associated with history in the upper case (as History, as Metanarrative) while the recognition that history is a self-referencing concept (it is the name given to the things historians make, i.e., historiography) means that history in the lower case (history as the study of the past for its own sake, i.e., as academic, professional history) is not "proper" history at all but merely the mythologizing way of legitimating a particular approach to the past *as if* it were the way that the past itself prefers to be read. This means, to put it simply, that both upper and lower case histories are literary genres, not epistemologies. In these ways postmodernism undercuts history as we have known it in both upper and lower case so that postmodernism can be held to signify "the end of history," not in the sense of the end of historical thinking as such, but historical thinking based on modernity's version of what history apparently was understood to be, namely history in upper and lower case versions. Postmodernism thus invites us to think of history as yet to be defined; that history is something that has "not yet been."

KEITH JENKINS

See also Foucault

Further Reading

Ankersmit, F.R., *Narrative Logic: A Semantic Analysis of the
Historian's Language*, The Hague: Nijhoff, 1983

Bauman, Zygmunt, *Intimations of Postmodernity*, London and New
York: Routledge, 1992

Berkhofer, Robert, Jr., *Beyond the Great Story: History as Text and
Discourse*, Cambridge, MA: Harvard University Press, 1995

Bertens, Hans, *The Idea of the Postmodern: A History*, London and
New York: Routledge, 1995

Callinicos, Alex, *Theories and Narratives: Reflections on the
Philosophy of History*, Durham, NC: Duke University Press, and
Oxford: Polity Press, 1995

Caplan, Jane, "Postmodernism, Poststructuralism, and
Deconstruction: Notes for Historians," *Central European History*,
3 (1989), 260–78

Docherty, Thomas, ed., *Postmodernism: A Reader*, London: Harvester Wheatsheaf, and New York: Columbia University Press, 1993

Elam, Diane, *Feminism and Deconstruction: Ms. en abyme*, London and New York: Routledge, 1994

Fish, Stanley, *Doing What Comes Naturally: Change, Rhetoric, and the Practice of Theory*, Durham, NC: Duke University Press, and Oxford: Oxford University Press, 1989

Harvey, David, *The Condition of Postmodernity: An Enquiry into the Origins of Cultural Change*, Oxford and Cambridge, MA: Blackwell, 1989

Jenkins, Keith, *On "What Is History"? From Carr and Elton to Rorty and White*, London and New York: Routledge, 1995

Jenkins, Keith, ed., *The Postmodern History Reader*, London and New York: Routledge, 1997

Lyotard, Jean-François, *La Condition postmoderne: rapport sur le savoir*, Paris: Minuit, 1979; in English as *The Postmodern Condition: A Report on Knowledge*, Manchester: Manchester University Press, and Minneapolis: University of Minnesota Press, 1984

Nicholson, Linda J., *Feminism/Postmodernism*, London and New York: Routledge, 1990

Norris, Christopher, *The Truth about Postmodernism*, Oxford and Cambridge, MA: Blackwell, 1993

Rorty, Richard, *Contingency, Irony, and Solidarity*, Cambridge and New York: Cambridge University Press, 1989

Scott, Joan Wallach, *Gender and the Politics of History*, New York: Columbia University Press, 1988

Spiegel, Gabrielle, "History, Historicism and the Social Logic of the Text in the Middle Ages," *Speculum* 65 (1990), 59–86

Wilson, Adrian, ed., *Rethinking Social History: English Society, 1570–1920 and Its Interpretation*, Manchester: Manchester University Press, 1993

Potter, David M. 1910–1971

US historian

David M. Potter was a historians' historian, whose unpretentious, economical, and closely argued books and essays had an influence on his field disproportionate to their number. He was known both for his mastery of detail and for his willingness to tackle extremely broad themes in United States history. Throughout his career Potter was preoccupied with two broad themes: the history of the South, the region where he was born, and broader themes dealing with the nature of American society and the character of the American people.

Potter's early work was on the proximate causes of the Civil War, and the question of whether the Civil War had in fact been inevitable. His well-received first book, *Lincoln and His Party in the Secession Crisis* (1942), was a revisionist study which argued that the outbreak of war owed more to blunders on the part of both president Abraham Lincoln and the southern secessionists than it did to any deep-laid plans on either side. He insisted that in order to gain an accurate appraisal of the situation at the time, one must abandon the insights provided by hindsight.

For much of the rest of his career, Potter was at work on *The Impending Crisis* (1976), a posthumously-published *magnum opus* that traced the roots of the Civil War back to the Mexican War and consequent controversies during the following thirteen years concerning the extension of slavery to United States territories acquired during the conflict. Again,

Potter rejected *ex post facto* knowledge in favor of restricting himself to the contemporary viewpoint of the participants in this struggle and, in the words of one reviewer, "tak[ing] no outcome for granted and see[ing] nothing as absolutely inevitable." He made it clear that many alternative courses of action existed at different points in time. His shorter essays on this theme are collected in *The South and the Sectional Conflict* (1968), and cover a wide array of topics, among them the nature of the South and of southern history, studies of Abraham Lincoln, John Brown, and Horace Greeley, the literature of the Civil War period, and studies of particular political episodes. These essays also won high praise from his peers for their meticulous preparation, subtlety, range, and readiness to challenge accepted truths. A series of lectures which he delivered at Louisiana State University in 1968, and later published as *The South and the Concurrent Majority* (1972), had broad implications for American political history from the late 19th to the mid-20th centuries, when, it argued, a southern majority with the power to block legislation displeasing to it effectively controlled the United States Congress, meaning that national policy had to take account of southern priorities and interests.

Potter's best-known book, *People of Plenty* (1954), tackled even more sweeping themes, attempting to relate the national character of the American people to the comparative plenty and the technological means to take advantage of this plenty that has historically characterized the United States. Potter drew on insights from the behavioral sciences, including cultural anthropology, psychology, and sociology, combining them with empirical historical methodology in an attempt to define the American national character and analyze his country's historical experience. He built upon Frederick Jackson Turner's thesis that the frontier and the ready availability of land had been the defining factor in creating the American character, expanding it to include natural resources and "the nation's system of production and distribution." Potter argued that their presence accounted for, among other things, the emergence of a consumer society, dominated by advertising; the relative social mobility of Americans and their definition by status rather than class, a trait which could create considerable psychological uneasiness; the permissiveness with which American children are reared, instilling a belief that Americans will always be able to attain their goals; and American-style democracy. He suggested that in foreign affairs Americans attempted to export their political institutions to countries which lacked the economic abundance to support them. In this work Potter placed himself with several historians of the 1950s, among them Daniel J. Boorstin, Louis Hartz, and Richard Hofstadter, who stressed the exceptionalism of the United States and those factors making for a political, social, and economic consensus as to their country's broader principles and goals, to which, they argued, the great majority of Americans throughout the course of United States history had subscribed. While attacked by some critics for ignoring the poor and those on the margins of society, in later life Potter himself felt that, with some exceptions, his thesis was still valid, and his book has had a substantial influence upon subsequent historians, despite a certain sense that when writing it he was inevitably affected by the prevailing material affluence of the 1950s.

Potter's concerns with the role and nature of freedom in the United States informed his Commonwealth Fund lectures of

1963, *Freedom and Its Limitations in American Life* (1976). Building on themes broached in *People of Plenty*, he suggested that, in a society without fixed status or classes, few individuals had the strength to withstand pressures for conformity. He also warned that Americans were routinely subjected to "noncoercive" manipulation from advertisers designed to persuade them to become biddable consumers. In numerous shorter essays published throughout his career, Potter wrote extensively on similarly general themes related to United States history, among them the national character, the question of whether the United States was a separate civilization, individualism, alienation, social cohesion, and the relationship between historians and nationalism. After his death these were collected in *History and American Society* (1973). In recent decades declining American economic growth and a new social and economic climate of scarcity, together with a sense that consumerism may not provide all the answers to US social and economic problems, have given his general works a revitalized cogency.

PRISCILLA M. ROBERTS

See also Hartz; United States: 19th Century; United States: Historical Writing, 20th Century

Biography

David Morris Potter. Born Augusta, Georgia, 6 December 1910. Received BA, Emory University, 1932; studied with Ulrich Bonnell Phillips, Yale University, MA 1933, PhD 1940. Taught at University of Mississippi, 1936–38; Rice University, 1938–42; Yale University, 1942–61; and Stanford University, 1961–71. Married 1) Ethelyn Elmer Henry, 1939 (marriage dissolved); 2) Dilys Mary Roberts, 1948 (died 1969; one daughter [committed suicide]). Died Palo Alto, California, 18 February 1971.

Principal Writings

Lincoln and His Party in the Secession Crisis, 1942
People of Plenty: Economic Abundance and the American Character, 1954
The South and the Sectional Conflict, 1968
The South and the Concurrent Majority, 1972
History and American Society: Essays of David M. Potter, 1973
Freedom and Its Limitations in American Life, 1976
The Impending Crisis, 1848–1861, completed by Don E. Fehrenbacher, 1976

Further Reading

Brogan, Denis William, "David M. Potter," in Marcus Cunliffe and Robin Winks, eds., *Pastmasters: Some Essays on American Historians*, New York: Harper, 1969
Carleton, Mark T., "David M. Potter," in Clyde N. Wilson, ed., *Twentieth-Century American Historians*, Detroit: Gale, 1983 [*Dictionary of Literary Biography*, vol. 17]
Collins, Bruce M., "David Potter's *People of Plenty* and the Recycling of Consensus History," *Reviews in American History* 16 (1988), 320–35
Degler, Carl N., "David Morris Potter," *American Historical Review* 76 (1971), 1273–75
Fehrenbacher, Don E., Howard R. Lamar, and Otis A. Pease. "David M. Potter: A Memorial Resolution," *Journal of American History*, 58 (1971), 307–10
Hartshorne, Thomas L., *The Distorted Image: Changing Conceptions of the American Character since Turner*, Cleveland: Press of Case Western Reserve University, 1968
Higham, John, with Leonard Krieger and Felix Gilbert, *History: The Development of Historical Studies in the United States*, Englewood Cliffs, NJ: Prentice Hall, 1965
Hofstadter, Richard, *The Progressive Historians: Turner, Beard, Parrington*, New York: Knopf, 1968; London: Cape, 1969
Johannsen, Robert W., "David M. Potter, Historian and Social Critic," *Civil War History* 20 (1974), 35–44
Kammen, Michael G., "On Predicting the Past: Potter and Plumb," *Journal of Interdisciplinary History* 5 (1974), 109–18
Kraus, Michael, and Davis D. Joyce, *The Writing of American History*, revised edition, Norman: University of Oklahoma Press, 1985
Morton, Marian J., *The Terrors of Ideological Politics: Liberal Historians in a Conservative Mood*, Cleveland: Press of Case Western Reserve University, 1972
Sternsher, Bernard, *Consensus, Conflict, and American Historians*, Bloomington: Indiana University Press, 1975
Tyrrell, Ian, *The Absent Marx: Class Analysis and Liberal History in Twentieth-Century America*, Westport, CT: Greenwood Press, 1986
Wise, Gene, *American Historical Explanations: A Strategy for Grounded Inquiry*, Homewood, IL: Dorsey Press, 1973; revised Minneapolis: University of Minnesota Press, 1980
Woodward, C. Vann, "David Morris Potter," in his *The Future of the Past*, New York: Oxford University Press, 1989, 353–58

Power, Eileen 1889–1940

British medievalist and economic and social historian

Eileen Power was the best-known medieval historian of the interwar years, and she brought medieval history into general culture. She wrote one of the most popular medieval histories, *Medieval People* (1924), which went into ten editions, and is still in print 70 years later. She taught economic history for nearly 20 years between 1921 and 1940 at the London School of Economics (LSE), and was the professor of economic history there for the last eight of those years. She was rare as a woman in reaching the pinnacles of mainstream academic success in the historical profession, and she was one of the first writers of women's history. The years when Power taught at the LSE were the most important years in the formation of the discipline of economic history, and during this time she brought a distinctive idea to the subject and its method. This idea was generated in her own formative educational and political experiences. Power fostered the development of a comparative and international economic history; she integrated economic and social history; and she pursued the comparative method as a special contribution which history could make to social scientific methodologies.

Power developed her discipline within the framework of medieval history. She avoided the contemporary traditions of legal and constitutional history, and initially followed an inclination toward literary history and the history of religious life. Her early work had a clear political framework in her commitment to the women's peace campaigns of the interwar years. Her book *Medieval English Nunneries* (1922), her major essays on medieval women's history, *Medieval Women* (1975), and her *Medieval People* were conceived and written in this framework. Her social history, which dwelt on themes of comparative and international history, became her response to World War I, and she spread her message in her teaching at the LSE, in debates on history teaching in schools and radio broadcasts to schools, and publishing initiatives in children's history books, including her very popular *Boys and Girls of History* (1926), written with her sister Rhoda Power.

At the LSE Power worked in partnership with R.H. Tawney to develop an extended course structure for economic history, as well as graduate seminars, social science discussion groups, and collaborative research projects. The keynote of Power's teaching was internationalism and comparative history, especially that between the East and the West. In a collaboration with Michael Postan (whom she later married) from the later 1920s she moved economic history forward into discussion with the social sciences, especially sociology and anthropology. She developed her comparative method through analogies between current under-developed economies, especially China and India and medieval societies, and she drew on the comparative regional studies developed by historians from the German historical school, especially of the Austrian historian Alfons Dopsch. Her project should be seen as parallel to the work in France of Marc Bloch and Lucien Febvre, founders of the *Annales*; Bloch and Power recognized the similarity of their goals.

Throughout this period Power concentrated on the study of long-distance trade and merchants. The inspiration on which she drew for this work, and the place she saw for it in explanations for the transition out of feudal economic limitations to capitalist development, were provided by Henri Pirenne. Pirenne had found in the medieval merchant entrepreneur the origins of the dynamism which would eventually lead to economic growth. For Power this position provided further connections between economic history and her internationalist political views. She associated trade and merchants with international connection and peace. Her research and publications over this period reflected this search for the origins of merchant capitalism before industrialization. *The Cambridge Economic History of Europe*, which she co-edited with J.H. Clapham, was the first great collaborative project in comparative economic history; it was also a great international enterprise which succeeded despite World War II.

Power's idea of social history from the time she came to the LSE developed away from simply revealing the lives of ordinary people toward offering a historical analysis of social structures. Thus she turned to the analysis of the underlying trends of medieval agrarian society and to comparative commercial and industrial development. This work took social history onto an altogether different plane, and bound it to the new discipline of economic history. She also took a professional attitude to the development of her discipline. She took a major role in the founding of a journal, the *Economic History Review*; she worked in archives, and started major new archive initiatives, such as the Business Archives Council. She developed research projects, set up her research seminar to pursue these, and left behind a group of research students who, in the following two decades, published work on medieval trade and commercial history. Other students and colleagues she influenced wrote the big books of social history and women's history that were not superseded until the 1970s and 1980s – Alice Clark, Dorothy George, Ivy Pinchbeck, Dorothy Marshall, and H.S. Bennett among them.

Soon after Power's death the types of history she stood for were no longer central. Women's history as an academic subject taught within the universities and incorporated within broader historical surveys was her creation, but it fell out of academic history after World War II, and re-emerged only in the 1970s. The broad comparative economic and social history informed by sociological and anthropological concepts she sought to foster with projects such as the *Cambridge Economic History* lost impetus in Britain, and economic approaches took priority. The achievement of social history was attributed to Tawney alone; the combined field with its international dimensions became a lost byway, and eventually a list of disconnected antiquarian pieces of social history. Women and many men with broader historical interests left the field and turned their attention to the founding of a separate social history.

MAXINE BERG

See also Economic; Knowles; Postan; Social

Biography

Eileen Edna Le Poer Power. Born Altrincham, Cheshire, 9 January 1889, daughter of a stockbroker. Educated at Oxford High School; Girton College, Cambridge, BA 1910; the Sorbonne, Paris; research student, London School of Economics, 1911–13. Director of studies, Girton College, 1913–21; Albert Kahn traveling fellow, 1920–21; taught at London School of Economics (rising to professor), 1921–40. Married historian Michael Postan, 1937. Died London, 8 August 1940.

Principal Writings

Medieval English Nunneries, c.1275–1535, 1922
Medieval People, 1924
Editor with R.H. Tawney, *Tudor Economic Documents*, 3 vols., 1924
With Rhoda Power, *Boys and Girls of History*, 1926
Editor with M.M. Postan, *Studies in English Trade in the Fifteenth Century*, 1933
The Wool Trade in English Medieval History, 1941
Editor with J.H. Clapham, *The Cambridge Economic History of Europe*, vol. 1, 1941
Medieval Women, edited by M.M. Postan, 1975

Further Reading

Berg, Maxine, "The First Women Economic Historians," *Economic History Review* 45 (1992), 308–29
Berg, Maxine, *A Woman in History: Eileen Power, 1889–1940*, Cambridge: Cambridge University Press, 1996
Melman, Billie, "Under the Western Historian's Eyes: Eileen Power and the Early Feminist Encounter with Colonialism," *History Workshop Journal* 42 (1996), 147–68

Prado Júnior, Caio 1907–1990
Brazilian historian and publisher

The influence of Caio Prado Júnior's historical work remains strong, and in the future he is likely to be remembered not only as one of the greatest Brazilian historians, but also, together with Roberto C. Simonsen (1889–1948) and Celso M. Furtado (b.1920), as one of the founding fathers of economic history in Brazil.

Almost a self-taught intellectual and scholar, Prado Júnior was more a man of action than a reading-room academician.

To be sure, he would have liked – and even attempted twice – to become a university professor, but, mainly for political reasons, this career never opened up for him. The consequent absence of formal pupils and disciples was, however, more than compensated for by the vast readership of his books and by the fundamental contribution of some of them to the intellectual formation of several generations of Brazilian historians, economists, and social scientists.

During the half century of his active life, from the early 1930s to the end of the 1970s, Prado Júnior published thirteen books. At the beginning of the 1980s, several others were added to them by his son and successor as director of Editora Brasiliense, the publishing house he founded during World War II, but these were merely reprints either of articles or chapters belonging to former books.

Chronologically and numerically, the apex of his intellectual work was reached in the 1950s. It was also during the 1950s that Prado began the bi-monthly publication of *Revista Brasiliense*, a political and cultural journal that lasted until the first months of 1964, after which the country remained for twenty years under the rule of a right-wing authoritarian military regime. In that journal Prado published dozens of important and interesting articles.

But his best historical books – those for which he will most probably be remembered in the future – are scattered throughout his lifetime and comprise no more than five titles. His other works included commentaries on new socialist states, products of trips to the Soviet Union, Czechoslovakia, Poland, China, and Cuba. Others represent his writings on philosophy and political economy. The first and last of these were elaborated as academic theses, by which Prado attempted – without success – to get a post at the University of São Paulo.

Evolução política do Brasil (Political Evolution of Brazil), his inaugural book, almost at once transformed the author into a celebrity. This was due not only to the novelty – at that time in Brazil – of its Marxian approach to history, but also – and perhaps mainly – to the work's high historiographical merits. In less than 200 pages, it opened completely new perspectives on the colonial and monarchic periods of Brazilian history (from the discovery in 1500 to the end of the 1880s). In its later editions, it was further enriched by the addition of several other essays written in the 1930s and 1940s that focused on the geographical factors affecting the development of the city of São Paulo, historiographical issues, and demographic and sociological treatment of the nature of rural settlement and immigration patterns.

In 1942 Prado Júnior published the book that would come to be recognized as his masterpiece, *Formação do Brasil contemporâneo Colônia*. It remains one of the best ever written on Brazil's colonial period, and is Prado Júnior's only book to get a full translation into English, as *The Colonial Background of Modern Brazil* (1967). Concentrating on the last decades of the colonial period, 16 of its 17 chapters, preceded by a short introduction, are grouped into three sets, dealing with patterns of settlement; main economic activities; and social and political institutions. A careful reader may discern not only traces of Prado Júnior's first book, but also elements of the next one, destined to be his bestseller.

The first edition of *História econômica do Brasil* (The Economic History of Brazil, 1945) was published simultaneously in Portuguese and in Spanish. More than half of the book, and certainly the best part, dealt with the colonial and the monarchical periods of Brazilian history. The years of the republic, from 1889 on, were viewed by him as a period of ongoing crisis. For political reasons, Prado Júnior always remained rather skeptical on the intensity and outcome of Brazilian industrialization.

In his opinion, the main obstacles to the country's economic independence and progress lay, on the one hand, in its rigid social and political structure, and on the other, in the yoke of imperialism – meaning not the domination of one nation by another, but the pervading and irresistible influence of the major multinational corporations of past and present days. This point of view appears more clearly in *A revolução brasileira* (The Brazilian Revolution, 1966). Although being technically a political study (and manifesto) rather than a piece of history, it helps us to understand better the nature and extent of his contribution to the latter.

Similar considerations apply to *A questão agrária no Brasil* (Brazil's Agrarian Problem), the last book issued by Prado himself. Although published in 1979, it contains articles written in the early 1960s. Through them, the author clarified not only the diversified nature and the very high degrees of economic concentration within the iniquitous agrarian structure of Brazil, but also its historical development and the mechanisms of its perpetuation.

TAMÁS SZMRECSÁNYI

See also Holanda; Latin America: National

Biography

Caio da Silva Prado Júnior. Born São Paulo, 11 February 1907, to a wealthy family. Studied at the Jesuit high school, Colégio São Luis, then in Eastbourne, England; received degree, São Paulo Law School (later part of University of São Paulo), 1928. Joined Brazilian Communist party, and traveled to the USSR, 1933; imprisoned for political activities, 1935–37; in exile in France, 1937–39. With José B. Monteiro Lobato, founded Editora Brasiliense publishing house, 1942. Elected to state assembly, served briefly before Brazilian Communist party was judicially dissolved, and he was imprisoned again, 1948. Founder/publisher, *Revista Brasiliense*. Jailed several more times, failed to gain an appointment to University of São Paulo, and occasionally fled country. Married several times. Died 24 November 1990.

Principal Writings

Evolução política do Brasil: ensaio de interpretação materialista da história brasileira (Political Evolution of Brazil: An Essay of Materialist Interpretation of Brazilian History), 1933; revised as *Evolução política do Brasil e outros estudos* (Political Evolution of Brazil and Other Studies)

URSS: um novo mundo (USSR: A New World), 1934

Formação do Brasil contemporâneo: colônia, 1942; in English as *The Colonial Background of Modern Brazil*, 1967

História econômica do Brasil (The Economic History of Brazil), 1945

Dialética do Conhecimento (Dialectic of Knowledge), 2 vols., 1952

Diretrizes para uma política econômica brasileira (Directives for a Brazilian Economic Policy), 1954

Notas introdutórias à lógica dialética (Introductory Notes to Dialectic Logic), 1955

Esbôço dos fundamentos da teoria econômica brasileira (Sketch of the Foundations of Brazilian Economic Theory), 1957

O mundo do socialismo (The World of Socialism), 1962

A revolução brasileira (The Brazilian Revolution), 1966
O estruturalismo de Levi-Strauss: O marxismo de Louis Althusser (The Structuralism of Levi-Strauss: The Marxism of Louis Althusser), 1971
História e desenvolvimento: a contribuição da historiografia para a teoria e a prática do desenvolvimento brasileiro (History and Development: the Contribution of Historiography to the Theory and Practice of Brazilian Development), 1972
A questão agrária no Brasil (Brazil's Agrarian Problem), 1979

Further Reading

Araújo, Braz José de, "Caio Prado Júnior e a questão agrária no Brasil" (Caio Prado Júnior and the Agrarian Problem in Brazil), *Temas de Ciências Humanas* 1 (1977), 47–89
Iglésias, Francisco, ed., *Caio Prado Júnior: História*, São Paulo: Ática, 1982
Incao, Maria Angela d', ed., *História e ideal: ensaios sobre Caio Prado Júnior* (History and Ideal: Essays on Caio Prado Júnior), São Paulo: Editora Brasiliense, 1989
Limongi, Fernando P., "Marxismo, nacionalismo e cultura: Caio Prado Júnior e a *Revista Brasiliense*" (Marxism, Nationalism, and Culture: Caio Prado Júnior and the *Revista Brasiliense*) *Revista Brasileira de Ciencias Sociais* 5 (1987), 27–46
Novais, Fernando A., "Caio Prado Júnior na historigrafia brasileira" (Caio Prado Júnior in Brazilian Historiography), in Reginald Moraes, Ricardo Antunes, and Vera B. Ferrante, eds., *Inteligência Brasileira*, São Paulo: Editora Brasiliense, 1986

Prebisch, Raúl 1901–1986

Argentine economist

Raúl Prebisch was one of the most important Argentine economists of the 20th century. He drew his critique of Argentina's economic problems from a historical analysis of the shaping of economic relations in the modern world. This assessment focused particularly on the role of technology in maintaining some regions as peripheral. His analyses have been widely used by historians examining modern economic systems.

Prebisch took up the subject at a very early age. His first writings date from 1918 and he quickly rose through the academic ranks. As a teacher during the 1920s he believed firmly in neoclassical theories. His career led him to responsible positions in public administration: he was appointed deputy director of statistics, where he introduced improvements to the system as a result of his experience abroad; and he later set up a department of economic research at the Argentine National Bank, and was its first director. Under his leadership, the department published a systematic analysis of the state of the country, which set forth for the first time the thesis of the deterioration in the terms of trade caused by international dealings between developed and underdeveloped countries. Later, Prebisch took an active part in the creation of the Central Bank and in drawing up its constitution. In 1943, he was forced to resign by the military government that had taken power.

From 1930 to 1943 Prebisch was a leading figure in Argentina's economic policy. He organized and led a think tank with members from broad sections of society, which gave shape to that policy, and with intelligence, wisdom, and prudence he made it possible to avoid the worst consequences of crisis and to achieve a rapid recovery. The Great Depression and World War II were critical events for capitalism, and Prebisch's attempts to deal with such events from the perspective of neoclassical economics led him to have serious doubts about the effectiveness of these theories when applied to reality. This was the start of a long period of "heresies," when he tried to explore new ideas in the field of economic development. Prebisch was a shrewd observer of reality, and with his broad theoretical knowledge – but without preconceptions – he established his analysis. Using this analysis with great imagination, he designed a set of measures, taking into consideration the problems of development and an equitable balance of the consequences for the different social groupings, especially the most vulnerable.

The changing reality and the widening of his own experience meant that his thinking was dynamic and passed through a number of phases. After he had to leave the Central Bank and later his university post for political reasons, in 1949 he joined the United Nations Economic Commission for Latin America (ECLA). From then on, his experience of Argentina and his theories about the causes of underdevelopment took on a greater maturity and widened to Latin America as a whole. His first work at ECLA was the Economic Report of 1949. This and other studies presented to the traditional school a lucid analysis and a range of suggested options.

His primary concern was to determine the modes of the spread of technological progress, which originated in Britain and spread through Europe with varying degrees of intensity, and to the United States with particular vigor. Around the *centers* there grew up a vast and heterogeneous *periphery* that received only a minor part of the improvements in productivity. Between these two distinct areas there developed a mode of production that may be described as an *international division of labor*, in which one part of the system is involved in industrial production and the other part is involved in the production of foodstuffs and raw materials. To a greater or lesser extent the periphery is restricted according to its ability to satisfy the center's needs for those goods in its process of production. Under such conditions, technological progress seeps through to the periphery in an irregular fashion, which creates distortions in the productive system and produces inequalities in the productivity and income of different economic sectors and regions. This analysis puts paid to the supposed universality of the doctrine that maintains that by means of international trade, the fruits of technological progress tend to spread evenly throughout the whole system. That may be true for the center, but not for the periphery.

Associated with this is low productivity and its consequence, the diminished savings and the precarious standard of living of the masses. This conclusion led Prebisch directly to his ideas about the worsening of terms of trade and the overriding repercussions on the process of accumulation of capital in the periphery. In this lies the main justification for Prebisch's proposal for industrialization in the peripheral countries. It is not a goal in itself, but rather the only means to obtain the benefits of technological progress and the improvements in the standard of living. From this analysis there followed other proposals: previously imported industrial goods should instead be manufactured domestically, under the protection of a light import tariff, assisted by a larger geographical area for trading between Latin American countries, created by means of common markets that would allow production on a larger scale more suited to the available technology. Indeed, in his report of 1949 Prebisch stressed the need for integration, and a few years later he was one of the creators of the Central American Common Market and the Latin American Free Trade Association. This indicates the need for planning to correct the imbalances created by the allocation of resources based exclusively on market forces, and allows growth to accelerate and maintain its pace, improves the distribution of income, and balances investments between those that lay off workers and those that employ them.

After serving for a long period at the Economic Commission for Latin America, in 1963 Prebisch became secretary general of the recently created UNCTAD. His duties did not allow him to undertake theoretical research, but all the experience that he had acquired in the preceding years enabled him to present a complete range of recommendations on economic policy that were the starting point of the debate between the member countries. This was the beginning of the North-South dialogue, but rather than a dialogue it was – and still is – a series of parallel monologues that do not lead to concrete action regarding the basic problems of international cooperation, which are, in Prebisch's own words, foreign trade, finance and technology.

In his later years, Prebisch was in charge of the journal of the Economic Commission for Latin America, where he made new contributions and published a very interesting analysis in *Capitalismo periférico* (Capitalism on the Periphery, 1981), in which he incorporated social and political aspects related to changes in the power structure into his economic approach, and provided an analysis of a new form of structural inflation. All his ideas have been widely employed by historians.

Oscar Julian Bardeci

See also Cardoso; Latin America: National

Biography

Born Tucumán province, Argentina, 17 April 1901. Attended school in the provinces of Tucumán and Jujuy; studied at Faculty of Economic Sciences, Buenos Aires, from 1918; scholarship in Australia and New Zealand to study the taxes on yields in agricultural countries. Taught in Faculty of Economic Sciences, University of Buenos Aires. Married 1) Adela Moll; 2) Eliana Diaz, 1962 (1 son). Died Santiago, Chile, 29 April 1986.

Principal Writings

Introducción a Keynes (Introduction to Keynes), 1947
El desarrollo económico de América Latina y sus principales problemas, 1949; ; in English as *The Economic Development of Latin America and Its Principal Problems*, 1950
Crecimiento, desequilibrio y disparidades: interpretación del proceso de desarrollo económico (Growth, Imbalance, and Difference: An Interpretation of the Process of Economic Development), 1950
Problemas teóricos y prácticos del crecimiento económico (The Theoretical and Practical Problems of Economic Growth), 1951
Hacia una dinámica del desarrollo latinoamericano con un apendice sobre el falso dilema entre desarrollo economico y estabilidad monetaria (Toward a Dynamic of Economic Development, with Appendix on the False Dilemma Between Economic Development and Monetary Stability), 1963
Transformación y desarrollo, la gran tarea de America-latina, 2 vols., 1970; in English as *Change and Development: Latin America's Great Task*, 1971
Capitalismo periférico: crisis y transformación (Capitalism on the Periphery: Crisis and Transformation), 1981

"Cinco etapas de mi pensamiento sobre el desarrollo" (My Five Levels of Thinking on Development), *Trimestre Económico* 50 (1983), 1077–96
La crisis del desarrollo argentino: de la frustración al crecimiento vigoroso (The Crisis of Argentine Development: From Frustration to Strong Growth),, 1986
Raúl Prebisch: obras completas, 1919–1948, 4 vols., 1991–93 [collected works]

Further Reading

Homenaje a Rául Prebisch (Homage to Raul Prebisch), Mexico City: Centro de Investigacion y Docencia Economicas, Colegio Nacional de Economistas, 1989
Marco, Luis Eugenio di, ed., *International Economics and Development: Essays in Honor of Raúl Prebisch*, New York: Academic Press, 1972

Prehistory

Prehistory is the long period of the human past prior to the appearance of written records, a period that can be reconstructed only using the techniques of archaeology and associated disciplines. Prehistory may be said to begin with the evolution of the first hominids in Africa about 5 million years ago, although the archaeological record is practically nonexistent before stone tools were manufactured from around 2.5 million years ago. Prehistory ended soon after 3000 BCE in Mesopotamia but continued until the 1930s in highland New Guinea.

The term *préhistorique* was used in 1833 by a French amateur geologist, Paul Tournal, and related terms have been confirmed in several other European languages in the 1830s and 1840s. The English word "prehistory" appears to have been coined, perhaps independently, by the Scottish antiquarian Daniel Wilson (1816–92) in his book *The Archaeology and Prehistoric Annals of Scotland* (1851). The term was popularized by John Lubbock in his bestselling *Pre-historic Times* (1865). However, the concept of a period of human history completely unrelated to the documentary sources was a revolutionary one, particularly in countries where religious beliefs were linked to the traditional written chronologies, and acceptance of what Glyn Daniel has called the "idea of prehistory" was a slow process. Gina Barnes recently noted that "one of the prerequisites in forming a pre-historical view of humankind was the acquired psychological ability to deal with the literary 'namelessness' of the people and places revealed through archaeological exploration." Another problem was how to interpret the apparently slow rate of change in prehistory. In the late 19th and early 20th centuries, prehistory was dominated by social evolutionism that served to deny the historicity of "primitive" peoples. If all societies evolved in the same sequence from primitive to civilized, then it followed that hunter-gatherer groups who still used stone tools had hardly evolved at all and could be studied in the present by ethnographers. It was only with the slow realization that apparently primitive societies, such as those in the New Guinea highlands, had in fact experienced considerable historical changes that a more dynamic view of prehistory developed.

Despite such advances, the concept of prehistory continues to remain controversial because of doubts over the utility of the split between prehistory and written history. Prehistoric archaeology cannot be said to have developed as a completely separate field within archaeology since many of the techniques and theories applied to historical archaeology are also used in prehistory. Differences between the period and region studied have usually been more important than the divide between prehistory and history *per se*. The major difference between prehistory and history is one of approach: in prehistory the individual and the event are invisible and only long-term processes of historical change can be reconstructed. While prehistory is thus in fact a different level of history, that difference has often been seen as the result of primitive, unchanging societies and in all historiographic traditions prehistory is still regarded as a poor cousin to "proper" written history. In this respect, however, a distinction needs to be made between countries in which there is a perceived basic continuity between the prehistoric and historic epochs and those in which the end of prehistory coincided with the arrival of (mainly European) colonial settlers. In the former countries – China, Japan, and much of Europe and West Asia – prehistory can be approached in terms of national history, whereas in the case of countries such as Australia and the US history was long seen as the story of white settlement and aboriginal (pre)history was largely confined to ethnography. As a result, in North America archaeology developed as a branch of anthropology with a strong antihistorical bias that reached its peak in the New Archaeology of the 1960s. In an influential paper on the Classic Maya collapse, for example, Binford argued that this event could be explained only in terms of universal laws of human behavior. Few if any Western prehistorians would now take such an extreme position, but it is still widely believed that prehistory should be a universally applicable generalizing science, a position that Glover (1993) has argued is alien to scholars in many non-Western countries who are mainly interested in the distinctive aspects of their national pasts.

Like archaeology, prehistory began first in Europe. Although it spread quite rapidly to some countries – to Japan, for example, by the 1870s – it is not until after World War II that we can begin to speak of a truly global prehistory. The development of radiocarbon and other scientific dating techniques in the 1950s revolutionized the field, making it possible to date cultures that lay outside the chronological or spatial borders of the ancient literate civilizations. One notable result was a completely new understanding of the prehistory of Australia and the Pacific as symbolized by Mulvaney's *The Prehistory of Australia* (1969) and Bellwood's *Man's Conquest of the Pacific* (1978). Another major postwar achievement was the confirmation that Africa rather than Asia was the original cradle of humankind. Grahame Clark's *World Prehistory* (1961) was an influential summary of the new global scope of the field. During the 1980s and 1990s there was growing debate over the political implications of the concept and conduct of prehistory particularly with respect to non-Western countries. At the same time, developments in genetic anthropology following the discovery of the molecular clock in the 1960s have continued to transform the study of human evolution and early prehistory.

MARK J. HUDSON

See also Archaeology; Trigger

Further Reading

Bailey, Geoff, "Concepts of Time in Quaternary Prehistory," *Annual Review of Anthropology* 12 (1983), 165–92

Barnes, Gina L., "The 'Idea of Prehistory' in Japan," *Antiquity* 64 (1990), 929–40

Bellwood, Peter, *Man's Conquest of the Pacific: The Prehistory of Southeast Asia and Oceania*, Auckland and London: Collins, and New York: Oxford University Press, 1978

Binford, Lewis R., "Some Comments on Historical versus Processual Archaeology," *Southwestern Journal of Anthropology* 24 (1968), 267–75

Chippindale, Christopher, "The Invention of Words for the Idea of 'Prehistory'," *Proceedings of the Prehistoric Society* 54 (1988), 303–14

Clark, Grahame, *World Prehistory: An Outline*, Cambridge and New York: Cambridge University Press, 1961; revised 1969

Clark, Grahame, *Space, Time and Man: A Prehistorian's View*, Cambridge and New York: Cambridge University Press, 1992

Daniel, Glyn, *150 Years of Archaeology*, London: Duckworth, 1950; revised 1976

Daniel, Glyn, and Colin Renfrew, *The Idea of Prehistory*, 2nd edition, Edinburgh: Edinburgh University Press, 1988 [1st edition, by Daniel only, 1962]

Gamble, Clive, ed., "Uttermost Ends of the Earth," special section of *Antiquity* 66 (1992)

Gamble, Clive, *Timewalkers: The Prehistory of Global Colonization*, Stroud: Sutton, 1993, Cambridge, MA: Harvard University Press, 1994

Glover, Ian, "Other Peoples' Pasts: Western Archaeologists and Thai Prehistory," *Journal of the Siam Society* 81 (1993), 45–52

Grayson, Donald K., *The Establishment of Human Antiquity*, New York: Academic Press, 1983

Lubbock, John, *Pre-historic Times, as Illustrated by Ancient Remains, and the Manners and Customs of Modern Savages*, London: Williams and Norgate, 1865; New York: Appleton, 1872

Mulvaney, Derek John, *The Prehistory of Australia*, London: Thames and Hudson, and New York: Praeger, 1969; revised 1975

Trigger, Bruce G., *Beyond History: The Methods of Prehistory*, New York: Holt Rinehart, 1968

Trigger, Bruce G., and Ian Glover, eds., "Regional Traditions of Archaeological Research," special issues of *World Archaeology* 13/2–3 (1981–82)

Trigger, Bruce G., *A History of Archaeological Thought*, Cambridge and New York: Cambridge University Press, 1989

Wilson, Daniel, *The Archaeology and Prehistoric Annals of Scotland*, Edinburgh: Sutherland and Knox, 1851

Prescott, William H. 1796–1859

US historian of imperial Spain and Latin America

William Hickling Prescott occupies a unique position in the historiography of Spain and Latin America. He was one of the first American writers seriously to study the history of Spain and Latin America, and he did so with such success that his works continue to influence the understanding of these subjects today. Best known for his grand narrative histories of the conquests of Mexico and Peru, he also wrote biographies of Ferdinand and Isabella and of Philip II that in many ways have yet to be surpassed.

Writing in the 1830s and 1840s Prescott was enveloped in the romantic view of history. His works display a keen grasp of the narrative and dramatic potential of the historical situation and vividly characterize the personalities of the main actors of the time. For Prescott, the consolidation of the

Spanish crown under Ferdinand and Isabella, Spain's rise to imperial greatness under Charles V and Philip II, and the conquest of the Aztec and Inca empires by the force of Spanish arms became a stage upon which the heroic dimension of the human character could be explored. He took as his task the depiction of the events of Spanish history as "an epic in prose, a romance of chivalry." Within this context he sought to depict the conditions of the human struggle with destiny and self-determination, and saw in these events confirmation of his belief that morality and civilization (both understood as subsets of Christianity) ultimately triumphed over the decadent forces of sensuality and barbarism.

Prescott's great accomplishment was to combine the skills of a novelist with the documentary discipline that lies at the core of modern historical scholarship. He understood how to bring the events of the past to life and to engage the reader's imagination and feeling as well as his or her intellect. In this regard he has few equals in the whole corpus of modern historical writing, and is unique within the field of Iberian history. It is this quality of his work that transcends the vagaries of historical fashion and gives it a lasting significance.

Prescott came to the study of Spanish history through the influence of his teacher and friend, George Ticknor. Burdened by weak eyesight, the result of having been hit in the eye with a piece of bread during a college brawl, he toiled for almost ten years on his *History of the Reign of Ferdinand and Isabella* (1838). To avoid further weakening his eyes, his secretary would read to him in a darkened room while Prescott made notes on a noctograph, a device that enabled him to write without looking at the page. Because of the difficulty of writing he would compose his chapters in his head, holding and refining the prose in his memory until he was ready to put the words on paper in their final form. In many ways *Ferdinand and Isabella* acted as a prelude to his subsequent and more famous work on the conquests of Mexico and Peru. In this study he discovered the dramatic themes of the transformation of a nation from the bonds of semibarbarism and chaos into the foremost power of Europe; a power, moreover, confident in its mission to spread the related goods of Christianity and civilization.

These themes were to be worked over in much more detail in *The History of the Conquest of Mexico* (1843). His most well-known work and by most critical accounts his best, it is tightly structured around the dichotomies that Prescott perceived to exist between the Aztecs and the Spaniards. In his narrative he emphasized the moral weaknesses of Aztec religion in contrast to the moral superiority of Christianity; the strength of character of Cortés in contrast to the vacillation and sensuality of Montezuma; and the inevitable triumph of civilization over the barbarism of the native peoples. Throughout his development of these contrasts Prescott used vivid descriptive language to convey a sense of place and to heighten the immediacy of the drama. *The Conquest of Mexico* is particularly effective because of the unity of its theme – the events themselves possess all the necessary character of the epic drama – and because of the character of its central actor, Hernando Cortés. For all the ambivalence that the personality of Cortés has aroused over the years, he possessed a stature and competence that readily lend themselves to hyperbole and idealization. Prescott capitalized on this raw material and placed Cortés in the pivotal heroic role, making of him the lens through which the significance of the events were refracted.

While *The History of the Conquest of Peru*, finished in 1846, carries through the same themes as those developed in *The Conquest of Mexico*, and possesses the same rhetorical and documentary solidity, this later work lacks some of the dramatic unity of the earlier. The contrast between the two is primarily the result of the different character of the events in Peru and of the actors who brought them about. Whereas Prescott clearly admired Cortés, he wished that Pizarro had been "more of a gentleman and less of a bandit." Also, where the events in Mexico fit Prescott's concept of European transcendence, the post-conquest turmoil in Peru was difficult to reconcile with this image. But despite these shortcomings, *The Conquest of Peru* holds its own as a solid piece of history and provides a necessary complement to the narrative from Mexico.

On completing *The Conquest of Peru*, Prescott turned his attention back to Spain itself, producing a 3-volume study of the life and reign of Philip II and writing a new conclusion to Robertson's *History of the Reign of the Emperor Charles V*. A fourth volume of Philip II was left uncompleted at Prescott's death. A forceful narrative of the political and military achievements of the Spanish empire at the moment of its apogee and the imminence of its decline, *Philip II* further demonstrated Prescott's dramatic skill. It also continued the documentary rigor that marked his previous works.

Making an assessment of Prescott and his works is a somewhat difficult task. He has unquestionably exerted a considerable influence on the writing of Iberian history from the time of his first publication up through the mid-20th century. But his work is marked by a number of cultural biases that require, at the least, the sympathetic indulgence of the modern reader, and for many people these biases undermine the effectiveness of his narrative. For all his interest in the events of the conquest of America, Prescott exhibits little understanding of the value of the historical experience of the Latin American people. His point of departure was almost exclusively Eurocentric. The pre-conquest Inca and Aztec cultures were analyzed in categories derived from the Christian understanding of the ancient Mediterranean pagan past, and, for Prescott, possessed few inherent virtues that would make their destruction a morally ambiguous event. Also, despite his sympathy for the Spanish culture, his Protestant understanding of Catholicism as an inferior and essentially superstitious form of Christianity colors his perceptions and descriptions of the characters of his histories. But if these biases, characteristic as they were of early 19th-century America, can be overlooked, and if his romantic methodology can be appreciated for its strengths, his works continue to provide a model of stimulating historical writing – a triumph of the combination of documentary scholarship with an effective literary intuition.

LINCOLN A. DRAPER

See also Latin America: Colonial; Spain: Islamic; Spain: Imperial

Biography

William Hickling Prescott. Born Salem, Massachusetts, 14 May 1796. Attended Harvard University where he was partially blinded in an accident outside a dining hall. Independent means allowed him to research and write. Married Susan Amory, 1820 (2 sons, 1 daughter). Died Boston, 28 January 1859.

Principal Writings

History of the Reign of Ferdinand and Isabella, 2 vols., 1838

The History of the Conquest of Mexico, with a Preliminary View of the Ancient Mexican Civilization, and the Life of the Conqueror, Hernando Cortez, 3 vols., 1843

Biographical and Critical Essays, 1845

The History of the Conquest of Peru, with a Preliminary View of the Civilization of the Incas, 2 vols., 1847

The History of the Reign of Philip the Second, King of Spain, 3 vols., 1855–58

The Complete Works of William Hickling Prescott, 16 vols., 1863–86

Further Reading

Cline, Howard F., C. Harvey Gardiner, and Charles Gibson, eds., *William Hickling Prescott: A Memorial*, Durham, NC: Duke University Press, 1959

Costeloe, Michael P., "Prescott's *History of the Conquest* and Calderón de la Barca's *Life in Mexico*: Mexican Reaction, 1843–1844," *The Americas* 47 (1991), 337–48

Cruz, Guillermo Felix, *El imperio español y los historiadores norteamericanos* (The Spanish Empire and the North American Historians), 2 vols., Santiago: Ediciones de los Anales de la Universidad de Chile, 1960

Darnell, Donald, *William Hickling Prescott*, Boston: Twayne, 1975

Gardiner, C. Harvey, *William Hickling Prescott: An Annotated Bibliography of Published Works, Prepared for the Library of Congress*, Washington, DC: Library of Congress Hispanic Foundation, 1958

Gardiner, C. Harvey, *William Hickling Prescott: A Biography*, Austin: University of Texas Press, 1969

Humphreys, R.A., "William Hickling Prescott: The Man and the Historian," *Hispanic American Historical Review* 39 (1959), 1–19

Levin, David, *History as Romantic Art: Bancroft, Prescott, Motley, and Parkman*, Stanford, CA: Stanford University Press, 1959

Peters, Edward, "Henry Charles Lea and the Abode of Monsters," in Angel Alcalá, ed., *The Spanish Inquisition and the Inquisitorial Mind*, Boulder, CO: Social Science Monographs, 1987

Ticknor, George M., *Life of William Hickling Prescott*, 1864

Procacci, Giuliano 1926–

Italian political historian

It is difficult to classify Procacci's main interests as an historian. At a very young age he joined the resistance movement in the Belluno district in northern Italy. He studied in Florence under Carlo Morandi, in Naples under Federico Chabod at the Istituto per gli studi storici, in Paris at the Centre National de la Recherche Scientifique, in Milan at the Istituto Feltrinelli, and finally in Rome. His professional development took him from Renaissance and early modern history to an increasing interest in and knowledge of 20th-century issues, particularly the history of the industrial working classes. His oeuvre and his uninterrupted activism in the Italian Communist party, accompanied by his independence of opinion, prompted Eric Hobsbawm to remark that Procacci was one of those Italian communist historians who consistently practiced historical research, while others – Hobsbawm's comparison is with French communists engaged in Stalinist militancy – returned to professional rigor only after the fall of communism.

Procacci is one of the most versatile and cultured Marxist-Gramscian scholars of his generation. In the 1950s, in the first phase of his scholarly activity, he published *Classi sociali e monarchia assoluta nella Francia della prima metà del secolo XVI* (Social Classes and Absolutism in France in the First Half of the 16th Century, 1955) and began to research the figure of Machiavelli. His studies on the International movement, the history of the industrial working classes, and of socialism were more closely tied to his interests as a militant communist. In this respect in the 1970s his interests focused in particular on the period from the Italian general election of 1874 to the strikes of 1904 and the international opposition to the fascist invasion of Ethiopia. His studies of class struggle in Italy at the beginning of the 20th century shed light on a social class which for the first time took a leading role in Italy during the Giolitti years, and linked the history of the working classes to that of the economic development of the country. Procacci wrote about the social history of Italy in a period of transformation, where the whole society, especially the old institutional and economic sectors, had to confront the new entity constituted by the working classes. Procacci's unique approach consisted in investigating the structure of industrial and agricultural workers' organizations, by analyzing the processes of their creation and the training of their cadres.

In the early 1960s he published works on Labriola and Karl Kautsky and began to research the history of the Soviet Union. His writings on the debate that took place in the USSR after the death of Lenin between Trotsky, Bukarin, Zinoviev, and Stalin, represented a real novelty in the cultural climate of those years. The same can be said of his study of the USSR Communist party's Statute of 1934, which revealed the structure of Soviet power at the beginning of Stalinism's last phase. The final stage of the historical development of the USSR and its Communist party were again analyzed by Procacci in the last part of his career.

The Ethiopian war was another topic that Procacci treated with great originality in the 1970s and in the 1980s. His new approach (neglected so far by other historians) to the study of socialism and decolonization consisted of analyzing that historical period from the point of view of the prewar anticolonialist movements, the Third World, and the International movement. The outcome of his research was provocatively entitled: *Dalla parte dell'Etiopia* (On the Side of Ethiopia, 1984). This reassessment of a much worked-over topic from a fresh point of view represents Procacci's most mature work, although the one with which he is most identified is his *Storia degli Italiani* (1969; *History of the Italian People*, 1970). This is another very innovative work, first because it analyzed the social history of a people over a very long span of time, and second, for its emphasis on the continuity of Italian culture, an indispensable element in the formation and definition of European civilization. According to Procacci that continuity began well before the advent of the *Respublica Christiana*, the new form of European vitality that dawned at the beginning of the second millennium, and of which Italy was an integral part, its origin going back to Etruscan and Greek pre-Roman Italy. Procacci stressed, together with other historians, the continuity of property, administrative structures, and regional balances, which neither the Christian revolution nor the modern era was able to overcome, and that still constitute the connective tissue of Italian society. Procacci pointed to deep-rooted "agrarian individualism" as one of the basic permanent features of the history of the Italians, limitation and strength of what Procacci ironically termed the "country of Pulcinella."

GENNARO CAROTENUTO

See also De Felice

Biography
Born Assisi, Perugia, 20 December 1926. Educated at the universities of Florence, Naples, Paris, Milan, and Rome. Fought in the resistance during World War II. Professor, University of Cagliari, 1966–69; and University of Florence, from 1969.

Principal Writings
Classi sociali e monarchia assoluta nella Francia della prima metà del secolo XVI (Social Classes and Absolutism in France in the First Half of the 16th Century), 1955
Studi sulla fortuna del Machiavelli (Essays on the Fortune of Machiavelli), 1965
Storia degli Italiani, 2 vols., 1969; in English as History of the Italian People, 1970
La lotta di classe in Italia agli inizi del secolo XX (The Class Struggle in Italy at the Beginning of the 20th Century), 1970
Il socialismo internazionale e la guerra d'Etiopia (International Socialism and the Ethiopian War), 1978
The Italian Working Class from the Risorgimento to Fascism, 1979
Dalla parte dell'Etiopia: l'aggressione italiana vista dai movimenti anticolonialisti d'Asia, d'Africa, d'America (On the Side of Ethiopia: The Italian Aggression as Seen by the Anti-Colonialist Movements of Asia, Africa, and America), 1984
Machiavelli nella cultura europea dell'età moderna (Machiavelli in the European Culture of the Modern Age), 1995

Procopius c.500–after 542
Byzantine historian

Procopius was one of the greatest historians of the Byzantine empire. Living in the reign of Justinian (527–65), he wrote a series of eight books describing the wars waged by that emperor against the Persians, Vandals, and Ostrogoths, many of which he witnessed in the company of the general Belisarius. His other surviving works are a hostile portrayal of aspects of the reign of the emperor and his wife Theodora, and an account of the buildings which Justinian could be given credit for having erected.

Like many Byzantine scholars, Procopius affected a remarkably traditional form of writing. The opening words of his Wars of Justinian echo phrases that Herodotus and Thucydides had used over a thousand years earlier when beginning the works in which they described the great wars of Greek antiquity, and they suggest the company to which Procopius thought he and his subject belonged. His tendency to avoid explicitly Christian vocabulary has sometimes been held to suggest that he was not a Christian, but it is now believed that he avoided such words because they were not employed by the classical authors he looked to as models. Similarly, in including speeches purportedly given by generals and other characters, he imitates a practice of classical historians.

The account Procopius provides of the early years of Justinian's wars is positive and full of optimism. These were heady days, in which large areas of Roman territory which had been lost to imperial power during the 5th century were reconquered, and Procopius must have been full of enthusiasm as he began the task of writing their history. Indeed, he sometimes tampered with the facts to make the successes seems greater than they were. But the victories that had carried the imperial armies relentlessly forward in the 530s proved impossible to sustain as the enemies of the empire, in particular the Ostrogoths, struck back. So it was that, as the writing of his long work proceeded, Procopius found himself looking with increased favor on Justinian's enemies and making the best of a topic he found increasingly distasteful.

It was against this background that Procopius composed, in 550, another, darker work, in the classical tradition of diatribe. Usually known in English as the Secret History, its Greek title, Anecdota, is better translated Unpublished, and it is easy to see why its author would have wished it to be kept under wraps. He begins by asserting that while the actors he described in the Wars were still alive he was afraid to tell the truth, a claim that suggests that he planned to publish the work after the deaths of Justinian and Theodora. The story he now told is famous for its pornographic descriptions of the empress Theodora, its allegations that Justinian was a demon, and the depiction of the emperor and Belisarius as controlled by their wives. Perhaps we have to deal here with the prejudices of a landowning class that turned against the government because of what it considered oppressive taxation as well as disillusionment with the wars. The starkness of the judgments in this book and their apparent incompatibility with those of the Wars are striking.

But some years later Procopius wrote another book, one redolent of panegyric. Like many other emperors, Justinian was an enthusiastic constructor of buildings, and the destruction caused by the Nika riots of 532 in Constantinople gave him the opportunity to rebuild much of his capital city. So it was that Procopius found himself writing the Buildings, an account of the buildings erected by the emperor in Constantinople and over much of the empire. But his attribution of buildings to Justinian was generous, and such details as his crediting Justinian with the solution of a problem in the building of Hagia Sophia which baffled its highly qualified architects reveal a determination to present him positively, at whatever cost to credibility. It is possible that this book was commissioned by Justinian.

That Procopius' books point in such different directions is disconcerting. In the Wars Justinian is described as the instigator of wars of major historical significance which began remarkably well but steadily went bad; in the Anecdota he is seen as the prince of demons; while in the Buildings he acts in the public interest under divine inspiration. These differences owe something to the different genres in which Procopius found himself writing, but they also reflect changes in his views.

Whatever the interest of his other writings, the Wars stands as his major historical work. If lacking in analysis, it is a detailed piece of military history, the work of one who was an eyewitness of much of what he recounts. For centuries the copious information the work provides led to its being given a privileged place in accounts of the reign of Justinian, and while its centrality may now be challenged by non-narrative sources, it remains a necessary means of approaching the 6th century.

JOHN MOORHEAD

See also Byzantium; Eastern Orthodoxy

Biography

Procopius or Prokopios. Born Caesarea, in Palestine, *c*.500, to a wealthy family. Educated classically. Served as secretary/aide to general Belisarius, accompanying him on his Persian, North African and Italian campaigns, 527–40; probably settled Constantinople, *c*.542. Date of death unknown.

Principal Writings

History of the Wars of Justinian, 550/1–554/5
Secret History, 550/1
On Justinian's Buildings, 553–55
Works (Loeb edition), translated by H.B. Dewing, 7 vols., 1914–40
History of the Wars, Secret History, and Buildings, translated by Averil Cameron, 1967

Further Reading

Cameron, Averil, *Procopius and the Sixth Century*, London: Duckworth, and Berkeley: University of California Press, 1985
Evans, James Allan Stewart, *Procopius*, New York: Twayne, 1972
Moorhead, John, *Justinian*, London and New York: Longman, 1994
Rubin, Berthold, *Prokopios von Kaisareia*, Stuttgart: Druckenmüller, 1954
Tinnefeld, Franz Hermann, *Kategorien der Kaiserkritik in der byzantinischen Historiographie von Prokop bis Niketas Choniates*, Munich: Fink, 1971
Ure, Percy Neville, *Justinian and his Age*, Harmondsworth: Penguin, 1951

Prosopography

Prosopography, which is collective biography spiced with analysis, is closely associated with the problems of causality and the writing of "scientific" history. Categories are created, and should biographical research reveal that the subjects in a group were Puseyites or Rotarians, or attended Oxford, or came from Devon, the implications can be explored.

At the heart of successful prosopography is taking considerable care as to which categories of information are to be gathered, as it will be difficult in the middle or the end of a study to go back and look for information for those that were missed. For example, the decision to omit as categories the place of death or church where confirmed, if they took on importance after the work was all done, might be irrevocable because country registers could not be searched again.

Lewis Namier (1888–1960) in *The Structure of Politics at the Accession of George III* (1929) and other works on British parliamentarians demonstrated the technique's effectiveness, but prosopography's proponents have often been attacked for claiming too much on basis of the study of too small a selection. The inherent problem is that prosopography is necessarily limited in the size of group that can be studied. The selection can be nonrepresentative and too small, but biographical analysis of large groups not only requires enormous resources but often is inconclusive. One of the best uses of prosopography is for the study of an elite group, such as the members of a legislature or club. A good example is R.S. Neale's *Class and Ideology in the Nineteenth Century* (1972) which examined the governors and executive councilors of the Australian colonies in 1788–1856.

Since Namier's time the technique has not featured prominently in the mainstream of historical writing. This neglect is unfortunate, because when the subject of study fits the criteria of not being too voluminous and of being fairly well-documented, it is a highly productive research tool.

PAUL JOHN RICH

See also Namier

Further Reading

Bidwell, Robin, "The Political Residents of Aden," *Arabian Studies* 5 (1979)
Fischer, David, *Historians' Fallacies: Toward a Logic of Historical Thought*, New York: Harper, 1970; London: Routledge, 1971
Himmelfarb, Gertrude, *The New History and the Old*, Cambridge, MA: Harvard University Press, 1987
Namier, Lewis, *The Structure of Politics at the Accession of George III*, London: Macmillan, 1929; New York: St. Martin's Press, 1957
Neale, R.S., *Class and Ideology in the Nineteenth Century*, London: Routledge, 1972
Neale, R.S., *History and Class: Essential Readings in Theory and Interpretation*, Oxford: Blackwell, 1983
Potter, David C., *India's Political Administrators, 1919–1983*, Oxford and New York: Oxford University Press, 1986

Protestantism

The term "Protestant" may be traced back to the Imperial Diet of Speyer in 1529, when adherents of the early German Reformation refused to bow to the religious demands of the emperor Charles V and vigorously "protested" their faith. This "protestation" (from the Latin *protestari* – to testify) was a positive testimony to the "Gospel" or the "Word of God," rather than a negative "protest against errors," though a sharp critique of the contemporary church was a natural corollary of their emphatic declarations.

Over time, however, Protestantism has developed into a comprehensive descriptive term embracing broadly all those Christian churches and groups which derived their origins as separate communities directly or indirectly from the Reformation of the 16th century which permanently divided the Western Catholic church.

In Continental Europe two distinctive patterns of Protestant Christianity emerged early – the "Evangelical" and the "Reformed" – deriving from the movements associated on the one hand with the German reformer Martin Luther, and on the other with the Swiss reformers Ulrich Zwingli and John Calvin. Outside its original German homeland the Evangelical (or Lutheran) movement was chiefly influential in Scandinavia, while the Reformed faith, especially in its Calvinist version, proved especially powerful in spreading across Europe, including France, the Netherlands, Scotland (where it eventually became the established faith), and parts of Eastern Europe.

"Evangelical" and "Reformed" patterns were influential in England at different stages in the gradual process by which the English church separated itself from Rome, though the emergent Anglican church as defined in the Elizabethan Settlement deliberately adopted a "middle way" between Rome and the more extreme versions of Reform, stressing its continuity with the historic English church through the centuries, and remaining ambivalent about whether or not to regard itself as Protestant.

Non Roman-Catholic Christians who dissented from the established church in England fragmented into a wide variety of religious groups which collectively came to be known as the English Free church tradition, all of which continued to trace their spiritual origins to the Reformation, despite their many differences from each other in matters of belief and practice. These groups included the English Presbyterians, the Independents or Congregationalists, the Quakers and the Baptists, and later the Methodists who separated from the Church of England following the 18th-century Evangelical revival. Through migration to the New World, Protestant communities expanded across the globe and further fragmentation occurred, especially in the United States.

As a subject for historical analysis, Protestantism is therefore marked by an extraordinary diversity of belief and practice which appears intrinsic rather than accidental and raises fundamental doubts about the possibility of a unified perspective. Can one in the end talk meaningfully of "Protestantism" at all, or only of numerous "Protestantisms"? On the other hand, the persistence of the singular term "Protestantism" implies that there is some significant common ground underlying its diverse expressions. The task of identifying that common ground has provided a major focal point for scholars from a variety of different perspectives.

Denominational histories represent a large genre of work within the general field, but in most cases they contribute little or nothing to the understanding of Protestantism, because they tend to limit their perspective to their immediate confessional frame of reference and avoid addressing the broader analytical themes.

Histories of the Reformation, on the other hand, have necessarily grappled with the issue of identifying key common themes at work in the thought of the various reformers and the life of the Protestant communities. Not all such historians, however, have used Protestantism as an overarching frame of reference or taken it upon themselves specifically to analyze it as a concept. Those especially who write from no committed religious standpoint have generally been content to explore the varied patterns of reformation in their diversity and to avoid comprehensive theorizing about Protestantism, while continuing to use it as a convenient umbrella term. By contrast, church historians and theologians with vital personal interests in the religious message of the Reformation (such as Robert McAfee Brown, John Dillenberger, and Claude Welch) have been more inclined to assume the theoretical task of explicating the meaning of Protestantism as a distinctive form of Christian thought and community life.

When Reformation Protestantism is subjected to specific analysis, by general consensus the two central themes identified have been the appeal to the authoritative role of Scripture as the "Word of God" (*sola scriptura*) and the doctrine of "justification by faith" – or more correctly of "salvation by grace, through faith" – the notion that mankind achieves salvation not through moral achievement but solely through the unmerited mercy of God, apprehended through faith (*sola gratia, sola fide*). Scripture may thus be regarded as the formal principle and salvation by grace through faith as the material principle of Protestantism. With differences in emphasis, all key reformers can be shown to have been united around these two themes.

Few would dispute the fundamental importance of these two unifying themes but their implications have been variously interpreted. A key issue has been whether the Protestant Reformation should be understood as inherently individualistic in its character. The assertion of the authority of Scripture against the teaching magisterium of the church soon raised the question – whose interpretation of Scripture? – and Roman Catholics were quick to claim that Protestantism asserted the authority of the individual Christian against the collective wisdom of centuries of church authority. The view that Protestantism enshrines "the right of private judgment" is widely entrenched and is a Roman Catholic assessment willingly acknowledged by some Protestants.

Historians of "classical" (that is, Reformation) Protestantism, however, emphatically reject the authenticity of such an interpretation, at least with respect to the early 16th century. The appeal to Scripture was an appeal not to "private judgment" but to the earliest traditions of the Christian church against the ecclesiastical and doctrinal novelties of more recent centuries. Early Protestants stood not for individualism but for a doctrine of the church as a community of the faithful under the headship of Christ, as a corporate "priesthood of believers," as a "reformed church always being reformed" (*ecclesia reformata semper reformanda*). According to this view the Reformation conflict was not between individualism and church authority but between two incompatible ecclesiologies.

Theologians and historians of doctrine have followed a parallel line of approach to church historians in identifying core Protestant doctrinal motifs, but with less interest in their original historical setting than in their capacity for contemporary reapplication. In the work of scholars as diverse as Karl Barth, Emil Brunner, Paul Tillich, and Reinhold Niebuhr, Protestant concepts and insights showed a capacity to take on fresh life in new and contemporary settings.

A large volume of the literature on Protestantism (and probably the least illuminating) could be characterized as ecclesiastical polemics, a form of writing by no means devoid of historical scholarship but directed fundamentally at polemical goals. Eschewing any search for common themes in Protestant thought, numerous Roman Catholic commentators from the 17th-century French scholar Jacques Bénigne Bossuet onwards have to varying degrees identified the wide differences of belief and practice among Protestants as evidence in themselves of fundamental error. Starting with the assumption that Christian truth is one and indivisible, variety is defined as virtually synonymous with heresy. Such analyses – with counter-arguments across the religious divide – have continued into recent times and have little historical value. Resting as they ultimately do on theological judgments, they are both unanswerable and at the same time unpersuasive in historical terms.

A more irenic version of this polemical approach, expressed in the writings of scholars such as Louis Bouyer, has been the interpretation of Protestantism as a diluted or attenuated form of Catholicism. Protestantism, it has been argued, has retained many elements of the historic Catholic faith but discarded other vital elements such as papal authority and major aspects of doctrine and practice, whereas the Roman Catholic tradition retains the fullness of the historic faith. Protestant critics have countered this argument by asserting on the basis of a different reading of tradition that Rome itself has both departed at key points from the historic faith and also grafted on to it unwarranted additions. Here again the discussion depends on theological judgments as much as historical analysis.

Exploring and articulating original Reformation principles, however, can take the task only so far. Histories of the Reformation present no more than the opening chapter in Protestant history, indispensable though that is to understanding Protestantism in its fullness. A sensitive historical understanding must take full account of the character of Protestantism as a developing historical movement. Every historical community undergoes development, and even the Roman Catholic church, notwithstanding its relative homogeneity and its firm authoritarian structure, exhibits change over time. Protestantism, without such constraints, has shown itself to be much more open to all kinds of influences for change within the developing modern world.

In the centuries since the Reformation, major theological and spiritual movements – such as Orthodoxy, Pietism, the Missionary movement, Fundamentalism, the Social Gospel movement, and the Ecumenical movement – have all left their mark on Protestantism, transforming its original character almost beyond recognition. Characteristically these movements, working within the various religious traditions, have created new possibilities for transcending denominational divisions, especially in the cases of the Missionary and Ecumenical movements. Yet with few exceptions traditional Protestant ecclesiastical boundaries have remained largely intact. Consequently, Protestantism as a movement has become even more widely differentiated than before, as diverse theological, spiritual, and social movements have spread across and interacted with continuing denominational structures.

Thus post-Reformation Protestant orthodoxy fostered a conception of Christianity based on rigid doctrinal confessions, while Pietism stressed the fundamental importance of religious experience in defining faith. Both movements were responses to and extensions of impulses rooted in the Reformation and exercised a continuing influence among diverse Protestant groups.

Not all developments within Protestantism, however, arose from fresh contact with its own past. Deep conflicts reflecting developments in modern secular thought emerged within the various church communities, with some Protestants for example welcoming the development of biblical criticism while others adopted a stance of implacable hostility towards the new "science." Such Protestant fundamentalists defiantly proclaimed a core of rigid doctrines based on a view of scriptural inspiration that appeared to echo the Reformation commitment to *sola scriptura* but which in reality arose out of the sharp ideological tensions of the 19th century, in particular the alleged conflict between science and religion. At the other end of the Protestant spectrum, the movements of "Christian socialism" in England and of the "Social Gospel" in America were responses to the crisis of modern industrial society reflecting a more liberal theological framework.

By the end of the 19th century Protestantism encompassed a vast range of institutional expressions, from a fundamentalist adherence to an infallible Bible at one extreme to so-called "neo-Protestantism" at the other, a liberal version of Christianity based on an attempt to accommodate Christianity to the tendencies of modern thought. The latter so distanced itself from "classical" Protestantism that it helped to trigger the neo-orthodox theological revival of the early 20th century that was notable for its strong reaffirmation of the perspectives of the early Reformation.

Modern Protestantism, therefore, is different from and vastly more complex than its first generation expression and accordingly any definition of Protestantism anchored to its 16th-century origins and its founding principles would be clearly inadequate. By the same token, any valid interpretation of the character of Protestantism must incorporate a recognition of those factors of change and growth, while continuing to acknowledge its original roots.

This makes it less likely that a satisfactory interpretation of Protestantism encompassing its whole history will emerge, based on some recognizable core of ideas and practices. An alternative approach, first clearly articulated by Paul Tillich and taken up by many other commentators since, has been to interpret Protestantism as a critical principle rather than a specific body of ideas.

According to this view, Protestantism is understood as a spirit of radical prophetic criticism, first evident in the original Reformation message directed against the medieval church and its claims to finality and absoluteness. The "Protestant principle" shows every religious institution, doctrinal statement, and pattern of liturgy to be deeply flawed and sharing in the distortions of human existence.

But the impact of this principle was not to set up a new core of absolute truths in place of the old. The Protestant principle is intrinsically self-critical, directed against Protestantism as much as against Catholicism, denying normative status and finality to any system of thought or ecclesiastical organization, and understanding reform as a never-ending process. Such an approach not only accommodates but anticipates change over time, yet its connections with its origins remain in that the starting-point of its prophetic critique is the scriptural norm and commitment to a never-ending process of reform within the church (*ecclesia semper reformanda*).

Interpreting Protestantism as a spirit or an attitude rather than a body of doctrine and practice provides an interesting link to a further range of interpretations that have emerged in the present century in secular scholarly circles and that focus on social context. Protestantism's vibrant interaction with the developing modern world has engaged the attention of scholars from a number of disciplines who have found intriguing connections with other historical movements and influences.

The coincidence in time of the definitive breakup of medieval Christian unity with the mature development of European nation-states has raised questions about the extent to which particular Protestant structures seem to relate positively to the process of state building in the differing countries and regions of Europe. Connections have been discerned between the authoritarian structure of the German territorial state and the political ideas of Luther, and between the more democratic structures of the urban reformed communities and the views of Zwingli and Calvin; while the relationship between English Protestant fortunes and the development of the English state has provided a particularly fruitful field of enquiry. In the interaction of religious and social life, Protestantism has been interpreted as both a product of the rising national state, and at the same time a stimulus to emerging national identity.

In the field of economics, the eminent sociologist Max Weber launched one of the more enduring concepts in modern historical scholarship by alleging close connections between what he called the "Protestant Ethic" and the emerging spirit of modern capitalism. Reformation scholars were easily able to question any such connections with 16th-century Protestantism, and such evidence as Weber was able to assemble came from a much later period, only tenuously related to its Reformation roots. At the same time this highlighted the extent to which later Protestantism had moved away from its origins.

The ambivalent relationship of Protestantism and the modern world was explored by scholars such as Wilhelm Dilthey and Ernst Troeltsch, the former identifying a positive connection between the two and the latter arguing – in *Bedeutung des Protestantismus für die Entstehung der modernen Welt* (1911; *Protestantism and Progress*, 1912) – that Protestantism represented a second blossoming of the authoritarian ecclesiastical culture of the Middle Ages which extended its influence for a further two centuries and devitalized the secular culture that had tentatively begun to emerge in the Renaissance. Accordingly, Troeltsch saw modern Protestantism as a contradiction rather than an authentic development of Reformation principles.

The American sociologist Richard Niebuhr, deeply influenced by Troeltsch, interpreted Protestantism in sociohistorical terms as the "religious phase of modern Western civilization," a movement both conservative in its transmission of traditional modes of thought and creative in its liberation of human interests. Building on Troeltsch's "Church-Sect" typology, Niebuhr distinguished within Protestantism three main sociological types – the "institutional," represented by Anglicanism and Lutheranism, the "sectarian," represented by early Anabaptism and the free-church traditions, and a "semi-institutional" type expressed in Calvinism. Under the institutional model, the church was conceived as coextensive with the community and as a divinely established guardian and teacher of faith, but subject to political control. The sectarian type, by contrast, regarded the church as a voluntary association of believers, separate from the state and democratic in its internal life. Calvinism adopted a median position, with the church understood as being coextensive with the general community but free of state control and maintaining clerical over lay authority.

Over time, Niebuhr argued, with the growth of religious pluralism, the separation of Church and State, and the decline of religious commitment, these types had necessarily become less sharply defined, as institutional churches developed into voluntary communities while sects assumed more institutional characteristics.

We may conclude, therefore, that a simple definition of Protestantism is clearly out of the question, and a comprehensive one problematical. The nature of Protestantism has been defined intellectually by reference to high theological principles and socially through analysis of its forms of secular organization. Its complex character has been shaped by the interaction between its historical foundations and the fresh agenda set by a continually changing society. It has expressed itself in a diversity of institutional forms and in a fundamental critique of all institutions. It has been since the 16th century and remains still an elusive but vital thread in the complex web of Western civilization.

JOHN TONKIN

See also Catholicism; Christianity; Counter-Reformation; Dilthey; Reformation; Religion; Religion, Comparative; Troeltsch; Weber, M.

Further Reading

Barth, Karl, *Die protestantische Theologie im 19. Jahrhundert*, Zurich: Evangelischer Verlag, 1947; in English as *Protestant Theology in the Nineteenth Century: Its Background and History*, London: SCM, 1972, Valley Forge, PA: Judson, 1973; partially translated as *From Rousseau to Ritschl*, London: SCM, 1959, and as *Protestant Thought: From Rousseau to Ritschl*, New York: Harper, 1959

Bouyer, Louis, *Du Protestantisme à l'Eglise*, Paris: Cerf, 1954; in English as *The Spirit and Forms of Protestantism*, London: Harvill, 1956; Westminster, MD: Newman, 1957

Brown, Robert McAfee, *The Spirit of Protestantism*, Oxford and New York: Oxford University Press, 1979

Brunner, Emil, *Christianity and Civilisation*, 2 vols., London: Nisbet, 1948–49; New York: Scribner, 1949

Dickens, A.G., and John Tonkin, *The Reformation in Historical Thought*, Cambridge, MA: Harvard University Press, and Oxford: Blackwell, 1985

Dillenberger, John, and Claude Welch, *Protestant Christianity Interpreted Through Its Development*, New York: Scribner, 1954

Hamilton, Kenneth, *The Protestant Way*, London: Epworth Press, 1956

Kattenbusch, Ferdinand, "Protestantismus," in *Protestantische Realenzyklopädie*, vol. 16

Kerr, Hugh Thomson, *Positive Protestantism: An Interpretation of the Gospel*, Philadelphia: Westminster Press, 1950

Niebuhr, H. Richard, *Christ and Culture*, New York: Harper, 1951; London: Faber, 1952

Niebuhr, Reinhold, "Protestantism," in Edwin R.A. Seligmann, ed., *Encyclopedia of the Social Sciences*, 15 vols., New York: Macmillan, 1930–35, vol. 12, 571–75

Pauck, W., *The Heritage of the Reformation*, Boston: Beacon Press, 1950; revised London and New York: Oxford University Press, 1968

Tillich, Paul, *The Protestant Era*, edited by James Luther Adams, Chicago: University of Chicago Press, 1948; London: Nisbet, 1951

Troeltsch, Ernst, *Die Bedeutung des Protestantismus für die Entstehung der modernen Welt*, Munich: Oldenbourg, 1906, 2nd edition 1911; 2nd edition in English as *Protestantism and Progress: A Historical Study of the Relationship of Protestantism to the Modern World*, London: Williams and Norgate, and New York: Putnam, 1912

Weber, Max, "Die protestantische Ethik und der Geist des Kapitalismus," *Archiv für Sozialwissenschaft und Sozialpolitik* 20–21 (1904–05), revised in *Gesammelte Aufsätze zur Religionssoziologie*, Tübingen: Mohr, 1920; in English as *The Protestant Ethic and the Spirit of Capitalism*, London: Allen and Unwin, 1930, New York: Scribner, 1958

Prucha, Francis Paul 1921–

US historian of Native Americans

Francis Paul Prucha, a Jesuit priest and professor emeritus at Marquette University, is the pre-eminent, albeit most controversial, scholar of Indian-White relations. However, even

Prucha's harshest critics praise his impeccable documentation, literary grace, and commitment to an impartial examination of the formulation and implementation of federal Indian policies.

Prucha's earliest works, such as *The Sword of the Republic* (1969), explored the multifaceted role that the United States Army played in paving the way for the settlement of the trans-Mississippi West. Soldiers were, remarked Prucha, "agents of empire" who assumed many guises. They served frontier communities as policeman, farmers, road builders, scientists, and lumbermen to help promote the social and economic development of the region. Prucha, along with leading members of the "Imperial school," Howard Lamar and William Goetzmann, perceived the West as America's first colonial empire, an empire that owed its development and its peculiar tensions to policies and plans formulated in the nation's capital.

Prucha's research regarding the "civilizing" aspects of the army introduced him to a new field of study, the relationship between American Indians and the federal government. He soon discovered that many areas of Indian-White relations had been neglected by other historians. *American Indian Policy in the Formative Years* (1962), *Lewis Cass and American Indian Policy* (1967), *Indian Peace Medals in American History* (1971), and *The Indian in American History* (1971) signaled Prucha's desire to shed light on previously unexplored topics.

Since the 1970s, Prucha has emerged as the foremost authority on the formation and implementation of US Indian policy. He was not, as his detractors have contended, an apologist for the federal government. Prucha repeatedly cautioned researchers not to let their own emotions or the "brilliance of hindsight" distort historical reality. In Prucha's opinion, scholars such as Francis Jennings, Virgil Vogel, Vine Deloria, Jr., Dee Brown, and Edward Pessen criticized the government's Indian policies too harshly, noting that the goal of all historical scholarship should be enlightenment and understanding and not the promotion of special causes.

Prucha does not deny that injustice took place. He demonstrated, however, that United States policy was not rooted in racism. In several works of the 1970s, including *Americanizing the American Indians* (1973) and *The Churches and the Indian Schools* (1979), Prucha surveyed the agenda of "self-righteous humanitarians" who endeavored to transform American Indians into "patriotic citizens indistinguishable from their white neighbors." Ironically, the well-intentioned reformers' ethnocentric policies – detribalization, allotment, education, Christianization, and reservations – ultimately proved disastrous for native peoples.

Not everyone agreed with Prucha's discussion of the reform programs he contended originated in evangelical Christianity. Critics noted that Prucha focused almost exclusively on the reformers' policies, but failed to explore the consequences of those actions at the reservation level. Vine Deloria, Jr., a Lakota scholar and activist, reported that Prucha suffered from reading documents divorced from involvement in the world in which people lived.

Prucha's seminal article, "Andrew Jackson's Indian Policy" (1969) generated a firestorm of controversy. Prucha argued that Jackson's removal policies grew out of the failure of previous efforts to "civilize" and assimilate American Indians into Euro-American society. By the 1820s, federal officials realized that native Americans had not been absorbed into the dominant society. To complicate matters, settlers were pressing westward in search of new lands and demanding that Indians be cleared from their path. Removal policies, wrote Prucha, represented a culmination of efforts to halt the continued encroachment onto tribal lands. President Jackson and other government officials advocated removing Indians west of the Mississippi to protect them from aggressive frontiersmen and enable them to move toward "civilization" at their own pace. To call Jackson an Indian hater, argued Prucha, was to mistake the tenor of the man and his times.

Prucha's interpretation challenged previous accounts of Jacksonian racism, treachery, and oppression. Virgil Vogel chastised Prucha for demolishing the image of Jackson as a contemptible racist. Vine Deloria, Jr., questioned Prucha's "incomprehensible interpretation" of Jackson as the beloved friend of the Indians. Michael Paul Rogin contended that Jackson's benevolent assertions were mere rhetoric disguising baser motives underlying removal policies. Prucha responded to his detractors by broadening his research interests and accumulating documentary evidence to support his views. He refined and expanded previous interpretations in a variety of writings.

The capstone of Prucha's scholarly career was *The Great Father* (1984), a comprehensive 2-volume history of Indian-White relations from the colonial period to 1980, that synthesized over thirty years of scholarship. The study, winner of the Ray Allen Billington award for the best book in American frontier history and a Pulitzer Prize finalist, won acclaim for its comprehensiveness, exemplary scholarship, balance, integration of existing sources, and editorial integrity. Prucha's survey portrayed natives and Europeans clashing from the earliest period of cultural contact. To protect the American Indians, Prucha demonstrated how public officials used their authority to guard Indians against the destructive forces of the dominant culture. Prucha called this paternalism, "a determination to do what was best for the Indians according to white norms, which translated into protection, subsistence of the destitute, punishment of the unruly, and eventually taking Indians by the hand and leading them along the path to white civilization and Christianity." Prucha condensed his findings in an abridged version of *The Great Father* (1986) and later distilled themes and patterns of Indian-White relations for nonspecialists in *The Indians in American Society* (1985).

In 1987 Prucha became a Fellow of the Society of American Historians in recognition of a lifetime of scholarship characterized by "literary distinction" and "scholarly merit." The invitation was a fitting reward for a historian whose dispassionate investigations moved historical debates beyond mere polemics and axe-grinding so prevalent in American Indian history. Few scholars have been as widely acclaimed, yet simultaneously attacked, for their historical interpretations. Through it all, however, Prucha has remained aloof from the historiographical fray, preferring instead to allow his meticulous research, thorough documentation, and well-argued positions stand on their own merits.

JON L. BRUDVIG

See also Native American

Biography

Born River Falls, Wisconsin, 4 January 1921. Received BS, Wisconsin State College, 1941; MA, University of Minnesota, 1947; PhD, Harvard University, 1950. Jesuit priest; taught at Marquette University, from 1960 (emeritus).

Principal Writings

Broadax and Bayonet: The Role of the United States Army in the Development of the Northwest, 1815–1860, 1953

American Indian Policy in the Formative Years: The Indian Trade and Intercourse Acts, 1790–1834, 1962

A Guide to the Military Posts of the United States, 1789–1895, 1964

Lewis Cass and American Indian Policy, 1967

"Andrew Jackson's Indian Policy: A Reassessment," *Journal of American History* 56 (1969), 527–39

The Sword of the Republic: The United States Army on the Frontier, 1783–1846, 1969

Editor, *The Indian in American History*, 1971

Indian Peace Medals in American History, 1971

Editor, *Americanizing the American Indians: Writings by the "Friends of the Indian," 1880–1900*, 1973

Editor, *The Dawes Act and the Allotment of Indian Lands*, by D.S. Otis, 1973

Editor, *Documents of United States Indian Policy*, 1975

American Indian Policy in Crisis: Christian Reformers and the Indian, 1865–1900, 1976

The Churches and the Indian Schools, 1888–1912, 1979

Indian Policy in the United States: Historical Essays, 1981

The Great Father: The United States Government and the American Indians, 2 vols., 1984; abridged 1986

The Indians in American Society: From the Revolutionary War to the Present, 1985

Atlas of American Indian Affairs, 1990

American Indian Treaties: The History of a Political Anomaly, 1994

Further Reading

Deloria, Vine, Jr., *Custer Died for Your Sins: An Indian Manifesto*, New York: Macmillan, and London: Collier Macmillan, 1969

Deloria, Vine, Jr., *Behind the Trail of Broken Treaties: An Indian Declaration of Independence*, New York: Delacorte Press, 1974

Rogin, Michael Paul, *Fathers and Children: Andrew Jackson and the Subjugation of the American Indian*, New York: Knopf, 1975

Vogel, Virgil, *This Country Was Ours: A Documentary History of the American Indian*, New York: Harper, 1972

Psellos, Michael 1018–after 1081

Byzantine writer and historian

The society that produced Michael Psellos highly valued education and learning in the classical Greek tradition. A proper education entitled one to admission into the quasi-mandarinate, the bureaucratic classes of the Byzantine state. Particular distinction as a scholar could lead not only to academic prominence, but to court positions of great political and ecclesiastical eminence.

Though not of aristocratic or privileged background himself, Psellos was able to enter this track of advancement thanks to his evident intellectual abilities. A student of the influential scholar John Mavropous, Psellos belonged to a coterie of young intellectuals who hoped to achieve important things through their prominence at court. Two of them, John Xiphilinos and

Constantine Leichoudes, were to become patriarchs of Constantinople, while another, Constantine Doukas, reached the throne itself. Psellos achieved his own high position, if an uneven one as a leading scholar and adviser. He exaggerated his actual political functions, but he did play an active (and often devious) role in events during the 1060s–70s, and he was tutor to his friend's son, the eventually ineffectual emperor Michael VII Doukas.

Of far more enduring substance was Psellos' intellectual achievement. Like all Byzantine intellectuals, Psellos aspired to the versatility of a polymath, leaving one of the most impressive records of this type. His surviving works (in Greek) range from poetry and letters through technical treatises on medicine, scientific topics, mathematics, theology, and, most of all, philosophy. His particular focus was on the thought of Plato, to whose importance he gave a new emphasis, helping to displace the earlier ascendancy of Aristotelian thought, and inclining subsequent Byzantine thought toward a crucial Platonic cast. Psellos' preoccupations with ancient philosophy brought suspicions of paganizing tendencies, but he was able to defend his Christian orthodoxy and avoid the later condemnation that his student, John Italos, was to suffer on these counts.

Psellos' one major historical work is still sufficient to win him one of the most prominent places in Byzantine literature. This is his *Chronographía* or *Chronography*, a record of events and personalities within the period 976–1078. (A shorter chronicle, the *Historia syntomos*, by Psellos on the earlier Roman empire has recently come to light as well, but is of limited importance.) It was a practice in Byzantine historiography for one writer to take up his account at the point where his most important literary predecessor had left off, and Psellos honors this tradition by linking his *Chronographía* to established accounts of the 10th century. Like the best authors in this tradition, too, Psellos understood his function as far more than mere chronicler of dry data, but as a writer in the classicizing high style that Byzantines thought continued the idiom of the great ancient historians. This idiom understood a strong sense of historical causality and set lofty standards of Greek literary expression. Unlike most in his tradition, however, Psellos slighted the broader scope of military and political events and concentrated on the immediate world of the capital and on the personalities of the court, filled with anecdotes and character sketches. His account up to the 1030s is relatively perfunctory, and comes alive only as he describes the episodes and individuals he knew so well from his personal contacts or observations. In addition, his own inflated pride prompted him to exaggerate his own importance and to shape his account around himself and his own perceptions. His account thus becomes as much a court memoir as a formal history, with something of an "Emperors-who-have-known-me" character.

That viewpoint acknowledged, however, Psellos' *Chronographía* is a remarkable work, still lively reading today. He reports that he began it as a short, skeletal chronicle account, requested of him by a friend; this no longer survives. He expanded and fleshed out this version as a literary work on a longer scale, carrying his account into the 1070s; there it breaks off abruptly, about the time of his own expulsion from court and public life, and is left formally unfinished.

For all its egomania and fussiness, the *Chronographía* is a work of remarkable lucidity, as the fashions of Byzantine literary style go. Its particular strength is Psellos' recognition of human individuality. His perception of personal emotions and motivations allows him to create believable portraits with a vividness not only striking in the context of Byzantium's genuine humanistic culture but utterly unparalleled by anything in the intellectually backward and stylistically impoverished world of medieval Western Europe of the time. Under his mask of pomposity, Psellos was a person of deep feelings, strong in his sense of friendship and firm in his sympathies or biases. He therefore could understand basic human impulses as far more causative than any abstract theories of Providence or Fortune so often favored in classical historiography. Despite conventional posturing, his Greek style shows a capacity for humor and irony. Within the parameters of the Byzantine literary pretensions he shared, Psellos brings to life his "warts-and-all" characters to a degree unknown in historical writing down to very modern times.

JOHN W. BARKER

See also Bury; Byzantium; Eastern Orthodoxy

Biography

Michael Psellos (Psellus). Born Constantine Psellos, Constantinople, 1018, of modest middle-class family. Received good education and, displaying evident talents, rapidly advanced in Byzantine cultural and court circles. With a group of intellectual colleagues, was instrumental in reviving higher education and Platonic studies in the capital, earning the title of Consul (*Hypatos*) of the Philosophers; fell into disfavor about 1054, retired for a while to a monastery on Mt. Olympus, taking the monkish name of Michael; returned to court and political posts, reached a peak of influence during reign of his school friend, Constantine X Doukas, and his son, Michael VII, Psellos' student; renewed disfavor drove him from office, if not also the capital. Died in obscurity at an unknown date, after 1081.

Principal Writings

Chronographia, c.1059–78; as *The Chronographia of Michael Psellus*, translated by E.R.A. Sewter, 1953, revised as *Fourteen Byzantine Rulers*, 1966

Further Reading

Angold, Michael, *The Byzantine Empire, 1025–1204: A Political History*, London and New York: Longman, 1984

Bury, J.B., "Roman Emperors from Basil II to Isaac Komnenos (AD 976–1057)," *English Historical Review* 4 (1889), 41–64, 251–85; reprinted in Harold Temperley, ed., *Selected Essays of J. B. Bury*, Cambridge: Cambridge University Press, 1930

Chamberlain, C., "The Theory and Practice of Imperial Panegyric in Michael Psellus: The Tension Between History and Rhetoric," *Byzantion* 56 (1986), 16–27

Hussey, Joan M., "Michael Psellos, the Byzantine Historian," *Speculum* 10 (1935), 81–90

Hussey, Joan M., *Church and Learning in the Byzantine Empire, 867–1185*, London: Oxford University Press, 1937; reprinted New York: Russell and Russell, 1963

Joannou, P., "Psellos et le Monastère Tà Narsoû," *Byzantinische Zeitschrift* 44 (1951), 283–90

Renaud, Emile, "Introduction," in Psellos, *Chronographie ou histoire d'un siècle de Byzance (976–1077)*, 2 vols., Paris: Belles Lettres, 1926–28; reprinted 1967

Snipes, Kenneth, "A Letter of Michael Psellos to Constantine the Nephew of Michael Cerularios," *Greek, Roman, and Byzantine Studies* 22 (1981), 89–107

Snipes, Kenneth, "A Newly Discovered History of the Roman Emperors by Michael Psellos," *Jahrbuch der Österreichischen Byzantinistik* 32 (1982), 53–61

Q

Quantitative Method

Quantitative method has had considerable impact on the direction of history since the early 1960s, as historians became more sensitive to the methods and approaches of social science as a whole. Thus the importance of statistics and statistical methods in areas of economics, political science, and sociology impinged on related branches of history. Historians in general became more interested in statistics and the manipulation and interpretation of data. Quantitative methods seemed to offer scientific and objective foundation to historical inference. A number of works emerged bringing together long-run time series of economic, demographic, and social indicators. This aggregative approach seemed to establish firmly the wider dynamics of the historical process. The normative approach complemented the former with detailed or case study statistical investigations allowing us to discover the complexity of historical relationships. Obviously by the 1970s the manipulation of data became greatly eased by the computer.

In the study of population, accurate knowledge of size of population is the *sine qua non*, and census, birth, death, and marriage registers are the principal source materials. The history of population was therefore transformed by this new departure. In 1965, Peter Laslett's *The World We Have Lost* shattered assumptions made about the family in English history. He found that the nuclear family predated the Industrial Revolution and that far from there being a static rural population there was considerable turnover of village inhabitants. This acted as catalyst to a whole generation of historical demographers and has elicited important debates about population, household, and family change.

Political history was also infected by quantitative concerns. The voting patterns at elections, and in representative assemblies, as well as membership statistics were all subjected to data analysis. This concern was dubbed new political history. In a recent example, Thomas Childers subjected statistics on the Nazi electorate to multiple regression analysis to demonstrate its age, gender, and class distribution. His results challenged some of the commonplaces held about the social base of the Nazis. The Nazi vote by 1932 was older, more female, and with greater numbers of upper middle class than was formerly supposed.

Its economic counterpart, "cliometrics" or new economic history, showed an even more ambitious enthusiasm for data and quantitative method. Indeed, this school applied the techniques of mathematical modeling of econometrics and economic forecasting to historical situations. In this way, the impact of specific historical variables could be singled out. New economic history was able to produce startling results. Curtin's *The Atlantic Slave Trade* (1969) revised downwards the accepted numbers involved in the slave trade. Fogel's study of the railroads in the United States postulated that they played a marginal role in America's industrialization. Fogel and Engerman's *Time on the Cross* (1974) sought to turn upside down the accepted view of slavery in the southern states, concluding that slave labor was highly productive, well-treated, and that their masters were imbued with economic rationalism. The ensuing furore demonstrated the way in which conclusions drawn from quantitative methods and from traditional sources could be extremely polarized. Indeed, in the early 1970s the debate over quantitative history "was the central preoccupation of theorists of history."

New economic history relies on the sophisticated input-output models – production, consumption, and investment functions of modern econometrics. This historical method has been able to plug gaps in our existing knowledge and to assess the impact of various variables. However, the problem is that the extravagance of their claims is based on models based on a set of assumptions about human behavior. Do humans always act as rational, profit-maximizing, individuals? Is a particular model informed by neoclassical, Keynesian, or Marxist economics? If the assumptions are wrong results are distorted, but, more importantly, if the assumptions are arbitary so are the results.

The advantages of quantitative methods are that they have dispelled some of our false assumptions about history. Knowledge of quantitative method has spread, particularly in the United States, through the journals *Historical Methods* and *Social Science History* and has gained increasing influence in some other journals such as the *Economic History Review* and the *Journal of Economic History*. However, new economic history's reliance on quantification assumes that historical phenomena are quantitative by nature. As Julian Hoppit argued in relation to the Industrial Revolution, in reality, quantity and quality are tightly entwined. Data assembled from socially constructed categories such as class or collected by particular institutions, be they states, trade unions, or employers, may pose as many questions as they answer.

By the late 1970s quantitative methods had considerably polarized historians. Indeed in 1983 it took the form of a debate between Elton and Fogel, *Which Road to the Past?* The premise of the book was that history had been divided into the traditional method of a subjective reconstruction from rigorous examination of the sources, and the objective "scientific" approach of cliometricians. Recent historical discourse on quantitative method has become more modest in its claims. Indeed, some historians have regretted that the polarization of debate has led to a too dismissive attitude to quantification. Floud and Kocka leveled similar cases respectively at History Workshop and the history of everyday life for being too complacent when it comes to quantitative and theoretical analysis.

Quantitative history did not supersede traditional history as some once claimed it would. It does, however, make an important contribution to selected areas of history. In general, quantitative methods are more freely used in the United States than Europe, more among economic and demographic historians than social or political ones and more in the study of modern than in early modern and premodern history. The irony has been noted by historians such as Middleton and Wardley that at a time when quantitative history seems to have lost momentum, the range of software, databases, statistical and econometric packages, and the increasing power of the humble PC, has grown prodigiously.

MATT PERRY

See also Curtin; Fogel; Industrial; Kocka

Further Reading

Childers, Thomas, *The Nazi Voter: The Social Foundations of Fascism in Germany, 1919–1933*, Chapel Hill: University of North Carolina Press, 1983

Curtin, Philip D., *The Atlantic Slave Trade: A Census*, Madison: University of Wisconsin Press, 1969

David, Paul, Herbert G. Gutman, Richard Sutch, Peter Temin, and Gavin Wright, *Reckoning with Slavery: A Critical Study in the Quantitative History of American Negro Slavery*, New York: Oxford University Press, 1976

Economic History Review, Oxford: Economic History Society, 1927–

Elton, G.R., and Robert William Fogel, *Which Road to the Past? Two Views of History*, New Haven: Yale University Press, 1983

Evans, Jeff, Ian Miles, and John Irvine, eds., *Demystifying Social Statistics*, London: Pluto Press, 1979

Floud, Roderick, "Quantitative History and People's History: Two Methods in Conflict," *History Workshop Journal* 17 (1984), 113–24

Fogel, Robert William, *Railroads and American Economic Growth: Essays in Econometric History*, Baltimore: Johns Hopkins Press, 1964

Fogel, Robert William, and Stanley L. Engerman, *Time on the Cross: The Economics of American Negro Slavery*, 2 vols., Boston: Little Brown, and London: Wildwood, 1974

Historical Methods, Washington, DC: Heldref, 1967–

Hoppit, Julian, "Counting the Industrial Revolution," *Economic History Review* 43 (1990), 173–93

Journal of Economic History, Wilmington, DE: Economic History Association, 1941–

Kocka, Jürgen, "Theories and Quantification in History," *Social Science History* 8 (1984), 169–78

Laslett, Peter, *The World We Have Lost*, London: Methuen, 1965, New York: Scribner, 1966; revised 1984

Middleton, Roger, and Peter Wardley, "Information Technology in Economic and Social History: The Computer as Philosopher's Stone or Pandora's Box?," *Economic History Review* 43 (1990), 667–96

Social Science History, Beverly Hills, CA: Sage, 1976–

Quinn, David B. 1909–

Irish historian

David Beers Quinn has been over the course of a long career the leading student of English maritime expansion during the Tudor and Stuart periods. Working alone and in collaboration with his wife Alison, Quinn has written prolifically and edited several important collections of primary source documents dealing first with English attempts to subdue Ireland and, later, with English efforts to explore, and then settle, the coast of North America.

Quinn began publishing on Irish history in 1933. In 1947 he completed *Raleigh and the British Empire*, and 19 years later *The Elizabethans and the Irish*, a study of English efforts to subdue, pacify, and colonize the island. Both works represented part of a renaissance of interest in Irish history, free of the intense partisanship between the North and the South which had existed earlier and which, Quinn recalled, "I was glad to play a small part in . . . and which I am glad to say has survived and flourished."

In both works, and in a number of influential essays, Quinn began to explore linkages between English efforts in Ireland and subsequent English attempts to settle North America. Working under the aegis of the Hakluyt Society, Quinn edited and published *The Voyages and Colonising Enterprises of Sir Humphrey Gilbert* (1940), a project that united his interest in what the English were up to in Ireland, with what they hoped to accomplish in North America. Fifteen years later the Hakluyt Society published *The Roanoke Voyages, 1584–1590*, an invaluable collection of documents, translated from several languages and culled from a wide variety of sources, charting the efforts of Sir Walter Ralegh to plant a colony on the North Carolina Outer Banks. The latter collection, especially, combining broad vision with a deft editorial touch, will continue to be used and respected by historians interested in English colonization and its effects upon Native American society.

Quinn included in *The Roanoke Voyages* a descriptive listing of the well-known John White drawings. In 1964, with the assistance of Paul Hulton, he oversaw the publication, for the first time, of *The American Drawings of John White*, thus providing students of early America with access to the only visual portrayal of Native American culture at the dawn of its encounter with European society.

Quinn's interest in English maritime expansion continued through the 1970s and 1980s. He co-edited *The New Found Land of Stephen Parmenius* (1972), based on the life and writings of Gilbert's ill-fated poet-chronicler, and in 1974 *The Hakluyt Handbook*, a convenient collection of essays by scholars working in a number of disciplines. Also in 1974 he published *England and the Discovery of America, 1481–1620*, a collection of previously published essays with some new material. In 1979, he edited *New American World*, a 5-volume collection of primary source documents. His involvement in the 350th anniversary of Maryland's founding led him to edit a useful volume of essays, *Early Maryland and a Wider World* (1982), and in commemoration of the 400th anniversary of the English arrival in North Carolina, Quinn wrote *Set Fair for Roanoke* (1985), the most comprehensive history of the subject.

In recent years, Quinn has described the "British" approach to early American history as one that is "warped and should be discarded, at least for the sixteenth and early seventeenth centuries." The British approach, advanced by J.G.A. Pocock, Bernard Bailyn and others, looks at the history of the English American colonies in a transatlantic context, viewing them as akin to Wales, Scotland, Ireland and the British West Indies in that they are peripheral areas, or frontiers, inextricably linked and bound in a dialectical relationship with the English metropolis. If, as Quinn said in 1952, he had tried through his work "to enlarge the picture of what the English did in these early days, it was as much to show how little they accomplished as how much." Still, Quinn's work has forced American colonial historians to broaden their perspective, to understand that events and developments in England could closely influence events in the New World, and that dramatic similarities exist between English activities in Ireland and America. That numerous scholars have followed Quinn in examining links between America, Ireland, and Britain and expanded upon his research demonstrates the enduring importance of his work.

MICHAEL L. OBERG

Biography

David Beers Quinn. Born Dublin, 24 April 1909. Received BA, Queen's University, Belfast, 1931; PhD, University of London, 1934. Taught at University College, Southampton, 1934–39; Queen's University, Belfast, 1939–44; University College, Swansea, 1944–57; and University of Liverpool, 1957–76. Married Alison Moffat Robertson (co-author of many of his books), 1937 (died 1993; 2 sons, 1 daughter).

Principal Writings

Editor, *The Voyages and Colonising Enterprises of Sir Humphrey Gilbert*, Hakluyt Society Series 2, vols. 88–89, 1940
"Sir Thomas Smith and the Beginnings of English Colonial Theory," *Proceedings of the American Philosophical Society* 85 (1945)
Raleigh and the British Empire, 1947
Editor, *The Roanoke Voyages, 1584–1590: Documents to Illustrate the English Voyages to North America under the Patent Granted to Walter Raleigh in 1584*, 2 vols., 1955
With Paul Hulton, *The American Drawings of John White*, 1964
The Elizabethans and the Irish, 1966
Editor with Neil M. Cheshire, *The New Found Land of Stephen Parmenius*, 1972
England and the Discovery of America, 1481–1620, from the Bristol Voyages of the Fifteenth Century to the Pilgrim Settlement at Plymouth: the exploration, Exploitation, and Trial-and-Error Colonization of North America by the English, 1974
Editor, *The Hakluyt Handbook*, 1974
North America from Earliest discovery to First Settlements: The Norse Voyages to 1612, 1977
Editor, *New American World*, 5 vols., 1979
Editor, *Early Maryland and a Wider World*, 1982
Set Fair for Roanoke: Voyages and Colonies, 1584–1606, 1985
Explorers and Colonies: America, 1500–1625, 1990

Further Reading

Andrews, Kenneth R., Nicholas P. Canny, and P.E.H. Hair, eds., *The Westward Enterprise: English Activities in Ireland, the Atlantic, and America, 1480–1650*, Liverpool: Liverpool University Press, 1978; Detroit: Wayne State University Press, 1979
Clough, Cecil H., and P.E.H. Hair, eds., *The European Outthrust and Encounter: The First Phase c.1400–c.1700: Essays in Tribute to David Beers Quinn on his 85th Birthday*, Liverpool: Liverpool University Press, 1994

R

Radzinowicz, Leon 1906–

British (Polish-born) legal historian

Leon Radzinowicz is the author of the monumental and magisterial 5-volume *History of English Criminal Law and Its Administration since 1750*, (1948–90). It comprises over 2,600 pages of text, over 300 pages of appendices, and a bibliography of over 500 pages.

Of Polish origin and trained in criminal law and criminology in Paris, Geneva, and Rome, Radzinowicz came to England in 1937 on behalf of the Polish government to study the English penal system, then widely regarded as the most progressive in Europe. The major influence in his career had been Enrico Ferri, the brilliant expositor of the Italian positivist school of criminology. When war broke out, Radzinowicz was invited to Cambridge where subsequently he became the first professor of criminology in Britain and director of the Institute of Criminology. He is widely regarded as the foremost criminologist of his generation: a figure of worldwide fame and influence. Nevertheless, it is as a historian that he has made his greatest contribution to scholarship.

The plan for the *History* grew from the recognition that previous histories of the criminal law – the prime example of which was Sir James Fitzjames Stephen's 3-volume *History of the Criminal Law of England* (1883) – had been content to describe the evolution of criminal statutes and procedures and to analyze the development of legal doctrine through trials and case-law. This approach had entirely neglected the social and political history of crime, law enforcement, and the administration of criminal justice. With the exception of the Webbs' *English Prisons under Local Government* (1922), almost no use had been made of the mine of information waiting to be excavated from the *Blue Books* – the reports of royal commissions and departmental committees, the annual reports of commissioners, inspectors, and public bodies, the mass of accounts and papers and statistical returns – and also from the parliamentary debates, newspaper reports, pamphlets, articles in Victorian periodicals, books, and the like. It was this mass of material that Radzinowicz mastered.

The title of this work somewhat obscures its scope, depth, and richness. It is less about criminal law *per se* and more about the realities of crime, the policies adopted to combat it, and the ways in which these policies were put into effect through the institutions of policing and punishment in the emerging modern liberal state. In other words it approached the subject from a criminological and social perspective.

Volume 1, *The Movement for Reform* (1948), dealt with capital punishment, a topic taken up again in volume 4 and brought to a conclusion in volume 5. This celebrated volume (for which the James Barr Ames prize of the Harvard Law School was awarded) traced how punishments were ameliorated under the pervasive influence of the liberal enlightenment and utilitarian social thought. Beginning with the vast range of offenses to which the death penalty could be applied in the 18th century, including the notorious Waltham Black Act, Radzinowicz vividly portrayed the way in which the statutes were applied and the nature, forms, and customs of execution. He analyzed the reasons why the policy of maximum severity, arbitrarily applied, held sway for so long in face of the reformers' attempts to create a system that ensured greater certainty of punishments by grading them in relation to the seriousness of the crime committed. It is a history of ideas, of social and political movements, and of the individual efforts of those who, like Sir Samuel Romilly, played so vital a part in the reform of the capital statutes. Volume 2, *The Enforcement of the Law*, and volume 3, *The Reform of the Police* (both published in 1956), were concerned with the emergence of public policing in place of private initiatives, and showed how the fears that the police would become a bastion of state control were eventually overcome. In volume 4, *Grappling for Control* (1968), the campaigns for the reform of the capital laws and the establishment of a public system of policing were traced up to the 1860s. Volume 5 *The Emergence of Penal Policy* (1986, with Roger Hood), explored 19th-century conceptions of crime and criminality, and revealed how a diversified state system of punishment was developed to deal with various categories of offender, such as juveniles, the mentally deficient, vagrants, political offenders, and habitual criminals. It also described how penal servitude replaced transportation, the difficulties this created, and how sentencing practices evolved to meet changing conceptions of crime and punishment.

There is no work to match Radzinowicz's *History* in scope and style. But, like all pioneering and authoritative works, it has not escaped criticism and controversy. In a period when there was a penchant for grand theoretical constructions, especially Marxist interpretations of the state and its controlling mechanisms, Radzinowicz's approach to understanding changes in criminal policy was accused of having failed to recognize that the criminal law was a vehicle for the repression of the lower orders. This was an exaggeration and, in any case, the Marxist interpretation proved to be unsustainable. Radzinowicz has also been labeled by some critics as a "Whig historian," a simplistic and misleading judgment. For while he does indeed chronicle some undisputable improvements in the way that offenders were treated, the *History*, taken as a whole, does not present the development of criminal policy as a seamless advance of progressive liberal reforms. Rather, it illustrates the tensions that have existed between the search for effective control of crime and the need to limit the power of the state's penal apparatus so as to preserve the rule of law, to protect innocent citizens, and to ensure just treatment for offenders.

Although recent scholarship has revealed more about the practices of law enforcement and punishment, particularly through the development of local studies, the major trends of "the great movements" (as he put it) in the growth and diversification of criminal policy, as revealed and analyzed by Radzinowicz, have remained largely intact. His work is enlivened by clarity of expression, telling turns of phrase, perceptive judgments of events and personalities, and an enormous range of sources: all of which make these formidable-looking volumes not only a pleasure to read but an outstanding resource for historians of the period.

ROGER HOOD

Biography
Born Lodz, Poland, 15 August 1906, son of a doctor. Educated in Kraków; at University of Paris, 1924–25; Licencié en Droit, University of Geneva, 1927; Doctor of Law, University of Rome, 1928. Lecturer, University of Geneva, 1928–31; Doctor of Law, Kraków, 1929; reported on working of penal system in Belgium, 1930; lecturer, Free University of Warsaw, 1932–36; came to England on behalf of Polish ministry of justice to report on working of English penal system, 1937; from 1939 helped establish criminological research unit, Cambridge University: Wolfson professor of criminology from 1959, and first director of the Institute of Criminology, 1973 (emeritus); fellow, Trinity College, from 1948. Naturalized British subject, 1947. Knighted 1970. Married 1) Irene Szerezewski, 1933 (marriage dissolved 1955); 2) Mary Ann Nevins, 1958 (marriage dissolved 1979; 1 son, 1 daughter); 3) Isolde Klarmann, née Doernenburg, 1979.

Principal Writings
A History of English Criminal Law and Its Administration since 1750, 5 vols., 1948–90 (vol. 5 written with Roger Hood)
Ideology and Crime: A Study of Crime in Its Social and Historical Context, 1966

Further Reading
Hood, Roger, ed., *Crime, Criminology and Public Policy: Essays in Honour of Sir Leon Radzinowicz*, London: Heinemann, and New York: Free Press, 1974

Raeff, Marc 1923–
US (Russian-born) social historian

One of the first American scholars to conduct a serious examination of the social and cultural life of the nobility of imperial Russia, Marc Raeff has made a significant contribution to the study of imperial Russian history and encouraged a generation of historians to re-examine previously accepted knowledge and assumptions about the Russian aristocracy. Unlike the work of his Russian predecessors, such as A. Romanovich-Slavatinskii and N. Pavlov-Silvanskii, who concentrated on the legal status of the nobility in relationship to other classes and the crown, most of Raeff's work focused on understanding the various social, cultural, and institutional elements that influenced this group's behavior and self-perception.

Raeff's most influential book was undoubtedly *Origins of the Russian Intelligentsia* (1966). Drawing on a wealth of primary and secondary material, including diaries, memoirs, and contemporary government sources, Raeff offered the first thorough study of the social dynamics and institutional factors that shaped the life and worldview of the Russian noble. In his book, Raeff described how the Russian noble, in contrast to his Western counterparts, had weak ties to his home estate and locality. Instead, the Russian noble's status and identity were derived primarily from his role in state service, a situation created by the strict service requirements of the Russian tsars. Thus, according to Raeff, the Russian nobility began to define itself primarily in terms of its service obligation, a tie that became particularly problematic after 1762, when compulsory service was ended by royal decree. The Russian elite was now expected to create a new personal and corporate identity based on life in the provinces and the management of estates, an existence wholly unfamiliar to the average noble who had spent the majority of his life away in service. In the end, these alienated nobles turned to their fellow aristocrats for a sense of security and belonging, organizing and participating in secret circles. Raeff emphasizes that this intelligentsia of the early 19th century grew directly out of the alienated nobility of the 18th century.

This book was only the first in a series of works by Raeff that examined questions of social history in 18th and early 19th century Russia. A subsequent work, for example, *Comprendre l'ancien régime russe* (1982; *Understanding Imperial Russia*, 1984), elaborated on his earlier argument. In this book, Raeff explored Russia's historical development under the Romanov dynasty. In particular, he concentrated on Russia's failure to develop a civil society based on legal rights. He argued that Peter the Great's westernization of the Russian elite severed it from the common people, and this, combined with the absolute control of the state, impeded the growth of the autonomous social forces that were necessary for the emergence of a modern society. The inability of subsequent rulers, such as Catherine II and Nicholas I, to compile a law code and reform the legal system signaled Russia's last chance to move toward a modern society. In the end, the failure to introduce timely reforms, the alienation between social groups, and the increasingly absolute nature of the tsarist regime made collapse inevitable.

Having looked at the development of Russian society through an examination of the nobility, Raeff then turned to a study of the origins of modern society from a comparative perspective. In *The Well-Ordered Police State* (1983), he examined the particular administrative practices and political attitudes of the 17th and 18th centuries which underlay the institutional and social changes in this formative period. His title was drawn from the central essay of his book which analyzed and interpreted those government and police regulations of the German states that expressed the philosophy and goals of the state and assisted in the creation of a modern society. The ability of the

German princes to combine state leadership with the enlistment of the cooperation and participation of the public eluded even Russia's most ambitious rulers, Peter and Catherine II, for Russia's social structure was too primitive to facilitate such a system. As a result, the overwhelming predominance of state power continued to inhibit the desired modernization.

Finally, in *Russia Abroad* (1990), Raeff presented a fascinating study of the first émigrés who left Russia as a result of the Revolution and the Civil War. In this valuable work, he focused on émigré life in Paris. Raeff described the education, culture, and religion of the émigrés who, in their belief that they would soon return to Russia, placed great emphasis on the need to preserve Russian culture.

Despite the influential nature of Raeff's works, he has not escaped criticism. On occasion, he has been criticized for excessive generalization, particularly in his characterization of the Russian elite and his failure sufficiently to distinguish between the various strata of noble society. Furthermore, Raeff's portrait of Russian émigré society has been called misleading and narrow. These criticisms aside, Raeff is without a doubt one of the most influential Russian historians of the 20th century and his contribution to the understanding of imperial Russia cannot be overestimated.

LEE A. FARROW

See also Russia: Modern

Biography
Born Moscow, 28 July 1923. Went to US, 1941 (naturalized 1943). Attended City College of New York, 1942–43. Served in US Army, 1943–46. Received MA, Harvard University, 1947, PhD 1950. Taught at Clark University, 1949–61; and Columbia University (rising to professor), from 1963.

Principal Writings
Siberia and the Reforms of 1822, 1956
Michael Speransky: Statesman of Imperial Russia, 1772–1839, 1957
"State and Nobility in the Ideology of M.M. Shcherbatov," *Slavic Review* 19 (1960), 363–79
The Decembrist Movement, 1966
Origins of the Russian Intelligentsia: The Eighteenth-Century Nobility, 1966
Imperial Russia, 1682–1825: The Coming of Age of Modern Russia, 1971
Comprendre l'ancien régime russe: état et société en Russie impériale: essai d'interprétation, 1982; in English as *Understanding Imperial Russia: State and Society in the Old Regime*, 1984
The Well-Ordered Police State: Social and Institutional Change Through Law in the Germanies and Russia, 1600–1800, 1983
Russia Abroad: A Cultural History of the Russian Emigration, 1919–1939, 1990
Political Ideas and Institutions in Imperial Russia, 1994

Ranger, Terence O. 1929–
British historian of Africa

Terence O. Ranger was among the pioneers of African historical studies. He has been a prolific scholar and a teacher on three continents, and his influence has been both far-reaching and pervasive. He has contributed to many areas of African historical research, including religion, politics, social history, and tradition.

Ranger is perhaps best known to many for his idea of the "usable past": the idea that history can be used to benefit the present. Ranger unashamedly admits that he was among the early conceptualizers of the African nationalist historiographical school. This school used history in order to strengthen the sense of nationhood of the newly independent African countries. In "Towards a Usable African Past" (1976) Ranger advocated studying the past to combat African poverty, better the condition of women, investigate cultural transmission, and arrive at a better understanding of African ecology and food production. He further stated that this can be done without a "radical" approach and need not criticize capitalism.

Religious studies has greatly benefited from Ranger's work. He has investigated religion in innovative ways. *Revolt in Southern Rhodesia* (1967) examined the role of MaShona and Ndebele prophetic leaders in resistance to British colonial conquest. While the methodology of this work has come under attack, no one can deny its value as a blueprint for examining resistance to colonialism. Ranger gave a place to religion in the investigation of resistance, a theme that had hitherto been neglected. He was among the first scholars to give the study of African religions a serious place in African historiography, as evidenced by *The Historical Study of African Religion* (1972). This work was organized under the principle that religion was a neglected aspect of study, but that it could also not be separated from politics, economics, and society. This was a rather revolutionary way to look at religion, because previous scholarship tended to study it as detached from the rest of African life. Ranger was also among the first scholars to give serious attention to syncretic religions, or those that combined indigenous and Christian beliefs in their practices. *The African Churches of Tanzania* (1969) is an examination of such religions.

Politics has also been a field of investigation for Ranger. Here again, he has analyzed the topic in inventive ways. *Peasant Consciousness and Guerrilla War in Zimbabwe* (1985) and "War, Violence and Healing in Zimbabwe" (1992) both examined the intersection of politics with religion. They dealt with colonial and postcolonial politics while simultaneously investigating the role of religious leaders in political protest, guerrilla war, and societal healing.

Ranger turned to social history in *The African Voice in Southern Rhodesia, 1898–1930* (1970). This work sets out to investigate Zimbabwean history from the "bottom up," especially in relation to the policy of Land Appointment. While largely an exposition of Zimbabwean politics, this work also looked at the role of churches, unions, and other institutions in Zimbabwean life.

Tradition, and the uses of it, has been a fairly recent research interest of Ranger. In "The Invention of Tradition in Colonial Africa" (1983) and "The Black Man's Burden" (1984) Ranger investigated the invention of tradition. It is Ranger's contention that colonial governments created traditions that they could use to control their subjects. The European regimes exploited these traditions in order to suggest that their policies were sympathetic to longstanding African social practices. These traditions not only affected political control, but were often projected back into African culture, often altering many other African cultural institutions.

Ranger has also sought to position African historiography within a larger historiographical context. In fact, in *The Emergence of African History at British Universities* (1995), Ranger described this as one of the duties of historians of Africa. In one of his latest edited works, *Epidemics and Ideas* (1992), his chapter on Africa is linked with essays from other parts of the world. The same is true of his chapter in *The Invention of Tradition* (1983). African history cannot exist in a vacuum unconnected to the rest of the historiographical world. Through his research on religion, politics, peasantry, and tradition, Ranger has done his share to ensure that the necessary connections are made.

TOYIN FALOLA and JOEL E. TISHKEN

See also Africa: Central; Africa: Eastern; Anthropology; Marks

Biography

Terence Osborn Ranger. Born London, 29 November 1929. Educated at Highgate School; BA, Oxford University, MA 1953, PhD 1960. Lecturer, Royal Naval College, Dartmouth, 1955–56; and College of Rhodesia and Nyasaland, 1957–63; professor, University of Dar es Salaam, 1963–69; University of California, Los Angeles, 1969–74; University of Manchester, 1974–87; and Oxford University, from 1987; fellow, St. Antony's College, Oxford, from 1987. Married Shelagh Campbell Clark, 1954 (3 daughters).

Principal Writings

Revolt in Southern Rhodesia, 1896–97: A Study in African Resistance, 1967
"Connexions between 'Primary Resistance' Movements and Modern Mass Nationalism in East and Central Africa," *Journal of African History* 9 (1968), 437–53; 631–41
The African Churches of Tanzania, 1969
The African Voice in Southern Rhodesia, 1898–1930, 1970
Editor with Isaria N. Kimambo, *The Historical Study of African Religion: With Special Reference to East and Central Africa*, 1972
Dance and Society in Eastern Africa, 1890–1970: The Beni Ngoma, 1975
"Towards a Usable African Past," in Christopher Fyfe, ed., *African Studies since 1945: A Tribute to Basil Davidson*, 1976
"The Invention of Tradition in Colonial Africa," in Eric J. Hobsbawm and Terence O. Ranger, eds., *The Invention of Tradition*, 1983
"The Black Man's Burden," *Wilson Quarterly* 8 (1984), 121–33
Peasant Consciousness and Guerrilla War in Zimbabwe: A Comparative Study, 1985
"Religious Movements and Politics in Sub-Saharan Africa," *African Studies Review* 29 (1986), 1–69
"Taking Hold of the Land: Holy Places and Pilgrimages in Twentieth-Century Zimbabwe," *Past and Present* 117 (1987), 158–94
Edited with Paul Slack, *Epidemics and Ideas: Essays on the Historical Perception of Pestilence*, 1992
"War, Violence and Healing in Zimbabwe," *Journal of Southern African Studies* 18 (1992), 698–707
Contributor, *The Emergence of African History at British Universities: An Autobiographical Approach*, edited by Anthony Kirk-Greene, Oxford: Worldview, 1995
Editor with Richard P. Werbner, *Postcolonial Identities in Africa*, 1996

Ranggawarsita, Raden Ngabei 1802–1873

Javanese court poet

Probably the most famous, though not necessarily the most widely read, poet at the Central Javanese courts of Surakarta in the 19th century was Raden Ngabei Ranggawarsita, great-grandson and grandson of the well-known court poets Yasadipura I and II, who likewise enjoyed the patronage of the Surakarta rulers. Ranggawarsita is generally regarded as "the last of the court poets" (*pujangga panutup*), yet it is not certain when this honorific title, used for the learned poet who was simultaneously an official scribe, a scholar, and a prolific writer of moralistic and didactic works as well as belles lettres in the service of the highest nobility of Surakarta, was bestowed upon him. While scholars such as J.A. Day have held that he came to be known as such after his death, others have argued that he was already called so during his lifetime; it is generally assumed that the title also referred to the poet's excellent qualities. Scholars such as George Quinn have considered this title as an indication of the condition of Javanese literature in general, that it implied that Ranggawarsita would never be equalled and that he would never have a successor – despite the fact that the Javanese courts remained in existence long after the great poet's death, and that men of letters continued to write for Javanese noblemen well into the 20th century.

The title of *pujangga* was used in Javanese writings during Hindu-Buddhist times to refer to a Brahman or other person of clerical rank. At the East Javanese court of Majapahit in the 14th century the term indicated a category of scholars or religious officials. The assumption was made by Vlekke that it was the task of a new king's *pujangga* to sanction the claim to legitimacy, each time the center of power shifted to a new place. Following an intermittent period in which newly emerging Islamic rulers in the Pasisir area along Java's north coast were strongly oriented toward international Islamic culture, the use of this title at the Islamic court of Surakarta signaled a renewed interest in the Hindu-Buddhist cultural and literary heritage, which the Dutch scholar Pigeaud termed the "renaissance of classical Javanese literature in the late eighteenth and nineteenth centuries." During this period court literati, primarily the members of the Yasadipura family, recomposed many of the ancient Old Javanese literary works in more modern poetic forms, which made a great impact on the flourishing of theatrical and musical art forms related to the traditional shadow puppet plays (*wayang*).

Ranggawarsita's major accomplishment was the monumental literary work in prose entitled *Pustaka Raja Purwa* (The Book of Kings of Ancient Times), intended as the first part of a "trilogy" covering the mythical past of Java, beginning with Adam and the Indian gods, from the (fictional) year 1 until the year 730. On account of correspondences in content and form, Drewes assumed that the *Pustaka Raja* was modelled after the great *Serat Kandha* ("Book of Tales") which was probably written by Yasadipura I and II in the second half of the 18th century. More recently, a relationship has been argued by Day with the prophecies of king Jayabaya, the legendary wise king of the medieval East Javanese kingdom of Kedhiri who features in eschatological prophecies of the Islamic period. Generally, the *Pustaka Raja* is considered to belong to the "books of tales" genre of the Pasisir literature of the 17th and 18th centuries, which had been continued in the major history of the court of Surakarta (*Babad Surakarta*) by Ranggawarsita's great ancestor, Yasadipura I.

Although the lengthy *Pustaka Raja* is often viewed as an attempt to write a comprehensive history of Java, according to Pigeaud the author's purpose apparently was not to write a historical chronicle, but rather to provide "encyclopedic knowledge of the whole of human history." The impression of a historical, linear development has been created by the arrangement of the myths and legends according to a chronology of solar and lunar years apparently of Ranggawarsita's own invention, starting from the *Paramayoga*, an introductory cosmogony or story of the gods, until the death of Arjuna's great-grandson, concluding the Mahabharata epic.

In Java, the *Pustaka Raja* was highly appreciated by Ranggawarsita's contemporaries and served as a source of inspiration to learned literati – including the well-known ruler and poet Prince Mangkunagara IV – as well as to following generations of learned authors and performers of the shadow puppet theater, *wayang kulit*. Epigones of the Mangkunagaran House wrote extensions entitled *Pustaka Raja Madya* and *Pustaka Raja Puwara*, with stories from supposedly later, post-epical times, including legends from the medieval East Javanese kingdoms, and thus covering the entire Hindu-Buddhist era in Java.

The appreciation for Ranggawarsita's work has not remained constant. Although he collaborated with Dutch contemporaries such as the linguist C.F. Winter in Surakarta and wrote a work on Javanese grammar, 19th-century Dutch scholars criticized Ranggawarsita's alleged lack of knowledge of Old Javanese. Even the western-educated Javanese scholar Poerbatjaraka was highly critical of the lack of reliable historical information in the *Pustaka Raja*. In Javanese society, the social criticism expressed in the poem *Kalatidha*, paraphrased as "the age of madness," has received much attention. This poetic complaint, meant as an elegy on social problems and lack of norms in the poet's own time, has often been interpreted as a prediction of the social upheaval in the following 20th century.

Lately, scholars both in Indonesia and abroad have paid much attention to Ranggawarsita's alleged prophetic qualities. Yet, most of the works of this typical 19th-century Javanese "man of letters" were of a didactic, moralistic, and philosophical nature. In spite of his fame, his works are not well-known to ordinary Javanese, probably because they are written in an ornate literary idiom that makes them rather inaccessible to modern Javanese readers.

CLARA BRAKEL-PAPENHUYZEN

Biography

Name also spelled Ronggawarsita and Ronggowarsito. Born Bagus Burham, 15 March 1802, grandson and great-grandson of court poets Yasadipura I and II; raised by his grandfather after his father was exiled. Educated at Tegalsari, near Panaraga, then traveled; although appointed court poet, he did not achieve the rank his grandfather had attained. Died 24 December 1873.

Principal Writings

Pustaka Raja Purwa (The Book of Kings of Ancient Times); various editions: *Poestaka Radja Poerwa* (Book of Kings of Ancient Times), 1884–1906; *Serat Pustaka Raja Purwa* (The Book of Kings of Ancient Times), 2 vols., 1912; *Lima Karya Pujangga Ranggawarsita* (Five Works by the Court Poet Ranggawarsita), edited by Kamadjaya, 1985

Further Reading

Day, John Anthony, *Meanings of Change in the Poetry of Nineteenth-Century Java*, doctoral dissertation, Ithaca, NY: Cornell University, 1981

Drewes, G.W.J., "Over werkeijke en vermeende Geschiedschrijving in de Nieuwjavaansche litteratuur" (Concerning Real and Supposed Historical Writing in New Javanese Literature), *Djawa* 19 (1939), 244–57

Drewes, G.W.J., "Ranggawarsita, the Pustaka Raja Madya and the wayang madya," *Oriens Extremus* 21 (1974), 199–215

Errington, J. Joseph, "To Know Oneself the Troubled Times: Ronggawarsita's Serat Kala Tidha," in Alton L. Becker, ed., *Writing on the Tongue*, Ann Arbor: Center for South and Southeast Asian Studies, University of Michigan, 1989

Kamadjaya, *Zaman edan: Suatu studi tentang buku Kalatida dari Ranggawarsita* (Times of Madness: A Study of the Kalatida by Ranggawarsita), Jogja: Indonesia University Press, 1964

Mulyanto, R.I., *Biografi Pujangga Ranggawarsita* (Biography of the Court Poet Ranggawarsita), Jakarta, 1990

Pigeaud, Theodore Gauthier Thomas, *Literature of Java*, 3 vols., The Hague: Nijhoff, 1967–70

Poerbatjaraka, Radan Mas Ngabei, *Kapustakan Djawi* (Javanese Literature), Djakarta: Djambatan, 1952

Quinn, George, *The Novel in Javanese*, Leiden: KITLV Press, 1992

Serat Paramayoga, Yogyakarta: Yayasan Centhini, 1992

Uhlenbeck, E.M., *A Critical Survey of Studies on the Languages of Java and Madura*, The Hague: Nijhoff, 1964

Vlekke, Bernard Hubertus Marius, *Nusantara: A History of the East Indian Archipelago*, The Hague: van Hoeve, and Cambridge, MA: Harvard University Press, 1943; revised as *Nusantara: A History of Indonesia*, 1959

Winter, C.F., *Javaansche zamenspraken* (Javanese Conversations), 2 vols., Amsterdam: Müller, 1848–58

Raniri, Nur ud-Din ar- d. 1658
Indian Islamic theologian and historian

Nur ud-Din ar-Raniri's family background was as varied as the scope of his influence. Born in Ranir, India, into a mixed Arab/Indian family with ties with the Malay world, ar-Raniri exerted an influence in various geographical locations and fields of learning.

Ar-Raniri saw himself first and foremost as an Islamic theologian. He is best known in this role, and the vast majority of his prolific writing relates to theological issues: the nature of God, the separation between God and creation, Islamic law and its application, traditions of the prophet Muhammad, and the application of Islamic mystical knowledge to what ar-Raniri considered to be orthodox theology.

Ar-Raniri also made a significant contribution to Malay and Islamic historiography through his *Bustan us-Salatin* (Garden of Kings, after 1638). This encyclopedic work consists of seven books, divided into forty sections, and was commenced in 1638 and probably never completed. It was commissioned by Sultan Iskandar Thani of Aceh and is eclectic in content, including sections on both theology and history. In preparing this work, ar-Raniri sought to mirror the writings of the great Arabic classical historian and exegete, at-Tabari.

The second of the seven books devotes its thirteen sections to wide-ranging topics of Muslim history, including the kings of Egypt to Alexander the great, the Arab rulers from the pre-Islamic period to Umar, the story of the prophet Muhammad and the first four caliphs, the history of the Arabs during the Umayyad and the Abbassid periods, the Muslim rulers of India, the kings of Malacca and Pahang, and the rulers and religious scholars of Aceh.

Just as significant a part of ar-Raniri's writings in the theological sphere was devoted to refuting the teachings of his scholarly predecessors in the Southeast Asian sultanate of Aceh; ar-Raniri wrote sections 12 and 13 of book 2 of the *Bustan us-Salatin* partly to compete with and supplant earlier historical works in the Malay world: the *Malay Annals* (*Sejarah Melayu*) and the *Hikayat Aceh*. Yet ar-Raniri owed much to the Malay Annals. A comparison of sections 12 and 13 of book 2 of *Bustan us-Salatin*, which focus on Malay and Acehnese history, with the *Malay Annals* shows that the *Bustan us-Salatin* drew extensively on this earlier work for its content. Like the *Malay Annals*, it manifests the penchant of Malay historical writers for glorifying rulers; the last two sections of book 2 sing the praises of sultan Iskandar Thani, ar-Raniri's great benefactor during his stay in Aceh from 1637 to 1644. Nevertheless, ar-Raniri's intention was clearly to write a definitive history of Islam in Malay for the benefit of Southeast Asian Muslims. In this he sought to emulate the contributions to Islamic historiography of the classical historians at-Tabari and ash-Shahrastani, whose writings served as important points of reference for ar-Raniri during his life.

Though the *Bustan us-Salatin* has been published only in parts, these published sections include parts of book 2 which relate to Malay history. Moreover, many of the stories in the historical sections of book 2 of *Bustan us-Salatin* have been adopted and presented to the Malay reading public through the "Bunga Rampai" literature, a form of popular literature among the Malays. Furthermore, other Malay classics such as the *Hikayat Hang Tuah* have drawn heavily on book 2 of the *Bustan us-Salatin*. Finally, historical sections of other books of this work have been published and distributed in recent decades.

Ar-Raniri's influence as a historian is not limited to recording Malay history. Those sections of the *Bustan us-Salatin* which record the history of other parts of the Muslim world have long served to open a window onto the broader Muslim world for Malay readers, and in this ar-Raniri was an important pioneer in terms of the broader historical education of Malays. This endeavor has not been free of controversy however; a lingering suspicion of ar-Raniri in the Malay world came to the fore at the turn of the 20th century, when Wilkinson's efforts to publish the *Bustan us-Salatin* in Singapore encountered opposition from local Malay religious scholars because of ar-Raniri's inclusion of cosmological and historical material that they considered of inappropriate and questionable authority. Nevertheless, ar-Raniri can rightly be considered an Islamic historian of some quality on the basis of his writings. His choice of Malay as the language of the *Bustan us-Salatin* necessarily restricted its potential readership but in this context, the recent efforts to translate his historical writings into English may in time increase his significance as a historian beyond Southeast Asia.

PETER G. RIDDELL

See also Islamic

Biography
Born Ranir, India. Flourished 1630s. Died 1658.

Principal Writings
Bustan us-Salatin (Garden of Kings), written after 1638

Further Reading
Attas, Syed M.N. al-, *Raniri and the Wujudiyyah of 17th Century Aceh*, Singapore: Malaysian Branch of the Royal Asiatic Society, 1966 (monograph 3)

Attas, Syed M.N. al-, *The Mysticism of Hamzah Fansuri*, Kuala Lumpur: University of Malaya, 1970

Attas, Syed M.N. al-, *A Commentary on the Hujjat al-Siddiq of Nur al-Din al-Raniri*, Kuala Lumpur: Ministry of Culture, 1986

Daudy, Ahmad, *Allah dan Manusia dalam konsepsi Syeikh Nuruddin ar-Raniri* (God and Mankind According to Nuruddin ar-Raniri), Jakarta: Rajawali, 1983

Drewes, G.W.J., "De Herkomst van Nuruddin ar-Raniri" (The Origin of Nuruddin ar-Raniri), *Bijdragen tot de Taal-, Land- en Volkenkunde* 111 (1955), 137–51

Grinter, C.A., *Book IV of the Bustan al-Salatin by Nuruddin ar-Raniri*, PhD thesis, School of Oriental and African Studies, London, 1979

Hooykaas, Christiaan, *Perintis Sastera* (Guide to Literature), Jakarta: Wolters, 1953

Iskandar, Teuku, *Nuruddin ar-Raniri Pengarang Abad ke–17* (Nuruddin ar-Raniri, a 17th-Century Author), Dewan Bahasa: October 1964, VIII, 10, 436–41

Iskandar, Teuku, *Nuru'd-din ar-Raniri Bustanu's-Salatin Bab II, Fasal 13*, Kuala Lumpur: Dewan Bahasa dan Pustaka, 1966

Iskandar, Teuku, "Three Malay Historical Writings in the First Half of the 17th Century," *Journal of the Malayan Branch of the Royal Asiatic Society* 40 (1967), 38–53

Ito, Takeshi, "Why Did Nuruddin ar-Raniri Leave Aceh in 1054 AH?," *Bijdragen tot de Taal-, Land- en Volkenkunde* 134 (1978), 489–91

Jones, Russell, *Nuru'd-din ar-Raniri Bustanu's-Salatin Bab IV Fasal 1: A Critical Edition and Translation of the First Part of Fasal 1, Which Deals with Ibrahim ibn Adham*, Kuala Lumpur: Dewan Bahasa dan Pustaka, 1974

Nieuwenhuijze, C.A.O. "Van, Nur al-Din al-Raniri als Bestrijder der Wugudiya," (Nur al-din al-Raniri as an opponent of the Wugudiya), *Bijdragen tot de Taal-, Land- en Volkenkunde* 76 (1920), 162–71

Salleh, Siti Hawa Haji, *Bustan al-Salatin*, Kuala Lumpur: Dewan Bahasa dan Pustaka, n.d.

Steenbrink, Karel A., "Jesus and the Holy Spirit in the Writings of Nur al-Din al-Raniri," *Islam and Christian Muslim Relations* 1/2 (1990), 192–207

Tudjimah, *Asrar al-insan fi ma'rifa al-ruh wa'l-rahman* (The Secrets for Mankind in Knowing the Spirit of the Merciful), Djakarta: Penerbitan Universitas, 1961

Voorhoeve, P., "Van en over Nuruddin ar-Raniri" (Of and About Nuruddin ar-Raniri), *Bijdragen tot de Taal-, Land- en Volkenkunde* 107 (1951), 353–68

Voorhoeve, P., "Lijst der Geschriften van Raniri" (List of Manuscripts of Works by Raniri), *Bijdragen tot de Taal-, Land-en Volkenkunde* 111 (1955), 152–61

Voorhoeve, P., "Short Note: Nuruddin ar-Raniri," *Bijdragen tot de Taal-, Land- en Volkenkunde* 115 (1959), 90–91

Wilkinson, Richard James, *Bustanu's-Salatin*, 2 vols., Singapore: Methodist Publishing House, 1899–1900

Ranke, Leopold von 1795–1886

German historian

The "father" of modern historical writing, Leopold von Ranke has been widely recognized as one of the world's great historians. He owed his success to his education in classical languages and literature as well as to his devotion to archival studies. In 1824 his first major work, *Geschichten der lateinischen und germanischen Völker* (*The Histories of the Latin and Teutonic Peoples*, 1887) appeared. It was the preface to this work that announced his often quoted dictum, to write history as it had actually occurred: "wie es eigentlich gewesen ist."

The success of his first book led to his appointment at the University of Berlin in 1825, where he remained until his retirement in 1871. At Berlin Ranke came in contact with Hegelian philosophy, but rejected it in favor of empirical research based on an exhaustive use of archival materials. The decline of empires stimulated his historical interests, as he began a study of the Ottoman and Spanish monarchies. Most of his research took him to Italy, particularly to Venice, where he became one of the first historians to use the reports of the Venetian ambassadors of the 16th century, documents which made it clear to him that the decline of these states could be attributed to internal causes. The ensuing work was published at intervals over several years: *Fürsten und Völker von Süd-Europa im sechzehnten und siebzehnten Jahrhundert* (1827–36; *The Ottoman and the Spanish Empires, in the Sixteenth and Seventeenth Centuries*, 1843).

After his return to Berlin in 1831, Ranke wrote his most famous book, *Die römischen Päpste in den letzten vier Jahrhunderten* (1834–36; *The Ecclesiastical and Political History of the Popes of Rome*, 1840). Hailed for its objectivity, it has often been reprinted. In it Ranke treats the papacy as a universal monarchy and presents succinct biographical sketches of the popes.

During the 1840s, Ranke returned to the study of ancient and medieval history. He came to believe that Roman history stood at the center of all world history and that the foundations of the modern world still rested on such ancient institutions as Roman law, the monarchy, and the church. These ideas represented the remnants of a German Romantic tradition which had begun to wane. The revolutionary upheavals of 19th-century Europe led Ranke to conclude that the idea of nationalism dominated modern history. His *Deutsche Geschichte im Zeitalter der Reformation* (1839–43; *History of the Reformation in Germany*, 1845–47) was, however, neither nationalist nor romantic. It focused on the political history of the reign of Charles V and on the German Reformation. His *Neun Bücher preussischer Geschichte* (1847; *Memoirs of the House of Brandenburg . . .*, 1849) was based on research in the royal archives and emphasized the importance of two notable Prussian rulers: Frederick William the Great Elector, and Frederick William I, the soldier king.

Ranke trained the first generation of genuinely professional historians at Berlin, including Georg Waitz, Theodor Mommsen, and Jakob Burckhardt. Maximilian II of Bavaria had also been Ranke's student and was moved to establish a special Historical Commission within the Bavarian Academy of Sciences. In 1854 he invited Ranke to give a series of private lectures, "Epochs of World History since the Fall of Rome." Ranke emphasized that history was not a matter of progress, and that the primary task of the historian was to study history itself and to find its honest truth.

Despite the strong theological coloring evident in many of his personal letters, Ranke was always a secular historian, devoted to appraising the major forces in history. He taught the necessity of juxtaposing important universal trends with particular details. Yet sometimes grand ideas seemed to work in a dialectical way, especially when confronted by a new set of ideas. Ranke viewed each nation and its people as unique entities producing forces of nationalism that no longer could be ignored.

During his later years Ranke wrote national histories for each of the major states of Europe. He put aside a project to study the French Revolution of 1789 in order to produce *Französische Geschichte, vornehmlich im sechzehnten und siebzehnten Jahrhundert* (1852–55; *Civil Wars and Monarchy in France*, 1852). He realized that the French Third Estate represented democratic ideas and that the French Revolution marked the beginning of a new age. Having married an Anglo-Irish woman, Clarissa Graves, Ranke was also able to devote some attention to learning English and to writing *Englische Geschichte vornehmlich im sechzehnten und siebzehnten Jahrhundert* (1859–68; *A History of England Principally in the Seventeenth Century*, 1875). The *Die deutschen Mächte und der Fürstenbund* (The German Powers and the Princes' League, 1871), and a revised Prussian history (1874) once more led him to reaffirm his Prussian patriotism and to realize that modern Prussian history, like modern French history, had to be understood in terms of its internal forces.

After he retired, Ranke resumed his interest in universal history and produced his *Weltgeschichte* (1881–88; *Universal History*, 1885). He was criticized because the vogue for writing comprehensive world histories had passed and the writing of national histories dominated the scene. Undeterred by such opposition, Ranke maintained a strict writing schedule, but died before he could complete his work. Although he was aware of the new theories of evolution, and did not reject them, he preferred to leave questions of human prehistory out of historical narratives. Ranke disliked despotism and vigorously denied taking the side of authority, but his conservative political interests have always been criticized and continue to provide grounds for further criticism by his American biographers. The Germans have continued to regard him as a founder of historism, and while the historicist interpretation usually understates Ranke's emphasis on the major tendencies and effective principles found in political forces, these constituted the true meaning of history for Ranke.

HELEN LIEBEL-WECKOWICZ

See also Annales regni; Burckhardt; Counter-Reformation; Diplomatic; Ecclesiastical; Gatterer; Germany: 1450–1800; Giesebrecht; Graetz; Guicciardini; Literature; Macaulay; Nietzsche; Philosophy of History; Reformation; Spain: Imperial; Universal

Biography

Born Wiehe, Thuringia in Saxony, 21 December 1795; descended from Lutheran pastors and lawyers. Studied at Schulpforta school; Donndorf monastery school; then universities of Halle and Leipzig.

Schoolmaster, Frankfurt, 1818–25; professor, University of Berlin, 1825–71. Married Clarissa Graves, 1843 (died 1870; 2 sons, 1 daughter). Ennobled 1865. Died Berlin, 23 May 1886.

Principal Writings

Geschichten der lateinischen und germanischen Völker, 1824; in English as *The Histories of the Latin and Teutonic Peoples*, 1887

Fürsten und Völker von Süd-Europa im sechzehnten und siebzehnten Jahrhundert, 4 vols., 1827–36; in English as *The Ottoman and the Spanish Empires, in the Sixteenth and Seventeenth Centuries*, 1843

Die römischen Päpste in den letzten vier Jahrhunderten, 3 vols., 1834–36; in English as *The Ecclesiastical and Political History of the Popes of Rome during the Sixteenth and Seventeenth Centuries*, 3 vols., 1840, and as *The History of the Popes*, 3 vols., 1907

Deutsche Geschichte im Zeitalter der Reformation, 5 vols., 1839–43; *History of the Reformation in Germany*, 3 vols., 1845–47

Neun Bücher preussischer Geschichte, 3 vols., 1847, revised 1874; in English as *Memoirs of the House of Brandenburg and History of Prussia during the Seventeenth and Eighteenth Centuries*, 3 vols., 1849, reprinted 1968

Französische Geschichte, vornehmlich im sechzehnten und siebzehnten jahrhundert, 3 vols., 1852–55; partially translated as *Civil Wars and Monarchy in France, in the Sixteenth and Seventeenth Centuries: A History of France Principally during That Period*, 2 vols., 1852

Englische Geschichte vornehmlich im sechzehnten und siebzehnten Jahrhundert, 7 vols., 1859–68; in English as *A History of England Principally in the Seventeenth Century*, 6 vols., 1875

Sämtliche Werke (Collected Works), 54 vols., 1867–90

Die deutschen Mächte und der Fürstenbund: deutsche Geschichte von 1780 bis 1790 (The German Powers and the Princes' League), 1871

Weltgeschichte, 9 vols., 1881–88; abridged in English as *Universal History*, 1885

Aus Werk und Nachlass (From Works and Legacies), 4 vols., 1964–75

The Theory and Practice of History, edited by Georg G. Iggers and Konrad von Moltke, 1973

The Secret of World History: Selected Writings on the Art and Science of History, edited by Roger Wines, 1981

Further Reading

Krieger, Leonard, *Ranke: The Meaning of History*, Chicago: University of Chicago Press, 1977

Laue, Theodore von, *Leopold von Ranke: The Formative Years*, Princeton: Princeton University Press, 1950

Mommsen, Wolfgang J., ed., *Leopold von Ranke und die moderne Geschichtswissenschaft* (Ranke and the Modern Science of History), Stuttgart: Klett Cotta, 1988

Powell, James M., and Georg G. Iggers, *Leopold von Ranke and the Shaping of the Historical Discipline*, Syracuse, NY: Syracuse University Press, 1990

Syracuse University, *The Leopold von Ranke Manuscript Collection of Syracuse University*, Syracuse: Syracuse University Press, 1958; revised and completed 1983

Rashīd al-Dīn, Fazlallah 1247–1318

Persian historian

In 1300, on the order of Ghazan Khan, Rashīd al-Dīn began the compilation of his universal history, *Jāmi al-tawārīkh* (The Collection of Chronicles). The plan of this work was based on the idea that the history of the Islamic world was only one of the rivers flowing into the sea of world history, and that world history had to include the history of all the known peoples, from the "Franks" in the West to the Chinese in the East; moreover, the history of non-Muslim peoples had to be based on their own historical traditions. Accordingly, the work was divided into four volumes: 1) the history of Turkic and Mongol tribes, the empire of Genghis [Chingis] Khan, and its successors, especially in Iran; 2) a general history of the world, including the pre-Islamic kings of Iran, Muhammad and the caliphs, the Islamic dynasties of Iran, the Oghuz and the Turks, the Chinese, the Jews, the Franks, and the Indians (with a lengthy account of Buddha); 3) *Shu'ab-i panjgāna* (The Five Branches [of the Human Race]), the genealogy of the ruling dynasties of "five peoples": Turks and Mongols, Muslims (that is, Arabs), Jews, Franks, and Chinese (originally it formed the second part of the second volume); and 4) *Suvar al-aqālīm* (The Pictures of the [Seven] Climes), geographical descriptions of the world and the routes of the Mongol empire. For the compilation of this work Rashīd al-Dīn used numerous assistants and collaborators, including prominent Mongols famous for their knowledge of Mongol historical tradition, two Chinese scholars, a Buddhist monk from Kashmir, and a French Catholic monk. Rashīd al-Dīn, apparently, wrote most of the first volume, and he edited the entire text, giving it the shape in which it came down to us. It is distinguished not only by the breadth of its design and its unbiased approach to its sources, but also by its simple prose, which favorably contrasts with the highly ornate style that became popular in Persian historiography during the Mongol period. This enterprise was unprecedented not only in Muslim, but also in world historiography, and the achievement of Rashīd al-Dīn remained unmatched during the Middle Ages.

Later Muslim historians, until modern times, never tried to write universal history modeled on Rashīd al-Dīn's work, but returned to the well established scheme of "general history," which was, essentially, the history of the Islamic world, with the addition of the history of four pre-Islamic Persian dynasties (including two mythical ones). But the information contained in the *Jāmi al-tawārīkh* was used in many later historical works in Persian and Turkic languages. *Jāmi' al-tawārīkh* was used by Rashīd al-Dīn's contemporary Banakati, whose short general history written in 1317 is largely an epitomized version of Rashīd al-Dīn's work; another short general history written by Rashīd al-Dīn's younger contemporary, Hamdallah Qazwini, in 1330, was also based mainly on the work. *Jāmi al-tawārīkh* was widely used by the historians of Timur and the Timurids, of whom Hafiz-i Abru (died 1430) wrote several historical compilations, some of which directly incorporated large portions of *Jāmi al-tawārīkh*, while others had to serve as its continuation. Two multivolume general histories of the late Timurid historians, *Rawżat al-ṣafā'* by Mirkhwand (died 1498) and *Ḥabīb al-siyar* by Khwandamir (died 1535), incorporated much of the material from *Jāmi al-tawārīkh*, especially on the history of the Turkic tribes and the Mongols; due to the great popularity of these two general histories in Iran and Central Asia, later historical works usually borrowed their information, which can be traced back to Rashīd al-Dīn, not from Rashīd al-Dīn directly, but from Mirkhwand and Khwandamir.

The fourth volume of Rashīd al-Dīn's work (the geographical part) has not come down to us, but references to it are found in the works of later Muslim authors. The third volume (*Shu'ab-i panjgāna*) has survived in a single manuscript in Istanbul; other parts exist in manuscripts in various libraries. There is no complete edition of the Persian text, but there are many text editions and European translations of separate parts (the most complete listing of these publications, as well as the extant manuscripts, is in Storey).

As well as the *Jāmi al-tawārīkh*, Rashīd al-Dīn wrote several theological works (preserved in a number of manuscripts), a treatise on agriculture, botany, architecture, and other subjects (an excerpt of which has been preserved and published in Iran as an anonymous work), and edited a collection of four books on Chinese medicine, Chinese and Mongol pharmaceutics, and the administration of the Chinese empire, of which the first volume includes a long introduction by Rashīd al-Dīn with a characterization of Chinese and Inner Asian culture (a unique manuscript of which exists in Istanbul). A collection of 53 letters, written by Rashīd al-Dīn to his sons, various officials, scholars, and other persons, has survived in several manuscripts and is a very important source for the history of Iran under the Mongols.

YURI BREGEL

See also Pelliot; World

Biography

Fazlallah [or Fadlallah] Rashīd al-Dīn. Born Hamadan, Iran, 1247; from a family of Jewish physicians, but converted to Islam. Began to serve the Mongol khans of Iran (*ilkhans*) some time between the mid-1260s and mid-1280s; court physician under Ghazan Khan (1295–1304); after 1298, a second *wazir* (chief minister); became the main adviser of Ghazan and the initiator of important administrative and financial reforms undertaken during Ghazan's reign. Under *ilkhan* Abu Sa'id he was removed from his post and in 1318 executed.

Principal Writings

Jāmi al-tawārīkh (The Collection of Chronicles), written c.1300, partially translated into Russian, French, German, and English; in English as *The Successors of Genghis Khan*, 1971

Further Reading

Bartol'd, Vasilii, "Review of: E. Blochet, *Introduction à l'histoire des Mongols de Fadl Allah Rashīd al-Dīn*," in his *Sochineniia*, vol. 8, Moscow: Izd-vo vostochnoi lit-ry, 1973

Boyle, John Andrew, "Rashīd al-Dīn: The First World Historian," *Journal of Pakistan Historical Society* 17 (1969), 215–27

Jahn, Karl, "The Still Missing Works of Rashīd al-Dīn," *Central Asiatic Journal* 9 (1964), 113–22

Jahn, Karl, "Rashīd al-Dīn as a World Historian," in *Yádnáme-ye Jan Rypka: Collection of Articles on Persian and Tajik Literature* Prague: Academia, 1967, 79–87

Jahn, Karl, "Some Ideas of Rashīd al-Dīn on Chinese Culture," *Central Asiatic Journal* 28 (1984), 161–75

Morgan, David, *The Mongols*, Oxford: Blackwell, 1986

Petrushevskii, Il'ia Pavlovich, "Rashīd al-Dīn i ego istoricheskii trud" (Rashīd al-Dīn and His Historical Work), in Rashīd al-Dīn, *Sbornik letopisei*, vol. 1, part 1, Moscow: Izdatel'stvo Akademii Nauk SSSR, 1952, 7–38

Storey, Charles Ambrose, *Persian Literature: A Bio-Bibliographical Survey*, in vol. 1, London: Luzac, 1935; revised in Russian with additions and corrections by Yuri Bregel, Moscow: Nauka, part 1, 306–318, and part 3, 1394–95

Togan, Ahmet Zeki Velidi, "The Composition of the History of the Mongols by Rashīd al-Dīn," *Central Asiatic Journal* 7 (1962), 60–72

Raynal, Guillaume-Thomas 1713–1796

French colonial historian

In his *Histoire Philosophique et politique des établissements et du commerce des Européens dans les deux Indes* (1772–81; *A Philosophical and Political History of the Settlements and Trade of the Europeans in the East and West Indies*, 1777) Abbé Guillaume-Thomas Raynal began his inquiry with the European discovery of the New World and the successful navigation of the Cape of Good Hope that established direct trade with India and the Spice Islands. Those events, Raynal said, "gave rise to a revolution in the commerce, and in the power of nations . . . in the manners, industry, and government of the whole world." Raynal introduced a new method of inquiry, an innovation in the writing of history. He began from the standpoint of the economic historian: industry and commerce were the most influential factors in the relations between states. Raynal's history was philosophical – we would say scientific – in the sense that he sought to discover the causes of historical events.

The *Histoire des deux Indes* consisted of 19 books, variously printed in three, five, seven, and ten volumes. Three editions, five translations, and 25 impressions appeared between 1772 and 1781, earning the author and publisher unusually large sums for that time. Raynal's method was scientific in the way that the *philosophes* understood the term; he made no appeals to divine causes or ends in order to explain historical phenomena. Raynal followed the chronological and geographical sequence of European exploration and colonization since the 15th century in order to explain the existing social orders rationally and scientifically, drawing inferences from the evidence, without recourse to metaphysics, theology, or Scripture. From the evidence Raynal inferred that significant changes in the volume of production or trade led to significant political changes. The sources of his fame among his contemporaries were his use of statistics and his plainspoken attacks on the royal administration. The sources of his statistics, and the reasons for their revisions in subsequent editions, are unknown.

It was not Raynal's purpose to provide a detailed economic analysis of the European colonial system, but to question "whether the revolutions that are passed, or those which must hereafter take place, have been, or can be of any utility to the human race." The thesis of the *Histoire des deux Indes* seems to be that world trade determined international politics but, while Raynal recounted the history of European trade and colonization, he did not prove or even seek to prove that thesis. Instead, he sought to answer the philosophical questions occasioned by the last 300 years of commercial history, questions that went beyond the issue of utility: what was the purpose of government; of society; what constituted a just social order? He began his answer by adopting the point of view of the economic historian: "The commercial states have civilized all others." The immediate context for Raynal's history was

France's recent defeat in the Seven Years' War. According to Raynal, the powerful, commercial states – the Greeks, Phoenicians, the Romans, and Spanish – had mismanaged their empires. Raynal therefore questioned whether Europeans understood the art of government. Like Montesquieu, Raynal used the history of empires to draw a lesson for contemporary France. Commerce was the source of luxury and civilization. It was also the source of power. By reminding his readers that "Commerce is finally destroyed by the riches it accumulates," Raynal warned them that France's recent defeat by England signified an important shift in the balance of power. Thus, Raynal's history was philosophical in two senses. It was scientific, and it was didactic. Raynal argued that France must break the cycle of history and establish an empire that would endure. He used the history of European colonization to argue for free trade, the abolition of mercantile policies and regulations, the abolition of slavery and the slave trade, and the superiority of the republican form of government. In his view, a republic was the only form of government able to ensure individual liberty, that is, the natural rights of freedom and property. Raynal's history was a warning that France's commercial, colonial, fiscal, and political policies were destructive of the nation's wealth and power. Despotism, mercantilism, and colonization by conquest were destroying liberty and property. After surveying the history of European colonization, Raynal argued that France should adopt a new colonial policy, reform the tax system, and revise its political system. The alternatives, he suggested, were revolution or permanent decline.

HUGH L. GUILDERSON

Biography

Abbé Guillaume-Thomas François Raynal. Born Saint-Geniez in the Rouergue, 12 April 1713. Educated by the Jesuits at Pézenas and took priest's orders, but was dismissed for unexplained reasons. He became a writer and traveled widely after his *Histoire* was banned in 1774; returned to France in 1784; was elected to the Etats Généraux, but did not take his seat on grounds of age. Lived in Passy and Montlhery until his death at Chaillot, 6 March 1796.

Principal Writings

Histoire Philosophique et politique des établissements et du commerce des Européens dans les deux Indes, 6 vols., 1772–81; in English as *A Philosophical and Political History of the Settlements and Trade of the Europeans in the East and West Indies*, 1777

Further Reading

Feugère, Anatole, *Un précurseur de la Révolution: Abbé Raynal* (Precursor of the Revolution: Abbé Raynal), Angoulême: Ouvrière, 1922
Kors, Alan Charles, *D'Holbach's Coterie: An Enlightenment in Paris*, Princeton: Princeton University Press, 1976
Wolpe, Hans, *Raynal et sa machine de guerre* (Raynal and His War Machine), Stanford, CA: Stanford University Press, 1957

The Reformation

The Reformation, in the form of the schisms in Western Christendom to which it gave rise, still commands a whole spectrum of sectarian allegiances. Even among academic historians, the freight of inherited prejudice, or the modish revisionisms to which sectarian evaluations can lead, distort historical perspectives, however demurely they are presented or however unwittingly modern values, incorporated into the vocabulary, are applied to events that took place nearly half a millennium ago. Phenomena such as "pluralism" or "absenteeism" have the built-in resonance of "abuses" requiring to be reformed. In fact, it can be argued that they were part of the intricate mechanism by which Europe's new nation-states drew, generally with papal acquiescence, on the only available source of talent, in order to allow high administrative offices to continue to be exercised by the same trained ecclesiastical administrators, financed from the same sources as before. It was a means of secularizing administration to accord with a new social and political reality, and need not have entailed abuse.

Furthermore, the Reformation inevitably had social and political as well as theological and spiritual, legal and philosophical, literary and visual dimensions. The sectarian affiliations and polemical intentions of historians of most of the arts and social science disciplines are often no less clear than those of the straightforward religious historians. There are therefore few areas of history in which some reference to the historiographical context in which the history was being written is more essential in assessing a historian's position than that involving the religious controversies of the Reformation. The result is that the historiography of the Reformation too readily resolves itself into the historical chronicle of the use of historical writing as a weapon of religious controversy or propaganda.

The early historians were crudely polemical in their attempts to discredit one another, and those favoring Lutheran or Zwinglian theologies, which came first and often had a millenarist tinge, at first sought to fit the 16th-century schisms into some divine plan for history. Johann Carion's popular 1532 *Chronica*, virtually rewritten by Melanchthon, saw the history of the world in terms of a 6,000-year scheme, with primitive, Mosaic, and Christian periods, and that of Luther inaugurating the final development of the third stage. The first major historian of the Reformation was Johannes Sleidan (1506–66), writing Latin "commentaries" in the manner of the chronicles of Froissart and Commines, both of whom he translated into Latin. They were published piecemeal, covering the period from 1517 to 1554, and the completed set of 24 books was published in a folio of 940 pages in 1555. Sleidan, secretary to the bishop of Paris before joining the liberal wing of the schism, followed the commentaries with a work in three books attempting to demonstrate the continuity between ancient Rome and the contemporary Holy Roman empire. He regarded the Reformation as the work of God, but was balanced in his views and in his use of source material, and was attacked by both sides. He wanted the emperor and the Protestant German princes to ally, and focused on princes and politicians rather than theologians, according lesser importance to the doings of popes and imperial Diets. He took sides against the peasants in writing of the Peasants' War.

Early, and roughly contemporaneous, Johannes Cochlaeus (1479–1552) and Friedrich Myconius (1491–1546) wrote from different sides. The 1549 commentaries of Cochlaeus give a year-by-year, strongly anti-Lutheran record of Luther's schism, depicting Luther as a sectarian pope-hater in league with Satan, morally decadent, and responsible for inciting the Peasants'

Revolt before turning against it. He regarded the Reformation as an ideological rather than a political battle. Myconius, on the other hand, a Franciscan who had joined the Swiss schism to become a married pastor, wrote a history of the Reformation, published only in 1715, that identified the papacy with anti-Christ, attacked its hypocrisy and immorality, and repudiated those aspects of medieval devotion, such as the cult of saints and pilgrimages, that were less immediately demanding of interior moral commitment. Like Sleidan, Myconius attached much importance to the conflicts within the cities, of which he gave lengthy and sometimes graphic accounts.

Accounts of the Reformation continued to be overtly partisan throughout the late 16th and the 17th centuries. Most influential was John Foxe (1516–87), who published the *Acts and Monuments* later to become known as the *Book of Martyrs* in an unfinished Latin version of 1559. The first English edition of 1563 was well over twice the size and was intended to be a general history of the church. A further enlarged edition appeared in 1570, and in 1576 a popular edition added the famous woodcuts depicting the atrocious sufferings of the Protestant martyrs. Foxe took the view that the English church was pure before its romanization by Augustine at the end of the 6th century, and saw a continuity between late medieval heresy and Protestantism. Becket, popularly considered in the 16th century to have been England's greatest saint, was a traitor, and Foxe saw history, governed by divine providence, as consisting of five ages, the apostolic, the age of the gentiles, corruption, the Reformation, and the coming age of Christ. Foxe hated violence, and looked forward to the triumph of the gospel, toleration, and freedom of the spirit.

The choice of Reformation history as a historical subject itself still denoted a propagandist approach, and influential attitudes to Reformation history are to be found in many writers who did not write specifically about the schisms, including those of Calvin and Henry VIII. The Latin history of the French wars of religion by Jacques-Auguste de Thou (1553–1617) was sufficiently impartial to be placed on the Roman index of forbidden books in 1609, while the Servite Paolo Sarpi (1552–1623), enlisted to defend Venice against the 1606 interdict of Paul V, demonstrated in his 1619 *Istoria del Concilio Tridentino* (*History of the Council of Trent*, 1620) just how harshly antipapalist it was possible to be while remaining in communion with Rome. Sarpi had gone so far as to declare obedience to the pope sinful, but, although excommunicated, continued to celebrate Mass to the end of his life.

History was still being used as a propagandist weapon later in the 17th century when Bossuet (1627–1704), whose intentions were truly ecumenical, published his *Histoire des variations des églises protestants* (1688; *The History of the Variations of the Protestant Churches*, 1742), attempting to demonstrate that the schismatic churches, lacking authority, could not preserve doctrinal unity. Only slightly less overtly polemical was Gilbert Burnet (1643–1715), a Whig bishop whose 3-volume *History of the Reformation* (1679–1714) again took the view that the Reformation was part of a grand historical development, separating the religious movement from the purely English matter of the annulment of Henry VIII's marriage to Catherine of Aragon, the proximate cause of the English schism. He called for a renewal of the radical continental origins of the Reformation.

Looking back from the 18th century, the age of Enlightenment, it is surprising to see how little weight had so far been attached to what were still to become the standard reasons later generations would give for the Reformation, centering on the corruption, nepotism, immorality, riches, and neglect of pastoral duties in the late medieval church. The highly coded attitudes of Bayle (1647–1706) at the very end of the 17th century are still controverted, but there is no serious reason to doubt the sincerity of his Huguenot religious views, and his desire to promote toleration is not only clear but intense. His *Dictionnaire historique et critique* (1697; *The Dictionary Historical and Critical*, 1734–44) disliked the radical Anabaptists for the civil disorder they provoked, was sympathetic towards Melanchthon and even Calvin, and rehabilitated Luther. Diderot's *Encyclopédie* can scarcely be considered as a whole because of the diversity of authorship, the threats of suppression, and the commercial considerations that impinged on the project in the course of its execution. Diderot had started by recruiting a number of priests to collaborate, and the final volumes are on the whole mild about Catholicism, defended in the article "Reformation," and harsh on Luther. The work firmly disliked superstition, and it is surprising that a fable satirizing the eucharist survived in the article "Ypain" at the end of the alphabet.

In the 19th century the historiography of the Reformation was dominated by German historical writing. It also became complex, partly on account of the work of historians such as Burckhardt and Michelet, as later of Pater and Huizinga, who produced global theories of the Renaissance that inevitably entailed views about the Reformation. Among the more important historians who directly took the Reformation as a subject were François Guizot (1787–1874), chiefly known for his 1833 public education act in France. In a series of Sorbonne lectures he concluded that Protestantism was an "enfranchisement of the human mind" rather than a purification of lax late medieval discipline, and that its concrete achievement lay in the destruction of the monopoly of clerical power. In England, the celebrated 1840 review by Thomas Babington Macaulay (1800–59) of Ranke's hostile *Die römischen Päpste in den letzten vier Jahrhunderten* (1834–36; *History of the Popes*, 1840) found a variety of political reasons in France, Spain, and Italy for the successes of the papacy, while various pieces by Thomas Carlyle (1795–1881) of 1837 and 1841 responded to the prevailing Romantic movement's need for the heroization that Carlyle bestowed on the Luther of "Here stand I. I can do no other." For Carlyle, Luther delivered Europe from its state of putrescence.

Leopold von Ranke (1795–1886) himself at first saw history in Hegelian terms, and the Reformation as a stage in the evolution of the human race marked by the triumph of the secular state. He later freed himself from Hegelian pantheism and, in *History of the Popes* regarded the German, but not the Swiss, Reformations and Counter-Reformations (for which he uses the plural) as having restored Christianity to a pristine purity. A serious historian who was perceptive about the causes of the Reformation, he paid little attention to the doctrinal issues involved. On the whole, the majority of the 19th-century German historians were liberals. Some, such as Albert Ritschl, were under the sway of Kant; others, such as Möhler (1796–1838), author of the 1832 *Symbolik*, and Döllinger (1799–1890), who refused to accept the dogma of papal infallibility and was excommunicated, were Catholic. Both Möhler and Ritschl were firmly opposed to dogmatism, although Ritschl's strictly historical approach to the Reformation enabled him to criticize Möhler's comparative study of creeds. Adolf von Harnack (1851–1930) concluded his *Lehrbuch der Dogmengeschichte* (1886–90; *History of Dogma*, 1896–99) with a study of Luther, who had released Christianity from excessive clericalism and moralism but strengthened the rest of its dogma. He thought Luther should have gone further in liberating Christianity from dogma, but should not have rejected monasticism or the notion of sacrifice. With the inception of sociology, Ernst Troeltsch (1865–1923) introduced another dimension, and began to see Protestantism's continuity with the Middle Ages. The Reformation simply produced new solutions to medieval problems.

Outside Germany, debate about the Reformation raged most vehemently in England, where the Tractarian movement took root, finally carrying Newman and some others into the Catholic church. E.B. Pusey (1800–82) changed his view, but remained an Anglican, conceding that Luther's error consisted only in going into schism and losing the apostolic succession, necessary for the sacramental powers of a hierarchical priesthood. Lord Acton (1834–1902), a born Catholic and a close friend of Döllinger, was shattered, like Döllinger, by the promulgation of papal infallibility as a dogma. Of particular interest was Philip Schaff (1819–93), the first great American historian of the Reformation, whose ecumenical 6-volume *History of the Christian Church* (1892) was for some time the best account of the Reformation available in English.

By the beginning of the 20th century, we have entered the era of critical editions, complete works, encyclopedic compilations, life-and-times biographies, and collections of letters, all of which, if not ways of writing history, belong in historiographical accounts, although virtually none can be mentioned here. Among the more important straightforward historians are certainly the Catholic Heinrich Denifle (1844–1905), a medievalist by profession, author of an important and highly critical *Luther und Luthertum* (1904–09; *Luther and Lutheranism*, 1917), Hubert Jedin (1900–80), historian of the Council of Trent, Pierre Imbart de la Tour (1860–1925), author of the 4-volume *Les Origines de la reforme* (1905–44), and Joseph Lortz (1887–1975), who believed that Luther had developed a neglected side of Catholicism.

During the final quarter of the 20th century, there have been two notable new developments. The first of these, primarily but not exclusively associated with a group of historians active at Cambridge, is revisionist in insisting on the deep popular conservatism that, especially in England in the 16th century, resisted not so much the theological innovations of the reformers as their liturgical changes. The laity are shown to have been deeply attached to the old rites and practices, with all the assurance accompanying what was conceived as the automatic and guaranteed *ex opere operato* efficacy of the sacramental bestowal of grace. The reformed rites, translations, prayer books, and antisacramental piety threatened the spiritual security of the faithful brought up in the tradition of late medieval Catholicism. Much importance has been attached by these historians to the overtly medieval piety centered on the commemoration of Christ's passion and death of such humanist clerics as John Fisher, bishop of Rochester, who was finally martyred under Henry VIII.

The second, and much more important change concerns the setting of Reformation history in its social and political context. Lucien Febvre (1878–1956), co-founder in 1929 with Marcel Bloch of the *Annales* review, inaugurated in the 1930s and 1940s an overdue historiographical revolution by seeing religious history in terms of *mentalités* rather than events, conditioned by all sorts of social, eonomical, and political constraints. The Reformation was essentially the response to a widely-felt cultural need that might have taken a different course.

Febvre has been shown to have gone too far in distinguishing religious history from ecclesiastical history, but the systematic deployment of his distinction between the religious and the ecclesiastic in discussions involving the Reformation has proved extremely fertile. In particular, Protestant theologians such as Steven Ozment have accounted for much pertaining to what Ozment still calls "the Reformation" with reference to its sociological and political roots, as if it were a single movement. Ozment's first really important book, *The Reformation in the Cities* (1975) saw the preoccupation with the realities of civic life as a reaction against earlier groups of historians, predominantly Catholic, who preserved a medieval perspective, from which to review the reform. Ozment identified the earlier groups with those of Lortz, extended to include Gilson, Leff, and Knowles, of the Protestant Heiko Augustinus Oberman, author of a brilliant study on the late medieval figure of Gabriel, and of what he calls "the romantic ecumenists" inspired by the Second Vatican Council, such as Hans Küng.

Ozment's second important book, *The Age of Reform, 1250–1550* (1980), emphasized the parts played by society and politics. The theological issues are identified in such a way as to make it doubtful whether Calvinists were really Protestants, although Ozment, like Roland Bainton, paid more serious attention to the radical Anabaptist wing of the Reformation than had hitherto been usual.

ANTHONY LEVI

See also Acton; Britain: 1066–1485; Britain: 1485–1750; Cantimori; Catholicism; Chadwick; Christianity; Counter-Reformation; Delumeau; Dickens; Ecclesiastical; Elton; France: 1450–1789; Froude; Germany: 1450–1800; Hegel; Janssen; Palacký; Protestantism; Ranke; Religion; Sarpi; Scotland; Scribner; Skinner; Thomas; Trevor-Roper; Troeltsch

Further Reading

Bainton, Roland, *Here I Stand: A Life of Martin Luther*, New York: Abingdon and Cokesbury Press, 1950; London: Hodder and Stoughton, 1951

Bainton, Roland, *The Reformation of the Sixteenth Century*, Boston: Beacon Press, 1952, London: Hodder and Stoughton, 1953; revised 1985

Bayle, Pierre, *Dictionnaire historique et critique*, 4 vols., Rotterdam, 1697; in English as *The Dictionary Historical and Critical of Mr. Peter Bayle*, 10 vols., London: Knapton, 1734–44, reprinted 5 vols., New York: Garland, 1984; abridged as *Selections from Bayle's Dictionary*, Princeton: Princeton University Press, 1952, and as *Historical and Critical Dictionary: Selections*, Indianapolis: Hackett, 1991

Bossuet, Jacques Bénigne, *Histoire des variations des églises protestantes*, Paris, 1688; in English as *The History of the Variations of the Protestant Churches*, 2 vols., Antwerp, 1742

Burnet, Gilbert, *The History of the Reformation of the Church of England*, 3 vols., London: Chiswell, 1679–1714; reprinted in 5 vols., Westmead: Gregg, 1969

Cameron, Euan, *The European Reformation*, Oxford and New York: Oxford University Press, 1991

Carion, Johann, *Chronica*, 1532; rewritten by Philipp Melanchthon as *Chronici absolvtissimi*, 1560–63

Cochlaeus, Johannes, *Commentaria de actis et scriptis Lutheri*, 1549; reprinted Farnborough: Gregg, 1968

Denifle, Heinrich, *Luther und Luthertum in der ersten Entwicklung: Quellenmässig dargestellt*, 2 vols., Mainz: Kirchheim, 1904–09; in English as *Luther and Lutheranism*, Somerset, OH: Torch, 1917

Dickens, A.G., *The English Reformation*, London: Batsford, and New York: Schocken, 1964; 2nd edition Batsford, 1989, University Park: Pennsylvania State University Press, 1991

Dickens, A.G., *Reformation and Society in Sixteenth-Century Europe*, New York: Harcourt Brace, and London: Thames and Hudson, 1966

Dickens, A.G., and John Tonkin, *The Reformation in Historical Thought*, Cambridge, MA: Harvard University Press, and Oxford: Blackwell, 1985

Diderot, Denis *et al.*, *Encyclopédie, ou, Dictionnaire raisonné des sciences, des arts et des métiers* (The Encyclopedia; or, Dictionary of the Sciences, the Arts, and the Professions), 17 vols., Paris, 1751–65

Döllinger, Johann Ignaz von, *Die Reformation* (The Reformation), 3 vols., Regensburg: Manz, 1846–48

Döllinger, Johann Ignaz von, *Christenthum und Kirche in der Zeit der Grundlegung*, Regensburg: Manz, 1860; as *First Age of Christianity*, London: Allen, 1866

Elton, G.R., ed., *The New Cambridge Modern History*, 2nd ed., vol. 2: *The Reformation*, Cambridge and New York: Cambridge University Press, 1990

Febvre, Lucien, *Au coeur religieux du XVIe siècle* (The Heart of 16th-Century Religion), Paris: Sevpen, 1957

Foxe, John, *Acts and Monuments*, 1563 and later revisions; subsequently known as *Book of Martyrs*

Gilson, Etienne, *History of Christian Philosophy in the Middle Ages*, New York: Random House, and London: Sheed and Ward, 1955

Greengrass, Mark, *The French Reformation*, Oxford and New York: Blackwell, 1987

Harnack, Adolf von, *Lehrbuch der Dogmengeschichte*, 3 vols., Freiburg: Mohr, 1886–90; in English as *History of Dogma*, 7 vols., London: Williams and Norgate, 1896–99; Boston: Roberts, 1897–99; reprinted 1961

Hillerbrand, Hans J., ed., *The Oxford Encyclopedia of the Reformation*, 4 vols., New York and Oxford: Oxford University Press, 1996

Hsia, R. Po-chia, ed., *The German People and the Reformation*, Ithaca, NY: Cornell University Press, 1988

Hsia, R. Po-chia, *Social Discipline in the Reformation: Central Europe, 1550–1750*, London and New York: Routledge, 1989

Imbart de la Tour, Pierre, *Les Origines de la reforme*, 4 vols., Paris: Hachette, 1905–44

Jedin, Hubert, *Katholische Reformation oder Gegenreformation? Ein Versuch zur Klärung der Begriffe nebst einer Jubiläumsbetrachtung über das Trester Konzil* (Catholic Reformation or Counter-Reformation? An Attempt to Clarify the Concepts), Lucerne: Stocker, 1946

Jedin, Hubert, "Catholic Reform and Counter Reformation," in Erwin Iserloh, Joseph Glazik, and Hubert Jedin, eds., *Reformation and Counter Reformation*, London: Burns and Oates, and New York: Seabury Press, 1980 [German original 1967]

Knowles, David, *The Religious Orders in England*, 3 vols., Cambridge: Cambridge University Press, 1948–59

Küng, Hans, *Strukturen der Kirche*, Freiburg: Herder, 1962; as *Structures of the Church*, New York: Nelson, 1964; London: Burns and Oates, 1965

Leff, Gordon, *Bradwardine and the Pelagians: A Study of His "De causa Dei" and Its Opponents*, Cambridge: Cambridge University Press, 1957

Lortz, Joseph, *Die Reformation in Deutschland*, 2 vols., Freiburg: Herder, 1949; in English as *The Reformation in Germany*, London: Darton Longman and Todd, 1968

McGrath, Alister E., *Reformation Thought: An Introduction*, Oxford and New York: Blackwell, 1988; revised 1993

Marshall, Sherrin, ed., *Women in Reformation and Counter-Reformation Europe: Public and Private Worlds*, Bloomington: Indiana University Press, 1989

Moeller, Bernd, *Reichsstadt und Reformation*, Gütersloh: Mohn, 1962; in English as *Imperial Cities and the Reformation: Three Essays*, Philadelphia: Fortress Press, 1972

Möhler, Johann Adam, *Symbolik*, Mainz, 1832; in English as *Symbolism*, New York: Crossroad, 1997

Myconius, Friedrich, *Historia reformationis vom Jahr Christi 1517 bis 1542* (History of the Reformation), Gotha: Schallen, 1715

Nicholls, David, "The Social History of the French Reformation: Ideology, Confession, and Culture," *Social History* 9 (1984), 25–43

Oberman, Heiko Augustinus, *Werden und Wertung der Reformation: vom Wegestreit zum Glaubenskampf*, Tübingen: Mohr, 1977; in English as *Masters of the Reformation: The Emergence of a New Intellectual Climate in Europe*, Cambridge and New York: Cambridge University Press, 1981

Oberman, Heiko Augustinus, *Wurzeln des Antisemitismus: Christenangot und Judenplage im Zeitalter von Humanismus und Reformation*, Berlin: Severin und Seidler, 1981; in English as *The Roots of Anti-Semitism in the Age of Renaissance and Reformation*, Philadelphia: Fortress Press, 1984

Ozment, Steven E., *Mysticism and Dissent: Religious Ideology and Social Protest in the Sixteenth Century*, New Haven: Yale University Press, 1973

Ozment, Steven E., *The Reformation in the Cities: The Appeal of Protestantism to Sixteenth-Century Germany and Switzerland*, New Haven: Yale University Press, 1975

Ozment, Steven E., *The Age of Reform, 1250–1550: An Intellectual and Religious History of Late Medieval and Reformation Europe*, New Haven and London: Yale University Press, 1980

Ozment, Steven E., ed., *Reformation Europe: A Guide to Research*, St. Louis: Center for Reformation Research, 1982

Pusey, E.B., *The Doctrine of the Real Presence*, Oxford: Parker, 1855

Ranke, Leopold von, *Die römischen Päpste in den letzten vier Jahrhunderten*, 3 vols., Leipzig: Duncker & Humblot, 1834–36; in English as *The Ecclesiastical and Political History of the Popes of Rome during the Sixteenth and Seventeenth Centuries*, 3 vols., London: Murray, 1840, Philadelphia: Lea and Blanchard, 1841; and as *The History of the Popes*, 3 vols., London: Bell, 1907

Ritschl, Albert, *Die christliche Lehre von der Rechtfertigung und Versöhnung* (Christian Teaching on Justification and Reconciliation), 3 vols., Bonn: Marcus, 1870–74

Roper, Lyndal, *The Holy Household: Women and Morals in Reformation Augsburg*, Oxford and New York: Oxford University Press, 1989

Sarpi, Paolo, *Istoria del Concilio Tridentino*, 1619; in English as *History of the Council of Trent*, 1620

Scarisbrick, J.J., *The Reformation and the English People*, Oxford: Blackwell, 1986

Schaff, Philip, *History of the Christian Church*, 6 vols., 1892

Scott, Tom, and R.W. Scribner, eds. and trans., *The German Peasants' War: A History in Documents*, Atlantic Highlands, NJ: Humanities Press, 1991

Scribner, R.W., *For the Sake of Simple Folk: Popular Propaganda for the German Reformation*, Cambridge and New York: Cambridge University Press, 1981

Scribner, R.W., *The German Reformation*, London: Macmillan, and Atlantic Highlands, NJ: Humanities Press, 1986

Scribner, R.W., *Popular Culture and Popular Movements in Reformation Germany*, London and Ronceverte, WV: Hambledon Press, 1987

Scribner, R.W., ed., *Germany: A New Social and Economic History*, vol. 1: *1450–1630*, London and New York: Arnold, 1996

Sleidan, Johannes, *Commentarii*, 1555

Strauss, Gerald, *Law, Resistance, and the State: The Opposition to Roman Law in Reformation Germany*, Princeton: Princeton University Press, 1986

Thomas, Keith, *Religion and the Decline of Magic: Studies in Popular Beliefs in Sixteenth- and Seventeenth-Century England*, London: Weidenfeld and Nicolson, and New York: Scribner, 1971

Thou, Jacques-Auguste de, *Historia sui temporis*, 4 vols., Paris, 1604–08

Troeltsch, Ernst, *Die Soziallehren der christlichen Kirchen und Gruppen*, Tübingen: Mohr, 1912; in English as *The Social Teaching of the Christian Churches*, 2 vols., New York: Macmillan, and London: Allen and Unwin, 1931; reprinted 1981

Wiesner, Merry E., "Beyond Women and the Family: Towards a Gender Analysis of the Reformation," *Sixteenth-Century Journal* 18 (1987), 311–21

Williams, George Huntston, *The Radical Reformation*, Philadelphia: Westminster Press, and London: Weidenfeld and Nicolson, 1962; revised edition, Kirksville, MO: Sixteenth Century Journal, 1992

Religion

The contemporary writing of the history of religion is the systematic gathering, arrangement, and interpretation of historical data on a comparative basis, rooted in both professional agnosticism and sympathetic understanding. The historian of religion must avoid the twin pitfalls of dogmatic apologetics on the one side and cynical atheism on the other. Added to this basic approach are a number of insights and methodological approaches taken from the social sciences (primarily anthropology, psychology, and sociology) and from the humanistic study of religion (comparative religion and the phenomenology of religion). This practice, however, is not merely a 20th-century invention. Historians have been writing about and commenting on religion since the beginning of Western civilization.

Prior to the modern era, Greco-Roman histories of religion focused on myths and founding stories, personalities – especially divine rulers – and cultic practices, tending towards description and cataloguing. One can see this practice in numerous authors between the 8th century BCE and the 2nd century CE: Homer, Herodotus, Strabo, and Plutarch. In writing their histories, these men most often applied a method of simple textual consensus. Plutarch, for example, argued that in order to reconstitute the ancient myths accurately, the records of poets, lawgivers, and philosophers must be consulted, with preference given to the philosophers in the case of contradictions.

Following the conversion of the Roman empire to Christianity in the 4th century, historical writers focused on the biographies of holy men as essential to the explanation and description of religion. The early study of the history of religion, first Roman religion and then Christianity, sought to describe and catalogue the practices, rites, structure, and belief system of a religious tradition. Christian writers sought to use the analysis and history of what was now referred to as paganism to refute its truth claims and assert the truth of Christianity. In his various writings, Basil of Caesarea used comparative and historical arguments to justify Christianity's ascendancy, arguing that pagan religions were a form of degenerate truth, a corruption of real religion. This argument, taking the form of the Christian religion as the standard against which all other religions beliefs were to be measured (and often found wanting) became the dominant manner in which histories of religion were written through the Middle Ages. In this vein, medieval authors emphasized ecclesiastical history, histories of heresies, and histories of monastic life, such as the 12th-century autobiography of Peter Abelard, *Historia calamitatum* (*The Story of My Misfortunes*, c.1140).

This tradition slowly began to undergo a serious transformation beginning in the 11th and 12th centuries, when travel literature introduced reports on the religious practices and histories of Africa and Asia to Western readers. The small beginnings of comparative study had a profound impact. By the time of the Renaissance of the 14th and 15th centuries, genuine interest in world religions contested with the previously exclusive focus on the history of Christianity. Nevertheless, most authors, such as Hugo Grotius in *De veritate religionis Christianae* (1632; *True Religion*, 1632), viewed non-Christian religions as degenerative, or, as in Francis Bacon's *Novum organum* (1620; *New Organon*) as allegories of nature and heroic men. Overall, Western writing on the history of religion from the 4th to the 18th centuries was dominated by the defense of Christianity and the dismissal of the truth claims of other religious traditions.

The modern historiography of religion begins with the effort of Enlightenment figures such as Bernard Fontenelle to move away from a model based on Christianity toward a concept of "natural religion." Under the influence of the natural sciences, the Protestant Reformation, and encounters with religious traditions in Asia and the Americas, many came to conceive of revealed religion as part of the childhood of humanity. In seeking the outlines of a natural religion, it was believed that the study of the history of religion, including all religions, both Western and Eastern, was essential. The translations of sacred texts of the religions of India and China in the 18th century were profoundly influential well into the next century. Comparative studies of Indian and Native American religions, for example, led Fontenelle in his *Entretiens sur la pluralité des mondes* (1686; *Conversations on the Plurality of Worlds*, 1715) to argue that all peoples have the same religious impulse, and would each arrive at a common religious truth given time and opportunity.

Despite these efforts, Enlightenment era writers regarded non-Christian religions as primitive and arising from psychological motives, most prominently the fear and ignorance of natural forces. Most of these efforts often blurred the line between historical investigation and apologetic or polemical purpose, as had much previous writing on the history of religion. Enlightenment writers understood the history of religion in twin terms: first as natural, including an innate knowledge of God, divine providence, and transcendence; and second as primitive, based on fear, superstition, irrationality, and polytheism. Although David Hume, author of *Dialogues Concerning Natural Religion* (1779), was one of the first explicitly to separate the empirical, historical analysis of religion from the normative evaluation of it, his example was rarely followed.

On the one hand, the rationalist approach to the history of religion, for some, lacked an appreciation for its subject. On the other hand, Romanticism, with its emphasis on emotion, imagination, spontaneity, and irrationalism as valued experiences and terms of analysis, appeared to open the door to an understanding of religion that did not reduce it to a need only for the primitive peoples still unenlightened. A precursor of this tradition, Giambattista Vico's *Orazioni inaugurali* (1699–1707, *On Humanistic Education*, 1993) argued that imagination had a central role in both the origins and study of religion. What separated Romantic era authors from other 18th- and 19th-century writers was their shared agreement with Friedrich Schleiermacher, author of *Hermeneutik und Kritik* (1838; *Hermeneutics and Criticism*, 1977) among other works, that emotion was the key to understanding religion.

Romantic writers also shared the view of Hegel's *Phänomenologie des Geistes* (1807; *The Phenomenology of Mind*, 1910) that God was active within history as the evolution of "spirit." For these men religion was a unique mode of consciousness separate from reason, and in many ways superior to it, both in its own value and as a key to understanding history. The 19th-century obsession with nationalism and the unity of language, myth, and culture in the creation of a common people influenced historical research in religion as well. In Johann Herder's *Ideen zur Philosophie der Geschichte der Menschheit* (1785–91; *Outlines of a Philosophy of the History of Man*, 1800) myth and language were the embodiment of human experience, and the task of the historian was to place oneself imaginatively within the soul of another people. Myths were best understood as a product of "the people," an expression of their efforts to understand the cosmos both emotionally and intellectually.

All of these traditions of historical writing on religion were challenged in the 19th century by new revelations in source materials: translations of unknown texts, especially the Rig-Veda of Brahminic India and the Avesta of the Persian Zoroaster; archaeological excavations revealing a lengthy prehistory for humanity; and ethnological and anthropological studies. All of these materials expanded knowledge of religious vocabularies and imageries. Historical writing on religion slowly began to look for commonalities and differences in religious practice, especially connections to the social, economic, political, familial, and gender structures of the community within which the religious belief was influential. The result of this, however, was a plethora of approaches to the historical study of religion, paralleling the increasing specialization and diversification of the social sciences and the humanities in the 19th and 20th centuries.

These new findings prompted renewed growth in the writing of the history of religion, especially as the influence of religion waned in the West and seemed most appropriately an object of historical interest. Many works, such as Theodor Mommsen's *Römische Geschichte* (1854–56; *The History of Rome*, 1864), were greatly influenced by both 19th-century historicism and evolutionary thinking, focusing on developmental stages in Roman religion. Others, under the influence of Auguste Comte's *Catéchisme positiviste* (1852; *The Catechism of Positive Religion*, 1858) pushed the stage of development model even further, linking it to a positivist sociology that saw religion as a dated, primitive remnant from the evolutionary

past. The agnosticism, if not atheism, of the 19th century also influenced views of religious history, especially in works such as Ludwig Feuerbach's *Das Wesen des Christentums* (1841; *The Essence of Christianity*, 1854) where religion was presented as merely the projection of human ideals, at best an intermediate stage between primitive non-religion and modern rationalism.

The latter half of the 19th and early part of the 20th centuries witnessed the fruition of these diverse historical interpretations of religion into two primary schools of thought. The first centered around social scientific approaches pioneered by Karl Marx, Emile Durkheim, and Max Weber. Marx, in "Die Judenfrage" (On the Jewish Question, 1843) and the "Economic and Philosophical Manuscripts" (1844), argued that religion was best understood as a support for the oppressive dominance of the social and economic structures of an era. The integral nature of religion as the ceremonial and expressive glue that binds any social organization together, or, put more baldly, religion as society's worship of itself, was Durkheim's essential insight in *Formes élémentaires de la vie religieuse* (1912; *The Elementary Forms of Religious Life*, 1915). Psychological and emotional needs were also part of Weber's analysis. In both "Die protestantische Ethik und der Geist des Kapitalismus" (1904; *The Protestant Ethic and the Spirit of Capitalism*, 1930) and "Religionssoziologie" (1922; *The Sociology of Religion*, 1963), Weber saw the need for a keystone that locks all of society's pieces in place as giving religion a certain autonomy from society, placing it as a variable in social analysis on the level of economics, politics, and culture. What all of these approaches had in common was a desire to root the understanding of the history of religion firmly in its social context.

The second school focused on the humanistic approach anticipated by Giambattista Vico and further developed by Wilhelm Dilthey in his argument in *Der Aufbau der geschichtlichen Welt in den Geisteswissenschaften* (1910; *Hermeneutics and the Study of History*, 1996) for the use of informed imagination in historical reconstruction. Their primary criticism of the social scientific approach was that it reduced religion to an economic, political, or social phenomenon. While not denying the importance of a social scientific approach, practitioners of *Religionswissenschaft* (loosely translated as "the science of religions") argued that religion must be understood on its own terms, without primary recourse to theological, philosophical, psychological or sociological explanations. This history of religions focuses on the intuitive understanding of descriptive and systematic matters.

The founders of this school of historical writing about religion in the late 19th and early 20th centuries thus focused their efforts on developing their skills in hermeneutics and textual interpretation rather than the social scientific approaches common among other historical schools. Rudolf Otto's *Das Heilige* (1918; *The Idea of the Holy*, 1923) and Friedrich Heiler's *Das Gebet* (1920; *Prayer*, 1932) elaborated an interpretation of the history of religion centered on the idea of "Holiness." Religious experience, especially that which occurred in the presence of the sacred, in the awe and mystery surrounding what Otto referred to as the "wholly Other," became the unifying theme that transcended all religious traditions. In this sense, the history of religions would concentrate on those comparative and interpretive issues that would help isolate each culture's experience of the "numinous," another of Otto's terms.

By the 1930s and after, the students of this historical-phenomenological school, Joachim Wach and Mircea Eliade, author of, among many others, *Histoire des croyances et des idées religieuses* (1976–83; *A History of Religious Ideas*, 1978–85), reinforced the hermeneutical approach of understanding as "re-cognition" or re-experiencing. They set the dominant standard for 20th-century research into the history of religion: non-normative, universal, structured, and inclusive of an element of personal experience. They looked for general patterns, broad generalizations, and common structures in religious experience, beliefs, and practices across cultures. Combining archaeological, anthropological, psychological, ethnographic, and sociological insights, they nevertheless rejected any efforts to "reduce" religion to any of these disciplines and attempted to create an autonomous discipline of religious studies rooted in intuitive understanding.

Although this school dominated the writing of the history of religion from the 1930s through the 1970s, it was not without critics or alternatives. The anthropologists Claude Lévi-Strauss and Clifford Geertz stressed a structuralist approach in distinction to the hermeneutic one. Through the decoding of myths, and the laying bare of the bipolar structures embedded in rites and familial ties, Lévi-Strauss, in works such as *Paroles données* (1984; *Anthropology and Myth*, 1987) and *La Pensée sauvage* (1962; *The Savage Mind*, 1966) sought to find the basic patterns within religious stories and traditions, rather than experiences. Geertz's *The Interpretation of Cultures* (1973) actually staked out a middle ground, looking for the "meaning" within religious symbols, but limiting his investigation to that which is public, rather than privately experienced. Structuralist approaches have influenced the writing of the history of religion, but the hermeneutic approach of Wach and Eliade is still the prevalent model.

DOUGLAS CREMER

See also Africa: Central; Africa: Eastern; Africa: North; African Diaspora; Astrology; Baron, S.; Bauer; Bodin; Breasted; Britain: 1066–1485; Britain: 1485–1750; Browne; Byzantium; Cantimori; Catholicism; Chadwick; Christianity; Collingwood; Counter-Reformation; Delumeau; Eastern Orthodoxy; Eberhard; Ecclesiastical; Egypt: Ancient; Feierman; France: 1450–1789; Fustel; Goitein; Greece: Ancient; Halecki; Halévy; Iran; Islamic; Italy: Renaissance; Jewish; Kołakowski; Kosambi; Maspero; Massignon; Merton; Middle East; Native American; Obolensky; Ortiz; Otsuka; Pagels; Poland: to the 18th Century; Poliakov; Protestantism; Ranger; Reformation; Rodinson; Russia: Early Modern; Southeast Asia; Sigerist; Slavery: Modern; Snorri; Tawney; Thomas; Toynbee; Trevor-Roper; Troeltsch; Universal; Watt; Women's History: Africa

Further Reading

Abelard, Peter, *Historia calamitatum*, c.1140; in English as *The Story of My Misfortunes*

Bacon, Francis, *Novum organum*, 1620; in English as *New Organon*, 1960

Bianchi, Ugo, *The History of Religions*, Leiden: Brill, 1975

Comte, Auguste, *Catéchisme positiviste, ou, sommaire exposition de la religion universelle de l'humanité*, Paris: Garnier, 1852; in English as *The Catechism of Positive Religion*, London: Chapman, 1858

de Vries, Jan, *The Study of Religion: A Historical Approach*, New York: Harcourt Brace, 1967

Dilthey, Wilhelm, *Der Aufbau der geschichtlichen Welt in den Geisteswissenschaften*, Berlin: Verlag der Königlichen Akademie der Wissenschaften, 1910; in English in *Hermeneutics and the Study of History*, Princeton: Princeton University Press, 1996 [*Selected Works*, vol. 4]

Durkheim, Emile, *Formes élémentaires de la vie religieuse: le système totémique en Australie*, Paris: Alcan, 1912; in English as *The Elementary Forms of Religious Life*, London: Allen and Unwin, 1915, New York: Macmillan, 1926

Eliade, Mircea, and Joseph M. Kitagawa, eds., *The History of Religions: Essays in Methodology*, Chicago: University of Chicago Press, 1959

Eliade, Mircea, *The Quest: History and Meaning in Religion*, Chicago: University of Chicago Press, 1969

Eliade, Mircea, *Histoire des croyances et des idées religieuses*, 3 vols., Paris: Payot, 1976–83; in English as *A History of Religious Ideas*, 3 vols., Chicago: University of Chicago Press, 1978–85

Feuerbach, Ludwig, *Das Wesen des Christentums*, Leipzig: Wigand, 1841; in English as *The Essence of Christianity*, London: Chapman, 1854

Fontenelle, Bernard le Bovier de, *Entretiens sur la pluralité des mondes*, Paris: Blageart, 1686; in English as *Conversations on the Plurality of Worlds*, London: Bettesworth, 1715

Geertz, Clifford, *The Interpretation of Cultures: Selected Essays*, New York: Basic Books, 1973; London: Hutchinson, 1975

Grotius, Hugo, *De veritate religionis Christianae*, 1632; in English as *True Religion, Explained and Defended Against the Archenemies Therof in These Times*, 1632; and as *The Truth of Christian Religion*, 1680

Hegel, G.W.F., *Die Phänomenologie des Geistes*, Bamberg: Goebhardt, 1807; in English as *The Phenomenology of Mind*, 2 vols., London: Sonnenschein, and New York: Macmillan, 1910, 2nd edition London: Allen and Unwin, and New York: Macmillan, 1931; as *Phenomenology of Spirit*, Oxford: Clarendon Press, 1977

Heiler, Friedrich, *Das Gebet: eine religionsgeschichtliche und religiös psychologische Untersuchung*, Munich: Reinhardt, 1920; in English as *Prayer: A Study in the History and Psychology of Religion*, London and New York: Oxford University Press, 1932

Herder, J.G., *Ideen zur Philosophie der Geschichte der Menschheit*, 4 vols., 1785–91; in English as *Outlines of a Philosophy of the History of Man*, London: Hansard, 1800; abridged as *Reflections on the Philosophy of the History of Mankind*, Chicago: University of Chicago Press, 1968

Hume, David, *Dialogues Concerning Natural Religion*, London, 1779

Kitagawa, Joseph M., ed., *The History of Religions: Essays on the Problem of Understanding*, Chicago: University of Chicago Press, 1967

Kitagawa, Joseph M., ed., *The History of Religions: Retrospect and Prospect*, New York: Macmillan, and London: Collier Macmillan, 1985

Lévi-Strauss, Claude, *La Pensée sauvage*, Paris: Plon, 1962; in English as *The Savage Mind*, Chicago: University of Chicago Press, 1966

Lévi-Strauss, Claude, *Paroles données*, Paris: Plon, 1984; in English as *Anthropology and Myth*, Oxford and New York: Blackwell, 1987

Mommsen, Theodor, *Römische Geschichte*, 3 vols., Berlin: Weidmann, 1854–56; in English as *The History of Rome*, 4 vols., 1864–75

Otto, Rudolf, *Das Heilige: über das Irrationale in der Idee des Göttlichen und sein Verhältnis zum Rationalen*, Breslau: Trewendt & Granier, 1918; in English as *The Idea of the Holy: An Inquiry into the Non-Rational Function in the Idea of the Divine and Its Relation to the Rational*, London and New York: Oxford University Press, 1923

Rudolph, Kurt, *Historical Fundamentals and the Study of Religion*, New York: Macmillan, 1985

Schleiermacher, Friedrich, *Hermeneutik und Kritik: mit besonderer Beziehung auf das Neue Testament*, Berlin: Reimer, 1838; in English as *Hermeneutics*, Missoula, MT: Scholars Press, 1977

Vico, Giambattista, *Orazioni inaugurali*, 1699–1707; in English as *On Humanistic Education: Six Inaugural Orations, 1699–1707*, Ithaca, NY: Cornell University Press, 1993

Wach, Joachim, *Essays in the History of Religions*, edited by Joseph M. Kitagawa and Gregory D. Alles, New York: Macmillan, 1988

Wach, Joachim, *Introduction to the History of Religions*, edited by Joseph M. Kitagawa and Gregory D. Alles, New York: Macmillan, 1988

Weber, Max, "Die protestantische Ethik und der Geist des Kapitalismus," *Archiv für Sozialwissenschaft und Sozialpolitik* 20–21 (1904–05), revised in *Gesammelte Aufsätze zur Religionssoziologie*, Tübingen: Mohr, 1920; in English as *The Protestant Ethic and the Spirit of Capitalism*, London: Allen and Unwin, 1930, New York: Scribner, 1958

Weber, Max, "Religionssoziologie" in *Wirtschaft und Gesellschaft*, Tübingen: Mohr, 1922; in English as *The Sociology of Religion*, Boston: Beacon Press, 1963, London: Methuen, 1965

Religion(s), Comparative History of

The term "history of religion(s)" is burdened with some ambiguity. First, the term has been used to describe the whole field of the scientific study of religions (i.e., *Religionswissenschaft*), and to describe a certain historical approach for characterizing different religious traditions, and modes of thinking and behavior. It is in this latter sense that the term is used here. Second, due to the ongoing debate concerning the sufficient and necessary characteristics of the concept of "religion," there exists a fundamental division between those scholars who argue that the object of the discipline is to examine the universal religious dimension of human existence through its empirical manifestations in the world, and those scholars who deny that a religious experience common to all humankind exists. Accordingly, the first group of scholars prefer to use the singular form "religion" to describe their research object, while the latter group opt for the plural "religions," in order to emphasize the empirical nature of their research. For the sake of clarity, the somewhat cumbersome "history of religion(s)" will be used throughout this essay to denote the approach as a whole.

The birth of the comparative history of religion(s) can be traced to the critique that scholars such as the 19th-century Dutch theologian Cornelius Petrus Tiele and the influential German Religionsgeschichtliche Schule, directed towards the – at time prevalent – historicist approach towards the past. They claimed that a simple ethnographic task was not enough for explaining and understanding religious phenomena. Instead, ethnographic materials collected from different religious traditions should be compared with each other in order to reveal the nature and structure of the underlying metaphysical category, like "god," "myth," "the sacred," etc. This classical version of the "religio-historical" method was firmly established by the early 20th-century Italian historian Raffaele Pettazzoni. Pettazzoni noted the dangers of using metaphysical categories in historical scholarship as religious phenomena are processes in continual change, and phenomenological categorization done on a semantic level might attach to religious phenomena meanings that simply are no longer there.

Since Pettazzoni the field has divided into two camps. First, there are those who have stayed close to the formulations of the classical approach. The most important representative of this approach is the American scholar Joseph Kitagawa and his method of "empirical phenomenology." According to him, the universal structures shared by different religious traditions are not based on metaphysical assumptions but on inductive generalizations. However, this approach has been severely criticized by more historically-minded scholars, who have argued that phenomenology is useless for historical scholarship, because the object of historical research cannot be any metaphysical or universal category of the human mind, but the different empirically observed patterns of behavior and thinking held to be religious. For these scholars the historical method is used for studying religions (in plural).

The Italian scholar Ugo Bianchi has been the leading authority of this second school of thought. He has argued that all claims concerning a common religious dimension of human existence are reductive, and the concept of religion is only a scholarly category born from the dialogue between individual scholars with their different backgrounds, and their target cultures and objects of research. Thus, according to Bianchi, the historical study of religions is largely an ethnographic project, although religious behavior could also be explained by linking it to the contextual cultural network of communication. In this respect, the "religio-historical" method is by nature always holistic.

Comparison is still held as fundamental to the method. Some scholars have argued that in Bianchi's model there is the danger of losing the comparative aspect of the "religio-historical" method. The American scholar Hans Penner has argued, however, that comparisons can and should be made in this model. The level of comparison is transferred from the level of single phenomena to the level of cultural or religious systems as a whole. Thus, instead of comparing, for example, the concept of "god" in European and Indian thinking, we should, according to Penner, compare how this concept has evolved in European thought, on the one hand, and Indian thought, on the other, and what these processes can tell us about the cultural histories of the two geographic areas.

The comparative-historical approach has its limitations, and it has drawn criticism on several counts. First, it has been argued that in spite of any neutral guise, there is no such thing as pure description or objectivity in the study of religions. Coincidentally, this same criticism was directed towards historicism by sociologists during the early decades of the 20th century. It is undoubtedly true that comparison is always a purposive selection of data from an endless array of possible items. As William Paden has clearly stated, the comparative method has historically been connected with quite different agendas. However, he goes on to argue that while there does not seem to be any absolutely value-free way to characterize and connect the structures of religions, the comparative framework nevertheless justifies its approach as a corrective both to uninformed or provincial ideas of religions, and to stances that view religions only in terms of their social and psychological functions.

A second criticism of comparativism asks, "What if there is no such thing as religion in any generic sense?" If "religion" is only a scholarly construction, as argued by, for example,

Bianchi, what is the explanatory value of the term in the first place? Comparative historians have tried to fend off this criticism by arguing that while the term itself is only a scholarly generalization, it does exist through its particular embodiments, and is useful in order to differentiate certain kind of cultural strategies from one another. After all, the same kind of critique has been directed at terms like "society" and "psyche" (or "mind"). Paden has argued that like these other verbal entities, "religion" can have either an explanatory or a descriptive slant, depending on the purpose of its user. Still, during the last decade, some historians of religions, such as the German scholar Kurt Rudolph, have started to question the methodological independence of their discipline, and argue that – in effect – the history of religion(s) belongs methodologically and theoretically in the field of historical anthropology in general.

Finally, there is the criticism that the comparative approach has nothing to say about the truth and validity of religions. It seems to have no evaluative capacity and to be hopelessly democratic. This seems to be a fair description of the method, although it is not necessarily a criticism. Things can be explained and described without normative claims concerning their nature. Indeed, this is something that the comparative history of religion(s) has in common with most of the other historical disciplines as well.

The comparative history of religion(s) is a well established field of historical scholarship. Until quite recently, its biggest problem has been its relative isolation from other historical disciplines, and with it, from the methodological and theoretical advances made in them after World War II. Fortunately this period of isolation appears to be over, and with it the comparative history of religion(s) can take its place as one of the many different approaches towards revealing the meaning of the past to the modern era.

TOM SJÖBLOM

See also Religion

Further Reading

Bianchi, Ugo, The History of Religions, Leiden: Brill, 1975
Bianchi, Ugo, "Current Methodological Issues in the History of Religions," in Joseph M. Kitagawa, ed., The History of Religions: Retrospect and Prospect, New York: Macmillan, and London: Collier Macmillan, 1985
Bianchi, Ugo, ed., The Notion of "Religion" in Comparative Research, Rome: Bretschneider, 1994
Dressel, Gert, Historische Anthropologie: Eine Einführung (Historical Anthropology: An Introduction), Vienna: Bölau, 1996
Idinopulos, Thomas A., and Edward A. Yonan, eds., Religion and Reductionism: Essays on Eliade, Segal and the Challenge of the Social Sciences for the Study of Religion, Leiden: Brill, 1994
Jenkins, Keith, Re-thinking History, London and New York: Routledge, 1991
Kitagawa, Joseph M., The History of Religions: Understanding Human Experience, Atlanta: Scholars Press, 1987
Leeuw, Gerardus van der, Phänomenologie der Religion, Tübingen: Mohr, 1933; in English as Religion in Essence and Manifestation, New York: Macmillan, and London: Allen and Unwin, 1938; reprinted Princeton: Princeton University Press, 1986
Mink, Louis, Historical Understanding, edited by Brian Fay, Eugene O. Golub, and Richard T. Vann, Ithaca, NY: Cornell University Press, 1987
Paden, William, Interpreting the Sacred: Ways of Viewing Religion, Boston: Beacon Press, 1992
Penner, Hans, "Why Does Semantics Matter to the Study of Religions," Method and Theory in the Study of Religions 7 (1995), 221–49
Pettazzoni, Raffaele, Essays on the History of Religions, Leiden: Brill, 1954
Reynolds, Frank E., and Joseph M. Ludwig, eds., Transitions and Transformations in the History of Religions, Leiden: Brill, 1980
Rudolph, Kurt, "Religionsgeschichtliche Schule," The Encyclopedia of Religion, vol. 12, New York: Macmillan, 1987
Rudolph, Kurt, Geschichte und Probleme der Religionswissenschaft (History and Problems in Comparative Religion), Leiden: Brill, 1992
Rudolph, Kurt, "Hvad religion er, fortaeller historien os" (What Religion is, History Reveals to Us), Religionsvidenskabeligt tidsskrift 23 (1993), 55–78
Sharpe, Eric J., Comparative Religion: A History, London: Duckworth, and New York: Scribner, 1975
Sjöblom, Tom, "Menneisyyden malleja" (Models of the Past), in Kimmo Ketola et al., Näköaloja uskontoon, Helsinki: Yliopistopaino, 1997
Tiele, Cornelius P., Inledning till religionsvetenskapen (Introduction to Comparative Religion), Stockholm: Fahlcrantz, 1903

Renaissance Historical Writing

The modern discipline of professional historical writing is a product of the Renaissance. In the Middle Ages, history was chronicle, time was linear, and progress was both invisible and incomprehensible. The educational, philosophical, and political changes of the Renaissance which are collectively called "humanism" explicitly rejected that schema, and the theological understanding of God's agency which lay at its heart. Humanist history was secular, practical, and the product of human action; it was designed to teach the lessons of moral philosophy and politics to its audience. This viewpoint is directly based on the assumption that a true understanding of the past necessitates a return to the sources. The choice of historical subjects as well as the manner of treatment was meant to be persuasive, to extol the virtues of the classical past, and to teach the lessons of the past so that the present could imitate and use them. In other words, like the other literary disciplines of the Renaissance studia humanitatis, history was rhetorical.

Two 20th-century works on Renaissance and humanist historiography deserve specific mention in this context: Donald J. Wilcox's The Development of Florentine Humanist Historiography in the Fifteenth Century (1969) and Eric Cochrane's Historians and Historiography in the Italian Renaissance (1981). Both discuss the attitudes and methods of Renaissance humanists and historians. Cochrane addressed not only the writing of history and historiography in the Renaissance, but also the study of those fields about the Renaissance. He noted the methodologies of the Italian and Italian-influenced Renaissance historians and historiographers beginning in the 15th century: humanist chronicles (medieval chronicles modified in language and style to fit humanist norms); humanist histories (conscious imitation of the ancient models); commentaries (on single events); "Livian-Brunian" histories (on a single political community); contemporary histories (dependent for style on either Thucydides or Polybius); universal histories (from the dawn of time to the present); and biographical histories. According to Cochrane, "humanist historiography was born fully grown"; it was characterized by organization based on themes rather than strictly on chronology and by being modeled on ancient paradigms. Beginning with Leonardo Bruni (c.1370–1444), authors of historical texts adopted the new principles in their ongoing quest to understand the glorious past that had existed before the decline of the "Dark Ages."

The first work of humanist historiography was Bruni's *Historiarum Florentini Populi* (History of the People of Florence, 1440s). In it, Bruni stressed the persuasive, educative function of history: it could teach prudent living and political wisdom. Bruni's style was adopted by such diverse humanist historians as Paolo Giovio, Cesare Baronio, Paolo Sarpi, and Antonio Possevino. Niccolò Machiavelli (1469–1527), Francesco Guicciardini (1483–1540), and Giorgio Vasari (1511–74) warrant particular attention. Machiavelli believed that humans, because they were always the same and always evil, were predictable; history was therefore circular. History provided contemporaries with a storehouse of *exempla* to study and either imitate or avoid. The study of history would enable an individual to control it. The medieval emphasis on the role of God was conspicuously and consciously absent in Machiavelli's historical writing; it was replaced by human agency. Guicciardini, though clearly humanist in his methodology, did break with the humanist theory of history. He accepted history as the history of politics, as totally secular, as the history of active participants in political process; but he stepped out of the local parochial outlook common to humanists, and saw Italy as whole (without advocating unification of the peninsula). He rejected the Machiavellian concept of constant human nature and the idea of history as a storehouse of *exempla*. There were no repetitive patterns in history, so there was also no possibility of finding historical laws.

Both of these historians were essentially political, though with different goals; but humanist history, like humanism itself, could also function to glorify individual human capacities. Vasari's *Le vite de' più eccellenti architetti, pittori et scultori italani* (1550, revised 1568; *Lives of the Most Eminent Painters, Sculptors and Architects*, 1912–15) clearly espoused a "Great Individuals" theory of cultural history. Giotto, Brunelleschi, and other luminaries revived the ancient glories of art and architecture through their personal genius and their study of the past. Modern historiography, while explicitly based on humanist methods of source study (though certainly espousing broader reading in sources), rejects the "Great Individuals" theory as well as the fundamentally rhetorical and political functions of history.

A final kind of Renaissance historical writing to consider is the personal account or memoir (*Ricordi*). Prominent men and families kept diaries of their lives and times; *Ricordi* generally contained political as well as personal information. The intention of such works was both to glorify the family in the present and to preserve the heritage for future generations. Among the most famous *Ricordi* are those by Bartolomeo Cerretani, Piero Parenti, and Guicciardini, who based his history of Florence in part on his family memoirs.

KATHLEEN COMERFORD

See also Baron, H.; Burckhardt; Cassirer; Chabod; Cipolla; Gilbert; Giovio; Guicciardini; Italy: Renaissance; Kristeller; Machiavelli; Martines; Sarpi; Vasari

Further Reading

Baron, Hans, *The Crisis of the Early Italian Renaissance: Civic Humanism and Republican Life in an Age of Classicism and Tyranny*, 2 vols., Princeton: Princeton University Press, 1955; revised 1966

Bietenholz, Peter G., ed., *Contemporaries of Erasmus: A Biographical Register of the Renaissance and Reformation*, 3 vols., Toronto: University of Toronto Press, 1985–87

Bondanella, Peter, and Mark Musa, eds., *The Portable Machiavelli*, New York: Penguin, 1979

Burckhardt, Jacob, *Die Cultur der Renaissance in Italien*, 2 vols., Basel: Schweighauss, 1860; in English as *The Civilization of the Renaissance in Italy*, 2 vols., New York: Macmillan, and London: Swan Sonnenschein, 1904

Cassirer, Ernst, Paul Oskar Kristeller, and John Herman Randall, Jr., eds, *The Renaissance Philosophy of Man*, Chicago: University of Chicago Press, 1948

Chabod, Federico, "The Concept of the Renaissance," in his *Machiavelli and the Renaissance*, London: Bowes and Bowes, and Cambridge, MA: Harvard University Press, 1958

Cipolla, Carlo M., "The Trends in Italian Economic History in the Later Middle Ages," *Economic History Review* 2 (1949), 181–84

Cochrane, Eric, *Historians and Historiography in the Italian Renaissance*, Chicago: University of Chicago Press, 1981

Croce, Benedetto, *Elementi di politica* (Elements of Politics), Bari: Laterza, 1925

D'Entreves, A.P., Introduction, in Federico Chabod, *Machiavelli and the Renaissance*, London: Bowes and Bowes, and Cambridge, MA: Harvard University Press, 1958

Ferguson, Wallace K., *The Renaissance in Historical Thought: Five Centuries of Interpretation*, Boston: Houghton Mifflin, 1948

Gilbert, Felix, *Machiavelli and Guicciardini: Politics and History in Sixteenth-Century Florence*, Princeton: Princeton University Press, 1965

Kristeller, Paul Oskar, *The Classics and Renaissance Thought*, Cambridge, MA: Harvard University Press, 1955; revised as *Renaissance Thought 1: The Classic, Scholastic, and Humanistic Strains*, New York: Harper, 1961

Martines, Lauro, *The Social World of the Florentine Humanists, 1390–1460*, Princeton: Princeton University Press, and London: Routledge, 1963

Martines, Lauro, *Power and Imagination: City-states in Renaissance Italy*, New York: Knopf, 1979; London: Allen Lane, 1980

Trinkaus, Charles, *The Scope of Renaissance Humanism*, Ann Arbor: University of Michigan Press, 1983

Vasari, Giorgio, *Le vite de' più eccellenti architetti, pittori et scultori italani*, 3 vols., Florence: H. Torrentino, 1550, revised 1568; in English as *Lives of the Most Eminent Painters, Sculptors and Architects*, 10 vols., London: Macmillan–Medici Society, 1912–15, reprinted New York: AMS, 1976

Vespasiano da Bisticci, *Viti di uomini illustri del secolo*, Rome, 1839; in English as *The Vespasiano Memoirs: Lives of the Illustrious Men of the XVth Century*, London: Routledge, and New York: Dial Press, 1926; reprinted as *Renaissance Princes, Popes, and Prelates*, New York: Harper, 1963

Wilcox, Donald J., *The Development of Florentine Humanist Historiography in the Fifteenth Century*, Cambridge, MA: Harvard University Press, 1969

Renouvin, Pierre 1893–1974

French historian

Pierre Renouvin's career demonstrates the strength of traditional French historiography at a time when it had to meet the competition of new intellectual approaches, such as those of the Annales school. In contrast to their development of social history, and of *l'histoire des mentalités*, Renouvin's subject was the oldest of all historical specializations, the history of relations between states, of diplomacy and war. This was an area slighted by the exponents of new types of history who criticized it under various headings, as being political rather than socioeconomic, as being concerned with individuals not social classes, as being quintessentially *histoire événementielle* as opposed to the *longue durée*. In fact Renouvin's work did embrace non-political forces and he did come to deal with long-term trends, without neglecting the exact and penetrating analysis of individual crises. In this way he deepened and extended the old, somewhat narrow and limited diplomatic history into the history of international relations. But this was still traditional in comparison to the explorations of the disciples of Bloch, Febvre, and Braudel. In another way also his career was traditional in that he did not work in one of the research institutions such as the Ecole des Hautes Etudes, or the "laboratories" of the Centre National de Recherche Scientifique, where most of the exponents of the new history were to be found, but in the university faculty of the Sorbonne where from 1921 to his retirement he taught as lecturer then professor and dean.

Renouvin was deeply marked by his experience of World War I. An infantry lieutenant, he was decorated and twice wounded, the second time in the terrible offensive of April 1917. He lost his left arm, and had other wounds, but he survived to resume the historical career that had begun before 1914 with research on the French Revolution under Aulard. He completed his thesis on the Provincial Assemblies of 1787 and was awarded his doctorate. But his attention had been turned from the Revolution to study of the origins and course of World War I, the topic that was to be the center of his life's work. After a brief period as a lycée teacher at Orléans, he was appointed in 1921 to teach a special course at the Sorbonne on the history of the war. He was also involved with the Bibliothèque de la Guerre, a comprehensive collection of books and documents from all of the belligerent powers that eventually formed the nucleus of the collections of the Bibliothèque de Documentation Internationale Contemporaine, now at the University of Nanterre.

In 1925 his work on the war led to the publication of two definitive studies, both eventually translated into English, *Les Origines immédiates de la guerre (28 juin-4 aôut 1914)* (*The Immediate Origins of the War*) and *Les Formes du gouvernement de guerre* (*The Forms of War Government in France*, 1927). The first was concerned with refuting German attempts to deny responsibility for the outbreak of war, enshrined in the war-guilt clause of the Treaty of Versailles. The second showed how France had preserved its parliamentary form of government throughout the war, in contrast to Germany, where military authoritarianism had strangled the small degree of responsible government existing in 1914. In both, but especially in the first work, Renouvin had to refute polemical charges from the French Left, as well as from German propagandists and their American converts. Such charges were epitomized in the slogan *Poincaré-la-guerre*, claiming that Poincaré had encouraged an aggressive Russian policy in 1912–14. Thus the German claim that they had been encircled by a threatening Franco-Russian combination could be supported. Close

analysis of the documentary sources already available allowed him to cast doubt on the German arguments; further documentary revelations, and historical analysis from that day to this has simply strengthened his original view. The second book went beyond administrative history, although it did provide a clear account of the administrative innovations of the war; it also explained the spirit of these arrangements, and showed that charges that the Clemenceau government of 1917–20 had been in any real sense dictatorial were unfounded.

There was need for careful analysis of the July 1914 crisis, because the German government had been quickest off the mark in producing its documentary collection, and had done so in a self-justificatory way. The other belligerents, or most of them, produced documents in subsequent years that nearly always confirmed and elaborated his original verdicts. Renouvin was able to incorporate this evidence in new editions of his original book, and in many articles on particular points. He himself was involved from the first in the publication of the French diplomatic documents, eventually becoming president of the two committees for the publication of French documents on the origins of the two world wars. A specialist review, the *Revue d'Histoire de la Guerre Mondiale*, was created, which devoted much attention to comment on the various documentary series; he frequently published in its columns. All of this work was incorporated in a much broader study of the war and its origins, *La Crise européenne et la grande guerre* (The European Crisis and the Great War), of which the first version was published in 1934. Subsequently revised and enlarged several times, it can be seen as his masterpiece, and has stood the test of time.

Although to the end of his life World War I remained a major focus of interest, and he published a substantial study of the 1918 armistice in 1969, Renouvin steadily broadened his concerns from the immediate origins of the war, to the study of the whole field of international relations in the 19th and 20th centuries. In 1946 came his study of *La Question d'Extrême Orient, 1840–1940* (The Question of the Far East), but the major achievement of his later years was editorship of an 8-volume *Histoire des relations internationales* (The History of International Relations, 1953–58), from the Middle Ages to 1945. Half of the whole work, four volumes covering 1815–1945, were written by Renouvin himself, and constituted a remarkable synthesis that has perhaps never been bettered. In 1964 he published jointly with J.-B. Duroselle, who was to be his successor in the chair of international history at the Sorbonne, a theoretical work, *Introduction à l'histoire des relations internationales* (Introduction to the History of International Relations). Thus, in some ways his work may be seen to have moved from the particular to the general, from minute analysis of five weeks in 1914 to general theories of international history. But this is only partially true, as he continued to write on detailed topics, and maintained his unrivalled mastery of the history of World War I.

Anyone who met Renouvin could not fail to be impressed by his authority, by something perhaps best conveyed by the Latin word *gravitas*, reinforced by the evidence of his old wounds. His views were incisive, but arrived at with all possible care. In the historical field that was the center of his research, and which was closest to his heart, France's struggle against Germany in the first half of the 20th century, he spoke as a deeply committed patriot, but without any bitterness. He defended French policies when they had been effective in warding off the attacks of the enemy, and criticized them when they were deficient, as in the tragic failure to uphold the peace settlement of 1919.

DAVID ROBIN WATSON

See also Diplomatic; World War I

Biography

Born Paris, 9 January 1893. Attended Lycée Louis-le-Grand, receiving his agrégation 1912. Traveled in Russia and Germany, 1912–14. Served in French infantry during World War I: wounded, losing his left arm and use of his right hand. Taught at Lycée d'Orléans, 1918–20; head, War History Library, Sorbonne, 1920–22, lecturer, 1922–33, professor from 1933, and dean, 1955–58; retired 1964. President, Fondation Nationale des Sciences Politiques. Elected to Académie des Sciences Morales et Politiques, 1946. Married Marie-Thérèse Gatialda, 1918. Died Paris, 7 December 1974.

Principal Writings

Les Formes du gouvernement de guerre, 1925; in English as The Forms of War Government in France, 1927
Les Origines immédiates de la guerre (28 juin–4 août 1914), 1925; in English as The Immediate Origins of the War, 28 June–4 August 1914, 1928
La Crise européenne et la grande guerre, 1904–1918 (The European Crisis and the Great War), 1934
La Question d'Extrême Orient, 1840–1940 (The Question of the Far East, 1840–1940), 1946
Editor, Histoire des relations internationales (The History of International Relations), 8 vols., 1953–58
Les Crise du XXe siècle, 2 vols., 1958–59; in English as War and Aftermath, 1914–1929, 1968; and World War II and Its Origins: International Relations, 1929–45, 1968
With Jean-Baptiste Duroselle, Introduction à l'histoire des relations internationales, 1964; in English as Introduction to the History of International Relations, 1967

Further Reading

Duroselle, Jean-Baptiste, "Pierre Renouvin," Revue d'Histoire Moderne et Contemporaine new series 27 (1975), 497–507
Halperin, S.W., Some Twentieth-Century Historians: Essays on Eminent Europeans, Chicago: University of Chicago Press, 1961, 143–70
Mélanges Pierre Renouvin: études d'Histoire des relations internationales (Pierre Renouvin Miscellany: Studies on the History of International Relations), Paris: Presses Universitaires de France, 1966 [includes bibliography]

Rhetoric and History

The words "rhetoric" and "history" have formed an uneasy linkage over the past 2,500 years in the West. Since Plato's critique of the Sophists, rhetoric has held a connotation of verbal artifice, or persuasive discourse. At the heart of this lies a tension between an image of language that is used factually to reflect events, on the one hand, and language that is richly mixed with personal viewpoints and ideology, on the other. Among historians, the former has often represented the unbiased pursuit of truth, while the latter has represented more or less extreme forms of subjectivity.

"Rhetoric" has by no means been a negative term for all thinkers, however. Aristotle presented a memorable defense, stating that "We must be able to employ persuasion . . . on opposite sides of a question, not in order that we may in practice employ it both ways (for we must not make people believe what is wrong) but in order that we may see clearly what the facts are, and that, if another man argues unfairly, we may be able to confute him." The art of rhetoric, he continues, "draws opposite conclusions impartially." By linking rhetoric to the pursuit of truth, Aristotle created a strong argument for its study. He nonetheless left the reader with an uneasy concern over one of its core features – it remains, at base, a persuasive device that is subject to grave abuse and that requires continued vigilance among fair-minded thinkers.

The tension between these two poles has been at the heart of varying conceptions of history and historical discourse over the past two millennia – from Herodotus and Thucydides to Vico and Ranke. There is a similar tension in Chinese thought that can best be summed up by a passage from Confucius' (Kong-zi's) Analects: "When there is a preponderance of (factual) substance over (literary) refinement, the result will be confusion; when there is a preponderance of refinement over substance, the result will be pedantry." Only when the two are mixed will one find balanced knowledge. The creative pull of this idea in Chinese historiography can be seen in the works of two of China's most influential historians. Sima Guang's Zizhi tongjian (Comprehensive Mirror for Aid in Government, completed 1084) is a detailed history of China over more than a millennium. Attention to detail and careful consideration of source materials are its strongest features. Zhu Xi, writing a century later, edited the work into an ethical textbook with historical examples. The former's wealth of detail and the latter's rigid ethics provide a parallel to Confucius' statement and the rhetorical concerns of writers half a world away.

The study of rhetoric in history and historiography has returned to prominence in the second half of the 20th century. Among the rhetorical works that have influenced historical thinkers are those by Kenneth Burke, whose notion of "dramatism" has had a profound impact, and by Mikhail Bakhtin, Wayne Booth, Fredric Jameson, and Wolfgang Iser. In particular, Hayden White's Metahistory (1973) has inspired many historians to examine rhetorical issues in historiography. White's introduction to that work, entitled "The Poetics of History," states his purpose forcefully, "I will consider the historical work as what it most manifestly is – a verbal structure in the form of narrative prose discourse that purports to be a model, or icon, of past structures and processes in the interest of explaining what they were by representing them." White further notes that the historical work lies at the intersection of a historical past, the historical record, and an audience. The manner in which records of the past are given new verbal forms – emplotted – lies at the heart of the historiographical operation.

Such emphasis on the constructive nature of historical knowledge and the literary nature of historical writing can also be found in, among others, Paul Veyne's Writing History (1984), Michel de Certeau's L'Ecriture de l'histoire (1975; The Writing of History, 1988), and Paul Ricoeur's Temps et récit (1983–85; Time and Narrative, 1984–88). Ricoeur in particular notes the profound connections between text and action: "The act of reading . . . is the final indicator of the world of action under the sign of the plot." For Ricoeur, the historical reader refigures the text through reading and carries the refigured "text" with him.

Because the study of rhetoric is of enormous importance to thinkers in a wide variety of fields, it is difficult to find a unified critical approach to rhetorical study. Nonetheless, it is possible to examine themes that many scholars share. To begin with, rhetorical analyses are relevant to an enormous range of public and private discourse, including legal cases, speeches, lectures, pamphlets, and even commercials. The double problem for historians is that they commonly employ a wide range of such "texts" in their research, even as they create new texts from their fragments.

Another feature of rhetorical criticism is that such discourse is subject to study not so much for the information or argument that it contains, but for the manner in which its contents shape the world beyond it. The writings of Karl Marx and Mao Zedong are just two notable examples of works that have been commonly analyzed for more than their literary, philosophical, or historical content. One could just as easily subject the works of far less prominent writers to the same analyses.

It is the *communicative* nature of discourse that lies at the heart of rhetorical criticism, and for historians this represents a double-edged sword. Language has the power (from the perspective of the rhetorical critic, if not the deconstructionist) to influence and create change – the kind of movements and events that are the very subject of the historian's study. But it is only through language that the historian can communicate such knowledge to readers. Whether this is a matter to be celebrated and studied in detail, as rhetorical critics would have it, or rather a problem requiring further research and greater care in composition, lies at the very heart of the historical discipline.

ROBERT A. LaFLEUR

See also Kong-zi; Marx; White, H.

Further Reading

Aristotle, "Rhetoric," in *The Complete Works of Aristotle: The Revised Oxford Translation*, vol. 2., Princeton: Princeton University Press, 1984

Bakhtin, Mikhail, *Voprosy literatury i estetiki: isseldovaniia let*, Moscow: Khudozh, 1975; in English as *The Dialogic Imagination: Four Essays*, Austin: University of Texas Press, 1981

Barilli, Renato, *La retorica*, Milan: Mondadori, 1983; in English as *Rhetoric*, Minneapolis: University of Minnesota Press, 1989

Booth, Wayne, *The Rhetoric of Fiction*, Chicago: University of Chicago Press, 1961

Burke, Kenneth, *Language as Symbolic Action: Essays on Life, Literature, and Method*, Berkeley: University of California Press, and Cambridge: Cambridge University Press, 1966

Certeau, Michel de, *L'Ecriture de l'histoire*, Paris: Gallimard, 1975; in English as *The Writing of History*, New York: Columbia University Press, 1988

Iser, Wolfgang, *Der implizite Leser: Kommunikationsformen des Romans von Bunyan bis Beckett*, Munich: Fink, 1972; in English as *The Implied Reader*, Baltimore: Johns Hopkins University Press, 1974

Jameson, Fredric, *Marxism and Form*, Princeton: Princeton University Press, 1971

Matsen, Patricia, Philip Rollinson, and Marion Sousa, *Readings from Classical Rhetoric*, Carbondale: Southern Illinois University Press, 1990

Ricoeur, Paul, *Temps et récit*, 3 vols., Paris: Seuil, 1983–85; in English as *Time and Narrative*, 3 vols., Chicago: University of Chicago Press, 1984–88

Veyne, Paul, *Comment on écrit l'histoire: essai d'epistémologie*, Paris: Seuil, 1971; in English as *Writing History: Essays on Epistemology*, Middletown, CT: Wesleyan University Press, and Manchester: Manchester University Press, 1984

White, Hayden V., *Metahistory: The Historical Imagination in Nineteenth-Century Europe*, Baltimore: Johns Hopkins University Press, 1973

Ritter, Gerhard A. 1888–1967

German political and cultural historian

Gerhard Ritter was known to many as the "final figure of an epoch." Ritter, perhaps one of the best known German historians of the 20th century, came from the tradition of the German political historians of the 19th century. To him, history was not only a subject of scientific research and discourse, but also a means of practical political education.

Ritter was a product of Wilhelmine Germany with its Prussian traditions and Lutheran faith. This provided the background for his first book, *Die preussischen Konservativen und Bismarcks deutsche Politik, 1858 bis 1876* (The Prussian Conservatives and Bismarck's German Policy, 1858 to 1876), completed as his dissertation in 1911 under the direction of professor Hermann Oncken in Heidelberg. In this book, Ritter traced the conflict between Bismarck's conservative party and the nobility which saw Bismarck's national policy as a threat to its rights and privileges. In particular, the nobility saw Bismarck's concessions to the southern German states as a threat to its power. This question of the limits of legitimate power would occupy Ritter again in his later works.

In 1914 as World War I began, Ritter, who had been working as a secondary school teacher in Magdeburg, volunteered for military service. The defeat of Germany in 1918 was very difficult for him, especially since he believed that it was a mistake to replace the monarchy and its long history with a republic in Weimar that had no strong traditions or claims to power.

To avoid thinking about the problems of the Weimar republic, Ritter took an assignment from the University of Heidelberg to write its history. It was in Heidelberg that in 1921 he completed his Habilitation, the last step to becoming a professor, on this same subject. In 1924, Ritter worked briefly in Hamburg, but in 1925 he accepted an offer to teach at the University of Freiburg where he remained until his retirement as a professor emeritus in 1956.

During this period, Ritter also published his now famous Luther biography (1925), in which he portrayed Luther as an "eternal German," prompting some critics to say that he was treading a fine line between the conservative and the fascist camp. Ritter, however, was far from a fascist and did not subscribe to the view that his statements could be interpreted as racist. His Luther was not the political opportunist portrayed by Max Weber and Ernst Troeltsch. He believed that the true worth of Luther's life lay in his ability to enlighten Germans to problems within the Roman Catholic church and to improve the self-confidence of churchgoers in order to make a difference in German society and eventually in the world. Luther taught that Christian moral codes could only be applied to the individual, not to the state that had to retain and protect its power and, therefore, could be guided only by the Christian sense of its politicians. Ritter not only supported this idea but also went further, using the ideas of Friedrich Patzel and Rudolf Kjelléns of the nation as a living organism to argue that the state had a right to life, meaning to territorial expansion and economic growth. From this point of view, Ritter saw Frederick the Great's conquest of Silesia as justified, no matter what the international law of the time said.

In 1931 Ritter completed his 2-volume biography of the Prussian liberal statesman and German nationalist Baron vom Stein, whom he saw as the almost total opposite of Bismarck with regard to power politics. If Bismarck was the power politician, the "Iron Chancellor," then Stein was the moralist whose contribution was rooted more in his political attempts than in his political successes. Ritter saw Stein as an example of a politician without a sense of politics who, despite his inability, could be successful on the basis of his strong personal character.

Adolf Hitler's assumption of the office of German chancellor in 1933 was not of great concern to Ritter, who initially approved of Hitler's foreign policy. But when Hitler began to reveal his true character, through his persecution of non-Aryans and the consolidation of his power through the "coordination" of the Lutheran church to meet his political needs, Ritter was not prepared to accept these moves. As a practicing Lutheran, he joined the Confessional church which brought him into contact with the resistance movement built around the leadership of the former lord mayor of Leipzig, Carl Friedrich Goerdeler, about whom Ritter later wrote a book.

In his biography of Frederick the Great, Ritter criticized Hitler's personality and political program by emphasizing the positive traits of Frederick as compared to Hitler. On this same topic of power and morality, Ritter published the pamphlet *Machtstaat und Utopie* (National Power and Utopia, 1940) in which he argued that only countries with military security (island empires such as the UK, for example) could promote personal freedoms, while continental powers such as Germany were constantly threatened and had to maintain discipline. In this work, it is difficult to disentangle Ritter's meaning as he mediated between his own beliefs and what was allowed by Nazi censors. It is, however, safe to say that Ritter, if not a National Socialist, was a nationalist who wanted to see Germany as a strong world power.

This is evident in his later work *Staatskunst und Kriegshandwerk: das Problem des "Militarismus" in Deutschland* (1954–68; published in English as *The Sword and the Scepter: The Problem of Militarism in Germany*, 1969) which he researched in the dark days of World War II as bombs were falling on Berlin. In this work, Ritter ignored the "common man" in history and concentrated on statesmen and military leaders. True to the tradition of 19th-century German political historians, he argued that militarism in the Prussian monarchy, in the Wilhelmine empire, and in the National Socialist era could not be compared and one must view each of these periods with a proper feeling for the spirit of the age.

Shortly before Ritter's third volume was published, Fritz Fischer released his *Griff nach der Weltmacht* (1961; *Germany's Aims in the First World War*, 1967) to which Ritter took vehement exception. Ritter did not believe that Germany had desired World War I but rather that politicians in Berlin had accepted the risk of war as a possibility and that it had caught them off guard. In volume 3 (1914–17), Ritter, therefore, tried to dispute Fischer's thesis by showing that the politician Bethmann Hollweg had attempted to slow the war aims of Ludendorff and other military leaders in the high command. This picture, however, said little historically and did little to refute Fischer.

Ritter's indifference towards social and economic questions became clear in the fourth volume (1917–18). His inability to relate the victory of military over civil leaders in relationship to these other issues weakens this volume substantially. A final chapter covering the period 1918 to 1945 was planned, but Ritter died before he could complete it.

Ritter remains one of the great post-World War II German historians despite his overemphasis on politics and individual political leaders. Although his work will probably speak less to coming generations than it did to his contemporaries, it is clear that his powerful, lively style will secure him a place in the pantheon of German historians. His life and work covered a vital period in German history from the Wilhelmine empire to chancellor Konrad Adenauer's Federal Republic. This in itself makes it impossible for historians of modern Germany to ignore him.

GREGORY WEEKS

See also Fischer; Germany: 1800–1945

Biography

Gerhard Albert Ritter. Born Bad Sooden, Allendorf, 6 April 1888, son of a Lutheran minister. Attended Gütersloh (near Bielefield) Westphalia Gymnasium; studied at the universities of Munich, Leipzig, and Heidelberg, from which he received a doctorate. Taught in Carsal, 1912–14; then at Magdeburg Oberrealschule. Served in the German infantry during World War I. Lecturer, University of Heidelberg, 1918–23; professor, University of Hamburg, 1924–25; and University of Freiburg, 1925–56; detained, 1944–45. Married Gertrud Reichardt, 1919 (3 children). Died Freiburg, 1 July 1967.

Principal Writings

Die preussischen Konservativen und Bismarcks deutsche Politik, 1858 bis 1876 (The Prussian Conservatives and Bismarck's German Policy, 1858 to 1876), 1913

Luther: Gestalt und Symbol, 1925; in English as *Luther: His Life and Work*, 1963

Stein: eine politische Biographie (Stein: A Political Biography), 2 vols., 1931

Friedrich der Grosse, 1936; in English as *Frederick the Great: A Historical Profile*, 1968

Machtstaat und Utopie: vom Streit um die Dämonie der Macht seit Machiavelli und Morus, 1940, revised as *Die Dämonie der Macht: Betrachtungen über Geschichte und Wesen des Machtproblems im politischen Denken der Neuzeit*, 1947; in English as *The Corrupting Influence of Power*, 1952

Europa und die deutsche Frage: Betrachtungen über die geschichtliche Eigenart des deutschen Staatsdenkens, 1948, revised as *Das deutsche Problem*, 1962; in English as *The German Problem: Basic Questions of German Political Life, Past and Present*, 1965

Carl Goerdeler und die deutsche Widerstandsbewegung, 1954; in English as *The German Resistance: Carl Goerdeler's Struggle against Tyranny*, 1958

Staatskunst und Kriegshandwerk: das Problem des "Militarismus" in Deutschland, 4 vols., 1954–68; in English as *The Sword and the Scepter: The Problem of Militarism in Germany*, 1969–73
Der Schlieffenplan: Kritik eines Mythos, 1956; in English as *The Schlieffen Plan: Critique of a Myth*, 1958

Further Reading

Dorpalen, Andreas, "Gerhard Ritter," in Hans-Ulrich Wehler, ed., *Deutsche Historiker*, Göttingen: Vandenhoeck & Ruprecht, 1973
Dorpalen, Andreas, "Historiography as History: The Work of Gerhard Ritter," *Journal of Modern History* 34 (1962), 1–18
Jäckel, Eberhard, "Gerhard Ritter, Historiker in seiner Zeit" (Gerhard Ritter, Historian of His Time), *Geschichte in Wissenschaft und Unterricht* 16 (1967), 705–15
Levine, Norman, "Gerhard Ritter's Weltanschauung," *Review of Politics*, 30 (1968), 209–27
Maehl, William H., "Gerhard Ritter," in Hans A. Schmitt, ed., *Historians of Modern Europe*, Baton Rouge: Louisiana State University Press, 1971
Schumann, Peter, "Gerhard Ritter und die deutsche Geschichtswissenschaft nach dem Zweiten Weltkrieg" (Gerhard Ritter and German Historical Study after World War II), in *Rudolf Vierhaus zum 60. Geburtstag*, Göttingen, 1982
Schwabe, Klaus, and Rolf Reichardt, eds., *Gerhard Ritter: Ein politischer Historiker in seinen Briefen* (Gerhard Ritter: A Political Historian in His Letters), Boppard am Rhein: Boldt, 1984

Robinson, James Harvey 1863–1936

US historian of European intellectual history

Amid the varied spheres of his career as professional historian and public intellectual, a single theme united James Harvey Robinson's life work. From his innovations in historical methodology and research to his revisions of secondary and undergraduate pedagogy, Robinson endeavored to reform the modern study of history, making it relevant and useful to contemporary peoples. A quintessential Progressive, he combined astute and erudite thinking with a penchant for activism in order to challenge his professional colleagues' "obsolete" conception of history and to demonstrate written history's potential for inspiring social improvement.

After completing doctoral studies at Freiburg, Germany in 1890, Robinson accepted an appointment as lecturer of European history at the University of Pennsylvania. The university's non-traditional history department allowed Robinson ample latitude to experiment with innovative, interdisciplinary instruction and research. Among his activities at Pennsylvania, Robinson cultivated a lifelong interest in original source materials. He translated *The Constitution of the Kingdom of Prussia* (1894), complete with introduction and explanatory notes. He also helped to translate and edit an inventive project called *Translations and Reprints from the Original Sources of European History* (1894).

In 1895, Robinson began a fruitful 24-year tenure at Columbia University. There, his numerous interests were sharpened and further developed under the influence of several important progressive-minded colleagues, including Charles Beard and John Dewey. The salient feature of Robinson's intellectual evolution at Columbia was his shift from Rankean objectivity – recounting the past "as it happened" – to historical

pragmatism – recounting the past in order to serve the present. Propelled by this pragmatic approach to historical knowledge, Robinson concentrated his efforts at Columbia on the tasks of reforming historical research methods and improving historical instruction.

Robinson is most commonly identified with the "New History," his bold prescription for modern historical thought and practice. In a collection of essays by the same name (published in 1912), he assailed older, traditionally accepted notions of the past. History, he asserted, encompasses all aspects of human existence and activity, not merely military and political achievements, as most historians seemed to indicate. Thus, *The New History* incorporated the newly emerging social sciences to understand the diverse arenas of human experience. "There are other fields," noted Robinson, "in which it is essential that the investigator should know everything that is being found out about man, unless he is willing to run the risk of superficiality and error."

The New History also chided the tendency of historians to become bogged down with detailed lists of archaic names and facts. Robinson deemed it senseless to study any past event or idea with no demonstrable bearing on modern times, rejecting concepts of historical research that resemble monastic scholasticism. His Progressive ethos suggested that modern intellectuals had an obligation to promote and extend the betterment of humankind in all their academic pursuits, and historians were no less obliged to carry this burden. If history was to achieve relevance in the lives of common people, argued Robinson, it must be constructed from their unique perspective and should seek to account for the origins of social problems. Thus, one of Robinson's essays in *The New History*, "History for the Common Man," urged the study of topics such as charity organizations in the Middle Ages (tracing an incipient version of social work) and the industrialization of Europe (showing both human progress and the plight of factory workers).

History teaching in the United States at the end of the 19th century was largely comprised of rote memorization and recitation, drawn from the pages of badly written, antediluvian textbooks. Robinson worked to change this dismal predicament by advocating new methods of classroom instruction and by producing an array of freshly conceived college and secondary texts. He continued to translate and edit original source materials because he believed that students would best understand and appreciate history through directly utilizing primary documents. Among the numerous such volumes edited and translated by Robinson during his years at Columbia was *Petrarch: The First Modern Scholar and Man of Letters* (1898), a collection of writings by the Renaissance figure. His incorporation of primary sources along with a provocative, sometimes irreverent style of lecture brought national recognition to Robinson's own courses in European intellectual history at Columbia.

Robinson's first and most famous college textbook, *An Introduction to the History of Western Europe*, appeared in 1903. It brought new life to historical pedagogy, an enterprise until then dominated by unimaginative sketches of political events and tedious surveys of military expeditions. The text offered perusals of social and cultural issues, incorporated actual historical research, and communicated by using lucid and interesting prose. Thereafter, Robinson continued to produce revised and new editions of college texts, including *The Last Decade of European History and the Great War* (1918) and *The Development of Modern Europe* (1907–08, with Charles Beard). He also authored secondary texts including *Medieval and Modern Times* (1916) and *A General History of Europe* (1921), revised as *Our World Today and Yesterday* (1924).

In 1919, Robinson left Columbia University to establish the New School for Social Research, an experimental project in higher education designed to provide a climate for social scientific research unfettered by usual constraints of academic institutions. Unfortunately the New School quickly faltered, and Robinson left his post as director in 1921. However, he continued to devote significant speaking and writing energy to promote the New School's ideals of educational reform, intellectual progress, and the scientific method, writing two successful popularized studies along these lines: *The Mind in the Making* (1921) and *The Humanizing of Knowledge* (1923).

Though Robinson never produced any major piece of original research, his place in the pantheon of historians in America is secure. With an unyielding faith in human progress, he endeavored to redefine history to facilitate social reform. In iconoclastic style, he rebuked and revised obsolete and counterproductive procedures of historical teaching and writing. His espousal of pragmatism, progressivism, and social science influenced a key generation of scholarship in America, and his ambitions keenly anticipated the radical historiography of the 1970s and 1980s.

JAY D. GREEN

See also Beard; United States: Historical Writing, 20th Century

Biography

Born Bloomington, Illinois, 29 June 1863. Studied briefly at Illinois State Normal School, then traveled in Europe and worked before earning BA, Harvard University, 1887; MA 1888; PhD, University of Freiburg, 1890. Taught history at University of Pennsylvania, 1891–95; and Barnard College/Columbia University, 1895–1918. Founding director, New School for Social Research, 1919–21. Married Grace Woodville Read, 1887. Died New York City, 16 February 1936.

Principal Writings

Editor and translator, *The Constitution of the Kingdom of Prussia*, 1894
Joint editor and translator, *Translations and Reprints from the Original Sources of European History*, 1894
Editor and translator, *Petrarch: The First Modern Scholar and Man of Letters*, 1898
An Introduction to the History of Western Europe, 1903
With Charles Beard, *The Development of Modern Europe*, 2 vols., 1907–08; enlarged 1929–30
The New History: Essays Illustrating the Modern Historical Outlook, 1912
Medieval and Modern Times, 1916; revised 1926
The Last Decade of European History and the Great War, 1918
A General History of Europe, 1921; revised as *Our World Today and Yesterday*, 1924
The Mind in the Making, 1921
The Humanizing of Knowledge, 1923

Further Reading

Barnes, Harry Elmer, "James Harvey Robinson," in Howard W. Odum, ed., *American Masters of Social Science: An Approach to the Study of the Social Sciences Through the Neglected Field of Biography*, Port Washington, NY: Kennikat Press, 1926
Braeman, John, "What Is the Good of History? The Case of James Harvey Robinson," *Amerikastudien/American Studies* 30 (1985), 75–89
Crunden, Robert Morse, *Ministers of Reform: The Progressives' Achievement in American Civilization, 1889–1920*, New York: Basic Books, 1982
Hendricks, Luther Virgil, *James Harvey Robinson: Teacher of History*, New York: King's Crown Press, 1946
Novick, Peter, *That Noble Dream: The "Objectivity Question" and the American Historical Profession*, Cambridge and New York: Cambridge University Press, 1988
Ross, Dorothy, *The Origins of American Social Science*, Cambridge and New York: Cambridge University Press, 1991
Skotheim, Robert Allen, *American Intellectual Histories and Historians*, Princeton: Princeton University Press, 1966
Strout, Cushing, *The Pragmatic Revolt in American History: Carl Becker and Charles Beard*, New Haven: Yale University Press, 1958
Whelan, Michael, "James Harvey Robinson: *The New History* and the 1916 Social Studies Report," *History Teacher* 24 (1991), 191–202
White, Morton, *Social Thought in America: The Revolt Against Formalism*, New York: Viking Press, 1949; Oxford: Oxford University Press, 1976

Rock, David 1945–

British historian of Latin America

David Rock has devoted his life to the study of Argentina. His work ranges from the analysis of Argentina's political economy in the 20th century to the study of the country's authoritarian past. Through the twists and turns of his research on Argentina, one sees illustrated the changes in approaches to the study of Latin American history during the last twenty years.

Rock's most notable work is *Politics in Argentina* (1975). He wrote and researched this book during the late 1960s and early 1970s when a military government ruled in Argentina. Thus the military coup of 1962 and the development of an armed revolutionary left shaped his research. Rock raised the question of why Argentina failed to develop a stable democratic system; in order to answer this question, he examined Argentina's democratically elected governments from 1890 to 1930.

Rock argued in *Politics in Argentina* that the middle class, which achieved control of the Argentine state from 1916 until 1930, was not an independent class and that it was highly dependent on the landed oligarchy. The implication of this argument is that the middle class never obtained an independent voice in the Argentine political system. Rock linked the absence of middle class autonomy to the failure of democracy in Argentina. He suggested that the Radical party – traditionally viewed as the middle class party – was in reality a coalition of the confederation of landed and middle-class sectors, which was based on a shared economic interest in maintaining an export-based economy.

Rock paid close attention to the importance of British economic interests, suggesting that the decline of British economic and political power brought about the loss of Argentina's privileged economic place in the world. Rock argued that the depression of the 1930s resulted in a military coup due to the diverging interests of the middle class and the landowning elite. It is clear that he strongly believed that Argentina's export-based economy determined its political structures, or, in other words, that Argentina's economic dependency led to its failed political development.

Rock's concern for Argentina's unfulfilled promise of economic development is a theme in his edited work *Argentina in the Twentieth Century* (1975): "Now she is more frequently seen as just another bankrupt and stagnant, weak and exploited corner of 'South America,' compelled to exist in the future, as she has now done for so long in the past, in a maelstrom of disorganization and decay." This quote illustrates Rock's conception that Argentina was somehow trapped in its deficient past. Rock belongs to the generation of scholars of the 1970s who resorted to the dependency paradigm to explain Latin America's political and economic problems. This paradigm suggested that Latin America's underdevelopment was a consequence of the development of other areas, such as Britain and the United States. According to this theory Latin American countries were assigned to a peripheral position in the world economy; "dependent economies" required a flawed political system under which there could be no real democratic participation.

Rock's next work, *Argentina, 1516–1982* (1985), ventured back in time to explore the roots of Argentina's problems. The military government's gross violations of human rights provided the context for this research. Rock did not enter into the debate on whether Perón's government was responsible for Argentina's economic decline and political troubles by the 1980s, although much of the controversy in Argentine historiography centers around the impact of Perón's regime. As he stated in his introduction, Rock wished to lay out the long-term patterns of Argentina's historical development. He characterized Argentina as an essentially "colonial" society. The themes of dependent elites and a weak middle class which Rock had begun to elaborate in *Politics in Argentina* were developed further in this monograph. Rock tried to make the case that because Argentine elites had always been dependent since the colonial era, the entire country was equally dependent.

Authoritarian Argentina (1993) represents a newer approach to history because Rock no longer centered his analysis on the political economy, but attempted to analyze the discourse and ideology of the nationalist right. In examining more than 100 years of nationalist ideology, Rock located the origins of the doctrine in Latin Europe, arguing against historians who linked the right in Argentina with Nazi Germany. He contended that the nationalist movement in Argentina never received much popular support and was unable to adapt to change. This weakness led the movement to resort to force and dictatorship. *Authoritarian Argentina* offered a new understanding of the emergence of the right through Rock's long-term perspective and sound research.

Some historians have criticized Rock for his *longue durée* approach and emphasis on continuities, arguing that agency and processes of change are overlooked. However, it is certain that Rock has made a solid contribution to the history of Argentina.

BRETT TROYAN

See also Argentina; Latin America: National

Biography

David Peter Rock. Born Blackburn, Lancashire, 8 April 1945. Taught briefly, Rosegrove School, Burnley, 1964. Attended St. John's College, Cambridge University, MA 1970, PhD 1971. Research officer, Institute of Latin American Studies, London, 1970–74, assistant secretary, 1974–77; taught, rising to professor, University of California, Santa Barbara, from 1978. Married Rosalind Louise Farrar, 1968 (2 sons).

Principal Writings

Editor, *Argentina in the Twentieth Century*, 1975
Politics in Argentina, 1890–1930: The Rise and Fall of Radicalism, 1975
Argentina, 1516–1987: From Spanish Colonization to Alfonsín, revised edition, 1987
Authoritarian Argentina: The Nationalist Movement, Its History, and Its Impact, 1993
Editor, *Latin America in the 1940s: War and Postwar Transitions*, 1994

Rodinson, Maxime 1915–

French Islamicist

Maxime Rodinson is a leading Orientalist, linguist, ethnographer, historian, philologist, sociologist, and historian who has specialized in Semitic languages (especially Old Ethiopic and Old South Arabian), and early Islamic history. An unusually eclectic scholar, he has written on the influence of Islamic countries on the West in the Middle Ages, on vehicles, on cookery, and even on the liver in Muslim countries.

His first major study, for which he received the *diplôme* in 1955, was *Magie, médecine, et possession à Gondar* (Magic, Medicine, and Possession in Gondar, 1967). This study was a translation of and commentary on an Amharic manuscript brought to France by a French anthropological mission that had traveled from Dakar to Djibouti in 1931–33. The manuscript was a register of people who performed magic and medical cures in Gondar, a town in Ethiopia. Rodinson later studied the *zar* (exorcism ceremonies) in Cairo.

Rodinson was a member of the Communist party until 1958, and his Marxist formation has influenced his historical and sociological thinking. His widely-read book, *Mahomet* (1961, *Mohammed*, 1971), an iconoclastic biography of the prophet Muhammad, demonstrates this most clearly. According to Rodinson himself, his interest in Muhammad at times drew inspiration from the lives of people such as Lenin and Stalin, men were men of conviction who became heads of state forced by circumstances to resort to the use of power to further their causes. To Rodinson the idea of reforming humanity, of establishing a community of believers as a political entity, was the project of both Muhammad and Stalin, God or no God.

In answer to a question much asked in the 1960s, "Is there something in Islam that impedes the spread of capitalism?", a question posed in response to Max Weber's famous though often oversimplified and misunderstood argument that Protestantism fostered the development of capitalism, Rodinson published *Islam et capitalisme* (1966, *Islam and Capitalism*, 1974). Rodinson argued that no religion was necessarily favorable or unfavorable to capitalism, because capitalism developed outside the sphere of religion. For example, when financial interests necessitated it, Muslim communities did not hesitate to collect interest, even though the Quran forbids it.

In *Marxisme et monde musulman* (1972, *Marxism and the Muslim World*, 1979), a compilation of his articles, he argued that dissension, protest, and ideas of revolt have always existed but that they need theories to shape them, to give birth to militant organizations and actions. So when Stalinist or Marxist ideas were in circulation they were as influential in Islamic countries as elsewhere. At present, he observes that Islamic or Islamist theories are shaping political protest movements in many Muslim societies.

His books *Israel and the Arabs* (1968) and *Israel: A Colonial-Settler State?* (1973), written in response to the events of 1967, were a critique of Zionism and its treatment of Palestinians. *Les Arabes* (1979, *The Arabs*, 1981), written in response to several rather superficial and stereotypic studies of Arab identity, was a erudite and carefully nuanced answer to the question "who are the Arabs?"

Rodinson's *Europe and the Mystique of Islam* (1980, translated 1987) consisted of the important essays "Western Views of the Muslim World" and "A New Approach to Arab and Islamic Studies." The first essay traced the evolution of Western views of the Muslim world and the development of Orientalism, the central tradition of Islamic studies. The second essay analyzed the current state of the field and encouraged students of Middle Eastern history to read the great Orientalist works. He urged students to study non-classical periods of history neglected by Orientalists, popular attitudes and customs, and to integrate current events into the history of the Middle East within the wider framework of world history, sociology, and anthropology.

Rodinson is currently writing his memoirs, compiling his articles on Islam and politics, and drafting a book comparing the political and organizational structure of Islam to that of other religious movements.

NANCY GALLAGHER

Biography
Born Paris, 26 January 1915. Studied at the Ecole des Langues Orientales, Paris, receiving his baccalauréat, 1936. Fellow, Caisse Nationale de la Recherche Scientifique, 1937–39. Member, Communist party, 1937–58. Served in French army, 1939–40. Worked in the (Free) French antiquities service for Syria and Lebanon, 1940–47; librarian, department of printed Oriental works, Bibliothèque Nationale, 1947–55; chair, Ethiopic and south Arabian studies, Ecole Pratique des Hautes Etudes, 1955–84. Married Geneviève Gendron, 1937 (2 sons, 1 daughter).

Principal Writings
Mahomet, 1961; in English as *Mohammed*, 1971
Islam et capitalisme, 1966; in English as *Islam and Capitalism*, 1974
Magie, médecine, et possession à Gondar (Magic, Medicine, and Possession in Gondar), 1967
Israël et le refus arabe: 75 ans d'histoire, 1968; in English as *Israel and the Arabs*, 1968
Marxisme et monde musulman, 1972; in English as *Marxism and the Muslim World*, 1979
Israel: A Colonial-Settler State?, 1973
Les Arabes, 1979; in English as *The Arabs*, 1981

La Fascination de l'Islam: suivi de, Le Seigneur bourguignon et l'esclave sarrasin, 1980; in English as *Europe and the Mystique of Islam*, 1987
Peuple juif ou problème juif? (Jewish People or Jewish Problem?), 1981
Cult, Ghetto and State: The Persistence of the Jewish Question, 1983
De Pythagore à Lénine: des activismes idéologiques (From Pythagoras to Lenin), 1993

Further Reading
Digard, Jean-Pierre, *Le Cuisinier et le philosophe: hommage à Maxime Rodinson* (The Chef and the Philosopher: Homage to Maxime Rodinson), Paris: Maisonneuve et Larose, 1982
Gallagher, Nancy, ed., *Approaches to the History of the Middle East: Interviews with Leading Middle East Historians*, Reading, Berkshire: Ithaca Press, 1994
Robin, Christian, ed., *Mélanges linguistiques offerts à Maxime Rodinson par ses élèves, ses collègues et ses amis* (Linguistic Selections Offered to Maxime Rodinson by His Students, Colleagues, and Friends), Paris: Geuthner, 1985

Rodney, Walter 1942–1980
Guyanese historian of Africa

Walter Rodney was a radical scholar who wed Marxist politics to historical scholarship. His writings helped to reverse some historical misconceptions held as a legacy from the colonial era. His works gave pride and self-respect to the demoralized peoples of Africa and the African diaspora who had been "dehistorified" by the slave trade and colonial eras. Even though Rodney was an intellectual, he also remained close to the working classes of Guyana and wrote about their plight. Despite his premature death by an assassin's bomb, he made many meaningful contributions to scholarship.

Rodney began his career as a historian of Africa. His first work, a revision of his doctoral thesis, *A History of the Upper Guinea Coast, 1545–1800* (1970), primarily examined the formation and consequences of the Atlantic slave trade in the area stretching from Cape Verde in contemporary Senegal to Cape Mount in contemporary Liberia. Rodney claimed that studying precolonial African history following the model of the nation-state had no justification. Nation-states were a late 19th-century creation, and colonial boundaries should not be projected backwards in time. He selected this region of Africa as his focus of study because of its precolonial history and its early contacts with Europeans.

The book began by describing the society and culture of the coast in the mid-16th century. It was Rodney's contention that it was European demand for slaves that created large reservoirs of slaves in the area. This in turn affected demography, diplomacy, society, culture, and nearly every aspect of Guinean life. The violent contradictions that resulted from African-European relations were resolved to the detriment of the societies of the region. Rodney's interpretation was a reversal of previous scholarship, which claimed that Europeans simply siphoned off pre-existing pools of slaves held by African elites. Rodney held that this interpretation was simply a means for Europeans, and colonial scholarship, to justify the slave trade by claiming that it was actually Africans who created it. Such an attempt at overturning existing beliefs was indeed considered radical for the time and fitted in with other scholarship of the 1960s which dispelled colonial myths.

Perhaps the work for which Rodney is best known is *How Europe Underdeveloped Africa* (1972); it was well received by scholars across the globe and has been translated into several languages including German, Portuguese, and Japanese. The work forms part of the foundation of Afro-Marxism because it rejected the Marxist idea that class struggle is the motive force behind history. Rodney picked up this idea from Amilcar Cabral and Che Guevara. Marxism states that history does not start until the existence of class struggle. These intellectuals stated that history can exist before class struggle, as is clear from much of the history of precolonial Africa. This is not to say that they did not find class struggle important, they just did not hold it to be evidence of possessing history. From this proposition, Rodney then demonstrated that Africa was involved in the process of development long before the arrival of Europeans. Further, the form of capitalism that took hold in Africa was of a much different character than that which evolved in Europe. Enslavement, forced labor, cash crops, and authoritarianism were the characteristics of capitalism in Africa which left a legacy of antidemocratic practice, poverty, food shortages, and technological stagnation. It was Europe that interrupted and stunted the path of Africa's development; Europe certainly did not initiate development. The only solution for contemporary African development, claimed Rodney, was a radical break with the international capitalist system. It was foreign investment that had kept Africa economically underdeveloped over the past five centuries, and only an alternate path would allow Africa to retrieve its means of self-development.

Rodney also wrote on the working classes of Guyana. *A History of the Guyanese Working People, 1881–1905* (1981) and *Guyanese Sugar Plantations in the Late Nineteenth Century* (1979) both investigated the material plight of Guyanese workers. Class struggle was analyzed within the framework of peasants, plantation workers, coolies, miners, and the emerging middle class. While Guyana did not experience colonialism in the same way that Africa did, Rodney contended that both were subject to control by a neocolonial elite which kept power from the masses. Moreover, Guyana was also split by the issue of race. Guyana received a large number of South Asian indentured workers in the late 19th and early 20th centuries, thus receiving another source of social division. Rodney claimed that race, like class, was also manipulated by the elite to maintain control of the country and ensure the exploitation of the working class. Race was a question of history and society, not of biology. Here too, Rodney differed from orthodox Marxist interpretation, in his use of race as a tool of analysis.

While Rodney's brief life did not permit him to be as prolific as some scholars, his legacy is a strong one. During the Cold War era his was among the most powerful radical voices to speak out against the capitalist system on behalf of Africa and its peoples. However, in the Caribbean, he did not limit his support of the lower classes to the people of African descent, but rather supported all Guyanese in their struggle for greater material wellbeing. While a Marxist, he did not entirely toe the orthodox party line, as evidenced by his study of race and class struggle. But he was more than an armchair radical and in his political involvement he practiced what he preached. Rodney laid the groundwork for much radical scholarship that has been written since the 1960s.

TOYIN FALOLA and JOEL E. TISHKEN

See also Imperial

Biography

Born British Guiana [now Guyana], 1942. Taught at the University College of the West Indies to 1968; University of Dar es Salaam, Tanzania, 1969–72; appointed professor, University of Guyana, 1972, but appointment revoked due to political pressure. Leader, Working People's Alliance, 1979–80. Assassinated by a car bomb, Georgetown, Guyana, 13 June 1980.

Principal Writings

"African Slavery and Other Forms of Social Oppression on the Upper Guinea Coast in the Context of the Atlantic Slave Trade," *Journal of African History* 7 (1966), 431–43

"European Activities and African Reaction in Angola," in Terence O. Ranger, ed., *Aspects of Central African History*, 1968

The Groundings with My Brothers, 1969

A History of the Upper Guinea Coast, 1545–1800, 1970

How Europe Underdeveloped Africa, 1972; revised edition 1981

"Africa in Europe and the Americas" and "The Guinea Coast," in Richard Gray, ed., *The Cambridge History of Africa*, vol. 4: *From c.1600 to c.1790*, 1975

Editor, *Guyanese Sugar Plantations in the Late Nineteenth Century: A Contemporary Description from the "Argosy,"* 1979

A History of the Guyanese Working People, 1881–1905, 1981

"People's Power, No Dictator," *Latin American Perspectives* 8 (1981), 64–78

Further Reading

Alpers, Edward A., and Pierre-Michel Fontaine, eds., *Walter Rodney: Revolutionary and Scholar: A Tribute*, Los Angeles: Center for Afro-American Studies and African Studies Center, 1982

Bly, Viola Mattavous, "Walter Rodney and Africa," *Journal of Black Studies* 16 (1985), 115–30

Campbell, Horace, "The Impact of Walter Rodney and Progressive Scholars on the Dar es Salaam School," *Social and Economic Studies* 40 (1991), 99–135

Campbell, Trevor A., "The Making of an Organic Intellectual: Walter Rodney (1942–1980)," *Latin American Perspectives* 8 (1981), 49–63

Hansen, William W., "Walter Rodney: An Exemplary Life," *Monthly Review* 32 (1981), 24–31

Lewis, Linden, "The Groundings of Walter Rodney," *Race and Class* 33 (1991), 71–82

Lewis, Rupert, "Walter Rodney Speaks: The Making of an African Intellectual," *Social and Economic Studies* 41 (1992), 223–27

Standing, Guy, "Walter Rodney: A Tribute," *Journal of Peasant Studies* 10 (1983), 250–52

Rodrigues, José Honório 1913–1987

Brazilian historian

The Brazilian historian José Honório Rodrigues was born in Rio de Janeiro in 1913. He attended the former National Law School in Rio de Janeiro from which he graduated in 1937. Additional advanced study in the United States (1943–44) and

Britain (1950) completed his formal education. He once described his training as basically Anglo-American.

Rodrigues' work spanned nearly five decades from 1940 to 1987, and is comparable to that of Francisco Adolfo de Varnhagen (1816–78) and João Capistrano de Abreu (1853–1927) in range and importance. Like his famous predecessors, Rodrigues was largely self-taught in Brazilian history – courses on the history of Brazil had not yet entered the curricula of national institutions of higher education when he was a student in the mid-1930s. Like them, he was an inexhaustible researcher with unrivaled knowledge of archival sources and historical methodology. Like them, he renovated and revised the writing of Brazilian history at a time when it was largely in the hands of amateurs or traditionalists committed to extoling the contributions of Brazil's political and economic elites. Rodrigues gets credit for having established a nationalist-populist school of history during the 1950s which made the Brazilian people – all of them – protagonists of history, and which exalted the right of historians to interpret and make judgments. By this time, he had come to believe that historians could not withdraw to redoubts of erudition, but had to participate in the great social and political movements of their time. The best history was contemporary history with the scholar projecting into the past the anxieties and popular aspirations of the present. Rodrigues never deviated from these views during the rest of his long and active intellectual life.

Rodrigues' contributions may be placed in three categories: as archivist and editor; as the writer of path-breaking, large-scale works on Brazilian historiography and historical methodology; and as the prolific author of well researched and often polemical essays and books. In each instance, he consistently demonstrated a mastery of thematic content and analysis, of sources primary and secondary, and of critical bibliographic and textual apparatus. Not the least of his gifts was the ability to express himself in vigorous, stimulating language that won him a place among Brazil's leading prose stylists.

As professor of diplomatic history at the Rio Branco Institute, Ministry of Foreign Affairs (1946–55), and director of the National Archive (1958–64), Rodrigues selected, edited, and oversaw publication of 39 volumes in the Documentos Históricos series. He also edited the collected works of Capistrano de Abreu. Rodrigues' high regard for Capistrano de Abreu is a key to understanding his own work. Capistrano de Abreu represented a reaction to Varnhagen who had been the first master of Brazilian historical writing, and who had used archival sources to write the magisterial, chronological História geral do Brasil (General History of Brazil, 1854–57), which aimed to show how the Portuguese overcame all obstacles in order to establish a productive and territorially immense Brazil. In criticizing Varnhagen, Capistrano de Abreu refocused attention away from European colonization and the Atlantic coast to settlement of the vast interior of South America and to the emergence of a Brazilian people comprised of indigenous, African, and Portuguese people. On this Brazilian frontier, and in a process that occurred over three centuries , these people, acting in close contact with one another, became something new and different. Rodrigues always honored Capistrano de Abreu as the first historian to decolonize the writing of Brazilian history, and to place the whole of the Brazilian people, not an elite minority, at the center of historical inquiry.

Rodrigues' contributions to Brazilian historiography are best seen in a trilogy of works: Teoria da história do Brasil (Theory of the History of Brazil, 1949), A pesquisa histórica no Brasil (Historical Research in Brazil, 1962), and História da história do Brasil (History of the History of Brazil, 1979–88). These are long and dense volumes of great erudition written for serious scholars. They may be said to constitute three enormous handbooks that summarize what Rodrigues felt had been done and needed still to be done in the production of Brazilian history, and what critical learning and skills were needed by researchers.

Finally, Rodrigues is the author of numerous essays and books for students of history and the general public. Brasil e Africa (1961; Brazil and Africa, 1965) studied Brazilian links to Africa and recalled that during Brazilian history, most of the population has not been white, but black and mestizo. Brazil and Africa virtually founded the field of Brazilian-African relations in Brazilian historiography. Two important books, Aspirações nacionais (1963; The Brazilians, 1967), and Conciliação e reforma no Brasil (Conciliation and Reform in Brazil, 1965) discussed Brazil's missing revolution. Rodrigues argued that Brazil has never experienced, during its independent existence since 1822, a revolution that would sweep aside the vestiges of colonialism and traditional elite resistance to necessary reforms, and would respond to the needs of the illiterate, impoverished, and almost completely unrepresented Brazilian majority. Elite interests – especially those of large landowners, and certainly slaveholders until 1888 – always prevailed or were protected. The government never dared to distribute uncultivated land to landless peasants while free public education has not been widely available to the masses, at least half of whom continued to be functionally illiterate. Meanwhile, poor or destitute people who rose in rebellions typically suffered cruel and murderous repression. All such theses were amply supported by myriad examples drawn from Brazilian history. A 5-volume, thematic history of the Brazilian independence period, Independência (Independence, 1975–76) is the major historical work of Rodrigues' late maturity and repels the argument that Brazilian independence was a peaceful and amicable divorce from Portugal. Rather it involved considerable bloodshed, and a mobilization of armed forces as numerous as in any Latin American war for independence.

Brazilian Marxist intellectuals from the mid-1950s to the mid-1980s sometimes looked on Rodrigues as a representative of petty bourgeois radical Jacobin thinking that came to prominence during a period of intense left-wing nationalism and popular mobilization between 1946 and 1964. However, his consistent emphasis on the importance of full liberty for all classes, on popular aspirations for education and land distribution, and on full participation for all groups, including the poor and illiterate, places his work at the center of present-day Brazilian political discourse. And his fervent economic and cultural nationalism, as well as his critique of a cruel and insensitive elite, maintain their contemporary resonance.

PHILIP EVANSON

See also Latin America: National

Biography

Born Rio de Janeiro, 20 September 1913. Received degrees in law and social science, University of Brazil, 1937, with some graduate study, Escola Superior de Guera, 1955. Director of publications, National Library, 1946–58; director, National Archive, 1958–64; executive director, Institute of International Relations, 1963–68. Parallel academic career: professor of diplomatic history and Brazilian history, Rio Branco Institute, Brazilian Ministry of Foreign Affairs, 1946–55; University of the State of Rio de Janeiro, 1953–83; professor, Federal University of Rio de Janeiro, 1979–87. Married Lêda Boechat, lawyer and writer, 1941. Died 1987.

Principal Writings

Civilização holandesa no Brasil (Dutch Civilization in Brazil), 1940

Teoria da história do Brasil: introdução metodológica (Theory of the History of Brazil), 1949; revised 1957

Brasil e Africa: outro horizonte, 1961; in English as *Brazil and Africa*, 1965

A pesquisa histórica no Brasil: sua evolução e problemas atuais (Historical Research in Brazil: Its Evolution and Present Day Problems), 1962

Aspirações nacionais: interpretação histórico-politico, 1963; in English as *The Brazilians: Their Character and Aspirations*, 1967

Conciliação e reforma no Brasil: um desafio histórico-cultural (Conciliation and Reform in Brazil), 1965

História e historiadores do Brasil (History and Historians of Brazil), 1965

Interêsse nacional e política externa (National Interest and Foreign Policy), 1966

Vida e História (Life and History), 1966

A Assembléia Constituinte de 1823, (The Constituent Assembly of 1823), 1974

Independência: revolução e contra-revolução (Independence: Revolution and Counter Revolution), 5 vols., 1975–76

História da história do Brasil (History of the History of Brazil), 2 vols. in 3, 1979–88

História combatente (Combative History), 1982

Tempo e sociedade (Time and Society), 1986

Further Reading

Rodrigues, Lêda Boechat, ed., *Bibliografia de José Honório Rodrigues*, Rio de Janeiro, 1956

Rodrigues, Lêda Boechat, and José Octávio de Arruda Mello, *José Honório Rodrigues: um historiador na trincheira* (José Honório Rodrigues: An Historian in the Trenches), Rio de Janeiro: Civilização Brasileira, 1994

Roger of Wendover d. 1236

English monastic chronicler

It is fitting that what little we know about the 13th-century chronicler Roger of Wendover should have come down to us from his successor at St. Albans, Matthew Paris, in whose long shadow Wendover's writings have since remained. Yet between them and those who continued to write history at St. Albans in the 13th and 14th centuries, they have furnished a significant proportion of our chronicles of medieval England. Despite being the effective founder of this important school of historical writing, little can be said with any certainty of either Roger himself or his chronicle. He wrote his one known work, the *Flores historiarum* (Flowers of History), during the first third of the 13th century in the monastery of St. Albans where he was a member of the Benedictine order. The *Flores* was a massive history, covering, in varied depth, the period from the Creation to the year 1235, and dealing with both England and Europe. It was probably begun after 1201 and possibly as late as 1231.

What Roger has left us is a complicated chronicle constructed from a tangle of sources. He is an original authority for events after about 1200, and most of what he has to say thereafter seems not to be drawn from other extant sources. Before 1200, much of the *Flores* was closely based on the work of chroniclers such as Roger of Hoveden and Ralph of Diceto, supplemented by the writings of Henry of Huntingdon and Ralph of Coggeshall among others. An added complication is that many historians have argued that Roger played no part in composing most of the pre-1200 sections of the *Flores*. Two abbots of St. Albans during the late 12th century, John de Cella and Walter of St. Albans, have been proposed as possible compilers of these portions and Roger has been cast as a copyist who borrowed the early text and transcribed it into the *Flores* to supply the narrative up to 1200. Other historians, notably Maurice Powicke and V.H. Galbraith, rejected the existence of such a rump "St. Albans compilation." Both the cases for and against its existence remain unproven.

Whether as the sole moving spirit or part-copyist, Roger of Wendover effectively founded the school of chronicle writing at St. Albans which was to flourish over the next two hundred years: it was Roger who wrote the sections of the *Flores* that are independent of other known sources, giving a largely original treatment of the reigns of John and Henry III. He said that he drew his material from many sources "just as flowers of many colours are gathered from many fields," telling his readers that he would "kindle in them a love of reading" and thus turn them into "diligent students." These phrases provided a justification for the writing of history that was commonly expressed by chroniclers: to instruct the faithful by supplying edifying examples. Roger noted in the preface, "the lives of good men are set forth for the imitation of succeeding times; and the examples of evil men, when they occur, are not to be followed, but to be shunned."

The complications of how the *Flores* was put together make it difficult to know when we are hearing Roger's voice or when we are hearing that of another compiler. In the sections for the period after 1200, when we can be confident that Roger himself is writing, a detailed narrative of political and ecclesiastical history unfurls. These two themes comprise the mainsprings of the narrative, but such preoccupations are shot-through with digressions and *marginalia* such as miracle stories, visions of the next world, tales about appearances of demons, and the evils of practicing magic. Roger, like so many of his contemporary chroniclers, seasoned his narrative liberally with tales of the marvelous, miraculous and demonic.

Roger had strong views on both secular and ecclesiastical politics. He was a trenchant critic of king John, using what Antonia Gransden has called "homiletic invective" in his attacks on him and backing baronial action to constrain the king. In particular, he singled out what he saw to be John's arbitrariness, bursts of temper, financial extortions, and willingness to be led astray by poor counsel. Roger could be similarly critical of the failings of his ecclesiastical superiors. Despite this, he was generally more measured in his criticisms and less given to outbursts of vitriol than his successor Matthew Paris. He is also a more difficult chronicler to read and understand, seldom explaining what he believed to be the cause of an event, being content simply to record it. His unwillingness to betray anything of himself in his writing and the lack of any distinct prose style combine with this to make him one of the more shadowy and enigmatic writers of English history.

CARL WATKINS

See also Britain: Anglo-Saxon; Paris

Biography

Probably from Wendover in Buckinghamshire. Took priestly orders; was prior of Belvoir, Leicestershire, an offshoot of St. Albans, before 1219; returned to St. Albans, where he became historiographer, c.1231. Died St. Albans, 6 May 1236.

Principal Writings

Flores historiarum, c.1201–31; in English as *Flowers of History*, 2 vols., 1849; reprinted 1968

The Rolls Series edition of Matthew Paris's *Chronica majora* prints Roger of Wendover's *Flores* in small print for the sections where Paris used Roger's material almost verbatim. This represents the most accurate edition to date of Roger.

Further Reading

Galbraith, Vivian Hunter, *Roger of Wendover and Matthew Paris*, Glasgow: Jackson, 1944

Gransden, Antonia, *Historical Writing in England*, vol. 1: c.550 to c.1307, London: Routledge, and Ithaca, NY: Cornell University Press, 1974

Holt, J.C., "The St. Albans Chroniclers and Magna Carta," *Transactions of the Royal Historical Society* 5th series, 14 (1964), 67–88

Kay, R., "Roger of Wendover's Last Annal," *English Historical Review* 84 (1969), 779–85

Roman Empire

Petrarch wrote that "all history was but the praise of Rome" and indeed, Western historical writing since the Renaissance has exhibited an obsession with Rome and its empire. Analysis of this subject began, of course, in the period itself with such writers as Polybius, Livy, Suetonius, Tacitus, Plutarch, and Cassius Dio, many of whom were provincials and others, such as Josephus and Luke, who represented the fringe. As a group they exhibited a variety of political, teleological, and pedagogical perspectives that, ultimately, laid foundations for modern historical analysis. Renaissance studies were focused on establishing the cultural, political, and religious roots of Europe. Analysis of texts, whether literary, legal, or Christian, emerged as central to this project. By the 18th century, however, historical analysis had taken on a more critical approach, stressing the otherness of the Roman past. English and German scholars became particularly interested in history as a "scientific" endeavor including new archaeological evidence. Yet, these same scholars, writing in the context of European imperialism, retained strong emphases on political and philosophical lessons not unlike those of their predecessors.

It was in this context that modern historical writing on the Roman empire began. Edward Gibbon wrote his ambitious work, *The History of the Decline and Fall of the Roman Empire* (1776–88), a 6-volume treatment covering the rise of Augustus to the Vandal sack of Rome in 410 CE. While he espoused an ideal of objective analysis, his "causes" of Rome's demise bore striking resemblance to the parliamentary politics of imperial Britain. Among these he identified an overextended empire, immoderate greatness, demagoguery, a loss of rule of law and, perhaps most importantly, the destruction of cultural unity through the influences of barbarians and a politicized Christianity. Gibbon's work reflected the politics of his day but, of broader importance, it represented the themes and assumptions that would dominate historical writing on the Roman empire well into the 20th century.

Similarly, the 19th-century German scholar Theodor Mommsen, a product of German nationalism, understood the study of Rome to be the study of the Roman state, its institutions and classes, rather than individuals or philosophies. His research included analysis of inscriptions as well as Justinian's *Corpus iuris civilis* and the *Res gestae* of Augustus. Hence, in his 3-volume work, *Römisches Staatsrecht* (Roman Penal Law, 1887–88), Mommsen provided a juridical analysis of republican and imperial Rome in which he produced what he understood to be the Roman constitution. Saller has shown that here he spoke of "parties," and of Scipio as "liberal" or Cato as "conservative," using language that reflected more his own political situation than the patronal system that would define imperial Roman politics. Yet Mommsen's influence was tremendous, as found in Eduard Meyer's *Caesars Monarchie und das Principat des Pompeius* (Caesar's Monarchy and Pompey's Principate, 1918), as well as the American L.R. Taylor's *Party Politics in the Age of Caesar* (1949). Mommsen provided much good scholarship while also cementing a legal-political perspective in the study of the empire that suggested a consistent, monolithic structure in it.

The most important challenge to Mommsen came in 1939 with the publication of Ronald Syme's *The Roman Revolution*. Syme utilized prosopography, a methodology known to Mommsen and developed in Germany by Edmund Groag and Arthur Stein's *Prosopographia Imperii Romani* (Prosopography of Imperial Rome, 1933–66) and Friedrich Münzer's *Römische Adelsparteien und Adelsfamilien* (Roman Noble Factions and Families, 1920). This approach focused on biographies of the ruling class, their marriages, friendships, and political debts, with the assumption that this class was most significant during the Augustan "revolution" at which time Rome became an imperial state. Syme rejected Mommsen's constitutional interpretation of innovation and postulated that the "revolution" had been a seizure of power perpetrated by a demagogue with aid and abetment from conspirators within the oligarchy. Syme's method influenced a number of scholars who (like M.W. Hoffman-Lewis) either sought a synthesis with the Mommsen approach or generally constituted a separate school like John Cook, Colin Wells, and Fergus Millar. Quite prominent in this method has been Géza Alföldy whose *Römische Statuen in Venetia et Histria* (Roman Statues in Venice and Romania, 1984), illustrated the attention to detail required by prosopography to build an adequate database of biographical material. Alföldy's *Römische Sozialgeschichte* (1975; *The Social History of Rome*, 1985) also revealed the tensions that have developed in the 20th century surrounding the extent to which this method might be considered social history.

Critics have noted the limited – elite – scope of evidence in prosopography and its essential affinity with the Mommsen approach.

Syme's definition of "revolution" has also been criticized because the oligarchy, largely contiguous with the pre-Augustan elite, retained control. Because little change came for the lower levels of society Santo Mazzarino in *L'impero romano* (The Roman Empire, 1973), identified this transformation as a "bourgeois revolution." In *The Senate of Imperial Rome* (1984), R.J.A. Talbert affirmed that, while membership changed, the senate remained the political organ of the elite, with mixed dependence on the emperor. It has also been broadly noted that Syme's work was heavily influenced by Hitler's rise to power. That Syme's second great study was a 2-volume work on *Tacitus* (1958) points to his bias against Augustus and the Principate, disregarding positive imperial voices as found in Claudia Kuntze's *Zur Darstellung des Kaisers Tiberius und seiner Zeit bei Velleius Paterculus* (The Portrayals of Tiberius and His Time According to Velleius Paterculus, 1985). Such questions regarding ancient political tensions and perceptions of the empire have been widely discussed in Ramsay MacMullen's *Enemies of the Roman Order* (1966) and Kurt Raaflaub's *Opposition et résistances à l'empire d'Auguste à Trajan* (Opposition and Resistance in the Empire from Augustus to Trajan, 1987).

Despite certain inadequacies, the prosopographic approach helped to establish broader discourse by steering the field toward more complex treatments of the empire. Even traditional studies, such as Arnaldo Momigliano's *Alien Wisdom* (1975), J.P.V.D. Balsdon's *Romans and Aliens* (1979), Fergus Millar's *The Emperor in the Roman World* (1977), and Andrew Lintott's *Imperium Romanum: Politics and Administration* (1993), illustrate the diversity of political and cultural relations within the empire. For example, the complexity of the imperial cult, or cults, has been adequately illustrated by S.R.F. Price's *Rituals and Power: The Roman Imperial Cult in Asia Minor* (1984) and Duncan Fishwick's *The Imperial Cult in the Latin West* (1987) against the older, monolithic model, L.R. Taylor's *The Divinity of the Roman Emperor* (1931). Even in numismatics, coins being an important vehicle of imperial propaganda, assumptions of central control and consistent themes have been re-evaluated by R.A.G. Carson and C.H.V. Sutherland, and by B. Levick. With this progression has come variety in methodology and in fields of interest. By the late 20th century legal/political topics ceased to dominate the study of imperial Rome.

Economic studies offered more complex pictures of the Empire. M.P. Charlesworth, Tenney Frank, as well as Michael Rostovtzeff began to illustrate the intricate network that existed between trading partners within and beyond the borders of Rome. Mortimer Wheeler's *Rome Beyond the Imperial Frontiers* (1954) assisted in developing a model of interaction with foreign partners that had begun as early as 1938 with O.H. Bedford's "The Silk Trade of China with the Roman Empire," and later detailed for India by Vimala Begley and R.D. DePuma's *Rome and India: The Ancient Sea Trade* (1991). These studies described an empire that was hegemonic rather than monolithic, balancing political and economic powers that covered a variety of cultures and geographic locations. It was a system that could be flexible and practical as well as unstable.

Such conclusions demanded reanalysis of the Roman military and frontier. While the military was certainly active in securing "borders" and in maintaining the power of the emperor, the interaction of economy, military, and frontier produced "border regions" that were complex, vibrant, and often shifting, rather than static and linear. The empire was more than a capital with provinces, it also contained cities, kingdoms, and states, generally positive toward Rome and the stability that it could offer. Despite attempts by Edward Luttwack in *The Grand Strategy of the Roman Empire* (1976) and others such as Jochen Bleicken to assert a consistent imperial modus operandi and administration, the empire has come to be seen by most, particularly Fergus Millar and A.D. Lee, as a serendipitous and pragmatic affair. Moving away from the Mommsen understanding of the empire, broader studies such as Barry Cunliffe's *Greeks, Romans and Barbarians* (1988) have produced more complex "spheres of interaction" and "center-peripheral" relationships.

While exploring these relationships scholarly interests also turned to other areas of economic activity. Slave labor was dominant in the empire along with the various forms of violence that maintained such a system. Yet slavery was only a part of the whole, with tenant farming and other possibilities making up a complex ancient economy.

And, of course, an important shift toward social history reflected the cultural concerns of late 20th-century Western society. The position of women in the economic and social structure of the Empire found expression in an idealistic study by J.P.V.D. Balsdon, *Roman Women: Their History and Habits* (1963). However, it was Sarah Pomeroy's work, *Goddesses, Whores, Wives, and Slaves* (1975), that initiated the application of feminist theory to the topic. Pomeroy's thesis that Roman women were thoroughly disadvantaged set the stage for further studies such as J.F. Gardner's that included mixtures of more traditional themes.

Social history also brought a surge in the analysis of the Roman family, particularly in works by Suzanne Dixon and Beryl Rawson. Such studies were often reconnected to the political themes of earlier years providing even more complete studies such as J.K. Evans' *War, Women and Children in Ancient Rome* (1991). At the same time, the politics of sexuality in the empire were being analyzed with traditional philological methods by J.N. Adams as well as through social and feminist theory in the work of Amy Richlin. All told, ventures such as C.A. Barton's into social and psychological theory and even J.D. Hughes' into environmental history brought new, fruitful discussion while also filling significant gaps of knowledge. Perhaps most interesting through all of this transition has been a continuation of the search for Western roots in the Roman past. Despite transitions in topics and methods, much of the early modern, pedagogical program informing the study of the Roman empire has remained. Rather then stressing the otherness of imperial Rome, modern historians continue to seek answers to the modern condition in this ancient material.

Remaining too has been an obsession with Rome's demise. What Augustine of Hippo began in his *De civitate dei* and Gibbon continued in his *Decline and Fall* has endured as a topic for hundreds of works, notably Mortimer Chambers' *The Fall of Rome: Can It be Explained?* (1963) and Lynn White's *The Transformation of the Roman World: Gibbon's Problem after*

Two Centuries (1966). First on the list of causes in this scholarship have been the traditional scapegoats, the "barbarians" or "Germanic tribes," as identified by British and French historians such as J.B. Bury and André Piganiol. Contrary to this view, German historians such as Wilhem Ensslin and Joseph Vogt have seen these groups as the Western inheritors and defenders of a spent empire. Other treatments of the topic have sought to emphasize the long-term relationships between the empire and its Germanic neighbors that certainly included conflict, but could also bring stability, security, and economic prosperity for all parties. Y.A. Dauge and others have provided insight into Roman perspectives while E.A. Thompson explored the "barbarian" side of these relationships. Finally, scholars such as J.M. O'Flynn and Ramsay MacMullen have also emphasized Rome's own contributions to the decline of the empire.

In response to Gibbonesque assertions of Christian responsibility in this demise, scholars have emphasized the position of this faith within a dynamic culture that had already incorporated a number of religious and philosophical influences. Rather than highlighting tensions alone, Christianity has been linked by E.R. Dodds and J.H.W. Liebescheutz to overall cultural transformations and even viewed by J.R. Fears as a preserver of certain aspects of Roman political tradition and by Jaroslav Pelikan as helping preserve Roman philosophical thought. As with the "barbarians," the study of Christian relations within the empire has been incorporated into broader studies of change by MacMullen.

Related to this is the religious-political "triumph" of Christianity explored by MacMullen, Marta Sordi, and Robin Lane Fox. Constantine's reign has been seen as complex and peculiar by Jacob Burckhardt, Andréas Alföldi, and T.D. Barnes. The resulting continuity and transformation in late antiquity from Roman, polytheistic universalism to Christian (and Islamic) monotheistic universalism has been explored by Garth Fowden.

Whether the division and demise of the empire is given broad study, as by A.H.M. Jones, or more narrow coverage, as by Stephen Williams and Gerard Friell, the discussion of how (or whether) the empire came to a close will remain a topic of research. Indeed, that the study of the Roman empire as a whole is by no means exhausted is exemplified in the excellent, continuing series edited by Hildegard Temporini and Wolfgang Haase, *Aufstieg und Niedergang der römischen Welt: Geschichte und Kultur Roms im Spiegel der neueren Forschung* (The Rise and Fall of the Roman World: The History and Culture of Rome as Reflected in the Most Recent Research, 1972–). Historical interest in the Roman empire shows little sign of weakening; it seems to have become a permanent fixture in the world of historical writing and in the Western search for self-understanding.

KENNETH R. CALVERT

See also Beloch; Burckhardt; Cassio Dio; Gibbon; Livy; Meyer; Mommsen, T.; Niebuhr; Plutarch; Polybius; Rostovtzeff; Suetonius; Syme; Tacitus; White, L.

Further Reading

Adams, James Noel, *The Latin Sexual Vocabulary*, Baltimore: Johns Hopkins University Press, and London: Duckworth, 1982

Alföldi, Andréas, *The Conversion of Constantine and Pagan Rome*, Oxford: Oxford University Press, 1948

Alföldi, Andréas, *Die monarchische Repräsentation im römischen Kaiserreiche* (Monarchical Representation in the Roman Principate), Darmstadt: Wissenschaftliche Buchgesellschaft, 1970

Alföldy, Géza, *Römische Sozialgeschichte*, Wiesbaden: Steiner, 1975; in English as *The Social History of Rome*, Totowa, NJ: Barnes and Noble, and London: Croom Helm, 1985

Alföldy, Géza, *Römische Statuen in Venetia et Histria: Epigraphische Quellen* (Roman Statues in Venice and Romania), Heidelberg: Winter, 1984

Arnheim, Michael T.W., *The Senatorial Aristocracy in the Later Roman Empire*, Oxford: Oxford University Press, 1972

Balsdon, J.P.V.D., *Roman Women: Their History and Habits*, London: Bodley Head, and New York: Day, 1963

Balsdon, J.P.V.D., *Life and Leisure in Ancient Rome*, London: Bodley Head, and New York: McGraw Hill, 1969

Balsdon, J.P.V.D., *Romans and Aliens*, London: Duckworth, and Chapel Hill: University of North Carolina Press, 1979

Barnes, Timothy David, *Constantine and Eusebius*, Cambridge, MA: Harvard University Press, 1981

Barnes, Timothy David., *The New Empire of Diocletian and Constantine*, Cambridge, MA: Harvard University Press, 1982

Barton, Carlin A., *The Sorrows of the Ancient Romans: The Gladiator and the Monster*, Princeton: Princeton University Press, 1993

Baynes, Norman H., *Constantine the Great and the Christian Church*, London: Oxford University Press, 1930

Bedford, O.H., "The Silk Trade of China with the Roman Empire," *China Journal* 28 (1938)

Begley, Vimala, and Richard Daniel DePuma, eds., *Rome and India: The Ancient Sea Trade*, Madison: University of Wisconsin Press, 1991

Bleicken, Jochen, *Zum Regierungsstil des römischen Kaisers: eine Antwort auf Fergus Millar* (The Government of the Roman Emperors: A Reply to Fergus Millar), Wiesbaden: Steiner, 1982

Boren, Henry Charles, *Roman Society: A Social, Economic, and Cultural History*, Lexington, MA: Heath, 1977

Bowersock, Glen Warren, *Augustus and the Greek World*, Oxford: Oxford University Press, 1965; Westport, CT: Greenwood Press, 1981

Bowersock, Glen Warren, *Greek Sophists in the Roman Empire*, Oxford: Clarendon Press, 1969

Bowersock, Glen Warren, *Julian the Apostate*, Cambridge, MA: Harvard University Press, and London: Duckworth, 1978

Bowersock, Glen Warren, *Roman Arabia*, Cambridge, MA: Harvard University Press, 1983

Bowersock, Glen Warren, *Martyrdom and Rome*, Cambridge and New York: Cambridge University Press, 1995

Bradley, Keith R., *Slaves and Masters in the Roman Empire: A Study in Social Control*, Brussels: Latomus, 1984; Oxford and New York: Oxford University Press, 1987

Bradley, Keith R., *Discovering the Roman Family: Studies in Roman Social History*, Oxford and New York: Oxford University Press, 1991

Braund, David C., *Rome and the Friendly King: The Character of the Client Kingship*, New York: St. Martin's Press, and London: Croom Helm, 1984

Brown, Peter, *The Social Context to the Religious Crisis of the Third Century AD*, Berkeley: University of California Press, 1975

Brown, Peter, *The Making of Late Antiquity*, Cambridge, MA: Harvard University Press, 1978

Brown, Peter, *The Body and Society: Men, Women, and Sexual Renunciation in Early Christianity*, New York: Columbia University Press, and London: Faber, 1988

Brown, Peter, *Power and Persuasion in Late Antiquity: Towards a Christian Empire*, Madison: University of Wisconsin Press, 1992

Brown, Peter, *Authority and the Sacred: Aspects of the Christianisation of the Roman World*, Cambridge and New York: Cambridge University Press, 1995

Brunt, Peter Astbury, *Roman Imperial Themes*, Oxford: Clarendon Press, and New York: Oxford University Press, 1990

Burckhardt, Jacob, *Die Zeit Constantins des Grossen*, Basel, 1853; in English as *The Age of Constantine the Great*, 1949

Bury, J.B., *The Invasion of Europe by the Barbarians*, London: Macmillan, 1928; New York: Russell and Russell, 1963

Cameron, Averil, *The Later Roman Empire, AD 284–430*, Cambridge, MA: Harvard University Press, 1993

Campbell, J. Brian, *The Emperor and the Roman Army, 31 BC–AD 235*, Oxford and New York: Oxford University Press, 1984

Carcopino, Jérôme, *La Vie quotidienne à l'apogée de l'Empire*, Paris: Hachette, 1939; in English as *Daily Life in Ancient Rome: The People and the City at the Height of the Empire*, New Haven: Yale University Press, 1940, London: Routledge, 1941

Carson, R.A.G., and C.H.V. Sutherland, eds., *Essays in Roman Coinage Presented to Harold Mattingly*, Oxford: Oxford University Press, 1956

Carson, R.A.G., *Coins of the Roman Empire*, London and New York: Routledge, 1990

Carter, J.M., *The Battle of Actium: The Rise and Triumph of Augustus Caesar*, London: Hamish Hamilton, and New York: Weybright and Talley, 1970

Chambers, Mortimer, ed., *The Fall of Rome: Can It be Explained?*, New York: Holt Rinehart, 1963

Charlesworth, Martin Percival, *Trade Routes and Commerce of the Roman Empire*, Cambridge: Cambridge University Press, 1924; revised 1926

Christensen, Torben, *Romermagt, hedenskab og Kristendom: en kulturkamp*, Copenhagen: Gad, 1970; in German as *Christus oder Jupiter: der Kampf um die geistigen Grundlagen des Römischen Reiches* (Christ or Jupiter: The Conflict of Beliefs in the Roman Empire), Göttingen: Vandenhoeck & Ruprecht, 1981

Chuvin, Pierre A., *Chronique des derniers païens: la disparition du paganisme dans l'Empire romain, du règne de Constantin à celui de Justinien*, Paris: Fayard, 1990; in English as *The Chronicle of the Last Pagans*, Cambridge, MA: Harvard University Press, 1990

Cochrane, Charles Norris, *Christianity and Classical Culture: A Study of Thought and Action from Augustus to Augustine*, Oxford and New York: Oxford University Press, 1940

Colish, Marcia L., *The Stoic Tradition from Antiquity to the Early Middle Ages*, 2 vols., Leiden: Brill, 1985

Colledge, Malcolm A.R., *The Parthians*, New York: Praeger, and London: Thames and Hudson, 1967

Cramer, Frederick Henry, *Astrology in Roman Law and Politics*, Philadelphia: American Philosophical Society, 1954

Crook, John Anthony, *Consilium Principis: Imperial Councils and Counsellors from Augustus to Diocletian*, Cambridge: Cambridge University Press, 1955; New York: Arno, 1975

Crook, John Anthony, *Law and Life of Rome*, Ithaca, NY: Cornell University Press, and London: Thames and Hudson, 1967

Cunliffe, Barry W., *Greeks, Romans and Barbarians: Spheres of Interaction*, London: Batsford, and New York: Methuen, 1988

Dauge, Yves Albert, *Le Barbare: recherches sur la conception romaine de la barbarie et de la civilisation* (The Barbarian: Studies in the Roman Conception of the Barbarians and Civilization), Brussels: Latomus, 1981

Dixon, Suzanne, *The Roman Mother*, Norman: University of Oklahoma Press, and London: Croom Helm, 1988

Dixon, Suzanne, *The Roman Family*, Baltimore: Johns Hopkins University Press, 1992

Dodds, Eric Robertson, *Pagan and Christian in an Age of Anxiety: Some Aspects of Religious Experience from Marcus Aurelius to Constantine*, Cambridge: Cambridge University Press, 1965; New York: Norton, 1970

Dodgeon, Michael H., and Samuel C.N. Lieu, *The Roman Eastern Frontier and the Persian Wars, AD 226–363: A Documentary History*, London and New York: Routledge, 1991

Drummond, Steven K., and Lynn H. Nelson, *The Western Frontiers of Imperial Rome*, Armonk, NY: Sharpe, 1994

Elton, Hugh, *Frontiers of the Roman Empire*, Bloomington: Indiana University Press, and London: Batsford, 1996

Ensslin, Wilhelm, *Theoderich der Grosse* (Theoderic the Great), Munich: Münchner, 1947

Evans, J.K., *War, Women and Children in Ancient Rome*, London and New York: Routledge, 1991

Fears, J. Rufus, *Princeps a Diis Electus: The Divine Election of the Emperor as a Political Concept at Rome*, Rome: American Academy, 1977

Ferrill, Arther, *The Fall of the Roman Empire: The Military Explanation*, London and New York: Thames and Hudson, 1986

Fishwick, Duncan, *The Imperial Cult in the Latin West: Studies in the Ruler Cult of the Western Provinces of the Roman Empire*, 2 vols., Leiden: Brill, 1987–92

Fowden, Garth, *Empire to Commonwealth: Consequences of Monotheism in Late Antiquity*, Princeton: Princeton University Press, 1993

Fox, Robin Lane, *Pagans and Christians*, Harmondsworth and New York: Viking, 1986

Frank, Tenney et al., eds., *An Economic Survey of Ancient Rome*, 6 vols., Baltimore: Johns Hopkins Press, 1933–40

Frier, Bruce W., *Landlords and Tenants in Imperial Rome*, Princeton: Princeton University Press, 1980

Gagé, Jean, *Les Classes sociales dans l'Empire romain* (Social Classes in the Roman Empire), Paris: Payot, 1964

Gagé, Jean, *Le Paganisme impérial à la recherche d'une théologie vers le milieu du IIIe siècle* (Imperial Paganism in the Third-Century Milieu), Mainz: Steiner, 1972

Gardner, Jane F., *Women in Roman Law and Society*, Bloomington: Indiana University Press, and London: Croom Helm, 1986

Garnsey, Peter, ed., *Non-Slave Labor in the Greco-Roman World*, Cambridge: Cambridge Philological Society, 1980

Garnsey, Peter, and C.R. Whittaker, eds., *Trade and Famine in Classical Antiquity*, Cambridge: Cambridge Philological Society, 1983

Geffcken, Johannes, *Der Ausgang des griechisch-römischen Heidentums*, Heidelberg: Winter, 1920; in English as *The Last Days of Greco-Roman Paganism*, Amsterdam and New York: North Holland, 1978

Gibbon, Edward, *The History of the Decline and Fall of the Roman Empire*, 6 vols., London: Strahan and Cadell, 1776–88

Groag, Edmund, and Arthur Stein, *Prosopographia Imperii Romani* (Prosopography of Imperial Rome), 4 vols., Berlin: de Gruyter, 1933–66

Hammond, Mason, *The Augustan Principate in Theory and Practice during the Julio-Claudian Period*, Cambridge, MA: Harvard University Press, and London: Oxford University Press, 1933; enlarged New York: Russell and Russell, 1968

Hannestad, Niels, *Romersk kunst som propaganda: aspekter af kunstens brug og funktion i det romerske sanfund*, Copenhagen: Berlingske, 1976; in English as *Roman Art and Imperial Policy*, Aarhus: Aarhus University Press, 1988

Heather, Pete J., *Goths and Romans, 332–489*, Oxford and New York: Oxford University Press, 1991

Hoffman-Lewis, Martha Wilson, *The Official Priests of Rome under the Julio-Claudians: A Study of the Nobility from 44 BC to 68 AD*, Rome: American Academy, 1955

Honoré, Tony, *Emperors and Lawyers*, London: Duckworth, 1981; revised Oxford and New York: Oxford University Press, 1994

Hughes, Johnson Donald, *Pan's Travail: Environmental Problems of the Ancient Greeks and Romans*, Baltimore: Johns Hopkins University Press, 1994

Isaac, Benjamin H., *The Limits of Empire: The Roman Army in the East*, Oxford and New York: Oxford University Press, 1990

Jaeger, Werner Wilhelm, *Early Christianity and Greek Paideia*, Cambridge, MA: Harvard University Press, 1961; London: Oxford University Press, 1962

Jones, A.H.M., *The Later Roman Empire, 284–602: A Social, Economic and Administrative Survey*, 3 vols., Oxford: Blackwell, and Norman: University of Oklahoma Press, 1964

Kuntze, Claudia, *Zur Darstellung des Kaisers Tiberius und seiner Zeit bei Velleius Paterculus* (The Portrayals of Tiberius and His Time According to Velleius Paterculus), Frankfurt and New York: Lang, 1985

Laistner, Max Ludwig Wolfram, *The Greater Roman Historians*, Berkeley: University of California Press, 1947

Lee, A.D., *Information and Frontiers: Roman Foreign Relations in Late Antiquity*, Cambridge and New York: Cambridge University Press, 1993

Levick, B., "Propaganda and the Imperial Coinage," in his *The Ancient Historian and His Materials: Essays in Honour of C.E. Stevens on His Seventieth Birthday*, Farnborough: Gregg, 1975

Lewis, Naphtadi, *Life in Egypt under Roman Rule*, Oxford and New York: Oxford University Press, 1983

Liebeschuetz, John Hugo Wolfgang Gideon, *Continuity and Change in Roman Religion*, Oxford and New York: Oxford University Press, 1979

Lintott, Andrew William, *Imperium Romanum: Politics and Administration*, London and New York: Routledge, 1993

Luck, Georg, *Arcana Mundi: Magic and the Occult in the Greek and Roman Worlds: A Collection of Ancient Texts*, Baltimore: Johns Hopkins University Press, 1985

Luttwak, Edward N., *The Grand Strategy of the Roman Empire from the First Century* AD *to the Third*, Baltimore: Johns Hopkins University Press, 1976

MacMullen, Ramsay, *Enemies of the Roman Order: Treason, Unrest, and Alienation in the Empire*, Cambridge, MA: Harvard University Press, 1966; London: Oxford University Press, 1967

MacMullen, Ramsay, *Paganism in the Roman Empire*, New Haven and London: Yale University Press, 1981

MacMullen, Ramsay, *Christianizing the Roman Empire*, AD 100–400, New Haven and London: Yale University Press, 1984

MacMullen, Ramsay, *Corruption and Decline of Rome*, New Haven and London: Yale University Press, 1988

MacMullen, Ramsay, *Changes in the Roman Empire: Essays in the Ordinary*, Princeton: Princeton University Press, 1990

Matthews, John F., *Political Life and Culture in Late Roman Society*, London: Variorum, 1985

Mattingly, Harold, and R.A.G. Carson, eds., *Coins of the Roman Empire in the British Museum*, 6 vols., London: British Museum, 1923–62

Mattingly, Harold *et al.*, eds., *The Roman Imperial Coinage*, 9 vols., London: Spink, 1923–

Mazzarino, Santo, *L'impero romano* (The Roman Empire), 3 vols., Rome: Laterza, 1973

Meyer, Eduard, *Caesars Monarchie und das Principat des Pompeius: innere geschichte Roms von 66 bis 44 v. Chr.* (Caesar's Monarchy and Pompey's Principate: The Core of Roman History from 66 to 44 BCE), Berlin: Cotta, 1918

Millar, Fergus, ed., *The Roman Empire and Its Neighbors*, New York: Delacorte Press, and London: Weidenfeld and Nicolson, 1967

Millar, Fergus, *The Emperor in the Roman World (31 BC–AD 337)*, London: Duckworth, and Ithaca, NY: Cornell University Press, 1977

Millar, Fergus, and Erich Segal, eds., *Caesar Augustus: Seven Aspects*, Oxford and New York: Oxford University Press, 1984

Millar, Fergus, *The Roman Near East, 31 BC to AD 337*, Cambridge, MA: Harvard University Press, 1993

Momigliano, Arnaldo, ed., *The Conflict Between Paganism and Christianity in the Fourth Century*, Oxford: Oxford University Press, 1963

Momigliano, Arnaldo, *Alien Wisdom: The Limits of Hellenization*, Cambridge and New York: Cambridge University Press, 1975

Mommsen, Theodor, *Römisches Staatsrecht* (Roman Constitutional Law), 3 vols., Leipzig: Hirzel, 1876–88

Münzer, Friedrich, *Römische Adelsparteien und Adelsfamilien* (Roman Noble Factions and Families), Stuttgart: Metzler, 1920

Niebuhr, B.G., *Römische Geschichte*, 3 vols., 1811–32; in English as *History of Rome*, 1828–42

North, J.A., "Novelty and Choice in Roman Religion," *Journal of Roman Studies* 70 (1980), 186–91

O'Flynn, John Michael, *Generalissimos of the Western Roman Empire*, Edmonton: University of Alberta Press, 1983

Pelikan, Jaroslav, *The Excellent Empire: The Fall of Rome and the Triumph of the Church*, San Francisco: Harper, 1987

Pelikan, Jaroslav, *Christianity and Classical Culture: The Metamorphosis of Natural Theology in the Christian Encounter with Hellenism*, New Haven and London: Yale University Press, 1993

Perowne, Stewart, *The End of the Roman World*, New York: Crowell, and London: Hodder and Stoughton, 1967

Piganiol, André, *Le Sac de Rome: vue d'ensemble* (The Sack of Rome: An Overview), Paris: Michel, 1964

Plass, Paul, *The Game of Death in Ancient Rome: Arena Sports and Political Suicide*, Madison: University of Wisconsin Press, 1995

Pohlenz, Max, *Die Stoa: Geschichte einer geistigen Bewegung* (The Stoa: A History of an Intellectual Moment), 2 vols., Göttingen: Vandenhoeck & Ruprecht, 1948–49

Pomeroy, Sarah B., *Goddesses, Whores, Wives, and Slaves: Women in Classical Antiquity*, New York: Schocken, 1975; London: Hale, 1976

Potter, D.S., *Prophets and Emperors: Human and Divine Authority from Augustus to Theodosius*, Cambridge, MA: Harvard University Press, 1994

Price, Simon R.F., *Rituals and Power: The Roman Imperial Cult in Asia Minor*, Cambridge and New York: Cambridge University Press, 1984

Raaflaub, Kurt, ed., *Opposition et résistances à l'empire d'Auguste à Trajan* (Opposition and Resistance in the Empire from Augustus to Trajan), Geneva: Hardt, 1987

Raaflaub, Kurt, and Mark Toher, eds., *Between Republic and Empire: Interpretations of Augustus and His Principate*, Berkeley: University of California Press, 1990

Rajak, Tessa, *Josephus: The Historian and His Society*, London: Duckworth, 1983; Philadelphia: Fortress Press, 1984

Rawson, Beryl, ed., *The Family in Ancient Rome: New Perspectives*, Ithaca, NY: Cornell University Press, and London: Croom Helm, 1986

Rawson, Beryl, ed., *Marriage, Divorce and Children in Ancient Rome*, Oxford and New York: Oxford University Press, 1991

Rawson, Beryl, and Paul Weaver, *The Roman Family in Italy: Status, Sentiment and Space*, Oxford and New York: Oxford University Press, 1997

Reinhold, Meyer, *Diaspora: The Jews among the Greeks and Romans*, Sarasota, FL: Stevens, 1983

Richlin, Amy, *The Garden of Priapus: Sexuality and Aggression in Roman Humor*, New Haven: Yale University Press, 1983; revised Oxford and New York: Oxford University Press, 1992

Richlin, Amy, ed., *Pornography and Representation in Greece and Rome*, Oxford and New York: Oxford University Press, 1992

Rostovtzeff, M.I., *The Social and Economic History of the Roman Empire*, 2 vols., Oxford: Oxford University Press, 1926

Rowlands, Michael, Mogens Larsen, and Kristian Kristiansen, eds., *Centre and Periphery in the Ancient World*, Cambridge and New York: Cambridge University Press, 1987

Saller, Richard P., *Personal Patronage under the Early Empire*, Cambridge and New York: Cambridge University Press, 1982

Schowalter, Daniel N., *The Emperor and the Gods: Images from the Time of Trajan*, Minneapolis: Fortress Press, 1993

Shahid, Irfan, *Rome and the Arabs: A Prolegomenon to the Study of Byzantium and the Arabs*, Washington, DC: Dumbarton Oaks, 1984

Sherwin-White, Adrian Nicolas, *The Roman Citizenship*, Oxford: Oxford University Press, 1939; reprinted 1973

Sherwin-White, Adrian Nicolas, *Racial Prejudice in Imperial Rome*, Cambridge and New York: Cambridge University Press, 1967

Simon, Marcel, *Verus Israel: étude sur les relations entre Chrétiens et Juifs dans l'Empire romain, 135–425*, Paris: Boccard, 1948; in English as *Verus Israel: A Study of the Relations Between Christians and Jews in the Roman Empire, 135–425*, Oxford and New York: Oxford University Press, 1986

Sordi, Marta, *I cristiani e l'impero romano*, Milan: Jaca, 1984; in English as *The Christians and the Roman Empire*, London: Croom Helm, and Norman: University of Oklahoma Press, 1986

Starr, Chester G., *The Roman Empire, 27 BC–AD 476: A Study in Survival*, Oxford and New York: Oxford University Press, 1982

Stevenson, George Hope, *Roman Provincial Administration till the Age of the Antonines*, Oxford: Blackwell, and New York: Stechert, 1939

Sutherland, C.H.V., *Coinage in Roman Imperial Policy, 31 BC to AD 68*, London: Methuen, 1951; New York: Barnes and Noble, 1971

Syme, Ronald, *The Roman Revolution*, Oxford and New York: Oxford University Press, 1939

Syme, Ronald, *Tacitus*, 2 vols., Oxford: Oxford University Press, 1958

Syme, Ronald, *Some Arval Brethren*, Oxford and New York: Oxford University Press, 1980

Syme, Ronald, *The Augustan Aristocracy*, Oxford and New York: Oxford University Press, 1986

Talbert, Richard J.A., *The Senate of Imperial Rome*, Princeton: Princeton University Press, 1984

Taylor, Lilly Ross, *The Divinity of the Roman Emperor*, Middletown, CT: American Philological Association, 1931

Taylor, Lilly Ross, *Party Politics in the Age of Caesar*, Berkeley: University of California Press, 1949

Temporini, Hildegard, and Wolfgang Haase, eds., *Aufstieg und Niedergang der römischen Welt: Geschichte und Kultur Roms im Spiegel der neueren Forschung* (The Rise and Fall of the Roman World: The History and Culture of Rome as Reflected in the Most Recent Research), 30 vols. to date, Berlin and New York: de Gruyter, 1972–

Thompson, E.A., *The Early Germans*, Oxford: Clarendon Press, 1965

Thompson, E.A., *Romans and Barbarians: The Decline of the Western Empire*, Madison: University of Wisconsin Press, 1982

Veyne, Paul, *Le Pain et le cirque: sociologie historique d'un pluralisme politique*, Paris: Seuil, 1976; in English as *Bread and Circuses: Historical Sociology and Political Pluralism*, London: Allen Lane, 1990

Vogt, Joseph, *Orbis romanus zur Terminologie des römischen Imperialismus* (Orbis Romanis: On Roman Imperial Technology), Tubingen: Mohr, 1929

Vogt, Joseph, *Römischer Glaube und römisches Weltreich* (Roman Confidence and Roman Empire), Padua: Milani, 1943

Vogt, Joseph, *Konstantin der Grosse und das Christentum: Ergebnisse und Aufgaben der Forschung* (Constantine the Great and Christianity), Zurich: Ordenssekretariates, 1960

Vogt, Joseph, *Der Niedergang Roms: Metamorphose der antiken Kultur*, Zurich: Kindler, 1965; in English as *The Decline of Rome: The Metamorphosis of Ancient Civilisation*, London: Weidenfeld and Nicolson, 1967, New York: New American Library, 1968

Walbank, Frank W., *The Awful Revolution: The Decline of the Roman Empire in the West*, Liverpool: Liverpool University Press, and Toronto: University of Toronto Press, 1969

Wells, Colin Michael, *The Roman Empire*, Stanford, CA: Stanford University Press, and London: Fontana, 1984

Wheeler, Mortimer, *Rome Beyond the Imperial Frontiers*, London: Bell, 1954; New York: Philosophical Library, 1955

White, Lynn Jr., ed., *The Transformation of the Roman World: Gibbon's Problem after Two Centuries*, Berkeley: University of California Press, and Cambridge: Cambridge University Press, 1966

Whittaker, C.R., *Les Frontières de l'Empire romain*, Paris: Belles Lettres, 1989; in English as *Frontiers of the Roman Empire: A Social and Economic Study*, Baltimore: Johns Hopkins University Press, 1994

Wiedemann, Thomas, *Adults and Children in the Roman Empire*, New Haven: Yale University Press, and London: Routledge, 1989

Wiedemann, Thomas, *Emperors and Gladiators*, London and New York: Routledge, 1995

Wilken, Robert L., *The Christians as the Romans Saw Them*, New Haven and London: Yale University Press, 1984

Williams, Stephen, *Diocletian and the Roman Recovery*, London: Batsford, and New York: Methuen, 1985

Williams, Stephen, and Gerard Friell, *Theodosius: The Empire at Bay*, London: Batsford, 1994; New Haven: Yale University Press, 1995

Wirszubski, Chaim, *Libertas as a Political Idea at Rome during the Republic and Early Principate*, Cambridge: Cambridge University Press, 1950

Wylie, John Kerr, *Roman Constitutional History from Earliest Times to the Death of Justinian: A Brief Outline Designed Mainly as a Preliminary to the Study of Roman Law*, Cape Town: African Bookman, 1948

Yavetz, Zvi, *Hamon u-manhigim be-Romi: be-shilhe ha-Republirkah uva-Kesarut ha-kedumah*, Tel Aviv: Devir, 1966; in English as *Plebs and Princeps*, London: Oxford University Press, 1968; revised New Brunswick, NJ: Transaction, 1988

Zanker, Paul, *The Power of Images in the Age of Augustus*, Ann Arbor: University of Michigan Press, 1988

Romeo, Rosario 1924–1987
Italian historian of the Risorgimento

Although relatively unknown in the English-speaking world, Rosario Romeo was perhaps the leading liberal historian of the postwar generation in Italy. He began to establish his reputation with a remarkable first book, *Il Risorgimento in Sicilia* (The Risorgimento in Sicily), published in 1950 when he was 26. In it, Romeo investigates the Risorgimento in Sicily as a process that reflected broader (European) cultural movements and was affected by a concomitant experience of economic and social change. The main, but not the only, focus of Romeo's work continued to be 19th-century Italy. His most important books after *Il Risorgimento in Sicilia* – *Risorgimento e capitalismo* (Risorgimento and Capitalism, 1959) and *Cavour e il suo tempo* (Cavour and His Time, 1969–84) – were concerned with the Risorgimento and its aftermath. His lengthy study of Cavour, without doubt his masterwork, is both a biography of the Piedmontese statesman and a detailed history of the intellectual, ideological, and economic climate of the time.

Romeo was born near Catania in Sicily and completed his formal training as a historian at the Institute of Historical Studies in Naples, where he studied under Federico Chabod. He spent much of his professional career as professor of history at Rome University. It was through Chabod and, in turn, Chabod's teacher, Benedetto Croce, that Romeo absorbed the philosophical idealism that was so characteristic of prewar antifascist historiography in Italy and which continued to influence Romeo's historical methodology throughout his career. Like his teachers Croce and Chabod, Romeo wholeheartedly rejected what he saw as the economic determinism and "classism" of Marxism. Unlike his teachers, however, Romeo was profoundly affected by non-Italian historiography and, in particular, by the new empirical research of American economic historians such as Kent Robert Greenfield and Alexander Gerschenkron.

A guiding principle of Romeo's work was that idealism and empiricism were not incompatible. When Greenfield's classic work on the Risorgimento, *Economics and Liberalism in the Risorgimento* (1934), was republished in Italy in 1964, Romeo wrote a new introductory essay. In this essay, one of the very few of Romeo's works to be translated into English, Romeo both acknowledged his debt to the older American historian and offered a thinly-veiled critique of idealist historiography. The "general insufficiency" of idealist historians was, in Romeo's view, demonstrated by their failure to grasp that Greenfield's "non-political" approach to the Risorgimento offered them an empirical basis on which to challenge Marxist determinism. Greenfield, according to Romeo, "placed at the center of historical life, within an empirically constructed cultural framework, that free creativity of consciousness and activity to which idealism was trying to restore all reality."

Between the publication of *Il Risorgimento in Sicilia* and the multivolume *Cavour*, another striking feature of Romeo's scholarship – a hostility to Marxist historiography in general and to certain Marxist historians in particular – becomes apparent. In a series of essays, notably those published in *Dal Piemonte sabaudo all'Italia liberale* (From Savoyard Piedmont to Liberal Italy, 1963) and *Italia moderna fra storia e storiografia* (Modern Italy Between History and Historiography, 1977), as well as in *Cavour* itself, Romeo defends the political and economic achievements of 19th-century Italian liberals and challenges the harsh judgments made by left-wing historians. In *Risorgimento e capitalismo*, Romeo replies to the Marxist interpretation of the Risorgimento as a failed agrarian revolution (*rivoluzione mancata*). Romeo uses a complex statistical analysis to argue that a peasant revolution in Italy could not and should not have happened. Whereas Marxists maintain that a successful peasant revolution in Italy would have overthrown the feudal order and created the conditions for capitalist development in Italy, Romeo seeks to show that its only effect would have been to prevent capital accumulation and thus frustrate industrial development in the North. When first published in article form, Romeo's thesis in *Risorgimento e capitalismo* created a great stir in historical circles in Italy, sparking off a series of debates among historians such as Pavone, Villari, Cafagna, and Gerschenkron.

Romeo was always a controversial historian. He was unhesitating in his denunciation of those he considered mistaken or to be his intellectual inferiors. The politicization of the historical profession in Italy was partly responsible for this tendency, although Romeo's willingness to engage in polemical debate and to make personal attacks on historians he disagreed with is striking even in this context. He became more conservative as he grew older. During his youth at the Naples institute, he was a supporter of innovation in historical research and methodology, yet as a professor in Rome in the 1970s and early 1980s he publicly criticized new methodologies and used his considerable influence to forestall new areas of research.

In the course of his career, Romeo's interests shifted from ideas and individuals toward a study of social structures and economic trends. He also became more interested in the "successful" modernization of northern Italy and progressively less interested in the "failed" experiences of the South. He became, in turn, less sympathetic to the fate of those who had lost. Thus, in *Il Risorgimento in Sicilia*, Romeo bemoans the fate of the Sicilian peasantry, for whom economic development in the Risorgimento was a major cataclysm. But by *Risorgimento e capitalismo* Romeo's sympathy all but disappeared and he depicted the suffering of the peasantry as merely a historical necessity in the industrialization of northern Italy.

It is hard to imagine the historiography of 19th-century Italy without Romeo's commanding presence. From the very beginning of his career, his arguments provided a series of benchmarks and starting points for future research. It was also Romeo who, in *Risorgimento e capitalismo*, introduced new ways of using official statistics for historical research in Italy. In particular, he showed idealist historians in Italy how to beat Marxist historians at their own game by carrying out empirical research. He led the way in the quality of his own research which is always faultless. Indeed, his command of the documentary evidence and secondary literature is sometimes breathtaking. Romeo's study of Cavour shows precisely the breadth of vision and grasp of historical detail that, in the introduction to Greenfield's *Economics and Liberalism in the Risorgimento*, he had recommended to readers as the way forward for historians of modern Italy. In this respect, if not always in others, Romeo fulfilled his early promise. He added vitality and interest to historical debate in Italy as well as controversy and rivalry.

LUCY RIALL

See also Mack Smith

Biography

Born Giarre, Catania, 11 October 1924. Educated in a classical high school before taking a degree in political science. Editor of *Treccani*, an encyclopedia, 1950–53; secretary, Institute of Historical Studies, Naples, 1953–58; dean and professor of history, Teacher Training Faculty, University of Messina, 1956–62; professor of history, University of Rome, 1963–87; also professor, European University, Florence. Died 1987.

Principal Writings

Il Risorgimento in Sicilia (The Risorgimento in Sicily), 1950

Le scoperte americane nella coscienza italiana del cinquecento (The American Discovery of Sixteenth-Century Italian Learning), 1954

Risorgimento e capitalismo (Risorgimento and Capitalism), 1959

Breve storia della grande industria in Italia (A Short History of Industrialization in Italy), 1961

Dal Piemonte sabaudo all'Italia liberale (From Savoyard Piedmont to Liberal Italy), 1963

Mezzogiorno e Sicilia nel Risorgimento (The Mezzogiorno and Sicily in the Risorgimento), 1963

Introductory essay to revised edition of Kent Robert Greenfield, *Economia e liberalismo nel Risorgimento: il movimento nazionale in Lombardia dal 1814 al 1848*, 1964; in English as *Economics and Liberalism in the Risorgimento: A Study of Nationalism in Lombardy, 1814–1848*, 1965

Cavour e il suo tempo (1842–1852) (Cavour and His Time), 3 vols., 1969–84

Italia moderna fra storia e storiografia (Modern Italy Between History and Historiography), 1977

L'Italia unita e la prima guerra mondiale (United Italy and the First World War), Rome, Laterza, 1978

Italia, democrazia industriali: del risorgimento alla Repubblica
(Italian Industrial Democracy: The Risorgimento of the Republic),
1986
Italia laica ed Europa unità (Lay Italy and United Europe), 1986
L'Italia liberale: sviluppo e contradizzioni (Liberal Italy:
Developments and Contradictions), 1987

Further Reading

Gerschenkron, Alexander, "Rosario Romeo and the Original
Accumulation of Capital," in his *Economic Backwardness in
Historical Perspective*, Cambridge, MA: Harvard University Press,
1962
Mori, G., "Rosario Romeo: un grande storico per una grande
illusione?" (Rosario Romeo: A Great Historian for a Great
Illusion?), *Passato e Presente* 13 (1987), 3–14
Pescosolido, Guido, *Rosario Romeo*, Rome: Laterza, 1990
Pescosolido, Guido, "Rosario Romeo e lo sviluppo economico
italiano" (Rosario Romeo and Italian economic development),
Storia Contemporanea 24 (1993), 631–60
Ramm, A., "The Risorgimento in Sicily: Recent Literature," *English
Historical Review* 87 (1972), 795–811
Salamone, A.W., "The Risorgimento Between Ideology and History:
The Political Myth of *rivoluzione mancata*," *American Historical
Review* 48 (1962), 39–56

Romero, José Luis 1909–1977

Argentine social historian

One of the most important Argentine intellectuals of the 20th
century, José Luis Romero was the leading figure in the revival
of historical studies in the country. An intellectual with a strong
and attractive personality, and a historian of considerable
erudition and originality, he was also a distinguished cultural
organizer committed to the ideas of humanistic socialism. His
main area of study was medieval history and his chosen field
that of the rise and development of the bourgeoisie. He also
carried out important research into Latin American and
Argentine history and he produced a far-reaching body of work
on the characteristics and conditions of historical knowledge.

One of the most original aspects of Romero's career was
his attempt to provide, from Argentina, an overview of the
historical process of the Western world. This ambitious project
was undertaken in a situation of double isolation: that of
the country from which Romero was writing, and that of the
prevailing tendency in Argentine historiography of the time,
which was marked by historical positivism and limited thematically to the area of national history.

The intellectual perspective of Romero's academic undertaking was closely connected to his experience of the world
situation in the interwar period, interpreted in terms of a crisis
of bourgeois civilization. The model that Romero used to interpret this crisis was based on a conception of cultural history
influenced by the perspectives of his principal teachers: the
philosopher Francisco Romero (his older brother), Alexander
Korn, and Pedro Henriquez Ureña.

Romero's research tended increasingly toward medieval
history and his approach tended toward social history – as he
put it, "of the play of real situations," and of that "other play
between these situations and the types of mentality that have
been brought about by the representation or image that each

group forms from them." This formulation can be seen in the
shift in his approach from systems of ideas to mentalities.

In his later years, Romero researched more extensively into
Latin American history, culminating in the publication of one
of his most important works: *Latinoamérica: las ciudades y
las ideas* (Latin America: Cities and Ideas, 1976). This book
brought together his interest in cities as a historical subject,
his knowledge of European urban history, and his awareness
of the distance that separated the experience of European cities
from that of American ones. Romero analyzed the role of
cities in the Latin American historical process from the time
of the conquest to the present, based on the dialectic between
"autonomous development" – arising from the internal development of urban societies – and "heteronomous development"
– relating to changes induced by external influences.

The influence of Romero was not limited to the impact of
his major works or that of his research papers. He also
succeeded in popularizing and disseminating history. On the
one hand, he wrote several books that reached a wide readership. Some of them, including *La edad media* (The Middle
Ages, 1949) and *Breve historia de la Argentina* (Brief History
of Argentina, 1965), were considerable publishing successes.
Romero's clear and precise prose contributed to such successes.
On the other hand, he was a notable cultural organizer. He
took part in the running of several journals and in 1955, as
rector of the University of Buenos Aires, he founded the Buenos
Aires University Press. At the faculties of Social History and
of Medieval History, and at the Center of Social History –
which he founded in 1958 – he undertook the translation and
publication of important papers and many articles by contemporary social historians. These works put Argentine students
in contact with the major historiographic currents of the time.
Romero's contribution as a researcher, educator, and cultural
organizer to the modern approach of the community of
scholars of history in Argentina has been decisive.

LUCAS J. LUCHILO

See also Argentina; Halperín-Donghi

Biography

Born Buenos Aires, 1909. Studied at the University of La Plata, PhD
1937. Taught at University of La Plata, 1937–46: member, Socialist
party, and expelled from the university for political reasons, 1946;
taught at University of the Republic, Montevideo, Uruguay, and
continued his research into the medieval bourgeoisie at Harvard
University; in 1955, after the fall of the Perón regime, appointed
rector of the University of Buenos Aires: dean, Faculty of
Philosophy and Humanities, 1962–65. Founder and editor, *Imago
Mundi*, 1953–56; editor, journal of the University of Buenos Aires,
1960–65. Member, Socialist party executive committee, 1956–60.
Member, Council of the United Nations University. Died Tokyo,
1977.

Principal Writings

*La crisis de la República Romana: los Gracos y la reception de la
politica imperial hellenistica* (The Crisis of the Roman Republic: The
Gracchi and the Reception of Hellenistic Imperial Politics), 1942
Maquiavelo historiador (Machiavelli, Historian), 1943
Sobre la biografía y la historia (On Biography and History), 1945
Las ideas políticas en Argentina, 1946; in English as *A History of
Argentine Political Thought*, 1963

El ciclo de la revolución contemporánea (The Cycle of Contemporary
   Revolution), 1948
La edad media (The Middle Ages), 1949
Argentina: imágenes y perspectivas (Argentina: Images and
   Perspectives), 1956
Breve historia de la Argentina (A Brief History of Argentina), 1965
La revolución burguesa en el mundo feudal, 1967
El pensamiento político de la derecha latinoamericana (The Political
   Thought of the Latin American Right), 1970
Latinoamérica: las ciudades y las ideas (Latin America: Cities and
   Ideas), 1976
Crisis y orden en el mundo feudoburgués (The Bourgeois Revolution
   in the Feudal World), 1980
La experiencia argentina y otros ensayos (The Argentine Experience
   and Other Essays), edited by Luis Alberto Romero, 1980
Situaciones e ideologías en Latinoamérica (Situations and Ideologies
   in Latin America), 1981
La vida histórica, edited by Luis Alberto Romero, 1988

Further Reading

De historia e historiadores: Homenaje a José Luis Romero (About
   History and Historians: A Tribute to Romero), Mexico City: Siglo
   XXI Editores, 1982
Devoto, Fernando J., ed., *La historiografía argentina en el siglo XX*
   (Argentine Historiography in the 20th Century), 2 vols., Buenos
   Aires: Centro Editor de América Latina, 1994
Halperín-Donghi, Tulio, "José Luis Romero y su lugar en la
   historiografía Argentina" (José Luis Romero and His Place in
   Argentina Historiography), *Desarrollo Económico: Revista de
   Ciencias Sociales* 20 (1980), 248–74
International Committee of Historical Sciences – Argentine
   Committee, *Historografía Argentina: una evaluación crítica*
   (Argentine Historiography: A Critical Evaluation), Buenos Aires:
   Comité Internacional de Ciencias Históricas, 1990

Rörig, Fritz 1882–1952
German medievalist

In 1942 Fritz Rörig produced a masterly critical account of
developments in the 20th-century German historiography
of the medieval Hanseatic towns, the principal subject of his
own scholarship over the preceding two and a half decades
and for the remainder of his life. In 1908 Dietrich Schaefer
had pronounced the Hansa virtually exhausted as a field of
historical research. Schaefer's own efforts, and the work he
inspired, fell entirely within the parameters of German
historism and so had held its focus firmly on the diplomatic
and military record of the Hansa. It interpreted the Hansa as
an "exceptional formation" necessitated by the process of
disintegration that overtook the Holy Roman Empire in the
late Middle Ages. The problem with viewing the Hansa from
this narrow political and constitutional historical perspective
was, complained Rörig, that it legitimated a perception of the
Hansa as a "second rate affair on the periphery" of German
history. Historically-minded economists had been still worse,
either ignoring the medieval towns, their merchants, and their
trade entirely, or denigrating their achievements. That the
Hansa subsequently came to be widely regarded both as pivotal
to an understanding of the medieval Reich and as a matter of
contemporary political and economic relevance to Germany
comprised a transformation that was chiefly ascribed to Rörig
himself and to the school he established. It was in large measure

a product of significant methodological shifts whose impact on
the interwar German historical profession has only recently
been recognized.

Rörig took the neglected subject of the Hansa in a new
direction by applying the questions and skills of the economic
and social historian. The paradigm he produced, and which
was to continue to influence research agendas at least into the
1980s, redirected historians' attention toward long-distance
trade and its practitioners – the mercantile upper classes. In a
series of studies, the most significant of which were eventually
to find their way into the two big collections of his essays,
Rörig sought first to provide a secure base for the historiographical monument he sought to erect to the elite of the
medieval German towns. Thus, in stark contrast to previously
dominant theses postulating an undercapitalized mercantile
class which owed its urban locations to princely initiatives, he
advanced the thesis that the foundation of urban centers such
as Lübeck and Rostock owed less to the granting of charters
than to the activities of "entrepreneurial consortiums." These,
he argued, not only financed but planned the new urban foundations. The particular role Rörig assigned to consortiums
aroused the suspicion of several other experts as soon as his
findings became widely known. It has subsequently been
exposed as a product of the historian's wishful thinking and
entirely unsupported by any archival evidence whatever. Yet
his critics on this one score have been equally consistent in
stressing that his general thesis was by no means dependent
on this one exaggeration.

Rörig established a significant distinction between *frequen-
tantes* and *manentes* – between the traveling traders who
merely visited developing ports such as that of Wisby on
Gothland, and their mature and literate successors who stayed
in the ports and contributed decisively to their expansion and
full urbanization. In his study of Lübeck he reconstructed the
networks that, notably through intermarriage, were pivotal to
the formation of a mercantile upper class and maximized its
human and financial resources. Marxist historians, especially
in the German Democratic Republic, were subsequently to
complain that Rörig, for all his interest in social and economic
questions, paid scant attention to producers. However, Rörig's
quarrel on this point was chiefly with an anti-urban – and
antimodern – tendency to downgrade mercantile activity and
render it either as a side interest of master craftsmen or as a
sort of sinecure that might, for instance, derive from tenure of
mayoral office. Rörig persuasively argued that the crafts were
subordinate to mercantile interests and that civic office was
attained as a consequence of success in trade.

Rörig's contribution to the 1932 edition of the *Propyläen
Weltgeschichte*, "Die europäische Stadt," was the most rounded,
widely read, and enduring statement of his thesis. An expanded
version of the essay, based on his original manuscript, was
published in the Federal Republic of Germany after his death as
a book in its own right and (badly) translated into English as
The Medieval Town in 1967. Its subscript was determinedly
political: the endeavor, as Rörig's correspondence reveals, of a
self-proclaimed "antifascist" to instill some "backbone" into
a middle class whose turn towards the Nazi party had worried
him for years. It was a hymn of praise to the medieval German
bourgeois and citizen, designed to inspire active citizenship
within a parliamentary democratic framework.

Many of the thematic and methodological characteristics of Rörig's work suggest that it should be seen in the context of a wider paradigm shift in interwar German historiography: the emergence of "folk history." Its advocates sought to jolt the discipline out of its fixation on the state and, as Rörig himself put it, to view history "from the perspective of the *Volk*." To this end, they encouraged interdisciplinarity – in the service of racially defined nationalism. Rörig's employment of some of the vocabulary of racist politics – of the terms *völkisch*, *Volk*-comrade and *Raum* (space) – was to provide one of the blocks on which he could continue to build his career in the Third Reich. But here his kinship with "folk history" ends, for Rörig did not share its penchant for praising the peasantry, still less its adulation of Germanic tribesmen.

"Folk history" was in most respects a parochial reaction to an isolated and isolationist German historical profession. Recent attempts to compare it with the work of the early Annales school in France is unconvincing. Certainly, Marc Bloch's contemporary reviews of "folk" historical writing were frequently withering. But Rörig provides an exception on both counts. Although he did not become acquainted with the work of the great Belgian historian Henri Pirenne until the early 1920s, he was quick to note the resemblances between Pirenne's and his own work and to acknowledge Pirenne's influence on him thereafter. When, on Bloch's invitation, Rörig published an article in the *Annales*, he became the first professional German historian to have done so, and remained the only one until after World War II.

Under the Nazi regime, ethnic triumphed over democratic values in Rörig's hitherto ambiguous historical thought. That he was under some pressure to conform ideologically is clear. In the mid-1930s, he found himself obliged to defend himself vigorously against the charge of purveying a materialist conception of history. He did so, ironically, with particular reference to his article for the *Annales*, by arguing that his research had shown that the Hanseatic traders and town-builders were "carriers of German blood" and its values. Ambition undoubtedly contributed to Rörig's self-coordination, and was rewarded when he took up a prestigious chair at Berlin in 1935. He remained willing to exploit the past for explicitly political purposes. Although he publicly expressed reservations about aspects of Nazi foreign policy through a critique of geopolitics, and privately became concerned that "*völkisch* energies" were being constrained by the overbearing practices of the state, positive notes predominated in his attitudes to Nazism. During World War II in particular, he enjoyed what he himself termed "an abundance of political influence," not least as a member of the Nord- und Ostdeutsche Forschungsgemeinschaft. He interpreted the Drang nach Osten as an extension and completion of the medieval German colonization of Eastern Europe and continued to volunteer his services as an historian for the war effort even into the final months of the war. Rörig's historically-grounded propaganda essays were written at the expense of his making progress on either of his two major intellectual projects: monographs on the Hansa and on Lübeck, which, indeed, he never did write.

The final twist in a long career riddled with paradoxes is that Rörig built bridges to Marxism, retaining his chair in the Soviet zone of occupation after the end of the war. He was the last "bourgeois" professor of history to remain in post in the German Democratic Republic, where his emeritation was eventually granted in 1950. His intellectual legacy was unique in that his posthumous influence straddled the Cold War divide: he left one school of Hanseatic historiography in West, and another in East German scholarship.

PETER A. LAMBERT

Biography

Friedrich Hermann Rörig. Born St. Blasien, Baden, 2 October 1882. Attended Barmen Gymnasium; University of Tübingen; University of Leipzig; and University of Göttingen, PhD 1908. Archivist, Metz and Lübeck, 1908–18; taught at University of Leipzig, 1918–23; and University of Kiel, 1923–35; professor, University of Berlin, 1935–50. Died 1952.

Principal Writings

Die Entstehung der Landeshoheit des Trierer Erzbischofs (The Origin of the Sovereignty of the Archbishops of Trier), 1906
"Die europäische Stadt," in Walter Goetz, ed., *Propyläen Weltgeschichte* 4 (1932), 279–392; expanded as *Die europäische Stadt und die Kultur des Bürgertums im Mittelalter*, 1955, 4th edition 1964; in English as *The Medieval Town*, 1967
Vom Werden und Wesen der Hanse (The Development and Nature of the Hanseatic League), 1940
Wirtschaftskräfte im Mittelalter: Abhandlungen zur Stadt- und Hansegeschichte (Economic Forces in the Middle Ages: Treatise on Town and Hanseatic History), edited by Paul Kaegbein, 1959 [includes bibliography]

Further Reading

Brandt, A. von, and Wilhelm Koppe, eds., *Stadtwesen und Bürgertum als geschichtliche Kräfte: Gedächtnisschrift für Fritz Rörig* (Town Character and the Bourgeoisie as Historical Forces: In Memory of Fritz Rörig), Lübeck: Schmidt-Römild, 1953 [includes bibliography]

Rosenberg, Arthur 1889–1943

German historian

Beginning his career as a typical and conventionally minded historian of ancient Roman society, Arthur Rosenberg was converted to Marxism by the revolutionary events that accompanied the end of World War I. Initially a conservative who admired the efficiency of the Imperial German Army, Rosenberg became a leading member and Reichstag representative of the German Communist party. Although he resigned from the party in 1927, he was to remain a dedicated Marxist historian for the rest of his life.

His most important works – *The Birth of the German Republic* (1928, translated 1931), *A History of the German Republic* (1935), *A History of Bolshevism* (1932, translated 1933), and *Democracy and Socialism* (1938) – attempted to synthesize his historical training and Marxist political beliefs. The resulting body of work is both engaging and provocative as Rosenberg followed the evidence to what he saw as the reasonable interpretation of events. In each work, he rejected the conventional wisdom of both the right and the left, attempting to develop his own understanding of historical phenomenon. This led him to reject right-wing conspiracy theories while he developed categories of historical analysis quite independent from those wielded by Comintern historians.

For example, he developed a unique theory to explain the birth of the Weimar republic as the culmination of two revolutions that took place during the war. He argued that the first was the establishment of the Hindenberg/Ludendorff defacto military dictatorship in 1916 which left both the Kaiser and the Reichstag as mere symbols. The second was in October 1918 when the military High Command collapsed, leaving power to the non-revolutionary middle strata of Germany. Oddly, Rosenberg completely ignored the revolutionary events of November and December 1918 which are more commonly the focus of Marxist scholarship on this period.

Although this may appear strange for an avowed Marxist historian, it is indicative of Rosenberg's commitment to following his own interpretation of momentous developments without allowing himself blindly to accept prevailing schools of thought. Of course, this has led Rosenberg's critics to charge that his work is marred by a personalized and individualistic approach that fails to recognize the contributions and insights of others. Some might even argue that his rejection of communist discipline after 1927 caused him to emphasize unique interpretive approaches beyond those supported by the evidence. For example, as late as 1934, Rosenberg would claim that Nazism added nothing new in principle to existing fascism which could even be traced back to the "victory of legal fascism" with the Cuno government of 1923. All the same, there is little doubt that Rosenberg's work offered a uncommonly rich mixture of Marxism and historical analysis.

WILLIAM A. PELZ

See also Germany: 1800–1945

Biography

Born Berlin, 1889. Attended a Berlin Gymnasium; studied history and classical philology, University of Berlin, doctorate, 1911. Lecturer, University of Berlin, 1913. Served with the War Press Department, 1914–18. Joined Communist party, 1920: local councillor, then Reichstag deputy, 1921–28; left party, 1928. Left Germany, 1933; taught at University of Liverpool, 1934–37; and Brooklyn College, 1937–43. Died Brooklyn, 7 February 1943.

Principal Writings

Die Entstehung der deutschen Republik, 1871–1918, 1928; in English as The Birth of the German Republic, 1871–1918, 1931
Geschichte des Bolschewismus, 1932; in English as A History of Bolshevism from Marx to the First Five Years' Plan, 1933
Entstehung und Geschichte der Weimarer Republik, 1935; in English as A History of the German Republic, 1935
Demokratie und Sozialismus: zur politischen Geschichte der letzten 150 Jahre, 1938; in English as Democracy and Socialism: A Contribution to the Political History of the Past 150 Years, 1938
Demokratie und Klassenkampf: ausgewählte Studien (Democracy and Class Struggle: Selected Studies), edited by Hans-Ulrich Wehler, 1974 [includes bibliography]

Further Reading

Carsten, Francis L., "Arthur Rosenberg: Ancient Historian into Leading Communist," Journal of Contemporary History 8 (1973), 63–75

Rosenberg, Charles E. 1936–

US historian of medicine and science

Charles E. Rosenberg is the leading American historian of medicine in the closing decades of the 20th century. The Cholera Years (1962), is the single most influential book in the new social history of medicine. Social history of medicine began before Rosenberg, but in The Cholera Years the shift of focus to the nature and meaning of disease and to the world of the patient is apparent. By evaluating the social, moral, political, and medical responses to three separate epidemics of cholera in 19th-century New York City, Rosenberg shows how experiences with epidemic disease can reveal much about medicine and medical knowledge of the era and open virtually every aspect of society and politics for the historian.

Rosenberg started toward a career in medicine, then shifted to history in the early 1960s. The social historian of medicine, Edwin Ackerknecht at the University of Wisconsin, was a crucial influence on his career. Rosenberg emerged at a time when medical historians were also physicians; scholarly works in the history of medicine by those not medically trained were regarded as suspect. American historians had not accepted the Annales school's theories and considered medicine a trivial element in the study of American history. Sigerist, Rosen, and Shryock had attempted to alter the patterns in the study of the history of medicine; Rosenberg changed the nature of the field. He expanded his studies beyond the history of medicine into the history of science and sociology. He has edited several series of books on the history of medicine and society and edited Isis, a journal devoted to the history of science, from 1986 to 1988.

Rosenberg's The Care of Strangers: The Rise of America's Hospital System (1987) did for medical institutions what The Cholera Years did for disease. This book narrates the development of hospitals in the United States and sees them as microcosms of the total society of cities in the United States. In this book Rosenberg is careful not to ignore medical science. As with The Cholera Years, Rosenberg's scholarship appealed to a wide audience, beyond historians of medicine.

Rosenberg in 1971 called for a new emphasis in the history of medicine, a shift away from looking at only the intellectual life of physicians to their activities as healers and as members of a profession. However he warned revisionist historians not to ignore the role of science in the history of medicine.

Rosenberg's work contains many personal statements about the work of the historian of medicine and science. One appears in the introduction to Explaining Epidemics (1992), in which he emphasizes the potential for the study of the history of medicine and science to integrate the disparate elements of social history by focusing on humankind's most basic struggle, life and death.

NANCY PIPPEN ECKERMAN

See also Medicine

Biography

Charles Ernest Rosenberg. Born New York City, 11 November 1936. Received BA, University of Wisconsin, 1956; MA, Columbia University, 1956, PhD 1961. Taught at University of Wisconsin,

1962–63; and University of Pennsylvania, from 1963. Married
1) Carroll Ann Smith, historian, 1961 (marriage dissolved 1977,
1 daughter); 2) Drew Gilpin Faust, historian, 1980 (1 daughter).

Principal Writings

The Cholera Years: The United States in 1832, 1849, and 1866,
    1962; revised 1987

*The Trial of the Assassin Guiteau: Psychiatry and Law in the
    Gilded Age*, 1968

No Other Gods: On Science and American Social Thought, 1976

The Care of Strangers: The Rise of America's Hospital System, 1987

With Janet Golden, *Pictures of Health: A Photographic History of
    Health Care in Philadelphia, 1860–1945*, 1991

Explaining Epidemics and Other Studies in the History of Medicine,
    1992

Editor with Janet Golden, *Framing Disease: Studies in Cultural
    History*, 1992

Rosenberg, Hans 1904–1988

German historian

Hans Rosenberg was 29 years old and well poised for a successful scholarly career when Hitler came to power in 1933. He was also a Jew with strong democratic and social sympathies, and he left for England immediately after the Reichstag fire of February 1933. He already enjoyed an enviable publication record. His "Theologischer Rationalismus und vormärzlicher Vulgärliberalismus" (Theological Rationalism and Popular Liberalism before March 1848, 1930) had appeared in 1930 in Germany's pre-eminent historical journal, the *Historische Zeitschrift*. The article drew on the research materials for his *Rudolf Haym und die Anfänge des klassischen Liberalismus* (Rudof Haym and the Beginnings of Classical Liberalism), published in 1933 by the prestigious Oldenbourg Press in a truncated form made necessary by the German political crisis and Rosenberg's flight. These works, which are still essential reading for those interested in early German liberalism and historiography, strongly bore the impress of his teacher Friedrich Meinecke. Meinecke defies easy description: always nationalist in outlook, he came to see the shadows in German nationalism and looked for what was different and deviant in German history. Meinecke did not leave Germany, though he and Rosenberg, reportedly, always remained friends. Another of Meinecke's star students, Hajo Holborn, did leave shortly after Rosenberg did, and both men – by themselves and through their students – fundamentally reshaped American study of Central European history.

Rosenberg's first works followed Meinecke's inasmuch as they studied Germany through its intellectual history, an intellectual history studied less for its own sake than for the sake of analyzing the larger national society. If that was true of intellectual history in general, it was true in particular of the intellectual history of Prusso-Germany. This belief in German exceptionalism could undergird a sense of German spiritual superiority, as it did in some of Meinecke's early works, but it also easily lent itself to German self-criticism and, thence, to inquiry into why Hitler happened in Germany. That was undoubtedly the major question for Rosenberg, both in his economic histories of Central Europe and in his work on the evolution of the Prussian state.

He pushed this inquiry more through economic and social history than through intellectual history. He reportedly never lost his esteem for Meinecke. However that may be, in exile Rosenberg soon began to write histories very different from his mentor's. Even his early work shows a greater interest in economic context than does Meinecke's, and he began to study economic theory and history even before leaving Germany. The turning point in the history of his publications came during his two-year stay in England, during which he was able to earn a modest stipend only in the final months. Back in 1928 Meinecke had helped Rosenberg to obtain a contract from the National Historical Commission (Historische Reichskommission) to prepare a critical bibliography of political literature in the period of Prussian Reawakening and national unification: *Die nationalpolitische Publizistik Deutschlands vom Eintritt der Neuen Ära in Preussen bis zum Ausbruch des deutschen Krieges* (National-Political Media in Germany from the Start of the New Era in Prussia to the Outbreak of the German War). Despite the interruptions of the early 1930s, the work was at last published in 1935. It remains a standard reference tool, especially useful because some of the works described in it did not survive World War II. Meanwhile, Rosenberg published in 1934 the then less noticed but methodologically more significant pioneering study *Die Weltwirtschaftskrise von 1857–1859* (The World Economic Crisis of 1857–1859).

His motives for writing it are easy to see. Rosenberg had personally witnessed the political convulsions that followed the German hyperinflation of 1923 and the special severity with which the world depression of 1929 struck his native Central Europe. That, again, was why he was living in England. Rosenberg also understood that the state of social science was opportune for such research. Economists had recently elaborated "crisis Theory," and he could consult empirically grounded studies of *Konjunktur*, the cyclic rise and fall of the market. In doing so, Rosenberg employed the "long wave" theories of Nicolai Kondratiev (also very important for the contemporaneous Annales school in France) and of Joseph Schumpeter. Rosenberg's intent was less to illustrate the operation of ongoing processes than to employ them to gain a particular understanding of the historical there-and-then of Germany 1859–66 – with the implicit hope of thus better understanding Germany 1929–33.

Rosenberg returned to this sort of inquiry much later in his career, with his 1967 publication as a professor at Berkeley of *Grosse Depression und Bismarckzeit* (The Great Depression and the Bismarck Era), which he wrote for the Berlin Historical Commission and specifically dedicated to the Berlin students he had taught in 1949–50 while he was a visiting professor. His revealing introduction to this work contained the complaint that the task was simply too ambitious to be more than an "essay," though this essay is 273 pages of carefully written, lucidly argued, and thoroughly documented text. He nonetheless thought that the task was too ambitious because it required a simultaneous study of all *Mitteleuropa*, by which he meant Cisleithian Austria and the German states, and because it called for detailed research that was possible, he felt, only for a professor with fewer teaching and administrative duties and more assistants than he had. Many professors have voiced similar complaints, but Rosenberg was undoubtedly right that his method and subject called for more time and energy than one scholar could likely possess.

Rosenberg could claim this because he had more than the usual amount of energy: he came to the United States in 1935, taught for two years at Illinois College, and then taught at Brooklyn College from 1938 to 1939, after which he was invited to the University of California at Berkeley as Shepard Professor of History. While still at Brooklyn he consistently taught overloads because he found it easy and needed the extra compensation. He could raise the claim for another reason: This "essay" was essentially a sideline to the much more ambitious but not completed effort at what he termed the "elucidation of the structure and dynamic of the social, economic and political system of stratification in German central Europe before the Reformation." This shift back into late medieval history was a further effort to understand modern Germany by reference to much longer-term German social peculiarities. The research for it overlapped with the preparation of his last major work, published in 1969, "Deutsche Agrargeschichte in alter und neuer Sicht" (German Agricultural History in Traditional and Recent Perspective). Research led to research, and his late medieval project was itself an offshoot from his major English-language publication, the genial *Bureaucracy, Aristocracy, and Autocracy* (1958). Curiously, the book – now a classic – was not translated into German.

During this postwar period, no doubt further prodded by his impressions while teaching at Berlin in 1949–50, Rosenberg had turned to the early history of the Prussian monarchy as a means to understand better German peculiarity and, so, the basis of later National Socialist rule. Rosenberg did not, however, oversimplify by reducing all earlier German history to a gestation process for Nazism. Instead, he applied modern sociology to the results of the thorough institutional studies of Prussian bureaucracy published by older scholars such as Otto Hintze. Rosenberg sought to write a collective biography that would be less a prosopography such as Lewis Namier had written on the English parliament and more a social portrait comparing and contrasting the Prussian with other bureaucracies. Rosenberg was, again, interested in what was exceptional in German history. He demonstrated the social evolution of the Prussian bureaucracy's sense of being a state-bearing order that had blended with the older hereditary aristocracy. This helped explain the relative weakness of liberalism in Germany in contrast to other modern bureaucratic states. *Bureaucracy, Aristocracy, and Autocracy* nicely embodies the typical traits of both his earlier and later works: analysis of the local and national from a broadly comparative perspective, an evident though not combative break with previous literature, and a powerful interest in the contemporary historical relevance of the past.

ROBERT FAIRBAIRN SOUTHARD

See also Germany: 1800–1945; Koselleck; Wehler

Biography

Hans Willibald Rosenberg. Born Hannover, 26 February 1904. Studied with Freidrich Meinecke: PhD, University of Berlin, 1927. Researcher, Bavarian Academy of Science, 1927–28; German Federal Historical Commission, 1928–34; and Institute of Historical Research, London, 1934–35; taught at Illinois College, 1936–38; Brooklyn College, 1938–59; and University of California, Berkeley, 1959–88. Died Freiburg, 1988.

Principal Writings

"Theologischer Rationalismus und vormärzlicher Vulgärliberalismus" (Theological Rationalism and Popular Liberalism before March 1848), *Historische Zeitschrift* 141 (1930), 497–541
Rudolf Haym und die Anfänge des klassischen Liberalismus (Rudolf Haym and the Beginnings of Classical Liberalism), 1933
Die Weltwirtschaftskrise von 1857–1859 (The World Economic Crisis of 1857–1859), 1934
Die nationalpolitische Publizistik Deutschlands vom Eintritt der Neuen Ära in Preussen bis zum Ausbruch des deutschen Krieges (National-Political Media in Germany from the Start of the New Era in Prussia to the Outbreak of the German War), 2 vols., 1935
Bureaucracy, Aristocracy, and Autocracy: The Prussian Experience, 1660–1815, 1958
Grosse Depression und Bismarckzeit: Wirtschaftsablauf, Gesellschaft und Politik in Mitteleuropa (The Great Depression and the Bismarck Era: Economic Flow, Society, and Politics in Central Europe), 1967
"Deutsche Agrargeschichte in alter und neuer Sicht" (German Agricultural History in Traditional and Recent Perspective), in his *Probleme der deutschen Sozialgeschichte*, 1969

Further Reading

Ritter, Gerhard, ed., *Entstehung und Wandel der modernen Gesellschaft: Festschrift für Hans Rosenberg* (Origin and Transformation of Modern Society: Festschrift for Hans Rosenberg), Berlin: de Gruyter, 1970
Ritter, Gerhard, "Hans Rosenberg, 1904–1988," *Geschichte und Gesellschaft* 15 (1989), 282–302
Wehler, Hans-Ulrich, *Sozialgeschichte heute: Festschrift für Hans Rosenberg zum 70. Geburtstag* (Social History Today: Festschrift for Hans Rosenberg on his 70th Birthday), Göttingen: Vandenhoek & Ruprecht, 1974
Winkler, Heinrich August, "Ein Erneuerer der Geschichtswissenschaft: Hans Rosenberg, 1904–1988" (A Reviver of the Science of History), *Historische Zeitschrift* 248 (1989), 529–55

Rostovtzeff, M.I. 1870–1952
Russian classical historian

M.I. Rostovtzeff was one of the most eminent ancient historians of the 20th century; his interests ranged from the economic structures of the Greco-Roman world to the Iranian nomads of the South Russian steppe. He is best known, however, for two works, *The Social and Economic History of the Roman Empire* (1926) and *The Social and Economic History of the Hellenistic World* (1941). These books were remarkable for their learning and their command of a broad spectrum of specialist areas such as papyrology, archaeology, epigraphy, and numismatics, and although Rostovtzeff's economic model for the ancient world has now been largely rejected, his impact on ancient history was enormous.

Born in Kiev in 1870, Rostovtzeff was 48 when the Russian Revolution forced him into exile. He was already known for his work on land tenure and taxation in the Hellenistic and Roman East: in 1910 he had published in German a monograph on the Roman Colonate which established his reputation. Less well known outside Russia was his research on the

Scythians and Sarmatians, but before his exile he had written the standard work on tomb painting in South Russia and he left behind him a manuscript on the Scythians that was published by the Soviet authorities in 1925, and then later revised and published by Rostovtzeff himself in 1931 in German.

After leaving the University of St. Petersburg, Rostovtzeff went first to Oxford and then to the University of Wisconsin where he published his *A Large Estate in Egypt in the Third Century* BC (1922) and completed his *The Social and Economic History of the Roman Empire*. The first was a study in agricultural economics based on the archive of Zenon, a Greco-Carian entrepreneur and agent of Apollonius, the vizier of king Ptolemy II Philadelphus. The *Social and Economic History*, however, was recognized immediately for its imagination and command of the evidence. It was modeled on the German school of Eduard Meyer, who imagined an ancient economic development that replicated that of modern Europe. Familiarity with tsarist Russia modified Meyer's model: the Roman social and economic world of Rostovtzeff was a civilization of the cities inhabited by a bourgeoisie who were a ruling elite. Peasants and slaves interested him only insofar as they contributed to urban life.

In 1925, Rostovtzeff was appointed Stirling professor of ancient history and archaeology at Yale University, and while there he directed the excavations at Dura-Europos, a Hellenistic, Parthian, and then Roman fortress on the Euphrates River discovered by the British army after World War I and already explored by the French scholar Franz Cumont. Ten seasons of excavations produced some remarkable finds, such as a pre-Constantinian Christian house of worship and a synagogue with wall paintings of biblical scenes with human figures; these furnished proof for the art historian that the characteristic frontal representation of the human form of late antiquity originated early in the 3rd century in the Roman East. Dura-Europos marked the culmination of Rostovtzeff's interest in urban life which ranged from Pompeii, which fascinated him, to the caravan cities of the east and even Kievan Russia.

The Social and Economic History of the Hellenistic World was his greatest work, ranging over the Greek world after Alexander the Great with a sure touch. Rostovtzeff had not abandoned his perception of an ancient capitalist economy, but he had learned from his critics. His final years were melancholy; nonetheless his last publication, a contribution to the Dura-Europos preliminary reports, appeared only four months before his death in 1952.

Rostovtzeff's concept of the ancient economy was overtaken by the work of Max Weber, Johannes Hasebrock, and, lately, Karl Polanyi. Polanyi emphasized the difference between the ancient city, which was a city of consumers, and its modern counterpart, the city of producers, and pointed out the links between the political life of the ancient world and the economy, which was (to use Polanyi's term) "embedded" in society. Moses Finley popularized Weber's views, and contributed to the eclipse of Rostovtzeff's. However Rostovtzeff's work still commands respect for its learning, and he remains one of the giants of historical scholarship.

J.A.S. EVANS

See also Greece: Ancient; Roman

Biography

Michael [Mikhail] Ivanovich Rostovtzeff [Rostovtsev]. Born Zhitomir, Ukraine, Russia, 10 November 1870. Studied at University of Kiev; BA, University of St. Petersburg, 1892, MA 1898, PhD 1903. Travelling fellowship in classical lands, 1895–98; taught ancient history and Latin, University of St. Petersburg, from 1893: professor, 1903–18; left Russia, 1918; taught at Queen's College, Oxford, 1918–20; professor of ancient history, University of Wisconsin, 1920–25; and Yale University, 1925–44 (emeritus). Married Sophie M. Kulczycki, 1901. Died New Haven, Connecticut, 20 October 1952.

Principal Writings

Studien zur Geschichte des römischen Kolonates (Studies on the History of the Roman Colonate), 1910

"The Foundations of Social and Economic Life in Egypt in Hellenistic Times," *Journal of Egyptian Archaeology* 6 (1920), 161–78

Iranians and Greeks in South Russia, 1922

A Large Estate in Egypt in the Third Century BC: *A Study in Economic History*, 1922

Ocherk istorii drevnego mira: Vostok-Gretsiia-Rim, 1924; in English as *A History of the Ancient World*, 2 vols., 1926–28; reprinted as *Rome*, 1960, and *Greece*, 1963

The Social and Economic History of the Roman Empire, 2 vols., 1926; 2nd edition 1957

Mystic Italy: The Colver Lectures at Brown University, 1927

The Animal Style in South Russia and China, 1929

Skythien und der Bosporus (The Scythians and the Bosporus), 1931

Caravan Cities, edited by D. Talbot Rice, 1932

The Social and Economic History of the Hellenistic World, 3 vols., 1941; revised 1953

Further Reading

Andreau, Jean, Introduction, to Rostovtzeff, *Histoire économique et sociale du monde hellénistique*, Paris: Laffont, 1989

Momigliano, Arnaldo, "M.I. Rostovtzeff," *Cambridge Journal* 7 (1954), 334–46; reprinted in his *Studies in Historiography*, London: Weidenfeld and Nicolson, and New York: Harper, 1966

Reinhold, Meyer, "Historian of the Classic World: A Critique of Rostovtzeff," *Science and Society* 10 (1946), 361–91

Welles, C. Bradford, "M.I. Rostovtzeff," *Gnomon* 25 (1953), 140–44

Rostow, W.W. 1916–

US economic historian

Walt Rostow is an internationally known economic historian whose academic eminence won him an important role in United States policymaking, particularly in the 1950s and 1960s, a period about which he has also written. His historical contributions therefore fall into two categories: extensive writings on broad themes in economic history, and materials in some way related to his own career as a historical protagonist. In all, the prolific Rostow has published thirty books and numerous articles on historical, political, and public themes.

Rostow's major professional efforts were devoted to attempting to explain the processes of economic growth, in the hope of developing a model that could be applied to other economies. His early works, *British Economy of the Nineteenth Century* (1948) and *The Growth and Fluctuation of the British Economy, 1790–1850* (with others, 1953), concentrated on

Britain, the first country to industrialize, in an attempt to explain why this should have been the first country to experience an industrial revolution. This effort resulted in *The Process of Economic Growth* (1953) and *The Stages of Economic Growth* (1960), works that purported to provide a gameplan which developing countries could follow in order to experience economic progress while avoiding revolution. In the 1970s and 1980s, Rostow reverted to these themes, in such volumes as *Politics and the Stages of Growth* (1971), *The World Economy* (1978), *Why the Poor Get Richer and the Rich Slow Down* (1980), *Rich Countries and Poor Countries* (1987), *Essays of a Half Century* (1988), and *History, Policy, and Economic Theory* (1990). His work made much use of such terms as "preconditions for growth," "take-off," "self-sustaining growth," and "leading sector," and of the theme that there exist long-term economic cycles, several decades in length. While many economists have criticized Rostow's use of these concepts, and the degree to which he emphasizes the nation-state as a unit of analysis and explanation, his writings gave rise to enormous discussion and speculation, in itself a tribute to the breadth of his thinking.

Rostow's analysis appealed to those American policymakers of the 1950s and 1960s who believed that it was possible to resolve international economic issues in a manner that would be favorable to their Cold War aims of preventing Third World revolution and promoting peaceful social change and economic growth. In 1961 he was invited to join the administration of the youthful, activist president John F. Kennedy as chairman of the State Department Policy Planning Council. In 1966 Rostow became special assistant to the president for National Security Affairs, and he remained in government service until 1969. Here he is best remembered for his insistence upon the escalation and continuation of the United States military commitment to South Vietnam, which made him possibly the strongest "hawk" in both the Kennedy and Johnson administrations. It was often alleged that Rostow's post-1969 relegation to a professorship at the University of Texas, rather than the prestigious Ivy League academic institutions he had previously adorned, was the direct consequence of the academic disfavor to which his Vietnam policies condemned him. He continued to defend the wisdom of United States policies in Vietnam in essays, most recently when reviewing Robert McNamara's memoirs of the Vietnam War period.

During the 1940s, well before he joined the Kennedy administration, Rostow served in the Office of Strategic Services and the State Department, and, later, on occasion served as a government consultant. In a series of short works on various key episodes during this period, Rostow drew on these experiences, and on his personal knowledge of many of the leading figures involved, to produce an interesting series of monographs on "Ideas and Action." All contained a useful appendix of relevant documents, many at the time still unpublished. A common theme of these studies was the degree to which initially sensible, rational proposals were diluted, altered, or rejected through the imperatives of bureaucratic politics and institutional and personal pressures, an outlook that no doubt reflected Rostow's frustrations as a public official and consultant. Although further works in this series were promised, none has yet appeared, possibly because their author turned his energies to other projects.

When dealing with Rostow, one should never forget the degree to which his academic preoccupations and his public service role were intertwined with and fed off each other. Overall, his oeuvre represents a fascinating combination of the professional economic historian, who attempted to influence the making of national and international policy through his specialized expertise and governmental connections, and the autobiographical recollections and reflections of the influential public servant.

PRISCILLA M. ROBERTS

See also Economic; Industrial Revolution

Biography

Walt Whitman Rostow. Born New York City, 17 October 1916. Received BA, Yale University, 1936, PhD 1940; Rhodes Scholar, Oxford University. Taught at Columbia University, 1940–41, before war service: in Office of Strategic Services, 1941–45, as a major, US Army, 1943–45, and as assistant chief, Division of German-Austrian Economic Affairs, Department of State, 1945–46; special assistant to executive secretary, Economic Commission for Europe, 1947–49; taught at Oxford University, 1946–47; Cambridge University, 1949–50; and Massachusetts Institute of Technology, 1951–61. At John F. Kennedy's election, returned to government service as deputy special assistant for National Security Affairs, 1961, chairman, Policy Planning Council, Department of State, 1961–66, and special assistant to the president, 1966–69; then taught at University of Texas, Austin. Married Elspeth Davies, 1947 (1 son, 1 daughter).

Principal Writings

British Economy of the Nineteenth Century: Essays, 1948
With Arthur D. Gayer et al., *The Growth and Fluctuation of the British Economy, 1790–1850*, 1953
The Process of Economic Growth, 1953
The Stages of Economic Growth: A Non-Communist Manifesto, 1960; 3rd edition 1990
Politics and the Stages of Growth, 1971
The Diffusion of Power, 1957–1972, 1972
The World Economy: History and Prospect, 1978
Why the Poor Get Richer and the Rich Slow Down: Essays in the Marshallian Long Period, 1980
The Division of Europe after World War II: 1946, 1981
Pre-Invasion Bombing Strategy: General Eisenhower's Decision of March 25, 1944, 1981
Europe after Stalin: Eisenhower's Three Decisions of March 22, 1953, 1982
Open Skies: Eisenhower's Proposal of July 21, 1955, 1982
Rich Countries and Poor Countries, 1987
Essays of a Half Century: Ideas, Policies, and Action, 1988
History, Policy, and Economic Theory, 1990

Further Reading

Dorfman, Robert, "Economic Development from the Beginning to Rostow," *Journal of Economic Literature* 29 (1991), 573–91
Halberstam, David, *The Best and the Brightest*, New York: Random House, and London: Barrie and Jenkins, 1972
Kindleberger, Charles P., and Guido di Tella, eds., *Economics in the Long View: Essays in Honor of W.W. Rostow*, 3 vols., London: Macmillan, and New York: New York University Press, 1982
Supple, Barry, "Revisiting Rostow," *Economic History Review* 37 (1984), 107–14

Rothschild, Joseph 1931–

US (German-born) historian of modern Eastern Europe

Joseph Rothschild's works have concentrated both on specific aspects of Eastern European history, as well as broader trends in that region and the world. He has distinguished himself by filling in important gaps in the historiography of Eastern Europe. *The Communist Party of Bulgaria* (1959) and *Pilsudski's Coup d'Etat* (1966) were two important works in this regard. In the former, a topic on which there had been no serious work, Rothschild traced the formation of the Bulgarian Socialist party in 1891 through its split in 1903 into the Broads and the Narrows, to the foundation of the Bulgarian Communist party in 1919, and its subsequent history to 1936. Throughout, Rothschild pointed to the close relationship the Narrows had with Russia. Indeed, Bulgarian communists were in the first Russian Marxist circles. This analysis is instrumental for understanding why the Bulgarian Communist party would later develop into Russia's most faithful ally.

With *Pilsudski's Coup d'Etat*, Rothschild entered the debate about interwar developments in Poland. In this portrayal of Pilsudski, Rothschild made two points that drew particular attention. First, he argued that Pilsudski was the forerunner of East European dictators of the 1930s, although he did point out that Pilsudski's form of dictatorship was preferable to totalitarianism. Second, Rothschild speculated that Pilsudski's importance for future Polish developments was crucial. He wrote: "Pilsudski must in justice be acknowledged as meriting primary credit for the fact that today the notion of Europe without a Polish state is no longer conceivable." Detractors have considered this both an overly flattering portrait of the man, and an exaggeration of his importance. This work has been widely praised, however, as a case study of the mechanics of a seizure of power and the destruction of a parliamentary system.

Rothschild has also written on broader issues dealing with Eastern Europe in both the interwar period and the post-1945 era. He discussed a variety of themes, such as the role of the bureaucracy and the intelligentsia, the political and socio-economic problems of the peasantry, and the problems of national minorities. In discussing the earlier period, Rothschild brought out several points about interwar Europe. He rejected the desirability of old multinational states and judged that the history of the new nation-states in Eastern Europe in the interwar period contributed to their development in the postwar period, although limited by the Cold War. He also firmly placed the blame for the failure of democratic institutions in the region on the Great Powers for not providing the economic aid necessary to ensure stability. His discussion of these various aspects in *East Central Europe Between the Two World Wars* (1974), delivered a more balanced approach than the earlier work by Hugh Seton-Watson *Eastern Europe Between the Wars, 1918–1941* (1945).

Rothschild carried many of his themes of interwar Eastern Europe into the postwar period and up to the collapse of communism. His main concern here was to trace the trend of increasing diversification in the region toward the plurality that existed in the interwar period. The failure of Stalinism to bring about a uniform political culture in the region, he suggested, was partly responsible for the divisions that emerged

towards the latter years of the Cold War. Rothschild also pointed out that the tendency toward authoritarian regimes in the interwar period might be a bad omen for future developments in Eastern Europe, hinting that throwing off Soviet rule would not automatically lead to parliamentary democracy. Rothschild's ideas are encapsulated in *Return to Diversity* (1989). Both this, and his earlier work on the interwar period, are ideal surveys of the history of East Central Europe and provide a framework in which to explore the issues further.

With the issue of national minorities in Eastern Europe as a starting point, Rothschild later developed his ethnicity concepts on a broader scale. In *Ethnopolitics* (1981) he argued that modernization mobilizes ethnic groups and turns them into political beings. His argument that modernization creates a feeling of alienation that leads to a reaffirmation of cultural identity has been disputed by historians who believe that class, rather than ethnicity, is a more dominant factor in political/historical development.

GARY S. BRUCE

See also Balkans; East Central Europe

Biography
Born Fulda, Germany, 5 April 1931; emigrated to US, 1940, naturalized 1945. Received BA, Columbia University, 1951, MA 1952; PhD, Oxford University, 1955. Taught political science (rising to professor), Columbia University, from 1958. Married Ruth Nachmansohn, art historian, 1959 (1 son, 1 daughter).

Principal Writings
The Communist Party of Bulgaria: Origins and Development, 1883–1936, 1959
Communist Eastern Europe, 1964
Pilsudski's Coup d'Etat, 1966
East Central Europe Between the Two World Wars, 1974
Ethnopolitics: A Conceptual Framework, 1981
Return to Diversity: A Political History of East Central Europe since World War II, 1989; revised 1993

Rowbotham, Sheila 1943–

British socialist-feminist historian

Sheila Rowbotham was a central figure in the emergence of women's history in the early 1970s. For her, writing women's history has been a part of the radical political activity that helped to create British second wave feminism from the late 1960s, and her influence as a politically engaged writer and activist has been more considerable outside the discipline of history rather than within it. Rowbotham set out to challenge ways of seeing women, both within socialism and in society as a whole, by demonstrating that women had their own history. This included women's participation in the creation of radical political movements in the past.

Along with several other female historians, including Sally Alexander and Anna Davin, she was part of the History Workshop movement that originated at Ruskin College in the 1960s. This sought to integrate the perspective of British Marxist historians with the labor movement tradition of workers' history. The emphasis on institutions of organized labor in traditional labor history was rejected in favor of research into popular movements of resistance. In spite of this, derisive incredulity was expressed at the History Workshop in 1969 when Rowbotham stood up to suggest a meeting of people working on women's history. This prompted the organization of the first national Women's Liberation conference in 1970, which has been seen as the formal beginnings of the movement in Britain.

Inspired by this, she began by writing about the role played by women and, in particular, working-class women, in revolutionary movements of the past. Her first book, *Women, Resistance and Revolution* (1972), was a trail-blazing exploration, primarily using secondary sources to uncover women's contribution to both historical and contemporary revolutionary movements. These stretched from the French Revolution to Maoist China. *Hidden from History* (1973), her best known work, was a Marxist analysis of the position of British women from the Puritans until 1930, in terms of industrialization, class, and the ongoing process of sexual discrimination. By concentrating on interpretation and analysis in structural terms rather than on the supporting detail, Rowbotham was able to trace a female consciousness through the complex webs of industrial and political change. The clarity and directness of her language, as well as her constant awareness of the potentially contradictory nature of women's desires and needs, ensured she reached a broad audience outside academia.

Rowbotham also challenged the theoretical resistance to feminism, and thus women's history, within Marxism. Socialists insisted that women's oppression was not separate from the oppression of the working classes, and that within communism sexual discrimination would not exist. In consequence of this, they asserted that any separate focus on women was a distraction. At the same time, women's domestic labor was not seen as part of the capitalist economy, as it did not produce surplus value. In *Women's Consciousness, Man's World* (1973), Rowbotham argued that women's domestic labor was a component of commodity production as it enabled the production and reproduction of male labor. However, she also insisted the family was never just the mediator of capitalism's need for discipline and hierarchy but always a potential refuge from the commodification of human relationships. Child-rearing and shared needs for sexuality and being comforted cannot be reduced to service commodities.

Having established a broad historical framework for women's history, Rowbotham moved on to look at earlier socialists who had refused to accept a materialistic definition of society, or a limiting approach to sexuality and the body. Edward Carpenter, the late 19th-century socialist and sexual radical, saw becoming a socialist as a spiritual rebirth, while Stella Browne, an early 20th-century socialist-feminist, campaigned for women's control over their fertility and insisted on the importance of sexual pleasure for women. Rowbotham asked how these people had lived and related to one another emotionally within their circles. Connecting these questions with their writing and other activities showed how new understandings emerged from a redefinition of aspects of life that had been previously seen as either political or personal, but never both.

Rowbotham rejected the radical feminist concept of patriarchy as essentialist and as denying the potential capacity of all human beings for transformation. She wanted to avoid a simple category of woman, including the imposition of such a category on women of other cultures. Nonetheless, her own work has remained within Marxist paradigms, while the feminism she helped to create has contributed to the destruction of those same theoretical certainties. This can be seen in *The Past Is Before Us* (1989), her chronicle of the British Women's Liberation movement over the last 25 years. Her sweeping up of changes – such as equal pay legislation – which were initiated by other groups, and indeed by parliamentarians of another, older generation, into the embrace of the Women's Liberation movement is confusing.

Although many of the questions that concern historians of women and gender in the 1990s were prefigured in her work during the 1970s, the wave of historical research in the field since then has meant that a mass of new information is now available. Yet Rowbotham's insistence on the importance of reproduction, sexuality, and domestic labor, as well as paid work, to the whole of society remains powerful. And *Hidden from History* remains a provocative historical synthesis of British women's experience over the last three centuries.

HERA COOK

Biography

Born Leeds, 27 February 1943. Educated at Hunmanby Hall, 1953–70; St. Hilda's College, Oxford, BA 1964; postgraduate work, Birkbeck College, University of London. Taught part-time in further education colleges and Workers' Educational Associations, 1960s and 1970s; visiting professor, Amsterdam, 1981–83; editor, *Jobs for Change* (Greater London Council newspaper), 1983–86; consultant, UN World Institute for Development and Economic Research, Helsinki, from 1986. Founder member, History Workshop movement, 1966. Has one son.

Principal Writings

Women, Resistance and Revolution, 1972
Hidden from History: 300 Years of Women's Oppression and the Fight Against It, 1973
Women's Consciousness, Man's World, 1973
A New World for Women: Stella Browne, Socialist Feminist, 1977
With Jeffrey Weeks, *Socialism and the New Life: The Personal and Sexual Politics of Edward Carpenter and Havelock Ellis*, 1977
With Lynne Segal and Hilary Wainwright, *Beyond the Fragments: Feminism and the Making of Socialism*, 1979
"The Trouble with 'Patriarchy,'" in Raphael Samuel, ed., *People's History and Socialist Theory*, 1981
Dreams and Dilemmas: Collected Writings, 1983
Friends of Alice Wheeldon, 1988
The Past Is Before Us, 1989
Women in Movement: Feminism and Social Action, 1992
Homeworkers Worldwide, 1993
Editor with Swasti Mitter, *Dignity and Daily Bread: New Forms of the Economic Organizing among Poor Women in the Third World and the First*, 1994
Editor with Swasti Mitter, *Women Encounter Technology: Changing Patterns of Employment in the Third World*, 1995
A Century of Women: The History of Women in Britain and the US, 1997

Further Reading

Vedder-Schultz, N., "Hearts Starve as Well as Bodies: Ulrike Prokop's *Production and the Context of Women's Daily Life*," *New German Critique*, 13 (1978), 5–17

Winslow, Barbara, Temma Kaplan, Rosalyn Baxandall, and Bryan D. Palmer, "Women's Revolutions: The Work of Sheila Rowbotham, A Twenty-Year Assessment," *Radical History Review* 63 (1995), 141–65

Rudé, George 1910–1993

British social historian

George Rudé became a convinced Marxist long before he became a practicing historian. Converted by reading the works of Marx and Lenin, as well as by a tour he made of the Soviet Union in 1932, Rudé believed that history progressed through a conflict of social classes that moved in a discernible pattern from lower to higher phases. Consequently he considered the common people as the basic force behind social change.

Not until his forties, however, after he had taken a degree from Cambridge University in modern languages and spent several years teaching in public schools, did Rudé undertake to study history. At the University of London he began research for his doctorate on Parisian wage earners during the insurrectionary movements from 1789 to 1791. He studied the course of popular violence, asking specific and hitherto unanswered questions about the individuals who captured the Bastille and marched on Versailles. In the French archives he made extensive use of public records to uncover the occupations, ages, and behavior of participants. But Rudé did not publish his dissertation until he had continued his research into the period 1792–95. Appearing as *The Crowd in the French Revolution* (1959), his book proved a model of erudition and established him as a leading authority on the period. Along with his friends and contemporaries Albert Soboul and Richard Cobb, Rudé was strongly influenced by Georges Lefebvre, who had done pioneering work on crowd behavior. Together they developed the concept of "History from Below," concentrating their research on the struggles of the lower classes to secure economic, social, and political rights.

During the 1960s Rudé began to explore popular movements in England. He applied the same methods of inquiry to the voluminous but largely neglected judicial records. In detailed studies of the Gordon riots of 1780 and the tumultuous career of the radical John Wilkes, he threw fresh light on the popular agitation that shook 18th-century London. Into his writings Rudé incorporated material culled from land tax registers, city directories, petitions, and poll books to identify the social condition of both rioters and their better-off victims. Rudé's work on the popular classes stood in sharp contrast to the efforts of Lewis Namier and his followers, who concentrated on the elites.

In his general synthesis, *The Crowd in History* (1964), Rudé compared popular disturbances, both rural and urban, on both sides of the Channel from the early 18th through the mid-19th centuries. He applied sociological methods to reveal the aims, structure, and conduct of "pre-industrial" crowds, analyzed their beliefs and motives, and why they triumphed or failed. He thus created a model for understanding the growth of a mass phenomenon that previous historians had largely neglected.

Until the last few years of his life, when serious illness prevented him from working, Rudé produced a variety of scholarly and general studies that demonstrated his mastery. He continually expanded understanding of crowds in history by conducting research into criminality and justice. In *Captain Swing* (1968), written in collaboration with E.J. Hobsbawm, he investigated the laborers' rising that swept across much of England in 1830. Two other investigations of crime and punishment, published while he himself was living "in exile" abroad, concerned the transportation of offenders to Australia. While making extensive use of court records and statistics to record offenses, Rudé nonetheless focused on the individuals who were condemned, and demonstrated noticeable sympathy for their unhappy fates.

He turned his hand to strictly urban history in *Hanoverian London* (1971), which incorporated examples of popular unrest into a detailed account of the growing metropolis in its economic, social, political, and cultural aspects. Written for a general audience, the volume demonstrated Rudé's ability to distill primary sources into a readable, informative text that concentrated on the human element.

In *Ideology and Popular Protest* (1980), he shifted from explaining the identity (the "who") of crowds to discussing their motives (the "why"). Employing concepts developed by the Italian Marxist Antonio Gramsci, Rudé traced the growth of class consciousness from medieval times to the mid-19th century. He contended that the ideology of common people was enriched by indoctrination, experience, and struggle that raised their awareness from lower to higher stages.

Rudé's books on Old Regime and revolutionary Europe showed his talent for synthesis. In them he compressed years of research on crowds and placed them in the larger framework of class structure, economic conditions, and political change. He made one lone venture into biography, a life of Maximilien Robespierre, intended less as the study of a personality than as a "political portrait," a sympathetic study of the "first great champion of democracy and the people's rights."

His final summation, *The French Revolution* (1988), a general history written to commemorate the 200th anniversary, brought him full circle. The book, which covered the period 1789–1848, indicated how far Rudé had matured as a scholar since he first entered the Parisian archives some forty years earlier.

Marxist as his outlook remained, Rudé was neither dogmatic in his historical judgments nor worshipful toward Marx's writings. Rather, he always based his conclusions on solid archival research and wide reading. He eagerly adopted new ideas concerning social structure, mass psychology, and political theory. Although his methodology and conclusions were not universally accepted, especially by non-Marxists, he refrained from attacking his critics and never engaged in personal polemics. The volume and variety of his scholarly production ensure his place as a leading authority on "History from Below."

JAMES FRIGUGLIETTI

See also Australia; Britain: since 1750; Cobb; France: French Revolution; History from Below; Marx; Marxist Interpretation

Biography

George Frederick Elliot Rudé. Born Oslo, Norway, 8 February 1910, son of an engineer. Educated at Shrewsbury School; Trinity

College, Cambridge, BA 1931; University of London, BA 1948, PhD 1950. Worked for London Fire Service during World War II. Teacher of modern languages and history in public schools, 1931–59: Stowe School, 1931–35; St. Paul's School, 1936–49; Sir Walter St. John's School, 1950–54; and Holloway School, 1954–59; taught (rising to professor), University of Adelaide, 1960–67; University of Stirling, 1968; Flinders University of South Australia, 1968–70; and Concordia University, 1970–87 (emeritus); founded Inter-University Centre for European Studies. Member of British Communist party, 1935–59. Married Doreen de la Hoyde, 1940. Died Battle, England, 8 January 1993.

Principal Writings

The Crowd in the French Revolution, 1959
Wilkes and Liberty: A Social Study of 1763 to 1774, 1962
The Crowd in History: A Study of Popular Disturbances in France and England, 1730–1848, 1964
Revolutionary Europe, 1783–1815, 1964
Editor, *The Eighteenth Century*, 1965
Editor, *Robespierre: A Life in Brief*, 1967
With E.J. Hobsbawm, *Captain Swing: A Social History of the Great English Agricultural Uprising of 1830*, 1968
Paris and London in the Eighteenth Century: Studies in Popular Protest, 1970
Hanoverian London, 1714–1808, 1971
Debate on Europe, 1815–1850, 1972
Europe in the Eighteenth Century: Aristocracy and the Bourgeois Challenge, 1972
Robespierre: Portrait of a Revolutionary Democrat, 1975
Protest and Punishment: The Story of Social and Political Protesters Transported to Australia, 1788–1868, 1978
Ideology and Popular Protest, 1980
Criminal and Victim: Crime and Society in Early Nineteenth-Century England, 1985
The French Revolution, 1988

Further Reading

Kaye, Harvey J., ed., *The Face of the Crowd: Studies in Revolution, Ideology, and Popular Protest: Selected Essays of George Rudé*, Atlantic Highlands, NJ: Humanities Press, and London: Harvester Press, 1988
Krantz, Frederick, ed., *History from Below: Studies in Popular Protest and Popular Ideology in Honour of George Rudé*, Montreal: Concordia University Press, 1985; Oxford: Blackwell, 1988

Runciman, Steven 1903–

British historian of Byzantium

Steven Runciman is an outstanding Byzantine historian. He received encouragement and some formal training in the field from the great British ancient historian J.B. Bury, who was one of the first historians to recognize the Byzantine empire's importance to western civilization. Bury also contributed significantly to Runciman's view of history, a view Runciman succinctly summarized in the preface of his 3-volume *A History of the Crusades* (1951–54): "I believe that the supreme duty of the historian is to write history, that is to say, to attempt to record in one sweeping sequence the greater events and movements that have swayed the destinies of man." He bemoaned the trend among contemporary historians to let "criticism overpower creation." In his opinion historians expended too much effort analyzing the past in a futile effort to "reduce history to a series of economic or sociological laws, and that however thoroughly you may analyze some special institution, or even some limited period, you must go further." That is, historians must study every aspect of their topic or risk losing some nuances of its sequence of cause and effect. Historians who bisect events either by applying theoretical models to an age, or by using quantitative methods, restrict our understanding of the past because these methods seek to reveal underlying forces that determine the course of history. Runciman feels that the number of variables possibly affecting the outcome of any given sequence of cause and effect are so numerous that no theoretical model can account for them all. Thus we can never predict even the immediate future because unforeseen events or "accidents" occur that alter the current "sequence of intelligible cause and effect." Accidents take civilization in different and unforeseen directions. Runciman argues that making sense of the past requires historians to study all available primary sources on their topic. After scrutinizing these sources carefully to determine their accuracy, the historian can reconstruct as completely as possible a segment of the past. In short, Runciman advocates striving for a total history as the only way to obtain accurate pictures of past events. Historians must also use narrative to write their total histories, rather than the jargon of social scientists. Although his theory of history has sparked controversy, Runciman has always practiced what he preached. He researches his topic thoroughly and subjects his primary sources to rigorous critical analysis.

Examples of Runciman's total history, although only on a much smaller scale than the *Crusades*, are *The Emperor Romanus Lecapenus and His Reign* (1929) and *The Fall of Constantinople, 1453* (1965). What both books have in common is a determination to remove the negative bias that surrounded Byzantine civilization before the 20th century. By considering the Byzantine empire in a favorable light, Runciman's writings have played a prominent role in attacking that prejudice. The first book, which Byzantine specialists consider his major contribution to the field, contains an authoritative account of the Byzantine empire during the 10th century's early decades. It also contributed greatly to the revival of interest in Byzantine studies. The second book's theme is the enthralling and occasionally thrilling story of the Byzantine empire's last days. Runciman presented it as a tragic struggle between the rising power of the Ottoman Turks and the feebleness of the Byzantine empire. Rather than merely analyze the military strategy and tactics of both sides, he offered a picture of war as involving primarily suffering and courage, even for the victors. In the end the old empire died with dignity.

The most impressive example of Runciman's narrative history is his general history of the Crusades. They studied the entire era, and are a monument to his rejection of the cautiously limited topics so popular among historians reaching for the definitive work. He approached the Crusades from a political perspective, and saw them as a force affecting the balance of power in the Levant. Consequently, the volumes offered little on institutional, legal, ecclesiastical, economic, or social structures. The work clearly revealed his admiration for the Byzantine empire, whose magnificence he compared unfavorably to the "intolerance and dishonorable barbarity of the

West." While this verdict corrected the anti-Byzantine bias of previous studies, critics have charged that portraying Byzantium as the hero and the West as the villain oversimplified the subject.

Runciman did not restrict his research to centuries when the Byzantine empire existed, but considered its legacy under the Ottoman Turks in *The Great Church in Captivity* (1968). This book was the first to pursue the fate of one of Byzantium's greatest cultural institutions, the Orthodox church, under the Ottoman Turks. It also filled a large gap in Greek history.

ROBERT F. FORREST

See also Balkans; Crusades

Biography

James Cochran Stevenson Runciman. Born Northumberland, 7 July 1903. Educated at Eton College; Trinity College, Cambridge, BA 1924, MA 1928; fellow, 1927–38. Press attaché, British Legation, Sofia, 1940; and British Embassy, Cairo, 1941; professor of Byzantine art and history, University of Istanbul, 1942–45; represented British Council in Greece, 1945–47. Independent scholar since 1947, with many advisory positions. Knighted 1958.

Principal Writings

The Emperor Romanus Lecapenus and His Reign: A Study of Tenth-Century Byzantium, 1929
A History of the First Bulgarian Empire, 1930
Byzantine Civilisation, 1933
The Medieval Manichee: A Study of the Christian Dualist Heresy, 1947
A History of the Crusades, 3 vols., 1951–54
The Eastern Schism: A Study of the Papacy and the Eastern Churches during the XIth and XIIth Centuries, 1955
The Sicilian Vespers: A History of the Mediterranean World in the Later Thirteenth Century, 1958
The White Rajahs: A History of Sarawak from 1841 to 1946, 1960
The Fall of Constantinople, 1453, 1965
The Great Church in Captivity: A Study of the Patriarchate of Constantinople from the Eve of the Turkish Conquest to the Greek War of Independence, 1968
The Last Byzantine Renaissance, 1970
The Orthodox Churches and the Secular State, 1971
Byzantine Style and Civilization, 1975
The Byzantine Theocracy, 1977
Mistra: Byzantine Capital of the Peloponnese, 1980

Russell, Conrad 1937–
British historian of early modern England

Conrad Russell has achieved fame as a revisionist historian of 17th-century Britain. He sees the English Civil War not as an inevitable result of constitutional conflict between the Parliament and the king, but as a result of inherent mistrust between the two sides, and of financial crisis, foreign affairs, religious conflict between Puritans and Arminians, and the attempt to unify England, Scotland, and Ireland in one nation. His focus is essentially political, although social factors do figure into his account. Russell's argument gives much less coercive power to Parliament than do previous historians' arguments. He links parliamentary power primarily to its financial

power over the king's revenue, but argues that this power was persuasive rather than coercive. The monarch had other means of getting money, such as forced loans, the sale of monastic lands, and the revenues that were granted for life, such as customs revenue and tonnage and poundage, and therefore had little need of Parliament's approval, except in times of great need, such as during war. Inflation strained this financial and administrative system, but it did not break down until the political crisis between king and Parliament arose in 1640.

Russell asserted that historians such as Wallace Notestein have overestimated Parliament's strength and influence in the early 17th century. Parliament was not a dynamic force trying to push for its own political goals in this time, but a tool of the king and his ministers. The constitutional conflict of the mid-17th century arose as a result of the political and social conflict, not vice versa. Because Parliament did not have much power on its own, its members tried to ally themselves with the king and his court in order to govern by cooperation rather than coercion. They did not cause the events leading up to the English Civil War, but reacted to them. The local provinces and outside influences such as Scotland, Ireland, and Spain did far more to cause war in England than Parliament did. Russell also moves away from discussing the Royalists and Parliamentarians as distinct, cohesive groups, arguing that ideological and class divisions do not hold up when members of the two sides are examined closely.

Russell has made an important contribution to historical theory by clearly explaining his revisionist philosophy, as well as his contributions to our understanding of the Civil War. Revisionism, according to Russell, is an attack on hindsight and teleology in history. It is an attempt to restore the political narrative to historical study and a resistance to the idea of English exceptionalism. It is also more complex than earlier history, he argues, because it does not rely on dualistic concepts such as court/country opposition. This view is currently being contested by historians such as Richard Cust and Ann Hughes, most notably in their edited collection of essays *Conflict in Early Stuart England* (1989).

KRISTEN D. ROBINSON

See also Britain: 1485–1750; Gardiner; Political

Biography

Conrad Sebastian Robert Russell, 5th Earl Russell. Born in Sussex, 15 April 1937, son of mathematician/philosopher Bertrand Russell. Studied at Merton College, Oxford, BA 1958, MA 1962. Taught at Bedford College, London, 1960–79; Yale University, 1979–84; University College, London, 1984–90; and King's College, London, from 1990. Married Elizabeth Franklyn Sanders, 1962 (2 sons). Succeeded to the family title, 1987; sits as Liberal Democrat, House of Lords.

Principal Writings

The Crisis of Parliaments: English History, 1509–1660, 1971
Editor, *The Origins of the English Civil War*, 1973
"Parliamentary History in Perspective, 1604–1629," *History* 61 (1976), 1–27
Parliaments and English Politics, 1621–1629, 1979
The Causes of the English Civil War, 1990
Unrevolutionary England, 1603–1642, 1990
The Fall of the British Monarchies, 1637–1642, 1991

Further Reading

Cust, Richard, and Ann Hughes, eds., *Conflict in Early Stuart England: Studies in Religion and Politics, 1603–1642*, London and New York: Longman, 1989

Wende, Peter, "Grundsatzkonflikt in der Konsensgesellschaft: Conrad Russells Analyse der englischen Krise des 17. Jahrhunderts" (Basic Conflict in a Consensus Society: Conrad Russell's Analysis of the English Crisis of the 17th Century, *Historische Zeitschrift 256* (1993), 387–95

Russia: Medieval

Medieval Russian history is generally subsumed chronologically between the period prior to the establishment of the Kievan state in the 11th century and the beginning of the reign of Peter the Great at the end of the 17th. Within this span of time, most historians have discerned five distinct periods, although their conceptualization sometimes varies. These five include, first, the foundation of the first notable state in the area known as Rus', Kievan Russia, which centered around the city of Kiev and flourished between the 9th and 11th centuries. The second was a period of disintegration following the decline of Kiev. Sometimes referred to as the "Period of Feudal Partition" it reached from the 12th to the 14th centuries, and was characterized by strong *boyar* (noble) families who went their own way, the predominance of the city of Novgorod, and by the pressures inflicted by the establishment of the "Golden Horde," under the descendants of Genghis Khan. It should be stressed that "feudalism" is too strong a term to describe either the Kievan state or its successors. Social organization still revolved around the clan and was more elastic than a feudal system might suggest. This era also saw disruption caused by invasions from the Mongol empire in the East, although the long-term impact was negligible. The third era (roughly the 14th and 15th centuries) saw first the organization of the Muscovite centralized state, its disintegration during the "Time of Troubles," and the enserfment of the peasants. Notable monarchs included Ivan III [the Great], Ivan IV [the Terrible], and Boris Godunov. The fourth period saw the establishment of the Romanov monarchy in the 15th and 16th centuries, while the fifth encompassed the formation of the autocratic state in the 16th and 17th centuries.

Very little formal study of medieval Russian history emerged until the establishment in 1725 of the Russian Academy of Sciences. Early academicians included Gerard Fridrikh Miller (1705–83), August Ludwig Schlözer (1735–1809), and Theophilus Siegfried Bayer (1694–1738) – all German by origin. They employed linguistic criticism and investigated various sources in order to create a chronicle of the Russian past from extant historical documents. This led to the Normanist Controversy, which sought an explanation for the emergence of early Rus' society. Some historians saw its origins in the eastern Slavic tribes which had predominated in the area, while others located the growth of some sort of state in the incursions of the Swedish Varangians (or Normans), who, it has been argued, were seeking to extend trade routes to the Byzantine empire in the 9th and 10th centuries. Studies of this question have been rooted in close textual examination of *Povest' vremennykh let* (*The Primary Chronicle*), especially by A.A. Shakhmatov (1864–1920), who established its multiple authorship over a century of time. This debate over origins fueled the first academic discussions in the Russian Academy of Sciences with opposition mounted by Mikhail Lomonosov (1711–65), who stressed Slavonic influences. Nikolai Karamzin's *Istoriia gosudarstva rossiiskogo* (History of Russian State, 1818–29) further developed the picture of the political development of Russia from the end of the 9th century up to the beginning of the 17th century, based on already familiar chronicles as well as on manuscripts opened in the late 18th and early 19th centuries. However, Karamzin's reputation rests more on his strength as a narrative historian than his insight as an analytical one; he has been described as the last Russian chronicler. Subsequent debate has focused on the origins of the Rus' themselves, with George Vernadsky (1887–1973) trying to reconcile Normanist and anti-Normanist positions and Soviet scholars clinging to an eastern Slav explanation.

After Karamzin historical debate on medieval Russia centered on the developmental aspects of the state. The tension replicated the more general intellectual trend to divide between Westernizers (supporters of Western civilization who saw its methods as necessary for Russian survival) and Slavophiles (those who wished to accentuate the internal or eastern influences on Russian development and to stress Russian particularity and originality). Although this debate did not emerge from historical study, it shaped the way historians interrogated sources on the Kievan and Muscovite states, among other things. These questions became unavoidable: how did the Russian Middle Ages basically differ from its Western counterparts? and were the peculiarities of Russian history exceptions to general historical laws or were they typical? In concert with this historians began to look beyond the elite to understand the growth of the state.

A second debate on the period searches for the origins of the Kievan state. Most historians long ago rejected the polarizing Normanist debate and have, like B.D. Grekov (1882–1953), found that the answer lies in the Varangian influence speeding processes already underway. Economic historians such as Kliuchevskii examined the importance of expanding trade networks in the development of the Kievan state, and argued that the inhabitants of Rus' were not primarily agriculturalists, but huntsmen and merchants. Grekov and others, however, disagreed and posited an agrarian society, whose growth had to do with agricultural prosperity. They discounted the importance of foreign trade, and recent archaeological evidence tends to confirm this part of Grekov's assessment. Historians have been less persuaded by his argument that a ruling class had been established within this framework.

The extent to which medieval Russian society can be termed feudal follows on from this debate. Although clearly there were already large-scale landowners, most historians have failed to find the type of social relations that characterize feudal organization. One of the first scholars to turn to the role of the common man was Nikolai Polevoi (1796–1846). In his work *Istoriia russkogo naroda* (The History of Russian People, 1829–30) he considered the question of whether Russian feudalism was similar to Western feudalism, or something very different. He concluded that the two were similar, but his conclusions exerted little influence on the historical establishment. Other areas that have sparked historical debate around this era include the beginnings of Russian Christianity, the "Golden Age" of Kievan culture, which began during the age of Iaroslav the Wise, and the state's decline after Iaroslav's death in 1054.

The decline of Kiev coincided with a period of external threat for the Rus'. On the one hand, the Mongol invasions loomed from the East, but the growth of the Crusades also saw Scandinavians and Teutonic knights moving through the region. Historians have focused on personalities such as Alexander Nevsky, who emerged to lead the military forces of Rus' in these years, as well as on the eventual rise of the Muscovite state.

The shift of power from Kiev to Moscow has evoked several explanations. Karamzin ascribed it to the influence of the Khanate of the Golden Horde. Pogodin saw geographical grounds as paramount. Solov'ev focused on Moscow as a crossroads of the communication network. Kliuchevskii stressed the commercial advantages and joined with P.N. Miliukov, S.F. Platonov, and others in stressing the forceful personalities of Muscovite princes. M.K. Liubavskii emphasized that as a center of migration, Moscow attracted a variety of people and this strengthened the population. Pokrovskii argued that a concentration of investment capital strengthened Moscow's position. Finally, Soviet historians stressed the breakdown of an inefficient feudal system.

The Muscovite state was severely challenged during the Time of Troubles, which was a direct result of the contradictory policies evolved under Ivan IV. He succeeded in destabilizing the existing aristocracy through his *oprichnina* (administrative elite), which Platonov treated at great length in his *Smutnoe vremia* (1923; *The Time of Troubles*, 1970).

Sergei Solov'ev and other representatives of the "State school" of Russian historiography such as Konstantin Kavelin (1818–85) and Boris Chicherin (1828–1904) also turned to the questions of medieval history of Russia. They were seeking to adduce historical laws which might explain long-term change both in Russia and in other countries. Their conclusion was that the shape of the contemporary Russian state was derived from what they termed the "ancestral state." This in turn was affected by the shifts in relationships between the tsar and his formal advisers, which had originally been rooted in personal relationships, sometimes based on family, but had come to be more formalized under Peter the Great. Solov'ev's own work stressed the importance of bringing the great estates under the control of the monarch, while V.O. Kliuchevskii and his students investigated the role of geography and the state.

In the late 19th and early 20th centuries analyses began to shift toward a Marxist approach that emphasized the economic structures of society in the work of Mikhail Pokrovskii (1868–1932) and Nikolai Rozhkov (1868–1927), although Grekov was probably the most influential of these historians. They were subsequently joined by Lev Cherepnin (1905–77), who focused on the Kievan state, Vladimir Pashuto (1918–79), who emphasized its foreign policy, and Mikhail Tikhomirov (1893–1965), who focused on the late medieval state.

DMITRY A. GOUTNOV

See also Eastern Orthodoxy; Karamzin; Kliuchevskii; Miliukov; Platonov; Schlözer; Solov'ev

Further Reading

Bakhrushin, Sergei Vladimirovich, *Ocherki po istorii remesla, torgovli i gorodov russkogo tsentralizovannogo gosudarstva XVI–nachala XVII vv* (Studies on the History of Handcraft, Trade, and Cities in the Russian Centralized State from the 16th to the beginning of the 17th century), Moscow: Akademii nauk SSSR, 1952

Cherepnin, Lev Vladimirovich, *Obrazovanie russkogo tsentralizovannogo gosudarstva v XIV–XV vv* (The Formation of the Russian Centralized State in the 14th and 15th Centuries), Moscow: Sotsial'no-ekon. lit-ry, 1960

Cherepnin, Lev Vladimirovich, Vladimir Terent'evich Pashuto, and Anatolii Petrovich Novosel'tsev, *Puti razvitiia feodalizma: Zakavkazie, Sredniaia Aziia, Rus, Pribaltika* (Paths of Feudal Development in the Caucasus, Middle Asia, Kievan Russia, and the Baltic Countries), Moscow: Nauka, 1972

Cherepnin, Lev Vladimirovich, *Zemskie sobory v russkogo gosudarstva v XVI–XVII vv* (Elective High Councils in the Russian State in the 16th and 17th Centuries), Moscow: Nauka, 1978

Chicherin, Boris Nikolaevich, *Opyty po istorii russkogo prava* (Experiences in the History of Russian Law), Moscow: Barfknecht, 1858

Chistiakova, Elena Viktorovna, *Gorodskie vosstaniia v Rossii v pervoi polovine XVII v* (Early 17th-Century Russian Town Revolts), Voronezh: Izd-vo Voronezhskogo universiteta, 1975

Crummey, Robert O., *The Formation of Muscovy, 1304–1613*, London and New York: Longman, 1987

Fennell, John L.I., *The Emergence of Moscow, 1304–1359*, Berkeley: University of California Press, and London: Secker and Warburg, 1968

Fennell, John L.I., *The Crisis of Medieval Russia, 1200–1304*, London and New York: Longman, 1983

Froianov, Igor' Iakovlevich, *Kievskaia Rus'* (Kievan Russia), 2 vols., Leningrad: Izd-vo Leningradskogo universiteta, 1974–80

Grekov, Boris Dmitrievich, *Kievskaia Rus'*, Moscow: Akademii nauk SSSR, 1939, originally published as *Feodal'nye otnosheniia v kievskom gosudarstve*, 1936; in English as *Kiev Rus*, Moscow: Foreign Languages Publishing House, 1959

Grekov, Boris Dmitrievich, *Krest'iane na Rusi s drevneishikh vremen do XVII veka* (Peasants in Russia from Ancient Times to the 17th century), 2 vols., Moscow: Akademii nauk SSSR, 1952–54

Karamzin, N.M., *Istoriia gosudarstva rossiiskogo* (History of the Russian State) 12 vols., St. Petersburg: Voennaia, 1818–29

Kavelin, Konstantin Dmitrievich, *Vzgliad na istoricheskoe razvitie russkogo poriadka zakonnago nasledovaniia . . .* (An Overview of the Historical Development of the Russian Lawful Order of Inheritance . . .), St. Petersburg: Wolf, 1860

Kliuchevskii, V.O., *Boiarskaia duma drevnei Rusi* (The Boyar Duma in Old Rus) Moscow, 1882

Kliuchevskii, V.O., *Kurs russkoi istorii*, vols. 1–3, Moscow: Sinodal'naia, 1904–21; vol. 3 in English as *A Course in Russian History: The Seventeenth Century*, Chicago: Quadrangle, 1968, and as *The Rise of the Romanovs*, London: Macmillan, 1970

Kochin, Georgii Evgen'evich, *Sel'skoe khoziaistvo na Rusi v periode obrazovaniia russkogo tsentralizovannogo gosudarstva, konets XIII–nachala XVI vv* (Agriculture in Russia from the 13th to the 16th Centuries), Leningrad: Nauka, 1965.

Liubavskii, Matvei Kuz'mich, *Lektsii po drevnei russkoi istorii* (Lectures on Russian History), Moscow, 1918

Mavrodin, Vladimir Vasil'evich, *Obrazovanie drevnerusskogo gosudarstva i formirovanie drevnerusskoi narodnosti* (Foundation of Ancient Russian State and Forming Ancient Russian Nationality), Moscow: Vyssh. shkola, 1971

Miliukov, Pavel, *Ocherki po istorii russkoi kul'tury*, 3 vols., St. Petersburg: Mir bozhii, 1896–1903; in English as *Outlines of Russian Culture*, 3 vols., Philadelphia: University of Pennsylvania Press, 1942; abridged as *The Origins of Ideology*, Gulf Breeze, FL: Academic International, 1974, and *Ideologies in Conflict*, Academic International, 1975

Pashuto, Vladimir Terent'evich, *Vneshnaia politika drevnei Rusi* (Foreign Policy of Ancient Russia), Moscow: Nauka, 1968

Pavlov-Sil'vanskii, Nikolai Pavlovich, *Feodalizm v drevnei Rusi* (Feudalism in Ancient Russia), St. Petersburg: Brokgauz-Efron, 1907; revised 1924

Pavlov-Sil'vanskii, Nikolai Pavlovich, *Feodalizm v udel'noi Rusi: izsledovanie* (Feudalism in Apanage Russia), St. Petersburg: Stasiulevich, 1910

Platonov, S.F., *Boris Godunov*, Petrograd: Ogni, 1921; in English as *Boris Godunov, Tsar of Russia*, Gulf Breeze, FL: Academic International Press, 1973

Platonov, S.F., *Ivan Groznyi*, Petrograd: Brokgauz-Efron, 1923; in English as *Ivan the Terrible*, Gulf Breeze, FL: Academic International Press, 1974

Platonov, S.F., *Smutnoe vremia*, Petrograd: Vremia, 1923; in English as *The Time of Troubles: A Historical Study of the Internal Crisis and Social Struggle in Sixteenth- and Seventeenth-Century Muscovy*, Lawrence: University of Kansas Press, 1970

Pogodin, Mikhail Petrovich, *Drevniaia russkaia istoriia, do mongol'skago iga* (Russian History to the Mongol Invasions), 3 vols., Moscow: Synolda'noi, 1871; reprinted The Hague: Mouton, 1971

Pokrovskii, Mikhail N., *Russkaia istoriia s drevneishikh vremen*, 5 vols., Moscow: Mir, 1910–13; abridged in English as *History of Russia, from the Earliest Times to the Rise of Commercial Capitalism*, New York: International Publishers, and London: Lawrence, 1931

Polevoi, Nikolai Alekseevich, *Istoriia russkogo naroda* (The History of Russian People), 6 vols., Moscow: Semena, 1829–30

Romanov, Boris Aleksandrovich, *Liudi i nravy drevnei Rusi* (People and Dispositions of Ancient Russia), Leningrad: Izd-vo Leningradskogo gos. ordena Lenina universiteta, 1947

Rozhkov, Nikolai Aleksandrovich, *Russkaia istoriia v sravnitel'no-istoricheskom osveshchenii* (Russian History in Comparative Perspective), 12 vols., St. Petersburg: Kniga, 1919–26

Rybakov, Boris Aleksandrovich, *Kievskaia Rus' i russkie kniazhestva XII–XIII vv*, Moscow: Nauka, 1982; in English as *Kievan Rus*, Moscow: Progress, 1989

Shakhmatov, Aleksei Aleksandrovich, *Izsledovanie o iazyke novgorodskikh gramot XIII–XIV vv* (Studies of the Language of 13th- and 14th-Century Novgorodian Deeds), St. Petersburg, 1887

Shmidt, Segurt Ottovich, *Stanovlenie rossiiskogo samoderzhavstva* (Foundation of Russian Serfdom), Moscow: Mysl, 1973

Skrynnikov, Ruslan G., *The Time of Troubles: Russia in Crisis, 1604–1618*, edited and translated by Hugh F. Graham, Gulf Breeze, FL: Academic International Press, 1988

Smirnov, Ivan Ivanovich, Arkadii Georgievich Mankov, E.P. Podiapolskaia, and Vladimir Vasil'evich Mavrodin, *Krest'ianskie voiny v Rossii XVII–XVIII vv* (Peasant Wars in 17th- and 18th-Century Russia), Moscow: Nauka, 1966

Solov'ev, S.M., *Istoriia Rossii s drevneishikh vremen*, 29 vols., Moscow: Soldatenkova, 1851–79; in English as *History of Russia*, 48 vols. planned, Gulf Breeze, FL: Academic International Press, 1976–

Tikhomirov, Mikhail Nikolaevich, *Rossiia v XVI stoletii* (Russia in the 16th Century), Moscow: Akademii nauk SSSR, 1962

Tikhomirov, Mikhail Nikolaevich, *Russkoe letopisanie* (Russian Chronicles), Moscow: Nauka, 1979

Vernadsky, George, *Ancient Russia*, New Haven: Yale University Press, 1943

Vernadsky, George, *The Origins of Russia*, Oxford: Oxford University Press, 1959

Veselovskii, S.B., *Feodal'noe zemlevladenie v severo-vostochnoi Rusi* (Feudal Landowning in Northeast Russia), Moscow: Akademii nauk SSSR, 1947

Zimin, Aleksandr Aleksandrovich, *Rossia na poroge novogo vremeni: ocherki politicheskoi istorii Rossii v pervoi treti XVI v* (Russia on the Threshold of Modern Time: Studies on the Political History of Russia in the First Third of the 16th century), Moscow: Mysl', 1972

Russia: Early Modern (1462–1689)

Russia's nation-state emerged with the end of Mongol suzerainty in 1480 and its expansion over the northern and central regions of European Russia under grand prince Ivan III (1462–1505). The Muscovite period lasted until the reign of Peter I (1689–1725) and the inception of the imperial era of St. Petersburg.

Gustave Alef assessed the beginning of the Muscovite state in *The Origins of Muscovite Autocracy* (1986). Alef attributed political power to the wisdom of Ivan III (1462–1505) and his manipulation of the old *boyars* (aristocrats) at court. The standard account of the reign of this grand prince remains that of John L.I. Fennell, *Ivan the Great of Moscow* (1961). Stressing Ivan's role as gatherer of the Russian lands, he provided a sound overview of events with an emphasis on territorial expansion. Nancy Shields Kollmann, in *Kinship and Politics* (1987), argued that primary ties of kinship were fundamental in shaping the nature of aristocratic and monarchical power in the rise of Muscovy.

The roots of Muscovite autocracy have stimulated much discussion. George Vernadsky, in two volumes of his *A History of Russia, Mongols and Russia* (1951) and *Russia at the Dawn of the Modern Age* (1969), catalogued the political legacies of the Mongol state within Muscovy. Charles J. Halperin, in *Russia and the Golden Horde* (1985), surveyed the Mongol and post-Mongol periods and described the effects of that alien domination on the emergence of Muscovite institutions. Robert Croskey, in *Muscovite Diplomatic Practice in the Reign of Ivan III* (1987), showed that the new Russian court was neither Western nor Oriental in its dealings with others, adopting Western forms when dealing with European powers, and Eastern forms when dealing with Oriental nations. Nevertheless, Croskey noticed that the diplomatic ritual of Moscow's traditional submission to Tatar rulers took a long time to overcome. Yet Moscow's adoption of an imperial ideology would justify Ivan IV's conquest of Tatar Kazan in the mid-16th century. Such a theme was developed by Jaroslaw Pelenski in *Russia and Kazan* (1974).

Dmitri Obolensky's *Byzantium and the Slavs* (1971) represented the Byzantine school. Church institutions appeared fundamental in his account, as also in James H. Billington's, *The Icon and the Axe* (1966). Billington likened Ivan the Terrible's arbitrariness to a perverse imitation of an abbot's rule over his monks. S.M. Solov'ev, in his account of the late 15th century in his mammoth *Istoriia Rossii s drevneishikh vremen* (1851–79; *History of Russia*, 1976–), devoted considerable space to the Byzantine court influence of Sophia Paleologue. Michael Cherniavsky's seminal essay, "Khan or Basileus" (1959) showed the continuity of both images of authority, Tatar and Byzantine, throughout the reign of Ivan IV, stressing the point that such images were not synthesized, but remained separate and powerful.

Notwithstanding the Mongol and Byzantine influences, most historians, when discussing the instruments of autocracy, followed the classic 19th-century historians Solovi'v and Vasilii Osipovich Kliuchevskii, *Kurs Russkoi istorii* (1904–10; *A History of Russia*, 1911–31). Discussion has focused on the *oprichnina* (administrative elite, and the territory assigned to this elite) of Ivan IV as the ultimate instrument of autocracy.

Solov'ev found Ivan's policies, despite his personal aberrations, progressive in centralizing the state against divisive aristocratic interests; but to Kliuchevskii the *oprichnina* was a product of Ivan's disordered mind. Sergei Fedorovich Platonov's *Ivan Groznyi* (1923; *Ivan the Terrible*, 1974) and A.A. Zimin's *Oprichnina Ivana Groznogo* (*Oprichnina of Ivan the Terrible*, 1964), adhered to Solov'ev's conclusion and, while admitting some irrational behavior in the tsar, accepted his rationale for state welfare.

Others followed the Kliuchevskii school, such as S.B. Veselovskii in *Issledovaniia po istorii oprichniny* (Investigations into the History of the Oprichnina, 1967), who regarded this institution as mainly designed to protect the person of Ivan IV. Robert O. Crummey's, *Reform in Russia and the USSR* (1989), applauded the governmental reforms of tsar Ivan but rejected the *oprichnina* as anything visionary, finding it rooted in Ivan's diseased mind.

Debates about the rule of Boris Godunov and his alleged involvement in the murder of tsarevich Dmitrii in Uglich have continued without resolution. Historians of the 19th century accepted the traditional version of the early Romanovs that Boris had sent agents to kill the tsarevich. However, Sergei Fedorovich Platonov in *Boris Godunov* (1921; English translation, 1973) defended Boris against that accusation and viewed his state policies as westernization. Ruslan G. Skrynnikov's *Boris Godunov* (1978; English translation, 1982) depicted his career similarly, and G. Edward Orchard, in his article "Boris Godunov" (1977), argued for the reliability of the investigating commission to Uglich dispatched by Godunov.

The resulting Time of Troubles from 1605 to 1613 was viewed by historians of the 19th century (Karamzin, Solov'ev, and Kliuchevskii) as introducing a new period of Russian history that revealed how previous state policies were successful in forming a popular conception of statehood. Platonov and Skrynnikov provided thorough accounts, the former in *Smutnoe vremia* (1923; *Time of Troubles*, 1970), and the latter in *The Time of Troubles* (1988). Platonov gave due respect to the class conflicts which he perceived in that turmoil. Skrynnikov's pages were nationalistic, critical of the aristocracy, and favorable to the common people.

Literature remains thin on the early Romanovs, and readers are largely left with the classic history of Kliuchevskii (*Kurs russkoi istorii*) whose account of the 17th-century developments was well told in a modern translation, *A Course in Russian History: The Seventeenth Century* (1968). Michael's reign was covered well in John L.H. Keep's essay in *The New Cambridge Modern History* (1970), wherein the author chronicled the revival of autocracy. Tsar Alexis (1645–76) was the subject of Philip Longworth's *Alexis, Tsar of all the Russias* (1984), a work that explained the nature of the tsar's struggle with patriarch Nikon, and Russia's territorial expansion. Sophia (1657–1704) received attention in the work by Lindsey A.J. Hughes' *Sophia, Regent of Russia* (1990), which exposed a number of myths about this older sister of Peter I and noted that she was less of a westerner than sometimes thought.

The *boyars* and *dvoriane* (service class) have been the subject of numerous analyses, particularly as they shed light on the nature of the autocracy, their promotion of peasant bondage, and their comparison with Western aristocratic counterparts. Works by Alef and Kollman, cited above, have delineated the personal relationships and rivalries among the aristocracy in the early Muscovite era. Crummey's *Aristocrats and Servitors* (1983) traced similar themes among Moscow nobles in the 17th century, noting how time altered those arrangements. Biographical work remains scant on individual noblemen, but Hughes' *Russia and the West* (1984) provided an intriguing story of an influential figure in the diplomatic service of the regency, noting that prince Golitsyn's love affair with Sophia enabled him to become powerful.

The *dvoriane* was treated in connection with the evolution of peasant bondage. Richard Hellie argued in *Enserfment and Military Change in Muscovy* (1971) that the "middle" service class, fearful of peasant flight when they were at war, pressured the state to adopt the "Forbidden Years" prohibiting peasant departures. Surveys of the peasant question remain provocative for the Muscovite period. Jerome Blum's *Lord and Peasant in Russia from the Ninth to the Nineteenth Century* (1961) traced the similarity of Russian peasant bondage to the evolution of serfdom in Western Europe, arguing that autocracy was incidental and that serfdom would have developed even under different political conditions – an argument that has not gone unchallenged. Another study by Hellie, *Slavery in Russia, 1450–1725* (1982), traced the evolution of serfdom into slavery, but noted that slaves had legal rights in the code of 1649.

Much energy has been devoted to town life in the Muscovite era. Samuel H. Baron asked "Who were the *Gosti*?" (1973). Baron concluded that there was little perception of an entrepreneurial spirit. Few great merchant families survived more than two or three generations and were often victims of arbitrary and destructive policies of the ruler. Paul Bushkovitch, in *The Merchants of Moscow* (1980), indicated that the *gosti* were a viable economic group within the Eastern European perspective but admitted that they never had the bargaining powers of Western merchant guilds. J. Michael Hittle in *The Service City* (1979) developed the thesis that Russian urban development was different from the European phenomenon in that Russian towns were more administrative and military centers than economic ones, and consequently more directly affected by actions of the monarch. Most Soviet writers, such as Pavel Petrovich Smirnov in *Posadskie liudi i ikh klassovaia bor'ba do serediny XVII veka* (The Urban Classes and Their Class Struggles until the Mid-17th Century, 1947–48), clung to the position that Russian towns had freed themselves from the feudal yoke, gaining special juridical status.

The standard account of religious history of Russia is still that of P.N. Miliukov in *Ocherki po istorii russkoi kul'tury* (1896–1903; *Outlines of Russian Culture*, 1942). Church institutions, religious ideology, and the schism of the 17th century were covered in this volume. Paul Bushkovitch's *Religion and Society in Russia* (1992) described the nature of the church and how the reforms of Peter I were prepared for by developments in this earlier period. Monastic authority, elite spirituality, public versus private religiosity, canonization, and rise of sermon are some of the topics that he discussed. David Goldfrank clarified the "Tale of the White Cowl" and its evolution into the doctrine of "Moscow, the Third Rome" (1981). Cherniavsky's "The Old Believers and the New Religion" (1970) described how the political theology of the Raskol was a response to secularist trends. Jack E. Kollman, Jr. in "The

Stoglav Council and Parish Priests" (1980) wrote about efforts to reform clerical education, clerical marriages, appointments, income, and responsibilities in the 16th century. Georges Florovsky in *Puti russkogo bogosloviia* (1957; *Ways of Russian Theology*, 1979) addressed the matter of church silence concerning theological questions, relating it in part to the timing of Russia's adoption of Christianity in the 10th century. Edward V. Williams' *The Bells of Russia* (1985) addressed a new subject when he demonstrated significant ties between Muscovite technology and religion.

Several specialized studies have broken new ground. Eve Levin's *Sex and Society in the World of the Orthodox Slavs, 900–1700* (1989) treated women's history from a broad chronological perspective, analyzing church influence, or sometimes the lack thereof, on a range of subjects affecting sexuality and marriage. Alexander A. Sydorenko's *The Kievan Academy in the Seventeenth Century* (1977) traced the academy's influence on both Ukrainian and Muscovite intellectual life. And Linda Gordon's *Cossack Rebellions* (1983) showed how economically unstable were Ukrainian and Cossack societies before the Khmelnytsky upheaval.

Imperialism was the subject of George V. Lantzeff's *Siberia in the Seventeenth Century* (1943). The author studied both central and local administrations and their interrelations with church and commerce. Lantzeff and Richard A. Pierce's *Eastward to Empire* (1973) explored some of the same themes but with greater attention to the role that individuals played in the Asiatic expansion.

A challenging literary controversy was begun by Edward L. Keenan, Jr. in *The Kurbskii-Groznyi Apocrypha* (1971). Arguing from linguistic evidence, he concluded that these supposedly 16th-century texts were written in the 17th century as either political or literary exercises, perhaps by one Semen Shakhovskii. Soviet scholars defended the authenticity of that correspondence. See, for example, Skrynnikov's *Perepiska Groznogo i Kurbskogo* (The Correspondence of Ivan the Terrible and Prince Kurbsky, 1973).

Ann M. Kleimola's *Justice in Medieval Russia* (1975) drew attention to emerging and evolving legal due process, including the role of testimony and written evidence in early Muscovite justice. She concluded that the system of law was workable and rational. Specific codes of Ivan III and IV were analyzed by Daniel Kaiser in *The Growth of Law in Medieval Russia* (1980), and that of Alexei by Hellie in "Early Modern Russian Law" (1988).

In the realm of popular culture historians are indebted to Russell Zguta's *Russian Minstrels* (1978). Zguta showed Skomorokhi contributions to Russian music, dance, and theater, including the puppet theater. Tsar Alexei banned their use of masques in dramatic presentations since they were thought to weaken moral and religious foundations within society. While historians of early modern Russia have broadened their themes of investigation, most social and even cultural studies continue to reflect the dominant concern with the phenomenon of the Russian state. This trend, no doubt, will continue.

JOHN D. WINDHAUSEN

See also Blum; Karamzin; Kliuchevskii; Obolensky; Platonov; Solov'ev; Vernadsky

Further Reading

Alef, Gustave, *Rulers and Nobles in Fifteenth-Century Muscovy*, London: Variorum, 1983

Alef, Gustave, *The Origins of Muscovite Autocracy: The Age of Ivan III*, Wiesbaden: Harrassowitz, 1986

Baron, Samuel H., "Who Were the *Gosti*?," *California Slavic Studies* 7 (1973), 1–40

Baron, Samuel H., *Muscovite Russia: Collected Essays*, London: Variorum, 1980

Baron, Samuel H., *Explorations in Muscovite History*, Aldershot: Variorum, 1991

Bater, James H., and R. A. French, eds., *Studies in Russian Historical Geography*, 2 vols., London and New York: Academic Press, 1983

Billington, James H., *The Icon and the Axe: An Interpretive History of Russian Culture*, New York: Knopf, and London: Weidenfeld and Nicolson, 1966

Blum, Jerome, *Lord and Peasant in Russia from the Ninth to the Nineteenth Century*, Princeton: Princeton University Press, 1961

Brown, William Edward, *A History of Seventeenth-Century Russian Literature*, Ann Arbor: Ardis, 1980

Bushkovitch, Paul, *The Merchants of Moscow, 1580–1650*, Cambridge and New York: Cambridge University Press, 1980

Bushkovitch, Paul, *Religion and Society in Russia: The Sixteenth and Seventeenth Centuries*, New York: Oxford University Press, 1992

Cherniavsky, Michael, "Khan or Basileus: An Aspect of Russian Medieval Political Theory," *Journal of the History of Ideas* 20 (1959), 459–76

Cherniavsky, Michael, "The Old Believers and the New Religion," in his *The Structure of Russian History: Interpretive Essays*, New York: Random House, 1970

Clements, Barbara Evans, Barbara Alpern Engel, and Christine D. Worobec, eds., *Russia's Women: Accommodation, Resistance, Transformation*, Berkeley: University of California Press, 1991

Croskey, Robert, *Muscovite Diplomatic Practice in the Reign of Ivan III*, New York: Garland, 1987

Crummey, Robert O., "Ivan the Terrible," in Samuel H. Baron and Nancy Whittier Heer, eds., *Windows on the Russian Past: Essays on Soviet Historiography since Stalin*, Columbus, OH: American Association for the Advancement of Slavic Studies, 1977

Crummey, Robert O., *Aristocrats and Servitors: The Boyar Elite in Russia, 1613–1689*, Princeton: Princeton University Press, 1983

Crummey, Robert O., *The Formation of Muscovy, 1304–1613*, London and New York: Longman, 1987

Crummey, Robert O., "Constitutional Reform during the Time of Troubles" and "Reform under Ivan IV: Gradualism and Terror," in Crummey, ed., *Reform in Russia and the USSR: Past and Prospects*, Urbana: University of Illinois Press, 1989

Domar, Evsey, "The Causes of Slavery or Serfdom: A Hypothesis," *Journal of Economic History* 30 (1970), 18–32

Fennell, John L.I., *Ivan the Great of Moscow*, London: Macmillan, and New York: St. Martin's Press, 1961

Florovsky, Georges, *Puti russkogo bogosloviia*, Paris: YMCA Press, 1957; in English as *Ways of Russian Theology*, Belmont, MA: Nordland, 1979

Goldfrank, David, "Moscow, the Third Rome," in Joseph L. Wieczynski, ed., *A Modern Encyclopedia of Russian and Soviet History*, vol. 23, Gulf Breeze, FL: Academic International Press, 1981

Gordon, Linda, *Cossack Rebellions: Social Turmoil in the Sixteenth-Century Ukraine*, Albany: State University of New York Press, 1983

Grobovsky, Antony N., *The "Chosen Council" of Ivan IV: A Reinterpretation*, Brooklyn, NY: Gaus, 1969

Halecki, Oskar, *Borderlands of Western Civilization: A History of East Central Europe*, New York: Ronald Press, 1952

Halperin, Charles J., *Russia and the Golden Horde: The Mongol Impact on Medieval Russian History*, Bloomington: Indiana University Press, 1985; London: Tauris, 1987

Hamilton, George Heard, *The Art and Architecture of Russia*, Harmondsworth and Baltimore: Penguin, 1954; 3rd edition 1983

Hellie, Richard, *Enserfment and Military Change in Muscovy*, Chicago: University of Chicago Press, 1971

Hellie, Richard, "The Stratification of Muscovite Society: The Townsmen," *Russian History* 5 (1978), 119–75

Hellie, Richard, "Muscovite Slavery in Comparative Perspective," *Russian History*, 6 (1979), 133–209

Hellie, Richard, *Slavery in Russia, 1450–1725*, Chicago: University of Chicago Press, 1982

Hellie, Richard, "Early Modern Russian Law: The Ulozhenie of 1649," *Russian History* 15 (1988), 155–80

Hittle, J. Michael, *The Service City: State and Townsmen in Russia, 1600–1800*, Cambridge, MA: Harvard University Press, 1979

Howes, Robert Craig, ed. and trans., *The Testaments of the Grand Princes of Moscow*, Ithaca, NY: Cornell University Press, 1967

Hrushevsky, Mykhailo, *A History of Ukraine*, New Haven: Yale University Press, 1941; reprinted Hamden, CT: Archon, 1970

Hughes, Lindsey A.J., *Russia and the West: The Life of a Seventeenth Century Westernizer, Prince Vasily Vasil'evich Golitsyn (1643–1714)*, Newtonville, MA: Oriental Research Partners, 1984

Hughes, Lindsey A.J., *Sophia, Regent of Russia, 1657–1704*, New Haven: Yale University Press, 1990

Kaiser, Daniel J., *The Growth of Law in Medieval Russia*, Princeton: Princeton University Press, 1980

Kami~ski, Andrzej, "The Cossack Experiment in *Szlachta* Democracy in the Polish-Lithuanian Commonwealth: The Hadiach (*Hadziacz*) Union," *Harvard Ukrainian Studies* 1 (1977), 178–97

Karamzin, N.M., *Istoriia gosudarstva rossiiskogo* (History of the Russian State) 12 vols., St. Petersburg: Voennaia, 1818–29

Kashtonov, S.M., "The Centralised State and Feudal Immunities in Russia," *Slavonic and East European Review* 49 (1971), 235–54

Keenan, Edward L., Jr., *The Kurbskii-Groznyi Apocrypha: the Seventeenth-century Genesis of the "Correspondence" Attributed to Prince A. M. Kurbskii and Tsar Ivan IV*, Cambridge, MA: Harvard University Press, 1971

Keenan, Edward L., Jr., "The Trouble with Muscovy: Some Observations upon Problems of the Comparative Study of Form and Genre in Historical Writing," *Medievalia et Humanistica: Studies in Medieval and Russian Culture* new series 5 (1974), 103–26

Keenan, Edward L., Jr., "Muscovite Political Folkways," *Russian Review* 45 (1986), 115–81

Keep, John L.H., "Russia, 1613-45," in J.P. Cooper, ed., *The New Cambridge Modern History*, vol. 4, Cambridge: Cambridge University Press, 1970

Kleimola, Ann M., *Justice in Medieval Russia: Muscovite Judgment Charters of the Fifteenth and Sixteenth Centuries*, Philadelphia: American Philosophical Society, 1975 (Transactions of the American Philosophical Society, new series, 65)

Kliuchevskii, V.O., *Kurs russkoi istorii*, 5 vols., Moscow, 1904–10; in English as *A History of Russia*, 5 vols., London: Dent, and New York: Dutton, 1911–31; selections as *A Course in Russian History: The Seventeenth Century*, Chicago: Quadrangle, 1968

Kollman, Jack E., Jr., "The *Stoglav* Council and Parish Priests," *Russian History* 7 (1980), 65–91

Kollmann, Nancy Shields, *Kinship and Politics: The Making of the Muscovite Political System, 1345–1547*, Stanford, CA: Stanford University Press, 1987

Lantzeff, George V., *Siberia in the Seventeenth Century: A Study of the Colonial Administration*, Berkeley: University of California Press, 1943; reprinted New York: Octagon, 1972

Lantzeff, George V., and Richard A. Pierce, *Eastward to Empire: Exploration and Conquest on the Russian Open Frontier to 1750*, Montreal: McGill-Queen's University Press, 1973

Lazarev, Viktor Nikitich, *Old Russian Murals and Mosaics from the Eleventh to the Sixteenth Century*, London: Phaidon, 1966

Levin, Eve, *Sex and Society in the World of the Orthodox Slavs, 900–1700*, Ithaca, NY: Cornell University Press, 1989

Lewitter, L.R., "Poland, the Ukraine, and Russia in the Seventeenth Century," *Slavonic and East European Review* 27 (1948-49), 157–71, 414–29

Longworth, Philip, *The Cossacks*, New York: Holt Rinehart, and London: Constable, 1970

Longworth, Philip, *Alexis, Tsar of all the Russias*, New York: Watts, and London: Secker and Warburg, 1984

Mancall, Mark, *Russia and China: Their Diplomatic Relations to 1728*, Cambridge, MA: Harvard University Press, 1971

Marker, Gary, "Literacy and Literacy Texts in Muscovy: A Reconsideration," *Slavic Review* 49 (1990), 74–89

Mazour, Anatole G., *An Outline of Russian Historiography*, Berkeley: University of California Press, 1939; revised as *Modern Russian Historiography*, Princeton, NJ: Van Nostrand, 1958; revised Westport, CT: Greenwood Press, 1975

Miasnikov, Vladimir Stepanovich, *Imperiia Tsin i russkoe gosudarstvo v XVII veke*, Moscow: Nauka, 1980; in English as *The Ch'ing Empire and the Russian State in the Seventeenth Century*, Moscow: Progress, 1985

Miliukov, Pavel, *Ocherki po istorii russkoi kul'tury*, 3 vols., St. Petersburg: Mir bozhii, 1896–1903; in English as *Outlines of Russian Culture*, 3 vols., Philadelphia: University of Pennsylvania Press, 1942; abridged as *The Origins of Ideology*, Gulf Breeze, FL: Academic International, 1974, and *Ideologies in Conflict*, Academic International, 1975

Obolensky, Dimitri, *Byzantium and the Slavs: Collected Studies*, London: Variorum, 1971

O'Brien, Carl Bickford, *Russia under Two Tsars, 1682–1689: The Regency of Sophia Alekseevna*, Berkeley: University of California Press, 1952

Orchard, G. Edward, "Boris Godunov," *Modern Encyclopedia of Russian and Soviet History*, vol. 5, Gulf Breeze, FL: Academic International Press, 1977

Pallot, Judith, and Dennis J. B. Shaw, *Landscape and Settlement in Romanov Russia, 1613–1917*, Oxford and New York: Oxford University Press, 1990

Pelenski, Jaroslaw, *Russia and Kazan: Conquest and Imperial Ideology, 1438–1560s*, The Hague: Mouton, 1974

Pelenski, Jaroslaw, "The Origins of the Official Muscovite Claims to the Kievan Inheritance," *Harvard Ukrainian Studies* 1 (1977), 29–52

Phillip, Werner, "Russia, the Beginning of Westernization," in J.S. Bromley, ed., *The New Cambridge Modern History*, vol. 6: *The Rise of Great Britain and Russia, 1688–1715/25*, Cambridge: Cambridge University Press, 1961

Pipes, Richard, *Russia under the Old Regime*, New York: Scribner, and London: Weidenfeld and Nicolson, 1974

Platonov, S.F., *Boris Godunov*, Petrograd: Ogni, 1921; in English as *Boris Godunov, Tsar of Russia*, Gulf Breeze, FL: Academic International Press, 1973

Platonov, S.F., *Ivan Groznyi*, Petrograd: Brokgauz-Efron, 1923; in English as *Ivan the Terrible*, Gulf Breeze, FL: Academic International Press, 1974

Platonov, S.F., *Smutnoe vremia*, Petrograd: Vremia, 1923; in English as *The Time of Troubles: A Historical Study of the Internal Crises and Social Struggle in Sixteenth- and Seventeenth-Century Muscovy*, Lawrence: University Press of Kansas, 1970

Presniakov, Aleksandr Evgen'evich, *Moskovskoe tsarstvo*, Petrograd: Ogni, 1918; in English as *The Tsardom of Muscovy*, Gulf Breeze, FL: Academic International Press, 1978

Pushkarev, Sergei Germanovich, *Dictionary of Russian Historical Terms from the Eleventh Century to 1917*, New Haven: Yale University Press, 1970

Pushkarevna, Natalia Lvovna, *Women in Russian History: From the Tenth to the Twentieth Century*, Armonk, NY: Sharpe, 1997

Rowland, Daniel, "The Problem of Advice in Muscovite Tales about the Time of Troubles," *Russian History* 6 (1979), 259–83

Skrynnikov, Ruslan G., *Perepiska Groznogo i Kurbskogo: paradoksy Edvarda Kinana* (The Correspondence of Ivan the Terrible and Prince Kurbsky: The Paradoxes of Edward Keenan), Leningrad: Nauka, 1973

Skrynnikov, Ruslan G., *Ivan Groznyi*, Moscow: Nauka, 1975; in English as *Ivan the Terrible*, Gulf Breeze, FL: Academic International Press, 1981

Skrynnikov, Ruslan G., *Boris Godunov*, Moscow: Nauka, 1978; in English as *Boris Godunov*, Gulf Breeze, FL: Academic International Press, 1982

Skrynnikov, Ruslan G., *The Time of Troubles: Russia in Crisis, 1604–1618*, edited and translated by Hugh F. Graham, Gulf Breeze, FL: Academic International Press, 1988

Smirnov, Pavel Petrovich, *Posadskie liudi i ikh klassovaia bor'ba do serediny XVII veka* (The Urban Classes and Their Class Struggles until the Mid-17th Century), 2 vols., Moscow: Academy of Sciences, 1947–48

Smith, Robert E.F., *Peasant Farming in Muscovy*, Cambridge and New York: Cambridge University Press, 1971

Solov'ev, S.M., *Istoriia Rossii s drevneishikh vremen*, 29 vols., Moscow: Soldatenkova, 1851–79; in English as *History of Russia*, 48 vols. planned, Gulf Breeze, FL: Academic International Press, 1976–

Subtelny, Orest, *Ukraine: A History*, Toronto: University of Toronto Press, 1988

Sydorenko, Alexander A., *The Kievan Academy in the Seventeenth Century*, Ottawa: University of Ottawa Press, 1977

Sysyn, Frank E., *Between Poland and Ukraine: The Dilemma of Adam Kysil, 1600–1653*, Cambridge, MA: Harvard Ukrainian Institute, 1985

Trubetzkoy, Nikolai Sergeevich, *The Legacy of Genghis Khan and Other Essays on Russia's Identity*, Ann Arbor: Michigan Slavic Publications, 1991

Vernadsky, George, *A History of Russia*, 5 vols., New Haven: Yale University Press, 1943–69

Vernadsky, George, *Russian Historiography: A History*, Belmont, MA: Nordland, 1978

Veselovskii, S.B., *Issledovaniia po istorii oprichniny* (Investigations into the History of the Oprichnina), Moscow: Nauka, 1967

Vipper, Robert Iur'evich, *Ivan Groznyi*, Moscow: Del'fin, 1922; in English as *Ivan the Terrible*, Moscow: Foreign Languages Publishing House, 1947

Volotskii, Iosif, *Dukhovnaia gramota prepodobnogo igumena Iosifa o monastyrskom*; in English as *Monastic Rule of Iosif Volotskii*, Kalamazoo, MI: Cistercian, 1983

Vucinich, Alexander, *Science in Russian Culture*, vol. 1: *A History to 1860*, Stanford, CA: Stanford University Press, 1963

Williams, Edward V., *The Bells of Russia: History and Technology*, Princeton: Princeton University Press, 1985

Zguta, Russell, *Russian Minstrels: History of the Skomorokhi*, Philadelphia: University of Pennsylvania Press, 1978

Zimin, Aleksandr Aleksandrovich, *Oprichnina Ivana Groznogo*, Moscow: Mysl, 1964; in English as *Oprichnina of Ivan the Terrible*, 1964

Russia: Modern (since 1690)

Since the late 17th century perhaps no European nation has experienced more political instability than Russia. Periods of authoritarian and totalitarian rule have been punctuated by dramatic reforms from above, by four revolutions from below, by foreign invasions, and by almost incessant peripheral wars. Historical writing on modern Russia has therefore focused broadly on the tension between the centralized state and its opponents, on the costs of empire and modernity in a multi-ethnic state, and on the difficulty of establishing democratic institutions in such a social-historical context.

For over two centuries the reign of Peter the Great has constituted a touchstone of historical scholarship. Peter's early critics, such as the conservative gentry historian M.M. Shcherbatov writing in his treatise *O povrezhdenii nravov v Rossii* (written 1780, published 1858; *On the Corruption of Morals in Russia*, 1969), accused Peter of violently destroying Russia's indigenous national culture for the sake of importing Western ways. Early admirers – for example, V.N. Tatishchev, writing in *Istoriia rossiiskaia* (Russian History, 1760–) – treated Peter's reforms as critical contributions to Russia's welfare; M.P. Pogodin's *Istoriko-kriticheskie otryvki* (Historical-Critical Fragments, 1846–57) credited Peter with imaginatively building on indigenous institutions and on borrowed foreign models to create qualitatively new, stable political and social institutions. Mid-19th-century liberal historians, such as B.N. Chicherin and S.M. Solov'ev, emphasized not so much the discontinuities attending the Petrine reforms as their historical and social continuities: Chicherin's *Oblastnye uchrezhdeniia Rossii v XVII-m veke* (Provincial Institutions of Russia in the 17th Century, 1856) declared that Peter's reformism was an organic outgrowth of Muscovite state-building; Solov'ev's *Publichnye chteniia o Petre Velikom* (Public Lectures on Peter the Great, 1872) asserted that the Petrine reforms were organic in two senses – as the logical outcome of 17th-century trends, and as a rational response to demands by Peter's own contemporaries. Virtually every Russian historian before 1890 credited Peter with strengthening Russia's military forces and using them to extend the empire's borders.

Late 19th-century historians were generally far more critical of Peter than their predecessors had been. V.O. Kliuchevskii's masterful portrait of Peter in lectures 64–79 of *Kurs russkoi istorii* (1904–21; *A History of Russia*, 1911–31; and *Peter the Great*, 1958) suggested that Peter's reforms were mostly improvisations adopted in response to particular military and financial emergencies. P.N. Miliukov's *Gosudarstvennoe khoziaistvo Rossii v pervoi chetverti XVIII stoletiia i reforma Petra Velikogo* (Russia's State Economy in the First Quarter of the 18th Century and the Reform of Peter the Great, 1890–92) and *Ocherki po istorii russkoi kul'tury* (1896–1903; partially translated as *The Origins of Ideology*, 1974, and *Ideologies in Conflict*, 1975), developed this argument further. Under Peter, he asserted, the government taxed the peasantry more onerously than before in order to finance Peter's military undertakings. The Petrine empire was built on the backs of peasant laborers.

Early Marxist historians, such as M.N. Pokrovskii, examined the Petrine reforms from a materialist perspective: thus, Pokrovskii's *Russkaia istoriia v samom szhatom ocherke* (1923; *Brief History of Russia*, 1933) saw Peter's economic reforms as an attempt to collaborate with the Russian bourgeoisie in the rapid creation of a mercantile economy capable of competing with other European economies. The determinist tinge of Pokrovskii's work failed to satisfy B.I. Syromiatnikov, whose *"Reguliarnoe" gosudarstvo Petra pervogo i ego ideologiia* ("Regular" State of Peter I and Its Ideology, 1943), treated Peter as a Russian Napoleon before the fact, whose "balancing" between declining gentry and rising bourgeoisie enabled him to chart a course largely independent of either social class. After 1934, Stalinist historians praised Peter as military leader and empire builder, but decried his exploitation of the Russian peasantry. According to this line, Peter was simultaneously a heroic leader and an "enemy of the people." Perhaps the most comprehensive and balanced treatment of Peter to emerge from within the Soviet historiographical tradition was N.I. Pavlenko's *Petr velikii* (Peter the Great, 1990). Pavlenko authoritatively analyzed Peter's social-economic reforms in the context of his state building, his successful extension of the empire, and his foreign policy.

After 1945 the "Peter question" occupied several important Western historians. Reinhard Wittram's *Peter I: Czar und Kaiser* (Peter I: Tsar and King, 1964) has been the standard biography for the past generation. In a series of books, especially his *The Well-Ordered Police State* (1983), Marc Raeff has argued that Peter was trying self-consciously to introduce into Russia a *Polizeistaat* of the Central European type; the absence in Russia of gentry institutions that could check the authority of the central bureaucracy ultimately led, in Raeff's opinion, to Russia's subsequent failure to develop into a *Rechtsstaat*. James Cracraft's *The Church Reform of Peter the Great* (1971) showed how Peter engineered the abolition of the patriarchate and brought about the bureaucratic submission of church to state.

The most lively recent work on Peter has come from E.V. Anisimov, whose book *Vremia petrovskikh reform* (1989; *The Reforms of Peter the Great*, 1993) depicted Peter as a "revolutionary on the throne," a dreamer who broke with his country's past in order to realize an unrealizable utopia. Anisimov provocatively included Peter in the line of "totalitarian" rulers extending from Ivan the Terrible to Stalin. Anisimov also rejected what other historians had considered Peter's greatest achievement – the extension of the empire.

Until recently, the period from 1725 to 1762 was perhaps the most underworked era in Russian historiography. The most authoritative survey of politics and foreign policy was written over a century ago by S.M. Solov'ev, in volumes 19 to 24 of his *Istoriia Rossii s drevneishikh vremen* (History of Russia since Ancient Times, 1869–74); V.O. Kliuchevskii's lectures 70–73 in *Kurs russkoi istorii* were perceptive popularizations based on Solov'ev's exhaustive labors. The mid-18th century interested Soviet historians insofar as they could locate there the roots of later peasant rebellions. Thus, P.K. Alefirenko's *Krest'ianskoe dvizhenie i krest'ianskii vopros v Rossii v 30–50-e gg. XVIII veka* (Peasant Movement and Peasant Question in Russia from the 1730s to the 1750s, 1958) and V.V. Mavrodin's *Klassovaia bor'ba i obshchestvenno-politicheskaia mysl' v Rossii v XVIII veka* (Class Struggle and Social-Political Thought in 18th-Century Russia, 1964) examined peasant protests and serfdom and the reaction of educated society to those protests. A revisionist picture of the period has been provided by E.V. Anisimov. His *Rossiia bez Petra* (Russia Without Peter, 1994) argued that, in 1730, court nobles missed a real chance to abolish the autocracy; his analysis of political crimes under Anna Ivanovna and her favorite Biron demonstrated that the number of prisoners did not much exceed that in other decades of the century. Anisimov's *Rossiia v seredine XVIII veka* (Russia in the mid-18th Century, 1986; as *Empress Elizabeth*, 1995) examined court politics and imperial affairs under Elizabeth.

Two Western scholars have written important monographs on the period: Brenda Meehan-Waters' *Autocracy and Aristocracy*

(1982) argued that the Muscovite elite not only survived the Petrine reforms, but accepted and learned to profit by them. John P. LeDonne departed sharply from the dominant Western paradigm that portrayed the state and the educated public as independent, often mutually hostile social formations. LeDonne's *Absolutism and Ruling Class* (1991) asserted that, despite differences in service rank, title, and landownership, the noble service elite constituted a coherent ruling class that largely determined Russia's political course through the early imperial period.

Scholarship on Russia from 1762 to 1801 has focused on Catherinian politics and on various dimensions of social life in the countryside. S.M. Solov'ev's *Istoriia Rossii s drevneishikh vremen*, vols. 25–29 (1875–79) interpreted the first half of Catherine II's reign as a time of comparative political toleration marred by the increasingly harsh social realities attendant on serfdom. David Ransel's *The Politics of Catherinian Russia* (1975) considered Nikolai Panin's 1762 attempt to modify tsarist administration through the creation of an imperial council; Ransel contended that Panin acted in the interest of a court "party" rather than out of an abstract desire to limit autocracy.

The 1773–74 Pugachev rebellion, which terminated Catherine's "enlightened" period, was first analyzed by the great poet A.S. Pushkin in his *Istoriia Pugacheva* (History of Pugachev, 1833). Pugachev's so-called "peasant war" against serfdom received its canonic treatment in Soviet historiography from V.V. Mavrodin, in *Krest'ianskaia voina v Rossii v 1773–1775 godakh: vosstanie Pugacheva* (Peasant War in Russia from 1773 to 1775: The Rebellion of Pugachev, 1961–65). Whereas Mavrodin interpreted the Pugachevshchina as a class-based revolt against serfdom, Marc Raeff's "Pugachev's Rebellion" (1970) read the episode as a "frontier" conflict in which various groups tried to preserve their traditional rights from encroachment by the central government.

The lamentable plight of the Russian peasantry under Catherine was analyzed exhaustively by the populist historian V.I. Semevskii in his *Krest'iane v tsarstvovanie imperatritsy Ekateriny II* (Peasants in the Reign of Empress Catherine II, 1881–1901). Michael Confino's classic study of the seigneurial economy, *Domaines et seigneurs en Russie vers la fin du XVIIIe siècle* (Estates and Masters in Russia at the End of the 18th Century, 1963) looked at efforts by the nobility to improve agriculture and modernize the rural economy; his sequel volume, *Systèmes agraires et progrès agricole* (Agrarian Systems and Agricultural Progress, 1969) traced the overall failure of these efforts to a structural impediment – namely, the prevalence of the three-field system which was well-suited to seigneurial economy.

The origins of Catherine's provincial reforms have been investigated by Iurii V. Got'e, whose *Istoriia oblastnogo upravleniia v Rossii ot Petra I do Ekateriny II* (History of Provincial Administration in Russia from Peter I to Catherine II, 1913–41) sought, without much success, to find glimmerings of provincial autonomy in the 18th century. Late Catherinian politics has been studied by Isabel de Madariaga, whose *Russia in the Age of Catherine the Great* (1981) authoritatively treated the government's increasingly conservative domestic policies. The freewheeling N.I. Eidel'man's *Mgnoven'e slavy nastaet: god 1789-i* (The Moment of Freedom Is At Hand: The Year 1789, 1989) looked at the collapse of Russian dreams of freedom during the French Revolution. Many historians have followed N.K. Shil'der's *Imperator Pavel pervyi* (Emperor Paul I, 1901), which portrayed Catherine's successor as a mad despot. However, the revisionists of Shil'der have had perhaps the better case. M.N. Klochkov's *Ocherki pravitel'stvennoi deiatel'nosti vremeni Pavla I* (Outlines of Government Activity under Paul I, 1916) and Eidel'man's brilliant *Gran' vekov* (Turn of the Century, 1982) both credited Paul with feeling his way toward social policies more generous to the peasantry than those embraced by Catherine.

Out of the political and economic crisis of the late 18th century, there emerged powerful cultural forces that would shape Russia's future. Marc Raeff's *Origins of the Russian Intelligentsia* (1966) argued that the Petrine nobility's "service mentality" was slowly transformed after 1762 into an abstract commitment to serve the Russian nation. The Soviet jurist P.S. Gratsianskii's *Politicheskaia i pravovaia mysl' Rossii vtoroi poloviny XVIII veka* (Political and Legal Thought of Russia in the Late 18th Century, 1984) made the case that A.N. Radishchev's desire to abolish serfdom and institute a Russian republic issued from Enlightenment ideals discussed by Russian nobles from the 1760s onward. The linkage of the nobility to cultural progress is explicit in Priscilla Roosevelt's *Life on the Russian Country Estate* (1995) and Iu. M. Lotman's *Besedy o russkoi kul'ture* (Conversations on Russian Culture, 1994). This last book contended flatly that the Russian nobility gave birth to "Russian national culture."

Scholarship on the period from 1801 to 1861 has investigated the struggle in the government between reformers and conservatives, the development of the Russian intelligentsia, and the slow genesis of the peasant emancipation.

Throughout the first half of the 19th century, enlightened bureaucrats pressed the government to reform itself and abolish serfdom. In the first years of his reign, Alexander I seriously considered how peasant emancipation might gradually be effected – a point made by Janet Hartley in *Alexander I* (1994) and by A.N. Bokhanov in *Rossiiskie samoderzhtsy 1801–1917* (Russian Autocrats, 1801–1917, 1993). In 1803 Alexander's visionary adviser, M.M. Speranskii, urged the tsar to free the peasants, a recommendation he later withdrew. According to Raeff's 1957 biography, Speranskii's famous 1809 legislative reform project was a cautiously reformist, even conservative plan calculated to preserve imperial authority while granting the formation of a consultative State Duma. Documents published by S.N. Valk in M.M. Speranskii's *Proekty i zapiski* (Legislative Drafts and Notes, 1961) have suggested that Speranskii was committed to a real limitation of the autocracy. Recently, N.V. Minaeva's *Pravitel'stvennyi konstitutsionalizm i peredovoe obshchestvennoe mnenie Rossii v nachale XIX veka* (Governmental Constitutionalism and Progressive Public Opinion in Early 19th-Century Russia, 1982) has portrayed Speranskii precisely as a progressive with ties to the future Decembrists. Alexander's early reformism was a casualty of forceful conservative opposition, such as that analyzed in Richard Pipes' outstanding essay on N.M. Karamzin in his translation of *A Memoir on Ancient and Modern Russia* (1959). It was also frustrated by international events, particularly by the Napoleonic invasion of 1812 – a traumatic event impressively analyzed by E.V. Tarlé in *Nashestvie Napoleona na Rossiiu: 1812 god* (Napoleon's Attack on Russia: The Year

1812, 1938) and L.G. Beskrovnyi in *Otechestvennaia voina 1812 goda* (Patriotic War of 1812, 1962).

Russia's success in overcoming Napoleon left Alexander the master of Europe, but also more uncertain than ever about his domestic policy. S.V. Mironenko's *Samoderzhavie i reformy: politicheskaia bor'ba v Rossii v nachale XIX v.* (Autocracy and Reforms: Political Struggle in Early 19th-Century Russia, 1989) showed that, after 1812, Alexander again considered abolishing serfdom and limiting his own authority by creating a State Duma; however, after authorizing N.N. Novosil'tsov to draft plans, the tsar changed his mind. The public's frustration with Alexander contributed to the Decembrist uprising, which has been variously analyzed. Anatole G. Mazour's *The First Russian Revolution 1825* (1937) portrayed the Decembrists in St. Petersburg mostly as moderate liberals, who favored limited monarchy and abolition of serfdom; the standard Soviet monograph by M.V. Nechkina, *Dvizhenie dekabristov* (Movement of the Decembrists, 1955), saw the Decembrists' center of gravity in the Jacobin-inspired Southern Society led by Pestel'. Although most historians have regarded the Decembrists as quixotic politicians, Mironenko has argued that their *coup d'état* almost succeeded. Soviet historians universally followed Aleksandr Herzen's famous memoirs, *My Past and Thoughts* (1921, translated 1924–26), in categorizing Nicholas I as a reactionary. A more balanced view informed W. Bruce Lincoln's *Nicholas I* (1978): Lincoln showed that in the early 1840s Nicholas recognized the need to abolish serfdom but hesitated publicly to authorize the fateful step.

Iuri M. Lotman's "Dekabrist v povsednevnoi zhizni" (1975, The Decembrist in Everyday Life, 1985) claimed that the *intelligent* as a psychological type appeared between 1812 and 1825. Isaiah Berlin's influential essays in *Russian Thinkers* (1978) put the origins of the intelligentsia in the "marvelous decade" from 1838 to 1848 – that is, in the middle of Nicholas I's reign. Berlin deplored the intelligentsia's tendency to reject autocracy in the name of some mastering, unitary theory – a tendency he found absent only in Aleksandr Herzen. Aileen Kelly's book *Mikhail Bakunin* (1982) demonstrated the unattractiveness of utopian thinking in the case of the famed Russian anarchist. Andrzej Walicki's *The Slavophile Controversy* (1964, translated 1975) argued that the period from 1812 to 1848 also gave rise to a retrospective, "conservative utopia" in the form of Slavophilism – a worldview that was anti-Westernism, antirevolutionary, and anticapitalist. Oddly enough, despite their anti-Westernism, the Slavophiles strongly agreed with the radical intelligentsia that serfdom should be abolished.

The legal emancipation of the serfs in 1861 has been bitterly debated by historians. The canonic Soviet interpretation by M.V. Nechkina, editor of a multivolume collaborative study *Revoliutsionnaia situatsiia v Rossii v 1859–1861 gg.* (Revolutionary Situation in Russia from 1859 to 1861, 1960–86), argued that the emancipation was prompted by a structural economic crisis that generated the threat of a peasant revolution, led radicals to criticize the serf order, and caused the ruling class to lose confidence in the existing political order. Both P.A. Zaionchkovskii's *Otmena krepostnogo prava v Rossii* (Abolition of Serfdom in Russia, 1954; revised 1968) and L.G. Zakharova's *Samoderzhavie i otmena krepostnogo prava v Rossii, 1856–1861* (Autocracy and the Abolition of Serfdom in Russia, 1856 to 1861, 1984) pointed out that Nechkina exaggerated the impact of radicalism on the monarchy. The American historian Terence Emmons' *The Russian Landed Gentry and the Peasant Emancipation of 1861* (1968) asserted that gentry liberalism had more to do with the emancipation than Nechkina acknowledged. Daniel Field's *The End of Serfdom* (1976) attributed the initiative for the reform squarely to the autocracy – a view also shared by W. Bruce Lincoln's *In the Vanguard of Reform* (1982). Recent documents published by Zakharova in *1857–1861: perepiska Imperatora Aleksandra II s Velikim Kniazem Konstantinom Nikolaevichem; Dnevnik Velikogo Kniazia Konstantina Nikolaevicha* (1857–1861: Correspondence of Emperor Alexander II with Grand Duke Konstantin Nikolaevich; Diary of Grand Duke Konstantin Nikolaevich, 1994) have proven that the royal family's concern over Russia's international prestige and competitiveness also drove the peasant reform.

Scholarship on Russia from 1861 to 1917 attempted to explain the growing tension between the government and educated society – tension that exploded in revolutions in 1905 and 1917. Liberal historians, such as B.N. Chicherin writing in his *Rossiia nakanune dvadtsatogo stoletiia* (Russia on the Eve of the 20th Century, 1900) and A.A. Kornilov writing in *Kurs istorii Rossii XIX veka* (Course of Russian History in the 19th Century, 1912–14; revised 1918), blamed extremists in the government and among radical youth for undermining Alexander II's "great reforms." The distinguished French observer Anatole LeRoy-Beaulieu, in *L'Empire des tsars et les Russes* (1881–96; *Empire of the Tsars and the Russians*, 1897–98), blamed the government's pro-Russian nationality policy and religious persecutions of non-Orthodox minorities for driving a wedge between the regime and society.

Not until the appearance of P.A. Zaionchkovskii and the so-called "Zaionchkovskii school" after 1945 did serious archival work on Russian internal policy occur. Zaionchkovskii himself published three classic books: *Krizis samoderzhaviia na rubezhe* (1964; *The Russian Autocracy in Crisis*, 1979) examined the government's vacillating reactions to Russian terrorism; *Rossiiskoe samoderzhavie v kontse XIX stoletiia* (1970; *Russian Autocracy under Alexander III*, 1976) traced Alexander III's "counter-reforms"; and *Pravitel'stvennyi apparat samoderzhavnoi Rossii v XIX v.* (Governmental Apparatus of Autocratic Russia in the 19th Century, 1978), which was the first prosopographical analysis of the state bureaucracy. Two of Zaionchkovskii's Soviet students explored additional dimensions of internal politics: L.G. Zakharova's *Zemskaia kontr-reforma 1890 g.* (Zemstvo Counter-Reform of 1890, 1968) looked at the interplay between state policy and the landed nobility; and V.A. Tvardovskaia's *Ideologiia poreformennogo samoderzhaviia: M.N. Katkov i ego izdaniia* (Ideology of the Reformed Autocracy: M.N. Katkov and His Publications, 1978) studied the ultra-nationalist Mikhail Katkov and his baneful influence on the regime. Zaionchkovskii also influenced the younger generation of Leningrad historians – B.V. Anan'ich, R. Sh. Ganelin, and V.S. Diakin. Their collective history, *Krizis samoderzhaviia v Rossii, 1895–1917* (Crisis of Autocracy, 1895–1917, 1984), was the first serious internal history of government policy under Nicholas II. It is worth noting that an entire generation of American scholars was inspired by Zaionchkovskii. Emmons' and Field's books on the peasant emancipation were written under his direction. Richard Robbins

book *The Tsar's Viceroys* (1987) applied Zaionchkovskii's prosopographical techniques and archival mastery to Russian provincial government. Works of the Zaionchkovskii school generally suggested that Russian officials were sharply divided on questions of internal policy between liberal reformers and Russian nationalist authoritarians, and that neither group developed an effective strategy to preserve social peace in a country rapidly developing industrial institutions.

A major consequence of the regime's failure to govern wisely was the alienation of the elites, although scholars have debated the degree and permanence of such alienation. N.M. Pirumova's *Zemskoe liberal'noe dvizhenie* (Zemstvo Liberal Movement, 1977) showed how a small portion of the landed nobility moved sharply to the left at the end of the 19th century. Terence Emmons, in *The Formation of Political Parties and the First National Elections in Russia* (1983), demonstrated that the social base of the Russian constitutional movement included both liberal gentry and many educated urbanites. However, Roberta Manning's *Crisis of the Old Order in Russia. Gentry and Government* (1982) suggested that the violence of 1905 provoked a conservative reaction among rural elites and a realignment of gentry and government under prime minister Stolypin. Manning wanted to understand the post-1905 rural gentry as Russia's ruling class. Thomas Owen's *Capitalism and Politics in Russia* (1981) suggested that Moscow's pre-1905 merchant elites were often politically conservative, but Robert Thurston's *Liberal City, Conservative State* (1987) saw the post-1905 merchantry as reformist and frustrated by the central government's conservative internal policies. Samuel Kassow's *Between Tsar and People* (1991) asserted that before 1917 the educated elites in Russia were beginning to coalesce in a "middle class" of sorts, and that the mood of civil society had turned oppositional.

The social roots of the revolutionary movement have sparked scholarly interest since the turn of the century. Early Marxist scholars, such as the Menshevik historians writing in Iurii V. Martov's *Obshchestvennoe dvizhenie v Rossii s nachala XX-ogo veka* (Social Movement in Russia since the Beginning of the 20th Century, 1908–11), traced social tensions to class antagonisms; this was the first publication systematically to examine the history of strikes and peasant disturbances in Russia. Historians during the Soviet period laid a broad documentary foundation for understanding conflicts between peasants and the regime; here the multivolume series *Krest'ianskoe dvizhenie v Rossii* (Peasant Movement in Russia, 1959–68), covering the entire century before 1905, was the landmark publication. P.N. Pershin's *Agrarnaia revoliutsiia v Rossii* (Agrarian Revolution in Russia, 1966) argued that peasant rebellion against the old regime between 1905 and 1917 was an essential component of the revolutionary process in Russia. Theodore von Laue's *Sergei Witte and the Industrialization of Russia* (1963) and *Why Lenin? Why Stalin?* (1964) argued that Russia's rapid industrialization entailed oppression of the peasantry, oppression which, in turn, provoked peasant violence against the regime. Laue saw Russia's social disorder as a historically determined result of global modernization.

Labor historians of Russia focused on the nexus between poverty and political mobilization in the cities. Allan Wildman's *Making of a Workers' Revolution* (1967) and Reginald Zelnik's *Labor and Society in Tsarist Russia* (1971) were pioneering attempts to analyze the origins of the working class in St. Petersburg, workers' participation in strikes, and their involvement in radical politics. Walter Sablinsky's *The Road to Bloody Sunday* (1976) and Gerald Suhr's *1905 in St. Petersburg* (1989) studied the roots of St. Petersburg labor violence in 1905. Laura Engelstein's *Moscow, 1905* (1982) linked Moscow's urban geography and workers' political organization. Charters Wynn's study of the Donbass, *Workers, Strikes, and Pogroms* (1992), argued that targets of worker violence were sometimes determined by ethnic and religious differences – an argument bolstered by evidence in Robert Weinberg's *Revolution of 1905 in Odessa* (1993).

Scholarship on the 1917 revolutions has been marked from the beginning by partisan divisions. The liberal P.N. Miliukov's *Istoriia vtoroi russkoi revoliutsii* (1921–24; *The Russian Revolution*, 1978–87) heralded the March 1917 overthrow of the tsarist government as a great act of statecraft, but blamed the October revolution on left utopianism. The Menshevik internationalist N.N. Sukhanov's *Zapiski o revoliutsii* (Notes on the Revolution, 1922–23) read the revolution as a spontaneous workers' revolution which Lenin captured in the Bolsheviks' name. Leon Trotskii's *Istoriia russkoi revoliutsii* (1931–33; *The History of the Russian Revolution*, 1932–33) argued that Bolshevik victory was the historically inevitable result of capitalism's sudden appearance in Russia and of the heroism of Lenin. The Bolshevik Central Committee's *History of the Communist Party of the Soviet Union: Short Course* (1939) credited Lenin and Stalin for the Bolshevik victory. The anti-Bolshevik S.P. Mel'gunov argued in his *Kak bol'sheviki zakhvatili vlast'* (1953; *The Bolshevik Seizure of Power*, 1972) that the October Revolution was a Leninist *coup d'état* without popular support.

Only in the wake of the XX Party Congress in 1956 did it become possible to move away from partisan scholarship on 1917. The Soviet historian E.N. Burdzhalov's *Vtoraia russkaia revolutsiia* (1967–71; *Russia's Second Revolution*, 1987) hinted that the February 1917 Revolution had not been inspired by the Bolsheviks after all. Burdzhalov's position was the starting point for T. Hasegawa's *The February Revolution: Petrograd 1917* (1981) which captured the dynamics of street protests in the capital in their interplay with party politics. Alexander Rabinowitch's *Prelude to Revolution* (1968) and *The Bolsheviks Come to Power* (1976) showed that in the July and October crisis the Bolshevik party was not the united force that revolutionary historians had once depicted. Rabinowitch explained the Bolshevik Revolution as the result of a complex interplay of worker radicalism, Bolshevik extremism, and Lenin's revolutionary intuition. Meanwhile, the Soviet historian V.I. Startsev emphasized that the Bolsheviks were not the only revolutionary actors in 1917: Startsev's *Krakh Kerenshchiny* (Collapse of the Kerenskii Regime, 1982) and *Oktiabrskaia bur'ia* (October Storm, 1987) implicitly challenged the October Revolution's inevitability. Stephen Smith's *Red Petrograd* (1983) and Diane Koenker's *Moscow Workers and the 1917 Revolution* (1981) moved the debate from party mobilization to the will of workers themselves. By the late 1980s the emerging consensus held that an internally divided Bolshevik party took advantage of labor radicalism and weak political opposition to make a revolution that was at once popular and partisan. However, Richard Pipes' *The Russian Revolution* (1990)

rejected this neo-orthodoxy by returning to something like the Mel'gunov line. Predictably, Pipes' revision stirred up a wave of protest, because he seemed to abandon any belief in labor activism as a major factor in the Revolution's origins.

The history of the Soviet regime has yet to assume definitive shape, partly because archives were inaccessible until 1991 and partly because Soviet historians were themselves subjected to stringent political oversight by the Communist party. Consequently, the finest histories of the Soviet period to date have been written by Russian émigrés, by Westerners, and by political dissidents – a fact noted with embarrassment and not a little irritation by the Russian historical establishment. The most compendious history of the 1920s and early 1930s was written by E.H. Carr and R.W. Davies. The Carr-Davies history was an unapologetic "history of the victors," valuable for its massive documentation from published sources. A trenchant attack on the Soviet system based partly on (former) insiders' access to little-known documents was written by Aleksandr Nekrich and Mikhail Geller, *Utopiia u vlasti* (1982; *Utopia in Power*, 1986). Martin Malia advertised his *The Soviet Tragedy* (1994), as the first history of the regime from its inception to its collapse. Like Nekrich and Geller, Malia assumed that Soviet socialism was inherently utopian, and hence that its tragic consequences and eventual collapse were foreordained.

The threshold question in historiography on the Soviet period has been the link between Leninism and Stalinism. Leonard Schapiro's *The Origin of the Communist Autocracy* (1956) and *The Communist Party of the Soviet Union* (1960) argued that Lenin established the Soviet dictatorship and that Stalin inherited and perfected it. Robert Conquest's *Great Terror* (1968), *Harvest of Sorrow* (1986), and *Stalin* (1993) all make a similar assumption. Richard Pipes' *Russia under the Bolshevik Regime* (1993) and his edition of unpublished documents from Lenin, *The Unknown Lenin* (1996) were intended to prove Lenin's responsibility for constructing the Soviet state terrorist apparatus. In the Russian literature, the most devastating indictment of Lenin can be found in Aleksandr Solzhenitsyn's *The Gulag Archipelago, 1918–1956*, 1973–76) – a book meant to destroy the intellectual and moral foundations of the Soviet regime. In *Lenin* (1994) D.A. Volkogonov came reluctantly to the conclusion that Lenin, like Stalin, had been a tyrant.

To some historians, the nexus between Lenin and Stalin has seemed not so straightforward. Moshe Lewin's *Le Dernier Combat de Lénine* (1967; *Lenin's Last Struggle*, 1968) made the case that, in the last year of his life, Lenin desperately tried to block Stalin's ascendancy in the party. R.A. Medvedev, in *Let History Judge* (1971) and *On Stalin and Stalinism* (1979), asserted a fundamental distinction between Leninism and Stalinism. Stephen F. Cohen's *Bukharin and the Bolshevik Revolution* (1973) argued that, before 1929, the party was far from monolithic and that Bukharin's gradual path to socialism represented a genuine Leninist alternative to Stalinism. Robert Tucker's multivolume biography of Stalin followed Cohen's line on Stalinism, but added that quirks in Stalin's personality – his need to be seen as a hero and his paranoia about opposition – were important in distinguishing Stalinism from Leninism.

The debate over Stalinism was part of a larger debate on whether the Soviet Union was a totalitarian society. The impetus for this debate came from various sources, chief among them being Hannah Arendt's *Origins of Totalitarianism* (1951) and Zbigniew Brzezinski and Carl J. Friedrich's *Totalitarian Dictatorship and Autocracy* (1956), which compared the Soviet and Nazi dictatorships. After Arendt and Brzezinski, it quickly became a hallmark of the totalitarian interpretation to insist on a fundamental continuity between Leninism and Stalinism. Thus, since 1985, when Stephen Cohen's *Rethinking the Soviet Experience* was published, many scholars have categorized Schapiro, Pipes, Conquest, and Malia as representatives of a so-called "Cold War school" of historiography; whereas Lewin, Tucker, and Cohen himself have considered themselves "revisionists." Recently, two historians have rethought the question of Soviet totalitarianism: in *Totalitarianism: The Inner History of the Cold War* (1995), Abbott Gleason showed that the intellectual history of the term "totalitarianism" has not been sufficiently understood by those historians who have brandished it as a weapon of struggle; in *Marxism and the Leap to the Kingdom of Freedom* (1995), Andrzej Walicki treated totalitarianism as that phase in early Soviet history when the Bolshevik party leadership attempted to realize the communist utopia. The effect of Gleason and Walicki may be to de-couple the Leninism-Stalinism debate from the wider controversy over totalitarianism.

Meanwhile, one of the most significant historians of the Soviet period, Sheila Fitzpatrick, has refused to accept the very terms of debate defining the field. Fitzpatrick has been far less interested in Lenin's and Stalin's personal contributions to the Soviet experiment than in cultural and institutional changes that occurred during the 1920s and 1930s. Her works shifted the focus from state terror to Soviet culture and to the formation of the first generation of Soviet citizens.

There have been relatively few good books by historians on the Soviet experience since 1939. The most reliable military history of the war against Nazism was written by John Erickson in *Stalin's War with Germany* (1975) and *The Road to Berlin* (1983). The German historian Omer Bartov's *The Eastern Front, 1941–1945* (1985) explained why the Nazi-Soviet war was decided not by the technical superiority of one side but by an elemental, almost atavistic struggle. Alexander Nekrich's *The Punished Peoples* (1978) showed that among the casualties of the war must be numbered the Soviet minorities which attracted Stalin's wrath for their alleged collaboration with Hitler. John Barber and Mark Harrison in *The Soviet Home Front* (1991) provided an excellent brief account of the much-neglected domestic impact of the war. Nina Tumarkin's *The Living and the Dead* (1994) demonstrated the ways that authorities manipulated memories of the war to strengthen the Soviet regime. To date, shockingly, there have been no first-rate studies of the Holocaust on Soviet territory. John Gordon Garrard's *Bones of Berdichev* (1996) demonstrated that some Soviet intellectuals were aware of Hitler's war against the Jews, but Garrard could not deal with the dimensions of this tragedy on the scale it deserved.

Stalin's legacy has been analyzed in David Holloway's *Stalin and the Bomb* (1994), which showed how the USSR became a superpower, and R.A. Medvedev's *Khrushchev* (1982), which explained Khrushchev's partly successful attempt to demolish state terrorism without destroying socialism. Meanwhile, Murray Feshbach's *The Soviet Union* (1982) and *Ecocide in the USSR* (1992) suggested that, from beginning to end, the Soviet experiment was a demographic and ecological disaster.

In view of the Chernobyl catastrophe of 1986, analyzed in scrupulous detail by Grigorii Medvedev in *The Truth about Chernobyl* (1991), Feshbach's pessimistic account of Soviet history seemed fully justified.

G.M. HAMBURG and THOMAS SANDERS

See also Berlin; Carr, E.; Conze; Davies, R.; Deutscher; Kliuchevskii; Lewin; Medvedev; Miliukov; Pipes; Raeff; Solov'ev; Zaionchkovskii

Further Reading

Alefirenko, Pelageia Kuz'minichna, *Krest'ianskoe dvizhenie i krest'ianskii vopros v Rossii v 30–50-e gg. XVIII veka* (Peasant Movement and Peasant Question in Russia from the 1730s to the 1750s), Moscow, 1958

Anan'ich, B.V., R. Sh. Ganelin, and V.S. Diakin, *Krizis samoderzhaviia v Rossii, 1895–1917* (Crisis of Autocracy, 1895–1917), Leningrad, 1984

Anisimov, Evgenii Viktorovich, *Rossiia v seredine XVIII veka: bor'ba za nasledie Petra*, Moscow, 1986; in English as *Empress Elizabeth: Her Reign and Her Russia, 1741–1761*, 1995

Anisimov, Evgenii Viktorovich, *Vremia petrovskikh reform*, Leningrad, 1989; in English as *The Reforms of Peter the Great: Progress Through Coercion in Russia*, Armonk, NY: Sharpe, 1993

Anisimov, Evgenii Viktorovich, *Rossiia bez Petra* (Russia Without Peter), St. Petersburg, 1994

Arendt, Hannah, *The Origins of Totalitarianism*, New York: Harcourt Brace, 1951; as *The Burden of Our Time*, London: Secker and Warburg, 1951

Barber, John, and Mark Harrison, *The Soviet Home Front, 1941–1945: A Social and Economic History of the USSR in World War II*, London and New York: Longman, 1991

Bartov, Omer, *The Eastern Front, 1941–1945: German Troops and the Barbarisation of Warfare*, Basingstoke: Macmillan, 1985; New York: St. Martin's Press, 1986

Berlin, Isaiah, *Russian Thinkers*, edited by Henry Hardy and Aileen Kelly, New York: Hogarth Press, and London: Viking, 1978

Beskrovnyi, Liubomir Grigorevich, *Otechestvennaia voina 1812 goda* (Patriotic War of 1812), Moscow, 1962

Bokhanov, Aleksandr Nikolaevich, *Rossiiskie samoderzhtsy, 1801–1917* (Russian Autocrats 1801–1917), Moscow: Mezhdunarodnye otnosheniia, 1993

Bolshevik Central Committee, *History of the Communist Party of the Soviet Union: Short Course*, Moscow: Foreign Language House, 1938; New York: International Publishers, 1939; London: Cobbett, 1943

Brzezinski, Zbigniew, and Carl J. Friedrich, *Totalitarian Dictatorship and Autocracy*, Cambridge, MA: Harvard University Press, 1956

Burdzhalov, Eduard Nikolaevich, *Vtoraia russkaia revoliutsiia*, 2 vols., Moscow, 1967–71; in English as *Russia's Second Revolution: The February 1917 Uprising in Petrograd*, Bloomington: Indiana University Press, 1987

Carr, E.H., *The Bolshevik Revolution, 1917–1923*, 3 vols., London and New York: Macmillan, 1950–53

Carr, E.H., *The Interregnum, 1923–1924*, 2 vols., London: Macmillan, and New York: St. Martin's Press, 1954

Carr, E.H., *Socialism in One Country, 1924–1926*, 3 vols., London and New York: Macmillan, 1958–64

Carr, E.H., and R.W. Davies, *Foundations of a Planned Economy, 1926–1929*, 2 vols., London and New York: Macmillan, 1969–78

Chicherin, Boris Nikolaevich, *Oblastnye uchrezhdeniia Rossii v XVII-m veke* (Provincial Institutions of Russia in the 17th Century), Moscow, 1856

Chicherin, Boris Nikolaevich, *Rossiia nakanune dvadtsatogo stoletiia* (Russia on the Eve of the 20th Century), Berlin: Shteinits, 1900

Cohen, Stephen F., *Bukharin and the Bolshevik Revolution: A Political Biography, 1888–1938*, New York: Knopf, and Oxford: Oxford University Press, 1973

Cohen, Stephen F., *Rethinking the Soviet Experience: Politics and History since 1917*, Oxford and New York: Oxford University Press, 1985

Confino, Michael, *Domaines et seigneurs en Russie vers la fin du XVIIIe siècle: étude des structures agraires et de mentalités économiques* (Estates and Masters in Russia at the End of the 18th Century), Paris: Institut d'Etudes Slaves de l'Université de Paris, 1963

Confino, Michael, *Systèmes agraires et progrès agricole: l'assolement triennal en Russie aux XVIIIe–XIXe siècles* (Agrarian Systems and Agricultural Progress), Paris: Mouton, 1969

Conquest, Robert, *The Great Terror: Stalin's Purge of the 1930s*, New York and London: Macmillan, and New York: Macmillan, 1968; revised 1973

Conquest, Robert, *The Harvest of Sorrow: Soviet Collectivization and the Terror-Famine*, New York: Oxford University Press, and London: Century Hutchinson, 1986

Conquest, Robert, *Stalin: Breaker of Nations*, New York: Viking, 1991; London: Weidenfeld and Nicolson, 1993

Cracraft, James, *The Church Reform of Peter the Great*, London: Macmillan, and Stanford, CA: Stanford University Press, 1971

Eidel'man, Natan Iakovlevich, *Gran' vekov: politicheskaia bor'ba v Rossii: konets XVIII–nachalo XIX stoletiia* (Turn of the Century), Moscow, 1982

Eidel'man, Natan Iakovlevich, *Mgnoven'e slavy nastaet: god 1789-i* (The Moment of Freedom Is at Hand: The Year 1789), Leningrad, 1989

Emmons, Terence, *The Russian Landed Gentry and the Peasant Emancipation of 1861*, Cambridge, MA: Cambridge University Press, 1968

Emmons, Terence, *The Formation of Political Parties and the First National Elections in Russia*, Cambridge, MA: Harvard University Press, 1983

Engelstein, Laura, *Moscow, 1905: Working-Class Organization and Political Conflict*, Stanford, CA: Stanford University Press, 1982

Erickson, John, *Stalin's War with Germany*, London: Weidenfeld and Nicolson, and New York: Harper, 1975

Erickson, John, *The Road to Berlin*, London: Weidenfeld and Nicolson, and Boulder, CO: Westview Press, 1983

Feshbach, Murray, *The Soviet Union: Population Trends and Dilemmas*, Washington, DC: Population Reform Board, 1982

Feshbach, Murray, *Ecocide in the USSR: Health and Nature under Siege*, New York: Basic Books, 1992

Field, Daniel, *The End of Serfdom: Nobility and Bureaucracy in Russia, 1855–1861*, Cambridge, MA: Harvard University Press, 1976

Fitzpatrick, Sheila, *Commissariat of Enlightenment: Soviet Organization of Education and the Arts under Lunacharsky, October 1917–1921*, Cambridge: Cambridge University Press, 1970

Fitzpatrick, Sheila, *Education and Social Mobility in the Soviet Union, 1921–1934*, Cambridge and New York: Cambridge University Press, 1979

Fitzpatrick, Sheila, *The Cultural Front: Power and Culture in Revolutionary Russia*, Ithaca, NY: Cornell University Press, 1992

Garrard, John, *Bones of Berdichev: The Life and Fate of Vasily Grossman*, New York: Free Press, 1996

Gleason, Abbott, *Totalitarianism: The Inner History of the Cold War*, New York: Oxford University Press, 1995

Got'e, Iurii Vladimirovich, *Istoriia oblastnogo upravleniia v Rossii ot Petra I do Ekateriny II* (History of Provincial Administration in Russia from Peter I to Catherine II), 2 vols., Moscow, 1913–41

Gratsianskii, Pavel Sergeevich, *Politicheskaia i pravovaia mysl' Rossii vtoroi poloviny XVIII veka* (Political and Legal Thought of Russia in the Late 18th Century), Moscow, 1984

Hartley, Janet, *Alexander I*, London and New York: Longman, 1994

Hasegawa, Tsuyoshi, *The February Revolution: Petrograd, 1917*, Seattle: University of Washington Press, 1981

Herzen, Aleksandr, *Byloe i dumy*, 5 vols., Berlin: Slovo, 1921; in English as *My Past and Thoughts*, 6 vols., New York: Knopf, 1924–26, London: Chatto and Windus, 1924–27

Holloway, David, *Stalin and the Bomb: The Soviet Union and Atomic Energy, 1939–56*, New Haven: Yale University Press, 1994

Karamzin, N.M., *O drevnei i novoi Rossii*, 1811; in English as *A Memoir on Ancient and Modern Russia*, Cambridge, MA: Harvard University Press, 1959

Kassow, Samuel, *Between Tsar and People: Educated Society and the Quest for Public Identity in Late Imperial Russia*, Princeton: Princeton University Press, 1991

Kelly, Aileen, *Mikhail Bakunin: A Study in the Psychology and Politics of Utopianism*, Oxford and New York: Oxford University Press, 1982

Kliuchevskii, V.O., *Kurs russkoi istorii*, 5 vols., Moscow, 1904–1921; in English as *A History of Russia*, 5 vols., London: Dent, and New York: Dutton, 1911–31; selections as *Peter the Great*, London: Macmillan, and New York: St. Martin's Press, 1958; and *The Rise of the Romanovs*, London: Macmillan, 1970

Klochkov, Mikhail Vasil'evich, *Ocherki pravitel'stvennoi deiatel'nosti vremeni Pavla I* (Outlines of Government Activity under Paul I), Petrograd: Senatskaia, 1916

Koenker, Diane, *Moscow Workers and the 1917 Revolution*, Princeton: Princeton University Press, 1981

Kornilov, Aleksandr Aleksandrovich, *Kurs istorii Rossii XIX veka* (Course of Russian History in the 19th Century), 3 vols., Moscow: Dom Sabashnikovnikh, 1912–14; revised 1918

Krest'ianskoe dvizhenie v Rossii (Peasant Movement in Russia), 7 vols., 1959–68

Laue, Theodore von, *Sergei Witte and the Industrialization of Russia*, New York: Columbia University Press, 1963

Laue, Theodore von, *Why Lenin? Why Stalin? A Reappraisal of the Russian Revolution, 1900–1930*, Philadelphia: Lippincott, 1964

LeDonne, John P., *Absolutism and Ruling Class: The Formation of the Russian Political Order, 1700–1825*, Oxford and New York: Oxford University Press, 1991

Lenin, V.I., *The Unknown Lenin: From the Secret Archive*, edited by Richard Pipes, New Haven: Yale University Press, 1996

LeRoy-Beaulieu, Anatole, *L'Empire des tsars et les Russes*, 3 vols., Paris: Hachette, 1881–96; in English as *Empire of the Tsars and the Russians*, 3 vols., New York and London: Putnam, 1897–98

Lewin, Moshe, *Le Dernier Combat de Lénine*, Paris: Minuit, 1967; in English as *Lenin's Last Struggle*, New York: Pantheon, 1968, London: Faber, 1969

Lincoln, W. Bruce, *Nicholas I: Emperor and Autocrat of All the Russias*, Bloomington: Indiana University Press, 1978

Lincoln, W. Bruce, *In the Vanguard of Reform: Russia's Enlightened Bureaucrats 1825–1861*, DeKalb: Northern Illinois University Press, 1982

Lotman, Iurii Mikhailovich, "Dekabrist v povsednevnoi zhizni," 1975; in English as "The Decembrist in Everyday Life," in Alexander D. Nakhimovsky and Alice Stone Nakhimovsky, eds., *The Semiotics of Russian Cultural History*, Ithaca, NY: Cornell University Press, 1985

Lotman, Iurii Mikhailovich, *Besedy o russkoi kul'ture* (Conversations on Russian Culture), St. Petersburg: Iskusstvo-SPB, 1994

Madariaga, Isabel de, *Russia in the Age of Catherine the Great*, London: Weidenfeld and Nicolson, and New Haven: Yale University Press, 1981

Malia, Martin Edward, *The Soviet Tragedy: A History of Socialism in Russia, 1917 to 1991*, New York: Free Press, 1994

Manning, Roberta Thompson, *Crisis of the Old Order in Russia: Gentry and Government*, Princeton: Princeton University Press, 1982

Martov, Iurii V., ed., *Obshchestvennoe dvizhenie v Rossii s nachala XX-ogo veka* (Social Movement in Russia since the Beginning of the 20th Century), 4 vols., St. Petersburg: Obschestvennaia Pol'za, 1908–11

Mavrodin, Vladimir Vasil'evich, *Krest'ianskaia voina v Rossii v 1773–1775 godakh: vosstanie Pugacheva* (Peasant War in Russia from 1773 to 1775: The Rebellion of Pugachev), 3 vols., Leningrad: Izd-vo Leningradskogo universiteta, 1961–65

Mavrodin, Vladimir Vasil'evich, *Klassovaia bor'ba i obshchestvenno-politicheskaia mysl' v Rossii v XVIII veka (1773–1790 gg): kurs lektsii* (Class Struggle and Social-Political Thought in 18th-Century Russia), Leningrad: Izd-vo Leningradskogo universiteta, 1964

Mazour, Anatole G., *The First Russian Revolution, 1825: The Decembrist Movement, Its Origins, Development, and Significance*, Berkeley: University of California Press, 1937

Medvedev, Grigorii, *The Truth about Chernobyl*, New York: Basic Books, 1991

Medvedev, Roy A., *K sudu istorii: genezis i posledstviia stalinizma*, 1971; in English as *Let History Judge: The Origins and Consequences of Stalinism*, New York: Knopf, 1971, London: Macmillan, 1972; revised edition, New York: Columbia University Press, and Oxford: Oxford University Press, 1989

Medvedev, Roy A., *On Stalin and Stalinism*, Oxford and New York: Oxford University Press, 1979

Medvedev, Roy A., *Khrushchev*, Oxford: Blackwell, 1982; Garden City, NY: Doubleday, 1983

Meehan-Waters, Brenda, *Autocracy and Aristocracy: The Russian Service Elite of 1730*, New Brunswick, NJ: Rutgers University Press, 1982

Mel'gunov, Sergei Petrovich, *Kak bol'sheviki zakhvatili vlast': oktiabr'skii perevorot 1917 goda*, Paris: La Renaissance, 1953; in English as *The Bolshevik Seizure of Power*, Santa Barbara, CA: ABC-Clio, 1972

Miliukov, Pavel, *Gosudarstvennoe khoziaistvo Rossii v pervoi chetverti XVIII stoletiia i reforma Petra Velikogo* (Russia's State Economy in the First Quarter of the 18th Century and the Reform of Peter the Great), St. Petersburg: Balasheva, 1890–92

Miliukov, Pavel, *Ocherki po istorii russkoi kul'tury*, 3 vols., St. Petersburg: Mir bozhii, 1896–1903; in English as *Outlines of Russian Culture*, 3 vols., Philadelphia: University of Pennsylvania Press, 1942; abridged as *The Origins of Ideology*, Gulf Breeze, FL: Academic International, 1974, and *Ideologies in Conflict*, Academic International, 1975

Miliukov, Pavel, *Istoriia vtoroi russkoi revoliutsii*, Sofia: Rossiisko-Bolgarskoe, 1921–24; in English as *The Russian Revolution*, 3 vols., Gulf Breeze, FL: Academic International, 1978–87

Minaeva, Nina Vasil'evna, *Pravitel'stvennyi konstitutsionalizm i peredovoe obshchestvennoe mnenie Rossii v nachale XIX veka* (Governmental Constitutionalism and Progressive Public Opinion in Early 19th-Century Russia), Saratov: Izd-vo Saratovskogo universiteta, 1982

Mironenko, Sergei V., *Samoderzhavie i reformy: politicheskaia bor'ba v Rossii v nachale XIX v.* (Autocracy and Reforms: Political Struggle in Early 19th-Century Russia), Moscow: Nauka, 1989

Nechkina, Militsa V., *Dvizhenie dekabristov* (Movement of the Decembrists), 2 vols., Moscow: Akademii nauk SSSR, 1955

Nechkina, Militsa V., ed., *Revoliutsionnaia situatsiia v Rossii v 1859–1861 gg.* (Revolutionary Situation in Russia from 1859 to 1861), 9 vols., Moscow: In-t istorii AN SSSR, 1960–86

Nekrich, Aleksandr, *Nakazannye narody*, New York: Khronika, 1978; in English as *The Punished Peoples: The Deportation and Fate of the Soviet Minorities at the End of the Second World War*, New York: Norton, 1978

Nekrich, Aleksandr, and Mikhail Geller, *Utopiia u vlasti: istoriia sovetskogo soiuza s 1917 goda do nashikh dnei*, 2 vols., London: Overseas Publications, 1982; in English as *Utopia in Power: A History of the Soviet Union from 1917 to the Present*, London: Hutchinson, 1986

Owen, Thomas, *Capitalism and Politics in Russia: A Social History of the Moscow Merchants, 1855–1905*, Cambridge: Cambridge University Press, 1981

Pavlenko, Nikolai Ivanovich, *Petr velikii* (Peter the Great), Moscow: Mysl', 1990

Pershin, Pavel Nikolaevich, *Agrarnaia revoliutsiia v Rossii* (Agrarian Revolution in Russia), Moscow: Nauka, 1966

Pipes, Richard, *The Russian Revolution*, New York: Knopf, and London: Collins, 1990; concise version, 1995

Pipes, Richard, *Russia under the Bolshevik Regime*, New York: Knopf, 1993; London: Harvill, 1994

Pirumova, Natal'ia Mikhailovna, *Zemskoe liberal'noe dvizhenie: sotsial'nye korni i evolutsiia do nachala XX veka* (Zemstvo Liberal Movement), Moscow: Nauka, 1977

Pogodin, Mikhail Petrovich, *Istoriko-kriticheskie otryvki* (Historical-Critical Fragments), 2 vols., Moscow: Sinodal'noi, 1846–57

Pokrovskii, Mikhail Nikolaevich, *Russkaia istoriia v samom szhatnom ocherke*, 4 vols., Moscow: Gosizdat, 1923; in English as *A Brief History of Russia*, 2 vols., London: Lawrence, and New York: International Publishers, 1933

Pushkin, Aleksandr, *Istoriia Pugacheva*, 1833; in English as *The History of Pugachev*, Ann Arbor, MI: Ardis, 1983

Rabinowitch, Alexander, *Prelude to Revolution: The Petrograd Bolsheviks and the July 1917 Uprising*, Bloomington: Indiana University Press, 1968

Rabinowitch, Alexander, *The Bolsheviks Come to Power: The Revolution of 1917 in Petrograd*, New York: Norton, 1976

Raeff, Marc, *Michael Speransky: Statesman of Imperial Russia, 1772–1839*, The Hague: Nijhoff, 1957

Raeff, Marc, *Origins of the Russian Intelligentsia: The Eighteenth-Century Nobility*, New York: Harcourt Brace, 1966

Raeff, Marc, "Pugachev's Rebellion," in Robert Forster and Jack P. Greene, eds., *Preconditions of Revolution in Early Modern Europe*, Baltimore: Johns Hopkins University Press, 1970, 161–202

Raeff, Marc, *The Well-Ordered Police State: Social and Institutional Change Through Law in the Germanies and Russia, 1600–1800*, New Haven: Yale University Press, 1983

Ransel, David, *The Politics of Catherinian Russia: The Panin Party*, New Haven: Yale University Press, 1975

Robbins, Richard, *The Tsar's Viceroys: Russia's Provincial Governors in the Last Years of the Empire*, Ithaca, NY: Cornell University Press, 1987

Roosevelt, Priscilla, *Life on the Russian Country Estate: A Social and Cultural History*, New Haven: Yale University Press, 1995

Sablinsky, Walter, *The Road to Bloody Sunday: Father Gapon and the St. Petersburg Massacre of 1905*, Princeton: Princeton University Press, 1976

Schapiro, Leonard, *The Origin of the Communist Autocracy: Political Opposition in the Soviet State, First Phase: 1917–1922*, Cambridge, MA: Harvard University Press, 1956

Schapiro, Leonard, *The Communist Party of the Soviet Union*, New York: Random House, 1960; London: Eyre and Spottiswoode, 1970

Semevskii, Vasilii Ivanovich, *Krest'iane v tsarstvovanie imperatritsy Ekateriny II* (Peasants in the Reign of Empress Catherine II), 2 vols., St. Petersburg: Sushchinskago, 1881–1901

Shcherbatov, Mikhail Mikhailovich, *O povrezhdenii nravov v Rossii*, written 1780, published London: Trübner, 1858; in English as *On the Corruption of Morals in Russia*, London: Cambridge University Press, 1969

Shil'der, N.K., *Imperator Pavel pervyi* (Emperor Paul I), St. Petersburg: Surovina, 1901

Smith, S.A., *Red Petrograd: Revolution in the Factories, 1917–1918*, Cambridge and New York: Cambridge University Press, 1983

Solov'ev, S.M., *Istoriia Rossii s drevneishikh vremen*, vols. 19–29, 1869–74; in English in *History of Russia*, 48 vols. planned, Gulf Breeze, FL: Academic International, 1976–

Solov'ev, S.M., *Publichnye chteniia o Petre Velikom* (Public Lectures on Peter the Great), Moscow: University Press, 1872

Solzhenitsyn, Aleksandr, *Arkhipelag Gulag, 1918–1956: Opyt khudozhestvennogo issledovaniia*, 3 vols., Paris: YMCA Press, 1973–76; in English as *The Gulag Archipelago, 1918–1956: An Experiment in Literary Investigation*, London: Collins, and New York: Harper, 1974–78

Speranskii, Mikhail Mikhailovich, *Proekty i zapiski* (Legislative Drafts and Notes), Moscow: Akademiia, 1961

Startsev, Vitalii Ivanovich, *Krakh Kerenshchiny* (Collapse of the Kerenskii Regime), Leningrad: Nauka, 1982

Startsev, Vitalii Ivanovich, *Oktiabrskaia bur'ia* (October Storm), Moscow: Molodaia gvardiia, 1987

Suhr, Gerald Dennis, *1905 in St. Petersburg: Labor, Society, and Revolution*, Stanford, CA: Stanford University Press, 1989

Sukhanov, N.N., *Zapiski o revoliutsii*, 7 vols., Berlin: Grzhebina, 1922–23; abridged in English as *The Russian Revolution, 1917: A Personal Record*, New York and Oxford: Oxford University Press, 1955

Syromiatnikov, B.I., *"Reguliarnoe" gosudarstvo Petra pervogo i ego ideologiia* ("Regular" State of Peter I and Its Ideology), Moscow: Akademiia nauk SSSR, 1943

Tarlé, E.V., *Nashestvie Napoleona na Rossiiu: 1812 god* (Napoleon's Attack on Russia: The Year 1812), Moscow, 1938

Tatishchev, Vasilii Nikitich, *Istoriia rossiiskaia* (Russian History), 5 vols., Moscow: Izd-vo Moskovskogo universiteta, 1760–1848

Thurston, Robert, *Liberal City, Conservative State: Moscow and Russia's Urban Crisis, 1906–1914*, New York: Oxford University Press, 1987

Trotskii, Leon, *Istoriia russkoi revoliutsii*, 3 vols., Berlin: Granit, 1931–33; in English as *The History of the Russian Revolution*, London: Gollancz, and New York: Simon and Schuster, 1932–33

Tucker, Robert W., *Stalin as Revolutionary, 1879–1929: A Study in History and Personality*, New York: Norton, 1973

Tucker, Robert W., *Stalin in Power: The Revolution from Above, 1928–1941*, New York: Norton, 1990

Tumarkin, Nina, *The Living and the Dead: The Rise and Fall of the Cult of World War II in Russia*, New York: Basic Books, 1994

Tvardovskaia, Valentina Aleksandrovna, *Ideologiia poreformennogo samoderzhaviia: M.N. Katkov i ego izdaniia* (Ideology of the Reformed Autocracy: M.N. Katkov and His Publications), Moscow: Nauka, 1978

Volkogonov, D.A., *Lenin: A New Biography*, New York: Free Press, 1994

Walicki, Andrzej, *W kregu konserwatywnej utopii: strutura, przemiany rosyjskieko slowianofilstwa*, Warsaw: Naukowe, 1964; in English as *The Slavophile Controversy: History of a Conservative Utopia in Nineteenth-Century Russian Thought*, Oxford: Oxford University Press, 1975

Walicki, Andrzej, *Marxism and the Leap to the Kingdom of Freedom: The Rise and Fall of the Communist Utopia*, Stanford, CA: Stanford University Press, 1995

Weinberg, Robert, *Revolution of 1905 in Odessa: Blood on the Steps*, Bloomington: Indiana University Press, 1993

Wildman, Allan, *Making of a Workers' Revolution: Russian Social Democracy, 1891–1903*, Chicago: University of Chicago Press, 1967

Wittram, Reinhard, *Peter I: Czar und Kaiser* (Peter I: Tsar and King), 2 vols., Göttingen: Vandenhoeck & Ruprecht, 1964

Wynn, Charters, *Workers, Strikes, and Pogroms: The Donbass-Dnepr Bend in Late Imperial Russia, 1870–1905*, Princeton: Princeton University Press, 1992

Zaionchkovskii, P.A., *Otmena krepostnogo prava v Rossii*, Moscow: Polit lit-ry, 1954, revised 1968; in English as *The Abolition of Serfdom in Russia*, Gulf Breeze, FL: Academic International Press, 1978

Zaionchkovskii, P.A., *Krizis samoderzhaviia na rubezhe 1878–1882*, Moscow: Izd-vo Moskovskogo universiteta, 1964; in English as *The Russian Autocracy in Crisis, 1878–1882*, Gulf Breeze, FL: Academic International Press, 1979

Zaionchkovskii, P.A., *Rossiiskoe samoderzhavie v kontse XIX stoletiia*, Moscow: Mysl', 1970; in English as *Russian Autocracy under Alexander III*, Gulf Breeze, FL: Academic International Press, 1976

Zaionchkovskii, P.A., *Pravitel'stvennyi apparat samoderzhavnoi Rossii v XIX v.* (The State Machinery in 19th-Century Russia), Moscow: Mysl', 1978

Zakharova, Larisa Georgievna, *Zemskaia kontrreforma 1890 g.* (Zemstvo Counter-Reform of 1890), Moscow: Izd-vo Moskovskogo universiteta, 1968

Zakharova, Larisa Georgievna, *Samoderzhavie i otmena krepostnogo prava v Rossii, 1856–1861* (Autocracy and the Abolition of Serfdom in Russia, 1856–1861), Moscow: Izd-vo Moskovskogo universiteta, 1984

Zakharova, Larisa Georgievna, *1857–1861: perepiska Imperatora Aleksandra II s Velikim Kniazem Konstantinom Nikolaevichem; Dnevnik Velikogo Kniazia Konstantina Nikolaevicha* (1857–1861: Correspondence of Emperor Alexander II with Grand Duke Konstantin Nikolaevich; Diary of Grand Duke Konstantin Nikolaevich), Moscow: Terra, 1994

Zelnik, Reginald, *Labor and Society in Tsarist Russia: The Factory Workers of St. Petersburg, 1855–1870*, Stanford, CA: Stanford University Press, 1971

Russia: Russian Revolution

The Russian Revolution remains a pivotal event in the history of Russia and the world in the 20th century. The revolutionaries claimed to be international socialists concerned to change not just Russia but the world. However by the 1930s a brutal dictatorship was in power which pursued a nationalist development program under the guise "socialism in one country." Whether this was any genuine kind of socialism and whether the regime that developed was a product of "continuity" or "discontinuity" with 1917 remains the basic frame of reference within which detailed debates about the Revolution take place.

The Russian Revolution began when the strain of World War I led to a general strike in February 1917 in Petrograd, overthrowing the tsarist dynasty and enabling the creation of a self-appointed bourgeois-liberal Provisional Government. When the Provisional Government vacillated over major reforms and delayed the calling of the Constituent Assembly it lost support, and in October 1917 it too was overthrown and a Bolshevik government took power, claiming legitimacy from its support in the factory committees and soviets that had grown up as organs of popular power in 1917. The immediate perspectives were to halt the war and to link up with the widely expected revolution in the West while beginning a process of revolutionary change in Russia itself. But it proved no less difficult to stabilize the post-October situation; the Left Socialist revolutionaries split from the government and open conflict broke out between the Bolsheviks and opponents of the Revolution, who were backed by Western governments. A catastrophic civil war developed which the revolutionaries won by 1921. Unfortunately in the process their urban working-class base had crumbled and there had been no successful revolution in the West.

Although many accounts of the Russian Revolution concentrate on 1917 itself, fuller accounts continue the analysis to at least 1921. How far the Revolution is seen as continuing after this date depends on the discontinuity-continuity debate.

Discontinuity theorists tend to argue that the Revolution ended with the triumph of Stalin, whereas continuity theorists on both the left and the right argue that elements of the revolutionary dynamic continued to be in place, sometimes up to the collapse of the USSR in 1991. Here, however, we will focus on the narrower period 1917–21.

In Russia the Revolution and civil war period gave little opportunity for reflective works on events. Early pro-revolutionary accounts tended to propagandize, stressing the popular nature of the October Revolution and the centrality of popular power. The end of the civil war allowed more proper historical work to begin. Major documentary and memoir collections were made in the 1920s which are still a vital resource for historians. But almost immediately the interpretation of the Revolution became embroiled in debates about its future. Trotsky and the left argued that the Revolution had been underpinned by internationalist aims, the drive for power from below and flexibility and debate within the Bolshevik party in which the leadership that came to power after Lenin's death in 1924 (and most notably Stalin) had not always distinguished themselves. As the power of Stalin and his supporters was consolidated they imposed a top-down view of the Revolution where Lenin (with Stalin's help) led the Revolution through a united Bolshevik party and a working class that answered its call. In the 1930s this view became official policy. Earlier revolutionary leaders and historians who might have contested it now lost their lives in the purges, the archives were closed, library stock removed to closed sections, and evidence selectively published or blatantly falsified to bolster the official view, which found crude canonical authority in *History of the Communist Party of the Soviet Union: Short Course*, (1938).

In 1956 Khrushchev denounced Stalin's crimes in his secret speech and this allowed a slightly more open discussion to develop, but the regime was anxious to limit any critique to Stalin and "the cult of personality." In a more relaxed atmosphere historians no longer feared arrest if they challenged these limits unless they moved to more open political opposition, as did some later dissidents. However, those who strayed too far could find their careers seriously damaged, as were those of E. Burdzhalov in 1956 and P.V. Volobuev in 1972, and until the development of glasnost' under Mikhail Gorbachev there were powerful pressures to conform to a modified version of the orthodoxy established under Stalin. Valuable documentary collections were again published after 1956 and important work was done in less political areas such as studies of the social composition of the working class by Rashin, Gaponenko, and others, but these still remained marked by the regime perspectives and had to be carefully sifted by Western historians.

The major debates on the Russian Revolution before the 1990s were therefore carried out in the West. Here, too, political issues were in the foreground. Many Western observers in Russia in 1917 fell under the spell of the Revolution, with John Reed's *Ten Days That Shook the World* (1919) being perhaps the greatest eyewitness account of any revolution. Originally an inspiration to Western communists, accounts like that of Reed became anathema as Stalinist history also came to dominate most left-wing thinking in the West. It was left to Trotskii, now in exile, to uphold the earlier interpretation in his historical masterpiece *Istoriia russkoi revoliutsii* (1931–33; *The History of the Russian Revolution*, 1932–33) before he too was silenced by Stalin's assassin.

The main interwar years debate was dominated by émigré accounts which were united in condemning the illegitimacy of the October Revolution but offered individually and politically self-serving accounts of the Revolution as the earlier battles continued to be fought from the main exile centers of Paris, Berlin, and Prague. But much of interest was produced by the defeated first and second rank leaders of 1917, and some important archive collections of memoirs were published. Aleksandr Kerenskii and some others continued this battle into the post 1945 period, but perhaps his most enduring contribution was to produce a major documentary collection with Robert Paul Browder's *The Russian Provisional Government, 1917* (1961).

Three more considered historical works remain from this early period. M.T. Florinsky analyzed the background to the February Revolution in *The End of the Russian Empire* (1931), part of a wider investigation into the impact of World War I. This was complemented by Bernard Pares' *The Fall of the Russian Monarchy* (1939), which focused much more on the top layers of Russian society. William Chamberlin, a Western journalist in Russia, published his *The Russian Revolution, 1917–1921* (1935), a work which, if it does not quite deserve the accolade of "a model of objectivity," remains a fundamental source for its period. It was only at the end of the 1930s that an attempt was made by Crane Brinton in his *Anatomy of Revolution* (1938) to put the events in Russia into a wider theoretical and comparative perspective.

After 1945 discussion of the Revolution came closer to the concerns of mainstream historians, but their approach was now heavily conditioned by the development of the Cold War. The Soviet Union was seen as the embodiment of "totalitarianism" with the Revolution prefiguring this. Accounts emphasized the manipulative dominance of Lenin and the Bolshevik party with workers, soldiers, and peasants forming at best a stage army and at worst an anarchic mob. Ironically although Western historians were aware of the distortions of Stalinist accounts in Russia, their interpretation had much in common with the official Soviet view save that what this saw as a triumph of "socialism" Western accounts saw as a triumph of a small unpopular minority by means of a *coup d'état*.

Although there were always historians who disagreed with the dominant perspective, it was only at the end of the 1960s that they began to gain a wider hearing, and even then they remained trapped within many of the early approaches. Alexander Rabinowitch produced a powerful study of the Bolshevik party and in France, Marc Ferro, a historian of the Annales school, produced the two insightful but eclectical and uneven volumes on the February and October revolutions.

In the 1970s and 1980s a new generation of historians began to develop what has been called "the social interpretation of the Russian Revolution." Their inspiration came in part from the analysis of the French Revolution, in part from the work of E.P. Thompson and the development of history from below, and in part from a more sympathetic approach to popular protest that emerged as a result of the upheavals of 1968 in Europe and the protests against the Vietnam War in America. Within a short period doctorates, articles, and books began to pour out exploring the experience of groups of workers, soldiers, peasants, and women, by town and region, which stressed not only the popular nature of 1917 but the richness of the institutional life, especially in the working class. Much of this was helpfully summarized in Daniel Kaiser in *The Workers' Revolution in Russia, 1917* (1987). Although this work did not entirely displace the more hostile view of the Revolution, it forced more traditional historians to redefine their arguments. However, even as many of these works were being published in the late 1980s, confidence in this perspective was beginning to be undermined. One aspect of this was the attraction of various postmodernist theories that began to flourish in some academic circles as the optimistic radicalism of the 1970s proved unfounded. The other was the collapse of the Soviet system in Eastern Europe in 1989 and in Russia in 1991.

In Russia itself the new-found freedom led many historians to insist on continuity between the Russian Revolution and the later development of Stalinism, often demonstrating a barely concealed distaste for what many thought of as a lumpen working class in 1917. Hostile Western accounts found a ready market in Russia, most notably the work of Richard Pipes, which had a more sympathetic audience than in the West. The result is that the immediate future direction of the historiography of the Russian Revolution remains problematic. For the first time since the 1920s the center of debate is likely to move to Russia, but it will be some time before a less overtly politicized history of the Revolution will be possible, in East or West.

MICHAEL HAYNES

See also Broué; Carr, E.; Davies, R.; Pipes

Further Reading

Acton, Edward, *Rethinking the Russian Revolution*, London: Arnold, 1990

Billington, James H., "Six Views of the Russian Revolution," *World Politics* 18 (1966), 452–73

Bolshevik Central Committee, *History of the Communist Party of the Soviet Union: Short Course*, Moscow: Foreign Language House, 1938; New York: International Publishers, 1939; London: Cobbett, 1943

Brinton, Crane, *Anatomy of Revolution*, New York: Norton, 1938, London: Allen and Unwin, 1939; revised 1965

Browder, Robert Paul, *The Russian Provisional Government, 1917*, 3 vols., Stanford, CA: Stanford University Press, 1961

Carr, E.H., *The Bolshevik Revolution, 1917–1923*, 3 vols., London and New York: Macmillan, 1950–53

Chamberlin, William Henry, *The Russian Revolution, 1917–1921*, 2 vols., London and New York: Macmillan, 1935

Ellison, Herbert J., "Soviet Historians and the Russian Revolution" in Lyman Howard Legters, ed., *Russia: Essays in History and Literature*, Leiden: Brill, 1972

Ferro, Marc, *La Révolution de 1917*, 2 vols., Paris: Aubier, 1967–76; vol. 1 in English as *The Russian Revolution of February 1917*, Englewood Cliffs, NJ: Prentice Hall, 1972

Florinsky, Michael T., *The End of the Russian Empire*, New Haven: Yale University Press, and London: Oxford University Press, 1931

Kaiser, Daniel H., ed., *The Workers' Revolution in Russia, 1917: The View from Below*, New York and Cambridge: Cambridge University Press, 1987

Karpovich, Michael, "The Russian Revolution of 1917," *Journal of Modern history*, 2 (1930), 258–80

Katkov, George, *Russia 1917: The February Revolution*, London: Longman, and New York: Harper, 1967

Pares, Bernard, *The Fall of the Russian Monarchy: A Study of Evidence*, London: Cape, and New York: Knopf, 1939

Pipes, Richard, *The Russian Revolution*, New York: Knopf, and London: Collins, 1990; concise version, 1995

Rabinowitch, Alexander, *Prelude to Revolution: The Petrograd Bolsheviks and the July 1917 Uprising*, Bloomington: Indiana University Press, 1968

Reed, John, *Ten Days That Shook the World*, New York: Boni and Liveright, 1919; London: Modern Books, 1928

Smith, Steve, "Writing the History of the Russian Revolution after the Fall of Communism," *Europe-Asia Studies* 46 (1994), 563–78

Sukhanov, N.N., *Zapiski o revoliutsii*, 7 vols., Berlin: Grzhebina, 1922–23; abridged in English as *The Russian Revolution, 1917: A Personal Record*, New York and Oxford: Oxford University Press, 1955

Suny, R.G. "Toward a Social History of the October Revolution," *American Historical Review* 88 (1983), 31–52

Suny, R.G. "Revision and Retreat in the Historiography of 1917: Social History and its Critics," *Russian Review* 53 (1994), 165–82; and response in *Russian Review* 54 (1995), 260–64

Trotskii, Leon, *Istoriia russkoi revoliutsii*, 3 vols., Berlin: Granit, 1931–33; in English as *The History of the Russian Revolution*, London: Gollancz, and New York: Simon and Schuster, 1932–33

Warth, Robert D., "On the Historiography of the Russian Revolution," *Slavic Review* 26 (1967), 247–64

White, James D., "Historiography of the Russian Revolution in the Twenties," *Critique* [Glasgow] 1 (1973), 42–53

S

Said, Edward W. 1935–

US (Palestinian-born) literary critic and historian

Edward Said has been profiled in *Time* as *the* leading Arab-American intellectual, and even mentioned as possible president of an independent Palestine. Much of his reputation rests on his bestselling *Orientalism* (1978), which has become part of the very fabric of postcolonial scholarship.

Born in Jerusalem and educated in the Middle East's leading secondary school, Victoria College in Cairo, before attending Princeton, Said is notable for his panache and style. His relevance to historians rests in his leadership of one side in the bitter divide between partisans of what was once called mainstream or Western history and proponents of greater immersion in the culture of a neglected "third world." His opponents accuse him of a blind enthusiasm for multiculturalism and political correctness that has skewed the historical record. Said, on the other hand, has unrepentantly and frequently returned to the themes which in *Orientalism* he made famous and which have made him famous. In his view, first and foremost is the need for recognizing imperialism for what it is and furthering decolonization. Said's views are challenged by authorities such as Paul Johnson, Lewis Gann, and Peter Duignan, who believe that the bad side of colonialism has been grossly overstated.

An ardent anti-victimizer, Said has attracted attention because of an exaggerated empathy for the marginal and anomalous he claims to represent. He has sought legitimacy for a plethora of nondescript noncanonical works. Or so this seems to his enemies. He warned in *Culture and Imperialism* (1993) that "The images of Western imperial authority remain – haunting, strangely attractive, compelling: Lawrence of Arabia, at the head of his Arab warriors, living the romance of the desert, inventing guerrilla warfare, hobnobbing with princes and statesmen, translating Homer, and trying to hold on to Britain's 'Brown Dominion'; Cecil Rhodes, establishing countries, estates, funds as easily as other men might have children or start businesses ... The list is long and its treasures massive."

Said is extremely outspoken. The New York *Times* (9 March 1993) has taken him to task for a "hectoring tone" accompanied by "angry, paranoid digressions about the Gulf war and America's imperial ambitions," as well as for "trying to shoehorn examples into a rigid theoretical structure." Ernest Gellner's review of *Culture and Imperialism* in the *Times Literary Supplement* (19 February 1993) brought forth a telling display of bad temper on Said's part: "Ernest Gellner is an academic Rumpelstiltskin, stamping his little feet ... For someone who, like Gellner, practices anthropology of a particularly antiquated and, yes, colonial kind, to make fun of 'lit crit' is symptomatically to exhibit that patronizing bad faith and complicity with imperial power which many, and a great deal more serious, anthropologists today, are trying to come to terms with in the history of their discipline. Not Gellner though, who can only resort to the puerile anti-American joke and piffling trivia of the Common Room."

Despite the impact of *Orientalism*, and despite virulent opposition by Said to positive statements about colonialism, there are signs of renewed discussion about the proposition that all cultures are *not* equal. Moreover, another difficulty with Said's sometimes shrill position is that "the West", to which he refers at times with a disdain as if it were a Dark Force, is a constantly changing phenomenon. Additions are made all the time to its canon; Western culture is eclectic.

For all of one's admiration for Said's accomplishments, the fact remains that the attack he has ably led seems to be faltering. That his opponents have regained their self-confidence is typified by Johnson's bald announcement in the *National Review* (14 December 1992) that "It's time to stop singing those 20th-century blues and start considering ways to secure global stability and extend prosperity. The first step: re-establish Western imperialism." Clearly the debate is not over.

PAUL JOHN RICH

See also Ileto; Imperial; Indigenous; Lewis, B.; Nationalism; Orientalism; Women's History: Asia

Biography

Born Jerusalem, 1 November 1935, son of a prosperous businessman. Attended St. George's School, before the family moved to Cairo, 1947; attended American School then Victoria College, before being sent to the Mount Hermon School, Massachusetts; received BA in English literature, Princeton University, 1957; MA, Harvard University, 1960, PhD 1964. Taught (rising to professor), Columbia University, from 1963. Member, Palestine National Council, from 1977. Married 1) Maire Jaanus, 1962 (marriage dissolved); 2) Mariam Cortas, 1970 (1 son, 1 daughter).

Principal Writings

Orientalism, 1978
The Question of Palestine, 1979
The World, The Text, and the Critic, 1983
After the Last Sky: Palestinian Lives, 1986

Editor with Christopher Hitchens, *Blaming the Victims: Spurious Scholarship and the Palestinian Question*, 1988
Culture and Imperialism, 1993
Representation and the Intellectual, 1994

Further Reading

Rich, Paul John, *The Invasions of the Gulf: Radicalism, Ritualism and the Shaikhs*, Cambridge: Alborough, 1991
Sprinker, Michael, ed., *Edward Said: A Critical Reader*, Oxford and Cambridge, MA: Blackwell, 1992

Sallust 86–35 BCE
Roman historian

Sallust's histories *Bellum Jugurthinum* (*The War with Jugurtha*), *Bellum Catilinae* (*The War with Catiline*) and *Historiae* (*Histories*) emphasize political biography, political and personal corruption, and party strife. The quality of these works ranks Sallust with the other two great Roman historians, Livy and Tacitus. Sallust was once credited with developing the style of the historical monograph. Today Lucius Coelius Antipater, who wrote historical monographs at the end of the 2nd century BCE, is credited as the founder of the genre, but Colelius' works are lost. Sallust's analytical historiography made his influence on later Roman historiography and biography greater than that of any other author. Livy reacted against his style. Tacitus refined it. Certainly, Sallust established the template for all Roman historical and biographical writers until Tacitus.

Quintilian (*c*.34–*c*.100 CE), a tutor of the Flavian emperors and a renowned orator, praised Sallust's work by comparing it to that of Thucycides. Martial the Roman epigrammist pronounced Sallust the "foremost" Roman historian. St. Augustine influenced generations of scholars by praising, erroneously, the accuracy of Sallust. Erasmus recommended him over Livy or Tacitus in 1511.

Criticism of Sallust's work has been directed at his strong expression of personal political views and his notion that Rome's perceived moral crisis arose spontaneously in the 2nd century BCE. He argued that the crisis had no roots in the past as he believed that the aristocratic or senatorial class, the knights or equestrians, and the common people or plebeians had worked in harmony, controlled by traditional virtues, such as self control and belief in the common good. Sallust is probably responsible for the popular notion that Roman politics was governed on the premise of two political parties, the Optimates and the Populares. This idea owes more to later interpreters' knowledge of the structure of politics in the 18th-century British parliament than to actual practice in ancient Rome.

The War with Catiline, covering events of 66 to 63, was written in 42/1 and established Sallust's favorite theme, the change in Rome's mentality and disturbing changes in Roman politics and personal morality. The conspiracy of Lucius Sergius Catilina is the first recorded threat to Roman stability by an internal enemy. Catiline rallied aristocrats deeply in debt, army veterans unhappy with their settlements, and impoverished peasants against the aristocracy in the Senate led by the famous orator Cicero. Sallust has no concern for what might be the legitimate complaints of the veterans and peasants, instead concentrating on the avarice and corruption of Cataline and his followers.

Sallust's second work, *The War with Jugurtha*, written *c*.41–40, is based on Carthaginian sources and Sallust's personal experience as governor of Numidia, where Jugurtha ruled. Surprisingly, Sallust reveals his ignorance of the geography and local chronology of Numidia. Once again his emphasis is on party politics in Rome. The rise of Gaius Marius, a new man, like Sallust and Cicero, was portrayed as contributing to political conflict detrimental to Rome's traditional institutions and morality. Marius was the enemy of Sallust's father-in-law, Sulla.

The surviving fragments of the *Histories* are Sallust's most important work. The work was originally five books or scrolls, covering Roman history from 78 BCE, and seems to have continued Sallust's theme of class and political conflict arising from personal corruption and avarice. Traditionally an ancient author set out in his first sentence the genre of his work, philosophy, history, literary criticism, etc. Sallust's opening lines of *The War with Jugurtha* ("Men have no right to complain that they are naturally feeble and short-lived, or that it is chance and not merit that decides their destiny") and *The War with Catiline* ("Every man who wishes to rise superior to the lower animals should strive his hardest to avoid living all his days in silent obscurity, like the beasts of the field, creatures which go with their faces to the ground and are the slaves of their bellies") have puzzled scholars. These lines, as translated by S.A. Handford, seem to indicate that a philosophical work follows. Did Sallust mean to announce he was writing not history but philosophy? If Sallust meant his work to be taken as philosophy, posterity has not remembered him as a philosopher.

What is remembered is that Sallust's writings strongly and sincerely reflected personal views. Like many Romans of his day he saw a gap widening between Rome's perceived Golden Age of the past and its condition in the late years of the republic and early years of the empire. Sallust's works convey the view that Rome suffered a moral crisis in the 2nd century BCE. When Rome defeated Carthage and no longer had a strong external enemy, the Roman people became weak and corrupt. Sallust believed that a man or nation without a purpose could feel little satisfaction in any activity.

Influenced by Thucycides and Polybius, Sallust searched for the causes of decadence and did some analysis of the general fate of empires as it was mirrored in the fate of Rome. History for Sallust was a didactic enterprise meant to set forth examples to be imitated and to be avoided.

NANCY PIPPEN ECKERMAN

See also Livy; Machiavelli

Biography

Gaius Sallustius Crispus. Born Amiternum (now San Vittorino, Italy), 86 BCE, to a family of equestrian rank. Became involved in imperial politics; supporter of the Populares; tribune, 52; expelled from the Senate, 50; joined Caesar and commanded a legion, 49; governor of Africa Nova, 46; on return to Rome charged with corruption, graft, and oppression as an administrator, but never tried; retired, 43. Married Fausta, daughter of Sulla. Died Rome, 35.

Principal Writings

Bellum Catilinae, c.42/1; in English as *The War with Catiline*
Bellum Jugurthinum, c.41–40; in English as *The War with Jugurtha*
Historiae; as *The Histories*, translated by Patrick McGushin, 2 vols.,
    1992–94
Works (Loeb edition; includes *The War with Catiline, The War with
    Jugurtha, Orations and Letters from the Histories, Pseudo-
    Sallustian Works*), translated by J.C. Rolfe, 1920

Further Reading

Breisach, Ernst, *Historiography: Ancient, Medieval, and Modern*,
    Chicago: University of Chicago Press, 1983; revised 1994
Büchner, Karl, *Sallust*, Heidelberg: Winter, 1960
Earl, Donald C., *The Political Thought of Sallust*, Cambridge:
    Cambridge University Press, 1961
Grant, Michael, ed., *Readings in the Classical Historians*, New
    York: Scribner, and London: Maxwell Macmillan, 1992
La Penna, Antonio, *Sallustio e la rivoluzione romana* (Sallust and
    the Roman Revolution), Milan: Feltrinelli, 1968
Latte, Kurt, *Sallust*, Leipzig: Teubner, 1935
Luce, T. James, ed., *Ancient Writers: Greece and Rome*, 2 vols.,
    New York: Scribner, 1982
McGushin, Patrick, *Sallust, The Conspiracy of Catline: A
    Companion to the Penguin Translation of S. A. Handford*,
    Bristol: Bristol Classical Press, 1987
Scanlon, Thomas Francis, *The Influence of Thucydides on Sallust*,
    Heidelberg: Winter, 1980
Syme, Ronald, *Sallust*, Berkeley: University of California Press,
    1964

Salvemini, Gaetano 1873–1957

Italian economic historian

Gaetano Salvemini was first appointed to a university lectureship in Messina in 1901 at the age of 28. He then taught at the
University of Pisa and in 1916 succeeded his mentor, the celebrated Pasquale Villari, to the chair of history at the University
of Florence. He taught there until 1925, when he renounced his
university position and chose to live abroad as an active antifascist refugee. In 1934 he was offered a lectureship in Italian
Civilization at Harvard, where he remained until his retirement,
although in 1949 he returned to Florence to teach for a
few years.

Salvemini combined a career as a distinguished historian
with an active, even passionate involvement in politics, first as
a socialist, then as a democratic radical and an antifascist close
to "Giustizia e Libertà" the movement created by his friend
Carlo Rosselli. At times his politics and his research sat
together uneasily, and Salvemini, with characteristic frankness,
was the first to recognize this. In his best work, however, he
managed to convey the strength of his convictions through an
accurate analysis of the past.

His early scholarship was devoted to the Middle Ages, and
in 1899 he published *Magnati e popolani in Firenze dal 1280
al 1295* (Prince and People in Florence, 1280–1295), in which
he focused on the class struggle between the nobility allied to
the wealthy bourgeoisie and the emerging middle classes, tied
to the corporations of the Commune. Salvemini thus turned a
conventional academic assignment into a refreshing work of
social and economic history, which soon acquired a path-
breaking influence on the younger generations of historians.

At this time he was under the influence of a somewhat basic
Marxism, and it was noted, particularly by the Russian historian Nicola Ottokar, in *Il Comune di Firenze alla fine del
Dugento* (The Commune of Florence at the End of the 13th
Century) (1926) that some of his causal connections were
simplistic and inaccurate. Marxists have charged him with an
insufficient theoretical grounding echoing a similar accusation
levelled against him by Benedetto Croce, the doyen of the idealistic school. Salvemini was quite unmoved, since he always
prided himself on being ill at ease in philosophical matters.

Having moved to the study of modern history, Salvemini
produced two important works on the French Revolution and
on Mazzini. The first, *La rivoluzione francese, 1788–1791*
(1905; *The French Revolution*, 1954) covered the causes and
the outbreak of the Revolution. Through what was basically
an advanced textbook reliant on published sources Salvemini
was nevertheless able to fill a serious gap in current Italian
historiography, given that the standard books on the topic were
still the French classics by Thiers, Tocqueville, and Michelet.
In the process he also advanced a reformist interpretation of
the Revolution, claiming that the excesses of the Jacobins could
have been avoided if the monarchy and the privileged classes
had been less selfish in the defence of their interests. Salvemini
had moved away from his youthful materialism and was now
prepared to make room for the role of elites and ideas in
shaping events. According to Stuart Hughes, Salvemini's book
was also a coded warning to the ruling classes in Italy that
they should accommodate reform rather than resist it.

Salvemini's book on Mazzini was a collection of essays,
falling short of a full-scale biography. It was written for the
centenary of Mazzini's birth, but it was far from an hagiography. Salvemini had very little time for Mazzini's spiritualism,
and he regarded his thinking as steeped in regressive anti-
Enlightenment values. No wonder, Salvemini later remarked,
Gentile had been able to hail Mazzini as Mussolini's precursor.
On the other hand, he admired Mazzini as a leader and recognized the part he had played in bringing about Italian unification. Salvemini's hero in the Risorgimento, however, was not
Mazzini, but Carlo Cattaneo, a selection of whose works he
edited in 1922.

In the last years of his stay in Italy, Salvemini concentrated
on the history of Italy's foreign policy after unification. He
was, according to Sestan, the first professional historian to
engage fully in this field. His main aim was to paint a critical
portrait of Italy's engagement in the Triple Alliance, which he
believed had served as a pillar of reaction and conservatism.
His research was never completed although extracts of it were
published on various occasions.

Once a refugee, Salvemini concentrated on writing about
fascism for a British, American, and French audience. He
produced a stream of books in all languages, which although
engaging, occasionally witty, and always well documented,
often fell short of proper historical standards, due to the
scarcity and biased nature of the sources he was able to draw
upon, as well as to the polemical purpose of his work, which
was designed primarily to counter the propaganda emanating
from the fascist regime. Nevertheless, as Roberto Vivarelli has
pointed out, there is much that is lasting and fruitful in his
analysis. *Under the Axe of Fascism* (1936), for example, is a
very detailed reconstruction of fascist corporatism, which not

only successfully punctured the myth of the "Third Way," but developed a subtle understanding of the oligarchical power-structure underpinning the regime. Equally, *Prelude to World War II* (1953) a scathing critique of appeasement, is full of valuable insight into the relationship between ideology and diplomacy during the 1930s.

Among Salvemini's lesser known works is *Historian and Scientist* (1939) in which, joining the contemporary Anglo-Saxon debate on the status of the social sciences, he staked out his neo-empiricist position. The historian, argued Salvemini, should be an empiricist, conducting experiments, and not a theologian, seeking to uncover grand designs in history. According to Bobbio, Salvemini represented the best of a positivist tradition that challenged the idealism prevailing in Italian culture. Most Italian intellectuals, Salvemini argued, are more prepared to dispute concepts rather than engage with positive facts.

RUGGERO RANIERI

See also Italy: since the Renaissance; Pieri

Biography
Born Molfetta, Bari, 8 September 1873, from a poor family. Studied with Pasquale Villari and Cesare Paoli at University of Florence, PhD 1894. Taught at Teachers College, Palermo, 1895–96; Lyceum of Faenza, 1896–97; Lyceum of Lodi, 1898–1900; Lyceum of Florence, 1900–01; University of Messina, 1901–10; University of Pisa, 1910–16; University of Florence, 1916–25; and after exile by fascist government in 1925, Harvard University, 1930, 1933–48. Lost his wife and five children in Messina earthquake, 1908; married 2) Fernande Dauriac, 1916. Died Capo di Sorrento, 6 September 1957.

Principal Writings
Magnati e popolani in Firenze dal 1280 al 1295 (Prince and People in Florence, 1280–1295), 1899

I partiti politici milanesi nel secolo XIX (Political Parties in Milan in the 19th Century), 1899

Studi Storici (Historical Studies), 1901

Il pensiero religioso, politico sociale di Giuseppe Mazzini (Mazzini's Religious, Political, and Social Thought), 1905

La rivoluzione francese, 1788–1791, 1905; revised in English as *The French Revolution, 1788–1792*, 1954

Mazzini, 1915; translated 1956

Editor, *Le piu' belle pagine di Carlo Cattaneo* (The Best Pages by Carlo Cattaneo), 1922

"L'Italia politica nel secolo XIX" (Italian Politics in the 19th Century) in D. Donati and F. Carli, eds., *L'Europa nel secolo XIX*, 1925

The Fascist Dictatorship in Italy, 1927

Mussolini diplomate, 1932

Under the Axe of Fascism, 1936

Italian Fascism, 1938

Historian and Scientist: An Essay on the Nature of History and the Social Sciences, 1939

La politica estera dell'Italia dal 1871 al 1915 (Italy's Foreign Policy Between 1871 and 1915), 1944

Prelude to World War II, 1953

Opere di Gaetano Salvemini (Works), 20 vols. to date, Milan: Feltrinelli, 1961–

The Origins of Fascism in Italy, edited by Roberto Vivarelli, 1973

Medioevo, risorgimento, fascismo: antologia di scritti storici (The Middle Ages, The Risorgimento, and Fascism: An Anthology of Historical Writings), edited by Enzo Tagliacozzo and Sergio Bucchi, Bari: Laterza 1992 [selected works]

Further Reading
Artifoni, Enrico, *Salvemini e il Medioevo: storici italiani tra Otto e Novecento* (Salvemini and the Middle Ages: An Essay on Italian Historians Between the 18th and 20th Centuries), Naples: Liguori, 1990

Associazione mazziniana italiana, *Gaetano Salvemini nella cultura e nella politica italiane* (Gaetano Salvemini Within History's Cultural and Political Life), Rome: Edizioni della Voce, 1968

Associazione mazziniana italiana, *Convegno di studi su Gaetano Salvemini, Faenza, 28–29 aprile 1973*, Faenza: Lega, 1973

Biscione, Michele, "Gaetano Salvemini e la polemica sulla storia come scienza" (Gaetano Salvemini and the Dispute on History as Science), *Rivista di storia della storiografia moderna* 1 (1980), 29–44

Bobbio, Norberto, "Salvemini e la democrazia" (Salvemini and Democracy), *Il Ponte* 21 (1975), 1254–78; reprinted in his *Maestri e compagni: Piero Calamandrei, Aldo Capitini, Eugenio Calorni, Leone Ginzburg, Antonio Giuriolo, Rodolfo Mondolfo, Augusto Monti, Gaetano Salvemini*, Florence: Passigli, 1984

Carocci, Giampiero, "Salvemini e la politica estera del fascismo" (Salvemini and Fascism's Foreign Policy), *Studi Storici* 9 (1968), 218–32

Cingari, Gaetano, ed., *Gaetano Salvemini tra politica e storia* (Gaetano Salvemini: Between Politics and History), Rome: Laterza, 1986

Cotroneo, Girolamo, "Croce e Salvemini: una polemica sulla storia" (Croce and Salvemini: A Polemic on the Nature of History), *Rivista di studi crociani* 17 (1980), 45–61

Croce, Benedetto, *Terze pagine sparse* (Essays and Notes), 2 vols., Bari: Laterza, 1955

De Felice, Renzo, *Le interpretazioni de fascismo*, Bari: Laterza, 1969; in English as *Interpretations of Fascism*, Cambridge, MA: Harvard University Press, 1977

Garrone, A.G., *Salvemini e Mazzini* (Salvemini and Mazzini), Messina: D'Anna, 1981

Hughes, H. Stuart, *The Sea Change: The Migration of Social Thought, 1930–1965*, New York: Harper, 1975

Maturi, Walter, "Gaetano Salvemini," in his *Interpretazioni del Risorgimento: lezioni di storia della storiografia*, Milan: Einaudi, 1962

Origo, Iris, "Gaetano Salvemini: The Man Who Would Not Conform" in her *A Need to Testify: Portraits of Lauro de Bosis, Ruth Draper, Gaetano Salvemini, Ignazio Silone and an Essay on Biography*, London: Murray, and San Diego: Harcourt Brace, 1984

Ottokar, Nicola, *Il Comune di Firenze alla fine del Dugento* (The Commune of Florence at the End of the Thirteenth Century), Florence: Vallechi, 1926

Puzzo, Dante A., "Gaetano Salvemini: An Historiographical Essay," *Journal of the History of Ideas* 20 (1959), 217–35

Ragionieri, Ernesto, "Gaetano Salvemini storico e politico" (Gaetano Salvemini's History and Politics), *Belfagor* 5 (1950), 514–36

Rodolico, Niccolao, "Gaetano Salvemini (1873–1957)," *Archivio Storico Italiano* 115 (1957), 378–79

Salvadori, Massimo L., *Gaetano Salvemini*, Turin: Einaudi, 1963

Sestan, Ernesto et al., *Gaetano Salvemini*, Bari: Laterza, 1959

Sestan, Ernesto, "Salvemini storico del Medioevo" (Salvemini Historian of the Middle Ages) in Ernesto Sestan, ed., *Atti del convegno su Gaetano Salvemini, Firenze 8–10 Novembre 1975*, Milan: Saggiatore, 1977

Tagliacozzo, Enzo, *Gaetano Salvemini nel cinquantennio liberale* (Gaetano Salvemini During the Fifty Years of Liberal Italy), Florence: La Nuova Italia, 1959

Venturi, Franco, "Salvemini storico" (Salvemini the historian), *Il Ponte* 13 (1957), 1794–1801

Vivarelli, Roberto, "Salvemini e il fascismo" (Salvemini and fascism), in Ernesto Sestan, ed., *Atti del convegno su Gaetano Salvemini, Firenze 8–10 Novembre 1975*, Milan: Saggiatore, 1977

Vivarelli, Roberto, "Salvemini e Mazzini" (Salvemini and Mazzini), and A.G. Garrone, "Mazzini e Salvemini: a Roberto Vivarelli," *Rivista Storica Italiana* 97 (1985), 42–85

Samuel, Raphael 1934–1996

British social historian

Raphael Samuel was a leading British social historian and the inspiration behind the History Workshop movement which he co-founded. Samuel's concerns as a historian and political activist were to open up the history of ordinary people and their lives in the last two centuries, experiences that he examined with a warm empathy. His career was truly unique. Committed to history as a collaborative process, he wrote only one major monograph of his own (*Theatres of Memory*, 1994) but his output was vast, ranging from articles and theoretical interventions to a number of important oral histories. He enlarged the possibilities of people's history, building on the work of left-wing historians such as E.P. Thompson and Eric Hobsbawm. Like them, he was passionately concerned with the politics of history, arguing not only about what kind of history should be written but also how it should be taught.

In a poignant series of articles in the *New Left Review*, Samuel described his communist upbringing that began with his mother and included his early activism in the party. At a young age, he joined the Communist Party Historians Group but left the party over the Soviet invasion of Hungary in 1956 and went on to become a leading figure in the New Left of the 1960s. Samuel taught at Ruskin College, Oxford (the trade union-backed college for mature students which trained them for university access). His students included Sally Alexander and Alun Howkins, who later became historians themselves, as well as John Prescott, the future Labour deputy prime minister. Adult education was Samuel's passion and the spur for the way in which he saw history. His teaching always began with primary sources rather than textbooks (in the 1960s, a radical departure) and his lecturing technique involved sharing his gleanings from archives with a generous delight. His publications had a similar quality in which example was followed by example sometimes in a rather unstructured way. Samuel would often talk about the way in which people found a voice, explaining his attraction to oral history. It was in this spirit that he co-founded History Workshop whose purpose was to give voice to those whose experiences had been silenced by authority (particularly women, blacks, and the working class).

As a historian, Samuel had wide interests. He was at home in economic and labor history but distrusted histories that simply concentrated on institutions such as trade unions. Perhaps his most influential piece was the 1977 article "Workshop of the World." This was one of the earliest statements of a revisionist position on the British Industrial Revolution. Samuel documented the persistence of hand technology in the age of steam, showing how the factory did not displace artisan modes of production until well after the mid-19th century. His research was characterized by a deep sense of place and love of community. This was true of the oral histories, *Village Life and Labour* (1975), *Miners, Quarrymen and Roughs* (1977), and *East End Underworld* (1981). The last was a superb evocation of the life of Arthur Harding, a gangster with whom Samuel collaborated. He had a huge knowledge of London and its history. His final project before he died was the creation of an institute for the study of East End history at the University of East London which granted him a professorship. This love of community was evident in his earliest research on the Irish in Britain but was also there in the oral history of the miners strike of 1984–85, published under the ironic title, *The Enemy Within* (1986).

Samuel's voice was at its most distinctive in his editorials and prefaces to History Workshop publications. He insisted that Britain's greatest contribution to Marxist thought was in the field of history, and yet was always concerned to reflect on new intellectual developments such as poststructuralism. He was particularly concerned with welcoming new theories about gender and race and provided a space for them. Curiously, for one so interested in theory, his own work often had an antiquarian flavor to it.

In the 1980s, he was both appalled and fascinated by Thatcherism and its appeals to national identity. It was in this spirit that he convened a History Workshop conference on national identity in 1984 and turned it into a 3-volume collection, *Patriotism* (1989), each prefaced by his lengthy introductions. He was particularly concerned during the Falklands crisis of 1982 at the apparent absence of the oppositional Englishness that had once protested against the Boer War and supported the Campaign for Nuclear Disarmament. Yet he was determined to understand the historical varieties of national identity which he treated with great sensitivity and respect.

Theatres of Memory, his most substantial book, should be read as a summary of his attempts to celebrate people's culture and to give it dignity. It was also the most sustained of the recent attempts of the left to think about the heritage industry. In the 1980s, most left-wing writers tended to attack the whole notion of heritage as intrinsically conservative. Samuel disagreed. His book celebrated the historical culture of ordinary people and argued that Britain in the 1990s was enjoying an expanding historical culture in which the past was being rendered accessible in all sorts of new ways. He documented the roots of the modern heritage industry, showing that it lay with progressive youth culture in the 1960s rather than Thatcherism in the 1980s. A sequel, *Island Stories*, was published in 1997.

Samuel was sometimes criticized for his deep romanticism about the working class. Though not naive, he did nevertheless place a high premium on understanding ordinary experience. He never wrote the sustained treatment of working-class history of the sort produced by Thompson or Hobsbawm and of which he was capable. What he did do was just as important. He acted as an enabler so that other people could find their voices and expanded the range of history so that it was forced to take seriously the history of everyday life. He was not only one of the important historians in postwar Britain; he was also one of its most significant democrats.

ROHAN McWILLIAM

See also Britain: since 1750; History Workshop; Oral

Biography

Born London, 26 December 1934. Educated at King Alfred's School, Hampstead; Balliol College, Oxford. Taught at Ruskin College, Oxford, 1962–96; professor, University of East London, 1996. Married Alison Light, historian and literary critic, 1987. Died London, 9 December 1996.

Principal Writings

"Comers and Goers" in H.J. Dyos and Michael Wolff, eds., *The Victorian City: Images and Realities*, vol.1, 1973

Editor, *Village Life and Labour*, 1975

Editor, *Miners, Quarrymen and Roughs*, 1977

"Workshop of the World: Steam Power and Hand Technology in Mid-Victorian Britain," *History Workshop Journal* 3 (1977), 6–72

"British Marxist Historians, 1880–1980," *New Left Review* 120 (March–April 1980), 21–96

Editor, *East End Underworld: Chapters in the Life of Arthur Harding*, 1981

Editor, *People's History and Socialist Theory*, 1981

"The Lost World of British Communism," *New Left Review* 154 (1985), 3–53

"The Roman Catholic Church and the Irish Poor," in Roger Swift and Sheridan Gilley, eds., *The Irish in the Victorian City*, 1985

Editor with Ewan McColl and Stuart Cosgrove, *Theatres of the Left, 1880–1935: Workers' Theatre Movements in Britain and America*, 1985

Editor with Barbara Bloomfield and Guy Boanas, *The Enemy Within: Pit Villages and the Miners' Strike of 1984–5*, 1986

Editor, *Patriotism: The Making and Unmaking of British National Identity*, 3 vols., 1989

Editor with Paul Thompson, *The Myths We Live By*, 1990

"Reading the Signs," *History Workshop Journal* 32 (1991), 88–109; and 33 (1992), 220–51

"The Discovery of Puritanism, 1820–1914: A Preliminary Sketch," in Jane Garnett and Colin Matthew, eds., *Revival and Religion since 1700: Essays for John Walsh*, 1993

Theatres of Memory: Past and Present in Contemporary Culture, 1994

Island Stories: Unravelling Britain, 1997

Further Reading

Thompson, Paul, "Raphael Samuel, 1934–96: An Appreciation," *Oral History* 25 (1997), 30–37

Sánchez-Albornoz, Claudio 1893–1984

Spanish medievalist

Claudio Sánchez-Albornoz, despite a career that involved him in the troubled politics of the Republican period of the 1930s and a long period in exile in Argentina, established himself as and remained for several decades the dominant figure in the study of Spanish medieval history, from the Visigothic period to the 12th century. His own training, which he frequently acknowledged, was at the hands of several of the leading medievalists of the preceding generation, including Eduardo Hinojosa and the German scholar Alfons Dopsch. His earliest work established many of the themes, primarily the legal and administrative history of the Asturian, Leonese, and early Castilian kingdoms, that he would pursue for the rest of his career. In particular his studies and publications of documents relating to the processes of the repopulation of areas of northern Spain in the centuries after the Arab conquest remain central to continuing debates on the subject. Similarly, although it is now, rather oddly, treated within Spanish universities as an aspect of ancient rather than medieval history, his work throughout his life on the previously neglected Visigothic period established its importance for the understanding of many of the institutional features of the kingdoms that followed it.

After a first publication in 1914 and the production of some important articles in the early 1920s, he became professor and then dean in the University of Madrid, and subsequently its rector. He founded and edited the *Anuario de Historia del Derecho Español*, which remains the most important journal of Spanish medieval legal history. His involvements as minister of education and then ambassador to Portugal made the 1930s almost completely unproductive as far as research was concerned, and in 1939 he went into exile. After a brief period in France he moved to Argentina, where he established the Instituto de Historia de España, which was effectively a personal fiefdom within the University of Buenos Aires. From it he published the *Cuadernos de Historia de España* (CHE), which for over four decades was the most regular and influential medieval history journal in the Spanish-speaking world. Although Sánchez-Albornoz was now far removed from the original sources for medieval research, his compendious notes taken during his work in Spanish archives in the 1910s and 1920s enabled him to renew his own scholarly output. He published numerous articles in CHE, as well as maintaining earlier contacts with French and Italian historians. With Spain itself largely isolated in Europe after World War II, he became the acceptable and authoritative face of the Spanish historiographical tradition as far as Europe was concerned, appearing frequently at conferences in Italy.

Through the Instituto he trained a new generation of pupils in South America, including Hilda Grassotti and Reyna Pastor de Togneri, who like most of his earlier Spanish disciples, continued to work in the areas and with the methods that he advocated. In the later 1940s and 1950s the Spanish scholars who had studied under him before the Civil War were also coming to the fore as the leading medieval historians in Spain, fully acknowledging their debts to him. Despite his political attachments in the 1930s, the late 19th century tradition of Spanish historiography to which he belonged, which was concerned pre-eminently with the rise of Castile and with the development of centralizing government and its institutions, was entirely acceptable to the Franco regime. Thus Sánchez-Albornoz continued to receive personal recognition and to exert an intellectual leadership in medieval historical studies in his homeland, which led in due course to his being able to make a triumphant return to Spain and to receive numerous honors there in the years leading up to his death in 1984.

His most famous, though ultimately least significant work of the Buenos Aires period was his 2-volume *España: un enigma histórico* (1956; *Spain: A Historical Enigma*, 1975), which challenged the broad interpretation advocated by Américo Castro of Spanish history as the fusion of different cultures. For Sánchez-Albornoz an essential "Spanishness" or "Hispanidad" transformed most of the alien cultural elements that entered the Iberian peninsula. His opinions on those, such as the Jews, whom he saw as resisting such hispanization, led to his later being accused of anti-Semitism. While the conflict between Sánchez-Albornoz and Castro was of major interest in the Spanish world for many years, with victory being accorded in Spain at least to the former, the presuppositions of his arguments now appear dated and irrelevant.

He was notorious as a polemicist. Intellectually his attitude to his former pupils, however personally warm, was always condescending. As numerous of his polemical articles show, in any scholarly argument, such as that with Antonio Ubieto Arteta over the Jimeno dynasty, if his opponent was a former pupil or even the pupil of a former pupil, this in itself was for Sánchez-Albornoz an argument against them – how could the pupil know better than the master? His style of debate in such published controversies was often highly patronizing, displaying an arrogance and a lack of openness to new ideas that can amaze the dispassionate reader. To his credit, he was also prepared to enter into debates in areas where caution might have kept him out. Thus, although not knowing the language, he stoutly defended his interpretations of the compositional history of such Arab historical texts as the *Ajbar maymu'a* against the criticisms of professional orientalists such as Evariste Lévi-Provençal and Pedro Chalmeta in some of the most polemical articles he ever wrote.

More significant and with enduring value are his numerous articles, some of considerable length, on medieval historiography and governmental and social institutions. Many of these were reprinted several times over in a variety of combinations quite bewildering to anyone trying to establish a bibliography of Sánchez-Albornoz's works. In such articles he often published texts taken from his early archival studies, which, unlike many of the footnotes in his work, prove to be remarkably accurate and exact. Although, like his predecessors, he remained wedded to a view that saw the medieval and modern Spanish state as the direct heir of an almost exclusively Castilian inheritance, his own partly Basque descent led him into publishing a small but significant corpus of articles on the then much neglected kingdom of Navarre. Here he was followed by his foremost Spanish pupil José Maria Lacarra. Unlike Lacarra, Sánchez-Albornoz never turned his attention to Aragón, let alone Catalonia. One consequence of this has been that in the post-Franco decades when there has been a marked shift away from the study of the centralizing Castilian tradition and towards regional studies, much of his work has gone out of fashion and hence out of print. In part, too, this is due to the appreciation by Spanish medievalists of new and more sophisticated methodologies, such as those offered by the French *Annales* school. However, through conferences and their publications the Fundación Sánchez-Albornoz in Avila continues to promote the study of many of the topics and periods that were his main interest.

ROGER COLLINS

See also Halperín-Donghi; Menéndez Pidal; Spain: Islamic; Spain: Medieval

Biography

Claudio Sánchez-Albornoz y Meduiña. Born Madrid, 7 April 1893. Taught at University of Barcelona, 1918–20; and University of Madrid, 1920–32: rector, 1932–33. Member, Chamber of Deputies, 1931–35; foreign minister, 1933; ambassador to Portugal, 1936. Taught at University of Bordeaux, 1937–40; and University of Buenos Aires, 1940–83. Exiled from Spain during the Franco era; returned 1983. Died Avila, 8 July 1984.

Principal Writings

La curia regia portuguesa, siglos XII y XIII (The Portuguese Royal Curia in the 12th and 13th Centuries), 1920
El "Ajbar maymu'a" cuestiones historiograficas que suscita (Historical Questions Raised by the *Ajbar maymu'a*), 1944

La España musulmana: según los autores islamitas y cristanos medievales (Muslim Spain According to Medieval Christian and Moslem Authors), 2 vols., 1946
Una ciudad hispano-cristiana hace un milenio, estampas de la vida en León (A Spanish Christian City a Millennium Ago: Aspects of Life in León), 1947; 10th edition as *Una ciudad de la España cristiana hace mil años*, 1984
España: un enigma histórico, 2 vols., 1956; in English as *Spain: A Historical Enigma*, 2 vols., 1975
Estudios sobre las instituciones medievales españolas (Studies on Medieval Spanish Institutions), 1965
La España cristiana de los siglos VIII al XI (Christian Spain from the 8th to the 11th Centuries), vol. 1: *El reino Astur-Leonés (772 a 1037)*, 1980

Further Reading

Carmen Carlé, María del, Hilda Grassotti, and German Orduna, eds., *Estudios en homenaje a Don Claudio Sánchez Albornoz en sus 90 anos* (Studies in Honor of Claudio Sánchez Albornoz on his 90th Birthday), 6 vols., Buenos Aires: Instituto de Historia de España, 1983–90
Clemente Ramos, Julián, "Entre el determenismo y la libertad: teoria historica y contradicciones internas en el systema albornociano" (Between Determinism and Liberty: Historical Theory and Internal Contradictions in the System of Claudio Sánchez Albornoz), *Cuadernos de Investigación Histórica* 10 (1986), 31–40

Sanctis, Gaetano de 1870–1957
Italian historian of Greece and Rome

Gaetano de Sanctis has been described as the most important Italian historian of antiquity since Carlo Sigonio, with whom he shared a vast historical vision, total control of the varied categories of sources, and a marvelous ability to bring the ancient world to life. Few historians have left us as vivid an account of the formative influences on their lives as he did in his *Ricordi della mia vita* (Memoirs, 1970). He has also been called by Aldo Ferrabino "the man of contradictions," which began with his own birth into a fiercely papal family in 1870, just after the capture of Rome. As with his own life, for de Sanctis history was full of contradictions which he attempted to reconcile (notably between the forces for freedom and independence as opposed to those for unity and hegemony). Life was for him the guide to history, not the other way around.

He is best remembered for *Storia dei Romani* (History of the Romans, 1907–64). The first two volumes, on the conquest of Italy, appeared in 1907, just after Theodor Mommsen's death. Trained by Beloch, de Sanctis attempted to devise and apply a "scientific" historiography. His own fundamental approach was conservative, but he was capable of bold views: he revived Perizonius' "ballad theory," used also by Niebuhr, which saw in songs the missing link in the earliest sources; he rejected the overthrow of the monarchy by revolution and modified Beloch's view of the dictator as the link between monarchy and republic to postulate a three-man college of praetors. In the unification of the peninsula, Rome was seen as engaged in a struggle for existence against inferior cultures such as the unoriginal Etruscans and even the Greeks; the battle of Sentinum (295 BCE) de Sanctis compared with Solferino (1895). His concept of a free state was admittedly founded on the formation of the modern Italian state.

The third volume (1916), on the Punic Wars, was written against the background of World War I, in which de Sanctis had been a fierce upholder of Italy's neutrality and loyalty to the Triple Alliance. Less pleasant aspects of his thought became apparent. He approved of Carthage's destruction, just as he approved of Italy's African imperialism in the 19th and 20th centuries, and there was a strange combination of Providence, xenophobia, and Hegelian necessity in his explanation of the defeat of this "parasitic" culture. He spoke of victories of Indo-Europeans over Semites.

The fourth volume (1923) was a turn to moral history: the Roman conquest of the East. This in de Sanctis' view was a fatal mistake. Rome should have directed her energies to conquering the backward West, instead of ending the brilliant Hellenistic age. The result was also the failure of the ruling aristocracy to address the various internal crises, so the middle class was destroyed, the citizen army was replaced by "mercenaries," and loyalty to the state by loyalty to military leaders. de Sanctis recognized the fate of his modern-day Italy. Here were his fatal contradictions, however, most notably the failure to see that his much loved struggle for freedom applied just as much to the Carthaginians and Spaniards as to the Romans. His notions of national unity were derived from the 19th century.

No further volumes of the history were to appear for 20 years. In the meantime, in 1931 de Sanctis was stripped of his chair for refusal to take an oath of loyalty to the regime, and during the 1930s he went blind. He became editor of the classical section of the *Enciclopedia Italiana* (Italian Encyclopedia). Yet he had been at work on the Gracchi as early as 1920. They were revolutionaries, but for him the real destroyers of the republic were the reactionaries who could provide no constructive alternative. Finally, just before de Sanctis' death appeared his description of Roman culture in the 2nd century BCE: literature, art, religion, and law. Chapters on the Social War published in 1976 show that he viewed that war as a turning point: Roman victory ensured decadence, then Sulla trampled on every constitutional norm. After crushing the freedom of others, the Romans *necessarily* lost their own.

De Sanctis also wrote on Greek history. *Atthis* (History of Athens, 1898), his first major work, and still of great value, traced the city's history from the remote tribal past down to the 5th century. It was, as even he admitted, too philological (utilizing the newly discovered Constitution of the Athenians) and neglectful of archaeology. *Storia dei Greci* (History of the Greeks, 1939) addressed the conflict in Greek history between the freedom of the city-state and the pursuit of national unity, as de Sanctis wrote on the eve of World War II. Within the city-state there was another tension: between the individual and the laws. de Sanctis obviously identified strongly with Socrates: the same tensions had been played out in his own life. His attempt to fit the very varied Greek states into a pattern was difficult. His *Perikle* (Pericles, 1944) studied the ruin brought to Athens through imperialism and war. The contemporary relevance was obvious. The great problem for de Sanctis was how any state could succeed, if Athens had failed, considering the level of her cultural achievements?

The main influences on de Sanctis could be summarized as his fervent Catholicism, his teacher Beloch, and the French philosopher Henri Bergson. As for his legacy, his Roman history remains the classic 20th-century account of the republic. It was composed as the Italians tried to create their own historical school – and De Sanctis' school at Rome, along with Pavia in the north retain their positions as the most influential in the country. De Sanctis' opposition to both Marxists, and popularizers such as Ferrero, was rooted in his belief that documents do not speak until the historian invests them with life. Perhaps, then, his most important legacy is the opinion that "where there is no freedom, there is no history."

RONALD T. RIDLEY

See also Beloch; Greece: Ancient; Momigliano

Biography
Born Rome, 15 October 1870. Studied at the Apollinare and at Rome University 1883–92. Professor of ancient history, Turin University, 1900–29; and of Greek history, Rome University, 1929–31; dismissed for refusal to take oath to fascist regime, 1931. Edited the classical articles of the *Enciclopedia Italiana*. Restored to his professorial chair, 1944. President of the Institute of the Italian Encyclopedia, 1947–54. Senator, 1950. Married Emilia Rosmina di Mondovi. Died Rome, 9 April 1957.

Principal Writings
Atthis: storia della Repubblica Ateniese dalle origini alla riforma di Clistene (History of Athens), 1898
Storia dei Romani (History of the Romans), 7 vols., 1907–64
Problemi di storia antica (Problems in Ancient History), 1932
Storia dei Greci (History of the Greeks), 2 vols., 1939
Perikle (Pericles), 1944
Studi di storia della storiografia greca (Studies in Greek historiography), 1951
Ricerche sulla storiografia siceliota (Researches in Sicilian history), 1958
Scritti minori (6 vols.), 1966–83
Ricordi della mia vita (Memoirs), 1970
La guerra sociale (The Social War), edited by Leandro Polverini, 1976

Further Reading
Cagnetta, Mariella, "Gaetano de Sanctis," in Ward W. Briggs and William M. Calder III, eds., *Classical Scholarship: A Biographical Encyclopedia*, New York: Garland, 1990
Treves, Piero, "Gaetano de Sanctis," *Dizionario biografico degli italiani*, 39 (1991), 297–309 [includes bibliography]

Sarpi, Paolo 1552–1623
Italian political and ecclesiastical historian

Author of a landmark in European post-Renaissance historiography, Paolo Sarpi was also a distinguished scholar and polemicist, as well as a scientist. While he conceived the writing of history as part of his vigorous and active antagonism to the Counter-Reformation church, his innovative method and style broke with the humanist tradition and inaugurated "problematic historiography," with its monographic approach to single issues. As a Servite friar, Sarpi promoted some reforms within his Order; later, as theologian canonist and juridical adviser of the Venetian government for 17 years, he led the republic's resistance to the temporal claims of the papacy. As a historian,

Sarpi enjoyed more freedom than as a spokesmen of the Venetian republic, and could learn from contemporary historians no less than from Guicciardini. His historical works are to be read in the context of the 16th- and 17th-century European wars of religion, as Sarpi himself was a European intellectual. In Venice, he became acquainted with Dutch merchants and members of the Jewish community. His friends and correspondents were the leading scientists, scholars, diplomats, and ecclesiastical men of his age, including Calvinists, Anglicans, and French Gallicans.

Sarpi's undisputed masterpiece is the *Istoria del Concilio Tridentino* (*History of the Council of Trent*, 1620). Because of its direct attack on the Roman church, it had to be published under pseudonym; sponsored by James I of England, the book was printed in London in 1619. In the so-called "pamphlet war" during the major confrontation between Venice and Rome, Sarpi had already demonstrated his awareness of the power of print as an instrument of propaganda. Though put on the *Index* of prohibited books within a few months, the *History* received a large positive response mostly but not exclusively in Reformation countries: in ten years, one revised edition and four translations appeared.

Unlike all the other historical works by Sarpi, the *History* did not originate from a particular circumstance; instead, it was the accomplishment of a lifetime effort in collecting sources, and in recognizing what had happened at Trent as crucial for the destiny of Europe – as "the Iliad of our century." The first part of the *History* dealt with the consolidation of the Lutheran and Calvinist reforms from 1520 to 1545, the decades preceding the Council of Trent; the rest of the book covered in details the 18 years of alternating sessions and suspensions of the Council (1545–63). Such a thorough examination of the Council's genesis and development was not intended to be a mere chronicle, but to uncover the hidden nature of this event. Sarpi showed how the Council had failed to fulfil its original purpose, that is, the reunion of Christendom, and how, in turn, it had resulted in the ultimate achievement of papal authority over bishops, and intrusion in secular affairs.

In order to stress the progressive transformation of a democratic means of settling ecumenical disputes into an oppressive tool in the hands of the papacy, the *History* opened with a brief overview of all Councils held since early Christianity. The recurrent opposition between the primitive and the contemporary church became explicit in the long-term chronological perspective adopted by Sarpi in the *Trattato delle materie beneficiarie* (*On Benefices*, 1610). The treatise was not finished and was possibly completed by Fulgenzio Micanzio, Sarpi's fellow and biographer. Stimulated by a contingent controversy between Rome and Venice, the book traced the history of ecclesiastic benefices, and thus presented church institutions as the product of human rather than divine will.

Sarpi's enduring influence was due also to his selfconscious originality in historical writing. From a rhetorical point of view, he dismissed Latin, preferring Italian, and used an unconventional style that was dry but clear, witty and extremely effective. From a methodological point of view, Sarpi's precision in handling chronological data and detail was not meant to imitate ancient annals as much as to attain an exact reconstruction leading to the establishment of truth and to historical understanding. This is most evident in the second part of the *History*, for which Sarpi drew on a variety of sources. Thanks to his connections he was able to acquire important printed and manuscript materials; had access to secret documents in Rome and in Venice; and could count on the oral reports of his friends who had taken part in the Council.

In his last work, Sarpi abandoned once and for all the celebratory character of "official historiography" in order to elucidate a burning contemporary issue. Published in this century but written at the end of 1619, the *Trattato di pace e accomodamento* (*On Peace and Settlement*) illustrated the diplomatic negotiations between Venice and the Habsburg empire over the problem of Uskok pirates in the Adriatic sea during the years 1615–19, and pointed to the responsibilities of Spain who stood behind the emperor.

Since its publication, Sarpi's *History* has been criticized by most Catholic historians for its supposedly biased use of the sources (some of which have been lost) – notable critics were the Jesuit Sforza Pallavicino (1607–67), who prepared the prompt, official answer to Sarpi's book, and, in the 20th century, Hubert Jedin. Some limits and errors notwithstanding, Sarpi's historical analysis has proved to be substantially correct; moreover, it marked a major turning-point in historical practice at a time when it was undergoing radical changes comparable to the 17th-century scientific revolution. Much more than Sarpi's accomplishments as a historian, his orthodoxy has often been called into question, especially on the basis of his correspondence and private notes – known as the *Pensieri filosofici e scientifici* (*Scientific and Philosophical Thoughts*). The majority of scholars, however, have increasingly disregarded this debate as a fruitless attempt to force Sarpi's very personal attitude towards the religious experience into a pre-existing reformed church or movement. Historians of political thought have generally considered Sarpi an early advocate of the separation between church and state; meanwhile, further research has investigated Sarpi's conceptions of possible cooperation between political and religious powers in the specific Venetian context.

FRANCESCA TRIVELLATO

See also Catholicism; Reformation; Renaissance Historical Writing

Biography

Born Venice, 1552. Joined Servite order, 1575, rising to vicar-general by 1599; but had strained relationship with the papal curia after several rejections for episcopal appointment and theological disputes, which ended in excommunication; became official theological adviser to Venetian government, 1606. Unsuccessful attempt on his life, 1607. Died Venice, 1623.

Principal Writings

Trattato delle materie beneficiarie (On Benefices), 1610
Istoria del Concilio Tridentino, 1619; in English as *History of the Council of Trent*, 1620
Trattatto di pace e accomodamento (On Peace and Settlement), written 1619
Opere, edited by Gateano and Luisa Cozzi, 1969

Further Reading

Acton, Lord, "Fra Paolo Sarpi," in his *Essays on Church and State*, edited by Douglas Woodruff, London: Hollis and Carter, 1952; New York: Crowell, 1968

Amerio, Romano, *Il Sarpi dei pensieri filosofici inediti*, Torino: Edizioni di Filosofia, 1950

Bouwsma, William J., *Venice and the Defense of Republican Liberty: Renaissance Values in the Age of the Counter Reformation*, Berkeley: University of California Press, 1968

Brown, Horatio F., "Paolo Sarpi," in *Studies in European Literature, Being the Taylorian Lectures, 1889–1899*, Oxford: Clarendon Press, 1900

Burke, Peter, "The Great Unmasker: Paolo Sarpi, 1552–1623," *History Today* 15 (1965), 426–32

Chabod, Federico, *La politica di Paolo Sarpi*, Rome: Istituto per la collaborazione culturale, 1962

Cochrane, Eric, *Historians and Historiography in the Italian Renaissance*, Chicago: University of Chicago Press, 1981

Cozzi, Gaetano, *Paolo Sarpi tra Venezia e l'Europa*, Turin: Einaudi, 1978

Frajese, Vittorio, *Sarpi scettico: stato e chiesa a Venezia tra cinque e seicento*, Bologna: Mulino, 1994

Getto, Giovanni, *Paolo Sarpi*, Pisa: Vallerini, 1941

Jedin, Hubert, *Das Konzil von Trient: Ein Überblick über die Erforschung seiner Geschichte*, Rome: Storia e Letteratura, 1948; in English as *A History of the Council of Trent*, 2 vols., London: Nelson, 1957

Lievsay, John Leon, *Venetian Phoenix: Paolo Sarpi and Some of His English Friends (1606–1700)*, Lawrence: University Press of Kansas, 1973

Prodi, Paolo, "The Structure and Organization of the Church in Renaissance Venice: Suggestions for Research," in J.R. Hale, ed., *Renaissance Venice*, London: Faber, and Totowa, NJ: Rowman and Littlefield, 1973

Salvatorelli, Luigi, "Paolo Sarpi," in *Contributi alla storia del Concilio di Trento*, Florence: Vallechi, 1948, 138–44

Wootton, David, *Paolo Sarpi: Between Renaissance and Enlightenment*, Cambridge: Cambridge University Press, 1983

Yates, Frances A., "Paolo Sarpi's 'History of the Council of Trent'," *Journal of the Warburg and Courtauld Institutes* 7 (1944), 123–43

Sarton, George 1884–1956
Belgian-American historian of science and Arabist

The objective of George Sarton's scholarly program was to justify the inclusion of the history of science in the roster of academic disciplines along with history proper and the histories of literature, art, law, and religion. This he called the "New Humanism." Science, which he defined as "systematized positive knowledge," was "the one essential phase of human civilization which has not received sufficient attention", as he wrote on the very first page of the *Introduction to the History of Science* (1927–48).

For Sarton, Greek science constituted a kind of "lay revelation." It had generally been undervalued as had that of the ancient Near East. Although writing very much in the neopositivist tradition of western science, Sarton understood the close relationship of science and theology that, "until relatively modern times . . . was an intrinsic part of science." From the medieval perspective, moreover, theology was also positive knowledge, though of a different kind than that now recognized. The habit cultivated by medieval theologians of studying things *sub specie aeternitatis* was also a scientific attitude. Sarton boasted that his work contained "the first tolerably complete account of mediaeval science." As with ancient science, he attempted to integrate Western and Eastern science into a single whole. He stressed the problems of the transmission of science in the Middle Ages, believing it to be a culturally original and creative process, obscured by excessive concentration by medievalists on scholastic philosophy. "Classical scholars," he concluded, "have no interest in science; mediaevalists have an erroneous concept of it, which is undoubtedly worse."

Another source of misconception was general ignorance of Arabic science. Sarton's scientific background was in mathematics. As a historian of science, although he was, by choice, an extreme generalist, he could well be considered an Arabist. To be sure, he was an autodidact, but when addressing Arabists, he referred to "our field." Virtually all of the great European Arabists of his generation were correspondents of his and through the three-pronged attack of the *Isis* critical bibliographies, the bio-bibliographical entries in the *Introduction*, and the further working-through of themes in correspondence with one or more experts, he set the agenda for the historiography of Arabic science in the 20th century and legitimized it as a central field of medieval intellectual and cultural history. He insisted that a medieval scholar who wanted to be up to date had to study Arabic. Medievalists who stressed the achievements of Europe while ignoring those of the Muslim world were reinforcing the notion of a "Dark Ages." Sarton even quantified the comparative importance of different scientific traditions up to 1400 CE: 362 figures from antiquity; 373 in the Latin West; 324 medieval Jews and Muslims; 189 from India and the Far East.

Sarton continually denied the absolute differentiation between East and West that seemed to underlay Western medievalism. "The majority of historians," he wrote, "have gradually evoked a conception of Western unity (at least spiritual unity) from which Eastern people were excluded." The whole process of the transmission of Greek science to the West through Arabic intermediaries belied any such essentialist conception of Western culture: "A Latin text may represent an Oriental tradition, and an Arabic one may represent a Western tradition." Because Sarton rejected cultural essentialism, he was not interested in distinguishing what might have been "Eastern" or "Western" about medieval science; rather he stressed what was universal. Sarton was an internationalist, and his impatience with cultural chauvinism was grounded in his understanding of those aspects of science that could be considered universal.

In explaining the subordination of science to theology in the Latin West, Sarton correctly identified a number of processes that ran counter to objective natural knowledge: the inability to test basic premises by experimentation or observation; the lack of any alternation between analysis and synthesis; and the habit of inserting such new experimental data as emerged not in the basic premises of science, "but somewhere in the superstructure of their theories." In a closed system such as scholasticism, new hypotheses cannot emerge. Sarton also characterized other premodern, nonwestern cultures – such as that of Neo-Confucian China or Vedantic India – as scholastic.

Sarton tried to draw a line between pure and applied science. Thus medicine and engineering were included in the *Introduction* only if the contribution was "original" or valuable from a "scientific" standpoint. It took an entire generation of historians to overcome Sarton's dictum and to recognize that science, medicine, and technology were cognate fields, with similar epistemologies.

Although an older generation of French historians such as Pierre Duhem and Paul Tannery may perhaps be regarded as the intellectual founders of 20th-century history of science, its foundation as a discipline was owing mainly to Sarton. In 1912, he put the first key institutional support of the new field in place by founding the journal *Isis* in Belgium. World War I obliged him to move both the journal and himself to the Untied States where he was supported by the Carnegie Institution. He was brought to Harvard in 1916 by L.J. Henderson and remained there until his death, but his appointment was always anomalous, with the majority of his support coming from the Carnegie Institution, not the university. A related project, his great bio-bibliographic *Introduction to the History of Science*, was to provide a bibliographical cornerstone for the new field (Robert K. Merton describes the work as "the pantheon which Sarton has created for the giants of science and learning"). He was able to bring the story only to 1400 CE, but the "critical bibliographies" that he established in *Isis* in part supplanted his grand project. In 1923, the History of Science Society was founded to finance *Isis* and to provide Sarton with a disciplinary pool of scholars for support.

THOMAS F. GLICK

See also Astrology; Merton; Natural Sciences; Science; Spain: Islamic; Spain: Medieval

Biography

George Alfred Leon Sarton. Born Ghent, Belgium, 31 August 1884, son of the chief engineer of the Belgian Railway. Briefly studied philosophy at University of Ghent, before switching to science, graduating DSc in physics and mathematics, 1911. Founder/editor, *Isis*, 1913–51. Emigrated 1914, eventually settling in the US. Temporary appointments led to lecturing (initially unofficially) at Harvard University, 1916–51, and to research position, Carnegie Institution, 1918–49. Married Eleanor Mabel Elwes, 1911 (1 daughter, the writer May Sarton). Died Cambridge, Massachusetts, 22 March 1956.

Principal Writings

Introduction to the History of Science, 3 vols. in 5 parts, 1927–48; reprinted 1975
The History of Science and the New Humanism, 1931
The Study of the History of Mathematics, 1936
The Life of Science: Essays in the History of Civilization, 1948
A History of Science, 2 vols., 1952–59
The Appreciation of Ancient and Medieval Science during the Renaissance (1450–1600), 1955
Six Wings: Men of Science in the Renaissance, 1957
Sarton on the History of Science, edited by Dorothy Stimson, 1962

Further Reading

"George Sarton Memorial Issue," *Isis* 48/3 (1957), 283–350 [includes bibliography]
Glick, Thomas F., "George Sarton and the Spanish Arabists," *Isis* 76 (1985), 487–99
Pyenson, Lewis, "Inventory as a Route to Understanding: Sarton, Neugebauer, and Sources," *History of Science* 33 (1995), 253–82
Thackray, Arnold, and Robert K. Merton, "On Discipline Building: The Paradoxes of George Sarton," *Isis* 63 (1972), 473–95

Sauer, Carl O. 1889–1975

US human geographer

Carl O. Sauer belonged to a small group of post-World War I human geographers in the United States who challenged the positivist orientation of their science. He also spoke out against the destructive consequences of large-scale development on rural communities and the environment.

Sauer's worldview was that of German historicism, acquired during his upbringing in a largely German-American town and his education at Central Wesleyan, then a largely German-American college, where his German-born father taught. Later, he was also influenced by the works of German geographers such as Friedrich Ratzel, and the German-American anthropologists Franz Boas and Alfred Kroeber. Sauer rejected the concept of progressive evolution according to universal laws in favor of a particularistic conception of cultures. He also liked rural societies for their stewardship of the land and balanced social structures. His worldview isolated him from the mainstream of Anglo-American geographers, which makes it difficult to assess his impact on the profession, especially as until his retirement Sauer published few monographs, relying more on teaching to promote his ideas.

Sauer first studied the shaping of the Midwest by 19th-century white settlers, notably in the Ozark Mountains. In "The Morphology of Landscape" (1925), he challenged the dominant environmental determinism of William Morris Davis and his school, who assumed that human societies reacted rationally, albeit with differing amounts of knowledge, to environmental stimuli through a Darwinian process. Their emphasis was on how subtle differences in the physical environment triggered different outcomes. Shocked by the devastation of midwestern forests by speculators, Sauer disagreed. He argued that people could act in irrational, destructive ways, and that to understand why, one had to study their "habitat and habit," as he put it, through their history, and fieldwork.

In the 1930s, his work became more explicitly historical when he began to work with periods during which, he thought, communities had been wiser in their husbandry of resources. He used as examples areas in the southwestern United States and Central America where traditional agriculture still existed. In several articles, and a collection of lectures published as *Agricultural Origins and Dispersals* (1952), Sauer argued notably that the origins of agriculture and animal husbandry owed more to the religious needs and the sheer playfulness of early humans, than the desire to maximize resources as materialist utilitarians would have it. But after World War II, there was a strong movement to change geography into a law-seeking "spatial science," with an epistemology and methodology based on modernization theory. There was dwindling tolerance for critics who ridiculed neoliberal assumptions of humans as rational profit-maximizers. Sauer resigned as dean at the University of California, though he continued to teach. Marxist scholars also criticized his work for side-stepping power relationships affecting cultural practices, and both sides attacked as unscientific his distaste for abstract theorizing. Indeed, Sauer was more interested in manifestations of culture than their deeper origins, and rejected theorizing as sophistry obscuring reality. To fight his critics, Sauer's students, including J.J. Parsons and W.L. Thomas, rallied his supporters at the 1956 symposium "Man's Role in Changing the Face of the Earth," and went on to shape the subfield of cultural geography, where many of Sauer's ideas survived.

To contrast native stewardship and destructive short-term development, Sauer focused on borderlands, where differences would be most apparent. But he published little after *Man in Nature: America before the Days of the White Man* (1939), until his retirement. He then wrote *The Early Spanish Main* (1966), *Sixteenth Century North America* (1971), and *Seventeenth Century North America* (1980), stirring controversy because of his sharp denunciation of European settlers for their senseless destruction of native cultures which had achieved a long-term balance with nature. Their historical scholarship was lauded by American historical journals, though reviewers such as David Hawke of Pace University complained that Sauer's favorite method, "to observe observation" by mulling over early travelogues somewhat lacked analytical rigor. In *Northern Mists* (1968), he looked at pre-Columbian European explorers and the physical constraints that had made their endeavors fail. With a touch of whimsy, he included Irish monks who may have landed in North America, and was criticized for it.

Sauer also was an active concerned citizen. At a time when it was not popular to do so, he criticized how the materialist conception of Western progress destroyed traditional cultures, as in his withering "Destructive Exploitation in Modern Colonial Expansion," which angered colleagues at the 1938 International Congress of Geography. He tried to interest the New Deal administration in promoting sustainable agriculture. Rebuffed, he wrote "Theme of Plant and Animal Destruction in Economic History" (1938), and other essays warning that unbridled development endangered human survival. They influenced the ecological movement of the 1960s.

Sauer's influence is difficult to gauge. His opposition to the materialistic conception of progress, his particularistic view of culture, and his historical-cultural methodology were at odds with the mainstream of American geography. But he shaped American cultural geography, and, together with such fellow critics of modernity as Lewis Mumford and Richard Hartshorne, ceaselessly reminded geographers of their responsibility for the social and ecological impact of their work. The rise of the postmodern "new ecology" approach in human geography has sparked new interest in Sauer's thought among geographers in general.

THOMAS REIMER

See also Borah; Latin America: Colonial; Semple

Biography
Carl Ortwin Sauer. Born Warrenton, Missouri, 24 December 1889. Received BA, Central Wesleyan College, 1908; studied at Northwestern University, 1908–09; PhD, University of Chicago, 1915. Assistant geologist, Illinois Geographical Survey, 1910–12; map editor, Rand McNally Publishers, 1912–13; taught at State Normal School, Salem, Massachusetts, 1913–14; University of Michigan (rising to professor), 1915–23; and University of California, Berkeley, 1923–57 (emeritus). Married Lorena Schowengerdt, 1913 (1 son, 1 daughter). Died 18 July 1975.

Principal Writings
The Geography of the Ozark Highland of Missouri, 1920
"The Morphology of Landscape," in *University Publications in Geography* [Berkeley, CA] 2 (1925), 19–54

"Destructive Exploitation in Modern Colonial Expansion," *Compte-rendus du Congrès International de Géographie, Amsterdam* 2 (1938), 494–99
"Theme of Plant and Animal Destruction in Economic History," *Journal of Farm Economics* 20 (1938), 765–75
Man in Nature: America before the Days of the White Man, 1939
Agricultural Origins and Dispersals, 1952
Land and Life: A Selection from the Writings of Carl Ortwin Sauer, edited by John Leighly, 1963
The Early Spanish Main, 1966
Northern Mists, 1968
Sixteenth Century North America: The Land and the People as Seen by the Europeans, 1971
Seventeenth Century North America, 1980

Further Reading
Billinge, Mark *et al.*, *Recollections of a Revolution: Geography as Spatial Science*, New York: St. Martin's Press, 1984
Blouet, Brian W., ed., *The Origins of Academic Geography in the United States*, Hamden, CT: Archon, 1981
Callahan, Bob, Introduction to Sauer, *Selected Essays, 1963–1975*, Berkeley, CA: Turtle Island Foundation, 1981
Kenzer, Martin S., "Milieu and the Intellectual Landscape: Carl Sauer's Undergraduate Heritage," *Association of American Geographers Annals* 75 (1985), 258–70
Kenzer, Martin S., ed., *Carl O. Sauer: A Tribute*, Corvallis: Oregon State University Press, 1987
Martin, Geoffrey J., "Paradigm Change: A History of Geography in the United States, 1892–1925," *National Geographic Research* 1 (1985), 217–35
Parsons, James J., "The Later Sauer Years," *Association of American Geographers Annals* 69 (1979), 9–15
Solot, Michael, "Carl Sauer and Cultural Evolution," *Association of American Geographers Annals* 76 (1986), 508–20
Speth, W.M., "Carl Ortwin Sauer on Destructive Exploitation," *Biological Conservation* 11 (1977), 145–60
Williams, M.,"The Apple of My Eye: Carl Sauer and Historical Geography," *Journal of Historical Geography* 9 (1983), 1–28
Zimmer, Karl S., "Human Geography and the New Ecology: The Prospect and Promise of Integration," *Association of American Geographers Annals* 84 (1994), 108–25

Savigny, Friedrich Karl von 1779–1861
German legal historian

Friedrich Karl von Savigny's legal education began early because of a personal tragedy. He was orphaned at age 13, but his aristocratic parents' friend von Neurath, the assessor to the Reichskammergericht at Wetzlar acted as von Savigny's guardian and personally taught him Roman law through rote memorization and catechistic questioning. Von Savigny then formally studied legal history in 1795 at Marburg and, in the next year, at Göttingen, where Gustav Hugo taught. Hugo's idea of law as organic growth became fundamental to what is called the "Historical School of Law," which von Savigny would continue and develop in the next generation. After receiving his doctorate in 1800, von Savigny taught briefly at Marburg and, then, declined professorships from Greifswald and Heidelberg. He was financially comfortable enough to travel widely in western Germany and France while researching the medieval history of Roman law.

The results of this research appeared later in his magisterial *Geschichte des römischen Rechts im Mittelalter* (History of Roman Law in the Middle Ages), which appeared in six volumes between 1815 and 1831. Then and now, this work was essential to the understanding of the post-imperial history of Roman law which, he showed, continued in force in the barbarian Germanic kingdoms and, from the time of the 12th-century legal scholar Irnerius, became the object of systematic study. In the first two volumes, von Savigny gave a very positive view of the Germanic invaders of Rome: far from destroying cities and rooting out Roman institutions, the German kings allowed urban Romans, who now enjoyed greater freedom than under the emperors, to retain and use their own institutions. Thus, von Savigny's book became a history of medieval institutional and legal life throughout the reaches of the former Roman empire, as well as an account of the scholarly exposition of Roman law between the 12th and 15th centuries.

The period before 1808 was not only one of travel and research. In 1803 von Savigny published his *Recht des Besitzes* (Property Law), which demonstrated that ancient Romans saw property more in terms of effective occupancy than absolute possession, and on its strength was appointed in 1808 to a professorship at Landshut. His real talent as a lecturer and his known German patriotism in a time of French invasion led Wilhelm von Humboldt to orchestrate Savigny's appointment to the new faculty at Berlin in 1810, which was charged with rebuilding Prussia through education in the wake of the calamitous defeat of the older absolutist Hohenzollern monarchy. Von Savigny would teach there until, in 1842, he left academic life for a cabinet-level appointment in Prussia as great chancellor (a revived title given a century before by Frederick the Great to a legal codifier). He was charged with codifying and revising certain areas of Prussian law, notably the laws of divorce. The actual results that von Savigny achieved were fairly modest, but there is some irony in his undertaking the work in the first place. This irony stems from his famous controversy with the great legal scholar Anton Friedrich Justus Thibaut at Heidelberg, in which von Savigny published an essay that was, in effect, the charter of the Historical school.

In 1814 Thibaut called for the codification of German law on the pattern of Napoleon's *Code civile*. This meant the rationalization of German laws and, in the process, their selective revision in accordance with reason and natural law. Von Savigny's instantly famous rebuttal, *Vom Beruf unserer Zeit für Gesetzgebung und Rechtswissenschaft* (1814; *On the Vocation of Our Age for Legislation and Jurisprudence*, 1831), would go through several revisions, but always maintained its basic argument: laws should not be made, except in small and inevitable increments because, properly, they evolve organically in accordance with the *Volksgeist* ("spirit of the people or nation"). As was to be expected, von Savigny argued this case with support from the history of medieval Roman law that he knew so well. This argument, which gathered force from German national resentment at the reforms of the French occupiers, also supported conservative resistance to middle-class demands for structural reforms and a sharing of power. Von Savigny's essay became a classic in political and historical theory and had a major future career in German political debate. In the shorter term, it led to his collaboration with Karl Friedrich Eichhorn – another pivotal figure in the school

– and Johann Friedrich Ludwig Göschen in the founding their journal *Zeitschrift für geschichtliche Rechtswissenschaft*, whose opening statement drew on arguments from *Vocation of Our Age*.

Von Savigny, however, did not decry all legal innovation. No historian could deny or delegitimate all change in history. In his correspondence, the politically active historian J.G. Droysen noted this fatal weakness in von Savigny's argument, since supposed "historical rights" and the "right of history" to effect radical change were reciprocal functions. All laws had been made some time, and later ages had the same right to create as had earlier ages. As if to illustrate this point, one of von Savigny's most successful students – Heinrich von Sybel – based his own politically charged theory of progressive change on the notion of an evolving *Volksgeist* that von Savigny taught him. These inconsistencies point up the theoretical weakness of von Savigny's outlook, but, if noticed, they probably did not bother him. He was alarmed at the prospect of sweeping change rather than change as such and disputed the sovereignty of reason in law rather than the use of any rational standards in legislation. He was a conservative pragmatist with deep learning and great respect for the past, which is what recommended him to the conservative romanticist Friedrich Wilhelm IV of Prussia in the first place.

This pragmatism was of a piece with his scholarship. There had never been anything merely antiquarian about von Savigny's vast erudition in Roman law. His 1803 book on property law was, in part, an attempt to demonstrate the use of Roman procedure. His history of Roman law in medieval times was a demonstration in six volumes of how later ages could appropriate and adapt, in keeping with their later needs and abilities, the laws of past times. His last major work, published between 1840 and 1849 in eight volumes, was *System des heutigen römischen Rechts* (System of Modern Roman Law). It was an approving demonstration of the continuing coherence and applicability of Roman law. His work as Prussian great chancellor in and after 1842 was a further demonstration of the continued vitality of Roman law and, so, of the ongoing relevance of its history.

ROBERT FAIRBAIRN SOUTHARD

See also Germany: Medieval; Niebuhr; Sybel

Biography
Born Frankfurt, 21 February 1779. Studied at the Universities of Göttingen and Marburg; degree, 1800. Professor of Roman law, University of Marburg, 1800–04; University of Landshut, 1808–10; and University of Berlin, 1810–42. Prussian minister for the revision of legislation, 1842–48. Married Kunigunde Brentano, 1803. Died Berlin, 25 October 1861.

Principal Writings
Recht des Besitzes: eine civilistische Abhandlung, 1803; in English as *Von Savigny's Treatise on Possession; or, the Jus Possessionis of the Civil Law*, 1848
Vom Beruf unserer Zeit für Gesetzgebung und Rechtswissenschaft, 1814; in English as *On the Vocation of Our Age for Legislation and Jurisprudence*, 1831
Geschichte des römischen Rechts im Mittelalter, 6 vols., 1815–31, 5th edition, 7 vols., 1986; vol. 1 translated as *The History of the Roman Law during the Middle Ages*, 1829

System des heutigen römischen Rechts, 8 vols., 1840–49; vol. 1 in
English as *System of the Modern Roman Law*, 1867; vol. 2 in
English as *Jural Relations; or, The Roman Law of Persons as
Subjects of Jural Relations*, 1884; vol. 8 in English as *Private
International Law: A Treatise on the Conflict of Laws, and
the Limits of Their Operation in Respect of Place and Time*,
1869

Further Reading
Schröder, Horst, *Friedrich Karl von Savigny: Geschichte und
Rechtsdenken beim Übergang vom Feudalismus zum Kapitalismus
in Deutschland* (Friedrich Karl von Savigny: History and Legal
Thought during the Transition from Feudalism to Capitalism),
Frankfurt and New York: Lang, 1984
Stoll, Adolf, *Friedrich Karl von Savigny*, 3 vols., Berlin: Heymann,
1927–39

Saxo Grammaticus *fl.* 1185–1208
Danish historian

Saxo Grammaticus was Denmark's most important medieval
writer, the only one with a European reputation; yet very little
is known about him. The only contemporary information is
that he was Sven Aggesen's colleague (*contubernalis*) and archbishop Absalon's clerk (*clericus*).

Commissioned by archbishop Absalon (d.1201), he wrote
a history of Denmark from the foundation of the state by a
mythical king "Dan" to *c*.1185. This large work (16 books,
filling some 550 quarto pages), first called *Gesta Danorum*
(GD) *c*.1300, consists of two more or less equal halves, one
dealing with pagan, the other with Christian times, suggesting
a conscious analogy with the Old and New Testaments. It has
been argued that in attempting to relate Danish history to that
of the church Saxo deliberately arranged his work in groups
of four books: the first (1–4) dealing with the period before
Christ, the second (5–8) ending with the coming of Christianity
to the Danes, the third (9–12) ending with the establishment
of a Danish archbishopric, while the last four books deal with
the archiepiscopal period (Skovgaard-Petersen).

Saxo drew on a wide variety of sources, such as Paul the
Deacon, Bede, Adam of Bremen, *Roskilde Chronicle*, and Sven
Aggesen, as well as the literature on St. Knud and Knut Lavard,
taking great liberties with them all. He also drew on oral traditions, mentioning both Icelanders and Absalon as informants.
Undoubtedly his account of contemporary history was deeply
influenced by traditions cherished by his patron's own family,
the powerful Hvides of Zealand.

Like Geoffrey of Monmouth's *Historia*, GD is a "national
history," reflecting the 12th-century renaissance and the revival
of interest in classical writers, who influenced not only Saxo's
vocabulary, syntax, and concepts, but also his poetry. He used
some twenty different meters, modeling himself, above all, on
Martianus Capella. It is hardly an exaggeration to say that
Saxo saw Danish history through Roman eyes. Even if the
language of GD is entirely secular it is clear that the received
opinion that he was anticlerical (Weibull) should be abandoned. It is true that he seems to have been remarkably cool,
almost hostile, towards monasticism, but he displays an active
interest in the church, albeit an interest in its political, moral,
and cultural rather than religious aspects.

Saxo has been considered a propagandist for royal political
ideas, but it can be shown that, thanks to a highly sophisticated technique of writing on two levels, implicitly questioning
what he explicitly states, Saxo was able to oppose what he
was commissioned to support. First, he offers very unflattering
portraits of the Valdemars, casting doubt on the worthiness of
their branch of the royal family. Second, he opposes hereditary kingship and strong royal power, emphasizing that with
one – disastrous – exception all Danish kings were elected by
the Danish people and teaching that society rested also on two
other pillars, namely church and aristocracy, including the aristocracy of talent. For Saxo it was not only noble birth and
glorious ancestry that counted, but, sometimes even more, wit,
eloquence, and ability.

Thus, rather than being propaganda for royal policies of
the time, Saxo's work is a *speculum principis*. But GD is more
than that; apart from being a "course-book" in such topics as
politics, warfare, and morals, it expresses criticism of society
and contemporary conditions (Johannesson). So, for example,
Saxo seriously questions the rights of women to inherit and
opposes the church demand for female consent to marriage
(Sawyer).

It is difficult to assess what contemporary influence Saxo had.
The fact that, from the end of the 13th until the beginning of
the 16th century, his work was known only in abbreviated
forms suggests that there cannot have been many people in
Denmark who could appreciate or even understand it. The most
comprehensive of the abbreviations, *Compendium Saxonis* (CS)
is one of the best preserved Danish medieval texts. It is interesting that, in contrast to GD, of which no complete manuscript
has been preserved, CS exists in no fewer than four Latin manuscripts and three manuscripts as well as one printed version
in Middle Low German, which were used and revised well
into the 17th century. Thus the printed editions of GD (1514
and 1575) apparently did not make the manuscripts of CS
redundant, which illustrates the great respect accorded to the
compendium.

There were obviously other reasons for abbreviating GD than
its length and complicated language; among other things, Saxo's
critical attitude to kings was not suitable in Denmark in the
1340s, when CS was compiled. The omissions made by the epit-
omator resulted in a work best described as a royal chronicle.
Thus, for many centuries Saxo's influence was mediated by other
writers and compilers who presented their interpretations of
GD, for example Albert Krantz (1445–1517), through whom
Shakespeare may have learned about prince Hamlet. It was not
until the 16th century that Saxo's own work reached a European
audience, and Saxo himself was recognized and highly praised as
a stylist, by Erasmus among others.

BIRGIT SAWYER

Principal Writings
Gesta Danorum, written *c*.1190–1210; as *History of the Danes*,
translated by Peter Fisher, 2 vols., 1979–80, and as *Danorum
regum heroumque historia* (includes translation), edited by Eric
Christiansen, 3 vols., 1980–81

Further Reading

Friis-Jensen, Karsten, ed., *Saxo Grammaticus: A Medieval Author Between Norse and Latin Culture*, Copenhagen: Museum Tusculanum Press, 1981

Friis-Jensen, Karsten, *Saxo Grammaticus as Latin Poet: Studies in the Verse Passages of the Gesta Danorum*, Rome: Bretschneider, 1987

Johannesson, Kurt, *Saxo Grammaticus: Komposition och världsbild i Gesta Danorum* (Saxo Grammaticus: Composition and Worldview in *Gesta Danorum*) Stockholm: Almqvist & Wiksell, 1978

Sawyer, Birgit, "Valdemar, Absalon and Saxo: Historiography and Politics in Medieval Denmark," *Revue Belge de Philologie et d'Histoire* 63 (1985), 685–705

Skovgaard-Petersen, Inge, *Da Tidernes Herre var nær: Studier i Saxos historieyn* (When the Lord of Time was Near: Studies in Saxo's Historical View) Copenhagen: Den danske historiske Forening, 1987

Strand [now Sawyer], Birgit, *Kvinnor och män i Gesta Danorum* (Women and Men in the *Gesta Danorum*), Gothenburg: Kvinnohistoriskt Archiv, 1980

Weibull, Curt, *Saxo: Kritiska undersökningar i Danmarks historia från Sven Estridsens död till Knut VI* (Saxo: Critical Studies in Denmark's History from Sven Estridsen's Death to Knut VI), Lund, 1915

Schama, Simon 1945–

British historian of early modern Europe

When Simon Schama published *Patriots and Liberators* in 1977, he was 32 years old. It was an astonishing debut for so young a historian. This study of the impact of the French Revolution on the Netherlands almost singlehandedly rescued late 18th-century Dutch history from the condescension of posterity. Far past their golden age of world power and cultural dynamism, and riven by conflicting parochialisms, the Dutch provinces could offer little in the way of active resistance to French hegemony. Yet in Schama's masterful reconstruction the story of their encounter with revolutionary France has its own drama. His first book not only made sense of the complex politics of adaptation and survival, it also offered a lively account of the hazards of occupation as they were experienced by ordinary people. In his preface to the book Schama thanked his mentors J.H. Plumb and Richard Cobb: with the former he shares an ability to render the maneuverings of politicians, the play of factions, as stirring narrative; with the latter, an interest in stubborn regional diversities and individual eccentricities that defy easy categorization. Like both of his mentors he writes in clear and sparkling prose that stakes a claim on history as art as well as craft.

After a remarkable detour into the history of Zionism, *Two Rothschilds and the Land of Israel* (1978), Schama produced the work that would consolidate his reputation as one of the most creative and ambitious historians of his generation. *The Embarrassment of Riches* (1987) offered a full-scale reassessment of Dutch culture at its zenith. One of the novelties here is the elaborate use of iconography: no surprise for art historians, to be sure, but unusual for a historian to use visual materials so extensively and brilliantly. The book is built around a series of unresolved oppositions in Dutch culture: between austerity and abundance, Calvinism and Erasmianism, domesticity and imperialism, prudence and prodigality, godliness and greed, the luminous silence of Vermeer and the bawdy exhibitionism of Steen. And Schama found traces of these oppositions not only in the visual arts, but in "moral geography," patriotic history, cookery, hydraulics, penology, economics, and child-rearing practices. Dazzled by their own vertiginous ascent, yet haunted by the perils of prosperity, the Dutch expressed the ambivalence of success in a wide variety of contexts. Schama's study of this ambivalence offers history on the grand scale in characteristically lively prose. The result is the kind of work that is rare in this century: a learned 700-page tome that retains on every page the freshness of an essay.

Simon Schama followed *The Embarrassment of Riches* with *Citizens: A Chronicle of the French Revolution* (1989). Here was another large-scale, lavishly illustrated volume that displayed narrative drive, analytical power, and an unerring eye for the telling anecdote. Firmly revisionist in orientation, the book not only offered a "chronicle" of events but also superb analyses of iconography and rhetoric. As in his study of the Dutch golden age, where a beached whale could provide the occasion for a fascinating inquiry into the history of mentalities, Schama ranged widely in his search for illuminating material: from popular physics and the first balloon flights to the politics of maternal breast-feeding in the *ancien régime*. More controversial was his treatment of the Revolution itself, which focused on the most sanguinary episodes and seemed to some critics to treat them with a Carlylean fatality.

More controversial still was a narrative experiment entitled *Dead Certainties* (1991), a work that mixed fact and fiction in recounting the deaths of an 18th-century British general and a 19th-century Boston Brahmin. However scandalous the book may have seemed to professional historians, it once again revealed Schama as a writer of extraordinary gifts. Its treatment of Benjamin West's memorable painting of the death of General Wolfe offered another brilliant example of Schama's skill as an analyst of iconography. And its account of the notorious murder trial of a Harvard professor not only demonstrated his forensic skills but also showed that he could practice microhistory as effectively as history on the grand scale.

Landscape and Memory (1995) brings to the fore once again Schama's concern with patriotic geography, the myths of national character that have been projected onto forests, mountains, and rivers. Just as the low-horizoned, boggy landscape of the Dutch had become a metaphor for a certain set of humble virtues, so Poles, Germans, and Americans have found usable self-images in their allegedly primeval forests; the French, the British, and the Italians have found the national character reflected in their principal rivers; and mountains have in the modern era become images of dreadful sublimity. What is extraordinary here is the chronological scope and geographical range of the argument, which extends from ancient Egypt to 20th-century America, or from the sacred hydraulics of Bernini's Rome to Anselm Kiefer's neo-Expressionist deconstructions of German history and mythology. This is perhaps Schama's most personal book, for it contains a moving evocation of his own family's history and its relation to the landscapes of Central and Eastern Europe, Britain, and North America.

In the conclusion of *Dead Certainties*, Schama invoked the models of Thucydides and Herodotus: politics and culture, analysis and anecdote, the rhetorical and the visual. His own work of course combines both of these models. In range, ambition, and style, he reminds one of the 19th-century masters of narrative history. Like Francis Parkman, about whom he has written a splendid chapter in *Dead Certainties*, he is a great and prolific student of the dialectic of nature and culture. But unlike Parkman, he has a sense of humor, and for sheer verve and brio his prose is hard to match. In mid-career, he has already earned a secure place among the modern masters of cultural history.

BRUCE THOMPSON

See also Consumerism; France: French Revolution; Low; Parkman; Political

Biography

Simon Michael Schama. Born London, 13 February 1945. Studied at Christ's College, Cambridge, BA 1966, MA 1969. Taught at Christ's College, 1966–76; Brasenose College, Oxford, 1976–80; Professor of history, Harvard University, 1980–93; and Columbia University from 1993. Art critic, the *New Yorker*, from 1995. Married Virginia Papaioannou, professor of anatomy and pathology, 1983 (1 son, 1 daughter).

Principal Writings

Patriots and Liberators: Revolution in the Netherlands, 1780–1813, 1977
Two Rothschilds and the Land of Israel, 1978
The Embarrassment of Riches: An Interpretation of Dutch Culture in the Golden Age, 1987
Citizens: A Chronicle of the French Revolution, 1989
Dead Certainties: Unwarranted Speculations, 1991
Landscape and Memory, 1995

Further Reading

Cobb, Richard, "Sitting Out the Revolution," *Times Literary Supplement* (29 July 1977), 906–07
Elliott, J.H., "From Bogs to Riches," *New Republic* 197 (24 August 1987), 28–31
Grafton, Anthony, "The Forest and the Trees," *New Republic* (7 August 1995), 37–42
Spitzer, Alan B., "Narrative Problems: The Case of Simon Schama," *Journal of Modern History* 65 (1993), 176–92
Steiner, George, "Two Hundred Years Young," *New Yorker* 65 (17 April 1989), 131–35

Schieder, Theodor 1908–1984

German historian

Theodor Schieder is one of the great German historians of the 20th century, praised by his colleagues as the Nestor of postwar practitioners of his vocation. His peers recognized his importance not only as an overarching historian, but also as one of Germany's foremost scholars, by inducting him into Germany's highest order of scholars and artists, Pour le Mérite.

Schieder became influential after 1948, when he was appointed to a chair at the University of Cologne. Schieder, whose love for the culture of Central Europe was his lifelong passion, had fled from East Prussia in 1944, where he had been professor at the University of Königsberg. In Cologne, Schieder influenced several generations of German historians, many of whom were his students, and contributed significantly to the survival of history as a venerable *Wissenschaft* through the turmoil of the late 1960s and early 1970s. Especially during those years, he defended rigorous, non-polemical research against those who sought to instrumentalize history. Influenced by the works of Jacob Burckhardt and others, he argued that the conflict between the investigation of the individual as a unique historical event and the quest of the social sciences to categorize all behavior by type permits the historian not only to evaluate any historical event by itself, but also to recognize its larger, lasting meaning. From 1957 until his death, Schieder edited Germany's oldest historical journal, *Historische Zeitschrift*. During his long career, he received scores of awards and honors. In addition to his membership in Pour le Mérite, he was president of Germany's premier historical academy, the Historical Commission of the Bavarian Academy of Sciences as well as a former president of the German Association of Historians and the Rhenish-Westphalian Academy of Sciences.

In an age where historians have become ever more specialized, Schieder was a committed generalist. The breadth of his research extended from the beginnings of the Prussian monarchy to the aftermath of World War II. Schieder's studies on the nation-state and nationalism in a European context, however, were his greatest historiographic contributions. In his essays on the subject, collected in *Nationalismus und Nationalstaat* (Nationalism and the Nation-State, 1991), Schieder attempted to reconcile his fundamental approval of the nation-state with the evils nationalism wrought on Europe. Influenced both by his studies and by his own experiences, Schieder frequently returned to the question of Germany's fate in Europe. In the end, he hoped for national reunification, which he did not live to witness. He believed that Germany could find a satisfying role for itself as one nation among equals in Europe, a role Schieder defined when he compared the German middle states of the 19th century with the European states of the 20th century, caught between the two superpowers. Schieder shared his vocation with a broader audience through his function as editor of the 7-volume *Handbuch der Europäischen Geschichte* (Handbook of European History, 1968–87). In the series, Schieder wrote the volume dealing with early 19th-century Europe and the volume addressing the height of European power before World War I.

For Schieder, World War II and the loss of his chosen home of Königsberg were the result of the exaggerated nationalism that occurred when a nation, in its quest for national self-fulfillment, ignored the European context of its development. Schieder, who was well-versed in all areas of German culture, considered the loss of Germany's eastern territories a great blow to Germany's cultural mission in Central Europe. Schieder collected the evidence of this catastrophe in his 5-volume *Dokumentation der Vertreibung der Deutschen aus Ost-Mitteleuropa* (1954–61; *Documents on the Expulsion of the Germans from Eastern-Central Europe*, 1956–61). Although flawed by the fact that Schieder and his staff did not start collecting the accounts of Germans refugees and expellees until ten years after the events themselves began, the number of documents and their intense quality, only slightly moderated by Schieder's judicious introductions, are incontrovertible proof that the horrors of World War II did not end with the cessation of hostilities.

While Schieder published numerous articles and books during his career, his greatest achievement was his 1983 biography of Frederick the Great of Prussia. This biography, which is a collection of essays rather than a strict narrative, perhaps most clearly shows his contribution to his profession. Above all, however, Schieder's sense of perspective and measure revealed themselves in his judiciousness which, more than anything else, established his authority as postwar Germany's foremost historian.

MARTIN R. MENKE

Biography

Born Bayrisch-Schwaben in Oettingen bei Nördlingen, 11 April 1908. Early education in Augsburg; studied history, German language, and geography, University of Munich to 1933, and University of Berlin to 1940. Taught at University of Konigsberg, 1942–44; and University of Cologne, 1948–84. Editor, *Historische Zeitschrift*, 1957–84. Married Eva Rogalsky, 1934 (4 children). Died 8 October 1984.

Principal Writings

Dokumentation der Vertreibung der Deutschen aus Ost-Mitteleuropa, 5 vols. in 8, 1954–61; reprinted 1984; in English as *Documents on the Expulsion of the Germans from Eastern-Central Europe*, 4 vols., 1956–61

Staat und Gesellschaft im Wandel unserer Zeit, 1958; in English as *The State and Society in Our Times: Studies in the History of the 19th and 20th Centuries*, 1962

Das Deutsche Kaiserreich von 1871 als Nationalstaat (The German Empire of 1871 as a Nation-State), 1961, 2nd edition 1992

Geschichte als Wissenschaft: Eine Einführung (History as Scholarship: An Introduction), 1965

Editor, *Handbuch der Europäischen Geschichte* (Handbook of European History), 7 vols., 1968–87

Zum Problem des Staatenpluralismus in der modernen Welt (Concerning the Problem of State Pluralism in the Modern World), 1969

Hermann Rauschnings "Gespräche mit Hitler" als Geschichtsquelle (Hermann Rauschning's "Conversations with Hitler" as Historical Evidence), 1972

Methodenprobleme der Geschichtswissenschaft (Methodological Problems in Historical Scholarship), 1974

Staatensystem als Vormacht der Welt, 1848–1918 (The System of State Alliances as Predominating Global Power, 1848–1918), 1977

Editor with Otto Dann, *Nationale Bewegung und soziale Organisationen: Vergleichende Studien zur nationalen Vereinsbewegung des 19. Jahrhunderts in Europa* (National Movement and Social Organizations: Comparative Studies on National Associations in 19th-Century Europe), 1978

"Die mittleren Staaten im System der Grossen Mächte (The Middle States within the Great Power System)," *Historische Zeitschrift* 232 (1981), 583–604

Friedrich der Grösse: Ein Königtum der Widersprüche (Frederick the Great: A Kingship of Contradictions), 1983

Über den Beinamen "der Grosse": Reflexionen über die historische Grosse (Concerning the Attribution "the Great:" Reflections on Historical Greatness), 1984

Editor with Otto Dann and Hans-Ulrich Wehler, *Nationalismus und Nationalstaat: Studien zum nationalen Problem im modernen Europa* (Nationalism and the Nation-State: Studies on the National Problem in Modern Europe), 1991

Further Reading

Allen, Peter, Wolfgang J. Mommsen, and Thomas Nipperdey, eds., *Geschichte und politisches Handeln: Studien zu europäischen*
Denkern der Neuzeit: Theodor Scheider zum Gedächtnis (History and Political Action: Studies on the European Thinkers of the Modern Age: In Memoriam Theodor Schieder), Stuttgart: Klett Cotta, 1985

Berding, Helmut, ed., *Vom Staat des Ancien Regime zum modernen Parteienstaat* (From the State of the Ancien Régime to the Modern Party State), Munich: Oldenbourg, 1978 [includes bibliography]

Broszat, Martin, "Nachruf auf Theodor Schieder" (Eulogy for Theodor Schieder), *Vierteljahrshefte für Zeitgeschichte* 32 (1984), 689–90

Gall, Lothar, "Theodor Schieder, 1908–1984," *Historische Zeitschrift* 241 (1985), 1–25

Hillgruber, Andreas, "Theodor Schieder zum 75. Geburtstag: Akademische Festveranstaltung in der Universität zu Köln am 16. April 1983" (On the Occasion of Theodor Schieder's 75th Birthday: Academic Celebration at Cologne University on 16 April 1983), Universität zu Köln, 1983

Kluxen, Kurt, and Wolfgang J. Mommsen, eds., *Politische Ideologien und nationalstaatliche Ordnung: Studien zur Geschichte des 19. und 20. Jahrhunderts: Festschrift für Theodor Schieder* (Political Ideologies and the Order of the Nation State: Studies in 19th- and 20th-Century History: *Festschrift* for Theodor Schieder), Munich: Oldenbourg, 1968

Mommsen, Wolfgang J., "Vom Beruf des Historikers in einer Zeit beschleunigten Wandels: Theodor Schieders historiographisches Werk" (The Historical Profession in a Time of Accelerated Change: The Historiographical Work of Theodor Schieder), *Vierteljahrshefte für Zeitgeschichte* 33 (1985), 387–405

Schlesinger, Arthur M., Jr. 1917–

US historian and biographer

Arthur M. Schlesinger, Jr., probably the best known and most controversial United States historian of the later 20th century, was literally born into the United States historical tradition. His father, Arthur M. Schlesinger, Sr., was for many years a distinguished professor of history at Harvard University, while his mother was descended from the eminent 19th-century historian George Bancroft. By the time he reached twenty their son had decided to emulate his forebears. He combined the narrative sweep and huge scale of Bancroft's works with a theory first expounded by his father, that the underlying pattern of United States history is a cyclical one of periods of conservatism, in which the power of business becomes dangerously strong, followed in approximately thirty-year intervals by bursts of reform designed to remedy the previous abuses.

Schlesinger was a diligent researcher and prolific writer of highly readable history. His lengthy, graceful volumes became prizewinning bestsellers and he was quickly recognized as the most distinguished American chronicler of what he perceived as the Democratic party's record of laudable centrist liberalism. A biography of Orestes A. Brownson (1939), his revised Harvard University senior undergraduate thesis, was followed by *The Age of Jackson* (1945); the three volumes of *The Age of Roosevelt* (1957, 1959, 1960); *A Thousand Days: John F. Kennedy in the White House* (1965); and *Robert Kennedy and His Times* (1978). Between them, these books give a record of the Democratic party's outstanding achievements, from the time of Andrew Jackson, when, according to Schlesinger, reformers embraced Hamiltonian, centralizing governmental powers in order to achieve Jeffersonian aims of equality and justice; through the New Deal of Franklin D. Roosevelt, which continued this process; to the tragically truncated careers of John F. Kennedy and his brother Robert. He structured his historical narratives around the careers of strong, heroic leaders, statesmen who, in his view, inspired their followers and the American people to rise to new challenges and overcome them.

Schlesinger's work, particularly his well-received early volumes on Jackson and Roosevelt, stressed the role of class conflict in American history. He argued that the Jacksonians included not simply disgruntled western farmers, but working men from the large eastern urban centers, allied with liberal intellectuals – a grouping that anticipated the New Deal coalition. This interpretation stressed the role of conflict in the emergence and adaptation of American political institutions and programs, an emphasis, as Schlesinger himself noted, at variance with the prevailing historiographical consensus school of American history in the 1950s, but in the tradition of such Progressive historians as Charles A. Beard and Vernon Parrington. Some critics, however, noted that in practice Schlesinger's interpretation focused on conflict but did so within a broader consensus as to the acceptable range of alternatives open to the United States. In those periods he studied, the successful reformers he clearly admired accepted the existing capitalist economic system and the United States Constitution as givens, and merely wished to adapt them to changing times.

Such an emphasis accorded well with Schlesinger's own political views and activities. He combined his academic career as a professor of history at Harvard University with deep involvement in Democratic party politics, and throughout his career wrote extensively on political matters for such influential journals of opinion as the *New York Times Magazine*, the *Saturday Evening Post*, *Harper's*, and the *Atlantic Monthly*. Over the years, he published several collections of such essays on topical themes, among them *The Vital Center* (1949), *The Politics of Hope* (1963), *The Bitter Heritage* (1967), and *The Crisis of Confidence* (1973), volumes that charted his course from an essentially optimistic outlook concerning his country's domestic and international policies to a qualified pessimism. A centrist, Schlesinger rejected the extremes of both conservatism and radical socialism or communism in favor of what he termed liberalism, essentially policies of New Deal reform at home and Cold War anticommunism abroad. Heavily influenced by the popular theologian Reinhold Niebuhr, he argued that practical politicians must be prepared to compromise and on occasion to use less than attractive means in order to attain at least part of their aims, and that it was necessary for the United States to combat the evil of totalitarianism abroad, even at the risk of war. In the 1940s, when Schlesinger first expressed his political credo, he was in accord with the prevailing Democratic party ethos. During the 1950s Schlesinger, seeking another heroic Democratic leader, attached himself first to Adlai Stevenson, in whose presidential campaigns he served as a speechwriter, and then to the young, Harvard-educated senator John F. Kennedy, whom he regarded as the embodiment of pragmatic liberalism. When the latter won election to the White House in 1960, he appointed Schlesinger to the ill-defined position of special assistant to the president, in which post Schlesinger gathered the raw material for his subsequent account of the Kennedy presidency.

It has often been suggested that Schlesinger's political activities and his close association with the Kennedy family were detrimental to his later historical writing. He himself strongly denied this, and alongside his two somewhat hagiographical volumes on the Kennedy brothers, he continued to write prolifically, producing many short pieces on history and politics. Even so, despite his frequent promises to return to it, his history of the Roosevelt administration is still incomplete, as the third volume ended in 1936. His study *The Imperial Presidency* (1973) drew attention to the dangerous increase in the powers of the presidency, but was criticized as too favorable in its treatment of Democratic presidents, even as he supported the impeachment of Richard Nixon. His collected historical essays, *The Cycles of American History* (1986), won high praise from his peers, while in *The Disuniting of America* (1991) he crossed swords with those who would misrepresent the past in the interests of political correctness and the enhanced self-esteem of particular minority groups. In his eighth decade, an unrepentant mid-20th-century liberal centrist who found himself out of sympathy with the prevailing political climate, Schlesinger remains the foremost American embodiment of a historian who combines academic concerns with political engagement.

PRISCILLA M. ROBERTS

See also Political; United States: 19th Century; United States: 20th Century; United States: Historical Writing, 20th Century; Williams, W.

Biography

Arthur Meier Schlesinger, Jr. Born Columbus, Ohio, 15 October 1917; son of historian Arthur Schlesinger, Sr. and descendant of George S. Bancroft. Educated at Cambridge Latin School; Phillips Academy; received BA, Harvard University, 1938; fellow, Peterhouse, Cambridge, 1938–39. Served in Office of War Information, 1942–43; Office of Strategic Services, 1943–45; US Army, 1945. Taught at Harvard University, 1946–60, then took leave to work in the John F. Kennedy presidential campaign; special assistant to the President of the US, Washington, DC, 1961–64; remained in Washington to write, 1964–66; professor, City University of New York, from 1966. Married 1) Marian Cannon, 1940 (marriage dissolved 1970; 2 sons, 2 daughters); 2) Alexandra Emmet, 1971 (1 son).

Principal Writings

Orestes A. Brownson: A Pilgrim's Progress, 1939
The Age of Jackson, 1945
The Vital Center: The Politics of Freedom, 1949
With Richard H. Rovere, *The General and the President*, 1951; as *General MacArthur and President Truman*, 1992
The Age of Roosevelt, 3 vols., 1957–60
The Politics of Hope, 1963
A Thousand Days: John F. Kennedy in the White House, 1965
The Bitter Heritage: Vietnam and American Democracy, 1941–1966, 1967
General editor, *History of American Presidential Elections, 1789–1968*, 4 vols., 1971; supplemental volume, 1972–1984, 1986
The Crisis of Confidence: Ideas, Power, and Violence in America, 1973
Editor, *History of US Political Parties*, 4 vols., 1973
The Imperial Presidency, 1973
Robert Kennedy and His Times, 1978

The Cycles of American History, 1986
The Disuniting of America, 1991

Further Reading

Brogan, Hugh, "The Uses of American History," *Reviews in American History* 15 (1987), 521–26

Cole, Donald B., "*The Age of Jackson*: After Forty Years," *Reviews in American History* 14 (1986), 149–59

Cunliffe, Marcus, "Arthur M. Schlesinger, Jr," in Marcus Cunliffe and Robin Winks, eds., *Pastmasters: Some Essays on American Historians*, New York: Harper, 1969

Depoe, Stephen P., *Arthur M. Schlesinger, Jr., and the Ideological History of American Liberalism*, Tuscaloosa: University of Alabama Press, 1994

Engelhardt, Carroll, "Man in the Middle: Arthur M. Schlesinger, Jr., and Postwar American Liberalism," *South Atlantic Quarterly* 80 (1981), 119–42

Kraus, Michael, and Davis D. Joyce, *The Writing of American History*, revised edition, Norman: University of Oklahoma Press, 1985

Lemisch, Jesse, *On Active Service in War and Peace: Politics and Ideology in the American Historical Profession*, Toronto: New Hogtown Press, 1975

Miles, Edwin A., "Arthur M. Schlesinger, Jr.," in Clyde N. Wilson, ed., *Twentieth-Century American Historians*, Detroit: Gale, 1983 [*Dictionary of Literary Biography*, vol. 17]

Morton, Marian J., *The Terrors of Ideological Politics: Liberal Historians in a Conservative Mood*, Cleveland: Press of Case Western Reserve University, 1972

Nuechterlein, James A., "Arthur M. Schlesinger, Jr., and the Discontents of Postwar American Liberalism," *Review of Politics* 39 (1977), 3–40

Reinitz, Richard, *Irony and Consciousness: American Historiography and Reinhold Niebuhr's Vision*, Lewisburg, PA: Bucknell University Press, 1980

Ross, Mitchell S., *The Literary Politicians*, Garden City, NY: Doubleday, 1978

Schlesinger, Arthur M., Jr., *In Retrospect: The History of a Historian*, New York: Harcourt Brace, 1963

Sternsher, Bernard, *Consensus, Conflict, and American Historians*, Bloomington: Indiana University Press, 1975

Schlözer, August Ludwig von 1735–1809

German historian

August Ludwig von Schlözer was a key figure among the leading historians of the German Enlightenment both as regards his methodological studies of universal history and his commitment to the reform of the study of history. Among his pupils were such eminent figures as von Humboldt, Hardenberg, Gentz, von Stein, and von Müller. Not only did he write influential historical, political, and pedagogical works, but he also founded several journals with large circulations: *Briefwechsel meist historischen und politischen Inhalts* (1778–81), succeeded by *Staatsanzeigen* (1782–95) and the later *Neueste Staatsanzeigen* (1796–1800). Empirically belonging more to the philosophy of the Enlightenment than to the historical thinking of the early 19th century, this journal in 1791 published the first German translation of the French Revolution's "Declaration of the Rights of Man and of the Citizen."

Schlözer can also be described as a publicist whose historico-political journals helped to develop a bourgeois public opinion. It was for this, probably more than as a historian, that he was best remembered during the 19th century. In his own time, however, he appeared most effective as a critical theorist of history. His famous 5-volume edition of Nestor's Russian annals (1802–09), studies of the history of northern Europe and of Russia, a history of Leipzig, studies of German expansion to the east, on statistics, universal history, and his famous world history for children (1779) are best understood in the context of his ideas on historical work.

Schlözer was deeply influenced by the development of the life sciences and their critique of traditional models of scientific explanation. Buffon's *Histoire naturelle* (1749–67) and Linnaeus' system of classification, for example, had an important impact on those who rejected existing mechanistic and empiricist modes of understanding. Herder, whom Schlözer considered to be a representative of conservative ideas famously expressed in his *Auch eine Philosophie der Geschichte der Bildung der Menschheit* (Also a Philosophy of History for the Education of Mankind, 1774), consequently wrote a critical review of Schlözer's *Vorstellung einer Universal-Historie* (Introduction to a Universal History, 1772–73). Other influences, apart from the Göttingen school and German historians such as Gatterer, Michaelis, Achenwall, Pütter, and Böhmer, came from the West European Enlightenment, in particular the French and Scottish theories of progress represented by the works of Montesquieu, Turgot, and Condorcet, as well as Ferguson, Millar, and Robertson. Further, Schlözer's *Vorstellung* is reminiscent of Voltaire's *Essai sur les moeurs et l'esprit des nations* (1756; *Essay on the Manner and Spirit of Nations*, 1780), an attempt to set a philosophy of history against the theologically based universal history of Bossuet. Finally, for his studies in northern European and Russian history Schlözer was indebted to Tatiscev and Lomonosov, and it was his interest in East European history that distinguished him from many of his colleagues.

More than any other 18th-century German works of historiography, Schlözer's studies are characterized by critical methods combined with an interest in the social, anthropological, geographical, ethnological, and linguistic aspects of universal history. Although he accepted political history as an important element of world history – he thought that the past could be relevant for the present – Schlözer devoted himself at least as much to social, economic, and cultural history as to the history of technology, of morals and manners, and of ideas. He no longer approved of an obsequious court-oriented historiography (*Regentengeschichte*). Instead, he demanded a comparative social, economic, cultural, even humanitarian perspective that mirrored the bourgeoisie's process of emancipation, and with which the bourgeoisie could identify. The history of tobacco or of the potato was as interesting to him as the history of kings. The history of mankind and the history of the bourgeoisie were equated; social history took the place of the history of monarchs. Regarding the historical process as a sequence of "revolutions," Schlözer first investigated the natural changes that had transformed man's living conditions. He then studied political upheavals on the one hand, and changes in civilization on the other. This approach allowed him to integrate a chronological method (*Zeitzusammenhang*) with a synchronic and analytical one (*Realzusammenhang*), rather as Gatterer had done.

It was more important for Schlözer for a systematic analysis to reveal causal connections than to establish sequences. He therefore constructed for historiography what had already been employed in the life sciences. His concept of universal history aimed to show how individual facts and general historical tendencies conditioned each other in historical experiences that could be described as conjunction and interaction. Accordingly, facts could not be seen in isolation but had to be regarded as part of a complex whole, a system of integrated events. The historical organization of the material, according to the links that different events generated, would consequently not follow a linear and mechanical order, but a complex order of inter-connections. The historian's task was to establish this context in order to make the singular understandable. His aim was to see the organic whole in order to appreciate the uniqueness of the singular. Schlözer's idea of history followed the historicization of the life sciences.

This can well be traced in his *Vorstellung einer Universal-Historie*, which makes an important theoretical contribution to 18th-century historiography, especially in its epistemological attempt to construct history as a science. In asking which peoples should be included in a world history, Schlözer addressed the problem of how to write a modern universal history. In the first edition of the *Vorstellung* he had distinguished between only two epochs of world history (ancient and modern), but in a later publication, *Weltgeschichte nach ihren Haupt-Theilen im Auszug und Zusammenhange* (Extracts and Overview of the Main Parts of a History of the World, 1785–89) he was receptive to new findings on systematizing a chronology.

Here it became obvious that he was looking for a "plan" for how to write a scientific, theoretically based history, distinct from the hitherto fashionable polyhistory, which merely assembled and described historical facts. He discussed his "plan" with his readers. It was intended to serve as an orientation for his students, and to contribute to the current scholarly debate. According to Schlözer, Enlightenment historiography could be applied to contemporary problems, since it was practical and characterized by open reflection and argument. This appreciation of open discourse distinguished him from the priestly demeanour of the next generation of historicists.

BENEDIKT STUCHTEY

See also Russia: Medieval; Universal

Biography

Born Gaggstadt, Hohenlohe-Kirchberg, 5 July 1735, descended from Protestant pastors. Studied theology at Wittenberg before turning to philology, Oriental linguistics, and medicine at University of Göttingen. Travelled to Sweden, where he served as a tutor, 1755–59; worked at the Academy of Sciences, St. Petersburg, 1761–67; professor, University of Göttingen, 1769–1804. Ennobled 1804. Married Caroline Roederer, 1769 (5 children). Died Göttingen, 9 September 1809.

Principal Writings

Versuch einer allgemeinen Geschichte des Handels und der Seefahrt in den ältesten Zeiten (An Attempt at the General History of Trade and of Seafaring in the Most Ancient Times), 1761 [originally written in Swedish, 1758]

Allgemeine Nordische Geschichte (General Nordic History), 2 vols., 1771

Vorstellung einer Universal-Historie (Introduction to a Universal History), 1772–73

Vorbereitung zur Weltgeschichte für Kinder (Introduction to World History for Children), 1779

Weltgeschichte nach ihren Haupt-Theilen im Auszug und Zusammenhange (Extracts and Overview of the Main Parts of a History of the World), 2 vols., 1785–89

Translator, *Nestor Russische Annalen in ihrer Slavonischen Grundsprache verglichen, übersetzt und erklärt* (Nestor's Russian Annals to 980 CE), 5 vols., 1802–09

Theorie der Statistik: nebst Ideen über das Studium der Politik überhaupt (Theory of Statistics and General Ideas about the Study of Political Science), 1804

Further Reading

Becher, Ursula A.J., *Politische Gesellschaft: Studien zur Genese bürgerlicher Öffentlichkeit in Deutschland* (Political Society: Studies on the Genesis of a Bourgeois Public Sphere in Germany), Göttingen: Vandenhoeck & Ruprecht, 1978

Becher, Ursula A.J., "August Ludwig von Schlözer," in Hans-Ulrich Wehler, ed., *Deutsche Historiker*, vol. 7, Göttingen: Vandenhoeck & Ruprecht, 1980

Becher, Ursula A.J., "August Ludwig von Schlözer – Analyse eines historischen Diskurses" (Schlözer: Analysis of a Historical Discourse), in Hans Erich Bödeker *et al.*, eds., *Aufklärung und Geschichte: Studien zur deutschen Geschichtswissenschaft im 18. Jahrhundert*, Göttingen: Vandenhoeck & Ruprecht, 1986

Butterfield, Herbert, *Man on His Past: The Study of the History of Historical Scholarship*, Cambridge: Cambridge University Press, 1955; Boston: Beacon Press, 1960

Hennies, Werner, *Die politische Theorie August Ludwig von Schlözers zwischen Aufklärung und Liberalismus* (The Political Theory of August Ludwig von Schlözer, Between Enlightenment and Liberalism), Munich: Tuduv, 1985

Mühlpfordt, Günter, "Völkergeschichte statt Fürstenhistorie: Schlözer als Begründer der kritisch-ethnischen Geschichtsforschung" (History of Peoples vs. History of Sovereigns: Schlözer as the Founder of Critical-Ethical History), *Jahrbuch für Geschichte* 25 (1982), 23–72

Mühlpfordt, Günter, "August Ludwig Schlözer und die 'Wahre Demokratie': Geschichts- und Obrigkeitskritik eines Anwalts der Unterdrückten unter dem Absolutismus" (August Ludwig Schlözer and the 'True Democracy': A Critique of History and Authority by a Lawyer of the Oppressed under Absolutism), *Jahrbuch des Instituts für Deutsche Geschichte* 12 (1983), 29–73

Saage, Richard, "August Ludwig Schlözer als politischer Theoretiker" (August Ludwig Schlözer as a Political Theoretician), in Hans-Georg Herrlitz and Horst Kern, eds., *Anfänge Göttinger Sozialwissenschaft: Methoden, Inhalte und soziale Prozesse im 18. und 19. Jahrhundert*, Göttingen; Vandenhoeck & Ruprecht, 1987

Warlich, B., *August Ludwig von Schlözer (1735–1809) zwischen Reform und Revolution: Ein Beitrag zur Pathogenese frühliberalen Staatsdenkens im späten 18. Jahrhundert* (Schlözer Between Reform and Revolution: A Contribution to the Pathogenesis of the Early Liberal Ideology of the State in the Late 18th Century), dissertation, University of Erlangen, 1972

Schnabel, Franz 1887–1966
German historian

Among the classic works of 20th-century German historical scholarship Franz Schnabel's *Deutsche Geschichte im neunzehnten Jahrhundert* (German History in the 19th Century, 1929–37) is not only of outstanding importance on academic grounds, but also of lasting popularity and instructiveness.

Until the relatively recent accounts of Thomas Nipperdey and Hans-Ulrich Wehler, Schnabel's studies on the 19th century were long unchallenged for their full descriptions, elegance of style, clarity of argument, and the variety of questions addressed both in terms of history in general and of German history in particular. Schnabel's history is, however, limited to the Vormärz period: he concentrated on and effectively restricted himself to the period between the late 18th and the early 19th century, the climax of the *Bürgertum*. What he understood by the bourgeois age was not only the economic and social predominance of a class but particularly the process of its political emancipation. That this emancipation was less successful in Germany than elsewhere in Western Europe gave German history its special image: here the collective was more strongly developed than the individual need for liberty. But Schnabel's skeptical interpretation of history reflected at the same time the necessity of believing in the idealistic nature of men regardless of historical failures.

A list of Schnabel's publications contains 521 entries covering a wide field of topics. Undoubtedly the four volumes of his *Deutsche Geschichte* are his masterpiece. This work gave him an international reputation and, in fact, came closest to fulfilling the task that Schnabel set himself: to write history on a large scale ("Geschichtsschreibung grossen Stils"). By this he meant describing all aspects of an epoch by combining political, religious, and cultural history, and – something that is probably most significant in the first volume of the *Deutsche Geschichte* – offering a European perspective, with which Schnabel overcame the Treitschkean national categories that were still quite fashionable in Weimar historiography. He aimed to show the context in which the single facts of history were rooted; the individual had to be deduced from the whole. In fact, Schnabel was the first after Treitschke to write a large-scale German history, and he certainly did not adopt an antinational approach. But unlike many historians of his time, Schnabel did not idealize the nation-state of 1871. That is why, in his *Deutsche Geschichte*, he put German *Geistesgeschichte* into a European context. Also, he was not an opponent of the Weimar republic, which was regarded by many as a symbol of national decline. Rather he was one of its defenders against, for example, von Papen whose politics in July 1932 – when he tried to abolish the federalist character of the republic – Schnabel strongly criticized using cultural and economic arguments.

Further he had a deep inner dislike for that which he regarded as characteristic of Bismarck's bureaucratic and military state: the bourgeoisie's lack of interest in self-government and of a sense of political responsibility. Here Schnabel's point of view was partly based on a tradition of liberalism from southwestern Germany to which he devoted *Geschichte der Ministerverantwortlichkeit in Baden* (History of Ministerial Responsibility in Baden, 1922) and two biographies, *Sigismund von Reitzenstein* (1927) and *Ludwig von Liebenstein* (1927). Before Schnabel went to the University of Munich, where he taught from 1947 to 1962, his academic positions were director of the Nordbadisches Kultur- und Unterrichtswesen (Cultural and Educational System in North Baden) and from 1922 the chair of history at the Technical University of Karlsruhe where he stayed until his forced retirement by the Nazis in 1936. Because he taught students in Karlsruhe who wanted to become engineers, architects, physicists, chemists, etc., he committed

himself to integrating natural history and the history of technology into his historical reflections, and thereby tried to make history accessible to a general community of students and readers. Without this personal background the famous third volume of the *Deutsche Geschichte* which dealt with the humanities and the sciences would hardly have been written.

Schnabel's academic and political philosophy was deeply rooted in a European humanism that searched for a comprehensive understanding of the world. His favorite age was the 19th century on which his work focused and from whose historicism he was never really free. Like Jacob Burckhardt's *The Civilization of the Renaissance in Italy*, Schnabel's major opus remained a torso, and for Schnabel, as for Burckhardt, it was the impact of the age of humanism on the emergence of the bourgeoisie in the 19th century that most interested him. In 1931 he published *Deutschlands geschichtliche Quellen und Darstellungen in der Neuzeit* (German Historical Sources and Accounts in the Early Modern Period). Believing in the values of humanism Schnabel also shared with Burckhardt a cultural skepticism (in the face of the events of the 20th century) which remained with him despite his idealism and his belief in the power of education.

Yet after World War II he published *Der Buchhandel und der geistige Aufstieg der abendländischen Völker* (The Book Trade and the Intellectual Rise of the Western People, 1951) and *Das humanistische Bildungsgut im Wandel von Staat und Gesellschaft* (Humanist Education in a Changing State and Society, 1956) in which he traced the history of education in Europe from the 16th century. A further characteristic Schnabel shared with Burckhardt was his neglect of the archives. With the exception of his studies on the history of Baden and his account of the history of the Historical Commission of the Bavarian Academy of Science – "Die Idee und die Erscheinung" (The Idea and the Manifestation, 1958) – Schnabel did not really work with archival material. He gave his students to understand that his pedagogical experiences of teaching in school had had a greater impact on his academic career than anything else. Schnabel used historical material that was already known, and when he talked of the "dust of the libraries" he meant that particularly important sources for the historian were the classical texts of former historians that needed to be looked at in a fresh light: a Burckhardtian declaration of highly professional amateurism.

In 1923 Schnabel published *1789–1919*, a schoolbook that ran into numerous editions. It was so successful because he worked out the central problems of the period he was describing rather than merely collecting facts as was common for textbooks at that time. By developing the interconnections between the political, social, economic, and intellectual aspects of his topic, Schnabel's synthesis had a much stronger impact, academic as well as educational, on his readership than a special study could achieve. This was also the formula for the success of his *Deutsche Geschichte*. Schnabel may be rightly called the first German historian to have achieved the aim of linking academic and general life. As a result he had a considerable influence on postwar German historiography. In addition his cultural-historical approach was more deeply developed than, for example, Meinecke's, whose concentration on the history of ideas basically remained politically oriented. On the other hand, Schnabel, with Burckhardt, rejected Karl

Lamprecht's methodological starting point of structuring cultural history via collective laws. Nor did he give priority to social and economic history.

But despite his closeness to Burckhardt, Schnabel was a political historian. His openness to cultural history was directed less toward the aesthetics of high art than to technology and the natural sciences. A work such as Johan Huizinga's *Herbst des Mittelalters* (*The Waning of the Middle Ages*) would have been an impossible undertaking for Schnabel. Schnabel devoted the second volume of the *Deutsche Geschichte* to the monarchy and constitutionalism. The national movement naturally deserved a volume to itself (which would have been the – unpublished – fifth, and the only one to go as far as the Revolution of 1848/49), but instead he studied the role of the Catholic and Protestant churches. All in all, his approach to history was a Christian, or to be more precise, a Catholic one, although his was definitely not *gross-deutsch* in the fashion of Heinrich von Srbik. This naturally distinguished him from Borussian admirers of Bismarck such as Erich Marcks.

BENEDIKT STUCHTEY

See also Germany: Modern

Biography

Born Mannheim, 18 December 1887. Attended Gymnasium, Mannheim; studied at the universities of Heidelberg and Berlin, receiving PhD. Professor, Technical University of Karlsruhe, 1922–36 (forced out by Nazis); and University of Munich, 1947–66. Died Munich, 25 February 1966.

Principal Writings

Der Zusammenschluss des politischen Katholizismus in Deutschland im Jahre 1848 (The Amalgamation of Political Catholicism in Germany in 1848), 1910

Geschichte der Ministerverantwortlichkeit in Baden (History of Ministerial Responsibility in Baden), 1922

1789–1919: Eine Einführung in die Geschichte der neuesten Zeit (1789–1919: Introduction to Modern History), 1923

Ludwig von Liebenstein: Ein Geschichtsbild aus den Anfängen des süddeutschen Verfassungslebens (Ludwig von Liebenstein: A Historical Picture from the Origins of South-German Constitutional Life), 1927

Sigismund von Reitzenstein: Der Begründer des badischen Staates (Sigismund von Reitzenstein: Founder of the State of Baden), 1927

Deutsche Geschichte im neunzehnten Jahrhundert (German History in the 19th Century), 4 vols., 1929–37

Deutschlands geschichtliche Quellen und Darstellungen in der Neuzeit: Das Zeitalter der Reformation, 1500–1550 (German Historical Sources and Accounts in the Early Modern Period: The Age of the Reformation, 1500–1550), 1931

Freiherr vom Stein, 1931

Der Buchhandel und der geistige Aufstieg der abendländischen Völker (The Book Trade and the Intellectual Rise of the Western People), 1951

Das humanistische Bildungsgut im Wandel von Staat und Gesellschaft (Humanist Education in a Changing State and Society), 1956

"Die Idee und die Erscheinung" (The Idea and the Manifestation), in his *Die Historische Kommission bei der Bayerischen Akademie der Wissenschaft* (The Historical Commission of the Bavarian Academy of Science), 1958

Alexander von Humboldt, 1959

Further Reading

Angermann, Erich, "Zum fünften Band von Franz Schnabels *Deutsche Geschichte im neunzehnten Jahrhundert*" (On the Fifth Volume of Franz Schnabel's *German History in the 19th Century*), *Historische Zeitschrift* 247 (1988), 603–12

Bahners, Patrick, "Kritik und Erneuerung: Der Historismus bei Franz Schnabel" (Criticism and Changing: The Historism of Franz Schnabel), *Tel Aviver Jahrbuch für deutsche Geschichte* 25 (1996), 117–53

Gall, Lothar, "Franz Schnabel," in Lothar Gall, ed., *Die grossen Deutschen unserer Epoche* (The Great Germans of Our Age), Berlin: Propyläen, 1985

Hertfelder, Thomas, *Franz Schnabel und die deutsche Geschichtswissenschaft: Geschichtsschreibung zwischen Historismus und Kulturkritik, 1910–1945* (Franz Schnabel and German Historical Science: Historiography Between Historism and Cultural Criticism, 1910–1945), Göttingen: Vandenhoeck & Ruprecht, 1998

Historische Kommission bei der Bayerischen Akademie der Wissenschaften, ed., *Franz Schnabel, Zu Leben und Werk (1887–1966): Vorträge zur Feier seines 100. Geburtstages* (Franz Schnabel, His Life and Work, 1887–1966: Lectures in Honor of his 100th Birthday), Munich: Oldenbourg, 1988

Lönne, Karl Egon, "Franz Schnabel," in Hans-Ulrich Wehler, ed., *Deutsche Historiker*, Göttingen: Vandenhoeck & Ruprecht, 1982, vol. 9, 81–101

Lutz, Heinrich, ed., *Franz Schnabel: Abhandlungen und Vorträge, 1914–1965* (Franz Schnabel: Transactions and Lectures, 1914–1965), Freiburg: Herder, 1970

Schubert, Friedrich Hermann, "Franz Schnabel und die Geschichtswissenschaft des 20. Jahrhunderts" (Franz Schnabel and Historical Science in the 20th Century), *Historische Zeitschrift* 205 (1967), 323–57

Straub, Eberhard, "Ein unzeitgemässer Chronist: Franz Schnabels Deutsche Geschichte des 19. Jahrhunderts" (An Old-Fashioned Chronicler: Franz Schnabel's *German History in the 19th Century*), *Die politische Meinung* 235 (1987), 83–90

Zeeden, Ernst Walter, "Das Jahrhundert des Bürgertums: Franz Schnabels *Deutsche Geschichte im neunzehnten Jahrhundert*" (The Century of the Bourgeoisie: Franz Schnabel's *German History in the 19th Century*), *Saeculum* 3 (1952), 509–21

Schorske, Carl E. 1915–
US cultural and intellectual historian

Carl E. Schorske has been among the most creative practitioners of interdisciplinary and cultural history in the late 20th century. After launching his career with a conventional political and intellectual study, *German Social Democracy, 1905–1917* (1955), Schorske, under the influence of Marxian and Freudian theory and amidst the political turmoil of the 1960s, when he taught at the University of California at Berkeley, began to publish on themes of generational rebellion and the rise of radical modernism in late 19th-century Europe. As a test case, he chose to focus on turn-of-the-century Vienna, capital of the multi-national Habsburg empire and seedbed of modernist trends in elite culture (psychoanalysis, logical positivism, expressionism, musical atonality) as well as political pathologies (strident rhetoric, ideological mobilization, extremist nationalism, anti-Semitism). In the 1960s and 1970s he published a series of imaginative essays on Vienna as a crucible for the aesthetic avante-garde and radical, antiliberal consciousness; his approach was a highly personalized blend of traditional cultural history and literary criticism, sociology of knowledge, and psycho-analytic interpretation. In article form, Schorske's ideas attracted mainly specialists in intellectual and Habsburg history, but in 1979 the scattered essays were combined with a methodological introduction and three previously unpublished pieces to produce a bestselling volume entitled *Fin-de-Siècle Vienna: Politics and Culture*. Schorske's significance for modern historiography rests mainly on this one work.

The book's introduction was both a personal testament and a statement of interdisciplinary purpose. As a new teacher in the late 1940s, Schorske recalled, he was drawn to the problem of linkages between high culture and social change. In the bleak aftermath of World War II he searched for new ways to understand this relationship. The optimistic terms that previous historians had often used for this purpose – rationalism, progress, liberalism – seemed inadequate to the task of one who wished to explain the roots of postwar disillusionment, and was himself a product of the modern temper of disenchantment. In place of the older, humanistic consensus that once surrounded the terms of cultural analysis, Schorske concluded, a series of separate disciplines had emerged – sociology, psychology, anthropology, art history, and musicology – each with its own specialized theories and vocabularies for explaining social and cultural change. He therefore turned to some of these disciplines in search of new interpretive paradigms, devising a "post-holing" strategy based on a series of methodologically and thematically distinct, essay-length inquiries. These included a reflection on cultural malaise in the tales and poetry of Arthur Schnitzler and Hugo von Hofmannsthal; a two-part meditation on the garden as symbol of social change in Austrian literature, painting, and music; a consideration of the rise of mass politics and anti-Semitism as mirrored in the lives of three charismatic personalities (Theodor Herzl, Karl Lueger, and Georg von Schönerer); an excavation of the roots of psychoanalysis in a dream of Freud; an interpretation of architectural styles employed along Vienna's circular boulevard, the Ringstrasse; and a study of the breakthrough to modern aestheticism in the paintings and murals of Gustav Klimt. Each essay was, in Schorske's words, a "separate foray into the terrain"; in each instance he tried to use the terms and concepts devised by disciplinary specialists – literary critics, art historians, psychoanalysts, etc. – to study diverse facets of high culture. Thus, to depict the rise of modernism in architecture and city planning (the Ringstrasse essay), he read city plans and urban structures as "texts," employing the terms of "specialized internal analysis" of fields such as architecture, art history, urban geography, and city planning. The end result of the combined essays was not a smooth narrative in the traditional sense, but a mosaic of pieces joined by Schorske's urge to explore high culture and sociopolitical change – especially the theme of art as an escape from politics – and by an alloy of Freudian and Marxian assumptions centering on the notions of "ideology" and oedipal revolt.

Though a commercial and critical success – it received a Pulitzer prize for general nonfiction – *Fin-de-Siècle Vienna* generated heated debate among scholars while arousing new interest in the hitherto under-researched field of late Habsburg history. Many agreed that Schorske's approach to elite cultural history was one of special significance and some predicted that the book would become a classic of the genre, in the tradition of Jacob Burckhardt's *The Civilization of the Renaissance in Italy* (1860, translated 1904) or Johan Huizinga's *The Waning of the Middle Ages* (1919, translated 1924). Conversely, much criticism centered on Schorske's post-holing technique, which required him to look intensely at a few select cases instead of viewing Vienna's cultural life as a whole. The result, from the standpoint of some of his critics, was not a sustained and comprehensive analysis, but a sampling of vignettes on subjects chosen merely according to the author's personal taste. It was, in fact, an extremely selective picture of Vienna's cultural life. In depicting the rebellion of the city's radical sons, for instance, Schorske displayed little interest in exploring the ethos of their liberal fathers – rather as if Turgenev, in his novel *Fathers and Sons*, had failed to take the older generation seriously. Yet Schorske's defenders countered by recalling the traditional rule that an author should be judged on the book he has written, not the one reviewers may wish him to write. Another contentious issue was Schorske's appeal to psychoanalytic theory. Critics objected that Freudian theory was now in disrepute, even in psychology itself, and that Schorske forced his data into a dubious oedipal framework. Others replied that critics of the book's Freudian underpinnings failed to credit its striking synthetic vision. Yet even admirers often found that Schorske's ideas in this specific regard lacked adequate factual basis. Still, *Fin-de-Siècle Vienna* was undoubtedly a major achievement of belletristic historiography. Despite its flaws, many would agree that Schorske's work stands as an impressive testament to one scholar's historical imagination, as one model of interdisciplinary reasoning, and as a legitimation of elite cultural history in an age of increasing emphasis on the study of popular culture.

HARRY RITTER

See also Austro-Hungarian; Cultural

Biography

Carl Emil Schorske. Born New York City, 15 March 1915. Received BA, Columbia University, 1936; MA, Harvard University, 1937; PhD 1950. Staff member, Office of Strategic Services, 1941–46; served in United States Naval Reserve, 1943–46. Taught at Wesleyan University, 1946–60; University of California, Berkeley, 1960–69; and Princeton University, 1969–80 (emeritus). Married Elizabeth Gilbert Rorke, 1941 (4 sons, 1 daughter).

Principal Writings

German Social Democracy, 1905–1917: The Development of the Great Schism, 1955

Fin-de-Siècle Vienna: Politics and Culture, 1979

Kandinsky in Munich, 1896–1914, 1982

Gustav Mahler: Formation and Transformation, 1991

Editor with Thomas Bender, *Budapest and New York: Studies in Metropolitan Transformation, 1870–1930*, 1994

Further Reading

Johnston, William M., "Cultivated Gardeners," *American Scholar* 50 (1981), 260–66

Roth, Michael S., "Performing History: Modernist Contextualism in Carl Schorske's *Fin-de-Siècle Vienna*," *American Historical Review* 99 (1994), 729–45

Schorske, Carl E., "A Life of Learning," American Council of Learned Societies, *Occasional Papers* 1 (1987)

Steinberg, Michael P., "'Fin-de-Siècle Vienna' Ten Years Later: *Viel Traum, Wenig Wirklichkeit,*" *Austrian History Yearbook* 22 (1991), 151–62

Schramm, Percy Ernst 1894–1970

German medievalist and military historian

Percy Ernst Schramm was a historian of several trades. He counts as one of the major representatives of the study of the medieval state and the founder of systematic research into the iconography of rulership, but also as a leading social historian of the Hanseatic city of Hamburg and – because of his position during World War II – one of the foremost experts on wartime German military history.

Schramm's first major project was *Kaiser, Rom und Renovatio* (Emperor, Rome and *Renovatio*), 1929), on the interrelation of ancient and medieval concepts in the formulation of imperial ideas in Carolingian and Ottonian times, particularly around 1000 CE. Schramm argued that the young "dreamer" Otto III, and his teacher Gerbert-Sylvester, were devoted adherents of a Christian "renewal" of Roman greatness, rather than engineers of a "German empire" as many political historians have argued. It was published in the famous Warburg Library in Hamburg, and not by coincidence, for the writings of the circle of Aby Warburg, including Ernst Cassirer, Fritz Saxl, and Erwin Panofsky, were crucial for Schramm's scholarly development. However, he contested several of their notions about the "survival of antiquity," finding it too mechanical and negligent of the medieval millennium.

While completing that book, Schramm embarked on a field that was to define five decades of his scholarly life. A famous illuminated double page of an Ottonian Gospel book, depicting the emperor presented with tributes and gifts, seemed not only to summarize the ideas inherent in Otto III's *renovatio*, but pointed to a series of problems central to the understanding of medieval rulership. Schramm abandoned as anachronistic the earlier approach that concerned itself with the likeness of the portrait and person. Most ruler images were not made to commemorate the individual features of a king or emperor, but were aimed at conveying certain essential traditional features that identified the ruler as ruler.

These inquiries drew Schramm's attention to those politically momentous "liturgical plays" in which the insignia of rulership were transferred to the new ruler. Schramm began to edit, date, and categorize the coronation *ordines* – the scripts and stage directions for these "constitutional" spectacles of the Middle Ages – of the West Frankish, Anglo-Saxon, and German kingdoms. During this research Schramm's attention was drawn to processes of intricate borrowing and returning, and the multifarious interrelationship between European kingdoms in transferring forms and ideas and adapting them to local conditions, themes that became central in Schramm's later work on the English coronation, in his *Der König von Frankreich* (The King of France, 1939), and in several articles on Spanish kingdoms.

After the war, an impressive collection of monumental evidence was assembled by Schramm for an all-European survey of royal symbology: three volumes on insignia, *Herrschaftszeichen und Staatssymbolik* (Ruler's Insignia and State Symbology,

1954–56). Having investigated the different functions of objects associated with the rulers and other persons in authority (judges, prelates, officers), Schramm suggested a classification of "signs" (*Zeichen*). As the medieval king "stood for" the authority that can be called the state, so the insignia "stood for" him. A special volume was devoted to one particular symbol – also an insignia – the orb (*Sphaira, Globus, Reichsapfel,* 1958). The subtitle of this book, "Wanderings and Metamorphoses of an Insigne from Caesar to Elizabeth II" was also meant as a commentary on his old controversy with the Warburg school: the survival of antiquity. One of Schramm's last medievalist works, prepared in collaboration with an art historian, is an impressive volume, widening the scope of the corpus he was about to assemble. The *Denkmale der deutschen Könige und Kaiser* (Monuments to German Kings and Emperors, 1962–78) contains a splendidly illustrated catalogue of several hundred objects related to Frankish-German rulers from the early Middle Ages to the time of Frederick II. The survey includes not only the "things" employed in royal presentation proper – that is, insignia in the widest sense – but everything that was in any way connected with the ruler. In his introductory study, Schramm reconstructed what constituted the "hoard" (*Hort*) of a ruler in the Middle Ages.

In retrospect, one might say that, with the *Denkmale* volume, the questions raised by the Otto-miniature received their answers. The program set out by Schramm fifty years before has been well-nigh fulfilled, at least for the medieval empire and – partially – for the major countries of Europe. Most of the objects, images, texts, and staged actions of kings and emperor were inspected and analyzed: a symbology of the medieval state had been outlined.

In addition to his work as a medievalist, Schramm studied the history of his home town, Hamburg. These studies began in his youth, and several articles and two volumes on Hanseatic burghers at home and overseas demonstrate the results of these "local patriotic" endeavors. But perhaps the most interesting – and certainly the most charming and eminently readable – book he wrote was the one on some 300 years of cultural history demonstrated by the fate of the Schramm family and its relatives.

As a *Rittmeister* (captain of the cavalry) in reserve, Schramm was mobilized during World War II, and friends of his, who knew about the Gestapo interest in him and his family for opposition to Hitler, secured him the position of keeper of the diary of the Army High Command (*Oberkommando der Wehrmacht*). As a historian, he resisted the order to destroy the record, and rescued most of the volumes and handed them over to the Allies. In 1960 these papers were returned to him for editing, and together with a number of pupils he published his war diaries and presented a number of studies connected to the German war effort. His writings on Hitler and his generals are characterized by the objectivity that was typical for his generation of German scholars. Hence, he was criticized and attacked by many, who expected a more passionate tone and stance against Nazism. But only Norman Cantor went so far as to accuse him of belonging to the company of war criminals.

JÁNOS M. BAK

See also France: to 1000; Germany: to 1450; Hillgruber

Biography

Born Hamburg, 14 October 1894, of a prominent burgher family. Received doctorate, University of Heidelberg, 1922. Professor of medieval and modern history, University of Göttingen, 1929–63. Married Elisabeth von Thadden (3 sons). Died Göttingen, 12 November 1970.

Principal Writings

Die deutschen Kaiser und Könige in Bildern ihrer Zeit, 1: Bis zur Mitte des 12. Jahrhunderts (751–1152) (The German Emperors and Kings in Images of Their Age, 1: To the Mid-12th Century, 751–1152), 2 vols., 1928

Kaiser, Rom und Renovatio: Studien und Texte zur Geschichte des römischen Erneuerungsgedankens vom Ende des karolingischen Reiches bis zum Investiturstreit (Emperor, Rome, and *Renovatio*: Studies and Texts to the History of the Roman Idea of Renewal from the End of the Carolingian Empire to the Investiture Conflict), 2 vols., 1929

"Die Ordines der mittelalterlichen Kaiserkrönung: Ein Beitrag zur Geschichte des Kaisertums" (The *Ordines* of the Medieval Imperial Coronation: A Contribution to the History of the Empire), *Archiv für Urkundenforschung* 11 (1930), 285–390

Geschichte des englischen Königtums im Lichte der Krönung, 1937; in English as *A History of the English Coronation*, 1937

"Die Erforschung der mittelalterlichen Symbole – Wege und Methoden" (The Study of Medieval Symbols: Means and Ways), preface to Berent Schwineköper, *Der Handschuh im Recht, Ämterwesen, Brauch und Volksglauben* (The Glove in Law, Office, Custom, and Popular Belief), 1938

Der König von Frankreich: Das Wesen der Monarchie vom 9. zum 16. Jahrhundert, ein Kapitel aus der Geschichte des abendländischen Staates (The King of France: The Essence of Monarchy from the 9th to the 16th Centuries, a Chapter from the History of the West European State), 2 vols., 1939

Hamburg, Deutschland und die Welt: Leistung und Grenzen hanseatischen Bürgertums in der Zeit zwischen Napoleon I. und Bismarck, Ein Kapitel deutscher Geschichte (Hamburg, Germany, and the World: Achievements and Limits of Hanseatic Burghers Between Napoleon I and Bismarck. A Chapter of German History), 1943

Herrschaftszeichen und Staatssymbolik: Beiträge zu ihrer Geschichte vom dritten bis zum sechzehnten Jahrhundert (Rulers' Insignia and State Symbology: Contributions to their History from the 3rd to the 16th Centuries), 3 vols., 1954–56

With Josef Deér and Olle Källeström, *Kaiser Friedrichs II: Herrschaftszeichen* (The Insignia of Emperor Frederick II), 1955

Sphaira, Globus, Reichsapfel: Wanderung und Wandlung eines Herrschaftszeichens von Caesar bis Elisabeth II (Wanderings and Metamorphoses of an Insigne from Caesar to Elizabeth II), 1958

Editor with Helmuth Greiner, *Kriegstagebuch des Oberkommandos der Wehrmacht (Wehrmachtführungsstab), 1940–1945* (War Diary of the High Command of the Wehrmacht 1940–1945), 4 vols. in 7, 1960

With Florentine Mütherich, *Denkmale der deutschen Könige und Kaiser* (Monuments of German Kings and Emperors), 2 vols., 1962–78

Hitler als militärischer Führer: Erkenntnisse und Erfahrungen aus dem Kriegstagebuch des Oberkommandos der Wehrmacht, 1962; in English as *Hitler: The Man and Military Leader*, 1971

Neun Generationen: Dreihundert Jahre deutscher "Kulturgeschichte" im Lichte der Schicksale einer Hamburger Bürgerfamilie, 1648–1948 (Nine Generations: Three Hundred Years of German 'Cultural History' in the Light of the Fate of a Hamburg Family of Burghers, 1648–1948), 2 vols., 1963–64

Kaiser, Könige und Päpste: Gesammelte Aufsätze zur Geschichte des Mittelalters (Emperors, Kings, Popes. Collected Studies on The History of the Middle Ages), 4 vols. in 5, 1968–71

Further Reading

Cantor, Norman F., *Inventing the Middle Ages: The Lives, Works, and Ideas of the Great Medievalists of the Twentieth Century*, New York: Morrow, 1991; Cambridge: Lutterworth Press, 1992

Ritter, A., "Veröffentlichungen von Professor Dr. Percy Ernst Schramm" (Publications of Professor Percy Ernst Schramm) in Peter Classen and Peter Scheibert, eds., *Festschrift Percy Ernst Schramm zu seinem siebzigsten Geburtstag von Schülern und Freunden zugeeignet* (Festschrift for Percy Ernst Schramm on his Seventieth Birthday, Presented by Friends and Pupils), 2 vols., Wiesbaden: Steiner, 1964 [includes bibliography to 1963]

Science, History of

The history of science originated with the writings of scientists, but it has increasingly become the domain of historians and philosophers. In the last two decades, new tools and techniques from sociology, anthropology, and feminist studies have transformed the history of science. Historians have used these tools and techniques to reshape the way they and society understand the workings of science and scientific communities. Emphasis has shifted from great ideas and great men to science as a social and cultural phenomenon. As Arnold Thackray noted in 1981, science, as an object of historical study, had changed from a "coherent, autonomous body of knowledge" to a "spectrum of activity." The shift in tools, emphases, and views paralleled shifts in the sciences that historians most often studied; the traditional subjects of mathematics, physics, chemistry, and astronomy were supplemented by the newer areas of biology, ecology, earth science, and computer science.

Practicing scientists dominated the early history of science up to the early 20th century. These early histories tended to be commentaries or introductions to scientific texts. Their aim was to make contemporary science understandable through an analysis of past developments and was almost always directed toward science students. Contemporary scientific categories, concepts, and standards were almost always imposed on past science.

History of science, as something distinct from the scope and methods of science, became noticeable in the early 20th century. The work of George Sarton, often called the "father" of the history of science, was instrumental in the establishment of this discipline as a field. Sarton studied science as a systematized body of knowledge. He and his contemporaries approached science as the triumphal advance of reason over superstition. Much of their early work is positivist – a linear, chronological story or description of unchallenged "facts" and discoveries of the "truths" of science. Biographies from this period often used the "great man" approach, with an internal focus on the individual practitioner of science, separate from – and unaffected by – the social and cultural settings in which they worked. A "Whiggish" approach – viewing history solely with respect to the present – was inherent in the goal of most of this early work: the clarification of contemporary science by description of its evolution. Thomas Kuhn succinctly pointed out in 1968 both the Whiggishness and the positivism of the early history of science when he described it as a "chronology of accumulating positive achievement in a technical specialty defined by hindsight."

The nature of the discipline changed with an influx of scholars trained in history (or the humanities and social sciences) rather than in the natural or physical sciences. These historians brought new questions, methods, and models; some were from history, but many were from other fields. Rather than focusing solely on the internal workings of science as a "search for truth," historians began to study science by situating it within social and cultural contexts. This new approach prompted a debate between the users of the "internalist" approach and those of the "externalist" approach. The externalist approach, in contrast to the internalist, focused on the role of non-intellectual factors, such as institutional and socioeconomic ones, in the development of science. Three important forms of external history are the study of scientific institutions, the impact of science on Western thought, and the interplay between specific cultural and national contexts and scientific development. Models from other fields, such as philosophy and sociology, were often influential in the development of an externalist approach.

Philosophy, particularly philosophy of science, provided many influential models for historians of science. The work of philosophers, such as A.O. Lovejoy, aided historians of science to view scientists with something other than pure reverence. Pierre Duhem's work on medieval physical thought challenged the "unchallengeable" views of the "novelty" of the scientific revolution of the 17th century. In the 1950s and 1960s, the work of philosopher Alexandre Koyré, primarily focused on ideas and the use of textual analysis, led to what Thackray in 1981 called the "Koyré paradigm" – a view of science as a "search for truth" with an "inherent and autonomous development." The influence of Lovejoy, Duhem, and Koyré infused the history of science with a new idealism that could redeem "pure" science from its association with the unpleasantness of nuclear destruction, state secrecy, and funding battles that came after World War II. This new idealist strategy often reinforced some of the main tenets of the Sarton approach: the importance of key ideas and figures, and the relative lack of importance of cultural and social contexts. The emphasis of the work in this area was on the roots and origins of scientific knowledge, with medieval science and the scientific revolution drawing most of the scholarly attention of this group (which included Koyré, Cohen, Hall, Kuhn, and Butterfield). While much of their work focused on the "great men" of science, these men were described as more complex than earlier "triumphal" biographies had described them.

The philosophy of Koyré, combined with that of Thomas Kuhn, and the sociology of Robert K. Merton, transformed the field of history of science in the post-World War II period. Just prior to the war, Merton began to ask questions about the influence of social forms and needs on the organization of science. The so-called "Merton thesis" dealt with essential questions in the history of science: the nature and origin of modern, Western science, and the special productivity of 17th-century science. Merton's work emphasized the relationship between science and practical arts (that is, technology) which brought forward new, practical problems and questions for scientists in the 17th century. Merton's thesis also argued that Puritanism was a primary stimulant for the new empirical, instrumental, and utilitarian tone of 17th-century science. The sociological approach that Merton used contributed to the spread of the externalist

approach. The work of Kuhn, particularly his highly influential *The Structure of Scientific Revolutions* (1962), continued the focus on the nature of modern scientific development by investigating the new fields that emerged after the 17th century. According to Kuhn (1968), in the early stages of the development of a scientific discipline, "social needs and values are a major determinant of the problems on which its practitioners concentrate." The Kuhnian approach, in part, aligned nicely with the externalists. However, Kuhn also argued that, once a science had matured (or established a reigning "paradigm"), internal challenges alone shaped the evolution. This concept aided the continued use of the internalist approach up to the 1980s when the new influences and models of social history, literary analysis, anthropology, and postmodernism overshadowed the influence of Kuhn's work.

Social history passed from the other fields of history into the history of science, particularly in studies of scientific communities and institutions. These institutions included professional societies, universities, laboratories, journals, disciplines, and funding agencies. Karl Marx and Friedrich Engels posed the question of the social roots of science in the 19th century, and Max Weber continued the discussion after the turn of the century. The work of Merton, discussed above, used statistical and prosopographical methods which influenced later social historians of science such as Jacob and Shapin, who sought explanations of science outside the internal developments. Historians such as Mendelsohn, Weingart, and Whitley also turned to the field of the sociology of knowledge as they treated science the same as any other form of knowledge, rather than as a privileged, unique form of communication. Derek Price pioneered work on the relationship between science and society in the form of science policy and its effects on the development of science.

The publication of Shapin and Schaffer's influential study, *Leviathan and the Air-Pump* (1985), has caused a dramatic reorientation of the field within the last decade. Shapin and Schaffer presented modern experimental science as contingent, with competing, alternative groups mobilizing material, social, and rhetorical techniques to put forward different messages about science. Recent work, such as that of Biagioli, Kay, Forman, and Latour and Woolgar, often has focused on power relationships, research programs, and the "truth content" of science; scientific ideas have been analyzed as "tools" used in the "politics of knowledge." As Jan Golinski noted, the new group of historians often considered scientific discourse as a kind of rhetoric and analyzed various genres of scientific writing, with the aim of showing in detail how they are constructed to serve specific, often non-scientific, aims. This work often centered on "techniques, instruments, and discourse, and their functions in the community of practitioners." These historians opened up new arenas for study, such as the public status of science.

In the last few decades, the work of scholars such as Michel Foucault, Michel Serres, and Clifford Geertz helped increase the interdisciplinarity of work in the field and, in some cases, have even changed the definition of the object of study. Epistemological, anthropological, and interpretive approaches often view history (or historical objects) as the result of construction by a community of scientists, politicians, and others during the period under study and by the historian. The purely literary training of many current historians of science has also affected the approach and the objects of study. With the works of scholars such as Haraway, Lynch, and Woolgar, history of science has often blurred into the newly emerging field of "science studies" which uses anthropological, sociological, and literary techniques for analysis of the practice and "construction" of science, both present and past, and for cultural critique.

The subjects of the study of history of science shifted somewhat in the 1980s and 1990s. Nineteenth- and 20th-century science, as well as non-Western science, drew more attention than the traditional areas of ancient science and the 17th and 18th centuries. Subjects explored by Galison, Kay, Kevles, and Leslie expanded to include physics, molecular biology, genetics, and the "big science" of postwar America. Historians had virtually ignored non-Western science, except for ancient Greek and Babylonian science, until the monumental work of Joseph Needham, beginning in the 1950s, on Chinese science. Alexander Vucinich pioneered the study of Russian science in the 1960s, and Loren Graham supplemented his work in the following decades with studies of Soviet science. Research on science in the Third World, for example Brown's or Stepan's work on South America and Africa, began to appear in the 1970s, although it often still focused on First World rather than native science until the 1980s and 1990s and the emergence of the work of Thomas-Emeagwali. Scholars such as Keller and Rossiter also paid more attention to other neglected areas, such as women in science.

Throughout the development of the history of science, the development of science itself affected the scope of the field and the approaches used. The rise of the importance of science after both world wars boosted the field. The disillusionment of society with science in the 1970s and 1980s contributed to the decline of the internalist and positivist approaches and the rise of more critical techniques of sociology and discourse analysis. A dramatic increase in the diversity of approaches in the history of science in the 1990s reflects the increased diversity of scientific disciplines and sub-disciplines. There is little consensus today in a field that is described variously as "eclectic," "diverse," and having "many faces."

Postwar interest in science spurred the growth of the history of science as an academic discipline. Over the course of the next four decades, historians of science eroded the idea of science as something separate from the common, ordinary concerns of mankind. The methods, questions, and goals of historians of science moved closer to those of historians studying other aspects of society and culture such as religion, art, politics, and literature. The diversity of the field, however, is still tied to the growing diversity of the subjects of study.

LINDA EIKMEIER ENDERSBY

See also al-Bīrūnī; Butterfield; Duhem; Foucault; Geertz; Kuhn; Lovejoy; A.; Medicine; Merton; Needham; Sarton; Weber, M.

Further Reading

Biagioli, Mario, *Galileo, Courtier: The Practice of Science in the Culture of Absolutism*, Chicago: University of Chicago Press, 1993

Boas, Marie, *The Scientific Renaissance, 1450–1630*, New York: Harper, and London: Collins, 1962

Brown, Alexander Claude, ed., *A History of Scientific Endeavour in South Africa*, Cape Town: Royal Society of South Africa, 1977

Buchwald, Jed, ed., *Scientific Practice: Theories and Stories of Doing Physics*, Chicago: University of Chicago Press, 1995

Butterfield, Herbert, *The Origins of Modern Science, 1300–1800*, London: Bell, 1949; New York: Macmillan, 1951

Clagett, Marshall, ed., *Critical Problems in the History of Science*, Madison: University of Wisconsin Press, 1959

Cohen, I. Bernard, *Franklin and Newton: An Enquiry into Speculative Newtonian Experimental Science and Franklin's Work in Electricity as an Example Therof*, Philadelphia: American Philosophical Society, 1956

Cohen, I. Bernard, "The Many Faces of the History of Science," in Charles F. Delzell, ed., *The Future of History*, Nashville: Vanderbilt University Press, 1977

Debus, Allen G., "Science and History: The Birth of a New Field," in Stephen A. McKnight, ed., *Science, Pseudo-Science, and Utopianism in Early Modern Thought*, Columbia: University of Missouri Press, 1992

Dhombres, Jean, "On the Track of Ideas and Explanations Down the Centuries: The History of Science Today," *Impact of Science on Society* 40 (1990), 187–206

Duhem, Pierre, *Etudes sur Léonard de Vinci* (Studies on Leonardo da Vinci), 3 vols., Paris: Hermann, 1906–13

Duhem, Pierre, *Le Système du monde: histoire des doctrines cosmologiques de Platon à Copernic*, 10 vols., Paris: Hermann, 1913–59; abridged in English as *Medieval Cosmology: Theories of Infinity, Place, Time, Void, and the Plurality of Worlds*, Chicago: University of Chicago Press, 1985

Forman, Paul, "Weimar Culture: Causality and Quantum Theory, 1918–1927: Adaptation by German Physicists and Mathematicians to a Hostile Intellectual Environment," *Historical Studies in the Physical Sciences* 3 (1971), 1–116

Foucault, Michel, *Les Mots et les choses: une archéologie des sciences humaines*, Paris: Gallimard, 1966; in English as *The Order of Things: An Archaeology of the Human Sciences*, London: Tavistock, 1970; New York: Pantheon, 1971

Galison, Peter, *How Experiments End*, Chicago: University of Chicago Press, 1987

Geertz, Clifford, *The Interpretation of Cultures: Selected Essays*, New York: Basic Books, 1973; London: Hutchinson, 1975

Geertz, Clifford, "The Legacy of Thomas Kuhn: The Right Text at the Right Time," *Common Knowledge* 6 (1997), 1–5

Golinski, Jan, *Science as Public Culture: Chemistry and Enlightenment in Britain, 1760–1820*, Cambridge: Cambridge University Press, 1992

Graham, Loren R., *Science and Philosophy in the Soviet Union*, New York: Knopf, 1972; London: Allen Lane, 1973

Hall, A. Rupert, *The Scientific Revolution, 1500–1800: The Transformation of Modern Scientific Attitude*, London and New York: Longman, 1954

Haraway, Donna J., *Primate Visions: Gender, Race, and Nature in the World of Modern Science*, New York: Routledge, 1989

Jacob, Margaret, *The Newtonians and the English Revolution, 1689–1720*, Ithaca, NY: Cornell University Press, and Hassocks, Sussex: Harvester Press, 1976

Kay, Lily E., *The Molecular Vision of Life: Caltech, the Rockefeller Foundation, and the Rise of the New Biology*, New York: Oxford University Press, 1993

Keller, Evelyn Fox, *Reflections on Gender and Science*, New Haven: Yale University Press, 1985

Kevles, Daniel J., *In the Name of Eugenics: Genetics and the Uses of Human Heredity*, New York: Knopf, 1985

Koyré, Alexandre, *Metaphysics and Measurement: Essays in Scientific Revolution*, Cambridge, MA: Harvard University Press, and London: Chapman and Hall, 1968

Kuhn, Thomas S., *The Copernican Revolution: Planetary Astronomy in the Development of Western Thought*, Cambridge, MA: Harvard University Press, 1957

Kuhn, Thomas S., *The Structure of Scientific Revolutions*, Chicago: University of Chicago Press, 1962; revised 1970

Kuhn, Thomas S., "The History of Science," in David L. Sills, ed., *International Encyclopedia of the Social Sciences*, 17 vols. [and supplements], New York: Macmillan, 1968, vol. 14, 74–83

Latour, Bruno, and Steve Woolgar, *Laboratory Life: The Construction of Scientific Facts*, Beverly Hills, CA: Sage, 1979

Leslie, Stuart W., *The Cold War and American Science: The Military-Industrial-Academic Complex at MIT and Stanford*, New York: Columbia University Press, 1993

Lovejoy, Arthur O., *The Great Chain of Being: A Study of the History of an Idea*, Cambridge, MA: Harvard University Press, 1936

Lynch, Michael, and Steve Woolgar, eds., *Representation in Scientific Practice*, Cambridge, MA: MIT Press, 1988

Mendelsohn, Everett, Peter Weingart, and Richard D. Whitley, eds., *The Social Production of Scientific Knowledge*, Boston: Reidel, 1977

Merton, Robert K., *Science, Technology and Society in Seventeenth-Century England*, Bruges: Saint Catherine Press, 1938; reprinted New York: Fertig, 1970

Needham, Joseph, *Science and Civilization in China*, 6 vols., Cambridge: Cambridge University Press, 1954–94

Price, Derek J. de Solla, *Little Science, Big Science*, New York: Columbia University Press, 1963; enlarged edition as *Little Science, Big Science . . . and Beyond*, 1986

Rossiter, Margaret W., *Women Scientists in America*, 2 vols., Baltimore: Johns Hopkins University Press, 1982–95

Sarton, George, *Introduction to the History of Science*, 3 vols., Baltimore: Williams and Wilkins, 1927–48

Schiebinger, Londa, *The Mind Has No Sex? Women in the Origins of Modern Science*, Cambridge, MA: Harvard University Press, 1989

Serres, Michel, general editor, *Elements d'histoire des science*, Paris: Bordas, 1989; in English as *A History of Scientific Thought*, Oxford and Cambridge, MA: Blackwell, 1995

Serres, Michel, with Bruno Latour, *Eclaircissements: cinq entretiens avec Bruno Latour*, Paris: Bourin, 1992; in English as *Conversations on Science, Culture, and Time*, Ann Arbor: University of Michigan Press, 1995

Shapin, Steven, "Phrenological Knowledge and the Social Structure of Early Nineteenth-Century Edinburgh," *Annals of Science* 32 (1975), 219–43

Shapin, Steven, "History of Science and Its Sociological Reconstructions," *History of Science* 20 (1982), 157–211

Shapin, Steven, and Simon Schaffer, *Leviathan and the Air-Pump: Hobbes, Boyle, and the Experimental Life*, Princeton: Princeton University Press, 1985

Stepan, Nancy, *Beginnings of Brazilian Science: Oswaldo Cruz, Medical Research and Policy, 1890–1920*, New York: Science History Publications, 1976

Thackray, Arnold, "History of Science," in Paul T. Durbin, ed., *A Guide to the Culture of Science, Technology, and Medicine*, New York: Free Press, 1980

Thackray, Arnold, "History of Science in the 1980s," *Journal of Interdisciplinary History* 12 (1981), 299–314

Thackray, Arnold, "The Pre-History of an Academic Discipline," in Everett Mendelsohn, ed., *Transformation and Tradition in the Sciences*, Cambridge: Cambridge University Press, 1984

Thomas-Emeagwali, Gloria, ed., *Science and Technology in African History with Case Studies from Nigeria, Sierra Leone, Zimbabwe, and Zambia*, Lewiston, ME: Mellen Press, 1992

Vucinich, Alexander, *Science in Russian Culture*, 2 vols., Stanford, CA: Stanford University Press, 1963–70

Weber, Max, "Die protestantische Ethik und der Geist des Kapitalismus," *Archiv für Sozialwissenschaft und Sozialpolitik* 20–21 (1904–05), revised in *Gesammelte Aufsätze zur Religionssoziologie*, Tübingen: Mohr, 1920; in English as *The Protestant Ethic and the Spirit of Capitalism*, London: Allen and Unwin, 1930, New York: Scribner, 1958

Westfall, Richard S., *Science and Religion in Seventeenth-Century England*, New Haven: Yale University Press, 1958

Whitley, Richard D., "From the Sociology of Scientific Communities to the Study of Scientists' Negotiations and Beyond," *Social Science Information* 22 (1983), 681–720

Scobie, James R. 1929–1981
US historian of Latin America

James R. Scobie was one of the early pioneers of Latin American urban and socioeconomic history. He examined the transformation of Argentina from a backwater region in the Spanish empire to a world supplier of agrarian products, and how this metamorphosis changed Argentina. Implicit in his analysis was an enduring model for how other Third World countries were plugged into the world economy, and remade in the process.

When Scobie wrote his undergraduate thesis (1950) at Princeton on Juan Bautista Alberdi as creator of the Argentine Constitution of 1853, and his dissertation (1954) at Harvard on the definitive formation of the Argentine nation in the period 1860–65, he was already working in a relatively unstudied period. Most Latin Americanists had concentrated on the conquest, colonial, and independence periods, and in Argentina's case, on the rule of the caudillo Juan Manuel de Rosas (1829–32, 1835–52). But Scobie wanted to study modern Latin American history and sought its roots in the second half of the 19th century. Lacking basic documentary sources taken for granted elsewhere, Scobie edited and published letters of the Argentine president Bartolomé Mitre that were essential for such a study. The result appeared in 1964 as the political history *La lucha por la consolidación de la nacionalidad Argentina, 1852–1862* (The Struggle for the Consolidation of Argentine Nationality, 1852–62) which covered the decade when Argentina finally coalesced as a nation. But two more of Scobie's books – very different from the first – appeared in the same year. They inaugurated the Latin American series at two distinguished academic presses and established Scobie's reputation.

Scobie's archival research in Argentina during 1949, 1952–54, 1959–60, and 1961 suggested that a history of the Argentine wheat zone would permit a social history of the rich Argentine pampas, for him the key to understanding Argentina's economic development. It would also help explain the dominant role of the city and province of Buenos Aires, the ignorance and poverty of the rural population, and the massive foreign immigration. At the time such a social history was a voyage into uncharted waters, but his discoveries eventually oriented a generation of Latin American scholars. Scobie's *Revolution on the Pampas: A Social History of Argentine Wheat, 1860–1910* (1964) initiated the University of Texas' monographs on Latin America, and his *Argentina: A City and a Nation* (1964) launched the Latin American Histories for Oxford University Press. As a general survey of Argentina the latter work reached a wide audience and was adopted as required reading in many surveys of modern Latin America. Its lucid prose, strong narrative style, rigorous analysis, and non-Marxist social, economic, and cultural focus proved to be a winning combination. Argentine history seemed to unfold in lock-step fashion as hides, salted meat, wool, mutton, beef, wheat, and corn each in turn brought an ever more intensive exploitation of the Argentine pampas and changes that resulted in the transformation of Argentina. Railroads and other infrastructure were built and converged on the great port of Buenos Aires to funnel agrarian commodities from the pampas to the world. While they ably served the export sector, their pattern obeyed the needs of a world economy rather than a nation requiring unity and more balanced development. Clearly the export sector seemed to be the decisive factor in the formation of a modern but skewed Argentina. The logic and clarity with which Scobie described the economic patterns and resulting social changes seemed to banish political history to a secondary role as historical explanation. Scobie's influence was magnified when he was named general editor of the Oxford series and asked to oversee the publication of histories with a similar social and economic focus on other Latin American countries. Volumes followed on Brazil, Mexico, Peru, Bolivia, the Caribbean, Central America, Chile, Cuba, and Venezuela. While none of these countries experienced the meteoric rise and rapid change to the same extent as Argentina, they had similar agrarian or mineral export commodities – coffee, sugar, bananas, copper, tin, oil – that benefited from a similar approach. Without a doubt many of the new approaches to Latin America's history resulted from this attention to structural factors and mega-forces such as geography, demography, and the transforming effects of exports that characterized Scobie's Oxford series.

Having examined the pampas and surveyed the country, Scobie was struck by how development had changed the very nature of urban life itself. He wanted to study in more detail the great city that dominated the nation and did so in *Buenos Aires: Plaza to Suburb, 1870–1910* (1974) where he dissected the astonishing urban growth and the creation of the metropolis where one third of the nation lived. In the process Scobie gave form and substance not only to Latin American but to urban history in general. He showed that the capital Buenos Aires took from the rest of the country, but did not give back in equal measure. He developed the concept of public versus private space. He peered inside the *conventillos* (slum housing estates) and described the essential role they played in acculturating the new immigrants. He showed that occupation was probably the best determinant of class and social structure. With findings obviously relevant to urban development elsewhere in the world, Scobie planned to extend them and do a cross-national study comparing Buenos Aires with an economically similar city in the United States and Australia. But first he felt that Buenos Aires was not the whole story of Argentina's urbanization, the completion of which would require a study of other Argentine cities. He chose Corrientes, Salta, and Mendoza and was well along with his *Secondary Cities of Argentina* (1988) when his untimely death required that it be completed and edited by his friend and colleague, the noted Latin Americanist Samuel L. Baily. As railroads or shipping connected the three cities to Buenos Aires, each found the metropolis weakening their ties to their hinterlands and restructuring a variety of relationships more directly to the capital. Only Mendoza with its vineyards supplying wine to a national market escaped emasculation, although colonial Salta with its tourism resisted more than Corrientes.

Scobie in the foreword to the second edition of his general survey *Argentina: A City and a Nation* (1971) recognized the need to return to political history in order to explain recent Argentine history, and he expressed a desire to provide a synthesis of post-1930 events. Argentina's precocious development had stalled, and everyone speculated on what had gone wrong. Argentina had become one of the most interesting case studies about development in general. Much of Scobie's work directly and indirectly concerned itself with patterns of development of the 19th and 20th centuries, with obvious implications for much of the rest of the world.

MAURICE P. BRUNGARDT

See also Argentina; Latin America: National

Biography

James Ralston Scobie. Born Valparaiso, Chile, 16 June 1929, to an American family. Studied at Princeton University, BA 1950; MA, Harvard University, 1951, PhD 1954. Taught at University of California, Berkeley, 1957–64; Indiana University, 1964–77; and University of California, San Diego, 1977–81. Married 1) Patricia Pearson Beauchamp, 1957 (died 1965; 1 son, 1 daughter); 2) Ingrid Ellen Winther, historian, 1967 (1 son, 1 daughter). Died Del Mar, California, 4 June 1981.

Principal Writings

Editor with Palmira S. Bollo Cabrios, *Correspondencia Mitre-Elizalde*, Buenos Aires: Universidad de Buenos Aires, 1960
Argentina: A City and a Nation, 1964; revised 1971
La lucha por la consolidación de la nacionalidad Argentina, 1852–1862 (The Struggle for the Consolidation of Argentine Nationality, 1852–1862), 1964
Revolution on the Pampas: A Social History of Argentine Wheat, 1860–1910, 1964
Editor with Dale L. Morgan, *Three Years in California: William Perkins' Journal of Life at Sonora, 1849–1852*, Berkeley: University of California Press, 1964
"Buenos Aires as a Commercial-Bureaucratic City, 1880–1910: Characterization of a City's Orientation," *American Historical Review* 77 (1972), 1035–73
Buenos Aires: Plaza to Suburb, 1870–1910, 1974
"The Growth of Latin American Cities, 1870–1930," in Leslie Bethell, ed., *The Cambridge History of Latin America*, vol. 4, Cambridge: Cambridge University Press, 1986
Secondary Cities of Argentina: The Social History of Corrientes, Salta, and Mendoza, 1850–1910, edited by Samuel L. Baily, 1988

Scotland

The turbulent character of Scotland's past has stimulated a historiography of considerable richness and complexity.

Writings on Scottish history from the very beginning reflected the perennially difficult question of national identity. This was provoked both by the fact of a striking ethnic heterogeneity within the kingdom and by the problem of restless neighbors without. One of the first extant genealogies, the *Senchus Fer nAlban* (History of the Men of Scotland), written in the 7th century, offers us a flickering image of a Gaelic warrior society struggling for survival on the northern fringes of Dark Age Europe. Other early texts, composed following the 9th-century political unification of the kingdom by Kenneth mac-Alpin and incorporating imaginary genealogies intended to establish the credentials of his successors, likewise illustrate the creative use of history to fashion in Scotland a workable identity for an otherwise diverse community.

Later ages were little different in their inventive approach to Scottish history. In particular, the disputes underlying the 14th-century wars of independence exercised a decisive influence over the subsequent treatment of Scotland's past. For commentators such as John of Fordun, Walter Bower, Andrew Wyntoun, and "Blind Hary," the English use of origin-myths and Arthurian legend to assert their sovereignty over Scotland, and the countervailing claims of the Scots to age-old independence – most majestically rendered in the Declaration of Arbroath (1320) – were central to an interpretation of the past. These factors established a specific historical frame of reference, emphasizing a proud record of vigorous self-government and even more vigorous self-defence, within which later commentators would think and write about the Scottish kingdom's precarious place in the world.

Such loaded interpretations of Scottish history duly registered the impact of the two greatest forces acting on early modern scholarship, the Renaissance and the Reformation. Scottish history was at this time given vibrant expression in Hector Boece's *Historiam Scottorum* (1527), a vehement criticism of political morality seriously weakened by its author's inattention to factual accuracy, and more studied treatment in John Mair's *Historia Majoris Britanniae* (1521), an attack on parochialism and aristocratic partiality. The same influences also produced the most controversial contribution ever made to the history of Scotland, George Buchanan's *Rerum Historia Scoticarum* (1582). Here, while replicating the medieval emphasis on national unity and independence, the greatest of Scottish humanists also skillfully recast the traditional material so as to deliver a stinging rebuke to recent royal absolutism. No less tendentious were the versions of the past offered by competing Catholic and Protestant historians. John Leslie's *De origine, moribus et rebus gestis Scotorum* (1578; in English in *The History of Scotland*, 1596) portrayed the Catholic monarchy as pious and patriotic. From the opposing wing, the architect of the Scottish Reformation, John Knox, gave the world a violently polemical, self-justificatory *History of the Reformation* (1644), in which the innumerable historical precedents and unmistakable evidence of divine approval for the Scottish people's resistance to papal supremacy were triumphantly adduced.

A train of committed churchmen – John Spottiswoode, David Calderwood, and Robert Wodrow among them – followed eagerly in their footsteps, establishing a tradition of unscrupulous and partisan religious historiography from which Scottish scholarship began properly to emerge only in the later 18th century. That period, however, saw the first great flowering of international interest in the Scottish past. Much of this was made possible by works of major intellectual significance, as scholars sought, in Bagehot's telling phrase, nothing less than to discover how man, "from being a savage, . . . became a Scotchman." William Robertson's magisterial *History of Scotland* (1759), with its pervasive air of reasonableness, and Hume's *History of Great Britain* (1754–56), a penetrating

analysis of constitutional history, were among the outstandingly readable products of Scottish Enlightenment thought. Yet no account of historical writing in Scotland should ignore the quite extraordinary influence exercised by the fictive talents of Sir Walter Scott (1771–1832). From *Waverley* (1814) to *The Fair Maid of Perth* (1828), Scott wove a tapestry on the themes of Scottish history whose sharply contrasting colors entirely bewitched his European contemporaries and continue today to lend exaggerated light and shade to the image in the wider world of Scotland's archetypally romantic past.

Since the middle of the 19th century, however, the study of Scottish history has also benefited both from a measure of welcome institutionalization and a great upsurge of academic and popular concern. Scottish history has, for example, been accepted as a distinctive discipline at university level, both in Scotland and in North America. Numerous academic journals have flourished, most notably the *Scottish Historical Review*. And a succession of much-esteemed organizations, such as the Maitland Club, the Bannatyne Club, the Abbotsford Club, and the Scottish Texts and Scottish History societies, have over the last century-and-a-half gradually made available the modern critical editions and textual sources – civic records, personal diaries, monastic charters, and so forth – on which the steady progress of historical understanding relies.

At the same time the range of scholarly approaches fruitfully brought to bear on Scottish subjects has been greatly extended. Scottish history was formerly marked by a predilection for the documentary study of political and religious history in the relatively remote past. But in the last fifty years research has produced exciting developments in our understanding of how intellectual life, radical political activity, industrialization, the urban experience, literary expression, gender difference, the presence of a living Gaelic community, and the broader movements of British and European history have each helped to define and enrich the Scottish past. Prominent works such as George Davie's *The Democratic Intellect* (1961) on the 19th-century anglicization of Scottish education, the writings of Sandy Grant and Jenny Wormald on the sophisticated political culture of 15th- and 16th-century Scotland, the provocative essays of Hugh Trevor-Roper, especially on the 18th-century Scottish Enlightenment, and the historical studies undertaken by political nationalists such as Tom Nairn and Christopher Harvie, have each helped open up new and fiercely contested fields of inquiry to which scholars, including English and American historians, have not been slow to flock.

Nor has scholarly history failed to provide general overviews of Scottish history to satisfy the needs of a voracious lay readership. One of the finest examples of genuinely accessible scholarship is Michael Lynch's *Scotland: A New History* (1991), a formidable performance both in entertainment and erudition that succeeds by conveying rather than evading the unresolved complexity and contentiousness of its fascinating material.

The fundamentally multidimensional character of Scottish history is, then, as clear now as at any time in its tortuous development. Whether as scholarly preoccupation or as popular culture, the discussion and dissection of Scotland's hotly disputed past remains resoundingly alive and well.

DAVID ALLAN

See also Britain; Hume; Trevor-Roper

Further Reading

Allan, David, *Virtue, Learning and the Scottish Enlightenment: Ideas of Scholarship in Early Modern History*, Edinburgh: Edinburgh University Press, 1993

Anderson, James, *Sir Walter Scott and History*, Edinburgh: Edina Press, 1981

Ash, Marinell, *The Strange Death of Scottish History*, Edinburgh: Ramsay Head Press, 1980

Bell, A.S., ed., *The Scottish Antiquarian Tradition: Essays to Mark the Bicentenary of the Society of Antiquaries of Scotland and Its Museum, 1780–1980*, Edinburgh: John Donald, 1981

Boece, Hector, *Historiam Scottorum*, 1527; reprinted in English as *Chronicle of Scotland*, Amsterdam: Theatrum Orbis Terrarum, and Norwood, NJ: Walter J. Johnson, 1977

Brown, Keith M., *Kingdom or Province? Scotland and the Regal Union, 1603–1715*, London: Macmillan, and New York: St. Martin's Press, 1992

Buchanan, George, *Rerum Historia Scoticarum*, Edinburgh: Arbuthnet, 1582; in English as *The History of Scotland*, London: Jones, 1690

Calder, Angus, *Revolving Culture: Notes from the Scottish Republic*, London and New York: Tauris, 1994

Cowan, Edward J., "Myth and Identity in Early Medieval Scotland," *Scottish Historical Review* 63 (1984), 111–35

Daiches, David, ed., *A Companion to Scottish Culture*, London: Arnold, 1981; New York: Holmes and Meier, 1982; revised as *The New Companion to Scottish Culture*, Edinburgh: Polygon, 1993

Davie, George, *The Democratic Intellect: Scotland and Her Universities in the Nineteenth Century*, Edinburgh: Edinburgh University Press, 1961

Devine, Thomas Martin, *Exploring the Scottish Past: Themes in the History of Scottish Society*, East Linton: Tuckwell Press, 1995

Dickinson, William C., *Scotland from the Earliest Times to 1603*, 3rd edition, edited by Archibald A. Duncan, Oxford: Clarendon Press, 1977

Donaldson, Gordon, general editor, *The Edinburgh History of Scotland*, 4 vols., Edinburgh: Oliver and Boyd, 1965–75, New York: Praeger/Barnes and Noble, 1966–75; reprinted Edinburgh: Mercat Press, 1992

Donnachie, Ian, and Christopher Whatley, eds., *The Manufacture of Scottish History*, Edinburgh: Polygon, 1992

Fearnley-Sander, Mary, "Philosophical History and the Scottish Reformation: William Robertson and the Knoxian Tradition," *Historical Journal* 33 (1990), 323–38

Goldstein, R. James, *The Matter of Scotland: Historical Narrative in Medieval Scotland*, Lincoln: University of Nebraska Press, 1993

Grant, Alexander, *Independence and Nationhood: Scotland, 1306–1469*, London: Arnold, 1984

Harvie, Christopher J., *Scotland and Nationalism: Scottish Politics and Society*, London: Allen and Unwin, 1977; revised London and New York: Routledge, 1994

Hume, David, *History of Great Britain*, 2 vols., 1754–56 [complete work published as *History of England*, 6 vols., 1754–62]

Knox, John, *History of the Reformation*, 1644

Lenman, Bruce, *Integration, Enlightenment and Industrialization: Scotland, 1746–1832*, London: Arnold, and Toronto: University of Toronto Press, 1981

Leslie, John, *De origine, moribus et rebus gestis Scotorum*, 1578; in English in *The History of Scotland*, 1596

Lynch, Michael, *Scotland: A New History*, London: Pimlico, 1991

McCrone, David, Angela Morris, and Richard Kiely, *Scotland – The Brand: The Making of Scottish Heritage*, Edinburgh: Edinburgh University Press, 1995

Mackie, John D., *A History of Scotland*, 2nd edition, edited by Bruce Lenman and Geoffrey Parker, Harmondsworth and New York: Penguin, 1978

Mair, John [John Major], *Historia Majoris Britanniae*, Paris: Badius, 1521

Mason, Roger A., "Kingship, Nobility and Anglo-Scottish Union: John Mair's *History of Greater Britain* (1521)," *Innes Review* 41 (1991), 182–222

Mitchison, Rosalind, ed., *Why Scottish History Matters*, Edinburgh: Saltire Society, 1991

Nairn, Tom, *The Break-up of Britain: Crisis and Neo-Nationalism*, London: NLB, 1977; revised 1981

Pittock, Murray G.H., *The Invention of Scotland: The Stuart Myth and Scottish Identity, 1638 to the Present*, London and New York: Routledge, 1991

Robertson, William, *History of Scotland*, 2 vols., London: Millar, 1759

Scott, Paul H., ed., *Scotland: A Concise Cultural History*, Edinburgh: Mainstream, 1993

Scottish Historical Review, 1904–27, 1947–

Smout, T.C., *A History of the Scottish People, 1560–1830*, London: Collins, 1969; New York: Scribner, 1970

Smout, T.C., *A Century of the Scottish People, 1830–1950*, London: Collins, and New Haven: Yale University Press, 1986

Trevor-Roper, Hugh, "The Scottish Enlightenment," *Studies on Voltaire and the Eighteenth Century* 58 (1967), 1635-58

Trevor-Roper, Hugh, "Scotland and the Puritan Revolution," in his *Religion, the Reformation and Social Change*, London: Macmillan 1967, 3rd edition, London: Secker and Warburg, 1984; as *The Crisis of the Seventeenth Century*, New York: Harper, 1968

Wormald, Jenny, *Court, Kirk and Community: Scotland, 1470–1625*, London: Arnold, and Toronto: University of Toronto Press, 1981

Scott, Anne Firor 1921–

US women's historian

In the early 1970s two events focused the attention of scholars on the history of women: Anne Firor Scott's *The Southern Lady* was published by University of Chicago Press (1970), and Scott taught her first formal college course on the social history of American women (1971). In writing a book about southern women, Scott faced considerable opposition from colleagues urging her to undertake a more conventional topic and criticism from those who accused her of practicing "female chauvinism." The product of nine years of research, Scott's *The Southern Lady* was met with critical acclaim as a thoughtful and innovative examination of the struggle of women to free themselves from the cultural expectations of ladyhood and find a way to individual and political self-determination.

Born nine months after the suffrage amendment was added to the US Constitution, Scott began her academic career studying political science. Together with her graduate school adviser, Oscar Handlin, Scott decided to write her dissertation not on American political thought, as she had originally planned, but on the southern progressive movement. Immersed in materials while researching at the Library of Congress, Scott "kept stumbling over women" speaking out on social and political issues – women that none of the historians who had studied the southern progressives (including Arthur S. Link and C. Vann Woodward) had bothered to mention. "Women *were* there," Scott argued, "and they made a difference."

The major themes of Scott's work are evident in *Making the Invisible Woman Visible* (1984), a collection of 21 essays on women's social, political, and cultural role in American history. In embarking on a study of women and their burgeoning political activism in the 19th-century South, Scott broke new ground for historians who followed. While researching *The Southern Lady*, Scott unearthed evidence of a topic that would become a central theme for her later work: women's voluntary organizations. In *Natural Allies* (1991), Scott argued that all-female voluntary associations, such as the Young Women's Christian Association and the National Council of Jewish Women, were important instruments of social change. While these organizations worked to identify and alleviate social problems, they also provided women with the opportunity to participate in public life. Barred from involvement in the state, the church, and higher education, a variety of women (black and white, working-class and wealthy) turned to voluntary organizations to work for the public good. By studying how women used voluntary organizations to make a place for themselves in public life and to bring about change in communities, Scott illuminated both the lives of women and the role of these associations in shaping American society.

Scott has advanced women's history by studying how women brought about change and how they were themselves changed by social and political developments in American society. She has been openly critical of the lack of interest shown by past historians in the female experience. "One day," she wrote in the introduction to *The American Woman* (1971), "perhaps an inquiring psychologist will explain the extreme reluctance of American historians to recognize that women have been here too, and when that time comes the answer will be, in part, that the historians were men." While criticizing the gap in scholarly endeavors that engulfed the lives of women, Scott worked to fill it, writing on education, religion, and social activism, and bringing a new perspective to sources and to the discipline as a whole. A woman's place, Scott argues, is in the history books: not in a few sentences inserted for the sake of what "very distinguished male historians" have called the fad of women's history, but in well-researched studies of how women were active players in the events, movements, and institutions of the past.

JENNIFER DAVIS McDAID

Biography

Anne Byrd Firor Scott. Born Montezuma, Georgia, 24 April 1921. Received BA, University of Georgia, 1941; MA, Northwestern University, 1944; PhD, Radcliffe College, 1958. Taught at Haverford College, 1957–58; University of North Carolina, 1959–69; and Duke University from 1961 (emeritus). Married Andrew M. Scott 1947 (3 children).

Principal Works

The Southern Lady: From Pedestal to Politics, 1830–1930, 1970
The American Woman: Who Was She?, 1971
With Andrew M. Scott, *One Half the People: The Fight for Woman Suffrage*, 1975; 2nd edition 1982
"Historians Construct the Southern Woman," in Joanne V. Hawks and Sheila L. Skemp, eds., *Sex, Race, and the Role of Women in the South*, 1983
Making the Invisible Woman Visible, 1984
With Jacquelyn Dowd Hall, "Women in the South," in John B. Boles and Evelyn Thomas Nolen, eds., *Interpreting Southern History: Historiographical Essays in Honor of Sanford W. Higginbotham*, 1987
Natural Allies: Women's Associations in American History, 1991
Editor, *Unheard Voices: The First Historians of Southern Women*, 1993

Further Reading

Malkiel, Nancy Weiss, "Invincible Woman: Anne Firor Scott," in Nancy A. Hewitt and Suzanne Lebsock, eds., *Visible Women: New Essays on American Activism*, Urbana: University of Illinois Press, 1993

Scott, James C. 1936–
US political theorist

James C. Scott is not a historian but a political scientist. As well, much of the body of his work and thought is concerned less with historical accounts than with modeling explanations of contemporary phenomena, most especially peasant rebellion and resistance. It is this latter project, worked out over three major works and several minor endeavors since the mid-1970s, that makes Scott's thought and analyses so useful for historians, in particular those concerned with the political life of what Eric Wolf has called "the people without history."

Scott began writing from within the sub-interdiscipline of peasant studies. In *The Moral Economy of the Peasant* (1976) he sought to locate and explain the bases of peasant revolutions. He did so in what are quite cultural terms bracketed by a vision of the disruptive potential of dominant class/dominated class relations in peasant societies. Scott's concerns at this time were symptomatic of the period in which he wrote. In the three decades after the end of World War II the Vietnamese reunification had been successfully concluded; peasant revolutionaries controlled Laos and Cambodia; peasant-based rebellions marked several other Asian polities, and also states in Africa and Mesoamerica. Seeking to account for these wars of national liberation in *The Moral Economy of the Peasant*, Scott argued that the founding of rebellious politics among peasants was almost involuntary. Fundamentally, he asserted that peasant revolution emerged from changes and troubles in social conditions and normative practices. This drew fire from Samuel Popkin, who made *The Moral Economy of the Peasant* the target of vigorous criticism in his book *The Rational Peasant* (1979), in which he counter-posed a rational choice model for understanding peasant politics.

Subsequently, Scott turned away from moral economies. In *Weapons of the Weak: Everyday Forms of Peasant Resistance* (1985) the age of peasant revolution was clearly over and Scott moved to a highly specific account of the ways in which Malay peasants cope with and resist local and national hegemons in modernizing Malaysia. At a time when intensive studies of local communities were quite out of vogue in the social sciences, Scott turned his eye on 74 Malay households during a period of significant economic change.

Here Scott seemed to reject the Gramscian vision of an underclass that was utterly ideologically suborned by the operations of hegemonic class culture and economies. Instead, he argued that seemingly trivial speech and other acts by peasants were in fact politically loaded. He found a politics of resistance in peasants' lies, minor sabotage, jokes, puns, laughter, disguise, and folktales, and he labeled them political acts of the everyday. Scott also suggested that his insights might be applicable to peasantry throughout the world and over time.

In the third of his major works, *Domination and the Arts of Resistance* (1990), Scott took his theory of peasant politics (re-named "infrapolitics") beyond the peasantry to encompass a much wider range of both rural and urban subordinate groups who are without history and seemingly without voice. He articulated a language for understanding underclass politics, making a distinction between public transcripts (the open dialogic and discursive relations between subordinates and hegemons) and hidden transcripts (discourses that take place out of the sight of the dominant classes and that more accurately represent the politics of the subordinate).

At this point Scott abandoned his hermeneutic anchors and the highly specific focus of his earlier work. Using examples from both Asian and European materials – European feudalism, land tenancy in Asia, labor camps, prisons, schools – he proceeded to a more theoretical and conceptual analysis and made general points about social relations and subordinate politics in a global and transhistorical fashion. He turned too to a closer encounter with the literary, examining canonical western texts for their negotiations of the tension between public and hidden transcripts.

Scott has made a very significant contribution to our theoretical cognizance of the material role language, symbols, and culture play in class struggle.

VIVIAN BLAXELL

See also Southeast Asia

Biography

James Campbell Scott. Born Mount Holly, New Jersey, 2 December 1936, son of a doctor. Received BA, Williams College, 1958; postgraduate study, University of Rangoon, 1958–59; Institut des Etudes Sciences Politiques, Paris, 1959–60; MA, Yale University, 1963, PhD 1967. Taught political science, Wesleyan College, 1967; University of Wisconsin, Madison, 1967–76; professor, Yale University, from 1976. Married Louise Goehring, art historian, 1961 (1 daughter, 2 sons).

Principal Writings

Political Ideology in Malaysia: Reality and the Beliefs of an Elite, 1968
The Moral Economy of the Peasant: Rebellion and Subsistence in Southeast Asia, 1976
Weapons of the Weak: Everyday Forms of Peasant Resistance, 1985
Domination and the Arts of Resistance: Hidden Transcripts, 1990

Further Reading

Evans, Grant, *From Moral Economy to Remembered Village: The Sociology of James C. Scott*, Clayton, Australia: Centre of Southeast Asian Studies, Monash University, 1986
Popkin, Samuel L., *The Rational Peasant: The Political Economy of Rural Society in Vietnam*, Berkeley: University of California Press, 1979

Scott, Joan Wallach 1941–

US historian of French gender and labor history

Joan Scott was trained as a social historian of France, and her most profound influence has been in her ground-breaking and sometimes controversial application of poststructuralism to historical and feminist theories. She has sought to salvage women's history from ghettoization by arguing cogently that gender, as a "useful category of analysis," must take center stage as crucial for any understanding of politics and society.

One of the pioneers of women's history, Scott played a significant role in developing a framework for analyzing patterns of women's work, stressing its close relationship with both family structure and economy. With Louise Tilly she made an important contribution to the debate, which had been inaugurated by Alice Clark, on the effect of industrialization on women. Scott and Tilly argued in *Women, Work, and Family*, published in 1978, that the development of women's waged work as a result of industrialization had neither brought about an improvement in women's social position nor altered their relationships to their families.

During the 1980s Scott became convinced that French poststructuralism – in particular Jacques Derrida's linguistic theory and Michel Foucault's work on power, knowledge, and discourse – could be developed to provide a more sophisticated analysis of the operation of gender, class, and race in past societies. In 1988 her essays on the uses of poststructuralism, influenced by discussions with other feminist historians including Denise Riley, were published together as *Gender and the Politics of History*. Scott defined gender as "knowledge about sexual difference," adopting Foucault's interpretation of knowledge as "the understanding produced by cultures and societies of human relationships." Such knowledge, she said, was "not absolute or true, but always relative," and was constructed, contested, and negotiated through discourse. Like Riley, she argued that it was impossible to separate gender as a discursive construct from any innate or fixed biological sex.

Scott criticized what she saw as the two dominant modes of women's history. The first, the writing of "her-story" had performed a valuable role in uncovering women's past lives but could all too easily lead to the treatment of women's history as an isolated discipline. The second approach, the compartmentalization of women's history as an aspect of social history, had led to the uncritical adaptation of existing historical methods and the failure to develop a theory of gender. Scott rejected Joan Kelly-Gadol's Marxist framework for women's history, considering the emphasis on economic factors inadequate as an explanation for the basis of the gender system.

Scott proposed that all history should be rewritten to take account of gender since it "is a primary way of signifying relations of power." Following Derrida, she argued that the western philosophical tradition rests on a system of normative concepts based on binary oppositions that construct meaning through difference. The meanings of masculinity and femininity have been constantly asserted to structure the "concrete and symbolic organization of all social life." Hence gender has been widely employed as a metaphor for all social and political relationships. Since normative concepts are unstable and open to contestation, the task for the historian must lie in deconstructing the terms of the debate, the meanings behind the use of gender.

Scott's essays went on to demonstrate how a poststructuralist theory of gender should be fitted into historical practice and the writing of history. She argued that historians E.P. Thompson and Gareth Stedman Jones, despite differing approaches, had both failed to integrate an awareness of gender into their analyses of the formation of 19th-century working-class consciousness. Although Thompson had included women, he had simply repeated the gendered notions of women's roles held by his 19th-century subjects. Jones, despite his interest in the "linguistic turn" and recognition of the discursive basis of class consciousness, had failed to deconstruct the concepts of difference which fomented identity. Scott then used her own research on 19th-century France to present a practical demonstration of how texts could be deconstructed to elucidate the formation of gendered identities, giving meticulous readings of three contrasting primary sources – the appeals made by male and female Parisian garment workers, official statistical reports, and texts on political economy.

Scott's poststructuralist approach has proved controversial, not least among feminist historians; she has been accused of neglecting the physical and material conditions of life, of relying on a very negative construction of identity through difference, of denying individual agency, and of ignoring women's experience (previously seen as the building block of feminist research). Fierce debates on the relevance of poststructuralism to feminist and labor history have ensued. Scott, however, has been quick to respond to her critics, continually developing her ideas about identity and experience and, moreover, challenging historians to question the philosophical bases of the very categories they choose to employ as tools of analysis.

LOUISE AINSLEY JACKSON

See also Family; Feminism; Gender; Gordon; Homosexuality; Labor; Social; Tilly, L.; Walkowitz; Women's History: European

Biography
Born Brooklyn, New York, 18 December 1941. Received BA, Brandeis University, 1962; MA, University of Wisconsin, Madison, 1964, PhD 1969. Taught at University of Illinois, Chicago, 1970–72; Northwestern University, 1972–74; University of North Carolina, Chapel Hill, 1977–80; Brown University from 1980; and currently Rutgers University. Married Donald M. Scott, 1965 (1 son, 1 daughter).

Principal Writings
The Glassworkers of Carmaux: French Craftsmen and Political Action in a Nineteenth-Century City, 1974
With Louise A. Tilly, *Women, Work, and Family,* 1978
With Jill Ker Conway and Susan C. Bourque, eds., *Learning about Women: Gender, Politics, and Power,* 1987
Gender and the Politics of History, 1988
Editor with Judith Butler, *Feminists Theorize the Political,* 1992
Editor, *Feminism and History,* 1996
Only Paradoxes to Offer: French Feminists and the Rights of Man, 1996

Further Reading
Downs, Laura Lee, "If 'Woman' is Just an Empty Category, then Why am I Afraid to Walk Alone at Night? Identity Politics Meets the Postmodern Subject," *Comparative Study of Society and History* 35 (1993), 414–37
Frader, Laura L., "Dissent over Discourse: Labor History, Gender, and the Linguistic Turn," *History and Theory* 34 (1995), 213–30
Gordon, Linda, "Book Review: Joan Scott, *Gender and the Politics of History*," *SIGNS: Journal of Women in Culture and Society* 15 (1990), 848–60

Hall, Catherine, "Politics, Poststructuralism, and Feminist History," *Gender and History* 3 (1991), 204–10
Hoff, Joan, "Gender as a Postmodern Category of Paralysis," *Women's History Review* 3 (1994), 149–68
Koonz, Claudia, "Postscripts," *Women's Review of Books* 6 (January 1989), 19–20
Palmer, Bryan D., Anson Rabinbach, and Christine Stansell, "Responses to Joan Scott," *International Labor and Working Class History* 31 (1987), 24–36
Sewell, William H., Jr., "Review Essay: *Gender and the Politics of History,*" *History and Theory* 29 (1990), 71–82

Scribner, R.W. 1941–1998
Australian historian of the Reformation

R.W. Scribner was one of a generation of gifted and articulate Australians who left their home country to make their careers in Britain. The best known – Clive James, Germaine Greer, and Robert Hughes (later in the US) – found fame in the public eye in the media and the arts, but others went on to establish themselves out of the limelight as scholars of the first rank. The creativity, energy, and irreverence that marked them all were, in Scribner's case, directed to a radical rethinking of his chosen historical subject, the German Reformation set in its wider social context.

Scribner's Catholic upbringing gave him insights into the fabric of religious belief that stood him in excellent stead when he came to study the origins of Protestantism, a creed whose apparent rationality and reliance upon literacy have sometimes been contrasted by its adherents with a sump of Catholic superstition. Scribner's involvement in student activism at the University of Sydney awakened his interest in political philosophers of the left, not only Marx, but later materialist thinkers, such as Gramsci, who were concerned with society and politics as cultural manifestations. In Britain, this intellectual orientation quickly brought Scribner into the orbit of the new social history (from 1976 he was a member of the editorial board of *Social History*), where he took an active part in the early years of the History Workshop movement. However, he never allowed himself to be ideologically pigeon-holed; indeed, one of his most engaging traits was his ability to get on with colleagues and scholars of very different persuasions, and his historical writing was admired by Catholics and Protestants alike. Following his BA and MA at Sydney, he began to research in Germany, eventually focusing on Erfurt (then in East Germany) for his doctoral work.

From the 1970s onwards a steady stream of articles appeared. At first they were chiefly concerned with the Reformation in German cities (including his classic discussion of the Reformation's "failure" in Cologne, "Why Was There No Reformation in Cologne?", 1976), but already Scribner was becoming fascinated by the mechanisms that underlie the transmission and reception of ideas. The communication of Reformation doctrines could not, he believed, be understood as a purely intellectual process: the assumptions and expectations of the audience itself counted for just as much, and these were located beyond mere intellectual curiosity in the deeper well-springs of psychological and cultural predispositions. Here Scribner was able to draw upon his formidable grasp of historical anthropology and cultural theory. The ritual and ludic elements of the Reformation as *enactment* were tellingly explored in "Reformation, Carnival, and the World Turned Upside-down" (1978).

These insights determined two central themes of his subsequent research: the startling continuities of ritual, belief, and popular culture before and after the Reformation; and the importance of nonliterary means of communicating ideas – oral, visual, or participatory – alongside the printed work. Scribner was not the first to recognize the significance of the enormous outpouring of pamphlets and broadsheets in helping to create a Reformation audience, but he was certainly the first to realize that their resonance derived as much from their style and language, satirical and often scatological, as from their arguments – and that their impact was heightened by visual means (the use of woodcuts as illustrations), as well as by recitation in taverns or on the street. This research came to fruition in Scribner's first book, *For the Sake of Simple Folk* (1981). The study was hailed as a breakthrough in Reformation research, spanning the disciplines of semiology, iconology, and the history of *mentalités*, as well as art history in general. It contains an extremely illuminating introduction that outlined the methodological issues underpinning the research.

In 1981, Scribner was appointed to a lectureship in Cambridge, and the next fifteen years were especially productive. More than fifty articles appeared, including forays into the world of vagrants, deviants, and witchcraft, as well as his remarkable investigation of Luther's transformation in Protestant circles from Reformer to quasi-saint – his "Incombustible Luther" (1986). The most important were reprinted in his collection of essays, *Popular Culture and Popular Movements in Reformation Germany* (1987). He also wrote two shorter introductions intended to guide students through the thickets of the rapidly changing historiography of the Reformation, *The German Reformation* (1986), and a particularly original and suggestive survey, *Varieties of Reformation* (1993).

From the outset, however, Scribner had always cast his net wider than the Reformation. In 1979 he edited a volume of essays with Gerhard Benecke, *The German Peasant War of 1525: New Viewpoints*, and in Cambridge he taught a Special Subject on the Peasants' War, translating all of the documents himself. This formed the bedrock of the first English-language edition of sources on the Peasants' War, compiled by Scribner and the present writer, which was published in 1991. He then embarked, with Sheilagh Ogilvie, on a magisterial survey of German social and economic history in two volumes from the late Middle Ages to the Napoleonic era, which were published in 1996 (a third volume up to the present day is in preparation).

At the end of the 1980s Scribner began a major project on the social history of the German Reformation from 1450 to 1580. This book, had it been completed, would undoubtedly have been the crowning achievement of his career, securing his reputation as the finest continental Reformation scholar of his generation. But it was not to be. Other projects demanded attention, and soon after his move to Harvard Divinity School in 1996, illness intervened. However, Scribner's body of work reveals him as one of the major scholars of the postwar era.

TOM SCOTT

See also Reformation

Biography

Robert Scribner. Born Sydney, 6 September 1941. Educated at University of Sydney, BA, MA 1967; studied in Marburg and Freiburg, 1967–69; PhD, Institute of Historical Research, University of London, 1972. Taught at Portsmouth Polytechnic, 1972–78; King's College, London, 1979–81; Cambridge University, 1981–96; and Harvard Divinity School, 1996–98. Married 1) Robyn Dasey, 1972 (marriage dissolved); 2) Lois Rutherford, 1989 (1 son, 1 daughter). Died Arlington, Massachusetts, 29 January 1998.

Principal Writings

"Why Was There No Reformation in Cologne?," *Bulletin of the Institute of Historical Research* 49 (1976), 217–41

"Reformation, Carnival, and the World Turned Upside-down," *Social History* 3 (1978), 281–329

Editor with Gerhard Benecke, *The German Peasant War of 1525: New Viewpoints*, 1979

For the Sake of Simple Folk: Popular Propaganda for the German Reformation, 1981

"Incombustible Luther: The Image of the Reformation in Early Modern Germany," *Past and Present* 110 (1986), 38–68

The German Reformation, 1986

Popular Culture and Popular Movements in Reformation Germany, 1987

Editor and translator with Tom Scott, *The German Peasants' War: A History in Documents*, 1991

Varieties of Reformation, 1993

With Paula Johnston, *The Reformation in Germany and Switzerland*, 1993

Editor with Roy Porter and Mikuláš Teich, *The Reformation in National Context*, 1994

Editor, *Germany: A New Social and Economic History*, vol.1: *1450–1630*, 1996

Editor with Trevor Johnson, *Popular Religion in Germany and Central Europe, 1400–1800*, 1996

Editor with Ole Peter Grell, *Tolerance and Intolerance in the European Reformation*, 1996

Editor with R. Po-Hsia, *Problems in the Historical Anthropology of Early Modern Europe*, 1997

Scriptores Historiae Augustae

Called "the most enigmatic work that Antiquity has transmitted" by Sir Ronald Syme, the text known commonly as the *Historia Augusta* (HA; Augustan History) – title devised by Isaac Casaubon in 1603 – consists of biographies of Roman emperors, pretenders, and usurpers covering the years 117 to 284 CE, with a gap for the years 244–59. Purportedly six authors (the *scriptores*: Aelius Spartianus, Julius Capitolinus, Aelius Lampridius, Vulcacius Gallicanus, Trebellius Pollio, and Flavius Vopiscus) wrote these biographies during the late 3rd and early 4th centuries. Although cited only once in antiquity, by Q. Symmachus, consul in 485 and father-in-law of Boethius, the work gained popularity during the Middle Ages and the Renaissance. Seventeen extant manuscripts in varying degrees of completeness derive from an original 9th-century codex. Understanding this mysterious work has proven to be a source of great consternation for historians, because, ironically, the HA provides one of the very few literary accounts of the 2nd and 3rd centuries, a period of great social, economic, and political change in the Roman world.

From Edward Gibbon in the 18th century on, concerns about the authorship, date, and reliability of the HA have plagued its use as a source. In 1889, Hermann Dessau argued that the work was a historical forgery, written a century later than it claimed (during the reign of Theodosius the Great, 379–95) and by one author posing as six. Scholars over the past hundred years have debated this thesis. Textual analysis and comparison of the HA with other authors have made it possible to establish certain characteristic features of the work however. While the biographies seem to be modeled after Suetonius' *De vita Caesarum* (Lives of the Caesars, early 2nd century CE) and fall within the tradition of Latin biography, they do not necessarily constitute a continuation of his work, even though some scholars postulate possible lost lives of Nerva and Trajan that would link the HA to Suetonius. Unlike Suetonius' work, the HA included lives of pretenders and usurpers in addition to emperors – the former group considered "secondary lives" by modern scholars, the latter "primary lives." Since more corroborating evidence from elsewhere exists for the primary lives, these are naturally viewed as more reliable than the secondary lives. Yet much inaccurate or imaginative information fills the work as a whole. Certain primary lives (e.g., Severus Alexander and Gallienus) portrayed the character and actions of the emperors in ways that bear almost no resemblance to modern historical assessments of them. Some 200 names and "authorities" attested nowhere else also appear throughout the work; many consider them highly suspect if not completely spurious. To these the HA adds invented speeches, letters, and documents, as well as some of the most hideous poetry in all antiquity. Even the names of the six authors suggest fabrication: no other source mentions them, and their playfulness seems contrived. For example, Vulcatius Gallicanus translates as "Fiery Frenchman," and its Latin abbreviation (V.C.) stands for *vir clarissimus*, the rank of a senator. What is more, the author couches his material in humor, witticisms, and tongue-in-cheek references, most of which are lost on a modern audience. The lives themselves vary in length, as does the degree to which they incorporate documents or other references. Furthermore, their merits as Latin literature are few.

Modern opinion concerning the proper use of the HA as a historical source is still evolving. Where previous generations consulted it, however reluctantly, we tend to dismiss it almost outright, relying instead on a growing body of archaeological, epigraphic, and numismatic evidence for the period. The general consensus now holds that an anonymous author composed the HA near the end of the 4th century, and recent investigations have abandoned questions of date and authorship, focusing instead on discerning the HA's sources and determining its historical worth. Its purpose, however, still evades us. While some detect in the lives senatorial sympathies, a dislike of hereditary monarchy, an aversion to the army's involvement in politics, and perhaps even a veiled animosity towards Christianity, these positions lack the uniformity necessary to serve as an agenda for the whole text. Syme's notion that some "rogue grammarian" wrote the biographies as sheer entertainment is appealing, especially since much ancient humor does not translate. The change in opinion over the past century, from viewing the HA as a quagmire to considering it a treasure trove of intriguing information about later Roman cultural sensibilities, is welcome. But as a historical source, this work must always be approached with caution. Indeed, one cannot escape the feeling that even if the author(s) did not intend it as a joke, the HA has nonetheless amounted to one played on posterity.

GAVIN A. SUNDWALL

See also Gibbon; Roman; Suetonius; Syme

Editions

Birley, Anthony R., ed. and trans., *Lives of the Later Caesars*, Harmondsworth: Penguin, 1976
Hohl, Ernst, ed., *Scriptores Historiae Augustae*, 2 vols., Leipzig: Teubner, 1927
Magie, David, *The Scriptores Historiae Augustae* (Loeb edition), 3 vols., Cambridge, MA: Harvard University Press, and London: Heinemann, 1922–32, reprinted 1960–61

Further Reading

Barnes, Timothy D., *The Sources of the Historia Augusta*, Brussels: Latomus, 1978
Baynes, Norman H., *The Historia Augusta: Its Date and Purpose*, Oxford: Oxford University Press, 1926
Birley, Anthony R., "The Augustan History," in Thomas Alan Dorey, ed., *Latin Biography*, New York: Basic Books, and London: Routledge, 1967
Dessau, Hermann, "Über Zeit und Persönlichkeit der Scriptores Historiae Augustae" (On the Time and Personality of the Scriptores Historiae Augustae), *Hermes* 24 (1889), 334
Honoré, Tony, "Scriptor Historiae Augustae," *Journal of Roman Studies* 77 (1987), 156–76
Matthews, John F., "Historia Augusta," in Simon Hornblower and Antony Spawforth, eds., *The Oxford Classical Dictionary*, 3rd edition, Oxford and New York: Oxford University Press, 1996
Momigliano, Arnaldo, "An Unsolved Problem of Historical Forgery: The Scriptores Historiae Augustae," in his *Studies in Historiography*, London: Weidenfeld and Nicolson, and New York: Harper, 1966
Syme, Ronald, *Ammianus and the Historia Augusta*, Oxford: Oxford University Press, 1968
Syme, Ronald, *Emperors and Biography: Studies in the Historia Augusta*, Oxford: Clarendon Press, 1971
Syme, Ronald, *The Historia Augusta: A Call of Clarity*, Bonn: Habelt, 1971; Oxford and New York: Oxford University Press, 1983
Syme, Ronald, *Historia Augusta Papers*, Oxford and New York: Oxford University Press, 1983
White, Peter, "The Authorship of the Historia Augusta," *Journal of Roman Studies* 57 (1967), 115–33

Seeley, J.R. 1834–1895

British historian

On the basis of bewildering credentials J.R. Seeley found himself appointed Regius professor of history at Cambridge University in 1869. Hitherto his only substantial publication had been an anonymous life of Christ. He soon came to be influential in the professionalization of historical study both in the university (the historical tripos was introduced four years after his appointment) and more widely through the medium of working men's colleges. In 1881 he began to work systematically on colonial history, most likely, it seems, lecturing to future members of the Indian Civil Service. Initially determined that his lectures should remain unpublished, he was persuaded otherwise in May 1882 by Florence Nightingale. *The Expansion of England* appeared the following year, coinciding with the British occupation of Egypt; by 1885 some 80,000 copies had been sold. Thereafter it remained in print, its reputation as an imperial primer established until 1956 – when Britain once more was bombarding Egypt. Now it is hardly read at all.

Seeley organized his account of the English nation in terms of its external dynamics: or better, he attempted to dismantle he dualism of "internal" and "external" by insisting on the necessary unity of the two, complaining of a historiography too exclusively European. He believed the central issue of early imperial Europe was the presence of the New World, which "does not lie outside Europe but exists inside it as a principle of unlimited political change." Or as he put it more pithily: in the 18th century "the history of England is not in England but in America and Asia."

In adopting this perspective Seeley was able to avoid some of the more usual hyper-idealizations of England. For him it is the authority of the English state that functions as the prime mover, an authority active as much in the colonies as in the metropolis. His own hopes were clear: that metropolitan rule would prove sufficiently benign, and colonialists sufficiently accommodating, for there to emerge throughout the empire a consensual unity founded on a shared recognition of English ethnicity. "If Greater Britain in the full sense of the phrase really existed, Canada and Australia would be to us as Kent and Cornwall."

Seeley was also concerned that his lectures should stand as an essay in the practice of history. He drew a fine distinction between history and politics – both, as he saw it, principally concerned themselves with the examination and organization of the state – believing history should "modify his [the reader's] view of the present." He railed against a historiography that peddled only "common sense" and worked by "the drowsy spell of narrative." He looked forward to a history based less on ethics and more on causes, which was analytical, rational, and true. History bereft of these qualities, and bereft of a properly masculine concern with politics, became merely "foppish . . . aiming only at literary display, which produces delightful books hovering between poetry and prose." A feminized history without politics could only alight upon such frivolities as "the ladies thronging to the toy-shops." He had a number of malefactors in sight. Scott was one, Macaulay another. But Thackeray he condemned most of all precisely because it was he who proclaimed that fiction could be historically truthful and history fictional, denying the possibilities (in Seeley's words) that "history can establish any solid or important truths." History in this scheme becomes only rhetoric. Thackeray, according to Seeley, "does not deny that history might be important if it were true, but he says it is not true." To this Seeley could only respond – one can imagine the tone – "Make it true and trustworthy."

Since the middle part of the 20th century Seeley has hardly been fashionable, regarded too often as an old relic of imperial Britain. But he remains a significant figure. He was crucial in introducing history as a subject worthy of serious intellectual study in the universities. He possessed an unusually sharp sense of the history of England having been formed by its colonies, and consequently proclaimed the need for a historiography that centered on the non-European world. And he

laid down, with great prescience, some of the philosophical issues that have come to dominate historiography in the subsequent century. Seeley's own intellectual code compelled him to adopt solutions to these dilemmas which, a hundred years on, might seem unpalatably positivistic in their inclination. But the issues he raised, of the relations between historical truth and the historical imagination, are still ours.

BILL SCHWARZ

See also British Empire; Political

Biography
John Robert Seeley. Born London, 10 October 1834, son of a publisher. Studied at Christ's College, Cambridge, BA 1857, MA 1860, fellow 1858–69. Taught Latin, University College, London, 1863–69; Regius professor of modern history, Cambridge University, 1869–95: fellow, Gonville and Caius College, 1882–95. Married Mary Agnes Phillot, 1869 (1 daughter). Knighted 1894. Died Cambridge, 13 January 1895.

Principal Writings
Ecce Homo: A Survey of the Life and Work of Jesus Christ, 1865
Lectures and Essays, 1870
Editor, *Livy: Book 1*, 1871
Life and Times of Stein; or, Germany and Prussia in the Napoleonic Age, 3 vols., 1878
The Expansion of England, 1883; abridged as *Our Colonial Expansion*, 1887
A Short History of Napoleon the First, 1886
Roman Imperialism, and Other Lectures and Essays, 1889
The Growth of British Policy: An Historical Essay, 2 vols., 1895
Introduction to Political Science, edited by Henry Sidgwick, 1896

Further Reading
Burroughs, Peter, "John Robert Seeley and British Imperial History," *Journal of Imperial and Commonwealth History* 1 (1973), 191–212
Herkless, John L., "Seeley and Ranke," *Historian* 43 (1980), 1–22
Rein, Gustav Adolf, *Sir John Seeley: A Study of a Historian*, Wolfeboro, NH: Longwood, 1987 (German original, 1912)
Wormell, Deborah, *Sir John Seeley and the Uses of History*, Cambridge: Cambridge University Press, 1980

Séguin, Maurice 1918–1984
French Canadian historian of Quebec

One of the founders of a professional history department at Quebec's largest university, Maurice Séguin produced an interpretation of Canadian history that gave rise to the influential neo-nationalist school. Rejecting the traditional clerical interpretation that emphasized French Canada's fight for survival as a Catholic peasant society dominated by a paternalistic elite, he focused on the British conquest of 1760 as the key event preventing the modernization of Quebec society.

Séguin had little formal training in history with only one sixty-hour lecture course (with no final exam) on Canadian history given by Quebec's "national historian," abbé Lionel Groulx. Groulx's charisma drew Séguin to history and he registered in a doctoral program in 1944. On completion of his thesis, he joined the newly created department of history at the University of Montreal alongside Guy Frégault and one year later was joined by Michel Brunet. Although Frégault was already an accomplished historian with two books to his credit, his interpretation of New France was radically transformed by Séguin's thesis and the younger colleague became the intellectual leader of the Montreal school. If Séguin was the inspiration, his ideas were circulated in scholarly circles largely through Frégault's writing, while Brunet's skill as an orator and polemicist enabled them to reach a wider audience.

Contrary to the prevailing Quebec historiography of the 1940s, Séguin's thesis did not glorify New France. The French colony was a nation in embryonic form that still required the protection, manpower, and capital of the metropolis to develop normally until it could become an independent nation. The British conquest of 1760 halted this development by depriving French Canada of its leadership and access to capital and resources, condemning it to vegetate or die. A new English Canada was born that benefited from the support of the mother country, and since it was impossible for two independent nations to share the same territory, the new nationality had to triumph. Eliminated from trade and industry, French Canada was forced to fall back on agriculture, the only economic sector under its control. This prevented its development as a normal nation. Relegated to an inferior economic status by the conquest, French Canada saw its subordination consolidated by the 1840 Act of Union, which condemned it to a provincial status within an English nation-state. Although federalists argued that Quebec could flourish within a larger unit, Séguin insisted that minority interests were always subordinated to those of the majority and that a normal nation must have complete control of a state, considered the main instrument for national development.

Séguin wrote little. His 1947 article laid down the essential points of his thesis but the complete text was published only in 1970. A short booklet drawn from a three-part television interview – *L'Idée d'indépendance au Québec* (The Idea of Independence in Quebec) – was published in 1968, the year the separatist Parti Québécois was founded. His reticence to publish stemmed from a personal conception of intellectual endeavor. Synthesis was the only proper form of expression; the rest was mere babble. Ideally a historian "should only publish one book that would set down what he had to say and where each word and each comma was either essential or should be edited out" (Comeau). Failure to publish was also linked to his preference for direct contact with his audience in a classroom setting where the nuances of thought could be made clear, ideas debated and arguments refined. Séguin was a captivating and convincing teacher, adulated by generations of students. His most influential course set out a theoretical model for the development of human societies and then illustrated why Quebec had not and could not develop as a normal society (Comeau). This vision influenced most of the teachers entering the rapidly expanding high school and college systems over three decades and became widely disseminated in textbooks.

Fifty years after its genesis, the Séguin thesis is still an essential reference for Quebec nationalism. In the preamble to the 1980 referendum question on sovereignty-association, the idea that New France would have become an independent nation had the conquest not intervened to deprive it of its leadership was clearly stated. In the 1995 referendum campaign, sovereigntists

continually harped on the necessity of independence for Quebec to become a "normal" society. Although Séguin believed that Quebec's complete emancipation was unlikely due to the opposition of the English majority in Canada, the transformation from a nationalism of survival to a dynamic nationalism is Séguin's most enduring contribution to Quebec intellectual life.

JOHN A. DICKINSON

See also Canada; Frégault

Biography
Born Horse Creek, Saskatchewan, 7 December 1918. Studied with the Jesuits, Collège Saint-Ignace and Collège Jean-de-Brébeuf, Montreal. Received BA, University of Montreal, 1942, PhD 1947. Taught at University of Montreal, 1948–84. Married Tatiana Demidoff, 1962 (1 son, 1 daughter). Died Montreal, 28 August 1984.

Principal Writings
"La Conquête et la vie économique des canadiens" (The Conquest and the Economic Life of the Canadians), *Action nationale* 28 (1947)
L'Idée d'indépendance au Québec: genèse et historique (The Idea of Independence in Quebec: Genesis and History), 1968
La "Nation canadienne" et l'agriculture (1760–1850): essai d'histoire économique (The "Canadian Nation" and Agriculture, 1760–1850: Essays in Economic History), 1970
Une Histoire du Québec: vision d'un prophète (A History of Quebec: The Vision of a Prophet), 1995

Further Reading
Blain, Jean, "Economie et société en Nouvelle-France: l'historiographie des années 1950–1960 – Guy Frégault et l'école de Montréal" (Economy and Society in New France: The Historiography of Guy Frégault and the Montreal School, 1950–1960), *Revue d'histoire de l'Amérique française*, 28 (1974), 163–86
Comeau, Robert, *Maurice Séguin, historien du pays québécois vu par ses contemporains* (Maurice Séguin, Quebec Historian: As Seen by His Contemporaries) Montreal: VLB, 1987
Lamarre, Jean, *Le Devenir de la nation québécoise selon Maurice Séguin, Guy Frégault et Michel Brunet, 1944–1969* (The Future of the Quebec Nation according to Maurice Séguin, Guy Frégault, and Michel Brunet, 1944–1969), Sillery, Quebec: Septentrion, 1993
Miquelon, Dale, ed., *Society and Conquest: The Debate on the Bourgeoisie and Social Change in French Canada, 1700–1850*, Toronto: Copp Clark, 1977
Nish, Cameron, ed., *The French Canadians, 1759–1766; Conquered? Half-Conquered? Liberated?*, Toronto: Copp Clark, 1966

Seignobos, Charles 1854–1942
French historian

One of the most prominent historians in Third Republic France, Charles Seignobos began his career as a medievalist. His work on contemporary Europe first brought him to public attention and he later proclaimed himself a "generalist." Yet his most lasting efforts are his elaborations of the methods that defined the so-called positivist (or "methodological") approach then dominant in historical inquiry. He worked to position and then strove to maintain history's privileged place among competing disciplinary approaches to describing human behavior. In his histories and in his methodological manifestos, Seignobos exemplified what adherents of the Annales school later derided as the "history of events."

Restricting his focus and that of the discipline of history to political and military incidents and individuals described in documents, Seignobos refused the abstract or structural. He rejected claims that historians should attempt to ascribe causality. The historian, Seignobos argued, needed to explain the past by exposing the significant accidents and linking them chronologically. For Seignobos, historians cannot recapture the past. In underlining the limitations of historical description he differed from fellow positivist historian Ernest Lavisse as well as from the Prussian "father" of historical science, Leopold von Ranke.

Seignobos was one of Lavisse's first students and he later trained in Prussia. Like that of Lavisse, Seignobos' vision of history became particularly important because of the close connections of the emerging discipline with the institutions of the nascent Third Republic, institutions to which he had access. Seignobos was instrumental both in placing the teaching of history at the center of the Republic's primary as well as secondary curriculums and in putting pedagogy on an equal basis with research for French historians. His most notable book, *Introduction aux études historiques* (1898; *Introduction to the Study of History*, 1898), which he co-wrote with the archivist Charles-Victor Langlois, was one part of his response to criticisms of history's pre-eminence among French academic disciplines.

The *Introduction* is a manifesto promoting the authority of historians and stating how descriptions of the past should be written. Seignobos, who authored most of the methodological chapters, described history as a utilitarian science. By this he meant that history is not the same as the natural sciences, for it cannot isolate laws. To do so for human activity, he wrote, is impossible. With this position, he effectively denied the underpinnings of social science. Seignobos and Langlois published their manifesto in the midst of numerous polemics, by François Simiand and other French Durkheimians, which claimed that sociology, with its attention to the recurrent and thus its ability to determine the laws governing human behavior, necessarily superseded history. Seignobos, in the *Introduction* and in various related articles, set a precedent for future historians by ignoring the substance of extra-disciplinary criticism. In response to Simiand's harsh attacks on the limits of history, Seignobos replied that "The difference between us is not that which exists between two generations: it is the natural divergence between a philosopher and a historian." According to Seignobos, only those individuals committed to and trained in historical research are qualified to evaluate the methods and claims of historians. History itself provides the common ground in which the insights of other disciplines which rely on documents could be brought together.

The *Introduction* defined what historians must do and how their work should be done. Seignobos described four stages of historical research: the collection and classification of documents ("heuristics"); the evaluation of these documents according to internal criteria ("hermeneutics"); the explanation, by analogy and deduction, of gaps between documented facts; and finally, the organization of established facts into logical constructions. He acknowledged that this process is subjective and that the historian operates from the supposition that past incidents are analogous to similar events in the present. Seignobos stated that this premise is never wholly true, that the past always remains somewhat opaque. Yet this technique allows the trained historian to write authoritatively, if cautiously, using documents that concern certain events and individuals. Historians should chronicle those people and incidents which participated in the series of accidents leading to the evolution of past institutions and understandings into their present more advanced forms.

Seignobos argued for histories of change, what he called "l'événement le plus intéressant de l'histoire" (the most interesting events in history). Thus, he suggested there is little the historian can contribute in examining the 17th century when, with the exception of the English Revolution, "nothing happened." Better to study the 18th, given that this was the century when the foundations of the French, American, Prussian, and other modern states emerged. Seignobos' writing situated history in the service of existing regimes. He admitted that as regimes changed, so would historians' focus. Writing in the democratic Third Republic, Seignobos explained history as evolutionary, guarding against the claims both of reactionaries who opposed all change and those who sought revolutionary upheaval. Seignobos himself began his career by producing the kind of monographs he later prescribed for younger scholars in the *Introduction*. He then turned to writing and directing large-scale general studies, the task which the *Introduction* advised senior scholars to undertake. His *L'Histoire politique de l'Europe contemporaine* (1897; *A Political History of Europe since 1814*, 1899) was the work that first brought Seignobos to the attention of the general public.

Seignobos saw history as cumulative and collaborative. Historians, he believed, collect and organize documents, contributing to the slow accumulation of facts. The monographs of younger historians provide the material for general histories. These should offer preliminary syntheses, yet can make no great explanatory claims. When all the documents have been analyzed, only then could historians offer insights into causality. Seignobos did not foresee this happening.

The *Introduction to the Study of History* remains the last guidebook introducing and codifying the study of history published in French. While what Marc Bloch and Lucien Febvre referred to as "l'histoire à la Seignobos" served as the antithesis for the Annales paradigm of historical research, the "new historians" produced no similar manifesto. In his almost genealogical approach to investigating the past, certain in practice while hesitant in claims, Seignobos offers intriguing methodological and analytic possibilities for our own uncertain age.

TODD DAVID SHEPARD

See also France: 1000–1450; Historiology; Simiand; Social

Biography
Born Lamastre, Ardèche, 10 September 1854. Studied at Ecole Normale Supérieure, 1874–77. Taught from 1879; professor of modern and political history, Sorbonne, 1925–42. Died Ploubozlanec, Côtes-du-Nord, 2 May 1942.

Principal Writings

Le Régime féodal en Bourgogne jusqu'en 1360: étude sur la société et les institutions d'une province française au Moyen-Age suivie de documents inédits tirés des archives des ducs de Bourgogne (The Feudal State in Burgundy before 1360: A Study of the Society and Institutions of a Medieval French Province According to the Archives of the Dukes of Burgundy), 1882

Histoire narrative et descriptive des anciens peuples de l'Orient: supplément à l'usage des professeurs (A Narrative and Descriptive History of the Ancient Peoples of the East: A Supplement), 1891

Contributor to Ernest Lavisse and Alfred Rambaud, eds., *Histoire générale du IVe siècle à nos jours* (A General History from the 4th Century until Today), 12 vols., 1892–1901

Histoire narrative et descriptive du peuple romain (A Narrative and Descriptive History of the Roman People), 1894

L'Histoire politique de l'Europe contemporaine, 1897; in English as *A Political History of Europe since 1814*, 1899

With Charles-Victor Langlois, *Introduction aux études historiques*, 1898; in English as *Introduction to the Study of History*, 1898

La Méthode historique appliquée aux sciences sociales (The Historical Method as Applied to the Social Sciences), 1901

L'Empire Russe jusqu' à Nicolas II (The Russian Empire before Nicholas II), 1905

L'Histoire de la France contemporaine (Contemporary French History), vols. 6–8, 1921–22

L'Histoire sincère de la nation française, 1933; in English as *The History of the French People*, 1932

Etudes de politique et d'histoire (Studies of Politics and History), 1934

Essai d'une histoire comparée des peuples de l'Europe (Essays on the Comparative History of the Peoples of Europe), 1938

Further Reading

Bloch, Marc, *Apologie pour l'histoire, ou, métier d'historien*, Paris: Colin, 1949; in English as *The Historian's Craft*, New York: Knopf, 1953, Manchester: Manchester University Press, 1954

Carbonell, Charles-Olivier, *Histoire et historiens: une mutation idéologique des historiens français, 1865–1885* (History and Historians: The Ideological Changes within the French Historical Profession, 1865–1885), Toulouse: Privat, 1976

Carrard, Philippe, "Disciplining Clio: The Rhetoric of Positivism," *Clio* 24 (1995), 189–204

Crubellier, Maurice, *L'Ecole républicaine 1870–1940* (Republican Schooling, 1870–1940), Paris: Christian, 1993

Davis, Natalie Zemon, "History's Two Bodies," *American Historical Review* 93 (1988)

Furet, François, *L'Atelier de l'histoire*, Paris: Flammarion, 1982; in English as *In the Workshop of History*, Chicago: University of Chicago Press, 1984

Keylor, William R., *Academy and Community: The Foundation of the French Historical Profession*, Cambridge, MA: Harvard University Press, 1975

Noiriel, Gérald, "Foucault and History: The Lessons of a Disillusion," *Journal of Modern History* 66 (1994), 547–68

Selden, John 1584–1654
English legal historian

John Selden, lawyer, scholar, antiquarian, political philosopher, historian, and a member of the parliamentary opposition to crown rule during the tumultuous years preceding the English Civil War, helped to revolutionize the study and writing of history in the early 17th century. Although according to Clarendon his writing could be described by "a little under-valuing the beauty of stile, and too much propensity to the language of antiquity," Selden played a role of fundamental importance in the transition of English historical writing from a medieval antiquarianism to a more modern understanding of the scope and function of history than had ever before been expressed in Renaissance England.

Selden was acquainted with the great antiquarians of the age, both in England and on the European continent, and as Hugh A. MacDougall has pointed out, there clearly existed a connection between antiquarianism and opposition politics in parliament. Selden was never a member of the Society of Antiquaries, however, and this may have provided him with the intellectual freedom to develop a more advanced sense of what history was, and how and why it should be studied, than any of his English contemporaries.

Selden completed his first historical work, the *Analecton Anglo-Britannicon* in 1607, though it was not published until 1615. In the *Analecton* Selden summarized the history of the successive nations which had inhabited Britain. *The Duello, or Single Combat* (1610), his first published work, traced the origins of this controversial practice from its ancient origins to the England of his own time. That same year he also published *Jani Anglorum facies altera*, a study of the development and changes in English laws from ancient times. Although he recognized the significant impact of the Norman Conquest upon English legal institutions, Selden never went so far as Saxonists such as Richard Verstegan, who celebrated all things Saxon. English law, Selden suggested, developed from the blending of pre- and post-Conquest innovations. As in earlier works, he relied primarily upon printed sources for his information.

Selden published *Titles of Honour* in 1613, an attempt, based on both printed and manuscript sources, to trace the development of nearly every conceivable title from its origins in antiquity. Selden organized the work along hierarchical lines, but for each rank in society he followed chronological principles. He included marginal references to document and identify his sources, as well as a bibliography of "the more speciall-autors" whom he had read.

Titles of Honour was an important book. It contains a more sophisticated understanding of the impact of the Norman Conquest on English landholding practices than had appeared in the *Jani Anglorum*. It was also more sophisticated methodologically than anything he had done before, and in it we can see the beginning of a conceptual shift in Selden's thinking regarding the purpose of history. In *Titles of Honour*, Selden recognized that the key to discovering truth, the purpose of all historical research, lay in the detailed analysis and close scrutiny of historical documents and other texts. This important rethinking of the scope and purpose of history would be developed more fully by Selden in his *The History of Tithes* (1618). Unlike the antiquarian studies of so many of his contemporaries, the *The History of Tithes* pointed no morals and no lessons. It was not about great men nor about great events. Rather, it was a study based on a careful examination of all relevant sources on the origins, development, and social consequences of tithing.

In *The History of Tithes*, Selden wondered whether tithes had always been paid to the clergy *jure divino*. In attacking this historical problem, he had little interest in the past for its own sake. Rather, he hoped to illuminate the entire institutional framework of tithing. As D.R. Woolf noted, Selden was less interested in "what hath been" than in its relevance to "the practice and doubts of the present."

It would be a grave mistake to view Selden as a precursor to the objective, scientific ideal pre-eminent in later historiography. His politics, which later would land him in jail twice, entered into his work. *The History of Tithes* directly challenged the clergy, because Selden argued that the canon law could be effective only when it had been incorporated, either through custom or expressly through statute, into the corpus of a given nation's laws. The clergy in England, he found, had hidden and distorted evidence in order to justify its claim to collect tithes *jure divino*. As Woolf pointed out, Selden "must have known that he was lighting a match to read the label on a barrel of gunpowder."

In 1631 Selden published an expanded *Titles of Honour*, with significant portions of the original rewritten. The expanded edition reveals Selden's progression from the antiquarian who composed *The Duello* and the *Analecton* to the historian who produced the *The History of Tithes* in an effort which discovered and presented facts about the past, and demonstrated their relevance to the present. One of Selden's contemporary critics, Sir James Sempill, argued in *Sacrilege Sacredly Handled* (1619) that history ought to be "a simple narration of what is done." Selden, through his historical studies, far transcended this narrowly constrained understanding of the scope of historical inquiry, and his great contribution lay in redefining the field in more modern terms. Selden wedded the antiquarian drive to collect records and texts from the past, with a desire to produce critically astute, methodologically sound historical narrative based upon the close interpretation of historical documents and the analysis of the motives of those who wrote them. History could no longer be understood as a dry collection of data from the past. History, under Selden's influence, became the dynamic study of continuity and change over time. Selden was not the only scholar responsible for this reformulation of history, but in it he played a very large role.

MICHAEL L. OBERG

See also Legal

Biography

Born West Tarling, Sussex, 1584; son of a yeoman. Educated at Oxford and the Inns of Court before briefly practicing law. Turned to scholarship, writing on medieval legal history, Syrian mythology, and Jewish law and institutions. Served as member of parliament preceding and during the Civil War. Died London, 1654.

Principal Writings

Analecton Anglo-Britannicon, written 1607, published 1615
The Duello; or, Single Combat, 1610
Jani Anglorum facies altera, 1610
Titles of Honour, 1613; expanded 1631
The History of Tithes, 1618
Tracts, 1683
Table Talk, Being the Discourses of John Selden, 1689
Opera omnia, edited by David Wilkins, 3 vols., 1726

Further Reading

Ferguson, Arthur M., *Clio Unbound: Perception of the Social and Cultural Past in Renaissance England*, Durham, NC: Duke University Press, 1979

Fussner, F. Smith, *The Historical Revolution: English Historical Writing and Thought, 1580–1640*, London: Routledge, and New York: Columbia University Press, 1962
Levine, Joseph M., *Humanism and History: Origins of Modern English Historiography*, Ithaca, NY: Cornell University Press, 1987
MacDougall, Hugh A., *Racial Myth in English History: Trojans, Teutons, and Anglo-Saxons*, Montreal: Harvest House, and Hanover, NH: University Press of New England, 1982
Pocock, J.G.A., *The Ancient Constitution and the Feudal Law: A Study of English Historical Thought in the Seventeenth Century*, Cambridge: Cambridge University Press, 1957; revised 1987
Woolf, Daniel R., *The Idea of History in Early Stuart England: Erudition, Ideology, and "The Light of Truth" from the Accession of James I to the Civil War*, Toronto: University of Toronto Press, 1990

Semple, Ellen Churchill 1863–1932
US environmental historian and geographer

Ellen Churchill Semple graduated from Vassar, then studied privately with Friedrich Ratzel in Leipzig. Ratzel (1844–1904), trained as a Darwinian zoologist, applied biological and ecological concepts to create an environmentally-determined view of human history, explicated in his famous *Anthropogeographie* (1882–91). He coined the concept of *Lebensraum*, the natural limits occupied by a state, viewed organically. Semple recast Ratzel's opus and published it in an abridged English version in 1911, in which she eliminated much of Ratzel's Spencerian organicism and replaced deterministic language with more general concepts of geographic "factors," "influences," and "controls" over human culture. However, Darwinian influences were still strongly in evidence. She used arguments very similar to those found in histories written by later evolutionary biologists, such as C.D. Darlington, who extended the findings of population biology (gene pools, genetic diversity) to social and cultural evolution.

Thus, in *Influences of Geographic Environment* (1911), Semple stressed the influence of natural conditions of variation, the environmental modification of physique, and the role of isolation in physical and cultural differentiation. She closely followed Moritz Wagner's analysis of the isolation of human groups in naturally defined regions which, when combined with periods of migration, produced the rapid development of "type forms." Eurasia had the greatest number and variety of segregated habitats and thus the best opportunities for vast historical movements. This was Wagner and Semple's appropriation of Darwin's view that divergence of character had been enhanced in the cases of large populations occupying large spaces with many niches that intragroup competition had forced them to fill. In human history, Darwin's concept became a *law* of anthropogeography. Many of the topics in the book's index under the rubric "Historical Movements" are overtly biogeographical (e.g., barriers to, climatic factors in, colonization as a form of, zonal limits of, and so forth). Semple was also interested in the effect of climate on natural character in the classical, Hippocratic sense that "air, water and places" exercised a formative influence on human culture.

In the 1920s and 1930s, environmental determinism came under attack by American anthropologists led by Franz Boas and, in France, by Lucien Febvre who sought to establish a more nuanced mating of geography and history; both attacked Ratzel and Semple explicitly. Nevertheless, the influence of her book in American geography was enormous even after World War II, as John K. Wright established by a questionnaire sent to geographers in 1961.

Semple's first book, *American History and Its Geographic Conditions* (1903), was a landmark in American historical geography, in which historical events were linked to physical environment. For example, Semple's analysis of the Civil War and the sectional conflict that led to it began with a consideration of environmental forces that encouraged slavery. Her work can indeed be viewed as a historical geography of sectionalism, stressing regional habitats and climate more than the natural resource base. She shared with Frederick Jackson Turner an evolutionary and environmental conception of the frontier. Both were recapitulationists (they argued that settlers in a wilderness recapitulated the history of mankind while civilizing it), although Turner's construction was more sensitive to cultural differentiation.

In her great work on the geography of the ancient Mediterranean (1931), Semple used a more sophisticated methodology (and an impressive mastery of both the primary and secondary literature of classical antiquity) to establish the relationship between environment and civilization in the ancient world. Here, the organization is strictly geographical: historical events are introduced only insofar as they illustrate points of geography, not the reverse. Semple wrote on a wide variety of topics: her world survey of "Mountain Peoples in Relation to Their Soil" (1905), grounded in her familiarity with Kentucky, anticipated a number of Fernand Braudel's findings with respect to the mountainous regions of the Mediterranean.

Semple was the first American cultural geographer, laying the groundwork for that field in her courses at the University of Chicago and, later, Clark University. She was also the first woman president of the Association of American Geographers, elected in 1921.

In order to drive a stake through the heart of environmental determinism, Boas suggested that Carl Sauer, founder of the Berkeley school of cultural geography, write biographies of both Ratzel and Semple in the *Encyclopedia of Social Sciences* (1934). There Sauer damned Ratzel with faint praise and wrote that Semple "had remained true to Ratzel in making no restriction as to kinds of cultural data taken under observation but in being interested in whatever data could be related to environmental conditioning. She did no more than Ratzel in solving the methodological difficulty as to how such a relationship could be evaluated scientifically."

THOMAS F. GLICK

See also Historical Geography

Biography

Born Louisville, Kentucky, 1863, to a wealthy family. Educated locally, then studied history and English literature at Vassar College, BA 1882, MA in history 1891. Taught in a private girls' school, Louisville, 1882–91; toured Europe, then studied with anthropologist Friedrich Ratzel, Leipzig, 1891–93. Died 1932.

Principal Writings

American History and Its Geographic Conditions, 1903; revised 1933
Influences of Geographic Environment, on the Basis of Ratzel's System of Anthropo-Geography, 1911
The Geography of the Mediterranean Region: Its Relation to Ancient History, 1931

Further Reading

Gelfand, Lawrence, "Ellen Churchill Semple: Her Geographical Approach to American History," *Journal of Geography* 53 (1954), 30–41
James, Preston, "Ellen Churchill Semple and the Development of a Research Paradigm," in Wilford A. Bladen and Pradyumna P. Karan, eds., *The Evolution of Geographic Thought in America: A Kentucky Root*, Dubuque, IA: Kendall Hunt, 1983
Sauer, Carl O., "Ellen Churchill Semple," in Edwin R.A. Seligmann, ed., *Encyclopedia of the Social Sciences*, vol. 13, New York: Macmillan, 1934
Wright, John K., "Miss Semple's 'Influences of Geographic Environment': Notes Towards a Bibliobiography," *Geographical Review* 52 (1962), 346–61

Seton-Watson, Hugh 1916–1984

British historian of Central and Southeastern Europe

Hugh Seton-Watson can be placed in a family milieu of eminent historians, being the son of the distinguished authority on Central and Southeastern Europe, R.W. Seton-Watson, and the brother of historian Christopher Seton-Watson. After receiving a first class honours degree from New College, Oxford, in 1938, he travelled widely in Central and Southeastern Europe. His family influence was reinforced by his experiences during World War II, when he was initially stationed in Romania and Yugoslavia, before being sent to Cairo to undertake intelligence work.

The development of Seton-Watson's interests and concerns can be traced with reference to his published works, the first of which, *Eastern Europe Between the Wars* (1945) was a political and social history of the region during the unstable interwar period, making use of an impressive knowledge and much primary material. Following the war, his experiences and knowledge of Eastern Europe were widened through his undertaking of numerous assignments as special correspondent for *The Times* in Bulgaria, Czechoslovakia, Greece, Hungary, Romania, and Yugoslavia, between 1946 and 1948. His personal experience of the communist takeover of power, and subsequent Stalinization process, was described in *The East European Revolution* (1950), in which he argued that the takeover process took place in three stages: a genuine coalition, in which the communists joined with other parties in a – given the presence of the Red Army – relatively free political system. The second stage, a façade coalition, was reached when the communist parties achieved a level of influence over their noncommunist opponents. The third and final stage of communist takeover saw the communist party unchallenged, and their former opponents reduced to mere ciphers, with no room for independent action. This experience was seminal for Seton-Watson, whose subsequent work was directed toward the study of Russian history, and an understanding of European communism. This new direction resulted in *The Decline of Imperial Russia* (1952); *The Pattern of Communist Revolution* (1953), which was among the first scholarly works to place communism in a worldwide context; and his major contribution to Russian history, *The Russian Empire, 1801–1917* (1967). Seton-Watson's interest in Russia was reflected in his appointment to the chair of Russian history at the University of London's School of Slavonic and East European Studies, in 1951.

The 1960s and 1970s were Seton-Watson's most productive period, in which he completed a number of more analytical and theoretical works dealing with the subjects of nationalism and communism. His *magnum opus, Nations and States: An Enquiry into the Origins of Nations and the Politics of Nationalism* (1977), was a pioneering work which drew upon his considerable learning and knowledge of languages, and allowed him to demonstrate his powers of insight and analysis, honed during his studies of Eastern Europe. Seton-Watson distinguished between the "old" nations, which had acquired a national identity or national consciousness before the advent of the doctrine of nationalism, and which were mainly characterized by an autochthonous ruling elite; and "new" nations, whose national consciousness was developed contemporaneously with the rise of nationalist movements in the 19th century. Seton-Watson felt that the distinction between "old" and "new" nations was more useful than the contrast between "historical" and "unhistorical" nations: he asserted that all nations have a history, which may be discontinued by conquest, whereas national consciousness frequently survives such ruptures.

MICHAEL ALMOND-WELTON

See also Balkans; Central Europe; East Central Europe; Frontiers

Biography

George Hugh Nicholas Seton-Watson. Born London, 15 February 1916, son of historian R.W. Seton-Watson. Educated at Winchester College; BA, New College, Oxford, 1938. Attached to British legations, Romania and Yugoslavia, 1940–41; served at Special Forces General Headquarters, Middle East, 1941–44. Fellow and praelector in politics, University College, Oxford, 1946–51; professor of Russian history, School of Slavonic and East European Studies, University of London, 1951–83 (emeritus). Married Mary Hope Rokeling, 1947 (3 daughters). Died Washington, DC, 19 December 1984.

Principal Writings

Eastern Europe Between the Wars, 1918–1941, 1945; 3rd edition 1962
The East European Revolution, 1950; 3rd edition 1956
The Decline of Imperial Russia, 1952
The Pattern of Communist Revolution, 1953
Some Myths of Marxism, 1954
Neither War nor Peace: The Struggle for Power in the Post-War World, 1960
The New Imperialism, 1961
The Russian Empire, 1801–1917, 1967
The "Sick Heart" of Modern Europe: The Problem of the Danubian Lands, 1975
Editor, with others, *R.W. Seton-Watson and the Yugoslavs: Correspondence, 1906–1941,* 1976
Nations and States: An Enquiry into the Origins of Nations and the Politics of Nationalism, 1977

The Imperialist Revolution, 1980
With Christopher Seton-Watson, *The Making of a New Europe: R.W. Seton-Watson and the Last Years of Austria-Hungary,* 1981
The Imperialist Revolutionaries, 1987

Seton-Watson, R.W. 1879–1951
British historian of Central and Southeastern Europe

The first British historian to venture into the "primeval jungle" of Central Europe and the Balkans, R.W. Seton-Watson came to be known as a champion of the small nationalities of the Habsburg empire. He was not only a dedicated propagandist for the Czechs, Slovaks, Romanians, and Yugoslavs, but a political force behind their national aspirations. Accordingly, throughout the interwar period he remained the most ardent British supporter of the territorial status quo in the "zone of small nations." He epitomized the moralistic, self-righteous liberal intellectual, whose judgment on foreign countries and their governments was based on conviction and personal experience as much as on historical arguments.

His preoccupation with Central Europe began on a trip to Hungary in 1905, which he recalled to be a "fearful eye-opener." The treatment of Slovaks and Romanians, and "the depth of chauvinism into which Hungary had fallen," shattered his illusions about Magyar liberalism. Writing in the *Spectator* under the pseudonym of "Scotus Viator," he heaped scorn on the Hungarian political elite. In response, the Magyar press launched a smear campaign against the "Scottish traveller." Seton-Watson left Budapest, as he put it, in a "blind fury." He wrote a succession of books exploding the liberal Hungarian myth in England. In *Political Persecution in Hungary* (1908) and *Corruption and Reform in Hungary* (1911) he pointed out the undemocratic features of Hungarian political life, while in *Racial Problems in Hungary* (1908) he denounced the policy of "Magyarization." Although his books were favorably reviewed by Oscar Jászi and a few radicals of the Hungarian opposition, Seton-Watson's views on Hungary echoed those of his Czech, Slovak, South Slav, and Romanian friends, among them Thomas Masaryk, the first president of Czechoslovakia. As a result, Hungarian historiography has consistently demonized Seton-Watson, blaming him for turning British public opinion against Hungary in the last decade of the Dual Monarchy.

By the time of World War I Seton-Watson had become the most powerful British advocate of national self-determination. From urging the federalization of the Danubian empire in *The Southern Slav Question and the Habsburg Monarchy* in 1911, he went on during the war to press for the Habsburg empire's "liquidation." His periodical *New Europe* (1916–20) became a forum for "oppressed nationalities."

Towards the end of the war Seton-Watson's authority on Central European issues was unrivaled in Britain. At the Peace Conference the experts of the British delegation, in Harold Nicolson's words, would "not move a yard" without his advice.

In the interwar years, however, the political influence of Seton-Watson diminished dramatically. In the Foreign Office he was regarded as a "propagandist," and by 1939 an old friend compared him to "a milchcow which is not being milked." In 1929, even an architect of the "New Europe," Sir John W. Headlam-Morley, the historical adviser of the Foreign Office, criticized Seton-Watson for being "blind" to the weaknesses of the Czechs.

In the 1930s Seton-Watson grew more critical of his Central European friends. Nevertheless, his affinity with Czechs and Romanians was still evident in *A History of the Roumanians* (1934) and *History of the Czechs and Slovaks* (1943), while his book *Disraeli, Gladstone and the Eastern Question* (1935) was revealing of "the author's lifelong sympathy with Balkan Christians."

By contrast Hungary was regarded by Seton-Watson as "the principal obstacle to European progress." Although in two pamphlets, *Treaty Revision and the Hungarian Frontiers* (1934) and *Transylvania: A Key-Problem* (1943), he alluded to the minority problems caused by the Treaty of Trianon, he remained firmly opposed to any frontier revision.

Seton-Watson's anti-Hungary views were first challenged in Britain by C.A. Macartney. The dispute between the two partisan Oxford scholars seriously undermined Seton-Watson's claim in his inaugural lecture in 1922 that "the British historian who does not belong to any of the rival nationalities which jostle each other throughout the wide area of Central Europe, is doubtless saved from the worst pitfall that threatens his continental colleagues."

Seton-Watson had a considerable impact on postwar British historical writing about Central Europe. His works were colored by partial judgments, but were also based on a thorough knowledge of documents and a personal acquaintance with some of the major players of interwar diplomatic history. He was particularly influential among historians of the anti-appeasement school. Along with G.P. Gooch, H.W. Temperley, and Lewis Namier, he passionately opposed and criticized any British attempts to come to terms with Nazi Germany. Seton-Watson remained a faithful ally of Czechoslovakia, which, even at the time of Munich, he viewed as the "keystone of Europe."

GÁBOR BÁTONYI

See also Balkans; Central Europe; East Central Europe

Biography

Robert William Seton-Watson. Born London, 20 August 1879. Educated at Winchester School; New College, Oxford, BA in modern history 1902, DLitt 1910; University of Berlin, 1903; the Sorbonne, 1903–04; University of Vienna, 1905. Served in the Intelligence Bureau of the War Cabinet, 1917; Enemy Propaganda Department, 1918; Foreign Research and Press Service, 1939–40; Political Intelligence Bureau, Foreign Office, 1940–42. Honorary lecturer in East European history, King's College, University of London, 1915–22; Masaryk professor of Central European history, University of London, 1922–45; Professor of Czechoslovak studies, Oxford University, 1945–49. Founder editor, *New Europe*, 1916–20; founder editor (with Sir Bernard Pares), *Slavonic Review*, 1922–49. Wrote under pseudonym Scotus Viator on Central European and Balkan history and politics. Married Marion Esther Stack, 1911 (2 sons, 1 daughter). Died Isle of Skye, 25 July 1951.

Principal Writings

As Scotus Viator, *Political Persecution in Hungary: An Appeal to British Public Opinion*, 1908
As Scotus Viator, *Racial Problems in Hungary*, 1908
Corruption and Reform in Hungary: A Study of Electoral Practice, 1911
The Southern Slav Question and the Habsburg Monarchy, 1911
German, Slav, and Magyar: A Study in the Origins of the Great War, 1916
A History of the Roumanians: From Roman Times to the Completion of Unity, 1934
Treaty Revision and the Hungarian Frontiers, 1934
Disraeli, Gladstone and the Eastern Question: A Study in Diplomacy and Party Politics, 1935
Britain and the Dictators: A Survey of Post-War British Policy, 1938
Munich and the Dictators, 1939
History of the Czechs and Slovaks, 1943
Transylvania: A Key-Problem, 1943

Further Reading

Bodea, Cornelia, and Hugh Seton-Watson, eds., *R.W. Seton-Watson and the Romanians 1906–1920*, Bucharest: Editura Stiintifica si Enciclopedica, 1988
Jeszenszky, Géza, *Az elveszett presztizs: Magyarország megítélésének megváltozása Nagy-britanniában, 1894–1918* (The Lost Prestige: A Change in the British View of Hungary), Budapest: Magvető, 1986
Péter, László, "Scotus Viator és a 'magyar kérdés' az első világháború előtt" (Scotus Viator and the "Hungarian Question" before World War I), in *Gesta Hungarorum III*, 1990
Seton-Watson, Hugh et al., eds., *R.W. Seton-Watson and the Yugoslavs: Correspondence, 1906–1941*, London: British Academy, and Zagreb: University of Zagreb Press, 1976
Seton-Watson, Hugh, and Christopher Seton-Watson, *The Making of a New Europe: R.W. Seton-Watson and the Last Years of Austria-Hungary*, London: Methuen, and Seattle: University of Washington Press, 1981
Seton-Watson, Hugh, "R.W. Seton-Watson and the Trianon Settlement," in Béla K. Király, Peter Pastor, and Ivan Sanders, eds., *Essays on World War I: Total War and Peacemaking, a Case Study of Trianon*, New York: Columbia University Press, 1982
Wingfield, Nancy, "The Historian as Political Force in East Central Europe: R.W. Seton-Watson and Anglo-American Public Opinion Concerning Czechoslovakia in the Interwar Period," in E. Schmidt-Hartmann and S.B. Winters, *Grossbritannien, die USA und die böhmischen Länder*, Munich: Oldenbourg, 1991

Sexuality

The development of the history of sexuality as a sub-discipline has been intimately related to the modern creation of the idea of a sexual "identity" and of sexual politics since the late 19th century. In part, the sub-discipline can be traced back to the rise of professional sexologists such as Havelock Ellis, and the development of Freud's psychoanalysis. Certainly, the sexologists created the typologies with which the modern history of sexuality is concerned. Homosexuality, lesbianism, and heterosexuality are all categories created and problematized in that period.

But, if the late 19th century named the categories and subdivisions that characterize the history of sexuality, it was the 1960s and 1970s that produced the beginnings of a coherent history of at least Western sexuality. This was gradually formed out of an amalgam of the history of the family, of homosexuality and lesbianism, of pornography, demography, of the body, gender, and medicine – disciplines which were themselves coming to maturity in this period. Perhaps the most significant of the early contributing literatures is that associated with pornography. Much of the early history of pornography occupied the rather shadowy borderland between academic writing and some forms of explicit pornography. Prior to the early 1960s a patina of academic research and style was often used to mask masturbatory aids. But in the process these pseudo-academic works encouraged and allowed the development of legitimate literary and historical enquiry, resulting in the development of a large body of meticulously researched literature on the history of pornography. In particular in the works of David Foxon and H. Montgomery Hyde, a selfconsciously academic approach was pursued that has more recently been extended and deepened by historians such as Peter Wagner, and, from a feminist perspective, Lynn Hunt.

Much of this literature is neutral if not celebratory, and charts the ever increasing amount and specialization of written and visual pornography. In the process this literature, and the content of Western pornography itself, has formed the basis for what might be characterized as the "liberation" school of the history of sexuality. One of the main characteristics of this approach is the belief that extreme repression and intolerance have been a traditional attribute of Western society, that this is in sharp contrast with non-Western and ancient societies, and that this extreme repression was gradually undermined from the 17th century onwards, facing only a temporary reversal during the height of Victorian prudery.

Other literatures that have either consciously or unconsciously tended to adopt this approach include much of the history of the family and of demography. In Lawrence Stone's *The Family, Sex and Marriage* (1977) and his more recent *Road to Divorce* (1990), a rise in sentimental attachment between men and women within marriage, and by extension, a greater degree of love in relation to sex, has been described. In particular, Stone has posited the development of a Western "companionate marriage" in the late 17th century. When this literature has been combined with the results of the work of the Cambridge Group for the History of Population and Social Structure, which has demonstrated a demographic transition toward earlier and more fecund marriages in the mid-18th century, an almost Whiggish model of increasing sexual pleasure and emotional intimacy has been depicted.

Historians of the Western experience have used this background to argue further that the process of increasing sexual pleasure and sophistication was continued and refined in the 19th and 20th centuries – pointing to the work of the sexologists and psychoanalysts as evidence.

Perhaps the most ardent, although in some ways atypical, advocate of this "liberationist" approach is Edward Shorter. In a series of articles and books published between the early 1970s and mid-1980s, Shorter argued that the 18th century witnessed a general European "sexual revolution" in which women, and plebeian women in particular, gained a greater sense of individual economic freedom, which they in turn used actively to pursue sexual pleasure. Newly independent urban working women naturally, in Shorter's view, found the opportunities for sex irresistible, resulting both in more sex and the demographic transition which had been by the early 1980s convincingly demonstrated by demographic historians.

Shorter has been roundly condemned by a number of critics who have pointed out that the demographic models do not support his peculiarly urban transition, and, more importantly, that he is dependent on an essentialist construction of the character of sexual desire. In a very real sense, what Shorter and other "liberationists" have assumed is there is an unlimited human need for sex, which is separate from the cultural construction of desire. In Shorter's view all that was needed to create a sexual revolution was opportunity – which according to Shorter was provided for early modern Europe by growing urbanization and economic well-being.

With the increasing intellectual importance of the history of mentalities and, in an anglophone context, the linguistic turn, this essentialism has generally fallen out of favor. It is not that a "liberationist" metahistory has in any way been overturned, but rather that it has been modified through the work of Michel Foucault, the historians of medicine and the body, and a more sophisticated approach to the nature of sexual desire derived to a large extent from the history of homosexuality.

Perhaps the greatest single influence can be found in the work of Foucault. In the three volumes of his *Histoire de la sexualité* (1976–84; *History of Sexuality*, 1978–86) he completed before his death, Foucault suggested that the very rise of discourses around sexuality, and the apparent increase in the repression of sexual behavior that seemed to characterize a Western experience in the 19th century, in fact created a whole new preoccupation with sex. In other words where Shorter saw a gradual decline in the repression of sex, Foucault saw the gradual growth of discourses around sexuality and hence the creation of a growing number of sites of sexual definition and behavior. By reformulating the history of sexuality, Foucault in effect allowed historians for the first time to see sexual desire itself as a creation of a particular moment and a particular culture. In the process he both reformulated a liberation hypothesis, and at the same time eliminated the essentialist basis of the ways in which sex and sexuality had been defined since the late 19th century. Foucault's influence has been profound and universal. But the areas of historical enquiry that have been most fully transformed by his work on the history of sexuality have been the study of homosexuality and of the body.

Since the rise of the Gay Rights movement in the late 1960s an increasingly complex historiography of homosexuality has developed. This has dealt primarily with the histories of Europe and America, but more than any other aspect of the history of sexuality has also incorporated world history, including the histories of aboriginal peoples and the classical world. The role of the *berdache* in native American culture, and of the sodomitical roles found in Japanese and Indian cultures, have been largely researched within this context. While the major themes of the work in these fields have been the rise of the homosexual "subculture," and the relative importance of nature versus nurture in the creation of homosexual behavior and identity, the literature itself has forced historians working in other fields to ask questions about the whole range of possible sexualities, including heterosexuality.

What has emerged from this literature is a complex amalgam of relationships in which sex is in many ways but a small part. Homosexuality in the classical world, for example, has been shown to form, not an identity, but the expression of a power relationship. In the work of historians such as Kenneth Dover, a set of homosexual relationships dependent largely on the relative social positions of the people involved has been described. So, to sodomize someone was seen in the classical world as a reflection of power, while to be sodomized a reflection only of powerlessness. Passive and active homosexuality were, in other words, quite separate.

In a modern Western context this idea has been used to argue that sodomy was a facet of "normal" sexual life for men up until the Renaissance – that the 16th-century image of the libertine with a whore on one arm and a catamite on the other reflected the extent to which modern boundaries between hetero- and homosexuality had yet to be drawn.

Within this context two separate and contradictory arguments have been made. First, that in the West the 17th and 18th centuries witnessed the creation of new boundaries, as reflected in the development of selfconscious homosexual subcultures in Amsterdam, London, and Paris. Or second, that the work of the sexologists and psychoanalysts of the late 19th century marked the significant point in the transition to a modern economy of sexuality, in which the male homosexual, in particular, could be viewed as the "other." The first argument, that the 18th century witnessed the significant transition, is contained within the work of historians such as Alan Bray, Randolph Trumbach, and Theo Van De Meer, while the second, supported by Foucault's own work, is best summarized by Jeffrey Weeks. The significance of these debates is that they have quite effectively disengaged the history of sexuality from a biologically reductive assumption about the naturalness of sexual desire, and in the process have helped to render problematic both sexual desire itself, and, most significantly, the normality of heterosexuality.

Equally important in undermining an essentialist approach to sexuality has been the history of the body. In the work of Londa Shiebinger and Thomas Laqueur, published since the early 1980s, many of the modern categories associated with gender and reproduction have been questioned. Both of these historians have suggested that the late 18th and early 19th centuries witnessed a transition from a "one body" model of sexual differentiation to a "two body" model. In other words, whereas prior to 1800 men and women were seen to be essentially the same, after this period they were viewed as fundamentally and "naturally" different. By making this distinction these historians, and others, have been able to question many of the assumptions that underlay the belief that heterosexual desire was itself "natural."

When the history of the body is combined with the creation of a homosexual subculture as a new phenomenon at the beginning the 18th century, a coherent story of the history of sexuality in the West begins to emerge. This history suggests that the West inherited an amorphous set of sexual categories, which although making sharp distinctions between the characteristics associated with men and women, assumed that sexual desire could be directed towards a wide range of objects. Sodomy, for example, was certainly a sin, and indeed a capital offence in most of Europe until the advent of the Napoleonic code, but it was a sin any man and some women might commit. With the decline of Galenic medicine, and the rise of the idea of a "natural" sexual differentiation in the 18th century, heterosexuality was gradually defined and imposed on both plebeian and elite cultures. "Normal" men and women from

this period onwards were assumed to find each other "naturally" attractive. And anyone whose sexual desires led down other paths, could now be viewed as "unnatural," a freak, an "other" against whom newly created heterosexuals could define themselves.

This process of the naturalization of heterosexuality reached its apotheosis with the medicalization of sexual desire at the end of the 19th century. As a result of the central role of sex in psychoanalysis and its variants, the 20th century has created a range of powerful normative models for sexual desire, any variation from which has generally been viewed as an illness.

In some ways historians are now turning away from a history of sexuality towards a history of desire. In the work of writers such as Henry Abelove and Thomas Laqueur the outline of a new approach, which takes as its starting point the cultural origins of sexual desire, has begun to emerge.

TIM HITCHCOCK

See also Corbin; Foucault; Homosexuality; Marriage; Stone

Further Reading

Abelove, Henry, "Some Speculations on the History of Sexual Intercourse during the Long Eighteenth Century in England," *Genders* 6 (1989), 125–30

Ariès, Philippe, and André Bejin, eds., *Sexualités occidentales*, Paris: Seuil, 1982; in English as *Western Sexuality: Practice and Precept in Past and Present Times*, Oxford and New York: Blackwell, 1985

Ariès, Philippe, and Georges Duby, eds., *Histoire de la vie privée*, 5 vols., Paris: Seuil, 1985–87; in English as *A History of Private Life*, 5 vols., Cambridge, MA: Harvard University Press, 1987–91

Bray, Alan, *Homosexuality in Renaissance England*, London: Gay Men's Press, 1982

Brown, Judith C., *Immodest Acts: The Life of a Lesbian Nun in Renaissance Italy*, Oxford and New York: Oxford University Press, 1986

Castle, Terry, *The Apparitional Lesbian: Female Homosexuality and Modern Culture*, New York: Columbia University Press, 1993

Cohen, David, "Law, Society and Homosexuality in Classical Athens," *Past and Present* 117 (1987), 3–21

Dekker, Rudolf, and Lotte C. van de Pol, *The Tradition of Female Transvestism in Early Modern Europe*, Basingstoke: Macmillan, and New York: St. Martin's Press, 1989

Donoghue, Emma, *Passions Between Women: British Lesbian Culture, 1668–1801*, London: Scarlet Press, 1993; New York: HarperCollins, 1995

Dover, Kenneth J., *Greek Homosexuality*, London: Duckworth, and Cambridge, MA: Harvard University Press, 1978

Duberman, Martin B., Martha Vicinus, and George Chauncey, Jr., eds., *Hidden from History: Reclaiming the Gay and Lesbian Past*, New York: New American Library, 1989; London: Penguin, 1991

Epstein, Julia, and Kristina Straub, eds., *Body Guards: The Cultural Politics of Gender Ambiguity*, London and New York: Routledge, 1991

Faderman, Lillian, *Surpassing the Love of Men: Romantic Friendship and Love Between Women from the Renaissance to the Present*, New York: Morrow, 1981; London: Women's Press, 1985

Feher, Michel, with Ramona Naddaff and Nadia Tazi, eds., *Fragments for a History of the Human Body*, 3 vols., New York: Zone, 1989

Foucault, Michel, *Histoire de la sexualité*, 3 vols., Paris: Gallimard, 1976–84; in English as *The History of Sexuality*, 3 vols., New York: Pantheon, 1978–86, London: Allen Lane, 1979–88

Foxon, David Fairweather, *Libertine Literature in England, 1660–1745*, London: Shevnal Press, 1964; New Hyde Park, NY: University Books, 1965

Gallagher, Catherine, and Thomas Laqueur, eds., *The Making of the Modern Body: Sexuality and Society in the Nineteenth Century*, Berkeley: University of California Press, 1987

Garber, Marjorie, *Vested Interests: Cross-Dressing and Cultural Anxiety*, New York: Routledge, 1992; London: Penguin, 1993

Hindley, Clifford, "Law, Society and Homosexuality in Classical Athens," with a reply by David Cohen, *Past and Present* 133 (1991), 167–94

Hitchcock, Tim, *English Sexualities, 1700–1800*, Basingstoke: Macmillan, and New York: St. Martin's Press, 1997

Hunt, Lynn, *The Invention of Pornography: Obscenity and the Origins of Modernity, 1500–1800*, New York: Zone, 1993

Hyde, H. Montgomery, *A Tangled Web: Sex Scandals in British Politics and Society*, London: Constable, 1986

Jacquart, Danielle, and Claude Thomasset, *Sexualité et savoir médical au Moyen-Age*, Paris: Presses Universitaires de France, 1985; in English as *Sexuality and Medicine in the Middle Ages*, Cambridge: Cambridge University Press, and Princeton: Princeton University Press, 1988

Laqueur, Thomas, *Making Sex: Body and Gender from the Greeks to Freud*, Cambridge, MA: Harvard University Press, 1990

Laqueur, Thomas, "Sex and Desire in the Industrial Revolution" in Patrick K. O'Brien and Roland Quinault, eds., *The Industrial Revolution and British Society*, Cambridge and New York: Cambridge University Press, 1993

Macfarlane, Alan, *Marriage and Love in England, 1300–1840: Modes of Reproduction*, Oxford and New York: Blackwell, 1986

McLaren, Angus, *A History of Contraception from Antiquity to the Present Day*, Oxford and Cambridge, MA: Blackwell, 1990

Maclean, Ian, *The Renaissance Notion of Woman: A Study in the Fortunes of Scholasticism and Medical Science in European Intellectual Life*, Cambridge and New York: Cambridge University Press, 1980

Mason, Michael, *The Making of Victorian Sexuality*, Oxford and New York: Oxford University Press, 1994

Meer, Theo van der, *De wesentlijke sonde van sodomie en andere vuyligheeden: sodomietenvervolgingen in Amsterdam, 1730–1811* (The Essential Probe of Sodomy and Other Filthinesses: Persecution of Sodomites in Amsterdam, 1730–1811), Amsterdam: Tabula, 1984

Norton, Rictor, *Mother Clap's Molly House: The Gay Subculture in England, 1700–1830*, London: GMP, 1992

Porter, Roy, and Mikuláš Teich, eds., *Sexual Knowledge, Sexual Science: The History of Attitudes to Sexuality*, Cambridge and New York: Cambridge University Press, 1994

Porter, Roy, and Leslie Hall, *The Facts of Life: The Creation of Sexual Knowledge in Britain, 1650–1950*, New Haven and London: Yale University Press, 1995

Roper, Lyndal, *Oedipus and the Devil: Witchcraft, Sexuality and Religion in Early Modern Europe*, London and New York: Routledge, 1994

Schiebinger, Londa, *Nature's Body*, Boston: Beacon Press, and London: Pandora Press, 1993

Shorter, Edward, *The Making of the Modern Family*, New York: Basic Books, 1975; London: Collins, 1976

Stone, Lawrence, *The Family, Sex and Marriage in England, 1500–1800*, London: Weidenfeld and Nicolson, and New York: Harper, 1977

Stone, Lawrence, *Road to Divorce: England, 1530–1987*, Oxford and New York: Oxford University Press, 1990

Tannahill, Reay, *Sex in History*, London: Hamish Hamilton, and New York: Stein and Day, 1980

Trumbach, Randolph, "Sodomitical Subcultures, Sodomitical Roles, and the Gender Revolution of the Eighteenth Century: The Recent Historiography," *Eighteenth-Century Life* 9 (1985), 109–21

Trumbach, Randolph, "Sex, Gender, and Sexual Identity in Modern Culture: Male Sodomy and Female Prostitution in Enlightenment London," *Journal of the History of Sexuality* 2 (1991), 186–203

Trumbach, Randolph, "The Origin and Development of the Modern Lesbian Role in the Western Gender System: Northwestern Europe and the United States, 1750–1990," *Historical Reflections/Réflexions Historiques* 20 (1994), 287–320

Wagner, Peter, *Eros Revived: Erotica of the Enlightenment in England and America*, London: Secker and Warburg, 1988

Weeks, Jeffrey, *Sex, Politics and Society: Regulation of Sexuality since 1800*, London and New York: Longman, 1981; revised 1989

Whitbread, Helena, ed., *I Know My Own Heart: The Diaries of Anne Lister, 1791–1840*, London: Virago, 1988; New York: New York University Press, 1992

Shigeno Yasutsugu 1827–1910

Japanese evidential historian

One of the pioneers of modern Japanese historiography, Shigeno was the founder of an influential school of *kōshō shigaku*, or evidential history. Shigeno's knowledge on evidential studies derived from Japanese, Chinese, and Western sources. When he was a student at the shogunal Confucian college in Edo he became interested in the Tokugawa tradition of evidential studies. Through contacts with Chinese scholars in Tokyo, he came to see that learning was best served not simply by conceptual thought and elegant composition, but also by evidential scholarship. He also paid much attention to modern Western historiography and archival studies, and believed that all the world's scholarship must ultimately resolve itself into induction and evidential studies.

As head of the Office of Historiography sponsored by the Meiji government, Shigeno was responsible for searching out and re-examining historical documents from all localities in Japan, which was part of the preparation for compiling the official chronological history of Japan. As a result, a large amount of primary material was collected and arranged in chronological order. The projects for the compilation and publication of these materials then started, and continue today at Tokyo University's Institute of Historiography. As research progressed, Shigeno and his colleagues began to adopt an objective attitude aimed at discovering facts. This marked a departure from the hortatory or moralistic history that had dominated premodern historical thinking and writing.

In 1889, at the suggestion of Ludwig Riess, a German historian belonging to the school of Ranke, Shigeno founded the Historical Society of Japan at Tokyo Imperial University to promote modern historical research. In his speech entitled "Those who engage in historical work must be fair and impartial in their hearts" at the inaugural meeting of the society, which was considered the founding declaration of evidential history, Shigeno presented a motto for historians which consisted of two quotations from the Chinese writings: *Chiu-cheng chia-an* (To make comments according to evidence) and *ju-shi zhi-shu* (To write bluntly based on facts). The journal of the society was then established, and it remains one of the most authoritative history journals in Japan.

With another evidential historian, Kume Kunitake (1839–1931), Shigeno tried to demonstrate, based on his findings in original sources, that some popular historical figures, including a loyal minister and several righteous persons, were fictitious.

For that reason, he was labeled "Dr. Expunger" by his opponents. But Shigeno responded fearlessly that he did not mind being the enemy of even a whole country, because he intended to establish history as a discipline independent from politics and ethics. He and his colleagues put together their research results in *Kōhon kokushigan* (A Survey of Japanese History, 1890), which was long used as a college textbook, exercising considerable influence on Japanese historical education. The project for compiling the official chronological history of Japan under Shigeno's leadership, however, was discontinued by the government in 1893, after strong opposition from a group of nationalistic scholars to the writing of Japanese history in Chinese, to evidential history, and to the very fact of historiography being undertaken by the government. Shigeno continued his study thereafter as an independent historian on a wide range of topics, such as the age of the gods, the Nara period, the Kamakura shogunate, Shintoism, Buddhism, Chinese studies in Japan, and the administrative district system in Japanese history. Some of his views are still the basis of commonly held points of view on modern Japanese history.

DE-MIN TAO

See also Japan

Biography

Shigeno Yasutsugu. Born 6 October 1827. Attended the domain school *Zōshikan* in Satsuma, studied at the shogunal college *Shōheikō* in Edo, and served as instructor at both institutions. Head of the Office of Historiography, 1877–88; professor, Tokyo Imperial University, 1888–93. Senator, 1888–90; member of House of Peers, 1890–1910. Died 6 December 1910.

Principal Writings

Kōhon kokushigan (A Survey of Japanese History), 1890
Seisai bun shoshū (The First Collection of Seisai's [Shigeno's] Essays), 1898
Seisai bun nishū (The Second Collection of Seisai's [Shigeno's] Essays), 1911
Seisai sensei ikō (Posthumous Works of Professor Seisai [Shigeno]), 1926
Shigeno hakase shigaku ronbunshu (A Collection of Dr. Shigeno's Historical Essays), 3 vols., 1939

Further Reading

Iwai Tadakuma, "Shigeno Yasutsugu," in Nagahora Keiji and Kano Masanao, eds., *Nihon no rekishika* (The Historians of Japan), Tokyo: Nihon hyōronsha, 1976
Nishimura Tokihiko, "Seisai sensei gyōjō shiryō" (Biographical Materials on Professor Seisai [Shigeno]), *Shigaku zasshi* (Journal of the Historical Society of Japan), 22:5 (1911)
Numata Jirō, "Shigeno Yasutsugu and the Modern Tokyo Tradition of Historical Writing," in William G. Beasley and Edward G. Pulleyblank, eds., *Historians of China and Japan*, London: Oxford University Press, 1961

Shiratori Kurakichi 1865–1942

Japanese historian of Asia

Shiratori was the principal founder of the modern study of Asian history (Tōyōshi) in Japan. As a young student, he was fortunate to be advised at Chiba High School by Naka Michiyo (1851–1908), the pioneer advocate of Asian history as an independent field, and at Tokyo Imperial University by Ludwig Riess, a Rankean historian of Germany who introduced modern Western historiography into Japan. Inspired by them and his own research experiences in Europe from 1910 to 1903, and encouraged by Japan's expansion through two wars against China and Russia around the turn of the century, Shiratori was determined to establish Asian history in Japan in order to catch up with, or even surpass the field in the West. His intention represented a kind of academic nationalism in Meiji Japan.

Shiratori chose Korea and Manchuria as his first subjects for research, because these two areas had been little studied in the West, where the focus had traditionally been on China, Mongol history, and Central Asia. He was also successful in shedding new light on the Xiongnu [Hsiung-nu] by tracing its Mongolian and Tungusic roots, an argument counter to the traditional view in the West that the Xiongnu was of Turkish origin. What increased the credibility of Shiratori's scholarship were his mastery of Western research methods and terminology and his free and creative use of abundant data from the Chinese dynastic histories. The former made it possible for him to communicate with Western Orientalists, while the latter ensured him the upper hand in the interpretation of Asian history. Shiratori's research interests, however, were not restricted to the history of Asian ethnic groups in the areas surrounding China. He also made several critical studies of the Chinese and Japanese classics, which had considerable influence on the Japanese academic world.

Perhaps Shiratori's most important contribution was his leadership in setting up several research institutions. He founded the Society for Asian Studies (Ajia gakkai) in 1905, which later became incorporated into the Society for Oriental Studies (Tōyō kyōkai, whose journal remains even today a major scholarly periodical in the field). In 1908, he was successful in persuading the president of the South Manchuria Railway Company to set up under his directorship a research department in its Tokyo branch to promote studies of Korean and Manchurian history and geography. The multivolume publications from the department, including those later in the name of Tokyo Imperial University, laid the foundations for the field. Shiratori was also successful in persuading the owner of the Mitsubishi Corporation to purchase the famous Morrison collection, which became the nucleus of the Oriental Library (Tōyō bunko, 1924), a key institution which Shiratori himself served as first director of research. The efforts of Shiratori's teacher Naka and Shiratori first came to fruition in 1894 when Tōyōshi began to be taught as one of the history subjects at middle schools, and in 1910 at the renaming of Tokyo Imperial University's Chinese history department as a Tōyōshi department.

DE-MIN TAO

Biography

Born 4 February 1865. Attended school in Chiba; studied history at Tokyo Imperial University, BA 1890. Taught at Gakushūin University, 1890–1921; and Tokyo Imperial University, 1904–25. Died 30 March 1942.

Principal Writings

Saiikishi kenkyū (A Study of Central Asian History), 2 vols., 1941–44; reprinted 1981

Shiratori Kurakichi zenshū (Complete Works of Shiratori Kurakichi), 10 vols., 1971

Further Reading

Goi Naohiro, *Kindai Nihon to tōyōshigaku* (Modern Japan and Oriental History), Tokyo: Aoki shoten, 1976

Ishida Mikinosuke, "Shiratori Kurakichi sensei shōden" (A Short Biography of Professor Shiratori Kurakichi), in *Shiratori Kurakichi zenshū* (Complete Works of Shiratori Kurakichi), vol. 10, Tokyo: Iwanami shoten, 1971

Oyama Masaaki, "Shiratori Kurakichi," in Nagahora Keiji and Kano Masanao, eds., *Nihon no rekishika* (The Historians of Japan), Tokyo: Nihon hyōronsha, 1976

Tanaka, Stefan, *Japan's Orient: Rendering Pasts into History*, Berkeley: University of California Press, 1993

Tsuda Sōkichi, "Shiratori hakase shōden" (A Short Biography of Doctor Shiratori), in *Tsuda Sōkichi zenshū* (Complete Works of Tsuda Sōkichi), vol. 24, Tokyo: Iwanami shoten, 1965

Sigerist, Henry E. 1891–1957

Swiss-American medical historian

It was Henry E. Sigerist who introduced the methods and approaches of the social history of medicine and disease into medical history – a discipline based on philological and bio-bibliographical grounds at that time. Sigerist was striving for a new medical history that would deepen the social commitment of physicians but would also remain fully integrated into medical science. During the 1930s and 1940s Sigerist fervently advocated a national health insurance system supposed to guarantee free medical care to the entire population of the United States. In addition, he fought for a comprehensive reform of the American healthcare system by means of a socialized medicine, in the way it was practised in the Soviet Union.

After studying medicine in Zurich and a short period of practicing as a doctor, Sigerist, born into a wealthy Swiss family, decided in 1917 to work as an independent scholar studying the history of medicine. On the recommendation of Karl Sudhoff, director of the Institute for the History of Medicine in Leipzig, and having mastered numerous Oriental languages, Sigerist started to study and edit medieval texts. Although later in life he turned to social history, Sigerist remained dedicated to the production of careful editions and translations of remote sources of medical history. He acquired his qualification as a university lecturer (Habilitation) for the history of medicine at Zurich with *Studien und Texte zur früh-mittelalterlichen Rezeptliteratur* (Studies and Texts on the Early Medieval Literature of Prescriptions, 1923). At the Institute for the History of Medicine in Leipzig, Sigerist's interest during the second half of the 1920s more and more shifted to transformations of culturally determined medical thinking (*Denkstil*) in different societies. Going beyond the limits of historicism, he employed Oswald Spengler's organismic metaphors such as growth, flourishing, and paralysis, in order to characterize phases of transformation. In his 1929 paper "William Harvey's Stellung in der europäischen Geistesgeschichte" (William Harvey's Position in the History of European Thought), Sigerist

related Harvey's discovery of blood circulation to a change in the attitude towards life of the Baroque era. In contrast to the relativism of his medical historiography of culture, Sigerist remained loyal to an idea of progress rooted in the continuous accumulation of medical facts. He argued that medical science originated from interpreting the actual facts.

In 1932 Sigerist left Germany for the Johns Hopkins Institute of the History of Medicine in Baltimore, where he made links between culture and medicine and sought to replace earlier vague metaphors. In a number of programmatic papers Sigerist called for the observation of the social, economic, and political roots of health and disease, of the doctor-patient relationship, of medical theory and practice. In *Civilization and Disease* (1943) he explained the interdependence of disease as a biological phenomenon and the historical contingencies within a given society. After studying Marxist theories, Sigerist began to focus on nutrition, housing, working conditions, and the standard of living in regard to the frequency and distribution of disease. Sigerist held that religion, philosophy, law, and politics had an impact on the social position of the patient. By changing an individual's predisposition these factors could influence the origin and course of certain diseases. Sigerist also examined the financial and demographic consequences of disease as well as alternating interpretations of it by religion, philosophy, art, and science. Despite this, he always claimed that the scientific interpretation could not be questioned by medical historiography. Sigerist argued that the contemporary explanation of disease evolved from magical and religious origins to philosophical and finally definite scientific stages. Sigerist's philosophy of history during the 1920s, dominated by cultural pessimism, had been transformed into an enthusiastic belief in scientific progress. His student George Rosen expanded this idea in order to base the comprehensive social history of medicine on sound case studies. Recent theoretical developments such as the history of the body and the social construction of disease further reveal the ideological components of the scientific model.

Sigerist increasingly committed himself to public health issues, using the social history of medicine as a tool to bring about radical reforms of the American healthcare system. His survey of medicine in capitalism *Amerika und die Medizin*, 1933 (*American Medicine*, 1934) was followed by *Socialized Medicine in the Soviet Union* (1937). Sigerist advocated the integration of preventive and curative medicine in socialism as a promising model of healthcare for any country. Health education was to control the entire life of the individual. Sigerist demanded that the physician be a social reformer whose task was to optimize the individual's social adaptation. A future society based on socialism would solve all its problems by science. Ideological errors of the past would become redundant as would infectious diseases and social medicine. Chronic diseases could be mastered by individual medical treatment. As a consequence of Sigerist's utopian vision of socialized medicine he was branded a Bolshevik, and he left the United States in 1947. Sadly, Sigerist's theories distracted attention from his pioneering findings on the social and cultural dependence of disease and medicine.

After his return to Switzerland, Sigerist started an immense project to publish the eight volumes of *A History of Medicine* (1951–61) which he did not live to complete. He expanded the focus of medical history from famous doctors and innovations of medical technology to the economic and social roots of disease in history, the role of doctors and patients within society, and the ideological background of medical concepts. He did not question, however, the objective truth of medical science, nor the progressive view of the role of the medical profession along with its power to interpret disease in a given society. It was not until the 1970s that this role was discussed along with the debate about professionalization and medicalization. Nevertheless, medical history would never have adopted modern historical methods and approaches or its critical function within medical science without Sigerist's scientific and political commitment.

RALF BRÖER

See also Medicine; Temkin

Biography

Henry Ernest Sigerist. Born Paris, 1891, to wealthy Swiss parents. Studied medicine, University of Zurich: appointed lecturer, 1917; briefly practiced before becoming an independent historian of medicine, achieving the Habilitation in 1923. Director, succeeding Karl Sudhoff, Institute for the History of Medicine, Leipzig, 1925–32; moved to Johns Hopkins Institute for the History of Medicine, 1932; returned to Switzerland, 1947. Married (2 daughters). Died Switzerland, March 1957.

Principal Writings

Studien und Texte zur frühmittelalterlichen Rezeptliteratur (Studies and Texts on the Early Medieval Literature of Prescriptions), 1923
Antike Heilkunde (Ancient Medicine), 1927
"William Harvey's Stellung in der europäischen Geistesgeschichte" (William Harvey's Position in the History of European Thought), *Archiv für Kulturgeschichte* 19 (1929), 158–82
Einführung in die Medizin, 1931; in English as *Man and Medicine: An Introduction to Medical Knowledge*, 1932
Grosse Ärzte: Eine Geschichte der Heilkunde in Lebensbildern, 1932; in English as *The Great Doctors: A Biographical History of Medicine*, 1933
Amerika und die Medizin, 1933; in English as *American Medicine*, 1934
Socialized Medicine in the Soviet Union, 1937; also published as *Medicine and Health in the Soviet Union*, 1947
Medicine and Human Welfare, 1941
Civilization and Disease, 1943
A History of Medicine, 8 vols., 1951–61
Landmarks in the History of Hygiene, 1956
Henry E. Sigerist on the History of Medicine, 1960

Further Reading

Beeson, Nora Sigerist, ed., *Autobiographical Writings*, Montreal: McGill University Press, 1966
Berg-Schorn, Elisabeth, *Henry E. Sigerist (1891–1957): Medizinhistoriker in Leipzig und Baltimore* (Henry E. Sigerist (1891–1957: Medical Historian of Leipzig and Baltimore), Cologne: Arbeiten der Forschungsstelle des Instituts für Geschichte der Medizin der Universität zu Köln, 1978
Brickman, Jane Pacht, "Science and the Education of Physicians: Sigerist's Contribution to American Medical Reform," *Journal of Public Health Policy* 15 (1994), 133–64
Fee, Elizabeth, "Henry E. Sigerist: His Interpretations of the History of Disease and the Future of Medicine," in Charles E. Rosenberg and Janet Golden, eds., *Framing Disease: Studies in Cultural History*, New Brunswick, NJ: Rutgers University Press, 1992

Fee, Elizabeth, and Edward T. Morman, "Doing History, Making Revolution: The Aspirations of Henry E. Sigerist and George Rosen," in Dorothy Porter and Roy Porter, eds., *Doctors, Politics and Society: Historical Essays*, Amsterdam: Rodopi, 1993
Fee, Elizabeth, and Theodore M. Brown, eds., *Making Medical History: The Life and Times of Henry E. Sigerist*, Baltimore: Johns Hopkins University Press, 1997
Wäspi, Marianne Christine, *Die Anfänge des Medizinhistorikers Henry E. Sigerist in Zürich* (Medical Historian Henry E. Sigerist's Beginnings in Zurich), Zurich: Juris, 1989

Sima Guang [Ssu-ma Kuang] 1019–1086
Chinese historian, statesman, poet, and essayist

Sima Guang was born in north China's Henan (now Shanxi) province and attained the rank of chief minister at the end of a long and distinguished political career. He was a conservative Neo-Confucian politician and policy critic who passionately opposed the regime of his southern Chinese opponent, Wang Anshi (1021–86). The hostility between the two factions led to Sima Guang's semi-retirement in Luoyang from 1070 to 1084, where he and his co-authors Liu Bin (1022–88) and Fan Zuyu (1041–98) completed a general history of China – *Zizhi tongjian* (Comprehensive Mirror for Aid in Government) – the magnum opus on which the reputation of Sima Guang as a seminal historian is based. A prolific writer, Sima Guang's extant historical works include *Jigu Lu* (Survey of Records Past) and *Sima wengong wenji* (Collected Writings of Sima Guang).

Together with Sima Qian's *Historical Records*, Sima Guang's *Comprehensive Mirror*, appearing more than a thousand years later, exerted great influence on premodern Chinese and East Asian historiography. Like the annals sections of *Historical Records*, *Comprehensive Mirror* is a chronicle presentation of the general history of China up to the historian's time. Sima Guang's historiography went beyond the traditional praise-and-blame format of historical criticism to the construction of a textbook of history lessons with which to instruct the emperor in rulership, the bureaucracy in statecraft, and the government in practice. It was for this particular reason that both traditional and modern historians acknowledge *Comprehensive Mirror* to be a pivotal and major advance in the history of Chinese historiography.

Comprehensive Mirror was actually first commissioned by the emperor, but the completed work, covering the period from 403 BCE to 959 CE and dwelling on the rise and fall of dynasties and the failures and successes of government, reflects Sima Guang's personal views on history and his practical experience in the government as a conservative Confucian statesman. The text, in 294 chapters, comes with an appendage entitled *Kaoyi* (Examining Discrepancies), where Sima Guang cites and evaluates 320 sources, many no longer extant and others with conflicting interpretations. By discussing alternative sources and views, Sima Guang explained his own interpretation while allowing the reader to concur or disagree. In the application of historical criticism, Sima Guang selected the events from history, extracted positive evidence from the sources, and used Confucian morality to reinforce the didactic import of history in order to guide the government of his day and that of the future.

Comprehensive Mirror considers hierarchy, morality, and rituals to be of crucial significance in good government, where the ruler plays a central role. Sima Guang accepted the unequal distribution of wealth in society, believing that government should not play an interfering role in the economy and warning that innovators such as Wang Anshi would destroy the structure of government and the backbone of the economy. Wang Anshi had the support of the emperor when he launched radical social, political, and economic reform by bringing in state capitalism and overhauling the civil service – a vision of reform deriving from Wang's concern for social justice and egalitarianism. When this emperor died, Wang Anshi lost power and Sima Guang, as chief minister, led the conservative faction that restored the previous status quo in 1086 by immediately and totally dismantling Wang's radical policies.

Published in 1086 in Hangzhou, *Comprehensive Mirror* circulated in nine editions in 11th- and 12th-century China, attesting to its seminal influence on Song and Chinese historiography. It inspired Sima Guang's admirers, contemporaries, and later historians to engage in a genre of *Comprehensive Mirror* scholarship, in the form of companion works, redactions, and sequels. Among companion volumes we note Hu Sanxing's (1230-87) annotated study in historical geography. The best known redaction that was extracted from *Comprehensive Mirror* is *Zizhi tongjian gangmu* (Outline History of Comprehensive Mirror), by the eminent Neo-Confucian philosopher and educator Zhu Xi (1130-1200). Bi Yuan's (1730-97) *Xu Zizhi tongjian* (The Continuation of Comprehensive Mirror) is one of several important sequels that updates the chronological narrative from Sima Guang's time to the author's.

Comprehensive Mirror circulated in East Asia by the 12th century as a textbook or guide to statecraft for the emperors, princes, and scholar-officials beyond Chinese territory. It became a model of official history-writing for Korea, Vietnam, and Japan. Among works deeply influenced by the historiography of *Comprehensive Mirror* one notes in particular Kim Pusik's *Samguk sagi* (History of the Three Kingdoms) in 12th-century Korea, Ngo Si Lien's *Dai Viet su ky toan thu* (Complete Book of the Historical Records of the Great Viet) in 15th-century Vietnam, and Hayashi Gaho's *Honcho tsugan* (The Comprehensive Mirror of This Court) in 17th-century Japan. Thus in both China and other East Asian civilizations, *Comprehensive Mirror* circulated widely and played a significant role in educating future policymakers as well as in providing the framework of history-writing.

JENNIFER W. JAY

See also China: Early and Middle Imperial; China: Historical Writing, Late Imperial; Rhetoric

Biography

Born Shaanzhou, Northern Song, now Xiaxian, Shanxi province, 1019. Read Confucian classics at age 6, passing scholar examination, 1038. In public office, 1039-86, except for semi-retirement in Luoyang, 1070-84; began *Zizhi tongjian* (Comprehensive Mirror for Aid in Government), 1067, and presented the completed work to the emperor, 1085; appointed chief minister, and completely dismantled the economic, political, and social policies set up by his rival, the visionary reformist Wang Anshi, 1086. Married Zhang, daughter of a chief minister (3 sons, 2 of whom died young). Died Bianjing, now Kaifeng, Henan, October 1086.

Principal Writings

Jigu Lu (Survey of Records Past)
Sima wengong wenji (Collected Writings of Sima Guang)
Sushi jiwen (Records and Notes of Sima Guang)
Zizhi tongjian (Comprehensive Mirror for Aid in Government), completed 1084; partially translated in *The Last of the Han*, 1969, chapters 58-68; and in *The Chronicle of the Three Kingdoms (220-265)*, 1965, chapters 69-78

Further Reading

Bol, Peter K., "Government, Society, and State: On the Political Visions of Ssu-ma Kuang and Wang An-shih," in Robert P. Hymes and Conrad Schirokauer, eds., *Ordering the World: Approaches to the State and Society in Sung Dynasty China*, Berkeley: University of California Press, 1993

Chan, Ming K., "The Historiography of the *Tzu-chih T'ung-chien*: A Survey," *Monumenta Serica* 31 (1974-75), 1-38

Faitler, Demerie Paula, "Confucian Historiography and the Thought of Ssu-ma Kuang," dissertation, University of Michigan, 1991

Hervouet, Yves, ed., *A Sung Bibliography*, Hong Kong: Chinese University Press, 1978

Nakai, Kate Wildman, "Tokugawa Confucian Historiography: The Hayashi, Early Mito School and Arai Hakuseki," in Peter Nosco, ed., *Confucianism and Tokugawa Culture*, Princeton: Princeton University Press, 1981

Pulleyblank, Edwin G., "The *Tzyjyh Tongjiann Kaoyih* and the Sources for the History of the Period 730-763," *Bulletin of the School of Oriental and African Studies* 13 (1950), 448-73

Pulleyblank, Edwin G., "Chinese Historical Criticism: Liu Chih-chi and Ssu-ma Kuang," in William G. Beasley and Edwin G. Pulleyblank, eds., *Historians of China and Japan*, London: Oxford University Press, 1961

Sariti, Anthony William, "Monarchy, Bureaucracy, and Absolutism in the Political Thought of Ssu-ma Kuang," *Journal of Asian Studies* 32 (1972), 53-76

Sima Qian [Ssu-ma Ch'ien], *c.*145–*c.*87 BCE

Chinese historiographer, prose stylist, and government official

As the most important name in traditional Chinese historiography and often compared to Herodotus in his pioneering role, Sima Qian is the subject of voluminous studies in both Chinese and Western scholarship. His *Shiji* (Historical Records), the first general or comprehensive history of China, circulated in the 1st century BCE, and was both an archetype of classical Chinese prose and a model for official histories in imperial China as well as in premodern Japan, Korea, and Vietnam. Its completion was set in an age of cultural and political prestige which witnessed Chinese expansion into Central Asia, the opening of the silk route, the consolidation of institutions at home, and cultural achievements at home and abroad.

Sima Qian's dates of birth and death are disputed, but it is indisputable that he lived in the entire reign of Emperor Wu (reigned 141–87 BCE) of the Han dynasty, a dynamic period of cultural growth and aggressive interaction with the frontier peoples. While in the combined position of the court astrologer and historian, a post held by his ancestral line including his father, Sima Qian defended a surrendering frontier general out of a sense of moral justice and incurred the wrath of the emperor. Imprisoned and sentenced to death but without adequate funds to have his punishment entirely mitigated, Sima

Qian was castrated, a surgical procedure that reduced him to a court eunuch and outcast of society. In a letter to his friend Ren An and in the autobiographical chapter of *Historical Records*, Sima Qian defended his choice of living a life of shame and serving as the emperor's private secretary and travelling companion, rather than honorably committing suicide, because he wanted to complete the general history project that his dying father had entrusted to him. This filial commitment was intensified by the sense of historical mission he shared with his father – to write and appraise the record of the past in order to construct and preserve moral lessons for the present and for posterity. On a personal level he wanted this project to vindicate his honor and remove the shame of his castration from the pages of history.

Historical Records, in 130 chapters and half a million characters, is a general history covering three millennia, with the 90 years of Sima Qian's period taking up half of the volume. Sima Qian was an innovator in organizing and presenting the records in five sections: chronicles or annals of the emperors, chronological tables of genealogies, treatises on topics such as astronomy and the economy, hereditary families, and biographies. All sections except that of hereditary families were retained by the dynastic histories that were compiled later and became known as the 25 official histories, with *Historical Records* considered as the first in the sequence.

The annals of Qin (221–208 BCE), the treatises, and the biographies that constitute 40 per cent of the work have attracted the most attention from historians and translators, among them Burton Watson. Watson characterized Sima Qian's historiography as rationalistic, eclectic, realistic, humanistic, and strongly assertive of the immortality of history.

In Sima Qian's time the fields of history and literature were not perceived as separate pursuits, and indeed *Historical Records* has long engaged the interest of scholars of Chinese literature. Devices such as irony and sarcasm, characterization, direct speech, juxtaposition of facts, and putting words into the mouth of contemporaries rather than applying the direct words of the historian-critic are reminiscent of historical fiction and reportage. Sima Qian has also been described as "historicizing" myths in history by providing actual dates for mythical rulers and ancient family lines, including that of his own, which he traced to the legendary emperors. Apart from historical sources, he used fictional and anecdotal accounts to supplement the gaps in the narratives. Sima Qian traveled widely and applied his personal knowledge to confirm or negate the sources available to him. Archaeological finds in the past decades are continuing to confirm the historical accuracy of *Historical Records*, particularly in confirming rulers' dates and tomb locations.

Sima Qian saw history as a comprehensive record of all people, a history not just confined to the succession of rulers and the rise and fall of dynasties. He was convinced that great men made history, and by selecting the subjects for biographies and exercising the grand historian's commentary to judge individuals and groups, he believed that he was fulfilling his historical mission for posterity. His experience as an official and the personal ordeal of castration deepened his belief that it was imperative for the ruler to distinguish constructive admonition from superficial flattery.

JENNIFER W. JAY

See also Ban; China: Ancient; China: Historical Writing, Early and Middle; China: Historical Writing, Late Imperial; World

Biography

Born Longmen, Xiagang district, now Hancheng, Shanxi province, *c.*145 BCE. Followed his court astrologer/grand historian father to the capital at age 8 and was immersed in Confucian classics at age 10. Traveled extensively through the provinces, including to Confucius' home. Employed as minor official, from 122, rising through ranks to be court astrologer/grand historian, 108; helped set up the new calendar and began writing *Historical Records* in 104; imprisoned and castrated for defending a surrendering general, 98; released and employed as private secretary and travel companion to the emperor, 96. Married (1 daughter). Died *c.*87. His grandson presented *Historical Records* to the court during 73–49 BCE.

Principal Writings

Shiji (*Historical Records*), completed 90 BCE

Translations

Records of the Grand Historian of China, translated by Burton Watson, 2 vols., New York: Columbia University Press, 1961; revised 1993

Ssu-ma Ch'ien's Historiographical Attitude as Reflected in Four Late Warring States Biographies, translated by Frank Algerton Kiernan, Jr., Wiesbaden: Harrassowitz, 1962

Les Mémoires historiques de Se-ma Ts'ien, translated by E. Chavannes, 5 vols., reprinted Paris, 1967

Historical Records, translated by Raymond Dawson, Oxford: Oxford University Press, 1994

The Grand Scribe's Records, edited by William H. Nienhauser, Jr., Bloomington: Indiana University Press, 1994–

Further Reading

Cohen, Alvin P., "Avenging Ghosts and Moral Judgment in Ancient Chinese Historiography: Three Examples from *Shih-chi*," in Sarah Allan and Alvin P. Cohen, eds., *Legend, Lore, and Religion in China: Essays in Honor of Wolfram Eberhard on His Seventieth Birthday*, San Francisco: Chinese Materials Center, 1979

Durrant, Stephen W., "Self as the Intersection of Traditions: The Autobiographical Writings of Ssu-ma Ch'ien," *Journal of the American Oriental Society* 106 (1986), 33–40

Hardy, Grant, "Can an Ancient Chinese Historian Contribute to Modern Western Theory? The Multiple Narratives of Ssu-ma Ch'ien," *History and Theory* 33 (1994), 20–38

Hou Wai-lu, "Ssuma Chien: Great Ancient Historian," *People's China* 12 (16 June 1956), 36–40

Hulsewé, Anthony F.P., "Founding Fathers and Yet Forgotten Men: A Close Look at the Tables of the Nobility in the *Shih chi* and the *Han shu*," *T'oung Pao* 75 (1989), 43–126

Jian Xiaobin, "Spatialization in the *Shiji*," dissertation, Ohio State University, 1992

Li Wai-Yee, "The Idea of Authority in the *Shih chi* (Records of the Historian)," *Harvard Journal of Asiatic Studies* 54 (1994), 345–405

Pokora, T., "Ironical Critics at Ancient Chinese Courts (*Shih Chi*, 126)," *Oriens Extremus* 20 (1973)

Watson, Burton, *Ssu-ma Ch'ien: Grand Historian of China*, New York: Columbia University Press, 1958

Wills, John Elliot, Jr., *Mountain of Fame: Portraits in Chinese History*, Princeton: Princeton University Press, 1994

Simiand, François 1873–1935

French sociologist and economic historian

François Simiand is notable to historians on two fronts: first, he was a peerless and merciless critic of the methodological bases of conventional French academic history; and second, he was a pioneer in advancing interdisciplinary history via his empirical studies on prices and wages. However, Simiand never viewed himself strictly as a historian. True to the imperial pretensions of his Durkheimian heritage he considered himself a social scientist *tout court*. From the Durkheimian perspective history was merely a handmaiden, a supplier of raw material, to the concept building and analysis performed by the genuine social scientist.

At the turn-of-the-century history as a discipline stood at the apex of the French academic hierarchy. According to the logic by which youthful disciplines such as sociology advanced in the French educational system, it was essential that the Durkheimians level a severe critique against the reigning discipline. It was only by weakening its rivals that the Durkheimians could carve out an independent position in the institutional structure. One of the Durkheimians' favored targets was Charles Seignobos, co-author of the influential *L'Introduction aux études historiques* (1898; *Introduction to the Study of History*, 1898). Seignobos acted as the defender of orthodox historical practice, and responded to persistent criticism of the academic and methodological sway of history in his essay, *La Méthode historique appliquée aux sciences sociales* (The Historical Method Applied to the Social Sciences, 1901). Seignobos was extremely skeptical of the notion of a unified social science, and had little positive to say of newly emerging disciplines such as sociology. Durkheim shot off an immediate rejoinder to Seignobos, but the real work of demolition was left to Simiand.

Simiand was the most youthful of the original contributors to Durkheim's *Année sociologique* (founded 1896), and his early career followed a pattern common among the Durkheimians. Although originally trained in philosophy at the Ecole Normale Supérieure, they were attracted by the promise of a rigorous science of society as promulgated by Durkheim. However, Simiand's philosophical training remained highly evident in his continued interest in formal methodological questions. The aggressiveness with which Simiand employed his critical and analytical skills were on full display in his 1903 article, "Méthode historique et science sociale" (Historical Method and Social Science).

Simiand opened with a blast against the academic historians. Historical method did not exist *per se*, but merely consisted of a set of procedures applied to the critical notation of documents. Simiand insisted on the centrality of causal explanation in all scientific studies. He was particularly scornful of Seignobos' argument that historical objectivity was founded on understanding the subjective motivations of individual historical actors. Simiand countered Seignobos' emphasis on discrete intentions, facts, and events with an explanatory science based on objective "social facts." In addition to offering a primer on Durkheimian method, Simiand made practical recommendations. He enjoined the historians to break some idols: the political idol, the individual idol, and the chronological idol.

Simiand's three idols furnished the base for what came to be known derisively as *histoire événementielle*. This notion was evoked by all the dissenting French historians of the 20th century, especially the *Annalistes*, who sought to broaden the purview of historical research. On the other hand, Simiand's abrasiveness and methodological rigor left many historians cold. Marc Bloch's reaction in *Apologie pour l'histoire, ou, métier d'historien* (1949; *The Historian's Craft*, 1953) was emblematic. Although Bloch had deep reservations about the methodological teachings of his mentor Seignobos, there was none of the personal rancor that one finds in Simiand. Furthermore, he was put off by the scientist posturing of the Durkheimians, and specifically Simiand's insistence on strict causal argumentation. According to Bloch, the narrow focus on causation was just as limiting as the conventional historians focus on the three idols.

Simiand was equally outspoken in territorial struggles with the discipline of economics. One of the principal weapons he deployed in his confrontation with orthodox economics was historical evidence. Simiand's concern was with the overly abstract character of economic thinking as manifested in concepts such as equilibrium and marginal-utility. The bulk of his work aimed at re-injecting society back into economics. To achieve this he focused on long-term price and wage fluctuations in which he identified rhythms of growth (alpha phase – A) and regression (beta phase – B). Among the Durkheimians he was the designated expert on statistics, and second generation *Annalistes* such as Ernest Labrousse and Fernand Braudel were deeply influenced by Simiand's employment of quantitative or serial data. Although Simiand viewed his own work as primarily economic in nature, his legacy carries much more weight in the historical field. His censure of conventional history combined with his empirical studies provided a powerful early example of what can be accomplished through interdisciplinary history.

JAMES MILLHORN

See also Annales School; Seignobos; Social

Biography

François Joseph Charles Simiand. Born in Gières, Isère, 18 April 1873. First in the agrégation de philosophie at the Ecole Normale Supérieure, 1896; defended his doctorat de droit, 1904. Held various academic and civil service positions, including librarian for the ministries of Commerce and Labor, aide to Albert Thomas as undersecretary of state for artillery and munitions during World War I, and lecturer at the Ecole Pratique des Hautes Etudes; chair of labor history, Collège de France, 1931–35. Died Saint-Raphael, Var, 17 April 1935.

Principal Writings

Introduction aux études historiques (Introduction to Historical Studies), 1898

La Méthode historique appliquée aux sciences sociales (The Historical Method Applied to the Social Sciences), 1901

"Méthode historique et science sociale" (Historical Method and Social Science), *Revue de synthèse historique*, 6 (1903), 1–22 and 129–157; reprinted in *Annales: ESC*, 15 (1960), 83–119

"La Causalité en histoire" (Causality in History), *Bulletin de la Société Française de philosophie*, 6 (31 May 1906), 243–90

Le Salaire des ouvriers des mines de charbon en France: contribution à la théorie économique du salaire (Workers' Salaries in French Coal Mines: Contributions to the Economic Theories of Salary), 1907

Les Fluctuations économiques à longue période et la crise mondiale (Long-term Economic Fluctuations and World Crisis), 1932

Recherches anciennes et nouvelles sur le mouvement général des prix du XVIe au XIX siècle (New Research and Old on the General Movement of Prices from the 16th to the 19th Century), 1932

Le Salaire, l'évolution sociale et la monnaie: essai de théorie expérimentale du salaire (Salary, Social Evolution, and Money: A Theoretical and Experimental Essay on Salary), 3 vols., 1932

Further Reading

Besnard, Philippe, ed., *The Sociological Domain: The Durkheimians and the Founding of French Sociology*, Cambridge and New York: Cambridge University Press, 1983

Bouvier, Jean, "Feu Francois Simiand?" *Annales ESC* 28 (1973), 1173–92

Braudel, Fernand, *Ecrits sur l'histoire*, Paris: Flammarion, 1969; in English as *On History*, Chicago: University of Chicago Press, 1980

Damalas, Basile, *L'Oeuvre scientifique de François Simiand* (The Scientific Work of François Simiand), Paris: Presses Universitaires de France, 1943

Lévy-Leboyer, Maurice, "L'Héritage de Simiand: prix, profit, et termes d'échange au XIXe siècle" (Simiand's Legacy: Price, Profit, and Terms of Exchange in the 19th Century), *Revue historique* 243 (1970), 77–120

Sée, Henri, "Interprétation d'une controverse sur les relations de l'histoire et de la sociologie" (An Interpretation of the Controversy on the Relations Between History and Sociology), *Archiv fur Sozialwissenschaft und Sozialpolitik* 65 (1931), 81–100

Simpson, A.W.B. 1931–

British legal historian

Brian Simpson has established an outstanding reputation, primarily as a legal historian, but also a legal theorist, both in England and in the US. Initially, this reputation was founded on two important early works on the history of the common law, the first of which was *A History of the Land Law* (1961). Simpson's text was intended to replace that by Holdsworth (1927), by that time out of print, and, moreover, was presaged on his belief that historical studies should "to some extent at least" be separated from the study of the modern law. Simpson's concern in this text was to emphasize the early history of the basic doctrines of the land law, although one finds also some analysis of the most important 19th-century reforms. Undoubtedly the most significant aspect of this monograph was Simpson's concern to make use not merely of the leading secondary materials, but also of cases in the Year Books and important editions of medieval materials prepared by the Selden Society.

A similar approach is reflected in Simpson's equally important monograph on contract law, *A History of the Common Law of Contract* (1975), which covers the period from the 13th century to the Statute of Frauds in 1677. A second volume, on the 18th and 19th centuries, was intended to follow but has never seen the light of day. The pervasive philosophy of this work is a concern with the development of legal ideas and doctrines, with a marked concentration on the development of the action of assumpsit, but also those of covenant, warranty, and debt. Earlier workings of some of the material had previously appeared in the *Law Quarterly Review*. The book includes a particularly thorough treatment on the vexed topic of consideration in contract; the author was especially at pains to emphasize here that "the conception of consideration was not that of a price for a promise, but a reason for a promise." At the time of its publication it was described by one reviewer as "*the* work on the history of contract," and this assessment of its value largely still stands, although some of its themes have been challenged (not always convincingly) and enlarged upon by those scholars who have sought to contribute further to scholarship on this facet of the history of the common law. Simpson himself has written at least three further learned articles on aspects of the subject.

Chronologically falling between the monographs on the land law and contract was *Oxford Essays in Jurisprudence* (1973) edited by Simpson and incorporating papers by the leading Oxford legal theorists, including Honoré, Finnis, Dworkin, MacCormick, and Hart. However no less important in this galaxy of stars is Simpson's own contribution to the volume, "The Common Law and Legal Theory," praised by one impressed reviewer as "the most intriguing of the lot."

In *Cannabalism and the Common Law* (1984), Simpson, in a much admired and highly original monograph, set out to examine the historical and legal context behind the famous criminal law case of *Regina* v. *Dudley & Stephens* ([1884] 14 Q.B.D. 273), in which the defendants, who had saved their own lives by killing the ship's cabin boy, were convicted of murder, later commuted to life imprisonment. One reviewer of the work praised it saying that he doubted "that a more civilized book has ever been written about a more gruesome topic."

In a related work, *In the Highest Degree Odious: Detention Without Trial in Wartime Britain* (1992), Simpson turned his attention away from the realm of private law and of theory to public law. The focus of the book was the detention of approximately two thousand British subjects during World War II, under Regulation 18B of the Defence Regulations. Simpson's approach, concentrating on the three main institutions involved in the program (the Security Service, the Home Office, and the legal profession), exhibits all the best hallmarks of his much-admired earlier work. Likewise, his most recent book, *Leading Cases in the Common Law* (1995), was written in a style "which will make them acceptable both to readers who are expert in the branch of law to which they belong, and to those who are not" (preface). The raison d'être of the book is Simpson's "philosophical interest in the casuistic processes of the common law, and a belief that the understanding of judicial decisions is little furthered by the elaboration of imaginative abstract theories, which have little connection with anything but themselves" (preface). This work in combination with the earlier work is bound to confirm Simpson's reputation as one of the leading legal historians of English law.

STEPHEN D. GIRVIN

See also Legal

Biography

Alfred William Brian Simpson. Born England, 17 August 1931, son of a clergyman. Educated at Oakham School, Rutland; Queen's College, Oxford, MA 1958. National Service with British Army, Royal West African Frontier Force, 1950–51. Junior research fellow, St. Edmund Hall, Oxford, 1954–55; fellow/tutor, Lincoln College, Oxford, 1955–73; dean, Faculty of Law, University of Ghana, 1968–69; professor, University of Kent, 1973–85; University of Chicago, 1984–87; and University of Michigan, from 1987. Called to the Bar, Gray's Inn, London, 1994. Married 1) Kathleen Anne Seston, 1954 (marriage dissolved 1968; 1 son, 1 daughter); 2) Caroline Elizabeth Ann Brown, 1969 (1 son, 2 daughters).

Principal Writings

A History of the Land Law, 1961

Editor, *Oxford Essays in Jurisprudence*, 2nd series, 1973

A History of the Common Law of Contract: The Rise of the Action of Assumpsit, 1975

Editor, *A Biographical Dictionary of the Common Law*, 1984

Cannibalism and the Common Law: The Story of the Tragic Last Voyage of the Mignonette and the Strange Legal Proceedings to Which It Gave Rise, 1984

Legal Theory and Legal History: Essays on the Common Law, 1987

In the Highest Degree Odious: Detention Without Trial in Wartime Britain, 1992

Leading Cases in the Common Law, 1995

Further Reading

Arnold, Morris S., "Transcending Covenant and Debt," *Yale Law Journal* 85 (1976), 990–99

Chase, Anthony, "Fear Eats the Soul," *Yale Law Journal* 94 (1985), 1253–69

Posner, Richard A., "Executive Detention in Time of War," *Michigan Law Review* 92 (1994), 1675–83

Twining, William, "Cannibalism and Legal Literature," *Oxford Journal of Legal Studies* 6 (1986), 423–30

White, Stephen, "Sailors, Savages and Civilisation: Professor Simpson's *Cannabalism and the Common Law*," *Criminal Law Journal* 10 (1986), 168–81

Sinclair, Keith 1922–1993

New Zealand historian

Certainly the most prominent New Zealand historian of the postwar period, Keith Sinclair was in many ways the most influential as well. He established fresh standards for New Zealand historical scholarship by his thorough research and vigorous writing and, by choosing to work in New Zealand history, he gave the field new significance. Appointed in 1947 to Auckland University College (from 1962 the University of Auckland), he taught there for forty years, but his interests and activities were neither insular nor parochial: he traveled widely, and spent several periods overseas, especially in Britain, Australia, and North America, often attending research seminars as well as carrying out his own research. He found the seminars at the Institute of Commonwealth Studies in London particularly stimulating, and its director, Sir Keith Hancock, became an important friend. Mercurial and opinionated, Sinclair was immensely energetic, impatient with careless work but quick to give generous encouragement to colleagues and students whose research displayed flair and originality, even when their views did not accord with his own.

In Britain on leave from the navy at the end of the war, Sinclair found an MA thesis topic in the papers of the Aborigines Protection Society, which had sought to promote British colonization of New Zealand in ways that would not be harmful to the indigenous Maori people. He discovered that research into "primary" materials was very much to his taste; nearly all his books and articles were to be based on close readings of manuscript sources in various archives and libraries, and he expected his postgraduate students to do likewise. His work on the Aborigines Protection Society also led Sinclair into examining the complex and volatile relationships between colonizers and colonized in 19th-century New Zealand. His substantial monograph, *The Origins of the Maori Wars*, originally published in 1957, was a scholarly benchmark for New Zealand historians in several ways: it was the first study of the subject; it was fully documented, based on personal and official records held in New Zealand and in Britain, including materials at the Public Record Office, London; and Sinclair placed the materials in a New Zealand perspective rather than a British or imperial one.

His experiences overseas during war service had made Sinclair very aware of the distinctiveness of New Zealanders; he also reacted against the uncritical adulation of empire by an earlier generation of New Zealanders, and considered the development of a New Zealand identity a central theme in New Zealand history. In *Imperial Federation* (1955), he argued that the support some New Zealand politicians had once given to ideas of imperial federation "was not evidence of the absence of nationalism but was itself an expression of an emergent New Zealand nationalism." *A Destiny Apart* (1986) was his fullest elaboration of this selfconscious "creole nationalism."

"The Search for Identity," as he entitled the epilogue, also informed Sinclair's most important work, *A History of New Zealand* (1959), which replaced William Pember Reeves' *The Long White Cloud: Ao Tea Roa* (1898) as the standard short account of New Zealand's past. In polished prose enlivened by sharp wit, Sinclair's *History* depicted the development of a young Pacific nation, emphasizing more the achievements of New Zealanders, Maori and Pakeha, than the British inheritance in the shaping of the new society. Sinclair confirmed, indeed strengthened Reeves' cautious suggestion that the advent of the Liberal government in 1891 marked a watershed in New Zealand's political and social history, and he saw the election of the Labour government in 1935 as similarly momentous, since "Labour had recaptured the New Zealand Liberal tradition of state humanitarianism." The book was a bestseller: a generation of New Zealanders, not just historians, drew their interpretive framework from Sinclair's *History*.

Sinclair explored both the Liberal and the Labour governments in more detail in major biographical works. In *William Pember Reeves* (1965), Sinclair insisted on the political importance of the intellectual Reeves and the radical nature of his legislation. Easily the best New Zealand historical biography published up to that time, Sinclair's *Reeves* demonstrated that biography could be significant history. *Walter Nash* (1976) provided as well as a political biography of the prominent Labour politician a richly detailed analysis of the first two Labour governments. John A. Lee, a dissident Labour politician, had so widely publicized his critical attitudes towards the Labour leaders of the late 1930s that his negative views had become the accepted orthodoxy. Sinclair, having weighed the evidence, characterized such views as "photographs taken through distorting lenses." Lee remarked that the victors always wrote history to suit themselves. "So do the losers," was Sinclair's riposte.

In the 1960s, Sinclair had acquired a reading knowledge of the Maori language, one of the first Pakeha historians to do so. This enabled him to make a preliminary assessment of some of the many 19th-century letters written by Maori in Maori, and to judge which were sufficiently pertinent to warrant translation by an expert in the language. Such materials formed a basis for *Kinds of Peace* (1991). Maori who "fought for the Queen" or were neutral in the conflicts, Sinclair claimed, had been "almost written out of our history. They are now written back." *Kinds of Peace*, his last historical work, provided a terse sequel to his first large study, the *Origins*.

Sinclair's enthusiasm for history was communicated in a variety of ways. His entertaining lectures aroused in many students their initial interest in New Zealand history. Some of his well-regarded poetry incorporated historical subjects. With Wendy Harrex, Sinclair produced *Looking Back: A Photographic History of New Zealand* (1978), almost the first illustrated history of New Zealand; later he edited the *Oxford Illustrated History of New Zealand* (1990). In 1967 he founded the *New Zealand Journal of History*, and oversaw it for twenty years: the *Journal* helped develop a sense of community among New Zealand historical scholars and between them and academic historians in other countries. He also wrote several lively school textbooks. In his later years he was something of a public figure, and his pronouncements upon matters historical raised the general awareness of history among New Zealanders: the accolades he received, including a knighthood in 1985, were an acknowledgment of his public contributions as well as his scholarship.

PETER GIBBONS

See also New Zealand; Popular

Biography

Born Auckland, 5 December 1922. Educated at Mount Albert Grammar School; BA, Auckland University College, 1945, MA 1946, PhD 1954. Served in New Zealand Army, 1941–44; Royal New Zealand Naval Reserve, 1944–45 (in England); New Zealand Army Reserve, 1951–53. Taught (rising to professor), Auckland University College (now University of Auckland), 1947–87. Knighted 1985. Married 1) Mary Edith Land, 1947 (marriage dissolved 1976; 4 sons); 2) Raewyn Mary Dalziel, historian, 1976. Died Canada, 20 June 1993.

Principal Writings

Imperial Federation: A Study of New Zealand Policy and Opinion, 1880–1914, 1955
The Origins of the Maori Wars, 1957; revised 1961
A History of New Zealand, 1959; 4th edition 1991
William Pember Reeves: New Zealand Fabian, 1965
Walter Nash, 1976
With Wendy Harrex, *Looking Back: A Photographic History of New Zealand,* 1978
A Destiny Apart: New Zealand's Search for National Identity, 1986
Editor, *Oxford Illustrated History of New Zealand,* 1990
Kinds of Peace: Maori People after the Wars, 1870–85, 1991

Further Reading

Oliver, W.H., "A Destiny at Home," *New Zealand Journal of History* 21 (1987), 9–15
Sinclair, Keith, *Halfway round the Harbour: An Autobiography,* Auckland and New York: Penguin, 1993

Skinner, Quentin 1940–
British historian of political thought

Over the course of his career thus far Quentin Skinner has had a tremendous impact upon the fields of intellectual history and political philosophy. He has gained recognition both for his ground-breaking interpretations of Renaissance political philosophy as well as for his more broadly theoretical and methodological writings. Along with fellow Cambridge professors J.G.A. Pocock and John Dunn, Skinner has led the way for scholars seeking a more contextual approach to the history of political philosophy. Distancing himself from older approaches to the "history of ideas" and political theory, which tended to treat concepts as having an independent, transcendent existence, he has consistently argued that the historical meaning of a text can be determined only through a thorough examination of the context in which that text was produced. Thus, unlike historians writing in the tradition of A.O. Lovejoy, who traced the history of "unit ideas" in works such as *Reflections on Human Nature* (1961), Skinner focuses his attention primarily on texts, their authors, and their use of language. His work is thus part of a broader trend among intellectual historians known as the "linguistic turn," a shift in methodology that, beginning in the late 1960s, transformed the old history of ideas into a history of discourse and of meaning.

Skinner's overriding concern with language as the key to understanding the past is evident in all of his scholarly endeavors. In 1978, the same year in which he was appointed to the position of professor of political science at the University of Cambridge, Skinner published his influential 2-volume survey, *The Foundations of Modern Political Thought*. Here, he examined the language used by writers engaged in political debates during the Renaissance and the Reformation. Far from positing a rigid dichotomy between a written text and a social or political context, Skinner conceived of context as largely discursive or linguistic. The context he finds most crucial to an understanding of any given text is the broader debate, carried on through other texts, of which it was a part. By paying attention to numerous minor figures and not just the acknowledged giants of political philosophy, Skinner established a richly textured discursive context for understanding what authors like Machiavelli were actually doing in writing in certain ways. In the case of Machiavelli, Skinner argued persuasively that Machiavelli's meaning in writing *The Prince* and the *Discourses* could best be understood as part of a larger debate at the time over the humanist ideal of republican liberty.

Although Skinner's own interests lie within the realm of political thought, his work has attracted the interest of scholars studying other aspects of politics and intellectual history, provoking vigorous debates over Skinner's theoretical perspective. Many of the critiques of Skinner's method have centered on his use of speech-act theory and his insistence that "words are deeds," a phrase borrowed from Wittgenstein. Skinner has developed these theoretical aspects of his work in a variety of publications, beginning with his article "Meaning and Understanding in the History of Ideas" (1969). Although the details and terminology of speech-act theory are complex, the essential element of this theory upon which Skinner bases his methods is a distinction between the locutionary or propositional meaning of a text (i.e., the substance of what is written) and the "illocutionary force" or intended meaning of the author's action in writing the text (i.e., why the text was written). Skinner contends that both types of meaning shape the historical meaning of a text; in other words, to comprehend the historical meaning of *The Prince* one must understand not only the argument Machiavelli advanced within the book but also the point he was trying to make in writing it.

While few scholars have disputed the notion that writers are performing an act by writing and thus engaging themselves in debate, not all share Skinner's conviction that an author's intentions in writing can be recovered by historians. Skinner himself draws nuanced distinctions among various types of intent in order to deflect the charge that he is claiming to read the minds of his historical subjects. On this particular issue, Skinner's theory is perhaps more controversial than his practice. In Skinner's exchanges with his critics, both sides have tended to focus on the role of the author and on intentions, whereas in Skinner's works on Renaissance political philosophy, these concerns are coupled with an interest in how texts were read, interpreted, and responded to by other authors. Even so, Skinner's critics are justified in arguing that, with respect to any individual philosopher, Skinner appears far more interested in determining what that thinker meant in writing his works than in examining how those same works have been interpreted either by the author's contemporaries or by subsequent generations.

Skinner's influence on historical scholarship extends beyond the books and articles he has written and the debates that these publications have sparked. Through his role as an editor he has actively promoted a language-based approach to contextual intellectual history, as well as scholarship on the theoretical dimensions of history. As an editor of the Cambridge University Press series Ideas in Context, he oversees the publication of monographs and collections of essays in intellectual history. The first volume in this series, *Philosophy in History*, which he co-edited with Richard Rorty and J.B. Schneewind, addresses many of the theoretical and methodological issues central to Skinner's own work. He has also edited or co-edited several other books, including *The Cambridge History of Renaissance Philosophy* (1988) and *The Return of Grand Theory in the Human Sciences* (1985), that unite revisionist scholarship and sophisticated theoretical discussions. In short, Skinner's impact on the study of political thought and other areas of scholarship has been immense. Even those scholars who reject his methods or dispute his interpretations must give him a large measure of credit for transforming and revitalizing the field of intellectual history.

DEIRDRE CHASE WEAVER

See also Begriffsgeschichte; Intellectual; Political

Biography

Quentin Robert Duthie Skinner. Born 26 November 1940. Attended Bedford School; Gonville and Caius College, Cambridge, BA 1962, MA 1965; fellow, Christ's College, from 1962. Lecturer in history, Cambridge University, 1967–78, professor of political science, from 1978. Married 2) Susan Deborah Thorpe James, 1979 (1 son, 1 daughter).

Principal Writings

"Meaning and Understanding in the History of Ideas," *History and Theory* 8 (1969); reprinted in James Tully, ed., *Meaning and Context: Quentin Skinner and His Critics*, 1988
The Foundations of Modern Political Thought, 2 vols., 1978
Editor, *The Return of Grand Theory in the Human Sciences*, 1985
Editor, with Charles B. Schmitt and Eckhard Kessler, *The Cambridge History of Renaissance Philosophy*, 1988
Reason and Rhetoric in the Philosophy of Hobbes, 1996

Further Reading

Dunn, John, "The Identity of the History of Ideas," *Philosophy* 43 (1968), 85–104
LaCapra, Dominick, and Steven L. Kaplan, eds., *Modern European Intellectual History: Reappraisals and New Perspectives*, Ithaca, NY: Cornell University Press, 1982
Rorty, Richard, Jerome B. Schneewind, and Quentin Skinner, eds., *Philosophy in History: Essays on the Historiography of Philosophy*, Cambridge and New York: Cambridge University Press, 1984
Skinner, Quentin, ed., *The Return of Grand Theory in the Human Sciences*, Cambridge: Cambridge University Press, 1985
Toews, John E., "Intellectual History after the Linguistic Turn: The Autonomy of Meaning and the Irreducibility of Experience," *American Historical Review*, 92 (1987), 879–907
Tully, James, ed., *Meaning and Context: Quentin Skinner and His Critics*, Princeton: Princeton University Press, and Cambridge: Polity Press, 1988

Slavery: Ancient

The beginning of a more-or-less disinterested historiographical treatment of ancient slavery came in the middle of the 19th century, at about the same time as Ranke's invention of a theory of history-writing that would ideally describe "exactly what happened," and also coinciding with the disappearance (forced or not) of "modern" slavery. Henri Wallon's *Histoire de l'esclavage dans l'Antiquité* (A History of Slavery in the Ancient World, 1847), has been identified as the first work to try to depict ancient slavery as an economic system that was neither "natural" nor inevitable, though Wallon was in fact following those unnamed sophists who, as early as the 4th century BCE, had opposed the better-known views of Aristotle. The latter part of the 19th and the 20th century first produced at least two contrasting approaches to ancient slavery: scholars following Marx's theory of a historical period dominated by a slaveholding "mode of production," and such factual-legal correlations and analyses as Buckland's *The Roman Law of Slavery* (1908). In fact comparatively few historians, with the understandable exception of certain Soviet Russian specialists in the history of slavery, have ever attempted fully to work out the Marxist theory of slavery-as-system (or, as an economic period dominated by chattel servitude as a mode of production). A recent exception to this pattern was made by the Oxford scholar G.E.M. de Ste. Croix, in *The Class Struggle in the Ancient Greek World* (1981), a massive work that has been accurately summarized as "more Marxist than Marx," and is probably best described, in terms of its theoretical substrate, as an oddity, though useful as a foil or target.

The scholar with a Marxist orientation (or at least a Marxist sensibility and base) who has been, arguably, the most influential modern writer on ancient slavery, is M.I. Finley, an American émigré to Great Britain. Finley devoted himself to analyzing the real social and economic origins of, and the complex interactional networks created by, the slave and the slaveholder involved together in the toils of ancient chattel servitude – that is, slavery strictly defined – but Finley also aimed to differentiate and explain other types and varieties of servitude. However, his most confrontational book on the subject is *Ancient Slavery and Modern Ideology* (1980), the first part of which consists of a vigorous attack on the ideas of the German scholar Joseph Vogt and his group of followers. Such emblematic works as Vogt's *Sklaverei und Humanität* (1965; *Ancient Slavery and the Ideal of Man*, 1974) laid out the thesis that the tremendous cultural contributions of the ancient Greeks in particular excused the minor aberration of human slavery, and also pointed to the "humanizing" effect of Christianity, to counter or modify the undeniable fact that slavery itself continued to exist long after the triumph of this faith. Finley's attack identified the Vogt school as, essentially, a regiment of idealist Cold Warriors opposed to any purely socioeconomic or "materialist" – i.e., Marxist-influenced – discussion of slavery. A much-modified Vogtian view of the influence on slavery and slaveholding of the Pauline injunction in I Corinthians 7 ("there is neither slave not free, but all one in Christ Jesus") will be found in Dale Martin's *Slavery as Salvation* (1990).

More recently new issues and attitudes have emerged, to be adapted and taken up in the historiographical process dealing with ancient slavery. What might be termed a psychosocial analytic has been suggested by Orlando Patterson, in his *Slavery and Social Death* (1982); this volume developed the idea of slavery as an ultimate defilement and pollution, with the slave categorized as the ultimate scapegoat. Patterson went much further into the theoretical battleground in his *Freedom in the Making of Western Culture* (1991), putting forth the notion that the concept of freedom itself, from the very inception of the idea, must rest on the presence and idea of the unfree: that the one presupposes and will always define the other. Patterson, a black scholar, clearly extrapolates the modern slave experience of blacks in both hemispheres back toward the general experience of all servile populations and individuals. Another view of the "racialist" aspect of ancient slavery is represented by Frank M. Snowden, Jr., whose *Before Color Prejudice* (1983) tries to demonstrate that the ancient world was, in fact, colorblind in respect to slavery. By and large this view has not held up, as witness such a work as Lloyd Thompson's *Romans and Blacks* (1989), where the antagonistic Roman attitude toward any anomalous, non-Mediterranean pigmentation is proven. The scholarly discussion of race in ancient slavery has not always been so enlightened; as late as the 1930s Tenney Frank, a respected American economic historian, was blaming "race mixing" (by way of African and Middle Eastern slaves) for the decline of Rome.

It is clear that modern historiographical views of ancient slavery continue to resonate to all the latest ideological developments, biases, quirks, and quarrels, responding favorably or unfavorably to Marxist ideas, confronting the problems of racism, and lately responding to feminist concerns: feminist writers have not hesitated to equate directly the situation and condition of free women in ancient Greece and Rome to the situation and condition of the slave. What might be called technical analyses of all the aspects of ancient slavery do continue to be written, however, and these analyses stand or fall, of course, on the analytic skill with which the sources are used, and the persuasiveness of their conclusions. The occurrence of slave rebellion, an important comparative problem because it was as rare in the ancient world as it was in the modern period, has been taken up in Keith Bradley's *Slavery and Rebellion in the Roman World* (1989). Another angle or aspect of the large subject of ancient slavery is discussed in Ellen Meiksins Wood's *Peasant-Citizen and Slave* (1988), which theorized that the servile element in Athens – Athens read as the city or as the closely-related countryside – was never particularly significant at all. Such books as that written by Wood often respond in some fashion to the ideological wars (as she responds to and criticizes St. Croix), but move off in pursuit of their own vectors, and make their own way.

DEAN MILLER

See also Daube; Finley; Roman

Further Reading

Badian, Ernst, "The Bitter History of Slave History," *New York Review of Books* (22 October 1981), 49–53

Bradley, Keith R., *Slaves and Masters in the Roman Empire: A Study in Social Control*, Brussels: Latomus, 1984; New York: Oxford University Press, 1987

Bradley, Keith R., *Slavery and Rebellion in the Roman World, 140 BC–70 BC*, Bloomington: Indiana University Press, and London: Batsford, 1989

Buckland, William Warwick, *The Roman Law of Slavery: The Condition of the Slave in Private Law from Augustus to Justinian*, Cambridge: Cambridge University Press, 1908; reprinted 1970

Davis, David Brion, *The Problem of Slavery in Western Culture*, Ithaca, NY: Cornell University Press, 1966; revised 1988

de Ste. Croix, G.E.M., *The Class Struggle in the Ancient Greek World, from the Archaic Age to the Arab Conquests*, London: Duckworth, and Ithaca, NY: Cornell University Press, 1981

Finley, Moses I., "Aulos Kapreilios Timotheos, Slave Trader," in his *Aspects of Antiquity: Discoveries and Controversies*, New York: Viking, and London: Chatto and Windus, 1968

Finley, Moses I., *Ancient Slavery and Modern Ideology*, London: Chatto and Windus, 1980; New York: Viking, 1981

Finley, Moses I., *Economy and Society in Ancient Greece*, edited by Brent D. Shaw and Richard P. Saller, London: Chatto and Windus, 1981; New York: Viking, 1982

Finley, Moses I., ed., *Classical Slavery*, London: Frank Cass, 1987

Frank, Tenney *et al.*, eds., *An Economic Survey of Ancient Rome*, 6 vols., Baltimore: Johns Hopkins Press, 1933–40

Garlan, Yvon, *Les Esclaves dans la Grèce ancienne*, Paris: Maspero, 1982; in English as *Slavery in Ancient Greece*, Ithaca, NY: Cornell University Press, 1988

Hopkins, Keith, *Conquerors and Slaves*, Cambridge and New York: Cambridge University Press, 1978

Martin, Dale, *Slavery as Salvation: The Metaphor of Slavery in Pauline Christianity*, New Haven and London: Yale University Press, 1990

Miller, Dean A., "Some Psycho-Social Perceptions of Slavery," *Journal of Social History* 18 (1985), 587–605

Patterson, Orlando, *Slavery and Social Death: A Comparative Study*, Cambridge, MA: Harvard University Press, 1982

Patterson, Orlando, *Freedom in the Making of Western Culture*, New York: Basic Books, 1991

Snowden, Frank M., Jr., *Before Color Prejudice: The Ancient View of Blacks*, Cambridge, MA: Harvard University Press, 1983

Thompson, Lloyd A., *Romans and Blacks*, Norman: University of Oklahoma Press, and London: Routledge, 1989

Vogt, Joseph, *Sklaverei und Humanität: Studien zur antiken Sklaverei und ihrer Erforschung*, Wiesbaden: Steiner, 1965; in English as *Ancient Slavery and the Ideal of Man*, Oxford: Blackwell, 1974; Cambridge, MA: Harvard University Press, 1975

Vogt, Joseph, and Norbert Brockmeyer, *Bibliographie zur antiken Sklaverei* (Bibliography on Slavery in the Ancient World), 2 vols., Bochum: Brockmeyer, 1971–83

Wallon, Henri, *Histoire de l'esclavage dans l'Antiquité* (A History of Slavery in the Ancient World), 3 vols., Paris: L'imprimerie royale, 1847; reprinted 1974

Watson, Alan, *Roman Slave Law*, Baltimore: Johns Hopkins University Press, 1987

Westermann, William L., *The Slave Systems of Greek and Roman Antiquity*, Philadelphia: American Philosophical Society, 1955

Wiedemann, Thomas, ed., *Greek and Roman Slavery*, Baltimore: Johns Hopkins University Press, and London: Croom Helm, 1981

Wood, Ellen Meiksins, *Peasant-Citizen and Slave: The Foundation of Athenian Democracy*, London and New York: Verso, 1988.

Slavery: Modern

Scholarship on slavery began as a response to the system of chattel slavery that developed in European colonies in the Americas, with the publication of such works as William Goodell's *Slavery and Anti-Slavery: A History of the Great Struggle . . .* (1853) marking the beginning of efforts to understand the institution that roused international debate and brought the United States to civil war. Thus, although various systems of unfree labor operated around the world throughout the era, the history and consequences of slavery in the Atlantic world, particularly in the American South, have dominated and shaped the scholarly discourse. The work of U.B. Phillips, *American Negro Slavery* (1918) and *Life and Labor in the Old South* (1929), was the first to take up the subject in post-emancipation America. A southerner himself, Phillips reassessed slavery as an essentially benign institution marked by paternalistic masters and generally contented slaves. The slave South, according to Phillips, produced a successful economy and an admirable elite culture. Phillips' focus on the impact of slavery on individuals and society was profoundly influential. Until the 1960s, the historical debate centered on the nature and extent of slavery's effects, though the judgment turned from positive to negative with the publication in 1956 of Kenneth M. Stampp's *The Peculiar Institution*. Stampp's condemnation of slavery seems gentle in retrospect, but Stanley Elkins' *Slavery: A Problem in American Institutional and Intellectual Life* (1959), published only a few years later, remains a forceful, if idiosyncratic indictment of slavery's devastating effect on the human psyche in its comparison of the peculiar institution to Nazi concentration camps. At the end of the 1950s, scholarship painted the institution as an unambiguous evil and portrayed the slave as its profoundly damaged, defeated victim.

The flowering of the Civil Rights movement in the 1960s, which depended on the heroic leadership of African Americans, elicited a fresh assessment of the experience of enslaved people, and a new body of scholarship appeared in the 1970s that portrayed the ability of slaves to surmount the crushing oppression of their condition through acts of creativity, social organization, and resistance. John Blassingame was among the earliest to challenge the Elkins thesis, with *The Slave Community*, originally published in 1972 and expanded in 1979. Together with Herbert Gutman's *The Black Family in Slavery and Freedom, 1750–1925* (1976), *The Slave Community* asserted the resilience and genius of enslaved people, recognizing their ability to sustain family and community ties and cultural richness in the face of constraint and oppression.

Working from a Marxist perspective, Eugene Genovese extended the recognition of slave agency and launched an important and enduring debate with his theory of Old South paternalism in *The Political Economy of Slavery* (1965) and in his magisterial *Roll, Jordan, Roll* (1974). Genovese contended that the southern economy was precapitalist and that planters and slaves engaged in a system of role-playing and mutual obligation that replicated relations of seigneurs and dependants. *Roll, Jordan, Roll* propelled slavery scholarship in a number of different directions. Historians, including James Oakes in *The Ruling Race* (1982) and Robert William Fogel and Stanley Engerman in *Time on the Cross* (1974), offered controversial rebuttals to Genovese's interpretation, arguing for the capitalist nature of the slave system. Others, beginning with Lawrence W. Levine in *Black Culture and Black Consciousness* (1977), explored the theme of slave agency and produced a rich literature on the cultural, economic, and social contributions of enslaved people. Scholarship on slave religion is especially well developed, moving from studies focused on the function of religion among bondpeople, as in Albert J. Raboteau's *Slave Religion* (1978), to complex assessments of how African American religious belief and practice steered broader currents in American religion, exemplified in the work of Mechal Sobel in *The World They Made Together* (1988) and Sylvia R. Frey and Betty Wood in *Come Shouting to Zion* (1998).

Resistance and rebellion, as the most potent manifestations of slave agency, have received substantial attention, beginning with Herbert Aptheker's *American Negro Slave Revolts* (1943). Peter Wood provided a detailed and nuanced description of the variety of slave resistance and the power of slave rebellion to shape planter thought and society in *Black Majority* (1974). Shipboard resistance during the middle passage has received attention primarily in journal articles, though Howard Jones' *Mutiny on the Amistad* (1987) chronicled a signally successful and notorious 19th-century revolt. While slave resistance constitutes a steady, though not preoccupying theme in American slavery scholarship, the historiography of Haiti (San Domingue) is dominated by examinations of the origins, progress, and aftermath of the only successful national slave revolution.

By shifting attention to the agency and varied contributions of enslaved people, slavery scholarship moved from a rather static, descriptive approach to a dynamic model that examined change over time. Peter Wood's *Black Majority* was a seminal work, illustrating how the presence of slaves shaped the course of low-country identity, culture, and economic development. Daniel C. Littlefield's *Rice and Slaves* (1981) and Gwendolyn Midlo Hall's *Africans in Colonial Louisiana* (1992) focused on the essential role that slaves played in creating successful plantation economies through the introduction of specific skills and knowledge.

Although interest in the developmental history of slavery has flowered only fairly recently, its origins have been examined and debated since the turn of the century. In 1902 James C. Ballagh's *A History of Slavery in Virginia* challenged a 19th-century consensus that slavery and racism appeared simultaneously in the 17th-century Chesapeake by pointing out that slavery did not exist in law in early Virginia and that blacks living as indentured servants or as free persons vitiated the conflation of African with slave. Ballagh's legal argument sowed the seeds of what Alden T. Vaughan has dubbed the "origins debate," in which racialist and economic theories of slavery's roots vie with one another. As desegregation and the civil rights movement got underway in postwar America, the attribution of slavery to economic imperatives, rather than to race prejudice, harmonized more closely with contemporary social goals. In this environment, Oscar and Mary F. Handlin's article "Origins of the Southern Labor System" (1950) was well received. Portraying slavery as an economic response to the promise of huge wealth through staple crop agriculture, which in turn required a large labor force, the Handlins asserted that slavery was the inevitable, tragic outcome of a demand for labor that could not be met in any other way. Permanently consigned to the most physically unpleasant and demeaning types of labor, slaves became the object of degradation. According to the Handlins, racism was a product, not a cause, of slavery. Edmund Morgan weighed in in favor of the Handlin thesis in his powerful study, *American Slavery, American Freedom* (1975), and T.H. Breen and Stephen Innes offered supporting evidence with their portraits of Virginia's free blacks in *"Myne Owne Ground"* (1980).

The Handlin thesis has been vigorously contested, beginning with Carl Degler's assertion of the primacy of racism in slavery's origins in "Slavery and the Genesis of American Race Prejudice" (1959) and subsequently with Winthrop D. Jordan's exhaustive study of European racialist thought in *White over Black* (1968). More recent scholarship, notably a special issue of the *William and Mary Quarterly* (1997), has probed the construction of race in the early modern Atlantic, delineating diverse strains in the long lineage of European racism. Kathleen Brown's *Good Wives, Nasty Wenches, and Anxious Patriarchs* (1996) portrayed the early modern Atlantic as an environment in which ideologies of identity turning on gender and race emerged and were molded at least partly in response to the dynamics of encounter and the demands of creating a viable colonial society. Although no explicit consensus has emerged, Brown's work paves the way for a dialectical model that recognizes the intersection of emerging racial ideologies with geographic and economic expansion as central to the development of slavery.

Economic historians and demographers helped to lay the essential groundwork for such a model by exposing the structural forces that inclined the Americas toward slavery. In his 1977 essay, "From Servants to Slaves," Russell R. Menard noted that the formalization of slave law and increased black bondage in the late 17th-century Chesapeake coincided with the declining availability of English indentured servants during this period, and David Galenson identified the same phenomenon at work in the low-country and the British Caribbean in *White Servitude in Colonial America* (1981). Peter Kolchin pushed the labor-supply thesis beyond the Americas in *Unfree Labor: American Slavery and Russian Serfdom* (1987), in which he linked the development of systems of bonded labor in the early modern world to the twinned phenomena of geographic expansion and a voluntary labor supply insufficient to the task of agricultural exploitation.

More recently, scholars have probed the sensitive topic of African participation in the evolution of New World slavery. John Thornton's compelling study, *Africa and Africans in the Making of the Atlantic World, 1400–1680* (1992), revealed the role of African culture, politics, and economics in the creation of a new form of human bondage, demonstrating how a confluence of European and African interests and imperatives spawned and nurtured modern chattel slavery. Others, beginning with Philip D. Curtin in *The Atlantic Slave Trade: A Census* (1969), have reconstructed the interior and transatlantic slave trade, detailing the function and effect of slaving on the African interior, the intersection of African and European traders on the West African coast, the mechanics of slave commerce, and its impact on African and European economies. Slave trade historians have also given attention to the demographics of the enslaved, which in turn speak to the nuances of the New World demand for specific ethnicities deemed particularly adapted to certain functions.

Scholars have, of course, moved beyond the morphology and developmental course of American slavery to ask more general questions about systems of forced labor, to focus on slave societies outside mainland North America, and to pose comparisons among various systems. David Brion Davis's *The Problem of Slavery in Western Culture* (1966) explored the broad intellectual underpinnings of modern slavery without focusing on particular examples. Orlando Patterson also moved beyond the specific in his *Slavery and Social Death* (1982), which attempted to isolate the features common to all systems of modern slavery. Focusing on divergences rather than commonalities, Frank Tannenbaum's *Slave and Citizen* (1946) suggested that there were significant differences between English and Spanish slave societies that sprang from divergent legal and religious cultures. A rich literature in comparative slavery and race relations has subsequently developed, in which a wide variety of factors are considered. Notable among recent scholarship is a collection edited by Ira Berlin and Philip D. Morgan, *Cultivation and Culture* (1993), which portrayed the diverse effects on slave life and culture of varying locales and staple crops.

Such comparative studies rest on a large body of specialized scholarship on slave societies in the Caribbean and South and Central America. The field of Brazilian scholarship is notably well developed, bracketed by Gilberto Freyre's *Casa-grande e senzala* (1933; *The Masters and the Slaves*, 1946) and Stuart Schwartz's *Slaves, Peasants, and Rebels: Reconsidering Brazilian Slavery* (1992), which examined a variety of factors that distinguished Brazilian slavery, including the influence of Catholicism and the huge numbers of enslaved Africans employed in the physically brutal cultivation of cane. Caribbean studies present a less coherent body of scholarship, largely owing to the diversity of colonizers, although the work of such scholars as Hilary McD. Beckles and David Geggus has brilliantly illuminated not only particular Caribbean experiences, but broader themes of master-slave relations, gender, resistance, and labor patterns.

The annual bibliographical supplement published in the journal *Slavery and Abolition* provides an overview of the diversity and depth of current scholarship. It divides work among eleven major categories, including general and comparative, North America, Spanish Mainland, Brazil, Caribbean, Africa, Muslim, slave trade, ancient, medieval, and early modern Europe, and "other." Within each major division there are as many as 16 sub-categories. Such breadth demonstrates that while slavery in the Americas launched the scholarship and continues to dominate the popular imagination, historians are engaged in demonstrating that systems of forced labor have pervaded nearly every place and society in the modern age.

EMILY CLARK

See also African American; Agricultural; Brazil; British Empire; Cardoso; Computing; Cuba; Curtin; Davis, D.; Degler; Economic; Elkins; Ethnicity; Family; Fogel; Foner, E.; Foner, P.; Franklin; Freyre; Genovese; Gutman; James; Jordan; Latin America: National; Levine; Litwack; Lovejoy; Marriage; Moreno Fraginals; Morgan; Phillips; Quantitative; Rodney; Stampp; Stein; Takaki; Tannenbaum; Thomas, H.; United States: Colonial; United States: American Revolution; United States: 19th Century; Watson; White, L.; Williams, E.; Women's History: North America; Women's History: African American; Woodson; Woodward

Further Reading

Aptheker, Herbert, *American Negro Slave Revolts*, New York: Columbia University Press, and London: King and Staples, 1943

Ballagh, James C., *A History of Slavery in Virginia*, Baltimore: Johns Hopkins University Press, 1902; reprinted 1968

Beckles, Hilary McD., ed., *Inside Slavery: Process and Legacy in the Caribbean Experience*, Kingston, Jamaica: Canoe Press, 1996

Berlin, Ira, and Philip D. Morgan, eds., *Cultivation and Culture: Labor and the Shaping of Slave Life in the Americas*, Charlottesville: University of Virginia Press, 1993

Berlin, Ira, "From Creole to African: Atlantic Creoles and the Origins of African-American Society in Mainland North America," *William and Mary Quarterly* 53 (1996), 251–88

Blassingame, John, *The Slave Community: Plantation Life in the Antebellum South*, New York: Oxford University Press, 1972; revised 1979

Breen, T.H., and Stephen Innes, *"Myne Owne Ground": Race and Freedom on Virginia's Eastern Shore, 1640–1676*, New York: Oxford University Press, 1980

Brown, Kathleen M., *Good Wives, Nasty Wenches, and Anxious Patriarchs: Gender, Race, and Power in Colonial Virginia*, Chapel Hill: University of North Carolina Press, 1996

Creel, Margaret Washington, *A Peculiar People: Slave Religion and Community-Culture among the Gullahs*, New York: New York University Press, 1988

Curtin, Philip D., *The Atlantic Slave Trade: A Census*, Madison: University of Wisconsin Press, 1969

Curtin, Philip D., *Economic Change in Precolonial Africa: Senegambia in the Era of the Slave Trade*, Madison: University of Wisconsin Press, 1975

Davis, David Brion, *The Problem of Slavery in Western Culture*, Ithaca, NY: Cornell University Press, 1966; revised 1988

Degler, Carl N., "Slavery and the Genesis of American Race Prejudice," *Comparative Studies in Society and History* 2 (1959), 49–66

Elkins, Stanley, *Slavery: A Problem in American Institutional and Intellectual Life*, Chicago: University of Chicago Press, 1959; 3rd edition 1976

Fogel, Robert William, and Stanley L. Engerman, *Time on the Cross: The Economics of American Negro Slavery*, 2 vols., Boston: Little Brown, and London: Wildwood, 1974

Frey, Sylvia R., and Betty Wood, *Come Shouting to Zion: African American Protestantism in the American South and British Caribbean to 1830*, Chapel Hill: University of North Carolina Press, 1998

Freyre, Gilberto, *Casa-grande e senzala: formação da família brasileira sob o regime de economia patriarcal*, 2 vols., Rio de Janeiro: Maia & Schmidt, 1933; in English as *The Masters and the Slaves: A Study in the Development of Brazilian Civilization*, New York: Knopf, 1946, London: Secker and Warburg, 1947

Galenson, David, *White Servitude in Colonial America: An Economic Analysis*, Cambridge and New York: Cambridge University Press, 1981

Gaspar, D. Barry, and David Geggus, eds., *A Turbulent Time: The Greater Caribbean in the Age of the Haitian and French Revolutions*, Bloomington: Indiana University Press, 1997

Geggus, David P, *Slavery, War and Revolution: The British Occupation of Saint Domingue, 1793–1798*, Oxford and New York: Oxford University Press, 1982

Genovese, Eugene D., *The Political Economy of Slavery: Studies in the Economy and Society of the Slave South*, New York: Pantheon, 1965; London: MacGibbon and Kee, 1968

Genovese, Eugene D., *Roll, Jordan, Roll: The World the Slaves Made*, New York: Pantheon, 1974; London: Deutsch, 1975

Goodell, William, *Slavery and Anti-Slavery: A History of the Great Struggle in Both Hemispheres; with a View to the Slavery Question in the United States*, New York: Goodell, 1853

Gutman, Herbert G., *The Black Family in Slavery and Freedom, 1750–1925*, New York: Pantheon, and Oxford: Blackwell, 1976

Hall, Gwendolyn Midlo, *Africans in Colonial Louisiana: The Development of Afro-Creole Culture in the Eighteenth Century*, Baton Rouge: Louisiana State University Press, 1992

Handlin, Oscar, and Mary F. Handlin, "Origins of the Southern Labor System," *William and Mary Quarterly* 7 (1950), 199–222

Jones, Howard, *Mutiny on the Amistad: The Saga of a Slaver Revolt and Its Impact on American Abolition, Law and Diplomacy*, Oxford and New York: Oxford University Press, 1987

Jordan, Winthrop D., *White over Black: American Attitudes toward the Negro, 1550–1812*, Chapel Hill: University of North Carolina Press, 1968; abridged as *The White Man's Burden: Historical Origins of Racism in the United States*, New York: Oxford University Press, 1974

Joyner, Charles W., *Down by the Riverside: A South Carolina Slave Community*, Urbana: University of Illinois Press, 1984

Kolchin, Peter, *Unfree Labor: American Slavery and Russian Serfdom*, Cambridge, MA: Harvard University Press, 1987

Levine, Lawrence W., *Black Culture and Black Consciousness: Afro-American Folk Thought from Slavery to Freedom*, Oxford and New York: Oxford University Press, 1977

Littlefield, Daniel C., *Rice and Slaves: Ethnicity and the Slave Trade in Colonial South Carolina*, Baton Rouge: Louisiana State University Press, 1981

Lovejoy, Paul E., *Transformations in Slavery: A History of Slavery in Africa*, Cambridge and New York: Cambridge University Press, 1983

McGiffert, Michael, "Constructing Race: Differentiating Peoples in the Early Modern World," *William and Mary Quarterly* 54 (1997), 3–6

Manning, Patrick, ed., *Slave Trades, 1500–1800: Globalization of Forced Labor*, Aldershot: Variorum, 1996

Menard, Russell R., "From Servants to Slaves: The Transformation of the Chesapeake Labor System," *Southern Studies* 16 (1977), 355–90

Morgan, Edmund S., *American Slavery, American Freedom: The Ordeal of Colonial Virginia*, New York: Norton, 1975

Oakes, James, *The Ruling Race: A History of American Slaveholders*, New York: Knopf, 1982

Parish, Peter J., *Slavery: History and Historians*, New York: Harper, 1989

Patterson, Orlando, *Slavery and Social Death: A Comparative Study*, Cambridge, MA: Harvard University Press, 1982

Phillips, Ulrich Bonnell, *American Negro Slavery: A Survey of the Supply, Employment, and Control of Negro Labor as Determined by the Plantation Regime*, New York: Appleton, 1918; reprinted Baton Rouge: Louisiana State University Press, 1966

Phillips, Ulrich Bonnell, *Life and Labor in the Old South*, Boston: Little Brown, 1929

Raboteau, Albert J., *Slave Religion: The "Invisible Institution" in the Antebellum South*, Oxford and New York: Oxford University Press, 1978

Schwartz, Stuart B., *Slaves, Peasants, and Rebels: Reconsidering Brazilian Slavery*, Urbana: University of Illinois Press, 1992

Sobel, Mechal, *The World They Made Together: Black and White Values in Eighteenth-Century Virginia*, Princeton: Princeton University Press, 1988

Stampp, Kenneth M., *The Peculiar Institution: Slavery in the Ante-Bellum South*, New York: Knopf, 1956; London: Eyre and Spottiswoode, 1964

Tannenbaum, Frank, *Slave and Citizen: The Negro in the Americas*, New York: Knopf, 1946

Thornton, John, *Africa and Africans in the Making of the Atlantic World, 1400–1680*, Cambridge and New York: Cambridge University Press, 1992

Vaughan, Alden T., "The Origins Debate: Slavery and Racism in Seventeenth-Century Virginia," *Virginia Magazine of History and Biography* 97 (1989), 311–54

Wood, Betty, *Women's Work, Men's Work: The Informal Slave Economies of Lowcountry Georgia*, Athens: University of Georgia Press, 1995

Wood, Peter H., *Black Majority: Negroes in Colonial South Carolina from 1670 Through the Stono Rebellion*, New York: Knopf, 1974

Smith, Henry Nash 1906–1986
US historian

A dominant theme in US western history is how the presence of an American frontier shaped national character. Rugged individualism and a thirst for pure democracy were but two traits attributed to Americans in Frederick Jackson Turner's 1893 *The Significance of the Frontier in American History*. Since publication of that famous essay, American exceptionalism has been a major debate among US historians, mostly among historians of the US West. Henry Nash Smith explored this theme in his seminal work, *Virgin Land: The American West as Symbol and Myth* (1950), through literature and popular culture, and, in so doing, kindled interest among historians in the neglected study of western literature and popular myth. In fact, he maintained that the myth of the West has been every bit as important as the reality. Although not a historian by training, this single book earned Smith a permanent place in the study of the history of the American West.

Publication of *Virgin Land* initiated a serious examination of the symbols and images of the West. The title of his book was itself an assertion of myth since the territory west of the Mississippi was hardly virgin in any sense of the word. On the contrary, it was peopled by a sizeable indigenous population, and, after 1492, by Spaniards in the area known as Spanish Borderlands. Nevertheless, the belief that America contained empty land fueled Manifest Destiny in the 1840s and encouraged a steady stream of white, European-American settlers intent upon developing this so-called empty, virgin space. In this instance, the myth of uninhabited land was more powerful than the fact. It dominated American desire to expand and occupy the continent, and it reinforced the Jeffersonian concept that the new republic offered an agricultural haven to a virtuous yeomanry. Furthermore, it spawned a vast literature that focused on notions of wilderness versus civilization.

In *Virgin Land*, Smith explored three versions of the American wilderness myth using literature written roughly between 1830 and 1900. He considered literary themes and characters from the Leatherstocking hero of James Fenimore Cooper to dime novels to Turner's frontier thesis, which he said, played as much into the Garden of Eden utopian myth of frontier as other less scholarly works. Perhaps most significant, Smith's work offered a new methodology to American historians, namely the analysis of literary symbol and popular culture.

Smith was a founder of the new school in the 1950s called American Studies, defined by him as the study of culture, which was simply the way subjective experience is organized. Thus, Buffalo Bill, the literary character of Deadwood Dick, even the whole Billy the Kid phenomenon were not to be ignored, but studied as part of the American culture. Although largely myth, these were as much a part of the American psyche as so-called reality, and, as a consequence, must be part of the scholarly historical study of the West.

This is a theme Smith returned to time and time again in his ongoing work on Mark Twain and in *Popular Culture and Industrialism, 1865–1890* (1967), which examined pseudo-ideas and stereotypes from fiction, art, and material culture relating to post-Civil War industrial growth and urbanization. In this book, Smith again examined the American character through its total culture, and concluded that by 1890, Americans saw themselves and their whole notion of progress in such unrealistic terms that it handicapped development of human resources. Thus, Smith continued a subtheme that runs through his works, specifically that Americans have chosen to focus so intently on factors that lead them away from Old World or European ideology that they have found it increasingly difficult to view themselves as part of a world community. This is one reason why, Smith suggests, comparative history has proven so elusive for US historians, even more so for historians of the US West.

Since its introduction in the 1950s, American Studies has been criticized as being too broad-based, unfocused, and obsessed with analysis and deconstruction. Despite this criticism, Smith's primary contribution to US history lay precisely in his belief that popular culture can indeed be examined for historical meaning and that, especially as it pertains to the so-called Wild West, myth can and should be studied for its own sake.

KATHLEEN EGAN CHAMBERLAIN

Biography

Born Dallas, 1906. Attended Southern Methodist University, BA in English 1925; Harvard University, MA in English 1926, PhD in American civilization 1940. Founded program in history of American civilization, Southern Methodist University, 1940; taught at University of Texas, 1941–47; University of Minnesota, 1947–53; University of California, Berkeley, from 1953. President, Modern Language Association, 1969. Married Elinor (1 son, 2 daughters). Died Elko, Nevada, 30 May 1986.

Principal Writings

Virgin Land: The American West as Symbol and Myth, 1950
"Can 'American Studies' Develop a Method?" *American Quarterly* 9 (1957), 197–208
Mark Twain: The Development of a Writer, 1962
Editor, *Popular Culture and Industrialism, 1865–1890*, 1967
"Virgin Land Revisited," *Indian Journal of American Studies* 3 (1973), 1–8
Democracy and the Novel: Popular Resistance to Classic American Writers, 1978
"Symbol and Idea in Virgin Land," in Sacvan Bercovitch and Myra Jehlen, eds., *Ideology and Classic American Literature*, 1986

Further Reading

Etulain, Richard W., "The American Literary West and Its Interpreters: The Rise of a New Historiography," *Pacific Historical Review* 45 (1976), 311–48
Etulain, Richard W., "Frontier, Region, and Myth: Changing Interpretations of Western Cultural History," *Journal of American Culture* 3 (1980), 268–84
Mitchell, Lee Clark, "Henry Nash Smith's Myth of the West," in Richard W. Etulain, ed., *Writing Western History: Essays on Major Western Historians*, Albuquerque: University of New Mexico Press, 1991
Veysey, Laurence R., "Myth and Reality in Approaching American Regionalism," *American Quarterly* 12 (1960), 31–43
Voloshin, Beverly R., ed., *American Literature, Culture, and Ideology: Essays in Memory of Henry Nash Smith*, New York: Lang, 1990 [includes select bibliography]

Smith, Merritt Roe 1940–

US historian of technology

As a leading historian of technology, Merritt Roe Smith pioneered an approach to the study of industrialization through the use of community studies and expanded the audience for the history of technology. His work provides a model for integrating technology and the community context. Smith takes the history of technology beyond the marginality it has acquired through an identification with antiquarianism by considering technical change in a wider social context that includes worker response to industrialization.

Harpers Ferry Armory and the New Technology (1977) is Smith's most influential book. It is a call to historians of technology to take an interest in worker response and the community setting of industrialization efforts. It also popularized the community study approach to industrialization used by several historians of technology during the 1980s. According to historian Carroll Pursell (1980), Smith "reminds us of the measure of social control over technological pace and direction exercised by such institutions as church, school, state, and business organizations."

In his book, Smith presents the push for interchangeable parts in terms of the conflict between the traditional customs and values of skilled artisans and the local landed elite at Harpers Ferry and the values of the Ordnance Department, which sought uniformity in managerial style as well as parts. Smith's work gives as much prominence to the view of the workers at the armory as to those of the local elite at Harpers Ferry and the Ordnance Department running the armory. *Harpers Ferry* was a challenge to many then-accepted notions about the American System of manufacturing; it showed that workers did not always welcome the system, and that the system did not necessarily lower production costs or necessarily involve interchangeability. This book, along with Anthony F.C. Wallace's *Rockdale* (1978), advanced the notion that the values and social configuration of communities partially determine the response to industrialization – acceptance or violence. The model at Harpers Ferry was conflictual, while the model at Rockdale was consensual. John Staudenmaier (1984) called *Harpers Ferry* and *Rockdale* "twin signals of increasing legitimation for the history of technology in the Organization of American Historians and in anthropological circles." Their nearly simultaneous publication was "taken as indicative of a breakthrough in the scholarly acceptance of technology."

The community study approach in *Harpers Ferry* is a compelling model for historians of how human culture and societal processes can shape technical design and how technologies, once designed, can influence later cultural and social developments. By the 1980s, historians of technology explicitly refer to *Harpers Ferry* as a model for social history of technology. For example, Judith McGaw in *Most Wonderful Machine* (1987) referred to *Harpers Ferry* as one of the "outstanding examples of work treating the social shaping of technology in 19th-century America."

Trained as an American historian at the Pennsylvania State University, Smith brought the history of technology to the attention of general historians. His work pushed against a trend toward the reduction of the relationship of the history of technology to general history; Brooke Hindle (1989) claimed that the reduction came with the professionalization of the history of technology. *Harpers Ferry* was the first work by an insider in the history of technology to receive national recognition by the wider audience of American historians through the Frederick Jackson Turner prize of the Organization of American Historians in 1977 and through a Pulitzer Prize in history nomination in the same year.

Smith continued his work on industrialization and the American System of manufactures, along with his work on the relationship between government, technology, and structure. This work on the military culminated with his edited volume *Military Enterprise and Technological Change* (1985). According to Staudenmaier (1985), the case studies in this volume represented "a significant early effort to test the assertion that US technological style would have turned out differently in a less militarized context by tracing causal connections between military bureaucracy, ideology and funding patterns, and the particular details of specific technologies." Smith's work in the history of technology also includes the strengthening of an international community in the history of technology, particularly in Sweden. In 1994, the Society for the History of Technology (SHOT) awarded Smith the Leonardo da Vinci medal – the highest honor the Society can bestow – for service to the field of the history of technology, both in academic circles and for general audiences.

Smith's work extends the history of technology beyond the academic community to a more general audience. During his term as vice president of SHOT, Smith and then-president Bruce Sinclair made the expansion of the audience for the history of technology a key priority. Smith was one of a group of SHOT members who considered how to accomplish this goal. These efforts led to the award of an National Science Foundation grant to a group of SHOT scholars and secondary school teachers to write an interdisciplinary curriculum aimed at bringing science and technology into social studies classrooms at secondary schools (completed in 1994); Smith acted as consultant to the project. He was also the primary consultant on "The Iron Road" segment of the television series *The American Experience* in 1990 and is currently on the board of advisers for the series *A Life of Science*. One of his most recent projects is a forthcoming textbook for use in general American history surveys in higher education; the goal is to integrate science and technology issues, where appropriate, into the study of American history alongside political, cultural, social, and ethnic issues. Smith's attempts to expand the audience for the history of technology also include service on numerous museum boards and as adviser to numerous exhibits, including several at the Smithsonian Institution.

Smith continues to use the community studies approach to the history of technology in his current research, a comparative study of early industrial communities in the United States.

LINDA EIKMEIER ENDERSBY

See also Technology

Biography

Born Waverly, New York, 14 November 1940. Studied at Georgetown University, BA 1963; Pennsylvania State University, MA 1965, PhD 1971. Taught at Ohio State University, 1970–78; and Massachusetts Institute of Technology, from 1978. Married Bronwyn Mellquist in 1974.

Principal Writings

"John H. Hall, Simeon North, and the Milling Machine: The Nature of Innovation Among Antebellum Arms Makers," *Technology and Culture* 14 (1973), 573–91

Harpers Ferry Armory and the New Technology: The Challenge of Change, 1977

"Eli Whitney and the American System," in C. W. Pursell, ed., *Technology in America*, 1981

With David Noble, "History of Technology in America," in Stephen H. Cutcliffe, ed., *The Machine in the University*, 1983

Editor, *Military Enterprise and Technological Change: Perspectives on the American Experience*, 1985

Editor with Everett Mendelsohn and Peter Weingart, *Science, Technology, and the Military*, 1988

With Steven C. Reber, "Contextual Contrasts: Recent Trends in the History of Technology," in Stephen H. Cutcliffe and Robert C. Post, eds., *In Context: History and the History of Technology*, 1989

"Industry, Technology, and the 'Labor Question' in 19th-Century America," *Technology and Culture* 32 (1991), 555–70

Editor with Leo Marx, *Does Technology Drive History? The Dilemma of Technological Determinism*, 1994

Further Reading

Daniels, George H., "The Big Questions in the History of American Technology," *Technology and Culture* 11 (1970), 1–21

Hindle, Brooke, "Historians of Technology and the Context of History," in Stephen H. Cutcliffe and Robert C. Post, eds., *In Context: History and the History of Technology: Essays in Honor of Melvin Kranzberg*, Bethlehem, PA: Lehigh University Press, 1989

Hughes, Thomas P., "Emerging Themes in the History of Technology," *Technology and Culture* 20 (1979), 697–711

Porter, Glenn, "A Historiographical Revolution: A.F.C. Wallace's *Rockdale* and Merritt Roe Smith's *Harpers Ferry*," Paper read at 22nd annual meeting of the Society for the History of Technology, Newark, NJ, October 1979

Pursell, Carroll W., Jr., "History of Technology," in Paul T. Durbin, ed., *A Guide to the Culture of Science, Technology, and Medicine*, New York: Free Press, 1980

Staudenmaier, John M., "What SHOT Hath Wrought and What SHOT Hath Not: Reflections on Twenty-five Years of the History of Technology," *Technology and Culture* 25 (1984), 707–30

Staudenmaier, John M., *Technology's Storytellers: Reweaving the Human Fabric* Cambridge, MA: MIT Press, 1985

Staudenmaier, John M., "Recent Trends in the History of Technology," *American Historical Review* 95 (1990), 715–25

Smith-Rosenberg, Carroll 1936–

US women's and gender historian

Since the publication in 1975 of her landmark essay "The Female World of Love and Ritual," Carroll Smith-Rosenberg has been a leading figure in the reconstruction of US women's history. Through the shifts in approach that have marked women's history over three decades, her work has continued to engage the vital issues in the field. The use of women's diaries and letters as central sources, the refusal to assume that women were merely victims, the insistence on examining women's views of gender as well as those of men – these are among the approaches that Smith-Rosenberg has helped to establish as central for historians in this field.

Smith-Rosenberg trained as a social historian before women's history became a recognized sub-discipline, and her earliest work focused on urban poverty in the 19th-century United States. The study of reform societies led her to focus on one reform organization that was explicitly anti-male: the American Female Moral Reform Society. By her own account in *Disorderly Conduct* (1985), it was the gender focus of this organization that convinced Smith-Rosenberg to recognize gender as a significant category for social analysis. Their protests against male sexual exploitation led her to an examination of other sites of sexual and gender conflict, examining medical literature among other traditional sources. The direction of her work changed drastically, however, with a shift of focus from such traditional, male-authored sources to diaries and letters written by women. The intense emotional world she discovered in these documents were the basis for her "Female World of Love and Ritual" essay, which is still required reading for anyone interested in women's history.

This essay explored women's homosocial relationships and the domestic sphere, using a wide range of women's documents. In Victorian America, Smith-Rosenberg argued, intense, loving friendships between women were widely accepted as compatible with heterosexual marriage. Such relationships were enabled by the rigid gender stratification of society that made men and women seem to each other like members of "an alien group." Female friendships served a number of roles. Most obviously, they served an emotional role in allowing women to share both joy and sorrow. In addition, kinship/friendship networks allowed for an apprenticeship system by which young women were educated for marriage and motherhood.

This work has been widely influential, and it has been interpreted in widely different ways. Some historians have seen it as uncovering a hidden world of lesbian activity, while others have seen it primarily as evidence of strong mother-daughter bonds. Still others have argued that the essay proves that lesbianism did not exist in this era. The essay has been criticized by some for ignoring the realities of oppression, while others have appreciated its focus on women's agency. Most importantly, though, the essay was central to opening debates about the meaning and origins of women's separate world.

Although highly influential, this essay should not be allowed to overshadow the larger body of Smith-Rosenberg's work. In 1985 a collection of previously published and new essays, *Disorderly Conduct*, demonstrated the range of her work. As a whole, the collection emphasized the ways in which psychosexual anxieties and social conflict are expressed in language, with special attention to metaphorical and symbolic discourse, an approach that is clearly influenced by anthropology and semiology. The essays ranged over a variety of types of discourse: from a discussion of how Davy Crockett tales reveal Victorian visions of masculinity, to an analysis of the relationship between the male discourse of medical professionalism and the criminalization of abortion. Taken as a whole, *Disorderly Conduct* provides both an overview of gender history and important specific case studies in the relation of discourse and social conflict over a hundred years of US history.

More recent work extended this attention to discourse to focus on the creation of an American national identity, and to include issues of race as well as gender. Two recent essays stand out. In "Dis-Covering the Subject of the 'Great Constitutional Discussion'" (1992) Smith-Rosenberg demonstrated how the new American subject was constructed in opposition to the subaltern figures of middle-class white women, Native Americans, and enslaved Africans. In "Subject Female: Authorizing American Identity" (1993) she argued that women writers who were fighting to attain liberal humanist subjectivity joined in the colonialist discourse of white men, but by the late 18th century, they had "learned to subvert the very discourses they helped construct." These and other recent essays reveal the power of gender and race analysis to reveal previously ignored but critical facets of nationalism and subjectivity. As it has done for decades, Smith-Rosenberg's work continues to challenge social history not merely to include the history of subaltern groups, but radically to reconstruct larger historical narratives from the new perspectives made possible by the recovery of those histories.

ANGELA VIETTO

See also Homosexuality; Women's History: North America

Biography

Born New York City, 15 March 1936. Received BA, Connecticut College for Women, 1957; MA, Columbia University, 1958, PhD 1968; postdoctoral study in psychiatry, University of Pennsylvania Medical School, 1968–71. Taught at University of Pennsylvania Medical School, in psychiatry department, 1969–76, and in history department, 1971–95; professor of history, women's studies, and American culture, University of Michigan, from 1996. Married Charles Ernest Rosenberg, historian, 1961 (marriage dissolved 1977; 1 daughter); partner from 1980: Alvia G. Golden.

Principal Writings

Religion and the Rise of the American City: The New York City Mission Movement, 1812–1870, 1971
"The Female World of Love and Ritual," *Signs* 1 (1975), 1–30
Disorderly Conduct: Visions of Gender in Victorian America, 1985
"Dis-Covering the Subject of the 'Great Constitutional Discussion'," *Journal of American History* 79 (1992), 841–73
"Subject Female: Authorizing American Identity," *American Literary History* 5 (1993), 481–511
"Black Gothics: Problematizing Identities in the New 'American' Nation," in Robert St. George, ed., *Possible Pasts*, Ithaca, NY: Cornell University Press, 1997

Further Reading

Dubois, Ellen Carol, Mari Jo Buhle, Temma Kaplan, Gerda Lerner, and Carroll Smith-Rosenberg, "Politics and Culture in Women's History: A Symposium," *Feminist Studies* 6 (1980), 26–64

Snorri Sturluson 1178/79–1241
Icelandic historian, poet, and statesman

Snorri Sturluson was one of the most outstanding personalities in medieval Icelandic history and literature. He belonged to the powerful Sturlunga family and held the important position of lawspeaker twice (1215–18 and 1222–31). His political activities and involvement in the family feuds that characterized his age are mainly known from the Íslendinga saga, one part of Sturlunga saga, which was written by his nephew. Early on Snorri sought patronage of the Norwegian court, he wrote praise poems in the skaldic tradition, and he supported Norwegian plans to annex Iceland. He visited Norway twice and had friendly relationships with Earl Skúli, who was first the regent for the young king Hákon Hákonarson, but later the king's rival. As a result Snorri too fell out of favor and was murdered at the instigation of the Norwegian king by his Icelandic enemies.

Among his contemporaries Snorri was most famous for his poetry, of which little is preserved. The works on history, mythology, and poetical theory which are known under his name were a highpoint in medieval Icelandic literature. *Snorra Edda* and *Heimskringla* are extremely valuable sources for our knowledge of the history of the medieval Norwegian kings, the pre-Christian Germanic religion, and the old Norse skaldic poetry. It is still debated whether Snorri was in fact the author of all parts. The precise dates for the composition of the works are not known but it is most likely that Snorri wrote them after his first visit to Norway during the relatively quiet period from 1220 to 1230. Snorri used his comprehensive knowledge of the skaldic tradition for these works.

Most editions of the *Edda* are based on the manuscript R (Codex Regius), written around 1325. The oldest complete manuscript of the *Edda* dates from around 1300. Only in this manuscript are title and author named. The meaning of the title is not clear; it has been interpreted as meaning poetry or poetics but there are linguistic problems. The suggestions connecting it with Oddi, the name of the farmstead where Snorri grew up, or with the word for great-grandmother, are also difficult to explain. The *Edda*, as Snorri stated himself, was written as a compendium for young skalds (court poets), so that they could learn about heathen poetry, its metrical rules, use of kenningar (metaphors) and heiti (synonyms), and read about the old Germanic gods and their myths, knowledge of which after 200 years of Christianization was vanishing. The work is divided into four parts. The main themes of the Prologue are the creation of the world, reminiscent of the first chapters of the Old Testament, an explanation of natural religion and the origins of the polytheistic religion in Scandinavia from an euhemeristic viewpoint. In *Gylfaginning* (tricking of Gylfi) Germanic mythology is explained comprehensively, including the ideas about the origin and the end of the world, creation of human beings and dwarfs, emergence of gods and giants, and the character of the gods and their deeds. Snorri gained his knowledge from eddic poems, such as Voluspá, Vafþrúðnismál, and Grímnismál, but also from oral traditions that would otherwise be lost. In *Skáldskaparmál* (Diction of Poetry) Snorri discussed the technique of skaldic poetry, especially the kenningar and the heiti, and as instruction he gave quotations from the poems of Norwegian and Icelandic poets of the 9th to the 12th centuries, many of which are otherwise lost. The last part, *Háttatal* (list of verse forms), is a praise poem to king Hákon Hákonarson and Earl Skúli. Using it as a model Snorri illustrated in 102 stanzas 100 different skaldic verse forms.

Snorri wrote in a Christian environment and it is controversial to what degree the traditions of the Nordic heathen past or Christian theological thinking from the south influenced his tales of the Germanic gods. He used a narrative framework that allowed him to tell the heathen myths not as narrator but in fictitious dialogues and thus distanced himself, as a Christian, from acknowledging any truth in the heathen stories. Snorri endeavored to link the heathen past, which formed an important foundation of historical identity, to the Christian present. Scandinavian pictorial sources as early as the Migration and Vendel periods have shown the authenticity and the age of at least some of Snorri's stories. Snorri's *Edda* was the only work of its kind in medieval literature.

The *Heimskringla* (The Orb of the World) recorded in a prologue and 16 sagas the history of the Norwegian and Swedish kings from their mythical origins until 1177. It is one of the last works in the genre of kings' sagas. Snorri used oral traditions from Norway and Iceland, but his most important sources were skaldic poems and prose writings. He strove to use his sources critically but he could not improve on them, and comparison with independent sources has shown numerous errors in his narrative. The first saga, the *Ynglinga saga*, relates the prehistory of Scandinavia and of the oldest Swedish royal dynasty, from which the first Norwegian king descended. The following sagas are about the fights of the Norwegian kings for the unity of their kingdom against external enemies and internal rivals. The longest saga is the story of king Olaf the Saint who Christianized Norway in the 11th century.

The *Heimskringla* is famous for its literary qualities, character studies, and attempts at historical explanation. Recurrent themes linked the different sagas, such as the good king who cared for the peasants and did not burden them unnecessarily with campaigns in foreign countries. Snorri sought to explain history in rational terms, and only occasionally told stories of miracles or deeds of monsters or sorcerers. The number of medieval manuscripts indicates the popularity of *Heimskringla*, which continued through the Renaissance and into the 19th and 20th centuries.

CHARLOTTE BEHR

Biography

Born Hvamm at Breidefjord, Iceland, 1178/79, part of the powerful Sturlungar family, raised by chieftain Jón Loftsson. Lived mainly in Reykjaholt from 1206; became chief and lawspeaker (president of the judicial assembly, the Althing), 1215–18, 1222–31; visited Norway, 1218–20, 1237–39, but failed to fulfil promise to king Hákon Hákonarson to bring Iceland under Norwegian rule, so his life was held forfeit. Married 1) Herdís Bersadóttir, 1199 (separated 1206/07; died 1233); 2) Hallveig Ormsdóttir, 1224; several children. Assassinated at his brother-in-law's commission: died Reykjaholt, 23 September 1241.

Principal Writings

Edda (prose), completed *c*.1223; as *The Prose Edda*, translated by A.G. Brodeur, 1916, Jean I. Young, 1954, and Anthony Faulkes, 1987

Heimskringla (The Orb of the World), completed 1230s; as *Heimskringla: Sagas of the Norse Kings*, translated by Samuel Laing, revised by Peter Foote, 1961, and as *Heimskringla: The Olaf Sagas*, translated by Samuel Laing, revised by Jacqueline Simpson, 2 vols., 1964

Further Reading

Bagge, Sverre, *Society and Politics in Snorri Sturluson's Heimskringla*, Berkeley: University of California Press, 1991

Ciklamini, Marlene, *Snorri Sturluson*, Boston: Twayne, 1978

Glendinning, Robert J., and Haraldur Bessason, eds., *Edda: A Collection of Essays*, Winnipeg: University of Manitoba Press, 1983

Gurevich, Aron, "Saga and History: The 'Historical Conception' of Snorri Sturluson," *Medieval Scandinavia* 4 (1971), 42–53

Holtsmark, Anne, *Studier i Snorres mytologi*, Oslo: Universitetsforlaget, 1964

Koht, Halvdan, "Snorri Sturluson," *Norsk biografisk Leksikon* (Norwegian Biographical Dictionary), vol.14, Christiana: Aschenhoug, 1923

Nordal, Sigurdur, *Snorri Sturluson*, Reykjavik: Tolaksson, 1920

Ross, Margaret Clunies, *Skáldskaparmál: Snorri Sturluson's ars poetica and Medieval Theories of Language*, Viborg: Odense University Press, 1987

See, Klaus von, *Mythos und Theologie im skandinavischen Hochmittelalter* (Myth and Theology in the Scandinavian High Middle Ages), Heidelberg: Winter, 1988

Sveinsson, Einar Ó., *The Age of the Sturlungs: Icelandic Civilisation in the Thirteenth Century*, Ithaca, NY: Cornell University Press, 1953; reprinted New York: Kraus, 1966

Whaley, Diana, *Heimskringla: An Introduction*, London: Viking Society for Northern Research, 1991

Wolf, Alois, ed., *Snorri Sturluson. Kolloquium anlässlich der 750. Wiederkehr seines Todestages* (Snorri Sturluson: Colloquium on the 750th Anniversary of His Death), Tübingen: Narr, 1993

Soboul, Albert 1914–1982

French historian

Albert Soboul has been a central figure in the debates over the reason for, and nature of, the French Revolution. His focus was on the Sans-Culottes, the Parisian masses who drove the Revolution in its most violent phase. For this reason, it has become commonplace to read about the rigid and sterile orthodoxy displayed in Albert Soboul's works. The so-called orthodoxy refers to the view that the French Revolution was a bourgeois revolution, an interpretation that has been under sustained attack since Alfred Cobban's lectures at the University of London in the late 1950s. Numerous historians have seized upon a reductionist view of Soboul's argument as developed in the *Précis d'histoire de la Révolution française* (1962; *The French Revolution*, 1974), which was written in a pedagogical spirit by its author for use by undergraduate students. These are hardly the right grounds for judging Soboul's contribution to French revolutionary studies. Indeed, contemporary historians in France and in English-speaking countries agree that Soboul's output has greatly enhanced the level of scholarship in revolutionary studies. They also accept that his doctoral thesis on the Parisian Sans-Culottes of the Year II, submitted in 1958, was an unprecedented achievement in that it brought to the fore the role of people hitherto left in some obscurity.

The sheer detail of the work and the remarkable amount of archival material consulted led to complex conclusions. Clearly, if the role of the Sans-Culottes was as crucial as Soboul implied, then the bourgeois revolution succeeded only with the help of other groups in French society. However, the Sans-Culottes were presented as diverse in their social composition and certainly not as a class that prefigured a coherent proletariat. Soboul viewed the Sans-Culottes as a complex body of people, from small independent artisans to journeymen and laborers. The work followed in Georges Lefebvre's tradition: it counted and quantified. In addition, it was an exercise in *Histoire des mentalités* and analyzed the behavior of Parisian Sans-Culottes. Soboul treated his readers to a sociological and ideological analysis of his subjects, as he portrayed their political practices and their rituals. He took his readers into the individual exponents (or sections) of the General Assemblies, evaluated the level of attendance, and discussed the issue of spontaneity in the decision-making process. In doing so, he was trying to understand the mentalities of the Sans-Culottes as well as the political, economic, and cultural structures within which they operated.

His work was also an analysis of the growing conflict between the popular movement – with its own dynamic and autonomous constitution – and central government. The relationship between the two goes a long way to explain the nature of the Terror and its limitations in scope and time. The proposition that the Terror was necessary was paralleled with a study of the tensions that existed between Sans-Culottes and government in their respective policies. Thus, the directed economic measures are contrasted with the liberal traditions of the representatives at the Assembly. In turn, dechristianization was seen as being opposed to a national religion, conceived as a moral necessity by members of the Convention, who were clearly influenced by Rousseau's views.

The choice of chronology for his study of the Sans-Culottes – fourteen months from May 1793 to July 1794 – placed Soboul at the heart of the debate which opposed Annales historians to other historical traditions. It is clear that he was wary of a long-term analysis that minimized or even ignored short-term political history. He worked tirelessly to defend the relevance of French revolutionary studies and feared that neglecting political events would ultimately lead to ignoring the Revolution itself as a significant moment in world history. This is not to say that Soboul's study of the Sans-Culottes should be seen as a piece of political writing in F.-A. Aulard's tradition. In fact, his work integrated social investigation and political analysis, resulting in a piece of "total social history," in the mold of Albert Mathiez and Lefebvre. It is with some justification that Soboul is remembered as the historian of the Parisian artisans, but his works also extended to other groups in French society.

In the tradition of his mentor Lefebvre, Soboul also wrote about the French peasantry. His concerns were with patterns of land ownership, but while Lefebvre had devoted his efforts to the study of the peasants of northern France, Soboul, the southerner, turned his attention to southern France and more specifically to the area around Montpellier. This did not distract him from emphasizing the progress of agrarian concentration in the northern plains. He identified the duality of the role of the peasants during the French Revolution, first as they struggled to free themselves from the yoke of despotism, and second as they helped to shape the slow transition from an agrarian to an industrial world.

Finally, Soboul contributed to the writing of cultural history. This was already clear in the way in which he had dissected the political activities and cultural rituals of the Parisian Sans-Culottes. He understood that the Sans-Culottes' aspirations for an equal society necessitated the creation of new rituals including changes in language practices, the use of *tu* instead of *vous*, of *citoyen* instead of *monsieur*. Clothing was to be changed too. So were all the usual points of reference of everyday occurrences. Thus the Sans-Culottes had no qualms about welcoming the revolutionary calendar. They also developed their own sense of conviviality as Soboul explained in presenting the purposes fulfilled by the Sociétés Fraternelles and the Sociétés Sectionnaires. This sense of common purpose was also found in the Armées Révolutionnaires. Following in Mathiez's footsteps, Soboul revisited religious history. In his 1957 article on holy martyrs for liberty, he showed how traditional practices were replaced by new symbols of communal life in the complex context of dechristianization in 1793–94. Soboul's concern for collective psychology reinforced the label of "social historian" bestowed upon him by some of his colleagues who related his approach to Ernest Labrousse's efforts toward a history of social structures and movements.

Thanks to Soboul, the Parisian masses arrived at the forefront of historical writing. *Les Sans-culottes parisiens en l'an II* (1958; *The Parisian Sans-Culottes and the French Revolution*, 1964) is a masterly demonstration of rich scholarship. In it, Soboul underlined the complexities of social realities in revolutionary France. Far from being sectarian, he was guided by a careful acknowledgment of the chronology, the facts and the archives. Flexible in his approach, his views on the nature of the Revolution and the debate concerning the transition from feudalism to capitalism evolved. In the end Soboul remained a Jacobin republican who successfully blended in his writings the heritage of Aulard, Mathiez, and Lefebvre.

MARTINE BONDOIS MORRIS

See also Cobb; France: French Revolution; Furet; Social

Biography

Albert Marius Soboul. Born Ammi Moussa, Oran, Algeria, 27 April 1914, to a peasant family from the Ardèche. Educated with state grants after his father's death in World War I, he was raised by his aunt in Nîmes in a strong tradition of French republican teaching; came to Paris to complete studies, 1931, agrégation in history and geography, 1938; doctorate 1958. Joined Communist Youth, 1932, and Communist party, 1935. Taught in Montpellier, 1940–42, before losing job under Vichy; then taught at various Paris schools, 1947–60; appointed to University of Clermont-Ferrand, 1960–67; professor of the history of the French Revolution, the Sorbonne, 1967–82. Succeeded Georges Lefebvre as director, *Annales Historiques de la Révolution Française*, 1959. Died Nîmes, 11 September 1982.

Principal Writings

"Sentiment religieux et cultes populaires pendant la Révolution: saintes patriotes et martyrs de la Liberté" (Religious Sentiment and Popular Cults during the Revolution: Patriotic Saints and Martyrs of Liberty), *Annales Historiques de la Révolution française* 29 (1952), 193–213

Les Campagnes montpelliéraines à la fin de l'Ancien Régime: propriété et cultures d'après les compoix (The Countryside of the Montpellier Area at the End of the *Ancien Régime*: Ownership and Cultivation According to the Land Registers), 1958

Les Sans-culottes parisiens en l'an II: mouvement populaire et gouvernement révolutionnaire, 2 Juin 1793–9 Thermidor An II, 1958; abridged and revised as *Mouvement populaire et gouvernement révolutionnaire en l'an II (1793–1794)*, 1973; in English as *The Parisian Sans-Culottes and the French Revolution, 1793-4*, 1964, and as *The Sans-Culottes: The Popular Movement and Revolutionary Government, 1793–1794*, 1972

Les Soldats de l'An II (The Soldiers of the Year II), 1959

Précis d'histoire de la Révolution française, 1962; expanded with a complete Soboul bibliography as *La Révolution française*, 1982; in English as *The French Revolution, 1787-1799: From the Storming of the Bastille to Napoleon*, 1974

La Civilisation et la Révolution française (Civilization and the French Revolution), 3 vols., 1970–83

"Some Problems of the Revolutionary State, 1789–1796," *Past and Present* 65 (1974), 52–74

Problèmes paysans de la Révolution, 1789–1848: études d'histoire révolutionnaire (Problems Concerning the Peasantry during the Revolution), 1976

Editor, *Contributions à l'Histoire paysanne de la Révolution française* (Contributions to Peasant History), 1977

Comprendre la Révolution: problèmes politiques de la Révolution française (1789–1797), 1981; in English as *Understanding the French Revolution*, 1988

Portraits de révolutionnaires (Biographies of Revolutionary Figures), 1986

Further Reading

Cobb, Richard, *People and Places*, Oxford: Oxford University Press, 1985

"Hommage à A. Soboul," *Annales Historiques de la Révolution française* 54 (1982), 513–653

Vovelle, Michel, "Albert Soboul et l'histoire des mentalités" (Albert Soboul and the History of Mentalities), *Bulletin d'Histoire de la Révolution française* (1992–93), 33–37

Social History

From an institutional standpoint, Adrian Wilson noted, "'Social' history first arose in England as a by-product of the professionalization of history from the 1860s onward." On the continent, it developed, haphazardly, as a reaction against the elitist, national, and political history of Ranke in Germany, and Lavisse and Monod in France. At the same time, the creation of provincial universities, and the beginnings of mass education and democracy, facilitated the emergence of a "people's history" which often found more congenial surroundings outside "the Academy," a circumstance that has persisted almost to the present day. Both R.H. Tawney and E.P. Thompson spent many years as extramural teachers. However, more important than its physical location was social history's intellectual and methodological *raison d'être*. Although obviously shaped by time, institutions, and national intellectual traditions, the professional practice of social history has been dominated by two historical sociologists, Karl Marx and Max Weber. Even when Marxism was rejected as too determinist, eminent social historians still felt obliged to pay homage to its founder, at least until the final quarter of the 20th century. Thus Fernand Braudel in *Ecrits sur l'histoire* (1969; *On History*, 1980) wrote: "Marx's genius, the secret of his long sway, lies in the fact that he was the first to construct true social models, on the basis of a historical *longue durée*." In 1973 Terrill argued that Tawney "took Marx seriously, and he chose his direction more than once under Marx's influence." This increasingly unholy (for some) alliance between positivistic scientism and empirical historical practice produced its own structural fault-line in the development of social history, again, one that has persisted to the present day. It was toward the end of the 19th century that this basic dilemma was first posed. According to H. Stuart Hughes, the premise on which the emerging social sciences began to operate involved a recognition of the "inevitable limitations on human freedom – whether by physical circumstance or through emotional conditioning." But, if the acts of men and women were simply to be dismissed as the product of material and psychological conditioning: "Were historians reduced to the necessity of becoming no more and no less than social scientists?" "Social" historians have never reached a consensus on the issue of freedom or determinism, which is the fundamental reason for the fact that social history has almost always been "in crisis." In essence, E.P. Thompson's attack on Louis Althusser in *The Poverty of Theory* (1978), was concerned with this fundamental issue. Almost a century earlier, Charles Seignobos and the economist François Simiand had conducted a similar battle over the integrity of history as a distinct discipline with its distinctive procedures and methodologies.

At the turn of the century, in almost every Western country, valiant efforts were made to bridge the gap between social history, history, and sociology, between "structures" and "human agency," general laws and contingency. In 1894 – two years before Emile Durkheim was appointed to the first chair in sociology in France – Henry Adams, in his presidential address to the recently formed American Historical Association, spoke of history as standing on the brink of creating "a great generalization." Fifteen years later, a successor declared the project to be chimerical. Romanticism (or what Durkheim would term "mysticism") was not dead. Veering between the two extremes of positivism and "romanticism," the 1900s would nonetheless prove to be a *Belle Epoque* for the advance of social history. In Germany, Max Weber, in his 1904–05 seminal study on capitalism and the work ethic, was making yet another attempt to bridge the epistemological gap by pleading for a rather speculative marriage of empirical and causal explanation and "understanding" or *verstehen* (a superior form of intuition). In France, Jean Jaurès rehabilitated Robespierre as the harbinger of socialism and democracy in his magisterial work, the *Histoire socialiste* (Socialist History, 1901–08). In his introduction, Jaurès offered his own solution to the problem of "structure" and "agency" by declaring that he was "materialist with Marx, but romantic with Michelet." A century later E.P. Thompson, in his final work, would declare his affinity with William Blake, "the founder of the obscure sect to which I belong, the Muggletonian Marxists." Both Jaurès and Thompson were activists and socialists, profoundly influenced by Marx, yet concerned as social *historians* to reject structuralist, "dehumanizing" history in favor of men and women forging, within existential limits, their own historical and "class" destiny. Finally in Russia, social historians such as Evgenii Tarlé were setting an agenda for the study of the French peasantry and the impact of industry on the countryside that would resurface in the 1970s as the debate on "protoindustrialization." The early links between social history and economics are being reforged today as some economic historians fall under the spell of the "cliometricians" – the old conflict between "structures" and "human agency" again?

Whatever momentous changes the two world wars of the 20th century wrought in the lives of individuals and nations, it could be argued that, as far as social history is concerned, they served to exacerbate rather than to ease the tensions and conflicts inherited from the historiography of the previous century, if only because the first precipitated the Russian Revolution of 1917, while the second increased the stature of the Soviet Union. Both appeared to many historians to validate the historical-materialist theory of Marx, as opposed to the more idealist approach of Weber and his followers, particularly after the Stock Market Crash of 1929. It is not coincidental, therefore, that the period from the 1920s to the 1960s proved to be one of increasing popularity, something of a Golden Age for Marxist social history. Understandably, given the titanic clash of ideologies – liberal-capitalist, fascist, and communist – and their disproportionate influence on different countries, social history would be defined in accordance with national political and intellectual traditions. In most countries, particularly after the Chinese and Latin American revolutions of the 1940s and 1950s, the analysis of revolutionary movements would bring a further shift towards *marxisant* theory.

In Britain, less traumatized by World War I and far less exercised by a revolutionary tradition than either France or Russia, social history would continue to pursue a broad agenda both within and without the universities, although one detects a shift to the left as the interwar years elapsed. This period strengthened the bonds between social history and organized labor, a distinguishing characteristic of British social history until the 1970s. The 1930s would also mark the publication of the first successful Marxist history of Britain: A.L. Morton's *A People's History of England* (1938). However, G.M. Trevelyan, despite a gradual move towards the "history of the people" tradition

in his *English Social History* (1942), continued along his Whiggish and literary way, being rewarded with the Regius professorship at Cambridge in 1927. His eminent pupil, J.H. Plumb, in a dedication to the master some thirty years later, would declare that for over fifty years, Trevelyan "maintained that history is literature"! Within the Academy was found that most formidable of the many pairs of British social and socialist historians, the Webbs, Sydney and Beatrice. Not only were they the co-founders of the Fabian Society and the London School of Economics, but, according to Royden Harrison, they were also "the founders of British Labor historiography." Further links in the chain which represented the labor movement in general were forged by G.D.H. Cole and, after World War II, Hugh Clegg. While R.H. Tawney – the English reply to Weber – and Eileen Power raised the profile of social and economic history from the London School of Economics, the extra-Academy tradition persisted with the major contributions of J.L. and Barbara Hammond (see *The Village Labourer*, 1911; *The Town Labourer*, 1917; *The Skilled Labourer*, 1919). We have noted above the contribution of several women historians to the social and socio-economic history in Britain: we could add many more among whom would be Dorothy George, Dorothy Marshall, Ivy Pinchbeck, Dorothy Thompson, and Maxine Berg. Inside the communist world, a "class" theory of history – suitably adapted by Lenin and then Stalin to fit the requirements of the Russian Bolshevik state – had assumed hegemonic proportions by the mid-1930s. However, "the relatively relaxed and pluralist regime of the 1920s" (see John Barber, *Soviet Historians in Crisis, 1928–32*, 1981) allowed influential historians such as Petrushevsky, and Pokrovsky, supported by Tarlé himself, to continue the tradition of the late 19th century which had focused on agrarian history as well as the impact of commercial capitalism. In France the interwar years witnessed an ever-widening interest in social history. The socialist historian Albert Mathiez not only re-edited Jaurès's *Histoire socialiste*, but, in 1927, published his *La Vie chère et le mouvement social sous la Terreur* (The High Cost of Living and the Social Movement during the Terror), a work focused on the *classes populaires* which was (according to Furet and Ozouf) to re-orient "the history of the Revolution towards research in social history." Mathiez thus paved the way for the classic social interpretation of the French Revolution along which Georges Lefebvre and Albert Soboul would tread from the 1930s to the 1980s. In 1929, one of the most influential history journals of the 20th century would make its first appearance as the *Annales d'histoire économique et sociale*. Under the influence of March Bloch, the review would be retitled the *Annales d'histoire sociale* during the 1930s. Similarly in America, as the Great Depression cut deeply into that increasingly divided society, there was a move toward social, sociological, and anthropological history, although political and intellectual history remained highly popular under the influence of respected historians such as Carl Becker. In Germany, the influence of Weber, and to some extent that of Karl Lamprecht's sociopsychological brand of history, promised to attract more converts, until Hitler's regime obliged most historians of the old school to emigrate.

The end of World War II heralded a new age for social history. In Britain, the period from 1945 to the 1970s marked the peak influence of the Communist Group of Historians, founded in 1946. Their work represented something of a "hidden revolution" since a generation of graduates, history teachers, and students would be profoundly influenced by Eric Hobsbawm, Rodney Hilton, Christopher Hill, and E.P. Thompson, although the more pragmatic and eclectic tradition of British social history continued to be defended by historians such as Arthur Marwick and Harold Perkin, for whom social history should be linked to unifying themes such as the Industrial Revolution. From the 1970s, the journal *History Workshop* provided space for Marxist and non-Marxist historians to pursue "history from below," while individualists such as Richard Cobb continued to pry, brilliantly, into the private lives of the powerless. Across the Channel, the influence of Marxism on history had been undermined in the 1950s and 1960s by the rise of the Annales school of historians. Led by the formidable Fernand Braudel, history in general would be stretched in time and intellectual space, posing formidable questions for the practitioners of "social history." Soon the phrase "total history" would trip lightly off the tongues of eager disciples around the world. In America, the "New History" fused, somewhat tenuously, with the work of labor historians such as Herbert Gutman and David Montgomery, already concerned with questions of ethnicity and gender. On the other hand, one of the most influential figures in American historiography, Charles Tilly, was making the most successful attempt to marry sociological theory to historical practice in his studies of popular and collective violence. In Britain, Keith Thomas led the charge in the 1960s with an appeal for closer links with the social sciences, particularly sociology and anthropology. A decade later, the ensuing epistemological and methodological confusion for old-style social historians would be aggravated by the increasing popularity of sociolinguistics and women's history. No social historian worth his or her professional salt would now feel complete without a nodding acquaintance with the works of Michel Foucault and Jacques Derrida. "Languages of class" were now to be heard in the corridors of the Academy more frequently than class language. However, it can persuasively be argued that women's history has made the more permanent impact upon social history. In Britain, the impact of women's history may be measured by the change in 1982 of the subtitle of *History Workshop* from "A journal of socialist historians" to "A journal of socialist and feminist historians." In America, historians as different as Joan Scott and Lynn Hunt would try to conceptualize the bewildering changes of the period. In addition, the association of social history with problems of race and ethnicity was more obvious and more productive in America than in Britain.

Recently there has been an attempt to create order out of what seems at times to be intellectual chaos, commonly explained away as "postmodernism." In France, *Annaliste* historians are rediscovering the importance of politics and elites. In America, labor historians such as Alan Dawley have integrated problems of political power, ethnicity, and gender into their work. In Britain, one detects a move to place culturalist explanations within a more social framework and to resist efforts to "textualize" the past, although any form of conceptualization remains suspect. For F.M.L. Thompson, the editor of the recent *Cambridge Social History of Britain*, "social history derives its appeal and fascination in no small measure from its open-endness, its freedom from the constraints of a formal tradition, its eclectic habits." The continuing battle over the soul of social history is poignantly reflected in the debate between a postcommunist Russian historian and a post-Braudelian editor of the journal *Annales, E.S.C.* Noting that in the 1960s and 1970s, "official" historians in Russia had tried to stop copies of the *Annales* coming in, Youri Bessmertny nonetheless appealed in 1992 to its editors not to throw out the "histoire totale" baby with the ideological bathwater. In their reply, the editors stated that "les grandes paradigmes qui unifiaient les sciences sociales ... se voyaient sévèrement ébranlés et avec eux, certaines des modalités de l'échange disciplinaires: ainsi, presque simultanément, du marxisme, du structuralisme et du fonctionalisme" (the great paradigms which used to unify the social sciences ... were seriously undermined, and with them, some of the methods of interdisciplinary exchange: thus, we saw, almost simultaneously, the attack on Marxism, Structuralism, and Functionalism). It seems that social history is in crisis – again!

GWYNNE LEWIS

See also Althusser; Annales School; Bloch; Braudel; Cobb; Cole; Conze; Corbin; Gutman; Hammond; Hill; Hilton; History Workshop; Hobsbawm; Hunt; Lamprecht; Lefebvre; Marx; Marxist Interpretation; Mathiez; Montgomery; Pinchbeck; Plumb; Power; Scott, Joan; Seignobos; Simiand; Soboul; Tawney; Thomas, K.; Thompson, E.; Thompson, F.; Tilly, C.; Trevelyan; Webb; Weber, M.

Further Reading

Barber, John, *Soviet Historians in Crisis, 1928–32*, New York: Holmes and Meier, and London: Macmillan, 1981

Berg, Maxine, *A Woman in History: Eileen Power, 1889–1940*, Cambridge: Cambridge University Press, 1996

Bessmertny, Youri, "Les *Annales* vues de Moscou" (The *Annales* as Seen from Moscow), *Annales: ESC* 47 (1992), 245–59; and response: Bernard Lepetit and Jacques Revel, "L'Expérimentation contre l'arbitraire" (Experimentation against the Arbitrary), *Annales, ESC* 47 (1992), 261–65

Braudel, Fernand, *Ecrits sur l'histoire*, Paris: Flammarion, 1969; in English as *On History*, Chicago: University of Chicago Press, 1980

Burke, Peter, and Roy Porter, eds., *The Social History of Language*, Cambridge and New York: Cambridge University Press, 1987

Burke, Peter, ed., *New Perspectives on Historical Writing*, Cambridge: Polity Press, 1991; University Park: Pennsylvania State University Press, 1992

Clark, Jon, Celia Modgil, and Sohan Modgil, eds., *Anthony Giddens: Consensus and Controversy*, London and New York: Falmer Press, 1990

Dawley, Alan, *Struggles for Justice: Social Responsibility and the Liberal State*, Cambridge, MA: Harvard University Press, 1991

Fink, Carole, *Marc Bloch: A Life in History*, Cambridge and New York: Cambridge University Press, 1989

Fogel, Robert William, and G.R. Elton, *Which Road to the Past? Two Views of History*, New Haven: Yale University Press, 1983

Furet, François, and Mona Ozouf, eds., *Dictionnaire critique de la Révolution française*, Paris: Flammarion, 1988; in English as *A Critical Dictionary of the French Revolution*, Cambridge, MA: Harvard University Press, 1989

Gilbert, Felix, and Stephen Grabard, *Historical Studies Today*, New York: Norton, 1972

Hammond, J.L., and Barbara Hammond, *The Village Labourer, 1760–1832: A Study in the Government of England before the Reform Bill*, London and New York: Longman, 1911

Hammond, J.L., and Barbara Hammond, *The Town Labourer, 1760–1832: The New Civilisation*, London and New York: Longman, 1917

Hammond, J.L. and Barbara, *The Skilled Labourer, 1760–1837*, London and New York: Longman, 1919

Himmelfarb, Gertrude, *The New History and the Old*, Cambridge, MA: Harvard University Press, 1987

Hobsbawm, Eric J., "From Social History to the History of Society," *Daedalus* 100 (1971), 20–45

Hughes, H. Stuart, *Consciousness and Society: The Reorientation of European Social Thought, 1890–1930*, New York: Knopf, 1958; London: MacGibbon and Kee, 1959; revised New York: Vintage, 1977

Jaurès, Jean, *Histoire socialiste* (Socialist History), 13 vols., Paris: Rouff, 1901–08

Kaye, Harvey J., *The British Marxist Historians: An Introductory Analysis*, Cambridge: Polity Press, 1984; New York: St. Martin's Press, 1995

Kocka, Jürgen, *Sozialgeschichte: Begriff, Entwicklung, Probleme* (Social History: Concept, Development, Problems), Göttingen: Vandenhoeck & Ruprecht, 1977

Mathiez, Albert, *La Vie chère et le mouvement social sous la Terreur* (The High Cost of Living and the Social Movement during the Terror), Paris: Payot, 1927

Morton, A.L., *A People's History of England*, London: Gollancz, and New York: Random House, 1938

Patterson, Thomas, "Post-structuralism, Post-modernism: Implications for Historians," *Social History* 14 (1988), 83–88

Perkin, Harold, *The Origins of Modern English Society, 1780–1880*, London: Routledge, 1969

Perkin, Harold, "Social History in Britain," *Journal of Social History* 10 (1976), 129–43

Plumb, J.H., ed., *Studies in Social History: A Tribute to G.M. Trevelyan*, London and New York: Longman, 1955

Pokrovskii, Mikhail N., *Russkaia istoriia s drevneishikh vremen*, 5 vols., Moscow: Mir, 1910–13; abridged in English as *History of Russia, from the Earliest Times to the Rise of Commercial Capitalism*, New York: International Publishers, and London: Lawrence, 1931

Schieder, Wolfgang, and Volker Sellin, *Sozialgeschichte in Deutschland: Entwicklungen und Perspektiven im internationalen Zusammenhang*, 4 vols., Göttingen: Vandenhoeck & Ruprecht, 1986–87

Scott, Joan Wallach, *Gender and the Politics of History*, New York: Columbia University Press, 1988

Tarlé, E.V., *L'Industrie dans les campagnes en France à la fin de l'ancien régime* (Industry in the French Countryside at the End of the *Ancien Régime*), Paris: Cornély, 1910

Terrill, Ross, *R.H. Tawney and His Times: Socialism as Fellowship*, Cambridge, MA: Harvard University Press, 1973; London: Deutsch, 1974

Thompson, E.P., *The Poverty of Theory and Other Essays*, London: Merlin Press, and New York: Monthly Review Press, 1978

Thompson, E.P., *Witness Against the Beast: William Blake and the Moral Law*, New York: New Press, and Cambridge: Cambridge University Press, 1993

Thompson, F.M.L., *The Cambridge Social History of Britain, 1750–1950*, 3 vols., Cambridge and New York: Cambridge University Press, 1990

Tilly, Charles, *As Sociology Meets History: Studies in Social Discontinuity*, New York: Academic Press, 1981

Trevelyan, G.M., *English Social History: A Survey of Six Centuries, Chaucer to Queen Victoria*, London and New York: Longman, 1942

Weber, Max, "Die protestantische Ethik und der Geist des Kapitalismus," *Archiv für Sozialwissenschaft und Sozialpolitik* 20–21 (1904–05), revised in *Gesammelte Aufsätze zur Religionssoziologie*, Tübingen: Mohr, 1920; in English as *The Protestant Ethic and the Spirit of Capitalism*, London: Allen and Unwin, 1930, New York: Scribner, 1958

Wilson, Adrian, ed., *Rethinking Social History: English Society 1570–1920 and Its Interpretation*, Manchester: Manchester University Press, 1993

Sociology and History

Sociologists and historians are often characterized as having incompatible research interests and agendas. This characterization stems from the traditional view (best expressed by Oakeshott and Erikson, respectively) that each discipline has a fundamentally different focus. For Oakeshott, history is an "ideographic" discipline, concerned with the study of how unique, or non-recurrent events in the past helped to shape the character of a given age, while for Erikson, sociology is a "nomothetic" discipline, concerned with developing abstract theories and empirical generalizations to explain recurrent events in contemporary society. Furthermore, according to this traditional view, while historians consider the use of *a priori* conceptual and theoretical frameworks an obstacle to the description and interpretation of historical events, sociologists consider them indispensable analytical tools for carrying out theory-driven research.

This image of the divergent theoretical and research interests separating historians and sociologists has never been universally accepted. Indicatively, in 1898, Emile Durkheim, one of the fathers of modern positivist sociology, argued that, "far from being antagonistic," sociology and history "tend naturally to converge." According to Wallerstein, Durkheim also predicted that eventually the two disciplines would "blend together into a common discipline in which elements from each would be combined and unified." Writing in the 1950s, C. Wright Mills similarly argued that the traditional disciplinary boundary separating sociology and history was illusionary and counter-productive. In his famous attack on the ahistorical bias of the functionalist approach that dominated American sociology in the 1950s, Mills reminded sociologists that "every well-considered social study . . . requires an historical scope of conception and a full use of historical materials." At the same time, he observed that history was "one of the most theoretical of the human disciplines." In England, the historian John H. Goldthorpe argued similarly in 1962 that the traditional (ideographic or nomothetic) disciplinary boundaries separating history and sociology could not be logically justified in light of the many overlapping interests and concerns that could be seen to bridge the two disciplines.

Beginning in the early 1960s, many sociologists turned to the study of "historical sociology." This development can be traced, at least in part, to the influential prescriptive writings of Mills and other historically-minded sociologists such as Cahnman and Boskoff, and Lipset and Hofstader, as well as to the exemplary historical studies that began to be published in the 1950s and 1960s by sociologists such as Bendix, Eisenstadt, Tilly, Moore, Skocpol, and Smith. During the same decade, an increasing number of historians, for example, Peter Burke and Gareth Stedman Jones, turned to the study of "social history" and to making more explicit use of sociological concepts and theories as heuristic tools for doing historical research. The period also witnessed the inception of several journals (such as *Social History*, *Journal of Interdisciplinary History*, and *Comparative Studies in Society and History*) which began to provide a common forum for the publication of work by members of both disciplines. Several interdisciplinary-minded commentators writing in the 1970s, most importantly, Burke, Erikson, and Goldthorpe, claimed to see many signs that pointed to the fact that sociology and history were beginning to converge, while others – significantly Runciman, Giddens, and Abrams – began to develop the more provocative argument that the two disciplines were, and always had been, logically and methodologically indistinguishable. While proponents of the "convergence thesis" claimed that the increasing unity of interests of sociologists and historians was most clearly reflected in their growing mutual interest in the study of social history, others – like Philip Abrams in 1982 – called upon members of the two disciplines to recognize the "unity of theoretical method between history and sociology" on the grounds that both disciplines already subscribed to "common rules of explanation and common conceptions of effective analysis."

More recent commentators have become considerably less optimistic about the extent to which sociologists and historians are open to exploring common ground. Although agreeing with Abrams' critique of the utopian view that saw sociology and history "progressively dissolving into a blissful social history," more recent commentators such as Abbott and Goldthorpe have argued that both proponents of the "convergence thesis" and opposing writers such as Giddens and Abrams, had failed adequately to grasp the complex and often rather tenuous nature of the relationship between the two disciplines. In this discussion of the "lost synthesis" of history and sociology, Abbott pointed out that, rather than being involved in a constant borrowing of ideas and methods, "most links between history and sociology come within limited areas – either within particular analytical approaches like Marxism and feminism or within particular substantive areas like demography, studies of the family, labor history, criminology, and so on." According to Abbott, "the story of history and sociology is the story of the mutual enlightenment that never happened." However, this is not to say that sociologists have given up on history. On the contrary, as Dennis Wrong noted, one of the most significant developments in contemporary sociology resides in the fact that comparative-historical sociology "has come to occupy a central place in the discipline." Wrong's contention that comparative-historical sociology is now competing for the center spot among the three major subfields of sociology (the other two being the "quantifiers" and "micro-sociological social constructionists"), is supported by a large number of references to recent commentaries and substantive work in the field by Badie, Eisenstadt, Goldthorpe, Kiser and Hechter, Mann, McMichael, and Tilly.

Of course, it is also well known that historians such as A.A. Van Den Braembussche share an interdisciplinary interest in comparative-historical research. However, it is also clear, in more general terms, that historians remain divided on the opinion of whether sociology has anything useful to offer history. According to some historians, the study of history is a broadly-based interdisciplinary enterprise. This has involved historians such as Marwick borrowing extensively from the repertoires of concepts and research techniques pioneered or developed in numerous other disciplines in the social sciences and humanities. Moreover, since the late 1970s, history has been inundated with new theoretical ideas from many different intellectual movements, including postmodernism, poststructuralism, postcolonialism, discourse analysis, and cultural studies, to list only the more prominent. Consequently, the common claim made by sociologists – that they can bring needed conceptual and theoretical tools to the study and writing of history – has been justifiably viewed with considerable skepticism by many historians.

With the exception of a small number of scholars who have managed to bridge the two disciplines, for the most part sociology and history remain quite separate and distinct. While they can often be seen to be sharing overlapping interests, members of the two disciplines are far from having arrived at any agreement about the contribution that sociology can make to the study of history. While historical-sociologists contend that they have a great deal to offer in the way of bringing sociological concepts and theories to bear on the study of history, many historians remain unconvinced of the legitimacy of this claim. Some of this reluctance to embrace sociology is no doubt due to the fact that historians have become aware of the divisive, and also arguably self-destructive, theoretical and ideological camps that exist within the discipline of sociology itself. These ideological divisions have made sociology vulnerable to both cutbacks in funding from governments and universities and an increasing skepticism among both sociologists and outsiders about the legitimacy and future of the discipline. Despite this, it is important for historians to remain open-minded about the work of historical-sociologists, especially in light of recent trends that indicate that comparative-historical sociology now occupies a central place in the discipline. Regardless of the reception they receive from historians, as long as the discipline continues in its present form, historical-sociologists will no doubt continue to bring their distinctive conceptual and theoretical approaches to bear on the study of historical phenomena.

RUSSELL C. SMANDYCH

See also Burke; Comte; Hofstadter; Jones, G.; Moore; Tilly, C.; Wallerstein

Further Reading

Abbott, Andrew, "History and Sociology: The Lost Synthesis," *Social Science History* 15 (1991), 201–38

Abrams, Philip, "History, Sociology, Historical Sociology," *Past and Present* 87 (1980), 3–16

Abrams, Philip, *Historical Sociology*, Ithaca, NY: Cornell University Press, and Shepton Mallet, Somerset: Open University Press, 1982

Ankersmit, F.R., "Historiography and Postmodernism," *History and Theory* 28 (1989), 137–53

Badie, Bertrand, "Comparative Analysis and Historical Sociology," *International Social Science Journal* 133 (1992), 319–27

Banks, J.A., "From Universal History to Historical Sociology," *British Journal of Sociology* 40 (1989), 521–43

Bendix, Richard, *Work and Authority in Industry: Ideologies of Management in the Course of Industrialization*, London: Chapman and Hall, 1956; New York: Wiley, 1957

Bonnell, Victoria E., "The Use of Theory, Concepts, and Comparison in Historical Sociology," *Comparative Studies in Society and History* 22 (1980), 156–73

Braembussche, A.A. Van Den, "Historical Explanation and Comparative Method: Towards a Theory of the History of Society," *History and Theory* 28 (1989), 1–24

Bryant, Joseph M., "Evidence and Explanation in History and Sociology: Critical Reflections on Goldthorpe's Critique of Historical Sociology," *British Journal of Sociology* 45 (1994), 3–19

Burke, Peter, *Sociology and History*, London and Boston: Allen and Unwin, 1980

Burke, Peter, *History and Social Theory*, Cambridge: Polity Press, 1992; Ithaca, NY: Cornell University Press, 1993

Cahnman, Werner J., and Alvin Boskoff, eds., *Sociology and History: Theory and Research*, Glencoe, IL: Free Press, 1964

Chirot, Daniel, "Thematic Controversies and New Developments in the Uses of Historical Materials by Sociologists," *Social Forces* 55 (1976), 232–41

Dirks, Nicholas, ed., *Colonialism and Culture*, Ann Arbor: University of Michigan Press, 1992

Eisenstadt, S.N., *The Political Systems of Empires: The Rise and Fall of the Historical Bureaucratic Societies*, New York: Free Press of Glencoe, 1963

Eisenstadt, S.N., "Frameworks of the Great Revolutions: Culture, Social Structure, History and Human Agency," *International Social Science Journal* 44 (1992), 385–402

Erikson, Kai T., "Sociology and the Historical Perspective," *American Sociologist* 5 (1970), 331–38

Giddens, Anthony, *Central Problems in Social Theory: Action, Structure, and Contradiction in Social Analysis*, London: Macmillan, and Berkeley: University of California Press, 1979

Göçek, Fatma Müge, "Whither Historical Sociology?", *Historical Methods* 28 (1995), 107–16

Goldthorpe, John H., "The Relevance of History to Sociology," *Cambridge Opinion* 28 (1962), 26–29; reprinted with postscript in Martin Bulmer, ed., *Sociological Research Methods: An Introduction*, London: Macmillan, 1977

Goldthorpe, John H., "The Uses of History in Sociology: Reflections on Some Recent Tendencies," *British Journal of Sociology* 42 (1991), 211–30

Goldthorpe, John H., "The Uses of History in Sociology – A Reply," *British Journal of Sociology* 45 (1994), 55–77

Gove, Walter R., "Is Sociology the Integrative Discipline in the Study of Human Behavior?" *Social Forces* 73 (1995), 1197–1206

Griffin, Larry J., "Narrative, Event-structure Analysis, and Causal Interpretation in Historical Sociology," *American Journal of Sociology* 98 (1993), 1094–1133

Griffin, Larry J., "How Is Sociology Informed by History?" *Social Forces* 73 (1995), 1245–54

Hall, J.R., "Where History and Sociology Meet: Forms of Discourse and Socio-historical Inquiry," *Sociological Theory* 10 (1992), 164–193

Harlan, David, "Intellectual History and the Return to Literature," *American Historical Review* 94 (1989), 581–609

Helmes-Hayes, R.C., "'From Universal History to Historical Sociology' by J.A. Banks: A Critical Comment," *British Journal of Sociology* 43 (1992), 333–44

Himmelfarb, Gertrude, "Some Reflections on the New History," *American Historical Review* 94 (1989), 661–70

Huber, Joan, "Institutional Perspectives on Sociology," *American Journal of Sociology* 101 (1995), 194–216

Hunt, Lynn, ed., *The New Cultural History*, Berkeley: University of California Press, 1989

Johnson, Bruce, "Missionaries, Tourists and Traders: Sociologists in the Domain of History," *Studies in Symbolic Interaction* (1982), 115–50

Jones, Gareth Stedman, "From Historical Sociology to Theoretical History," *British Journal of Sociology* 27 (1976), 295–305; reprinted in his *Languages of Class: Studies in English Working-Class History, 1832–1982*, Cambridge and New York: Cambridge University Press, 1983

Joyce, Patrick, "History and Post-Modernism," *Past and Present* 133 (1992), 204–09

Kiser, Edgar, and Michael Hechter, "The Role of General Theory in Comparative-historical Sociology," *American Journal of Sociology* 97 (1991), 1–30

Leca, Jean, "Postface: Has Historical Sociology Gone Back to Its Infancy? or, 'When Sociology Gave Up to History,'" *International Social Science Journal* 44 (1992), 403–15

Lipset, Seymour Martin, and Richard Hofstadter, eds., *Sociology and History: Methods*, New York: Basic Books, 1968

McMichael, Philip, "Incorporating Comparison within a World-Historical Perspective: An Alternative Comparative Method," *American Sociological Review* 55 (1990), 385–97

McMichael, Philip, "Rethinking Comparative Analysis in a Post-developmentalist Context," *International Social Science Journal* 44 (1992), 351–65

Mann, Michael, "In Praise of Macro-Sociology: A Reply to Goldthorpe," *British Journal of Sociology* 45 (1994), 37–54

Marwick, Arthur, *The Nature of History*, London: Macmillan, 1970; New York: Knopf, 1971

Mills, C. Wright, "The Uses of History," in his *The Sociological Imagination*, New York: Oxford University Press, 1959

Moore, Barrington, Jr., *Social Origins of Dictatorship and Democracy: Lord and Peasant in the Making of the Modern World*, Boston: Beacon Press, 1966; Harmondsworth: Penguin, 1967

Oakeshott, Michael, "The Activity of Being an Historian," in his *Rationalism in Politics*, New York: Basic Books, 1962; revised Indianapolis: Liberty Press, 1991

Palmer, Bryan D., *Descent into Discourse: The Reification of Language in the Writing of Social History*, Philadelphia: Temple University Press, 1990

Platt, Jennifer, "Evidence and Proof in Documentary Research," *Sociological Review* new series 29 (1981), 31–66

Prakash, Gyan, "Subaltern Studies as Postcolonial Criticism," *American Historical Review* 99 (1994), 1475–90

Rock, Paul, "Some Problems of Interpretive Historiography," *British Journal of Sociology* 27 (1976), 353–69

Roy, W.G., "Time, Place, and People in History and Sociology: Boundary Definitions and the Logic of Inquiry," *Social Science History* 11 (1987), 53–62

Runciman, W.G., "Sociology in Its Place," in his *Sociology in Its Place, and Other Essays*, Cambridge: Cambridge University Press, 1970

Said, Edward W., *Orientalism*, New York: Pantheon, and London: Routledge, 1978

Said, Edward W., *Culture and Imperialism*, New York: Knopf, and London: Chatto and Windus, 1993

Schottler, Peter, "Historians and Discourse Analysis," *History Workshop: A Journal of Socialist and Feminist Historians* 27 (1989), 37–65

Skocpol, Theda, and Margaret Somers, "The Uses of Comparative History in Macrosocial Inquiry," *Comparative Studies in Society and History* 22 (1980), 174–97

Skocpol, Theda, ed., *Vision and Method in Historical Sociology*, Cambridge and New York: Cambridge University Press, 1984

Smith, Dennis, "Social History and Sociology: More than Just Good Friends," *Sociological Review* 30 (1982), 286–308

Smith, Dennis, *The Rise of Historical Sociology*, Philadelphia: Temple University Press, 1991

Stinchcombe, A.L., *Theoretical Methods in Social History*, London: Tavistock, and New York: Academic Press, 1978

Stone, Lawrence, "History and the Social Sciences in the Twentieth Century," in Charles F. Delzell, ed., *The Future of History*, Nashville: Vanderbilt University Press, 1977

Stone, Lawrence, "History and Post-Modernism," *Past and Present* 135 (1992), 189–94

Sztompka, Piotr, "The Renaissance of Historical Orientation in Sociology," *International Sociology* 1 (1986), 321–37

Tilly, Charles, *The Vendée*, London: Arnold, 1964; Cambridge, MA: Harvard University Press, 1968

Tilly, Charles, *As Sociology Meets History: Studies in Social Discontinuity*, New York: Academic Press, 1981

Tilly, Charles, *Big Structures, Large Processes, Huge Comparisons*, New York: Russell Sage Foundation, 1984

Tilly, Charles, "Prisoners of the State," *International Social Science Journal* 44 (1992), 329–42

Tuchman, Gaye, "Historical Social Science: Methodologies, Methods, and Meanings," in Norman Denzin and Yvonne Lincoln, eds., *Handbook of Qualitative Research*, Thousand Oaks, CA: Sage, 1994

Valverde, Mariana, "Poststructuralist Gender Historians: Are We Those Names?" [review essay], *Labour/Le Travail* [Canada] 25 (1990), 227–36

Wallerstein, Immanuel, "Sociology and History" [Letter from the President], *International Sociological Association Bulletin* (Summer 1995), 1–2

Williamson, John, David Karp, and John Dalphin, "Historical Analysis," in Williams, Karp, and Dalphin, eds., *The Research Craft: An Introduction to Social Science Methods*, Boston: Little Brown, 1977

Wrong, Dennis, "The Present Condition of American Sociology," *Comparative Studies in Society and History* 35 (1993), 183–96

Wurgaft, Lewis D., "Identity in World History: A Postmodern Perspective," *History and Theory* 34 (1995), Beiheft 67–85

Zaret, David, "Sociological Theory and Historical Scholarship," *American Sociologist* 13 (1978), 114–21

Solov'ev, S.M. 1820–1879

Russian historian

This renowned historian and moralist from Moscow University wrote a magisterial account of Russia's past in 29 volumes. In 1851 S.M. Solov'ev began work on *Istoriia Rossii s drevneishikh vremen* (History of Russia from Earliest Times), completing one volume each year until his death in 1879. His account reached to 1775 and the exhaustive treatment earned for him the sobriquet, "Russia's Herodotus."

Although Solov'ev refrained from a present-minded approach to the past, he held that Russia was European, unique in its absence of natural barriers that allowed repeated attacks from the nomad South. Revealing his debt to Hegel, he eschewed rigid periodization in historical narration, treating each era as part of an evolutionary system. He broke with the tradition of dividing historical narration by reigns of rulers, following the scientific approach then popular in the West. Hence he minimized the Varangian effects on early Russia (as he later minimized that of the Mongols), and explained the evolution of state institutions from Kiev to Muscovy by the internal forces of society. Later, endeavoring to connect Muscovy to Peter I's Russia, he affirmed specifically that the preparation for the new order of things began under the first of the Romanovs.

His unique contribution was the development of the clan theory of Russian history. Comparing Russian clans with the patriarchal modes of other peoples, he countered the Slavophile theory of an exclusive, distinct Russian development. Solov'ev refuted that theory of contrasting "origins," demonstrating that Russian developments began just like the Germans from the clan mode of life, thereby taking the first step toward a scientific convergence of Russian and Western history.

In 1864 Solov'ev outlined new viewpoints, revealing the influences of the English historian, Henry Thomas Buckle. Solov'ev's scheme of Russian history in volume 13 began with an overall view of the spread of European civilization from the West to the East. He sharply separated the life of each people into two ages, likening the "organic" life of a nation with that of a separate individual. In the first stage of life, people live chiefly under the influence of feeling; in the second, feeling yields little by little to the dominance of reason. This second stage of growth is marked by the flourishing of science and education. Solov'ev found in all nations the moment when the stage of feeling developed into that of reason. That transition was perfected whenever a people came into contact with those more highly developed, more educated.

Influenced as well by Buckle's belief in geographical pressures, Solov'ev argued that a nation particularly submits to natural conditions in the time of its infancy. Already in 1851, six years before the appearance of the first volume of Buckle's *History of Civilization in England*, Solov'ev's own first volume began with the words of Herodotus: "Tribes learn the form of life which the nature of the country has directed," and he asserted that "the course of events constantly is subordinated to the conditions of nature." In 1843 Solov'ev had listened to Karl Ritter's lectures in Berlin, and at Moscow University he was captivated by the lectures of a protégé of Ritter, Alexander I. Chivilev who, like Ritter, described how natural conditions of a country affected a nation's evolution.

Buckle's work reinforced those views on this subject and Solov'ev opened volume 13 with an exposition of Buckle's ideas. His new history was especially evident in his discussion of Peter's reforms which marked the Russian transition from the stage of feeling to a life governed by reason. The Petrine reform was Russia's Renaissance and it was accompanied by the development of industry and commerce. Western nations passed from one stage of growth to the next in the 15th and 16th centuries; Russia under Peter did so in 1700, two centuries later. To Solov'ev, this was not backwardness, but delayed development, explained by geographical conditions. The favorable geographical conditions were concentrated in Western Europe, but for Russians there were vast plains, far from the sea. "Nature for Western European peoples was a mother; for the Eastern European peoples, amid the lands which fate destined them to labor, it was a step-mother."

For example, from rocky mountains Westerners built castles and from there controlled the peasants who, in time, enclosed themselves by stone and so acquired freedom and independence. Russia had few stones for use in building, and the constant threat of fire provided little stability for town existence. Hence a Russian would more easily leave for the open frontiers with little to bind him to the more settled existence. Among Russians, he argued, everything was precarious, unstable. In the West "all was durable and certain, thanks to stone."

In the West the transition from youth to maturity was constantly made ready by the growth of public power, social organization, and the growth of trade and industry. Russians, he wrote, developed otherwise and reached the stage of transition to maturity "morally and economically bankrupt." After an 8th-century eastward orientation, Russians were bound to turn sharply to the West; hence the necessity of Peter the Great.

Finally, looking at the bottom rather than the top of society, Solov'ev saw Western feudal elements in Russia. Those very institutions associated with feudalism in Europe survived longer in Russia owing to unfavorable natural conditions in a poor, agricultural, under-populated, undeveloped country. This last position was advanced by Solov'ev in a series of articles in 1872 and marked a reversal from views expressed earlier in 1864. Solov'ev wrote other works, including numerous articles on historiography; he revealed an anti-Catholic bias in his *Istoriia padeniia Pol'shi* (History of the Fall of Poland, 1863), gave little space to non-Russians in his *Uchebnaia kniga russkoi istorii* (Textbook of Russian History, 1860), and published his lectures on Alexander I in 1877. But he is remembered for his *History*, which, with its Great Russian orientation, was so successful that it replaced that of Nikolai Karamzin as the most widely read history of the Russian people.

JOHN D. WINDHAUSEN

See also Russia: Medieval; Russia: Early Modern; Russia: Modern

Biography

Sergei Mikhailovich Solov'ev. Born Moscow, 17 May 1820, to a clerical family. Educated at Moscow University, 1838–42, PhD 1847; and at universities of Paris, Berlin, and Heidelberg, 1842–44. Professor, Moscow University, 1847–79: dean of History/Philology Department, 1864–70; rector, 1871–77. Died Moscow, 16 April 1879.

Principal Writings

Istoriia Rossii s drevneishikh vremen, 29 vols., 1851–79; in English as *History of Russia*, 48 vols. planned, 1976–

Uchebnaia kniga russkoi istorii (Textbook of Russian History), 1860; reprinted 1996

Istoriia padeniia Pol'shi (History of the Fall of Poland), 1863

Publichnye chteniia o Petre Velikom (Public Lectures on Peter the Great), 1872

Imperator Aleksandr Pervyi: politika, diplomatiia (Emperor Alexander I: Politics and Diplomacy), 1877

Moi zapiski dlia detei moikh, a esli mozhno, i dlia drugikh (Notes to My Children, and, If Possible, Also for Others), 1914; reprinted 1980

Further Reading

Black, Joseph Laurence, "The State School Interpretation of Russian History: A Reappraisal of Its Genetic Origins," *Jahrbücher Geschichte Osteuropas* (1973), 509–30

Graham, Hugh F., "Introduction" to S.M. Solov'ev, *A History of Russia: The Age of Vasily III*, Gulf Breeze, FL: Academic International Press, 1976

Illeritskii, V.E., *Sergei Mikhailovich Solov'ev*, Moscow: Progress, 1980

Kliuchevskii, V.O., "Pamiati S.M. Solov'eva" (In Remembrance of S.M. Solov'ev), in his *Istoricheskie portrety* (Historical Portraits), Moscow: Pravda, 1990

Mazour, Anatole G., *An Outline of Russian Historiography*, Berkeley: University of California Press, 1939; revised as *Modern Russian Historiography*, Princeton, NJ: Van Nostrand, 1958; revised Westport, CT: Greenwood Press, 1975

Mirsky, D.S., Prince, *A History of Russian Literature*, New York: Knopf, and London: Routledge, 1927; abridged 1969

Pavlov-Sil'vanskii, Nikolai Pavlovich, *Feodalizm v drevnei Rusi* (Feudalism in Ancient Rus), St. Petersburg: Brokgauz-Efron, 1907; revised 1924

Reddel, Carl W., "Solov'ev, Sergei Mikhailovich," in Joseph L. Wieczynski, ed., *Modern Encyclopedia of Russian and Soviet History*, vol. 36, Gulf Breeze, FL: Academic International Press, 1984

Vernadsky, George, *Russian Historiography: A History*, Belmont, MA: Nordland, 1978

Zilper, Nadezhda, "Introduction" to reprint of S.M. Solov'ev, *Moi zapiski dlia detei moikh, a esli mozhno, i dlia drugikh* (Notes to My Children, and, If Possible, Also for Others), Newtonville, MA: Oriental Research Partners, 1980

South Africa

South African historiography was from its inception characterized by division into highly polarized, politicized camps. This is largely due to South Africa's fractured past, and the lack of a unified minority "white" English and Afrikaner (Dutch-descended) identity, let alone the broader "South African" consciousness promised by the coming of the post-apartheid state in the 1990s.

The so-called "settler" school had its roots in the early 19th century, in polemical articles, histories of frontier wars, and Donald Moodie's documentary compilation, *The Record* (1838–41). All sought to undermine claims against white settlers by missionaries and philanthropists, especially those made in the missionary John Philip's *Researches in South Africa* (1828), which, in attempting a pro-black account of relations between whites and the indigenous Khoisan, provided the remote ancestor of liberal and radical scholarship. Such an approach had to wait almost a century to find new champions.

The settler tradition was consolidated by the Canadian George Theal (1837–1919), who tried to balance both Afrikaner and English perspectives. Theal published numerous primary sources on the early colonial period and wrote the first really comprehensive history of the country. Drawing on the earlier polemical works, he canonized a series of assumptions that became axiomatic in later conservative histories, especially those of Afrikaner scholars: South Africa was allegedly essentially vacant when the whites arrived, the natives were distinct, endlessly warring peoples, and the many frontier wars were caused by black raiding.

Theal influenced several generations, from his disciple George Cory, historian of the Eastern Cape, to Afrikaner nationalists such as Gustav Preller and Floris van Jaarsveld, who cited him as a major source as late as 1975. Only in 1927 did William Macmillan's *The Cape Colour Question* revive a liberal approach, empathizing with missionaries such as Philip and viewing black Africans more as victims than villains. Britain seemed a benevolent referee in his work and that of his successors, C.W. de Kiewiet and Eric Walker. De Kiewiet also wrote the first socioeconomic history of South Africa (1941), foreshadowing the materialist explanations of the 1970s. Another major contemporary showing such an unusual focus was P.J. van der Merwe, the first Afrikaner nationalist historian to concentrate on everyday frontier life.

The liberal school, despite its novel voice, was limited by its increasing preoccupation with politics and diplomacy, a comparative naivety regarding the role of the British (which encouraged adherence by English-speaking scholars), and its relegation of blacks to a secondary role. Occasionally, radical or black intellectuals such as Hosea Jaffe challenged not only settler myths, but even liberal assumptions, attacking the missionaries and other liberals as British or capitalist agents. But, lacking the liberals' and Afrikaner nationalists' institutional base in the universities, their work failed to make much impact.

Only in the 1960s did a new generation of "Africanist" liberals at last try to put blacks at the center of South African history. Led by Leonard Thompson, this group had barely made its voice heard when it was besieged by bitter attacks from left and right. The *Oxford History of South Africa* (1969–71), edited by Thompson and anthropologist Monica Wilson, was criticized by Afrikaner nationalists like van Jaarsveld as anti-Afrikaner and as not so much history as a potpourri of anthropology, linguistics, archaeology, and political science. Shula

Marks and other Marxist-influenced "revisionists" queried the lack of chronological continuity, the many authors, the self-congratulatory liberal bias, and the lack of a deeper socio-economic analysis.

But while Afrikaner nationalists remained engrossed in dutifully researched, primarily political histories imbued with the spirit of Ranke, barred by language from contact with a wider audience or the emergence of a broader, explicitly "African" history, the revisionists made their critique the manifesto of a whole new school. Thompson and the liberals, centered at Yale and Wesleyan universities' Southern Africa Research Program, continued to produce nuanced, rigorously empirical studies with an African focus, from Thompson's life of Moshweshwe to Richard Elphick's pioneering study of the Khoisan. But the Marxists, led by Stanley Trapido at Oxford and Shula Marks at London's School of Oriental and African Studies, tended to dominate the field.

The Oxford-based *Journal of Southern African Studies* was the latter's standard-bearer, focusing on class rather than race, and shifting blame for the country's woes from the Afrikaner – the liberals' *bête-noire* – to capitalism. Although the revisionists did produce some excellent studies of initial white-African interaction, the chief focus was on the mineral revolution and industrialization. The trend was to demonize the role of London and English-speakers in general, and to blur the divide between post-1948 apartheid and earlier segregationist schemes. Although there were heated debates between theoretically oriented Althusserian structuralists such as Dan O'Meara and more empirical social historians such as Charles van Onselen, their shared remoteness from the liberals seemed almost as great as from the Afrikaner nationalists.

In the 1980s, however, this gap became less marked, as liberals began selectively to incorporate revisionist insights. The demise of Soviet communism and growing interest in the construction of ethnicity, intellectual and women's history, and postmodernism also undermined the old split. Both Marxists and liberals began to overlap in working on neglected areas such as slavery and the early 19th-century upheavals known as the *Mfecane*. Even a few Afrikaner historians, such as Hermann Giliomee and André du Toit, produced work that is difficult to identify with any one camp.

The end of apartheid has created a far greater crisis of identity for a historiography predicated on the struggle to preserve, reform, or destroy white rule. Black historians, sadly so markedly absent from this discussion, will likely become more common, and many scholars may be drawn into the new regime's "nation-building" project. This may well produce mediocre hagiography, but the dire lack of funding may be still more threatening, and finding appropriate themes now will be as hard for those steeped in oppositional traditions as for Afrikaner historians reduced to analyzing the apparent failure of a communal past.

PATRICK J. FURLONG

See also Foner, E.; Marks; Thompson, L.

Further Reading

Bank, Andrew, "The Great Debate and the Origins of South African Historiography," paper presented to biennial meeting of the South African Historical Society, Grahamstown, July 1995

Cory, George Edward, *The Rise of South Africa: A History of the Origin of South African Colonisation and Its Development Towards the East from the Earliest Times to 1857*, 6 vols., London and New York: Longman, 1910–40

Elphick, Richard, *Kraal and Castle*, New Haven: Yale University Press, 1977; 2nd edition as *Khoikhoi and the Founding of White South Africa*, Johannesburg: Ravan Press, 1985

Foner, Eric, "'We Must Forget the Past': History in the New South Africa," *South African Historical Journal* 32 (May 1995), 163–76

Jaarsveld, Floris van, *The Afrikaner's Interpretation of South African History*, Cape Town: Simondium, 1964

Jaffe, Hosea, *European Colonial Despotism: A History of Oppression and Resistance in South Africa*, London: Karnak, 1994

Kiewiet, Cornelius William de, *A History of South Africa: Social and Economic*, London: Oxford University Press, 1941

Macmillan, William, *The Cape Colour Question: A Historical Survey*, London: Faber, 1927

Marks, Shula, "The Historiography of South Africa: Recent Developments," in Bogumil Jewsiewicki and David Newbury, eds., *African Historiographies: What History for Which Africa?*, Beverly Hills, CA: Sage, 1986

Marks, Shula, and Stanley Trapido, eds., *The Politics of Race, Class, and Nationalism in Twentieth-Century South Africa*, London and New York: Longman, 1987

Moodie, Donald, *The Record; or, A Series of Official Papers Relative to the Condition and Treatment of the Native Tribes of South Africa*, 1838–41; reprinted Amsterdam: Balkema, 1960

O'Meara, Dan, *Volkskapitalisme: Class, Capital and Ideology in the Development of Afrikaner Nationalism, 1934–1948*, Cambridge and New York: Cambridge University Press, 1983

Philip, John, *Researches in South Africa*, London: Duncan, 1828; reprinted New York: Negro Universities Press, 1969

Preller, Gustav Schoeman, *Historiese Opstelle* (Historical Essays), Pretoria: Van Schaik, 1925

Saunders, Christopher, "Liberal Historiography before 1945," in Jeff Butler, Richard Elphick, and David Welsh, eds., *Democratic Liberalism in South Africa: Its History and Prospect*, Cape Town: Philip, and Middletown, CT: Wesleyan University Press, 1987

Saunders, Christopher, *The Making of the South African Past: Major Historians on Race and Class*, Cape Town: David Philip, and Totowa, NJ: Barnes and Noble, 1988

Smith, Ken, *The Changing Past: Trends in South African Historical Writing*, Johannesburg: Southern Book Publishers, 1988; Athens: Ohio University Press, 1989

Theal, George, *History of Southern Africa under the Administration of the Dutch East India Company (1652–1795)*, 2 vols., London: Sonnenschein, 1897; reprinted New York: Negro Universities Press, 1969

Thompson, Leonard, *Survival in Two Worlds: Moshoeshoe of Lesotho, 1786–1870*, Oxford: Clarendon Press, 1975

Van der Merwe, Petrus Johannes, *Die trekboer in die geskiedenis van die Kaapcolonie, 1657–1842*, Cape Town: Nasionale pers, 1938; in English as *The Migrant Farmer in the History of the Cape Colony*, Athens: Ohio University Press, 1995

Van Onselen, Charles, *Studies in the Social and Economic History of the Witwatersrand, 1886–1914*, 2 vols., Johannesburg: Ravan Press, 1982

Walker, Eric, *A History of Southern Africa*, London and New York: Longman, 1928; revised 1957

Wilson, Monica, and Leonard Thompson, eds., *The Oxford History of South Africa*, 2 vols., Oxford: Clarendon Press, 1969–71

Wright, Harrison M., *The Burden of the Present: Liberal-Radical Controversy over South African History*, Cape Town: David Philip, and London: Rex Collings, 1977

Southeast Asia

The study of Southeast Asian history is still developing as a regional specialization among historians in the West and Asians trained in modern historical analysis. There has been much greater interest during the past century in understanding the development of the neighboring, densely populated Chinese, Japanese, and South Asian civilizations, in part because the documentary records and historiographical traditions are far more comprehensive and accessible. But recent decades have seen a resurgence of scholarship on Indonesia, Vietnam, Thailand, the Philippines, and other lands of the Southeast Asian subcontinent and archipelago, based on both indigenous sources and Western colonial records and writings.

Many Southeast Asian societies had a tradition of historiography or quasi-history writing, including chronicles (such as the Javanese verse chronicles, *babad*) and prose narratives (*hikayat*), as well as inscriptions and literary works containing historical material; these narrated or suggested the course and meaning of histories of, or recent events in, states or ethnocultural entities. The earliest known written materials are inscriptions from the Vietnam region that date from the 2nd or 3rd centuries CE, while the first surviving chronicles and literary works come from the 14th century; these historiographical traditions continued into the 19th century. The historical accuracy of these sources has been a matter of much debate among scholars, since indigenous writings were chiefly rooted in societal worldviews and maintained an elite bias, focusing on and legitimizing rulers, dynasties, principalities, wars, religious values, and moral orders. For example, the *Babad Tanah Jawi* (1647) celebrated the 17th-century Javanese kingdom of Mataram. In some cases these were composed in later centuries, to memorialize a glorious past undermined by contemporary difficulties. Hence the *Hmannan maha yazawintawkyi* (*The Glass Palace Chronicle*, 1923), reconstructing the great classical Burman kingdom of Pagan (11th–13th century), were compiled by Burman traditionalists in the 19th century as British power increasingly subordinated their society.

The writing and interpretation of broader regional histories commenced only in the 20th century, when a more sophisticated and analytical historical sensibility became available. The Western colonial enterprise that began in the 16th century and intensified in the 19th brought Europeans (and later Americans) into the region and a few of them developed scholarly interests in the history of these societies. A case in point was the British imperialist Thomas Stamford Raffles, who compiled a history of Java, in part to justify interventionist British activities in the Dutch colonial sphere. In the decades before World War II several scholars began researching and writing about interregional themes, although the conception of Southeast Asia as a coherent region was slow to develop. Eurocentrism or patronizing attitudes were implicit in many of these writings but a few were able to develop a broader vision. The French scholar George Coèdes examined the evolution of the region during the classical period, helping popularize the notion of "Hinduization" (later termed Indianization by others) as a motive process in the development of great classical states such as Angkor. Coèdes' major writings were later translated into English and had a profound effect on Anglo-American scholars. While most historians, like Coèdes, stressed external influences

on Southeast Asian civilizations, several emphasized indigenous forces and structures. Paul Mus, who spent much of his early life in Indochina, developed notions of a distinctive Southeast Asian cultural substratum, while the Dutchman J.C. van Leur argued that outside influences – Indian, Islamic, and European – were chiefly superficial glazes superimposed on indigenous structures that retained their essential shape; to van Leur Southeast Asians were proactive in adopting and adapting those external institutions and ideas they found attractive. A variation on this theme stressed the "local genius" of Southeast Asian peoples.

The scholarship of prewar historians such as Coèdes, Mus, van Leur, H.G. Quartich-Wales, G. H. Luce, Lennox Mills, C.C. Berg, Bertram Schrieke, and Clive Day established a framework for the Southeast Asian field. But the momentous events of the 1940s and 1950s – war, nationalist upsurge, revolution, decolonization – also changed the equation, sparking the increasing interest in political, social, and economic questions as well as a new appreciation of modern and contemporary history. For the first time scholars also began to conceive of a heterogeneous Southeast Asia (like a heterogeneous Europe or South Asia) as a coherent region requiring a larger macroview, although the debate about which modern states constituted Southeast Asia would remain lively for some years. A persistent dialogue matched those who emphasized diversity and variation, rendering Southeast Asia an arbitrary geographical expression, and those who perceived an inherent and underlying unity in the obvious diversity of the region. The debate over perspective initiated by van Leur and Mus also continued. In the 1960s John Smail argued strongly (and, to many, persuasively) for an autonomous history, a view from the shore rather than the foreign ship that understands Southeast Asian events on their own terms rather than through forces emanating from outside the region (including European contact and colonialism); but he was opposed by those who contended that Western expansion and colonialism constituted dramatic watersheds, fundamentally restructuring Southeast Asian life.

In the 1940s Southeast Asian history began a slow rise to increased prominence in North America, Australia, and Europe. Yale University established a Southeast Asian Studies program in 1947; in the 1950s Cornell University rapidly became the major American center for scholarship and graduate education in history and other fields. Later, universities such as Wisconsin, Michigan, Hawaii, Australian National, Monash, Leiden, and the London School of Oriental and African Studies would develop international reputations in shaping the history field through their research and graduate training. Concurrently, various Southeast Asian universities and research institutes were moving away from narrowly nationalistic concerns toward a broader interest in the historical development of the region as a whole; in 1960 Singapore University began publishing the *Journal of Southeast Asian History*. Historians would be able to make use of the seminal works by social scientists such as anthropologist Clifford Geertz, sociologist W.F. Wertheim, and political scientists James Scott and Benedict Anderson. Geertz's writings on Indonesian religion, political economy (agricultural involution), and traditional political structures (the theater state), Wertheim's analysis of Indonesian society, Scott's work on the moral economy of the peasantry, everyday resistance, and rebellion, and Anderson's studies of Javanese culture and nationalism all had a profound influence, stimulating vigorous controversies that ultimately prompted much denser research.

In 1955 the first comprehensive general history appeared, D.G.E. Hall's magisterial *A History of South-East Asia*. Hall, a former British official in Burma who later taught at the School of Oriental and African Studies at London University, provided a detailed synthesis of the growing literature. A year earlier Brian Harrison had published a short survey, but Hall's project was much more ambitious. Hall also helped convene a series of multinational seminars in the late 1950s that explored the status and future of Southeast Asian historical writing, setting an agenda for future work. Three consequent general overviews stand out. In 1964 John Cady finished his *Southeast Asia: Its Historical Development*; this readable work presented an accessible summary suitable as an undergraduate textbook. In 1971 the six-author *In Search of Southeast Asia: A Modern History*, supervised by David J. Steinberg, became available; this fruitful collaborative study of the period since the 17th century represented a brilliant synthesis of the work of the new generation of US-based historians and social scientists, with a more concerted emphasis on identifying themes and patterns. The book proved to be an intellectual breakthrough in tying together the complex social, economic, political, and cultural history. The Steinberg volume acknowledged that the region had changed profoundly since the 18th century but also argued that Southeast Asians were never passive receptors, since local contexts reshaped imported forms. Later, the Australian Milton Osborne would publish a shorter interpretive study that effectively summarized many of the key themes in the region's history.

In 1992 the massive, 2-volume *The Cambridge History of Southeast Asia* appeared, involving mostly Western scholars, under the editorship of Nicholas Tarling; the collection of ambitious thematic essays utilized the literature appearing over the past three decades and reflected a maturity in the field. Just as valuable as these broad surveys have been the intraregional studies of others, especially Harry Benda, Anthony Reid, and Peter Bellwood, that are more modest in scope but have proved seminal influences nonetheless. In addition to important studies on colonialism, Islam, and rebellion, Benda offered a brief examination of the structure of Southeast Asia's past that provided a basis for integrating the history of the region; this work helped shape the intellectual agenda. More recently Reid's brilliant 2-volume *tour de force*, *Southeast Asia in the Age of Commerce, 1450–1680* (1988–93), attempted the sort of comparative, interlinked, and multifaceted exposition of the entire region that Fernand Braudel had provided for the Mediterranean realm. Reid offered many valuable insights into everyday life, with many common regional patterns, while also drawing a complex tapestry of a dynamic era marked by commerce, urbanization, absolute monarchy, and religious revolutions. Inevitably Reid's work sparked a vigorous debate as to its applicability to varied societies. Bellwood summarized the scholarship in archaeology and prehistory. Many valuable collections of essays on intraregional patterns also appeared. Excepting texts aimed at local secondary schools, Southeast Asia-based scholars have been more reluctant to engage in the sort of grand regional synthesis exemplified by Hall, Cady, Steinberg, Osborne, Benda, Reid, Bellwood, and the Cambridge history.

Most historians have understandably chosen to concentrate on more manageable topics; over the past 50 years, especially since the late 1960s, the scholarship on geopolities, regions, and ethnocultural groups has flourished. So have the debates over the appropriate perspectives and conceptual schemes as well as the value of foreign as opposed to indigenous approaches. The substantial majority of published scholarship concerns the modern period (since 1750 or 1800), when the documentary record becomes much more voluminous; work on earlier eras is necessarily but regrettably thinner and based on sparser sources which must sometimes be creatively interpreted. While political, institutional, and economic history have particularly thrived, social, intellectual, and cultural history also attracted increasing attention. Studies by Western and Western-trained scholars have tended to dominate the discourse, partly due to their accessibility for global audiences.

Pioneering publications from the 1950s through the mid-1970s greatly expanded our knowledge or stimulated later research agendas. For Indonesia and Malaysia the most influential writings included Paul Wheatley on the Malay world and trading systems in the 14th–15th centuries, Oliver Wolters on the great mercantile empire of Srivijaya, John Legge on interpreting Indonesian history, M.A.P. Meilinck-Roelofsz on trade in the early Dutch period, Robert van Niel on colonial Javan economic patterns, Bernhard Dahm on 20th-century Indonesia, George McT. Kahin on the Indonesian Revolution, Ruth McVey on the rise of Indonesian communism, John Legge on Sukarno, Donald Brown on the Brunei sultanate, John Gullick on precolonial Malay sociopolitical patterns, Nicholas Tarling on piracy and politics, Robert Pringle on the Ibans of Sarawak, and William Roff on the rise of Malay nationalism. For the Philippines John Phelan on the Hispanization process, John Larkin on the socio-economic history of a province, and Edgar Wickberg on Chinese economic activity were critical. For the mainland, seminal works included Lawrence Briggs on Angkor, Cady and Emanuel Sarkisyanz on modern Burma, G. William Skinner on Chinese society in Thailand, Walter Vella on Thai kingship, David Wyatt on late 19th-century Thai education, Joseph Buttinger on Vietnam's general history, Alexander Woodside on 19th-century Vietnamese government, and David Marr and Truong Buu Lam on Vietnamese anticolonialism and nationalism.

Most of these scholars would later publish other important works, such as Wolters' analysis of the structure and mindset of early Southeast Asian society, Wyatt's general history of Thailand, Woodside's study of themes in 20th-century Vietnamese history, Kahin's explication of the origins of the Vietnam War, and Larkin's examination of the roots of the Philippine sugar economy. It should be noted that historians based in Southeast Asia also contributed to the emerging framework. Among the more influential of the earlier generation have been the Malaysian Khoo Kay Kim (on political-economic change and Malay society), the Thai specialist on the premodern era Charnvit Kasetsiri, and the Indonesian Sartono Kartodirdjo (on anticolonial peasant rebellion). Southeast Asian historiography benefited from becoming an increasingly transnational enterprise.

By the later 1970s and early 1980s these path-breakers had been joined by a younger generation of Western and Southeast Asian scholars who would expand the dialogue. Among the most important of the many excellent books to appear in the past two decades on the archipelago realm are Merle Ricklefs on the traditional Javanese political system, Robert Elson on the 19th-century Javanese economy, Heather Sutherland on the colonial Javanese elite, Takashi Shiraishi on the nationalist movement, Reid on the Indonesian Revolution, Nancy Florida on Javanese literary history and worldviews, Laurie Sears on the politics of Javanese shadow plays, Leonard and Barbara Watson Andaya on precolonial and modern Malay and Indonesian political history, Shaharil Talib on colonization of Trengganu, Lim Teck Ghee on the Malayan colonial economy, Carl Trocki on Malayan Chinese, Anthony Milner on Malay nationalism and political thinking, and C.M. Turnbull's survey of Singapore history. Major contributions to Philippine history include William Henry Scott on precolonial Filipino society, Vicente Rafael on Spanish colonialism, James Warren on maritime trade and marauding, Norman Owen on economic history, Ken De Bevoise on epidemic disease, Reynaldo Ileto on religion and revolution, and Ben Kerkvliet on the Huk rebellion, as well as a collection (edited by McCoy and de Jesus) on regional socio-economic history. For Theravada Buddhist societies, David Chandler and Ian Mabbett on the history of Cambodia, Thongchai Winichakul on Thai intellectual history, Benjamin Batson on the political decline of the Thai monarchy, Michael Aung-Thwin on Pagan, Victor Lieberman on pre-modern Burmese political history, and Michael Adas on the colonial economy in British Burma are especially valuable. A renaissance of scholarship on Vietnam produced such valuable books as Keith Taylor on ancient history, Thomas Hodgkin's synthesis of the work of Vietnamese historians, William Duiker on 20th-century nationalism, Ngo Vinh Long on rural society under colonialism, Huynh Kim Khanh on the rise of communism, and Hue-Tam Ho Tai on Vietnamese radicalism. Several scholars addressed regional themes, such as Kenneth Hall's survey of pre-modern maritime trade and politics, and Robert Elson's examination of changing peasantry in the past two centuries.

To be sure, the writing, study, and teaching of Southeast Asian history remains relatively marginal in North America and Britain, although it has enjoyed impressive growth in Australian education; it remains the most understaffed of the regional specializations in US higher education, despite extensive American involvement in the region since World War II. Some critics have raised questions about the Western (especially Anglo-Australian-American-Dutch) domination of graduate education and widely accessible scholarship, seeing in this an "Orientalism" that bends Southeast Asian realities to Western preconceptions and (witting or unwitting) agendas; by shaping the narrative and intellectual framework, Western and Western-trained scholars also influence the view of Southeast Asia and its past. This perspective merits debate even if few critics have yet offered substantial alternative views. In any case the writing of Southeast Asian history persists as a continuing dialectic between Western and Asian voices, imported and indigenous influences, modern and premodern foci, and transregional and national preoccupations.

CRAIG A. LOCKARD

See also Anderson, B.; Geertz; Islamic; Malay Annals; Scott, James; Vietnam; Vietnamese Chronicles; Yamin

Further Reading

Adas, Michael, *The Burma Delta: Economic Development and Social Change on an Asian Rice Frontier, 1852–1941*, Madison: University of Wisconsin Press, 1974

Andaya, Barbara Watson, and Leonard Y. Andaya, *A History of Malaysia*, New York: St. Martin's Press, and London: Macmillan, 1982

Andaya, Barbara Watson, *To Live as Brothers: Southeast Sumatra in the Seventeenth and Eighteenth Centuries*, Honolulu: University of Hawaii Press, 1993

Andaya, Leonard Y., *The Kingdom of Johor, 1641–1728: Economic and Political Developments*, Kuala Lumpur and New York: Oxford University Press, 1975

Andaya, Leonard Y., *The World of Maluku: Eastern Indonesia in the Early Modern Period*, Honolulu: University of Hawaii Press, 1993

Anderson, Benedict, *Java in a Time of Revolution: Occupation and Resistance, 1944–1946*, Ithaca, NY: Cornell University Press, 1972

Anderson, Benedict, *Imagined Communities: Reflections on the Origin and Spread of Nationalism*, London and New York: Verso, 1983; revised 1991

Anderson, Benedict, *Language and Power: Exploring Political Cultures in Indonesia*, Ithaca, NY: Cornell University Press, 1990

Aung-Thwin, Michael, *Pagan: The Origins of Modern Burma*, Honolulu: University of Hawaii Press, 1985

Babad Tanah Jawi (Chronicle of the Land of Jawa), 1647

Bastin John, and Harry Benda, *A History of Modern Southeast Asia*, Englewood Cliffs, NJ: Prentice Hall, 1968

Batson, Benjamin, *The End of the Absolute Monarchy in Siam*, Singapore and New York: Oxford University Press, 1984

Bellwood, Peter, *Man's Conquest of the Pacific: The Prehistory of Southeast Asia and Oceania*, Auckland and London: Collins, 1978; New York: Oxford University Press, 1979

Benda, Harry, *Continuity and Change in Southeast Asia: Collected Journal Articles*, New Haven: Yale University Press, 1972

Berg, C.C., *De evolutie der Javaanse geschiedschrijving* (The Evolution of Javanese Historical Writing), Amsterdam: Mededelingen der Koninklijke Nederlaandse Akademie van Wetenschappen, 1951

Briggs, Lawrence Palmer, *The Ancient Khmer Empire*, Philadelphia: American Philosophical Society, 1951

Brown, D.E., *Brunei: The Structure and History of a Bornean Malay Sultanate*, Brunei: Brunei Museum, 1970

Buttinger, Joseph, *Vietnam: A Political History*, New York: Praeger, 1968; London: Deutsch, 1969

Cady, John F., *A History of Modern Burma*, Ithaca, NY: Cornell University Press, 1958

Cady, John F., *Southeast Asia: Its Historical Development*, New York: McGraw Hill, 1964

Cady, John F., *The History of Post-War Southeast Asia*, Athens: Ohio University Press, 1974

Chandler, David P., *A History of Cambodia*, Boulder, CO: Westview Press, 1983

Chandler, David P., *The Tragedy of Cambodian History: Politics, War, and Revolution since 1945*, New Haven: Yale University Press, 1991

Charnvit Kasetsiri, *The Rise of Ayudhya: A History of Siam in the Fourteenth and Fifteenth Centuries*, Kuala Lumpur and New York: Oxford University Press, 1976

Coèdes, George, *Les Peuples de la péninsule indochinoise: histoire, civilisations*, Paris: Dunod, 1962; in English as *The Making of South East Asia*, Berkeley: University of California Press, and London: Routledge, 1966

Coèdes, George, *Histoire ancienne des Etats hinouises d'Extrême Orient*, Hanoi: Imprimerie d'Extrême-orient, 1944; in English as *The Indianized States of Southeast Asia*, Honolulu: East-West Center Press, 1968

Cribb, Robert, and Colin Brown, *Modern Indonesia: A History since 1945*, London and New York: Longman, 1995

Dahm, Bernhard, *History of Indonesia in the Twentieth Century*, New York: Praeger, and London: Pall Mall Press, 1971

Day, Clive, *The Policy and Administration of the Dutch in Java*, New York: Macmillan, 1904; reprinted as *The Dutch in Java*, Kuala Lumpur: Oxford University Press, 1966

De Bevoise, Ken, *Agents of Apocalypse: Epidemic Disease in the Colonial Philippines*, Princeton: Princeton University Press, 1995

Duiker, William J., *The Rise of Nationalism in Vietnam, 1900–1941*, Ithaca, NY: Cornell University Press, 1976

Elson, Robert Edward, *Village Java under the Cultivation System, 1830–1870*, Sydney: Allen and Unwin, 1994

Elson, Robert Edward, *The End of the Peasantry in Southeast Asia: A Social and Economic History of Peasant Livelihood, 1800–1990s*, London: Macmillan, 1997

Florida, Nancy, *Writing the Past, Inscribing the Future: History as Prophecy in Colonial Java*, Durham, NC: Duke University Press, 1995

Geertz, Clifford, *The Religion of Java*, Glencoe, IL: Free Press, 1960

Geertz, Clifford, *Agricultural Involution: The Process of Ecological Change in Indonesia*, Berkeley: University of California Press, 1963

Geertz, Clifford, *Negara: The Theatre State in Nineteenth-Century Bali*, Princeton: Princeton University Press, 1980

Gullick, J.M., *Indigenous Political Systems of Western Malaya*, London: Athlone Press, 1958; New York: Humanities Press, 1965; revised 1988

Hall, D.G.E., *A History of South-East Asia*, London: Macmillan, and New York: St. Martin's Press, 1955; 4th edition 1981

Hall, D.G.E., ed., *Historians of South East Asia*, London: Oxford University Press, 1961

Hall, Kenneth R,. and John K. Whitmore, eds., *Explorations in Early Southeast Asian History: The Origins of Southeast Asian Statecraft*, Ann Arbor: Center for South and Southeast Asian Studies, University of Michigan, 1976

Hall, Kenneth R., *Maritime Trade and State Development in Early Southeast Asia*, Honolulu: University of Hawaii Press, 1985

Harrison, Brian, *South-East Asia: A Short History*, London: Macmillan, and New York: St Martin's Press, 1954; 3rd edition, 1966

Hmannan maha yazawintawkyi; in English as *The Glass Palace Chronicle of the Kings of Burma*, London: Oxford University Press, 1923; reprinted New York: AMS Press, 1976

Hodgkin, Thomas, *Vietnam: The Revolutionary Path*, London: Macmillan, and New York: St. Martin's Press, 1981

Huynh Kim Khanh, *Vietnamese Communism, 1925–1945*, Ithaca, NY: Cornell University Press, 1982

Ileto, Reynaldo C., *Pasyon and Revolution: Popular Movements in the Philippines, 1840–1910*, Quezon City: Ateneo de Manila University Press, 1979

Ingleson, John, *The Road to Exile: The Indonesian Nationalist Movement, 1927–1934*, Singapore: Heinemann, 1979

Journal of Southeast Asian History, Singapore: Department of Southeast Asian Studies, 1960–69

Journal of Southeast Asian Studies, Singapore: Far Eastern Publishers International, 1970–

Kahin, George McTurnan, *Nationalism and Revolution in Indonesia*, Ithaca, NY: Cornell University Press, 1952

Kahin, George McTurnan, *Intervention: How America Became Involved in Vietnam*, New York: Knopf, 1986

Kartodirdjo, Sartono, *Protest Movements in Rural Java: A Study of Agrarian Unrest in the Nineteenth and Early Twentieth Centuries*, Singapore and New York: Oxford University Press, 1973

Kerkvliet, Benedict J., *The Huk Rebellion: A Study of Peasant Revolt in the Philippines*, Berkeley: University of California Press, 1977

Keyes, Charles F., *The Golden Peninsula: Culture and Adaptation in Mainland Southeast Asia*, New York: Macmillan, 1977

Khoo Kay Kim, *The Western Malay States, 1850–1873: The Effects of Commercial Development on Malay Politics*, Kuala Lumpur and New York: Oxford University Press, 1972

Lam, Truong Buu, *Patterns of Vietnamese Response to Foreign Intervention, 1858–1900*, New Haven: Center for Southeast Asian Studies, Yale University, 1967

Larkin, John A., *The Pampangans: Colonial Society in a Philippine Province*, Berkeley: University of California Press, 1972

Larkin, John A., *Sugar and the Origins of Modern Philippine Society*, Berkeley: University of California Press, 1993

Legge, John David, *Indonesia*, Englewood Cliffs, NJ: Prentice Hall, 1964; 3rd edition, Sydney: Allen and Unwin, 1980

Legge, John David, *Sukarno: A Political Biography*, New York: Praeger, and London: Allen Lane, 1972; revised 1985

Leur, J.C. van, *Indonesian Trade and Society: Essays in Asian Social and Economic History*, The Hague: van Hoeve, 1955

Lieberman, Victor B., *Burmese Administrative Cycles: Anarchy and Conquest, c.1580–1760*, Princeton: Princeton University Press, 1984

Lim Teck Ghee, *Peasants and Their Agricultural Economy in Colonial Malaya, 1874–1941*, Kuala Lumpur and New York: Oxford University Press, 1977

Lockard, Craig A., *From Kampung to City: A Social History of Kuching, Malaysia, 1820–1970*, Athens: Ohio University Press, 1987

Lockard, Craig A., *The Rise and Changing Status of the Southeast Asian History Field in the United States: An Analytical Study*, Madison: Center for Southeast Asian Studies, University of Wisconsin, 1989

Luce, G.H., and Pe Maung Tin, eds. and trans., *The Glass Palace Chronicle of the Kings of Burma*, London: Oxford University Press, 1923

Mabbett, Ian, and David Chandler, *The Khmers*, Oxford and Cambridge, MA: Blackwell, 1995

McCoy, Alfred W., and Ed C. de Jesus, eds., *Philippine Social History: Global Trade and Local Transformations*, Quezon City: Ateneo de Manila University Press, and Honolulu: University of Hawaii Press, 1982

McVey, Ruth T., *The Rise of Indonesian Communism*, Ithaca, NY: Cornell University Press, 1965

Marr, David G., *Vietnamese Anticolonialism, 1885–1925*, Berkeley: University of California Press, 1971

Marr, David G., *Vietnamese Tradition on Trial, 1920–1945*, Berkeley: University of California Press, 1981

Marr, David G., and A.C. Milner, eds., *Southeast Asia in the 9th to 14th Centuries*, Singapore: Institute of Southeast Asian Studies, 1985

Meilink-Roelofsz, Marie Antoinette Petronelli, *Asian Trade and European Influence in the Indonesian Archipelago Between 1500 and about 1630*, The Hague: Nijhoff, 1962

Mills, Lennox Algernon, "British Malaya, 1824–1867," *Journal of Malayan Branch, Royal Asiatic Society*, 3 (1925); reprinted New York: AMS Press, 1971

Milner, A.C., *The Invention of Politics in Colonial Malaya: Contesting Nationalism and the Expansion of the Public Sphere*, Cambridge and New York: Cambridge University Press, 1995

Mus, Paul, "Cultes indiens et indigenes au Champa," *Bulletin de l'Ecole Française d'Extrême Orient* 33 (1933), 367–410; reprinted as *Inde vue de l'Est: cultes indiens et indigenes au Champa*, Hanoi, 1934; in English as *India Seen from the East: Indian and Indigenous Cults in Champa*, Clayton: Monash University Papers on Asia, 3, 1975

Ngo Vinh Long, *Before the Revolution: The Vietnamese Peasants under the French*, Cambridge, MA: MIT Press, 1973

Niel, Robert van, *Java under the Cultivation System: Collected Writings*, Leiden: KITLV Press, 1992

Osborne, Milton, *Southeast Asia: An Illustrated Introductory History*, Sydney, London, and Boston: Allen and Unwin, 1979; 6th edition 1995

Owen, Norman G., *Prosperity Without Progress: Manila Hemp and Material Life in the Colonial Philippines*, Berkeley: University of California Press, 1984

Phelan, John L., *The Hispanization of the Philippines: Spanish Aims and Filipino Responses, 1565–1700*, Madison: University of Wisconsin Press, 1959

Pringle, Robert M., *Rajahs and Rebels: The Ibans of Sarawak under Brooke Rule, 1841–1941*, Ithaca, NY: Cornell University Press, and London: Macmillan, 1970

Quaritch-Wales, Horace Geoffrey, *Ancient Siamese Government and Administration*, London: Bernard Quaritch, 1934; reprinted New York: Paragon, 1965

Quaritch-Wales, Horace Geoffrey, *The Making of Greater India: A Study in South-East Culture Change*, London: Bernard Quaritch, 1951; revised 1974

Rafael, Vicente L., *Contracting Colonialism: Translation and Christian Conversion in Tagalog Society under Early Spanish Rule*, Ithaca, NY: Cornell University Press, 1988

Raffles, Thomas Stamford, *The History of Java*, 2 vols., London: Murray, 1817; reprinted Kuala Lumpur: Oxford University Press, 1965–78

Reid, Anthony, *Indonesian National Revolution, 1945–50*, Hawthorn, Victoria: Longman, 1974

Reid, Anthony, and Lance Castles, eds., *Pre-colonial State Systems in Southeast Asia: The Malay Peninsula, Sumatra, Bali-Lombok, South Celebes*, Kuala Lumpur: Malaysian Branch of the Royal Asiatic Society, 1976

Reid, Anthony, and David G. Marr, eds., *Perceptions of the Past in Southeast Asia*, Singapore: Heinemann, 1979

Reid, Anthony, *Southeast Asia in the Age of Commerce, 1450–1680*, 2 vols., New Haven: Yale University Press, 1988–93

Reid, Anthony, ed., *Southeast Asia in the Early Modern Era: Trade, Power, and Belief*, Ithaca, NY: Cornell University Press, 1993

Ricklefs, Merle Calvin, *Jogjakarta under Sultan Mangkubumi, 1749–1792: A History of the Division of Java*, London: Oxford University Press, 1974

Roff, William R., *The Origins of Malay Nationalism*, New Haven: Yale University Press, 1967

Sarkisyanz, Emanuel, *Buddhist Backgrounds to the Burmese Revolution*, The Hague: Nijhoff, 1965

Schrieke, Bertram, *Indonesian Sociological Studies: Selected Writings*, 2 vols., The Hague: van Hoeve, 1955–57

Scott, James C., *The Moral Economy of the Peasant: Rebellion and Subsistence in Southeast Asia*, New Haven: Yale University Press, 1976

Scott, James C., *Weapons of the Weak: Everyday Forms of Peasant Resistance*, New Haven: Yale University Press, 1985

Scott, William Henry, *Looking for the Prehispanic Filipino and Other Essays in Philippine History*, Quezon City: New Day, 1992

Sears, Laurie J., *Shadows of Empire: Colonial Discourse and Javanese Tales*, Durham, NC: Duke University Press, 1996

Shaharil Talib, *After Its Own Image: The Trengganu Experience, 1881–1941*, Singapore and New York: Oxford University Press, 1984

Shiraishi, Takashi, *An Age in Motion: Popular Radicalism in Java, 1912–1926*, Ithaca, NY: Cornell University Press, 1990

Skinner, G. William, *Chinese Society in Thailand: An Analytical History*, Ithaca, NY: Cornell University Press, 1957

Smail, John R.W., "On the Possibility of an Autonomous History of Modern Southeast Asia," *Journal of Southeast Asian History* 2 (1961), 72–103

Smith, Ralph Bernard, and William Watson, eds., *Early South East Asia: Essays in Archaeology, History, and Historical Geography*, Kuala Lumpur and New York: Oxford University Press, 1979

Steinberg, David Joel, ed., *In Search of Southeast Asia: A Modern History*, Kuala Lumpur: Oxford University Press, New York: Praeger, and London: Pall Mall Press, 1971; revised edition, Honolulu: University of Hawaii Press, 1987

Sutherland, Heather, *The Making of a Bureaucratic Elite: The Colonial Transformation of the Javanese Priyayi*, Singapore: Heinemann, 1979

Tai, Hue-Tam Ho, *Radicalism and the Origins of the Vietnamese Revolution*, Cambridge, MA: Harvard University Press, 1992

Tarling, Nicholas, *Piracy and Politics in the Malay World: A Study of British Imperialism in Nineteenth-Century South-East Asia*, Singapore: Moore, and Melbourne: Cheshire, 1963

Tarling, Nicholas, ed., *The Cambridge History of Southeast Asia*, 2 vols., Cambridge: Cambridge University Press, 1992

Taylor, Keith Weller, *The Birth of Vietnam*, Berkeley: University of California Press, 1983

Thongchai Winichakul, *Siam Mapped: A History of the Geo-Body of a Nation*, Honolulu: University of Hawaii Press, 1994

Trocki, Carl A., *Opium and Empire: Chinese Society in Colonial Singapore, 1800–1910*, Ithaca, NY: Cornell University Press, 1990

Turnbull, Constance Mary, *A History of Singapore, 1819–1975*, Kuala Lumpur and New York: Oxford University Press, 1977

Vella, Walter F., *Siam under Rama III, 1824–1851*, Locust Valley, NY: Augustin, 1957

Warren, James F., *The Sulu Zone: The Dynamics of External Trade, Slavery, and Ethnicity in the Transformation of a Southeast Asian Maritime State*, Singapore: Singapore University Press, 1981

Wertheim, Willem Frederik, *Indonesian Society in Transition: A Study in Social Change*, The Hague: van Hoeve, 1956; revised 1964

Wheatley, Paul, *The Golden Khersonese: Studies in the Historical Geography of the Malay Peninsula Before AD 1500*, Kuala Lumpur: University of Malaya Press, 1961

Wickberg, Edgar, *The Chinese in Philippine Life, 1850–1898*, New Haven: Yale University Press, 1965

Wolters, O.W., *Early Indonesian Commerce: A Study of the Origins of Srivijaya*, Ithaca, NY: Cornell University Press, 1967

Wolters, O.W., *History, Culture, and Region in Southeast Asian Perspectives*, Singapore: Institute of Southeast Asian Studies, 1982

Woodside, Alexander B., *Vietnam and the Chinese Model: A Comparative Study of Nguyen and Ch'ing Civil Government in the First Half of the Nineteenth Century*, Cambridge, MA: Harvard University Press, 1971

Woodside, Alexander B., *Community and Revolution in Modern Vietnam*, Boston: Houghton Mifflin, 1976

Wyatt, David K., *The Politics of Reform in Thailand: Education in the Reign of Chulalongkorn*, New Haven: Yale University Press, 1969

Wyatt, David K., *Thailand: A Short History*, New Haven: Yale University Press, 1984

Southern, R.W. 1912–

British medieval historian

Few British historians of the 20th century have written with the grace and power of Richard Southern. He combines, in a way that may owe something to his having spent his working life at Oxford, an extraordinary ability to represent the thoughts of his subjects in evocatively precise English with an eye for suggestive examples. Many of his finest passages are pieces of commentary on issues that may seem of small import but which are shown to illumine whole areas of understanding and have widened the horizons of generations of readers. His *The Making of the Middle Ages* (1953) has remained in print for more than four decades, been translated into some two dozen foreign languages, and suggested the title of more than one recent book.

Southern began his historical work laying the groundwork for an edition of the letters of St. Anselm (*c.*1033–1109), an Italian who became a monk in northern France and finished his days as archbishop of Canterbury. Significantly, he had been attracted to Anselm by his letters of friendship. The edition came to nothing, for another scholar was already working on an edition of Anselm, but this early interest led to a major book on Anselm that approached its subject by way of his relationships with other people, in particular monks, among them his biographer Eadmar, and an investigation of his intellect. Hence, Anselm's responses to the problems that he encountered when archbishop are interpreted in the light of his wrestling with philosophical problems of liberty and obedience. Not only does the book provide a most lucid and sympathetic account of Anselm, but it admirably conveys a sense of the difficulty in approaching its subject and the limitations of the evidence, so that when Southern produced a much revised version of it in 1990 he included a discussion of Anselm's sexual orientation which precisely indicated just how far the facts at our disposal will take us.

The Making of the Middle Ages, the book for which Southern is best known, is an extraordinarily felicitous account of aspects of the central Middle Ages. It is divided into four chapters, which successively examine Latin Christendom and its neighbors (a theme also pursued in a 1962 book on *Western Views of Islam in the Middle Ages*), the bonds of society, the ordering of the Christian life, and the tradition of thought. The result is a most vivid view of the period which seems to be almost that of an insider. A similar way of organizing the material is evident in his contribution to the Pelican History of the Church, *Western Society and the Church in the Middle Ages* (1970), but it is possible to feel that Southern is less happy with this topic. In a pointer to his chief interests, he warns readers that the theme of this book, the connections between the church and its social environment, must exclude "a great part of that spiritual and intellectual activity which must form the best memorial to the medieval church and its chief claim to our regard."

A concern that has remained prominent in Southern's thought is relations between England and the continent. He has written challengingly on the role of England in the 12th-century Renaissance, while his book on Robert Grosseteste, with its significant subtitle "The growth of an English mind in medieval Europe," developed a theme anticipated in earlier works. It argued, against the prevailing view, for Grosseteste's intellectual formation having been more English than continental, and placed his scientific activities against a background of earlier English empirical thought.

Another sustained interest has been humanism, a hard-to-define concept that Southern sees in a positive way. Against a widely-held view of humanism having come to flourish during the Italian Renaissance, he has argued for some decades for the claims of intellectuals of the central Middle Ages to be seen as exponents of it. Again, one is struck by a sensitivity to the limits of the evidence. For example, against a long-standing tradition that emphasizes the contributions of a "school of Chartres," Southern has shown how slender the evidence for such a school is.

It is too early to offer a full appreciation of Southern's work, which is still very much in progress, with a major account of scholasticism in course of publication. Doubtless it can be supplemented in some respects. A general history of the church which identifies that body with the clergy and professed religious may be found problematic, particularly in that it necessarily excludes almost all women. While Southern succeeds brilliantly in presenting the thoughts of medieval writers, it could be argued that the intuitive enthusiasm with which he approaches the spiritual, intellectual, and personal concerns of an elite group of professed religious authors may incline his readers to over-estimate their importance and encourage them to accept the writers' own explanations for what they did too readily. But one can only admire the achievement of the most influential English medieval historian of his generation. He has brought many to love the study of the Middle Ages, and his original work has had an extremely powerful impact on the way scholars understand a period whose importance he has taught them to see.

JOHN MOORHEAD

Biography

Richard William Southern. Born 8 February 1912. Educated at Royal Grammar School, Newcastle upon Tyne; Balliol College, Oxford, BA 1932. Served in the British Army, 1940–44; in the political intelligence department, Foreign Office, 1943–45. Junior research fellow, Exeter College, Oxford, 1933–37; studied in Paris, 1933–34, and Munich, 1935; at Oxford University: fellow/tutor, Balliol College, 1937–61; professor, 1961–69; president, St. John's College, 1969–81. Married Sheila Cobley Crichton-Miller, 1944 (2 sons). Knighted 1974.

Principal Writings

The Making of the Middle Ages, 1953
Western Views of Islam in the Middle Ages, 1962
Saint Anselm and His Biographer: A Study of Monastic Life and Thought, 1963; revised as *Saint Anselm: A Portrait in a Landscape*, 1990
Memorials of St. Anselm, 1969
Medieval Humanism and Other Studies, 1970
Western Society and the Church in the Middle Ages, 1970
Robert Grosseteste: The Growth of an English Mind in Medieval Europe, 1986
"Anselm: an Examination of the Foundations," *Albion* 20 (1988), 181–204
Scholastic Humanism and the Unification of Europe, 1995

Further Reading

Davis, R.H.C., and J.M. Wallace-Hadrill, eds., *The Writing of History in the Middle Ages: Essays Presented to Richard William Southern*, Oxford and New York: Oxford University Press, 1981
Thomson, Rodney M., "England and the Twelfth-Century Renaissance," *Past and Present* 101 (1983), 3–21
Vaughn, Sally N., *Anselm of Bec and Robert of Meulan: The Innocence of the Dove and the Wisdom of the Serpent*, Berkeley: University of California Press, 1987
Vaughn, Sally N., "Anselm: Saint and Statesman," *Albion* 20 (1988), 205–20

Spain: Islamic

The history of Islamic Spain, or al-Andalus as it is properly called, charts the increasing ability to conceptualize that society as a normative Islamic one whose culture and social structure are divorced from that of Christian Spain. Nineteenth-century narratives were the first to be based on Arabic texts, beginning with José Antonio Conde (1765–1820) and then

Pascual de Gayangos (1809–97). Gayangos, a political liberal exiled in England, produced an English abridgment of al-Maqqarī's history which influenced Hispanists in both America and England, including Richard Ford, Washington Irving, and William Henry Prescott. Ford, whose findings were published in his famous *Hand-Book for Travellers in Spain* (1845), was nevertheless the first scholar who made a documented case for the vast influence of Islamic upon Christian culture. The Dutch scholar Reinhart Dozy (1820–83) produced, at mid-century, the first modern history of al-Andalus based on his study of the Arabic sources. Dozy was also the author of a "supplement" to Arabic dictionaries which is a gold mine of Andalusi variants still useful. Francisco Codera (1836–1917) imported Dozy's methods and perspectives to Spain and edited an important series of medieval Andalusi texts.

Francisco Javier Simonet (1829–1897) in his mid-century history of Spanish Mozarabs (Christians under Islamic rule) exaggerated the role that Christians had played in Andalusi society and culture. He denied to the great Andalusi Arab historians any legitimacy in the representation of Islamic or Arab culture, claiming that most of them were really "Spaniards," descended from Hispano-Romans. However, in his glossary of Latinate words in Andalusi Arabic, he made a solid contribution to the linguistic history of Andalusi culture.

Codera's student Julián Ribera (1858–1934) drew attention to the impact of Arabic on medieval Spanish culture and institutions; he studied the Christian assimilation of Muslim juridical institutions, and carried out parallel studies on the educational system and music. Miguel Asín Palacios (1871–1944) was most noted for his studies of Islam and its impact on Christian theology and literature, in particular his famous study of the influence of Islam on Dante. At the same time, a French scholar, Evariste Lévi-Provençal (1894–1956), produced the first modern narrative of the history of al-Andalus through the 10th century, based on his knowledge of the Arabic sources. Dozy had emphasized the role of tribal politics (particularly the Qaysi-Yemeni split among the early Arab settlers of the peninsula). In reaction Lévi-Provençal stressed the role of the Umayyad state in counteracting tribalism to establish a centralized state, in particular 'Abd al-Rahmān III's success in pacifying the country and establishing the Caliphate of Córdoba. More recently, Pierre Guichard has recast the role of tribalism in the social history of al-Andalus by analyzing the segmentary nature of Andalusi society and identifying the role of clan groups in the social organization of the countryside.

In the late 1920s, José Millás Vallicrosa (1897–1970), a student of Ribera, began a career of research on the history of Arabic science in al-Andalus. Millás was from the start a correspondent of George Sarton, founder of the academic discipline of the history of science, to whose doctrine of science as "new humanism" he keenly subscribed. Millás's first book on the subject, his *Assaig d'història les idees físiques i matemàtiques a la Catalunya medieval* (1931) was an analysis of MS Ripoll 225, a scientific miscellany of the 10th century, which showed the monastery of Ripoll in Catalonia to have played a precocious role in the transmission of Arabic science to Latin Europe. The *Assaig* served as an agenda for the rest of Millás' career, as he proceeded to study the Arabic antecedents, particularly in astronomy, of the Ripoll manuscript, carrying the story forward to the 11th century and the work of al-Zarqālluh

and his school. Millás' student Juan Vernet continued the same line of research and institutionalized a distinctive scholarly tradition in medieval Andalusi science known as the "school of Barcelona." The research line could perhaps be characterized as the study of the reception of Eastern science in al-Andalus, in the case of astronomy its adaptation, via new observational data, to the latitude of Spain, and the transmission of this science to Latin Europe. Associated, directly or indirectly, with the school of Barcelona have been a large number of foreign historians working on questions of transmission (M. T. d'Alvernhy, Guy Beaujouan, Georg Bossong, Charles Burnett) or on Arabic astronomy (Paul Kunitzsch, Emmanuelle Poule, John D. North, G. J. Toomer).

In the 1950s there erupted a tremendous polemic ("the polemic of Spanish history") in reaction to the publication in 1948 of Américo Castro's *España en su historia* (*The Structure of Spanish History*, 1954). According to Castro, the culture that we call "Spanish" came into existence in the Middle Ages through the interaction (*convivencia* was his term) of three competing "castes" – Christians, Muslims, and Jews. To make his point, he marshaled a great deal of evidence – much of it from literary sources – bearing on the influence that the ideas, customs, and values of Jews and Muslims had on Christian culture. He was opposed by his old friend and political ally Claudio Sánchez-Albornoz, who argued for the autochthonous nature of Spanish culture, asserting that Islamic influence was superficial, and retrieving most of the ageless arguments for the perduring nature of Spanish character traits that can be dated back to the Numantines. Castro had scant influence on historians, because he was a professor of literature, and his followers lacked the sophistication or knowledge of social sciences required to plead his case. Nevertheless, his advocacy of the autonomous nature of Andalusi culture legitimized the claims of the next generation of Spanish Arabists. At the same time, Sánchez-Albornoz in his dotage became a promoter of the Franco regime, which was in its own dotage. Although the polemic was largely confined to literary historians, it did have the effect of drawing attention to Andalusi culture and further legitimizing its role as a normative Islamic society. Coincidentally, in the same year as Castro's book was first published, there appeared an enormously influential article by S.M. Stern, documenting the presence of Romance vernacular couplets (*kharja*/s) in Arabic and Hebrew poetry (the genre of *muwashshaha*). The coincidence appeared to underscore Castro's argument and promoted an alliance between Arabists and medieval literary scholars.

Al-Andalus is a severely under-documented society; the circumstances of its termination clearly resulted in a tremendous loss of recorded information. Thus after Lévi-Provençal had blocked out the narrative history of al-Andalus, there was nothing left except to fill in the lacunae, on the basis of the same roster of sources. Therefore a historiographical revolution made by medieval archaeologists in the 1980s was both radical (because it upset the methodological bases on which the received view was based) and innovative (because it opened up for research whole areas of Andalusi culture and society that had heretofore been neglected).

A meeting on *incastellamento* organized by Pierre Toubert in Rome in 1978 had a dramatic effect on studies of al-Andalus, stimulating a turn from urban to rural civilization and from cultural to material history. From the early 1980s an increasing number of scholars has been involved in "extensive archaeology" of medieval sites (the methods are those of site inspection and superficial collection of archaeological remains, saving the costs of stratigraphic digs). Data from two study areas – Sharq al-Andalus and Almería – generated a distinctive model of rural settlement in al-Andalus, a subject undocumented in Arabic sources and about which virtually nothing was known before. The model describes mainly mountainous castral districts whose focal point is a castle (Arabic, *hisn*), around which are grouped as many as ten villages (*qurā*; singular *qarya*). Unlike feudal castles, however, the *hisn* in general did not dominate the villages but served as a refuge in times of insecurity and was not normally garrisoned. In most cases, moreover, there is a further association with irrigation agriculture, which, along with arboriculture, was the key to the rural economy in the zones studied.

Another contribution of medieval archaeology has been to define a distinctive "paleoandalusi" culture, extending from the conquest of 711 to around 1000 CE, characterized by the survival of late Roman pottery forms and irrigation systems on the Mediterranean littoral (not yet developed into the peri-urban *huertas* of later medieval times), associated with social phenomena characteristic of societies undergoing an extended process of religious conversion. In a chapter on Islamic Spain in a 1979 book on religious conversion, Richard Bulliet suggested that the revolt of Ibn Hafsūn (880–928), viewed as a rallying point of oppressed neo-Muslims and Christians against the Umayyad emirate, was a phenomenon characteristic of the "early majority" phase of conversion, similar to revolts throughout the Islamic world by indigenous groups at the point when they perceived the Islamic state as "a permanent fact and a threat to the continued existence of the non-Muslim communities." Recently Manuel Acién presented a more finely-tuned assessment of the significance of Ibn Hafsūn, uniting archaeological and historical perspectives. By studying the pattern formed by the castles of the rebels Acién argued that Ibn Hafsūn was actually rallying the remnants of Gothic nobility – now converted to Islam – in southern Spain in defense of their protofeudal privileges. Another "early majority" dynamic – the mid-9th-century martyrdoms of Córdoba – has been analyzed by Jessica Coope in terms of Bulliet's "curve of conversion." She found that most of the martyrs came from families deeply divided by conversion to Islam, a phenomenon in line with Bulliet's curve and which accounts for the explosive psychological context of the martyrdoms.

The economic history of al-Andalus has been studied in the context of the wider economic horizons of the Islamic world and, within it, the western Mediterranean. Thus S.D. Goitein showed, by analyzing the activities of Jewish traders, that merchants from al-Andalus took advantage of the entire Islamic "common market" all the way to India. Olivia Constable demonstrated the commercial linkages of al-Andalus with the Christian Mediterranean, particularly Genoa. These studies link up nicely to Charles-Emmanuel Dufourcq's monumental study of late medieval relationships between Catalonia and the Maghreb. As for agriculture, Andrew Watson and Lucie Bolens have argued that the regionalization of the economy under the Party Kingdoms of the 11th century favored the development of the great *huertas* with their distinctive mix of eastern and western crops. The irrigation systems of al-Andalus have been shown by Thomas F. Glick to have been organized along eastern lines, a concomitant, according to Watson, of the water needs of the roster of Indian crops that the Arabs introduced. Andalusi hydraulic systems have been studied archaeologically by Miquel Barceló and others.

The society and culture of subject Muslims (Mudéjars) in medieval Christian Spain have generally been studied with reference to Christian society rather than in the context of Andalusi history. An exception is L.P. Harvey who has analyzed Mudéjar society of the 14th and 15th centuries in tandem with the fully Islamic culture of the kingdom of Granada. However, given the constraints on contact between the two populations, there are bound to be more contrasts than parallels. The discussion of Mudéjars has to a certain extent turned on the historian's evaluation of the quality of acculturation and assimilation. On one end of the spectrum, Elena Lourie presents a negative assessment of the role of both Muslim and Jewish minorities, to the point of negating any positive value of *convivencia* whatever, and adducing evidence to demonstrate the near universal intolerance of the Christian majority in Aragón. A different approach, largely institutional, is that of Robert I. Burns who analyzed the institutional and social deculturation of Valencian Mudéjars of the 13th century whereby Muslim institutions were made to fit into specific organizational forms of Christian governance. Mark Meyerson adopted a similar stance in his study of late medieval Valencian Mudéjars who, through long acquaintance and habitual use of Christian institutions and particularly the legal system, had in fact achieved a substantial level of cultural and social adjustment, if not assimilation. In view of the enormous pressures placed on Muslims to abandon the remnants of segmentary social organization, Meyerson emphasized the positive role of interfamiliar feuding in the maintenance of social cohesion among Mudéjars.

THOMAS F. GLICK

See also Castro; Goitein; Lévi-Provençal; Sarton

Further Reading

Acién Almansa, Manuel, *Entre el feudalismo y el Islam: 'Umar Ibn Hafsūn en los historiadores, en las fuentes y en la historia* (Between Feudalism and Islam: 'Umar Ibn Hafsūn in the Historians, in the Sources, and in the History), Jaén: Universidad de Jaén, 1994

Barceló, Miquel, *Arqueología medieval: En las afueras del "medievalismo"* (Medieval Archaeology: On the Edge of "Medievalism"), Barcelona: Crítica, 1988

Bazzana, André, Patrice Cressier, and Pierre Guichard, *Les Châteaux ruraux d'Al-Andalus: histoire et archéologie des husun du sud-est de l'Espagne* (Rural Castles in Islamic Spain: History and Archaeology of Fortresses of Southeastern Spain), Madrid: Casa de Velázquez, 1988

Bulliet, Richard W., *Conversion to Islam in the Medieval Period: An Essay in Quantitative History*, Cambridge, MA: Harvard University Press, 1979

Castro, Américo, *España en su historia: cristianos, moros y judíos*, Buenos Aires: Losada, 1948; in English as *The Structure of Spanish History*, Princeton: Princeton University Press, 1954, revised as *The Spaniards: An Introduction to Their History*, Berkeley: University of California Press, 1971

Cirre, Manuela Manzanares, *Arabistas españoles del siglo XIX* (Spanish Arabists of the 19th Century), Madrid: Instituto Hispano-Arabe de Cultura, 1972

Constable, Olivia Remie, *Trade and Traders in Muslim Spain: The Commercial Realignment of the Iberia Peninsula, 900–1500*, Cambridge: Cambridge University Press, 1994

Coope, Jessica, *The Martyrs of Córdoba: Community and Family Conflict in an Age of Mass Conversion*, Lincoln: University of Nebraska Press, 1995

Ford, Richard, *Hand-Book for Travellers in Spain*, 1845

Glick, Thomas F., *From Muslim Fortress to Christian Castle: Social and Cultural Change in Medieval Spain*, Manchester: Manchester University Press, 1995

Jayyusi, Salma K., ed., *The Legacy of Muslim Spain*, Leiden: Brill, 1992

Millás Vallicrosa, José, *Assaig d'història les idees físiques i matemàtiques a la Catalunya medieval* (History of the Ideas in Physics and Mathematics in Medieval Catalunya), Barcelona: Institut Patxot, 1931

Monroe, James T., *Islam and the Arabs in Spanish Scholarship*, Leiden: Brill, 1970

Watt, W. Montgomery, *A History of Islamic Spain*, Edinburgh: Edinburgh University Press, and Chicago: Aldine, 1965

Journals

Arqueología Medieval (Mértola, Portugal), 1992–

Boletín de Arqueología Medieval (Madrid), 1987–

Al-Qantara (Madrid), 1980–

Sharq al-Andalus (Alicante), 1984–

Spain: to 1450

After the composition of the *Primera Crónica General* in the reign of king Alfonso X the Wise (1252–84) Castilian chroniclers, writing in the vernacular, favored broad views of the history of the kingdom, locating the origins of its inhabitants and of its royal line in the Visigothic period. This somewhat anachronistic approach helped validate the aspirations of the Castilian monarchy to authority over the whole peninsula. By the time this was actually achieved by the Habsburg kings in the 16th century, a rather more sophisticated historiography, albeit of an antiquarian kind, had already established itself in Spain. Under the patronage of Philip II (reigned 1556–98) an important library of Spanish manuscripts was formed in his monastery palace of El Escorial, and he commissioned his Cronista Real (Historiographer Royal), Ambrosio de Morales (1513–91), to undertake an extended voyage to the north in 1572 to report on the historical materials to be found in the lands of the earlier kingdoms of the Asturias and León. Although his account was not published until 1765, his journey led him to find and publish texts, such as the works of Eulogius of Córdoba (died 859), whose sole manuscript would later be lost. Another important, and more accurate, transcriber of now vanished manuscript sources in this period was Juan Bautista Pérez (1534–97), bishop of Segorbe from 1591, who also successfully detected the forged chronicles that were being circulated by Román de la Higuera. The materials collected by Morales and Pérez were used in 1592 by Juan de Mariana (1536–1624) to write a general history of Spain, *Historia de Rebus Hispaniae* (History of Spanish Affairs; an amended vernacular version appeared in 1601).

The 17th century was in these respects less productive than its predecessor, though it saw the publication of important local histories, such as Francisco de Pisa's *Descripción de la Imperial Ciudad de Toledo* (Description of the Imperial City of Toledo, 1605), and the 1633 *Historia de la Ciudad de Mérida* (History of the City of Mérida) by Bernabé Moreno de Vargas. A by-product of French ambitions at recovering royal authority over Catalunya, formally lost in the 12th century, was the expedition to the region undertaken in 1644 by Pierre de Marca (1584–1662), later archbishop of Narbonne. The appendices to his *Marca Hispanica* (The Spanish March, 1688), edited after his death by Etienne Baluze, contain the first published selection from the extraordinarily rich 9th to 12th century Catalan charter collections.

In the 18th century large-scale projects for the recording of inscriptions and documents, often containing engravings of monuments, became popular. The greatest of these was the series of volumes entitled *España Sagrada* (Sacred Spain, 1751–), initiated by Enrique Flórez (1702–73), and continued after his death by Manuel Risco (1735–1801). A few more volumes were added in the 19th century, and a final trio on the church in Granada came out as recently as 1961. This series was organized by episcopal diocese, and contained a history of each see, reports on notable antiquities, accounts of the individual bishops and the main monasteries of the diocese, and was usually accompanied by appendices of documents. Many historical texts, such as the *Historia Silense* (The Silos History) and numerous charters were first brought to light in this way. On a smaller scale and more topographical was Antonio Ponz's *Viage de España* (Spanish Journey, 1772–94). This was organized geographically and cast in the form of a series of letters to the reader. While Ponz's work is primarily important as a record of archaeological materials since lost, the 22 volumes of Jaime Villanueva's *Viage literario a las iglesias de España* (Literary Journey to the Churches of Spain, 1803–52) constitute a major source for the history of Catalonia. Their appendices contain large numbers of documents, several of which have since been lost, or like so many of the Catalan texts, have never otherwise been published. He also recorded some of bishop Pérez's manuscripts in Segorbe that would later be destroyed in the Civil War of 1936–39.

The writing of accounts of regional centers and their archives was also matched by the publication of documents of central government and of the earliest records of the Spanish church. The writings of the leading ecclesiastical luminaries of the Visigothic period and of the 13th-century archbishop of Toledo, Rodrigo Jiménez de Rada, were edited in four volumes under the patronage of Cardinal Lorenzana, who was also interested in the early Spanish liturgy. Various attempts were also made in the late 18th and early 19th centuries to edit the great collection of canon law known as the *Hispana*. The Visigothic law code, often called the *Forum Iudicum* or in its vernacular form the *Fuero Juzgo*, whose rules continued to apply in some regions of the peninsula up to the 13th century, was first edited in 1815 on the initiative of the Spanish Royal Academy.

After the splendid achievements of late Enlightenment period, the middle of the 19th century was an anticlimax, with hardly any work of note being undertaken, other than in Arab studies. The most notable achievement was the publication of Tomás Muñoz y Romero's *Colección de fueros municipales y cartas pueblas* (Collection of Municipal *fueros* and *cartas pueblas*, 1847), still the only attempt at a comprehensive edition of the medieval *fueros*, the local law codes and deeds of urban foundation. But local antiquarian studies continued to prosper; thus, some very valuable work was done in recording the numerous medieval Asturian inscriptions in the 2-volume *Asturias monumental, epigráfica y diplomática* of Ciriaco Miguel Vigil (Epigraphic and Documentary Monuments of the Asturias), published in 1887. He also produced a pioneering edition of medieval town charters in his *Colección histórico-diplomática del Ayuntamiento de Oviedo* (The Historical Documents of the Town Council of Oviedo, 1889). By this time there was a major revival in historical studies well under way, to which both Spanish and other European scholars contributed. One of the most neglected of these is Eduardo Pérez Pujol, whose 4-volume *Historia de las instituciones sociales de la España goda* (History of the Social Institutions of Gothic Spain) was published posthumously in 1896. This was groundbreaking, as the first sustained attempt to analyze the evidence relating to the Visigothic period, but it did not accord well with the era of introspection and pessimism in Spanish intellectual circles that was ushered in by defeat in the Spanish-American War of 1898.

Interest in such materials followed developments elsewhere in Europe, notably in Germany, where the *Monumenta Germaniae Historica* was extending its editorial activities into ever new fields. One of these was the publication of the law codes of the successor states to Rome. Karl Zeumer (1849–1914) undertook the study of the Visigothic ones, producing an edition of Reccessuinth's version of the *Forum Iudicum* (The Judges' Book) in 1894 and another one of all the versions of that code, together with the preceding one of Euric, in 1902. Other German scholars, notably Paul Ewald in 1878–79, visited Spain to trawl for manuscripts relevant to the *Monumenta*'s editorial plans. Later, Paul Kehr (1860–1944) came to look for papal decretals in Spanish archives, which he then published. Manuscript collections began to be catalogued, such as the Latin codices in the Escorial, described by Guillermo Antolín in five volumes published from 1910, and the manuscripts formerly belonging to the Catalan abbey of Ripoll were painstakingly studied by Rudolf Beer in 1907–08. The medieval vernacular chronicles in the Royal Library in Madrid were first catalogued in 1898 by one of the rising stars of a new generation of medievalists, Ramón Menéndez Pidal (1869–1968), who in the course of a very long life went on to edit the earliest of them, the *Primera Crónica General* (First General Chronicle, 1906), and to produce an enormous body of studies and editions of medieval texts, as well as a classic history of the Spanish language.

These collecting and editorial activities inevitably aroused interest in the distinctive handwriting of early medieval Spanish codices, the so-called Visigothic script, which continued in use in some centers at least until the 13th century. Extracts and transcribed facsimiles began to be published, of which Paul Ewald and G. Loewe's *Exempla scripturae Visigoticae* (Examples of Visigothic Script, 1883) was one of the earliest and best. The first attempts at comprehensive guides to medieval Spanish paleography were those published in 1881 and 1889 by Jesús Muñoz y Rivero, covering the periods of Visigothic and post-Visigothic scripts respectively. These were superseded by the 2-volume *Paleografía Española* (Spanish Paleography, 1923) of Zacarías García Villada, who also catalogued the rich collection of medieval manuscripts in the cathedral of León and began

publishing a history of the Spanish church. This was cut short when he, like a number of other clerical scholars, was murdered in the opening phase of the Spanish Civil War. The authoritative treatment of Spanish medieval paleography is now the three volumes of Agustín Millares Carlo's *Tratado de paleografía española* (Treatise of Spanish Paleography, reprinted 1983), to be supplemented by the numerous codicological studies of Manuel Díaz y Díaz.

Menéndez Pidal, who had been a pupil of the great literary historian Marcelino Menéndez y Pelayo (1856–1912), had in the meantime turned from cataloguing manuscripts to the study of Rodrigo Díaz de Vivar, better known as "El Cid," a mercenary of genius who managed to make himself ruler of Valencia in 1094. Although long known as the subject of a 13th-century verse epic, which Menéndez Pidal edited in three volumes between 1908 and 1912, it was his book on the subject, *La España del Cid* (1929; *The Cid and His Spain*, 1934), that transformed the Cid into a modern Castilian folk hero. In the process he confirmed the view that saw the modern Spanish state as the direct heir of the old Castilian kingdom, validating a tradition of scholarship that concentrated exclusively on the history of the latter and on the two preceding phases of the Asturian (718–910) and Leónese (910–1037) monarchies. This was entirely endorsed by scholars of the next generation such as Claudio Sánchez-Albornoz (1893–1984) and Justo Pérez de Urbel (1895–1976), author of a 3-volume *Historia del Condado de Castilla* (History of the County of Castile, 1945), who became abbot of the monastery founded by Franco to commemorate the Nationalist dead of the Civil War. While their interpretations were based upon a peculiarly inward-looking and exclusively Castilian interpretation of the national history, Pérez de Urbel's book, like that of Menéndez Pidal on the Cid, included large quantities of hitherto unpublished texts in a substantial documentary appendix.

Although the Castilian view of Spanish history was that favored both by the government in Madrid and its approved historians such as Luís García de Valdeavellano, and was also propagated from exile by Sánchez-Albornoz, some regional studies flourished after the Civil War of 1936–39. In Catalunya Fernando Valls-Taberner and Ramón d'Abadal produced a series of important editions of charters and books on the history of the region up to the 12th century. Federico Udina Martorell and his son Antoni Udina i Abelló have followed them in this, and new interpretations of the emergence of Catalunya in the 9th to 11th centuries are being developed by Josep M. Salrach and others. A particularly important contribution to this subject, from outside Spain, is Pierre Bonnassie's thesis *La Catalogne du milieu du Xe à la fin du XIe siècle* (Catalonia from the Middle of the 10th to the End of the 11th Century, 1975–76). Similarly, José María Lacarra, a pupil of Sánchez-Albornoz, published extensively on the medieval history of the Pyrenean regions, and two of his pupils, Angel Martin Duque and Antonio Ubieto Arteta, followed him, producing editions of texts, notably charters, and publishing monographs on the medieval history of Navarre and Aragón respectively. Similar regional schools have developed in Cantabria, the Asturias, Galicia, and León under José Angel García de Cortázar, Juan Ignacio Ruiz de la Peña, Ermelindo Portela, and José María Fernández Catón respectively. All of these have benefited from the intense regionalization of historical studies, together with the growth of political autonomy and localized funding for research and publication that have developed in Spain since the death of Franco in 1975. In some cases this has led to the publication of works in regional dialects, and there has been an outpouring of new editions of texts from regional archives.

While French regional theses of the Annales school are currently highly influential among Spanish medievalists, since the Civil War it has been British and American historians who have been the most active non-Spaniards to engage in the study of Spanish medieval history. The way was led by Evelyn Procter, Derek Lomax, and Peter Russell, who initially devoted themselves to the reign of Alfonso X of Castile (1252–84), the Spanish knightly Order of Santiago, and late 14th-century Anglo-Spanish relations respectively. Jocelyn Hillgarth has written on both the Visigothic and late medieval periods, also editing texts from both, while Peter Linehan began his research into Hispano-papal dealings in the 13th century before writing a major study of Spanish medieval historiography. Alan Forey has worked extensively on the military orders in the peninsula, and on the Templars in the Kingdom of Aragón in particular. Richard Fletcher published a thesis on the bishops of León in the 12th century, and has since turned to the more controversial figures of archbishop Gelmírez of Santiago and the Cid. The first large-scale British contribution to Visigothic studies was E.A. Thompson's *The Goths in Spain* of 1969, which was criticized in Spain for its lack of attention to the views of Sánchez-Albornoz – possibly one of its virtues. Since then Roger Collins has written on the Visigothic period, which in recent Spanish scholarship is being increasingly relegated to the field of ancient rather than medieval history, and on the early medieval period more generally. Among the leading American historians of medieval Spain are Bernard F. Reilly, who has contributed ground-breaking studies of the reigns of the Castilian monarchs Alfonso VI (1072–1109) and Urraca (1109–26) and Thomas N. Bisson, who has unraveled the fiscal and administrative complexities of 11th and 12th century Catalan government, as well as writing a synoptic history, *The Medieval Crown of Aragon* (1986). Robert Ignatius Burns has opened up an entirely new field in his books and editions of documents relating to later 13th-century Valencia.

ROGER COLLINS

See also Burns; Menéndez Pidal; Sánchez-Albornoz

Further Reading

Abadal y Vinyals, Ramón d', *Els primers comtes catalans* (The First Catalan Counts), Barcelona: Teide, 1958

Antolín, Guillermo, *Catálog de los códices latinos de la Real Biblioteca del Escorial* (Catalogue of the Latin Manuscripts of the Royal Library of the Escorial), 5 vols., Madrid: Imprenta Helénica, 1910–23

Beer, Rudolf, *Die handschriften des klosters Santa Maria de Ripoll*, 2 vols., Vienna: Hölder, 1907–08; in Spanish as *Los manuscrits del monastir de Santa María de Ripoll* (The Manuscripts of the Monastery of Santa Maria de Ripoll), Barcelona: Casa Provincial de Caritat, 1910

Bisson, Thomas N., *The Medieval Crown of Aragon: A Short History*, Oxford: Oxford University Press, 1986

Bonnassie, Pierre, *La Catalogne du milieu du Xe à la fin du XIe siècle* (Catalonia from the Middle of the 10th to the End of the 11th Century), Toulouse: Association des Publications de l'Université de Toulouse, 1975–76

Burns, Robert Ignatius, *The Crusader Kingdom of Valencia: Reconstruction of a Thirteenth-Century Frontier*, Cambridge, MA: Harvard University Press, 1967

Collins, Roger, *Early Medieval Spain: Unity in Diversity, 400–1000*, Basingstoke: Macmillan, and New York: St. Martin's Press, 1983

Díaz y Díaz, Manuel C., *Códices visigóticos en la monarquía leonesa* (Visigothic Manuscripts in the Leonese Kingdom), León: Consejo Superior de Investigaciones Científicas, 1983

Ewald, Paul, and Gustavus Loewe, *Exempla scripturae Visigoticae* (Examples of Visigothic Script), Heidelberg, 1883

Fernández Catón, José María, ed., *León y su Historia* (León and Its History), 8 vols., León: Centro de Estudio San Isidoro, 1969–97

Fletcher, Richard, *The Quest for El Cid*, London: Hutchinson, and New York: Knopf, 1989

Flórez, Enrique, and Manuel Risco, *España Sagrada* (Sacred Spain), 56 vols., 1751–1961

Forey, Alan, *The Templars in the "Corona de Aragón,"* London: Oxford University Press, 1973

García de Cortázar, José Angel, and Carmen Díez Herrera, *La formación de la sociedad hispano-cristiana del Cantábrico al Ebro en los siglos VIII al XI* (The Formation of Hispano-Christian Society Between Cantabrio and the Ebro in the 8th to the 11th Centuries), Santander: Estudio, 1982

García Villada, Zacarías, *Paleografía Española* (Spanish Palaeography), 2 vols., Madrid: Revista de Filología Española, 1923

Hillgarth, J.N., *The Spanish Kingdoms, 1250–1516*, 2 vols., Oxford: Oxford University Press, 1976–78

Historia Silense (The Silos History), Madrid: Rivadeneyra, 1921

Kehr, Paul, *Das Papsttum und der katalanische Prinzipat bis zur Vereinigung mit Aragon* (The Papacy and the Principality of Catalonia up to the Union with Aragon), Berlin: de Gruyter, 1926

Lacarra, José María, *Vasconia medieval*, San Sebastián: Diputación Provincial de Gupázcoa, 1951

Linehan, Peter, *History and the Historians of Medieval Spain*, Oxford and New York: Oxford University Press, 1993

Lomax, Derek, *La orden de Santiago, 1170–1275* (The Order of Santiago), Madrid: Consejo Superior de Investigaciones Científicas, 1965

Marca, Pierre de, *Marca Hispanica* (The Spanish March), edited by Etienne Baluze, 1688; reprinted Barcelona: Base, 1972

Mariana, Juan de, *Historia de Rebus Hispaniae* (History of Spanish Affairs), 1601

Mariana, Juan de, *Historia general de España* (A General History of Spain), 2 vols., Toledo: Rodriguez, 1601

Martín Duque, Angel J., ed., *Documentación medieval de Leire (siglos IX al XII)* (The Medieval Documents of the [Monastery of] Leire, 9th to 12th Centuries), Pamplona: Diputación Foral de Navarra, 1983

Menéndez Pidal, Ramón, ed., *Primera Crónica General: estoria de España que mondó componer Alfonso el Sabio y se continuaba bajo sancho 4 en 1289* (First General Chronicle), Madrid: Bailly-Bailliére, 1906

Menéndez Pidal, Ramón, *La España del Cid*, 2 vols., Madrid: Plutarco, 1929; in English as *The Cid and His Spain*, London: Murray, 1934

Miguel Vigil, Ciriaco, *Asturias monumental, epigráfica y diplomática: datas los para la historia de la provincia* (Epigraphic and Documentary Monuments of the Asturias), Oviedo: Valdés, 1887

Miguel Vigil, Ciriaco, *Colección histórico-diplomática del Ayuntamiento de Oviedo* (The Historical Documents of the Town Council of Oviedo), Oviedo: Imprimerie de Pardo, Gusano y compa, 1889

Millares Carlo, Agustín, *Tratado de paleografía española* (Treatise of Spanish Paleography), 3 vols., Madrid: Hernando, 1929, revised 1932; reprinted 1983

Moreno de Vargas, Bernabé, *Historia de la Ciudad de Mérida: dedicada à la misma ciudad* (History of the City of Mérida), Madrid: Taso, 1633; reprinted 1892

Muñoz y Rivero, Jesús, *Paleografía visigoda* (Visigothic Paleography), Madrid: Guirnalda, 1881; reprinted 1919

Muñoz y Romero, Tomás, *Colección de fueros municipales y cartas pueblas de las[sic] reinos de Castilla, León Crono de Aragón y Navarra* (Collection of Municipal *fueros* and *cartas pueblas* of the Kingdoms of Castile, León, Aragon, and Navarra), Madrid: Alonso, 1847

Pérez de Urbel, Justo, *Historia del Condado de Castilla* (History of the County of Castile), 3 vols., Madrid: Consejo Superior de Investigaciones Científicas, Escuela de Estudios Medievales, 1945

Pérez Pujol, Eduardo, *Historia de las instituciones sociales de la España goda* (History of the Social Institutions of Gothic Spain), 4 vols., Valencia: Vives Mora, 1896

Pisa, Francisco de, *Descripción de la Imperial Ciudad de Toledo* (Description of the Imperial City of Toledo), Toledo: Rodriguez, 1605

Ponz, Antonio, *Viage de España, o cartas en que sedá noticia de las cosas masappreciables, y dignas de saberse que hay en ella* (Spanish Journey), 18 vols., Madrid: Ibarra, 1772–94

Portela, Ermelindo, "La propriedad, el trabajo y los frutos de la tierra en la Galicia medieval, 900–1300" (Property, Work, and the Fruits of the Earth in Medieval Galicia), *Estudios Compostelos* 5 (1978), 156–200

Procter, Evelyn S., *Curia and Cortes in León and Castile, 1072–1295*, Cambridge and New York: Cambridge University Press, 1980

Reilly, Bernard F., *The Kingdom of León-Castilla under Queen Urraca, 1109–1126*, Princeton: Princeton University Press, 1982

Ruiz de la Peña, Juan Ignacio, *Las "polas" asturianas en la Edad Media estudio y diplomatano* (The Asturian "polas" in the Middle Ages), Oviedo: Universidad de Oviedo, 1981

Russell, Peter Edward, *The English Intervention in Spain and Portugal in the Time of Edward III and Richard II*, Oxford: Oxford University Press, 1955

Salrach i Marbes, Josep M., *El procés de formació nacional de Catalunya* (The Process of National Formation in Catalunya), 2 vols., Barcelona: Edicions 62, 1978

Sánchez Alonso, Benito, *Historia de la historiografía española: ensayo de un examen de conjunto* (History of Spanish Historiography), 2 vols., Madrid: Sánchez de Ocaña, 1941–50

Sánchez-Albornoz, Claudio, *Estudios sobre las instituciones medievales españolas* (Studies on Medieval Spanish Institutions), Mexico City: Universidad Nacional Autonoma de Mexico, Instituto de Investigaciones Historicas, 1965

Thompson, E.A., *The Goths in Spain*, Oxford: Oxford University Press, 1969

Ubieto Arteta, Antonio, *Coleción diplomatica de Pedro I de Aragón y Navarra* (The Documents of Pedro I of Aragon and Navarra), Zaragoza: Consejo Superior de Investigaciones Cientícas, 1951

Udina i Abelló, Antoni M., *La successió testada a la Catalunya altomedieval* (Inheritance by Will in Early Medieval Catalonia), Barcelona: Fundació Noguera, 1984

Udina i Martorell, Frederic, *El archivo condal de Barcelona en los siglo IX–X* (The Comital Archive of Barcelona in the 9th and 10th Centuries), Barcelona: Consejo Superior de Investigaciones Cientícas, 1951

Valdeavellano, Luís García de, *Historia de España*, vol. 1: *De los orígenes a la baja edad media* (History of Spain, vol. 1: From the Origins to the Late Middle Ages), Madrid: Revista de Occidente, 1952

Valls-Taberner, Fernando, ed., *Los usatges de Barcelona* (The Customs of Barcelona), Barcelona: Imprenta de la Casa Provinciale Caritat, 1913; reprinted 1984

Villanueva, Jaime, *Viage literario a las iglesias de España: le publica con algunas observaciones Don Joachquin Lorenzo Villanueva* (Literary Journey to the Churches of Spain), 22 vols., Madrid: Imprenta Real, 1803–52

Zeumer, Karl, ed., *Forum Iudicum* (The Judges' Book), 1894

Zeumer, Karl, ed., *Leges Visigothorum* (Laws of the Visigoths), 1902

Spain: Imperial

Few topics are of more importance to the history of the Western world than is the narrative of imperial Spain. While the Iberian peninsula played only a marginal role in defining the character of medieval Christendom, the unification of the crowns of Aragon and Castile – brought about by the marriage of Ferdinand and Isabella in 1469 – combined with the final destruction of an organized Moorish polity in Europe to catapult Castile into a pivotal role in European politics. This prominence was transformed into a veritable hegemony a generation later when Charles V inherited the imperial title of the Holy Roman empire and became the monarch of a unified Spain.

Added to this, the discovery of the Americas by a Castilian agent (Christopher Columbus) and the conquest of the Aztec and Inca empires by Castilian adventurers provided Spain with a vast geographical reach and with hitherto incomparable resources. During the 16th and 17th centuries the Spanish experience directly and indirectly influenced political events, economic trends, and social and cultural developments throughout Europe and the Americas.

As may be expected, such a complex experience has generated a rich and diverse literature as scholars have struggled to come to terms with the significance and depth of imperial Spanish history. Studies on imperial Spain have figured prominently in the key interpretive models that have defined the historical understanding of early modern Europe and of colonial America. These models can be divided into several different categories: 1) institutional, political, and intellectual studies delimited by the nation-state with a focus on the causality of events, actors, and ideas; 2) studies rooted in the assumption that material/economic forces provide the most effective measure of historical causality and those that attempt to identify the long-term trends influencing the Spanish experience; and 3) studies seeking to bring the methodologies and insights of the two previous modes of interpretation to investigations of the structures, trends, and qualities of Spanish society – frequently identifying a specific social sector or professional caste as the locus of study.

In general, all these studies have taken as their subject either European Spain or the Spanish colonies with only occasional examples looking effectively at both sides of the Atlantic. In recent years the reciprocal impact of Spain on the Americas and the Americas on Spain has begun to be studied with more interest, and the trend is toward identifying key tendencies and structures that betray the intercontinental influences on the Spanish experience – and by extension on that of Europe in general.

Studies inspired by the scientific mode of historical inquiry, pioneered by the 19th-century liberal historians, focused on the political narrative and the institutional structures of imperial Spain. These studies established the outline of what happened, who was responsible for the most notable events of the period and the institutional structures within which major governmental decisions were made. The classic studies of this type are Merriman's *The Rise of the Spanish Empire in the Old World and the New* (1918–34) and Ranke's *Fürsten und Völker* (1827–36; *The Ottoman and the Spanish Empires, in the Sixteenth and Seventeenth Centuries*, 1843). W.H. Prescott's *History of the Reign of Ferdinand and Isabella* (1838) remains a noteworthy source on this important period of consolidation. For Spain in America, C.H. Haring's *The Spanish Empire in America* (1947) is the standard institutional study, while J.H. Parry's *The Age of Reconnaissance* (1963) is essential reading for an understanding of the Hispanic expansion into the New World. On the establishment of the Catholic church in Spanish America, Robert Ricard's *La "conquête spirituelle" du Mexique* (1933; *The Spiritual Conquest of Mexico*, 1966) provides the starting point for all future discussions of the church. For the church in Spain, H.C. Lea's *A History of the Inquisition in Spain* (1906–07) placed ecclesiastical institutional history on an impeccable documentary footing; this work remains an indispensable source for researches into the Inquisition and the Catholic church in Spain. His work on the Inquisition in the Americas is also an important source.

Closely related to this institutional approach are the investigations into the intellectual history of the period – typically emphasizing the impact on Spain of the dominant philosophical currents of the period and identifying the individuals who were the most influential in articulating an Iberian response to these trends. The most notable example of this type of examination is Marcel Bataillon's *Erasmo y España* (Erasmus and Spain, 1950) an expanded translation of his *Erasme et l'Espagne* (1937). This work looked at the impact of the humanist tradition on Spanish intellectual life and pointed to its influence on such pivotal events as the reforms of Cisneros and on the formation of the ideology of the Franciscan friars who undertook the initial evangelization of Mexico. Studies of the American intellectual and religious environment have been strongly influenced by the work of Lewis Hanke, in particular his examination of the ideas and impact of Bartolomé de Las Casas in *The Spanish Struggle for Justice in the Conquest of America* (1949). Silvio Zavala has also written extensively on this subject; his *La filosofía política en la conquista de América* (1947; *The Political Philosophy of the Conquest of America*, 1953) is a comprehensive and erudite source that complements the work of Hanke.

These studies of the institutional, political, and intellectual structures of imperial Spain mapped out the essential contours of the Spanish experience of this period. But they typically paid little or no attention to the economic and social forces that were also at play. The importance of economic trends came to provide one of the key themes by which Spanish history was integrated into the European experience and into an understanding of historical processes extending beyond the bounds of the Spanish nation-state. One of the first economic studies, was Earl J. Hamilton's *American Treasure and the Price Revolution in Spain, 1501–1650* (1934). In this work he identified the impact that the influx of American silver had on the economy of Spain and Europe and pointed the way to looking at America, Spain, and Europe as integral parts of an economic system that transcended the individual boundaries of each.

Hamilton's focus on economic causality added an important dimension to the picture offered by the traditional institutional studies, but he stopped short of identifying it as an essential historical process. This latter point of view, inspired by Marxist philosophy, underlay the methodology of the Annales school and gave an impetus to the creation of several seminal works on imperial Spain. In *La Méditerranée et le monde méditerranéen à l'époque de Philippe II* (1949; revised 1966; *The Mediterranean and the Mediterranean World in the Age of Philip II*, 1972–73) Fernand Braudel examined the material, economic, and social structures that gave shape to the apogee of Spain's influence. And while he used the Spanish context as his focal point, he effectively articulated the character of the multilayered material processes – social, economic, and political – that influenced every aspect of life in early modern Europe.

Working within the same conceptual framework, Pierre and Huguette Chaunu in *Séville et l'Atlantique* (Seville and the Atlantic, 1955–60) extended the circle of influences to incorporate the interaction between the twin economic spheres of Spain and its American empire. The Chaunus' work also updated many of Hamilton's observations on the inflationary impact of American silver. Elaborating an even broader conceptual framework, Wallerstein in *The Modern World-System* (1974–89) pointed to the era of Spain's hegemony as the key era in the formation of the modern global economy. This he characterized as being divided between the core states (initially Spain but moving to Holland and eventually to Great Britain) and the peripheral arenas (the fringes of Europe, America, and eventually the rest of the world); with the balance of power residing decisively within the core areas.

Related to these broad economic histories in their focus on material historical causality are several works whose goal was to establish the character of the demographic movements of this period. In Spain, reliable population figures were developed by Jorge Nadal in *La población española* (The Spanish Population, 1973). The impact of the epidemic of 1596–1602 is laid out by Bartolomé Bennassar, *Recherches sur les grandes épidémies dans le Nord de l'Espagne à la fin du XVIe siècle* (Research on the Great Epidemics of Northern Spain at the End of the 16th Century, 1969). Also useful are works by Bernard Vincent, Halperín Donghi, and Caro Baroja. In America, the devastating post-conquest population decline of the indigenous population in Mexico was traced by Sherburne F. Cook and Woodrow Borah in their *Essays in Population History* (1971–79). The parallel decline in the highlands of Peru and Bolivia has been studied by Noble David Cook in *Demographic Collapse* (1981) and by Nicolás Sánchez Albornoz in *La población de América Latina* (1973; *The Population of Latin America*, 1974).

While the economic historians established the manner in which Spain interacted with large impersonal historical processes, other historians began to look in other directions to map out some of the details of local society and the characteristics of specific social classes. The numerous works of Antonio Domínguez Ortiz provide the core of this type of study. Most notable are his *The Golden Age of Spain, 1516–1659* (1971), *El Antiguo Régimen* (The Ancien Régime, 1973), and *La sociedad española en el siglo XVII* (Spanish Society in the 17th Century, 1963–70). Bartolomé Bennassar's *L'Homme espagnol* (1975; *The Spanish Character*, 1979) took an anecdotal look at the peculiarities of the inner life of "typical" Spanish social types in an attempt to define the elusive quality of national character. In a more analytical style, Richard L. Kagan's *Students and Society in Early Modern Spain* (1974) and his *Lawsuits and Litigants in Castile, 1500–1700* (1981) examined the social origins, stature, and prospects of the *letrado* or clerical class – the clerks who staffed the imperial bureaucracy, and identified the role they played within the larger dynamic of Spanish society.

The technique of examining social processes by focusing on a narrowly defined geographical region or social group also has been employed with significant success for the Spanish empire in America. The pioneering studies of Charles Gibson – *Tlaxcala in the Sixteenth Century* (1952) and *The Aztecs under Spanish Rule* (1964) – possessed the dual distinction of articulating on the one hand the dynamism and significance of the social forces active at the municipal level of political organization and on the other of incorporating sophisticated ethnographic material into the analysis. James Lockhart, inspired by this model, demonstrated the effectiveness of collective biography in his *Men of Cajamarca* (1972) and developed a sophisticated picture of the social networks characteristic of the viceregal capital of Peru in *Spanish Peru, 1532–1560* (1968). William B. Taylor's *Landlord and Peasant in Colonial Oaxaca* (1972) carried this type of micro-regional analysis into the south of Mexico, while his *Drinking, Homicide, and Rebellion in Colonial Mexican Villages* (1979) demonstrated the possibility of identifying the social functions and values associated with antisocial behaviors. Also of vital importance in the development of a complete picture of colonial society are the recent studies on the role of women. The works of Asunción Lavrin, *Sexuality and Marriage in Colonial Latin America* (1989); Irene Silverblatt, *Moon, Sun, and Witches* (1987); and Susan Socolow and Louisa Hoberman, *Cities and Society in Colonial Latin America* (1986), among others, have laid the groundwork for an investigation into gender issues and their impact on societal processes.

As valuable as these micro-analyses are in bringing to life the patterns and details of imperial and colonial society, their very conception points to the necessity of weaving the details of the locality into a larger pattern that encompasses the whole of the imperial experience. Several authors have begun the difficult process of developing a synthesis of material that integrates the American and the European experiences. The pioneering work of this type is John Elliott's brief but portentous *The Old World and the New* (1970). A more traditional effort at synthesis is John Lynch's *Spain under the Habsburgs* (1964–69). Lockhart and Schwartz's *Early Latin America* (1983) looked to the cultural structures inherited from Spain and from indigenous America to explain the character of the colonial experience. Lyle McAlister's *Spain and Portugal in the New World, 1492–1700* (1984) integrated the European and indigenous American experience into his comprehensive analysis of the first 200 years of Iberian hegemony in America. Other works, most notably Anthony Pagden's *The Fall of Natural Man* (1982) and *Spanish Imperialism and the Political Imagination* (1990), and David Brading's *The First America* (1991), through an examination of the intellectual context of imperial Spain have emphasized the intimate linkages between metropolis and colony and have pointed to the necessity of understanding the quality of the experience on both sides of the Atlantic.

LINCOLN A. DRAPER

See also Borah; Braudel; Domínguez Ortiz; Elliott; European Expansion; Gibson; Hanke; Las Casas; Latin America: Colonial; Lavrin; Lea; Prescott; Ranke; Sánchez-Albornoz

Further Reading

Bataillon, Marcel, *Erasme et l'Espagne* (Erasmus and Spain), Paris: Droz, 1937; expanded as *Erasmo y España*, 2 vols., Mexico City: Fondo de Cultura Económica, 1950

Bennassar, Bartolomé, *Recherches sur les grandes épidémies dans le Nord de l'Espagne à la fin du XVIe siècle: problèmes de documentation et de méthode* (Research on the Great Epidemics of Northern Spain at the End of the 16th Century: Problems of Documentation and Method), Paris: SEVPEN, 1969

Bennassar, Bartolomé, *L'Homme espagnol: attitudes et mentalités du XVIe au XIXe siècle*, Paris: Hachette, 1975; in English as *The Spanish Character: Attitudes and Mentalities from the Sixteenth to the Nineteenth Century*, Berkeley: University of California Press, 1979

Brading, David A., *The First America: The Spanish Monarchy, Creole Patriots, and the Liberal State, 1492–1867*, Cambridge and New York: Cambridge University Press, 1991

Braudel, Fernand, *La Méditerranée et le monde méditerranéen à l'époque de Philippe II*, 2 vols., Paris: Colin, 1949, revised 1966; in English as *The Mediterranean and the Mediterranean World in the Age of Philip II*, 2 vols., London: Collins, and New York: Harper, 1972–73

Chaunu, Pierre, and Huguette Chaunu, *Séville et l'Atlantique, 1504–1650* (Seville and the Atlantic), 8 vols., Paris: Colin, 1955–60

Cook, Noble David, *Demographic Collapse: Indian Peru, 1520–1620*, Cambridge and New York: Cambridge University Press, 1981

Cook, Sherburne F., and Woodrow Borah, *Essays in Population History: Mexico and the Caribbean*, 3 vols., Berkeley: University of California Press, 1971–79

Domínguez Ortiz, Antonio, *La sociedad española en el siglo XVII* (Spanish Society in the 17th Century), 2 vols., Madrid: Consejo Superior de Investigaciones Científicas, 1963–70; reprinted 1992

Domínguez Ortiz, Antonio, *The Golden Age of Spain, 1516–1659*, London: Weidenfeld and Nicolson, and New York: Basic Books, 1971

Domínguez Ortiz, Antonio, *El Antiguo Régimen: los Reyes Católicos y los Austrias* (The *Ancien Régime*: The Catholic Kings and the Habsburgs), Madrid: Alianza, 1973

Elliott, J.H., *The Old World and the New, 1492–1650*, Cambridge: Cambridge University Press, 1970

Gibson, Charles, *Tlaxcala in the Sixteenth Century*, New Haven: Yale University Press, 1952

Gibson, Charles, *The Aztecs under Spanish Rule: A History of the Indians of the Valley of Mexico, 1519–1810*, Stanford, CA: Stanford University Press, 1964

Hamilton, Earl J., *American Treasure and the Price Revolution in Spain, 1501–1650*, Cambridge, MA: Harvard University Press, 1934

Hanke, Lewis, *The Spanish Struggle for Justice in the Conquest of America*, Philadelphia: University of Pennsylvania Press, 1949

Haring, Clarence Henry, *The Spanish Empire in America*, New York: Oxford University Press, 1947

Kagan, Richard L., *Students and Society in Early Modern Spain*, Baltimore: Johns Hopkins University Press, 1974

Kagan, Richard L., *Lawsuits and Litigants in Castile, 1500–1700*, Chapel Hill: University of North Carolina Press, 1981

Lavrin, Asunción, ed., *Sexuality and Marriage in Colonial Latin America*, Lincoln: University of Nebraska Press, 1989

Lea, Henry Charles, *A History of the Inquisition in Spain*, 4 vols., New York and London: Macmillan, 1906–07

Lockhart, James, *Spanish Peru, 1532–1560: A Colonial Society*, Madison: University of Wisconsin Press, 1968

Lockhart, James, *Men of Cajamarca: A Social and Biographical Study of the First Conquerors of Peru*, Austin: University of Texas Press, 1972

Lockhart, James, and Stuart B. Schwartz, *Early Latin America: A History of Colonial Spanish America and Brazil*, Cambridge and New York: Cambridge University Press, 1983

Lynch, John, *Spain under the Habsburgs*, 2 vols., New York: Oxford University Press, and Oxford: Blackwell, 1964–69

McAlister, Lyle, *Spain and Portugal in the New World, 1492–1700*, Minneapolis: University of Minnesota Press, 1984

Merriman, Roger Bigelow, *The Rise of the Spanish Empire in the Old World and the New*, 4 vols., New York: Macmillan, 1918–34; reprinted 1962

Nadal Oller, Jorge, *La población española (siglos XVI a XX)* (The Spanish Population from the 16th to the 20th Centuries), Barcelona: Ariel, 1973

Pagden, Anthony, *The Fall of Natural Man: The American Indian and the Origins of Comparative Ethnology*, Cambridge and New York: Cambridge University Press, 1982

Pagden, Anthony, *Spanish Imperialism and the Political Imagination: Studies in European and Spanish-American Social and Political Theory, 1513–1830*, New Haven: Yale University Press, 1990

Parry, J.H., *The Age of Reconnaissance*, Cleveland: World, and London: Weidenfeld and Nicolson, 1963

Prescott, William H., *History of the Reign of Ferdinand and Isabella*, 2 vols., New York: Burt, 1838; London: Routledge, 1841

Ranke, Leopold von, *Fürsten und Völker von Süd-Europa im sechzehnten und siebzehnten Jahrhundert*, Hamburg: Perthes, 1827–36; in English as *The Ottoman and the Spanish Empires, in the Sixteenth and Seventeenth Centuries*, London: Whittaker, 1843; New York: AMS, 1975

Ricard, Robert, *La "conquête spirituelle" du Mexique: essai sur l'apostolat et les méthodes missionaires des ordres mendicants en nouvelle Espagne de 1523–24 à 1572*, Paris: Institut d'ethnologie, 1933; in English as *The Spiritual Conquest of Mexico: A Essay on the Apostolates and the Evangelizing Methods of the Mendicant Orders in New Spain, 1523–1572*, Berkeley: University of California Press, 1966

Sánchez Albornoz, Nicolás, *La población de América Latina: desde los tiempos pre-colombinos al año 2000*, Madrid: Alianza, 1973; in English as *The Population of Latin America: A History*, Berkeley: University of California Press, 1974

Silverblatt, Irene, *Moon, Sun, and Witches: Gender Ideologies and Class in Inca and Colonial Peru*, Princeton: Princeton University Press, 1987

Socolow, Susan Migden, and Louisa Schell Hoberman, *Cities and Society in Colonial Latin America*, Albuquerque: University of New Mexico Press, 1986

Taylor, William B., *Landlord and Peasant in Colonial Oaxaca*, Stanford, CA: Stanford University Press, 1972

Taylor, William B., *Drinking, Homicide, and Rebellion in Colonial Mexican Villages*, Stanford, CA: Stanford University Press, 1979

Wallerstein, Immanuel, *The Modern World-System*, 3 vols., New York and London: Academic Press, 1974–89

Zavala, Silvio, *La filosofía política en la conquista de América*, Mexico City: Fondo de Cultura Económica, 1947; in English as *The Political Philosophy of the Conquest of America*, Mexico City: Cultura, 1953

Spain: Modern (since 1808)

The historiography of modern Spain has long labored in the shadow of its more popular siblings, the medieval and early modern periods. In fact, until quite recently the historiography of modern Spain was largely ignored. The topics favored by Spanish historians treated Spain's rise and fall as a world power based on the creation, growth, eventual decline, and loss of its vast overseas empire. Moreover, the methodologies used to study Spanish history were dated, focusing on traditional narratives that highlighted political, diplomatic, and intellectual history. Rafael Altamira y Crevea's 5-volume *Historia de España y de la civilización española* (1900–30; *A History of Spanish Civilization*, 1930) and Américo Castro's *La realidad histórica de España* (The Realities of Spanish History, 1954) are examples of this traditional methodology.

The root causes of such a historical tradition are many, but two are particularly important when we refer to the modern period. First, from 1939 to 1975 Spain suffered under the intellectual oppression of the Franco dictatorship. As a result the writing of history and the topics deemed suitable for historical research were under fairly close government scrutiny. According to Shubert and Kagan in their introduction to the Spain and Portugal section of *The American Historical Association's Guide to Historical Literature* (1995), centralized control of research funding and *catedráticos* (senior professors who direct research projects and act as patrons for young scholars) who were apologists for, or subservient to, the regime, combined to curtail new historical approaches and contrary historical interpretations by marginalizing them. Second, historians developed an interest in explaining Spain's apparent failure to modernize as other European countries such as Britain, Germany, and France had done. They pointed to the 19th century and Spain's comparative economic stagnation, near constant political upheaval, and rebellious national character to advance the idea of Spanish exceptionalism. In short, Spaniards and their political culture were fundamentally different from other Europeans. Shubert and Kagan contended that the Franco regime used this idea "as a means of self-justification: their people were ill-suited for such 'foreign' inventions as democracy and required a different political solution, more congruent with national traditions." This resulted in the development of a national historiography isolated from the broader European context.

The traditional historiography of modern Spain began to change with the work of Jaime Vicens Vives and his "Barcelona school," especially his ground-breaking *Aproximación a la historia de España* (1952; *Approaches to the History of Spain*, 1967). Vicens Vives was Spain's first "modern historian," meaning his work was less polemic, less narrative than his predecessors and it was based on intensive archival research. Vicens Vives introduced Spanish historiography to research methods long used by historians outside of Spain. He believed history was more than a stylish prose narrative of great men and great events embellished by rhetorical virtuosity. Vicens Vives did this in three ways: first, he sought to verify historical events by testing them quantitatively against the social and economic developments of the period. Second, he never lost sight of the interpretive nature of the historian's craft. He did not select facts which fit his own interpretation, rather he interpreted the facts his archival research turned up. Finally, he was acutely aware of the impact of the past on the present and future (as Joan Connelly Ullman argued in the foreword to the second edition of *Approaches*). Thus, his history is political in the sense that it inevitably confronts the reader with the problem of historical relevance. In short, his work revolutionized the way history was conceived and carried out in Spain. Vicens Vives' work was cut short by his death in 1960. Josep Fontana continues the work of Vicens Vives' Barcelona school with its attention to archival resources, quantitative rigor, and the relationship between socio-economic development and Spanish politics.

Fontana's key contribution in this regard is his *La quiebra de la Monarquia Absoluta, 1814–1820* (The Failure of the Absolute Monarchy, 1971).

In the 1960s foreign scholarship, particularly English-language scholars, continued the evolution of modern Spanish history. Here, the seminal work was Raymond Carr's exhaustive *Spain, 1808–1975* (1966; revised as *Spain, 1808–1975*, 1982). In it, Carr examined the birth and development of liberalism from the Napoleonic interlude through the end of the Franco regime. Carr's work represented the first systematic effort (in English) to place Spanish history in its broader European context while fusing the political, social, and economic history of the period into one sensible narrative. Despite its age, and its biases, the work still stands as the best single-volume survey of modern Spain.

Other notable scholars of the period are Stanley Payne, Richard Herr, Pierre Vilar, Gabriel Jackson, and Hugh Thomas. Of these, the most prolific is Payne who has tackled a wide variety of topics from a conservative perspective. His work has consistently elucidated the motivations of the Spanish political right. Payne's writings have responded to a tradition in Spanish historiography that offered sympathetic treatments of the Spanish political left. Therefore, Payne's contributions have "balanced" the narrative and broadened the discourse of modern Spanish history. A less pessimistic approach than Carr and Payne is found in Richard Herr's classic *Spain* (1971; revised as *An Historical Essay on Modern Spain*, 1974). Herr, best known for his examination of the Spanish Enlightenment in *The Eighteenth Century Revolution in Spain* (1958), also attempted to explain the trials and tribulations of the efforts to implant lasting representative government in Spain by Spanish liberals. On this subject Herr's survey was not as extensive as Carr's but profited from an astute synthesis of personal experience and command of the secondary literature. Pierre Vilar wrote *Crecimiento y desarrollo* (Growth and Development, 1964) and *Histoire de L'Espagne* (1947; *Spain: A Brief History*, 1967) which combined the tradition of the Barcelona school with the reflective, geosocial approach of the Annales school of French historians pioneered by Fernand Braudel and Marc Bloch. Together, Carr, Payne, and Herr revolutionized Spanish historiography by moving away from the quantitative approach of Vicens Vives and the Barcelona school. Their work highlighted the human element in history and represented the earliest attempts at what would become the social and cultural history approaches of the 1970s and later.

While Carr and Herr surveyed the modern period as a whole and Payne dealt with the political right, Gabriel Jackson and Hugh Thomas were writing more specific and, perhaps, more polemic histories of the most controversial period in Spanish history – the 1930s. Jackson's *The Spanish Republic and the Civil War, 1931–1939* (1965) and Thomas' *The Spanish Civil War* (1961; revised 1977) opened the national calamity of the Second Republic and the Spanish Civil War to "modern" historical scrutiny. Of the two, Thomas' account is a more comprehensive treatment of the war, its battles, and the military strategy of both sides in the conflict. Thomas also strove for an even-handed treatment of the Loyalist (the legitimate Republican government) and Nationalist (Franco's right-wing insurgents) and was reasonably successful, no small feat given a topic that still arouses heated debate today. Conversely,

Jackson made no attempt at historical objectivity. He persuasively demonstrated, from a Marxist perspective, the complicity of the political right in the downfall of the Second Republic and in the Civil War. While slightly dated, Jackson's treatment remains fundamental to any serious study of the period because of its passionate style, brilliant analysis of the conflict's causes, and his portrayal of the international situation in which the Spanish Second Republic struggled.

Since the 1970s historical research on modern Spain has grown dramatically, in no small part owing to the more relaxed intellectual and social environment of the post-Franco years (the old dictator died in 1975). Historians of the last quarter-century have furthered the close, analytical studies of relatively narrow historical periods pioneered by Jackson, including the notion of the historian as subjective interpreter of historical events. Moreover, these historians have introduced new methods (social and cultural history, especially political culture) and fresh perspectives (a less pessimistic comparative evaluation of Spain since 1808), including opening up the 19th century to more intensive scholarly research. Notable among them are Manuel Tuñon de Lara and his now-famous Pau colloquia, David Ringrose, Edward Malefakis, Carolyn P. Boyd, and Martin Blinkhorn.

Manuel Tuñon de Lara was a journalist in Spain and was active in the socialist youth groups during the Spanish Civil War. He left Spain for France during the repressive years of the Franco regime and turned to history, studying and producing his thesis under the direction of Pierre Vilar. His first book, *La España del siglo XIX* (19th-Century Spain, 1960; revised 1981), was an overview of the 19th century written from a Marxist perspective. It was an immediate success with members of the anti-Franco opposition in Spain. As a result, beginning around 1970, Tuñon organized regular meetings of historians of the opposition, called the Pau colloquia, from his post at the University of Pau in southern France. These colloquia produced a number of books, for example, on the agrarian question and the crisis of the *ancien régime*, and Tuñon continued his own work on 19th-century Spain. However, the greater significance of the Pau colloquia was that they brought together a number of the country's great historians in an intellectually friendly environment. A list of the attendees includes Antonio Maria Calero, Manuel Perez Ledesma, Miguel Artola, and José Luis Delgado, and reads like a who's who of modern Spanish history. Furthermore, the colloquia provided an important base of contact with Catalan historians such as Josep Termes, Albert Balcells, and Josep Fontana. These colloquia kept the historical profession current during a time when serious historical study was not encouraged.

While the Pau colloquia put its stamp on Spanish history, foreign scholars continued to investigate previously under-explored topics. David Ringrose exposed the dominance of Madrid and its effects on the Spanish economy in two important works, *Transportation and Economic Stagnation in Spain, 1750–1850* (1970) and *Madrid and the Spanish Economy, 1560–1850* (1983). His recently published *Spain, Europe, and the "Spanish Miracle," 1700–1900* (1996) is a masterful synthesis of the latest research in the field and revised long outmoded paradigms about the economic, social, and political backwardness of Spain, focusing on the 19th century as a period of steady growth. The Spanish economy was also the subject of Edward Malefakis' insightful *Agrarian Reform and Peasant Revolution in Spain* (1970) in which he lucidly wove together the historical roots of the agrarian question, land tenure patterns, a hopelessly divided political system, and the deleterious effect of the agrarian crisis on the Second Republic. Ringrose and Malefakis are necessary reading for a complete understanding of contemporary Spain. For an analysis of the origins of the Spanish military's involvement in the nation's politics, of which the Spanish Civil War and the Franco regime are but the latest example, see Carolyn P. Boyd's excellent study, *Praetorian Politics in Liberal Spain* (1979). An understanding of the political opposition faced by the Second Republic is found in Martin Blinkhorn's *Carlism and Crisis in Spain, 1931–1939* (1975) and *Spain in Conflict, 1931–1939* (1986). Of these, the earlier work is better for its elucidation of the political machinations of the Carlists just prior to the outbreak of civil war.

During the 1980s Spain's transition to democracy (acknowledged by Spain's admittance into the EEC [later the European Union] in 1986) substantively changed the climate for historical research. A number of historians seized the opportunity to produce monographs of major importance, books that would have been impossible to write a mere decade sooner. The most prolific writer of this generation is Paul Preston. Preston's work provides a nice counterpoint to Stanley Payne's conservative treatment of Spanish history. Preston is a liberal historian whose efforts highlight the Spanish political left, which is apparent from the earliest works in his career, *Revolution and War in Spain, 1931–1939* (1984) and *The Triumph of Democracy in Spain* (1986), to his latest, *The Coming of the Spanish Civil War* (revised 1994). The differences in historical perspective and methodology between Preston and Payne are never more apparent than in their treatment of the Franco regime: Preston excoriated the regime, while Payne was almost apologetic about the Franco era. Preston's work, however, is methodologically standard political narrative.

The work of Adrian Shubert and José Alvarez Junco approached modern Spanish history from more challenging historical perspectives. Shubert has extended the influence of the social history approach to Spain in his *The Road to Revolution in Spain* (1987), *A Social History of Modern Spain* (1990), and *Spain at War* (with George Esenwein, 1995). Shubert's work also highlights the importance and formative nature of the 19th century, a period conspicuously neglected by previous historians of Spain. Similarly, José Alvarez Junco's work has also opened up the 19th century to more extensive scholarly research. His specialty is the development of Spanish political culture, especially of the working class. Alvarez Junco's compiled volumes, *Populismo, caudillaje y discurso demagógico* (Populism, Political Bossism, and Demagogic Discourse, 1987) and *El movimiento obrero en la historia de Cádiz* (The Workers' Movement in the History of Cádiz, 1988), and his monographs *La ideología política del anarquismo español, 1868–1910* (The Political Ideology of Spanish Anarchism, 1976), and *El emperador del Paralelo* (The Emperor of the Paralelo, 1990) have underscored the political education of the Spanish working classes that began in the last third of the 19th century.

Given the preceding pedigree, the future of modern Spanish history is bright. The modern period will no longer be overshadowed by the historians and histories of the medieval and early modern periods. The 1990s, in fact, will witness a further extension of the methodological experimentation evident in the work cited here. A new crop of talented scholars is at work in the Spanish archives and the recently published work of Jesus Cruz, *Gentlemen, Bourgeois, and Revolutionaries* (1996), and Pamela B. Radcliff, *From Mobilization to Civil War* (1996) attest to the quality and diversity of their work. Moreover, new edited volumes such as Helen Graham and Jo Labanyi's *Spanish Cultural Studies* (1995) promise to introduce Spanish history to interdisciplinary research, while bringing it to a wider, popular reading audience. Undoubtedly the most important element of the recent scholarship on modern Spain, evident in the latest publications of Shubert and Ringrose and an integral assumption of the newest scholarship of Cruz and Radcliff, is its attempt to normalize Spain's past. This work will permanently lay to rest the shopworn popular historical adage that "Europe ends at the Pyrenees." Spain will be written back into the mainstream history of modern Europe, a history too often thought of as encompassing only the national histories of Britain, France, and Germany. This more inclusive version of European history is welcome and long overdue.

DAVID ORTIZ, JR.

See also Carr, R.; Castro; Thomas, H.

Further Reading

Altamira y Crevea, Rafael, *Historia de España y de la civilización española*, 5 vols., Barcelona: Gili, 1900–30; in English as *A History of Spanish Civilization*, London: Constable, 1930

Alvarez Junco, José, *La ideología política del anarquismo español, 1868–1910* (The Political Ideology of Spanish Anarchism), Madrid: Siglo XXI de España Editores, 1976

Alvarez Junco, José, *Populismo, caudillaje y discurso demagógico* (Populism, Political Bossism, and Demagogic Discourse), Madrid: Centro de Investigaciones Sociológicas: Siglo XXI de España, 1987

Alvarez Junco, José, ed., *El movimiento obrero en la historia de Cádiz* (The Workers' Movement in the History of Cádiz), Cádiz: Diputacion Provincial de Cádiz, 1988

Alvarez Junco, José, *El emperador del Paralelo: Lerroux y la demagogia populista* (The Emperor of the Paralelo: Lerroux and Populist Demagoguery), Madrid: Alianza, 1990

Blinkhorn, Martin, *Carlism and Crisis in Spain, 1931–1939*, Cambridge and New York: Cambridge University Press, 1975

Blinkhorn, Martin, ed., *Spain in Conflict, 1931–1939: Democracy and Its Enemies*, Beverly Hills, CA: Sage, 1986

Boyd, Carolyn P., *Praetorian Politics in Liberal Spain*, Chapel Hill: University of North Carolina Press, 1979

Carr, Raymond, *Spain, 1808–1939*, Oxford: Oxford University Press, 1966; revised as *Spain, 1808–1975*, 1982

Castro, Américo, *La realidad histórica de España* (The Realities of Spanish History), Mexico City: Porrúa, 1954, revised 1962; 8th edition, 1982

Cruz, Jesus, *Gentlemen, Bourgeois, and Revolutionaries: Political Change and Cultural Persistence among the Spanish Dominant Groups, 1750–1850*, Cambridge: Cambridge University Press, 1996

Fontana i Làzard, Josep, *La quiebra de la Monarquia Absoluta, 1814–1820* (The Failure of the Absolute Monarchy), Barcelona: Ariel, 1971

Graham, Helen, and Jo Labanyi, *Spanish Cultural Studies, An Introduction: The Struggle for Modernity*, Oxford and New York: Oxford University Press, 1995

Herr, Richard, *The Eighteenth Century Revolution in Spain*, Princeton: Princeton University Press, 1958

Herr, Richard, *Spain*, Englewood Cliffs, NJ: Prentice Hall, 1971; revised as *An Historical Essay on Modern Spain*, Berkeley: University of California Press, 1974

Jackson, Gabriel, *The Spanish Republic and the Civil War, 1931–1939*, Princeton: Princeton University Press, 1965

Malefakis, Edward, *Agrarian Reform and Peasant Revolution in Spain: Origins of the Civil War*, New Haven: Yale University Press, 1970

Payne, Stanley, *Falange: A History of Spanish Fascism*, Stanford, CA: Stanford University Press, and London: Oxford University Press, 1961

Payne, Stanley, *Politics and the Military in Modern Spain*, Stanford, CA: Stanford University Press, 1967

Payne, Stanley, *Basque Nationalism*, Reno: University of Nevada Press, 1975

Payne, Stanley, *Spanish Catholicism: An Historical Overview*, Madison: University of Wisconsin Press, 1984

Payne, Stanley, *The Franco Regime, 1936–1975*, Madison: University of Wisconsin Press, 1987

Payne, Stanley, *Spain's First Democracy: The Second Republic, 1931–1936*, Madison: University of Wisconsin Press, 1993

Payne, Stanley, *The Spanish Revolution*, London: HarperCollins, 1993; New York: Basic Books, 1994

Preston, Paul, *The Coming of the Spanish Civil War: Reform, Reaction, and Revolution in the Second Republic, 1931–1936*, London: Macmillan, and New York: Barnes and Noble, 1978; revised London and New York: Routledge, 1994

Preston, Paul, *Revolution and War in Spain, 1931–1939*, Oxford and New York: Oxford University Press, 1984

Preston, Paul, *The Spanish Civil War, 1936–1939*, London: Weidenfeld and Nicolson, and New York: Grove Press, 1986

Preston, Paul, *The Triumph of Democracy in Spain*, London and New York: Methuen, 1986

Preston, Paul, *Salvador de Madariaga and the Quest for Liberty in Spain*, Oxford: Oxford University Press, 1987

Preston, Paul, *The Politics of Revenge: Fascism and the Military in Twentieth Century Spain*, London and Boston: Unwin Hyman, 1990

Preston, Paul, ed., *Franco: A Biography*, London and New York: Methuen, 1993

Radcliff, Pamela B., *From Mobilization to Civil War: The Politics of Polarization in the Spanish City of Gijón, 1900–1937*, Cambridge and New York: Cambridge University Press, 1996

Ringrose, David, *Transportation and Economic Stagnation in Spain, 1750–1850*, Durham, NC: Duke University Press, 1970

Ringrose, David, *Madrid and the Spanish Economy, 1560–1850*, Berkeley: University of California Press, 1983

Ringrose, David, *Spain, Europe, and the "Spanish Miracle," 1700–1900*, Cambridge and New York: Cambridge University Press, 1996

Shubert, Adrian, *The Road to Revolution in Spain: The Coal Mines of Asturias, 1860–1934*, Urbana: University of Illinois Press, 1987

Shubert, Adrian, *A Social History of Modern Spain*, London and Boston: Unwin Hyman, 1990

Shubert, Adrian, and Richard L. Kagan, "Spain and Portugal," in Mary Beth Norton, ed., *The American Historical Association's Guide to Historical Literature*, New York and Oxford: Oxford University Press, 1995

Shubert, Adrian, and George Esenwein, *Spain at War: The Spanish Civil War in Context, 1931–39*, London and New York: Longman, 1995

Thomas, Hugh, *The Spanish Civil War*, New York: Harper, and London: Eyre and Spottiswoode, 1961; 3rd edition, Harper and London: Penguin, 1977

Tuñon de Lara, Manuel, *La España del siglo XIX, 1808–1914* (19th-Century Spain), Paris: Club del libro Español, 1960; revised 1981

Tuñon de Lara, Manuel, *Medio siglo de cultura Española* (Half a Century of Spanish Culture), Madrid: Tecnos, 1970

Tuñon de Lara, Manuel, *Estudios sobre el siglo XIX español* (Spanish 19th-Century Studies), Madrid: Siglo XXI de España, 1971

Tuñon de Lara, Manuel, ed., *La Cuestion agraria en al España contemporánea* (The Agrarian Question in Contemporary Spain), Madrid: Cuadernos Para el Diálogo, 1976

Tuñon de Lara, Manuel, ed., *De la crisis del antiguo régimen al franquismo* (From the Crisis of the Old Regime to Francoism), Madrid: Cuadernos Para el Diálogo, 1977

Vicens Vives, Jaime, *Aproximación a la historia de España*, Barcelona: Viñetas de J.M. Rovira Brull, 1952; in English as *Approaches to the History of Spain*, Berkeley: University of California Press, 1967; revised 1970

Vilar, Pierre, *Crecimiento y desarrollo: economia e historia, reflexiones sobre el caso español* (Growth and Development: Economy and History, Reflections on the Spanish Case), Barcelona: Ariel, 1964

Vilar, Pierre, *Histoire de L'Espagne*, Paris: Presses Universitaires de France, 1947; in English as *Spain: A Brief History*, Oxford and New York: Pergamon Press, 1967

Spence, Jonathan D. 1936–

British historian of China

Jonathan Spence is an academic historian of great erudition whose works cross the boundary into popular history, an author whose wide-ranging output and interests cover the entire spectrum of Chinese history, with a strong early concentration on the Manchu period. An Englishman, a product of Winchester and Cambridge, in 1959 Spence came to Yale University to pursue graduate work in history and – apart from extensive periods as a visiting professor at assorted prestigious institutions – has spent the remainder of his career there. In 1988 his work was also recognized by a MacArthur Foundation "genius" award.

While Spence's work is extremely broad in scope, ranging over all periods and aspects of Chinese history, one continuing theme has been the encounter between China and the West, from the time of Marco Polo to the present. An examination of this interaction lies at the heart of several of his works, including *To Change China* (1969), *The Memory Palace of Matteo Ricci* (1984), *The Question of Hu* (1988), and *God's Chinese Son* (1996), and plays an important role in *The Gate of Heavenly Peace* (1981) and *The Search for Modern China* (1990).

A pronounced feature of much of Spence's oeuvre is his stress on the biographical. Indeed, his critics and detractors have claimed that he has overemphasized the exploration of fascinating individual histories and offbeat anecdotes and details to the detriment of broader analysis, while his admirers have argued that his sensitivity to the interplay of the individual and society is a particular strength of his writing. His first work, *Ts'ao Yin and the K'ang-hsi Emperor: Bondservant and Master* (1966), explored the relationship between one of the most prominent Manchu emperors and one of his leading officials, not only depicting the two protagonists but giving a broad-brush picture of the early Ch'ing state and society. Spence made the emperor's own writings available in *Emperor of China: Self-Portrait of K'ang-hsi* (1974). *To Change China* con-centrated upon the generally ill-fated and often ill-considered attempts of Westerners from the 16th century onward to bring about major change in China, while *The Memory Palace of Matteo Ricci* focused upon one of first Jesuits to attempt to win the Chinese over to Western ways. The latter was also distinguished by the stylistic device of structuring the book around assorted images linked to Ricci's own mnemonic system. *The Death of Woman Wang* (1978) employed a legal case involving the 17th-century murder of an adulterous Chinese wife to illuminate the entire legal and social system of an obscure province of the time. *The Question of Hu* was an imaginative reconstruction of the story of a 17th-century Chinese Roman Catholic convert who, when brought to France by his Jesuit patron, appeared overcome by madness, and was ultimately repatriated to China. Spence's penchant for inventing interior monologues and ascribing thoughts and actions to his main characters in the two latter and highly readable works led some historians to question his methodology and suggest that such works constituted novels rather than history. The most recent of such biographical works was *God's Chinese Son*, a study of the life and times of the 19th-century Chinese peasant rebel who claimed to be Jesus Christ's younger brother and came close to overturning the Ch'ing dynasty.

Spence's bestselling *The Gate of Heavenly Peace* was a much broader work, attempting to illuminate the entire sweep of the Chinese reform movement from the mid-19th century until 1980 through the careers of three Chinese intellectuals, the political activist and theorist Kang Youwei, the writer Lu Xun, and the novelist and feminist Ding Ling, together with some of their associates. It was followed by a still more ambitious narrative account of the past 400 years of Chinese history, *The Search for Modern China*. Like its predecessor this immensely readable and entertaining volume, a treasure-trove of odd and entertaining facts and snippets of information which synthesized a whole field of scholarship, became a bestseller, winning several major prizes and awards, though some academic historians criticized it for emphasizing narrative rather than analysis and in some cases suggested that it took too kind a view of the years of Mao Zedong's rule. Spence's recent pictorial history of the last century of Chinese history won high praise for both its informative text and its excellent selection of photographs.

Today Spence is one of the most prominent and oft-cited historians of China, his expertise drawn on by such popular journals as *Time*, *Newsweek*, and the *New York Times*. He frequently writes reviews for the *New York Review of Books* which range over the entire span of Chinese history with, it seems, a particular concentration upon those relating to contemporary or near-contemporary Chinese affairs. His articles on the current Chinese scene are also published in the *New Yorker*. An assortment of Spence's essays on widely disparate subjects were collected in *Chinese Roundabout* (1992). Among contemporary sinologists he is distinguished by his appeal to a non-academic audience, to whom he has made the history of China accessible; the breadth of his interests; and his refreshing readiness to break new ground and follow unconventional and unexplored historical trails wherever they may lead.

PRISCILLA M. ROBERTS

See also China: Late Imperial; China: Modern

Biography

Jonathan Dermot Spence. Born Surrey, England, 11 August 1936. Educated at Winchester College; BA, Cambridge University, 1959; PhD, Yale University, 1965. Taught at Yale University from 1965. Served in the British Army, 1954–56. Married 1) Helen Alexander, 1962 (marriage dissolved 1993; 2 sons); 2) Chin Ann-ping, 1993.

Principal Writings

Ts'ao Yin and the K'ang-hsi Emperor: Bondservant and Master, 1966; 2nd edition 1988

To Change China: Western Advisers in China, 1620–1960, 1969; in UK as *The China Helpers: Western Advisers in China, 1620–1960*, 1969

Emperor of China: Self-Portrait of K'ang-hsi, 1974; as *K'ang-hsi: Emperor of China*, 1974

The Death of Woman Wang, 1978

The Gate of Heavenly Peace: The Chinese and Their Revolution, 1895–1980, 1981

The Memory Palace of Matteo Ricci, 1984

The Question of Hu, 1988

The Search for Modern China, 1990

Chinese Roundabout: Essays in History and Culture, 1992

The Chinese Century: A Photographic History of the Last Hundred Years, 1996

God's Chinese Son: The Taiping Heavenly Kingdom of Hong Xiuquan, 1996

The Chan's Great Continent: China in Western Minds, 1998

Further Reading

Mazlish, Bruce, "The Question of The Question of Hu," *History and Theory* 31 (1992), 143–52

Mirsky, Jonathan, review of *Chinese Roundabout*, *New York Review of Books* 39/18 (5 November 1992), 51–53

Nathan, Andrew J., "A Culture of Cruelty: Review of *The Search for Modern China*," *New Republic* 203 (30 July 1990), 30–34

Spengler, Oswald 1880–1936

German historian

Oswald Spengler gained fame and notoriety with the publication of his *Der Untergang des Abendlandes* (1918–22; *The Decline of the West*, 1926–28). With these two volumes, he significantly transformed German historiography and, to a lesser extent, altered the philosophical landscape of Western historiography.

In 1911 Spengler gave up teaching and began working on *The Decline of the West*. Almost immediately, the work became widely popular within Germany. More than 100,000 copies were quickly sold. Spengler's rejection of historical morality and his message of prophetic doom found a receptive audience in the minds of Germans reeling from the humiliation of defeat in World War I and fearful of the future. His work emphasized the hollowness of the Allied victory and absolved human guilt by consigning events to the workings of a fate-driven cycle of history. As the full extent of the catastrophe of the war became evident, Spengler's work spread throughout the West. His forceful message especially appealed to the angst-driven societies of the postwar years because he articulated the fears and doubts of the era and offered a vision of the future. Although his popular reception declined after about 1924 and none of his other works were even remotely as successful as

The Decline of the West, these first two volumes continued to influence Western historiography.

Spengler was not a trained historian. At best, his status was that of amateur historian, and his work reflects this. When he formed his ideas, he borrowed Goethe's intuitive approach to history and his organic analogy of cultures. However, Spengler developed these approaches into a forceful system that rejected the benefits of scientific methodology and in general attacked the Hegelian system. Spengler adamantly opposed the concept of Hegel's progressive world history that would supposedly culminate in a divinely ordained realization of "freedom" based on a universal acceptance of right and law. Following in Nietzsche's footsteps, he also disavowed Hegel's reliance on reason and logic. Spengler claimed there was no such thing as an "absolute truth." Truth was relative and based solely on the criteria of individual cultures. Instead, Spengler argued that history was composed of flux and development and therefore, by its very nature, could not be measured in terms of quantitative analysis. By his definition a true historian could not be trained. He believed that history had to be interpreted through an innate, intuitive process, that bypassed logic, yet revealed the spirit of the culture studied.

Spengler also rejected a linear concept of history that was composed of ancient, medieval, and modern eras. He described this system as a "linear tapeworm" blindly attaching epochs one after the other. Instead, he stressed that each culture was a distinct human expression with its own spirit and its own unique abilities. Each culture had to be studied as a separate entity and not as a forerunner to the modern world.

All of these tenets were synthesized into one philosophy of history in Spengler's *The Decline of the West*. In that work he presented eight separate "high cultures" of the human race: the Egyptian, the Chinese, the Babylonian, the Indian, the Mayan, the Magian (Semitic and Islamic), the Greco-Roman and the ominously labeled Faustian (the modern West). All of these cultures were presented as distinct entities, fundamentally separate from each other. Each culture was no less important than any other and each was presented in a morphological manner. Each culture was treated as a living organism with a limited life cycle of approximately one thousand years. Using the analogy of a plant, Spengler described a culture's development as originating in the unique matrix of its mother soil, followed by growth, blossoming with creativity, and then eventually fading into death. Civilization itself was a final manifestation marked by the death of creativity, the erosion of the ideals and morality that energized that culture, the spread of materialism, the growth of cities that broke down the community spirit of the population, and the spread of tyrannies and endemic warfare. In prophetic fashion, Spengler explained that our modern world was now in the phase of decay and that our cultural demise was both inevitable and imminent.

Spengler's philosophy immediately attracted criticism. His message, methodology, and dogmatic style were all attacked. Critics claimed that his fatalistic philosophy ignored the divine and that it seemed an invitation to barbarism. Later, both proponents and opponents of Nazism saw his philosophy as a contributing factor in the rise of fascism and totalitarianism. His methodology was ravaged by professional historians who correctly pointed out the many historical errors present in his work, the misuse of comparative analogies between cultures,

the flaws inherent in his cyclical morphological model, and his exaggeration of the separateness of all eight cultures. His pretentious style was described as too rigid and inflexible and wholly unacceptable for an academic work. In fact, many historians now view his work as mainly allegorical poetry and little else.

Despite these significant criticisms, Spengler's work still exerts a substantial influence. His masterwork does address a substantial change in the philosophy of history and the world at large. His attack on the progressive, positive outlook toward the future was not an aberration. Instead, it proved to be the clarion call of the 20th century. Few historians today continue to present an idealistic portrayal of the future without, at least, acknowledging the dangers inherent in our technology and our industrial lifestyle. Furthermore, historians now realize that an all-encompassing world history is probably impossible. They concede that individual cultures do exhibit certain unique qualities and expressions that can be accurately evaluated only within the context of that particular culture. Western norms, and even Western logic cannot be blindly superimposed over other cultures. This realization illustrates the continuing worth of Spengler's flawed, yet pioneering, masterwork.

FRED HOOVER

See also Comparative; Febvre; McNeill; Metahistory; Nietzsche; Philosophy of History; Toynbee; Universal; World

Biography

Oswald Arnold Gottfried Spengler. Born Blankenburg am Harz, Prussia, 29 May 1880, son of a postal inspector. Studied mathematics, natural sciences, and philosophy, universities of Hamburg, Berlin, and Halle; received PhD, 1904. Schoolteacher in Düsseldorf, 1906–07; and Hamburg, 1908–11; independent writer from 1911. Died Munich, 8 May 1936.

Principal Writings

Der Untergang des Abendlandes: Umrisse einer Morphologie der Weltgeschichte, 2 vols., 1918–22; in English as *The Decline of the West*, 2 vols., 1926–28
Der Mensch und die Technik: Beitrag zu einer Philosophie des Lebens, 1931; in English as *Man and Technics: A Contribution to the Philosophy of Life*, 1932
Jahre der Entscheidung, 1933; in English as *The Hour of Decision*, 1934

Further Reading

Fischer, Klaus P., *History and Prophecy: Oswald Spengler and The Decline of the West*, Durham, NC: Moore, 1977
Hughes, H. Stuart, *Oswald Spengler: A Critical Estimate*, New York: Scribner, 1952

Sport, History of

Most sports history offers perspectives on the cultural history of ordinary people. Perhaps this is why for many years academics shied away from the subject, leaving the field to journalists and enthusiastic amateurs whose celebratory, nostalgic, often anecdotal, and generally uncritical approach helped sustain the belief that sports history was part of the historical baggage not wanted on any serious academic voyage. Later, especially in the United States and Australasia, physical educators embraced the subject but again many of them were untrained as historians leading to works of narrative rather than analysis, though their empirical bricks contributed to the foundations of the academic sub-discipline status to which sports history can now lay claim. Although, as in any branch of history, pedestrian, unanalytic studies still abound, the overall standard of sports history has risen significantly, an improvement appreciated by university presses and quality commercial publishers.

The transformation has resulted from a combination of factors: the general move toward "history from below"; the boom in social history toward which sports history gravitates despite contributions from economic and political historians; and the expansion of the sports industry coupled with a growing awareness of its impact on society.

In North America sports history emerged out of physical education, perhaps because of the important role that sport has in American tertiary educational institutions. Much of the early work was synthesized in John R. Betts' *America's Sporting Heritage* (1974). Australia too had a tradition of sports history by physical educators, although historian Bill Mandle undertook a pioneering role with his study of sporting nationalism. In contrast, despite individual exceptions such as Peter McIntosh, physical educators in Britain have not been to the fore in sports history. This is partly a reflection of the British approach to sport which has tended to define it as competitive games rather than general physical culture. European sports history has had the advantage of regional and national government involvement both in sport itself (which has resulted in the existence of substantial state archives) and in sports history where inquiries into the origin and development of sport have been officially sanctioned and subsidized.

Sports history has accrued the trappings of academic credibility via the establishment of societies with associated journals and conferences. The North American Society for Sports History (NASSH) was founded in 1972 and publishes the *Journal of Sports History*, one of the most cited historical journals in the United States. Also published in North America is the *Canadian Journal of the History of Sport* which predated the *Journal of Sports History* by a year and emanated from the University of Windsor until 1995, when its editorship switched to the University of Western Ontario and its title changed to *Sports History Review*. NASSH also launched an international book award whose winners provide a quality English-language bibliography. Beginning in 1989 with Wray Vamplew's *Pay Up and Play the Game* (1988), successive awards have gone to Warren Goldstein's *Playing For Keeps* (1989), Harold Seymour's *Baseball: The People's Game* (1990), Allen Guttmann's *Women's Sports* (1991), Peter Levine's *Ellis Island to Ebbets Field* (1992), Robert Edelman's *Serious Fun* (1993), Susan Cahn's *Coming on Strong* (1994), Robin Lester's *Stagg's University* (1995), and Bruce Kidd's *The Struggle for Canadian Sport* (1996).

The International Society for the History of Physical Education and Sport (ISHPES) emerged in 1989 from the amalgamation of two distinct organizations – the International Committee for the History of Physical Education and Sport (ICOSH) and the International Association for the History of

Physical Education and Sport (HISPA). ICOSH had been founded in Prague in 1967 and HISPA in Zurich in 1973. The two groups came to represent the East and the West and their widely different approaches both to history and to sport. Today ISHPES acts as an umbrella organization for sports historians around the world, uniting all national and regional bodies. In particular it works to promote exchanges of information and cooperative research across national boundaries.

Although founded in 1983, the British Society for Sport History did not possess its own journal, *The Sports Historian*, until 1993, but it had issued a Bulletin of Conference Proceedings from its inception. That the *British Journal of Sports History* (the *International Journal of Sports History* from 1987) was a separate commercial venture has hindered the development of BSSH. In 1994 the Association of Sports Historians was formed to cater for academic and amateur sports historians with the publication of *Sporting Heritage*.

The current pacesetter is the proactive Australian Society for Sports History, founded in 1983 and beginning the publication of *Sporting Traditions* a year later. Collectively its members have established a Studies in Sports History series, participated in television documentary production and written *The Oxford Companion to Australian Sport*, edited by Vamplew et al. (1992).

That sports history is a relatively recent arrival on the academic scene means that, despite considerable progress, there are still many major gaps to be filled – not least, particularly outside North America – the role of race and gender. Attention should also be given to losing, the most typical sports experience, as a counterbalance in a historical world often obsessed with winners. More comparative work needs to be undertaken. Of course sports historians have made temporal comparisons but there has been a reluctance to undertake inter-sport and international comparisons, so that the sports-specific can be distinguished from the cultural-specific.

Another aspect of sports history is the sports museum. Unfortunately most are of the Hall of Fame variety, and like the commercial ventures associated with professional sports clubs, tend to emphasize ludic rather than social history. Generally they present champions without warts and championships with no political or social context.

Finally, despite criticisms levied earlier, the contribution of the amateur sports historian should not be denigrated. The work of such enthusiasts, be they compilers of cricket statistics, supporters of particular football clubs, or collectors of local sports minutiae, can provide the empirical evidence for testing academic hypotheses. Moreover, it is often these writers and their journalistic counterparts, rather than the academic sports historian, who best convey the drama and excitement of sport.

WRAY VAMPLEW

See also Leisure

Further Reading

Baker, William J., *Sports in the Western World*, Totowa, NJ: Rowman and Littlefield, 1982; revised Urbana: University of Illinois Press, 1988

Betts, John Rickards, *America's Sporting Heritage, 1850–1950*, Reading, MA: Addison Wesley, 1974

Cahn, Susan K., *Coming on Strong: Gender and Sexuality in Twentieth-Century Women's Sport*, New York: Free Press, 1994

Edelman, Robert, *Serious Fun: A History of Spectator Sports in the USSR*, New York: Oxford University Press, 1993

Eisenberg, Christiane, "The Middle Class and Competition: Some Considerations on the Beginnings of Modern Sport in England and Germany," *International Journal of the History of Sport* 7 (1990), 265–82

Goldstein, Warren, *Playing for Keeps: A History of Early Baseball*, Ithaca, NY: Cornell University Press, 1989

Guttmann, Allen, *From Ritual to Record: The Nature of Modern Sports*, New York: Columbia University Press, 1978

Guttmann, Allen, *Women's Sports: A History*, New York: Columbia University Press, 1991

Holt, Richard, *Sport and the British: A Modern History*, Oxford and New York: Oxford University Press, 1989

Holt, Richard, "Sport and History: The State of the Subject in Britain," *Twentieth Century British History* 7 (1996), 231–52

Kidd, Bruce, *The Struggle for Canadian Sport*, Toronto: University of Toronto Press, 1996

Lester, Robin, *Stagg's University: The Rise, Decline, and Fall of Big-Time Football in Chicago*, Urbana: University of Illinois Press, 1995

Levine, Peter, *Ellis Island to Ebbets Field: Sport and the American Jewish Experience*, New York: Oxford University Press, 1992

McIntosh, Peter C., *Sport in Society*, London: C.A. Watts, 1963

Mandell, Richard, *The Nazi Olympics*, New York: Macmillan, 1971; London: Souvenir Press, 1972

Mandle, William F., "Cricket and Australian Nationalism in the 19th Century," *Transactions: The Journal of the Royal Australian Historical Society* 59 (1973), 225–46

Mason, Tony, ed., *Sport in Britain: A Social History*, Cambridge and New York: Cambridge University Press, 1989

Seymour, Harold, *Baseball: The People's Game*, New York: Oxford University Press, 1990

Vamplew, Wray, *Pay Up and Play the Game: Professional Sport in Britain, 1875–1914*, Cambridge and New York: Cambridge University Press, 1988

Vamplew, Wray, Katharine Moore, John O'Hara, Richard Cashman, and Ian Jobling, eds., *The Oxford Companion to Australian Sport*, Oxford, Melbourne and New York: Oxford University Press, 1992

Vamplew, Wray, and Brian Stoddart, eds., *Sport in Australia: A Social History*, Cambridge and New York: Cambridge University Press, 1994

Vigarello, Georges, *Une Histoire culturelle du sport* (A Cultural History of Sport), Paris: Robert-Laffont, 1988

Spriano, Paolo 1925–1988
Italian political historian

At a very young age Paolo Spriano joined the resistance movement of Giustizia e Libertà, and in 1946 the Italian Communist party (PCI), to which he bound his public and academic life. Spriano belonged to that generation of historians who traveled to historical research from antifascism and the resistance. This seemed to confirm Croce's affirmation that history is always contemporary history, perhaps even rooted in personal experience or *Erlebnis*. The best proof of that can be found in his choice of research topics. Spriano started his career as a journalist. From 1948 he wrote for the PCI official newspaper, *L'Unità*, reaching academia late in life. His first studies were on Gobetti, Gramsci, and working-class Turin, approached from a broader cultural awareness than that acquired from the orthodox texts of Third International Marxism.

His beginnings were in Turin, where he trained as a historian and focused his research on the local industrial working class, influenced by the legacy of the local writers Italo Calvino and Primo Levi. He concentrated particularly on the period from 1892 to the occupation of factories by the workers in 1920, on the eve of the birth of the PCI. His method was rooted in archival research: he compared primary material in the State Central Archive in Rome (especially police reports), and that at the PCI archive.

Spriano moved to Rome in 1955 and combined his political activism with journalism. He collected the memoirs of his most important period of political militancy in *Le passioni di un decennio, 1946–1956* (Passions of a Decade, 1946–1956, 1986). In it he evaluated what he considered to be the most important years in his life. This work was followed by the unfinished study, later published by *L'Unità*, about the efforts to save Gramsci from death in the fascist prisons. *Le passioni* deals with his experiences on the cultural weekly *Il contemporaneo*, which lasted from 1954 to 1957, his dissent from the PCI when it approved of the Soviet invasion of Hungary, and his firm decision to remain in the party when so many intellectuals took that opportunity to resign. From 1957 he focused his efforts as a scholar and a political activist on the anti-Stalinist debate and on the centrality of the PCI in its fight against fascism, its involvement in the resistance movement, the building of the Republic, and the establishment of democracy.

Spriano continued to operate in this cultural and political environment, conceiving and carrying out what remains his great achievement: *Storia del Partito Comunista Italiano* (History of the Italian Communist Party, 1968–75). From today's perspective, this work may look dated, if not hagiographic; it was certainly part of a militant agenda. When it was first published, concurrently with Renzo de Felice's work on Mussolini, it served to restore to their proper place leaders such as Bordiga or Tasca, who until then had often been erased from the official histories of the PCI. In this work Spriano explored primary sources, but was criticized by the communist leader Giorgio Amendola for having shown more interest in the party's ruling establishment than in the rank and file. Nevertheless the *Storia* was innovative, if not from a methodological point of view, then from its critical knowledge of communist primary sources. Spriano achieved this by exploiting his position as both a PCI executive and as a scholar. He could make use of the archival resources of the PCI (generally closed to outsiders); this served his needs as a historian, and put an end to the subordination of historical truth to the "official" version. In spite of his revisionism Spriano was often described by the press as the "official historian of the PCI" (the word "official" concealing a critical reservation) and as a "liberal communist," partly heterodox and partly revisionist, for which he was looked upon with suspicion by the communist orthodoxy of Eastern Europe which, without censuring his works, tried to limit their diffusion.

In his final years Spriano devoted himself to teaching. As a lecturer he had a special relationship with his students, which included members of the PCI youth organization, the FGCI. To them, through his real enjoyment of teaching, he left a legacy of love for political democracy as a universal value and the rejection of Soviet socialism. Later he redirected his attention to key postwar periods of socialist history from a historiographical and autobiographical point of view. He continued to exploit his political expertise, as a long-standing member of the Central Committee of the PCI, and his intellectual acumen to promote historical research on the themes that always fascinated him: the "New Party," the "Turning-point of 1956," and the "Italian way to socialism."

GENNARO CAROTENUTO

Biography

Born Turin, 30 November 1925. Member, Italian Communist party (PCI), 1946–88. Journalist, *L'Unità*, from 1948; and *Il contemporaneo*, 1954–57. Professor, University of Cagliari. Died 1988.

Principal Writings

L'occupazione delle fabbriche, Settembre 1920, 1964; in English as *The Occupation of the Factories: Italy, 1920*, 1975

Storia del Partito Comunista Italiano (History of the Italian Communist Party), 5 vols., 1968–75

Gramsci in carcere e il Partito, 1977; in English as *Antonio Gramsci and the Party: The Prison Years*, 1979

I comunisti europei e Stalin, 1983; in English as *Stalin and the European Communists*, 1985

Le passioni di un decennio, 1946–1956 (Passions of a Decade, 1946–1956), 1986

Spruill, Julia Cherry 1899–1986

US women's historian

Julia Cherry Spruill published one book in her career as a historian: *Women's Life and Work in the Southern Colonies* (1938). After graduating with a master's degree in history from the University of North Carolina, Spruill secured a grant from the Institute for Research in the Social Sciences and began a study of women's daily lives and their status in the English colonies of the South. In her research, Spruill answered the call of Arthur M. Schlesinger, Sr., who observed in his *New Viewpoints in American History* (1922) that "if the silence of the historians is taken to mean anything, it would appear that one-half of our population have been negligible factors in our country's history."

Spruill's work was path-breaking since it addressed the lives of ordinary women. By using colonial newspapers, court records, and manuscript materials to reconstruct colonial society, she crafted a classic work in early American social history. Spruill's scholarship was unique on at least two fronts: first, in addressing the lives of women and their families, and second, in the type of research she conducted in original materials. The women who emerged as a result of Spruill's work were strikingly different from those who had occasionally appeared in earlier histories. Keepers of the home, women were also active participants in public life, teaching schools, managing plantations and businesses, and practicing medicine. Spruill pioneered a tactic in her writing now widely used by social historians: using the words of individuals and their contemporaries to tell the story of the past. By finding out so much from such a variety of sources about women in the colonial South, Spruill showed tenacity, patience, and innovation.

More than a decade of research went into the creation of *Women's Life and Work in the Southern Colonies*, which was preceded by five articles. Each corresponded with a segment or chapter of Spruill's book, which was published to critical acclaim from reviewers including Eudora Ramsay Richardson and Mary R. Beard. Philip Davidson, writing for the *Journal of Southern History*, praised the book as the product of "serious, prolonged research . . . presented clearly, lucidly, and soberly." Spruill's work, he concluded, was "a grand study of women, and by women, but for everybody." "Here is a book for which the feminists have been waiting," proclaimed Eudora Ramsay Richardson, director of the New Deal's Virginia Writers Project. Reviewing for the *William and Mary Quarterly*, Richardson heralded the book as a welcome antidote to the existing works on colonial history, written by men interested primarily in "martial matters and in statecraft" who had effectively "expunged women's work from the record." Richardson urged historians to read Spruill's work for enjoyment, then keep it nearby for reference: "It should be in the libraries of all intelligent women," she concluded, "where husbands may have easy access to the entertaining and profitable information it contains."

Women's Life and Work in the Southern Colonies was Spruill's only book. After its publication, she occasionally reviewed books for scholarly periodicals and taught part-time at the University of North Carolina. This classic work of social history was the first comprehensive study of women in the colonial South. Spruill's meticulous research opened the way for the study of women and of colonial society as a whole, marking the path for Anne Firor Scott and others who followed.

JENNIFER DAVIS MCDAID

Biography

Born Rocky Mount, North Carolina, 8 January 1899. Attended North Carolina State Normal and Industrial School, 1915–20; received MA, University of North Carolina, 1923. Taught at Rocky Mount High School, 1920–22; and Chapel Hill High School, 1924; research assistant, Institute for Research in the Social Sciences, 1923: part-time instructor in social sciences to 1949. Married Corydon Spruill, economist, 1922. Died Chapel Hill, 27 January 1986.

Principal Writings

"Mistress Margaret Brent, Spinster," *Maryland Historical Magazine* 29 (1934), 259–68

"The Southern Lady's Library, 1770–1776," *South Atlantic Quarterly* 34 (1935), 23–41

"Virginia and Carolina Homes before the Revolution," *North Carolina Historical Review* 12 (1935), 320–40

"Southern Housewives before the Revolution," *North Carolina Historical Review* 13 (1936), 25–46

"Women in the Founding of the Southern Colonies," *North Carolina Historical Review* 13 (1936), 202–18

Women's Life and Work in the Southern Colonies, 1938

Further Reading

Hall, Jacquelyn Dowd, and Anne Firor Scott, "Women in the South," in John B. Boles and Evelyn Thomas Nolen, eds., *Interpreting Southern History: Historiographical Essays in Honor of Sanford W. Higginbotham*, Baton Rouge: Louisiana State University Press, 1987

Scott, Anne Firor, "Historians Construct the Southern Woman," in Joanne V. Hawks and Sheila L. Skemp, eds., *Sex, Race, and the Role of Women in the South: Essays*, Jackson: University Press of Mississippi, 1983

Scott, Anne Firor, ed., *Unheard Voices: The First Historians of Southern Women*, Charlottesville: University Press of Virginia, 1993

Srbik, Heinrich von 1878–1951

Austrian historian, founder of the *gesamtdeutsch* (Pan-German) school of historical writing

Heinrich Ritter von Srbik's father was a high-ranking imperial civil servant and his mother came from a distinguished academic family. His family background represented a fusion of German and Austrian traditions. His father's family were Germanized Czechs from Bohemia, while his mother's family migrated from Westphalia to Vienna, where her father founded the historical seminar at the University of Vienna.

In the 1890s Srbik attended the University of Vienna where he joined a radically Pan-German fraternity and participated in the violent riots that convulsed Vienna. He also attended lectures by the economic historian Alfons Dopsch, which emphasized the central importance of the *Reichsidee* ("idea of the Reich") in German history. According to Dopsch, Germanic barbarians supplanted Rome with the founding of Charlemagne's Holy Roman empire and were entrusted with the preservation of Western Christian civilization in a chaotic world.

After he earned a doctorate in 1902, Srbik remained at the University of Vienna as an academic assistant. He published a number of works in medieval economic history. When World War I broke out, Srbik was a professor at the University of Graz. Although exempt from military service, he volunteered, serving with distinction on the Tyrolian front as an artillery officer. When the Austro-Hungarian empire collapsed in 1918, Srbik was profoundly shocked. The lack of German unity weighed on his soul and his writings focused on how the *Volk* could extricate themselves from their national catastrophe.

In 1920 Srbik published *Wallensteins Ende* (Wallenstein's End), ostensibly a biographical study of the 17th-century Bohemian condottiere Albrecht von Wallenstein. Srbik portrayed Wallenstein as a great leader in the Thirty Years' War who failed because of shifting allegiances. Molded by Czech and German culture, Wallenstein was torn between Protestantism and Catholicism. These unresolved tensions continued to plague *Mitteleuropa*, even after 1918, producing accelerating political and cultural anarchy.

Srbik's 1925 biography of Austrian chancellor Clemens von Metternich addressed the same problem. Long regarded by historians as a narrow-minded reactionary and foe of all humane ideals, Metternich was revealed as a brilliant statesman whose conservative beliefs were firmly based on profound philosophical and theological insights. Srbik's Metternich was a visionary leader whose vehement rejection of popular sovereignty kept social barbarism at bay. Metternich's concept of a multinational state under strong German leadership would create stability in Central Europe, Srbik maintained. Sharply criticized by liberals, democrats, and Marxists, Srbik's rehabilitation of Metternich was enthusiastically received by Austria and Germany's antidemocratic intelligentsia.

By 1930 Srbik was recognized as the undisputed leader of the Pan-German school of historical writing which included Wilhelm Schüssler, Harald Steinacker, Erich Keyser, Gustav Roloff, and Helmut Rössler. His growing renown in academic and political circles was responsible for Srbik's appointment as Austrian minister of education in 1929. When the Third Reich was born in 1933, Srbik was the undisputed leader of conservative *völkisch* historical writing. Nazi historian Walter Frank praised Srbik for his reliance on the Great Man theory of history and for his unique understanding of the role of *Geist* (spirit) in German history.

In 1936 Srbik continued his role as a public figure as well as a renowned scholar. Austrian chancellor Kurt von Schuschnigg briefly considered appointing Srbik to the post of vice-chancellor to appease growing Nazi sentiments. At the same time he was offered (and declined to accept) the chair of modern history at the University of Berlin – the most prestigious history professorship in Germany. He was invited to lecture throughout the Reich, and his ideas were enthusiastically received in Nazi Germany and praised by Joseph Goebbels' newspaper *Der Angriff*. Srbik's assertions were very popular. For example he stated that the Danzig-Trieste-Odessa-Riga quadrilateral "rightfully" belonged to the German Reich whose mission was to "civilize" the East. Such notions provided intellectual respectability for Nazi Germany's claims to those areas.

Srbik published a massive 2-volume study, *Deutsche Einheit* (German Unity) in 1935, which culminated with two further volumes appearing in 1942. In this monumental work he examined the development of German unity within an idealistic and *völkisch* frame of reference. Emphasizing the supranational aspects of German historical evolution since the Holy Roman empire, Srbik delineated a clear line of progression in German history which moved from chaos to unity. For almost all of German history, unity was little more than an idea or a concept. But now, in the first years of Adolf Hitler's Third Reich, unity had finally become a reality. Influenced by Friedrich Meinecke's work in the history of ideas, Srbik argued in *Deutsche Einheit* that the most powerful idea in German history was the *Reichsidee*, an eternal and universal concept of a unified people living in harmony in one powerful Reich.

When the Austro-German *Anschluss* took place in 1938, it appeared that the ideas Srbik presented in *Deutsche Einheit* and other writings had come to fruition. Pan-Germanism had leapt from the pages of books and journals to become a euphoric reality. Srbik shared glory and honor with the Nazis who now ruled Austria. He was elected President of Vienna's Academy of Sciences (now "purified" of Jews and anti-Nazis, a purge he did not oppose), and became a member of the Nazi party. Other honors included a sumptuous *Festschrift* for his 60th birthday and election to the Reichstag of Greater Germany. In March 1939, he heralded the Nazi occupation of Bohemia and Moravia as the glorious start of a new age of German leadership in Central Europe.

This period of triumph was short-lived as Srbik's views were increasingly rejected by radical Nazi historians and ideologues after 1940. They saw him as overly sympathetic to the conservative ideals of Catholic, Habsburg "Old Austria." Nazi militants found Srbik's ideas were not radical enough for a Germany at war. In 1944 his home was searched to seek evidence of his association with the anti-Hitler conspirator Carl Goerdeler.

At the end of World War II Srbik was briefly imprisoned and then expelled from the University of Vienna faculty. Living in straitened circumstances in the town of Ehrwald, Tyrol, he continued to write and publish. His last major work was *Geist und Geschichte vom deutschen Humanismus bis zur Gegenwart* (1950–51; The Spirit and History of German Humanism to the Present). Although he denounced Nazi excesses, he tenaciously defended a Pan-German perspective that emphasized ideas and peoples rather than dynasties and states. Unlike most other post-1945 Austrian historians, he never accepted the notion of a uniquely Austrian national identity.

Srbik's death marked the end of the *gesamtdeutsch* school of history. Although much of his work remains under a cloud due to its close associations with National Socialism, Srbik's historical agenda was a bold one. His rehabilitation of Metternich and his belief in the value of a supranational Central European state stimulated vigorous debate that led to important work by other scholars.

JOHN HAAG

See also Germany: 1450–1800

Biography

Heinrich Ritter von Srbik. Born Vienna, 10 November 1878, grandson of the historian Wilhelm Heinrich Grauert, first director of the Historisches Seminar, University of Vienna. Studied with Alfons Dopsch, University of Vienna, PhD 1902. Served in the Austrian Army during World War I. Taught Austrian history, University of Vienna, 1902–12; professor of modern and economic history, University of Graz, 1912–22; professor of modern history, University of Vienna, 1922–45; minister of education in Austrian government, 1929–30; dismissed from academic post, 1945; retired to Ehrwald, 1945–51. Died Ehrwald, Tyrol, 15 February 1951.

Principal Writings

Der staatliche Exporthandel Österreichs von Leopold I bis Maria Theresia (Austrian Export Trade from Leopold I to Maria Theresa), 1907

Wilhelm von Schroeder: Ein Beitrag zur Geschichte der Staatswissenschaften (Wilhelm von Schroeder: A Contribution to the History of Political Science), 1910

Studien zur Geschichte des österreichischen Salzwesens (Studies on the History of the Austrian Salt Industry), 1917

Die Wiener Revolution des Jahres 1848 in sozialgeschichtlicher Beleuchtung (The Viennese Revolution of 1848 Viewed in the Light of Social History), 1919

Wallensteins Ende: Ursachen, Verlauf und Folgen der Katastrophe (Wallenstein's End: Cause, Chronology, and Consequences of the Catastrophe), 1920

Metternich: Der Staatsmann und Mensch (Metternich: Statesman and Man), 1925

Deutsche Einheit: Idee und Wirklichkeit vom heiligen Reich bis Königgratz (German Unity: Ideal and Reality from the Holy Empire to Königgratz), 4 vols., 1935–42

Wien und Versailles, 1692–1697: Zur Geschichte von Strassburg, Elsass, und Lothringen (Vienna and Versailles, 1692–97: On the History of Strasbourg, Alsace, and Lorraine), 1944

Geist und Geschichte vom deutschen Humanismus bis zur Gegenwart (The Spirit and History of German Humanism to the Present), 1950–51

Further Reading

Agnelli, Arduino, *Heinrich Ritter von Srbik*, Naples: Guida, 1975

Breuning, Klaus, *Die Vision des Reiches: Deutscher Katholizismus zwischen Demokratie und Diktatur (1929–1934)* (The Vision of the Reich: German Catholicism Between Democracy and Dictatorship (1929–1934)), Munich: Hueber, 1969

Broszat, Martin, and Klaus Schwabe, eds., *Die Deutschen Eliten und der Weg in den Zweiten Weltkrieg* (The German Elites and the Path to the Second World War), Munich: Beck, 1989

Dachs, Herbert, *Österreichische Geschichtswissenschaft und Anschluss, 1918–1930* (The Austrian Historical Profession and the Anschluss, 1918–1930), Vienna: Geyer, 1974

Ebneth, Rudolf, *Die österreichische Wochenschrift "Der Christliche Ständestaat": Deutsche Emigration in Österreich, 1933–1938* (The Austrian Weekly *Der Christliche Ständestaat*: German Emigrés in Austria, 1933–1938), Mainz: Grünewald, 1976

Engel-Janosi, Friedrich, *. . . aber ein stolzer Bettler: Erinnerungen aus einer verlorenen Generation* (. . . But a Proud Beggar: Memoirs from a Lost Generation), Graz: Styria, 1974

Eppel, Peter, *Zwischen Kreuz und Hakenkreuz: Die Haltung der Zeitschrift "Schönere Zukunft" zum Nationalsozialismus in Deutschland, 1934–1938* (Between Cross and Swastika: The Position Taken by the Journal *Schönere Zukunft* toward National Socialism in Germany, 1934–1938), Vienna: Böhlau, 1980

Gesamtdeutsche Vergangenheit: Festgabe für Heinrich Ritter von Srbik zum 60. Geburtstag am 10. November 1938 (The Pan-German Past: Commemorative Volume for Heinrich Ritter von Srbik on his Sixtieth Birthday on 10 November 1938), Munich: Bruckmann, 1938

Heiss, Gernot et al., eds., *Willfährige Wissenschaft: Die Universität Wien, 1938–1945* (Compliant Scholarship: The University of Vienna, 1938–1945), Vienna: Verlag für Gesellschaftskritik, 1989

Heiss, Gernot, "Pan-Germans, Better Germans, Austrians: Austrian Historians on National Identity from the First to the Second Republic," *German Studies Review* 16 (1993), 411–33

Kämmerer, Jürgen, ed., *Heinrich Ritter von Srbik: Die wissenschaftliche Korrespondenz des Historikers, 1912–1945* (Heinrich Ritter von Srbik: The Historian's Scholarly Correspondence, 1912–1945), Boppard am Rhein: Boldt, 1988

Kolnai, Aurel, *The War Against the West*, London: Gollancz, and New York: Viking, 1938

Luza, Radomir, *Austro-German Relations in the Anschluss Era*, Princeton: Princeton University Press, 1975

Pasteiner, Josef M., "Die Gesamtdeutsche Geschichtsauffassung Heinrich von Srbiks und Ihr Beitrag zur Geschichtstheorie" (The Pan-German Historical Conception of Heinrich von Srbik and Its Contribution to Historical Theory), dissertation, University of Vienna, 1979

Pasteiner, Josef M., "Das freiheitliche Porträt: Heinrich Ritter von Srbik, der grosse österreichische Historiker" (The Liberal Portrait: Heinrich Ritter von Srbik, the Austrian Historian), *Freie Argumente* 13 (1986), 243–51

Pitcher, John Harold, "Heinrich Ritter von Srbik and the Evolution of *Gesamtdeutsch* Historiography," dissertation, Tulane University, 1975

Reimann, Viktor, *Fünf ungewöhnliche Gespräche: Jörg Haider, Emil Jannings, Bruno Kreisky, Karl Roman Scholz, Heinrich von Srbik* (Five Unusual Conversations: Jörg Haider, Emil Jannings, Bruno Kreisky, Karl Roman Scholz, Heinrich von Srbik), Vienna: Ueberreuter, 1991

Reinalter, Helmut, "Heinrich Ritter von Srbik," in Hans-Ulrich Wehler, ed., *Deutsche Historiker*, vol. 8, Göttingen: Vandenhoeck & Ruprecht, 1982

Rosar, Wolfgang, *Deutsche Gemeinschaft: Seyss-Inquart und der Anschluss* (German Community: Seyss-Inquart and the Anschluss), Vienna: Europa, 1971

Ross, Ronald J., "Heinrich Ritter von Srbik and 'Gesamtdeutsch' History," *Review of Politics* 31 (1969), 88–107

Schleier, Hans, *Die bürgerliche deutsche Geschichtsschreibung der Weimarer Republik* (German Bourgeois Historical Writing in the Weimar Republic), Berlin: Akademie, 1975

Stadler, Friedrich, ed., *Kontinuität und Bruch 1938–1945–1955: Beiträge zur österreichischen Kultur- und Wissenschaftsgeschichte* (Continuity and Breakup 1938–1945–1955: Contributions to Austrian Cultural and Scientific History), Vienna: Jugend und Volk, 1988

Sweet, Paul R., "The Historical Writing of Heinrich von Srbik," *History and Theory* 9 (1970), 37–58

Talos, Emmerich, and Wolfgang Neugebauer, eds., *"Austrofaschismus": Beiträge über Politik, Ökonomie und Kultur, 1934–1938* ("Austro-fascism": Contributions to Politics, Economics, and Culture, 1934–1938), 4th edition, Vienna: Verlag für Gesellschaftskritik, 1988

Wandruszka, Adam, "Heinrich Ritter von Srbik: Leben und Werk" (Heinrich Ritter von Srbik: Life and Work), *Anzeiger der Österreichischen Akademie der Wissenschaften, philosophisch-historische Klasse 1978*, Vienna, 1979

Stampp, Kenneth M. 1912–

US historian

Kenneth Stampp's ability to challenge cherished myths in US historiography may be tied to the fact that his roots in a socialist and pacifist German-American community in Milwaukee were outside mainstream US society. For whatever reason, Stampp's writings during the 1950s and 1960s on US slavery and Reconstruction overturned the dominant interpretations of the time. Stampp's major works focus on US history from 1857 to 1877, but he remains best known for *The Peculiar Institution* (1956), which established his reputation as one of the leading historians in the country.

Stampp earned his PhD at the University of Wisconsin at Madison in 1942 under the guidance of well-known Civil War historian William Best Hesseltine. The economic determinism of Stampp's dissertation, subsequently published as *Indiana Politics during the Civil War* (1949), suggests the influence of Charles A. Beard, but in rehabilitating the reputation of Indiana's Democrats, the study hints at the revisionary tone that would mark most of Stampp's scholarship. Interestingly, Stampp's second book, *And the War Came* (1950), is among the more detached surveys of this pivotal event in US history. It deliberately avoided the issue of whether the Civil War was irrepressible, although it suggested that the US political system was severely strained by deepening divisions between North and South. Although Stampp was sympathetic to northern war aims, he concluded that the war failed to accomplish what it ought to have.

Stampp's *magnum opus*, *The Peculiar Institution*, was published only two years after the US Supreme Court ruled that racial segregation in public schools was illegal. It marked a great turning point in the historiography of slavery because it was the first major study of slavery free of the racist assumptions that influenced earlier work. Indeed, Stampp's provocative statement "Negroes *are*, after all, only white men with black skins, nothing more, nothing less," which has been interpreted as patronizing – must be understood in this context.

The Peculiar Institution took aim at the work of Ulrich Bonnell Phillips (1877–1934), especially his *American Negro Slavery* (1918). Using primarily plantation records, the very sources upon which Phillips' work was based, Stampp aimed to refute Phillips' arguments that for blacks slavery was a paternalistic and benign institution, and that slavery was conducive to racial harmony in the South, but that it was unprofitable for southern slaveholders, and a hindrance to southern economic development. In contrast, *The Peculiar Institution* depicted slavery as a psychological and physically brutal system of labor that destroyed families and stripped slaves of their African cultures. It argued that slaves were routinely overworked, underfed, poorly housed, and inadequately clothed. According to Stampp the relationship between slaveholder and slave was marked by continuous conflict, with the slave population in a state of constant semi-rebellion. Nevertheless, slaveholders made a very satisfactory profit from their slaves and showed no sign of abandoning slavery at the beginning of the Civil War. Thus Stampp questioned the major assumptions about US slavery at the time. Subsequent work, particularly that of Robert Fogel and Stanley L. Engerman, Eugene Genovese, and Herbert Gutman has superseded the book in some respects, but *The Peculiar Institution* remains the starting point for modern studies of US slavery.

Written during the "Second Reconstruction" in the United States, *The Era of Reconstruction* (1965), like *The Peculiar Institution*, turned the dominant historiography on its head. In *The Era of Reconstruction*, however, Stampp's arguments were based on secondary sources, particularly the scholarship of earlier black historians such as W.E.B. Du Bois, whose research had been largely overlooked. Stampp aimed to refute the work of William A. Dunning (1857–1922) and the so-called "Dunning school." *The Era of Reconstruction* argued that Abraham Lincoln died before devising a firm plan for Reconstruction; that his successor, Andrew Johnson, was an inflexible racist who acquiesced in the South's plans to establish a quasi-slavery system after the Civil War; and that southern Republican governments during Reconstruction were not dominated by blacks, and were not particularly incompetent or corrupt. Furthermore, it argued that "carpetbaggers" (northerners who relocated South during the Reconstruction) were often Union soldiers who were already in the South at the end of the Civil War, and "scalawags" (southerners who cooperated with Reconstruction) were often southerners who had always sympathized with the North. Thus, Stampp concluded that the South was not "redeemed" in 1877, but that the North abandoned its program of Reconstruction before completing it. Still, although Stampp was disappointed with the results of Reconstruction, he argued that the passage of the Fourteenth and Fifteenth amendments to the Constitution made it a success. These arguments stood in stark contrast to the dominant interpretation of the time.

America in 1857 (1990) is a narrative survey of 1857. For Stampp "1857 was probably the year when the North and South reached the political point of no return" in their descent toward war. He argued that at the beginning of 1857 the people of the US hoped the newly elected president, James Buchanan, could help heal the divisions within the country. Instead, by the end of the year Buchanan's inflexibility and incompetence had so divided the Democratic party that the stage was set for the triumph of the Republican party in the election of 1860.

Although written decades ago, Stampp's studies of US slavery and Reconstruction remain important milestones in the historiography of those fields. His studies of Civil War history are also very well regarded. Stampp has also been praised for his excellence in teaching. As a professor at the University of California at Berkeley for 37 years he influenced many undergraduate and graduate students.

THEODORE BINNEMA

See also African American; Dunning; Fogel; Franklin; Litwack; Slavery: Modern; United States: 19th Century

Biography

Kenneth Milton Stampp. Born Milwaukee, Wisconsin, 12 July 1912. Received BS, University of Wisconsin, 1935, MA 1937, PhD 1942. Taught at University of Arkansas, 1941–42; University of Maryland, 1942–46; and University of California, Berkeley, 1946–83.

Principal Writings

Indiana Politics during the Civil War, 1949
And the War Came: The North and the Secession Crisis, 1860–1861, 1950
The Peculiar Institution: Slavery in the Ante-Bellum South, 1956
The Causes of the Civil War, 1959; revised 1991
The Era of Reconstruction, 1865–1877, 1965
Editor with Leon F. Litwack, Reconstruction: An Anthology of Revisionist Writings, 1969
America in 1857: A Nation on the Brink, 1990

Further Reading

Abzug, Robert H., and Stephen E. Maizlish, eds., New Perspectives on Race and Slavery in America: Essays in Honor of Kenneth M. Stampp, Lexington: University of Kentucky Press, 1986
Sproat, John G. "Kenneth M. Stampp," in Clyde N. Wilson, ed., Twentieth-Century American Historians, Detroit: Gale, 1983 [Dictionary of Literary Biography, vol. 17]

The State

The "state," though it is central to the study of political power, is "as abstract as time, yet as real as a firing squad," to paraphrase Kaufman and Jones. What is the state? Is it simply a set of formal institutions? Is it principally characterized by its monopoly of coercive powers? Does it represent the "national interest" or more sectional interests? Does the state have any interests of its own? Where does it fit in to the global order of nation-states?

The state, many observers contend, may be understood as a set of central and co-ordinated institutions that exercise a monopoly of coercive and rule-making powers in a given territory. From this definition it may be seen that the study of the state has been largely in the hands of political theorists, political scientists, and political sociologists, whose various aims have been to advance not only empirical and theoretical accounts of the state but also normative theories as to what the role of the state *ought* to be. Yet in recent years the state has become a key area of historical research. Historians have begun to reflect on the peculiarities of the state and its capacity to introduce change at any given period of time.

The earliest selfconscious development of the state or sovereignty as a concept appeared in the works of the 16th-century French political thinker Jean Bodin, and in the writings of the 17th-century English theorist Thomas Hobbes. Writing in the context of civil wars, both writers sought to develop a theory of the state that would promote social peace by providing an intellectual justification for the notion that the sovereign was above the law and beyond challenge by the "people." John Locke also used the notion of sovereignty, but suggested that it lay with the "people," who ceded certain of their powers to a limited central government that would protect property and individual liberty and rule with the consent of the governed. If the state became oppressive, however, the "people" retained an inalienable right to revolution.

Lockean suspicions of state power have been shared by Marxists and some pluralists. Karl Marx and Friedrich Engels argued in *Manifesto der kommunistischen Partei* (1848; *The Communist Manifesto*) that the state was but "an executive committee for managing the common affairs of the whole bourgeoisie," i.e., an instrument of capitalist class rule. But, later, in analyzing the *coup d'état* of Louis Bonaparte, Marx suggested that the emperor had exercised autonomy, and was the instrument of no particular class. Marx's economistic theory was further adapted by Lenin in the era of monopoly capitalism, but after the failure of the post-1918 socialist revolutions in the West, Antonio Gramsci, the Italian communist leader, argued that an adequate understanding of the state required recognition that the state was also a political and ideological phenomenon. Its role was not only to coerce the working class but also to organize and perpetuate bourgeois hegemony through the construction of historical blocs – coalitions that included representatives of all major social classes, with each group accepting the need to sacrifice certain of their interests to further a broader "national interest." Gramsci therefore placed greater emphasis on the state's role in actively constituting the social, economic, political, and ideological orders, as opposed to considering the state to be an instrument in the hands of capitalists. Up to the 1970s, it was the state-as-instrument and state-as-relatively-autonomous that dominated intra-Marxist debates.

A differing line of research and normative theory has viewed the existence of independent groups (guilds, churches, trade unions) as a counterweight to state power and as a means of influencing policymaking, i.e., pluralism as embodied in the works of J.N. Figgis and F.W. Maitland, and of Arthur F. Bentley and David Truman. American pluralism dominated the state debate from the 1950s to the 1970s, especially in the wake of Robert Dahl's modern classic, *Who Governs?* (1961), on the historical evolution of democracy in New Haven, Connecticut. Dahl and his supporters concluded that there was no ruling class or power elite that had usurped political power in the United States, on the grounds that significant governmental decisions had been influenced by a variety of interests and not by the business community alone.

Ironically, despite their obvious differences, pluralism and Marxism share two defects. They both tend to see the state as an instrument of groups or classes and as domestically-oriented; thus allowing little or no room for state autonomy or for the fact that states exist in an international system of states. Yet the statist tradition has a long history, especially in the neglected works of Otto Hintze. More recently, Theda Skocpol and Michael Mann have shown how determining state power has been historically, because of its special position at the interface of domestic and global affairs. Empowered to promote the national interest, the state dominated foreign affairs. In order better to prepare the nation for military and / or economic competition, the state may develop the capacity to reorder society and the economy despite the resistance of dominant economic classes. The state, therefore, is not a passive vehicle; it is proactive in developing its own goals, defining its own interests and, most importantly, in mobilizing nominally private groups for the pursuit of those interests. Skocpol and Mann both insisted that the state had to be understood in historical terms. John Brewer, using the insights of statist thought and applying them to 18th-century Britain, argued that it was precisely state-led reforms in the collection of taxes and in the financing and administration of modern warfare that were integral to Britain's emergence as a global power in the period. Brewer described this phenomenon as the "fiscal-military state." Such conclusions have been borne out by the social and historical explorations of Geoffrey Ingham and of D.C.M. Platt, and by the US foreign economic policy studies of Stephen Krasner, further undermining the society-based Marxist and pluralist viewpoints. Gender and the family have been integrated into the history of state formation.

The rise of the "New Right" in the 1980s revived the popularity of Lockean ideas on limited government, under the slogan of "rolling back the frontiers of the state." This political and ideological development curiously tied in with the idea of the globalization of many aspects of life that appeared to be in vogue and which called into question the future of the nation-state, as transnational corporations and inter-state bodies (for example, the United Nations and the European Community), have begun to take power out of the hands of individual states. Such developments demanded new conceptualizations and more empirical analyses in order to determine the dynamics of what remains of state power today.

Although the theoretical work has been mostly left to political scientists and sociologists, historians have always been concerned with the state, particularly in the fields of political, administrative, and legal history. For example, in British history, a history of state formation can be distilled from Maitland's excavation of the Anglo-Saxon and Norman states, G.R. Elton's argument about the Tudor revolution in government, and Oliver MacDonagh's thesis about the 19th-century revolution in government. Similarly, historians have produced an extensive literature on the absolutist state in Europe. The contributors to John Miller's edited collection *Absolutism in Seventeenth-Century Europe* (1990) debated the meaning of absolutism and considered its applicability in different countries. In terms of the last hundred years, historians have been concerned with the origins of the welfare state in different countries (for example, Susan Pedersen's comparison of Britain and France). Much debate has focused on the question of whether situations of total war helped to create the welfare state. As John Brewer's work shows, war has important links to state-building.

Although the stance of much of this work has been strongly empirical, there have also been important theoretical debates among historians. Of particular importance is the work of Perry Anderson, whose *Passages from Antiquity to Feudalism* (1974) and *Lineages of the Absolutist State* (1974) are two of

the most ambitious and theoretically informed treatments of state formation that have ever been written. Equally important was Anderson's earlier debate with E.P. Thompson. In "Origins of the Present Crisis" (1964) Anderson claimed that the failure of the English state to modernize could be attributed to the demise of the English revolution in the 17th century. The monarchy and aristocracy remained in control, creating a supine bourgeoisie with the result that British society was constructed around deference. E.P. Thompson's "The Peculiarities of the English" (1978) responded by arguing that the bourgeoisie had been far more successful in constructing a modern state than Anderson allowed. In a not dissimilar vein, David Blackbourn and Geoff Eley's *Mythen deutscher Geschichtsschreibung* (1980; *The Peculiarities of German History*, 1984) critiqued the idea of the allegedly supine 19th-century bourgeoisie. Their assault on the idea of German exceptionalism included extended passages on the specifics of state formation. The Anderson/Thompson debate also fed into Philip Corrigan and Derek Sayer's account of a thousand years of English state formation, *The Great Arch* (1985). Influenced by historical sociology, Corrigan and Sayer examined the waves of power that had helped create the actual idea of the state. They interpreted the state as a cultural as well as a political phenomenon.

This turn towards state formation among historians in recent years represents a disenchantment with the social history of the 1960s and 1970s, which frequently ignored the complexities of state power, public finance, and political structure. Reductionist accounts of state formation have been replaced by a stress on the relative autonomy of the state. The structure of the state, it is becoming clear, helped shape the social and political agenda at any given historical moment.

INDERJEET PARMAR

See also Anderson, P.; Conze; Elton; Engels; Gramsci; Hintze; Maitland; Marx; Marxist Interpretation; Thompson, E.

Further Reading

Anderson, Perry, "Origins of the Present Crisis," *New Left Review* 23 (1964), 26–54; reprinted in his *English Questions*, London: Verso, 1992

Anderson, Perry, *Lineages of the Absolutist State*, London: NLB, 1974

Anderson, Perry, *Passages from Antiquity to Feudalism*, London: NLB, 1974

Bentley, Arthur F., *The Process of Government: A Study of Social Pressures*, Chicago: University of Chicago Press, 1908; reprinted 1967

Blackbourn, David and Geoff Eley, *Mythen deutscher Geschichtsschreibung: die gescheiterte bürgerliche Revolution von 1848*, Frankfurt: Ullstein, 1980; revised in English as *The Peculiarities of German History: Bourgeois Society and Politics in Nineteenth-Century German History*, Oxford: Oxford University Press, 1984

Block, Fred, "Beyond Relative Autonomy: State Managers as Historical Subjects," *The Socialist Register 1980*, 227–42

Brewer, John, *The Sinews of Power: War, Money, and the British State, 1688–1783*, London: Unwin Hyman, and New York: Knopf, 1989

Corrigan, Philip, and Derek Sayer, *The Great Arch: English State Formation as Cultural Revolution*, Oxford and New York: Blackwell, 1985

Dahl, Robert, *Who Governs? Democracy and Power in an American City*, New Haven: Yale University Press, 1961

Elton, G.R., *The Tudor Revolution in Government: Administrative Changes in the Reign of Henry VIII*, Cambridge: Cambridge University Press, 1953

Evans, Peter B., Dietrich Rueschemeyer, and Theda Skocpol, eds., *Bringing the State Back In*, Cambridge and New York: Cambridge University Press, 1985

Figgis, John Neville, *Churches in the Modern State*, London and New York: Longman, 1913

Gamble, Andrew, *The Free Economy and the Strong State: The Politics of Thatcherism*, London: Macmillan, and Durham, NC: Duke University Press, 1988

Gilpin, Robert, "Three Models of the Future," *International Organization* 29 (1975), 37–62

Gramsci, Antonio, *Quaderni del carcere*, 6 vols., written 1926–37, published Turin: Einaudi, 1948–51, critical edition, 4 vols., 1975; in English as *Selections from the Prison Notebooks*, London: Lawrence and Wishart, 1971, New York: International Publishers, 1972

Hall, John A., ed., *States in History*, Oxford and New York: Blackwell, 1986

Hall, John A., and G. John Ikenberry, *The State*, Milton Keynes: Open University Press, 1989

Hall, John A., ed., *The State: Critical Concepts*, 3 vols., London and New York: Routledge, 1994

Hayek, Friedrich August, *The Road to Serfdom*, Chicago: University of Chicago Press, 1944; reprinted 1994

Hayek, Friedrich August, *The Constitution of Liberty*, London: Routledge, and Chicago: University of Chicago Press, 1960

Hintze, Otto, *The Historical Essays of Otto Hintze*, edited by Felix Gilbert, New York: Oxford University Press, 1975

Ingham, Geoffrey, *Capitalism Divided? The City and Industry in British Social Development*, London: Macmillan, and New York: Schocken, 1984

Jessop, Bob, *The Capitalist State*, Oxford: Robertson, and New York: New York University Press, 1982

Kaufman, Herbert, and Victor Jones, "The Mystery of Power," *Public Administration Review* 14 (1954), 205–12

Krasner, Stephen D., *Defending the National Interest: Raw Materials Investments and US Foreign Policy*, Princeton: Princeton University Press, 1978

Lenin, V.I., *Gosudarstvo i revolutsia*, 1917; in English as *The State and Revolution*, Moscow: Progress, 1970

Lindblom, Charles E., *Politics and Markets: The World's Political and Economic Systems*, New York: Basic Books, 1977

MacDonagh, Oliver, "The Nineteenth-Century Revolution in Government: A Reappraisal," *Historical Journal* 1 (1958), 52–67

Maitland, Frederic William, "Introduction" to Otto von Gierke, *Political Theories of the Middle Ages*, Cambridge: Cambridge University Press, 1900

Mann, Michael, *The Sources of Social Power*, 2 vols., Cambridge and New York: Cambridge University Press, 1986

Mann, Michael, ed., *States, War and Capitalism: Studies in Political Sociology*, Oxford and New York: Blackwell, 1988

Marx, Karl, and Friedrich Engels, *Manifesto der kommunistischen Partei*, London: Burghard, 1848, Chicago: Hofmann, 1871; in English as *Manifesto of the Communist Party*, London: Reeves, 1888, Chicago: Kerr, 1902; generally known as *The Communist Manifesto*

Marx, Karl, *Der achtzehnte Brumaire des Louis-Bonaparte*, Hamburg: Meissner, 1869; in English as *The Eighteenth Brumaire of Louis Bonaparte*, London: Allen and Unwin, 1924; New York: International Publishers, 1926

Miliband, Ralph, *The State in Capitalist Society*, London: Weidenfeld and Nicolson, and New York: Basic Books, 1969

Miliband, Ralph, *Divided Societies: Class Struggle in Contemporary Capitalism*, Oxford and New York: Oxford University Press, 1989

Miller, John, ed., *Absolutism in Seventeenth-Century Europe*, Basingstoke: Macmillan, and New York: St. Martin's Press, 1990

Nicholls, David, *Three Varieties of Pluralism*, London: Macmillan, and New York: St. Martin's Press, 1974

Nozick, Robert, *Anarchy, State and Utopia*, Oxford: Blackwell, and New York: Basic Books, 1974

Pedersen, Susan, *Family, Dependence and the Origins of the Welfare States: Britain and France, 1914–1945*, Cambridge and New York: Cambridge University Press, 1993

Platt, Desmond Christopher Martin, *Finance, Trade and Politics in British Foreign Policy, 1815–1914*, Oxford: Oxford University Press, 1968

Polsby, Nelson, *Community Power and Political Theory*, New Haven: Yale University Press, 1963

Poulantzas, Nicos, "The Problem of the Capitalist State," *New Left Review* 58 (1969), 67–78

Sklair, Leslie, *Sociology of the Global System*, London: Harvester Wheatsheaf, and Baltimore: Johns Hopkins University Press, 1991

Skocpol, Theda, *States and Social Revolutions: A Comparative Analysis of France, Russia and China*, Cambridge and New York: Cambridge University Press, 1979

Skocpol, Theda, *Protecting Soldiers and Mothers: The Political Origins of Social Policy in the United States*, Cambridge, MA: Harvard University Press, 1992

Strange, Susan, "Supranationals and the State," in John A. Hall, *States in History*, Oxford and New York: Blackwell, 1986

Thompson, E.P., "The Peculiarities of the English," in his *The Poverty of Theory and Other Essays*, London: Merlin, and New York: Monthly Review Press, 1978

Truman, David, *The Governmental Process: Political Interests and Public Opinion*, New York: Knopf, 1951; reprinted 1993

Stavrianos, Leften Stavros 1913–

US (Canadian-born) historian of the Balkans

Leften Stavrianos grew up during the 1930s in depression-ravaged Vancouver. The contrast between the poverty of many Canadians and the wealth of British Columbia prompted him to conclude that societies always promise more than they can deliver. He became a historian in order to expose this gap and has criticized historians who can find no more significance for history than introducing people to their cultural heritage. Stavrianos has also actively focused his efforts on current issues rather than attempting to fashion definitive histories at the cost of ignoring history's deeper philosophic implications.

As a graduate student he became interested in the Balkans. To present a more realistic version of Balkan history, he studied the region as a whole from the perspective of its inhabitants. By using this method he avoided the ethnocentricity common to most native Balkan historians and the tendency of Western historians to concentrate on Europe's Great Powers at the expense of the Balkan peoples. He published several books on Balkan history, culminating in 1958 with a still important textbook, *The Balkans since 1453*. Balkan unity and stability were the main themes of these books, and Stavrianos' research – supplemented by his experience during 1944–45 as head of Greek affairs for the American wartime intelligence agency, the Office of Strategic Services (OSS) – convinced him that the Great Powers' imperialistic interventions into Balkan affairs bore most of the responsibility for the peninsula's disunity and instability.

By the end of the 1950s, Stavrianos had decided to expand into world history. His belief that no group of people is superior to another, as well as events such as decolonization and the expansion of the Cold War into Asia, persuaded him that the search for reality required historians to emancipate themselves and their students from the now antiquated Western orientation of history. In a series of pioneering textbooks, he adopted the view that world history must focus on issues, values, achievements, and prospects affecting everyone at a particular time rather than just produce a series of loosely related national or cultural histories. Called global, rather than world history, it echoed his earlier attack on history as cultural revelation, his emphasis on unification, and stability, and his conviction that history should illuminate the current situation. While de-emphasizing Western civilization, he still adopted center-periphery theory to explain the West's importance as the vital center of innovation for global civilization since it had developed capitalism at the end of the Middle Ages. Consequently, much of his global history concentrated on the expansion of Western civilization throughout the world, but with more sympathy for the periphery's plight than previous historians had displayed. However, in *Global Rift* (1981), Stavrianos noted that capitalism's dynamic technology was rendering the center-periphery theory obsolete by blurring the distinctions between the industrial center and the Third World.

In two provocative monographs, *The Promise of the Coming Dark Age* (1976) and *Lifelines from Our Past* (1989; revised 1997), Stavrianos summarized the significance of his research for contemporary life. Starting from the premise that human nature is plastic, he reasoned that its flexibility has allowed people to create their own environment. That effort suggested three stages of history dominated by different societies: prehistoric kinship based on cooperation among family members, a pre-Renaissance tributary based on an elite's exploitation of the masses, and capitalist. The last has evolved from commercial through industrial phases into high technology capitalism dominated by multinational corporations. It is currently causing serious ethnic, political, ecological, and economic disruptions throughout the world. However, Stavrianos is an optimist because, although there are no guarantees for the future, the destroyers of the previous stages of civilization have also created new, higher forms of civilization. He believes that making people aware of the destructive-constructive nature of change is one of the most important challenges currently facing world historians.

ROBERT F. FORREST

See also Balkans; World

Biography

Born Vancouver, British Columbia, 5 November 1913. Received BA, University of British Columbia, 1933; MA, Clark University, 1934, PhD 1937. Taught at Queen's University, Kingston, Ontario, 1937–38; Smith College, 1939–46; rose to professor, Northwestern University, 1946–73 (emeritus). Naturalized US citizen, 1940. Served in Office of Strategic Services during World War II. Married Bertha Kelso, psychologist, 1940 (1 son, 1 daughter).

Principal Writings

Balkan Federation: A History of the Movement toward Balkan Unity in Modern Times, 1944

Greece: American Dilemma and Opportunity, 1952

The Balkans since 1453, 1958

Editor, *The Epic of Modern Man: A Collection of Readings*, 1966

The World since 1500: A Global History, 1966; 7th edition 1995
The World to 1500, 1970; 6th edition 1995
The Epic of Man to 1500, 1971
The Promise of the Coming Dark Age, 1976
Global Rift: The Third World Comes of Age, 1981
Lifelines from Our Past: A New World History, 1989; revised 1997

Stein, Stanley J. 1920–
US historian of Latin America

Throughout his work, Stanley Stein has emphasized the economic aspects of history. Writing about the economy of Latin America was for Stein the best way to understand and discover the distinctive development of this region. However, he did not limit himself to commenting only on the economic structures, but sought to shed light on Latin American society as a whole. His first monograph, *The Brazilian Cotton Manufacture* (1957), dealt with the development of the textile sector. Stein's interest in this sector of the economy derived from his view that the cotton enterprise was a developed area in contrast to Brazil's overall economic underdevelopment. Stein viewed the Brazilian style of development, which relied on the exports of primary products such as coffee and sugar, as flawed. He aimed to refute the traditional view of economic historians that Brazil, and Latin America in general, owed its underdevelopment to its late start in industrialization. He argued that Brazil's policies in regards to industrialization during the late 19th and early 20th centuries actually paralleled those of the United States and European countries. He located the root of Brazil's problems in the rural areas: "The problem of textile entrepreneurs was indissolubly linked with the national economy; a sound cotton manufacture could not exist alongside a sick rural economy." This quotation sums up Stein's conclusions and his particular succinct style. He failed to foresee Brazil's tremendous industrialization, which was to occur in the 1960s and 1970s despite "archaic" land tenure patterns. However, Brazil does continue to grapple with structural problems of land tenure and Stein rightly pointed out the magnitude and endurance of this trend.

In 1957 Stein also published *Vassouras*, a study of one *municipio*-county in the Paraiba Valley near Rio de Janeiro. His use of notarial records, oral interviews, and municipal documents sets this monograph apart from those of other members of his generation of scholars who were sometimes content to rely on published primary sources. However Stein's abrupt style and his absence of generalizations perhaps played a part in consigning his work to relative obscurity. A paperback version of *Vassouras* appeared only in 1985. The author in his new preface explained that the title of his book: *Vassouras, A Brazilian Coffee County, 1850–1900*, led librarians and perhaps reviewers to overlook the subtitle, *The Roles of Planter and Slave in a Plantation Society*. As he pointed out in the reprinted edition (1985), he debunked the notion advanced by the Brazilian sociologist Gilberto Freyre that slavery in Brazil was somehow a gentle form of servitude in comparison to North American slavery. However, Stein in his usual unassuming style did not trumpet his original findings about the conditions of slavery or try to provoke a debate. At a time when many economic historians were trapped in a debate over whether Latin America was feudal or not, to paraphrase Stein's introduction, his close analysis of the evidence of the archives allowed him to portray the planters as rational agents who were neither feudal nor precapitalistic. However one might conclude that Stein adopted too fatalistic a tone in this work: there was a sense that Brazil would always be trapped in this cycle of dependence, only able to export agricultural products, that it would go eternally from boom to bust. In this monograph little possibility of change was foreseen.

This tendency to overemphasize the patterns of dependency was particularly evident in Stein's last major work, *The Colonial Heritage of Latin America* (1970). Stein's collaboration with his wife Barbara Stein came to fruition in this work, a series of essays that explored the economic dependency of the region. The essays sought to show how a colonial heritage restricted Latin America's development. This heritage, the Steins argued, was essentially a negative one, since Portugal and Spain themselves were economically dependent on England and France. The origins of an inefficient bureaucracy and the unequal distribution of land were traced back to the colonial times. Although the Steins had the merit of succinctly showing the enduring structures of Latin America, the agency of the people and change were sometimes overlooked in this narrative. In particular, indigenous peoples were characterized as "submissive," a characterization that denied the multiple ways in which they sought to combat the Spanish colonial state.

Stein sought to stress the importance of the 19th century and in particular the period from 1850 to the first half of the 20th century. The bibliography which he compiled with Roberto Cortes Conde is testimony to his insistence on the necessity of studying this period.

BRETT TROYAN

See also Brazil; Latin America: National

Biography
Born New York City, 8 June 1920. Received BA, City College of New York, 1941; MA, Harvard University, 1948, PhD in history 1951. Taught (rising to professor), Princeton University, from 1953 (emeritus). Married Barbara H. Stein, historian and bibliographer, 1943 (2 daughters, 1 son).

Principal Writings
The Brazilian Cotton Manufacture: Textile Enterprise in an Underdeveloped Area, 1850–1950, 1957
Vassouras, A Brazilian Coffee County, 1850–1900: The Roles of Planter and Slave in a Plantation Society, 1957
"The Historiography of Brazil, 1808–1889," *Hispanic American Historical Review* 40 (1960), 234–78
With Barbara H. Stein, *The Colonial Heritage of Latin America: Essays on Economic Dependence in Perspective*, 1970
Editor with Roberto Cortés Conde, *Latin America: A Guide to Economic History, 1830–1930*, 1977

Stenton, F.M. 1880–1967
British Anglo-Saxonist

Sir Frank Stenton spent most of his working life, save a brief period at Oxford, at the University of Reading, rising from the position of research fellow, to lecturer, then professor, and finally to become vice-chancellor before his retirement in 1950. His reputation at the time was very considerable and he accumulated no fewer than eight honorary degrees. The turn of the century had seen a revolution in the detailed study of Anglo-Saxon England. Excellent editions were made available for the first time of much of the primary source material, not simply of the writings of historians, but also of collections of documents. Moreover, a start was made in such fields as the study of place-names. There was as yet, however, no major synthesis of this new work. Existing textbooks, except for the best, perhaps Hodgkin's *History of the Anglo-Saxons* (1935), were mainly rehashings of Bede, with Chronicles thrown in for good measure but not much else. Even Hodgkin failed to produce a complete answer since his survey stopped at the time of king Alfred.

Stenton was well placed to fill the gap. His strength was in the production of no-nonsense, comprehensive surveys, as he demonstrated right from his first book, *William the Conqueror* (1908). Nonetheless, he was also close to the new standards of rigor in the use of documents, exemplified in his pioneering employment of charters in the writing of *The Early History of the Abbey of Abingdon* (1913). He was also interested in new areas of evidence, as in his *Place-Names of Berkshire* (1911). The latter was to prove a particular forte, and he co-edited 14 volumes of the English Place Name Society's works from 1925 to 1950. He was also greatly involved with other enterprises, such as the Pipe Roll Society, the Lincolnshire and Northamptonshire Record Societies and the History of Parliament.

Anglo-Saxon England (1943), although it was planned as a free-standing work, finally appeared in the Oxford History of England series; it is in every way a big book. It can be seen as the culmination of Stenton's work to that point, and in its successive editions, he maintained it as his greatest achievement. His aim in this book was to attain a form and depth of synthesis on Anglo-Saxon culture and events that had not previously been reached. To that end he tried to encompass as many fields of evidence as possible; starting with literary accounts, but encompassing place-names, coins, charters, wills, archaeology, and laws. He took the story through to the immediate post-Conquest period, the evidence of which he considered important for our understanding of what had gone before.

Stenton did not stop writing in his later years and the variety as well as the scale of his output can be best gauged by the commemorative collection edited by his widow, *Preparatory to Anglo-Saxon England*, which appeared in 1970. Reviewing his wider production, impressions of his thoroughness of view, forged in reading *Anglo-Saxon England*, are confirmed. It is true that for modern tastes his work is lacking in the use of pictures, maps, and diagrams, and his concern with archaeology was far less than it could, and perhaps should, have been. Furthermore, Stenton was never over-interested, or indeed it may appear really at all interested, in linking Anglo-Saxon history with continental developments. But then some Anglo-Saxon generalists, even today, appear to pride themselves on both their purely literary erudition and their geographical insularity. However, if Stenton exemplified a little of the worst of Early English studies in Britain in the 20th century, he nevertheless represented far more of the best.

DOMINIC JANES

See also Britain: Anglo-Saxon

Biography

Frank Merry Stenton. Born 17 May 1880. Educated at Southwell Grammar School; University College, Reading; Keble College, Oxford, MA 1902. At University of Reading: professor of modern history, 1912–46, deputy vice-chancellor, 1934–46, and vice-chancellor, 1946–50. Married Doris Mary Parsons, historian, 1919. Knighted 1948. Died 15 September 1967.

Principal Writings

William the Conqueror and the Rule of the Normans, 1908
The Place-Names of Berkshire: An Essay, 1911
The Early History of the Abbey of Abingdon, 1913
The First Century of English Feudalism, 1066–1166, 1932
Anglo-Saxon England, 1943
The Free Peasantry of the Northern Danelaw, 1969

Further Reading

Stenton, Doris Mary, "Memoir: Frank Merry Stenton," *Proceedings of the British Academy* 54 (1968), 315–423
Stenton, Doris Mary, ed., *Preparatory to Anglo-Saxon England, Being the Collected Papers of Frank Merry Stenton*, Oxford: Clarendon Press, 1970

Stone, Lawrence 1919–

British early modern historian

Lawrence Stone is the author of major works such as *The Crisis of the Aristocracy* (1965), *The Family, Sex and Marriage in England, 1500–1800* (1977), and more recently *Road to Divorce* (1990) and *Uncertain Unions* (1992), and his focus has been on the collection of massive amounts of data into large books that ask questions and make generalizations about the political power, economics, and family structure of the English aristocracy. His enthusiastic interest in new approaches to history fueled this research.

Although Stone had written earlier books on medieval sculpture and on Palavincino, *The Crisis of the Aristocracy* was his first major foray into the area of history that has dominated his output from the mid-1960s to the present – the English aristocracy from the 16th through the 18th centuries. *The Crisis of the Aristocracy* was part of the ongoing argument started by R.H. Tawney and Hugh Trevor-Roper, both influences on Stone, about whether or not the English aristocracy was undergoing economic decline in the period after 1550. In this first book, he presented not only a wealth of statistical data, but a detailed picture of aristocratic life. While critics such as D.C. Coleman attacked his somewhat unsophisticated use of the statistics, generally historians agreed with J.H. Hexter that the book was a major contribution to the secondary historical literature on early modern England.

Although Stone produced some other volumes after *The Crisis of the Aristocracy* on such subjects as education and the causes of the English Civil War, his next major effort, *The Family, Sex and Marriage in England*, was even more controversial. One of the main points of contention was Stone's statement that love within marriage could not have existed before the 18th century. Medieval historians in particular disagreed with Stone and pointed out that he had either been unaware of or ignored evidence from the period before 1500. Alan Macfarlane's *Marriage and Love in England: Modes of Reproduction, 1300–1840* (1986) was written, in part, to refute Stone's thesis. Stone has, over the years, become willing to abandon this argument himself.

While *The Crisis of the Aristocracy* put Stone on the map, and his later studies of family kept him there, his book reviews and historiographical essays have given insight into what he has considered the important theoretical and methodological questions facing the historical profession. These essays (collected in *The Past and the Present*, 1981) have been influential in shaping historical discourse over the last 20 years. The essay "History and the Social Sciences in the Twentieth Century" (1977; in *The Past and the Present*, 1981) was Stone's reassessment of the uses of social science theory in history. Using these theories was a methodology to which he had become committed while still an undergraduate at Wadham College, Oxford. In the essay, he first looks at the influence of Max Weber's ideas on the writing of history in the 1960s. He goes on to assess the many contributions that social science theories have made to historians willing to use them. Methodology is yet another contribution, although perhaps the most contentious, since he mainly discusses quantification, which is a technique that not many traditional historians are interested in pursuing. Stone is an advocate of testing common-sense assumptions and literary evidence with quantitative data. He also sees the social sciences as providing hypotheses that can be used by the historian. These hypotheses are then tested against the evidence provided by the primary source materials. However, Stone is not an advocate of turning history into a social science. Indeed, his argument is a practical one – use the methods created by the social sciences, but only as they pertain to the traditional agenda of the historian. He argues that history is not science. The historian may make hypotheses and generalizations about a particular period, but the formation of general laws is not on Stone's agenda. He is particularly cautious about the over-quantification of history and the use of psychology, which he argues is fundamentally ahistorical in its approach. He is also not convinced by Fernand Braudel's explanation as a "one-way hierarchy of causation," seeing historical explanation as a messy process that leaves, by the incompleteness of documentation, many loose ends.

While Stone's essay on prosopography may be seen as a way of bringing together various forms of historical writing, his essay "The Revival of Narrative" (1979; in *The Past and the Present*, 1981) was the one that caused the most comment in the profession. Certainly traditional historians were not comforted by his use of the word "narrative." Stone's description of the new narrative history did not sound much like the old narrative history. Traditional critics such as Gertrude Himmelfarb warned of the dangers of Stone's storytelling/analytical approach. E.J. Hobsbawm, while agreeing with Stone's methods, disagreed with the use of the term narrative, feeling that it carried so much traditional baggage that the new definition would be ignored. Although in his discussion of narrative Stone deals with such topics as quantification, the broadening of the audience for history, the young "antiquarian-empiricist historians," and the like, Stone's major focus is on the idea of the *mentalité* approach to history – a methodology also favored by some of the French Annales school. He is also interested in the anthropological approach of "thick description" formulated by Clifford Geertz, although Stone argues that unlike anthropology, where the study is of a particular group at a particular time in a particular place, like a fly in amber, the historian is interested in looking at change over time.

Stone brings an elegance to the writing of history that can serve as a model for other writers. He is also intellectually stimulating and open-minded. Although he does tear down old conceptions, he also tries to build, if not consensus, at least dialogue. Unlike those who would like to see traditional historians and cliometricians go their separate ways, Stone tries to bring them together. While many historians of different orientations do not agree with his theories and methodologies, Stone has, in his writings, established the plane on which historical discourse must now take place. Although Stone has a "hunter-gatherer" approach to history, he asks the big questions, and, if he cannot always answer them, he has at least set the agenda for the cultivators to follow.

SHARON D. MICHALOVE

See also Brenner; Britain: 1485–1750; Crime; Family; Legal; Marriage; Mentalities; Sexuality; Tawney

Biography

Born Epsom, Surrey, 4 December 1919. Educated at Charterhouse School, 1933–38; the Sorbonne, Paris, 1938; Christ Church, Oxford, 1938–40, 1945–46, BA 1946. Served as Lieutenant, Royal Naval Volunteer Reserve, 1940–45. Taught at Oxford University, 1946–47, at Corpus Christi College, Oxford, 1947–50, and at Wadham College, 1950–63; Institute for Advanced Study, Princeton, 1960–61, and Princeton University, 1963–90; director, Shelby Cullom Davis Center for Historical Studies, 1968–90 (emeritus). Married Jeanne Caecilia Fawtier, 1943 (1 son, 1 daughter).

Principal Writings

The Crisis of the Aristocracy, 1558–1641, 1965
The Causes of the English Revolution, 1529–1642, 1972
Family and Fortune: Studies in Aristocratic Finance in the Sixteenth and Seventeenth Centuries, 1973
The Family, Sex and Marriage in England 1500–1800, 1977
The Past and the Present, 1981; revised as The Past and the Present Revisited, 1987 [collected essays]
With Jeanne C. Fawtier Stone, An Open Elite? England, 1540–1880, 1984
Road to Divorce: England, 1530–1987, 1990
Uncertain Unions: Marriage in England, 1660–1753, 1992
Broken Lives: Separation and Divorce in England, 1660–1857, 1993
Editor, An Imperial State at War: Britain from 1689 to 1815, 1994

Further Reading

Beier, A.L., David Cannadine, and James M. Rosenheim, eds., The First Modern Society: Essays in English History in Honour of Lawrence Stone, Cambridge: Cambridge University Press, 1989 [includes bibliography]
Berlatsky, Joel, "Lawrence Stone: Social Science and History," in Walter L. Arnstein, ed., Recent Historians of Great Britain: Essays on the Post-1945 Generation, Ames: Iowa State University Press, 1990
Coleman, D.C., "The 'Gentry Controversy,'" History 51 (1966), 165–78
Hexter, J.H., On Historians: Reappraisals of Some of the Makers of Modern History, Cambridge, MA: Harvard University Press, and London: Collins, 1979

Himmelfarb, Gertrude, The New History and the Old, Cambridge, MA: Harvard University Press, 1987
Hobsbawm, Eric J., "The Revival of Narrative: Some Comments," Past and Present, 86 (1980), 3–8
Kenyon, John, The History Men: The Historical Profession in England since the Renaissance, London: Weidenfeld and Nicolson, 1983; Pittsburgh: University of Pittsburgh Press, 1984

Stubbs, William 1825–1901
British medievalist

After experiencing a rather turbulent, frustrating, and disappointing early academic career, William Stubbs was appointed Regius professor of modern history at Oriel College, Oxford in 1866. It was at Oxford that Stubbs developed his reputation as a meticulous scholar who was committed to his students and his church; Stubbs was ordained into the Anglican priesthood in 1850. During his tenure at Oriel and in the years that followed while serving as bishop of Chester and Oxford, Stubbs demonstrated that he was a prolific historian. Indeed, while he enjoyed some renown among his contemporaries for his 3-volume The Constitutional History of England in Its Origin and Development (1874–78), his reputation as a substantive contributor to English historiography rests on his labors as the tireless editor of the Rolls Series (Chronicles and Memorials of Great Britain and Ireland during the Middle Ages), his hundreds of entries written for the Dictionary of Christian Biography (1877–87), his recognition that continental, especially German, historical methods should be emulated in Britain, and his enduring influence on generations of British historians.

Stubbs' work ethic and interest in history was evident in his youth. His father, William Morley Stubbs, was a solicitor who trained his first son, William, in the methodology of charter and deed research. During his formative years Stubbs exhibited values which he sustained throughout his life: an interest in British history and historical methodology, an unquestioned affinity to the Church of England, and support for Tory/Conservative politics. Stubbs was educated at the Ripon Grammar School and Christ Church, Oxford; he held a fellowship at Trinity College, Oxford until 1850. Stubbs' academic life in Oxford was interrupted when he was ordained; from 1850 to 1866, he was a vicar in Navestock in Essex. In addition to his clerical duties, Stubbs' interest in history remained active; in 1858, he published his first scholarly work, Registrum Sacrum Anglicanum, which focused on English episcopal history. This work and his subsequent minor publications resulted in his appointment as librarian of Lambeth Palace in 1862; while still retaining his vicarship in Essex, Stubbs focused most of his energy on studying the vast manuscript depositories of Lambeth. In the next year, he was appointed the editor of the Rolls Series; from his initial volume, Chronicle Memorials of Richard I, to his 2-volume work on William of Malmesbury, Stubbs exercised meticulous care and demonstrated the value of primary archival materials.

During his 17 years as a Regius professor at Oxford, Stubbs succeeded in producing a formidable body of work that contributed to a transformation of historical scholarship in Britain. Along with Mandell Creighton, C.H. Firth, and many others, Stubbs introduced new exacting standards in history. Initially he had hoped to establish a formal "school of history" along the lines of the German universities. While he failed to achieve that objective, he did succeed in pointing the way to a more sophisticated understanding of history and its methodology. In 1870 Stubbs published *Select Charters and Other Illustrations of English Constitutional History from the Earliest Times to the Reign of Edward VI*. Stubbs' emphasis on the use of primary texts brought considerable attention to this work and its author. In *Select Charters* Stubbs also revealed his penchant for the era of the reign of Henry II. This work was followed shortly by the publication of the first volume of the *Constitutional History*. The critically acclaimed *Constitutional History* was the first historical analysis of the development of the English constitution based on primary sources; it was considered definitive until after World War I when a generation of new historians challenged Stubbs' account as a static interpretation lacking in creativity and directed by 19th-century "German" historical values. After the success of the *Constitutional History*, Stubbs returned to his work on the *Rolls Series*. In 1884 he resigned his position at Oxford University and accepted the appointment of bishop of Chester where he served with distinction as an active pastoral bishop who was committed to his people and to orthodox Anglican doctrine. In 1888 Stubbs was appointed Bishop of Oxford and served in that capacity until his death.

William T. Walker

See also Britain: 1066–1485; Cam; France: 1000–1450; Maitland; Nationalism; Political

Biography

Born Knaresborough, 21 June 1825, son of a lawyer. Educated privately at Knaresborough; Ripon Grammar School; attended Christ Church, Oxford, 1844–48, BA in classics and mathematics, 1848, MA 1851. Took orders; vicar, Navestock, Essex, 1850–66; librarian, Lambeth Palace, 1862–68; rector, Cholderton, 1876–79; canon, St. Paul's Cathedral, 1879–84; bishop of Chester, 1884–89; bishop of Oxford, 1889–1901. Regius professor of modern history, Oxford University, 1866–84. Married Catherine Dellar, 1859. Died Cuddesdon, 22 April 1901.

Principal Writings

Registrum Sacrum Anglicanum: An Attempt to Exhibit the Course of Episcopal Succession in England from the Records and Chronicles of the Church, 1858

Select Charters and Other Illustrations of English Constitutional History, 1866; 9th edition, 1913

With Arthur West Haddan, *Councils and Ecclesiastical Documents Relating to Great Britain and Ireland*, 3 vols. in 4, 1869–78

The Constitutional History of England in Its Origin and Development, 3 vols., 1874–78; reprinted 1979

Editor, with others, *Chronicles and Memorials of Great Britain and Ireland during the Middle Ages (Rerum Britannicarum medii aevi scriptores)*, commonly referred to as the *Rolls Series* [Stubbs edited 19 of the 243 volumes], 1876–

The Early Plantagenets, 1876; 10th edition 1901

Seventeen Lectures on the Study of Mediaeval and Modern History and Kindred Subjects, 1886; reprinted 1967

Historical Introductions to the Rolls Series, edited by Arthur Hassall, 1902; reprinted 1968

Germany in the Early Middle Ages, 476–1250 and Later Middle Ages, 1200–1500, edited by Arthur Hassall, 2 vols., 1908

Further Reading

Cantor, Norman F., ed., *William Stubbs on the English Constitution*, New York: Crowell, 1966

Hutton, William Holden, ed., *Letters of William Stubbs, Bishop of Oxford, 1825–1901*, London: Constable, 1904

Petit-Dutaillis, Charles, and Georges Lefebvre, *Studies and Notes Supplementary to Stubbs's Constitutional History*, 3 vols., Manchester: Manchester University Press, 1908–29

Richardson, Henry Gerald, and George Osborne Sayles, *The Governance of Medieval England: From the Conquest to Magna Carta*, Edinburgh: Edinburgh University Press, 1963

Subaltern Studies

Before the 1980s the English word "subaltern" was only occasionally used (following the Italian Marxist Antonio Gramsci) to describe subordinate social groups such as peasants. The term gained far wider usage, especially in the historiography of the non-Western world, with the publication from the 1982 onwards of a series of volumes, entitled *Subaltern Studies: Writings on South Asian History and Society*. The first six volumes (1982–89) were edited by the Bengali historian Ranajit Guha, the school's founding father, and drew mainly on the work of a small group of Indian and British historians; subsequent volumes have been edited by other members of the Subaltern Studies "collective." In his "Preface" to the first volume Guha gave *Subaltern Studies* a wide remit by defining "subaltern" as "a name for the general attribute of subordination in South Asian society whether this is expressed in terms of class, caste, age, gender, and office or in any other way." He added: "We recognize ... that subordination cannot be understood except as one of the constitutive terms in a binary relationship of which the other is dominance," for "subaltern groups are always subject to the activity of ruling groups, even when they rebel and rise up." The approach was to be broadly historical, but due attention was to be given to "the politics, economics and sociology of subalternity as well as the attitudes, ideologies and belief systems – in short, the culture – informing that condition."

The early volumes of *Subaltern Studies* closely reflected Guha's concern with relations of power between "elite" and "subaltern" groups, and in focusing especially on episodes of popular rebellion and resistance showed the influence of recent events in India as well as the work of English social historians such as E.P. Thompson and E.J. Hobsbawm. India's subalterns – peasants, tribals, urban workers – were shown to have a history of resistance and a capacity for self-mobilization (at a time when these were denied or the evidence for them overlooked). *Subaltern Studies* attacked three of the dominant strands in Indian history writing at the time – the triumphalist nationalist historiography (which subsumed popular politics within the history of the nationalist movement and the creation of the nation state); "elite" interpretations of Indian history (associated with the "Cambridge school" of British South Asian historians based at Cambridge University), which assumed that political leadership and initiative came from Indian elites, not from the masses, and which drew upon a Namerian understanding of political factionalism and self-interest; and the heavily economistic class analysis favored by many Indian

Marxist historians at the time. The main focus in the early *Subaltern Studies* essays was on the politics and culture of popular resistance and the ways in which this illuminated the "autonomy" or "relative autonomy" of the subaltern classes. Subsequent volumes showed a shift away from this original agenda toward a broader (in part more Gramscian) set of issues including gender relations and middle-class mentalities, with greater emphasis on hegemony and modes of domination, as well as the use of deconstructionist techniques and text-based explorations of how the history of the subordination classes could (or could not) be written.

The initial appeal of *Subaltern Studies* was its emphatic declaration in favor of what Guha in 1982 termed "the politics of the people," and the possibility this opened up of exploring new sources and new kinds of history-writing. The predominantly Indian composition of the group gave it an additional cachet: historical schools originating outside Europe and North America have rarely had such an impact on wider trends in historical writing and analysis. But the "Subalternists" were almost from the outset criticized for focusing too heavily (and, it was felt, unrealistically, even romantically) on moments of peasant or tribal rebellion, and thus seeming to ignore the everyday life and structural subordination of subaltern groups and, more generally, for replacing the language of class with a crude binary division between elites and subalterns (this in a society renowned for its complex hierarchy of social and economic relations). It was asked whether it was even possible for historians to recover the consciousness of Indian subalterns without, in effect, imposing post-Enlightenment ideals of individuality and freedom upon them. *Subaltern Studies* was also criticized for dealing almost exclusively with the colonial period of India's history and thus failing to address the issue of relations of power in earlier times, for largely ignoring gender and women as a subaltern group, and for turning from the original attempt to write the history of the masses in terms of their own experiences and consciousness to a historical approach based on literary theory and the use of middle-class texts and colonial source materials. In its later phases, *Subaltern Studies* has become as much preoccupied with "the subalternity of non-Western histories" as with the subalternity of the actual social groups caught up in those histories.

Despite continuing doubts about how far a history that is sharply dichotomized between elites and subalterns, domination and resistance, Western and non-Western can continue to generate fresh historical insights, since the late 1980s the term "subaltern" has gained remarkably wide usage in the writing of "postcolonial" or "post-Orientalist" history. Despite its origins in the historiography of colonial South Asia, the vocabulary of subalternity has been freely applied to other once-colonized societies – Africa and Latin America especially. While the original momentum and sense of direction may have been lost, the promise and the dilemmas involved in subaltern studies continue to provoke lively debates and a critical approach to the writing of history in, and for, the non-Western world.

DAVID ARNOLD

See also Gramsci; Guha; India; Marxist Interpretation; Masculinity; Mexico; Nationalism; Native American; Orientalism; Pacific; Political; Turner, V.; Women's History: Asia; Women's History: Latin America

Further Reading

Arnold, David, "Gramsci and Peasant Subalternity in India," *Journal of Peasant Studies* 11 (1984), 155–77

Arnold, David, and David Hardiman, eds., *Essays in Honour of Ranajit Guha*, Delhi and New York: Oxford University Press, 1994 [*Subaltern Studies* 8]

Bayly, C.A., "Rallying around the Subaltern," *Journal of Peasant Studies* 16 (1988), 110–20

Chatterjee, Partha, and Gyanendra Pandey, eds., *Subaltern Studies* 7, Delhi: Oxford University Press, 1992

Cooper, Frederick, "Conflict and Connection: Rethinking Colonial African History," *American Historical Review* 99 (1994), 1516–45

Guha, Ranajit *et al.*, eds., *Subaltern Studies: Writings on South Asian History and Society*, 9 vols to date, Delhi and Oxford: Oxford University Press, 1982–

Guha, Ranajit, and Gayatri Spivak, eds., *Selected Subaltern Studies*, New York: Oxford University Press, 1988

Hobsbawm, Eric J., "Peasants and Politics," *Journal of Peasant Studies* 1 (1973), 3–22

Mallon, Florencia E., "The Promise and Dilemma of Subaltern Studies: Perspectives from Latin American History," *American Historical Review* 99 (1994), 1491–1515

O'Hanlon, Rosalind, "Recovering the Subject: Subaltern Studies and Histories of Resistance in Colonial South Asia," *Modern Asian Studies* 22 (1988), 189–224

Prakash, Gyan, "Writing Post-Orientalist Histories of the Third World: Perspectives from Indian Historiography," *Comparative Studies in Society and History* 32 (1990), 383–408

Prakash, Gyan, "Subaltern Studies as Postcolonial Criticism," *American Historical Review* 99 (1994), 1475–90

Spivak, Gayatri, "Subaltern Studies: Deconstructing Historiography," in Ranajit Guha, ed., *Subaltern Studies* 4, Delhi: Oxford University Press, 1985

Sudhoff, Karl 1853–1938

German medical historian

Karl Sudhoff played a crucial role in establishing medical history as a field of research and teaching. As a result of his pioneering work, medical history in Germany and in many other countries following the German model has its institutional place within the medical faculty.

Until the 19th century medical knowledge as handed down from ancient times was the core of medical training at universities. During the early modern period, however, more and more new knowledge was added. At the end of the 18th century, the new knowledge had so increased that some university teachers saw a need to consider the traditional doctrines separately and began to publish the first specialized books on history of medicine. Their aim was to help the students decide what parts of the ancient knowledge were still useful for them. Additionally, this was a time when scholars and scientists developed new interests in the temporal aspects of such phenomena as nature and disease as well as of politics and culture and introduced a historical approach in their respective fields. In the German-speaking countries medical history became part of the university syllabus from 1810 onwards. It was part of the propedeutics to medicine, taught by teachers of other fields, often in conjunction with subjects such as theory and methodology of medicine. Later in the 19th century, medical training became increasingly based on the natural sciences and medical history came to be regarded as insignificant. As a result, the subject was taught only sporadically and studied only on a voluntary basis.

Toward the end the 19th century, some medical faculties began to rediscover history as a resource for the education of future doctors. At a time when the medical profession was subject to radical change, the study of medical tradition could give medical students a sense of the general ethical implications of their occupation and help to maintain a professional identity.

One of the people who tried to attain a higher status for medico-historical teaching and research was Karl Sudhoff. Until 1905 Sudhoff worked as a country doctor. During his 27 years of medical practice he devoted his spare time to the study of the history of medicine. His first major contribution to the field was his 2-volume *Bibliographia Paracelsia* (1894–99), a guide to the Paracelsian printed and manuscript source material. This made him a renowned expert in the history of medicine.

Because of Sudhoff's efforts the most important German scientific association, Gesellschaft der Naturforscher und Ärzte (Society of Scientists and Physicians), organized a section on the history of medicine and science at its 70th annual convention in Düsseldorf in 1898. In 1901 the Deutsche Gesellschaft für Geschichte der Medizin und der Naturwissenschaften (German Society for the History of Medicine and Science) was organized under Sudhoff's chairmanship. The society's journal was founded in the following year and became instrumental in forming a community of interested scholars. In 1905 Sudhoff chaired the foundation of an international commission for the history of science in Rome.

In 1906, at the age of 52, Sudhoff, the physician and amateur historian, became professor of the history of medicine at the University of Leipzig where he founded the first Institute for the History of Medicine in the world. This was possible because the widow of the Vienna medical historian Theodor Puschmann left her fortune to the University of Leipzig for the promotion of the study of medical history. With this institute, medical history was established as a discipline within the context of the medical faculty. Teaching was directed at medical students, of whom 170 wrote their dissertations on historical subjects under Sudhoff's guidance.

Sudhoff's research was concerned chiefly with ancient, medieval, and early modern medicine, epidemiology, hygiene, and dentistry. He traveled widely to examine medieval manuscripts, which he photographed and edited. He was particularly concerned with medical and anatomical iconography. He edited a large number of medieval texts on medicine, surgery, dietetics, and anatomy, and called attention to the significance of the Salernitan school as a center of medical lore and training in the Latin West. In Renaissance studies, he returned to the works of Paracelsus in 1922 and began the critical edition that he finished 11 years later; he also published facsimile editions of early modern anatomical tables. In epidemiology, Sudhoff edited important source materials on the early history of syphilis and the plague.

Sudhoff wrote two textbooks, an innovative history of dentistry, and a medical history that continued Julius Leopold Pagel's introduction to the subject. He also edited a number of important periodicals: the *Mitteilungen zur Geschichte der Medizin und der Naturwissenschaften* (from 1902), the *Studien zur Geschichte der Medizin* (1907), *Sudhoffs Klassiker der Medizin* (1919), and the *Archiv für die Geschichte der Medizin* (1907) that was later renamed *Sudhoffs Archiv für die Geschichte der Medizin*.

Sudhoff did much to create a secure source basis for further studies. His chief contribution lies in his espousal of a strict historical and philological method, based upon thorough studies of the original sources. He argued that ideas were the driving forces of historical change. He took Leopold von Ranke as his model, and his theoretical approach was historicist. His aim was to come to a true and objective picture of the medical thinking over time. Though Sudhoff tried to be part of the community of professional history, historians never accepted him as their equal.

According to the medical tradition he inherited, Sudhoff justified medical history through its contribution to the education of future doctors. He argued that history enhanced the respect for the achievements of the past and called attention to possible errors of the present, and that knowledge about the past could promote ethical ideals among the medical students.

Sudhoff's Leipzig institute was a center of medico-historical research and served as a model for other such departments all over the world. Though Sudhoff was acknowledged as a leading expert, he himself did not found a school of his own. In 1925 he was succeeded by the Swiss medical historian Henry E. Sigerist (1891–1957) as director of the Leipzig institute, but he resumed his directorship (1932–34) when Sigerist went to Johns Hopkins University. As a pioneer in the field, Sudhoff shaped for many decades the methodological approach, the main topics, and the form of institutionalization of the field of the history of health and medicine.

THOMAS SCHLICH

See also Medicine

Biography

Karl Friedrich Jakob Sudhoff. Born Frankfurt, 26 November 1853, son of a Protestant minister. Educated in Frankfurt, Zweibrückern, and Kreuznach, then studied medicine at the universities of Erlangen, Tübingen, and Berlin, receiving MD in 1875 before postgraduate study in Augsburg and Vienna. General practice in Bergen near Frankfurt, 1877–83, then at Hochdahl near Düsseldorf, 1883–1905. Chairman and founder, Institute for the History of Medicine, University of Leipzig, 1906–25; retired, but returned as acting director, 1932–34. Died Salzwedel, 8 October 1938.

Principal Writings

Bibliographia Paracelsia, 2 vols., 1894–99
Tradition und Naturbeobachtung in den Illustrationen medizinischer Handschriften und Frühdrucke vornehmlich des 15. Jahrhunderts (Tradition and Observation of Nature in the Illustrations of Medical Manuscripts and Incunabula Mainly from the 15th Century), 1907
Ein Beitrag zur Geschichte der Anatomie im Mittelalter speziell der anatomischen Graphik und Handschriften des 9. bis 15. Jahrhunderts (A Contribution to the History of Anatomy in the Middle Ages Especially of Anatomical Drawings and Manuscripts of the 9th to the 15th Centuries), 1908
Ärztliches aus griechischen Papyrus-Urkunden: Bausteine zu einer medizinischen Kulturgeschichte des Hellenismus (Medical Issues from Greek Papyrus Documents: Elements of a Medical History of Hellenistic Culture), 1909

Aus dem antiken Badewesen (Of Ancient Balneology), 1910

Aus der Frühgeschichte der Syphilis (Of the Early History of Syphilis), 1912

Beiträge zur Geschichte der Chirurgie im Mittelalter (Contributions to the History of Surgery in the Middle Ages), 2 vols., 1914–18

Geschichte der Zahnheilkunde (History of Dentistry), 1921

Skizzen, 1921; in English as *Essays in the History of Medicine*, 1925

Kurzes Handbuch der Geschichte der Medizin (Short Handbook of the History of Medicine), 1922 [new edition of J.L. Pagel, *Einführung in die Geschichte der Medizin* (Introduction to the History of Medicine), 1902]

Paracelsus: Theophrast von Hohenheim ... Medizinische, naturwissenschaftliche und philosophische Schriften (Paracelsus: Theophrast of Hohenheim ... Medical, Scientific, and Philosophical Works), 14 vols., 1922–33 [critical edition]

Erstlinge der pädiatrischen Literatur (First Works in Pediatric Literature), 1925

With Arnold Klebs, *Die ersten gedruckten Pestschriften* (The First Printed Pest-Tracts), 1926

Autobiographical note: "Aus meiner Arbeit: Eine Rückschau" (From My Work: A Review), *Sudhoffs Archiv* 21 (1929), 333–87

Further Reading

Brocke, Bernhard vom, *Wissenschaftsgeschichte als historische Disziplin* (History of Science as a History Discipline), Berlin: Akademie, 1996

Garrison, Fielding H., "Karl Sudhoff as Editor and Bibliographer," *Bulletin for the History of Medicine* 2 (1934), 7–9

Herbrand-Hochmuth, G., "Systematisches Verzeichnis der Arbeiten Karl Sudhoffs," *Sudhoffs Archiv* 27 (1934), 131–86; 31 (1938), 343–44; and 32 (1939), 279–84 [critical bibliography]

Keil, Gundolf, "Sudhoffs Sicht vom deutschen medizinischen Mittelalter" (Sudhoff's View of the German Medical Middle Ages), *Nachrichtenblatt der Deutschen Gesellschaft für Geschichte der Medizin, Naturwissenschaft und Technik e.V.* 31 (1981), 94–129

Mani, Nikolaus, "Sudhoff, Karl Friedrich Jakob," *Dictionary of Scientific Biography*, vol. 13 (1976), 141–43

Oliver, John Rathbone, "Karl Sudhoff as a Classical Philologian," *Bulletin for the History of Medicine* 2 (1934), 10–15

Roelcke, Volker, "Die Entwicklung der Medizingeschichte seit 1945" (The Development of Medical History since 1945), *NTM, Internationale Zeitschrift für Geschichte und Ethik der Naturwissenschaften, Technik und Medizin*, new series 2 (1994), 193–216

Sigerist, Henry E., "Karl Sudhoff, the Man and the Historian," *Bulletin for the History of Medicine* 2 (1934), 3–6

Sigerist, Henry E., "Karl Sudhoff the Mediaevalist," *Bulletin for the History of Medicine* 2 (1934), 22–5

Temkin, Owsei, "Karl Sudhoff, the Rediscoverer of Paracelsus," *Bulletin for the History of Medicine* 2 (1934), 16–21

Thom, Achim, "75 Jahre wissenschaftsgeschichtliche Forschung und Lehre am Karl-Sudhoff-Institut für Geschichte der Medizin und der Naturwissenschaften in Leipzig" (75 Years of Research and Teaching in the History of Science at the Karl-Sudhoff-Institute for the History of Medicine and Science in Leipzig), *Wissenschaftliche Zeitschrift, Karl-Marx-Universität Leipzig, Gesellschafts- und Sprachwissensschaftliche Reihe* 29 (1980), vol.6, 525–45

Suetonius *c.*70–*c.*140 CE

Roman biographer

A scholar and secretary of the Roman emperor Hadrian, Suetonius wrote about Roman manners, customs, dress, grammar, chronology, and many other subjects. However, only his biographies have been preserved. Notable among these are lives of the poets Terence, Horace, Virgil, and Lucan included in his *De viris illustribus* (*Lives of Illustrious Men*), and the twelve Caesars from Julius through Domitian covered in his fascinating *De vita Caesarum* (*Lives of the Caesars*). This latter work especially established Suetonius as a pioneer in analytical, critical biography independent both from the chronological and narrative pattern common for history in his day (for example, Tacitus' *Histories* and *Annals*) and from the elaborate, eulogistic praise style characteristic of classical biography before and during his own life (for example, Plutarch's *Lives*). Suetonius was also the earliest Latin biographer whose works are now extant (aside from the relatively undistinguished Cornelius Nepos, d.24 BCE), and his biographical concerns and methods became a pattern for several authors from the 2nd century to the Renaissance. Perhaps most important, his relatively objective portrayal of the personalities of the emperors, using stories that related to their private lives, helped direct history away from a dry chronicle of public events and toward a more comprehensive consideration of the motives and influences at work in the people involved in those events.

As with most writers, Suetonius' methodology was shaped by his background. He was a member of the Roman equestrian rank, practised law, and enjoyed several official posts under Trajan and Hadrian. He lost his most important position, in charge of Hadrian's correspondence, in 122, and seems also to have lost access to the imperial archives at that time. Just before that, perhaps around the time of the death of Trajan in 117, Tacitus completed his *Annals* covering the emperors from Tiberius to Nero. Suetonius, then working in Rome and writing primarily for an equestrian audience, seems to have decided not to compete with the great literary talent and style of Tacitus. Instead, the *Lives of the Caesars* was designed as a biographical supplement to Tacitus that deliberately avoided the normal structure, subject matter, and style of history at that time.

In structure, Suetonius usually avoided chronology and historical narrative, and instead presented events under subject headings or rubrics. For example, rather than describe successively the major events of Julius Caesar's conquest of Gaul, he gives an analysis of Caesar's military leadership by describing Caesar's personal energy, his caution and daring, his attitude toward omens, and his personal participation and example in battle.

Next, instead of concentrating on the traditional historical subjects of politics and war, Suetonius thought that intimate, personal, or even trivial items best showed the emperors as real people living in a social as well as a political environment. For example, he believed it was pertinent under various headings to mention that Augustus decorated his house with the bones of prehistoric animals, that he liked green figs, that he sometimes relaxed by fishing or playing dice, that he wrote a collection of *Epigrams* in the baths, and that he always carried a piece of sealskin as a protective amulet against lightning. In fact, Suetonius includes hundreds of such details for each emperor under headings covering their appearance, cultural interests, eating and drinking habits, religious practices, sexual behavior, virtues and vices, and many other things.

Some modern writers have complained that Suetonius is primarily interested in gossip, scandals, and prurient details.

Of course, anecdotal information is included quite indiscriminately according to standards today, but the objective presentation of such material seems intended primarily to inform rather than titillate the reader. For example, information about Augustus' frequent adulteries and his passion for deflowering virgins, some of whom were found for him by his wife Livia, is included without particular comment by Suetonius, along with the many other personal habits and interests of Augustus. The real problem with such information is that in the absence of other sources it is frequently impossible now to determine its accuracy.

Finally, Suetonius' style also differed from the norm for history in his day. Rather than using poetry, epigrams, or other rhetorical devices to elevate the tone and pathos of the narrative, Suetonius was straightforward, objective, and even somewhat monotonous in his use of the organizational rubrics. According to Wallace-Hadrill, this businesslike method and scholarly style can be seen in Suetonius' use of technical vocabulary, Greek transliterations, and verbatim citation of documents. This inclusion of exact quotation was highly unusual, if not unprecedented, among ancient historians. Unfortunately, most of the quotations are found in the life of Augustus, probably indicating that the later lives were composed after Suetonius lost favor with Hadrian. If so, the shorter and perhaps less accurate character of the later lives may be explained in part by Suetonius' lack of access to sources during their composition.

Suetonius' methods influenced many later biographical and historical works. Marius Maximus, writing in the late 2nd century, picked up where Suetonius left off, and patterned his biographies of the emperors from Nerva through Elagabalus on Suetonius' model. The 3rd- and early 4th-century *Historia Augusta*, covering the emperors from 117 to 284, explicitly cited Suetonius as its model, sometimes using organizational rubrics, and occasional quotations from sources such as letters and speeches, although much of the information is falsified or pure conjecture. The church father Jerome used Suetonius' *Lives of Illustrious Men* as a source and a pattern for his own work. The Frankish scholar Einhard's 9th-century biography of Charlemagne, was clearly based on Suetonius. Several phrases used by Suetonius to describe the appearance and habits of Julius, Augustus, and Tiberius were borrowed by Einhard and applied to Charlemagne, and Suetonian style was closely followed throughout. From the early Renaissance onward biographers such as Petrarch tended to use Suetonius more as a source than a model to be followed. Nevertheless, his scholarly interest in the personal lives and characteristics of important leaders continues among historians, biographers, and writers in various other fields, even if his style is no longer imitated.

Daniel L. Hoffman

See also Einhard; Roman; Scriptores

Biography

Gaius Suetonius Tranquillus. Born possibly Hippo Regius, Numidia, c.70 CE, into a family of equestrian rank. Entered imperial service, holding important offices including chief correspondence secretary in Latin, after 117; dismissed from office and retired from public career, 122. Died Hippo Regius, c.140.

Principal Writings

De viris illustribus, 113; part of *De grammaticis et rhetoribus* survives; in English as *The Lives of Illustrious Men*
De vita Caesarum, c.121–22; in English as *The Lives of the Caesars* and *The Twelve Caesars*
Works (Loeb edition), translated by J.C. Rolfe, 2 vols., 1913–14

Further Reading

Baldwin, Barry, "Suetonius: Birth, Disgrace and Death," *Acta Classica* 18 (1975), 61–70
Baldwin, Barry, *Suetonius*, Amsterdam: Hakkert, 1983
Cizek, Eugen, *Structures et idéologie dans "Les Vies des douze Césars" de Suétone* (Structures and Ideas in Suetonius' *Lives of the Twelve Caesars*), Paris: Belles Lettres, 1977
Della Corte, Francesco, *Suetonio, eques Romanus* (Suetonius, Roman Equestrian), Milan: Istituto editoriale cisalpino, 1958
Gascou, Jacques, *Suétone historien* (Suetonius, Historian), Rome: Ecole Française de Rome, 1984
Lounsbury, Richard Cecil, *The Arts of Suetonius: An Introduction*, New York: Lang, 1987
Mouchová, Bohumila, *Studie zu Kaiserbiographien Suetons* (Studies on Suetonius, Biographer of the Caesars), Prague: Universita Karlova, 1968
Pliny the Younger, *Letters* [1.18, 24; 3.8; 5.10; 9.34; 10.94]
Steidle, Wolf, *Sueton und die antike Biographie* (Suetonius and Biography in the Ancient World), Munich: Beck, 1951
Syme, Ronald, "The Travels of Suetonius Tranquillus," *Hermes* 109 (1984), 105–17
Townsend, G.B., "The Date of Composition of Suetonius' *Caesars*," *Classical Quarterly* 53 (1959), 285–93
Townsend, G.B., "Suetonius and His Influence" in Thomas Alan Dorey, ed., *Latin Biography*, New York: Basic Books, and London: Routledge, 1967
Wallace-Hadrill, Andrew, *Suetonius: The Scholar and His Caesars*, London: Duckworth, and New Haven: Yale University Press, 1983 [includes bibliography]

Sugar, Peter F. 1919–

Hungarian historian of East Central Europe

Peter Sugar's distinguished reputation as a historian rests on his activities as an author and editor of works on East Central Europe. Two of the three monographs he has written have focused on the Balkans, while, with the exception of a history of Hungary, the volumes he has edited have concentrated on the related themes of nationalism, ethnicity, and fascism. The goal of his editorial work has been to arrive at a clearer understanding of the similarities and contrasts among the various cultures of East Central Europe through the collaborations of experts with diverse academic and linguistic skills. Such an approach overcomes the formidable problems that historians face from the numerous East Central European languages and enriches history by integrating the efforts of social scientists with those of historians. The result has been both stimulating and controversial.

In 1963 Sugar published his first book, *Industrialization of Bosnia-Hercegovina, 1878–1918*, a study of Balkan economic development that remains important today for the light it sheds on Bosnia-Hercegovina's Ottoman era and how the Austro-Hungarians neglected Bosnia-Hercegovian modernization out of selfish motives. Sugar based his conclusion on the Austro-Hungarian refusal to develop an adequate railroad network for Bosnia-Hercegovina, and their failure to exploit either its potential for heavy industry or its income-producing light industry.

Southeastern Europe under Ottoman Rule, 1354–1804 (1977) is Sugar's most important book. It is volume 5 of *A History of East Central Europe*, a projected 11-volume series that he has co-edited. Unlike most non-Turkish historians, Sugar used Ottoman sources for this monograph largely to break free of the ethnocentricity characteristic of Balkan historiography and its conflict model that bases the history of Ottoman rule in Europe on a struggle between the Christian Balkan nations and their alien Muslim exploiters. The text contains an excellent description of the Ottoman state and the Porte's diplomatic relations with the Habsburg empire and Poland along with a pioneering analysis of the Ottoman impact on the economic, social, political, and cultural development of the Balkans, Hungary, and Transylvania. The material on Transylvania is especially good and should be read in conjunction with Sugar's chapter on that complex territory in *A History of Hungary* (1990), a book that he co-edited.

As an editor, Sugar has striven for a comprehensive history of East Central Europe and Hungary for nonspecialists and students in the above-mentioned projects. He has also used the comparative method for the difficult but necessary task of elucidating nationalism's role in East Central Europe. In 1969, he and Ivo Lederer edited the frequently cited *Nationalism in Eastern Europe*. The contributions of eight specialists on different East Central European countries led Sugar to conclude that the complex political environment of the region altered Western nationalism into four types – bourgeois, aristocratic, popular, and bureaucratic. Sugar expanded this investigation in *Eastern European Nationalism in the Twentieth Century* (1995), with a different set of specialists to trace the evolution and continuity of East Central European nationalism through the pre-Communist, Communist, and post-Communist eras.

Two concepts associated with nationalism – fascism and ethnicity – also received Sugar's attention in a pair of books that he edited. The first of these interdisciplinary studies, *Native Fascism in the Successor States, 1918–1945* (1971), sought rather unsuccessfully to produce a precise definition of fascism that is applicable to East Central Europe. Although scholars have disputed the book's theoretical conclusion, they have also praised it for providing useful historical information on fascist groups in the region.

The second study, *Ethnic Diversity and Conflict in Eastern Europe* (1980), realized its goal of defining East Central European ethnicity. Sugar maintained that the three main elements of ethnicity – religion, ethnic community, and language – joined with East Central European nationalism to form "ethnonationalism." It suspended East Central Europe in "semimodernism," meaning that ethnonationalism prevented the region from moving from a pre-modern (spiritual, rural, agrarian) to a modern (secular, urban, industrial) culture. In short, ethnonationalism contributed greatly to stagnation in East Central Europe, which is just another example of the original and important contributions that Sugar's efforts have bestowed on the history of this region.

ROBERT F. FORREST

See also Balkans; East Central Europe; Nationalism; Ottoman

Biography

Peter Frigyes Sugar. Born Budapest, 5 January 1919. Received BA, City College of New York, 1954; MA, Princeton University, 1956, PhD 1959. Taught at Princeton University, 1957–59; University of Washington, Seattle, 1959–89 (emeritus). Married Sally Bortz, 1955 (1 son, 2 daughters).

Principal Writings

Industrialization of Bosnia-Hercegovina, 1878–1918, 1963
Editor with Ivo J. Lederer, *Nationalism in Eastern Europe*, 1969
Editor, *Native Fascism in the Successor States, 1918–1945*, 1971
Editor with Donald Treadgold, *A History of East Central Europe*, 9 vols. to date, 1974–
Southeastern Europe under Ottoman Rule, 1354–1804, 1977 [*A History of East Central Europe*, vol.5]
Editor, *Ethnic Diversity and Conflict in Eastern Europe*, 1980
Editor with Gunther E. Rothenberg and Béla K. Király, *East Central European Society and War in the Prerevolutionary Eighteenth Century*, 1982
Editor with Péter Hanák, *A History of Hungary*, 1990
Editor, *Eastern European Nationalism in the Twentieth Century*, 1995
Nationality and Society in Habsburg and Ottoman Europe, 1997

Sweden

The historiography of Sweden is dominated by two strands: studies of the rise of the Swedish state, evident in conflicts between rulers and aristocracy, and studies of Sweden's relationship with the surrounding nations of Denmark, Norway, Finland, and, increasingly, Russia. Its position at the center of the Baltic and in a central spot on the Scandinavian peninsula have also been crucial. This essay will trace historiographical developments from prehistoric times to the present.

Although there is some evidence that Scandinavia was inhabited as early as 2000 BCE, by the early Iron Age most people had probably been forced out by the increasingly cold climate. The first written account of the region concerned a migration from the island of Scandza, mentioned in the *Getica* (The Gothic History) of the 6th-century chronicler Jordanes, whose linguistic analysis raised doubts early about this movement of people. The migration remains controversial and recently both archaeologists and more traditional historians such as Lars Hermodsson in *Goterna* (The Goths, 1993) have extended the debate in the light of new research.

However, by the Roman Iron Age the area was certainly settled and forging links with the Roman empire. In *Roman Reflections in Scandinavia* (1996) much of the recent archaeological evidence is presented in context. Much of this material probably originated with Erulian, Lombard, and Gothic returnees to present-day southern Sweden after their service in the Roman army (as described in Rhodin et al., *Gudaträd och västgötska skottkungar: Sveriges bysantiska arv* [Trees of God and Kings of West Gothia], 1994). Pliny the Elder and Tacitus also referred to an island in the north. Suiones (Swedes) are mentioned in these writings for the first time.

This period of migration was followed by one from which Viking society emerged. Centers of population included Uppland, around Uppsala, and the Goth strongholds of Östergötland and Västergötland, each of which were separate political entities. Historians have debated their character and importance as precursors of the Swedish state. Dag Stålsjö was, until his early death, the leading proponent of the Västgöta school. In his *Svearikets vagga* (The Cradle of the Svear Kingdom, 1983), he raised doubts about the central role of Uppsala and the Svear in early Swedish state formation and called for a more nuanced understanding of this problem. However, Peter Sawyer in *The Making of Sweden* (1989) described the crucial events that led to a united Sweden under the rule of the Svear. As Sawyer pointed out, in this period kingdoms were located in both Gothorum and Sweorum. These two kingdoms later merged (in the 13th century) and the Svear became the rulers of the unified state. Sweden was named the Svear kingdom (Svea rike, Sverige).

In this period the Swedes – with the Danes and Norwegians – emerged as Viking raiders and settlers. Much historical attention has been focused on this period, examining the limits of Viking influence and mobility. Herman Lindqvist's *Historien om Sverige* (History of Sweden, 1992–95) pointed out that Swedish Vikings travelled further to the east than any other Europeans: to Jerusalem, the Caspian Sea, Constantinople, and Baghdad. M.G. Larsson in *Rusernas rike* (Realm of the Rus, 1993) stressed the links between the Vikings and Russia.

This link with the region that would become Russia dominates an important strand of historiography, as Russian territorial aims were constantly at odds with those of Sweden. Aleksandr Kan argued in *Sverige och Ryssland* (Sweden and Russia, 1996) that the Swedish influence on the rise of Russia was crucial. His book is well-researched, but not conclusive.

Historians have also focused on the 11th century as a time of crucial change. Sweden had resisted Christianity longer than most and the pagan temple in Uppsala survived until the 11th century. Christianity was instrumental in the political instability of the century as rival families vied for control. Religion lay at the base of much of the conflict of this period although the ruling family was baptized. Birger Jarl of the Folkung family emerged as ruler in 1266 after a struggle with other magnates for the throne. He was also the founder of Sweden's capital, Stockholm. Birger Jarl's eldest son, Valdemar, was elected king in 1250, but after his father's death in 1266, he failed to retain the throne. In 1275 Valdemar's brother, Magnus Ladulås, overthrew him. Magnus Ladulås reshaped the Swedish state, formalizing the power of the magnates by creating a council of nobles, bishops, and lawmen, and creating three important officials: the Lord High Steward, the Chancellor, and the Marshal. Although this was a move toward a feudal system, the Swedish peasants were never subjected to serfdom.

This was also a period of Swedish expansion under the guise of meeting the papal call for crusades. The Swedes chose to invade and christianize Finland; this foreshadowed an ongoing confrontation with Russia, which saw the area as part of its sphere of influence. The conflict was resolved by the establishment of formal borders between Sweden, Finland, and Russia, under the Peace of Nöteborg of 1323. This is treated at length in Kan's *Sverige och Ryssland*.

Throughout the 14th century, Sweden's throne remained the object of struggles among the powerful nobility who elected and deposed kings frequently. These struggles were resolved when the nobles requested help from Margaret I, the powerful regent of Denmark and Norway, who sent her troops to settle the argument about who was to rule. Her great-nephew Erik of Pomerania was crowned king in 1397 as a result of the Kalmar Union, uniting for the first time Denmark, Norway, and Sweden. Margaret's role has been explored in a collection celebrating the 600th anniversary of the union, *Unionsdrottningen* (The Union Queen, 1997).

Unfortunately, the union was strong only during Margaret's lifetime. In the 1430s, the Swedes revolted against Erik, mainly due to his appointment of Danes and Germans to administrative posts, his interference with the church, and his imposition of heavy taxes to fund a bellicose foreign policy. The revolt of peasants and miners in 1434 was led by Engelbrekt Engelbrektsson, who was elected regent but soon murdered by the nobles. The latest treatment on him is L.O. Larsson's *Engelbrekt Engelbrektsson* (1984) while B. Waldén's *Engelbrektsfejdén* (The Engelbrekt Strife, 1934) explored the struggle between Engelbrekt and the nobles. Engelbrekt's death was succeeded by another period of unrest in which the headship of the Kalmar Union was generally contested, and seldom to Sweden's advantage. There was also continuing civil strife in Sweden as various rulers failed to find the support of nobles, church, or peasants. This was exacerbated by a conflict between the old landowning class, who preferred rule by council, and new commercial interests who favoured a strong local monarch.

This situation continued into the late 15th and early 16th centuries, when Christian II (of Denmark) invaded Sweden, took Stockholm, and executed 82 of the leading supporters of the Swedish regent, Sten Sture the Younger. The Swedes revolted under the leadership of Gustav Eriksson Vasa, of whom the leading biography, *Gustav Vasa* (1950), is that by Ivan Svalenius. Vasa succeeded not only in driving Christian II out of Sweden, but also from the throne of Denmark. In 1523, Vasa was elected king of Sweden and the Kalmar Union was officially dissolved. The official book celebrating the 500th anniversary of the birth of Gustav, *Gustav Vasa 500 år* (1996) by Alf Åberg, is a bilingual presentation of the king and his country. Åberg located Gustav among the great kings of Sweden. Ingvar Andersson explored the complexity of Gustav's son in *Erik XIV* (1948), which is probably the best account of this renaissance figure. Erik, who ruled from 1560 to 1568, was one of the most controversial figures in Swedish history.

The years following Gustav Vasa's election as king in 1523 saw the increasing strength of Sweden as an independent nation, often at odds with a Denmark that wished to re-establish the union of the Scandinavian states. For the next century, Sweden increased its economic power through its dominance of the Baltic, and the 17th century must be seen as the golden age of Sweden as a major power. This was halted only when it threatened European interests in the late 17th century. The Peace of Copenhagen settled the frontiers between Sweden, Denmark, and Norway that remain today, and guaranteed the failure of Sweden's dream of Baltic domination.

Recently this golden age has been thoroughly re-evaluated. Herman Lindqvist's *Historien om Sverige: När Sverige blev stormakt* (History of Sweden: When Sweden Became a Great Power, 1994) was a straightforward account of this complex period in Swedish history. He focused on Gustavus Adolphus' intentions in Germany: was he seeking an emperor's crown for himself? Jörg-Peter Findeisen's *Das Ringen um die Ostseeherrschaft* (The

Struggle over the Baltic Sea Area, 1992) provided a good overview of the struggle for supremacy in the Baltic and of Sweden's kings during these crucial years. Peter Englund's *Ofredsår* (Years of War, 1993) focused on the leading Swedish artist, war leader, and architect, Erik Dahlberg, but also recounted the rise of Sweden from a small kingdom on the northern edge of Europe to one of the great powers that influenced the fate of the continent. Sweden's international influence is the subject of *New Sweden in America* (1995), edited by Carol E. Hoffecke *et al.* and published on the 350th anniversary of the founding of the first Swedish colony in America. New Sweden, the first European settlement in the Delaware River valley, was a subject long ignored by American colonial historians.

Gustavus II Adolphus (1594–1632), who was instrumental in establishing Sweden's dominant position in Scandinavia, was probably best examined by Michael Roberts in his two works: *Gustavus Adolphus* (1953–58), which is still the unsurpassed treatment, and *Gustavus Adolphus and the Rise of Sweden* (1973). Both present the wide and complex range of activities of the king and his chancellor, Axel Oxenstierna. Göte Göransson's *Gustav Vasa och hans folk* (Gustavus Adolphus and His People, 1983) presented a broad picture of the social situation in Sweden during Gustav's reign. The complex character of Gustavus Adolphus' daughter, Christina, was well presented in *Christina von Schweden* (Christina of Sweden, 1992) by Jörg-Peter Findeisen. He provided new interpretations of Christina's break with tradition and her search for eternal truths in an era of profound change.

Charles XI (ruled 1672–97) was known for breaking the power of the nobility by reclaiming estates for the crown (*reduktionen*) and carrying out reforms of the economy, the penal code, the church, education, and defence. He was also the defender of the Swedish conquests from Denmark of Skåne, Halland, and Blekinge. Alf Åberg's *Kampen om Skåne under försvenskningstiden* (The Struggle for Scania during the Era of Swedenization, 1994) described in detail the Swedenization process and the bloody guerrilla warfare waged against the Swedish occupiers by the "friskyttar" and "snapphanar" (pro-Danish guerrillas and mercenaries), which began in Charles XI's reign. When his son, Charles XII, succeeded to the throne, Sweden had the largest army in its history. And Charles XII and his policies of expansion, not only within Scandinavia, but in Poland and along the Baltic, have been the subject of a tremendous literature.

One of the latest books on Charles XII is Findeisen's *Karl XII von Schweden* (Charles XII of Sweden, 1992). Findeisen attempted to go beyond the myth in discerning the driving force behind Charles. But Ragnhild Marie Hatton's *Charles XII of Sweden* (1968) is still regarded by many as the foremost of the biographies of the "warrior king."

Charles XII's reign signalled the end of Swedish greatness. The wars he conducted – which began well, but ended in defeat – have been studied intensively. An Estonian perspective was added in *Segern vid Narva* (The Victory at Narva, 1996) by Margus Laidre, the former Estonian ambassador in Stockholm. Laidre examined the beginning of the decline in Swedish power and showed how the Great Northern War was not only a conflict between Sweden and Russia, but a power struggle among groups and individuals. The initial Swedish military

campaign in Estonia (1700–01) reflected this tension. Peter Englund's *Poltava* (1988; *The Battle of Poltava*, 1992) was a detailed account of the 1709 battle in the Ukraine with an hour-by-hour chronology of events. It illustrates why, even today, this catastrophe influences Swedish views on war. An important aspect of the ramifications for Sweden of the defeat at Poltava was treated in Alf Åberg's *Fångars elände* (Prisoners' Misery, 1991): the fate of the 30,000 Swedes defeated in the Ukraine. For many of these men, women, and children it took ten to fifteen years before they could return home, and many never saw Sweden again.

After the death of Charles XII, absolute monarchy was replaced by parliamentary power. Power devolved to a 24 member council responsible to parliament (*riksdagen*). Two parties emerged to fight for power, generally known by their nicknames of "Nightcaps" and "Hats." Both were pro-mercantile, and might best be characterized by the allies they sought.

In 1741 Sweden started a war against Russia which in 1743 resulted in a loss of territory. What has been called the age of liberty ended with deflation, party intrigues, and economic failure. But the era also fostered great men of science (Linnaeus, Celsius, Polhem, and Swedenborg). Land reforms were introduced and Sweden took a step toward parliamentary democracy. Michael Roberts' *The Age of Liberty* (1986) provides the best introduction to this era, emphasizing among other things Sweden's new influence in European culture.

In 1771, Gustav III carried out a coup, and increased the power of the king. In the beginning his rule was successful and he stabilized the economy. However, in 1788 he started a war against Russia to regain the provinces lost earlier. Stig Jägerskiöld's *Svensksund* (Svensksund, 1990) was published on the 200th anniversary of one of Sweden's greatest naval victories, Svensksund, off the southern Finnish coast. The war ended in 1790 with reconquest of territory lost in 1745, but in 1792 Gustav was assassinated at a masked ball in Stockholm. Gardar Sahlberg's *Murder at the Masked Ball* (1969, translated 1974) attempted to reveal the web of aristocratic conspiracy behind the crime.

During Gustav's reign culture flowered and among other institutions the Swedish Academy was established in 1786. Gustav IV, his son, sided with Britain during the Napoleonic Wars. This resulted in a Russian invasion of Finland in 1808 followed by Sweden's loss of the whole of Finland in 1809. Finland became a Grand Duchy of the Russian empire. Allan Sandström's *Sveriges sista krig* (Sweden's Last War, 1994) provided a short and dramatic account of this final war with Russia.

In 1814 one of Napoleon's marshals, Jean-Baptiste Bernadotte, was named heir to the Swedish throne, to which he succeeded as Karl XIV Johan in 1818. Alan Palmer's *Bernadotte* (1990) is perhaps the best recent introduction to the French marshal, who was also the father of Sweden's policy of non-alignment.

The 19th century was successful for Sweden, a viewpoint reflected in Stig Hadenius' *Svensk politik under 1900-talet* (1984; *Swedish Politics during the Twentieth Century*, 1985). However, before the introduction of industrialization by the end of the century, a weak economy had forced millions of Swedes to emigrate to the United States, beginning in 1846.

The 20th century has been more problematic. During World War II, Sweden maintained a neutral stance. It became a haven for Danes and Norwegians escaping Nazi occupation, but at the same time it signed a transit agreement with Nazi Germany allowing for transport of German troops to Norway. Unlike many other countries Sweden has yet to come to terms with its World War II policies. Swedish non-alignment policy during the Cold War has also been criticized. Indeed Sweden was in reality secretly preparing for cooperation with NATO as demonstrated in *Had There Been a War . . . Preparations for the Reception of Military Assistance, 1949–1969* (1994). Bo Petersson based his *Med Moskvas ögon* (With the Eyes of Moscow, 1994) on archival studies in Moscow and revealed the intricacies of Russian and Swedish diplomacy in the postwar era. In 1970 the bicameral riksdag (established in the 1870s), was replaced with a single chamber elected through proportional representation. The monarch was retained, but with ceremonial duties only. In 1995 Sweden joined the European Union after a referendum. Hard hit by recession and mass unemployment, the Social Democratic government since 1994 has been forced to introduce cuts in its welfare programs. The history of this period is only beginning to be written.

BERTIL HÄGGMAN

Further Reading

Åberg, Alf, *Sveriges historia i fickformat*, Stockholm: LTS, 1985; in English as *A Concise History of Sweden*, Stockholm: Natur & Kultur, 1991

Åberg, Alf, *Folket i Nya Sverige: vår koloni vid Delaware floden, 1638–1655*, Stockholm: Natur & Kultur, 1987; in English as *The People of New Sweden: Our Colony on the Delaware River 1638-1655*, 1988

Åberg, Alf, *Fångars elände: Karolinerna i Ryssland 1700–1723* (Prisoners' Misery: Caroline Soldiers in Russia, 1700–1723), Stockholm: Natur & Kultur, 1991

Åberg, Alf, *Kampen om Skåne under försvenskningstiden* (The Struggle for Scania during the Era of Swedenization), Stockholm: Natur & Kultur, 1994

Åberg, Alf, *Gustav Vasa 500 år, 1496–1996: Stora jubileumsboken* (Gustav Vasa: 500 years, 1496–1996: Official Anniversary Book), Stockholm: Norstedt, 1996

Ahnlund, Nils, ed., *Den svenska utrikespolitikens historia* (History of Swedish Foreign Policy), 5 vols. in 10, Stockholm: Norstedt, 1951–61

Amelunxen, Clemens, *Jean-Baptiste Bernadotte: Marschall Napoleons, König von Schweden* (Jean-Baptiste Bernadotte: Napoleon's Marshal, King of Sweden), Cologne: Heymann, 1991

Ander, Oscar Fritiof, *The Building of Modern Sweden: The Reign of Gustav V, 1907-1950*, Rock Island, IL: Augustana, 1958

Andersson, Ingvar, *Sveriges historia*, Stockholm: Natur & Kultur, 1944; in English as *A History of Sweden*, New York: Praeger, and London: Weidenfeld and Nicolson, 1956

Andersson, Ingvar, *Erik XIV*, Stockholm: Wahlström & Widstrand, 1948

Andrén, Nils, *Modern Swedish Government*, Stockholm: Almqvist & Wiksell, 1961

Andrén, Nils, *Power Balance and Non-Alignment: A Perspective on Swedish Foreign Policy*, Stockholm: Almqvist & Wiksell, 1967

Bengtsson, Frans Gunnar, *The Life of Charles XII, King of Sweden, 1697-1718*, London: Macmillan, and New York: St. Martin's Press, 1960

Bergengren, Erik, *Alfred Nobel*, Stockholm: Geber, 1960; in English as *Alfred Nobel: The Man and His Work*, London and New York: Nelson, 1962

Berner, Felix, *Gustav Adolf: der Löwe aus Mitternacht* (Gustavus Adolphus: The Lion Out of Midnight), Stuttgart: Deutsche Verlags-Anstalt, 1982

Carlgren, Wilhelm M., *Svensk utrikespolitik, 1939-45*, Stockholm: Almänna, 1973; in English as *Swedish Foreign Policy during the Second World War*, London: Benn, and New York: St. Martin's Press, 1977

Carlsson, Sten Carl Oscar, and Jerker Rosén, *Svensk historia* (Swedish History), 2 vols., Stockholm: Svenska Bokförlaget, 1961–62

Den svenska historien (Swedish History), 15 vols., Stockholm: Bonnier, 1977–79

Derry, Thomas Kingston, *The History of Scandinavia: Norway, Sweden, Denmark, Finland and Iceland*, London: Allen and Unwin, and Minneapolis: University of Minnesota Press, 1979

Elder, Neil, *Government in Sweden: The Executive at Work*, Oxford and New York: Pergamon Press, 1970

Englund, Peter, *Poltava: Berättelsen om en armés undergång*, Stockholm: Atlantis, 1988; in English as *The Battle of Poltava: The Birth of the Russian Empire*, London: Gollancz, 1992

Englund, Peter, *Ofredsår: om den svenska stormaktstiden och en man i dess mitt* (Years of War: On the Swedish Era of Greatness and a Man in Its Midst), Stockholm: Atlantis, 1993

Findeisen, Jörg-Peter, *Christina von Schweden: Legende durch Jahrhunderte* (Christina of Sweden: Legends Through the Centuries), Frankfurt: Societäts, 1992

Findeisen, Jörg-Peter, *Karl XII von Schweden: Ein König, der zum Mythos wurde* (Charles XII of Sweden), Berlin: Duncker & Humblot, 1992

Findeisen, Jörg-Peter, *Das Ringen um die Ostseeherrschaft: Schwedens Könige der Grossmachtzeit* (The Struggle over the Baltic Sea Area: Sweden's Kings from the Era of Great Power), Berlin: Duncker & Humblot, 1992

Fritz, Martin, *German Steel and Swedish Iron Ore 1939-1945*, Gothenburg: Institute of Economic History, 1974

Geoffrey, Auguste Mathieu, *Gustave III et la Cour de France suivi d'une étude critique sur Marie-Antoinette et Louis XVI apocryphes* (Gustavus III and the French Court), 2 vols., Paris: Didier, 1867

Goldsmith, Margaret Leland, *Christina of Sweden: A Psychological Biography*, London: Barker, and Garden City, NY: Doubleday, 1933

Göransson, Göte, *Gustav Vasa och hans folk* (Gustavus Adolphus and His People), Stockholm: Trevi, 1983

Grimberg, Carl Gustaf, *A History of Sweden*, Rock Island, IL: Augustana, 1935

Had There Been a War . . . Preparations for the Reception of Military Assistance, 1949–1969: Report of the Commission on Neutrality Policy, Stockholm: Fritzes, 1994

Hadenius, Stig, *Svensk politik under 1900-talet: konflikt och samförstånd*, Stockholm: Tidens, 1984, revised 1997; in English as *Swedish Politics during the Twentieth Century*, Stockholm: Swedish Institute, 1985

Hatton, Ragnhild Marie, *Charles XII of Sweden*, New York: Welbright and Talley, and London: Weidenfeld and Nicolson, 1968

Heckscher, Eli F., Kurt Bergendahl, Wilhelm Keilhau, Einar David Cohn, and Thorsteinn Thorsteinsson, *Sweden, Norway, Denmark, and Iceland in the World War*, New Haven: Yale University, and London: Oxford University Press, 1930

Hermodsson, Lars, *Goterna: ett krigarfolk och dess bibel* (The Goths: A Warrior People and Its Bible), Stockholm: Atlantis, 1993

Hoffecker, Carol E., Richard Waldron, Lorraine E. Williams, and Barbara E. Benson, eds., *New Sweden in America*, Newark: University of Delaware Press, 1995

Hovde, Brynjolf Jakob, *Diplomatic Relations of the United States with Sweden and Norway, 1814-1905*, Iowa City: University of Iowa, 1920

Jägerskiöld, Stig, *Svensksund: Gustaf III's krig och skärgårdsflottan, 1788–1790* (Svensksund: The War of Gustav III and the Archipelago Fleet, 1788–1790), Stockholm: Atlantis, 1990

Jansson, Sven Birge Fredrik, *The Runes of Sweden*, Stockholm: Norstedt & Förlag, London: Phoenix, and New York: Bedminster, 1962

Jordanes, *Getica: Om goternas ursprung och bedrifter* (Getica: On the Origin of the Goths and Their Deeds), written 6th century; in English as *The Gothic History*, Princeton: Princeton University Press, 1908, Stockholm: Atlantis, 1997

Kan, Aleksandr Sergeevich, *Sverige och Ryssland: ett 1200-årigt förhållande* (Sweden and Russia: A 1200-Year Relationship), Stockholm: Almquist & Wiksell, 1996

Kirby, David G., *Northern Europe in the Early Modern Period: The Baltic World, 1492–1772*, London and New York: Longman, 1990

Koblik, Steven, *Sweden, The Neutral Victor: Sweden and the Western Powers, 1917-1918: A Study in Anglo-American-Swedish Relations*, Stockholm: Läromedelsförlagen, 1972

Koblik, Steven, ed., *Från fattigdam till överflöd*, Stockholm: Wahlström & Widstrand, 1973; in English as *Sweden's Development from Poverty to Affluence, 1750–1970*, Minneapolis: University of Minnesota Press, 1975

Laidre, Margus, *Segern vid Narva: Början till en stormakts fall* (The Victory at Narva: Beginning of the Fall of a Great Power), Stockholm: Natur & Kultur, 1996

Larsson, Lars Olof, *Engelbrekt Engelbrektsson och 1430-talets Svenska uppror* (Engelbrekt Engelbrektsson and the Swedish Uprising of the 1430s), Stockholm: Norstedt, 1984

Larsson, Mats G., *Rusernas rike: Nordborna och Rysslands födelse* (Realm of the Rus: Scandinavians and the Birth of Russia), Stockholm: Atlantis, 1993

Lindberg, Folke Adolf, *Scandinavia in Great Power Politics, 1905–1908*, Stockholm: Almqvist & Wiksell, 1958

Lindgren, R.E., *Norway-Sweden: Union, Disunion, and Scandinavian Integration*, Princeton: Princeton University Press, 1959

Lindqvist, Herman, *Historien om Sverige* (History of Sweden), 4 vols., Stockholm: Norstedt, 1992–95

Lisk, Jill, *The Struggle for Supremacy in the Baltic, 1600–1725*, London: University of London Press, 1967; New York: Funk and Wagnalls, 1968

Metcalf, Michael F., ed., *The Riksdag: A History of the Swedish Parliament*, Stockholm: Bank of Sweden Tercentenary Foundation, 1988

Misgeld, Klaus, *Sozialdemokratie und Aussenpolitik in Schweden: Sozialistische Internationale, Europapolitik und die Deutschlandfrage, 1945–1955* (Social Democracy and Foreign Policy in Sweden: The Socialist International, European Politics, and the German Question), Frankfurt: Campus, 1984

Munch-Petersen, Thomas, *The Strategy of Phoney War: Britain, Sweden and the Iron Ore Question 1939–1940*, Stockholm: Militärhistoriska, 1981

Nissen, Henrik, ed., *Scandinavia during the Second World War*, Oslo: Universitetsforlaget, and Minneapolis: University of Minnesota Press, 1983

Nordstrom, Byron J., ed., *Dictionary of Scandinavian History*, Westport, CT: Greenwood Press, 1986

Oakley, Stewart, *War and Peace in the Baltic, 1560–1790*, London and New York: Routledge, 1993

Palmer, Alan, *Bernadotte: Napoleon's Marshal, Sweden's King*, London: Murray, 1990

Petersson, Bo, *Med Moskvas ögon: Bedömningar av svensk utrikespolitik under Stalin och Chrusjtjov* (With the Eyes of Moscow: Analysis of Swedish Foreign Policy during the Rule of Stalin and Khrushchev), Stockholm: Arena, 1994

Pulsiano, Phillip, and Kirsten Wolf, eds., *Medieval Scandinavia: An Encyclopedia*, New York: Garland, 1993

Rhodin, L., V. Lindblom, and K. Klang, *Gudaträd och västgötska skottkungar: Sveriges bysantiska arv* (Trees of God and Kings of West Gothia: Sweden's Byzantine Heritage), 1994

Roberts, Michael, *Gustavus Adolphus: A History of Sweden, 1611–1632*, 2 vols., London: Longman, 1953–58

Roberts, Michael, *The Early Vasas: A History of Sweden, 1523–1611*, Cambridge: Cambridge University Press, 1968

Roberts, Michael, *Sweden as a Great Power, 1611–1697: Government, Society, Foreign Policy*, London: Arnold, and New York: St. Martin's Press, 1968

Roberts, Michael, *Gustavus Adolphus and the Rise of Sweden*, London: English Universities Press, 1973; reprinted as *Gustavus Adolphus*, London and New York: Longman, 1992

Roberts, Michael, *Sweden's Age of Greatness, 1632–1718*, London: Macmillan, and New York: St. Martin's Press, 1973

Roberts, Michael, *The Swedish Imperial Experience, 1560–1718*, Cambridge and New York: Cambridge University Press, 1979

Roberts, Michael, *British Diplomacy and Swedish Politics, 1758–1773*, Minneapolis: University of Minnesota Press, and London: Macmillan, 1980

Roberts, Michael, *The Age of Liberty, Sweden 1719–1772*, Cambridge and New York: Cambridge University Press, 1986

Roberts, Michael, *From Oxenstierna to Charles XII: Four Studies*, Cambridge and New York: Cambridge University Press, 1991

Roman Reflections in Scandinavia, Rome: Bretschneider, 1996

Rystad, Göran, ed., *The Swedish Armed Forces and Foreign Influence, 1870–1945*, Stockholm: Militärhistoriska, 1992

Sahlberg, Gardar, *Den aristokratiska Ligan: Sammanvärjningen mot Gustaf III*, Stockholm: Bonnier, 1969; in English as *Murder at the Masked Ball: The Assassination of Gustavus III of Sweden*, London: Macdonald and Jane's, 1974

Samuelsson, Kurt, *Från Stormakt till välfärdsstat: Svensk samhällsutveckling und 300 år*, Stockholm: Rabén e Sjögren, 1968; in English as *From Great Power to Welfare State: 300 Years of Swedish Social Development*, London: Allen and Unwin, 1968

Sandström, Allan, *Sveriges sista krig: de dramatiska åren, 1808–1809* (Sweden's Last War: The Dramatic Years, 1808–1809), Stockholm: Libris, 1994

Sawyer, Peter H., *The Age of the Vikings*, London: Arnold, and New York: St. Martin's Press, 1962

Sawyer, Peter H., *Kings and Vikings: Scandinavia and Europe AD 700–1100*, London and New York: Methuen, 1982

Sawyer, Peter H., *The Making of Sweden*, Alingsås: Viktoria, 1989

Sawyer, Peter H., and Birgit Sawyer, *Medieval Scandinavia: From Conversion to Reformation circa 800–1500*, Minneapolis: University of Minnesota Press, 1993

Scott, Franklin D., *Sweden: the Nation's History*, Minneapolis: University of Minnesota Press, 1977; revised edition, Carbondale: Southern Illinois University Press, 1988

Sletten, Vebard, *Five Northern Countries Pull Together*, Copenhagen: Nordic Council, 1967

Stiles, Andrina, *Sweden and the Baltic, 1523–72*, London: Hodder and Stoughton, 1992

Stålsjö, Dag, *Svearikets vagga: en historia i gungning* (The Cradle of the Svear Kingdom: A History in Unbalance), Skövde: Karlstedts, 1983

Sundin, Sven Z., *Efter Poltava: Karoliner i Sibirien* (After Poltava: Caroline Soldiers in Siberia), Stockholm: Fischer, 1993

Svalenius, Ivan, *Gustav Vasa*, Stockholm: Wahlström & Widstrand, 1950

Swedish Historical Bibliography 1971–1975, Stockholm: Almqvist & Wiksell, 1988

Tolf, Robert W., *The Russian Rockefellers: The Saga of the Nobel Family and the Russian Oil Industry*, Stanford, CA: Hoover Institution Press, 1976

Unionsdrottningen: Margareta I och Kalmar Unionen (The Union Queen), Stockholm: Föreningen Norden, 1997

Voltaire, *Histoire de Charles XII, roi de Suède*, Basel: Revis, 1731; in English as *The History of Charles XII, King of Sweden*, London: Alexander Lyon, 1732

Waldén, B., *Engelbrektsfejdén: ett femhundraarsminne* (The Engelbrekt Strife), Stockholm: Saxon & Lindstrom, 1934

Switzerland

As the oldest republic, founded in 1291, Switzerland's historiography is both extensive and confusing. The problem centers around the nation's federalist tradition, which emphasizes the individuality of each canton or region. This sociopolitical tradition did not spare the Swiss historical profession, which consists of a mosaic of various historical publications and traditions. Nevertheless, there exist certain distinguishable historical trends. These originated in medieval religious chronicles and regional (cantonal) records.

Early historical writings exist in 11th-century religious records such as the chronicles of the St. Gallen convent, which were used legally to sanction the convent's independence from the bishop of Constance. By the 14th century, archival storage was established as cities gained in territorial importance and influence. Such records were essential to confirm legally claims made in chroniclers' accounts. It was not until the advent of printing, however, that such archival practices truly spread. During the Renaissance, humanism, personified among others in Tschudi's work (from Canton Glarus) sought to justify the political system of the republic and its independence in historical terms. The author of several works notable more for their endeavor than historical rigor, Tschudi is most remembered for his *Chronicon Helveticum* (Swiss Chronicles, 1734–36), which surveyed Swiss history from 1000 to 1470. This work epitomized the chronicling practice that other Swiss historians adopted extensively.

By the 18th century, the "Enlightened" critical approach was adopted in many historical accounts, and came through in the questioning of foundational legends by such historians as Gottlieb Emanuel von Haller. Haller also wrote the first bibliographic guide for the history of Switzerland: *Conseils pour former une bibliothèque historique de la Suisse* (Advice for Establishing a Historical Library of Switzerland, 1771). The work surveyed some 250 works on Switzerland. It is now obsolete, even in its descriptions, but it set a precedent for better works, such as Georg von Wyss' *Geschichte der Historiographie in der Schweiz* (Survey of Swiss Historiography, 1895), which constitutes one of the classic works of Swiss history writing. In the 18th century a Swiss trend of writing world histories rather than regional ones also came about. Accounts such as those of Johannes von Müller (1752–1809) served to emphasize nationalist tendencies over cantonal accounts. Müller's *Der Geschichten schweizerischer Eidgenossenschaft* (Histories of the Swiss Confederation) presented the history of a small people with a common will whose evolution is disrupted by conquest; interestingly, it is not optimistic, for it makes no claim to discern any kind of historical progression.

With the 19th century the first Swiss historical society, the Schweizerische Geschichtsforschende Gesellschaft, was established (1811–38; it published *Der Schweizerische Geschichtsforscher*). It was soon followed by the Société générale suisse d'histoire (1841). Generally, a positivist trend appeared in Swiss historical thought, in line with German historiography. The result of this was an emphasis, present well into the 20th century, on historical accounts of the founding era presenting multiple theories and explanations for the successful conglomeration of small states into a confederation. In parallel, Reformation history gained momentum, eventually developing into its own historical field. On the other hand, historical investigations of the period between the 16th and 18th centuries remained few. As for the historical crises of 1798 (the Napoleonic invasion) and 1848 (the year of the first federal constitution), these were often set aside by liberal historians (such as Wilhelm Oechsli and Johannes Dierauer), who felt that 1848 had accomplished the nation's goal of constitutional federalization and thus did not require analysis. Conservative scholars (such as Gonzague de Reynold and Richard Feller) acted likewise, as they set about to rehabilitate the *ancien régime* period, including the last period of Swiss mercenary duty under Louis XVI. As for histories of Catholic Switzerland, these were also set aside in favor of local histories. This has recently been remedied by encompassing investigations by Urs Altermatt.

Histories of Switzerland often emphasized politics at the expense of social and cultural research. Also legal studies of the country were popular because Switzerland represented an interesting example of the application of Germanic law (as presented by Eugen Huber), thus prompting investigations of the Middle Ages prior to 1291.

In the 20th century, a clearer interest in business and social history appeared, pioneered by Eduard Fueter and especially William Rappard. By the 1930s, this had receded somewhat in favor of nationalist studies. After World War II, however, following the example of French historiography, a renewed interest in social, cultural, and economic (Jean François Bergier) aspects of all time periods ensued. The acceptance of new methodologies has thus prompted a resurgence of interest in Switzerland as a whole. Political histories also gained in importance in response to world events. Most notable in its scope, Edgar Bonjour's multivolume history of Swiss neutrality linked together Swiss political history with the nation's place in Europe. Later on, special attention was given in the work of Daniel Bourgeois, and later Jean-Claude Favez and André Lasserre, to Switzerland's role in World War II, especially in terms of its relationship to Germany. Accounts of Switzerland's relationships with other nations, however, are few, except for occasional university theses.

The celebration of Switzerland's 700th anniversary occasioned considerable critical analysis of the nation's place in history and is likely to carry on into the new millennium as the country re-evaluates its identity in both domestic and foreign terms. In parallel, signs of a new trend have appeared, as English-speaking historians move to analyze the sociopolitical and cultural aspects of various Swiss events and reframe them in their wider European context. This practice may prove a valuable impulse to rejuvenate Swiss historical writing as new hypotheses are tested in the analysis of Swiss history.

GUILLAUME DE SYON

Further Reading

Most writings on Swiss history appear in German, but many are now translated into French, and a few into English. The leading Swiss history journal, the trilingual *Zeitschrift für schweizerische Geschichte*, founded in 1921, also provides a valuable selection from the various subfields that form Swiss historiography, in the form of articles and bibliographical surveys. The annual *Etudes et travaux* reports on new research by members of the Swiss Federal Archives.

Altermatt, Urs, *Le Catholicisme au défi de la modernité* (Catholicism and the Challenge of Modernity), Lausanne: Payot, 1994

Baker, J. Wayne, "Church, State and Dissent: The Crisis of the Swiss Reformation, 1531–1536," *Church History* 57 (1988), 135–52

Barber, Benjamin R., *The Death of Communal Liberty: A History of Freedom in a Swiss Mountain Canton*, Princeton: Princeton University Press, 1974

Bendix, Regina, "National Sentiment in the Enactment and Discourse of Swiss Political Ritual," *American Ethnologist* 19 (1992), 768–90

Bergier, Jean François, *Histoire économique de la Suisse* (An Economic History of the Swiss), Paris: Colin, 1983

Bibliographie der Schweizer Geschichte, published yearly by the Swiss national library

Billigmeier, Robert Henry, *A Crisis in Swiss Pluralism: The Romansh and Their Relations with the German- and Italian-Swiss in the Perspective of a Millennium*, The Hague: Mouton, 1979

Bonjour, Edgar, *Geschichte der schweizerischen Neutralität: Drei Jahrhunderte eidgenössischer Aussenpolitik* (A History of Swiss Neutrality: Three Centuries of Confederation Foreign Policy), 8 vols., Basel: Helbing & Lichtenhahn, 1946, revised 1967–75; in French as *Histoire de la neutralité suisse* (A History of Swiss Neutrality), Neuchâtel: Baconnière, 1949

Bourgeois, Daniel, *Le Troisième Reich et la Suisse, 1933–1941* (Switzerland and the Third Reich, 1933–1941), Neuchâtel: Baconnière, 1974

Bouvier, Nicholas, Gordon A. Craig, and Lionel Gossman, *Geneva, Zurich, Basel: History, Culture, and National Identity*, Princeton: Princeton University Press, 1994

Brady, Thomas A., *Turning Swiss: Cities and Empire, 1450–1550*, Cambridge and New York: Cambridge University Press, 1985

Craig, Gordon, *The Triumph of Liberalism: Zurich in the Golden Age, 1830–1869*, New York: Scribner, 1988

Dierauer, Johannes, *Geschichte der schweizerischen Eidgenossenschaft* (A History of the Swiss Confederation), 4 vols., Gotha: Perthes, 1887; in French as *Histoire de la Confederation Suisse*, 5 vols., Lausanne: Payot, 1910–19

Fahrni, Dieter, *Schweizer Geschichte: ein historischer Abriss von den Anfängen bis zur Gegenwart*, Zurich: Pro Helvetica, 1982; in English as *An Outline History of Switzerland*, 1983

Feller, Richard, and Edgar Bonjour, *Geschichtsschreibung der Schweiz: vom Spätmittelalter zur Neuzeit* (Swiss Historiography: From the Late Middle Ages to the Present), 2 vols., Basel: Schwabe, 1962; revised Basel: Helbing & Lichtenhahn, 1979

Haller, Gottlieb Emanuel von, *Conseils pour former une bibliothèque historique de la Suisse* (Advice for Establishing a Historical Library of Switzerland, 1771)

Head, Randolph C., *Early Modern Democracy in the Grisons: Social Order and Political Language in a Swiss Mountain Canton, 1470–1620*, Cambridge and New York: Cambridge University Press, 1995

Kohn, Hans, *Nationalism and Liberty: The Swiss Example*, London: Allen and Unwin, and New York: Macmillan, 1956

Lasserre, André, *La Suisse des années sombres: courants d'opinion pendant la Deuxième Guerre mondiale, 1939–1945*, Lausanne, Payot, 1989

Meier, Heinz K., *Friendship under Stress: US–Swiss Relations, 1900–1950*, Bern: Lang, 1970

Müller, Johannes von, *Die Geschichte schweizerischer Eidgenossenschaft* (Histories of the Swiss Confederation), 5 vols., Leipzig: Weidman, 1805–08

Oechsli, Wilhelm, *History of Switzerland, 1499–1914*, Cambridge: Cambridge University Press, 1922

Remak, Joachim, *A Very Civil War: The Swiss Sonderbund War of 1847*, Boulder, CO: Westview Press, 1993

Scribner, R.W., "Communalism: Universal Category or Ideological Construct? A Debate in the Historiography of Early Modern Germany and Switzerland," *Historical Journal* 37 (1994), 199–207

Steinberg, Jonathan, *Why Switzerland?*, Cambridge and New York: Cambridge University Press, 1976

Tschudi, Gilg (or Aegidius), *Chronicon Helveticum* (Swiss Chronicles), 2 vols., 1734–36; reprinted in 11 vols., Bern: Selbstverlag der Allgemeinen Geschichtsforschenden Gesellschaft der Schweiz, 1968

Wyss, Georg von, *Geschichte der Historiographie in der Schweiz* (Survey of Swiss Historiography), Zurich: Fasi & Beer, 1895

Sybel, Heinrich von 1817–1895

German historian

Heinrich von Sybel was both a social interpreter for Germans of the French Revolution of 1789 and a prominent member of the Prussian or *kleindeutsch* ("little German") school. The school's members combined careful scholarship and energetic partisanship to demonstrate the historical ineluctability and political desirability of German unification under a Prussian aegis. These contributions of Sybel's appeared in, respectively, his multivolume *Geschichte der Revolutionszeit* (1853–79; *History of the French Revolution*, 1867–69) and his multivolume *Die Begründung des deutschen Reiches durch Wilhelm I* (1889–94; *The Founding of the German Empire by William I*, 7 vols., 1890–97). Both were heavily narrative works, based on archival research, and in both cases official archives were open to him because of his ideological congeniality to the regimes that, ultimately, controlled them. Thus, Napoleon III of France was delighted to help a German intent on showing the destructiveness of the Paris mob, and the Prussian government under Wilhelm I and Bismarck was pleased to open its papers to a repentant liberal nationalist who celebrated their accomplishments in his triumphalist narrative. Indeed, it appointed him director of its state archives in 1875.

Sybel, nonetheless, was not as consistently or singlemindedly a Prussian patriot as his Prussian school colleagues Johann Gustav Droysen (1808–86), Max Duncker (1811–86), or Heinrich von Treitschke (1834–96). Thus, in the early weeks of the German Revolution of 1848, which frightened him into the fear of mobs evinced in his French revolutionary history, he warned against unification under Prussia except as a last resort. The continual defeats of liberal and nationalist hopes in the following months evidently convinced him, in the now fashionable spirit of *Realpolitik* being proclaimed by the like-minded August von Rochau, that Prussia was Germany's last hope. Sybel's resigned acceptance of the inevitable evolved into genuine admiration for Prussia after he left Munich for Bonn in the Prussian Rhineland in 1861. His political views, which consistently penetrated his historiography, were always complex. While still in Munich, for example, he founded the *Historische Zeitschrift* (still Germany's most prestigious historical journal) and trumpeted its progressive and pro-Protestant, liberal and national outlook. Later, as a Prussian deputy, he opposed Bismarck on army reform before national unification and, true to his social conservatism, on universal manhood suffrage during it. Sybel's occasional oppositionalism, however, was always tempered by his profound respect for the state which, he believed, should represent but not be controlled by its citizens.

Sybel's characteristic ideological mix dates from his earliest works. Unlike many of his contemporaries and intellectual allies, he was not much affected by the ideas of G.W.F. Hegel

(1770–1831). By his own route, however, he arrived at a fairly Hegelian conception of the state as the carrier of ethical ideas. Sybel had matriculated at the University of Berlin in 1834, and in his three years there set a record by attending the famous *Historische Seminar* of Leopold von Ranke (1795–1886) for six consecutive semesters. Sybel later claimed that the seminar began his academic life. Sybel was also much influenced by his teacher Friedrich von Savigny (1779–1861), the founder of the Historical School of Law. Both Ranke and Savigny exerted conservative influences upon Sybel, which set him somewhat apart from such later historical-political collaborators as Droysen. No doubt their influence predisposed him to his profound admiration of Edmund Burke and the evolutionary quality of British constitutional history, and Sybel always distrusted crowds and firm constitutional guarantees. Still, he was not instinctively conservative, and from the first he rejected the relatively conservative Rankean pose.

For example, in the theses appended to his 1838 dissertation on Jordanes and the Getae, he reversed the Tacitean tag to argue that *scriptor historiae scribat cum ira et studio*: The historian should write *with*, not without, "anger and passion." He acted accordingly, and all his histories have a polemical, more or less progressive edge. Thus, his 1841 *Geschichte des ersten Kreuzuges* (History of the First Crusade) and, even more, his 1844 *Die Entstehung des deutschen Königthums* (Origins of German Kingship) were controversial inasmuch as they invidiously compared old Germany to the more polished nations of Europe, and older to more modern Germany. This was deeply upsetting to Romantics and even more sober nationalist historians such as Sybel's friend Georg Waitz. For Sybel it was just evidence of historical dynamism that he hoped to see continue, peacefully, in his own age.

In the 1840s, therefore, he undertook to educate Germans politically. Partly he did so through instructive examples, for instance his long essays on Edmund Burke in Adolf Schmidt's liberal-minded *Zeitschrift für Geschichtswissenschaft*. (The *Historische Zeitschrift*, which Sybel helped found a decade and a half later, really continued Schmidt's work.) In a similar spirit, and based on his equation of Catholicism with un-national political reaction, Sybel collaborated in a scholarly attack on the genuineness of Christ's robe at Trier Cathedral. He continued this attack in his prerevolutionary foray into political reportage and analysis, his *Die politischen Parteien im Rheinland in ihrem Verhältnis zur preusschen Verfassung geschildert* (Political Parties in the Rhineland, 1847), which was essentially an attack on the "feudal-clerical party" for seeking to reverse the historical process, with which he aligned himself. Thus, old institutions might continue only if sanctioned by history. He parted company with Savigny by taking his idea of "national spirit" (*Volksgeist*) and seeing it less as a bar to change than as a forward national evolution. This accommodationist view of history sanctioned change, even revolutionary change. On the other hand, and along with his social anxiety, he argued in 1848 against democratic control over the state and against attempts to separate state powers. As he later argued in his lectures on politics, the state was an ethical entity that was its own justification.

ROBERT FAIRBAIRN SOUTHARD

See also Germany: 1800–1945; Giesebrecht; Savigny

Biography

Born Düsseldorf, 2 December 1817. Attended Düsseldorf Gymnasium; studied with Ranke and Savigny at University of Berlin, took degree, 1834. Taught (rising to professor), University of Bonn, 1841–45; University of Marburg, 1845–56; University of Munich, 1856–61; and University of Bonn, 1861–75. Director, Prussian State Archives, Berlin, 1875–95. Founder/editor, *Historische Zeitschrift*, 1859–95. Married (2 sons). Died Marburg, 1 August 1895.

Principal Writings

Geschichte des ersten Kreuzuges, 1841; partially translated as *The History and Literature of the Crusades*, 1861
Die Entstehung des deutschen Königthums (Origins of German Kingship), 1844
Die politischen Parteien im Rheinprovinz in ihrem Verhältnis zur preussichen Verfassung geschildert (Political Parties in the Rhineland), 1847
Geschichte der Revolutionszeit von 1789 bis 1800, 5 vols., 1853–79; in English as *History of the French Revolution*, 4 vols., 1867–69
Die Begründung des deutschen Reiches durch Wilhelm I, 7 vols., 1889–94; in English as *The Founding of the German Empire by William I*, 7 vols., 1890–97; reprinted 1968

Further Reading

Schleier, Hans, *Sybel und Treitschke: Antidemokratismus und Militarismus im historischen-politischen Denken grossburgeoiser Geschichtsschreibung* (Sybel and Treitschke: Anti-Democratic Thought and Militarism in the Historical-Political Thought of Bourgeois Historiography), Berlin: Akademie, 1965
Seier, Hellmut, *Die Staatsidee Heinrich von Sybels in den Wandlungen der Reichsgründungszeit* (Sybel's Idea of State in the Transformations of the Age of National Unification), Lübeck: Matthieson, 1961

Syme, Ronald 1903–1989
British (New Zealand-born) classicist and prosopographer

In 1939 a young New Zealander named Ronald Syme published his first and most influential work, *The Roman Revolution*, which challenged the dominant Mommsen (constitutional) approach to Roman politics. In this work Syme introduced to classical studies an emerging biographical method called prosopography. Responding, in great part, to the rise of totalitarian regimes in Europe, he cast the Augustan "revolution" or transformation of the republic to a principate as the work not of a savior and preserver, but of a cynical, fraudulent, and bloody revolutionary who utilized various, similarly ambitious, conspirators as well as the redistribution of property to seize power. Focusing on the elite factions of ancient Rome, Syme built upon the work of Friedrich Münzer, Edmund Groag and Arthur Stein all of whom had studiously gathered the names, lives, and relationships of the known players in Roman politics. Through this multi-biographical approach Syme identified the family-history as well as the cadres of conspirators that furthered the elevation of Augustus to ultimate power. Rejecting the "great man" approach, Syme meticulously dissected the oligarchy that had formed Augustus' political "party."

Syme studied classics as well as French language and literature at the University of Auckland before entering Oxford University in 1925. During the 1920s and 1930s he traveled widely in Europe, examining the Roman frontiers, particularly in the Danube and Balkan regions. While there he mastered a number of European languages, including Serbo-Croatian, as well as a broad range of historical skills. There can be no doubt that these travels permanently affected both his scholarly abilities and the strong political opinions that were certainly shaped by his firsthand observations of the emerging political scene in Europe. During these years he delved into military history, epigraphy as well as the application of prosopography to classical studies. His early publications, touching on Roman legions, provinces, frontiers, and, finally, senators of the late republic, suggest the emerging direction of his interests. The result of these experiences was a decidedly critical view of Augustus and, by extension, all absolutism and totalitarianism no matter how skillfully it was established. Scholarly appreciation of *The Roman Revolution* was immediate and widespread, particularly in its relevance to the emerging war in Europe.

The general critical responses to Syme's work, not surprisingly, addressed both the anachronistic tendency in his work as well as the limitations of prosopography as a historical method. Mortimer Chambers criticized him for developing an overly-harsh opinion of Augustus that was rooted too much in Syme's own political position and experience. Yet Chambers also admitted that such value judgment was not outside the purview of the historian and that, until tyranny is eradicated on earth, Syme will "remain contemporary."

Regarding his methodology, Syme did not consider himself a social historian nor did he give great credence to social theory. Nevertheless, his use of prosopography broke ground for the use of these methods among classicists and helped lay the foundations for similar methods such as the use of network theory. Yet, although A.H.M. Jones and others followed Syme's lead, prosopographic studies of elites and oligarchic factions have shown their limitations when faced with the variety of textual and archaeological evidence that demands broader interpretations of Roman politics.

Despite these criticisms Syme went on to produce an impressive series of works that furthered his project. His second book was a complex and thorough treatment of Tacitus, with whom Syme must have felt a close political kinship. This masterful and influential 2-volume examination of the great Roman historian included a breadth and depth that inspired a number of scholars to produce similar studies of ancient authors in their historical contexts. Syme's own further work on Sallust and Ovid were additions to a growing genre that has now come to include most, if not all, the writers of the ancient Greco-Roman world. These works were accompanied by controversial studies of the *Historia Augusta*, which Syme deemed to have been written by a single author, and by his final monograph, *The Augustan Aristocracy* (1986), which returned to the personnel of the Roman "revolution."

In addition to his publications this prodigious historian also added his voice to a number of scholarly societies including the Roman Society and the American Philosophical Society. He participated in events beyond his field as well, laboring as a press attaché in Belgrade during World War II and then as a professor in classical philology in Istanbul where he apparently did more than simply lecture. G.W. Bowersock has conjectured that his espionage activities during this period helped to earn Syme membership in the prestigious Order of Merit. In addition, Syme's tremendous linguistic skills and great integrity allowed him to participate in a number of international organizations, including the UNESCO International Council for Philosophy and Humanistic Studies.

That historians have now placed the work of Ronald Syme alongside that of Tacitus, Edward Gibbon, and Theodor Mommsen suggests the great influence that he wielded in his field. The independence, complexity, and thoroughness of his work was consistently praised by friends and detractors alike. Most importantly, his work has now become required reading for every student of Roman history as well as every serious historian of the Augustan age.

KENNETH R. CALVERT

See also Roman; Scriptores

Biography

Born Eltham, Taranaki, New Zealand, 11 March 1903, son of a lawyer. Studied at Victoria University, Wellington, 1921–23; University of Auckland, 1922–25 (extramurally 1922–24); Oriel College, Oxford, BA 1927. Fellow, Trinity College, Oxford, 1929–49. Press attaché with rank of first secretary, British Legation, Belgrade, 1940–41; and British Embassy, Ankara, 1941–42. Professor of classical philology, University of Istanbul, 1942–45; professor of ancient history, Oxford University, 1949–70 (emeritus); fellow, Brasenose College, Oxford, 1949–70; and Wolfson College, Oxford, 1970–89. Knighted 1959. Order of Merit, 1976. Died Oxford, 4 September 1989.

Principal Writings

The Roman Revolution, 1939
Colonial Elites: Rome, Spain and the Americas, 1958
Tacitus, 2 vols., 1958
Sallust, 1964
Ammianus and the Historia Augusta, 1968
Ten Studies in Tacitus, 1970
Emperors and Biography: Studies in the Historia Augusta, 1971
The Historia Augusta: A Call for Clarity, 1971
Danubian Papers, 1971
History in Ovid, 1978
Roman Papers, 7 vols., 1979–91
Some Arval Brethren, 1980
Historia Augusta Papers, 1983
The Augustan Aristocracy, 1986
Anatolica: Studies in Strabo, edited by Anthony Birley, 1995

Further Reading

Alföldy, Géza, *Sir Ronald Syme, "Die römische Revolution" und die deutsche Althistorie* (Sir Ronald Syme: *The Roman Revolution* and German Classical History), Heidelberg: Winter, 1983
Bowersock, Glen Warren, "Ronald Syme," *Proceedings of the American Philosophical Society* 135 (1991), 119–22
Chambers, Mortimer, *Greek and Roman History*, 2nd edition, in Service Center for Teachers of History, no. 11, Washington, DC: American Historical Association, 1965, 28–30
Galsterer, H., "A Man, a Book, and a Method: Sir Ronald Syme's Roman Revolution after Fifty Years," in Kurt Raaflaub and Mark Toher, eds., *Between Republic and Empire: Interpretations of Augustus and His Principate*, Berkeley: University of California Press, 1990

Grant, M., "Sir Ronald Syme," *Journal of Roman Studies* 80 (1990), xi–xiv

Linderski, J., "Mommsen and Syme: Law and Power in the Principate of Augustus," in Kurt Raaflaub and Mark Toher, eds., *Between Republic and Empire: Interpretations of Augustus and His Principate*, Berkeley: University of California Press, 1990

Millar, Fergus, "Style Abides," *Journal of Roman Studies* 71 (1981), 144–52

Yavetz, Zvi, "The Personality of Augustus: Reflections on Syme's Roman Revolution," in Kurt A. Raaflaub and Mark Toher, eds., *Between Republic and Empire: Interpretations of Augustus and His Principate*, Berkeley: University of California Press, 1990

Szekfű, Gyula 1883–1955

Hungarian historian of ideas

Undoubtedly ranking among the greatest scholarly achievements of Hungarian historiography, Gyula Szekfű's works defy traditional classification. Although he has been regarded as one of the founders of the Hungarian school of *Geistesgeschichte*, together with Bálint Hóman, his co-author on the 5-volume *Magyar történet* (Hungarian History, 1935–36), Szekfű was not merely a historian of ideas but the historian of the Magyar state, the "political nation," and the declining middle class. He was renowned for his strikingly original, highly controversial, and frequently shifting interpretations. As his former student Domokos Kosáry has argued, Szekfű challenged the national demagogy and narrow constitutional approach of the liberal school of Hungarian historians, infusing his narratives on political history with a refined and idealistic "humanistic nationalism." In the finest example of his scholarship, the three volumes of the *Magyar történet* spanning the 15th to the 20th centuries, he managed to strike a balance between the intellectual, political, social, economic, and demographic aspects of history. Moreover, in his historical portraits he departed from the romantic school's idealization of national heroes such as prince Rákóczi, the leader of the war of independence, and Gábor Bethlen, the Transylvanian sovereign idolized in Magyar Protestant historiography.

In his first substantial work, *A száműzött Rákóczi* (Rákóczi in Exile, 1913), Szekfű characterized the old Kuruc (anti-Habsburg) leader as a tragic figure, a devout Catholic, a man of principle who was not however without vanity, naivety, or political illusions. He shocked many patriotic readers with the embarrassing revelation that the Kuruc exiles established a gambling house in Paris to finance their political activities. The book was publicly burnt by nationalists, and the young historian, who worked as an archivist at the Haus-, Hof-, und Staatsarchiv in Vienna, was branded as a pro-Austrian traitor. Indeed, he was accused of tarnishing the memory of all exiled champions of Hungarian independence. Szekfű was badly bruised by the vicious recriminations but stood firm, defending his views in a series of polemical articles.

In 1917 at the request of a German publisher, he wrote *Der Staat Ungarn* (The Hungarian State), a brief overview of Hungarian history to explain the status of Hungary within the Habsburg empire. He set out to illustrate to German readers the continuity of Hungarian statehood, from the reign of St. Stephen to the *Ausgleich* in 1867. He refuted the Austrian view that the collapse of Hungary in 1526 resulted in the loss of the "individuality of the Magyar state." At the same time he emphasized that Hungary was part of "German-Christian" civilization, carefully avoiding any allusions to Hungarian independence and favoring the term "national autonomy" when referring to Hungary's status within the Habsburg monarchy. Consequently, he was once again censured for shifting the interpretation of Hungarian history more closely toward a pro-Habsburg Catholic point of view.

In the interwar period Szekfű became a semi-official historian of Hungary and editor of the *Magyar Szemle* (Hungarian Review). His reputation was established by another polemical work, *Három Nemzedék* (Three Generations, 1920), which launched a bitter attack on Hungarian liberalism. He described the whole era from the middle of the 19th century to World War I as the "age of decline." The book gives a particularly damning view of the romantic nationalists who ignored István Széchenyi's conservative reformist heritage and embarked on a distorted and peculiarly Magyar form of liberalism. Further fierce criticism is reserved for the second and third generations of Kossuth's successors, whom Szekfű blamed for the steady deterioration of Hungarian culture and the corruption of political life. Finally, he held the liberals responsible for the disasters of two revolutions, and the collapse of the old Magyar state. In 1934 he added a new chapter to the book, a separate essay, reproaching a "fourth generation," this time his own. The essay and his other writings of the 1930s reflect his increasing alarm at the growing popularity of Nazi Germany and the policy of extremist groups.

His final study of the "decay of Hungarian society," *Forradalom Után* (After the Revolution, 1947), signalled yet another U-turn in Szekfű's views. In this work, the former pro-Habsburg historian, one of the most prominent conservatives of the Bethlen era, argued that social revolution was an unavoidable necessity. In his capacity as Hungarian ambassador in Moscow, he condemned Hungary's wartime leaders for delaying peace negotiations with the Soviets, and for ignoring the obvious geopolitical fact that an Allied victory would secure a dominant position in Central Europe for the Soviet Union. In spite of this, Szekfű distanced himself from Marxism; even in the isolation of his last years he remained a Catholic thinker from the politically extinct Hungarian middle class.

GÁBOR BÁTONYI

See also Central Europe; East Central Europe

Biography

Born Székesfehérvár, 1883. Staff member, Hungarian National Museum, 1904, Hungarian National Archives, 1909–13, and Haus-, Hof- und Staatsarchive, Vienna, 1913–16; professor, University of Budapest, from 1916. Hungarian ambassador to Moscow, 1945. Died Budapest, 28 June 1955.

Principal Writings

A száműzött Rákóczi (Rákóczi in Exile), 1913
Der Staat Ungarn (The Hungarian State), 1917
Három Nemzedék (Three Generations), 1920; revised 1934
With Bálint Hóman, *Magyar történet* (Hungarian History), 5 vols., 1935–36
Forradalom Után (After the Revolution), 1947

Further Reading

Bibó, István, "Németh László kelet-európai koncepciója és Szekfű Gyulával folytatott vitája" (The Eastern European Concept of László Németh and His Controversy with Gyula Szekfű), in Bibó István, *Válogatott tanulmányok* (Selected Essays), vol. 3, Budapest: Magvető Kiadó, 1986

Dénes, Zoltán Iván, A *"realitás" illúziója: a históríkus Szekfű Gyula pályafordulója* (The Illusion of "Reality": The Historian Gyula Szekfű's volte-face), Budapest: Akadémiai Kiadó, 1976

Glatz, Ferenc, *Történetíró és politika* (The Historian and Politics), Budapest: Akadémiai Kiadó, 1980

Gunst, Péter, *A magyar történetírás története* (The History of Hungarian Historiography), Debrecen: Csokonai Kiadó, 1995

Kosáry, Domokos, "A magyar történetírás a két világháború között" (Hungarian Historical Writing Between the Two World Wars), in Domokos Kosáry, *A történelem veszedelmei* (The Perils of History), Budapest: Magvető Kiadó, 1987

Kosáry, Domokos, "The Idea of a Comparative History of East Central Europe: The Story of a Venture," in Dennis Deletant and Harry Hanak, eds., *Historians as Nation-Builders*, London: Macmillan, 1988

Németh, László, *Szekfű Gyula*, Budapest: Bólyai Akadémia, 1940

T

Tacitus *c.*56–after 118 CE

Roman historian

Tacitus is among the foremost stylists of the Silver Age of Latin literature and ranks next to or ahead of Livy and Sallust as the foremost Roman historian. Tacitus' reputation as a historian has waxed and waned, usually with the relevance of his works to contemporary politics. His style is terse, fluid, and direct.

By the time of the 3rd-century CE emperor Tacitus – who may have been a relative of the historian – only an imperial edict kept Tacitus' works from being lost. During the Carolingian Renaissance of the 7th and 8th centuries his works were considered important enough to be copied, and current knowledge of them comes primarily from one manuscript. During the Renaissance Tacitus was read and admired. His histories inspired plays by Ben Jonson and Racine. Thomas Jefferson found his works cautionary tales for the new North American republic. They warned that despotism could triumph over freedom and virtue could be routed by corruption and decadence if a nation was not of strong character. Also, Tacitus' comparison of the tribes of Germans to the Romans served as an example for Anglo-American relations with Native Americans. Napoleon was less convinced: "Tacitus! Don't talk to me about that sensation-monger! He has libeled the emperors." Tacitus' mood of pessimism attracted modern scholars to his work after World War II. Despite their biases, Tacitus' works remain an important literary source for knowledge of 1st-century Rome and ancient Germany and Britain. They are more dependable than those of Suetonius or Dio Cassius.

Tacitus' use of conditional sentences and rhetorical questions suggests less eagerness to "explain" events than is found in Sallust's works. Professing to write "sine ira et studio" (without hatred and partisan purpose) Tacitus maintained an anti-imperial, pro-senatorial bias in his works.

Scholars now believe that Tacitus' first historical work was *De vita Iulii Agricolae* (On the Life of Julius Agricola). Agricola was Tacitus' father-in-law and by Tacitus' account conqueror of all Britain. Writing about 98 CE, Tacitus depicted Agricola as a noble subject. The *Agricola* includes passages on British geography, ethnography, and the effect of Roman civilization on the natives of Britain. The final sections may have been actual funeral oratory for Agricola.

Also published in 98 CE was *De origine et situ Germanorum* (The Origins and Country of the Germans) or *Germania*.

Although Tacitus used ten sources, he seems to have had no firsthand experience with the Germans. Using out-of-date materials from the reign of Augustus, he failed to incorporate current events from the reign of Domitian. He contrasted the upright freedom-loving German barbarians with the now corrupt and servile Romans. Both works illustrate the moral philosophy underlying Tacitus' historical writings. Although he dramatized the triumph of corruption, he realized that there are always men and women who manage to maintain standards of courage and morality.

Dialogus de oratoribus (Dialogue on Orators) is now dated after 100 CE instead of the 80s. The *Dialogue* is an inquiry into the decadence of oratory and is both fascinating and thought-provoking. The work is more Ciceronian than *Germany* or *Agricola* but its subject matter may account for its style, not its proximity to Tacitus' active political career as a legal advocate.

Tacitus' best writing is found in the *Historiae* (The Histories) which covered the years 68–96 CE and the *Annals* which treated 14 to 68 CE. Both works were completed by 109 CE and numbered some 30 books or scrolls, the equivalent of about five modern books. Only about half of these two works survives. Missing is the reign of Domitian, a tyrant, during whose reign the senatorial class was subject to persecution. Some think that the well-known invective Tacitus directed toward the earlier emperor, Tiberius, was in part influenced by his own experience with the emperor Domitian. Velleius may have produced a more accurate portrait of Tiberius in his *Histories of the Romans*.

The *Annals* followed the old Roman tradition of recording events by years, hence its name. Tacitus, however, superbly drew three-dimensional characters in his annals. He argued that only a myriad of minor events had occurred since Augustus's reign. Accordingly, he replaced the telling of epic events with character studies. Tacitus firmly expressed his ideas on character and politics. He believed character rather than the form of government determined the fate of nations, including Rome. Character was revealed in dedication to civic duties and in the integrity of leaders who overcame ambition and greed. Although Tacitus referred intermittently to gods, fortune, and fate in the history of Rome, he never formulated an explanation for their relation to the actions of humans.

All his works reflected Tacitus' own life, especially the trauma of the year of four emperors. In the *Annals*, Tacitus defined history's purpose as follows: "The principal office of history I take to be this: to prevent virtuous actions from being forgotten, and that evil words and deeds should fear an infamous reputation with posterity."

NANCY PIPPEN ECKERMAN

See also Germany: to 1450; Roman; Suetonius; Syme; Velleius

Biography

Publius or Gaius Cornelius Tacitus. Born c.56 CE, Narbonese Gaul, present-day Provence or northern Italy. Studied in Rome where he knew Pliny the Younger. Served as an advocate at law. Served in various provincial capacities, returning to Rome, where he held several offices including praetor, 88, consul, 97, and proconsul of Asia, 112/13. Married in 77 daughter of Gnaeus Julius Agricola, later governor of Britain. Died after 118 CE.

Principal Writings

De origine et situ Germanorum, 98 CE; in English as Germania
De vita Iulii Agricolae, 98 CE; in English as Agricola
Dialogus de oratoribus, 101/2 CE; in English as Dialogue
Annales ab excessu divi Augusti, 109 CE; in English as The Annals
Historiae, c.109/10 CE; in English as The Histories
Tacitus in Five Volumes (Loeb edition; includes Agricola, Germania, Dialogus, The Histories, The Annals), 5 vols., 1969–80

Further Reading

Dorey, Thomas Alan, ed., Latin Historians, New York: Basic Books, and London: Routledge, 1966

Dorey, Thomas Alan, ed., Tacitus, New York: Basic Books, and London: Routledge, 1969

Dudley, Donald Reynolds, The World of Tacitus, Boston: Little Brown, and London: Secker and Warburg, 1968

Duff, J.W., A Literary History of Rome in the Silver Age, from Tiberius to Hadrian, London: Unwin, 1927; New York: Scribner, 1935; 3rd edition London: Benn, 1964

Goodyear, Francis Richard David, Tacitus, Oxford: Oxford University Press, 1970

Grant, Michael, Greek and Latin Authors, 800 BC–AD 1000, New York: Wilson, 1980

Henry, Elisabeth, The Annals of Tacitus: A Study in the Writing of History, Manchester: Manchester University Press, 1952; reprinted New York: Arno, 1981

Laistner, Max Ludwig Wolfram, The Greater Roman Historians, Berkeley: University of California Press, 1947

Luce, T. James, ed., Ancient Writers: Greece and Rome, 2 vols., New York: Scribner, 1982

Luce, T. James, and A.J. Woodman, eds., Tacitus and the Tacitean Tradition, Princeton: Princeton University Press, 1993

Martin, Ronald H., Tacitus and the Writing of History, Berkeley: University of California Press, and London: Batsford, 1981

Mendell, C.W., Tacitus: The Man and His Work, New Haven: Yale University Press, 1957

Momigliano, Arnaldo, Essays in Ancient and Modern Historiography, Middletown, CT: Wesleyan University Press, and Oxford: Blackwell, 1977

Scott, Russell T., Religion and Philosophy in the Histories of Tacitus, Rome: American Academy Press, 1968

Smith, Robert W., and Donald C. Bryant, eds., Ancient Greek and Roman Rhetoricians: A Biographical Dictionary, Columbia, MO: Artcraft, 1968

Syme, Ronald, Tacitus, 2 vols., Oxford: Oxford University Press, 1958

Syme, Ronald, Ten Studies in Tacitus, Oxford: Oxford University Press, 1970

Takaki, Ronald 1939–

US ethnic and social historian

Ronald Takaki is best known as the foremost exponent of the history of Asian Americans in the United States, a field the development of which his pioneering work made a large contribution. He has also made path-breaking contributions to the history of American racism. He is among the large number of historians who from the early 1970s onwards expanded the range of US history, focusing upon previously neglected groups, including women and nonwhite Americans. His work belongs to the new social history of this period, heavily emphasizing the day-to-day experiences of nonelite groups and figures, rather than focusing upon the prominent. It consciously attempts to incorporate previously excluded groups and issues into the generally accepted US historical tradition. Readable and lively, but based on wide research and models of scholarship, Takaki's work crosses the divide between academic and popular history; his later volumes on Asian Americans and on multicultural immigrant history have attracted a large nonprofessional audience.

Takaki began his career working in southern and African American history. His first book, A Pro-Slavery Crusade (1971), studied in depth the previously neglected determination of antebellum southerners to regain access to their supply of slaves from African sources. He analyzed the dynamics of class hegemony, racial relations, and a sense of national and international beleaguerment in creating this movement, themes that would be of continuing interest to Takaki. Shortly afterwards, in Violence in the Black Imagination (1972), Takaki moved from whites to blacks to study the direct experiences and thought of African Americans as exemplified in 19th-century literature.

Takaki's interests broadened over time. His next and most ambitious work, Iron Cages (1979), a tour de force of interdisciplinary historical scholarship, was "a comparative analysis of racial domination within the context of the development of capitalism and class divisions in nineteenth-century American society" which sought "to understand how the domination of various peoples of color in America had cultural and economic bases which involved as well as transcended race." Much influenced by the theories of Antonio Gramsci and Max Weber, the book gave an overview of the nature of white racism in the United States, its generalisms supplemented by specific studies of 14 prominent political and intellectual figures. Takaki focused upon the manner in which the constricting three "iron cages" of American republican ideology, bureaucratic capitalism, and "demonic" imperialistic violence affected the nature of racism in the United States. Comparing the ways in which racism affected blacks, ethnic Americans, Mexicans, and Asians, Takaki showed how the sometimes differing experiences of these various groups were in fact interrelated and the product of the same overriding white outlook.

Takaki, himself of Japanese American extraction, then turned to the history of Asian Americans in the United States. Pan Hana (1983), a specialized study of the life of Asian laborers on Hawaiian plantations, was followed by Strangers from a Different Shore (1989), an overview of the Asian immigrant experience in the United States. His next book, the prizewinning and widely acclaimed A Different Mirror (1993), continued to mine the vein of immigrant history, attempting to provide a comprehensive "multicultural history" of the United States through the varying experiences of whites, ethnic Americans, African Americans, Chinese, Japanese, Chicanos, Jews, and Irish. Takaki combined his previous interests in racial and ethnic relations and the immigrant experience, in a conscious effort to answer such critics of multiculturalism as Allan Bloom and E.D. Hirsch by producing a history that reflected the diversity of the experiences of numerous ethnic groups in the United States. His work gave particular attention to the development of slavery and racism and to social and labor history, in an attempt to convey the reality of life in the United States for average men and women from many cultures.

Most recently, Takaki entered the ongoing and highly topical debate on the dropping of atomic bombs on Japan in 1945, inspired by the 1994 controversy over a proposed Smithsonian exhibition. In *Hiroshima: Why America Dropped the Atomic Bomb* (1995), published to mark the 50th anniversary of the event, he drew on his past research on racism and the frontier tradition in United States to suggest that "racialized rage" against the Japanese played a large part in the decision to use the bomb. Clearly opposed to the decision, Takaki argued that it was unnecessary, that other alternatives were not properly explored, and that the frontier-generated combativeness of the American character, which leading American policymakers of the time displayed, bore much of the responsibility for their decision to employ atomic weapons. This short volume also demonstrated Takaki's desire that historical research and writing should escape the academy and address major contemporary political and social concerns, a theme that has informed the entire career of a man always deeply engaged with current public issues.

PRISCILLA M. ROBERTS

Biography

Ronald Toshiyuki Takaki. Born Honolulu, 12 April 1939. Received BA, College of Wooster, 1961; MA, University of California, Berkeley, 1962, PhD 1967. Taught at College of San Mateo, 1965–67; University of California, Los Angeles, 1967–72; and University of California, Berkeley, from 1972. Married 1961 (2 children).

Principal Writings

A Pro-Slavery Crusade: The Agitation to Reopen the African Slave Trade, 1971
Violence in the Black Imagination: Essays and Documents, 1972
Iron Cages: Race and Culture in Nineteenth-Century America, 1979
Pan Hana: Plantation Life and Labor in Hawaii, 1835–1920, 1983
Strangers from a Different Shore: A History of Asian Americans, 1989
A Different Mirror: A History of Multicultural America, 1993
Hiroshima: Why America Dropped the Atomic Bomb, 1995

Tannenbaum, Frank 1893–1969

US (Polish-born) historian of Latin America

More than a Latin American historian, Frank Tannenbaum was a socially conscious academic who used his own activism to advance the understanding of history. Tannenbaum made the teaching of history as important as conducting research. He was responsible for the creation of the University Seminars at Columbia University, which brought about a new interdisciplinary approach to history.

In the early years of the 20th century, he was concerned with the problems of the poor and the working class, and became a member of the Industrial Workers of the World ("Wobblies"). He was arrested for organizing unemployed workers in New York City, and spent time in prison for his activities. It was these experiences that provided the foundation for Tannenbaum's lifelong commitment to the concerns of labor. These experiences were also the basis for his first book, *The Labor Movement* (1921). Tannenbaum saw the labor movement as basis for stability in society, and given his intimate involvement with the movement, he showed a high level of professionalism in his objective approach to the subject. His experiences in jail were the basis for his second work, *Wall Shadows* (1922). In this book Tannenbaum chronicled the mechanics of the criminal justice system, and made a plea for the reform of a prison system he described as "medieval."

Tannenbaum next turned to a study of Latin America, specifically, Mexico, the subject of six books written between 1928 and 1962. These works provide a great insight into the problems of Latin America in the 20th century and reflect Tannenbaum's social concerns for the people of the region, and the problems they faced. Two of these works, *Slave and Citizen* (1946) and *Ten Keys to Latin America* (1962) are especially noteworthy.

Slave and Citizen examined the common theme of the historical experiences of two disparate cultures. In this work, Tannenbaum presented a three point argument concerning the nature of slavery. First, he felt that slavery was both a moral and legal relationship. Second, abolition as a process of emancipation could have been a peaceful process, and third, the acknowledgment of a slave's moral existence was dependent on the social and religious history of the slaveholder, and the slaveholder's conception of the relationship of man to God.

Ten Keys to Latin America is unusual in that it is written without footnotes and is the summation of Tannenbaum's thirty years of experience in trying to understand the region. It won the Bolton prize in history in 1963 for showing a grasp of the unique issues that confronted and affected Latin America.

In addition to his influential works on Latin America and labor history, Tannenbaum is also known for his work in creating the University Seminars at Columbia University. The Seminars evolved just before the end of World War II as a means finding solutions to what were termed "going concerns." This meant problems related to such things as peace, religion, or issues of state. The Seminars were designed to be fluid in nature. They were also meant to be interdisciplinary, bringing together academics from different institutions and people from the private sector. Tannenbaum also initiated a series of seminars that focused on the problems confronting Latin America.

DREW PHILIP HALEVY

See also Brazil; Cuba; Elkins; Freyre; Latin America: National; Mexico; Slavery: Modern

Biography

Born Poland, 4 March 1893; moved with his family to the US in 1905, settling in Great Barrington, Massachusetts. Moved to New York City, 1914, where he worked in a variety of jobs, joined the Industrial Workers of the World, and served a prison term for labor organizing; entered Columbia University through the recommendation of Thomas Mott Osborne, governor of Sing-Sing Prison, graduating with honors, 1921. Travelled through Mexico before serving in the US Army; received PhD from the Brookings Institution, 1927; then took part in an economic and social survey of Puerto Rico, 1927–30, a survey of education in rural Mexico, 1930–31, and travelled in Latin America. At Columbia University: taught criminology, 1932; taught history (rising to professor), 1935–61. Married 1) Esther Abramson (marriage dissolved); 2) Jane Belo, 1940 (died 1968). Died June 1969.

Principal Writings

The Labor Movement: Its Conservative Functions and Social Consequences, 1921
Wall Shadows: A Study in American Prisons, 1922
Darker Phases of the South, 1924
The Mexican Agrarian Revolution, 1929
Peace by Revolution: An Interpretation of Mexico, 1933
Whither Latin America? An Introduction to Its Economic and Social Problems, 1934
Crime and the Community, 1938
Slave and Citizen: The Negro in the Americas, 1946
Mexico: The Struggle for Peace and Bread, 1950
The American Tradition in Foreign Policy, 1955
Ten Keys to Latin America, 1962
The Balance of Power in Society, and Other Essays, 1969

Further Reading

Cowie, Jefferson R., *The Emergence of Alternative Views of Latin America: The Thought of Three US Intellectuals, 1920–1935,* Durham, NC: Duke–University of North Carolina Program in Latin American Studies, 1992
Delpar, Helen, "Frank Tannenbaum: The Making of a Mexicanist, 1914–1933," *Americas* 4 (1988), 153–71
Foner, Laura, and Eugene D. Genovese, eds., *Slavery in the New World: A Reader in Comparative History,* Englewood Cliffs, NJ: Prentice Hall, 1969
Maier, Joseph, and Weatherhead, Richard W., *Frank Tannenbaum, A Biographical Essay,* New York: University Seminars, Columbia University, 1974

Tawney, R.H. 1880–1962

British historian of early modern Britain

As a Christian, a socialist, and an ardent supporter of the Workers' Education Association movement, R.H. Tawney was primarily interested in the ethical dimensions attached to the production of wealth. His *Acquisitive Society* (1920) and *Equality* (1931), both sought to provide broad historical explanations for the inequality and stress on private income which, in his view, epitomized contemporary Britain: both were enormously influential. As the *Times* obituarist noted, Tawney was, "the most distinguished English economic historian of his generation," and his early writings in particular treated history as a branch of philosophy. Like his contemporary G.D.H. Cole, he placed moral judgments at the center of his historical work. Since his death his reputation has declined under the relentless

critique of those who, not sharing his values, accused him of allowing them to distort historical reality. Nevertheless, Tawney's work was central to three great 20th-century historical debates about the nature of early modern Britain.

In 1911 John and Barbara Hammond published *The Village Labourer,* characterizing the 18th-century enclosure movement as ruthlessly exploitative and greedy. The following year Tawney, writing from a similar political perspective, presented an identical view of the earlier enclosure movement in his *The Agrarian Problem in the Sixteenth Century* (1912). Tawney himself accepted that there were flaws in his book – this is why he would not allow it to be reprinted unrevised in his own lifetime – but the passion and conviction with which it was written served to heighten its impact on the world of 16th-century scholarship. Critics nibbled away at his arguments over the years, often along lines suggested by Tawney himself, but the most substantial demolition came more than half a century after the book's first appearance: Eric Kerridge comprehensively rejected Tawney's view that in the Tudor period ruthless agrarian capitalists swept aside a helpless peasantry. Tawney the politician, he concluded, had got in the way of Tawney the scholar, thereby leading generations of students into "grievous error."

In 1926 Tawney's best known work appeared, *Religion and the Rise of Capitalism.* The book was translated into several foreign languages with sales running into six figures, and the brilliance and power of its writing have remained substantially undiminished by the passage of time. It addressed the hypothesis advanced by Max Weber that in the course of the 16th and 17th centuries the social and economic values inherent in Calvinism facilitated the rise of capitalism in western Europe. Tawney pointed out that capitalism was nothing new in the 16th century and not so exclusively Protestant thereafter as Weber implied. Inverting Weber, Tawney argued that Calvinism in fact provided a religious rationale for capitalism, a process which, as he made all too evident for some of his critics, he viewed as a perversion of Christian values. The book concluded with an attack on modern capitalism for neglecting the truism that "even quite common men have souls and that no economic system was satisfactory that did not allow for the satisfaction of other than purely material wants." It was inevitable that such a bold and wide-ranging book should invite and receive well-founded critical comment and amendment: in particular Tawney's assertion that the values inherent in puritanism had led to a declining sense of social obligation was much discussed. The most powerful of his critics was Geoffrey Elton, who deplored Tawney's work for its present-mindedness and accused him of weakening both Protestantism and capitalism. Elton was still harping on this theme some 15 years after Tawney's death, reviling *Religion and the Rise of Capitalism* as a prime example of selective history, written to prove an already existing conviction.

The problems of economic morality received rather less attention in Tawney's later and perhaps most controversial publication, "The Rise of the Gentry, 1558–1640." In this article, he argued that the land seized by the Tudor monarchy from the monasteries in the 1530s eventually passed, along with its associated political power, from the aristocracy into the hands of the gentry. Crown efforts to check this development ultimately led to the Civil War. This interpretation won immediate acceptance, partly because of its persuasive writing and partly because it fitted so well with other work, notably J.E. Neale's analyses of the rise of the Elizabethan House of Commons. Seven years later it received powerful support in an article by Lawrence Stone. However, Stone's paper was demolished almost at once in a vitriolic counter from Hugh Trevor Roper who then turned his fire on Tawney himself, accusing him of statistical misinterpretation and selective use of ancillary evidence. The ensuing debate dragged on for years, turning largely on the evidence for social change in the 17th century. If Tawney's original hypothesis is now largely discredited, one positive outcome was the production of several important local studies of the gentry showing that the story was considerably more complex and diverse than either Tawney or his critics had appreciated. Furthermore, the debate succeeded in laying to rest a long-standing interpretation of the 17th century that had been based mainly on parliamentary politics and the constitution.

Tawney himself was not unduly perturbed by the criticism that his major works attracted: he believed that the task of the historian was to raise questions in the hope that the collective input of the historical community would go some way towards providing answers. Thus he expected his work to be challenged and refined. What he did not relish was the personal tone that many of the attacks assumed. There is no doubt that both his choice of subjects and his interpretations of them were colored by his own beliefs. In that sense his critics were right when they accused him of being an ideologue: but in essence such charges really reflect much deeper disagreements among historians about the purpose for which history should be studied and how the past relates to the present.

KENNETH D. BROWN

See also Britain: 1485–1750; Economic; Hill; Power; Social; Stone; Thirsk; Thomas, K.

Biography

Richard Henry Tawney. Born Calcutta, 30 November 1880. Educated at Rugby School; Balliol College, Oxford, BA in classics 1903. Teacher and executive member, Workers' Educational Association, 1905–47: president, 1928–44; assistant, Glasgow University, 1906–08; teacher, Tutorial Classes Committee, Oxford, 1908–14; taught (rising to professor of economic history), London School of Economics, 1920–49. Served in the British Army, 1915–16, rising to sergeant; wounded. Member of many commissions and committees. Married Annette Jeanie Beveridge, 1909 (died 1958). Died London, 16 January 1962.

Principal Writings

The Agrarian Problem in the Sixteenth Century, 1912
The Assessment of Wages in England by Justices of the Peace, 1913
The Acquisitive Society, 1920
Editor with Eileen Power, *Tudor Economic Documents*, 3 vols., 1924
The British Labor Movement, 1925
Religion and the Rise of Capitalism, 1926
Equality, 1931; revised 1952
Land and Labour in China, 1932
"The Rise of the Gentry, 1558–1640," *Economic History Review* 11 (1941), 1–38
Business and Politics under James I: Lionel Cranfield as Merchant and Minister, 1958
History and Society: Essays, edited by Jay M. Winter, 1978

Further Reading

Court, William Henry Bassano, *Scarcity and Choice in History*, London: Arnold, and New York: A.M. Kelley, 1970
Fisher, Frederick Jack, ed., *Essays in the Economic and Social History of Tudor and Stuart England in Honour of R.H. Tawney*, Cambridge: Cambridge University Press, 1961
Kenyon, John, *The History Men: The Historical Profession in England since the Renaissance*, London, Weidenfeld and Nicolson, 1983; Pittsburgh: University of Pittsburgh Press, 1984
Ormrod, David, "R.H. Tawney and the Origins of Capitalism," *History Workshop Journal* 18 (1984), 138–59
Parker, Christopher, *The English Historical Tradition since 1850*, Edinburgh: John Donald, 1990
Reisman, David, *State and Welfare: Tawney, Galbraith, and Adam Smith*, London: Macmillan, and New York: St. Martin's Press, 1982
Terrill, Ross, *R.H. Tawney and His Times: Socialism as Fellowship*, Cambridge, MA: Harvard University Press, 1973; London: Deutsch, 1974
Wright, Anthony, *R.H. Tawney*, Manchester: Manchester University Press, 1987

Taylor, A.J.P. 1906–1990
British historian

A leading political and diplomatic historian, A.J.P. Taylor was nothing less than the public face of history in Britain in the second half of the 20th century and a teacher of genius. Taylor prided himself on having founded no school of history nor having made any significant historical discoveries. He displayed an unfashionable love of events and great men at a time when social history was in the ascendant. He believed that history was primarily a matter of accident, rather than the product of profound forces. His work was read extensively by the general public, although he felt slighted by the historical profession as a whole. Taylor was a great narrative historian. His skills were honed in journalism and his style easily recognizable for its short, staccato sentences and its playful love of paradox.

Taylor's books were devoted mainly to European history in the 19th and 20th centuries. His early research in the Staatsarchiv in Vienna led to a lasting concern with European foreign policy. After writing two detailed monographs, his acclaimed book, *The Habsburg Monarchy, 1815–1918* (1941) reached out to a popular audience with its cynical, epigrammatic style influenced by his friend Malcolm Muggeridge, though its judgments were shaped partly by his colleague, Lewis Namier. Having investigated *Germany's First Bid for Colonies, 1884–1885* (1938), he was drawn into a series of works that examined the German problem in diplomacy more generally. *The Course of German History* (1945) was uncharacteristically determinist, arguing that Nazism was produced by the peculiarities of the German state: absolutism became totalitarianism. The German people as a whole were to blame for Hitler. In the 1961 edition, he wrote that "it was no more a mistake for the German people to end up with Hitler than it is an accident when a river flows into the sea." However, his short biography of Bismarck praised the statesman for his moderation, noting that he reacted to events rather than worked to a predetermined strategy. This analysis was also applied to Hitler in *The Origins of the Second World War* (1961), but with more controversial results. Taylor attempted to view Hitler as a statesman rather than as a master criminal. The war was the result of diplomatic blunders on both sides. Taylor never sought to excuse Hitler but to view him historically. His was simply the traditional German foreign policy. It should be remembered that the book was written in the shadow of the atom bomb. For Taylor, accidents in diplomacy could happen and the deterrent might not always deter. The debate over the volume caused some damage to his reputation.

His two most important books were his Oxford histories: *The Struggle for Mastery in Europe, 1848–1918* (1954) and *English History, 1914–45* (1965). These became standard works, based on extensive research and brilliant though sometimes maverick judgments. The former examined the balance of power in Europe which prevented a major war until the system broke down in 1914. Although widely admired, it has been criticized for its exclusive focus on a narrow group of policymakers. Taylor's extensive research in published editions of diplomatic documents (which he often reviewed) gave his work scholarly distinction. *English History, 1914–45* contributed to a reappraisal of the 1930s, noting the economic success of the decade alongside the appalling social conditions. As he was to put it later on: "which was more significant for the future – over a million unemployed or over a million private cars?" Taylor considered World War II a just war and Churchill "the saviour of his country." In a number of works, he contributed to a more positive appraisal of the career of David Lloyd George whose reputation was then in the doldrums. His friendship with Lord Beaverbrook led to a biography of the newspaper magnate, his final major work.

Taylor's favorite book was *The Trouble Makers* (1957), based on his 1955 Ford lectures at Oxford and a celebration of critics of British foreign policy from Cobden onwards. It was a tradition to which he wholeheartedly belonged. Taylor came from radical dissenting stock in Lancashire and received a Quaker education that provided him with both the habit of industry and a hostility toward the establishment that never left him. Essentially a Little Englander, he was always on the left (though this did not influence his historical works to any discernible extent). He once claimed his were "extreme views weakly held." For most of his life, Taylor was a critical supporter of the Labour party. He was a critic of Suez and helped launch the Campaign for Nuclear Disarmament. He showed an admiration (without illusions) for the achievement of the Soviet Union under Stalin and claimed that his favorite historian was E.H. Carr. By contrast, he disliked the United States, a country he refused to visit partly because of its role in the Cold War. Taylor's politics were more evident in his journalism (he was a regular contributor to the *Sunday Express*) and in his brilliant book reviews for the *Observer*, many of which were later re-published. It was apparently Taylor's journalism that resulted in his failure to obtain the Regius professorship of history at Oxford University in 1957 (which was given to Hugh Trevor-Roper).

Taylor's reputation soared on the television screen. He became a political commentator on the programs *In the News* and *Face the Press*. Already a popular teacher at Oxford (his talks had to be scheduled for 9 am on a Monday morning to prevent overcrowded lecture halls), he became famous for his live half-hour talks on television where he dissected historical problems without aid of notes or maps and was always able

to finish exactly on time. As with his books, his style was often impish, recreating historical events and stressing the role of chance. One lecture claimed that World War I started only because the Archduke Franz Ferdinand's driver had taken the wrong turning at Sarajevo. These talks were also subsequently reprinted in book form. A generation of schoolchildren was encouraged by watching him to study history at university. It is a measure of his reputation that he received no fewer than three *Festschriften*. Taylor was distinguished for his insistence that history should always be readable and accessible to all. He was the people's historian.

ROHAN McWILLIAM

See also Austro-Hungarian; Diplomatic; Germany: 1800–1945

Biography

Alan John Percivale Taylor. Born Birkdale, Lancashire, 25 March 1906, son of a cotton merchant. Educated at Bootham School, York; Oriel College, Oxford, BA 1927; researched in Vienna, 1928–30. Lecturer in history, Manchester University, from 1930; fellow/tutor, Magdalen College, Oxford, 1938–76; freelance journalist from 1963. Married 1) Margaret Adams, 1931 (marriage dissolved 1951; 2 sons, 2 daughters); 2) Eve Crosland, 1951 (marriage dissolved 1974; 2 sons); 3) W. Eva Haraszti, historian, 1976. Died London, 7 September 1990.

Principal Writings

The Italian Problem in European Diplomacy, 1847–1849, 1934
Germany's First Bid for Colonies, 1884–1885: A Move in Bismarck's European Policy, 1938
The Habsburg Monarchy, 1815–1918: A History of the Austrian Empire and Austria-Hungary, 1941; revised [with dates 1809–1918] 1948
The Course of German History: A Survey of the Development of Germany, 1945
The Struggle for Mastery in Europe, 1848–1918, 1954
Bismarck: The Man and the Statesman, 1955
The Trouble Makers: Dissent over Foreign Policy, 1792–1939, 1957
The Origins of the Second World War, 1961
English History, 1914–45, 1965
From Sarajevo to Potsdam, 1966
Beaverbrook, 1972
How Wars End, 1985
From Napoleon to the Second International: Essays on Nineteenth-Century Europe, edited by Chris Wrigley, 1993

Further Reading

Cole, Robert, *A.J.P. Taylor: The Traitor within the Gates*, London: Macmillan, and New York: St. Martin's Press, 1993
Gilbert, Martin, ed., *A Century of Conflict, 1850–1950: Essays for A.J.P. Taylor*, London: Hamish Hamilton, and New York: Atheneum, 1966
Louis, William Roger, ed., *The Origins of the Second World War: A.J.P. Taylor and His Critics*, New York: Wiley, 1972
Martel, Gordon, ed., *The Origins of the Second World War Reconsidered: The A.J.P. Taylor Debate after Twenty-Five Years*, Boston: Allen and Unwin, 1986
Robertson, Esmonde M., ed., *The Origins of the Second World War: Historical Interpretations*, London: Macmillan, 1971
Sisman, Adam, *A.J.P. Taylor: A Biography*, London: Sinclair Stevenson, 1994
Sked, Alan, and Chris Cook, eds., *Crisis and Controversy: Essays in Honour of A.J.P. Taylor*, London: Macmillan, and New York: St. Martin's Press, 1976

Taylor, A.J.P., Donald Cameron Watt, Oswald Hauser, and John W. Boyer, *Journal of Modern History* 49 (1977), 1–72 [special issue on Taylor]

Williams, H. Russell, "A.J.P. Taylor," in Hans A. Schmitt, ed., *Historians of Modern Europe*, Baton Rouge: Louisiana State University Press, 1971

Wrigley, Chris, ed., *A.J.P. Taylor: A Complete Annotated Bibliography and Guide to His Historical and Other Writings*, Brighton: Harvester Press, and New York: Barnes and Noble, 1980

Wrigley, Chris, ed., *Warfare, Diplomacy and Politics: Essays in Honour of A.J.P. Taylor*, London: Hamish Hamilton, 1986

Technology

The history of technology has been a neglected area of study while more glamorous sub-disciplines such as political, military, economic, and social history have been elevated within the profession. Ironically, the history of technology exerts a crucial influence on the more heavily studied fields. It is nearly impossible fully to interpret a society without possessing at least a rudimentary understanding of its technology. From the highest levels of government to the most minute aspects of daily life, technology shapes the way individuals interact with one another, thus making the study of technology increasingly important. The history of technology also plays an important multidisciplinary role by bringing together divergent practitioners in fields such as science, cultural studies, and archaeology.

Perhaps the major reason that the history of technology has not been more widely studied and championed among scholars is that it requires a vast degree of both historical and technical expertise. In fact, the first historians of technology were usually engineers, scientists, or archaeologists. The history of technology was not widely embraced as an academic discipline by historians until the mid to latter half of the 20th century, even though it is an old field of scholarship. The first general history of technology is said to have been written by Polydore Virgil in 1499. Later studies, however, mainly developed as narrow lists of inventors and inventions rather than analytical examinations.

The modern study of the history of technology developed when engineers entered the discipline in the late 19th and early 20th centuries, especially in Germany. The interaction between engineers and specialists in related fields played a crucial role in the growth of the field. From the 1910s through the 1940s, numerous scholars became interested in aspects of technological change in the United States, including Louis C. Hunter, Lewis Mumford, Joseph W. Roe, Abbott P. Usher, and Lynn White, Jr. These individuals were pioneers long before the history of technology was recognized as a field of specialization or accepted within history departments.

When the Society for the History of Technology (SHOT) was founded in 1958 more than half of its members were either engineers or had mechanical training. Thus, the history of engineering and the social role of engineering in history has always had an important role in the history of technology. During the 1950s major steps were made to modernize the discipline. New manuscript collections were investigated, critical monographs written, and myths regarding technological innovation were destroyed. SHOT's quarterly journal, *Technology and Culture*, under the guidance of Melvin Kranzberg, gained a reputation for important scholarship that defined the field. The Dexter prize, the society's annual outstanding book award, has become one of the profession's major prizes. A number of Pulitzer prize winners have also won the Dexter prize for their contributions to the history of technology.

The history of technology has split into two major schools of thought in the last 25 years. One group of scholars has concentrated on the concept of design and emphasized technological detail and changes in design over time, with little discussion of the political or cultural contexts in which new technologies developed. The history of technology, according to these historians, centers on the esoteric knowledge and special study required to understand technology. The second group, on the other hand, has placed increasing importance on the social, political, and economic factors that influence and are affected by technological evolution. Known as "contextualists," these scholars have insisted that the history of technology be framed within the larger universal picture. The latter group has been influenced by the large impact social historians have made on the profession since the 1960s.

Despite the success historians of technology have experienced, the field has not been without criticism. David F. Noble and Leo Marx have publicly questioned the need for SHOT at all. They claim that the organization exists simply as a means for self-promotion to fulfill careerist goals. Noble believes that SHOT adds little scholarly value to the larger field. He believes that the articles and essays that appear in *Technology and Culture* could be written without the society and if done well, would be accepted within the wider parameters of the profession. Adding weight to this critique is the lack of a defining textbook that sums up the important research of the last four decades. Because the history of technology has exerted such a minimal influence in textbooks and historical literature in general, historians outside the field have not widely incorporated its findings. Alex Roland, 1996 SHOT president, admitted, "While we have concentrated over the last quarter century on explaining the nature of technological change, other historians want to understand technology as an engine of historical change."

Along with many other historical fields, the history of technology is integrating the methodologies that have been popularized in the last 25 years. Obviously when an overhaul within the field takes place there are going to be disputes. Some scholars may frown upon the open insertion of "the little people" and other forms of social history into the history of technology, but to remain vigorous historians of technology should continue to refigure the field using all the available historical and interdisciplinary material at their disposal. Bringing new methodologies and information to light will energize the history of technology and help it to gain a stronger foothold within the larger profession.

ROBERT P. BATCHELOR

See also America: Pre-Columbian; Anthropology; Business; Cipolla; Computers; Computing; de Vries; Ecology; European Expansion; Habakkuk; Habermas; Hughes, T.; Industrial Revolution; Keegan; Kosambi; Landes; Merton; Military; Mumford; Needham; Parker; Science; Smith, M.; White, L.; World; Worster

Further Reading

Baldwin, Neil, *Edison: Inventing the Century*, New York: Hyperion, 1995

Billington, David, *Robert Maillart's Bridges: The Art of Engineering*, Princeton: Princeton University Press, 1979

Burlingame, Roger, *The March of the Iron Men: A Social History of Union Through Invention*, New York: Scribner, 1938

Cochran, Thomas C., *Frontiers of Change: Early Industrialism in America*, New York: Oxford University Press, 1981

Constant, Edward W., *The Origins of the Turbojet Revolution*, Baltimore: Johns Hopkins University Press, 1980

Cowan, Ruth Schwartz, *More Work for Mother: The Ironies of Household Technology from the Open Hearth to the Microwave*, New York: Basic Books, 1983; London: Free Association, 1989

Finn, Bernard S., *The History of Electrical Technology: An Annotated Bibliography*, New York: Garland, 1991

Flink, James J., *The Automobile Age*, Cambridge, MA: MIT Press, 1988

Heinrich, Thomas R., *Ships for the Seven Seas: Philadelphia Shipbuilding in the Age of Industrial Capitalism*, Baltimore: Johns Hopkins University Press, 1997

Hindle, Brooke, *Technology in Early America: Needs and Opportunities for Study*, Chapel Hill: University of North Carolina Press, 1966

Hounshell, David A., *From the American System to Mass Production, 1800–1932: The Development of Manufacturing Technology in the United States*, Baltimore: Johns Hopkins University Press, 1984

Hughes, Thomas P., *Networks of Power: Electrification in Western Society, 1880–1930*, Baltimore: Johns Hopkins University Press, 1983

Hughes, Thomas P., *American Genesis: A Century of Invention and Technological Enthusiasm, 1870–1970*, New York: Viking, 1989

Hurt, R. Douglas, and Mary Ellen Hurt, *The History of Agricultural Science and Technology: An International Bibliography*, New York: Garland, 1994

Kelly, Patrick, and Melvin Kranzberg, eds., *Technological Innovation: A Critical Review of Current Knowledge*, San Francisco: San Francisco Press, 1978

Kranzberg, Melvin, and Carroll W. Pursell, Jr., eds., *Technology in Western Civilization*, 2 vols., New York: Oxford University Press, 1967

Landes, David S., *The Unbound Prometheus: Technological Change and Industrial Development in Western Europe from 1750 to the Present*, Cambridge: Cambridge University Press, 1969

Layton, Edwin T., Jr., *The Revolt of the Engineers: Social Responsibility and the American Engineering Profession*, Cleveland: Case Western Reserve University Press, 1971

Marcus, Alan I., and Howard P. Segal, *Technology in America: A Brief History*, San Francisco: Harcourt Brace, 1989

Marx, Leo, *The Machine in the Garden: Technology and the Pastoral Ideal in America*, New York and London: Oxford University Press 1964

Noble, David F., *America by Design: Science, Technology, and the Rise of Corporate Capitalism*, New York: Knopf, 1977; Oxford: Oxford University Press, 1979

Noble, David F., *Forces of Production: A Social History of Industrial Automation*, New York: Knopf, 1984

Pursell, Carroll W., Jr., ed., *Technology in America: A History of Individuals and Ideas*, Cambridge, MA: MIT Press, 1981

Pursell, Carroll W., Jr., *White Heat: People and Technology*, Berkeley: University of California Press, 1994

Rothenberg, Marc, *The History of Science and Technology in the United States*, 2 vols., New York: Garland, 1982–93

Segal, Howard P., *Technological Utopianism in American Culture*, Chicago: University of Chicago Press, 1985

Smith, Merritt Roe, *Harpers Ferry Armory and the New Technology: The Challenge of Charge*, Ithaca, NY: Cornell University Press, 1977

Staudenmaier, John M., *Technology's Storytellers: Reweaving the Human Fabric*, Cambridge, MA: MIT Press, 1985

Wallace, Anthony F.C., *The Social Context of Innovation: Bureaucrats, Families and Heroes in the Early Industrial Revolution*, Princeton: Princeton University Press, 1982

White, Lynn, Jr., *Medieval Technology and Social Change*, Oxford and New York: Oxford University Press, 1962

Temkin, Owsei 1902–

US (Russian-born) historian of medicine

Owsei Temkin was educated as a physician, and his work reflects his view that the history of medicine is part of the discipline of medicine. A pupil of Henry Sigerist at the University of Leipzig Institute for the History of Medicine, Temkin produced scholarship that reflected the German tradition of the history of medicine, in which physicians trained in the classics and humanities studied the history of their profession. His objective was to inform current medical scholarship and practice. He recognized that the cultural context of medicine was necessary to any study of it. The philosophical systems underlying medical practice are prominent in his work.

Temkin followed Sigerist to the Johns Hopkins University Institute for the History of Medicine in 1932. Although a highly skilled scholar of languages, Temkin resisted his mentor's lead in making "literary" studies of medical texts; also, he did not agree with Sigerist on the importance of medical sociology. Temkin's authoritative study of epilepsy, *The Falling Sickness* (1945), illustrates both his idea of the history of medicine and the breadth of his scholarship. His purpose in writing the book was to help neurologists by providing a historical explication of epilepsy. One of the work's strongest points is its examination of the body (*soma*) and mind (*psyche*) dichotomy in Western culture.

From 1932 to 1947 Temkin taught and researched various topics. The Johns Hopkins Institute had not succeeded in establishing the history of medicine as a part of the curriculum in medical schools. Therefore, the Institute and Temkin were educating ever more non-medically trained scholars as historians of medicine. In 1947 Sigerist left Johns Hopkins. Richard H. Shryock, a historian not a physician, became director of the Institute. Shryock was not interested in producing physician historians but rather in the social history of medicine. Temkin was the editor of the *Bulletin of the History of Medicine* from 1948 to 1968. During these years, he strove to maintain a place in the *Bulletin* for publications by practicing physicians, though he recognized that few physicians had the necessary historical background to write first-rate history. He tried to shape the study of the history of medicine with his editorial policies, perhaps as Karl Sudoff had shaped the history of medicine in Germany with his publication, *Sudhoffs Archiv: Zeitschrift für Geschichte der Medizin* (Sudhoff's Archive: Journal on the History of Medicine).

Seeing medicine as a manifestation of a culture, Temkin believed medical history should concern itself with the rise of the profession and the analysis of medical thought, rather than socio-economic studies that could have no influence on the practicing physician. Retiring in 1968, Temkin published many works based on research begun years before. His publishing record after his retirement suggests how much research was done in his teaching years. Reviews emphasize the range of knowledge he displayed in his books and their readability. In his collection of essays *The Double Face of Janus, and Other Essays in the History of Medicine* (1976), Temkin offered a personal and intellectual autobiography: "There will be those for whom historiography will be an integral part of medicine, where a substantive, technical knowledge that can hardly be acquired from books alone is essential. Others, in the manner of Shryock, without personal involvement in medicine, will take it as a social phenomenon that concerns us all, or, as historians of science, will cultivate the basic medical sciences. A last group (I may cite Edelstein [a classical scholar who studied medicine as an aspect of classical civilization] as an example) may view medicine as an institution within a particular period medicine." *The Double Face of Janus* is frequently used as a 1-volume history of medicine, since the new social historians have not produced one.

In the United States the study of the history of medicine became dominated by historians rather than physicians during Temkin's career. Temkin recognized a place for those who study medicine as a social phenomenon, but he clearly saw the history of medicine as part of medicine, not as a social science. Nor could he agree that the history of medicine was part of the history of science. For him it was a totally separate enterprise – and not applied biology.

NANCY PIPPEN ECKERMAN

See also Medicine

Biography

Born Minsk, Belarus, 6 October 1902; naturalized US citizen. Earned a medical degree, University of Leipzig, 1927; intern, St. Jacob Hospital, Leipzig, 1927–28. Lecturer, University of Leipzig Institute for the History of Medicine, 1928–32; taught (rising to professor), Johns Hopkins University, 1932–58; civilian with the Division of Medical Sciences of the National Research Council, 1943–44; William H. Welch professor and director of the Institute for the History of Medicine, 1958–68 (emeritus). Married in 1932 (2 daughters).

Principal Writings

The Falling Sickness: A History of Epilepsy from the Greeks to the Beginnings of Modern Neurology, 1945; revised 1971
Editor with Lillian Temkin, *Ancient Medicine: Selected Papers of Ludwig Edelstein*, 1967
Galenism: Rise and Decline of a Medical Philosophy, 1973
The Double Face of Janus, and Other Essays in the History of Medicine, 1976
Respect for Life in Medicine, Philosophy, and the Law, 1977
Hippocrates in a World of Pagans and Christians, 1991

Further Reading

Stevenson, Lloyd G., and Robert P. Multhauf, eds., *Medicine, Science, and Culture: Historical Essays in Honor of Owsei Temkin*, Baltimore: Johns Hopkins Press, 1968

Thapar, Romila 1931–
Indian historian

The pre-eminent interpreter of ancient Indian history today, Romila Thapar has definitively reformulated central questions and issues in the field. Her work on Indian social history in the 1st millennium BCE, the period of the Aryan expansion in North India, has been instrumental in deconstructing the stereotypes of ancient Indian culture propagated by earlier historians with particular ideological biases. In the colonialist view, ancient Indian society was characterized by stagnation, resulting from a preoccupation with religion, a rigid social structure (embodied in the caste system), and a complete lack of historical consciousness. Indian nationalist historians tended to discover in the data of the ancient period evidence of an idealized, but equally static, civilization. In writings spanning nearly forty years (in addition to her books, see the collections of her essays, *Ancient Indian Social History* [1978] and *Interpreting Early India* [1992]) Thapar has effectively argued the case for a dynamic transition, spurred by a number of socioeconomic factors, from Vedic society to the social formations represented in the two Sanskrit epics, early Buddhist texts, and the records of the Mauryan empire of Aśoka (3rd century BCE). She has also identified complex forms of historical consciousness in the (mainly literary) sources available for the ancient period, including the genre known as "traditional narrative" (Purāna). Among the major historians of ancient India in recent times, Thapar's emphasis on social history differentiates her approach from that of the cultural historian A.L. Basham, while her rejection of ideological frames of reference sets her work apart from that of the Marxist scholar D.D. Kosambi.

Thapar's central argument, which she elaborates in *From Lineage to State* (1984) and elsewhere, is that Indian society underwent a major change in the course of the spread of the Aryans in the Gangetic plain, with an older, lineage-based social formation gradually giving way to a state-centered society. The shift from lineage to state was not simply a political process, but reflected and recorded profound changes in the entire social structure, involving, for instance, a shift from loyalty to the lineage, a unilineal kin-group, to loyalty to the larger, more complex, nonlineal social grouping known as caste. The epics *Rāmāyana* and *Mahābhārata* need to be carefully examined by the historian, since the central narratives of these epics, which are concerned with the expansion of warrior lineages over North India and the establishment of kingdoms in the Gangetic plain, provide imaginative insights into the attitudes and processes involved in the movement towards a state-centered, caste-oriented, settled society. In fact, the compendious and poetic character of the Indian epics, which were transmitted from oral to written traditions, and which were edited over a period of nearly a thousand years, has allowed them to preserve historical memory as well as to juxtapose depictions of a variety of anachronistic social formations. In her studies of the two epics, she offered the first comprehensive social historical interpretation of the epic material, and she showed that the transition from lineage to state encompassed a number of distinct forms of social stratification, and variant models of the state as well. At every point in her study of the texts of the ancient period, she has also taken into account ongoing archaeological discoveries regarding life in the Ganges valley in the 1st millennium and earlier.

A second focus of Thapar's writings, and one that is related to her study of social formations, is the identification of indigenous expressions of historical consciousness. Modern historians have tended to dismiss large portions of the epics and Purānas, which contain traditional genealogies, origin myths, and other legendary material, as being ahistorical. Thapar suggests that myth and genealogy, generally associated with lineage societies, ought to be read as forms of "embedded history," whereas epic and related forms are "externalized" forms of historical expression. Editing the epic narratives, brahmins (members of the priestly class) appropriated both forms of historical material from bardic, oral traditions, and used them to confer elite (usually "warrior") status on, and to legitimate the claims of, aspirants to power of diverse social origins. According to Thapar the appearance of externalized forms of historical expression in ancient India, in the epics as well as in Buddhist texts, is in large measure related to the rise of state systems and monarchies, along with concomitant factors such as urbanization and trade. The core of Thapar's argument is that the historian must establish causal relationships between social, political, and institutional change and changing forms of historical expression.

Among Thapar's lasting contributions to the study of ancient India is her thorough revaluation of *a priori* assumptions regarding ancient Indian society. Her work on the epics and Purānas has been important, for example, in deconstructing the idea of caste as a fundamental, monolithic, and unchanging category. Her analysis of the texts has revealed caste in the ancient period as an evolving concept, functioning not as a rigid marker of identity but as a flexible, multivalent instrument of social change and social mobility. Likewise, her work shows that the identities and status indicated by terms such as "Aryan," *mleccha* ("outsider"), and *katriya* ("warrior," one of the four major subdivisions of the caste system at the macro-level) changed throughout the ancient period. Characterized by an integrative approach to social history, an impressive command of the sources, rigorous attention to methodological issues, and a persistent rejection of ideologically-driven presuppositions, Thapar's scholarship continues to set the standard for a new generation of historians of ancient India.

INDIRA VISWANATHAN PETERSON

See also Women's History: India

Biography
Born India, 30 November 1931. Received BA, Punjab University, 1952; BA, University of London, 1955, PhD 1958. Taught at School of Oriental and African Studies, University of London, 1959–61; Kurukshetra University, 1961–63; and Delhi University, 1963–70; professor of ancient Indian history, Jawaharlal Nehru University, New Delhi, 1970–93 (emeritus).

Principal Writings
Aśoka and the Decline of the Mauryas, 1961; revised 1997
Editor, with Sarvepalli Gopal, *Problems of Historical Writing in India*, 1963
A History of India, 2 vols., 1965–66
"History of the Indian Sub-continent, 1500 BC–AD 200," in *Encyclopaedia Britannica*, 15th edition, 1974 (revised 1992)
"Ideology and the Interpretation of Ancient Indian History," in K.S. Krishnaswamy, ed., *Society and Change: Essays in Honour of Sachin Chaudhuri*, 1977; reprinted in *Interpreting Early India*, 1992
Exile and the Kingdom: Some Thoughts on the Ramayana, 1978
Ancient Indian Social History: Some Interpretations, 1978

From Lineage to State: Social Formations in the mid-First Millennium BC *in the Ganga Valley*, 1984
Editor with Sabyasachi Bhattacharya, *Situating Indian History: For Sarvepalli Gopal*, 1986
"Society and Historical Consciousness: The *Itihāsa-purāna* Tradition," in S. Bhattacharya and Romila Thapar, eds., *Situating Indian History*, 1986
Interpreting Early India, 1992
"Archaeology and Language at the Roots of Early India," *Journal of the Royal Asiatic Society of Bombay* new series 64–66, 249–68
"Sacrifice, Surplus, and the Soul," *History of Religions* 33 (1994), 305–24
"The First Millennium BC in Northern India," in her *Recent Perspectives of Early Indian History*, 1995
Editor, *Recent Perspectives of Early Indian History*, 1995
"The Search for a Historical Tradition," *Transactions of the International Conference of Eastern Studies* [Kyoto] 60 (1995)
Time as a Metaphor of History: Early India, 1996

Theatre

The academic discipline of theatre history seeks to understand performance in its aesthetic, political, and economic dimensions. It includes histories of individual theatres (such as Shakespeare's Globe) and the development of performance styles as well as the lives of individual actors. It can also include an archaeological dimension as represented by the excavation of old theatres, such as the recently discovered Elizabethan Rose Theatre in London and the various attempts to recreate the Globe.

Theatrical history has enjoyed a complex relationship with the study of literature and drama, from which it emerged. Literary scholars have tended to privilege the written text as the main source of inquiry but theatrical history aims to go beyond texts by looking at all aspects of performance: theatre architecture, the role of actors and directors, settings and scenery, the reception of a play by the first-night critics (whose reviews and descriptions of performance are themselves a form of theatre history), and the composition of theatre audiences. But theatre by its very nature is ephemeral, and even filmed performances cannot wholly capture the nature of the event, in particular the relationship between actor and audience.

While theatre historians have been required to know about larger historical trends that affected their subject, historians have typically known very little about the theatre. This has begun to change. Not only is theatre history flourishing as an academic discipline in its own right but it has begun to intrude into wider historical questions. Mainstream historians have not only become interested in the way in which the stage mirrored wider social trends but they have started to consider the ways in which theatricality and the conventions of the theatre helped to structure language and everyday life in a variety of societies.

Theatre history has been studied since antiquity. According to the theatre historigrapher, R.M. Vince, the first recorded historian was King Juba II of Mauretania (*c.*50 BCE– *c.*23 CE) whose *Theatriké historia* is sadly lost to us. The study of theatrical forms began to take shape in the Renaissance, as scholars needed to account for the conditions that produced the theatres of ancient Greece and Rome. By the 18th century, it was necessary to explain the transition from the medieval mystery play to the flowering of the drama during the 16th and 17th centuries in England. Shakespeare's works alone have generated a scholarly industry of textual critics. Theatre history did not, however, really become distinct from literary history until the later 19th century, and even today, the disciplines continue to overlap.

The 20th century has been characterized by the attempt to construct a distinct discipline of theatre history based on rigorous work in the archives. For example, Allardyce Nicoll's magisterial *A History of English Drama* (originally begun in 1923) is a major work of reference with its elaborate handlists of plays, documenting past productions and theatrical trends. Organizations such as the British Society for Theatre Research and the French Société d'Histoire du Théâtre have also been founded to promote the systematic investigation of performing arts in all their aspects.

The major works of such 20th-century scholar-historians as Arthur Pickard-Cambridge, Glynne Wickham, and Richard Southern, among others, have greatly illuminated the stage conditions of classical and medieval theatre. While new evidence continues to come to light, increasing our understanding of the physical conditions of earlier theatrical periods, the work of such scholars has formed the backbone for the kind of succinct, 1-volume studies during the last 25 years that have sought to combine the essentials in terms of historical evidence with a more contemporary interest in the sociology of theatre, the relation between the dramatic text, theatrical conventions, and the production of meaning, and the composition and expectations of theatre audiences. Notable examples of these studies include Walcot, Walton, and Beacham on classical theatre; Wickham (1974) and Harris on the medieval stage; Gurr and Powell on Renaissance and Restoration theatre; and Taylor on the Victorian stage.

Another important development since the 1970s has been the emergence of a number of historical overviews in English of theatre traditions – or major periods thereof – from around the world, whose authors draw on the available scholarship in other languages to provide useful introductory narratives. Examples of these studies include Carlson's volumes on Europe, Patterson on Germany, McKendrick and Holt on Spain, the Markers on Scandinavia, and Mackerras on China. A global perspective on theatre culture – as opposed to just the history of dramatic writing – is also represented by the most ambitious theatrical encyclopedia that has appeared to date, the Italian *Enciclopedia dello spettacolo* (1954–62), an invaluable resource to be found now only in larger libraries. A widely available, 1-volume companion with a determinedly postcolonial and multicultural perspective is the *Cambridge Guide to Theatre* (new edition, 1995) under the general editorship of Martin Banham, which, in its coverage of theatre in the developing world, and interest in theatre anthropology and popular entertainment, tugs the definition of "theatre history" further away from the more scholarly, literary-historical, and English-cultural priorities of its long-established competitor, Phyllis Hartnoll's *The Oxford Companion to Theatre* (4th edition, 1983). Two helpful spin-offs (with extended coverage) from the *Cambridge Guide* in effect provide English-language surveys of a wide range of the theatrical phenomena in Africa and the Caribbean (Banham *et al.*, 1994) and Asia (Brandon, 1993).

The evolution of genres has been a particular modern concern. For example, Michael Booth and David Grimsted (in separate works) have investigated the growth of melodrama in Britain and the United States. Melodrama was formerly considered an embarrassment in the history of drama, a primitive form that was eventually banished by the rise of naturalism in the late 19th century. The modern wave of writing on the subject has retrieved melodrama's reputation and insisted that it be taken seriously as a theatrical form in its own right, arguing, for instance, the view that the acting style of melodrama was not as artificial as often thought (with its grand gestures) but a form of heightened realism.

One of the most common forms of theatre history is the biography. Full-scale biographies of individual actors, such as Charles Gildon's *Life of Mr. Thomas Betterton* (1710), and autobiographies, such as Cibber's *An Apology for the Life of Mr. Colley Cibber, Comedian* (1740) – the first theatrical autobiography in English – contributed to theatre writing by providing anecdotal information on the theatrical trade. These "memoirs of the green room" flourished in the 19th century as demonstrated by Charles Dickens' *Memoirs of Joseph Grimaldi* (1838), based on the life of the famous clown. Like Dickens, Thomas Frost explored an area of performance about which his contemporaries knew little in his study *Circus Life and Circus Celebrities* (1876), a collection of anecdotes, publicity, press reports, and biography, which brought together journalism and theatrical writing. While an eccentric interest in this demi-monde of the theatrical trade motivated these and other writers, scholarship remained focused on the stage. James Robinson Planché's important work on theatrical practice, *The Recollections and Reflections of J.R. Planché* (1872), was based on his experience in London's theatres. Shortened biographies in *The Green Room Book* (1906–09) continued as *Who's Who in the Theatre* (from 1912, edited by John Parker) provided a more comprehensive record of the contemporary theatrical trade. Modern biographies can be anecdotal but they can also be immensely scholarly, as in Nina Auerbach's study of Ellen Terry.

The study of theatre is of course not restricted to Europe and America. For example, of recent works, Benito Ortolani's examination of the Japanese theatrical arts includes popular forms such as puppet theatre and even acts that one might commonly associate with the circus, such as juggling and acrobats. Nor has theatre history been restricted to the conventional theatre. It also includes the study of opera, dance, and all aspects of the performing arts from grand guignol to the music hall. Peter Bailey and Jacqueline S. Bratton have become major figures in the study of the English music hall. Bailey in *Leisure and Class in Victorian England* (1978) examined why the increase of capital investment within the performance world, particularly in Victorian London, was central to the development of new performance genres, such as music hall. Through their study of music hall, Bailey, Bratton, and others have examined working-class attitudes toward everyday life on such matters as war, empire, and trade unionism.

Professionalization is also a major theme in the historiography of the mainstream theatre. J.R. Stephens' *The Profession of the Playwright* (1992) explored the playwright's relationship to artists and theatre managers in Victorian Britain. The playwright's precarious financial and social status made him a vulnerable partner in this relationship, a point that also emerged from Stephens' earlier work, *The Censorship of English Drama, 1824–1901* (1980). Tracy C. Davis provided a feminist analysis of professionalization during the same period in her study *Actresses as Working Women* (1991). Viewing the experience of Victorian actresses in terms of pay, working conditions, and training, Davis balanced the economically and socially precarious life of actresses with their struggle for respectability. The feminization of the theatre has also been explored in Viv Gardner and Susan Rutherford's edited volume, *The New Woman and Her Sisters* (1992), which offered some interesting case studies and analyses of women crossing gender lines, a theme that was earlier examined by Peter Ackroyd in his study *Dressing Up: Transvestism and Drag* (1979), and by Corrinee Holt Sawyer in her article "Men in Skirts and Women in Trousers from Achilles to Victoria Grant" (1987). The question of "camp" is considered historically by Marybeth Hamilton in her study of Mae West's vaudeville and film career.

In the last three decades, social historians have shifted the discipline away from an antiquarian focus on technical aspects of production work, acting, and management and integrated it into cultural history. There has been a new focus on the theatrical dimensions of popular culture. Some historians have studied the crowd and the meanings attached to their theatrical – or performance – rituals. E.P. Thompson's influential essay "Rough Music" (1991), and Natalie Zemon Davis' *Society and Culture in Early Modern France* (1975) examined the extent to which the "world turned upside down" at carnival time reinforced the social fabric of the community. Increasingly, historians have come to view the theatre as an integral part of the construction of the public sphere. Jean-Christophe Agnew's *Worlds Apart* (1986) argued that the theatre did not simply mirror the emergence of the market in early modern England and America but actually helped to construct the culture of the market as both employed similar representational strategies. David Blackbourn considered German high politics as a form of theatre in his revisionist article about metaphors of the stage in German history.

The relationship between politics and the stage – or the festival – is another crucial area that historians have recently investigated in their examinations of culture and society. Mona Ozouf's *Festivals and the French Revolution* (1976, translated 1988) analyzed the forces of conflict and change, creativity and inventiveness, modernity and secularization in the 1790s. In a related way, works on the theatre, such as Frederick Brown's *Theater and Revolution* (1980) and Graham E. Rodmell's *French Drama of the Revolutionary Years* (1990), have also made the link between politics and the stage by treating specific productions in revolutionary Paris. The political realm was also integral to the Spanish theatrical world at the start of the 19th century, as examined by David Thatcher Gies in *Theatre and Politics in Nineteenth-Century Spain* (1988). In a more recent volume, Gies revealed how Spanish theatre was influenced by important political and social changes, such as the transition from war to dictatorship, rebellion to reaction, and the growth of a small, but powerful middle class. Spanish influences greatly affected the development of the Latin American theatre, as Adam Versenyi's *Theatre in Latin America* (1993) demonstrated. Other important works on politics and the stage have included Marc Baer's *Theatre and Disorder in Late Georgian London* (1992), which investigated the Old Price Riots in London in Covent Garden in 1809. It was that rare work: a study of the audience as much as the actors. More recently, Jared Brown's *The Theatre in America during the Revolution* (1995) provided an important study of the British theatrical influence on the American stage, particularly in terms of staged military battles, at a time when cultural exchange between the two countries was far from straightforward.

The theatre is becoming a key part of modern social history. These changes have not only affected the writing of British theatrical history, but also that of Europe, Latin America, North America, Asia, and Africa. No longer a subject for antiquarians, as it had been in the 19th and early 20th centuries, theatre history has helped scholars to answer some mainstream questions that have emerged from the recent historiography on society and culture.

BRENDA ASSAEL

See also Davis, N.; Leisure; Ozouf; Thompson, E.

Further Reading

Ackroyd, Peter, *Dressing Up: Transvestism and Drag: The History of an Obsession*, London: Thames and Hudson, and New York: Simon and Schuster, 1979

Agnew, Jean-Christophe, *Worlds Apart: The Market and the Theatre in Anglo-American Thought, 1550–1750*, Cambridge and New York: Cambridge University Press, 1986

Auerbach, Nina, *Ellen Terry: Player in Her Time*, New York: Norton, and London: Phoenix House, 1987

Baer, Marc, *Theatre and Disorder in Late Georgian London*, Oxford and New York: Oxford University Press, 1992

Bailey, Peter, *Leisure and Class in Victorian England: Rational Recreation and the Contest for Control, 1830–1885*, Toronto and Buffalo: University of Toronto Press, and London: Routledge, 1978; revised London and New York: Methuen, 1987

Bailey, Peter, ed., *Music Hall: The Business of Pleasure*, Milton Keynes: Open University Press, 1986

Banham, Martin, ed., *The Cambridge Guide to World Theatre*, Cambridge and New York: Cambridge University Press, 1988; revised edition, as *The Cambridge Guide to Theatre*, 1992; new edition, 1995

Banham, Martin, Errol Hill, and George Woodyard, eds., *The Cambridge Guide to African and Caribbean Theatre*, Cambridge and New York: Cambridge University Press, 1994

Beacham, Richard C., *The Roman Theatre and Its Audience*, London and New York: Routledge, 1991

Benson, Eugene, and L.W. Conolly, eds., *The Oxford Companion to Canadian Theatre*, Oxford and New York: Oxford University Press, 1989

Berthold, Margot, and Felicia Londré, *The History of World Theater*, New York: Ungar/Continuum, 1994

Blackbourn, David, "Politics as Theatre: Metaphors of the Stage in German History, 1848–1933," *Transactions of the Royal Historical Society* 37 (1987), 149–67

Booth, Michael, *English Melodrama*, London: Jenkins, 1965

Brandon, James R., ed., *The Cambridge Guide to Asian Theatre*, Cambridge and New York: Cambridge University Press, 1993

Bratton, Jacqueline S., ed., *Music Hall: Performance and Style*, Milton Keynes: Open University Press, 1986

Brown, Frederick, *Theater and Revolution: The Culture of the French Stage*, New York: Viking, 1980

Brown, Jared, *The Theatre in America during the Revolution*, Cambridge and New York: Cambridge University Press, 1995

Carlson, Marvin, *The French Stage in the Nineteenth Century*, Metuchen, NJ: Scarecrow Press, 1972

Carlson, Marvin, *The German Stage in the Nineteenth Century*, Metuchen, NJ: Scarecrow Press, 1972

Carlson, Marvin, *The Italian Stage from Goldoni to D'Annunzio*, Jefferson, NC: McFarland, 1981

Chambers, E.K., *The Medieval Stage*, 2 vols, Oxford: Oxford University Press, 1903

Cibber, Colley, *An Apology for the Life of Mr. Colley Cibber, Comedian*, London: Dodsley, 1740

Davis, Natalie Zemon, *Society and Culture in Early Modern France: Eight Essays*, Stanford, CA: Stanford University Press, and London: Duckworth, 1975

Davis, Tracy C., *Actresses as Working Women: Their Social Identity in Victorian Culture*, London and New York: Routledge, 1991

Dickens, Charles, ed., *Memoirs of Joseph Grimaldi*, 2 vols., London: Bentley, 1838; reprinted London: MacGibbon and Kee, and New York: Stein and Day, 1968

Easterling, P.E., ed., *The Cambridge Companion to Greek Tragedy*, Cambridge and New York: Cambridge University Press, 1997

Enciclopedia dello spettacolo, 9 vols., Rome: Le Maschere, 1954–62; supplementary volume, Rome: Unione, 1966

Frost, Thomas, *Circus Life and Circus Celebrities*, London: Tinsley, 1876; reprinted 1970

Gardner, Viv, and Susan Rutherford, eds., *The New Woman and Her Sisters: Feminism and the Theatre, 1850–1914*, Hemel Hampstead: Harvester Press, 1992

Gies, David Thatcher, *The Theatre in Nineteenth-Century Spain*, Cambridge and New York: Cambridge University Press, 1994

Gies, David Thatcher, *Theatre and Politics in Nineteenth-Century Spain: Juan de Grimaldi as Impresario and Government Agent*, Cambridge and New York: Cambridge University Press, 1988

Gildon, Charles, *The Life of Mr. Thomas Betterton*, London: Gosling, 1710; reprinted London: Cass, and New York: A.M. Kelley, 1970

Grimsted, David, *Melodrama Unveiled: American Theater and Culture, 1800–1850*, Chicago: University of Chicago Press, 1968

Gurr, Andrew, *The Shakespearean Stage, 1574–1642*, Cambridge: Cambridge University Press, 1970; 3rd edition, Cambridge and New York: Cambridge University Press, 1992

Hamilton, Marybeth, *"When I'm Bad, I'm Better": Mae West, Sex, and American Entertainment*, New York: HarperCollins, 1995; in UK as *The Queen of Camp: Mae West, Sex, and Popular Culture*, London: HarperCollins, 1996

Harris, John Wesley, *Medieval Theatre in Context*, London and New York: Routledge, 1992

Hartnoll, Phyllis, ed., *The Oxford Companion to Theatre*, London and New York: Oxford University Press, 1951, 4th edition 1983

Hattaway, Michael, *Elizabethan Popular Theatre*, London and Boston: Routledge, 1982

Holt, Marion Peter, *The Contemporary Spanish Theater, 1949–1972*, Boston: Twayne, 1976

McKendrick, Melveena, *Theatre in Spain, 1490–1700*, Cambridge and New York: Cambridge University Press, 1989

Mackerras, Colin, *Chinese Theater from Its Origins to the Present Day*, Honolulu: University of Hawaii Press, 1983

Marker, Frederick, and Lise-Lone Marker, *The Scandinavian Theatre: A Short History*, Oxford: Blackwell, and Totowa, NJ: Rowman and Littlefield, 1975

Nicoll, Allardyce, *A History of English Drama, 1660–1900*, revised edition, 6 vols., Cambridge: Cambridge University Press, 1952–59

Ortolani, Benito, *The Japanese Theater: From Shamanistic Ritual to Contemporary Pluralism*, Princeton: Princeton University Press, 1990; revised 1995

Ozouf, Mona, *La Fête révolutionnaire, 1789–1799*, Paris: Gallimard, 1976; in English as *Festivals and the French Revolution*, Cambridge, MA: Harvard University Press, and Cambridge: Cambridge University Press, 1988

Parker, John, ed., *The Green Room Book; or, Who's Who on the Stage*, London, 1906–09 [1906 vol. edited by Bampton Hunt], continued as *Who's Who in the Theatre: A Biographical Record of the Contemporary Stage*, London, 1912–

Patterson, Michael, *The Revolution in German Theatre, 1900–1933*, London and Boston: Routledge, 1981

Pickard-Cambridge, Arthur, *The Dramatic Festivals of Athens*, Oxford: Oxford University Press, 1953; 2nd edition, revised by John Gould and D.M. Lewis, 1968; corrected edition, 1988

Planché, James Robinson, *The Recollections and Reflections of J.R. Planché*, 2 vols., London Tinsley, 1872; reprinted New York: Da Capo Press, 1978

Powell, Jocelyn, *Restoration Theatre Production*, London and Boston: Routledge, 1984

Rodmell, Graham E., *French Drama of the Revolutionary Years*, London and New York: Routledge, 1990

Rudnitskii, Konstantin, *Russian and Soviet Theatre: Tradition and the Avant Garde*, London: Thames and Hudson, 1988

Sawyer, Corinee Holt, "Men in Skirts and Women in Trousers from Achilles to Victoria Grant: One Explanation of a Comedic Paradox," *Journal of Popular Culture* 21 (1987), 1–16

Southern, Richard, *The Medieval Theatre in the Round*, London: Faber, 1957; New York: Theatre Arts, 1958; 2nd edition, Faber, 1975

Southern, Richard, *The Seven Ages of the Theatre*, New York: Hill and Wang, 1961; London: Faber, 1962

Stephens, John Russell, *The Censorship of English Drama, 1824–1901*, Cambridge and New York: Cambridge University Press, 1980

Stephens, John Russell, *The Profession of the Playwright: British Theatre, 1800–1900*, Cambridge: Cambridge University Press, 1992

Taylor, George, *Players and Performances in the Victorian Theatre*, Manchester: Manchester University Press, 1989

Thompson, E.P., "Rough Music," in his *Customs in Common*, London: Merlin Press, and New York: New Press, 1991

Versenyi, Adam, *Theatre in Latin America: Religion, Politics, and Culture from Cortés to the 1980s*, Cambridge and New York: Cambridge University Press, 1993

Vince, R.M., "Theater History as an Academic Discipline" in Thomas Postlewait and Bruce A. McConachie, eds., *Interpreting the Theatrical Past: Essays in the Historiography of Performance*, Iowa City: University of Iowa Press, 1987, 1–18

Walcot, Peter, *Greek Drama in Its Theatrical and Social Context*, Cardiff: University of Wales Press, 1976

Walton, J. Michael, *Greek Theatre Production*, Westport, CT: Greenwood Press, 1980; revised edition, London: Methuen, 1991

Walton, J. Michael, *The Greek Sense of Theatre: Tragedy Reviewed*, London and New York: Methuen, 1984; 2nd edition, Amsterdam: Harwood, 1996

Wickham, Glynne, *Early English Stages, 1300–1600*, 4 vols., London: Routledge, and New York: Columbia University Press, 1959–80

Wickham, Glynne, *The Medieval Theatre*, London: Weidenfeld and Nicolson, and New York: St. Martin's Press, 1974; 3rd edition, Cambridge and New York: Cambridge University Press, 1987

Wickham, Glynne, *A History of the Theatre*, Oxford: Phaidon Press, 1985; 2nd edition, Cambridge and New York: Cambridge University Press, 1992

Yates, Frances A., *Theatre of the World*, Chicago: University of Chicago Press, and London: Routledge and Kegan Paul, 1969

Thierry, Augustin 1795–1856

French liberal historian

Augustin Thierry was a leading French liberal historian from the 1820s to the 1850s who initiated more popular and nationally focused forms of historical writing. He was a major contributor to the creation of a successful liberal paradigm and practice of history, which replaced conservative founding myths by the invention of a liberal history of medieval and early modern French progress toward individual freedom. Thierry's critiques of his predecessors decisively revealed the political roles of historians and the ideological character and function of their writing. His public challenge to Catholic and royalist historians was announced in an innovative series of essays, "Lettres sur l'histoire de France" (Letters on the History of France), first published in 1820 in the journal *Le Courrier Français* and collected as a book in 1827. The essays argued for reform in both the research and the writing of history. Historians were urged to consult the original sources and to cite them in their footnotes in order to ensure accuracy in their historical reconstructions, rather than relying on later accounts by church or court apologists. The "true" meaning of history, as the story of the development of individual liberty, could then be presented. For Thierry both the science of history and literary art were necessarily combined in the creation of historical narrative, as in Walter Scott's contemporary historical novels such as *Ivanhoe* (1819), or Chateaubriand's historical volume *Les Martyrs, ou, le triomphe de la religion chrétienne* (1809).

Thierry applied his liberal-revisionist model of the research and writing of history in his 2-volume work, *Histoire de la conquête de l'Angleterre par les Normands* (1825; *History of the Conquest of England by the Normans*, 1825). He explained that "The essential aim of this history is to contemplate the destiny of peoples, and not that of certain famous men, to recount the adventures of social life and not those of individual life." These adventures were dominated by the central role of conquest in medieval history, as in the Norman Conquest of England from 1066. In practice "social life" was superseded in Thierry's text by the political conflicts of powerful individuals and groups. Racial and class conflict were seen as central. Karl Marx referred sarcastically to Thierry in 1854 as "the father of the class struggle in French historiography." The progress of modern history was measured by Thierry in terms of the distance from the conflicts and the wrongs inflicted on people in medieval times. His story of the Norman Conquest was his most significant contribution to the Romantic revival of medieval history.

The 1830 Revolution and the July Monarchy opened up French public life to greater influence by liberal politicians and historians such as François Guizot (1787–1874), and renewed Thierry's enthusiasm for the cause of history as the story of the growing liberty of the people. In 1836 Thierry was appointed by Guizot to a commission responsible for the collection of unpublished documents of the history of the Third Estate, by whom Thierry meant the great majority of the French people, excluding only the clergy and the nobility. The publication and interpretation of these documents, from petitions, "cahiers," and charters to municipal and royal ordinances, was an essential step in the legitimation of a liberal reading of the French past. Thierry's role as a historian in the 1830s was also illustrated in his articles for the leading journal *Revue des Deux Mondes* from 1833 to 1837, collected as the *Récits des temps mérovingiens* (1840; *Narratives of the Merovingian Era*, 1845). These narratives are among Thierry's best known work, creating vivid and dramatic portraits of leading figures in 6th-century Gaul, "teeming with curious facts, eccentric characters, and such a variety of dramatic incidents that one's only difficulty is to impose some order on the mass of details." He emphasized the civilizing Gallo-Roman origins of France triumphing over the barbarism of the Franks.

Thierry's emphasis on dramatic, readable history was explicitly justified again in 1834 in a published collection of his early essays, *Dix ans d'études historiques* (*The Historical Essays*, 1845), where he was "ambitious to display art as well as science, to write dramatically with the aid of materials furnished by sincere and scrupulous erudition." This emphasis on the fusion of art and "science" in historical writing was shared by other Romantic historians of the 1830s and 1840s such as Jules Michelet. From 1846 to 1850 Thierry wrote a number of articles for the *Revue des Deux Mondes* on the Third Estate, which were published in 1853 as *Essai sur l'histoire de la formation et des progrès du Tiers Etat* (*Formation and Progress of the Tiers Etat*, 1855). The alliance of the middle class and the monarchy was seen as essential to the French nation until the reign of Louis XIV. The Constituent Assembly of 1789–91 was represented as the source of 19th-century progress. For Thierry, as for Michelet, the liberal myth of modern French unity and the common interests of classes was founded on this first phase of the French Revolution, a myth renewed by succeeding generations of liberal historians.

The February 1848 Revolution was seen by Thierry as a catastrophe for France, threatening the unity of the Third Estate by setting workers against the bourgeoisie. He remained an 1820s liberal to the end. Thierry's reputation declined with the rise of more scientistic and professional models of history from the 1860s, but there has been a revival of interest in his work since the 1950s. For Lionel Gossman, "the patterns and the dilemmas . . . in Thierry's writing are intimately connected with the liberal and rational tradition of which we are still, despite the debacle of 1848, the heirs." Thierry's project to write a popular, literary history, to situate historical writing at the center rather than at the monographic margins of culture, has continued to resonate for those historians seeking to transcend the hyper-specialization of much recent historical research.

JOHN HOOPER

See also France: to 1000

Biography

Jacques-Nicolas-Augustin Thierry. Born Blois, 1795. Educated at Ecole Normale; secretary to the social reformer Claude Saint-Simon, 1814–17; journalist, *Censeur Européen*, 1817–20, and *Courrier Français*, 1820–21; dismissed because of his liberal ideas, he turned to historical studies. His eyesight worsened throughout 1820s, and he eventually went blind. Elected to Académie des Inscriptions et Belles-Lettres, 1831. Died Paris, 22 May 1856.

Principal Writings

Histoire de la conquête de l'Angleterre par les Normands, 1825; in English as *History of the Conquest of England by the Normans*, 1825
Lettres sur l'histoire de France (Letters on the History of France), 1827
Dix ans d'études historiques, 1834; in English as *The Historical Essays*, 1845
Récits des temps mérovingiens, 3 vols., 1840; in English as *Narratives of the Merovingian Era*, 1845
Essai sur l'histoire de la formation et des progrès du Tiers Etat, 1853; in English as *Formation and Progress of the Tiers Etat*, 1855

Further Reading

Carroll, Kieran Joseph, *Some Aspects of the Historical Thought of Augustin Thierry (1795–1856)*, Washington DC: Catholic University of America Press, 1951

Crossley, Ceri, *French Historians and Romanticism: Thierry, Guizot, the Saint-Simonians, Quinet, Michelet*, London and New York: Routledge, 1993

Engel-Janosi, Friedrich, *Four Studies in French Romantic Historical Writing*, Baltimore: Johns Hopkins Press, 1955

Gossman, Lionel, *Augustin Thierry and Liberal Historiography*, Middletown, CT: Wesleyan University Press, 1976

Jullian, Camille, "Augustin Thierry et le mouvement historique sous la Restauration" (Augustin Thierry and the Historical Movement during the Restoration), *Revue de Synthèse Historique* 12 (1906), 129–42

Smithson, Rulon Nephi, *Augustin Thierry: Social and Political Consciousness in the Evolution of a Historical Method*, Geneva: Droz, 1973

Walch, Jean, *Les Maîtres de l'histoire, 1815–1850: Augustin Thierry, Mignet, Guizot, Thiers, Michelet, Edgar Quinet*, Paris: Champion, 1986

Thietmar, bishop of Merseburg 975–1018

Saxon historian

Thietmar was born into an important east Saxon aristocratic family, that of the counts of Walbeck, in 975, during the reign of Otto II. He was always destined for a clerical career, and after being educated at Magdeburg he became successively provost of the family house of canons at Walbeck, a member of the cathedral chapter at Magdeburg, and a member of the royal chapel. In 1009 Henry II, to whom he was distantly related, made him bishop of the recently restored see of Merseburg, a post he held until his death in 1018.

Thietmar began work on his *Chronicon* (Chronicle) around 1012. Like Widukind of Corvey, whose work Thietmar drew on extensively for the early part of the Chronicle, Thietmar conceived his work as a history of the Saxons, but whereas Widukind began his work with early Saxon history and allowed this to flow into the successful contemporary history of its kings, Thietmar's much larger work was conceived from the beginning as a history of the Saxon rulers: each of the first four books is devoted to a single ruler (Henry I, Otto I, Otto II, Otto III), and prefaced by verses on them, with the remaining four books being devoted to the history of Thietmar's friend and patron Henry II. Unusually for a medieval historical work, Thietmar's own autograph manuscript has survived, though it was badly damaged by fire and water in 1945 and is now best viewed in the facsimile edition made in 1905. Thietmar wrote much of it himself, constantly correcting, amplifying, and rewriting. In 1013 he acquired additional material in the form of a set of annals from Quedlinburg, which allowed him to make substantial additions to the first five books. He also added extensive anecdotes at the end of each book about contemporaries of the rulers whose reigns he was covering. The last entries in the 8th book deal with events of the summer of 1018; it would seem that Thietmar was still working on his Chronicle right up to the final illness which led to his death.

Though Thietmar's work is formally structured by the reigns of kings, these were by no means his only concern. His bishopric, Merseburg, had been founded only shortly before his birth, and for more than twenty years, between 981 and 1004, it had been merged with the archbishopric of Magdeburg. Thietmar was only the second bishop to hold the see following its restoration in 1004, and it was understood at his appointment that he would not only use his inherited wealth to strengthen the bishopric's shaky finances, but also pursue a vigorous policy of recuperation. Thietmar's Chronicle is part of this policy: its first book begins with an account of the alleged foundation of the city of Merseburg by Julius Caesar, and the fortunes of the bishopric (and the misfortunes of those who harmed it or suffered it to be amalgamated with Magdeburg) run through the work as a constant thread.

Yet neither the history of Merseburg nor that of the Saxon *Reich* account fully for the content and tone of the Chronicle. Much of it is best described as memorial in function. The lives of Thietmar's ecclesiastical colleagues, friends, ancestors, and kinsmen are here recorded, not only for posterity but for God: it is the historiographical equivalent of the contemporary practice of recording the names of the dead in a "Book of Life," and indeed just such a necrology survives from Thietmar's own period of office in Merseburg, including an injunction to his successors who read the necrology to "remember your colleague Thietmar, an unworthy sinner." Thietmar's sense of his own personal sinfulness and unworthiness as a cleric and a bishop runs in counterpoint to his fierce devotion to the cause of the bishopric of Merseburg.

This conjuncture of regal history, episcopal history, and family history created a remarkable work, unlike that of almost any other historian of the early and high Middle Ages (except perhaps for the Norman Ordericus Vitalis' *Ecclesiastical History*, written about a century later, which offers a similar mixture). It is best compared to the great aristocratic memoirs of the 17th and 18th centuries. Thietmar's highly discursive narrative not only provides unusually rich coverage of the politics of his own time – his account of the election of Henry II in 1002 is far more detailed than any other description of an early medieval kingmaking – but even more importantly it gives an insight into the strange mentality of the east Saxon aristocracy and church of his period. Thietmar seems startlingly pious and self-accusatory to those for whom a true inner religion did not appear until the 12th-century renaissance. But the *Chronicle* is not only the memoirs of a bishop very conscious of his own unworthiness; it also gives an intimate view of the aristocratic world of which Thietmar was a part, with its strong sense of family, its mistrust of the world beyond the borders of Saxony – especially, but not only, of the Slav peoples and princes to the east – and its addiction to the defence of honor and status through feud, matched in medieval historical writing only by the ethos of the Icelandic family and kings' sagas.

Only two manuscripts of the Chronicle are known (though a short fragment of a third manuscript has recently been discovered), but the work was nevertheless used extensively by later Saxon historians from the 12th to the 16th centuries, and it is the central source for the history of the German kingdom in the reigns of Otto III and Henry II; all modern accounts must to a large extent be a gloss and commentary on Thietmar's narrative.

TIMOTHY REUTER

Biography

Born Walbeck, 25 July 975; descended from a noble family. Educated at the monastery of Berge near Magdeburg. Entered cathedral chapter, Magdeburg, c.1000; ordained as priest, 1004; appointed bishop of Merseburg, 1009. Died Merseburg, 1 December 1018.

Principal Writings

Chronicon (Chronicle), written from 1012

Text in *Monumenta Germaniae historica: Scriptores*, new series 9, 1935

Further Reading

Fickermann, Norbert, "Thietmar von Merseburg in der lateinischen Sprachtradition" (Thietmar of Merseburg's Place in the Latin Linguistic Tradition), *Jahrbuch für die Geschichte Mittel- und Ostdeutschlands* 6 (1957), 21–57

Leyser, Karl, "Three Historians" and "The Ascent of Latin Europe," in his *Communications and Power in Medieval Europe*, vol. 1: *The Carolingian and Ottonian Centuries*, edited by Timothy Reuter, London and Rio Grande, OH: Hambledon Press, 1994

Lippelt, Helmut, *Thietmar von Merseburg, Reichsbischof und Chronist* (Thietmar of Merseburg, Imperial Bishop and Historian), Cologne: Böhlau, 1973

Warner, David, "Thietmar of Merseburg on Rituals of Kingship," *Viator* 26 (1995), 53–76

Wattenbach, Wilhelm, and Robert Holtzmann, eds., *Deutschlands Geschichtsquellen im Mittelalter: die Zeit der Sachsen und Salier* (Germany's Historical Sources of the Middle Ages: The Era of the Saxons and Salians), new edition, 3 vols., Darmstadt: Wissenschaftliche Buchgesellschaft, 1967–71

Thirsk, Joan 1922–

British economic and social historian

Although Joan Thirsk would modestly describe the distinctive character of her work as approaching history from a woman's point of view, her fellow historians regard her as one of the leading proponents of the revisionist approach to agrarian history which has been taking place since the 1950s. Thirsk has greatly influenced the direction and methodology of recent research, particularly of the early modern period.

After her own postgraduate research (1947–50) in London where she was a leading light in the Tawney seminars, and a brief spell as assistant lecturer in sociology at London School of Economics, Thirsk was appointed by W.G. Hoskins in 1951 to the position of senior research fellow in agrarian history in the Department of English Local History at Leicester University. She continued there some 14 years before succeeding Hoskins as reader in economic history at Oxford University in 1965. Since her retirement from this post in 1983, Thirsk has remained active in research and publications and continues to challenge received opinions and to support young scholars in their research.

Thirsk combined the tradition of Tawney's rigorous research on the 16th century with Hoskins' refreshing approach to the countryside and his emphasis on localities, and from this base she delved into previously untapped sources and constructed new interpretations. Thirsk was a major force in shifting agricultural history from a reliance on the printed source as led by Ernle and others, toward a large-scale and detailed reconstruction of manuscript sources held in local record offices throughout the country. Her imaginative research into probate inventories not only highlighted the value of this type of source but demonstrated the variety of ways in which such material could be used, and thus provided direction to young researchers. Throughout her work Thirsk has emphasized the importance of constructing rural communities from the "inside" and has demonstrated the significance of these local findings for a fuller understanding of the dynamics of development at national level. Her early researches on Fenland farming and the Isle of Axholme published in 1953 provided the basis for a re-evaluation of methodology. This revision of accepted doctrine has reverberated through agricultural history in the succeeding decades. As a result of her findings she has removed many of the preconceptions about premodern rural society. For example, she challenged the idea of inexorable agricultural progress and demonstrated that the coherence, logic, and significance of local structures and events meant that the adoption of the "progressive" ideas in the 18th century did not necessarily result in improvement or advancement in a particular locality. Similarly, her work on open fields challenged the idea of communality of such systems. Her extensive researches have resulted in a recognition of diversity of experience and a reassessment of regions and regionalization that, in turn, has informed recent interpretations of national trends.

Another of Thirsk's strengths is the breadth of perspective which, as a result of her undergraduate studies in French, German, and Spanish, has enabled her to place the British experience in a European context. This breadth of scholarship has been particularly fruitful in demonstrating that many elements of what formerly had been accepted as peculiarly English were to be found in other countries.

The fresh approach taken by Thirsk to rural society in the 16th century has resulted in other historians reassessing Tawney's findings concerning the conflict between capitalism and custom. This debate is ongoing and has been taken up by rural historians of other periods with the increasing recognition of the importance of endogenous local factors and the extent of their linkage with external national demands.

A further major contribution to scholarship has been the study of the interrelationship between agriculture and industries in rural areas. Largely through her researches into probate records, Thirsk demonstrated both the symbiotic nature of this relationship and the importance of inheritance of customs which she linked with her researches into the development of the family. The work on agriculture and industry has resulted in a major reassessment of the location and dynamics of industry in the pre-industrial period. She extended this revisionism through her later work on the knitting industry which identified the level of adoption and long-term impact of innovations that occurred in the 16th and 17th centuries. In respect of innovation, adoption, and diffusion, by undertaking detailed local research instead of following previous scholars whose conclusions were based solely on patents and publications, Thirsk has successfully challenged received views on the relationship between published theory and farming practice. Again, other scholars have followed her lead and the debate on the vectors of innovation continues.

Thirsk has also forayed into other related subjects. For example, she has usefully contributed to the debate on the role of women in English economy and society and more recently she has concentrated upon the role of women historians, publishing "The History Women" as a response to John Kenyon's *The History Men*. A further topic of her research which has led to a reassessment is her study of the role of the horse in 16th- and 17th-century England.

Thirsk possesses that rare combination of being both an intuitive researcher and an excellent communicator. The ability to communicate her enthusiasms and findings, through both her teaching (particularly of postgraduates) and the written word, has led to a wide dissemination of her work and her research techniques.

Apart from her own impressive list of published works, throughout her career Thirsk has been a major contributor in an editorial capacity to many publications. One of her most significant achievements has been her contributions to and editorship of volumes 4, 5, and 6, of *The Agrarian History of England and Wales* published by Cambridge University Press at various dates since 1967. She received further endorsement of the quality of her work when, in 1974, she was appointed general editor of the series.

Throughout her career she has been a major force in the development of the British Agricultural History Society, of which she was made president for an unprecedented second time in 1995. As editor of the Society's journal, *Agricultural History Review* (1964–72), Thirsk has ensured that the study of agrarian history has remained rigorous and challenging.

Although almost exclusively based in rural society, the breadth of Thirsk's researches has been extensive in terms of temporal, geographical, and topic range. Further, her influence, whether through the Tawney seminars, or at Leicester or Oxford universities, or her publications, has been far-reaching, and agrarian scholars of all periods have been directly or indirectly stimulated by her approach, her research and her revisionist findings. These achievements were acknowledged by her election to the British Academy in 1974, by the publication of her *Festschrift* in 1990, and by the award of the Companion of the British Empire in 1995 for her services to agrarian history. Her enormous contribution to the development of agricultural history, and particularly the early modern period, in the latter part of the 20th century is such that her achievements will have a significant influence on future generations of rural historians.

CHRISTINE S. HALLAS

Biography

Irene Joan Watkins Thirsk. Born London, 19 June 1922. Attended Camden School for Girls; MA, Westfield College, University of London, PhD. Subaltern, Auxiliary Territorial Service (ATS), Intelligence Corps, 1942–45. Assistant lecturer in sociology, London School of Economics, 1950–51; senior research fellow in agrarian history, University of Leicester, 1951–65; reader in economic history, Oxford University, 1965–83: fellow, St. Hilda's College, 1965–83. Married James Wood Thirsk (1 son, 1 daughter), 1945.

Principal Writings

English Peasant Farming: The Agrarian History of Lincolnshire from Tudor to Recent Times, 1957

Editor, *The Agrarian History of England and Wales*, vols. 4–6, 1967–81

General editor, *History of Lincolnshire*, 1970–

Editor with J.P. Cooper, *Seventeenth-Century Economic Documents*, 1972

Editor with Jack Goody and E.P. Thompson, *Family and Inheritance: Rural Society in Western Europe, 1200–1800*, Cambridge: Cambridge University Press, 1976

The Restoration, 1976

Economic Policy and Projects: The Development of a Consumer Society in Early Modern England, 1978

The Rural Economy of England: Collected Essays, 1984

Agricultural Regions and Agrarian History in England, 1500-1750, 1987

"The History Women," in Mary O'Dowd and Sabine Wichert, eds., *Chattel, Servant or Citizen: Women's Status in Church, State and Society*, Belfast: Institute of Irish Studies, 1995

Further Reading

Chartres, John, and David Hey, eds., *English Rural Society, 1500–1800: Essays in Honour of Joan Thirsk*, Cambridge and New York: Cambridge University Press, 1990

Thomas, Hugh 1931–
British European and world historian

Hugh Thomas is a prime example of the non-academic historian who specializes in well-researched blockbuster works on major themes, aimed at the general public. A brief spell in the Foreign Office in the 1950s, from which he resigned on a matter of principle, was followed by several years as a freelance writer, during which he produced the first of his massive tomes. Although he spent ten years as professor of history at Reading University, he found the routine of the academic world unappealing. Early in his writing career Thomas produced novels; he also wrote many essays and short pieces on a variety of political and other subjects, and displayed a wide familiarity with the cultural and artistic world. His work was recognized by his ennoblement as Lord Thomas of Swynnerton, an elevation which his timely espousal of free-market conservatism during the Thatcher years certainly did not hinder.

Thomas first won attention with *The Spanish Civil War* (1961), a 1-volume narrative account of that conflict, which became a bestseller. While critical of both sides, and perhaps most friendly to the anarchists, he was clearly unsympathetic to the continuing dictatorship of General Franco, and the book was banned in Spain, a tactic which failed to prevent large-scale smuggling of copies into the country.

A decade later, Thomas' Hispanic interests led him to produce a still more gigantic 1-volume narrative history, *Cuba: The Pursuit of Freedom* (1971), a survey of that island's troubled past as a Spanish colony, a United States quasi-dependency, and an independent communist state. Like his work on the Spanish Civil War, the Cuban volume gave much attention to social and economic history, in particular to the compelling effects of slavery and the sugar trade on Cuban history. While admiring the social progress and sense of hope that the Castro government gave, Thomas clearly had reservations as to the arbitrary nature of the regime. He finally concluded that, at the time of writing, Cuba was, as throughout its history, in many ways still controlled by outside economic forces beyond the government's power to change.

A shorter work by Thomas, *Goya: The Third of May, 1808* (1973), again focused on revolutionary Hispanic events. Over time, however, his interests became broader. In the mid-1960s he published a study, *The Suez Affair* (1966), severely critical of British, French, Israeli, and United States policy in that international imbroglio. He also wrote a short and largely favorable biography of the left-wing British journalist and political thinker John Strachey (1973), who edited the *Spectator* in the 1920s and 1930s. In *Europe: The Radical Challenge* (1973), Thomas attempted to influence contemporary politics, welcoming British entry into the European Economic Community, but arguing that the aim of British policy must be "to achieve a federal and democratic united community of Europe, in which the needs of different regions and classes are creatively realized."

Shortly afterward Thomas' political outlook, like that of various other once left-wing British and American intellectuals, moved distinctly to the right, so that in the 1980s he became a strong supporter of British prime minister Margaret Thatcher's free-enterprise conservatism, and in 1979 chairman of her Centre for Policy Studies. His political shift can perhaps be regarded as the logical development of his left-wing dislike of the British establishment, documented in his edited works, *The Establishment* (1959), and *Crisis in the Civil Service* (1968), which condemned the existing British power structure as fossilized, antidemocratic, and hostile to change, and even in his shorter commissioned volume, *The History of Sandhurst* (1961). His expression of these themes reached its apogee in *History, Capitalism and Freedom* (1979), a lecture he delivered before the 1978 Conservative party conference at Brighton.

Thomas' subsequent books, as well as his refusal to accept a lucrative but government-funded prize for one of them, reflected this viewpoint. *A History of the World* (1979) was a vast account of world history, from the perspective of economic, technological, cultural, and social developments rather than the narrative of the rise and fall of individual governments and states. Thomas clearly deprecated government intervention in the economy, commerce, and industry, regarding this as counterproductive and the enemy of genuine progress. It seems likely that this huge, stimulating, over-stuffed work, the distillation of a lifetime's thought on broad historic themes, will be regarded as his masterpiece.

Thomas then embarked on what is potentially as ambitious a project, a multivolume history of the Cold War. So far, only the first part of this, *Armed Truce* (1987), has appeared in print. In general, it reflected not only his continuing European perspective, concentrating upon developments in Europe rather than in the United States, but also his neoconservative sympathies, being highly condemnatory of Soviet policies, which he largely blamed for the Cold War's onset. Thomas strongly suggested that at that time an expansionist Soviet state posed a moral threat to European civilization, and gave a graphic, well-researched account of the extension of Soviet power through much of Central Europe during these years. On the whole, Thomas focused more on the individual quirks of the leading personalities involved than on broader historical forces – something of a change in emphasis from his previous work.

Thomas then abandoned this project, at least temporarily, to return to his Hispanic roots, with another huge narrative, *The Conquest of Mexico* (1993), a work that inevitably recalled the massive classic of his predecessor, W.H. Prescott. As one might expect from Thomas' previous interests, this ambitious study was firmly grounded in Hispanic sources and gave full weight to social, economic, and technological aspects. Nor does Thomas attempt to minimize the cruelties and near-genocide which the native population suffered. Even so, at heart it is an old-fashioned, stirring narrative epic, focused primarily upon the heroic figure of the conquistador Hernando Cortés.

Overall, Thomas can be regarded as a master of well-written, excellently researched, narrative histories, and as a model of the increasingly rare old-fashioned gentleman scholar.

PRISCILLA M. ROBERTS

See also Pérez; Spain: Modern

Biography

Hugh Swynnerton Thomas. Born 21 October 1931. Educated at Sherborne School; Queens' College, Cambridge; the Sorbonne, Paris. President, Cambridge Union, 1953; staff member, Foreign Office, 1954–57; lecturer, Royal Military Academy, Sandhurst, 1957; professor of history, University of Reading, 1966–76; chairman, Centre for Policy Studies, 1979–91. Married Vanessa Jebb, daughter of 1st Baron Gladwyn, 1962 (2 sons, 1 daughter). Created Baron Thomas of Swynnerton of Notting Hill in Greater London (life peer), 1981.

Principal Writings

Editor, *The Establishment*, 1959
The History of Sandhurst, 1961
The Spanish Civil War, 1961; 3rd edition, 1977
The Suez Affair, 1966
Crisis in the Civil Service, 1968
Cuba: The Pursuit of Freedom, 1971, abridged as *The Cuban Revolution*, 1977
Europe: The Radical Challenge, 1973
Goya: The Third of May, 1808, 1973
John Strachey, 1973
History, Capitalism and Freedom, 1979
A History of the World, 1979
Armed Truce: The Beginnings of the Cold War, 1945–46, 1987
The Conquest of Mexico, 1993, in US as *Conquest: Montezuma, Cortés, and the Fall of Old Mexico*, 1993
The Slave Trade: The History of the Atlantic Slave Trade, 1440–1870, 1997

Further Reading

Annan, Noel, *Our Age: Portrait of a Generation*, London: Weidenfeld and Nicolson, 1990; also published as *Our Age: English Intellectuals Between the World Wars, a Group Portrait*, New York: Random House, 1991
Cormack, Patrick, *Right Turn: Eight Men Who Changed Their Minds*, London: Leo Cooper, 1978
Harbutt, Fraser J., "Cold War Origins: An Anglo-European Perspective," *Diplomatic History* 13 (1989), 123–33
Haseler, Stephen, *The Battle for Britain: Thatcher and the New Liberals*, London: Tauris, 1989

Thomas, Keith 1933–

British social historian

Keith Thomas has been inextricably associated with the rise of social history in Britain since the early 1960s, a development he inspired both in precept, through a series of articles in the mid–1960s, and in practice, above all in *Religion and the Decline of Magic* (1971) and *Man and the Natural World* (1983). Although these books have reached a wide public, his career has been a highly orthodox Oxford one, culminating in the presidencies of Corpus Christi College and of the British Academy, and his leading role as an editor and delegate for Oxford University Press.

Like that of his Balliol tutor Christopher Hill, Thomas' work has been based on a prodigious grasp of the printed output of the early modern period, together with forays into the manuscript collections of the Bodleian and British libraries, rather than extensive archival research. In Thomas' case, this has been supplemented by encyclopedic familiarity with the social sciences and humanities, reflecting his belief that history requires a constant dialogue with other disciplines committed, as history should be, to a holistic understanding of human society. His programmatic pleas for this, expressed most trenchantly in his article "The Tools for the Job" (1966), earned him the hostility of historical traditionalists such as Geoffrey Elton, but have also been questioned by other social historians for their positivistic tone and apparent willingness to see historians as the passive recipients of the insights of other disciplines. His particular debt – especially in his work on witchcraft – is to the social anthropology of E.E. Evans-Pritchard, which drew him into debates between functionalist and hermeneutic anthropologists. This prefigured the shift of social history itself away from economic or social-structural forms of explanation toward cultural history. It is easy to see Thomas as a pioneer in this shift, leading the interest in popular culture and mentalities, and his work undoubtedly inspired many others to explore such subjects. Yet as late as 1991 in "Ways of Doing Cultural History," he confessed he had never thought of himself as a cultural historian. Instead his preferred self-image has been as a historical or "retrospective" ethnographer.

Thomas' "field-work" – the reading of the printed survivals of early modern England "until we can hear the people" – has explored every aspect of thought and life. Accumulated examples recorded on index-cards have been characteristically developed into a lecture, then extended into an essay; even his two books can be read as collections of essays, with *Man and the Natural World* arising from the Trevelyan lectures at Cambridge in 1979. In 1991 he summarized his other output as "shorter studies of literacy, numeracy, childhood, schoolboy life, women, sexual morality, attitudes to the past and the future" and promised future studies of "dress, speech, bodily comportment, dirt and cleanliness, taste and possessions." Such studies pioneered historical analysis by gender, age, and culture, as opposed to class, which had dominated earlier social history. Yet placing Thomas in this context is problematic, not least because he rarely refers to the arguments of other historians: the influence of other social sciences is much more overt. Where historiographical debts are acknowledged, they are to an older generation, in particular to that "most influential historian" R.H. Tawney, who sought to develop within English historiography the analytic insights of European social science, both Marxist and Weberian. The title of Thomas' greatest work, *Religion and the Decline of Magic*, is surely a deliberate echo of Tawney's *Religion and the Rise of Capitalism* (1926), which he dubbed "one of the century's greatest historical works" and

"an unforgettable account," while the core theme of both his books is the Weberian "disenchantment of the world" and the roots of this "great historical divide" in the post-Reformation centuries. Fundamentally, Thomas has remained true to the Tawney-Hill view of the Protestant Reformation as implicitly revolutionary in its effects, even if followed by a transitional century in which a hierarchical society sought to control such forces. The revolution that followed brought out their full implications, but also engendered the Restoration backlash in which such forces were either defeated, or secularized and molded into new forms, leaving modern British history the "result of the peculiar compromise implicit in the half-achieved revolution of the mid-17th century."

Such historical schemata are, however, rarely prominent in Thomas' work, which characteristically has dwelt on the complexities and paradoxes of historical development, just as it has focused on the anxieties and dilemmas of human behavior and choice facing people in the past. His writings have therefore been freely appropriated by historians of all types, including revisionists who have found, in *Religion and the Decline of Magic* in particular, evidence for "slow Reformation" and popular conservatism which has been turned against the Tawney-Hill view. Thomas has succeeded in his primary goal of opening up the whole of human experience to historical enquiry: the subsequent specialization and fragmentation of social history may disappoint, but perhaps not surprise, this detached observer of mental habits.

JONATHAN BARRY

See also Astrology; Britain: 1485–1750; Mentalities; Social

Biography

Keith Vivian Thomas. Born Wick, Glamorganshire, Wales, 2 January 1933, son of a farmer. Educated at Barry County Grammar School. Served in the Royal Welch Fusiliers, 1950–52. Studied at Balliol College, Oxford, BA 1955, MA 1959. At Oxford University: senior scholar, St. Antony's College, 1955; fellow, All Souls College, 1955–57, fellow/tutor, St. John's College, 1957–86; reader in modern history, 1978–85, and professor, from 1986; president, Corpus Christi College, from 1986. Married Valerie Little, 1962 (1 son, 1 daughter). President, British Academy, 1993. Knighted 1988.

Principal Writings

"Women and the Civil War Sects," *Past and Present* 13 (1958), 42–62

"The Double Standard," *Journal of the History of Ideas* 20 (1959), 195–216

"History and Anthropology," *Past and Present* 24 (1963), 3–24

"The Social Origins of Hobbes's Political Thought," in Keith Brown, ed., *Hobbes Studies* (1965), 185–236

"The Tools for the Job," *Times Literary Supplement* (1966), 275–76

"Another Digger Broadside," *Past and Present* 42 (1969), 57–68

Religion and the Decline of Magic: Studies in Popular Beliefs in Sixteenth- and Seventeenth Century England, 1971

With Hildred Geertz, "An Anthropology of Religion and Magic: Two Views," *Journal of Interdisciplinary History* 6 (1975–76), 71–109

"Age and Authority in Early Modern England," *Proceedings of the British Academy* 62 (1976), 205–48

Man and the Natural World: Changing Attitudes in England, 1500–1800, 1983; in US as *Man and the Natural World: A History of the Modern Sensibility*, 1983

The Perception of the Past in Early Modern England, 1984
"The Meaning of Literacy in Early Modern England," in Gerd
  Baumann, ed., *The Written Word: Literacy in Transition*, 1986,
  97–131
"Numeracy in Early Modern England," *Transactions of the Royal
  Historical Society* 5th series, 37 (1987), 103–32
History and Literature, 1988
"Children in Early Modern England," in Gillian Avery and Julia
  Briggs, eds., *Children and their Books: A Celebration of the
  Work of Iona and Peter Opie*, 1989, 45–77
"Ways of Doing Cultural History," in Rik Sanders and others, eds.,
  *Balans en perspectif van der Nederlandse cultur geschiedenis: de
  verleiding van de overvloed*, 1991, 65–81
"Cases of Conscience in 17th-century England," in John Morrill,
  Paul Slack, and Daniel Woolf, eds., *Public Duty and Private
  Conscience in Seventeenth-century England: Essays Presented to
  G.E. Aylmer*, 1993, 29–56
"Cleanliness and Godliness in Early Modern England," in Anthony
  Fletcher and Peter Roberts, eds., *Religion, Culture and Society in
  Early Modern Britain: Essays in Honor of Patrick Collinson*,
  1994, 56–83

Further Reading

Barry, Jonathan, "Introduction: Keith Thomas and the Problem of
  Witchcraft," in Jonathan Barry, Marianne Hester, and Gareth
  Roberts, eds., *Witchcraft in Early Modern Europe: Studies in
  Culture and Belief*, Cambridge and New York: Cambridge
  University Press, 1996, 1–45

Thompson, E.P. 1924–1993

British social historian

One of the pioneers of British social history after 1945,
E.P. Thompson recast the histories of labor, crime, protest, and
popular culture – areas that came to be known collectively as
"History from Below." Thompson epitomized the politically
engaged intellectual moving from his studies to condemn the
contemporary state, particularly in his work on behalf of the
peace movement. He insisted that history was not a neutral
pursuit and throughout his life was unafraid to take sides,
writing passionately on behalf of the English laboring poor
and their leaders in the 18th and 19th centuries, whom he
perceived to be the victims of the emerging market economy.
His excavation of a variety of English radical traditions not
only influenced the writing of social history around the world
but (along with the work of Raymond Williams and Richard
Hoggart) helped found English cultural studies. He enjoyed
a creative intellectual partnership with his wife, Dorothy
Thompson, a distinguished historian of Chartism and of
Victorian women.

Thompson was one of a remarkable group of historians who
emerged from the Communist party Historians Group under the
mentorship of Dona Torr. Other members included Christopher
Hill, E.J. Hobsbawm, and John Saville. Thompson left the
Communist party in 1956 over the Soviet invasion of Hungary,
a move that also signalled the search for a "socialist humanism"
that led him to assist in the creation of the New Left. His work
thereafter was characterized by a non-reductive Marxism that
changed the way in which labor history was written. Rather than
insisting on the overriding determinism of the economic base
in society, Thompson invoked the category of "culture" and

insisted that class was inseparable from class consciousness.
Thus it was necessary to reconstruct the lived experience of
historical participants, investigating folk customs and rituals.
Thompson's work was also distinctive in its passion for literature, especially the Romantics with their critique of industrialism. His first book was a study of the poet and artist William
Morris, whom he established as a major socialist thinker, while
his last was devoted to William Blake, placing him in the context
of radical religion and heretical thought.

Thompson's most influential book was undoubtedly *The
Making of the English Working Class* (1963). This proved to
be a clarion call for a new labor history, rejecting older interpretations that reduced the working class to dry statistics and
institutions, or assumed that it was the passive recipient of
change. The book argued that class was a determining feature
of experience and insisted that by 1832 a working-class movement had been created that was "the most significant factor
in British politics." Thompson also pushed forward the boundaries of labor history by taking seriously groups that had previously been dismissed or neglected by earlier scholars. In his
most famous sentence, he announced that he was "seeking to
rescue the poor stockinger, the Luddite cropper, the 'obsolete'
hand-loom weaver, the 'utopian' artisan and even the deluded
follower of Joanna Southcott, from the enormous condescension of posterity." This emphasis on the marginalized inspired
many studies of proletarian figures who had not been taken
seriously before.

The book celebrated the Jacobin political inheritance among
artisans in London and the West Riding of Yorkshire, tracing
the influence of Paineite ideas and insisting on the existence of
a revolutionary underground in the 1790s that emerged after
1815 to provide the basis for the working-class political plat-
form. The Industrial Revolution was interpreted as a cataclysm
in the lives of the poor. Thompson made an important contribution to the debate on whether working-class standards of
living rose or fell during the Industrial Revolution. He resisted
the claims of statistical series and instead urged attention to
the lived experience of the new proletariat, taking into account
environmental factors and (in a later study) the time discipline
of the new factory system.

This combination of a materialist analysis with cultural history also influenced labor history not just in Britain (where his
followers included Gareth Stedman Jones, Iowerth Prothero,
and the History Workshop movement) but throughout the
world. The American labor historians David Montgomery,
Herbert Gutman, and Eugene Genovese have all acknowledged
their debt to him. Thompson's influence was also felt in studies of African and Asian peasant communities.

Having dealt with the period between 1780 and 1832,
Thompson moved further back in time to open up the then
neglected field of 18th-century social history. He launched a series
of studies on custom, crime, and the penal code which were
published in *Whigs and Hunters* (1975), *Customs in Common*
(1991), and an influential collection of work with his students
at the University of Warwick, *Albion's Fatal Tree* (1975).
Thompson argued that certain kinds of crime such as poaching
and riot could be interpreted as social protest against the patrician oligarchy and the new commercial order. In a much-
discussed article, he posited the existence of a "moral economy"
among the plebeian crowd that resisted the imperatives of the

market in favor of a just price, legitimated by custom and tradition. Thompson's bipolar model of social relations in the 18th
century was based on a struggle between the plebeians and the
patricians which anticipated the class struggle documented in his
earlier works. In the wake of Thompson's research came numerous studies of early modern crime and the law, many of which
were structured by a critical engagement with his work. It was to
Thompson's credit that he took criticism seriously, always adding
postscripts to later editions of his books in which he responded
at length to reviewers and others. He also engaged in debate with
Perry Anderson over the neofeudal nature of British social development, with Leszek Kołakowski over communism, and with
Louis Althusser over the claims of structural Marxism. All these
writings were published in *The Poverty of Theory* (1978).

As important as Thompson's books were the debates they
produced. He was frequently criticized for exaggerating the
revolutionary potential of working-class politics and devoting
insufficient attention to popular conservatism. His hostile treatment of early Methodism, which he saw as facilitating the
work-discipline of industrial England and which he likened to
"psychic masturbation," was contested. More generally,
Thompson has been criticized for his lack of attention to
women, to the middle classes, and to the political history of
the elite. What is indisputable, however, is the way in which
Thompson shaped the paradigms and established the agenda
for historians of 18th- and 19th-century England, whether or
not they agreed with his work.

ROHAN MCWILLIAM

See also Anderson, P.; Annales School; Anthropology; Britain: since
1750; Commons; Crime; Economic; Europe: Modern; Geertz;
Gutman; History from Below; History Workshop; Hobsbawm;
Labor; Legal; Moore; Scott, Joan; Social; State; Subaltern; Theatre;
United States: Historical Writing, 20th Century

Biography

Edward Palmer Thompson. Born 3 February 1924, son of a
Methodist missionary. Studied at Corpus Christi College,
Cambridge, BA 1946. Served in the British Army in Italy during
World War II. Youth brigade volunteer, helping construct railways in
Yugoslavia and Bulgaria, 1946–47; teacher in extra-mural
department, University of Leeds, 1948–65; reader in social history,
University of Warwick, 1965–71: assisted in establishment of Centre
for the Study of Social History. Active in the UK peace movement,
especially against Korean War; member of the British Communist
party until 1956, and served on Yorkshire District Committee; a
leader of END, the European Nuclear Disarmament movement.
Married Dorothy Towers (i.e., Dorothy Thompson, the historian of
Chartism), 1948 (2 sons, 1 daughter). Died Worcester, 28 August
1993.

Principal Writings

William Morris: Romantic to Revolutionary, 1955
The Making of the English Working Class, 1963
Editor with Eileen Yeo, *The Unknown Mayhew: Selections from
    "The Morning Chronicle"* 1971
Whigs and Hunters: The Origin of the Black Act, 1975
Editor with Douglas Hay and Peter Linebaugh, *Albion's Fatal Tree:
    Crime and Society in Eighteenth-Century England*, 1975
Editor, with Jack Goody and Joan Thirsk, *Family and Inheritance:
    Rural Society in Western Europe, 1200–1800*, 1976
The Poverty of Theory and Other Essays, 1978

Customs in Common, 1991
Witness Against the Beast: William Blake and the Moral Law, 1993
Persons and Polemics, 1994
Making History: Writings on History and Culture, 1995
*Beyond the Frontier: The Politics of a Failed Mission – Bulgaria,
    1944*, 1997

Further Reading
Anderson, Perry, *Arguments within English Marxism*, London:
    Verso, 1980
Chandavarkar, Rajnarayan, "The Making of the Working Class:
    E.P. Thompson and Indian History," *History Workshop Journal*
    43 (1997), 177–96
Fine, R., "The Rule of Law and Muggletonian Marxism: The
    Perplexities of Edward Thompson," *Journal of Law and Society*
    21 (1994), 193–213
Johnson, Richard, "Thompson, Genovese and Socialist-Humanist
    History," *History Workshop Journal* 6 (1978), 79–100
Kaye, Harvey J., *The British Marxist Historians: An Introductory
    Analysis*, Cambridge: Polity Press, 1984; New York: St. Martin's
    Press, 1995
Kaye, Harvey J., and Keith McClelland, eds., *E.P. Thompson:
    Critical Perspectives*, Cambridge: Polity, and Philadelphia: Temple
    University Press, 1990
Palmer, Bryan D., *The Making of E.P. Thompson: Marxism,
    Humanism, and History*, Toronto: New Hogtown Press, 1981
Palmer, Bryan D., *E.P. Thompson: Objections and Oppositions*,
    London and New York: Verso, 1994
Rule, John, and Robert Malcolmson, eds., *Protest and Survival: The
    Historical Experience: Essays for E.P. Thompson*, London: Merlin
    Press, and New York: New Press, 1993
Schwarz, Bill, "'The People' in History: The Communist Party
    Historians' Group, 1946–56" in Richard Johnson *et al.*, eds.,
    Making Histories: Studies in History-Writing and Politics,
    London: Hutchinson, and Minneapolis: University of Minnesota
    Press, 1982

Thompson, F.M.L. 1925–
British economic and social historian

Although Michael Thompson's specific research area is
landownership and agriculture and particularly the landed
estate in the 19th century, his contribution to the development
of agrarian history as a subject has been very important. His
postgraduate research was supervised by Sir John Habakkuk
and resulted in the seminal book *English Landed Society in
the Nineteenth Century* (1963). Thompson's work inspired
scholars to reassess the role of the landed in both the 19th
and 20th centuries while other historians have revisited the
subject for earlier periods. Although some of Thompson's work
on landed society in the 19th century, such as the extent of
its decline, has been subject to revision, the depth of research
and analysis and the inherent incisiveness remain and the book
is still the standard text on the subject.

The development from the landed estate to more general
agrarian history was demonstrated in several articles and particularly in Thompson's research into the role of the horse in the
19th century. He furthered his interest in the structure of
the landed community in his work on the development of the
profession of chartered surveyors. He subsequently moved
closer to the city with his study of Hampstead from the 17th to
20th centuries and later through his editorship of the *Rise of*

Suburbia (1982). This theme was expanded in his research on the urban middle and working classes in Victorian Britain and the resultant publication, *The Rise of Respectable Society* (1988), and through his editorship of the 3-volume *Cambridge Social History of Britain, 1750–1950* (1990). Thompson's views on the dynamics of society have added fuel to the debate on class that has been a lively issue in the 1990s. In particular, by emphasizing "respectability" and by demonstrating that this operated across class boundaries thus providing a stabilizing counterbalance to the societal upheavals of the period, he challenged the Marxist view on class and the inevitability of class conflict.

Although his primary interest was in the Victorian period, Thompson's work ranged more broadly and included a history of the University of London and his editorship of a *Festschrift* for John Habakkuk in 1994. Although largely concerned with social and economic issues, political history also came under his purview and his interest in both rural England and the different strata of society was further developed in his research and subsequent publications on Whigs and liberals in the West Riding of Yorkshire and on land and politics in the 19th century.

Thompson's ability to range beyond his main foci in terms of both period and topic and his facility for drawing into center stage aspects that may have been regarded as peripheral (for example, the role of the horse and the development and influence of chartered surveyors) has been of great benefit to a new generation of historians. He has demonstrated the importance of identifying context and continuum in interpreting history and has forced a revisionist approach in many areas. Throughout his research he has not shied from entering the cutting edge of the debate and has challenged some of Lawrence Stone's conclusions and W.D. Rubinstein's research. His work on social control challenged received opinion and has resulted in recent historians opening up new areas of research into the topic.

Thompson's influence on succeeding generations of historians is extensive. He has provided an anchor for scholars in encouraging them always to seek the essence of issues by asking simple but searching questions, identifying themes and, above all, undertaking detailed research. His method is sound and pragmatic, his findings have been both innovatory and confirmatory. He is a formidable supervisor, examiner, and conference delegate. He has an unerring eye for the kernel of issues and, as scholars have sometimes found to their cost, quickly disregards the chaff. His lively sense of humor is to be found in his publications and his flowing literary style has ensured that his research is easily accessible to the interested reader.

Thompson's international reputation is impressive and while his research interests are concentrated in specific areas, his breadth of knowledge and understanding of issues mean that he is frequently called upon in international fora, as is demonstrated by his contributions to the European Science Foundation and to the British National Committee of the International Congress of Historical Sciences.

As a result of Thompson's contributions to social and economic history, particularly of rural England in the 19th and 20th centuries, the study of the subject has been greatly enhanced, new questions concerning the impact and role of the landed have been raised, and the potential for further research has been highlighted. The historical community still benefits from his successful struggles of the 1980s, as the Institute of Historical Research continues to thrive. His pragmatic and gently reformist approach to history will continue to provide direction for new generations of historians.

CHRISTINE S. HALLAS

Biography

Francis Michael Longstreth Thompson. Born 13 August 1925. Educated at Bootham School, York; Queen's College, Oxford, MA 1949, PhD 1956. Served in the Indian Artillery, 1943–47. Taught at University of London: at University College, 1951–68; at Bedford College, 1968–77; and as director, Institute of Historical Research, 1977–90 (emeritus). Married Anne Challoner (2 sons, 1 daughter).

Principal Writings

English Landed Society in the Nineteenth Century, 1963
Chartered Surveyors: The Growth of a Profession, 1968
Hampstead: Building a Borough, 1650–1964, 1974
"Social Control in Victorian Britain," *Economic History Review* 34 (1981), 189–208
Editor, *The Rise of Suburbia*, 1982
Editor, *Horses in European Economic History: A Preliminary Canter*, 1983
The Rise of Respectable Society: A Social History of Victorian Britain, 1830–1900, 1988
Editor, *The Cambridge Social History of Britain, 1750–1950*, 3 vols., 1990
Editor, *The University of London and the World of Learning, 1836–1986*, 1990
Editor, *Landowners, Capitalists and Entrepreneurs: Essays for Sir John Habakkuk*, 1994

Further Reading

Beckett, J.V., *The Aristocracy in England, 1660–1914*, Oxford and New York: Blackwell, 1986
Howell, David W., *Land and People in Nineteenth Century Wales*, London and Boston: Routledge, 1977
Koditschek, Theodore, "A Tale of Two Thompsons," *Radical History Review* 56 (1993), 69–84
Quinault, Roland, and N.B. Harte, *Land and Society in Britain, 1700–1914, Essays in Honour of Michael Thompson*, Manchester: Manchester University Press, and New York: St. Martin's Press, 1996

Thompson, Leonard 1916–
British-born historian of South Africa

One of the greatest historians of South Africa, Leonard Thompson has produced more work of quality, over a longer period, than any other professional historian of that country. His central importance is that he, more than any other historian, was responsible for moving South African history in an Africanist direction in the 1960s. Through his teaching and writing at that time, he argued that South African history should abandon its predominantly Eurocentric approach and take account of the past of all the people of the country. In calling, in particular, for the history of Africans to be written, Thompson set South African history on a course on which it must, given the demographic composition of the country, always remain. The Africanist perspective that he did so much to promote helped usher in a "golden age" of South African historical studies.

Before Thompson became an Africanist, he wrote mainly political history. His magisterial monograph, *The Unification of South Africa* (1960), was published as South Africa commemorated fifty years of Union. While that book did not pick up on the social and economic insights of the two leading historians of the previous generation, William Macmillan and C.W. de Kiewiet, it was at once the standard work on its subject, and it showed Thompson to be a historical craftsman of the first rank, able to order a mass of material and present detailed and complex arguments with admirable clarity and lucidity.

Thompson became an Africanist at the time of the decolonization of tropical Africa, and in reaction against the apartheid policies of his country, which he deplored. The intensification of apartheid led him to emigrate to the United States in 1961, and it was there that he emerged as a central figure in the "liberal Africanist" school of South African historical writing. He did so, above all, as editor of, and contributor to, the 2-volume *The Oxford History of South Africa* (1969–71) and a collection of essays entitled *African Societies in Southern Africa* (1969). In the preface to the *Oxford History*, co-authored with the anthropologist Monica Wilson, and more extensively in his introductory chapter in the *African Societies* collection, Thompson pointed the way to a new history, only partially achieved in those volumes, one that would draw on other disciplines for evidence, in particular for South Africa's early history, where written evidence was nonexistent. In the late 1960s this was a novel methodological approach for a historian of South Africa.

The *Oxford History* especially, but also other of his writings, was strongly criticized by conservative, pro-apartheid Afrikaner historians for being pro-black and anti-Afrikaner. Proud of his anti-apartheid credentials, Thompson scorned such criticism. But the *Oxford History* also became the main target for a new generation of historians of a radical, materialist persuasion. They too were Africanists, but they criticized liberal history for ignoring class analysis, for placing too much stress on race, for not explaining racism, and for remaining essentially elitist in approach. Thompson's relations with these critics, many of whom were not historians by training and approached history with clearly political agendas, were often strained, but he recognized the force of some of what they said, and gradually incorporated some of their insights into his own work.

Before he did so, however, he published three very different books, on topics considered unfashionable by revisionists when they appeared. His *Survival in Two Worlds* (1975), a biography of Moshoeshoe of Lesotho, remains one of the greatest biographies ever written of any southern African figure. Conceived in the nationalist period of African historiography and written out of a deep sympathy with its subject, it included a surprising amount of material on the social and economic context of Moshoeshoe's life, and drew upon pioneering oral research. After moving from UCLA to Yale, Thompson co-edited *The Frontier in History* (1981) with a historian of America, Howard Lamar. Some critics said that this volume did not advance the study of the frontier history of the US and South Africa beyond rather obvious juxtapositions, but the volume was a pioneering attempt at comparative history, and one that has not, to date, been superseded. Then in *The Political*

Mythology of Apartheid (1985), Thompson traced how particular racial myths had developed and been used for racist and nationalist ends. Afrikaner critics accused him of viewing Afrikaners in general as backward and myth-prone and exclusively responsible for apartheid. Other critics agreed that the book did not distinguish sufficiently an Afrikaner nationalist from an apartheid mythology, and maintained that it exaggerated the role of racial prejudices and myths in its historical development. But again the book remains the best treatment of its theme.

Thompson's *A History of South Africa* (1990) is widely regarded as the best recent synthesis of South Africa's history. He offered no bold new overarching interpretation, but a masterly survey of the state of knowledge of the field. His approach was as always essentially pluralist and empirical, emphasizing the importance of the political, but Thompson now incorporated insights from some of the best of the work of the previous two decades in social and economic history. Some said he placed too much importance on the 18th century in the development of the "racial order," and not enough on the degree to which the mineral revolution of the late 19th century transformed South African society, while others faulted him for a too authoritative tone and for failing to make clear how contested much of South African history was. Like almost all of his work, his *History* was written in exceptionally lucid prose. Indeed, only C.W. de Kiewiet among professional historians of South Africa equals Thompson for elegance of style. Now that the ideological battles of the 1970s and 1980s have passed, Thompson's stature should grow, as one of the most influential historians of South Africa of his generation.

CHRISTOPHER SAUNDERS

See also Curtin; South Africa

Biography

Leonard Monteath Thompson. Born Cranborne, England, 6 March 1916. Received BA, Rhodes University, South Africa, 1935, MA 1938; BA, Oxford University, 1939, MA 1943. Lectured at the University of Cape Town, 1946–61; Professor of African History, University of California, Los Angeles, 1961–68; and Yale University, 1968–85 (emeritus): founder/director, Southern African Research Program, Yale University. Married 1950 (2 children).

Principal Writings

The Cape Coloured Franchise, 1949
The Unification of South Africa, 1902–1910, 1960
"Afrikaner Nationalist Historiography and the Policy of Apartheid," in *Journal of African History*, 1962
Politics in the Republic of South Africa, 1966
Editor, *African Societies in Southern Africa: Historical Studies*, 1969
Editor with Monica Wilson, *The Oxford History of South Africa*, 2 vols., 1969–71
Editor with Richard Elphick and Inez Jarrick, *Southern African History before 1900: A Select Bibliography of Articles*, 1971
Editor with Jeffrey Butler, *Change in Contemporary South Africa*, 1975
Survival in Two Worlds: Moshoeshoe of Lesotho, 1786–1870, 1975
Editor with Howard Lamar, *The Frontier in History: North America and Southern Africa Compared*, 1981
With Andrew Prior, *South African Politics*, 1982
The Political Mythology of Apartheid, 1985
A History of South Africa, 1990

Further Reading

Keegan, Timothy, "The Long Journey of Leonard Montieth [sic] Thompson," *Southern African Review of Books*, (June/July 1990)

Saunders, Christopher, *The Making of the South African Past: Major Historians on Race and Class*, Cape Town: David Philip, and Totowa, NJ: Barnes and Noble, 1988

Saunders, Christopher, "Leonard Thompson's Historical Writing on South Africa: An Appreciation," *South African Historical Journal* 30 (1994), 3–15

Smith, Ken, *The Changing Past: Trends in South African Historical Writing*, Johannesburg: Southern Book Publishers, 1988; Athens: Ohio University Press, 1989

Thorne, Samuel E. 1907–

US legal historian of medieval and early modern England

A teacher of lawyers and legal historians, Thorne is one of the premier American legal historians of medieval and early modern England from the 12th to the late 16th century. Thorne's academic career at Northwestern, Yale, and Harvard law schools spanned more than half a century, and his scholarly writing underwent three phases, from the early canon and common law to the legal renaissance of the 16th century, and then to the era of Bracton's treatise in the 13th century for which he has become best known. His earliest work in the 1930s was on St. Germain and the canon law of medieval England, with several articles published in the late 1930s on Heydon's case, Dr. Bonham's case, and the legal controversies of the late 16th and early 17th centuries. The development of his interests in this period were furthered in his work as an associate member of the research staff of the Henry E. Huntington Library in San Marino, California, during the summers of 1937–39, where he began to research legal education at the Inns of Court and the interpretation of statutes.

At the Huntington Library Thorne discovered two manuscript copies of a discourse on the interpretation of statutes in the Ellesmere manuscripts, which he later meticulously edited, with a long introduction on the history of statutory interpretation, and published as *A Discourse upon the Exposicion and Understandinge of Statutes* (1942). Discerning the attempts of the author's annotations to preserve a balance between parliamentary authority and the administration of justice, he pursued this subject in future editing and writing (such as his *Prerogativa regis*, 1949), and opened up its study for future legal historians. Thorne then went on to write provocatively on Sir Edward Coke, Edward Hake, and the legal-constitutional problems of the era. Throughout, his focus was on the original manuscripts and their interpretation. In the end, he produced one of the most thoughtful essays on the interface of law, society, and economy in the 16th century ("Tudor Social Transformation," 1951).

In moving back to the first formative period in the history of English law, Thorne re-examined early feudalism. In several articles he identified the major changes in the law of real property that led to the restructuring of English feudal society. Other articles on the coronation oath of Henry I and Magna Carta placed these constitutional events within the context of feudal society. Thorne was equally interested, however, in the canon law. Early work on the assize *utrum*, canon law, and the post-glossators lay behind his interest in the convergence of Roman civil and English common law, and formed perhaps the foundations of his later interest in the pivotal document named Bracton's treatise.

Thorne's major work from the 1960s centered on his study of Henry Bracton, the mid-13th-century judge and alleged author of the famous common law treatise, *De legibus et consuetudinibus Angliae* (Of the Laws and Customs of England). Although Thorne started out to produce only a translation of Woodbine's edited Latin text of that treatise, he ended up producing his own new edition as well as the first English translation. Even more important for scholars was the fact that his work on the text led him to a significant revision of previous conclusions about the date of the writing of the original text as well as the likely author and authors. He was able to show that Henry Bracton was only the final reviser of the text and not its original author. Thorne also challenged the conventional view of the relationship between the treatise and the collection of copies of plea roll enrollments to which F.W. Maitland had given the name of "Bracton's NoteBook." The major value of Thorne's text is that it provides historians with a valuable source through which to examine the intellectual and social history of the common law in this era, thereby merging the subjects of social and legal change that had marked the advent of Thorne's academic career.

LOUIS A. KNAFLA

See also Maitland

Biography

Samuel Edmund Thorne. Born New York City, 14 October 1907. Received BA, City College of New York, 1927; LLB, Harvard University, 1930. Taught at Northwestern University Law School, 1932–45; professor, Yale University Law School, 1945–55; professor, Harvard University Law School, from 1955.

Principal Writings

Editor, *A Discourse upon the Exposicion and Understandinge of Statutes*, 1942

Editor, *Prerogativa regis: tertia lectura Roberti Constable de Lyncolnis Inne anno 11 Henry VII* (Robert Constable of Lincoln's Inn, 11 Henry VII, His Third Lecture on the Statute of the Royal Prerogative), 1949

"Tudor Social Transformation and Legal Change," *New York University Law Review* 26:10 (1951)

Editor, *Readings and Moots at the Inns of Court in the Fifteenth Century*, 1954

Translator and editor, *Bracton on the Laws and Customs of England*, 4 vols., 1968–77

Essays in English Legal History, 1985

Further Reading

Arnold, Morris S., Thomas A. Green, Sally A. Scully, and Steven D. White, eds., *On the Laws and Customs of England: Essays in Honor of Samuel E. Thorne*, Chapel Hill: University of North Carolina Press, 1981

Thucydides c.460/455–c.399 BCE

Greek historian

Thucydides wrote one work, usually known as *The Peloponnesian War* (the author did not give it a title), which was left unfinished at his death. It describes the war fought between the Athenians and their allies on the one side, and the Peloponnesians, led by the Spartans, on the other. The war lasted from 431 to 404 BCE, but Thucydides' narrative breaks off abruptly in 411. Thucydides served as an Athenian general during the war, but was exiled for his failure in a campaign of 424, and spent the rest of the war outside Athens, during which time he was able to travel around Greece and research his work.

In the preface to the work, Thucydides claims that he conceived the idea of writing a history as soon as the war broke out. At that time, in all probability, the only substantial work of history to have been written was that of Herodotus. Thucydides never names Herodotus, but it is clear that he knew the work. He criticizes a number of Herodotus' statements, and the brief account of Greek history before the war that Thucydides gives begins at exactly the point that Herodotus' narrative stops. Thucydides' claim that he will not include *to muthôdes* (a term difficult to translate, but referring to legendary or fabulous material) is also taken to mark a deliberate contrast with Herodotus. Athenian culture of this period was in general "agonistic," with writers, including playwrights, setting themselves up in competition with their predecessors. The inclusion of several pairs of antithetical speeches, in which rival generals or politicians set out opposing arguments about the same issues, is part of the same cultural tradition. It is in this light that Thucydides' criticisms of Herodotus should be read, rather than as a wholesale rejection of his historical approach. However, since antiquity, writers have identified Herodotus and Thucydides as representing two distinct approaches to the writing of history.

Thucydides' work reflects a number of preoccupations. His concentration on war and politics as the proper subject for a historian distinguishes him from his predecessor and set a trend. So too did his interest in writing about his own times. It is an important claim of his work that he is offering an analysis of the causes and course of the Peloponnesian War in the belief that such events will recur in the future, and that people in the future can learn from their past. It is clearly with this in view that he presents certain individuals and events in considerable detail, as representing general types. Thus, for example, he gives a long and powerful description of civil war in Corcyra, and comments that, after this, civil war became widespread in Greece; he also concentrates on the Athenian general Cleon, who is presented as a typical demagogue.

Thucydides is often characterized as a "scientific historian." As well as indicating some of his intellectual affinities (discussed below), this reflects his interest in *akribeia*, meaning "precision" or "accuracy." Numbers are often given very precisely in the work, and this must in part indicate careful research; however, this kind of precision can also be used to heighten the dramatic impact of the narrative. His concern with chronology, and the way he establishes a clear chronological framework for his narrative, counting by summers and winters, is also taken as an indication of a scientific approach.

A strong interest in causation is a feature of Thucydides' work. Famously, in the discussion of the causes of the Peloponnesian War he makes a distinction between the events that immediately led up to the outbreak of the war, and the "truest cause", which he identified as the growth of Athenian power and the fear this caused for Sparta. However, it is important to note that although Thucydides' ideas of causation are more developed than simply identifying the actions of individuals (whether human or divine) as the causes of events, his discussion of states as causal agents attributes to them human emotions and intentions.

Thucydides' writing was influenced by the intellectual climate of the Greek cities in the second half of the 5th century. In particular his description of the effects of plague on Athens, with its methodical description of the range of symptoms, is closely related to the works on *Epidemics* in the Hippocratic corpus. The speeches in the work are written in a dense style that owes much to contemporary ideas about rhetoric. Parallels to some of the arguments used by speakers, for example in the so-called "Melian Dialogue," can be found in the writings of the Sophists, who were prominent in Athens in the period in which Thucydides grew up and was active. Commentators have also recognized affinities with Greek tragedy in Thucydides' work. Tragedies were written by members of the same Athenian intellectual and political elite in which Thucydides moved, and they were influenced by the same intellectual developments; it is unsurprising to find Thucydides using the techniques of tragedy in the presentation of events in his work.

Thucydides' narrative was carried on by a number of writers, including Xenophon, whose *Hellenica* is the only continuation to survive. His work was read in the centuries after his death, but its literary style was considered difficult, and before the Roman imperial period it was not as popular as the works of Herodotus and Xenophon. Even after that it was read more for its style than for its contribution to an understanding of the past. In the modern period Thucydides' status as "the first scientific historian," and his apparently conservative attitude to democracy meant that the reliability of his information and of his judgment were for a long time unchallenged. It is only recently that scholars have begun to recognize the power of his literary techniques and at the same time to raise some questions about his veracity.

HUGH BOWDEN

See also Diodorus; Greece: Ancient; Memory; Military; Universal; Xenophon

Biography

Born Athens, c.460/455 BCE, descendant (through his father), of royal Thracian family. Caught the plague c.430/27, but recovered. Elected military magistrate, with task of protecting Thracian coast, but failed to rescue besieged Amphipolis, 424; exiled to family lands at Skape Hyle, Thrace, 424; recalled from exile, 404. Died c.399.

Principal Writings

Works (Loeb edition), translated by C.F. Smith, revised edition, 4 vols., 1928–30
The Peloponnesian Wars, translated by Benjamin Jowett, revised by P.A. Brunt, 1963
History of the Peloponnesian War, translated by Richard Crawley, edited by W. Robert Connor, 1993

Further Reading

Adcock, Frank E., *Thucydides and His History*, Cambridge: Cambridge University Press, 1963; Hamden, CT: Archon, 1973

Connor, W. Robert, *Thucydides*, Princeton: Princeton University Press, 1984

Cornford, Francis Macdonald, *Thucydides Mythistoricus*, London: Arnold, 1907

Gomme, Arnold Wycombe, Antony Andrewes, and Kenneth J. Dover, *A Historical Commentary on Thucydides*, 5 vols., Oxford: Oxford University Press, 1945–81

Grundy, George Beardoe, *Thucydides and the History of His Age*, 2 vols., London: Murray, 1911; reprinted Oxford: Blackwell, 1948

Hornblower, Simon, *Thucydides*, London: Duckworth, and Baltimore: Johns Hopkins University Press, 1987

Hornblower, Simon, ed., *Greek Historiography*, Oxford and New York: Oxford University Press, 1994

Hornblower, Simon, *A Commentary on Thucydides*, Oxford and New York: Oxford University Press, 1991–

Hunter, Virginia, *Thucydides the Artful Reporter*, Toronto: Hakkert, 1973

Kosso, Peter, "Historical Evidence and Epistemic Justification: Thucydides as a Case Study," *History and Theory* 32 (1993), 1–13

Rawlings, Hunter R. III, *The Structure of Thucydides' History*, Princeton: Princeton University Press, 1981

Romilly, Jacqueline de, *Histoire et raison chez Thucydide* (History and Reason in Thucydides), Paris: Belles Lettres, 1956

Schwartz, Eduard, *Das Geschichtswerk des Thukydides* (The Historical Work of Thucydides), Bonn: Cohen, 1929

Stahl, Hans-Peter, *Thukydides: die Stellung des Menschen im geschichtlichen Prozess* (Thucydides: The Position of Individuals in the Historical Process), Munich: Beck, 1966

Westlake, H.D., *Individuals in Thucydides*, Cambridge: Cambridge University Press, 1968

Westlake, H.D., *Studies in Thucydides and Greek History*, Bristol: Bristol Classical Press, 1989

Tilly, Charles 1929–

US social historian of modern Europe

It is testimony to Charles Tilly's cross-disciplinary influence that he is simultaneously one of the most widely cited American historians of modern Europe and one of the half-dozen most influential sociologists in the English-speaking world. From the time of his graduate work at Harvard in the 1950s where he worked with the macrosociologists Barrington Moore and Pitirim Sorokin and the social historian G.W. Homans, through his professorships at Toronto, Michigan, the New School for Social Research, and Columbia Tilly has always excelled in interdisciplinary research. His students have worked in anthropology, economics, and political science as well as history and sociology. His most well-known scholarly work has been on collective action and state-making – indeed, he played a major role in defining these as topics of contemporary historical study. He has also published widely on urbanization, labor history, and migration. Among historians, he has been a pioneer in the use of quantification and the testing of social theory. At the same time, he has helped introduce archival research and a sensitivity to chronology among sociologists, and thereby to rejuvenate "historical sociology." In addition to his impressive activity as an editor and project director, Tilly has had a major influence through his students, both those who formally studied

with him and those at other institutions whom he has helped – Janet Abu-Lughod, Ronald Aminzade, Ron Aya, William Christian, Michael Hanagan, Rudy Koshar, Ted Margadant, Douglas McAdam, John Merriman, Leslie Moch, William Roy, David Snyder, and Olivier Zunz, for example.

Much of Tilly's scholarship has been devoted to challenging what he has seen as the implicitly Durkheimian or structural-functional tradition in Anglo-American historiography and social science. In this view, societies are presumed to have a certain coherence. Protest and conflict against the dominant social order come from maladjusted groups. In contrast, Tilly has pointed out that "societies" are in fact simply the people within political units. Conflict arises when holders of political power oppose disadvantaged groups who have real grievances.

Tilly has argued this most broadly in the area of what he terms "collective action," that is, concerted public acts by identifiable groups. For much of the 20th century, many scholars followed the hallowed tradition of seeing collective action by ordinary people – protests, strikes, riots – as emotional outbursts, fueled by simple deprivation or psychological maladjustments. Along with the British Marxist historians such as E.J. Hobsbawm, George Rudé, and E.P. Thompson and social scientists such William Gamson, Tilly has argued in contrast that ordinary people's actions are often motivated by their own sense of justice and follow complex strategies. Collective action, even collective violence, is not random, but aimed at specific targets. Often it has flowed through carefully chosen forms that the surrounding society could understand. The forms of collective action available at any one time Tilly calls "repertoires." Repertoires have changed as politics and the economy have changed. The petition drive, the demonstration, and labor strike, Tilly argues, have their own history. Thus, a political rally would have been meaningless in the 17th century, just as a shaming ritual would be in the 20th. New forms of protest arose within urban and economic settings in which governments, elites, or employers were forced to confront the grievances of ordinary people.

The most important ways in which collective action has changed, according to Tilly, are tied to the two most fundamental transformations of modern history – the rise of the state and the growth of capitalism. As governments took on new powers such as taxation and conscription and capitalistic markets penetrated more into the lives of lower-class people, the typical forms of collective protest changed in Europe; while common people began by reacting against the intrusion of the state and capitalist methods, they gradually acquired the ability to organize themselves and influence the action of the state and capitalism. Tilly's arguments have been based on empirical investigations that are unusual among both historians and social scientists. He and his large group of collaborators have created huge data bases of collective action in France, Britain, Italy, and Germany.

Based on his work on collective action, Tilly has criticized prevailing models of revolution and strike activity. The "revolutions" on which most scholars focus are often only stages in larger struggles between contenders for power. Demonstrations and collective violence were more widespread after the French Revolution of July 1830, for example, than during the 1789 Revolution itself. Workers, peasants, and middle-class groups struggled over the shape of the new government, and the state frequently responded with violent repression. Revolution, Tilly also argues, should not be seen as a phenomenon completely apart from normal political struggle. Instead, it is the mix of repression, the balance of power between contending groups, and divisions within elites that determine whether conflict develops from mobilization into revolution. Similarly, scholars had previously argued that strikes occurred because workers were isolated or alienated from the mainstream of society. Tilly showed that French strikes were actually more common in large urban areas where workers had access to allies and resources. Collective action, in other words, was not a sign of simple maladjustment or alienation: it arose where people with real grievances had the opportunity and ability to make demands.

Tilly's interest in the long-run factors shaping collective action led him naturally into a concern with what he terms "state-making," the process by which governments exerted their power over people and territory. According to Tilly, the keys to the rise of states in European history have been coercion and capital: power-holders had to succeed in monopolizing the means of violence and in controlling a substantial portion of moveable wealth. Armed force allowed governments to repel rival states and to repress those who opposed taxation or conscription. Access to capital allowed states to maintain armed forces as well as a state bureaucracy. At the same time, states were usually forced to accommodate those with large amounts of capital: penetration of state power into the daily lives of common people and into remote territory usually came to serve the interests of capital as well as the state.

Aided by states, capitalism, according to Tilly, created a wage-earning population much earlier than traditional historiography has argued. Centuries before the Industrial Revolution, large numbers of rural people became dependent on wages through working in domestic industry or the "proto-industrial" system. Thus, the 19th-century migration to European cities and to the Western Hemisphere was not a movement of peasants who became members of a capitalist system for the first time. Instead, these people's ancestors in the countryside had already begun living in a capitalist system and changing their economic and demographic behavior.

Tilly's work on state-making in particular has led him in his more recent work to a greater interest in the complex interactions between political actors' forms of identity and the opportunities created by short-term political changes. Confrontations can more easily turn into revolutionary situations when power-holders and challengers are redefining their political identities. At the same time, the chances for successful collective action are greatly enhanced when short-lived, contingent weaknesses appear on the side of those who hold power.

By studying collective action, state-making, revolution, and capitalism over the whole span of modern European history, Tilly has played an almost unique role in demonstrating how historians can integrate political and social theory with historical sensitivity. In an age where many decry increasing specialization, Tilly, along with Perry Anderson, S.N. Eisenstadt, and Immanuel Wallerstein, has helped re-create a wide-ranging historical social science that sweeps across disciplines.

CARL STRIKWERDA

See also Crime; France: French Revolution; Labor; Military; Mousnier; Social; Sociology

Biography

Born Lombard, Illinois, 27 May 1929. Trained as a sociologist, Harvard University, BA 1950, PhD 1958; also studied at Balliol College, Oxford, 1950–51; Facultés Catholiques de l'Ouest, 1955–56. Taught sociology and/or history at University of Delaware, Newark, 1956–62; Princeton University, 1962–63; Harvard University, 1963–65; University of Michigan, 1964–65 and 1969–84; University of Toronto, 1965–69; New School for Social Research, 1984–96; and Columbia University from 1996. Married Louise Audino (i.e. Louise Tilly, q.v.), 1953 (1 son, 3 daughters).

Principal Writings

The Vendée, 1964

With James B. Rule, *Measuring Political Upheaval*, 1965

"Collective Violence in European Perspective," in Hugh Davis Graham and Ted Robert Gurr, eds., *Violence in America: Historical and Comparative Perspectives*, 1969

Editor with David S. Landes, *History as Social Science*, 1971

"How Protest Modernized in France," in William Aydelotte, Allan Bogue, and Robert Fogel, eds., *The Dimensions of Quantitative Research in History*, 1972

With Lynn Lees, "Le Peuple de juin 1848" (The People in June 1848), *Annales: ESC* 29 (1974), 1061–91

With Edward Shorter, *Strikes in France, 1830–1968*, 1974

"Food Supply and Public Order," in Charles Tilly, ed., *The Formation of National States in Western Europe*, 1975

With Louise Tilly and Richard Tilly, *The Rebellious Century, 1830–1930*, 1975

From Mobilization to Revolution, 1978

Editor, *Historical Studies of Changing Fertility*, 1978

"Migration in Modern European History," in William H. McNeill and Ruth S. Adams, eds., *Human Migration: Patterns and Policies*, 1978

As Sociology Meets History: Studies in Social Discontinuity, 1981

Big Structures, Large Processes, Huge Comparisons, 1984

"The Demographic Origins of the European Proletariat," in David Levine, ed., *Proletarianization and Family History*, 1984

"Social Movements and National Politics," in Charles Bright and Susan Harding, eds., *Statemaking and Social Movements: Essays in History and Theory*, 1984

The Contentious French, 1986

Coercion, Capital, and European States, AD 990–1990, 1990

European Revolutions, 1492–1992, 1993

Editor with Wim P. Blockmans, *Cities and the Rise of States in Europe*, AD 1000 to 1800, 1994

Editor, *Citizenship, Identity, and Social History*, 1995

Popular Contention in Great Britain, 1758–1834, 1995

Roads from Past to Future, 1997 [includes bibliography]

Further Reading

Hanagan, Michael, Leslie Page Moch, and Wayne Brake, eds., *Challenging Authority: The Historical Study of Contentious Politics*, Minneapolis: University of Minnesota Press, 1997

Hunt, Lynn, "Charles Tilly's Collective Action," in Theda Skocpol, ed., *Vision and Method in Historical Sociology*, Cambridge and New York: Cambridge University Press, 1984

Skocpol, Theda, "Sociology's Historical Imagination" and "Emerging Agendas and Recurrent Strategies in Historical Sociology," in Theda Skocpol, ed., *Vision and Method in Historical Sociology*, Cambridge and New York: Cambridge University Press, 1984

Tarrow, Sidney, *Power in Movement: Social Movements, Collective Action, and Politics*, Cambridge and New York: Cambridge University Press, 1994

Tilly, Louise A. 1930–

US social historian of European labor and women

Louise Tilly has been one of the leaders in the growth of scholarship on women's history, the history of the family, and social history in the late 20th century, helping to create an interdisciplinary approach to the study of social change that combines anthropology, sociology, economics, and demography with traditional archival and historical research. Her central contributions have been in demonstrating the historical importance of women's labor, showing the crucial effect of demographic change on the work of women and children, and documenting the interrelations between economic developments and family life. Beyond these concerns, she has also contributed to the study of food riots, collective action, social movements, and social welfare.

In contrast to the prevailing view up until the 1970s that women's work was a relatively recent phenomenon linked to increasing political and social freedom for women, Tilly demonstrated that the vast majority of women in pre-industrial Western families had worked, sometimes in the home, sometimes outside. Indeed, the distinction between waged labor outside the home and unwaged labor within the household, she argued, was often misleading in understanding how preindustrial and industrial workers' families managed their lives. In an important article and subsequent book, Tilly and Joan Wallach Scott borrowed the concept of "household economy" from the turn of the century Russian economist A.V. Chayanov, who had concluded that peasant families had pooled the labor and household resources of all family members in order to maximize their welfare. Tilly argued that like peasant families, the artisanal and working-class households in which many women lived in the pre-industrial period combined the work of men, women, and children and combined working outside the home and within the home in differing proportions as their opportunities and resources changed. The Industrial Revolution created more opportunities to work at waged labor outside the home, but the logic of a household pooling its labor to its collective advantage did not change radically. Furthermore, Tilly pointed out that the previous literature in economic history had implicitly used a male perspective in emphasizing the revolutionary quality of industrialization. The major areas of women's employment – textiles, garments-making, and domestic service – were all closely connected to work that women had traditionally done before the Industrial Revolution. The decline in women's waged labor in the early 20th century, Tilly and Scott argued, came as real wages finally rose for men along with government welfare expenditures and as workers became increasingly attracted to the middle-class lifestyle of homemaking.

Tilly also explored the crucial role that demography played in this story by showing how economic developments tended to create new family patterns. The first step toward women's increasing participation in waged work in Europe was the growth during the early modern era of employment in proto-industrial or rural industrial work in which women and children did simple tasks such as spinning or carding. Proto-industrial work was much more prevalent in areas where surplus population provided a ready labor force, while proto-industry itself encouraged a lower age of marriage and thus higher fertility. In the 19th century, too, Tilly argued, the level of women's waged work and the kinds of work that women did were closely tied to the demographic structure of an area. Textile cities provided employment for women and created higher rates of marriage. Fertility rose until families adjusted to a new urban world and adopted birth control. Coal-mining areas and large commercial cities with domestic service were interesting exceptions to this pattern, according to Tilly. Typically, there was little work available for women in the mines – especially as children's and women's work in mining was gradually banned across Europe in the 19th century. Consequently, mining areas often saw relatively high rates of fertility and low levels of women's waged work. Large cities meanwhile drew thousands of young women to be servants, but as long as they were servants women usually were not allowed to marry. Along with crowded housing, rising educational levels, and knowledge of birth control, domestic service, too, lowered levels of fertility. With fewer children, working-class women had more invested in each individual child and, where possible, withdrew more from waged work. With John Gillis and David Levine, Tilly edited a major study of modern European demography, *The European Experience of Declining Fertility* (1992), which argued that the watershed decline in the birthrate occurred at different times in various "demographic provinces" across Europe and had been caused by new attitudes toward children, which Europeans had adopted in reaction to social and economic change. In her address entitled "Connections" as president of the American Historical Association in 1992, Tilly pointed out that industrialization in England in the 18th and 19th centuries had profound effects on family life in France and as far away as India. More agricultural than England, France still created an industrial sector of working-class women similar to that of England, while, because of colonialism and competition from officially promoted British mechanized industry, hand-spinning for textiles declined in India. Industrialized textile production provides a key example of how factories created ripple effects of migration, population growth, and dramatically changed families in places around the world.

Beyond these concerns, Tilly has also contributed to the study of food riots, collective action, social movements, and social welfare. Her interest in the effects of industrialization led her to publish work on how the early effects of capitalism spawned food riots and how migration and factory work in cities shaped demonstrations and the rise of socialism. Her interest in women's work has led her in her most recent scholarship to an interest in "social citizenship" – the economic and social rights that countries grant – and how the process of European integration has affected social welfare. Tilly has been a leader among historians in moving easily between national specialties, in joining social scientific theories and methods to archival research, and in connecting contemporary concerns to a study of long-run historical change. She has done research and published on French, Italian, American, and English history; she has worked as closely with sociologists, anthropologists, and economists as with historians; she has helped to create the influential Social Science History Association of which she was also elected president; and, at the national level in the United States, she served as chair of the National Research Council and National Academy of Sciences Panel on Technological Change and Women's Employment.

CARL STRIKWERDA

See also Crime; Family; Feminism; Labor; Scott, Joan; Women's History: Europe

Biography

Louise Audino Tilly. Born Orange, New Jersey, 13 December 1930, daughter of an engineer and an artist. Received BA, Douglass College, 1952; MA, Boston University, 1955; PhD, University of Toronto, 1974. Taught at University of Michigan, Flint, 1971–72; Michigan State University, 1972–75; University of Michigan (rising to professor), Ann Arbor, 1977–84; and New School for Social Research, from 1984. Married Charles Tilly (q.v.), 1953 (1 son, 3 daughters).

Principal Writings

"The Food Riot as a Form of Political Conflict in France," *Journal of Interdisciplinary History* 2 (1971), 32–57

"I fatti di maggio: The Working Class of Milan and the Rebellion of 1898," in Robert Bezucha, ed., *Modern European Social History*, 1972

With Joan Wallach Scott, "Women's Work and Family in Nineteenth-Century Europe," *Comparative Studies in Society and History* 17 (1975), 36–64

With Charles Tilly and Richard Tilly, *The Rebellious Century, 1830–1930*, 1975

With Joan Wallach Scott and Miriam Cohen, "Nineteenth-Century European Fertility Patterns and Women's Work," *Journal of Interdisciplinary History* 6 (1976), 447–76

With Joan Wallach Scott, *Women, Work, and Family*, 1978

"The Family Wage Economy of a French Textile City: Roubaix, 1872–1906," *Journal of Family History* 4 (1979), 381–94

"Paths of Proletarianization: The Sex Division of Labor and Women's Collective Action in Nineteenth-Century France," *Signs: Journal of Women in Culture and Society* 7 (1981), 400–17

Editor with Charles Tilly, *Class Conflict and Collective Action*, 1981

Editor with Vivian Patraka, *Feminist Re-Visions: What Has Been and Might Be*, 1983

Editor with Heidi I. Hartmann and Robert E. Kraut, *Computer Chips and Paper Clips: Technology and Women's Employment*, 2 vols., 1986–87

"Gender, Women's History, and Social History," *Social Science History* 13 (1989), 439–62

Editor with Patricia Gurin, *Women, Politics, and Change*, 1990

Politics and Class in Milan, 1881–1901, 1992

Editor with John R. Gillis and David Levine, *The European Experience of Declining Fertility, 1850–1970*, 1992

"Industrialization and Gender Equality," in Michael Adas, ed., *Islamic and European Expansion: The Forging of a Global Order*, 1993

"Connections," *American Historical Review* 99 (1994), 1–20

"Women, Work, and Citizenship," *International Labor and Working Class History* 52 (1997), 1–26

Edited with Jytte Klausen, *European Integration in Social and Historical Perspective*, 1997

Tocqueville, Alexis de 1805–1859
French historian

Alexis de Tocqueville is one of the world's best known historical writers, but his historical work was relatively small, came late in his life, and was unfinished. His major historical work, *L'Ancien Régime et la Révolution* (*The Ancien Régime and the Revolution*, 1966) was published in 1856, three years before his early death. It was only the first part of his project, and

dealt with France before 1789 – the *ancien régime* – not with the Revolution itself. He had been researching the subject since 1850, although the main lines of his interpretation had been outlined as early as 1836, in an article that was translated by John Stuart Mill and published in the *London and Westminster Review*. Tocqueville himself said in the preface that his book was not a history of the Revolution, but a "study" of the Revolution. What he meant was that, unlike the narrative histories such as those by Thiers and Michelet, which were the bestsellers of the day, he totally avoided narrative. This makes his book seem in many ways remarkably modern. Like many products of 20th-century academic research it consists of analysis, and discussion of hypotheses, with the historical evidence organized to support the argument, without a narrative line. It is possible that if he had been able to complete his plan, the pages on the Revolution itself might have included more about the unrolling of events. But this is doubtful, as the fragments and notes of the continuation, which have been published in the modern edition of his collected works, suggest that he would have continued along the same lines.

Tocqueville belonged to a noble family with landed estates in Normandy, and with connections to the pre-1789 *noblesse de robe*, including the eminent Malesherbes. His father – who was also a historian, but a totally forgotten one – served as a prefect under the restoration, and had Legitimist opinions. This tradition of political and administrative service of the monarchy meant that it was not surprising that as a young man his son would take up a post in the legal system. The 1830 revolution and the subsequent Orléanist monarchy were not to the taste of his family, and in 1831 Tocqueville resigned his post to carry out a governmental mission of enquiry into the penal system of the United States. He used this opportunity to look in a much broader way at the political system and the society of the United States, the investigation that resulted in *De la démocratie en Amérique* (1835–40; *Democracy in America*, 1835–40).

From this time onward his main activity was intellectual, the research and reflection that led to his two major works, and the correspondence with his numerous acquaintances, the publication of which in his modern collected works has revealed the immense scope of his intellectual interests. In addition he engaged in politics as an opposition deputy in the last years of the Orléans monarchy, and then as a deputy, and later as foreign minister under the Second Republic. Louis Napoleon's coup d'état of 1851 ended his participation in active politics, and confirmed the pessimistic analysis of French history that underpinned the studies of the Revolution on which he now embarked.

These studies were a development of the reflections about the long-term evolution of modern society and politics which he had begun during his visit to the United States. Naturally he was most concerned about France, but he thought that France could best be understood on a comparative basis. Comparison with France was an underlying theme of *Democracy in America*; in Tocqueville's mind the comparison was really between France and the Anglo-Saxon countries as a whole; he treated the United States as revealing the completion of tendencies that had not yet worked themselves out in Britain, but which had British roots. He had many intellectual contacts in England, and also an English wife.

He lived before the age of academic specialization, being, like Marx, one of the great speculative polymaths. But *Democracy in America* can be seen as prefiguring modern sociology. His 1836 article on the state of France before and after 1789 was also abstract sociological analysis although it prefigured the main lines of *The Ancien Régime*, but it was only in the work which he began in 1850, after the collapse of his own political career, and the foreshadowing of the failure of the Second Republic to whose success he was committed, that he turned himself into a historian.

This came with his exploration of the archives of the pre-1789 royal administration, beginning with the year he spent in Tours, working in the departmental archives, which preserved the documents of the old *généralité*. Taking one small area as a case study, Tocqueville adopted a very modern approach. He worked in central government archives as well, and used other sources, some of them printed, but it was this exploration of the Tours archives that provided the nucleus and the real novelty of his work.

He was not the first to use government archives; Michelet (and others) had done so, but in a very different way, and in a way that did not fundamentally alter their narrative histories derived from secondary sources and memoirs. Perhaps a parallel would be in the archival research already being conducted by medievalists, although it is unlikely that he had any knowledge of this. In any case the medieval work was antiquarian in character, and lacked the analytical framework that Tocqueville combined with his exploration of the archives. It is this combination which identifies Tocqueville as the historical genius and path-breaker that he surely is.

What was the great hypothesis that guided his research? It was the idea that although the men of 1789 had tried to make a totally new beginning, to build a new world that would be totally different from France before 1789, there had in reality been a great continuity. The main element of this continuity was the centralization of the absolute state. Absolutism, in contrast to the English tradition of parliamentary liberties and local "self-government," had produced the violent Revolution in 1789. However, the ingrained mental characteristics of the French had ensured that after the anarchy and excesses of the brief revolutionary period the final result was the Napoleonic state, which simply extrapolated and completed the centralization and absolutism of the *ancien régime*; Napoleon was Louis XIV writ large. The Second Empire showed, as Tocqueville was writing, that the attempt to avert this destiny with a constitutional monarchy copied from England, had failed. The revolution had come again in 1848 – "and it was always the same Revolution" – and had resulted again in Napoleonic despotism.

Although not so central to his thought, and probably not as startling a hypothesis as the centralization theory, was another insight to which he came in the course of his study of the Revolution, which can perhaps be called the Tocqueville law on the causes of revolutions. His conviction was that revolution came – and he framed this as a general rule of which France before 1789 was only one example – not when misery and oppression were at their worst, but when conditions were improving. As he put it "the worst moment for a bad government is when it begins to reform," and he drew attention to the many reforming actions of Louis XVI's reign. Another expression of the same insight is his formulation that the French

peasantry before 1789 resented the remaining seigneurial dues precisely because they had long since ceased to be serfs, under the daily control of their manorial lords. A fully operating manorial (or feudal) system would be accepted because it was functional, and was thus seen as a necessary part of social and political life. That was still the position in Central and Eastern Europe in the 18th century, and even in Tocqueville's own lifetime; he visited Germany to investigate the conditions of peasant life there, seeking to establish this point. But in France precisely because the peasants were no longer either oppressed or controlled by the seigneurial lords, they felt all the more resentment at the arbitrary payments that could still be exacted on occasion. It was this that led to the passion for equality that he saw as the guiding motif of 1789, and of the subsequent history of France.

The Ancien Régime posed questions that would take generations of subsequent research, not to solve, but even to explore thoroughly. It is no longer consulted on questions of fact, but its abiding interest derives from two features. The first is the way in which Tocqueville pioneered the methods of archival research followed by later generations of historians. The second is the general framework of explanation which he provided for the French Revolution, and for revolutions in general; that is that a revolution is always a parenthesis – in spite of the most desperate attempts to wipe out the old, there will be some continuity; and that revolutions come not from oppression, but at times of reform.

DAVID ROBIN WATSON

See also Bailyn; Commager; France: since 1789

Biography
Alexis Charles-Henri-Maurice Clérel de Tocqueville. Born Paris, 29 July 1805, to an aristocratic family. Studied law. Magistrate, Versailles tribunal, 1827–32; traveled in US, 1831–32; elected to parliament, 1839; briefly minister of foreign affairs, 1849; retired from public life, 1851. Elected to Académie Française, 1841. Married Mary Mottley, 1836. Died Cannes, 16 April 1859.

Principal Writings
De la démocratie en Amérique, 2 vols., 1835–40; in English as *Democracy in America*, 1835–40
"The Political and Social Condition of France," *London and Westminster Review* 3 & 25 (April 1836), 137–69; reprinted in *Memoirs, Letters, and Remains*, 2 vols., 1861
L'Ancien Régime et la Révolution, 1856; in English as *The Ancien Régime and the Revolution*, 1966
Oeuvres complètes (Complete Works), edited by G. de Beaumont, 9 vols., 1864–66
Souvenirs, 1893; in English as *Recollections: The Revolution of 1848*, 1948
Oeuvres complètes (Complete Works), edited by J.P. Mayer, 18 vols. to date, 1951–

Further Reading
Bergin, Martin J., Jr., *Tocqueville as Historian: An Examination of the Influences on His Thought, and on His Approach to History*, Ann Arbor: University of Michigan Press, 1986
Centre National de la Recherche Scientifique, *Alexis de Tocqueville, livre du centenaire, 1859–1959* (Centenary Volume), Paris: Centre National de la Recherche Scientifique, 1960

Cox, Marvin R., "Tocqueville's Bourgeois Revolution," *Historical Reflections* 19 (1993), 279–307

Furet, François, "Tocqueville," in Furet and Mona Ozouf, eds., *Dictionnaire critique de la Révolution française*, Paris: Flammarion, 1988; in English as *A Critical Dictionary of the French Revolution*, Cambridge, MA: Harvard University Press, 1989

Herr, Richard, *Tocqueville and the Old Regime*, Princeton: Princeton University Press, 1962

Jardin, André, *Alexis de Tocqueville, 1805–59*, Paris: Hachette, 1984; in English as *Tocqueville: A Biography*, New York: Farrar Straus, and London: Halban, 1988

Mélonio, François, *Tocqueville et les Français* (Tocqueville and the French), Paris: Aubier, 1993

Mitchell, Harvey, *Individual Choice and the Structures of History: Alexis de Tocqueville as Historian Re-Appraised*, Cambridge: Cambridge University Press, 1996

Siedentop, Larry, *Tocqueville*, New York and Oxford: Oxford University Press, 1994

Todorov, Tsvetan 1939–

Bulgarian literary theorist

One of the leading thinkers in 20th-century poetics, Tsvetan Todorov was born in Bulgaria before settling in France in the early 1960s. He studied literature with Roland Barthes at the University of Paris, undertaking a doctoral thesis on Laclos' novel *Les Liaisons dangereuses*, which was published in 1967 as *Littérature et signification* (Literature and Meaning). He received a research appointment at the Centre National de la Recherche Scientifique in Paris, and served for a decade as editor of the influential journal *Poétique*.

Todorov's many influences can be traced to the Russian formalism of Vladmir Propp, Roman Jakobson, and Mikhail Bakhtin, as well as the structuralism of Claude Lévi-Strauss and the poststructuralist work of Roland Barthes and Jacques Derrida. His poetics is grounded in the search for structures inherent in literature, not in meaning as such, and it is perhaps for that reason that his work has found a larger audience among scholars interested in issues of genre and rhetoric than among mainstream historians.

Among the most prominent of his writings are *Poétique de la prose* (1971; in English as *The Poetics of Prose*, 1977), *Poétique* (1968; *Introduction to Poetics*, 1981) and *Théories du symbole* (1977; *Theories of the Symbol*, 1982). These works help the historian to find new approaches to history as text, since Todorov's main concern is the manner in which narratives are constructed from the smallest units to the largest, and the problems encountered in various readings of such texts.

In particular, his *Introduction to Poetics* describes three aspects of literary discourse – the semantic, the verbal, and the syntactic. Todorov notes that semantic questions have been jumbled into what he terms "formal" and "substantial" – "how does a text signify?" and "what does a text signify?" The first confines itself too narrowly to "meaning" and the second is overly concerned with a "reality" that lies outside of the text itself. Todorov, however, refines a distinction between sign and symbol, and in particular examines "registers of discourse" – language patterns and preliterary materials that are conceptually prior to the finished work. Among these are

relationships between concrete and abstract, "figurality" and repetition, and references to anterior discourses, or "intertextual valences," as well as the subjectivity of language.

In discussing the verbal aspect of literature, Todorov argues against the "representative illusion" that holds sway over many readers – "there is not *first of all* a certain reality, *and afterward*, its representation by the text." It is the text, maintains Todorov, that is the "given," and the verbal aspect of its discourse concerns mode, time, perspective, and voice. Finally, literary syntactics concerns the various logical, temporal, and spatial relationships between units of thematic structure. Todorov notes that the orders encountered in actual literature represent a rich mixture of these aspects. What the reader encounters is not the minimal units of narrative, but rather the entire text made up of multiple sequences that are combined through processes of embedding, linking, and alternation.

Since the mid-1980s, Todorov's work has taken a turn toward fuller treatment of the philosophical and historical issues that lie at the heart of contemporary French thought. A number of works, including *La Conquête de l'Amérique* (1982; *The Conquest of America*, 1984), *Nous et les autres* (1989; *On Human Diversity*, 1993), *Les Morales de l'histoire* (1991; *The Morals of History*, 1995), and *Face à l'extrême* (1991; *Facing the Extreme*, 1996), represent a wider range of questions than can be found in his earlier writing on poetics. In *The Morals of History*, Todorov discusses a broad array of eclectic topics, from the relationship between truth, fiction, and lies, to the role of intellectuals in society. A theme that runs through this and many of his other recent works is that ethics and values need a prominent place in society, and that intellectuals must assume a larger public role in discussing them.

Facing the Extreme focuses on "moral life in the concentration camps," examining the power of basic goodness in the face of inhumanity. Todorov stressed that his "object of inquiry [is] the moral life of the individual," and that what interests him is "not the past *per se* but rather the light it casts upon the present." It is a solid core of goodness – "simple daily virtues" – that Todorov carefully separates from acts of charity, purely moral acts, acts of solidarity, and acts of self-sacrifice. In the testimony of camp survivors Todorov finds a distinction between acts of heroism and a simpler, unpretentious goodness that has little to do with personal glory. Simple goodness is socially configured and deeply contextual. Unlike acts of heroism, it is often not distinctly remembered – it does not, as Todorov notes, lend itself well to stories. Todorov's philosophical and historical analysis of these themes gives them a narrative dimension they once lacked.

On Human Diversity analyzed prominent French writers – among them Rousseau, Montesquieu, and Lévi-Strauss – who have treated issues of cultural understanding. His work represents an attempt to create appreciation for diversity without settling for a simplistic relativism, asking how people can maintain deep commitment to their own cultural experiences while developing respect for others. Todorov criticized both ethnocentrism and simple relativism, finding instead in the works of Enlightenment humanists a way of understanding what brings cultures together and what separates them. In both his early work on structuralist poetics and his more recent work on what might broadly be called social thought, Todorov presented an interpretive challenge for historians. His works represent a complex vision of the historical past and the historical text that is difficult to categorize, but which creates a compelling case for a genuinely interdisciplinary approach to the past.

ROBERT A. LaFLEUR

See also European Expansion; Mexico

Biography

Born Sofia, 1 March 1939, son of a university professor. Received MA in philology, University of Sofia, 1963; doctorates, University of Paris, 1966, 1970. Taught at Centre National de la Recherche Scientifique, from 1968. Married Martine van Woerkens, writer, 1972 (2 sons, 1 daughter).

Principal Writings

Littérature et signification (Literature and Meaning), 1967

Poétique, 1968; in English as Introduction to Poetics, 1981

Introduction à la littérature fantastique, 1970; in English as The Fantastic: A Structural Approach to a Literary Genre, 1973

Poétique de la prose, 1971; in English as The Poetics of Prose, 1977

Théories du symbole, 1977; in English as Theories of the Symbol, 1982

Symbolisme et interprétation, 1978; in English as Symbolism and Interpretation, 1982

Mikhail Bakhtine: le principe dialogique, 1981; in English as Mikhail Bakhtin: The Dialogical Principle, 1984

La Conquête de l'Amérique: la question de l'autre, 1982; in English as The Conquest of America: The Question of the Other, 1984

Critique de la critique: un roman d'apprentissage, 1984; in English as Literature and Its Theorists: A Personal View of Twentieth-Century Criticism, 1984

Nous et les autres: la réflexion française sur la diversité humaine, 1989; in English as On Human Diversity: Nationalism, Racism, and Exoticism in French Thought, 1993

Face à l'extrême, 1991; in English as Facing the Extreme: Moral Life in the Concentration Camps, 1996

Les Morales de l'histoire, 1991; in English as The Morals of History, 1995

Les abus de la mémoire (Tricks of Memory), 1995

Toynbee, Arnold J. 1889–1975

British historian

Arnold J. Toynbee was perhaps the leading philosopher of history during the middle of the 20th century. His massive A Study of History (12 volumes, 1934–61), brought him to the world's attention after World War II. Toynbee had been active as a specialist in Greek and Near Eastern affairs before he commenced his study. It was in part a reply to the gloomy speculations of Oswald Spengler's Decline of the West, which had aroused such a sensation after World War I. Toynbee's work was directed toward the problem of the rise and fall of civilizations. He had become highly critical of the kind of monographic writing that had come to dominate professional history; the universal history he advocated proved to be less an exercise in international history than an analytical study of some 20 (or, later, 30) civilizations or societies. A civilization was, in fact, a society in which a high degree of culture had been attained. At such a stage, a universally recognized religion

existed, and written records were used to help define a recognizable people or group of peoples. Most of Toynbee's civilizations include a wide range of societies and not a single nation. This marks a break with 19th-century traditions which emphasized the writing of national histories. At times, as is evident from his debate with Pieter Geyl, the word "civilization" did seem to include a "national civilization."

Most of the civilizations included in the original Study could be located in time, between 3500 BCE and the present. Further observations on the more recent archaeological research were discussed in his 1976 work, Mankind and Mother Earth. In essence, Toynbee distinguished between two types of civilizations. There were 1) "full blown" civilizations, and 2) abortive or arrested civilizations. The latter group involved societies which were later eclipsed by more powerful cultures. He had in mind the shift from medieval European civilization to the modern, technological "world" civilization. Toynbee relied heavily on his education in Greek and Roman classics. His basic model for the development of civilization from a state of political plurality to the emergence of a universal state, is derived from his understanding of Egyptian and Roman history. Although he was able to include the Sumerian, Akkadian, and Hittite civilizations, he was not familiar with the preceding Hatti. Most of his independent civilizations were familiar to his readers: Egyptian, Aegean, Indus, Orthodox Christian, Western, and Islamic. Some American Indian cultures were included – the Mexican and Andean. The satellite civilizations he described were less well known. They included the national Tibetan, Japanese, and Korean. He raised these to a dominant Sinic or Chinese civilization. Perhaps he failed to make some basic distinctions in East Asian culture created by the language variations. Almost all Asian societies were placed in the Chinese-related group.

Although he was sharply criticized for some of his more sweeping generalizations, Toynbee did reduce his arguments to simple principles. Growth was related to a stimulus and response model that he described in terms of challenge and response. Many civilizations had the potential for continuing indefinitely, yet did not. They could survive if they successfully rallied in the face of crisis and decline. There was no set pattern to the number of times a rally could occur. If, as in the case of Western Christian culture, a former civilization such as the Roman one, collapsed, then a surviving elite could provide leadership for the civilization which arose from the ruins of the first one. Western European civilization arose because of the dynamic leadership offered by an effective minority of Roman Christians.

Once dominated by the notion of a plan of God in history, historians had relinquished it by the 18th century, in favor of the idea of the indefinite progress of mankind. The 19th century had interpreted progress in a materialist sense which emphasized the study of nation-states. Toynbee considered nationalist historiography to have had a detrimental effect and deplored its influence. The rise of sociological studies produced a new kind of social science that focused on the role played by elites and bureaucrats in the development of nations. Toynbee made full use of the conceptual apparatus arising from that discipline. Even more important was Toynbee's conception of a universal church, an idea that represented an extension of the medieval idea of Christian unity. His work continued to reflect the importance of the British belief in progress as typically Western.

The older cyclical theories of the Indians and Greeks were rejected. The stimulus of a crisis could result in progress proceeding from learning and new knowledge.

Many of Toynbee's conclusions were debated between himself and Pieter Geyl of the University of Utrecht in early 1948 and broadcast on BBC radio. Geyl congratulated Toynbee for not having proclaimed a doom and gloom theory like Spengler's. Toynbee believed that the issue at hand was the nature of history, and that the "fate of the world" depended on finding the answer to it. He once more emphasized the importance of spiritual over material problems. Geyl doubted that historians could make a chart of history as Toynbee had suggested. Yet he did believe that history had some meaning. He doubted Toynbee's claim that the history of the Netherlands – as one of a hard country rising to the challenge of North Sea floods – proved his "challenge and response" interpretation. Yet Geyl believed that the future of Western society remained open, while Toynbee only partly concurred in that view.

Toynbee continued to defend his ideas at international congresses, especially in 1958 and 1961. Despite his original interest in the spiritual aspects of civilization, he did admit the need for economic surpluses to sustain society. Modern technology was praised for having made the subdivision of society into social classes unnecessary. He was forced to give a better definition of what he meant by a "breakdown of civilization." Such a disruption of human cooperation could occur even before a civilization had reached its peak. As a more effective elite emerged, a new spirit could open the way to the future. He knew very well that any regularities described in his theories lacked the rigor of scientific law and acknowledged that they were of an intellectual and moral nature.

At a conference in Salzburg held in 1961, Toynbee revealed that he remained uncertain about his earlier holism. He did not know whether a civilization represented a real entity or not. He envisioned a movement toward a world culture. In it were identifiable elements showing the influence of psychology. He realized that human affairs were unpredictable because there was a subconscious component in them. He continued to believe in free will and human choice.

Just prior to World War II, Toynbee had modified his theory of civilization. The basic unit of society was not really a civilization, it was religion. He appreciated the cultural importance of the world's great religions and hoped for a fusion of them at some time in the future. On the whole, Toynbee remained devoted to the traditions of his own Western civilization, and its religious and political attitudes. His basic explanatory model for the changeover from one civilization to another had been derived from his study of its history. The Roman empire had declined, in part, because its internal proletariat had been excluded from power. Its state had been destroyed by invading barbarians who constituted an external proletariat. Whether this model can be extended to any and all of 21 or more civilizations seems doubtful.

After World War II, Toynbee revised some of his theories and expanded the number of civilizations in his study to 31. His focus shifted to the religious and cultural achievements of many peoples. Rigid determinism was rejected and his faith in human spiritual revival remained high.

HELEN LIEBEL-WECKOWICZ

See also Burke; Comparative; Egypt: Ancient; Febvre; Geyl; Kedourie; McNeill; Philosophy; Universal

Biography

Arnold Joseph Toynbee. Born London, 14 April 1889. Educated at Winchester College; Balliol College, Oxford. Fellow/tutor, Balliol College, 1912–15; Koraes professor of Byzantine and modern Greek language, literature and history, University of London, 1919–24; director of studies, Royal Institute of International Affairs, 1925–55; research professor of international history, University of London, 1925–55. Various government work in connection with war, 1915–19; with Political Intelligence Department, Foreign Office, April 1918; member of Middle Eastern Section, British delegation, Peace Conference, 1919; director, Foreign Research and Press Service, Royal Institute of International Affairs, 1939–43; director, Research Department, Foreign Office, 1943–46; delegate, Paris Peace Conference, 1946. Married 1) Rosalind Murray (daughter of Gilbert Murray), 1913 (marriage dissolved 1946; 2 sons); 2) Veronica Marjorie Boulter, 1946. Died York, 22 October 1975.

Principal Writings

Editor and translator, *Greek Historical Thought from Homer to the Age of Heraclius*, 1924
A Study of History, 12 vols, 1934–61; vols. 1–10 abridged by D.C. Somervell, 2 vols., 1946–57
Civilization on Trial, 1948
The World and the West, 1953
An Historian's Approach to Religion, 1956
Hannibal's Legacy: The Hannibalic Wars' Effect on Roman Life, 2 vols., 1965
Constantine Porphyrogenitus and His World, 1973
Mankind and Mother Earth: A Narrative History of the World, 1976

Further Reading

Gargan, Edward T., ed., *The Intent of Toynbee's History: A Cooperative Appraisal*, Chicago: Loyola University Press, 1961
McIntire, C.T., and Marvin Perry, eds., *Toynbee: Reappraisals*, Toronto: University of Toronto Press, 1989
McNeill, William H., *Arnold J. Toynbee: A Life*, Oxford and New York: Oxford University Press, 1989
Montagu, M.F. Ashley, ed., *Toynbee and History: Critical Essays and Reviews*, Boston: Sargent, 1956
Morton, S. Fiona, *A Bibliography of Arnold J. Toynbee*, Oxford and New York: Oxford University Press, 1980

Treitschke, Heinrich von 1834–1896

German political historian

Heinrich von Treitschke was one of the greatest German nationalist historians of the 19th century, his works constituting a major part of the "Prussian School" of German historiography. His theory of German nationalism was centered on the notion of the *Volk* (people), and the desirability of unifying all German states under Prussian leadership. In certain ways his ideas resembled those of another prominent German philosopher J.G. Herder. Treitschke believed that a united Germany was one in which its people would obey one ruler, for only in that way would a *Machtstaat* (a unified German state) be achieved. Treitschke's political philosophy was based on his dismay at the state of "Germany" during his early years when the smaller principalities were hostile to Prussia. According to

Treitschke, during that time most "Germans" saw Prussia as a military dictatorship where equality did not exist.

Perhaps Treitschke's thoughts are best explained by reference to his early academic years, where he excelled in literature and history, becoming a specialist in political and intellectual history. He believed that both literature and history had their own special social significance. Following other prominent German historians, Treitschke preferred to be remembered as one who influenced the course of history rather than one who simply related the events that had happened. Treitschke's teachings included an emphasis on mythology, which reflected his own attraction to Romanticism and early liberalism. Furthermore, Treitschke was overwhelmed by the glory associated with war, arguing that "war is just and moral." However, as Prussia developed, his earlier liberal thoughts gave way to more authoritarian ones.

Treitschke's most influential work was his 5-volume *Deutsche Geschichte im neunzehnten Jahrhundert* (1879–94; *History of Germany in the Nineteenth Century*, 1915–19). The first volume dealt with the historical tradition of the new empire that came into existence in 1815, and as historian Gordon A. Craig has noted, the *History* identified "the history of Prussia with that of Germany." The final volume covered events until the revolution of 1848. Treitschke had certainly hoped to cover a greater series of events but his untimely death did not allow him to do so. The *History*'s main aim was to enlighten the German people politically. Treitschke believed that the essence of the state was power, emphasizing that the state was a means to promote and preserve moral values. In order to achieve this, a degree of freedom had to exist. "A mature people," argued Treitschke, "must therefore demand these things of the State for the assurance of its personal liberty: The most fruitful outcome of the metaphysical fights for freedom during the past century, namely, the truth that the citizen must never be utilized by the State merely as a means, should be recognized as a true fundamental principle." Treitschke was so obsessed with the power of the state that he did not realize that such great power brought danger rather than a means of protecting the liberty of the German people.

Treitschke's ideas were promulgated through his university lectures on politics at the University of Freiburg. These lectures were repeated annually to large audiences of mixed social composition. In his lectures, Treitschke emphasized the centrality of the state. Furthermore, he argued that big powerful states were the victors and small states the losers. As mentioned earlier, the glory associated with war remained undisputed in Treitschke's ideas – and in his lectures. These lectures, published after his death, formed the 2-volume *Politik* (1911–13; *Politics*, 1916). Following the trends of his *History*, Treitschke's *Politics* emphasized the importance of a strong nationalism, calling for the unity of the German people, and for them to strive to be superior over all other peoples.

YEONG-HAN CHEONG

See also Europe: Modern; Germany: 1800–1945; Graetz; Meinecke; Mommsen, T.; Nationalism

Biography

Heinrich Gotthard von Treitschke. Born Dresden, Saxony, 15 September 1834, from a military family. Studied at universities of Bonn, Leipzig, Tübingen, and Heidelberg. Taught at University of Leipzig; University of Freiburg, 1863–66; University of Kiel, 1866–67; University of Heidelberg, 1867–73; and University of Berlin, 1873–96. Reichstag member, 1871–84. Editor with Hans Delbrück, *Preussische Jahrbücher*, 1883–90. Died Berlin, 28 April 1896.

Principal Writings

Historische und politische Aufsätze (Historical and Political Essays), 4 vols., 1863–97
Zehn Jahre deutscher Kämpfe, 1865–1874: Schriften zur Tagespolitik (The Ten Years' War in Germany, 1865–1874: Writings on Day-to-Day Politics), 2 vols., 1874; revised as *Deutsche Kämpfe: neue Folge: Schriften zur Tagespolitik* (German Battles: New Results), 1896
Deutsche Geschichte im neunzehnten Jahrhundert, 5 vols., 1879–94; in English as *Treitschke's History of Germany in the Nineteenth Century*, 7 vols., 1915–19
Politik, 2 vols., 1911–13; in English as *Politics*, 2 vols., 1916

Further Reading

Bussmann, Walter, *Treitschke: sein Welt- und Geschichtsbild*, Göttingen: Musterschmidt, 1952; in English as *Treitschke: His Life and Works*, London: Jarrold, 1914
Davis, Henry William Carless, *The Political Thought of Heinrich von Treitschke*, London: Constable, 1914; New York: Scribner, 1915
Dorpalen, Andreas, *Heinrich von Treitschke*, New Haven: Yale University Press, 1957
Guilland, Antoine, *L'Allemagne nouvelle et ses historiens: Niebuhr, Ranke, Mommsen, Sybel, Treitschke*, Paris: Alcan, 1899; in English as *Modern Germany and Her Historians*, London: Jarrold, 1915, reprinted Westport, CT: Greenwood Press, 1970
Schleier, Hans, *Sybel und Treitschke: Antidemokratismus und Militarismus im historischen-politischen Denken grossburgeoiser Geschichtsschreibung* (Sybel and Treitschke: Anti-Democratic Thought and Militarism in the Historical-Political Thought of Bourgeois Historiography), Berlin: Akademie, 1965

Trevelyan, G.M. 1876–1962
British historian

Probably no other English historian after World War I was as successful and popular, and received so many honors as G.M. Trevelyan. His numerous books, mainly on English and Italian history, sold extremely well. He could be classified as an intellectual aristocrat who had his finger in almost every political and academic pie. Descended from an old and influential English family, Trevelyan could virtually claim that for him writing English history meant to a certain extent writing the history of his own family. He found disciples in such eminent historians as Owen Chadwick and J.H. Plumb. However, Trevelyan was often strongly criticized because he thought and wrote in an anachronistic, Victorian manner. He was a fierce opponent of modern, Rankean "scientific history," which he saw represented by J.B. Bury, F.W. Maitland, Lewis Namier, and J.R. Seeley. As a student at Cambridge Trevelyan was taught by Seeley that Thomas Babington Macaulay and Thomas Carlyle were "charlatans."

Because he could not and would not accept the scientific-historical atmosphere of Cambridge, Trevelyan withdrew from the university between 1903 and 1927. In these 24 years he published 13 books (further to his first study: his fellowship dissertation, *England in the Age of Wycliffe*, 1899) among which are the important *Garibaldi* trilogy (1907–11), his *British History in the Nineteenth Century* (1922), and his *History of England* (1926). The latter made him the most widely read of all English historians. In this respect Trevelyan did more than most of his contemporaries in catching the popular mood and in bringing history to the people. His books sought to combine literary interest with a Victorian concern for social matters and a post-Boer War romantic patriotism. In fact, Trevelyan wrote only a few lengthy articles. Instead he mostly concentrated on producing shorter contributions for learned journals, and only his later publications are based on detailed archival work. His numerous books, on the other hand, demonstrate an admirable technique of presentation.

Among Trevelyan's critics were Herbert Butterfield (particularly in his *The Whig Interpretation of History*, 1931), G.R. Elton, Lewis Namier (with his ideas of structural analysis as an alternative to narrative), and J.B. Kenyon, who noted that Trevelyan tried to restore old-fashioned concepts of history. It was also claimed that Trevelyan was not critically reflective about what he wrote. Certainly the verdict of his professional colleagues was in many respects more critical than that of the public or of amateur historians. In his own and his contemporaries' opinion Trevelyan was the last Whig historian. He therefore saw himself in the tradition of early 19th-century "literary history," regarding historiography as a narrative art for which analytical qualities were of only secondary importance. Trevelyan knew that his Whiggism was out of tune with his times. In his person he thus combined an essential "Englishness" with cultural pessimism. As a Whig he glorified English common sense, toleration, and the liberal institutions naturally identified with upper- and middle-class values.

In Trevelyan's view history's task was to instruct, to teach moral and ethical values, and to entertain the general public. Thus history should be poetic, educative, and compassionate. It could be a training in citizenship in order to remove prejudice and to provide people with inspiring ideas. This was a program diametrically opposed to that expressed by Bury in his inaugural lecture on the science of history in 1903. In his famous polemical essay in answer to Bury, "Clio: A Muse" (1903), Trevelyan listed a number of authors (J.A. Froude, J.R. Green, W.E.H. Lecky, John Morley, and Leslie Stephen) who, as he thought, carried on the liberal tradition of "literary history" founded by Macaulay and Carlyle. The only "scientific" aspect of history Trevelyan would accept was the collecting of facts. This function, however, in contrast to the speculative and the literary, was of only minor relevance.

Trevelyan held Macaulay, his great-uncle, in the highest esteem. He wanted to follow in Macaulay's footsteps, in what he regarded "the family tradition of literary history," in order to maintain the readability of his writing and continue his Whiggish belief in the value of historical lessons for the present. But, as he admitted, he had to be careful not to fall into "Macaulayese." Beginning his other trilogy, *England under Queen Anne* (1930–34), in the late 1920s, Trevelyan declared that he took up the story where his great-uncle had left off. He wanted to do justice to Marlborough after Macaulay's misinterpretation. These books, the only ones for which Trevelyan

undertook archival work, fostered his reputation in the academic world. As did Macaulay, Trevelyan visited the places that he described. He went on long walking tours through England and Italy, retracing Garibaldi's campaign of 1860. He thereby reinforced his conviction that the prerequisite of a historian was the power of imagination to develop his ideas in a grand narrative. The *Garibaldi* trilogy is thus a great epic story, full of romantic and passionate images. However, this imagination worked only on the material Macaulay would already have used. This placed definite limits on Trevelyan's idea of social history, which he defined as "history with the politics left out."

His last great and most successful work, in fact one of the bestselling history books ever and now almost a classic, *English Social History: A Survey of Six Centuries* (1942), demonstrates this nostalgia. It is a patriotic description of England from Chaucer to Queen Victoria's death, designed as a contribution to the war effort. Further, it is an indictment against mass society and a threnody for a Paradise Lost. Like no other of his works this book, another tribute to Macaulay, shows how far Trevelyan had distanced himself from academic historiography, when he claimed to write a social history, although he hardly dealt with social trends, statistical evidence, or sociological theory. Instead he was mainly occupied with the decline and fall of the British aristocracy. Trevelyan's last important published piece was an article for the *Times* in December 1959. Commemorating Macaulay's death in 1859, Trevelyan still loyally defended the Macaulayian historical tradition.

Naturally an individual or a whole people provides the best material for a history written as drama. Consequently Trevelyan predominantly chose individual biographies (e.g., *The Life of John Bright*, 1913; *Lord Grey of the Reform Bill*, 1920; *Manin and the Venetian Revolution of 1848*, 1923) or the history of the English people as the subjects for his historiography. Here the influence of Carlyle, his hero-worship and moral attitudes, his work ethos and hatred of modern industrialized society, can be traced in Trevelyan's works. But unlike Carlyle Trevelyan praised individuals who fought for liberty, not military despotism. He also owed to Carlyle his concern for "social history." His literary interest and his feeling for imaginative, poetic descriptions of the past, especially as regards his books on Italy, stimulated his admiration for George Meredith, the only living person Trevelyan ever wrote a book about (*The Poetry and Philosophy of George Meredith*, 1906). Here his belief in an inseparable union of literature and history was strengthened. His essentially literary view of the past went back to his belief that Shakespeare and Milton, Tennyson and Browning were equally relevant to history and literature. In many respects, therefore, Trevelyan remained a representative of Victorian attitudes.

BENEDIKT STUCHTEY

See also Europe: Modern; Italy: since the Renaissance; Literature; Mack Smith; Political; Social

Biography

George Macaulay Trevelyan. Born Welcombe, Warwickshire, 16 February 1876, son of historian/biographer, George Otto Trevelyan, and great-nephew of Thomas Babington Macaulay. Educated at Harrow School; Trinity College, Cambridge, BA 1896. Tutor/fellow, Trinity College, Cambridge, 1896–1903; moved to London to research and write; Regius professor of modern history, Cambridge University, 1927–40; master, Trinity College, Cambridge, 1940–51; chancellor, University of Durham, 1949–57. Married Janet Penrose Ward, daughter of the novelist Mrs. Humphry Ward, 1904 (died 1956; 1 son, 1 daughter). Died Cambridge, 21 July 1962.

Principal Writings

England in the Age of Wycliffe, 1899
England under the Stuarts, 1904
The Poetry and Philosophy of George Meredith, 1906
Garibaldi's Defence of the Roman Republic, 1848–49, 1907
Garibaldi and the Thousand: Naples and Sicily, 1859–60, 1909
Garibaldi and the Making of Italy, June–November 1860, 1911
Clio: A Muse, and Other Essays Literary and Pedestrian, 1913; enlarged as *The Recreations of a Historian*, 1919
The Life of John Bright, 1913
Scenes from Italy's War, 1919
Lord Grey of the Reform Bill, Being the Life of Charles, Second Earl Grey, 1920
British History in the Nineteenth Century, 1782–1901, 1922
Manin and the Venetian Revolution of 1848, 1923
History of England, 1926
Editor, *Macaulay's Lays of Ancient Rome and Other Historical Poems*, 1928
England under Queen Anne, 3 vols., 1930–34
Sir George Otto Trevelyan: A Memoir, 1932
Grey of Fallodon, Being the Life of Sir Edward Grey, 1937
The English Revolution, 1688–89, 1938
English Social History: A Survey of Six Centuries, Chaucer to Queen Victoria, 1942
An Autobiography and Other Essays, 1949
Editor, *Carlyle: An Anthology*, 1953

Further Reading

Arnstein, Walter L., "George Macaulay Trevelyan and the Art of History: A Centenary Appraisal," *Midwest Quarterly* 18 (1976), 78–97

Cannadine, David, *G.M. Trevelyan: A Life in History*, London: HarperCollins, 1992; New York: Norton, 1993

Clark, George, "George Macaulay Trevelyan, 1876–1962," *Proceedings of the British Academy* 49 (1963), 375–86

Hernon, J.M., "The Last Whig Historian and Consensus History: George Macaulay Trevelyan, 1876–1962," *American Historical Review* 81 (1976), 66–97

Moorman, Mary, *George Macaulay Trevelyan: A Memoir*, London: Hamilton, 1980

Plumb, J.H., *G. M. Trevelyan*, London and New York: Longman, 1951

Winkler, Henry R., "George Macaulay Trevelyan," in S.W. Halperin, ed., *Some 20th-Century Historians*, Chicago: University of Chicago Press, 1961

Trevor-Roper, Hugh 1914–

British historian

Hugh Trevor-Roper's long and varied career has been marked by his desire to elucidate a historical philosophy. He is a prolific and diverse writer who has published works on topics ranging from Adolf Hitler's fall to the life of Sir Edmund Backhouse, an English sinologist, to a study of Desiderius Erasmus' impact on European history. Trevor-Roper justifies this range by explaining that he is interested in explaining the process of history. In order to do that, he asserts he needs to examine areas outside his particular specialty to see if his ideas about process apply there as well. He is dedicated to the idea of a universal human nature, which he believes transcends time and place.

Trevor-Roper, despite his forays into other areas of history, concentrates on 16th- and 17th-century Europe. He sees the central unifying theme of this period as expansion. He does not believe in an inevitable, continuous progression toward a perfect state of humanity, but he does believe that there is such a perfect state. That state can be attained, but it is not inevitable; people sometimes move toward it, and sometimes away from it. He asserts that individuals influence history and can change it, and was, early in his career, a proponent of the "great man" theory of history which asserts that history is created by the actions of great men. Trevor-Roper also recognizes the impact of social forces on history, but concentrates on individualistic ideas.

Trevor-Roper mixes his concentration between social, political, spiritual, and intellectual causes in his study of history. He sees these causes as interrelated and finds it difficult, if not impossible, to separate them from each other. For example, in his essay "The General Crisis of the Seventeenth Century" (1959), he argued that the revolutions and attempted revolutions of the mid-17th century were the result of structural problems in society stemming from the political changes and intellectual and religious innovations of the Renaissance and Reformation, rather than the result of a constitutional struggle or an economic crisis, although those factors certainly helped create the mood necessary for revolutionary action.

Religion is a political as well as spiritual creation in Trevor-Roper's mind. In his study of the English Civil War, he argued that although the conflict between the Arminians and the Puritans helped cause the war, that conflict was not over ideology, but over the political structure and use of the church. The Arminians, led by Laud, wanted a hierarchical, apostolic church with bishops, a dedication to divine right, and a concentration on good works. The Puritans, however, wanted a less hierarchical church emphasizing the faith of the laity. Trevor-Roper saw this opposition as one of social policy rather than religion, at least on the part of Laud.

Trevor-Roper's dedication to the idea of expansion in the 17th century has been constant throughout his work. He saw external expansion in the European explorations of the New World and Africa and internal expansion in the religious reformations, the Enlightenment, and the growth of nationalism. In keeping with his refusal to believe in linear progress, however, he saw the witch-crazes of the 17th century as a backlash against that progress. In his theory, the conflict between the spiritual ideals of the Reformation and the rationalism of Erasmus and other humanist scholars became manifest in the hysteria and fear of the witch-hunts. To support his theory, he points to the reluctance of the established church to support the witch-hunts.

Trevor-Roper's contributions to historical theory are as great as his contributions to history. He asserts that history is an art, not a science, and therefore, the imagination is an indispensable element in the study of history. He links the imagination with free will, which he considers the dynamic element of human nature. In his view, the outcome of events is not fixed; history is not the culmination of a predetermined path of events. It is constantly being changed and created by people. Therefore, history must be interpreted by asking what might have been as well as what has been. The imagination, rather than scientific study, is his key to understanding history.

KRISTEN D. ROBINSON

See also Britain: 1485–1750; Scotland; Stone; Tawney

Biography
Hugh Redwald Trevor-Roper. Born Glanton, Northumberland, 15 January 1914. Educated at Charterhouse School; Christ Church, Oxford, BA 1936; research fellow, Merton College, Oxford, 1937–39, MA 1939. British Army intelligence officer, 1939–45. Taught at Christ Church, Oxford, 1945–57; Regius professor of modern history and fellow, Oriel College, Oxford, 1957–80; master, Peterhouse, Cambridge, 1980–87. Married Lady Alexandra Howard-Johnston, daughter of Field Marshal Earl Haig, 1954. Created Baron Dacre of Glanton in the County of Northumberland (life peer), 1979.

Principal Writings
Archbishop Laud, 1573–1645, 1940
The Last Days of Hitler, 1947
Historical Essays, 1957; in US as *Men and Events: Historical Essays*, 1957
"The General Crisis of the Seventeenth Century," *Past and Present* 16 (1959), 31–64
The Rise of Christian Europe, 1965
Religion, the Reformation and Social Change, and Other Essays, 1967, 3rd edition 1984; in US as *The Crisis of the Seventeenth Century*, 1968
Editor, *The Age of Expansion: Europe and the World, 1559–1660*, 1968
Queen Elizabeth's First Historian: William Camden and the Beginnings of English "Civil History", 1971
A Hidden Life: The Enigma of Sir Edmund Backhouse, 1976, in US as *Hermit of Peking: The Hidden Life of Sir Edmund Backhouse*, 1977
Princes and Artists: Patronage and Ideology at Four Habsburg Courts, 1517–1633, 1976
History and Imagination: A Valedictory Lecture Delivered before the University of Oxford on 20 May 1980, 1980
Renaissance Essays, 1985
Catholics, Anglicans, and Puritans: Seventeenth Century Essays, 1987
From Counter-Reformation to Glorious Revolution, 1992

Further Reading
Lloyd-Jones, Hugh, Valerie Pearl, and Blair Worden, eds., *History and Imagination: Essays in Honor of H.R. Trevor-Roper*, London: Duckworth, 1981; New York: Holmes and Meier, 1982
Saleh, Zaki, *Trevor-Roper's Critique of Arnold Toynbee: A Symptom of Intellectual Chaos*, Baghdad: Al-Ma'eref Press, 1958

Trigger, Bruce G. 1937–
Canadian anthropologist, archaeologist, and ethnohistorian

As practitioner and theorist Bruce Trigger has been one of the most influential scholars in defining and promoting the sub-discipline of ethnohistory. Trigger's academic training and interests are diverse: while completing his PhD in African anthropology at Yale University – a revised version of which was published as *History and Settlement in Lower Nubia* in 1965, he was also researching and publishing on the Huron and Iroquois of eastern Canada. His work in these areas of research holds great theoretical significance, particularly in the theory of archaeology and of ethnohistory.

Trigger himself traces the origins of ethnohistory to A.G. Bailey's *The Conflict of European and Eastern Algonkian Cultures, 1504–1700* (1937), although Bailey's work did not receive widespread acclaim until it was reprinted by the University of Toronto Press in 1969. After World War II a number of American anthropologists and ethnologists began studying the acculturation of Natives in the period following European settlement. By the 1950s such studies became known as ethnohistory and were defined by works such as Ralph Linton's *Acculturation in Seven American Tribes* (1940) and E.H. Spicer's influential *Cycles of Conquest* (1962). As an approach, ethnohistory is now flourishing in North America, Australia, and the Pacific region. Within European studies its closest affinities are to the study of folklore and folk culture. It has emerged as an aggressively interdisciplinary approach that combines methods and sources familiar to anthropologists, archaeologists, linguists, and historians. It employs written and oral traditions and anthropological knowledge to study nonliterate peoples and their encounters with Europeans. Trigger's *The Children of Aataentsic* (1976) is a monumental contribution to ethnohistory. In it Trigger challenged the views of historians such as C.H. McIlwain and George T. Hunt, who had assumed that Native societies were static before the arrival of Europeans. He also questioned what he saw as the excessive economic determinism of these historians. Trigger's emphasis on rational calculations and material preoccupations as factors influencing behavior in Native societies, in this study and in his subsequent work, challenges the idealist and romantic interpretations that are now common among ethno-historians.

Trigger's most influential work is arguably *Natives and Newcomers* (1985). Distinctly interdisciplinary in nature, Trigger's study uses historical, archaeological, and anthropological research available in both principal Canadian languages and transcends colonial political boundaries. Aiming to re-examine the "framework within which the whole of Canadian history must be considered," Trigger reacted against the 19th-century historian Francis Parkman's "colourful but biased portrayals" and the work of the economic historian Harold Innis who saw Natives as "economic stereotypes only minimally disguised in feathers." This tradition tended to dismiss or under-rate the role and vitality of Natives in the early historical period; in contrast, Trigger presented indigenous cultures as dynamic, rather than static, and as integral participants in the social, intellectual, and economic environment of New France. Further, his emphasis on the utility of anthropological and archaeological evidence for the ethnohistorian has resulted in a significant reevaluation of the working relationship between colonial Europeans and Native people. Trigger argues that the traditional interpretation of Euro-Canadian history has paid too much attention to the activities of priests and government officials, who left many of the written records; indeed, he argues that it was traders and their employees who were the most significant participants in forging alliances and providing the material goods that inevitably changed Native societies.

Trigger has been especially influential in several regards. His work represents a sustained synthesis of a variety of disciplines. He has urged historians and anthropologists to bridge the methodological gaps separating them. In addition, works such as *Natives and Newcomers* and *The Huron* (1969) are written for the general reader, as well as the specialist, and have contributed greatly to correcting the myth that Natives were merely part of the natural setting against which the dynamics of a colonial society developed. As past president of the American Society for Ethnohistory and as the author of a prodigious number of influential articles and books, Trigger has been a significant figure in initiating the complex task of studying the history of smaller-scale, nonliterate societies.

BRIAN GOBBETT and THEODORE BINNEMA

See also America: Pre-Columbian; Archaeology; Canada; Ethnohistory; Indigenous; Near East; Prehistory

Biography
Bruce Graham Trigger. Born Cambridge, Ontario, 18 June 1937. Educated locally, then at St. Mary's Public School and College Institute to 1951; attended Stratford Collegiate Institute, 1951–55; University of Toronto, BA 1959; Yale University, PhD 1964. Taught anthropology, Northwestern University, 1963–64; and McGill University (rising to professor), from 1964.

Principal Writings
History and Settlement in Lower Nubia, 1965
The Late Nubian Settlement at Arminna West, 1967
Beyond History: The Methods of Prehistory, 1968
The Huron: Farmers of the North, 1969
The Children of Aataentsic: A History of the Huron People to 1660, 2 vols., 1976
Nubia under the Pharaohs, 1976
Time and Traditions: Essays in Archaeological Interpretation, 1978
Gordon Childe: Revolutions in Archaeology, 1980
Natives and Newcomers: Canada's "Heroic Age" Reconsidered, 1985
A History of Archaeological Thought, 1989
Early Civilizations: Ancient Egypt in Context, 1993

Troeltsch, Ernst 1865–1923
German philosopher of history, theologian, and sociologist

Strictly speaking Ernst Troeltsch was not a historian since he made no independent study of primary historical sources and was content to interpret other scholars' findings; yet few modern intellectuals have had a more influential impact on the study of history.

After an early attraction to jurisprudence and classical philology, Troeltsch turned to theology because of its unique ability to unite metaphysical and historical questions, the two sets of highly significant problems which he found challenging in themselves and in their interaction. His commitment to radical historical criticism posed major problems for a theological tradition based on divine revelation. As professor of theology at Heidelberg from 1894 to 1915, Troeltsch turned to the study of religion as a comparative science, treating Christianity psychologically and historically in the same way as other religions, arguing that the investigation and assessment of Christianity had to find its place within the framework of religious and cultural history. His move to a personal chair in philosophy at Berlin from 1915 until his death in 1923 indicated that he had outgrown the narrower interests of the theological faculty, and provided him with a broader context for the pursuit of his interests in social and intellectual reconstruction; yet he remained passionately interested in the religious questions that had engaged him from the beginning.

Troeltsch saw theology as the setting in which man's relations with the eternal and unconditioned met the historical and relative. Acutely aware of the flux of history, he made clear his distance from both Marxist and orthodox Christian dogmatic approaches to history, insisting against Marx that religion was a primal force in the human spirit, and against orthodox dogmatic Christianity that religious life interacted with political structures, social institutions, and ethical and cultural concerns. Throughout his life he sought a synthesis that could provide understanding without destroying the manifold variety of human life.

In a major article, "Historiography," in Hastings' *Encyclopedia of Religion and Ethics* (1914), Troeltsch distinguished sharply between the causality of natural science and that of historical science, the former having to do with general laws, the latter having to do with individual and concrete reality and "almost exclusively a matter of psychological motivation," though having recourse to natural causation as well. Historical science selects from the flux of phenomena that which is qualitatively and uniquely individual, and makes this intelligible in its concrete and specific relations. Its conceptual processes are different from those of the natural sciences, as is its principle of development, which denotes "the working out of the consequences that are latent in the earliest beginnings."

Troeltsch's critical historical thought had major implications for his principal interest in religion. It implied that the findings of history were always open to revision and therefore could never claim more than probability. It assumed that events of the past were analogous to those of the present and that reported events such as miracles which had no analogy in our own experience must be deemed inherently improbable. It asserted that all events are of the same order within a continuous causal nexus, and accordingly ruled out the claim of any historical event or phenomenon to finality or absoluteness. The impact of this critical approach was to strip Christianity of its supernatural aspects and reject its claim to finality or absoluteness, and though Troeltsch continued to argue for some time that Christianity was the climax of religious development so far, he later asserted that it could claim definitive status only within its particular historical culture.

Perhaps the most enduring aspect of Troeltsch's influence on historical studies was his reassessment of the place of the Reformation in history and theology, presented in its most accessible form in *Protestantism and Progress* (1906, translated 1912) Approaching history as a means to understanding his own time, he was profoundly conscious of the great gulf between the Reformation and the modern world. Accordingly, he challenged the widely accepted assumption that Protestantism represented the dawn of the modern era and argued that modern Protestantism amounted to a contradiction rather than an authentic development of Reformation principles.

To Troeltsch, the Reformation was a fundamental reshaping of the medieval idea and proposed new solutions to medieval problems, keeping intact the basic features of the medieval system – the preoccupation with individual salvation, the ideal of a total Christian culture, the notion of the church as a divine institution, and the recognition of absolute authority. Far from being the dawn of modern times, the Reformation represented a second blossoming of medieval civilization for two centuries more and a corresponding devitalization of the secular culture that had tentatively begun to emerge in the Renaissance. While Luther's ideas may have been essentially destructive of the medieval system, their impact remained limited to the religious sphere and brought no basic change to social life. For Troeltsch the real watershed between medieval and modern times was the Enlightenment, which saw the assertion of human autonomy carried forward by an alliance of the secular state with study of science.

The same perception of the Reformation as a conservative reshaping of the medieval idea received a definitive statement in Troeltsch's major work *Die Soziallehren der christlichen Kirchen und Gruppen* (1912; *The Social Teaching of the Christian Churches*, 1931), which showed the strong influence of Max Weber's sociological ideas, in particular his distinction between church and sect, to which Troeltsch added a third category – mysticism. Originating as a book review, this work grew to over one thousand pages, covering in diffuse style but with massive documentation the social history of Christendom from the beginnings to his own time.

In this his largest work Troeltsch argued that the Christian Gospel was essentially a message of personal piety and spiritual fellowship, that no particular institutional form was intrinsic to it, but that it took varied forms in the process of its compromise with the world. All three types of social organization – church, sect and mysticism – were present from the beginning, and Christian history showed the complex unfolding of this variety. Thus medieval Catholicism was inclusive and universal, with the church incorporating the life of the world, while medieval sectarianism presented the other face of the Middle Ages, in its rejection of the world. The Reformation maintained the medieval Catholic unity of church and state, yet sectarianism grew within and was responsible for most of Protestantism's internal tensions. In due course many of the Protestant sects became Free churches and abandoned radicalism for another kind of compromise with the world.

For all his uncompromisingly intellectual approach to his subject and the complexity of his arguments, Troeltsch passionately believed that the primary purpose of history was the practical task of clarifying the problems of the present. This preoccupation motivated most of his major writings and was expressed also in his own involvement in public life. He held political office concurrently with his academic post during the early years of Weimar republic, testimony to his conviction about the close relationship of theory and practice, knowledge and ethics, the past and the present.

JOHN TONKIN

See also Protestantism; Reformation

Biography

Born Haunstetten, Bavaria, 17 February 1865, son of a doctor. Educated in Augsburg; studied theology at universities of Erlangen, 1884–85; Berlin, 1885–86; and Göttingen, 1886. Lutheran curate, Munich, 1887–90; professor of theology, University of Bonn, 1892–94; and University of Heidelberg, 1894–1915; professor of philosophy, University of Berlin, 1915–23. Married Marta Fick, 1901 (1 son). Member, Prussian Landtag and Bavarian legislature; under-secretary of state, Ministry of Public Worship. Died Berlin, 1 February 1923.

Principal Writings

Vernunft und Offenbarung bei Johann Gerhard und Melanchthon (Reason and Revelation in Johann Gerhard and Melanchthon), 1891

Die Absolutheit des Christentums und die Religionsgeschichte, 1902; in English as *The Absoluteness of Christianity and the History of Religions*, 1971

"Protestantisches Christentum und Kirche in der Neuzeit" (Protestant Christianity and the Church in the Modern Age), in Paul Hinneberg, ed., *Die Kultur der Gegenwart: ihre Entwicklung und ihre Ziele*, 1905

Die Bedeutung des Protestantismus für die Entstehung der modernen Welt, 1906, 2nd edition 1911; 2nd edition in English as *Protestantism and Progress: A Historical Study of the Relation of Protestantism to the Modern World*, 1912

"Historiography," in James Hastings, ed., *Encyclopedia of Religion and Ethics*, 1908–26; reprinted in John Macquarrie, ed., *Contemporary Religious Thinkers*, 1968

Die Soziallehren der christlichen Kirchen und Gruppen, 1912; in English as *The Social Teaching of the Christian Churches*, 2 vols., 1931

Gesammelte Schriften, 4 vols., 1913–25; selections in English as *Writings on Theology and Religion*, 1977

Augustin, die christliche Antike, und das Mittelalter (Augustine, Christian Antiquity, and the Middle Ages), 1915

Der Historismus und seine Probleme, 1922; selections in English as *Historism and Its Problems: First Book, The Logical Problem of the Philosophy of History*, 1922

Der Historismus und seine Überwindung, 1924; in English as *Christian Thought: Its History and Application*, 1923

Glaubenslehre, 1925; in English as *The Christian Faith: Based on Lectures Delivered at the University of Heidelberg in 1912 and 1913*, 1991

Religion in History, 1991 [collected essays]

Further Reading

Bodenstein, Walter, *Neige des Historismus: Ernst Troeltschs Entwicklungsgang* (The Decline of Historicity: Ernst Troeltsch's Path of Development), Gütersloh: Mohn, 1959

Kasch, Wilhelm F., *Die Sozialphilosophie von Ernst Troeltsch* (The Social Philosophie of Ernst Troeltsch), Beiträge zur historischen Theologie 34, Tübingen: Mohr, 1963

Mackintosh, Hugh Ross, *Types of Modern Theology: Schleiermacher to Barth*, New York: Scribner, and London: Nisbet, 1937

Macquarrie, John, *Twentieth Century Religious Thought: The Frontiers of Philosophy and Theology, 1900–1960*, London: SCM, and New York: Harper, 1963; revised 1971, 1981, 1988

Morgan, Robert, "Ernst Troeltsch on Theology and Religion," introduction to Ernst Troeltsch, *Writings on Theology and Religion*, London: Duckworth, and Atlanta: John Knox Press, 1977

Niebuhr, H. Richard, introduction to Ernst Troeltsch, *The Social Teaching of the Christian Churches*, London: Allen and Unwin, and New York: Macmillan, 1931

Reist, Benjamin A., *Towards a Theology of Involvement: The Thought of Ernst Troeltsch*, Philadelphia: Westminster Press, 1966

Renz, Horst, and Friedrich Wilhelm Graf, *Troeltsch-Studien*, 7 vols., Gütersloh: Mohn, 1982–93

Turner, Frederick Jackson 1861–1932

US historian of the frontier

The 1890s were a decade of nostalgia and anticipation for the United States. Americans looked back wistfully on a disappearing past dominated by Indians and the wild lands they controlled. At the same time they looked forward to 20th-century global military and political dominance with the pivotal conquest of the remnants of the Spanish New World empire. In this age of ambivalence Frederick Jackson Turner emerged as a founder of the modern discipline of American historical scholarship. He played an important role in shaping the nature of contemporary historical research, trained a generation of students to proselytize his creed, and framed an analytical theory of American history that has dominated the field for over a century.

Turner was trained at Johns Hopkins University where he learned about the "germ theory" of American history, then the dominant explanation of the American past. The germ theory proposed that immigrants from Europe implanted on American soil the institutions of Old World life, where those ways of life sprouted and thrived. America was an imitation of Europe, especially England, slowly becoming more like the mother country. Upon his return to the University of Wisconsin to take up a professor's chair, Turner rejected this analysis in favor of American exceptionalism. In 1893, after only a few years at his post, the historian presented a paper which proved to be his most influential contribution to American history. At the American Historical Association meeting that year, held in conjunction with the extravagant Chicago World's Columbian Exposition celebrating the 400th anniversary of Columbus' visit to the New World, Turner delivered a lecture entitled "The Significance of the Frontier in American History." The thesis of this lecture has dominated historians' explanations of the American past ever since.

Rejecting the germ theory, Turner argued at Chicago that the experience of living on a frontier that moved steadily westward for three centuries had created an American identity unique in the world. Living in primitive conditions far from ordered society, fighting Indians, and wresting civilization from a wilderness landscape had forced Americans to reinvent society:

> The existence of an area of free land, its continuous recession, and the advance of American settlement westward, explain American development ... to the frontier the American intellect owes its striking characteristics. That coarseness and strength combined with acuteness and inquisitiveness; that practical, inventive turn of mind, quick to find expedients; that masterful grasp of material things, lacking in the artistic but powerful to effect great ends; that restless, nervous energy; that dominant individualism, working for good and for evil, and withal that buoyancy and exuberance which comes with freedom – these are traits of the frontier.

Turner's analysis of American history as an infinitely repeated reinvention on the frontier both expressed the popular mood of the early 20th century and engendered it. His was a heroic creation myth, a story of common folks grimly facing up to the challenges of a savage people and an inhospitable wild landscape, and then, through perseverance and hard work, introducing civilization while inventing a new national character devoted to the ideal of democracy. Turner's approach touched the way books, movies, and television would portray the West, and how non-historians would view their heritage. The thesis quickly became the dominant paradigm within the discipline of American history.

The frontier thesis pervaded American history for three decades almost without challenge. While Turner published little – two unremarkable monographs and two collections of essays, and three of those essays only posthumously – his great strength was teaching. A generation of graduate students at Wisconsin and later at Harvard regarded him as their mentor, and went on in their own careers to elaborate the details of Turner's basic framework. Many of these disciples were more absolute in their devotion to the frontier thesis than the master himself, and that exaggeration was the root of later attacks on the theory.

Soon after Turner's death in 1932 critiques of the frontier thesis appeared. In the face of the Great Depression many Americans became less sanguine about their nation. Some scholars felt that the frontier had little to do with the questions and problems of urban, industrial, capitalist America. They argued that Turner discounted the importance of economic systems that were really central to explaining human activity. With the gates open to criticism, the flood came. Scholars pointed out numerous flaws in Turner's idea. Since the frontier had ceased to exist around 1890, there was no way to make sense of history since then. Many western settlers had in fact copied democratic institutions from their homes in the East, rather than creating them anew. Even the frontier did not move westward as a straight line; it jumped the Great Plains and Rocky Mountains to the California gold fields and Oregon Territory in the 1840s and 1850s, then backtracked into Colorado, the Dakotas, and other backwaters as mineral and grain booms pulled settlers unevenly around the West. New Western Historians of the 1990s point out that Turner excluded many people: women, children, diverse Indian peoples, Hispanics, blacks, and Asians. In fact the US West was one of the most cosmopolitan places on earth in the 19th century, but Turnerian history recognizes only white men.

American historians responded to these attacks on Turner's basic premise in uneven ways. The frontier approach was in clear decline through the 1930s and 1940s, but as America emerged from the Great Depression and World War II to become a global political, economic, and military power, optimism returned, and the frontier idea regained popularity. Led by Walter Prescott Webb and Ray Allen Billington, among others, historians continued to publish books based on Turner, including the most widely used textbooks. Thus the frontier model remained entrenched in the popular mind. The New Western History school has released another barrage against Turner in the 1990s, and this may be the end for the thesis. However, no unifying analysis or narrative with such poetic power has replaced Turner's seductive theory, and he is still defended by many who acknowledge faults in details of his original essay. Turner has been the single most influential American historian, guiding both scholarly and popular attitudes toward the history of the United States.

GEOFF CUNFER

Biography

Born Portage, Wisconsin, 14 November 1861. Received BA, University of Wisconsin, 1884, MA 1888; PhD, Johns Hopkins University, 1891. Taught at University of Wisconsin, 1885–1910, and Harvard University, 1910–24; senior research associate, Huntington Library, 1927–32. Married Caroline Mae Sherwood, 1889 (3 children). Died Pasadena, California, 14 March 1932.

Principal Writings

The Significance of the Frontier in American History, 1894 [as lecture, 1893]
Rise of the New West, 1819–1829, 1906
The Frontier in American History, 1920
The Significance of Sections in American History, 1932
The United States, 1830–1850: The Nation and Its Sections, 1935
The Early Writings of Frederick Jackson Turner, 1938
Frederick Jackson Turner's Legacy: Unpublished Writings in American History, edited by Wilbur R. Jacobs, 1965

Further Reading

Billington, Ray Allen, *The Frontier Thesis: Valid Interpretation of American History?*, New York: Holt Rinehart, 1966
Billington, Ray Allen, ed., *"Dear Lady": The Letters of Frederick Jackson Turner and Alice Forbes Perkins Hooper, 1910–1932*, San Marino, CA: Huntington Library, 1970
Billington, Ray Allen, *Frederick Jackson Turner: Historian, Scholar, Teacher*, New York: Oxford University Press, 1973
Cronon, William, "Revisiting the Vanishing Frontier: The Legacy of Frederick Jackson Turner," *Western Historical Quarterly* 18 (1987), 157–76
Cronon, William, George Miles, and Jay Gitlin, eds., *Under an Open Sky: Rethinking America's Western Past*, New York: Norton, 1992
Faragher, John Mack, *Rereading Frederick Jackson Turner: The Significance of the Frontier in American History, and Other Essays*, New York: Holt, 1994
Hofstadter, Richard, *The Progressive Historians: Turner, Beard, Parrington*, New York: Knopf, 1968; London: Cape, 1969
Jacobs, Wilbur R., ed., *The Historical World of Frederick Jackson Turner, with Selections from His Correspondence*, New Haven: Yale University Press, 1968
Limerick, Patricia Nelson, Clyde A. Milner II, and Charles E. Rankin, eds., *Trails: Toward a New Western History*, Lawrence: University Press of Kansas, 1991
Malin, James C., *Essays on Historiography*, Lawrence, KS, 1946
Marion, William E., and Vernon E. Mattson, *Frederick Jackson Turner: A Reference Guide*, Boston: Hall, 1985
Milner, Clyde A. II, ed., *Major Problems in the History of the American West: Documents and Essays*, Lexington, MA: Heath, 1989
Pomeroy, Earl, "Toward a Reorientation of Western History: Continuity and Environment," *Mississippi Valley Historical Review* 41 (1955), 579–600
Taylor, George Rogers, ed., *The Turner Thesis: Concerning the Role of the Frontier in American History*, Boston: Heath, 1949, 1972

Turner, Victor 1920–1983

US (British-born) anthropologist

Victor Turner, although often described as a symbolic anthropologist, contributed to the increased interest in the place of ritual systems in history, rescuing, to use a happy phrase of Ronald Grimes in *Research in Ritual Studies* (1985), symbolism and metaphor as concepts from the exclusive provenance of literary critics and linguists. Ritual studies as a discipline owes Turner an immense debt. His work has made historians more aware of the centrality of symbolism and the power of myth and ritual in history. For Turner, rituals were the creators of dominance, hierarchy, and integration. They were the constraints necessary for civilization: imperative boundaries whose creation was essential for society's development. Society itself, he wrote in *The Ritual Process* (1969), "seems to be a process rather than a thing, a dialectical process with successive phases of structure and communitas."

Although Turner came out of the Durkheimian tradition, much of his vocabulary was developed from field study among the Ndembu tribes of Central Africa: social drama, rite of passage, liminality, anti-structure. He became in the 1970s and early 1980s the preferred cultural theorist for many scholars. Despite a decline in interest in his work, it continues to push historians toward constructing more fluid and interdisciplinary models. Turner believed in the drama of history. "Drama was in his blood" his widow explained.

Turner has been criticized, notably by Renato Rosaldo, for a lack of attention to the social control implicit in the rituals of the majority. This perhaps misinterprets his view that ritual was a mechanism by which the obligatory became the desirable and moralism became virtue. For example, the use made of Turner by Kay Warren illustrated that ritualist and subaltern studies are not exclusive. Turner was well aware that ritual was a way in which power relationships were maintained and he has not received the attention he deserves for his awareness of the "marginals," the social groups who refuse to be part of the ritual consensus. He was aware of the lack of attention they had from historians and was curious about those who rejected the egalitarianism and stability of the main ritual process of a society. However, it is true that a historical approach drawing on Turner, and which emphasizes ritual, is one that focuses attention on consensus rather than individualism. Moreover, Turner felt that political structures nurtured division while ritual was inclusive, a view which is clearly subject to reservations.

Turner's legacy to historians is not any particular paradigm, although in the last years of his life he was regarded as something of a visionary-shaman, but rather is that of an advocate of ritual research and of the exploration of the ritual process. All societies make use of ritual, and Turner observed in *The Ritual Process* that "The structurally inferior aspire to symbolic structural superiority in ritual; the structurally superior aspire to symbolic communitas and undergo penance to achieve it." If historians are more sensitive than they once were to the ways in which even a supposedly modern technological society is heavily dependent on rituals, it is partly because of Turner's work. His essays in *Dramas, Fields, and Metaphors* (1974) and the Symbol, Myth, and Ritual series he edited for Cornell University Press (1972–83) are lasting memorials.

PAUL JOHN RICH

See also Africa: Central; Anthropology; Indigenous

Biography

Victor Witter Turner. Born Glasgow, 28 May 1920, son of an actress. Received BA in anthropology, University College, London, 1949; PhD, University of Manchester, 1955. Research officer, Rhodes-Livingston Institute, Lusaka, 1950–54; research fellow, University of Manchester, 1955–57, then taught, 1958–64; professor, Cornell University, 1964–68; University of Chicago, 1968–77; and University of Virginia, 1977–83. Married Edith Lucy Brocklesby Davis, 1943 (4 sons, 1 daughter). Died Charlottesville, Virginia, 18 December 1983.

Principal Writings

The Lozi Peoples of North-Western Rhodesia, 1953
Schism and Continuity in an African Society: A Study of Ndembu Village Life, 1957

Editor with Marc J. Swartz and Arthur Tuden, Political Anthropology, 1966
The Forest of Symbols: Aspects of Ndembu Ritual, 1967
The Drums of Affliction: A Study of Religious Processes among the Ndembu of Zambia, 1968
The Ritual Process: Structure and Anti-Structure, 1969
Dramas, Fields, and Metaphors: Symbolic Action in Human Society, 1974
On the Edge of the Bush: Anthropology as Experience, edited by Edith Turner, 1985
The Anthropology of Performance, 1986
Blazing the Trail: Way Marks in the Exploration of Symbols, 1992

Further Reading

Grimes, Ronald, Research in Ritual Studies: A Programmatic Essay and Bibliography, Metuchen, NJ: Scarecrow Press, 1985
Mach, Zdzislaw, "The Symbolic Construction of Identity," in his Symbols, Conflict and Identity, Krakow: UJ, 1989; Albany: State University of New York Press, 1993
Rosaldo, Renato, Culture and Truth: The Remaking of Social Analysis, Boston: Beacon Press, 1989
Warren, Kay, The Symbolism of Subordination: Indian Identity in a Guatemalan Town, Austin: University of Texas Press, 1989

U

Ullman, Berthold L. 1882–1965

US paleographer and historian of the Renaissance

Berthold L. Ullman was a pioneer in Renaissance studies. He was trained as a Latinist and paleographer, and his classicism was the predominant influence on his interest in Renaissance thought. While working on a degree in classics at the University of Chicago, Ullman studied paleography in Munich with Ludwig Traube and at the School of Classical Studies in Rome. He immersed himself in the reading of medieval and Renaissance Latin while researching the sources of a 1566 edition of the Roman poet Catullus and an edition of Propertius. This work led him to become the first American fluent in the study of the material evidence of medieval and Renaissance writing, and expert in the sciences of codicology, philology, and paleography developed by European archivists and librarians. While Ullman taught in the United States, he spent much time in European libraries throughout his life, especially in Florence and Rome, and discussed the formation of libraries in the Renaissance in his final work. His keen interest in and erudition about the material practices of writing is the common thread in his work.

Ullman's legacy is difficult to define. This is largely because he was less interested in situating humanism in a philosophical or political context, than in clarifying its relation to classical antecedents. Erudition often seems to outweigh contextualization in his two masterful general works, *Ancient Writing and Its Influence* (1932), a wide-ranging study of practices of writing from ancient Greece to the rediscovery of uncial cursive in the Renaissance, and *The Origin and Development of Humanistic Script* (1960), a study of the varieties of styles of writing among humanists after Petrarch. In both studies of the practices of lettering, he dwelled little on the transmission of the cursive or Gothic of the Middle Ages, and privileged the rediscovery of the "antiqua lettera" of humanists as a "movement in the history of civilization." Both, however, suggest the broad notions of intellectual influences and traditions that shaped Ullman's work. In later studies and articles, Ullman developed his interest in the transmission of classical writings, and the reception of history as defined by Ciceronian conventions. His concern with the humanists' avid interest in classics led to a study of the Florentine chancellor Coluccio Salutati, through his writings, transcriptions, and collection of classical manuscripts.

Perhaps the main reason for the difficulty in placing Ullman's work in a tradition of American scholarship is that his concerns placed him in difficult relation to the generation of émigré scholars whose work came to define much of Renaissance studies in America. Ullman was of the same generation as Hans Baron and Paul Oskar Kristeller, both Europeans trained in Germany who emigrated to the United States after World War II. But while Baron devoted considerable attention to the politics of Renaissance city-states in the 14th and 15th centuries, and Kristeller emphasized traditions of Renaissance philosophy, chiefly in Florence, Ullman devoted attention to the use of Latin in private writings and public communication, and rooted all discussion of humanists in an appreciation of their classical idiom. If the notion of a "Renaissance" was important to Ullman, he was loathe to give it a purely political or intellectual sense, and doing so defined his distance from Baron and Kristeller. Instead Ullman looked at a central figure of the early Florentine Renaissance, Salutati, an avid reader of the Latin authors whose work set the stage for the Florentine Renaissance. Ullman wanted to document the ways in which humanists from the 13th to 15th centuries defined their relations to Latin writers. He defined the place of classical literature in humanism and to the Renaissance in the early essays collected in *Studies in the Italian Renaissance* (1955); and he later studied the collection of classical texts in the public Florentine library of San Marco, in the posthumously published *The Public Library of Renaissance Florence* (1972). The ways in which he did so combined an American pragmatism that was confident of the relation of language to social claims with a strong commitment to the importance of manuscript research. The lines on which Ullman sketched the intellectual development of humanist thought were always rooted in locating the significance of neoclassical models of communication in humanists' intellectual life.

Interest in Latin writers and strong adherence to neoclassical principles of composition were, for Ullman, loosely associated with a "reform of morals" and an ethics of public life. He gained considerable expertise in reading neo-Latin handwriting and an appreciation of late medieval and Renaissance hands. Knowledge of Latin and of the usefulness of this knowledge in public life became his lifelong concern as an academic and as a public citizen. His much reprinted text on Latin for Americans illustrates his commitment to establishing the study of Latin in the United States; this interest no doubt motivated admiration for the intensity with which men of the Renaissance devoted themselves to writing and speaking in Latin as a demonstration and illustration of their commitment to public life. Whereas Renaissance intellectual historians such as Kristeller and Baron saw humanist philology as intertwined with intellectual or political interests, Ullman valorized humanists' immersion in classical styles in itself. He understood this immersion as the humanists' way of life, rather than embedding it in philosophical or political interests.

Ullman's interest in the uses of Latin among Italian humanists after Petrarch may have helped prepare interest in the United States for the work of Kristeller and Baron. Ullman's work, together with the broader studies of Wallace Ferguson, stimulated interest among Americans in the Italian Renaissance as the origin of liberal discourse. Ullman never fully organized his theory of the place of classical study in Renaissance culture, but he described the commitment to collecting and reading historical and political writings as a profoundly public act. Through close attention to the works of Renaissance men, Ullman sought to document the importance of Latin for the 15th-century writers out of a firm belief in the place of the Renaissance in American education. Ullman's liberal optimism about the revival of Latin classical studies largely followed Georg Voigt and Jacob Burckhardt, but no doubt helped define the place of Renaissance studies in the United States. While the specialization of much of his work prevented it from reaching a wider audience, he was committed both to classical erudition and to understanding the Renaissance as a cultural phenomenon. His affirmation of philological and textual studies in Renaissance history influenced the reception of European scholarship in the United States, and the concerns of paleographers of both the classical and Renaissance worlds.

DANIEL BROWNSTEIN

Biography
Berthold Louis Ullman. Born Chicago, 18 August 1882. Received BA, University of Chicago, 1903, PhD 1908; also studied at University of Munich and American School of Classical Studies, Rome. Taught at University of Chicago, 1906–09; University of Pittsburgh, 1909–19; University of Iowa, 1919–25; University of Chicago, 1925–44; and University of North Carolina, 1944–59 (emeritus). Married (1 son, 1 daughter). Died Vatican City, 21 June 1965.

Principal Writings
Ancient Writing and Its Influence, 1932; reprinted 1965
Studies in the Italian Renaissance, 1955; reprinted 1973
The Origin and Development of Humanistic Script, 1960
The Humanism of Coluccio Salutati, 1963
With Philip A. Stadter, *The Public Library of Renaissance Florence*, 1972

Ullmann, Walter 1910–1983
British (Austrian-born) medievalist

As one of the many scholars who emigrated from continental Europe during the period of National Socialist ascendancy, Walter Ullmann was instrumental in introducing anglophone medievalists to continental methods, such as the use of liturgical and theological materials as sources for political history. Ullmann particularly advocated an increased emphasis on jurisprudential issues and legal sources, an approach which

accorded well with the established traditions in anglophone medieval historiography. However, he went further than any of his English predecessors in deeming the law to be "the one unimpeachable, unassailable and reliable source." Furthermore, Ullmann insisted on the addition of biblical and especially of canonistic materials to the medievalist's legal evidentiary base, at a time when such sources were largely ignored in anglophone scholarship. Beginning with his first major monograph, *The Origins of the Great Schism* (1948), he worked to publicize the importance of medieval canon lawyers to the so-called "Western Tradition" by, for example, tracing fundamental principles of representative government to their activities. At Cambridge University, he trained a number of graduate students, many of whom have become legal historians and, near the end of his career, he produced a thorough, accessible introduction to medieval legal sources aimed at students of all levels (*Law and Politics in the Middle Ages*, 1975). Beyond the spur he gave to the use of the legal approach in medieval historiography, Ullmann also stimulated – particularly through his students – research on the continental early Middle Ages, a period previously neglected by anglophone historians.

Looking back over his body of work in 1977, Ullmann stressed that a grasp of medieval history "presupposes a virtually constant preoccupation with, and immersion in, the sources" (*Scholarship and Politics in the Middle Ages*, 1978). Perhaps paradoxically, Ullmann's commitment to sources coexisted with an idealist approach to the construction of historical narratives, an approach that manifested itself in a number of concrete ways. First, he adapted to an ecclesiastical context the ethno- and state-centered narratives of 19th-century German philosophers of history such as Wilhelm von Humboldt and G.W.F. Hegel, arguing that the papacy was a stable "idea" (or unchanging program) which slowly "realized itself" in institutional form. Ullmann believed in the reality – and the legitimacy – of the Roman church as an effective central governing authority in Europe, largely through canonistic mechanisms; rather than support the legitimizing genealogies of secular states such as the modern German empires, he insisted that the medieval empire was itself merely a creation of the medieval papacy. Second, Ullmann's work remained untouched by any materialist currents in 20th-century historiography, either explicitly Marxian or otherwise. It was his idealist bent that permitted him to see "the law" as an "objective" source for historical knowledge, rather than as a socially-embedded human institution which results from and reproduces sociopolitical power relations. Finally, historical development was, for Ullmann, driven entirely by (decontextualized) ideas, and particularly by the political ideas of the learned; considerations such as the practical limitations – technological and otherwise – to the exercise of centralized authority did not enter into his discussions. As a result of all these tendencies, Ullmann's synthetic works (*Medieval Papalism*, 1949; *The Growth of Papal Government in the Middle Ages*, 1955; *A History of Political Thought*, 1965; and the non-academic *A Short History of the Papacy in the Middle Ages*, 1972) are currently out of favor among the majority of medievalists.

Along with David Knowles, Ullmann was among the first scholars to write, in the English language, in a positive manner concerning medieval ecclesiastical institutions. Even if his specific arguments are not accepted by most academic historians,

Ullmann's sympathetic approach to "the" medieval church has nevertheless been influential. Through more than 400 repeatedly reprinted and vigorously argued works, decades of captivating lecturing, and his work with graduate students, Ullmann helped anglophone medievalists move away from anachronistic assumptions concerning the supposedly nefarious effects of ecclesiastical "meddling" in secular "politics." There is now widespread recognition of the inadequacy of dichotomous, binary categories such as "religion" and "politics" – or "Church" and "State" – to describe the European past, although there is not, nor can there be, widespread scholarly lauding of the benefits which Ullmann himself believed to have resulted from "the contribution of ecclesiastics to problems of public government" (*The Carolingian Renaissance and the Idea of Kingship*, 1969).

Ullmann was a person of strong convictions who expressed himself with characteristic hyperbole, often staking out extreme positions. In *The Medieval Papacy: St. Thomas and Beyond* (1960), he came close to asserting the near-omnipotence of the popes in medieval Europe. Whereas most of the scholars exiled from Nazi-dominated Europe were considered to be unwilling refugees, Ullmann is said to have refused to cooperate with the German authorities who courted his favor. The tone of his published work was normally quite pugnacious, despite his eschewal of *ad hominem* attacks; a classic example of Ullmann's dismissive attitude towards the generality of his colleagues and predecessors may be found in the preface to his *Medieval Foundations of Renaissance Humanism* (1977). The effects of his non-conciliatory personality have combined with those of his now-outdated idealist methodology to rob much of his own scholarship – outside of legal-historical studies narrowly defined – of recognized credibility. His writings, whether in the original or in translation, are almost entirely out of print. Nevertheless, through his numerous students, who work in all fields of medieval history, Ullmann's legacy remains considerable; a sense of the influence he continues to exercise can be gained by reading the contributions of some of those students to his 1980 *Festschrift*.

FELICE LIFSHITZ

See also Barraclough; France: to 1000

Biography

Born Pulkau, Austria, 1910, son of a physician. Studied law at universities of Vienna and Innsbruck, then did postgraduate work at Cambridge University. Briefly a schoolmaster, then taught at University of Vienna, 1935–38. Emigrated to Britain, 1938; naturalized 1947. Served in the British Army, Royal Pioneer Corps and Royal Engineers, 1940–43. Taught at Ratcliffe College, Leicester, 1943–47; University of Leeds, 1947–49; and Cambridge University, 1949–78 (emeritus): fellow, Trinity College, Cambridge, 1959–83. Married Mary Elizabeth Finnemore Knapp, 1940 (2 sons). Died Cambridge, 18 January 1983.

Principal Writings

The Origins of the Great Schism: A Study in Fourteenth-Century Ecclesiastical History, 1948
Medieval Papalism: The Political Theories of the Medieval Canonists, 1949
The Growth of Papal Government in the Middle Ages: A Study in the Ideological Relation of Clerical to Lay Power, 1955

The Medieval Papacy: St. Thomas and Beyond, 1960
"Reflections on the Medieval Empire," *Transactions of the Royal Historical Society* 5th series, 14 (1964), 89–108
A History of Political Thought: The Middle Ages, 1965; reprinted as *Medieval Political Thought*, 1975
The Carolingian Renaissance and the Idea of Kingship, 1969
A Short History of the Papacy in the Middle Ages, 1972
The Future of Medieval History: An Inaugural Lecture, 1973
The Church and the Law in the Earlier Middle Ages: Selected Essays, 1975
Law and Politics in the Middle Ages: An Introduction to the Sources of Medieval Political Ideas, 1975
The Papacy and Political Ideas in the Middle Ages, 1976
Medieval Foundations of Renaissance Humanism, 1977
Scholarship and Politics in the Middle Ages: Collected Studies, 1978
Jurisprudence in the Middle Ages, 1980
Gelasius I (492–496): Das Papsttum an der Wende der Spätantike zum Mittelalter (Gelasius I: The Papacy during the Transition from Late Antiquity to the Middle Ages), 1981
Law and Jurisdiction in the Middle Ages, 1988 [includes bibliography]

Further Reading

Tierney, Brian, and Peter Linehan, eds., *Authority and Power: Studies on Medieval Law and Government Presented to Walter Ullmann on His Seventieth Birthday*, Cambridge and New York: Cambridge University Press, 1980 [includes bibliography]

Ulrich, Laurel Thatcher 1938–

US historian of women's history and colonial social history

Laurel Thatcher Ulrich shaped the concerns, issues, methods, and theories of the fields of colonial American history and women's history. Ulrich challenged scholars to find women in the silences of traditional historical sources and to search out new sources that bring women's lives to light. Her work demonstrates her own success at doing just that. The focus of Ulrich's work is the history that went unwritten and hence unremarked for centuries: daily life in the colonial past and specifically colonial women's place in it.

Good Wives (1982), Ulrich's first work, stands as one of the richest treatments of women's lives in colonial New England. In her research Ulrich mined sources where women were assumed silent, but under her craft the sources reverberate with women's experiences. She drew on probate, court, and church records as well as family papers which to previous historians told the stories only of male heads of household. Ulrich's historical skill turns a probate inventory of household contents into a fascinating trove of material culture evidence, enabling her to describe the ordinary tasks and surroundings of colonial housewives. It is with the minutiae of such details that Ulrich bridges the gulf between the image and reality of colonial womanhood. To great effect she used role theory and biblical paragons to understand women's position in puritan communities.

Ulrich describes women's roles in colonial family and community life, concluding that the colonial good wife could undertake virtually any task so long as it furthered her family's interest. In their husbands' absences wives performed economic transactions and made decisions that might typically fall under the purview of men. Sphere, Ulrich demonstrated, is an inappropriate metaphor for colonial women's social position. They performed diverse tasks and duties and while domestically oriented, their arena of activity included much of the village, not just their own home. Individual women's lives were intimately connected with their communities. Networks of neighbors provided both protection and standards of behavior. Neighboring women engaged in trade, aid, friendship; gossip was a primary tool of social control. Ulrich proposed that connection and communication among women served to mitigate the hierarchial relations between men and women in colonial society.

To understand the crucial importance of women to colonial social and community life, Ulrich turned to the extraordinary women celebrated in New England sermons and histories – those who emerged from anonymity because of acts of bravery and physical aggression. Her discussion of "Jaels" – heroic women – and viragoes – potentially dangerous women – illustrate the ambiguous potential of women's strength – essential for community and family survival, yet a threat to the ordered relations within that society.

While amply demonstrating the diversity of women's work and the breadth of their domain in preindustrial New England, *Good Wives* exposes the continuities between colonial and 19th-century womanhood: Ulrich contends that motherhood, romantic love, and female piety were already established ideals in the 17th and 18th centuries.

In *A Midwife's Tale* (1990), Ulrich continued her mission of rescuing women's experiences in the past from obscurity. In this case she reclaimed the diary of a Maine woman, Martha Ballard, long dismissed by historians as trivial, and through exceptional detective work showed how much it reveals of community life and women's lives in New England. *A Midwife's Tale* tracked a busy Maine midwife, noting the varied boundaries of her life and work. Ulrich structured her biographical history around the diary entries of Ballard over 27 years. She suggested that men and women had both shared and separate worlds in postrevolutionary New England. Through Ballard's diary we follow legal scandals, births, deaths, and learn of the impact of harsh winters on mobility as well as the wax and wane of New England households over the life cycle. Ulrich explicitly compared the complexity and thoroughness of Ballard's diary with other surviving documents to emphasize the necessity of including women's side of the story in the study of the past. Indeed, Ballard's diary revealed more about the town and its family life than the surviving diary of the county clerk, Henry Sewall.

As in *Goodwives*, in *A Midwife's Tale*, Ulrich emphasized the varied nature of women's work and economic roles in the colonial household, concluding that two distinct but interdependent economies operated in the Ballard household: her husband Ephraim's, and Martha's. In addition to her midwifery, Ballard belonged to a female network of barter and trade in both goods and services. She presided over her daughters' weaving through much of her middle age. Production and reproduction went hand in hand for colonial women. Ulrich's work prevents historians from taking at face value the domestic "private" sphere. Clearly Ballard, though deeply embroiled in women's worlds, operated in a very public and economically essential capacity.

Ulrich's work won praise for its detailed, intimate portrait of colonial family and community life over the life cycle, but it also contributed to the understanding of a neglected facet of history – the work of women as midwives and healers. Midwives left few records of their lives and practices. In this respect Ballard's diary is unique. The diary was as much her professional record and account book as it was a personal reminiscence. Ballard presided and helped in more than 800 births during the 27 years encompassed in her diary and saw only five women die, a maternal death rate that rivals that of the late 20th-century United States. But her practice included much more than just attending births, as busy as that kept her. Neighbors called on her to minister to other needs as well. She was practised in the uses of the herbal pharmacopeia that Maine gardens and woods provided, mixing teas and poultices for various neighbors. Ballard's profession made her an integral part of her community, turned to at every stage of the life cycle.

By example Ulrich showed the breadth and depth that attention to women's lives and daily experience lends to historical understanding of the past. Through Ballard's diary we learn the history of a community – its households, scandals, and politics in the early years of United States – and women's part in that community and its economy. Silent though the sources may seem on the surface, Ulrich reminds historians that "women were everywhere" in the colonial past. Her challenge to scholars is that they sift through detailed, often dull documents – needlework, material culture, and women's writings of all kinds – for clues to the human past.

JESSICA WEISS

See also Medicine; United States: American Revolution; Women's History: North America

Biography
Born 1938. Received BA, University of Utah, 1960; MA, Simmons College, 1971; PhD, University of New Hampshire, 1980. Professor, University of New Hampshire until 1996; professor, Harvard University, from 1996. Married Gail Ulrich (2 sons, 2 daughters).

Principal Writings
Good Wives: Image and Reality in the Lives of Women in Northern New England, 1650–1750, 1982
A Midwife's Tale: The Life of Martha Ballard, Based on Her Diary, 1785–1812, 1990
"Of Pens and Needles: Sources in Early American Women's History," *Journal of American History* 77 (1990), 200–07

United States: Colonial

For a great many years, the writing of American colonial history has focused on the activities of Englishmen in America: the institutions they constructed, the ideas they believed in, the wars they fought, and, ultimately, the process through which they became Americans. As Charles McLean Andrews wrote in *The Colonial Period of American History* (1934–38), "the 17th century shows us an British world in America, with but little in it that can strictly be called American." Only the 18th, he said, "everywhere presents to the view an Anglo-American conflict."

Their eyes fixed firmly on the apparatus of British empire and the relationship between that apparatus and the onset of the American Revolution, Andrews, Herbert L. Osgood, and George Louis Beer – together the "Imperial school" of colonial historians – dominated the field through much of the first half of the 20th century. Viewing the developing British colonial system from the broad perspective of Whitehall and Westminster, the Imperial historians included Nova Scotia and the West Indies in their analysis. They studied public law and the administration of imperial policy, and they increasingly directed their studies toward explaining why this system broke down in the 1760s.

The Progressive historians – Frederick Jackson Turner, Charles Beard, and, later, Merrill Jensen and his students at the University of Wisconsin – relied heavily on what the Imperial historians had to say about the colonial period. Interested primarily in colonial history only insofar as it explained the origins of the American Revolution, few of the Progressives, with some notable exceptions, ventured deeply into the colonial past. When they did, however, they rejected the Imperial school's emphasis on the British Atlantic, on law, and on administration. Instead they sought explanations for the social development of pre-Revolutionary America and the contours of Revolutionary-era politics in class and sectional conflicts in American society. Rapid westward expansion during the colonial period created conflicts between the seaboard and the backcountry, while the growth of colonial economies generated tension between the haves and the have-nots. These tensions would explode in the conflagration of 1776.

The Progressive paradigm, however, faced a serious challenge beginning in the 1950s. "Consensus" historians, such as Robert E. Brown, who published *Middle-Class Democracy and the Revolution in Massachusetts, 1691–1780* in 1955, argued that most white males could participate in politics if they chose, that property was easily acquired, and that class conflict in America was virtually nonexistent. Brown's work quickly came under attack. Some challenged his data on wealth and voting. Others, such as J.R. Pole and Charles S. Sydnor, interested in why ordinary colonists consistently chose their social betters to govern them, used the concept of deference to explain that widespread voter participation and democracy were not necessarily the same thing. Later, a group of younger historians used quantitative methods to analyze wealth and political participation in Massachusetts and found a much less democratic society than that described by Brown. While few found Brown's work persuasive, however, he did direct the attention of colonial historians toward affairs in the colonies, and away from the larger imperial relationship. Studies of colonial politics multiplied as historians tested different components of the Brown thesis.

The proliferation of scholarship on the colonial period has in recent years generated calls for synthesis. Increasing numbers of colonial historians have spoken of the need to integrate social and political developments in the colonies back into their Atlantic context. In fact, as Bernard Bailyn and Philip Morgan have recently pointed out, "there has been a resurgence of interest in the Atlantic dimensions of American colonization." Stephen Saunders Webb's controversial work on "garrison government" and the military nature of British imperialism, published as *The Governors-General* (1979) and *1676* (1984); Bernard Bailyn's far-reaching study, *Voyagers to the West*

(1986); Donald Meinig's *The Shaping of America* (1986); and Jack P. Greene's *Pursuits of Happiness* (1988), have all viewed developments in colonial America as part of a broader story of British expansion in the 17th and 18th centuries. Yet these works are only the first steps in an effort to make sense of an enormously diverse and complex field.

Since the middle of the 1960s, as in other fields of American history, historical writing about the colonial period has undergone significant transformation. Family and community studies, such as those published by John Demos, Kenneth Lockridge, Philip Greven, and Michael Zuckerman in 1970, which in turn built upon the earlier work of Darret Rutman, Sumner Chilton Powell, and Charles Grant, all raised important questions about the contours of everyday life in early America. Influenced by the work of French demographers and the Cambridge Group for the History of Population and Social Structure, these works delineated the nature of family life, highlighted attitudes toward economic and political activity, and analyzed the process and cultural assumptions behind town formation. These community studies not only helped legitimize a historical approach that viewed ordinary people as worthy subjects of inquiry, but also identified important continuities between English village life and the cultural life of the American colonies.

The community studies demonstrated the variety of rural life in early America. Other historians attempted to explain why so many Europeans left their homelands for British North America and the Caribbean in the 17th and 18th centuries. A large number of the migrants, perhaps half, came as bond labor, usually young British males, serving a term of years in exchange for passage to America. The vast majority of these came hungry for work, with few skills, and even fewer prospects in the places from which they came. Social and economic conditions in England and on the continent, in fact, played a large role in pushing Europeans westward across the Atlantic. Bad harvests, increasing landlessness, a spate of plague years, and the pressures of population growth combined in England with growing religious and political turmoil in the first decades of the 17th century to create what looked like an increasingly bleak future at home. The promoters of British colonization may have seen their settlements as a "cittie upon a hill," but even their motives were mixed. The decision to emigrate to America was a complex one, and it is abundantly clear that even in Puritan New England, religious considerations were only one among many determining factors.

While even bound European immigrants enjoyed an element of choice in the decision to come to British America, such was not the case for the 2.34 million Africans who were dragged across the Atlantic into a life of slavery in the mainland colonies and, especially, in the Caribbean. The study of slavery in the colonial world occupied an increasing amount of attention from colonial historians, and has resulted in the publication of some of the most exciting scholarship in the field. Works such as Winthrop Jordan's *White over Black* (1968), David Brion Davis' *The Problem of Slavery in Western Culture* (1966), and Edmund S. Morgan's *American Slavery, American Freedom* (1975) examined the process through which Africans came to occupy a status very different from British bound laborers. Other studies, such as Peter Wood's *Black Majority* (1974), have examined interactions between blacks and whites in early America, and the significance of this for the development of Anglo-American and African American culture. Initially, these studies found, race relations in early America were characterized by a degree of flexibility and fluidity. The legal status of blacks in areas where the institution was as yet marginal, such as Virginia prior to the 1670s, was often uncertain. Furthermore, the range of economic activities engaged in by Africans was wider, and Africans in places could contribute skills important to the development of a colonial society, as Wood has shown in his study of early South Carolina. Finally, social interaction between blacks and whites occurred openly and often as black and white servants ran away together, conceived children together, and apparently overlooked racial differences.

Only when slavery became central to the economic functioning of a given colonial society did racial lines harden. Where the legal status of slaves previously had been ambiguous, now elaborate legal codes eliminated any uncertainty regarding the slave's position in colonial society, or of that slave's offspring. Opportunities for acquiring freedom narrowed for blacks as well. To a great extent, with some important regional exceptions, the bulk of the slave force was directed toward the drudgery of field labor and the production of agricultural staples. While blacks living under the restrictions of full-blown slavery were able, at certain times and in certain places, to carve out spaces where they could exercise a degree of autonomy, in general race relations in societies where slavery constituted the essential social institution were filled with tension, deeply polarized between black and white, potentially explosive, and characterized by a pervasive brutality. Studies such as Edmund Morgan's on early Virginia and Peter Wood's on South Carolina have brilliantly demonstrated this shift. These works, however, have also pointed out that Africans were not merely objects acted upon by their enslavers. Africans always retained a degree of autonomy and preserved important parts of their African culture. The interaction of African and British cultures affected the development of both.

Both the Europeans who freely migrated to the Americas and Africans carried over against their will interacted with a great variety of Native American groups. Since 1957, when the Institute of Early American History and Culture published William M. Fenton's *American Indian and White Relations to 1830*, ethnohistorians have moved to restore Native Americans to their critically important role in the development of Anglo-American society. Drawing upon insights from anthropology and ethnology, ethnohistorians have produced an enormous body of work describing the consequences of what Francis Jennings would call "The Invasion of America," in his very important 1975 book.

One result of their work has been an awareness of the sheer loss of human life in Native American societies resulting from their encounter with European settlers. Everywhere in British America, enormous numbers of natives died during the initial contact period. As Alfred Crosby and scores of others have pointed out, Europeans carried with them to the Americas diseases against which Indians had no natural immunity. In many areas, these "virgin-soil epidemics" killed 90 per cent of the native population, leaving behind what Jennings called "a widowed land."

Other studies have emphasized the rapacity, land hunger, and greed which characterized Anglo-Indian relations. Jennings,

Bernard Sheehan, and others have found the intellectual justifications for the callous treatment of natives in British "perceptions" of the Indians. Though far too many studies of British attitudes toward the Indians have tended to ignore the violent arena of intercultural contact where these attitudes were forged, there can be no doubt that the Indians were thought of as backwards and barbaric by frontier settlers who had few scruples about dispossessing the Indians they settled among and driving them off the land.

Yet more recent studies have shown persuasively that Indians were much more than the passive victims of British imperialism. Frederick Jackson Turner may have seen the frontier "as the outer edge of the wave, the meeting point between savagery and civilization," but so simple a definition of the encounter between Indians and Englishmen has long since been discarded. Indians did not disappear. They resisted British settlement. They played different groups of Europeans off each other as they pursued their goals against rivals both Native American and European.

Colonial historians increasingly have recognized the importance of divisions both among and between a variety of Native American and European groups, and the concept of a bipolar Indian-white exchange has been shown to be simply inadequate for describing the vast complexity of Anglo-Indian relationships. Competition between Europeans and Indians for control of and access to a limited supply of frontier resources, as William Cronon showed in *Changes in the Land* (1983), shaped the historic development of both Native American and Anglo-American societies in North America. Against this backdrop of environmental and cultural conflict, however, Indians and Europeans were able to create for a time what Richard White called a "Middle Ground" based on mutual accommodation and "an ongoing ritual of surrender and redemption." This "Middle Ground" resulted from the inability of either Europeans or Indians to dictate independently the nature of the relationships that developed along the frontier. Cronon and White have done much to recast the history of Native Americans in the colonial period. Any work viewing Indians simply as pawns in a game of imperialism is grossly oversimplified. Indians were important participants in American colonial history who, through the aggressive pursuit of their own goals played a significant role in shaping the structure of provincial society.

All this work has served to broaden the scope of American colonial history, placing the field in the broad context, as Bailyn and Morgan described it, of "the expansion of the European world outward into a number of alien peripheries or marchlands." American colonial history has become increasingly transatlantic and multicultural in approach, tracing relations between peoples in the colonies and between the frontier and the metropolis. In these marchlands, numerous studies have shown, complex societies developed, shaped by the interaction of British men and women with the environment, the indigenous population, and with a great diversity of others who migrated freely or who were imported into the American colonies. The relationships that developed between different peoples in the marchlands dramatically shaped the religious, political, economic, and military history of the colonies, as well as the link between the provinces and an English metropolis which throughout the colonial period sought to bend the colonies to serve imperial needs. The writing of American colonial history, the history of the First British Empire, in short is beginning to move toward answering T.H. Breen's call in 1986 for a history that "will focus on the movement of peoples and the clash of cultures, on common folk rather than on colonial administrators, on processes rather than on institutions, on aspects of daily life that one would not regard as narrowly political. It will," Breen continued, "be an integrated story, neither American nor English, but an investigation of the many links that connected men and women living on both sides of the Atlantic Ocean."

MICHAEL L. OBERG

See also Andrews; Bailyn; Cott; Cronon; Greene; Jordan; Morgan; Native American; Osgood; Turner

Further Reading

Andrews, Charles McLean, *The Colonial Period of American History*, 4 vols., New Haven: Yale University Press, 1934–38

Bailyn, Bernard, *Voyagers to the West: A Passage in the Peopling of America on the Eve of the Revolution*, New York: Knopf, 1986; London: Tauris, 1987

Bailyn, Bernard, and Philip D. Morgan, eds., *Strangers within the Realm: Cultural Margins of the First British Empire*, Chapel Hill: University of North Carolina Press, and London: Tauris, 1991

Brown, Robert Eldon, *Middle-Class Democracy and the Revolution in Massachusetts, 1691–1780*, Ithaca, NY: Cornell University Press, 1955

Brown, T.H., "An Empire of Goods: The Anglicization of Colonial America, 1690–1776," *Journal of Interdisciplinary History* 25 (1986)

Cronon, William, *Changes in the Land: Indians, Colonists, and the Ecology of New England*, New York, Hill and Wang: 1983

Crosby, Alfred W., Jr., *The Columbian Exchange: Biological and Cultural Consequences of 1492*, Westport, CT: Greenwood Press, 1972

Davis, David Brion, *The Problem of Slavery in Western Culture*, Ithaca, NY: Cornell University Press, 1966; revised 1988

Demos, John, *A Little Commonwealth: Family Life in Plymouth Colony*, New York: Oxford University Press, 1970

Fenton, William, *American Indian and White Relations to 1830, Needs and Opportunities for Study: An Essay*, Chapel Hill: University of North Carolina Press, 1957

Grant, Charles S., *Democracy in the Connecticut Frontier Town of Kent*, New York: Columbia University Press, 1961

Greene, Jack P., and J.R. Pole, eds., *Colonial British America: Essays in the New History of the Early Modern Era*, Baltimore: Johns Hopkins University Press, 1984

Greene, Jack P., *Pursuits of Happiness: The Social Development of Early Modern British Colonies and the Formation of American Culture*, Chapel Hill: University of North Carolina Press, 1988

Greven, Philip J., *Four Generations: Population, Land, and Family in Colonial Andover, Massachusetts*, Ithaca, NY: Cornell University Press, 1970

Jennings, Francis, *The Invasion of America: Indians, Colonialism, and the Cant of Conquest*, Chapel Hill: University of North Carolina Press, 1975

Jordan, Winthrop D., *White over Black: American Attitudes toward the Negro, 1550–1812*, Chapel Hill: University of North Carolina Press, 1968; abridged as *The White Man's Burden: Historical Origins of Racism in the United States*, New York: Oxford University Press, 1974

Lockridge, Kenneth A., *A New England Town, the First Hundred Years: Dedham, Massachusetts, 1636–1736*, New York: Norton, 1970; revised 1985

Meinig, D.W., *The Shaping of America: A Geographical Perspective on 500 Years of History*, 2 vols., New Haven: Yale University Press, 1986–93

Morgan, Edmund S., *American Slavery, American Freedom: The Ordeal of Colonial Virginia*, New York: Norton, 1975

Powell, Sumner Chilton, *Puritan Village: The Formation of a New England Town*, Middletown, CT: Wesleyan University Press, 1963

Rutman, Darrett Bruce, *Winthrop's Boston: Portrait of a Puritan Town, 1630–1649*, Chapel Hill: University of North Carolina Press, 1965

Sheehan, Bernard W., *Savagism and Civility: Indians and Englishmen in Colonial Virginia*, Cambridge and New York: Cambridge University Press, 1980

Webb, Stephen Saunders, *The Governors-General: The English Army and the Definition of the Empire, 1569–1681*, Chapel Hill: University of North Carolina Press, 1979

Webb, Stephen Saunders, *1676: The End of American Independence*, New York: Knopf, 1984

White, Richard, *The Middle Ground: Indians, Empires, and Republics in the Great Lakes Region, 1650–1815*, Cambridge and New York: Cambridge University Press, 1991

Wood, Peter H., *Black Majority: Negroes in Colonial South Carolina from 1670 Through the Stono Rebellion*, New York: Knopf, 1974

Zuckerman, Michael, *Peaceable Kingdoms: New England Towns in the Seventeenth Century*, New York: Knopf, 1970

United States: American Revolution

Americans actually experienced two revolutions during the final quarter of the 18th century. As Carl Becker put it in his famous essay of 1909, the first involved the struggle to establish "home rule," the second a contest to determine "who should rule at home." Perhaps because the revolutionaries themselves regarded it as their central achievement, the quest for national liberation – both in terms of obtaining independence from Britain and as a matter of establishing new systems of government – traditionally framed scholarly discussions of the revolution's general significance. Nonetheless, for most of this century – and particularly in the period since the end of World War II – historians have tended to treat the social changes wrought by the revolution as the more interesting and important. Indeed, no issue has proved more vexing for modern scholars than the question of exactly what sort of larger transformation resulted from the political act of declaring independence.

Probably the most widely accepted answer is the one favored by historians of constitutional and political thought like Caroline Robbins, J.R. Pole, J.G.A. Pocock, and Bernard Bailyn. According to the "neo-Whig" school – as it is sometimes called – the greatest change precipitated by the revolution involved the intellectual terms in which Americans understood both themselves and their political culture. In *The Ideological Origins of the American Revolution* (1967), for example, Bailyn traced the revolution's origins to the opposition thought of Augustan England and the heightened fears of despotism which Americans gleaned from the works of radical Whigs like John Trenchard and Thomas Gordon. Largely because of their familiarity with this literature, Americans came to regard any concentration of political power – whether in the hands of the British ministers who sought to assert parliamentary sovereignty in the colonies, or in those of their own leaders – as a dangerous threat to their liberties. The result, according to Bailyn, was a self-actualizing language of revolution, one where ordinary men and women "found in the defiance of traditional order the firmest of all ground for their hope for a freer life."

No doubt this formulation has continued to hold sway partly because it offers a ready explanation for why Americans should have wished to declare independence from a government which was almost universally regarded as the freest in the world. Of equal importance, however, is the light which the neo-Whig thesis shed on the history of the revolution after 1775. As Gordon Wood argued in *The Creation of the American Republic* (1969), the distrust of energetic, intrusive government ultimately proved so strong that the federal Constitution of 1788 contained an elaborate system of checks and balances in order to prevent Congress from dominating the other two, less democratic branches of government. In a similar manner, historians of religion like Jon Butler, Patricia Bonomi, and Nathan Hatch have pointed out the close relationship between the resistance to Parliament's absolutist claims and the assault on established churches which swept every state outside of New England during the 1780s. Furthermore students of American slavery have frequently noted the blow that the revolutionary injunctions against the figurative dangers of political bondage dealt to the legitimacy of more literal varieties of enslavement.

For all its explanatory power, however, the neo-Whig interpretation has always been vulnerable to charges of favoring those men and women who were sufficiently literate and articulate to express themselves in writing. For this reason, the late 1960s witnessed a growing effort to recover the experience of the "lesser sort" – artisans, small farmers, even landless laborers and servants – whose involvement in urban crowds, patriot associations, and local militias was just as instrumental in triggering the Revolution. In his study of popular resistance to the Stamp Act, for example, Gary Nash argued that the colonial assemblies' defiance of Parliament's fiscal authority in 1765 set the stage for much more far-reaching social protests over the growing disparities of wealth in cities like Boston, New York, and Newport, Rhode Island. In a similar manner, Eric Foner and Edward Countryman documented the emergence of nascent working-class movements in Philadelphia and New York during the latter stages of the revolution. Indeed, according to Rhys Isaac's path-breaking *Transformation of Virginia* (1982), such tensions were even present in rural areas like the Chesapeake, where the planters' challenge to British sovereignty ultimately helped undermine the supremacy which they had long enjoyed over their poorer white neighbors.

Without question, the "neo-Progressive" interpretation – as it came to be known – has provided a useful counterpoint to the textual analysis favored by students of constitutional theory or radical political thought. What is less clear is exactly how the political conflicts which the Revolution occasioned contributed to later social transformations. In recent years, Joyce Appleby and Gordon Wood have both suggested that the intellectual triumph of laissez-faire economic theory amounted to a social revolution of sorts, as genteel republicans like Jefferson managed to overlook the corrupting effects of manual labor and unbridled commerce in order to win the votes of the artisans and small farmers who increasingly held the balance of

political power in state and national elections. The problem with this argument, however, is that it implicitly discounts the extent to which colonial society on the eve of the revolution already sanctioned what Jack Greene has termed "the quest for the good life, defined as the pursuit of individual happiness and material achievement." Although American politics were certainly less deferential and more democratic, it remains an open question whether the underlying social assumptions at Washington's first inaugural address differed significantly from those at the close of the Seven Years' War.

Perhaps this is why historians seeking a broader perspective have turned increasingly to those groups – women, free and enslaved blacks, Native Americans – whom the new republic continued to exclude from the formal exercise of political power. In the case of women, historians like Linda Kerber and Mary Beth Norton have suggested that the revolution provided "liberty's daughters" with a new measure of civic involvement through the cult of "republican motherhood." On the other hand the adoption of a much broader franchise for white males also established new markers of inequality. As Gary Nash has noted, this pattern proved especially debilitating for African Americans, a substantial number of whom gained their freedom during the revolution, but who were usually deprived of civil rights such as sitting on juries or voting in elections. It is likewise clear that the democratic project of making lands on the frontier available for settlement by poor whites in the East directly threatened the rights of the Indians who still occupied them. Indeed, a kind of counter-Whig thesis seems to have taken shape in recent years, one where the democratic liberation which the revolution achieved for the republic's white citizens produced correspondingly detrimental effects for those on its margins.

Like any topic, the literature on the American revolution has always reflected changing concerns within the historical discipline. More than most, however, the revolution is also a subject which continues to attract a much wider public, at least in the United States. For this reason alone, the republic's founding moment promises to remain one of the livelier fields of American history.

Eliga H. Gould

See also Bailyn; Foner, E.; Greene; Kerber; Nash; Pocock; Ulrich; Wood, G.S.

Further Reading

Appleby, Joyce, *Capitalism and a New Social Order: The Republican Vision of the 1790s*, New York: New York University Press, 1984

Bailyn, Bernard, *The Ideological Origins of the American Revolution*, Cambridge, MA: Harvard University Press, 1967; revised 1992

Becker, Carl, *The History of Political Parties in the Province of New York, 1760–1776*, Madison: University of Wisconsin Press, 1909

Bonomi, Patricia U., *Under the Cope of Heaven: Religion, Society, and Politics in Colonial America*, Oxford and New York: Oxford University Press, 1986

Butler, Jon, *Awash in a Sea of Faith: Christianizing the American People*, Cambridge, MA: Harvard University Press, 1990

Clark, Jonathan C.D., *The Language of Liberty, 1660–1832: Political Discourse and Social Dynamics in the Anglo-American World*, Cambridge and New York: Cambridge University Press, 1994

Countryman, Edward, *A People in Revolution: The American Revolution and Political Society in New York, 1760–1790*, Baltimore: Johns Hopkins University Press, 1981

Countryman, Edward, "Indians, the Colonial Order, and the Social Significance of the American Revolution," *William and Mary Quarterly*, 3rd series, 53 (1996), 342–62

Davis, David Brion, *The Problem of Slavery in the Age of Revolution, 1770–1823*, Ithaca, NY: Cornell University Press, 1975

Egnal, Marc, *A Mighty Empire: The Origins of the American Revolution*, Ithaca, NY: Cornell University Press, 1988

Foner, Eric, *Tom Paine and Revolutionary America*, New York and London: Oxford University Press, 1976

Greene, Jack P., *Peripheries and Center: Constitutional Development in the Extended Polities of the British Empire and the United States, 1607–1788*, Athens: University of Georgia Press, 1986

Greene, Jack P., *Pursuits of Happiness: The Social Development of Early Modern British Colonies and the Formation of American Culture*, Chapel Hill: University of North Carolina Press, 1988

Hatch, Nathan O., *The Sacred Cause of Liberty: Republican Thought and the Millennium in Revolutionary New England*, New Haven: Yale University Press, 1977

Isaac, Rhys, *The Transformation of Virginia, 1740–1790*, Chapel Hill: University of North Carolina Press, 1982

Kerber, Linda K., *Women of the Republic: Intellect and Ideology in Revolutionary America*, Chapel Hill: University of North Carolina Press, 1980

McDonald, Forrest, *Novus Ordo Seclorum: The Intellectual Origins of the Constitution*, Lawrence: University Press of Kansas, 1985

Maier, Pauline, *From Resistance to Revolution: Colonial Radicals and the Development of American Opposition to Britain, 1765–1776*, New York: Knopf, 1972; London: Routledge, 1973

Maier, Pauline, *American Scripture: Making the Declaration of Independence*, New York: Knopf, 1997

Nash, Gary B., *The Urban Crucible: Social Change, Political Consciousness, and the Origins of the American Revolution*, Cambridge, MA: Harvard University Press, 1979; abridged as *The Urban Crucible: The Northern Seaports and the Origins of the American Revolution*, 1986

Nash, Gary B., *Forging Freedom: The Formation of Philadelphia's Black Community, 1720–1840*, Cambridge, MA: Harvard University Press, 1988

Norton, Mary Beth, *Liberty's Daughters: The Revolutionary Experience of American Women, 1750–1800*, Boston: Little Brown, 1980; revised 1996

Pocock, J.G.A., *The Machiavellian Moment: Florentine Political Thought and the Atlantic Republican Tradition*, Princeton: Princeton University Press, 1975

Pole, Jack Richon, *Political Representation in England and the Origins of the American Republic*, London: Macmillan, and New York: St. Martin's Press, 1966

Robbins, Caroline, *The Eighteenth-Century Commonwealthman: Studies in the Transmission, Development, and Circumstance of English Liberal Thought from the Restoration of Charles II until the War with the Thirteen Colonies*, Cambridge, MA: Harvard University Press, and Oxford: Oxford University Press, 1959

Ulrich, Laurel Thatcher, "'Daughters of Liberty': Religious Women in Revolutionary New England," in Ronald Hoffman and Peter J. Albert, eds., *Women in the Age of the American Revolution*, Charlottesville: University Press of Virginia, 1989

White, Richard, *The Middle Ground: Indians, Empires, and Republics in the Great Lakes Region, 1650–1815*, Cambridge and New York: Cambridge University Press, 1991

Wood, Gordon S., *The Creation of the American Republic, 1776–1787*, Chapel Hill: University of North Carolina Press, 1969

Wood, Gordon S., *The Radicalism of the American Revolution*, New York: Knopf, 1992

Young, Alfred, ed., *Beyond the American Revolution: Explorations in the History of American Radicalism*, DeKalb: Northern Illinois University Press, 1993

United States: 19th Century

General

American historiography has evolved in its own distinctive way, and much of its emphasis has always been on the unique, or at least distinctive, features of the American experience. This has been especially characteristic of historical writing on the 19th century, in so many ways the key formative period in the making of the US, and the shaping of American society. In the course of that century, the infant agrarian republic of 1800 grew into the greatest industrial power on earth; a country with a population of a few million, mainly scattered along the Atlantic seaboard, expanded into a continental power with a population of 75 million stretching from the Atlantic to the Pacific; the fragile union of the Jeffersonian era survived the life-threatening challenge of the Civil War and developed into a consolidated nation.

It is small wonder that much American historical writing on the 19th century has been celebratory, even triumphalist, in tone. The mid-19th-century patrician men of letters writing their multi-volume histories focused their attention mainly on the colonial and Revolutionary periods. The great exemplar of this school, George Bancroft, author of a 10-volume *History of the United States from the Discovery of the American Continent* (1834–74), did much to set a pattern of presenting American history as a narrative of the onward and upward march of liberty and democracy. In the later 19th century, the natural successors to the Bancroft generation were the members of the nationalist school, including Hermann von Holst, James Schouler, and James Ford Rhodes, who saw in the outcome of the Civil War the consolidation of the American national state. This was the last generation of gentleman scholars to dominate American historical writing, because the late 19th century also witnessed the steady professionalization of American history, with the emergence of graduate schools in a number of universities, the establishment of the American Historical Association and the *American Historical Review*, and the adoption of new standards of scholarship. Before 1890, almost all the major writings on American history had been the work of gentlemen scholars; from the early 1900s, professional, university-trained scholars dominated the field.

The most significant figure of this turn-of-the-century period – and arguably the single most influential figure in American historiography – was Frederick Jackson Turner. No historian who has written so little has achieved so much. His most influential books were collections of his essays, many of them variations on the same basic theme. In its simplest form, his "frontier thesis" announced that "the existence of an area of free land, its continuous recession, and the advance of American settlement westward, explain American development." American democracy, individualism and nationalism were all shaped by the frontier experience. A century later, Turner's star has waned; over the years, numerous critics have challenged the logic of his argument and listed other formative influences that Turner ignored. In recent years, the concept of the advance of American settlement has given way to talk of "the legacy of conquest," and to emphasis on other peoples – Native Americans and Hispanics, for example – who were a part of western history. But, whatever the diminution of the influence of his frontier thesis, Turner has left a crucially important double legacy. First, he provided a continental American perspective on the American past to replace, or at least challenge, the European-Atlantic perspective of the gentlemen scholars. Second, he shifted American historical writing from preoccupation with political and institutional history to social history, and the life of the people.

Turner is often placed, somewhat uncomfortably perhaps, in the progressive tradition of American historiography. A much more representative figure among progressive historians is Charles A. Beard, but most of his more specialized writings were devoted to the late 18th century or to the role of the US in the 20th-century world. However, with his wife Mary Ritter Beard, he wrote a widely-read and influential survey of American history, *The Rise of American Civilization* (1927–42). They treated the 19th century as an arena of conflict between the forces of agriculture and industry, and interpreted the Civil War as a second American Revolution, in which industrial interests triumphed, with far-reaching consequences for the whole of American society. This is a classic text of progressive history in its emphasis on change and development – what one commentator has called an "aggregative" view of American history – and its view of conflict between competing interests as the engine of progress. The progressive approach maintained its domination at least until the end of World War II. One of its last major products was Arthur Schlesinger's *The Age of Jackson* (1945); both here and in various essays, Schlesinger defined the major theme of American history as the struggle between the many and the few, the people and the interests.

The most comprehensive and searching critique of the pioneers of progressive history – specifically Turner, Beard and also Vernon Louis Parrington – is to be found in Richard Hofstadter's *The Progressive Historians* (1968). Curiously, Hofstadter has often been labeled as the herald of the new consensus school of American history which emerged in the 1950s. Certainly his first major book, *The American Political Tradition and the Men Who Made It* (1948), made an enormous impact and has remained hugely popular for half a century. It takes the form of a series of biographical sketches of major figures; it is usually challenging and often iconoclastic in tone, and always brilliantly written. However, apart from a brief comment in his introduction on the importance of a "common climate of opinion" in the American political tradition, the book was scarcely an unambiguous advertisement for consensus history. If Hofstadter identified a common thread in the American political tradition, it was the tendency to look for a golden age in the past; even reform movements, he suggested, were engaged in a forward-looking return to the past.

The complex and sometimes frightening postwar world after 1945 weakened faith in progress, and encouraged a closing of ranks against external dangers. Instead of conflict and change, the emphasis shifted to consensus, continuity, and often conservatism. Much more than Hofstadter, historians such as Daniel Boorstin and Louis Hartz typified the new approach. In his three volumes on *The Americans* (1958–73), Boorstin rejoiced in consensus as he ranged far and wide over the American past to demonstrate the uniqueness of the American experience, and the impossibility of exporting American democracy and the American way of life.

Even the most enthusiastic champion of consensus had difficulty in coping with divisive features of American history, such as the Civil War or recurring ethnic and racial conflict. Amid the turmoil of the 1960s, consensus history had a very limited expectation of life. The reaction against it was vigorous and vocal and came most stridently from the New Left historians, strongly influenced by their guru, William Appleman Williams, most of whose own work was devoted to American foreign policy and the expansion of the American "empire." Many of the New Left historians took a strongly presentist view of the past and were primarily interested in recent history, but others – Eugene Genovese, for example, on slavery, and Stephan Thernstrom on social mobility – redefined key questions in 19th-century history. More enduringly, the backlash against consensus history ushered in a new period of ferment in American historiography, characterized by complexity, diversity, and fragmentation – and a much wider range of subject matter. The new social history, which often owed at least as much to new research techniques as to the New Left, overshadowed conventional political history, although pronouncements about the death of political history proved distinctly premature. However, social history itself was rapidly fragmenting into various sub-fields, dealing separately with such topics as class and labor, race (especially black history), immigration and ethnicity, and gender (especially women's history). "Race, class, and gender" became the mantra of the new breed of historians. This was social history without much sense of society as a whole. Fragmentation and ever greater specialization made it increasingly difficult to discern any unifying theme in American history, in the 19th century as in other periods. Some historians demanded a new synthesis with increasing desperation; others gave up the quest as impossible. By the 1980s and 1990s, social history itself was giving some ground to cultural history, and a surge of enthusiasm for the study of popular culture, which again reflected a presentist approach to the past, and a predilection for the recent past. If 19th-century history felt in any way neglected, at least it was spared some of the excesses of rapidly changing historiographical fashions.

There are a number of illuminating guides to successive stages in the history of 19th-century history, and the accelerating rate of change from one school to another. For historical writings up to the 1950s, Kraus and Joyce's *The Writing of American History* (revised edition, 1985) is extremely helpful, particularly for its critical summaries of the work of scores of individual historians. For more recent trends, three collections of historiographical essays are invaluable. Among the 25 essays in William H. Cartwright and Richard L. Watson's *The Reinterpretation of American History and Culture* (1973), there are discussions of Native American, African American, and women's history, and even chapters on Chicanos and on Asian Americans, as well as reviews of work on successive periods of history. What this volume did for historical writing in the 1960s, Michael Kammen's *The Past before Us* (1980) did for the 1970s, although it also includes some coverage of non-American history and of new techniques and methods, including psychohistory and the use of quantitative methods. Eric Foner's *The New American History* (1990), like the Kammen volume sponsored by the American Historical Association, is the best available review of recent trends in American historiography. Seven essays deal with periods of American history – four of them covering the 19th century – while six deal with major themes, five of them on social history.

The most ambitious recent critique of American historiography is Peter Novick's *That Noble Dream* (1988). Focusing on the problem of objectivity in historical study, he argued that the late 19th-century recognition of objectivity as the norm of the historical profession was challenged by the historical relativism of the interwar years, revived in more modest guise after World War II, and then collapsed in face of the confusion, polarization, and uncertainty of the period since the 1960s. He made pointed comments on Turner, Beard, Hofstadter, Genovese, and other historians of the 19th century, and was particularly severe in his criticism of "present chaos," as he called it.

This introductory section has concentrated mainly on the long-term evolution of the historiography of the 19th century. In contrast, the three more specialized sections that follow will give priority to more recent work in each of three periods. The need to subdivide the discussion in this way is itself a reflection of the fragmentation of the subject and the intense specialization within the American historical profession. Attempts to write a synthesis of the whole of 19th-century American history have become rare indeed. One particular challenge facing 19th-century historians is to integrate what have tended to become two distinct histories of the period. On the one hand, there is the history dominated by the dramatic events relating to slavery and its further expansion, North–South rivalry, the Civil War, the emancipation of the slaves, and the troubled years of postwar Reconstruction. On the other hand, there is the history that examines the broad, continuing development of the American economy and American society – westward expansion, large-scale immigration, urban growth, the advance of industrial capitalism, and the emergence of a complex modern society. In this second history, the Civil War often appears only as a minor distraction; in the first history, it is often difficult to connect the most profound and threatening crisis of the Union with the long-term continuous flow of the alternative account. The historical literature discussed in the following sections reflects this problem but does not solve it.

From the Early Republic to the Age of Jackson, c.1790–1840

For many years, the pervasive influence of what Thomas Cochran called "the presidential synthesis" encouraged a view of this period as constructed around the two poles of Jefferson and Jackson, with a vaguely defined interlude of two decades between them. More recently, in search of a more comprehensive and rounded interpretation, scholars have looked beyond conventional political history, and, predictably perhaps, have seized upon themes of growth and expansion, in one form or another, as the key to understanding of the period.

The most wide-ranging, and the most complex and demanding, of these overviews is Robert H. Wiebe's *The Opening of American Society* (1984), which sweeps through the whole period from the making of the Constitution to the coming of the Civil War. Defining his subject as "the process of creating a national society in the United States where none existed," he traced the change from a republic run by an elite minority to a much more open democratic society, in which seemingly boundless space, an abundance of resources, and expanding opportunities offered Americans ever wider choices in every aspect of their lives.

A very different synthesis, more rigidly based on one central concept, is presented in Charles Sellers' *The Market Revolution* (1991). Sellers emphasized the transformation of American society wrought by the increasing domination of the market, and the social and economic capitalist system associated with it. The great conflict of the period was between the republican values of a stable agrarian society and the entrepreneurial spirit of the new capitalist order. For Sellers, democracy was born in tension with capitalism, not as its natural political expression. His book covers the period from 1815 to 1840, but its implications spread more widely, and some critics have claimed that the market revolution was underway well before 1815. A much older survey of the whole period from 1815 to 1860, which has acquired the status of a classic, foreshadowed many of the themes of Sellers' book, but without the ideological baggage. This was George Rogers Taylor's *The Transportation Revolution* (1951), which traced the consequences of developments in roads, bridges, canals, steamboats, and railroads for domestic and foreign trade, manufacturing, industrial workers, the financial system, and the role of government.

The most recent overview of the period speaks from a geographical, or geopolitical, perspective. D.W. Meinig's *Continental America, 1800–1867* (1993) is the second volume in his series *The Shaping of America*. The expansion of the US is the clear central theme, in multiple meanings of the term: the growth of a "continental empire" from the Louisiana Purchase to the mid-century acquisitions from Mexico, the growth of population and the actual process of settlement, and the growth of towns and cities. Meinig analyzed the stresses and strains of expansion, but pointed to elements of continuity as well as change.

The most vigorous recent debate among historians of the early years of the republic has revolved around the concept of republicanism. Following the work of Bernard Bailyn, Gordon Wood, and others on the Revolution itself, various historians have pursued into the early national period the discussion of republican ideology and the concept of a republic based on the virtue of its citizens. Drew McCoy, for example, in *The Elusive Republic* (1980) sought to show that republican virtue could be reconciled with commercial pursuits. In various writings including *Capitalism and a New Social Order* (1984), Joyce Appleby, the most persistent critic of the republican synthesis, argued the case for liberalism as a rival ideology that eventually prevailed. The most challenging study of the process by which republicanism gave ground to the forces of popular democracy during and after the Revolution is Gordon Wood's *The Radicalism of the American Revolution* (1992). As his title implies, he believes that, far from being limited or moderate or even conservative in character, the Revolution wrought a huge transformation in American political, economic, and social life.

The interpretation of the early republic based on the ideology of republicanism informs two recent general works on the 1790s. James Roger Sharp's *American Politics in the Early Republic* (1993) stressed the seriousness of the political divisions of the period and the dangers that they created for the survival of the republic. Stanley Elkins and Eric McKitrick's *The Age of Federalism* (1993) is narrative history on the grand scale, but includes analysis of the early achievements of the new government, the erosion of the Federalist vision of the American future, and the rise of an opposition, led by Jefferson and

Madison, drawing on increasing popular support. In an imaginative attempt to break away from concentration on elite politics, David Waldstreicher's *In the Midst of Perpetual Fetes* (1997), looks to popular celebrations and festivities for an answer to the question of how patriotic ardor and a desire for national unity could coexist with deepening political divisions.

The first quarter of the 19th century has attracted less recent attention from political historians. The giant figure of Thomas Jefferson still bestrides the early 1800s, but much of the heat seems to have gone out of the protracted historiographical debate about the causes of the War of 1812. The 1810s and 1820s were in many respects crucial decades in the growth of the US, and from Frederick Jackson Turner to George Dangerfield and on to Charles Sellers a number of ambitious interpreters of the early republic have underlined their importance, but this significant period awaits a major new synthesis.

In sharp contrast, the years to which Andrew Jackson has given his name, have attracted unrelenting attention – and indeed may serve to display changing fashions in American historiography in microcosm. The phrase "Jacksonian democracy" has been variously applied to a political party, a popular movement, the spirit of a particular age, or the period as a whole, and interpretations of it have been just as diverse. Turner offered a sectional interpretation, depicting Jackson as the symbol of the rise of the new west. In his highly influential *Age of Jackson*, Schlesinger emphasized class rather than section. For him, the political contests of the period reflected the clash between laboring people and business interests, and he gave new prominence to the workingmen's movements of the northeastern cities. Never afraid to link his historical writing to his own partisan commitments, Schlesinger portrayed Jackson as a kind of prototype Franklin Roosevelt. Two rival interpretations emerged during the 1950s and 1960s. Richard Hofstadter and Bray Hammond saw in the Jacksonian period the emergence of a democracy of men on the make, imbued with the entrepreneurial spirit and eager to grasp new economic opportunities. Using quantitative techniques in a detailed study of New York state, Lee Benson's *The Concept of Jacksonian Democracy* (1961) found no clear class difference in support for the Democratic and Whig parties, and offered instead an "ethnocultural" interpretation, based on ethnic background and religious affiliation.

Charles Sellers subsumed elements of earlier interpretations into his presentation of the Jackson years as a conflict between the agrarian, communal, republican values of the Democrats, with Jackson at their head, and the acquisitive, entrepreneurial, and socially repressive spirit of the Whigs – in essence a battle between democracy and capitalism in which democracy lost out. The two most recent overviews of the Jacksonian era offer contrasting views. In his *Liberty and Power* (1990), Harry Watson shared much of the Sellers' market revolution interpretation, but was more temperate and less apocalyptic (and much more concise) in expounding it. But he did point to the stresses and strains of rapid economic and social change as well as the new opportunities that were created. On the other hand, Daniel Feller's *The Jacksonian Promise* (1995) drew attention to the enterprise and dynamism of the period, and to the confidence and optimism shared by many Americans. His discussion ranged over business, labor, law, religion, education, gender, and social reform, as well as politics.

Economic and social historians, less tied to specific events or dominant personalities, have found it easier to discern themes that run through this whole half century from 1790 to 1840 – and indeed on through much of the 19th century. Westward expansion, early industrial development, the rise of towns and cities, the democratization of many (but by no means all) aspects of American life, the gradual evolution of a stronger sense of national identity – all of these provide a backdrop to important studies in particular fields. Only a sampling is possible here (and African American history is considered in the next section). In labor history, Sean Wilentz's *Chants Democratic* (1984) traced the growth of working-class consciousness among artisans in New York City, examined working-class politics in detail, and discussed the use of republican rhetoric by workers facing the challenge of new industrial development. On the other hand, Peter Way's *Common Labor* (1993), described the miserable, insecure, and often violent lives of the men who dug America's canals. All too aware of their own powerlessness, they lived and worked far beyond the world of conventional politics and commitment to republican values. Way's book extended the scope of labor history in the first half of the 19th century into areas hitherto little known or little understood.

In the rapidly growing literature on women's history, two works may be cited to indicate different approaches and shifting emphases. A pioneering work in its day, Nancy Cott's *The Bonds of Womanhood* (1977) showed how, as a result of the increasing separation of male work from home, women assumed control of the domestic environment, and with it a large measure of responsibility for the moral and social well-being of the community. The book concentrated on middle-class women, in New England, and occupied a very different world from the subjects of Christine Stansell's *City of Women* (1986), a study of working-class women in New York who combined the roles of industrial worker, housewife, and mother, and who knew little or nothing of "separate spheres" or the "cult of domesticity." Stansell discussed many different aspects of the lives and relationships of working-class women, always stressing the sheer struggle for survival, and integrating class and gender skillfully into her analysis.

The opening-up of American society described by Wiebe and others stretched far beyond the realm of politics. Some historians regard the Second Great Awakening of the early 1800s as one of the formative events in 19th-century American history, and, in *The Democratization of American Christianity* (1989), Nathan Hatch interpreted it, not as some kind of conservative reaction, but as a popular mass movement that rejected traditional religious authority and assigned greater importance to private judgment and individual commitment.

It is an obvious criticism of the emphasis on the democratic and egalitarian trends of the early national period that they were not shared by large sections of American society – women, blacks, Indians, immigrants, and many poorer whites. Even in strictly economic terms, equality of opportunity may have been an aspiration but equality of condition was very far from a reality. One of the great iconoclasts among historians of the period, Edward Pessen, wrote several books, including a general work on Jacksonian democracy, in which he punctured what he saw as the myths surrounding Jackson and his supporters. In *Riches, Class, and Power before the Civil War* (1973), he maintained that the gap between rich and poor was widening, that upward social mobility was very limited indeed, and that the wealthy had not in most cases risen from humble beginnings. Critics claim that some of his assumptions, and his concentration on the very rich, distorted his findings, but he offered a healthy corrective to over-enthusiastic talk about an age of egalitarianism.

Some of the clearest insights into a rapidly changing American society are to be found in excellent community studies, which manage to weave issues of class, ethnicity, race, gender, religion, social mobility, and economic opportunity into their accounts. Many of these works focus on communities in the northeast, especially in New England. Both Jonathan Prude's *The Coming of Industrial Order* (1983) and Christopher Clark's *The Roots of Rural Capitalism* (1990) examine the impact of capitalist enterprise and industrialization on small towns and rural communities in Massachusetts. Clark traced with great insight and subtlety the gradual transition from household production to more complex market relationships, and both books demonstrated the stresses and strains involved in the process. Elsewhere, two outstanding studies of communities in Illinois highlight crucial issues. Don Doyle's history of Jacksonville between 1825 and 1870, *The Social Order of a Frontier Community* (1978), contrasted a core group who settled and promoted a sense of community and a genuine community life, with others who came and went during a period of headlong western expansion. John Mack Faragher's *Sugar Creek: Life on the Illinois Prairie* (1986) focused on a group of neighboring small communities, and is equally illuminating on their struggle to make a living and on such matters as marriage and family, the role of women, sickness and health, and education. Both Doyle and Faragher excel in relating local community concerns to the wider national scene and the evolution of a sense of national identity. Studies of this kind reveal more of the real stuff of 19th-century American life than many larger-scale accounts.

Slavery, Civil War, and Reconstruction

No period or topic in modern history has attracted greater attention than the Civil War and all its attendant issues of slavery and race, which threatened the very survival of the Union. If any clear pattern can be discerned in the evolution of this mass of historical writing, it runs along the following lines. In the aftermath of the war, and down to the early 20th century, the dominant influence was the nationalist school, which deplored slavery, condemned secession, and celebrated the triumph of a reinvigorated Union. Then, from the 1910s to the 1940s, revisionist historians painted a quite different picture. Slavery was presented as a paternalist system to which southern slaveowners adhered despite its economic burdens. The Civil War became a needless war that inadequate statesmanship allowed to happen, and Reconstruction involved the imposition of a punitive peace on the defeated South, and gave rights and liberties to the freed slaves, for which they were ill-prepared and unfitted. Later generations of historians since the 1950s have judged slavery to be economically successful, but racially oppressive and morally unjustifiable. This in turn restored a sense of purpose to a war that saved the Union and freed the slaves, and Reconstruction became "an unfinished revolution" that failed to live up to its early promise.

Slavery

Historians' understanding of southern slavery has been transformed during the last forty years. Until the 1950s, the most influential historian of slavery was Ulrich B. Phillips, who combined painstaking archival research with traditional white southern attitudes to race. In *American Negro Slavery* (1918) and his other writings, slavery is presented as a patriarchal but unprofitable system, and a legitimate instrument for the preservation of white supremacy. It was not until forty years later that the growing challenge to this view culminated in Kenneth Stampp's *The Peculiar Institution* (1956), which used the same research methods as Phillips to arrive at totally opposite, and generally convincing, conclusions. For Stampp, slavery was economically viable and usually profitable, but commonly harsh and brutal in its treatment of the slaves. Neither Phillips nor Stampp paid much attention to slavery as seen and experienced by the slaves themselves. Slave culture, the slave personality, and the slave community were not yet part of the debate, but all that was soon to change, in the aftermath of World War II and the social and racial concerns of mid-20th-century America.

The trigger for much of this new debate was the publication of Stanley Elkins' highly controversial *Slavery: A Problem in American Institutional and Intellectual Life* (1959; 3rd edition 1976). In place of the assumption of racial inferiority that was central to the Phillips interpretation, Elkins depicted slaves as psychic casualties of unrelenting repression, which had reduced the slave to the stock image of the compliant, submissive, irresponsible childlike "Sambo." Elkins highlighted his argument by a notorious comparison with the effects of Nazi concentration camps upon their inmates. The backlash against Elkins did much to set a new agenda for studies of slavery. The very title of John W. Blassingame's *The Slave Community* (1972; revised 1979) is indicative of this change. Blassingame described the interior life of the slave community, which, he claimed, became the slaves' primary environment, as opposed to the secondary environment of their work experience and their contact with whites.

The mid-1970s saw an explosion of new work on slave culture and the slave community, which made extensive use of source material – hitherto neglected or dismissed – emanating directly or indirectly from the slaves themselves. The seminal work of these years was Eugene Genovese's *Roll, Jordan, Roll: The World the Slaves Made* (1974), much influenced by Antonio Gramsci's concept of hegemony. Genovese described an elaborate balance between accommodation and resistance in the relationship between slaves and their masters, and offered a vivid, complex, and sensitive picture of the world of the slaves in all its many aspects – not least their religion, to which he attached special importance.

Before the 1970s, the notion of a substantial study of the slave family, stressing its positive role within the slave community, would have seemed completely out of the question, but that is what Herbert Gutman provided in *The Black Family in Slavery and Freedom* (1976). Gutman may have claimed too much for the "autonomy" of the slave family, and subsequent work has modified his conclusions, but the family, like religion, was now established as a central institution of the slave community. Since the 1970s, a large number of local or more specialized studies have filled out the picture of slave life, clarified, corrected, and consolidated earlier work, and added greatly to knowledge and understanding of slave culture, slave religion, the slave family, slave women, the internal slave trade, the diversity of slave experience in an urban or industrial setting, and many other topics.

The 1970s also witnessed a revival of the debate over the economics of slavery. In 1974 Robert W. Fogel and Stanley L. Engerman created a sensation with their *Time on the Cross*, which claimed not only that southern agriculture, based on slave labor, was more profitable and more efficient – 35 per cent more efficient, to be precise – than northern agriculture using free labor, but that southern planters were capitalists with all the acquisitive instincts of their kind, who happened to rely on a different kind of labor extremely well adapted to their purposes. The authors intended their work as a demonstration model of what could be achieved by the use of quantitative methods in history, but, in the furore aroused by their book, other quantitative historians often took the lead in challenging their methods and their conclusions. Among the most effective was Gavin Wright whose own *The Political Economy of the Cotton South* (1978) offered an alternative picture of the southern antebellum economy that attributed its successes more to its peculiar advantages in supplying the world market for cotton than to the supposed efficiency of slave labor. Few scholars would now accept in full the arguments of *Time on the Cross*, but Fogel returned to the subject in his *Without Consent or Contract* (1989), in which he modified some of his earlier judgments but for the most part remained surprisingly unrepentant.

The argument over the economics of slavery and the debate over the character of southern slave society are of course interrelated. Genovese's picture of a paternalist or "pre-capitalist" society is completely at odds for example with James Oakes' portrayal of profit-hungry slaveowning capitalists in *The Ruling Race* (1982). However, Genovese has pointed out that it is not only capitalists who prefer profits to losses, and Oakes has modified his position in his more recent work. There has often been a tendency to present issues relating to slavery in terms of sharp dichotomies: paternalism or profit, slave resistance or slave docility, the "autonomy" of the slave community or the total authority of the master. The actual history of southern slavery is more complicated, and there are signs of the emergence of a more balanced view that does not descend into equivocation or bland compromise. Those in search of handy guides to a complex subject may turn to two brief and readable books. The best brief recent overview is Peter Kolchin's *American Slavery, 1619–1877* (1993). A critic of an excessively "cosy" view of the slave community, which belittled the power of the master, Kolchin is judicious and authoritative in his evaluation of controversial topics. A brief critical assessment of the modern historiography of slavery may be found in Peter J. Parish's *Slavery: History and Historians* (1989).

Civil War

The major modern attempts at an overview of the whole Civil War era reflect changing historiographical fashions. J.G. Randall and David Donald's *The Civil War and Reconstruction* (1961, 1969) held sway for at least a generation as the most comprehensive and dependable single-volume history. But it had its own revealing history. The book was first published in 1937, with Randall as sole author, and in places it reflected his own revisionist inclinations, for example in its gentle treatment of the South. In the revised 1961 edition, Donald incorporated more recent research, and adopted a more even-handed stance, although some sections, notably on Reconstruction for example, still showed strong signs of the book's provenance. The revival of the nationalist interpretation found its fullest and most impressive voice in the eight volumes of Allan Nevins' *The Ordeal of the Union* and *The War for the Union* (1947–71). Nevins absorbed many different approaches into his massive study, although he usually placed slavery and race at the core of the crisis of the Union. The four volumes on the war years concentrate heavily on the North, and pursue with great determination the central argument that the war transformed an unorganized, "invertebrate" society into one that was much more complex, structured, and interdependent. Much the most successful recent synthesis is James M. McPherson's *Battle Cry of Freedom* (1988) which combines a nationalist approach with an appreciation of the multiple meanings of freedom involved in the conflict between North and South. The book concentrates heavily on the war years, including detailed accounts of the actual fighting, which enable McPherson to stress the role of contingency in Civil War history. He also brings African Americans into the center of his interpretation more than any previous general account.

The literature devoted to the causes of the war is enormous. Thomas J. Pressly's *Americans Interpret Their Civil War* (1954) is a judicious appraisal of that literature from the era of the war itself down to 1950. Because of its clarity in style and argument, Avery Craven's *The Coming of the Civil War* (1942, 1957) may serve as a good example of the work of the revisionist school. Craven is unabashed in his southern sympathies, and gives short shrift to those whom he regarded as northern agitators and extremists. During the last thirty years, slavery and antislavery, and all their repercussions, have been at center stage, and if the "needless war" of the revisionists has not quite become the inevitable war, it certainly appears as a conflict over real issues in which, ultimately, the resort to arms was extremely difficult to avoid. In his masterly *The Impending Crisis* (1976), David Potter combined an appreciation of the deepening differences between North and South over slavery, with an understanding of the unintended or unforeseen consequences of particular events or decisions.

Many recent studies have underlined the relentlessly mounting pressures at work within both North and South. In *Free Soil, Free Labor, Free Men* (1970), Eric Foner showed how the Republican party's basic policy of opposition to any further extension of slavery was sustained by a whole range of northern interests, aspirations, anxieties, ideals, and emotions. For their part, Genovese and others have seen secession and a bid for independence as the last desperate throw of a distinctive precapitalist southern elite, threatened by the onward march of an expanding capitalist North, and worried by threats from within. In *The Road to Disunion* (1990), the first volume of an intended 2-volume study, William Freehling has portrayed slavery as increasingly the peculiar institution of the deep South, and has pointed to deepening divisions between upper and lower South – again encouraging a "now or never" attitude in the latter. Michael A. Morrison's *Slavery and the American West* (1997) underlined the point that the dispute over the further extension of slavery, far from being trivial or unreal, was of fundamental importance to both North and South. Among briefer accounts of the origins of the war, Bruce Levine's *Half Slave and Half Free* (1991) stands out for its skill in relating the foreground issues surrounding slavery to the whole development of American society from the Revolution onwards. An alliance between free labor and slave labor communities had secured independence and backed the Constitution, but the subsequent growth of both sections led to ever-widening divergence, and massive popular commitment on each side.

Of course there have been dissenters from the dominant view of the coming of the war. The ethnocultural historians challenged the notion of the primacy of slavery in political debate in the 1840s and 1850s, and pointed to other factors – ethnic and religious identity, hostility to immigrants (especially Irish Catholic immigrants), the persistence of antipartyism and of cherished republican values – in order to explain the party political upheaval of the 1850s. In *The Political Crisis of the 1850s* (1978) and his challenging book of essays, *Political Parties and American Political Development* (1992), Michael Holt has been one of the most forceful exponents of this point of view. The difficulty of attempts by such historians to minimize the significance of the widely accepted causes of the Civil War is that the war did nevertheless happen. They have to confront what one historian has called "the massive inconvenient reality of the Civil War." It is noteworthy that, in the latest overview of the coming of the war, *The Origins of the American Civil War* (1996), Brian Holden Reid did not wholeheartedly embrace the Holt approach, but he did emphasize the role of contingency and of specific events, and he devoted more than half the book to the years from 1858 to 1861. Perhaps, a new era of revisionism is at hand.

The literature on the war years matches or exceeds in volume that on the coming of the war. There is no scope here for discussion of the huge volume of works on military history, but there has also been a marked increase of interest in the politics of war and more generally in the home front. The former owes a good deal to the unflagging fascination with the personality and leadership of Abraham Lincoln, while the latter was greatly stimulated by the monumental work of Allan Nevins. Lincoln biography is a genre all of its own, and its most authoritative modern exponent is David Herbert Donald, whose *Lincoln* (1995) offered many insights into the politics of the North at war. Its most surprising feature is its insistence on portraying Lincoln as an essentially passive figure, reacting to events rather than shaping them. Phillip Shaw Paludan's *The Presidency of Abraham Lincoln* (1994) is the outstanding modern study of the politics of the Union at war. Paludan insists that saving the Union and freeing the slaves were not two separate challenges for Lincoln, but were interwoven into one common task – the salvation of a Union that was worth the saving.

Paludan's earlier book, *"A People's Contest": The Union and Civil War, 1861–1865* (1988) is a valuable survey of northern politics and society, with sections on agriculture, industry, religion, and the methods and burdens of war-making, as well as perceptions of the meaning and purpose of the conflict. It draws together the results of various studies of the home front, but does not offer any bold new interpretation. Among more specialized studies, one of the most striking is Iver Bernstein's *The New York City Draft Riots* (1990), which uses one set of violent events to explore and illuminate longer-term social and political developments during the Civil War period, involving race, class, ethnicity, business interests, and party politics at local and national level.

Studies of the internal history of the Confederacy have tended to revolve around the questions, first, whether the establishment of the Confederacy amounted to a revolution, and, second, whether any kind of Confederate nationalism was able to develop in the face of devotion to the concept of states' rights. It is widely believed that Emory Thomas, the main proponent of "the Confederacy as a revolutionary experience," marred his case by overstatement, but George C. Rable, in *The Confederate Republic: A Revolution Against Politics* (1994), developed a more subtle and elaborate argument. Hoping to restore the purity – more myth than fact – of the early American republic, the Confederates rebelled against party politics and what they saw as the corrupt and divisive northern political culture of the antebellum years, but many of them were surprised and disillusioned by the bickerings and divisions within their own ranks during the war. On the nationalism issue, Paul Escott is one historian who has argued that the Confederacy was undermined first by the states' rights mentality of many Southerners, and then by class divisions, in particular by the grievances of the nonslaveholding majority, complaining about a rich man's war and a poor man's fight. On the other hand, in a brief but provocative study, *The Creation of Confederate Nationalism* (1988), Drew Gilpin Faust pointed to political and religious efforts to promote a strong sense of cultural identity, which had some success at least in the earlier part of the war. In *The Confederate War* (1997), Gary Gallagher mounted a strong defence of popular commitment to the Confederate cause and the strength of Confederate national loyalties.

One other area of rapidly growing interest to historians, which embraced both military and social history, lies in the experience and the motivation of common soldiers on both sides. Here the key work is Gerard F. Linderman's *Embattled Courage* (1987), which closely analyzed the battlefield experience, and suggested that initial idealism and romantic attachment to the cause often gave way, in face of the horror of the new warfare, to a simple instinct for survival. Other scholars, including Reid Mitchell, set greater store by the continuing ideological commitment of soldiers on both sides, and this line of argument is pushed much further – too far, some might think – in James M. McPherson's *For Cause and Comrades* (1997). Basing his conclusions on prodigious research in soldiers' letters and diaries, McPherson recognized that soldiers fought for their comrades and to avoid appearing as cowards in front of those comrades, but he insisted that motives of patriotism, honor, duty, and devotion to their respective causes impelled most of them to go on fighting. In any event, it is clear that questions of morale and commitment, on the home front as well as the battlefront, stand out as one area of Civil War history where further study would be welcome.

Reconstruction

The most remarkable feature of Reconstruction historiography is that it was written for so long from the point of view of the losers in the war itself. What Ulrich B. Phillips did for slavery William A. Dunning did for Reconstruction. His *Reconstruction: Political and Economic, 1865–1877* (1907) blended a modicum of scholarship, political and constitutional conservatism, and early 20th-century racism to build up a picture of extremist northern Republicans bent on revenge against the white South. They flouted the Constitution, gave civil rights and political power to former slaves totally unfitted for them, and established corrupt and incompetent regimes in the southern states, which humiliated white Southerners and led to violence, misery, and economic disaster. For adherents of the Dunning school, the recovery of white control was the "redemption" of the southern states. Extraordinarily, this "Birth-of-a-Nation" view of Reconstruction held sway at least until the 1940s, fuelled by state studies written by Dunning disciples, and by more lurid popular accounts written in the interwar years by Claude Bowers (*The Tragic Era*, 1929) and George Fort Milton (*The Age of Hate*, 1930).

There was one early and powerful voice of dissent, but it was largely ignored. It came from the leading black intellectual and activist, W.E.B. Du Bois. Writing from a Marxist perspective in his *Black Reconstruction* (1935), he not only paid much more attention to the former slaves themselves, but suggested that the Reconstruction years witnessed a short-lived alliance between northern capitalists and the freed slaves and poor whites of the South. But, in the 1870s, northern business returned to an alliance with the southern white elite who regained local control in the South in return for acceptance of northern business domination nationwide.

It was not, however, until the 1950s that the long overdue challenge to the Dunning interpretation came to fruition. Two brief interpretive surveys, reflecting the civil rights concerns of their time, stood the received view on its head. Kenneth M. Stampp's *The Era of Reconstruction, 1865–1877* (1965) took a much more favorable view of the motives and direction of Republican Reconstruction policy, and regretted that, far from being too radical, it was not radical enough. John Hope Franklin's *Reconstruction: After the Civil War* (1961) gave greater emphasis to Reconstruction on the ground in the South. He refuted many of the charges of corrupt and extravagant misrule leveled against the "radical" governments there, and stressed their reforming achievements in very difficult circumstances. However, in the longer run, it was not enough simply to challenge the pernicious and outdated assumptions, and to reverse, point by point, the arguments of the Dunning school. Gradually, over the following generation, a more complex and realistic (if not always a clearer) picture emerged, on the one hand of the evolution of Republican Reconstruction policy, and then its loss of impetus, and on the other of the tangled history of Reconstruction in the southern states. On the making of Reconstruction policy, historians such as Eric McKitrick, Hans Trefousse, Herman Belz, and Michael Les Benedict were sharply critical of president Andrew Johnson, and demonstrated that the so-called "Radical Reconstruction" program in fact took shape through a series of compromises between various groups within the Republican party – and often proved to be not very radical at all. For example, in *A Compromise of Principle: Congressional Republicans and Reconstruction* (1974), Benedict argued that most Republicans genuinely wanted to secure the basic rights of black Americans, but conservatives, moderates, and radicals disagreed on how far they could and should go in pursuit of that goal. On Reconstruction in the South, Dan Carter, Michael Perman, and others have described the complexities of politics in the southern states and there have now been a number of state studies that highlight the diverse Reconstruction experience of many parts of the South.

By the 1980s, Reconstruction was crying out for a new synthesis, and it came in the shape of Eric Foner's massive study, *Reconstruction: America's Unfinished Revolution, 1863–1877* (1988). The title itself revealed one of the basic themes – that the Reconstruction program was in many ways radical, and its achievements should not be overshadowed by the backlash that followed in the later 19th century. Foner pointed out that, among slave societies, it was only in the US that emancipation was followed within a year or two by the enfranchisement of the former slaves. He does not ignore congressional and presidential politics, but he is anxious to take the broadest possible view of the whole Reconstruction process, and gives close attention to social and economic aspects. In particular, he placed African Americans at the center of his account to an unprecedented extent. Foner suggested that, during Reconstruction, the Republican party sought to spread its free labor ideology into the South, only to see the freed slaves – and various groups in the North, including workers and women – push that ideology in new directions for their own purposes. Northern business interests were sufficiently alarmed to abandon support for Reconstruction and to compromise with southern conservatives. Foner's emphasis on class and on economic factors has its critics, but, for the moment, the Foner synthesis remains supreme. One superb example of "post-Foner" Reconstruction history is Laura F. Edwards' *Gendered Strife and Confusion: The Political Culture of Reconstruction* (1997). Rejecting the conventional separation of the private and the public spheres, she focused on the household as the focal point of social and political relationships. Edwards wove class and race, as well as gender, into her study of one North Carolina county. Giving special prominence to African Americans and poorer whites, as well as women, she opened up a fresh perspective on life during the Reconstruction years. It would be unwise to jump to the conclusion that the reconstruction of Reconstruction history is over and done with.

The Later Nineteenth Century, c.1865–1900

It was during the later decades of the 19th century that many long-term economic and social trends came to a climax and shaped a new and recognizably modern America. Politics, at least in its conventional forms, was slow to catch up, and it was not until the turn of the century that the progressive movement offered even a limited response to a new political agenda. The presidential and congressional politics of the later 19th century were fiercely and evenly contested by the two main parties, but often with more noise than substance. Some recent attempts have been made to rescue the politics of the 1880s and 1890s from obscurity, but most surveys give strong precedence to economic transformation and social upheaval over the uninspiring Washington politics of the "Gilded Age."

Technological advance, industrial growth, the rise of big business, the swelling population of the great cities, tidal waves of immigration, the growth of the industrial working class, the rise of a new managerial and professional middle class, the special problems of the West and the South: these are the central themes of the history of the period, which have dominated textbook surveys and more ambitious interpretive studies. The 1950s and 1960s saw a rash of such surveys. One of the first and best was Samuel P. Hays' *The Response to Industrialism, 1885–1914* (1957) which, like some others, treated the late 19th and early 20th centuries as one period. Hays pursued the theme stated in his title consistently and perceptively. In a broadly based but very concise study, he saw the political protests and movements of the period as an anxious reaction by many different sections of American society to sweeping economic and social change. In a more sharply critical style, and from a more radical political stance, Ray Ginger's *Age of Excess* (1965) painted a not dissimilar picture of huge material progress, based on mass production and mass consumption, which left many people helpless and powerless, handed control of government and politics to the great corporations, and destroyed much that was worthwhile about an older America.

The most brilliant and influential reinterpretation of the period came from Robert H. Wiebe in *The Search for Order, 1877–1920* (1967). Making use of the *gemeinschaft/gesellschaft* distinction expounded by European social theorists, he saw in headlong urban-industrial growth the destruction of an America based on the life of small communities, leaving a "society without a core." Gradually, new groups and new forces moved in to fill the gap – managers and professionals, corporations and bureaucracies – all emphasizing regularity, efficiency, and organization in the new and much more impersonal social order that they established. The Wiebe interpretation became the dominant synthesis of the period, though challenged twenty years later, not altogether persuasively, by Nell Irvin Painter in *Standing at Armageddon: The United States, 1877–1917* (1987). She highlighted the role of the main casualties of rapid change – industrial workers, western and southern farmers, women, and ethnic and racial minority groups – and claimed that their protests in various forms alarmed the more affluent and comfortable sections of society sufficiently to extract some limited reforms during the progressive era. She saw in the period a competition between the forces of prosperity and democracy, in which the former won, but not completely.

Even if congressional and presidential politics have not roused the interest of many modern historians of this period, there has been important work on the structure and institutions of government and politics. Morton Keller's *Affairs of State* (1977) examined politics, law, and government as component parts of the national public life of the late 19th-century US. He analyzed the decentralizing tendencies of the "postwar polity" from 1865 to 1880, and then the confrontation of American public life with industrialism in the "industrial polity" of the period 1880–1900. Public life still confronted the long-standing struggle between the desire for a more effective and more unified national state, on the one hand, and traditions of localism and deep suspicion of government, on the other. In confronting the problems of a new era, state governments, courts, and administrative agencies often became more important than presidents and congresses. In *Building a New American State: The Expansion of National Administrative Capacities, 1877–1920*

(1982), Stephen Skowronek addressed similar questions, and showed how limited was the effectiveness of government attempts to regulate business during the Gilded Age, until greater political will and growing administrative capacity produced some improvement during the early 20th century. The cities have commonly been regarded as one of the most conspicuous failures of American government, dominated as they apparently were by corrupt bosses and party machines. In *The Unheralded Triumph: City Government in America, 1870–1900* (1984), Jon C. Teaford attempted, with some measure of success, to provide a much more favorable picture. Much of the real story, he insisted, lay in the practical business of city government and the work of professional experts and managers who brought about huge improvements in water supply, sewage systems, paved streets, and the provision of city parks.

The true test of the power of the state lay in its relationship with the large corporations that threatened to overpower the limited institutional muscle of government at any level. A vividly written and highly critical work of popular history, Matthew Josephson's *The Robber Barons* (1934), established a stereotype of the business leaders of the age which has proved remarkably durable. In more restrained fashion, Thomas C. Cochran and William Miller's *The Age of Enterprise: A Social History of Industrial America* (1942, 1961) offered a more judicious but still critical view, written from a post-New Deal perspective. Although now outdated in many ways, it still provides a very readable and thoughtful survey, and it too has had a long shelf life. Biographies, some of them voluminous, of the great captains of industry have often tried to transform them from robber barons to wealth creators and industrial statesmen. Harold C. Livesay's *Andrew Carnegie and the Rise of Big Business* (1975) avoided the extremes of this kind of argument, but insisted upon the crucial role of the individual entrepreneur in the rise of the great corporations. However, the scholar who now bestrides this whole topic is Alfred D. Chandler, whose prolific writings have analyzed the structure of American business, and revealed how it responded to rapidly changing circumstances from the mid-19th century onward by moving toward vertical integration and economies of scale. His seminal work, *The Visible Hand: The Managerial Revolution in American Business* (1977), focused on administrative structure, management, and competition, rather than individual business leaders. Chandler has sometimes been criticized for inadequate attention to the broader social, political, and moral issues that preoccupied many earlier writers.

Social historians have kept such matters clearly in their sights, as they investigated the consequences and the casualties of headlong urban-industrial growth. Mass immigration, the ethnic mix of the urban population and the industrial labor force, and the problems of industrial workers, organized and unorganized, are three interlocking issues that have commanded much attention. On immigration and ethnicity, Stephan Thernstrom's *Harvard Encyclopedia of American Ethnic Groups* (1980) is a massive and authoritative guide, though it is now almost twenty years old, and needs updating. It contains essays on more than 100 different ethnic groups as well as illuminating discussion of many controversial issues. John Bodnar's *The Transplanted: A History of Immigrants in Urban America* (1985) pointed to the diversity of the immigrant experience in facing up to American capitalist society. He questioned some of the common assumptions about that experience – for example, how drastic a break was necessarily involved in the move from the homeland to America, or how far the immigrants were in reality acculturated or Americanized. Bodnar evoked clearly many aspects of the everyday life and culture of immigrant communities, as did Roger Daniels in *Coming to America* (1990). Daniels was less committed to an ideological framework than Bodnar, and organized his treatment of the 19th century mainly around the experience of various ethnic groups. One notable feature of his work was the attention given to Chinese and Japanese immigration. There is no modern study of nativist hostility to immigration to replace the standard work by John Higham, *Strangers in the Land* (1955, 1988). He identified anti-Catholicism, anti-radicalism, and racism as the three main elements in nativism, and discussed fluctuations in the relative importance of each of them. He also suggested that upsurges of nativism at particular times were often symptoms of broader and deeper unease or unrest.

The ethnic diversity of the industrial workforce is one of the main factors in the labor history of this period. Perhaps the single most influential scholar in the field has been Herbert Gutman, whose collection of essays, *Work, Culture, and Society in Industrializing America* (1976) – and especially the long essay of the same title – did much to set a new agenda. Among many important points, Gutman urged that labor history must embrace far more than the small minority of workers who belonged to trade unions. The large majority of unorganized workers included many immigrants, and Gutman suggested that each succeeding wave of immigrants "re-made" the working class, as it adapted, often reluctantly, to the demands and disciplines of industrial labor. In *The Fall of the House of Labor* (1987), David Montgomery, another very influential labor historian, sought to put into practice the new approach to labor and working-class history by placing his study of labor activism in this much broader context. J. Carroll Moody and Alice Kessler-Harris' *Perspectives on American Labor History* (1989) is an important collection of papers from a major conference where the shape and direction of labor history were fiercely debated. One of the editors, Kessler-Harris, launched an onslaught on the failure of labor historians to address the problems of women, and other contributors deplored the neglect of race. In another collection of essays, *Towards the Abolition of Whiteness* (1994), David R. Roediger pursued this latter point and urged the need to integrate race and class in the serious study of labor and working-class history. The field of labor history has been in ferment in recent years, and in no other field has the debate on class, race, and gender been more vigorously conducted.

Race has of course also been close to the center of the discussion of the post-Reconstruction South. The classic study of the later 19th-century South, which has influenced all subsequent work, is C. Vann Woodward's *Origins of the New South, 1877–1913* (1951, 1971), which ranged widely over industrial development, agricultural crisis, political protest, and social and cultural life. However, the most contentious argument of this book, and even more clearly of Woodward's later *The Strange Career of Jim Crow* (1955, 1974), was that, after the end of Reconstruction, there was a period of fluidity in race relations before the apparatus of segregation and disfranchisement was fastened upon the black population in the 1890s.

More recent work by Howard Rabinowitz, Joel Williamson, and others has suggested that the picture is much more complicated, that *de facto* and even some legal segregation was in place well before the 1890s – and even that formal segregation represented an improvement for most black southerners over the exclusive regime that preceded it. The debate goes on, with the eyes of many participants as much on the racial situation in the late 20th century as in the late 19th. Perhaps it was partly in reaction against this preoccupation that the most recent attempt at a synthesis of southern history in this period, Edward L. Ayers' *The Promise of the New South* (1992), took a much broader view, stressed the complexity and diversity of southern society, and dwelt on the life of ordinary southerners of all kinds. For Ayers, the promise of the new South endured but remained far from fulfillment, amid continuing economic and social change.

If perspectives on southern history have changed, the whole character of western history has been transformed. For many years, Turner's frontier thesis maintained its grip, and his forebodings about the consequences of the "closing of the frontier" in the 1890s were widely shared. Walter Prescott Webb's *The Great Plains* (1931) was a wonderful evocation of that region, in some respects very much in the Turner mold, but in others – notably its feeling for the whole environment of the plains – a precursor of much more recent approaches to the subject. Patricia Nelson Limerick's *The Legacy of Conquest* (1987) is a prime example of the so-called "new western history," which treats the frontier as a region or a whole environment, and not as a process, and embraces all the peoples who were part of the population of the region, including Indians, Hispanics, Asians, and African Americans, as well as the whites who "settled" in the West. Richard White's *"It's Your Misfortune and None of My Own": A New History of the American West* (1991) placed particular emphasis on the complex ethnic mixture of the West, and noted with a nice sense of irony the extent to which this homeland of American rugged individualism depended on the support and intervention of the federal government.

It was agrarian distress and discontent in the West and the South, rather than militancy among industrial workers, that gave birth to the main popular protest movements of the late 19th century. For many years, John D. Hicks' *The Populist Revolt* (1931) was the standard work. In a sympathetic account, Hicks depicted the populist movement as a genuine response to serious hardship, placed it firmly in the American reform tradition, and saw its program as the precursor, even the progenitor, of 20th-century reforms. In *The Age of Reform* (1955), Richard Hofstadter developed his "status revolution" explanation of turn-of-the-century reform movements. In his view, the populist movement reflected the concerns of farmers about their loss of status in American society. He criticized them for their alleged racism and anti-Semitism, and argued that they should have concentrated on demands for redress of real economic grievances. Many of Hofstadter's claims have been hotly disputed, and the pendulum has swung back to a more sympathetic view of the movement, for example in Lawrence Goodwyn's *Democratic Promise: The Populist Movement in America* (1976), which presented it as an active radical movement. One aspect of Goodwyn's major reappraisal of the movement was his shift of focus from the West to the South. Hicks, and even Hofstadter, had portrayed populism as primarily a western movement, with particular strength in the plains states and in mining areas. Woodward had noted the strength of populism in much of the South, but Goodwyn pushed this point much further, unfortunately to the point of becoming almost dismissive about the western contribution.

The last two decades have seen such intense debate on so many aspects of the history of the later 19th century – from big business to agrarian discontent, and from the new labor history to the new western history – that the case for a new synthesis appears to be overwhelming. However, there are so many divergent strands in the history of these decades that the task would be formidable indeed.

PETER J. PARISH

See also African American; Bancroft; Blassingame; Boorstin; Chandler; Cott; Cronon; Du Bois; Dunning; Elkins; Foner, E.; Franklin; Genovese; Gutman; Hofstadter; Meier; Montgomery; Native American; Nevins; Owsley; Pessen; Phillips; Schlesinger; Stampp; Turner; Wiebe; Wood, G.S.

Further Reading

Appleby, Joyce, *Capitalism and a New Social Order: The Republican Vision of the 1790s*, New York: New York University Press, 1984

Ayers, Edward L., *The Promise of the New South: Life after Reconstruction*, New York: Oxford University Press, 1992

Bancroft, George, *History of the United States from the Discovery of the American Continent*, Boston: Little Brown, 10 vols., 1834–74

Beard, Charles, and Mary Ritter Beard, *The Rise of American Civilization*, 4 vols., New York: Macmillan, and London: Cape, 1927–42

Belz, Herman, *Reconstructing the Union: Theory and Policy during the Civil War*, Ithaca, NY: Cornell University Press, 1969

Benedict, Michael Les, *A Compromise of Principle: Congressional Republicans and Reconstruction, 1863–1869*, New York: Norton, 1974

Benson, Lee, *The Concept of Jacksonian Democracy: New York as a Test Case*, Princeton: Princeton University Press, 1961

Bernstein, Iver, *The New York City Draft Riots: Their Significance for American Society and Politics in the Age of the Civil War*, New York: Oxford University Press, 1990

Blassingame, John, *The Slave Community: Plantation Life in the Antebellum South*, New York: Oxford University Press, 1972; revised 1979

Bodnar, John, *The Transplanted: A History of Immigrants in Urban America*, Bloomington: Indiana University Press, 1985

Boorstin, Daniel J., *The Americans*, 3 vols., New York: Random House, 1958–73; London: Cardinal, 1988

Carter, Dan T., *When the War Was Over: The Failure of Self-Reconstruction in the South, 1865–1867*, Baton Rouge: Louisiana State University Press, 1985

Cartwright, William H., and Richard L. Watson, Jr., eds., *The Reinterpretation of American History and Culture*, Washington, DC: National Council for Social Studies, 1973

Chandler, Alfred D., Jr., *The Visible Hand: The Managerial Revolution in American Business*, Cambridge, MA: Harvard University Press, 1977

Clark, Christopher, *The Roots of Rural Capitalism: Western Massachusetts, 1780–1860*, Ithaca, NY: Cornell University Press, 1990

Cochran, Thomas C., and William Miller, *The Age of Enterprise: A Social History of Industrial America*, New York: Macmillan, 1942; revised New York: Harper, 1961

Cochran, Thomas C., "The 'Presidential Synthesis' in American History," *American Historical Review* 53 (1948), 748–59

Cott, Nancy F., *The Bonds of Womanhood: "Woman's Sphere" in New England, 1780–1835*, New Haven and London: Yale University Press, 1977

Craven, Avery O., *The Coming of the Civil War*, New York: Scribner, 1942; revised Chicago: University of Chicago Press, 1957

Cronon, William, *Nature's Metropolis: Chicago and the Great West*, New York: Norton, 1991

Dangerfield, George, *The Awakening of American Nationalism, 1815–1828*, New York: Harper, 1965

Daniels, Roger, *Coming to America: A History of Immigration and Ethnicity in American Life*, New York: HarperCollins, 1990

Donald, David Herbert, *Lincoln*, New York: Simon and Schuster, and London: Cape, 1995

Doyle, Don Harrison, *The Social Order of a Frontier Community: Jacksonville, Illinois, 1825–70*, Urbana: University of Illinois Press, 1978

Du Bois, W.E.B., *Black Reconstruction: An Essay toward a History of the Part Which Black Folk Played in the Attempt to Reconstruct Democracy in America, 1860–1880*, New York: Harcourt Brace, 1935; as *Black Reconstruction in America*, Cleveland: World, 1964, London: Cass, 1966, reprinted New York: Atheneum, 1992

Dunning, William A., *Reconstruction: Political and Economic, 1865–1877*, New York: Harper, 1907

Edwards, Laura F., *Gendered Strife and Confusion: The Political Culture of Reconstruction*, Urbana: University of Illinois Press, 1997

Elkins, Stanley, *Slavery: A Problem in American Institutional and Intellectual Life*, Chicago: University of Chicago Press, 1959; 3rd edition 1976

Elkins, Stanley, and Eric McKitrick, *The Age of Federalism: The Early American Republic, 1788–1800*, New York: Oxford University Press, 1993

Escott, Paul D., *After Secession: Jefferson Davis and the Failure of Confederate Nationalism*, Baton Rouge: Louisiana State University Press, 1978

Faragher, John Mack, *Sugar Creek: Life on the Illinois Prairie*, New Haven: Yale University Press, 1986

Faust, Drew Gilpin, *The Creation of Confederate Nationalism: Ideology and Identity in the Civil War South*, Baton Rouge: Louisiana State University Press, 1988

Feller, Daniel, *The Jacksonian Promise: America, 1815–1840*, Baltimore: Johns Hopkins University Press, 1995

Fogel, Robert William, and Stanley L. Engerman, *Time on the Cross: The Economics of American Negro Slavery*, 2 vols., Boston: Little Brown, and London: Wildwood, 1974

Fogel, Robert William, *Without Consent or Contract: The Rise and Fall of American Slavery*, New York: Norton, 1989

Foner, Eric, *Free Soil, Free Labor, Free Men: The Ideology of the Republican Party before the Civil War*, New York: Oxford University Press, 1970

Foner, Eric, *Reconstruction: America's Unfinished Revolution, 1863–1877*, New York: Harper, 1988; abridged as *A Short History of Reconstruction*, 1990

Foner, Eric, ed., *The New American History*, Philadelphia: Temple University Press, 1990

Franklin, John Hope, *Reconstruction: After the Civil War*, Chicago: University of Chicago Press, 1961; 2nd edition 1994

Freehling, William W., *The Road to Disunion: Secessionists at Bay, 1776–1854*, New York: Oxford University Press, 1990

Gallagher, Gary W., *The Confederate War*, Cambridge, MA: Harvard University Press, 1997

Genovese, Eugene D., *The Political Economy of Slavery: Studies in the Economy and Society of the Slave South*, New York: Pantheon, 1965; London: MacGibbon and Kee, 1968

Genovese, Eugene D., *Roll, Jordan, Roll: The World the Slaves Made*, New York: Pantheon, 1974; London: Deutsch, 1975

Ginger, Ray, *Age of Excess: The United States from 1877 to 1914*, New York: Macmillan, 1965

Goodwyn, Lawrence, *Democratic Promise: The Populist Moment in America*, New York: Oxford University Press, 1976; abridged as *The Populist Moment: A Short History of the Agrarian Revolt in America*, 1978

Gutman, Herbert G., *The Black Family in Slavery and Freedom, 1750–1925*, New York: Pantheon, and Oxford: Blackwell, 1976

Gutman, Herbert G., *Work, Culture, and Society in Industrializing America: Essays in American Working-Class and Social History*, New York: Knopf, 1976; Oxford: Blackwell, 1977

Hammond, Bray, *Banks and Politics in America, from the Revolution to the Civil War*, Princeton: Princeton University Press, 1957

Harris, William C., *With Charity for All: Lincoln and the Restoration of the Union*, Lexington: University Press of Kentucky, 1997

Hartz, Louis, *The Liberal Tradition in America: An Interpretation of of American Political Thought since the Revolution*, New York: Harcourt Brace, 1955

Hatch, Nathan O., *The Democratization of American Christianity*, New Haven: Yale University Press, 1989

Hays, Samuel P., *The Response to Industrialism, 1885–1914*, Chicago: University of Chicago Press, 1957; 2nd edition 1995

Hicks, John D., *The Populist Revolt: A History of the Farmers' Alliance and the People's Party*, Minneapolis: University of Minnesota Press, 1931

Higham, John, *Strangers in the Land: Patterns of American Nativism, 1860–1925*, New Brunswick, NJ: Rutgers University Press, 1955, corrected reprint 1963; 2nd edition 1988

Hofstadter, Richard, *The American Political Tradition and the Men Who Made It*, New York: Knopf, 1948; London: Cape, 1962

Hofstadter, Richard, *The Age of Reform: From Bryan to FDR*, New York: Knopf, 1955; London: Cape, 1962

Hofstadter, Richard, *The Progressive Historians: Turner, Beard, Parrington*, New York: Knopf, 1968; London: Cape, 1969

Holden Reid, Brian, *The Origins of the American Civil War*, London and New York: Longman, 1996

Holt, Michael F., *The Political Crisis of the 1850s*, New York: Wiley, 1978

Holt, Michael F., *Political Parties and American Political Development: From the Age of Jackson to the Age of Lincoln*, Baton Rouge: Louisiana State University Press, 1992

Howe, Daniel Walker, *The Political Culture of the American Whigs*, Chicago: University of Chicago Press, 1979

Hyman, Harold M., and William M. Wiecek, *Equal Justice under Law: Constitutional Development, 1835–1875*, New York: Harper, 1982

Josephson, Matthew, *The Robber Barons: The Great American Capitalists, 1861–1901*, New York: Harcourt Brace, 1934

Kammen, Michael G., ed., *The Past before Us: Contemporary Historical Writing in the United States*, Ithaca, NY: Cornell University Press, 1980

Keller, Morton, *Affairs of State: Public Life in Late Nineteenth Century America*, Cambridge, MA: Harvard University Press, 1977

Kolchin, Peter, *American Slavery, 1619–1877*, New York: Hill and Wang, 1993; London: Penguin, 1995

Kraus, Michael, and Davis D. Joyce, *The Writing of American History*, revised edition, Norman: University of Oklahoma Press, 1985 [earlier editions, by Kraus only, as *A History of American History*, 1937, and *The Writing of American History*, 1953]

Levine, Bruce, *Half Slave and Half Free: The Roots of Civil War*, New York: Hill and Wang, 1991

Limerick, Patricia Nelson, *The Legacy of Conquest: The Unbroken Past of the American West*, New York: Norton, 1987

Linderman, Gerald F., *Embattled Courage: The Experience of Combat in the American Civil War*, New York: Free Press, and London: Collier Macmillan, 1987

Livesay, Harold C., *Andrew Carnegie and the Rise of Big Business*, Boston: Little Brown, 1975

McCoy, Drew R., *The Elusive Republic: Political Economy in Jeffersonian America*, Chapel Hill: University of North Carolina Press, 1980

McKitrick, Eric, *Andrew Johnson and Reconstruction*, Chicago: University of Chicago Press, 1960

McPherson, James M., *Battle Cry of Freedom: The Civil War Era*, New York and Oxford: Oxford University Press, 1988

McPherson, James M., *For Cause and Comrades: Why Men Fought in the Civil War*, New York: Oxford University Press, 1997

Meier, August, and Elliott M. Rudwick, *Black History and the Historical Profession, 1915–1980*, Urbana: University of Illinois Press, 1986

Meinig, D.W., *The Shaping of America: A Geographical Perspective on 500 Years of History*, vol. 2: *Continental America, 1800–1867*, New Haven and London: Yale University Press, 1993

Mitchell, Reid, *Civil War Soldiers: Their Expectations and Their Experiences*, New York: Viking, 1988

Montgomery, David, *The Fall of the House of Labor: The Workplace, the State, and American Labor Activism, 1865–1925*, Cambridge and New York: Cambridge University Press, 1987

Moody, J. Carroll, and Alice Kessler-Harris, eds., *Perspectives on American Labor History: The Problems of Synthesis*, DeKalb: Northern Illinois University Press, 1989

Morrison, Michael A., *Slavery and the American West: The Eclipse of Manifest Destiny and the Coming of the Civil War*, Chapel Hill: University of North Carolina Press, 1997

Nevins, Allan, *The Ordeal of the Union*, 8 vols.: vols. 1–2, *The Ordeal of the Union*; vols. 3–4, *The Emergence of Lincoln*; vols. 5–8, *The War for the Union*, New York: Scribner, 1947–71; reprinted 4 vols., New York: Maxwell Macmillan, 1992

Novick, Peter, *That Noble Dream: The "Objectivity Question" and the American Historical Profession*, Cambridge and New York: Cambridge University Press, 1988

Oakes, James, *The Ruling Race: A History of American Slaveholders*, New York: Knopf, 1982

Painter, Nell Irvin, *Standing at Armageddon: The United States, 1877–1919*, New York: Norton, 1987

Paludan, Phillip Shaw, *"A People's Contest": The Union and the Civil War, 1861–1865* New York: Harper, 1988

Paludan, Phillip Shaw, *The Presidency of Abraham Lincoln*, Lawrence: University Press of Kansas, 1994

Parish, Peter J., *Slavery: History and Historians*, New York: Harper, 1989

Parrington, Vernon Louis, *Main Currents in American Thought: An Interpretation of American Literature from the Beginnings to 1920*, 3 vols., New York: Harcourt Brace, 1927–30

Perman, Michael, *The Road to Redemption: Southern Politics, 1869–1879*, Chapel Hill: University of North Carolina Press, 1984

Pessen, Edward, *Riches, Class, and Power before the Civil War*, Lexington, MA: Heath, 1973

Phillips, Ulrich Bonnell, *American Negro Slavery: A Survey of the Supply, Employment, and Control of Negro Labor as Determined by the Plantation Regime*, New York: Appleton, 1918; reprinted Baton Rouge: Louisiana State University Press, 1966

Potter, David M., *The Impending Crisis, 1848–1861*, completed by Don E. Fehrenbacher, New York: Harper, 1976

Pressly, Thomas J., *Americans Interpret Their Civil War*, Princeton: Princeton University Press, 1954

Prude, Jonathan, *The Coming of Industrial Order: Town and Factory Life in Rural Massachusetts, 1810–1860*, Cambridge and New York: Cambridge University Press, 1983

Rabinowitz, Howard N., *Race Relations in the Urban South, 1865–1890*, New York: Oxford University Press, 1978

Rable, George C., *The Confederate Republic: A Revolution Against Politics*, Chapel Hill: University of North Carolina Press, 1994

Randall, James G., and David Herbert Donald, *The Civil War and Reconstruction*, Boston: Heath, 1961, revised 1969 [original edition, by Randall only, 1937]

Rhodes, James Ford, *History of the United States from the Compromise of 1850*, 7 vols., New York: Harper, 1893–1906

Roediger, David R., *Towards the Abolition of Whiteness: Essays on Race, Politics and Working Class History*, London and New York: Verso, 1994

Ryan, Mary P., *Civic Wars: Democracy and Public Life in the American City during the Nineteenth Century*, Berkeley: University of California Press, 1997

Schlesinger, Arthur M., Jr., *The Age of Jackson*, Boston: Little Brown, 1945; London: Eyre and Spottiswoode, 1946

Sellers, Charles, *The Market Revolution: Jacksonian America, 1815–1846*, New York: Oxford University Press, 1991

Sharp, James Roger, *American Politics in the Early Republic: The New Nation in Crisis*, New Haven: Yale University Press, 1993

Skowronek, Stephen, *Building a New American State: The Expansion of National Administrative Capacities, 1877–1920*, Cambridge and New York: Cambridge University Press, 1982

Stampp, Kenneth M., *The Peculiar Institution: Slavery in the Ante-Bellum South*, New York: Knopf, 1956; London: Eyre and Spottiswoode, 1964

Stampp, Kenneth M., *The Era of Reconstruction, 1865–1877*, New York: Knopf, and London: Eyre and Spottiswoode, 1965

Stansell, Christine, *City of Women: Sex and Class in New York, 1789–1860*, New York: Knopf, 1986

Taylor, George Rogers, *The Transportation Revolution, 1815–1860*, New York: Holt Rinehart, 1951

Teaford, Jon C., *The Unheralded Triumph: City Government in America, 1870–1900*, Baltimore: Johns Hopkins University Press, 1984

Thernstrom, Stephan, *The Other Bostonians: Poverty and Progress in the American Metropolis, 1880–1970*, Cambridge, MA: Harvard University Press, 1973

Thernstrom, Stephan, ed., *Harvard Encyclopedia of American Ethnic Groups*, Cambridge, MA: Harvard University Press, 1980

Thomas, Emory M., *The Confederacy as a Revolutionary Experience*, Englewood Cliffs, NJ: Prentice Hall, 1971

Thomas, Emory M., *The Confederate Nation, 1861–1865*, New York: Harper, 1979

Trefousse, Hans L., *The Radical Republicans: Lincoln's Vanguard for Racial Justice*, New York: Knopf, 1968

Trefousse, Hans L., *Andrew Johnson: A Biography*, New York: Norton, 1989

Turner, Frederick Jackson, *The Frontier in American History*, New York: Holt, 1920

Waldstreicher, David, *In the Midst of Perpetual Fetes: The Making of American Nationalism, 1776–1820*, Chapel Hill: University of North Carolina Press, 1997

Warner, Sam Bass, *The Urban Wilderness: A History of the American City*, New York: Harper, 1972

Watson, Harry L., *Liberty and Power: The Politics of Jacksonian America*, New York: Hill and Wang, 1990

Way, Peter, *Common Labor: Workers and the Digging of North American Canals, 1780–1860*, Cambridge and New York: Cambridge University Press, 1993

Webb, Walter Prescott, *The Great Plains*, Boston: Ginn, 1931

White, Richard, *"It's Your Misfortune and None of My Own": A New History of the American West*, Norman: University of Oklahoma Press, 1991

Wiebe, Robert H., *The Search for Order, 1877–1920*, New York: Hill and Wang, and London: Macmillan, 1967

Wiebe, Robert H., *The Opening of American Society: From the Adoption of the Constitution to the Eve of Disunion*, New York: Knopf, 1984

Wilentz, Sean, *Chants Democratic: New York City and the Rise of the American Working Class, 1788–1850*, New York: Oxford University Press, 1984

Williamson, Joel, *The Crucible of Race: Black–White Relations in the American South since Emancipation*, New York: Oxford University Press, 1984; abridged as *A Rage for Order*, 1986

Wood, Gordon S., *The Radicalism of the American Revolution*, New York: Knopf, 1992

Woodward, C. Vann, *Origins of the New South, 1877–1913*, Baton Rouge: Louisiana State University Press, 1951; updated by Charles B. Dew, 1971

Woodward, C. Vann, *The Strange Career of Jim Crow*, New York: Oxford University Press, 1955; 3rd edition 1974

Wright, Gavin, *The Political Economy of the Cotton South: Households, Markets, and Wealth in the Nineteenth Century*, New York: Norton, 1978

United States: 20th Century

The historiography of the 20th-century United States has been enormously varied, but overall one characteristic has remained constant: the degree to which the recent past has been viewed through the prism of the present, reflecting the contemporary concerns and biases of historians and society in general. To a considerable extent this is a trait common to all US historiography, but the obvious temporal proximity of the 20th century and the involvement of historians in the affairs of their own time have tended to mean that the historiography of this period is more clearly informed by the preoccupations and fashions prevailing when a given work was written and published. As a rule, the further away in time that historians were from the period of which they were writing, the greater their detachment, but, even at the distance of several decades, works on the 20th-century US have tended to mirror essentially contemporary concerns. One can trace this pattern in the historiography on liberal reform periods, including progressivism, the New Deal, and the 1960s; on African Americans, women, and ethnic minorities; and perhaps most of all in studies of US diplomacy. These changing approaches to the history of the 20th-century US suggest that there is at least a modicum of truth in the hotly contested arguments of deconstructionist and poststructuralist theoreticians such as Michel Foucault, that those subjects that historians choose to study and the manner in which they do so reflect both their own biases and priorities, and those of contemporary society.

Progressivism, the multifarious liberal reformist movement of the late 19th and early 20th centuries, offers the most long-term example of the evolving interpretation of a particular issue. Initially, fundamentally sympathetic historians such as Benjamin Parke De Witt and Harold U. Faulkner presented a rather simplistic picture of enlightened and virtuous reformers battling against entrenched special interests, especially big business. In doing so, they relied heavily on the writings, memoirs, and personal recollections of the period's most articulate participants, who tended to be liberal political activists, social workers, and journalists, essentially middle- or upper-class reformers. By the mid-1950s a more nuanced picture began to emerge. Richard Hofstadter's *The Age of Reform* (1955), which embodied many of the views and concerns of the consensus school of American history, presented progressivism as an essentially backward-looking movement that wished to restore the outdated values of a small-scale society. He drew attention to the limited commitment to reform of many of the period's middle-class activists, their desire to reaffirm their own social status by reining in the super-wealthy and big business, and their lack of sympathy for the immigrant urban working class, characteristics that he contrasted with those of the supposedly far more class-based New Deal. Hofstadter's seminal work inaugurated a broad range of studies that would bring about a greater appreciation of the complexity of progressivism. While Hofstadter still focused on educated, middle-class professionals, John D. Buenker and J. Joseph Huthmacher among others concentrated on the significant input of urban political elements, including the immigrant machines, labor unions, and the working class, whose views and activities were less well represented in the written record and had previously been ignored, yet whose support and votes underpinned most successful progressive legislation. Robert H. Wiebe, James Weinstein, and Gabriel Kolko demonstrated that business interests, whether large or small, were far from united in opposition to reform and that they tended to favor measures that they believed would be advantageous to themselves or, conversely, detrimental to their competitors. Kolko and Weinstein, leading exemplars of the New Left, went so far as to suggest that virtually all progressive measures were the product of a corporate strategy designed to protect the status quo and to pre-empt radical social change by making limited and modest concessions, a strategy that owed more to the demands of big business for order, stability, and social regimentation than to genuine altruism. While less overtly conspiratorial in interpretation, others such as Wiebe, John Whiteclay Chambers II, Samuel P. Hays, Martin J. Sklar, and Alan Trachtenberg, perceived progressive measures as part of a broader "search for order" and rationalization that was almost inevitable in a mass urban, industrial society, one with parallels in other industrializing countries. They also drew attention to the elitist outlook of many reformers, their concern for efficiency, their respect for specialized expertise and their disregard of the views of ordinary Americans, themes popular in the anti-elitist 1960s. Numerous studies of progressivism in particular states and cities, for example, those of Carl H. Chrislock on Minnesota and David P. Thelen on Wisconsin, attempted to draw general conclusions as to the nature of progressivism, but in practice were most successful in illuminating the movement's differing rural and urban characteristics. Important variations in the regional experience of the South in particular, and of the western and northeastern sections, began to emerge. From the 1960s onward historians increasingly undertook studies of the role in progressivism of women, particular ethnic groups, and African Americans, both as actors and as objects to whom politicians responded, a reflection of the new importance of feminist, racial, and ethnic themes. Nell Irvin Painter's 1987 synthesis *Standing at Armageddon* gave particular weight to the factors of race, class, and gender, and stressed the contributions of the disadvantaged, including farmers and industrial workers, as well as women, African Americans, and minorities. She showed that their demands for change galvanized an alarmed middle class to take reformist action.

The treatment of such sociopolitical issues as prohibition can serve as a case study of the evolving historiography on progressivism. Temperance supporters, whom sophisticated intellectuals such as Hofstadter initially ridiculed for their alleged anti-urban and anti-immigrant mentality, were perceived to have varied backgrounds and motives. James H. Timberlake and K. Austin Kerr presented prohibition as part of the broader progressive concern for rationalization and social efficiency, which would be enhanced by the eradication of alcohol. While these scholars tended to emphasize the nostalgia and anti-industrial outlook of some temperance advocates, others, such as Jack S. Blocker, Jr., demonstrated the support for prohibition by some wealthy industrialists, as likely to provide them with better-disciplined and more reliable workers. In a less pejorative vein than Hofstadter, Joseph H. Gusfield elucidated the symbolic functions, especially the attempt to recapture an idealized and more manageable past, that the advocacy of temperance served for its supporters. Pointing to the central role of women in the temperance movement, Kenneth D. Rose showed that prohibition not only provided them with the opportunity to demand that society as a whole conform to their personal values and high standards of behavior, but also gave them the opportunity to participate in a form of political activism that, if presented as the natural outcome of their concern to protect their families, could be reconciled with and even depicted as fundamental to their role as wives and mothers. As Blocker's synthesis revealed, prohibition was a movement in which many different and sometimes mutually conflicting groups played a part and which fulfilled a variety of functions for its supporters. In this sense it is a miniature of the progressive period, the overall historiography of which now offers a far more complex picture, in which liberal reformist elements were only one among many participating in a multifaceted social, political, and economic adjustment to the new demands of a large-scale industrial and urban nation.

The voluminous historiography of the New Deal has tended to replicate this pattern. This period, which Carl N. Degler termed "the third American revolution," can plausibly claim to be the time when the US government and political economy assumed the shape it still bears today, and, although the 1930s have attracted even more historical attention than the progressive period, it was in the latter that at least some of its new intellectual and political antecedents undoubtedly lay. Initial assessments of the New Deal, pre-eminent among them being Arthur M. Schlesinger's 3-volume *Age of Roosevelt* (1957–60) and Frank Freidel's unfinished multivolume biography of Roosevelt, tended to be highly favorable, reflecting the liberal reformist post-World War II consensus to which many historians subscribed. The period was depicted as one of major accomplishments in the direction of social justice, masterminded by Franklin D. Roosevelt, who presided benevolently over a broker state, a welfare state that catered to all the varied large-scale competing interest groups of a modern pluralist society. James MacGregor Burns' biography, though also fundamentally friendly to Roosevelt, criticized him for providing insufficiently liberal leadership in the mid-1930s and for an inadequate commitment to Keynesian economic policies, which might have mitigated the impact of the Great Depression. The rise of the New Left in the 1960s brought far fiercer criticism of the New Deal, as the radical revisionists Barton J. Bernstein, Thomas Ferguson, Ronald Radosh, Harvard Sitkoff, and others, in many ways the heirs of Charles A. Beard and other progressive historians of the first half of the century, condemned what they regarded as its failures and its betrayal of the socially disadvantaged. They argued that the major New Deal measures were limited in scope and accomplishment, and that they failed to implement a radical redistribution of wealth or deep-rooted social change. Pointing to the role of various business interests in the development of such programs as Social Security, they suggested that New Deal policies represented a conscious and essentially conservative attempt to stave off revolution and radical social change at the cost of minor and often cosmetic concessions. From this time onward, New Deal historiography, while rarely accepting the New Left analysis *in toto*, tended to incorporate some of its insights and to demonstrate a greater appreciation of the period's complexity and the limits as well as the accomplishments of the New Deal. From a more sympathetic perspective than that of the New Left, one that emphasized the political constraints on Roosevelt, James T. Patterson also drew attention to the New Deal's limited accomplishments, but he ascribed them to conservative congressional opposition to more radical reform, an opposition that drew its strength in part from the very nature of the existing American political system. Kenneth Finegold and Theda Skocpol, discussing the evolution of social security policy, likewise suggested that the exclusion of domestic servants and agricultural workers from coverage by the Social Security Act of 1935 was dictated by the need to secure the political support of conservative southern Democrats, who would have rejected legislation extending its benefits to categories that included substantial numbers of African Americans. Ellis W. Hawley focused upon the inconsistencies of New Deal policies toward big business and their possible consequent ineffectiveness, while Colin Gordon, Kim McQuaid, and Stanley N. Vittoz demonstrated the role that business interests played in policymaking. From the early 1970s onward the growing strength of conservatism in the US also led to attacks on New Deal policies, but for attempting too much rather than too little, a break with the liberal consensus of approval for the welfare state and 20th-century reform efforts that until then had generally informed the views of most American historians. Anna Jacobson Schwartz, Murray N. Rothbard, Milton Friedman, for example, suggested that the handling of the money supply by the Federal Reserve Board and the passage of banking and securities legislation in the 1930s acted as a brake on economic recovery. More recently, and by contrast, Michael A. Bernstein held that the failure wholeheartedly to embrace national economic planning was responsible for the New Deal's limited success in bringing about recovery. Gary Dean Best, however, investigated the reasons underlying business criticism of New Deal policies, and suggested that the program's inability to win business confidence represented a major weakness. Even historians sympathetic to the New Deal, such as Albert U. Romasco, pointed out the many economic inconsistencies in its program, though they tended to suggest that in practice these had much to do with its political success.

John M. Allswang produced the best documented study of the New Deal's political effects on the US. Relying heavily on massive quantitative data, he demonstrated its role in the creation of the Democratic electoral coalition that would dominate the mid-third of the 20th century. As with progressivism, municipal, state, and regional studies and monographs concentrating on the role of African Americans, ethnic groups, labor, women, bureaucratic and administrative imperatives, and specific government agencies also began to proliferate. Patterson investigated the overall relationship between the federal government and the states that were responsible for administering

and even formulating many of the New Deal programs. A pioneering work by Jordan A. Schwarz demonstrated the degree to which New Deal policies precipitated and funded the economic development of the South and West, bringing these regions into the national mainstream. Douglas L. Smith explored the extent to which the New Deal transformed the South and the degree to which southern politicians and interests were still able to retain control and use federal largesse to promote their own agenda. Whereas earlier 1-volume surveys, such as those of William Leuchtenburg and Paul Conkin, tended to concentrate primarily on politics and economics, recent syntheses, notably that of Anthony Badger, gave more prominence to labor, farmers, race, class, and gender, concluding that, despite its undoubted weaknesses, the New Deal often enabled disadvantaged groups to survive the Great Depression. Similar conclusions underlay Nancy Weiss' study of blacks and the New Deal, Irving Bernstein's survey of labor, and the works of Theodore Saloutos and James N. Gregory on American farmers and agricultural migrants. Lizabeth Cohen's study of both black and white Chicago industrial workers put New Deal policies in the broader context of urban working-class culture and experience from 1919 onward. While the New Deal did little specifically to assist women, Susan Ware depicted the manner in which it furthered the development of an influential female network in Washington, one that played an important part in developing New Deal policies. Eleanor Roosevelt, the most prominent member of this group, has recently received particular attention from historians such as Doris Kearns Goodwin, Joan Hoff-Wilson and Marjorie Lightman, and Blanche Wiesen Cook, as she developed into a feminist icon whom Hillary Rodham Clinton would regard as a role model. As with progressivism, New Deal historiography has evolved from a somewhat simplistic Manichaean taxonomy of virtuous reformers battling against entrenched interests to an exceedingly complicated picture that draws on almost every variety of historical specialization to demonstrate the breadth and complexity of the forces at work in the US of the 1930s.

It has come to be seen as almost inevitable that within a few decades the reputations of particular presidents should be subjected first to revisionist scrutiny, reversing the initial historical judgment upon them, and then to some form of postrevisionism. Franklin D. Roosevelt has to some extent escaped this fate, perhaps because, as William E. Leuchtenburg has demonstrated, he bestrides 20th-century US history like a colossus, the only president to serve four terms and the one under whose leadership the country took the decisive moves to develop a large-scale activist federal government and to assume a major role in world affairs. While some recent historians, notably Frederick Marks, have vehemently questioned his diplomatic abilities, on the whole Roosevelt's pre-eminent stature has remained unchallenged even by those who have deprecated his policies. Most other presidents have been less fortunate; those whose reputations have undergone often dramatic changes include Theodore Roosevelt, Woodrow Wilson, Harry S. Truman, Dwight D. Eisenhower, John F. Kennedy, Lyndon B. Johnson, Richard Nixon, and Jimmy Carter. Beginning with Howard K. Beale's 1954 study of his foreign policies and John M. Blum's assessment of his presidency, from the 1950s onward Theodore Roosevelt, once regarded as a somewhat comic buffoon, regained the respect of historians as a tough and realistic statesman, the first modern president, whose policies represented a conscious effort to enable his country to face the domestic and foreign challenges of the 20th century. The reputation of his rival Woodrow Wilson, derided or pitied as a failure when he left office, underwent a similar metamorphosis. The results of World War II gave Wilson's international policies new credibility, and historians such as Thomas A. Bailey now presented him as a prescient statesman, disregard of whose advice had brought on the war. After the war the prodigious work of Arthur S. Link, the president's biographer and editor of 69 volumes of his papers, transformed his historical image. Link revealed Wilson to have been a shrewd and even ruthless politician, one of the remarkably few 20th-century presidents successfully to push through Congress a major reform program, and a visionary but shrewd international statesman whose policies represented one major strand of American internationalist thought. A dual biography by John Milton Cooper, Jr., gave an enlightening picture of the many resemblances of Roosevelt and Wilson, as well as their crucial differences, while numerous works by, among others, Edmund Morris, David McCullough, Marks, and H.W. Brands on Roosevelt, and Link himself, Lloyd Ambrosius, J.W. Schulte Nordholt, and Kendrick A. Clements on Wilson, testified to their new status as important historical figures. Once his papers were open to research, the more uninspiring Herbert Hoover was revealed as decidedly less conservative than his popular image, an exemplar, according to Joan Hoff-Wilson, Martin Fausold, and others, not only of progressivism's business wing and the period's search for order, efficiency, and rationalization, but even, in Hoff-Wilson's New Left-inspired outlook, of a highly desirable restraint in foreign affairs and of prescient fears of the growth of dangerous government interventionism in the US.

Truman's stock began to rise with the publication in the 1970s of Merle Miller's oral reminiscence *Plain Speaking* (1974). In the subsequent scandal-riddled decades of carefully packaged and marketed politicians, the man once thought to be a political hack and an accidental president who failed to measure up to his predecessor assumed near-iconic popular status as, in Dean Acheson's words, "a great little man" who met great international challenges and rose to them while remaining personally modest, unassuming and, most of all, himself. This view was enshrined in the enormous bestselling biographies by McCullough and Alonzo L. Hamby, which, while not uncritical, presented a generally favorable picture of a liberal, reformist Truman, giving special praise to his Cold War policies, which were portrayed as farsighted, wise, and prudent, while blaming his failures primarily on domestic political constraints and the rise of McCarthyism. Eisenhower's standing in the presidential stakes likewise improved, as Fred I. Greenstein and Stephen E. Ambrose presented him as an engaged and able chief executive, who deliberately preferred to exercise leadership indirectly and who eschewed unwise foreign adventures, qualities that won new admiration after America's divisive involvement in Vietnam. Extremes characterized historical writing on John F. Kennedy. The unqualified adulation that followed his untimely death, exemplified in admiring works by such aides as Arthur M. Schlesinger and Theodore Sorensen, was soon tempered by more sobering assessments of his presidency. Often these were written by

disillusioned liberals and former admirers, whose personal bitterness only made their criticisms more acerbic. Critics such as Thomas G. Paterson and others of a New Left pedigree questioned every aspect of JFK's image, highlighting his somewhat conservative political outlook and minimal commitment to reform, often inflated foreign policy rhetoric, and reckless international behavior, while more scandalous accounts such as those of Nigel Hamilton and Seymour Hersh focused on Kennedy's indisputable personal flaws, his womanizing, health problems, plagiarism, manipulation of the press, and cynical readiness to conceal the truth. Over time a more balanced approach began to prevail, exemplified in the recent biography by Hugh Brogan. Tapes of the Cuban missile crisis revealed that Kennedy had been considerably more cautious than critics alleged, while historians such as William H. Chafe and Carl M. Brauer gave him credit for his domestic attainments in such areas as civil rights and for his ability to inspire Americans to try to accomplish idealistic objectives. Even so, it seems unlikely that the passionate responses Kennedy provoked will fade until all those who either idolized or lost faith in him are themselves dead. It was symptomatic of his relentless hold on the American imagination that in 1988, 25 years after his death, Thomas Brown published a monograph on the evolution of his historical image.

Despite the bitter divisiveness caused by the Vietnam War, Lyndon B. Johnson stirred fewer emotions. Robert A. Caro's ferociously one-sided condemnation of him as a totally corrupt and almost worthless politician was countered by more rounded portraits by Irving Bernstein and Robert Dallek, who presented an undeniably flawed but able and genuinely idealistic president whose tragedy was that his vision exceeded the grasp even of his gigantic political skills, and whose domestic policies were stymied not only by the Vietnam War but also by his own reluctance to make the American people pay the necessary taxes to support them. Richard Nixon, once hated by American liberals as the apotheosis of McCarthyite evil, has won historians' respect for his undoubted political abilities. He is increasingly viewed as a complex and even tragic character whose personal failings undercut and destroyed him, despite his substantial domestic and international achievements. Stanley I. Kutler and Fred Emery concentrated on his role in the Watergate scandal and the manner in which it diminished all political trust in the US, contributing to the prevailing disillusionment of the 1970s. By contrast, Ambrose and Hoff both admired Nixon's domestic achievements in creating a centrist Republican coalition and pre-empting many formerly Democratic positions. Although many had reservations as to Nixon's Vietnam and Cambodian policies, his foreign policy skills won him wide public and international admiration before and after his disgrace, and praise from his biographers, including Ambrose, Roger Morris, and Tom Wicker. A more critical appraisal was William Bundy's *A Tangled Web* (1998), and the final verdict must clearly await the opening of Nixon's own papers and those of such close associates as Henry A. Kissinger. As with Nixon, the reassessment of Jimmy Carter's record owed much to a sustained campaign by a rejected president to rehabilitate himself publicly by amassing a record of commendable international activity and expertise and, at least in Carter's case, good works. New biographical studies by Peter G. Bourne, Douglas Brinkley, and Kenneth Earl Morris and the work of Irwin C. Hargrove and Burton I. Kaufman on his presidency undoubtedly offer a more favorable and almost certainly more balanced picture of this once derided president than that current immediately after he left office, but as with other recent incumbents, it will probably be several more decades before anything approaching a final historical verdict can be rendered.

The same is true of the most recent reform movements in the US, essentially those of the 1960s, which have so far attracted relatively little in-depth study and have given rise to a less complex, rich, and extensive historiography than their predecessors. Many Americans' memory of the time is still green, archives often remain closed, and serious scholarly accounts, such as those of John M. Blum and Allen Matusow, began to appear only in the mid-1980s, while many participants, such as Robert McNamara and David Halberstam, are still producing first-hand accounts of the period. Since the 1970s conservatives such as Gertrude Himmelfarb have tended to cite the period's social upheavals and the shortcomings and limited achievements of Johnson's Great Society reforms in support of their arguments that such activist state social policies are inherently flawed and that the government should reduce its intervention in society and the economy. Americans remain deeply divided in their assessment of the 1960s: while conservatives regard the decade as the fount of all the evils – family breakdown, drugs, declining educational standards, disrespect for moral values, and the absence of social order – that in their view characterize the US today, others look back to those years nostalgically as an optimistic era of social change, when women and blacks began to achieve greater equality and all ideals seemed possible of fulfillment. One effect of the political shift to the right in the US since 1970 has also been an increasing number of serious historical studies of aspects of American conservatism, both the far right and mainstream conservatism, as exemplified in the works of William C. Berman, Dan T. Carter, and Walter H. Capps. These provided a counterpoint to the prevailing mid-century liberal consensus whose assumptions had previously tended to dominate not only American politics but historical writing on and of the time, a tradition and outlook whose changing fortunes were traced by Alonzo L. Hamby.

As with domestic affairs, fierce debates characterized the historiography of 20th-century American diplomacy and the expanded international role of the US. In the 1920s and even more the 1930s, revisionist historians such as Harry Elmer Barnes attacked American intervention in World War I as a mistake, which, they often implied, their country would be most unwise to repeat in the event of another European conflict. During World War II and the succeeding Cold War most historians rallied round and endorsed the policies of the official leadership. Even though they sometimes criticized particular episodes or tactics, such exemplars of the prevailing Realist school of diplomatic history as Hans J. Morgenthau and Norman A. Graebner generally endorsed the broad thrust of "internationalist" US foreign policies in the 1940s and 1950s and reserved their real condemnation for the "isolationist" 1920s and 1930s. From the late 1950s, however, the influential Wisconsin school of New Left radical revisionist historians led by William Appleman Williams – a group whose impact would soon be greatly magnified by the polarizing and fragmenting

effect of the Vietnam War on all aspects of American intellectual life – began to assail the country's diplomatic past. Heirs to the Beardian dissenting tradition, the New Left charged that, since the late 18th century US diplomacy had been motivated not by idealism, democratic values, or concern for other nations, but by the desire of American big-business interests to find and exploit overseas export markets, sources of raw materials, and foreign investment opportunities, objectives for which official enunciations of more altruistic or benevolent goals merely provided a convenient smokescreen. Heated debates ensued between the New Left and more orthodox historians, disputes often further envenomed by personal dislikes and by fervent differences of opinion over the rights and wrongs of American intervention in Vietnam. As late as the 1990s remnants of this bitterness were much in evidence in the reception given to Robert McNamara's memoir *In Retrospect* (1995), only one example of continuing fierce historiographical and political debate over the feasibility and morality of American policies in Vietnam. Such lingering resentments still infected criticisms by such radical historians as Bruce Cumings of the new National Security school of American diplomatic history, in many respects a more sophisticated restatement of the Realist position. Its exponents, including John Lewis Gaddis and Melvyn P. Leffler, argued that the protection of American strategic interests justified and indeed demanded American intervention in both world wars and involvement in the Cold War, albeit with caveats as to the wisdom of American policies in Vietnam and other peripheral areas. Insights derived from the newly available Soviet and other former communist-bloc sources led at least some historians to argue that US Cold War policies were entirely justified and to ascribe to Stalin principal responsibility for the development of Soviet–American antagonism. By the mid-1990s the National Security approach dominated the field, yet various New Left insights had also been incorporated into the prevailing interpretation, particularly the Corporatist approach to interwar and post-World War II diplomacy exemplified in the works of Leffler and Michael J. Hogan, which stressed the significant contribution of large transnational business on such matters as the economic diplomacy of the 1920s and the evolution of the Marshall Plan. Meanwhile leading radical revisionist historians, Lloyd Gardner, for example, or Walter LaFeber (whose book *The Clash* won the Bancroft Prize for 1997), had become respected pillars of their profession.

By the late 1980s debates over the history of American foreign policy found new foci. Michael Hunt and the British scholar Christopher Thorne even more condemned the propensity of many American diplomatic historians to write international history from an Americo-centric viewpoint, using largely American sources and assuming that Americans had controlled all the important decisions, an outlook that, they argued, magnified the significance of their own country at the expense of the contributions of other states and their nationals. The pervasive rhetoric of globalization and ease of international communication and interchange in the late 20th century perhaps also had some effect in encouraging comparative history. American intellectual and politico-economic historians, such as James Kloppenberg and Martin J. Sklar for the progressive period, began to question their country's claims to exceptionalism and to explore possible parallels and comparisons between its 20th-century experience and that of other nations, while Gaddis followed in the footsteps of the New Left by suggesting that the 20th-century US had acquired an empire that, however distinctive, should be viewed against the broad context of the imperial ventures of other nations. Paul M. Kennedy's bestselling *The Rise and Fall of the Great Powers* (1987) placed the international predominance of the US in the broad context of five centuries of changing world hegemons, suggesting that ultimately economic weaknesses would force the country to relinquish much of its global supremacy. The relationship between war and domestic reform attracted attention. Whereas Hofstadter's *The Age of Reform* famously argued that "war has always been the nemesis of reform," several historians, among them David M. Kennedy and Ronald Schaffer for World War I and Richard Polenberg and Alan Brinkley for World War II, demonstrated the effects of war in promoting greater social equity and reform and enhancing the role of government. J.A. Thompson brought out the often ambiguous attitudes of progressive intellectuals and reformers to World War I and its potential for domestic and international change, while Michael S. Sherry focused more broadly on the domestic impact from the 1930s onward both of the experience of war and the possibility of war. American diplomatic historians also now devoted much of their energies to the vexed questions of the role of such categories as gender, ethnicity, ideology, and material culture in their own sub-field.

The pervasive anti-elitism of the 1960s and the growing social, political, and economic status of women, blacks, and ethnic minorities brought demands that historians give less attention to the study of elites and traditional political and diplomatic questions and more to social history in general, to the dispossessed or those of low social standing, to questions of gender, race, and ethnicity, and to non-traditional and non-written sources. Such studies often brought out aspects of history once ignored, presenting familiar events from a new, fresh, and illuminating perspective, but they sometimes tended to be monographic, to stand in isolation from the broader historical narrative, and on occasion perhaps to exaggerate the overall influence and significance of their subjects. By the late 1990s each specialization had produced a substantial and varied body of work, which historians of any period or aspect of 20th-century US history could no longer disregard or discount. Women's history was just one example of the prevailing trends in social history. Such textbooks and readers as Teresa Amott and Julie Matthaei's *Race, Gender, and Work* (1991) or Ellen Carol DuBois and Vicki L. Ruiz's *Unequal Sisters* (1990) synthesized much of the previous two or three decades' scholarship and approaches in social history as a whole, as did broad histories of 20th-century American women, such as that of William H. Chafe. As shown above, the participation of women in such political coalitions as progressivism and the New Deal and the benefits that they obtained from these movements attracted new attention. As was to be expected, from the late 1960s there appeared numerous studies of the suffrage movement, those of Eleanor Flexner and Ellen Fitzpatrick, Aileen Kraditor, and William L. O'Neill, for example, and the feminist movement itself generated an even larger literature, among others works by Flora Davis, Sara M. Evans, and Cynthia Harrison. Marjorie Spruill Wheeler focused on the southern suffrage movement, revealing its intimate interconnection with issues of race, civil rights, and

reform. Significantly, women were often perceived not simply as battling for their rights, but also in the social context of their attainment of skills and knowledge or their working experience, all aspects of life that at least to some degree crossed gender lines, in the sense that education and work were important common denominators in the careers of men and women alike. Barbara Miller Solomon's account of the history of American women's education described the interplay between women and those institutions that assisted in their empowerment and which they themselves in turn helped to mold. The interrelationships between women, whether black or white, the work they did, and their community and political roles and self-perception were the subject of studies by Barbara Hilker Andolsen, Susan Porter Benson, Jacqueline Jones, and Alice Kessler-Harris. Numerous historians, of whose works *Unequal Sisters* provides merely a sampling, described the lives and activities of black, ethnic, and immigrant women and the sometimes complicated interrelationships between gender, class, and race or ethnicity. Should anyone be tempted to discount the significance of such conservative women as Phyllis Schlafly, the volumes by Elinor Burkett, Glen Jeansonne, and Rebecca E. Klatch, which concentrated on the role of women in right-wing movements, serve as a salutary corrective to the sometimes romanticized 1980s and 1990s portrayal of women as naturally socialist, pro-labor, anti-racist, and generally liberal in outlook. Far from being exceptional, the richness and multi-facetedness of 20th-century women's history and its contributions to every aspect of US history typified virtually all the newer fields of social history, which in turn contributed to the regeneration of more traditional political, institutional, and diplomatic history.

US history remains in an untidy but stimulating state of flux, with scholars, politicians, and the general public engaged in fierce debate as to the relative weighting deserved by traditional diplomatic and political history, as opposed to the newer social history focusing on ethnic, racial, and feminist concerns. In the late 20th century the role of history as a means by which the US defined itself and its priorities won the discipline much popular and media attention, not all of it favorable. Public history, for example a 1995 Smithsonian Institution exhibit marking the 50th anniversary of Hiroshima, could easily become controversial – politicians, the general public, and some historians condemned the accompanying text as insufficiently pro-American and pro-bomb and far too sympathetic to the Japanese position. In the 1990s attempts to arrive at a generally accepted broad narrative of the American past proved fraught, as conservatives assailed a proposed national history curriculum for devoting too much space to blacks, ethnic Americans, minorities, and women, and to unflattering aspects of the American historical experience. This debate was paralleled by lengthy disputes as to precisely which works deserved inclusion in the "Western canon" of significant literary classics. Such episodes reflected the manner in which, to a degree unprecedented in other countries, Americans have used versions of their past history and perhaps especially that of the 20th century to state, affirm, and reinforce those contemporary values that they hope or believe should characterize their existing polity. While prophecy is always dangerous, it seems safe to predict that, while emphases may change, for the foreseeable future the history of the 20th-century US will continue to reflect and embody the priorities and preoccupations of the times in which it is written.

PRISCILLA M. ROBERTS

See also African American; Ambrose; Degler; Foner, P.; Kessler-Harris; Kolko; LaFeber; Leuchtenburg; Link; Williams, W.

Further Reading

Allswang, John M., *The New Deal and American Politics: A Study in Political Change*, New York: Wiley, 1978

Ambrose, Stephen E., *Eisenhower*, 2 vols., New York: Simon and Schuster, 1983–84; London: Allen and Unwin, 1984

Ambrose, Stephen E., *Nixon*, 3 vols., New York: Simon and Schuster, 1987–91

Ambrosius, Lloyd E., *Woodrow Wilson and the American Diplomatic Tradition: The Treaty Fight in Perspective*, Cambridge and New York: Cambridge University Press, 1987

American Historical Review 94 (June 1989) [entire issue]

Amott, Teresa L., and Julie Matthaei, eds., *Race, Gender, and Work: A Multicultural Economic History of Women in the United States*, Boston: South End Press, 1991

Andolsen, Barbara Hilker, *Good Work at the Video Display Terminal: A Feminist Ethical Analysis of Changes in Clerical Work*, Knoxville: University of Tennessee Press, 1989

Appleby, Joyce, Lynn Hunt, and Margaret Jacob, *Telling the Truth about History*, New York: Norton, 1994

Badger, Anthony J., *The New Deal: The Depression Years, 1933–40*, London, Macmillan, and New York: Hill and Wang, 1989

Bailey, Thomas A., *Woodrow Wilson and the Great Betrayal*, New York: Macmillan, 1945

Barnes, Harry Elmer, *The Genesis of the World War: An Introduction to the Problem of War Guilt*, revised New York: Knopf, 1929

Beale, Howard K., *Theodore Roosevelt and the Rise of America to World Power*, Baltimore: Johns Hopkins Press, 1956

Benson, Susan Porter, *Counter Cultures: Saleswomen, Managers, and Customers in American Department Stores, 1890–1940*, Urbana: University of Illinois Press, 1986

Berman, William C., *America's Right Turn: From Nixon to Bush*, Baltimore: Johns Hopkins University Press, 1994

Bernstein, Barton J., ed., *Towards a New Past: Dissenting Essays in American History*, New York: Pantheon, 1968

Bernstein, Irving, *A Caring Society: The New Deal, the Worker, and the Great Depression: A History of the American Worker, 1933–1941*, Boston: Houghton Mifflin, 1985

Bernstein, Irving, *Guns or Butter: The Presidency of Lyndon Johnson*, New York: Oxford University Press, 1996

Bernstein, Michael A., *The Great Depression: Delayed Recovery and Economic Change in America, 1929–1939*, Cambridge and New York: Cambridge University Press, 1987

Best, Gary Dean, *Pride, Prejudice, and Politics: Roosevelt versus Recovery, 1933–1938*, New York: Praeger, 1991

Blocker, Jack S., Jr., *Retreat from Reform: The Prohibition Movement in the United States, 1890–1913*, Westport, CT: Greenwood Press, 1976

Blum, John Morton, *The Republican Roosevelt*, 2nd edition, Cambridge, MA: Harvard University Press, 1977

Blum, John Morton, *Years of Discord: American Politics and Society, 1961–1974*, New York: Norton, 1991

Bourne, Peter G., *Jimmy Carter: A Comprehensive Biography from Plains to Post-Presidency*, New York: Scribner, 1997

Brands, H.W., *T.R.: The Last Romantic*, New York: Basic Books, 1997

Brauer, Carl M., *John F. Kennedy and the Second Reconstruction*, New York: Columbia University Press, 1977

Breisach, Ernst A., *American Progressive History: An Experiment in Modernization*, Chicago: University of Chicago Press, 1993

Brinkley, Alan, *The End of Reform: New Deal Liberalism in Recession and War*, New York: Knopf, 1995

Brinkley, Douglas, *The Unfinished Presidency: Jimmy Carter's Journey Beyond the White House*, New York: Viking, 1998

Brogan, Hugh, *Kennedy*, London and New York: Longman, 1996

Brown, Thomas, *JFK: History of an Image*, Bloomington: Indiana University Press, 1988

Buenker, John D., *Urban Liberalism and Progressive Reform*, New York: Norton, 1978

Buhle, Paul, ed., *History and the New Left: Madison, Wisconsin, 1950–1970*, Philadelphia: Temple University Press, 1990

Buhle, Paul, and Edward Rice-Maximin, *William Appleman Williams: The Tragedy of Empire*, New York: Routledge, 1995

Bundy, William, *A Tangled Web: The Making of Foreign Policy in the Nixon Presidency*, New York: Hill and Wang, 1998

Burkett, Elinor, *The Right Women: A Journey Through the Heart of Conservative America*, New York: Scribner, 1998

Burns, James MacGregor, *Roosevelt: The Lion and the Fox*, New York: Harcourt Brace, and London: Secker and Warburg, 1956

Capps, Walter H., *The New Religious Right: Piety, Patriotism, and Politics*, Columbia: University of South Carolina Press, 1990

Caro, Robert A., *The Years of Lyndon Johnson*, 2 vols., New York: Knopf, 1982–90; vol. 1 London: Collins, 1983, vol. 2 London: Bodley Head, 1990

Carter, Dan T., *The Politics of Rage: George Wallace, the Origins of the New Conservatism, and the Transformation of American Politics*, New York: Simon and Schuster, 1995

Chafe, William H., *The Paradox of Change: American Women in the Twentieth Century*, New York: Oxford University Press, 1991

Chafe, William H., *The Unfinished Journey: America since World War II*, 3rd edition, New York: Oxford University Press, 1995

"The Challenge of American History," *Reviews in American History* 26:1 (March 1998), 1–328 [special issue]

Chambers, John Whiteclay II, *The Tyranny of Change: America in the Progressive Era, 1890–1920*, 2nd edition, New York: St. Martin's Press, 1992

Chrislock, Carl H., *The Progressive Era in Minnesota, 1899–1918*, St. Paul: Minnesota Historical Society, 1971

Clements, Kendrick A., *The Presidency of Woodrow Wilson*, Lawrence: University Press of Kansas, 1992

Cohen, Lizabeth, *Making a New Deal: Industrial Workers in Chicago, 1919–1939*, Cambridge and New York: Cambridge University Press, 1990

Cohen, Warren I., *The American Revisionists: The Lessons of Intervention in World War I*, Chicago: University of Chicago Press, 1967

Combs, Jerald A., *American Diplomatic History: Two Centuries of Changing Interpretations*, Berkeley: University of California Press, 1983

Conkin, Paul K., *The New Deal*, 3rd edition, Arlington Heights, IL: Harlan Davidson, 1992

Cook, Blanche Wiesen, *Eleanor Roosevelt*, vol. 1: *1884–1933*, New York: Viking, and Harmondsworth: Penguin, 1993

Cooper, John Milton, Jr., *The Warrior and the Priest: Woodrow Wilson and Theodore Roosevelt*, Cambridge, MA: Harvard University Press, 1983

Cumings, Bruce, *The Origins of the Korean War*, 2 vols., Princeton: Princeton University Press, 1981–90

Dallek, Robert, *Flawed Giant: Lyndon Johnson and His Times, 1961–1973*, New York: Oxford University Press, 1998

Davis, Flora, *Moving the Mountain: The Women's Movement in America since 1960*, New York: Simon and Schuster, 1991

Degler, Carl N., *Out of Our Past: The Forces That Shaped Modern America*, New York: Harper, 1959; 3rd edition 1984

De Witt, Benjamin Parke, *The Progressive Movement: A Non-Partisan, Comprehensive Discussion of Current Tendencies in American Politics*, New York: Macmillan, 1915

Diggins, John Patrick, *The Rise and Fall of the American Left*, New York: Norton, 1992 [original edition as *The American Left in the Twentieth Century*, 1973]

Dubofsky, Melvyn, *The New Deal: Conflicting Interpretations and Shifting Perspectives*, New York: Garland, 1992

DuBois, Ellen Carol, and Vicki L. Ruiz, eds., *Unequal Sisters: A Multicultural Reader in US Women's History*, New York: Routledge, 1990; 2nd edition 1994

Emery, Fred, *Watergate: The Corruption and Fall of Richard Nixon*, London: Cape, 1994; as *Watergate: The Corruption of American Politics and the Fall of Richard Nixon*, New York: Times Books, 1994

Evans, Sara M., *Born for Liberty: A History of Women in America*, New York: Free Press, 1989

Faulkner, Harold U., *The Quest for Social Justice, 1898–1914*, New York: Macmillan, 1931

Fausold, Martin L., *The Presidency of Herbert C. Hoover*, Lawrence: University Press of Kansas, 1985

Ferguson, Thomas, "From Normalcy to New Deal: Industrial Structure, Party Competition, and American Public Policy in the Great Depression," *International Organization* 38:1 (Winter 1984), 41–94

Finegold, Kenneth, and Theda Skocpol, *State and Party in America's New Deal*, Madison: University of Wisconsin Press, 1995

Flexner, Eleanor, and Ellen Fitzpatrick, *Century of Struggle: The Woman's Rights Movement in the United States*, enlarged edition, Cambridge, MA: Harvard University Press, 1996

Fowler, Robert Booth, *Believing Skeptics: American Political Intellectuals, 1945–1964*, Westport, CT: Greenwood Press, 1978

Freidel, Frank, *Franklin D. Roosevelt*, 4 vols., Boston: Little Brown, 1952–73

Friedman, Milton, and Anna Jacobson Schwartz, *A Monetary History of the United States, 1867–1960*, Princeton: Princeton University Press, 1963

Gaddis, John Lewis, *We Now Know: Rethinking Cold War History*, Oxford and New York: Oxford University Press, 1997

Gardner, Lloyd C., *Safe for Democracy: The Anglo-American Response to Revolution, 1913–1923*, New York: Oxford University Press, 1984

Goodwin, Doris Kearns, *No Ordinary Time: Franklin and Eleanor Roosevelt: The Home Front in World War II*, New York: Simon and Schuster, 1994

Gordon, Colin, *New Deals: Business, Labor, and Politics in America, 1920–1935*, Cambridge and New York: Cambridge University Press, 1994

Graebner, Norman A., *Cold War Diplomacy: American Foreign Policy, 1945–1960*, Princeton: Van Nostrand, 1962

Greenstein, Fred I., *The Hidden-Hand Presidency: Eisenhower as Leader*, New York: Basic Books, 1982

Gregory, James N., *American Exodus: The Dust Bowl Migration and Okie Culture in California*, New York: Oxford University Press, 1989

Gusfield, Joseph H., *Symbolic Crusade: Status Politics and the American Temperance Movement*, Urbana: University of Illinois Press, 1963

Halberstam, David, *The Children*, New York: Random House, 1998

Hamby, Alonzo L., *Liberalism and Its Challengers: From FDR to Bush*, 2nd edition, New York: Oxford University Press, 1992

Hamby, Alonzo L., *Man of the People: A Life of Harry S. Truman*, New York: Oxford University Press, 1995

Hamerow, Theodore S., *Reflections on History and Historians*, Madison: University of Wisconsin Press, 1987

Hamilton, Nigel, *JFK: Reckless Youth*, New York: Random House, and London: Century, 1992

Hargrove, Erwin C., *Jimmy Carter as President: Leadership and the Politics of the Public Good*, Baton Rouge: Louisiana State University Press, 1988

Harlan, David, *The Degradation of American History*, Chicago: University of Chicago Press, 1997

Harrison, Cynthia, *On Account of Sex: The Politics of Women's Issues, 1945–1968*, Berkeley: University of California Press, 1988

Hartshorne, Thomas L., *The Distorted Image: Changing Conceptions of the American Character since Turner*, Cleveland: Press of Case Western Reserve University, 1968

Harwit, Martin, *An Exhibit Denied: Lobbying the History of the Enola Gay*, New York: Copernicus, 1996

Hawley, Ellis W., *The New Deal and the Problem of Monopoly: A Study in Economic Ambivalence*, Princeton: Princeton University Press, 1966

Hays, Samuel P., *The Response to Industrialism, 1885–1914*, 2nd edition, Chicago: University of Chicago Press, 1995

Hersh, Seymour M., *The Dark Side of Camelot*, Boston: Little Brown, 1997

Higham, John, "The Cult of the American Consensus: Homogenizing American History," *Commentary* 27 (February 1959), 93–101

Higham, John, with Leonard Krieger and Felix Gilbert, *History: The Development of Historical Studies in the United States*, Englewood Cliffs, NJ: Prentice Hall, 1965

Himmelfarb, Gertrude, *The De-Moralization of Society: From Victorian Virtues to Modern Values*, New York: Knopf, 1995

Hoff, Joan, *Nixon Reconsidered*, New York: Basic Books, 1994

Hoff-Wilson, Joan, *Herbert Hoover: Forgotten Progressive*, Boston: Little Brown, 1975

Hoff-Wilson, Joan, and Marjorie Lightman, eds., *Without Precedent: The Life and Career of Eleanor Roosevelt*, Bloomington: Indiana University Press, 1984

Hofstadter, Richard, *The Age of Reform: From Bryan to FDR*, New York: Knopf, 1955; London: Cape, 1962

Hogan, Michael J., *The Marshall Plan: America, Britain, and the Reconstruction of Western Europe, 1947–1952*, Cambridge and New York: Cambridge University Press, 1987

Hogan, Michael J., ed., *America in the World: The Historiography of American Foreign Relations since 1941*, Cambridge and New York: Cambridge University Press, 1995

Hogan, Michael J., ed., *Hiroshima in History and Memory*, Cambridge: Cambridge University Press, 1996

Hunt, Michael H., *Ideology and US Foreign Policy*, New Haven: Yale University Press, 1987

Huthmacher, J. Joseph, *Senator Robert F. Wagner and the Rise of Urban Liberalism*, New York: Atheneum, 1968

Jeansonne, Glen, *Women of the Far Right: The Mothers' Movement and World War II*, Chicago: University of Chicago Press, 1996

Jones, Jacqueline, *Labor of Love, Labor of Sorrow: Black Women, Work, and the Family from Slavery to the Present*, New York: Basic Books, 1985

Kammen, Michael G., ed., *The Past Before Us: Contemporary Historical Writing in the United States*, Ithaca, NY: Cornell University Press, 1980

Kammen, Michael G., *In the Past Lane: Historical Perspectives on American Culture*, New York: Oxford University Press, 1997

Kaufman, Burton I., *The Presidency of James Earl Carter, Jr.*, Lawrence: University Press of Kansas, 1993

Kennedy, David M., *Over Here: The First World War and American Society*, New York: Oxford University Press, 1980

Kennedy, Paul M., *The Rise and Fall of the Great Powers: Economic Change and Military Conflict from 1500 to 2000*, New York: Random House, 1987; London: Unwin Hyman, 1988

Kerr, K. Austin, *Organized for Prohibition: A New History of the Anti-Saloon League*, New Haven: Yale University Press, 1985

Kessler-Harris, Alice, *Out to Work: A History of Wage-Earning Women in the United States*, New York and Oxford: Oxford University Press, 1982

Klatch, Rebecca E., *Women of the New Right*, Philadelphia: Temple University Press, 1987

Kloppenberg, James T., *Uncertain Victory: Social Democracy and Progressivism in European and American Thought, 1870–1920*, New York: Oxford University Press, 1986

Kolko, Gabriel, *The Triumph of Conservatism: A Reinterpretation of American History, 1900–1916*, New York: Free Press, and London: Collier Macmillan, 1963

Kraditor, Aileen S., *The Ideas of the Woman Suffrage Movement, 1890–1920*, 2nd edition, New York: Norton, 1981

Kraus, Michael, and Davis D. Joyce, *The Writing of American History*, revised edition, Norman: University of Oklahoma Press, 1985 [earlier editions, by Kraus only, as *A History of American History*, 1937, and *The Writing of American History*, 1953]

Kutler, Stanley I., and Stanley N. Katz, "The Promise of American History: Prospects and Progress," *Reviews in American History*, 10:4 (December 1982), 1–330

Kutler, Stanley I., ed., *Abuse of Power: The New Nixon Tapes*, New York: Free Press, 1997

LaFeber, Walter, *The Clash: A History of US–Japan Relations*, New York: Norton, 1997

Leffler, Melvyn P., *A Preponderance of Power: National Security, the Truman Administration, and the Cold War*, Stanford, CA: Stanford University Press, 1992

Lemisch, Jesse, *On Active Service in War and Peace: Politics and Ideology in the American Historical Profession*, Toronto: New Hogtown Press, 1975

Leuchtenburg, William E., *Franklin D. Roosevelt and the New Deal, 1932–1940*, New York: Harper, 1963

Leuchtenburg, William E., *In the Shadow of FDR: From Harry Truman to Bill Clinton*, revised Ithaca, NY: Cornell University Press, 1993

Linenthal, Edward T., and Tom Engelhardt, eds., *History Wars: The Enola Gay and Other Battles for the American Past*, New York: Metropolitan Books, 1996

Link, Arthur S., *Wilson*, 5 vols., Princeton: Princeton University Press, 1947–65

Lipset, Seymour Martin, *American Exceptionalism: A Double-Edged Sword*, New York: Norton, 1996

McCullough, David, *Mornings on Horseback*, New York: Simon and Schuster, 1982

McCullough, David, *Truman*, New York: Simon and Schuster, 1992

McNamara, Robert S., with Brian VanDeMark, *In Retrospect: The Tragedy and Lessons of Vietnam*, New York: Times Books, 1995

McQuaid, Kim, *Big Business and Presidential Power: From FDR to Reagan*, New York: Morrow, 1982

Maddox, Robert James, *The New Left and the Origins of the Cold War*, Princeton: Princeton University Press, 1973

Marks, Frederick W. III, *Velvet on Iron: The Diplomacy of Theodore Roosevelt*, Lincoln: University of Nebraska Press, 1979

Marks, Frederick W. III, *Wind over Sand: The Diplomacy of Franklin Roosevelt*, Athens: University of Georgia Press, 1988

Matusow, Allen J., *The Unravelling of America: A History of Liberalism in the 1960s*, New York: Harper, 1984

May, Ernest R., and Philip D. Zelikow, eds., *The Kennedy Tapes: Inside the White House during the Cuban Missile Crisis*, Cambridge, MA: Harvard University Press, 1997

Miller, Merle, *Plain Speaking: An Oral Biography of Harry S. Truman*, New York: Berkley, 1974

Morgenthau, Hans J., *In Defense of the National Interest: A Critical Examination of American Foreign Policy*, New York: Knopf, 1951

Morris, Edmund, *The Rise of Theodore Roosevelt*, New York: Coward McCann, and London: Collins, 1979

Morris, Kenneth Earl, *Jimmy Carter, American Moralist*, Athens: University of Georgia Press, 1996

Morris, Roger, *Richard Milhous Nixon: The Rise of an American Politician*, New York: Holt, 1990

Morton, Marian J., *The Terrors of Ideological Politics: Liberal Historians in a Conservative Mood*, Cleveland: Press of Case Western Reserve University, 1972

Nordholt, J.W. Schulte, *Woodrow Wilson: A Life for World Peace*, Berkeley: University of California Press, 1991

Novick, Peter, *That Noble Dream: The "Objectivity Question" and the American Historical Profession*, Cambridge and New York: Cambridge University Press, 1988

O'Neill, William L., *Everyone Was Brave: A History of Feminism in America*, Chicago: Quadrangle, 1971

Painter, Nell Irvin, *Standing at Armageddon: The United States, 1877–1919*, New York: Norton, 1987

Paterson, Thomas G., ed., *Kennedy's Quest for Victory: American Foreign Policy, 1961–1963*, New York: Oxford University Press, 1989

Patterson, James T., *Congressional Conservatism and the New Deal: The Growth of the Conservative Coalition in Congress, 1933–1939*, Lexington: University of Kentucky Press, 1967

Patterson, James T., *The New Deal and the States: Federalism in Transition*, Princeton: Princeton University Press, 1969

Polenberg, Richard, *War and Society: The United States, 1941–1945*, Philadelphia: Lippincott, 1972

Radosh, Ronald, and Murray N. Rothbard, eds., *A New History of Leviathan: Essays on the Rise of the American Corporate State*, New York: Dutton, 1972

Riemer, Neal, *The Democratic Experiment*, Princeton: Van Nostrand, 1967 [*American Political Theory*, vol. 1]

Romasco, Albert U., *The Politics of Recovery: Roosevelt's New Deal*, New York: Oxford University Press, 1983

Rose, Kenneth D., *American Women and the Repeal of Prohibition*, New York: New York University Press, 1996

Rothbard, Murray N., *America's Great Depression*, 2nd edition, Los Angeles: Nash, 1972

Saloutos, Theodore, *The American Farmer and the New Deal*, Ames: Iowa State University Press, 1982

Schaffer, Ronald, *America in the Great War: The Rise of the War Welfare State*, New York: Oxford University Press, 1991

Schlesinger, Arthur M., Jr., *The Age of Roosevelt*, 3 vols., Boston: Houghton Mifflin, 1957–60

Schlesinger, Arthur M., Jr., *A Thousand Days: John F. Kennedy in the White House*, Boston: Houghton Mifflin, and London: Deutsch, 1965

Schwarz, Jordan A., *The New Dealers: Power Politics in the Age of Roosevelt*, New York: Knopf, 1993

Sherry, Michael S., *In the Shadow of War: The United States since the 1930s*, New Haven: Yale University Press, 1995

Siracusa, Joseph M., *New Left Diplomatic Histories and Historians: The American Revisionists*, Port Washington, NY: Kennikat Press, 1973; revised Claremont, CA: Regina, 1993

Sitkoff, Harvard, *A New Deal for Blacks: The Emergence of Civil Rights as a National Issue*, Oxford and New York: Oxford University Press, 1978

Sitkoff, Harvard, ed., *Fifty Years Later: The New Deal Evaluated*, Philadelphia: Temple University Press, 1985

Sklar, Martin J., *The Corporate Reconstruction of American Capitalism, 1890–1916: The Market, the Law, and Politics*, Cambridge and New York: Cambridge University Press, 1988

Smith, Douglas L., *The New Deal in the Urban South*, Baton Rouge: Louisiana State University Press, 1988

Solomon, Barbara Miller, *In the Company of Educated Women: A History of Women and Higher Education in America*, New Haven and London: Yale University Press, 1985

Sorensen, Theodore C., *Kennedy*, New York: Harper, and London: Hodder and Stoughton, 1965

Sternsher, Bernard, *Consensus, Conflict, and American Historians*, Bloomington: Indiana University Press, 1975

Thelen, David P., *The New Citizenship: Origins of Progressivism in Wisconsin, 1885–1900*, Columbia: University of Missouri Press, 1972

Thelen, David P., Jonathan Wiener, John D'Emilio, Herbert Aptheker, Gerda Lerner, Christopher Lasch, John Higham, Carl Degler, and David Levering Lewis, "A Round Table: What Has Changed and Not Changed in American Historical Practice?" *Journal of American History* 76 (1989), 393–478

Thompson, J.A., *Progressivism*, London: British Association of American Studies, 1979

Thompson, John A., *Reformers and War: American Progressive Publicists and the First World War*, New York and Cambridge: Cambridge University Press, 1987

Thorne, Christopher, *Border Crossings: Studies in International History*, Oxford and New York: Blackwell, 1988

Timberlake, James H., *Prohibition and the Progressive Movement, 1900–1920*, Cambridge, MA: Harvard University Press, 1963

Trachtenberg, Alan, *The Incorporation of America: Culture and Society in the Gilded Age*, New York: Hill and Wang, 1982

Tucker, Robert W., *The Radical Left and American Foreign Policy*, Baltimore: Johns Hopkins Press, 1971

Tyrrell, Ian, *The Absent Marx: Class Analysis and Liberal History in Twentieth-Century America*, Westport, CT: Greenwood Press, 1986

Veysey, Laurence R., "The 'New' Social History in the Context of American Historical Writing," *Reviews in American History* 7 (March 1979), 1–12

Vittoz, Stanley N., *New Deal Labor Policy and the American Industrial Economy*, Chapel Hill: University of North Carolina Press, 1987

Ware, Susan, *Beyond Suffrage: Women in the New Deal*, Cambridge, MA: Harvard University Press, 1981

Weinstein, James, *The Corporate Ideal in the Liberal State, 1900–1918*, Boston: Beacon Press, 1968

Weiss, Nancy J., *Farewell to the Party of Lincoln: Black Politics in the Age of FDR*, Princeton: Princeton University Press, 1983

Wheeler, Marjorie Spruill, *New Women of the New South: The Leaders of the Woman Suffrage Movement in the Southern States*, New York and Oxford: Oxford University Press, 1993

Wicker, Tom, *One of Us: Richard Nixon and the American Dream*, New York: Random House, 1991

Wiebe, Robert H., *The Search for Order, 1877–1920*, New York: Hill and Wang, and London: Macmillan, 1967

Williams, William Appleman, *The Tragedy of American Diplomacy*, Cleveland: World, 1959; revised New York: Dell, 1972

Wise, Gene, *American Historical Explanations: A Strategy for Grounded Inquiry*, Homewood, IL: Dorsey Press, 1973; revised Minneapolis: University of Minnesota Press, 1980

United States: Historical Writing, 20th Century

"Recent history," always a difficult region for scholarly explorations, lengthened only with the century itself into a scholarly retrospect on coherent, long-term historical developments. Trends within the historical profession, from progressivism to liberalism to New Leftism and neorealism and from economic and political history to social and cultural history, inevitably played a large role in defining subjects and approaches to them. But the study of the near-present has also had its own unique and defining features.

During the latter quarter of the century, just as a greater sense of detachment from the experiences of participants in the great political events of the world wars, the Depression, and Cold War had been gained, interest in "recent history" expanded more rapidly than any other field of US history. That history, however, also grew very distant from the old standard of "history as past politics." Culture (especially popular culture), gender, race, and ethnicity among other largely recent subjects, occupied an attention and commanded a scholarly dignity that transformed the study of the century and, in all likelihood, US history as a whole. As "public history," the rapidly growing sector of museums, historically-based media treatments, historical recreations or re-enactments, occupied a steadily larger role in American culture, the understanding of the 20th century as a culmination and inner meaning of US history offered a zone of inquiry and presentation hotly contested from Congress to the Smithsonian museum and from the *New York Times* to the presidential race.

The American section of the historical scholarship, before 1930, was ironically known among insiders as a "Turner-verein." A play at once upon the *Turnverein* – the German immigrant gymnastic and educational institution that conveyed *Kultur* to the masses – and the historian Frederick Jackson Turner, the joke suggested that Turner's theme of the frontier dominated the writing of all US history. That theme suggested a decisive watershed had been passed during the 1890s, with the close of the frontier, but proposed no necessary successor influence or direction. It also suggested with intuitive shrewdness that Turner's 1893 essay, "The Significance of the Frontier in American History," might still somehow remain for a very long time the most influential piece of history writing in the entire field.

Thus Woodrow Wilson, the most prominent former historian (until 1972 presidential candidate George McGovern and 1994–95 Congressional leader Newt Gingrich) within American public life, suggested that the close of continental frontiers implied the need for economic and political internationalism under the guidance of an enlightened elite. The progressive historians, led by Charles A. Beard in their skepticism toward the outcome of US participation in World War I, drew nearly opposite conclusions. The differences between these two positions remained vitally important for decades. Indeed, the coming retrospect on 20th-century developments and the methodologies suitable to grasp them found the two in a virtual dyad of possible interpretations, closing off other alternatives until both had been bypassed (or at least set aside) for other and very different areas of interest.

Supporters of Wilson's position tended toward the study of leadership policies, often with an emphasis on political history; and they based themselves increasingly within the prestigious Ivy League schools. Successors to Beard's positions often stressed economic and regional history, and their proponents could be found frequently, especially after World War II, in the midwestern and western states. James Harvey Robinson, who taught history at Columbia University (from which Charles Beard had resigned, protesting the persecution of antiwar faculty members), meanwhile urged an influential middle term: a "new history" drawing upon social sciences, charting progress in thought as well as institutions and re-measuring history's meaning in each generation through the changing frame of reference. Turner had suggested as much in his first published essay in 1890, but without placing a stamp upon the methodology to follow.

Beard, the single most influential historian of the 1910s to the 1930s, in concert with his wife, Mary Beard, formulated the progressive view that economic interests indeed played a central role, but not in the ways that most liberals, conservatives, or Marxists had imagined. The Beards, in their acclaimed *The Rise of American Civilization* (first 2 vols., 1927), the only history book to reach a large minority of educated Americans' homes, maintained that "interests" rather than class as such had ruled society at most stages, but these interests had been often far from benign. Democratic struggles had sometimes, but only temporarily, overwhelmed the influence of the ostensible rulers, and war helped to make their rule near complete. World war hardened class positions and created a dangerous bureaucratic tendency in the national state, an estimate that the Beards softened in subsequent editions of the same volume, shaped by hopeful moments of the New Deal. If the best of national history featured a repudiation of European class systems, the uniqueness of the American experience might yet permit an escape from the trauma of the century.

In the shadow of the Depression, other and related newer trends of historical study took shape, often the product of highly influential nonacademics. For the last time, these nonprofessionals may be said to have dominated the general history interests of the reading public (and not merely in specific subject areas, such as the Civil War, where nonprofessional scholarship remained prominent). Usually, these works placed recent history in the domain of culmination, recasting the longer historical trends but with ends distinctly different from Wilsonianism or Beardianism. Drawing much inspiration from V.L. Parrington's *Main Currents in American Thought* – published in 1927, it did not reach the 20th century due to the author's death – a writer such as V.F. Calverton's *The Liberation of American Literature* (1932) or English professor Granville Hicks' *The Great Tradition* (1933) treated as general cultural history American literature's advance from Puritan influences to vigorous realism and on to the progressive modernism of current dissenting artists and intellectuals.

Lewis Mumford, Van Wyck Brooks, Waldo Frank, Malcolm Cowley, and others interested primarily in cultural questions constituted a veritable school built around the similar criticism of past blighted democratic promise and the proposal that a modernist transformation had given the 20th century new hope and meaning. Meanwhile, in the popular iconography of the New Deal, notably marking thousands of public spaces with images of the national past, a certain vein of nostalgic Americana promised the recovery and updating of democratic traditions in the current era. Within the history profession proper, Merle Curti's *The Growth of American Thought* (1943), influenced by pacifism and a fondness for the political dissident, capped a parallel trend and also nearly marked its eclipse.

Only a few historians, and most of those on the distant Left, appreciated at the time the historical classic of that age destined to have the greatest influence on future generations of scholars: W.E.B. Du Bois' *Black Reconstruction* (1935). Its implication that 20th-century history as well as civilization would be measured "by the color line" was a dramatic attack on the failure of society to encompass and empower ex-slaves, and on academic historians for failing to recognize the consequences. So politically unwelcome, as American intellectuals of nearly all kinds laid stress upon common traditions preparing Americans to embrace antifascism, and in some cases so exaggerated his specific historical claims, that only scholarly generations in the last third of the century could accept Du Bois' corresponding emphasis on hopeful elements in national culture. His earlier quasi-historical work, *Souls of Black Folk* (1903), on black religion, culture, politics, and history as vitally significant to their study, predicted better than historians of the 1930s–50s what the interests and pursuits of innovative future scholars would be.

Meanwhile, as the war years dramatically changed the nation, the limitations of progressive history and its popular recuperation during the 1930s became more evident, while the political urge to banish its influence grew into a historiographical crusade. The war and the outbreak of Cold War had a sudden and traumatic effect upon the reputation of Charles Beard in particular. Increasingly resisting the pull toward intervention, and insisting in current historical terms that Roosevelt had maneuvered the nation toward the inevitable Japanese strike on Pearl Harbor, the erstwhile dean of American history faced a wave of hostility unprecedented toward a leading American scholar of any kind. His severest critics, liberal and conservative historians directly active in the war or in related information and intelligence agencies, now treated the "relativism" or "frame of reference" approach adopted by progressive historians as intellectually and morally suspect, if not actually treasonous. In its place, they sought absolutes.

Thus, in his 1950 American Historical Association presidential address, Samuel Eliot Morison derided Beard's "scornful attitude" toward American accomplishments and called for history to be rewritten "from a sanely conservative point of view" honoring appropriate leaders of various eras including the current one. Likewise, Columbia University's prestigious economic historian Allan Nevins, writing in *Fortune* magazine, repudiated the "feminine idealism" of progressive historians and called for a major history in which industrial barons derided during the 1930s would be seen as the virile "builders of an indispensable might." America's role in defending world civilization against communism had been made possible by the geographical and economic expansion of national influence, and the recent victory over fascism had decisively demonstrated the nation's democratic destiny. For these and many less ideologically driven historians, the New Deal was in any case the culmination of modern (and perhaps premodern) American history; all else afterward was merely the necessary defense of the gains made.

In a deeper historiographical sense, as keen observer Warren Susman would remark decades later, the end of the 1930s marked a definitive crisis in progressive interpretations. Some of the newer leading historians had indeed become more skeptical about dramatic social change of any kind, present or past. If immigration historian Oscar Handlin and a host of business historians such as Alfred Chandler celebrated economic dynamism, ethnic mobility, and 20th-century meritocracy as the proof of national uniqueness, others judged the same apparent consensus from a more distaff angle. Richard Hofstadter, whose *American Political Tradition* (1948) and *The Age of Reform* (1955) won great acclaim and reached a wide nonscholarly audience, cast doubt on reformers' motives but also treated cupidity and ideological self-deception as virtual national traits. Scholars and commentators to the center and right of the political spectrum enjoyed his attack on Populism as a deeply irrational precursor to the safe and sane farm lobby of the 20th century. But in contrast to Arthur Schlesinger, Jr., and his fellow liberal historians, Hofstadter ridiculed the reform temperament of Wilsonianism and the New Deal as genteel self-interest in disguise.

This view could not prevail among a scholarly community that still recalled the Roosevelt years as the most hopeful ones in recent history. More than consensus as such, the leading trends during the 1950s and early 1960s continued along lines evident in Schlesinger's *The Crisis of the Old Order,*

1919–1933 (1957) or various studies of the progressive era, especially those by Wilson scholar Arthur S. Link. The two presidential fathers of modern liberalism had sought the proper balance of various social forces, including the regulation of business, and had triumphed (or met the inevitable defeat of their ultimate democratic quest) in the great moments of international crisis. Republican eras, such as the 1920s, seemed by contrast lamentable throwbacks to less enlightened times, or in the case of the present-day Eisenhower years, a bland acceptance of the course laid out by others better suited to the task. Not so much triumphal or congratulatory, this body of work might be called liberal and "ironic" for the spin that rightward turning theologian-popularizer Reinhold Niebuhr had placed on the modern condition. In this view, distant from Hofstadter's skepticism, the pluralistic consensus successfully reached within America could not be attained worldwide, and the use of even immoral means to achieve merely acceptable ends – a balance of power, the internationalist version of pluralism – made for a built-in tragedy of the present era. The outcome of a unique national past was, therefore – and in no way due to shortcomings of the United States – less than happy.

The limits of consensus history became increasingly evident as the years of the high Cold War passed and national consensus passed into open conflicts on issues involving race, international policy, cultural, and – to a lesser degree – class differences. But on its often hidden side of a skepticism toward the fruits of consensus, the trend had at least one more very large contribution to make. William Appleman Williams' *Tragedy of American Diplomacy* (1959), destined to be one of the most influential history books in the second half of the American 20th century, readily accepted consensus as the reality of national life and the premise of foreign policy.

Williams had, however, subtly turned the proposition around to suggest that American policymakers (like other Americans) viewed their national self-interest as the inherent good of the world, and that they practised "Open Door Imperialism," imposing their system upon often unwilling populations and seeking to crush all efforts to escape from US global plans. Unable to confront the contradictions of their own past and to see themselves in the reflection of the national quest of other peoples, Americans high and low increasingly engaged in military and ideological excess on a global scale, threatening all human existence. Among the dozens of notable scholars trained in whole or part by Williams, Walter LaFeber and Lloyd Gardner labored to fill out the picture with a new view of 20th-century internationalism in Latin America and Asia, an unpleasant culmination indeed of American history. Historians of the US engagement in Vietnam, growing into a large-scale industry of academics and journalists, mostly followed in the wake of this interpretation. At best the Southeast Asian engagement had been a tragedy all around; at worst, it was something far more telling of flaws in national judgment or even character.

Such views evoked considerable rage in the academic establishment, from diplomatic to political historians, but spoke vividly to the younger generations of scholars who were active in political movements and who focused their undergraduate and graduate education in history. Those alert to historiography, whether friendly or hostile to Williams, identified the roots of his work in Charles Beard's tradition and in the pockets of Beardianism that remained in the Midwest and Plains States universities.

Younger scholars sympathetic to Williams' broader approach (including his clever adaptation of business historians' use of "corporate" models) put themselves to work elaborating the themes of modern America as a corporate society sufficiently unlike the European class models as to demand a unique interpretive thrust. Guided by the studies of Gabriel Kolko, they portrayed the progressive era as the successful imposition of stable rule by an interlocked business and administrative class. Woodrow Wilson, rather than a champion of democracy, now became the figure who epitomized both reform and repression (as well as lily-white values in the nation's capital). Franklin Roosevelt assumed much the countenance he had in Beard's later writings, as a Lincoln-like figure who introduced a third American Revolution (as Lincoln had introduced a second Revolution) which firmly established a worldwide domain for American hegemony to command. Later scholarly interpretations of the New Deal, like those widely-read studies of Alan Brinkley, added ballast but did little conceptually to change the overall view of Roosevelt's rule as emanating from the top down.

The historiographical transformation precipitated by Williams also reorganized the broad study of the West, leading up into the 20th century and occupying one of the most contentious scholarly areas of the 1980s–90s. *The Great Frontier* (1952) by the dean of western historians, Walter P. Webb, had forecast this drift by suggesting that expansionism had its own inherent logic beyond any economic, social, or ethical purpose. Later historians of the West, including Richard White, Patricia Limerick and John Mack Faragher, assumed that rather than a moving line of democratic inclusion, westward movement brought contest with existing inhabitants of the open spaces and conquest of them, in a far-from-happy ending. This same trend also shaped most of the new scholarly area of environmental history, which dealt mostly with pre-20th-century themes but which had special importance for continuing land policies. If, as Richard White in particular argued, the progressive era had seen large-scale depredations even amid the establishment of national parks, then subsequent ill-considered and ecologically destructive activity across large areas from California to Florida by the Army Corps of Engineers and the abuse of Indian lands for toxic and nuclear dump-sites were disturbingly normal aspects of economic development, security, and energy policies.

But even Williams' careful readers did not usually see at work in him yet other methodological influences of the 1950s, including a multidisciplinary interest in psychology and the social sciences, warmly greeted by leading historians in the writings of David Potter and others. The quasi-historical and quasi-psychological reading of an American "character" emerging from the reading of Freud, the "culture and personality" interdisciplinary studies of the 1920s–40s, and the intense engagement of anthropologists, psychologists, sociologists such as Columbia's Margaret Mead and Yale's John Dollard, were all attempts to understand the meaning of group behavior and tradition. The Cold War had placed a premium on the favorable reading of the American character as a model for other societies to follow. But only some (such as Potter) were persuaded that the "culture of abundance" had been the dominant experience, or that the classes left out of abundance – above all, African Americans – had fallen behind due to cultural and psychological dysfunctions rather than the baneful effects of the social system at large.

Coming scholars of great importance drew different inferences from a growing body of interdisciplinary data. Labor historian Herbert Gutman, who by the early 1970s had become an enormously admired advocate and essayist in the social history of working-class populations, had been greatly influenced by the work of anthropologists such as Sidney Mintz and of various statisticians. David Montgomery, destined to become the doyen of labor history, looked to various sociological workplace studies and early versions of what might be called the social history uses of quantitative history.

The influence of Gutman and Montgomery on the next generation of US historians had a great deal to do with the changed political atmosphere of the day (the two had been either members of or close to Communist party circles in early Cold War days), but almost as much to do with the influence of the British historian E.P. Thompson. *The Making of the English Working Class* (1963) had a somewhat delayed but finally overwhelming impact upon the study of history, and not only of working-class subjects. Devotees of Thompson included those whom his study hardly included, but who represented classes of citizens to be newly considered in depth by historians: women and nonwhites. Thompson's emphasis on "history from the bottom up", and on the subjectivity of the ordinary participant in historical events, precipitated impulses that liberal scholars active in the civil rights movement had rarely transferred into their intellectual work. History would be remade, refitted for broader democratic (not merely Democratic) purposes.

The drastically increased size of undergraduate and graduate classes during the 1960s and much of the 1970s also played a significant role in this equation. If history had long been considered a gentlemen's profession, the entrance of GI Bill students had helped bring in more children of European ethnic groups (especially Jews) and inspired a thin but significant strain of immigrant history. The expansion of the universities and the demands made upon them for more inclusion of outsiders accelerated this trend for later generations of European ethnics and working-class descendants, but also for women, African Americans, and to a lesser extent Chicanos and Asians.

Many of the newer entrants, notably until the later 1960s, chose the path of mobility studies, with its familiar and satisfying American success stories. But more and more saw, instead, a rough path of forward and backward movement, periods of crisis marked by actual violence and bruising ridicule or scapegoating, and few happy endings. The 19th century remained a comfortable arena for testing many of the newer methodologies. But those who pursued women's labor and political activities into the 20th century, such as Alice Kessler-Harris, Linda Gordon, and Mari Jo Buhle, pointed to repeated and courageous efforts which had met with crushing opposition. Such writers, and, even more so, prestigious newer authors on gay and lesbian history such as John D'Emilio and Estelle B. Freedman, sought to depict spaces in which a degree of autonomy had been successfully carved out and maintained, making future advance possible.

The same spirit prevailed across broad ranges of African American history in particular. The popular historian-journalist Manning Marable's *Black American Politics* (1985) and Robin D.G. Kelley's multiple award-winning *Hammer and Hoe* (1990) may be said to mark culminations of lengthy trends in assessing the precursors and the after effects of the civil rights movement. Scholarly and semi-scholarly but highly popular biographical writings on such figures as W.E.B. DuBois, Paul Robeson, Langston Hughes, Martin Luther King, Jr., and Malcolm X underlined this trend and gave it a readership far beyond normal scholarly circles.

Kelley's much-admired *Race Rebels* (1994) bore the stamp of yet another and vital trend in 20th-century historical scholarship, tending further and further toward the domains of American Studies. George Lipsitz, whose *Class and Culture in Cold War America* (1981, revised as *Rainbow at Midnight*, 1994) might almost be called a manifesto of popular culture scholarship, supplied a preface to *Race Rebels* suggesting that good history could provide readers with "pictures of people as they actually are rather than as others wish them to be" and that "allows people to openly acknowledge the things that divide them even as they rally together for common goals."

Lipsitz's own work best made the point that hundreds of younger historians sought to elaborate, criticize, or refine in scholarly presentations, essays, and above all in college courses aimed at the "post-literate" generations of graduates and undergraduates. The study of modern media at its most vernacular levels, television and "B" films, the search for pockets of interracial exchange in street carnivals and certain music, the hopes for democratic memory in an age of seeming amnesia – all carried the postmodern scholar to the extreme of intellectual engagement that many would not undertake comfortably, but others would make into a model of the 21st-century historian.

Further alternatives to the older standard historical efforts could be found, for instance, in the popular treatments of themes. The sheer excess of history PhDs produced during the 1960s–70s and the urge toward social history melded with the opportunities presented for public history. Ever since D.W. Griffith's *Birth of a Nation* (1915) film had treated historical themes, but for almost fifty years, "historical" movies had been largely costume dramas such as *Gone with the Wind* (1939), biopics such as *Wilson* (1944), or film documentaries, mostly government-funded projects during World War II and the Cold War aiming to justify official actions. The 1960s–90s saw an increasing rush of episodes and more or less historical events cinematically reconstructed with the close assistance of scholarly advisers, including *The Molly Maguires* (1970) and *Glory* (1989), the extensive documentary treatment among many other subjects of working women and blue-collar life generally, sports, and inevitably the Civil War. *Roots* (1977), twenty years later still the most watched miniseries of television history, demonstrated with both its popularity and its scholarly improbability (for slavery's documentation to be so exact) the ambivalences of new quasi-scholarly presentation. The emergence of US television's History Channel promised nothing better and probably more of the same. At least for the nonscholarly observer, the era of the amateur (not an essayist now, but a television writer or producer) had come again.

Other remarkable phenomena of historical presentation, such as the "historical corridors" of vanished industry in Pennsylvania and Rhode Island or islands of vanished (and recreated) colonial life in Williamsburg and Old Sturbridge, grew rapidly with the expanse of state and federal public monies. Hardly a district seeking tourism lacked a historical zone by the 1990s, and the varieties of re-enactments or historical costume events continued to climb steadily. Whether this series of phenomena derived more from the rapid increase of college-educated retirees or the deep sense of loss for green space, community, lifetime jobs, and extended families (or, less pleasantly, a majority white America) remained very much to be seen.

Yet for 20th-century historians at the end of "their" century, viable alternatives to ambiguous postmodernism seem to have grown scarce indeed. Perhaps the Reagan years with their effectively constructed mythic golden national past – reputedly squandered by generations of liberal bureaucrats and amoral youths – had closed off more intelligent conservative challenges, much as the virtual collapse of the contemporary labor movement had eclipsed the lure of labor history, or the decline in African American leadership made histories of civil rights movements seem exercises in nostalgia, or as the endless wars and stalemates after the Cold War had deflated upbeat neorealist treatments of diplomatic history. Scholarly volumes continued to appear at a staggering rate, of course. But beyond the social history impulse of the 1970s–80s lay only cultural history, and that which captured the attention of young intellectuals as well as students appeared steadily less likely to bridge the gap between the history of Rock 'n' Roll and the history of the Presidency.

PAUL BUHLE

See also Beard; Du Bois; Foner, E.; Gutman; Hofstadter; Kessler-Harris; LaFeber; Montgomery; Schlesinger; Williams, W.

Further Reading

Beard, Charles, and Mary Ritter Beard, *The Rise of American Civilization*, vols. 1–2, New York: Macmillan, and London: Cape, 1927

Benson, Susan Porter, Stephen Brier, and Roy Rosenzweig, eds., *Presenting the Past: Essays on History and the Public*, Philadelphia: Temple University Press, 1986

Calverton, Victor Francis, *The Liberation of American Literature*, New York: Scribner, 1932

Curti, Merle, *The Growth of American Thought*, New York: Harper, 1943; 4th edition 1982

D'Emilio, John, *Sexual Politics, Sexual Communities: The Making of a Homosexual Minority in the United States, 1940–1970*, Chicago: University of Chicago Press, 1983

Du Bois, W.E.B., *Souls of Black Folk: Essays and Sketches*, Chicago: McClurg, 1903; London: Constable, 1905

Du Bois, W.E.B., *Black Reconstruction: An Essay toward a History of the Part Which Black Folk Played in the Attempt to Reconstruct Democracy in America, 1860–1880*, New York: Harcourt Brace, 1935; as *Black Reconstruction in America*, Cleveland: World, 1964, London: Cass, 1966, reprinted New York: Atheneum, 1992

Foner, Eric, ed., *The New American History*, Philadelphia: Temple University Press, 1990

Gutman, Herbert G., *Work, Culture, and Society in Industrializing America: Essays in American Working-Class and Social History*, New York: Knopf, 1976; Oxford: Blackwell, 1977

Hicks, Granville, *The Great Tradition: An Interpretation of American Literature since the Civil War*, New York: Macmillan, 1933; revised 1935

Higham, John, *Writing American History: Essays on Modern Scholarship*, Bloomington: Indiana University Press, 1970

Hofstadter, Richard, *The American Political Tradition and the Men Who Made It*, New York: Knopf, 1948; London: Cape, 1962

Hofstadter, Richard, *The Age of Reform: From Bryan to FDR*, New York: Knopf, 1955; London: Cape, 1962

Hofstadter, Richard, *The Progressive Historians: Turner, Beard, Parrington*, New York: Knopf, 1968; London: Cape, 1969

Kelley, Robin D.G., *Hammer and Hoe: Alabama Communists during the Great Depression*, Chapel Hill: University of North Carolina Press, 1990

Kelley, Robin D.G., *Race Rebels: Culture, Politics, and the Black Working Class*, New York: Free Press, 1994

Kessler-Harris, Alice, *Out to Work: A History of Wage-Earning Women in the United States*, New York and Oxford: Oxford University Press, 1982

Kolko, Gabriel, *The Triumph of Conservatism: A Reinterpretation of American History, 1900–1916*, New York: Free Press, and London: Collier Macmillan, 1963

LaFeber, Walter, *Inevitable Revolutions: The United States in Central America*, New York: Norton, 1983; revised 1993

Lipsitz, George, *Class and Culture in Cold War America*, New York: Praeger, 1981; revised as *Rainbow at Midnight: Labor and Culture in the 1940s*, Urbana: University of Illinois Press, 1994

Marable, Manning, *Black American Politics: From the Washington Marches to Jesse Jackson*, London: Verso, 1985

Montgomery, David, *Workers' Control in America: Studies in the History of Work, Technology, and Labor Struggles*, Cambridge and New York: Cambridge University Press, 1979

Parrington, Vernon Louis, *Main Currents in American Thought: An Interpretation of American Literature from the Beginnings to 1920*, 3 vols., New York: Harcourt Brace, 1927–30

Schlesinger, Arthur M., Jr., *The Crisis of the Old Order, 1919–1933*, Boston: Houghton Mifflin, and London: Heinemann, 1957

Susman, Warren, *Culture as History: The Transformation of American Society in the Twentieth Century*, New York: Pantheon, 1984

Thompson, E.P., *The Making of the English Working Class*, London: Gollancz, 1963; New York: Pantheon, 1964

Webb, Walter Prescott, *The Great Frontier*, Austin: University of Texas Press, 1952

White, Richard, *"It's Your Misfortune and None of My Own": A New History of the American West*, Norman: University of Oklahoma Press, 1991

Williams, William Appleman, *The Tragedy of American Diplomacy*, Cleveland: World, 1959; revised New York: Dell, 1972

Wise, Gene, *American Historical Explanations: A Strategy for Grounded Inquiry*, Homewood, IL: Dorsey Press, 1973; revised Minneapolis: University of Minnesota Press, 1980

Universal History

The tradition of universal history has long been associated with Western conceptions of history. It has complex relations with the writing of history and with the emergence in the 19th century of the historical discipline. Originally, the tradition's core idea was that there exists a single history of all humankind and that this history, in the form of a story having a beginning, middle, and end, is already known to us. The founders of Western historiography, the Greeks, did not have the notion that there exists a single history. The first sentence of Herodotus (484–c.425 BCE) is "These are the histories of Herodotus of Halicarnassus," but for Herodotus the Ionian word *historie* meant only "researches" or "investigations." The term was in the plural: there was no conception in Herodotus of an overarching "History" out there, some universal narrative of history of which the *Histories* would be a part: indeed, one is struck by the often conflicting character of the stories that Herodotus recounted. His successor, Thucydides (*c*.460–*c*.400 BCE), was dismissive of Herodotus' willingness to tolerate a multiplicity of often fantastic stories (*mythodes*), but while Thucydides hinted in his account of the Peloponnesian War that there are recurring patterns in human interaction, he likewise had no notion of a single History into which these patterns might fit.

Christianity later came on the scene, with its claim to be a universal religion. Augustine of Hippo (354–430), in *The City of God* (413–26), interpreted all worldly events as leading by divine plan to judgment day, when the *civitas divina* would triumph over the *civitas terrena*. Other writers took *The City of God* as inspiration for writing universal history: these include Paulus Orosius (*c*.385–420) in his *Seven Books of History Against the Pagans*, in which world history is treated as proof of the apocalyptic visions in the Bible, and Isidore of Seville (*c*.560–636) in his *Etymologies*. The notion of universal history is thus deeply embedded in the Christian tradition. As is shown by the *Muqaddima* of Ibn Khaldūn (1332–1406), the notion also has a presence in Islam, another monotheistic religion making universal claims.

However, universal history first became an institutionally grounded tradition in Germany in the 16th century. The time and place are significant, for in early modern Germany Western Christianity experienced its most troubling schism, while, in contrast to the situation in France, a nation-state failed to develop. Consequently, for Protestant Germans in particular, universal history provided a vision of unity in a situation where unity did not exist in either the ecclesiastical or the political realms. The founder of the institutionally grounded tradition was the Reformation humanist Philip Melanchthon (1497–1560). Melanchthon, who had a great impact on German education, lectured on universal history at the University of Wittenberg in the mid-16th century, and the idea soon caught on at the other Protestant German universities. Even today in Germany there still exist professorial chairs devoted, at least in name, to *Universalgeschichte*.

Christian universal history emphasized the Hebrews and took its chronology and periodization from the Bible. A well known contribution to the tradition was *Discours sur l'histoire universelle* (1681; *Discourse on Universal History*, 1976) by the French prelate Jacques Bénigne Bossuet (1627–1704). But as Adalbert Klempt has shown, in the 16th century a secularization of the tradition was already underway, for the biblical narrative proved inadequate to accommodate what Europeans were learning about the non-European world. Especially in Germany, where professors were paid to cultivate the subject, universal history continued to be taught and written with great enthusiasm. A famous essay by the philosopher Immanuel Kant (1724–1804), "Idee zu einer allgemeinen Geschichte in welt-bürgerlicher Absicht" ("Idea for a Universal History with a Cosmopolitan Purpose," 1784), is explicitly a contribution to the universal history tradition. Inspired by Kant, in May 1789 Friedrich Schiller (1759–1805) delivered his inaugural lecture as professor of history at the University of Jena on the topic "Was heisst und zu welchem Ende studiert man Universalgeschichte?" (What Is and Why Do We Study Universal History?). He saw the European state system as an interlinked community – indeed, as a family – in which no state could be fundamentally at odds with the other states.

The upheavals of the French Revolutionary and Napoleonic periods made such complacency difficult, but they did not destroy the universal history tradition. Rather, historians ranging from Leopold von Ranke to Lord Acton and J.B. Bury still saw universal history as the ideal toward which historical research was directed, an ideal they hoped would eventually be realized. Only with the further upheavals of the 20th century was the notion that historians should aim at the writing of a universal history pushed out of the historical discipline. It came to be generally held that historians were united not by the single Story that they aspired to tell, but only by commitment to a common historical method. To be sure, in the 20th century the notion of universal history continued to live in at least two contexts, but these lay outside the discipline. First, in the 19th century, the philosopher G.W.F. Hegel was one of many writers who lent authority to the idea that there is a single History, and Hegel's influence persisted, most notably among Marxists but also in the neo-Hegelianism of Alexandre Kojève and some other philosophers and publicists. Second, some historians writing outside the discipline, such as Oswald Spengler, H.G. Wells, and Arnold Toynbee, also continued to write universal history.

But by the early 1990s such projects had few adherents in the wider intellectual world. In a much-noticed book, *La Condition postmoderne* (1979; *The Postmodern Condition*, 1984) the French philosopher Jean-François Lyotard offered a challenge to "grand narrative" – a notion closely akin to universal history – that seemed to accord with the widespread experience of personal and sociological discontinuity in the contemporary world. The collapse of the Soviet imperium in 1989–91 reoriented the political order in unexpected, and often particularizing, ways, and the postcolonial impulse in general seems to have had a similar effect. At the same time, economic and communicative interconnections between different parts of the world are continuing to tighten. There have been some attempts to revive universal history (see Fukuyama, 1992), but it seems unlikely that it will return in the near future, at least not in its old form of a story having a beginning, middle, and end. Two historians, Michael Geyer and Charles Bright, have suggested ("World History in a Global Age," 1995) that although the contemporary world "has come into its own as an integrated globe, . . . it lacks narration and has no history"; at most it has "narrative residues from previous eras." One historiographical strategy in what is now called "world history" is the making of limited comparisons between different parts of the world that the historian selects for comparison in the hope of generating insight. Such work, however, is clearly not universal history as it was known in the past, but a mark of its absence.

ALLAN MEGILL

See also Acton; Bury; Hegel; Ibn Khaldūn; Koselleck; Postmodernism; Ranke; Schlözer; Spengler; Toynbee

Further Reading

Augustine, St., *De civitate dei*, written 413–26; in English as *The City of God*

Bossuet, Jacques Bénigne, *Discours sur l'histoire universelle*, Paris: Mabre Cramoisy, 1681; in English as *Discourse on Universal History*, 1976

Breisach, Ernst, "Universal History: A Troubled Tradition," in his *Historiography: Ancient, Medieval, and Modern*, Chicago: University of Chicago Press, 1983; revised 1994

Curtin, Philip D., "Graduate Teaching in World History," *Journal of World History* 2 (1991), 81–89

Fukuyama, Francis, *The End of History and the Last Man*, New York: Free Press, and London: Hamish Hamilton, 1992

Gatterer, Johann Christoph, *Handbuch der Universalhistorie* (Handbook of Universal History), 2 vols., Göttingen: Vandenhoeck, 1761–65

Geyer, Michael, and Charles Bright, "World History in a Global Age," *American Historical Review* 100 (1995), 1034–60

Hübinger, Gangolf, Jürgen Osterhammel, and Erich Pelzer, eds., *Universalgeschichte und Nationalgeschichten* (Universal History and National Histories), Freiburg: Rombach, 1994

Ibn Khaldūn, *Muqaddima*, written 1375–78; in English as *The Muqaddimah: An Introduction to History*, 2nd edition, Princeton: Princeton University Press, 1967, London: Routledge/Secker and Warburg, 1978

Isidore of Seville, *Etymologiae* (Etymologies), written c.620

Kant, Immanuel, "Idee zu einer allgemeinen Geschichte in weltbürgerlicher Absicht," written 1784, in Hans Reiss, ed., *Kants politisches Denken*, Frankfurt: Lang, 1977; in English as "Idea for a Universal History with a Cosmopolitan Purpose," in Hans Reiss, ed., *Kant: Political Writings*, Cambridge: Cambridge University Press, 1970; revised and enlarged 1991

Klempt, Adalbert, *Die Säkularisierung der universalhistorischen Auffassung: Zum Wandel des Geschichtsdenkens im 16. und 17. Jahrhundert*, Göttingen: Musterschmidt, 1960

Koselleck, Reinhart, "Die Entstehung des Kollektivsingulars" (section V.1.a. of "Geschichte"), in Otto Brunner, Werner Conze, and Reinhart Koselleck, eds., *Geschichtliche Grundbegriffe: historisches Lexikon zur politisch-sozialen Sprache in Deutschland*, Stuttgart: Klett, 1972–, vol. 2

Koselleck, Reinhart, "On the Disposability of History," in Koselleck, *Futures Past: On the Semantics of Historical Time*, Cambridge, MA: MIT Press, 1985

Lyotard, Jean-François, *La Condition postmoderne: rapport sur le savoir*, Paris: Minuit, 1979; in English as *The Postmodern Condition: A Report on Knowledge*, Manchester: Manchester University Press, and Minneapolis: University of Minnesota Press, 1984

Megill, Allan, "'Grand Narrative' and the Discipline of History," in F.R. Ankersmit and Hans Kellner, eds., *A New Philosophy of History*, Chicago: University of Chicago Press, and London: Reaktion, 1995

Mink, Louis O., "Narrative Form as a Cognitive Instrument" (1978) in his *Historical Understanding*, edited by Brian Fay, Eugene O. Golob, and Richard T. Vann, Ithaca, NY: Cornell University Press, 1987

Müller, Johannes von, *Vierundzwanzig Bücher allgemeiner Geschichten besonders der europäischen Menschheit*, Tübingen, 1810

Orosius, Paulus, *Historiae adversum Paganos*, written c.417 CE; in English as *Seven Books of History Against the Pagans*, Washington, DC: Catholic University of America Press, 1964

Ranke, Leopold von, "Idee der Universalhistorie" [lecture script of 1831–32], in *Aus Werk und Nachlass*, edited by Walther Peter Fuchs and Theodor Schieder, 4 vols., Munich: Bayerischen Akademie, 1964–75, vol. 4: *Vorlesungseinleitungen*; abridged in English as "On the Character of Historical Science (A Manuscript of the 1830s)," in *The Theory and Practice of History*, edited by Georg G. Iggers and Konrad von Moltke, Indianapolis: Bobbs Merrill, 1973

Ranke, Leopold von, "Die Notwendigkeit universalgeschichtlicher Betrachtung," in *Aus Werk und Nachlass*, edited by Walther Peter Fuchs and Theodor Schieder, 4 vols., Munich: Bayerischen Akademie, 1964–75, vol. 4: *Vorlesungseinleitungen*; in English as "The Role of the Particular and the General in the Study of Universal History (A Manuscript of the 1860s)," in *The Theory and Practice of History*, edited by Georg G. Iggers and Konrad von Moltke, Indianapolis: Bobbs Merrill, 1973

Schiller, Friedrich, "Was heisst und zu welchem Ende studiert man Universalgeschichte?" (What Is and Why Do We Study Universal History?) in Wolfgang Hardtwig, ed., *Über das Studium der Geschichte*, Munich: Deutscher Taschenbuch, 1990

Schlözer, August Ludwig von, *Vorstellung seiner Universal-Historie* (Introduction to Universal History), 2 vols., Göttingen, 1772–73

Schulin, Ernst, ed., *Universalgeschichte* (Universal History), Cologne: Kiepenheuer & Witsch, 1974

Toynbee, Arnold J., *A Study of History*, 12 vols., Oxford and New York: Oxford University Press, 1934–61

Wells, Herbert George, *The Outline of History*, 2 vols., London: Newnes, and New York: Macmillan, 1920 [and later revisions]

Urban History

As a historical discipline, urban history has always been peculiarly unsure of its own identity. H.J. Dyos, the father of British urban history, described it as a "portmanteau subject," a "field of knowledge" rather than a discipline as traditionally defined. Much of the history of towns and cities is written outside the confines of the academy, merging into the genres of "local history" or topography. Although it would claim a greater degree of historical rigor than such writings, urban history has never established its own identifiable theories and methodologies, being instead a promiscuous borrower of concepts and procedures from other fields of history and from the disciplines of the social sciences. Urban historians also remain acutely aware of the difficulty of defining the "urban" (not least the inconsistency of definition between countries and continents), and are troubled by the degree to which, particularly in modern industrial societies, the extent of town- and city-dwelling means that most history of any sort is "urban" in that it occurs either in towns and cities, or in the context of a predominantly urban society.

This uneasiness is reflected in the profusion of introspective surveys of the nature and identity of urban history, and in its slow and uncertain institutional development. The sense of urban history as a discipline emerged first in the United States in the years around World War II, prompted by the works of Arthur Meier Schlesinger and Richard C. Wade which integrated the city into Turner's frontier thesis, and thus made cities central to the development of American nationhood. An Urban History Group of the American Historical Association was established in the early 1950s. At this time, despite the important work on medieval towns published by Henri Pirenne in the 1920s, there was still little or no interest in the study of urban history *per se*. In Britain, the publication of Asa Briggs' *Victorian Cities* (1963) was an important step forward. However, it was two conferences, in 1961 in the US, and 1966 in Britain, that produced the two foundational programs of urban history, Handlin and Burchard's *The Historian and the City* (1963) and *The Study of Urban History* (1968) edited by Dyos.

Even then, institutional formalization occurred only hesitantly. In North America, an *Urban History Newsletter* was published from the 1950s, eventually superseded in 1974 by the *Journal of Urban History*. But it was not until the establishment of the Urban History Association in 1988 that urban historians could claim an associational base. In Europe it was not until the mid-1970s that the first urban history journals were established, and not until the early 1990s that the European Association of Urban Historians was formed; in Britain, it took 20 years to convert the *Urban History Newsletter* into a semiannual journal, *Urban History*, and in the mid-1990s there was still no formal urban history association. Outside these two continents, although it has been possible to trace an increasingly amount of urban history research, little or no progress towards the institutionalization of the discipline has taken place.

Such unevenness illustrates the degree to which the development of urban history in different national and regional contexts has been strongly influenced by their own histories of urbanization. It is possible to discern a distinction between those countries (including Italy, Spain, and Holland) where the dominance of the city from an early date has made it more difficult to distinguish urban history from general political and administrative histories, or works of economic and social history where the city was the most convenient unit of analysis of essentially national problems, those areas (such as Eastern Europe, China, or Latin America) where the dominance of the rural economy and lack of major industrial centers worked against the development of a strong urban history, and those countries (United States, Britain) where the Industrial Revolution brought rapid urbanization to essentially rural societies, and where concern from the early 19th century onwards with the problems of urban growth created the basis for a strong urban history, albeit dominated by notions of the city as pathology.

This pattern reflects in turn the dominance of the industrial town and city in the discipline (not merely in America where the opportunities for pre-industrial urban history are dwarfed by those of the industrial city). In some senses this is surprising: for historians of classical Greece, of Rome, and of much of medieval Europe, cities were the basic administrative and political unit; urban history merged into political history; the growth of cities was coterminous with the development of civilization, of law, of national polities. In the later 19th century studies such as F.W. Maitland's *Township and Borough* (1898) discovered in the emergence of the town the administrative underpinnings of national institutions and laws. However, as political and purely economic approaches were challenged in the 20th century by broader social perspectives, the preoccupations (and limited source-bases) of pre-industrial urban history came to be seen as increasingly restricted, despite Pirenne's attempt to develop a more socioeconomic framework for the study of medieval cities. From the 1950s through to the 1980s pre-industrial towns were marginal to urban historians. Only in the 1980s, often through the creation of a new generation of networks of urban historians, such as the Early Modern Towns Group in Britain, were there signs of a lessening of this imbalance.

Of course, in one sense, this revival only reunited urban history with the longstanding tradition of urban biography, which originated as early as the 16th century in countries such as France and Italy. Methodologically, this work was rather naive, such studies being frequently celebratory or centenary accounts, written by antiquaries or amateur historians for the purpose of civic boosterism, or the preservation of local knowledge. Into the 20th century they were often merely compilations of documents, put together in "scissors and paste" form, or straightforward chronicles, with hagiographic accounts of founding fathers and local worthies. More recently this work has been supplemented by more sophisticated descriptive and analytical works, often the result of collective local history projects derived from adult education classes.

For all its greater sophistication, and to the frustration of many of its champions, urban history has never entirely escaped the pull of the biographical frame. The overwhelming preponderance of urban history has taken the single urban center as its focus, from early classic studies such as Bayrd Still's *Milwaukee* (1948), to modern series such as the Bellhaven World Cities histories. Nevertheless, it is possible to trace a development of urban history in the 20th century through various approaches. Adopting – as is common – descriptions borrowed from the natural sciences, these might be described, in addition to the biographical, as pathological, anatomical, and ecological approaches.

What might be called the pathological approach emerged during the 19th century, when the established tradition of civic boosterism was challenged by the perception of the city as a social and cultural problem, exemplified by Friedrich Engels' *Die Lage der arbeitenden Klasse in England* (1845; *The Condition of the Working Class in England in 1844*, 1887), by the analyses of Louis Wirth and the Chicago school of sociology which was a fundamental influence on early American urban studies, and by Lewis Mumford's *The Culture of Cities* (1938). This perspective had the advantage of shifting the scope away from the narratives of city life to studies, if not of the workings of the city as a social system, then at least of problems of pollution, disease, poverty, and planning, and the attempts of reformers to provide solutions. Such a focus allowed urban historians to work closely with planners, urban sociologists, and policymakers, and provided it with a seductively utilitarian justification.

Until the 1960s, urban historians lacked the capacity to move effectively beyond the symptoms of urban malaise, comprehensively to reconstruct the social and economic anatomy of the city. Here, as elsewhere, developing computer technologies provided the tools needed to harness to the task the masses of statistical data in census, rating and local government files. For a decade or two, the possibilities illustrated by works such as Stephan Thernstrom's *Poverty and Progress* (1964), captured the imagination of urban historians, encouraging the strong influence of social science methodologies and preoccupations, especially concerned with questions of demography and geography.

During the 1970s, however, increasing dissatisfaction was voiced at the limitations of the new urban history, and the preoccupations which it shared with early pathological approaches. There were two main lines of criticism. One emphasized the extent to which urban history continued to concentrate on the nature of the urban experience rather than on the causes of urbanization, on structures rather than processes, on the internal examination of individual localities, rather than on comparative studies of urban ecologies in general. The pioneering comparative study of urbanization, Adna F. Weber's *The Growth of Cities* was published as early as 1899, followed by Pierre Lavedan's *Histoire de l'urbanisme* (A History of

Urbanism, 1926–52); but it was only in the 1980s that these models prompted more sustained attention to comparative studies of urbanization, and to national and international urban history syntheses, most significantly Jan de Vries' *European Urbanization, 1500–1800* (1984), and P.M. Hohenberg and L.H. Lees' *The Making of Urban Europe, 1000–1950* (1985).

At the same time, a second trajectory of development repudiated the definition of the city as problem, and what were seen as the rather narrow and even arid range of questions raised by the new urban history, moving beyond production and reproduction to a focus on consumption, raising a series of questions about religion, leisure, literature and the arts, about the cultural life of cities, and the place of urban centers in wider cultural processes. The most important early example of this new approach, which gathered momentum from the expanding influence of postmodernism and the spread of cultural studies, was *The Victorian City* (1973) edited by H.J. Dyos and Michael Wolff. During the 1980s and 1990s, this concern with the construction and reading of images and "texts" of the city renewed a link between urban history and art and architectural history which, once strong, had been lost during the emergence of urban history as a distinct discipline, and encouraged the forging of new links with literary studies.

As a result, urban history, always a "multidisciplinary space," reaches the end of the century influenced by a greater diversity of theoretical and methodological approaches than ever before. This eclecticism carries with it the dangers of fragmentation that have long worried its practitioners, and that continue to inhibit the development of the kind of large-scale interpretive frameworks that might integrate the discipline and push forward the recent advances toward greater comparison and synthesis. It also ensures the vitality of urban history and its safety from being captured by any one of its methodological or conceptual frames.

MARTIN HEWITT

See also Briggs; de Vries; Duby; Engels; Handlin; Local; Maitland; Mumford; Pirenne; Rörig

Further Reading

Blumin, Stuart M., "City Limits: Two Decades of Urban History in the *Journal of Urban History*," *Journal of Urban History*, 21 (1994), 7–30

Briggs, Asa, *Victorian Cities*, London: Odhams Press, 1963; New York: Harper, 1965

Cannadine, David, and David Reeder, eds., *Exploring the Urban Past: Essays in Urban History by H.J. Dyos*, Cambridge and New York: Cambridge University Press, 1982

de Vries, Jan, *European Urbanization, 1500–1800*, Cambridge, MA: Harvard University Press, and London: Methuen, 1984

Duby, Georges, ed., *Histoire de la France urbaine* (A History of Urban France), 5 vols., Paris: Seuil, 1980–83

Dyos, H.J., *Victorian Suburb: A Study of the Growth of Camberwell*, Leicester: Leicester University Press, 1961

Dyos, H.J., ed., *The Study of Urban History*, London: Arnold, and New York: St. Martin's Press, 1968

Dyos, H.J., and Michael Wolff, eds., *The Victorian City: Images and Realities*, 2 vols., London: Routledge, 1973

Engeli, Christian, and Horst Matzerath, eds., *Modern Urban History Research in Europe, USA and Japan: A Handbook*, Oxford and New York: Berg, 1989

Engels, Friedrich, *Die Lage der arbeitenden Klasse in England*, Leipzig: Wigand, 1845; in English as *The Condition of the Working Class in England in 1844*, New York: Lovell, 1887, London: Sonnenschein, 1892

Ferreira, John Vincent, and Shashi Shekhar Jha, *The Outlook Tower: Essays on Urbanization in Memory of Patrick Geddes*, Bombay: Popular Prakashan, 1976

Fraser, Derek, and Anthony Sutcliffe, *The Pursuit of Urban History*, London: Arnold, 1983

Gillette, Howard, and Zane Miller, eds., *American Urbanism: A Historiographical Review*, New York: Greenwood, 1987

Handlin, Oscar, and John Burchard, eds., *The Historian and the City*, Cambridge, MA: MIT Press, 1963

Hershberg, Theodore, ed., *Philadelphia: Work, Space, Family and Group Experience in the Nineteenth Century: Essays Toward an Interdisciplinary History of the City*, Oxford and New York: Oxford University Press, 1980

Hohenberg, Paul M., and Lynn Hollen Lees, *The Making of Urban Europe, 1000–1950*, Cambridge, MA: Harvard University Press, 1985

Jackson, Kenneth, *Crabgrass Frontier: The Suburbanization of the United States*, New York and Oxford: Oxford University Press, 1985

Jacobs, Jane, *The Death and Life of Great American Cities*, New York: Random House, 1961; London: Cape, 1962

Journal of Urban History, 1974–

Lampard, Eric, "American Historians and the Study of Urbanization," *American Historical Review* 67 (1961), 49–61

Lavedan, Pierre, *Histoire de l'urbanisme* (A History of Urbanism), 3 vols., Paris: Laurens, 1926–52

Lees, Lynn Hollen, "The Challenge of Political Change: Urban History in the 1990s," *Urban History*, 21 (1994), 7–19

Maitland, F.W., *Township and Borough*, Cambridge: Cambridge University Press, 1898

Monkkonen, Eric H., *America Becomes Urban: The Development of US Cities and Towns, 1780–1980*, Berkeley: University of California Press, 1988

Mumford, Lewis, *The Culture of Cities*, New York: Harcourt Brace, 1938; London: Secker and Warburg, 1940

Mumford, Lewis, *The City in History: Its Origins, Its Transformations, and Its Prospects*, New York: Harcourt Brace, and London: Secker and Warburg, 1961

Olsen, Donald J., *The City as a Work of Art: London, Paris, Vienna*, New Haven and London: Yale University Press, 1986

Pinol, Jean-Luc, *Le Monde des villes au XIXe siècle* (The World of Cities in the 19th Century), Paris: Hachette, 1991

Pirenne, Henri, *Medieval Cities: Their Origins and the Revival of Trade*, Princeton: Princeton University Press, 1925; French version as *Les Villes du Moyen-Age: essai d'histoire économique et sociale*, Brussels: Lamertin, 1927

Rodger, Richard, *European Urban History: Prospect and Retrospect*, Leicester: Leicester University Press, and New York: St. Martin's Press, 1993

Schlesinger, Arthur Meier, *The Rise of the City, 1878–1898*, New York: Macmillan, 1933

Still, Bayrd, *Milwaukee: The History of a City*, Madison: State Historical Society, 1948

Thernstrom, Stephan, *Poverty and Progress: Social Mobility in a Nineteenth Century City*, Cambridge, MA: Harvard University Press, 1964

Thernstrom, Stephan, and Richard Sennett, *Nineteenth Century Cities: Essays in the New Urban History*, New Haven: Yale University Press, 1969

Urban History/Urban History Yearbook, 1974–91, 1992–

Wade, R.C., *The Urban Frontier: The Rise of Western Cities, 1790–1830*, Cambridge, MA: Harvard University Press, and Oxford: Oxford University Press, 1959

Warner, Sam Bass, *Streetcar Suburbs: The Process of Growth in Boston, 1870–1900*, Cambridge, MA: Harvard University Press, 1962

Weber, Adna Ferrin, *The Growth of Cities in the Nineteenth Century: A Study in Statistics*, New York: Columbia University Press, 1899

Wirth, Louis, *On Cities and Social Life: Selected Papers*, Chicago: University of Chicago Press, 1964

Woude, A.M. van der, Akira Hayzmi, and Jan de Vries, eds., *Urbanization in History: A Process of Dynamic Interactions*, Oxford and New York: Oxford University Press, 1990

V

Vagts, Alfred 1892–1986

US (German-born) military historian

Few scholars have written about their own turbulent times with the same degree of sophisticated historical insight as Alfred Vagts. A Prussian officer in World War I, Vagts abandoned the military and joined the ranks of the "Lost Generation," devoting his life to peace by understanding war. It is logical that a scholar with Vagts' life experience would emerge as the most eloquent commentator on the phenomenon of militarism. After taking part in the cultural wars of the Weimar republic, Vagts left to study in America and decided to stay after Hitler's consolidation of power. Vagts is most important for his groundbreaking scholarship regarding civil-military relations. Decades before scholars such as Michael Howard and Peter Paret introduced military history into universities as a legitimate scholarly subject, Vagts laid the groundwork by demonstrating the pivotal role militaries play in diplomatic, political, and even social discourse. He helped elevate topics once studied only in staff colleges to the forefront of academia.

Vagts' seminal work, *A History of Militarism* (1937) delineated the role of the officer corps within the state from feudal times to the 20th century. He devoted more attention to Germany than to other nations, but, given the Prussian officer corps' example of displaying the "state within a state" mentality which is partly responsible for militarism, Vagts' consistent reference to Germany is understandable. Sections on World War II and the Third World were included in the 2nd edition published in 1959. Vagts influenced a generation of scholars with his definition of militarism. He described a militaristic society as one that "ranks military institutions and ways above the prevailing attitudes of civilian life and carries the military mentality into the civilian sphere." Vagts was most compelling when revealing that this atmosphere actually subverts the original purpose of the military. Professional officers lose their singular status in a militaristic society. The frustrations of German officers forced to submit to National Socialism and Hitler's "generalship" was his best example. Fellow German émigré Gerhard Ritter and historian Michael Geyer are among the more influential authors to expand upon Vagts' arguments.

Other works by Vagts originated during his period with the US Office of Economic Warfare during World War II. These include *Hitler's Second Army* (1943) and *Landing Operations* (1946). Vagts demonstrated a talent for addressing current affairs while remaining the quintessential historian. He was especially interested in the interaction between diplomats and military officers assigned to politically sensitive posts. *Defense and Diplomacy* (1956) is both a history and a prescription. Using history as evidence, Vagts concluded that only a strong civilian executive branch capable of utilizing military expertise could avoid sliding into militarism on one hand and inefficiency on the other. *The Military Attaché* (1967) was the first book of its kind to focus exclusively on this special breed of soldier-diplomat that has wielded so much influence throughout modern European history.

Vagts' earlier works were accused of being "too German," that is dense and inartistic. This deficiency was remedied over time as Vagts wrote with greater confidence on subjects with which he had personal experience. Occasionally his personal experience led him to condemn military institutions collectively; this tendency made some of his more passionate arguments disingenuous. Moreover, some of the prominent works contain relatively slim bibliographies and infrequent citations. His scholarship, however, addresses one of the most important issues facing 20th-century society – the precarious relationship between civilians and soldiers. The frequency with which Vagts is cited in current literature and the fact that his personal papers have been organized into a valuable research collection is a testament to the strength of his legacy.

BRIAN CRIM

Biography

Alfred Hermann Friedrich Vagts. Born Basbeck, 1 December, 1892. Officer in German forces, 1914–18. Attended universities of Munich and Hamburg, PhD 1927. Voluntary military service against right-wing organizations, 1923. Emigrated to US, 1924; naturalized 1933. Foreign relations assistant, Institute of Foreign Affairs, 1923–32; taught at Harvard University and Radcliffe College, 1938; member, Institute for Advanced Study, Princeton, 1938–42. Worked in the US Office of Economic Warfare during World War II. Independent researcher and writer, from 1942. Married Miriam Beard, writer, and daughter of historians Charles and Mary Beard, 1927 (1 son). Died 16 June 1986.

Principal Works

Deutschland und die Vereinigten Staaten in der Weltpolitik (Germany and the United States in World Politics), 2 vols., 1935

A History of Militarism: Romance and Realities of a Profession, 1937; revised 1959

Hitler's Second Army, 1943

Landing Operations: Strategy, Psychology, Tactics, Politics, from Antiquity to 1945, 1946

*Defense and Diplomacy: The Soldier and the Conduct of Foreign
    Relations,* 1956
*Deutsch-Amerikanische Rückwanderung: Probleme, Phänomene,
    Statistik, Politik, Soziologie, Biographie* (German-American
    Remigration: Problems, Phenomenon, Statistics, Politics, Sociology,
    Biography), 1960
The Military Attaché, 1967

Vansina, Jan 1929–
Belgian historian of Africa

Jan Vansina set the pace in African historical studies from the
1950s into the 1990s, in what one observer termed a methodological "decathlon of the social sciences." He was trained in
the rigors of medieval history in Belgium, but by 1953 found
himself appointed a researcher in anthropology in the late-
colonial Belgian Congo. Extended fieldwork there among the
Kuba people there led to a doctoral dissertation defying canonical authority in the profession by proposing a formal historical
method employing African "oral traditions" as evidence.
Further research in Belgian central Africa, involving linguistics
and archaeology in Rwanda and Burundi, as well as study of
British social anthropology at the University of London, honed
Vansina's path-breaking interdisciplinary recovery of the early
history of African regions almost entirely lacking in the written
records then regarded as essential to the historian's craft.

Vansina's published dissertation in 1961 amounted to a
methodological manifesto on behalf of the then-emergent field
of African history. Its appearance coincided with an invitation
to join Philip Curtin's program in Comparative Tropical
History, including Africa, at the University of Wisconsin,
Madison, in 1961. With Curtin and later with Steven Feierman,
Vansina trained numerous students subsequently prominent in
African history and wrote more than a dozen monographs and
methodological treatises and over 150 articles and other shorter
works in English, French, Flemish, German, and Italian. These
illuminated the past of what he once, ironically, called "lost
corners of the world" and continually advanced the standards
of historical research on Africa's unwritten past.

Vansina almost single-handedly added the "kingdoms" of
central Africa to the galaxy of early African polities being celebrated in "trade and politics" studies typical of historical work
on Africa during the 1960s. His first two monographs, one on
Rwanda and the other on the Kuba, revealed the subtle politics
of alliance, the power of ideology, and the pluralism of African
polities behind the prevailing emphasis on centralization and
royal courts. *Kingdoms of the Savanna,* his 1966 synthesis of
written evidence for the political history of southern central
Africa, became an immediate classic and eventually stimulated
a generation of monographs by students and others, exploring
in greater detail the states it introduced. In the early 1970s,
Vansina published two further monographs in this series of
political works, both venturing further into the originality
of African dispersed political systems and setting each one in
its cultural and ideological contexts.

The interdisciplinary bases of Vansina's work grew steadily
in complexity and rigor, both as applied to the historical problems at hand and as formal methodology. *The Tio Kingdom*
(1973) broke through the presentism still prevalent in

Africanist anthropology of the 1960s by practicing what
Vansina termed a "historical ethnography," firmly dated to the
late 19th century. Throughout the 1970s he teased out a record
of the past visible through Bantu historical linguistics, as
linguists continued to define relationships among the 400 or
so Bantu languages now spoken in central Africa, as well as
historicizing other related disciplines (prominently in *Art
History in Africa,* 1984). He became his own leading critic
when, in 1978, he returned to the topic of his first field research
in a linguistically enriched history of the Kuba peoples, in
which he made clear his growing skepticism of the literal readings that he had given oral traditions in earlier studies. He
incorporated two decades of sometimes intense criticism from
anthropologists, particularly Lévi-Straussian structuralists, in a
new methodological overview defending *Oral Tradition as
History* (1985) on grounds reflecting more the then-maturing
field of African studies than the Belgian philosophy of history
available to him as a disciplinary anchor in the 1950s. Vansina
has not formally acknowledged the deconstructionist, historical memory, and the cultural-historical studies that have subsequently come to dominate the study of oral traditions.

Instead, in *Paths in the Rainforests* (1990) Vansina emphasized the creation of cultures underlying political traditions, then
emerging as a prominent theme throughout African studies.
Applying historical linguistic methodologies ("words and
things") to the Bantu-speaking peoples of the central African
forest, in a tour de force of characteristic methodological rigor,
wide-ranging interdisciplinary skill, linguistic virtuosity, and
subtle conceptualization, he sketched the innovations that more
than 200 Bantu-speaking communities had created out of a
shared cultural heritage in until-then "darkest Africa" during
more than 3000 years, illuminating the only region in Africa still
substantially without a known past, owing to its lack of early
written records, shallow oral traditions, and undeveloped
archaeology. Dozens of technical essays flowed from the
research and thinking behind Vansina's monographs. One
approach interpreted developments in Bantu historical linguistics for historians, and another reflected on the interaction of
archaeology and history in recovering Africa's past. Vansina's
defining influence in the field extended beyond his reconstruction
of what seems to have happened to a setting out the historical
applications of most other relevant academic disciplines and
providing formal methodological rationales for the practice.

Professionally during these years Vansina became a central
figure in the planning and editing of the massive UNESCO
General History of Africa (1981–93) and informally facilitated
communications among historians and scholars in the other disciplines in which he worked, in Africa, Britain, Europe, the
United States, and beyond. Following the departures of Curtin
(1975) and Feierman (1990) from Wisconsin, he became the
key historian of Africa there, as Vilas professor and MacArthur
fellow until his retirement in 1994. Throughout Vansina's
career, he remained particularly dedicated to the development
of autonomous history programs at institutions of higher education in Africa. Vansina's decisive influence on the methodology of modern history in Africa reaches well beyond the public,
written record outlined here to a worldwide range of informal
inspiration and instruction to many other scholars, particularly
students at universities in Africa. Like Vansina's creative techniques of teasing unexpectedly rich historical evidence from

·novel sources, his professional vision has also tapped the diverse contributions of promising new contributors to the field.

JOSEPH C. MILLER

See also Africa: Central; Africa: West; Memory; Oral

Biography

Jan Maria Jozef Vansina. Born Antwerp, 14 September 1929, son of painters. Received PhD, Catholic University of Louvain, 1957. Researcher, Institute and Center for African Research, Belgium, 1952–60: director, 1957–60; taught history and anthropology (rising to professor), University of Wisconsin, Madison, 1961–94 (emeritus). Married Claudine Marie-Jeanne Herman, 1954 (1 son).

Principal Writings

De la tradition orale: essai de méthode historique, 1961; in English as *Oral Tradition: A Study in Historical Methodology*, 1965
L'Evolution du royaume Rwanda des origines à 1900 (The Evolution of the Kingdom of Rwanda from Its Origins to 1900), 1962
Geschiedenis van de Kuba van ongeveer 1500 tot 1904 (History of the Kuba from 1500 to 1904), 1963
Le Royaume Kuba (The Kuba Kingdom), 1964
Kingdoms of the Savanna, 1966
La Légende du passé: traditions orales du Burundi (Legends of the Past: Oral Traditions of Burundi), 1972
The Tio Kingdom of the Middle Congo, 1880–1892, 1973
The Children of Woot: A History of the Kuba Peoples, 1978
Art History in Africa: An Introduction to Method, 1984
Oral Tradition as History, 1985
Paths in the Rainforests: Toward a History of Political Tradition in Equatorial Africa, 1990
Living with Africa, 1994

Further Reading

Harms, Robert W., Joseph C. Miller, David Newbury, and Michele D. Wagner, eds., *Paths to the African Past: African Historical Essays in Honor of Jan Vansina*, Atlanta: African Studies Association Press, 1994

Varnhagen, Francisco Adolfo de

1816–1878

Brazilian historian

One of the most influential historians of Second Empire Brazil (1840–89), Varnhagen has been considered the founder of Brazilian historiography. His *História geral do Brasil* (General History of Brazil, 1854–57), inspired by his reading the Brazilian studies of the German natural historian K.F. Martius, is the most complete collection of facts about early Brazilian history. It is a study of the culture and customs of the Indians and of the colonial system. Varnhagen brought attention to Frei Vicente do Salvador's early *História do Brasil (1500–1627)*, and eclipsed Robert Southey's classic *History of Brazil* (3 vols., 1810–19).

However, praise for Varnhagen has not been wholehearted. Although he conducted archival reasearch, revealing numerous new documents on early Brazilian history, he was less reliable in giving credit to the work of fellow historians. At the same time, he set a standard of scientific rigor, for establishing detail, the authenticity of the sources, and clarifying contradictions. He was much more concerned with creating a chronological narrative than with grouping, interpreting, and contextualizing the product of his research. Finally, it must be said that stylistically his work lacked life and tended to be overstuffed with sometimes irrelevant information.

Varnhagen ignored periodization. He thus missed the opportunity to create a major historiographical work. Although revealing facts and events never before thought to be relevant for Brazilian history, he was unable to understand them as part of a system and to formulate a theory explaining the sequence. This task was reserved for João Capistrano de Abreu (1853–1927), responsible for the annotated edition of the major work of Varnhagen. But Abreu himself, considered the first major figure in modern Brazilian historiography, never wrote a general history of Brazil. The four general histories of Frei Vicente do Salvador, José Inácio de Abreu e Lima, Robert Southey, and Varnhagen constitute the basis on which the modern historiography of Brazil has been established. With Abreu e Lima, Varnhagen engaged in the most important debate in Brazilian historiography.

Varnhagen made his first contribution to the intellectual life of the Second Empire with the publication of *Florilégio da poesia brasileira* (The Flourishing of Brazilian Poetry, 1850–53), the first comprehensive critical collection of Brazilian poetry. The collection was profoundly nationalistic, in the sense of giving priority to works with Brazilian motifs, and as a result Varnhagen entered into a confrontation with Portuguese critics. But he always revealed a positive attitude toward Portugal, and this is evident in his approach to the history of Brazil. He was a controversial intellectual, extremely conservative and an admirer of the Portuguese colonial rule. He has even been accused of having praised the House of Braganza with the objective of being recognized by the reigning emperor, Dom Pedro II, who indeed eventually elevated him to viscount.

Varnhagen, as viscount of Porto Seguro, embarked on a diplomatic career and spent much of his life in Europe. This gave him an opportunity to look into the best archives of Europe and to write the most well-documented history of Brazil. The research leading to this scholarly work also resulted in the publication of a letter of Columbus to Santangel (1493) and on comments on Americo Vespucci, which resulted in a polemical exchange with the historian Armand d'Avezac-Macaya. Varnhagen also edited the diaries of Pero Lopes de Sousa (1530) and Gabriel Soares de Sousa (1587), as well as Mauricio de Heriarte's *Descripção do estado do Maranhão, Pará, Corupá e Rio das Amazonas* (A Description of the States of Maranhão, Pará, and Corupá, and the Amazon River, 1662), and Bernardo José da Gama's *Informação sobre a capitania do Maranhão* (Information on the Captaincy of Maranhão, 1813).

The historical writing of Varnhagen focused essentially on colonial history and he was meticulous in dealing with this period. His careful research of dates, places, and individuals is recognized as having established what might be called the "official" Brazilian history. Also recognized has been his sympathy for colonialism, and his choosing to ignore the movement for independence.

UBIRATAN D'AMBROSIO

See also Latin America: National; Rodrigues

Biography

Born São João de Ipanema, State of São Paulo, 17 February 1816, son of a German engineer and his Portuguese wife. Went to Portugal with family, 1824; studied at Real Colegio da Luz, Portugal, 1825–33; Academia da Marinha, Brazil, 1832–33. Took Brazilian citizenship, 1841; served in corps of engineers; secretary, Brazilian legation, Lisbon; ambassador to Madrid, 1847, Latin America, 1859–68, and Vienna, 1869–78. Created baron, 1872; and viscount of Porto Seguro, 1874. Died Vienna, 29 June 1878.

Principal Writings

Florilégio da poesia brasileira (The Flourishing of Brazilian Poetry), 3 vols., 1850–53

História geral do Brasil (General History of Brazil), 6 vols., 1854–57

História das lutas com os holandêses no Brasil desde 1624 a 1654 (History of the Conflicts with the Dutch in Brazil from 1624 to 1654), 1871

L'origine touranienne des Américains Tupis-Caribes et des anciens Egyptiens, indiquée principalement par la philologie comparée: traces d'une ancienne migration en Amérique, invasion du Brésil par les Tupis, 1876

História da independência do Brasil (History of the Independence of Brazil; unknown up to 1916), 1917; 6th edition 1972

Further Reading

Abreu, João Capistrano de, "A Critique of Francisco Adolfo de Varnhagen," in E. Bradford Burns, ed., *Perspectives on Brazilian History*, New York: Columbia University Press, 1967

Calman, Pedro, "Varnhagen," *Revista do Instituto Histórico e Geográfico Brasileiro* 338 (1983), 249–58

Cámara, José Gomes Bezerra, "Varnhagen: O Homen e o historiador" (Varnhagen: The Man and the Historian), *Revista do Instituto Histórico e Geográfico Brasiliero* 328 (1980), 161–87

Martinière, Guy, "Problemes du developpement de l'historiographie Bresiliene" (Problems in the Development of Brazilian Historiography), *Storia della storiografia* 19 (1991), 117–47

Rodrigues, José Honório, "Varnhagen: O primeiro mestre de Historografia Brasileira" (Varnhagen: The First Master of Brazilian Historiography), *Revista do Instituto Histórico e Geográfico Brasiliero* 328 (1980), 135–60

Schwartz, Stuart B., "Francisco Adolfo de Varnhagen: Diplomat, Patriot, Historian," *Hispanic American Historical Review* 48 (1967), 185–202

Vasiliev, A.A. 1867–1953

Russian historian of Byzantium

Raised in a great Russian tradition of scholarship, A.A. Vasiliev was an important intellectual émigré from the early Soviet Union. Transplanted to the USA, he became a pioneer of Byzantine history as a serious field of study in American scholarly and academic life.

Impressed by Vasiliev's early mastery of languages, including Arabic, his mentor, V.G. Vasilievskii, directed him into study of Byzantium and its relations with the medieval Arab world. That theme of interstate and intercultural relations colored Vasiliev's life's work as a scholar; his wide linguistic facility augmented his voracious love for travel and a cosmopolitan outlook. He did not ignore institutions or internal social and economic developments, but his background in the Tsarist academic tradition led him to take for granted its positive model of a centralized and authoritarian imperial system,

which he never challenged or scrutinized unduly. Thus, his writings on "Byzantine feudalism" reflected the assumption that such institutional developments were, though indigenous, essentially a negative and ultimately a weakening factor in Byzantine society. Generally, however, Vasiliev focused on political and cultural history and on Byzantium's relations with its neighbors, and through the entire thousand-year span of Byzantine history, rather than in any single period.

Vasiliev's first major scholarly achievement, published during his thirties, was his 2-volume exposition of the interactions between Byzantium and the Abbassid Caliphate which, especially in its subsequent French translation, remains fundamental. The books themselves were supplemented over the years by a number of short studies and articles on related diplomatic and textual topics, beginning a prolific record of publication that was to span six decades.

Vasiliev wrote a subsequent synthesis of his work in the form of a chapter in the "Byzantine" volume 4 of *The Cambridge Medieval History* (1923), his first venture into print in English. And, late in his life, he did contemplate work on the Arabs during the 7th century and in the pre-Islamic era, but, in fact, he never did return to this original focus of work. Instead, his publications (in Russian up to 1923, then variously in French, German, and Italian, with an eventual commitment predominantly to English) reflected his widely ranging curiosity. He was recurrently interested in textual and manuscript studies, reflecting his early training in classics, but he also dealt occasionally with matters of art and archaeology. His subjects ran in time from the 4th through the 15th centuries, and included aspects of late Byzantine involvement with Italy, France, and England in the 14th and 15th centuries.

Though medieval Russia had not figured in his writings before he left his homeland, it emerged in a number of short articles and in two of his most important monographs: his study of a medieval society left over from earlier folk migrations, *The Goths in the Crimea* (1936), which was foreshadowed by two of his Russian articles published just before his emigration; and *The Russian Attack on Constantinople in 860* (1946), representative of several examinations of relations between Byzantium and Kievan Rus'. On the other hand, recurrent attention to 6th-century Byzantium led to the writing of his last major monograph, on the epoch of Emperor Justin I, a classic example of a regnal study, for which he won the Mediaeval Academy of America's prestigious Haskins medal.

In the optimism of his unfailing good health and unflagging energy, Vasiliev planned more major projects: not only the aforementioned one on the early Arabs, but treatment of the society and economy of the Roman empire in the 3rd and 4th centuries, and a study of that fascinating and neglected Byzantine byway, the empire of Trebizond. He published two preliminary articles (1936, 1941) on the latter subject but never realized these larger intentions.

Nevertheless, at the end of the his life he gave final form to his most widely influential publication, his general *History of the Byzantine Empire, 324–1453* (revised 1952). In his earliest years, following established European tradition, he published (in Russian) the formal texts of his course lectures (in several segments, 1917–25) in Byzantine history. More systematically assembled and revised, these surveys were translated into English and published in two volumes by the University of Wisconsin

Press in 1928–29, not long after his establishment in Madison. Thereafter, this work was translated into French, Turkish, and Spanish with a subsequent version in modern Greek. In the late 1940s, it was arranged that the University of Wisconsin Press would publish, not a reprint, but a newly revised and updated English version which, issued in 1952, was to be its definitive embodiment. Even though it was soon challenged by the German and then English editions of George Ostrogorsky's *History of the Byzantine State*, Vasiliev's work offered unique features within a comprehensive, 1-volume overview that Ostrogorsky's book lacked. Still in print (as a 2-volume paperback), and though dated on some counts, Vasiliev's work remains a valuable treatment as well as a landmark of its kind.

Vasiliev's achievement involves no single focus nor any profound theoretical or interpretive direction. In his day, the field of Byzantine history was not as developed nor as ripe for revision and rethinking as were other areas of historical study. A late arrival to recognized scholarly fields, it still required basic spadework in establishing the fundamentals of knowledge. The seeming diffuseness of Vasiliev's activities reflects such a situation, but also testifies to his own tireless range and productivity. There are few areas of Byzantine historical studies where Vasiliev did not leave a lasting mark. The first scholar to teach Byzantine history on the American academic scene, he produced only one doctoral student (Peter Charanis), but he exercised a wide influence through undergraduate teaching, through his active involvement in the academic community of medieval scholarship, and through his lively international contacts. He died on the 500th anniversary of the fall of Constantinople in 1453.

JOHN W. BARKER

See also Byzantium

Biography

Aleksandr Aleksandrovich Vasiliev. Born St. Petersburg, 22 September (old style) 1867. Studied music, languages, and history, 1887–92; PhD, St. Petersburg University, 1902. Taught at St. Petersburg Gymnasium; University of Dorpat; St. Petersburg Pedagogical Institute for Women; St. Petersburg University; traveled widely; professor of history, University of Wisconsin, Madison, 1925–38; resident scholar, Dumbarton Oaks, Washington, DC, 1944–53. Died Washington, DC, 30 May 1953.

Principal Writings

Vizantiia i araby (Byzantium and the Arabs), 2 vols., 1900–02; in French as *Byzance et les Arabes*, 3 vols., 1935–68
"The Struggle with the Saracens (867-1057)," in H.M. Gwatkin and J.P. Whitney, eds., *The Cambridge Medieval History*, vol. 4: *The Eastern Roman Empire, 717-1453*, Cambridge: Cambridge University Press, 1923, 138–50
Istoriia Vizantii, 3 vols., 1923; in English as *History of the Byzantine Empire*, 2 vols., 1928–29; revised as *History of the Byzantine Empire, 324-1453*, 1952
The Goths in the Crimea, 1936
The Russian Attack on Constantinople in 860, 1946
Justin the First: An Introduction to the Epoch of Justinian the Great, 1950

Further Reading

Anastos, Milton V., "Alexander A. Vasiliev: A Personal Sketch," *Russian Review* 13 (1954), 59–63
Grégoire, Henri, "Alexandre Alexandrovic Vasiliev," *Byzantion* 22 (1952–53), 526–31
Nersesasian, Sirarpie Der, "Alexander Alexandrovich Vasiliev (1867-1953)," *Dumbarton Oaks Papers* 9–10 (1955–56), 3–21 [includes bibliography]
Topping, Peter, "Alexandros A. Basilieph," *Helleniká* 13 (1954), 496–99
Vernadsky, George, "A.A. Vasiliev: on His Seventieth Birthday," *Annales de l'Institut Kondakov* 10 [*Mélanges A.A. Vasiliev*] (1938), 1–17

Velleius Paterculus *c.*20/19 BCE–after 30 CE
Roman historian

Velleius Paterculus's importance as a historian lies in his sympathetic portrait of the emperor Tiberius in some 40 books based upon his own experience serving as an army officer under the future emperor. Tacitus, who lived a generation later, in his portrait of Tiberius may be telling us more about the Flavian emperors of his own time. The unflattering portrait of Tiberius given by Tacitus has been the preferred one for centuries. Velleius' portrait of Tiberius needs the careful attention of scholars to prove whether or not it is uncritical flattery.

Velleius wrote *Historiae Romanae* (Histories of the Romans), an abridgment of Roman history, to celebrate the consulship of Velleius' friend Marcus Vinicius who married Julia Livilla, granddaughter of the Roman emperor Tiberius. Histories of the Romans consists of two books. The first book ends with the destruction of Carthage in 146 BCE and the second book covers the period 147–30 BCE.

Velleius' haste in composing his compendium resulted in an oversimplification of the material, and the work has long been the object of derision for several reasons. It is amateurish, offering shallow interpretations and crude characterizations; Velleius unsuccessfully attempted to employ antithesis, epigram, and rhetorical embellishments, the style of the Silver Age of Latin literature. However, the target of most criticism is the author's flattering portrait of Tiberius, and this criticism deserves some consideration. Velleius had served under Tiberius in the army, so he had first-hand knowledge of the future emperor's character, unlike the later Tacitus who found in Tiberius little to admire. Some experts now believe that Velleius' portrait is perhaps more accurate than "the venomous hostility" of Tacitus.

To the credit of Histories of the Romans it provides the only continuous record of long early epochs of Roman history and it covers periods of the lost books of Livy's *History*. The work also provides information about the colonizing of Italy by Rome, the administration of the Roman provinces, and the principates of Augustus and Tiberius. Its passages on literature are also unique.

Critics have derided Velleius for believing that Augustus' *restituta respublica* was a sincere effort to restore the republic. Histories of the Romans gives us a nonsenatorial point of view, while writers such as Tacitus, Dio Cassius, and Suetonius were of the senatorial class. Velleius' attitude toward the new empire may represent that of the administrative officers of the equestrian order, a class of men that may have broadly supported the empire. For Velleius the transition from the Roman republic to empire was smooth.

In spite of Velleius' faults, Lord Macaulay noted that he "seems to be a remarkably good *epitomes*. I hardly know of any work of which the scale is so small and the subject so extensive." De Quincey also praised Velleius. Velleius mentioned Cato the Elder (the Censor, 234–149 BCE) and the orator Quintus Hortensius Hortalus (114–50 BCE) as sources. If Velleius used Livy's *History* as a source, he disagreed with him on many points.

The reader new to Velleius, or any other ancient historian, must always be vigilant for factual errors and mistakes in chronology. Those unaware of the recognized errors in the work must rely on commentaries written by classicists and historians for guidance. However, the recognized shortcomings of Velleius in literary style or objectivity should not be deemed more important that his contribution to our knowledge of ancient Rome. Only in recent decades has Velleius' portrait been seen as worthy of consideration among scholars. Likewise, Velleius' bias as a nonaristocrat in itself is interesting to modern scholarship. As a source of thought and experience Velleius should be taken as seriously as diarists of other eras. His status as a historian may be low but as an eyewitness to history he produced work that is important.

NANCY PIPPEN ECKERMAN

See also Roman; Tacitus

Biography
Born into a prominent but not aristocratic Campanian family, probably in Capua, Italy, *c*.20/19 BCE. Served in the Roman army in Thrace, Macedonia, and Greece from *c*.1 CE; cavalry officer in Germany under the future emperor Tiberius, 4–12 CE; held the post of quaestor, 7 CE, and praetor, 15 CE. Died after 30 CE.

Principal Writings
Historiae Romanae (Histories of the Romans), 30 CE
Compendium of Roman History (Loeb edition), translated by
    Frederick W. Shipley, 1924

Further Reading
Dorey, Thomas Alan, ed., *Latin Historians*, New York: Basic Books,
    and London: Routledge, 1966
Duff, J.W., *A Literary History of Rome in the Silver Age, from
    Tiberius to Hadrian*, London: Unwin, 1927; New York: Scribner,
    1935; 3rd edition London: Benn, 1964
Sumner, G.V., "The Truth about Velleius Paterculus: prolegomena,"
    Harvard Studies in Classical Philology 74 (1970), 257–97
Woodman, A.J., "Questions of Date, Genre, and Style in Velleius:
    Some Literary Answers," *Classical Quarterly* 69 (1975), 272–306

Venturi, Franco 1914–
Italian historian of the Enlightenment

In an era of increasingly specialized scholarship, narrow subjects, and dry prose with a somewhat overbearing focus on detail (often at the expense of a broader perspective), Italian historian Franco Venturi remains within the tradition of the great European historians of the 19th century as a brilliant scholar whose works combine refined analysis with masterful narrative description. His scholarship is invariably concerned with monumental topics, which Venturi approaches conceptually: he depicts main historical trends and illuminates them with elegantly integrated tales and memorable episodes that are invariably revealing and characteristic of the general themes under study.

Venturi is considered by many to be the century's leading scholar of the European Enlightenment. His approach to the subject is that of a cosmopolitan, which requires him to take the Enlightenment across the parameters dictated by political boundaries and distinct national cultures. The most extended of all his typically voluminous works is the multivolume epic *Settecento riformatore* (1969–90; *The First Crisis*, 1989–). In this opus containing close to 4,000 pages, Venturi, according to one of his reviewers, while focusing on different parts of Italy, moves outward and "ranges from North America in the west to Russia in the east, from Sweden in the north to Spain and Greece in the south. Few are the historians who have the linguistic competence to range so widely; fewer still possess the imagination and the learning to join such distant parts in a single connected enquiry."

Nor does Venturi limit his analysis to strictly philosophical or even generally intellectual aspects of the 18th century; rather, he is concerned with the variety of ways in which ideas influenced social and political phenomena. Venturi's *a priori* assumption is that ideas have value not only as cultural, spiritual, and intellectual abstractions; they play an instrumental role in socio-political processes, including those of reforms and revolutions. Critics noted that in his volumes on the Enlightenment, one of Venturi's key themes is the crisis and the eventual downfall of the *ancien régime*, which the historian attributed largely to the interplay between ideas and political actions. Venturi used the same general pattern of explication dealing with other historical movements, most notably the phenomenon of Russian Populism, to which he devoted his famous 1952 study *Il populismo russo* (*Roots of Revolution*, 1960).

Roots of Revolution stands out as a classic in the sea of scholarly literature on Russian 19th-century radicalism in part because of Venturi's methodological success in integrating intellectual and political history. The result is a comprehensive picture, in which general political trends are viewed (and become discernible) through the many prisms of personal intellectual development, as Venturi traces the spiritual and ideological maturation of key thinkers and practitioners in the Russian opposition movement. Thus Venturi's beautifully depicted portraits of Russian political leaders are first and foremost intellectual biographies of individuals whose ideals and ideas left a profound impact on the entire course of the revolution.

The historian's unequivocally sympathetic attitude *vis à vis* the causes of the Russian liberation movement and its representatives has been partly attributed to his personal background in politics, namely his participation in the antifascist movement in the years of Mussolini's regime in Italy and especially his involvement with the partisans after 1943. A tendency to formulate a link between his lifelong fascination with the Enlightenment and his commitment to liberal ideals may be seen as early as the late 1930s, when the young Venturi was conducting research on Denis Diderot, the topic of his first book, published in 1939. His war experiences strengthened his adherence to liberal ideals and democratic institutions against all shades of despotism and simultaneously enhanced the connection between contemporary politics and his mode of historical inquiry. In the words of a commentator, Venturi's engagement with the principles of liberty in Russia "arises not from a Whiggish complacency about the superiority of liberal values, but from a passionate admiration for those who sacrifice their lives to the cause of freedom." This is what "gives even his most detailed discussions the resonance of moral fervor."

Studies in Free Russia (1982), while integrating several of Venturi's shorter writings on Russian history, emphasized the continuity of the country's intellectual tradition. Experts stress that the common theme in this eclectic work is liberty, to which so many distinguished Russian intellectuals – from the 18th-century writer Aleksandr Radishchev to the dauntless Soviet scholar Lev Gordon – were selflessly devoted. In terms of an apparently endless historiographic debate as to whether Russia belongs to the family of European nations, essential is Venturi's conviction that Russia's political trends are inseparable from the great intellectual tradition of Europe, with populism, for instance, being "a page in the history of European socialism."

True to his primary concern with ideas and consciousness, Venturi has been charged with overemphasizing the elevated ideals of liberals and socialists at the expense of the less-than-lofty methods employed by the practitioners of the Russian Revolution. Because of his preoccupation with the European cultural legacy, he has also been criticized for not sufficiently differentiating between the Russian and the West European variants of socialism, and more specifically, Populism. Notwithstanding the validity of these judgments, Venturi's excellent writings on the 18th and 19th centuries manifest the penetrating intelligence, phenomenal learning, exceptional scholarship, and outstanding spiritual refinement of a great "Europeanist."

ANNA GEIFMAN

See also Italy: since the Renaissance

Biography
Born Rome, 16 May 1914. Entered exile with his father, 1931; studied at the Sorbonne, 1930s. Interned by fascists during World War II. After the war, served as Italy's cultural attaché at Moscow embassy; returned to Italy and held chairs at Cagliari, Genoa, and Turin universities. Married Gigliola Spinelli (1 child).

Principal Writings
La Jeunesse de Diderot (Young Diderot), 1939
Dalmazzo Francesco Vasco, 1732–1794, 1940
L'antichà svelata e l'idea del progresso in N.A. Boulanger (1722–1759) (Uncovered Antiquity and the Idea of Progress in N.A. Boulanger), 1947
Il populismo russo, 1952; in English as *Roots of Revolution: A History of the Populist and Socialist Movements in Nineteenth-Century Russia*, 1960
Settecento riformatore, 6 vols., 1969–90; in English as *The First Crisis*, 1989–
Utopia e riforma nell'Illuminismo, 1970; in English as *Utopia and Reform in the Enlightenment*, 1971
Italy and the Enlightenment: Studies in a Cosmopolitan Century, 1972
Studies in Free Russia, 1982

Further Reading
Diaz, Furio, Luciano Guerci, and Carlo Capra, "Settecento riformatore" (The Reforming Eighteenth Century), *Passato e Presente* 8 (1985), 13–31
Robertson, John, "Franco Venturi's Enlightenment," *Past and Present* 137 (1992), 183–206

Vergil, Polydore 1470?–1555?
Italian historian of early modern England

Polydore Vergil may, without too much exaggeration, be called the father of modern English history. Writing in the 16th century, he introduced new, more rigorous criteria for historical research and documentation, criteria that dramatically changed the course of historical investigation in England.

Prior to Vergil, the study of history in England was primarily the domain of monkish chroniclers who geared their writing toward their own community, usually dominating their discourse with a concern for illustrating and recording only those events that had an impact upon their own existence. It was left up to the writers and recorders of the Renaissance to establish new rules of historical writing and criticism, but it was not until 1502, with the arrival in England of Vergil, that this Renaissance scholasticism came to Britain.

Vergil had already created a reputation as a scholar prior to his arrival with the publication of his *Proverbiorum libellus* (1498) and his *De inventoribus rerum* (1499), but it was after he moved to England that he made his greatest impact on the writing of history with his *Anglica historia*. The *Anglica historia* (The History of the English, 1534, 1555) challenged the perceived wisdom of the pre-eminent 12th-century Welsh chronicler, Geoffrey of Monmouth, whose *Historia regum Britanniae* dominated English historical thought.

In *Historia regum Britanniae*, Geoffrey had proposed a curious mixture of myth and legend for the creation of the English state, tracing the establishment back to refugee Trojans, and proceeding from there to deal with the mythic adventures of King Arthur. Although it is probable that Geoffrey based his work on other sources, there was little mention in the *Historia regum Britanniae* of any evaluation of these sources. It may be because of this bland acceptance of myth as historical fact that Vergil seems to have placed little credence in Geoffrey's work when writing his own history, relying instead upon sources that he judged to be more reliable. Indeed, Vergil was extremely disparaging about the writings of most of the medieval chroniclers, referring to them as "bald, uncouth, chaotic and deceptive." Vergil's own writing reflected this insistence upon verifiable sources, often commenting upon the believability of differing sources and generally implying that his work relied completely upon accurate sources while other authors may have been more carefree in their approach to historical fact.

The reaction of Vergil's contemporaries, most of them followers or adherents of Geoffrey of Monmouth's tale, was anything but happy, as Vergil challenged the historical basis of some of the most cherished of the English legends. As one of the primary sources used for the study of the reign of Richard III, he has also come under attack as a Tudor propagandist, and a vilifier of the good name of that monarch. Of course, Vergil's position as a Catholic Italian, with connections to the papal bureaucracy, meant that he stood apart from his contemporaries at the court of Henry VIII. Nonetheless, it is a fascinating measure of his impact on the writing of history in England, that even those who affected to despise Vergil's works were forced to adapt his methodology in order to challenge his conclusions. As Denys Hay pointed out in his biography of Vergil, one Elizabethan courtier, Sir Philip Sidney, would later attack Vergil for introducing the historian's critical judgment of sources, claiming it created a historian "loden with old Mouse-eaten records, authorising himselfe (for the most parte) upon other histories, whose greatest authorities are built upon the notable foundation of Heare-say."

Of course, those writers who could not successfully dispute Vergil's writings with their own research would claim that Vergil had destroyed records once he was finished with them, but this calumny did not repress the impact of his critical innovation. By 1618, Vergil's portrait was painted upon the wall of the Bodleian Library at Oxford University as one of the great scholars. His influence lived on, and even though his *Anglica historia* has often fallen into disrepute, his methodology has continued, and may be witnessed in every text of history written about Britain, as no serious work of history today is accepted without some form of evaluative examination of the sources employed. This was the legacy of Polydore Vergil to the writing of British history.

DANIEL M. GERMAN

Biography
Born Urbino, 1470?, to an academic family. Studied at Padua. Served Duke of Urbino as secretary; chamberlain to pope Alexander VI, 1492–1502; went to England as deputy to Adriano Castellesi, bishop of Hereford, 1502; held a series of clerical appointments (including as archdeacon of Wells, 1508–54), but fell into disfavor with Cardinal Wolsey and was imprisoned; afterwards lived mainly in England although regularly traveled to Italy. Died Urbino, 1555?

Principal Writings
Proverbiorum libellus, 1498
De inventoribus rerum, 1499
Anglica historia (The History of the English), 1534, 1555

Further Reading
Clough, Cecil H., "Federigo Veterani, Polydore Vergil's *Anglica Historia* and Baldassare Castiglione's *Epistola . . . ad Heurlam Angliae regnum*," *English Historical Review* 82 (1967), 772–83
Copenhaver, Brian P., "The Historiography of Discovery in the Renaissance," *Journal of the Warburg and Courtauld Institutes* 41 (1978), 192–214
Ellis, Sir Henry, Preface to *Polydore Vergil's English History*, 2 vols., London: Camden Society, 1844–46
Gabrieli, V., "L'Anglica Historia di Polydoro Vergilio" (The *English History* of Polydore Vergil), *La Cultura* 24 (1986), 64–97
Hanham, Alison, *Richard III and His Early Historians, 1483–1535*, Oxford: Clarendon Press, 1975
Hay, Denys, *Polydore Vergil: Renaissance Historian and Man of Letters*, Oxford: Clarendon Press, 1952

Vernadsky, George 1887–1973
US (Russian-born) medievalist

A product of the great liberal Russian intelligentsia tradition, George Vernadsky explored a whole range of topics in Russian history during his career of nearly sixty years, from Russian Freemasonry in the time of Catherine the Great to the life and politics of V.I. Lenin. His most influential and well-known works, however, discussed the significance of the Mongols in Russian history and the theory of Eurasianism. In these areas Vernadsky made his greatest contribution to the field of Russian history and to the historical debate of Russia's place between East and West.

The first signs of Vernadsky's theory of Eurasianism, the theory that Russia was a world unto itself, distinct from Europe and Asia, can be detected in a series of articles he produced between 1913 and 1915. These early works concentrated on the subject of Russia's expansion to the east, and in particular, the settlement of Siberia. Echoing in many ways the arguments of previous historians such as V.O. Kliuchevskii, Vernadsky argued that the Russian national character had changed as the Russians moved eastward. Unlike Kliuchevskii, however, Vernadsky attributed to Asia and Asians a far greater role in the political and cultural transformation of Russia. The Mongols and their conquest, for example, were presented as pivotal factors in Russia's historical development, allowing Russia to continue its expansion eastward and placing Russia in contact with the non-Slavic peoples of the Near East and Central Asia. In these first articles, Vernadsky anticipated a number of the basic tenets of Eurasianism, namely, that the Mongol conquest was both a pivotal and positive event in Russian history, and that Russian history was indisputably influenced by contact with and expansion into Asia.

It was only after his emigration to the West that Vernadsky came to accept what would be a crucial axiom of Eurasianism – that there was an inherent hostility and incompatibility between Europe and Russia. Leaving Russia after the Revolution, Vernadsky made his way to Constantinople, Athens, and finally Prague, where he became associated with the Eurasian school of thought founded by P.N. Savitskii and N.S. Trubetskoi. Like many of their liberal intellectual brethren, these early Eurasianists saw the catastrophe of the Russian Revolution as the fatal result of Russia's uncritical embracing of Western ideas and failure to respect native institutions. The Eurasian school argued that Eurasia was a definable geographical unit with boundaries roughly coinciding with those of the Russian empire of 1914. Russia, then, was neither European nor Asian and thus should reject all Western political and cultural forms, not the least of which was Marxism, which was viewed as another product of decadent European civilization. Furthermore, the historical roots of Russia's tragic descent into Western decadence could be traced to Peter the Great, who had diverted Russia from its true path. In the 1920s and 1930s, Vernadsky explored the theory of Eurasianism in a number of articles and books. In an article on the Orthodox and Roman Catholic churches, for example, Vernadsky criticized all historical attempts at union, emphasizing the special place of Orthodoxy in Russian history and culture. In other works he argued the importance of the Mongol conquest and the uniqueness of Russia.

After moving to the United States and arriving at Yale University, Vernadsky began work on the major project that dominated his research for the next thirty years – a multivolume history of Russia to 1682. The first volume, entitled *Ancient Russia*, appeared in 1943, followed by *Kievan Russia* (1948), *The Mongols and Russia* (1953), *Russia at the Dawn of the Modern Age* (1959) and *The Tsardom of Muscovy, 1547–1682* (1969). Particularly in the earlier volumes, Vernadsky's Eurasianism is still apparent, though he softened the militancy of his arguments in subsequent volumes. The collected history has been considered one of the most influential and important contributions in English to the study of early and medieval Russia. Written in the grand narrative style of 19th-century historiography and containing useful maps, glossaries, and bibliographies, these volumes are both scholarly and accessible to the non-specialist.

Vernadsky was an extremely important and influential figure in the field of Russian history. During his years in New Haven, he worked to increase the library's holdings, thus helping to make Yale one of the centers for the study of Russia in the United States. More importantly, his works on early and medieval Russia contributed to a better understanding of this difficult period and his emphasis on the Eurasian principle in Russian history added much to a debate that goes on even at the end of the 20th century.

LEE A. FARROW

See also Mongol; Russia: Medieval; Russia: Early Modern

Biography

Born St. Petersburg, 20 August 1887. Attended Fifth Classical Gymnasium, Moscow, 1899–1905; University of Moscow, 1905–10; PhD, University of St. Petersburg, 1917. Taught at University of St. Petersburg, 1914–17; University of Perm, 1917–18; University of Tauride, Simferpol, Crimea, 1918–20; and Russian School of Law, Prague, 1922–27; emigrated to US, 1927 (naturalized 1933); rose to professor, Yale University, 1927–56 (emeritus). Married Nina Ilyinski, 1908. Died New Haven, 12 June 1973.

Principal Writings

Russkoe masonstvo v tsarstvovanie Ekateriny II (Russian Freemasonry in the Reign of Catherine II), 1917
A History of Russia, 1929 [and subsequent revisions]
Lenin, Red Dictator, 1931
The Russian Revolution, 1917–1932, 1932
Political and Diplomatic History of Russia, 1936
Bohdan, Hetman of Ukraine, 1941
A History of Russia, 5 vols., 1943–69 [not same as 1929 book]
Translator, *Medieval Russian Laws*, 1947
The Origins of Russia, 1959
Editor with Ralph Talcott Fisher, Jr., *Dictionary of Russian Historical Terms from the Eleventh Century to 1917*, by S.G. Pushkarev, 1970
Russian Historiography: A History, 1978

Further Reading

Halperin, Charles J., "George Vernadsky, Eurasianism, the Mongols, and Russia," *Slavic Review* 41 (1982), 477–93
Obolensky, Dimitri, "George Vernadsky as a Historian of Ancient and Medieval Russia," in Alan D. Ferguson and Alfred Levin, eds., *Essays in Russian History: A Collection Dedicated to George Vernadsky*, Hamden, CT: Archon, 1964

Vernant, Jean-Pierre 1914–

French classical historian

Jean-Pierre Vernant is most famous for his structuralist analyses of ancient Greek myths and his explorations of the function of the Greek pantheon. His work is, however, far broader in scope than this and, at the Centre des Recherches Comparées sur les Sociétés Anciennes, now the Centre Louis Gernet, he has not only brought together a group of young French classical scholars but also attracted many postgraduate students and other visitors both from France and from around the world. Among the most distinguished of his colleagues and sometime collaborators are Pierre Vidal-Naquet, Marcel Detienne, and Nicole Loraux.

Vernant's mentors were Ignace Meyerson and Louis Gernet, and in his earliest work he set out to apply to ancient Greek studies Meyerson's historical psychology in order to discover "a history of the inner being," a history that takes up Gernet's interests in sociology and anthropology. All areas of ancient society, from its religion and philosophy to its art and technology, are seen as equally the creations of the human mind; Vernant is interested not only in the development of the idea of the individual, but also in that individual as "a being inseparable from the social and cultural environment of which he is at once the creator and the product." Zeitlin has pointed out that Vernant's concern with the society and the individual extended into all areas of his life. After World War II, Vernant's exploits in the French Resistance were recognized by his being honored as a Compagnon de la Libération. Much of his work was concerned with the "Greek miracle," the shift from mythical to rational thought, but he recognized first that the Greeks invented only one type of rationality, specific to their own culture, and second that myth has its own "reason," or logic.

Vernant's best-known studies are those based on close textual analysis of myths, combining the structuralist view of myth as a language with the methods of traditional philology, while remaining aware of the cultural context in which such texts are produced. For example, his "Le Mythe prométhéen chez Hésiode" ("The Myth of Prometheus in Hesiod") carries out three levels of analysis: formal analysis of Hesiod's two versions of the myth, analysis of the semantic components, and a study of the sociocultural context in which the myth was used. Vernant shows how "the grammar of the narrative" works around the opposition between giving and not-giving/withholding, and uses the myth as a way into the constellation of features the Greeks believed characterized their world: agricultural labor, a specific diet, marriage, sacrifice and the use of fire. Later collaborative work at the Centre des recherches comparées sur les sociétés anciennes developed Vernant's identification of sacrifice, as a central institution in Greek self-definition, one that permitted communication from men to gods while simultaneously reminding men of the lost golden age in which sacrifice was unnecessary, because gods and men ate together.

In his studies of the Greek pantheon, Vernant argued that a Greek god's "mode of operation" should be seen as the key unifying the apparently diverse facets of any deity's activities; in contrast to traditional diachronic methods which argue that these facets should be understood as the result of the fusion of various local cults over time, Vernant's synchronic approach enables us to understand how Artemis or Poseidon was perceived as "one" deity. By looking at the different deities associated with an area of life such as marriage, navigation, or space it is possible to define what is specific to each one. For example, when Vernant looks at the operation of Hestia and Hermes in terms of ideas about space, he demonstrates that Hestia is consistently associated with the fixed point, Hermes with movement around it; he is then able to draw out parallels with female and male roles in society. Much of Vernant's work is concerned with boundaries; not only those explored in myth between god, man, and beast, but also those that society presents for individuals to cross. "Marriage is to the girl what war is to the boy: for each, they mark the fulfillment of their respective natures, by quitting a state in which each has still some of the characteristics of the other." A similar concern with boundaries informs his scholarship on memory, time, work, and mirrors and doubles, while his study with Marcel Detienne of the semantic field of *mètis* or "cunning intelligence" investigates the differences between ancient and modern ideas of a particular kind of intelligence that thrives on the margins.

HELEN KING

See also Greece: Ancient

Biography

Born Provins, Seine-et-Marne, 4 January 1914, son of a newspaper proprietor. Studied at the Lycée Carnot; Lycée Louis-le-Grand; and the Sorbonne, receiving the agrégation in philosophy. Taught philosophy at a lycée in Toulouse, 1940–46; Lycée Jacques Decour, Paris, 1946–48; Centre National de la Recherche Scientifique, 1948–58; and Ecole Pratique des Hautes Etudes, 1958–75; professor, Collège de France, 1975–84. Married Lida Nahimovitek, 1939 (1 daughter).

Principal Writings

Les Origines de la pensée grecque, 1962; in English as *The Origins of Greek Thought*, 1982

Mythe et pensée chez les grecs: études de psychologie historique, 1965; in English as *Myth and Thought among the Greeks*, 1983

With Pierre Vidal-Naquet, *Mythe et tragédie en Grèce ancienne*, 2 vols., 1972–86; in English as *Myth and Tragedy in Ancient Greece*, 1988

Mythe et société en Grèce ancienne, 1974; in English as *Myth and Society in Ancient Greece*, 1980: includes "Le Mythe prométhéen chez Hésiode" (The Myth of Prometheus in Hesiod)

With Marcel Detienne, *Les Ruses de l'intelligence: la mètis des Grecs*, 1974; in English as *Cunning Intelligence in Greek Culture and Society*, 1978

Religions, histoires, raisons (Religions, Histories, Reasons), 1979

La mort dans les yeux: figures de l'autre en Grèce ancienne (Death in the Eyes: Figures of the Other in Ancient Greece), 1985

L'individu, la mort, l'amour: soi-même et l'autre en Grèce ancienne (The Individual, Death, and Love: The Self and the Other in Ancient Greece), 1989

Figures, idoles, masques (Figures, Idols, Masks), 1990

Mortals and Immortals: Collected Essays, edited by Froma I. Zeitlin, 1991

Further Reading

Ellinger, P., "Vingt ans de recherches sur les mythes dans la domaine de l'antiquité grecque" (Twenty Years of Research in Ancient Greece), *Revue des Etudes Grecques* 86 (1984), 7–29

Gordon, Richard Lindsay, ed., *Myth, Religion and Society: Structuralist Essays*, Cambridge and New York: Cambridge University Press, 1981

"La mythologie grecque change de sens: un entretien avec J.-P. Vernant" (Greek Mythology Changing Meaning: An Interview with Vernant), *Sciences et Avenir* 419 (1982), 105–06

Vico, Giambattista 1668–1744
Italian cultural historian and philosopher

The most original historical thinker of the 18th century, Giambattista Vico sought new ways to understand and to write history. His greatest book, *La scienza nuova* (1725; *The New Science*, 1948), is the pioneering work of modern cultural history. Indeed, the origins of all the social sciences are to be found in this seminal book.

His early life gave no hint of future greatness. Sick and fragile as a child, Vico grew up in a poor section of Naples where his impoverished bookseller father could barely provide for the family. Despite these disadvantages, Vico persevered and excelled as a student, although for most of his childhood he taught himself. He thoroughly mastered Latin and rhetoric, and because of these achievements secured a tutoring position, which lasted from 1686 to 1695. During that period Vico frequented the literary salons and private academies of the city, engaging in the intellectual debates of the day over the rationalist and skeptical ideas of René Descartes (1596–1650).

His tutoring job ended when he was 27, and for the next four years he led a hand-to-mouth existence as a Latinist, doing translations and composing Latin verse for ceremonial occasions. In 1699, the same year that Vico married, the University of Naples hired him to teach rhetoric, but at a very low salary. Soon the father of a large family, he continued to give private lessons and to provide translations, commemorative verse, and epigraphs on commission.

University tradition mandated that the professor of rhetoric open the academic year with a Latin oration, and Vico's first professional publication, *De nostri temporis studiorum ratione* (1709; *On the Study Methods of Our Time*, 1965) was expanded from one of his inaugural lectures. In it he presented a defense of the humanities against the Cartesian charge that nonmathematical knowledge was a contradiction in terms. Vico, denouncing the encroachment of mathematical methods in nonscientific fields, held that the prudent conduct of life required a much broader base of knowledge than the one provided by Descartes' geometric formulas. This polemic against Descartes serves as the main intellectual point of departure for the rest of Vico's work.

In *On the Study Methods of Our Time* Vico had insisted on the importance of the humanities in principle, but he later acknowledged that they had fallen into decline because of confused, inconsistent, and unconvincing methodologies. In *The New Science* he set about to strengthen the humanities by laying down appropriate procedures of inquiry for them. An outline of Vico's plan of reorganization had appeared in a 2-volume legal treatise, *Diritto universale* (1720–21, Universal Law), in a chapter entitled "The New Science Is Attempted." On the basis of this outline, Vico secured a promise of financial support for a book on the subject from the Florentine cardinal Lorenzo Corsini, the future Pope Clemente XII. The cardinal soon withdrew support, but at great personal economic sacrifice Vico managed to publish the book.

Trying to advance the sphere of historical study beyond the traditional boundaries of mere politics into the realms of language, fable, legend, popular customs and mores, myth, literature, art, law, and religion, Vico argued – again contra Descartes – that education was too important to be left exclusively in the hands of the mathematicians. Education had to consist of all these diverse elements, for which history served as the mother academic discipline, lest human intelligence become lopsided and destructive.

Moral concerns governed Vico's thinking in *The New Science*. A deeply conservative Catholic, he stands out in the intellectual history of 18th-century Europe as an archetypal anti-Enlightenment thinker. At the core of his thought lay Augustine's distinction between the City of God and the City of Man. Perfect justice and divine harmony eternally pervaded the City of God, but here below a cyclical progression of birth and death prevailed in all things. Thus, he strenuously opposed the rationalist model of linear historical development that became the gospel of the Enlightenment. According to Vico, the only honest and realistic explanation of human history in its entirety hinged on divine Providence, operating according to laws God alone understood, although man could know and was obliged to know the part of history that he himself had made – "the world of civil society."

Few great books have had a more inauspicious reception than *The New Science*. Coming so soon after an embittering 1723 rejection of his candidacy for a much higher paying chair in Roman law and the critical failure of *Diritto universale*, the disastrous reviews of *The New Science* left him profoundly demoralized, but not for long. He convinced himself that the problem lay not with his ideas, but with the obscure style of the book. Vico set about to restructure and to rewrite it, while completing the first part of his invaluable *Autobiografia* (1729; *The Autobiography of Giambattista Vico*, 1944), a supplement to which he added in 1731, although it was not published until 1818. The second edition of *The New Science* came out in 1730, again to uncomprehending notices by the critics and to the general indifference of the public. Vico persisted and spent the rest of his life, through worsening health and growing family misfortunes, working on the third edition, which appeared posthumously in 1744. A 1735 appointment as royal historian eased Vico's economic difficulties during his last years.

Despite two rewrites, Vico never succeeded in systematizing and clarifying the insights that lay hidden in *The New Science*. Two centuries of scholarship and some simplified translations have rendered the book accessible to today's readers, but Vico's contemporaries could not get past his unmediated prolixity. Nearly a hundred years passed before the French historian Jules Michelet (1798–1874) rediscovered Vico's book, translated it, and pronounced it a masterpiece. A major theme in modern European intellectual history concerns the process by which the rest of the scholarly world has caught up with and shared Michelet's judgment of *The New Science* as a work of Promethean genius that called attention to the need for historical research into the full social context of human development.

RICHARD DRAKE

See also Berlin; Enlightenment; Historiology; Italy: since the Renaissance; Manzoni; Michelet; Philosophy; Religion

Biography

Giovan Battista or Giambattista Vico. Born Naples, 23 June 1668, son of a bookseller. Early study with the Jesuits gave way to self-education. Professor of rhetoric, University of Naples, 1699–1742; royal historian, 1735–44. Married Teresa Destito, 1699 (8 children, 5 surviving infancy). Died Naples, 23 January 1744.

Principal Writings

Orazioni inaugurali, 1699–1707; in English as *On Humanistic Education: Six Inaugural Orations, 1699–1707*, 1993
De nostri temporis studiorum ratione, 1709; in English as *On the Study Methods of Our Time*, 1965
Diritto universale (Universal Law), 1720–21
La scienza nuova, 1725; revised 1730, 1744; in English as *The New Science*, 1948
Autobiografia, 1729; in English as *The Autobiography of Giambattista Vico*, 1944

Further Reading

Lilla, Mark, *G.B. Vico: The Making of an Anti-Modern*, Cambridge, MA: Harvard University Press, 1993
Mali, Joseph, *The Rehabilitation of Myth: Vico's "New Science,"* New York: Cambridge University Press, 1992
Pompa, Leon, *Vico: A Study of the New Science*, Cambridge and New York: Cambridge University Press, 1975
Verene, Molly Black, *Vico: A Bibliography of Works in English from 1884 to 1994*, Bowling Green, OH: Philosophy Documentation Center, 1995
Wilson, Edmund, *To the Finland Station: A Study in the Writing and Acting of History*, New York: Harcourt Brace, and London: Secker and Warburg, 1940

Vietnam

Europeans and especially North Americans are apt to think of Vietnam largely in terms of its recent history, which included a century of French colonialism followed by revolutionary wars pitting ultimately successful Vietnamese nationalists against French colonizers, Japanese occupiers, and finally Americans pursuing Cold War-driven strategies of combating communist revolutions. In this Western view, Vietnam is perceived largely through the prism of what the French termed the "Indochina wars" and Americans called the "Vietnam War," but which many Vietnamese considered the American War or the wars of national liberation. But Vietnam's history is very ancient, and it can be argued that had Americans and their leaders known more about that legacy they might have been warier about committing themselves to a war that proved unwinnable. Indeed, Vietnamese tend to take a much longer view of their historical development, and forged the richest tradition of historiography in premodern Southeast Asia. In Vietnam history has long been taken very seriously, with the general population highly conscious of their own historical and literary traditions to a much greater extent than most societies.

Imbued with this worldview, Vietnamese Marxist scholars contend that the August Revolution of 1945, which first brought the communists to power in the North, can be understood only in the context of 4000 years of Vietnamese history. Similarly, perhaps the most fruitful way of looking at the Vietnam War is as a brief albeit exceptionally violent episode in Vietnam's long history, particularly its well-documented struggle for independence and the long search for social justice. The Vietnamese are no strangers to the notion of struggle, for much of their history has been one of struggle, most importantly against foreign invaders, but sometimes against their own rulers or each other. In addition, and unlike most premodern peoples, the Vietnamese constructed a well-developed sense of national identity, which no doubt aided their survival of numerous catastrophes including a millennium-long colonization by China (which profoundly reshaped society and culture), a similarly disruptive hegemony by the French (who progressively annexed the country beginning in the mid-19th century), and nearly forty years of persistent warfare from the 1940s through the 1970s, during which several million Vietnamese were killed and many millions more were injured or experienced severe life disruptions.

Thanks in part to Chinese sources, including dynastic histories, we know more about Vietnam's early history than for the rest of Southeast Asia. The earliest local inscriptions date from sometime between the 2nd and 5th centuries CE, but these can be supplemented by the Chinese records, among them biographies of or reminiscences by colonial officials, and administrative data, as well as an increasingly rich Vietnamese historiographical tradition, the earliest surviving examples of which date from the 14th and 15th centuries. These official and unofficial sources look back on the colonial years as well as documenting the centuries following the re-establishment of an independent Vietnamese polity a millennium ago. Not surprisingly, the Vietnamese historians were preoccupied with the volatile Sino-Vietnamese relationship, the dominant reality from the 2nd century BCE until the 10th century CE and an ever-present influence afterward. The Vietnamese historians were concerned with justifying a separate Vietnamese identity as well as, for the most part, reflecting elite views of order and supporting the authority of the royal courts. Hence, there was a close connection between history-writing and politics, a tradition of selectively redeeming the past that would be maintained by Vietnamese historians in the 20th century, concerned with legitimizing or attacking revolutionary nationalism and collectivist ideologies. But Western scholars studying Vietnam in the 20th century have also seldom been divorced from political considerations as they engaged or reflected the realities of Western imperialism in the region.

The multifaceted Vietnamese historiographical tradition has been analyzed by scholars such as Nguyen The Anh, David Marr, Keith Taylor, John Whitmore, O.W. Wolters, and various authors in Taylor and Whitmore's collection. Vietnamese (and sometimes Chinese) sources have also been utilized by various scholars in preparing general histories, including Joseph Buttinger, Jean Chesneaux, Thomas Hodgkin, and Le Khanh Khoi. Khoi is the standard work on the precolonial era. Buttinger's work (especially *The Smaller Dragon*, 1958) provides the most useful general overview in English, although Hodgkin (who summarized the writings of Vietnamese Marxist scholars) offers more detailed coverage of the entire premodern period. Chesneaux stressed socio-economic change. Indigenous sources have also been integral to those scholars reconstructing the era of Chinese colonization and its aftermath, including Taylor (the most comprehensive

treatment of the entire Chinese colonial period), Whitmore (the outstanding student of the 14th–15th centuries, when Confucianism became a more prominent influence among the elites), Alexander Woodside (the major Western specialist on 18th- and 19th-century Vietnam), and Nguyen Thanh Nha (on socioeconomic patterns). There has been a lively scholarly debate involving, among others, Whitmore, Woodside, Taylor, and Wolters as to whether Vietnam should be situated within the East Asian or Southeast Asian orbit of civilization, or as a transition point between the two.

Useful briefer overviews of Vietnamese history include those by Woodside, André Masson, Truong Buu Lam (who emphasized various forms of struggle over the centuries), Nguyen Khac Vien (who identified traditional influences on Vietnamese communism), Ralph Smith (a 1968 collection of essays linking traditional and modern themes), D.S. Sar Desai, and Arlene Bergman (a feminist interpretation of women's experience). Good summaries can also be found in Southeast Asia survey texts by scholars such as George Coèdes, D.G.E. Hall, John Cady, and David Steinberg. On the premodern period, the various essays in the edited collections by Hall and Whitmore, Marr and Milner, Taylor and Whitmore, Lam, Tarling, and Wickberg, as well as Michael Cotter's interesting analysis of the southward expansion of Vietnamese civilization into the Mekong delta and Lockard's speculations on national identity, should also be noted. Given the importance of literature in the Vietnamese tradition, the excellent anthologies of Vietnamese poetry by Nguyen Ngoc Bich and Huynh Sanh Thong along with Nguyen Du's famous *The Tale of Kieu* – often considered the quintessential local novel, a critique of Confucian society published in the early 19th century – provide excellent introductions to the Vietnamese worldview.

Historical writing becomes much richer for the modern period. There are several good surveys of this era, including those by Woodside, Buttinger, Neil Jamieson, and Ngo Vinh Long as well as the essays collected by David Elliott and Walter Vella. The gradual colonization by French imperialism, and the (often negative) impacts this had on Vietnam's political evolution, social structure, and economic patterns, generated a number of studies. The French imperial enterprise has been analyzed by, among others, John Cady, Milton Osborne, and Pierre Brocheux and Daniel Hémery. But even after conquest it took the French an additional fifteen years of bloody repression to "pacify" the country against a heroic resistance; this opposition has been well studied by Truong Buu Lam, Helen Lamb, and David Marr.

The social and economic aspects of French colonialism, including the effects on village life, have been the subject of numerous studies, including those by Ngo Vinh Long, Hy V. Luong, and Pham Cao Duong (all writing on the transformation of the peasantry), Brocheux (a study of the Mekong delta), Nguyen Van Phong (early colonial social change), Donald Lancaster, and Martin Murray (on capitalist development). Both Marr and Woodside have brilliantly deciphered the complex intellectual and cultural developments of the period, while Osborne has outlined political change. The nationalist surge that commenced after the turn of the century and accelerated before World War II, most significantly in the form of the communist movement, has generated a considerable literature. William Duiker's various books constitute an essential baseline for understanding, augmented by Huynh Kim Khanh's incisive study of Vietnamese communism. The best biography of communist leader Ho Chi Minh is by Jean Lacouture. Mention should also be made of the works by John T. McAlister and Paul Mus, Ken Post (an exhaustive 5-volume study of the Vietnamese revolution), Hémery, Hodgkin, and Hue-Tam Ho Tai (who writes on noncommunist radical traditions).

The Japanese occupation of the early 1940s, followed by the First Indochina War pitting the French against the revolutionary nationalist coalition headed by Ho, changed the shape of Vietnam. The best studies of this period include those by McAlister (on wartime occupation), Marr (on the crucial year of 1945), Philippe Devillers (who offers a liberal French perspective), Lancaster, Fall, and Hammer (all writing on the French-Vietnamese political and military struggle). The American commitment began in the early 1940s and accelerated during the First Indochina War, escalating during the later 1950s and early 1960s into a full-fledged commitment to suppress militarily revolutionary nationalism while protecting the pro-US regime in South Vietnam. Among others, Duiker, George Kahin, Gabriel Kolko, Lloyd Gardner, and Anthony Short have ably traced the evolution of this policy.

The Vietnam War (or the American War) has generated a massive scholarship by historians, social scientists, military officers, journalists, and others, from many nations and all political positions. Few authors have been completely detached from the passions of the controversial conflict. Only a few of the dozens of valuable sources can be mentioned here. The handbook by James Olson provides a good general introduction to the historiography and debates of the war from an American vantage point. The Vietnamese context is explored by Duiker and Buttinger. Many excellent surveys of the war in English exist, most of them emphasizing US activities and decisions. The most useful include those by George Herring (the best product of research in US archives), Gary Hess and Patrick Hearden (both strong on the US background), Olson and Randy Roberts (a highly readable synthesis), Stanley Karnow (a journalistic account), Marilyn Young (a good combination of American and Asian expertise), James Harrison and William Turley (the most knowledgeable on Vietnam), Smith (which emphasized the overall international context), Frances Fitzgerald (a flawed but provocative cross-cultural approach), George Moss (strongest on military history), T. Louise Brown and Hugh Higgins (both of which offer an antiwar British perspective), Kahin, and Kolko. There are also many fine collections of essays and documents, including those edited by Robert McMahon, Allen and Long (antiwar), and Werner and Huynh (which incorporates both American and Vietnamese perspectives). An essay by Lockard attempted to place the conflict in a broader historical perspective.

The dramatic developments in Vietnam since the end of the war in 1975 await intensive historical scrutiny, but there are several good general studies, including those by Duiker, Kolko, Gareth Porter, and Melanie Beresford, as well as many edited collections and specialized analyses. Modern and premodern Vietnamese history, and the persisting connections between past and present, will no doubt remain rich fields of inquiry.

CRAIG A. LOCKARD

See also Kolko; Southeast Asia; United States: 20th Century

Further Reading

Allen, Douglas, and Ngo Vinh Long, eds., *Coming to Terms: Indochina, the United States, and the War*, Boulder, CO: Westview Press, 1991

Beresford, Melanie, *Vietnam: Politics, Economics and Society*, London and New York: Pinter, 1988

Bergman, Arlene Eisen, *Women of Viet Nam*, San Francisco: Peoples Press, 1974

Bich, Nguyen Ngoc, ed., *A Thousand Years of Vietnamese Poetry*, New York: Knopf, 1975

Brocheux, Pierre, and Daniel Hémery, *Indochine la colonisation ambigüe, 1858–1954* (Indochina: An Ambiguous Colonization), Paris: Découverte, 1995

Brocheux, Pierre, *The Mekong Delta: Ecology, Economy, and Revolution, 1860–1960*, Madison: Center for Southeast Asian Studies, University of Wisconsin, 1995

Brown, T. Louise, *War and Aftermath in Vietnam*, London: Routledge, 1991

Buttinger, Joseph, *The Smaller Dragon: A Political History of Vietnam*, New York: Praeger, and London: Atlantic, 1958

Buttinger, Joseph, *Vietnam: A Dragon Embattled*, 2 vols., New York: Praeger, 1967

Buttinger, Joseph, *Vietnam: A Political History*, New York: Praeger, 1968; London: Deutsch, 1969

Buttinger, Joseph, *A Dragon Defiant: A Short History of Vietnam*, New York: Praeger, 1972

Cady, John F., *The Roots of French Imperialism in Eastern Asia*, Ithaca, NY: Cornell University Press, 1954

Chesneaux, Jean, *Contribution à l'histoire de la nation Vietnamienne*, Paris: Editions Sociales, 1955; revised in English as *The Vietnamese Nation: Contribution to a History*, Sydney: Current Book Distributors, 1966

Coèdes, George, *Les Peuples de la péninsule indochinoise: histoire, civilisations*, Paris: Dunod, 1962; in English as *The Making of South East Asia*, Berkeley: University of California Press, and London: Routledge, 1966

Cotter, Michael G., "Towards a Social History of the Vietnamese Southward Movement," *Journal of Southeast Asian History* 9 (1968), 12–24

Devillers, Philippe, *Histoire du Viêt-Nam, de 1940 à 1952* (A History of Vietnam), Paris: Seuil, 1952

Duiker, William J., *The Rise of Nationalism in Vietnam, 1900–1941*, Ithaca, NY: Cornell University Press, 1976

Duiker, William J., *Historical Dictionary of Vietnam*, Metuchen, NJ: Scarecrow Press, 1989

Duiker, William J., *US Containment Policy and the Conflict in Indochina*, Stanford, CA: Stanford University Press, 1994

Duiker, William J., *Sacred War: Nationalism and Revolution in a Divided Vietnam*, New York: McGraw Hill, 1995

Duiker, William J., *Vietnam: Revolution in Transition*, 2nd edition, Boulder, CO: Westview Press, 1995

Duiker, William J., *The Communist Road to Power in Vietnam*, 2nd edition, Boulder, CO: Westview Press, 1996

Elliott, David P. *et al.*, *Vietnam: Essays on History, Culture, and Society*, New York: Asia Society, 1985

Fall, Bernard, *The Two Vietnams: A Political and Military Analysis*, New York: Praeger, 1958; revised 1964

Fall, Bernard, *Street Without Joy: Indochina at War, 1946–1954*, Harrisburg, PA: Stackpole, 1961; reprinted 1994

Fitzgerald, Frances, *Fire in the Lake: The Vietnamese and the Americans in Vietnam*, Boston: Little Brown, and London: Macmillan, 1972

Gardner, Lloyd C., *Approaching Vietnam: From World War II Through Dienbienphu, 1941–1954*, New York: Norton, 1988

Hall, D.G.E., *A History of South-East Asia*, London: Macmillan, and New York: St. Martin's Press, 1955; 4th edition 1981

Hall, Kenneth R., and John K. Whitmore, eds., *Explorations in Early Southeast Asian History: The Origins of Southeast Asian Statecraft*, Ann Arbor: Center for South and Southeast Asian Studies, University of Michigan, 1976

Hammer, Ellen J., *The Struggle for Indochina, 1940–1955*, Stanford, CA: Stanford University Press, 1954

Harrison, James P., *The Endless War: Fifty Years of Struggle in Vietnam*, New York: Free Press, 1982

Hearden, Patrick J., *The Tragedy of Vietnam*, New York: HarperCollins, 1991

Hémery, Daniel, *Révolutionnaires vietnamiens et pouvoir colonial en Indochine* (Vietnamese Revolutionaries and Colonial Power in Indochina), Paris: Maspero, 1975

Herring, George C., *America's Longest War: The United States and Vietnam, 1950–1975*, New York: Wiley, 1979; 3rd edition, New York: McGraw Hill, 1996

Hess, Gary R., *Vietnam and the United States: Origins and Legacy of War*, Boston: Twayne, 1990

Higgins, Hugh, *Vietnam*, London: Heinemann, 1975

Hodgkin, Thomas, *Vietnam: The Revolutionary Path*, London: Macmillan, and New York: St. Martin's Press, 1981

Huynh Kim Khanh, *Vietnamese Communism, 1925–1945*, Ithaca, NY: Cornell University Press, 1982

Huynh Sanh Thong, ed., *An Anthology of Vietnamese Poems from the Eleventh Through the Twentieth Centuries*, New Haven: Yale University Press, 1996

Jamieson, Neil L., *Understanding Vietnam*, Berkeley: University of California Press, 1993

Kahin, George McTurnan, *Intervention: How America Became Involved in Vietnam*, New York: Knopf, 1986

Karnow, Stanley, *Vietnam: A History*, New York: Viking, and London: Century, 1983; revised 1991

Kolko, Gabriel, *Anatomy of a War: Vietnam, the United States, and the Modern Historical Experience*, New York: Pantheon, 1985; as *Vietnam: Anatomy of a War, 1940–1975*, London: Unwin, 1987

Kolko, Gabriel, *Vietnam: Anatomy of a Peace*, London and New York: Routledge, 1997

Lacouture, Jean, *Ho Chi Minh*, Paris: Seuil, 1967; in English as *Ho Chi Minh: A Political Biography*, London: Allen Lane, and New York: Vintage, 1968

Lam, Truong Buu, *Patterns of Vietnamese Response to Foreign Intervention, 1858–1900*, New Haven: Center for Southeast Asia Studies, Yale University, 1967

Lam, Truong Buu, *Resistance, Rebellion, Revolution: Popular Movements in Vietnamese History*, Singapore: Institute of Southeast Asian Studies, 1984

Lam, Truong Buu, ed., *Borrowings and Adaptations in Vietnamese Culture*, Honolulu: Southeast Asian Studies, University of Hawaii, 1987

Lamb, Helen B., *Vietnam's Will to Live: Resistance to Foreign Aggression from Early Times to the Nineteenth Century*, New York: Monthly Review Press, 1972

Lancaster, Donald, *The Emancipation of French Indochina*, London and New York: Oxford University Press, 1961

Le Thanh Khoi, *Histoire du Viet Nam, des origines à 1858* (A History of Vietnam), Paris: Sudestasie, 1981

Lockard, Craig A., "Meeting Yesterday Head-on: The Vietnam War in Vietnamese, American, and World History," *Journal of World History* 5 (1994), 227–70

Lockard, Craig A., "The Unexplained Miracle: Reflections on the History of Vietnamese National Identity and Survival," *Journal of Asian and African Studies* 29 (1994), 10–35

Luong, Hy V., *Revolution in the Village: Tradition and Transformation in North Vietnam, 1925–1988*, Honolulu: University of Hawaii Press, 1992

McAlister, John T., *Vietnam: The Origins of Revolution, 1885–1946*, Washington, DC: Center for Research in Social Systems, 1968

McAlister, John T., and Paul Mus, *The Vietnamese and Their Revolution*, New York: Harper, 1970

McMahon, Robert J., ed., *Major Problems in the History of the Vietnam War*, Lexington, MA: Heath 1990; revised 1995

Marr, David G., *Vietnamese Anticolonialism, 1885–1925*, Berkeley: University of California Press, 1971

Marr, David G., "Vietnamese Historical Reassessment, 1900–1944," in Anthony Reid and David G. Marr, eds., *Perceptions of the Past in Southeast Asia*, Singapore: Heinemann, 1979

Marr, David G., *Vietnamese Tradition on Trial, 1920–1945*, Berkeley: University of California Press, 1981

Marr, David G., and A.C. Milner, eds., *Southeast Asia in the 9th to 14th Centuries*, Singapore: Institute of Southeast Asian Studies, 1985

Marr, David G., *Vietnam 1945: The Quest for Power*, Berkeley: University of California Press, 1995

Masson, André, *Histoire de l'Indochine* (History of Indochina), Paris: Presses Universitaires de France, 1950; reprinted as *Histoire du Vietnam* (History of Vietnam), 1960

Moss, George D., *Vietnam: An American Ordeal*, Englewood Cliffs, NJ: Prentice Hall, 1990; revised 1994

Murray, Martin J., *The Development of Capitalism in Colonial Indochina (1870–1940)*, Berkeley: University of California Press, 1980

Ngo Vinh Long, *Before the Revolution: The Vietnamese Peasants under the French*, Cambridge, MA: MIT Press, 1973

Ngo Vinh Long, "Communal Property and Peasant Revolutionary Struggles in Vietnam," *Peasant Studies* 17 (1990), 121–27

Ngo Vinh Long, "Vietnam," in Douglas Allen and Ngo Vinh Long, eds., *Coming to Terms: Indochina, the United States, and the War*, Boulder, CO: Westview Press, 1991

Nguyen Du, *Kim-Vân Kiêu*; in English as *The Tale of Kieu*, New York: Vintage, 1973

Nguyen Thanh Nha, *Tableau Economique du Viêt-Nam aux dix-septième et dix-huitième siècles* (Economic Picture of Vietnam in the 17th and 18th Centuries), Paris: Cujas, 1970

Nguyen The Anh, "Historical Research in Vietnam: A Tentative Survey," *Journal of Southeast Asian Studies* 26 (1995), 121–32

Nguyen Van Phong, *La Societé vietnamienne de 1882 à 1902* (Vietnamese Society from 1882 to 1902), Paris: Presses Universitaires de France, 1971

Olson, James S., and Randy Roberts, *Where the Domino Fell: America and Vietnam, 1945–1995*, New York: St. Martin's Press, 1991; revised 1996

Olson, James S., *The Vietnam War: Handbook of the Literature and Research*, Westport, CT: Greenwood Press, 1993

Osborne, Milton, *The French Presence in Cochinchina and Cambodia: Rule and Response (1859–1905)*, Ithaca, NY: Cornell University Press, 1969

Pham Cao Duong, *Vietnamese Peasants under French Domination, 1861–1945*, Berkeley: University of California Press, 1989

Porter, Gareth, *Vietnam: The Politics of Bureaucratic Socialism*, Ithaca, NY: Cornell University Press, 1993

Post, Ken, *Revolution, Socialism and Nationalism in Viet Nam*, 5 vols., Belmont, CA: Wadsworth, and Aldershot: Dartmouth, 1989–94

Sar Desai, D.R., *Vietnam: The Struggle for National Identity*, 2nd edition, Boulder, CO: Westview Press, 1992

Short, Anthony, *The Origins of the Vietnam War*, London and New York: Longman, 1989

Smith, Ralph Bernard, *Viet Nam and the West*, London: Heinemann, 1968; Ithaca, NY: Cornell University Press, 1971

Smith, Ralph Bernard, *An International History of the Vietnam War*, 3 vols., London: Macmillan, and New York: St. Martin's Press, 1983–91

Steinberg, David Joel, ed., *In Search of Southeast Asia: A Modern History*, Kuala Lumpur: Oxford University Press, New York: Praeger, and London: Pall Mall Press, 1971; revised edition, Honolulu: University of Hawaii Press, 1987

Tai, Hue-Tam Ho, *Millenarianism and Peasant Politics in Vietnam*, Cambridge, MA: Harvard University Press, 1983

Tai, Hue-Tam Ho, *Radicalism and the Origins of the Vietnamese Revolution*, Cambridge, MA: Harvard University Press, 1992

Tarling, Nicholas, ed., *The Cambridge History of Southeast Asia*, 2 vols., Cambridge: Cambridge University Press, 1992

Taylor, Keith Weller, *The Birth of Vietnam*, Berkeley: University of California Press, 1983

Taylor, Keith Weller, and John K. Whitmore, eds., *Essays into Vietnamese Pasts*, Ithaca, NY: Southeast Asia Program, Cornell University, 1995

Turley, William S., *The Second Indochina War: A Short Political and Military History, 1954–1975*, Boulder, CO: Westview Press, and London: Gower, 1986

Vella, Walter F., ed., *Aspects of Vietnamese History*, Honolulu: Asian Studies Program, University of Hawaii, 1975

Vien, Nguyen Khac, *Traditional Vietnam: Some Historical Stages*, special issue of *Vietnam Studies*, 21, Hanoi: Foreign Language Press, 1969

Vien, Nguyen Khac, *Tradition and Revolution in Vietnam*, Berkeley, CA: Indochina Resource Center, 1974

Werner, Jayne S., and Luu Doan Huynh, eds., *The Vietnam War: Vietnamese and American Perspectives*, Armonk, NY: Sharpe, 1993

Whitfield, Danny J., *Historical and Cultural Dictionary of Vietnam*, Metuchen, NJ: Scarecrow, 1976

Whitmore, John K., "Social Organization and Confucian Thought in Vietnam," *Journal of Southeast Asian Studies* 15 (1984), 296–306

Whitmore, John K., *Vietnam, Ho Quy Ly, and the Ming (1371–1421)*, New Haven: Southeast Asia Studies, Yale University, 1985

Wickberg, Edgar, ed., *Historical Interaction of China and Vietnam: Institutional and Cultural Themes*, Lawrence: Center for East Asian Studies, University of Kansas, 1969

Wolters, O.W., *History, Culture, and Region in Southeast Asian Perspectives*, Singapore: Institute of Southeast Asian Studies, 1982

Woodside, Alexander B., *Vietnam and the Chinese Model: A Comparative Study of Nguyen and Ch'ing Civil Government in the First Half of the Nineteenth Century*, Cambridge, MA: Harvard University Press, 1971

Woodside, Alexander B., *Community and Revolution in Modern Vietnam*, Boston: Houghton Mifflin, 1976

Woodside, Alexander B., "Vietnamese History: Confucianism, Colonialism, and the Struggle for Independence," in David P. Elliott *et al.*, *Vietnam*, New York: Asia Society, 1985

Young, Marilyn Blatt, *The Vietnam Wars, 1945–1990*, New York: Harper, 1991

Vietnamese Chronicles

The Confucian influence was a mixed blessing in Vietnam. On the one hand, it meant that court historians were carefully chosen and historical writing was regarded as a prestigious activity. From the Tran dynasty (1225–1400) onwards, the affairs of the king were recorded and arranged in chronological sequence and thus each reign compiled historical materials for its successor. This bureaucratic insistence on the careful organization of materials left Vietnam with more ordered sources than any of its Southeast Asian neighbors could possibly imagine. On the other hand, the Confucian concept of historiography held that the ultimate duty of the historian was to define what was right and wrong and thus teach the lessons of the past to future generations. Official historians, who were always Confucian scholars, adhered to orthodox rules for establishing legitimacy, and took it upon themselves to determine what should be recorded and how it was to be recorded. They therefore tended to edit their material to emphasize the norms rather than the realities of Vietnamese society. These principles still influence official historical writing

in contemporary Vietnam, though today they are devoted to exemplifying the different ideals of legitimacy and morality.

The most important Vietnamese chronicle is *Dai Viet Su Ky Toan Thu* (Complete Historical Records of Great Viet). Although published in 1697, it was actually a conflation of earlier official annals by Le Van Huu (1272) and Ngo Si Lien (1479), with additions up to 1662 by Pham Cong Tru and to 1675 by Le Hi. Scholars have commented that there were direct relationships between Le Van Huu's *Dai Viet Su Ky*, which was later incorporated into the *Dai Viet Su Ky Toan Thu* under Ngo Si Lien's revision, and *Viet Su Luoc* (Abbreviated History of Viet), a 13th-century Vietnamese official source taken away during the Ming invasion that survived under Chinese custodianship.

Since no historical work was printed in Vietnam before 1697, manuscripts of *Dai Viet Su Ky Toan Thu* made by previous historians had been frequently reduced, revised, and corrected by later historians in attempts to confirm to contemporary needs. From this point of view, the *Dai Viet Su Ky Toan Thu* best reflected the judgments of 17th-century Vietnamese literatis on Vietnamese history, and their desire to legitimize the dominant position of the bureaucracy in the state, rather than a genuine perspective held by those of the previous periods. Interventions made by the later historians to the earlier history is characteristic of Vietnamese historiography.

The official history of 19th-century Vietnam is contained in *Dai Nam Thuc Luc* (True or Vertical Records of Greater Vietnam), with 560 chapters, compiled from 1821 to 1909 by official scholars at the Nguyen court's Bureau of Historiography under the supervision of very senior court figures. This source traced the history of the southern Nguyen lords from 1558 to 1777, and was edited as *Tien Bien* (Premier Period of the Nguyen), while the dynastic history, from the rise of Nguyen Anh (1778) to the end of Dong Khanh reign (1889), was compiled as *Chinh Bien* (Principal Period). In addition to this detailed chronological account of government, the Nguyen also produced *Dai Nam Liet Truyen*, a 3-volume compilation of biographies of queens, princes and princesses, and high office holders, as well as noteworthy subjects, including exemplary women and important rebels. *Liet Truyen* also used an interesting range of sources – oral tradition, family records, inscriptions, and questionnaires sent to local officials.

The Nguyen Bureau of Historiography also sought to reconstruct Vietnamese history from its mythical origin in 2879 BCE to 1789 CE, from a 19th-century perspective. Under the guidance of Emperor Tu Duc (reigned 1847–83), an accomplished Confucian scholar and poet, the Bureau compiled *Kham Dinh Viet Su Thong Giam Cuong Muc* (Imperially Ordered Annotated Text Completely Reflecting the History of Viet), in part to demonstrate the historical legitimacy of Nguyen rule. The content was divided into two categories: *cuong* (key links), followed and complemented by *muc* (detailed items), sometimes with the emperor's annotations which set down his convictions on the past. As it was dominated by moralistic evaluations, no records of the Tay Son reign (1789–1801) were provided.

Official Vietnamese historiography differed from Chinese practice, where composite standard histories were compiled by official historians. Rather, the chronicle form was the mainstream in Vietnamese historiography. The only composite histories that survived in opposition to the chronicle history was

Le Quy Don's *Le Trieu Thong Su* (Complete History of the Le Dynasty, 1749).

Hundreds of unofficial histories (*da su*) were created by individual scholars throughout centuries, sometimes as variations of official history, sometimes as independent sources and adopted partly for the compilation of the later official history (*chinh su*). In addition, local histories and inscriptions (*van bia*), geographical records (*dia chi*), village regulations (*huong uoc*), and family genealogies (*gia pha*) were constantly compiled by this social group. Many thousands still remain today, a treasure trove for Vietnamese historiography.

The French colonial conquest (1860–1954) introduced Western historiographical concepts and forms. Narrative history appeared, initially as reinterpretations of earlier chronicles, as by Truong Vinh Ky in his influential *Cours d'histoire annamite* (A Course of History of Annam, 2 vols., 1875–77). Seeking to account for Western dominance, nationalist scholars from Phan Boi Chau onwards turned to Western analytical tools, replacing the old cyclical concept of history with the idea of linear progress, and experimenting with sociologically derived categories and periodizations. This culminated in the 1930s with new historians such as Dao Duy Anh who consciously applied dialectical methods to historical analysis.

Postcolonial North Vietnamese historical writing developed by using a narrow Marxist dialectic for political purposes. History was meant to demonstrate the people's national struggle against foreign aggression and their own ruling class. In the Socialist Republic of Vietnam, this became the official historiographical approach for almost all published studies until the late 1980s. Thus, ironically, official historical writing under communist rule resembles pre-19th century official Vietnamese historiography more than its colonial past of the 1930s and 1940s, when uniquely, non-official historians explored the Vietnamese past not to legitimize authority, but to explain why the government had failed.

LI TANA

Further Reading

Chen Ching-ho, "Daietsu Shiki Zensho no Senshu to Denpon" (On *Dai Viet Su Ky Toan Thu*'s author and its editions), *Tonan Ajia: Rekishi to Bunka* 7 (1977), 3–36

Durand, Maurice, and Nguyen Tran Huan, *Introduction à la littérature vietnamienne*, Paris: Maisonneuve et Larose, 1969; in English as *An Introduction to Vietnamese Literature*, New York: Columbia University Press, 1985

Gaspardone, Emile, "Bibliographie annamite," *Bulletin de l'Ecole Française d'Extrême Orient*, 34 (1934), 1–18, 49–85

Le Quy Don, *Le Trieu Thong Su* (Complete History of the Le Dynasty); also known as *Dai Viet Thong Su* (Complete History of the Dai Viet), 50 vols., 1749

Marr, David G., *Vietnamese Tradition on Trial, 1920–1945*, Berkeley: University of California Press, 1981

Nguyen The Anh, "Historical Research in Vietnam: A Tentative Survey," *Journal of Southeast Asian Studies* 26 (1995), 121–32

Phan Huy Le, "Historical Research in Vietnam," *Vietnamese Studies* 71 (1983) 100–32

Taylor, Keith Weller, "Appendix O: Sources for Early Vietnamese History," in his *The Birth of Vietnam*, Berkeley: University of California Press, 1983

Taylor, Keith Weller, "The Literati Revival in Seventeenth-century Vietnam," *Journal of Southeast Asian Studies* 18 (1987), 1–23

Tran Van Giap, *Tim Hieu Kho Sach Han-Nom* (Understanding the Chinese and Nom Collections), vol.1, Hanoi: Van Hoa, 1984

Truong Vinh Ky [Petrus Jean-Baptiste Vinh-Ky Truong], *Cours d'histoire annamite* (A Course of History of Annam), 2 vols., Saigon: Imprimerie du Gouvernement, 1875–77

Whitmore, John K., "Vietnamese Historical Sources for the Reign of Le Thanh-tong (1460–1497)," *Journal of Asian Studies*, 29 (1970), 373–89

Wolters, O.W., "Le Van Huu's Treatment of Ly Than Ton's Reign (1127–1137)," in C.D. Cowan and O.W. Wolters, eds., *Southeast Asian History and Historiography: Essays Presented to D.G.E. Hall*, Ithaca, NY: Cornell University Press, 1976

Wolters, O.W., "What Else May Ngo Si Lien Mean? A Matter of Distinctions in the Fifteenth Century," in Anthony Reid, ed., *Sojourners and Settlers: Histories of Southeast Asia and the Chinese, in Honour of Jennifer Cushman*, St. Leonards, Australia: Allen and Unwin, 1996

Woodside, Alexander B., "Conceptions of Change and of Human Responsibility for Change in Late Traditional Vietnam," in David K. Wyatt and Alexander B. Woodside, eds., *Moral Order and the Question of Change: Essays on Southeast Asian Thought*, New Havevn: Yale University Press, 1982

Villani, Giovanni 1276–1348

Medieval Italian chronicler

Giovanni Villani claimed to have obtained the inspiration for his chronicle of Florence when he visited Rome as a pilgrim in the Jubilee Year of 1300. Rome's fortunes, he perceived, were declining while those of his native city rose. This version of the genesis of the *Cronica* (or *Cronaca*) need not be discounted, but it is not thought that the work began to be written down before the 1320s. It was essential to Villani's conception that it should be a universal chronicle: among his most important sources was a widely known example of the genre, the chronicle of Martinus Polonus.

Following existing Florentine tradition, he established Florence's status as a "daughter of Rome," whose most worthy inhabitants preserved their inheritance of Roman blood. It has recently been argued that the legend recounted by Villani of Florence's refoundation by Charlemagne, after its destruction by Totila (confused by Villani and his sources with Attila), was in fact his own invention. This can be seen as an historical endorsement of the close links between Florence and the royal house of France. As a young man working out his business apprenticeship during the first decade of the 14th century, Villani spent extended periods in France, as is apparent from the chronicle itself. As historian, he vindicated Florence's alignment, with its rapidly developing banking and commercial interests, on the axis that linked the Angevin kingdom of Naples with the papacy, now established at Avignon; as a moderate Black Guelf (the party that in 1302, with the aid of the king of France's brother, Charles of Valois, had triumphed in Florence's internal power struggles), and as office-holder and businessman, he was himself, in his prime, identified with the regime. This did not obviate disillusionment with Philip IV of France, or with the conduct of Florentine affairs, in his later years.

The chronicle as we have it begins with a declaration of intent: Villani was going to rectify the lack of any coherent account of Florence's origins and development, whether it arose from the negligence of man or from the destruction of ancient records. The work achieved a quasi-official status even while it was being written, and Villani undertook a revision of his own text, which has been recently re-edited under the title *Nuova cronica*; a new edition of the first version is awaited. Subsequent Florentine chroniclers depended heavily on it. A long debate as to whether a chronicle supposedly written in the late 13th century by Ricordano Malispini was a source for Villani, or in fact a later compilation largely derived from him, seems to have ended with the majority acceptance of the latter view. Villani's work was known also outside Florence; Sienese chroniclers, for example, used it as a quarry. It constituted a major source for Leonardo Bruni's *Historia Florentina*, completed in 1444, even if the humanist unsurprisingly re-evaluated some of Villani's historical and moral standpoints.

Villani's relationship with his great older contemporary Dante has attracted extensive comment. He read, admired, and derived ideas from Dante, but his political experience and affiliations differed markedly. Not only had the poet been a casualty of the ruin of the rival White Guelfs in 1302, but, as a member of one of the greater guilds, the Calimala (the cloth importers), Villani could scarcely share Dante's spiritually conservative attitudes to the commercial and financial concerns that were shaping Florentine policy. To a large extent, he spoke for those who took it for granted that the greater guildsmen, such as the members of the Calimala, represented the real interests of the city. This was not just a matter of "politics" narrowly defined, but of urban amenities and all that made the city conspicuous in the eyes of mankind. Recording the commission to the sculptor Andrea Pisano to make the first set of bronze doors for the Baptistery of San Giovanni in 1330, Villani praises their great beauty and adds, "And I the author, was the official in charge of this work on behalf of the merchants of the Calimala, guardians of the works of San Giovanni."

The inclusion of such entries, and the descriptions of comets, miracles, and the acquisition of relics, may help to define Villani for us as "chronicler," rather than "historian," but he himself claimed a part in the heritage of the classical authors whose names came into his mind when he contemplated the decline of Rome. The ambivalence he intermittently expressed in the face of material wealth and power may also seem to us consonant with a "medieval" cast of mind, but it has been contended that Villani's outlook was fundamentally optimistic, that the story of Florence that he told is above all a success story. His readers can scarcely fail to see in him a representative of a literate culture compounded of many influences, Latin and vernacular, biblical, classical, astrological, and mercantile. Among his most quoted passages is a statistical profile of Florence in the 1330s, in which, it is generally felt, he ministers to the modern appetite for quantitative data more reliably than most medieval chroniclers.

It is however arguable that Villani's own tribulations in later life, as well as those experienced by Florence, cast a shadow on his worldly optimism. Books 12 and 13, written after the great Florentine flood of 1333, stand a little apart from the rest and have their own manuscript tradition. In the last chapter that he was able to write before he died – a victim of the great plague of 1348 – Villani suggested that the earthquakes which had occurred in many regions in 1347 might be reckoned among the signs which Christ had warned his disciples would herald the end of the world. His brother Matteo continued the

chronicle down to 1363. For modern students of the Italian 13th and 14th centuries it is an inescapable presence, vividly documenting both factual realities and *mentalités*.

DIANA WEBB

Biography
Born Florence, 1276. Partner and associate, Peruzzi and Buonaccorsi companies, international bankers; traveled to Flanders, Rome, and Naples; settled in Florence to write, 1308; also held civic offices. His brother Matteo (1285–1363) and nephew Filippo (d.1405) were also historians. Died Florence, 1348, in the Black Death.

Principal Writings
Cronaca fiorentina (Florentine Chronicle), 12 vols., c.1300–48; Villani's revision edited by Giuseppe Porta as *Nuova cronica*, 3 vols., 1990–91; selections in English as *Villani's Chronicle*, 1906

Further Reading
Davis, Charles T., *Dante's Italy and Other Essays*, Philadelphia: University of Pennsylvania Press, 1984
Green, Louis, *Chronicle into History: An Essay on the Interpretation of History in Florentine Fourteenth-Century Chronicles*, Cambridge: Cambridge University Press, 1972
Holmes, George, *Florence, Rome and the Origins of the Renaissance*, Oxford and New York: Oxford University Press, 1986
Maissen, Thomas, "Attila, Totila e Carlo Magno fra Dante, Villani, Boccaccio e Malispini: Per la genesi di due leggende erudite" (Attila, Totila, and Charlemagne in Dante, Villani, Boccaccio, and Malispini: On the Origins of Two Learned Legends), *Archivio Storico Italiano* 152 (1994), 56–639
Najemy, John, *Corporatism and Consensus in Florentine Electoral Politics, 1280–1400*, Chapel Hill: North Carolina University Press, 1982
Rubinstein, Nicolai, "The Beginnings of Political Thought in Florence: A Study in Medieval Historiography," *Journal of the Warburg and Courtauld Institutes* 5 (1942), 198–227
Rubinstein, Nicolai, "Some Ideas on Municipal Progress and Decline in the Italy of the Communes," in Donald James Gordon, ed., *Fritz Saxl, 1890–1948: A Volume of Memorial Essays from His Friends in England*, London and New York: Nelson, 1957

Villari, Pasquale 1827–1917
Italian historian, biographer, and political figure

Through English, French, and German translations, Pasquale Villari became one of the most internationally famous Italian historians of his time. He combined scholarship with an active involvement in politics as a cabinet minister and member of parliament as well as being a reform-minded commentator on public issues (see especially *Le lettere meridionali ed altri scritti sulla questione sociale in Italia*; Southern Letters and Other Writings on the Social Question in Italy, 1875, revised 1885). He moved back and forth between these two spheres over a long and enormously productive career that began in the 1840s with the sharp acceleration of Italy's Risorgimento struggle against foreign occupation and the old regime. With Francesco De Sanctis, his revered teacher, Villari participated in the 1848 uprising against the Bourbon government in their native Naples. Villari's youthful experiences in the Risorgimento exerted a lifelong influence on his politics and scholarship.

Condemned thereafter to exile, Villari fled to Florence where for the next ten years he continued his studies and familiarized himself with the city's historical archives. To these researches he brought a mind basically shaped by De Sanctis who, as one of the leading Hegelians in Naples, had taught his students that the true spirit of a nation was to be found in the masterpieces of its literature.

Educated in the philosophy of dialectical idealism, Villari launched his career as a publishing scholar with two studies, on the medieval history of Italy and on the philosophy of history, but the book that gave him a national reputation was *La storia di Girolamo Savonarola e de' suoi tempi* (1859–61; *Life and Times of Girolamo Savonarola*, 1888). Critics praised the book for the originality and depth of its research as well as its graceful style. The year it appeared Villari accepted a teaching appointment at the University of Pisa where he remained until 1865. Thereafter he began a nearly fifty-year-long association with the Royal Istituto di Studi Superiori in Florence.

The methodological principles to which Villari adhered all of his life underlay the Savonarola biography. In "La filosofia positiva e il metodo storico" (Positivist Philosophy and the Historical Method, 1866), he would profess admiration for historical positivism, a scientific approach to the writing of history then primarily associated with the work of Henry Thomas Buckle. Yet Villari's embrace of positivism did not fundamentally alter his Hegelian notions about the centrality of the great man of virtuous resolve in the historical process. The scientific rigor of positivism appealed to the researcher in him, and it was strictly in a methodological sense that he can be said ever to have been a positivist. The patriotic and ethical values, manifestly driving Villari's interpretation of Savonarola and all of his other books, came not from positivism, but from the strong convictions that he held about the Risorgimento faith of liberalism and the social necessity of religion.

Villari, inconsistently describing Savonarola as a representative man of the Renaissance while showing him as an intransigent defender of medieval Christianity, reconstructed the 15th-century Dominican friar's life in the light of "his sermons, his writings and . . . the real history of events." Combining a traditional historian's concern for context with the critical theory of De Sanctis, he tried to end the confusion left behind by partisans on both sides of the debate over the fiery preacher's spectacular and still controversial career in Renaissance Florence. Villari sought the balance point between these two schools of thought, mainly defending Savonarola as a sublime moral leader at a time of unparalleled decadence and cynicism in Italian life, but commenting negatively on historians who by going too far in exalting him imparted "a polemical rather than a historical character to their work."

Even in the Savonarola biography, Villari made prominent mention of Niccolò Machiavelli, the subject of the other major work on which his immense international fame, particularly in England, rested. "The great difference between these two almost antagonistic characters," represented for Villari the polar extremes of the Italian national character.

In *Niccolò Machiavelli e i suoi tempi* (1877–82; *Life and Times of Niccolò Machiavelli*, 1878–83), Villari began the biography proper with an account of the indelible impression that the Savonarola episode had made on the 29-year-old Florentine

secretary. In a 1498 letter, Machiavelli characterized Savonarola as the "weaponless prophet." Savonarola's fall from power illustrated for Machiavelli the main premise of his still-forming political philosophy, that without recourse to efficacious military force no political leader can long survive. Villari then analyzed virtually every line Machiavelli ever wrote, "with the strict justice that is the chief purpose of history," in the context of his political career and private life. As in the Savonarola biography, he gave evidence of prodigious research, discovering many new documents in the archives, poring over a mass of unpublished letters, and mastering the even then staggering secondary literature on the subject.

Villari expressly disavowed the role of apologist, but his admiration for Machiavelli as a piercing and wonderfully lucid political writer and his sympathy for him as a man pervaded the book. While conceding that Machiavelli had much to answer for, particularly the gross immorality of *The Prince*, Villari concluded that the thwarting circumstances of his life and the national tragedy of conquest that befell Renaissance Italy went far toward exculpating him. Ever enamored of the Risorgimento's ideals, Villari celebrated Machiavelli for his patriotism, above all for being the first person to recognize the necessity of Italian unity. He interpreted Machiavelli's major books as the signposts of a heroic quest to save Italy from invasion and destruction, by discovering the secret inner workings of politics and the most successful methods of war and governance: "Never, in short, was there a less Machiavellian man than Machiavelli."

Villari continued to publish major historical works at a prolific rate until the end of his life. Among the most significant of them were *I primi due secoli della storia di Firenze* (1893–94; *The First Two Centuries of Florentine History*, 1894), *Le invasioni barbariche in Italia* (1901; *The Barbarian Invasions of Italy*, 1902), and *L'Italia da Carlo Magno ad Arrigo VII* (1910; *Medieval Italy from Charlemagne to Henry VII*, 1910). To the end, he thought that by transcending historiography's indispensable scientific basis the greatest historians always aimed at the improvement and spiritualization of humanity through a celebration of its capacity for good.

RICHARD DRAKE

Biography

Born Naples, 3 October 1827, son of a lawyer. Studied under Francesco De Sanctis. Supported revolution of 1848, then exiled from Neapolitan kingdom; settled Florence where he researched independently in archives, 1849–59. Professor, University of Pisa, 1859–65; and Royal Istituto di Studi Superiori, Florence, 1865–1913. Member, Chamber of Deputies, 1870–76, 1880–82; senator, from 1884: held several government posts. President, Dante Alighieri Society, 1896–1903. Married Linda White (died 1915). Died Florence, December 1917.

Principal Writings

La storia di Girolamo Savonarola e de' suoi tempi, 2 vols., 1859–61; in English as *Life and Times of Girolamo Savonarola*, 2 vols., 1888
"La filosofia positiva e il metodo storico" (Positivist Philosophy and the Historical Method), 1866; reprinted in his *Saggi di storia, di critica e di politica*, 1868
Le lettere meridionali ed altri scritti sulla questione sociale in Italia (Southern Letters and Other Writings on the Social Question in Italy), 1875; revised 1885

Niccolò Machiavelli e i suoi tempi, 3 vols., 1877–82; in English as *Life and Times of Niccolò Machiavelli*, 4 vols., 1878–83; new translation in 2 vols., 1891

I primi due secoli della storia di Firenze, 1893–94; in English as *The First Two Centuries of Florentine History: The Republic and Parties at the Time of Dante*, 1894

Le invasioni barbariche in Italia, 1901; in English as *The Barbarian Invasions of Italy*, 2 vols., 1902

L'Italia da Carlo Magno ad Arrigo VII, 1910; in English as *Medieval Italy from Charlemagne to Henry VII*, 1910

Studies: Historical and Critical, 1907

Further Reading

Baldasseroni, Francesco, *Pasquale Villari, profilo biografico e bibliografia degli scritti* (Pasquale Villari's Biographical Profile and Bibliography of Writings), Florence: Galileiana, 1907

Barbagallo, Francesco, Introduction to Pasquale Villari, *Le lettere meridionali* (Southern Letters), Naples: Guida, 1979

Cicalese, Marialuisa, *Note per un profilo di Pasquale Villari* (Notes for a Profile of Pasquale Villari), Rome: Istituto Storico Italiano, 1979

Coppola, Nunzio, ed., *Carteggi di Vittorio Imbriani: gli hegeliani di Napoli ed altri corrispondenti, letterati, ed artisti* (The Correspondence of Vittorio Imbriani: The Hegelians of Naples and Other Correspondents, Literary Men, and Artists), Rome: Istituto per la Storia del Risorgimento Italiano, 1964

Coppola, Nunzio, ed., *Carteggi di Vittorio Imbriani: voci di esuli politici meridionali: lettere e documenti dal 1849 al 1861* (The Correspondence of Vittorio Imbriani: Voices of Southern Political Exiles: Letters and Documents from 1849 to 1861), Rome: Istituto per la Storia del Risorgimento Italiano, 1965

Croce, Benedetto, *Storia della storiografia italiana nel secolo decimonono* (The History of Italian Historiography in the 19th Century), 2 vols., Bari: Laterza, 1921

De Aloysio, Francesco, "Il vichismo di Pasquale Villari: un itinerario nelle regioni dello storicismo" (The Viconianism of Pasquale Villari: An Itinerary in the Regions of Historicism), *Nuova rivista storica* 62 (1978), 29–81

De Sanctis, Francesco, *Lettere a Pasquale Villari* (Letters to Pasquale Villari), Turin: Einaudi, 1955

Garin, Eugenio, *La cultura italiana tra '800 e '900: studi e ricerche* (Italian Culture Between the 19th and 20th Centuries), Bari: Laterza, 1963

Gentile, Giovanni, *Gino Capponi e la cultura toscana nel secolo decimonono* (Gino Capponi and Tuscan Culture in the 19th Century), Florence: Valecchi, 1922

Russo, Luigi, *Francesco De Sanctis e la cultura napoletana, 1860–1885* (Francesco De Sanctis and Neapolitan Culture, 1860–1885), Venice: Nuova Italia, 1928

Vinogradoff, Paul 1854–1925

British (Russian-born) legal historian

After graduating from Moscow University in 1875, Paul Vinogradoff received a scholarship to study in Berlin under Heinrich Brunner and Theodor Mommsen. Developing an interest in the Germanic school of history, he moved to Italy, where he researched an MA thesis on feudal relations in Italy, which he completed at Moscow in 1880. He first visited England in 1883, where the treasures of the Public Record Office attracted him to English medieval social and legal history. In this first trip he discovered Bracton's "Note Books," which had a profound influence on early legal history.

Returning to Moscow, he received his doctorate in 1884 and was appointed professor of history in 1887, founding a program for Western European historical methods. His interest in the subject of emancipation in Russian history, and in the legal records in England, drew him to his first major work, *Villainage in England* (1892), based on "scientific" Germanic research and an encyclopedic knowledge.

These years in Russia were marked by intellectual repression, and Vinogradoff was deeply touched by the riots in St. Petersburg and Moscow in 1899. Having married Louise Stang, the daughter of a Norwegian judge, he took an active political role in shaping the country by defining its problems and suggesting solutions. But he resigned his position in 1901 when one of his reports was not accepted by the government. Appointed a lecturer at Oxford University in 1902, he moved his family to England and was elected Corpus Christi chair of jurisprudence in 1903, a position held until his death in 1925. Still, he went to Moscow often, giving lectures and contributing to the reform movement, and was elected a member of the Imperial Academy of Sciences in 1915. Disillusioned with the Bolshevik Revolution in 1917 and the drift away from "democracy," he took British citizenship in 1918 and never returned to his native land.

Vinogradoff followed Henry Maine and Frederick Pollock in the Oxford chair. He regarded Maine as his teacher of ancient law and legal theory, and Frederic Maitland as the formative influence on his research. His second major work, *The Growth of the Manor* (1905), was inspired by Pollock and Maitland's *The History of English Law* (1895), and by J.H. Round and Frederick Seebohm, who had sought to raise the manor to the forefront of any understanding of medieval society. Vinogradoff's third major work, *English Society in the Eleventh Century* (1908), used Old English, Danish, and Norman customs, together with public law, to explore contrasting influences on the development of private law and class. In this work his views on feudal and democratic society came to the fore along with long, tedious, and often confusing passages on the events that had shaped his life in Russia.

Other, later work revealed more of his deficiencies. The edition of the *Year Books of Edward II* (1917) was excellent in its editing of the records, but was inadequate in explaining their meaning and context. Similar problems occurred in the *Survey of the Honour of Denbigh* (1914). However, when his medium was narrative writing, as it was in *Roman Law in Mediaeval Europe* (1909) and chapters for the *Cambridge Medieval History*, Vinogradoff was more able to focus on general ideas, such as the decline of medieval, and the origins of modern, society. Perhaps Vinogradoff's most typical work was *Outlines of Historical Jurisprudence* (1920–22), where his cosmopolitan and comparative law background enabled him to write poignantly on the origins of tribal, civic, feudal, and canon law. The problem was that he tried to carry it to the age of Socialism.

Vinogradoff saw himself as a "European" historian of jurisprudence, where law, like logic and psychology, was a science. He wrote from first principles, which he sought to demonstrate by hard work in the archives. His general writing was much more lucid than his scholarly work, and articles such as "Comparative Jurisprudence," "Custom and Right," and "Common-sense in Law" were widely read in his day. He was never, however, quite at home in Oxford, and had less influence on students than contemporary lecturers. This may have been due in part to his background: he had lectured in Moscow until 1911, when he found government spies in his classes. Many students considered him antiquarian, while his peers admired him as a great scholar who was also a fine musician and patriot. Vinogradoff preferred the seclusion of his country garden home in nearby Iffley, where he worked 12-hour days. Amiable, perceptive, with a satirical humor, he was tough and courageous. He had an unflinching belief in free men, communal life, and Teutonic institutions, all of which he saw in the law books and cartularies of the medieval world. A liberal, he had a clear vision of the cultural evolution of society that was rooted in his studies of the ancient tribes and civilizations of Eurasia.

In Russia, Vinogradoff's convictions led him to try to form a school of historians trained in methods of Western historiography, and to create educational reform from elementary school to university. He wrote Russian elementary textbooks on history, and organized teachers to discuss problems and changes. Fluent in twelve languages, he had few peers in comparative law. More analytical than creative, he could write eloquently on a theme, but never wrote any sustained, readable narrative. Much of his writing was in essay form. He was a prodigious translator, translating many of what he saw as the great authors of the West – Dicey, Guizot, Maine, Montesquieu, and Tocqueville – into Russian. He also wrote a large number of book reviews, in Russian- and English-language journals, on historical subjects ranging from ancient to modern, Europe to North America. In addition, he contributed numerous articles to periodicals and encyclopedias, and was director of publications for the British Academy and the Selden Society.

The dilemma throughout his life was Russia. He had fought an increasingly reactionary government which closed down Moscow University in 1899. He had believed fervently that Russia would develop a democracy as had England and Germany. The Russian problem, as he saw it, was that villages were losing communal organization and their hold on the land, and the state was not providing public assistance to maintain them nor creating conditions for an industrial economy. He wrote copiously on these subjects in 1914–17. Thus the Russian Revolution broke his heart, and the Red Terror shattered his lifetime of patriotic aspirations. Hurt badly by his friends' suffering in 1917–19, and suffering from failing eyesight, he spent his later years in travel. While his people had failed him, he had demonstrated to the world what a well-educated Russian could do in the West.

LOUIS A. KNAFLA

See also Economic; Legal

Biography

Paul Gavrilovich Vinogradoff. Born Kostroma, Russia, 1 December 1854, son of a historian schoolmaster. Graduated from Moscow University, 1875; studied with Theodor Mommsen and Heinrich Brunner at the University of Berlin; received PhD, University of Moscow, 1884. Taught at University of Moscow, 1887–1901; left Russia for Britain, 1903; Corpus Christi chair of jurisprudence, Oxford University, 1903–25. Became British citizen. Knighted, 1917. Married Louise Stang, 1897 (1 son; 1 daughter). Died Paris, 19 December 1925.

Principal Writings

Villainage in England: Essays in English Mediaeval History, 1892
The Growth of the Manor, 1905; revised 1911
English Society in the Eleventh Century: Essays in English Mediaeval History, 1908
Roman Law in Mediaeval Europe, 1909
Common-sense in Law, 1914
Editor, *Essays in Legal History Read before the International Congress of Historical Studies Held in London in 1913*, 1913
Editor with Frank Morgan, *Survey of the Honour of Denbigh, 1334*, 1914
The Russian Problem, 1914
Editor, *Year Books of Edward II*, 1917
"Introduction" to Rudolf Hübner, *A History of Germanic Private Law*, 1918; reprinted 1968
Outlines of Historical Jurisprudence, 2 vols., 1920–22; reprinted 1971
Custom and Right, 1925
The Collected Papers of Paul Vinogradoff, with a Memoir, edited by H.A.L. Fisher, 2 vols., 1928

Further Reading

Holdsworth, W.S., *The Historians of Anglo-American Law*, New York: Columbia University Press, 1928
Krader, Lawrence, ed., *Anthropology and Early Law: Selected from the Writings of Paul Vinogradoff, and Others*, New York: Basic Books, 1966

Voltaire 1694–1778
French philosopher and historian

Probably the most famous figure of the Enlightenment, Voltaire recast historiography in both factual and analytical terms. Not only did he reject traditional biographies and accounts that claimed the work of supernatural forces, but he went so far as to suggest that earlier historiography was rife with falsified evidence and required new investigations at the source. Such an outlook was not unique and echoed the scientific spirit that 18th-century intellectuals perceived themselves as invested with. A rationalistic approach was key to rewriting history.

Voltaire's first historical work was a *Histoire de Charles XII* (1731; *The History of Charles XII*, 1732). Clearly written and documented, it signaled Voltaire as the promoter of a new historical genre. He apparently started writing it while in England, studiously collecting evidence from supporters and enemies of the Swedish king, who had recently died. The result of Voltaire's endeavor was a noncommittal and free account of the sovereign, which contrasted substantially with the detail-laden and pointless biography of the same king written by his chaplain. Voltaire's style matured, too, as did his views on religion and the state. Unfortunately, much of the first edition was seized by French authorities upon publication; yet it became an instant success on the black market. Encouraged by his first try as a historian, Voltaire persevered, and began work the following year on his historical masterpiece.

Le Siècle de Louis XIV (1751 – two chapters of which had been printed in 1739, but suppressed by the authorities, before reappearing in the enlarged edition in 1779–81; *The Age of Louis XIV*, 1753) confirmed the originality of Voltaire's historical thought. In it, Voltaire rejected the theological view of history, which Bossuet had used in his *Discours sur l'histoire universelle* (*Discourse on Universal History*, 1681). Rather, he sought to understand what elements had made Louis XIV's times truly great. In so doing, he distanced himself from traditional chronologies by seeking out themes that contributed to a clarification of the context surrounding major events. The result of this quest was a highly researched, yet highly subjective investigation. Nevertheless, this constituted a radical departure from traditional accounts by emphasizing the selection of cultural and intellectual facts rather than a mere listing of events. While noting Louis XIV's achievements and rarely mentioning his failures, Voltaire actually focused on the success of the French as a nation.

Voltaire's thoughts on history are also reflected in another monumental study, the *Encyclopédie* (1751–72), published by Diderot. The multivolume endeavor confirmed the new 18th-century outlook on history. Not only was Voltaire's account of Jansenism under Louis XIV transcribed quasi-verbatim into Jeaucourt's entry on the papal bull *unigenitus*, but the concern with man throughout the entries related to civil and intellectual history implied that while the enlightened intellectuals may have claimed to disdain history, they concerned themselves with it in order to understand the path humanity had followed. The lessons learned from history, especially modern history, were central to improving humankind; history could therefore double as a propaganda tool for the Enlightenment. In his encyclopedia entry on history, Voltaire appeared ambivalent about the lessons of history, arguing that the primary message one could receive from it was a hatred of mankind. He pointed out, however, that to ignore the study of history and its value as a teacher would be dangerous. To interpret the past beyond the factual was a duty, which Voltaire summarized in his other great historical work.

In 1756, Voltaire published his first version of the *Essai sur les moeurs et l'esprit des nations* (*Essay on the Manners and Spirit of Nations*, 1780) followed 13 years later by the definitive edition. This work reflects the secular and liberal spirit of Voltaire as applied to a world history, and was the first of its kind to treat of topics outside of Europe. Voltaire's purpose was clearly stated, as he moved from a brief survey of antiquity to a description of China, India, and Persia, followed by a focus on the establishment and consolidation of Christianity, and eventually on the Europe of Charlemagne (the rest of the account was actually a reprint of his work on Louis XIV). Time and again Voltaire used the opportunity of historical events to condemn fanaticism and war and uphold the value of learning. Of great importance in the work is its 1765 introduction, *La Philosophie de l'histoire* (*The Philosophy of History*). Voltaire was the first to coin the phrase, which he intended to mean a rational history of civilization independent of divine intervention. In the process, he implicitly attacked past historians for ignoring non-Western topics, but it is in his *Le Pyrrhonisme de l'histoire* (The Pyrrhonism of History, 1768) that he openly did so, questioning not only such predecessors as Herodotus and Bossuet, but moving on to expose dubious sources. Such a doctrine of doubting history while professing its value was typical of the philosopher.

Overall, Voltaire's legacy as a historian is remarkable, equal to that of his contemporaries Hume and Gibbon. Voltaire owed much to the dexterity of his writing and his ability to depart from established convention. Replacing divine tradition with reports on China and India, or recasting history within a conflict between clerical and secular power characterizes the Voltairian spirit. This very spirit has often been attacked as reflective of petty bickering and negativity. The fact is that Voltaire's pioneering methodology was anchored in the idea of progress while distrusting its reality. This awkward contrast between human success and human misery should in fact be recognized as a stepping stone toward later philosophies of history.

GUILLAUME DE SYON

See also Delumeau; Enlightenment; France: to 1000; France: 1450–1789; Gatterer; Gay; Philosophy; World; Zinn

Biography

François Marie Arouet. Born Paris, 21 November (possibly 21 February) 1694. Attended the Jesuit Collège Louis-le-Grand, 1704–11; studied law, 1711–13. First incurred trouble with the Paris authorities because of some political writings, 1716; imprisoned in the Bastille for several months in 1717 (after which he used the name Voltaire) and 1726; lived in exile in England, 1726–29; lived intermittently on the Cirey estate of his companion Marquise du Châtelet, 1734–49; had love affair with Mme. Denis from 1744; guest at the court of Frederick II of Prussia, 1750–53; settled at Les Délices, Geneva, 1755–64; lived on his own estate at Ferney, near Geneva, 1759–78. Adopted Marie Corneille, 1760. Returned to Paris a few weeks before his death, 30 May 1778.

Principal Writings

Histoire de Charles XII, roi de Suède, 1731; in English as *The History of Charles XII, King of Sweden*, 1732
Le Siècle de Louis XIV, written 1732–34; published 1751, enlarged edition 1779–81; in English as *The Age of Louis XIV*, 1753
Histoire de la guerre de 1741, 1745; in English as *The History of the War of 1741*, 1756
Annales de l'Empire depuis Charlemagne, 1753; in English as *Annals of the Empire from the Reign of Charlemagne*, 1781
Essai sur les moeurs et l'esprit des nations, 1756; revised 1761–63, 1769; in English as *Essay on the Manners and Spirit of Nations*, 1780
Histoire de l'empire de Russie sous Pierre le Grand, 1759–63; in English as *The History of the Russian Empire under Peter the Great*, 1763
La Philosophie de l'histoire, 1765; in English as *The Philosophy of History*, 1766
La Défense de mon oncle (A Defence of My Uncle), 1767
Le Pyrrhonisme de l'histoire (The Pyrrhonism of History), 1768
Histoire du parlement de Paris (A History of the Parlement of Paris), 1769
Fragments pour servir à l'histoire de la guerre présente en Amérique (A Fragmentary Account of the Present War in America), 1777

Further Reading

Ayer, A.J., *Voltaire: An Intellectual Biography*, London: Weidenfeld and Nicolson, and New York: Random House, 1986
Besterman, Theodore, *Voltaire*, New York: Harcourt Brace, and London: Longman, 1969
Brumfitt, J.H., *Voltaire: Historian*, London: Oxford University Press, 1958
Brumfitt, J.H., "History and Propaganda in Voltaire," *Studies on Voltaire and the Eighteenth Century* 24 (1963), 271–87
Church, William F., *Louis XIV in Historical Thought: From Voltaire to the Annales School*, New York: Norton, 1976

Gay, Peter, *The Enlightenment: An Interpretation*, 2 vols., New York: Knopf, 1966–69

Gossman, Lionel, "Voltaire's *Charles XII*: History into Art," *Studies on Voltaire and the Eighteenth Century* 25 (1963), 691–720

Kölving, Ulla, *Provisional Table of Contents to the Oeuvres Complètes de Voltaire*, London: Oxford University Press, 1983

Kotta, Nuci, "Voltaire's *Histoire du Parlement de Paris*," *Studies on Voltaire and the Eighteenth Century* 41 (1966), 219–30

Mason, Haydn, *Voltaire: A Biography*, Baltimore: Johns Hopkins University Press, and London: Elek, 1981

Schargo, Nelly Noémie, *History in the "Encyclopédie,"* New York: Columbia University Press, 1947

Vovelle, Michel 1933–

French historian of mentalities

Best known for his monumental work on the French Revolution, Michel Vovelle belongs to a group of 20th-century French historians who have revolutionized modern historiography – Marc Bloch, Lucien Febvre, Fernand Braudel, and Georges Duby. An unconventional Marxist historian who claimed to be of Ernest Labrousse's school, Vovelle independently reconciled the study of change (*histoire événementielle*) and of continuity (*longue durée*). Although Vovelle did not associate himself directly with the Annales school, he nonetheless rejuvenated its premises by combining opposite approaches to history, while elevating the history of mentalities to the rank of an influential, cutting-edge academic field. In a dialectical fashion, he established dynamic relations between superstructures and infrastructures, ideologies and mentalities. Further, by putting his faith into the pervasive influence of collective mental attitudes on historical change, he introduced wider parameters of cultural history to popular expression and ethnology. In this regard, Vovelle's approach has paralleled that of his colleague and friend, Maurice Agulhon. Vovelle has also been an active participant in the renewal of older historical genres, such as political history (as seen through his magisterial study of the French Revolution, carried through, according to him, by a fundamental mutation of popular mental habits) and historical biography (as seen in his studies on Viala, Théodore Desorgues, and Joseph Sec).

Vovelle's vast scholarship – internationally disseminated and translated into several languages, including Russian and Japanese – combined mind and action in historical developments. His first major contribution emerged in the early 1970s, and dealt with the concept of death in the *ancien régime*. He extended the thesis of Philippe Ariès, pioneer of the study of sentiment of death in history, by applying quantitative methods as well as ethnographic sources to mental facts, and integrating the common people into the frame of his enquiry, by amassing and computerizing 30,000 wills. The numbers pointed to significant mutations over time as indicated by changing patterns and trends of collective mental habits, thus preparing the field for an event of enduring consequences: the French Revolution. The originality of this method and its promising results were to inspire a new generation of historians, such as medievalist Jacques Chiffoleau in his *La Comptabilité de l'au-delà* (The Accounting of the Afterlife, 1980).

Indisputably, Vovelle has first and foremost left an indelible mark on the history of the French Revolution, a political event that he always studied against the background of religious and cultural changes. Since the publication of *La Chute de la monarchie, 1787–1792* in 1972, he has written extensively on the subject, while organizing several international conferences and collections of essays in relation to the Bicentennial celebrations in 1989 (*Les Images de la Révolution française* [Images of the French Revolution], 1988, was the result of the Sorbonne conference of 1985 attended by more than one hundred scholars). Here again, Vovelle's most important contribution lies in his epistemological originality. It is his use of a vast array of sources and approaches that lends Vovelle's interpretation of history a personal uniqueness. This is well illustrated in the biographical genre where he exhibits – notwithstanding his Marxist inclination – his most creative treatment of history. *L'Irrésistible ascension de Joseph Sec*, an early publication (1975), exemplifies the solidity of his efforts toward a global approach of a single historical character. Here, in the study of one private funeral monument – founded by a late 18th-century *nouveau-riche* from Aix-en-Provence – he cleverly tied together art description and symbolism, biography, and social, spiritual, religious, and political history, thus providing a multifaceted mirror of a collective transformation. In this work, as in others based on ethnographical evidence, Vovelle also attempted to bridge classical and popular culture, too often viewed as opposites in traditional historiography.

Vovelle's profound influence in France and abroad cannot be disputed, either among Marxist or non-Marxist historians. This is not to say that he is without his detractors. He has been criticized for exaggerating the importance of the secular transformation of society over revolutionary action, and for using interchangeably concepts such as "secularization" and "dechristianization." His approach to the history of religious mentalities has also been questioned with regard to social consciousness leading to radical transformation, particularly in reference to the French Revolution. However, Vovelle's work remains a cornerstone of late 20th-century historiography, thanks to his brilliant combination of erudition and creativity.

FRANCINE MICHAUD

See also Mentalities

Biography

Michel Luc Vovelle. Born Gallardon, Eure-et-Loir, 6 February 1933, son of two teachers. Educated at Lycée Marceau, Chartres, and Louis-le-Grand and Henri-IV, Paris, before receiving his agrégation in history from the Ecole Normale Supérieure, Saint-Cloud, and doctorate from the Faculté des Lettres, Paris. Taught at Saint-Cloud, 1956–65, and the University of Aix-en-Provence (rising to professor), 1965–82; succeeded Soboul as professor of the history of the French Revolution, the Sorbonne, 1983. Married 1) Gaby Cérino (died; 2 daughters); 2) Monique Rebotier, university teacher, 1971.

Principal Writings

With Gaby Vovelle, *Vision de la mort et de l'au-delà en Provence, d'après les autels des âmes du purgatoire, XVe–XXe siècles* (Vision of Death and Afterlife in Provence, 15th–20th Centuries), 1970

La Chute de la monarchie, 1787–1792, 1972; in English as *The Fall of the French Monarchy, 1787–1792*, 1984

Piété baroque et déchristianisation en Provence au dix-huitième siècle: les attitudes devant la mort d'après les clauses des testaments (Baroque Piety and Dechristianization in 18th-Century Provence: Attitudes Towards Death According to Testamentary Clauses), 1973

Mourir autrefois: attitudes collectives devant la mort aux XVIIe et XVIIIe siècles (Death in Other Times: Collective Attitudes Towards Death in the 17th and 18th Centuries), 1974

L'Irrésistible ascension de Joseph Sec, bourgeois d'Aix, suivi de quelques clefs pour la lecture des "Naïfs" (The Irresistible Rise of Joseph Sec, Bourgeois of Aix), 1975

Les Métamorphoses de la fête en Provence, de 1750 à 1820 (The Metamorphosis of Festivals in Provence Between 1750 and 1820), 1976

Religion et révolution: la déchristianisation de l'an II, 1976

De la cave au grènier: un itinéraire en Provence au XVIIIe siècle, de l'histoire sociale à l'histoire des mentalités (From the Cellar to the Attic: An Itinerary in 18th-Century Provence, from Social History to the History of Mentalities), 1980

Ville et campagne au 18e siècle: Chartres et la Beauce (City and Countryside in the 18th Century: Chartres and Beauce), 1980

Idéologies et mentalités, 1982; in English as *Ideologies and Mentalities*, 1990

La Mort et l'Occident de 1300 à nos jours (Death in the Western World from 1300 to the Present), 1983

Théodore Desorgues, ou, La désorganisation: Aix-Paris, 1763–1808 (Théodore Desorgues; or, "The Désorganisation"), 1984

La Mentalité révolutionnaire: société et mentalités sous la Révolution française (The Revolutionary Mentality: Society and Mentality during the French Revolution), 1985

La Révolution française: images et récits, 1789–1799 (The French Revolution: Images and Narratives, 1789–1799), 5 vols., 1986

Editor, *Les Images de la Révolution française* (Images of the French Revolution), 1988

1793, la Révolution contre l'Eglise: de la raison à l'être suprême, 1988; in English as *The Revolution Against the Church: From Reason to the Supreme Being*, 1991

"Reflections on the Revisionist Interpretation of the French Revolution," *French Historical Studies* 16 (1990), 749–55

La Révolution française, 1789–1799 (The French Revolution, 1789–1799), 1992

La Découverte de la politique: géopolitique de la Révolution française (The Discovery of Politics: Geopolitical Implications of the French Revolution), 1993

Further Reading

Burke, Peter, *The French Historical Revolution: The Annales School, 1929–89*, Cambridge: Polity Press, and Stanford, CA: Stanford University Press, 1990

Carrard, Philippe, *Poetics of the New History: French Historical Discourse from Braudel to Chartier*, Baltimore: Johns Hopkins University Press, 1992

Gordon, Daniel, "Review Essay: Michel Vovelle's *Ideologies and Mentalities*," *History and Theory* 32 (1993), 196–213

Hunt, Lynn, "French History in the Last Twenty Years: The Rise and Fall of the Annales Paradigm," *Journal of Contemporary History* 21 (1986), 209–24

W

Waitz, Georg 1813–1886

German medievalist

Georg Waitz was one of the most important German historians of the 19th century and contributed considerably to the institutionalization of medieval history. Waitz was not only a famous historian and teacher, but also a well-known politician in his younger days, an interest reflected in his historical works.

Waitz was a student of Ranke, Savigny, Wilken, and Lachmann, all of whom influenced historiography in the 19th century. Deeply influenced by Ranke, Waitz used the philological method of "text critique." He declared that a researcher should analyze the sources, but should find new ways of interpretation at the same time. His final aim was objectivity in historical writing.

Waitz's first important work was his study of the German king Henry I. He was also very interested in German constitutional history and published eight volumes that dealt with the period until the 12th century. He planned to write a history of Schleswig-Holstein in three volumes, but was able to finish only two of them prior to his sudden death in 1886. In 1864 he published an abridged version. During the research for this book, he discovered much material that he used in his 3-volume study of Lübeck.

Following on from his career as a politician (he represented Kiel in 1848–49 at the national parliament in Frankfurt), he continued to be interested in politics and published a study on the federal system, *Das Wesen des Bundesstaats* (The Nature of the Federal State, 1853) and a general book on politics, *Grundzüge der Politik nebst einzelnen Ausführungen* (Basic Political Trends and Particular Implementations, 1862). At the same time he continued his research on constitutional history and published several articles and book reviews.

As a successor to Dahlmann he published in 1869 the third edition of a source manual (*Quellenkunde der deutschen Geschichte*) to which he added an index and a register and which he enlarged considerably. Dahlmann had included only 617 entries, Waitz had in his edition 3753. This work was continuously enlarged and re-edited by his successors and is still in use in Germany. At the same time, it served as a model for the French historical bibliography published by Waitz's student Gabriel Monod in 1888.

Waitz was also an influential teacher, especially during his long stay at the University of Göttingen. His teaching covered a wide range including an introduction in German history, German politics, constitutional history, medieval history, German history in the 16th century, modern German history since the 18th century, and German history of the 19th century. Most famous was his lecture course on general constitutional history, which treated the development of the constitutions of different countries since their beginnings. Each week he gave two lectures, and not only students in history but also those in law and philology flocked to them.

Another of his teaching methods came to serve as a model for some of his students. These were the so-called "historical exercises" (*historische Übungen*) which took place in his study at home and included two groups of no more than ten students each and which lasted for about two hours. He discussed different sources and also the individual work of his students. Some of them, such as Monod, copied this type of class when they themselves began teaching. Both German and foreign students in history, law, and philology participated. Many (like Monod) became famous in later years, as professors in different universities in Germany and abroad, and occupying important posts in academic institutions, academies, and archives.

During Waitz's stay in Göttingen (1849–75), that university became one of the most important centers of historical study, and Waitz became very well-known and respected in Germany and abroad. As early as 1851, Maximilian II of Bavaria tried to convince Waitz to accept a chair at the University of Munich; over the next twenty years he refused offers of chairs from Munich, Tübingen, and Berlin. Göttingen rewarded his devotion by electing him vice-rector twice. Although his university commitments were great, Waitz also was member of several societies and governing bodies. From 1862 to 1886 he directed the periodical *Historische Forschungen*, which became very quickly one of the most eminent historical reviews. In 1876, after his retirement, he became director of the newly reorganized *Monumenta Germaniae Historica* where in his early career he had been employed as a researcher.

RAPHAELA AVERKORN

See also France: to 1000; Germany: to 1450; Ranke

Biography

Born Flensburg in Schleswig, 9 October 1813, son of a merchant. Studied law at University of Kiel, 1832–33; then history with Karl von Savigny, Karl Lachmann, and Leopold von Ranke, University of Berlin, PhD 1836. Staff member, *Monumenta Germaniae Historica*, 1836–42: chief director, 1875–86; professor, University of Kiel, 1842–47; University of Göttingen, 1849–75; and University of

Berlin, 1875–86. Representative for Kiel in national parliament, 1848–49. Married 1) Clara Schelling, daughter of philosopher Wilhelm Schelling, 1842; 2) the daughter of General von Hartmann, 1858. Died Berlin, 24 May 1886.

Principal Writings

Jahrbücher des Deutschen Reichs unter der Herrschaft König Heinrichs I (Year Books of the German Empire under Henry I), 1837

Deutsche Verfassungsgeschichte (German Constitutional History), 8 vols., 1844–78

Das alte Recht der salischen Franken: eine Beilage zur deutschen Verfassungsgeschichte (The Former Rights of the Salian Franks: A Supplement on German Constitutional History), 1846

Schleswig-Holsteins Geschichte (The History of Schleswig Holstein), 2 vols., 1851–54; abridged as *Kurze Schleswig-Holsteinische Landesgeschichte* (A Short History of Schleswig Holstein), 1864

Das Wesen des Bundesstaats (The Nature of the Federal State), 1853

Lübeck unter Jürgen Wullenwever und die europäische Politik (Lübeck under the Rule of Jürgen Wullenwever and European Politics), 3 vols., 1855–56

Grundzüge der Politik nebst einzelnen Ausführungen (Basic Political Trends and Particular Implementations), 1862

Editor, *Quellenkunde der deutschen Geschichte* (The Study of the Sources of German History), 3rd edition, 1869

Further Reading

Jordan, K., "Georg Waitz als Professor in Kiel," in Peter Classen and Peter Scheibert, eds., *Festschrift Percy Ernst Schramm zu seinem siebzigsten Geburtstag*, 2 vols., Vienna: Steine, 1964

Steindorff, E., *Bibliographische Übersicht über Georg Waitz's Werke* (Bibliographic Overview of Waitz's Works), Göttingen, 1886

Waitz, E., *Georg Waitz, Ein Lebens- und Charakterbild* (Georg Waitz: A Life and Character Portrait), Berlin, 1913

Walkowitz, Judith R. 1945–

US historian of British cultural and women's history

Judith Walkowitz is one of the most important and influential historians of gender in the United States. Not only has she been a major pioneer of women's history, but in recent years her work has included some of the most constructive responses in the historical profession to postmodernism and the linguistic turn. Her carefully researched and scholarly articles on prostitution in Plymouth and Southampton in England began to appear in the 1970s and she established an enviable reputation based on the book that resulted from this work, *Prostitution and Victorian Society* (1980). It placed particular emphasis upon the Contagious Diseases Acts of the 1860s, the repeal campaigns, the consequent defence of the Acts, and the impact of the administration of the Acts upon the lives of prostitutes and the working class in general. Walkowitz linked her study firmly to the very considerable quantity of "history from below" that was documenting the "new enthusiasm for state intervention into the lives of the unrespectable poor"; increased state control of prostitution was an essential part of such state expansion. Methodologically complex, her book was distinguished by her attempt to "examine how sexual and social ideology became embedded in laws, institutions, and social policy." Eschewing simple, chronological narrative, Walkowitz used her study of

prostitution as a point of entry into an exploration of wider social, institutional, medical, and political developments.

Its major conclusions have not been disputed by the historians who have come after her. Her discovery of cross-class, cross-gender cooperation in the repeal campaigns provided an important balance to the conventional view of a class- and gender-divided Victorian world. The clear outline of the radical ways in which women were prepared to speak about sex in Victorian England has been followed up by much feminist writing about women and sexuality in a period that had been considered by historians to be sexually "repressed." While Michel Foucault has frequently been considered to be the founding voice of the challenge to the conventional understanding of Victorian sexuality, Walkowitz's work is evidence that feminist historiography was building more complex and nuanced stories about Victorian sexuality at the same time that Foucault was conceiving his analysis. Walkowitz's conclusion that the positive elements in the early critique mounted by the Ladies' Association for the Repeal of the Contagious Diseases Acts were defeated by the co-option of this critical energy into conservative social-purity crusades has been taken up by other historians such as Lucy Bland in her book *Banishing the Beast* (1995). Walkowitz concluded that the draconian administration of the Contagious Diseases Acts transformed the loose and flexible structure of prostitution, labeling women clearly as prostitutes for the first time, thereby making it more difficult for women to move invisibly in and out of prostitution as economic necessity dictated. No one has disputed the implication that the Acts were an important element in the development of modern structures in the trade.

Walkowitz's next major work, *Sex and Class in Women's History* (1983), involved cooperation with two other editors on a collection in the History Workshop series. This book brought to a wider audience a number of important essays written by scholars in both Britain and the US, which had originally appeared in the US journal *Feminist Studies*, thus emphasizing the Anglo-American connection within feminist historical scholarship. These papers were sophisticated and "cutting-edge" both in their field, and in social and radical history as a whole; many of them remain very influential. The collection is indeed impressive from today's perspective and is powerful evidence for how quickly feminist history moved from a fairly crude enterprise dedicated to "rescuing" invisible women, and highlighting the depths of women's victimization and oppression, to a far more challenging and diverse historiography. One of the many ways in which the volume captured the richness of feminist theory at this time is in the interdisciplinary influences that are evident throughout: history, sociology, anthropology, and psychology in particular are woven in different patterns – though it is interesting that the important influence of literary studies on historical scholarship, that would fundamentally affect the approach taken by Walkowitz in her next book, was not particularly evident in this 1983 collection.

By 1992, when *City of Dreadful Delight* was published, the "literary turn" had become a highly contentious theoretical development in historical studies. Within feminist history, Joan Wallach Scott's germinal theoretical justification of poststructuralist approaches had been published in the *American Historical Review* (1986) while other historians, both feminist and conservative, hotly contested the relevance of the approach.

But all of this proceeded at the theoretical level: interested scholars waited with frustration for a concrete example of "poststructuralist history."

With the publication of *City of Dreadful Delight*, the waiting was over. History for Walkowitz is fundamentally about narrative, but not the sort of single, linear narrative of times past. Walkowitz tells stories about narratives, and in the process weaves her way through labyrinths of dispersed, decentered power effects, through contested, shifting, contradictory meanings to explore many ways in which narrative and power are related. She has located the 1880s as a key moment when feminist sexual politics developed in ways that were integrally related to narratives of "sexual danger." Feminist political mobilization over sexual issues (the campaigns against the Contagious Diseases Acts) were part of the historical conditions that enabled the narratives of sexual danger that exploded in the 1880s. And these narratives themselves (about youthful prostitution and Jack the Ripper) were multifaceted, and could be translated or resisted with different political and material effects. There were parallel stories of gender and sex that conflicted with the media scandals about sexual vulnerability and crime. In 1880s London, a redefined public domain provided middle-class women with new political networks and spaces where they "were enabled to speak publicly about sexual passion and sexual danger." Middle-class women's heterosexual expectations were expanded by such discourse. The intricate links between sexuality and gender relations ensured that this had considerable implications for power relations between women and men.

Walkowitz had embraced poststructuralist theory, but not discarded the notion of historical agency. Many people came alive in her subtle studies. And it is through such detailed focus on individuals that we come to understand one way in which people could exercise power in late 19th-century London: through constructing and controlling narratives about gender and sex. W.T. Stead emerged as an enterprising journalist who wrote his sensational stories about vice with a very clear practical purpose (though the powerful effects of his narrative may in the end have been unintended). Karl Pearson and other freethinkers of the Men and Women's Club met to talk about sex and through their different narratives affected relations between women and men. In the comic tale of Georgina Weldon, a courageous female spiritualist fought successfully against her incarceration in a lunatic asylum, demonstrating the possibilities that could exist for middle-class women in 1880s London.

But while searching for dispersed operations of power, Walkowitz retained her fundamental awareness of inequalities, especially those based upon gender and class. The central thesis of the book, after all, was about representations of women as victims of the danger that lurks in the streets; so power worked against women in very material ways through acts of sexual violence as horrendous as those of the Ripper, but also through the discourses that were constructed around such violence. Although of course there were complexities, multiple effects, and resistances, it also cannot be denied that women were portrayed as powerless victims who needed protection, and who should remain within restricted, "safe," places. The real challenge was both to recognize the material violence, and to construct narratives that empower women – and that is a political task for the present, to which Walkowitz's book contributes.

The author also did not discard her deep understanding of the complex interrelationships of the social, economic, and political dimensions that were so carefully wrought in *Prostitution and Victorian Society*. The interweaving of theoretical cultural analysis with her earlier insights has produced what one reviewer called "stunning" results. Interested scholars wait to see how her present research on the history of Soho develops her work.

MARGARET L. ARNOT

See also Crime; Gender

Biography
Judith Marion Rosenberg Walkowitz. Born New York City, 13 September 1945. Received BA, University of Rochester, 1967, MA 1969, PhD 1974. Taught (rising to professor) at Rutgers University, 1971–89; and Johns Hopkins University, from 1989. Married Daniel J. Walkowitz, historian, 1965 (1 daughter).

Principal Writings
Prostitution and Victorian Society: Women, Class, and the State, 1980
Editor with Judith L. Newton and Mary P. Ryan, *Sex and Class in Women's History*, 1983
City of Dreadful Delight: Narratives of Sexual Danger in Late-Victorian London, 1992

Wallerstein, Immanuel 1930–
US social scientist

Immanuel Wallerstein is the founding father of the "world-system school," which has its genesis at the Fernand Braudel Center for the Study of Economies, Historical Systems, and Civilization in the State University of New York at Binghamton. He is also the editor of a new journal entitled *Review*, which calls for the primacy of analysis of economies over long historical time and large space, the holism of the sociohistorical process, and the transitory (heuristic) nature of theories. Under Wallerstein's guidance, the world-system school holds a professional meeting every year and publishes its conference papers. Although its roots were in sociology, the world-system school has now extended its impact to history, anthropology, archaeology, geography, political science, economics, and urban planning.

Wallerstein's world-system analysis has drawn on two major intellectual sources. His book *The Capitalist World-Economy* (1979) incorporated many concepts from neo-Marxist literature, including unequal exchange, core-peripheral exploitation, and the world-market. Wallerstein also adopted many neo-Marxist tenets, such as the argument that the feudal forms of production characteristic of much of Latin American history are not persistent from the past but rather products of Latin America's historical relations with the core. However, at a later stage, Wallerstein was strongly influenced by Fernand Braudel and the French Annales school, especially by their focus on total history, *la longue durée* (the long-term), and problem-oriented history. The Annales school has provided the foundation on which Wallerstein formulated his world-system analysis.

In *Unthinking Social Sciences* (1991), Wallerstein protested against the ways in which social scientific inquiry itself was structured since its inception in the 19th century. First, Wallerstein questioned whether academic disciplines can be separated from one another in the first place. Can the economy, the polity, and the society have, even hypothetically, autonomous activity? For instance, as markets are sociopolitical creations, can a true economic price somehow be stripped of its political and social bases? As an alternative, Wallerstein proposed a new historical social science that encouraged researchers to examine the interactions among economics, politics, and society.

Second, Wallerstein's world-systems analysis fought a war on two fronts regarding the concept of time: against traditional historians who aimed to provide a narrative, episodic history unique only in its own terms; and against social scientists who searched for eternal laws applicable across time. To go beyond these 19th-century conceptions of time, Wallerstein called for a shift of focus from the historian's episodic time and the social scientist's eternal time to the historical social scientist's study of structural time (the *longue durée*) and cyclical time (*conjonctures*).

Third, Wallerstein questioned the treatment of the state/society as the unit of analysis, asking where and when do the entities within which social life occurs exist? Thus Wallerstein insisted on taking the large-scale historical world-system, rather than the state/society, as the unit of scientific inquiry. For Wallerstein, this was more than a mere semantic substitution because the term "historical world-system" rids us of the connotation that society is linked to the state, and that the nation-state represents a relatively autonomous society that develops over time.

In his multivolume *The Modern World-System* (1974–89), Wallerstein put forward a set of hypotheses concerning the nature of historical systems. The defining boundaries of a historical system are those within which the system and the people within it are regularly reproduced by means of some kind of ongoing division of labor. In human history, Wallerstein argued that there have been three known forms of historical systems – the mini-systems, the world-empires, and the world-economies.

In the preagricultural era, there was a multiplicity of mini-systems that were small in space and brief in time (a life-span of about six generations). The mini-systems were highly homogeneous in terms of cultural and governing structures, and they split up when they became too large. The basic logic was one of reciprocity in exchange.

In the period between 8000 BCE and 1500 CE, the world-empires were the dominant form of historical system. The world-empires were vast political structures, encompassing a wide range of cultural patterns. The basic logic was the extraction of tribute from otherwise locally self-administered direct producers that was passed upward to the center and redistributed to a network of officials.

Around 1500, the capitalist world-economies were born. These world-economies were vast uneven chains of integrated production structures dissected by multiple political structures. The basic logic was that the accumulated surplus was distributed unequally in favor of those able to achieve monopolies in the market networks. By their inner logic, the capitalist world-economies then expanded to cover the entire globe, absorbing in the process all existing mini-systems and world-

empires. Hence by the late 19th century, for the first time ever, there existed only one historical system on the globe.

To conclude, Wallerstein's world-systems analysis provided a new mode of thinking that stressed large-scale, long-term, and holistic social change: the instantaneous interactions among politics, economics, and culture. In addition, Wallerstein formulated many innovative concepts for examining the historical origins and transformation of the modern world-system. Nevertheless, he has been criticized for being overly economistic, Eurocentric, and state-centrist, and for paying too little attention to class, culture, and gender. In the 1990s Wallerstein and his followers have begun to address these issues. Some recent world-system school's research topics are: women, households, and gender in world-system analysis; the intricate relationship among class, ethnicity, nation, and personhood; East Asia and precapitalist world-systems; and the role of culture in the world economy.

ALVIN Y. SO

See also Annales School; Comparative; Imperial; Inalcık; Indigenous; Poland: to the 18th Century; Sociology; Spain: Imperial; World

Biography

Born New York City, 28 September 1930. Received BA, Columbia University, 1951, MA 1954, PhD 1959; postgraduate study, Oxford University, 1955–56. US military service, 1951–53. Taught sociology, Columbia University, 1958–71; professor of sociology, McGill University, 1971–76; and State University of New York, Binghamton, from 1976; director, Fernand Braudel Center for the Study of Economics, Historical Systems, and Civilizations, from 1976. Married Beatrice Friedman, 1964 (1 daughter).

Principal Writings

The Modern World-System, 3 vols., 1974–89
The Capitalist World-Economy, 1979
Africa and the Modern World, 1986
Unthinking Social Sciences: The Limits of Nineteenth-Century Paradigms, 1991

Further Reading

Chase-Dunn, Christopher, and Peter Grimes, "World-Systems Analysis," *Annual Review of Sociology* 21 (1995), 387–417
Hall, Thomas D., "The World-System Perspective: A Small Sample from a Large Universe," *Sociological Inquiry* 66 (1996), 440–54
Kaye, Harvey J., "Totality: Its Application to Historical and Social Analysis by Wallerstein and Genovese," *Historical Reflections* 6 (1979), 405–19
Martin, William G., "The World-Systems Perspective in Perspective," *Review* 18 (1994), 145–85
Ragin, Charles, and Daniel Chirot, "The World System of Immanuel Wallerstein: Sociology and Politics as History," in Theda Skocpol, ed., *Vision and Method in Historical Sociology*, Cambridge: Cambridge University Press, 1984
Skocpol, Theda, "Wallerstein's World Capitalist System: A Theoretical and Historical Critique," *American Journal of Sociology* 82 (1977), 1075–90
So, Alvin Y., and Mohammad Hikam, "'Class' in the Writings of Wallerstein and Thompson," *Sociological Perspectives* 32 (1989), 453–67
So, Alvin Y., *Social Change and Development: Modernization, Dependency, and World-System Theories*, Newbury Park, CA: Sage, 1990

Wang Fuzhi [Wang Fu-chih] 1619–1692
Chinese historian

One of the most important philosophers of the 17th century, Wang Fuzhi was born in Hengyang prefecture, Hunan province, where he lived until the proclamation of a new dynasty by the Manchus in 1644. After a period of opposition to the Qing troops in Hunan province, he returned to his native place in 1651 and retired into seclusion, devoting himself to a life of scholarship. His collected work comprises more than 70 titles, including works of poetry, literary criticism, and historical research.

A virulent critic of the Qing, Wang Fuzhi expressed loyalist views in favor of the last dynasty and exalted historical figures such as Yue Fei and Zong Ze, who had resisted foreign invasions in previous dynasties. In general, the historiographical scholarship of that period was implicitly concerned with the fall of the Ming and the foundation of the Qing by the Manchus. Leading figures of this movement were Huang Zongxi (1610–95), Gu Yanwu (1613–82) and Wang Fuzhi, who had all been involved in some way in the organization of local defence groups against the Qing armies. Many philosophical differences separated these three scholars, but they were united in their commitment to the previous dynasty and in their refusal to serve the new conquerors. Their search for an explanation of the collapse of the Ming also produced similar political theories, in particular their condemnation of autocracy and centralization. Similar conclusions were also reached through their attempts to invoke historical evidence in the condemnation of Song philosophy, seen to be at the roots of the decay of China under the Ming. In order to adduce evidence for his historical hypothesis that the country had flourished most when its provinces were strong and its central government relatively weak, Wang Fuzhi turned to historical events, in particular in two of his more popular works, *Dutong jianlun* (On Reading the Comprehensive Mirror) and *Songlun* (On the History of the Song Dynasty). In these historical works, Wang Fuzhi incorporated his views on contemporary issues in the form of judgments on historical events.

Wang Fuzhi distanced himself from the "praise and blame" tradition which had marked most historiographical work so far and insisted that no individual could be seen to be entirely good or bad, as the moral character of an important figure was only one factor in the complex circumstances of a historical crisis. He proposed a vision of history in which human beings were endowed with a capacity to adjust to a certain degree to broader processes of change. Advocating a measure of control over historical forces, he believed that important figures could influence universal change and avoid certain historical disasters. Within this particular theory of historical development, Wang Fuzhi accused orthodox scholars of having failed to adapt classical learning and ancient institutions to the concrete problems of later ages. Although his writings remained virtually unknown outside his home province for two centuries – some manuscripts expressed a vivid hatred for the new conquerors that would not have survived later literary inquisitions – his political ideas attracted many admirers by the end of the Qing. His historical work in particular circulated among reform-minded intellectuals in the last decades of the 19th century, a testimony to the influence of earlier intellectual movements that may have been underestimated by later historians.

FRANK DIKÖTTER

See also China: Historical Writing, Late Imperial

Biography
Born Hengyang prefecture, Hunan, 7 October 1619. Passed provincial civil service examination, receiving the *ju ren* degree, 1642; part of resistance to Qing conquest, 1644–50; withdrew from society to write at Mount Shichuan from 1651. Died Hengyang, 18(?) February 1692.

Principal Writings
Chuanshan ishu (Bequeathed Writings of Chuan-shan)
Dutong jianlun (On Reading the *Comprehensive Mirror*)
Songlun (On the History of the Song Dynasty)
Tuo shi (The History of Tuo)
Yongli shilu (The Veritable Records of the Yong-li Reign)

Further Reading
Beasley, William G., and Edwin G. Pulleyblank, eds., *Historians of China and Japan*, London: Oxford University Press, 1961
Black, Alison H., *Man and Nature in the Philosophical Thought of Wang Fu-chih*, Seattle: University of Washington Press, 1989
McMorran, Ian, *The Passionate Realist: An Introduction to the Life and Political Thought of Wang Fuzhi*, Hong Kong: Sunshine, 1992
Vierheller, Ernstjoachim, *Nation und Elite im Denken von Wang Fu-chih (1619–1692)* (Nation and Elite in the Philosophical Thought of Wang Fuzhi), Hamburg: Gesellschaft für Natur- und Völkerkunde Ostasiens, 1968

Watson, Alan 1933–
British historian of Roman and comparative law

As the author or editor of at least 27 books and many more scholarly articles in leading law journals, Alan Watson is one of the most prolific scholars in the Anglo-American tradition of writing in his area, which has embraced traditional scholarship in the field of Roman law, as well as Roman law in its later life in continental Europe. His work has been in the nature of a crusade: "My ambition is not less than to put forward, in terms accessible to beginner and professional law teacher alike, the proposition that comparative (and within it, Roman) law is so vital to understanding the relation of law to society that no law school in the Western world will fail to make it a core subject in the curriculum." The sad fact is that despite the vivid and enriching work of scholars such as Watson, the study of Roman law, once an important component of law curricula in the medieval English and Scottish universities, has practically disappeared from the compulsory curriculum.

Watson's early scholarship in Roman law on the law of obligations, succession, persons, and property during the later Roman republic has received wide acclaim. His approach in each was to undertake a detailed examination of those texts directly concerned with republican law and then to reach certain general conclusions about the state of law and the attitude to it in the later republic. Even here, the central characteristic of Watson's writing throughout his academic career first made its appearance: his fearless challenge of the accepted or dominant view and his own encyclopedic knowledge of the abundant continental literature of Roman law. In his primary work as a Romanist of the first order, the author has frequently acknowledged his debt to his Oxford teacher, David Daube; in one of his early monographs, Watson expressed his wish that "nothing could give me greater pleasure than for it to be obvious to everyone that I am his pupil." This debt was in part repaid when Watson edited a collection of Roman law essays for Daube in honor of the latter's 65th birthday in 1974 and more recently expressed in the dedication of Watson's treatise, *The Spirit of Roman Law* (1995), itself being a summation of Watson's work in this area. Other important work, hitherto largely ignored by Roman law scholars – Buckland aside – has included an influential study, *Roman Slave Law* (1987). Here Watson's intention was to offer a succinct account of the relevant law seen as a whole, with the view of demonstrating that its rules aimed at "maximising the profit (economic, social and political), and . . . minimising the risk (economic and physical)" for the slaveowners. The reviewer in the *Journal of Legal History* of a more recent study (*The State, Law and Religion: Pagan Rome*, 1992) considered that Watson had deliberately "gone beyond the bounds of definite knowledge about the [XII] Tables to produced a disciplined and consistent, if imaginative and provocative, theory of their origins and importance, a theory which deserved the careful attention of students of Roman law and from which important new perspectives will undoubtedly emerge."

While Watson's acutely critical and informed approach to scholarship has been generally welcomed, certain of his more controversial, provocative, and often uncompromising propositions have generated considerable debate. He has written highly critical reviews of the work of others; indeed "he savages old shibboleths and not infrequently their authors." In one scathing review he wrote: "Against these judgments [of other academics] I must protest, for the dignity of the subject. The [book] is not a work of learning. [The author] does not know at first hand the most basic primary sources, let alone the secondary literature. And he is remarkably careless. The book's publication, especially by an academic press, is a defeat for scholarship." His incisive review of a book by Mark Tushnet on the American law of slavery written from a Marxist perspective inspired him to write his own monograph on the subject, *Slave Law in the Americas* (1989), a successor to his earlier masterly study of the Roman law.

The second major strand in Watson's work has been to offer a view of the structure of the private law of those countries, especially – but not limited to – continental Europe, which have been affected by Roman law. In *The Making of the Civil Law* (1981), the first of a series of books on this subject, Watson argued that "the acceptance of Justinian's *Corpus iuris civilis*, in whole or in part, as authoritative or at least as directly highly persuasive, determined the future nature of civil law systems and made so distinctive." Later books, such as *Sources of Law, Legal Change, and Ambiguity* (1984), *The Evolution of Law* (1985), and *Failures of the Legal Imagination* (1988), and learned articles have returned to this as well as a wider theme, expressed by Watson as an interest in two relationships: "the relationship between legal rules and the society in which they operate, and the relationship between sources of law and the way law evolves." This work has been of such importance that no comparative lawyer or legal historian with an interest in civilian systems can afford to ignore it.

STEPHEN D. GIRVIN

Biography

William Alexander Jardine Watson. Born Hamilton, Scotland, 27 October 1933. Received MA, University of Glasgow, 1954, LLB 1957; BA, Oxford University, 1957, MA 1958, DPhil 1960, DCL 1973. Lecturer, Wadham College, Oxford, 1957–59; lecturer/fellow, Oriel College, Oxford, 1959–65, and pro-proctor, Oxford University, 1962–63; professor of civil law, University of Glasgow, 1965–68; University of Edinburgh, 1968–79; University of Pennsylvania, 1979–89 (director, Center for Advanced Studies in Legal History, 1980–89); and University of Georgia, from 1989. Married 1) Cynthia Betty Balls, 1958 (marriage dissolved; 1 son, 1 daughter); 2) Harriett Camilla Emanuel, 1986 (1 daughter).

Principal Writings

Contract of Mandate in Roman Law, 1961
The Law of Obligations in the Later Roman Republic, 1965
The Law of Persons in the Later Roman Republic, 1967
The Law of Property in the Later Roman Republic, 1968
The Law of the Ancient Romans, 1970
The Law of Succession in the Later Roman Republic, 1971
Roman Private Law around 200 BC, 1971
Editor, *Daube Noster: Essays in Legal History for David Daube*, 1974
Law Making in the Later Roman Republic, 1974
Legal Transplants: An Approach to Comparative Law, 1974
Rome of the XII Tables: Persons and Property, 1976
The Nature of Law, 1977
Society and Legal Change, 1977
The Making of the Civil Law, 1981
"Slave Law: History and Ideology," *Yale Law Journal* 91 (1982), 1034–47 [review]
"Legal Change: Sources of Law and Legal Culture," *University of Pennsylvania Law Review* 131 (1983), 1121–57
Sources of Law, Legal Change, and Ambiguity, 1984
Editor, *Digest of Justinian*, 4 vols., Philadelphia: University of Pennsylvania Press, 1985
The Evolution of Law, 1985
"The Evolution of Law: Continued," *Law and History Review* 5 (1987), 537–70
Roman Slave Law, 1987
Failures of the Legal Imagination, 1988
Slave Law in the Americas, 1989
Legal Origins and Legal Change, 1991
Roman Law and Comparative Law, 1991
Studies in Roman Private Law, 1991
Joseph Story and the Comity of Errors: A Case Study in Conflict of Laws, 1992
The State, Law and Religion: Pagan Rome, 1992
International Law in Archaic Rome: War and Religion, 1993
Jesus and the Jews, 1995
The Spirit of Roman Law, 1995
The Trial of Jesus, 1995
Jesus and the Law, 1996
The Trial of Stephen, 1996

Further Reading

Abel, Richard L., "Law as Lag: Inertia as Social Theory of Law," *Michigan Law Review* 80 (1982), 785–809
Dawson, John P., "The Making of the Civil Law," *University of Chicago Law Review* 49 (1982), 595–604

Donahue, Charles, Jr., "Roman Law Influence on the Civil Law," *Michigan Law Review* 81 (1983), 972–76

Donahue, Charles, Jr., "Translating the *Digest*," *Stanford Law Review* 39 (1987), 1057–77

Frier, Bruce W., "Why Law Changes," *Columbia Law Review* (1986), 888–900

Hoeflich, Michael H., "Law, Society and Reception: The Vision of Alan Watson," *Michigan Law Review* 85 (1987) 1083–94

Oberdiek, Hans, "The Nature of Law," *University of Pennsylvania Law Review* 130 (1981), 229–58

Watt, W. Montgomery 1909–

British Islamicist

Known primarily for his work on the history of Islamic theology and on the life of Muhammad, W. Montgomery Watt has combined an attention to detailed textual work with the skill of making the results of his research available to both the scholarly and general reading communities.

A unified view of history underlies all of Watt's work, whether on early Islamic history, Islamic theology, or the contemporary dialogue between Islam and Christianity. A minister in the Anglican church, Watt is convinced of the necessity of a firm historical grounding to Christianity, a vision that is fully compatible with the contemporary critical historical sense. For Watt, that same critical sense can, and indeed must, tackle all religions worth their muster, if religion is going to be a viable and valuable vehicle for contemporary humanity. Clearly, Islam is no exception to this.

Watt's study of Islam reached an early prominence with his doctoral dissertation on the theological controversy in early Islam over the doctrines of free will and predestination. While the point had been made previously in scholarship, Watt lucidly emphasized the political arenas in which these topics were debated and the effect that politics and political alignments had on the stances being taken. In the words of Josef van Ess, the history of theology was treated by Watt not "as an impersonal fight of ideas or, even worse, as a catalogue of notions and values, but as an expression of the way specific persons or groups reacted to the demands of their time."

In a similar manner, Watt's biographies of Muhammad – works that have become standard sources in the field – positioned Muhammad as "prophet and statesman" (as the title of one of his shorter volumes has it) within the prophet's life in Mecca and Medina. However, underlying this work was another more substantial and influential theory that evoked a great deal of debate. This was a picture of Muhammad as a socialist reformer who was concerned with the process of rapid social change which he saw his society going through as a result of a conflict between economic evolution and unchanging ideology. As a result, Muhammad tailored his deeply felt religious message to that context of societal upheaval. Sociology and economics became the tools with which Watt analyzed the situation.

Watt has not written a great deal about the methodological principles which underlie his work, although he has, on occasion, attempted to develop his position in light of critical work taking place in related fields in Islamic studies. The critiques of Ignaz Goldziher and Joseph Schacht, who argued that the ascription of legal material to Muhammad was a back-projection on the part of the later Muslim community, were dismissed as inconsequential in so far as they might be thought to apply to historical materials dealing with the life of Muhammad. The possibility of "tendential shaping" of the accounts is real, according to Watt, but buried within the material must be a historical kernel of truth; it is up to the historian and his/her ability to consider how something "must have" taken place (in accord with the logic of the historical period and the general behavior of human beings) and to write history accordingly, minus the tendentious fabrications of the sources.

Watt has also, on occasion, expressed his historical views through his repudiation of contrary approaches, especially the more skeptical approaches to the sources which have recently emerged in the field and which argue that "early" historical data are, in fact, later back-projections. Of those approaches, Watt has taken the view that they require a conspiracy view of history, because they seem to suggest that people lost all sense of "what really happened" within one hundred years of the death of Muhammad when Muslim history began to be written down. Furthermore, the sheer bulk of the material which is available (for example, thousands of biographies) suggests to Watt that it is inconceivable that fabrication could have taken place on such a scale.

The most substantial scholarly debate that has emerged surrounding the work of Watt is concerned with the rise of Islam and the socioeconomic picture that he has painted. Patricia Crone's *Meccan Trade and the Rise of Islam* (1987) re-examined Watt's textual bases, especially those related to the economic factors, and noted the exaggerated stress placed on isolated pieces of information. Where some earlier critiques may have questioned Watt's premises, Crone's work pointed to the difficulties of the process of constructing history on the basis of the data available altogether.

Watt's position as a Christian scholar of Islam has never been in doubt. He has produced popular works of Christian thought alongside his scholarly works on Islam, and has pursued the middle path between the two vigorously as well. His concern has not only been to see what the Christian can gain from being exposed to another way of God's message being present in the world (something he clearly believes about Islam), but also what both sides can gain from a dialogue between the two religions when they are treated seriously and historically. Watt's works on dialogue between the two religions may be viewed as the culmination of his studies, being, for him, the expression of the significance and meaning of the historical study of religion as a vital part of human existence.

ANDREW RIPPIN

See also Middle East; Spain: Islamic

Biography

William Montgomery Watt. Born Ceres, Fife, 14 March 1909. Attended George Watson's College, Edinburgh; MA, University of Edinburgh, 1930, PhD 1944; BA, Balliol College, Oxford, 1932, BLitt 1933, MA 1936; graduate study: University of Jena; Cuddeston College. Assistant lecturer in moral philosophy, University of Edinburgh, 1934–38; curate, St. Mary Boltons, London, 1939–41; curate, Old St. Paul's, Edinburgh, 1941–43; Arabic specialist to Anglican bishop in Jerusalem, 1943–46; taught (rising to professor of Arabic and Islamic studies), University of Edinburgh, 1946–79 (emeritus). Married Jean Macdonald Donaldson, 1943 (1 son, 4 daughters).

Principal Writings

Free Will and Predestination in Early Islam, 1948
Translator, *The Faith and Practice of al-Ghazali*, 1953
Muhammad at Mecca, 1953, and *Muhammad at Medina*, 1956; abridged as *Muhammad: Prophet and Statesman*, 1961
Islam and the Integration of Society, 1961
Islamic Philosophy and Theology, 1962; revised 1985
Muslim Intellectual: A Study of al-Ghazali, 1963
A History of Islamic Spain, 1965
Islamic Political Thought: The Basic Concepts, 1968
What Is Islam?, 1968
Editor, *Bell's Introduction to the Qur'an*, 1970
The Influence of Islam on Medieval Europe, 1972
The Formative Period of Islamic Thought, 1973
The Majesty That Was Islam: The Islamic World, 661–1100, 1974
Islamic Fundamentalism and Modernity, 1988
Muhammad's Mecca: History in the Qur'an, 1988
Early Islam: Collected Articles, 1990
Muslim-Christian Encounters: Perceptions and Misperceptions, 1991
A Short History of Islam, 1996

Further Reading

Bousquet, G.H., "Une Explication marxiste de l'Islam par un ecclésiastique épiscopalien" (A Marxist Explanation of Islam by an Episcopal Minister), *Hesperis* 41 (1954), 231–47
Crone, Patricia, *Meccan Trade and the Rise of Islam*, Princeton: Princeton University Press, 1987
Ess, Josef van, "A Tribute to William Montgomery Watt," in Alford T. Welch and Pierre Cachia, eds., *Islam: Past Influence and Present Challenge*, Edinburgh: Edinburgh University Press, and Albany: State University of New York Press, 1979
McDonald, Michael V., "A Bibliography of W. Montgomery Watt," in Alford T. Welch and Pierre Cachia, eds., *Islam: Past Influence and Present Challenge*, Edinburgh: Edinburgh University Press, and Albany: State University of New York Press, 1979
Rodinson, Maxime, "La Vie de Mahomet et le problème sociologique de l'Islam," *Diogène*, 20 (1957), 37–64; in English as "The Life of Muhammad and the Sociological Problem of the Beginnings of Islam," *Diogenes* 20 (1957), 28–51
Rodinson, Maxime, "Bilan des études mohammadiennes," *Revue historique* 229 (1963), 169–220; revised in English as "A Critical Survey of Modern Studies on Muhammad," in Merlin Swartz, ed., *Studies on Islam*, Oxford and New York: Oxford University Press, 1981

Webb, Beatrice 1858–1943
and Sidney Webb 1859–1947
British social, labor, and administrative historians

Prominent writers and public intellectuals of the late 19th and early 20th centuries, Beatrice and Sidney Webb were pioneers in social, labor, and administrative history. Best conceived of as a partnership, the Webbs' lifelong collaboration as historians was an integral part of their prodigious political activism. Leaders of the Fabian Society, the Webbs viewed themselves as members of a new class of experts trained in the management of public affairs. Toward that end Sidney played an instrumental role in founding the London School of Economics and Political Science, an institution dedicated to research in the social sciences. The Webbs pursued their investigations in the history of English "social institutions," a special interest, as a foundation for the work of social reform. They were convinced collectivists, although averse to the main tenets of Marxism, and their scholarly approach, like their politics, was marked by a belief in "the inevitability of gradualness," the virtue of piecemeal reform and a corporatist conception of society anchored in the traditions of Benthamite utilitarianism.

The Webbs are widely acknowledged as founders of labor history. Their first major study, *The History of Trade Unionism*, published in 1894, characteristically emerged from their political involvements. The study broke with the conventional wisdom of the age, that trade unions had origins in medieval guilds. Instead, they conceived of trade unions as the resort of small producers separated from the means of production during the ascent of capitalism. *The History of Trade Unionism* traced the development of the trade union movement from the proliferation of local clubs in the early 18th century to the great national organizations and system of institutionalized collective bargaining in their own day, a trend that the Webbs admired. According to the Webbs, the years around 1850 marked a "watershed" in the development of trade unions. With the defeat of the radical political aspirations represented by Owenism and Chartism, "New Model Unions" came to the forefront of the labor movement. These politically quiescent bodies, sectionalist and exclusive in nature, championed a new moderate and conciliatory approach in industrial relations with a highly centralized and bureaucratic form of organization. This interpretation, stressing sharp discontinuity in the character of 19th-century trade unionism, has been heatedly disputed by modern labor historians. However, it remains of enduring importance.

The History of Trade Unionism displayed the Webbs' signature methodology, an approach they would refine in the next four decades. Greatly influenced by positivist sociology, they were practitioners of a meticulous empiricism based upon "the precise observation of actual facts." They wrote narratives constructed "piece by piece" from file cards, joined to close argumentation and analysis.

The companion volume to *The History of Trade Unionism* was *Industrial Democracy* (1897). An ambitious work of historical sociology and political theory, this study examined the evolution of trade union structure and function. For the Webbs, a critical turning point in the evolving structure of trade unions was the abandonment of "primitive" or direct democracy by key trade unions for representative control through elected councils and the administration of civil servants. The Webbs likewise posited a three-stage development in the instruments used by trade unions to enforce regulations, a gradualist account that emphasized the role of leadership and organization. *Industrial Democracy* also presented a theory of trade unions in a democratic society. Here, the Webbs wrote with a clear political agenda, seeking to end the disruptive conflicts between capital and labor and to establish a new framework for relationships that would promote efficiency and cooperation. With the goal of uniting the distinct interests of producers, consumers, and citizens into a coherent whole, they argued that democracy must address economic as well as political relationships and further challenged Victorian orthodoxy in their insistence that trade unions had an important role in modern society. Envisioning trade unions as "democracies of the producers," they saw these bodies as vital representatives of workers' interests, responsible for securing "the National Minimum" of employment conditions and acting as a counterweight to state power.

Thereafter, the Webbs turned from the study of voluntary institutions to the study of local government – subjects virtually ignored by previous historians. This engagement would occupy their scholarly efforts for the next three decades. They had initially planned a single work on the contemporary problems of local government with a preliminary chapter on the pre-1835 antecedents to modern institutions. However, they soon found themselves delving deeper into history after concluding that present local government was firmly rooted in the past. Gradually conceived as a systematic and comprehensive treatment, they eventually published 11 volumes on the history of *English Local Government* (1906–29). The studies concentrated on the years 1689 to 1835, significant because of the absence of intervention by national governments in local affairs. With the aim of delineating the origin of efficient, centralized, and bureaucratic local government, the Webbs took a particular interest in the ad hoc bodies examined in *Statutory Authorities for Special Purposes* (1922). These institutions, not the county, parish, or borough, were the source of crucial innovations such as land drainage, town sewers, highways, and police, the forerunners of Webbian "municipal socialism." Also noteworthy was their history of the Poor Law, studies that grew out of Beatrice's work as a member of the Royal Commission on the Poor Law, 1905–09.

Late in life the Webbs developed an attraction for Stalin's Soviet Union, producing *Soviet Communism: A New Civilisation?* (1935). Written at a time when western capitalism was in apparent collapse, it nevertheless did little for their reputations.

By the 1960s, with the emergence and success of the New Social History, the Webbs came under sustained attack. Many historians derided their work as elitist, excessively empiricist, and teleological. Others rejected what they described as the Webbs' narrow institutionalism and seeming lack of interest in either noninstitutional forms of association or issues of culture. But any balanced assessment must credit the Webbs for their immense contribution as historians. Combining pioneering vision and extraordinary productivity, their massive works of scholarship are of lasting value. One critic has called their work "a magnificent ruin."

RICHARD J. SODERLUND

See also Britain: 1066–1485; Britain: since 1750; Economic; Hobsbawm; Labor; Social

Biography

Martha Beatrice Potter Webb. Born Standish House, near Gloucester, 22 January 1858, daughter of a railway magnate. Educated privately. Investigator/contributor, Charles Booth's *Life and Labour of the People of London*; member, Royal Commission on Poor Law and Unemployment, 1905–09: joint author of minority report; member of many government committees; Justice of the Peace, London, 1919–27. Married Sidney Webb, 1892. Died Passfield Corner, near Liphook, Hampshire, 30 April 1943.
Sidney James Webb. Born London, 13 July 1859. Educated at private schools in London, Switzerland, and Mecklenburg-Schwerin;

Birkbeck Institute; City of London College. Clerk, colonial broker's office, London, 1875–78; civil servant: War Office, 1878–79; Surveyor of Taxes Office, 1879–81; and Colonial Office, 1881–91. Called to the Bar, 1885. Received LLB, University of London, 1886. Member, London County Council, 1892–1910. Occasional lecturer on political economy, City of London College and Working Men's College; honorary professor of public administration, London School of Economics, 1912–27. Labour member of parliament for Seaham, 1922–29. Married Beatrice Potter, 1892. Created 1st Baron Passfield of Passfield Corner, 1929. Died Passfield Corner, near Liphook, Hampshire, 13 October 1947.

Principal Writings

The History of Trade Unionism, 1894; revised 1920
Industrial Democracy, 2 vols., 1897
The History of Liquor Licensing in England, Principally from 1700 to 1830, 1903; as vol. 11 of *English Local Government*, 1963
English Local Government from the Revolution to the Municipal Corporations Act, 9 vols, 1906–29; with 2 additional vols., 11 vols., 1963
Editors, *The Minority Report of the Poor Law Commission*, 2 vols., 1909
English Poor Law Policy, 1910; as vol. 10 of *English Local Government*, 1963
Soviet Communism: A New Civilisation?, 2 vols., 1935

Other works by Beatrice Webb
My Apprenticeship, 1926
Our Partnership, 1948
The Diary of Beatrice Webb, 4 vols., 1982–85

Further Reading

Clegg, Hugh, "The Webbs as Historians of Trade Unionism, 1874–1894," *Bulletin of the Society for the Study of Labour History* 4 (1962)
Harrison, Royden, "The Webbs as Historians of Trade Unionism," in Raphael Samuel, ed., *People's History and Socialist Theory*, London and Boston: Routledge, 1981
Johnson, Richard, "Culture and the Historians," in John Clarke, Chas Critcher, and Richard Johnson, eds., *Working Class Culture: Studies in History and Theory*, London: Hutchinson, and New York: St. Martin's Press, 1979
Kidd, Alan J., "Historians or Polemicists? How the Webbs Wrote Their History of the Poor Laws," *Economic History Review* 40 (1989), 400–17
MacKenzie, Norman, and Jeanne MacKenzie, *The First Fabians*, London: Weidenfeld and Nicolson, 1977; as *The Fabians*, New York: Simon and Schuster, 1977
Musson, A.E., "The Webbs and Their Phasing of Trade-Union Development Between the 1830s and the 1860s," *Bulletin of the Society for the Study of Labour History* 4 (1962)
Nord, Deborah Epstein, *The Apprenticeship of Beatrice Webb*, Amherst: University of Massachusetts Press, and London: Macmillan, 1985
O'Day, Rosemary, "Before the Webbs: Beatrice Potter's Early Investigations for Charles Booth's Inquiry," *History* 78 (1993), 218–42
Price, Richard, "Rethinking Labor History: The Importance of Work," in James Cronin and Jonathan Schneer, eds., *Social Conflict in the Political Order in Modern Britain*, London: Croom Helm, and New Brunswick, NJ: Rutgers University Press, 1982
Seymour-Jones, Carole, *Beatrice Webb: Woman of Conflict*, London: Allison and Busby, 1992; as *Beatrice Webb: A Life*, Chicago: Dee, 1992
Zeitlin, Jonathan, "From Labour History to the History of Industrial Relations," *Economic History Review* 40 (1987), 159–84

Weber, Eugen 1925–

Romanian-born historian of modern France

As a student at Emmanuel College, Cambridge shortly after World War II, Eugen Weber was inspired by the rich scholarship of his tutors, Denis Brogan and David Thomson, and by the fresh ideas that Lucien Febvre, Marc Bloch, and other *annalistes* had recently swept into history's stuffy house. They brought the quotidian and the dead to life. The Annales school lost its luster in the decades that followed, but the founding spirit of the enterprise – the imagination and empathetic reach, the pursuit of the particular, the meticulous archival research, the clear and vigorous writing style – endures in the "incurably curious" Weber.

Weber's scholarship – more than a dozen books and 400 articles, essays, and reviews to date – resists neat taxonomy, though the landscape is most often France and the time is the Third Republic. *The Nationalist Revival in France, 1905–1914* (1959) signaled the young historian's interest in the new atmosphere of integral nationalism on the eve of World War I; it ventured beyond traditional political history to probe the literature of national regeneration; and it confirmed Weber's predilection for the detailed stories of individuals and events. "History is about people," he would later write, "theory is about theory." Slim but provocative, *The Nationalist Revival* became a prologue of sorts to the magisterial book that secured Weber's international reputation as a leading historian of modern Europe. *Action Française* (1962) remains the definitive study of the extreme neoroyalist organization that, born of the Dreyfus affair, helped give birth to Vichy. Through the 1960s and beyond, Weber, like historian René Rémond, challenged colleagues to recognize the crucial differences between radical fascism and reactionary authoritarianism – a quest for nuance that also informed *Varieties of Fascism* (1964). And in 1970, at an international conference in Moscow, Weber kindled yet another controversy (and helped inspire the later work of Zeev Sternhell and others) when he made the seemingly outlandish suggestion that "fascism and communism were not antithetical but *frères ennemis*."

By that time Weber had taken to the playing fields of politics. Seminal articles in the *Journal of Contemporary History* (1970) and the *American Historical Review*, (1971) analyzed the efflorescence of organized athletics in the decades on either side of 1900, and, specifically, the relationship of games and sports to ideology and politics. Sound bodies defended sound nations, contemporaries argued, and decadence harbored defeat. Weber's pioneering work prompted a wave of scholarship that brought sports and leisure in from the margins to the center of social and political history.

After years of focusing on Paris, Weber probed a dozen departmental archives and uncovered a treasure trove of material for the book that would become his most influential to date: *Peasants into Frenchmen* (1976). Close analysis of rural schools, migration, military service, and the national market economy across the 19th century demonstrated that France was not truly unified until the middle decades of the Third Republic. With its integration of history, cultural anthropology, sociology, and political science, the book charted a nation-in-the-making. Widely acclaimed in the academic and popular press, it also drew salvos from some social historians who praised the wit and erudition, but questioned the accuracy of "bourgeois" and folkloric sources, and challenged the conclusions; above all, they insisted that much of rural France had been radicalized long before the Third Republic. Weber responded in articles published through the early 1980s, but the journey toward a more complicated story had always mattered more than the arrival at a rigid rule. So it had gone with fascism and sport. Opening a new door into France's past, he had prompted yet another vigorous debate.

Six years as dean of UCLA's College of Letters and Science led to essays on higher education in historical context. But France and its archives beckoned. *France: Fin de Siècle* (1986) wove a tapestry of the period's paradoxes: the "decadence" and scientific progress, the social unrest and rising standard of comfort. *My France* (1991) assembled previously published articles and a new autobiographical essay on the author's love affair with France and even longer love of history, from the Daco-Roman epics he devoured as a boy in Romania to the reading always on the horizon. Most recently, *The Hollow Years* (1994) has the atmosphere of Marc Bloch's *Strange Defeat* about it. Indeed it clothes with scholarly evidence the broad issues that Bloch had only sketched before his execution as a *résistant*. Recreating the mood of the decade, Weber demonstrated the ways in which fear bred impotence in some, pacifism in others, and courage in very few. The book carried the essence of its author's skills and priorities; searching out evidence with the expertise of Simenon's detective Maigret, it orders the myriad details that, says Weber, make history; studying the personalities who shaped the ideologies, it tackles the topics of honor and cowardice; and consistent with four decades of scholarship, it brings to every individual – high, low, and middling – the empathy that Charles Péguy deemed essential to the historian's craft.

Though enthused by the *annalistes* of the first hour, Weber never joined a "school" of history. He never had the temperament to embrace even the ones he admired. In that regard, and in his crystaline prose, he is much like A.J.P. Taylor, without the irascibility. Neither the leader of a methodological movement nor the follower of a trend, he sets examples rather than rules (though he adheres to the belief that if history does not repeat itself, historians should not do so either). Through the post-World War II decades, as history has migrated from the humanities to the social sciences, Weber has persisted in the art of telling stories that, fastidiously researched and elegantly written, elucidate the variety, nuance, paradox, and particularity of the French and European past.

MICHAEL BURNS

See also Agrarian; France: since 1789

Biography

Eugen Joseph Weber. Born Bucharest, Romania, 24 April 1925. Attended school at Ashville College, Windermere, England. Served in the British Army in Belgium, India and Germany, 1943–47. Studied at the Sorbonne and Institut d'Etudes Politiques, Paris; Emmanuel College, Cambridge, BA 1950, MA 1954, MLitt 1956. Taught at Emmanuel College, 1953–54; University of Alberta, 1954–55; University of Iowa, 1955–56; and (rising to professor), University of California, Los Angeles, 1956–93 (emeritus). Married Jacqueline Brument-Roth, 1950.

Principal Writings

The Nationalist Revival in France, 1905–1914, 1959
Action Française: Royalism and Reaction in Twentieth Century France, 1962
"Nationalism, Socialism and National-Socialism in France," *French Historical Studies* 2 (1962), 273–307
Satan Franc-Maçon: la mystification de Leo Taxil, 1964
Varieties of Fascism: Doctrines of Revolution in the Twentieth Century, 1964
Editor with Hans Rogger, *The European Right: A Historical Profile,* 1965
"Pierre de Coubertin and the Introduction of Organized Sports in France," *Journal of Contemporary History* 5 (1970), 3–26
"Gymnastics and Sports in Fin-de-Siècle France: Opium of the Classes?," *American Historical Review* 76 (1971), 70–98
A Modern History of Europe: Men, Cultures, and Societies from the Renaissance to the Present, 1971; abridged as *Europe since 1715: A Modern History,* 1972
Peasants into Frenchmen: The Modernization of Rural France, 1870–1914, 1976
"Comment la politique vint aux paysans: A Second Look at Peasant Politicization," *American Historical Review* 87 (1982), 357–89
"Reflections on the Jews in France," in Frances Malino and Bernard Wasserstein, eds., *The Jews in Modern France,* Hanover, NH: University Press of New England, 1985
France: Fin de Siècle, 1986
My France: Politics, Culture, Myth, 1991
The Hollow Years: France in the 1930s, 1994

Further Reading

Amato, Joseph A., "Eugen Weber's France," *Journal of Social History* 25 (1992), 879–82

Weber, Hermann 1928–

German historian

Hermann Weber, a West German political historian at the University of Mannheim, has focused his studies on the history of German communism, the theories of socialism and communism, the international workers' movement, and the history of the German Democratic Republic. In the areas of GDR history and the history of German communism in particular, Weber's contributions have considerably advanced historical research. He was the first to uncover the complete protocols of the founding of the German Communist party (KPD) while researching in the papers of Paul Levi in New York, and eventually published them in *Der Gründungsparteitag der KPD* (The Founding Party Conference of the KPD, 1969). The protocols revealed for the first time who took part at the founding, and the variety of ideas on communism that the founders represented. Of particular importance was the information that the KPD was dominated by anti-parliamentarians who distanced themselves from Soviet-style communism. These various factions and their development in the Weimar era were detailed in *Die Wandlung des deutschen Kommunismus* (The Transformation of German Communism, 1969), the most comprehensive treatment of the KPD during this period. In this work Weber used a sociological structural method to trace the manner in which Stalin's concepts were brought to dominate the party. In so doing, he proved that the far left of the KPD, which fought against social democracy and the parliamentary system, did not have roots in the German workers' movement.

Weber's background in the study of German communism, influenced largely by his own membership in the KPD/Socialist Unity party (SED) from 1945 until his flight to the West in 1954, was well suited for his later studies of the GDR. He was one of the first to portray the SED not as an unchanging monolith, but as a complex entity made up of various persuasions. In this regard, he introduced the term "Stalinism" into GDR studies to differentiate between German communists. Weber himself always believed in a "third way" socialist option, one that he felt Marx had proposed, but that Stalin had dislodged. He felt that the "third way" opposition lived on, however, as demonstrated by the events in Czechoslovakia in 1968. Weber also saw the history of the GDR as circular, varying between a hard and soft policy, and between stability and instability. This phenomenon arose from the difficulty of a Soviet system imposed from outside and the contradiction within Marxism-Leninist ideology that it both justified power relationships and political norms. In the 1970s and 1980s, he felt that the SED had succeeded in creating a relatively stable society with good education and health systems, but that the SED would still be forced to reform towards a "democratic Communism," something that Weber felt was, at least, a theoretical possibility.

Weber should also be applauded for his contributions in the publication of documents. His collection and dissemination of often difficult to access documents, has facilitated the study of German communism and the history of the GDR.

Weber's analysis of the GDR has not been without criticism, however. His emphasis on the relative success of the GDR, apparent in his comment in *Geschichte der DDR* (History of the GDR, 1985) that the GDR is one of the stablest countries of recent German history, led to considerable questioning in the historical field even before the revolutions of 1989. Additionally, much of his work focuses on the GDR as a closed entity, without exploring the dynamic relationship that it had with the Federal Republic of Germany. His interpretation of the SED as a democratic Communist party that was not Stalinist from the outset but only became so around 1947–48 due to the Cold War, has been questioned by Dietrich Staritz in particular.

Weber deserves credit, however, for his dispassionate analysis of the GDR during the Cold War.

GARY S. BRUCE

See also Germany: since 1945

Biography

Born Mannheim, 23 August 1928. Studied political science and history at the universities of Marburg and Mannheim, 1964–68; received doctorate, 1968; Habilitation, 1970. Taught (rising to professor), University of Mannheim, from 1970. Married Gerda Röder, 1951.

Principal Writings

With Gerda Weber, *Lenin: Ausgewählte Schriften,* 1963; in English as *Lenin: Life and Works,* 1974
Der Gründungsparteitag der KPD: Protokoll und Materialien (The Founding Party Conference of the KPD), 1969
Die Wandlung des deutschen Kommunismus: Die Stalinisierung der KPD in die Weimarer Republik (The Transformation of German Communism), 1969

Die Generallinie: Rundschreiben des Zentralkomitees der KPD an die Bezirke, 1929–1933 (The General Line: Circulars of the Central Committee of the KPD to the Districts, 1929–1933), 1981

Parteiensystem zwischen Demokratie und Volksdemokratie: Dokumente und Materialien zum Funktionswandel der Parteien und Massenorganisationen in der SBZ/DDR, 1945–1950 (The System of Parties between Democracy and People's Democracy), 1982

Geschichte der DDR (History of the GDR), 1985

DDR: Dokumente zur Geschichte der Deutschen Demokratischen Republik, 1945–1985 (GDR: Documents on the History of the German Democratic Republic), 1986

Die DDR, 1945–1986 (The GDR, 1945–1986), 1988; revised [with dates 1945–1990], 1993

Editor with Dietrich Staritz, *Einheitsfront, Einheitspartei: Kommunisten und Sozialdemokraten in Ost- und Westeuropa, 1944–1948* (United Front, United Party: Communists and Social Democrats in Eastern and Western Europe, 1944–1948), 1989

Aufbau und Fall einer Diktatur: kritische Beiträge zur Geschichte der DDR (The Construction and Fall of a Dictatorship: Contributions on the History of the GDR), 1991

Editor, *Die Gründung der KPD: Protokolle und Materialien des Gründungsparteitages der Kommunistischen Partei Deutschlands, 1918–1919* (The Founding of the KPD: Protocols and Material of the Founding Party Conference of the Communist Party of Germany), 1993

Further Reading

Müller, Werner, "Hermann Weber 60 Jahre" (Hermann Weber: Sixty Years), *Internationale Wissenschaftliche Korrespondenz zur Geschichte der Deutschen Arbeiterbewegung*, 24 (1988), 357–71

Schonhoven, Klaus, and Dietrich Staritz, eds., *Sozialismus und Kommunismus im Wandel: Hermann Weber zum 65. Geburtstag* (Socialism and Communism in Transition: Hermann Weber on His 65th Birthday), Cologne: Bund Verlag, 1993

Spittmann, Ilse, "Die wahre Geschichte der DDR wurde zuerst im Westen geschrieben" (The True History of the GDR Was First Written in the West), *Deutschland Archiv* 24 (1991), 1–4

Weber, Max 1864–1920

German historical sociologist

A fundamental problem confronts us at the outset: in what sense is it proper to speak of Max Weber as a historian? His undergraduate and graduate studies were principally in law, while his university appointments (1894–1902, 1918–20) were in the faculty of "National Economy." Furthermore, apart from two dissertations that were the product of his early legal studies, there is only one work of his maturity that might in any sense be called a work of historical research – "Die protestantische Ethik und der Geist des Kapitalismus" (1904–05, revised 1920; *The Protestant Ethic and the Spirit of Capitalism*, 1930) – and this, when published in the *Archiv für Sozialwissenschaft* (a journal of which Weber was co-editor), was deemed to merit excuse as something exceptional to its (and his) ordinary range. Nonetheless, there can be no doubt of the significance of Weber's historical concerns. His primary focus was indeed on the present, a premise that underlay a good deal of empirical research into the social life of his own day, and which readily explains his absence from any history faculty. On the other hand, he believed, as much as any orthodox

historian, that present-day phenomena should be understood in terms of their previous history. In the case of East Elbean rural society this took him back 50 or 60 years, but in the case of fundamental structures, such as law, the state, and religion, he returned to classical antiquity and pre-Christian Judaism. As a result, there is immense historical content in both his empirical and his "sociological" (or typological) writings, which are all readily accessible to the historically minded reader. In his methodological writings, too, Weber argued with exemplary clarity that, while the investigator should be looking out for typical and recurrent elements in social phenomena, the unique element underlying these was irreducible. In thinking thus, he was little different from many historians in the post-Enlightenment mainstream who used the foundation supplied by historically unique evidence as the basis for wider and even timeless generalizations (which might be called "philosophical" or "sociological"), except that the balance between these concerns was tipped rather more toward the latter. To use Weber's own words, he saw himself as a historian in the "broad" if not in the "narrow" sense.

Weber's eccentric relation to orthodox history helps to explain both the originality of his thinking and also why it made so little impact before the 1960s. The historiographical context to which he responded was that evoked by Nietzsche in his tract "Vom Nutzen und Nachtheil der Historie für das Leben" (1874) – literally On the Uses and Drawbacks of Historical Writing for Life. Publication of accurately researched "scientific" historical writing in the Rankean mold had already produced (to Nietzsche's discerning eye) a fundamental disenchantment with the study of the past akin to that which we now recognize as "post-modern": such literature was in principle infinite in extent and was, even at its best, based on a number of irreconcilable worldviews; at worst, it was wholly vacuous, but in either case, it had little meaning or use "for life". By definition, then, the prevalent "philosophic" schemes that claimed absolute validity for their (various) organizations of world history were to be discarded – utilitarian, Hegelian, Marxist, progressive, or evolutionary. Weber's version of these dilemmas laid particular stress on the clash of national values and on the seepage of any meaning for "life" out of the post-Hegelian Protestant culture amid which he grew up – dilemmas that led him to the brink of psychic collapse in 1898. However, he achieved a partial resolution or understanding of these difficulties in the methodological writings of 1902–07 and *The Protestant Ethic*, texts of fundamental importance for all historians. In the former he "overcame" his doubts about the worth and viability of history (and indeed of all humane or social scientific inquiry) by accepting a radical relativism in values, offset by the defense of a qualified objectivity in academic discussion. Moreover, in *The Protestant Ethic* Weber deployed an array of new methodological devices deriving from other disciplines, in an attempt to cope with the essentially infinite nature of historical data. The best known, though by no means the most original, was the reduction or grouping of historical phenomena into types: these might be either timeless and universal (and "sociological"), or else unique and genetic (and "historical") They were dubbed "ideal type" since besides offering schematic presentations of complex historical phenomena such as modern capitalism, they also encoded the individual and relative values (or Ideas) of the investigator who set them up. The innovation was daring enough as it stood, but Weber could not resist the hubris of asserting that such schemas did not "really" exist in any one literal exemplar, which had the effect of turning a potentially useful shorthand into a liability (to say nothing of its tendency to impenetrable theoretical elaboration). In addition, *The Protestant Ethic* flagrantly ignored conventional chronology in its organization, and displayed no qualms about yoking historical investigation firmly to present-day issues: it was thus all too easily read as a sustained assault on traditional historical method.

It is no surprise, then, that in Germany before 1933 *The Protestant Ethic* was of more interest to historians in the "broad" sense (social scientists, historical economists, comparative historians) than faculty historians in the "narrow" sense. After its translation into English (1930) Anglo-Saxon empiricism found a new way of marginalizing its ideas and approach by contending that it was "wrong" about 17th-century Calvinism. Sociologists compounded the felony by defending one whom they claimed as their own (often with scant justification) as "right". No doubt Weber is "wrong," just as Gibbon is "wrong" about Rome or Burckhardt is "wrong" about the Renaissance: Weber himself was well aware that empirical investigation is always yielding new results. But this is grotesquely irrelevant to the conceptual model presented by the essay, based on the interaction between psychological and rational modes of behavior, and also to its wider theses, which simultaneously offered a trenchant cultural criticism of the "Occidental" present and also one of the most sophisticated, and perhaps the last plausible, exposition of a Eurocentric version of world history. Weber has enjoyed a much more sympathetic reception in (West) Germany since 1960, where many of his concepts and categories have achieved something like hegemonic status. Even so, an obvious narrowing of his thought is still apparent, in that this hegemony applies principally to German history for the period 1870–1940 – thus it centers on his lifetime, where his concepts and local interpretations can easily be used in a familiar context. Again, the lavish *Gesamtausgabe* of his writings that began in the 1980s has been criticized as an inappropriate monument, for embodying a Rankean approach that directs the reader's attention towards the empirical and specific contexts of his work at the expense of its conceptual breadth and universality.

Nonetheless, the existence of both the edition and its critics testifies to the extraordinary prestige that Weber enjoys today throughout Europe and America. It is safe to say that the time for some of his central ideas must come – though whether we will think of them as Weberian is another matter. In epistemology it is clear that "scientific" objectivity is impossible but so, too, is limitless relativism; thus the only option is the Weberian one of negotiating a middle way between these two poles. In this respect his manifesto text on "Die 'Objektivität' sozialwissenschaftlicher und sozialpolitischer Erkenntnis" (The "Objectivity" of Knowledge in Social Science and Social Policy, 1904) is of exceptional importance, since it represents an epistemological model *designed for* history and social science, unlike most "postmodern" thinking, which is literary or philosophical in derivation. Again, the problems posed by the infinite proliferation of historical data are so obvious – though the range of recorded history is as yet microscopic – that typological thinking must necessarily advance, even if typologies are more likely to be local than universal (as Weber supposed).

The increasing acceptance of historical sociology and comparative history in the past 25 years may perhaps be read as symptoms of this. A surer prediction is that a fuller, more flexible, and less restricted understanding of Weber's general concepts within the historical community can only grow.

PETER GHOSH

See also Comparative; Hill; Historiology; Intellectual; Merton; Mommsen, W.; Protestantism; Religion; Science; Social; Stone; Tawney; Thomas, K.

Biography
Born Erfurt, 21 April 1864. Studied at universities of Heidelberg, Strasbourg, and Berlin; Habilitation in law, 1892. Professor of Economics at Freiburg and then Heidelberg, 1894–98, but a nervous collapse in 1898 led to resignation of his chair in 1902, the date of his partial recovery. With Werner Sombart and Edgar Jaffé took over the editorship of the *Archiv für Sozialwissenschaft und Sozialpolitik*, 1904, his principal academic outlet thereafter. Served as a reserve officer in charge of hospitals in the Heidelberg area, 1914–15; visiting professor, University of Vienna, 1918; full-time professor of economics, University of Munich, 1919–20. Died Munich, 14 June 1920.

Principal Writings
Die römische Agrargeschichte in ihrer Bedeutung für das Staats- und Privatrecht, 1891
Die Lage der Landarbeiter im ostelbischen Deutschland, 1893
"Die 'Objektivität' sozialwissenschaftlicher und sozialpolitischer Erkenntnis" (The "Objectivity" of Knowledge in Social Science and Social Policy), *Archiv für Sozialwissenschaft und Sozialpolitik* 19 (1904)
"Die protestantische Ethik und der Geist des Kapitalismus," *Archiv für Sozialwissenschaft und Sozialpolitik* 20–21 (1904–05), revised in *Gesammelte Aufsätze zur Religionssoziologie*, 1920; in English as *The Protestant Ethic and the Spirit of Capitalism*, 1930
"Die Wirtschaftsethik der Weltreligionen" (The Economic Ethics of the World Religions), *Archiv für Sozialwissenschaft und Sozialpolitik* 41–46 (1915–19)
Wissenschaft als Beruf (Science as a Vocation), 1917
Politik als Beruf, 1919; in English as *Politics as a Vocation*, 1946
Wirtschaft und Gesellschaft, 1922, revised 1925, 1956; in English as *Economy and Society: An Outline of Interpretive Sociology*, 3 vols., 1968
Wirtschaftsgeschichte, 1923; in English as *General Economic History*, 1927

Further Reading
Ghosh, Peter, "Some Problems with Talcott Parsons' Version of *The Protestant Ethic*," *Archives Européennes de Sociologie* 35 (1994), 104–23
Hennis, Wilhelm, *Max Weber: Essays in Reconstruction*, London and Boston: Allen and Unwin, 1988
Kocka, Jürgen, ed., *Max Weber, Der Historiker* (Max Weber, the Historian), Göttingen: Vandenhoeck & Ruprecht, 1986
Lehmann, Hartmut, and Günther Roth, eds., *Weber's Protestant Ethic: Origins, Evidence, Contexts*, Cambridge and New York: Cambridge University Press, 1993
Marshall, Gordon, *In Search of the Spirit of Capitalism: An Essay on Max Weber's Protestant Ethic Thesis*, London: Hutchinson, and New York: Columbia University Press, 1982
Mommsen, Wolfgang J., *Max Weber und die deutsche Politik, 1890–1920*, Tübingen: Mohr, 1959, revised 1974; in English as *Max Weber and German Politics, 1890–1920*, Chicago: Chicago University Press, 1984

Mommsen, Wolfgang J., and Jürgen Osterhammel, eds., *Max Weber and His Contemporaries*, Boston and London: Unwin Hyman, 1987

Mommsen, Wolfgang J., *The Political and Social Theory of Max Weber: Collected Essays*, Oxford: Polity Press, and Chicago: University of Chicago Press, 1989

Roth, Günther, "History and Sociology in the Work of Max Weber," *British Journal of Sociology* 27 (1976), 306–18

Roth, Günther, and Wolfgang Schluchter, *Max Weber's Vision of History: Ethics and Methods*, Berkeley: University of California Press, 1979

Weber, Marianne, *Max Weber: ein Lebensbild*, Tübingen: Mohr, 1926; in English as *Max Weber: A Biography*, New York: Wiley Interscience, 1975

Wedgwood, C.V. 1910–1997
British biographer and historian

C.V. Wedgwood introduced generations of children and adults to the history of early modern Europe. Her writing is subtle, sympathetic, and passionate, reverberating with sheer delight in primary sources. Serious scholarship takes an imaginative leap, the elements of literary style being in her own words "the natural concomitants of the clear, enquiring, disciplined, and imaginative mind needed for historical research."

To Wedgwood, the origin of all economic trends and social movements lies in the individual: "human life is essentially dramatic; it is born and exists in conflict, conflict between men, conflict between men and circumstances, or conflict within the confines of a single human skull." Biography provides insights unavailable to a quantitative sociological approach to the past. "The individual – stupendous and beautiful paradox – is at once infinitesimal dust and the cause of all things. . . . I prefer this overestimate to the opposite method which treats developments as though they were the massive anonymous waves of an inhuman sea or pulverizes the fallible surviving records of human life into the grey dust of statistics."

Her work is largely biographical, its narrative style influenced by G.M. Trevelyan and A.L. Rowse. Her best-known book is the 2-volume *The Great Rebellion* (1955–58), which recounts the events of Charles II's reign. It restores the immediacy of the experience of the people involved. The highly detailed nature of her work makes it eminently readable. Her books were reprinted regularly until the mid-1970s; many are still in print, although they are no longer as widely read as they used to be. Her concentration on narrative at the expense of theory has been criticized. For Wedgwood, "the whole value of the study of history is for me its delightful undermining of certainty, its cumulative insistence of the differences of point of view . . . it is not lack of prejudice which makes for dull history, but lack of passion." Her autobiographical essay "The Velvet Study" (1946) begins, "If I was not born a historian, I was an aspirant at six and a practitioner at twelve," and goes on to set out many of her motivations and inspirations. One of these was F.W. Maitland, in whom she found "the whole architecture of a period built up from the analysis of its detail." The same could be said of Wedgwood's own work. She is a popularist in the best possible sense: a historian attentive to the education of her public (the phrase is from her essay "The Historian and the World"). She lectured widely, and many lectures were individually published as pamphlets before being included in one of her three volumes of collected essays, themselves collated in *History and Hope* (1987). Articles appeared originally in *Time and Tide*, for which she served as literary editor, the *Times Literary Supplement*, the *Spectator*, and many other periodicals. Many of her books in their original editions appeared in series with titles such as the Teach Yourself History Library and the Home University Library.

Wedgwood kept her distance from more traditional universities. Although a special lecturer at many universities, she declined all opportunities to take a regular teaching post, preferring to maintain her independence. (As a member of the famous china manufacturing family, she had no pressing need for an academic post.) Wedgwood's last and most ambitious work, *The Spoils of Time* (1984), a short history of the world initially planned for two volumes, was a unique attempt by a specialist historian to make sense of the "vast and confused record of world history" up to her own day and in different parts of the world. The one volume completed is as entertaining and elegant as any of her prose.

AMY LOUISE ERICKSON

Biography
Cicely Veronica Wedgwood. Born Stocksfield, Northumberland, 20 July 1910. Educated privately and at Lady Margaret Hall, Oxford, BA 1931. Literary adviser, Jonathan Cape publishers, 1941–44; literary editor of the weekly *Time and Tide*, 1944–50: director 1948–58; member, Institute for Advanced Study, Princeton, 1953–68. Dame of British Empire (DBE), 1968. Died London, 9 March 1997.

Principal Writings
Strafford, 1593–1641, 1935
The Thirty Years War, 1938
Oliver Cromwell, 1939
Translator, *The Emperor Charles V*, by Karl Brandi, 1939
William the Silent: William of Nassau, Prince of Orange, 1944
Translator, *Auto da fé*, by Elias Canetti, 1946; as *The Tower of Babel*, 1947
Velvet Studies, 1946
Richelieu and the French Monarchy, 1949
Seventeenth-Century English Literature, 1950; revised 1970
The Last of the Radicals: Josiah Wedgwood, MP, 1951
Montrose, 1952
The Great Rebellion: The King's Peace, 1637–41, 1955
The Great Rebellion: The King's War, 1641–47, 1958
Poetry and Politics under the Stuarts, 1960
Truth and Opinion: Historical Essays, 1960; as *The Sense of the Past*, 1967
Thomas Wentworth, 1st Earl of Strafford 1593–1641: A Revaluation, 1961
The Trial of Charles I, 1964; in US as *A Coffin for King Charles: The Trial and Execution of Charles I*, 1966
The Spoils of Time: A Short History of the World, vol. 1: *From the Earliest Times to the Sixteenth Century*, 1984
History and Hope: The Collected Essays of C.V. Wedgwood, 1987

Further Reading
Johnson, E., "C.V. Wedgwood and Her Historiography," *Contemporary Review* 201, 1962
Ollard, Richard and Pamela Tudor-Craig, eds., *For Veronica Wedgwood These: Studies in Seventeenth-Century History*, London: Collins, 1986

Wehler, Hans-Ulrich 1931–

German social historian

Hans-Ulrich Wehler has been one of the most productive and innovative historians of his generation. Not only as a prolific writer, but also as an administrator at the University of Bielefeld, and as editor of numerous series and the journal *Geschichte und Gesellschaft*, he has exerted a major influence on the direction of German historiography of the 19th and 20th centuries since the mid-1960s.

Belonging to the first generation of Germans who had lived through the Nazi period without actively being involved, Wehler started his career in the 1960s in Cologne with Theodor Schieder. The explanation of the disasters of Nazism and the war – commonly suppressed by the older generation and put back on the agenda by the student movement of the 1960s – loomed behind most modern German societal history. The problem of Germany's *Sonderweg* (special path) was ever present in the historical studies of the society even when not explicitly addressed.

Together with Jürgen Kocka, Wehler developed a conception and program of social history that is known under the labels of Gesellschaftsgeschichte, Sozialgeschichte and Geschichte als (kritische) historische Sozialwissenschaft in books such as *Geschichte als historische Sozialwissenschaft* (History as Historical Social Science, 1973) and *Modernisierungstheorie und Geschichte* (Modernization Theory and History, 1975). He stressed the need for a synthetic history that used social science – quantitative and comparative – methods and theories. At the same time Wehler criticized traditional German historiography as basically conservative, anti-social scientific and narrative, oriented towards individuals and not capable of explaining modern mass phenomena, and finally, affirmative of the status quo. In its stead he promoted German émigré historians (especially Hans Rosenberg and Eckart Kehr) as the appropriate "role models" for modern German historians in books such as *Historische Sozialwissenschaft und Geschichtsschreibung* (Historical Social Science and the Writing of History, 1980). Rosenberg and Kehr had fled Nazi Germany and had experimented in the US with the integration of history and the social sciences. By supporting their methods Wehler helped to found a liberal and left-wing countertradition based on "outsiders" of the historical profession in a conscious opposition to the national-conservative historical establishment.

Using these methodological and political approaches, Wehler and others developed a counter-interpretation of modern German history in the aftermath of the so-called Fischer debate on the origins of World War I. Instead of the traditional glorification of the German national state and of Bismarck as its founder, they emphasized the historical "costs" of the German empire of 1871 as seen from the viewpoint of 1933. After all, only the 14 years of the Weimar republic separated the downfall of the second German empire in 1918 from the rise of the Third empire in 1933. Therefore the continuities between both undemocratic and authoritarian political systems were stressed by Wehler, and characteristics of the first system were put forward as explanatory factors for the latter.

His widely read *Habilitationschrift*, *Bismarck und der Imperialismus* (Bismarck and Imperialism, 1969), was the first step on this historiographical track. With this book Wehler pursued two goals. First, he looked for the origins of authoritarian and aggressive policies in imperial Germany. He found them in the political alliance between the German aristocracy and the German bourgeoisie, who were threatened by a severe economic crisis and the political mobilization of the working class in the last quarter of the 19th century. Second, he tried to demonstrate the potential of a history informed by social science. Wehler experimented with economic theories and social psychological theories of ingroup/outgroup mechanisms and explored their explanatory power. His book was simultaneously acclaimed as innovative and criticized as "unhistorical." Soon he was offered a chair in Bielefeld – in 1971 – where he would stay until his official retirement in 1996.

Because the analysis of the German empire of 1871 was crucial for the interpretation of 19th- and 20th-century German history in general, Wehler chose this historiographical battleground for a frontal attack on the established interpretations of historians such as Gerard Ritter, Ludwig Dehio, Andreas Hillgruber, and Klaus Hildebrand. In his widely read *Das Deutsche Kaiserreich* (1973; *The German Empire*, 1985), he developed a critical and social interpretation of modern German political history. The illiberal, undemocratic, and authoritarian character of German politics was interpreted as a consequence of "partial modernization": while Germany's economy and society modernized rapidly during the industrialization, the modernization (that is: democratization) of politics – such as took place in Western Europe and North America – was blocked by an alliance of major parts of the bourgeoisie and aristocracy. In Germany, therefore, liberalism and liberal values remained much weaker than elsewhere in the West. According to Wehler the tensions generated by this "untimely" blockade of democratization were channeled by the state toward scapegoats inside and outside the German borders. The Germans, therefore, were already used to reducing societal problems to minority issues, and were accustomed to discriminatory politics long before the Nazis took over the German state (*Krisenherde des Kaiserreichs 1871–1918* [Crisis Points of the Empire, 1871–1918], 1973).

Wehler's interpretation of modern Germany from the viewpoint of "1933" has been debated extensively and was severely criticized by Thomas Nipperdey as reductionistic, teleological, and deterministic. According to Nipperdey, Wehler's interpretation suggested that the German empire of 1871 had led directly and inevitably to the Third Reich, and ignored the possibility that German history after 1918 could have taken many different turns. According to other critics, especially Geoff Eley and David Blackbourn, Wehler's idea of a "blocked" political modernization in Germany is based on an untenable, idealized view of modern Western history.

In Wehler's view, reflecting on and accounting for the social and political aspects of historical knowledge is part of "doing history." He therefore regularly commented on public issues concerning modern German history. His last major project will result in his *magnum opus*: a 4-volume history of Germany from 1700 until 1989. The first three volumes of his *Deutsche Gesellschaftsgeschichte* (German Society in History, 1987–) have already been published. These volumes reveal how Wehler has refined his view under the influence of numerous critiques, although his general ideas remain little changed. For

Wehler, the "problem of modern German history" is still the problem of "defensive modernization." Now, however, imperial Germany appears as more modern and bourgeois than before and as less influenced by aristocratic or feudal "premodern" traditions. German politics is not longer interpreted as a manipulative "reaction" of the elite to perceived threats to the status quo.

Although Wehler's *Gesellschaftsgeschichte* constitutes a landmark in modern German historiography, it is doubtful that it will satisfy the recent critics of social history. Inspired by cultural anthropology and postmodernism, they have criticized social history for not integrating the cultural and symbolic dimensions of history adequately and for clinging to a unilinear and monolithic view of modernization. In the same vein social history has been criticized for a fixation on the social-economic aspects of history – a criticism already formulated by proponents of the history of everyday life (*Alltagsgeschichte*) – and for not taking ethnicity, nationality, and gender seriously. Therefore, to all appearances, the debate on the merits and deficits of Wehler's *Gesellschaftsgeschichte* will continue for some time to come.

CHRIS LORENZ

See also Europe: Modern; Germany: 1450–1800; Germany: 1800–1945; Kocka

Biography

Born Freudenberg, 11 September 1931. Attended universities of Cologne, Bonn, and Ohio, 1952–58; PhD, University of Cologne, 1960, Habilitation. Taught at University of Cologne, 1968–70; Free University of Berlin, 1970–71; and University of Bielefeld, 1971–96 (emeritus). Married Renate Pflitsch, 1958 (3 sons).

Principal Writings

Bismarck und der Imperialismus (Bismarck and Imperialism), 1969

Editor, *Deutsche Historiker* (German Historians), 1971–

Das Deutsche Kaiserreich, 1871–1918, 1973; in English as *The German Empire, 1871–1918*, 1985

Geschichte als historische Sozialwissenschaft (History as Historical Social Science), 1973

Krisenherde des Kaiserreichs, 1871–1918 (Crisis Points of the Empire, 1871–1918), 1973

Modernisierungstheorie und Geschichte (Modernization Theory and History), 1975

Historische Sozialwissenschaft und Geschichtsschreibung (Historical Social Science and the Writing of History), 1980

Preussen is wieder chic: Politik und Polemik in zwanzig Essays (Prussia is Fashionable Again: Politics and Polemics in Twenty Essays), 1983

"Historiography in Germany Today," in *Observations on "The Spiritual Situation of the Age": Contemporary German Perspectives*, edited by Jürgen Habermas, 1984

Deutsche Gesellschaftsgeschichte (German Society in History), 3 vols. to date, 1987–

Entsorgung der deutschen Vergangenheit: ein polemischer Essay zum "Historikerstreit" (Discharge of the German Past: A Polemical Essay on the "Historians' Quarrel"), 1988

Editor with Otto Dann and Theodor Schieder, *Nationalismus und Nationalstaat: Studien zum nationalen Problem im modernen Europa* (Nationalism and the Nation-State: Studies on the National Problem in Modern Europe), 1991

Die Gegenwart als Geschichte (The Present as History), 1995

Further Reading

Eley, Geoff, and David Blackbourn, *Mythen deutscher Geschichtsschreibung: die gescheiterte bürgerliche Revolution von 1848*, Frankfurt: Ullstein, 1980; revised and expanded as *The Peculiarities of German History*, Oxford and New York: Oxford University Press, 1984

Nipperdey, Thomas, *Nachdenken über die deutsche Geschichte* (Reflecting on German History), Munich: Beck, 1986

Wellhausen, Julius 1844–1918

German religious historian

Like many 19th-century German historians, Julius Wellhausen was a Protestant pastor's son. Born in Hameln, he studied at nearby Göttingen under Heinrich Ewald – author of the multi-volume *Geschichte des Volkes Israel* (1851–59; *The History of Israel*, 1869–86) and much biblical criticism – and served there as lecturer from 1870 to 1872. Wellhausen's training was in theology and Semitics, but, as an Ewald student, his central interest was historical. Largely for that reason, he would resign from the faculty of theology at Greifswald in 1882 to become, first, an assistant professor of Semitics at Halle and, later, a professor of Semitics at Marburg, which he left for Göttingen in 1892. Wellhausen simply felt ill-equipped to train pastors for the ministry, and, in any case, his Greifswald colleagues found his interpretation of the Bible too unorthodox. Though very Christian in culture and outlook, Wellhausen was not, in fact, conventionally religious, and, for him, Hebrew scriptures were only historical sources for tracking and understanding the very interesting early history of the Israelite people.

At age 19 a reading of Ewald's history of Israel had decided Wellhausen on his course of study, and as a student and young scholar he was deeply interested by Ferdinand Christian Baur's technique of "tendency criticism," a historically-based method for resolving internal textual problems by reference to the historical context of the work. Much of Wellhausen's critical achievement consisted in applying this technique, which Baur had used on Christian sources, to Hebrew scriptures. Wellhausen did not, however, disdain older, more purely textual methods. His *Der Text der Bücher Samuelis* (The Text of the Book of Samuel, 1871), for example, used the Greek Septuagint text in an attempt to find the original text of Samuel, whose tales of David's time delighted and fascinated him. Moreover, Wellhausen dedicated his crowning work, *Prolegomena zur Geschichte Israels* (1882; *Prolegomena to the History of Israel*, 1885) to his teacher Ewald, but acknowledged at the outset his deep indebtedness to the research of W.M.L. De Wette, Wilhelm Vatke, Eduard Reuss, and K.H. Graf. The debt was very real, and Lothar Perlitt in *Vatke and Wellhausen* (1965) persuasively dismissed the once common accusation that Wellhausen merely applied Hegel's notions by lucidly demonstrating how Vatke and, before him, J.G. Herder shaped Wellhausen's vision of Israelite history.

Like Herder and Vatke, Wellhausen was strongly impressed with the historical uniqueness and beauty of each people. The people he chose for study were those of Israel, not in his own or in any post-exilic time but in their early, presumably unspoiled youth. This presumption, of course, meant that the trajectory of Jewish history had been downward, a track of departure from a beautiful original condition. If reinterpreting scripture to find this happy childhood offended Lutherans at Griefswald, Wellhausen's injury to Lutheran orthodoxy was slight in contrast to its affront to modern Judaism. Wellhausen claimed that the priestly rule (theocracy) in particular and *halakha* – Mosaic law – in general were post-exilic alterations, or even corruptions, of original Israelite culture. This claim was necessarily offensive to Jewish scholars. The contemporaneous *Jewish Encyclopedia*, for example, celebrated his achievements but lamented that they "were marred by unmistakable anti-Jewish bias." There were excellent grounds for offense because Wellhausen lent his enormous prestige as the foremost Bible scholar of Wilhelmine Germany to a critique of post-exilic Judaism that was consistent with his scholarly findings but was really a secularized Pauline polemic against Judaism. Jewish law, which he considered adventitious in any case, takes "the soul out of religion and spoils morality." He followed this outlook to its logical conclusion by arguing that gospel Christianity was a necessary and very positive revolt against pharisaic Judaism. Wellhausen himself drew the obvious conclusion: theologically liberal Jewish scholars such as Abraham Geiger were wrong in supposing that Judaism was at all compatible with the modern world, as Christianity was. Jewish assimilation, therefore, would lead to Jewish disappearance.

This mildly judaeophobic view of an Israelite history that Wellhausen loved appeared progressively in his publications. He followed his study of Samuel with *Die Pharisäer und die Sadducäer* (The Pharisees and the Sadducees, 1874) for which he adduced evidence from Josephus' histories and New Testament texts to understand the fights between the two Jewish parties. He revisited the topic later in his career by portraying the allegedly legalist Pharisees as the logical outgrowth of post-exilic Judaism. He then returned to the study of Hebrew scriptures. His *Die Composition des Hexateuchs* (The Composition of the Hexateuch, 1889) plausibly claimed that the "Book of Joshua" belonged with the five traditional Mosaic books. Wellhausen reached this conclusion by re-identifying the four sources discussed in the "textual interpretation" of Hebrew scripture. Beginning in 1886, he also published successive editions of Bleek's *Einleitung in das alte Testament* (Introduction to the Old Testament). Here he studied historical context to arrive at findings that began to appear in the contemporaneous *Geschichte Israels* (The History of Israel, 1878), later revised and expanded into his *Prolegomena* and, subsequently, his more comprehensive and narrative *Israelitische und jüdische Geschichte* (Israelite and Jewish History, 1895). The central claim in these writings, a claim that is fundamental to his argument, is that the legal texts of the Pentateuch and the historical accounts of theocratic rule in Chronicles are not, as they seem, the earliest Jewish texts. To the contrary, they are self-justifying priestly screeds written after the return from exile proclaimed by Cyrus the Great in 538 BCE. The real ancient Israel that Wellhausen imagined and loved was earlier and could be found in the stories of books such as Samuel's. That version of Israelite history was Wellhausen's subject, and that Israelite history moved him to research and write, in 1887, *Reste arabischen Heidentumes* (Remnants of Arabian Paganism) and, in 1902, his more synthetic *Das arabische Reich und sein Sturz* (*The Arab Kingdom and Its Fall*, 1927). He believed that Semitic peoples were enough alike for one early Semitic history,

the Arabian, to throw light on another, the Hebrew. Although Wellhausen's conclusions have fallen before later studies of the ancient Near East, he remains an important source for understanding historic Protestant views of biblical and post-biblical Judaism.

ROBERT FAIRBAIRN SOUTHARD

See also Meyer

Biography

Born Hameln, Hannover, 17 May 1844. Studied at University of Göttingen, where he received his degrees and taught, 1870–72. Professor of theology, University of Greifswald, 1872–82; professor of Oriental languages, University of Halle, 1882–85; University of Marburg, 1885–92; and University of Göttingen, 1892–1918. Died Göttingen, 7 January 1918.

Principal Writings

Der Text der Bücher Samuelis (The Text of the Book of Samuel), 1871
Die Pharisäer und die Sadducäer (The Pharisees and the Sadducees), 1874
Geschichte Israels (The History of Israel), 2 vols., 1878
Prolegomena zur Geschichte Israels, 1882; in English as *Prolegomena to the History of Israel*, 1885
Editor, *Einleitung in das alte Testament* (Introduction to the Old Testament), by Friedrich Bleek, 1886
Reste arabischen Heidentumes (Remnants of Arabian Paganism), 1887
Die Composition des Hexateuchs und der historischen Bucher des Alten Testaments (The Composition of the Hexateuch and the Historical Books of the Old Testament), 1889
Israelitische und jüdische Geschichte (Israelite and Jewish History), 1895
Die religiös-politischen Öppositionsparteien im alten Islam, 1901; in English as *The Religio-Political Factions in Early Islam*, 1975
Das arabische Reich und sein Sturz, 1902; in English as *The Arab Kingdom and Its Fall*, 1927

Further Reading

Boschwitz, Friedemann, *Julius Wellhausen: Motive und Masstäbe seiner Geschichtsschreibung* (Julius Wellhausen: Motive and Measures of His Historiography), Darmstadt: Wissenschaftliche Buchgesellschaft, 1968
Meyer, Michael A., *Response to Modernity: A History of the Reform Movement in Judaism*, New York and Oxford: Oxford University Press, 1988
Perlitt, Lothar, *Vatke und Wellhausen: Geschichtsphilosophische Voraussetzungen und historiographische Motive für die Darstellung der Religion und Geschichte Israels durch Wilhelm Vatke und Julius Wellhausen* (Vatke and Wellhausen: The Historical-Philosophical Presupposition and Historiographical Motives for the Pesentation of the Religion and History of Israel by Wilhelm Vatke and Julius Wellhausen), Berlin: Thopelmann, 1965

Whewell, William 1794–1866
British historian of science, mathematician, and moral philosopher

In October 1811 William Whewell began a long tedious journey from Lancaster to Cambridge. It was the beginning of a trip that would take him from being the son of a carpenter and joiner to master of Trinity College. When he first arrived in Cambridge the war with revolutionary France was still raging, and the English physical and mental landscape was gradually changing to meet the needs of a developing industrial economy. For many it was heralding a new morality expunged of religion and a very real threat to the English Constitution. It was in this context that Whewell became assimilated into the traditional Anglican culture of the 18th century.

Within the walls of Trinity College Whewell labored to protect it from the illusionary and destructive effects of French abstract reason, as well as the growing interests stemming from the new industrial cities such as Manchester. Indeed, he devoted his life to ensuring that political and intellectual changes did not adversely affect the constitutional marriage between church and state, and the intrinsic role Oxford and Cambridge universities played in this holy alliance. Intrinsic to Whewell's historical approach was a variation of the German historical method and philology.

Whewell was an important exponent of the inclusion of German idealism and historiography in the philosophy of science and political economy. He was part of a group of undergraduates which included Julius Hare (whose uncle was the philologist Sir William Jones), Connop Thirlwall, and Hugh Jones Rose all of whom imported German Romanticism into Cambridge. Their initial resource was a recent publication by Barthold Georg Niebuhr, entitled *Romanische Geschichte* (1811–32; *History of Rome*, 1828–42), which they used as a textbook. Through his "Critical Method," Niebuhr set out to analyze written accounts that had survived from the past, and subject them to a philosophical investigation that would unlock an inner meaning that had faded over time and was subsequently no longer suspected. He dwelt upon the critical evaluation of sources – especially traditional accounts – using language itself as historical evidence.

Niebuhr further maintained a kind of "evolutionary" interpretation of the history and development of all human societies, under which practical comparisons might be drawn between nations and epochs. The history of the Greek and Roman world was revised by the new approaches of Niebuhr, and through the work of others such as August Boeckh and Karl Otfried Müller. Their work was a reaction in part to the "rationalist" school of David Hume and Edward Gibbon, which drew upon Locke's principles to posit a kind of uniformitarianism of the human mind, seeing man in all times and places to be the same psychological creature, and viewing social development as a continual, linear progression toward material and moral progress.

Whewell worked with the Coleridgean Germanist Hare, and Thirlwall, in the activities of the Etymological Society and its journal the *Philological Museum*, established in 1831 at Cambridge. Their target was the nominalism of English etymologists such as Horne Tooke and more generally as a potent antidote to Ricardianism and utilitarianism. A "fact," for Whewell, was a product of the particular circumstances and history of a particular society. Philology would awaken the forgotten consciousness of former generations and present vital clues to social, economic, and political arrangements. History and not abstract laws was the key to deciding the best arrangement.

For Whewell, induction set the intellectual conditions necessary for the long hard road to truth and salvation. To reason downwards was to fall from grace by placing one's faith internally, instead of externally within the divine world. The physical universe provided signposts for this path to God in collaboration with the written word. To place one's faith internally expelled the need for scripture or indeed the church to make sense of this world. Morally and politically this congealed in utilitarian and commercial notions of self-interest, which had in many ways eclipsed 18th-century notions of virtue and corruption.

The godless internal deductivists concentrated their faith on man's ability to invent and reason from the erection of abstract terms into principles. For Whewell, this manifested itself in French analytical mathematics, Benthamite utilitarianism, radical views on morphology, and Ricardian political economy. He presented this way of thinking as manufacturing a "destructive" morality destined to destroy the traditional fabric of English society as engraved in the church and state and its accompanying social hierarchy. He fought hard to safeguard this world by defining an appropriate science characterized by induction, and fortified by installing this notion of intelligence into a liberal education at Cambridge. Whewell's work in the history of the inductive sciences, philology, political economy, mathematics, and his overall construction of a system of morality operated to promote this end. In short, Whewell turned to history to counter abstract reason and to seek an appropriate scientific morality.

For Whewell, language was intrinsic to permanent knowledge, and history was the tool to finding it. In his metascientific project, Whewell did not seek to ground rules of science, but rather to generalize through the history of science the pattern in which subjects were translated into scientific disciplines. For Whewell, science had to be assimilated into the traditional structure of a liberal education. Discovery was not part of a university education, which should, rather, form the basis of an equilibrium between new and old knowledge. Whewell's moral philosophy, in particular, was designed to restore this balance through a correct training of the Cambridge mind. He used it both to legitimate a particular stance (as opposed to the use of pure reason), and to show that science did not progress through sudden changes with the past, but rather accommodated old claims within a new perspective. Scientific progress operated through a philosophy of induction in which advances still retained old truths revealed in a new point of view.

WILLIAM ASHWORTH

Biography

Born Lancaster, 24 May 1794, eldest of 7 children of a master-carpenter. Attended the "Blue school" in Lancaster; studied at Trinity College, Cambridge, BA 1817, MA 1819, DD 1844: fellow from 1817; ordained priest, Church of England, 1825. At Cambridge University: professor of mineralogy, 1825–32 and moral philosophy, 1838–1855, and master of Trinity College, 1841–66. Married 1) Cordelia Marshall, 1841 (died 1855); 2) Lady Evering Affleck, 1858. Died Cambridge, 6 March 1866 from a horse-riding accident.

Principal Writings

An Elementary Treatise on Mechanics, 1819

"Mathematical Exposition of Some Doctrines of Political Economy," *Transactions of the Cambridge Philosophical Society* 3 (1830), 191–230

Astronomy and General Physics Considered with Reference to Natural Theology, 1833

"On the Uses of Definitions," *Philological Museum* 2 (1833), 263–72

The History of the Inductive Sciences, from the Earliest to the Present Time, 3 vols., 1837

On the Principles of English University Education, 1837

The Mechanical Euclid, 1838

The Philosophy of the Inductive Sciences, Founded on Their History, 2 vols., 1840

The Elements of Morality, Including Polity, 2 vols., 1845

Of a Liberal Education in General; and with Reference to the Leading Studies of the University of Cambridge, 1845

Lectures on the History of Moral Philosophy in England, 1852

Of the Plurality of Worlds: An Essay, 1853

On the Philosophy of Discovery, 1860

Further Reading

Ashworth, William, ed., *A Calendar of the Correspondence of William Whewell*, Cambridge: Trinity College, 1996

Becher, Harvey, "William Whewell and Cambridge Mathematics," *Historical Studies in the Physical Sciences* 11 (1980), 1–48

Fisch, Menachem, and Simon Schaffer, eds., *William Whewell: A Composite Portrait*, Oxford and New York: Oxford University Press, 1991

Fisch, Menachem, *William Whewell: Philosopher of Science*, Oxford and New York: Oxford University Press, 1991

Morrell, Jack, "William Whewell: Rough Diamond," *History of Science* 34 (1994), 345–59

Stair Douglas, Janet Mary, *The Life and Selections from the Correspondence of William Whewell DD*, London: Kegan Paul, 1881

Todhunter, Isaac, *William Whewell, DD, Master of Trinity College, Cambridge: An Account of His Writings with Selections from His Literary and Scientific Correspondence*, 2 vols., London: Macmillan, 1876; reprinted 1970

Yeo, Richard, *Defining Science: William Whewell, Natural Knowledge and Public Debate in Early Victorian Britain*, Cambridge and New York: Cambridge University Press, 1993

Whig Interpretation of History

The term derives from the book of this title published by Herbert Butterfield in 1931. By it he meant to stigmatize "certain fallacies to which all history is liable," since they were intrinsic to the psychology of all historians, except perhaps pure researchers. These were: the assessment of the past not on its own terms but from the standpoint of the historian's alien present; writing history as if the present was the teleological endpoint of that process; and assuming that the historical process could be studied from the perspective of one side only – those who temporarily prevailed in the present day – rather than as the outcome of an infinitely complicated dialectic. His critique has been enormously successful, having been adopted in just the spirit in which it was intended and any form of historical inquiry may now be criticized as "Whiggish": it is the commonest form of historiographical criticism (or abuse). The limitations of Butterfield's approach are less frequently noted. His was the protest of the empirical researcher, justifiably aggrieved at the flabbiness of later 19th-century "abridgments" of history according to the prescriptions of evolution, or absolute progress (in various forms).

However, he put nothing in their place. The upshot of *The Whig Interpretation* was that any truthful "abridgment" of history – he seems unaware that it might be *conceptually* ordered – was held to be impossible except by abandoning a historical perspective for a theological one. The historical process was so complex, it could only be construed as Christian Providence at work. The conceptual poverty of this stance is clear: Butterfield's European and American contemporaries had also seen through secular historical theodicies, and accepted that, if there were no absolute pattern to history, they must grapple with the problem of historical relativism. He, by contrast, used the observation that historical judgments were "merely relative to time and circumstances" as a buttress to his Christian fundamentalism: it was simply another illustration of the triviality of historical study in a large perspective. Butterfield's problems were not only abstract. Having demoted historians to the passive station of "expert witnesses," he knowingly consigned the interpretive shaping and public utilization of their work to the tender mercies of "the economist, the politician, the diplomat, ... the strategist ... the ecclesiastic and the administrator."

A further weakness of *The Whig Interpretation* was that it had been a polemic against an extremely ill-defined target: "the great patriarchs of history-writing, so many of whom seem to have been Whigs and gentlemen when they have not been Americans." In *The Englishman and His History* (1944, first given as lectures in 1938) he turned to more precise historiographical analysis, and attached a second, quite distinct meaning to the phrase "Whig interpretation": "now it was an aspect of the English mind and as a product of the English tradition" (i.e., something specific and not universal). Aided by his good empirical practice, he at last awoke to the fact that history was something more than either rank empiricism or the object of mystical contemplation; that it had a public role as the principal codifier of English national identity, and that if history did have to be conceptually organized, there was a good deal more to be said for Whig history than he had previously realized. This book has had much more measurable, because more concrete, influence than *The Whig Interpretation*, having sired a whole seam of monographic literature on what is "really the 'English' interpretation" of history. Butterfield's overall schema has proven remarkably durable, and most of the scholarly debates have concerned issues of detail – was Hume a Whig? what was Macaulay's relation to the Whig tradition? – and no adequate synthesis has either taken its place or brought it up to date. The salient features of Whiggism in this guise were: its partisan roots in the constitutional struggles of the mid-17th century, the subsequent development of a bipartisan, national reverence for the libertarian, parliamentary, and "ancient constitution," which represented a unique medieval survival in post-1688 Europe; and the entrenching of that reverence as a result of the French Revolution, the revolutions of 1848, and those between 1917 and 1939. These stood in forcible contrast to the peculiar and benign English way, where liberty and order, compromise and tolerance, respect for tradition and capacity for continuous, evolutionary innovation were all united without bloodshed or civil strife.

The Whig interpretation is distinctive because it is not merely a historiographical construct, but the embodiment of the English political tradition c.1688–1940. Being a national and not a partisan history, there is no such thing as a competing "Tory" interpretation, and being grounded in central realities of present experience it was, if not "right," certainly inescapable. As Butterfield stated with only mild exaggeration: "it will always be true that ... in yesterday's meaning of the term at least – we are all of us exultant and unrepentant Whigs." But by the same reasoning, the Whig interpretation is not marked by a series of great scholarly monuments, especially before Macaulay: rather, it is an outstanding example of a widely diffused, historiographical *mentalité*. Since Butterfield wrote, many factors have worked to bury the "Whig" view: relative British economic decline, the prevalence of stable democracy throughout Western Europe, and the rise of extra-European powers with no respect for, or reference to, European cultural norms and traditions. But the vehemence of the disputes about England's national identity and position in Europe show that even today the legacy of "Whiggism" exerts a powerful effect on British politics and historical writing; and in the scholarly treatment of the period of its cultural hegemony, the full import of English exceptionalism is only just beginning to be appreciated.

PETER GHOSH

See also Butterfield

Further Reading

Anderson, Perry, "Components of the National Culture," *New Left Review* 50 (1968), 3–58

Blaas, P.B.M., *Continuet en anachronisme: het beeld van de Engelse parlementaire en constitutionele ontwikkeling in de Whig geschiedschrijving en de Kritiek hierop in die jaren, 1890–1930*, Amsterdam: Universiteit, 1974; in English as *Continuity and Anachronism: Parliamentary and Constitutional Development in Whig Historiography and the Anti-Whig Reaction Between 1890 and 1930*, The Hague: Nijhoff, 1978

Burrow, John Wyon, *A Liberal Descent: Victorian Historians and the English Past*, Cambridge and New York: Cambridge University Press, 1981

Butterfield, Herbert, *The Whig Interpretation of History*, London: Bell, 1931; New York: Scribner, 1951

Butterfield, Herbert, *The Englishman and His History*, Cambridge: Cambridge University Press, 1944; Hamden, CT: Archon, 1970

Cannadine, David, *G.M. Trevelyan: A Life in History*, London: HarperCollins, 1992; New York: Norton, 1993

Fisher, H.A.L., "The Whig Historians," *Proceedings of the British Academy* 14 (1928), 297–339

Forbes, Duncan, "Scientific Whiggism: Adam Smith and John Millar," *Cambridge Journal* 7 (1954), 643–70

Forbes, Duncan, *Hume's Philosophical Politics*, Cambridge and New York: Cambridge University Press, 1975

Hamburger, Joseph, *Macaulay and the Whig Tradition*, Chicago: University of Chicago Press, 1976

Kelley, Donald R., "History, English Law and the Renaissance," *Past and Present* 65 (1974), 24–51

Kidd, Colin, *Subverting Scotland's Past: Scottish Whig Historians and the Creation of an Anglo-British Identity, 1689–c.1830*, Cambridge and New York: Cambridge University Press, 1993

Pocock, J.G.A., *The Ancient Constitution and the Feudal Law: A Study of English Historical Thought in the Seventeenth Century*, Cambridge: Cambridge University Press, 1957; New York: Norton, 1967; revised 1987

Pocock, J.G.A., "The Varieties of Whiggism from Exclusion to Reform," in his *Virtue, Commerce, and History: Essays on Political Thought and History, Chiefly in the Eighteenth Century*, Cambridge and New York: Cambridge University Press, 1985

Thompson, E.P., "The Peculiarities of the English," *Socialist Register* 2 (1965), 311–62; reprinted in his *The Poverty of Theory and Other Essays*, London: Merlin Press, and New York: Monthly Review Press, 1978

Trevor-Roper, Hugh, Introduction to Thomas Babington Macaulay, *The History of England*, Harmondsworth: Penguin, 1979

White, Hayden V. 1928–

US intellectual historian and literary theorist

Hayden White has been a leader in late 20th-century efforts to define the role of language and narrative form in historical understanding. After publishing on a variety of topics in the 1960s, White found his field of inquiry in the history of historical consciousness itself. In 1973 he attracted international, cross-disciplinary attention with his book *Metahistory*. He then extended his ideas in numerous essays, many of which were collected in *Tropics of Discourse* (1978) and *The Content of the Form* (1987).

Inspired by the Italian neo-idealism of Benedetto Croce and by Friedrich Nietzsche's late 19th-century attack on institutionalized history, *Metahistory* was written under the influence of continental structuralist philosophy and linguistics and the North American literary criticism of Northrop Frye and Kenneth Burke. The book was an often cumbersome but nonetheless ingenious anatomy of the "deep structure of the historical imagination" as exemplified in the work of several social philosophers and historians: Hegel, Michelet, Ranke, Tocqueville, Burckhardt, Marx, Nietzsche, and Croce. Although it focused on 19th-century authors, the book contained challenging and – to many readers – profoundly disturbing, subjectivist implications for historical knowledge in general.

In evaluating accounts of the past, previous historians had naturally addressed such salient issues as logic, thoroughness, accuracy, and the handling of evidence. White, however, studied the ways historians use words, or the ways words use them. He approached his authors' books as imaginative constructs, much like works of fiction (he later wrote an essay on "The Fictions of Factual Representation"), analyzing each as "what it most manifestly is: a verbal structure in the form of a narrative prose discourse." The underlying meanings of these texts were, he maintained, controlled by rhetorical conventions that sprang from the structures of language itself. Advancing a complex taxonomy of historical representation, he defined three basic explanatory strategies that his authors used: explanation by formal argument, by emplotment, and by ideological implication. Under each of these headings he distinguished four possible types of articulation: formism, organicism, mechanism, and contextualism (for arguments); romance, comedy, tragedy, and satire (for emplotments); anarchism, conservatism, radicalism, and liberalism (for ideological implication). The *style* of a given historical author, he concluded, is the product of that writer's personal mix of these possible strategies and modes of articulation. The entire theory was built on the hypothesis that there is a deep level of consciousness from which historians – in various ways, intentionally or (more often) unintentionally – derive the conceptual frameworks they use to explain their evidence. To designate these "types of prefiguration" or "frames of mind," White drew on ancient and Renaissance rhetoric to identify four "tropes" of figurative language: metaphor, metonymy, synecdoche, and irony. In poetic theory, the word trope (from the Greek *tropein*, to turn, to swerve) means turns (or figures) of speech – metaphor, simile, etc. White extended this idea to designate alleged deep-level "turns of thought." The "dominant tropological mode and its attendant linguistic protocol," he argued, "comprise the irreducibly 'metahistorical' basis of every historical work." Thus, the texts produced by his authors actually represented "the working out of the possibilities of tropological prefiguration of the historical field contained in poetic language in general."

More broadly, White suggested that virtually *any* historical text rests on such a deep poetic undergirding and that this constitutes its "metahistorical" (i.e., formal, narrative, nonempirical) basis, which is (in contrast to the work's manifest content) the essential ground for understanding its meaning. Since the ultimate basis and meaning of any representation of the past is nonempirical, he concluded, "the best grounds for choosing one perspective on history rather than another are ultimately aesthetic or moral rather than epistemological."

White's theory of the historical imagination seemed radically to contradict the commonsense notion that many historians and their readers shared, that is, that the past they write about is real rather than invented, and that the historian's task is simply to retell its story as it actually happened. Partly because his book challenged such fundamental beliefs, and partly because its abstract and demanding argument was not presented in a clear or graceful style, it was at first ignored or dismissed out of hand by most historians, attracting mainly the interest of literary theorists. Those historians who took the book seriously tended to reject its relativist message, while complaining that White's highly schematic argument failed adequately to relate such writers as Ranke and Tocqueville to the specific historical settings in which they operated. Yet some reviewers found that White had inaugurated a new way of thinking about history as a process of writing: "That historians are to some extent poets as well has been a commonplace since classical times," wrote John Clive, "But White is the first to have tried to grapple systematically with the manner in which literary artistry is not merely decorative or ancillary but integral to the historical work in hand." Indeed, it was possible to separate White's radically subjectivist theory of historiographical cognition from selected aspects of his poetics and employ the latter as a model for further study of the 19th-century historical imagination – although this potential was generally disregarded. In recent years White's views have become better known among historians, while remaining highly controversial. This is because his theory is widely viewed as the prime example of an untenable "rhetorical relativism" – that is, the doctrine that the knowledge content of historical accounts is controlled by the literary forms in which they are cast. Thus the interpretations of historians are cognitively incomparable, since the poetic forms they employ are ultimately matters of aesthetic or political taste.

HARRY RITTER

See also Film; Historiology; Intellectual; Literature; Metahistory; Philosophy; Rhetoric; Vico

Biography

Born 12 July 1928. Received BA, Wayne State University, 1951; MA, University of Michigan, 1952, PhD 1956. Taught at Wayne State University, 1955–58; University of Rochester, 1958–68; and University of California, Los Angeles, 1968–73, director, Center for Humanities, Wesleyan University, 1973–78; taught at University of California, Santa Cruz, from 1978. Married in 1952.

Principal Writings

Metahistory: The Historical Imagination in Nineteenth-Century Europe, 1973
Tropics of Discourse: Essays in Cultural Criticism, 1978
The Content of the Form: Narrative Discourse and Historical Representation, 1987

Further Reading

Dray, W.H., "Review of Hayden White, *The Content of the Form*", *History and Theory* 27 (1988), 282–87
Friedlander, Saul, ed., *Probing the Limits of Representation: Nazism and the "Final Solution,"* Cambridge, MA: Harvard University Press, 1992
Himmelfarb, Gertrude, *On Looking into the Abyss: Untimely Thoughts on Culture and Society*, New York: Knopf, 1994
Kansteiner, Wulf, "Hayden White's Critique of the Writing of History," *History and Theory*, 32 (1993), 273–95
Konstan, David, "The Function of Narrative in Hayden White's Metahistory," *Clio* 11 (1981), 65–78
Kramer, Lloyd S., "Literature, Criticism, and Historical Imagination: The Literary Challenge of Hayden White and Dominick La Capra," in Lynn Hunt, ed., *The New Cultural History*, Berkeley: University of California Press, 1989
"*Metahistory*: Six Critiques," *History and Theory*, Beiheft 19 (1980)
Mink, Louis O., "Narrative Form as a Cognitive Instrument" (1978) in his *Historical Understanding*, edited by Brian Fay, Eugene O. Golob, and Richard T. Vann, Ithaca, NY: Cornell University Press, 1987
Ostrowski, Donald, "A Metahistorical Analysis: Hayden White and Four Narratives of 'Russian' History," *Clio* 19 (1990), 215–36
Ritter, Harry, "Progressive Historians and the Historical Imagination in Austria," *Austrian History Yearbook* 19–20 (1983–84), part 1, 45–90
Roth, Michael S., "Cultural Criticism and Political Theory: Hayden White's Rhetorics of History," *Political Theory* 16 (1988), 636–46
Storia della Storiografia 24 (1993) and 25 (1994)

White, Lynn, Jr. 1907–1987

US medievalist and historian of technology

Lynn White, Jr. was a student of Charles Homer Haskins at Harvard at a time in the late 1920s when Haskins' studies of medieval science were attracting great attention. He wrote his dissertation, however, on a standard topic: Latin monasticism in Norman Sicily. In the mid-1930s his perspective took a turn towards material culture under the influence Alfred L. Kroeber's *Anthropology*, which he read in 1933, and which stimulated him to read a number of classics in the history of medieval technology, including works by Marc Bloch and Richard Lefèbvre des Noëttes. His first publication on medieval technology was a 1940 article entitled "Technology and Invention in the Middle Ages" in which he sketched out a number of problems that, in effect, became a blueprint for the next phase of his career. This resulted in his influential 1962 volume, *Medieval Technology and Social Change*.

The theme of this work is, first, the substitution of horse-power for that of man in military and agricultural technology and, second, the introduction of water power for milling in the early Middle Ages. With regard to horsepower, the key innovations – the stirrup in military technology, the nailed horse shoe, padded horse collar, and heavy, wheeled plow – all reached Western Europe through the chain of barbarian nomads or semi-nomads extending out into Central Asia. With regard to the stirrup, White's most controversial conclusion was that its introduction set off a chain of events that led to a central element of feudalism: the grant of land in return for military service. The stirrup made it possible for a mounted knight to deliver a lance thrust with the combined weight of rider and horse; this in turn required heavy armor and created financial needs that could not be met with salaries in the money-poor dark ages. Thus Charles Martel began to grant his senior officers land in return for military duty in 732, the year before the decisive battle against the Muslims at Poitiers. The agricultural developments were analogous. Horses could not be used for plowing before the availability of horse shoes and padded collars, which allowed the horse to throw his entire weight into drawing the plow. Horses are more efficient when fed oats, and this need stimulated the switch from two- to three-course rotations, wherein a spring crop of oats, peas, beans, and barley was added to complement winter wheat. The oat crop also filled demand emanating from feudal cavalry. These innovations in agriculture, which made it possible to cultivate the rich, clay-laden soils of the alluvial valleys of northern Europe produced unprecedentedly high yields that underwrote the growth of cities and the revival of the European economy. White's conclusions were influential, although controversial because of their multicausal nature. We now know that the transformation from two- to three-field agriculture took place more slowly than he had imagined and that the replacement of oxen by horses as the plow beast of choice was considerably delayed.

White's analysis of the application of water power reflected the current thinking on the problem which, following Marc Bloch, presumed that rural slavery acted to impede the diffusion of the water-powered grist mill. White thought the grist mill was possibly a barbarian invention associated with Jutland, even though a horizontal mill is documented in China of the 1st century CE. He regarded as incomprehensible the thousand-year interval between the first appearance of the water mill and its wider application, but his solution to the problem was an overly-general appeal to the prevailing views of man's relationship with nature and the reluctance to improve upon the "natural" resolution of technical problems. But Vitruvius also understood steam power and therefore White was reluctant to attribute the Romans' unwillingness to substitute mechanical for human power to social reasons, such a slavery, alone.

In all these separate arguments, White displayed an ingenious range of source material, including archaeological, iconographical, and linguistic evidence to fill in the vast lacunae where no direct documentation exists.

White was fascinated by the West's technological superiority and the reasons for it. He asserted that Western Europe was "technologically dynamic" by the early 14th century and that the Byzantine and Islamic worlds were, by contrast, passive with respect to invention. All three zones had similar needs yet necessity was not everywhere the mother of invention. White also doubted the old theory that slavery was a necessary obstacle to technological advance. More significant, in this respect, were the values of elites as reproduced in educational establishments that were rhetorical in nature. He further stipulated that values relating to technology were linked to religious ones – those that governed peoples' personal relationships with nature.

In 1967, at the height of the American environmental movement, White published an essay titled "The Historical Roots of Our Ecologic Crisis" whose immediate notoriety and tremendous influence surprised its author who (he was fond of telling) had written it as a kind of light aperçu by a medievalist of currently fashionable issues. He argued that the European value system with respect to the environment had changed around 1000 CE to reflect the tremendous productive power unleashed by the agricultural revolution of the 9th and 10th centuries. As a result the traditional concept of stewardship was replaced by an imperative to subdue the earth.

THOMAS F. GLICK

See also Environmental; Roman; Technology

Biography

Lynn Townsend White, Jr. Born San Francisco, 29 April 1907. Received BA, Stanford University, 1928; MA, Union Theological Seminary, New York, 1929; MA, Harvard University, 1930, PhD 1934. Taught at Princeton University, 1933–37; and Stanford University, 1937–43; president, Mills College, 1943–58; professor, University of California, Los Angeles, 1958–72 (emeritus). Married Maude McArthur, 1940 (1 son, 3 daughters). Died 30 March 1987.

Principal Writings

"Technology and Invention in the Middle Ages," *Speculum* 15 (1940), 141–59

Medieval Technology and Social Change, 1962

Editor, *The Transformation of the Roman World: Gibbon's Problem after Two Centuries*, 1966

"The Historical Roots of Our Ecologic Crisis," *Science* 155 (1967), 1203–07

Machina ex Deo: Essays in the Dynamism of Western Culture, 1968; reprinted as *Dynamo and Virgin Reconsidered: Essays in the Dynamism of Western Culture*, 1971

"Cultural Climates and Technical Advance in the Middle Ages," *Viator* 2 (1971), 171–202

Medieval Religion and Technology: Collected Essays, 1978

Further Reading

Clagett, Marshall, Richard H. Rouse, and Edward Grant, "Lynn White, Jr., 29 April 1907–30 March 1987," *Speculum* 63 (1988), 769–71

Widukind of Corvey c.925–after 973

Saxon historian

We know virtually nothing about Widukind except what he reveals in his one surviving work, the *Rerum gestarum Saxonicarum libri tres* (Three Books of the Deeds of the Saxons, cited henceforth as *Deeds of the Saxons*). Born into a noble Saxon family – he was a relative of Otto I's mother Mathilda – he entered the Westphalian royal monastery of Corvey shortly before the death of Abbot Folcmar in 942. He wrote some hagiographical works, which have not survived, and then in the mid-960s he composed the *Deeds of the Saxons*.

This deals with the history of the Saxon people from its beginnings – much of the first part of the first book is devoted to an account of the Saxon conquest of Britain and of the return of some of them to the continent and their conflicts with the Thuringians – down to Widukind's own time. The first book covers the Saxons' origins, their conversion to Christianity under Charlemagne, the emergence of their leader as the dominant figure in the politics of the emergent east Frankish/German kingdom by the early 10th century, and finally the election of the first Saxon king, Henry I, in 919, and his reign. The second book extends from the election of Henry's son Otto I as king in 936 down to the death of Otto's wife Edith in 946; the third covers Saxon history from 946 to about 958/9, with some passages relating to more recent events. The manuscript tradition allows us to see that the work circulated in two "editions," the first written around 967/8, the second with an epilogue extending to the death of Otto I in 973: the *Deeds of the Saxons* in this version closes with a stately and moving account of Otto's death at the height of his power, his funeral, and the acknowledgement of his son Otto II as king. The view once held that these two editions had been preceded by an earlier one written around 957/8 was shown by Beumann (1950) to be false.

Beumann's monograph on Widukind marked a watershed in the study and understanding of the author. Before its appearance, Widukind – a historian of central importance for our knowledge of early Ottonian history – had been seen as a somewhat artless writer, given to reproducing the tone, narrative style, and material of oral poems and sagas about contemporary events, the existence of which was in turn posited on the basis of Widukind's work. Beumann showed that Widukind's writing was deeply rooted in a specifically Latin literary tradition, and that it owed much to earlier writers, notably Sallust and Einhard; Widukind was revealed as a stylist and narrator of great power, whose apparent silences and imbalances were deliberate and meaningful. He was also revealed as far more a representative of the views held by many of the Saxon aristocracy than a purely monastic historian. A further stage in our understanding of the work was marked by Althoff's recent explanation of why Widukind should have written the work for the young Mathilda, abbess of Quedlinburg (to whom all three books are dedicated): it was intended to serve her as an *aide-mémoire* for her political conduct after the deaths of Otto I's son William, archbishop of Mainz, and of his mother. Mathilda was left as the only representative of the Ottonian house north of the Alps during Otto I's long absence in Italy in the late 960s.

This also explains why some matters which were undoubtedly of great importance in the 960s (for example Otto I's imperial coronation in 962, or the canon-law background to the founding of the archbishopric at Magdeburg in 967) are passed over in silence by Widukind: these were not things whose details it was necessary for the young princess to know, whereas it was vital that she should be fully informed about the history of the Saxons' aristocratic feuds (not least with members of the royal house), to which she devotes much attention, lest she make any errors through ignorance in handling the magnates.

Widukind's *Deeds of the Saxons*, like the work of any engaged contemporary historian, is highly problematic if it is viewed merely as a source of neutral and reliable "facts," and his work has been criticized down to the present day as "unreliable," the work of a *romancier*. Yet as a coherent attempt by a Saxon aristocrat to make historical sense of the remarkable transformation that had brought Saxons in less than two centuries from being pagans beyond the Frankish borders to being the people who gave the east Frankish kingdom its kings, emperors, and military power it deserves high praise, both for its literary merit and its intellectual level. It also provides important insights into the mores of the Saxon aristocracy of which Widukind was a part, notably its refusal to condemn rebellion against the ruler outright. According to Leyser, Widukind was conscious of the fact that "the king did not stand outside the circle of feud and revenge," something which modern historians have only slowly rediscovered in recent decades. His work was used extensively by later historians, from Thietmar of Merseburg and Frutolf of Michelsberg through the later medieval historians up to the writings of the German humanists and antiquaries, and Widukind's narrative has shaped all attempts by modern historians to retell the rise of the Ottonian dynasty.

TIMOTHY REUTER

See also Thietmar

Biography
Born Westphalia, c.925, descended from Saxon nobility. Entered Corvey monastery, on the Weser, c.940. Died Corvey, after 973.

Principal Writings
Rerum gestarum Saxonicarum libri tres (Three Books of the Deeds of the Saxons), written mid-960s; revised 973
German and Latin text in *Quellen zur Geschichte der sächsischen Kaiserzeit*, edited by Albert Bauer and Reinhold Rau, 1971, 3–183

Further Reading
Althoff, Gerd, "Widukind von Corvey: Kronzeuge und Herausforderung" (Widukind of Corvey: Key Witness and Challenge), *Frühmittelalterliche Studien* 27 (1993), 253–72

Beumann, Helmut, *Widukind von Korvei: Untersuchungen zur Geschichtsschreibung und Ideengeschichte des 10. Jahrhunderts* (Widukind of Corvey: Studies on 10th-Century Historiography and Intellectual History), Weimar: Böhlau, 1950

Beumann, Helmut, "Historiographische Konzeption und politische Ziele Widukinds von Corvey" (Widukind of Corvey's Historiographical Conception and Political Aims), in his *Wissenschaft vom Mittelalter: Ausgewählte Aufsätze*, Cologne: Böhlau, 1972

Beumann, Helmut, *Ausgewählte Aufsätze aus den Jahren 1966–1986: Festgabe zu seinem 75. Geburtstag* (Selected Articles Published 1966–1986, Presented on His 75th Birthday), edited by Jürgen Petersohn and Rodrich Schmidt, Sigmaringen: Törbecke, 1987

Brundage, James A., "Widukind of Corvey and the 'Non-Roman' Imperial Idea," *Mediaeval Studies* 22 (1960)

Hill, Boyd H., Jr., *The Rise of the First Reich: Germany in the Tenth Century*, New York: Wiley, 1969

Karpf, Ernst, *Herrscherlegitimation und Reichsbegriff in der ottonischen Geschichtsschreibung des 10. Jahrhunderts* (Legitimation of the Ruler and Conceptions of the Kingdom in 10th-Century Ottonian Historiography), Wiesbaden: Steiner, 1985

Keller, Hagen, "Widukinds Bericht über die Aachener Wahl und Krönung Ottos I." (Widukind's Account of the Election and Coronation of Otto I at Aachen), *Frühmittelalterliche Studien* 29 (1995), 390–453

Leyser, Karl, *Rule and Conflict in an Early Medieval Society: Ottonian Saxony*, London: Arnold, and Bloomington: Indiana University Press, 1979

Leyser, Karl, "Three Historians" and "Ritual, Ceremony and Gesture: Ottonian Germany" in his *Communications and Power in Medieval Europe*, vol. 1: *The Carolingian and Ottonian Centuries*, edited by Timothy Reuter, London and Rio Grande, OH: Hambledon Press, 1994

Wattenbach, Wilhelm, and Robert Holtzmann, eds., *Deutschlands Geschichtsquellen im Mittelalter: die Zeit der Sachsen und Salier* (Germany's Historical Sources of the Middle Ages: The Era of the Saxons and Salians), new edition, 3 vols., Darmstadt: Wissenschaftliche Buchgesellschaft, 1967–71

Wiebe, Robert H. 1930–

US historian

Robert Wiebe defies labeling. In a profession where historians eagerly define themselves as specialists in particular fields, he is a "generalist" in the best sense of the word. Wiebe has spent his career synthesizing ideas regarding politics, culture, organization, and community. In fact, he has joined the ranks of other prominent historians such as Richard Hofstadter, Christopher Lasch, Ernest May, and Michael Katz, who have written for a general audience and hoped to influence intellectual debate outside the bounds of academe. Wiebe's focus has been on democracy, and his works have pondered the rise, decline, and future prospects of democracy as a political institution.

Wiebe's first book, *Businessmen and Reform* (1962), argued that the Progressive era served as a transformational period between agrarian and urban America. During the time, people born on farms and in small towns with traditional rural views began a modernization that led to the first experiments in reorganizing into an industrial society. The demands for reform came largely from middle-class citizens who established a new social structure, thus leading to a redistribution of leadership and privilege. Wiebe examined the way businessmen influenced the Progressive era and were affected by it. Instead of examining individuals, Wiebe studied organized self-interest groups and businessmen as a whole.

The Search for Order (1967) is considered a classic text. In the book, Wiebe explored the rise of loose-knit "bureaucracies" and the dominance that such groups exerted over the American economy, culture, and values. The traditional community was replaced by the modern bureaucratic state, according to Wiebe. The triumph of the "new middle class" and its ideals of organized life placed the group at the front of the Progressive movement. The rise of large corporations, rapid urbanization, and widespread industrialization bewildered the middle class, which then sought security and regulation by building elaborate bureaucratic institutions. These measures were taken by the new professional and engineering elite to bring the chaotic situation under control.

Wiebe's reaction to the turbulence of the 1960s was embodied in *The Segmented Society* (1975). The Vietnam era called into question the "order" imposed by bureaucratic organizations, so he looked for other basic tenets that tied the country together. He investigated the division of society into "segments" or "units of life" defined by distinctive organizations and customs. He thought the fundamental enduring quality of America was its "segmentation," which made the country unlike Europe. While relying less on bureaucracy than previously, Wiebe retained his organizational perspective. What made the United States unique was that democracy survived in a society full of opposing groups, each with its own individual customs and traditions.

The next subject Wiebe explored was the "great transformation" of the United States from the Constitution to the eve of the Civil War. He discussed the democratization of America between the two tumultuous periods in *The Opening of American Society* (1984). Invoking the Turner thesis, he declared that the "most powerful influence in the shaping of American society was space." The relationship between space and authority contributed to the spread of democracy and led America from gentry leadership in the colonial era to the beginnings of Jeffersonian egalitarianism. Once again, Wiebe looked at how "a distinctive American society did appear, however ambiguously; a democracy did develop, however brutally; and a national expansion did occur, however costly in lives." He addressed these "not as triumphs but as challenges to our understanding."

Wiebe's latest book, *Self-Rule* (1995), was a survey tracing the history of democracy in the United States. Not only did Wiebe summarize democracy's condition, but he critiqued a vast number of social and political commentators, who usually approached the subject ahistorically. He believed that adding "an awareness of history" to critiques of democracy would "plant our feet once again on the original piece of common ground, popular self-government. Here is democracy's heartland." Wiebe called for democracy's reinvigoration through local empowerment and a wariness of central government. People also needed to be energized about politics, not just by going to the polls, but actively participating on a number of levels. Only when people care deeply about democracy, and begin to act on those feelings, will democracy flourish.

Throughout his career, Wiebe has made important contributions to the study of American history. His books, taken as a whole, have covered the entire sweep of the nation's past. His writing has been marked by incisive analysis and comprehensive interpretations. Early in his career, however, Wiebe was criticized for concentrating too heavily on organizations and bureaucracies at the expense of historical actors. More recently, like most generalists, he has been censured for being too broad. Nevertheless, historians who take on popular subjects, like Wiebe, serve an important role in current debate precisely because they think and analyze themes in historical terms. They show a larger audience that historical thinking has relevance outside academe and can serve to enlighten contemporary approaches to political thinking. In retrospect, Wiebe's central theme has been an important one: the fate of democracy in the modern world.

ROBERT P. BATCHELOR

See also United States: 19th Century; United States: 20th Century

Biography

Robert Huddleston Wiebe. Born Amarillo, Texas, 22 April 1930. Received BA, Carleton College, 1951; PhD, University of Rochester, 1957. Taught at Michigan State University, 1957–58; Columbia University 1958–60; and Northwestern University, from 1960. Married Allene Davis, 1952 (3 sons).

Principal Writings

Businessmen and Reform: A Study of the Progressive Movement, 1962

The Search for Order, 1877–1920, 1967

The Segmented Society: An Introduction to the Meaning of America, 1975

The Opening of American Society: From the Adoption of the Constitution to the Eve of Disunion, 1984

Self-Rule: A Cultural History of American Democracy, 1995

Further Reading

Cmiel, Kenneth, "Destiny and Amnesia: The Vision of Modernity in Robert Wiebe's *The Search for Order*," *Reviews in American History* 21 (1993), 352–68

Wilamovitz-Möllendorff, Ulrich von

1848–1931

German classical historian

Arguably the greatest figure in the history of classical scholarship, Wilamovitz, in his long and productive career, combined the tradition of literary analysis and textual criticism with the study of religion, art, epigraphy, prosody, and history to become the finest representative of a new comprehensive science of antiquity (*Altertumswissenschaft*). The various disciplines thus linked together were in theory on equal footing, but in practice they were held together by a single branch of study – history. In conscious opposition to the aestheticism of a previous generation of classicists, he insisted on a systematic application of the historical perspective to every subject of study, and he saw this method as the sole guarantee of elevating belle lettres, or mere esoteric scholarship, to the rank of science.

His dissatisfaction with classicism, however, did not drive him to the strong and populous camp of the positivists. For he never thought of his *Altertumswissenschaft* as a branch of, or a handmaiden to, natural science. Minute facts in themselves, which the positivists were so fond of accumulating, he considered dead matter. The ghostlike spirits of the tradition "which we evoke demand the blood of our hearts," he said. His intellectual roots connected him with the German Golden Age and, in it, with a trend of thinking outside the confines of the academy (*Fachphilosophie*), a trend started by Lessing and continued by Herder and Goethe.

His general outlook showed the influence of the nationalistic tradition represented by men such as Bismarck and Droysen. From the latter's works Wilamovitz inherited not only the underestimation of post-Periclean democracy and the political ideals of Demosthenes and Aristotle, but also the overestimation of the historical role of Alexander the Great. However, while he emphasized the necessity of an omnipotent state – an

article of faith for his contemporary Eduard Meyer – he did so mainly in his polemic against the "enemies of the state" such as the left-wing socialists and the Nietzschean anarchists. This brand of conservative nationalism derived mostly from his distrust of democracy and liberalism. His political thought is best summed up in his *Platon* (Plato, 1919).

At the close of World War I, after the destruction of the empire, his voice became more decidedly antidemocratic and antirepublican. He was convinced more than ever that only an enlightened elite could save the state. Traces of hero-worship, a mythical conception of personality – Carlyle's influence – is also detectable in his general outlook. His most imposing historical contribution was his *Aristoteles und Athen* (Aristotle and Athens, 1893). It consisted of three books, the first of which presented an analysis of Aristotle's text (*Politeia*) and the history it treats, while the remaining two books dealt with special problems; in the course of brilliant descriptions and analyses nearly everything in Athenian history seems to be worked in somewhere – a truly impressive product of *Altertumswissenschaft*.

The fact that to some extent Wilamovitz shared with the Romantics their cult of individuality and their subjectivism helps explain his strong inclination to biography on the one hand, and the unmistakable autobiographical undertones of these biographies on the other. His *Herakles* (Heracles, 1889) which he clearly intended to be his *magnum opus* (it has not been recognized as such), is a case in point. He perceived the life of Heracles, and his own life, as parallel exemplary phenomena (he saw the connection between classical Athens and 19th-century German civil society in the same light). The labors of Heracles, which none of his peers would dare to attempt, echoed Wilamovitz's wrestling with the forbidding problems of contemporary scholarship: the historical Euripides, the Homeric question, or the religion of the Greeks. In Wilamovitz's mind, Heracles achieved greatness by the distinctly Prussian ethic of hard work.

Ironically, there was someone of his own generation, a rival and a hated intellectual foe, with whom Wilamovitz shared important features, enough for a perhaps even more convincing parallel biography. This someone was Nietzsche. Their lives were connected through their education at the same illustrious Gymnasium (Schulpforta) and university (Bonn); their show of exceptional promise at an early age and their fulfillment of it even without producing a magnum opus; their aristocratic distrust of the masses, of democracy, of liberalism, and their idealization of the elite; their monk-like devotion to scholarship and the realm of ideas; and through their equally exalted devotion to an idol (Wilamovitz's to Mommsen, Nietzsche's to Wagner) followed in both cases by bitter disillusionment and hostility (the dark side of hero-worship). Wilamovitz's marriage to the daughter of Mommsen at the time when he still perceived the historian to be divine can hardly be considered a break of his monk's vow.

It is a further irony that Wilamovitz's best students (Paul Friedländer, Karl Reinhardt, Eduard Fraenkel, Wolfgang Schadewaldt, and Werner Jaeger) in their respective careers abandoned the course outlined for them by the master's method largely as a result of yielding in various degrees to the powerful influence of Nietzsche. The author of *The Birth of Tragedy* was subjected to annihilating criticism by Wilamovitz's

Zukunftsphilologie! (The Future of Philology!, 1872–73). But, as Karl Reinhardt noted, Nietzsche survived the onslaught, not indeed as a champion of research (*Erforschung*) but of exploration (*Erschliessung*). The greatness of Wilamovitz as a scholar was never questioned by even his most rebellious disciples. They were convinced, however, that the meaning and justification of the science of antiquity as their master conceived it could not be obtained within the discipline itself. Their solution was to extend *Altertumswissenschaft* in the direction of psychology, metaphysics, and philosophy.

The unquestionable and lasting merit of Wilamovitz is that he was able to breathe life into the inert data of history by letting his personality, his humanism, blend with his subject matter. His last book, *Der Glaube der Hellenen* (The Belief of the Greeks, 1931–32), is perhaps the best example of this. The data he commanded was vast, his personality forceful, and his humanism sincere. All of this enabled him to transcend the classicist view of antiquity, but he wanted to attach his name to more than just another stage in the history of scholarship. As the greatest interpreter of the Greeks' immortal achievements he wished to be a messenger of immortality, or eternity itself. But in this ambition he ran into his own limitations.

JANOS SALAMON

Biography

Friedrich Richard Ulrich von Wilamovitz-Möllendorff. Born Markowitz, Prussia, 22 December 1848. Attended school at Schulpforta; studied at the universities of Bonn and Berlin. Served in the Franco-Prussian war, 1870. Taught at universities of Greifswald, 1876–83; and Göttingen, 1883–97; chair of Greek studies, University of Berlin, 1897–1921. Married Marie Mommsen (daughter of historian Theodor Mommsen), 1878. Editor of Inscriptiones Graecae, 1902; and of the series Philologische Untersuchungen (Philological Investigations), 1880–1925. Died Berlin, 25 September 1931.

Principal Writings

Zukunftsphilologie! Eine Erwidrung auf Friedrich Nietzsches ... "Geburt der Tragödie" (The Future of Philology! An Analysis of Nietzsche's *The Birth of Tragedy*), 2 vols., 1872–73
Herakles (Heracles), 1889
Aristoteles und Athen (Aristotle and Athens), 2 vols., 1893
Platon (Plato), 1919
Geschichte der Philologie, 1921; in English as *History of Classical Scholarship*, 1982
Der Glaube der Hellenen (The Belief of the Greeks), 2 vols., 1931–32

Further Reading

Bierl, Anton, William M. Calder III, and Robert L. Fowler, eds., *The Prussian and the Poet: The Letters of Ulrich von Wilamovitz-Moellendorff to Gilbert Murray (1894–1930)*, Hildesheim: Weidmann, 1991
Calder, William M. III, *The Wilamovitz-Nietzsche Struggle: New Documents and a Reappraisal*, Berlin: Internationales Jahrbuch für die Nietzsche Forschung, 1983
Calder, William M. III, Hellmut Flascher, and Theodor Lindken, eds., *Wilamovitz nach 50 Jahren*, Darmstadt: Wissenschaftliche Buchgesellschaft, 1985
Goldsmith, Ulrich, *Wilamovitz and the "Georgekreis": New Documents*, New York: Lang, 1989
Lloyd-Jones, Hugh, Introduction, to Wilamovitz-Möllendorff, *History of Classical Scholarship*, London: Duckworth, and Baltimore: Johns Hopkins University Press, 1982
Mansfeld, Jaap, *The Wilamovitz-Nietzsche Struggle: Another New Document and Some Further Comments*, Berlin: Internationales Jahrbuch für die Nietzsche Forschung, 1986
Zelle, Carsten, *Der Abgang des Herakles: Beobachtungen zur mythologischen Figurkonstellation in Hinsicht auf Friedrich Nietzsche und Ulrich von Wilamovitz-Möllendorff* (The Passing of Herakles: Observations on Mythological Figure Grouping with Regard to Nietzsche and Wilamovitz), Berlin: Internationales Jahrbuch für die Nietzsche Forschung, 1994

William of Malmesbury c.1090–c.1143
English chronicler

William of Malmesbury was certainly the greatest English historian to emerge after Bede, and, arguably, the first of England's "professional" historians. His most famous and ambitious historical writings are the *Gesta regum Anglorum* (Deeds of the Kings of the English, c.1118–25; revised 1135–40), a history of England from the Anglo-Saxon settlements to 1120; the *Gesta pontificum Anglorum* (Deeds of the Archbishops and Bishops of the English, c.1120–25; revised 1135–40), an ecclesiastical history of England from the conversion to 1125; and the *Historia novella* (Recent History, c.1140–c.1143), a history of England from 1126 to 1142. Remarkably, his thought processes can be followed through the phases of writing and revision, for each of these major works survives in several early manuscripts, some of them autograph. The *Historia novella*, though involving certain difficulties of interpretation, is an independent and highly valued contemporary history, especially for the first seven years of king Stephen's reign; while the *Gesta pontificum* retains lasting importance because some of the written sources William used have perished, and many of the churches he described have been destroyed or much altered.

His influence on the development of medieval English historiography was important for two basic reasons: his method of inquiry laid unprecedented stress on deploying the totality of available information; and his historical writing set new standards of critical analysis and evaluation in the handling of evidence. In both respects, he fully deserves to be regarded as a leading figure of the 12th-century Renaissance, with its relentless quest for knowledge and emphasis on rational thought. As a researcher, he used not only annals, biographies, chronicles, and hagiographies, but also documentary sources in the form of letters and charters (title deeds). In addition, he was the first English historian to make systematic use of non-written materials, including topographical, architectural, and archaeological evidence. For both the *Gesta regum* and the *Gesta pontificum*, he travelled widely in England, perhaps as far north as Hexham and Carlisle, to visit most of the major monasteries and cathedrals, because he realized that only organized and intensive searches could produce the evidence required. As a writer, he was naturally influenced by earlier historiographical traditions; but he found the brief, annalistic writings of the Anglo-Saxon past unsatisfactory, and he distrusted classical models, which treated history merely as a branch of rhetoric. He thus castigated previous writers for their superficial and inaccurate reconstructions: "I grope," he wrote, "within the thick dark clouds of ignorance, making my own path, with no lantern of history to guide the way." Above all, he insisted that the historian was duty-bound "to write the truth of things without any concession to dislike or favour." He tried to distinguish between fact and fantasy, carefully collated different texts, drew attention to their inconsistencies, and sometimes dealt authoritatively with motivation and causation. He rarely employed imaginary speeches; he was cautious in using oral evidence, as can be seen from his efforts to discriminate between eyewitness reports and hearsay or gossip; and he was conscious of the risk that too much emphasis on literary embellishments might distort historical truth. Moreover, it was a mark of his historical feel that he was acutely aware of the special challenges of writing contemporary history.

All in all, William gave a considerable stimulus to English historical studies at a time when they had only marginal relevance, and in many respects his precocious grasp of the historian's craft helped to lay the foundations of modern historiography. But while his approaches broke fresh ground, his work nevertheless had obvious limitations. He was in fact far from achieving the accuracy and impartiality he aspired to. He wrote to entertain, and could not altogether resist borrowing from the inflated rhetoric of classical writers – though in later life he was increasingly self-critical and tried to concentrate more on careful scholarly presentation. He also wrote to please his patrons, notably Robert, Earl of Gloucester. As a result, the veracity of his account in the *Historia novella* of Gloucester's political maneuvers has been seriously doubted – though to reject it as wholly unhistorical is surely to overstate the case. Worse still, his recognition of the value of documents did not prevent him from occasionally tampering with the texts, or even passing off forged charters as genuine. He also wrote to give vent to his own quirks and prejudices. In particular, he displayed excessive bias against the Welsh, Scots, and Irish. He regarded them as racially inferior and "barbarous," and he bears a significant responsibility for the emergence of an imperialist "anti-Celtic" English culture – with long-range consequences for the future course of British history. It would, however, be wrong to stress his shortcomings at the expense of his overall achievement and usefulness. His output was prodigious; the more serviceable and rational frames of reference he developed were widely adopted by later medieval chroniclers; and his faults and limitations provide today's historians with invaluable insights into the mind-world of his age.

K.J. STRINGER

See also Britain: Anglo-Saxon; Britain: 1066–1485

Biography

Born Wiltshire, c.1090. Entered Malmesbury Abbey as oblate, c.1100; became scholar/monk; served as librarian; precentor, from c.1137; unsuccessful candidate for abbot, 1140. Died Malmesbury, c.1143.

Principal Writings

Gesta regum Anglorum (Deeds of the Kings of the English), written c.1118–25; revised 1135–40; translated 1815
Gesta pontificum Anglorum (Deeds of the Archbishops and Bishops of the English), c.1120–25; revised 1135–40
De antiquitate Glastoniensis ecclesiae (On the Antiquities of the Church of Glastonbury), written 1129–39

Vita Sancti Dunstani (Life of St. Dunstan), written c.1130
Historia novella (Recent History), c.1140–c.1143; translated 1815 and 1955

Further Reading

Crouch, David, "Robert, Earl of Gloucester, and the Daughter of Zelophehad," *Journal of Medieval History* 11 (1985), 227–43
Farmer, Hugh, "William of Malmesbury's Life and Works," *Journal of Ecclesiastical History* 13 (1962), 39–54
Gillingham, John, "Foundations of a Disunited Kingdom," in Alexander Grant and Keith J. Stringer, eds., *Uniting the Kingdom? The Making of British History*, London and New York: Routledge, 1995
Gransden, Antonia, "Realistic Observation in 12th-Century England," *Speculum* 47 (1972), 29–51
Gransden, Antonia, *Historical Writing in England*, vol. 1: c.550 to c.1307, London: Routledge, and Ithaca, NY: Cornell University Press, 1974
Gransden, Antonia, "Prologues in the Historiography of 12th-Century England," in Daniel Williams, ed., *England in the Twelfth Century*, Woodbridge, Suffolk: Boydell and Brewer, 1990
Hay, Denys, *Annalists and Historians: Western Historiography from the Eighth to the Eighteenth Centuries*, London: Methuen, and New York: Harper, 1977
Leedom, Joe W., "William of Malmesbury and Robert of Gloucester Reconsidered," *Albion* 6 (1974), 251–65
Patterson, Robert B., "William of Malmesbury's Robert of Gloucester: A Re-evaluation of the *Historia Novella*," *American Historical Review* 70 (1965), 983–97
Southern, R.W., "Aspects of the European Tradition of Historical Writing, 4: The Sense of the Past," *Transactions of the Royal Historical Society* 5th series, 23 (1973), 243–63
Thomson, Rodney, *William of Malmesbury*, Woodbridge, Suffolk: Boydell and Brewer, 1987

William of Tyre c.1130–1186
Historian of the Latin East

William II, archbishop of Tyre from 1175 until his death in 1186, wrote at least three works of history: an account of the Third Lateran Council of 1179, a history of the Muslim world, and a history of the crusader states in the Middle East. The last is the only one that has survived, and is regarded as an indispensable guide to the history of the crusader states in the 12th century.

William's history seems to have been incomplete on his death, and after Saladin's victory over the forces of the kingdom of Jerusalem in 1187 any message William might have intended to convey was superseded by events. Nevertheless his history enjoyed great success and was used by a wide variety of European writers. The English abbey of St. Albans possessed copies of both the history of the crusader states and the history of the Muslims, which were used by the chronicler Matthew Paris. As William's work broke off before the final disaster hit the crusader states, continuations were written to bring it up to date. A Latin continuation seems to have been known in England by 1220, and a number of continuations were composed in French.

In Latin, William's work remained inaccessible to all but the best educated. Some time in the early 13th century it was translated and partly rewritten in French, the language of secular culture. Through the French version of his work

William became the best known historian of the Latin East in the Middle Ages; it was this version that William Caxton partly translated into English and published in 1481 as *The History of Godefrey of Boloyne and of the Conquest of Jerusalem.*

William's education and fine Latin style ensured the survival of his reputation through the Reformation period, despite Reformation and Enlightenment writers' disapproval of the crusades. An edition of his Latin chronicle was published at Basel in 1549; another edition was published by J. Bongars in 1611 in his *Gesta Dei per Francos* (Deeds of God through the French). Thomas Fuller had a high opinion of his work and made great use of it in his *Historie of the Holy Warre* (1639). In his *Decline and Fall of the Roman Empire* (1776–88) Edward Gibbon remarked that William of Tyre was the only historian of the crusades who had any knowledge of classical antiquity.

A new edition of the chronicle appeared in 1844 as volume 1 of the *Recueil des historiens des croisades: historiens occidentaux* (The Collected Works of the Historians of the Crusades: Western Historians). Yet there were few critical examinations of William's work. Although it was possible to tackle certain limited problems such as William's chronology or his treatment of the Knights Templar, it was a daunting task to produce a detailed analysis of the vast chronicle as a whole. On a purely practical level, the *Recueil* edition is too large and cumbersome for easy reading; and perhaps William's scholarly reputation was too hallowed to question.

Scholarship received a welcome stimulus in 1943 with the publication of Emily Babcock and August Krey's translation, *A History of Deeds Done Beyond the Sea.* Their introduction waxes lyrical on William's virtues: his historical method was superior to any of his contemporaries; his impartiality is "scarcely less impressive than his critical skill." Ironically their translation has facilitated studies that have undermined this view of William as a historian.

As well as valuable studies on individual aspects of William's work and the man himself, his personality, life, and career, historians have set out to examine William's work as a whole, seeking unifying themes in an attempt to identify his motives in writing. While William informs his readers that he wrote out of love for his country, he also appears to have had a wider agenda. In 1973 R.H.C. Davis suggested that William was trying to convince Europeans that only the peaceful policies of the Christian settlers in the Latin East would save the crusader states; European readers enjoyed his picturesque tales but largely ignored his message. Peter Edbury and John Rowe's *William of Tyre: Historian of the Latin East* (1988) concluded that William set out both to inspire his fellow-Latins in the East and to win sympathy in Europe. He wanted to show that the rulers of the kingdom of Jerusalem were legitimate and fit to rule and that the kingdom deserved the assistance of Europeans. Yet he also questioned why this kingdom created through God's favor had suffered so many setbacks.

William's value as a historian and long-held interpretations of his work have been thoroughly reassessed. In 1973 D.W.T.C. Vessey demonstrated convincingly in his "William of Tyre and the Art of Historiography" that William was not impartial, but was a "master of propaganda and subtle suggestion." More recently, in "Propaganda and Faction in the Kingdom of Jerusalem" (1993), Peter Edbury argued that not

only has William's propaganda misled historians, but historians have read more into his account than he intended.

In 1986 R.B.C. Huygens published the first critical edition of William's history of the crusader states, the final outcome of many years of research in which he has clarified and discovered a great deal about William and his writing. At the same time interest is growing in the French versions of William's work as it becomes clear that the translator did not simply translate but also rewrote. Yet despite recent advances in scholarship, old habits die hard and historians of the crusades and the Latin East are still apt to quote William's history uncritically, even where he has been shown to be unreliable.

HELEN J. NICHOLSON

Biography

Born Jerusalem, c.1130, of a crusader family settled there. Studied from 1146 in Paris, Orléans, and Bologna, returning to Jerusalem, 1165. Canon of Acre, 1165; archdeacon of Tyre, 1167, and of Nazareth, c.1173/4; served king Amalric of Jerusalem as ambassador to Manuel I of Byzantium, 1168, and as tutor to the future Baldwin IV; appointed chancellor of the Latin kingdom of Jerusalem, 1174, then archbishop of Tyre, 1175; attended third Lateran Council, 1179. Died 29 September 1186.

Principal Writings

Chronicon (in Latin); as *A History of Deeds Done Beyond the Sea*, edited and translated by Emily Atwater Babcock and A.C. Krey, 1943
Chronique, edited by R.B.C. Huygens, 1986

Further Reading

Davis, R.H.C., "William of Tyre," in Derek Baker, ed., *Relations Between East and West in the Middle Ages*, Edinburgh: Edinburgh University Press, 1973

Edbury, Peter W., and John Gordon Rowe, "William of Tyre and the Patriarchal Election of 1180," *English Historical Review* 93 (1978), 1–25

Edbury, Peter W., and John Gordon Rowe, *William of Tyre: Historian of the Latin East*, Cambridge and New York: Cambridge University Press, 1988

Edbury, Peter W., "Propaganda and Faction in the Kingdom of Jerusalem: The Background to Hattin," in Maya Shatzmiller, ed., *Crusaders and Muslims in Twelfth Century Syria*, Leiden: Brill, 1993

Hiestand, R., "Zum Leben und zur Laufbahn Wilhelms von Tyrus," *Deutsches Archiv für Erforschung des Mittelalters* 34 (1978), 345–80

Huygens, R.B.C., "Guillaume de Tyr étudiant: un chapitre (XIX, 12) de son *Histoire* retrouvée," *Latomus* 21 (1962), 811–29

Huygens, R.B.C., "Editing William of Tyre," *Sacris Erudiri: Jaarboek voor Godsdienstwetenschappen* 27 (1984), 461–73

Krey, A.C., "William of Tyre," *Speculum* 16 (1941), 149–66

Pryor, J.M., "The 'Eracles' and William of Tyre," in Benjamin Z. Kedar, ed., *The Horns of Hattin*, Jerusalem: Yad Yzhak Ben-Zvi, and London: Variorum, 1992

Schwinges, Rainer Christoph, *Kreuzzugsideologie und Toleranz: Studien zu Wilhelm von Tyrus* (Crusade Ideology and Tolerance: Studies on William of Tyre), Stuttgart: Hiersemann, 1977

Vessey, D.W.T.C., "William of Tyre and the Art of Historiography," *Medieval Studies* 35 (1973), 433–55

Williams, Eric 1911–1981

Trinidadian historian

Eric Williams, brilliant historian and putative "father of his nation," driven and irascible, was always sure of the truth of his own convictions. He was of that generation which won independence from colonial power by hard intellect and guts of steel. His sense of history was inseparable from his vision of a Trinidad free from colonial rule and purposeful in its dignity.

The tiny island of Trinidad produced two fine historians in the mid-20th century: C.L.R. James and his star pupil, Eric Williams. Williams himself, by virtue of his schooling in a strongly anglicized educational culture, was inducted into a mentality effortlessly convinced of its own superiority and of its own decency. His intellectual and political life was charged by his determination to break from this inheritance and to discover new historical truths appropriate for a newly independent people. At school, he always claimed, "what I knew of slavery and the plantation economy came from Roman history."

Williams arrived at Oxford University in the middle of the 1930s, where he attended Vincent Harlow's imperial history seminars and where, eventually, Harlow was to supervise his thesis on slavery during the time of the Industrial Revolution. The clash between the mentality of this dispossessed black Trinidadian and the intellectual milieu of Oxford was profound. Williams consciously set out to break the entire historiographical tradition that Oxford represented.

In 1938 Williams completed his thesis. (This was the same year that James published his own *The Black Jacobins*: indeed, the two had been drawn to the same archive in Bordeaux.) Williams' thesis was published, in the United States, as *Capitalism and Slavery* in 1944. A British edition did not appear until 1964.

The principal theme of the book rested on the conviction that the rise and collapse of slavery were driven by economic forces, and had precious little to do with either iniquitous human behavior (in its formation) or with virtuous philanthropy (in its collapse). Four overriding propositions emerged. First, slavery was an economic phenomenon, and thus racism was a consequence, not a cause, of slavery. Second, Williams argued that slavery was a decisive causal factor in the making of the Industrial Revolution in Britain – and, anticipating the more philosophical insights of Frantz Fanon – he suggested at the same time that the Third World had effectively *made* Europe. Third, he attempted to demonstrate that after the wars of the American revolution, the slave economies declined in profitability. And fourth, he insisted that the abolition of slavery could be explained in terms of this declining profitability.

The challenge was formidable. Here was a thesis written in powerful, lucid prose, deeply researched, that took on an entire national historiography. It gave no quarter. For almost sixty years, Williams influenced the terms of the debate. In 1987 Cambridge University Press published the proceedings of a symposium, *British Capitalism and Caribbean Slavery: The Legacy of Eric Williams*, edited by Barbara Solow and Stanley Engerman, evidence of the continuing vitality of Williams' provocation.

After Oxford, Williams moved to the more congenial environment of Howard University in the United States. Through the 1950s his career took him into politics rather than into academic life – devoted to the same project, though by different means. He became a proponent of West Indian federation; he became a national leader; and – in 1962 – as prime minister he led Trinidad and Tobago to independence.

With the exception of his devastating, compelling and characteristically irascible *British Historians and the West Indies* (1964), Williams' historiographical concerns henceforth moved into a more popular idiom. On the very eve of his nation's independence he sat down to write his *History of the People of Trinidad and Tobago*. He began the project on 25 July 1962 and completed it (bar the index, he tells us) on 25 August. Copies reached street vendors on the morning following independence.

Williams warned that this was not a book conforming to established "scholastic canons." "The aim was to provide the people of Trinidad and Tobago on their Independence Day with a National History, as they have already been provided with a National Anthem, a National Coat of Arms, National Birds, a National Flower and a National Flag" – all, in other words, simply the product of another day's work for Trinidad's philosopher-king.

This was followed, in 1970, by a similar intervention: his *From Columbus to Castro: The History of the Caribbean*, a history which, a quarter of a century on, though lacking in many obvious respects, is still perfectly serviceable.

For a man who – for most of his life – history-writing occurred as a merely secondary, or extramural, activity, Williams' legacy is extraordinary, putting entire rafts of professionals to shame. Intellectually, there have been many advancements within the discipline of history that suggest that Williams' explanations were too simple or one-dimensional. The key thesis that has dominated his historiography – the belief that slavery produced capitalism – is contentious, to say the least, and too mechanical by half. But even so, the clarity of his history-writing – the lucid prose, the drive of his argument – contained a kind of unsettling beauty, that made his histories dazzle. Even if later generations, quite properly, find him wanting, he more than any other single individual broke the hegemony of an English, Whiggish, imperial historiography.

BILL SCHWARZ

See also British Empire; James

Biography

Eric Eustace Williams. Born Port of Spain, Trinidad, 25 September 1911, son of a postal clerk. Attended Tranquillity Boys' School; Queen's Royal College, Trinidad, 1922–31; BA, St. Catherine's College, Oxford University, 1935, PhD 1938. Taught (rising to professor) at Howard University, Washington, DC, 1939–55. Member, Caribbean Commission, from 1943; deputy chair, Caribbean Research Council, 1948–55; founder, Peoples' National Movement, 1956; chief minister, Trinidad, 1956–62 (also minister of finance); first prime minister of independent Trinidad and Tobago, 1962–81 (also foreign minister). Married 1) Elsie Ribeiro, *c*.1939 (marriage dissolved 1951; 1 son, 1 daughter); 2) Soy Moyeau, *c*.1951 (marriage dissolved 1953; 1 daughter); 3) Mayleen Mook Soong, 1957 (marriage dissolved 1958). Died St. Anne, Trinidad, 29 March 1981.

Principal Writings
Capitalism and Slavery, 1944
History of the People of Trinidad and Tobago, 1962
British Historians and the West Indies, 1964
From Columbus to Castro: The History of the Caribbean,
   1492–1969, 1970

Further Reading
Solow, Barbara, and Stanley L. Engerman, eds., *British Capitalism
   and Caribbean Slavery: The Legacy of Eric Williams*, Cambridge
   and New York: Cambridge University Press, 1987

Williams, Raymond 1921–1988

British cultural critic

In no formal sense was Raymond Williams a historian. He himself preferred the simple denomination "writer." Not that such a deliberately understated term begins to encompass the prodigious range of his literary output, which included six novels, five works of drama criticism, several more of literary criticism, studies of film, television, and communications, numerous contributions to the debates around Marxism, modernism, and postmodernism, not to mention film and television scripts and innumerable reviews. He was a thinker, an intellectual.

He was also at the heart of the transformation of British cultural studies, and British cultural history, from the aridities of 1930s vulgar Marxism to the subtleties and complexities of the 1980s. He is generally acknowledged as the seminal figure in the development of that brand of marxisante historical analysis known as "cultural materialism," and his *Marxism and Literature* (1977) contained one of the clearest expressions of this approach. Williams rejected the Marxist grand narrative of history, and the base/superstructure model on which it was founded; instead he argued for the materiality of culture and the determinance not merely of economic modes of production, but of the "the whole social process." He was fiercely critical of capitalism and its cultural impact, but argued that despite its hegemony, there existed residual and emergent cultural practices within which a challenge to capitalism might gradually be nurtured. His 1973 study *The Country and the City* can be taken as an example of his historicist approach to English literature, and the way in which he was able to deploy what in other hands might have remained quite conventional literary criticism to uncover the almost imperceptible influence of characteristic modes of seeing the world (as the town v. country dichotomy) and their ability to promote certain ways of seeing, and inhibit others.

Williams was particularly sensitive to the self-sustaining system of meanings and values that underpinned capitalist society and that, he argued, must in turn be defeated by the creation and cultivation of alternative conceptions and values. At the center of this creation of meanings was language. Not in any deterministic sense, but recognizing that in the processes by which particular languages were invested at particular times with particular meanings, certain ways of comprehending the world were encouraged, and others inhibited. The most direct expression of this concern was *Keywords* (1976), an exercise in historical semantics; but this was a characteristic mode of analysis that infused almost all of Williams' work.

Five of these *Keywords* – culture, industry, democracy, class, and art (especially culture) – had served as the primary focus of Williams' first major historical study, *Culture and Society* (1958). In this volume Williams traced the history of the idea of culture as a record of the reactions to social and economic change in, during, and after the Industrial Revolution in Britain. Analyzing the writings of social commentators from Coleridge to Orwell, he identified a tradition of social criticism that opposed the mechanical spirit of industrial society with calls for the renewal of culture. In doing so, he demonstrated that the most-cited text of this criticism, Matthew Arnold's *Culture and Anarchy*, derived from a line of criticism stretching back through Carlyle to the Romantics. He further established that the exclusive view of culture embodied in this tradition was expanded in the 20th century, and the central problem of civilization reformulated: concern for the defence of culture against industrialism and democracy was superseded by concern for the extension of culture from an elite to the people generally.

As Williams recognized, this was above all a problem of communication, a problem posed in acute form by the rise of "mass-communication." The concern lay at the heart of Williams' second major work of historical interpretation, *The Long Revolution* (1961). The "long revolution" was Williams' description of the cultural change, and especially the extension of learning, literacy, and forms of advanced communication to all groups in society, that he saw as concomitant to the political and industrial revolutions which together engrossed most of the attention of historians. Williams' study began with four seminal chapters for the framing of subsequent cultural history; these developed his working definition of culture as a "way of life" and an associated "structure of feeling." Its heart consisted of a series of historical studies of the growth of education, the emergence of the reading public, the rise of the press, the growth of standard English, and social histories of English writers and dramatic forms. In Williams' hands these histories traced the origins of a fragmented culture, the constructions of "cultured elites" and "degraded masses."

Williams' contributions to historical writing lay not in primary research, notwithstanding the close analysis of literary texts that marked *Culture and Society* and *The Country and the City*. Even *The Long Revolution*, the most "historical" of his works, is not an exercise in research, but in interpretation. The significance of Williams' work was that it lay down the foundations of modern cultural history, concerned not just with individual elements of "culture," but in the complex inter-relations between modes of life and modes of economic and political action. Williams' work has been surprisingly neglected by cultural historians. Nevertheless, cultural history has become, as he said it must, "more than the sum of the particular histories, for it is with the relations between them, the particular forms of the whole organization, that it is especially concerned."

MARTIN HEWITT

See also Cultural; Ecology; Jones, G.; Leisure; Literature; Media

Biography
Raymond Henry Williams. Born Pandy, near Abergavenny, Wales, 31 August 1921, son of a railway signalman. Educated at Abergavenny Grammar School; entered Trinity College, Cambridge,

1939, BA 1946. Served, ending as captain, 21st Anti-Tank Regiment, Guards Armoured Division, 1941–46. Staff tutor in literature, Extra-Mural Department based in East Sussex, Oxford University, 1946–61; fellow, Jesus College, Cambridge, 1961–88; university reader in drama, Cambridge University, 1967–74, professor, 1974–83. Married Joyce Mary Dalling, 1942 (2 sons, 1 daughter). Died Saffron Walden, 26 January 1988.

Principal Writings

Culture and Society, 1780–1950, 1958
The Long Revolution, 1961; revised 1966
Communications, 1962; revised 1966
The Country and the City, 1973
Keywords: A Vocabulary of Culture and Society, 1976; revised 1983
Marxism and Literature, 1977
Problems in Materialism and Culture: Selcted Essays, 1980
Writing in Society, 1983
Resources of Hope: Culture, Democracy, Socialism, 1989

Further Reading

Eagleton, Terry, "Resources for a Journey of Hope: The Significance of Raymond Williams," *New Left Review* 168 (March–April 1988), 3–11
Eagleton, Terry, *Raymond Williams: Critical Perspectives*, Cambridge: Polity Press, and Boston: Northeastern University Press, 1989
Eldridge, John Eric Thomas, *Raymond Williams: Making Connections*, London and New York: Routledge, 1994
Gorak, Jan, *The Alien Mind of Raymond Williams*, Columbia: University of Missouri Press, 1988
Inglis, Fred, *Raymond Williams*, London and New York: Routledge, 1995
Johnson, Lesley, *The Cultural Critics: From Matthew Arnold to Raymond Williams*, London and Boston: Routledge, 1979
O'Connor, Alan, *Raymond Williams: Writing, Culture and Politics*, Oxford and New York: Blackwell, 1989
Pinkney, Tony, *Raymond Williams*, Bridgend, Wales: Seren, and Chester Springs, PA: Dufour, 1991
Ward, John Powell, *Raymond Williams*, Cardiff: University of Wales Press, 1981

Williams, William Appleman 1921–1990

US diplomatic and intellectual historian

The most influential American historian since Frederick Jackson Turner and Charles A. Beard, William Appleman Williams was a widely read scholar, an extremely productive mentor to scholars of foreign policy, and a figure of central importance to historians of the American West. Often acknowledged as the father of diplomatic "revisionism," he placed expansionism at the center of American history and the corporate state as the consequence of this development. A political rebel who drew on his own experience as a former naval commander to explore the *mentalité* of the elite, Williams wrapped his critical and anti-imperial studies in the flag of progressive patriotism. The Vietnam War and associated disillusionment with government made him (with Herbert Marcuse) perhaps the most important American intellectual in an era of crucial change in historical scholarship.

Williams' intellectual genealogy can readily be found in the "Wisconsin school" of Progressive historians. Tracing their roots in turn back to Wisconsin native Frederick Jackson Turner and the egalitarian spirit of "Fighting Bob" LaFollette, these historians privileged social and economic history over intellectual history (long considered the domain of the Ivy League), collected and delved into the common records of state historical agencies, and insisted on the importance of the westward movement for American uniqueness. As a group, they also shared the widespread popular revulsion at World War I, and nurtured a mounting suspicion of the leviathan national state as an agency for imperial aims.

Following Charles Beard's political legacy and the scholarly work of diplomatic historian Fred Harvey Harrington, Williams wrote as his first book *American–Russian Relations, 1781–1947* (1952), a brisk revisionist account of US actions. As in his controversial essays for the *Nation* magazine during the 1950s, Williams stressed that US aims of international economic expansion and of blocking potential competitors had remained largely stable over time, and had been in place long before the Russian Revolution. Williams' book, received by many scholars as a welcome "realist" antidote to Cold War rhetoric, enjoyed a limited circulation, although two subsequent volumes of diplomatic documents and historical studies by other writers, edited and introduced by Williams, were widely used in foreign affairs history courses of the later 1950s and 1960s.

Williams' *The Tragedy of American Diplomacy*, published in 1959 with several significantly revised later editions, had, by contrast, an explosive effect among both scholars and most careful observers of foreign affairs. Just as "consensus" history had begun to fade and civil rights events stirred academic liberalism, Williams argued for a distinctly left-wing view of consensus. Americans had failed in foreign policy, even in their own terms, he argued, because their successful expansionism had blinded them to wider realities. On the basis of this book, Williams was invited by Adolph Berle into the Kennedy State Department (he politely declined), and on the basis of rumors of a volume to follow, called for questioning by Cold Warriors on the House Committee on un-American Activities.

The Contours of American History (1961) lived up to its advanced billing. A sweeping view of US history at large, it began with the aims of mercantilism and the rise of an semi-independent mercantilist colony demanding its own right to empire. In Williams' view, the Founding Fathers had foreseen an ever-expanding empire as the only means to avoid the internal crises that European societies perennially faced. They did not foresee the human costs of mass cupidity set loose by laissez-faire frontiersmen such as Andrew Jackson or the ways in which even an antislavery crusade could be fought in alliance with the mighty railroad corporations so as to accelerate the expansion of empire. Neither radicals nor conservatives (with the possible exception of Henry Adams, one of Williams' favorites) had taken the measure of empire a century after the Constitution, and the ways that the immense tragedy of the next century had already been set into motion.

Traditionalists of the center and the right, such as Arthur Schlesinger, Jr., and Oscar Handlin, met Williams's work with great hostility. For the antiwar generation of graduate students (not only in history, but other fields as well), on the contrary, his work quickly became a touchstone of scholarly acuity and political idealism. Williams had explained, to their satisfaction at any rate, the sources of the national crisis of conscience experienced over Vietnam. By 1970–72 *Tragedy* became one of the most widely-read books of any kind on inflamed American campuses.

Even before the widening of the war, however, Williams had also set into motion the scholarship that would long outlast his personal study. For a decade from the later 1950s, when he returned to Madison, he trained more than forty graduate students and taught thousands of undergraduates. Among those who counted themselves students or devotees were Gar Alperowitz, Walter LaFeber, Lloyd Gardner, Thomas McCormick, and a half-dozen others (including scholarly popularists such as Saul Landau) who with him drastically reshaped diplomatic history. Indeed, it was often said later that every study after *Tragedy* and *Contours* was in some sense an attempt to deal with the "revisionist" thesis that Williams proposed and that others detailed so closely with regard to US dealings in Asia, Africa, and Latin America. Japanese and German historians applied his lessons to their own nations, with much similar "revisionist" effect. Moreover, as noted scholars of US westward movements acknowledged in later decades, he had successfully turned the familiar themes of democratic expansionism upside-down. In the work of John Mack Faragher, Patricia Limerick and others, the continuously moving frontier of contest and conquest contained the undoing of egalitarian hopes rather than their realization.

None of Williams' subsequent books proved nearly so influential, although a small work, *Some Presidents* (1972) had wide circulation as a series of essays originally published in the *New York Review of Books*. His *Empire as a Way of Life* (1980) was excerpted in the *Nation* magazine, and distributed to delegates at the Democratic convention of that year. A last, philosophical-minded summation of themes, it reached print as Williams became president of the Organization of American Historians.

This estimable honor ironically placed Williams as the representative of a scholarly generation younger than himself, writing history quite unlike that which he had undertaken – more social, more interested in the lower classes, women, and nonwhites than in the upper-class *mentalité* of Williams' favorite characters. His spirited attempts to create a national fund for historians (especially the underemployed women and nonwhites), and to open or preserve security files of the FBI and State Department from secrecy and destruction, were only partly successful. But in these as many other ways, he had left an indelible stamp on the writing of US history.

PAUL BUHLE

See also United States: 19th Century; United States: 20th Century; United States: Historical Writing, 20th Century

Biography

Born Atlantic, Iowa, 12 June 1921. Attended public schools; Kemper Military Academy; US Naval Academy, BS 1944; University of Wisconsin, MA 1948, PhD 1950. Served as commander of landing vessel in the Pacific during World War II: suffered serious spinal injury, 1945. Active in the civil rights movement in Texas, 1946. Taught at Washington and Jefferson College, 1950–51; Ohio State University, 1951–52; University of Oregon, 1952–57; University of Wisconsin, 1957–68; and Oregon State University, 1968–85. Frequent speaker against Vietnam War and other US interventions. Columnist, Portland *Oregonian*, 1980s. Married. Died Newport, Oregon, 5 March 1990.

Principal Writings

American–Russian Relations, 1781–1947, 1952
Editor, *The Shaping of American Diplomacy, 1750–1955*, 2 vols., 1956; revised 1972
The Tragedy of American Diplomacy, 1959; revised 1972
The Contours of American History, 1961; new edition, 1989
The United States, Cuba, and Castro, 1962
The Great Evasion: An Essay on the Contemporary Relevance of Karl Marx and on the Wisdom of Admitting the Heretic into the Dialogue about America's Future, 1964
The Roots of the Modern American Empire: A Study of the Growth and Shaping of Social Consciousness in a Marketplace Society, 1969
Some Presidents: Wilson to Nixon, 1972
History as a Way of Learning, 1974
Empire as a Way of Life: An Essay on the Causes and Character of America's Present Predicament along with a Few Thoughts about an Alternative, 1980
A William Appleman Williams Reader: Selections from His Major Historical Writings, 1992

Further Reading

Abelove, Henry *et al.*, eds., *Visions of History*, by MARHO: The Radical Historians Organisation, Manchester: Manchester University Press, and New York: Pantheon, 1983
Buhle, Paul, ed., *History and the New Left: Madison, Wisconsin, 1950–1970*, Philadelphia: Temple University Press, 1990
Buhle, Paul, and Edward Rice-Maximin, *William Appleman Williams: The Tragedy of Empire*, New York: Routledge, 1995
Gardner, Lloyd C., ed., *Redefining the Past: Essays in Diplomatic History in Honor of William Appleman Williams*, Corvallis: Oregon State University Press, 1986
Noble, David W., *The End of American History*, Minneapolis: University of Minnesota Press, 1985
Said, Edward W., *Culture and Imperialism*, New York: Knopf, and London: Chatto and Windus, 1993

Wilson, Charles H. 1914–1991

British economic historian

Respected for a breadth of historical knowledge that transcended specialty and period, Charles H. Wilson established business history in Britain with his multivolume work, *The History of Unilever* (1954–68). Other studies explored Anglo-Dutch relations in the 16th and 17th centuries, immigration history, mercantilism, and the Industrial Revolution. He sought to analyze long-term economic trends in his work without losing sight of the impact of the individual. He highlighted this point in his inaugural lecture at Cambridge University, published as *History in Special and in General* (1964): "To reduce great historic dramas to graphs and curves, to purge them of human values, is merely to substitute one kind of myopia for another. It is to deny the basic principle that history is a true counterpoint between man and his circumstances."

Wilson studied at Jesus College, Cambridge, where he came under the influence of Bernard Manning, Kenneth Pickthorn, and Edward Welbourne. In his first research project, *Anglo-Dutch Commerce and Finance in the Eighteenth Century* (1941), he became the first scholar to examine the growth of Dutch lending to England. He demonstrated how the shift from domestic investment to international finance underwrote England's wars while undermining Amsterdam's economic position. The war interrupted his professional career with a stint at the Admiralty, which may have given him the insight into the workings of institutions that made his writings so distinctive. A slim book, *Holland and Britain* (1946), with chapters on law and culture as well as economics, reinforced his status as a scholar of Anglo-Dutch relations.

The opportunity that changed his career came shortly after the war, when he had taken up a University Lectureship in history at Cambridge. Through the intercession of G.N. Clark, Wilson was invited to write the history of the Anglo-Dutch business group, Unilever. The result was a lengthy case study that unraveled a highly complicated story. *The History of Unilever* focused first on the development of England's Lever Brothers company, which dominated the soap market in England and on the Continent by the early 20th century, and then took up the Margarine Unie in the Netherlands, which similarly controlled a large part of Europe's edible fats market. Wilson then described the merger of the companies in 1929, and carried the narrative through the years of World War II. A third volume traced the multinational corporation's adaptation to the postwar environment. One of the first scholarly studies of a consumer-oriented business, *The History of Unilever* broke into a field dominated by histories of banks and heavy industries. In this, as in all his subsequent works, Wilson spotlighted the role of the individual entrepreneur in business development, which also allowed him to show how frequently corporate development was no rational, orderly affair. For example, in examining the role played by advertising in the growth of business in a way no previous business historian had, he demonstrated that business leaders were slow to appreciate the use of advertising to create demand for their products, considering it merely a means of attracting the attention of existing consumers.

Wilson added to his reputation with accounts of a range of businesses, from an engineering company, D. Napier, to the bookseller W.H. Smith. Nor were his interests limited to company case studies. Wilson also wrote provocative work on the relationship of state finance and national power, on mercantilism, on Anglo-Dutch relations in the 16th and 17th centuries, and on the British Industrial Revolution.

Wilson's work in business history inspired not only W.J. Reader's own work on Imperial Chemical Industries, Metal Box, Bowater, and the Weiter Group, but also Peter Mathias' research on the English brewing industry and on retailing in the food trades, plus Ronald Ferrier's work on British Petroleum, and many others.

Wilson held the chair of modern history at Cambridge from 1965 until 1979, and spent five years at the newly formed European University Institute in Florence. The latter appointment reflected the truly international insight brought to historical scholarship by a man whose interests ranged from the role of enterprise in the creation of the Dutch state in the 17th century through its place in the development of industry in England and to its continuing function in the modern multinational corporation.

MARYBETH CARLSON

Biography

Charles Henry Wilson. Born 16 April 1914. Attended De Aston Grammar School, Lincolnshire; Jesus College, Cambridge; then studied in the Netherlands and Germany, 1937–38. Served in Royal Naval Volunteer Reserve and in the Admiralty, 1940–45. Taught (rising to professor), at Cambridge University, 1945–79; and at European University Institute, Florence, 1976–79, 1980–81. Fellow of Jesus College, Cambridge, 1938–91. Married 1) Angela Marshman, 1939 (marriage dissolved 1972; 1 daughter); 2) Alena Kouril, 1972. Died Sydney, Australia, 1 August 1991.

Principal Writings

Anglo-Dutch Commerce and Finance in the Eighteenth Century, 1941
Holland and Britain, 1946
The History of Unilever: A Study in Economic Growth and Social Change, 3 vols., 1954–68
Profit and Power: A Study of England and the Dutch Wars, 1957
With William J. Reader, *Men and Machines: A History of D. Napier and Sons, Ltd., Engineers, 1809–1958*, 1958
History in Special and in General: An Inaugural Lecture, 1964
England's Apprenticeship, 1603–1763, 1965
The Dutch Republic and the Civilisation of the Seventeenth Century, 1968
Queen Elizabeth and the Revolt of the Netherlands, 1970
The Transformation of Europe, 1558–1648, 1976
First with the News: The History of W.H. Smith, 1792–1972, 1985

Further Reading

Coleman, D.C., and Peter Mathias, eds, *Enterprise and History: Essays in Honour of Charles Wilson*, Cambridge and New York: Cambridge University Press, 1984
Mathias, Peter, "Charles Wilson, 1914–1991: A Retrospect for an Historian," *Journal of European Economic History* 22 (1993), 143–54

Winckelmann, J.J. 1717–1768

German art historian

J.J. Winckelmann is often called the "Father of Art History." He is not the only one to whom this title is given, but his claim to it is considerable – he was the first to use the phrase "History of Art" as the title of a monumental work. Previous works were largely compilations of artworks or biographies of artists; Winckelmann was the first to attempt to perceive and categorize the historical development of art.

Winckelmann's love of Greco-Roman culture led him to abandon his work as a schoolteacher and librarian to move in 1755 from his native Germany to Rome, where he had access to the vast Italian collections of Greco-Roman art and the excavations of Pompeii and Herculaneum. His major work, *Geschichte der Kunst des Altertums* (1764; *The History of Ancient Art*, 1849–73), was a vast undertaking. The work is divided into separate volumes. The first was theoretical, dealing with the diversity of art in the ancient world. Winckelmann briefly presented the essential aspects of the art of the Egyptians, Phoenicians, Persians, Etruscans, Greeks, and Romans, and considered how such diversity occurred. He identified Greek art as being superior, and discusses the probable causes, examining all aspects of Greek society and civilization in the process. The second volume focused on Greek art specifically, and applied his theories within a concrete framework. In the same way that he held Greek art to be superior to the art of other ancient cultures, he promoted the art of the classical period of the 5th and 4th centuries BCE as the most perfect manifestation of Greek artistic achievement. Through careful analysis based as much as possible on the surviving ancient works themselves, he traced the development, culmination, and decline of the Greek style of art, identifying, in turn, various styles within it that help define its chronological evolution: the archaic style, the sublime style (early classical), the beautiful style (classical), and the imitative style (Hellenistic and Roman decline). Winckelmann was the first to establish such periodization. In fact, he was the first to use the term "style" in its modern sense.

The model of origin-growth-climax-decline imbedded itself deeply into art historical method. It was seen as a paradigm that repeated itself, and could, for instance, be clearly seen in the art of the Renaissance as well. An extension of this idea is that all of art history is similarly cyclical; classical Greek art provided the ideal, and periods that evoke its principles are the periods of climax (the Italian Renaissance, 18th- and 19th-century Neoclassicism), while the periods that reject it (the Middle Ages, the Baroque) are periods of decline. Winckelmann consciously supported the development of Neoclassicism in his own time. Ironically, his focus on the ideal also had considerable significance to the Romantic movement in that he sanctioned (even celebrated) subjective responses to art.

Winckelmann's idealization of the classical style of the 5th and 4th centuries BCE is now widely rejected within the study of ancient Greek art, although it remained at the core of "classical" studies for over a century; the periods/styles that he identified within Greek art have been retained in a general sense, but have been refined and stripped of his valuations; and most of the conclusions that he drew from his analysis of Greek art have long since been superseded. Nevertheless, the structure that Winckelmann developed remains significant. His focus on analysis of original artworks and his attempts to combine that information with ancient writings about art and a thorough understanding of the Greek culture as a whole had profound influence on the way that the fledgling discipline of art history developed. Even his championship of the classical ideal signified an attempt to infuse aesthetics into a historical structure on the same grounds as in other cultural considerations. His work stands as the first systematic approach to a history of art, one upon which – whether in imitation or reaction – all others have been built.

JULIET GRAVER ISTRABADI

See also Archaeology; Art

Biography

Johann Joachim Winckelmann. Born Stendal, in Prussian Saxony, 9 December 1717, son of a cobbler. Studied classical languages at a Berlin Gymnasium; Protestant theology, University of Halle, 1738; and medicine, University of Jena, 1741–42. Private tutor and teacher, Seehausen, 1743–48; librarian of Count Heinrich von Bünau, from 1748; converted to Catholicism, 1755; moved to Rome where he worked at the prefecture of antiquities, the Vatican scrittore, and as librarian to Cardinal Albani. Murdered in Trieste, 8 June 1768.

Principal Writings

Gedanken über die Nachahmung der griechischen Werke in der Malerei und Bildhauerkunst, 1755; in English as *Reflections on the Imitation of Greek works in Painting and Sculpture*, 1765

Sendschreiben über die herkulanischen Entdeckungen (Letters on the Herculaneum Discoveries), 1762

Geschichte der Kunst des Altertums, 1764; in English as *The History of Ancient Art*, 4 vols., 1849–73

Monumenti antichi inediti, 2 vols., 1767

Sämtliche Werke (Collected Works), 12 vols., 1825–29

Further Reading

Häsler, Berthold, ed., *Beiträge zu einem neuen Winckelmannbild* (Essays on a New Perspective on Winckelmann), Berlin: Akademie, 1973

Hatfield, Henry Caraway, *Winckelmann and His German Critics, 1755–1781: A Prelude to the Classical Age*, New York: Kings Crown Press, 1943

Justi, Carl, *Winckelmann und seine Zeitgenossen* (Winckelmann and His Contemporaries), 3 vols., Leipzig: Vogel, 1866–72

Leppmann, Wolfgang, *Winckelmann*, New York: Knopf, 1970

Potts, Alex, *Flesh and the Ideal: Winckelmann and the Origins of Art History*, New Haven: Yale University Press, 1994

Women's History: Africa

The history of African women has emerged since 1970 as a vibrant and steadily expanding area of research and study, motivated, as with other areas of women's history, by the development of the international feminist movement. African women's history also paralleled the expansion of African history following World War II, as scholars inside and outside of Africa began to focus on historical transformations on the African continent. This essay will consider sub-Saharan Africa only, following the practice of African studies in general which treats North Africa as a separate entity culturally and historically.

Before the 1970s there was little available research on African women's history. Information on women in Africa was more often found in anthropological and ethnographic studies. This focus has continued in the preponderance of research on African women appearing in development studies rather than history *per se*. The first publications in the 1970s dealt with women and economic change and with women as political activists. By the mid-1980s a number of important extended studies began to appear. Nina Mba's *Nigerian Women Mobilized* (1982), Claire C. Robertson's *Sharing the Same Bowl* (1984), and Margaret Strobel's *Muslim Women in Mombasa* (1979) still primarily focused on women's public lives. However, with Kristin Mann's *Marrying Well* (1985) and Luise White's *The Comforts of Home* (1990), studies of family and sexuality were also beginning to appear. Only in the 1990s did a substantial number of monographs on specific topics begin to appear, although the bulk of new research continues to be found in journal and anthology articles.

Earlier eras were initially neglected, in part a result of the difficulty in obtaining historical sources that dealt with women before the 19th century. Because many African communities were decentralized and nonliterate, written materials on earlier eras, especially from an African woman's perspective, were scarce. While some historians have turned to women's life histories and the use of oral testimony to fill lacunae in published sources, as Susan Geiger has noted, this has limitations in researching earlier periods. Topics that have useful source materials included such elite women as Queen Nzinga, a 16th-century ruler in what became Angola and wealthy traders along the West African coast. Source availability also influenced one of the most studied 19th-century topics: slave women, which was important, but did not represent the experience of most women. As Robertson and Klein's *Women and Slavery in Africa* (1983) demonstrated, slaves within Africa were more likely to be women, a reflection of their productive and reproductive contributions to their communities. With creative use of sources, scholars have retrieved further important information on women in the 19th century: Elizabeth Eldredge on women's work in Lesotho, Nakanyike Musisi on elite women in Buganda, Marcia Wright on women's vulnerability in Central Africa, Edward Alpers on Swahili women's spirit possession cults, Agnes Aidoo on Asante queen mothers' political influence, and Jean Boyd and Murray Last on religious women in West Africa.

Turning to more unusual sources has enabled historians to retrieve further details about women's experiences. Leroy Vail and Landeg White analyzed Tumbuka women's songs from Malawi to suggest a new periodization of history. For those women the late 19th century was marked by a loss of power resulting from a shift away from matrilineal descent patterns, an issue ignored in the conventional regional histories of Ngoni raids. Colleen Kriger's analysis of weaving techniques found in 19th-century fabrics from Sokoto in West Africa suggests that women's weaving was more varied, had a higher value, was more organized, and was better known than earlier studies indicated. African women's history has been taken further into the past by scholars such as Christine Ahmed and David L. Schoenbrun who use historical linguistics to examine changing patterns in women's roles as wives and mothers within pastoralist and agricultural communities.

Re-examining familiar issues from a woman's perspective has altered African history more generally. For example, studies of women's work during the colonial period often showed how they had lost power and economic autonomy with the arrival of cash crops and their exclusion from the global marketplace, in contrast to men who were more likely to benefit from these economic changes. This research also exhibits a common tension between women as victims and women as powerful agents within their communities, as female agricultural innovations were described by Margaret Jean Hay and Maud Shimwaayi Muntemba as essential to community survival, and according to Cora Ann Presley, as women became politically active because of their experiences. Others such as Jane L. Parpart have investigated women's changing position in arenas formerly seen as exclusively male, such as mining compounds. Studies of political activism changed previously accepted ideas of women's passivity in the face of such changes. Judith Van Allen demonstrated in an influential article that women drew on precolonial practices to make clear their displeasure with the colonial powers. Susan Geiger's study of the leadership of illiterate Muslim women in Dar es Salaam fundamentally changed the view that the Tanzanian anticolonial movement was led solely by men who were products of Christian mission education. Analysis by Martin Chanock of the development of legal systems under colonialism has shown that women were at a disadvantage as "customary" laws were established based on male testimony that gave men, especially elite men, advantages over women in issues of marriage and divorce.

As women were primarily responsible for agricultural labor, studies of the formal sector of the economy eclipsed women's actual economic activity. In Africa, studying women's economic contributions meant paying attention to rural agricultural work as well the urban efforts of market vendors, both sectors previously neglected in African labor history. Studies of women and religion have included work by Bennetta Jules-Rosette on the role of women in developing local churches that were often offshoots of larger denominations, and by Iris Berger on the sources of female spiritual power in local religions.

Although an 1987 overview by Claire Robertson suggested that African women's history had shifted to include a more economic perspective, or as Margaret Jean Hay argued, had shifted from the study of elites to the study of more ordinary women, the most notable change has been an increasing level of analysis. The earliest works, with some exceptions, tended to be descriptive, as scholars worked to prove that African women were there, and had made an impact on their societies. More recently studies have provided much more nuanced descriptions of the complexities of women's lives, of the changes over time, and of local and outsider ideologies about women in Africa. Cheryl Johnson did not simply describe the market women's associations in Lagos, but discussed why three different organizations formed, serving different groups of women.

A recent re-analysis of the role of the adolescent girl Nongqawuse in the Xhosa cattle-killing of the 1870s, has demonstrated that taking women's testimony seriously and centering women's experience and expression of history can fundamentally change the explanation for an event. Bradford convincingly suggests that issues of changing sexuality and possibly abuse or incest were of central importance to understanding people's motivations, and conventional reliance on broader economic and political reasons for the upheaval is not completely satisfactory.

Among the issues continuing to appear in writings on African women's history are those of representation (who is writing this history and for what audience), sources and methodology, and periodization, as well as the usual areas of productive work, family life, and public activities such as politics and religion. The absence of African women historians is frequently commented on, as there are regrettably few who publish regularly (Kanogo, Musisi, and Awe are among them). Often work by African scholars is not published, or is available only in African publications, which can be difficult to obtain in Europe and North America. Recently work has expanded on gender, masculinity, and ideologies, as in Timothy Burke's examination of ideas about consumption and cleanliness in Zimbabwe and as noted in Nancy Rose Hunt's overview of gender in Africa, which refers to a number of important French studies. The history of women in precolonial Africa continues to be a weak point, while the history of the colonial era (c.1880 to the 1960s for most of the continent) has shifted from examining the impact of colonialism on women (assessed as mostly negative) to investigating African communities and history from their own perspective, with an emphasis on African women's agency and efforts to present African women's own voices in the work of Jean Allman, Jane Turrittin, and in collections edited by Karen Hansen and Kathleen Sheldon. Even studies of European and American women travelers, government agents, researchers, and missionaries assess their position within their own societies as well as their interaction with African communities as can be seen in Margaret Strobel's *European Women and the Second British Empire* (1991). These approaches both re-examine territory already covered and open new topics while infusing the research with the voices of African women as both subjects and scholars, indicating the direction African women's history will take in the near future.

KATHLEEN SHELDON

See also Coquery-Vidrovitch

Further Reading

Ahmed, Christine Choi, *Before Eve Was Eve: 2200 Years of Gendered History in East-Central Africa*, dissertation, University of California, Los Angeles, 1996

Aidoo, Agnes, "Asante Queen Mothers in Government and Politics in the Nineteenth Century," in Filomina Chioma Steady, ed., *The Black Woman Cross-Culturally*, Cambridge, MA: Shenkman, 1981

Allman, Jean, "Rounding Up Spinsters: Gender Chaos and Unmarried Women in Colonial Asante," *Journal of African History* 37 (1996), 195–214

Alpers, Edward A., "'Ordinary Household Chores': Ritual and Power in a Nineteenth-Century Swahili Women's Spirit Possession Cult," *International Journal of African Historical Studies* 17 (1984), 677–702

Awe, Bolanle, ed., *Nigerian Women in Historical Perspective*, Ibadan: Sankore, 1992

Berger, Iris, "Fertility as Power," in David M. Johnson and Douglas H. Anderson, eds., *Revealing Prophets: Prophecy in Eastern African History*, London: Currey, and Athens: Ohio University Press, 1995

Boyd, Jean, and Murray Last, "The Role of Women as 'Agents Religieux' in Sokoto," *Canadian Journal of African Studies* 19 (1985), 283–300

Bradford, Helen, "Women, Gender, and Colonialism: Rethinking the History of the British Cape Colony and its Frontier Zones, c.1806–70," *Journal of African History* 37 (1996), 351–70

Brooks, George, Jr., "The *Signares* of Saint-Louis and Gorée: Women Entrepreneurs of Eighteenth-Century Senegal," in Nancy J. Hafkin and Edna G. Bay, ed., *Women in Africa: Studies in Social and Economic Change*, Stanford, CA: Stanford University Press, 1976

Burke, Timothy, *Lifebuoy Men, Lux Women: Commodification, Consumption, and Cleanliness in Modern Zimbabwe*, Durham, NC: Duke University Press, and Leicester: Leicester University Press, 1996

Chanock, Martin, "Making Customary Law: Men, Women, and Courts in Colonial Northern Rhodesia," in Margaret Jean Hay and Marcia Wright, eds., *African Women and the Law: Historical Perspectives*, Boston: African Studies Center, Boston University, 1982

Eldredge, Elizabeth A., "Women in Production: The Economic Role of Women in Nineteenth-Century Lesotho," *Signs* 16 (1991), 707–31

Geiger, Susan, "Women's Life Histories: Method and Content," *Signs* 11 (1986), 334–51

Geiger, Susan, "Women in Nationalist Struggle: TANU Activists in Dar es Salaam," *International Journal of African Historical Studies* 20 (1987), 1–26

Geiger, Susan, "Tanganyikan Nationalism as 'Women's Work': Life Histories, Collective Biography, and Changing Historiography," *Journal of African History* 37 (1996), 465–78

Hafkin, Nancy J., and Edna G. Bay, ed., *Women in Africa: Studies in Social and Economic Change*, Stanford, CA: Stanford University Press, 1976

Hansen, Karen Tranberg, ed., *African Encounters with Domesticity*, New Brunswick, NJ: Rutgers University Press, 1992

Hay, Margaret Jean, "Queens, Prostitutes and Peasants: Historical Perspectives on African Women, 1971–1986," *Canadian Journal of African Studies* 22 (1988), 431–47

Hunt, Nancy Rose, "Placing African Women's History and Locating Gender," *Social History* 14 (1989), 353–79

Hunt, Nancy Rose, "Introduction," special issue on "Gendered Colonialism in African History," *Gender and History* 8 (1996), 323–337

Johnson, Cheryl, "Class and Gender: A Consideration of Yoruba Women during the Colonial Period," in Claire C. Robertson and Iris Berger, eds., *Women and Class in Africa*, New York: Holmes and Meier, and London: Africana, 1986

Jules-Rosette, Bennetta, ed., *The New Religions of Africa: Priests and Priestesses in Contemporary Cults and Churches*, Norwood, NJ: Ablex, 1979

Kanogo, Tabitha, "Kikuyu Women and the Politics of Protest: Mau Mau," in Sharon Macdonald, Pat Holden, and Shirley Ardener, eds., *Images of Women in Peace and War: Cross-Cultural and Historical Perspectives*, Basingstoke: Macmillan, 1987; Madison: University of Wisconsin Press, 1988

Kriger, Colleen, "Textile Production and Gender in the Sokoto Caliphate," *Journal of African History* 34 (1993), 361–401

Mann, Kristin, *Marrying Well: Marriage, Status, and Social Change among the Educated Elite in Colonial Lagos*, Cambridge and New York: Cambridge University Press, 1985

Mba, Nina Emma, *Nigerian Women Mobilized: Women's Political Activity in Southern Nigeria, 1900–1965*, Berkeley: Institute of International Studies, University of California, 1982

Miller, Joseph C., "Nzinga of Matamba in a New Perspective," *Journal of African History* 16 (1975), 201–16

Muntemba, Maud Shimwaayi, "Women and Agricultural Change in the Railway Region of Zambia: Dispossession and Counterstrategies, 1930–1970," in Edna G. Bay, ed., *Women and Work in Africa*, Boulder, CO: Westview Press, 1982

Musisi, Nakanyike B., "Women, 'Elite Polygyny,' and Buganda State Formation," *Signs* 16 (1991), 757–86

Parpart, Jane L., "Sexuality and Power on the Zambian Copperbelt, 1926–1964," in Sharon B. Stichter and Jane L. Parpart, eds., *Patriarchy and Class: African Women in the Home and the Workforce*, Boulder, CO: Westview Press, 1988

Presley, Cora Ann, "Labor Unrest among Kikuyu Women in Colonial Kenya," in Claire C. Robertson and Iris Berger, eds., *Women and Class in Africa*, New York: Holmes and Meier, and London: Africana, 1986

Robertson, Claire C., and Martin A. Klein, *Women and Slavery in Africa*, Madison: University of Wisconsin Press, 1983

Robertson, Claire C., *Sharing the Same Bowl: A Socioeconomic History of Women and Class in Accra, Ghana*, Bloomington: Indiana University Press, 1984

Robertson, Claire C., "Developing Economic Awareness: Changing Perspectives in Studies of African Women, 1976–1985," *Feminist Studies* 13 (1987), 97–135

Robertson, Claire C., "Never Underestimate the Power of Women: The Transforming Vision of African Women's History," *Women's Studies International Forum* 11 (1988), 439–53

Schoenbrun, David L., "Gendered Histories Between the Great Lakes: Varieties and Limits," *International Journal of African Historical Studies* 29 (1996), 461–92

Sheldon, Kathleen, ed., *Courtyards, Markets, City Streets: Urban Women in Africa*, Boulder, CO: Westview Press, 1996

Strobel, Margaret, *Muslim Women in Mombasa, 1890–1975*, New Haven: Yale University Press, 1979

Strobel, Margaret, "African Women: Review Essay," *Signs* 8 (1982), 109–31

Strobel, Margaret, *European Women and the Second British Empire*, Bloomington: Indiana University Press, 1991

Thornton, John, "Legitimacy and Political Power: Queen Njinga, 1624–1663," *Journal of African History* 32 (1991), 25–40

Turrittin, Jane, "Aoua Kéita and the Nascent Women's Movement in the French Soudan," *African Studies Review* 36 (1993), 59–89

Vail, Leroy, and Landeg White, "The Possession of the Dispossessed: Songs as History among Tumbuka Women," in Vail and White, eds., *Power and the Praise Poem: Southern African Voices in History*, Charlottesville: University Press of Virginia, and London: Currey, 1991

Van Allen, Judith, "'Aba Riots' or Igbo 'Women's War'? Ideology, Stratification, and the Invisibility of Women," in Nancy J. Hafkin and Edna G. Bay, eds., *Women in Africa: Studies in Social and Economic Change*, Stanford, CA: Stanford University Press, 1976

White, Luise, *The Comforts of Home: Prostitution in Colonial Nairobi*, Chicago: University of Chicago Press, 1990

Wright, Marcia, "Women in Peril: A Commentary on the Life Stories of Captives in Nineteenth-Century East Central Africa," *African Social Research* 20 (1975), 800–19

Women's History: African American

The field of African American women's history grew out of historical developments in the 1960s and 1970s and the growing interest in social history since the 1960s. The civil rights movement and black nationalism motivated extensive research into African American history. Likewise the women's liberation movement spurred interest in women's history.

Pioneers in the field of African American women's history charged historians of African Americans with neglecting gender and contended that most women's historians had omitted the study of race from their research. Scholars of African American women's history have thus sought to correct these errors of omission and to challenge once-dominant historical narratives regarding slavery, Reconstruction, 19th-century gender ideology, women's work, and women's social movements.

Scholars of African American women's history have followed at least two different paths. Primarily through writing biographies of notable African American women, some historians have focused on the outstanding achievements of individual black women. Influenced by social history, other scholars have attempted to understand the experiences of "anonymous" African American women in slavery, freedom, work, religion, and social movements.

In the early 1970s, a few historians and other scholars began to illuminate the experiences of African American women in history. Their earliest efforts were primarily collections of documents by and about African American women: Gerda Lerner's *Black Women in White America: A Documentary History* (1972) and Bert James Loewenberg and Ruth Bogin's *Black Women in Nineteenth-Century American Life* (1976). In the early 1980s, Dorothy Sterling compiled another set of documents: *We Are Your Sisters* (1984).

Analytical articles and monographs soon followed these documentary anthologies. In the late 1970s and the early 1980s, several works addressed images of black women in history, including Rosalyn Terborg-Penn and Sharon Harley's *The Afro-American Woman* (1978); Angela Davis' *Women, Race, and Class* (1981); and Bettina Aptheker's *Woman's Legacy* (1982). Davis and Aptheker took issue with the images of black women and black family life portrayed by Daniel

Patrick Moynihan in *The Negro Family* (1965), written when he was assistant secretary of labor. In what came to be called "The Moynihan Report," the future senator had contended that a greater number of female-headed households in the black community had mired black families in a "tangle of pathology" and poverty. Davis and Aptheker as well as Jacqueline Jones in *Labor of Love, Labor of Sorrow* (1985) accused Moynihan of "blaming the victim" and of distracting Americans from the real economic problems of African Americans.

In the mid-1980s, several significant works addressed African American women's experiences in slavery, the work force, and social movements. Deborah Gray White's *Ar'n't I a Woman?* (1985) challenged prior scholarship into slave households and families. Asserting that historians Herbert Gutman, Eugene Genovese, and John Blassingame had slighted the importance of women in the slave family, White argued that African American women slaves were self-reliant and central to slave households. White also contended that because slavery undermined the role of men as providers and allowed slave women greater independence, slave families did not mimic white middle-class gender roles of the time.

Jones' *Labor of Love, Labor of Sorrow* examined women's work in both slavery and freedom. She argued that the daily work of black women in both racially segregated and gender-specific employment led to the creation of a distinct black women's culture, independent of both black male culture and white women's social networks. Darlene Clark Hine, in a series of essays written in the 1980s, also added to a discussion of African American women's work by studying black women in the medical and nursing professions.

Another significant work of the mid-1980s, Paula Giddings' *When and Where I Enter* (1984) explored the political activities of African American women, especially black clubwomen, at the turn of the century. Giddings argues that instilling middle-class notions of female respectability among poorer and less educated black women was of great importance to these clubwomen. In an important article, "Discontented Black Feminists" (1983), Rosalyn Terborg-Penn studied the political activities of black suffragists, analyzing the discrimination they suffered at the hands of white feminists in the women's suffrage movement.

In the early 1990s, Evelyn Brooks Higginbotham concentrated on black women's role in religion in *Righteous Discontent* (1993). Like Giddings' study of black clubwomen, Higginbotham found evidence of black churchwomen's attempts to spread middle-class gender conventions to poor or less educated blacks. Higginbotham's work also explored black churchwomen's "biculturalism," their socialization into and role in shaping both mainstream and African American culture.

Another field of study within African American women's history has probed relations between African American and white women. Jacquelyn Dowd Hall's *Revolt Against Chivalry* (1979), while ostensibly a biography of Jessie Daniel Ames, also included discussion of how white and black women worked together and separately in their attempts to eradicate lynching. Elizabeth Fox-Genovese's *Within the Plantation Household* (1988) examined the intricate relationships that developed between white mistresses and their slaves.

In the late 1980s and early 1990s, several African American women's historians were influential in opening new theoretical debates in women's history and African American history. Evelyn Brooks Higginbotham's article, "Beyond the Sound of Silence" (1989), challenged all American historians to give more attention to the growing field of African American women's history. Darlene Clark Hine's essays, gathered together in *Hine Sight* (1994), argued that the study of African American women in history has necessarily changed "larger" narratives about slavery, Reconstruction, and women in American history. Hine also served as editor of a multivolume series, *Black Women in United States History* (1990), which collected hundreds of articles on African American women's history, and also published several biographies of African American women.

MARGARET D. JACOBS

See also Hine; Lerner

Further Reading

Aptheker, Bettina, *Woman's Legacy: Essays on Race, Sex, and Class in American History*, Amherst: University of Massachusetts Press, 1982

Davis, Angela, *Women, Race, and Class*, New York: Random House, 1981; London: Women's Press, 1982

Fox-Genovese, Elizabeth, *Within the Plantation Household: Black and White Women of the Old South*, Chapel Hill: University of North Carolina Press, 1988

Giddings, Paula, *When and Where I Enter: The Impact of Black Women on Race and Sex in America*, New York: Morrow, 1984

Hall, Jacquelyn Dowd, *Revolt Against Chivalry: Jessie Daniel Ames and the Women's Campaign Against Lynching*, New York: Columbia University Press, 1979

Higginbotham, Evelyn Brooks, "Beyond the Sound of Silence: Afro-American Women in History," *Gender and History* 1 (1989), 50–67

Higginbotham, Evelyn Brooks, *Righteous Discontent: The Women's Movement in the Baptist Church, 1880–1920*, Cambridge, MA: Harvard University Press, 1993

Hine, Darlene Clark, ed., *Black Women in United States History*, 16 vols., New York: Carlson, 1990

Hine, Darlene Clark, *Hine Sight: Black Women and the Re-Construction of American History*, New York: Carlson, 1994

Jones, Jacqueline, *Labor of Love, Labor of Sorrow: Black Women, Work, and the Family from Slavery to the Present*, New York: Basic Books, 1985

Lerner, Gerda, ed., *Black Women in White America: A Documentary History*, New York: Pantheon, 1972

Loewenberg, Bert James, and Ruth Bogin, eds., *Black Women in Nineteenth-Century American Life*, University Park: Pennsylvania State University Press, 1976

Sterling, Dorothy, *We Are Your Sisters: Black Women in the Nineteenth Century*, New York: Norton, 1984

Terborg-Penn, Rosalyn, and Sharon Harley, eds., *The Afro-American Woman: Struggles and Images*, Port Washington, NY: Kennikat Press, 1978

Terborg-Penn, Rosalyn, "Discontented Black Feminists: Prelude and Postscript to the Passage of the Nineteenth Amendment," in Lois Scharf and Joan M. Jensen, eds., *Decades of Discontent: The Women's Movement, 1920–1940*, Westport, CT: Greenwood Press, 1983

White, Deborah Gray, *Ar'n't I a Woman? Female Slaves in the Plantation South*, New York: Norton, 1985

Women's History: Asia

The designation "women of Asia" has meaning only when one looks from the outside in: the women in Asia do not call themselves such. For this reason, the writing of histories of Asian women has always been entangled with the larger history of international relations and the politics of cultural perceptions. Indeed, references to "Asian" family values or "traditional oppression of women in Asia" so prevalent in the daily news are more statements about the multi-ethnic societies in Europe and the US than the worlds that the immigrants left behind.

So diverse are the histories of women in Asia and the historiographical traditions that produced them that there is no treatment of the subject under one cover. Even the common subdivisions of South Asia, Southeast Asia and Northeast Asia are woefully inadequate in imparting coherence onto the experiences of groups of women uncovered by national and community histories. As early as the 16th century, European missionaries and traders remarked on how different women from various regions of Asia looked: they saw Chinese and Japanese women as fair-skinned, similar to Europeans, whereas women from areas close to the tropics were dark-skinned. The same missionary letters that laid the foundation of knowledge about Asia among the reading public in early modern Europe also introduced a powerful religious-philosophical lens through which the lives of East Asian women have been understood henceforth: Confucianism.

Confucianism is a useful category of gender analysis in China, Korea, and, to a lesser extent, Japan and Vietnam, because its unity derives from the formidable canonical tradition shared by these East Asian countries. In the 18th and 19th centuries, these Confucian classics and didactic texts were translated into European languages, conveying the lofty images of elite East Asian women as morally upright, domestic, and leading lives in strict gender segregation. In the same period, artists and writers, fascinated by the trope of the hidden cloistered women, perpetuated images of the Oriental harem. The women of "Asia" acquired a common identity only as a result of this erotic and exotic imagination.

Neither the chaste domestic woman nor the forlorn creatures of the harem – frozen in time and barred from the public sphere – were considered fitting subjects of history. It is thus no accident that the writing of women's history, and the writing of women into history, emerged as projects integral to the anticolonial nationalistic struggles in late 19th- and early 20th-century China, Korea, and Japan. In fact, the establishment of women's history as a legitimate field was the most visible achievement of the emergent feminist movements in these countries.

In China a revolutionary martyr, Xu Tianxiao, pioneered the genre of general women's history by extolling the military virtues of women warriors in successive dynasties. His work, *Shenzhou nüzi xinshi* (A New History of Women of the Divine Land, 1913), was published two years after the dynastic order fell. In Korea, the development of the women's movement in the 1920s coincided with the publication of ethnographies of women's lives; the foremost example was Yi Nŭng-hwa's *Chosŏn yŏsok-ko* (Customs of Korean Women, 1926). In Japan, the famous feminist scholar Takamure Itsue established a Marxist-feminist historiographical tradition with her influential *Bokeisei no kenkyū* (Studies in Matriarchy, 1938). The central question raised by Takamura – did the transition from a classless to a class society in ancient Japan lead to the rise of patriarchy? – remained the central problematic issue in the field until the 1970s.

In short, the very concept of women's history in East Asia was born of the political necessities of mobilizing the female half of the population and transforming women into productive modern citizens. The threat of colonialism rendered the liberation of women an urgent task of national survival. Highly iconoclastic in tone, these women's histories were written in terms of the vocabularies of progress, rights, equality, liberation, and community of nations. The attacks on Confucian gender norms as misogynist and the Confucian vision of a hierarchical society as authoritarian were particularly fierce in China and Korea. In Japan, where nationalists saw themselves as at once victims of Euro-American imperialism and welcomed colonizers of the peoples in Korea and Taiwan, the relationship between tradition and women's liberation was more ambivalent.

The tropes of this nationalistic tradition of women's history-writing, all the more poignant because they were written by Asian men and women themselves, retained a powerful grip on professional historians and the reading public until the present day. Foremost is the trope of Asian-woman-as-victim, who was denied freedom of choice in marriage, career, and residence. A related problem is the separation of "tradition" from "modernity." When women's history is written as part-and-parcel of a history of national liberation, it is natural to construe it as linear history: a history of progress and retrenchments toward the final goal of freedom and equality.

The assumption of linear progression is particularly dominant in the writing of women's history in Japan, where Marxist historiography has ruled supreme in the modern period. From early debates on the economic basis of an ancient matriarchy and the marriage patterns that supported it, Japanese women's history has developed into a flourishing enterprise. In the immediate postwar years of the late 1940s and early 1950s, the history of Japanese women was woven into the twin themes of victimization and liberation, as exemplified by Inoue Kiyoshi's *Nihon josei-shi* (A History of Japanese Women, 1949). Inoue spoke for his generation of anticapitalist intellectuals in believing that women's liberation could be achieved only in a democratic-socialist society.

A number of voices were heard beginning in the late 1960s, when courses on women's history were being offered in schools and grassroots study groups gained momentum. Embracing locale- and time-specific studies, scholars produced finely textured local histories that complicated the Marxian periodization scheme and historical materialism. In the area of feminist theory, too, Japanese scholars made contributions by rethinking the intersection between class and gender. Scholars and activists debated the relationship between production and reproduction and the related issue of the housewife's role and power in the household economy. Turning away from the liberationist rhetoric, feminists began to write and teach women's history shaped by three categories: family, prostitution, and labor. Building on these developments, the vintage decades of 1980s and 1990s saw the publication of monumental anthologies and general women's histories in Japan.

The global radicalization in the late 1960s and 1970s had a different impact on the writing of Asian women's history in the US and Europe. Feminist scholars sympathetic to the Chinese socialist revolution created a new field of Chinese women's history in the anglophone world in the 1970s. Inspired by the Maoist utopian visions of the then-raging Cultural Revolution, these scholars combined the strict tradition-modernity divide with a Marxian focus on forces and relations of economic production. As a result, beginning with the pioneering *Women in China* (1973) edited by Marilyn Young, these histories tended to focus on women active in the communist movement that led to the establishment of the People's Republic of China in 1949. These feminist historians identified the socialist liberation of forces of production and the destruction of the bourgeois family as prerequisite for women's liberation. In the late 1970s to early 1980s, such scholars as Phyllis Andors, Elisabeth Croll, and Kay Ann Johnson illuminated the intricate and not always salutary relationship between women, family reform, and socialist revolution in post-1949 China. Other feminist historians, notably Gail Hershatter and Emily Honig, focused on the social and economic lives of female factory workers as well as the difficulties of organizing them for political action before 1949.

Another pioneering anthology, *Women in Chinese Society* (1975) edited by the anthropologist Margery Wolf and the historian Roxane Witke, heralded a different tradition in the writing of East Asian women's history: the application of anthropological paradigms to historical inquiry. As social history became prevalent in the anglophone scholarly world, the pursuit of women's history gained respectability and visibility. The lives of women in Asia were construed as part of the history of humanity, and could be illuminated by theoretical constructs believed to be universally applicable: marriage, kinship, inheritance patterns, family rituals, power and pollution, literacy and education, physical and social mobility, and so on.

The social history tradition has produced the bulk of Chinese and Korean women's histories found in the English language today, although its influence on the Japan field is less pronounced. For China, Patricia Ebrey has published articles and books on concubinage, daughter's inheritance, and family rituals from the 10th to 13th centuries. Focusing on the 17th to 19th centuries, Susan Mann has pioneered research on women's learning, work and household economy, and the emotional contours of domestic life. Ann Waltner has studied women as producers of kinship relations in a comparative perspective. For Korea, Martina Deuchler has illuminated the profound changes in elite women's lives as a result of the introduction of Confucian kinship structures and agnatic principles at the beginning of the Chosŏn dynasty (1392–1910).

Besides anthropology, historians of East Asian women have collaborated closely with literature specialists in a blossoming subfield: the retrieval and analysis of women's writings. Although Japanese women diarists and novelists have long been recognized for their unique contributions to the country's literary history, women's writings in China and Korea were ignored as unworthy or ghostwritten by men. Since the late 1980s, the burst of academic interest in Chinese women's poetry written before the 19th century has opened up questions about women's voice, class, and literacy, the formation of the canon, as well as the negotiation of power relations. Landmarks of this research by a close community of US-based scholars are a forthcoming 1000-page translation, *Chinese Women Poets*, edited by Kang-i Sun Chang and Haun Saussy, and a recent anthology, *Writing Women in Late Imperial China*, edited by Ellen Widmer and Chang. Similarly, the novels and songs written by Korean women were brought to the attention of feminist scholars, notably by JaHyun Kim Haboush.

When "traditional" East Asian women began to speak of the emotional contours of their everyday life, albeit in a mediated and indirect voice, the Confucian world ceased to appear as entirely restrictive of women's creativity, nor does the tradition-modernity divide seem as immutable as before. The research on women's literature, however, has made it painfully obvious that only a tiny minority of women (and indeed, men) could read and write. Although scholars have realized that womanhood was always fragmented by other hierarchies such as age, class, and ethnicity, the exact terms in which class and gender identities intersected remained vague. Research on law and spirituality, which promises to shed light on the lives of illiterate women, has only begun.

Never before has "women of Asia" seemed so elusive and yet so necessary as a category of knowledge as in the 1990s. A host of divergent forces has led to a basic rethinking of disciplinary boundaries and the nature of knowledge itself; these forces include the growing economic prowess of East Asia, the end of the Cold War, and the heightened pace of intellectual interactions between disparate parts of the globe, as well as the advent of cultural studies and the postcolonial critique. The writing of women's history has become a contentious ground on which disagreements on epistemology, the reading of texts, as well as the relationship between history and political activism are being fought.

Most significant is the increasingly visible presence of Asian women in the anglophone academy as professors, creative writers, and students. This, together with the emergence of gender studies in the People's Republic of China, the explosion of the women's movement in Taiwan after the lifting of martial law, the growth of women's studies as a grassroots movement in Japan, and the increasing vocalness of Korean feminists, as well as nascent women's studies programs in Vietnam, have created unprecedented opportunities for Euro-American scholars to learn from their former subjects of study. This has complicated the question of "who is speaking, and for whom?"

Some "Asian" scholars are explicit in denouncing paradigms of "Western feminism" as hegemonic and irrelevant, to the point of rejecting the labels of "feminist" and "women's studies" in favor of male-inclusive categories such as "gender studies." Ironically, their nationalistic stance is often manifested in the ferocity with which they hold on to antiquarian ideals of national self-determination and the writing of women's histories in terms of a tradition-modernity rupture, even as they assert that "modernity" is not the prerogative of the "West." In any case, their critique of Eurocentric frameworks has prompted new research on Asia-centered women's history, often taking the form of a repudiation of Japanese imperialism before World War II. In particular, the problem of "comfort women" (*wi'anbu* in Korean; *ianfu* in Japanese) – women from the Japanese colonies who were forced to serve as prostitutes for the Japanese army – has produced oral histories and theoretical investigations into sexuality and empire, as well as the transnational traffic in women.

In the US, these global developments have led to two intellectual shifts. First is the growing theoretical sophistication and self-reflexiveness on the parts of scholars of Asian women's history. The warnings in Edward Said's *Orientalism* (1978) were often evoked, and debates raged on Gayatri Spivak's famous question: "Can the subaltern speak?" Instead of socioeconomic structures such as kinship or economic production, scholars have turned to understanding the forces shaping women's lives in terms of linguistic and visual constructs. Cultural critics and historians have raised new questions about power, bodies, and sexuality. In particular, the history of medicine figures as a focal point for rethinking about the construction of gender differences and notions of subjectivity.

The second development is an increasing awareness that the history of women in Asia is essential to the history of Asian American women and their place in US society. This coalescence of disparate historigraphical traditions reverses a longstanding practice among "Asian American" historians of drawing clear boundaries between Asian history and US history, thought by many to be necessary to signal to the public that they are bona fide "Americans." Historians of Asian women and American women will have much to learn from each other in historical methods, sharing of sources, and pedagogical strategies. As to what kind of global history that will emerge from this collaboration, only time will tell.

As bewildering as these disparate voices may seem, in light of the stark singularity of distorted vision with which the history of Asian women was being written centuries ago, one would have to conclude that the cacophony signifies progress in both historical methods and our understanding of the pasts of over one-tenth of the population in the present world: East Asian women.

DOROTHY KO

See also Said

Further Reading

Andors, Phyllis, *The Unfinished Liberation of Chinese Women, 1949–1980*, Bloomington: Indiana University Press, 1983

Bernstein, Gail Lee, ed., *Recreating Japanese Women, 1600–1945*, Berkeley: University of California Press, 1991

Chang, Kang-i Sun, and Haun Saussy, eds., *Chinese Women Poets: An Anthology of Poetry and Criticisms from Ancient Times to 1911*, Stanford, CA: Stanford University Press, forthcoming

Croll, Elisabeth J., *Feminism and Socialism in China*, London and Boston: Routledge, 1978

Deuchler, Martina, *The Confucian Transformation of Korea: A Study of Society and Ideology*, Cambridge, MA: Council on East Asian Studies, Harvard University, 1992

Ebrey, Patricia Buckley, *The Inner Quarters: Marriage and the Lives of Chinese Women in the Sung Period*, Berkeley: University of California Press, 1993

Gilmartin, Christina, Gail Hershatter, Lisa Rofel, and Tyrene White, eds., *Engendering China: Women, Culture and the State*, Cambridge, MA: Harvard University Press, 1994

Haboush, JaHyun Kim, "Filial Emotions and Filial Values: Changing Patterns in the Discourse of Filiality in Late Chosŏn Korea," *Harvard Journal of Asiatic Studies* 55 (1995), 129–77

Haboush, JaHyun Kim, *The Memoirs of Lady Hyegyong: The Autobiographical Writings of a Crown Princess of Eighteenth-Century Korea*, Berkeley: University of California Press, 1996

Hershatter, Gail, *Dangerous Pleasures: Prostitution and Modernity in Twentieth-Century Shanghai*, Berkeley: University of California Press, 1997

Hicks, George, *The Comfort Women: Japan's Brutal Regime of Enforced Prostitution in the Second World War*, New York: Norton, and London: Souvenir Press, 1995

Honig, Emily, *Sisters and Strangers: Women in the Shanghai Cotton Mills, 1919–1949*, Stanford, CA: Stanford University Press, 1986

Inoue Kiyoshi, *Nihon josei-shi* (A History of Japanese Women), Tokyo: Sanichi Shobo, 1949

Johnson, Kay Ann, *Women, the Family and Peasant Revolution in China*, Chicago: University of Chicago Press, 1983

Kendall, Laurel, and Mark Peterson, eds., *Korean Women: View from the Inner Room*, New Haven: East Rock Press, 1983

Ko, Dorothy, *Teachers of the Inner Chambers: Women and Culture in Seventeenth-Century China*, Stanford, CA: Stanford University Press, 1994

Kondo, Dorinne, *Crafting Selves: Power, Gender, and Discourses of Identity in a Japanese Workplace*, Chicago: University of Chicago Press, 1990

Kristeva, Julia, *Des Chinoises*, Paris: Editions de Femmes, 1974; in English as *About Chinese Women*, London: Boyars, and New York: Urizen, 1977

Mann, Susan, *Precious Records: Women in China's Long Eighteenth Century*, Stanford, CA: Stanford University Press, 1997

Matsumoto, Valerie J., *Farming the Home Place: A Japanese American Community in California, 1919–1982*, Ithaca, NY: Cornell University Press, 1993

Said, Edward W., *Orientalism*, New York: Pantheon, and London: Routledge, 1978

Smith, Robert John, and Ella Lury Wiswell, *The Women of Suye Mura*, Chicago: University of Chicago Press, 1982

Spivak, Gayatri, "Can the Subaltern Speak?", in Cary Nelson and Lawrence Grossberg, eds., *Marxism and the Interpretation of Culture*, Urbana: University of Illinois Press, 1988, 271–313

Takamure Itsue, *Bokeisei no kenkyū* (Studies in Matriarchy), Tokyo: Kōseikaku, 1938

Waltner, Ann, *Getting an Heir: Adoption and the Construction of Kinship in Late Imperial China*, Honolulu: University of Hawaii Press, 1990

Watson, Rubie S., and Patricia Buckley Ebrey, eds., *Marriage and Inequality in Chinese Society*, Berkeley: University of California Press, 1991

Widmer, Ellen, and Kang-i Sun Chang, eds., *Writing Women in Late Imperial China*, Stanford, CA: Stanford University Press, 1997

Wolf, Margery, and Roxane Witke, eds., *Women in Chinese Society*, Stanford, CA: Stanford University Press, 1975

Xu Tianxiao [Hsu Tien-hsiao], *Shenzhou nüzi xinshi* (A New History of Women of the Divine Land), 1913

Yamakawa Kikue, *Buke no josei*, Tokyo: Iwanomi shoten, 1983; in English as *Women of the Mito Domain: Recollections of Samurai Family Life*, Tokyo: University of Tokyo Press, 1992

Yi Nŭng-hwa, *Chŏson yŏsok-ko* (Customs of Korean Women), 1926

Young, Marilyn Blatt, ed., *Women in China: Studies in Social Change and Feminism*, Ann Arbor: Center for Chinese Studies, University of Michigan, 1973

Zito, Angela, and Tani E. Barlow, eds., *Body, Subject and Power in China*, Chicago: University of Chicago Press, 1994

Women's History: Australia and New Zealand

In Australia and New Zealand, as in Europe and the United States, second-wave feminism heralded the emergence of women's history. Prior to the 1970s, and apart from such notable exceptions as Helen M. Simpson's 1940 study, *The Women of New Zealand*, Australian and New Zealand historiography focused on white men's experiences in such public realms as party politics, trade unions, and the formal economy. The Women's Liberation movement stimulated academic as well as popular interest in retrieving women's past, an undertaking that also benefited from the simultaneous development of social history. Patricia Grimshaw's pioneering study, *Women's Suffrage in New Zealand*, appeared in 1972; the establishment of women's history as an academic discipline in Australia occurred during 1975 and 1976 with a series of major publications, most notably Anne Summers' *Damned Whores and God's Police* (1975), Beverley Kingston's *My Wife, My Daughter and Poor Mary Ann* (1975), and Miriam Dixson's *The Real Matilda* (1976).

Much of the energies of early feminist historians in Australia and New Zealand were devoted to the retrieval function of women's history. Women were added to existing historical categories and specialties such as labor history, without directly challenging them. From the 1980s, however, there was increasing recognition of the need to move beyond such compensatory history to embrace what Australian Jill Julius Matthews defined as feminist history "which seeks to change the very nature of traditional history by incorporating gender into all historical analysis and understanding." The development of gender relations studies expanded the range of topics subjected to feminist scrutiny from those that related specifically to "women's sphere" to all aspects of society. It encouraged the analysis of men, as well as women, as gendered actors.

The diversity of offerings from feminist historians in the 1980s and 1990s reflected a strong tendency toward specialization in this period, a direct contrast to the pioneering overviews of Australian feminists in the 1970s. Feminist labor history emerged as a particularly fertile field with studies of women's involvement in the labor movement, their experiences of paid and unpaid work, and the gendered nature of the economy. Women's roles within the family and state intervention in families became a significant strand within feminist historiography. Investigation of relations between the state and women was also undertaken within the context of welfare history. Women's political mobilizations attracted considerable interest. Both Australian and New Zealand feminist historians contributed to the study of crime, analyzing its gendered dimensions and women's involvement as perpetrators and victims. Research into citizenship, female subjectivity, and sexuality, including lesbian perspectives, was also undertaken.

While the subjects explored by feminist historians in Australia and New Zealand became increasingly diverse during the 1980s, they usually remained concentrated on nonindigenous women. The histories of Aboriginal and Maori women emerged instead primarily through race relations studies and biography/autobiography. The very different experiences of these women undermined the viability of a unitary history of women. Additionally, recognition of the significance for women of colonialism and race relations prompted examinations of white women's roles as colonizers and of the racial dimensions of Australian feminism.

In both New Zealand and Australia, historians of gender relations are exploring the issue of "difference," recognizing the multiple and often conflicting histories of women in those countries. This emphasis reflects in part the challenge posed by the histories of non-European women and also the influence of postmodernism. Moreover, increasingly sophisticated analyses are recognizing both the historical constraints on women's experiences and the extent to which women were nevertheless active agents in their own lives. Kay Saunders and Raymond Evans' *Gender Relations in Australia* (1992) exemplified these trends with its recognition of the diverse histories of women and men and its analysis of the interpenetration of race, class, and gender relations in Australian history.

By the 1990s, feminist history was a flourishing field within Australian and New Zealand historiography, yet its potential to transform basic paradigms had not always been realized. General histories of the two countries remained largely impervious to the insights of two decades of feminist historiography. The publication in 1994 of *Creating a Nation* by four leading Australian feminist historians, however, signalled that even this conservative forum was subject to challenge. *Creating a Nation* is the first general history of Australia to foreground women's experiences and gender relations.

JOANNE SCOTT

See also Grimshaw; Lake

Further Reading

Australian Feminist Studies 19 (1994) [special issue on women and citizenship]

Australian Historical Studies 106 (1996) [special issue on women's history]

Brookes, Barbara, Charlotte Macdonald, and Margaret Tennant, eds., *Women in History: Essays on European Women in New Zealand*, Wellington: Port Nicholson Press, 1986

Brookes, Barbara, "Women's History," in Colin Davis and Peter Lineham, eds., *The Future of the Past: Themes in New Zealand History*, Department of History, Massey University, 1991, 76–97

Brookes, Barbara, Charlotte Macdonald, and Margaret Tennant, eds., *Women in History 2*, Wellington: Bridget Williams Books, 1992

Damousi, Joy, and Marilyn Lake, eds., *Gender and War: Australians at War in the Twentieth Century*, Cambridge, Melbourne, and New York: Cambridge University Press, 1995

Dixson, Miriam, *The Real Matilda: Woman and Identity in Australia, 1788–1975*, Ringwood: Penguin, 1976; revised 1984

Frances, Raelene, and Bruce Scates, eds., *Women, Work and the Labour Movement in Australia and Aotearoa/New Zealand*, Sydney: Australian Society for the Study of Labour History, 1991

Grimshaw, Patricia, *Women's Suffrage in New Zealand*, Auckland: Auckland University Press, 1972

Grimshaw, Patricia, Marilyn Lake, Ann McGrath, and Marian Quartly, *Creating a Nation*, Melbourne: McPhee Gribble, and New York: Viking, 1994

Huggins, Rita, and Jackie Huggins, *Auntie Rita*, Canberra: Aboriginal Studies Press, 1994

Kingston, Beverley, *My Wife, My Daughter and Poor Mary Ann: Women and Work in Australia*, Melbourne: Nelson, 1975

Macdonald, Charlotte, *A Woman of Good Character: Single Women as Immigrant Settlers in Nineteenth-Century New Zealand*, Wellington: Bridget Williams Books, 1990

Magarey, Susan, Sue Rowley, and Susan Sheridan, eds., *Debutante Nation: Feminism Contests the 1890s*, St. Leonards: Allen and Unwin, 1993

Matthews, Jill Julius, *Good and Mad Women: The Historical Construction of Femininity in Twentieth-Century Australia*, North Sydney: Allen and Unwin, 1984

New Zealand Journal of History 23, 1 (April 1989) [special issue on women's history]

New Zealand Journal of History 27, 2 (October 1993) [special issue on women and politics]

Reiger, Kerreen, *The Disenchantment of the Home: Modernizing the Australian Family, 1880–1940*, Melbourne and New York: Oxford University Press, 1985

Saunders, Kay, and Raymond Evans, eds., *Gender Relations in Australia: Domination and Negotiation*, Sydney and Fort Worth: Harcourt Brace, 1992

Saunders, Kay, "From Women's History to Gender Relations Studies in Australia: The Decade Reviewed," *Australian Journal of Politics and History* 41 (1995), 17–32

Simpson, Helen M., *The Women of New Zealand*, Wellington: Department of Internal Affairs, 1940

Summers, Anne, *Damned Whores and God's Police: The Colonization of Women in Australia*, Melbourne: Penguin, and London: Allen Lane, 1975

Swain, Shurlee, with Renate Howe, *Single Mothers and Their Children: Disposal, Punishment and Survival in Australia*, Melbourne: Cambridge University Press, 1995

Women's History: Europe

Research in the history of European women on a significant scale was inspired by second-wave feminism. Early studies focused on the lives and achievements of outstanding individuals who could serve as role models for the current generation of feminists. Equally marked was the concern with ideas (feminism, sexism) and institutions (female emancipation movements).

Following the ascendance of social history, attention shifted from individuals to groups of women. The use of quantification methodologies and details from everyday life, along with interdisciplinary borrowings from sociology, demography, and ethnography made aspects of ordinary women's lives available to historical analysis. Previously consigned to obscurity, family relationships, fertility, and sexuality were conceptualized as historical phenomena. Furthermore, by dealing with large-scale social processes as they are realized in many dimensions of human experience, social history has rendered legitimate a focus – central to the project of women's history – on groups customarily excluded from historical consideration.

Thus the wide variety of working-class women's involvement in paid work, both inside and outside the home, on a casual or regular basis, part-time or full-time, has been disclosed by increasingly sophisticated research into sources constructed so as to obscure women. Since the seminal work of Tilly and Scott, it has been amply demonstrated that the form of women's involvement in paid work, which was crucial for securing family survival, depended on both the composition of, and their various obligations to, the family in which they lived.

The focus on female collectives has illuminated the central role played by women (mainly plebeian) in popular movements of protest such as rebellions, food riots, charivaris, or revolutions. Drawing on anthropology and semiotics, Natalie Zemon Davis read the rebellious woman of the early modern period as the symbolic agent of fundamental social change. Further research has revealed a more varied picture. Women were mainly involved in economic and religious riots, both of which could be part of a political context: they acted together with other women, or in the society of men, or merely instigated the riot, leaving all further action to men. They used little, if any, violence themselves, driving men on with their taunts. In food riots, women were present in the marketplace, rather than interfering with shipments of grain. With few exceptions, rioting women aimed at reinstating an old order, including gender relations in which the man protected his family from the adverse impact of change. In doing this, women possibly gave expression to grievances widely felt in the community. At least in the closing decades of the 18th century, the rebellious woman emerged as a conservative figure. Although in popular protest women appear to have acted as members of their communities rather than as individuals in their own right, these studies helped to undermine the prevalent view of women as the helpless victims of male dominance.

Certain historical periods were singled out to illustrate the persistent victimization of women by men. Thus, the witch-hunt in early modern Europe was presented as a particularly bloody phase in the male quest, variously to assert domination over women, suppress female sexuality, and eradicate female knowledge of natural remedies, including abortifacients, by cruelly torturing and executing large numbers of women. The timing of the witch-hunt led Honegger even to claim that, because the oppression of nature was the basis of modernity, the mass killings of women as witches was a precondition of occidental rationalization.

Further research has revealed marked geographical variations in the intensity of the persecution of witches, showing that wide stretches of Europe remained untouched. Recourse to the methods and findings of anthropology and social history has produced an understanding of witchcraft as a gender-related rather than a gender-specific crime. While misogynist notions inspired by the church or ancient Greek philosophy may have influenced the establishment members involved in witch trials, witchcraft accusations, arising as they did from bad neighbor relationships, usually originated from below. Frequently, the witch was an elderly, unattached woman who relied on neighbors for help to fend off poverty, when customary obligations to the local poor were being eroded. The curse uttered when help was denied was the only means of intimidation available to a powerless individual. Indigent – and hence more likely to be female than male – yet refusing deference, as Larner argued, the witch, too, has been shown to some extent to have been the agent of her own history.

In Germany, the debate about women's historical agency has been particularly virulent with regard to National Socialism, that touchstone of the country's history. While early studies consistently portrayed women as the victims of a type of misogyny that had reached its apogee during the Third Reich, more recent work has ceased to conceive of women as a homogeneous group, emphasizing instead the sufferings inflicted as well as the opportunities afforded by National Socialism's impact on groups of women distinguished by race, class, religion, political allegiance, and sexual orientation, among other things.

Without neglecting the social structures and socioeconomic processes that circumscribed women's opportunities at any one time, the focus on women has led to a reassessment of some of the key periods and long-term processes of history. Close scrutiny of the effects on women's lives of the transition from feudalism to capitalism, the Renaissance, the Reformation, industrialization, modernization, or rationalization has led away from both an uncritical hallowing of modernity and the notion of a "golden age" located either in the Middle Ages or in the distant period of supposed matriarchy.

Drawing on historical anthropology, the history of mentalities and the family, practitioners of women's history have convincingly historicized even those aspects of women's lives, such as the female body, female sexuality, and women's reproductive behavior, that used to be cited in justification of women's consignment to the realm of biology. Adopting an interdisciplinary approach has allowed historians to abandon the narrow focus on the 19th and early 20th centuries and extend the investigation of women's lives via the Middle Ages as far back as antiquity.

JUTTA SCHWARZKOPF

See also Bock; Clark; Davis, N.; Duby; Engels; Hufton; Kelly; Koonz; Pieroni Bortolotti; Pinchbeck; Rowbotham; Scott, Joan; Tilly, L.; Walkowitz

Further Reading

Allen, Peter S., and A. Lily Macrakis, eds., *Journal of Modern Greek Studies* 1 (1983) [special issue on women's history]

"Auf den Spuren weiblicher Vergangenheit / A la recherche du passé féminin" (Tracing Women's Past), *Itinera* (Switzerland) 2/3 (1985)

Clio: histoire, femmes et sociétés (Clio: History, Women and Societies), Toulouse: University Press of Mirail, 1995

Davis, Natalie Zemon, *Society and Culture in Early Modern France: Eight Essays*, Stanford, CA: Stanford University Press, and London: Duckworth, 1975

Duby, Georges, and Michelle Perrot, general editors, *Storia delle donne in Occidente*, 5 vols., Bari: Laterza, 1990–92; in English as *A History of Women in the West*, 5 vols., Cambridge, MA: Harvard University Press, 1992–94

Historievidenskab (Copenhagen) 21 (1980) [Special issue on women's history]

Historisk Tidskrift (Stockholm) 1, 3 (1987, 1990) [special issues on women's history]

Historisk Tidsskrift (Norway) 69 (1990) [special issue on women's history]

L'Homme: Zeitschrift für feministische Geschichtswissenschaft, Vienna: Böhlau, 1990–

Honegger, Claudia, ed., *Die Hexen der Neuzeit* (Witches of the Modern Period), Frankfurt: Suhrkamp, 1978

Hufton, Olwen F., *The Prospect before Her: A History of Women in Western Europe*, vol. 1, London: HarperCollins, 1995

Irish Historical Studies 28 (1992) [special issue on women's history]

Jaarboek voor Vrouwengeschiedenis (Women's History Yearbook), Nijmegen: Socialistiese Uitgererij Nijmegen, 1980–

Kyle, Gunhild, ed., *Handbok i svensk kvinnohistoria* (Handbook of Swedish Women's History), Stockholm: Carlsson, 1987

Larner, Christina, *Witchcraft and Religion: The Politics of Popular Belief*, Oxford and New York: Blackwell, 1984

Memoria: Rivista di storia delle donne, Turin: Rosenberg & Sellier, 1981–91

Saldern, Adelheid von, "Victims or Perpetrators: Controversies about the Role of Women in the Nazi State," in David F. Crew, ed., *Nazism and German Society, 1933–45*, New York and London: Routledge, 1994

Seminario de estudios de la mujer de la Universidad Autonoma de Madrid, Actas (Proceedings of the Seminar of Women's Studies at the Universidad Autonoma of Madrid), 1982–

Sextant, Université Libre de Bruxelles, 1991–

Tilly, Louise A., and Joan Wallach Scott, *Women, Work, and Family*, New York: Holt Rinehart, 1978; London: Methuen, 1987

Women's History Review, Wallingford, Oxfordshire: Triangle, 1992–

Women's History: India

The study of women's history in India is a field that has been assuming increasing significance in recent times. The study of the past has been visualized as a means of understanding the sources of women's oppression and hence of removing those sources. This perspective has proved extremely useful both in terms of theoretical insights, as well as in terms of detailed empirical studies. By and large women have been invisible in Indian historical writing and this invisibility varies vastly over time and space according to differences in social and cultural practices. In the Indian context women's history is still at its infancy. This does not mean that serious thinking regarding women's problems did not exist in the earlier centuries or until recent times. But women's history as a mature and independent discipline has still not materialized.

There is no denying the fact that the perception of the Indian past has been from a male point of view. Indian history writing has consistently relegated women to the background. Although many books do have a chapter on women, often at the end, entitled, "Position of women in Vedic/later Vedic/Medieval/Vijayanagara Society," this in no way does justice to the role of women in Indian history. Conventional history has concentrated mainly on male-dominated activities such as politics, war, or diplomacy where women had little impact. When women like Razia Sultan or Rani Jhansi have been brought within the purview of history, it has been because they were performing male roles. Men's history has been presented as universally human rather than as exclusively male, while activities that are mainly female such as child bearing, cooking, women's work in agriculture, husbandry, magic, and folk art and tradition have been generally regarded as unimportant and unworthy of study and as such outside the purview of the academic discipline of history.

Another important reason for this neglect has been the source material used for the writing of history. Numismatics, archaeology, inscriptions, and literary texts reflect an elite world and, coupled with the preoccupation with political history, have completely ignored women. Now with the increasing democratization of history, new areas such as people's history and social history have been brought into the center of debates, and although a welcome expansion, male concerns have also dominated these new approaches. Gender, like any group, class, or race has been a powerful operating factor in history. This is a lesson still being learned in Indian history.

In the 19th century Europeans began to take an interest in the ancient history of India, and they included some consideration of women's role in their studies. Initially, Orientalists reconstructed the glory of Indian civilization in the ancient past. Later historians have pointed out that this was part of a romantic search for a distant edenic world, a utopia to escape the bewildering changes taking place in 19th century. On the other hand, the utilitarians and evangelicals attacked contemporary Indian society, especially the visibly low status of the women. In response nationalists quoted extensively from ancient texts to show that earlier women had enjoyed a high status.

Orientalists such as William Jones and H.T. Colebrook of the Asiatic Society of India gazed back to the glory of the past and treated a wide range of themes in Sanskrit literature on history and philosophy. Women, however, were marginal to their discussion. Jones made only a passing reference to Gargi as a woman of great piety and learning and paid no attention to *Sati*, the practice of widow immolation. Conversely, Colebrook explored the textual representations of *Sati* and elevated text over custom. The past was presented as a homogeneous whole and *Sati* epitomized the retrograde role of Hindu women in a land where a widow would voluntarily and cheerfully mount the pyre of her husband.

In her unanalytical and often contradictory monograph *La Femme dans l'Inde antique* (1864; *Women in Ancient India*, 1925), Clarisse Bader examined the role played by women in the Hindu pantheon from the time of the Aryans. She depicted an idyllic past. Bader argued that Western women had much to learn from the ancient Aryan civilization, where women were characterized by spiritual and ascetic tenderness, complete denial of self-interest, and unlimited devotion to the family. For Bader, this awe-inspiring spiritual courage was still evident in the women who mounted the funeral pyre of their husbands to commit *Sati*. Women in the Vedic age were unfettered in their movements and listened to discourses of men, though decorum did not permit them to answer directly. How decorum could serve as a "fetter" is not understood at all. Bader also tried to explain the preference for a son over a daughter in terms of the need for a son to perform funeral rites. When the Vedic culture later absorbed non-Aryan practices, traditionally referred to as Vishnawa, Bader found Vedic culture degenerating and women's status also changing. This reached its nadir with the coming of Islam.

Horner's work *Women under Primitive Buddhism* (1930) was based primarily on Buddhist Pali literature. This work indicated a slight shift, because while most work on women in early India dealt with categories of daughters, wives, mothers, and widows, Horner recognized a new category: women workers. This was a conceptual advance in its attempt to see women outside the domestic sphere in kinship relations and in the context of the wider society. However, the majority of this work focused on courtesans while laboring women were given less attention, although women in the Sangha who were pursuing nonfamilial goals were also mentioned.

It was James Mill, with his *History of British India* (1817), who defined the parameters of the 19th-century discourse on history. Mill deemed Hindu civilization to be very crude because of the status of its women. According to him the Hindus had little respect for their women. They excluded women from sacred texts, while depriving them of education, of a share in paternal property, and held them as unworthy to eat with their husbands. According to Mill the practice of segregating women did not come with the Muslims but was the consequence of the whole spirit of Hindu society, where women needed constant guarding for fear of their innate tendency towards infidelity. The degeneration of Hindu civilization and the abject position of Hindu women required the protection and intervention of the colonial state. Besides this Hindu men were seen to be "effeminate" and unfit for self-rule.

Mill's observations were echoed and elaborated in the writings of many British administrators and politicians. British fiction, journalism, and travel writing in the 19th century became accounts of the moral lapses or of sensational practices. The widow burning on the funeral pyre or the child bride became equated with India in Western imagination. Katherine Mayo's *Mother India* (1927), which provided a detailed and indignant account of the sexual excesses of Indian men and the terrible sufferings of their child wives became a bestseller with different translations and numerous editions. This book provided pornographic titillation and moral indignation, and served the colonial interest. As a reviewer put it in the *New Statesman and Nation* (1927), Mayo's book made the claim for *Swaraj* (self-government) seem nonsense and the wish to grant it almost a crime.

Western scholars depended largely on textual sources for their information and many of these are Brahminical in origin. These texts are heavily preoccupied with religious and legal questions such as the right of the widow to remarry, of women to hold property, of childless widows to adopt, of a woman's right to perform sacrifices with or without her husband, of the inclusion or exclusion of women from public assemblies, and of women's right to education. Here too, women are viewed mainly within the family context, and the relationship between husband and wife is the main concern. These texts reflected the precepts of the Brahmins, rather than the actual practices of the people and confined themselves only to the upper caste. Thus they were bound to give only a partial picture of the existing society.

These Western reconstructions of the past were not meant to provide the Indian people themselves an analysis of their *Shastras* or sacred writings, but to reshape the past for imperial purposes. The woman question became crucial in colonial ideology in order to establish a psychological advantage over imperial subjects. The high morality of the imperial masters could be effectively established by highlighting the low status of the women among the subject population.

This construction of the past also became the context for the fabrication of a particular kind of womanhood. The account was itself a creation of the compulsions of the present and these compulsions determined which elements were to be highlighted and which receded from the conscious object of concern in historical writing. The entire focus in the 19th century centered around the high caste Hindu woman, whether it was to highlight her high status in the past or to reveal her low status in the present. Women of other castes and sections were totally omitted from scrutiny and were not a matter of concern.

The emerging Indian intelligentsia in the first half of the 19th century also became an active agency in the reconstruction of the past. They were aware of the "glorious past" through Orientalist scholarship and yet countered a strong negative perception of women in the present. The social reform movements of the 19th century all advocated reform of Hindu society whose twin evils were seen as the existence of the caste system and the low status of women perceived through institutions like *Sati*, child marriage, female infanticide, and enforced widowhood. The preoccupation with these questions was derived from the dominance of Sanskritic models, and the sanction of the *Shastras* were used by both proponents and opponents of reform.

A very important work, which proved influential in shaping popular perception of the problem, was A.S. Altekar's *Position of Women in Hindu Civilization* (1938), which was exclusively based on Brahminical sources. It revealed the details of an entire body of opinion of lawmakers on such areas as education of women, marriage, divorce, the position of widows, women in public life, and proprietary rights of women. Altekar's theoretical framework is spelt out on the very first page of his work: "One of the best ways to understand the spirit of a civilization and to appreciate its excellence and to realize its limitations is to study the status of women in it. The marriage laws and customs enable us to realize whether men regard women as market commodities or war prizes or whether they realize that the wife is after all her husband's valued partner whose cooperation was indispensable for happiness and success of family life." Thus women are seen only in the context of family.

Altekar even provided a psychological argument to explain existing biases against women. He stated that the Hindu preference for a son over daughter was mainly because a widowed daughter is a cause of endless misery and worry for her parents and it broke their hearts to see her burn alive as remarriage was impossible. Women were unable to hold property because they were powerless to defend it against actual or potential rivals and enemies. To Altekar the lowering of the age of marriage was a reaction to maidens joining the Buddhist and Jain orders. He noted a connection between the fall of the Aryan woman and the subjugation of the Sudras, when Aryan women ceased to be producing members of society and thus lost their esteemed position. Thus Altekar painted a picture of the idyllic conditions of the Aryans in the Vedic age and within it the high status of its women. This set the tone for almost all the works on women that followed for a decade and it crippled the emergence of an analytically rigorous study of women in ancient India.

Devaki Indra's *Status of Women in Ancient India* (1940) stated that Vedic literature suggested that women in early Aryan society enjoyed a much better social, religious, and political position than they did in the later age of the Dharmasastras. J.B. Chaudhuri's *Position of Women in the Vedic Ritual* (1956) found women to have conservative natures and therefore generally to wish to stick together. In *The Status of Women in the Epics* (1966), Shakambari Jayal perceived an initial high status for women, and a general decline in the post-Vedic phase, after the non-Aryan wife came into the picture.

Despite a recognition of the inadequacies of these studies, little discussion on women took place on a rigorous level. Most Marxist scholars, with their focus on traditional political history, paid little attention to women. Thus D.D. Kosambi hardly touched on women and R.S. Sharma's *Perspectives in Social and Economic History of Early India* (1983) and *Material Culture and Social Formations in Early India* (1983), discussed eight types of marriage without ever considering what this meant for women. Even Romila Thapar, who has done remarkable work on the concept of lineage, did not incorporate an analysis of gender.

Moti Chandra's *World of Courtesans* (1973) was somewhat different, as its subjects were examined from outside the sociolegal framework. But there was no analysis of this institution or its placement within the patriarchal system, and the book is limited to a listing of references to courtesans in various texts. The degradation of this institution is traced to the medieval period when courtesans began caring only for money and not for art, and to the low characters who visited them who were reduced to mere pimps and abject flatterers. This implied that earlier contacts had been noble.

Medievalists such as Saroj Gulati and Kamala Gupta have shown there are many distortions in the way women are represented when they held political power. Women such as Razia who wielded political power are often viewed as potentially dangerous and much emphasis has been placed on their moral failings. Some texts emphasized how when she was mounting a horse the slave Yakut would hold her arm, which implied moral laxity. This was despite the recognition that Razia was wise, just, generous, a protector of her subjects, and leader of her armies. Nurjahan, who wielded power for her husband, is ridiculed, and we have numerous accounts in history books which talk of petticoat government, the effete rule of an emasculated king, and the manipulation by a power-hungry woman. This is in spite of the recognition of the fact that medieval Indian political history is replete with examples of men manipulating for the sake of power.

In contrast, historical discourse has praised women who acted as regents and thus combined the mother role with that of the ruler. Hence women such as Chandbibi and Rani Lakshmi Bai became mythified and glorified. Works such as Rekha Misra's *Women in Mughal India* (1967) highlighted the political participation of women during Mughal rule. The book mainly concentrated on the aristocracy, and on the social, religious, and cultural lives of women. Saroj Gulati's *Women and Society: Northern India* (1985) presented a detailed analysis of women's role within the family and in rituals, while women's role in the production process was totally ignored. Kamala Gupta's *Social Status of Hindu Women in Northern India* (1987) explored the impact of social customs of Muslims among the Hindu women.

In the modern period there have been a number of books and articles on the social reform movement and the woman question. The social reform movement was the first that organized a pan-Indian response to the challenges posed by the colonial rule. It was initiated by an urban educated elite who, although a small proportion of the population, because of their contact with new Western ideas, redefined the woman question. The Indian intellectual reformer, sensitive to the implicit power of the colonial cultural domination, responded to Western ideas of rationalism, liberalism, and civilized society, and at the same time sought ways and means of resisting this colonial hegemony, resorting to a "cultural defense" as a means of resistance.

This cultural defense resulted in a paradoxical situation. The social reformers questioned the traditional order both because of the new intellectual climate and as a strategy of cultural defense. As a result the intellectual context of the social reform movement was a curious mixture of 19th-century European ideas of individualism, rationalism, progress, scientific thought, and the reaffirmation of the basic tenets of Hinduism which were redefined to meet the challenges of colonialism. Thus there was an attempt to create a new society, modern and yet rooted in the Indian tradition. In the creation of this new ethos, the reformers sought reference points in the past and sanctions from a period in Indian tradition which they believed did not manifest these aberrations. The fight against social evil was also defined in the light of the past. Hence, they fought against *Sati*, essentially in the belief that it was not sanctioned by the *Shastras*.

In the case of women, the ambivalence of social reform is evident. The attempt was to create a new Indian woman, truly Indian and yet sufficiently educated and tutored in 19th-century values to suit the needs of the emerging bourgeois society. In doing this women were brought more securely into the ambit of the culture being shaped in the 19th century – a culture whose definitions and contours were laid down by the Indian male social reformer.

In *The Reluctant Debutante* (1983) Ghulam Murshid argued that the cultural politics of nationalism glorified the past and tended to demand that everything traditional or Indian be defended. Any questioning of traditional practices began to be regarded as Western and antinational, and therefore, as far as women were concerned, nationalism was clearly retrogressive.

Joanna Liddle and Rama Joshi's *Daughters of Independence* (1986) brought imperialism to the center of analysis. They argued that a great limitation to the woman question was that it was caught between the political agendas of the British rulers and Indian nationalists. Women could not envisage an independent program, for they had to find their understanding of women's oppression within the conceptual framework of the national movement.

Partha Chatterjee's article in Sangari and Vaid's *Recasting Women* (1989), also revealed the relation between nationalism and the woman question, and how "nationalism" resolved the woman question in complete accordance with its preferred goals. The nationalist discourse set out to establish a series of oppositions between male and female, inner and outer, public and private, material and spiritual. The new woman was now a product of a new patriarchy formed along class lines.

We usually find that when women are written about they are either seen as passive, secondary, supportive, and inert, or are glorified as heroines in some movement or revolt. A refreshing change, however, can be seen in a few recent books which put women center stage, and talk from a woman's point of view. In Ke Lalita's 1989 collection on women's role in an important postwar insurrectionary peasant struggle in India – the Telangana arms struggle – contributors discussed the different kinds of activity and levels of consciousness coexisting among women. Another collection edited by Tharu and Lalita, *Women Writing in India* (1991–93), offered an account of women's real experiences, which are transparently available in women's writing, especially in realist fiction and in lyric poetry. By making women the center of these works, an attempt has been made to see how women articulated and responded to ideologies from complexly constituted and decentralized positions within them. Manushi's *Women Bhaktas* (1989) also exposed the lives and poetry of a whole range of extraordinarily courageous and creative women who have asserted their rights to their own life as they define it.

All these are useful in building a new comprehensive history in which women are given a proper place on a par with men. But much still needs to be done. The influence of women as a group in the socioeconomic changes of a particular period, or the changing patterns of their lives in accordance with the changes in the polity, society, and religion are not sufficiently examined, and only when this is accomplished will we be able to get a total picture, moving away from the male and elite perspective that has dominated the writing of history.

REKHA PANDE

See also Kosambi

Further Reading

Altekar, Anant Sadashiv, *Position of Women in Hindu Civilization: From Prehistoric Times to the Present Day*, Benares: Benares Hindu University Press, 1938; reprinted 1958

Bader, Clarisse, *La Femme dans l'Inde antique: études morales et littéraires*, Paris, 1864; in English as *Women in Ancient India: Moral and Literary Studies*, London: Kegan Paul, 1925; reprinted Varanasi: Chowkhamber, 1986

Bagachi, Jasodhara, ed., *Indian Women: Myth and Reality*, Hyderabad and London: Sangam, 1995

Basu, Aparna, and Bharati Ray, *Women's Struggle: A History of the All-India Women's Conference, 1927–1990*, New Delhi: Manohar, 1990

Bhattacharya, Nandini, *Reading the Splendid Body: Gender and Consumerism in Eighteenth-Century Writing on India*, Newark: University of Delaware Press, 1998

Borthwick, Meredith, *The Changing Role of Women in Bengal, 1849–1905*, Princeton: Princeton University Press, 1984

Chandra, Moti, *World of Courtesans*, New Delhi: Vikas, 1973

Chandra, Sudhir, *Enslaved Daughters: Colonialism, Law and Women's Rights*, Delhi, Oxford, and New York: Oxford University Press, 1998

Chaudhuri, Jatindra Bimal, *Position of Women in the Vedic Ritual*, Calcutta: privately printed, 1956

Ghosh, S.K., *Indian Women Through the Ages*, Delhi: Ashish, 1989

Ghulam Murshid, *Reluctant Debutante: Response of Bengali Women to Modernization, 1849–1905*, Rajashahi: Rajashahi University Sahitya Sansad, 1983

Guha, Ranjit, "Chandra's Death," in Ranjit Guha, ed., *Subaltern Studies 5*, Delhi and Oxford: Oxford University Press, 1987

Gulati, Saroj, *Women and Society: Northern Indian in 11th and 12th Centuries*, Delhi: Chanakya, 1985

Gupta, Kamala, *Social Status of Hindu Women in Northern India, 1206–1707 AD*, New Delhi: Inter-India, 1987

Horner, Isabel Bleu, *Women under Primitive Buddhism: Kywomen and Almswomen*, New York: Dutton, and London: Routledge, 1930; reprinted Delhi: Motilal Barnarsidass, 1975

Indra, Devaki, *Status of Women in Ancient India: A Vivid and Graphic Survey of Women's Position, Social, Religious, Political and Legal, in India*, Lahore: Minerva, 1940; reprinted 1955

Jayal, Shakambari, *The Status of Women in the Epics*, Delhi: Motilal Barnarsidass, 1966

Kaur, Manmohan, *Women in India's Freedom Struggle*, Delhi: Sterling, 1985

Kosambi, D.D., *An Introduction to the Study of Indian History*, Bombay: Popular Book Depot, 1956

Kosambi, D.D., *Myth and Reality: Studies in the Formation of Indian Culture*, Bombay: Popular Prakasan, 1962; London: Sangam, 1983

Krishnamurty, Jayasankar, ed., *Women in Colonial India: Essays on Survival, Work, and the State*, Delhi, Oxford, and New York: Oxford University Press, 1989

Kumar, Radha, *The History of Doing: An Illustrated Account of Movements for Women's Rights and Feminism in India, 1800–1990*, London and New York: Verso, 1993

Lalita, Ke et al., *"We Were Making History": Life Stories of Women in the Telangana People's Struggle*, New Delhi: Kali for Women, and London: Zed, 1989

Liddle, Joanna, and Rama Joshi, *Daughters of Independence: Gender, Caste and Class in India*, Delhi: Kali for Women, London: Zed, and Totowa, NJ: Biblio, 1986

Mayo, Katherine, *Mother India*, London: Cape, and New York: Harcourt Brace, 1927

Mill, James, *History of British India*, 3 vols., London: Baldwin Cradock and Joy, 1817

Minault, Gail, ed., *The Extended Family: Women and Political Participation in India and Pakistan*, Delhi: Chanakya, and Columbia, MO: South Asia Books, 1981

Minault, Gail, *Secluded Scholars: Women's Education and Muslim Social Reform in Colonial India*, Delhi, Oxford, and New York: Oxford University Press, 1998

Misra, Rekha, *Women in Mughal India, 1526–1748 AD*, Delhi: Munshiram Manoharlal, 1967

Mukherjee, Prabhati, *Hindu Women: Normative Models*, Calcutta: Orient Longman, 1978; revised 1994

Nand, Lokesh Chandra, *Women in Delhi Sultanate*, Allahabad: Vohra, 1989

Nanda, Bal Ram, ed., *Indian Women: From Purdah to Modernity*, New Delhi: Vikas, 1976

Niranjana, Tejaswini, P. Sudhir, and Vivek Dhareshwar, eds., *Interrogating Modernity: Culture and Colonialism in India*, Calcutta: Seagull, 1993

Raman, Sita Anantha, *Getting Girls to School: Social Reform in Tamil Districts, 1870–1930*, Calcutta: Stree, 1996

Ray, Bharati, ed., *From the Seams of History: Essays on Indian Women*, Delhi, Oxford, and New York: Oxford University Press, 1995

Sangari, Kum Kum, and Sudesh Vaid, eds., *Recasting Women: Essays in Colonial History*, New Delhi: Kali for Women, 1989

Sharma, R.S., *Material Culture and Social Formations in Early India*, New Delhi: Macmillan, 1983

Sharma, R.S., *Perspectives in Social and Economic History of Early India*, New Delhi: Munshiram Manoharlal, 1983

Thadani, Giti, *Sakhiyani: Lesbian Desire in Ancient and Modern India*, London and New York: Cassell, 1996

Thapar, Romila, *Ancient Indian Social History: Some Interpretations*, Delhi: Orient Longman, 1978

Thapar, Romila, *From Lineage to State: Social Formations in the mid-First Millennium BC in the Ganga Valley*, Bombay: Oxford University Press, 1984

Tharu, Susie, and Ke Lalita, eds., *Women Writing in India: 600 BC to the Present*, 2 vols., New York: Feminist Press, 1991–93; Oxford: Oxford University Press, 1993–95

Women's History: Latin America

Stereotypical representations of Latin American women as passive, tradition-bound, and dominated by *machismo* have undergone intense historical scrutiny in the last two decades. Early attempts to include women in Latin American historical narratives began during the mid-20th century. Mostly based on written records by elites, these analyses tended to focus on the experiences of extraordinary women, including writers, artists, and renowned political figures of the colonial and modern periods. Access to a wider variety of sources and the critical use of the concept of gender not only allowed the eventual examination of ethnically diverse women of different classes of society, but also initiated a global reevaluation of male-oriented historical narratives. Scholars were no longer analyzing the neglected voices of women to fill a void, but rather to assess how gendered social relations of power between and among the sexes contributed to the historical development of the region. Approaching patriarchy as a point of departure, historians now asked how gender definitions were constructed and experienced in daily life and, more importantly, how they were contested. In this historiographical context, women's active participation in the formation and transformation of Latin American societies became increasingly evident.

Anthropological tools and historical methodologies have both contributed to the growth of studies on pre-Columbian gender relations. Emphasizing the interconnection between gender, power, and culture, Irene Silverblatt's *Moon, Sun, and Witches* (1987) explored how parallel lines of descent and common worship of *Pachamama* (Earth Mother) structured a world in which both Andean men and women played separate yet equally relevant social roles at both material and symbolic levels. Andean gender complementarity vanished as the Inca established a new "conquest hierarchy" which, in turn, was later used by the Spaniards to achieve political power in the region. Analysis of gender relations was also central in Susan Kellogg's examination of the cultural and social transformation of Aztec society in the post-conquest era.

Strict legislation limited the role of women during the 300 years of Spanish rule. According to the law of the *Siete Partidas*, women were under the tutelage of male members of the family until reaching adulthood. In addition, they were not eligible to vote or to hold public office. Yet, recent studies on women of the colonial era indicate that legal restriction converged with diverse instances of legal protection. Lavrin's analysis of official records, financial reports, and diaries, suggested that, as parent's responsibility included granting daughters a dowry, upper-class women were often able to secure certain economic independence. Although this was uncommon, Cartier demonstrated that some women owned and managed their own landed properties. Observance of the "pledge to marry" also protected women against deception. Using the techniques of discursive analysis on recorded prenuptial disputes, Patricia Seed's *To Love, Honor, and Obey in Colonial Mexico* (1988) examined how legal precepts, the participation of the church, and cultural understandings of concepts of honor safeguarded women's status, at least during the early colonial period. Second to marriage, the convent became an important means of escaping male domination. A growing scholarship – including work by both Lavrin and Gallagher – uncovering female worlds suggested that, although enclosed and limited, and initially available only to members of the elite, nunneries proved to be instrumental in allowing women to expand their areas of influence. Not all women remained at home or in convents, however. Arrom showed that single women and widows of the popular classes increasingly participated in the labor market after 1799. Both the church and the state established rigorous moral and social codes of behavior, but the essays in Lavrin's *Sexuality and Marriage in Colonial Latin America* (1989) noted that the prevalence of illegitimacy, consensual unions, and heterodox sexual relations between men and women of all social extractions effectively thwarted the reach of secular and ecclesiastical control. Women's resistance to colonial patriarchal rule found alternative, if more muted, venues of expression. Using feminist and anthropological concepts to read critically inquisitorial records, Ruth Behar examined the rich symbolic language of beliefs that allowed women of different ethnicities and classes to use sexual witchcraft as means to resist, punish, and even control men's behavior. Silverblatt argued that politically disruptive poor women in colonial Peru were also condemned as witches. In Central Mexico, subaltern women forged important roles in popular political culture through their prominent participation in riots. According to Steve Stern's *The Secret History of Gender* (1995), in the wake of social and political emergencies women skillfully used their reputations as defenders of their kin to voice their own versions of community and citizenship.

Most Latin American countries achieved independence from Spain by 1825. Recent scholarship strongly suggests that the legal, economic, and social redefinition of women's place in society importantly influenced the processes of nation formation. Florencia Mallon's use of the theory of articulation of modes of production placed women's domestic activities within the larger context of economic modernization. Empirical research by Donna Guy has demonstrated that, in Argentina, the emergence of industrialization allowed women to participate in growing numbers in the urban labor market, yet the concomitant decline of the cottage industry, in which the female participation had been paramount, led women to concentrate in low status and poorly paid jobs as laundresses, ironers, and maids in the provinces. Meanwhile, Arrom has revealed how family codes issued in the late 19th century extended *patria potestad* (authority over children) to women, yet legal double-standards remained in distinctive punishments for adultery along gender lines.

Social constructions of gender underwent increasing debate as Latin America engaged in the process of modernization. Both French and Ramos-Escandon have established that while intersecting crucial definitions of class and ethnicity, the cult of female domesticity helped to further values of discipline, temperance, and morality in an increasingly urbanized and politically centralized milieu. Concomitantly, concerns with the damaging moral and economic effects of prostitution became central in both medical and civil discourses of the late 19th century. Based on a novel and careful analysis of public health records, Donna Guy's *Sex and Danger in Buenos Aires* (1991) examined state concerns with the economic functions of the popular classes embedded in Argentina's regulation of prostitution. Lauderdale-Graham has demonstrated that medically-based definitions of gender and race were also taking place in Brazil. These ground-breaking studies in Latin American historiography manifested the relevance of gender in the construction of modernity.

Incipient feminist organizations also emerged during this era. Women of Latin America started to organize international congresses as early as 1910. In the 1916 Feminist Congress of Yucatan, social activists and middle-class journalists and teachers concerned with "the social question" voiced their gender-related demands. A vast scholarship, including work from Miller, Lavrin, Macias, Stoner, and Hahner, has demonstrated that women of most Latin American countries extended their sphere of influence to the public arena by defending women's right to education, and demanding equal opportunities and fair treatment at work, as well as women's recognition as citizens through the right to vote. An increasing number of testimonies, particularly those by Menchu and by Barrios, have allowed a critical revision of women's participation in the Latin American revolutions and social mobilizations in the 20th century. Rather than mere accessories in the search for social justice and democratization, peasant and working-class women brought with them a rich arsenal of practices and interpretations rooted in their everyday experiences, both as women and as citizens, which questioned the legitimacy of male-dominated state power. More importantly, research by Bouvard and by Agosin on women-led grassroots mobilization against the military regimes of Argentina and Chile has demonstrated that, in opposing governmental policies, women incorporated an innovative political style by deliberately invoking the ethical and political relevance of long-standing symbols of femininity. Increasing emphasis on female strategies of resistance has resulted in the exploration of the languages and practices of ordinary, tradition-bound women. In *Translated Woman* (1993), as author Ruth Behar attentively and respectfully listened to Esperanza's life story, reified images of Third World women as merely submissive victims of patriarchy and capitalism underwent a compelling theoretical and empirical revision. Esperanza's narrative contained all the predictable tropes of her poor, rural, lower-class, and mestizo Mexican origins. Yet, organized in three evolving stages – suffering, rage, and redemption – her story unveiled the paradoxical and active ways in which women from the margins of society simultaneously used and defied prescribed gender definitions in order to empower themselves. Further use of interdisciplinary conceptual and methodological tools will enable historians to pay close attention to similar stories in the near future. Engendering the history of modern Latin America will also include a more rigorous study of women in the borderlands.

CRISTINA RIVERA-GARZA

See also Lavrin

Further Reading

Agosin, Marjorie, *Tapestries of Hope, Threads of Love: The Arpillera Movement in Chile, 1974–1994*, Albuquerque: University of New Mexico Press, 1996

Arrom, Silvia, "Change in Mexican Family Law in the Nineteenth Century: The Civil Codes of 1870 and 1884," *Journal of Family History* 10 (1985), 305–17

Arrom, Silvia, *The Women of Mexico City, 1790–1857*, Stanford, CA: Stanford University Press, 1985

Barrios de Chungara, Domitila, with Moema Vizzier, *Si me permit en hablar . . .: testimonio di Domitila, una mujer de las minas de Bolivia*, Mexico City: Siglo XXI, 1977; in English as *Let Me Speak! Testimony of Domitila, a Woman of the Bolivian Mines*, New York and London: Monthly Review Press, 1978

Behar, Ruth, "Sexual Witchcraft, Colonialism, and Women's Powers: Views from the Mexican Inquisition," in Asunción Lavrin, ed., *Sexuality and Marriage in Colonial Latin America*, Lincoln: University of Nebraska Press, 1989

Behar, Ruth, *Translated Woman: Crossing the Border with Esperanza's Story*, Boston: Beacon Press, 1993

Bouvard, Marguerite Guzman, *Revolutionizing Motherhood: The Mothers of the Plaza de Mayo*, Wilmington, DE: Scholarly Resources, 1994

Courtier, Edith, "Women in a Noble Family: the Mexican Counts of Regla, 1750–1830," in Asunción Lavrin, ed., *Latin American Women: Historical Perspectives*, Westport, CT: Greenwood Press, 1978

Franco, Jean, *Plotting Women: Gender and Representation in Mexico*, New York: Columbia University Press, 1989

French, William, "Prostitutes and Guardian Angels: Women, Work and the Family in Porfirian Mexico," *Hispanic American Historical Review* 72 (1992), 529–53

Gallagher, Ann Miriam, "The Indian Nuns of Mexico City's Monasterio of Corpus Christi, 1724–1821," in Asunción Lavrin, ed., *Latin American Women: Historical Perspectives*, Westport, CT: Greenwood Press, 1978

Guy, Donna J., *Sex and Danger in Buenos Aires: Prostitution, Family, and Nation in Argentina*, Lincoln: University of Nebraska Press, 1991

Hahner, June Edith, *Emancipating the Female Sex: The Struggle for Women's Rights in Brazil, 1850–1940*, Durham, NC: Duke University Press, 1990

Kellogg, Susan, *Law and the Transformation of Aztec Culture, 1500–1700*, Norman: University of Oklahoma Press, 1995

Kellogg, Susan, "The Woman's Room: Some Aspects of Gender Relations in Tenochtitlan in the Late Pre-Hispanic Period," *Ethnohistory* 42 (1995), 563–76

Lau, Ana, and Carmen Ramos, eds., *Mujeres y Revolución, 1900–1917*, Mexico City: Instituto Nacional de Antropología e Historia, 1993

Lauderdale-Graham, Sandra, *House and Street: The Domestic World of Servants and Masters in Rio de Janeiro*, Cambridge and New York: Cambridge University Press, 1988

Lavrin, Asunción, ed., *Latin American Women: Historical Perspectives*, Westport, CT: Greenwood Press, 1978

Lavrin, Asunción, "Female Religious," in Louisa Schell Hoberman and Susan Migden Socolow, eds., *Cities and Society in Colonial Latin America*, Albuquerque: University of New Mexico Press, 1986

Lavrin, Asunción, ed., *Sexuality and Marriage in Colonial Latin America*, Lincoln: University of Nebraska Press, 1989

Lavrin, Asunción, *Women, Feminism, and Social Change in Argentina, Chile, and Uruguay, 1890–1940*, Lincoln: University of Nebraska Press, 1995

Macías, Ana, *Against All Odds: The Feminist Movement in Mexico to 1940*, Westport, CT: Greenwood Press, 1982

Mallon, Florencia E., "Gender and Class in the Transition to Capitalism: Household and Mode of Production in Central Peru," *Latin American Perspectives* 13 (1986), 147–74

Menchu, Rigoberta, with Elizabeth Burgos-Debray, *Me llamo Rigoberta Menchú y así me nació la conciencia*, Barcelona: Argos Vergara, 1983; in English as *I, Rigoberta Menchu: An Indian Woman in Guatemala*, London: Verso, 1984

Miller, Francesca, *Latin American Women and the Search for Social Justice*, Hanover, NH: University Press of New England, 1991

Radaku, Verena, *Por la debilidad de nuestro ser: mujeres del pueblo en la paz Porfiriana* (Through the Weakness of Our Very Being: Women of the People during the Porfirian Peace), Mexico City: Cuadernos de la Casa Chata 168, 1989

Ramos Escandon, Carmen, "Senoritas Porfirianas: mujer e ideologia en el Mexico progresista, 1880–1910" (Porfirian Women: Women and Ideology in Progressive Mexico, 1880–1910), in Carmen Ramos Escandon, ed., *Presencia y Transparencia: la mujer en la historia de México*, Mexico City: El Colegio de México, 1987

Salas, Elizabeth, *Soldaderas in the Mexican Military: Myth and History*, Austin: University of Texas Press, 1990

Seed, Patricia, *To Love, Honor, and Obey in Colonial Mexico: Conflicts over Marriage Choice, 1574–1821*, Stanford, CA: Stanford University Press, 1988

Silverblatt, Irene, *Moon, Sun, and Witches: Gender Ideologies and Class in Inca and Colonial Peru*, Princeton: Princeton University Press, 1987

Stern, Steve J., *The Secret History of Gender: Women, Men, and Power in Late Colonial Mexico*, Chapel Hill: University of North Carolina Press, 1995

Stoner, K. Lynn, *From the House to the Streets: The Cuban Women's Movement for Legal Reform, 1898–1940*, Durham, NC: Duke University Press, 1991

Tutino, John, "Power, Class, and Family: Men and Women in the Mexican Elite, 1750–1810," *The Americas* 39 (1983), 359–82

Women's History: North America

The roots of women's history in North America lie with the beginnings of women's activism. The explosion of women's history in the 1970s which accompanied the postwar feminist revival was preceded by an earlier flowering of women's scholarship during the first wave of feminism which culminated in the suffrage movement. Early 20th-century women's history scholars sought to reclaim women's contributions to society or to understand women's disadvantaged position in society. The best known "foremother" of American women's history was Mary Ritter Beard. Beard examined women's voluntarism and activism as early as 1915, and went on to co-author major works in American history with her husband, the noted historian Charles Beard. Her *magnum opus* would not appear until 1946. Beard's views grew out of early 20th-century expansion of women's roles, female reform, and her own suffrage activism. Troubled by an emphasis on women's second-class citizenship, Beard demonstrated the integral role women had played since ancient times in shaping and creating human society. Her *Women as Force in History* (1946) would not receive a warm reception until a new generation of historians took up her call to give "the personalities, interests, ideas and activities of women . . . an attention commensurate with their energy in history." Beginning in the late 1960s, this is exactly what historians of women have done.

Second-wave feminism's contribution to the history of women in North America is the understanding of gender as a social category that is historically constructed and that shapes the experiences of women in family, community, and workplace, and in relation to the state. Yet women's historians have had to shape their analysis of gender to include an understanding of race, class, and ethnicity and their impact on the female experience.

Barbara Welter's "The Cult of True Womanhood" (1966), a pioneering work in North American women's history, set the paradigm for later historians by defining women's sphere. Welter analyzed prescriptive literature's message for 19th-century women, delineating the concept of separate spheres. The home, woman's sphere, became the repository of virtue in the burgeoning nation. Piety, purity, and submissiveness were the watchwords of femininity. Welter's work raised a series of questions that shaped research into women's history. If women's sphere was so confining, and industrialization was one cause of this development, were women's lives less constrained in the colonial era? Within women's sphere were there satisfactions and sources of power? Did Welter's definition of women's sphere apply beyond the white, Protestant northeastern United States?

The constraints on 19th-century women prompted research into early America. "Golden Age" theories characterized the first forays into American women's past. In preindustrial North America the home, as a site of production, economically essential to the family, engaged women in crafts, barter, and trade, in contrast to their seemingly diminished role in 19th-century households. Laurel Thatcher Ulrich explored colonial American women's position in society further. "Goodwife" summed up the lives of most women, and those who took charge of farms and businesses did so as "deputy husbands" – surrogates for the men in their lives. Cornelia Dayton Hughes' research on Connecticut courts revealed the mitigating effect that Puritan community life had on patriarchal English legal tradition. Dayton shows the uses New Haven women made of the courts in the 17th century. But women's use of the courts faded with the maturation of colonial New England society in the 18th century. Evidence from wills shows that women in the Chesapeake during the 17th century experienced greater autonomy than in England. Skewed sex ratios, indentured servitude, and high mortality rates led to late marriages, smaller families, and premature widowhood, increasing women's social status. Essential to the transfer of property to the next generation, women carved a unique position in colonial Chesapeake. European women in New France shared the experience of small numbers in the 17th century. A majority of female immigrants migrated alone. One significant group of women in New France were the nuns, arriving first to convert the Native Americans, and ultimately to minister to the French community and educate generations of Canadian women in their convent schools. High rates of intermarriage in New France placed indigenous women in the role of cultural intermediaries. In late 18th-century Upper Canada, women's roles as wives, mothers, and workers within and outside the home made them essential contributors to colonial development.

In the 1980s and 1990s, historians turned increasingly to the study of the "first women" of North America, Native American women. Despite tremendous regional, language, and cultural diversity, scholars agreed that women's crucial role in community survival was recognized in Native American societies, reflected in considerable social, economic, and political influence. Tribes were organized both matrilineally and matrilocally. Native American women held responsibility for husbanding, processing, and distributing the tribes' diet. Consequently women exercised tribal power over in community decisions, the selection of leaders, and war making.

From early rosy views of colonial womanhood, women's historians assumed the American Revolution had a negative impact on American women. It resulted in a diminution of social status and exploitation by market capitalism, according to Joan Hoff Wilson. Mary Beth Norton studied Tory women and discovered, however, that disruption resulted in increased competence among women. Linda Kerber delved into the impact of revolutionary rhetoric on American women. She found that the potential of equality and liberty was not lost on educated elite women. The new nation bestowed a political function on women – as mothers of citizens.

Further inquiry illustrated that women's sphere in the 19th century was not as narrow or private as Welter had assumed. According to historians Nancy Cott and Carroll Smith Rosenberg, women's family worlds provided an important source of sisterhood. Cott showed how women took the social directive of piety and channeled it into religion and reform, arguing that domestic ideology could be a launching pad for public activity as well as domestic power. Smith Rosenberg posed a "female world of love and ritual" defined by life cycle and close relationships among women. She found evidence of romantic friendships among women, perhaps the most emotionally important ties in women's lives.

The impact of industrialization provided another area for study. In the New England textile mills young women found their first opportunity to live outside the family. Working together on the mill floors, and living together in boarding houses, this homogenous work force began some of the earliest industrial labor protests in American history. These mills provided jobs for Canadian and Southern European immigrant women later in the century. In antebellum New York City, Christine Stansell found that wages in an urban setting weakened the patriarchal family and conferred a new status on working-class daughters. Working-class women shared a female world, a "city of women" but one that spilled out into the workshops and streets and that offered the dangers of sexual and economic exploitation as well as the possibility of mutual support and collective action.

Historians of African American women's history built on the signposts of white women's history but reshaped the questions to fit the experience of coerced migration, enslavement, and institutionalized racism. Work and reproduction defined the parameters of African American women's lives on southern plantations. According to Deborah White, slave women shared a female community that eased the burdens and exploitation of their condition. Despite white views that denied African American women's motherhood and derided their sexuality, family relationships and child rearing offered solace and esteem. After slavery, family and community survival channeled African American women's entry into the domestic labor force, education, and reform activity. Political goals like suffrage were race- as well as sex-based demands.

Eleanor Flexner's pioneering *Century of Struggle* (1959), an institutional history of the suffrage movement, was followed by Ellen DuBois' exploration of feminism and suffrage, which applied social movement theory to women's grassroots activism. The single-issue focus of the suffrage movement won the passage of the 19th amendment but served to camouflage the divergent interests of American women. Feminism and women's activism seemed to unravel after 1920, however, Cott's 1987 study of feminism in the 1920s revealed a profusion of activity and a tremendous diversity of interest.

Turn-of-the-century urbanization, immigration, and industrialization raised once again the question of women's role in the family economy. The city and its economic opportunities drew women from the countryside, and single women away from the family. Joanne Meyerowitz's study of Chicago and its "women adrift" described women's residential and work communities. Industrial wages provided independence for daughters. The gendered pay scale nonetheless placed young women at a distinct disadvantage in their social and sexual relationships with male peers, a position they navigated with aplomb and ingenuity, shaping North American dating patterns for most of the century, according to Kathy Peiss. North American cities not only abetted youthful heterosexuality but also provided an arena for the expression of homosexuality, from the lifelong liaisons of middle-class female reformers, to the selfconscious sexual autonomy of African American blues singers in 1920s Harlem.

Of central concern to both Canadian and American women's historians is the impact of World War II and developments in women's lives in the post-World War II era. Married women became a major factor in the labor force during the 1940s, and have increased their presence with each decade since. Ruth Milkman studied the position of women in the electronics industry, their job descriptions, wages, and union representation, or lack thereof. Her study showed the tremendous flexibility of definitions of men's and women's work, with one caveat: inferior wages and lack of advancement accompanied women into their industrial frontiers.

Until recently Betty Friedan's portrayal of the 1950s held sway: government and media beckoned women back into the home after the war with promises of complete fulfillment in homemaking and child rearing. Joanne Meyerowitz and other scholars question that depiction, noting its narrow middle-class, white parameters and its one-dimensional treatment of middle-class women. Their work uncovered a more varied image of women in the popular media, the proliferation of organizational activity among working-class, Mexican American, and African American women in their struggle for justice, and the subversive uses of the cultural conception of motherhood. Political experience, not just discontent, primed postwar women for the 1960s feminist revival.

Sara Evans pinpointed the civil rights and student movements as the crucibles of radical feminism, providing theories of oppression, political and leadership skills, and consciousness of gender oppression to young women activists. Alice Echols exposed the crosscurrents within radical feminism that pulled against unity even as feminists professed universal sisterhood. After 1960, immigration reshaped North American society tremendously. Scholars such as Evelyn Nakano Glenn analyzed the position of women of color and immigrant women in the economy, noting the connections between prewar domestic service and the postwar expansion of the service sector. Glen's work and the work of scholars such as Linda Gordon illustrate the important contributions of women's history to our understanding of gender role in shaping the state. Pioneering work on the welfare state uncovers the deep cultural notions of motherhood and family that influenced the construction, and, in the 1990s, the dismantling of the welfare state. Other scholars assert the importance of women's history to political history more broadly defined, in the essays in *US History as Women's History* edited by Kerber, Alice Kessler-Harris, and Kathryn Kish Sklar.

Having created gender as a category of historical analysis, women's historians have redefined its centrality in order to understand the impact of race, class, and ethnicity on women's status and experience. Feminism prompted the study of women's history, informs its analysis, and garners much of its attention. But in Canada and the US family relationships, racial and ethnic allegiance, labor force participation, and other forms of activism have proven to be crucial aspects of women's experience, past and present. With attention to the variables that shape the lives of all women, women's historians are creating new understandings of female experiences in North America.

JESSICA WEISS

See also Beard, M.; Cott; Degler; Kerber; Kessler-Harris; Smith-Rosenberg; Ulrich

Further Reading

Anderson, Karen, *Chain Her by One Foot: The Subjugation of Native Women in Seventeenth Century New France*, London and New York: Routledge, 1993

Beard, Mary Ritter, *Woman as Force in History: A Study in Traditions and Realities*, New York: Macmillan, 1946

Carr, Lois Green and Lorena Walsh, "The Planter's Wife: The Experience of White Women in Seventeenth Century Maryland," *William and Mary Quarterly* 34 (1977), 542–71

Cott, Nancy F., *The Bonds of Womanhood: "Woman's Sphere" in New England, 1780–1835*, New Haven and London: Yale University Press, 1977

Cott, Nancy F., *The Grounding of Modern Feminism*, New Haven: Yale University Press, 1987

Dayton, Cornelia Hughes, *Women before the Bar: Gender, Law, and Society in Connecticut, 1639–1789*, Chapel Hill: University of North Carolina Press, 1995

Degler, Carl N., *At Odds: Women and the Family in America from the Revolution to the Present*, New York and Oxford: Oxford University Press, 1980

Dubinsky, Karen, *Improper Advances: Rape and Heterosexual Conflict in Ontario, 1880–1929*, Chicago: University of Chicago Press, 1993

DuBois, Ellen Carol, *Feminism and Suffrage: The Emergence of an Independent Women's Movement in America, 1848–1869*, Ithaca, NY: Cornell University Press, 1978

DuBois Ellen Carol, and Vicki L. Ruiz, eds., *Unequal Sisters: A Multicultural Reader in US Women's History*, New York: Routledge, 1990; 2nd edition 1994

Echols, Alice, *Daring to Be Bad: Radical Feminism in America, 1967–1975*, Minneapolis: University of Minnesota Press, 1989

Errington, Elizabeth Jane, *Wives and Mothers, Schoolmistresses and Scullery Maids: Working Women in Upper Canada, 1790–1840*, Montreal: McGill University Press, 1995

Evans, Sara M., *Personal Politics: The Roots of Women's Liberation in the Civil Rights Movement and the New Left*, New York: Knopf, 1979

Flexner, Eleanor, *Century of Struggle: The Woman's Rights Movement in the United States*, Cambridge, MA: Harvard University Press, 1959; enlarged edition, with Ellen Fitzpatrick, 1996

Friedan, Betty, *The Feminine Mystique*, New York: Norton, and London: Gollancz, 1963

Giddings, Paula, *When and Where I Enter: The Impact of Black Women on Race and Sex in America*, New York, Morrow, 1984

Glenn, Evelyn Nakano, *Issei, Nisei, War Bride: Three Generations of Japanese American Women in Domestic Service*, Philadelphia: Temple University Press, 1986

Gordon, Linda, *Pitied but Not Entitled: Single Mothers and the History of Welfare, 1890–1935*, New York: Free Press, 1994

Hoff, Joan, *Law, Gender, and Injustice: A Legal History of US Women*, New York: New York University Press, 1991

Kerber, Linda K., *Women of the Republic: Intellect and Ideology in Revolutionary America*, Chapel Hill: University of North Carolina Press, 1980

Kerber, Linda K., Alice Kessler-Harris, and Kathryn Kish Sklar, eds., *US History as Women's History: New Feminist Essays*, Chapel Hill: University of North Carolina Press, 1995

Meyerowitz, Joanne, *Women Adrift: Independent Wage Earners in Chicago, 1880–1930*, Chicago: University of Chicago Press, 1988

Meyerowitz, Joanne, *Not June Cleaver: Women and Gender in Postwar America*, Philadelphia: Temple University Press, 1994

Milkman, Ruth, ed., *Women, Work, and Protest: A Century of US Women's Labor History*, Boston and London: Routledge, 1985

Norton, Mary Beth, *Liberty's Daughters: The Revolutionary Experience of American Women, 1750–1800*, Boston: Little Brown, 1980; revised 1996

Peiss, Kathy, *Cheap Amusements: Working Women and Leisure in Turn-of-the-Century New York City*, Philadelphia: Temple University Press, 1986

Prentice, Alison *et al.*, *Canadian Women: A History*, Toronto: Harcourt Brace Jovanovich, 1988

Schlissel, Lillian, Vicki L. Ruiz, and Janice Monk, eds., *Western Women: Their Land, Their Lives*, Albuquerque: University of New Mexico Press, 1988

Smith-Rosenberg, Carroll, *Disorderly Conduct: Visions of Gender in Victorian America*, New York: Knopf, 1985

Stansell, Christine, *City of Women: Sex and Class in New York, 1789–1860*, New York: Knopf, 1986

Ulrich, Laurel Thatcher, *Good Wives: Image and Reality in the Lives of Women in Northern New England, 1650–1750*, New York: Knopf, 1982

Welter, Barbara, "The Cult of True Womanhood, 1820–1860," *American Quarterly* 8 (1966), 151–74; also in her *Dimity Convictions: The American Woman in the Nineteenth Century*, Athens: Ohio University Press, 1976

White, Deborah Gray, *Ar'n't I a Woman? Female Slaves in the Plantation South*, New York: Norton, 1985

Wood, G.A. 1865–1928
Australian (British-born) historian

G.A. Wood was the first professor and incumbent of the Challis chair of history at the University of Sydney from 1891 until his death. During his long teaching career he exerted considerable influence over many students who became leading citizens in a variety of fields such as law, education, government service, and the church. Five students became either professors of history or of history and political science. Coming from a Manchester nonconformist family and educated at Oxford in the school of history founded by Bishop Stubbs, Wood invested his teaching and writing with a strong Whiggish and moralistic bias. Following the British radical anti-aristocratic political tradition traceable back to Milton and Cromwell, Wood was convinced that the best elements in British history were represented by their ideological successors such as W.E. Gladstone and Lloyd George. These great liberals were exemplary for the British empire and its dominions as well as for the world in general. Wood believed in the singularity of British history in that its course, above all others, evinced the triumph of humane, progressive, and democratic political principles. Indeed, what had begun in Britain would be continued with even greater prospects for success in the dominions because they were not encumbered by a traditional aristocracy.

As a professional historian trained in the Oxford school which did so much to import the methodology of Leopold von Ranke from Germany, Wood was earnest in his emphasis of the importance of primary sources. However, in contrast to Ranke, Wood did not regard every age of the past as of equal importance. In his inaugural lecture (22 May 1891) Wood frankly averred that some ages of the past were dead, that is, they held nothing of value for the present. Others lived, producing individuals of great humanitarian vision and influence. It was these which the historian had to reveal to the current generation for their political and cultural edification. History was thus a storehouse of culturally valuable examples that were essential for the education of well-rounded, humane, and public-spirited individuals. If anything, Wood became more vigorous in this political-cultural pedagogy with the passage of time, as his 1901 public lecture, "The Study of History in Relation to Culture" illustrates.

No doubt the experience of the Boer War, which Wood vehemently opposed as thoroughly unworthy of the British empire, intensified his commitment to Whig historiography. He regarded the campaign against the Boer republics as a blatant example of aristocratic imperialist politics, and so he used all the influence he could muster to oppose the use of Australian troops as part of the imperial force. Wood's anti-Boer war activity brought him the threat of dismissal for "disloyal utterances." Following the example set by Gladstone, Wood championed the rights of "small" peoples. Ironically, this passion led Wood to fervent support of Britain against Germany in 1914 because of the latter's violation of Belgian neutrality. Consequently, he was an advocate of conscription in Australia, but at the same time a champion of Home Rule for Ireland because he believed that this would lead Irish Australians to drop their reservations about the imperial war effort against the Kaiser's Germany and support conscription.

Wood was an avowedly political historian, as his many occasional publications and lectures, especially those on World War I, show. At the base of his mindset was his nonconformist Christianity, which enabled many 19th-century liberals to combine deep religious conviction with intellectual radicalism. Wood taught history at Sydney entirely on his own until 1916 when the first assistant lecturer was appointed, and this workload, as well as his penchant for becoming involved in causes such as the South African War and World War I, account for his relatively small output of books. He was a trained documentary historian, and it was clear he would never be able from his Sydney base to work again on a European topic, so he devoted himself to the collection of sources on the discovery and settlement of Australia. Out of this he published in 1922 *The Discovery of Australia* (reissued 1969), his *magnum opus*. It was essentially a work of nautical history which became controversial because it obscured the Portuguese contribution. Wood followed this by a smaller and popular work inspired by the figure of Captain Cook, *The Voyage of the Endeavour* (1926). Given other circumstances, Wood might have produced much more about the foundations of New South Wales, as he had amassed a great deal of the primary source material. However, all that appeared from this preliminary work was a series of articles in the *Journal of the Royal Australian Historical Society* on key personages such as Richard Johnson, the colony's first chaplain, naval officers, and early colonial governors. In 1920 Wood wrote a long essay, "Australia and Imperial Politics" in which he explained Australian independence of mind as deriving essentially from the British radical democratic tradition. Wood perceived himself as an "Englishman Australianate" serving the country of his adoption as a pioneer in the new environment of the values enshrined in that democratic tradition.

JOHN A. MOSES

Biography

George Arnold Wood. Born Salford, England, 7 June 1865, son of a cotton merchant. Attended Bowden College, Cheshire; Owens College, Manchester University, BA 1885; Balliol College, Oxford, BA 1888, MA 1890; University of Marburg, Germany, 1889; Mansfield College, Oxford, 1890–91. Emigrated to Australia, 1891; Challis chair of history, University of Sydney, 1891–1928. Married Eleanor Madeline Whitfeld, 1898 (3 sons, 1 daughter). Died Sydney, 14 October 1928.

Principal Writings

"Australia and Imperial Politics," in Meredith Atkinson, ed., *Australia: Economic and Political Studies*, 1920

The Discovery of Australia, 1922

"Foundations of Australia, 1788–1855," extracts in *Journal of the Royal Australian Historical Society*, 1922–30

The Voyage of the Endeavour, 1926

Further Reading

Caine, Barbara *et al.*, eds., *History at Sydney, 1891–1991: Centenary Reflections*, Sydney Studies in History, University of Sydney, 1992

Crawford, Raymond Maxwell, *A Bit of a Rebel: The Life and Work of George Arnold Wood*, Sydney: Sydney University Press, 1975

Moses, John A., "The Christian Basis of George Arnold Wood's Historiographical Assumptions," *St. Mark's Review* (Canberra) (1991), 17–24

Moses, John A., *Prussian-German Militarism, 1914–18 in Australian Perspective: The Thought of George Arnold Wood*, Bern: Lang 1991

Wood, Gordon S. 1933–
US historian

Over the last three decades, Gordon S. Wood has been among the most prominent figures involved in re-evaluating the causes and meaning of the American Revolution. In interpreting this critical period of US history, Wood has stressed the importance and widespread nature of changing political and social beliefs. Despite criticism from the New Left, Wood's work has been influential among scholars and has reached a broad general audience through his Pulitzer prize-winning *The Radicalism of the American Revolution* (1992).

The title of an early essay, "Rhetoric and Reality in the American Revolution" (1966), revealed a consistent tension in Wood's work. While examining the rhetoric of the period, Wood attempted to go beyond ideological explanations to search for the roots of the American Revolution in real social conflict; yet, throughout his career, his analysis has typically focused on discourse to reveal ideology, *through which* the "reality" of social conflict may be explored.

Perhaps Wood's most widely acclaimed book was *The Creation of the American Republic* (1969). Following in the ideological tradition of his mentor Bernard Bailyn, Wood in this early masterpiece traced the changes in American perceptions of politics during the Revolutionary years. A dramatic shift in political thought paralleled changes in actual forms of government. Wood outlined these concurrent changes by looking at the new state constitutions and the federal constitution of 1787–88. The new constitutions reflected new political thought: they provided not for the old English mixed government, but for a tripartite government in which all parts depended on the people. The development of this democratic republic was, he argues, "not the revolution that had been intended but it was a real revolution nonetheless, marked by a momentous upheaval in the understanding of politics." The radicalism of the revolution, as he later called it, was the result of revolutionary ideas slipping out of the control of patrician leaders, who had little choice but to adapt to popular notions of democracy they had never intended to adopt.

The notion of an unintentionally radical revolution connects the early classic *The Creation of the American Republic* to the more recent landmark *The Radicalism of the American Revolution*. This study argued that, far from the conservative coup that some would make it out to be, the American Revolution was an event of social and political transformation that was indeed radical in its 18th-century context. The three sections into which Wood divided the book pointed to his interpretation of the progress of the Revolution: monarchy, republicanism, democracy. While monarchy in the colonies was never the impressive force it was within England, it was an important facet of colonial life and established the basis for a patriarchal, vertically organized society that was a truncated version of hierarchical society in Europe. The intent of the revolutionary leaders was to reorganize this society along republican lines, replacing patronage and dependence with virtue and disinterestedness – a society that would still need a patrician class, though it had no nobility. The seeds of egalitarianism had been sown, however, and the republican revolution gave way to a more dramatic democratic revolution. Conceptions of property, labor, and social equality all changed drastically. Despite its failure to abolish slavery or enfranchise women, the Revolution also unleashed the forces that would eventually lead to abolitionism and the suffrage movement. Wood's revolution is thus a long revolution, the results of which are still making themselves known today.

Critics have varied in their notion of how *Radicalism* relates to *Creation*; some have seen the later book as demolishing the earlier, while others consider *Radicalism* a "reprise" of Wood's earlier work. What seems clear is that at least since *The Creation of the American Republic*, Wood viewed the American Revolution as moving through republicanism toward greater democracy and as turning out to be more radical than intended. The use of the term *radical* itself seems to have been the issue that has drawn the most violent criticism; critics on the left have argued that the use of the term is inappropriate given the continuing inequalities in American society, particularly the continuation of slavery after the Revolution. Wood's Revolution has been renamed "adequate," his radicalism labeled "genteel." In response, Wood has reminded us that his intention was to reconstruct the context in which the Revolution was indeed radical – that is, a monarchical society in which the vast majority of people, white men as well as women and slaves, were subordinated within a long chain of hierarchies that defined their place in society. While the oppression experienced by the average white working man was not comparable to that experienced by the slave, Wood contended that the abolition of the former was a prerequisite for the destruction of the latter. It is this reconstruction of the social world out of which the American Revolution arose that is perhaps the most important contribution of this work, helping us to place the Revolution and its rhetoric within its historical context in a more meaningful way.

ANGELA VIETTO

See also Bailyn; United States: American Revolution; United States: 19th Century

Biography

Gordon Stewart Wood. Born Concord, Massachusetts, 27 November 1933. Received BA, Tufts University, 1955; MA, Harvard University, 1959, PhD 1964. Served in the US Air Force, 1955–58. Taught at College of William and Mary, 1964–66; Harvard University, 1966–67; University of Michigan, Ann Arbor, 1967–69; and Brown University (rising to professor), from 1969. Married Louise Goss, 1956 (2 daughters, 1 son).

Principal Writings

The Creation of the American Republic, 1776–1787, 1969
With others, *The Great Republic: A History of the American People*, 1977; 4th edition, 1992
The Radicalism of the American Revolution, 1992

Further Reading

Appleby, Joyce, Barbara Clark Smith, Michael Zuckerman, and Gordon S. Wood, "How Revolutionary Was the Revolution? A Discussion of Gordon S. Wood's *The Radicalism of the American Revolution*," *William and Mary Quarterly* 51 (1994), 677–716

Woodson, Carter G. 1875–1950
US historian

The "Father of Negro History" was born in 1875 in New Canton, Virginia, the son of James Henry Woodson, a sharecropper, and Anne Eliza Riddle Woodson. Carter G. Woodson was the first and only black American descended from slave parents to earn a PhD in history, and his parents' background influenced him to write about slavery.

Woodson's philosophy of history and ideas about how education could influence society and improve race relations were shaped by his experiences at Frederick Douglass High School, Berea College, the University of Chicago, and Harvard University. His doctoral dissertation, which was directed at Harvard by Albert Bushnell Hart, Edward Channing, and Frederick Jackson Turner, focused on the events leading to the secession of counties in western Virginia and the creation of the state of West Virginia after the Civil War broke out.

In 1915 Woodson founded the Association for the Study of Negro Life and History and began the work that sustained him for the rest of his career. He established the *Journal of Negro History* in 1916 and Associated Publishers in 1921 to publish materials in African American History. The *Journal* served as the centerpiece for Woodson's research program, and not only provided black scholars with a medium in which to publish their research, but also served as an outlet for white scholars, when their interpretations differed from their colleagues in the mainstream of the historical profession. To bring his message to a broader audience of schoolteachers and the general public, Negro History Week was launched in 1926, and the *Negro History Bulletin* was published as a monthly, beginning in 1937.

Woodson's research and programmatic objectives were to write the social history of African Americans and to counter the racism in the work published by white historians. With several young black assistants, Woodson used new interdisciplinary methods and sources, combining anthropology, archaeology, sociology, and history, and moved away from interpreting African Americans as victims of white oppression and racism. Instead, they were viewed as major actors in American history with a separate and rich cultural past. From 1915, when his first book, *The Education of the Negro prior to 1861*, came out, until 1947, when the 9th edition of his textbook, *The Negro in Our History* appeared, Woodson published four monographs, five textbooks, five edited collections of source materials, and thirteen articles, as well as five sociological studies that were collaborative efforts.

Topically, Woodson's work covered all aspects of the African American experience: slavery, the slave trade, culture, the family, religion, work, and the building of black institutions. Among the first scholars to study slavery from the slaves' perspective, Woodson also gave attention to the comparative study of slavery as an institution in the United States and Latin America. His work prefigured the interpretations of contemporary scholars of slavery by several decades, since he examined resistance to slavery, miscegenation, and black achievements during slavery. In his work Woodson also noted the African cultural influences on African American culture. Woodson devoted several books to work, examining both the black working class and black professionals. He also pioneered in the study of black religious history and was drawn to an examination of the black church because it functioned as an institutional center in the community, serving as the foundation for the rise of an independent black culture.

JACQUELINE GOGGIN

See also African Diaspora

Biography

Carter Godwin Woodson. Born New Canton, Virginia, 19 December 1875. Educated at Frederick Douglass High School, 1895–99; received BLitt, Berea College, 1903; taught English in the Philippines, 1903–07; MA in European history, University of Chicago, 1908; studied at University of Paris, 1908; PhD, Harvard University, 1912. Founder, Association for the Study of Negro Life and History, 1915; founder/editor, *Journal of Negro History*, 1916–54; founder, *Negro History Bulletin*, 1937. Died Washington, DC, 3 April 1950.

Principal Writings

The Education of the Negro prior to 1861: A History of the Education of the Colored People of the United States from the Beginning of Slavery to the Civil War, 1915
A Century of Negro Migration, 1918
The History of the Negro Church, 1921
The Negro in Our History, 1922
The Rural Negro, 1930
The Mis-Education of the Negro, 1933
The Negro Professional Man and the Community, with Special Emphasis on the Physician and the Lawyer, 1934
The African Background Outlined; or, Handbook for the Study of the Negro, 1936

Further Reading

Franklin, John Hope, "The New Negro History," *Journal of Negro History* 42 (1957), 89–97
Goggin, Jacqueline, *Carter G. Woodson: A Life in Black History*, Baton Rouge: Louisiana State University Press, 1993
Klingberg, Frank J., "Carter G. Woodson, Historian, and His Contribution to American Historiography," *Journal of Negro History* 41 (1956), 66–68
Meier, August, and Elliott M. Rudwick, *Black History and the Historical Profession, 1915–1980*, Urbana: University of Illinois Press, 1986
Thorpe, Earl E., *Negro Historians in the United States*, Baton Rouge, LA: Fraternal Press, 1958; revised as *Black Historians: A Critique*, New York: Morrow, 1971

Woodward, C. Vann 1908–

US historian of the American South

C. Vann Woodward's writings have dominated the post-World War II historiography of the modern American South. Such scholarly eminence is particularly remarkable given that Woodward's major works were published in the 1950s; yet in the case of his *magnum opus*, *Origins of the New South* (1951), no significant challenges have yet overturned his central premises and conclusions.

Woodward's first work, *Tom Watson: Agrarian Rebel* (1938), reflected interests and positions that characterized Woodward's entire oeuvre. Writing in the midst of the worst economic depression in American history, Woodward was influenced by the historiography of Charles Beard and others who emphasized the dynamic of conflict as the driving force in American history. Woodward sought to bring this approach to his reading of the South in the wake of the Civil War. Previous generations of southern historians had emphasized the continuities between the Old South and the New: slavery was viewed as a benign institution, replaced later by an equally benign world of "Jim Crow" segregation. Planter aristocrats became the robber barons of New South industrialism.

In his interpretation of Tom Watson, a leader of the Populist party in Georgia, Woodward argued that Watson, and Populism, embodied all of the class and racial tensions that characterized the truly "New" South. The Populists rejected the leadership of the middle-class industrialists, and in some cases openly supported class-based, rather than racially divided, alliances, threatening to overturn the entire edifice of white political and economic supremacy. Watson was at the forefront of these efforts, according to Woodward.

This interpretation was also a significant corrective to prevailing opinions of Populism at large, suggesting that it was more southern, and more radical in its diagnosis and remedy for the ills of burgeoning industrial American capitalism, than had previously been thought. Purchasing cooperatives, a "Farmers Alliance" attempted to combat the emerging forces of "bigness" in American life: railroads, banks, and politics, for example. In Woodward's hands Watson became a tragic figure, one who passed from constructive political leader to a disillusioned racist demagogue.

Woodward deepened many of these insights in his prize-winning *Origins of the New South* (1951). Beginning in the year 1877, the official terminus of Reconstruction, Woodward argued that the Redeemers, those who sought economic and political power in the period of restoration of southern political power, were not legatees of the Old South ruling class, but were quite new in interests and background: "In the main they were of middle-class, industrial, capitalistic outlook, with little but nominal connection with the planter regime." Thus these pro-business, pro-commercial forces were – in Woodward's words – representatives of "more innovation than restoration, more break than continuity with the past."

Woodward told a bitter story of the oppression of poor whites, black disfranchisement, and growing impoverishment, the continuing colonization of southern resources at the hands of the industrial North, all enriching this emerging class of New South industrialists. In politics as well, corruption and racism dominated the tableau, with the occasional outburst of a doomed democratic impulse, such as the Populists.

Woodward's enduring interest in the twists and turns of southern history manifested itself in his best-known, most controversial book, *The Strange Career of Jim Crow* (1955). The book was written in the same year as the landmark school desegregation case, *Brown* v. *Board of Education*, in which Woodward served as an academic adviser for the counsel for the plaintiffs seeking desegregation, and in it he sought to answer the question of what the history of segregation actually had been in the South.

Woodward maintained that rigid segregation should be understood as *de jure*, and such legal actions had not immediately taken root in the post-Reconstructionist South, but rather had emerged only gradually, culminating in the spate of Jim Crow statutes and state constitutions of the 1890s and early 1900s. This phase replaced "an era of experiment and variety in race relations . . . in which segregation was not the invariable rule." Subsequent historians took issue with this emphasis on the legal phase of segregation, arguing that legal measures merely formalized informal, customary, yet ultimately exclusivist practices in manifold public facilities. Ironically then, segregation may have fostered a legitimate, if second-class, status to black access to these facilities. In recent writings Woodward has conceded that more segregation existed earlier in the postbellum South, while the segregation of the early 20th century may have been less all-encompassing than he maintained.

Woodward's significance as a historian of American history remains despite his largely regionally focused scholarship. It is also the case that in one of his later books, *The Burden of Southern History* (1960), he explicitly sought to illuminate American life through the lens of the southernist. In a series of essays, particularly "The Irony of Southern History" (1958) and "The Search for Southern Identity" (1953), Woodward – as he explicitly acknowledged – explored Reinhold Niebuhr's notion of "irony" as a useful way to understand the South and its relation to American civilization.

Woodward's notion of irony was designed to help the South reconsider its own identity in light of its history. The South had a different history of race relations, as well as of economic and social patterns. In an age of increasing national homogeneity, Woodward sought a viable means of ensuring a positive, enduring southern distinctiveness. For him, it should not be the tragic legacy of slavery and racial division, nor the New South's creation of an industrial elite and a downtrodden working class. It would rather be the South's sense of that historical record, with its various accomplishments and failures.

This notion of southern history in turn could inform the American present. American culture included the mythology of innocent origins; its historical trajectory was a path to world power. Woodward recast this cultural dissonance by asserting that America's story of overwhelming success placed it largely outside the experience of the rest of the world, thereby endangering its ability to lead a world with which it had little in common. The American South, by contrast, had experienced manifest defeat, rather than destiny, poverty and exploitation, occupation and humiliation. Hence it could fairly be said that its history constituted a teaching for America about life as it truly was for most people and countries throughout the world. Such a history – ironically prescient in light of events in the 1960s – might prevent America from behaving with hubris in spite of its manifold powers.

DAVID B. STARR

See also African American; United States: 19th Century

Biography

Comer Vann Woodward. Born Vanndale, Arkansas, 13 November 1908. Received PhB, Emory University, 1930; MA in political science, Columbia University, 1932; PhD in history, University of North Carolina, 1937. Taught English, Georgia Institute of Technology, 1930–31, 1932–33; social science, University of Florida, 1937–39; and history, University of Virginia, 1939–40; and Scripps College, 1940–43; professor, Johns Hopkins University, 1946–61; and Yale University, 1961–77 (emeritus). Served in naval intelligence, 1942–46. Married Glenn Boyd MacLeod, 1937 (died 1982; 1 son).

Principal Writings

Tom Watson: Agrarian Rebel, 1938
Origins of the New South, 1877–1913, 1951; updated by Charles B. Dew, 1971
Reunion and Reaction: The Compromise of 1877 and the End of Reconstruction, 1951
"The Search for Southern Identity," *Journal of Southern History* 19 (1953), 3–19
The Strange Career of Jim Crow, 1955; 3rd edition 1974
"The Irony of Southern History," *Virginia Quarterly Review* 34 (1958), 321–38
The Burden of Southern History, 1960
American Counterpoint: Slavery and Racism in the North-South Dialogue, 1971
Editor, *Mary Chestnut's Civil War*, 1981
Thinking Back: The Perils of Writing History, 1986
The Future of the Past, 1989
The Old World's New World, 1991

Further Reading

Kousser, J. Morgan, and James M. McPherson, eds., *Religion, Race, and Reconstruction: Essays in Honor of C. Vann Woodward*, New York: Oxford University Press, 1982 [includes bibliography]
Roper, John Herbert, *Comer Vann Woodward, Southerner*, Athens: University of Georgia Press, 1987

World History

World or global history is of relatively recent origin as a coherent field of study. To be sure, even in ancient times historians such as Herodotus (Greece) and Sima Qian (Han China) introduced a broad framework, examining the peoples on the fringes of their own civilizations, while the 13th-century Persian Rashid al-Din offered a multicultural approach, and the 14th-century Arab Ibn Khaldun explained the behavior of varied societies. Their preoccupation with supernatural intervention in temporal affairs necessarily gave some premodern Hebrew, Christian, Muslim, Buddhist, and Hindu thinkers a universal outlook. There was a persistent concern over the centuries with larger questions, including the consequences of the interaction between diverse and competitive peoples. During the European Enlightenment Voltaire developed an interest in Asian civilizations for purposes of comparison with

Europe and compiled a universal history that broadened the rigid historiographical tradition. Later Karl Marx articulated a world historical approach. In late 19th-century China the reformist scholar Liang Qichao called for the study of world history to address his country's national humiliation at the hands of the West. But the sort of global history accepted today was impossible for centuries; historians lacked sufficient information about other societies while worldviews were still largely parochial.

A truly analytical and comprehensive history with a universal perspective became feasible only with the great increase of knowledge and the evolution of a more international orientation during the past century. Social scientists and humanists learned much more about the peoples and traditions of Asia, Africa, and Latin America, while Western critical historiography spread. The context of the current era, including devastating world wars, colonization and decolonization, revolutions, nuclear threats, environmental crises, and rapid changes in all aspects of life also fostered a realization that the widest possible angle of vision was most appropriate for understanding Spaceship Earth and the Global Village. This required a history that was more than the sum of its parts. And yet, world history has remained relatively marginal as a field of study worldwide, criticized as requiring a grand synthesis involving vast amounts of knowledge and sweeping generalizations. Nor was there agreement on whether world history commenced with the Western voyages of exploration in the 15th–16th centuries or millennia earlier. Heated debates persisted between those identifying a progressive evolution or directionality of humankind (e.g., toward socialism, liberal capitalism, freedom, or religion) and those mistrusting broad theoretical or ideological thrusts.

The pioneers of world history in the West during the first half of this century were philosophers of history, Oswald Spengler and Arnold Toynbee; along with other universalist scholars of the period, such as H.G. Wells, Christopher Dawson, Karl Jaspers, Pitirim Sorokin, and Karl Lamprecht, they sought for the most part to comprehend the principles of history rather than narrate events or analyze processes. Spengler, an eclectic German, and Toynbee, a British classicist, were particularly interested in understanding "civilizations" and "cultures," large complexes defined by shared features and orientations, rather than national states. The foreordained rise and fall of Western Christendom or Hindu India were deemed the appropriate focus for studying the larger forces of history such as "challenge and response." But although their work was valuable in establishing some key frameworks and posing stimulating questions, most historians found it wanting on various counts; all too often they were forced to conform their material to their explanatory framework. Furthermore, their ideas were based largely on European (especially ancient) and, to a lesser extent, Asian experience, betraying little understanding of other regions. The same was true for the efforts of French Orientalist René Grousset, although his work, along with the informed musings of the Indian nationalist leader Jawaharlal Nehru, restored Asia to a position of historical primacy.

The writing of world history changed dramatically from the 1950s onwards, with less emphasis on the meaning of history and more on processes and comparisons. No doubt this reflected the increasing interaction and sometimes confrontation of nations, as well as the globalization of education in the United States. Whereas most earlier studies were by Europe-based scholars, Americans now came to the forefront. Furthermore, there was a gradual movement toward a more comprehensive approach that incorporated all world regions. The study of Western civilizations became entrenched in American universities in the years following World War I and it remained a dominant pattern well into the 1970s. But beginning in the 1950s, Asian, African, Middle Eastern, and Latin American studies developed. Furthermore the writings of non-Western scholars such as the Indian K.M. Panikkar (on Western expansion) were becoming more accessible. Concurrently UNESCO commissioned the preparation of a noncentric history of humankind. The project came to involve hundreds of scholars from around the world, including Louis Gottschalk of the University of Chicago; he struggled to overcome his own entrenched Eurocentrism in discussing the period from 1300 to 1700 while also recruiting a number of young scholars into the effort. The UNESCO project was completed in 1963, under the editorship of Ralph Turner.

By the 1970s the study of Western civilizations no longer seemed sufficient to prepare American and European students for life in a pluralistic world as well as increasingly multicultural nations. As historians examined China's long-lasting Golden Age, scientific thinking in early India, vibrant Asian trade routes, the florescence of Islamic civilization, mercantile societies in black Africa, long-forgotten pre-Columbian peoples, and the substantial European import of technologies and ideas from Asia and North Africa, among other topics, it was no longer intellectually defensible to view the mainstream of history as invariably European. Clearly world history was far more complex, with major contributions from and achievements attributed to many different peoples. A pronounced internationalism and a dissatisfaction with the long-entrenched Eurocentrism of the history profession became the hallmark of world historians; there was also the realization, articulated most strongly perhaps by Geoffrey Barraclough, that global history necessarily constituted much more than a collection or compilation of national and regional narratives. World history also increasingly became differentiated from international history, the study of interstate, diplomatic, and strategic concerns (especially for the 20th century).

Out of this intellectual ferment came several major historians whose influence has been pervasive. Some of the major figures can be loosely grouped together under the rubric of the "Chicago school," since they taught at universities in the Chicago area and took up the study of world history in the 1950s; they also began publishing their most important works in the 1960s. The doyen was Canada-born William McNeill, a Europeanist whose work, borrowing from cultural anthropology, emphasized diffusion, especially of technology, and the impact this had on various societies. McNeill's scholarship was inspired by Toynbee, with whom he collaborated for a time, but was far more nuanced, sophisticated, and rooted in broadbased research. McNeill's *The Rise of the West* (1963), the first major American synthesis of the broad sweep of world history, was probably the most influential book in invigorating global studies. It incorporated Toynbee's emphasis on large-scale patterns of change but also provided a more comprehensive framework emphasizing processes transcending regions; indeed, Toynbee's "civilizations" seemed increasingly timebound and outdated as concepts in a world marked by global influences and forces. To McNeill, change was produced by contacts and collisions between societies. He pursued this theme in a series of brilliant books analyzing various aspects of diffusion and interaction, including epidemic diseases, parasitism, military and industrial technologies, and human migrants. In the process McNeill became the role model for a younger generation of world historians and the chief influence on the founding of the World History Association in 1983.

The other key figures of the "Chicago school" were Marshall Hodgson and L.S. Stavrianos. Hodgson was trained as an Islamicist and his ideas were certainly shaped by his focus on the Middle East, the pivotal intersection between East and West. His hemispheric interregional approach offered the concept of the Afro-Eurasian Historical Zone, a single field of interaction linking much of Asia, Europe, and large chunks of Africa into a comprehensible whole. Hodgson also pioneered the idea of "ecumenes," periods when transregional trade and contact became commonplace. Stavrianos, a Canada-born Balkanist, became a strong proponent of globalizing the high school and college curriculum, devoting his early energies to promoting the study of "global history" (as opposed to a Europe-based history) through his World History Project at Northwestern University and then writing textbooks for use in secondary and higher education; by the late 1960s his 2-volume world history survey had become the major text for teachers seeking a fresh approach. Stavrianos was particularly interested in the evolution and spread of technology, as well as the consequences when various peoples interact. Later in his career he employed world-system ideas to write a stimulating modern history of the "Third World" and also offered an interpretive framework for understanding world history.

A second American strand of world history study was associated with the University of Wisconsin at Madison. Philip Curtin became the most influential exponent of the comparative framework that provided the heart of the "Wisconsin school." Curtin began his career as a Caribbeanist and economic historian of West Africa; later he pioneered the concept of the Atlantic system linking the Americas, Europe, and Africa, focusing his writing on trans-Atlantic interaction (such as the slave trade), plantation systems, and kindred themes as well as on global trade patterns. Curtin also trained a number of younger world historians.

An interest in world history emerged across the Atlantic. The British scholar John Roberts, a Europeanist, contributed synthetic overviews emphasizing the rise of the West, not just as a technological and economic triumph but as a confirmation of the power of Western ideas. Barraclough stressed themes, especially for the modern period. Also influential have been Eric Hobsbawm, whose most recent study examined the 20th-century world, and C.R. Boxer and J.H. Parry (both writing on European expansion and empires). Fernand Braudel and the larger Annales school had a profound influence on world historians, especially Braudel's analysis of the rise of a global economy. Among German historians Imanuel Geiss was notable for arguing that world history commenced in deep antiquity. Italian scholar Carlo Cipolla helped pioneer demographic history.

Historically-oriented social scientists contributed greatly to the world history field. The Chicago school was influenced by concepts (such as societal typology) from anthropologists such as Alfred Kroeber and Robert Redfield. In the 1950s and 1960s the writings of modernization theorists, chiefly sociologists, and their notions of systemic change became the mainstream in American scholarship, reflected in the comparative history of Cyril Black. But the modernization concept was later perceived as rooted in American ideology and lost its credence. In the 1970s and 1980s some scholars turned to the world-system ideas of sociologist Immanuel Wallerstein and his followers, who postulated the rise after 1500 of a global economy embracing and affecting all societies as the essential framework for understanding the experiences of individual nations. Later Janet Abu-Lughod and Andre Gunder Frank (who earlier helped formulate dependency theory) would extend these ideas back to the pre-Columbian era, while Giovanni Arrighi and others would refine them for the past several centuries. Political scientist Benedict Anderson's provocative analysis of nationalism and anthropologist Eric Wolf's effort to shift the focus of world history away from Western elites to non-Western masses should also be noted.

The past two decades have seen a flourishing, heterogeneous scholarship on various themes in world history by a younger generation of scholars based chiefly in North America, Britain, and Oceania. Much of it has focused on the past thousand years, especially the centuries since 1400 CE; earlier centuries remain insufficiently studied. Scholars such as Fred Spier argue for a "big history" that begins with the Big Bang that created our universe, and places human beings in the broader context of the evolution of the Earth. Among the most important recent studies have been Jerry Bentley's examination of Eurasian interaction prior to the 16th century, Arnold Pacey's comprehensive survey of the history of technology, Paul Kennedy's tour de force on the rise and fall of empires, K.N. Chaudhuri's explorations in the evolution of the Indian Ocean trading networks, Ross Dunn's evocation of the Islamic realm of the 14th century, the various studies on environmental and agricultural history by David Arnold, Alfred Crosby, Henry Hobhouse, Clive Ponting, and Sidney Mintz, various accounts of African contributions to the emerging Atlantic world (e.g., Franklin Knight, John Thornton), the analyses by Daniel Headrick and Michael Adas of technology's role in Western expansion, the assessment of the spreading industrial revolution by Peter Stearns and Tom Kemp, James Tracy's study of early medieval world trade, books on revolutions and rebellions by Adas, Wolf, Barrington Moore, Jack Goldstone and Theda Skocpol, and the revisionist presentations of the rise of the West by Alan Smith and E.L. Jones.

As courses on world history proliferated in North American universities, the writing of surveys and overviews became more sophisticated and comprehensive; by the 1990s there were more than a dozen texts with a global focus surveying the broad sweep of history, with those by Bulliet and his colleagues, Duiker and Spielvogel, Esler, McNeill, Stavrianos, Stearns, and Upshur et al. particularly notable for non-Eurocentrism and inclusiveness. An increasing number of surveys of modern history and the 20th century by American (for example, Strayer, Chirot, Findley and Rothney, Brower, Von Laue), British (Grenville, Howarth) and Commonwealth (Robertson, Vadney) historians also appeared. Along with western historians such as Peter Gran, some Third World scholars have criticized much Western writing on world history as rooted in a Eurocentric or Americocentric hegemonic dimension. For example, India's Claude Alvares attacked the prevailing interpretation of technology and culture as imperialistic, while Egypt-born Samir Amin critiqued the Eurocentric bias and neglect of the Arab-Islamic world in the discussion of the rise of the West. And yet attempts to comprehend world history and relate it to national experiences have lately developed in China, South Africa, and elsewhere.

To be sure, there remain major controversies among world historians over many issues, including periodization, definitions, the balance between Western and non-Western societies at various periods of history, the most appropriate methodological and pedagogical approaches (chronological treatment, comprehensive or more restricted focus, comparison, thematic studies, etc.), the relationship between global and regional or national histories, whether global history constitutes a separate form that examines 20th-century globalization, and the possibility of non-centric viewpoints. World history remains a lively and increasingly international field expanding in both breadth and depth.

CRAIG A. LOCKARD

See also Barraclough; Boxer; Braudel; Chaudhuri; Cipolla; Crosby; Curtin; Herodotus; Hobsbawm; Hodgson; Ibn Khaldūn; Lamprecht; McNeill; Marx; Moore; Sima Qian; Spengler; Stavrianos; Toynbee; Voltaire; Wallerstein

Further Reading

Abu-Lughod, Janet L., *Before European Hegemony: The World System, AD 1250–1350*, New York: Oxford University Press, 1989

Adas, Michael, *Prophets of Rebellion: Millenarian Protest Movements Against the European Colonial Order*, Cambridge: Cambridge University Press, and Chapel Hill: University of North Carolina Press, 1979

Adas, Michael, *Machines as the Measure of Men: Science, Technology, and Ideologies of Western Dominance*, Ithaca, NY: Cornell University Press, 1989

Adas, Michael, ed., *Islamic and European Expansion: The Forging of a Global Order*, Philadelphia: Temple University Press, 1993

Alvares, Claude, *Decolonizing History: Technology and Culture in India, China and the West, 1492 to the Present Day*, Goa: Other India Press, and New York: Apex, 1991

Amin, Samir, *L'Eurocentrisme: critique d'une idéologie*, Paris: Anthropos, 1988; in English as *Eurocentrism*, New York: Monthly Review Press, 1989

Anderson, Benedict, *Imagined Communities: Reflections on the Origin and Spread of Nationalism*, London and New York: Verso, 1983; revised 1991

Arnold, David, *Famine: Social Crisis and Historical Change*, Oxford and New York: Blackwell, 1988

Arrighi, Giovanni, *The Long Twentieth Century: Money, Power and the Origins of Our Times*, London: Verso, 1994

Barraclough, Geoffrey, *An Introduction to Contemporary History*, London: Watts, and New York: Basic Books, 1964

Barraclough, Geoffrey, *Main Trends in History*, New York: Holmes and Meier, 1979

Barraclough, Geoffrey, *Turning Points in World History*, London: Thames and Hudson, 1979

Bentley, Jerry, *Old World Encounters: Cross-Cultural Contacts and Exchanges in Pre-Modern Times*, New York: Oxford University Press, 1993

Bentley, Jerry, *Shapes of World History in 20th Century Scholarship*, Washington, DC: American Historical Association, 1996

Black, Cyril E., *The Dynamics of Modernization: A Study in Comparative History*, New York: Harper, 1966

Boxer, C.R., *The Dutch Seaborne Empire, 1600–1800*, New York: Knopf, and London: Hutchinson, 1965

Boxer, C.R., *The Portuguese Seaborne Empire, 1415–1825*, London: Hutchinson, and New York: Knopf, 1969

Braudel, Fernand, *Civilisation matérielle et capitalisme, XVe–XVIIIe siècle*, Paris: Colin, 1967, reprinted as vol. 1 of *Civilisation matérielle, économie et capitalisme, XVe–XVIIIe siècle*, 1979; in English as *Capitalism and Material Life, 1400–1800*, New York: Harper, and London: Weidenfeld and Nicolson, 1973

Braudel, Fernand, *Grammaire des civilisations*, Paris: Flammarion, 1987; in English as *A History of Civilizations*, London and New York: Allen Lane, 1994

Brower, Daniel R., *The World in the Twentieth Century: The Age of Global War and Revolution*, 3rd edition, Englewood Cliffs, NJ: Prentice Hall, 1996

Bulliet, Richard W. *et al.*, *The Earth and Its Peoples: A Global History*, Boston: Houghton Mifflin, 1997

Cahiers d'histoire mondiale/Journal of World History, Paris: UNESCO, 1953–72

Chaudhuri, K.N., *Trade and Civilisation in the Indian Ocean: An Economic History from the Rise of Islam to 1750*, Cambridge and New York: Cambridge University Press, 1985

Chaudhuri, K.N., *Asia before Europe: Economy and Civilisation of the Indian Ocean from the Rise of Islam to 1750*, Cambridge and New York: Cambridge University Press, 1990

Chirot, Daniel, *Social Change in the Modern Era*, San Diego: Harcourt Brace, 1986

Cipolla, Carlo M., *The Economic History of World Population*, Harmondsworth: Penguin, 1962

Conniff, Michael, and Thomas J. Davis, *Africans in the Americas: A History of the Black Diaspora*, New York: St. Martin's Press, 1994

Costello, Paul, *World Historians and Their Goals: Twentieth Century Answers to Modernism*, DeKalb: Northern Illinois University, 1993

Crosby, Alfred W., Jr., *The Columbian Exchange: Biological and Cultural Consequences of 1492*, Westport, CT: Greenwood Press, 1972

Crosby, Alfred W., Jr., *Ecological Imperialism: The Biological Expansion of Europe, 900–1900*, Cambridge and New York: Cambridge University Press, 1986

Crosby, Alfred W., Jr., *Germs, Seeds, and Animals: Studies in Ecological History*, Armonk, NY: Sharpe, 1994

Curtin, Philip D., *Cross-Cultural Trade in World History*, Cambridge and New York: Cambridge University Press, 1984

Curtin, Philip D., *The Rise and Fall of the Plantation Complex; Essays in Atlantic History*, Cambridge and New York: Cambridge University Press, 1990

Duiker, William J., and Jackson Spielvogel, *World History*, 2 vols., Minneapolis: West, 1994

Dunn, Ross E., *The Adventures of Ibn Battuta: A Muslim Traveller of the 14th Century*, Berkeley: University of California Press, 1980; London: Croom Helm, 1986

Esler, Anthony, *The Human Venture: A World History from Prehistory to the Present*, 3rd edition, Englewood Cliffs, NJ: Prentice Hall, 1995

Findley, Carter V., and John Rothney, *Twentieth Century World*, 3rd edition, Boston: Houghton Mifflin, 1994

Frank, Andre Gunder, *World Accumulation, 1492–1789*, New York: Monthly Review Press, 1978

Frank, Andre Gunder, and Barry Gills, eds., *The World System: Five Hundred Years or Five Thousand?* London and New York: Routledge, 1994

Geyer, Michael, and Charles Bright, "World History in a Global Age," *American Historical Review* 100 (1995), 1034–60

Goff, Richard *et al.*, *The Twentieth Century: A Brief Global History*, New York: Wiley, 1983

Goldstone, Jack A., *Revolution and Rebellion in the Early Modern World*, Berkeley: University of California Press, 1991

Gran, Peter, *Beyond Eurocentrism: A New View of Modern World History*, Syracuse: Syracuse University Press, 1996

Grenville, John Ashley Soames, *A History of the World in the Twentieth Century*, Cambridge, MA: Harvard University Press, 1994

Grousset, René, *Bilan d'histoire*, Paris: Plon, 1946; in English as *The Sum of History*, Westport, CT: Hyperion, and Hadleigh, Essex: Tower Bridge, 1951

Headrick, Daniel R., *The Tools of Empire: Technology and European Imperialism in the Nineteenth Century*, New York: Oxford University Press, 1981

Headrick, Daniel R., *The Tentacles of Progress: Technology Transfer in the Age of Imperialism, 1850–1940*, New York: Oxford University Press, 1988

Hobhouse, Henry, *Seeds of Change: Five Plants That Transformed Mankind*, London: Sidgwick and Jackson, 1985; New York: Harper and Row, 1986

Hobhouse, Henry, *Forces of Change: An Unorthodox View of History*, New York: Arcade, 1989; also as *Forces of Change: Why We Are the Way We Are Now*, London: Sidgwick and Jackson, 1989

Hobsbawm, Eric J., *The Age of Extremes: The Short Twentieth Century, 1914–1991*, London: Joseph, 1994; as *The Age of Extremes: A History of the World, 1914–1991*, New York: Pantheon, 1994

Hodgson, Marshall G.S., *The Venture of Islam: Conscience and History in a World Civilization*, 3 vols., Chicago: University of Chicago Press, 1974

Hodgson, Marshall G.S., *Rethinking World History: Essays on Europe, Islam and World History*, edited by Edmund Burke III, Cambridge and New York: Cambridge University Press, 1993

Howarth, Tony, *Twentieth Century History: The World since 1900*, London and New York: Longman, 1979

International Commission for a History of the Scientific and Cultural Development of Mankind, *History of Mankind*, 6 vols., London: Allen and Unwin, and New York: Harper, 1963–

Jones, E.L., *The European Miracle: Environments, Economies and Geopolitics in the History of Europe and Asia*, Cambridge and New York: Cambridge University Press, 1981

Journal of World History, Honolulu: University of Hawaii Press, 1990–

Kemp, Tom, *Historical Patterns of Industrialization*, London and New York: Longman, 1978

Kennedy, Paul M., *The Rise and Fall of the Great Powers: Economic Change and Military Conflict from 1500 to 2000*, New York: Random House, 1987; London: Unwin Hyman, 1988

Keylor, William R., *The Twentieth Century World: An International History*, 3rd edition, New York: Oxford University Press, 1996

Knight, Franklin W., *The African Dimension in Latin American Societies*, New York: Macmillan, 1974

Laue, Theodore von, *The World Revolution of Westernization: The Twentieth Century in Global Perspective*, New York: Oxford University Press, 1987

Lockard, Craig A., "Global History, Modernization, and the World-System Approach," *History Teacher* 14 (1981), 489–515

Lockard, Craig A., "The Contributions of Philip Curtin and the 'Wisconsin School' to the Study and Promotion of Comparative World History," *Journal of Third World Studies* 11 (1994), 180–223

McNeill, William H., *The Rise of the West: A History of the Human Community*, Chicago: University of Chicago Press, 1963

Mason, Philip, *Patterns of Dominance*, London: Oxford University Press, 1970

Mazlish, Bruce, and Ralph Buultjens, eds., *Conceptualizing World History*, Boulder, CO: Westview Press, 1993

Mintz, Sidney W., *Sweetness and Power: The Place of Sugar in Modern History*, New York: Viking, and London: Sifton, 1985

Moore, Barrington, Jr., *Social Origins of Dictatorship and Democracy: Lord and Peasant in the Making of the Modern World*, Boston: Beacon Press, 1966; Harmondsworth: Penguin, 1967

Nehru, Jawaharlal, *Glimpses of World History*, London: Drummond, 1939; New York: Day, 1942

Pacey, Arnold, *Technology in World Civilization: A Thousand-Year History*, Oxford: Blackwell, and Cambridge, MA: MIT Press, 1990

Panikkar, Kavalam M., *Asia and Western Dominance: A Survey of the Vasco da Gama Epoch of Asian History, 1498–1945*, London: Allen and Unwin, 1953; New York: Day, 1954

Parker, Geoffrey, ed., *The World: An Illustrated History*, New York: Harper, and London: Times Books, 1986

Parry, J.H., *Europe and a Wider World*, London: Hutchinson, 1949, revised 1961; as *The Establishment of the European Hegemony, 1415–1715: Trade and Exploration in the Age of the Renaissance*, New York: Harper, 1961

Parry, J.H., *The Age of Reconnaissance*, Cleveland: World, and London: Weidenfeld and Nicolson, 1963

Parry, J.H., *The Spanish Seaborne Empire*, New York: Knopf, and London: Hutchinson, 1966

Pomper, Philip, William McNeill, Francis Fukuyama, Ashis Nandy, Lewis D. Wurgaft, Janet L. Abu-Lughod, and William Green, eds., "World Historians and Their Critics," special issue of *History and Theory*, 34 (1995)

Ponting, Clive, *A Green History of the World: The Environment and the Collapse of Great Civilizations*, London: Sinclair Stevenson, 1991; New York: St. Martin's Press, 1992

Powell, Philip W. *et al.*, *Essays on Frontiers in World History*, Austin: University of Texas Press, 1981

Reilly, Kevin, *The West and the World: A History of Civilization*, 2 vols., New York: Harper, 1980; revised 1989

Roberts, J.M., *The Hutchinson History of the World*, London: Hutchinson, 1976, revised 1987; as *History of the World*, New York: Knopf, 1976, Oxford: Oxford University Press, 1993; also revised as *The Pelican History of the World*, Harmondsworth and New York: Penguin, 1980, and *The Penguin History of the World*, Harmondsworth and New York: Penguin, 1990, 3rd edition 1995

Roberts, J.M., *The Triumph of the West: The Origins, Rise, and Legacy of Western Civilization*, London: BBC, and Boston: Little Brown, 1985

Robertson, R.T., *The Making of the Modern World: An Introductory History*, London: Zed, 1986

Skocpol, Theda, *States and Social Revolutions: A Comparative Analysis of France, Russia and China*, Cambridge and New York: Cambridge University Press, 1979

Smith, Alan K., *Creating a World Economy: Merchant Capital, Colonialism, and World Trade, 1400–1825*, Boulder, CO: Westview Press, 1991

Spengler, Oswald, *Der Untergang des Abendlandes: Umrisse einer Morphologie der Weltgeschichte*, 2 vols., Munich: Beck, 1918–22; in English as *The Decline of the West*, 2 vols., London: Allen and Unwin, and New York: Knopf, 1926–28

Spier, Fred, *The Structure of Big History from the Big Bang until Today*, Amsterdam: Amsterdam University Press, 1996

Stavrianos, Leften Stavros, *The World since 1500: A Global History*, Englewood Cliffs, NJ: Prentice Hall, 1966; 7th edition 1995

Stavrianos, Leften Stavros, *The World to 1500*, Englewood Cliffs, NJ: Prentice Hall, 1970; 6th edition 1995

Stavrianos, Leften Stavros, *Global Rift: The Third World Comes of Age*, New York: Morrow, 1981

Stavrianos, Leften Stavros, *Lifelines from Our Past: A New World History*, New York: Pantheon, 1989; revised 1997

Stearns, Peter N., *The Industrial Revolution in World History*, Boulder, CO: Westview Press, 1993

Stearns, Peter N., *World History: Patterns of Change and Continuity*, 2nd edition, New York: Harper, 1995

Stearns, Peter N., Michael Adas, and Stuart B. Schwartz, *World Civilizations: The Global Experience*, 2 vols., 2nd edition, New York: HarperCollins, 1996

Strayer, Robert W., ed., *The Making of the Modern World: Connected Histories, Divergent Paths, 1500 to the Present*, 2nd edition, New York: St. Martin's Press, 1995

Thornton, John, *Africa and Africans in the Making of the Atlantic World, 1400–1680*, Cambridge and New York: Cambridge University Press, 1992

Toynbee, Arnold J., *A Study of History*, 12 vols., Oxford and New York: Oxford University Press, 1934–61

Toynbee, Arnold J., *The World and the West*, New York: Oxford University Press, 1953

Tracy, James D., ed., *The Rise of Merchant Empires: Long Distance Trade in the Early Modern World, 1350–1750*, Cambridge and New York: Cambridge University Press, 1990

Tracy, James D., ed., *The Political Economy of Merchant Empires: State Power and World Trade, 1350–1750*, Cambridge: Cambridge University Press, 1991

Upshur, Jiu-Hwa Lo *et al.*, *World History*, 2 vols., 2nd edition, Minneapolis: West, 1995

Vadney, Thomas E., *The World since 1945*, Harmondsworth and New York: Penguin, 1987

Wallerstein, Immanuel, *The Modern World-System*, 3 vols., New York and London: Academic Press, 1974–89

Wallerstein, Immanuel, *The Capitalist World-Economy*, Cambridge: Cambridge University, 1979

Wolf, Eric R., *Peasant Wars of the Twentieth Century*, New York: Harper, 1969

Wolf, Eric R., *Europe and the People Without History*, Berkeley: University of California Press, 1982

World War I (1914–1918)

The battle over the origins of World War I began soon after the war itself. In the 1920s and 1930s, most of the major belligerents fired hefty salvoes intended to show that, individually, they had nothing to be ashamed of in the slide towards war. Germany, Britain, Austria, France, and Russia published immense collections of documents to prove that their own political, military, and diplomatic machinations were no better or worse than any other state's. At the same time, historians engaged in a certain amount of finger-pointing: Pierre Renouvin blamed Germany and Austria for the coming of war, Alfred von Wegerer blamed Russia and Britain, and Harry Elmer Barnes blamed France and Russia. In the midst of these mutual recriminations, it was hard to disagree with G. Lowes Dickinson, who argued that the war had stemmed from the general bankruptcy of European diplomacy.

International relations remained the focus of most accounts of the war's origins, but in 1961 the debate exploded with the publication of Fritz Fischer's *Griff nach der Weltmacht* (*Germany's Aims in the First World War*, 1967). The book created a storm of controversy by arguing that there had been a strong will for war in the German leadership before 1914; stressing domestic rather than external factors, he pinned blame squarely on an antidemocratic military autocracy that provoked war to satisfy its own expansionist aims. The response to Fischer's painstaking study was quick and forceful, largely because of its implications for the accepted interpretation of the place of the Nazi era in German history, and the historian was attacked as much as his work.

Despite its rancor, the long debate did allow historians to hammer out a workable and broadly accepted interpretation of the events of July 1914. Indeed, when James Joll published *The Origins of the First World War* in 1984, he largely accepted the position that had evolved during the Fischer controversy. Joll did, however, bring new dimensions to an understanding of the underlying causes of the war. Weaving together imperialism, militarism, the alliance system, the international economy, domestic politics, armaments, strategy, and psychological factors, he produced a provocative and textured account of the years leading up to August 1914 that will point future historians in new directions.

While the history of the war's origins has been confined largely to academic historians working on traditional political and diplomatic matters, the history of the war itself has seen an explosion of interest among professional and amateur historians working with a variety of methodologies. This evolution has taken time, but since the 1970s World War I has emerged as a growth industry.

The interwar period was the era of the official history, when many belligerent nations published exhaustive accounts (of varying degrees of quality and detachment) of their own war effort. In the Australian official history, C.E.W. Bean crystallized the myth of the "digger" as the embodiment of all that was great about Australia. Canadian official historian A.F. Duguid, after a strenuous debate over how his British counterpart James Edmonds would describe the Second Battle of Ypres in the British history, never got beyond a first volume. At the same time, the great political and military leaders of the war were the subjects of a huge body of literature that ranged from genuine attempts at critical analysis – perhaps the best being Basil Liddell Hart's *Reputations Ten Years After* (1928) – to shallow personal attacks to hagiography.

Not until the late 1950s was there a comparable boom in studies of the war, this time inaugurated by Alan Moorehead's *Gallipoli* (1956). Over the next ten years, a spate of bestselling books – mostly by nonacademic historians – brought the war firmly to the fore. Alan Clark popularized an apocryphal metaphor (attributed to Falkenhayn's memoirs), that the British Army was an army of lions commanded by donkeys; the same notion had been implicit in Leon Wolff's earlier book on the 1917 offensives. Against this panoply of dull generals and misled soldiers, John Terraine was beginning to stake out his turf as almost the sole defender of Sir Douglas Haig and his strategic vision.

If some of these books were dubious in their methodology and historical detachment, they at least served to rekindle interest in the war among amateur and academic historians alike. Indeed, the decades of uncritical literature that reduced the war to a series of one-sided stereotypes have provided modern historians with exceptional scope for research.

There has been greater effort to understand the motivation of the individual soldier. A ground-breaking study by Eric Leed on the identity of the individual soldier led other scholars to examine how the Tommy, *poilu*, or doughboy interacted with his comrades and his army at the front. Leonard Smith used techniques adapted from French social history to discern the group dynamics within the mutinous French 5th Division, while Stéphane Audoin-Rouzeau and J.G. Fuller studied trench newspapers in an effort to understand what sustained the man at the front.

Tactical history, dismissed by some as a necessary evil in the historiography of World War I, has also yielded a number of important studies. Bruce Gudmundsson detailed the evolution of German infantry tactics that occurred as a product of both improvisation and desperation on the Western Front, while Tim Travers and William Rawling have added considerably to our understanding of the relationship between technology and tactics.

At the same time, scholars have turned their attention away from the Western Front to examine the war in a broader context. Akinjide Osuntokun and Albert Grundlingh have described the war's impact in Africa, while Paul Halpern has written a detailed and much-needed synthesis of the war at sea. Among the best of the new studies of the home front is Angela Woollacott's examination of munitions workers.

Perhaps more importantly, scholars have begun to look at the war not simply as a political or military event, but as a cultural and philosophical force. Paul Fussell, Samuel Hynes, John Keegan, and George Mosse have worked from the assumption that perceptions of the war were at least as important as its reality. Borrowing fruitfully from psychology, literary theory, anthropology, sociology, and other disciplines, they have encouraged new generations of historians to consider World War I, not simply as an episode, but also as an idea.

JONATHAN F. VANCE

See also Bean; Conze; Fischer; Halecki; Hillgruber; Howard; Keegan; Military; Mosse; Taylor

Further Reading

Audoin-Rouzeau, Stéphane, *14–18: les combattants des tranchées: à travers leurs journaux*, Paris: Colin, 1986; in English as *Men at War, 1914–1918: National Sentiment and Trench Journalism in France during the First World War*, Oxford: Berg, 1992
Barnes, Harry Elmer, *The Genesis of the World War: An Introduction to the Problem of War Guilt*, revised edtion, New York: Knopf, 1929
Bean, C.E.W., *The Story of Anzac*, 2 vols., Sydney: Angus and Robertson, 1921–24; reprinted St. Lucia: University of Queensland Press, 1981
Bond, Brian, ed., *The First World War and British Military History*, Oxford and New York: Oxford University Press, 1991
Clark, Alan, *The Donkeys*, London: Hutchinson, 1961; New York: Morrow, 1962
Dickinson, G. Lowes, *The International Anarchy, 1904–1914*, London: Allen and Unwin, and New York: Century, 1926
Duguid, A. Fortescue, *Official History of the Canadian Forces in the Great War, 1914–1919*, Ottawa: Patenaude, 1938
Falls, Cyril, *War Books: A Critical Guide*, London: P. Davies, 1930; revised by R.J. Wyatt as *War Books: An Annotated Bibliography of Books about the Great War*, London: Greenhill, 1989
Fischer, Fritz, *Griff nach der Weltmacht: die Kriegszielpolitik des kaiserlichen Deutschland, 1914–18*, Düsseldorf: Droste, 1961; in English as *Germany's Aims in the First World War*, London: Chatto and Windus, and New York: Norton, 1967
Fuller, J.G., *Troop Morale and Popular Culture in the British and Dominion Armies, 1914–1918*, Oxford and New York: Oxford University Press, 1991
Fussell, Paul, *The Great War and Modern Memory*, Oxford and New York: Oxford University Press, 1975
Grundlingh, Albert, *Fighting Their Own War: South African Blacks and the First World War*, Johannesburg: Ravan Press, 1987
Gudmundsson, Bruce I., *Stormtroop Tactics: Innovation in the German Army, 1914–1918*, Westport, CT: Praeger, 1989
Halpern, Paul G., *A Naval History of World War I*, Annapolis, MD: Naval Institute Press, 1994

Henig, Ruth B., *The Origins of the First World War*, London and New York: Routledge, 1989
Hynes, Samuel Lynn, *A War Imagined: The First World War and English Culture*, London: Bodley Head, 1990; New York: Atheneum, 1991
Joll, James, *The Origins of the First World War*, London and New York: Longman, 1984
Keegan, John, *The Face of Battle*, London: Cape, and New York: Viking, 1976
Langdon, John W., *July 1914: The Long Debate, 1918–1990*, Oxford: Berg, 1991
Leed, Eric J., *No Man's Land: Combat and Identity in World War I*, Cambridge and New York: Cambridge University Press, 1979
Liddell Hart, B.H., *Reputations Ten Years After*, Boston: Little Brown, 1928; as *Reputations*, London: Murray, 1928
Moorehead, Alan, *Gallipoli*, New York: Harper, and London: Hamish Hamilton, 1956
Mosse, George L., *Fallen Soldiers: Reshaping the Memory of the World Wars*, Oxford and New York: Oxford University Press, 1990
Osuntokun, Akinjide, *Nigeria in the First World War*, London: Longman, and Atlantic Highlands, NJ: Humanities Press, 1979
Rawling, William, *Surviving Trench Warfare: Technology and the Canadian Corps, 1914–1918*, Toronto: University of Toronto Press, 1992
Renouvin, Pierre, *Les Origines immédiates de la guerre (28 juin–4 août 1914)*, Paris: Costes, 1925; in English as *The Immediate Origins of the War, 28 June–4 August 1914*, New Haven: Yale University Press, and London: Oxford University Press, 1928
Robertson, John, *Anzac and Empire: The Tragedy and Glory of Gallipoli*, London: Leo Cooper, 1990
Smith, Leonard V., *Between Mutiny and Obedience: The Case of the Fifth French Infantry Division during World War I*, Princeton: Princeton University Press, 1994
Terraine, John, *Douglas Haig, The Educated Soldier*, London: Hutchinson, 1963
Travers, Tim, *The Killing Ground: The British Army, the Western Front and the Emergence of Modern Warfare, 1900–1918*, London and Boston: Allen and Unwin, 1987
Travers, Tim, "Allies in Conflict: The British and Canadian Historians and the Real Story of Second Ypres (1915)," in *Journal of Contemporary History* 24 (1989), 301–25
Travers, Tim, *How the War Was Won: Command and Technology in the British Army on the Western Front, 1917–1918*, London: Routledge, 1992
Wegerer, Alfred von, *Die Widerlegung der Versailler Kriegsschuldthese*, Berlin: Hobbing, 1928; in English as *A Refutation of the Versailles War Guilt Thesis*, New York: Knopf, 1930
Wolff, Leon, *In Flanders Fields: The 1917 Campaign*, New York, Viking, 1958
Woodward, David R., and Robert Franklin Maddox, *America and World War I: A Selected Annotated Bibliography of English-Language Sources*, New York: Garland, 1985
Woollacott, Angela, *On Her Their Lives Depend: Munitions Workers in the Great War*, Berkeley: University of California Press, 1994

World War II (1939–1945)

World War II was the most extensive and the bloodiest war ever fought. The scale of the conflict was so great that for the first and, perhaps, last time, the belligerents mobilized almost their entire populations to contribute to the war effort. It should come as no surprise therefore that the literature is vast and covers virtually every aspect of individual and collective participation.

British and American historiography has, to a large extent, followed the same pattern. At first, major political and military figures produced their memoirs, which were often used as tools to refurbish reputations or disparage wartime rivals. American soldiers were first off the mark when generals Dwight D. Eisenhower and Omar Bradley published their respective memoirs, *Crusade in Europe* (1948) and *A Soldier's Story* (1951). Their disparaging remarks about the British gave the Allies' most controversial soldier, Field-Marshal Montgomery, the excuse to criticize publicly his former comrades, particularly Eisenhower, as well as the conduct of allied armies during the war, which caused lasting resentment. Less quarrelsome, but still tendentious, was Winston Churchill's multivolume *The Second World War* (1948–54). The only major allied leader to write his account of the war, Churchill also sought to ameliorate the effects of his 1945 election defeat and to show himself once again in an heroic light.

The wartime perceptions of both the British and American peoples were largely formulated by official mythmaking and propaganda. In Britain these began to be unraveled from the 1960s. Montgomery's military aura was attacked by Correlli Barnett in *The Desert Generals* (1960); the bomber offensives were criticized on both military and moral grounds by Stephen A. Garrett in his *Ethics and Airpower in World War II* (1993), although Richard Overy's *Why the Allies Won* (1995) restated the success of the bombing campaign. Peter Elphick's book *Singapore, the Pregnable Fortress* (1995) added to the corpus of literature devoted to Britain's biggest defeat of the war, a defeat that has poisoned relations with Australia ever since. Elphick concluded that although the British did not take the Japanese threat seriously, did not make adequate preparations, and did not provide strong leadership following the Japanese invasion, the conduct of Australian troops and their leaders was rarely any better. In short, the fall of Singapore remains a highly emotive subject in both Britain and Australia. With regard to the home front, the wartime view of a united people all pulling together was dispelled in Angus Calder's *The People's War* (1969) and *The Myth of the Blitz* (1991). Calder explained that there was panic during the Blitz and that rural people often resented the evacuation of children and civilians from the cities into the countryside.

Similarly, the American experience has come under critical investigation. Martin V. Melosi has examined the heated political arguments that followed the defeat at Pearl Harbor in his *The Shadow of Pearl Harbor* (1977). On the home front, the sanitized view that World War II was a "good war" in which the American people pulled together has been revised. William L. O'Neill's *A Democracy at War* (1993) argued that America fought under several handicaps, not least the failure to mobilize more of the population for military and industrial purposes (America did not compare favorably with Britain in this regard), and prejudice against minorities, such as Jews, blacks, and Japanese Americans, which wasted manpower and talent. Furthermore, Michael C.C. Adams' *The Best War Ever* (1994) explained that the war has been idealized by censorship and Hollywood, especially compared with Vietnam, and that the experiences of American troops have never really been appreciated.

A historiographical trend evident in both Britain and America is the considerable interest in the wartime experiences of women. In Britain, earlier historiography agreed that war work changed women's lives for the better, but disagreed on how far these changes continued after the war. More recently, Penny Summerfield, in her *Women Workers in the Second World War* (1984), has argued that detrimental prewar attitudes continued to thrive in the war industries, with the implication that women did not benefit from the war as much as first thought. In America, historiography continues to stress that the war gave many women, especially minorities, greater opportunities, which were then more or less lost afterwards; see for example Sherna Berger Gluck's *Rosie the Riveter Revisited* (1987).

For those countries under Nazi occupation the historiography has naturally focused on the twin issues of resistance and collaboration. Fifty years on, these subjects remain controversial and are reawakened every time an old Nazi is put on trial for war crimes. In France, the Germans established a puppet regime in Vichy which collaborated effectively with its Nazi overlords, and has meant that the history of this period has been steeped in controversy. For recent works see *Collaboration in France* edited by Gerhard Hirschfeld and Patrick Marsh (1989), and *In Search of the Maquis* by H.R. Kedward (1993). For other occupied countries, see for example *Holland and the War Against Hitler* edited by M.R.D Foot (1990), and *The Czechs under Nazi Rule* by Vojtech Mastny (1971).

The part played by the Soviet Union in what the Russians term the "Great Patriotic War" was until 1990 written within the confines imposed by the communist regime, such as the necessity to praise Stalin and communism as the saviors of the Soviet peoples. Discussion of more sensitive issues such as the regime's culpability for the Nazi attack was not permitted. Since the collapse of communism and the release of documents, western scholars are now finding out more about the Soviet war effort and life under Nazi occupation. John and Carol Garrard's collection of essays in *World War Two and the Soviet People* (1993), discussed issues such as the role of the secret police, collaboration, and the disregard of soldiers' lives by the Soviet high command. Although the Soviet Union did most to defeat the Germans, and suffered appalling losses as a result, it is only now that the terrible treatment of the Soviet peoples by Stalin's regime is coming to light. Only when the Soviet archives are fully researched will perhaps the last secrets of the war be revealed.

Of the German political leadership, Albert Speer, Hitler's architect and armaments minister, was the only one to leave his account in *Inside the Third Reich* (1970), in which he distanced himself from Nazi atrocities. However, Speer's role has been questioned by Gitta Sereny in her *Albert Speer: His Battle with Truth* (1995). Much of the literature on Nazi Germany has examined the Nazi state in its entirety, from its inception to its collapse, and much of the material on World War II is subsumed by other considerations. Nevertheless, works have appeared which examine Germany during the war years, for example Martin Kitchen's *Nazi Germany at War* (1995) and Eleanor Hancock's *The National Socialist Leadership and Total War 1941–1945* (1991). Otherwise, there are two main historiographical trends related to the war years. The role of the German army as an instrument of Nazi policy has always been controversial. During the postwar years, surviving generals suggested that the army was forced into committing atrocities by Nazi political power and was essentially "obeying orders." Since the 1960s, the role of the leading generals has been investigated and the army has been shown to be more culpable than its apologists would suggest. More recently, Omer Bartov in his *The Eastern Front* (1985) and *Hitler's Army* (1991), has shown how Nazified the army became, owing to the savage warfare against the Russians and because of the influx of recruits who were more imbued with the Nazi ethos than their predecessors. Theo J. Schulte's *The German Army and Nazi Policies in Occupied Russia* (1989) has examined the relationship between Nazi policies and the army in a more wide-ranging fashion. The other trend deals with the performance of the German economy and particularly the relationship between the Nazi and big business leaderships. Debate has centered on which side held the dominant position, or if either did. After analyzing the various arguments, Ian Kershaw in his *The Nazi Dictatorship* (1985) argued that from 1936 the Nazis dominated the relationship as economic and military strategic factors became interlocked. The primary role of the Nazi leadership is evident, it is argued, by the fact that they were able to waste so much human and material resources pursuing their exterminationist policies.

Unlike that on the European theater, writing on the Pacific and East Asian wars is not so prolific. The communist takeover of China in 1949 has meant that the Chinese role is not particularly well-documented. For the Japanese, whose war against China began in 1936 and continued after the attack on the Americans and British in 1941, World War II remains a controversial and contentious issue. In a country which still plays down its often savage conduct of the war against China, its role as an aggressor against the western, imperialist powers has not found universal acceptance in Japan itself. Indeed, according to *The Cambridge History of Japan: The Twentieth Century*, edited by Peter Duus (1988), following the end of the American occupation in 1952, Japanese accounts began to use the term "Greater East Asia War" to describe the conflict, a term previously banned and replaced by the "Pacific War." The latter term for many Japanese does not really include the long war against China and centers too much on the conflict with America. Since the 1950s and 1960s, Japanese historiography has fallen into two main interpretive camps; those who acknowledge Japanese "guilt" in starting an aggressive war against the Americans and European powers, which was the result of the government producing a heavily militaristic society; and those who prefer to see the Japanese reacting either against western, imperialistic pressure, or conducting a war of liberation against western imperialism. Any attempt by the Japanese to whitewash or play down their role in the war has met with increased concern not only by many Japanese themselves, but also by those countries occupied or attacked by Japan between 1941 and 1945.

KEITH SURRIDGE

See also Ambrose; Broszat; Central Europe; Davies, R.; East Central Europe; Fischer; Halecki; Hillgruber; Holocaust; Keegan; Meinecke; Military; Schieder; Schramm; Seton-Watson, R.; Simpson; Taylor

Further Reading

Adams, Michael C.C., *The Best War Ever: America and World War II*, Baltimore: John Hopkins University Press, 1994

Anderson, Karen, *Wartime Women: Sex Roles, Family Relations and the Status of Women during World War II*, Westport, CT: Greenwood Press, 1981

Barber, John, and Mark Harrison, *The Soviet Home Front, 1941–1945: A Social and Economic History of the USSR in World War II*, London and New York: Longman, 1991

Barnett, Correlli, *The Desert Generals*, London: Kimber, 1960; New York: Viking, 1961

Bartov, Omer, *The Eastern Front, 1941–1945: German Troops and the Barbarisation of Warfare*, London: Macmillan, 1985; New York: St. Martin's Press, 1986

Bartov, Omer, *Hitler's Army: Soldiers, Nazis, and War in the Third Reich*, Oxford and New York: Oxford University Press, 1991

Blum, John Morton, *V Was for Victory: Politics and American Culture during World War II*, New York: Harcourt Brace, 1976

Bradley, Omar, *A Soldier's Story*, New York: Holt, and London: Eyre and Spottiswoode, 1951

Bunting, Madeleine, *The Model Occupation: The Channel Islands under German Rule, 1940–45*, London: HarperCollins, 1993

Calder, Angus, *The People's War*, London: Cape, and New York: Pantheon, 1969

Calder, Angus, *The Myth of the Blitz*, London: Cape 1991

Calvocoressi, Peter, Guy Wint, and John Pritchard, *Total War: The Causes and Courses of the Second World War*, London: Allen Lane, 1972; revised 1989

Cashman, Sean Dennis, *America, Roosevelt, and World War II*, New York: New York University Press, 1989

Churchill, Winston, *The Second World War*, 6 vols., London: Cassell, and Boston: Houghton Mifflin, 1948–54

Clark, Alan, *Barbarossa: The Russian–German Conflict, 1941–45*, London: Hutchinson, and New York: Morrow, 1965

Costello, John, *Love, Sex and War: Changing Values, 1939–45*, London: Collins, 1985

Crosby, Travis L., *The Impact of Civilian Evacuation*, London and Dover, NH: Croom Helm, 1986

Cruickshank, Charles Greig, *The German Occupation of the Channel Islands*, London and New York: Oxford University Press, 1975

Day, David, *The Great Betrayal: Britain, Australia and the Onset of the Pacific War, 1939–42*, London: Angus and Robertson, 1988; New York: Norton, 1989

Dear, I.C.B., ed., *The Oxford Companion to the Second World War*, Oxford and New York: Oxford University Press, 1995

De Gaulle, Charles, *Mémoires de guerre*, 3 vols., Paris: Plon, 1954–59; in English as *War Memoirs*, 3 vols., London: Collins, 1954–59; New York: Simon and Schuster, 1955–60

Dockrill, Saki, ed., *From Pearl Harbor to Hiroshima: The Second World War in Asia and the Pacific, 1941–1945*, London: Macmillan, and New York: St. Martin's Press, 1994

Dower, John, *War Without Mercy: Race and Power in the Pacific War*, New York: Pantheon, and London: Faber, 1986

Duus, Peter, ed., *The Cambridge History of Japan*, vol. 6: *The Twentieth Century*, Cambridge and New York: Cambridge University Press, 1988

Eisenhower, Dwight D., *Crusade in Europe*, New York: Doubleday, and London: Heinemann, 1948

Elphick, Peter, *Singapore, the Pregnable Fortress: A Study in Deception, Discord, and Desertion*, London: Hodder and Stoughton, 1995

Erickson, John, *The Road to Stalingrad*, London: Weidenfeld and Nicolson, and New York: Harper, 1975

Erickson, John, *The Road to Berlin*, London: Weidenfeld and Nicolson, and Boulder, CO: Westview Press, 1983

Foot, M.R.D., ed., *Holland and the War Against Hitler, 1940–1945*, London: Cass, 1990

Garrard, John, and Carol Garrard, *World War Two and the Soviet People*, New York: St. Martin's Press, 1993

Garrett, Stephen A., *Ethics and Airpower in World War II: The British Bombing of German Cities*, New York: St. Martin's Press, 1993

Girdner, Audrie, and Anne Loftis, *The Great Betrayal: The Evacuation of Japanese-Americans during World War II*, New York: Macmillan, 1969

Gluck, Sherna Berger, *Rosie the Riveter Revisited: Women, the War, and Social Change*, Boston: Twayne, 1987

Hancock, Eleanor, *The National Socialist Leadership and Total War 1941–1945*, New York: St. Martin's Press, 1991

Havens, Thomas Robert Hamilton, *Valley of Darkness: The Japanese People and World War Two*, New York: Norton, 1978

Hildebrand, Klaus, *Das Dritte Reich*, Munich: Oldenbourg, 1979; in English as *The Third Reich*, London and Boston: Allen and Unwin, 1984

Hinsley, Francis Harry, ed., *British Intelligence in the Second World War*, 5 vols., London: HMSO, and New York: Cambridge University Press, 1979–90

Hirschfeld, Gerhard, *Fremdherrschaft und Kollaboration: die Niederlande unter deutscher Besatzung, 1940–1945*, Stuttgart: Deutsche Verlags-Anstalt, 1984; revised and expanded in English as *Nazi Rule and Dutch Collaboration: The Netherlands under German Occupation, 1940–1945*, Oxford and New York: Berg, 1988

Hirschfeld, Gerhard, and Patrick Marsh, eds., *Collaboration in France: Politics and Culture during the Nazi Occupation*, Oxford and New York: Berg, 1989

Kedward, H.R., *In Search of the Maquis: Rural Resistance in Southern France, 1942–44*, Oxford and New York: Oxford University Press, 1993

Kershaw, Ian, *The Nazi Dictatorship: Problems and Perspectives of Interpretation*, London: Arnold, 1985; 3rd edition 1993

Kitchen, Martin, *Nazi Germany at War*, London and New York: Longman, 1995

Klemperer, Klemens von, *German Resistance Against Hitler: The Search for Allies Abroad, 1938–45*, Oxford and New York: Oxford University Press, 1992

Liddell Hart, B.H., *History of the Second World War*, London: Cassell, 1970; New York: Putnam, 1971

Mastny, Vojtech, *The Czechs under Nazi Rule: The Failure of National Resistance, 1939–42*, New York: Columbia University Press, 1971

Melosi, Martin V., *The Shadow of Pearl Harbor: Political Controversy over the Surprise Attack, 1941–46*, College Station: Texas A & M University Press, 1977

Milward, Alan S., *The German Economy at War*, London: Athlone Press, 1965

Montgomery, Bernard Law (1st Viscount Montgomery of Alamein), *Memoirs*, London: Collins, and Cleveland: World, 1958

Mulligan, Timothy Patrick, *The Politics of Illusion and Empire: German Occupation Policy in the Soviet Union, 1942–43*, New York: Praeger, 1988

Noakes, Jeremy, ed., *The Civilian in War: The Home Front in Europe, Japan, and the USA*, Exeter: University of Exeter Press, 1992

O'Neill, William L., *A Democracy at War: America's Fight at Home and Abroad in World War II*, New York: Free Press, and Oxford: Maxwell Macmillan, 1993

Overy, Richard, *Why the Allies Won*, London: Cape, 1995

Reynolds, David, *Rich Relations: The American Occupation of Britain, 1942–45*, London: HarperCollins, and New York: Random House, 1995

Rich, Norman, *Hitler's War Aims: Ideology, the Nazi State and the Course of Expansion*, 2 vols., New York: Norton, and London: Deutsch, 1973–74

Sainsbury, Keith, *Churchill and Roosevelt at War: The War They Fought and the Peace They Hoped to Make*, New York: New York University Press, and London: Macmillan, 1994

Schulte, Theo J., *The German Army and Nazi Policies in Occupied Russia*, Oxford and New York: Berg, 1989

Sereny, Gitta, *Albert Speer: His Battle with Truth*, London: Macmillan, and New York: Knopf, 1995

Sheridan, Dorothy, *Wartime Women: An Anthology of Women's Wartime Writing for Mass Observation, 1939–45*, London: Heinemann, 1990

Shirer, William L., *The Rise and Fall of the Third Reich: A History of Nazi Germany*, New York: Simon and Schuster, and London: Secker and Warburg, 1960

Speer, Albert, *Erinnerungen*, Berlin: Propyläen, 1969; in English as *Inside the Third Reich: Memoirs*, London: Weidenfeld and Nicolson, and New York: Macmillan, 1970

Summerfield, Penny, *Women Workers in the Second World War*, London: Croom Helm, 1984

Worster, Donald 1941–

US environmental historian

One of the leading historians of the American West, Donald Worster has played a key role in the development of the field of environmental history – the historical study of the human relationship with the world of plants and animals, of water and air and land. He has argued forcefully for the importance of "an ecological perspective" in intellectual and civic life. In books and essays often described as eloquent, passionate, and provocative, he has contributed to public debate about the important issues of our time. "Environmental history ought to have a few ideas to offer the public," he explained in the preface to his book *The Wealth of Nature* (1993), "and those ideas ought to have a little conviction in them as well as reason and evidence."

Worster first made a mark on the historical profession with *Dust Bowl* (1979), awarded the Bancroft prize in American history. The book argued that the history of the dust storms that devastated the southern Great Plains in the 1930s offered profound lessons about the environmental insensitivities of American culture and capitalist economics: the Dust Bowl was a consequence of human arrogance, greed, and recklessness, not simply a natural disaster. The immediate cause of the disaster lay in "the great plow-up" of the 1920s. Eager to capitalize on the high price of grain after World War I, farmers used new technology to turn five million acres of grassland into wheat fields; when the price of wheat plummeted, thousands of farmers simply abandoned the newly plowed ground, and so left the land without the vegetative cover needed to protect against the ill-effects of drought and wind. But the dust storms of the 1930s also had important cultural causes. The settlers on the southern Plains shared with most Americans a powerful drive to conquer nature – a drive exemplified in pioneer boasts about "busting" and "breaking" the earth. The region's wheat farmers also lacked a deep sense of place, a rootedness that would have encouraged a more careful and far-sighted way of farming. Instead, they valued the main chance, and they saw the land solely as a resource, a potential source of capital and consumer goods. In Worster's view, however, the fault was general. The Dust Bowl suggested that "a capitalist-based society has a greater resource hunger than others, greater eagerness to take risks, and less capacity for restraint."

Though the professional acclaim for *Dust Bowl* testified to Worster's skill as a writer, the Bancroft prize also recognized the power of Worster's ecological perspective. By attending to the human relationship with the nonhuman world, Worster had changed the way historians viewed a significant event. In his next book, *Rivers of Empire* (1985), Worster went further, offering a major reinterpretation of the most analyzed and mythologized of American regions: the West.

The heart of the West receives little rain, and Worster argued that the effort to overcome water scarcity had shaped much of the region's history. It helped to consolidate the power of the Mormon church, for example, and to concentrate population in the cities. In part, Worster built on the work of Walter Prescott Webb, the first historian to see aridity as the region's defining characteristic, yet Worster rejected Webb's argument that the struggle with water scarcity had ennobled the West's inhabitants. Instead, he concluded that the region's history revealed the costs of relying on complex and capital-intensive technology to remake the landscape. The extraordinary growth of the West depended to a great extent on the expertise and power of government – only state and federal agencies could marshal the vast resources needed to dam rivers and redirect water to farms, factories, and cities. Yet the reliance on a technocratic elite undermined democracy. Though unelected, the region's water managers soon had enormous power, and they often used that power to increase the wealth and influence of large corporations. The elaborate water-control infrastructure also came at considerable environmental cost. The dams destroyed important ecosystems, Worster concluded, and the widespread use of irrigation threatened to turn healthy soils into salty wastelands.

Rivers of Empire provoked heated debate among specialists in the history of water use in the West. Yet the book quickly became one of the exemplars of the "new" western history, which seeks to face squarely the region's contradictions and failures. As Worster wrote in the opening essay in *Under Western Skies* (1992), the field could only be vital if western historians refused to stand aloof from political and moral controversy. The response to the new western history in both scholarly and popular forums suggests that Worster was right: the field is once again a subject of lively discussion.

Environmental history owes even more to Worster's work. In the mid-1970s, Worster helped found the American Society for Environmental History. Though his own research has focused on American agriculture, he has inspired scholarship on a wide array of topics in American environmental history. He also has supported a comparative and global approach to the subject: he co-edits a Cambridge University Press series on environment and history with a truly international scope, and he has spoken about environmental history in dozens of countries around the world.

For Worster, indeed, the field offers a path across a variety of boundaries, including the intellectual boundary that "separates nature from culture, science from history, matter from mind." Like almost all environmental historians, Worster has used the research of scientists to weigh the human impact on nature, yet, more uncommonly, he has worked to place scientific ideas in historical context. His first major work, *Nature's Economy* (1977), was a history of ecological thought in England and America since the 18th century. What were the cultural and scientific roots of modern ways of perceiving the workings of nature? Worster's answers to that question were stimulating, yet *Nature's Economy* had a broader import:

the book made clear that history could shed light on the modern environmental crisis.

ADAM W. ROME

See also Ecology; Environmental

Biography

Donald Eugene Worster. Born Needles, California, 14 November 1941, son of a railway worker. Received BA, University of Kansas, 1963, MA 1964; MPhil, Yale University, 1970, PhD 1971. Taught at Brandeis University, 1971–74; University of Hawaii (rising to professor), 1975–83; Brandeis University, 1983–89; and University of Kansas, from 1989. Married Beverly Marshall, 1964 (1 son, 1 daughter).

Principal Writings

Nature's Economy: The Roots of Ecology, 1977; 2nd edition [with subtitle *A History of Ecological Ideas*], 1994
Dust Bowl: The Southern Plains in the 1930s, 1979
Rivers of Empire: Water, Aridity, and the Growth of the American West, 1985
Editor, *The Ends of the Earth: Perspectives on Modern Environmental History*, 1988
Under Western Skies: Nature and History in the American West, 1992
The Wealth of Nature: Environmental History and the Ecological Imagination, 1993
An Unsettled Country: Changing Landscapes of the American West, 1994

Wrigley, E.A. 1931–
British demographic and economic historian

Tony Wrigley has been a central figure in both demographic and economic history since the 1960s. His major achievement is *The Population History of England, 1541–1871: A Reconstruction*, published in 1981 and co-authored with Roger Schofield. The authors amassed an enormous amount of statistical data to study the interplay between economic and population trends. This relationship might be seen as the central focus of Wrigley's research.

Wrigley was a founding member of the Cambridge Group for the History of Population and Social Structure in 1964. Shortly before this he started the first English demographic reconstitution, of the parish of Colyton in Devon, by following the principles of family reconstitution established in France. He began to publish results from the Colyton project in the mid-1960s. The most startling was the evidence of family limitation in 17th-century Colyton, which has, by his own admission, subsequently seemed to rest on less secure foundations. Following Louis Henry's work, Wrigley has been influential in determining the rules of historical demography in England through works such as *An Introduction to English Historical Demography* (1966) and *Nineteenth Century Society: Essays in the Use of Quantitative Methods for the Study of Social Data* (1972). More broadly, Wrigley has succeeded in placing demographic patterns at the center of economic and social history.

The major objective of Wrigley's research could be described as the search for the logic of a connection between fertility and mortality. Since his first book, *Industrial Growth and Population Change* (1961), which looked at demographic change in coalfield industrial areas of western Europe in the late 19th century, he has been interested in raw materials. His background in geography has influenced his advocacy of a regional approach. Subsequently, he has moved backwards in time to the 18th century to center on the Industrial Revolution. *Continuity, Chance and Change* (1988), his published Ellen McArthur lectures, discusses the nature of the Industrial Revolution within the process of modernization, dismissing industrialization as a cumulative and slow process and presenting a "model" of the way in which change happened in an organic economy. The main intellectual thrusts of Wrigley's endeavor are contained in his essays published in *People, Cities and Wealth* (1987) which review population change through marriage and reproduction, urban growth, and the processes by which the material needs of society were met by the Industrial Revolution. Much of his work reflects his deep interest in the writings of classical economists and demographers such as Adam Smith and Thomas Malthus. A tempered approach has also characterized his work since his first book when he warned against the dangers of quantitative history "producing causal rabbits out of correlation top hats."

PAMELA SHARPE

See also Cambridge Group; Computing; Demography; Economic; Henry; Industrial Revolution

Biography

Edward Antony Wrigley. Born 17 August 1931. Educated at King's School, Macclesfield; then studied at Peterhouse, Cambridge, MA, PhD. Research fellow, University of Chicago, 1953–54; at Cambridge University: fellow of Peterhouse; lecturer in geography, 1958–74; co-director, Cambridge Group for the History of Population and Social Structure, from 1974; professor of population studies, London School of Economics, 1979–88; president, Manchester College, Oxford, 1987–94; master, Corpus Christi College, Cambridge, from 1994. Married Maria Laura Spelberg, 1960 (1 son, 3 daughters). Knighted 1996.

Principal Writings

Industrial Growth and Population Change, 1961
Editor with D.E.C. Eversley and Peter Laslett, *An Introduction to English Historical Demography*, 1966
Population and History, 1969
Editor, *Nineteenth Century Society: Essays in the Use of Quantitative Methods for the Study of Social Data*, 1972
Editor, *Identifying People in the Past*, 1973
Editor with Paul Abrams, *Towns in Societies: Essays in Economic History and Historical Sociology*, 1978
With Roger S. Schofield, *The Population History of England, 1541–1871: A Reconstruction*, 1981
People, Cities and Wealth: The Transformation of Traditional Society, 1987
Continuity, Chance and Change: The Character of the Industrial Revolution in England, 1988
Editor, with Julian Hoppit, *The Industrial Revolution in Britain*, 1994
Editor, with others, *English Population History from Family Reconstitution, 1580–1837*, 1997

X

Xenophon *c.428–c.354* BCE

Greek historian

Xenophon, son of Gryllus, was born into an affluent Athenian family and as a young man was a follower of Socrates; like many of Socrates' disciples, he found democracy uncongenial, and left Athens to join the force of 10,000 Greek mercenaries who supported Cyrus' rebellion (401 BCE) against his brother, the Persian king Artaxerxes II. Later (after 371) Xenophon related the adventures of the Ten Thousand and their escape after Cyrus' defeat and death at Cunaxa in his *Anabasis* (*The Persian Expedition*). He entered Spartan service after his return to Greece and became an admirer of the Spartan king Agesilaus, who procured an estate for him at Scillus near Olympia after he was exiled from Athens for his Spartan sympathies. He lived there until he was expelled when Spartan hegemony collapsed after its defeat by Thebes at Leuctra (362), and he spent the remainder of his life in Corinth. Athens rescinded his exile before his death, but he seems not to have returned, though his last work, the "Ways and Means," is an attempt to draw up an economic plan for Athens with the aim of providing her with the wherewithal for leadership in a renewed Greek world.

His chief contributions to political science were the *Hiero*, the *Cyropaedia*, the "Constitution of the Spartans," and the *Agesilaus*, the first two of which were cited by Niccolò Machiavelli who read Xenophon in a Latin translation of 1490. In the *Hiero*, a dialogue between the poet Simonides and the tyrant of Syracuse, Hiero, is, according to Leo Strauss, as "as near to the teaching of [Machiavelli's] *Prince* as the teaching of any Socratic could possibly come." The *Cyropaedia* is a utopian novel that presents Cyrus, the founder of the Old Persian empire, as an ideal monarch, and is a forebear both of the Greek novel and of numerous mirrors of princes in the Middle Ages. The 1st-century novelist Xenophon of Ephesus borrowed vocabulary and possibly also his name from the Athenian Xenophon. According to Cicero, Scipio Africanus, the conqueror of Hannibal, took Cyrus as depicted by Xenophon as his model, and in the Renaissance, to judge by the number of editions, the *Cyropaedia* outranked both Herodotus and Thucydides in popularity. The *Agesilaus* continued the theme of ideal monarchy, for it is an encomium presenting Xenophon's friend, Agesilaus, king of Sparta as a perfectly good man, and it marked the beginning of a new literary genre, the biographical essay, which Plutarch was later to make his forte. The "Constitution of the Spartans" presented us for the first time with the myth of the great Spartan reformer and ideal statesman Lycurgus, who was to be admired and emulated long afterwards by French *philosophes* and revolutionaries and, in the 20th century, by German Nazis.

The *Anabasis* is an adventure story, much favored by teachers of classical Greek, but it also illustrated Xenophon's political thought, for the Ten Thousand Greeks, stranded in the Persian empire after the defeat at Cunaxa and the treacherous murder of their officers from the Persians, formed themselves into a sort of utopian city-state, which elected new leaders to take them out of Persia. The work also has overtones of panhellenism, for its subtext was that Greece should unite to attack Persia, and also of Orientalism, for the Asians were presented as treacherous, and inferior soldiers. Xenophon the soldier reappeared in his "Cavalry Commander," which dealt with the management of the Athenian horse, and the commander's duties; warfare, Xenophon claimed, is the most profitable art for a man, far surpassing gymnastics. His essay "On Horsemanship," a manual for horse trainers, described many of the movements still used by modern equestrians, and a technical treatise "On Hunting" dealt comprehensively with the chase. The favored quarry was the hare; Xenophon disapproved of hunting foxes.

The *Hellenica*, Xenophon's effort to write history in the manner of Thucydides, has won him a reputation as a historian neither in ancient nor modern times. He seems to have begun it with the intention of completing Thucydides' history of the Peloponnesian War until the defeat of Athens in 404, but later continued it until the Spartan defeat at Mantineia in 362. George Grote's judgement, written in 1850, is one that the 19th century shared: "To pass from Thucydides to the *Hellenica* of Xenophon is a descent truly mournful . . ." Xenophon's reputation, which remained high until the end of the 18th century, declined sharply thereafter. He was neither profound nor original, but he was well attuned to the intellectual currents of his day, and he planted the seeds of a number of ideas and literary genres that were to have important later developments.

J.A.S. EVANS

See also Greece: Ancient; Military

Biography

Born Athens, *c.*428 BCE. Associate of Socrates in Athens, 404–403. Joined Cyrus' unsuccessful rebellion against Artaxerxes II, 402–401; after the defeat of Cyrus at Cunaxa, 401, led the survivors to

Trapezus, and served under the Thracian Seuthes; joined Spartan camp, under Thibron, 399; under Agesilaus fought with Sparta against Athens at Coronea, 394; exiled from Athens (although exile possibly later revoked); lived on an estate (granted by the Spartans) near Olympia for 20 years; settled in Corinth after 371. Married Philesia (2 sons). Died Corinth, c.354 BCE.

Principal Writings

Anabasis; as *The Persian Expedition*, translated by Rex Warner, 1949
Hellenica, 380s and 350s; as *History of My Times*, translated by Rex Warner, 1966
Hiero; in English as *Hiero*, 1713, and *On Tyranny*, 1948
Cyropaedia, completed 362; in English as *Cyropaedia*, 1632
Works (Loeb edition; includes *Hellenica*; *Anabasis*; *Symposium* and *Apology*; *Memorabilia* and *Oeconomicus*; *Cyropaedia*; *Scripta minora*), translated by Carleton L. Brownson *et al.*, 7 vols., 1914–25

Further Reading

Anderson, J.K., *Xenophon*, London: Duckworth, and New York: Scribner, 1974
Bertrand-Dagenbach, Cecile, "Histoire et mythologie grecques dans l'oeuvre de Machiavel" (Greek History and Mythology in the Works of Machiavelli), *Antike und Abendland* 37 (1991), 126–43
Burke, Peter, "A Survey of the Popularity of Ancient Historians," *History and Theory* 5 (1966), 135–52
Dillery, John, *Xenophon and the History of His Times*, London and New York: Routledge, 1995
Gray, Vivienne, *The Character of Xenophon's Hellenica*, London: Duckworth, and Baltimore: Johns Hopkins University Press, 1989
Higgins, W.E., *Xenophon the Athenian: The Problem of the Individual and the Society of the Polis*, Albany: State University of New York Press, 1977
Hirsch, Steven W., *The Friendship of the Barbarians: Xenophon and the Persian Empire*, Hanover, NH: University Press of New England, 1985
Nussbaum, G.B., *The Ten Thousand: A Study in Social Organization and Action in Xenophon's Anabasis*, Leiden: Brill, 1967
Proietti, Gerald, *Xenophon's Sparta: An Introduction*, Leiden: Brill, 1987
Richard, Carl J., *The Founders and the Classics: Greece, Rome and the American Enlightenment*, Cambridge, MA: Harvard University Press, 1994
Strauss, Leo, *On Tyranny: An Interpretation of Xenophon's Hiero*, Glencoe, IL: Free Press, 1948; revised 1963, 1991; Oxford: Maxwell Macmillan, 1991
Tigerstedt, Eugene Napoleon, *The Legend of Sparta in Classical Antiquity*, Stockholm: Almqvist & Wiksell, 1965–78, vol. 1: 159–79

Y

Yamin, Muhammad 1903–1962

Indonesian nationalist, politician, and writer

Muhammad Yamin was born in 1903 in the village of Talawi, in Sawah Lunto in West Sumatra. His family was connected with the local nobility. Most of his schooling was in Java, and after graduating from high school he studied law in Jakarta.

Yamin was eclectic in terms of his talents. He was to become one of the greatest names in the Indonesian nationalist movement, a significant figure on the political stage after independence, a historical writer of some reputation, and a poet of considerable skill. Nevertheless, his wide-ranging talents were all to be firmly grounded in the primary force that drove him throughout his life; that is, a commitment to his ideology of nation building and Indonesian nationalism.

Yamin rose to the leadership of the youth movement Indonesia Muda and by the mid-1920s he had firmly established himself as one of the principal names in the emerging Indonesian nationalist movement. As a result, he was invited to deliver the keynote address to the 1928 Congress of Indonesian Youth, where he argued strongly for the acceptance of Bahasa Indonesia as the national language. In 1937 Yamin was one of the principal founders of the Gerakan Rakyat Indonesia (Indonesian People's Movement), a nationalist organization with strong socialist underpinnings which aimed for a full parliament for Indonesia but was prepared to cooperate with Dutch authorities in opposing the rise of fascism. The following year Yamin was elected to the Volksraad, the consultative body established by the Dutch colonial authorities and consisting of various representatives from diverse Indonesian groups.

He was also prominent during the period of Japanese occupation. When the Japanese established advisory councils at central and regional levels in August 1943 as part of their plan for Indonesian participation in government, Yamin benefited by being appointed, along with Sukarno, as a top-level adviser. He was also appointed by the Japanese in early 1945 as a lecturer at the State Training Institute for young leaders. In the last months of Japanese rule, leading Indonesian nationalists were assembled into a Committee for the Investigation of Independence (BPKI), which met for the first time in late May 1945. Yamin was one of the nationalist representatives on this committee, alongside representatives from various other groupings, including Islamic spokesmen.

The several meetings of the BPKI in mid-1945 provided Yamin with a further forum for expounding on his ideas as to the future shape of the Indonesian nation. He committed himself to a concept of a Greater Indonesia, and called for the new state to include all of the island of New Guinea, Portuguese Timor, British Borneo and Malaya, and Patani (ruled by Thailand). Yamin's vision was shared by many, and his proposal won when it was put to the vote in the BPKI Committee. Yamin was also instrumental in the formulation of the Jakarta Charter which represented a compromise between nationalist and Muslim forces during the process of drafting the Indonesian constitution and which prevented Islam from being declared as the state religion.

Nevertheless, Yamin was to have a chequered career in political life. He was to experience arrest and imprisonment under both the Japanese and the Indonesian republican forces during the mid-1940s. His arrest by the latter resulted from his opposition to the willingness of the republican forces to negotiate and compromise with the Dutch regarding the scope of Indonesian independence.

Yamin's political star rose again after independence. He was a member of the Indonesian delegation which took part in the 1949 conference in The Hague to ratify Indonesia's independence from the Netherlands. He served as justice minister and minister for education and culture under successive cabinets in the early 1950s. His support for Sukarno's move towards Guided Democracy was to pay further dividends, and in August 1959 Yamin was appointed chairman of the National Planning Commission which met to draw up an eight-year plan. This plan, presented some 12 months later, focused upon the development of Indonesia on a very grandiose scale consistent with Yamin's expansive view.

Yamin's writing was varied in its emphasis, though much of his output concerned itself with history. He quite overtly saw historical writing as a function of nation-building; indeed, in a paper delivered to a history seminar in 1957, Yamin argued forcefully that the requirements of nation-building necessitated that history be based on nationalism.

Yamin sought to portray a former Golden Age as a model for the future nation. To this end, he glorified early historical writings such as the *Sejarah Melayu* (The Malay Annals), which he described as one of the greatest historical works produced in the East, and calling on Indonesian historians to follow the example of the author of the *Sejarah Melayu* in developing the literature of the new nation. Moreover, he extolled the grandeur of former empires, principally those of Srivijaya and Majapahit, emphasizing their role in uniting far-flung territories throughout the archipelago and arguing that their very existence pointed to an

Indonesian national identity dating back several millennia. He wrote two works specifically designed to glorify early Javanese heroes whom he portrayed as nation-builders: namely *Gadjah Mada: Pahlawan Persatuan Nusantara* (1953; Gadjah Mada: Hero of the United Archipelago) and *Sejarah Peperangan Dipanegara* (1950; The History of the War of Dipanegara).

His interest was not so much focused on the greatness of Islamic Indonesia; rather, he focused on those elements of Indonesian history, regardless of religious or regional considerations, that could be used to portray a national history dating back many millennia. To this end, the history of the great Hindu Buddhist kingdoms such as Srivijaya served his purposes just as well as did local Islamic kingdoms.

Yamin had a particular fascination with the medieval Javanese kingdom of Majapahit. His play *Ken Arok dan Ken Dedes* focused on the contribution of Ken Arok in uniting two Javanese kingdoms, an act that ultimately led to the emergence of the greater kingdom of Majapahit. For Yamin, this served as a model for postcolonial Indonesia which promised to unite far-flung territories in the formation of a single national entity.

Arguably Yamin's most tendentious piece of historical writing is *6000 Tahun Sang Merah-Putih* of 1954 (6000 Years of the Red and White Flag), in which the author claims that the colors red and white, which form the flag of modern Indonesia, can in fact be traced back 6000 years, pointing to the existence of a national identity in the region from the earliest historical period. Yamin also produced a historical atlas which again focused on the contribution of past empires to the formation of an Indonesian national identity.

Those of his writings that were not specifically devoted to an exposé of his view of Indonesian history were nevertheless dominated by his preoccupation with nation building. In the last months of Japanese rule, Yamin wrote an essay extolling the virtues of the socialist leader Tan Malaka, calling him the father of the Indonesian republic and claiming that he was superior to Plato as a political philosopher.

In the field of poetry, Yamin also made a considerable impact in terms of the development of modern Indonesian literature, abandoning traditional poetic forms and producing the first truly modern Indonesian poetry. He published a collection of poems when he was barely 20, entitled *Tanah Airku* (My Country of Birth) which looked beyond his own immediate ethnic environment of the Minangkabau region to the island of Sumatra in nationalist terms. By the time he published the collection *Indonesia Tumpah Darahku* (Indonesia, Land of My Birth) in 1929, his nationalist horizons had extended to encompass the entire Indonesian archipelago and beyond.

While several detailed studies have been made of other leading nationalists such as Sukarno and Sjahrir, a detailed academic study of the life and contribution of Yamin has not yet been carried out. This is long overdue, given his contribution to literature, historical writing, and above all the ideology of Indonesian nation building that underpinned his wide-ranging activities.

PETER G. RIDDELL

Biography

Born Talawi, West Sumatra, 1903. Traditionally educated before attending Dutch schools, graduating in law, 1932. Held a number of political and government posts including minister of education and minister of information, 1951–62. Died Jakarta, 17 October 1962.

Principal Writings

Sejarah Peperangan Dipanegara (The History of the War of Dipanegara), 1950
Gadjah Mada: Pahlawan Persatuan Nusantara (Gadjah Mada: Hero of the United Archipelago), 1953
6000 Tahun Sang Merah-Putih (6000 Years of the Red and White Flag), 1954
Atlas Sejarah (Historical Atlas), 1956

Further Reading

Dahm, Bernard, *History of Indonesia in the Twentieth Century*, New York: Praeger, 1971
Kahin, George McTurnan, *Nationalism and Revolution in Indonesia*, Ithaca, NY: Cornell University Press, 1952
Noer, D., "Yamin and Hamka: Two Routes to an Indonesian Identity," in Anthony Reid and David G. Marr, eds., *Perceptions of the Past in Southeast Asia*, Singapore: Heinemann, 1979
Ricklefs, Merle Calvin, *A History of Modern Indonesia, c.1300 to the Present*, London: Macmillan, and Bloomington: Indiana University Press, 1981; 2nd edition Macmillan, and Stanford, CA: Stanford University Press, 1993
Sastrawiria, Tatang, and Haksan Wirasutisna, *Ensiklopedi Politik*, Jakarta: Perpustakaan Perguruan, 1955
Teeuw, A., *Modern Indonesian Literature*, vol. 1, Dordrecht: Foris, 1967

Yates, Frances A. 1899–1981

British historian of the Renaissance

Frances Yates was a brilliant and original scholar. Drawing on a vast range of learning, she made complex ideas accessible through an amazing series of interdisciplinary works. These transformed knowledge of Renaissance thought in the 16th and 17th centuries and opened out many new areas of study. She revealed that hermetic magic, Jewish Cabala, and Renaissance Neoplatonism were vital links between the medieval world and the rise of science in the 17th century.

Friends and colleagues believed that her originality resulted from her early life. The family moved around following their father's work as a naval architect. The youngest of four children, Yates was educated largely at home. In her later years her sister Ruby, a retired missionary teacher, became her companion. Yates warmly acknowledged her support in her books. She did not follow a conventional academic path: she took her degree in French externally from London University. After her MA, she taught at North London Collegiate School for girls, while pursuing her research privately. During this period she produced her first two books. These anticipated her future scholarship and introduced two of her heroes, William Shakespeare, and Giordano Bruno, a former Dominican friar and intellectual exile from Italy.

Yates may have had an affinity with exiles because of her early rootlessness. Certainly studying the transmission of ideas from one group of thinkers to another was an important aspect of her work. Very significant for her own intellectual development was her association with the circle of Jewish refugee scholars around the Warburg Institute from about 1940. Aby Warburg was a German Jew who used his banking family fortune to establish a library in Hamburg. After his death his associates, perceiving the Nazi threat, moved his library to

London in 1933. Warburg was the founder of modern art history, through his interpretation of images in their cultural context. The attempt to reconstruct lost mental worlds has been a feature of various schools of 20th-century history. One strand descended from Warburg to Yates. In *The Valois Tapestries* (1959) she brilliantly evoked a moment when enlightened thinking might have transformed the subsequent history of war and bloodshed. This was a theme to which she returned in *The Rosicrucian Enlightenment* (1972) unravelling the complex intellectual strands that led ultimately to the scientific revolution. In her work on Ramon Lull, Giordano Bruno, and John Dee, she had the courage to make a serious study of a subject previously shunned by academics, the contribution of the occult sciences to Western European civilization. In the hermetic tradition of astrology and alchemy, and in the Jewish mystical Cabala are the origins, later rejected, of mathematics and modern scientific disciplines. In the religious quest of the magus for self-mastery and power over nature lies the origin of the modern secular mentality. Her final book, *The Occult Philosophy of the Elizabethan Age* (1979), written when she was 80, incorporated many aspects of this work into a broad panorama. Perhaps her most original contribution was *The Art of Memory* (1966). Before the advent of printing, the trained memory was an invaluable asset to scholarly and public life. Her ground-breaking work rescued a forgotten field of knowledge from oblivion. She traced this subject from the Greeks and Romans through the Middle Ages to the Renaissance.

Yates took her readers on a voyage of discovery as exciting as any detective story. Her intellectual clarity made accessible the reconstruction of patterns of thought from complex and obscure sources, for general reader and specialist alike. She was renowned for her formidable learning, her dislike of academic pomposity, and her generosity toward colleagues and students. Her contribution to our understanding of Renaissance literature, imagery, and ritual, and philosophy and science has been profoundly innovative and enduring.

VIRGINIA R. BAINBRIDGE

See also Astrology; Germany: 1450–1800; Heilbron

Biography

Frances Amelia Yates. Born Portsmouth, 28 November 1899, daughter of a naval architect. Educated Laurel Bank School, Glasgow; Birkenhead High School; BA, University College, London, 1924, MA 1926. Private researcher and writer, with some teaching at North London Collegiate School, 1926–39; ambulance attendant, 1939–41; part-time research assistant, Warburg Institute, University of London, 1941–44, lecturer and publications editor, 1944–56, reader in history of the Renaissance, 1956–67, and honorary fellow, 1967–81. Dame of the British Empire (DBE), 1977. Died 29 September 1981.

Principal Writings

John Florio: The Life of an Italian in Shakespeare's England, 1934
The French Academies of the Sixteenth Century, 1947
The Valois Tapestries, 1959; 2nd edition 1975
Giordano Bruno and the Hermetic Tradition, 1964
The Art of Memory, 1966
Theatre of the World, 1969
The Rosicrucian Enlightenment, 1972
Astraea: The Imperial Theme in the Sixteenth Century, 1975
The Occult Philosophy of the Elizabethan Age, 1979
Collected Essays, 3 vols., 1982–84
Ideas and Ideals in the North European Renaissance, 1984

Further Reading

Frances A. Yates, 1899–1981, London: Warburg Institute, 1982 [includes bibliography]

Z

Zaionchkovskii, P.A. 1904–1983

Soviet historian of modern Russia

P.A. Zaionchkovskii's contribution to Russian historiography is as a specialist in the history of the state and of the domestic policy of the Russian monarchy in the second half of 19th century. In exploring this theme he suggested several new approaches based on new historical sources unearthed by him. These new approaches inspired both Soviet and foreign historiography.

Zaionchkovskii began his investigations by looking at the history of reform and revolution. His master's thesis, written in 1939, traced the history of one mid-19th century Russian revolutionary society. He then turned to late 19th-century domestic policy, particularly in his monograph devoted to the reform of the peasants in 1861, *Otmena krepostnogo prava v Rossii* (1954; *The Abolition of Serfdom in Russia*, 1978). This work was the first attempt in Soviet historiography to bring together the existing documents on this question. For the first time in the post-revolutionary period, Zaionchkovskii looked beyond the economic and social bases of capitalist development to an understanding of the political roots of reform. He also illuminated the motives that sparked the decisions of contemporary leaders as they pursued reform.

The other aspect of reform that attracted Zaionchkovskii was that by Milutin in the 1870s. Zaionchkovskii's doctoral thesis, *Voennye reformy 1860–1870* (Military Reforms, 1860–1870, 1952), and one of his last monographs, *Samoderzhavie i russkaia armiia na rubezhe 19–20 stoletii, 1881–1903* (Autocracy and the Russian Army, 1881–1903, 1973), were devoted to this theme. Evaluating the significance of these reforms, he argued that they were much deeper than had been generally accepted. Earlier historians had held that reform only shifted the military from an emphasis on recruitment to one of service. Zaionchkovskii examined many previously unknown documents concerning the organizational structure, recruitment system, education of personnel, and arming of military forces. These changes were also apparent in the officers' corps. Zaionchkovskii's general conclusion was that due to Milutin's reform the Russian army was transformed from a tool of autocratic monarchy to a tool of bourgeois monarchy. However, political reaction after the assassination of Alexander II terminated the reforms and halted changes in the army. The result was the defeat of Russia in the 1904–05 war with Japan.

Zaionchkovskii's work on domestic policy and the growth of the state at the end of the 19th century was the logical continuation of his interest in the reforms of the 1860s and 1870s. He posited several arguments that were very important to the study of Russian domestic policy. First, he refuted the generally accepted theory that peasants rebellion had caused the crisis of the monarchy in 1870s and 1880s. Archival research had revealed to him the limited nature of the military suppression of these revolts. Instead, he saw the roots of the crisis in revolutionary terrorist activity. This conclusion broke the accepted scheme of Soviet historians and is widely accepted today. His revision of Alexander III's assassination into the context of the clash of democratic change was very progressive for Soviet historiography. His employment of ranking lists to elucidate the power structure of late 19th-century Russia was also an important contribution. Zaionchkovskii used a range of documents to reveal the changing social hierarchies within the ruling class.

Finally, Zaionchkovskii's role as bibliographer and editor was important, and under his direction the diaries and letters of 19th-century politicians such as Milutin, Valuev, and Polovtsev reached a wider audience. He also helped shaped historical discourse through his many bibliographic guides. The most famous among them are *Spravochniki po istorii dorevoliutsionnoi Rossii* (Research Guides to Prerevolutionary Russia, 1971) and *Istoriia dorevoliutsionnoi Rossii v dnevnikakh i vospominaniiakh* (Prerevolutionary Russian History in Diaries and Recollections, 1976–89).

DMITRY A. GOUTNOV

See also Russia: Modern

Biography

Petr Andreevich Zaionchkovskii. Born Ural'sk, 5 September 1904 to a medico-military family. Educated in the Moscow cadet corps from 1914; had several jobs in 1920s and 1930s; studied history, Moscow Institute of History, Philosophy and Literature, from 1937, wrote master's thesis under Yuri Gotie, 1939, received PhD, 1951. Volunteered for army, 1941, retired with rank of major, 1944. Archivist, Department of Rare Manuscripts, Lenin State Library; director, Scientific Library, Moscow University; head, Scientific Council, 1952–54. Taught at Moscow Teachers Institute; and Moscow University, 1948–83. Died 1983.

Principal Writings

Editor, *Dnevnik D.A. Milutina, 1873–1875* (The Diaries of D.A. Milutin), 4 vols., 1947–50
Voennye reformy 1860–1870 (Military Reforms, 1860–1870), 1952

Otmena krepostnogo prava v Rossii, 1954; in English as *The Abolition of Serfdom in Russia*, 1978
Editor, *Dnevnik P.A. Vallueva* (The Diaries of P.A. Valluev), 2 vols., 1961
Krizis samoderzhaviia na rubezhe, 1870–1880, 1964; in English as *The Russian Autocracy in Crisis, 1878–1882*, 1979
Editor, *Krest'ianskoe dvizhenie v Rossii v 1870–1880 gg.* (The Russian Peasants' Movement, 1870–1880), 1968
Rossiiskoe samoderzhavie v kontse XIX stoletiia, 1970; in English as *The Russian Autocracy under Alexander III*, 1976
General editor, *Spravochniki po istorii dorevoliutsionnoi Rossii* (Research Guides to Prerevolutionary Russia), 1971
Samoderzhavie i russkaia armiia na rubezhe 19–20 stoletii, 1881–1903 (Autocracy and the Russian Army, 1881–1903), 1973
General editor, *Istoriia dorevoliutsionnoi Rossii v dnevnikakh i vospominaniiakh* (Prerevolutionary Russian History in Diaries and Recollections), 1976–89
Pravitel'stvennyi apparat samoderzhavnoi Rossii v XIX v. (The State Machinery in 19th-Century Russia), 1978

Further Reading

Anan'ich, B.V., "Istoriia Rossii vtoroi poloviny XIX veka v trudakh P.A. Zaionchkovskogo (k 80-letiiu so dnia rozhdeniia)" (The History of Russia in the Second Half of the 19th Century in the works of P.A Zaionchkovskii (1804–83) on the 80th anniversary of his birth), *Istoriia SSSR* 5 (1984), 80–88
Field, Daniel, "Petr Andreevich Zaionchkovskii," *Russian Review* 42 (1983), v–vii
Mironenko, Sergei, "P.A. Zaionchkovskii: arkheograf and bibliograf" (P.A. Zaionchkovskii: Scholar of Early Texts and Bibliographer), *Arkheograficheskii ezhegodnik 1979*, Moscow, 1981, 177–80
Strelkova, A., and I. Fillimonova, *Petr Andreevich Zaionchkovskii, biobibliografiia: k semidesiatiletiiu so dnia rozhdeniia* (P.A. Zaionchkovskii: A Bio-bibliography on the 70th Anniversary of His Birth), Moscow: Moskva un-ta, 1974
Strelkova, A., and Larisa Georgievna Zakharovoi, eds., *Petr Andreevich Zaionchkovskii: bibliograficheskii ukazatel'* (P.A. Zaionchkovskii: A Bibliographical Index), Moscow: Izd-vo Moskovskogo Universiteta, 1995
Zakharova, Larisa Georgievna, "Petr Andreevich Zaionchkovskii: uchenyi i uchitel'" (P.A. Zaionchkovskii: Scholar and Teacher), *Voprosy istorii* 5 (1994), 171–79

Zaydān, Jurjī 1861–1914

Lebanese social and literary historian

Jurjī Zaydān used historical novels, linguistic historical research, and historical investigation in order to write Arab/Islamic history. Zaydān was the son of a Lebanese Christian, and after the deterioration of the social/economic conditions in the Arab East during the late Ottoman period, he left Lebanon for Egypt – after having started his education at the Syrian Protestant College (later to become the American University of Beirut).

Intellectually, Zaydān was principally occupied by two complementary topics. The first one was the history of the Arabs in both the pre-Islamic period as well as the Islamic period, and the history of the Arabic language. In the field of history he wrote a 2-volume book dealing with the pre-Islamic history of the Arabs, their kingdoms, kings, ethics, languages, customs, religions, geographies, and social conditions. His approach to history was, as he states in the introduction to

al-'Arab qabla al-Islam (The Pre-Islamic Arabs, 1908), a critical one. He was looking not just to see what happened, but also to see why events in history took place the way they did. He went beyond description to a more critical investigatory approach to history, an approach that was missing to some extent from the literature of his time. One may argue that Zaydān's approach to history, through his works on the history of Arabic language, had an impact on the development of the political events in the Arab East with regard to the Arab relationship to the non-Arabic speaking Ottomans.

In addition to the *al-'Arab qabla al-Islam*, Zaydān wrote the multivolume *Tārīkh al-tamaddun al-Islāmī* (1902–06; vol. 4 as *Zaidan's Umayyads and Abbasids*, 1982), in which he focused on the history of political institutions such as the caliphate, the financial and tax system, the salaries of viziers and judges, the sources of the elite's wealth and its disappearence, Arabic and non-Arabic sciences, the social system, and even the position of women during both the pre-Islamic and the Abbasid period.

Zaydān introduced the notion of social history, which for him dealt with social conditions and social divisions among the population of the caliphate. For example, he introduced the notion of the elite (*al-khasa*) who were divided into the caliph and his aides, and the army officers.

He clearly stated that by social division he meant "class division," though such analysis should not suggests that Zaydān saw Islamic history from a Marxist point of view, although the class factor in his analysis was present. In this regard one might add that Zaydān's intellectual background was not different from other Christian Arabs such as Shibli Shumayyil, Farah Antun, Ya'qub Sarruf, and Faris Nimr, who had migrated to Eygpt at the end of the 19th century and, with the contributions of their Egyptian colleagues, were the leading figures in propagating Darwinism and secularism.

As a Christian Arab, Zaydān emphasized the importance of pre-Islamic Arab achievements, in order to situate the Arab Christians within Arab/Islamic heritage. Zaydān attempted to articulate an approach to the history of the Arabs grounded in language and culture, an approach that led him to consider the Babylonian Hamourabi as Arabs. For Zaydān, language was a living entity, passing through processes of change until its "final" formation. Zaydān's historical and linguistic approach had an impact on the political scene not only in his time but also today, an implication well articulated by Albert Hourani: that Jurji Zaydān "did more than any other to create a consciousness of the Arab past, by his histories and still more by his series of historical novels."

Zaydān's works carried a strong political dimension at a time when the Arab cultural identity, based on language and common history, was in a process of formation within the Arab-speaking population of the Ottoman empire.

ISKANDAR MANSOUR

Biography

Born Beirut, 14 December 1861, to an Arab Greek Orthodox family. Studied medicine, Syrian Protestant College (later American University of Beirut), 1881–83, but left without taking a degree. Settled in Egypt, 1883; worked in publishing, Cairo, then became a historical novelist, 1891; editor, *al-Hilāl* (The Crescent), 1892–1914; declined a university professorship, 1910. Died Cairo, 21 July 1914.

Principal Writings

Fatat Ghassan (The Girl of Ghassan), 1898

al-Tārīkh al-ʿamm (The General History), 1899

Tārīkh al-yunan wa al-ruman (The History of the Greeks and the Byzantine), 1899

Tārīkh al-tamaddun al-Islāmī (The History of Islamic Civilization), 5 vols., 1902–06; vol. 4 in English as *Zaidan's Umayyads and Abbasids*, 1982

Fath al-andalus (The Conquest of Andalusia), 1903

al-ʿArab qabla al-Islam (The Pre-Islamic Arabs), 2 vols., 1908

Tārīkh Misr al-Hadith (The History of Modern Egypt), 1911

Tārīkh ādāb al-lugha al-ʿarabiyah (The History of Arabic Language and Literature), 4 vols., 1911–12

Salah al-din al-ayyubi (Saladdin), 1913

The Autobiography of Jurji Zaidan, translated and edited by Thomas Philipp, 1990

Further Reading

Alkhayat, Hamdi, *Gurji Zaidan: Leben und Werk* (Life and Work), Cologne: Orient Mercur, 1973

Philipp, Thomas, "Language, History, and Arab National Consciousness in the Thought of Jurji Zaidan," *IJMES* 4/1 (1973), 3–22

Philipp, Thomas, *Gurji Zaidan: His Life and Thought*, Beirut: Orient-Institute, 1979

Ware, Lewis Beier, "Jurji Zaidan: The Role of Popular History in the Formation of a New Arab World-View," thesis, Princeton University, 1973

Zeldin, Theodore 1933–

British social and cultural historian of modern France

Theodore Zeldin is a leading historian of post-1840s France who has created original and popular histories based largely on the lives of individuals rather than communities or social classes. His focus on France is based on the view that "All human passions can be seen at play in France, which means that to recognize the French is to recognize something in oneself, also" (*The French*, 1982). Zeldin emphasized the subjective nature of history, indeed he regards it as a form of autobiography for both author and reader. He challenged the dominance of the Annales school in French and European historiography, and rejected models of historical writing either as social science or as expressions of Marxism. For Zeldin, historical writing stands at the center of modern culture, with a commitment to innovation in perspective, in subject, and in genre. Histories are seen as potentially liberating texts for individual readers, as aids to selfconsciousness, to detachment, and to different choices in life. These controversial views challenge professional models, especially because of his public success and recognition in a wide range of media and markets.

Zeldin established his professional reputation in the 1950s and 1960s with two books, *The Political System of Napoleon III* (1958) and *Emile Ollivier and the Liberal Empire of Napoleon III* (1963), along with two supporting volumes of extracts from Ollivier's *Journal 1846–1869* (1961). These books on aspects of French politics from the 1850s to the 1870s demonstrated a mastery of unpublished primary sources, and developed a revisionist interpretation of the Liberal empire – as a successful break with the cycle of revolution and reaction in France from 1789 to 1848. Zeldin refuted the myth of the Second empire as a gap or aberration in the political history of France; and emphasized the complexity and diversity of local politics and public opinion, a theme that became even more dominant in his later work. The study of Emile Ollivier (1825–1913) affirmed the importance of biography – the weakest branch of French historical writing – in understanding the past. Zeldin's early stress on the importance of understanding the individual in history was exemplified in Ollivier's own independent and idealistic nature, the key to his liberal Bonapartist politics, which had been misunderstood both by contemporaries and later historians.

The first volume of Zeldin's most influential work so far, *France, 1848–1945*, was published in 1973, with the intriguing subtitle *Ambition, Love and Politics*, and the second volume appeared in 1977, as *Intellect, Taste and Anxiety*. This was a rather idiosyncratic contribution to the Oxford History of Modern Europe series, structured thematically rather than chronologically, integrating an extraordinary range of data about the French, and emphasizing "understanding values, ambitions, human relationships and the forces which influenced thinking." It retained his central emphasis on the individual. *France, 1848–1945* was awarded a prestigious Wolfson Historical prize, but there was strong criticism by some historians of Zeldin's move away from the chronological imperatives of political and economic history, and his rejection of theoretical models. Some found fragmentation rather than illumination in "particle-history." For Zeldin there was "a kind of *pointillisme* reducing complex phenomena into their most elementary forms." His writing was characteristically lucid and accessible and the book was exceptionally successful, with an unusually wide readership in many countries. This was extended further by the unprecedented Oxford Paperbacks republication in five volumes (1979–81), and a new 2-volume edition retitled *A History of French Passions* (1993).

In 1982 Zeldin's analysis *The French* was published, with French, German, Russian, and Japanese translations. This thematic account of 20th-century French social life and customs became a bestseller in France. "Guide Zeldin" aimed to demythologize "the French" through an exploration of their differences as individuals. The premises were that "individuals are the basic atom," and "now individuals are emerging as infinitely varied permutations of qualities and choices." Biographical case studies provided the structural foundation, within a thematic framework (regionalism, aspects of family life, work, taste, language, etc.). The view of intellectuals was both historical and apparently self-referential: "The most important influence intellectuals have had has been to cultivate individualism . . . [to] encourage even greater variation between individuals." Zeldin welcomed the role of public intellectual-historian, contributing extensively to the popular media (television, radio, journalism) and to conferences, congresses, and meetings in France and elsewhere.

In 1988 Zeldin's satirical novel *Happiness* was published in simultaneous French translation, as "an attempt to develop a more imaginative kind of history," with a revealing paperback subtitle: *An Exploration of the Art of Sleeping, Eating, Complaining, Postponing, Sympathising, and, Above All, Being Free*. This Voltairean exploration of the history of Paradise included penetrating criticisms of the university world, which was represented as far from free. The function of historians, and historical writing, was implicitly questioned as part of the critique of "academic" knowledge in this entertaining and provocative novel. Zeldin's ambitious *An Intimate History of Humanity* (1994) also broke decisively with conventional historical scholarship, extending the methods and the themes of *The French*, but with contemporary female biographies ("portraits") introducing explorations of emotional themes (e.g., hope, desire, respect, fear) across historical time. All "thirty-four major human civilisations" were prospective sources in this *Intimate History*, for "you belong with those people with whom you can sympathise, in whatever century they lived, in no matter what civilisation."

An Intimate History of Humanity is worlds away from *The Political System of Napoleon III*, but there is a continuity of liberal ideas about history, including the importance of the individual as the central character, which gives a unity to Zeldin's work. Curiosity about individuals has been the driving force of his research, and curiosity is valued as "the key to freedom" in *An Intimate History of Humanity*. Preconceived ideas and systems of thought are seen as concealed obstacles to individual freedom, which historians can uncover. Thus historians too can be useful, but in Zeldin's view academic historians must extricate themselves from the blind alley of hyper-specialization. Zeldin's views and his books will continue to be controversial, and a challenge to readers and writers in both public and private life.

JOHN HOOPER

See also France: since the Revolution

Biography

Born 1933 of Russian parents. Attended boarding school, Cairo; received BA in philosophy, Latin and history, Birkbeck College, University of London; BA from Christ Church, and DPhil from St. Antony's College, Oxford. Scholar at Christ Church and held research fellowship, St. Antony's College, 1957–63: fellow since 1963. Married Deirdre Wilson, professor of linguistics.

Principal Writings

The Political System of Napoleon III, 1958
Editor with Anne Troisier de Diaz, *Journal d'Emile Ollivier, 1846–1869*, 2 vols., 1961
Emile Ollivier and the Liberal Empire of Napoleon III, 1963
Editor, *Conflicts in French Society: Anticlericalism, Education and Morals in the Nineteenth Century*, 1970
France, 1848–1945, 2 vols., 1973–77; revised in 5 vols., 1979–81; as *A History of French Passions*, 2 vols., 1993
"Social History and Total History," *Journal of Social History*, 10 (1976), 237–45
The French, 1982
Happiness, 1988 [novel]
An Intimate History of Humanity, 1994

Further Reading

Hardyment, Christina, "Zeldin and the Art of Human Relationships," *Oxford Today*, 7/2 (1995), 28–30

Zhang Xuecheng [Chang Hsueh-ch'eng]

1738–1801

Chinese philosopher and historian

Zhang Xuecheng may be called a theorist of history or a philosophically-minded historian by our standard today. In his own time, however, he was known to his friends as a Confucian scholar with special interests in history and literature. But his was an age in which philologically-oriented classical scholarship dominated the Chinese intellectual world. In the 18th century philology was a newly discovered instrument in the hands of Confucian classicists, who claimed that they alone had access to the Confucian *Dao* ("Way" or "Truth") by way of philological explication of Confucian and pre-Confucian texts. For it was only in these early texts, they argued, that the subtle wealth of meaning in the messages of ancient sages was to be found. Since classicists were concerned typically with permanence rather than change and process, they naturally considered history, especially postclassical history, to be of no importance. It was against this intellectual background that Zhang developed his theories of history.

In the opening chapter of his *magnum opus, Wenshi tongyi* (General Principles of Literature and History), he propounded his famous thesis "The Six Classics Are All History." He argued that in pre-Confucian antiquity (the period from Emperor Yao to the Duke of Zhou) the very notion of putting thought in writing never occurred to the sages who, according to tradition, were also rulers. Therefore every thought worthy of being kept in writing must have been translated into practice in order to make the world better for the people to live under the sagely rule. He then went on with his analysis, work by work, to show that each of the so-called Six Classics is a truthful recording of what the sages actually did and said in connection with their work as dutiful administrators. The term "classic" did not even exist in pre-Confucian times; it was coined by later scholars to name these early documents which are all historical in nature.

To support this thesis he also disputed with classicists over the definition of *Dao*. In a well-known essay "On the *Dao*," he suggested that ancient sages did not create the *Dao* from their own minds and then impose it on the people. On the contrary, the *Dao* as order arose originally from the "daily activities" of the common people, and the sages' contribution consisted primarily in the discovery and continuing perfection of that order. This is precisely why he insisted that "the sages learned from the common people." The *Dao* is therefore in an ever-growing process and cannot be conceived as being fully revealed in the Six Classics which are but historical records of high antiquity. Thus Zhang historicized not only the Confucian classics but the *Dao* as well. This historicization worked both ways for him: On the one hand he demolished the classicists' monopolistic claim to the *Dao* and on the other hand he made history central and sacred in the Confucian scheme of things.

On the grounds of historical epistemology, Zhang also challenged the classicist's philological theory of reading and understanding. The philologist insisted that the only way to decipher a classical text is to start from the etymological root of every single word and then move on to discover the grammatical structure of a sentence. To this methodological individualism

Zhang opposed his holistic approach. He gave philology credit where it was due. But he pointed out the danger, as shown in the work of many contemporary philologists, that it is quite easy to get lost in the process of philological analysis. On his part he emphasized the importance of the ability to grasp holistically the central significance of a text. From his point of view, a grasp of the whole did not necessarily require grasp of every detail. He raised Chinese hermeneutics to a new height.

Because of his strong criticism of classical philologism of his own day, his work was largely ignored by his contemporaries. He remained a relatively obscure man in the world of learning. With the help of Western ideas and methods, he was rediscovered by Japanese and Chinese scholars in the early years of the 20th century. Since then his influence on Chinese philosophy and historiography has been enormous, and is still growing. Today he is generally recognized as one of two towering figures in the intellectual history of 18th-century China, the other one being Dai Zhen (1724–77), the arch-philologist and his chief rival.

YING-SHIH YU

See also China: Historical Writing, Late Imperial

Biography
Born Guiji, now Shaoxing, Zhejiang province, 1738. Rejected role as part of historical establishment; lectured independently and wrote. Died 1801.

Principal Writings
Hubei tongzhi (A History of Hubei Province), 1794
Wenshi tongyi (General Principles of Literature and History), written 1772–1800; printed 1832
Jiao-chou-gong-yi (General Textual Criticism)

Further Reading
Demieville, Paul, "Chang Hsueh-ch'eng and His Historiography," in William G. Beasley and Edwin G. Pulleyblank, eds., *Historians of China and Japan*, London: Oxford University Press, 1961
Momose, Hiromu, "Chang Hsüeh-ch'eng," in Arthur W. Hummel, ed., *Eminent Chinese of the Ch'ing Period, 1644–1912*, Washington, DC: US Government Printing Office, 1943
Nivison, David S., *The Life and Thought of Chang Hsueh-ch'eng (1738–1801)*, Stanford, CA: Stanford University Press, 1966
Yü Ying-shih, "Zhang Xuecheng versus Dai Zhen: A Study in Intellectual Challenge and Response in Eighteenth-Century China," in Philip J. Ivanhoe, ed., *Chinese Language, Thought, and Culture: Nivison and His Critics*, Chicago: Open Court, 1996

Zinn, Howard 1922–
US historian

As the relatively tranquil 1950s gave way to the turbulent 1960s in the United States, so the dominant consensus-and-continuity paradigm of historical writing gave way to a new emphasis on conflict and change. A new group of scholars – referred to variously as radical, New Left, neo-Progressive, revisionist, or conflict historians – approached history, as one put it, "from the bottom up." Their emphasis was on minorities, women, common people. They were also quite critical of America's history of military adventures abroad. William Appleman Williams is sometimes considered the "founder" of this "New Left school" of historians; other prominent members included Staughton Lynd, Eugene Genovese, and Howard Zinn.

To discuss Zinn's major writings is also to discuss some of the major events of his/our time, especially the civil rights and anti-Vietnam War movements. His first book, however, was an admiring study of the congressional career (1917–33) of the crusading reformer Fiorello La Guardia, best known as the mayor of New York during the New Deal era. Zinn followed this with an edited work, *New Deal Thought* (1965). He carefully tried to include all points of view, including La Guardia's, but his own came through clearly. Although the New Deal's accomplishments were "considerable," he said, still, "when it was over, the fundamental problem remained – and still remains – unsolved: how to bring the blessings of immense natural wealth and staggering productive potential to every person in the land." These two volumes in a sense prepared the way for Zinn's later work.

One of Zinn's unique contributions was an in-depth chronicling of the events of his own time, a kind of advocacy-journalism-as-history. Two works, both published in 1964, represent this style: *The Southern Mystique* and *SNCC: The New Abolitionists*. At the time Zinn was teaching at a college for African American women in Atlanta, and he had participated in the events he described. In *The Southern Mystique*, he insisted that racism in the South was not instinctive but circumstantial, and could therefore be changed. He also insisted that southern exceptionalism was a myth, that the South instead was a mirror, the essence of the nation, containing "in concentrated and dangerous form, a set of characteristics which mark the country as a whole." Among these were racism, violence, religious fundamentalism, nativism, hypocrisy in the elevation of women, suppression of class grievances, and poverty.

SNCC, the Student Nonviolent Coordinating Committee – the "New Abolitionists" of Zinn's title – was one of the most important and radical organizations to emerge from the civil rights movement. Zinn himself became an "adult adviser" to SNCC, and praised its members: "For the first time in our history a major social movement, shaking the nation to its bones, is being led by youngsters . . . All Americans owe them a debt for . . . releasing the idealism locked so long inside a nation that has not recently tasted the drama of a social upheaval."

Zinn next turned his attention to the war in Vietnam. The title of one book he published in 1967 is self-explanatory: *Vietnam: The Logic of Withdrawal*. Its influence is suggested by the fact that it quickly went through eight printings. Zinn broadened his field with *Disobedience and Democracy* (1968). His starting point here was the widely-circulated essay by Supreme Court Justice Abe Fortas, *Concerning Dissent and Civil Disobedience*. "For the crisis of our time, the slow workings of American reform, the limitations on protest and disobedience and innovation set by liberals like Justice Fortas," wrote the radical Zinn, "are simply not adequate. We need devices . . . to resist the government's actions against the lives and liberties of its citizens; to pressure, even to shock the government into change; to organize people to replace the holders of power, as one round in the continuing cycle of political renewal which alone can prevent tyranny."

Zinn's two most important books appeared after the 1960s: *The Politics of History* (1970) and *A People's History of the United States* (1980). The former was a ringing call for history to be relevant, and even more "for the notion of the historian as actor." Significantly, Zinn began the volume by quoting Diderot on Voltaire: "Other historians relate facts to inform us of facts. You relate them to excite in our hearts an intense hatred of lying, ignorance, hypocrisy, superstition, tyranny; and the anger remains even after the memory of the facts has disappeared."

A People's History has served as a sort of radical textbook for some fifteen years now; a new edition (1995), up to date through president Clinton, assures that it will continue to do so. Perhaps the key to the book is found in Zinn's statement that

in that inevitable taking of sides which comes from selection and emphasis in history, I prefer to try to tell the story of the discovery of America from the viewpoint of the Arawaks, of the Constitution from the standpoint of the slaves, of Andrew Jackson as seen by the Cherokees, of the Civil War as seen by the New York Irish, of the Mexican war as seen by the deserting soldiers of Scott's army, of the rise of industrialism as seen by the young women in the Lowell textile mills, of the Spanish-American war as seen by the Cubans, the conquest of the Philippines as seen by black soldiers on Luzon, the Gilded Age as seen by southern farmers, the First World War as seen by socialists, the Second World War as seen by pacifists, the New Deal as seen by blacks in Harlem, the postwar American empire as seen by peons in Latin America. And so on, to the limited extent that any one person, however he or she strains, can "see" history from the standpoint of others.

Zinn's work, in *A People's History of the United States* and elsewhere, has gone far toward accomplishing that goal; it provides a useful corrective to mainstream American historical writing.

DAVIS D. JOYCE

Biography

Born New York City, 24 August 1922. Received BA, New York University, 1951; MA, Columbia University, 1952, PhD 1958. Taught history and political science at Upsala College, 1953–56; Spelman College, 1956–63; and Boston University from 1964. Married in 1944 (2 children).

Principal Writings

La Guardia in Congress, 1959
SNCC: The New Abolitionists, 1964
The Southern Mystique, 1964
Editor, *New Deal Thought*, 1965
Vietnam: The Logic of Withdrawal, 1967
Disobedience and Democracy: Nine Fallacies on Law and Order, 1968
The Politics of History, 1970
Editor with Noam Chomsky, *The Pentagon Papers: Critical Essays*, 1972
Postwar America, 1945–1971, 1973
Editor, *Justice in Everyday Life: The Way it Really Works*, 1974
A People's History of the United States, 1980; revised 1995
Declarations of Independence: Cross-Examining American Ideology, 1990
Failure to Quit: Reflections of an Optimistic Historian, 1993
You Can't Be Neutral on a Moving Train, 1994

Further Reading

Bernstein, Barton J., ed., *Towards a New Past: Dissenting Essays in American History*, New York: Pantheon, 1968

Davis, Allen F., and Harold D. Woodman, eds., *Conflict and Consensus in Early American History*, Lexington, MA: Heath, 1968; 8th edition 1992

Higham, John, "The Cult of the American Consensus: Homogenizing Our History," *Commentary* 27 (1959), 93–101

Higham, John, "Beyond Consensus: The Historian as Moral Critic," *American Historical Review* 67 (1962), 609–25

Hollingsworth, J. Rogers, "Consensus and Continuity in Recent American Historical Writing," *South Atlantic Quarterly* 61 (1962), 40–50

Kraus, Michael, and Davis D. Joyce, *The Writing of American History*, revised edition, Norman: University of Oklahoma Press, 1985

Novick, Peter, *That Noble Dream: The "Objectivity Question" and the American Historical Profession*, Cambridge and New York: Cambridge University Press, 1988

Skotheim, Robert Allen, ed., *The Historian and the Climate of Opinion*, Reading, MA: Addison Wesley, 1969

Sternsher, Bernard, *Consensus, Conflict, and American Historians*, Bloomington: Indiana University Press, 1975

Unger, Irwin, ed., *Beyond Liberalism: The New Left Views American History*, Toronto: Xerox College Publishing, 1971

INDEXES

TITLE INDEX

This index lists all the titles in the Principal Writings sections of the entries on individual historians. The name in parentheses directs the reader to the appropriate entry, where fuller information is given. The date given is that of first publication; revised titles and published English-language translations are listed, with their dates.

15. századi magyar aristokrácia mobilitása (Fügedi), 1970
894 (1488–1489) yılı cizyesinin tahsılatına âit muhasebe bilânçoları (Barkan), 1964
1070–1071 (1660–1661) tarihli Osmanlı bütçesi ve bir mukayese (Barkan), 1955
1079–1080 (1669–1670) mâlî yılına âit bir Osmanlı bütçesi ekleri (Barkan), 1955
1789–1919 (Schnabel), 1923
1793, la Révolution contre l'Eglise (Vovelle), 1988
1848 (Meinecke), 1948
1848 (Namier), 1944
1914 (Mosse), 1966
1914 Debate Continues (Joll), 1972
1917: Before and After (Carr, E), 1969
6000 Tahun Sang Merah-Putih (Yamin), 1954
XV. ve XVI. asırlarda Osmanlı imparatorluğunda ziraî ekonominin hukukî ve malî esasları (Barkan), 1943
XVI. asrın ikinci yarısında Türkiye'de fiyat hareketleri (Barkan), 1970
XVIe et XVIIe siècles (Mousnier), 1953

À propos de nos écoles (Lavisse), 1895
Ab urbe condita (Livy), 31 BCE
Abbot Suger on the Abbey Church of St-Denis and Its Art Treasures (Panofsky), 1946
ABC of Communism (Carr, E), 1969
Abendländisches Geschichtsdenken (Brunner), 1954
Aberdeenshire to Africa (Hargreaves), 1981
Abhandlung über den Ursprung der Sprache (Herder), 1772
Abhandlung vom Standort und Gesichtspunkt des Geschichtsschreibers (Gatterer), 1768
Abolition of Serfdom in Russia (Zaionchkovskii), 1978
Aboriginal Population of Central Mexico on the Eve of the Spanish Conquest (Borah), 1963

Abraham Lincoln and the Union (Handlin), 1980
Abram S. Hewitt (Nevins), 1935
Abriss der Chronologie (Gatterer), 1777
Abriss der Diplomatik (Gatterer), 1778
Abriss der Geographie (Gatterer), 1775
Abriss der Universalhistorie (Gatterer), 1765
Absoluteness of Christianity and the History of Religions (Troeltsch), 1971
Absolutheit des Christentums und die Religionsgeschichte (Troeltsch), 1902
Abus de la mémoire (Todorov), 1995
Aby Warburg (Gombrich), 1970
Academia de Jurisprudencia y la vida de su fundador, Manuel Antonio de Castro (Levene), 1941
Academic Discourse (Bourdieu), 1994
Academies of Art, Past and Present (Pevsner), 1940
Achzehnte Brumaire des Louis-Bonaparte (Marx), 1869
Acquisitive Society (Tawney), 1920
Acta Sanctorum (Bolland), 1643
Acta sanctorum ordinis sancti Benedicti (Mabillon), 1668
Actes normands de la Chambre des comptes sous Philippe de Valois (Delisle), 1871
Action Française (Weber, E), 1962
Acton and History (Chadwick), 1998
Acts and Monuments (Foxe), 1563
Adam, Eve, and the Serpent (Pagels), 1988
Adelchi (Manzoni), 1822
Adeliges Landleben und europäischer Geist, 1612–1688 (Brunner), 1949
Admiral Farragut (Mahan), 1892
Admiral of the Ocean Sea (Morison), 1942
Adolf Hitler und der 9. November 1923 (Mommsen, H), 1994
Affaire de la Compagnie des Indes (Mathiez), 1921
Affluence and Anxiety (Degler), 1968
Afghani and Abduh (Kedourie), 1966
Africa (Coquery-Vidrovitch), 1988
Africa: History of a Continent (Davidson), 1966

Africa: A Voyage of Discovery (Davidson), 1984
Africa and Africans (Curtin), 1971
Africa and Empire (Marks), 1989
Africa and the Modern World (Wallerstein), 1986
Africa and the Victorians (Gallagher), 1961
Africa and the West (Curtin), 1972
Africa en America Latina (Moreno Fraginals), 1977
Africa from the Sixteenth to the Eighteenth Century (Ogot), 1992
Africa in Europe and the Americas (Rodney), 1975
Africa in History (Davidson), 1967
Africa in Latin America (Moreno Fraginals), 1984
Africa in Modern History (Davidson), 1978
Africa in the Iron Age, c.500 BC to AD 1400 (Oliver), 1975
Africa in the Nineteenth Century until the 1880s (Ajayi), 1989
Africa Remembered (Curtin), 1967
Africa since 1800 (Oliver), 1967
Africa since 1935 (Mazrui), 1993
Africa under Colonial Domination, 1880–1935 (Boahen), 1985
Africaines (Coquery-Vidrovitch), 1994
Africains (Julien), 1977
African Awakening (Davidson), 1955
African Background Outlined (Woodson), 1936
African Churches of Tanzania (Ranger), 1969
African Civilization Revisited (Davidson), 1991
African Experience (Oliver), 1991
African Experience with Higher Education (Ajayi), 1996
African Exploration and Human Understanding (Ayandele), 1972
African Genius (Davidson), 1970
African Historical Studies (Ayandele), 1979
African Histories and the Dissolution of World History (Feierman), 1993

FURTHER READING INDEX

Books and articles cited in the Further Reading sections of the entries are listed here by author / editor name. The page number refers to the Further Reading lists themselves, where full publication information is given.

NOTES ON ADVISERS
AND CONTRIBUTORS

Abalahin, Andrew J. Doctoral candidate in history, Cornell University. Author of articles on Indonesian and Philippine ethnic groups for *Encyclopedia of Cultures and Daily Life* (forthcoming). **Essay:** Ileto.

Adamo, Phillip C. Doctoral candidate and teaching associate, Ohio State University. Contributor to *Journal of the History of the Behavioral Sciences, Clio,* and *Undergraduate Historical Review.* **Essay:** Burke

Allan, David. Lecturer in Scottish history, University of St. Andrews. Author of *Virtue, Learning and the Scottish Enlightenment: Ideas of Scholarship in Early Modern History* (1993), *Philosophy and Politics in Later Stuart Scotland: Neo-Stoicism, Culture and Ideology in an Age of Crisis* (forthcoming), and of numerous articles on Scotland's cultural and intellectual life in *History of European Ideas* and *Comparative Studies in Society and History.* **Essays:** Hume; Scotland.

Almond-Welton, Michael. Research student, Oxford Polytechnic. **Essays:** Macartney; Nationalism (with Catherine Carmichael); Hugh Seton-Watson.

Alpers, Edward A. Professor of history, University of California, Los Angeles. Author of *Ivory and Slaves: Changing Patterns of Trade in East Central Africa to the Late Nineteenth Century* (1975), and of many articles in the *Journal of African History, International Journal of African Historical Studies, Canadian Journal of African Studies,* and *African Economic History.* Editor of *Walter Rodney: Revolutionary and Scholar: A Tribute* (1982). President, African Studies Association, 1994. **Essay:** Ajayi.

Arnold, David. Professor of South Asian history, School of Oriental and African Studies, University of London. Author of *The Congress of Tamilnad: Nationalist Politics in South India, 1919–1937* (1977), *Police Power and Colonial Rule: Madras, 1859–1947* (1986), *Famine: Social Crisis and Historical Change* (1988), *Colonizing the Body: State Medicine and Epidemic Disease in Nineteenth-Century India* (1993), and *The Problem of Nature: Culture and European Expansion* (1996). Editor or co-editor of *Imperial Medicine and Indigenous Societies* (1988), *Subaltern Studies 8: Essays in Honour of Ranajit Guha* (1994), *Nature, Culture, Imperialism: Essays on the Environmental History of South Asia* (1995), and *Warm Climates and Western Medicine: The Emergence of Tropical Medicine, 1500–1900* (1996). **Essays:** Environmental History; Subaltern Studies.

Arnot, Margaret L. Senior lecturer in history, Roehampton Institute, London. Author of a number of articles on gender and crime in 19th-century England and of a forthcoming book on infanticide in Victorian England. Editor (with Cornelie Usborne) of *Gender and Crime in Modern Europe* (1999). **Essays:** Davidoff; Walkowitz.

Ashworth, William. Customs and Excise research fellow, Department of Economic and Social History, University of Liverpool. Editor of *A Calendar of the Correspondence of William Whewell* (1996). **Essay:** Whewell.

Assael, Brenda. Lecturer in history, University of Wales, Swansea. Author of *The Circus and Victorian Society* (forthcoming). **Essay:** Theatre.

Atallah, Samira Ali. Lecturer in Arab studies, Boston University. Writer/researcher on Middle Eastern societies, especially as related to gender, development, and international relations. **Essay:** Hodgson.

Averkorn, Raphaela. Assistant professor of history, University of Hannover, Germany. Author of *Adel und Kirche in der Grafschaft Armagnac* (1997) and several articles on French, Spanish, and German history and historiography. **Essay:** Waitz.

Bainbridge, Virginia R. V.H. Galbraith fellow, St. Hilda's College, University of Oxford. Author of *Gilds in the Medieval Countryside: Social and Religious Change in Cambridgeshire, c.1350–1558* (1996). **Essays:** Britain: 1066–1485; Camden; Froissart; Hilton; Huizinga; Knowles; Maitland; Pirenne; Postan; Yates.

Bak, János M. Professor, Central European University, Budapest, and emeritus professor, University of British Columbia, Vancouver. Author of *Königtum und Stände in Ungarn im 14.–16. Jahrhundert* (1973) and *Medieval Narrative Sources: A Chronological Guide* (1987). Editor of *The German Peasant War of 1525* (1976), *From Hunyadi to Rákóczi: War and Society in Late Medieval and Early Modern Hungary* (1982), *Religion and Rural Revolt* (1984), *Coronations: Medieval and Early Modern Monarchic Ritual* (1990), and the English edition of *The Hungarian Revolution of 1956: Reform, Revolt, and Repression, 1953–1963* (1996). **Essay:** Schramm.

Bardeci, Oscar Julian. Former director, Centro Latinoamericano de Demografía, United Nations. Author of many works on Latin America. **Essay:** Prebisch.

Barker, John W. Professor of history, University of Wisconsin, Madison. Author of *Justinian and the Later Roman Empire* (1966), *Manuel II Palaeologus (1391–1425): A Study in Late Byzantine Statesmanship* (1969), and *The Use of Music and Recordings for Teaching about the Middle Ages* (1988), and many articles and reviews in *Speculum, Byzantinische Zeitschrift, American Historical Review, Balkan Studies, Classical World, Renaissance Quarterly, Manuscripta, Modern Greek Studies Yearbook, Italica, Reviews in American History*, and other journals. **Essays:** Komnene; Psellos; Vasiliev.

Barnett, Robert E. Associate professor of history, Lee College, Tennessee. Contributor to *Nineteenth Century, American National Biography*, and *Memories to Memoirs* (1992). **Essay:** Boorstin.

Barrett, T.H. Professor of East Asian history, School of Oriental and African Studies, University of London. Author of *Singular Listlessness: A Short History of Chinese Books and British Scholars* (1989), *Li Po: Buddhist, Taoist or Neo-Confucian?* (1992), *Taoism under the T'ang* (1996); contributor to *Journal of the Royal Asiatic Society* and *Buddhist Forum*. Editorial board member, *Modern Asian Studies* and *Bulletin of the School of Oriental and African Studies*. **Essays:** Maspero; Naitō.

Barry, Jonathan. Senior lecturer in history, University of Exeter, England. Editor of *The Tudor and Stuart Town, 1530–1688: A Reader in English Urban History* (1990). Co-editor of *Medicine and Charity before the Welfare State* (1991), *Culture in History: Production, Consumption, and Values in Historical Perspective* (1992), *The Middling Sort of People: Culture, Politics and Society in England, 1550–1800* (1994), *Reformation and Revival in Eighteenth-Century Bristol* (1994), and *Witchcraft in Early Modern Europe: Studies in Culture and Belief* (1996). **Essay:** Keith Thomas.

Barton-Kriese, Paul. Assistant professor of political science, Indiana University East. Author of *Truth-Speaking and Power: Ethical Alternatives and Political Consequences* (1987), *The Politics of Diversity in the United States: Positive Dreams and Pyrrhic Victories* (1993), *Nonviolent Revolution* (1995), and articles on nonviolence, confrontation, and human rights. **Essay:** Cassirer.

Batchelor, Robert P. Historian, History Factory/Temple University. Author of entries on business and the economy in *The Encyclopedia of American Decades* (1996). **Essays:** Technology; Wiebe.

Bátonyi, Gábor. Lecturer in modern European history, Department of European Studies, University of Bradford. Author of *Britain and Central Europe, 1918–1932*. **Essays:** Central Europe; Frontiers; Marczali; R.W. Seton-Watson; Szekfű.

Baxell, Richard. Doctoral candidate researching British volunteers in the Spanish Civil War, London School of Economics, and adjunct lecturer in history and computing, Middlesex University and Queen Mary and Westfield College, University of London. **Essays:** Cambridge Group; Computing and History.

Beecher, Jonathan. Professor of history, University of California, Santa Cruz. Author of *Charles Fourier: The Visionary and His World* (1987; French edition, 1993) and contributor to *History Workshop Journal, Journal of Modern History, American Historical Review, Nineteenth-Century French Studies, Utopian Studies*, and other journals. Editor and translator (with Richard Bienvenu) of *The Utopian Vision of Charles Fourier* (1971). **Essays:** Berlin; Cobb.

Behr, Charlotte. Lecturer in early medieval history, Roehampton Institute, London. **Essays:** Ammianus Marcellinus; Annales regni Francorum; Snorri Sturluson.

Berg, Maxine. Reader in history, and director of the Warwick Research Centre in Eighteenth-Century Studies, University of Warwick. Author of *The Machinery Question and the Making of Political Economy, 1815–1848* (1980), *The Age of Manufactures, 1700–1820* (2nd edition, 1994), *A Woman in History: Eileen Power, 1889–1940* (1996), and numerous articles. **Essays:** Halévy; Power.

Berger, Carl. Professor of history, University of Toronto. Author of *The Sense of Power: Studies in the Idea of Canadian Imperialism, 1867–1914* (1970), *The Writing of Canadian History* (1976), *Science, God, and Nature in Victorian Canada* (1983), and *Honour and Search for Influence: A History of the Royal Society of Canada* (1996).

Berkeley, Christopher. Formerly faculty member, Framingham State College. Contributor to *Oxford Companion to United States History, The Encyclopedia of New England Culture*, and many other publications. **Essays:** Adams; Curti.

Binnema, Theodore. Doctoral candidate, University of Alberta. Contributor to *American Indian Quarterly, Prairie Forum*, and *Canadian Historical Review*. Former editor, *Past Imperfect*, and assistant editor, *Chronology of Native North American History*. **Essays:** Stampp; Trigger (with Brian Gobbett).

Black, Jeremy. Professor of history, University of Exeter, England. Author of several books, including *Culloden and the '45* (1990), *The War for America* (1991), *Pitt the Elder* (1992), *European Warfare, 1660–1815* (1992), *Maps and History: Constructing Images of the Past* (1997), and *America or Europe? British Foreign Policy, 1739–63* (1998). Editor of *Archives*. **Essays:** Elton; Enlightenment Historical Writing; Historical Geography; Historical Maps and Atlases; Plumb.

Blackwood, Lee. Assistant professor of history, and associate chair, Council on Russian and East European Studies, Yale University. Author of *European Socialists on the Road to Locarno and Munich: The Democratic Left and the Roots of Appeasement Between the Wars, 1918–38* (forthcoming). **Essays:** Kuczynski; Kula.

Blaxell, Vivian. Professor of history, Marlboro College, Vermont. **Essay:** James C. Scott.

Blumberg, Laurie Robyn. Doctoral student, Near Eastern and Judaic studies, Brandeis University. **Essay:** Marrus.

Blyth, Stuart. Doctoral candidate and visiting lecturer in history, University of Wolverhampton. **Essay:** Raymond Carr.

Bogle, Lori Lyn. Doctoral candidate, University of Arkansas. Contributor to *Missouri Historical Review, Ozark Historical Review, Historical Journal of Massachusetts, Chronicles of Oklahoma,* and *Arkansas State University Museum Occasional Papers.* **Essay:** Pipes.

Bolton, Geoffrey. Emeritus professor of history, Edith Cowan University, Western Australia. Author of *Alexander Forrest* (1958), *A Thousand Miles Away: A History of North Queensland to 1920* (1963), *The Passing of the Irish Act of Union* (1966), *A Fine Country to Starve In* (1972), *Britain's Legacy Overseas* (1973), and *The Middle Way, 1942–1988* (1990). General editor, *The Oxford History of Australia*; section editor, *Australian Dictionary of Biography.* **Essay:** Blainey.

Borges, Dain. Associate professor of history, University of California, San Diego. Author of *The Family in Bahia, Brazil, 1870–1945* (1992). **Essay:** Freyre.

Bowden, Hugh. Lecturer in ancient history, King's College, University of London. Author of *Apollo and Athena: The Classical Athenian Democracy and the Delphic Oracle* (forthcoming). **Essays:** Greece: Ancient; Thucydides.

Boyd, Kelly. Lecturer in modern British and women's history, Middlesex University, London. Author of articles on masculinity and juvenile literature in modern Britain. Editor, *Encyclopedia of Historians and Historical Writing* (1999). **Essay:** Family.

Boyden, James M. Associate professor of history, Tulane University. Author of *The Courtier and the King: Ruy Gómez de Silva, Philip II, and the Court of Spain* (1995). **Essay:** Maravall.

Brakel-Papenhuyzen, Clara. Senior researcher, Leiden University, and research fellow, Institute of Asian and African Studies, Hebrew University of Jerusalem. Author of *The Bedhaya Court Dances of Central Java* (1992) and *Classical Javanese Dance* (1995), and editor or author of numerous articles on the cultural history of Indonesia, especially of Java. **Essays:** Babad; Ranggawarsita.

Bregel, Yuri. Professor of Central Eurasian studies, Indiana University. Author of *Khorezmskie turkmeny v XIX veke* (1961), a revised and enlarged Russian edition of C.A. Storey's *Persian Literature: A Bio-Bibliographical Survey* (1972), and *Bibliography of Islamic Central Asia* (1995). **Essays:** Bartol'd; Rashīd al-Dīn.

Breisach, Ernst. Professor of history, Western Michigan University. Author of *Introduction to Modern Existentialism* (1962), *Caterina Sforza* (1969), *Renaissance Europe* (1973), *Historiography: Ancient, Medieval, and Modern* (1983, 1994), and *American Progressive History* (1993). Editor of *Classical Rhetoric and Medieval Historiography* (1985). **Essays:** Beard; Becker.

Brett, Michael. Senior lecturer in the history of North Africa, School of Oriental and African Studies, University of London. Author of *The Moors: Islam in the West* (1980) and *The Berbers* (with Elizabeth Fentross, 1996). **Essays:** Africa: North and the Horn; Egypt: since the 7th Century CE; Julien; Laroui; Middle East: Medieval; Oliver.

Bröer, Ralf. Member, Institute of the History of Medicine, University of Heidelberg. Author of *Salomon Reisel (1625–1701): Barocke Naturforschung eines Leibarztes im Banne der mechanistischen Philosophie* (1995). **Essay:** Sigerist.

Bromley, Marilynne. Director of classical studies, St. Mary's University College, University of Surrey, England. Editor of *St. Thomas More* (1990) and contributor to *Bulletin of the Institute of Classical Studies, Classical and Modern Literature, Journal of the T.E. Lawrence Society,* and *Classical Review.* **Essays:** Julius Caesar; Diodorus Siculus.

Brown, Kenneth D. Professor of economic and social history, and dean of the Faculty of Legal, Social and Educational Sciences, Queen's University, Belfast. Author of *Labour and Unemployment, 1900–1914* (1971), *John Burns* (1977), *The English Labour Movement, 1500–1951* (1985), *A Social History of the Nonconformist Ministry in England and Wales, 1800–1930* (1988), *The British Toy Business: A History since 1700* (1995), and *A Comparative Economic and Social History of Britain and Japan since 1900* (1998). Editor of *Essays in Anti-Labour History* (1971). **Essays:** Clapham; Cole; Tawney.

Brownstein, Daniel. Specialist in Renaissance history and early modern science. Associate researcher, History of Cartography Project, Department of Geography, University of Wisconsin. Author of reviews in *Medievalia et Humanistica* and *Sixteenth-Century Studies.* **Essays:** Fleck; Poliakov; Ullman.

Bruce, Gary S. Lecturer, University of New Brunswick, Canada. Contributor to *Conflict Quarterly, Historische Zeitschrift,* and *Journal of Conflict Studies.* **Essays:** Germany: 1800–1945; McNeill; Rothschild; Hermann Weber.

Brudvig, Jon L. Assistant professor of history, University of Mary, Bismarck, North Dakota. Contributor to *American National Biography, Encyclopedia of North American Indians, Censorship: A World Encyclopedia, Dictionary of Women's Education,* and *Virginia Archaeological Bulletin.* **Essay:** Prucha.

Brunelle, Gayle K. Associate professor of history, California State University, Fullerton. Author of *The New World Merchants of Rouen, 1559–1630* (1991), and contributor to *French Historical Studies, Sixteenth Century Journal,* and *Terra Incognita.* **Essay:** Indigenous Peoples.

Brungardt, Maurice P. Associate professor of history, Loyola University, New Orleans. Contributor to *American Business History: Case Studies* (1987), *Latin American Population History Bulletin* (1990), *Reform and Insurrection in Bourbon New Granada and Peru* (1990), *Global Education and the Study Abroad Program* (1991), and *Memorias* vol.3: *Cultura* *politica, movimentos sociales y violencia en la historia de Colombia* (1993). **Essays:** Elliott; Latin America: Colonial; Latin America: National; Scobie.

Bugos, Glenn E. Historian, Prologue Group, California. Author of *Engineering the F-4 Phantom II: Parts into Systems* (1996). **Essay:** Thomas P. Hughes.

Buhle, Paul. Visiting associate professor of history, Department of American Civilization, Brown University, and director, Oral History of the American Left, Tamiment Library, New York University. Author of *Marxism in the United States* (1987), *C.L.R. James: The Artist as Revolutionary* (1988), *William Appleman Williams: The Tragedy of Empire* (1995), *A Dreamer's Paradise Lost: Louis C. Fraina/Lewis Corey* (1995), and (with Patrick McGilligan) *Tender Comrades: A Backstory of the Hollywood Blacklist* (1997). Editor or co-editor of *The Concise History of Woman Suffrage* (1978), *C.L.R. James: His Life and Work* (1986), *Popular Culture in America* (1987), *History and the New Left: Madison, Wisconsin, 1950–1970* (1990), *C.L.R. James's Caribbean* (1992), *The American Radical* (1994), *Images of American Radicalism* (1998), and *Encyclopedia of the American Left* (2nd edition 1998). Editor of the journals *Radical America* (1967–73) and *Cultural Correspondence* (1976–81). **Essays:** James; United States: Historical Writing, 20th Century; William Appleman Williams.

Bulliet, Richard W. Director, Middle East Institute, Columbia University. Author of *The Patricians of Nishapur: A Study in Medieval Islamic Social History* (1972), *The Camel and the Wheel* (1975), *Conversion to Islam in the Medieval Period: An Essay in Quantitative History* (1979), *The Gulf Scenario* (1984), *Islam: The View from the Edge* (1994), and *The Columbia History of the Twentieth Century* (1998).

Burns, Michael. Professor of modern European history, Mount Holyoke College. Author of *Rural Society and French Politics: Boulangism and the Dreyfus Affair* (1984), "Families and Fatherlands: The Lost Provinces" in *Nationhood and Nationalism in France* (1991), "L'Honneur incarné" in *Les Cahiers Naturalistes* (1995), and *Dreyfus: A Family Affair, 1789–1945* (1991). Editor, *Main Trends in History* (1991). **Essay:** Eugen Weber.

Burrell, David T. Doctoral candidate in history, University of Chicago. Former curator, Buffalo Bill Memorial Museum. **Essay:** Dunning.

Buttafuoco, Annarita. Professor of the history of contemporary Europe, Siena University. Author of *Le Mariuccine: storia di un istituzione laica* (1985), *Cronache femminili: temi e momenti della stampa emancipazionista in Italia* (1988), and *Questioni di cittadinanza: donne e diritti sociali nell'Italia liberale* (1995). **Essay:** Pieroni Bortolotti.

Caldwell, I.A. Lecturer in Malay language and literature, University of Hull; former lecturer, Department of Malay Studies, National University of Singapore. Author of "The Myth of the Exemplary Centre: Shelly Errington's *Meaning and Power in a Southeast Asian Realm*," *Journal of Southeast Asian Studies*

(1991), "The Holy Footprints of the Venerable Gautama: A New Translation of the Pasir Panjang Inscription," *Bijdragen tot de Taal-, Land- en Volkenkunde* (with A. Hazelwood, 1994), and "Power, State and Society among the pre-Islamic Bugis," *Bijdragen tot de Taal-, Land- en Volkenkunde* (1995). **Essays:** Bugis and Makasar Chronicles.

Calmard, Jean. Director of research, Centre National de la Recherche Scientifique (CNRS), Paris. Editor of *Etudes Safarides* (1993) and contributor to *Encyclopaedia of Islam*. **Essay:** Cahen.

Calvert, Kenneth R. Assistant professor of history, Hillsdale College, Michigan. **Essays:** Bernal; Haskins; Polybius; Roman Empire; Syme.

Carlson, Marybeth. Assistant professor of history, University of Dayton. Author of "A Trojan Horse of Worldliness? Maidservants in the Burger Household in Rotterdam at the End of the Seventeenth Century" in *Women in the Golden Age* (1994). Assistant editor, *Documentary History of the Ratification of the Constitution*, vols. 8–10. **Essays:** Fruin; Geyl; Low Countries; Motley; Wilson.

Carmichael, Catherine. Lecturer in Central European history, Middlesex University, London. **Essay:** Nationalism (with Michael Almond-Welton).

Carotenuto, Gennaro. Research associate, University of Buenos Aires and University of Macerata. Freelance journalist with *RAI* (Italian Broadcasting Company) and *El Pais* (Madrid), literary translator, and contributor to numerous academic journals, including *Latinoamerica*, *Cinema Sessanta*, *Spagna Contemporanea*, *Scrivere*, *Vevy Europe Editore*, and *Quaderni di filologia e lingue romanze*. **Essays:** Portelli; Procacci; Spriano.

Carroll, Stuart. Lecturer in history, University of York, England. Author of *Noble Power during the French Wars of Religion: The Guise Affinity and the Catholic Cause in Normandy* (1998). **Essay:** Le Roy Ladurie.

Chakrabarty, Dipesh. Professor of history, South Asian studies, and history of culture, University of Chicago. Author of *Rethinking Working-Class History: Bengal, 1890–1940* (1989), and articles in *Representations*, *History Workshop Journal*, *Past and Present*, and *Public Culture*. Founding member of the editorial collective of *Subaltern Studies*, and editor (with Shahid Amin) of *Subaltern Studies*, vol. 9 (1991). **Essay:** Guha.

Chamberlain, Kathleen Egan. Assistant professor of US history, Castleton State College, Vermont. Author of "Competition for the Native American Soul" in *Religion in the West* (1996) and contributor to *New Mexico Historical Review*, *Journal of the West*, and *Communications Magazine*. **Essays:** Bancroft; Bolton; Debo; Handlin; Henry Nash Smith.

Chang, Chun-shu. Professor of history, University of Michigan, Ann Arbor, and honorary professor of history, China. Author (in English) of *Premodern China* (1971), *The Making of China* (1975), *South China in the Twelfth Century* (1981), *Crisis and*

Transformation in Seventeenth-Century China (1992), *The Stained Mirror of History* (1997), *Redefining History* (1997), and (in Chinese) of *Handai bianjiangshi lunji* (Studies in Han Frontier History, 1977), *Hanjian yu Hanjian de shijie* (The World of Han China in Han Wooden Documents, 1997), and *Zhongguo jinshi zhi renwu sixiang yu wenhua jingshen* (The Intellectuals and Their Cultural World in Early Modern China, 1998). **Essays:** China, Historical Writing (3 entries).

Chenault, Stephen K. Doctoral candidate in history, University of Arkansas. **Essays:** Austro-Hungarian Empire; Brunner; Niethammer.

Cheong, Yeong-han. Faculty member, National Institute for Law, Ethics, and Public Affairs (NILEPA), Griffith University, Australia. Co-author, *America's Australia, Australia's America: A Guide to Issues and References* (1997). **Essays:** Manning Clark; Treitschke.

Choe, Yŏng-ho. Professor of history, University of Hawaii at Manoa. Author of *The Civil Examinations and the Social Structure in Early Yi Korea* (1987), "An Outline History of Korean Historiography," *Korean Studies* (1980), and "Reinterpreting Traditional History in North Korea," *Journal of Asian Studies* (1981). Co-editor of *Sources of Korean Civilization* (1993). **Essay:** Korea.

Chryssavgis, John. Professor of theology, Holy Cross School of Theology. Author of *Fire and Light* (1987), *Ascent to Heaven* (1989), *The Desert Is Alive* (1990), *Repentance and Confession* (1990), and *Love, Sexuality, and Marriage* (1996). Editorial board member, *Phronema* (1986–95) and *Greek Orthodox Theological Review* (from 1988). **Essay:** Eastern Orthodoxy.

Clark, Emily. Mellon research fellow in American history, University of Cambridge. Author of "'By All the Conduct of Their Lives': A Laywoman's Confraternity in New Orleans, 1730–1744," *William and Mary Quarterly* (1997). **Essay:** Slavery: Modern.

Clendinnen, Inga. Emeritus reader in anthropology, La Trobe University, Australia. Author of *Ambivalent Conquests: Maya and Spaniard in Yucatan, 1517–1570* (1987) and *Aztecs: An Interpretation* (1991). **Essay:** Geertz.

Clough, Cecil H. Reader in Italian Renaissance studies, University of Liverpool. Recent publications include "Federico da Montefeltro e l'Umanesimo," *Res Publica Litterarum* (1993), "Love and War in the Veneto: Luigi da Porto and the True Story of Giulietta e Romeo" in *War, Culture and Society in Renaissance Venice* (1993), and "Art as Power in the Decoration of the Study of an Italian Renaissance Prince," *Artibus et Historiae* (1995). **Essays:** Cantimori; Giannone; Giovio; Guicciardini; Kantorowicz; Kristeller; Machiavelli; Pieri.

Coates, Ken. Dean, Faculty of Arts, University of New Brunswick at Saint John. Author of *Best Left as Indians: Native–White Relations in the Yukon* (1991); joint author with William Morrison of *Land of the Midnight Sun: A History of the Yukon* (1988), *The Sinking of the Princess Sophia: Taking the North Down with Her* (1990), *The Alaska Highway in World War II: The US Army of Occupation in Canada's Northwest* (1992), *The Forgotten North* (1992), and *Working the North: Labor and the Northwest Defense Projects, 1942–1946* (1994). Editor of *Aboriginal Land Claims: Canada* (1992). Editorial board member, *Northern Review* and University of Alaska Press. **Essays:** Crosby; Morton; Popular History (with William Morrison).

Cobb, Adam. Doctoral candidate in history, St. John's College, University of Cambridge. Contributor to *Pacific Defence Reporter* and *China Journal*. **Essays:** E.H. Carr; Intelligence and Espionage.

Cohen, Alvin P. Professor of Chinese and chair of the Department of Asian Languages and Literatures, University of Massachusetts at Amherst. Editor of *Selected Works of Peter A. Boodberg* (1979) and *Legend, Lore, and Religion in China: Essays in Honor of Wolfram Eberhard on His Seventieth Birthday* (with Sarah Allan, 1979); author of "Solar Eclipses Recorded in China During the Tang Dynasty," in *Monumenta Serica* (with Robert R. Newton, 1981–83) and "Chinese Religion: Popular Religion" in *The Encyclopedia of Religion* (1987); translator of *Tales of Vengeful Souls: A Sixth Century Collection of Chinese Avenging Ghost Stories* (1982). Associate editor, *East Asia* (1975–78) and *Journal of the American Oriental Society*. **Essay:** Eberhard.

Collins, Roger. Fellow of the Institute of Advanced Studies, University of Edinburgh. Author of *Early Medieval Spain, 400–1000* (1983; revised 1995), *The Basques* (1986), *The Arab Conquest of Spain, 710–797* (1989), *Early Medieval Europe, 300–1000* (1991), *Law, Culture and Regionalism in Early Medieval Spain* (1992), *The Oxford Archaeological Guide to Spain* (1998), *Charlemagne* (1998), and of numerous articles. Editor of *Charlemagne's Heir* (with Peter Godman, 1991), *The Ecclesiastical History* by Bede (1994), and *Fredegar* (1996). **Essays:** Bede; Britain: Anglo-Saxon; Bury; France: to 1000; Germany: to 1450; Gsell; Pelliot; Sánchez-Albornoz; Spain: to 1450.

Comerford, Kathleen. Assistant professor of history, Benedictine College, Kansas. Author of "Clement VIII," in *Notable Popes: A Biocritical Sourcebook* (forthcoming), and articles in *Erasmus of Rotterdam Society Yearbook* (1996), *Catholic Historical Review*, *Sixteenth Century Journal*, and *Libraries and Culture*. Book review editor, H-Italy, 1996–97. **Essays:** Cipolla; Delumeau; Gurevich; Italy: Renaissance; Italy: since the Renaissance; Renaissance Historical Writing.

Constantelos, Demetrios J. Charles Cooper Townsend distinguished professor of history and religion, Richard Stockton College of New Jersey. Author of *Byzantine Philanthropy and Social Welfare* (1968), *Understanding the Greek Orthodox Church* (1982), *Poverty, Society and Philanthropy in the Late Medieval Greek World* (1992), and *Christian Hellenism* (1995). Editor, *Greek Orthodox Theological Review*, 1965–71, and *Orthodox Theology and Diakonia*, 1981; associate editor, *Journal of Ecumenical Studies*, from 1974. **Essay:** Byzantium.

Coodley, Lauren. Professor, Napa Valley College. Author of an article on Upton Sinclair and contributor to *Encyclopedia of Violence in America*. Essays: Lerner; Painter.

Cook, Hera. Doctoral candidate, University of Sussex; Leverhulme fellow, University of Sydney. Essay: Rowbotham.

Coon, Timothy P. Curriculum manager, Connecticut Police Academy; captain, US Army Reserve. Essay: Comte.

Crampton, R.J. Professor of East European history, and fellow of St. Edmund Hall, University of Oxford. Author of *The Hollow Detente: Anglo–German Relations in the Balkans, 1911–1914* (1981), *Bulgaria, 1878–1918: A History* (1983), *A Short History of Modern Bulgaria* (1987), *Eastern Europe in the Twentieth Century* (1994), and *Atlas of Eastern Europe in the Twentieth Century* (1996).

Cremer, Douglas. Assistant professor of history, and chair, Department of Natural and Social Sciences, Woodbury University. Author of "Protestant Theology in Early Weimar Germany: Barth, Tillich, Bultmann," *Journal of the History of Ideas*. Essays: Christianity; Religion.

Crim, Brian. Doctoral candidate, Rutgers University. Author of several articles on military history. Essays: European Expansion; Parker; Vagts.

Cunfer, Geoff. Doctoral candidate, University of Texas, Austin. Essays: Malin; Frederick Jackson Turner.

Curry, Patrick. Independent scholar. Author of *Prophecy and Power: Astrology in the Early Modern World* (1989), *A Confusion of Prophets: Victorian and Edwardian Astrology* (1992), and *Defending Middle Earth: Tolkien, Myth, and Modernity* (1997). Editor of *Astrology, Science and Society* (1987). Essay: Astrology.

D'Ambrosio, Ubiratan. Professor emeritus, University of Campinas (UNICAMP), Brazil. Essays: Febvre; Varnhagen.

Davis, Belinda. Assistant professor of history, Rutgers University. Author of *Home Fires Burning: Daily Life and Politics in World War I Berlin* (1999). Essay: Lüdtke.

Deslippe, Dennis A. Lecturer in history, Australian National University. Author of "'We Had an Awful Time with Our Women': Iowa's United Packinghouse Workers of America, 1945–75," *Journal of Women's History* (1993) and "Organized Labor, National Politics, and Second-Wave Feminism in the United States, 1965–74," *International Labor and Working-Class History* (1996). Essay: Kessler-Harris.

Dickinson, John A. Professor, Département d'histoire, Université de Montréal and Professeur associé à mi-temps, Université de Versailles St-Quentin-en-Yvelines. Former directeur scientifique, *Revue d'histoire de l'Amérique française*. Author or co-author of *Justice et Justiciables: la procédure civile à la Prévôté de Québec, 1667–1759* (1982), *A Short History of Quebec* (1988, 1993), *1492: Les Européens découvrent l'Amérique* (1992),

Brève histoire socio-économique du Québec (1992, 1995) and *Les Français en Amérique* (1993). Essays: Eccles; Séguin.

Diesener, Gerald. Director, Karl Lamprecht Institute, Leipzig. Author of *Propaganda in Deutschland: zur Geschichte der politischen Massenbeeinflussung im 20. Jahrhundert* (1996). Editor of *Karl Lamprecht weiterdenken: Universal- und Kulturgeschichte heute* (1993). Essay: Lamprecht.

Dikötter, Frank. Senior lecturer in the history of medicine, School of Oriental and African Studies, University of London; director, Contemporary China Institute. Author of *The Discourse of Race in Modern China* (1992), *Sex, Culture and Modernity in China* (1995), and *Imperfect Conceptions: Medical Knowledge, Birth Defects and Eugenics in China* (1998). Editor of *The Construction of Racial Identities in China and Japan: Historical and Contemporary Perspectives* (1997). Editorial board member, *Nations and Nationalism*. Essays: China: Modern; Wang Fuzhi.

Domenico, Roy Palmer. Associate professor of history, University of Scranton. Author of *Italian Fascists on Trial, 1943–1948* (1991), "Impressioni anglo-americane riguardo ai partigiani sulla Linea Gotica: il caso del Patriots Branch" in *Al di qua e al di là della Linea Gotica* (1993), and "America, the Holy See, and the War in Vietnam" in *Papal Diplomacy in the Modern Age* (1994). Essay: De Felice.

Dorsett, Mark Richard. Parish priest, Church of England. Author of "Populistischer konservatismus und elitärer Liberalismus: Margaret Thatcher und die Führungskräfte der Church of England 1979 bis 1990" in *Christentum und Demokratie in 20. Jahrhundert* (1992). Essay: Chadwick.

Drake, Richard. Professor of history, University of Montana. Author of *Byzantium for Rome: The Politics of Nostalgia in Umbertian Italy, 1878–1900* (1980), *The Revolutionary Mystique and Terrorism in Contemporary Italy* (1989), and *The Aldo Moro Murder Case* (1995). Essays: Burckhardt; De Sanctis; Vico; Villari.

Draper, Lincoln A. Independent scholar. Author of "Archbishops, Canons and Priests: The Interaction of Religious and Social Values in the Clergy of Seventeenth-Century Bolivia" (doctoral dissertation, University of New Mexico, 1989). Research assistant, *Hispanic American Historical Review*, 1984–85. Essays: Boxer; Central America; Ecclesiastical History; Gibson; Lea; Prescott; Spain: Imperial.

Dreifus, Erika. Doctoral candidate in history, Harvard University. Contributor to *Boston Book Review*, *French Politics and Society*, *Dictionary of Hispanic Biography*, and *Contemporary Authors*. Essays: Guizot; Michelet.

Drescher, Seymour. Professor of history, University of Pittsburgh. Author of *Econocide: British Slavery in the Era of Abolition* (1977), *Capitalism and Antislavery: British Mobilization in Comparative Perspective* (1986), *The Abolition of Slavery and the Aftermath of Emancipation in Brazil* (with others, 1988), and articles in *American Historical Review*,

History and Theory, Past and Present, Journal of American History, Journal of Interdisciplinary History, Social Science History, Journal of Economic History, Political Theory, Journal of Modern History, Immigrants and Minorities, Journal of the History of Ideas, and *Hispanic American Historical Review.* Editor (with Stanley L. Engerman) of *A Historical Guide to World Slavery* (1998). Co-editor, *Journal of Contemporary History* (from 1991). **Essay:** David Brion Davis.

Dunne, John. Senior lecturer in history, University of Greenwich, England. Author of *Grands Notables du Premier Empire: Seine Inférieure* (with Jérôme Decoux, 1993) and "The Nobility's New Clothes: Revisionism and the Survival of the Nobility during the French Revolution" in *The French Revolution of 1789 and Its Impact* (1995). **Essay:** Cobban.

Dursteler, Eric R. Instructor, Brigham Young University. Author of "Identity and Coexistence in the Eastern Mediterranean, c.1600: Venice and the Ottoman Empire," in *New Perspectives on Turkey* (1998). Translator (with Christopher Lund) of *Columbus, Da Gama and Cabral, c.1501: Angelo Trevisan's Letters on the European Age of Expansion* (1999). **Essay:** Chabod.

Dyke, Carl. Doctorate, University of California, La Jolla, 1995. **Essays:** Bourdieu; Garin.

Eckerman, Nancy Pippen. Special collections librarian, Ruth Lilly Medical Library, Indiana University School of Medicine. Contributor to *Indiana Libraries, AB Bookman's Weekly,* and *Encyclopedia of Indianapolis* (1994). **Essays:** Cassius Dio; Dionysius of Halicarnassus; Livy; Medicine; Charles E. Rosenberg; Sallust; Tacitus; Temkin; Velleius Paterculus.

Edmonds, Anthony O. Professor of history, Ball State University. Author of *Joe Louis* (1973), *Resources for Teaching the Vietnam War: An Annotated Guide* (1992), and articles on Vietnam and sports. **Essay:** Ambrose.

Eley, Geoff. Professor of history, University of Michigan. Author of *Reshaping the German Right: Radical Nationalism and Political Change after Bismarck* (1980), *From Unification to Nazism: Reinterpreting the German Past* (1986), and (with David Blackbourn) *Mythen deutscher Geschichtsschreibung: die gescheiterte bürgerliche Revolution von 1848* (1980), in English as *The Peculiarities of German History: Bourgeois Society and Politics in Nineteenth-Century Germany* (1984). Co-editor of *Culture/Power/History: A Reader in Social Theory* (1994), *Becoming National: A Reader* (1996), and *Society, Culture, and the State in Germany, 1870–1930* (1996).

Elliot-Meisel, Elizabeth B. Assistant professor of history, Creighton University. Author of "Sovereignty and the North: Canadian–American Cooperation, 1939–45" in *Three Northern Wartime Projects* (1996) and *Arctic Diplomacy: Canada and the United States in the Northwest Passage* (1998). **Essays:** Franklin; Kolko.

Elliott, J.H. (Sir John Elliott). See his own entry.

Endersby, Linda Eikmeier. Doctoral candidate, Massachusetts Institute of Technology. Contributor to *IA: The Journal of the Society for Industrial Archaeology* and *The Biographical Encyclopedia of Science.* **Essays:** Computers and Computing; Science; Merritt Roe Smith.

Erickson, Amy Louise. Research fellow, University of Sussex, England. Author of *Women and Property in Early Modern England* (1993), an introduction to the 1992 edition of Alice Clark's *Working Life of Women in the Seventeenth Century,* and many articles. **Essays:** Alice Clark; Wedgwood.

Estebanez, Maria Elina. Researcher, Center of Advanced Studies, University of Buenos Aires. Author of works on the links between industry and higher education in Latin America. **Essay:** Germani.

Evans, J.A.S. Professor emeritus, University of British Columbia. Author of *A Social and Economic History of an Egyptian Temple in Greco-Roman Egypt* (1961), *Procopius* (1972), *Herodotus* (1982), *Herodotus, Explorer of the Past: Three Essays* (1991), *The Age of Justinian: The Circumstances of Imperial Power* (1996), and many articles on Greek, Roman, and Byzantine studies. **Essays:** Egypt: Ancient; Plutarch; Rostovtzeff; Xenophon.

Evans, Jennifer V. Doctoral candidate in German history, State University of New York, Binghamton. **Essay:** Hausen.

Evanson, Philip. Associate professor of history, Temple University. Author of *Latin America* (1984) and numerous articles and reviews in *Caribbean Studies, Studies in Latin American Popular Culture, Hispanic American Historical Review, South Atlantic Quarterly, Georgia Review,* and *Southeastern Latinamericanist.* **Essays:** Basadre; Rodrigues.

Everett, Nicholas. Research fellow in history, University of Queensland, Australia. **Essays:** Croce; Manzoni.

Falola, Toyin. Professor of history, University of Texas, Austin. Author of *Development Planning and Decolonization in Nigeria* (1996). Editor of *Modern Nigeria* (1990), *African Historiography* (1993), and *Pawnship in Africa: Debt Bondage in Historical Perspective* (with Paul E. Lovejoy, 1994). Editor of the journal *African Economic History* and associate editor, *Environment and History.* **Essays** (with Joel E. Tishken): Africa: Central; Africa: Eastern and Southern; Coquery-Vidrovitch; Davidson; Feierman; Iliffe; Mazrui; Ogot; Ranger; Rodney.

Farrow, Lee A. Doctoral candidate, Tulane University. Contributor to *Russian Review* and *Legal and Political Values in History* (1997). **Essays:** Raeff; Vernadsky.

Fast, Susan. Associate professor, McMaster University. Author of *Johannis de Muris Musica Speculativa* (1994) and articles in *Plainsong and Medieval Music* and *Canadian University Music Review.* **Essay:** Musicology.

Figueirôa, Silvia. Assistant professor, University of Campinas (UNICAMP), Brazil. Author of three books on the geological sciences in Latin America; contributor to *Earth Sciences History*, *Interciência*, *Cuadernos Americanos*, and *Rostocker Wissenschaftshistorische Manuskripte*. Editor-in-chief, *Cadernos IG-UNICAMP*. President, Latin American Society on the History of Science and Technology, 1995–98. Member, International Commission on the History of Geological Sciences (INHIGEO). Essays: Holanda; Natural Sciences.

Finley-Croswhite, Annette. Assistant professor of history, Old Dominion University. Author of several articles, including "Engendering the Wars of Religion: Female Agency during the Catholic League in Dijon," *French Historical Studies* and "Urban Identity and Transitional Politics: The Transformation of Political Allegiance inside Amiens before and after the City's 1594 Capitulation to Henry IV," *Proceedings of the Annual Meeting of the Western Society for French History* (1993), and of *Henry IV and the Towns: Power and Authority in French Urban Society, 1589–1610* (forthcoming). Essay: Mousnier.

Fisher, James. Doctoral candidate, Kent State University. Author of "A Forgotten Hero Remembered, Revered, and Revised: The Legacy and Ordeal of George Rogers Clark," *Indiana Magazine of History* (1996). Essays: America: Pre-Columbian; Andrews; Axtell.

Fisher, Michael H. Professor of history, Oberlin College. Author of *A Clash of Cultures: Awadh, the British, and the Mughals* (1987), *Indirect Rule in India: Residents and the Residency System, 1764–1858* (1991), *The Politics of British Annexation of India, 1757–1857* (1993), and *The First Indian Author in English* (1996). Editor of *The Travels of Dean Mahomet* (1997). Essay: Eaton.

Fletcher, Brian H. Bicentennial professor of Australian history, University of Sydney. Author of *Landed Enterprise and Penal Society* (1976), *Colonial Australia before 1850* (1976), *Ralph Darling: A Governor Maligned* (1984), *The Grand Parade: A History of the Royal Agricultural Society of New South Wales* (1988), *Australian History in New South Wales, 1888–1938* (1993), and of numerous articles in journals and edited collections. Essay: Bean.

Flynn, John F. Professor of history, University of the South. Author of "The Split in the Reichstag Caucus of the National Liberal Party over the German Military Budget of 1871" (1982) and "At the Threshold of Dissolution: The National Liberals and Bismarck 1877/1878," (1988), both in *Historical Journal*, and "Some Archival Sources for the Study of the European Community," *The European Community Today* (1986). Essay: Kehr.

Forrest, Robert F. Associate professor of history, McNeese State University, Louisiana. Author of "The *Courier de Moldavie* and *Der Kriegsbote*: Two Views of the French Revolution for Romanians," *East European Quarterly* (1991), "Eighteenth-Century Romanian Institutions and the Impact of the French Revolution," *Revue des Etudes Sud-Est Européennes* (1992), and "Romanian–American Economic Relations, 1947–1975" in *Romania between East and West* (1982), and contributor to *Proceedings* of the Consortium on Revolutionary Europe.

Essays: Balkans; Dopsch; Obolensky; Ostrogorsky; Palacký; Runciman; Stavrianos; Sugar.

Foster, John Bellamy. Associate professor of sociology, University of Oregon. Author of *The Theory of Monopoly Capitalism* (1986) and *The Vulnerable Planet: A Short Economic History of the Environment* (1994). Co-editor of *In Defense of History: Marxism and the Postmodern Agenda* (1997) and *Capitalism and the Information Age: The Political Economy of the Global Communication Revolution* (1998). Editorial board member, *Capitalism, Nature, Socialism*; feature editor, *Organization and Environment*. Essay: Ecology.

Foster, Robert Wallace. Doctoral candidate, Department of East Asian Languages and Civilizations, Harvard University. Author of "Seeking a Tradition: Lu Jiuyuan's Attempt to Define *Ru* Approaches to Education, Politics, and Philosophy in Southern Song," *Papers on Chinese History* (1992) and "A Bibliography of English Language Sources, 1987–1990, on the Five Dynasties, Sung, Liao, Chin, and Yuan," *Journal of Sung-Yuan Studies* (1990–92). Translator of Kumamoto Takashi's "Review of Japanese Bibliography in 1990: Five Dynasties, Song, and Yuan," *Journal of Sung-Yuan Studies* (1995). Essay: Liu Zhiji.

Frank, Billy. Research student, Edge Hill University College, Lancashire. Essay: Dutt.

Franklin, James E. Doctoral candidate, University of Wisconsin, Madison. Essays: Keegan; Mosse; Napoleonic Wars.

Friguglietti, James. Professor of history, Montana State University, Billings. Author of *Albert Mathiez, Historien Révolutionnaire (1874–1932)* (1974). Editor or co-editor of *The Shaping of Modern France* (1969) and *Bibliographie de Georges Lefebvre* (1972). Co-translator of Georges Lefebvre's *The French Revolution, 1793–1799* (1964). Contributor to *French Historical Studies*. Essays: Godechot; Rudé.

Frucht, Richard. Professor of history, Northwest Missouri State University. Author of *Dunărea Noastră: Romania, the Great Powers and the Danube Question* (1982) and articles in *Balkanistica, Access, Revue des Etudes Sud-Est Européennes*, and *War and Society in East Central Europe*. Editor of *Labyrinth of Nationalism, Complexities of Diplomacy: Essays in Honor of Barbara and Charles Jelavich* (1992) and *Encyclopedia of Modern East Europe, 1815–1989*. Essay: Jelavich.

Furlong, Patrick J. Associate professor of history, Alma College, Michigan. Author of *The Mixed Marriages Act: An Historical and Theological Study* (1983), *Between Crown and Swastika: The Impact of the Radical Right on the Afrikaner Nationalist Movement in the Fascist Era* (1991), and articles in *Journal of Theology for Southern Africa, Ufahamu, African Affairs*, and *South African Historical Journal*. Essays: Marks; South Africa.

Gallagher, Nancy. Professor of history, University of California, Santa Barbara. Author of *Medicine and Power in Tunisia, 1780–1900* (1983), *Egypt's Other Wars: Epidemics and the Politics of Public Health* (1990), and *Approaches to the History* *of the Middle East: Interviews with Leading Middle East Historians* (1994). Editor (with Rahma Bourquia and Mounira Charrad) of *Femmes, culture et société au Maghreb* (1996). Book review editor, *International Journal of Middle East Studies*, 1984–88. **Essays:** Inalcık; Issawi; Postcolonialism; Rodinson.

Garay, Kathleen E. Associate professor of history and acting director, Women's Studies Programme, McMaster University. Contributor to *Mystics Quarterly*, *Florilegium*, *The New Dictionary of National Biography*, and *Women in World History*. **Essays:** Cam; Fügedi; McLuhan.

Geifman, Anna. Assistant professor of history, Boston University. Author of *Thou Shalt Kill: Revolutionary Terrorism in Russia, 1894–1917* (1993). **Essays:** Miliukov; Venturi.

George, Gene. Director of institutional research, Butler County Community College, Kansas. Doctorate in Russian and Eastern European history, University of Kansas. **Essay:** Lelewel.

German, Daniel M. Archivist, National Archives of Canada. Author of "John Wildman and Rushworth's *Historical Collections*: An Editor Identified?" in *Fontanus* (1990) and other articles. **Essays:** Darnton; Pocock; Vergil.

Ghosh, Peter. University lecturer and fellow in modern history, St. Anne's College, University of Oxford. Author of several articles in *English Historical Review*, *Journal of Roman Studies*, and *Archives Européennes de Sociologie*. **Essays:** Gibbon; Max Weber; Whig Interpretation.

Gibbons, Peter. Senior lecturer in history, University of Waikato, New Zealand. Contributor to *The Oxford History of New Zealand* (1981, 1992) and *The Oxford History of New Zealand Literature in English* (1991, 1998). **Essays:** Beaglehole; New Zealand; Sinclair.

Gilley, Sheridan. Reader in theology, University of Durham, England. Author of *Newman and His Age* (1990). Editor (with W.J. Sheils) of *A History of Religion in Britain* (1994). **Essays:** Dyos; Macaulay.

Girvin, Stephen D. Senior lecturer in law, University of Nottingham, England. Contributor to *South African Law Journal*, *Juridical Review*, *Journal of the Law Society of Scotland*, *Journal of Legal History*, *Irish Jurist*, *Anglo-American Law Review*, *Company Law Monitor*, *Tijdschrift voor Rechtsgeschiedenis*, *Lloyd's Maritime and Commerical Law Quarterly*, *Journal of Business Law*, *European Law Review*, and *Law and History Review*. **Essays:** Holdsworth; Milsom; Simpson; Watson.

Glick, Thomas F. Professor of history, Boston University. Author of *Irrigation and Society in Medieval Valencia* (1970), *Islamic and Christian Spain in the Early Middle Ages* (1979), *From Muslim Fortress to Christian Castle* (1995), and *Irrigation and Hydraulic Technology: Medieval Spain and Its Legacy* (1996). **Essays:** Burns; Castro; Comparative History; Feudalism; Goitein; Guichard; Ibn Khaldūn; Lévi-Provençal; Menéndez Pidal; Merton; Sarton; Semple; Spain: Islamic; Lynn White, Jr.

Gobbett, Brian. Doctoral candidate, University of Alberta. Co-author of *Introducing Canada: An Annotated Bibliography of Canadian History in English* (1998). **Essay** (with Theodore Binnema): Trigger.

Goggin, Jacqueline. Development officer, Harvard University. Author of *Carter G. Woodson: A Life in Black History* (1993) and articles in *American Historical Review* and *Journal of Negro History*. Editor (with Morey Rothberg) of *John Franklin Jameson and the Development of Humanistic Scholarship in America* (2 vols to date; 1993–); editor, J. Franklin Jameson Papers. **Essay:** Woodson.

Goodrich, Robert. Doctoral candidate, University of Wisconsin, Madison. **Essay:** Europe: Modern.

Górecki, Piotr. Associate professor of history, University of California, Riverside. Author of *Economy, Society, and Lordship in Medieval Poland, 1100–1250* (1992), *Parishes, Tithes, and Society in Earlier Medieval Poland, c.1100–c.1250* (1993), and articles in *Transactions of the American Philosophical Society*, *Oxford Slavonic Papers*, *Slavic Review*, and *Law and History Review*. **Essay:** Poland: to the 18th Century.

Gould, Eliga H. Assistant professor of history, University of New Hampshire. Author of *The Persistence of Empire: British Political Culture in the Age of the American Revolution* (1999). Co-editor of *Empire and Nation: The American Revolution in an Atlantic World*. Contributor to *Past and Present*, *American Historical Review*, and *Historical Journal*. **Essay:** United States: American Revolution.

Goutnov, Dmitry A. Member, Russian Academy of Sciences. Author of *Podgotovka kadrov istorikov v Moskovskom universitete* (1991), *Ludi i sobutia smutnogo vremeni* (1994), and *Biografischeskii slovar kuratov* (1995). **Essays:** Kliuchevskii; Platonov; Russia: Medieval; Zaionchkovskii.

Graham, Jeanine. Senior lecturer in history, University of Waikato, and researcher in New Zealand and childhood history. Author of *Frederick Weld: A Biography* (1983) and *My Brother and I: Glimpses of Childhood in Our Colonial Past* (1992); contributor to *The Oxford Illustrated History of New Zealand* (1990) and *The Oxford History of New Zealand* (1992). **Essay:** Childhood.

Grant, Jonathan A. Assistant professor of history, Florida State University. Contributor to *Central Asian Survey*, *Comparative Studies in Society and History*, and *Journal of World History*. **Essay:** Central Asia.

Gray, Christopher. Assistant professor of history, Florida International University. Author of *Conceptions of History in the Works of Cheikh Anta Diop and Théophile Obenga* (1989); contributor to *History in Africa* and *Islam et Société au Sud du Sahara*. **Essay:** Diop.

Green, Jay D. Assistant professor, Covenant College, Georgia. Author of "'Nothing to Advertise Except God': Christian Radio and the Creation of an Evangelical Subculture in Northeast Ohio, 1958–1972," *Ohio History* (1997). **Essay:** Robinson.

Grele, Ronald J. Director, Oral History Research Office, Columbia University. Author of *Envelopes of Sound: The Art of Oral History* (1988). Editor of *Subjectivity and Multiculturalism in Oral History* (1991); editor-in-chief, *International Journal of Oral History* (1980–85). **Essay:** Oral History.

Gudermann, Rita. Wissenschaftliche Mitarbeiterin, Free University of Berlin. **Essay:** Ennen.

Guilderson, Hugh L. Adjunct professor of history, Boston College. Author of *From the State of Nature to the Empire of Reason: Civilization in the French Enlightenment* and contributor to *Theory and Society, Journal of Social History,* and *Comparative Civilizations Review.* **Essays:** Montesquieu; Raynal.

Guy, Donna J. Professor of history, University of Arizona. Author of *Argentine Sugar Politics: Tucumán and the Generation of Eighty* (1980) and *Sex and Danger in Buenos Aires: Prostitution, Family, and Nation in Argentina* (1991). Co-editor of *Sex and Sexuality in Latin America* (1997) and *Contested Ground: Comparative Frontiers on the Northern and Southern Edges of the Spanish Empire* (1998).

Haag, John. Associate professor, University of Georgia. Contributor to *Who Were the Fascists?* (1980), *Journal of Contemporary History, Leo Baeck Institute Year Book, Central European History,* and *Contemporary Austrian Studies.* **Essays:** Susanne Miller; Srbik.

Häggman, Bertil. Director, Center for Research on Geopolitics, Sweden. Author of *Sweden's Maoist "Subversives": A Case Study* (1975), *Industrispionage i Sverige och i utlandet* (Industrial Espionage in Sweden and Abroad, 1975), *Terrorism* (1978), and *Desinformation* (Disinformation, 1990). **Essay:** Sweden.

Hahn, H. Hazel. Doctoral candidate in history, University of California, Berkeley. **Essays:** Consumerism and Consumption; Film; Media; Pevsner.

Halevy, Drew Philip. Doctoral candidate in history, University of Arkansas. **Essays:** Díaz del Castillo; Tannenbaum.

Hall, Stephen Gilroy. Doctoral candidate, Ohio State University. **Essays:** Hanke; David Levering Lewis.

Hallas, Christine S. Head of School of Humanities and Cultural Studies, Trinity and All Saints College, University of Leeds. Contributor to *Agricultural History Review, Local Population Studies, Textile History, PUSH (Public Sector History) Journal, Northern History, Yorkshire Archaeological Society Journal, Journal of Regional and Local Studies,* and *Journal of Transport History.* **Essays:** Thirsk; F.M.L. Thompson.

Halpern, Rick. Reader in the history of the United States, University College, London. Author of *Meatpackers: An Oral History of Black Packinghouse Workers* (1996) and *Down on the Killing Floor: Black and White Workers in Chicago's Packinghouses* (1997). Editor of *Race and Class in the Ameri-*

can South (1993). Contributor to *Journal of American Studies, International Review of Social History, Journal of American History,* and *Ethnic and Racial Studies.* **Essay:** Du Bois.

Hamburg, G.M. Professor of history, University of Notre Dame. Author of *Politics of the Russian Nobility, 1881–1905* (1984), *Boris Chicherin and Early Russian Liberalism, 1828–1866* (1992), and articles in *Slavic Review, Russian Review, Jahrbücher für Geschichte Osteuropas,* and *Canadian American Slavic Studies.* **Essay:** Russia: Modern (with Thomas Sanders).

Hauner, Milan. Fulbright visiting professor, University of Leipzig. Author of *Eight Months of One Spring* (in Czech, 1979), *India in Axis Strategy: Germany, Japan, and Indian Nationalists in the Second World War* (1981), *Hitler: A Chronology of His Life and Time* (1983), *Afghanistan and the Soviet Union: Collision and Transformation* (1989), *The Soviet War in Afghanistan: Patterns of Russian Imperialism* (1991), *What Is Asia to Us? Russia's Asian Heartland Yesterday and Today* (1990, 1992), "The Meaning of Czech History: Masaryk versus Pekař" in *T.G. Masaryk: Statesman and Cultural Force* (1987), "Josef Pekař: Interpreter of Czech History" in *Czechoslovak and Central European Journal* (1991), and many other articles. **Essay:** Pekař.

Haynes, Michael. Senior lecturer in European studies, University of Wolverhampton. Author of *Nikolai Bukharin and the Transition from Capitalism to Socialism* (1985). **Essays:** R.W. Davies; Deutscher; Lewin; Russia: Russian Revolution.

Helt, J.S.W. Assistant professor of history, Hollins College. Contributor to *Sixteenth Century Journal.* **Essay:** Hexter.

Hepburn, A.C. Professor of Modern Irish history and director of the Graduate Research School, University of Sunderland. Author of *The Conflict of Nationality in Modern Ireland* (1980) and *A Past Apart: Studies in the History of Catholic Belfast, 1850–1950* (1996). Joint editor of *Ethnic Identity in Urban Europe* (1992). **Essay:** Lyons.

Hessenbruch, Arne. Research fellow, Dibner Institute for the History of Science and Technology, Massachusetts Institute of Technology. Editor of *Reader's Guide to the History of Science* (1999). **Essays:** Heilbron; Needham.

Hewitt, Martin. Principal lecturer in history, Trinity and All Saints College, University of Leeds. Author of *The Emergence of Stability in the Industrial City: Manchester, 1832–67* (1996) and articles in *Historical Journal, Acadiensis, British Journal of Canadian Studies, Historical Research, Nineteenth Century Prose,* and *Urban History.* Editor of *Journal of Victorian Culture.* **Essays:** Briggs; Carlyle; Gallagher; Hobsbawm; Gareth Stedman Jones; Urban History; Raymond Williams.

Hirst, John. Professor of history, La Trobe University. Author of *Adelaide and the Country, 1870–1917: Their Social and Political Relationship* (1973), *Convict Society and Its Enemies: A History of Early New South Wales* (1983), *The Strange Birth of Colonial Democracy: New South Wales, 1848–1884* (1988),

The World of Albert Facey (1992), and *A Republican Manifesto* (1994). Co-editor of *Oxford Companion to Australian History* (1998).

Hitchcock, Tim. Reader in history, University of Hertfordshire. Author of *English Sexualities, 1700–1800* (1996). Co-editor of *Stilling the Grumbling Hive* (1991) and *Chronicling Poverty: The Voices and Strategies of the English Poor, 1640–1840* (1997). Contributor to *History Workshop Journal*. **Essay:** Sexuality.

Hoffman, Daniel L. Assistant professor of history, Lee College, Tennessee. Author of *The Status of Women and Gnosticism in Irenaeus and Tertullian* (1995) and articles in *Journal of the Evangelical Theological Society* and *Trinity Journal*. **Essays:** Bauer; Suetonius.

Holguín, Sandie. Assistant professor of history, University of Oklahoma. **Essay:** Feminism.

Holloran, Peter C. Secretary, New England Historical Association. Author of *Boston's Wayward Children: Social Services for Homeless Children, 1830–1930* (1989). **Essay:** Parkman.

Hood, Roger. Professor of criminology, director, Centre for Criminological Research, and fellow, All Souls College, University of Oxford. Author of *Borstal Re-Assessed* (1965) and (with Sir Leon Radzinowicz) *A History of English Criminal Law*, vol. 5: *The Emergence of Penal Policy* (1986). General editor of Clarendon Studies in Criminology. **Essay:** Radzinowicz.

Hooper, John. Dean of the Graduate School, Australian National University. Author (with Pat Jalland) of *Women from Birth to Death: The Female Life Cycle in Britain, 1830–1914* (1986). Contributor to *Journal of European Studies*, *Australian Journal of Politics and History*, and *Teaching History*. **Essays:** Joll; Thierry; Zeldin.

Hoover, Fred. Sandra Myers graduate research assistantship, Center for Greater Southwestern Studies and the History of Cartography, University of Texas at Arlington. Editor, *E.C. Barksdale Essays in History*, vol.25. **Essays:** Giesebrecht; Hegel; Spengler.

Hudson, Mark J. Lecturer in archaeology, Okayama University, Japan. Co-editor of *Multicultural Japan: Palaeolithic to Postmodern* (1997). Contributor to *Anthropological Science*, *Japanese Journal of Religious Studies*, and *Monumenta Nipponica*. **Essay:** Prehistory.

Hudson, Pat. Professor of history, University of Wales, Cardiff. Author of *The Genesis of Industrial Capital* (1986) and *The Industrial Revolution* (1992). Editor of *Regions and Industries: A Perspective on Britain's Industrial Revolution* (1989), and (with W.R. Lee), *Women's Work and the Family Economy in Historical Perspective* (1990). **Essays:** Economic History; Polanyi.

Hutton, Patrick H. Professor of history, University of Vermont. Author of *The Cult of the Revolutionary Tradition: The Blanquists in French Politics* (1981) and *History as an Art of Memory* (1993). Editor of *An Historical Dictionary of the Third French Republic* (1986). Contributor to *History and Memory*, *Journal of the History of Ideas*, *Historical Reflections*, *History and Theory*, *Psychohistory Review*, *New Vico Studies*, *Journal of Aesthetics and Art Criticism*, *Journal of Contemporary History*, *Journal of Modern History*, and *French Historical Studies*. **Essay:** Mentalities.

Istrabadi, Juliet Graver. Assistant curator, Valparaiso University Museum of Art, Indiana. Contributor to *Beyond Black and White: Chiaroscuro Prints from Indiana Collections* (1989), *Indiana University Bookman* (1988), and *The Valparaiso University Inaugural Catalogue* (1995). **Essays:** Art History; Gombrich; Panofsky; Winckelmann.

Jackson, Louise Ainsley. Lecturer in history, Leeds Metropolitan University. Author of a number of articles and a forthcoming monograph on child sexual abuse and the law in Victorian England. **Essays:** Gordon; Kelly-Gadol; Joan Wallach Scott.

Jacobs, Margaret D. Assistant professor, New Mexico State University. Author of *Engendered Encounters: Feminism and Pueblo Cultures, 1879–1934*, several articles on interactions between white women and Native Americans, and entries in the *Encyclopedia of the American West* and *Encyclopedia of African-American Culture and History*. **Essay:** Women's History: African American.

Janes, Dominic. Research fellow, Pembroke College, University of Cambridge. Author of *God and Gold in Late Antiquity* (1998) and articles on Roman and medieval history. **Essays:** Brown; Cameron; Finley; Kathleen Hughes; A.H.M. Jones; Stenton.

Jantzen, Kyle. Sessional instructor, University of Saskatchewan. Contributor to *"Für Deutschland": Die Männer des 20. Juli* (1994), *Modern Germany: An Encyclopedia of History, People and Culture, 1871–1990* (1998), and *Documents of Resistance to National Socialism in Germany, 1933–1945*. **Essay:** Butterfield.

Jardine, Nicholas. Professor of history and philosophy of the sciences, and fellow of Darwin College, University of Cambridge. Author of *The Birth of History and Philosophy of Science: Kepler's "A Defence of Tycho Against Ursus" with Essays on Its Provenance and Significance* (1984), *The Fortunes of Inquiry* (1986), and *The Scenes of Inquiry: On the Reality of Questions in the Sciences* (1991). Co-editor of *Romanticism and the Sciences* (1990), *Cultures of Natural History* (1996), *History of the Sciences*, and *History of the Book* (forthcoming). Editor of the journals *Studies in History and Philosophy of Science* and *Studies in History and Philosophy of Biological and Biomedical Sciences*.

Jay, Jennifer W. Associate professor of history, University of Alberta. Author of *A Change of Dynasties: Loyalism in Thirteenth-Century China* (1991) and articles in *Journal of the*

American Oriental Society, *Canadian Journal of History*, *Han-hsüeh yen-chiu*, *Harvard Journal of Asiatic Studies* and *T'ang Studies*. **Essays:** Sima Guang; Sima Qian.

Jazayery, M.A. Professor emeritus, Center for Middle Eastern Studies, University of Texas, Austin. Editor (with Werner Winter) of *Languages and Cultures* (1988). **Essay:** Kasravi.

Jeay, Madeleine. Professor of history, McMaster University. Editor of *Les Evangiles des quenouilles* (1985) and author of *Donner la parole: l'histoire-cadre dans les recueils de nouvelles des XVe–XVIe siècles* (1992). **Essay:** Natalie Zemon Davis.

Jenkins, Keith. Senior lecturer in history, Chichester Institute, England. Author of *Re-Thinking History* (1991), *On "What Is History?" From Carr and Elton to Rorty and White* (1995), and articles in *Literature and History*, *Welsh Historians*, and *Teaching History*. Editor of *The Postmodern History Reader* (1997). **Essays:** Metahistory; Postmodernism.

Jensen, Lionel. Director, Chinese Studies Progam, University of Colorado, Denver. Author of "The Invention of 'Confucius' and His Chinese Other, 'Kong Fuzi'," *Positions: East Asia Cultures Critique* (1993), "Wise Man of the Wilds: Fatherlessness, Fertility, and the Mythic Exemplar, Kongzi," *Early China* (1995), "Among Fallen Idols and Noble Dreams: Notes from the Field of Chinese Intellectual History," *Studies in Chinese History* (1997), and *Manufacturing Confucianism: Chinese Traditions and Universal Civilization* (1997). **Essay:** China: Ancient.

Johnson, William T. Science librarian, Texas Tech University. Contributor to *Encyclopedia of the History of Science and Technology and Medicine in Non-Western Cultures* (1995); author of several journal articles on digital initiatives in library science and the role of electronic information in scholarly communication. **Essays:** Bīrūnī; Chaudhuri; Gopal.

Johnston, Robert D. Assistant professor of history, Yale University. Author of "'Beyond the West': Regionalism, Liberalism, and the Evasion of Politics in the New Western History" in the journal *Rethinking History* (1998). **Essay:** Lasch.

Jones, Colin. Professor of history, University of Warwick, England. Author of *Charity and Bienfaisance* (1983), *The Charitable Imperative* (1989), *The Cambridge Illustrated History of France* (1993), and (with Lawrence Brockliss) *The Medical World of Early Modern France* (1997). **Essay:** Hufton.

Joyce, Davis D. Soros professor of American studies, Kossuth University, Hungary. Author of *Edward Channing and the Great Work* (1974), *History and Historians* (1983), *The Writing of American History* (with Michael Kraus, revised 1985), and articles in *Teaching History*, *History Teacher*, *Social Science*, *American National Biography*, *Dictionary of Afro-American Slavery*, *Dictionary of Literary Biography* and *Encyclopedia USA*. Editor of *A History of the United States* by Edward Channing (1993) and *I Had Never Seen Before: Alternative Views of Oklahoma History* (1994). **Essay:** Zinn.

Kaiser, Thomas E. Professor of history, University of Arkansas at Little Rock. Author of articles in *Journal of Modern History*, *French Historical Studies*, *Eighteenth Century Studies*, and *Studies on Voltaire and the Eighteenth Century*. Contributor to *The French Idea of Freedom: The Old Regime and the Declaration of Rights of 1789* (1994) and *From the Royal to the Republican Body: Incorporating the Political in Seventeenth- and Eighteenth-Century France* (1998). **Essay:** France: 1450–1789.

Kallis, Aristotle A. Tutor, Departments of Politics and History, University of Edinburgh. **Essays:** Greece: Modern; Wolfgang Mommsen.

Katzenellenbogen, Simon. Senior lecturer in economic history, University of Manchester. Author of *Railways and the Copper Mines of Katanga* (1973), *South Africa and Southern Mozambique: Labour, Railways and Trade in the Making of a Relationship* (1982), and articles in *Business Archives*, *African Affairs*, *African Economic History*, *Business History*, *Clio*, and several collections. **Essay:** Hargreaves.

Keddie, Nikki R. Professor of history, University of California, Los Angeles. Founding editor of *Contention*. Author of *Religion and Rebellion in Iran: The Tobacco Protest of 1891–1892* (1966), *An Islamic Response to Imperialism: Political and Relgious Writings of Sayyid Jamal ad-Din "al-Afghani"* (1968), *Sayyid Jamal ad-Din "al-Afghani": A Political Biography* (1972), *Iran: Religion, Politics and Society* (1980), *Roots of Revolution: An Interpretive History of Modern Iran* (1981), *Iran and the Middle East: Resistance and Revolution* (1995), and many other edited works and articles. **Essay:** Iran: since 1500.

Kelsey, Sean. Postdoctoral fellow, King's College, University of London. Author of *Inventing a Republic: The Political Culture of the English Commonwealth, 1649–1653* (1997). **Essay:** Britain: 1485–1750.

King, Helen. Senior lecturer in history, Liverpool Institute of Higher Education. Contributor to *Hysteria Beyond Freud* (1993), *Women in Ancient Studies* (1994), *British Museum Book of Mythical Beasts* (1995) and to the journals *Arethusa*, and *Helios*. **Essay:** Vernant.

Klein, Dennis B. Professor of history and Jewish studies, Kean College. Senior publications consultant, US Holocaust Memorial Museum. Founding director, Braun Center for Holocaust Studies and its Hidden Child Foundation. Author of "The Fate of Holocaust Literature" in *The Handbook of Holocaust Literature* (1993). Editor of *The Holocaust in Books and Films* (with J. M. Muffs, 1986) and *Hidden History of the Kovno Ghetto* (forthcoming) and of *Dimensions: A Journal of Holocaust Studies*. **Essay:** Holocaust.

Knafla, Louis A. Professor of history, University of Calgary. Author of *Law and Justice in a New Land: Essays in Western Canadian Legal History* (1989), *Kent at Law 1602: The County Jurisdiction: Assizes and Sessions of the Peace* (1994), and *Crime History and Histories of Crime: Studies in the*

Historiography of Crime and Criminal Justice in Modern History (1995). Editor of *Law, Society and the State* (with Susan Binnie, 1995). Editor of the journal *Criminal Justice History*, and editorial board member, *Canadian Journal of Law and Society*. **Essays:** Bodin; Crime and Deviance; Legal History; Plucknett; Thorne; Vinogradoff.

Knight, Franklin W. Professor of history, Johns Hopkins University. Author of *Slave Society in Cuba* (1970), *African Dimension of Latin American Societies* (1974), *The Caribbean: Genesis of a Fragmented Nationalism* (1990). Editor of *Slave Societies of the Caribbean* (1997). President, Latin American Studies Association, 1998–2000. **Essay:** Moreno Fraginals.

Ko, Dorothy. Associate professor of history and women's studies, Rutgers University. Author of *Teachers of the Inner Chambers: Women and Culture in Seventeenth-Century China* (1994) and numerous articles on women in late imperial China. **Essay:** Women's History: Asia.

Kramer, Martin. Director, Moshe Dayan Center, Tel Aviv University. Author of *Islam Assembled* (1986) and *Arab Awakening and Islamic Revival* (1996). Editor of *Shiism, Resistance and Revolution* (1987), *Middle Eastern Lives* (1991), and *Middle Eastern Lectures*. **Essays:** Kedourie; Bernard Lewis.

LaFleur, Robert A. Assistant professor of history and chair of Asian studies, Beloit College. Author of "The Historiography of Utopia: Images of Moral Rule in Early Chinese History," *Comparative Civilizations Review* (1999). **Essays:** China: Early and Middle Imperial; China: Late Imperial; Rhetoric and History; Todorov.

Lambert, Andrew. Lecturer in war studies, King's College, University of London. Author of *The Crimean War: British Grand Strategy against Russia, 1853–1856* (1990) and *The Last Sailing Battlefleet: Maintaining Naval Mastery, 1815–1850* (1990). **Essay:** Naval History.

Lambert, Peter A. Lecturer in history, University of Wales, Aberystwyth. **Essays:** Haller; Rörig.

Laughran, Michelle A. Lecturer, University of Maryland University College, European Division. **Essay:** Body.

Laurie, Ross. Lecturer in contemporary studies, University of Queensland. Contributor to *Journal of Australian Studies*. **Essay:** Masculinity.

Lee, David D. Teaching fellow, University of California, Los Angeles. Author of "Sigmund Freud und Oskar Pfister: Entstehung und Dynamik ihrer Beziehung" in *Untersuchungen zur Geschichte der Psychologie und Psychotechnik* (1996), "Oskar Pfister, Sigmund Freud, and the Creation of the First Psychoanalytic Psychology of Religion" in *Issues in the History of Psychology of Religion* (1998), and articles in *Dictionnaire de la psychanalyse* (1997) and *Epoche*. **Essay:** Erickson.

Leupp, Gary P. Associate professor of history, Tufts University. Author of *Servants, Shophands and Laborers in the Cities of Tokugawa Japan* (1992) and contributor to *Female and Male Role Sharing in Japan: Historical and Contemporary Constructions of Gender* (1996), *Japan Forum*, *Jiendaa no Nihonshi* (History of Gender in Japan), *Japan Foundation Newsletter*, and *Gest Library Journal*. **Essays:** Arai Hakuseki; Gunki monogatari; Hayashi School; Japan; Japanese Chronicles; Kitabatake Chikafusa; Mito School.

Levi, Anthony. Professor emeritus of French, University of St. Andrews. Author of numerous works, including *French Moralists: The Theory of Passions, 1585–1649* (1964), *Religion in Practice* (1966), *Guide to French Literature* (2 vols., 1992–94), and *Renaissance and Reformation: The Intellectual Genesis* (forthcoming). Editor of several scholarly editions of the works of Erasmus and contributor to numerous volumes and scholarly journals. **Essay:** Reformation.

LeVos, Ernest A. Instructor in history, Grant MacEwan Community College, Edmonton. Author of "Robert Duff: A British Seigneur in Kelantan, 1892–1932," in *Journal of the Malaysian Branch of the Royal Asiatic Society* (1997), and reviews for *Crossroads*, *China Information*, and *Canadian Social Studies*. **Essay:** Furnivall.

Lewis, Gwynne. Professor of modern history and chair of the Centre for Social History, University of Warwick, England. Author of *Life in Revolutionary France* (1971), *The Second Vendée* (1978), *The Advent of Modern Capitalism in France* (1993), and *The French Revolution: Rethinking the Debate* (1993). President, Society for the Study of French History, 1990–93. **Essays:** Annales School; Braudel; France: French Revolution; Social History.

Li Tana. Lecturer in history and politics, University of Wollongong. Author of *Peasants on the Move* (1996) and *Nguyen Cochinchina: Southern Vietnam in the Seventeenth and Eighteenth Centuries* (1998). Editor (with Anthony Reid) of *Southern Vietnam under the Nguyen* (1993). **Essays:** Le Quy Don; Vietnamese Chronicles.

Liebel-Weckowicz, Helen. Emeritus professor of history, University of Alberta, Canada. Author (with Thaddeus E. Weckowicz) of *A History of Great Ideas in Abnormal Psychology* (1990). **Essays:** Habermas; Herder; Ranke; Toynbee.

Lifshitz, Felice. Associate professor of history, Florida International University. Author of *The Norman Conquest of Pious Neustria: Historiographic Discourse and Saintly Relics, 684–1090* (1995) and articles in *Early Medieval Europe*, *Journal of Medieval History*, *Viator*, *Analecta Bollandiana*, *Haskins Society Journal*, *Revue d'Histoire Ecclésiastique*, *Annales de Normandie*, *History and Memory*, and several edited collections. Translator of Dudo of St. Quentin's *Gesta Normannorum* in On-Line Resource Book for Medieval Studies and of Bede's *Martyrology* in *Medieval Hagiography: A Sourcebook*. **Essays:** Barraclough; Krusch; Levison; Lopez; Ullmann.

Lockard, Craig A. Rosenberg professor of history, University of Wisconsin, Green Bay. Author of *From Kampung to City: A Social History of Kuching, Malaysia, 1820–1970* (1987), *The*

Rise and Changing Status of the Southeast Asian History Field in the United States: An Analytical Study (1989), *Reflections of Change: Sociopolitical Commentary and Criticism in Malaysian Popular Music since 1950* (1991), *Dance of Life: Popular Music and Politics in Southeast Asia* (1998), and articles in *Journal of World History, Journal of Third World Studies,* and *History Teacher.* **Essays:** Southeast Asia; Vietnam; World History.

Lorenz, Chris. Professor of philosophy of history, University of Leiden and Free University of Amsterdam. Author of *De constructie van het verleden* (1987, 1998), *Het historisch atelier* (1990), and *Konstruktion der Vergangenheit* (1997). Contributor to *History and Theory, Journal of Contemporary History,* and *Geschichte und Gesellschaft.* **Essays:** Broszat; Kocka; Wehler.

Luchilo, Lucas J. Professor of contemporary Latin American history, University of Buenos Aires. Co-author of *Historia Argentino* (1995) and *Historia 3: El mundo contemporáneo* (1996). **Essay:** Romero.

Lund, Erik A. Independent scholar. Author of "The Industrial History of Strategy: Re-evaluating British Aircraft Production in Comparative Perspective, 1939–45," *Journal of Military History* (1997). **Essay:** Germany: 1450–1800.

McBride, Ian. Lecturer in early modern history, University of Durham, England. Author of *The Siege of Derry in Ulster Protestant Mythology* (1997) and *Scripture Politics: Ulster Presbyterians and Irish Radicalism in the Late Eighteenth Century* (1998). Editor (with Tony Claydon), *Protestantism and National Identity: Britain and Ireland, c.1650–c.1850* (1998). **Essay:** Ireland.

McBride, Lawrence W. Professor of history, Illinois State University. Author of *People, Space, and Time: An Introduction to Community Studies* (1986), *The Greening of Dublin Castle* (1991), and articles in *New Hibernia Review, History Teacher, Teaching History,* and *Social Education.* **Essays:** Froude; Green.

McCarthy, Joseph M. Professor of history, Suffolk University, Massachusetts. Author of *Humanistic Emphases in the Educational Thought of Vincent of Beauvais* (1976), *An International List of Articles on the History of Education* (1977), *Pierre Teilhard de Chardin: A Comprehensive Bibliography* (1981), "Ecclesiology in the Letters of St. Ignatius of Antioch," *American Benedictine Review,* and "The Pastoral Practice of the Sacraments of Cleansing in the Legislation of Visigothic Spain," *Classical Folia.* Advisory editor, Garland Publishing, 1978–93. **Essays:** Bolland; Catholicism; Fustel de Coulanges; Gilson; Mabillon; Mansi; Medieval Chronicles.

McDaid, Jennifer Davis. Assistant editor, *Virginia Cavalcade,* Library of Virginia. Contributor on women's history to *The Chronology of Women's History, Dictionary of Virginia Biography,* and *Historical Dictionary of Women's Education in the United States.* **Essays:** Anne Firor Scott; Spruill.

McPherson, James M. Professor of history, Princeton University. Author of *The Struggle for Equality: Abolitionists and the Negro in the Civil War and Reconstruction* (1964), *Ordeal by Fire: The Civil War and Reconstruction* (1982, 1993), *Battle Cry of Freedom: The Civil War Era* (1989), and *For Cause and Comrades: Why Men Fought in the Civil War* (1997).

McPherson, Ken. Faculty member, Indian Ocean Centre, Curtin University. Author of *The Muslim Microcosm: Calcutta, 1918 to 1935* (1974), *Jinnah* (1980), and *The Indian Ocean: A History of People and the Sea* (1993). **Essay:** Indian Ocean Region.

McWIlliam, Rohan. Senior lecturer in Modern British and American history, Anglia Polytechnic University. Author of *Popular Politics in Nineteenth-Century England* (1998) and articles in *Currents of Radicalism* (1991), *Living and Learning* (1996), and *Social History.* **Essays:** Acton; Britain: since 1750; History Workshop; Political and Constitutional History; Samuel; Taylor; E.P. Thompson.

Maiolo, Joseph. Former tutorial fellow in international history, London School of Economics and currently lecturer in modern history, University of Leicester. Author of *The Royal Navy and Nazi Germany, 1933–39: A Study in Appeasement and the Origins of the Second World War* (1998). **Essay:** Kennedy.

Mansour, Iskandar. Author (with Elie Chalala) of "Elias Khoury on Politics and Culture," *JUSUR* (1990). Editorial board member, *JUSUR.* **Essay:** Zaydān.

Marshall, P.J. Emeritus professor of history and senior research fellow, King's College, London. President, Royal Historical Society. Author of *Problems of Empire* (1968), *East Indian Fortunes: The British in Bengal in the Eighteenth Century* (1976), *The Great Map of Mankind: British Perceptions of the World in the Age of the Enlightenment* (with Glyndwr Williams, 1982), *Bengal – The British Bridgehead: Eastern India, 1740–1828* (volume in The New Cambridge History of India, 1988), and *Trade and Conquest: Studies on the Rise of British Dominance in India* (1993). Editor of *The Writings and Speeches of Edmund Burke,* vols. 5–6 (1991), *The Cambridge Illustrated History of the British Empire* (1996), and *The Oxford History of the British Empire,* vol. 2: *The Eighteenth Century* (1998). **Essay:** India: since 1750.

Martin, Geoffrey H. Professor of history, University of Essex. Author of *The Town: A Visual History* (1961), *Ipswich Recognizance Rolls, 1294–1327* (1973), *Knighton's Chronicle, 1337–96* (1995), and *Portsmouth Royal Charters, 1194–1974* (1995). **Essays:** France: 1000–1450; Medieval Historical Writing.

Martin, R.N.D. Doctorate in history of science, London School of Economics. Author of *Pierre Duhem: Philosophy and History in the Work of a Believing Physicist* (1991), and other works on Duhem. **Essay:** Duhem.

Mason, Herbert W. Professor of history and religion, Boston University; also novelist and poet. Author of *Two Statesmen of Mediaeval Islam: A Study* (1972), *Memoir of a Friend: Louis Massignon* (1988), *Testimonies and Reflections* (1989), *Hallaj:*

Mystic and Martyr (1995). Translator/editor of *The Passion of al-Hallaj* by Louis Massignon (1983). **Essays:** Massignon; Near East: Ancient.

Matsumoto, Saho. Doctorate in social history, University of Warwick, England. **Essay:** Diplomatic History.

Mazrui, Ali A. See his own entry.

Megill, Allan. Professor of history, University of Virginia. Author of *Prophets of Extremity: Nietzsche, Heidegger, Foucault, Derrida* (1985) and articles in *American Historical Review*, *History and Theory*, *Journal of Modern History*, *Journal of the History of Ideas*, and other journals. Co-editor of *The Rhetoric of the Human Sciences* (1987) and editor of *Rethinking Objectivity* (1994). **Essays:** Historiology; Literature and History; Memory; Philosophy of History; Universal History.

Meier, David A. Associate professor of history, Dickinson State University, North Dakota. Contributor to *German Studies Review*, *European Studies Journal*, and *The Historian*. **Essay:** Nietzsche.

Menke, Martin R. Assistant professor, Rivier College, Nashua, New Hampshire. Co-author of *Discussion Guide for Readings in European History* (1993). **Essays:** Gall; Koonz; Hans Mommsen; Schieder.

Michalove, Sharon D. Assistant to the chair, Department of History, and adjunct assistant professor, Department of Educational Policy Studies (History of Education), University of Illinois, Urbana. Editor (with A. Compton Reeves) of *Estrangement, Enterprise, and Education: Chapters in Fifteenth-Century English History*. Contributor to *The Ricardian*, *Thematica*, *The ACADV Electronic Journal* (1993), *Educational Forum*, *Ricardian Register*, and *Medieval History*. **Essays:** Holinshed; Stone.

Michaud, Francine. Associate professor of history, University of Calgary. Author of *Un Signe des temps: accroissement des crises familiales autour du patrimoine à Marseille à la fin du XIIIe siècle* (1994). Contributor to *Revue historique*, *Annales du Midi*, and *Provence historique*. **Essay:** Vovelle.

Miller, Dean. Professor emeritus of history, University of Rochester. Author of *The Byzantine Tradition* (1966) and *Imperial Constantinople* (1969). **Essay:** Slavery: Ancient.

Miller, Joseph C. T. Cary Johnson, Jr. professor of history, University of Virginia and 1998 president, American Historical Association. Author of *Kings and Kinsmen: Early Mbundu States in Angola* (1976), *The African Past Speaks: Essays on Oral Tradition and History in Africa* (1980), and *Way of Death: Merchant Capitalism and the Angolan Slave Trade, 1780–1880* (1988). Editor (with Paul Finkelman) of *Macmillan Encyclopedia of World Slavery* (1998). Editor, *Journal of African History* (1990–96). **Essays:** Curtin; Vansina.

Millhorn, James. Social sciences librarian, Founders Memorial Library, Northern Illinois University. Co-author of "Cardin Le

Bret and Lese Majesty," *Law and History Review* (1986). **Essay:** Simiand.

Minichillo, Matthew A. Doctoral candidate, Kent State University. **Essay:** Jensen.

Moore, R. Scott. Graduate teaching associate, Ohio State University. Contributor to *De Imperatoribus Romanis* website, *Journal of Women's History*, and *History Reviews On-Line*. **Essay:** Kazhdan.

Moorhead, John. Reader in history, University of Queensland, Australia. Author of *Theoderic in Italy* (1992) and *Justinian* (1994). Translator of *History of the Vandal Persecution* by Victor of Vida (1992), and (with Richard Cusimano) of *The Deeds of Louis the Fat* by Abbot Suger (1992). Corresponding editor of *Early Medieval Europe*. **Essays:** Cassiodorus; Gregory of Tours; Momigliano; Procopius; Southern.

Moran, Seán Farrell. Associate professor of history, Oakland University. Author of *Patrick Pearse and the Politics of Redemption: The Mind of the Easter Rising, 1916* (1994) and articles in *The Irish Terrorism Experience* (1991), *Journal of the History of Ideas*, *Journal of Modern History*, *American Historical Review*, *The Historian*, and *Journal of British Studies*. **Essays:** Bultmann; Collingwood; Intellectual History; Arthur O. Lovejoy; Moody.

Morgan, Gwenda. Reader in history, University of Sunderland. Author of *The Hegemony of the Law: Richmond County, Virginia, 1692–1776* (1989), *Rogues, Thieves and the Rule of Law* (with Peter Rushton, 1998), and articles in *Journal of American Studies*, *Virginia Magazine of History and Biography*, and *Slavery and Abolition*. **Essays:** Greene; Osgood.

Morris, Martine Bondois. Senior lecturer in history, Middlesex University, London. Author of *Myth and Realities of French Republicanism* (forthcoming). **Essays:** France: since the Revolution; Labrousse; Lefebvre; Mathiez; Soboul.

Morrison, William. Professor of history, University of Northern British Columbia. Author of *Showing the Flag: The Mounted Police and Canadian Sovereignty in the North, 1894–1925* (1985) and *True North: The Yukon and Northwest Territories* (1998); joint author with Ken Coates of *Land of the Midnight Sun: A History of the Yukon* (1988), *The Sinking of the Princess Sophia: Taking the North Down with Her* (1990), *The Alaska Highway in World War II: The US Army of Occupation in Canada's Northwest* (1992), *The Forgotten North* (1992), *Working the North: Labor and the Northwest Defense Projects, 1942–1946* (1994), and several co-edited works. **Essay:** Popular History (with Ken Coates).

Moses, John A. Adjunct professor, St. Mark's National Theological Centre, Canberra. Author of *The Politics of Illusion: The Fischer Controversy in German Historiography* (1975), *Trade Unionism in Germany from Bismarck to Hitler, 1869–1933* (1982), *Prussian-German Militarism in Australian Perspective* (1991), and *Trade Union Theory from Marx to Walesa* (1990). Editor, *Australian Journal of Politics and History*, 1988–93. **Essays:** Fischer; G.A. Wood.

Moye, J. Todd. Doctoral candidate, University of Texas at Austin. Contributor to *American National Biography*, *Jazz and American Culture*, *Southern Cultures*, and *Africa Today*. **Essays:** Boahen; Eric Foner; Leuchtenburg.

Murray, James M. Associate professor of history, University of Cincinnati. Author of *The Notarial Instrument in Flanders* (1995) and numerous articles. **Essay:** Ganshof.

Nelson, Janet L. Professor of medieval history, King's College, London. Author of *Politics and Ritual in Early Medieval Europe* (1986), *Charles the Bald* (1992), and *The Frankish World* (1996). Co-editor of *Charles the Bald: Court and Kingdom* (1981, 1992) and *Alfred the Wise* (1997). Translator of *The Annals of St-Bertin* (1991).

Neumann, Caryn E. Managing editor, *Journal of Women's History*. Author of "Grounded: American Women Aviators in the Great War," *Journal of the League of World War One Aviation Historians* (1995) and "The End of Gender Solidarity: A History of the Women's Organization for National Prohibition Reform," *Journal of Women's History* (1997). **Essays:** Hine; Lavrin.

Nicholson, Helen J. Lecturer in medieval history, University of Wales College of Cardiff. Author of *Templars, Hospitallers and Teutonic Knights: Images of the Military Orders, 1128–1291* (1993) and *Chronicle of the Third Crusade: A Translation of the Itinerarium Peregrinorum et Gesta Regis Ricardi* (1997), and of articles in *Monastic Studies 1: The Continuity of Tradition* (1990), *The Military Orders: Fighting for the Faith and Caring for the Sick* (1994), *Medieval History*, and *History Today*. Editor of *The Military Orders*, vol. 2: *Welfare and Warfare* (1998). **Essays:** Crusades; Duby; Paris; William of Tyre.

Noonkester, Myron C. Associate professor of history, William Carey College, Missouri. Author of articles in *Harvard Theological Review*, *Historical Research*, *Sixteenth Century Journal*, *Notes and Queries*, *English Language Notes*, and *New England Quarterly*. **Essay:** Gardiner.

Oberg, Michael L. Assistant professor of history, Montana State University. Editor (with James Roger Sharp) of *Understanding America: Episodes in the American Past, 1607–1860* (1993), and contributor to *Montana Education Association Journal*, *History Review*, *Hanoverian England: An Encyclopedia*, *American National Biography*, and *Virginia Magazine of History and Biography*. **Essays:** Jordan; Levine; Quinn; Selden; United States: Colonial.

Olson, Robert. Professor of Middle East history, University of Kentucky. Author of *The Siege of Mosul and Ottoman–Persian Relations, 1718–1743: A Study of Rebellion in the Capital and War in the Provinces of the Ottoman Empire* (1975), *The Ba'th and Syria, 1947 to 1982: The Evolution of Ideology, Party, and State, from the French Mandate to the Era of Hafiz al-Asad* (1982), *The Emergence of Kurdish Nationalism and the Sheikh Said Rebellion, 1880–1925* (1989), and *The Kurdish Question and Turkish–Iranian Relations: From World War I to 1998* (1998). Editor of *The Kurdish Nationalism Movement in the 1990s: Its Impact on Turkey and the Middle East* (1996). **Essays:** Barkan; Köprülü; Naima; Ottoman Empire.

Ortiz, David, Jr. Assistant professor of history, University of Arizona. Author of *The Strange Birth of Liberal Spain: The Press and Power in an Authoritarian State, 1885–1902* (forthcoming) and contributor to *Spanish Writers on Gay and Lesbian Themes: A Biographical Sourcebook* (forthcoming). **Essays:** Spain: Modern.

Palm, Donald R. Professor, Sierra College, California. Author of "Intellectuals and the Presidency: Eric Goldman in the L.B.J. White House," *Presidential Studies Quarterly*. **Essays:** Bailyn; Commons; Elkins; Fogel; Gipson.

Palmer, Bryan D. Professor of history, Queen's University, Canada. Author of several works, including *Descent into Discourse: The Reification of Language and the Writing of Social History* (1990), *Working-Class Experience: Rethinking the History of Canadian Labour, 1800–1991* (1992), and *E.P. Thompson: Objections and Oppositions* (1994). **Essays:** Gutman; Montgomery.

Pande, Rekha. Lecturer in history, University of Hyderabad. Author of *Succession in the Delhi Sultanate* (1990) and articles on Indian religious and gender history. **Essays:** Kosambi; Women's History: India.

Parish, Peter J. Director of the Institute of United States Studies, University of London, 1983–92; now Mellon senior research fellow in American history, University of Cambridge. Author of *The American Civil War* (1975) and *Slavery: History and Historians* (1989). Editor of *Abraham Lincoln: Speeches and Letters* (Everyman edition, 1993) and *Reader's Guide to American History* (1997). **Essay:** United States: 19th Century.

Parmar, Inderjeet. Lecturer in government, University of Manchester. Author of "Intellectuals, Foreign Policy and the State," *Manchester Papers on Intellectuals, the State and Society* (1994), "Chatham House, the Foreign Policy Process, and the Making of the Anglo-American Alliance" in *Chatham House and British Foreign Policy, 1919–1945* (1994), *Special Interests, the State, and the Anglo-American Alliance, 1939–1945* (1995), "The Issue of State Power: A Case Study of the Council on Foreign Relations," *Journal of American Studies* (1995), and many other articles. **Essay:** State.

Pascoe, Robert. Dean of arts, Victoria University, Melbourne. Author of *The Manufacture of Australian History* (1979), *A Place of Consequence: A Pictorial History of Fremantle* (1983), *Peppermint Grove: Western Australia's Capital Suburb* (1983), *Buongiorno Australia: Our Italian Heritage* (1987), *The Recollections of Luigi Grollo* (1988), *In Old Kalgoorlie* (1989), *Open for Business* (1990), *We Work with Grollo* (1992), *The Winter Game* (1995), and *The Seasons of Treviso* (1995). **Essays:** Australia; Dening; Ethnicity; Ginzburg.

Patrouch, Joseph F. Assistant professor of history, Florida International University. Author of *Negotiated Settlement: The Counter-Reformation in the Habsburg Province of Upper*

Austria (forthcoming) and several articles on early modern Austrian religious history. **Essays:** Counter-Reformation; Holy Roman Empire.

Pedersen, Frederik J.G. Lecturer in history, University of Aberdeen. Author of "Romeo and Juliet of Stonegate: A Medieval Marriage in Crisis," *Borthwick Paper 87* (1996), *Legal Culture and Marriage in the North of England, 1300–1450* (forthcoming), and articles on marriage and family in *Bulletin of the Institute of Historical Research, Continuity and Change*, and various edited volumes. **Essay:** Marriage.

Peers, Douglas. Associate professor of history, University of Calgary. Author of *Between Mars and Mammon: Colonial Armies and the Garrison State in India, 1819–1835* (1995) and of articles in *Modern Asian Studies, Journal of Imperial and Commonwealth History, International History Review, Medical History, Radical History Review, Criminal Justice History*, and *Historical Journal*. Editor or co-editor of *Warfare and Empire* (1995), *John Stuart Mill and India* (1996), and *Space, Text, Identity: Negotiating India in the Periodical Press, 1840–1914*. **Essays:** Imperialism; Military History; Orientalism.

Pelz, William A. Director, Social Sciences Program, DePaul University. Author of *The Spartakusbund and the German Working Class Movement, 1914–1919* (1988), *Wilhelm Liebknecht and German Social Democracy: A Documentary History* (1994), *The Revolutionary Left in Europe, 1871–1921* (1996), *Working Class Movements, Politics and Culture in Western Europe: An Annotated Bibliography* (1997), and articles in *Left History, German History* and *This Fine Place So Far From Home*, 1995. **Essays:** Broué; Engels; Gramsci; Marx; Arthur Rosenberg.

Pérez, Carlos. Assistant professor of humanities, University of New England. Author of "NAFTA and the Crisis of the Mexican State," *Proceedings of the Twelfth Annual Meeting, Association of Third World Studies* (1994), "The Export Roots of Bolivian Caudillo Politics," *Bolivian Studies* (1996), "Cascarilleros y comericantes en cascarilla durante las insurrecciones populares de Belzu en 1847 y 1848," *Revista de Humanidades y Ciencias Sociales* (1996), and "D'Orbigny and Bolivia's Crisis of the Mexican State," *Bolivian Studies* (1997). **Essays:** Argentina; Borah; Brazil; Cardoso; Cuba; Halperín-Donghi.

Perry, John R. Professor of Persian, Department of Near Eastern Languages and Civilizations and the Center for Middle Eastern Studies, University of Chicago. Author of *Karim Khan Zand: A History of Iran, 1747–1779* (1979). **Essay:** Browne.

Perry, Matt. Lecturer in modern European history, University of Sunderland. Articles on unemployment in *Radical Statistics*. **Essays:** History from Below; Mason; Mayer; Quantitative Method.

Peterson, Indira Viswanathan. Professor of Asian studies, Mount Holyoke College. Author of *Poems to Śiva: The Hymns of the Tamil Saints* (1989) and *Design and Rhetoric in a Sanskrit Court Epic: The Kirātārjunīya of Bhāravi* (1997).

Editor, Indian literature section, *Norton Anthology of World Masterpieces* (6th edition 1995). Contributor to *Journal of the American Oriental Society, History of Religions, Literature East and West, South Asian Social Scientist, Indo-Iranian Journal, Journal of South Asian Literature, Encyclopedia of Religion*, and *The HarperCollins Dictionary of Religion*. **Essay:** Thapar.

Pfitzer, Gregory M. Associate professor of American studies, Skidmore College. Author of *Samuel Eliot Morison's Historical World: In Quest of a New Parkman* (1991). **Essay:** Morison.

Phelps, Christopher. Assistant professor of history, Simon Fraser University. Author of articles in *Monthly Review, Science and Society, New Politics*, and *Left History*. Editorial board member, *Against the Current* (from 1994). **Essay:** Philip S. Foner.

Philippon, Daniel J. Assistant professor of rhetoric, University of Minnesota, Twin Cities. Co-editor of *The Height of Our Mountains: Nature Writing from Virginia's Blue Ridge Mountains and Shenandoah Valley* (1998). **Essay:** Merchant.

Pickus, Keith H. Assistant professor of history, Wichita State University. Author of *Constructing Modern Identities: Jewish University Students in Germany, 1848–1914*. Contributor to *Jewish Social Studies, Leo Baeck Institute Yearbook*. **Essays:** Graetz; Hilberg.

Pinnock, Katherine. Doctoral candidate, School of Languages and European Studies, University of Wolverhampton. **Essay:** Medvedev.

Pipes, Richard. See his own entry.

Polikanov, Dmitri. Doctoral student, Moscow State Institute of International Relations. Author or co-author of a Russian–Swahili dictionary (1997), *Crisis in the Great Lakes Region: Rwanda, Burundi, Zaire* (1997), and *Conflicts in Africa and Conflict Management Activities of the International Organizations* (1998). **Essay:** Mongol Empire.

Porter, Joy. Lecturer in American history, Anglia Polytechnic University, England. Contributor to *Reader's Guide to American History* (1997), *Over-Here* and *Journal of American Studies*. **Essay:** Native American History.

Prosser, Gareth. Doctorate, University College, London. Author of a forthcoming book on noble opposition to Louis XI; researching Norman customary law, provincial institutions, French 15th-century political culture, and the War of the Bien Public. **Essay:** Delisle.

Racine, Karen. Assistant professor of history, Valparaiso University, Indiana. Author of "Alberto Masferrer and the Vital Minimum: The Life and Thought of a Salvadoran Journalist" in *The Americas* (1997). Editor (with Ingrid E. Fey) of *Strange Pilgrimages: Travel, Exile and Foreign Residence in the Creation of Latin American Identity* (forthcoming). **Essays:** Góngora; Ortiz.

Radzilowski, John. Doctoral candidate, Arizona State University; secretary, Polish American Historical Association. Author of *Out on the Wind: Poles and Danes in Lincoln County, Minnesota, 1880–1905* (1992), *Bell Across the Prairie: 125 Years of Holy Trinity Catholic Church* (1995), *Prairie Town: A History of Marshall, Minnesota, 1872–1997* (1997), *The Eagle and the Cross: A History of the Polish Roman Catholic Union of America, 1872–1997,* and articles in *The Historian, Polish American Studies,* and *American Heritage of Invention and Technology.* Editor of *Follow Me: The Memoirs of a Polish Priest* (1997). **Essays:** Agrarian History; Norman Davies; Dubnov; East Central Europe; Halecki; Local History; Poland: since the 18th Century.

Ranger, Terence O. See his own entry.

Ranieri, Ruggero. Lecturer in European economic history, University of Manchester. Articles on antifascist movements in *Prospettive Settanta, Il Ponte* and *The Frontier of National Sovereignty: History and Theory, 1945–1992* (1993). **Essays:** Industrial Revolution; Salvemini.

Reher, David. Professor, Facultad de Ciencias Políticas y Sociología, Universidad Complutense de Madrid. Author of *Familia y sociedad en la provincia de Cuenca, 1750–1970* (1988), *Town and Country in Pre-industrial Spain: Cuenca, 1550–1870* (1990), and *Perspectives on the Family in Spain: Past and Present* (1997). Co-editor of *The Decline of Mortality in Europe* (1991) and *Old and New Methods in Historical Demography* (1993). **Essay:** Domínguez Ortiz.

Reid, Anthony. Professor of Southeast Asian history, Research School of Pacific and Asian History, Australian National University. Author of *The Contest for North Sumatra: Atjeh, the Netherlands, and Britain, 1858–1898* (1969), *The Indonesian National Revolution, 1945–1950* (1974), *The Blood of the People: Revolution and the End of Traditional Rule in Northern Sumatra* (1979), and *Southeast Asia in the Age of Commerce, 1450–1680* (2 vols., 1988–93). Editor or co-editor of *Perceptions of the Past in Southeast Asia* (1979), *Southern Vietnam under the Nguyen* (1993), *Southeast Asia in the Early Modern Era: Trade, Power, and Belief* (1993), *The Last Stand of Asian Autonomies: Responses to Modernity in the Diverse States of Southeast Asia and Korea, 1750–1900* (1997), *Essential Outsiders: Chinese and Jews in the Modern Transformation of Southeast Asia and Central Europe* (1997), and *Asian Freedoms: The Idea of Freedom in East and Southeast Asia* (1998).

Reid, John G. Professor of history, Saint Mary's University, Halifax, Nova Scotia. Author of *Maine, Charles II, and Massachusetts* (1977), *Acadia, Maine, and New Scotland* (1981), *Six Crucial Decades: Times of Change in the History of the Maritimes* (1987), and *The New England Knight: Sir William Phips, 1651–1695* (1998). Co-editor of *Social History of Higher Education* (1989), *Youth, University and Canadian Society* (1989), and *The Atlantic Region to Confederation: A History* (1994). **Essay:** Ethnohistory.

Reimer, Chad. Assistant professor of history, University College of the Fraser Valley, Canada. Contributor to *Pacific Northwest*

Quarterly, Prairie Forum, Journal of Canadian Studies, and *Canadian Journal of History.* **Essays:** Canada; Ormsby.

Reimer, Thomas. Doctorate, Syracuse University, 1996. Freelance historian and indexer. Author of "Vanished Villages: The Story of the Carpathian Germans," *Manas-Peace* (1991) and "Distant Thunder: The German-American Clergy of Schenectady, New York, and the Great War, 1914–1917," *New York History* (1992). Columnist, *New Yorker Staatszeitung,* 1996–97. **Essays:** Mach; Sauer.

Reins, Thomas D. Lecturer in history, California State University at Fullerton. Author of "Reform, Nationalism, and Internationalism: The Opium Suppression Movement in China and the Anglo-American Influence, 1900–1908," *Modern Asian Studies* (1991). Editor, *Chinese-Americans in Orange County, California: An Oral History* (1995). Contributor, *Asian-American Encyclopedia, Asian Pacific Migration Review, History,* and *Asian Affairs.* **Essays:** Fairbank; Liang Qichao.

Reisman, David. Doctoral candidate in the Department of Near East Studies at Yale University, where he researches on Mamluk historiography and intellectual history. **Essay:** Ibn al-Athīr.

Reuter, Timothy. Professor of medieval history, University of Southampton, England. Author or editor of *The Medieval Nobility: Studies in the Ruling Classes of France and Germany from the Sixth to the Twelfth Centuries* (1978), *The Greatest Englishman: Essays on St. Boniface and the Church at Crediton* (1980), *Wortkonkordanz zum Decretum Gratiani* (with Gabriel Silagi, 1990), *Germany in the Early Middle Ages, c.800–1056* (1991), *The Annals of Fulda* (1992), and *Warriors and Churchmen in the High Middle Ages: Essays Presented to Karl Leyser* (1992); editor of several collections of works by Karl Leyser. **Essays:** Leyser; Thietmar; Widukind.

Riall, Lucy. Lecturer in modern European history, Birkbeck College, University of London. Author of *The Italian Risorgimento: State, Society, and National Unification* (1994) and *Sicily and the Unification of Italy: Liberal Policy and Local Power, 1859–66* (1998). Editorial board member, *Modern Italy.* **Essays:** Mack Smith; Romeo.

Rich, Paul John. Professor of international relations and history, Universidad de las Américas, Mexico, and visiting fellow, Hoover Institution, Stanford University, since 1993. Author of *Elixir of Empire: The English Public Schools, Ritualism, Freemasonry and Imperialism* (1989), *Chains of Empire: The English Public Schools, Historical Causality, Masonic Cabalism, and Imperial Clubdom* (1991), *The Invasions of the Gulf: Radicalism, Ritualism and the Shaikhs* (1991), *The Mexican and American Presidencies: Ritual, Secrecy, Power* (1996), and many articles. **Essays:** Namier; Prosopography; Said; Victor Turner.

Richards, Eric. Professor of history, Flinders University, Australia. Author of *The Leviathan of Wealth: The Sutherland Fortune in the Industrial Revolution* (1973), *A History of the Highland Clearances* (2 vols., 1982–85), and *Cromartie: Highland Life, 1650–1914* (with Monica Clough, 1989). Editor,

Flinders History of South Australia (1986), *Poor Australian Immigrants* (1991), *Visible Women: Female Immigrants in Colonial Australia* (1995), and *The Australian Immigrant in the Twentieth Century* (1998). **Essay:** Migration.

Riddell, Peter G. Director, Centre for Islamic Studies, London Bible College (Brunel University). Author of *Transferring a Tradition: 'Abd al-Ra'ūf al-Singkilī's Rendering into Malay of the Jalālayn Commentary* (1990), and articles in *Journal of the Malaysian Branch of the Royal Asiatic Society*, *Archipel*, *Indonesia Circle*, and *Australian Religion Studies Review*. Co-editor of *Islam: Essays on Scripture, Thought and Society* (1997). **Essays:** Ali Haji; Islamic Nations and Cultures; Malay Annals; Raniri; Yamin.

Ridley, Ronald T. Holds a personal chair in history, University of Melbourne. Author of *The Unification of Egypt* (1973), *Gibbon's Complement: Louis de Beaufort* (1986), *History of Rome* (1989), *The Eagle and the Spade: The Archaeology of Rome in the Napoleonic Period* (1992), *The Historical Observations of Jacob Perizonius* (1992), *Jessie Webb: A Memoir* (1994), *Melbourne's Monuments* (1996), and *Napoleon's Proconsul in Egypt: The Life and Times of Bernardino Drovetti* (1998). **Essays:** Beloch; Breasted; Sanctis.

Rielly, Edward J. Professor of English and director of the honors program, Saint Joseph's College, Maine. Editor of *Approaches to Teaching Swift's Gulliver's Travels* (1988); author of seven books of poetry, many short stories and book reviews, and a variety of articles on 18th-century literature, the Middle Ages, the Vietnam War, and sports literature; a book in preparation on baseball and popular culture. **Essay:** Anglo-Saxon Chronicle.

Rippin, Andrew. Professor of religious studies, University of Calgary. Author of *Muslims: Their Religious Beliefs and Practices* (2 vols., 1990–93). Associate editor, *Encyclopedia of the Qur'an* (forthcoming). **Essay:** Watt.

Ritter, Harry. Professor of history, Western Washington University. Author of *Dictionary of Concepts in History* (1986) and articles on German and Austrian history in *Central European History*, *Austrian History Yearbook*, and *German Studies Review*. **Essays:** Begriffsgeschichte; Schorske; Hayden V. White.

Rivera-Garza, Cristina. Assistant professor, DePauw University. Her doctoral dissertation was entitled "The Masters of the Streets: Bodies, Power, and Modernity in Mexico, 1867–1930." **Essay:** Women's History: Latin America.

Roberts, Priscilla M. Lecturer in history, and director, Centre of American Studies, University of Hong Kong. Editor of *Sino–American Relations since 1900* (1991), and articles in *Diplomatic History*, *Business History*, *Journal of Oriental Studies*, *Journal of American Studies*, and *Diplomacy and Statecraft*. **Essays:** Chandler; Commager; Degler; Goldman; Hartz; LaFeber; Link; Nash; Nevins; Owsley; Parrington; Pessen; Potter; Rostow; Schlesinger; Spence; Takaki; Hugh Thomas; United States: 20th Century.

Robinson, Kristen D. Doctoral candidate in history, University of Kentucky. **Essays:** Russell; Trevor-Roper.

Rome, Adam W. Assistant professor of history and geography, Pennsylvania State University. Author "Building on the Land: Toward an Environmental History of Residential Development in American Cities and Suburbs, 1870–1990," *Journal of Urban History* (1994) and "Coming to Terms with Pollution: The Language of Environmental Reform, 1865–1915," *Environmental History* (1996). **Essay:** Worster.

Romero, Tom I. II. Doctoral candidate, University of Michigan School of Law and Department of History. **Essay:** Horwitz.

Rubinstein, W.D. Professor of history, University of Wales, Aberystwyth. Author of *Men of Property: The Very Wealthy in Britain since the Industrial Revolution* (1981), *Capitalism, Culture, and Decline in Britain, 1750–1990* (1993), *A History of the Jews in the English-Speaking World: Great Britain* (1995), *The Myth of Rescue: Why Democracies Could Not Have Saved More Jews from the Nazis* (1997), and many articles. Editor of *Journal of the Australian Jewish Historical Society*, 1988–95. **Essay:** Braham.

Rudin, Ronald. Professor of history, Concordia University. Author of *Banking en français* (1985), *The Forgotten Quebecers* (1985), *In Whose Interest: The Caisses Populaires of Quebec, 1900–1945* (1990), and *Making History in Twentieth-Century Quebec* (1997). **Essays:** Groulx; Ouellet.

Ruggiero, Guido. Josephine Berry Weiss chair in the humanities and professor of Renaissance history, Pennsylvania State University. Author of *Violence in Early Renaissance Venice* (1980), *The Boundaries of Eros: Sex, Crime and Sexuality in Renaissance Venice, 1290–1500* (1985), *Binding Passions: Tales of Magic, Marriage, and Power at the End of the Renaissance* (1993), and of many articles. Series editor, *Studies in the History of Sexuality* (Oxford University Press), since 1985. **Essay:** Martines.

Rushton, Peter. Reader in historical sociology, School of Social and International Studies, University of Sunderland. Author of "Idiocy, the Family and the Community in Early Modern England" in *From "Idiocy" to "Mental Deficiency": Historical Perspectives on People with Learning Disabilities* (1996) and (with Gwenda Morgan), of *Rogues, Thieves and the Rule of Law* (1998). **Essays:** Ariès; Foucault.

Salahub, Jennifer E. Doctoral candidate in design history, Royal College of Art/Victoria and Albert Museum, London. Author of *Quebec Samplers: ABCs of Embroidery* (1994). **Essay:** Design History.

Salamon, Janos. Doctoral candidate in philosophy, Graduate School of City University of New York. Author of several articles in *Nappali Haz*. **Essays:** Dilthey; Freud; Kuhn; Wilamovitz-Möllendorff.

Salamone, Frank A. Professor of sociology and anthropology, Iona College, New Rochelle, New York. Author of *Gods and*

Goods in Africa: Persistence and Change in Ethnic and Religious Identity in Yauri Emirate, North-Western State, Nigeria (2 vols., 1974), *The Hausa People: A Bibliography* (2 vols., 1983), and *The Yanomani and Their Interpreters: Fierce People or Fierce Interpreters?* (1997). Editor of *Art and Culture in Nigeria and the Diaspora* (1991), *The Fulbright Experience in Nigeria* (1995), and *Bridges to Humanity: Narratives on Anthropology and Friendship* (1995). **Essays:** Afigbo; Africa: West; African Diaspora; Ayandele; Paul E. Lovejoy.

Saliba, Gloria Ibrahim. Moderator, Syria-Net and author of many articles on Syria. **Essay:** Hourani.

Salisbury, Joyce E. Professor of history, University of Wisconsin, Green Bay. Author of *Iberian Popular Religion, 600 BC to 700 AD: Celts, Romans, and Visigoths* (1985), *Medieval Sexuality: A Research Guide* (1990), *Church Fathers, Independent Virgins* (1991), *A Short History of Western Civilization: A Study Guide* (1994), *The Beast Within: Animals in the Middle Ages* (1994), *Perpetua's Passion: The Death and Memory of a Young Roman Woman* (1997), and articles in *Journal of Medieval History, Teaching History, Journal of Religious History*, and *Manuscripta*. Editor of *Sex in the Middle Ages* (1991) and *The Medieval World of Nature* (1993). **Essays:** Einhard; Eusebius; Pagels.

Samson, Jane. Assistant professor of history, University of Alberta; former fellow, University of British Columbia and Institute of Commonwealth Studies, University of London. Author of *Imperial Benevolence: Making British Authority in the Pacific Islands* (1998). **Essays:** Maritime History; Pacific/Oceanic History.

Sanders, Thomas. Associate professor of history, United States Naval Academy. Editor of *Imperial Russian Historiography* (1997), and contributor to *Slavic Review, Jahrbücher für Geschichte Osteuropas, World Futures Journal*, and *Problems of Communism*. **Essay:** Russia: Modern (with G.M. Hamburg).

Saunders, Christopher. Associate professor of history, University of Cape Town. Author of *The Making of the South African Past* (1988), *Historical Dictionary of South Africa* (1983, 1998), and articles in *South African Historical Journal* and *History in Africa*. Editor, *Reader's Digest Illustrated History of South Africa* and *An Illustrated Dictionary of South African History* (1994). **Essay:** Leonard Thompson.

Sawyer, Birgit. Associate professor of history, Gothenburg University, Sweden. Author of *Kvinnor och män i Gesta Danorum* (1980), *Property and Inheritance in Viking Age Scandinavia: The Runic Evidence* (1988), *Medieval Scandinavia: From Conversion to Reformation, c.800–1500* (with Peter Sawyer, 1993), and "Historiography and Politics in Medieval Denmark," *Revue Belge de Philologie et d'Histoire*. Co-editor of *The Christianization of Scandinavia* (1987) and *Manliga strukturer och kvinnliga strategier* (1987). **Essay:** Saxo Grammaticus.

Schlich, Thomas. Research officer, Institut für Geschichte der Medizin der Robert Bosch Stiftung. Author of *Marburger jüdische Medizin- und Chirurgiestudenten, 1800–1832* (1990),

"Changing Disease Identities: Coetinism, Politics and Surgery (1844–1892)," *Medical History* (1994), "How Gods and Saints Became Transplant Surgeons: The Scientific Article as a Model for the Writing of History," *History of Science* (1995), and "Medicalization and Secularization: The Jewish Ritual Bath as a Problem of Hygiene," *Social History of Medicine* (1995). Co-editor of *Neue Wege in der Seuchengeschichte* (1995). **Essay:** Sudhoff.

Schuurmans, Frank. Associate lecturer, University of Wisconsin. Contributor to *Skript Historisch Tydschrift* and *German History*. **Essays:** Hartung; Koselleck.

Schwarz, Bill. Reader in communications and cultural studies, Goldsmiths' College, University of London. Editor of *Crises in the British State, 1880–1930* (1985) and *The Expansion of England: Race, Ethnicity and Cultural History* (with Mary Langan, 1996). **Essays:** Cultural History; Seeley; Eric Williams.

Schwarzkopf, Jutta. Lecturer in history, University of Hannover, Germany. Author of *Women in the Chartist Movement* (1991) and "Die soziale Konstruktion von Qualifikation: Eine historische Untersuchung der Weberei von Lancashire zwischen 1885 und dem Ersten Weltkrieg," in *Prokla* (1993). Co-editor of *Nichts also Unterdrückung? Geschlecht und Klasse in der englischen Sozialgeschichte* (1991). **Essays:** Gender; Women's History: Europe.

Scott, Joanne. Lecturer in Australian studies, University of the Sunshine Coast. Contributor to *Journal of Australian Studies* and *Labour History*. **Essays:** Grimshaw; Lake; Women's History: Australia and New Zealand.

Scott, Tom. Reader in medieval history, University of Liverpool. Author of *Freiburg and the Breisgau: Town-Country Relations in the Age of Reformation and the Peasants' War* (1986), *Thomas Müntzer: Theology and Revolution in the German Reformation* (1989), and *Regional Identity and Economic Change: The Upper Rhine, 1450–1600* (1997). Editor (with E.I. Kouri) of *Politics and Society in Reformation Europe: Essays for Sir Geoffrey Elton on His Sixty-fifth Birthday* (1986); translator of *The German Peasants' War: A History in Documents* (with R.W. Scribner, 1991) and *The Peasantries of Europe: From the Fourteenth to the Eighteenth Centuries* (1998). **Essay:** Scribner.

Scribner, Christopher MacGregor. Adjunct professor of history, Tennessee State University. **Essays:** Documentary Film; Mumford.

Seed, John. Senior lecturer in history, Roehampton Institute, London. Author of essays and articles on 18th- and 19th-century British history, and writer on poetry, including studies of Basil Bunting and George Oppen. Co-editor of *The Culture of Capital: Art, Power, and the Nineteenth-Century Middle Class* (1988) and *Cultural Revolution: The Challenge of the Arts in Britain in the 1960s* (1992). **Essays:** Althusser; Perry Anderson; Hammond; Marxist Interpretation.

Sewell, Sara Ann. Doctoral candidate, University of Wisconsin. Her dissertation is entitled "From the Lives of Workers:

Everyday Politics and Everyday Life in the Writings of Communist Worker Correspondents in Cologne, 1924–1933." **Essays:** Hunt; Leisure.

Sharpe, Pamela. Lecturer in economic and social history, University of Bristol, England. Author of *Adapting to Capitalism: Working Women in the English Economy, 1700–1850* (1995) and of articles in *Economic History Review, Continuity and Change, Urban History,* and *Rural History.* Co-editor of *Chronicling Poverty: The Voices and Strategies of the English Poor, 1640–1840* (1997), and editor of *Women's Work: The English Experience* (1998). **Essays:** Demography; Habakkuk; Henry; Wrigley.

Sheldon, Kathleen. Research scholar, Center for the Study of Women, University of California, Los Angeles. Editor of *Courtyards, Markets, City Streets: Urban Women in Africa* (1996). Contributor to *African Encounters with Domesticity* (1992), *Women and Revolution in Africa, Asia, and the New World* (1994) and to *Signs* and *Women's Studies International Forum.* **Essay:** Women's History: Africa.

Shepard, Todd David. Doctoral candidate in history, Rutgers University. **Essays:** Chartier; Homosexuality; Lavisse; Seignobos.

Shifrin, Susan. Independent scholar and consultant; former curator of textiles and costumes, Paley Design Center, Philadelphia College of Textiles and Science. Contributor to *Black Women in America: An Historical Encyclopedia* (1993), *Chronology of Women's History* (1996), and to *Dress: The Journal of the Costume Society of America* and *Transactions and Studies of the College of Physicians of Philadelphia.* **Essay:** Dress.

Shively, Charles. Professor of American studies, University of Massachusetts, Boston. Editor of *Calamus Lovers: Walt Whitman's Working-Class Camerados* (1987) and *Drum Beats: Walt Whitman's Civil War Boy Lovers* (1989). **Essay:** Perry Miller.

Shkimba, Margaret. Faculty member, York University, Canada. **Essays:** Foxe; Pinchbeck.

Siegel, Mona L. Doctoral candidate and Detling fellow, University of Wisconsin, Madison. **Essays:** Corbin; Ozouf.

Sjöblom, Tom. Independent researcher. Author of *Celtica Helsingiensia* (1996) and *Näköalosa Uskontoon* (Perspectives on Religion, 1997). Editorial board member, *Sfks-Newsletter* (The Newsletter for the Finnish Society of Celtic Studies). **Essay:** Religions, Comparative.

Smandych, Russell C. Associate professor of sociology, University of Manitoba. Co-editor of *Canadian Criminal Justice History: An Annotated Bibliography* and *Dimensions of Childhood: Essays on the History of Children and Youth in Canada* (1991). Contributor to *Manitoba Law Journal, Manitoba Law Annual, Native Studies Review, Criminologie, Canadian Journal of Criminology, International Criminal Justice Review, Criminal Justice History: An International*

Annual, Canadian Journal of Sociology, and *Canadian Journal of Social Policy.* **Essay:** Sociology and History.

Smith, John David. Graduate Alumni distinguished professor of history, North Carolina State University. Author of *Window on the War* (1976), *Black Slavery in the Americas* (1982), *An Old Creed for the New South* (1985, 1991), *Dictionary of Afro-American Slavery* (1988, 1997), *Ulrich Bonnell Phillips* (1990), *Anti-Black Thought* (1993), and *Black Voices from Reconstruction* (1996). **Essays:** Genovese; Phillips.

So, Alvin Y. Professor of sociology, University of Hawaii. Author of *The South China Silk District* (1986) and *Social Change and Development* (1990) and co-author of *East Asia and the World Economy* (1995). Co-editor of *Hong Kong–Guangdong Link* (1995) **Essay:** Wallerstein.

Soderlund, Richard J. Assistant professor of history, Illinois State University. Contributor to *A Dictionary of Nineteenth-Century World History* (1993). **Essays:** Hill; Kiernan; Webb.

Southard, Robert Fairbairn. Professor of history, Earlham College, Indiana. Author of *Droysen and the Formation of the Prussian School* (1995). **Essays:** Salo Wittmayer Baron; Droysen; Jewish History; Meyer; Theodor Mommsen; Otto; Hans Rosenberg; Savigny; Sybel; Wellhausen.

Spenser, Daniela. Research fellow, Centro de Investigaciones y Estudios Superiores en Antropolgía Social, Mexico City. Co-author of *Los empresarios alemanes* (1988), *El Partido Socialista de Chiapas* (1989), and *El triangulo imposible* (1998) as *The Impossible Triangle: Mexico, Soviet Russia and the United States in the 1920s* (forthcoming). Editor of the documentary series *History of the Communist International in Mexico.* **Essays:** Cosío Villegas; González Casanova; Las Casas; Léon-Portilla; O'Gorman.

Starr, David B. Instructor in history, Hebrew College, and adjunct lecturer, Brandeis University. Author of "We Cannot Escape History: Solomon Schechter and Zionism," *Proceedings of the Rabbinical Assembly* (1993), "'This Is Only the Fact, but We Have the Idea': Solomon Schechter's Path to Zionism," *Jewish Political Studies Review* (1997), and "Call Me Ishmael? A Midrash for Conservative Judaism," *Conservative Judaism.* **Essays:** Hofstadter; Katz; Woodward.

Stevens, Amy. Independent scholar. **Essay:** Kerber.

Stokes, Raymond G. Senior lecturer in economic and social history, University of Glasgow. Author of *Opting for Oil: The Political Economy of Technological Change in the West German Chemical Industry, 1945–1961* (1994), *Divide and Prosper: The Heirs of I.G. Farben under Allied Authority, 1945–1951* (1988), and articles in *German History, Central European History, Technology and Culture, Journal of European Economic History,* and *Business History Review.* Contributor to the collections *American Policy and the Reconstruction of West Germany, 1945–1955* (1993), *Technology Transfer Out of Germany after 1945* (1996), *The United States and the Integration of Europe: Legacies of the Postwar Era* (1996), and *Science under Socialism.* **Essay:** Business History.

Stoutenburg, Dennis. Professor of biblical studies, Providence College, Manitoba, Canada. Author of *With One Voice – B'Qol Echad: The Sermon on the Mount and Rabbinic Literature* (1996) and articles in *Didaskalia, Journal of the Evangelical Theological Society, Critical Review of Books in Religion*, and *Journal of Biblical Literature*. **Essay:** Archaeology.

Strikwerda, Carl. Professor of history and associate dean of the College of Liberal Arts and Sciences, University of Kansas. Author of *A House Divided: Catholics, Socialists, and Flemish Nationalists in Nineteenth-Century Belgium* (1997) and articles in *Comparative Studies in Society and History, American Historical Review, Journal of Social History*, and *Urban History Yearbook*. Co-editor of *The Politics of Immigrant Workers: Labor Activism and Migration in the World Economy since 1830* (1993, 1998). **Essays:** deVries; Labor History; Landes; Charles Tilly; Louise A. Tilly.

Stringer, K.J. Senior lecturer in history, University of Lancaster, England. Author of *Earl David of Huntingdon, 1152–1219: A Study in Anglo-Scottish History* (1985) and *The Reign of Stephen: Kingship, Warfare and Government in Twelfth-Century England* (1993). Editor or co-editor of *Essays on the Nobility of Medieval Scotland* (1985), *Medieval Scotland: Crown, Lordship and Community: Essays Presented to G.W.S. Barrow* (1993), *Social and Political Identities in Western History* (1994), and *Uniting the Kingdom? The Making of British History* (1995). **Essays:** Cheney; William of Malmesbury.

Stuchtey, Benedikt. Research fellow, German Historical Institute, London. Author of "The Lecky Papers in Trinity College, Dublin," *Europa: European Review of History* (1994) and *W.E.H. Lecky (1838–1903)* (1997). **Essays:** Conze; Gatterer; Lecky; Niebuhr; Schlözer; Schnabel; Trevelyan.

Sundwall, Gavin A. Visiting professor of history, University of North Carolina, Chapel Hill. Author of "Ammianus Geographicus," *American Journal of Philology* (1996). **Essay:** Scriptores Historiae Augustae.

Surridge, Keith. Lecturer in modern British history, University of Notre Dame London Program. Author of *Politicians and Generals: Managing the South African War, 1899–1902: A Study in Civil-Military Relations* (1998) and of articles on the South African War in *History* (1997) and *Small Wars and Insurgencies* (1997). **Essays:** British Empire; World War II.

Syon, Guillaume de. Assistant professor of history, Albright College, Pennsylvania. Author of *Zeppelin! Germany and the Airship Experience, 1900–1939* (forthcoming); contributor to *American National Biography*. Contributing editor, *The Collected Papers of Albert Einstein*, vol. 8: *The Berlin Years: Correspondence, 1914–1919* (1996). **Essays:** Switzerland; Voltaire.

Szmrecsányi, Tamás. Professor of social history of science and technology, Department of Science Policy, University of Campinas (UNICAMP), Brazil. Author of articles on Brazilian economic history and contributor to *Foreign Investment in Latin America: Impact on Economic Development, 1850–1930* (1994). **Essays:** Heckscher; Prado Júnior.

Tao, De-min. Associate professor, Faculty of Letters, Kansai University, Japan. Author of *Kaitokudō shushigaku no kenkyū* (A Study of the Kaitokudō Neo-Confucianism, 1994) and articles in *Shisō, Tōhōgaku, Rikkyō Hōgaku, Gest Library Journal, Sino-Japanese Studies*, and other journals. **Essays:** Maruyama Masao; Niida Noboru; Otsuka Hisao; Shigeno Yasutsugu; Shiratori Kurakichi.

Tarver, H. Micheal. Assistant professor of Latin American history, McNeese State University, Louisiana. Author or co-author of "Salamander Territoriality: Pheromonal Markers as Advertisement by Males," *Animal Behaviour* (1986), "Skeletal Biology and the History of Native Americans and African Americans," *Latin American Population History Bulletin* (1992), and "Administrative Corruption: The Case of Carlos Andrés Pérez," *Current World Leaders* (1994). **Essays:** Garcilaso de la Vega; Pérez.

Ten Dyke, Elizabeth A. Adjunct assistant professor, Hunter College. Author of "The Politics of Memory and Moral Righteousness: A Case Study from Dresden, Germany," in *POLAR* (Political and Legal Anthropology Review) (1995), "Memory, History and Remembrance Work in Dresden" *Altering States: Ethnographies of Transition in Eastern Europe and the Former Soviet Union* (forthcoming), and *Paradoxes of Memory in History: Dresden, Germany after 1989* (forthcoming). **Essay:** Anthropology.

Thomas, Jack Ray. Professor of history, Bowling Green State University. Author or co-author of *Latin America* (1972), *Varieties and Problems of Twentieth-Century Socialism* (1981), *Biographical Dictionary of Latin American Historiography and Historians* (1984), *Essays on Socialism* (1992), and articles in *Americas: A Quarterly Review of Inter-American Cultural History, Revista/Review Interamericana, Americas (OAS), Journal of Library History, Social Science, Hispanic American Historical Review*, and *Journal of Inter-American Studies and World Affairs*. **Essays:** Levene; Mitre.

Thompson, Bruce. Lecturer in history, University of California, Santa Cruz. Contributor to *Stanford Humanities Review* and *Environmental History*. **Essays:** Blum; Brenner; Gilbert; Kołakowski; Mattingly; Moore; Schama.

Tishken, Joel E. Doctoral candidate, University of Texas, Austin. Author of "Central Africa: People and States" in *African History and Culture to 1885*; contributor to *African Economic History*. **Essays** (with Toyin Falola): Africa: Central; Africa: Eastern and Southern; Coquery-Vidrovitch; Davidson; Feierman; Iliffe; Mazrui; Ogot; Ranger; Rodney.

Tonkin, John. Professor of history, University of Western Australia. Author of *The Church and the Secular Order in Reformation Thought* (1971) and (with A.G. Dickens) of *The Reformation in Historical Thought* (1985). Editor of *Religion and Society in Western Australia* (1987). **Essays:** Dickens; Janssen; Protestantism; Troeltsch.

Trivellato, Francesca. Doctoral candidate, Brown University. Author of "La missione diplomatica a Venezia del fiorentino

Giannotto Manetti a metà Quattrocento," *Studi Veneziani* (1995) and "Salaires et justice dans le monde comparatif à Venise au XVII siècle," *Annales*. **Essays:** Bloch; Sarpi.

Troup, Kathleen. Lecturer in medieval history, University of Waikato, New Zealand. Author of *The Houses of History: A Critical Reader in Twentieth-Century History and Theory* (with Anna Green, 1998) and *Wakefield Court Rolls, 1338–1342*. **Essay:** Orderic Vitalis.

Troyan, Brett. Doctoral candidate, Cornell University. Author of "Aventuras de una gringa," *Estrategía* (1988). **Essays:** Chevalier; Mexico; Rock; Stein.

Usborne, Cornelie. Senior lecturer in history, Roehampton Institute, London. Author of *The Politics of the Body in Weimar Germany: Women's Reproductive Rights and Duties* (1992), *Frauenkörper - Volkeskörper* (1994), "The New Woman and Generational Conflict: Perceptions of Young Women's Sexual Wars in the Weimar Republic" in *Generations in Conflict: Youth Revolt and Gender Formation in Germany, 1770–1968* (1995), and various articles on the culture of abortion in the 20th century. Editor (with Margaret L. Arnot) of *Gender and Crime in Modern Europe* (1999). **Essay:** Bock.

Vamplew, Wray. Professor of sports history, De Montfort University. Author of *The Turf: A Social and Economic History of Horse Racing* (1976), *Pay Up and Play the Game* (1988), *The Oxford Companion to Australian Sport* (1991, 1994), *Sport in Australia: A Social History* (1994), and *Sport in Australian History* (1997). **Essay:** Sport.

Van Beek, Elizabeth T. Assistant professor, San Jose State University. Author of "A Coventry Backdrop: Davenport's and Eaton's Old World Roots," *Journal of the New Haven Colony Historical Society* (1994) and a forthcoming book on the Puritan founders of the colony of New Haven. **Essay:** Morgan.

Vance, Jonathan F. Assistant professor of history, University of Western Ontario. Author of *Objects of Concern: Canadian Prisoners of War Through the Twentieth Century* (1994), *A Gallant Company: The Men of the Great Escape* (1997), and *Death So Noble: Memory, Meaning and the First World War* (1997), and articles in *Journal of Contemporary History, War and Society, Journal of Military History, Material History Review*, and *Canadian Military History*. Editor of *National History: A Canadian Journal of Enquiry and Opinion*. **Essays:** Creighton; Frégault; Innis; Lower; World War I.

van Dijk, Ruud. Doctoral candidate, Contemporary History Institute, Ohio University. Author of "The 1952 Stalin Note Debate: Myth or Missed Opportunity for German Unification?" (Cold War International History Project Working Paper, 1996) and articles for various encyclopedias and handbooks. **Essays:** Bracher; Hillgruber.

Verney, Kevern J. Senior lecturer in history, Edge Hill University College, Lancashire. His research interests include Booker T. Washington, W.E.B. Du Bois, and Marcus Garvey. **Essays:** African American History; Litwack; Meier.

Vietto, Angela. Doctoral candidate, Pennsylvania State University. Contributor to *Reader's Guide to Literature in English* (1996) and *Encyclopedia of American Literature*. Assistant editor, *American Women Prose Writers to 1820* (forthcoming). **Essays:** Benedict Anderson; Smith-Rosenberg; Gordon S. Wood.

Walbank, F.W. Emeritus professor of ancient history and classical archaeology, University of Liverpool. Author of *Aratos of Sicyon* (1933), *Philip V of Macedon* (1940), *The Decline of the Roman Empire in the West* (1946; as *The Awful Revolution*, 1969), *A Historical Commentary on Polybius* (3 vols; 1957–79), *Polybius* (1972), *The Hellenistic World* (1981, 1992), *Selected Papers: Studies in Greek and Roman History and Historiography* (1985), *A History of Macedonia*, vol. 3: *336–168 BC* (with N.G.L. Hammond, 1988), and *Timaios und die westgriechische Sicht der Vergangenheit* (1992).

Walker, William T. Professor of humanities and history, Philadelphia College of Pharmacy and Science. Author of *Disraeli: An Annotated Bibliography*; contributor to *Encyclopedia of Revolutions and Civil Wars in the Twentieth Century*. **Essays:** Buckle; Stubbs.

Watkins, Carl. Research fellow, Magdalene College, University of Cambridge. **Essay:** Roger of Wendover.

Watson, David Robin. Senior lecturer in history, University of Dundee. Author of *The Life of Charles I* (1972; new edition 1993), *Georges Clemenceau: A Political Biography* (1974), and articles in *European History Quarterly, Revolutionary Russia, Cahiers du Monde Russe et Soviétique, Historical Journal, English Historical Review, Modern Language Review*, and *Past and Present*. **Essays:** Furet; Renouvin; Tocqueville.

Weaver, Deirdre Chase. Assistant professor of history, West Texas A&M University. Author of "'Words are the True Masks of Our Ideas': Counter-Revolutionary Discourse and Fourier's Critique of the Jacobins," in *Consortium on Revolutionary Europe: Selected Papers 1997*; contributor to *Makers of Western Culture, 1800–1914*. **Essay:** Skinner.

Webb, Diana. Lecturer in history, King's College, University of London. Author of *Patrons and Defenders: The Saints in the Italian City States* (1996). **Essays:** Muratori; Villani.

Weeks, Gregory. Doctoral candidate in history, University of Graz, Austria. Author of articles on German history and US popular culture of the 1960s in *The Encyclopedia of Propaganda, Geschichte und Gegenwart, Chronology of 20th-Century History: Arts and Culture, Women in World History*, and *Popular Musicians*. **Essays:** Delbrück; Gay; Howard; Mahan; Popper; Ritter.

Weiss, Jessica. Visiting lecturer in history, University of California, Berkeley. **Essays:** Cott; Ulrich; Women's History: North America.

Windhausen, John D. Professor of history, Saint Anselm College, Manchester, New Hampshire. Editor and translator of

History of Russia: The Reign of Ivan the Great by S.M. Solov'ev (1978) and *History of Russia: Russian Society in the Age of Ivan III* by Solov'ev (1979). Contributor to *Studies in Soviet Thought, History of European Ideas,* and *Great Lives in History.* **Essays:** Karamzin; Russia: Early Modern; Solov'ev.

Wise, Edward M. Professor of law, Wayne State University. Co-author of *Anglo-American Criminal Justice* (1967) and *Aut Dedere Aut Judicare* (1995). Editor or co-editor of *International Criminal Law* (1965), *Studies in Comparative Criminal Law* (1975), *Criminal Science in a Global Society* (1994), and *Comparative Law: Cases-Text-Materials* (1998). Translator of *The Italian Penal Code* (1976). Editorial board member, *American Journal of Comparative Law* and *International Criminal Justice Review*; editor-in-chief, American Series of Foreign Penal Codes. **Essay:** Daube.

Witt, Ronald G. Professor of history, Duke University. Author *Coluccio Salutati and His Public Letters* (1976), *Hercules at the Crossroads: The Life, Works and Thought of Coluccio Salutati* (1983), and *In the Footsteps of the Ancients: The Origins of Italian Humanism from Lovato to Bruni* (1999); co-author of *Cultural Roots and Continuities,* (5th edition 1997). Co-editor of *The Earthly Republic: Italian Humanists on Government and Society* (1976). **Essay:** Hans Baron.

Wyatt, Don J. Professor of history, Middlebury College. Author of "Chu Hsi's Critique of Shao Yung: One Instance of the Stand Against Fatalism," *Harvard Journal of Asiatic Studies* (1985), "A Language of Continuity in Confucian Thought" in *Ideas across Cultures: Essays on Chinese Thought in Honor of*

Benjamin I. Schwartz (1990), *The Recluse of Loyang: Shao Yung and the Moral Evolution of Early Sung Thought* (1996), and "Bonds of Certain Consequence: The Personal Responses to Concubinage of Wang Anshi and Sima Guang" in *Presence and Presentation: Women in the Chinese Literati Tradition* (1998). **Essays:** Kong-zi; Ma Huan.

Xiao-bin Ji. Assistant professor of history, Rutgers University, Camden. **Essays:** Ban Gu; Gu Jiegang.

Yamauchi, Edwin M. Professor of history, Miami University, Ohio. Author of *Greece and Babylon* (1967), *The Stones and the Scriptures* (1972), *Foes from the Northern Frontier* (1982), and *Persia and the Bible* (1990). Contributor to *Berytus, Biblical Archaeologist, Fides et Historia, Journal of the American Oriental Society, Journal of Near Eastern Studies,* and *Journal of Semitic Studies.* **Essays:** Herodotus; Josephus.

Yu, Ying-shih. Professor of East Asian studies, Princeton University. Author (in English) of *Trade and Expansion in Han China: A Study in the Structure of Sino-Barbarian Relations* (1967) and of many works in Chinese. **Essays:** Chen Yinke; Zhang Xuecheng.

Zimmer, Matthias. DAAD German studies professor, University of Alberta. Author of *Nationales Interesse und Staatsräson: Zur Deutschlandpolitik der Regiesüng Kohl, 1982–1989* (1992) and (with Udo Margedant) of *Eigentum und Freiheit* (1993). Editor (with Angelika E. Sauer) of *A Chorus of Different Voices: German–Canadian Identities* (1998). **Essays:** Germany: since 1945; Hintze; Meinecke.